AutoCAD
and Its Applications
C O M P R E H E N S I V E

by

Terence M. Shumaker
Faculty Emeritus
Former Chairperson
Drafting Technology
Autodesk Premier Training Center
Clackamas Community College, Oregon City, Oregon

David A. Madsen
Faculty Emeritus, Former Department Chair Drafting Technology
Autodesk Premier Training Center
Clackamas Community College, Oregon City, Oregon
Director Emeritus, American Design Drafting Association

David P. Madsen
Vice President, Madsen Designs Inc.
Computer-Aided Design and Drafting Consultant and Educator
Autodesk Developer Network Member
American Design Drafting Association Member

Craig P. Black
Instructor, Mechanical Design
Manager, Autodesk Premier Training Center
Fox Valley Technical College, Appleton, Wisconsin

2008

Publisher
The Goodheart-Willcox Company, Inc.
Tinley Park, Illinois
www.g-w.com

Manufactured in the United States of America.

Library of Congress Catalog Card Number 2007022480

ISBN 978-1-59070-834-7

1 2 3 4 5 6 7 8 9 – 08 – 12 11 10 09 08 07

The Goodheart-Willcox Company, Inc. Brand Disclaimer: Brand names, company names, and illustrations for products and services included in this text are provided for educational purposes only and do not represent or imply endorsement or recommendation by the author or the publisher.

The Goodheart-Willcox Company, Inc. Safety Notice: The reader is expressly advised to carefully read, understand, and apply all safety precautions and warnings described in this book or that might also be indicated in undertaking the activities and exercises described herein to minimize risk of personal injury or injury to others. Common sense and good judgment should also be exercised and applied to help avoid all potential hazards. The reader should always refer to the appropriate manufacturer's technical information, directions, and recommendations; then proceed with care to follow specific equipment operating instructions. The reader should understand these notices and cautions are not exhaustive.

The publisher makes no warranty or representation whatsoever, either expressed or implied, including but not limited to equipment, procedures, and applications described or referred to herein, their quality, performance, merchantability, or fitness for a particular purpose. The publisher assumes no responsibility for any changes, errors, or omissions in this book. The publisher specifically disclaims any liability whatsoever, including any direct, indirect, incidental, consequential, special, or exemplary damages resulting, in whole or in part, from the reader's use or reliance upon the information, instructions, procedures, warnings, cautions, applications, or other matter contained in this book. The publisher assumes no responsibility for the activities of the reader.

Library of Congress Cataloging-in-Publication Data

Shumaker, Terence M.
    AutoCAD and Its Applications Comprehensive 2008 / by
Terence M. Shumaker, David A. Madsen, David P. Madsen.
– 15th ed.
      p. cm.

    Includes index.
    ISBN 978-1-59070-834-7
    1. Computer graphics. 2. AutoCAD. I. Madsen, David A.. II.
Madsen, David P. III. Craig P. Black

T385.S46123   2008
620'.00420285536—dc22   2007022480

AutoCAD
and Its Applications
B A S I C S

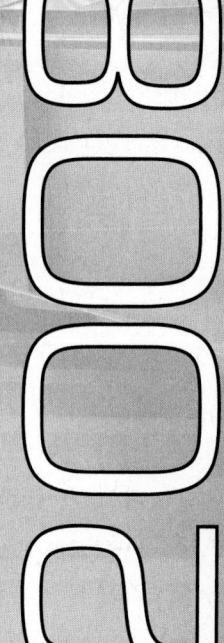

2008

by

Terence M. Shumaker
Faculty Emeritus
Former Chairperson
Drafting Technology
Autodesk Premier Training Center
Clackamas Community College, Oregon City, Oregon

David A. Madsen
Faculty Emeritus, Former Department Chair Drafting Technology
Autodesk Premier Training Center
Clackamas Community College, Oregon City, Oregon
Director Emeritus, American Design Drafting Association

David P. Madsen
Vice President, Madsen Designs Inc.
Computer-Aided Design and Drafting Consultant and Educator
Autodesk Developer Network Member
American Design Drafting Association Member

Publisher
The Goodheart-Willcox Company, Inc.
Tinley Park, Illinois
www.g-w.com

Manufactured in the United States of America.

Library of Congress Catalog Card Number 2007022481

ISBN 978-1-59070-830-9

1 2 3 4 5 6 7 8 9 – 08 – 12 11 10 09 08 07

Library of Congress Cataloging-in-Publication Data

Shumaker, Terence M.
  AutoCAD and Its Applications BASICS 2008 / by Terence M. Shumaker, David A. Madsen, David P. Madsen. – 15th ed.
    p. cm.

  Includes index.
  ISBN 978-1-59070-830-9
    1. Computer graphics. 2. AutoCAD. I. Madsen, David A. II. Madsen, David P.

T385.S461466   2008
620'.00420285536--dc22   2007022481

Introduction

AutoCAD and Its Applications—Basics is a textbook providing complete instruction in mastering fundamental AutoCAD® 2008 commands and drawing techniques. Typical applications of AutoCAD are presented with basic drafting and design concepts. The topics are covered in an easy-to-understand sequence and progress in a way that allows you to become comfortable with the commands as your knowledge builds from one chapter to the next. In addition, *AutoCAD and Its Applications—Basics* offers the following features:

- Step-by-step use of AutoCAD commands.
- In-depth explanations of how and why commands function as they do.
- Extensive use of font changes to specify certain meanings.
- Examples and descriptions of industry practices and standards.
- Actual screen captures of AutoCAD and Windows features and functions.
- Professional tips explaining how to use AutoCAD effectively and efficiently.
- More than two hundred exercises to reinforce the chapter topics. These exercises also build on previously learned material.
- Chapter tests for review of commands and key AutoCAD concepts.
- A large selection of drafting problems supplementing each chapter. Problems are presented as industrial drawings, engineering sketches, or architectural, civil, electrical, or other related industry drawings.

With *AutoCAD and Its Applications—Basics*, you learn AutoCAD commands and become acquainted with information in other areas:

- Office practices for firms using AutoCAD systems.
- Preliminary planning and sketches.
- Drawing geometric shapes and constructions.
- Special editing operations that increase productivity.
- Making multiview drawings (orthographic projection).
- Dimensioning techniques and practices, based on accepted standards.
- Drawing section views and designing graphic patterns.
- Creating shapes and symbols for different uses.
- Creating and managing symbol libraries.
- Sketching with AutoCAD.
- Plotting and printing drawings.

Learning Objectives identify key items you will learn in the chapter.

Command Entry Graphics show command prompt, toolbar, and pull-down menu entry options. Command options are also shown where applicable.

Prompt Sequences highlight procedures for entering commands and options.

Illustrations, including AutoCAD "screen shots" and line art illustrations, make learning easy.

New Feature Graphics identify new and updated features for AutoCAD 2008.

Running Glossary Entries define key terms.

Professional Tips increase your productivity in using AutoCAD commands and techniques.

Cautions alert you to potential problems.

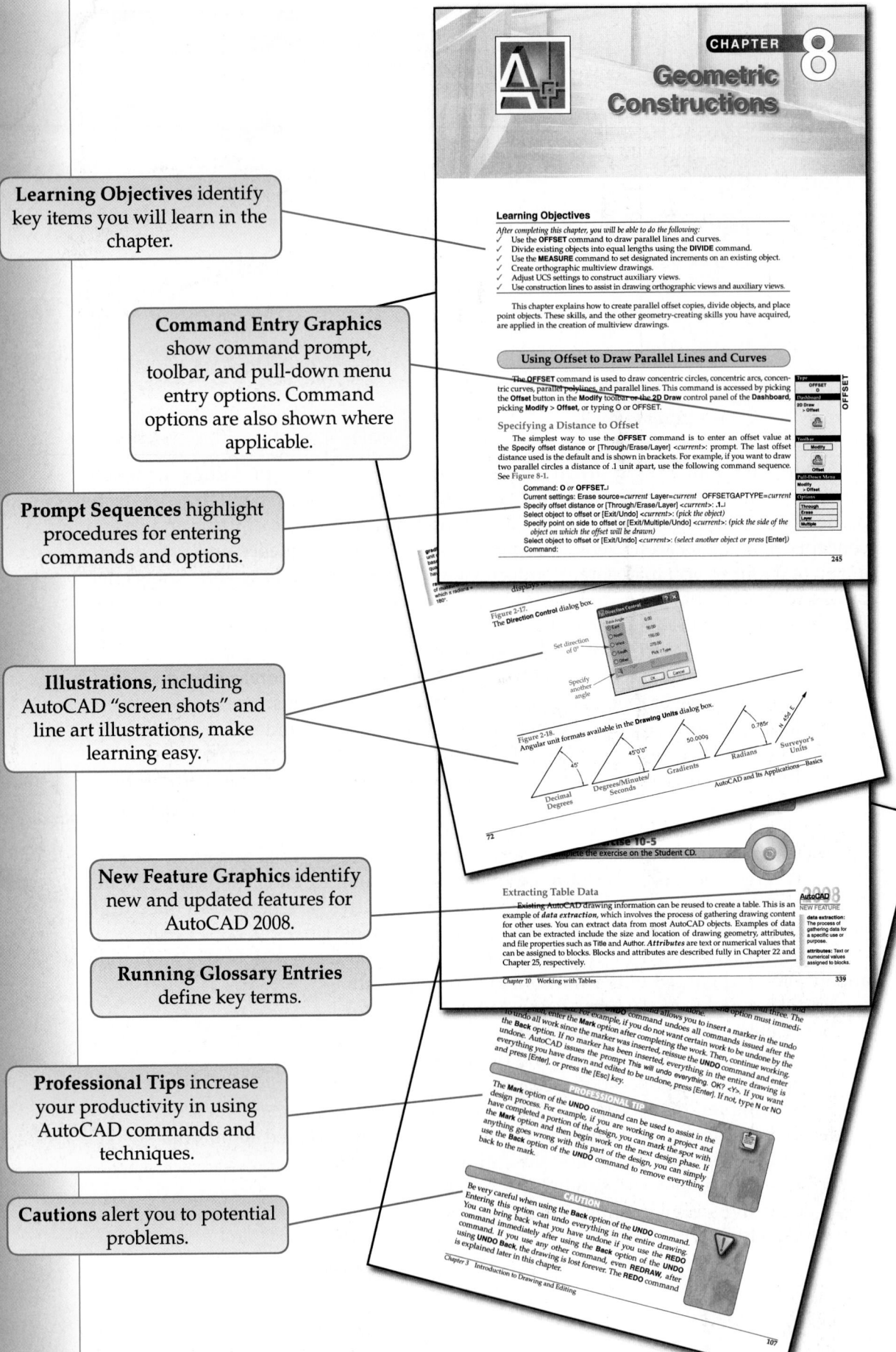

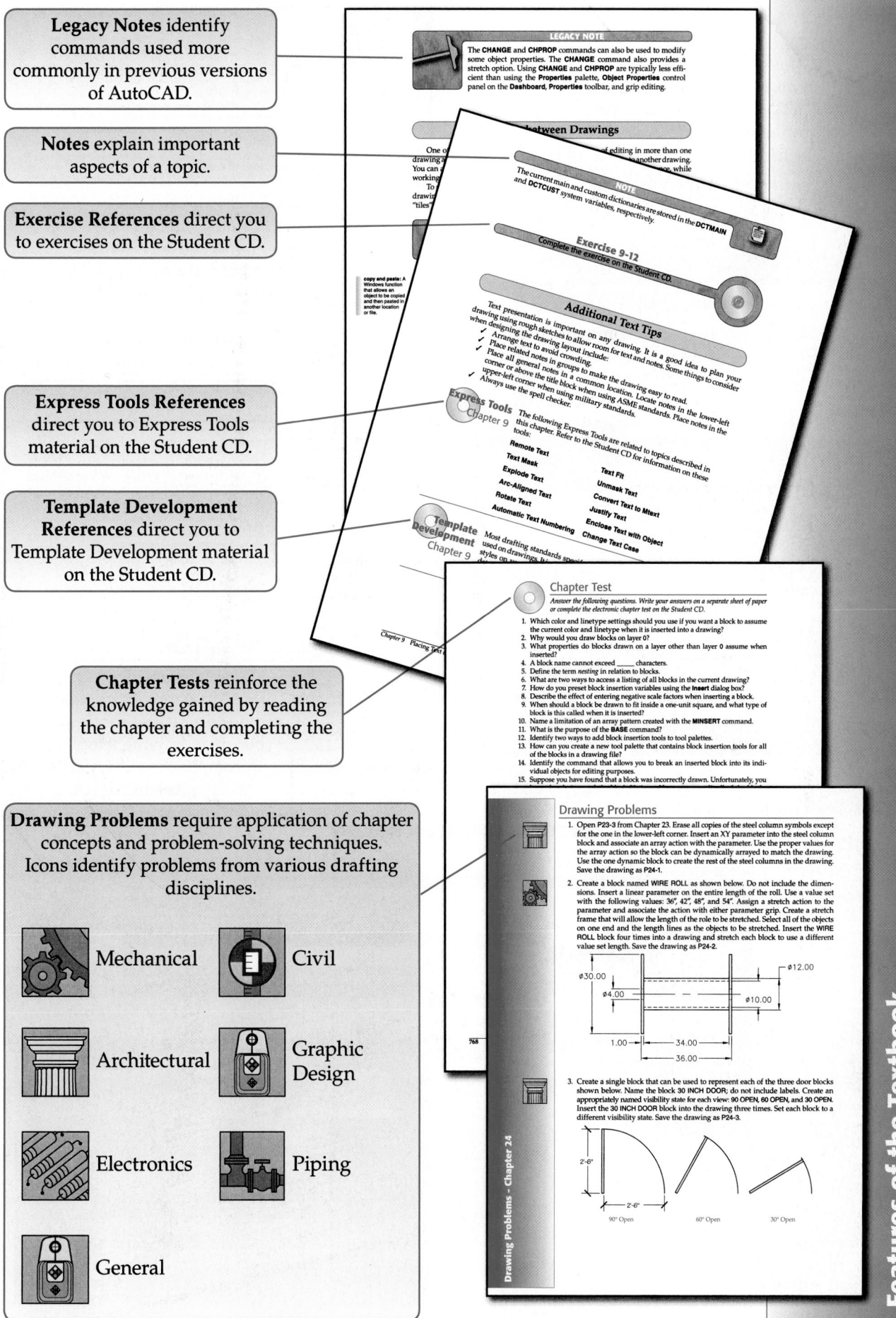

Legacy Notes identify commands used more commonly in previous versions of AutoCAD.

Notes explain important aspects of a topic.

Exercise References direct you to exercises on the Student CD.

Express Tools References direct you to Express Tools material on the Student CD.

Template Development References direct you to Template Development material on the Student CD.

Chapter Tests reinforce the knowledge gained by reading the chapter and completing the exercises.

Drawing Problems require application of chapter concepts and problem-solving techniques. Icons identify problems from various drafting disciplines.

Mechanical

Civil

Architectural

Graphic Design

Electronics

Piping

General

Features of the Textbook

AutoCAD Software. Pick this button to link to access a Web site from which you can download the AutoCAD Electrical software at no cost for use with this book.

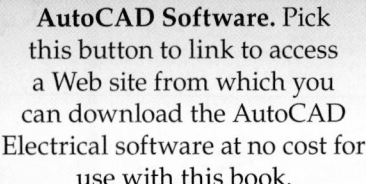

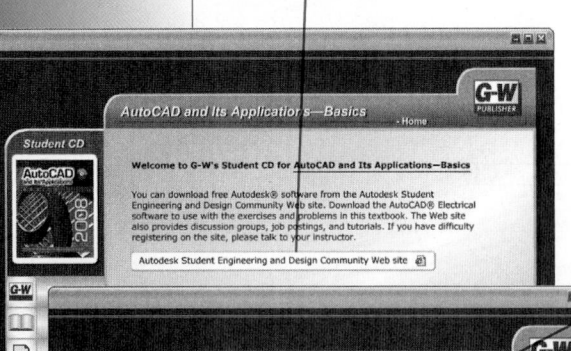

Using Text Express Tools

The **Express** pull-down menu includes a **Text** cascading menu with several commands. These commands offer extended functionality for text in AutoCAD. See Figure ET9-1.

Using Remote Text

Remote text is text created from an ASCII text file or DIESEL expression. *ASCII* (American Standard Code for Information Interchange) is a code in which letters, numbers, and other characters are represented numerically for transmission and display via computer. ASCII text editors such as Windows Notepad can be used to write text and save the file as a TXT file. A *DIESEL expression* (Direct Interpretively Evaluated String Expression Language) is a type of programming code that evaluates AutoCAD variables to determine a function.

To use the **Remote Text** command, select **Express > Text Remote > Text** from the pull-down menu, or type RTEXT. The following sequence is used

Copyright by Goodheart-Willcox Co., Inc.

Express Tools Material. Express Tools are supplemental AutoCAD functions that may be available to you. Notes in the textbook refer to these components.

Adding Layers

Template Development Objectives

You will complete the following tasks during this stage of template development:
✓ Adjust default lineweight settings.
✓ Load linetypes.
✓ Create layers.

The next stage of template development includes adjusting default lineweight settings, loading linetypes, and creating layers. The templates you create in this book focus on specific drafting disciplines and use exact lineweights, linetypes, and layers set according to drafting industry standards.

Adjusting Default Lineweight Settings

Often templates co... of layers added to a m... layers in the template u... value. Layers that use... change each layer's line... lineweight for specifyi... default lineweight to a... Follow these steps to s...

Copyright by Goodheart-Willcox Co., Inc.

Template Development. These in-depth instructions provide guidelines for creating your own drawing templates in compliance with ASME and other related drafting standards.

Related Web Sites. Use this to access a wide variety of CAD/Drafting Web sites.

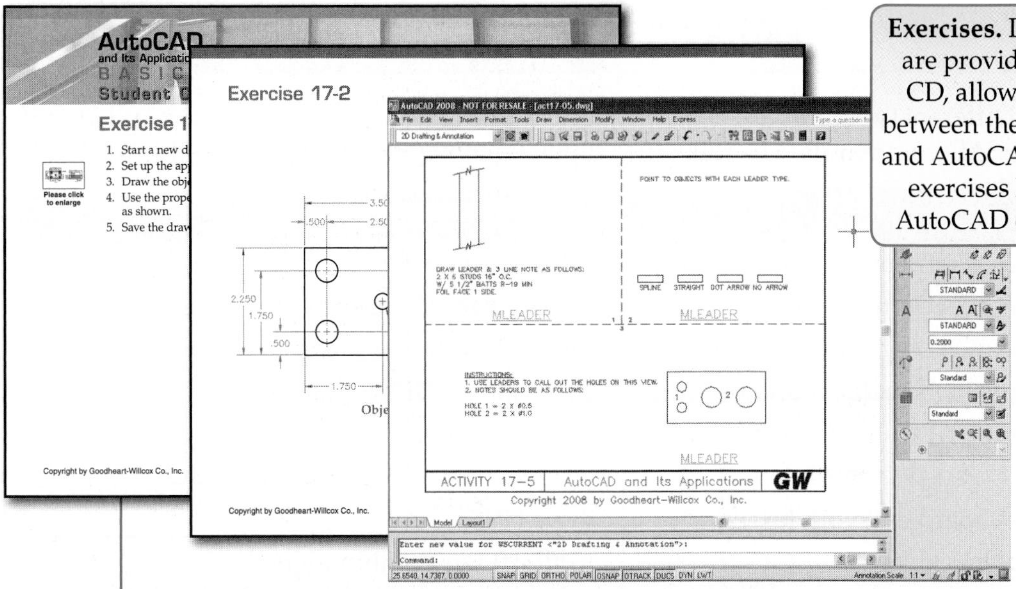

Features of the Student CD

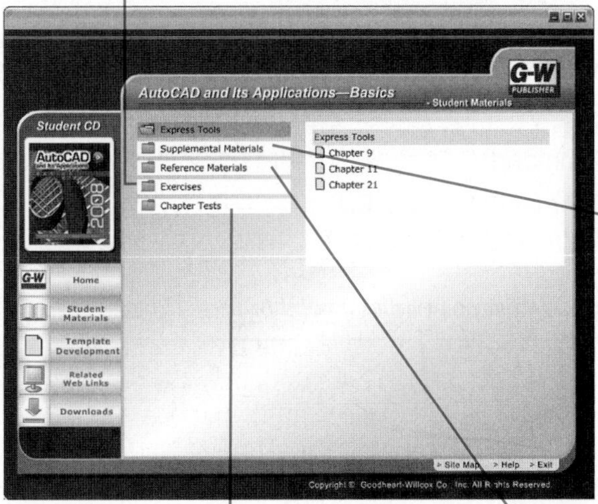

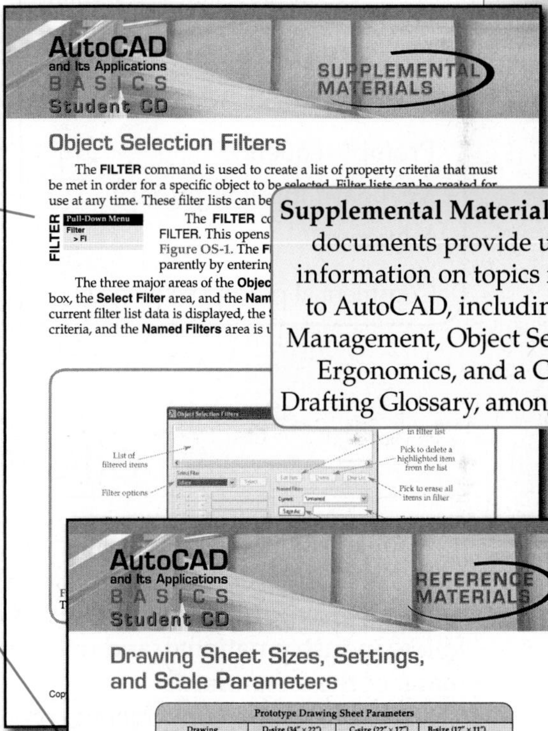

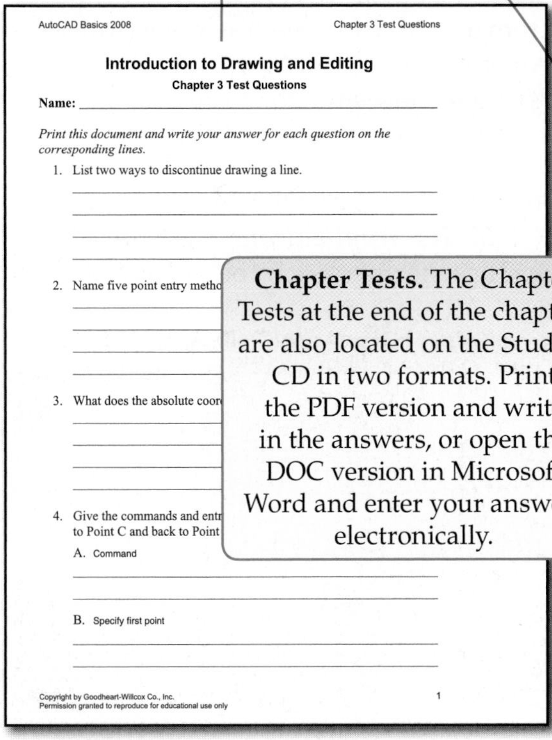

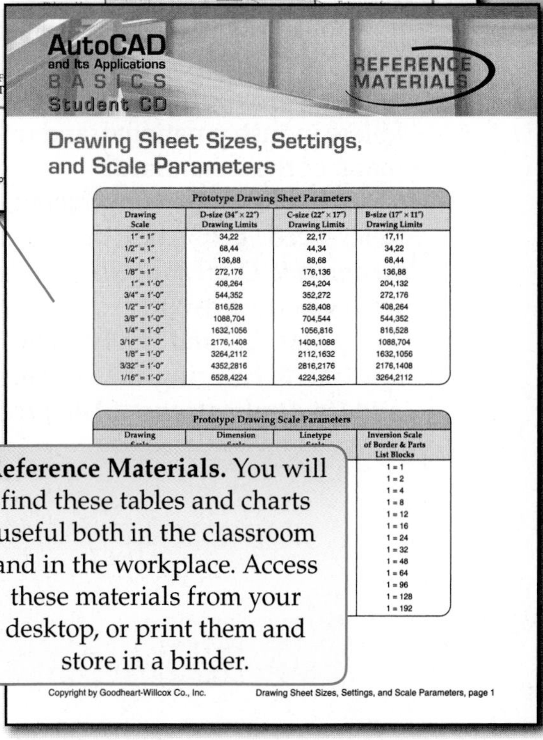

Fonts Used in This Textbook

Different typefaces are used throughout this textbook to define terms and identify AutoCAD commands. The following typeface conventions are used in this textbook:

Text Element	Example
AutoCAD commands	**LINE** command
AutoCAD pulldown menus	**Draw > Arc> 3 Points**
AutoCAD system variables	**FILEDIA** system variable
AutoCAD toolbars and buttons	**Edit** toolbar, **Offset** button
AutoCAD dialog boxes	**Insert Table** dialog box
Keyboard entry (in text)	Type LINE
Keyboard keys	[Ctrl]+[1] key combination
File names, folders, and paths	C:\Program Files\AutoCAD 2008\my drawing.dwg
Microsoft Windows features	Start menu, Programs folder
Prompt sequence	Command:
Keyboard input at prompt sequence	Command: **L** *or* **LINE**↵
Comment at prompt sequence	Specify first point: *(pick a point or press* [Enter]*)*

Other Text References

For additional information, standards from organizations such as ANSI (American National Standards Institute) and ASME (American Society of Mechanical Engineers) are referenced throughout the textbook. Use these standards to create drawings that follow industry, national, and international practices. The Student CD includes a list of many of these standards.

Also for your convenience, other Goodheart-Willcox textbooks are referenced. Referenced textbooks include *AutoCAD and Its Applications—Advanced* and *Geometric Dimensioning and Tolerancing*. These textbooks can be ordered directly from Goodheart-Willcox.

AutoCAD and Its Applications—Basics covers basic AutoCAD applications. For a textbook covering the advanced AutoCAD applications, please refer to *AutoCAD and Its Applications—Advanced*.

Contents in Brief

About the Authors

Terence M. Shumaker is Faculty Emeritus, the former Chairperson of the Drafting Technology Department, and former Director of the Autodesk Premier Training Center at Clackamas Community College. Terence taught at the community college level for over 25 years. He has professional experience in surveying, civil drafting, industrial piping, and technical illustration. He is the author of Goodheart-Willcox's *Process Pipe Drafting* and coauthor of the *AutoCAD and Its Applications* series.

David A. Madsen is Faculty Emeritus and former Chairperson of Drafting Technology at the Autodesk Premier Training Center at Clackamas Community College in Oregon City Oregon. David was a member of the Board of Directors and was awarded Director Emeritus of the American Design and Drafting Association. His education includes a Bachelor of Science degree in Technology Education and a Master of Education in Vocational Administration. During his teaching career, David was an instructor and a department chair at Clackamas Community College for nearly thirty years. In addition to community college teaching experience, David was a Drafting Technology instructor at Centennial High School in Gresham, Oregon. David also has extensive experience in mechanical drafting, architectural design and drafting, and construction practices. He is the author of several Goodheart-Willcox drafting and design textbooks, including *Geometric Dimensioning and Tolerancing*, and coauthor of the *AutoCAD and Its Applications* series, *Architectural Drafting Using AutoCAD*, and *Architectural Desktop and Its Applications*.

David P. Madsen holds a Master of Science degree in Educational Policy, Foundations, and Administrative Studies with a specialization in Postsecondary, Adult, and Continuing Education; a Bachelor of Science degree in Technology Education; and an Associate of Science degree in General Studies and Drafting Technology. Dave has been involved in providing Drafting and Computer-Aided Design and Drafting instruction to adult learners since 1999. Dave has extensive and varied experience in the drafting, design, and engineering fields. He has worked in the drafting industry for over ten years and has created everything from mechanical and electronic to architectural and civil drawings.

Acknowledgments

Special thanks from Terence Shumaker to contributing author Craig Black for his expert reviews, technical assistance, and contribution of new material for several chapters in this book. Craig is manager of the Autodesk Premier Training Center at Fox Valley Technical College in Appleton, Wisconsin.

Technical Assistance and Contribution of Materials

Margo Bilson of Willamette Industries, Inc.
Fitzgerald, Hagan, & Hackathorn
Bruce L. Wilcox, Johnson and Wales University School of Technology

Contribution of Photographs or Other Technical Information

Arthur Baker
Autodesk
CADalyst magazine
CADENCE magazine
Chris Lindner
EPCM Services, Ltd.
Harris Group, Inc.

International Source for Ergonomics
Jim Webster
Kunz Associates
Myonetics, Inc.
Norwest Engineering
Schuchart & Associates, Inc.
Willamette Industries, Inc.

Contents

Introduction to AutoCAD

Basic Drawing and Printing

Creating Text and Tables

Editing Drawings

Polylines, Multilines, and Splines

Dimensioning and Tolerancing

Additional AutoCAD Applications

Using Layouts

Student CD Content

Using the Student CD

Student Materials

Textbook Exercises
Express Tools
Chapter Tests
Supplemental Materials
Reference Materials

Template Development

Chapter-Related Development Tasks
Industry-Standard Templates

Download Student AutoCAD

Related Web Links

CHAPTER 1

Introduction to AutoCAD Features

Learning Objectives

After completing this chapter, you will be able to do the following:

✓ Describe the methods and procedures used in computer-aided drafting.
✓ Explain the value of planning your work and system management.
✓ Load AutoCAD from the Windows desktop.
✓ Describe the AutoCAD screen layout and user interface.
✓ Describe the function of dialog boxes.
✓ Identify the function of palettes.
✓ Use control keys and function keys.
✓ Describe various methods of entering commands in AutoCAD.
✓ Use the features found in the **AutoCAD Help** window.

The computer and software are the principal components of the present-day design and drafting workstation. These tools make up a system referred to as *CAD*—computer-aided design or computer-aided drafting, or *CADD*—computer-aided design and drafting. Drafters, designers, and engineers use CAD to develop designs and drawings and to plot them on paper or film. Additionally, drawings and designs can be displayed as three-dimensional (3D) models and animations or used in analysis and testing.

CAD: Computer-aided design or computer-aided drafting.

CADD: Computer-aided design and drafting.

CAD has surpassed the use of manual drafting techniques because of the increase in speed, power, accuracy, and flexibility. However, designing with computers is not totally without its attendant problems and trade-offs. Although the uses of CAD designs are limited only by the imagination, it should be remembered that computer hardware is sensitive to the slightest electrical impulses and the human body is sensitive to the repetitive motions required when using this modern method.

The Tools of AutoCAD

Drawings and models are constructed in AutoCAD using XYZ coordinates. The *Cartesian (rectangular) coordinate system*, which is based on selecting distances from three intersecting axes, is used most often. AutoCAD tools are available for drawing objects of any size or shape. Objects can be given colors, patterns, and textures. Drawings can be annotated with text and described with a variety of dimensioning techniques. AutoCAD also provides you with the tools to create *isometric drawings* and powerful 3D solid and surface models.

Establishing an AutoCAD Drawing Method

All aspects of the project must be considered when developing a drawing plan. Careful use of the CAD system is required for the planning and drawing process. Therefore, it is important to be familiar with the AutoCAD tools and to know how they work and when they are best suited for a specific job. There is no substitute for knowing the tools of AutoCAD, beginning with the Cartesian coordinate system.

Learning the XYZ Coordinate System

The XYZ coordinate system provides a method for constructing an AutoCAD drawing. The locations of points are described with XYZ coordinate values. These values are called *rectangular coordinates* and locate any point in 3D space. XY coordinates locate any point on a flat plane, such as a sheet of paper. The *origin* of the coordinate system is where the axes meet. See **Figure 1-1**. A distance measured horizontally from the origin is an X value. A distance measured vertically from the origin is a Y value.

Rectangular coordinates can also be measured in three-dimensional space. The third dimension rises up from the surface of the paper and is given a Z value. When describing coordinate locations, the X value is first, the Y value is second, and the Z value is third. Each value is separated by a comma. For example, the coordinate location of 3,1,6 represents three units from the origin in the X direction, one unit from the origin in the Y direction, and six units from the origin in the Z direction. A detailed explanation of rectangular coordinates is provided in Chapter 3.

AutoCAD Applications

Using AutoCAD software and this textbook, you will learn how to construct, lay out, dimension, and annotate two-dimensional (2D) drawings. If you want to expand your study into the topics of three-dimensional (3D) modeling, 3D rendering, and customization, *AutoCAD and Its Applications—Advanced* can provide you with detailed instruction. Your studies can allow you to create a wide variety of drawings, designs, and 3D models in any of the drafting, design, and engineering disciplines.

Figure 1-1.
A 3D model shown as an exploded assembly. (Thomas Short, Anthony Dudek)

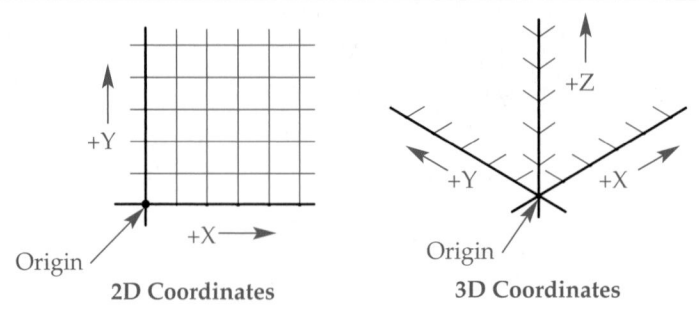

2D Coordinates   **3D Coordinates**

Figure 1-2.
An exploded
assembly. (Autodesk,
Inc.)

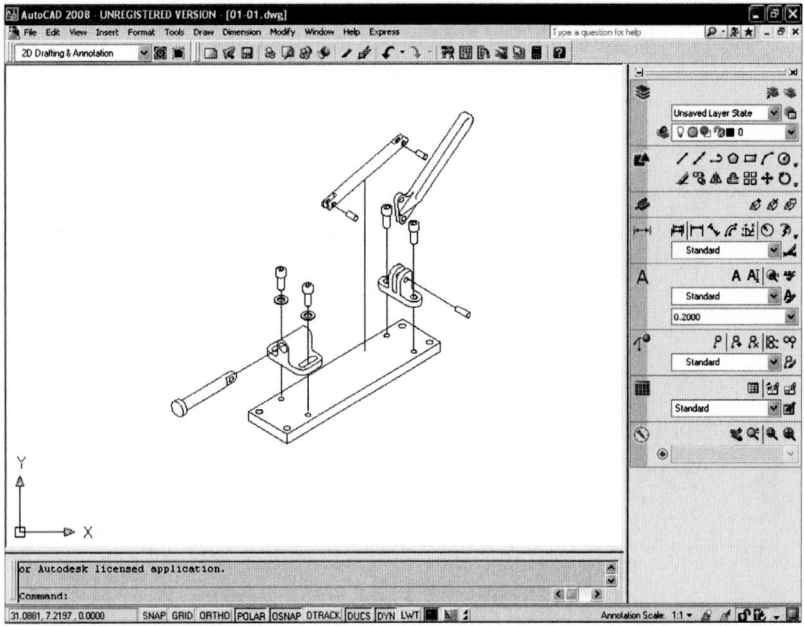

AutoCAD drawings can have hundreds of properties, such as layers, which contain different kinds of object information. Objects can also be shown as 2D, 3D, or exploded assemblies. See Figure 1-2. In addition, objects in the drawing can be given "intelligence" in the form of *attributes*. These attributes are various kinds of data that turn a drawing into a graphical database. For example, a door in a drawing may have attributes that define the type of wood, door manufacturer, and price. You can then ask questions of your drawing and receive a variety of information.

attributes: Text items that may be displayed in the drawing that are assigned to a specific object.

Using AutoCAD, you have the ability to construct 3D models that appear as wireframes or have surface colors and textures. The creation of solid models having physical properties, such as mass and density, that can be used for analysis is also possible with AutoCAD. The display in Figure 1-3 is an example of a solid model created in AutoCAD. You can view 3D drawings and models in several ways. These models can also be colored and shaded, or *rendered*, to appear in a realistic format.

A powerful application of CAD software and 3D models is animation. The simplest form of animation is to rotate the model dynamically in order to view it from any

rendered: Displayed in a realistic format with coloring and material textures and lighting.

Figure 1-3.
A welding fixture model. Models can be displayed in many formats, including the wireframe and rendered formats shown here. (Autodesk, Inc.)

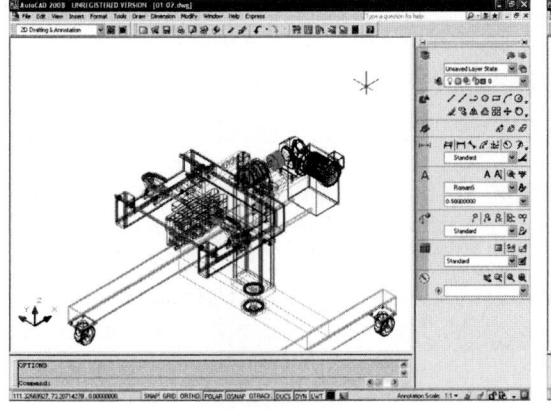

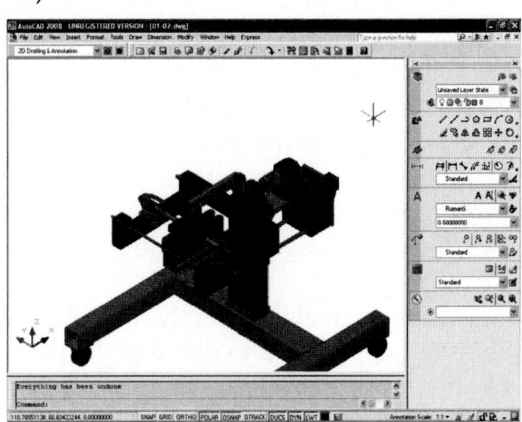

Wireframe   Rendering

Figure 1-4.
A model can be rotated, zoomed in and out, and viewed from any location in 3D space.

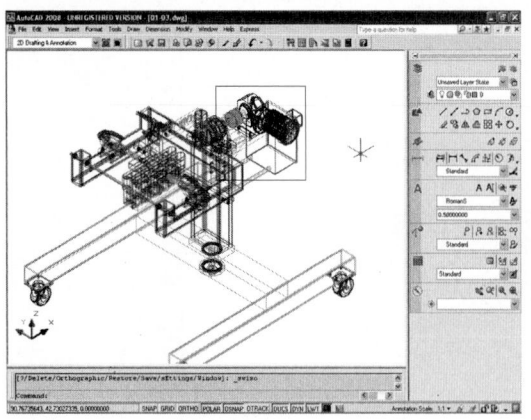

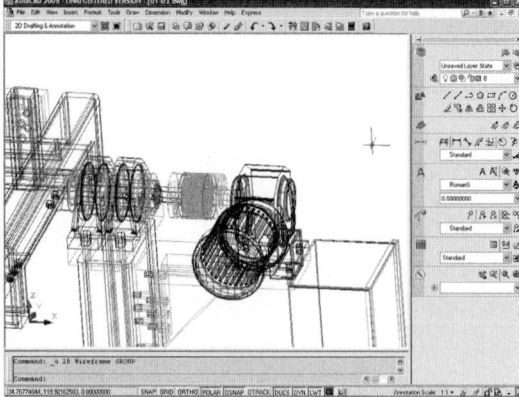

Initial Display   Highlighted Area Rotated and Zoomed In

direction. See **Figure 1-4.** Drawings and models can also be animated so the model appears to move, rotate, and even explode into its individual components. An extremely useful form of animation is called a *walkthrough*. Using the **WALK** and **FLY** commands, you "walk" a path through or around a model and "fly" above it. These concepts are described in *AutoCAD and Its Applications—Advanced*. The logical next step in viewing the model is to actually be inside it and have the ability to manipulate and change the objects in it. This is called *virtual reality*, and it is achieved through the use of 3D models and highly specialized software and hardware.

walkthrough: A simulation that follows a path through or around a model.

virtual reality: A simulation that responds to the viewer's physical movements.

Planning Your Work

As you begin your CAD training, plan your drawing sessions thoroughly to organize your thoughts. Sketch the problem or design, noting the sizes and locations of features. List the drawing commands needed in the order they are to be used. Schedule a regular time to use the computer and adhere to that time. Follow the standards your school or firm has set. These might include specific drawing names, project planning sheets, project logs, drawing layout procedures, special title blocks, and a location for drawing storage. Everyone using the computers in your school or company must follow the standards and procedures. Confusion may result if your drawings do not have the proper name, are stored in the wrong place, or have the wrong title block.

You should develop methods of managing your work. This is critical to computer drafting and is described throughout this textbook. Keep the following points in mind as you begin your AutoCAD training:

✓ Plan your work and organize your thoughts.
✓ Learn and use your classroom or office standards.
✓ Save your work often.

If you remember to follow these three points, your grasp of the tools and methods of CAD will be easier. In addition, your experiences with the software will be more enjoyable.

When you feel the need to dive blindly into a drawing or project, restrain yourself. Take the time needed to develop the project goals. Then proceed with the confidence of knowing where you are heading.

During your early stages of AutoCAD training, write down all the instructions needed to construct your drawing, especially for your first few assignments. This means documenting every command and every coordinate point (dimension) needed. Develop a planning sheet for your drawings. Following these suggestions can make your time with AutoCAD more productive and enjoyable.

Planning a Drawing

Drawing planning involves looking at the entire process or project in which you are involved. A plan determines how a project will be approached. It includes the drawings to be created, the title and numbering conventions, the information to be presented, and the types of symbols needed to show the information.

More specifically, drawing planning applies to how you create and manage a drawing or set of drawings. This includes which view or feature you draw first and the coordinates and AutoCAD commands you use to draw it. Drafters who begin constructing a drawing from the seat of their pants—creating symbols and naming objects, shapes, and views as they go—do not possess a good drawing plan. Those who plan, use consistent techniques, and adhere to school or company and industry standards are developing good drawing habits.

Aids are provided throughout this textbook to help you develop good drawing habits. The importance of planning cannot be emphasized enough. There is no substitute.

Using Drawing Standards

Standards are guidelines for operating procedures, drawing techniques, and record keeping. Most drafting fields, schools, and companies have established standards. It is important that standards exist and are used by all CAD personnel. Drawing standards may include the following items:

standards: Guidelines containing procedures and techniques.

- Methods of file storage (location and name)
- File naming conventions
- File backup methods and times
- Drawing templates with predefined settings
- Layouts
- Borders and title blocks
- Drawing symbols
- Dimensioning styles and techniques
- Text styles
- Table styles
- Layer settings
- Plot styles

Your standards may vary in content, but the most important aspect of standards is that they are used. When standards are used, your drawings are consistent, you become more productive, and the classroom or office functions more efficiently.

Saving Your Work

Develop the habit of saving your work regularly—at least every ten to fifteen minutes. The automatic save tool can be set to automatically save your drawings at predetermined intervals. Automatic save is covered in detail in Chapter 2. Drawings may be lost due to a software error, hardware malfunction, power failure, or your own mistakes. This is not common, but you should still be prepared for such an event.

Using Drawing Plan Sheets

A good work plan can save drawing time. Planning should include sketches. A rough preliminary sketch and a drawing plan can help by:

- Determining the drawing layout.
- Setting the overall size of the drawing by laying out the views and required free space.
- Confirming the drawing units, based on the dimensions provided.
- Predetermining the point entry system and locating the points.
- Establishing drawing settings.
- Presetting some of the drawing variables, such as layers, linetypes, and line widths.
- Establishing how and when various activities are to be performed.
- Determining the best use of AutoCAD, resulting in an even workload.
- Providing maximum use of equipment.

Planning Checklist

In the early stages of your AutoCAD training, it is best to plan your drawing projects carefully. There is a tendency to want your applications to happen immediately or to be automatic, but if you hurry and do little or no planning, you can become increasingly frustrated. Therefore, as you begin each new project, step through the following planning checklist so the execution of your project goes smoothly:

- ✓ Analyze the problem.
- ✓ Study all engineering sketches.
- ✓ Locate all available resources and list for future use.
- ✓ Determine the applicable standards for the project.
- ✓ Sketch the problem.
- ✓ Decide on the number and kinds of views required.
- ✓ Determine the final plotted scale of the drawing and of all views.
- ✓ Determine the drawing sequence, such as lines, features, dimensions, and notes.
- ✓ List the AutoCAD commands to be used.
- ✓ Follow the standards and refer to resources as you work.

PROFESSIONAL TIP

AutoCAD is designed so you can construct drawings and models using the actual dimensions of the object. *Always draw in full scale.* The proper text and dimension size is set using scale factors. This is covered in detail in later chapters. The final scale of the drawing should be planned early and displayed on the plot.

Working Procedures Checklist

As you begin learning AutoCAD, you will realize that several skills are required to become a proficient CAD user. The following checklist provides you with some hints to help you become comfortable with AutoCAD. These hints will also allow you to work quickly and efficiently. The following actions are described in detail in later chapters:

- ✓ Plan all work with pencil and paper before using the computer.
- ✓ Constantly check object and drawing settings, such as layers, styles, and properties, to see which object and drawing aids are in effect.
- ✓ Read the prompts displayed by AutoCAD. Constantly check for the correct commands, instructions, or keyboard entry of data.

- ✓ Right-click to access shortcut menus; review available options.
- ✓ Think ahead. Know your next move.
- ✓ Learn new commands every day. Do not rely on just a few that seem to work. Find commands that can speed your work and do it more efficiently.
- ✓ Save your work every ten to fifteen minutes, in case a power failure or system crash deletes the drawing held in computer memory.
- ✓ If you are stumped, learn to use available resources, such as this textbook, to help solve problems and answer questions. You should also become familiar with the AutoCAD help system.

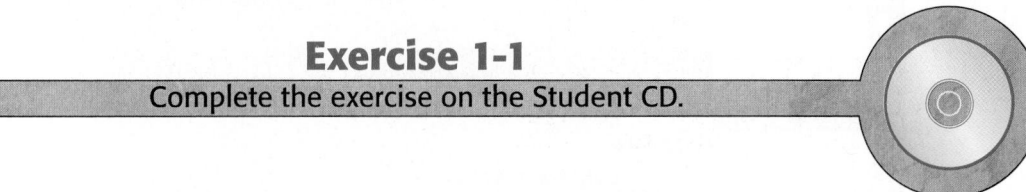

Exercise 1-1
Complete the exercise on the Student CD.

Starting AutoCAD

AutoCAD 2008 is designed to operate with Windows Vista, Windows XP Professional, Windows XP Home, and Windows 2000 Professional. If you see illustrations in this textbook that appear slightly different from your screen, do not be concerned, as the AutoCAD feature is the same.

When AutoCAD is first installed, Windows creates a program icon, which is displayed on the desktop and in the list of programs available from the Start menu. An *icon* is a small graphic representing an application, accessory, file, or command.

icon: Small graphic representing an application or file.

AutoCAD can be started using several different techniques. One of the quickest ways to start AutoCAD is to double-click on the AutoCAD 2008 icon on the Windows desktop. See Figure 1-5.

A second method for starting AutoCAD is to pick the Start button at the lower-left corner of the Windows desktop. Move the cursor to Programs and hold it there or pick. Pick Autodesk, AutoCAD 2008, and AutoCAD 2008 to start the program. See Figure 1-6.

Figure 1-5.
Double-click the AutoCAD 2008 icon on the Windows desktop to start AutoCAD.

Double-click to start AutoCAD

Figure 1-6.
Pick AutoCAD 2008 in the AutoCAD 2008 menu to load the program.

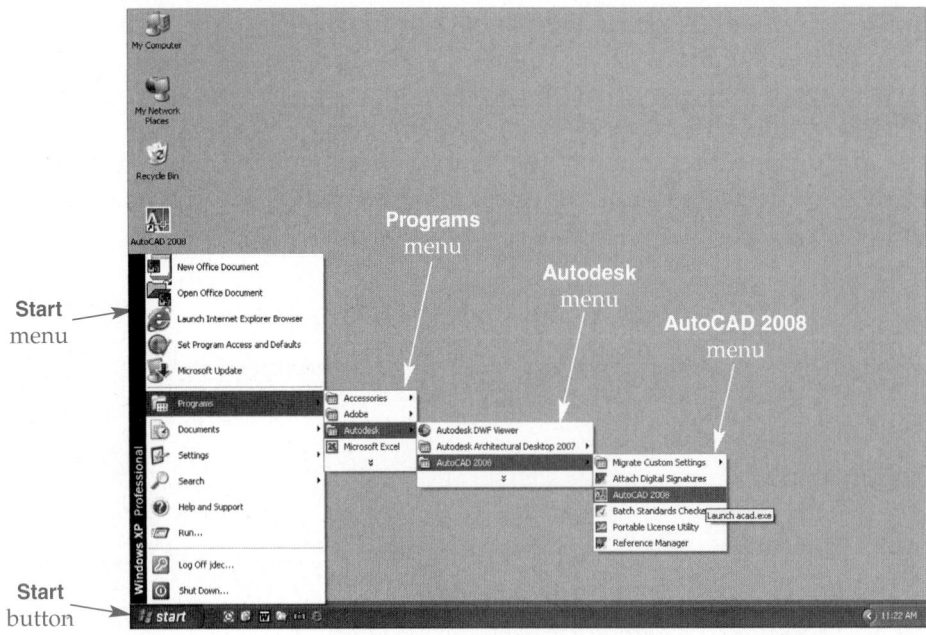

The AutoCAD Interface

Interface, also known as *user interface,* is a term describing the tools and techniques used to provide and receive information to and from a computer application. Interface items include devices to input data, such as the keyboard and mouse, and devices to receive information, such as the monitor. The interface also includes on-screen features, commonly referred to as the *graphical user interface (GUI).* AutoCAD uses the familiar Windows-style interface with buttons, pull-down menus, and dialog boxes.

Figure 1-7 displays the AutoCAD window shown when you first launch AutoCAD. Each of the interface items shown in **Figure 1-7** and others are described in this chapter and throughout this textbook. Become familiar with the unique AutoCAD interface. Learning the layout, appearance, and proper use of interface items allows you to quickly master AutoCAD.

Exercise 1-2
Complete the exercise on the Student CD.

Understanding Terminology

The following terms are used throughout the textbook and will help you select AutoCAD functions. You should become familiar with them.

- **Default.** A value maintained by the computer until you change it.
- **Pick or click.** Use the mouse to select an item on the screen.
- **Button.** One of the screen toolbar or mouse buttons.
- **Key.** A key on the keyboard.
- **Function key.** One of the keys labeled [F1]–[F12] along the top of the keyboard.
- **[Enter] (↵).** The [Enter] key on the keyboard.
- **Command.** An instruction issued to the computer.
- **Option.** An aspect of a command that can be selected.

Figure 1-7.
The default AutoCAD window with the **2D Drafting & Annotation** workspace active.

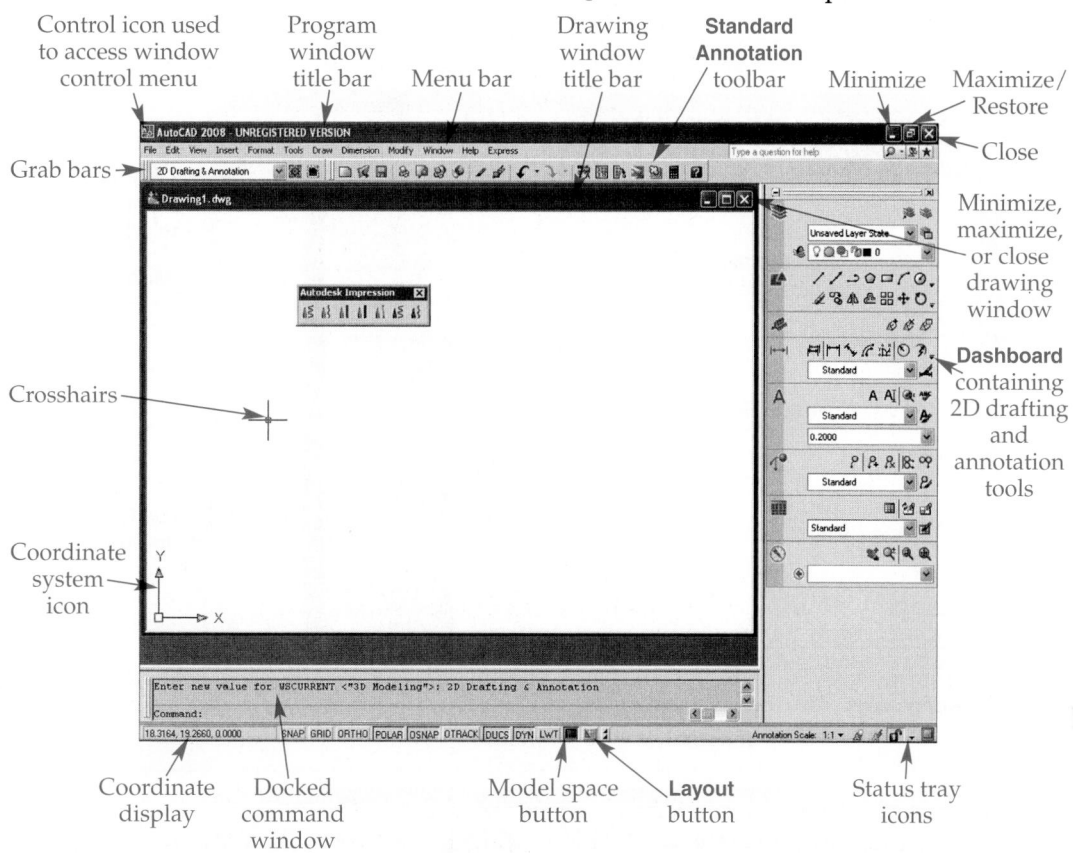

Workspaces

A *workspace* is a preset work environment that displays interface items specific to your drafting requirements and use of AutoCAD. For example, if you only create 2D drawings, you can establish a workspace that only displays 2D drawing tools; or if you do not prefer to use certain interface items, such as toolbars, you can develop a workspace that does not display toolbars. *Toolbars* are interface items containing buttons used to start commands. Interface items and AutoCAD tools and options that are not shown in a workspace are still available and can be added to the workspace at any time.

workspace: Preset work environment containing specific interface items.

toolbars: Interface items containing buttons or drop-down lists.

Three workspaces are available by default: **2D Drafting & Annotation**, **AutoCAD Classic**, and **3D modeling**. The **2D Drafting & Annotation** workspace is displayed when you first launch AutoCAD. See **Figure 1-7.** The **2D Drafting & Annotation** workspace contains a large drawing area, two toolbars above the drawing area, the command line below the drawing area, and the **Dashboard** displaying only specific 2D drafting and annotation tools. The *command line* is an interface area where commands and their subsequent options may be entered by using the keyboard. The **AutoCAD Classic** workspace, shown in **Figure 1-8,** displays a large drawing area, toolbars above, to the left, and to the right of the drawing area, and the command line below the drawing area. The **Tool Palettes** window is also shown. The **AutoCAD Classic** workspace contains interface items, tools, and options that can be used for a variety of 2D and 3D drawing applications. The **3D Modeling** workspace, also shown in **Figure 1-8,** contains a large drawing area, three toolbars above the drawing area, and the command line below the drawing area. The **Tool Palettes** window and the **Dashboard** displaying only specific 3D modeling tools are also provided.

NEW FEATURE

command line: Area where commands and options may be typed.

Figure 1-8.
Each workspace displays different components on the AutoCAD window.

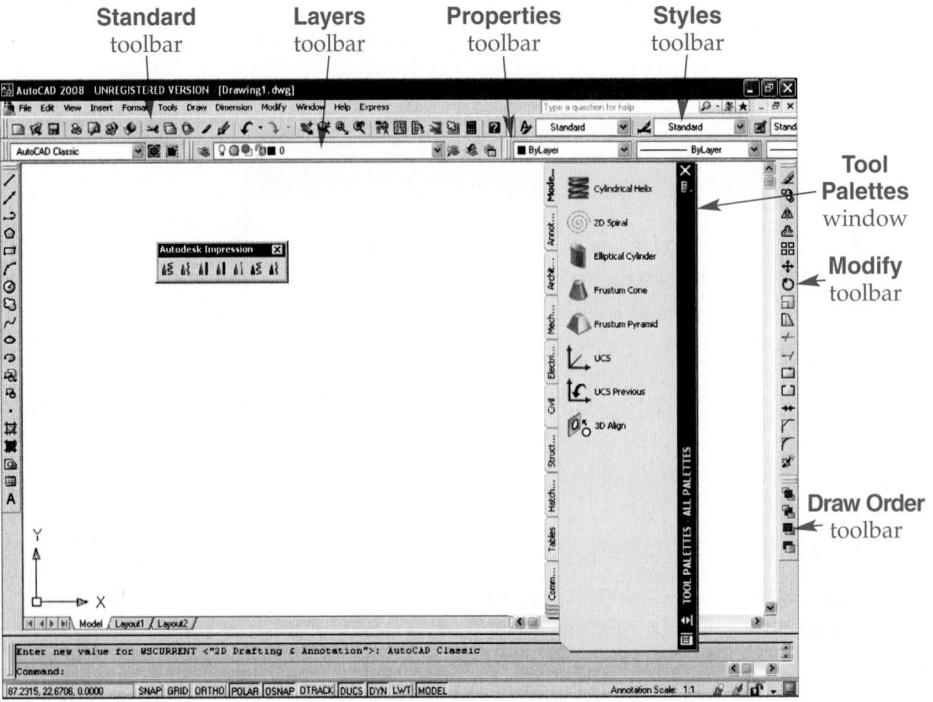

AutoCAD Classic Workspace

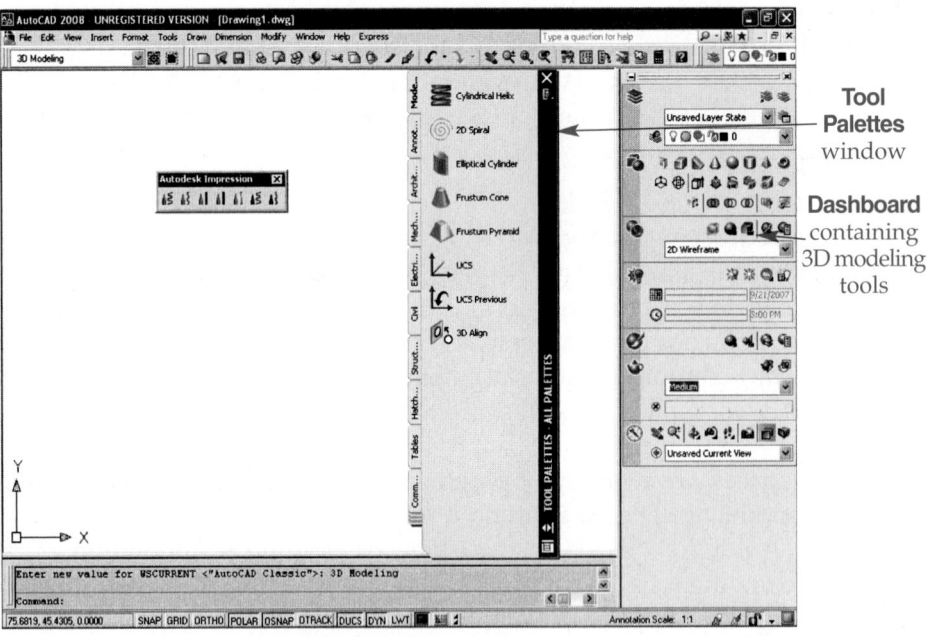

3D Modeling Workspace

WSCURRENT

Type
WSCURRENT
Pull-Down Menu
Tools
> Workspaces

To change workspaces, type WSCURRENT, or select the workspace you want to enter from the **Tools** > **Workspaces** pull-down menu or from the drop-down list located in the **Workspaces** toolbar. See Figure 1-9. *AutoCAD and Its Applications—Advanced* demonstrates how to create custom workspaces and adjust workspace settings.

Figure 1-9.
Control the workspace settings with the **Workspaces** toolbar.

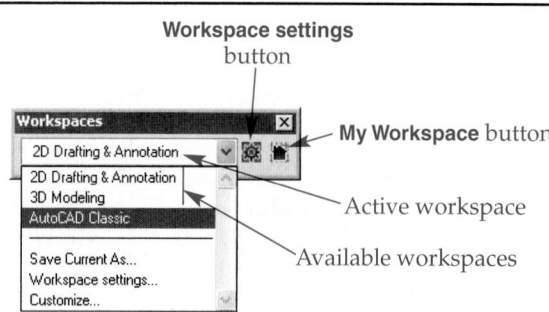

Workspace settings button

My Workspace button

Active workspace

Available workspaces

NOTE

The proportional size of the AutoCAD window features may vary depending on the display resolution of your computer system.

Crosshairs

The AutoCAD crosshairs is your primary means of pointing to objects or locations within a drawing. The crosshairs changes to the familiar Windows cursor when you move the crosshairs outside of the drawing area or over an interface item, such as a toolbar.

Controlling AutoCAD Windows

The AutoCAD program and drawing windows are similar to other windows within the Windows operating system. Minimizing, maximizing, and closing the program window or individual drawing windows is done by picking the small control icon in the upper-left corner, which displays a standard window control menu, or picking one of the appropriate icons in the upper-right corner. Window sizing operations are done as with any other window. **Figure 1-10** shows a summary for standard window control functions available for drawing windows.

Floating and docking interface items

Several AutoCAD interface items, including the program and drawing windows, can float or can be docked. *Floating* means the item can be freely resized or moved about the screen into a new position. Floating features are contained within a standard Windows border and display a title bar at the top or side, depending on the item. When you run AutoCAD for the first time, the AutoCAD program window is displayed in a floating position on the desktop. A smaller window inside the AutoCAD window displays the drawing area for the currently open drawing file. Floating windows are moved and adjusted for size in the same manner as any other window. However, the drawing windows can only be adjusted and positioned within the AutoCAD window.

Docking a floating item means the feature is moved to one of the edges of the AutoCAD window (top, bottom, left, or right) until it snaps into position. Once docked, the feature loses its title bar and gains a grab bar. The term *grab bar* refers to the two thin bars at the top or left edge of a docked feature.

Locking interface items

AutoCAD interface items, including the program and drawing windows, can be moved around to suit your work environment. To prevent items from being accidentally moved, each feature can be locked in either a floating or docked state. To access the locking options, select **Window** > **Lock Location** from the pull-down menu, pick the **Toolbar/Window Positions** icon from the system tray, or right-click over the item and select **Lock Location** from the shortcut menu. The **Lock Location** menu options are displayed in **Figure 1-11**.

floating: Toolbars or palettes that can be freely resized or moved about the screen.

docking: Moving a toolbar or palette to an edge of the AutoCAD window until it snaps into position.

grab bar: Two thin bars at the top or left edge of a docked feature.

Figure 1-10.
Drawing window control options.

Window Control Buttons		
Button	**Function**	**Description**
 ▬	Minimize	Displays window as a button along bottom of drawing window space in AutoCAD window.
 ⟳	Restore	Returns window to floating state, at previous size and position, displays title bar.
 ☐	Maximize	Displays window at largest possible size, hides title bar.
 ✕	Close	Closes drawing, provides option to save drawing if any changes remain unsaved.
 ⊞	Display window control menu	Displays pull-down menu with window control options.

Resizing Controls		
Cursor	**Function**	**Usage**
 ↕	Size window vertically	Press and hold pick button while pointing at top or bottom border of window, then move mouse.
↔	Size window horizontally	Press and hold pick button while pointing at left or right border of window, then move mouse.
 ⤢	Size window diagonally	Press and hold pick button while pointing at any corner on border of window, then move mouse.
 ⬀	Move window	Press and hold pick button while pointing at title bar of window, then move mouse.

Figure 1-11.
Toolbars and windows can be locked in position.

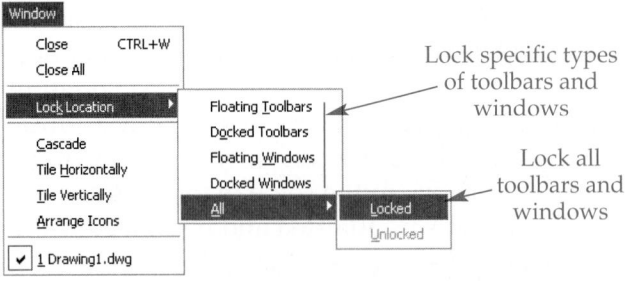

Select an option to lock the interface items that reside in that group as floating or docked. To unlock a group, select the option again. To quickly lock or unlock all of the interface items, select **Locked** or **Unlocked** from the **All** cascading menu. A locked feature can be moved without unlocking it by holding down the [Ctrl] key while moving the feature.

Menu Bar

The AutoCAD menu bar appears just below the title bar and displays menu names. As with standard Windows menus, use the cursor to point at a menu name and press the pick button to display a pull-down menu. A *pull-down menu* is an interface object under the menu bar that lists commands or options. The default menu bar has twelve pull-down menus: **File**, **Edit**, **View**, **Insert**, **Format**, **Tools**, **Draw**, **Dimension**, **Modify**, **Window**, **Help**, and **Express**.

pull-down menu: List of related commands or options available by picking the menu bar.

NOTE

The **Express** pull-down menu includes additional tools for improved functionality and productivity during your drawing processes. Express Tools are described on the Student CD and referenced where appropriate throughout this textbook.

Menu items and commands are easily selected by picking a menu item with your mouse. Some commands in the pull-down menu have a small arrow to the right. When one of these items is selected, a *cascading menu* appears, providing additional options. Some of the menu selections are followed by an ellipsis (…). If you pick one of these items, a dialog box is displayed.

cascading menu: Contains options related to chosen pull-down menu item.

It is also possible to use the keyboard to access pull-down menu items by typing shortcuts. These shortcut keystrokes are called *menu accelerator keys*. The [Alt] key turns on the menu accelerator keys. To access any pull-down menu selection, use an [Alt]+[*key*] combination on the keyboard. For instance, the **View** pull-down menu can be accessed by first pressing the [Alt] key and then pressing the [V] key.

menu accelerator keys: Shortcut keystrokes used to access pull-down menu items.

One character of each pull-down menu title or command is underlined after you press the [Alt] key. Once a pull-down menu is displayed, a menu item can be selected using that single character key. For example, to zoom in closer to your work, press [Alt]+[V] to access the **View** pull-down menu. Then, press [Z] to select the **Zoom** command, and [I] to select the **In** option.

The **InfoCenter** also resides in the menu bar. The **InfoCenter** contains a text box where you can search for helpful information. It also includes shortcut buttons to the **Communication Center** and a **Favorites** list.

PROFESSIONAL TIP

Once a pull-down menu is displayed, you can use the up, down, right, and left arrow keys to move to different items in the menus. Press [Enter] to select a highlighted item.

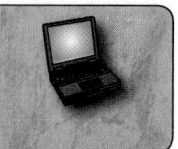

NOTE

Many individual character key and key combination shortcuts are available for Windows and Windows-based applications. Refer to the *Reference Materials* on the Student CD for a complete list of keyboard shortcuts.

Exercise 1-3

Complete the exercise on the Student CD.

Toolbars

tool buttons: Interface items used to start commands.

drop-down lists: Lists containing various options.

Toolbars contain *tool buttons*, which are interface items used to start commands. In some cases, toolbars contain other items, such as *drop-down lists*, which are lists containing settings that can be changed. Toolbars group commands and options into similar drawing tasks. For example, the **Workspaces** toolbar contains tools for controlling and modifying workspaces. Each button on a toolbar displays an image that indicates an AutoCAD command or command option. As you move your cursor across a toolbar button, a 3D border is displayed around the previously flat button. Holding the cursor motionless over a button for a moment displays a *tooltip*, which shows the name of the button in a small box at the cursor location. While the tooltip is visible, a brief explanation of what the button does is displayed along the status bar at the bottom-left edge of the window. Selecting a toolbar button activates the command.

tooltip: Name of a button, displayed when holding the cursor over a button.

> **NOTE**
>
> AutoCAD 2008 installs an **Autodesk Impression** toolbar, which is displayed in each default workspace. To use any of the commands from this toolbar, you must first install the Autodesk Impression software.

Toolbars can be resized, modified, hidden, floating, and docked as needed. Some toolbar buttons show a small black triangle in the lower-right corner. These buttons are called *flyouts*. Press and hold the pick button while pointing at a flyout to display a set of related buttons.

flyout: Set of related buttons displayed by picking certain toolbar buttons.

The toolbars displayed in AutoCAD by default vary according to the active workspace. Depending on the active workspace, the **Standard** toolbar or the **Standard Annotation** toolbar is located just below the menu bar and contains a series of buttons that provide access to several of AutoCAD's drawing setup and control commands. The **Workspaces** toolbar is located below the menu bar or the **Standard** toolbar, depending on the active workspace. The **Workspaces** toolbar contains a drop-down list and two buttons that are used to change workspaces, create new workspaces, and customize workspace settings.

You can display other toolbars by right-clicking on any existing toolbar and selecting the toolbar you want to display from the menu, or by using the **Customize User Interface** dialog box. *AutoCAD and Its Applications—Advanced* demonstrates how to create custom toolbars and adjust toolbar settings.

> **NOTE**
>
> Additional default toolbars are displayed when the **AutoCAD Classic** and **3D Modeling** workspaces are active.

COMMANDLINEHIDE

Type
COMMANDLINEHIDE
[Ctrl]+[9]

Pull-Down Menu
Tools
> Command Line

The Command Line

By default, the **Command Line** window is docked at the bottom of the AutoCAD window, above the status bar. It displays the Command: prompt and reflects any command entries you make. It also displays prompts that supply information or that request input. The command line displays communications to and from AutoCAD, including the steps necessary to complete a specific task, so watch for any information shown on this line.

The command line is displayed in each default AutoCAD workspace, and can float and be docked, resized, and locked. To hide it, type COMMANDLINEHIDE, select **Tools** > **Command Line** from the pull-down menu, or press [Ctrl]+[9].

The Status Bar

The status bar is divided into areas that display and control a variety of drawing aids and tools. The coordinate display field, found on the left side of the status bar, shows the XYZ crosshairs location. The buttons to the right of the coordinate display field show the current state of specific drawing control features and allow access for changing the settings of these features. Additional drawing control feature buttons and a tray with icons are located on right side of the status bar. These icons represent the presence of various drawing conditions. When a pull-down menu item is highlighted or you are pointing at a toolbar button, the status bar changes to display a brief explanation of the item. Look for this information along the left side of the status bar.

Dialog Boxes

One of the most common components of the graphical user interface is the dialog box. A *dialog box* is a box that may contain a variety of information and settings. You can set variables and select items in a dialog box using your cursor. This eliminates typing, which may save time and increase productivity.

dialog box: Part of the user interface that contains different kinds of information and settings.

Picking any pull-down selection or button displaying an ellipsis (…) activates a dialog box. An example of a dialog box is shown in **Figure 1-12**. This dialog box is displayed when you pick **Insert** > **Block...** from the pull-down menu.

Buttons in a dialog box that are followed by an ellipsis (…) display another dialog box when they are picked. You must make a selection from the second dialog box before you return to the original dialog box. A button in a dialog box with an arrow icon requires you to make a selection in the drawing area.

Some features are standard to all dialog boxes. Knowing these parts will make it much easier to work with the dialog boxes.

- **Command buttons.** When you pick a command button, something happens immediately. The most common buttons are **OK**, **Cancel**, and **Help**. See **Figure 1-12**. If a button has a dark border, it is the default. Pressing the [Enter] key accepts the default. If a button is "grayed-out," it cannot be selected.
- **Text box.** You can type a name or single line of information using the text box. Refer to the text box in **Figure 1-12**.
- **Check box.** A check box, or toggle, displays a "✓" when it is on (active). If the box is empty, the option is off. See **Figure 1-13**.

Figure 1-12.
A dialog box is displayed when you pick an item that is followed by an ellipsis. The dialog box shown here appears after you select **Insert** > **Block...** from the pull-down menu. You can type a name, number, or single line of information in a text box.

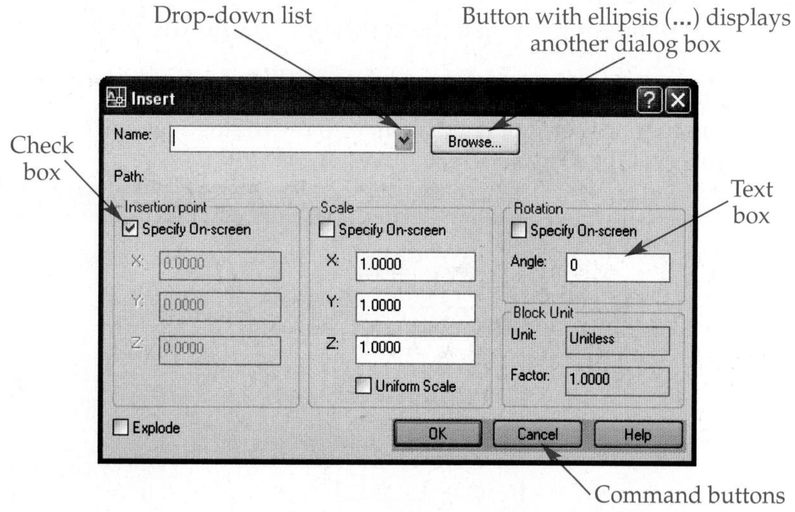

Figure 1-13.
Dialog boxes often contain radio buttons, check boxes, tabs, and other organization features.

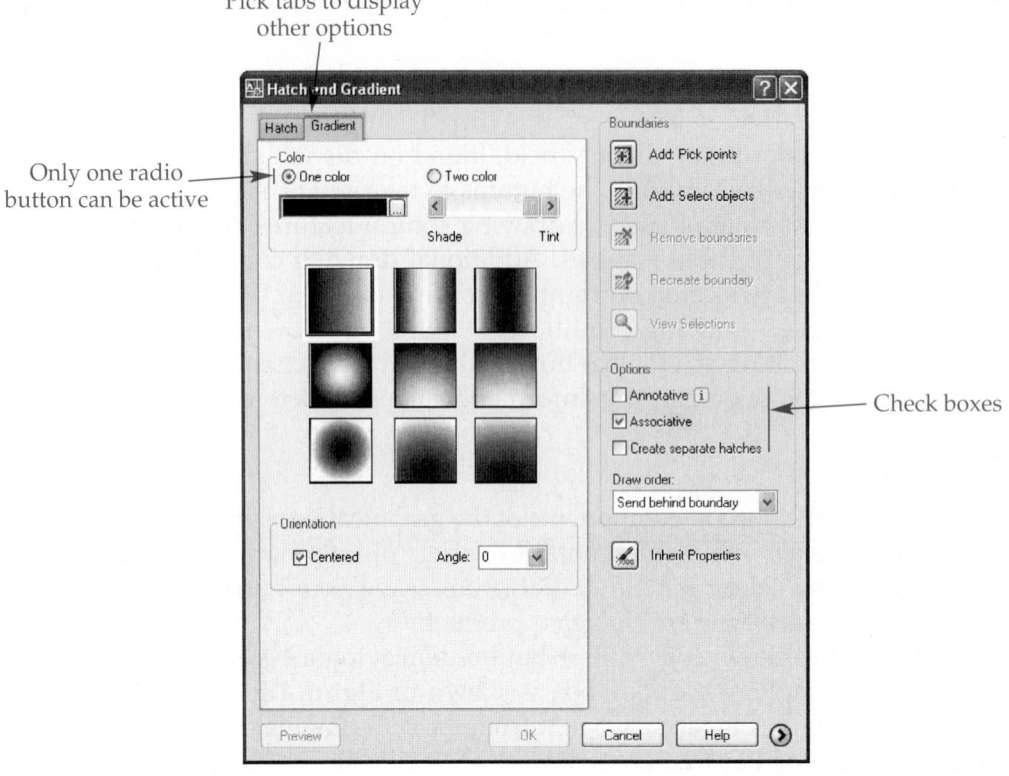

Pick tabs to display other options

Only one radio button can be active

Check boxes

- **Radio buttons.** Only one item in a group of radio buttons can be highlighted or active at one time. See **Figure 1-13.**
- **Tab.** A dialog box tab is much like an index tab used to separate sections of a note-book or the label tab on the top of a file folder. Many dialog boxes in AutoCAD contain two or more "pages," each with a tab at the top. See **Figure 1-13.**
- **List box.** A list box contains a list of items or options that you can scan through using the scroll bar (if present) or the keyboard arrow keys. Either highlight the desired item with the arrow keys and press [Enter] or select it with the mouse. See **Figure 1-14.**
- **Drop-down list box.** The drop-down list box is similar to the standard list box, except only one item is initially shown. The remaining items are hidden until you pick the drop-down arrow. When you pick the drop-down arrow, the drop-down list is displayed below the initial item. You can then pick from the expanded list or use the scroll bar to find the item you need. See **Figure 1-14.**

Figure 1-14.
A list box contains a list of items related to the dialog box. A drop-down list is displayed when you pick the drop-down arrow.

List box

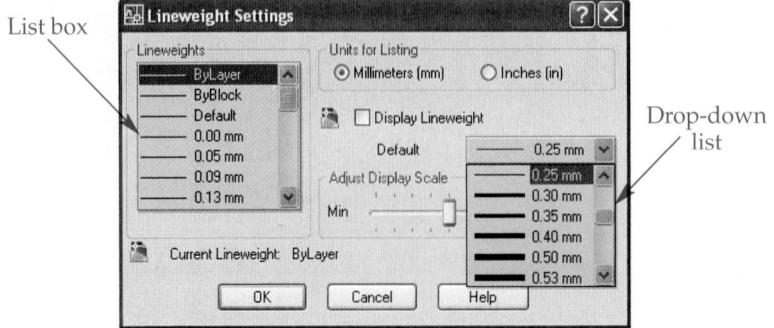

Drop-down list

Figure 1-15.
The **Select File** dialog box provides a simple means of locating files. A **Preview** box displays the selected setting or file.

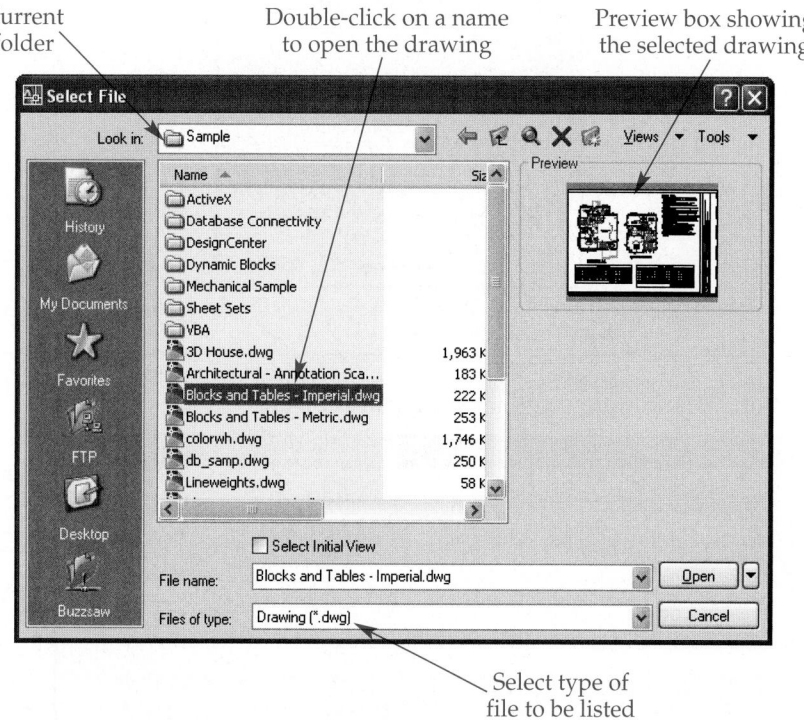

Current folder

Double-click on a name to open the drawing

Preview box showing the selected drawing

Select type of file to be listed

- **Preview box.** A preview box is an area of a dialog box that displays a "picture" of the item you select. See **Figure 1-15**.
- **Scroll bars and buttons.** Vertical scroll bars and buttons allow you to scroll up or down a list of items. Pick the up or down arrows. Horizontal scroll bars and buttons operate in the same manner. **Figure 1-16** shows the operation of a scroll bar.
- **Alerts.** Alerts may appear in the lower-left corner of the original dialog box, or as a separate alert dialog box. See **Figure 1-17**.
- **Help.** If you are unsure of any features of a dialog box, pick the question mark button in the upper-right corner of the dialog box. When the question mark appears next to your cursor, you can pick any feature in the dialog box to see a description of what that feature does. See **Figure 1-18**.
- **... (Ellipsis button).** Some dialog box features have an ellipsis button that provides access to a related dialog box.

Figure 1-16.
Use scroll bars and buttons to scroll through a listing or to view sections of a drawing.

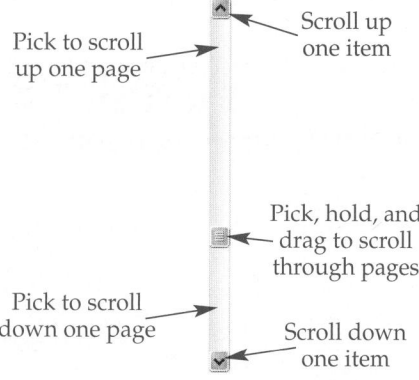

Pick to scroll up one page

Scroll up one item

Pick, hold, and drag to scroll through pages

Pick to scroll down one page

Scroll down one item

Figure 1-17.
An alert may appear as a separate dialog box.

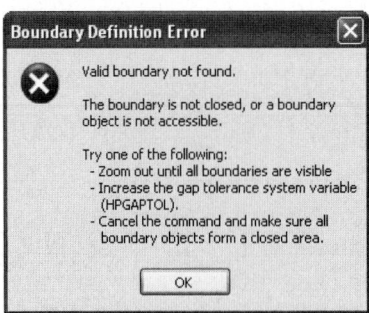

Figure 1-18.
Pick the question mark button to get help in a dialog box

Pick to access a dialog box

Pick to view information about a dialog box component

Question mark cursor appears after picking help button

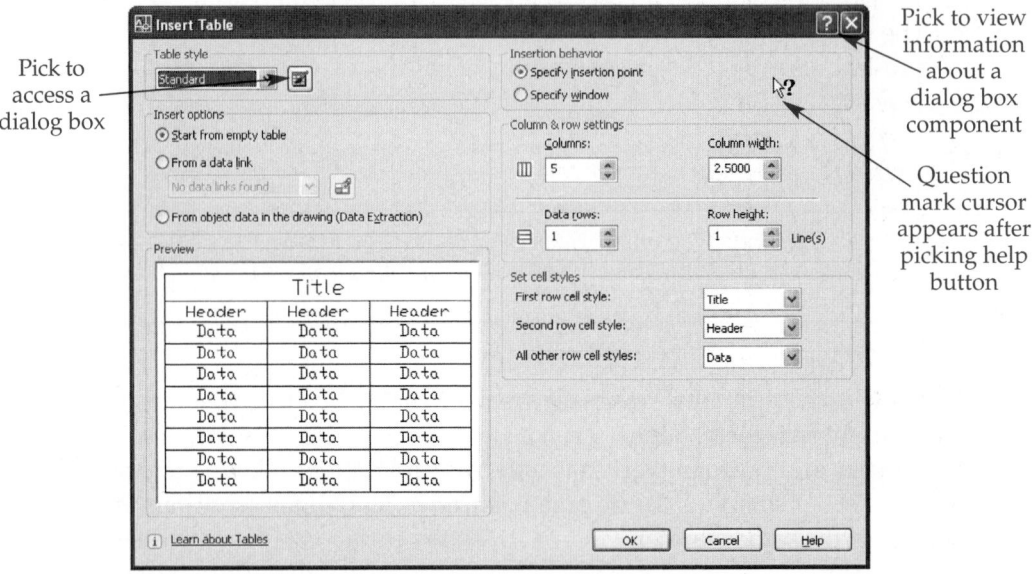

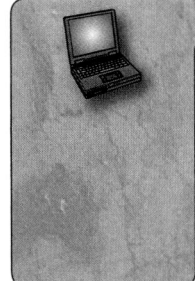

PROFESSIONAL TIP

system variable:
Setting that lets you change the way AutoCAD works.

The appearance of dialog boxes is controlled by the **FILEDIA** system variable. A *system variable* is a setting that lets you change the way AutoCAD works. System variables are remembered by AutoCAD and remain in effect until you change them again. If the **FILEDIA** system variable is set to 1 (the default), dialog boxes are displayed at the appropriate times. If **FILEDIA** is set to 0, dialog boxes do not appear. You must then type the desired information at the command line.

Exercise 1-4
Complete the exercise on the Student CD.

Palettes

Many AutoCAD features are presented in a special type of window known as a *palette*. A palette may also be referred to as a *modeless dialog box*. Palettes can look like extensive toolbars or more like dialog boxes, depending on the function of the palette. The **Dashboard** shown in **Figure 1-19** is an example of one of the many palettes available in AutoCAD. Palettes may contain tool buttons and many of the same features found in dialog boxes, such as list boxes, drop-down list boxes, and scroll bars. Some palettes are divided into *control panels*, or *panels*, separated by a line, that group commands for certain drawing tasks. Large palettes may be divided into separate "pages" or "windows" that function much like dialog box tabs.

Palettes function more like toolbars than dialog boxes because they can float; be docked, resized, or locked; and do not need to be closed in order to type commands and work within the drawing. If a palette is docked, as the **Dashboard** is in the default **2D Drafting & Annotation** workspace, double-click the grab bar to change it to the floating state. Double-click the title bar to return to the docked position. When a palette is docked, the resizing bar allows you to adjust the size to suit your needs.

The **Auto-hide** button allows the palette to minimize out of your way when the cursor is away from the window. Each palette also contains a **Properties** button, which allows you to control how the palette operates and displays within AutoCAD. The **Properties** button includes a **Transparency...** option, which allows drawing geometry behind the palette to be viewed, as shown in **Figure 1-20**.

Palettes are available from the **Tools** > **Palettes** pull-down menu, or by using palette-specific access techniques. *AutoCAD and Its Applications—Advanced* demonstrates how to create custom palettes and adjust palette settings.

PROFESSIONAL TIP

You can move palettes to the side of the AutoCAD window without docking them by holding the [Ctrl] key while positioning the palette.

Figure 1-19.
Palettes, such as the **Dashboard**, remain displayed on-screen as you work in the drawing area.

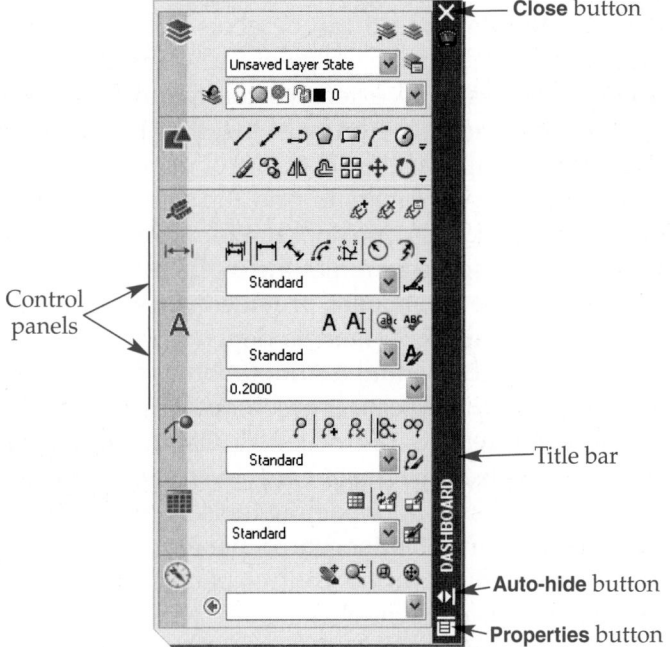

Control panels

Close button

Title bar

Auto-hide button

Properties button

Figure 1-20.
Tool palettes can be
made transparent
by picking the
Properties button in
the title bar.

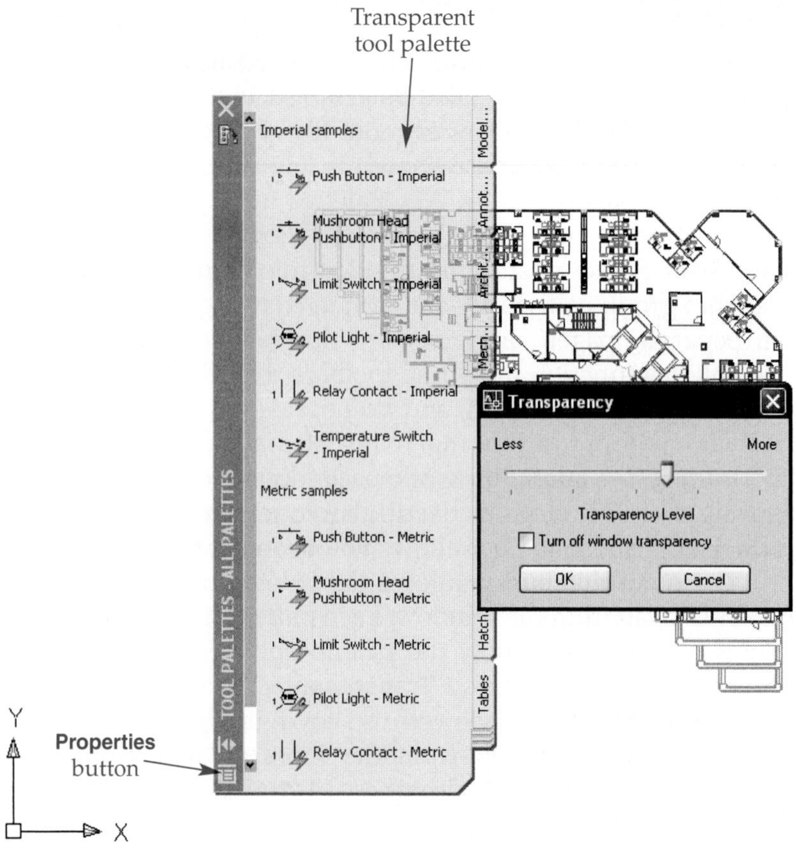

Transparent
tool palette

Properties
button

Dashboard

The **Dashboard**, shown in Figure 1-19, is used to access AutoCAD commands. The **Dashboard** is divided into control panels, separated by a line, that group tools and options for certain drawing or modeling tasks. For example, the **Text** control panel provides tools for creating, modifying, and formatting text. The same commands provided in the **Dashboard** can be accessed using the command line, toolbars, and pull-down menus. The advantage of using the **Dashboard** is that several commands, traditionally accessed by extensive command line entries or from multiple toolbars and pull-down menus, are brought together in one location in the **Dashboard**. Using the previous example of the **Text** control panel, you would need to access three pull-down menus or two toolbars to find the same text commands. The **Dashboard** often allows you to spend less time looking for tools and options, while increasing valuable drawing window space by removing toolbars.

By default, the **Dashboard** provides you with a list of design tools available for creating 2D drawings or 3D models, depending on the active workspace. The **Dashboard** shown when the **2D Drafting & Annotation** workspace is active provides easy access to 2D drawing tools from the **2D Draw**, **Annotation Scaling**, **Text**, **Dimensions**, **Multileaders**, **Tables**, and **2D Navigate** control panels. **Object Properties** and **Block Attributes** control panels can be added. The **Dashboard** shown when the **3D Modeling** workspace is active provides easy access to 3D modeling tools from the **3D Make**, **3D Navigate**, **Visual Styles**, **Lights**, **Materials**, and **Render** control panels.

You can remove unused control panels or add control panels by selecting the **Properties** button or right-clicking anywhere on the **Dashboard**, and picking the control panels to add or remove from the **Control panels** cascading submenu. Specific **Dashboard** command and options are described throughout the textbook where applicable.

Properties

The **Properties** palette lets you manage the properties of new and existing objects in a drawing. The actual use of the **Properties** palette is explained where it applies throughout this textbook.

Tool Palettes

The **Tool Palettes** window provides access to frequently used commands, block symbols, and hatch patterns. These items can be organized into palette categories for easy management and use. **Figure 1-21** shows some sample tool palettes. Tool palettes can be customized with your own symbols, hatch patterns, or commands, and new palettes can be created. This process is explained in *AutoCAD and Its Applications—Advanced*.

QuickCalc

The **QuickCalc** calculator allows you to perform mathematical, scientific, and trigonometric calculations. It also contains a units-of-measurement converter and allows variables to be created and saved for later use. The **QuickCalc** calculator is described in detail in Chapter 13.

DesignCenter

DesignCenter is a powerful drawing information manager that provides an excellent tool for effectively reusing and sharing drawing content. One of the primary productivity benefits of using CAD is that once something has been created, you can use it repeatedly in any number of drawings or drawing projects. Many types of drawing

Figure 1-21.
Block symbols, hatch patterns, and commands can be organized into palettes. Mechanical fasteners and electrical symbols are available in these palettes.

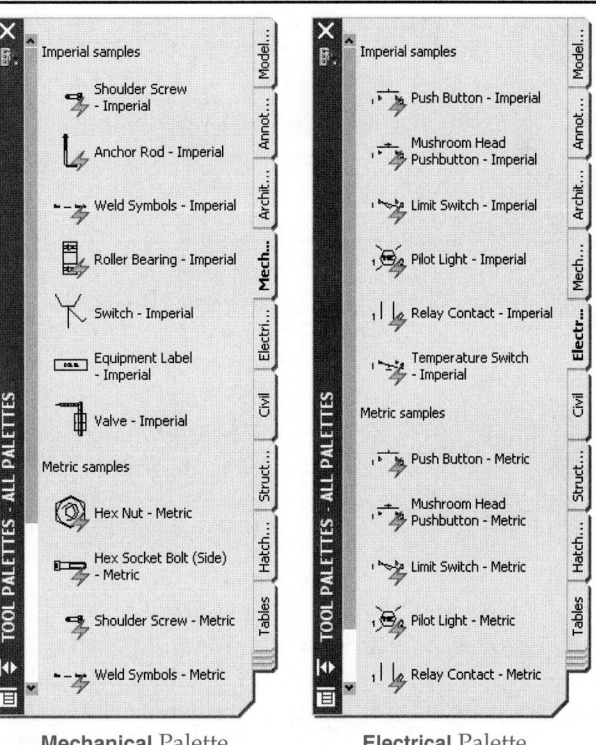

Mechanical Palette   Electrical Palette

elements are similar or the same in numerous drawings, such as common drawing details, frequently used subassemblies or parts, and drawing layouts. **DesignCenter** lets you conveniently "drag and drop" drawing content to add it from one drawing to another. The use of this powerful information management system is described in more detail in Chapter 5 and additionally throughout the textbook where it applies.

NOTE

Several other palettes are available, including the **External References**, **Sheet Set Manager**, **Markup Set Manager**, and 3D modeling palettes. These palettes are described when applicable throughout this textbook or in *AutoCAD and Its Applications—Advanced*.

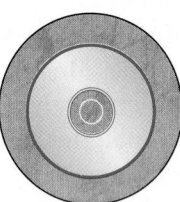

Exercise 1-5
Complete the exercise on the Student CD.

Shortcut Menus

AutoCAD makes extensive use of *shortcut menus* to simplify and accelerate command entries. Sometimes referred to as *cursor menus* because they are displayed at the cursor location, these context-sensitive menus are accessed by right-clicking. Because they are context sensitive, the shortcut menu content varies based on the location of the cursor when you right-click and the current conditions, such as whether a command is active or whether an object is selected.

When you right-click in the drawing area with no command active, the first item displayed on the shortcut menu is typically an option to repeat the previously used command or operation. If you right-click while a command is active, the shortcut menu contains options specific to the command. See **Figure 1-22**.

Exercise 1-6
Complete the exercise on the Student CD.

Figure 1-22.
Shortcut menus provide instant access to commands and options related to the current drawing or editing operation.

Shortcut Menu When
No Active Command

ZOOM Command
Shortcut Menu

Keyboard Keys

AutoCAD provides several ways of performing a given task. Many keys on the keyboard allow you to quickly perform many functions. Become familiar with these keys to help improve your performance with AutoCAD.

The [Esc] key

Anytime it is necessary to cancel a command or dialog box, press the *escape key* [Esc] on your keyboard. This key is found on the upper-left corner of most keyboards and is typically labeled Esc. Some command sequences may require the [Esc] key to be pressed twice to completely cancel the operation.

escape key: Key used to cancel a command or exit a dialog box.

Control keys

Most computer programs use *control key* functions to perform common tasks. Control key functions are used by pressing and holding the [Ctrl] key while pressing a second key. These keys are also called *accelerator keys*. If a control key is a "toggle," it is either on or off—nothing else.

control key (accelerator key): Functions with a second key to perform common tasks.

Function keys

Function keys provide instant access to commands. They can also be programmed to perform a series of commands. The function keys are located along the top of the keyboard and are numbered from [F1] to [F12].

> **NOTE**
>
>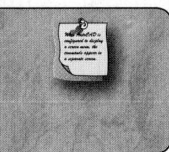
>
> The *Reference Materials* section of the Student CD includes lists of control key shortcuts and function key commands. Keep printouts of these reference sheets handy while you are learning AutoCAD.

Selecting AutoCAD Commands

AutoCAD commands are selected using one of four primary ways:
- Picking a toolbar or palette button
- Selecting a pull-down menu item
- Selecting a shortcut menu item
- Typing at the keyboard

Accessing commands using toolbars, palettes, pull-down menus, and shortcut menus may offer advantages over typing commands at the keyboard. One benefit is that you do not need to remove your eyes from the screen. Commands and your drawing activities are shown on-screen as you work, using visual icons, tooltips, prompts, and command titles. As you work with AutoCAD, you will become familiar with the display and location of commands.

If you choose to type commands, you may have to turn your eyes from the screen, and you may also need to memorize command names or aliases. As an AutoCAD drafter, you will decide which command selection technique works best for you. A combination of command selection methods may prove most effective.

Using Dynamic Input

Dynamic input is an area at the crosshairs where commands may be typed and context-specific information may be given. It allows you to keep your focus at the point where you are drawing. When dynamic input is on, a temporary area for command input and command information is displayed at the crosshairs in the drawing area. When you type a command, it is displayed in the lower-right corner of the crosshairs. See Figure 1-23. To start a command, pick the command from a toolbar, palette, pull-down menu, shortcut menu, or type the command name and press the [Enter] key. When a command is in process, the next action needed to proceed with the command is displayed, along with additional command options, an input area, and additional information. Depending on your working preference, dynamic input can be used at the same time as the command line or can be disabled if you use the command line. Dynamic input can be toggled on and off by either picking the **DYN** button on the status bar or using the [F12] function key. If dynamic input is turned off, the command line is used for command input and information.

Depending on the command that is in process, different information and options are available in the dynamic input area. In Figure 1-24, the **RECTANG** command has been started. The first part of the dynamic input area is the tooltip, which reads Specify first corner point or. In this case, you need to pick in the drawing area or type coordinates to specify the first corner of the rectangle, or use the arrow keys.

Pressing the down arrow key displays the available options associated with the current command. See Figure 1-25. Options in the list can be selected at any time using your cursor. Pressing the down arrow again cycles through the available options, which is indicated by a bullet next to the option. To select an option once it is bulleted, press [Enter]. The next available options and additional information are then displayed in the dynamic input area.

Figure 1-23.
Using dynamic input, commands can be typed in or selected from a temporary input area next to the crosshairs.

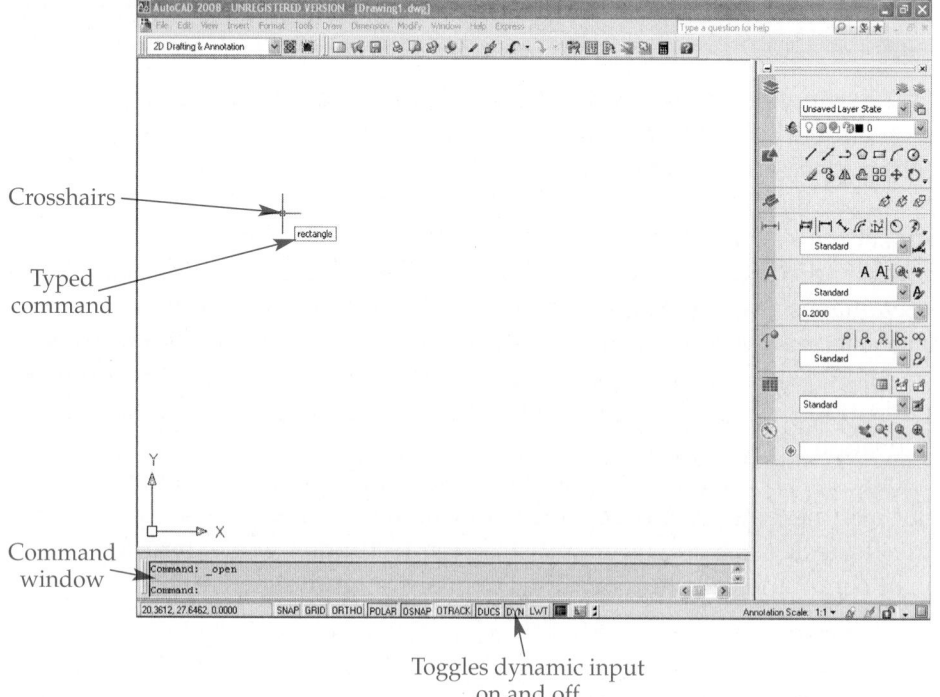

Figure 1-24.
The dynamic input fields after the **RECTANG** command has been started.

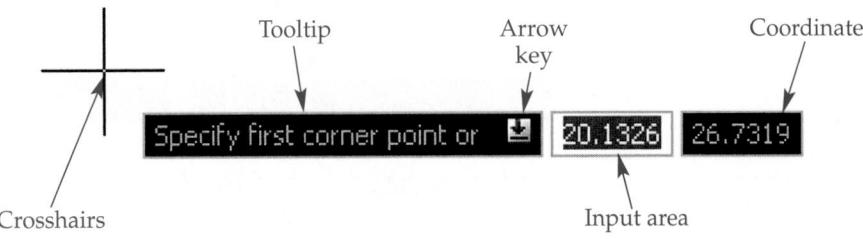

Figure 1-25.
Using the down arrow key exposes additional options for the current command. Pick an option with your cursor, or use the up and down arrow keys to position the bullet at the desired option and press the [Enter] key to select that option.

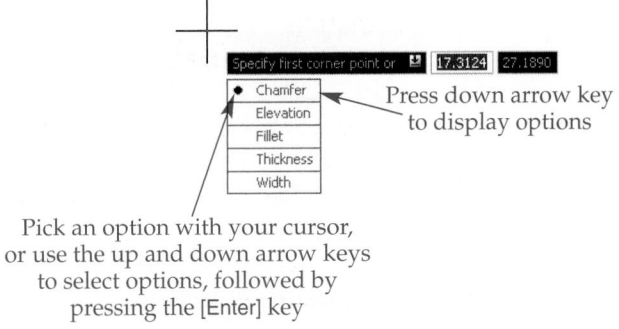

Once a command is started, the dynamic input area displays the appropriate tooltip, input field, and any other additional information for the current command. This information changes during the command depending on the action. **Figure 1-26** shows the dynamic input display during a typical **LINE** operation. Additional options for dynamic input are described in Chapter 3.

Using the Command Line

Commands can be typed and command information can be read within the command line when it is turned on. When a command is started, whether from a toolbar, palette, pull-down menu, shortcut menu, or by typing, AutoCAD either performs the specified operation or prompts you for any additional information. AutoCAD commands have a standard format, structured as follows:

Command: **COMMANDNAME**↵
Current settings: Setting1 Setting2 Setting3
Instructional text [Option1/oPtion2/opTion3/...] <default option or value>:

If the command has associated settings or options, these are displayed as shown. The instructional text indicates what you should do at this point, and all available options are shown within the square brackets. Each option has a unique combination of uppercase characters that can be entered at the prompt rather than typing the entire option name. If a default option is displayed in the angle brackets (<>), you can press [Enter] to accept it rather than typing the value again.

Depending on your working preference, the command line can be used at the same time as dynamic input or can be disabled if you only use dynamic input. To disable the command line, select **Tools** > **Command Line** or use the [Ctrl]+[9] key combination. If the command line is turned off, dynamic input is used for command input and information. The floating command line contains the **Auto-hide** and **Properties** buttons found on palettes. The **Command Line** window can also be dragged into the drawing area and resized in the same manner as a toolbar or palette.

Figure 1-26.
The dynamic input fields change while a command is active. When you pick the first endpoint of a line, the coordinates of the crosshairs are displayed. After the first endpoint is picked, the distance and angle of the crosshairs relative to the first endpoint are displayed.

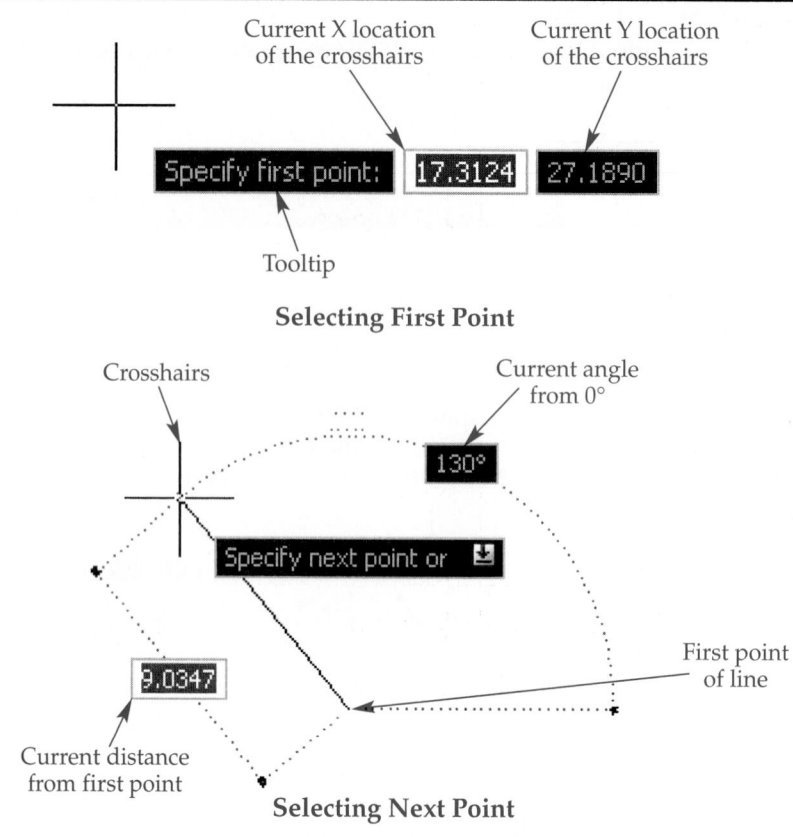

Current X location of the crosshairs

Current Y location of the crosshairs

Specify first point: 17.3124 27.1890

Tooltip

Selecting First Point

Crosshairs

Current angle from 0°

130°

Specify next point or

First point of line

9.0347

Current distance from first point

Selecting Next Point

PROFESSIONAL TIP

AutoCAD provides a set of abbreviated commands called *command aliases*. Command aliases are also called *keyboard shortcuts* because they reduce the amount of typing needed when entering a command at the keyboard. Using command aliases allows you to enter commands more quickly. For example, instead of typing LINE, you can type L, which takes less time. Becoming familiar with the available command aliases can help you become more productive with AutoCAD.

Command Entry Shortcuts

AutoCAD provides you with the ability to select previously used commands by using the up and down arrow keys. When no command is active, press the up arrow key on the keyboard to display the previously used command. If dynamic input is active, previously used commands are displayed near your cursor by default. To display previously used commands at the command line, you must pick the command line, or turn off dynamic input. If you continue to press the up arrow key, AutoCAD continues to backtrack through the commands you have used. Then press [Enter] to activate a displayed command.

Right-clicking in the drawing area displays a shortcut menu with a **Recent Input** cascading menu showing a list of commands you have used recently. See **Figure 1-27.** Pick a command name from the list to use that command again.

In addition, you can type the first letter (or several letters) of the command or system variable you want to use, and press the [Tab] key. This displays the first command or system variable beginning with the entered letter(s). Continue to press the [Tab] key to display all of the commands and system variables. When the desired command is displayed, press the [Enter] key.

Figure 1-27.
The shortcut menu displayed when you right-click in the drawing area offers a cascading menu listing commands you have used recently.

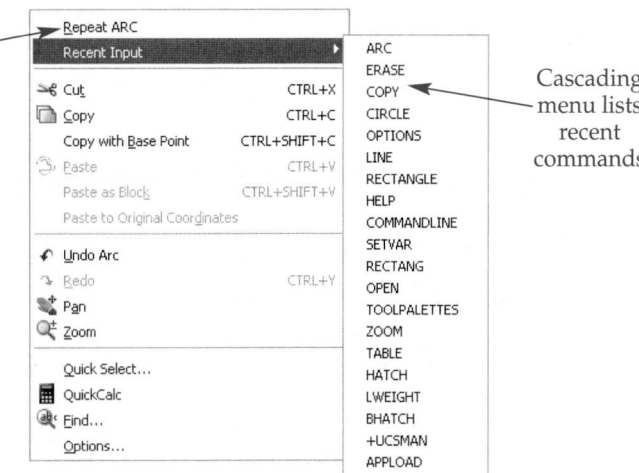

Repeat most recent command

Cascading menu lists recent commands

While learning AutoCAD, it is highly recommended that you pay close attention to the prompts displayed in the command line and the dynamic input area.

Getting Help

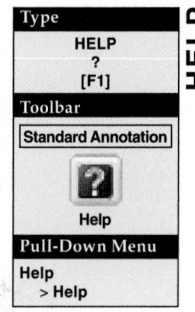

HELP	
Type	
HELP	
?	
[F1]	
Toolbar	
Standard Annotation	
Help	
Pull-Down Menu	
Help	
> Help	

If you need help with a specific command, option, or program feature, AutoCAD provides a powerful and convenient help system. There are several ways to access this feature. The fastest method is to press the [F1] function key. You can also pick the **?** button at the right end of the **Standard** or **Standard Annotation** toolbar, select **Help > Help** from the pull-down menu, or type **?** or HELP. Each of these methods displays the **AutoCAD Help** window.

If you are unfamiliar with how to use a Windows help system, it is suggested you spend time now exploring all the topics under **AutoCAD Help** in the **Contents** tab of the **AutoCAD Help** window.

The **AutoCAD Help** window consists of two frames. See **Figure 1-28.** The left frame, which has three tabs, is used to locate help topics. The right frame displays the selected help topics. The tabs in the left frame are as follows:

- **Contents.** This tab displays a list of book icons and topic names. The book icons represent the organizational structure of books of topics within the AutoCAD documentation. Topics contain the actual help information; the icon used to represent a topic is a sheet of paper with a question mark. To open a book or a help topic, double-click on its name or icon. The **Contents** tab lists each of the help documents within the AutoCAD help system. The documents available are **AutoCAD Help; User's Guide; Command Reference; Driver and Peripheral Guide; Installation and Licensing Guides; Customization Guide; AutoLISP, Visual LISP, and DXF;** and **ActiveX Automation and VBA.**

Figure 1-28.
The **AutoCAD Help** window.

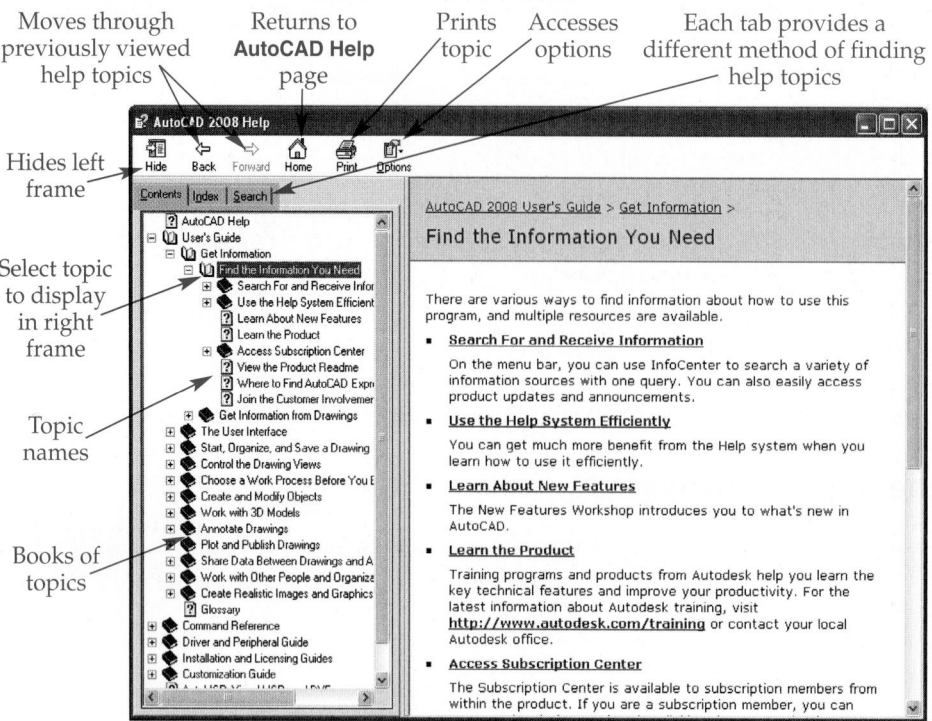

Moves through previously viewed help topics

Returns to **AutoCAD Help** page

Prints topic

Accesses options

Each tab provides a different method of finding help topics

Hides left frame

Select topic to display in right frame

Topic names

Books of topics

- **Index.** Although the **Contents** tab of the **AutoCAD Help** window is useful for displaying all the topics in an expanded table of contents manner, it is not very useful when you are searching for a specific item. In this case, most people refer to the index. This is the function of the **Index** tab.
- **Search.** This tab is used to search the help documents for specific words or phrases.

In addition to the two frames and four tabs, six buttons reside at the top of the **AutoCAD Help** window. The **Hide/Show** button controls the visibility of the left frame. The **Back** button is used to view the previously displayed help topic. The **Forward** button is used to go forward to help pages you viewed before pressing the **Back** button. The **Home** button takes you to the AutoCAD Help page. The **Print** button is used to print a help topic. The **Options** button contains a cascading menu with a variety of items used to control other aspects of the **AutoCAD Help** window.

PROFESSIONAL TIP

AutoCAD's help function can also be used while you are in the process of using a command. For example, suppose you are using the **ARC** command and forget what type of information AutoCAD requires for the specific prompts on-screen. If you press [F1] function key or the **?** button, the help information for the currently active command is displayed. This *context-oriented help* saves valuable time, since you do not need to scan through the help contents or perform any searches to find the information.

context-oriented help: Help information for the active command.

Exercise 1-7

Complete the exercise on the Student CD.

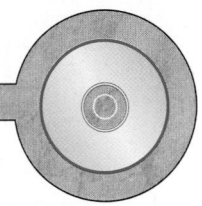

Using the InfoCenter

AutoCAD's **InfoCenter** feature is located in the menu bar. **InfoCenter** allows you to search for topics without first displaying the **AutoCAD Help** window. It also provides buttons for access to the **Communication Center** and the **Favorites** list. To search for topics, you can type a question in the text box. Then, select the appropriate topic from the list to display it in the **AutoCAD Help** window. To add a topic to the **Favorites** list, pick the star next to the topic. Pick the **Communication Center** button to access content on a variety of help topics. Pick the **Favorites** button to access any help topics you have stored.

Using the Support Knowledge Base

AutoCAD's product support extends beyond the locally installed help system. The Autodesk Web site provides additional support resources. To access this information, pick **Help** > **Additional Resources** > **Support Knowledge Base**. Your computer must have an Internet connection to access this information. Enter the topic in the text box to search the database.

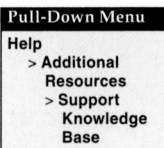

Exercise 1-8

Complete the exercise on the Student CD.

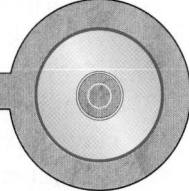

Exiting AutoCAD

The **EXIT** command is the primary way to end an AutoCAD session. You can close the program by picking **File** > **Exit** or by typing EXIT or QUIT. If you attempt to exit before saving your work, AutoCAD gives you a chance to decide what you want to do with unsaved work.

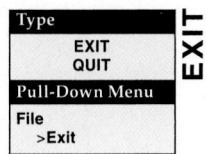

Chapter Test

Answer the following questions. Write your answers on a separate sheet of paper or complete the electronic chapter test on the Student CD.

1. What system is used to construct drawings and models in AutoCAD?
2. Using the system referred to in Question 1, what is the proper notation for the values Z = 4, X = 2, and Y = 5?
3. What is drawing planning?
4. What are standards?
5. Why should you save your work every ten to fifteen minutes?
6. What is the first thing you should do as part of your planning checklist?
7. What scale should you use to draw in AutoCAD?
8. What is the quickest method for starting AutoCAD?
9. Give the name for the interface that includes on-screen features.
10. Define or explain the following terms:
    A. Default
    B. Pick or click
    C. Button
    D. Key
    E. Function key
    F. [Enter] (↵)
    G. Command
    H. Option
11. What is a workspace?
12. How do you change workspaces?
13. What is the difference between a docked toolbar and a floating toolbar?
14. How do you select the locking options to lock the toolbars and windows in both their floating and docked states?
15. What type of pull-down menu item has an arrow to the right?
16. What are menu accelerator keys? How are they used?
17. What is a flyout menu?
18. How do you hide the command line?
19. Briefly discuss the function of the status bar, and identify the items found in the status bar.
20. What is the function of tabs in a dialog box?
21. What is the function of the ... (ellipsis) button?
22. Identify the appearance of a palette and give another name for the palette.
23. Briefly discuss the basic advantage of using the **Dashboard**.
24. Give the basic function of tool palettes.
25. Give the basic function of **DesignCenter**.
26. How do you access a shortcut menu?
27. Briefly explain the function of the [Esc] key.
28. What are the functions of the following control keys? (Refer to the *Shortcut Keys* document in the *Reference Materials* section of the Student CD.)
    A. [Ctrl]+[B]
    B. [Ctrl]+[C]
    C. [Ctrl]+[D]
    D. [Ctrl]+[G]
    E. [Ctrl]+[O]
    F. [Ctrl]+[S]
29. Name the function keys that execute the same tasks as the following control keys. (Refer to the *Shortcut Keys* document in the *Reference Materials* section of the Student CD.)

A. [Ctrl]+[B]
B. [Ctrl]+[D]
C. [Ctrl]+[G]
D. [Ctrl]+[L]
E. [Ctrl]+[T]
30. Briefly describe the function of dynamic input.
31. How do you access previously used commands?
32. Give the purpose and function of right-clicking in the drawing area.
33. Identify the quickest way to access the **AutoCAD Help** window.
34. Describe the purpose of the book icons in the **Contents** tab of the **AutoCAD Help** window.
35. What is context-oriented help, and how is it accessed?

Problems

1. Interview your drafting instructor or supervisor and try to determine what type of drawing standards exist at your school or company. Write them down and keep them with you as you learn AutoCAD. Make notes as you progress through this textbook on how you use these standards. Also note how the standards could be changed to better match the capabilities of AutoCAD.

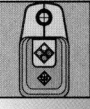

2. Research your drawing department standards. If you do not have a copy of the standards, acquire one. If AutoCAD standards have been created, make notes as to how you can use these in your projects. If no standards exist in your department or company, make notes as to how you can help develop standards. Write a report on why your school or company should create CAD standards and how they would be used. Discuss who should be responsible for specific tasks. Recommend procedures, techniques, and forms, if necessary. Develop this report as you progress through your AutoCAD instruction and as you read through this textbook.

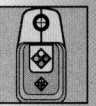

3. Develop a drawing planning sheet for use in your school or company. List items you think are important for planning a CAD drawing. Make changes to this sheet as you learn more about AutoCAD.

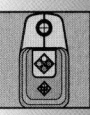

4. Launch AutoCAD and perform the following tasks:
   A. Open the **AutoCAD Help** window.
   B. In the **Contents** tab, expand the User's Guide category.
   C. In the right pane, pick the Get Information, Find the Information You Need, and Use the Help System Efficiently topics.
   D. If you have access to a printer, print the topic.
   E. Close the **AutoCAD Help** window, and then close AutoCAD.

5. Launch AutoCAD using the Start button on the Windows task bar.
   A. Move the cursor over the buttons in the **Standard** toolbar and read the notes on the status bar at the bottom of the screen.
   B. Slowly move the cursor over each of the buttons on the **Workspace** and **Standard** toolbars and read the tooltips.
   C. Pick the **File** pull-down menu to display it. Using the right arrow key, move through all the pull-down menus. Use the left arrow key to return to the **Draw** pull-down menu. Use the down arrow key to move to the **Circle** command, then use the right arrow key to display the **Circle** options in the cascading menu.
   D. Press the [Esc] key to dismiss the menu.
   E. Close AutoCAD.

6. Draw a freehand sketch of the screen display. Label each of the screen areas. To the side of the sketch, write a short description of each screen area's function.

Learning Objectives

After completing this chapter, you will be able to do the following:

✓ Start a new drawing.
✓ Use various save commands and options.
✓ Open a saved drawing.
✓ Manage multiple drawings.
✓ Use the **CLOSE** command.
✓ Create a template drawing.
✓ Determine settings for linear and angular units and precision.
✓ Adjust grid and snap settings.

When using AutoCAD, you work with drawing files. In this chapter, you will learn how to create new drawing files, save drawing files, and open existing drawing files.

Some of the basic drawing aids used in AutoCAD are discussed in this chapter. As you begin working with drawing files, you will find these and other types of settings a very useful starting point.

Starting a New Drawing

In AutoCAD, new drawings are typically started from templates. ***Drawing templates*** store standard drawing settings and objects. All settings and contents of the template file are included in the new drawing.

drawing templates:
Files of standard drawing settings and objects.

Templates can be incredible productivity boosters. The provided template files may meet some needs, but the ability to create new custom templates provides the greatest benefit. Custom templates allow you to use an existing drawing as a starting point for any new drawing. This option is extremely valuable for ensuring that everyone in a department, class, school, or company uses the same standards within their drawings.

When you are using a template, values defining the drawing settings are automatically set. Templates usually have the following values and drawing elements:

✓ Drawing units and angle values
✓ Grid, snap, and other drawing aid settings
✓ Standard layouts with a border and title block
✓ Text styles
✓ Table styles
✓ Dimension styles
✓ Layer definitions and linetypes
✓ Plot styles
✓ Commonly used symbols and blocks
✓ General notes

These items are discussed later in this textbook.

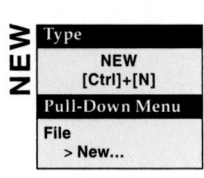

To start a drawing, select **File** > **New...**, type NEW, or use the [Ctrl]+[N] key combination. This displays the **Select template** dialog box, **Figure 2-1**.

The **Select template** dialog box lists the templates found in the default template folder. A variety of templates is included with AutoCAD. You will notice all the files have a .dwt extension, which stands for "drawing template." If you just want to open a blank file, use the acad.dwt template for English settings or the acadiso.dwt template for metric settings. To open a template file, double-click on the file or select the file and then pick the **Open** button.

Starting a Drawing Quickly

AutoCAD also provides methods of starting a new drawing from a preset template. This allows you to begin a drawing more quickly.

Before using the "quick start" feature, you must specify the template to be used for quick starts. This is done in the **Options** dialog box. To access the dialog box, pick **Tools** > **Options...** from the pull-down menu. In the **Files** tab, expand Template Settings, and then expand Default Template File Name for QNEW item. Either a template file name or None is displayed. See **Figure 2-2**. Pick the **Browse...** button to select a template.

Figure 2-1.
The **Select template** dialog box allows you to begin a new drawing by selecting a template.

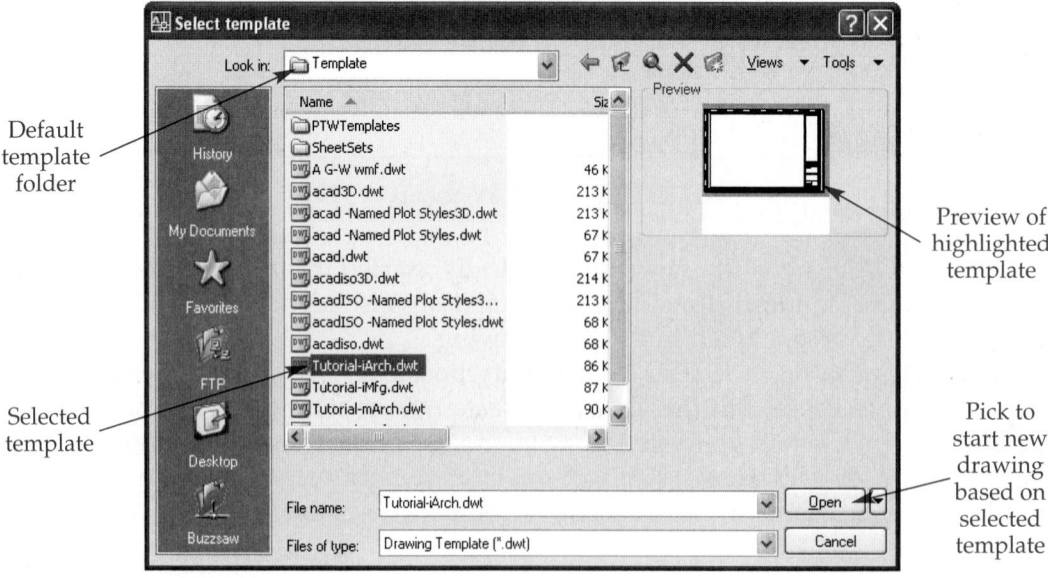

Figure 2-2.
Specifying a template file for the **QNEW** command.

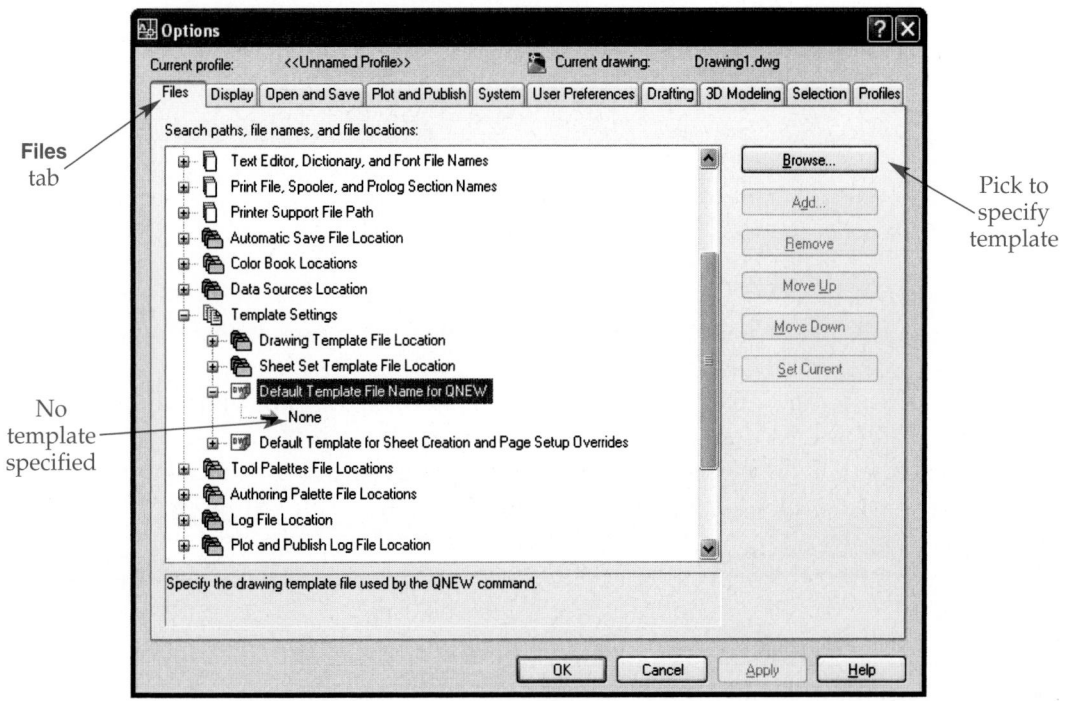

Files tab

No template specified

Pick to specify template

To start a new drawing using this template, pick the **QNew** button from the **Standard** or **Standard Annotation** toolbar or type QNEW. If the Default Template File Name for QNEW setting is None, typing QNEW or picking the **QNew** button opens the **Select template** dialog box.

Type	
	QNEW
Toolbar	
Standard Annotation	
	QNew

QNEW

PROFESSIONAL TIP

When you begin a session of AutoCAD, a new drawing is started. If a template is specified for the **QNEW** command, it is used for the initial drawing. If no template is specified for the **QNEW** command, the initial drawing is based on the acad.dwt template.

Starting a Drawing from Scratch

You can also start a drawing without using a template. This is also called starting a drawing "from scratch." Doing so provides a "blank" drawing without a title block, layouts, or customized drawing settings. Use this option to "play it by ear" when you are just sketching or when the start or end of a drawing project is unknown.

To create a new drawing from scratch, pick the arrow next to the **Open** button in the **Select template** dialog box. See Figure 2-3. Select one of the **Open with no Template** options. Pick the option corresponding to the type of units to be used in the drawing.

Figure 2-3.
Starting a drawing without a template.

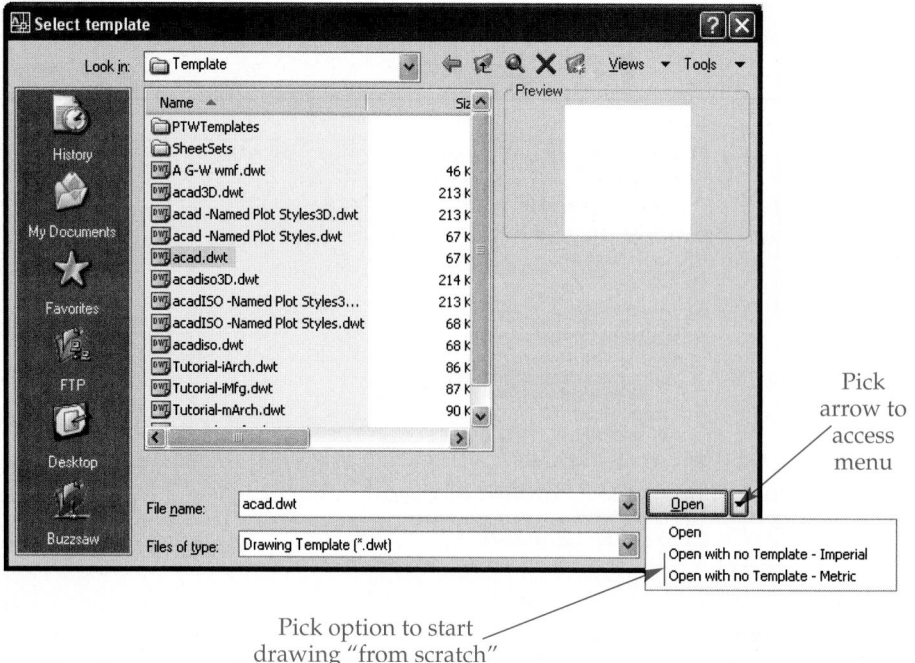

Pick arrow to access menu

Pick option to start drawing "from scratch"

Saving Drawings

After starting a drawing, you need to assign a name to the new drawing and save it. The following discussion provides you with detailed information about saving and closing a drawing.

You must save your drawing periodically to protect your work. While working in AutoCAD, you should save your drawing every 10 to 15 minutes. This is very important! If there is a power failure, a severe editing error, or another problem, all the work saved prior to the problem will be usable. If you save only once an hour, a power failure could result in an hour of lost work. Saving your drawing every 10 to 15 minutes results in less lost work if a problem occurs.

The **QSAVE**, **SAVEAS**, and **SAVE** commands allow you to save your work. Also, any command or option ending the AutoCAD session provides a warning asking if you want to save changes to the drawing. This gives you a final option either to save or not save changes to the drawing.

Naming Drawings

Drawing names may be chosen to identify a product by name and number—for example, VICE-101, FLOORPLAN, or 6DT1005. Your school or company probably has a drawing numbering system you can use. Drawing names should be recorded in a part numbering or drawing name log. Such a log serves as a valuable reference long after you forget what the drawings contain.

It is important to set up a system that allows you to determine the content of a drawing by the drawing name. Although it is possible to give a drawing file an extended name, such as Details for Top Half of Compressor Housing for ACME, Inc., Part Number 4011A, Revision Level C, this is normally not a practical way of sorting drawing information. Drawing titles should be standardized and may be most effective when they contain a clear and concise reference to the project, part number, process, sheet number, and revision level.

When a standardized naming system exists, a shorter name like ACME.4011A.C provides all the necessary information. If additional information is desirable for easier recognition, it can be added to the base name, for example: ACME 4011A.C Compressor Housing.Top.Casting Details. Always record drawing names and provide information related to the drawings. The following rules and restrictions apply to naming all files, including AutoCAD drawings:

- A maximum of 256 characters can be used.
- Alphabetical and numeric characters and spaces, along with most punctuation symbols, can be used.
- The following characters cannot be used: quotation mark ("), asterisk (*), question mark (?), forward slash (/), and backward slash (\).

Using the Qsave Command

Of the three available save commands, the most frequently used is the **QSAVE** command. **QSAVE** stands for *quick save*. The **QSAVE** command is accessed by picking the **Save** button from the **Standard** or **Standard Annotation** toolbar, picking **File > Save** from the pull-down menu, typing QSAVE, or pressing [Ctrl]+[S].

The **QSAVE** command response depends on whether or not the drawing already has a name. If the current drawing has a name, the **QSAVE** command updates the file based on the current state of the drawing. In this situation, **QSAVE** issues no prompts and displays no dialog boxes.

If the current drawing has not yet been named, the **QSAVE** command displays the **Save Drawing As** dialog box. See Figure 2-4. You must complete three steps in order to save your file:

1. Select the folder in which the file is to be saved.
2. Select the type of file to save, such as drawing (.dwg) or template (.dwt).
3. Type a name for the file.

quick save: Tool that allows you to save a named drawing without a dialog box.

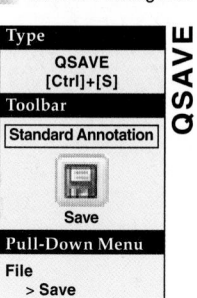

Figure 2-4.
The **Save Drawing As** dialog box.

Select folder where drawing will be saved

Move up one level from current folder

Create a new folder

Enter name

Select type of file to save as

When you are selecting the folder in which the file will be stored, first select the disk drive from the **Save in:** drop-down list. To move upward from the current folder, pick the **Up one level** button. To create a new folder in the current location, pick the **Create New Folder** button and type the name for the folder.

The **Files of type:** drop-down list offers options to save the drawing file in alternative formats. For most applications, this should be set to AutoCAD 2007 Drawing (*.dwg) when you are saving drawings. When you save a template file, this is set as AutoCAD Drawing Template (*.dwt).

> **NOTE**
>
> Drawings created in AutoCAD 2008 are saved as AutoCAD 2007 drawings. You will not see an option for saving a drawing as an AutoCAD 2008 drawing file in the **Files of type:** drop-down list.

If the drawing has not yet been named, the name Drawing1 appears in the **File name:** text box. Change this to the desired drawing name. You do not need to include the .dwg extension.

Once you have specified the correct location and file name, pick the **Save** button to save the drawing file. Keep in mind that you can either pick the **Save** button or just press the [Enter] key to activate the **Save** button and save the drawing.

> **NOTE**
>
> The **Save Drawing As** dialog box is a standard file selection dialog box. The features of this dialog box are discussed more thoroughly later in this chapter.

Using the Saveas Command

The **SAVEAS** command is used when:
- The current drawing already has a name and you need to save it under a different name.
- You need to save the current drawing in an alternative format, such as a previous AutoCAD release format.
- You open one of your drawing template files as a basis for another drawing. This leaves the drawing template unchanged and ready to be used for other drawings.

The **SAVEAS** command is accessed by picking **File** > **Save As...** from the pull-down menu or by typing SAVEAS. This command always displays the **Save Drawing As** dialog box. If the current drawing has already been saved, the current name and location are displayed. Confirm that the **Save in:** drop-down list displays the current drive and directory folder you want and that the **Files of type:** drop-down list displays the desired file type. Type the new drawing name in the **File name:** text box and pick the **Save** button.

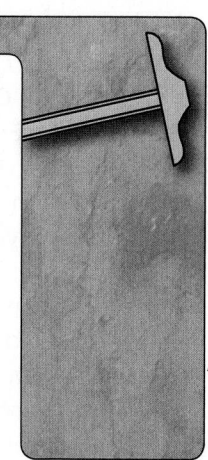

The third command provided for saving a drawing is the **SAVE** command. The **SAVE** command is not commonly used and is only available by typing SAVE. The **SAVE** command displays the **Save Drawing As** dialog box, regardless of whether the drawing has been previously saved. Because of this, the **QSAVE** command is better for saving a drawing in progress, and the **SAVEAS** command is better for saving a drawing with a new name or location.

When you are saving a drawing to a different name, the **SAVE** command saves the drawing file with a different name, but leaves you in the current drawing. The **SAVEAS** command discards all changes to the original drawing file up to the last save.

Saving Your Work Automatically

AutoCAD can create an automatic backup copy of the active drawing. The backup file has a .bak extension and is created in the same folder where the drawing is located. When you save the drawing, the DWG file is updated, and the BAK file is overwritten by the old DWG file. Therefore, the backup file is always "one save behind" the drawing file.

This feature is on by default and can be controlled using the **Create backup copy with each save** check box in the **Open and Save** tab of the **Options** dialog box. See **Figure 2-5.**

Before you can access a backup file, you must rename it. Use Windows Explorer to rename the file and change the file extension from .bak to .dwg. Refer to the *Supplemental Materials* on the Student CD for more information on Windows Explorer. Once the file has been renamed, it can be opened in AutoCAD.

Figure 2-5.
Use the **Open and Save** tab in the **Options** dialog box to save backup files and set the autosave feature.

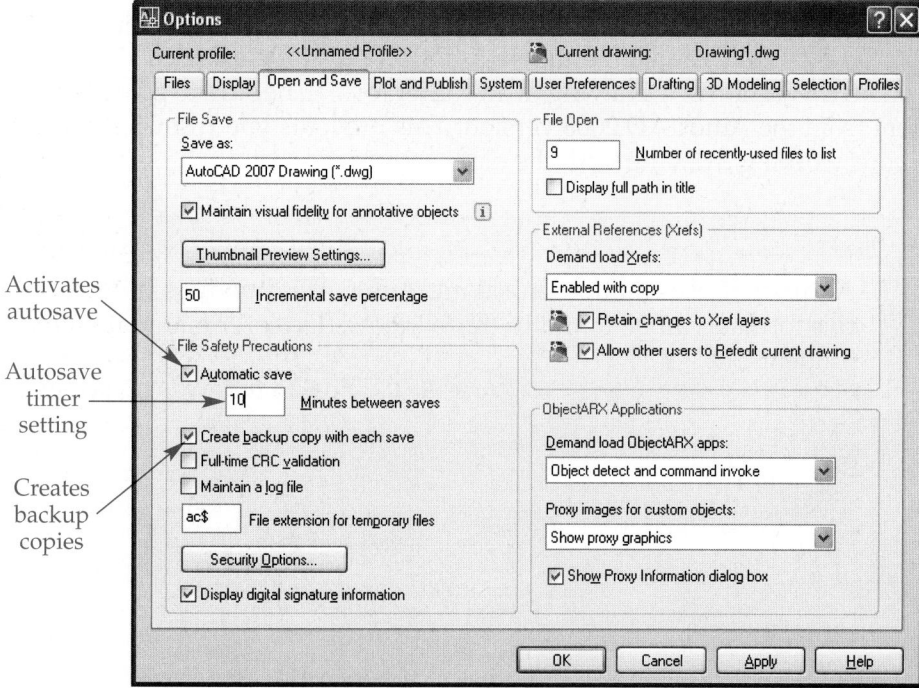

AutoCAD provides you with another automatic work-saving tool called *automatic save (autosave)*. Type the amount of time (in minutes) between saves in the **Open and Save** tab of the **Options** dialog box. The value is typed in the **Minutes between saves** text box in the **File Safety Precautions** area. In Figure 2-5, the setting is 10 minutes.

The autosave timer starts as soon as a change is made to the drawing. The timer is reset when the drawing is saved. The drawing is automatically saved when the first command is given after the autosave timer has been reached. For example, if you set the timer to 10 minutes, work for 9 minutes, and then let the computer remain idle for 5 minutes, an automatic save is not executed until you return and execute a command. Therefore, be sure to save your drawing manually if you plan to be away from your computer for an extended period of time.

The autosave feature is intended to be used in case AutoCAD shuts down unexpectedly. Therefore, when you close a drawing file, the autosave file associated with that drawing is automatically deleted. If AutoCAD does shut down unexpectedly, the autosave file remains and can be used. The autosave drawing is always saved with the name of *DrawingName_n_n_nnnn*.sv$. If you need to use the autosave file, you must rename it with a .dwg extension using Windows Explorer.

NOTE

The **Automatic Save File Location** listing in the **Files** tab of the **Options** dialog box determines the folder where the autosave files are saved.

Saving Drawings to Older Release Formats

The drawing file type saved by AutoCAD 2008 is a different file format from the file types saved by some previous releases of AutoCAD. AutoCAD 2008 drawings can be saved in a different file format, such as the AutoCAD 2004 format. This allows you to send AutoCAD 2008 drawings to businesses where older releases of AutoCAD are being used.

To save a drawing to an older release format, use the **SAVEAS** command. The **Save Drawing As** dialog box appears. Using the **Files of type:** drop-down list, select the AutoCAD 2004/LT2004 Drawing (*.dwg) option to save the drawing in the AutoCAD 2004 format. AutoCAD 2004, 2005, and 2006 all use AutoCAD 2004 format files.

When you save a version of a drawing in an earlier format, be sure to give it a name that is different from the AutoCAD 2008 version. This prevents you from accidentally overwriting your working drawing with the older format file.

NOTE

Additional information on saving AutoCAD drawings in alternative formats can be found in the Windows Explorer material on the Student CD.

Opening Existing Drawings

An existing drawing is one that has been previously saved. Existing drawings can be opened in various ways. You can use the **OPEN** command, select from the **File** pull-down menu, or open a drawing from Windows Explorer. These methods are discussed in the following sections.

Using the Open Command

You can easily access any existing drawing with the **OPEN** command. To use the **OPEN** command, pick the **Open** button on the **Standard** or **Standard Annotation** toolbar, select **File > Open...** from the pull-down menu, press the [Ctrl]+[O] key combination, or type OPEN. The **Select File** dialog box appears. See **Figure 2-6**. This dialog box contains a list of folders and files. Double-click on a file folder to open it, and then double-click on the desired file to open it. In **Figure 2-6**, the AutoCAD 2008\Sample folder is shown open, with the sample drawings displayed.

When you select an existing drawing, an image of the drawing is displayed in the **Preview** area. This provides an easy way for you to get a quick look at the drawing without loading it into AutoCAD. You can view each drawing until you find the one you want.

After picking a drawing file name to highlight it, you can quickly highlight another drawing in the list using the keyboard arrow keys. Use the up and down arrow keys to move vertically between files and use the left and right arrow keys to move horizontally. This enables you to scan through the drawing previews very quickly.

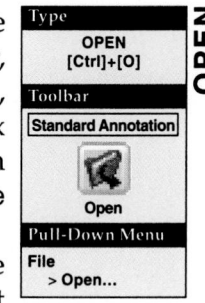

Type
OPEN
[Ctrl]+[O]

Toolbar
Standard Annotation

Open

Pull-Down Menu
File
> Open...

Exercise 2-1
Complete the exercise on the Student CD.

Figure 2-6.
The **Select File** dialog box is used to select a drawing to open. Notice that the db_samp drawing has been selected from the file list box and appears in the **File name:** text box.

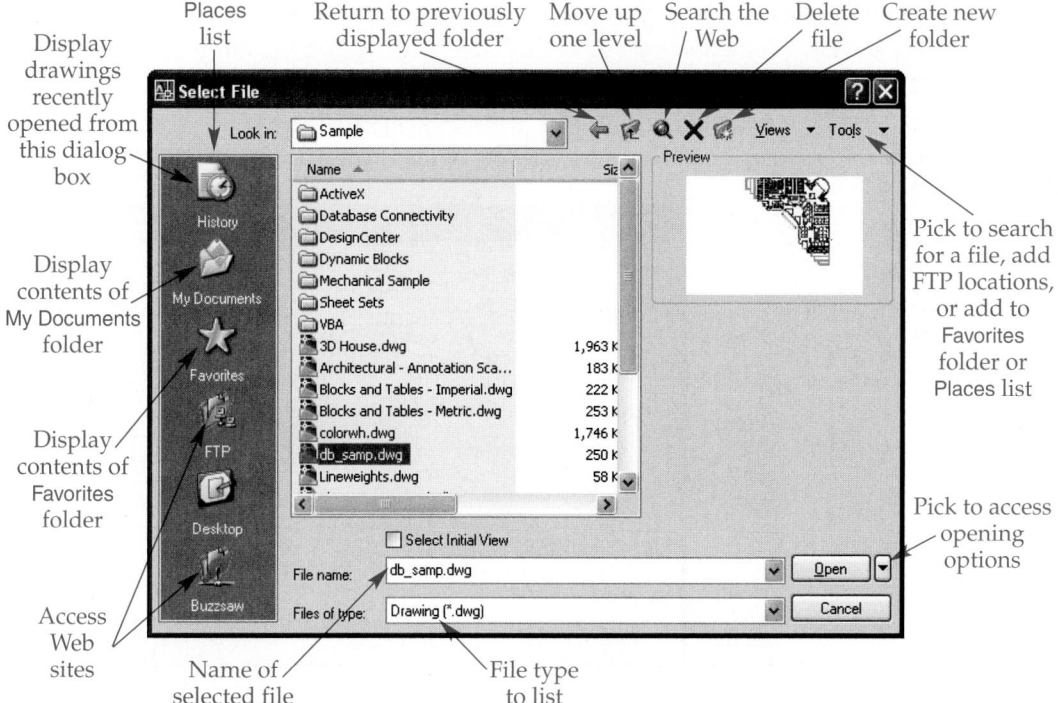

The Select File Dialog Box

The **Select File** dialog box includes a list along its left side. The list provides instant access to certain folders. The following buttons are available:

- **History.** Lists drawing files opened recently from the **Select File** dialog box.
- **My Documents.** Displays the files and folders contained in the My Documents folder for the current user.
- **Favorites.** Displays files and folders located in the Favorites folder on your hard drive.
- **FTP.** Displays available FTP (file transfer protocol) sites. To add or modify the listed FTP sites, select **Add/Modify FTP Locations** from the **Tools** menu in the **Select File** dialog box.
- **Desktop.** Lists the files, folders, and drives located on your desktop.
- **Buzzsaw.** Displays projects on the Buzzsaw Web site. Buzzsaw.com is designed for the building industry. After setting up a project hosting account, users can access drawings from a given construction project on the Web site. This allows the various companies involved in the project to have instant access to the drawing files.

The **Select File** dialog box includes other features for selecting folders and files:

- **Back button.** Shows the previously displayed folder contents.
- **Up one level button.** Displays the contents of the folder containing the currently displayed file or folder.
- **Search the Web button.** Accesses the **Browse the Web** dialog box, from which you can open files found on the Internet.
- **Delete button.** Deletes the selected file or folder.
- **Create New Folder button.** Creates a new folder within the folder being displayed.
- **Views menu.** Provides options for how file names are displayed in the **Select File** dialog box.

Finding files

You can search for files from the **Select File** dialog box by picking **Find...** in the **Tools** menu. This accesses the **Find** dialog box, Figure 2-7. If you know the file name for the drawing, type it in the **Named:** text box. If you do not know the name, you can use wildcard characters, such as *, to narrow the search.

Figure 2-7.
The **Find** dialog box is used to locate drawing files.

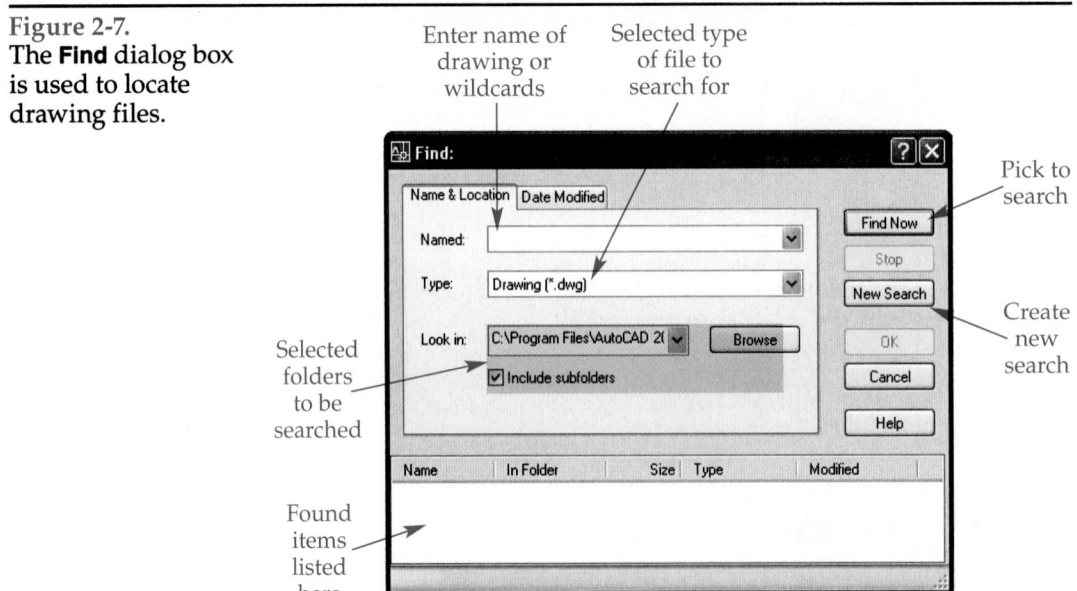

Choose the type of file from the **Type:** drop-down list. You can search for DWG, DWS, DXF, or DWT files from the **Find** dialog box. If you are searching for another type of file, use the Windows Explorer search tool.

A search can be completed more quickly if you do not search the entire hard drive. If you know the folder in which the file is located, specify the folder in the **Look in:** text box. Pick the **Browse** button to select a folder from the **Browse for Folder** dialog box. Check the **Include subfolders** check box if you want the subfolders within the selected folder to be searched.

You can also search for files based on when they were last modified. The **Date Modified** tab provides options to search for files modified within a certain time period. This option is very useful if you wish to list all drawings modified within a specific week or month.

PROFESSIONAL TIP

While working in file dialog boxes, certain file management capabilities are available, similar to when you are using Windows Explorer. To rename an existing file or folder, pick it once and pause for a moment, then pick the name again. This places the name in a text box for editing. Type the new name and press [Enter].

For a full listing of all the available options, point to a desired file folder, and then right-click. This displays a shortcut menu of available options for working with the file folder. Use one of the options or pick somewhere off the menu to close it.

CAUTION

Use extreme caution when you are deleting or renaming files and folders. Never delete or rename anything if you are not absolutely certain you should. If you are unsure, ask your instructor or system administrator for assistance.

Opening drawings from previous releases of AutoCAD

In AutoCAD 2008, you can open drawing files created in AutoCAD Release 12 or later. When you open a drawing from a previous release and work on it, AutoCAD automatically updates the drawing to the AutoCAD 2007 file format when you save. After the older release drawing is saved in AutoCAD 2008, it can be viewed in the **Preview** image tile in the **Select File** dialog box during future applications.

NOTE

When you open a drawing file created in a previous release of AutoCAD while using AutoCAD 2008, the file is automatically updated to the new file format. In order for it to be viewed in its original format, you must use the **SAVEAS** command and change the file format appropriately.

Opening drawings as read-only

When a drawing is opened as read-only, the drawing changes cannot be saved to the original file. This ensures that the original drawing file remains unchanged.

To open a drawing as read-only, select the drawing in the **Select File** dialog box, and pick the **Open Read-Only** option from the **Open** drop-down menu. You can also select **Partial Open Read-Only** to use the **Partial Open** option with a read-only file. You can make changes to a drawing opened as read-only, but AutoCAD will not allow you to save the changes to the original file. However, you can use the **SAVEAS** command to save the modified drawing file using a different name.

NOTE

When working with large drawings, you can use the **Partial Open** option to open only part of a drawing by selecting specific views and layers to be opened. Views and layers are discussed later in this textbook.

Exercise 2-2
Complete the exercise on the Student CD.

Opening Drawings from the File Pull-Down Menu List

By default, AutoCAD stores the names and locations of the last nine drawing files opened. These file names are listed at the bottom of the **File** pull-down menu, as shown in **Figure 2-8.** Any one of these files can be quickly opened by picking the file name.

Figure 2-8.
The **File** pull-down menu contains a list of the last nine edited drawings.

Pick to open drawing

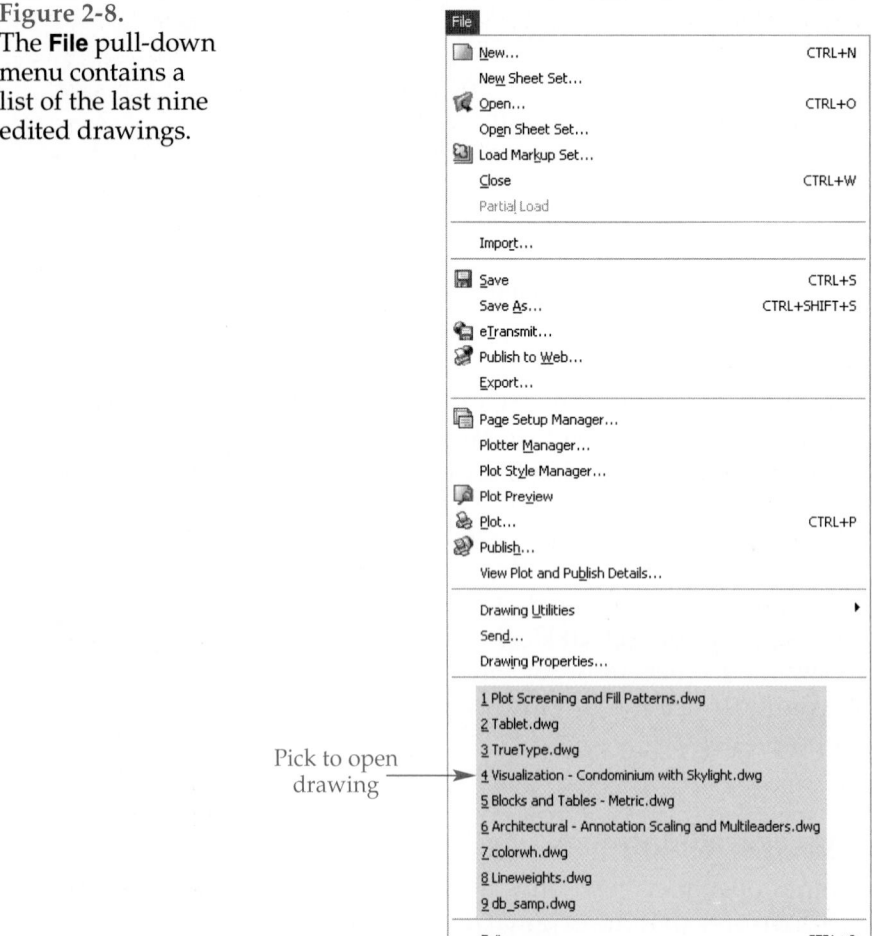

AutoCAD and Its Applications—Basics

If you try to open one of these drawing files after it has been deleted or moved to a different drive or directory, AutoCAD is unable to locate it. AutoCAD displays the message Cannot find the specified drawing file. Please verify that the file exists. AutoCAD then opens the **Select File** dialog box.

PROFESSIONAL TIP

You can specify the number of previous drawings displayed in the **File** pull-down menu by accessing the **Open and Save** tab of the **Options** dialog box. The setting that controls this function is the **Number of recently-used files to list** value in the **File Open** area.

Using Windows Explorer to Open Drawings

You can open drawing files through Windows Explorer in either of two ways. You can double-click on the file, and it opens in AutoCAD. If AutoCAD is not already running, it starts and the file opens. You can also drag-and-drop a file to the AutoCAD command line, and AutoCAD opens it. If AutoCAD is not running, you can drag-and-drop the file to the AutoCAD 2008 icon on your desktop. AutoCAD then starts and opens the drawing file. Refer to the Student CD for more information about Windows Explorer.

Working with Multiple Drawings

AutoCAD allows you to have multiple drawings open at the same time. Most drafting projects are composed of a number of drawings, where each presents different aspects of a project. For example, in an architectural drafting project, required drawings might include a site plan, a floor plan, electrical and plumbing plans, and assorted detail drawings. Consider a mechanical assembly composed of several unique parts. The required drawings might include an overall assembly view, plus individual detail drawings of each component part. The drawings in such projects are closely related to one another. By opening two or more of these drawings at the same time, you can easily reference information contained in existing drawings while working in a new drawing. AutoCAD even allows you to copy all or part of the contents from one drawing directly into another, using a simple drag-and-drop operation.

When multiple drawings are open, display can be controlled by several methods. Controlling the arrangement of multiple drawing windows will help you avoid confusion.

Each drawing you open or start in AutoCAD is placed in its own drawing window. Based on AutoCAD's default behavior, drawing windows are displayed in a floating state. This means the drawing area is displayed within a smaller window inside the main AutoCAD window. When multiple drawings are open at the same time, they are placed in a cascading arrangement by default. The name of each drawing is displayed on the left side of its title bar.

AutoCAD's drawing windows have the same control options as program windows on your desktop. They can be resized, moved, minimized, maximized, restored, and closed, using the same methods used for program windows on your desktop.

The drawing windows and the AutoCAD window have the same relationship that program windows have with the Windows desktop. When a drawing window is maximized, it fills the available area in the AutoCAD window. Minimizing a drawing window displays it as a reduced size title bar along the bottom of AutoCAD's drawing area. Drawing windows cannot be moved outside the AutoCAD window. **Figure 2-9** illustrates drawing windows in a floating state and minimized.

Figure 2-9.
Drawing windows can be displayed in several ways. By default, drawings are displayed in floating windows. Minimized drawing windows are displayed as reduced size title bars. Pick the title bar drawing icon to display a window control menu.

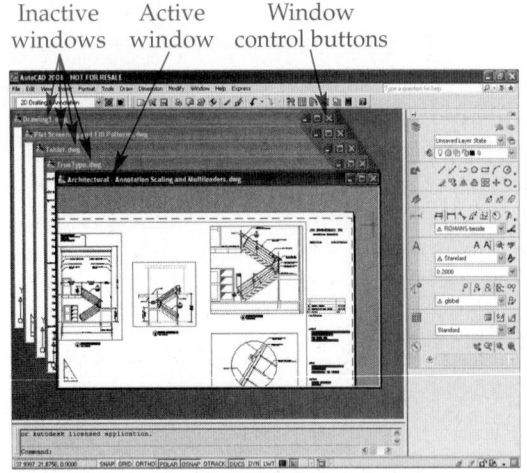
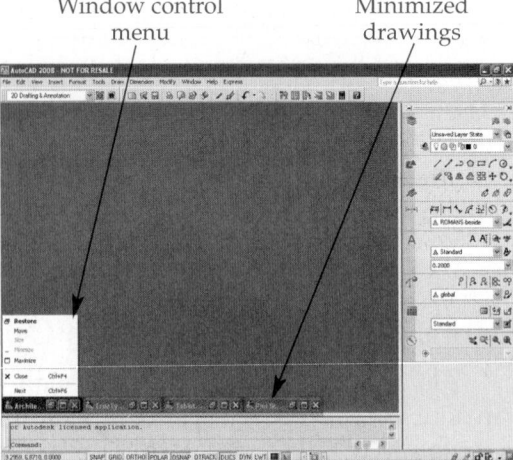

Inactive windows   Active window   Window control buttons   Window control menu   Minimized drawings

Floating Windows   **Minimized Windows**

To work on any currently open drawing, just pick its title bar if it is visible. Pressing the [Ctrl]+[F6] key combination allows you to cycle through all open drawings. To go directly to a specific drawing when the title bars are not visible, access the **Window** pull-down menu in AutoCAD. The name of each open drawing file is displayed, and the active drawing shows a check mark next to it. See **Figure 2-10A**. Pick the name of the desired drawing to make it current. Up to nine drawing names are displayed on this menu. If more than nine drawings are open, a **More Windows...** selection is displayed. Picking this displays the **Select Window** dialog box, **Figure 2-10B**.

The additional control options available in the **Window** pull-down menu include:

- **Close.** Closes the active drawing.
- **Close All.** Closes all open drawings.
- **Cascade.** Arranges the drawing windows that are not currently minimized in a cascade of floating windows, with the active drawing placed at the front.
- **Tile Horizontally.** Tiles the drawing windows that are not currently minimized in a horizontal arrangement, with the active drawing window placed in the top position.
- **Tile Vertically.** Tiles the drawing windows that are not currently minimized in a vertical arrangement, with the active drawing window placed in the left position.
- **Arrange Icons.** Arranges minimized drawings neatly along the bottom of the AutoCAD drawing window area.
- **Lock Location.** Prevents toolbars and windows from being moved in the drawing area.

The effects of tiling the drawing windows vary, based on the number of windows being tiled and whether they are tiled horizontally or vertically. See **Figure 2-11**.

NOTE

Typically, you can change the active drawing as desired. In some situations, however, you cannot switch between drawings. For example, you cannot switch drawings while a dialog box is open. You must either complete the operation or cancel the dialog box before switching is possible.

Figure 2-10.
Selecting the active drawing window. A—Pick the name of a drawing displayed on the **Window** pull-down menu to make it current. This menu also offers additional drawing window control options. B—When more than nine drawings are open, pick **More Windows…** from the **Window** pull-down menu to display the **Select Window** dialog box.

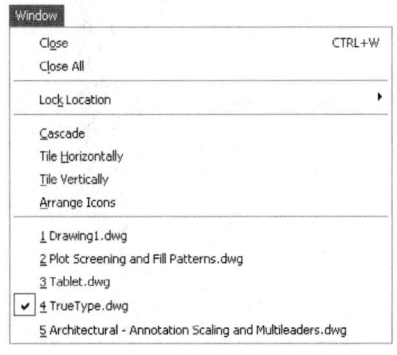

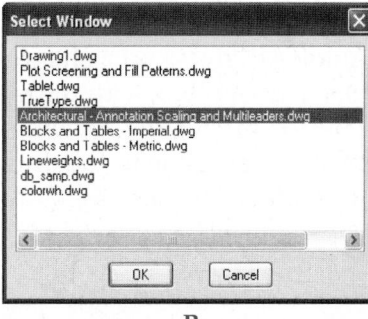

A

B

Figure 2-11.
Tiled drawing windows.

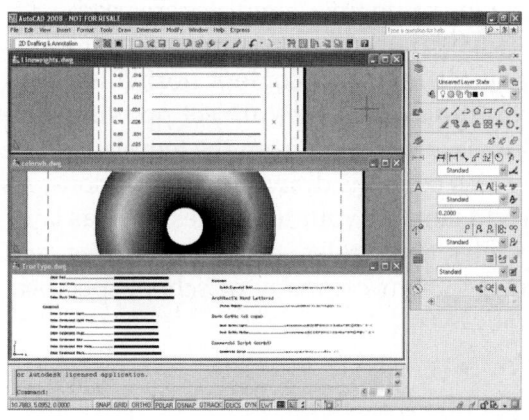

Horizontal Tiling

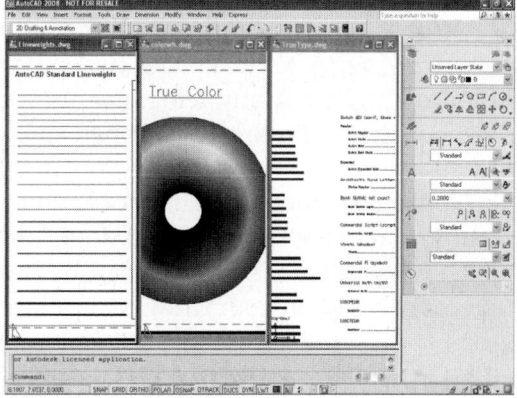

Vertical Tiling

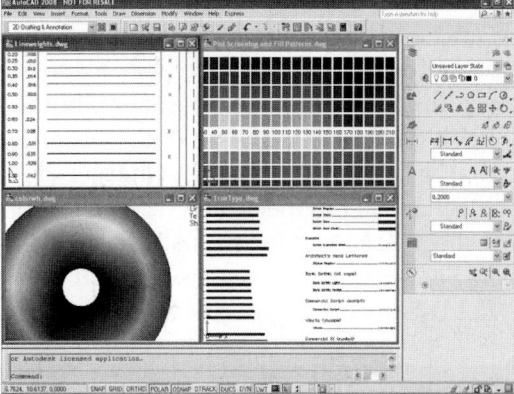

Horizontal or Vertical Tiling

Exercise 2-3

Complete the exercise on the Student CD.

Closing a Drawing

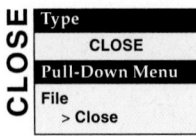

CLOSE

Type
   CLOSE
Pull-Down Menu
File
  > Close

The **CLOSE** command is the primary way to exit a drawing file without ending the AutoCAD session. You can close the current drawing file by picking **File** > **Close** pull-down menu or by typing CLOSE. If you enter the **CLOSE** command before saving your work, AutoCAD gives you a chance to decide what you want to do with unsaved work. An AutoCAD alert box with the message Save Changes to *drawing*.dwg? appears. Pick the **Yes** button to save the drawing. You can also pick the **No** button if you plan to discard any changes made to the drawing since the previous save. Pick the **Cancel** button if you decide not to close the drawing and want to return to the drawing area.

Creating and Using Drawing Templates

Depending on the types of drawing projects with which you work, many settings may be the same from one drawing to the next. These may include drawing aids, such as snap and grid, and drawing settings, such as units. In most companies, standard borders and title blocks are used in all drawings. To save drawing setup time, templates are used.

When you use a template, all the settings saved in the template are applied to your new drawing. A template file can supply any settings and content normally saved in a drawing file. Many templates used by drafting companies are set up with standard borders and title blocks. When a new drawing is created from the template, these objects appear on screen. A template drawing also contains drawing setup options. As you continue through this textbook, you can add items to your templates, such as layer settings, company information, logos, text styles, plot styles, dimension styles, and table styles. All these settings can be designed to your company or school specifications and based on your drawing applications.

Standard Sheet Sizes

sheet size: Size of the paper used to lay out and plot drawings.

Drafters often think of the drawing size as sheet size. The *sheet size* is the size of the paper you will use to lay out and plot the final drawing. It takes into account the size of the drawing and additional space for dimensions, notes, and clear space between the drawing and border lines. The sheet size also includes room for the title block, the revision block, zoning, and an area for general notes. In AutoCAD, the sheet size is specified in the **Page Setup** dialog box when you are defining your drawing layout. The **Page Setup** dialog box is discussed in Chapter 25.

American Society of Mechanical Engineers (ASME) and American National Standards Institute (ANSI) standard sheet sizes and formats are specified in the documents ASME Y14.1, *Decimal Inch Drawing Sheet Size and Format*, and ASME Y14.1M, *Metric Drawing Sheet Size and Format*. ASME Y14.1 lists sheet size specifications in inches, as follows:

Size Designation	Size (in inches)
A	8 1/2 × 11 (horizontal format) 11 × 8 1/2 (vertical format)
B	11 × 17
C	17 × 22
D	22 × 34
E	34 × 44
F	28 × 40
Sizes G, H, J, and K are roll sizes.	

ASME Y14.1M provides sheet size specifications in metric units. Standard metric drawing sheet sizes are designated as follows:

Size Designation	Size (in millimeters)
A0	841 × 1189
A1	594 × 841
A2	420 × 594
A3	297 × 420
A4	210 × 297

Longer lengths are referred to as elongated and extra-elongated drawing sizes. These are available in multiples of the short side of the sheet size. **Figure 2-12** shows standard ASME/ANSI sheet sizes.

All generic templates provided with AutoCAD are based on decimal inches as the unit of measure. Architectural templates may be set up for measurements in inches and feet, which is typical in architectural applications.

NOTE

Although ANSI and ASME standards may be used to set up templates, other standards may be considered. *DIN* refers to the German standard *Deutsches Institut Für Normung*, which was established by the German Institute for Standardization. *Gb* refers to Guo Biao (Chinese) standards, *ISO* is the International Organization for Standardization, and *JIS* is the Japanese Industry Standard. DIN, Gb, ISO, and JIS template files are based on metric measurement settings.

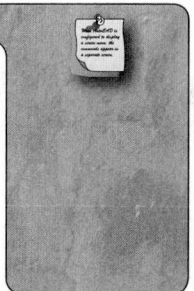

DIN (Deutsches Institut Für Normung): Standard established by the German Institute for Standardization.

Gb: Guo Biao (Chinese) standards.

ISO: International Organization for Standardization.

JIS: Japanese Industry Standard.

The Tutorial templates for architecture and manufacturing are provided with imperial and metric units. The architectural templates provide a title block on the right side of the sheet, which is common in the architectural industry. The Template folder also contains the acad.dwt template, for starting a drawing using feet and inches, and the acadiso.dwt template, for using metric units. These options do not have layouts or title blocks.

PROFESSIONAL TIP

If you want to change the default template folder, you can do so in the **Options** dialog box. To access this dialog box, pick **Tools** > **Options...** from the pull-down menu. In the **Files** tab of the **Options** dialog box, expand Template Settings, and then expand Drawing Template File Location.

Exercise 2-4

Complete the exercise on the Student CD.

Figure 2-12.
A—Standard drawing sheet sizes (ASME Y14.1). B—Standard metric drawing sheet sizes
(ASME Y14.1M).

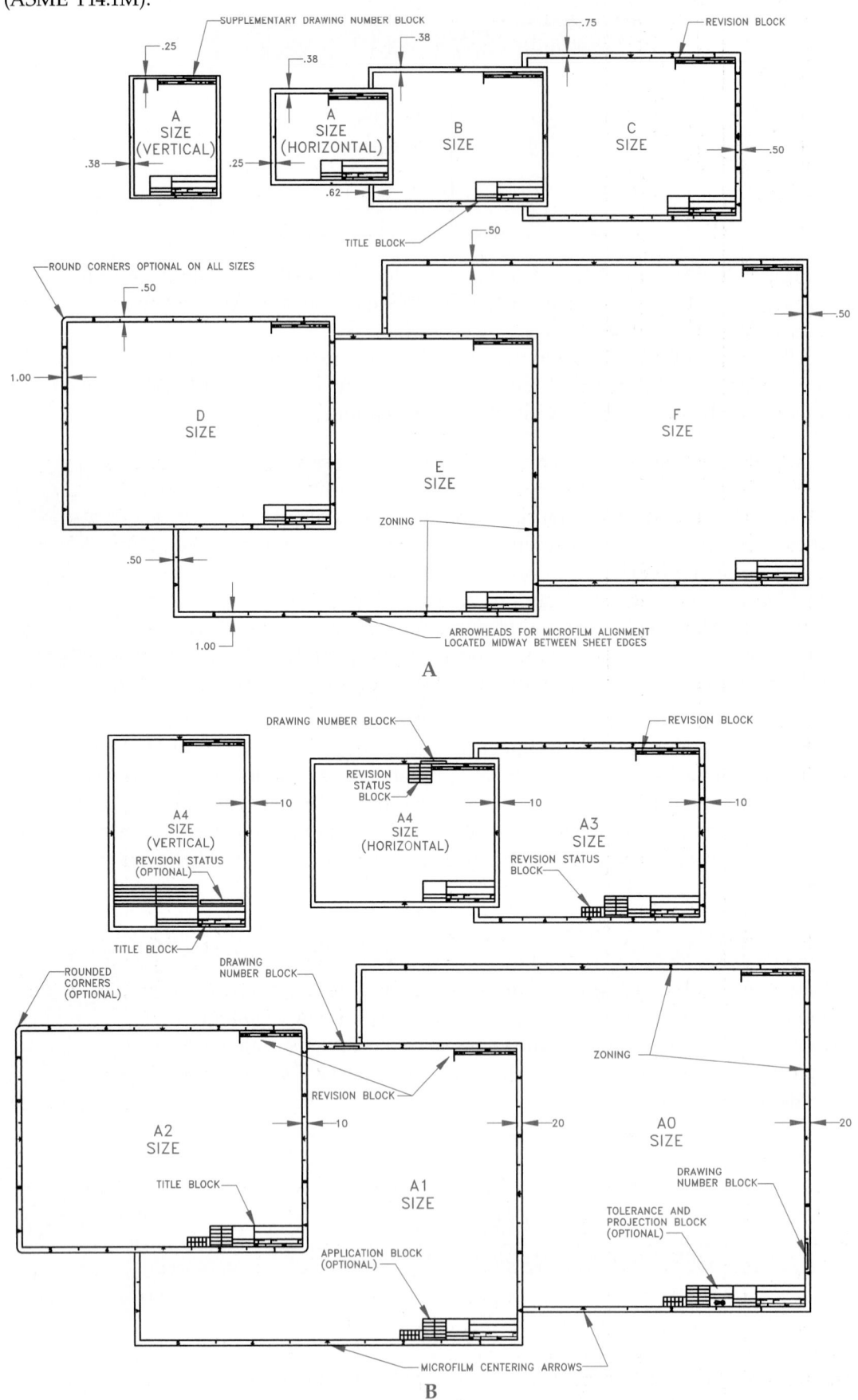

ANSI/ASME Drawing Templates

Although most companies maintain their own templates for employee use, there may be times when you need to create a drawing using the ASME Y14.1 or ASME Y14.1M standard. The *Template Development* section of the Student CD contains several templates that you can use to create drawings in accordance with ANSI/ASME standards.

- **MECHANICAL-INCH.dwt.** Use this template for mechanical drawings dimensioned in decimal inches. This template contains four layout options: **A-SIZE**, **B-SIZE**, **C-SIZE**, and **D-SIZE**.
- **MECHANICAL-METRIC.dwt.** Use this template for mechanical drawings dimensioned using metric units. This template contains four layout options: **A4-SIZE**, **A3-SIZE**, **A2-SIZE**, and **A1-SIZE**.
- **ARCHITECTURAL-US.dwt.** Use this template for architectural drawings dimensioned in feet and inches. This template contains two layout options: **ARCH C-SIZE** and **ARCH D-SIZE**.
- **ARCHITECTURAL-METRIC.dwt.** Use this template for architectural drawings dimensioned using metric units. This template contains two layout options: **ARCH A2-SIZE** and **ARCH A1-SIZE**.
- **CIVIL-US.dwt.** Use this template for civil drawings dimensioned in decimal inches. This template contains two layout options: **C-SIZE** and **D-SIZE**.
- **CIVL-METRIC.dwt.** Use this template for civil drawings dimensioned using metric units. This template contains two layout options: **A2-SIZE** and **A1-SIZE**.

In addition to defining units, layers, and other settings, each template provides appropriate borders and title blocks for laying out drawings. See Chapter 25 for more information about laying out a drawing for plotting. As you proceed through this book, you will learn how to apply the settings and create similar templates of your own. The *Template Development* section at the end of several chapters refers you to the Student CD for important template creation topics and procedures.

Creating Your Own Templates

If none of the predefined AutoCAD templates meet your needs, you can create and save your own custom templates. Some existing AutoCAD templates may be close to what you need and simply need fine-tuning. AutoCAD allows you to save *any* drawing as a template. A drawing template should be developed whenever several drawing applications require the same setup procedure. The template then allows the setup to be applied to any number of future drawings. Creating templates increases drafting productivity by decreasing setup requirements.

Some basic parameters that can be specified in a drawing template include settings for units, snap, and grid. These functions are discussed later in this chapter. You can also draw your own border and title block.

As you learn more about working with AutoCAD, you will find many other settings that can be included in your drawing templates. When you have everything needed in the template, the template is ready to save. Use the **SAVEAS** command to save a drawing template. This command displays the **Save Drawing As** dialog box. To specify that the drawing is to be saved as a drawing template, pick AutoCAD Drawing Template (*.dwt) from the **Files of type:** drop-down list. The file list window then shows all the drawing templates currently found in the Template folder. See **Figure 2-13**. You can store custom templates in another location, but it is recommended that they be stored in the Template folder so they will appear in the **Select template** dialog box. After specifying the name and location for the new template file, pick the **Save** button in the **Save Drawing As** dialog box. The **Template Options** dialog box is now displayed. See **Figure 2-14**. Use the **Description** area to type a description of the template file you are saving. A brief description usually works best. In the **Measurement** drop-down list, specify whether the units used in the template are English or Metric, and then pick the **OK** button.

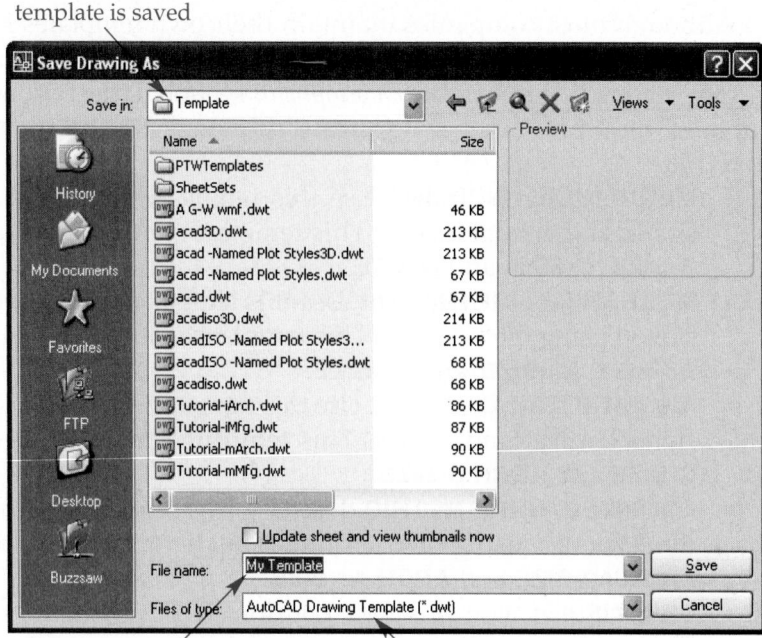

Figure 2-13.
Saving a template in the AutoCAD Template folder.

Folder where template is saved

Enter name for template

Set to save as template

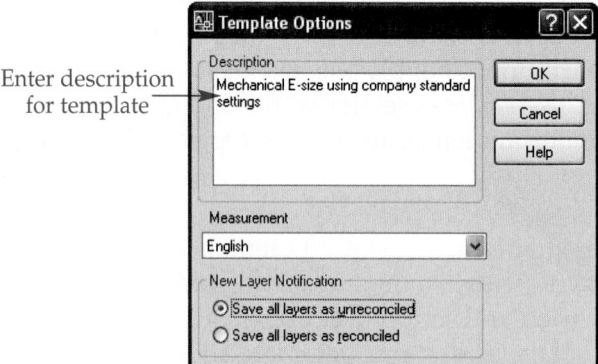

Figure 2-14.
Type a description of the new template in the **Template Options** dialog box.

Enter description for template

The template name should relate to the template, such as Mechanical A size, for a mechanical drawing on an A-size sheet. The template might be named for the drawing application, such as Architectural floor plans. The template name might be as simple as Template 1. The name should be written in a reference manual, along with documentation about what is included in the template. This provides future reference for you and other users. The template drawing you create is saved for you to open and use whenever it is needed. Once you exit AutoCAD and start it up again, the template you created is ready for you to use for preparing a new drawing.

Planning Your AutoCAD Templates

Effective planning can greatly reduce the amount of time it takes to set up and complete a drawing. By creating a variety of templates with various setups, the basic drawing aids and drawing settings are already set when you begin the drawing.

The following sections discuss the most basic drawing aids for inclusion in your templates. These are the basic units, Grid mode, and Snap mode drawing settings. Additional items to be included in templates are discussed throughout this textbook.

Drawing Settings

Drawing settings determine the general characteristics of a drawing. These include the type of units used for linear and angular measurements and the precision to which these measurements are displayed. The drawing units can be changed within a drawing, but it is best to use the settings defined in the template.

Drawing Units

Drawing units are set in the **Drawing Units** dialog box. See Figure 2-15. To access this dialog box, pick **Format** > **Units...** or type UN or UNITS.

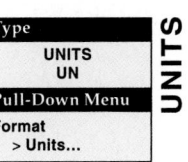

Both linear and angular units are set in the **Drawing Units** dialog box. Linear units are specified in the **Length** area. Select the desired linear units format from the **Type:** drop-down list and use the **Precision:** drop-down list to specify the linear unit's precision. The following options are illustrated in Figure 2-16:

- **Decimal.** Decimal units are used to create drawings in decimal inches or millimeters. Decimal units are normally used on mechanical drawings for manufacturing. This option conforms to the ASME Y14.5M dimensioning and tolerancing standard. The initial default precision is four decimal places.
- **Engineering.** Engineering units are often used in civil drafting projects, such as projects involving maps, plot plans, dam and bridge construction, and topography. The initial default precision is four decimal places.

Figure 2-15.
The **Drawing Units** dialog box.

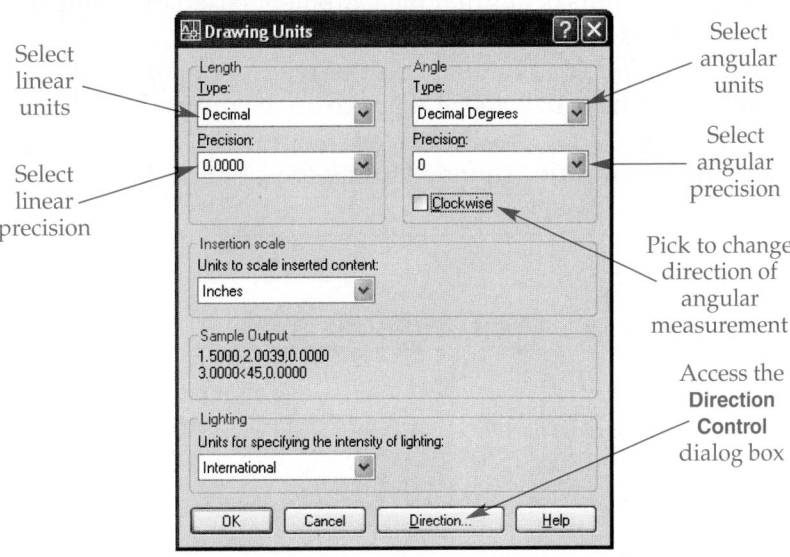

Figure 2-16.
Linear unit formats available in the **Drawing Units** dialog box.

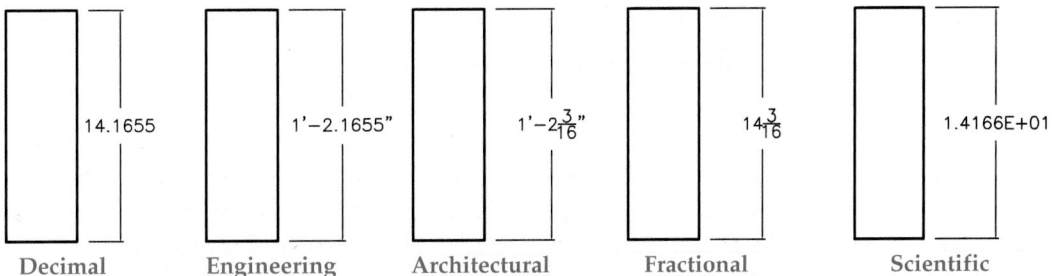

- **Architectural.** Architectural, structural, and other drawings use architectural units when measurements are in feet, inches, and fractional inches. The initial default precision is 1/16″.
- **Fractional.** This option is used for drawings having fractional parts of any common unit of measure. The initial default precision is 1/16.
- **Scientific.** Scientific units are used when very large or small values are applied to a drawing. They are used in industries such as chemical engineering and astronomy. The initial default precision is four decimal places. The unit precision E+01 means the base number is multiplied by 10 to the first power.

The angular unit format and precision is set in the **Type:** and **Precision:** drop-down lists in the **Angle** area of the **Drawing Units** dialog box. Selecting the **Clockwise** check box changes the direction for angular measurements to clockwise from the default setting of counterclockwise.

Pick the **Direction...** button to access the **Direction Control** dialog box. See **Figure 2-17.** The standard **East**, **North**, **West**, and **South** options are offered as radio buttons. Pick one of these buttons to set the compass orientation. The **Other** radio button activates the **Angle:** text box and the **Pick an angle** button. The **Angle:** text box allows you to enter an angle for zero direction. The **Pick an angle** button allows you to pick two points on the screen to establish the angle zero direction.

The angular unit formats available are illustrated in **Figure 2-18** and include:
- **Decimal Degrees.** This is the initial default setting. It is normally used in mechanical drafting, where degrees and decimal parts of a degree are commonly used.
- **Deg/Min/Sec.** This style is sometimes used in mechanical, architectural, structural, and civil drafting. There are 60 minutes in 1 degree and 60 seconds in 1 minute.
- **Grads.** *Grad* is the abbreviation for *gradient*. The angular value is followed by a g. Gradients are units of angular measurement based on one-quarter of a circle having 100 grads. A full circle has 400 grads.
- **Radians.** A *radian* is an angular unit of measurement in which 2π radians = 360° and π radians = 180°. Pi (π) is approximately equal to 3.1416. For example, a 90° angle has $\pi/2$ radians and an arc length of $\pi/2$. Changing the precision displays the radian value rounded to the specified decimal place.

gradient: Angular unit of measurement based on one-quarter of a circle having 100 grads.

radian: Angular unit of measurement in which π radians = 180°.

Figure 2-17.
The **Direction Control** dialog box.

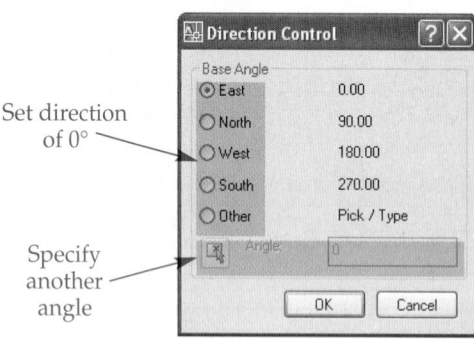

Set direction of 0°

Specify another angle

Figure 2-18.
Angular unit formats available in the **Drawing Units** dialog box.

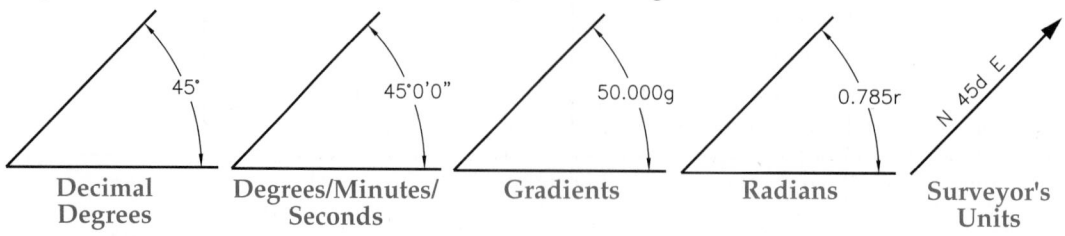

- **Surveyor.** Surveyor angles are measured using bearings. A *bearing* is the direction of a line with respect to one of the quadrants of a compass. Bearings are measured clockwise or counterclockwise (depending on the quadrant), beginning from either north or south. Bearings are measured in degrees, minutes, and seconds. An angle measuring 55°45′22″ from north toward west is expressed as N55°45′22″W. An angle measured 25°30′10″ from south toward east is expressed as S25°30′10″E. Use the **Precision:** drop-down list to set measurement to degrees, degrees/minutes, or degrees/minutes/seconds, or use it to set decimal display accuracy of the seconds part of the measurement.

After selecting the linear and angular units and precision, pick the **OK** button to exit the **Drawing Units** dialog box.

LEGACY NOTE

Every drawing has defined model space drawing limits. These limits are set using the **LIMITS** command. Model space drawing limits are intended to define the space in which all drawing objects are located. The drawing limits can be used to define an area to be plotted and to limit the area in which grid points are displayed.

The **LIMITS** command asks you to specify the coordinates for the lower-left corner and the upper-right corner of the drawing area. The lower-left corner is usually 0,0, but you can specify a different value. The upper-right corner setting usually identifies the upper-right corner of the drawing area. The first value is the horizontal measurement, and the second value is the vertical measurement of the limits. A comma separates the values.

Exercise 2-5

Complete the exercise on the Student CD.

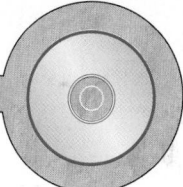

Establishing a Grid on the Screen

AutoCAD provides a grid, or pattern of dots, on the screen to help you lay out a drawing. When the Grid mode is activated, this pattern of dots appears in the drawing area, as shown in **Figure 2-19.** By default, the grid pattern displays only within the drawing limits to help clearly define the working area. The spacing between dots can be adjusted.

Though many ways exist to control whether the grid is displayed on-screen, one of the most efficient ways is to pick the **GRID** button on the status bar. Using this method means no typing is necessary because the grid can be toggled on or off with a mouse click.

Figure 2-20 shows the **Snap and Grid** tab of the **Drafting Settings** dialog box. This dialog box can be used to turn the grid on and off and to set the grid spacing and display. To access the **Drafting Settings** dialog box, right-click on the **GRID** or **SNAP** button in the status bar and select **Settings...** from the shortcut menu.

The grid spacing can be set in the **Grid spacing** area of the **Drafting Settings** dialog box. If the grid spacing you choose is too dense, AutoCAD adjusts the display automatically for the grid to be shown on-screen.

Figure 2-19.
Dots represent the grid spacing when Grid mode is activated.

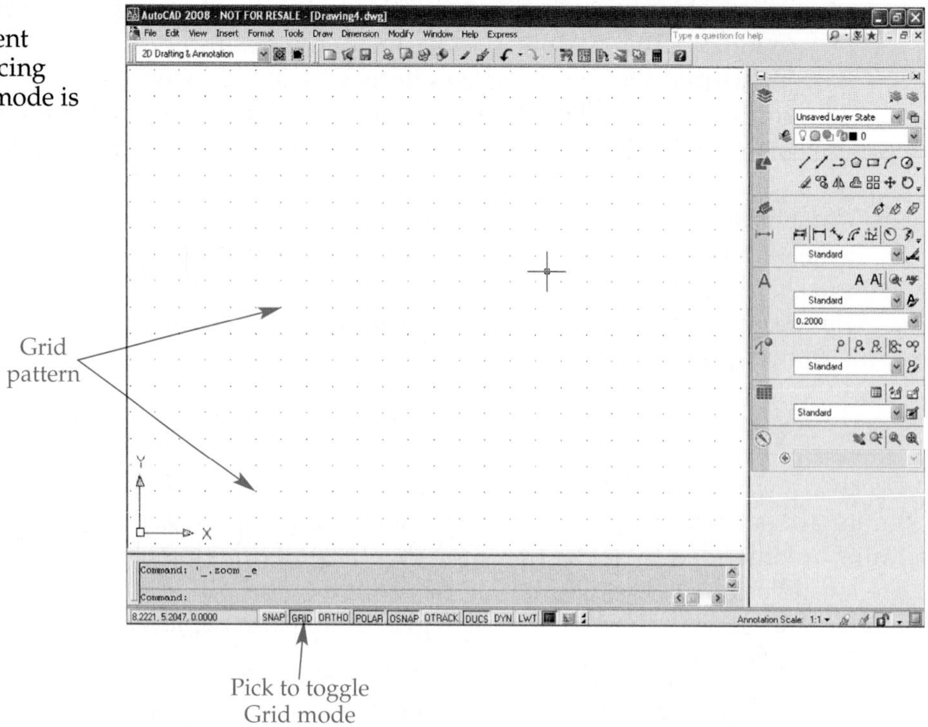

Grid pattern

Pick to toggle Grid mode

NOTE

You can access the **Drafting Settings** dialog box by selecting **Tools > Drafting Settings...** or by typing DSETTINGS, DS, or SE. The grid may be turned on or off by checking the **Grid On** check box inside the **Drafting Settings** dialog box. Other methods for turning the grid on and off include using the **ON** and **OFF** options of the **GRID** command, using the [Ctrl]+[G] key combination, and pressing the [F7] function key.

Figure 2-20.
Grid settings can be made in the **Snap and Grid** tab of the **Drafting Settings** dialog box.

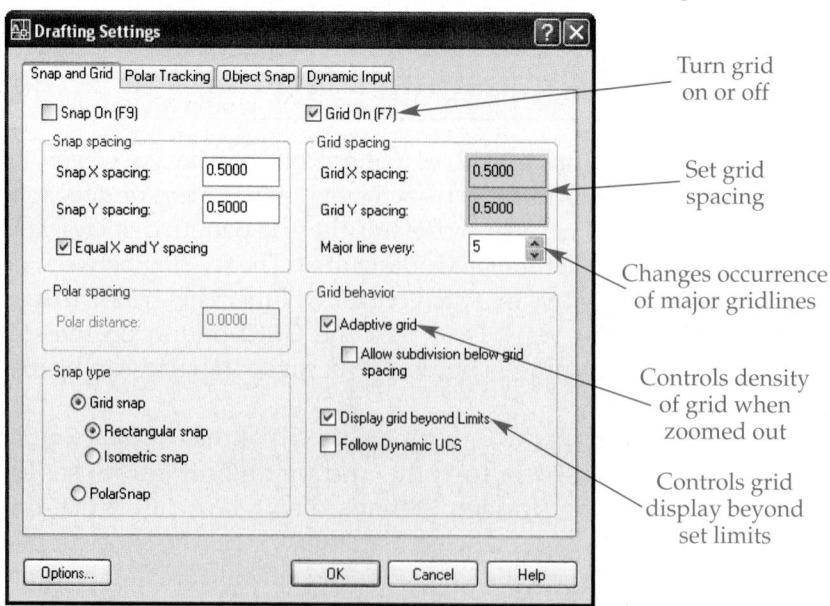

Turn grid on or off

Set grid spacing

Changes occurrence of major gridlines

Controls density of grid when zoomed out

Controls grid display beyond set limits

Figure 2-21.
The X and Y grid spacing units can be set to different values. Notice that, here, the horizontal spacing is greater than the vertical spacing.

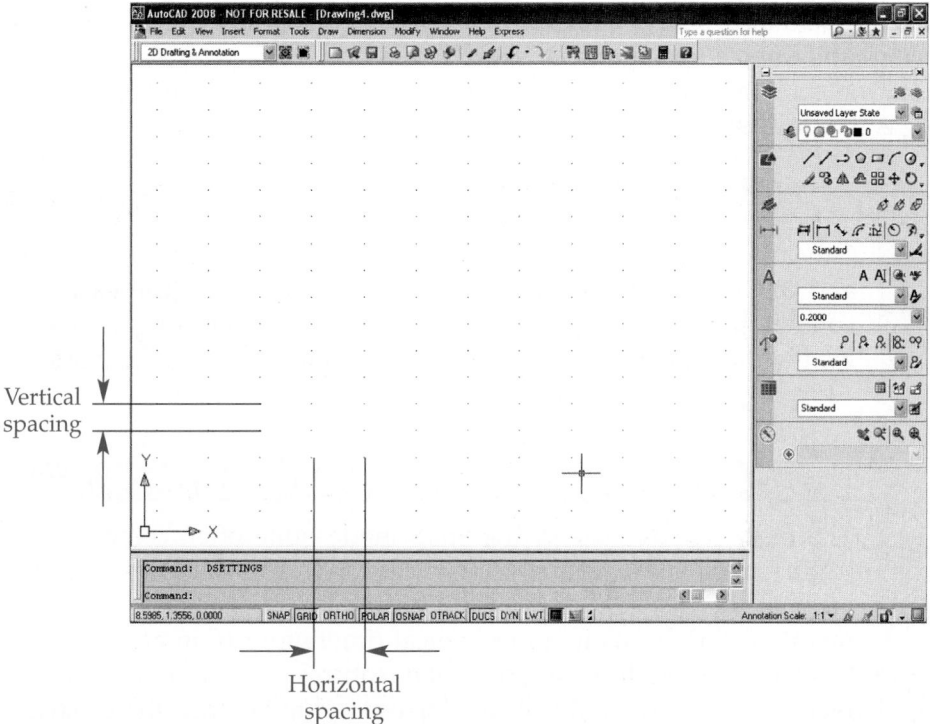

Setting Different Horizontal and Vertical Grid Units

When you are setting different values for horizontal and vertical grid spacing, first be sure the **Equal X and Y spacing** check box in the **Snap spacing** area of the **Drafting Settings** dialog box is turned off. Then, type the appropriate values in the **Grid X spacing:** and **Grid Y spacing:** text boxes. For example, Figure 2-21 shows a horizontal spacing of 1 and a vertical spacing of .5.

Changing the Grid Display

The options in the **Grid behavior** area of the **Drafting Settings** dialog box allow you to set how the grid appears on the screen. When the **Adaptive Grid** check box is turned on, dense grids with small spacing values can be displayed when zoomed out. The **Display grid beyond Limits** option determines whether or not the grid shows only within the set drawing limits. The **Allow subdivision below grid spacing** and **Follow Dynamic UCS** options are used for 3D applications.

Setting Increments for Cursor Movement

When you move your pointing device, the crosshairs move freely on the screen. Sometimes it is hard to place a point accurately. You can set up an invisible grid that allows the crosshairs to move only in exact increments. This is called the *snap grid*, or *snap resolution*. Using the snap grid is different from using Grid mode. The snap grid controls the movement of the crosshairs, while Grid mode is only a visual guide. The grid and snap grid settings can, however, be used together. The AutoCAD defaults provide the same settings for both.

snap grid (snap resolution): Invisible grid that allows the crosshairs to move only in exact increments.

Picking the **SNAP** button on the status bar is an easy way to turn Snap mode on or off at any time. Properly setting the snap grid can greatly increase your drawing speed and accuracy. The snap grid spacing can be set in the **Snap and Grid** tab of the **Drafting Settings** dialog box. See **Figure 2-22**. Type the snap spacing values in the **Snap X spacing:** and **Snap Y spacing:** text boxes.

The value you set remains the same until changed. If you turn snap off, the same snap spacing is in effect when you turn snap on again.

NOTE

Other methods for turning the snap on and off include using the **ON** and **OFF** options of the **SNAP** command, pressing the [Ctrl]+[B] key combination, pressing the [F9] function key, or selecting or deselecting the **Snap On** check box in the **Drafting Settings** dialog box.

PROFESSIONAL TIP

The most effective use of the Snap mode quite often comes from setting an equal X and Y spacing to the lowest, or near lowest, increment of the majority of the feature dimensions. For example, this might be .0625 units in a mechanical drawing or 6″ in an architectural application. If many horizontal features conform to one increment and most vertical features correspond to another, then a snap grid can be set up using different X and Y values.

Setting the Snap Type and Style

The **Snap type** area of the **Drafting Settings** dialog box allows you to select one of two types of snap grids: **Grid snap** or **PolarSnap**. **PolarSnap** allows you to snap to precise distances along alignment paths when you use polar tracking. Polar tracking is discussed in Chapter 7. **Grid snap** has two styles: **Rectangular snap** and **Isometric snap**. **Rectangular snap** is the standard style. **Isometric snap** is useful when you are creating

Figure 2-22.
Snap grid settings can be made in the **Snap and Grid** tab of the **Drafting Settings** dialog box.

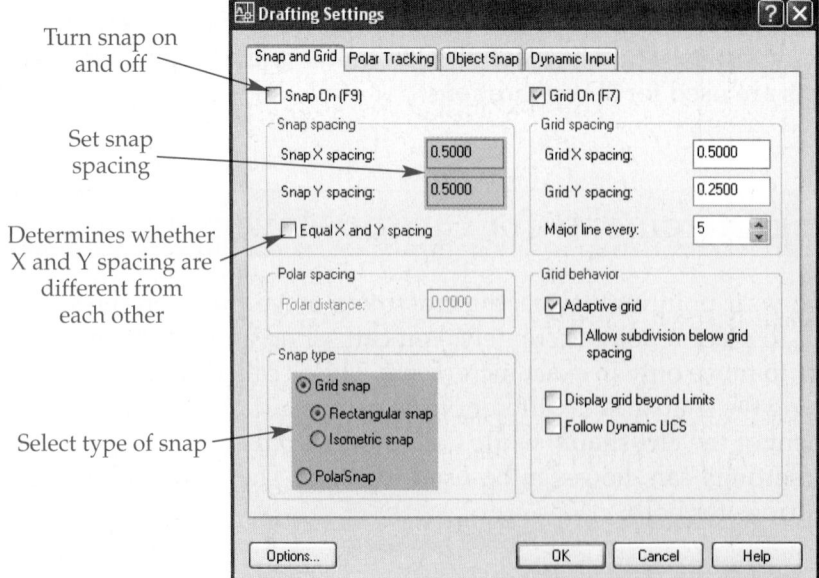

isometric drawings (discussed in Chapter 22). Select the radio button(s) for the snap type and style you desire and pick the **OK** button. You can also use the **Type** and **Style** options of the **SNAP** command to change these settings. Use the **Type** option to select **Polar** or **Grid** and use the **Style** option to select **Standard** (rectangular) or **Isometric**.

Factors to Consider When Setting Drawing Aids

The following factors influence the drawing aid settings you choose to use:

✓ **The drawing units.** If the units are decimal inches, set the grid and snap values to standard decimal increments, such as .0625, .125, .25, .5, and 1 or .05, .1, .2, .5, and 1. For architectural units, use standard increments, such as 1, 6, and 12 (for inches) or 1, 2, 4, 5, and 10 (for feet).

✓ **The drawing size.** A very large drawing might have a grid spacing of 12 (one foot), or 120 (ten feet), while a small drawing may use a spacing of .125 or less.

✓ **The value of the smallest dimension.** If the smallest dimension is .125, then an appropriate snap value would be .125, with a grid spacing of .25.

✓ **The ability to change the settings.** You can change the snap and grid values at any time without changing the location of points or lines already drawn. This should be done when larger or smaller values would assist you with a certain part of the drawing. For example, suppose a few of the dimensions are in .0625 multiples, but the rest of the dimensions are .250 multiples. Change the snap spacing from .250 to .0625 when laying out the smaller dimensions.

✓ **Sketches prepared before starting the drawing.** Use the visible grid to help you place views and lay out the entire drawing.

✓ **Efficiency.** Use whatever method works best and quickest for you when setting or changing the drawing aids.

Exercise 2-6
Complete the exercise on the Student CD.

Template Development
Chapter 2

The development of a drawing template requires much thought and consideration. Many factors and settings need to be defined, and appropriate standards should be consulted. Refer to the Student CD for detailed instructions to begin the development of drawing templates for use in mechanical, architectural, and civil drafting.

Chapter Test

Answer the following questions. Write your answers on a separate sheet of paper or complete the electronic chapter test on the Student CD.

1. What is a drawing template?
2. What does the .dwt file extension stand for?
3. By default, what is the name of the dialog box that opens when using the **NEW** command?
4. How often should work be saved?
5. Name the system variable allowing you to control the dialog box display.
6. Name the command allowing you to quickly save your work without displaying a dialog box.
7. How do you set AutoCAD to automatically save your work at designated intervals?
8. Name the pull-down menu where the **SAVE**, **SAVEAS**, and **OPEN** commands are located.
9. What appears in the **Name** list box when you pick the **Favorites** button in the **Select File** dialog box?
10. What does the term *read-only* mean?
11. From which pull-down menu can you select the name of a recently opened drawing file and open it?
12. How can you set the number of files listed in the pull-down menu described in Question 13?
13. How do you quickly cycle through all the currently open drawings in sequence?
14. How can you simultaneously close all open drawing windows?
15. Identify the command you would use if you wanted to exit a drawing file, but remain in the AutoCAD session.
16. What is sheet size?
17. What are the dimensions of an ASME/ANSI B-size sheet?
18. Is the size of an ASME/ANSI A2 sheet specified in inches or millimeters?
19. How can you access the **Drawing Units** dialog box?
20. Name three settings that can be specified in the **Drawing Units** dialog box.
21. Name the command used to place a pattern of dots on the screen.
22. How do you set a grid spacing of .25?
23. Name three ways to access the **Drafting Settings** dialog box.
24. How do you activate the Snap mode?
25. How do you set a snap spacing of .125?

Drawing Problems

1. Create a new drawing based on one of the templates supplied by AutoCAD. Save the new drawing as a file named P2-1.dwg.

The following problems can be done if the AutoCAD 2008\Sample file folder is loaded. All drawings listed are found in that folder.

2. Locate and preview or open the Lineweights drawing. Describe the drawing in your own words.

3. Locate and preview or open the TrueType drawing. Describe the drawing in your own words.

4. Locate and preview or open the Tablet drawing. Describe the drawing in your own words.

5. Locate and preview or open the 3D House drawing. Describe the drawing in your own words.

The following problems can be saved as templates for future use.

6. Create a template with decimal units with 0.0 precision, decimal degrees with 0.0 precision, default angle measure and orientation, a snap setting of .1, and a grid setting of .5. Save the template as P2-6.dwt. Enter an appropriate description for the template.

7. Create a template with architectural units with 0'-0" precision, decimal degrees with 0 precision, a snap setting of 1", and a grid setting of 6". Save the template as P2-7.dwt. Enter an appropriate description for the template.

AutoCAD includes many standard templates. These templates include settings and title blocks for many standard sheet sizes. Three such templates are shown here.

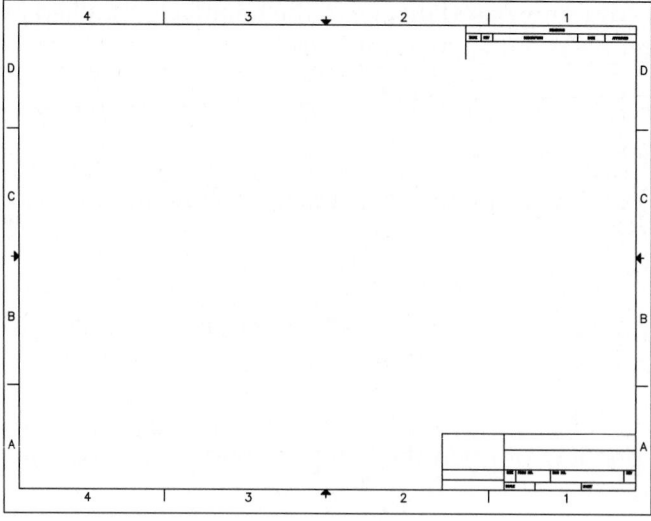

ANSI C Title Block

Architectural Title Block

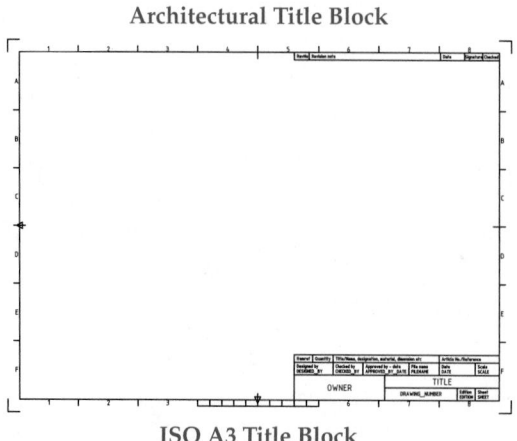

ISO A3 Title Block

CHAPTER 3

Introduction to Drawing and Editing

Learning Objectives

After completing this chapter, you will be able to do the following:

✓ Select the **LINE** command to draw various objects.
✓ Use various point entry methods.
✓ Use **Ortho** mode, direct distance entry, and polar tracking.
✓ Use dynamic input for efficient entry.
✓ Revise objects using the **ERASE** command and its options.
✓ Create selection sets using various selection options.
✓ Cycle through stacked objects.
✓ Use the **OOPS** command to bring back an erased object.
✓ Use the **U** command to undo a command.
✓ Explain the functions of the **UNDO** and **REDO** commands.

This chapter introduces drawing and editing using the **LINE** and **ERASE** commands. Although you will learn many other commands in later chapters, you can learn much about AutoCAD using these two basic commands. Like all drawing commands, **LINE** requires you to enter points in the drawing area. Similarly, like nearly all editing commands, **ERASE** requires you to select one or more objects. This chapter introduces point entry methods, such as coordinate entry, crosshairs selection, and direct distance entry, as well as many methods of object selection.

point entry:
Identifying a point location in AutoCAD's coordinate system.

Drawing Lines with AutoCAD

Individual line segments are drawn between two points on the screen. The process of specifying the endpoints of the line is referred to as *point entry*. Point entry is the simplest form of drafting. After selecting the **LINE** command, simply type the coordinates for each end of the line. Picking the **Line** button in the **2D Draw** control panel of the **Dashboard** or in the **Draw** toolbar, picking **Draw > Line**, or typing L or LINE accesses the **LINE** command.

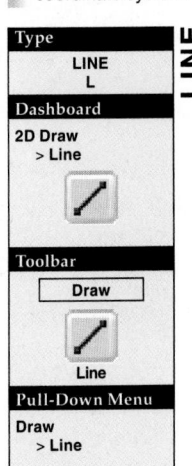

Type
LINE
L

Dashboard
2D Draw
> Line

Toolbar
Draw

Line

Pull-Down Menu
Draw
> Line

LINE

Using the Line Command

To use the **LINE** command, select a start point. When the next Specify next point or [Undo]: prompt appears, continue selecting additional points if you want to connect a series of lines. Then, press the [Enter] key or the space bar or right-click and select **Enter** to end the command.

Responding to AutoCAD Prompts with Numbers

Many of the AutoCAD commands require specific types of numeric data. Some of AutoCAD's prompts require you to enter a whole number. Other entries require whole numbers that may be positive or negative. AutoCAD understands that a number is positive without the plus sign (+) in front of it. The minus sign (–) must, however, precede a negative number.

Much of your data entry may not be whole numbers. In these cases, any real number can be used and expressed as a decimal, as a fraction, or in scientific notation. These numbers may be positive or negative. Examples of acceptable real numbers include:

4.250
-6.375
1/2
1-3/4
2.5E+4 *(25,000)*
2.5E-4 *(0.00025)*

For fractions, the numerator and denominator must be whole numbers greater than zero. For example, 1/2, 3/4, and 2/3 are all acceptable fraction entries. Fractional numbers greater than one must have a hyphen between the whole number and the fraction. For example, 2-3/4 is typed for two and three quarters. The hyphen (-) separator is needed because a space acts just like pressing [Enter] and automatically ends the input. The numerator may be larger than the denominator, as in 3/2, *only* if a whole number is not used with the fraction. For example, 1-3/2 is not a valid input for a fraction.

When you enter coordinates or measurements, the values used depend on the units of measurement.

- AutoCAD understands that values on inch drawings are in inches without placing the inch marks (") after the numeral. For example, 2.500 is automatically understood to be 2.500".
- When your drawing is set up for metric values, any entry is automatically expressed as millimeters.
- If you are working in an engineering or architectural environment, any value greater than 1' is expressed in inches, feet, or feet and inches. The values can be whole numbers, decimals, or fractions.
  - For measurements in feet, the foot symbol (') must follow the number, as in 24'.
  - If the value is in feet and inches, there is no space between the feet and inch value. For example, 24'6 is the proper input for the value 24'-6".
  - If the inch part of the value contains a fraction, the inch and fractional part of an inch are separated by a hyphen, such as 24'6-1/2.
  Never mix feet with inch values greater than one foot. For example, 24'18" is an invalid entry. In this case, you should type 25'6.

Point Entry Methods

Several point entry techniques exist for drawing lines. Becoming skillful with these methods is very important. A combination of point entry techniques should be used to help reduce drawing time.

Each of the point entry methods uses the Cartesian, or rectangular, coordinate system. The *Cartesian coordinate system* is based on selecting distances from three intersecting axes. The point's distance from the intersection point, the *origin*, in respect to each of these axes defines a *location*. In standard 2D drafting applications, you draw objects in the XY plane without referencing the Z axis. Using the Z axis is discussed in *AutoCAD and Its Applications—Advanced*.

In 2D drafting, the origin divides the coordinate system into four quadrants within the XY plane. Points are located in relation to the origin, or (0,0), where X = 0, and Y = 0. **Figure 3-1** shows the X,Y values of points located in the Cartesian coordinate system.

In 2D applications of AutoCAD, the origin (0,0) is usually at the lower-left corner of the drawing. This setup places all points in the upper-right quadrant, where both X and Y coordinate values are positive. See **Figure 3-2**. Methods of establishing points in the Cartesian coordinate system include using absolute coordinates, relative coordinates, and polar coordinates.

Cartesian coordinate system: A rectangular system based on selecting distances from three intersecting axes.

origin: The intersection point of the axes.

location: The point's distance from the origin.

Picking points using the crosshairs

Typically, object snaps are used to select points using the crosshairs. These tools are discussed in Chapter 7. Situations may also arise where **Snap** mode can be a useful aid in using the crosshairs for point entry. This assists in drafting presentation and maintains accuracy when using a mouse. With **Snap** mode on, the crosshairs move in designated increments without any guesswork.

Figure 3-1.
The Cartesian coordinate system.

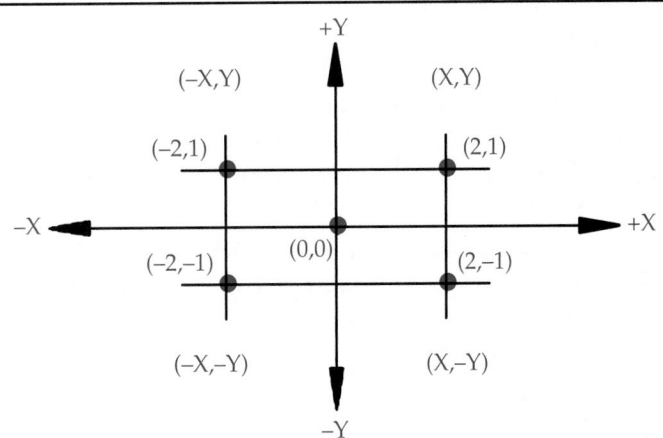

Figure 3-2.
The XY coordinate
axes on the screen.

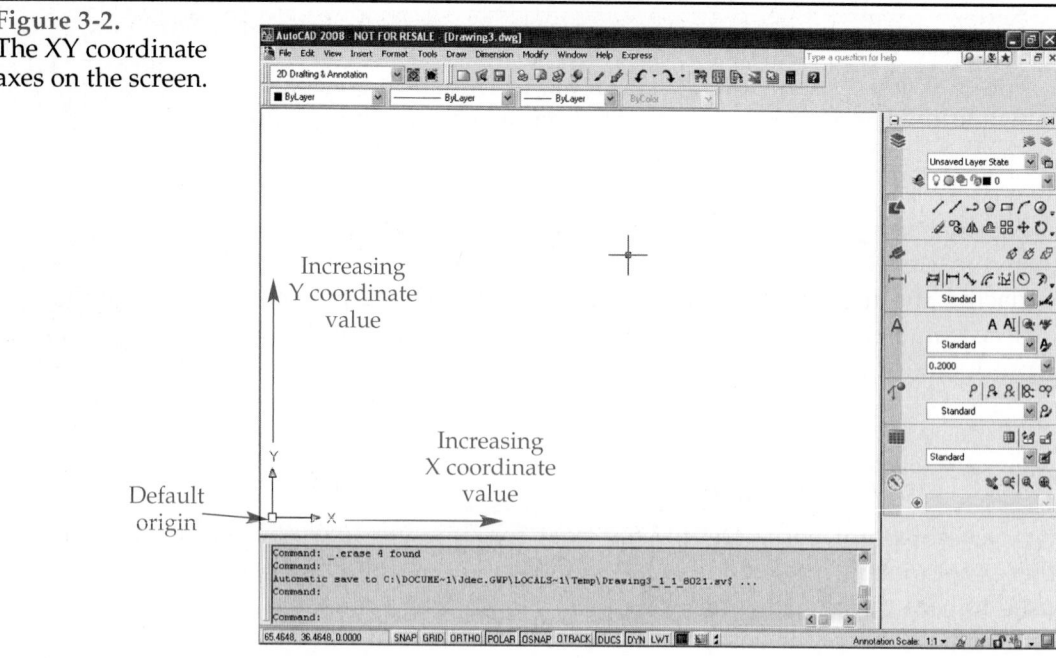

When you use a mouse, the command sequence is the same as when you use coordinates. Points are picked when the crosshairs are at the desired location. After the first point is picked, the distance to the second point and the point's coordinates are displayed on the status line for reference. When picking points in this manner, there is a *rubberband* line connecting the first point and the crosshairs. The rubberband line moves as the crosshairs are moved, showing where the new line will be placed.

rubberband: A stretch line that extends from the crosshairs during certain drawing commands.

Using absolute coordinates

Points located using the absolute coordinate system are measured from the origin (0,0). For example, when X = 4 and Y = 2 (4,2), a point is located four units horizontally and two units vertically from the origin, as shown in Figure 3-3. The coordinate display on the status bar registers the location of the selected point in XYZ coordinates.

The discussion and examples in this chapter reference only the XY coordinates for 2D drafting. Also note that the coordinate display reflects the current system of working units. Remember, when the absolute coordinate system is used, each point is located from 0,0. Follow these commands and point placements in the command line as you refer to Figure 3-4:

Command: **L** *or* **LINE.**↵
Specify first point: **4,2.**↵
Specify next point or [Undo]: **7,2.**↵
Specify next point or [Undo]: **7,6.**↵
Specify next point or [Close/Undo]: **4,6.**↵
Specify next point or [Close/Undo]: **4,2.**↵
Specify next point or [Close/Undo]: ↵
Command:

The command sequence above will work only if dynamic input is disabled. If you are entering absolute coordinates using dynamic input with default settings, you must enter the pound sign (#) before the absolute coordinate value. Dynamic input is discussed later in this chapter.

AutoCAD and Its Applications—Basics

Figure 3-3.
Locating points with
absolute coordinates.

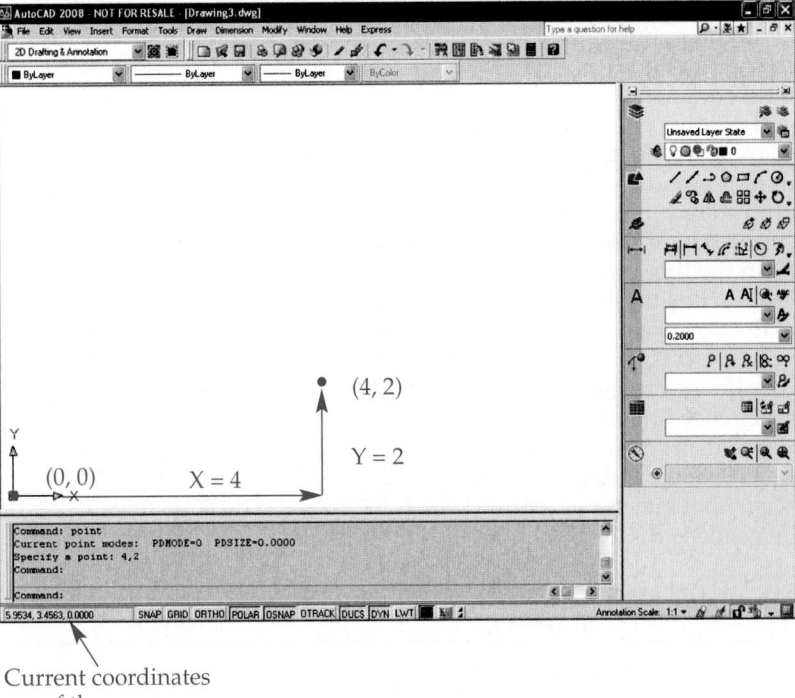

Current coordinates
of the cursor

Figure 3-4.
Drawing simple
shapes using the
LINE command and
absolute coordinates.

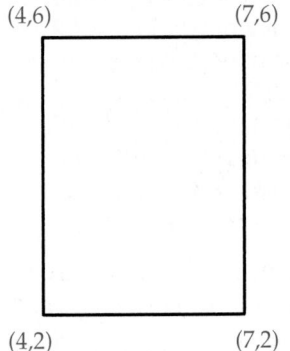

(4,6)   (7,6)

(4,2)   (7,2)

Exercise 3-1

Complete the exercise on the Student CD.

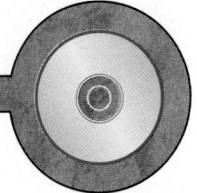

Using relative coordinates

Relative coordinates are located from the previous position, rather than from
the origin. The relationship of points in the Cartesian coordinate system, shown in
Figure 3-1, must be clearly understood before using this method. When you enter relative coordinates at the command window, the @ symbol must precede your entry.
Holding the [Shift] key and pressing the [2] key at the top of the keyboard selects this
symbol. Follow these commands and relative coordinate point placements as you refer
to Figure 3-5:

**relative
coordinates:**
Coordinates
specified from the
previous position,
rather than from the
origin.

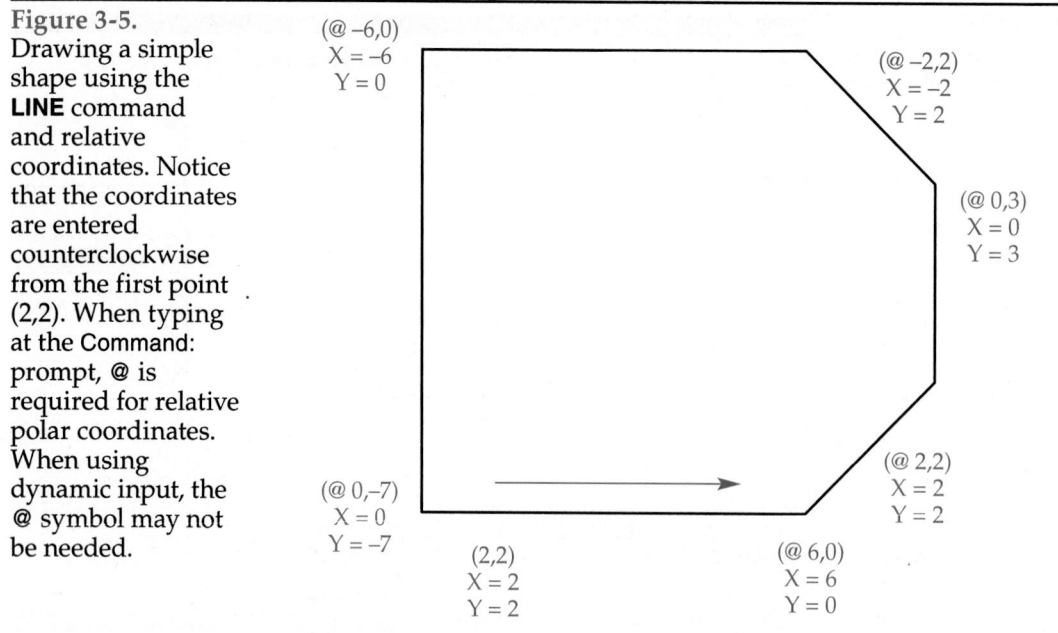

Figure 3-5. Drawing a simple shape using the **LINE** command and relative coordinates. Notice that the coordinates are entered counterclockwise from the first point (2,2). When typing at the Command: prompt, @ is required for relative polar coordinates. When using dynamic input, the @ symbol may not be needed.

(@ –6,0)
X = –6
Y = 0

(@ –2,2)
X = –2
Y = 2

(@ 0,3)
X = 0
Y = 3

(@ 2,2)
X = 2
Y = 2

(@ 0,–7)
X = 0
Y = –7

(2,2)
X = 2
Y = 2

(@ 6,0)
X = 6
Y = 0

```
Command: L or LINE⏎
Specify first point: 2,2⏎
Specify next point or [Undo]: @6,0⏎
Specify next point or [Undo]: @2,2⏎
Specify next point or [Close/Undo]: @0,3⏎
Specify next point or [Close/Undo]: @-2,2⏎
Specify next point or [Close/Undo]: @-6,0⏎
Specify next point or [Close/Undo]: @0,-7⏎
Specify next point or [Close/Undo]: ⏎
Command:
```

This command sequence will work only if dynamic input is disabled. If you are using dynamic input with default settings, relative coordinate entry is assumed for "next point" selections. The @ symbol is therefore not required.

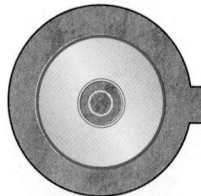

Exercise 3-2
Complete the exercise on the Student CD.

Using polar coordinates

polar coordinates: Coordinates based on the distance from a fixed point at a given angle.

A point located using *polar coordinates* is based on the distance from a fixed point at a given angle. The distance is entered, then the angle. A < symbol separates the two values.

The angular values used for the polar coordinate format are shown in Figure 3-6. Consistent with standard AutoCAD convention, 0° is to the right, or east. Angles are measured counterclockwise.

When preceded by the @ symbol, a polar coordinate point is measured relative to the previous point. If the @ symbol is not included, the coordinate is located relative to the origin. If you want to draw a line four units long from point (1,1) at a 45° angle, type the following information in the command line:

Figure 3-6.
Angles used in the
polar coordinate
system.

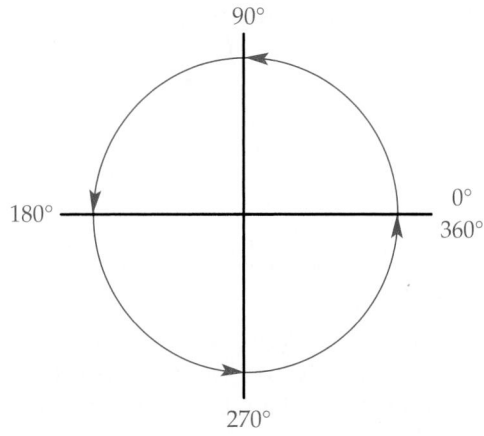

```
Command: L or LINE↵
Specify first point: 1,1↵
Specify next point or [Undo]: @4<45↵
Specify next point or [Undo]: ↵
Command:
```

Figure 3-7 shows the result of this command. The entry @4<45 means the following:
- **@.** Tells AutoCAD to measure from the previous point. This symbol must precede all relative coordinate inputs in the command line. If you are using dynamic input with default settings, this symbol does not need to be entered.
- **4.** Gives the distance, such as 4 units, from the previous point.
- **<.** Establishes that a polar or angular increment is to follow.
- **45.** Specifies the angle, such as 45°, from 0°.

Now, follow these command window entries and polar coordinate points on your computer, as you refer to **Figure 3-8:**

```
Command: L or LINE↵
Specify first point: 2,6↵
Specify next point or [Undo]: @2.5<0↵
Specify next point or [Undo]: @3<135↵
Specify next point or [Close/Undo]: 2,6↵
Specify next point or [Close/Undo]: ↵
Command: ↵
LINE Specify first point: 6,6↵
Specify next point or [Undo]: @4<0↵
```

Figure 3-7.
Using polar
coordinates for the
LINE command.

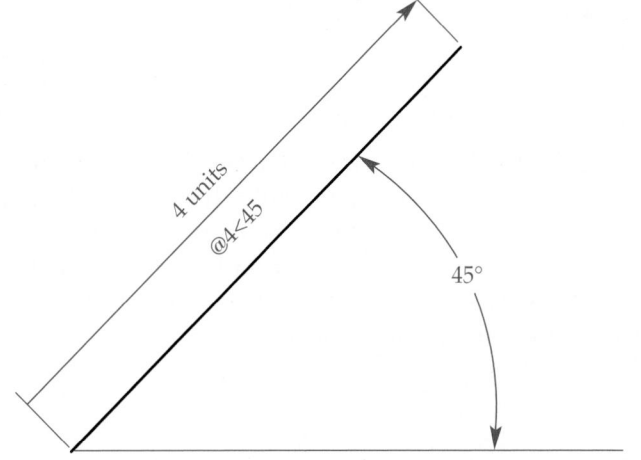

4 units
@4<45

45°

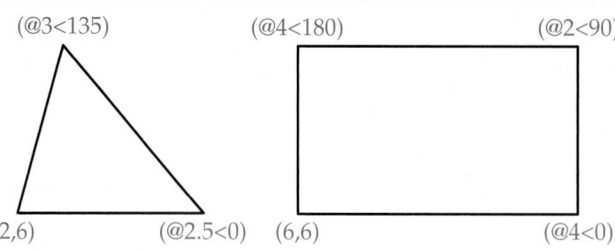

Figure 3-8.
Using polar coordinates to draw.

(@3<135)   (@4<180)   (@2<90)

(2,6)   (@2.5<0)   (6,6)   (@4<0)

Specify next point or [Undo]: **@2<90**↵
Specify next point or [Close/Undo]: **@4<180**↵
Specify next point or [Close/Undo]: **@2<270**↵
Specify next point or [Close/Undo]: ↵
Command:

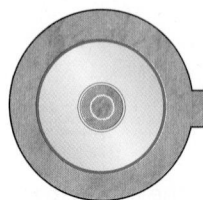

Exercise 3-3
Complete the exercise on the Student CD.

The Coordinate Display

The area to the left side of the status bar shows the coordinate display window. The drawing units setting determines the format and precision of the coordinate display. The coordinate display changes to represent the location of the crosshairs in relation to the origin. Each time a new point is picked or the crosshairs is moved, the coordinates are updated.

Picking the coordinate display in the status bar toggles the coordinate display on and off. With coordinates on, the coordinates constantly change as the crosshairs move. With coordinates off, the coordinate display is "grayed out," but still updates to display the coordinates of the last point selected.

Absolute and polar coordinate display modes may be used. Both display the current crosshairs location. When a command is active, the polar mode displays the crosshairs position as polar coordinate relative to the previously picked point.

Exercise 3-4
Complete the exercise on the Student CD.

Drawing in Ortho Mode

ortho: Orthogonal, at right angles.

The term *ortho* comes from *orthogonal*, which means "at right angles." The **Ortho** mode constrains points selected while drawing and editing to be only horizontal or vertical. See **Figure 3-9**. To activate or deactivate **Ortho** mode, pick the **ORTHO** button on the status bar; use the [F8] function key or the [Ctrl]+[L] key combination; or type ORTHO. If **Ortho** mode is turned off, it can be temporarily turned on when drawing an object by holding down the [Shift] key.

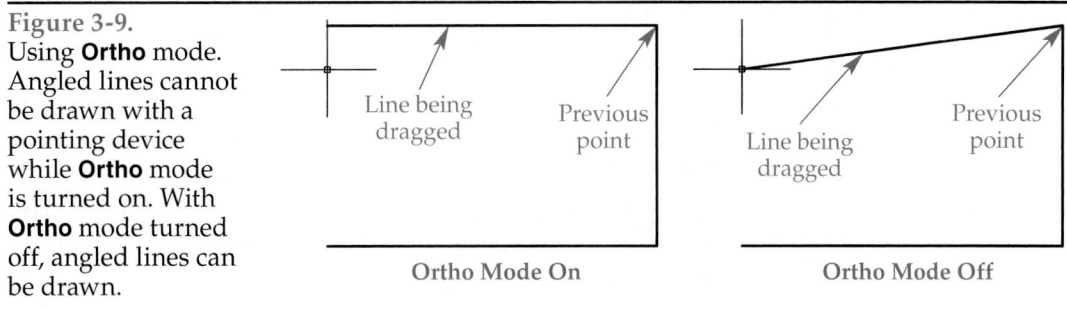

Figure 3-9.
Using **Ortho** mode. Angled lines cannot be drawn with a pointing device while **Ortho** mode is turned on. With **Ortho** mode turned off, angled lines can be drawn.

Ortho Mode On   Ortho Mode Off

Using Direct Distance Entry

Direct distance entry is a method of entering points by dragging the crosshairs to indicate direction and typing a number to specify distance. To draw a line using this point entry method, drag the crosshairs in any desired direction from the first point of the line. Type a numerical value indicating the distance from that point.

The direct distance entry method works best in combination with the **Ortho** mode or polar tracking. **Figure 3-10** shows how to draw a rectangle using direct distance entry. Note that the **Ortho** mode is on for this example:

Command: **L** *or* **LINE**↵
Specify first point: **2,2**↵
Specify next point or [Undo]: *(drag the crosshairs to the right)* **3**↵
Specify next point or [Undo]: *(drag the crosshairs up)* **2**↵
Specify next point or [Close/Undo]: *(drag the crosshairs to the left)* **3**↵
Specify next point or [Close/Undo]: *(drag the crosshairs down)* **2**↵
Specify next point or [Close/Undo]: ↵
Command:

PROFESSIONAL TIP

Direct distance entry is a convenient way to find points quickly and easily with a minimum amount of effort. Use direct distance entry with **Ortho** mode or polar tracking to draw objects with perpendicular lines. Direct distance entry can be used whenever AutoCAD expects a point coordinate value, including drawing and editing commands.

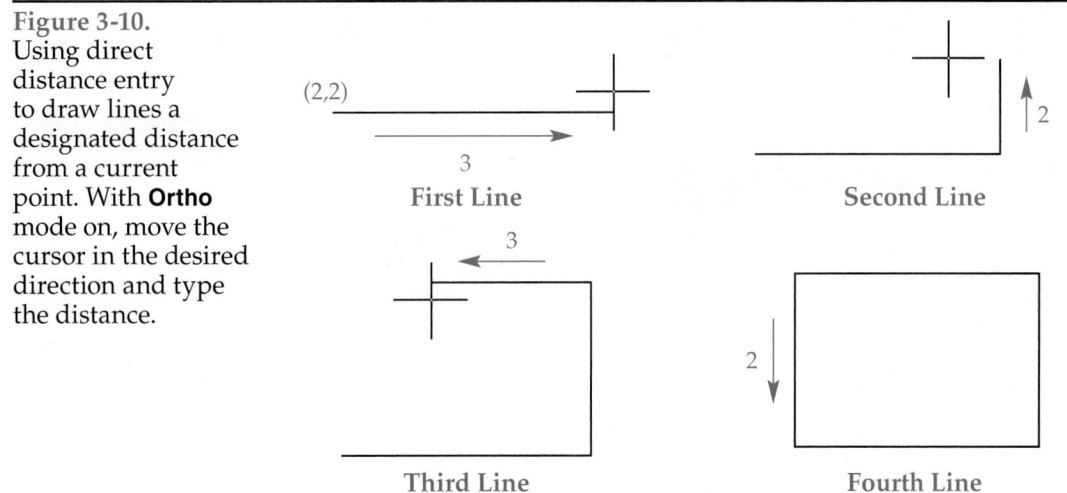

Figure 3-10.
Using direct distance entry to draw lines a designated distance from a current point. With **Ortho** mode on, move the cursor in the desired direction and type the distance.

(2,2)

3

First Line   **Second Line**

2

3

2

Third Line   **Fourth Line**

Introduction to Polar Tracking

Polar tracking is similar to **Ortho** mode, except you are not limited to 90° angles. With polar tracking toggled on, you can cause the drawing crosshairs to "snap" to any predefined angle increment. To turn on polar tracking, pick the **POLAR** button on the status bar or use the [F10] function key. Polar tracking provides visual aids. As you move the crosshairs in the desired direction, AutoCAD displays an alignment path and tooltip at the default polar angle increments of 0°, 90°, 180°, or 270°. Setting different polar alignment angles is explained in Chapter 7.

After you have specified a start point in the **LINE** command and moved the crosshairs in alignment with a polar tracking angle, you only need to type the desired distance value and press [Enter] to draw the line. Polar tracking is used as follows to draw the lines shown in **Figure 3-11**:

> Command: **L** *or* **LINE**↵
> Specify first point: **2,2**↵
> Specify next point or [Undo]: **2** *(drag the crosshairs while watching the tooltip; at 0°, press [Enter])*
> Specify next point or [Undo]: **3** *(drag the crosshairs while watching the tooltip; at 90°, press [Enter])*
> Specify next point or [Close/Undo]: ↵
> Command:

Polar tracking is discussed in detail in Chapter 7.

Using Previously Picked Points

In some cases, you will need to specify a point that has already been picked. AutoCAD provides several methods for picking previously selected points.

Typing @ and pressing [Enter] at a point selection prompt automatically picks the last point selected. In addition, you can access a list of recently picked points by right-clicking and picking the **Recent Input** cascading menu.

Figure 3-11.
Using polar tracking to draw lines at predefined angle increments.

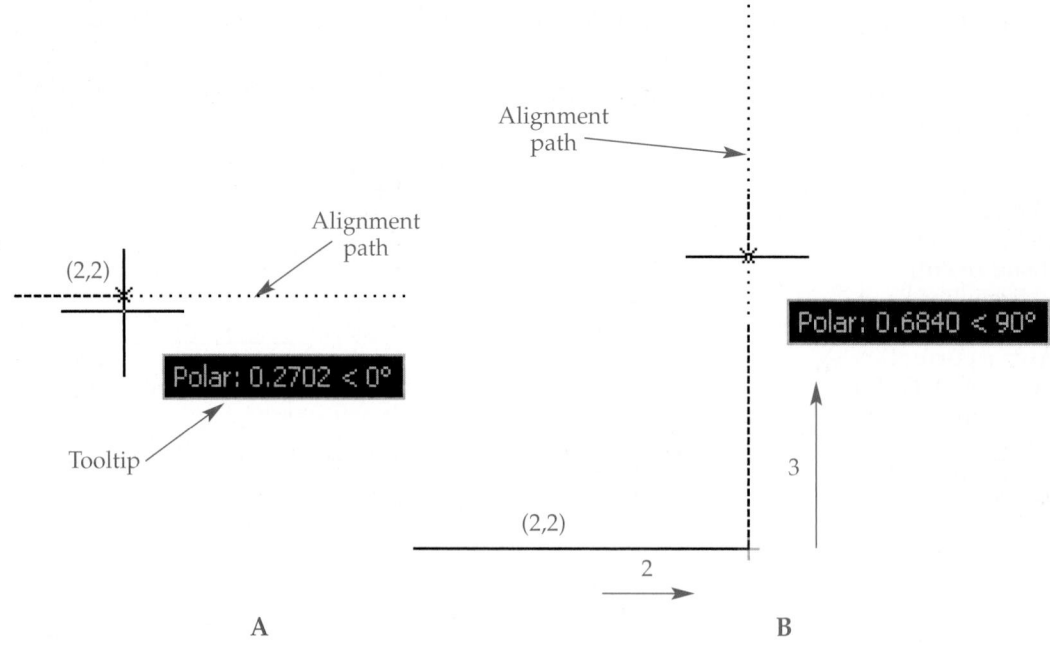

When you use dynamic input, pressing the up arrow key at a point selection prompt displays the coordinates of the last picked point. You can continue to press the up arrow key to cycle through other previously picked points. As you scroll through the point coordinates in this way, a symbol appears at the displayed point's location. This is a useful tool for reselecting points.

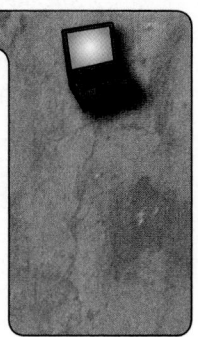

PROFESSIONAL TIP

Practice using the different point entry techniques and decide which method works best for certain situations. Keep in mind that you may mix methods to help enhance your drawing speed. For example, absolute coordinates may work best to locate an initial point or to draw a simple shape. These calculations are easy. Polar coordinates may work better to locate features in a circular pattern or at an angular relationship. Practice with **Ortho** mode, polar tracking, and direct distance entry to see the advantages and disadvantages of each.

Exercise 3-5
Complete the exercise on the Student CD.

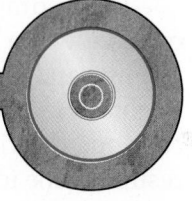

Using the Close Line Option

A *polygon* is a closed plane figure with at least three sides. Triangles and rectangles are examples of polygons. After you have drawn two or more line segments of a polygon, the endpoint of the last line segment can be connected automatically to the first line segment using the **Close** option. To use this option, type C or CLOSE. In Figure 3-12, the last line is drawn using the **Close** option, as follows:

polygon: Closed plane figure with at least three sides.

> Command: **L** *or* **LINE**↵
> Specify first point: *(pick Point 1)*
> Specify next point or [Undo]: *(pick Point 2)*
> Specify next point or [Undo]: *(pick Point 3)*
> Specify next point or [Close/Undo]: *(pick Point 4)*
> Specify next point or [Close/Undo]: **C**↵
> Command:

Using the Line Continue Option

Suppose you draw a line, then exit the **LINE** command, but decide to go back and connect a new line to the end of the previous one. Type L to begin the **LINE** command. At the Specify first point: prompt, simply press the [Enter] key or space bar or right-click the mouse. This action automatically connects the first endpoint of the new line

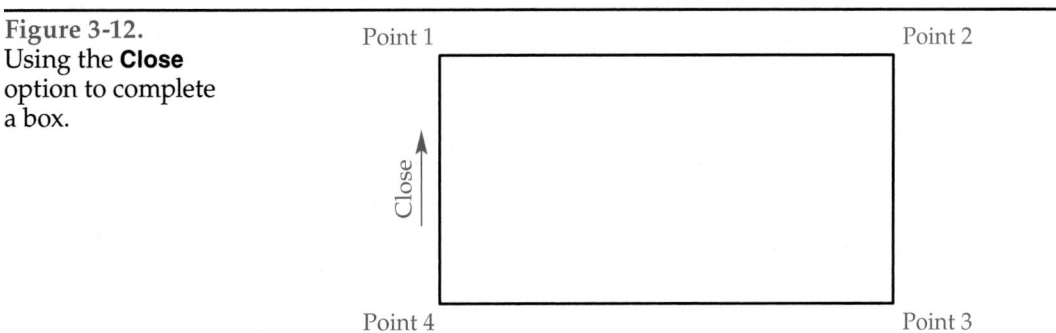

Figure 3-12.
Using the **Close** option to complete a box.

Point 1　　　　Point 2

Close

Point 4　　　　Point 3

segment to the endpoint of the previous one. The **Continue** option can also be used for drawing arcs, as discussed in Chapter 4. The following command sequence is used for continuing a line:

Command: **L** *or* **LINE**⏎
Specify first point: *(press [Enter] or the space bar, and AutoCAD automatically picks the last endpoint of the previous line)*
Specify next point or [Undo]: *(pick the next point)*
Specify next point or [Undo]: *(press [Enter] to exit the command)*
Command:

PROFESSIONAL TIP

Pressing the space bar or [Enter] repeats the previous command.

Undoing the Previously Drawn Line

When drawing a series of lines, you may find you made an error. To delete the mistake while still in the **LINE** command, type U at the Specify next point or [Undo]: prompt and press [Enter]. This removes the previously drawn line and allows you to continue from the previous endpoint. You can use the **Undo** option repeatedly to continue deleting line segments until the entire line is gone. See **Figure 3-13** for the results of the following prompt sequence:

Command: **L** *or* **LINE**⏎
Specify first point: *(pick Point 1)*
Specify next point or [Undo]: *(pick Point 2)*
Specify next point or [Undo]: *(pick Point 3)*
Specify next point or [Close/Undo]: *(pick Point 4)*
Specify next point or [Close/Undo]: **U**⏎
Specify next point or [Close/Undo]: **U**⏎
Specify next point or [Undo]: *(pick Point 5)*
Specify next point or [Close/Undo]: *(press [Enter] to exit the command)*
Command:

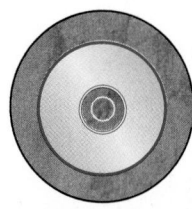

Exercise 3-6
Complete the exercise on the Student CD.

Figure 3-13.
Using the **Undo** option while in the **LINE** command.

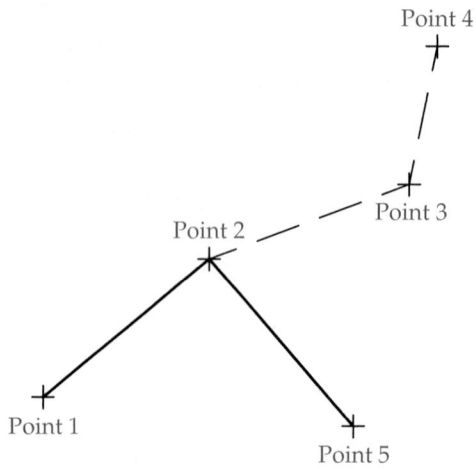

Point 4

Point 3

Point 2

Point 1

Point 5

Dynamic Input

Earlier in this chapter, absolute, relative, and polar coordinates were discussed, and the command line method was used to demonstrate inputting values. Typing the same values when dynamic input is enabled produces the same results, but some additional techniques are available when using dynamic input.

Dynamic Input and Coordinate Input

When you start the **LINE** command, the dynamic input tooltip reads Specify first point:, the X coordinate value is active, and the Y coordinate value is displayed. See **Figure 3-14**. At this point, the X and Y coordinates can be typed using the same method as with the command line. For example, typing 4,2 and pressing [Enter] starts the line 4 units on the X axis and 2 units on the Y axis. The 4 is typed into the X coordinate field, and when the comma (,) is typed, the Y coordinate field becomes active. The 2 is then typed into the Y coordinate field. If you type the @ symbol before an entry to specify relative coordinates or typing the less than symbol (<) to specify polar coordinates, the dynamic input fields automatically change to anticipate the next entry, just as when a comma is entered. **Figure 3-15** shows the dynamic input fields when using relative and polar coordinates.

PROFESSIONAL TIP

The [Tab] key on the keyboard can be used to cycle through the dynamic input fields. You may find this more convenient than using characters such as the comma (,) and the less than symbol (<).

Figure 3-14.
After you start the **LINE** command, dynamic input displays these items.

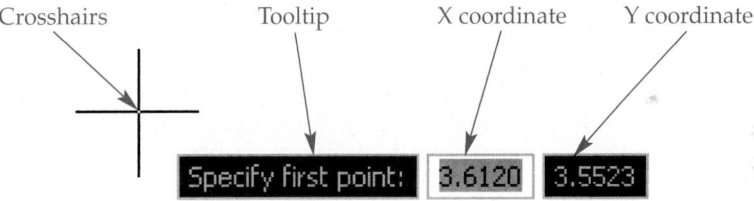

Figure 3-15.
A—After you type the @ symbol, it is displayed in the tooltip. B—When using the polar coordinates, the less than symbol (<) is displayed in the tooltip just before the angle.

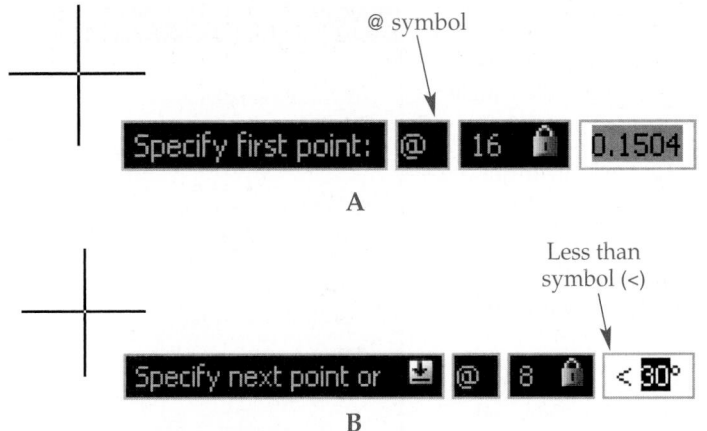

Dynamic Input Settings

Options for dynamic input can be found on the **Dynamic Input** tab of the **Drafting Settings** dialog box. To access this dialog box, right-click on the **DYN** button from the status bar, and then select **Settings**; pick **Tools** > **Drafting Settings...** from the pull-down menu; or type DSETTINGS or DS. **Figure 3-16** shows the **Dynamic Input** tab of the **Drafting Settings** dialog box.

When **Enable Pointer Input** is checked, commands are entered into the pointer input field next to the crosshairs. The X and Y coordinates are also displayed in the tooltip area, and values can be typed directly into these fields. When **Enable Pointer Input** is unchecked, typing occurs at the command line. Picking the **Settings...** button in the **Pointer Input** area displays the **Pointer Input Settings** dialog box. See **Figure 3-17**.

Figure 3-16.
Dynamic input settings are found on the **Dynamic Input** tab of the **Drafting Settings** dialog box.

When this box is checked, commands are entered into the pointer input field

Diplays the **Pointer Input Settings** dialog box

Displays the **Tooltip Appearance** dialog box

When this box is checked, the dimension and angle values are displayed

Displays the **Dimension Input Settings** dialog box

Determines whether or not the command prompts and tooltips appear next to the crosshairs

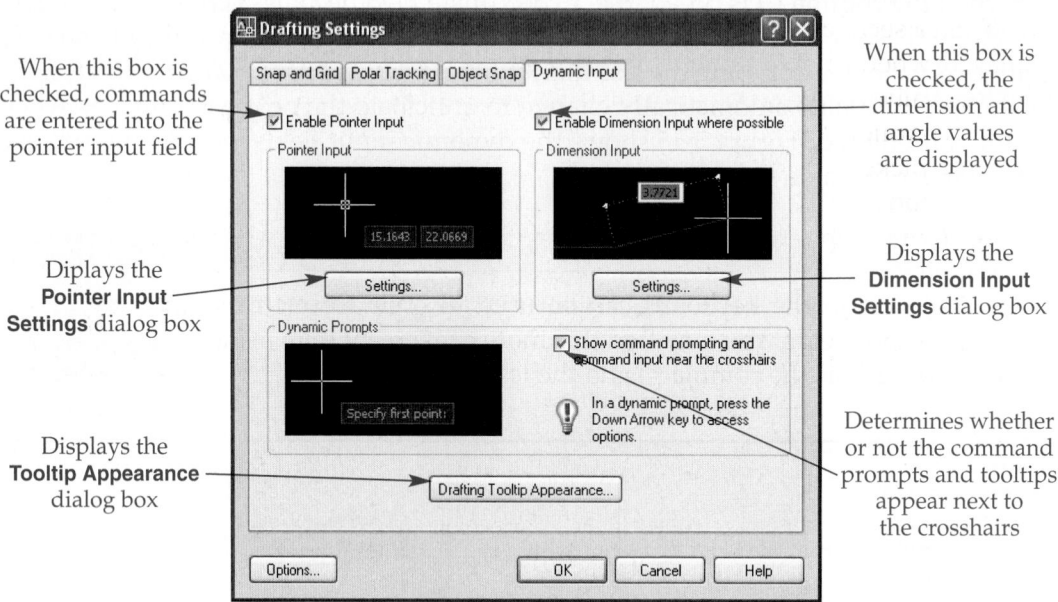

Figure 3-17.
The **Pointer Input Settings** dialog box controls the format and visibility of the tooltip.

Tooltip values are displayed as a distance and an angle

Tooltip values are displayed as X and Y values

Tooltip values do not appear until a value is typed

X and Y coordinates are always displayed

Tooltip values are displayed relative to the last point picked

Tooltip values are displayed as absolute coordinate values

Tooltip values appear when a command is in progress and prompt for a point to be selected

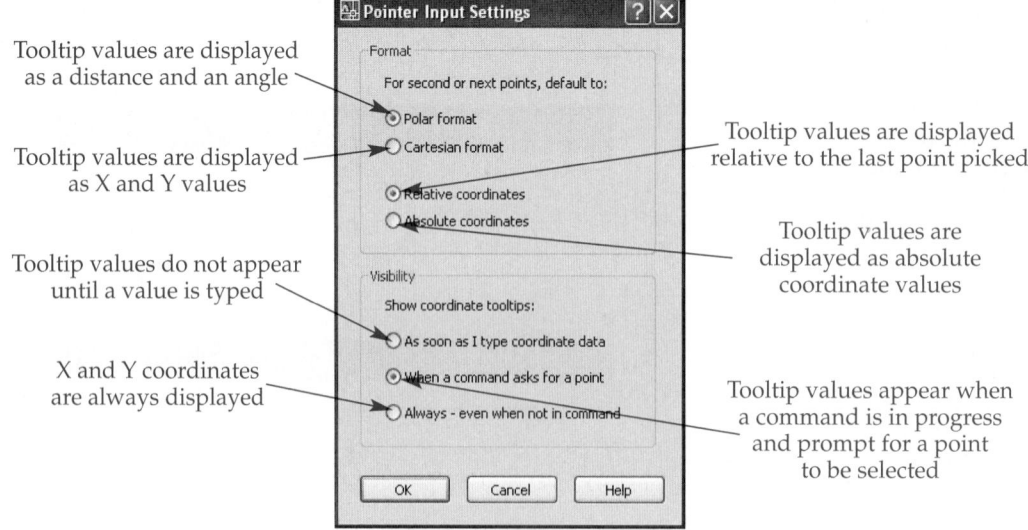

In the **Format** area, default options can be specified for selecting a second or next point. The following options are available:

- **Polar format.** Tooltip values are displayed in the polar format (distance and angle).
- **Cartesian format.** Tooltip values are displayed in the Cartesian format (X and Y values).
- **Relative coordinates.** Tooltip values are displayed relative to the last point picked.
- **Absolute coordinates.** Tooltip values are displayed in the absolute coordinate values.

The **Visibility** area of the **Pointer Input Settings** dialog box controls when the tooltip values appear next to the crosshairs. When **As soon as I type coordinate data** is selected, the tooltip values do not appear until a value is typed. If **When a command asks for a point** is selected, the tooltip values appear when a command is in progress and the command is prompting for a point to be selected. To have the X and Y coordinates always displayed, select **Always - even when not in a command**.

When a second point or distance is requested, the dimension and angle values are displayed when **Enable Dimension Input where possible** is checked on the **Dynamic Input** tab. Values can be typed directly into these fields. As you move the crosshairs, the values dynamically update to reflect the current crosshairs location relative to the last point picked. Pick the **Settings...** button in the **Dimension Input** area to open the **Dimension Input Settings** dialog box. This dialog box is shown in **Figure 3-18**. For the most part, these options apply to grip editing, which is discussed in Chapter 12. The following options are available in the **Visibility** area:

- **Show only 1 dimension input field at a time.** Displays only the distance dimension value when creating and grip-editing objects.
- **Show 2 dimension input fields at a time.** Displays the distance and the angle value when creating and grip-editing objects.
- **Show the following dimension input fields simultaneously.** Lets you select any of the items to display when applicable for grip-editing objects.
  - **Resulting Dimension.** Displays the dynamic distance value while you move the crosshairs when grip-editing an object.
  - **Length Change.** Displays the change in length when you grip-edit an object.
  - **Absolute Angle.** Displays the absolute angle during grip-editing.
  - **Angle Change.** Displays the change in angle during grip-editing.
  - **Arc Radius.** Displays the radius of an arc while it is being grip-edited.

Figure 3-18.
Different dimension values can be specified to display as tooltips from the **Dimension Input Settings** dialog box.

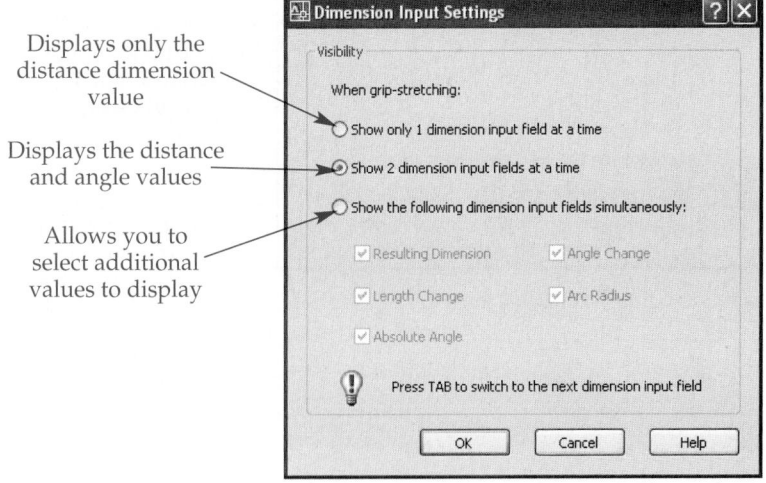

Displays only the distance dimension value

Displays the distance and angle values

Allows you to select additional values to display

In the **Dynamic Prompts** area of the **Dynamic Input** tab, the **Show command prompting and command input near the crosshairs** setting determines whether the command prompts and tooltips appear next to the crosshairs. If this option is turned off, the down arrow key on the keyboard can be pressed to show the command prompting and inputs. Picking the **Drafting Tooltip Appearance...** button at the bottom of the **Dynamic Input** tab displays the **Tooltip Appearance** dialog box. See **Figure 3-19**. The **Colors...** button presents the **Drawing Window Colors** dialog box, allowing you to change the background color for drafting tooltips. The **Context:** list box displays the various applications for drafting tooltips. Pick the context, such as **2D model space**, and then pick in the **Color:** box to display a drop-down list of available colors. In the **Size** area, you can type a value or drag the slider bar to change the overall size of the dynamic input fields. The **Transparency** setting can be changed so you can see through the dynamic input fields to the drawing area. Increasing the transparency value allows you to see through the dynamic input fields, but the fields are less visible. Two options exist in the **Apply to:** area that determine the tooltips where the settings are applied. If **Override OS settings for all drafting tooltips** is selected, the appearance options are applied to all tooltips, overriding the operating system settings. When **Use settings only for Dynamic Input tooltips** is selected, the appearance options are applied only to tooltips controlled by dynamic input.

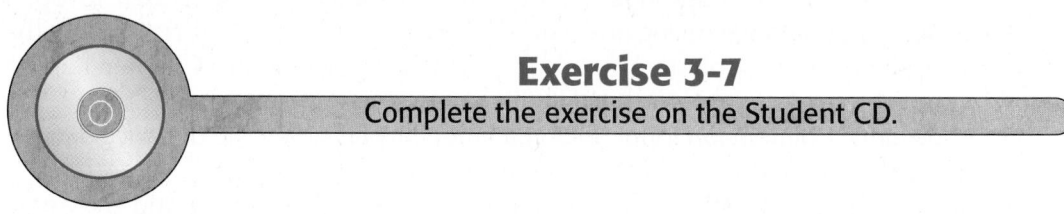

Exercise 3-7
Complete the exercise on the Student CD.

Figure 3-19.
The tooltip color, size, and transparency settings can be specified in the **Tooltip Appearance** dialog box.

Changes the background color of tooltips

Changes the overall size of dynamic input fields

Changes the transparency of dynamic input fields

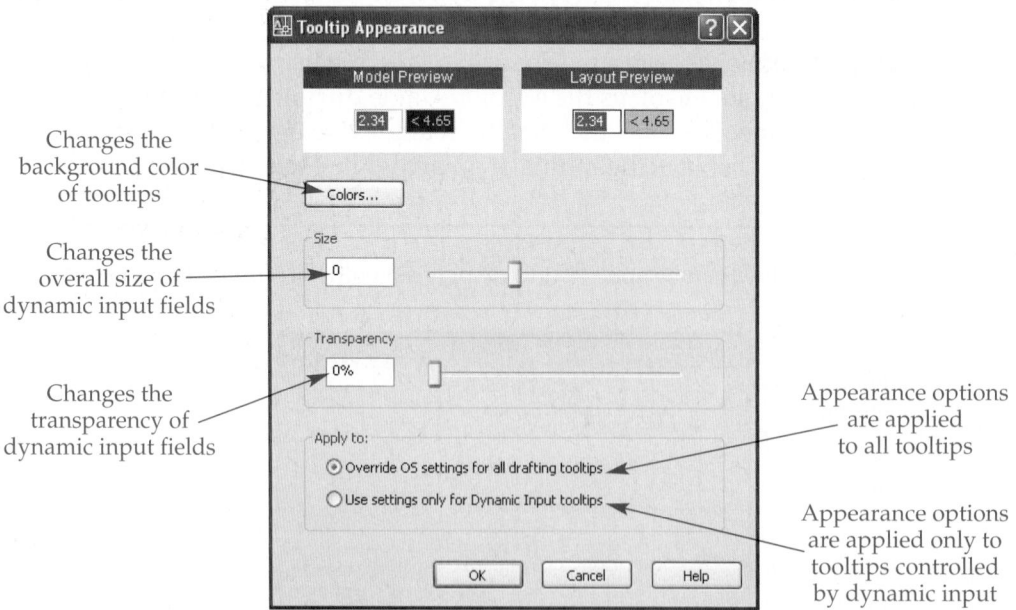

Appearance options are applied to all tooltips

Appearance options are applied only to tooltips controlled by dynamic input

Canceling a Command

If you press the wrong key or misspell a word when typing a command or answering a prompt, use the [Backspace] key to correct the error. This works only if you notice your mistake *before* you press the [Enter] key. If you do enter an incorrect option or command, AutoCAD usually responds with an error message. The error message tells you what has happened.

Previous messages displayed in the command window may not be visible. Press the [F2] function key to display AutoCAD's text screen. This allows you to read the entire message. Also, you will be able to review the commands and options you entered. This may help you understand the reason for the error message. You can press the [F2] key again to return to the graphics screen or use your cursor to pick any visible portion of the graphics screen to make it current again.

It is often necessary to stop the currently active command to either reenter a command or use another command. This can occur if you make an incorrect entry and need to restart the command using the correct method or even if you simply decide to do something different. Pressing the [Enter] key or the space bar discontinues some commands, such as the **LINE** command. This does not work in all situations.

You can cancel any active command or abort any data entry and return to the Command: prompt by pressing the [Esc] key. This key is located in the upper-left corner of your keyboard. It may be necessary to press the [Esc] key twice to cancel certain commands completely. Most of the toolbar buttons and pull-down menu options automatically cancel any currently active command before entering the new command. If you wish to abort the current command and start a new one, simply pick the appropriate toolbar button or pull-down menu option.

Introduction to Editing

Editing is the procedure used to correct mistakes or revise an existing drawing. Many editing functions exist to help increase productivity. The basic editing operations **ERASE**, **OOPS**, **U**, **UNDO**, and **REDO** are introduced in the next sections.

editing: Procedure used to modify an existing object.

To edit a drawing, you must select items to modify. The Select objects: prompt appears whenever you need to select items in the command sequence. Whether you select only one object or hundreds of objects, a *selection set* is created. You can create a selection set using a variety of selection options, including the following:

selection set: A group of one or more drawing objects, typically defined to perform an editing operation.

- Window selection
- Crossing selection
- Window polygon selection
- Crossing polygon selection
- Selection fence

When you become familiar with the selection set options, you will find they increase your flexibility and productivity.

In the following discussion and examples, several of the selection set methods are introduced using the **ERASE** command. Keep in mind, however, that these techniques can be used with most of the editing commands in AutoCAD whenever the Select objects: prompt appears. Any of the selection set methods can be enabled from the command line or dynamic input.

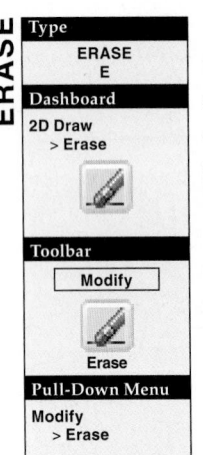
Using the Erase Command

The **ERASE** command is similar to using an eraser in manual drafting to remove unwanted information. With the **ERASE** command, however, you have a second chance. If you erase the wrong item, you can bring it back with the **OOPS** or **UNDO** command. Picking the **Erase** button in the **2D Draw** control panel of the **Dashboard** or in the **Modify** toolbar, typing E or ERASE, or picking **Modify > Erase** accesses the **ERASE** command.

When you enter the **ERASE** command, you are prompted to select an object. When the Select objects: prompt appears, a small box replaces the screen crosshairs. This box is referred to as the *pick box*. Move the pick box over the item to be erased and pick that item. The object is highlighted, and the Select objects: prompt is redisplayed. You can then select another object to erase. If you are finished selecting objects, erase the selected objects by pressing the space bar, right-clicking and selecting **Enter** from the shortcut menu, or pressing [Enter]. See **Figure 3-20**.

pick box: Small box that replaces the screen crosshairs when objects are to be selected.

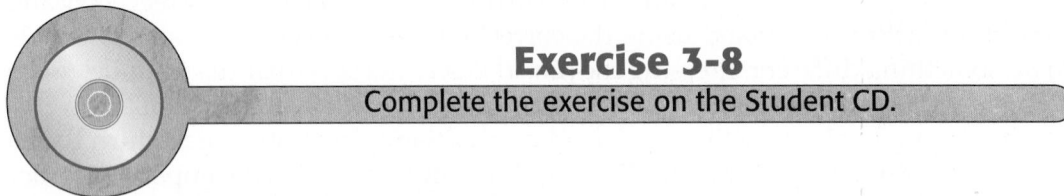

Exercise 3-8
Complete the exercise on the Student CD.

Using the Window selection option

The **Window** option can be used at any Select objects: prompt. This option allows you to draw a box, or "window," around an object or group of objects to select for editing. Everything entirely within the window is selected at the same time. If portions of objects project outside the window, those objects are not selected.

When the Specify first corner: prompt is shown, select a point clearly below and to the left of the object to be erased. The crosshairs is replaced by a selection box. This box grows as you move the corner to the right of the first point. By default, the box is a solid line with a light blue background.

The Specify opposite corner: prompt is shown. Move the pointing device up and to the right so the box completely covers the object(s) to be erased. Pick to locate the second corner, as shown in **Figure 3-21**. All objects within the box become highlighted. Press [Enter] or pick the right mouse button to complete the **ERASE** command.

Figure 3-20.
Using the **ERASE** command to erase a single object.

Screen crosshairs before
the **ERASE** command

A

Crosshairs change to
a pick box during the
ERASE command

B

Selected object
becomes highlighted

C

After pressing [Enter],
the selected object is
erased, and the
crosshairs return

D

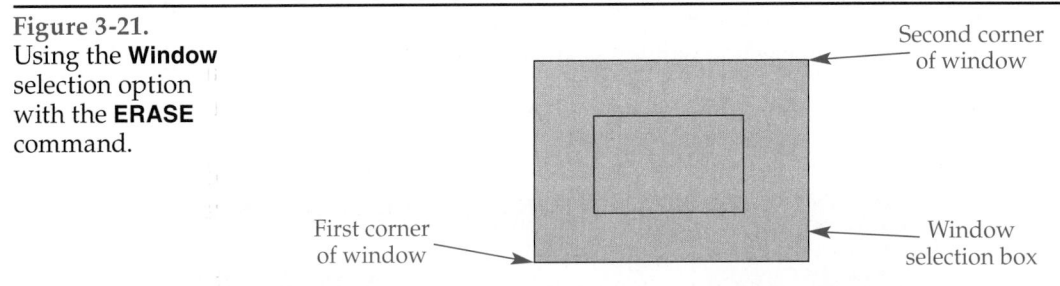

Figure 3-21.
Using the **Window** selection option with the **ERASE** command.

First corner of window

Second corner of window

Window selection box

You can also specify the **Window** selection option manually from the command line. You need to do this if the **PICKAUTO** variable (discussed later in this chapter) is set to 0. Type W at the Select objects: prompt to use the **Window** selection option. When you enter the **Window** option manually, you do not need to pick the first point to the left of the object(s) being erased. The box remains the **Window** box whether you move the cursor to the left or right.

Using the Crossing selection option

The **Crossing** selection option is similar to the **Window** option. With the **Crossing** option, however, objects contained within the box *and object crossing the box* are selected. The **Crossing** box outline is dotted with a light green background to distinguish it from the the **Window** box.

To use the **Crossing** option, select a point to the right of the object to be erased when the Select objects: prompt is shown. After you select the first point, the cursor expands in size as you move the pointing device to the left.

Remember, the crossing box does not need to enclose the entire object to erase it, as the window box does. The crossing box needs only to cross part of the object. **Figure 3-22** shows how to erase three of the four lines of a rectangle using the **Crossing** option.

You can also specify the **Crossing** option manually by typing C at the Select objects: prompt. When you enter the **Crossing** option manually, you do not need to pick the first point to the right of the object(s) being erased. The box remains the **Crossing** box whether you move the cursor to the left or right.

Window and Crossing display options

By default, the **Window** selection window has a transparent blue background, and the **Crossing** selection window has a transparent green background. These colors and other selection window settings can be modified in the **Visual Effect Settings** dialog box. To access this dialog box, select **Tools** > **Options...** from the pull-down menu or type OP or OPTIONS. You can also right-click in the drawing area and select **Options...** from the shortcut menu. In the **Options** dialog box, pick the **Selection** tab. In the **Selection Preview** area, pick the **Visual Effect Settings...** button. The **Visual Effect Settings** dialog box is shown in **Figure 3-23**.

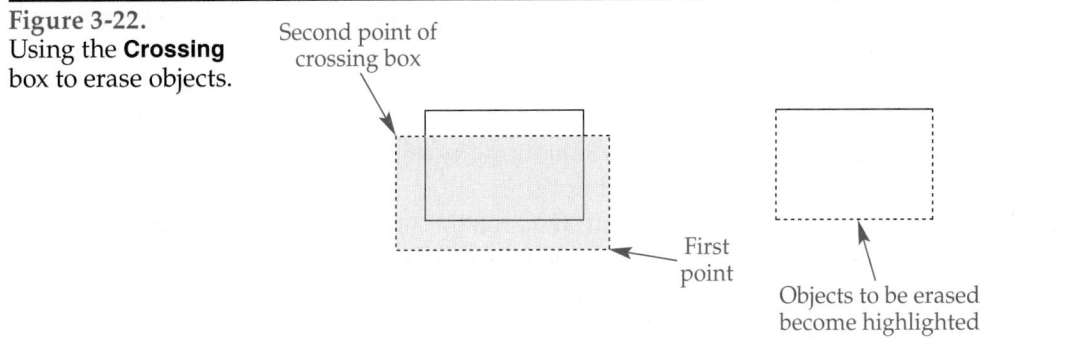

Figure 3-22.
Using the **Crossing** box to erase objects.

Second point of crossing box

First point

Objects to be erased become highlighted

Figure 3-23.
Display options for the selection windows can be set in the **Visual Effect Settings** dialog box.

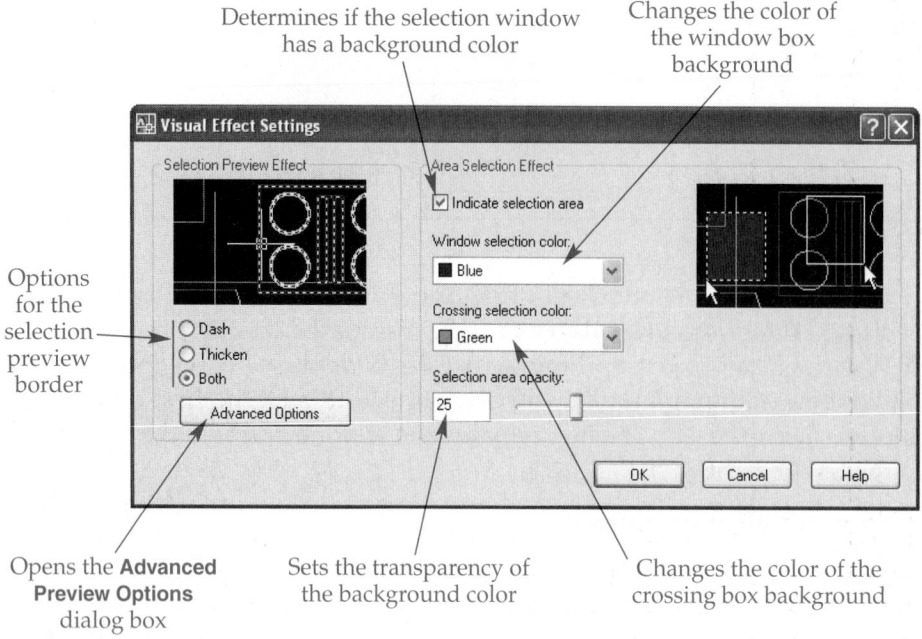

Determines if the selection window has a background color

Changes the color of the window box background

Options for the selection preview border

Opens the **Advanced Preview Options** dialog box

Sets the transparency of the background color

Changes the color of the crossing box background

The **Indicate selection area** option determines whether the selection window has a background color. If this option is checked, the window is filled with a background color. If it is unchecked, there is no background color, and only the solid and dashed border lines are displayed. The color of the window box background can be changed by selecting a different color from the **Window selection color:** drop-down list. The **Crossing selection color:** sets the background color for the crossing box. The transparency of the background color can be set in the **Selection area opacity:** field. To make the background more opaque, type a larger value or move the slider bar to the right. To make it more transparent, type a smaller value or move the slider bar to the left.

Object selection preview

You may have noticed that when you move the crosshairs over an object and pause for a moment, the object changes to a thicker lineweight. When the crosshairs are moved off the object, its lineweight goes back to normal. This allows you to preview the object before you select it. When many objects are in a small area, this feature helps you select the correct object the first time.

In the **Selection** tab of the **Options** dialog box, the **Selection Preview** area contains settings for this feature. If **When a command is active** is checked, the selection preview works in the middle of a command, and if **When no command is active** is checked, the preview works when no command is being used. If you find the selection preview distracting while you move the crosshairs around the drawing area, you can uncheck these boxes to turn the preview feature off.

The selection preview border can be set to **Dash**, **Thicken**, or **Both**. This setting can be accessed by picking the **Visual Effect Settings...** button in the **Selection Preview** area. Select one of the options in the **Selection Preview Effect** area. **Figure 3-24** illustrates the results of the three different options.

Picking the **Advanced Options** button opens the **Advanced Preview Options** dialog box. In this dialog box, certain types of objects can be excluded from using the selection preview settings.

Figure 3-24.
Before selecting an object, you can hover over it to have it display as dashed, thickened, or both.

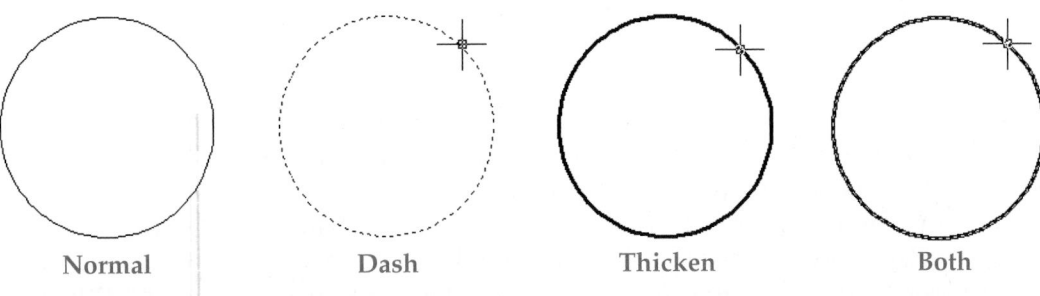

| Normal | Dash | Thicken | Both |

implied windowing: Automatic windowing that allows you to select multiple objects at one time.

Exercise 3-9
Complete the exercise on the Student CD.

Using the WPolygon and CPolygon selection option

The **Window** selection option is a rectangle selection box, which may not allow you to select the items you need to erase. You can also draw a polygon as the selection set boundary by using the **WPolygon** selection option.

To use the **WPolygon** option, type WP at the Select objects: prompt. Draw a polygon enclosing the objects. As you pick corners, the polygon drags into place. The command sequence for erasing the five middle squares in **Figure 3-25** is as follows:

    Command: E *or* ERASE↵
    Select objects: WP↵
    First polygon point: (pick Point 1)

Figure 3-25.
Using the **WPolygon** selection option to erase objects.

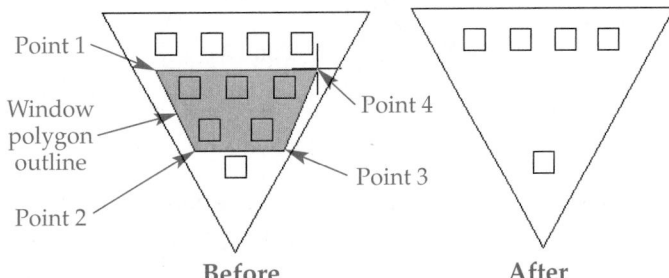

Point 1

Window polygon outline

Point 4

Point 3

Point 2

Before   After

```
Specify endpoint of line or [Undo]: (pick Point 2)
Specify endpoint of line or [Undo]: (pick Point 3)
Specify endpoint of line or [Undo]: (pick Point 4)
Specify endpoint of line or [Undo]: ↵
Select objects: ↵
Command:
```

If you do not like the last polygon point you picked, use the **Undo** option by typing U at the Specify endpoint of line or [Undo]: prompt.

The **CPolygon** selection option is similar to the **WPolygon** selection option. With the **CPolygon** option, however, a crossing window is created. Type **CP** at the Select objects: prompt to access this selection option. **Figure 3-26** illustrates the **CPolygon** selection option.

PROFESSIONAL TIP

When using **WPolygon** or **CPolygon**, AutoCAD does not allow you to select a point that causes the lines of the selection polygon to intersect each other. Pick locations that do not result in an intersection. Use the **Undo** option if you need to go back and relocate a preceding pick point.

Using the Fence selection option

Fence is another selection option used to select several objects at the same time. When using the **Fence** option, you simply place a fence through the objects you want to select. Only the objects the fence passes through are included in the selection set. The fence can be straight or staggered, as shown in **Figure 3-27**. Type F at the Select objects: prompt to use the **Fence** option:

```
Command: E or ERASE↵
Select objects: F↵
Specify first fence point: (pick Point 1)
Specify next fence point or [Undo]: (pick Point 2)
Specify next fence point or [Undo]: (pick Point 3)
Specify next fence point or [Undo]: (pick Point 4)
Specify next fence point or [Undo]: (pick Point 5)
Specify next fence point or [Undo]: (pick Point 6)
Specify next fence point or [Undo]: ↵
Select objects: ↵
Command:
```

Figure 3-26.
Using the **CPolygon** selection option. Everything enclosed within and crossing the polygon is selected.

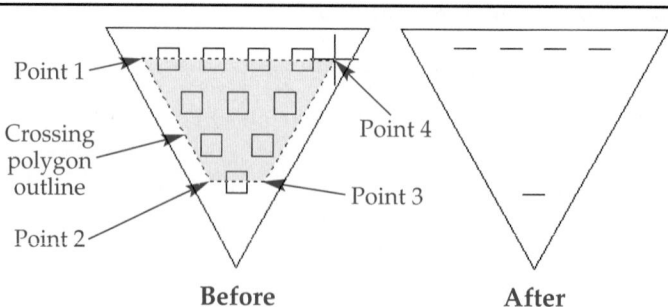

Point 1

Crossing polygon outline

Point 2

Point 4

Point 3

Before

After

Figure 3-27.
Using the **Fence** selection option to erase objects. The fence can be either straight or staggered.

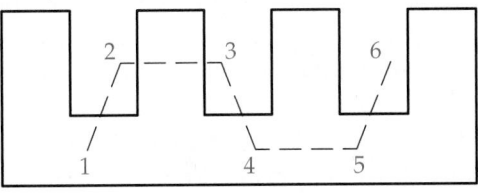

Before

After

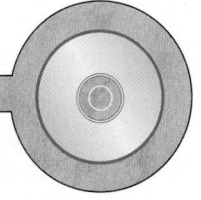

Exercise 3-10
Complete the exercise on the Student CD.

Removing from and adding to the selection set

When editing a drawing, a common mistake is to accidentally select an object you do not want to select. The simplest way to remove one or more objects from the current selection set is to hold down the [Shift] key and reselect the objects. This is possible only for individual picks and implied windows. For an implied window, the [Shift] key must be held down while picking the first corner and then can be released while picking the second corner. If you accidentally remove the wrong object from the selection set, release the [Shift] key and pick it again.

To use other methods for removing objects from a selection set or for specialized selection needs, you can switch to the **Remove** option by typing R at the Select objects: prompt. This changes the Select objects: prompt to Remove objects:. The command sequence is as follows:

    Command: **E** or **ERASE**↵
    Select objects: (*pick several objects, using any technique*)
    Select objects: **R**↵
    Remove objects: (*pick the objects you want removed from the selection set*)
    Remove objects: ↵
    Command:

Switch back to the selection mode by typing A (for the **Add** option) at the Remove objects: prompt. This restores the Select objects: prompt and allows you to select additional objects.

Using the Last Selection

The **ERASE** command's **Last** option saves time if you need to erase the last entity drawn. For example, suppose you draw a line and then want to erase it. The **Last** option automatically selects the line. Typing L at the Select objects: prompt selects the **Last** option:

    Command: **E** or **ERASE**↵
    Select objects: **L**↵
    1 found
    Select objects: ↵
    Command:

Keep in mind that using the **Last** option only highlights the last item drawn. You must press [Enter] to erase the object. If you need to erase more than just the last object, you can use the **ERASE** command and **Last** option repeatedly to erase items in reverse order. This is not as quick, however, as using the **ERASE** command and selecting the objects.

Using the Previous Selection

The object selection options given up to this point in the chapter have used the example of the **ERASE** command. These selection options are also used when moving objects, rotating objects, and performing other editing functions. These basic editing commands are explained in Chapter 11.

Often, more than one sequential editing operation needs to be carried out on a specific group of objects. In this case, the **Previous** selection option allows you to select the same object(s) you just edited. You can select the **Previous** selection set by typing P at the Select objects: prompt. In the following example, a group of objects is erased, and the **OOPS** command is used to recover them. The **ERASE** command is then issued again, this time using the **Previous** selection option to access the previously selected objects:

> Command: **E** *or* **ERASE.⏎**
> Select objects: *(pick several items, using any selection technique)*
> Select objects: ⏎
> Command: **OOPS.⏎**
> Command: **E** *or* **ERASE.⏎**
> Select objects: **P.⏎**
> Select objects: ⏎
> Command:

Selecting All Objects in a Drawing

Sometimes, you may want to select every object in the drawing. To do this, type ALL at the Select objects: prompt, as follows:

> Command: **E** *or* **ERASE.⏎**
> Select objects: **ALL.⏎**
> Select objects: ⏎
> Command:

This procedure erases everything in the drawing. You can use the **Remove** option at the second Select objects: prompt to remove certain objects from the set. You can also type ALL after typing R to remove all objects from the set.

Exercise 3-11
Complete the exercise on the Student CD.

Cycling through Stacked Objects

stacked objects:
Objects that overlap in the drawing; when you pick with the mouse, the topmost object is selected by default.

cycling: Repeatedly selecting one item from a series of stacked objects until the desired object is highlighted.

One way to deal with *stacked objects* is to let AutoCAD cycle through the overlapping objects. *Cycling* is repeatedly selecting one item from a series of stacked objects until the desired object is highlighted. This works best when several objects cross at the same place or are very close together.

To cycle through stacked objects, first access a command, such as **ERASE**. Next, with the Select objects: prompt shown, hold-down the [Shift] key and the space bar and pick near the intersection of the stacked objects. This process will turn cycling on as indicated by <Cycle On>. Once cycle is on you can release the [Shift] key and the space bar, and pick anywhere in the drawing window to cycle through the stacked objects. Every time you pick, another object becomes highlighted. When the desired object is highlighted, press [Enter] to end the cycling process and return to the Select objects: prompt. The following command sequence is used to erase one of the circles in Figure 3-28, but you can use this for any editing function:

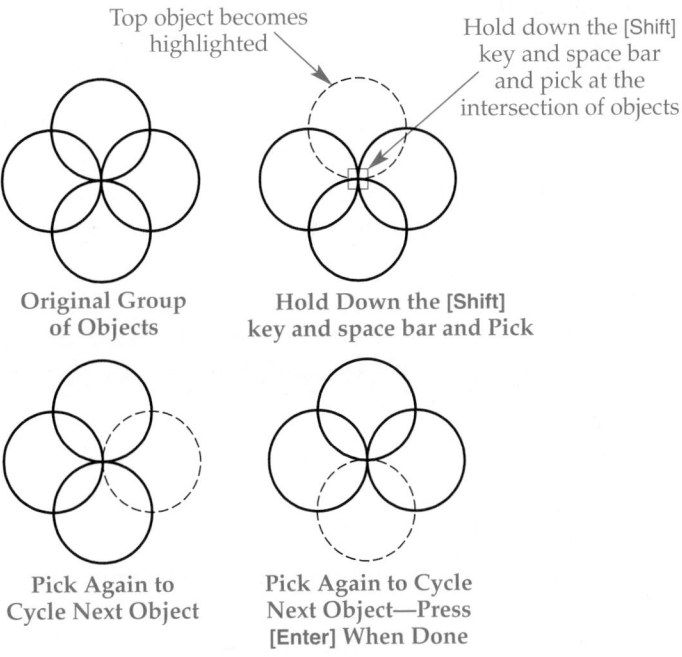

Figure 3-28.
Cycling through a series of stacked circles until the desired object is highlighted.

Top object becomes highlighted

Hold down the [Shift] key and space bar and pick at the intersection of objects

Original Group of Objects

Hold Down the [Shift] key and space bar and Pick

Pick Again to Cycle Next Object

Pick Again to Cycle Next Object—Press [Enter] When Done

Command: **E** *or* **ERASE**↵
Select objects: *(hold down the* [Ctrl] *key and pick)* <Cycle on> *(pick until you highlight the desired object and press* [Enter]*)*
<Cycle off>1 found
Select objects: *(select additional objects or press* [Enter]*)*
Command:

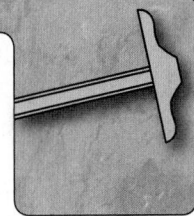

LEGACY NOTE

The **MULTIPLE** command causes AutoCAD to continue to reissue a command until you press the [Esc] key. The **MULTIPLE** command is no longer practical, since you can repeat a command more easily by pressing the space bar or [Enter] key, or by right-clicking and picking **Repeat** *COMMAND* from the top of the shortcut menu.

Using the Oops Command

The **OOPS** command brings back the last object you erased. It is issued by typing OOPS. If you erased several objects in the same command sequence, all are brought back to the screen. Only the objects erased in the most recent procedure can be returned using **OOPS**.

Using the U Command

While the **OOPS** command brings back the last object you erased, the **U** command undoes the effects of the previously entered command. The **U** command is different from the **Undo** option of the **LINE** command and the **Undo** option available while using certain other tools. After a command has been completed, pick the **Undo** button on the **Standard Annotation** toolbar, pick **Edit > Undo** *current*, press the [Ctrl]+[Z] key combination, or type U. The **U** command can also be activated by right-clicking in the drawing area and selecting **Undo** *current* from the shortcut menu. AutoCAD indicates which command was undone on the prompt line:

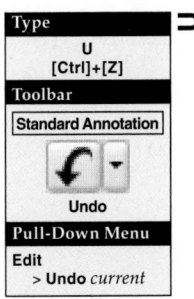

Type
U
[Ctrl]+[Z]
Toolbar
Standard Annotation

Undo
Pull-Down Menu
Edit
> **Undo** *current*

```
Command: U↵
LINE
Command:
```

In this example, the **LINE** command was the last command. Therefore, it was the command whose actions were undone. You can reissue the **U** command to continue undoing commands, but you can only undo one command at a time. The commands must be undone in the order in which they were used.

Exercise 3-12
Complete the exercise on the Student CD.

Using the Undo Command

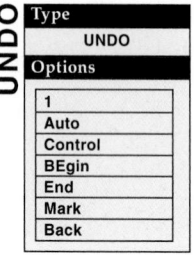

Type	
	UNDO
Options	
1	
Auto	
Control	
BEgin	
End	
Mark	
Back	

The **UNDO** command is different from the **U** command. The **UNDO** command offers several options that allow you to undo a single command or a number of commands at once. When you enter the command, the prompt reads Enter the number of operations to undo or [Auto/Control/BEgin/End/Mark/Back] <1>:. The default option allows you to designate the number of previous command sequences to remove. For example, if you enter 1, the previous command sequence is undone. If you enter 2, the previous two command sequences are undone. AutoCAD tells you which commands were undone with a message on the prompt line.

Undo options

The **UNDO** command contains several other options. When the **Auto** option is on, any commands that are part of a group and used to perform a single operation are removed together. For example, when a command contains other commands, all the commands in that group are removed as one single command. The **Auto** option is active by default. If it is turned off, each command in a group of commands is treated individually.

The **Control** option allows you to specify how many of the **UNDO** command options you want active. You can even disable the **UNDO** command altogether. To use the **Control** option, type C after issuing the **UNDO** command. Selecting the **All** suboption keeps the full range of **UNDO** command options active. This is the default setting. The **None** suboption disables the **U** and **UNDO** commands. When the **U** command is entered, the prompt indicates the command is disabled. It then tells you to reactivate the **U** and **UNDO** commands by entering the **All** suboption of the **UNDO** command.

The **One** suboption limits **UNDO** to one operation only. If you attempt to enter a number higher than one when this suboption is active, you get an error message. You can type C at the Enter an option [Control] <1>: prompt to display the **Control** suboptions.

The **Combine** option determines whether or not **PAN** and **ZOOM** operations are combined together.

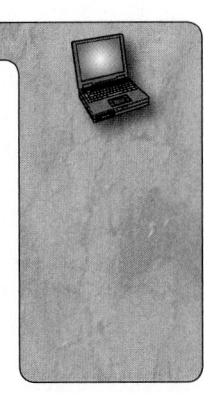
The **BEgin** and **End** options of the **UNDO** command are used together to perform several undo operations at once. They allow you to group a series of commands and treat them as a single command. Once the group is defined, the **U** command is then used to remove the commands that follow the **BEgin** option, but precede the **End** option. These options are useful if you can anticipate the possible removal of several commands entered consecutively. For example, if you think you may want to undo the next three commands altogether, start by entering the **BEgin** option of the **UNDO** command. Execute the three drawing commands. Then, enter the **End** option of the **UNDO** command. Since the three commands were executed between the **BEgin** and **End** options, the **U** command treats them as one command and undoes all three. The **BEgin** option must precede the command sequence and the **End** option must immediately follow the last command in the group to be undone.

The **Mark** option of the **UNDO** command allows you to insert a marker in the undo file. The **Back** option of the **UNDO** command undoes all commands issued after the marker was inserted. For example, if you do not want certain work to be undone by the **Back** option, enter the **Mark** option after completing the work. Then, continue working. To undo all work since the marker was inserted, reissue the **UNDO** command and enter the **Back** option. If no marker has been inserted, everything in the entire drawing is undone. AutoCAD issues the prompt This will undo everything. OK? <Y>. If you want everything you have drawn and edited to be undone, press [Enter]. If not, type N or NO and press [Enter], or press the [Esc] key.

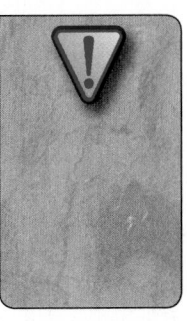

Using the Undo list

The **Undo** list allows you to graphically select a number of commands to undo. Using this feature performs the same function as using the **UNDO** command and entering a number. Access the **Undo** list by picking the down arrow to the right of the **Undo** button on the **Standard** toolbar. A small window containing a sequential list of commands is displayed below the button. See **Figure 3-29.** The first (top) command in the list is the most recent command. Commands must be undone in reverse order. To select a number of commands, move the cursor down. The commands that will be undone are highlighted. To execute the undo operation, pick the last command to undo. All commands executed after the one selected will be undone, along with the selected command. Using this list is an easy way to undo back to an exact command without having to figure out how many commands have been issued since.

Redoing the Undone

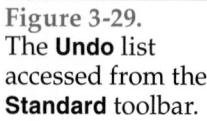

The **REDO** command is used to reverse the action of the **UNDO** and **U** commands. Type REDO, pick **Edit** > **Redo**, press the [Ctrl]+[Y] key combination, or pick the **Redo** button from the **Standard Annotation** toolbar to activate the command. The **REDO** command works only *immediately* after undoing something. The **REDO** command does *not* bring back line segments that were removed using the **Undo** option of the **LINE** command.

If multiple undos are performed, any or all of the commands that were undone can be redone using the **REDO** list. Pick the down arrow next to the **Redo** button on the **Standard** toolbar. The list window is displayed, which shows the commands that were undone and can be redone. This list functions in the same way as the **UNDO** list discussed earlier.

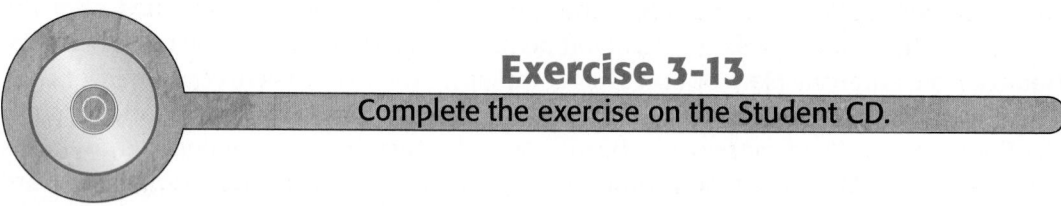

Exercise 3-13
Complete the exercise on the Student CD.

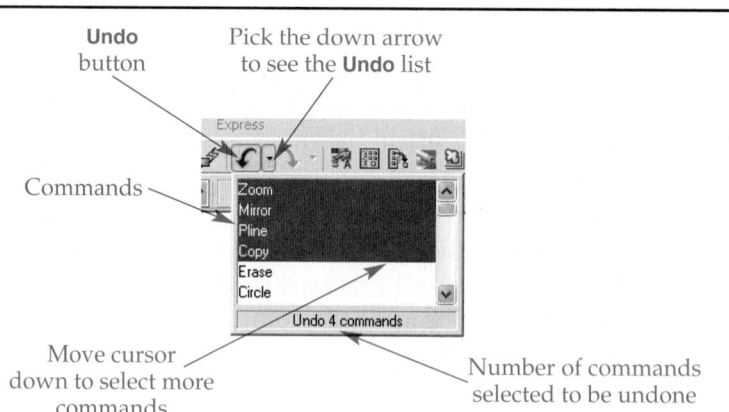

Figure 3-29.
The **Undo** list accessed from the **Standard** toolbar.

Undo button

Pick the down arrow to see the **Undo** list

Commands

Express

Zoom
Mirror
Pline
Copy
Erase
Circle

Undo 4 commands

Move cursor down to select more commands

Number of commands selected to be undone

Chapter Test

Answer the following questions. Write your answers on a separate sheet of paper or complete the electronic chapter test on the Student CD.

1. List two ways to discontinue drawing a line.
2. Name five point entry methods.
3. What does the absolute coordinate display 5.250,7.875 mean?
4. Give the commands and entries to draw a line from Point A to Point B to Point C and back to Point A. Return to the Command: prompt:
   A. Command: _____
   B. Specify first point: _____
   C. Specify next point or [Undo]: _____
   D. Specify next point or [Undo]: _____
   E. Specify next point or [Close/Undo]: _____
5. What does the polar coordinate display @2.750<90 mean?
6. How can you turn on the coordinate display?
7. How can you turn on the **Ortho** mode?
8. Explain, in general terms, how direct distance entry works.
9. What are the default angle increments for polar tracking?
10. Explain how you can continue drawing another line segment from a previously drawn line.
11. Where does the result of typing occur when dynamic input is turned on?
12. When dynamic input is enabled, what are the four options for selecting your next point?
13. When you access the **ERASE** command, what replaces the crosshairs?
14. How do the appearances of a window and a crossing box differ?
15. List five ways to select an object to erase.
16. Define *stacked objects*.
17. Name the command used to bring back the last object(s) erased before issuing another command.
18. How many commands can you undo at one time with the **U** command?
19. What is the difference between picking **Edit** > **Undo** and entering the **UNDO** command?
20. Name the command used to bring back an object that was previously removed using **UNDO**.

Drawing Problems

1. Open one of your templates. Draw the specified objects as accurately as possible with grid and snap turned off. Use the **LINE** command and draw the following objects on only the left side of the screen:
   - Right triangle.
   - Isosceles triangle.
   - Rectangle.
   - Square.

   Save the drawing as P3-1.

2. Draw the same objects specified in Problem 1 on the right side of the screen. This time, make sure the snap grid is turned on. Observe the difference between having snap on for this problem and off for the previous problem. Save the drawing as P3-2.

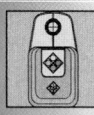

3. Draw an object by connecting the following point coordinates. Save your drawing as P3-3.

Point	Coordinates	Point	Coordinates
1	2,2	8	@-1.5,0
2	@1.5,0	9	@0,1.25
3	@.75<90	10	@-1.25,1.25
4	@.1.5<0	11	@2<180
5	@0,-.75	12	@-1.25,-1.25
6	@3,0	13	@2.25<270
7	@1<90		

4. With the absolute, relative, and polar coordinate entry methods, draw the following shapes. Set the units to decimal; grid spacing to .5; and snap spacing to .0625. Draw Object A three times, using a different point entry system each time. Draw Object B once, using at least two methods of coordinate entry. Do not draw dimensions. Save the drawing as P3-4.

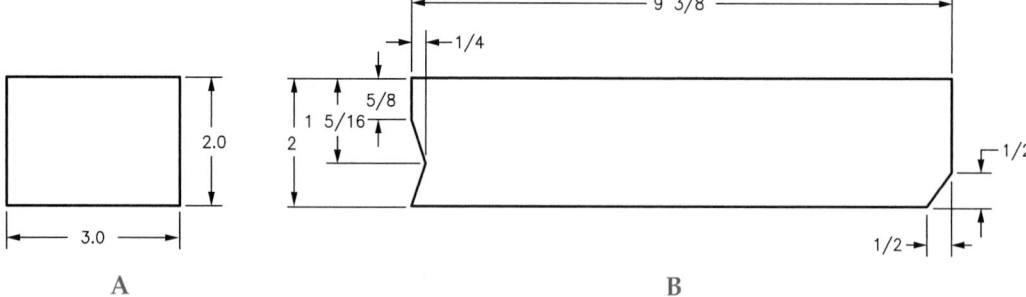

5. Use **Ortho** mode and direct distance entry to draw the outline shown. Each grid square is one unit. Do not draw the grid lines. Save the drawing as P3-5.

6. Use polar coordinate entry to draw the hexagon shown. Each side of the hexagon is 2 units. Begin at the start point, and draw the lines in the direction indicated by the arrows. Do not draw dimensions. Save the drawing as P3-6.

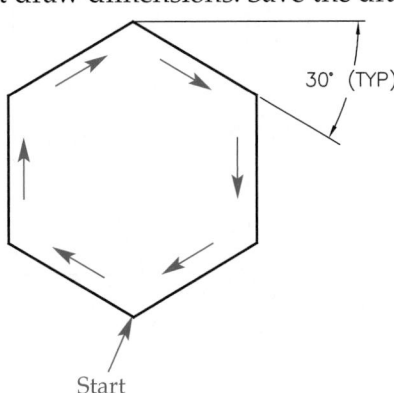

7. Draw the objects shown in A and B. Begin at the start point and then discontinue the **LINE** command at the point shown. Complete each object using the **Continue** option. Do not draw dimensions. Save the drawing as P3-7.

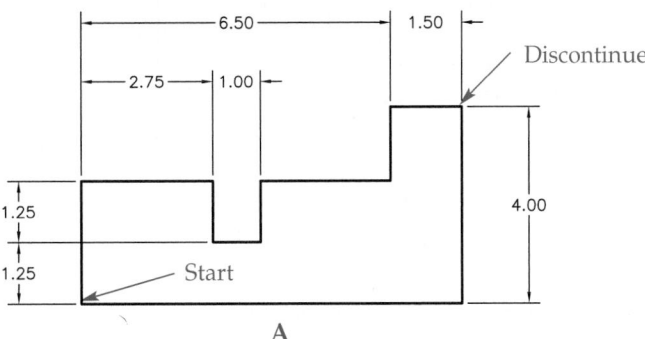

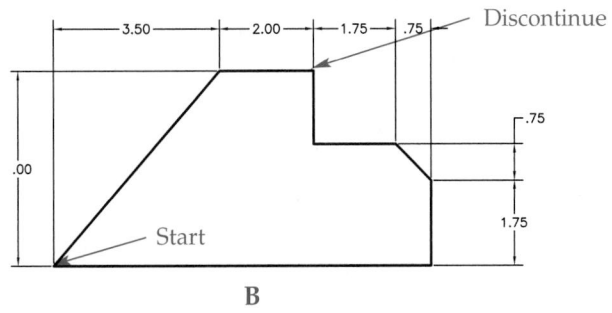

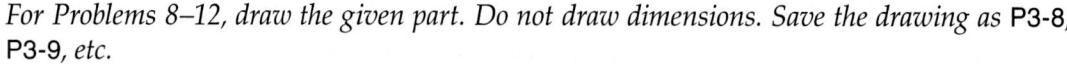

For Problems 8–12, draw the given part. Do not draw dimensions. Save the drawing as **P3-8**, **P3-9**, *etc.*

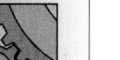

8.

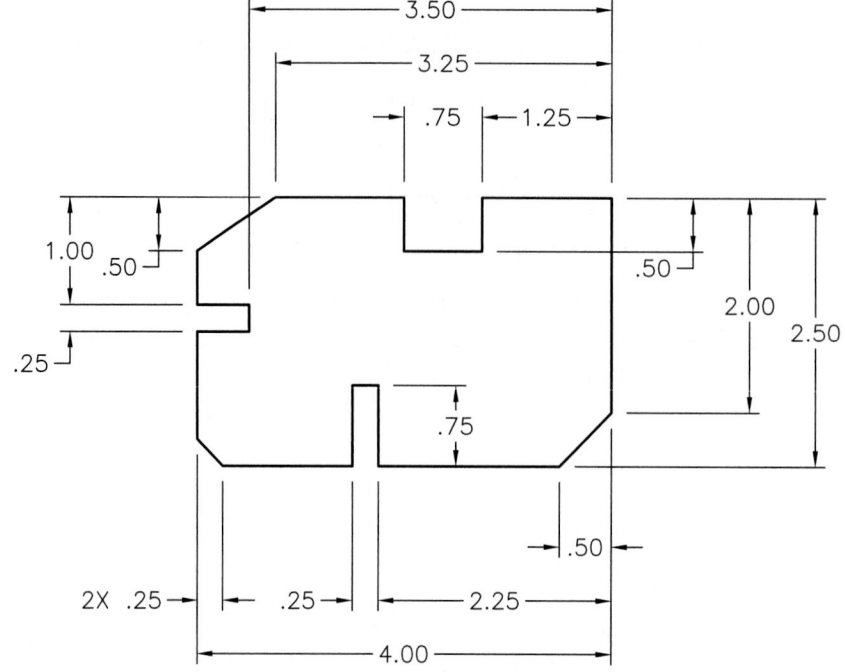

9.

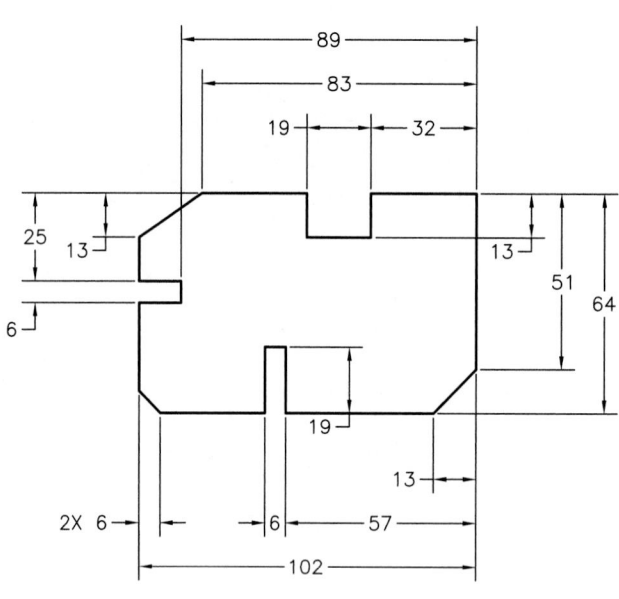

10.

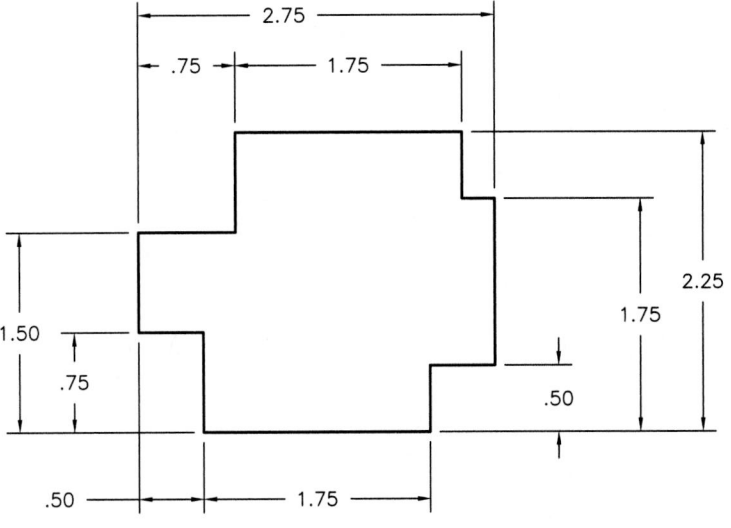

11.

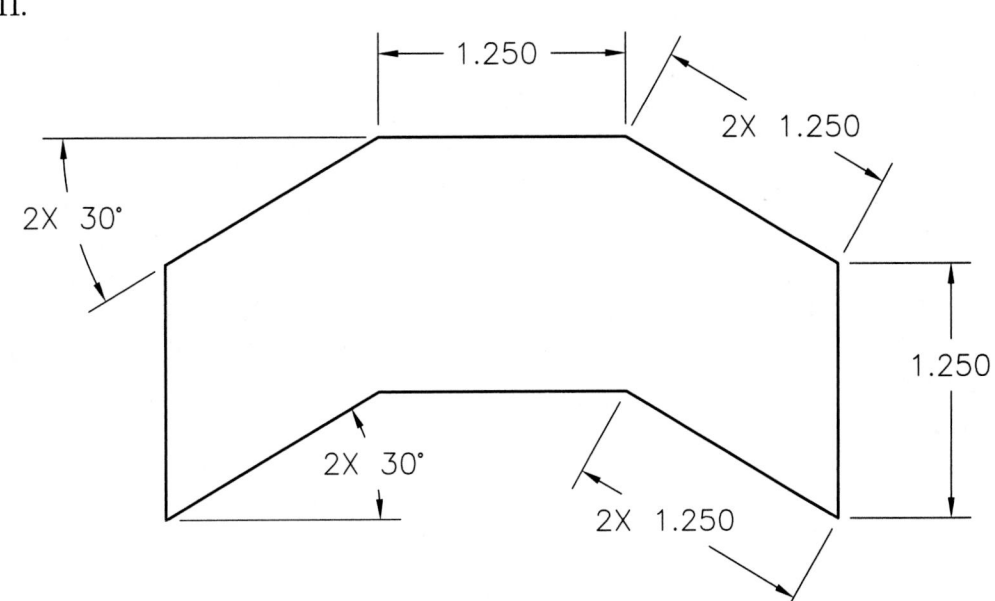

12.

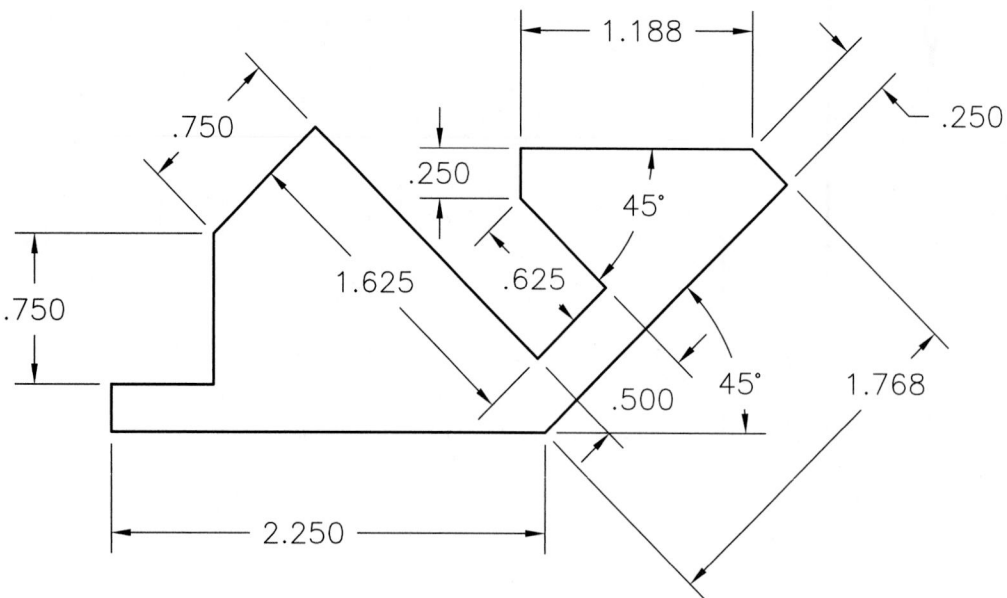

CHAPTER 4

Drawing Basic Shapes

Learning Objectives

After completing this chapter, you will be able to do the following:

✓ Use **DRAGMODE** to observe an object being dragged into place.
✓ Draw circles using the **CIRCLE** command options.
✓ Draw arcs using the **ARC** command options.
✓ Use the **ELLIPSE** command to draw ellipses and elliptical arcs.
✓ Draw polygons using the **POLYGON** command.
✓ Draw rectangles using the **RECTANG** command options.
✓ Draw donuts using the **DONUT** command.

The decisions you make when drawing circles and arcs with AutoCAD are similar to those you would make when drawing the items manually. AutoCAD provides many ways to create circles and arcs using the **CIRCLE** and **ARC** commands. These methods require specifying the center location and radius or diameter or entering where the outline of the circle or arc should be located. AutoCAD includes additional drawing tools, such as the **ELLIPSE**, **POLYGON**, **RECTANG**, and **DONUT** commands, to draw a wide variety of shapes.

Dragging Objects into Place

Chapter 3 showed how the **LINE** command displays an image that is "dragged" across the screen before the second endpoint is picked. This image is called a *rubberband*. The **CIRCLE**, **ARC**, **ELLIPSE**, **POLYGON**, and **RECTANG** commands also display a rubberband image to help you decide where to place the object.

For example, when you draw a circle using the **Center, Radius** option, a circle image appears on the screen after you pick the center point. This image gets larger or smaller as you move the pointer. When you pick the desired circle size, a circle replaces the dragged image. See **Figure 4-1**.

The **DRAGMODE** command affects the visibility of the rubberband. The options are **ON**, **OFF**, and **Auto**. To change the setting, type DRAGMODE:

> **rubberband:** A stretch line that extends from the crosshairs during certain drawing commands.

Command: **DRAGMODE**↵
Enter new value [ON/OFF/Auto] <Auto>: *(type* ON, OFF, *or* A, *and press* [Enter])

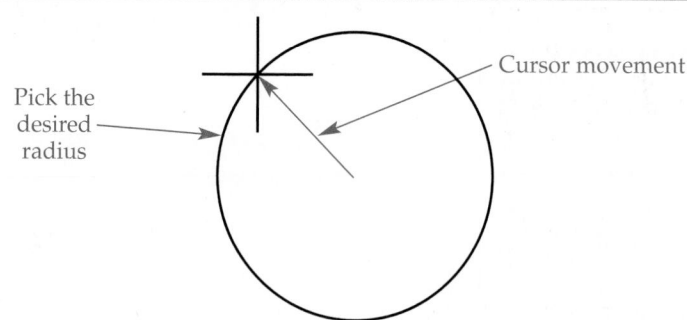

Figure 4-1.
Dragging a circle to its desired size. The circle attached to the crosshairs stretches like a rubberband until you pick a point to define the radius.

Pick the desired radius

Cursor movement

The current (last used) mode is shown in brackets. The **Auto** option is the default. Pressing the [Enter] key keeps the existing status. When the setting is **On**, you must enter DRAG during a command sequence to see the objects drag into place.

Drawing Circles

CIRCLE

Type	
CIRCLE	
C	

Dashboard

2D Draw
> Circle

Toolbar

Draw

Circle

Pull-Down Menu

Draw
> Circle

Options

3P
2P
Ttr (tan tan radius)

The **CIRCLE** command is activated by picking the **Circle** button in the **2D Draw** control panel of the **Dashboard** or the **Draw** toolbar. You can also select **Draw > Circle** or type C or CIRCLE. The options available in the **Circle** cascading menu are shown in Figure 4-2.

Drawing a Circle by Radius

A circle can be drawn by specifying the center point and the radius. After accessing the **Center, Radius** option, you are asked to specify the center point, followed by the radius. You can enter the center point coordinates and a radius value by typing or by picking with the crosshairs. The following command sequence is used to draw the circle shown in Figure 4-3:

Figure 4-2.
The **Circle** cascading menu in the **Draw** pull-down menu.

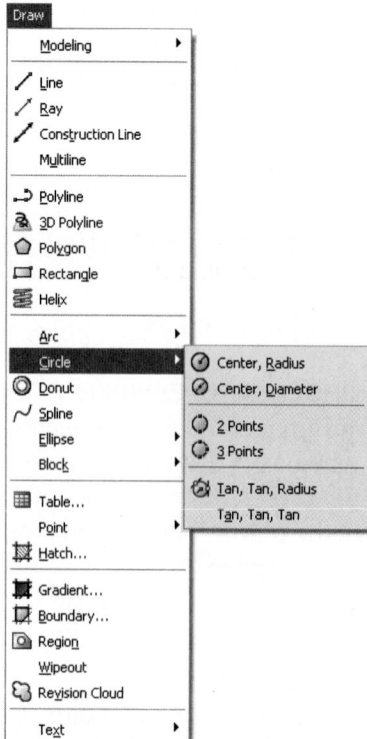

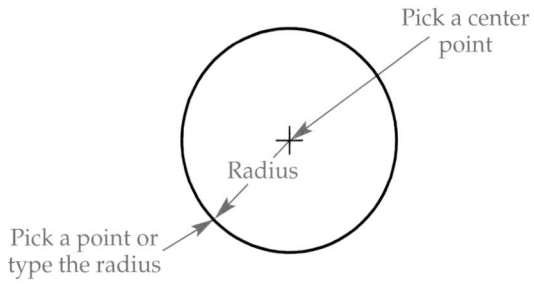

Figure 4-3.
Drawing a circle by specifying the center point and radius.

Pick a center point

Radius

Pick a point or type the radius

Command: **C** *or* **CIRCLE**↵
Specify center point for circle or [3P/2P/Ttr (tan tan radius)]: *(select a center point)*
Specify radius of circle or [Diameter] *<current>*: *(drag the circle to the desired radius and pick, or type the radius size and press* [Enter]*)*

NOTE

The radius value you enter is stored in the **CIRCLERAD** system variable. This system variable defines the default radius setting. Its value will appear in angle brackets the next time you use the **CIRCLE** command. If **CIRCLERAD** is set to 0, no default radius is provided the next time you use the **CIRCLE** command.

Drawing a Circle by Diameter

A circle can also be drawn by specifying the center point and the diameter. The command sequence for the **Center, Diameter** option is as follows:

Command: **C** *or* **CIRCLE**↵
Specify center point for circle or [3P/2P/Ttr (tan tan radius)]: *(select a center point)*
Specify radius of circle or [Diameter] *<current>*: **D**↵
Specify diameter of circle *<current>*: *(drag the circle to the desired diameter and pick, or type the diameter size and press* [Enter]*)*

Watch the screen carefully when using the **Center, Diameter** option. The crosshairs measures the diameter, but the rubberband circle passes midway between the center and the crosshairs. See **Figure 4-4**. The **Center, Diameter** option is convenient because most circular holes, shafts, and features are specified by the diameter.

After you draw a circle, its radius becomes the default for the next circle. If you use the **Radius** option to draw a circle after using the **Diameter** option, AutoCAD changes the default to a radius measurement based on the previous diameter. If you set **CIRCLERAD** to a value such as .50, the default for a circle drawn with the **Diameter** option is automatically 1.00 (twice the default radius).

Figure 4-4.
When you use the **Center, Diameter** option, AutoCAD calculates the circle's position as you move the crosshairs.

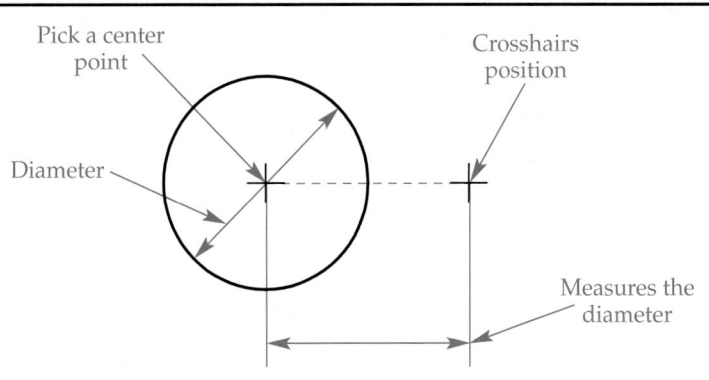

Pick a center point

Crosshairs position

Diameter

Measures the diameter

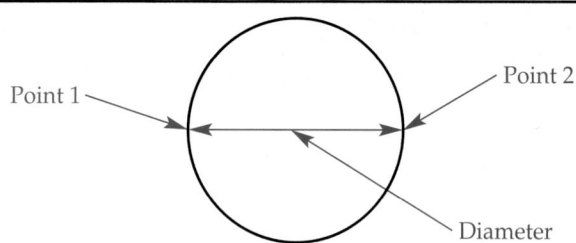

Figure 4-5.
Drawing a circle by selecting two points.

Point 1

Point 2

Diameter

Drawing a Two-Point Circle

A two-point circle is drawn by picking two points on opposite sides of the circle to define its diameter. See **Figure 4-5.** The **2 Points** option is useful if the diameter of the circle is known, but the center is difficult to find. One example of this is locating a circle between two lines. The command sequence is as follows:

Command: **C** *or* **CIRCLE⏎**
Specify center point for circle or [3P/2P/Ttr (tan tan radius)]: **2P⏎**
Specify first end point of circle's diameter: *(select a point)*
Specify second end point of circle's diameter: *(select a point)*

AutoCAD automatically calculates the radius of the circle. This is the default radius the next time the **CIRCLE** command is used.

Drawing a Three-Point Circle

If three points on the circumference of a circle are known, the **3 Points** option is the best method to use. The three points can be selected in any order. See **Figure 4-6.** The command sequence is as follows:

Command: **C** *or* **CIRCLE⏎**
Specify center point for circle or [3P/2P/Ttr (tan tan radius)]: **3P⏎**
Specify first point on circle: *(select a point)*
Specify second point on circle: *(select a point)*
Specify third point on circle: *(select a point)*
Command:

AutoCAD automatically calculates the radius of the circle. This becomes the default radius the next time the **CIRCLE** command is used.

Drawing a Circle Tangent to Two Objects

tangent: A line, circle, or arc that comes into contact with another circle or arc at only one point.

point of tangency: The point shared by tangent objects.

The term *tangent* refers to a line, circle, or arc that comes into contact with another circle or arc at only one point. That point is called the *point of tangency.* When a line is tangent to a circle, a line drawn from the circle's center to the point of tangency is perpendicular to the tangent line. A line drawn between the centers of two tangent circles passes through the point of tangency. You can draw a circle tangent to given lines, circles, or arcs.

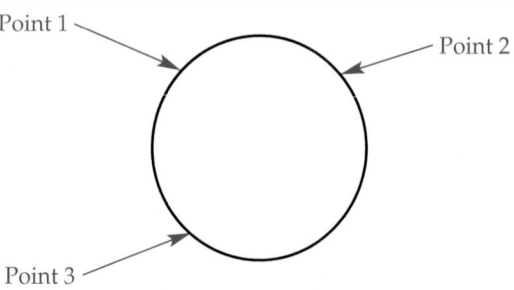

Figure 4-6.
Drawing a circle by picking three points that lie on the circle.

Point 1

Point 2

Point 3

The **Tan, Tan, Radius** option creates a circle of a specified radius tangent to two objects. After selecting the **Tan, Tan, Radius** option, select two lines, arcs, or circles to which the new circle will be tangent. Then enter the radius of the circle.

To create a circle that is tangent to other objects, you must pick points that lie directly on the tangent objects. To assist you in picking a point exactly on the objects, AutoCAD uses an *object snap* known as **Deferred Tangent**. (Object snaps are covered in Chapter 7.) You will see the deferred tangent symbol when you move the crosshairs near the objects you want to pick.

object snap: A tool that snaps to exact points, such as endpoints or midpoints, when you pick a point near these locations.

The command sequence is as follows:

> Command: **C** *or* **CIRCLE**↵
> Specify center point for circle or [3P/2P/Ttr (tan tan radius)]: **T**↵
> Specify point on object for first tangent of circle: *(pick the first line, circle, or arc)*
> Specify point on object for second tangent of circle: *(pick the second line, circle, or arc)*
> Specify radius of circle <current>: *(type a radius value and press* [Enter]*)*

Two examples of this option are shown in **Figure 4-7**. As with other **CIRCLE** options, AutoCAD automatically calculates the radius of the circle. This is the default radius the next time the **CIRCLE** command is used. If the radius you enter is too small, AutoCAD displays the message Circle does not exist.

Drawing a Circle Tangent to Three Objects

The **Tan, Tan, Tan** option allows you to draw a circle tangent to three existing objects. This option creates a three-point circle using the three points of tangency. See **Figure 4-8**. Selecting the pull-down option is the same as using the **3 Points** option and specifying the **Tangent** object snap:

> Command: **C** *or* **CIRCLE**↵
> Specify center point for circle or [3P/2P/Ttr (tan tan radius)]: **3P**↵
> Specify first point on circle: **TAN**↵
> to *(pick an object)*
> Specify second point on circle: **TAN**↵
> to *(pick an object)*
> Specify third point on circle: **TAN**↵
> to *(pick an object)*
> Command:

Figure 4-7.
Two examples of drawing circles tangent to two given objects using the **Tan, Tan, Radius** option.

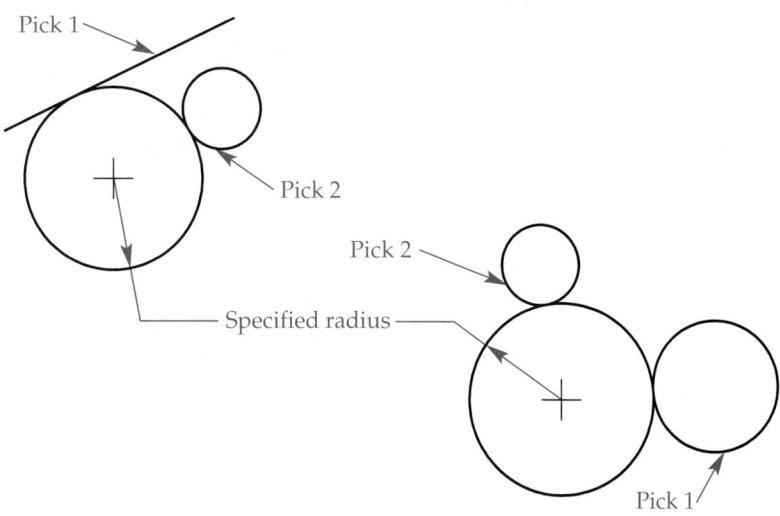

Pick 1
Pick 2
Pick 2
Specified radius
Pick 1

Figure 4-8.
Two examples of
drawing circles
tangent to three
given objects.

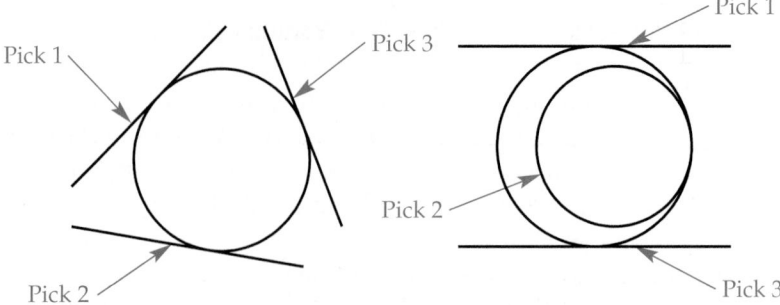

Pick 1   Pick 3   Pick 1

Pick 2

Pick 2   Pick 3

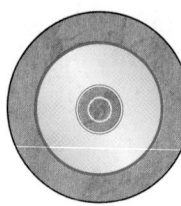

NOTE

Unlike the **Tan, Tan, Radius** option, the **Tan, Tan, Tan** option does
not automatically recover when a point prompt is answered with a
pick where no tangent exists. In such a case, the **Tangent** object snap
must be manually reactivated for subsequent attempts to make that
pick. The **Tangent** object snap is one of the object snaps discussed in
Chapter 7 of this textbook. For now, if this happens, type TAN and
press [Enter] at the point selection prompt. This returns the pick box
so you can pick again.

Exercise 4-1
Complete the exercise on the Student CD.

Drawing Arcs

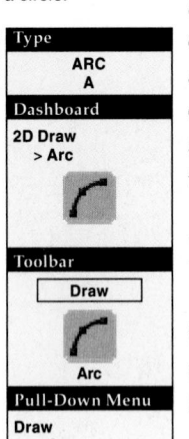

arc: Any portion of
a circle.

Type
ARC
A

Dashboard
2D Draw
> Arc

Toolbar
Draw

Arc

Pull-Down Menu
Draw
> Arc

An *arc* is defined as any portion of a circle. Arcs are commonly dimensioned with
a radius, but they can be drawn by a number of different methods. The **ARC** command
can be accessed by selecting **Draw > Arc**. The **Arc** cascading menu contains eleven
arc construction options. See **Figure 4-9**. This is the easiest way to access the **ARC**
command and an arc option. The **ARC** command and its options, however, also can be
accessed by picking the **Arc** button in the **2D Draw** control panel of the **Dashboard** or in
the **Draw** toolbar or by typing A or ARC. The **3 Points** option is the default.

Drawing a Three-Point Arc

The **3 Points** option asks for the start point, a second point along the arc, and
the endpoint. See **Figure 4-10**. The arc can be drawn clockwise or counterclockwise
and is dragged into position as the endpoint is located. The command sequence is as
follows:

Command: **A** *or* **ARC**↵
Specify start point of arc or [Center]: *(select the first point on the arc)*
Specify second point of arc or [Center/End]: *(select the second point on the arc)*
Specify end point of arc: *(select the arc's endpoint)*
Command:

Figure 4-9.
The **Arc** cascading menu in the **Draw** pull-down menu.

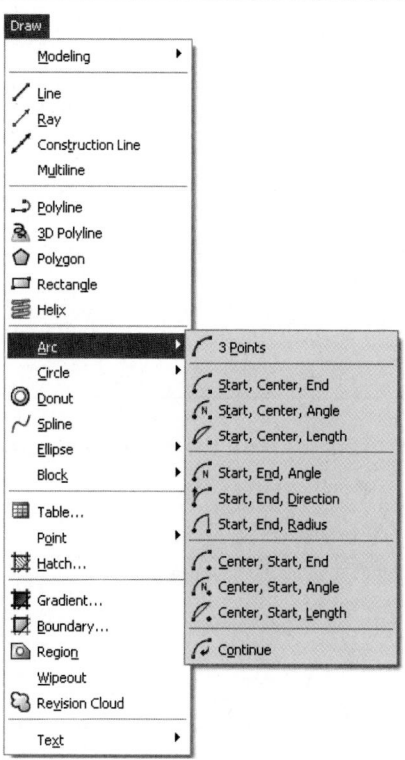

Figure 4-10.
Drawing an arc by picking three points.

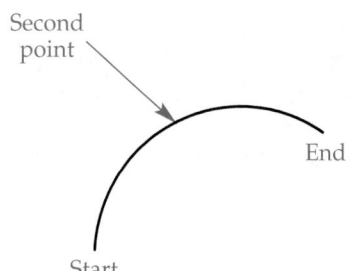

Drawing Arcs Using the Start, Center, End Option

Use the **Start, Center, End** option when you know the start, center, and endpoint locations for the arc. With this method, arcs are drawn counterclockwise. Picking the start and center points establishes the arc's radius. The point selected for the endpoint determines the arc length. The selected endpoint does not have to be on the radius of the arc. See **Figure 4-11.** The command sequence is as follows:

> Command: **A** *or* **ARC**↵
> Specify start point of arc or [Center]: *(select the first point on the arc)*
> Specify second point of arc or [Center/End]: **C**↵
> Specify center point of arc: *(select the arc's center point)*
> Specify end point of arc or [Angle/chord Length]: *(select the arc's endpoint)*
> Command:

Drawing Arcs Using the Start, Center, Angle Option

When the arc's included angle is known, the **Start, Center, Angle** option may be the best choice. The *included angle* is an angle formed between the center, start point, and endpoint of the arc. The arc is drawn counterclockwise, unless a negative angle is specified. See **Figure 4-12.**

included angle:
The angle formed between the center, start point, and endpoint of the arc.

Figure 4-11.
Using the **Start, Center, End** option. Notice that the endpoint does not have to be on the arc.

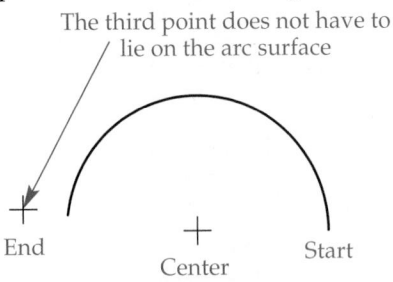

The third point does not have to lie on the arc surface

End   Center   Start

Figure 4-12.
Positive and negative angles with the **Start, Center, Angle** option.

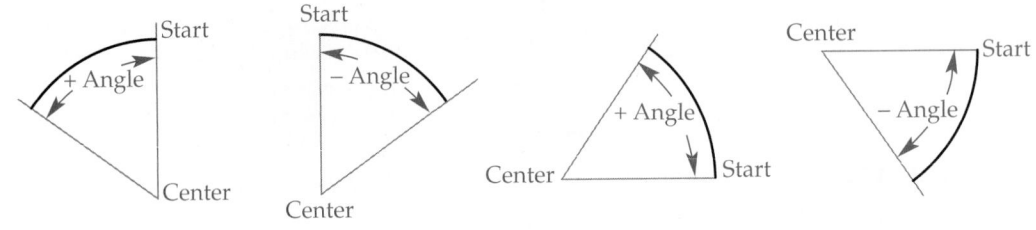

The following shows the command sequence with a 45° included angle:

Command: **A** *or* **ARC**↵
Specify start point of arc or [Center]: *(select the first point on the arc)*
Specify second point of arc or [Center/End]: **C**↵
Specify center point of arc: *(select the arc's center point)*
Specify end point of arc or [Angle/chord Length]: **A**↵
Specify included angle: **45**↵
Command:

Drawing Arcs Using the Start, Center, Length Option

<table>
<tr><td>

chord length: The linear distance between two points on a circle or arc.

</td><td>

The *chord length* of an arc is the linear distance between its two endpoints. This distance can be determined using a chord length table. (A chord length table is provided in the *Standard Tables* document in the *Reference Materials* section of the Student CD.) For example, a one-unit radius arc with an included angle of 45° has a chord length of .765 units.

</td></tr>
</table>

You can use the **Start, Center, Length** option to specify the chord length of an arc. With this method, arcs are drawn counterclockwise. A positive chord length gives the smallest possible arc with that length. A negative chord length results in the largest possible arc. See **Figure 4-13.** The following shows the command sequence with a chord length of .765:

Command: **A** *or* **ARC**↵
Specify start point of arc or [Center]: *(select the first point on the arc)*
Specify second point of arc or [Center/End]: **C**↵
Specify center point of arc: *(select the arc's center point)*
Specify end point of arc or [Angle/chord Length]: **L**↵
Specify length of chord: *(type .765 for the smaller arc or –.765 for the larger arc, and press [Enter])*
Command:

Figure 4-13.
Positive and
negative chord
lengths with the
Start, Center, Length
option.

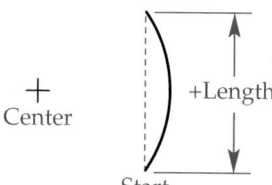

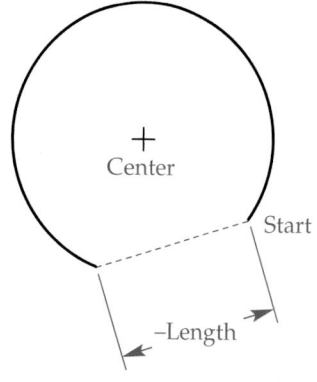

Exercise 4-2

Complete the exercise on the Student CD.

Drawing Arcs Using the Start, End, Angle Option

An arc can also be drawn by picking the start point and endpoint and entering the included angle. A positive included angle draws the arc counterclockwise, while a negative angle produces a clockwise arc. See **Figure 4-14**. The command sequence is as follows:

> Command: **A** *or* **ARC**↵
> Specify start point of arc or [Center]: *(select the first point on the arc)*
> Specify second point of arc or [Center/End]: **E**↵
> Specify end point of arc: *(select the arc's endpoint)*
> Specify center point of arc or [Angle/Direction/Radius]: **A**↵
> Specify included angle: *(type a positive or negative angle and press* [Enter]*)*
> Command:

Drawing Arcs Using the Start, End, Direction Option

An arc can be drawn by picking the start point and endpoint and then using the mouse to specify the direction of rotation. The distance between the points and the direction the crosshairs is moved determine the arc's location and size. The arc is started tangent to the direction specified, as shown in **Figure 4-15**. The command sequence is as follows:

> Command: **A** *or* **ARC**↵
> Specify start point of arc or [Center]: *(select the first point on the arc)*
> Specify second point of arc or [Center/End]: **E**↵
> Specify end point of arc: *(select the arc's endpoint)*
> Specify center point of arc or [Angle/Direction/Radius]: **D**↵
> Specify tangent direction for the start point of arc: *(pick the direction from the start
>   point, or type the direction in degrees and press* [Enter]*)*
> Command:

Figure 4-14.
Positive and
negative angles with
the **Start, End, Angle**
option.

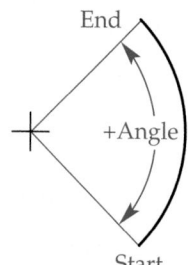

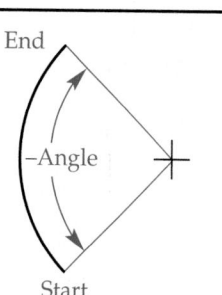

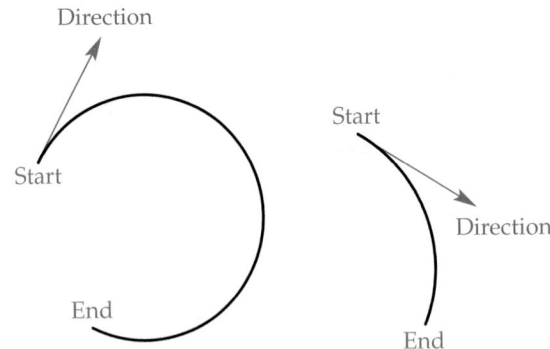

Figure 4-15.
Using the **Start, End, Direction** option.

Drawing Arcs Using the Start, End, Radius Option

A positive radius value for the **Start, End, Radius** option results in the smallest possible arc between the start point and endpoint. A negative radius gives the largest arc possible. See Figure 4-16. Arcs can only be drawn counterclockwise with this option. The command sequence is as follows:

Command: **A** *or* **ARC**↵
Specify start point of arc or [Center]: *(select the first point on the arc)*
Specify second point of arc or [Center/End]: **E**↵
Specify end point of arc: *(select the arc's endpoint)*
Specify center point of arc or [Angle/Direction/Radius]: **R**↵
Specify radius of arc: *(pick or type a positive or negative radius and press [Enter])*
Command:

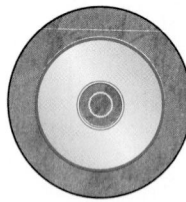

Exercise 4-3
Complete the exercise on the Student CD.

Drawing Arcs Using the Center, Start, End Option

The **Center, Start, End** option is a variation of the **Start, Center, End** option. See Figure 4-17. Use the **Center, Start, End** option when it is easier to begin by locating the center. The command sequence is as follows:

Command: **A** *or* **ARC**↵
Specify start point of arc or [Center]: **C**↵
Specify center point of arc: *(pick the center point)*
Specify start point of arc: *(pick the start point)*
Specify end point of arc or [Angle/chord Length]: *(pick the arc's endpoint)*
Command:

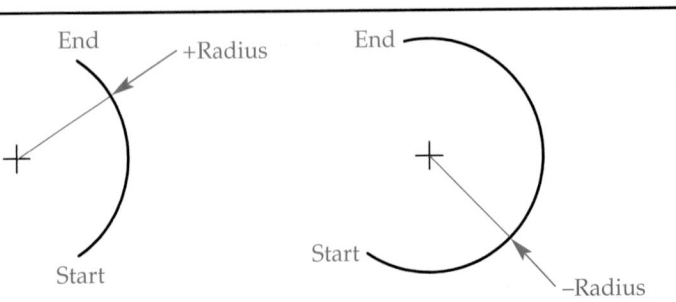

Figure 4-16.
Using the **Start, End, Radius** option with a positive and negative radius.

Figure 4-17.
Using the **Center, Start, End** option. Like the **Start, Center, End** option, this option does not require the endpoint to be on the arc.

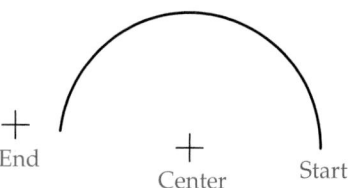

Drawing Arcs Using the Center, Start, Angle Option

The **Center, Start, Angle** option is a variation of the **Start, Center, Angle** option. Use the **Center, Start, Angle** option when it is easier to begin by locating the center. Figure 4-18 shows how positive and negative angles work with this option. The command sequence is as follows:

Command: **A** *or* **ARC**⏎
Specify start point of arc or [Center]: **C**⏎
Specify center point of arc: *(pick the center point)*
Specify start point of arc: *(pick the start point)*
Specify end point of arc or [Angle/chord Length]: **A**⏎
Specify included angle: *(pick the included angle, or type a positive angle or negative angle and press [Enter])*
Command:

Drawing Arcs Using the Center, Start, Length Option

The **Center, Start, Length** option is a variation of the **Start, Center, Length** option. Use the **Center, Start, Length** option when it is easier to begin by locating the arc's center. Figure 4-19 shows how positive and negative chord lengths work with this option. The command sequence is as follows:

Command: **A** *or* **ARC**⏎
Specify start point of arc or [Center]: **C**⏎
Specify center point of arc: *(pick the center point)*
Specify start point of arc: *(pick the start point)*
Specify end point of arc or [Angle/chord Length]: **L**⏎
Specify length of chord: *(pick or type the chord length, and press [Enter])*
Command:

Figure 4-18.
Positive and negative angles with the **Center, Start, Angle** option.

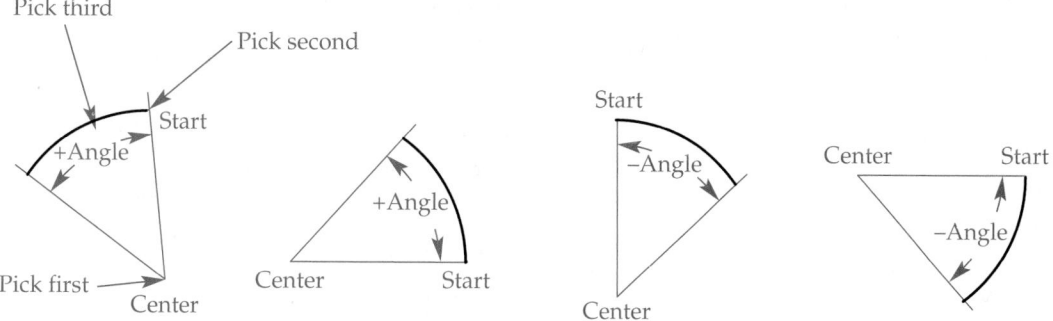

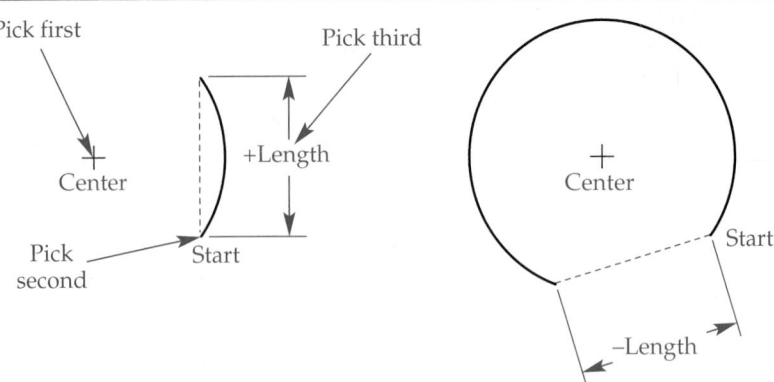

Figure 4-19.
Positive and negative chord lengths with the **Center, Start, Length** option.

Pick first
Pick third
Center
+Length
Pick second
Start
Center
Start
−Length

Continuing Arcs from a Previously Drawn Arc or Line

An arc can be continued from the previous arc or line. To do so, select **Draw** > **Arc** > **Continue**. The **Continue** option can also be accessed by beginning the **ARC** command and then pressing the [Enter] key, pressing the space bar, or selecting **Enter** from the shortcut menu when prompted to specify the start point of the arc.

When a series of arcs are drawn in this manner, each consecutive arc is tangent to the object before it. The start point and direction are taken from the endpoint and direction of the previous arc. See **Figure 4-20.**

The **Continue** option can also be used to quickly draw an arc tangent to the endpoint of a previously drawn line. See **Figure 4-21.** The command sequence is as follows:

Command: **L** *or* **LINE**↵
Specify first point: *(select a point)*
Specify next point or [Undo]: *(select a second point)*
Specify next point or [Undo]: ↵
Command: **A** *or* **ARC**↵
Specify start point of arc or [Center]: *(press the space bar or* [Enter] *to place the start point of the arc at the end of the previous line)*
Specify end point of arc: *(select the endpoint of the arc)*
Command:

Exercise 4-4
Complete the exercise on the Student CD.

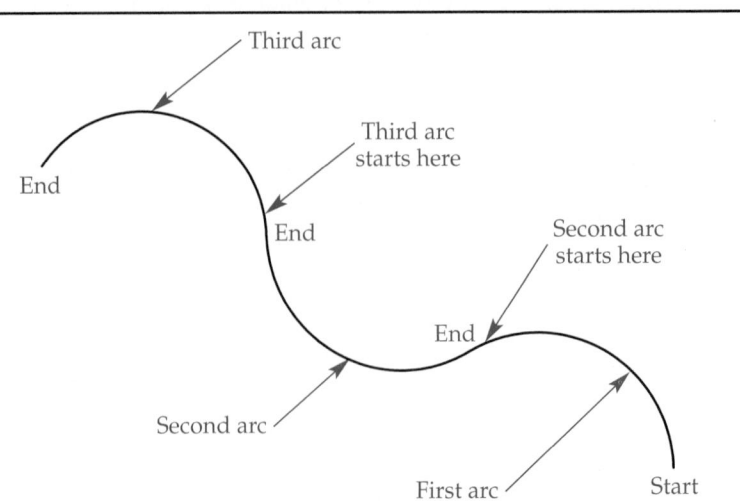

Figure 4-20.
Using the **Continue** option to draw three tangent arcs.

Third arc
Third arc starts here
End
End
Second arc starts here
End
Second arc
First arc
Start

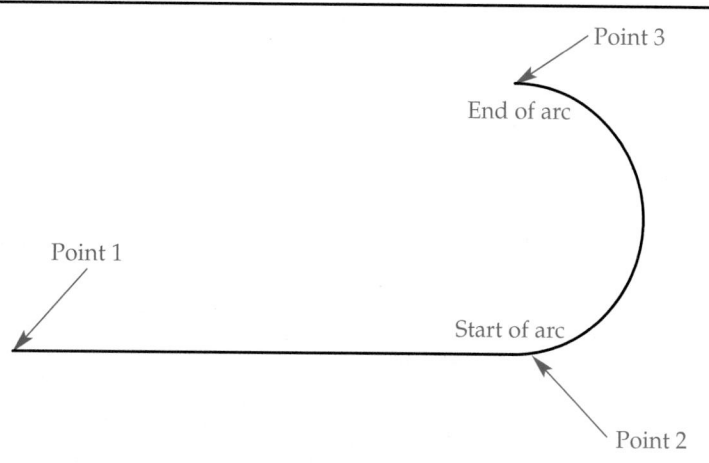

Figure 4-21.
An arc continuing from the previous line. Point 2 is the start of the arc, and Point 3 is the end of the arc.

Drawing Ellipses

When a circle is viewed at an angle, an elliptical shape is seen. For example, a 30° ellipse is created if a circle is rotated 30° from the line of sight. An *ellipse* is an oval shape that has two centers of equal radius and contains a *major axis* and a *minor axis*. The parts of an ellipse are shown in **Figure 4-22**. The **ELLIPSE** command can be accessed by selecting **Draw > Ellipse**, picking the **Ellipse** button in the **2D Draw** control panel of the **Dashboard** or the **Draw** toolbar, or typing EL or ELLIPSE.

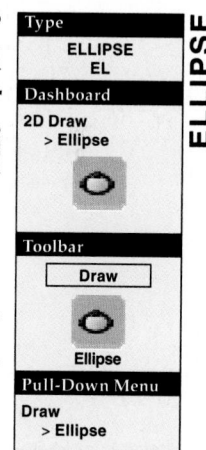

Drawing an Ellipse Using the Center Option

An ellipse can be constructed by specifying the center point and one endpoint for each of the two axes. See **Figure 4-23**. The **Center** option is used to draw an ellipse in this manner. The command sequence for this option is as follows:

> Command: **EL** *or* **ELLIPSE**↵
> Specify axis endpoint of ellipse or [Arc/Center]: **C**↵
> Specify center of ellipse: *(select a center point)*
> Specify endpoint of axis: *(select the endpoint of one axis)*
> Specify distance to other axis or [Rotation]: *(select the endpoint of the other axis)*

If you respond to the last prompt with R for **Rotation**, AutoCAD assumes you have selected the major axis with the first axis endpoint. The next prompt requests the angle at which the corresponding circle is rotated from the line of sight to produce the ellipse. The command sequence is as follows:

> Specify distance to other axis or [Rotation]: **R**↵
> Specify rotation around major axis: **30**↵
> Command:

ellipse: An oval shape that contains two centers of equal radius.

major axis: The longer of the two axes in an ellipse.

minor axis: The shorter of the two axes in an ellipse.

Figure 4-22.
The parts of an ellipse.

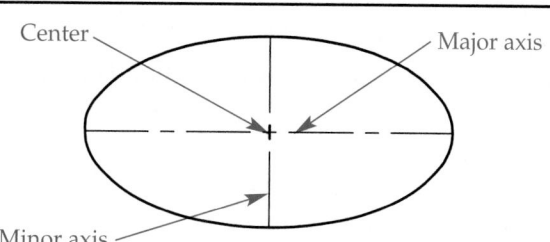

Figure 4-23.
Drawing an ellipse by picking the center and an endpoint for each axis.

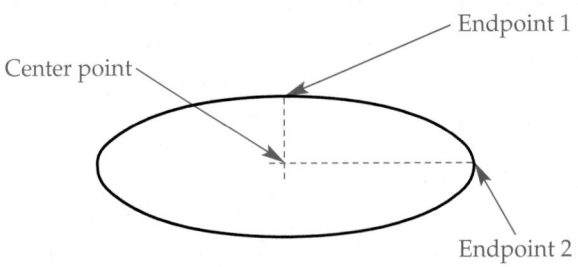

The **30** response draws an ellipse that is created when a circle is rotated 30° from the line of sight. A **0** response draws an ellipse with the minor axis equal to the major axis—that is, a circle. AutoCAD rejects any rotation angle between 89.99994° and 90.00006° or between 269.99994° and 270.00006°. **Figure 4-24** shows the relationship among several ellipses having the same major axis length, but different rotation angles.

Drawing an Ellipse Using the Axis, End Option

The **Axis, End** option establishes the first axis and one endpoint of the second axis. The first axis may be either the major or minor axis, depending on what you enter for the second axis. After you pick the first axis, the ellipse is dragged with the crosshairs until you pick a point. The command sequence for the ellipses in **Figure 4-25** is as follows:

Command: **EL** *or* **ELLIPSE**⏎
Specify axis endpoint of ellipse or [Arc/Center]: *(select an axis endpoint)*
Specify other endpoint of axis: *(select the other endpoint of the axis)*
Specify distance to other axis or [Rotation]: *(select a distance from the midpoint of the first axis to the end of the second axis and press* [Enter]*)*
Command:

Figure 4-24.
Ellipse rotation angles.

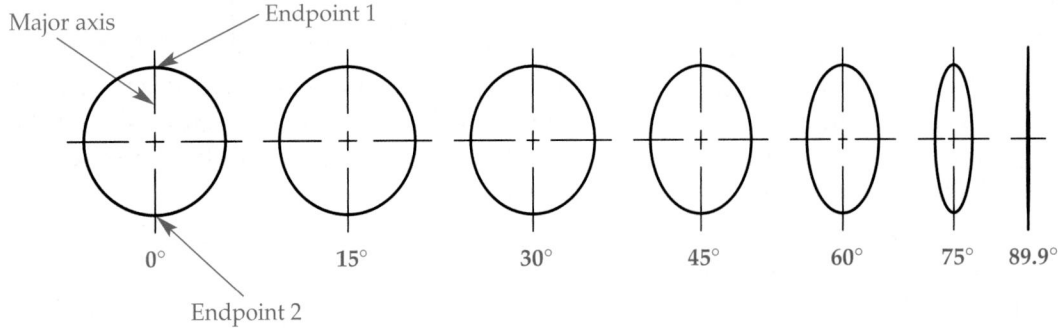

Figure 4-25.
Constructing the same ellipse by choosing different axis endpoints.

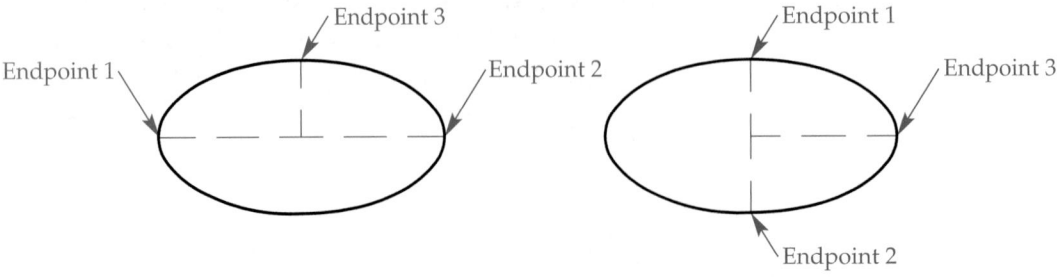

AutoCAD and Its Applications—Basics

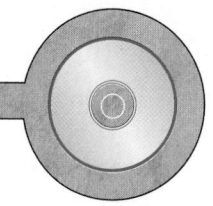

Drawing Elliptical Arcs

The **Arc** option of the **ELLIPSE** command is used to draw elliptical arcs. The **Arc** option can be specified from within the **ELLIPSE** command, or it can be entered directly by picking the **Ellipse Arc** button on the **2D Draw** control panel of the **Dashboard** or the **Draw** toolbar. The command sequence for the **Arc** option is as follows:

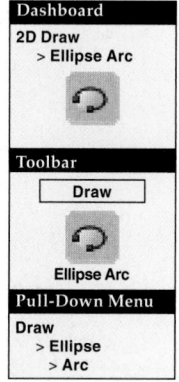

Dashboard
2D Draw
> Ellipse Arc

Toolbar
Draw
Ellipse Arc

Pull-Down Menu
Draw
> Ellipse
> Arc

> Command: **EL** *or* **ELLIPSE.**↵
> Specify axis endpoint of ellipse or [Arc/Center]: **A**↵
> Specify axis endpoint of elliptical arc or [Center]: *(pick the first axis endpoint)*
> Specify other endpoint of axis: *(pick the second axis endpoint)*
> Specify distance to other axis or [Rotation]: *(pick the distance for the second axis)*
> Specify start angle or [Parameter]: **0**↵
> Specify end angle or [Parameter/Included angle]: **90**↵
> Command:

After selecting the second endpoint of the first axis, you can drag the shape of a full ellipse. This can help you visualize the other axis. The distance for the second axis is from the ellipse's center to the point you pick. Enter a start angle. The start and end angles are the angular relationships between the ellipse's center and the arc's endpoints. The angle of the elliptical arc is established from the angle of the first axis. A 0° start angle begins the arc at the first endpoint of the first axis. A 45° start angle begins the arc 45° counterclockwise from the first endpoint of the first axis. End angles are also established counterclockwise from the start point. **Figure 4-26** shows the elliptical arc drawn with the previous command sequence and displays sample arcs with different start and end angles.

Using the Parameter option

With the **Parameter** option, AutoCAD uses a different means of vector calculation to create the elliptical arc. The **Parameter** option requires the same input used for drawing other elliptical arcs, until the Specify start angle or [Parameter]: prompt. The results are similar, but the command sequence is as follows:

> Specify start angle or [Parameter]: **P**↵
> Specify start parameter or [Angle]: *(pick the start point or enter a value)*
> Specify end parameter or [Angle/Included angle]: *(pick the endpoint or enter a value)*
> Command:

Figure 4-26.
Drawing elliptical arcs. Note the three examples at the bottom created by three different angle settings.

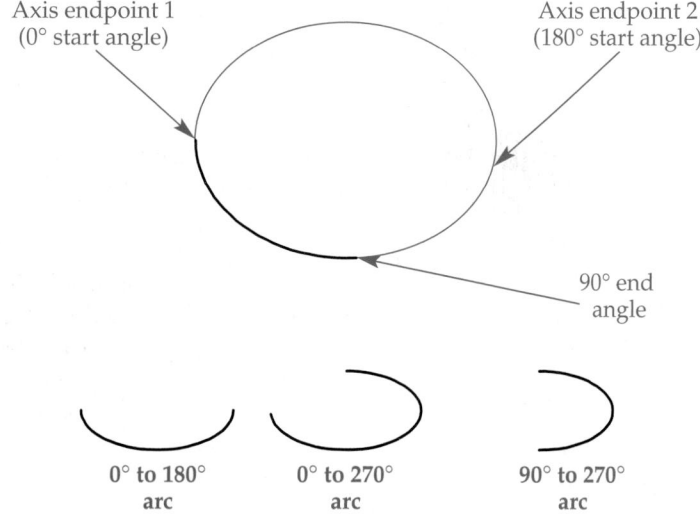

Using the Included angle option

The **Included angle** option establishes an included angle beginning at the start angle. This option requires the same input used for drawing other elliptical arcs until the Specify end angle or [Parameter/Included angle]: prompt. The command sequence is as follows:

Specify end angle or [Parameter/Included angle]: **I**↵
Specify included angle for arc <*current*>: *(enter the included angle)*
Command:

Rotating an elliptical arc around its axis

The **Rotation** option for drawing an elliptical arc is similar to the **Rotation** option for drawing a full ellipse, which was discussed earlier. This option allows you to rotate the elliptical arc about the first axis by specifying a rotation angle. Refer to **Figure 4-24** for examples of various rotation angles. This option requires the same input used for drawing other elliptical arcs, until the Specify distance to other axis or [Rotation]: prompt. The command sequence is as follows:

Specify distance to other axis or [Rotation]: **R**↵
Specify rotation around major axis: *(enter rotation value)*
Specify start angle or [Parameter]: *(enter start angle)*
Specify end angle or [Parameter/Included angle]: *(enter end angle)*
Command:

Drawing an elliptical arc using the Center option

The **Center** option for drawing an elliptical arc lets you establish the center of the ellipse. See **Figure 4-27**. This option requires the same input used for drawing other elliptical arcs, until the Specify axis endpoint of elliptical arc or [Center]: prompt. The command sequence is as follows:

Specify axis endpoint of elliptical arc or [Center]: **C**↵
Specify center of elliptical arc: *(select the ellipse's center point)*
Specify endpoint of axis: *(select the endpoint of the axis)*
Specify distance to other axis or [Rotation]: *(select the endpoint of the other axis)*
Specify start angle or [Parameter]: *(enter start angle)*
Specify end angle or [Parameter/Included angle]: *(enter end angle)*
Command:

Figure 4-27.
Drawing elliptical arcs with the **Center** option.

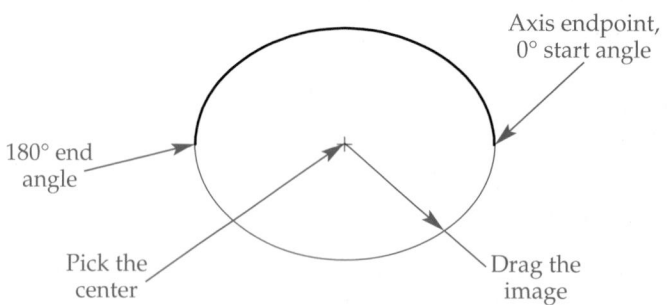

Axis endpoint, 0° start angle

180° end angle

Pick the center

Drag the image

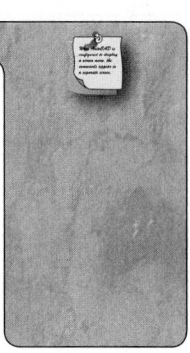

NOTE

The setting of the **PELLIPSE** system variable affects the way an ellipse can be edited. An ellipse drawn when **PELLIPSE** is set at 0 is a true elliptical object, while an ellipse drawn when **PELLIPSE** is set at 1 is a polyline ellipse. A true elliptical object maintains its elliptical shape during grip editing, which is discussed in Chapter 12 of this text. The vertices of a polyline ellipse can be moved out of the elliptical shape. The **Arc** option of the **ELLIPSE** command is not available when **PELLIPSE** is set to 1.

Exercise 4-6

Complete the exercise on the Student CD.

Drawing Regular Polygons

A *regular polygon* is any closed-plane geometric figure with three or more equal sides and equal angles. For example, a hexagon is a six-sided regular polygon. The **POLYGON** command is used to draw any regular polygon with up to 1024 sides.

The **POLYGON** command can be accessed by selecting **Draw > Polygon**, picking the **Polygon** button in the **2D Draw** control panel of the **Dashboard** or the **Draw** toolbar, or typing POL or POLYGON. Regardless of the method used to select the command, you are first prompted for the number of sides. For example, if you want an octagon (a polygon with eight sides), enter 8.

regular polygon: A closed geometric figure with three or more equal sides and equal angles.

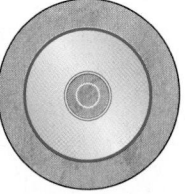

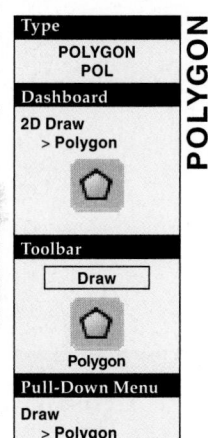

NOTE

The number of sides you enter becomes the default for the next time you use the **POLYGON** command. This value is saved in the **POLYSIDES** system variable.

Next, AutoCAD prompts for the center or edge of the polygon. If you reply by picking a point on the screen, this point becomes the center of the polygon.

You are then asked if you want to have the polygon inscribed within or circumscribed outside of an imaginary circle. An *inscribed polygon* is one that is drawn inside an imaginary circle so that its corners touch the circle. A *circumscribed polygon* is drawn outside of an imaginary circle so that the sides of the polygon are tangent to the circle. See Figure 4-28. The **I** (inscribed) or **C** (circumscribed) option you select becomes the default for the next polygon. With either option, you must specify the radius of the circle. Finally, you must pick the center or specify an edge for the polygon. Notice that picking the center is the default.

inscribed polygon: A polygon that is drawn inside an imaginary circle so that its corners touch the circle.

circumscribed polygon: A polygon that is drawn outside of an imaginary circle so that the sides of the polygon are tangent to the circle.

Figure 4-28.
Polygons can be inscribed in a circle (left) or circumscribed around a circle (right).

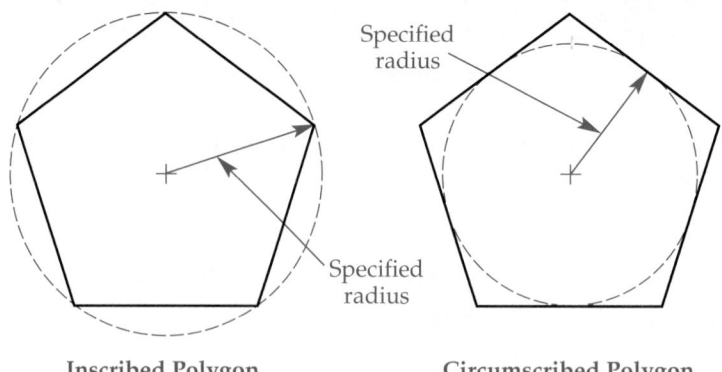

Specified radius

Specified radius

Inscribed Polygon   Circumscribed Polygon

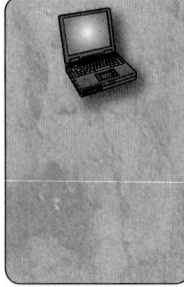

PROFESSIONAL TIP

Hexagons (six-sided polygons) are commonly drawn to represent bolt heads and nuts on mechanical drawings. Keep in mind that these features are normally dimensioned across the flats. To draw a polygon to be dimensioned across the flats, circumscribe it. The radius you enter is equal to one-half the distance across the flats. The distance across the corners is specified when the polygon must be confined within a circular area. In this case, use an inscribed polygon.

polyline: A series of lines and arcs that constitute a single object.

Polygons are *polylines* and can be easily edited using the **PEDIT** (polyline edit) command. The **PEDIT** command is discussed in Chapter 14 of this textbook.

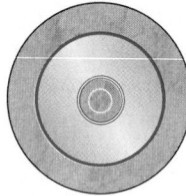

Exercise 4-7

Complete the exercise on the Student CD.

Drawing Rectangles

RECTANGLE

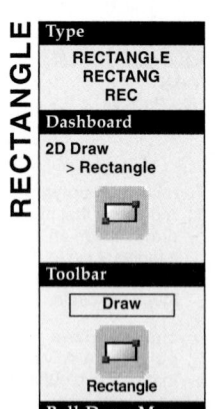

Type
RECTANGLE
RECTANG
REC
Dashboard
2D Draw
> Rectangle

Toolbar
Draw

Rectangle
Pull-Down Menu
Draw
> Rectangle

The **RECTANG** command allows you to draw rectangles easily. To use this command, pick one corner and then the opposite diagonal corner to establish the rectangle. See **Figure 4-29.** The **RECTANG** command can be accessed by picking the **Rectangle** button in the **2D Draw** control panel of the **Dashboard** or in the **Draw** toolbar; by selecting **Draw > Rectangle**; or by typing REC, RECTANG, or RECTANGLE.

Rectangles are polylines and can be edited using the **PEDIT** command. Since a rectangle is a polyline, it is treated as one entity until it is exploded. After it is exploded, the individual sides can be edited separately. The **EXPLODE** command is discussed in Chapter 14 of this textbook.

Drawing Rectangles with Line Width

The **Width** option of the **RECTANG** command is used to adjust the width of the rectangle in the XY plane. The following sequence is used to create a rectangle with .5 wide lines:

Command: **REC, RECTANG,** *or* **RECTANGLE.**↵
Specify first corner point or [Chamfer/Elevation/Fillet/Thickness/Width]: **W.**↵
Specify line width for rectangles <*current*>: **.5.**↵
Specify first corner point or [Chamfer/Elevation/Fillet/Thickness/Width]:

Figure 4-29.
Using the **RECTANG** command.

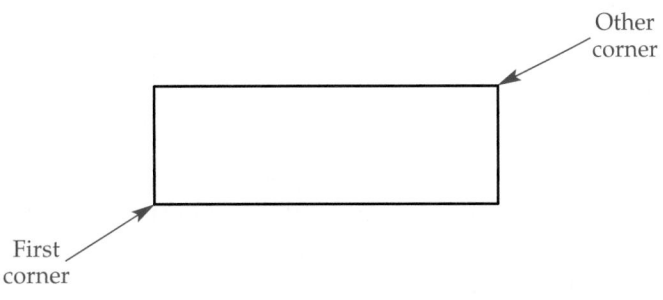

Other
corner

First
corner

After setting the rectangle width, you can either select another option or draw the rectangle. Continue selecting options until you have set the characteristics correctly, and then draw the rectangle. If a width is set, any new rectangles drawn use the width you entered. To reset the width to the initial default, enter the **Width** option, and then specify a width of 0. Now, new rectangles are drawn using a standard "0 width" line.

Drawing Chamfered Rectangles

The **RECTANG** command has a **Chamfer** option that includes chamfered corners in the initial rectangle construction. A *chamfer* is an angled corner on an object. Drawing chamfers is covered in detail in Chapter 11 of this textbook.

chamfer: In mechanical drafting, a small angled surface used to relieve a sharp corner.

The **Chamfer** option requires you to specify chamfer distances, or distances from the corner. See **Figure 4-30.** The command sequence is as follows:

> Command: **REC**, **RECTANG**, *or* **RECTANGLE.**↵
> Specify first corner point or [Chamfer/Elevation/Fillet/Thickness/Width]: **C**↵
> Specify first chamfer distance for rectangles <*current*>: *(enter the first chamfer distance)*
> Specify second chamfer distance for rectangles <*current*>: *(enter the second chamfer distance)*
> Specify first corner point or [Chamfer/Elevation/Fillet/Thickness/Width]:

After setting the chamfer distances, you can either draw the rectangle or select another option. If you select the **Fillet** option, the chamfers will not be drawn.

The default chamfer distances are the chamfer distances used to draw the previous rectangle. If the default for the first chamfer distance is zero, and you enter a different value, the new distance becomes the default for the second chamfer distance. If the default chamfer distances are nonzero values, however, a new value entered for the first distance does *not* become the default for the second distance. As with the **Width** option, if you set the **Chamfer** option's distances to a value greater than 0, any new

Figure 4-30.
Rectangles can be chamfered or rounded when they are created.

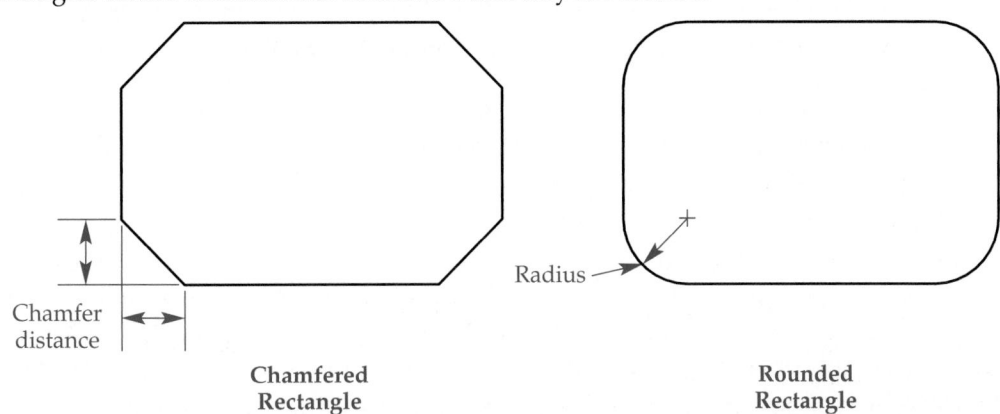

Chamfer
distance

Radius

Chamfered
Rectangle

Rounded
Rectangle

rectangles created are automatically chamfered. New rectangles continue to be created with chamfers until you reset the chamfer distances to 0 or use the **Fillet** option to create rounded corners.

Drawing Rounded Rectangles

A *fillet* is a rounded interior corner on an object and a *round* is a rounded exterior corner. AutoCAD uses the term *fillet* to describe both fillets and rounds. See **Figure 4-30.** Drawing fillets and rounds is covered in detail in Chapter 11 of this textbook. This is a brief introduction to drawing rounds on rectangles.

Rounds can be automatically drawn on rectangles using the **Fillet** option of the **RECTANG** command. After selecting the option, you must enter the round radius:

Command: **REC, RECTANG,** *or* **RECTANGLE.**↵
Specify first corner point or [Chamfer/Elevation/Fillet/Thickness/Width]: **F**↵
Specify fillet radius for rectangles *<current>*: *(enter a round radius or press* [Enter] *to accept the default)*
Specify first corner point or [Chamfer/Elevation/Fillet/Thickness/Width]:

The default round radius is the radius of the rounds in the previous rectangle. Once a radius is specified, the **RECTANG** command automatically draws rounds on all new rectangles. In order to draw rectangles without rounds, the radius must be set to 0.

Specifying Rectangle Areas

When you know the area of a rectangle and the length of one of its sides, the rectangle can be drawn using the **Area** option. This option is available after the first corner point of the rectangle is picked:

Specify other corner point or [Area/Dimensions/Rotation]: **A**

You are then prompted to enter the total area for the rectangle. Enter a value that corresponds to the current units. The following sequence is used to draw a rectangle with an area of 45 in² when the length is known:

Enter area of rectangle in current units *<current>*: **45**↵
Calculate rectangle dimensions based on [Length/Width] *<current>*: **L**↵
Enter rectangle length *<current>*: **10**↵
Command:

After you enter the length, AutoCAD calculates the width dimension automatically and draws the rectangle.

Specifying Rectangle Dimensions

AutoCAD provides a **Dimensions** option for the **RECTANG** command. The option is available after the first corner of the rectangle is picked.

Enter D to access the **Dimensions** option. You are then prompted to enter the length and width of the rectangle. In the following example, a 5 × 3 rectangle is specified:

Specify other corner point or [Area/Dimensions/Rotation]: **D**↵
Specify length for rectangles *<current>*: **5**↵
Specify width for rectangles *<current>*: **3**↵
Specify other corner point or [Area/Dimensions/Rotation]: *(move the crosshairs to the desired quadrant and pick a point)*
Command:

After specifying the length and width, AutoCAD asks for the other corner point. If you wish to change the dimensions, select the **Dimensions** option again. If the dimensions are correct, you can specify the other corner point to complete the rectangle. The second corner point determines which of four possible rectangles is drawn. See **Figure 4-31.**

AutoCAD and Its Applications—Basics

Figure 4-31.
The orientation of the rectangle relative to the first corner point is determined by the second corner point.

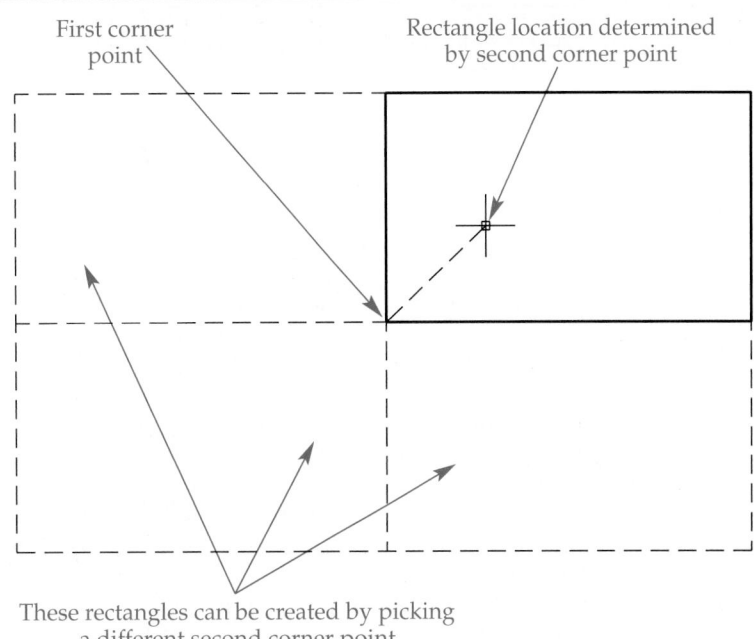

First corner point

Rectangle location determined by second corner point

These rectangles can be created by picking a different second corner point

Drawing a Rotated Rectangle

A rectangle can be drawn at an angle by specifying a rotation angle after selecting the first point. To do so, use the **Rotation** option as follows:

Specify other corner point or [Area/Dimensions/Rotation]: **R**↵
Specify rotation angle or [Pick points] <*current*>: *(enter an angle, pick a point, or enter P to pick two reference points)*
Specify other corner point or [Area/Dimensions/Rotation]: *(pick the second point)*
Command:

If you select the **Pick points** option, you are prompted to select two points to define the angle. When a new value is specified for the **Rotation** option, it becomes the default angle.

Additional Rectangle Options

Two other options are available for the **RECTANG** command. These options remain effective for multiple uses of the command:

- **Elevation.** This option sets the elevation of the rectangle along the Z axis. The default value is 0.
- **Thickness.** This option gives the rectangle depth along the Z axis. The default value is 0.

NOTE

A combination of rectangle settings can be used to draw a single rectangle. For example, you can enter a width value, chamfer distances, and length and width dimensions, all to create a single rectangle.

Exercise 4-8
Complete the exercise on the Student CD.

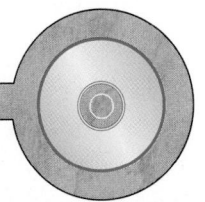

Drawing Donuts and Solid Circles

DONUT

Type

DONUT
DOUGHNUT
DO

Pull-Down Menu

Draw
> Donut

The **DONUT** command allows you to draw a thick circle. It can have any inside and outside diameters or be completely filled. See **Figure 4-32.** Donuts drawn in AutoCAD are actually polyline arcs with width. Polylines are covered in detail in Chapter 14.

The **DONUT** command can be accessed by selecting **Draw** > **Donut** or by typing DO, DONUT, or DOUGHNUT as follows:

Command: **DO**, **DONUT**, *or* **DOUGHNUT**.↵
Specify inside diameter of donut *<current>*: **3**.↵
Specify outside diameter of donut *<current>*: **5**.↵
Specify center of donut or <exit>: *(select the donut's center point)*
Specify center of donut or <exit>: *(select the center point for another donut, or press* [Enter] *to end the command)*

The current diameter settings are shown in brackets. New diameters can be entered, or the current value can be accepted by pressing the [Enter] key. An inside diameter of 0 produces a solid circle.

After you select the center point, the donut appears on the screen. You may pick another center point to draw the same size donut in a new location. The **DONUT** command remains active until you press [Enter] or cancel by pressing [Esc].

When the **FILL** mode is turned off, donuts appear as segmented circles or concentric circles. **FILL** can be used transparently by entering 'FILL while inside the **DONUT** command. Enter ON or OFF as needed. The fill display for previously drawn donuts is updated when the drawing is regenerated.

NOTE

The setting for the inside diameter of a donut is stored in the **DONUTID** system variable. The setting for the outside diameter is stored in the **DONUTOD** system variable. If the value of **DONUTID** is greater than the value of **DONUTOD**, the values are switched when the next donut is drawn.

Exercise 4-9

Complete the exercise on the Student CD.

Figure 4-32.
The appearance of a donut depends on its inside and outside diameters and the current **FILL** mode.

Fill On

Fill On
I.D. = 0

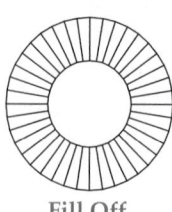

Fill Off

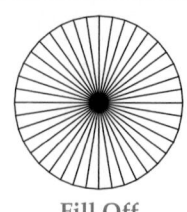

Fill Off
I.D. = 0

Chapter Test

Answer the following questions. Write your answers on a separate sheet of paper or complete the electronic chapter test on the Student CD.

1. Which command controls the visibility of the rubberband image that appears by default when you create objects?
2. Name the system variable used to set the default radius when drawing circles.
3. Explain how to create a circle with a diameter of 2.5 units.
4. Define the term *point of tangency*.
5. What option of the **CIRCLE** command creates a circle of a specific radius that is tangent to two existing objects?
6. Identify how to access the option that allows you to draw a circle tangent to three objects.
7. Briefly explain how to create a three-point arc.
8. Define the term *included angle* as it applies to an arc.
9. Explain the procedure to draw an arc beginning with the center point and having a 60° included angle.
10. List the three input options that can be used to draw an arc tangent to the endpoint of a previously drawn arc.
11. What is the default option if the **ARC** command is entered at the keyboard?
12. Briefly describe the procedure to draw an ellipse using the **Axis, End** option.
13. What is the **ELLIPSE** rotation angle that causes you to draw a circle?
14. Identify two ways to access the **Arc** option for drawing elliptical arcs.
15. Name the AutoCAD system variable that lets you draw a true ellipse or a polyline ellipse with the **ELLIPSE** command.
16. Name at least three commands you could use to create a rectangle.
17. Explain how to draw a hexagon measuring 4″ (102 mm) across the flats.
18. Given the distance across the flats of a hexagon, would you use the **Inscribed** or **Circumscribed** option to draw the hexagon?
19. Name the control panel on the **Dashboard** where the **RECTANG** command is found.
20. Name the command option designed specifically for drawing rectangles with a specific line thickness.
21. Name the command option used to draw rectangles with rounded corners.
22. Explain how to draw two donuts with an inside diameter of 6.25 and an outside diameter of 9.50.
23. Describe a method for drawing a solid circle.
24. Explain how to turn the **FILL** mode off.
25. Give the easiest keyboard shortcut for the following commands:
    A. **CIRCLE**
    B. **ARC**
    C. **ELLIPSE**
    D. **POLYGON**
    E. **RECTANG**
    F. **DONUT**

Drawing Problems

Start AutoCAD and use a template or a setup option of your choice. Do not draw dimensions or text. Use your own judgment and approximate dimensions if needed.

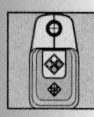

1. You have just been given the sketch of a new sports car design (shown below). You are asked to create a drawing from the sketch. Use the **LINE** command and selected shape commands to draw the car. Do not be concerned with size and scale. Consider the commands and techniques used to draw the car, and try to minimize the number of objects. Save your drawing as P4-1.

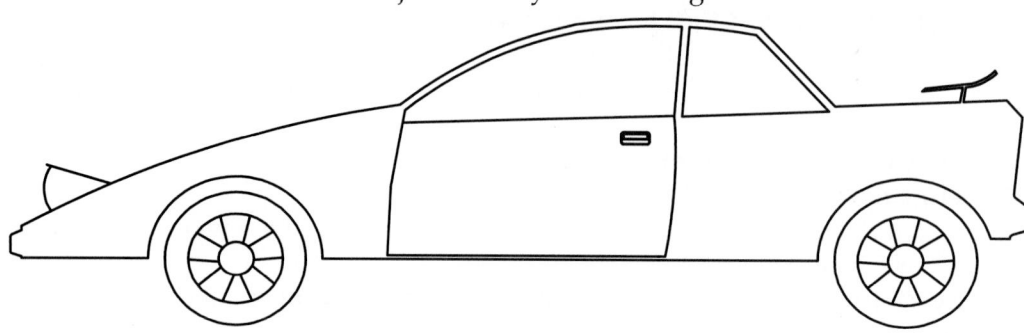

2. You have just been given the sketch of an innovative new truck design (shown below). You are asked to create a drawing from the sketch. Use the **LINE** command and selected shape commands to draw a truck resembling the sketch. Do not be concerned with size and scale. Save your drawing as P4-2.

3. Use the **LINE** and **CIRCLE** command options to draw the objects below. Do not include dimensions. Save the drawing as P4-3.

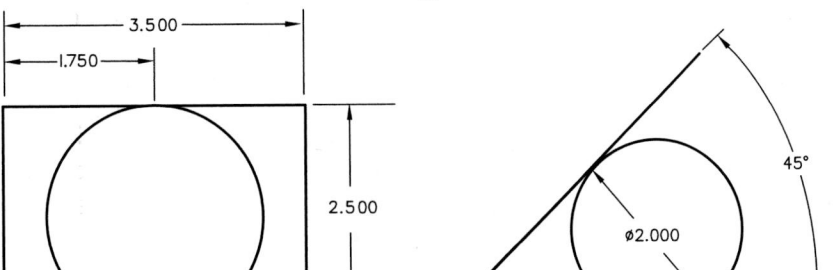

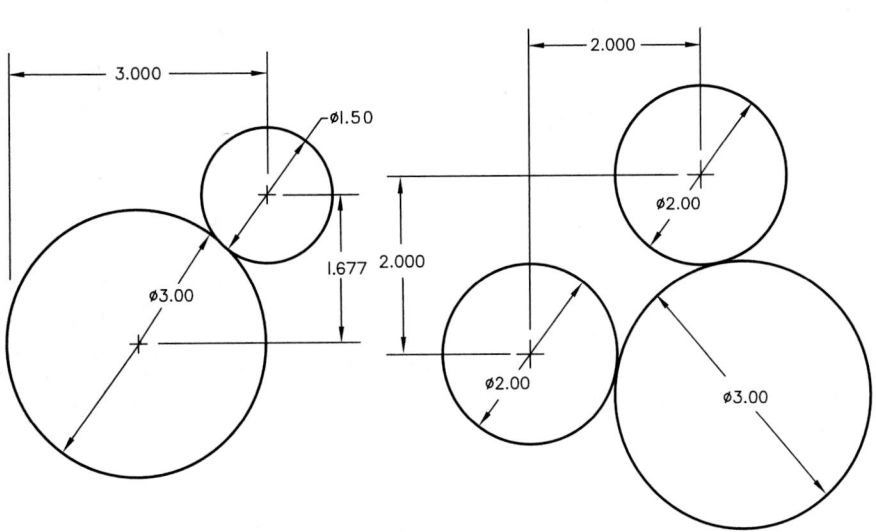

4. Use the **CIRCLE** and **ARC** command options to draw the object below. Do not include dimensions. Save the drawing as P4-4.

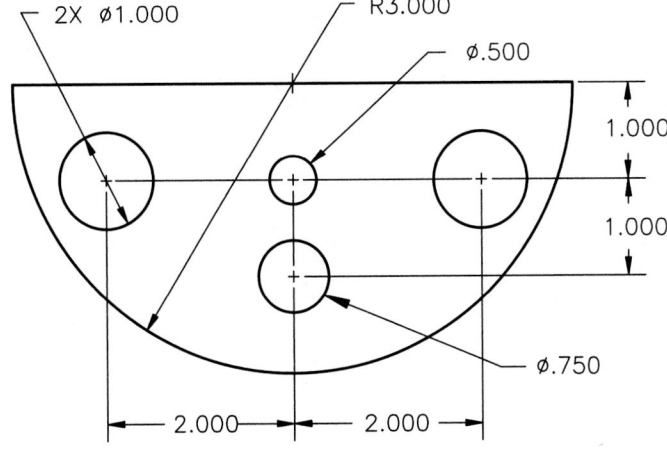

5. Draw the following object. Do not include centerlines or dimensions.

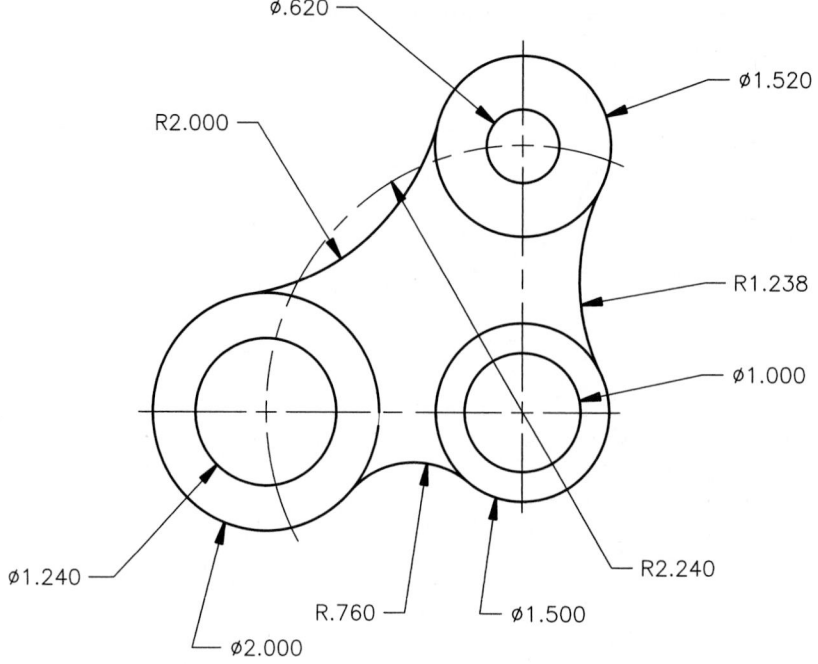

ø.620

ø1.520

R2.000

R1.238

ø1.000

ø1.240

R2.240

R.760   ø1.500

ø2.000

(Art courtesy of Bruce L. Wilcox)

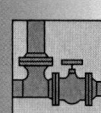

6. Draw the pressure cylinder shown below. Use the **Arc** option of the **ELLIPSE** command to draw the cylinder ends. Do not include the dimensions. Save the drawing as **P4-6**.

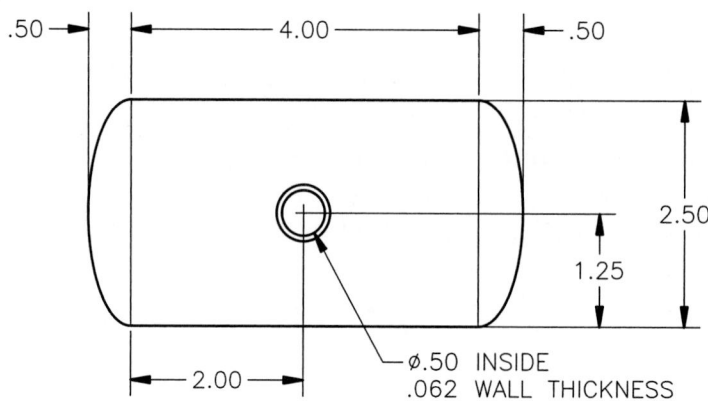

.50   4.00   .50

2.50

1.25

2.00   ø.50 INSIDE
.062 WALL THICKNESS

7. Draw the spacer below. Do not draw the centerlines or dimensions. Save the drawing as **P4-7**.

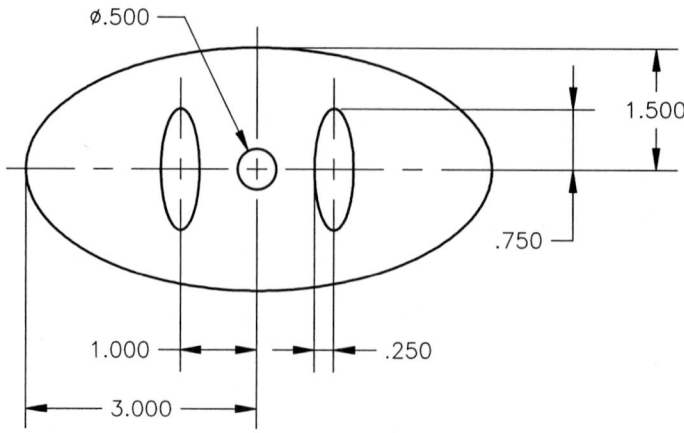

ø.500

1.500

.750

1.000   .250

3.000

8. Draw the following object. Do not draw the dimensions. Save the drawing as P4-8.

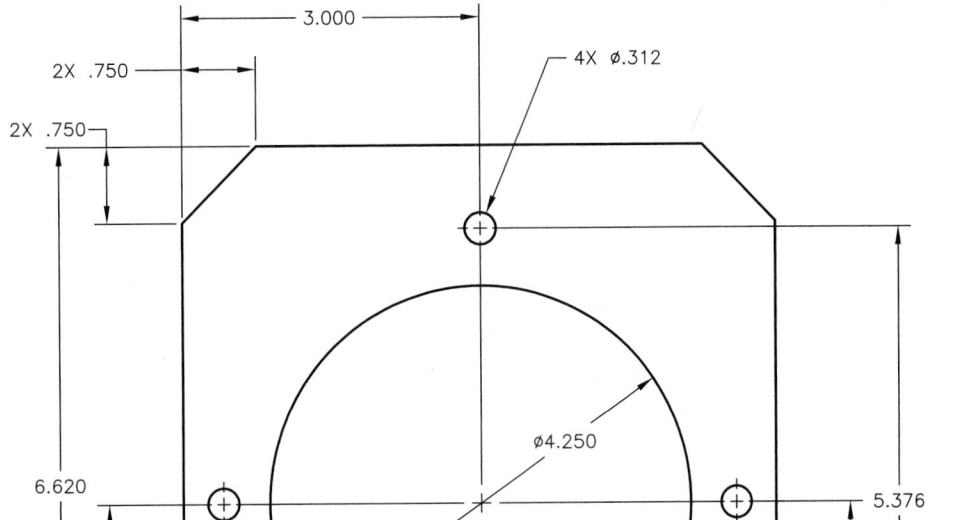

9. Draw the following object. Do not draw the centerlines or dimensions. Save the drawing as P4-9.

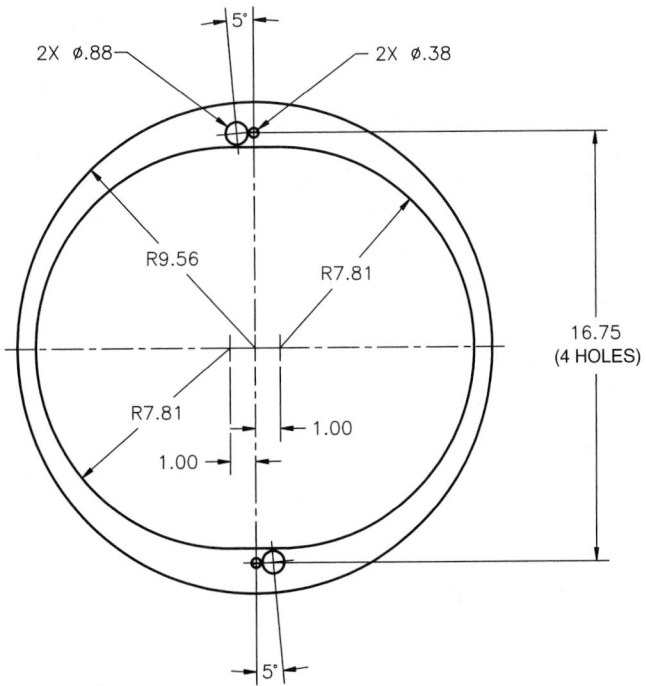

10. Draw this elevation using the **ARC**, **CIRCLE**, and **RECTANG** commands. Do not be concerned with size and scale. Save the drawing as P4-10.

11. Draw the object shown below. Do not draw the centerlines or dimensions. Save the drawing as P4-11.

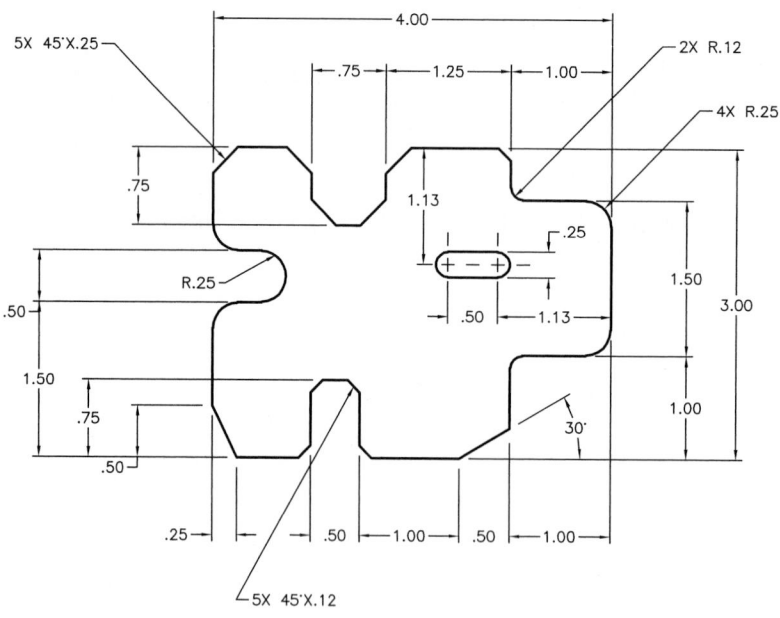

12. Draw the gasket shown below. Do not draw the dimensions. Save the drawing as P4-12.

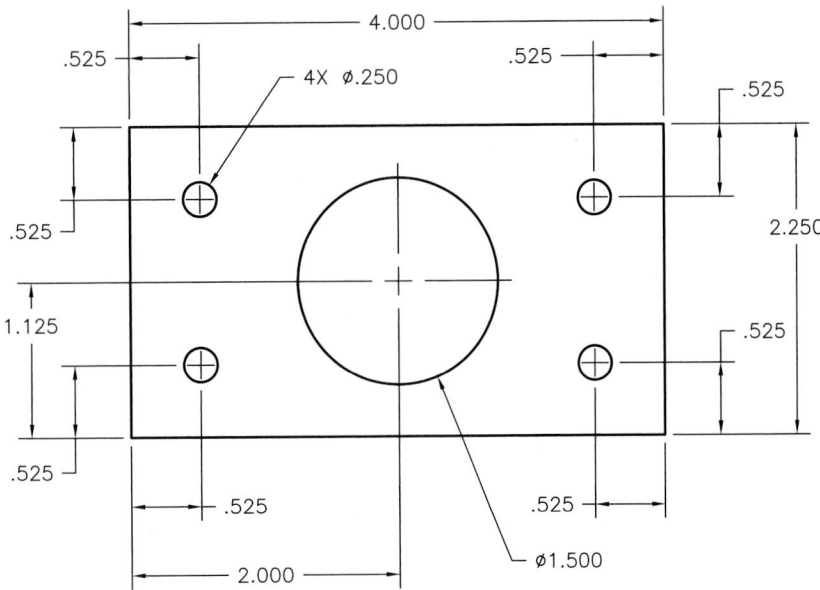

For Problems 13–16, draw the part shown. Do not draw centerlines or dimensions. Save your drawing as P4-(problem number).

13.

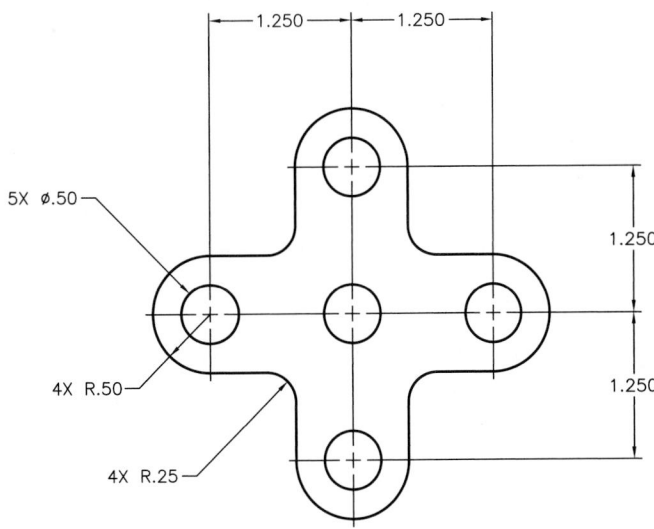

14.

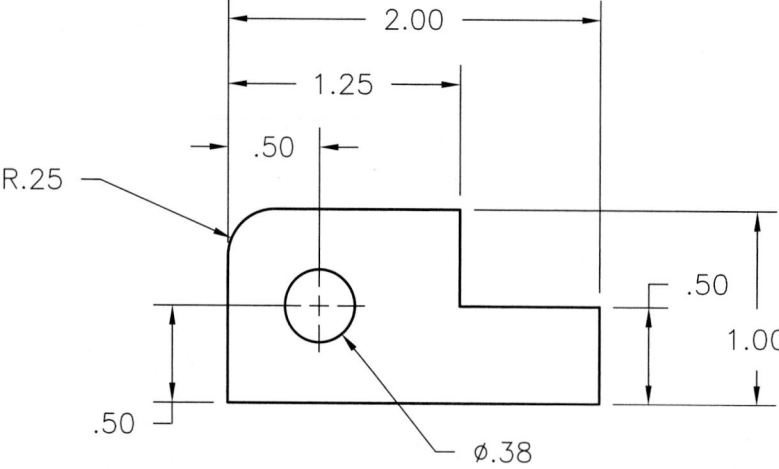

15.

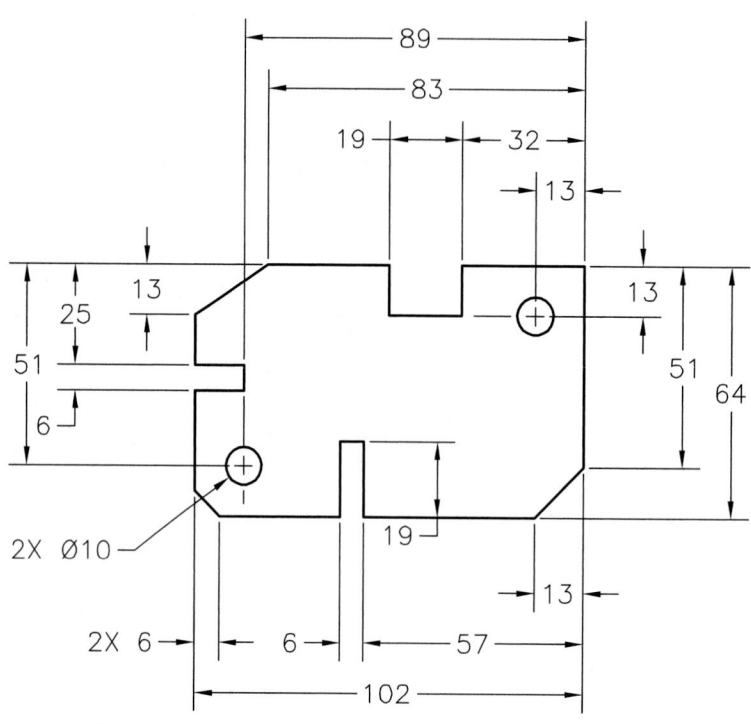

16.

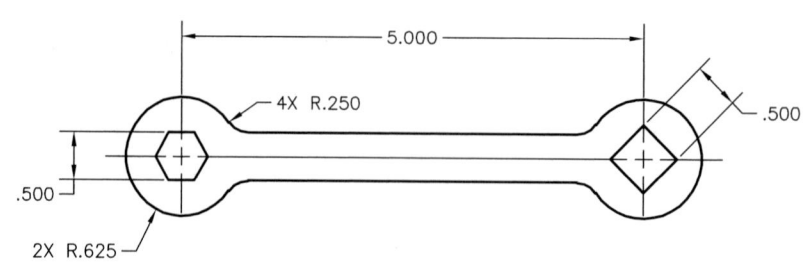

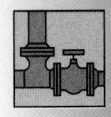

17. Draw the pipe fitting shown. Save the drawing as P4-17.

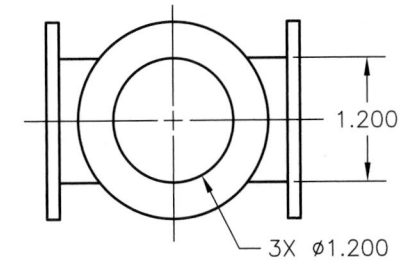

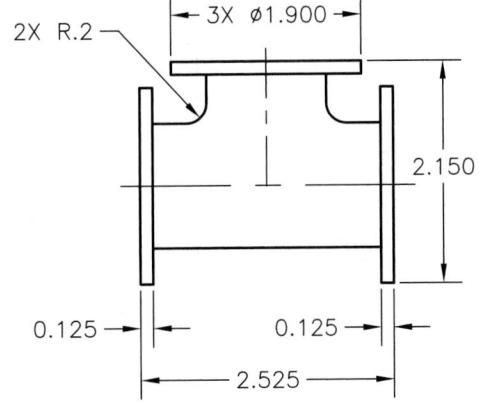

18. Draw the ellipse template shown. Save the drawing as P4-18.

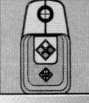

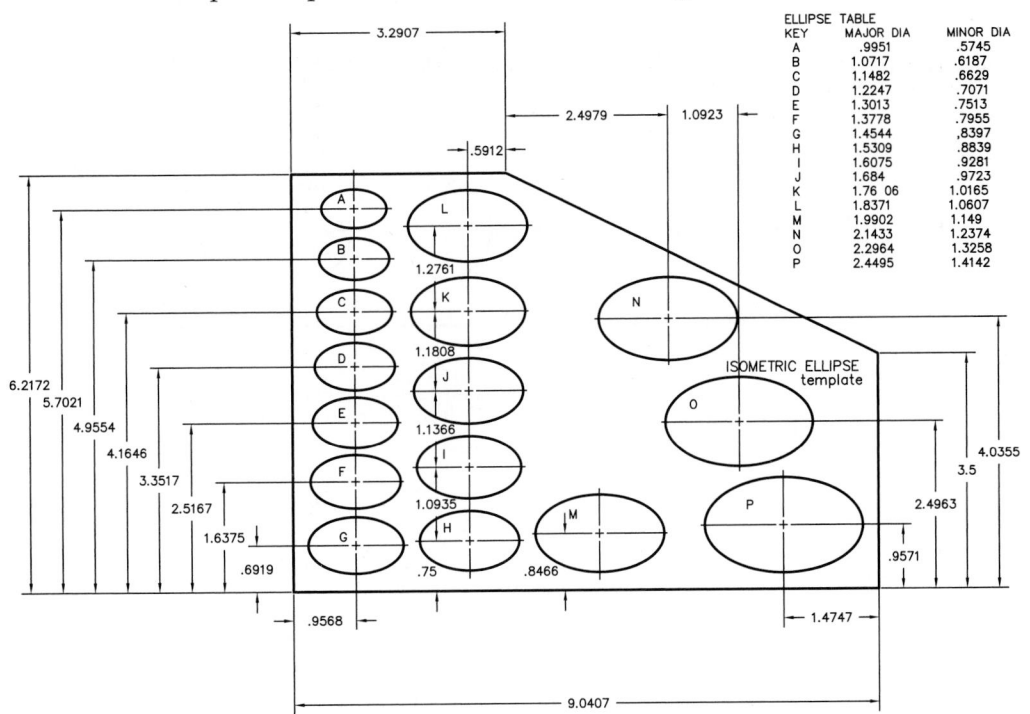

| ELLIPSE TABLE | | |
KEY	MAJOR DIA	MINOR DIA
A	.9951	.5745
B	1.0717	.6187
C	1.1482	.6629
D	1.2247	.7071
E	1.3013	.7513
F	1.3778	.7955
G	1.4544	.8397
H	1.5309	.8839
I	1.6075	.9281
J	1.684	.9723
K	1.76 06	1.0165
L	1.8371	1.0607
M	1.9902	1.149
N	2.1433	1.2374
O	2.2964	1.3258
P	2.4495	1.4142

19. Draw the gasket shown. Do not include the dimensions. Save the drawing as P4-19.

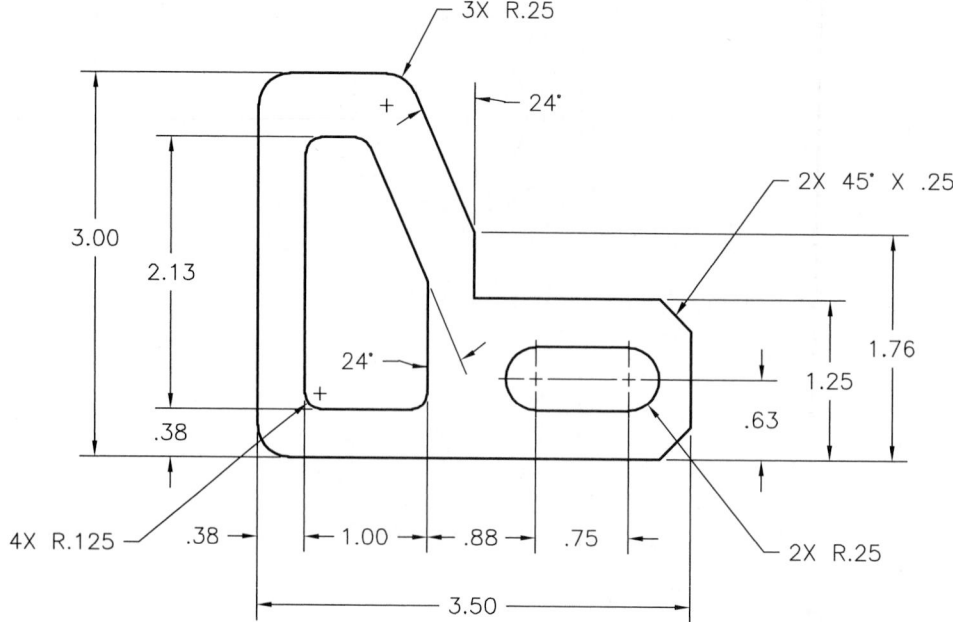

20. Draw the pipe spacer shown. Do not include the dimensions. Save the drawing as P4-20.

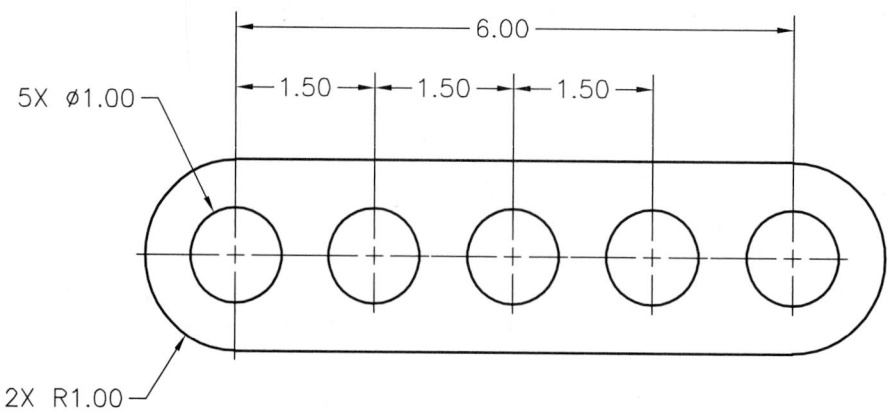

Line Standards, Drawing Format, and Printing

Learning Objectives

After completing this chapter, you will be able to do the following:
- ✓ Describe basic line conventions for drafting.
- ✓ Create and manage drawing layers.
- ✓ Set up and use a variety of linetypes.
- ✓ Draw objects on separate layers.
- ✓ Filter a list of layers.
- ✓ Use **DesignCenter** to copy layers and linetypes between drawings.
- ✓ Make prints of your drawings.

An important part of basic drawing setup consists of assigning and organizing linetypes and other object properties to conform to accepted standards and conventions. AutoCAD uses a layer system to simplify the process of assigning and modifying object properties. In addition, you can use layer display options to create several different drawing sheets, views, and displays from a single drawing.

This chapter introduces line conventions and AutoCAD's layer system. It also provides a brief introduction to printing and plotting. Printing and plotting is covered in greater detail in Chapter 25.

Line Standards

Drafting is a graphic language using lines, symbols, and words to describe products to be manufactured. Line conventions are standards based on line thickness and type. These standards are designed to enhance the readability of drawings. This section introduces the line standards that you will apply later in this chapter when you begin loading linetypes and defining layers, as well as throughout your drafting career.

The American Society of Mechanical Engineers (ASME) is responsible for the drafting standards approved by the American National Standards Institute (ANSI). These standards recommend two line widths to establish contrasting lines in a drawing. Lines are described as thick or thin. For manual drafting, thick lines are twice as thick as thin lines, with recommended widths of 0.6 mm and 0.3 mm, respectively. However, a single line width for all types of lines is acceptable on drawings prepared with a CAD system. **Figure 5-1** shows recommended line width and type as defined in ASME Y14.2M, *Line Conventions and Lettering*.

Figure 5-1.
Line conventions. (Adapted from ASME Y14.2M)

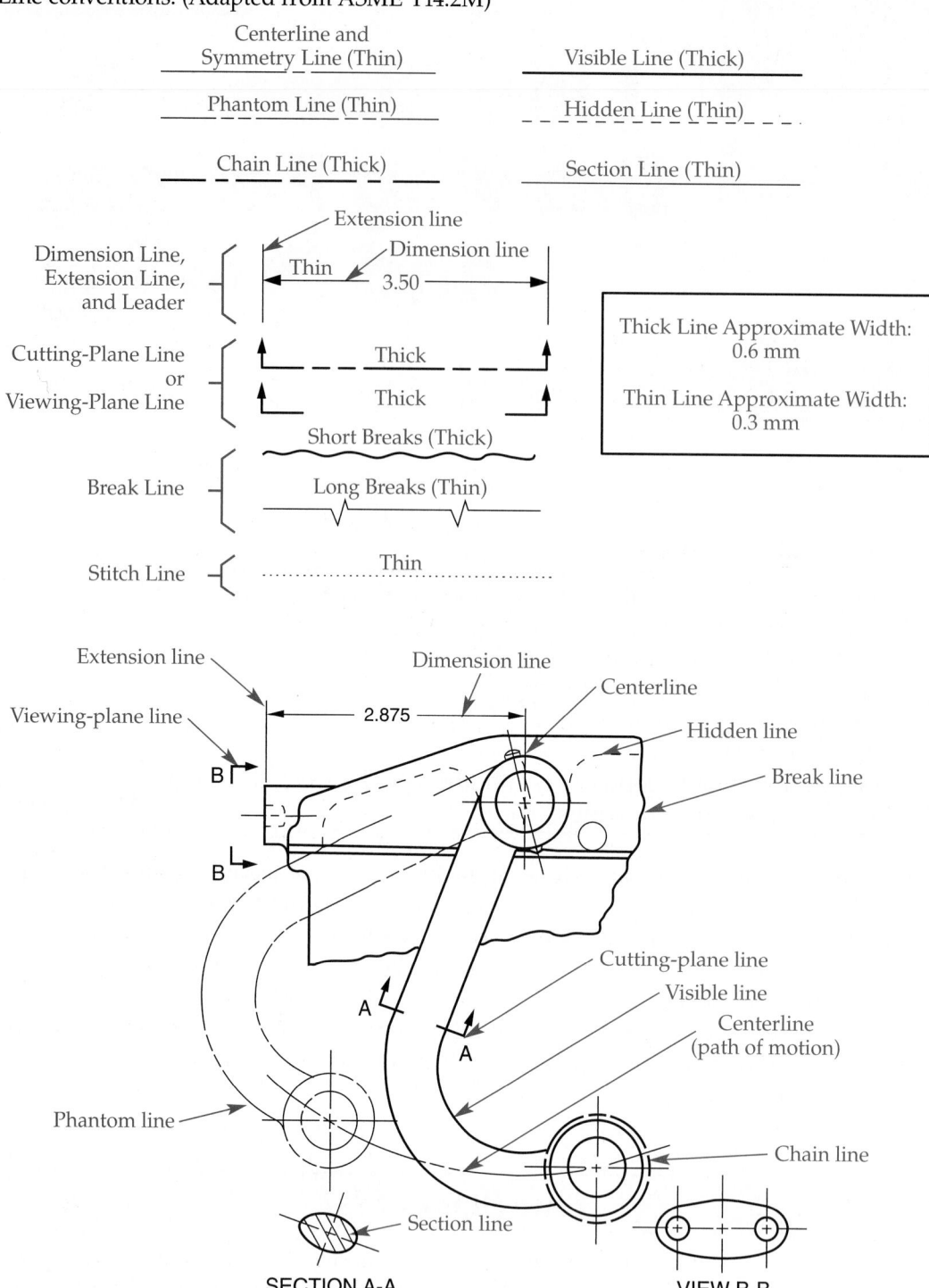

Object Lines

Object lines, also called *visible lines*, are thick lines used to show the outline or contour of an object. See **Figure 5-2**. Object lines are the most commonly used type of lines in drawings. These lines should be twice as thick as thin lines.

Hidden Lines

Hidden lines, often called *dashed lines,* are used to represent invisible features of an object, as shown in **Figure 5-2**. They are drawn thin to contrast clearly with thick

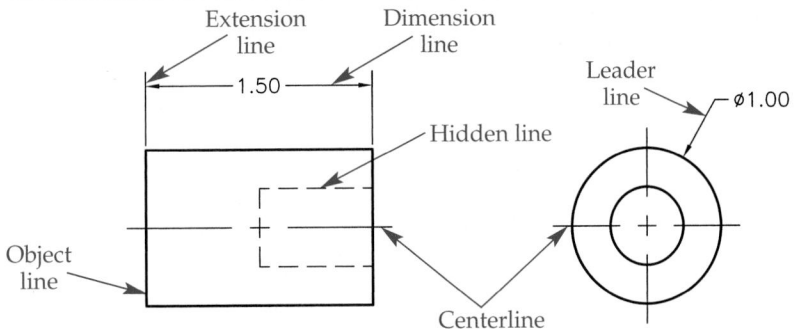

Figure 5-2.
This simple drawing shows standard line styles and line thicknesses used in drafting.

object lines. When properly drawn at full size, the dashes are .125" (3 mm) long and spaced .06" (1.5 mm) apart. Be aware that if the drawing is to be greatly reduced or scaled down during the plotting process, the dashes may appear too small.

Centerlines

Centerlines are thin lines consisting of alternating long and short dashes that locate the centers of circles and arcs and show the axis of a cylindrical or symmetrical shape. See **Figure 5-2.** The recommended dash lengths are .125" (3 mm) for the short dashes and .75" to 1.5" (19 mm to 38 mm) for the long dashes. These lengths can be altered, depending on the size of the drawing. Spaces approximately .06" (1.5 mm) long should separate the dashes. The small centerline dashes should cross only at the center of a circle. Centerlines should extend .125" to .25" (3 mm to 6 mm) past objects.

centerlines: Lines made up of alternating long and short dashes, representing a center point or axis of symmetry.

Extension Lines

Extension lines are thin lines used to show the "extent" of a dimension, as shown in **Figure 5-2.** They begin a short distance from an object and extend .125" (3 mm) beyond the last dimension line. Extension lines may cross object lines, hidden lines, and centerlines, but they may not cross dimension lines. Centerlines become extension lines when they are used to show the extent of a dimension. When this is done, there is no space where the centerline joins the extension line.

extension lines: Lines that extend from the object being measured to the dimension line to show the extent of the dimension.

Dimension Lines

Dimension lines are thin lines placed between extension lines to indicate a measurement. In mechanical drafting, the dimension line is normally broken near the center for placement of the dimension numeral, as shown in **Figure 5-2.** The dimension line normally remains unbroken in architectural and structural drawings. The dimension numeral is placed on top of an unbroken dimension line. Arrows terminate the ends of dimension lines, except in architectural drafting, where slashes (ticks) or dots are often used.

dimension lines: Thin lines placed between extension lines to show the distance being measured.

Leader Lines

Leader lines are thin lines used to connect a specific note to a feature on a drawing. A leader line terminates with an arrowhead at the feature and has a small shoulder at the note. See **Figure 5-2.** Dimension and leader line usage is discussed in detail in Chapters 16 and 17.

leader lines: Thin lines used to connect a note to a feature on a drawing.

Cutting-Plane and Viewing-Plane Lines

Cutting-plane lines are thick lines identifying the location of a section. See **Figure 5-3.** *Viewing-plane lines* are drawn in the same style as cutting-plane lines, but identify the location of a view. Cutting-plane and viewing-plane lines can be drawn one of two ways, as shown in **Figure 5-1.** The uses of viewing-plane and cutting-plane lines are discussed in detail in Chapters 7 and 21.

cutting-plane lines: Thick lines that identify the location and viewing direction of a section view.

viewing-plane lines: Thick lines that identify the location of a view.

Figure 5-3.
Section lines and cutting-plane lines.

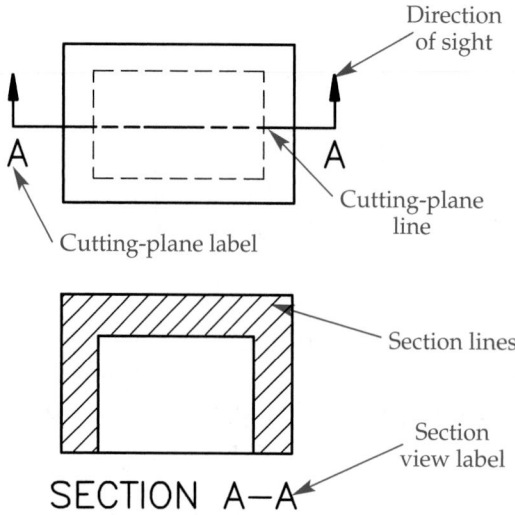

Section Lines

section lines: Thin lines, usually drawn in a regular pattern, that show cut surfaces.

Section lines are thin lines drawn in a section view to show where material has been cut away. See **Figure 5-3.** Types of section lines and applications are discussed in Chapter 21.

Break Lines

break lines: Lines that show where a portion of an object has been removed.

Break lines show where a portion of an object has been removed for clarity or convenience. For example, the center portion of a very long part can be broken out so the two ends can be moved closer together for a more convenient representation. Several types of break lines are shown in **Figure 5-4.**

Phantom Lines

phantom lines: Thin lines that identify repetitive details, alternate positions of moving parts, and locations of adjacent parts.

Phantom lines are thin lines with two short dashes alternating with long dashes. The short dashes are .125″ (3 mm) long, and the long dashes range from .75″ to 1.5″ (19 mm to 38 mm) in length, depending on the size of the drawing. Spaces between dashes are .06″ (1.5 mm). Phantom lines identify repetitive details, show alternate positions of moving parts, and locate adjacent positions of related parts. See **Figure 5-5.**

Chain Lines

chain lines: Thick lines that indicate special features or unique treatment for a surface.

Chain lines are thick lines of alternating long and short dashes. They show that the portion of the surface next to the chain line has special features or receives unique treatment. See **Figure 5-6.**

Figure 5-4.
Standard break lines.

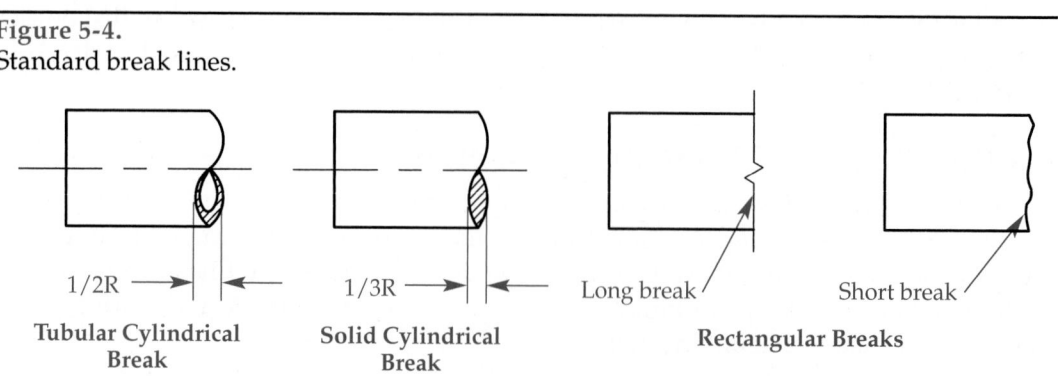

Figure 5-5.
Phantom lines.

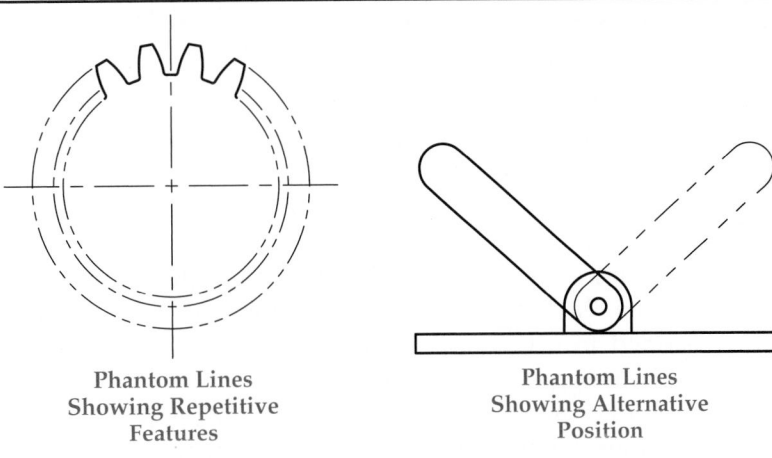

Phantom Lines
Showing Repetitive
Features

Phantom Lines
Showing Alternative
Position

Figure 5-6.
Chain lines.

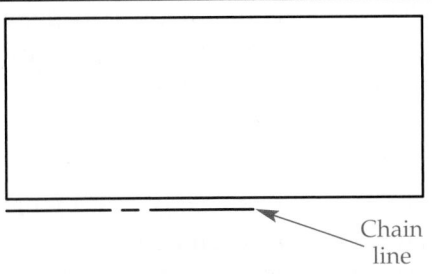

Chain
line

Introduction to Layers

In manual drafting, different elements or components of a drawing might be separated by placing them on different sheets. When each sheet is perfectly aligned with the others, you have what is called an *overlay system*. In AutoCAD, the components of this overlay system are referred to as *layers*. All the layers can be reproduced together to reflect the entire design drawing. Individual layers might also be reproduced to show specific details or components of the design. Using layers increases productivity in several ways:

✓ Specific information can be grouped on separate layers. For example, the floor plan can be drawn on one layer, the electrical plan on another, and the plumbing plan on a third.

✓ Several plot sheets can be created from the same drawing file by modifying layer visibility.

✓ Drawings can be reproduced in individual layers, or the layers can be combined in any desired combination. For example, the floor plan and electrical plan can be reproduced together and sent to an electrical contractor for a bid. The floor plan and plumbing plan can be reproduced together and sent to a plumbing contractor.

✓ Each layer can be assigned a different color, linetype, and lineweight to correspond to line conventions and to help improve clarity.

✓ Each layer can be plotted in a different color, linetype, or lineweight, or it can be set not to plot at all.

✓ Selected layers can be turned off or frozen to decrease the amount of information displayed on the screen or to speed screen regeneration.

✓ Changes can be made to a layer promptly, often while the client watches.

overlay system:
A system of separating drawing components by layer.

layers:
Components of AutoCAD's overlay system that allow users to separate objects into logical groups for formatting and display purposes.

Layers Used in Different Drafting Fields

Typically, the type of drawing you create determines the function of each layer. In mechanical drafting, each different type of line or object is usually assigned to a specific layer. For example, visible object lines might be drawn on an Object layer that is black in color and uses a solid (continuous) linetype that is 0.6 mm wide. Hidden lines might be drawn on a green Hidden layer that uses a 0.3 mm hidden linetype. Architectural and civil drawings may have over one hundred layers in a drawing, each used to produce a specific item. For example, full-height walls on a floor plan might be drawn on a black A-WALL-FULL layer that uses a 0.6 mm solid linetype. Plumbing fixtures added to a floor plan might be drawn on a blue P-FIXT layer that uses a 0.3 mm solid linetype.

Layers can be created for any type of drawing, including detail parts, assemblies, floor plans, foundation plans, partition layouts, plumbing systems, electrical systems, structural systems, roof drainage systems, reflected ceiling systems, HVAC systems, site plans, profiles, topographic maps, and details. Interior designers may use floor plan, interior partition, and furniture layers. In electronics drafting, each level of a multilevel circuit board can be drawn on its own layer.

Naming Layers

Layers should be given names to reflect what is drawn on them. Layer names can have up to 255 characters and can include letters, numbers, and certain other characters, including spaces. Some examples of typical mechanical, architectural, and civil drafting layer names are as follows:

Mechanical	Architectural	Civil
Object	A-WALL-FULL	C-BLDG
Hidden	A-GLAZ	C-WATR
Center	A-DOOR	C-TOPO
Dimension	E-LITE	C-PROP
Construction	P-FIXT	C-NGAS
Section	S-FNDN	C-SSWR
Border	M-FURN	C-ELEV

Layers are usually named according to specific industry or company standards. However, for very simple drawings, layers might be named by linetype and color. For example, the layer name Continuous-White may have a continuous linetype drawn in white. The layer usage and color number, such as Object-7, can also be used to indicate an object line with color 7. Another option is to assign the linetype a numerical value. For example, object lines can be 1, hidden lines can be 2, and centerlines can be 3. If you use this method, keep a written record of your numbering system for reference.

Layers can also be given more complex names. The name might include the drawing number, color code, and layer content. The layer name Dwg100-2-Dimen, for example, could refer to drawing DWG100, color 2, and the fact that this layer is used for dimensions. The American Institute of Architects (AIA) has established a layer naming system for architectural and related drawings. This standard is found in the document *CAD Layer Guidelines*, published by AIA.

AutoCAD and Its Applications—Basics

The Layer Properties Manager

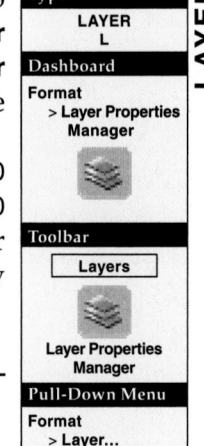

The **LAYER** command opens the **Layer Properties Manager**, which is used to create and delete layers and layer properties. To display this dialog box, pick the **Layer Properties Manager** button in the **Layers** control panel of the **Dashboard** or the **Layer Properties Manager** button from the **Layers** toolbar, select **Format > Layer...** from the pull-down menu, or type LA or LAYER. See **Figure 5-7.**

Only one layer is required in an AutoCAD drawing. This default layer is named 0 and cannot be renamed or purged from the drawing. See **Figure 5-8.** However, the 0 layer is primarily reserved for drawing blocks. Each object should be drawn on a layer specific to the object. For example, draw visible object lines on an Object layer, or draw floor plan walls on an A-WALL layer.

Figure 5-7.
The layer name appears in the Layer Control drop-down list in the Layers control panel of the Dashboard. Layer 0 is AutoCAD's default layer and should be reserved for creating blocks.

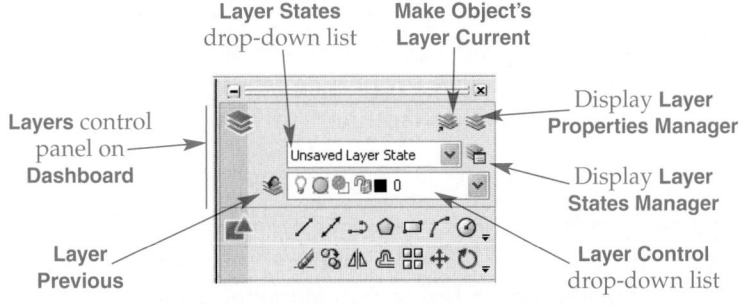

Figure 5-8.
The **Layer Properties Manager**.

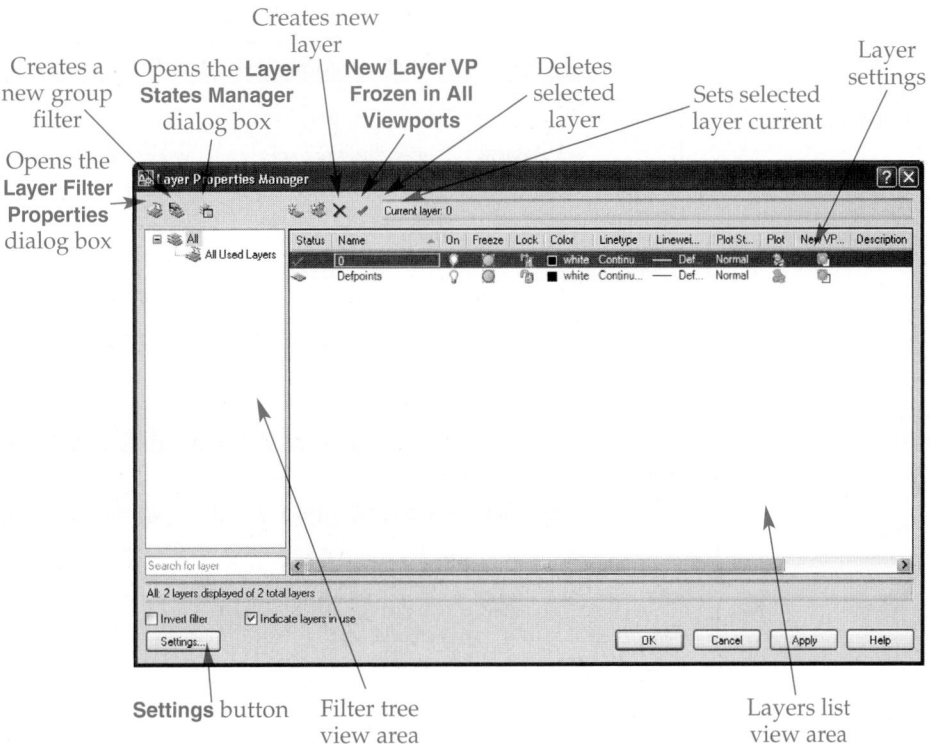

Creating Layers

Layers should be added to a drawing to meet the needs of the current drawing project. To add a new layer, select an existing layer that contains properties similar to those that you want to assign to the new layer. If this is the first new layer in a default template, only the 0 layer is available to reference. Then pick the **New Layer** button from the **Layer Properties Manager**, right-click and select the **New Layer** menu option, or press [Alt] + [N]. A new layer listing appears, using a default name of Layer1. See **Figure 5-9**. The layer name is highlighted when the listing appears, allowing you to type a new name.

Typing a layer name and then pressing the comma key enters the first layer name and creates and moves on to a new layer name. Entering several layer names in this manner saves time because it keeps you from having to pick the **New Layer** button each time. Pick the **Apply** button to alphabetize the new layer names, as shown in **Figure 5-10**. Pick the **OK** button to exit the **Layer Properties Manager**. If you did not pick the **Apply** button after creating new layers, the new layer names are alphabetized when you reopen the **Layer Properties Manager**.

NOTE

Selecting the headings in the layer names window controls sorting. Each time the **Layer Properties Manager** is reopened, however, the layers are sorted alphanumerically by default.

PROFESSIONAL TIP

To exit the **Layer Properties Manager** after creating layers, pick the **OK** button to accept the creation of the new layers. Picking the **Close** button (**X**) causes the dialog box to be closed without saving the list of layers you created.

Figure 5-9.
A new layer is named Layer1 by default.

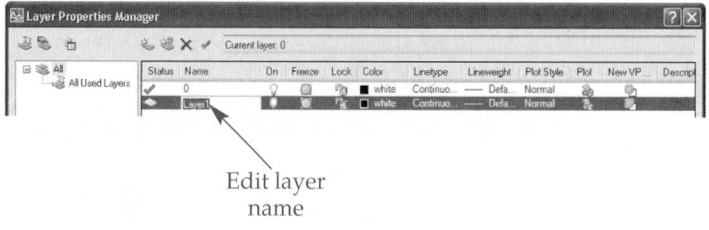

Edit layer name

Figure 5-10.
Layer names are placed in alphanumerical order when you pick **Apply** or reopen the **Layer Properties Manager**.

Layer names sort automatically

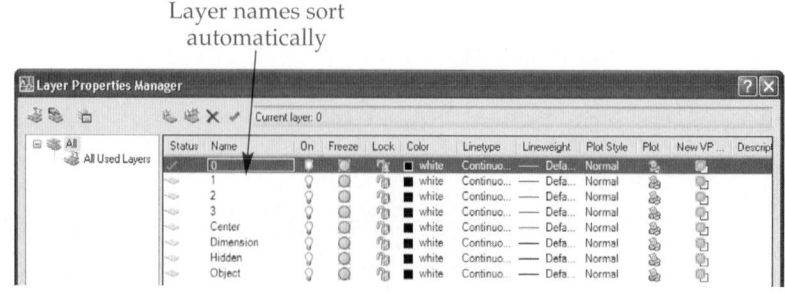

Deleting Layers

To delete a layer using the **Layer Properties Manager**, select the layer and then pick the **Delete Layer** button, or right-click on the layer and choose the **Delete Layer** menu option. Picking **Delete Layer** only selects the layer for deletion. You must then select the **Apply** button to remove the layer from the list. Layers selected for deletion can be deselected by repicking **Delete Layer**. The following layers cannot be deleted or purged from a drawing:

- The 0 layer
- The current layer
- Layers that contain objects
- Layers associated with an external reference

Setting the Current Layer

The *current layer* is the layer that is active at a given time. Whatever you draw is placed on the current layer. It is useful to think of the current layer as the top layer. Layer 0 is AutoCAD's default layer. Until another layer is defined and set current, all objects drawn are placed on and belong to layer 0. As mentioned earlier, however, you should create and draw on other layers, reserving layer 0 for block creation. Block creation is discussed later in this textbook.

current layer: The active layer.

To set a different layer current using the **Layer Properties Manager**, double-click the layer name, pick the layer name in the layer list and select the **Set Current** button, or right-click on the layer and choose the **Set Current** menu option. To highlight the layer name, pick the name. The current layer is specified in the status line above the layer list in the **Layer Properties Manager** and the **Layer Control** drop-down list in the **Layers** control panel of the **Dashboard**.

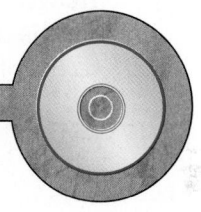

Exercise 5-1
Complete the exercise on the Student CD.

Layer Properties

Layer properties are displayed in a column format in the **Layer Properties Manager** with icons to the right of the layer name. See **Figure 5-11**. Picking the icons changes layer settings. The following layer properties are available:

- **Status.** The icon in this field indicates the status of the layer. A green check mark indicates that this is the current layer. The **Indicate layers in use** check box, located in the lower-left corner of the **Layer Properties Manager**, controls the function of the display status icon. When **Indicate layers in use** is not checked, all status icons appear as a blue sheet of paper. When **Indicate layers in use** is checked and there are objects on the layer, the icon is a blue sheet of paper. A white sheet of paper indicates that there are no objects on the layer.
- **Name.** The layer name column lists all the layers in the drawing. To change an existing name, pick the name once to highlight it, pause for a moment, and then pick it again. When you pick the second time, the layer name is highlighted, allowing you to type a new layer name. Layers can also be renamed by picking the name once to highlight it and then pressing the [F2] key, or by right-clicking and selecting the **Rename Layer** menu option. Layer 0 and layers associated with an external reference cannot be renamed.

Figure 5-11.
Layer settings can be changed by picking the icons in the **Layer Properties Manager**.

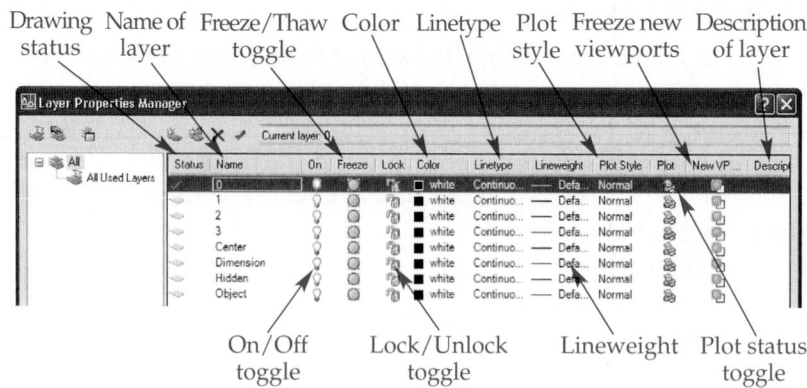

On   Off

- **On.** The light bulb shows whether a layer is on or off. The yellow light bulb means the layer is on. Objects on that layer are displayed on-screen and can be selected and plotted. If you pick on a yellow light bulb, it turns gray, turning the layer off. If a layer is off, the objects on it are not displayed on-screen and are not plotted. Objects on a layer that has been turned off can still be edited when using advanced selection techniques and are regenerated when a drawing regeneration occurs.

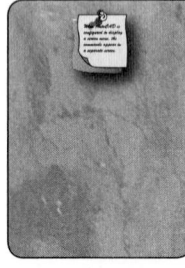
Thawed   Frozen

- **Freeze.** Layers are further classified as thawed or frozen. Frozen layers are similar to turned off layers: They are not displayed and do not plot. Objects on a frozen layer, however, cannot be edited and are not regenerated when the drawing regenerates. Freezing layers containing objects that do not need to be referenced for current drawing tasks can greatly speed up system performance. The snowflake icon is displayed when a layer is frozen. Layers are normally thawed, which means objects on the layer are displayed on-screen. The sun icon is displayed for thawed layers. Picking the sun/snowflake icon toggles it to the other icon.

> **NOTE**
> It is important to note that objects on frozen layers cannot be modified, but objects residing on layers that have been turned off can be modified. For example, if you turn off half your layers and use the **All** selection option with the **ERASE** command, even the objects on the turned-off layers will be erased! The **ERASE** command does not, however, affect frozen layers.

Lock   Unlock

- **Lock.** The unlocked and locked padlock symbols are for locking and unlocking layers. Layers are unlocked by default, but you can pick on an unlocked padlock to lock it. A locked layer remains visible and new objects can be added to it, but existing objects cannot be edited.

> **NOTE**
> When you rest the crosshairs over an object on a locked layer, the lock icon appears.

- **Color.** The color swatch shows the current default color for objects created on each layer. When you need to change the color of an existing layer, pick the swatch to display the **Select Color** dialog box. Working with colors is described later in this chapter.

- **Linetype.** The current linetype setting for each layer is shown in the **Linetype** list. Picking the linetype name opens the **Select Linetype** dialog box, where you can specify a new linetype. Working with linetypes is described later in this chapter.
- **Lineweight.** The current lineweight setting for each layer is shown in the **Lineweight** list. Picking the lineweight name opens the **Lineweight** dialog box, where you can specify a new lineweight. Working with lineweights is described later in this chapter.
- **Plot Style.** This setting changes the plot style associated with the selected layers. The plot style setting is disabled when you are working with color-dependent plot styles (the **PSTYLEPOLICY** system variable is set to 1). Otherwise, picking the plot style displays the **Select Plot Style** dialog box. Plot styles are described in Chapter 25.
- **Plot.** Select this toggle to turn off plotting for a particular layer. The "no plot" symbol is displayed over the printer image when the layer is not available for plotting. The layer is still displayed and selectable, but it is not plotted.

Plot   No Plot

- **New VP Freeze.** This property controls freezing or thawing of layers when a new viewport is created. When the sun and viewport icon is displayed and a new viewport is added to a layout, objects on the layer are thawed in the new viewport. When the snowflake and viewport icon is displayed and a new viewport is added to a layout, objects on the layer are frozen in the new layout viewport. A layer can be frozen in all layout viewports, including those created before picking the **New VP Freeze** icon, by right-clicking and picking the **VP Freeze Layer in All Viewports** menu option. A layer can be thawed in all layout viewports by right-clicking and selecting the **VP Thaw Layer in All Viewports** menu option. Layouts are described in Chapter 25.

- **Description.** Provides an area to type a short description for the layer. To add or change a description, pick the description once to highlight it, pause for a moment, and then pick it again. When you pick the second time, the layer description is highlighted, allowing you to type a description. Layer description can also be defined by right-clicking and selecting the **Change Description** menu option.

The following layer options appear only in layout mode. These properties are used to display layers and override layer settings in layout viewports.

- **VP Freeze**
- **VP Color**
- **VP Linetype**
- **VP Lineweight**
- **VP Plot Style**

Adjusting column size

The layer properties columns in the **Layer Properties Manager** can be adjusted in size and customized to display only the columns you want to display. To resize a column, move your cursor over the column edge to display the resize icon and drag the column to the desired width. The width of an individual column can be maximized to show the longest value in the column list by right-clicking on the property column heading and selecting the **Maximize column** menu option. To maximize the width of all columns in the **Layer Properties Manager**, right-click on any property column heading and select the **Maximize all columns** menu option.

Hiding and displaying columns

You can hide columns in the **Layer Properties Manager** by right-clicking on any property column heading and deselecting the property column name from the menu. Another option is to right-click on any property column heading and select the **Customize...** menu option to display the **Customize Layer Columns** dialog box. This dialog box can be used to hide property columns by the associated check boxes. The **Customize Layer Columns** dialog box can also be used to rearrange columns by picking the column name and selecting the **Move Up** or **Move Down** button to move the column left or right in the **Layer Properties Manager**. Reset the display of all property columns to default settings by right-clicking on any property column heading and selecting **Restore all columns to defaults**.

Exercise 5-2
Complete the exercise on the Student CD.

Selecting Layers

Any layer property you change in the **Layer Properties Manager** affects all currently selected layers. Selecting layer names uses the same techniques used to select files. You can highlight a single name by picking it. Picking another name deselects the previous name and highlights the new selection. You can use the [Shift] key to select two layers and all layer names between them on the listing. Holding the [Ctrl] key while picking layer names highlights or deselects each selected name without affecting any other selections. The following additional layer selection options are provided in a shortcut menu available by right-clicking in the layer list area of the **Layer Properties Manager**.

- **Select All.** Selects all layers.
- **Clear All.** Deselects all layers.
- **Select All but Current.** Selects all layers except the current layer.
- **Invert Selection.** Deselects all selected layers and selects all deselected layers.

Exercise 5-3
Complete the exercise on the Student CD.

Setting Layer Color

Each layer can be assigned a unique color to help distinguish the objects drawn on those layers. Layer colors can be used purely to differentiate drawing items on-screen, as is the case when drawings are plotted using black ink only. Alternatively, layer colors can affect the appearance of drawings plotted in color and can control object properties such as lineweight.

The number of layer colors available depends on your graphics card and monitor. Color systems usually support at least 256 colors, while many graphics cards support up to 16.7 million colors. Layer colors should highlight the important features on the drawing and not cause eyestrain. AutoCAD allows you to assign colors to layers by selecting a color from the **Select Color** dialog box.

Figure 5-12.
The **Select Color** dialog box.

Index Color tab
255 colors

True Color tab
24-bit color

Color Books tab
Pantone colors

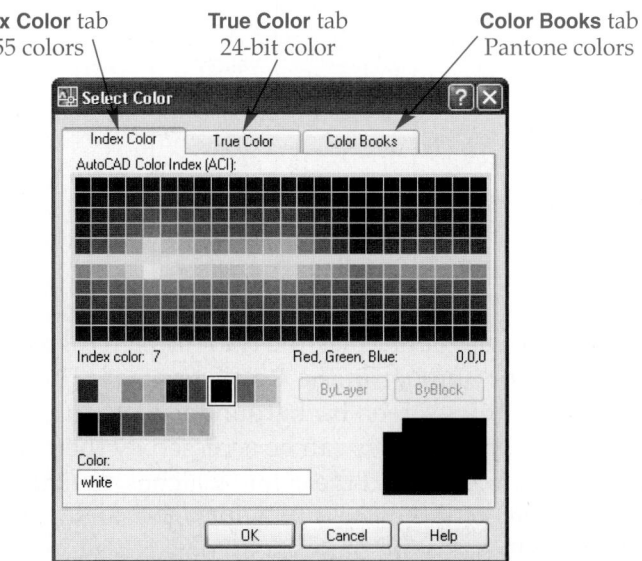

To assign a color to a layer, pick the current color swatch associated with the layer name in the **Layer Properties Manager**, or right-click on the color swatch and pick the **Select Color** menu option. This displays the **Select Color** dialog box, shown in **Figure 5-12.** This dialog box includes three different tabs from which a color can be selected: the **Index Color** tab, the **True Color** tab, and the **Color Books** tab. Each tab uses a different method of obtaining colors for assignment to a layer.

Index Color tab

This tab includes 255 color swatches from which you can choose. See **Figure 5-13.** This tab is commonly referred to as the AutoCAD Color Index (ACI) because layer colors are coded by name and number. The first seven colors in the ACI include both a numerical index number and a name:

Figure 5-13.
The **Index Color** tab contains 255 indexed colors.

Selected color

Color index
number

Standard
colors #1–9

Selected
color index
number

Red, green, and blue
colors mixed to make
selected color

Previous
selected color

New selected
color

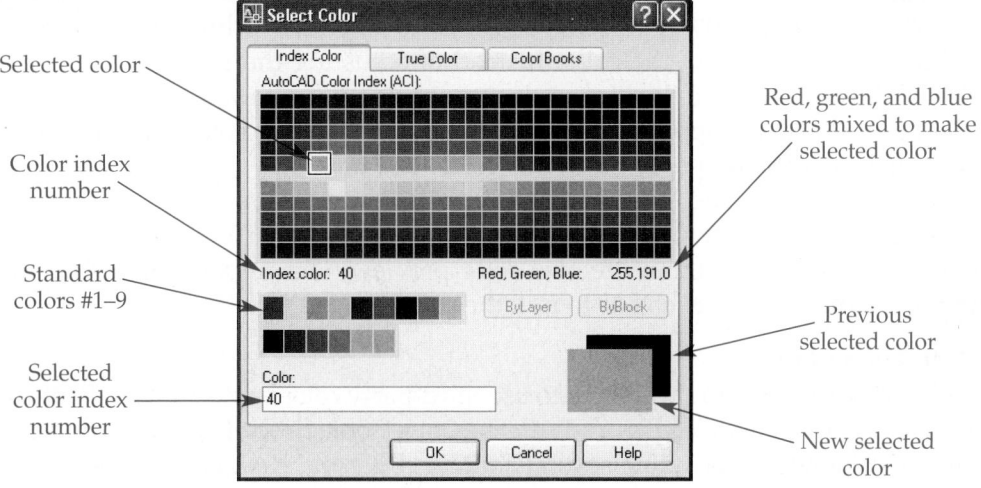

Number	Color
1	red
2	yellow
3	green
4	cyan
5	blue
6	magenta
7	white

To select a color, you can either pick the color swatch displaying the desired color or type the color name or number in the **Color:** text box. The color white (number 7) refers to white if the graphics screen background is black, and it refers to black if the background is white. All other colors can be accessed by their ACI numbers.

As you move the cursor around the color swatches, the **Index color:** note updates to show you the number of the color over which the cursor is hovering. Beside the **Index color:** note is the **Red, Green, Blue:** (RGB) note. This indicates the RGB numbers used to mix the highlighted color. When you pick a color, the **Index color:** note is entered into the **Color:** text box. A preview of the newly selected color and a sample of the previously assigned color appear in the lower right of the dialog box. An easy way to investigate the ACI numbering system is to pick a color swatch and see what number appears in the **Color:** text box.

After selecting a color, pick the **OK** button. The color you picked is now displayed as the color swatch for the highlighted layer name in the **Layer Properties Manager**.

True Color tab

The **True Color** tab allows you to specify a true color (24-bit color) using either Hue, Saturation, and Luminance (HSL) or Red, Green, and Blue (RGB) color models. **Figure 5-14A** shows the **True Color** tab with the **HSL** color model selected. The **True Color** tab is shown in **Figure 5-14B** with the **RGB** color model selected.

The **HSL** color model includes three text boxes allowing you to control the properties of the color. The **Hue:** value represents a specific wavelength of light within the visible spectrum. Valid hue values range from 0°–360°. The **Saturation:** value refers to the purity of the color. Valid saturation values range from 0%–100%. Finally, the **Luminance:** value specifies the brightness of the color. Valid luminance values range from 0%–100%, where 0% represents black, 100% represents white, and 50% represents the optimal brightness of the color. Instead of adjusting the HSL colors through the text boxes, you can move the cursors in the spectrum preview screen and luminance slider bar and pick the approximate color you want. The true color is then translated to RGB values, which are displayed in the **Color:** text box.

The **RGB** color model includes four text boxes and three slider bars. Adjusting the values in the **Red:**, **Green:**, and **Blue:** text boxes causes the slider bars to adjust, with the mixed color displayed in the new color preview. The cursors can also be used to slide the markers along each bar to mix the colors.

Color Books tab

The **Color Books** tab allows you to use third-party color books, such as Pantone color books, to specify a color. See **Figure 5-15**. The **Color Book:** drop-down list includes several different color books, including several Pantone, DIC, and RAL books. Once a book has been selected, the available colors within the book are displayed. (RAL colors, which were developed in Germany, are used internationally.) You can pick an area on the color slider or use the up and down keys to browse through the book. To select a color, pick one of the color book swatches. As a color is selected, the equivalent RGB values are displayed on the right side of the dialog box, and the color is updated in the new color preview.

Figure 5-14.
The **True Color** tab uses 24-bit color. A—HSL color model. B—RGB color model.

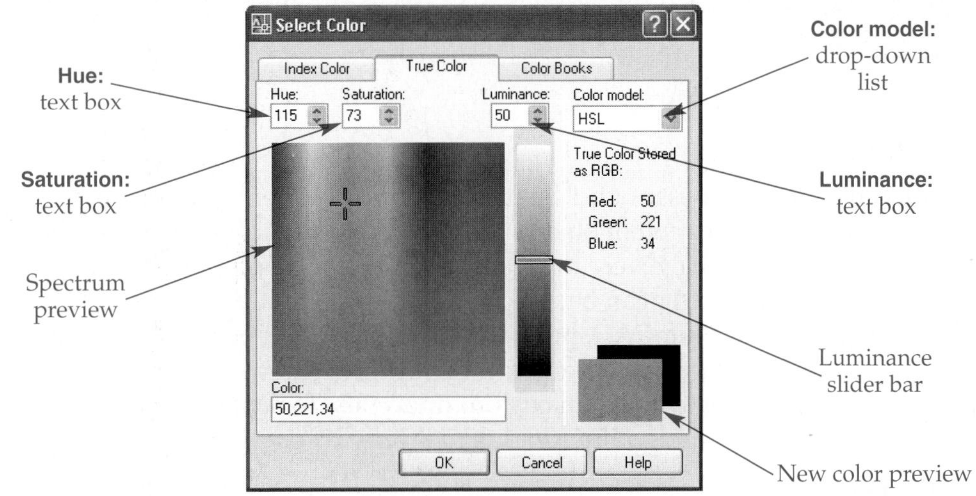

Hue: text box

Saturation: text box

Spectrum preview

Color model: drop-down list

Luminance: text box

Luminance slider bar

New color preview

HSL Color Model
A

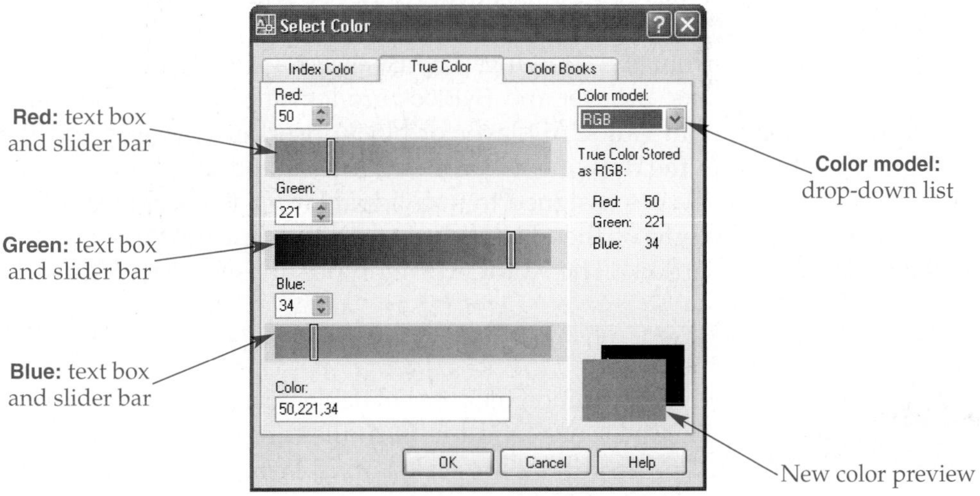

Red: text box and slider bar

Green: text box and slider bar

Blue: text box and slider bar

Color model: drop-down list

New color preview

RGB Color Model
B

Figure 5-15.
The **Color Books** tab uses Pantone, DIC, and RAL colors.

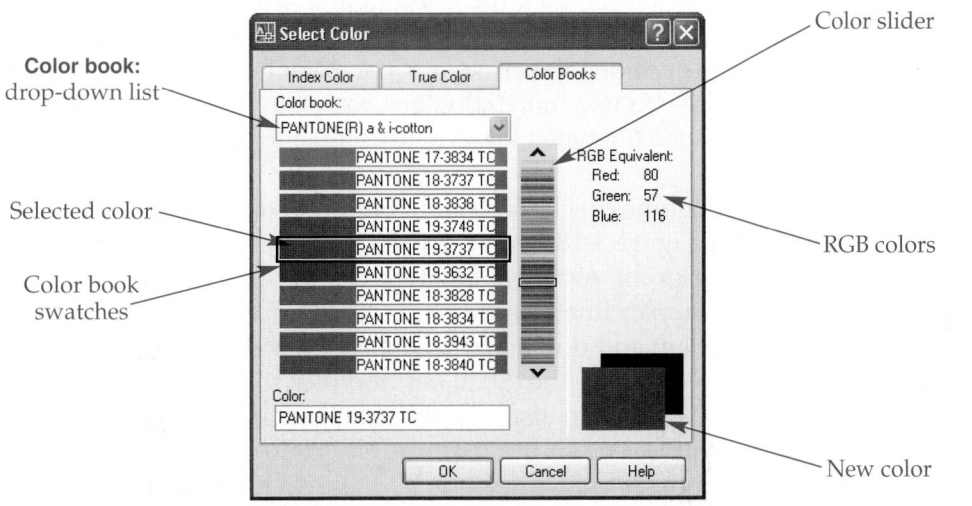

Color book: drop-down list

Selected color

Color book swatches

Color slider

RGB colors

New color

Setting Layer Linetype

Different line thicknesses and linetypes are used to enhance the readability of drawings and illustrate different objects. The line conventions described earlier in this chapter can be applied selectively to objects by applying linetypes and thicknesses to individual layers. Each layer can be assigned a linetype that corresponds to a specific drawing requirement. AutoCAD provides standard linetypes that can be used to match the ASME standards or the standards for other drafting applications you are using. You can also create your own custom linetypes. To achieve different line thicknesses, it is necessary to assign lineweights to layers.

AutoCAD linetypes

AutoCAD maintains its standard linetypes in external linetype definition files. Before any of these linetypes can be used, they must be loaded, and then they must be set current or assigned to a layer. Three of AutoCAD's linetypes are required and cannot be deleted from the drawing. The Continuous linetype represents solid object lines with no breaks. ByLayer and ByBlock are logical linetypes that represent the linetype assigned to an AutoCAD layer or block insertion. ByLayer and ByBlock are assigned to objects in the drawing and cannot be assigned to layers because they already represent the linetypes assigned to individual layers. ByLayer means "use the linetype, color, or lineweight of the object's layer." ByBlock means "use the linetype assigned to the block insertion." The AutoCAD linetypes are shown in **Figure 5-16.**

PROFESSIONAL TIP

Two linetype definition files are available, acad.lin and acadiso.lin. The ACAD ISO linetypes found in both files are identical, but the non-ISO linetype definitions are scaled up 25.4 times in the acadiso.lin file. The scale factor of 25.4 is used to convert from inches to millimeters. The ACAD ISO linetypes are for metric drawings.

Changing linetype assignments

To assign a linetype to a layer, pick the linetype that is currently associated with the layer name in the **Layer Properties Manager,** or right-click on the linetype and pick the **Select Linetype** menu option. This displays the **Select Linetype** dialog box. See **Figure 5-17.** The first time you use this dialog box, you may find only the Continuous linetype listed in the **Loaded linetypes** list box. You must load any other linetypes to be used in the drawing.

If you need to add linetypes, pick the **Load...** button to display the **Load or Reload Linetypes** dialog box. See **Figure 5-18.** The ACAD ISO, standard, and complex linetypes are named and displayed in the **Available Linetypes** list. Standard linetypes use only dashes, dots, and gaps. Complex linetypes can also contain special shapes and text.

Use the scroll bars or up and down arrow keys to look at all the linetypes. Select the linetypes you want to load. Use the [Shift] key and pick to select linetypes between your two picked linetypes. You can also use the [Ctrl] key and pick to select nonconsecutive linetypes. Quickly select all the linetypes by right-clicking and picking the **Select All** menu option, or deselect all linetypes by right-clicking and picking the **Clear All** menu option. Pick the **OK** button to return to the **Select Linetype** dialog box, where

Figure 5-16.
AutoCAD's linetype library contains ACAD ISO, standard, and complex linetypes.

Linetype		Linetype	
Continuous	————————	Acad_iso02w100	– – – – – –
Border	— — — — —	Acad_iso03w100	— — — —
Border2	— — — — — —	Acad_iso04w100	—·—·—·—
Borderx2	— — — —	Acad_iso05w100	—··—··—··—
Center	—— — —— — ——	Acad_iso06w100	—··—··—··
Center2	— – — – —	Acad_iso07w100	····················
Centerx2	—— — ——	Acad_iso08w100	—— · —— · ——
Dashdot	— · — · — · —	Acad_iso09w100	—— · · —— · · ——
Dashdot2	–·–·–·–·–	Acad_iso10w100	—·—·—·—
Dashdotx2	—— · —— · ——	Acad_iso11w100	—— · —— · ——
Dashed	— — — — —	Acad_iso12w100	—··—··—··
Dashed2	– – – – –	Acad_iso13w100	—··—··—··
Dashedx2	—— —— —— ——	Acad_iso14w100	—·—·—·—
Divide	— · · — · · —	Acad_iso15w100	—··—··—··

Linetype	
Divide2	–··–··–··–
Dividex2	—— · · —— · · ——
Dot	· · · · · · · · ·
Dot2	····················
Dotx2	· · · · · · ·
Hidden	– – – – – – – – –
Hidden2	– – – – – – – – – – –
Hiddenx2	—— —— —— ——
Phantom	— – – — – – —
Phantom2	—– – – —– – – —–
Phantomx2	—— — — ——

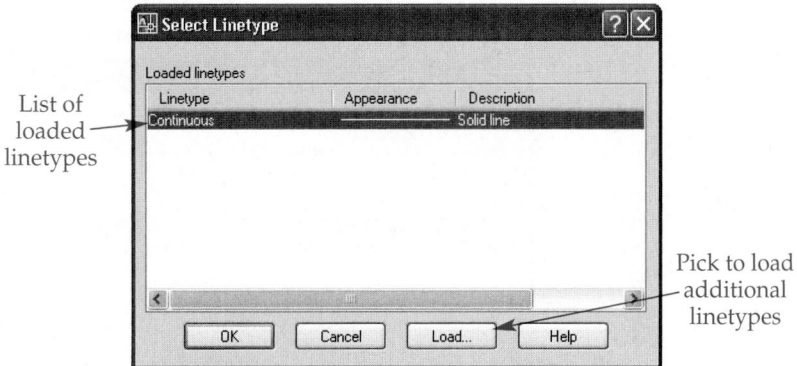

Fenceline1	—o———o———o—
Fenceline2	—□———□———□—
Gas_line	—— GAS —— GAS ——
Hot_water_supply	—— HW —— HW ——
Tracks	++++++++++++++
Zigzag	/\/\/\/\/
Batting	⧢⧢⧢⧢⧢⧢⧢⧢

Figure 5-17.
The **Select Linetype** dialog box.

List of loaded linetypes

Pick to load additional linetypes

Figure 5-18.
The **Load or Reload Linetypes** dialog box.

Select file where linetype definitions are stored

Select linetypes to load into drawing

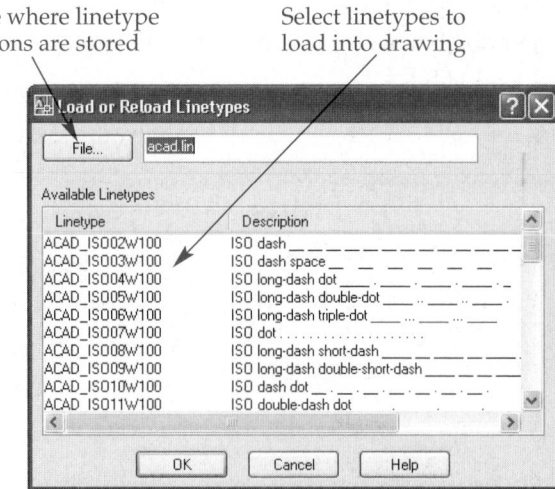

the linetypes you selected are listed, as shown in **Figure 5-19**. In the **Select Linetype** dialog box, pick the desired linetype, and then pick **OK**. The HIDDEN linetype selected in **Figure 5-19** is now the linetype assigned to the layer named Hidden, as shown in **Figure 5-20**.

NOTE

The acad.lin file is used by default. You can switch to the ISO library by picking the **File...** button in the **Load or Reload Linetypes** dialog box. This displays the **Select Linetype File** dialog box, where you can select the acadiso.lin file.

Managing linetypes

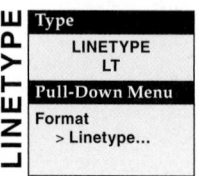

Type	
	LINETYPE
	LT
Pull-Down Menu	
Format	
> Linetype...	

The **Linetype Manager** dialog box is a convenient place to load and access linetypes. This dialog box can be accessed by selecting **Format** > **Linetype...** from the pull-down menu, selecting **Other...** in the **Linetype Control** drop-down list in the **Properties** toolbar or the **Object Properties** control panel of the **Dashboard**, or typing LT or LINETYPE. See **Figure 5-21**.

This dialog box is similar to the **Layer Properties Manager**. Picking the **Load...** button opens the **Load or Reload Linetypes** dialog box. Picking the **Delete** button deletes any selected linetypes that are not in use in the drawing.

Figure 5-19.
Linetypes loaded from the **Load or Reload Linetypes** dialog box are added to the **Loaded linetypes** list box.

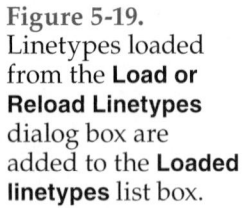

Loaded linetypes

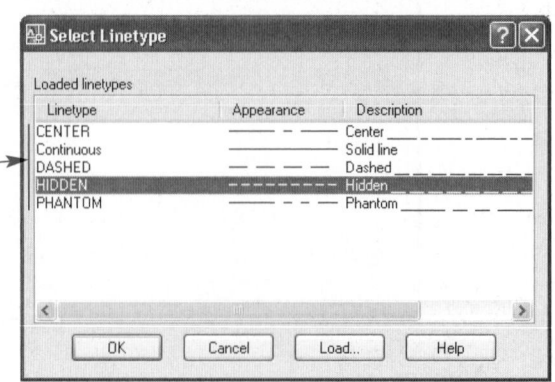

Figure 5-20.
Objects drawn on the Hidden layer now have a HIDDEN linetype.

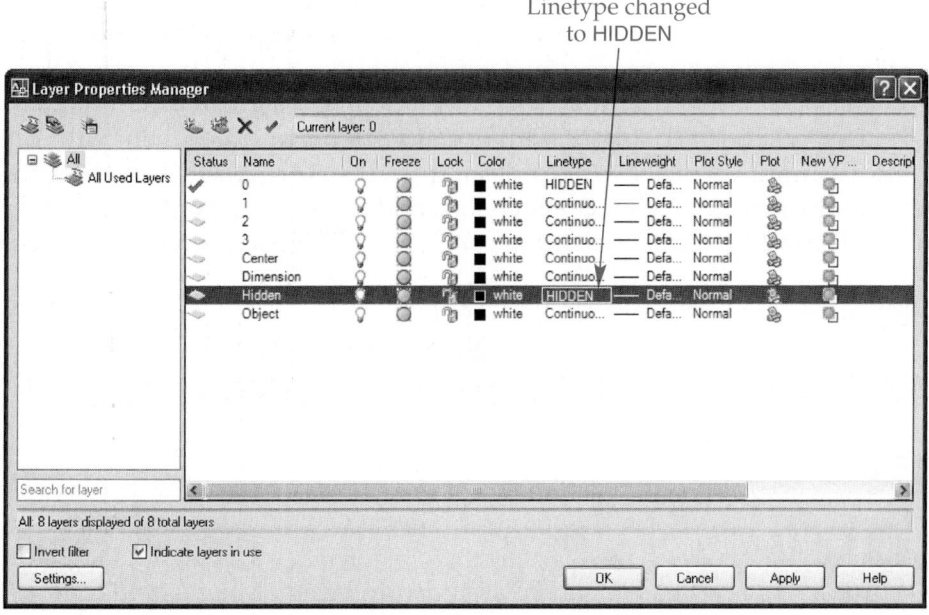

Figure 5-21.
The **Linetype Manager** dialog box.

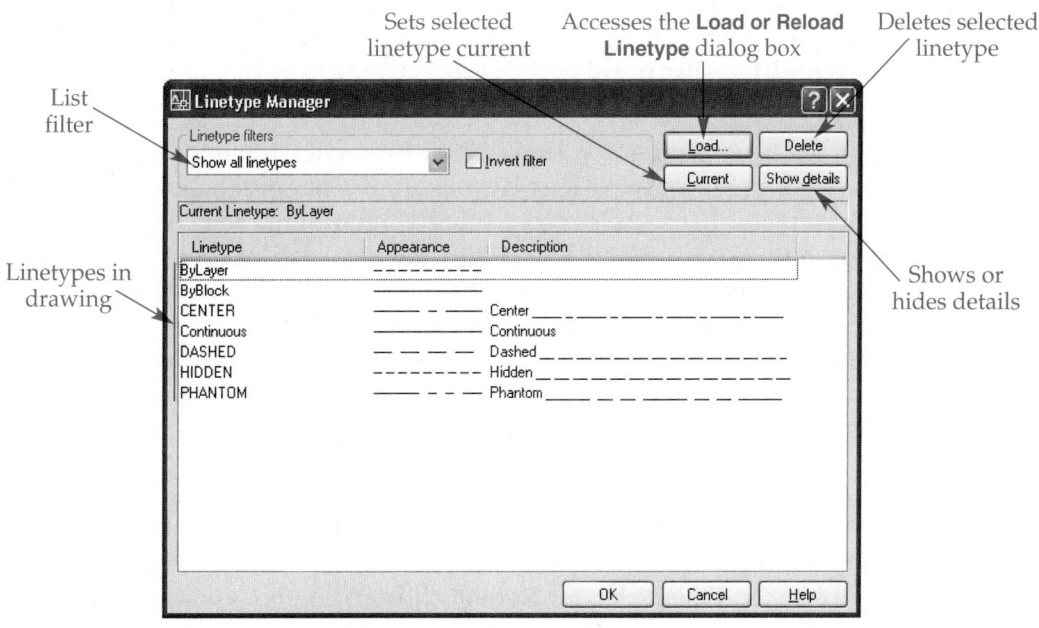

Setting linetype scale

The *linetype scale* sets the lengths of dashes and spaces in linetypes. When you start AutoCAD with a wizard or template, the *global linetype scale* is automatically set to match the units you select. The global linetype scale can be changed to increase or decrease the lengths of dashes and spaces in linetypes in order to make your drawing more closely match standard drafting practices. A global change is the preferred method for adjusting linetype scale, though it is possible to change the linetype scale of individual objects.

linetype scale: The lengths of dashes and spaces in linetypes.

global linetype scale: A linetype scale applied to every linetype in the current drawing.

The **LTSCALE** system variable can be used to make a global change to the linetype scale. The default global linetype scale factor is 1.0000. Any line with dashes initially assumes this factor. To change the linetype scale for the entire drawing, type LTSCALE. The current value is listed. Enter the new value and press [Enter]. The drawing regenerates as the global linetype scale is changed for all lines on the drawing. A value less than 1.0 makes the dashes and spaces smaller, and a value greater than 1.0 makes the dashes and spaces larger. Using this information, you can experiment with different linetype scales until you achieve your desired results. Be careful when changing linetype scales to avoid making your drawing look odd and not in accordance with drafting standards. **Figure 5-22** shows a diagram comparing different linetype scale factors.

Exercise 5-5
Complete the exercise on the Student CD.

Setting Layer Lineweight

lineweight: The assigned width of lines for display and plotting.

Like linetypes, lineweights can be assigned to layers. *Lineweight* adds width to objects for display and plotting. Assigning lineweights to layers allows you to draw objects on specific layers to manage their lineweights. You can control the display of line thickness to match ASME or other standards related to your drafting application.

The layer lineweight settings are displayed on the screen when the lineweight display is turned on. To toggle screen lineweights, pick the **LWT** button on the status bar.

Changing lineweight assignments

To assign a lineweight to a layer, pick the lineweight currently associated with the layer name in the **Layer Properties Manager**, or right-click the lineweight and pick the **Select Lineweight** menu option. This displays the **Lineweight** dialog box. Scroll through the **Lineweights:** list to select the desired lineweight. See **Figure 5-23**. The **Lineweight** dialog box displays fixed lineweights available in AutoCAD. The Default lineweight is the lineweight initially assigned to a layer when it is created.

The area near the bottom of the **Lineweight** dialog box lists the original lineweight (the lineweight previously assigned to the layer) and the new lineweight (the new lineweight assigned to the layer). In **Figure 5-23**, the **Original:** and **New:** specifications are the same because the initial layer lineweight has not been changed from the default.

Lineweight settings

Current lineweights are set in the **Lineweight Settings** dialog box, shown in **Figure 5-24**. The **Lineweight Settings** dialog box can be accessed by right-clicking the **LWT** button on the status bar and then selecting **Settings...** from the shortcut menu; typing LW, LWEIGHT, or LINEWEIGHT; or picking **Format > Lineweight...** from the pull-down menu. The following describes the features of the **Lineweight Settings** dialog box:

LINEWEIGHT

Type
LINEWEIGHT
LWEIGHT
LW

Pull-Down Menu
Format
> Lineweight...

Figure 5-22.
The CENTER linetype at different linetype scales.

Scale Factor	Line
0.5	― ― ― ― ― ― ― ― ― ― ― ― ― ― ― ― ― ― ― ―
1.0	―――― ― ―――――― ― ―――――― ― ――――
1.5	――――――― ― ―――― ― ―――――――

Figure 5-23.
The **Lineweight**
dialog box.

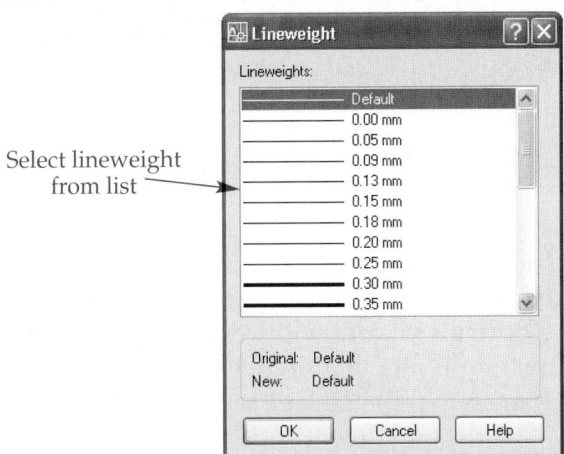

Select lineweight
from list

Figure 5-24.
The **Lineweight**
Settings dialog box.

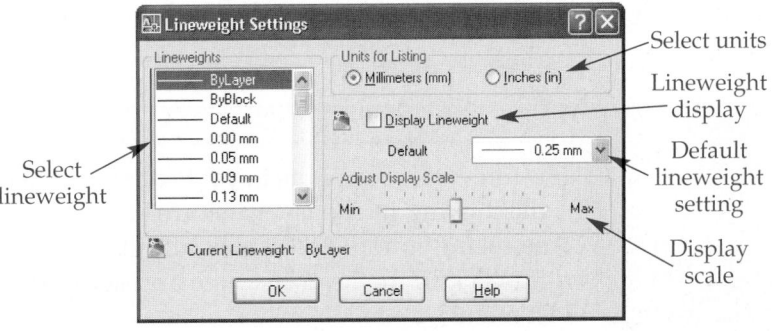

Select
lineweight

Select units

Lineweight
display

Default
lineweight
setting

Display
scale

- **Lineweights.** Set the current lineweight by selecting the desired setting from the list. If lineweight is set to ByLayer, the object lineweight corresponds to the lineweight assigned to its layer. The Default option lineweight width is controlled by the Default list options. Settings other than ByLayer, ByBlock, or Default are used as overrides for lineweights of objects drawn with the selected option.
- **Units for Listing.** This area allows you to set the lineweight thickness to **Millimeters (mm)** or **Inches (in)**.
- **Display Lineweight.** This is another way to turn lineweight thickness on or off. Check this box to turn lineweight on.
- **Default.** Select a lineweight default value from the drop-down list. This becomes the default lineweight for layers. The initial default setting is 0.010" or 0.25 mm. The default setting is stored in the **LWDEFAULT** system variable.
- **Adjust Display Scale.** This scale allows you to adjust the lineweight display scale to improve the appearance of different lineweight widths. Adjusting the lineweight display scale toward the **Max** value can reduce AutoCAD performance. A setting near the middle of the scale or toward **Min** may be preferred.
- **Current Lineweight.** This indicates the current lineweight setting.

NOTE

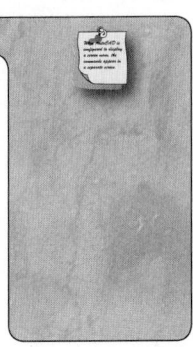

An object's individual properties, such as color, linetype, and lineweight, can be assigned "by layer" or "by object." It is important to note that assigning properties "by object" overrides any assignments made "by layer." For example, if a line's color property is ByLayer, the line obtains its color from the color of the layer on which it is drawn. If that same line's color is changed "by object" to a green color, however, the line is green regardless of the layer color. This is also true for linetype and lineweight.

Layer Filters

In some applications, large numbers of layer names are used to assist in drawing information management. Having all layer names showing at the same time in the layer list can make it more difficult to work with your drawing layers. *Layer filters* are used to screen, or filter, out any layers you do not want to display in the **Layer Properties Manager**. The filter tree area in the **Layer Properties Manager** is used to manage layer filters. See **Figure 5-25**. Selecting the **All** node of the filter tree area displays all layers in the drawing. Layer filters are displayed in alphabetical order inside the **All** node. The **All Used Layers** filter is a default filter created by AutoCAD and cannot be removed or modified. Selecting the **All Used Layers** filter hides all the layers that have no objects on them.

layer filters: Filters that screen out layers you do not want to display.

> **NOTE**
>
> The filter tree area of the **Layer Properties Manager** can be hidden by right-clicking in the layer list area and deselecting the **Show Filter Tree** menu option. To display all filters and layers in the layer list, right-click in the layer list area and select the **Show Filters in Layer List** menu option.

Figure 5-25.
Layer filters can be created and restored from the filter tree view area of the **Layer Properties Manager**.

Pick to create a new property filter   Pick to create a new group filter

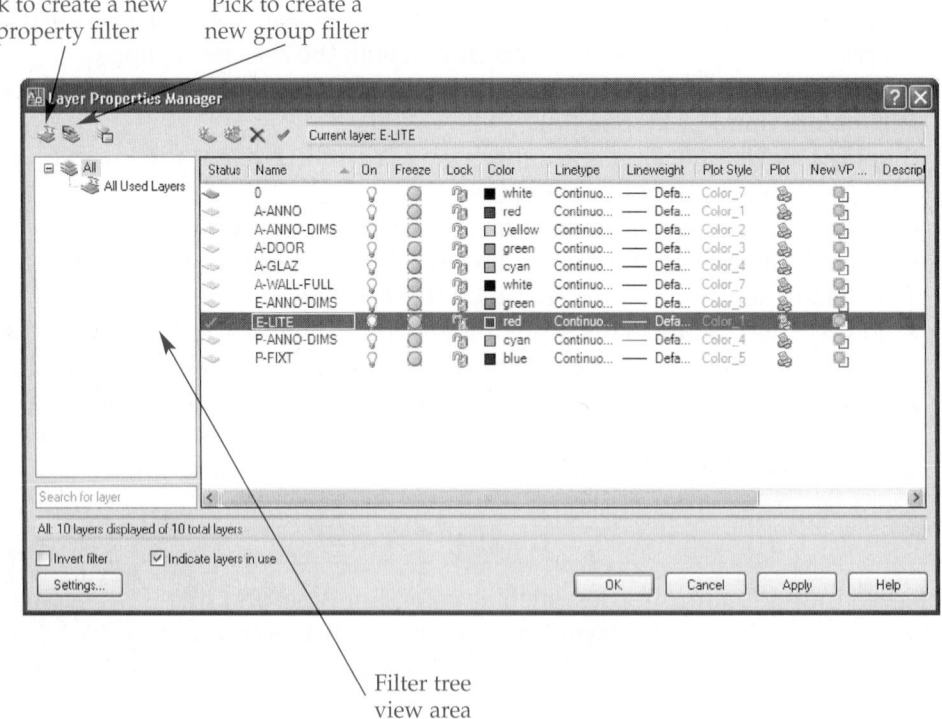

Filter tree view area

You can create two different types of layer filters, a property filter or a group filter. A *property filter* screens layers according to specific layer properties. For example, a property filter can filter all layers that are turned on, or have a name beginning with the letter *A*, or both. The default **All Used Layers** filter is an example of a property filter that filters layers according to layer status. A *group filter* is created by adding layers to the filter without defining individual layer properties. For example, to filter all layers used to draw an electrical plan you drag and drop the electrical layers into the group filter, instead of using properties, such as all layer names beginning with the letter *E*.

To create a property filter, pick the **New Property Filter** button or right-click in the filter tree area and select the **New Properties Filter...** menu option. This displays the **Layer Filter Properties** dialog box. See **Figure 5-26**. Enter a name for the new filter in the **Filter name:** text box. The **Filter definition** area is where the properties are defined to hide the unwanted layers from the **Layer Properties Manager**, the **Layer Control** drop-down list on the **Layers** toolbar, and the **Layers** control panel of the **Dashboard**. To create a definition, pick in any of the layer settings fields. The appropriate options become available for the selected layer setting. Options can be entered in the text edit box, selected from a drop-down list, or accessed using a dialog box. The following filter definition options are available for each setting:

- **Status.** Use this filter to display the names of all layers, used layers only, or unused layers only.
- **Name.** This is a text edit box in which you can type a layer name or a partial layer name using the * wildcard character. If you want to see all the layers that start with an *A*, type a*.
- **On.** Use this filter to display only the names of layers that are on or only those that are off.
- **Freeze.** Use this filter to display frozen layers only or thawed layers only.
- **Lock.** Use this filter to display locked layers only or unlocked layers only.
- **Color.** Type a color number or name or pick the **...** button to select a color from the **Select Color** dialog box.

property filter: A filter that screens layers according to property.

group filter: A filter created by adding layers to the filter definition.

Figure 5-26.
New property filters are created in the **Layer Filter Properties** dialog box.

Edit the layer properties to define the layer filter

Enter name for filter

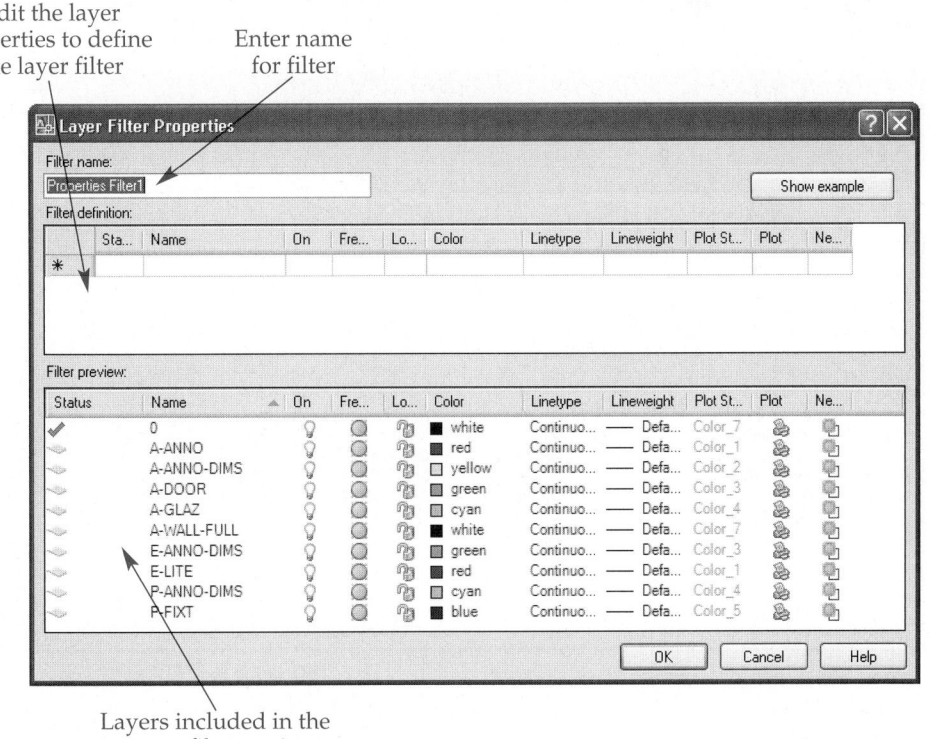

Layers included in the current filter settings

- **Linetype.** Type a linetype name or pick the **...** button to select a linetype from the **Select Linetype** dialog box.
- **Lineweight.** Type a lineweight or pick the **...** button to select a lineweight from the **Lineweight** dialog box.
- **Plot Style.** Type a plot style name or pick the **...** button to select a plot style from the **Select Plot Style** dialog box. This option is only available if the current drawing uses named plot style tables. Plot styles are described in Chapter 25.
- **Plot.** Use this filter to display the names of layers that plot or the names of layers that do not plot.
- **New VP Freeze.** Use this filter to display only frozen or only thawed layers applied when a new layout viewport is created. This option is only available in paper space.

The following layer filter options appear only in paper space layout mode. These properties are used to filter layers according to layout viewport layer display and overrides. Layouts are described in Chapter 25.

- **VP Freeze**
- **VP Color**
- **VP Linetype**
- **VP Lineweight**
- **VP Plot Style**

Once a property filter definition has been edited, another row is added to the **Filter definition:** area. This allows you to create simple to advanced filters. **Figure 5-27** shows a filter named Floor Plan, in which two rows are used to filter out all the layers except the P-FIXT layer and layers beginning with the letter A. To save the filter, pick the **OK** button. The new filter now displays in the filter tree view area.

To create a group filter, select the **New Group Filter** button or right-click in the filter tree area and select the **New Group Filter...** menu option. A group filter can be created from outside the **Layer Properties Manager** using the **Dashboard** by right-clicking in the **Layer Filters** drop-down list in the expanded **Layers** control panel and selecting

Figure 5-27.
Multiple rows in the **Filter definition:** area can be used to create a filter.

Layer filter definitions   Filter name

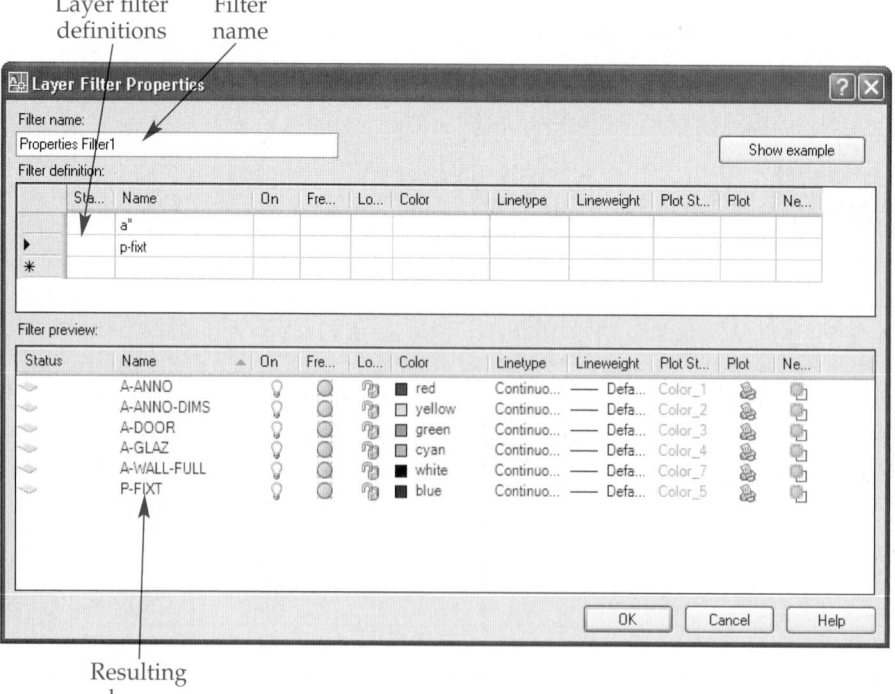

Resulting layers

AutoCAD and Its Applications—Basics

the **New Group Filter...** menu option. A new group filter is created in the filter tree view area. After you create the group filter, you may want to select the **All** node at the top of the filter tree area to display all the layers in the drawing. Then, to add a layer to a group filter, select a layer in the layer list and drag and drop it onto the group filter name. You can also add layers to a group filter by selecting the group filter, right-clicking, and choosing the **Select Layers** menu option. Pick **Add** from the **Select Layers** cascading menu to hide the **Layer Properties Manager** temporarily, allowing you to select objects on the layers you wish to add to the group filter. After you have selected the objects, right-click or press the [Enter] key to add the layers to the group filter.

Pick **Replace** from the **Select Layers** cascading menu to hide the **Layer Properties Manager** temporarily, allowing you to select objects on the layers to replace all other layers in the group filter. After you have selected the objects, right-click or press the [Enter] key to add the layers to the group filter. The **Select Layers** menu option is also available by right-clicking in the **Layer Filters** drop-down list in the expanded **Layers** control panel of the **Dashboard**.

> **NOTE**
>
> A layer can be removed from a group filter by right-clicking on the layer in the layer list area of the **Layer Properties Manager** and choosing the **Remove From Group Filter** menu option.

Activating layer filters

To activate a layer filter using the **Layer Properties Manager**, select the filter from the filter tree area or right-click in the layer list area and select the filter from the **Layer Filters** cascading submenu. A layer filter can be activated from outside the **Layer Properties Manager** using the **Dashboard**. The **Dashboard** contains a **Layer Filters** drop-down list in the expanded **Layers** control panel from which filters can be made current. When a layer filter is current, only those layers associated with the filter are shown in the layer list area. To view all the layers again, pick the **All** node at the top of the filter tree area.

> **NOTE**
>
> A description of the active layer filter settings is provided in the lower **Layer Properties Manager** status bar.

Inverting layer filters

Layer filter settings can be inverted to display filtered layers. For example, selecting the **All Used Layers** filter shows only the layers that have objects on them, but what if you want to show all unused layers? In this case, you can invert, or reverse, your choice to show all unused layers without creating an additional filter. To invert a layer filter using the **Layer Properties Manager**, pick the **Invert filter** check box located in the lower-left corner or right-click in the layer list area and select the **Invert Layer Filter** menu option. You can invert a layer filter from outside the **Layer Properties Manager** using the **Dashboard** by picking the **Invert** option from the **Layer Filters** drop-down list in the expanded **Layers** control panel.

Additional layer filter options

Other options associated with filters are accessible from a shortcut menu. To display the shortcut menu, right-click in the filter tree view area **Layer Properties Manager** or right-click in the **Layer Filters** drop-down list of the expanded **Layers** control panel of the **Dashboard**. Most of the options in the shortcut menu are the same for the filter types, but some options are available only for a certain filter. The following options are available and are applied to the layers associated with the filter only:

- **Visibility.** Allows you to change the **On/Off** and **Thawed/Frozen** states of the unfiltered layers.
- **Lock.** Locks or unlocks the unfiltered layers.
- **Viewport.** Allows you to freeze or thaw the unfiltered layers in the current layout viewport.
- **Isolate Group.** Freezes all layers except those associated with the filter and the current layer.
- **New Properties Filter.** Opens the **Layer Filter Properties** dialog box.
- **New Group Filter.** Creates a new group filter.
- **Convert to Group Filter.** Converts a property filter to a group filter.
- **Rename.** Allows you to rename the selected filter.
- **Delete.** Deletes the selected filter.
- **Properties.** Allows you to edit a property filter.
- **Select Layers.** Provides options to add layers or replace layers in an existing group filter.

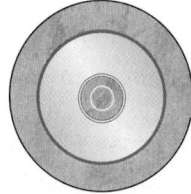

Exercise 5-7
Complete the exercise on the Student CD.

Layer States

Layer settings, such as on/off, frozen/thawed, plot/no plot, and locked/unlocked, determine whether objects drawn on a layer are displayed, plotted, and editable. The status of layer settings for all layers in the drawing can be saved as a named *layer state*. Once a layer state is saved, you can readjust layer settings to meet your needs, with the option to restore the previously saved layer state at any time.

layer state: A saved status of layer settings for all layers in a drawing.

For example, a basic architectural drawing uses the layers shown in **Figure 5-25**. From this drawing file, three different drawings are plotted: a floor plan, a plumbing plan, and an electrical plan. The following chart shows the layer settings for each of the three drawings:

Layer	Description	Floor Plan	Plumbing Plan	Electrical Plan
0		Off	Off	Off
A-ANNO-DIMS	Floor Plan Dimensions	On	Frozen	Frozen
P-ANNO-DIMS	Plumbing Plan Dimensions	Frozen	On	Frozen
E-ANNO-DIMS	Electrical Plan Dimensions	Frozen	Frozen	On
A-ANNO	Floor Plan Notes	On	Frozen	Frozen
A-DOOR	Doors	On	Frozen	Locked
A-GLAZ	Windows	On	Frozen	Locked
A-WALL-FULL	Full Height Walls	On	Locked	Locked
P-FIXT	Plumbing Plan Fixtures	Locked	On	Locked
E-LITE	Electrical Plan Lights	Frozen	Frozen	On

Each of the three groups of settings can be saved as an individual layer state. Once the layer state is created, the settings can be restored by restoring the layer state. This is easier than changing the settings for each layer individually.

A layer state can be saved in the **Layer States Manager** or by using menu options in the **Layer Properties Manager** or the **Layers** control panel of the **Dashboard**. To save a layer state outside the **Layer States Manager**, right-click in the layer list area of the **Layer Properties Manager** and select the **Save Layer States** menu option, or pick the **New Layer State...** option from the **Layer States** drop-down list in the **Layers** control panel of the **Dashboard**. The **New Layer State to Save** dialog box appears, as shown in **Figure 5-28.** Type a name for the layer state in the **New layer state name:** field and enter a description if necessary. Pick the **OK** button to save the new layer state.

To save a layer state using the **Layer States Manager**, pick the **Layer States Manager** button from the **Layer Properties Manager**, the **Layers** toolbar, or the **Layers** control panel of the **Dashboard**. You can also access the **Layer States Manager** by picking the **Manage Layer States...** option from the **Layer States** drop-down list in the **Layers** control panel of the **Dashboard**; right-clicking in the layer list area of the **Layer Properties Manager** and selecting the **Restore Layer State** menu option; selecting **Format > Layer States Manager...** from the pull-down menu; or typing LAYERSTATE. The **Layer States Manager** dialog box appears as shown in **Figure 5-29.** To create a new layer state, pick the **New...** button to display the **New Layer State to Save** dialog box.

Figure 5-28.
Creating a new layer state.

Enter the layer
state name

If necessary, enter a description of the layer state

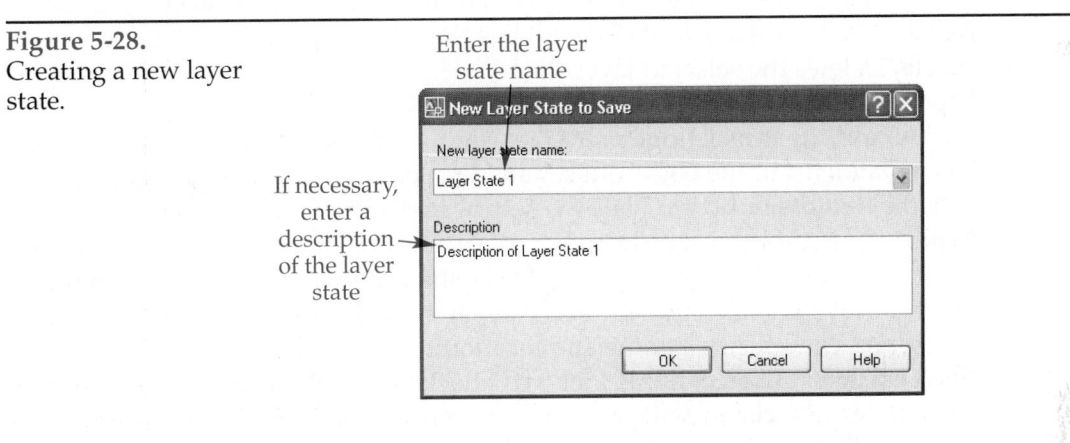

Figure 5-29.
The **Layer States Manager** allows you to save, restore, and manage layer settings.

Select to create a new layer state

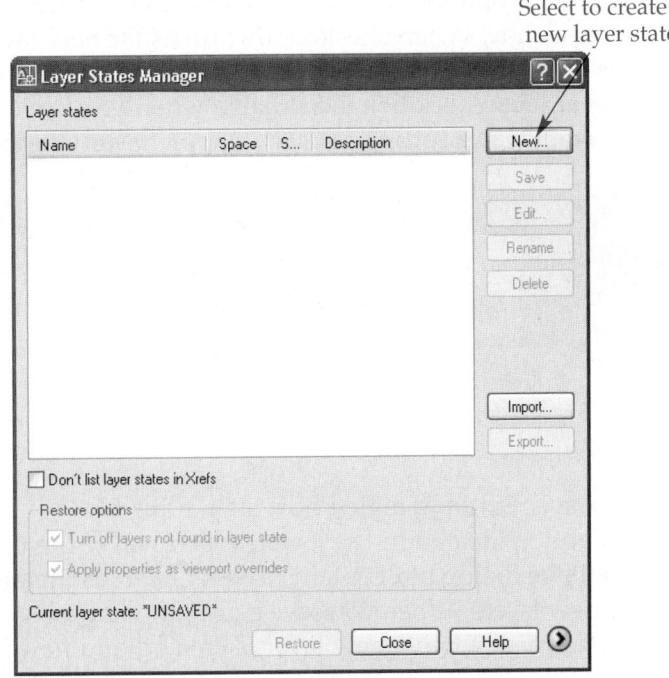

Once you save a layer state, you can adjust layer properties as needed and then restore layer properties to the settings saved in the layer state. To activate a layer state quickly using the **Dashboard**, select the layer state from the **Layer States** drop-down list in the **Layers** control panel. Otherwise, you can restore a layer state using the **Layer States Manager** by selecting the layer state from the list and picking the restore button.

The following areas, options, and buttons are available in the **Layer States Manager** to control layer states:

- **Layer states.** This list box displays saved layer states. The **Name** list provides the name of the layer state. The **Space** column indicates whether the layer state was saved in model space or paper space. The **Same as DWG** column indicates whether the layer state is the same as the current layer properties. The **Description** column lists the layer state description added when the layer state was saved.
- **Save.** Pick this button to resave and override the selected layer state according to the current layer properties.
- **Edit.** Pick this button to access the **Edit Layer State** dialog box, where you can adjust layer properties without exiting the **Layer States Manager**. The **Edit Layer State** dialog box contains a **Remove layer from layer state** button that can be used to delete a layer from the layer state, as well as an **Add layer to layer state** button that can be used to add new or removed layers to the layer state.
- **Rename.** Activates a text box that allows the current layer state to be renamed.
- **Delete.** Deletes the selected layer state.
- **Import.** Accesses the **Import layer state** dialog box, where you can select an LAS file containing an existing layer state. Imported layer states are listed in the **Layer states** list in the **Layer State Manager**. Select the imported layer state and pick the **Restore** button to have the settings restored.
- **Export.** Saves the layer state as an LAS file and allows it to be imported into other drawings. This allows you to share layer states between drawings containing identical layers. Pick this button to access the **Export layer state** dialog box, where you can specify a name and location for the LAS file.
- **Don't list layer states in Xrefs.** Pick this check box if you do not want to display layer states associated with external reference drawings. External references are described in Chapter 28.
- **Restore options.** This area contains the **Turn off layers not found in layer state** check box. When checked, this turns off new layers or layers removed from a layer state when the layer state is restored. The **Apply properties as viewport overrides** check box is available when you are adjusting layer states within a layout viewport and is used to apply layer viewport overrides.

PROFESSIONAL TIP

If you have a drawing that does not contain layer names, importing a layer state file (.las) causes the layers from the layer state to be added to your drawing.

Layer Settings

The **Layer Settings** dialog box, shown in **Figure 5-30**, is accessed by picking the **Settings** button located in the lower-left corner of the **Layer Properties Manager**. The **Layer Settings** dialog box contains a **New Layer Notification Settings** area used to help manage new layers. When you save a drawing file, a list of the layers in the drawing is also saved. Then, when a new layer is created or a new layer comes into the drawing

Figure 5-30.
The **Layer Settings** dialog box provides options for processing new layers.

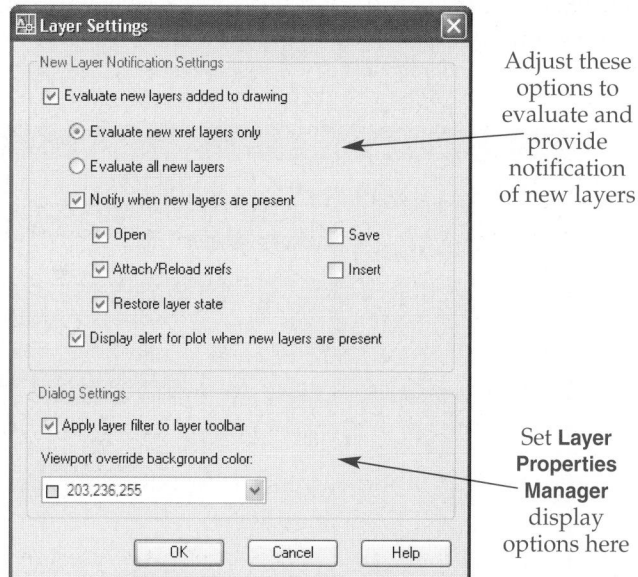

Adjust these options to evaluate and provide notification of new layers

Set **Layer Properties Manager** display options here

from another drawing, the new layer can be evaluated against the existing list of layers. If you choose to evaluate new layers, those that are not found in the existing list of layers are known as *unreconciled layers*.

To evaluate new layers, you must pick the **Evaluate new layers added to drawing** check box or set the **LAYEREVAL** system variable to 1. You can choose to evaluate all new layers or only those associated with external references by picking the appropriate radio button. You can also specify whether you are notified in the status bar when a new layer is evaluated. Pick the **Notify when new layers are present** check box and select the appropriate check boxes to specify when you want to be notified. For example, pick the **Open** check box if you want to be notified of new layers every time you open the file. The **LAYERNOTIFY** system variable can also be used to set notification preferences. **Figure 5-31** shows what happens when a new layer is evaluated and notification is provided. To add the new layer to the list of existing layers, right-click on the new layer in the layer list area of the **Layer Properties Manager** and select the **Reconcile Layer** menu option.

unreconciled layers: Layers not found in the existing layer list when new layers are evaluated.

PROFESSIONAL TIP

Evaluating and providing notification about new layers is not necessary, but it can be helpful for managing layers.

The **Dialog Settings** area of the **Layer Settings** dialog box is used to set **Layer Properties Manager** display options. Check **Apply layer filter to layer toolbar** if you want only the layers matching the current filter displayed in the **Layers** toolbar and the **Layers** control panel of the **Dashboard**. Left unchecked, all layers are available in the **Layers** toolbar and the **Layers** control panel of the **Dashboard**. The **Viewport override background color** option is used to select the background color for layers that have layout viewport overrides associated with them.

Figure 5-31.
Reconciling a new layer.

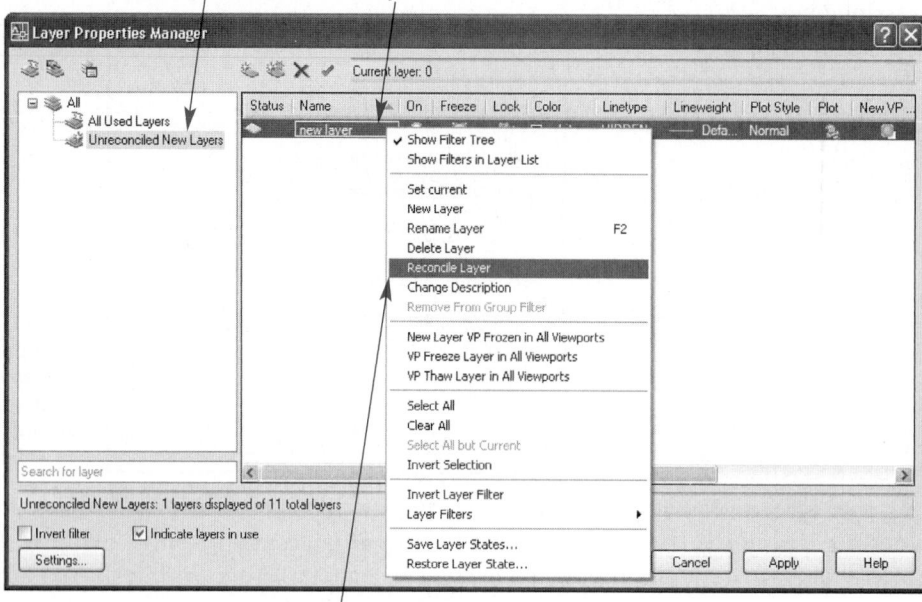

Pick to add the layer to
the list of existing layers

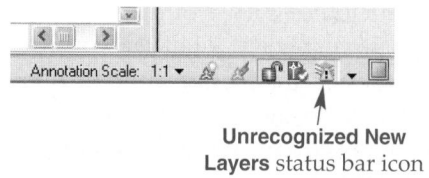

Unrecognized New
Layers status bar icon

Quickly Setting a Layer Current

You can quickly make another layer current by using the **Layer Control** drop-down list located in the **Layers** toolbar or the **Layers** control panel of the **Dashboard**. The name of the current layer is displayed in the box. Pick the drop-down arrow to display a layer list, as shown in **Figure 5-32.**

Pick a layer name from the list to set that layer. When many layers are defined in the drawing, the vertical scroll bar can be used to move up and down through the list. Selecting a layer name to set as current automatically closes the list and returns you to the drawing. When a command is active, the drop-down button is grayed out, and the list is not available. The **Layer Control** drop-down list has the same status icons as the **Layer Properties Manager**. By picking an icon, you can change the state of the layer.

PROFESSIONAL TIP

Layers are meant to simplify the drafting process. They separate different details of the drawing and can reduce the complexity of what is displayed. If you set color and linetype by layer, do not reset and mix object linetypes and color on the same layer. Doing so can mislead you and your colleagues when you try to find certain details. Always maintain accurate records of your template drawings.

AutoCAD and Its Applications—Basics

Figure 5-32.
The **Layer Control** drop-down list.

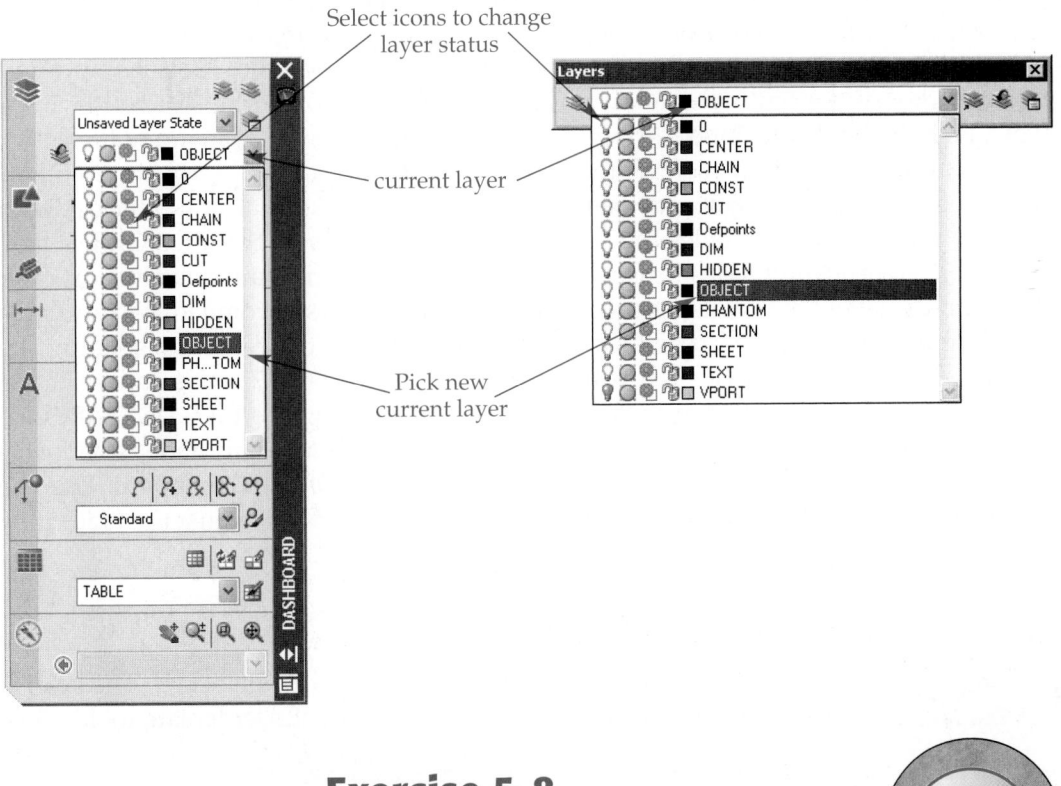
Select icons to change layer status

current layer

Pick new current layer

Exercise 5-8
Complete the exercise on the Student CD.

Additional Layer Tools

Several other layer tools are available in addition to the standard layer tools described throughout this chapter. The following additional layer tools are available from **Format** > **Layer tools**, the **Layers** control panel of the **Dashboard**, and either the **Layers** toolbar *or* the **Layers II** toolbar.

Making an Object's Layer Current

Another quick way to set the current layer is to reference an object in your drawing that is drawn on the layer you want to make current. This is accomplished using the **Make Object's Layer Current** tool. Pick the **Make Object's Layer Current** button to select the tool and pick an object on the layer you want to make current to set the object's layer current.

Returning to the Previous Layer

After changing layer properties, you can restore the previous layer settings by accessing the **Layer Previous** tool. The **Layer Previous** tool affects layer operations only. Therefore, after using commands to draw, modify, and zoom, you can use the **Layer Previous** button to restore the last layer state without affecting any other functions. All layer properties are restored. The **Layer Previous** tool does not affect layer name changes. It does not recreate layers that have been purged or delete layers that have been added.

Isolating Layers

The **Layer Isolate** tool can be used to turn off or lock and fade all the layers in the drawing, except for the layer of an object or objects you choose. When you access the **Layer Isolate** tool, the Select objects on the layer(s) to be isolated or [Settings]: prompt appears. Choose the **Settings** option to describe how to isolate the selected layer or layers. Pick the **Lock and Fade** setting to lock and fade the layers that are not isolated, or pick the **Off** option to turn off all the layers that are not isolated.

When you select the **Lock and Fade** setting, AutoCAD asks for a fade value between 0 and 90. A fade value of 0 fades the display of unisolated layers the least, while a fade value of 90 significantly fades unisolated layers. After entering a fade value, pick the objects on the layers that you want to isolate. All other layers become locked and fade according to the specified fade value. **Figure 5-33** displays the result of isolating the layer used to draw the floor plan walls, using a fade value of 75. You can reset the fade value by repeating the **Layer Isolate** tool, or by entering the **LAYLOCKFADECTL** command. However, the most effective way to work with lock and fade isolation is to use the options in the expanded **Layers** control panel of the **Dashboard**. Use the **Locked layer fading** slide bar or edit box, shown in **Figure 5-34**, to adjust the fade value and see the results in real time on-screen.

NOTE

Locked layer fading is applied to any layer that is locked. The layer does not have to have been locked using the **Layer Isolate** tool.

When you choose the **Off** setting, the In paper space viewport use [Vpfreeze/Off]: prompt appears. Pick the **VPfreeze** setting to freeze all the unisolated layers in the active layout viewport, or pick the **Off** setting to turn off all the unisolated layers. Next, pick the objects on the layers that you want to isolate. All other layers become frozen or are turned off according to the specified settings. **Figure 5-35** displays the result of isolating the layer used to draw the floor plan walls, using the **Off** setting.

Figure 5-33.
The **Layer Isolate** tool isolates layers by fading unisolated layers or hiding them from view.

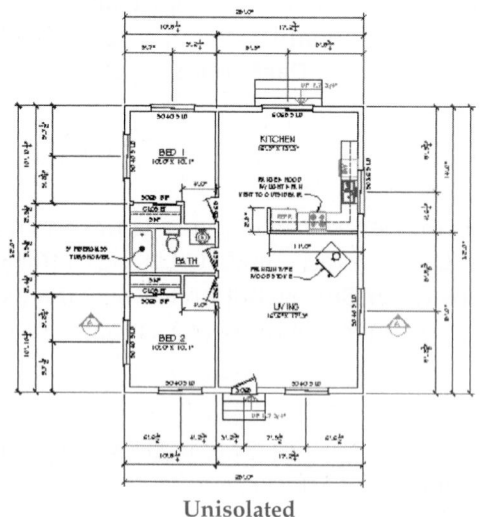

Unisolated

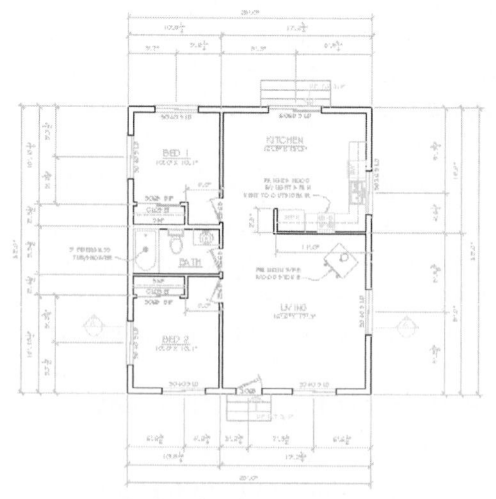

Isolated using **Lock and fade** with a fade value of 75

Figure 5-34.
Using the **Dashboard**
to adjust fade values.

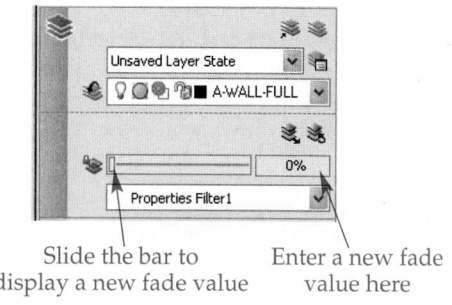

Slide the bar to Enter a new fade
display a new fade value value here

Figure 5-35.
When the **Off**
isolation option is
active, unisolated
layers are hidden on
the screen.

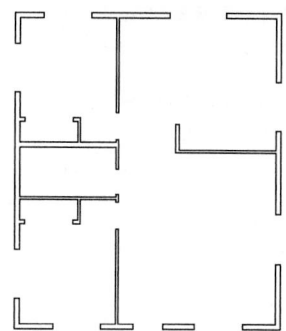

Unisolating Layers

The **Layer Unisolate** tool restores layers to the state before a layer was isolated. Any changes made during **Layer Isolate** are kept after using this tool. **Layer Unisolate** only restores layers locked or turned off during **Layer Isolate** function. Layers that were locked or turned off individually using the **Layer Properties Manager** or by other means are not affected. The simplest way to use **Layer Unisolate** is to pick the button in the **Layer** control panel on the **Dashboard**.

Walking Through Layers

Selecting the **Layer Walk...** tool opens the **LayerWalk - Layers:** *n* dialog box, as shown in Figure 5-36A. This tool provides a list box showing all the layers in the drawing. Selecting a layer name in the list causes all the layers to be turned off except for the selected layer. This provides a means for you to "walk" through a drawing full of layers to see which objects are drawn on which layers. To access this tool, pick the **Layer Walk** button on the **Layers II** toolbar, pick **Format** > **Layer Tools** > **Layer Walk...**, or enter LAYWALK. You can select multiple layers to be displayed. You can also pick the **Select object** button to enter the drawing window and select an object to isolate the layer used to draw the object.

The **LayerWalk - Layers:** *n* dialog box contains other functions, including a **Purge** button that can be used to purge an unused layer from the drawing file. You can also enter a character in the filter list to filter for layers with specific characters. Layers meeting your filter criteria are displayed in the list box. See Figure 5-36B. Deselecting the **Restore on exit** check box sets layer status according to the settings you specify using the **Layer Walk** tool.

Matching Layers

The **Layer Match** tool allows you to change the layer of selected objects to match the layer of another selected object. To use this tool, select the objects whose layers you want to change, and enter those selections. Then select an object on the layer you want to match. The layers of the objects you pick first are matched to the layer of the object

Figure 5-36.
The **LayerWalk - Layers:** *n* dialog box. A—Selected layers are displayed in the drawing area.
B—Entering a filter in the filter drop-down lists only those layers that match the filter criteria.

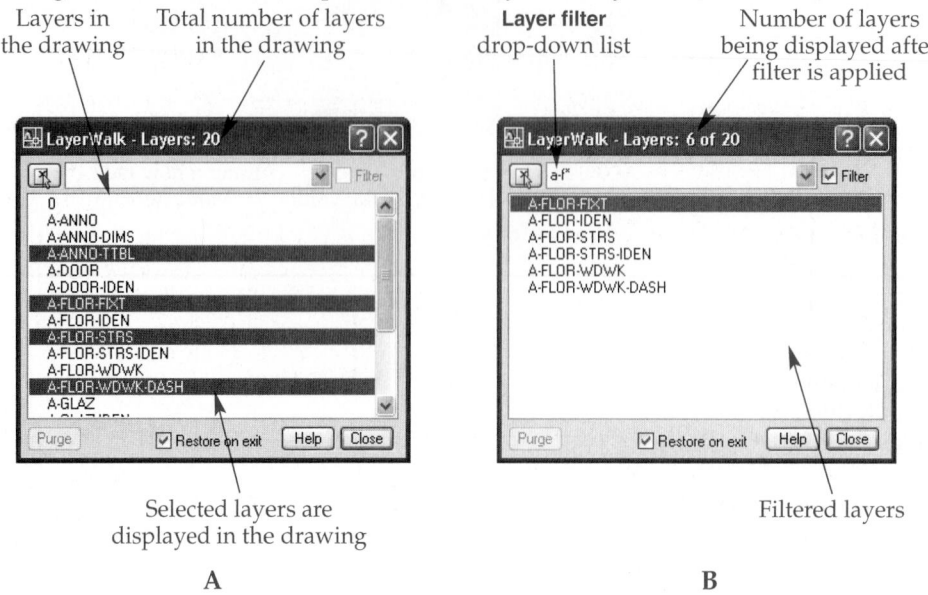

Layers in the drawing · Total number of layers in the drawing · **Layer filter** drop-down list · Number of layers being displayed after filter is applied

Selected layers are displayed in the drawing

Filtered layers

A   B

you pick second. An alternative is to enter the **Name** option after selecting and entering the objects whose layers will be changed. This option displays the **Change to Layer** dialog box, where you can select the layer to which the objects will be matched.

Changing Objects to the Current Layer

The **Change to Current Layer** tool allows you to pick objects on other layers to change them to the current layer. This process can also be accomplished by selecting an object, then picking a layer from the **Layer Control** drop-down list on the **Layers** toolbar or the **Layers** control panel of the **Dashboard**.

Copying Objects to a New Layer

The **Copy Objects to New Layer** tool combines a copy tool and the **Layer Match** tool. Use this command to copy objects to a new location and simultaneously match the object's layer to another object's layer. To use this tool, select the objects whose layers will be changed, and enter those selections. Then enter the **Name** option to select a layer name using the **Change to Layer** dialog box, or select an object whose layer will be matched. The layers of the objects you pick first are matched to the layer of the object you pick second. After selecting the layer, you have the option of choosing a base point from which to copy the objects and a displacement point, or new location, for the copied objects.

Other helpful layer tools include:

- **Isolate Layer to Current Viewport.** This command is similar to **Layer Isolate**, except it freezes the selected layer in all layout viewports other than the current viewport. Layer control for layout viewports is described in Chapter 25.
- **Layer Off.** Use this command to turn off a layer by selecting an object whose layer you want to turn off.
- **Turn All Layers On.** This command turns on all layers that have been turned off.
- **Layer Freeze.** Similar to the **Layer Off** command, this command freezes the layer of an object you select.
- **Thaw All Layers.** This command thaws all frozen layers in the drawing.

- **Layer Lock.** Use this command to lock the layer of an object you select.
- **Layer Unlock.** Use this command to unlock any locked layers in the drawing.
- **Layer Merge.** This command can be used to change all objects on an existing layer to a different selected layer and delete the original layer from the drawing. To merge layers, first select the objects on the layers you want to change and delete. Then, enter the **Name** option to select a layer name using the **Change to Layer** dialog box, or select an object on the layer onto which you want the first selected objects to be merged. After you select the merge layer, AutoCAD warns you of the pending merge operation and prompts you to continue.
- **Layer Delete.** This command deletes all objects on a layer you choose and deletes the selected layer from the drawing. To delete layers using this technique, enter the **Name** option to select a layer name using the **Change to Layer** dialog box, or select an object on the layer to be deleted. After you select the layer, AutoCAD warns you of the pending deletion and prompts you to continue.

NOTE

The additional layer tools described in this section are shortcuts to help you work more efficiently with layers. Most of the tasks accomplished by these tools can also be accomplished using the **Layer Properties Manager**. Be sure you are comfortable performing these tasks using the **Layer Properties Manager** before using the additional layer tools.

Exercise 5-9
Complete the exercise on the Student CD.

Reusing Drawing Content

In nearly every drafting discipline, individual drawings created as part of a given project are likely to share a number of common elements. All the drawings within a specific drafting project generally have the same set of standards. Drawing features, such as layer names and properties, text size and font used for annotation, standardized dimensioning methods and appearances, drafting symbols, drawing layouts, and even typical drawing details, are often duplicated in many different drawings. These and other components of CAD drawings are referred to as *drawing content*. One of the most fundamental advantages of CAD systems is the ease with which content can be shared between drawings. Once a commonly used drawing feature has been defined, it can be used again as needed in any number of drawing applications.

drawing content: All of the objects, settings, and other components that make up a drawing.

The creation and use of drawing template files was covered in Chapter 2. Drawing templates represent one way to reuse drawing content that has already been defined. Creating your own customized drawing template files provides an effective way to start each new drawing using standard settings.

Drawing templates, however, provide only a starting point. During the course of a drawing project, you may need to add content to the current drawing that has been defined previously in another drawing. Some drawing projects may require you to revise an existing drawing rather than start a completely new drawing. For other projects, you may need to duplicate the standards used in a drawing a client has supplied.

AutoCAD provides a powerful drawing content manager called **DesignCenter**. **DesignCenter** allows you to reuse drawing content defined in previous drawings by using a drag-and-drop operation. **DesignCenter** was introduced in Chapter 1.

DesignCenter can be used to manage several types of drawing content, including layers, linetypes, blocks, dimension styles, layouts, table styles, text styles, and externally referenced drawings. Layers and linetypes are described in this chapter; the other content types are introduced in the chapters where they apply. The following discussion details the features of **DesignCenter** and shows how layer and linetype content from existing drawings can be reused in other drawing projects.

Using DesignCenter to Copy Layers and Linetypes

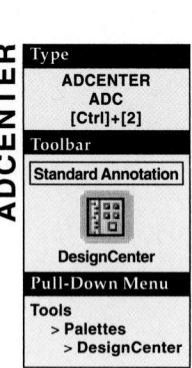

DesignCenter is activated by picking the **DesignCenter** button on the **Standard** or **Standard Annotation** toolbar, picking **Tools** > **Palettes** > **DesignCenter**, typing ADC or ADCENTER, or using the [Ctrl]+[2] key combination. The main features of **DesignCenter** are shown in **Figure 5-37**.

It is not necessary to open a drawing in AutoCAD in order to view or access its content. **DesignCenter** allows you to load content directly from any accessible drawing. You can also use **DesignCenter** to browse through existing drawing files and view their contents, or you can use its advanced search tools to look for specific drawing content.

DesignCenter allows you to share content easily between drawings that are currently open in AutoCAD. To copy content, first use the tree view pane to select the drawing from which the content is to be copied. If the tree view is not already visible, toggle it on by picking the **Tree View Toggle** button in the **DesignCenter** toolbar. The first three tabs on the **DesignCenter** toolbar control the tree view display:

- **Folders.** Pick this tab to display the folders and files found on the hard drive and network.
- **Open Drawings.** Pick this tab to list only drawings that are currently open.
- **History.** Pick this tab to list recently opened drawings.

Figure 5-37.
DesignCenter is used to copy content from one drawing to another.

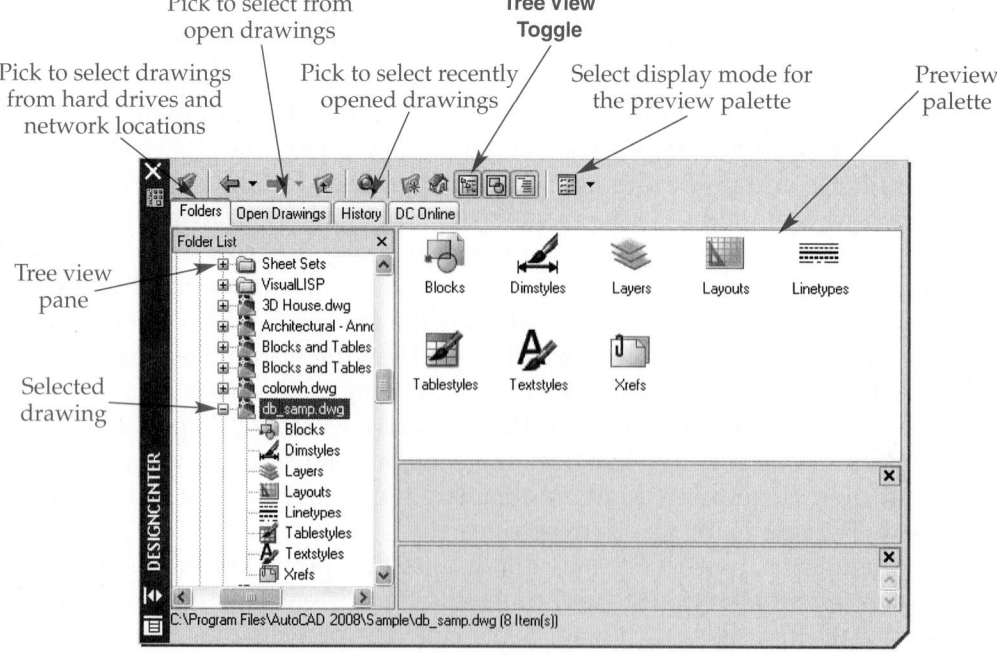

Pick the plus sign (+) next to a drawing icon to view the content categories for the drawing. Each category of drawing content is listed with a representative icon. Pick the Layers icon to load the palette with the layer content found in the selected drawing. The preview palette now displays all the layers defined in the selected drawing. See **Figure 5-38.**

To select layers from the palette, use standard Windows selection methods. Use the [Shift] and [Ctrl] keys for selecting multiple items. In this example, the drawing is selected first, and the **Layers** content is picked. The preview palette displays the available content. Select the desired layers and use one of the following options to import them into the current drawing:

- **Drag and drop.** Move the cursor over the desired icon in the preview palette. Press and hold down the pick button on your pointing device. Drag the cursor to the open drawing. See **Figure 5-39.** When you release the pick button, the selected content is added to your current drawing file.
- **Add from shortcut menu.** Select the desired icon(s) in the preview palette and right-click to open the shortcut menu. Pick the **Add Layer(s)** option to add the selected content to your current drawing.
- **Copy from shortcut menu.** This option is identical to the **Add Layer(s)** option, except you select **Copy** from the shortcut menu instead of **Add Layer(s)**. Now, move the cursor to the drawing in which you want the content added and right-click to open the shortcut menu. Select **Paste** to add the selected contents to the current drawing.

To select more than one icon at one time, hold down the [Shift] key and pick the first and last icons in a group. You can also hold down the [Ctrl] key to select multiple icons individually. The copied layers are now available in the active drawing. If the name of a layer being loaded already exists in the destination drawing, that layer name and its settings are ignored. The existing settings for the layer are preserved, and a message is displayed at the command line indicating that duplicate settings were ignored.

Linetypes can be copied using the same procedure. In the tree view, select the drawing containing the linetypes to be copied. Select **Linetypes** to display the linetypes in the preview palette. Select the linetypes to be copied, and then use drag and drop or the shortcut menu to add the linetypes to the current drawing.

Figure 5-38.
Displaying the layers found in a drawing using **DesignCenter**.

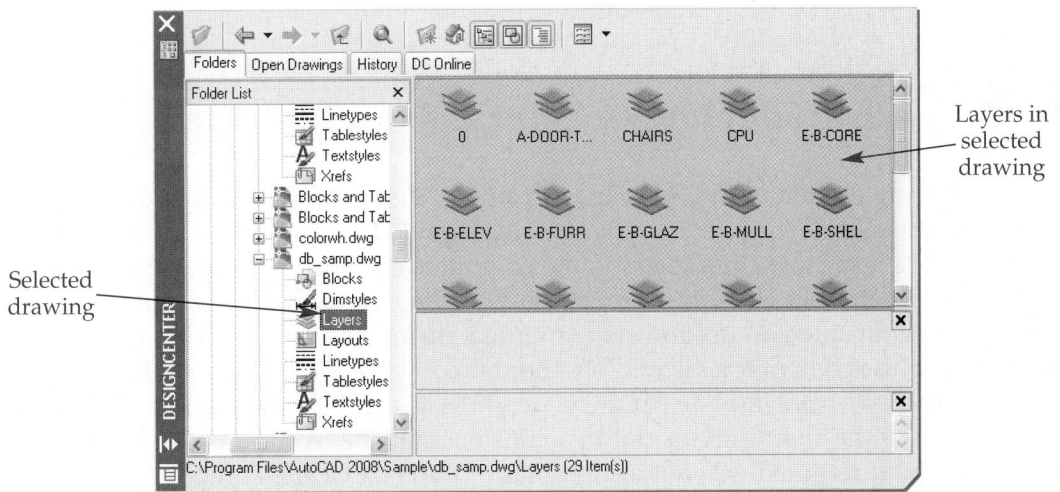

Figure 5-39.
To copy layers shown in **DesignCenter** into the current drawing, first select the layers to be copied, and then drag and drop them into the drawing area of the current drawing.

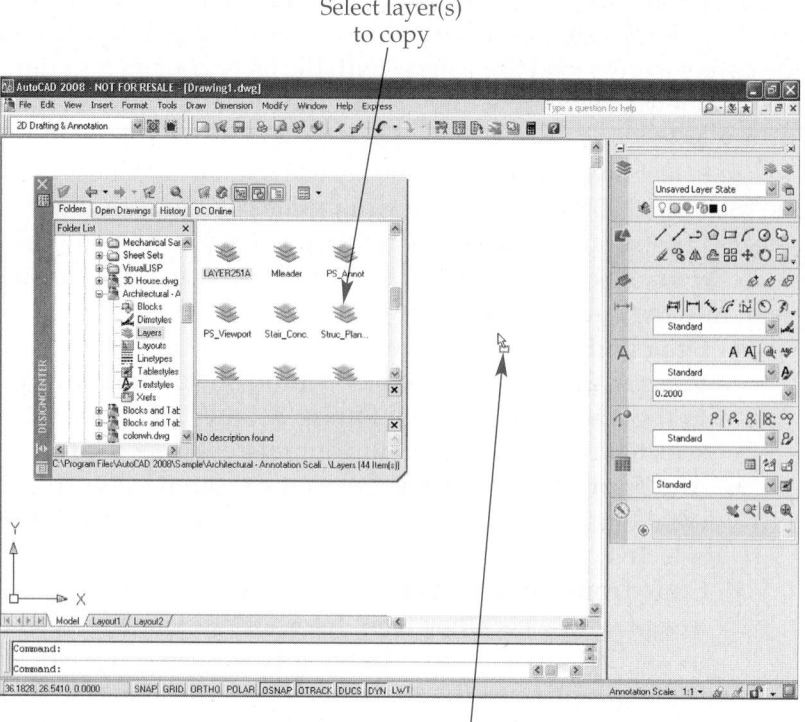

Select layer(s) to copy

Cursor appearance during drag-and-drop operation

NOTE

DesignCenter is a very powerful tool. Specific applications of **DesignCenter** are provided throughout this text.

Exercise 5-10

Complete the exercise on the Student CD.

Introduction to Printing and Plotting

A drawing created with CAD can exist in two distinct forms: hard copy and soft copy. The term *hard copy* refers to a physical drawing a printer or plotter produces on paper. The term *soft copy* refers to the computer software version of the drawing, or the actual data file. The soft copy can only be displayed on the computer monitor, making it inconvenient to use for many manufacturing and construction purposes. If the power to the computer is turned off, the soft copy drawing is not available.

A hard copy drawing is extremely versatile. It can be rolled up or folded and taken down to the shop floor or out to a construction site. A hard copy drawing can be checked and redlined without a computer or CAD software. Although CAD is the standard throughout the world for generating drawings, the hard copy drawing is still a vital tool for communicating the design.

hard copy: A physical drawing produced by a printer or plotter.

soft copy: The electronic data file of a drawing.

Hard copy drawings are created by printers or plotters. These terms can be used interchangeably, although *plotter* typically refers to a large-format printer. Printers take the soft copy images you draw in AutoCAD and transfer them onto paper.

There are two general classifications of printers: desktop printers and large-format printers. Desktop printers generally print 8 1/2" × 11" or possibly 11" × 17" drawings. These are the printers common to computer workstations. Desktop printers are used to print small drawings and to print reduced-size test prints. Large-format printers can print larger drawings, such as C-size and D-size drawings. The most common types of both desktop and large-format printers are inkjet and laser printers. Pen plotters, which "draw" with actual ink pens, are still in use, but are not as common as they were in the past.

The information in this chapter is provided to give you only the basics, so you can make your first plot. Chapter 25 explores the detailed aspects of printing and plotting. Prints and plots are made using the **Plot** dialog box. Access this dialog box by picking the **Plot** button in the **Standard Annotation** toolbar, selecting **File** > **Plot...** from the pull-down menu, pressing the [Ctrl]+[P] key combination, or typing PLOT.

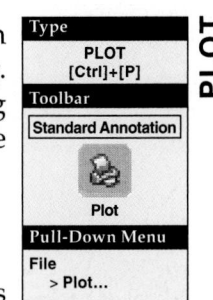

Model Space and Paper Space

The first step in making an AutoCAD drawing is to create a model. The *model* is composed of various objects, such as lines, circles, and text. The term model has more meaning when working in 3D, but you can consider any drawing as a model, even if it is 2D. The model is created in an environment called *model space*. Model space can be thought of as the space in AutoCAD where you draw and design. See **Figure 5-40.** Model space can be accessed by picking the **Model** button on the **Status** bar, or if the layout and model tabs are displayed, you can pick the **Model** tab at the bottom of the drawing area or the **Model** button on the **Status** bar.

Once the model is completed, a layout can be created. A *layout* is used to lay out a drawing or model to be plotted and can contain various views of the model, a border and title block, and other annotations. In addition, the layout includes page setup information (such as paper size and margins) and plotter configuration data

model: A 2D or 3D drawing, usually created at full size.

model space: The environment in AutoCAD where drawings and designs are created.

layout: An arrangement of a drawing or model for plotting.

Figure 5-40.
Model space is the environment in which drawings and designs are created.

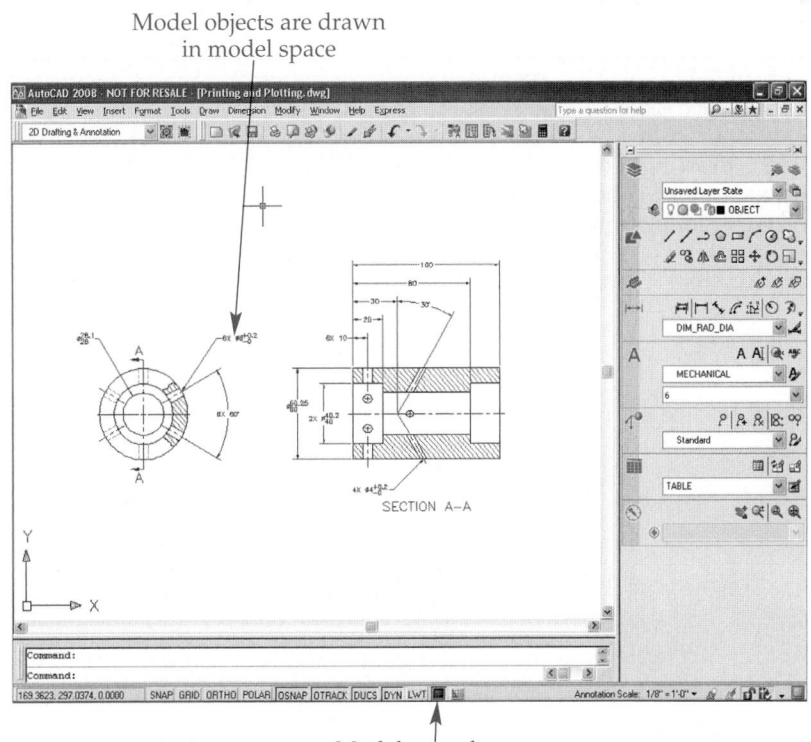

Model objects are drawn in model space

Model space button

(information related to the specific model of printer or plotter being used). A single drawing can have multiple layouts. Layouts are created in an environment called *paper space*. Paper space represents the sheet of paper used to lay out and plot a drawing or model. Paper space can be accessed by picking one of the **Layout** buttons on the **Status** bar, or if the layout and model tabs are displayed, by picking one of the **Layout** tabs at the bottom of the drawing area or the **Layout** button on the **Status** bar. See **Figure 5-41.**

Do not be confused by model space and paper space. Drawings can be plotted from model space or from a layout. The following information describes plotting from model space only. Creating and plotting layouts is addressed in Chapter 25.

Making a Plot

In this section, one of the many methods for creating a plot from the **Model** tab is described. Refer to **Figure 5-42** as you read through the following plotting procedure:

1. Access the **Plot** dialog box. If the column on the far right of the dialog box shown in **Figure 5-42** is not displayed, pick the **More Options** button (**>**) in the lower-right corner.
2. Check the plot device and paper size specifications in the **Printer/plotter** and **Paper size** areas.
3. Select what is to be plotted in the **Plot area** section. The following options are available:
   - **Display.** This option plots the current screen display.
   - **Extents.** This option plots only the area of the drawing where objects are drawn.
   - **Limits.** This option plots everything inside the defined drawing limits.
   - **Window.** This option allows you to select a rectangular area of the drawing to plot. When you pick the **Window** option, the drawing area is displayed so you can specify a window to plot. After you select the second corner of the window, the **Plot** dialog box returns.
4. Select an option in the **Drawing orientation** area. Choose **Portrait** or **Landscape** to orient your drawing vertically (*portrait*) or horizontally (*landscape*). The **Plot upside-down** option rotates the paper 180°.

Figure 5-41.
Paper space is the environment in which drawings and designs are laid out on paper for plotting.

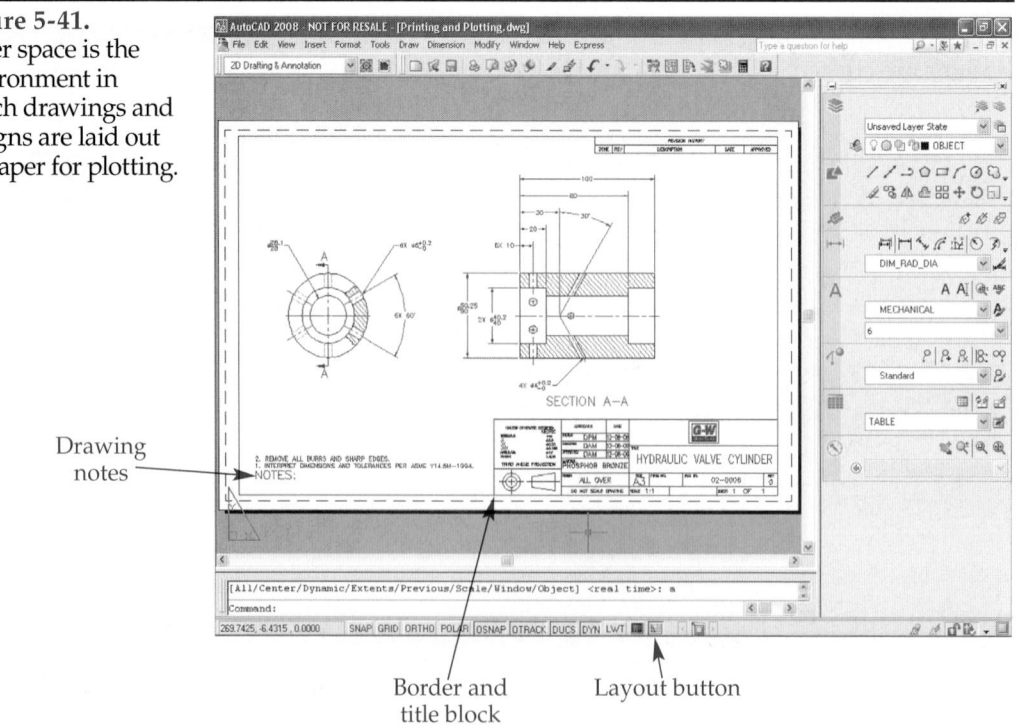

Drawing notes

Border and title block

Layout button

AutoCAD and Its Applications—Basics

Figure 5-42.
The **Plot** dialog box.

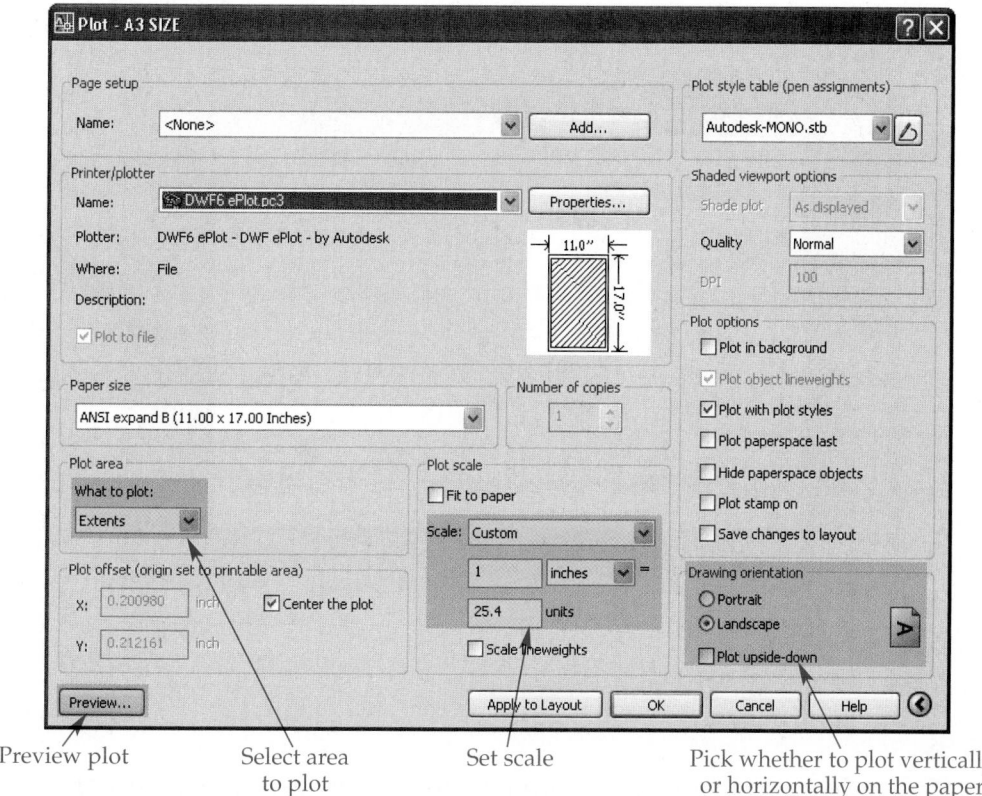

Preview plot   Select area to plot   Set scale   Pick whether to plot vertically or horizontally on the paper

5. Set the scale in the **Plot scale** area. Because you draw full-scale in AutoCAD, you typically need to scale drawings either up or down to fit the paper. Scale is measured as a ratio of either inches or millimeters to drawing units. Select a predefined scale from the **Scale:** drop-down list or enter your own values into the custom fields. Choose the **Fit to paper** check box to let AutoCAD automatically shrink or stretch the plot area to fill the paper.

6. If desired, use the **Plot offset (origin set to printable area)** area to set additional left and bottom margins around the plot or to center the plot.

7. Preview the plot. Pick the **Preview...** button to display the sheet as it will look when it is plotted. See **Figure 5-43.** The cursor appears as a magnifying glass with + and − symbols. The plot preview image zooms if you hold the left mouse button and move the cursor. Press [Esc] to exit the preview.

8. Pick the **OK** button in the **Plot** dialog box to send the data to the plotting device.

Before you pick the **OK** button to send your drawing to the plotter, you should check the following items:

    ✓ The printer or plotter is plugged in
    ✓ The cable from your computer to the printer or plotter is secure
    ✓ The printer has paper
    ✓ Paper is properly loaded in the plotter, and grips or clamps are in place
    ✓ The plotter area is clear for paper movement

Exercise 5-11

Complete the exercise on the Student CD.

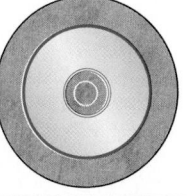

Figure 5-43.
A preview of the plot shows exactly how the drawing will appear on the paper.

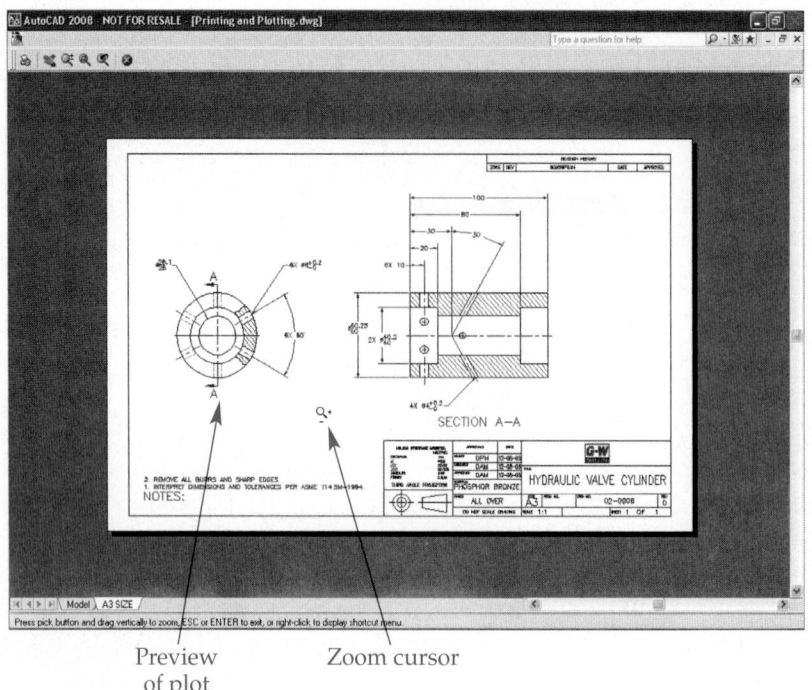

Preview
of plot

Zoom cursor

Template Development

Chapter 5

Lineweight, linetype, and layer definitions are important elements of most drawing templates. Refer to the Student CD for detailed instructions to add these elements to your mechanical, architectural, and civil drawing templates.

Chapter Test

Answer the following questions. Write your answers on a separate sheet of paper or complete the electronic chapter test on the Student CD.

1. Identify the following linetypes:

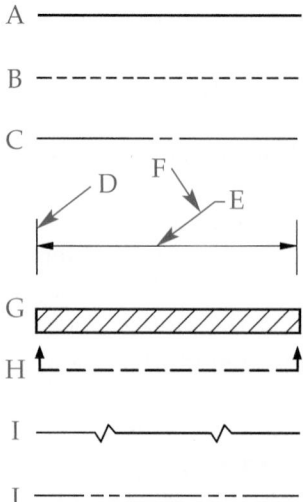

2. Identify three ways to access the **Layer Properties Manager**.
3. How can several new layer names be entered consecutively without using the **New Layer** button in the **Layer Properties Manager**?
4. Should you draw on layer 0? Explain.
5. How do you make another layer current in the **Layer Properties Manager**?
6. Identify at least three layers that cannot be deleted from a drawing.
7. List and identify at least three layer selection options provided in the short-cut menu that appears when you right-click in the layer list area of the **Layer Properties Manager**.
8. How can you tell if a layer is off, thawed, or unlocked by looking at the **Layer Properties Manager**?
9. What is the state of a layer *not* displayed on the screen and *not* calculated by the computer when the drawing is regenerated?
10. Identify the following layer status icons:

A.   💡

D.   ❄️

B.   💡

E.   🔓

C.   ◯

F.   🔒

11. Explain the purpose of locking a layer.
12. How is the **Select Color** dialog box displayed from the **Layer Properties Manager**?
13. List the seven standard color names and numbers.
14. What is the default linetype in AutoCAD?
15. What condition must exist before a linetype can be used in a layer?
16. Describe the basic procedure to change a layer's linetype to HIDDEN.
17. What is the function of the linetype scale?
18. Explain the effects of using a global linetype scale.
19. Why do you have to be careful when changing linetype scales?
20. How do you change a layer's linetype in the **Layer Properties Manager**?
21. Why is ByLayer referred to as a logical color, linetype, and lineweight?
22. Which button in the **Layer Properties Manager** allows you to save layer settings so they can be restored at a later time?
23. Describe the purpose of layer filters.
24. Name the two basic types of filters.
25. How do you make another layer current using the **Dashboard**?
26. How do you make the layer of an existing object current?
27. Define *global change*.
28. Discuss the basic function of the New Layer Notification Settings area of the Layer Settings dialog box.
29. In the tree view area of **DesignCenter**, how do you view the content categories of one of the listed open drawings?
30. How do you display all the available layers in a drawing using the **DesignCenter** preview palette?
31. Briefly explain how drag and drop works.
32. Define *hard copy* and *soft copy*.
33. Identify four ways to access the **Plot** dialog box.
34. Describe the difference between the **Display** and **Window** options in the **Plot area** section of the **Plot** dialog box.
35. What is the major advantage of doing a plot preview?

Drawing Problems

Before beginning these problems, set up template drawings with layer names, colors, linetypes, and lineweights for the type of drawing you are creating. Do not draw dimensions. Be sure to do preliminary planning for each drawing as described in this chapter.

1. Draw the plot plan shown below. Use the linetypes shown, which include Continuous, HIDDEN, PHANTOM, CENTER, FENCELINE2, and GAS_LINE. Make your drawing proportional to the example. Save the drawing as P5-1.

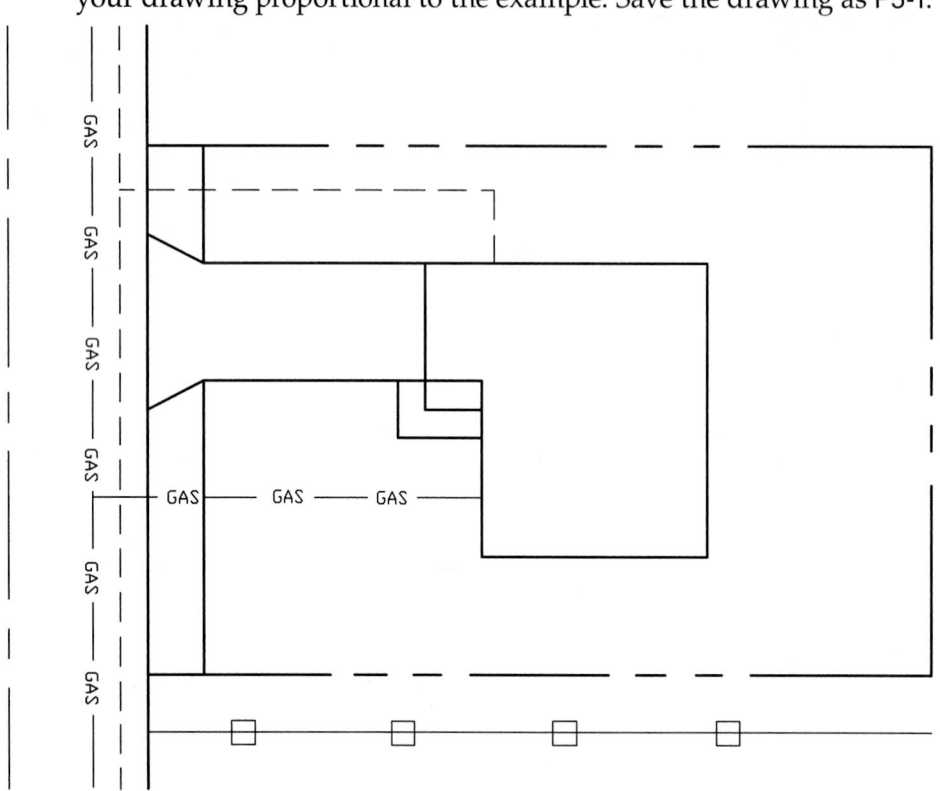

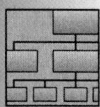

2. Draw the line chart shown below. Use the linetypes shown, which include Continuous, HIDDEN, PHANTOM, CENTER, FENCELINE1, and FENCELINE2. Make your drawing proportional to the given example. Save the drawing as P5-2.

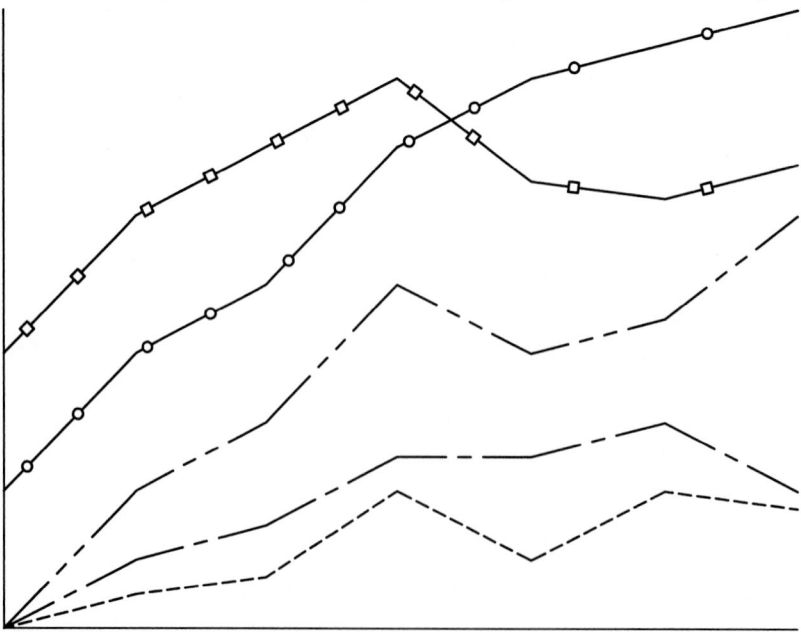

3. Draw the hex head bolt pattern shown below. Save the drawing as P5-3.

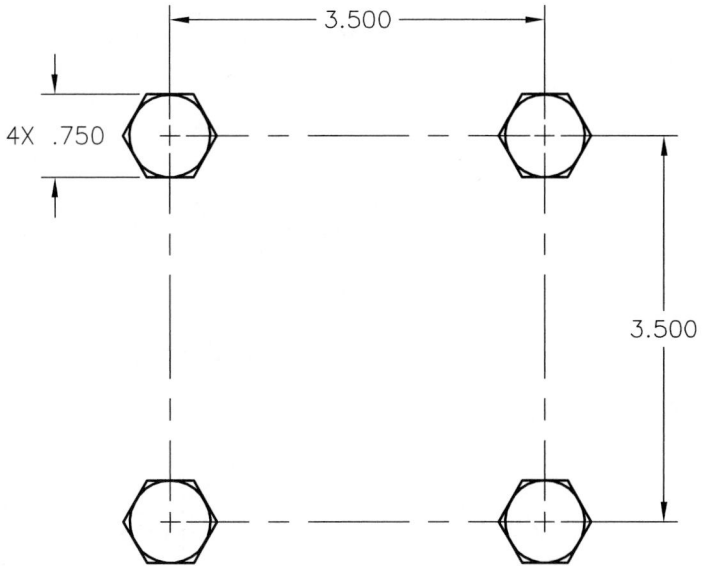

4. Create the controller integrated circuit diagram. Use a ruler or scale to keep the proportion as close as possible. Do not include the text. Save the drawing as P5-4.

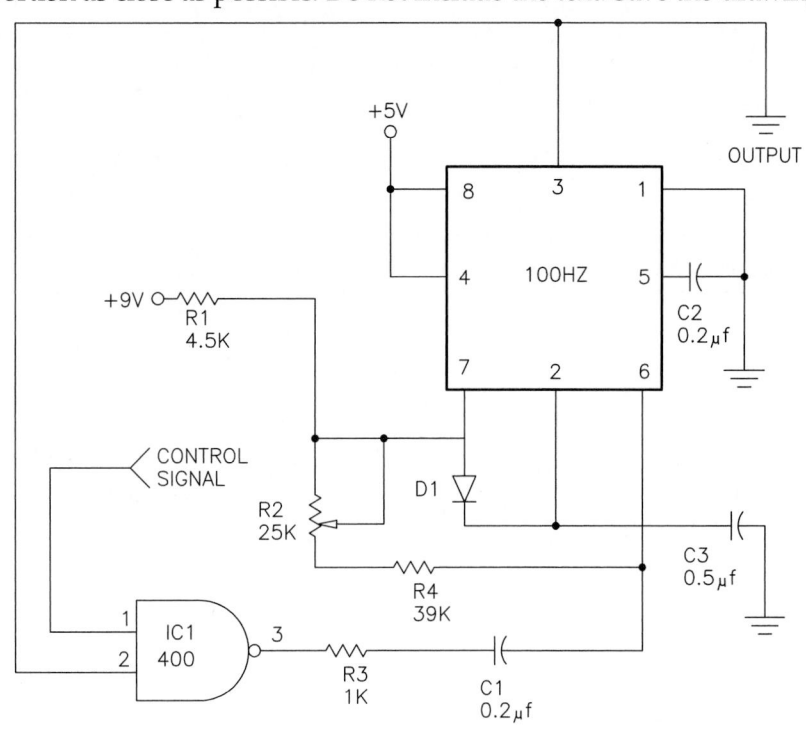
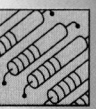

5. Create a 1/2″ hex nut with 3/4″ across the flats and a .422″ root diameter as shown. Save the drawing as P5-5.

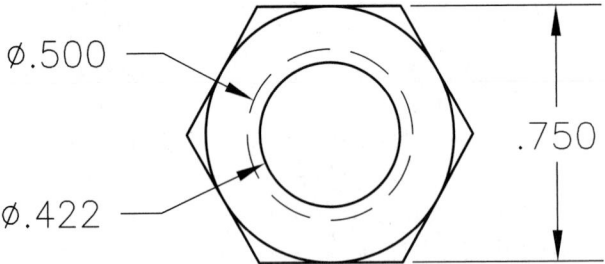

6. Draw the part shown below. Save the drawing as P5-6.

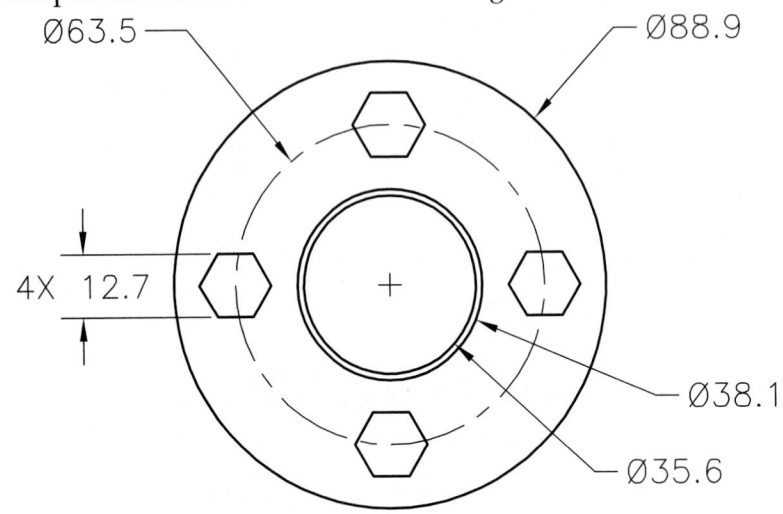

7. Draw the part shown below. Save the drawing as P5-7.

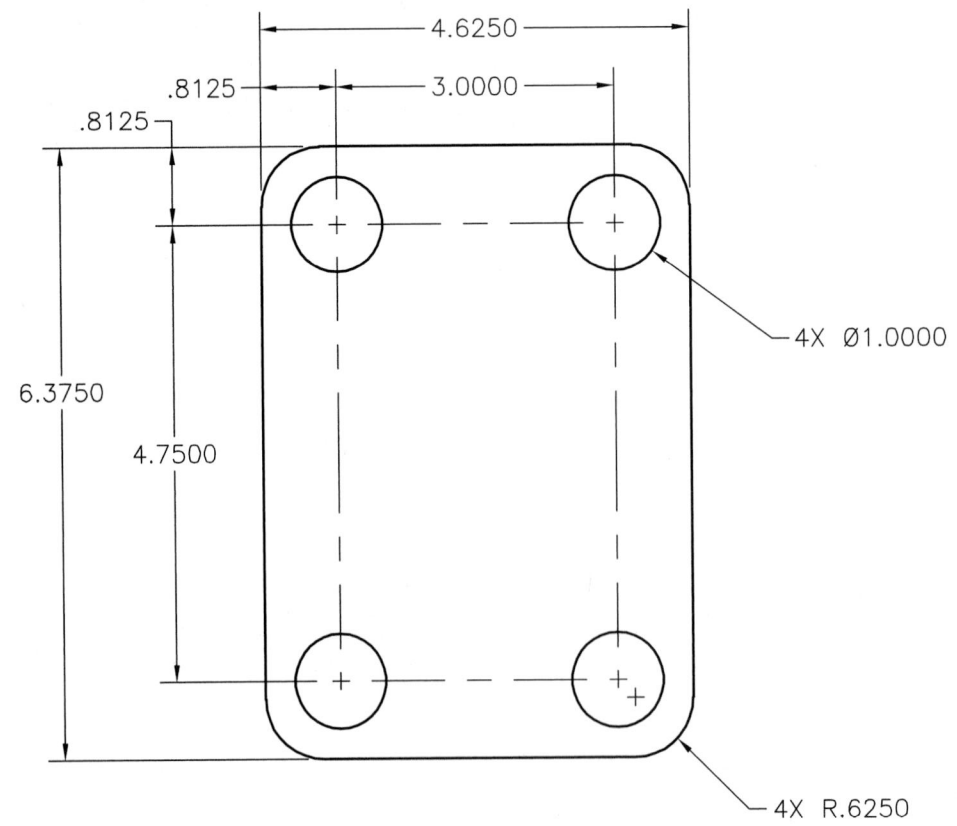

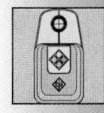

8. Open P4-5, create a new layer for centerlines, and insert the centerlines. Save the drawing as P5-8.

9. Open P4-7, create a new layer for centerlines, and insert the centerlines. Save the drawing as P5-9.

10. Open P4-9, create a new layer for centerlines, and insert the centerlines. Change the global linetype scale to achieve an effect similar to the centerlines shown in Chapter 4. Save the drawing as P5-10.

11. Draw a drift boat similar to the one shown below. Estimate dimensions. Save the drawing as P5-11.

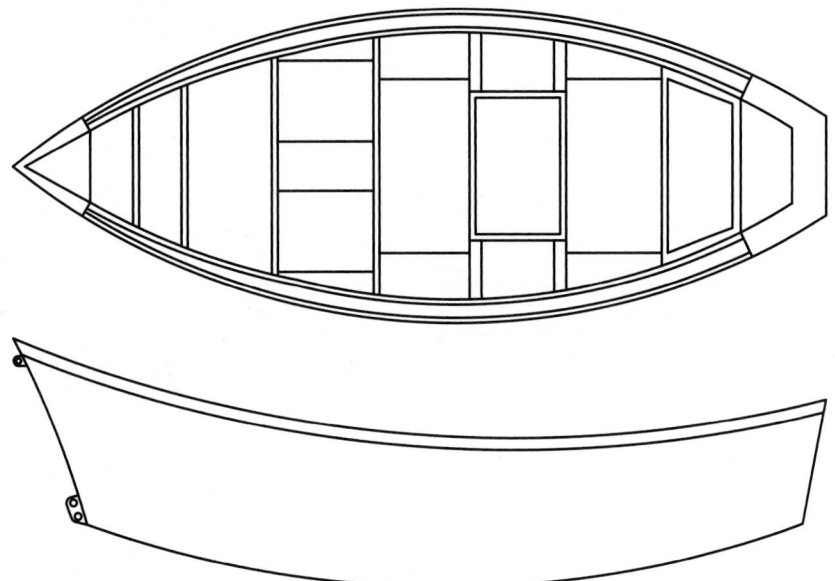

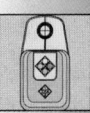

12. Draw the fishing boat shown. Save the drawing as P5-12.

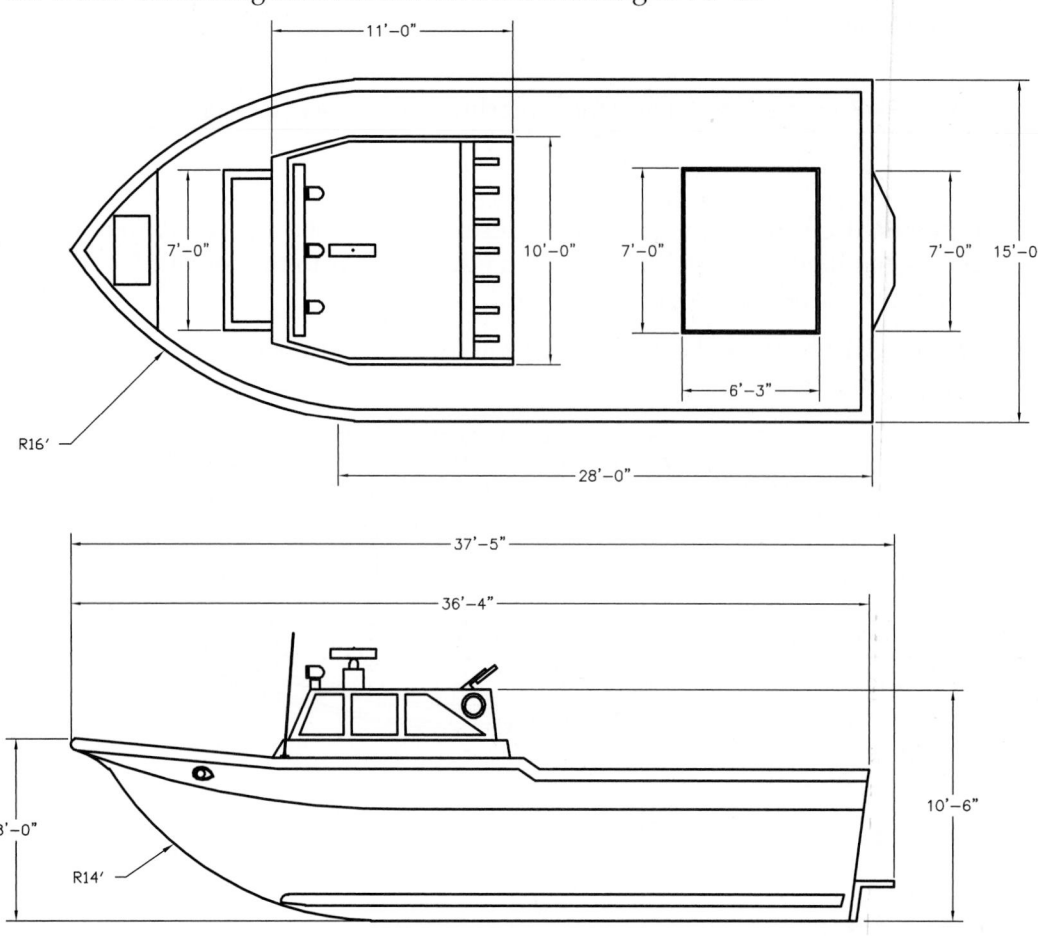

Display Options

Learning Objectives

After completing this chapter, you will be able to do the following:

- ✓ Magnify a small part of a drawing to work on details.
- ✓ Move the display window to reveal portions of the drawing outside the boundaries of the monitor.
- ✓ Explain the differences between the **REDRAW** command and the **REGEN** command.
- ✓ Create named views that can be recalled instantly.
- ✓ Create multiple viewports in the graphics window.
- ✓ Control display order.

You can view a specific portion of a drawing using the AutoCAD display commands. The **ZOOM** command magnifies objects so that you can see them more clearly. The portion of a zoomed drawing that is displayed on-screen can be changed using the **PAN** command. Use the **View Manager** to create and name specific views of the drawing. When further drawing or editing operations are required, the view can be quickly and easily recalled.

While you work on a drawing, you may need to refresh the screen display. This chapter discusses the options for refreshing the screen and optimizing both display speed and drawing quality.

Getting Close to Your Work

Zooming is the process of making objects appear bigger or smaller on the screen without affecting their actual sizes. Zooming gives designers the ability to create extremely small items, such as the electronic circuits found in a computer. The **ZOOM** command is a helpful tool that you will use often. The various options of the **ZOOM** command are discussed in the next sections.

zooming: Making objects appear bigger or smaller on the screen without affecting their actual sizes.

The Zoom Options

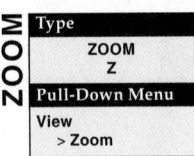

Each of the **ZOOM** options can be accessed by selecting the option in the **Zoom** cascading menu from the **View** pull-down menu. If you are working in the **AutoCAD Classic** workspace, the options are also available as a **Zoom** flyout in the **Standard** toolbar. All the buttons in the **Zoom** flyout are also found in the **Zoom** toolbar. See **Figure 6-1**. All **ZOOM** options except **In** and **Out** are available when Z or ZOOM is typed:

Command: **Z** *or* **ZOOM**⌐
Specify corner of window, enter a scale factor (nX or nXP), or
[All/Center/Dynamic/Extents/Previous/Scale/Window/Object] <real time>:

> **NOTE**
>
> The **Zoom** buttons are not available on the **Standard Annotation** toolbar in the **2D Drawing and Annotation** workspace. However, the **Realtime**, **Window**, and **Extents** options are available in the **2D Navigate** control panel of the **Dashboard**.

The **ZOOM** options are as follows:
- **Realtime.** This interactive zooming is the default option. Zooming is done by holding down the left mouse button while moving the cursor up or down.
- **All.** Zooms to the edge of the drawing limits. If objects are drawn beyond the limits, the **All** option zooms to the edges of your geometry. Always use this option after you change the drawing limits.

Figure 6-1.
ZOOM command options. A—The **Zoom** flyout button on the **Standard** toolbar. B—The **Zoom** cascading menu. C—The **Zoom** toolbar.

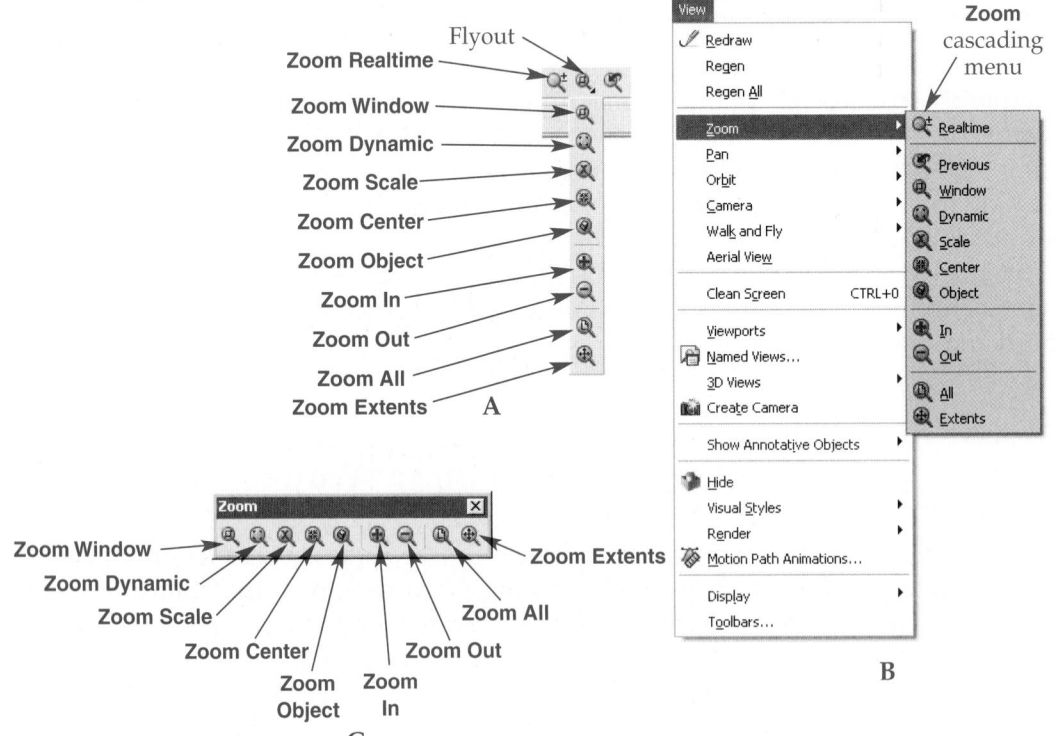

- **Center.** Zooms the center of the display screen to a picked point. If you want to zoom to the center of an area of the drawing and want to magnify the view as well, then pick the center and height of the area in the drawing. Rather than a height, a magnification factor can be entered by typing a number followed by an X, such as 4X. The current value represents the height of the screen in drawing units. Entering a smaller number enlarges the image size, while a larger number reduces it.
- **Dynamic.** Allows for a graphic pan and zoom with the use of a view box that represents the screen. This option is discussed in detail later in the chapter.
- **Extents.** Zooms to the extents (or edges) of the geometry in a drawing. This is the portion of the drawing area that contains drawing objects.
- **Window.** Allows you to pick opposite corners of a box. Objects in the box enlarge to fill the display. The **Window** option is the default if you pick a point on the screen upon entering the **ZOOM** command.
- **Scale.** The following prompt appears when you select the **Scale** option:

  Enter a scale factor (nX or nXP):

  The **nX** option scales the display relative to the current display. To use this option, type a positive number, then X, and then press [Enter]. For example, enter 2X to magnify the current display "two times." To reduce the display, enter a number less than 1. For example, if you enter .5X, objects appear half as large as they did in the previous display.

  The **nXP** option is used in conjunction with model space and paper space. It scales a drawing in model space relative to paper space and is used primarily in the layout of scaled multiview drawings.

  Both of the **Scale** options can be entered at the initial **ZOOM** command prompt. For example, enter the following sequence to enlarge the current display by a factor of three:

  Command: **Z** *or* **ZOOM**⏎
  [All/Center/Dynamic/Extents/Previous/Scale/Window/Object] <real time>: **3X**⏎
  Command:

- **Previous.** Returns to the previous display. You can go back ten displays, one at a time.
- **Object.** Allows you to select an object or set of objects. The selection is zoomed and centered to fill the display area.
- **In.** This option is available only on the toolbar and the pull-down menu. It automatically executes a 2X zoom scale factor.
- **Out.** This option is available only on the toolbar and the pull-down menu. It automatically executes a .5X zoom scale factor.

View Transitions

When you use the **ZOOM** command or any of its associated options, the zoom operation is performed in a smooth transition from the current display to the new display. This feature is controlled by the **VTENABLE** system variable. To turn off smooth transitions, type VTENABLE and enter a value of 0. To turn on smooth transitions, type VTENABLE and enter a value of 3, which is the default setting.

The **VTENABLE** system variable also is used to change the smooth transitions for changes of view angle and for scripts. This variable can be changed in the **View Transitions** dialog box, which is accessed by typing VTOPTIONS. See **Figure 6-2.**

Figure 6-2.
The **View Transitions** dialog box is used to change the smooth transitions for zooming and panning operations, changes of view angle, and scripts.

Turn smooth transitions on and off

Speed control for transitions

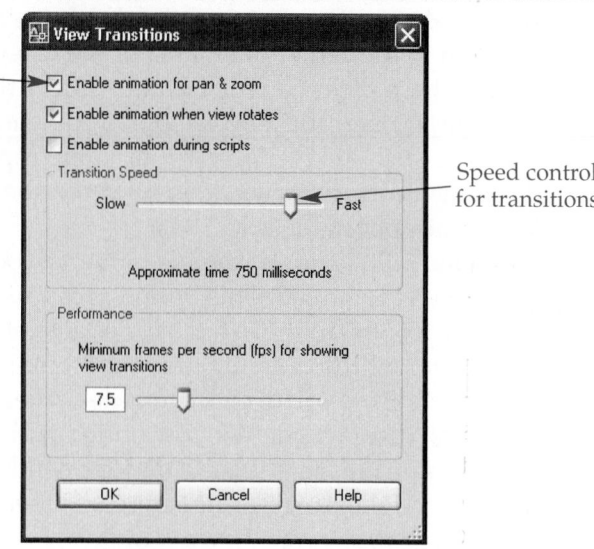

Performing Realtime Zoom

When using the command line, the default option of the **ZOOM** command is **Realtime**. A *realtime zoom* can be viewed as it is performed. It is activated by pressing [Enter] at the **ZOOM** command prompt, by picking the **Zoom Realtime** button in the **2D Navigate** control panel of the **Dashboard** or in the **Standard** toolbar, by picking **View** > **Zoom** > **Realtime**, or by right-clicking in the drawing area and selecting **Zoom** in the shortcut menu.

Realtime zooming allows you to see the model move on the screen as you zoom. The Zoom cursor (a magnifying glass icon with a plus and minus) is displayed when realtime zoom is executed. Press and hold the left mouse button (pick button) and move the pointer up to zoom in (enlarge) and down to zoom out (reduce). When you have achieved the display you want, release the button. If the display needs further adjustment after the initial zoom, press and hold the left mouse button again and move the pointer to get the desired display. To exit realtime zooming, press the [Esc] key or the [Enter] key, or right-click and pick **Exit**.

If you right-click while the Zoom cursor is active, a shortcut menu is displayed. This menu appears at the Zoom cursor location and contains six viewing options.

- **Pan.** Activates the **PAN Realtime** option. This allows you to adjust the placement of the drawing on the screen. If additional zooming is required, right-click again to display the shortcut menu and pick **Zoom**. In this manner you can toggle back and forth between **PAN** and **ZOOM Realtime** to accurately adjust the view. A detailed explanation of the **PAN** command is given later in this chapter.
- **Zoom.** Activates the **ZOOM Realtime** option. A check appears to the left of this option if it is active.
- **3D Orbit.** This option is used to move around a 3D object. When this is selected, your point of view around the drawing can change. A detailed explanation of **3D Orbit** is provided later in this chapter.
- **Zoom Window.** Activates the **ZOOM Window** option and changes the cursor display. See **Figure 6-3.** You can pick opposite corners of a window but, unlike the typical zoom window, you must press and hold the pick button while dragging the window box to the opposite corner, then release the pick button.
- **Zoom Original.** Restores the previous display before any realtime zooming or panning occurred. This is a handy function if the current display is not to your liking, and it would be easier to start over rather than to make further adjustments.

Figure 6-3.
The cursor changes when **Zoom Window** is selected from the shortcut menu.

- **Zoom Extents.** Zooms to the extents of the drawing geometry. This can also be accomplished by double-clicking a wheel mouse.

PROFESSIONAL TIP

AutoCAD supports most mice that have a scroll wheel. This is a wheel between the two mouse buttons that usually scrolls the display up or down. Within AutoCAD, the scroll wheel has these basic functions:
- Roll the wheel forward (away from you) to zoom in.
- Roll the wheel backward (toward you) to zoom out.
- Press and hold the wheel button and move the mouse to pan.
- Double-click the wheel to zoom to the drawing extents.

The **ZOOMFACTOR** system variable controls the incremental movement of the wheel. By default, the zoom factor is set to 60 percent.

Accurate Displays with a Dynamic Zoom

The **ZOOM Dynamic** option allows you to use a *view box* to specify the portion of the drawing you want to display. This view box is proportional to the size of the display area of your screen. If you are looking at a zoomed-in view when **ZOOM Dynamic** is selected, the entire drawing is displayed on the screen.

> **view box:** A small box that allows you to adjust the current zoom magnification visually.

To practice using this command, load any drawing into AutoCAD. Then select the **ZOOM Dynamic** option. The screen is now occupied by three boxes. See **Figure 6-4.** The third box (panning view box) changes to a zooming view box during the process. Each box has a specific function:
- **Drawing extents.** (blue dotted line) This box shows the area of the drawing that is occupied by drawing objects. It is the same area that is displayed with **ZOOM Extents**.
- **Current view.** (green dotted line) This is the view that was displayed before you selected **ZOOM Dynamic**.
- **Panning view box.** (X in the center) Move the pointing device to find the center point of the desired zoomed display. When you press the pick button, the zooming view box appears.
- **Zooming view box.** (arrow on right side) This box allows you to reduce or enlarge the area you wish to zoom. Move the pointer to the right to increase the size of the box. Move the pointer to the left to shrink the box. You can also pan up or down with the zooming view box. The only restriction is that you cannot move the box to the left.

The **ZOOM Dynamic** command is not complete until you press [Enter]. If you press the pick button to select the zooming view box, you can resize the viewing area. Press the pick button again and the panning view box reappears. The panning view box can then be repositioned over the area desired. In this manner, you can fine-tune the exact display needed. This is also helpful in defining permanent views, which is discussed later in this chapter.

Figure 6-4.
Features of the **ZOOM Dynamic** option.

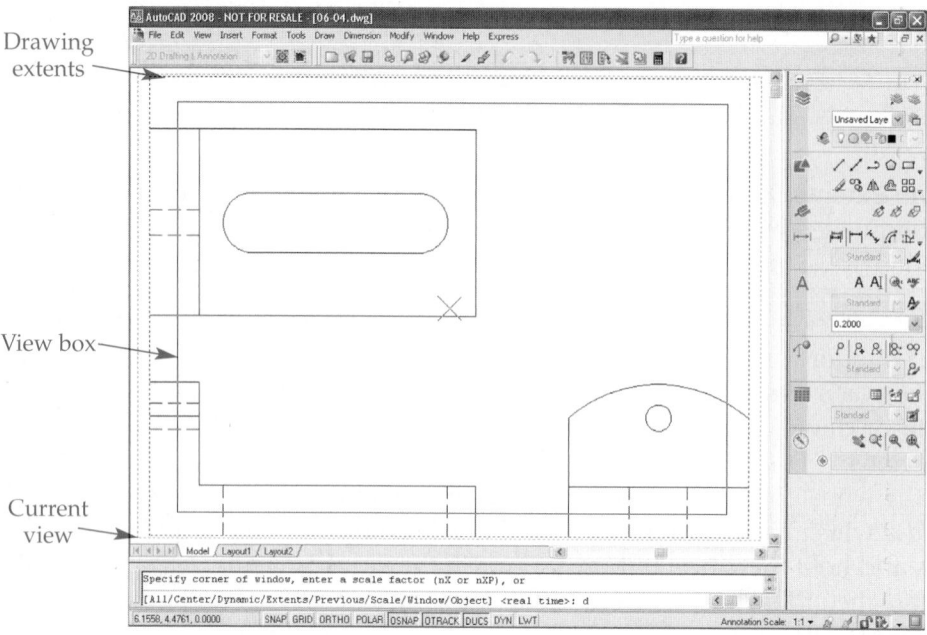

Drawing extents

View box

Current view

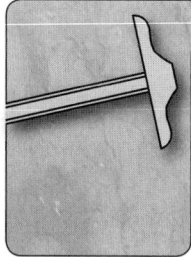

Aerial View is a navigation tool that uses a separate window to specify the display. The **Aerial View** window is accessed by picking **View > Aerial View**. Use the box displayed within the **Aerial View** window to define the display. Realtime zooming and panning are typically more effective and do not occupy any of your screen area (as the **Aerial View** window does).

Exercise 6-1
Complete the exercise on the Student CD.

panning: Moving a zoomed drawing around so that different parts of it are visible on-screen.

realtime pan: A panning operation in which you can see the drawing move on the screen as you pan.

Moving around the Display Screen

The **PAN** command is used to move your viewpoint around the drawing without changing the magnification factor. *Panning* is similar to looking through a camera lens and moving the camera across the drawing. It is typically used in conjunction with the **ZOOM** command to change the display.

Performing Realtime Pan

A *realtime pan* allows you to see the drawing move on the screen as you pan. It is the quickest and easiest method of adjusting the view around the objects on the screen. To activate realtime panning, pick **View > Pan > Realtime**, pick the **Pan Realtime** button on the **2D Navigate** control panel of the **Dashboard**, or type P or PAN.

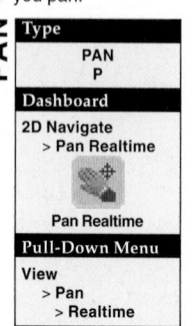

PAN

Type
PAN
P

Dashboard
2D Navigate
> Pan Realtime

Pan Realtime

Pull-Down Menu
View
> Pan
> Realtime

AutoCAD and Its Applications—Basics

The **Realtime Pan** button is also available on the **Standard** toolbar in the **AutoCAD Classic** workspace. It is not available on the **Standard Annotation** toolbar in the **2D Drawing and Annotation** workspace. Instead, it is located in the **2D Navigate** control panel of the **Dashboard**.

After starting the command, press and hold the pick button and move the pointing device in the direction you wish to pan. The pan icon of the hand is displayed when a realtime pan is used. A right-click displays the same shortcut menu available for realtime zooming.

Using Scroll Bars to Pan

The scroll bars at the bottom and to the right of the drawing area can also be used to pan the display. See **Figure 6-5**. Pick the arrows at the end of the scroll bar to pan in small increments. Select the scroll bar itself to pan in larger increments. Position the cursor over the box in the scroll bar, pick and hold the left mouse button, and then move the mouse to see realtime panning in the horizontal or vertical direction.

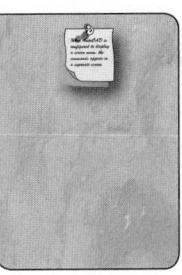

The drawing area scroll bars can be activated and deactivated by selecting the **Display scroll bars in drawing window** option in the **Window Elements** area of the **Display** tab of the **Options** dialog box. To access this dialog box, select **Tools** > **Options...** from the pull-down menu or right-click in the drawing area and select **Options...** from the shortcut menu.

Figure 6-5.
The drawing area scroll bars can be used for panning operations.

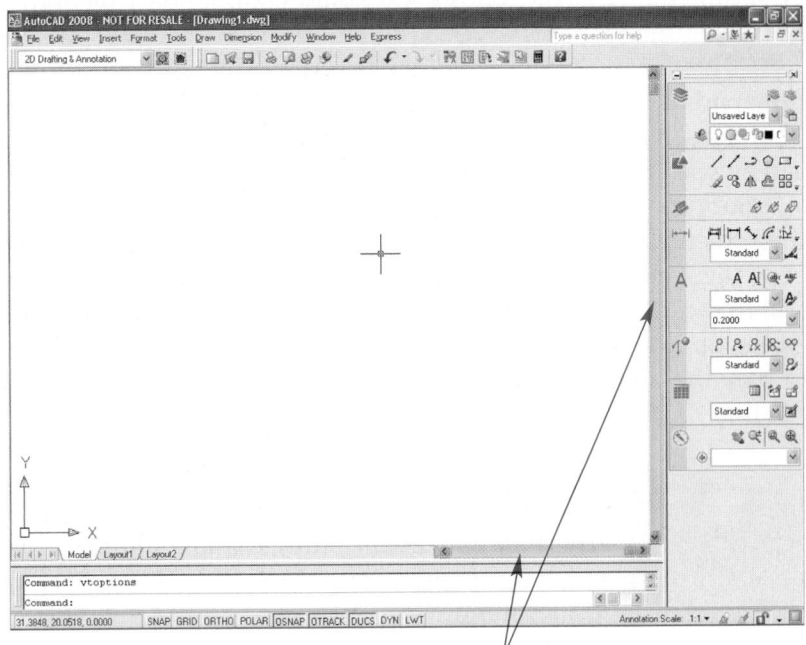

Use vertical and horizontal
scroll bars to pan drawing

Undoing Pan and Zoom Operations

There are times when you are working in one area of a drawing and you need to reference another area for information. It may take a few zoom and pan operations to get to the other area. By using the **UNDO** command, you can get back to the working area of the drawing in just one undo. This is because AutoCAD groups together pan and zoom commands that are operating at the same time. This allows you to pan and zoom around the drawing and then get back to the original view quickly. To use this feature, select **Edit** > **Undo**, pick the **Undo** button from the **Standard Annotation** toolbar, type UNDO, or right-click and select **Undo** from the shortcut menu. This feature is controlled by the **Combine zoom and pan commands** option in the **Undo/Redo** area of the **User Preferences** tab of the **Options** dialog box. Deactivating this option makes each pan and zoom operation count as an individual undo even if they are performed at the same time.

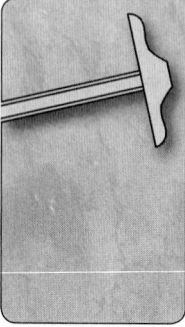

LEGACY NOTE

AutoCAD provides two additional panning tools: pan displacement and pan presets. These options are available in the **View** > **Pan** cascading menu. You specify the pan displacement by picking two points, with the drawing panning so that the first point is relocated to the second point. Pick the **Point** option to specify a pan displacement. The pan presets options—**Left**, **Right**, **Up**, and **Down**—pan the drawing in the selected direction by a set increment. Realtime panning is more efficient than pan displacement and pan presets.

Using Transparent Display Commands

To begin a new command, you usually need to complete or cancel the current command. Most menu picks automatically cancel the command in progress before initiating the new one. However, some commands function without canceling an active command.

transparent command: A command that can be used while another command is in progress.

A *transparent command* temporarily interrupts the active command. After the transparent command is completed, the command that was interrupted is resumed. Therefore, it is not necessary to cancel the initial command. Many display commands can be used transparently, including **REDRAW**, **PAN**, and **ZOOM**.

Suppose that while drawing a line, you need to place one end somewhere off the screen. One option is to cancel the **LINE** command, zoom out to see more of the drawing, and select **LINE** again. A more efficient method is to use **PAN** or **ZOOM** while still in the **LINE** command. To do so, begin the **LINE** command and pick the first point. At the Specify next point: prompt, pick the **Pan** or **Zoom** button or use the wheel mouse to pan and zoom. When the drawing is displayed correctly, pick the second point of the line.

PROFESSIONAL TIP

The **Pan** and **Zoom** buttons and pull-down menu selections activate commands transparently. The wheel mouse also works transparently.

You can also activate commands transparently by typing. To do so, type an apostrophe (') before the command name. For example, to enter the transparent **ZOOM** command, type 'Z or 'ZOOM.

A transparent redraw is executed when **Redraw** is picked from the **View** pull-down menu. Commands such as **GRID**, **SNAP**, and **ORTHO** can be used transparently, but it is quicker to activate these modes with the appropriate function keys or from the status bar.

Redrawing and Regenerating the Screen

The **REDRAW** command is used to refresh the display of objects. To redraw the screen, select **View** > **Redraw** or type R or REDRAW. The **REDRAW** command simply refreshes the current screen. To recalculate all drawing object coordinates and regenerate the display based on the current zoom magnification, regenerate the screen with the **REGEN** command. For example, if you have zoomed in and curved objects appear as straight segments, use **REGEN** to smooth the curves. To access the **REGEN** command, pick **View** > **Regen** or type RE or REGEN. The screen is immediately regenerated.

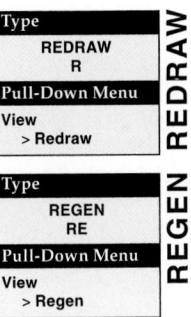

Type
REDRAW
R
Pull-Down Menu
View
> Redraw

REDRAW

Type
REGEN
RE
Pull-Down Menu
View
> Regen

REGEN

Setting View Resolution

AutoCAD can save you time on zooming and panning at the expense of display accuracy. AutoCAD can also provide a highly accurate display at the expense of zoom and pan speed. The main factor is the view resolution.

The *view resolution* controls the number of lines used to draw circles and arcs. High resolution values display smooth circles and arcs. Low resolution values display segmented approximations of circles and arcs. The view resolution can be set in the **Options** dialog box. To access this dialog box, pick **Tools** > **Options...** from the pull-down menu and pick the **Display** tab. In the **Display resolution** area in the upper-right corner of the dialog box is the **Arc and circle smoothness** text box. This contains the current **VIEWRES** setting. See **Figure 6-6**.

The **VIEWRES** setting can vary between 1 and 20000. The default setting is 1000, which produces relatively smooth circles. A number smaller than 1000 causes circles and arcs to be drawn with fewer vectors (straight lines). See **Figure 6-7**. A number larger than 1000 causes more vectors to be included in the circles.

It is important to remember that the **VIEWRES** setting is a display function only and has no effect on the plotted drawing. A drawing is plotted using an optimum number of vectors for circles and arcs. In other words, even if a circle you draw looks like a polygon in the drawing area before **REGEN** is used, it will still look like a circle when the drawing is plotted.

view resolution: A setting that controls the number of line segments AutoCAD uses to create circles and arcs.

You can change the **VIEWRES** setting by typing VIEWRES. A Do you want fast zooms? prompt appears. This prompt is no longer useful, but remains in AutoCAD so programs written for earlier versions will still function properly.

Figure 6-6.
The view resolution (**VIEWRES** variable) can be set in the **Options** dialog box.

Change number to change the view resolution (**VIEWRES**)

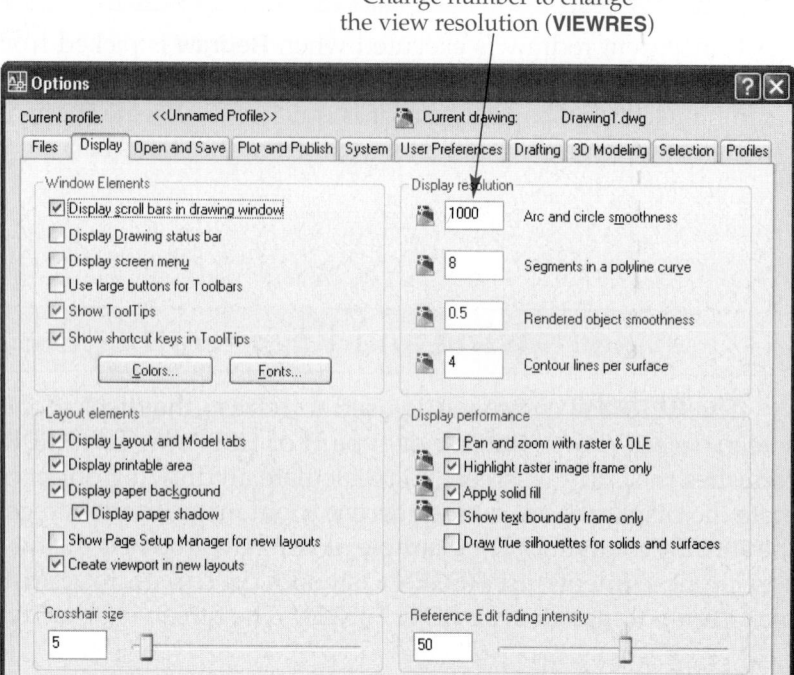

Figure 6-7.
The higher the **VIEWRES** value, the smoother a circle will appear.

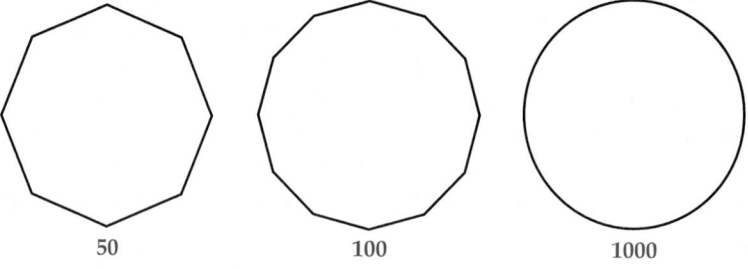

50   100   1000

Exercise 6-2
Complete the exercise on the Student CD.

Creating Your Own Working Views

On a large drawing with a number of separate details, using the **ZOOM** and **PAN** commands can be time-consuming. Being able to specify a certain part of the drawing quickly is much easier. This is possible with the **View Manager**, which allows you to create named views of any area of the drawing. A view can be a portion of the drawing, such as the upper-left quadrant, or it can represent an enlarged area. After the view is created, you can instruct AutoCAD to display it at any time.

View Manager

The **View Manager** can be accessed by picking the **Named Views** button in the **View** toolbar, selecting **View** > **Named Views...** from the pull-down menu, or typing V, VIEW, or DDVIEW. The left side of the **View Manager** contains a list of view types, or nodes. See **Figure 6-8**. Each node can be expanded, except **Current**, to reveal any saved views:

- **Current.** Displays the properties of the current view.
- **Model Views.** Contains a list of saved model views.
- **Layout Views.** Contains a list of saved layout views.
- **Preset Views.** Lists all preset orthogonal and isometric views.

Picking one of the view nodes displays information about the view type. The right side of the **View Manager** contains buttons to control or modify the selected view or view type. These actions are also available in a shortcut menu when you right-click on the view or view type. Select the **New...** option to open the **New View** dialog box.

Picking one of the view names causes the middle area of the dialog box to display information related to the current view. See **Figure 6-9**. The first section, **General**, contains details such as the name of the view, layer settings saved with the view, and other settings pertinent to the type of view. This section is not visible while the **Current** node is selected. The settings in the **View** section include camera position, target position, and perspective status. The **Clipping** section controls front plane and back plane location and the clipping status. Some of these items will be covered in more detail in this chapter; others are reserved for later chapters, where the information is more relevant.

The lower-right corner of the **View Manager** shows a preview image of the selected view. This image is only visible when one of the named model or layout views is selected.

Preset views

The **Preset Views** node is used to choose one of the ten preset views. Notice in **Figure 6-9** that the icons highlight the side of the drawing that will be viewed. The orthogonal views include Top, Bottom, Front, Back, Left, and Right. Picking any of these icons and pressing the **Set Current** button changes the view in AutoCAD so you are looking at your drawing from the selected direction. The preset isometric

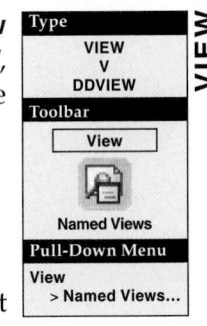

Figure 6-8.
The view nodes of the **View Manager** dialog box help organize saved and preset drawing views.

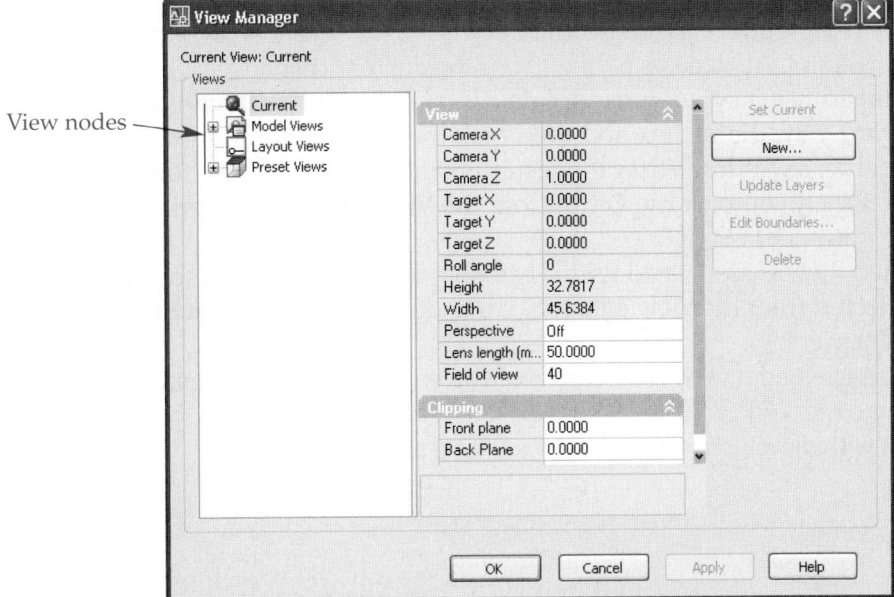

Figure 6-9.
Select a named view to see its properties and a preview image.

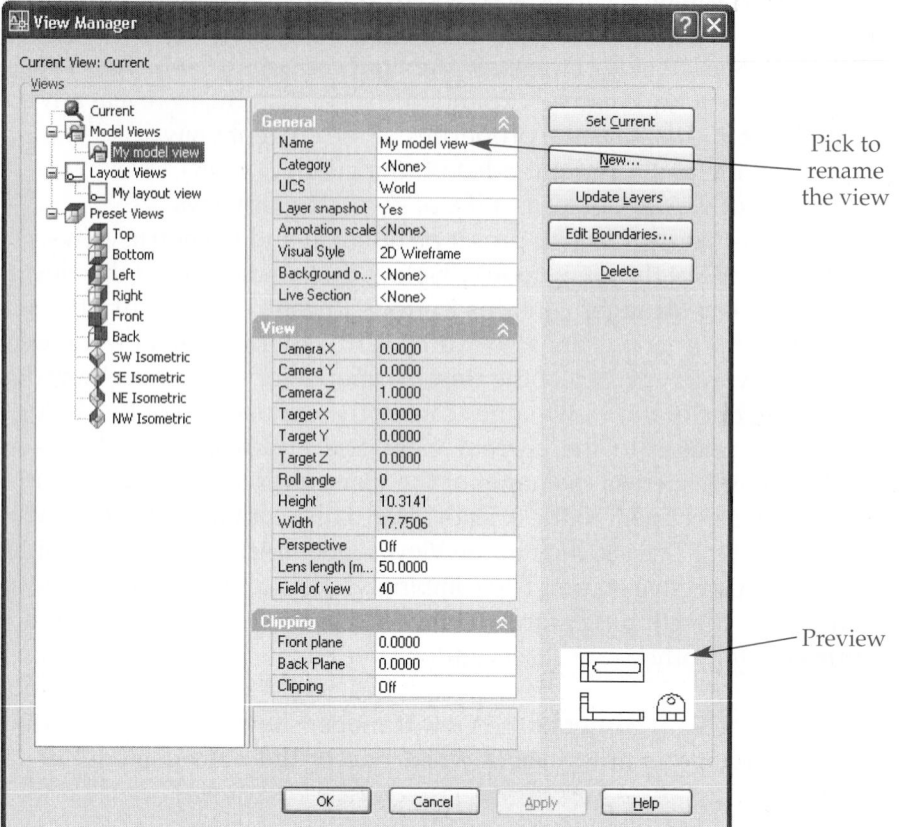

Pick to
rename
the view

Preview

views include Southwest, Southeast, Northeast, and Northwest. These views can also be selected from the **View** > **3D Views** cascading menu or from the **View** toolbar. See **Figure 6-10.** Selecting any of these icons displays a 3D (isometric) view of the drawing. Orthogonal and isometric views are covered in greater depth in *AutoCAD and Its Applications—Advanced.*

New view

If you want to save the current display as a view, pick the **New...** button to access the **New View** dialog box. Type the desired view name in the **View name:** edit box. The **Current display** radio button is the default. See **Figure 6-11.** Click **OK** to add the view name to the list. AutoCAD creates a view from the current display.

If you want to use a window to define the view, pick the **Define window** radio button in the **New View** dialog box and then pick the **Define view window** button. Pick two points to define a window. After the second corner is selected, the **New View** dialog box reappears. When you pick the **OK** button, the **View Manager** is updated to reflect the new view.

If the named view is associated with a category in the **Sheet Set Manager**, the category can be selected from the **View category** drop-down list. The **Sheet Set Manager** is discussed in Chapter 29.

When you save a new view, you can save the current layer settings with it. These layer settings are recalled each time the view is set current. To do this, check the **Save layer snapshot with view** check box.

Figure 6-10.
Preset orthographic and isometric views can also be selected in the **3D Views** cascading menu in the **View** pull-down menu or from the **View** toolbar.

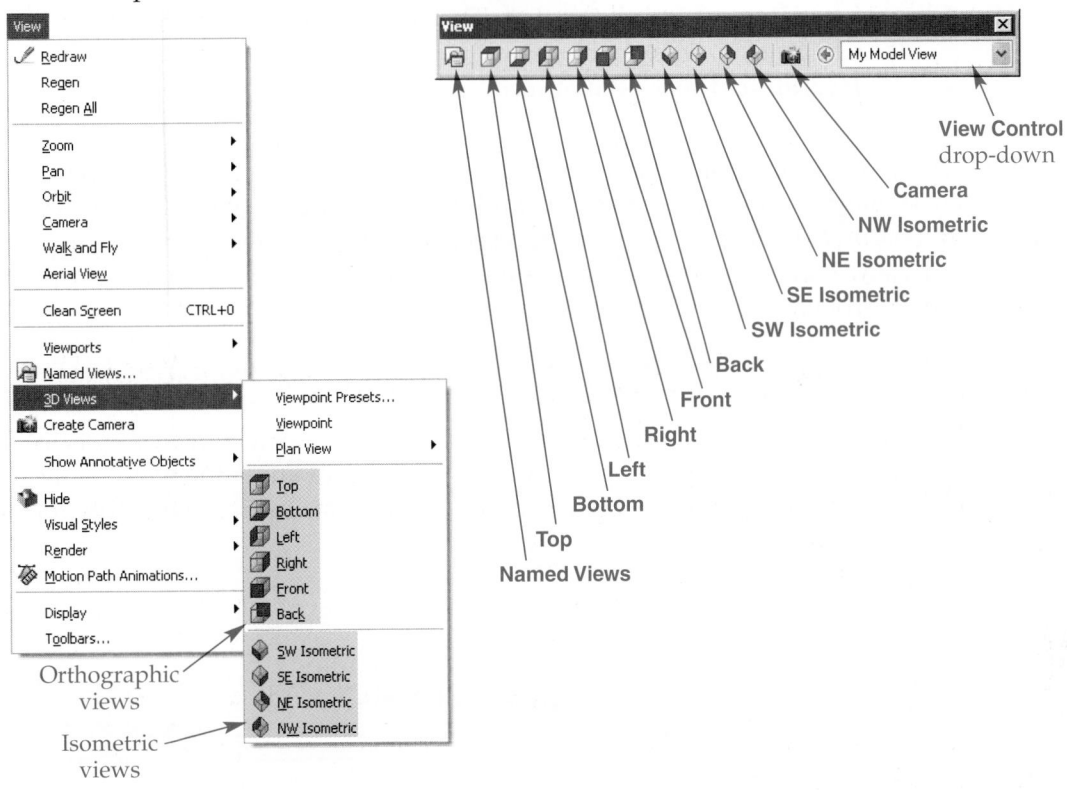

Figure 6-11.
In the **New View** dialog box, you can save the current display as a view or define a window to create a view.

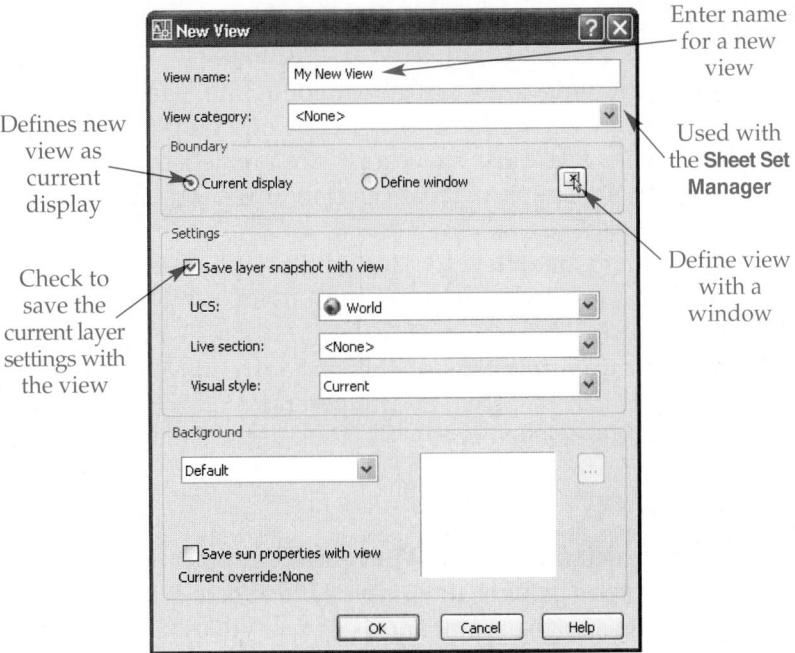

NOTE

It is possible to save a named UCS (user coordinate system) to a new view when it is created. The **UCS** command is introduced in Chapter 8 of this textbook and covered in depth in *AutoCAD and Its Applications—Advanced.*

To display one of the listed views, pick its name from the list in the **Views** area of the **View Manager** and pick the **Set Current** button. The name of the current view appears in the **Current View:** label above the **Views** area. Pick the **OK** button to display the selected view. You can also select a named view using the drop-down list in the **2D Navigate** control panel of the **Dashboard**.

PROFESSIONAL TIP

Part of your project planning should include view names. A consistent naming system guarantees that all users know the view names without having to list them. The views can be set as part of the template drawings.

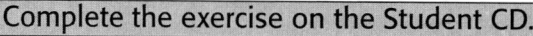

Exercise 6-3

Complete the exercise on the Student CD.

Tiled Viewports

The model space drawing area can be divided into various viewports. These viewports are called *tiled viewports*. Another type of viewport, *floating viewports*, can be created in a layout tab. Tiled viewports are created in model space; floating viewports are created in paper space. Floating viewports and layouts are described in Chapter 25.

tiled viewports:
Viewports created in model space.

floating viewports:
Viewports created in paper space.

By default, there is only one viewport in the drawing area. Additional viewports can be added. The edges of tiled viewports butt against one another like floor tile. Tiled viewports cannot overlap.

Viewports contain different views of the same drawing, displayed at the same time. Only one viewport can be active at any given time. The active viewport has a bold outline around its edges. See **Figure 6-12**.

Creating Tiled Viewports

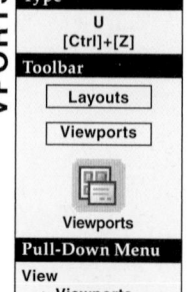

Viewports can be created using the **Viewports** dialog box. See **Figure 6-13**. You can access this dialog box by picking the **Display Viewports Dialog** button from either the **Layouts** or **Viewports** toolbar. You can also type VPORTS, or select **View** > **New Viewports** > **Viewports...** from the pull-down menu.

The **New Viewports** tab is shown in **Figure 6-13**. The **Standard viewports:** list contains many preset viewport configurations. The configuration name identifies the number of viewports and the arrangement or location of the largest viewport. These configurations are shown in **Figure 6-14**. When you select one, a preview appears in the **Preview** area. Select *Active Model Configuration* to preview the current configuration.

Figure 6-12.
An example of three tiled viewports in model space. All viewports contain the same objects, but the display in each viewport can be unique.

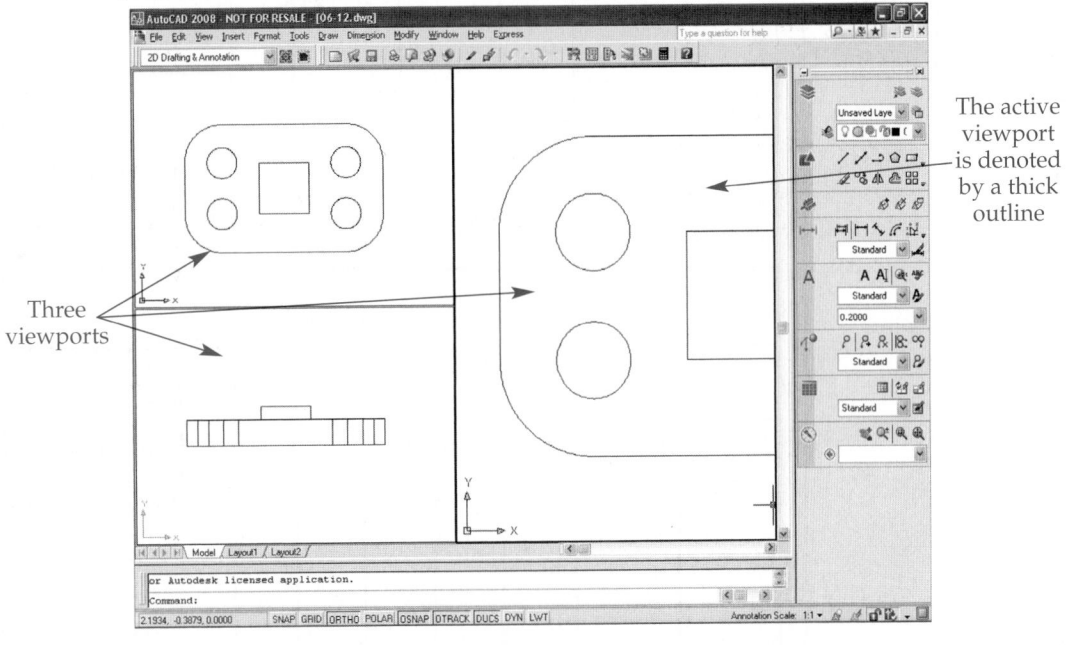

The active viewport is denoted by a thick outline

Three viewports

Figure 6-13.
Specify the number and arrangement of tiled viewports in the **New Viewports** tab of the **Viewports** dialog box.

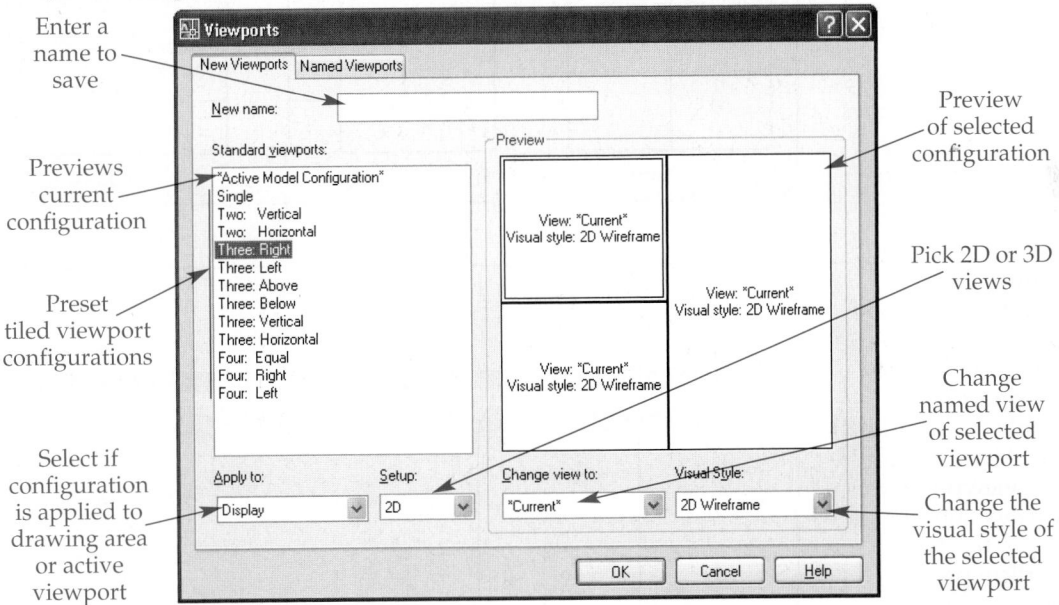

Enter a name to save

Previews current configuration

Preset tiled viewport configurations

Select if configuration is applied to drawing area or active viewport

Preview of selected configuration

Pick 2D or 3D views

Change named view of selected viewport

Change the visual style of the selected viewport

If none of the preset configurations fits your needs, you can create a unique viewport configuration and save it. Enter a name in the **New name:** text box. When you pick the **OK** button, the new named viewport configuration is recorded in the **Named Viewports** tab. Use a descriptive name. For example, if you are going to configure four viewports, you might name this as Four Viewports.

The **Apply to:** drop-down list allows you to specify whether the viewport configuration is applied to the graphics window or to the active viewport only. Select **Display** to have the configuration applied to the entire drawing area. Select **Current Viewport** to apply the new configuration in the active viewport only. See **Figure 6-15.**

Figure 6-14.
Preset tiled viewport configurations are available in the **New Viewports** tab of the **Viewports** dialog box.

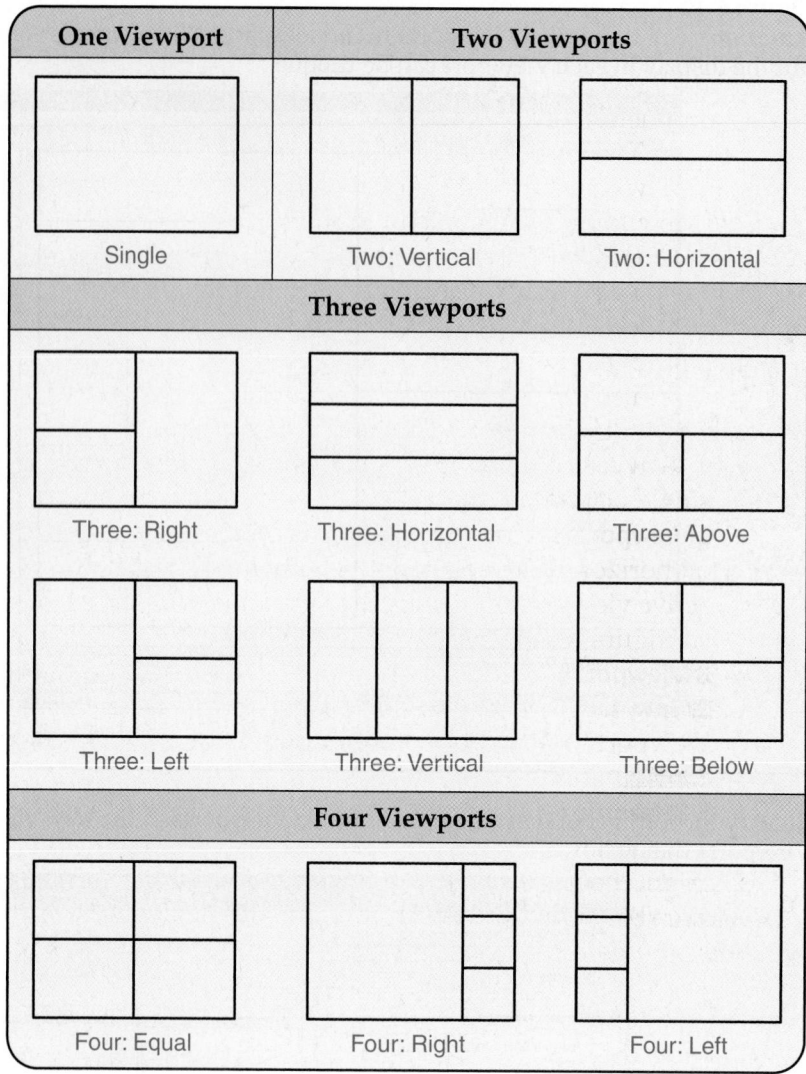

Figure 6-15.
You can subdivide a viewport by choosing **Current Viewport** in the **Apply to:** drop-down list. Here, the top-left viewport was further subdivided using the **Two: Vertical** preset configuration.

Configuration applied to active viewport

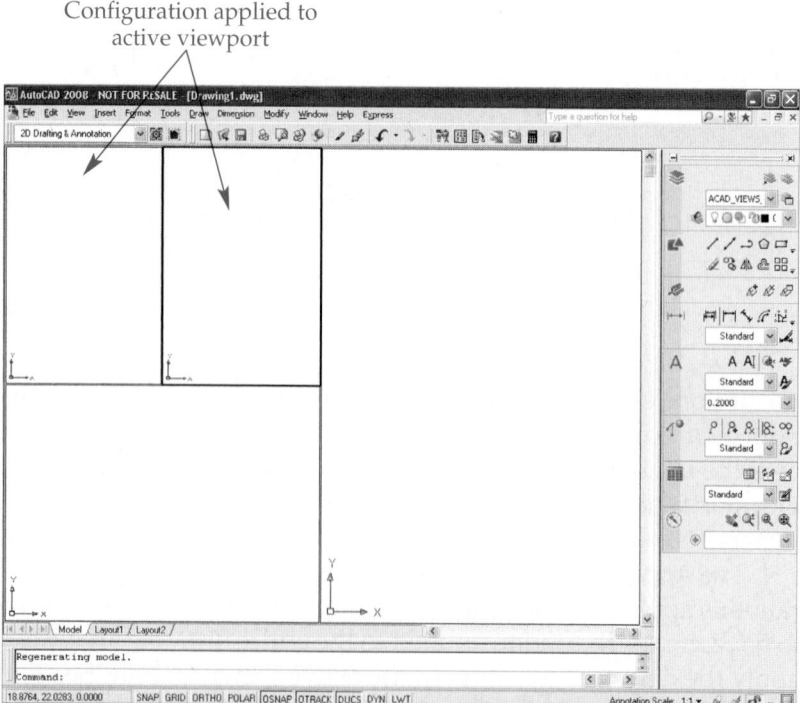

The default setting in the **Setup:** drop-down list is **2D**. When this is selected, all viewports show the top view of the drawing. If the **3D** option is selected, the different viewports display various 3D views of the drawing. At least one viewport is set up with an isometric view. The other viewports have different views, such as a top view or side view. The viewpoint is displayed within the viewport in the **Preview** image. To change a view in a viewport, pick the viewport in the **Preview** image and then select the new viewpoint from the **Change view to:** drop-down list.

The **Named Viewports** tab displays the names of saved viewport configurations and gives you a preview of each. See **Figure 6-16.** Select the named viewport configuration and pick **OK** to apply it to the drawing area. Named viewport configurations cannot be applied to the active viewport only.

You can also select a viewport configuration from the **View** > **Viewports** cascading menu, shown in **Figure 6-17.** The following configuration options are available:

- **1 Viewport.** This option replaces the current viewport configuration with a single viewport.
- **2 Viewports.** When you select this option, you are prompted to select a vertical or horizontal arrangement. The arrangement you choose is applied to the active viewport only. This configuration does not replace the current viewport configuration.
- **3 Viewports.** The following options are available: **Horizontal**, **Vertical**, **Above**, **Below**, **Left**, and **Right**. The arrangement you choose is applied to the active viewport only. This configuration does not replace the current viewport configuration.
- **4 Viewports.** This option creates four equal viewports within the active viewport.

Once you have selected the viewport configuration and returned to the drawing area, move the pointing device around and notice that only the active viewport contains crosshairs. The cursor is an arrow in the other viewports. To make a different viewport active, move the pointer into it and pick.

As you draw in one viewport, the image is displayed in all viewports. Try drawing lines and other shapes and notice how the viewports are affected. Use a display command, such as **ZOOM**, in the active viewport and notice the results. Only the active viewport reflects the use of the **ZOOM** command.

Figure 6-16.
The **Named Viewports** tab displays custom viewports.

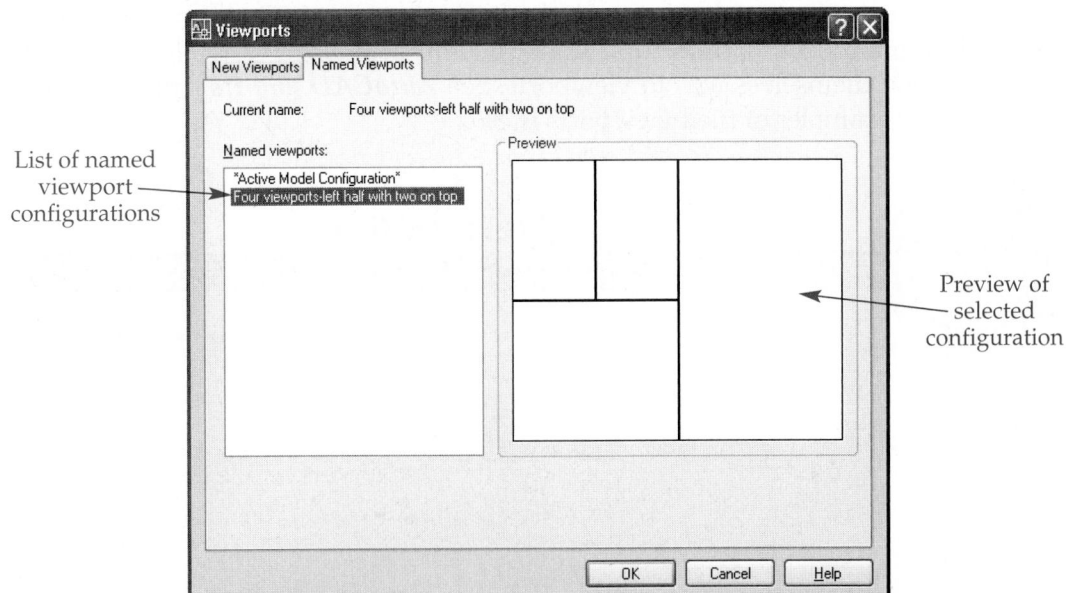

List of named viewport configurations

Preview of selected configuration

Figure 6-17.
Some **Viewports** options are available from the **View** pull-down menu.

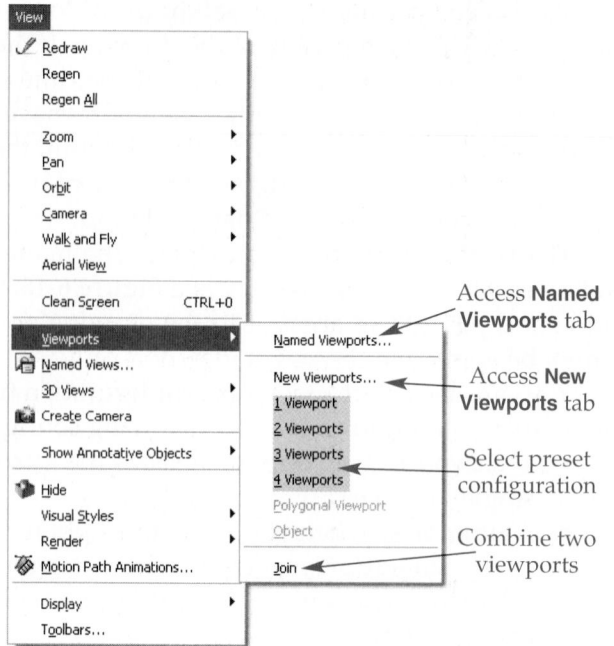

Access **Named Viewports** tab

Access **New Viewports** tab

Select preset configuration

Combine two viewports

If you want to join two viewports together, you can do so by picking **View** > **Viewports** > **Join**. AutoCAD prompts you to select the dominant viewport. Select the viewport that has the view you want to keep in the joined viewport. Next, select the viewport that you want to join with the dominant viewport. AutoCAD "glues" the two viewports together and retains the dominant view.

NOTE

The two viewports you are joining cannot create an L-shape viewport. In other words, the adjoining edges of the viewports must be the same size in order to join them.

Uses of Tiled Viewports

Viewports in model space can be used for both 2D and 3D drawings. They are limited only by your imagination and need. The nature of 2D drawings, whether mechanical multiview, architectural construction details, or unscaled schematic drawings, lend themselves well to viewports. See *AutoCAD and Its Applications—Advanced* for examples of tiled viewports in 3D.

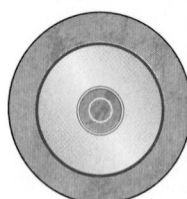

Exercise 6-4
Complete the exercise on the Student CD.

Redrawing and Regenerating Viewports

Since each viewport is a separate screen, you can redraw or regenerate a single viewport at a time without affecting the others. In fact, the **REGEN** and **REDRAW** commands work only in the current viewport. To redraw all viewports, use the **REDRAWALL** command or pick **View > Redraw**. If you need to regenerate all viewports, use the **REGENALL** command or pick **View > Regen All**.

Controlling Automatic Regeneration

When developing a drawing, you may use a command that changes certain aspects of the objects. When this occurs, AutoCAD does an automatic regeneration to update the objects. This may not be of concern when you work on small drawings, but this regeneration may take considerable time on large and complex drawings. In addition, it may not be necessary to have a regeneration of the drawing at these times. If this is the case, set the **REGENAUTO** command to off.

> Command: **REGENAUTO**↵
> Enter mode [ON/OFF] <*current*>: **OFF**↵
> Command:

Some of the commands that may automatically cause a regeneration are **PLAN**, **HIDE**, and **VIEW Restore**.

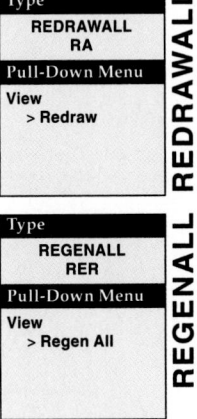

Controlling the Order of Display

Drawings can have objects that overlap each other, but since most objects are made of thin lines, the overlap is unseen. Controlling the order of display is better illustrated with an object that has some width, such as a donut. See **Figure 6-18**. The bracket was drawn before the donuts were added. The donuts, and all other objects, can be moved above or below selected objects and to the front or back of all objects.

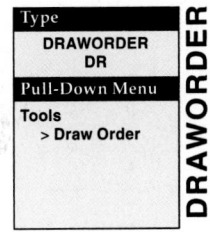

Figure 6-18.
The order of objects can be changed to put them in under or above the other objects.

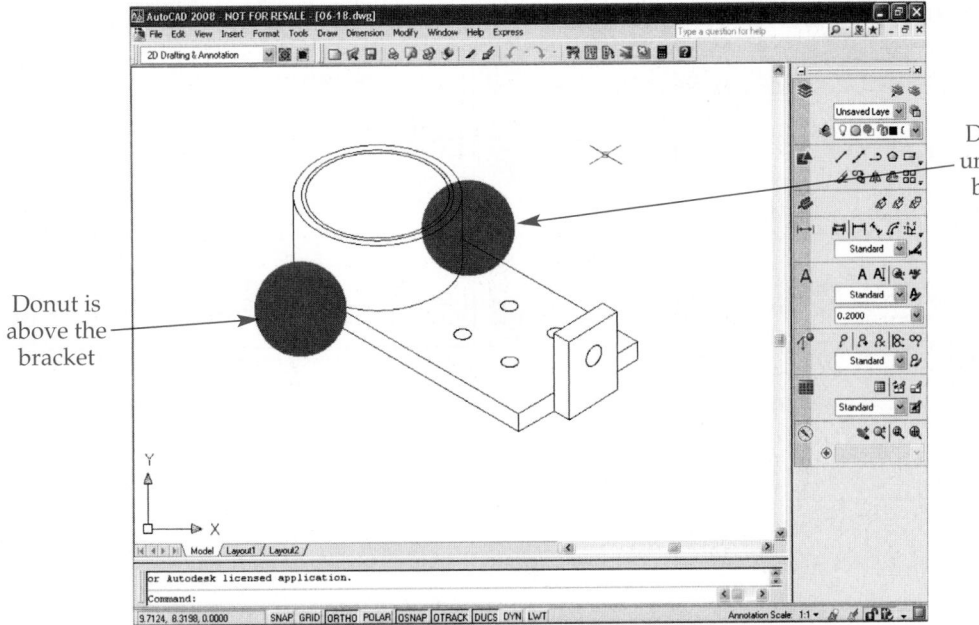

Donut is under the bracket

Donut is above the bracket

To change the order of an object, use the **DRAWORDER** command, pick **Tools** > **Draw Order** from the pull-down menu, pick a button in the **Draw Order** toolbar, or type DR or DRAWORDER. You can also just pick an object to select it, right-click, and select **Draw Order** from the shortcut menu. The order and arrangement functions are handled by the following **DRAWORDER** options:

- **Above objects.** The selected object is moved above the reference object.
- **Under objects.** The selected object is moved below the reference object.
- **Front.** The selected object is placed at the front of the drawing.
- **Back.** The selected object is placed at the back of the drawing.

Clearing the Screen

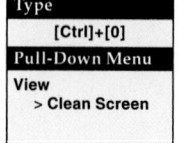

The AutoCAD window can become crowded in the course of a drawing session. Each toolbar and palette displayed reduces the size of the drawing area. As the drawing area gets smaller, less of the drawing is visible. This can make drafting difficult. You can quickly maximize the size of the drawing area using the **Clean Screen** tool.

This tool clears the AutoCAD window of all toolbars, modeless dialog boxes, and title bars. See **Figure 6-19.** The **Clean Screen** tool is accessed by picking **View** > **Clean Screen** or using the [Ctrl]+[0] (zero) key combination. You can also pick the **Clean Screen** button at the right end of the status bar. To return to the normal display, use the [Ctrl]+[0] (zero) key combination or pick the **Clean Screen** button in the status bar.

PROFESSIONAL TIP

The **Clean Screen** tool can be helpful when you have multiple drawings displayed. Only the active drawing is displayed when the **Clean Screen** tool is used. This allows you to work more efficiently within one of the drawings. You can use the **Window** pull-down menu options to switch between drawings.

Figure 6-19.
Using the **Clean Screen** tool. A—Initial display with toolbars and **Dashboard** displayed. B—Display after using the **Clean Screen** tool.

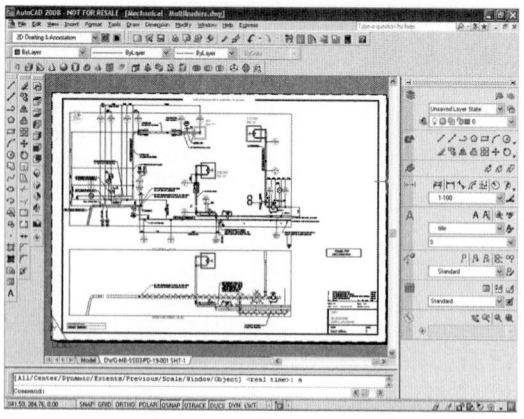
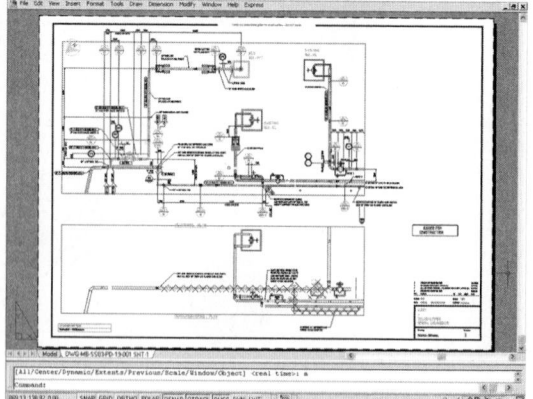

A   B

Template Development
Chapter 6

Drawing templates are easier to use if they show the entire drawing extents when they are first opened. View resolution may also need to be increased for some drawing applications. Refer to the Student CD for detailed instructions to incorporate these elements into your mechanical, architectural, and civil drawing templates.

Chapter Test

Answer the following questions. Write your answers on a separate sheet of paper or complete the electronic chapter test on the Student CD.

1. Give the proper command option and value to automatically zoom to a 2X scale factor.
2. What is the difference between **ZOOM Extents** and **ZOOM All**?
3. During the drawing process, when should you use **ZOOM**?
4. How many different boxes are displayed during the **ZOOM Dynamic** command?
5. When using the **ZOOM Dynamic** option, what represents the current view?
6. What is the purpose of the **PAN** command?
7. Explain how scroll bars can be used to pan the drawing display.
8. How is a transparent display command entered at the keyboard?
9. What is the difference between the **REDRAW** and **REGEN** commands?
10. What is *view resolution*?
11. In which dialog box is circle smoothness set?
12. How do you create a named view of the current screen display?
13. How do you display an existing view?
14. How would you obtain a listing of existing views?
15. What type of viewport is created in model space?
16. What type of viewport is created in paper space?
17. What is the purpose of the **Preview** area of the **Viewports** dialog box?
18. Explain the procedures and conditions that need to exist when joining viewports.
19. Which command regenerates all of the viewports?
20. Which command changes the order in which objects are displayed in a drawing?

Drawing Problems

1. Open the drawing named 3D House.dwg found in the AutoCAD 2008\Sample folder.
   Perform the following display functions on the drawing:
   A. **ZOOM Extents**.
   B. Create a view named Rendering.
   C. Replace the view with the Top view.
   D. Create a view named Plan using **Define Window** in the **New View** dialog box.
   E. Use realtime pan and realtime zoom to create a display of the dining room in the top-right area of the Plan view.
   F. Create a view of this display named Dining Room.
   G. Display the view named Rendering.
   H. Save the drawing as P6-1.

2. Use the **Select Template** dialog box to load the Tutorial-iMfg.dwt template or another mechanical template you have access to that contains a border and title block. Do the following:
   A. Zoom into the title block area. Create and save a view named Title.
   B. Zoom to the extents of the drawing and create and save a view named All.
   C. Determine the areas of the drawing that will contain notes, parts list, and revisions. Zoom into these areas and create views with appropriate names such as Notes, Partlist, and Revisions.
   D. Divide the drawing area into commonly used multiview sections. Save the views with descriptive names such as Top, Front, Rightside, and Leftside.
   E. Restore the view named All.
   F. Save the drawing as P6-2.

3. Use the Select **Template dialog** box to load the Tutorial-iArch.dwt template or another architectural drafting template you have access to that contains a border and title block. Do the following:
   A. Zoom into the title block area. Create and save a view named Title.
   B. Zoom to the extents of the drawing and create and save a view named All.
   C. Determine the area of the drawing that will contain notes, schedules, or revisions. Zoom into these areas and create views with appropriate names such as Notes, Schedules, and Revisions.
   D. Restore the view named All.
   E. Save the drawing as P6-3.

Object Snaps and AutoTracking

Learning Objectives

After completing this chapter, you will be able to do the following:

✓ Use object snap to create precision drawings.
✓ Use object snap overrides for single point selections.
✓ Set running object snap modes for continuous use.
✓ Use the AutoSnap features to speed up point specifications.
✓ Adjust marker size.
✓ Use AutoTrack and temporary tracking modes to locate points relative to other points in a drawing.

This chapter explains how the powerful object snap and AutoTrack™ features are used when creating and editing your drawing. *Osnap* means *object snap*. Object snap can be used to visually preview and confirm point options prior to selection. AutoTrack creates and deletes construction lines automatically. After these features are explained, you will learn how to take advantage of their strengths when you create geometry.

Object Snap

Object snap is one of the most useful tools in AutoCAD. It increases your drafting performance and accuracy. *Snapping* is the process of picking a point near the intended position to have the crosshairs "snap" exactly to the specific point.

Object snap modes identify the object snap point. For instance, the **Endpoint** object snap mode automatically selects a line's endpoint, and the **Midpoint** object snap mode automatically selects a line's midpoint. The AutoSnap™ feature provides visual cues related to the active object snap modes. There are two methods of activating object snap modes: running object snaps and snap overrides. These topics are covered in more detail in the following sections.

The AutoSnap feature is enabled by default. With AutoSnap active, visual cues are displayed while snapping. This helps you visualize and confirm candidate points for object snap. These visual cues appear as *markers* displayed at the current selection point. **Figure 7-1** shows two examples of visual cues provided by AutoSnap. The visual cue for an **Endpoint** object snap is a square that appears when the crosshairs is

snapping: Picking a point near the intended position to have the crosshairs "snap" exactly to the specific point.

markers: Visual cues to confirm points for object snap.

Figure 7-1.
AutoSnap displays markers and related tooltips for object snap modes.

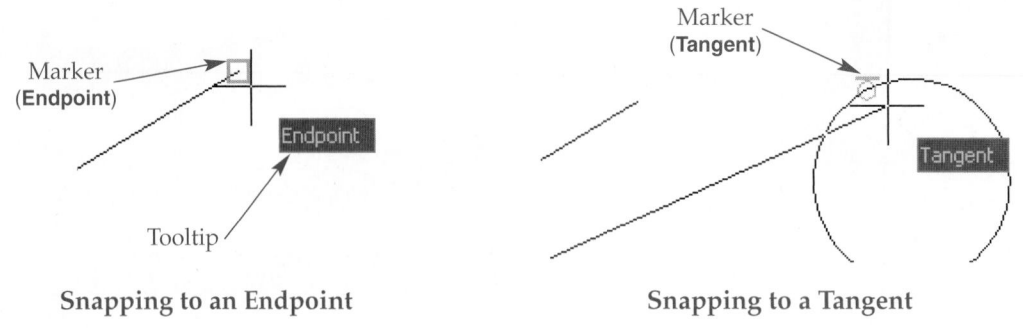

Snapping to an Endpoint   Snapping to a Tangent

placed close to the line object. After a brief pause, a tooltip is displayed, indicating the object snap mode. The AutoSnap symbol for a tangency point is shown as a circle with a tangent horizontal line.

Object Snap Modes

The table in **Figure 7-2** summarizes the object snap modes. Included with each mode is the marker that appears on-screen and its button from the **Object Snap** toolbar. Each object snap mode selects a different portion of an object.

> **PROFESSIONAL TIP**
>
> Remember that object snap overrides are not commands. They are, however, used in conjunction with commands. If you type MID when no command is active, for example, AutoCAD displays the following error message: Unknown command "MID". Press F1 for help.

Practice with the different object snap modes to find the ones that work best in various situations. Be sure to clear the previous object snap mode before activating the next one. Object snaps can be used during many commands, such as **LINE**, **CIRCLE**, **ARC**, **MOVE**, **COPY**, and **INSERT**. The most common uses for object snaps are discussed in the following sections.

Endpoint object snap

In many cases, you need to connect new geometry to the endpoint of an existing line or arc. Select the **Endpoint** object snap mode and move the crosshairs past the midpoint of the line or arc, toward the end to be picked. A small square marks the endpoint that will be picked. Pick to begin drawing the new object. See **Figure 7-3.**

The **Endpoint** object snap can be used to quickly select the endpoints of all types of lines and arcs. It is often selected as a running object snap.

Midpoint object snap

The **Midpoint** object snap mode finds and picks the midpoint of a line, a polyline, or an arc. During a command, type MID, pick the **Snap to Midpoint** button on the **Object Snap** toolbar, or select **Midpoint** from the **Object Snap** shortcut menu to activate this object snap mode. Position the crosshairs near the midpoint of the object. See **Figure 7-4.**

Exercise 7-1
Complete the exercise on the Student CD.

Figure 7-2.
The object snap modes.

Object Snap Modes			
Mode	**Marker**	**Button**	**Description**
Endpoint	□		Finds the nearest endpoint of a line, arc, polyline, elliptical arc, spline, ellipse, ray, solid, or multiline.
Midpoint	△		Finds the middle point of any object having two endpoints, such as a line, polyline, arc, elliptical arc, polyline arc, spline, ray, solid, xline, or multiline.
Center	○		Locates the center point of a radial object, including circles, arcs, ellipses, elliptical arcs, and radial solids.
Quadrant	◇		Picks the closest of the four quadrant points that can be found on circles, arcs, elliptical arcs, ellipses, and radial solids. (Not all of these objects may have all four quadrants.)
Intersection	✕		Picks the closest intersection of two objects.
Apparent Intersection	⊠		Selects a visual intersection between two objects that appear to intersect on screen in the current view, but may not actually intersect each other in 3D space.
Extension	+		Finds a point along the imaginary extension of an existing line, polyline, arc, polyline arc, elliptical arc, spline, ray, xline, solid, or multiline.
Insertion	⊐		Finds the insertion point of text objects and blocks.
Perpendicular	⊢		Finds a point that is perpendicular to an object from the previously picked point.
Parallel	⫽		Used to find any point along an imaginary line parallel to an existing line or polyline.
Tangent	◯		Finds points of tangency between radial and linear objects.
Nearest	⋈		Locates the point on an object closest to the crosshairs.
Node	⊗		Picks a point object drawn with the **POINT**, **DIVIDE**, or **MEASURE** command.
None			Temporarily turns running object snap off during the current selection.

Center object snap

The **Center** object snap mode allows you to snap to the center point of a circle, donut, ellipse, elliptical arc, polyline arc, or arc. During a command, type CEN, pick the **Snap to Center** button on the **Object Snap** toolbar, or pick **Center** from the **Object Snap** shortcut menu.

Be sure to move the crosshairs near the perimeter, not the center point, of the object. For example, when you locate the center of a large circle, the **Center** object snap mode will *not* locate the center if the crosshairs is not near the perimeter of the circle. See **Figure 7-5**.

Figure 7-3.
Using **Endpoint** object snap.

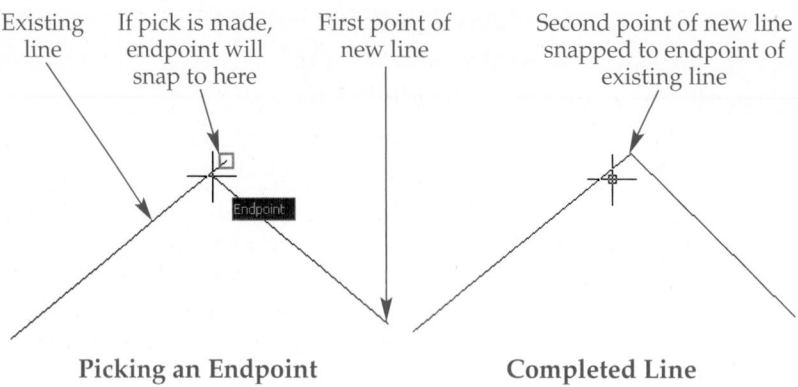

Existing line

If pick is made, endpoint will snap to here

First point of new line

Second point of new line snapped to endpoint of existing line

Picking an Endpoint   **Completed Line**

Figure 7-4.
Using **Midpoint** object snap.

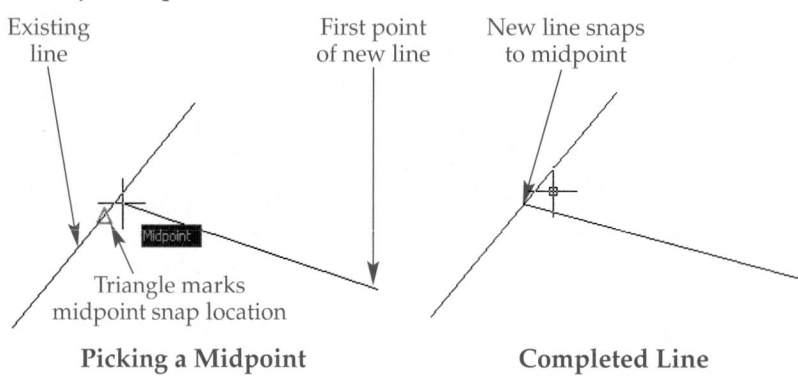

Existing line

First point of new line

New line snaps to midpoint

Triangle marks midpoint snap location

Picking a Midpoint   **Completed Line**

Figure 7-5.
Using **Center** object snap.

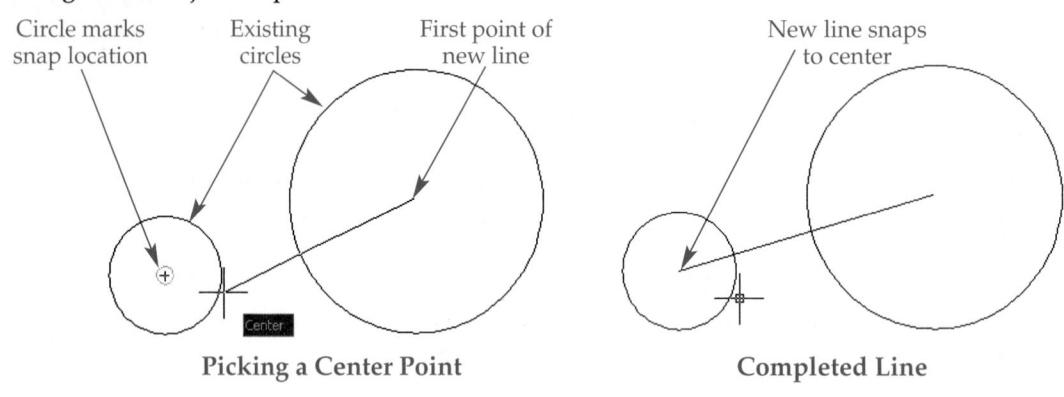

Circle marks snap location

Existing circles

First point of new line

New line snaps to center

Picking a Center Point   **Completed Line**

Quadrant object snap

quadrant: Quarter section of a circle, a donut, or an ellipse.

A *quadrant* is a quarter section of a circle, donut, or ellipse. The **Quadrant** object snap mode finds the 0°, 90°, 180°, and 270° positions on a circle, donut, ellipse, elliptical arc, polyline arc, or arc. See **Figure 7-6.** When picking quadrants, move the crosshairs near the intended quadrant on the circle, donut, ellipse, or arc.

Figure 7-6.
The four quadrant points of a circle can be selected with the **Quadrant** object snap.

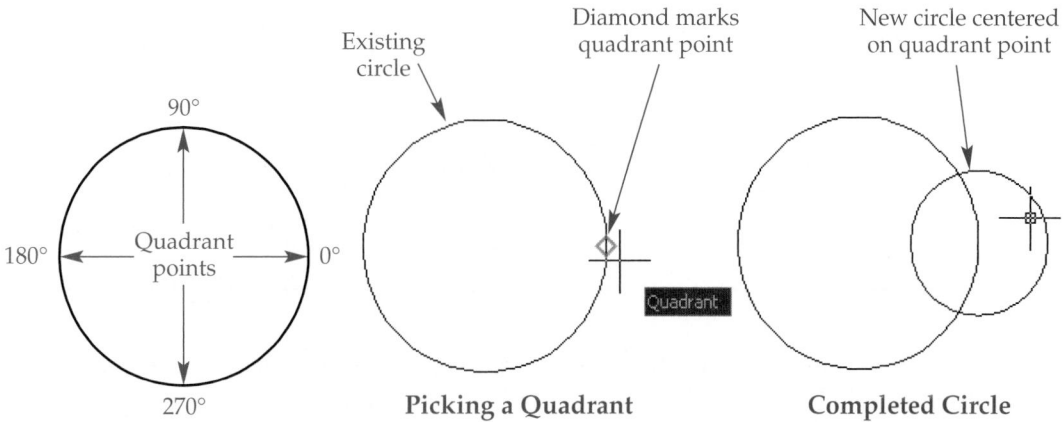

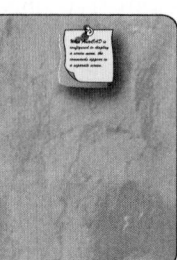

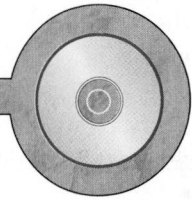

NOTE

Quadrant positions are unaffected by the current angle zero direction, but they always coincide with the current world coordinate system (WCS). The WCS is discussed in Chapter 8. The quadrant points of a circle, a donut, or an arc are at the top, bottom, left, and right, regardless of the rotation of the object. The quadrant points of ellipses and elliptical arcs, however, rotate with the objects.

Exercise 7-2
Complete the exercise on the Student CD.

Intersection object snap

The **Intersection** object snap mode is used to snap to the intersection of two or more objects. This mode is activated by typing INT at the selection prompt, picking the **Snap to Intersection** button on the **Object Snap** toolbar, or picking **Intersection** from the **Object Snap** shortcut menu. Move the crosshairs near the intersection to cause a small "X" to appear at the intersection. See **Figure 7-7.**

Apparent Intersection object snap

The *apparent intersection* is the point where two objects created in 3D space appear to intersect based on the current view. Three-dimensional objects that are far apart may appear to intersect when viewed from certain angles. Whether they intersect or not, this option returns the coordinate point where the objects appear to intersect. This is a valuable option when working with 3D drawings. Creating and editing 3D objects is discussed in *AutoCAD and Its Applications—Advanced*.

apparent intersection: The point where two objects created in 3D space appear to intersect based on the current view.

Extension object snap

The **Extension** object snap mode is used to find any point along the imaginary extension of an existing line, polyline, or polyline arc. This mode is activated by typing EXT at the selection prompt, picking the **Snap to Extension** button on the **Object Snap** toolbar, or picking **Extension** from the **Object Snap** shortcut menu. The **Extension** object snap differs from most other snaps because it requires more than one selection point. The initial point, called the *acquired point*, is not selected in the typical manner,

acquired point: The initial point picked when using object snaps.

Figure 7-7.
Using **Intersection** object snap.

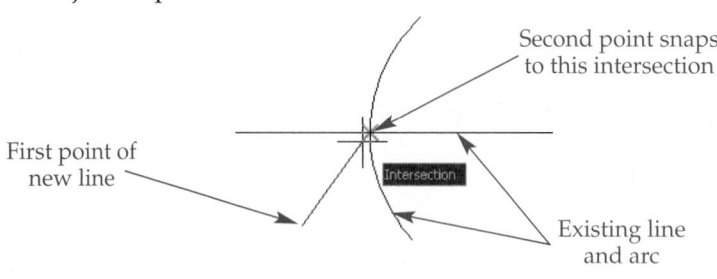

but is found by simply moving the crosshairs over the line, polyline, or polyline arc from which the new object is to be extended. When the object is found, a + symbol marks the location. If the new object is to be created at the intersection of extensions from two objects, the crosshairs must be placed over the second object to locate its extension path. The last point, which is the actual snap point, can be placed anywhere along the extension path, including the intersection of two extension paths. The *extension path*, represented by a dashed line or arc, extends from the acquired point to to the current location of the crosshairs.

extension path:
Dashed line or arc that extends from the acquired point to the current location of the crosshairs.

Figure 7-8 shows an example of how the **Extension** object snap can create a new line anywhere along the extension of an existing object. The first acquired point is found by moving the crosshairs directly over the upper-right corner of the rectangle. The tooltip for the extension is displayed, and the + marker becomes visible at the end of the line. While the dotted extension line is displayed, the first point can be picked. The second acquired point is found in the same manner at the endpoint of the line on the right. Pick near the intersection of the extension lines to locate the start point of the new line.

The **Extension** object snap can also be used to create the new line a specific distance away from the end of the old line. In **Figure 7-9**, the distance (.8) is typed while the first extension is displayed.

Figure 7-8.
The **Extension** object snap can be used to create a line from an extended intersection to an extended endpoint.

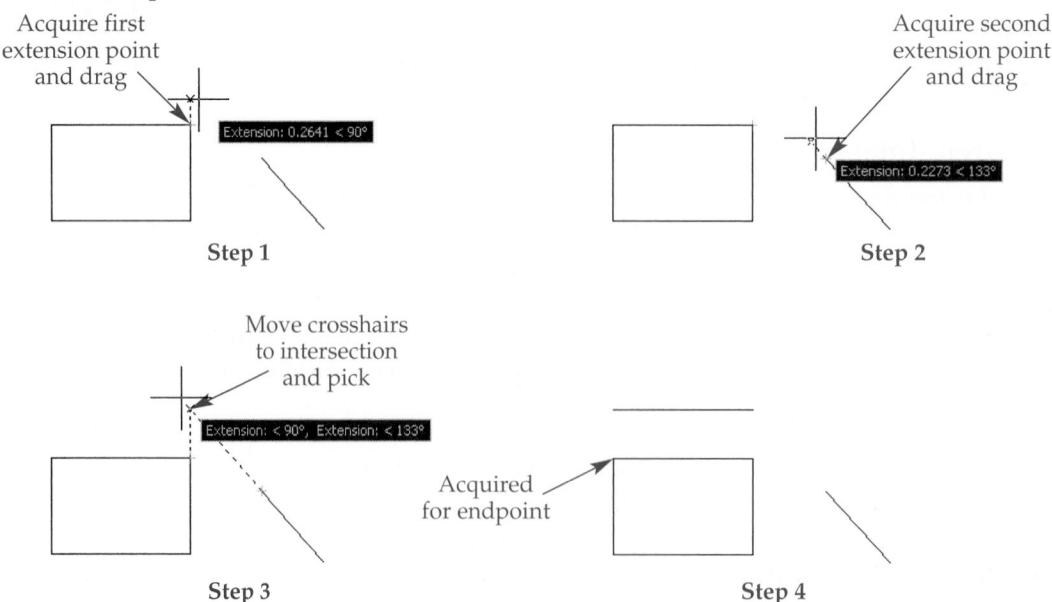

Figure 7-9.
Using the **Extension** object snap to create a line .8 units away from a rectangle.

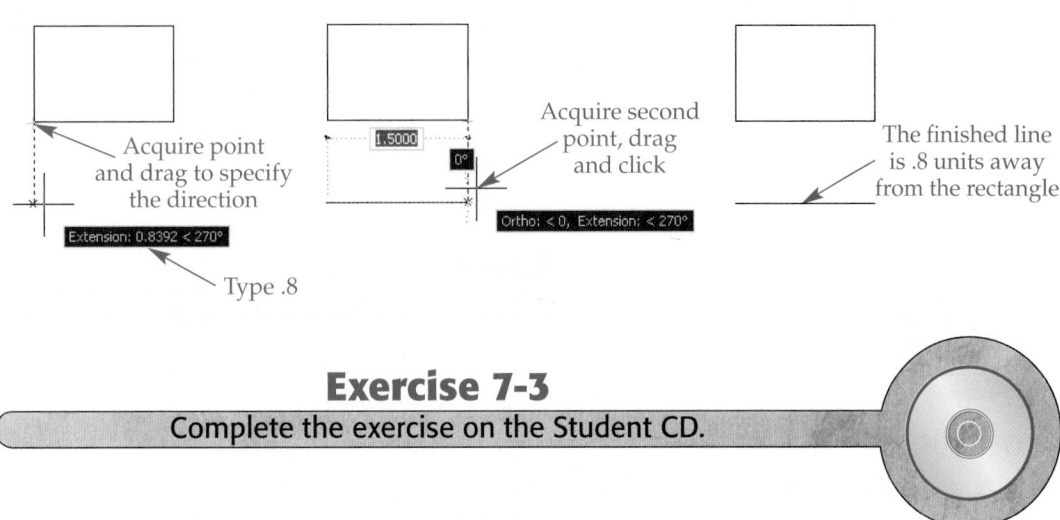

Acquire point and drag to specify the direction

Type .8

Acquire second point, drag and click

The finished line is .8 units away from the rectangle

Exercise 7-3
Complete the exercise on the Student CD.

Extended Intersection object snap

One object snap—*extended intersection*—is available only as a snap override. When using **Extended Intersection**, you select the objects one at a time, and the intersection point is automatically located. This is useful when two objects do not actually intersect and you need to access the point where these objects would intersect if they were extended.

To activate **Extended Intersection**, select the **Intersection** object snap override and pick an object (rather than an intersection). If the crosshairs is near an object, but not close to an actual intersection, the tooltip reads Extended Intersection, and the AutoSnap marker is followed by an ellipsis (…). **Figure 7-10** shows the use of **Extended Intersection** to find an intersection point between a line and an arc.

extended intersection: Object snap override in which the objects are selected one at a time, and the intersection point is automatically located.

Figure 7-10.
Finding the extended intersection of two objects. A—Select the first object. B—When the second object is selected, the extended intersection becomes the snap point. C—The completed line.

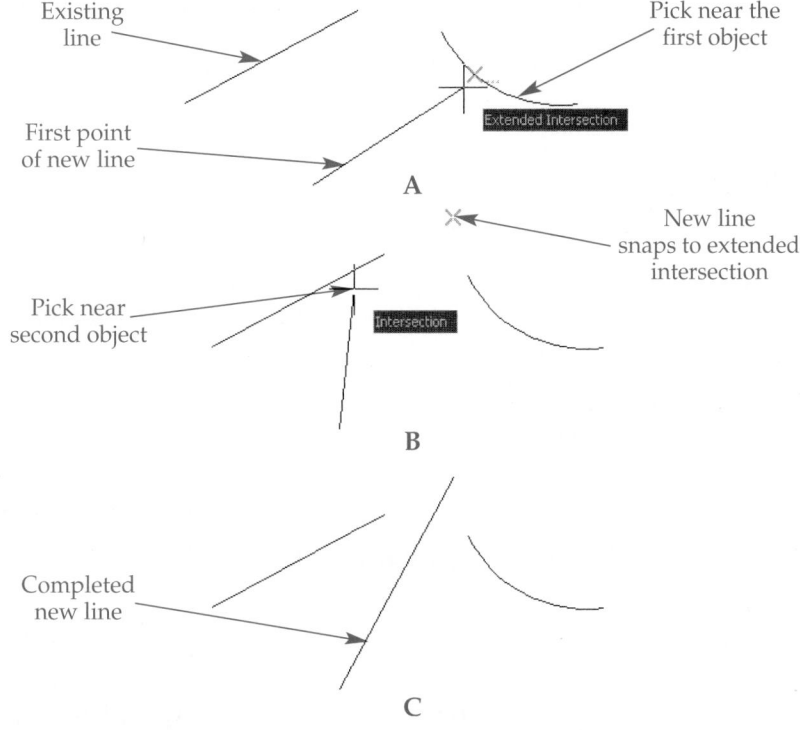

Existing line

Pick near the first object

First point of new line

A

New line snaps to extended intersection

Pick near second object

B

Completed new line

C

If the intersection point is not in the currently visible screen area, the AutoSnap marker is not displayed when you select the second object. You can still confirm the point before picking, however. Keeping the crosshairs motionless over the second object displays the tooltip, which confirms that the objects intersect somewhere beyond the currently visible area. When selecting two objects that could not intersect, no AutoSnap marker or tooltip is displayed, and no intersection point is found if the pick is made.

Exercise 7-4
Complete the exercise on the Student CD.

Perpendicular object snap

In geometric construction, it is common to draw one object perpendicular to another. This is done using the **Perpendicular** object snap mode. To activate this mode, type PER at the selection prompt, pick the **Snap to Perpendicular** button in the **Object Snap** toolbar, or pick **Perpendicular** from the **Object Snap** shortcut menu. A small right-angle symbol appears at the snap point. This mode can be used with arcs, elliptical arcs, ellipses, splines, xlines, multilines, polylines, solids, traces, or circles.

Figure 7-11 shows the **Perpendicular** object snap being used to locate the second point of a line perpendicular to a vertical line. In **Figure 7-12**, the object snap is used to start the line perpendicular to each object. The tooltip reads Deferred Perpendicular, and the AutoSnap marker is followed by an ellipsis (...). The term *deferred perpendicular* means the calculation of the perpendicular point is delayed until another point is picked. The second endpoint determines the location of the entire line.

It is important to understand that perpendicularity is calculated from points picked and not as a relationship between objects. Also, perpendicularity is measured at the point of intersection. Therefore, it is possible to draw a line perpendicular to a circle or arc.

deferred perpendicular: Calculation of the perpendicular point is delayed until another point is picked.

Figure 7-11. Drawing a line from a point perpendicular to an existing line. The **Perpendicular** object snap mode is used to select the second endpoint.

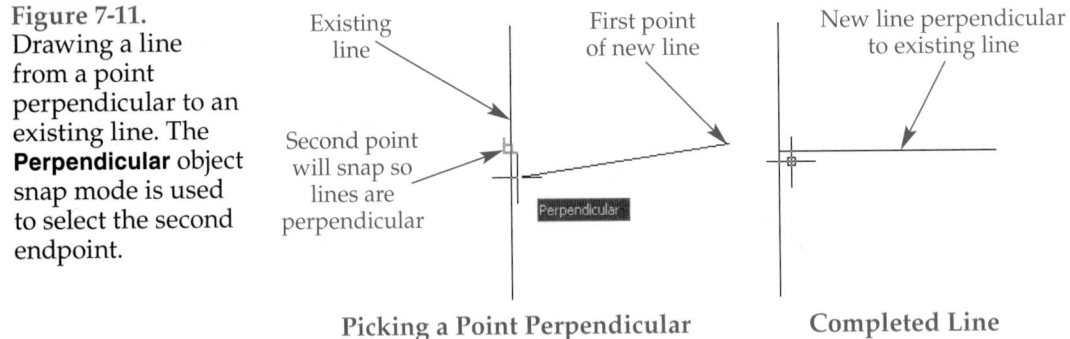

Figure 7-12. Deferring the perpendicular location until the second point is selected. The **Perpendicular** object snap mode is used to select the first endpoint.

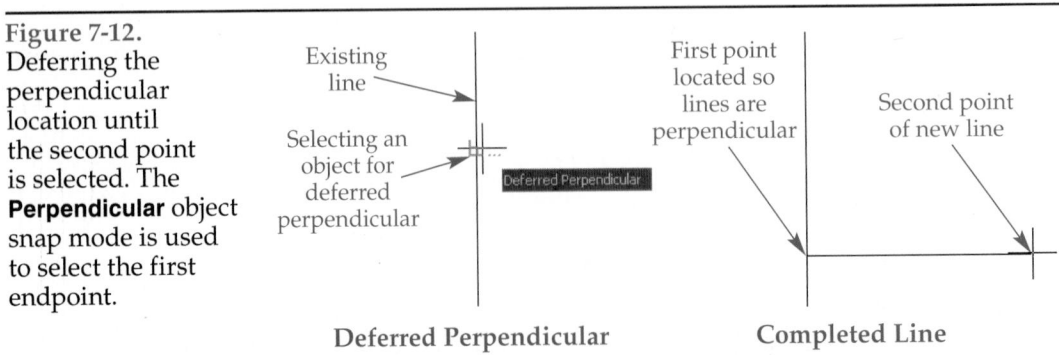

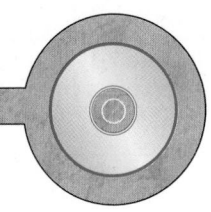

Exercise 7-5
Complete the exercise on the Student CD.

Tangent object snap

The **Tangent** object snap is used to align objects tangentially to an arc, circle, ellipse, elliptical arc, and spline. To activate this mode, type TAN at the selection prompt, pick the **Snap to Tangent** button on the **Object Snap** toolbar, or pick **Tangent** from the **Object Snap** shortcut menu.

In **Figure 7-13**, the endpoint of a line is located using the **Tangent** object snap mode. The first point is selected normally. As the crosshairs is placed near the tangent point on the circle, AutoCAD determines the tangent point and places the snap point there.

When you are creating an object tangent to another object, you may need to pick multiple points to fix the tangency point. For example, the point at which a line is tangent to a circle cannot be found without knowing the locations of both ends of the line. Until both points have been specified, the object snap specification is for *deferred tangency*. Once both endpoints are known, the tangency is calculated, and the object is drawn in the correct location. In **Figure 7-14**, a line is drawn tangent to two circles.

deferred tangency: Calculation of the point of tangency is delayed until both points have been picked.

Exercise 7-6
Complete the exercise on the Student CD.

Parallel object snap

The process of drawing, moving, or copying objects that are not horizontal or vertical is improved with the **Parallel** object snap mode. This option is used to find any point along an imaginary line that is parallel to an existing line or polyline. To activate the **Parallel** object snap mode, type PAR at the selection prompt, pick the **Snap to Parallel** button on the **Object Snap** toolbar, or pick **Parallel** from the **Object Snap** shortcut menu.

The **Parallel** object snap is similar to the **Extension** object snap because it requires more than one selection point. The acquired point is found by pausing the crosshairs over any point on the line to which the new object is to be parallel. When the object is found and you move the crosshairs in a direction parallel to the existing line, a (//) symbol marks the existing line. A dashed line, parallel to the existing line, extends from

Figure 7-13.
Using **Tangent** object snap.

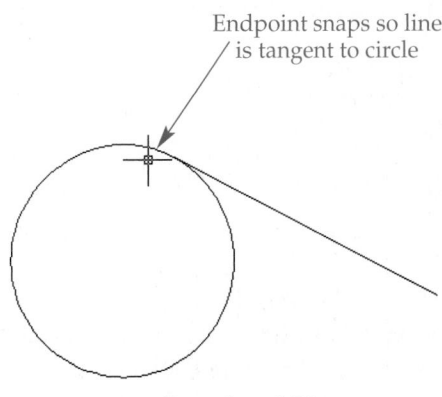

Existing circle   Point of tangency   First point of new line   Endpoint snaps so line is tangent to circle

Picking a Tangent Point   Completed Line

Figure 7-14.
Drawing a line
tangent to two
circles.

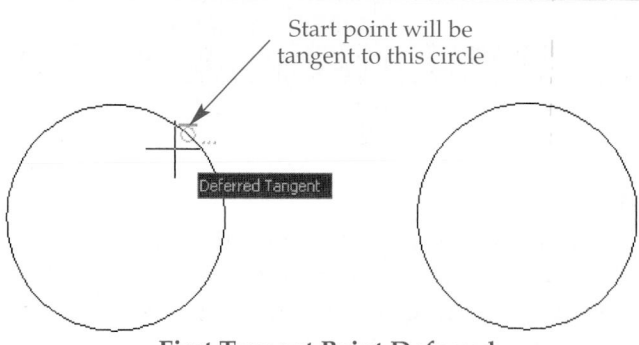

Start point will be
tangent to this circle

First Tangent Point Deferred

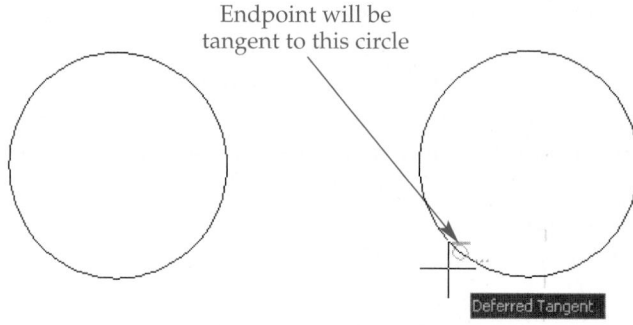

Endpoint will be
tangent to this circle

Picking Second Tangent Point

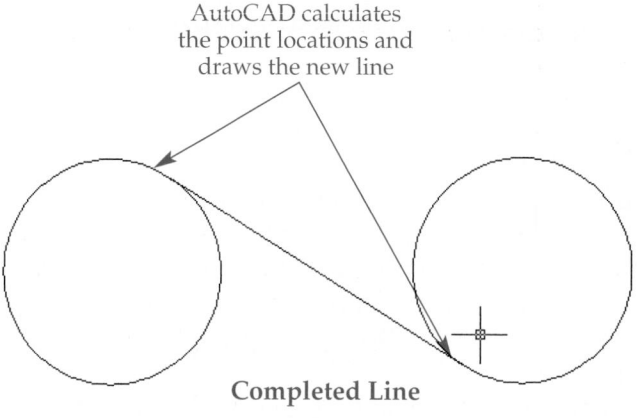

AutoCAD calculates
the point locations and
draws the new line

Completed Line

parallel alignment path: A dashed line, parallel to the existing line, that extends from the location of the crosshairs.

the location of the crosshairs. This line is known as the *parallel alignment path*. The last point, which is the actual snap point, can be placed anywhere along the parallel alignment path. When the alignment path is displayed, the **Parallel** snap marker appears on the line from which the parallel is used. Picking any location along the parallel alignment path creates the second point of the parallel line. **Figure 7-15** shows an example of the **Parallel** object snap being used to draw a line parallel to an existing line.

Exercise 7-7
Complete the exercise on the Student CD.

Node object snap

You can snap to point objects using the **Node** object snap mode. In order for object snap to find the point object, the point must be in a visible display mode. Controlling the point display mode is covered in Chapter 8.

Figure 7-15.
Using the **Parallel** object snap option to draw a line parallel to an existing line. A—Select the first endpoint for the new line, select the **Parallel** object snap, and then move the crosshairs near the existing line to acquire a point. B—After the parallel point is acquired, move the crosshairs near the location of the parallel line, and an extension path appears.

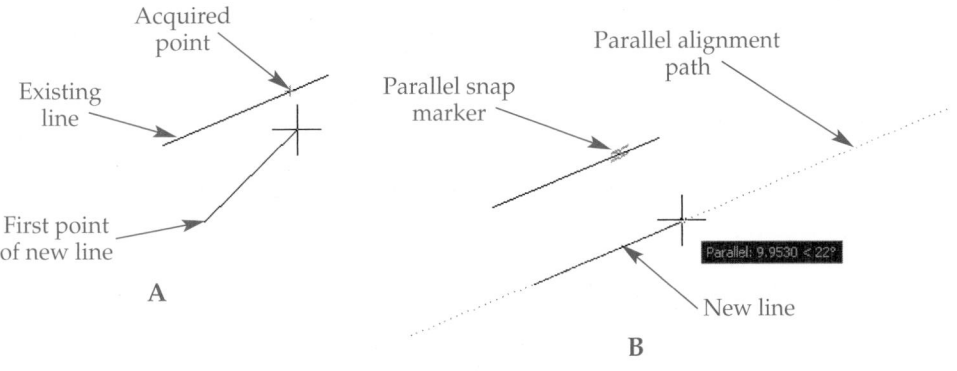

Nearest object snap

When you need to specify a point that is on an object, but cannot be located with any of the other object snap modes, you can use the **Nearest** mode. This object snap locates the point on the object closest to the crosshairs location. Use it when you want an object to touch an existing object, but the location of the intersection is not critical.

Consider drawing a line object that is to end on another line. Trying to pick the point with the crosshairs is inaccurate because you are relying only on your screen and mouse resolution. The line you draw may fall short or extend past the line. Using **Nearest** ensures that the point is precisely on the object.

Object Snap Overrides

When you want to activate an object snap mode for a single point selection, use an *object snap override*. Enter the object snap override when you are prompted to select a point. This temporarily suspends any running object snap modes (which are defined later in this chapter). After you select the point, the running object snap modes are reactivated.

object snap override: A single, selected object snap mode that temporarily suspends any running object snap modes.

After you enter a command, an object snap override can be activated in any of three ways:

- **Object Snap shortcut menu.** This shortcut menu lists the object snap modes. See **Figure 7-16.** To access the **Object Snap** shortcut menu when selecting a point, right-click and pick **Snap Overrides** or hold the [Shift] key and right-click.
- **Object Snap toolbar.** The **Object Snap** toolbar includes a button for each object snap mode. See **Figure 7-17.** Pick the appropriate button to activate the snap override. To access this toolbar, right-click on any toolbar button and select **Object Snap** from the shortcut menu.
- **Keyboard entry.** Each object snap override can be activated by typing a three-letter abbreviation at a point selection prompt.

PROFESSIONAL TIP

Use the object snap modes not only when drawing, but also when editing. With practice, using object snaps becomes second nature, greatly increasing your productivity and accuracy.

Figure 7-16.
The **Object Snap**
shortcut menu
provides quick
access to object snap
overrides.

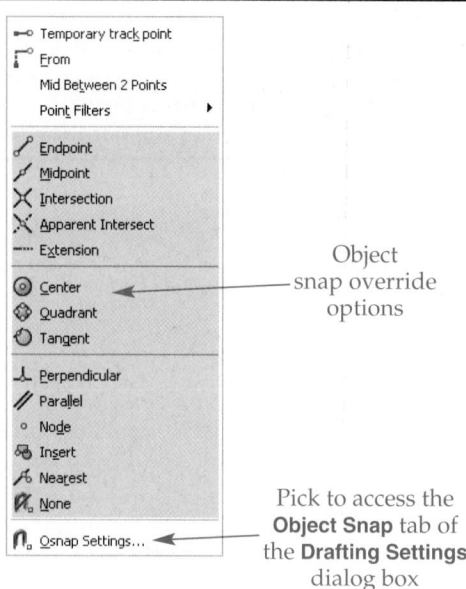

Object
snap override
options

Pick to access the
Object Snap tab of
the **Drafting Settings**
dialog box

Figure 7-17.
The **Object Snap**
toolbar.

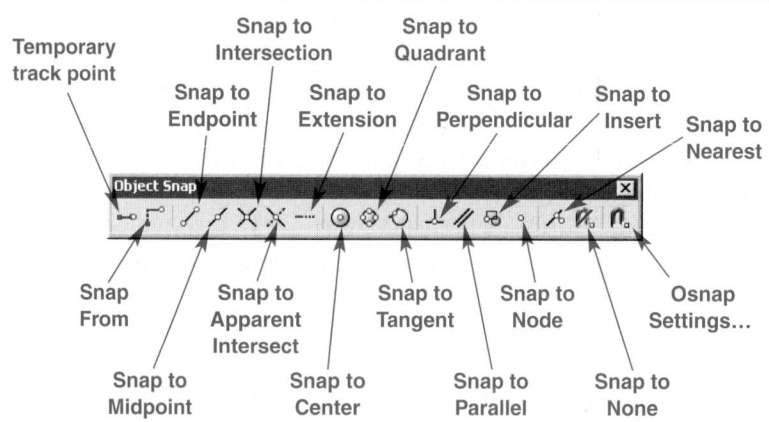

Running Object Snaps

Type
DDOSNAP
OSNAP
OS
Toolbar
Object Snap

Osnap Settings...
Pull-Down Menu
Tools
  > Drafting
    Settings...

**running object
snaps:** Object
snaps that are
always active for
drawing commands.

You can set an object snap mode using the **Object Snap** tab in the **Drafting Settings** dialog box. To access this dialog box, pick the **Osnap Settings...** button from the **Object Snap** toolbar; pick **Tools** > **Drafting Settings...** from the pull-down menu; right-click on the **OSNAP** or **OTRACK** button on the status bar and select **Settings...** from the shortcut menu; or type OS, OSNAP, or DDOSNAP. You can also type DSETTINGS to access the **Drafting Settings** dialog box.

The **Object Snap** tab of the **Drafting Settings** dialog box is shown in **Figure 7-18**. Notice that the **Endpoint, Intersection, Extension,** and **Parallel** modes are active. The object snaps that are selected in this dialog box are called *running object snaps*. You can use this dialog box at any time to discontinue a running object snap or to set additional modes.

When you need to make several point specifications without the aid of object snap, you can toggle running object snaps off by picking the **OSNAP** button on the status bar. The advantage of this method is that you can make several picks and then restore the same running object snap modes by picking the **OSNAP** button again. You can also pick the **Object Snap On (F3)** check box in the **Drafting Settings** dialog box or press the [F3] key on your keyboard. Any of these options can be used to toggle running object snaps.

You can remove the active checks in the **Drafting Settings** dialog box as needed to disable running object snaps. You can also pick the **Clear All** button to disable all running modes. Select desired running object snaps by picking the associated boxes or pick the **Select All** button to activate all object snaps.

Figure 7-18.
Running object snap modes can be set in the **Drafting Settings** dialog box.

Running object snaps activate when checked

Running object snap modes are checked

Access the **Drafting** tab of the **Options** dialog box

Activates all modes

Deactivates all modes

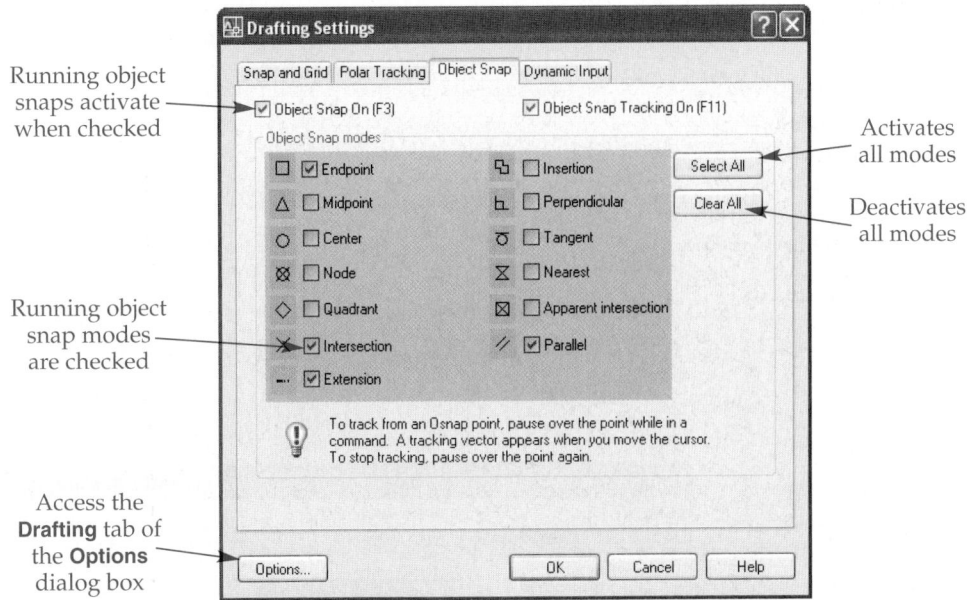

PROFESSIONAL TIP

By default, a keyboard entry overrides any currently running object snap modes. This behavior can be changed in the **Priority for Coordinate Data Entry** area in the **User Preferences** tab of the **Options** dialog box.

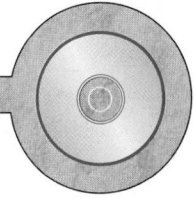

Exercise 7-8
Complete the exercise on the Student CD.

AutoSnap Settings

To customize the appearance and functionality of the AutoSnap feature, access the **Object Snap** tab of the **Drafting Settings** dialog box and pick the **Options...** button in the lower-left corner. This opens the **Drafting** tab of the **Options** dialog box, shown in **Figure 7-19.** To activate an AutoSnap option, check the corresponding check box:

- **Marker.** Toggles the AutoSnap marker display.
- **Magnet.** Toggles the AutoSnap magnet. When active, the magnet snaps the crosshairs to the object snap point.
- **Display AutoSnap tooltip.** Toggles the tooltip display.
- **Display AutoSnap aperture box.** Toggles the display of the aperture.

The marker color and size can also be adjusted to suit your needs. For example, the default marker color is yellow, but this is difficult to see if you have the graphics screen background set to white. Pick the **Colors:** button to access the **Drawing Window Colors** dialog box. Highlight the **2D model space** selection in the **Context:** list and the **Autosnap marker** in the **Interface element:** list. Access the **Color:** drop-down list, and select the desired color. Pick **Apply & Close** to return to the **Options** dialog box.

At higher screen resolutions, a larger marker size improves visibility. While the **Drafting** tab of the **Options** dialog box is still open, move the slider in the **AutoSnap Marker Size** area to change the size. **Ignore hatch objects** determines whether you can snap to hatch patterns. Hatching is discussed in Chapter 21.

Figure 7-19.
Setting AutoSnap features.

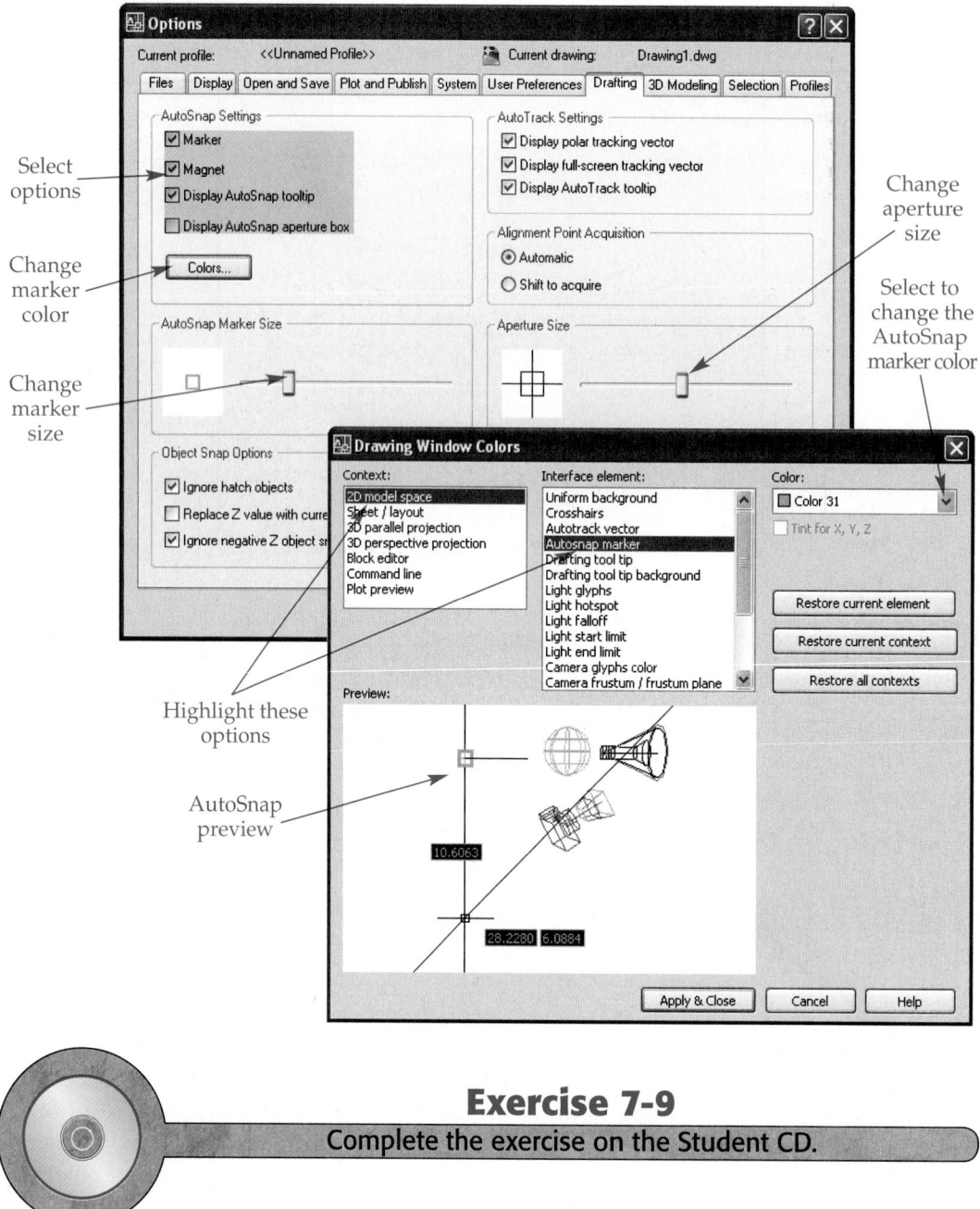

Select options

Change marker color

Change marker size

Highlight these options

AutoSnap preview

Change aperture size

Select to change the AutoSnap marker color

Exercise 7-9
Complete the exercise on the Student CD.

Changing the aperture size

When you select a point using object snaps, the crosshairs must be within a specific range of a candidate point before the point is located. The object snap detection system finds everything within a square area centered at the crosshairs location. This square area is called the *aperture* and is invisible by default.

aperture: The square area within which objects are detected by object snap.

To display the aperture, open the **Drafting Settings** dialog box and pick the **Options...** button from the **Object Snap** tab. The **Drafting** tab of the **Options** dialog box appears. Activate the **Display AutoSnap aperture box** check box. Having the aperture visible may be helpful when you are first learning to work with object snap.

To change the size of the aperture, move the slider in the **Aperture Size** area. Various aperture sizes are shown in **Figure 7-20.**

Figure 7-20.
Aperture box size is measured in pixels. The three examples here are not shown in actual size, but they are provided to show the size relationships among different settings.

5 Pixels   10 Pixels   20 Pixels

Keep in mind that the *aperture* and the *pick box* are different. The aperture is displayed on the screen when object snap modes are active. The pick box appears on the screen for any command that activates the Select objects: prompt.

Exercise 7-10
Complete the exercise on the Student CD.

AutoTrack

Creating geometry that lines up with existing geometry is very common in drafting and design. AutoTrack makes this procedure straightforward and accurate by creating alignment paths and tracking vectors when needed. *Alignment paths* are temporary lines and arcs that coincide with the position of existing objects. *Tracking vectors* are temporary lines that are displayed at specific angles, typically 0°, 90°, 180°, and 270°.

The two AutoTrack modes are object snap tracking and polar tracking. Any commands requiring a point selection, such as the **COPY**, **MOVE**, and **LINE** commands, can make use of these modes.

Object Snap Tracking

Object snap tracking is always used in conjunction with object snaps. When this mode is active, placing the crosshairs near an AutoSnap marker acquires the point. After a point is acquired, horizontal and vertical alignment paths are available for locating points.

The [F11] function key and the **OTRACK** button on the status bar toggle object snap tracking on and off. This mode is only available for points selected by the currently active object snap modes. When running object snaps are active, all selected object snap modes are available for object snap tracking. These modes are not available for object snap tracking, however, if running object snaps are deactivated.

In **Figure 7-21**, object snap tracking is used in conjunction with the **Perpendicular** and **Midpoint** running object snaps to draw a line that is 2 units long and perpendicular to the existing, slanted line. The running object snap modes are set before the following command sequence is initiated. The **OSNAP** and **OTRACK** buttons on the status bar are active.

alignment paths: Temporary lines and arcs that coincide with the position of existing objects.

tracking vectors: Temporary lines that are displayed at specific angles.

object snap tracking: Mode that gives horizontal and vertical alignment paths for locating points once a point is acquired with object snap.

Figure 7-21.
Using object snap tracking to draw a line. A—The first endpoint is located at the midpoint of the existing line. The alignment path is displayed when the crosshairs are near. B—The completed line, with the second endpoint identified using direct distance entry along the alignment path.

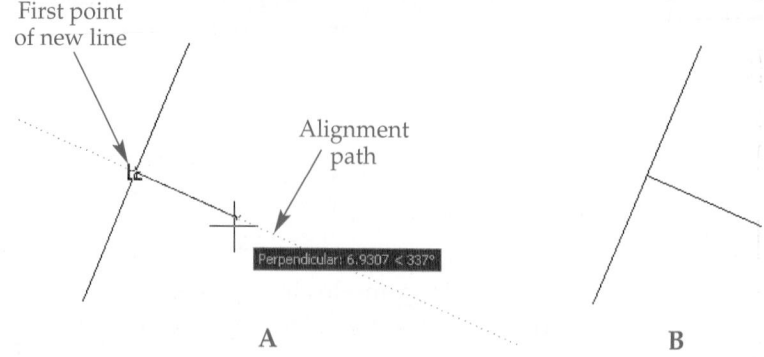

Command: **L** *or* **LINE.**↵
Specify first point: *(pick the midpoint of the existing line)*
Specify next point or [Undo]: *(pause the crosshairs near the first point to acquire it, and then position the crosshairs as shown in* Figure 7-21A *to activate the perpendicular alignment path)* **2**↵
Specify next point or [Undo]: ↵
Command:

Object snap tracking can also be used to position new geometry based on the locations of existing geometry. In Figure 7-22, object snap tracking is used to position a circle directly above the midpoint of a horizontal line and to the right of the midpoint of an angled line, with only the **Midpoint** running object snap on. The **OSNAP** and **OTRACK** buttons on the status bar are active.

Figure 7-22.
Object snap tracking is used to position this circle in line with the midpoints of each line.

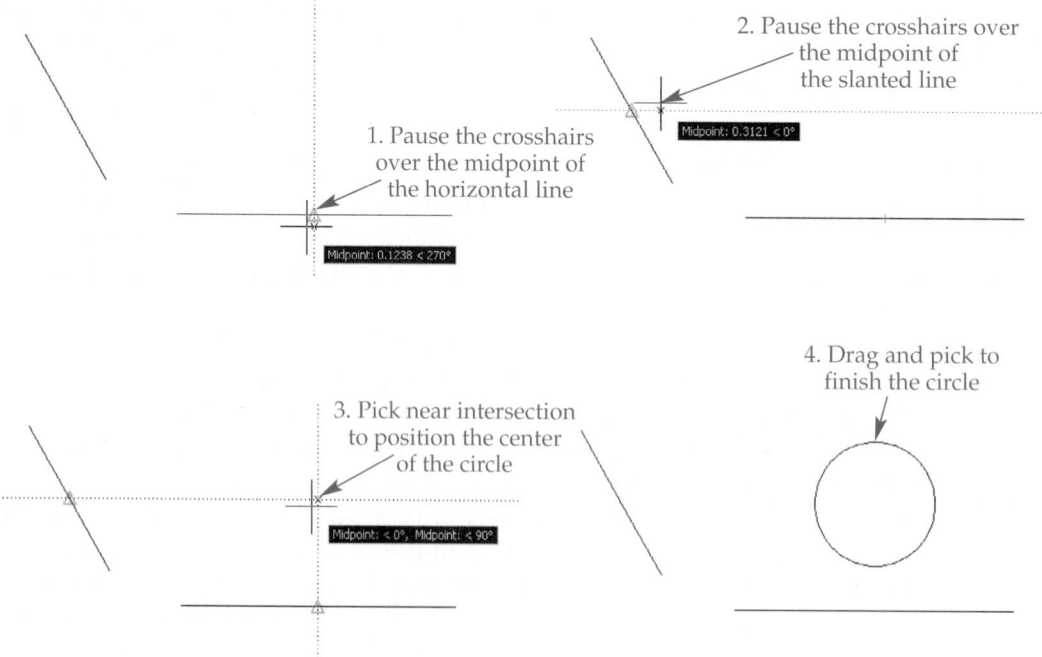

Command: **C** *or* **CIRCLE**⏎
Specify center point for circle or [Undo]: *(pause the crosshairs near the midpoint of the horizontal line to acquire it, and then pause the crosshairs near the midpoint of the angled line to acquire it. Move the crosshairs to the position as shown in the second step of* Figure 7-22 *until two tracking vectors appear. Pick to locate the center of the circle.)*
Specify radius of circle or [Undo]: *(drag the crosshairs to specify any radius and pick to complete the circle)*
Command:

PROFESSIONAL TIP

AutoTracking is similar in performance to the **Extension** object snap. Experiment with a combination of just the **Endpoint** object snap mode and AutoTracking. Try a combination of **Endpoint** and **Extension** object snap modes without AutoTracking to see the difference. Notice that without object snap tracking, you cannot drag in a direction perpendicular to an endpoint.

Exercise 7-11
Complete the exercise on the Student CD.

Polar Tracking

Ortho mode, discussed in Chapter 3, forces the crosshairs movement to orthogonal (horizontal and vertical) orientations. When Ortho mode is turned on and the **LINE** command is in use, all new line segments are drawn at 0°, 90°, 180°, or 270°. *Polar tracking* works in much the same way, but it allows for a greater range of angles.

Selecting the **POLAR** button from the status bar or using the [F10] function key turns polar tracking on and off. You cannot use polar tracking and Ortho at the same time. AutoCAD automatically turns Ortho off when polar tracking is on, and it turns polar tracking off when Ortho is on.

When polar tracking mode is turned on, the crosshairs snaps to preset incremental angles if a point is being located relative to another point. For example, in the **LINE** command, polar tracking is not active for the first endpoint selection, but it is available for the second and subsequent point selections. Polar tracking vectors are displayed as dashed lines whenever the crosshairs aligns with any of these preset angles.

To set incremental angles, use the **Polar Tracking** tab in the **Drafting Settings** dialog box. To access this dialog box, right-click on the **POLAR** button from the status bar, and then select **Settings**; pick **Tools > Drafting Settings...** from the pull-down menu; or type DSETTINGS or DS. Figure 7-23 shows the **Polar Tracking** tab of the **Drafting Settings** dialog box.

The following features are found in the **Polar Tracking** tab:
- **Polar Tracking On (F10).** Turns polar tracking on.
- **Polar Angle Settings area.** Sets the desired polar angle increments. It contains the following items:
  - **Increment angle.** Sets the angle increments at which polar tracking vectors occur. Open the drop-down list to select from a variety of preset angles. The default increment is 90, which provides angle increments every 90°. The setting in Figure 7-23 provides polar tracking in 30° increments.

polar tracking: Mode that allows the crosshairs to snap to preset incremental angles if a point is being located relative to another point.

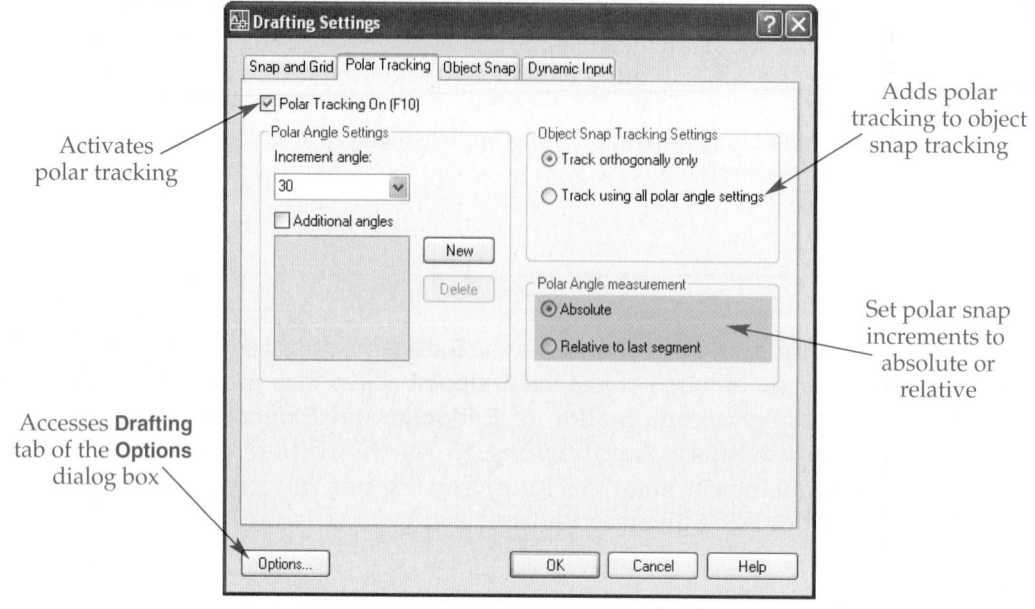

Activates polar tracking

Accesses **Drafting** tab of the **Options** dialog box

Adds polar tracking to object snap tracking

Set polar snap increments to absolute or relative

- **Additional angles.** Activates your own angle increments. To do this, pick the **New** button to open a text box in the window. Type the desired angle. Pick the **New** button each time you want to add another angle. The additional angles are used together with the increment angle setting when you use polar tracking. Use the **Delete** button to remove angles from the list. You can make the additional angle(s) inactive by turning off the **Additional angles** check box.
- **Object Snap Tracking Settings area.** Sets the angles available with object snap tracking. If **Track orthogonally only** is selected, only horizontal and vertical alignment paths are active. If **Track using all polar angle settings** is selected, alignment paths for all polar snap angles are active.
- **Polar Angle measurement area.** This setting determines whether the polar snap increments are constant or relative to the previous segment. If **Absolute** is selected, the polar snap angles are measured from the base angle of 0° set for the drawing. If **Relative to last segment** is selected, each increment angle is measured from a base angle established by the previously drawn segment.

Figure 7-24 shows a parallelogram being drawn with polar tracking active and set for 30° angle increments and absolute polar angle measurements. The following command sequence creates the parallelogram:

Command: **L** or **LINE.**↵
Specify first point: (*select the first point*)
Specify next point or [Undo]: (*drag the crosshairs to the right while the polar alignment path indicates <0°*) **3.**↵
Specify next point or [Undo]: (*drag the crosshairs to the 60° polar alignment path*) **1.5.**↵
Specify next point or [Close/Undo]: (*drag the crosshairs to the 180° polar alignment path*) **3.**↵
Specify next point or [Close/Undo]: **C.**↵
Command:

Exercise 7-12
Complete the exercise on the Student CD.

Figure 7-24.
Using polar tracking with 30° angle increments to draw a parallelogram. A—After the first side is drawn, the alignment path and direct distance entry are used to create the second side. B—A horizontal alignment path is used for the third side. C—The parallelogram is completed with the **Close** option.

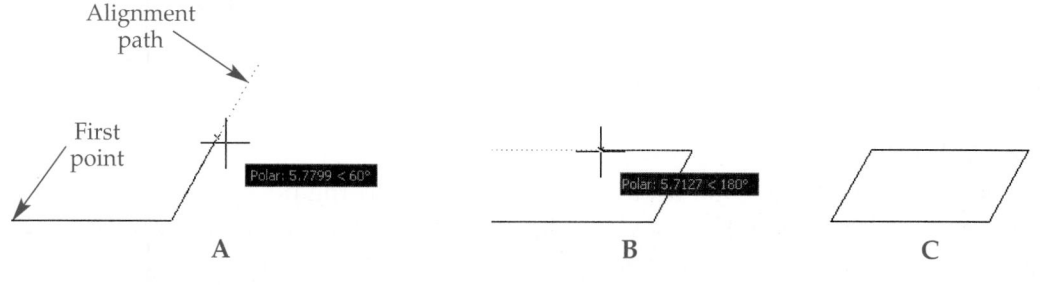

Polar tracking with polar snaps

Polar tracking can also be used in conjunction with polar snaps. If polar snaps are used when drawing the parallelogram in **Figure 7-24**, there is no need to type the length of the line, because you set both the angle increment and a length increment. The desired angle and length increments are established in the **Snap and Grid** tab of the **Drafting Settings** dialog box. You can open this dialog box as previously described, or you can right-click on the status bar **SNAP** button and pick **Settings...** from the shortcut menu. This opens the **Drafting Settings** dialog box, as shown in **Figure 7-25**.

To activate polar snap, pick the **PolarSnap** button in the **Snap type & style** area of the dialog box. Picking this button activates the **Polar spacing** area and deactivates the **Snap** area. The length of the polar snap increment is set in the **Polar distance:** box. If the **Polar distance:** setting is 0, the polar snap distance will be the orthogonal snap distance. **Figure 7-26** shows a parallelogram being drawn with 30° angle increments and length increments of .75. The lengths of the parallelogram sides are 1.5 and .75.

Figure 7-25.
The **Snap and Grid** tab of the **Drafting Settings** dialog box is used to set the polar snap spacing.

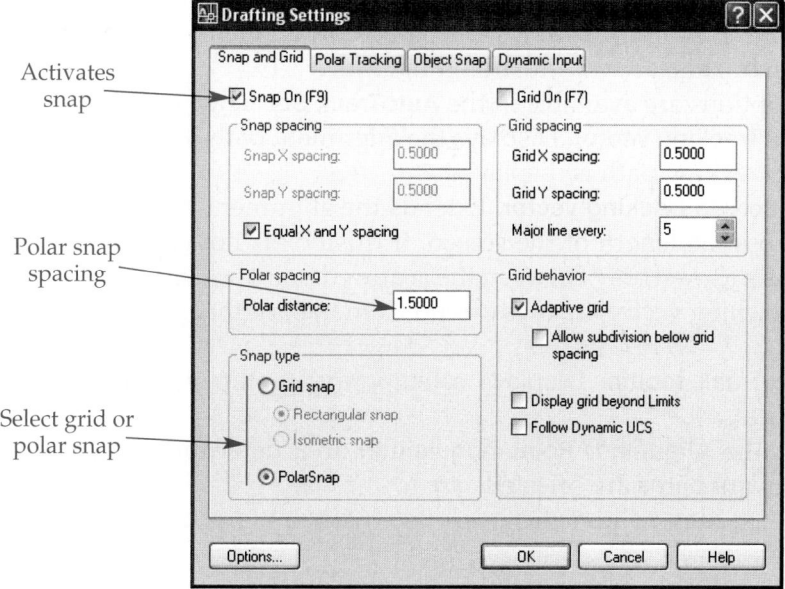

Figure 7-26.
Drawing a parallelogram with polar snap.

A   B   C   D

Using polar tracking overrides

It takes some time to set up the polar tracking and the polar snap options, but it is worth the effort if you have several objects to draw that can take advantage of this feature. If you want to perform polar tracking for only one point, you can use the polar tracking override to do this easily. This works for the specified angle whether polar tracking is on or off. To activate a polar tracking override, type a left angle bracket (<) followed by the desired angle when AutoCAD asks you to specify a point. The following command sequence uses a 30° override to draw a line 1.5 units long:

```
Command: L or LINE↵
Specify first point: (pick a start point for the line)
Specify next point or [Undo]: <30↵
Angle Override: 30
Specify next point or [Undo]: (move the crosshairs in the desired 30° direction) 1.5↵
Specify next point or [Undo]: ↵
Command:
```

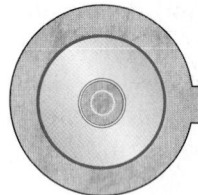

Exercise 7-13
Complete the exercise on the Student CD.

AutoTrack Settings

The settings that control the function of AutoTracking can be accessed through the **Options...** button on the **Drafting Settings** dialog box. This opens the **Options** dialog box to the **Drafting** tab. This tab was illustrated in **Figure 7-19.**

The following options are available in the **AutoTrack Settings** area:
- **Display polar tracking vector.** Displays the alignment path. When this option is off, no polar tracking path is displayed.
- **Display full-screen tracking vector.** Extends the alignment path for object snap tracking across the length of the screen. If this box is not checked, the alignment paths are shown only between the acquired point and the crosshairs location. Polar tracking vectors always extend from the original point to the extents of the screen.
- **Display AutoTrack tooltip.** Displays a temporary tooltip with the AutoTrack alignment paths.

The options in the **Alignment Point Acquisition** area determine how the object snap tracking alignment paths are selected:
- **Automatic.** Acquires points whenever the crosshairs is paused over an object snap point.
- **Shift to acquire.** Requires the [Shift] key to be pressed to acquire an object snap point and use object snap tracking. AutoSnap markers are still displayed, and normal object snap can be used without pressing the [Shift] key. If many running object snaps are set, you may want to use this option to reduce the number of paths displayed across the screen.

Other tracking modes are available in addition to those listed in the **Object Snap** tab of the **Drafting Settings** dialog box. These modes may be used whether object snap tracking is on or off. These modes are **Temporary track point**, **From**, and **Mid Between 2 Points**.

Temporary Track Point

Object snap tracking has two requirements: running object snap mode must be active and the crosshairs must pause over the selected point long enough to acquire it. Temporary track point can produce tracking vectors without either of these conditions.

To activate temporary tracking, pick the **Temporary track point** button from the **Object Snap** toolbar, type TT at the selection prompt, or pick **Temporary track point** from the **Object Snap** shortcut menu. For example, temporary tracking can be used to place a circle at the center of a rectangle. See **Figure 7-27**. The X coordinate of the rectangle's center corresponds to the midpoint of the horizontal lines. The Y coordinate of the rectangle's center corresponds to the midpoint of the vertical lines. Temporary tracking can be used to combine these two points to find the center of the rectangle using this sequence:

> Command: **C** or **CIRCLE**↵
> Specify center point for circle or [3P/2P/Ttr (tan tan radius)]: **TT**↵
> Specify temporary OTRACK point: **MID**↵
> of *(pick one of the vertical lines and move the crosshairs horizontally)*
> Specify center point for circle or [3P/2P/Ttr (tan tan radius)]: **TT**↵
> Specify temporary OTRACK point: **MID**↵
> of *(pick one of the horizontal lines and move the crosshairs vertically)*
> Specify center point for circle or [3P/2P/Ttr (tan tan radius)]: *(select the point where the two alignment paths intersect)*
> Specify radius of circle or [Diameter] <*current*>: ↵
> Command:

The direction of the orthogonal line determines whether the X or Y component is used. In the previous example, after picking the first tracking point, the crosshairs is moved horizontally. This means the Y axis value of the previous point is being used, and tracking is now ready for an X coordinate specification.

After moving the crosshairs horizontally, you may notice movement is locked in a horizontal mode. If you need to move the crosshairs vertically, move it back to the previously picked point, and then drag vertically. Use this method whenever you need to switch between horizontal and vertical movements.

Figure 7-27.
Using temporary tracking to locate the center of a rectangle. A—The midpoint of the left line is acquired. B—The midpoint of the bottom line is acquired. C—The center point of the circle is located at the intersection of the alignment paths.

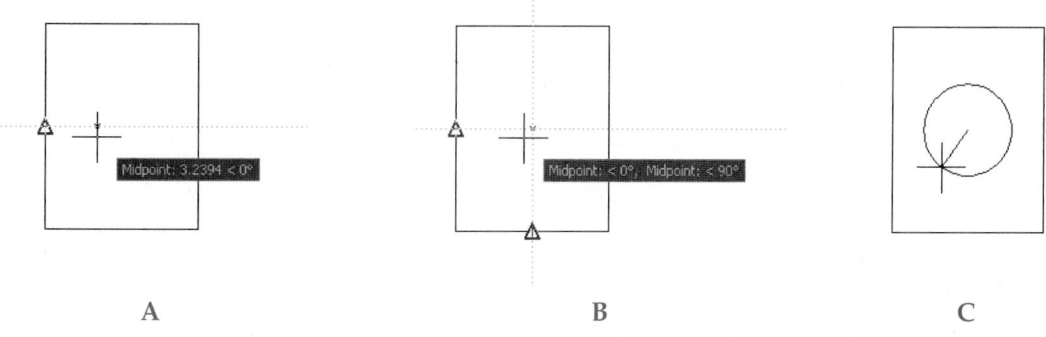

A   B   C

Using the From Point Selection Option

The **From** point selection option is another tracking tool that can be used to locate points based on existing geometry. It allows you to establish a relative coordinate, polar coordinate, or direct distance entry from a specified reference base point. Access the **From** option by selecting the **Snap From** button in the **Object Snap** toolbar, selecting **From** in the **Object Snap** shortcut menu, or typing FRO at a point selection prompt. The example in **Figure 7-28** shows the center point for a circle being established as a polar distance from the midpoint of an existing line. The command sequence is shown here:

> Command: **C** *or* **CIRCLE**↵
> Specify center point for circle or [3P/2P/Ttr (tan tan radius)]: **FRO.**↵
> Base point: **MID.**↵
> of *(pick line)*
> <Offset>: **@2<45.**↵
> Specify radius of circle or [Diameter] <*current*>: *(pick a radius)*
> Command:

Using the Mid Between 2 Points Option

A point can be located at the midpoint of two picks by using the **Mid Between 2 Points** feature. This is different from the **Midpoint** object snap, which finds the midpoint of a selected object. **Mid Between 2 Points** picks the midpoint between any two points in the drawing area and can be used in conjunction with object snap modes.

Mid Between 2 Points can only be accessed from the **Object Snap** shortcut menu or by typing M2P at a point selection prompt. The example in **Figure 7-29** locates the center of a circle between two line endpoints:

> Command: **C** *or* **CIRCLE**↵
> Specify center point for circle or [3P/2P/Ttr (tan tan radius)]: **M2P**↵
> First point of mid: *(select first point)*
> Second point of mid: *(select second point)*
> Specify radius of circle or [Diameter] <*current*>: *(pick a radius)*
> Command:

Figure 7-28.
Using the **From** point selection mode, following the command sequence given in the text.

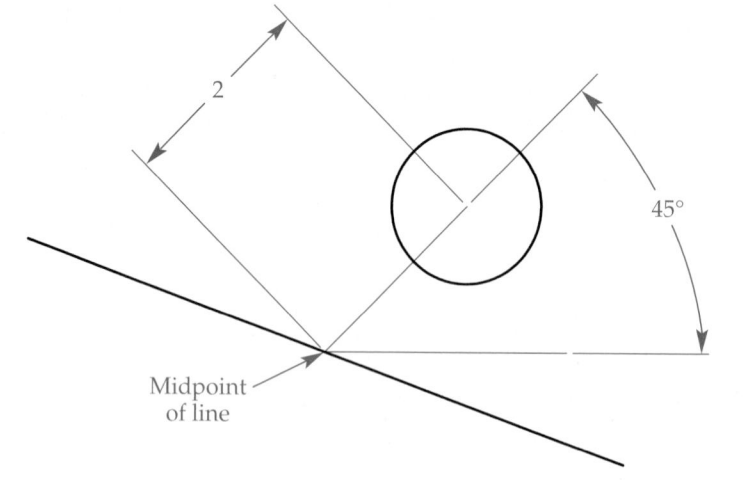

Figure 7-29.
Creating a circle, in which the center is an exact equal distance between two points, using the **Mid Between 2 Points** option.

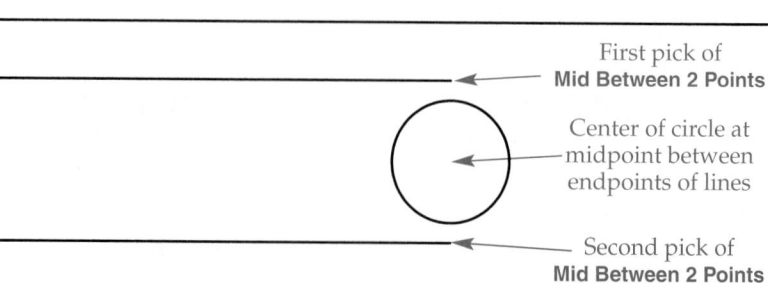

AutoCAD and Its Applications—Basics

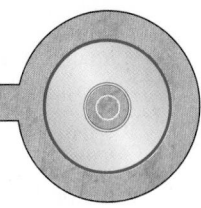

Exercise 7-14

Complete the exercise on the Student CD.

Template Development

Chapter 7

You will find that you need different object snaps and polar tracking settings depending on the type of drawing you are creating. These settings can be specified in your drawing templates to save time and increase efficiency. Refer to the Student CD for detailed instructions to add these settings to your mechanical, architectural, and civil drawing templates.

Chapter Test

Answer the following questions. Write your answers on a separate sheet of paper or complete the electronic chapter test on the Student CD.

1. Define the term *object snap*.
2. What is an AutoSnap tooltip?
3. Name the following AutoSnap markers:

   A.   B.   C.

   D.   E.   F.

   G.   H.   I.

   J.   K.   L.

4. Give the command and entries needed to draw a line to the midpoint of an existing line:
   A. Command: _____
   B. Specify first point: _____
   C. Specify next point or [Undo]: _____
   D. of _____
5. Define the term *quadrant*.
6. What is the situation when the tooltip reads Extended Intersection?
7. Give the command and entries needed to draw a line tangent to an existing circle and perpendicular to an existing line:
   A. Command: _____
   B. Specify first point: _____
   C. to _____
   D. Specify next point or [Undo]: _____
   E. to _____
8. What does it mean when the tooltip reads Deferred Perpendicular?
9. What conditions must exist for the tooltip to read Tangent?
10. What is a deferred tangency?
11. Which object snaps depend on "acquired points" to function?

12. Describe the object snap override.
13. If you are using running object snaps and you want to make a single point selection without the effects of the running object snaps, what do you do?
14. How do you activate the **Object Snap** shortcut menu?
15. Define the term *running object snap mode*.
16. How do you set running object snaps?
17. How do you access the **Drafting Settings** dialog box to change object snap settings?
18. If you are using running object snaps and want to make several point specifications without the aid of object snap, but want to continue the same running object snaps after making the desired point selections, what is the easiest way to turn off the running object snaps temporarily?
19. Define the term *AutoSnap*.
20. How do you change the color of the AutoSnap marker?
21. How do you change the aperture size?
22. Define the term *AutoTracking*.
23. Which feature should be used in conjunction with AutoTracking?
24. When are polar tracking vectors displayed as dashed lines?
25. What are the two requirements to use object snap tracking?

Drawing Problems

Load AutoCAD for each of the following problems, and use one of your templates or start a new drawing using your own variables.

1. Draw the object below using the object snap modes. Do not draw the dimensions. Save the drawing as P7-1.

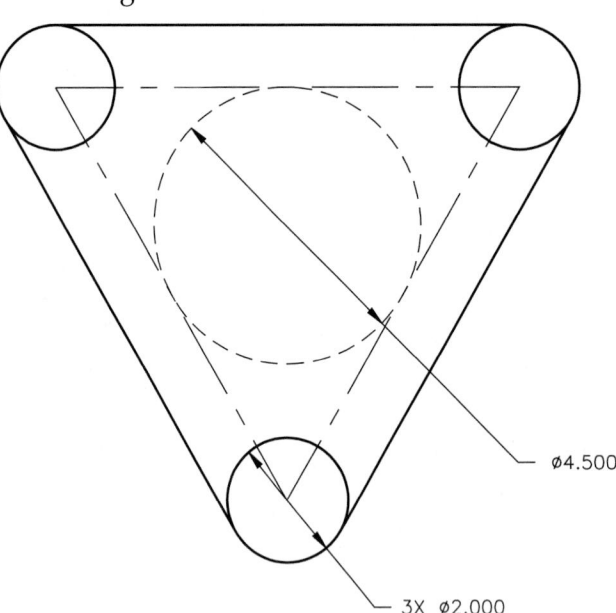

ø4.500

3X ø2.000

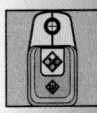

2. Draw the highlighted objects below, and then use the object snap modes indicated to draw the remaining objects. Save the drawing as P7-2.

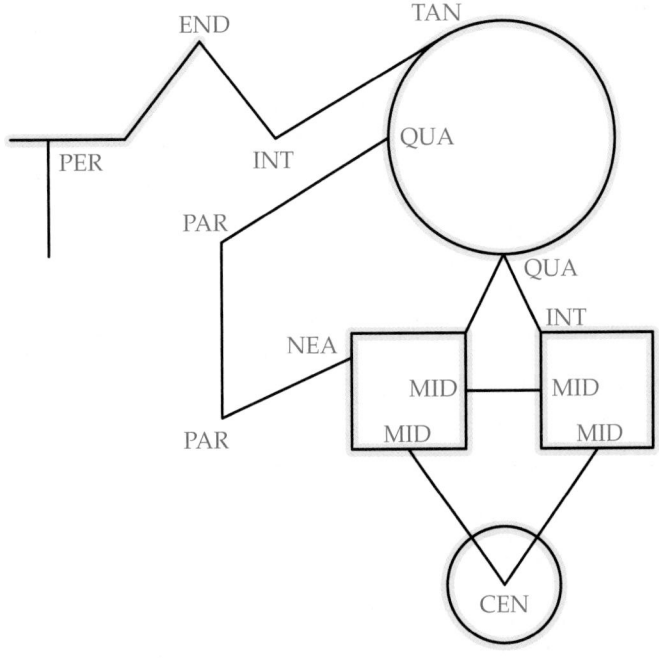

3. Draw the object below using the **Endpoint**, **Tangent**, **Perpendicular**, and **Quadrant** object snap modes. Save the drawing as P7-3.

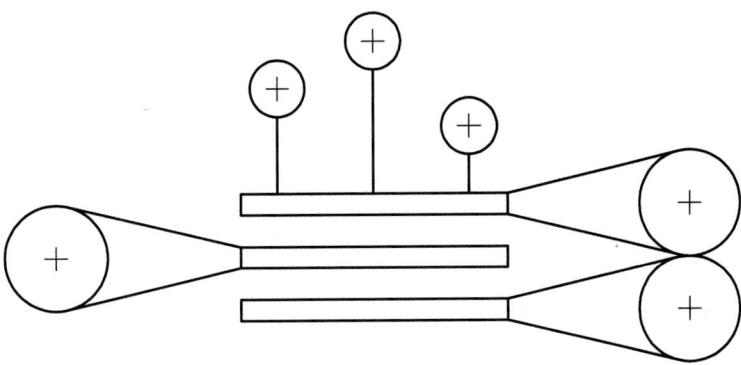

4. Use the **Midpoint**, **Endpoint**, **Tangent**, **Perpendicular**, and **Quadrant** object snap modes to draw these electrical switch schematics. Do not draw the text. Save the drawing as P7-4.

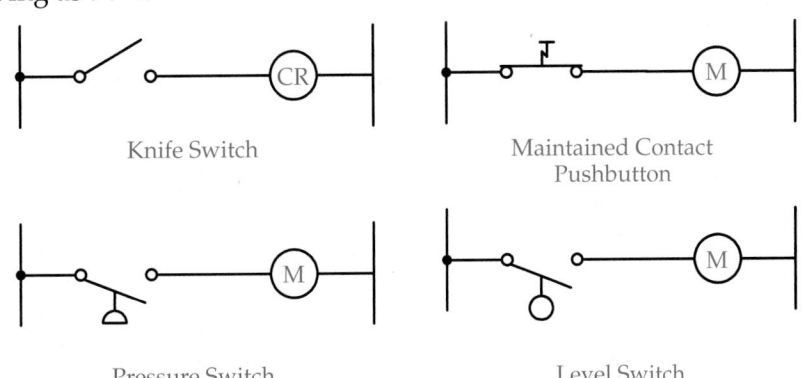

Knife Switch

Maintained Contact
Pushbutton

Pressure Switch
(Start on Rise in Pressure)

Level Switch
(Start on High Level)

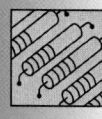

5. Use object snap modes to draw this elementary diagram. Do not draw the text. Save the drawing as P7-5.

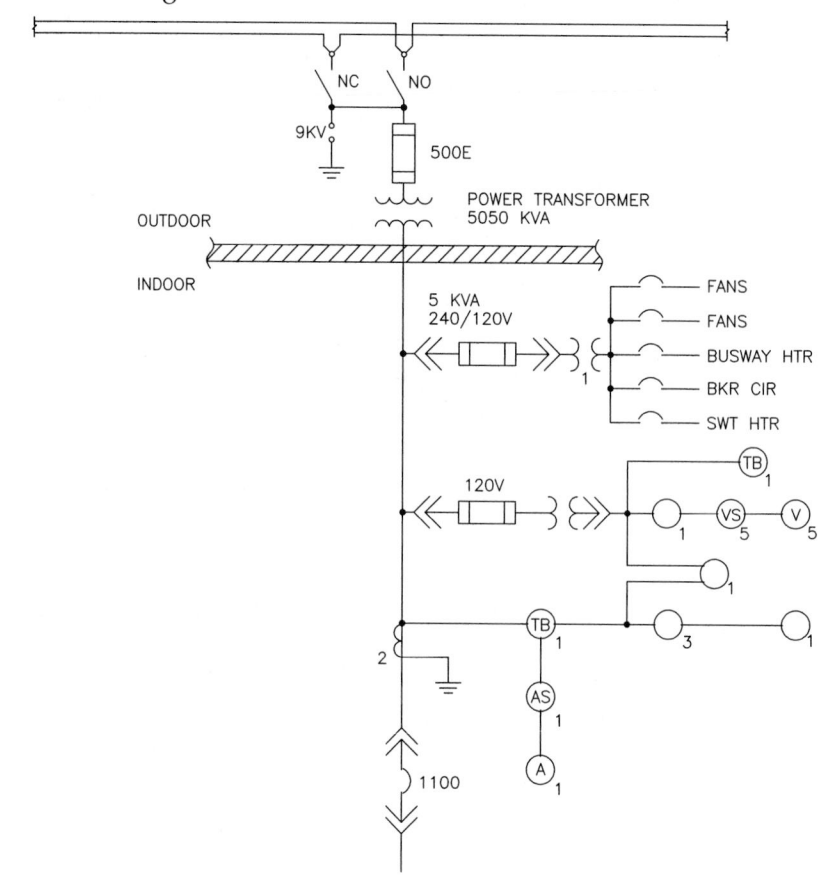

6. Draw the elbow shown. Save the drawing as P7-6.

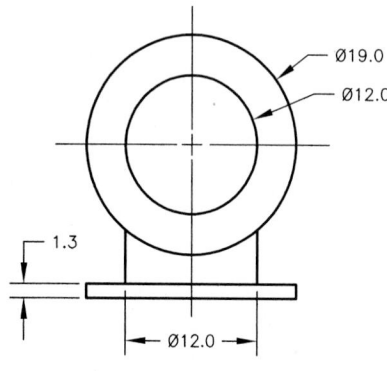
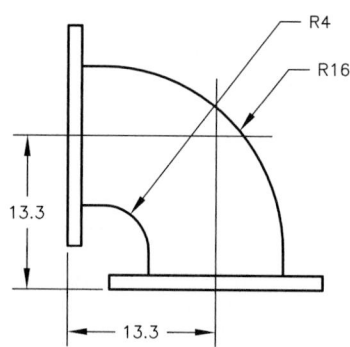

7. Draw the elbow shown. Save the drawing as P7-7.

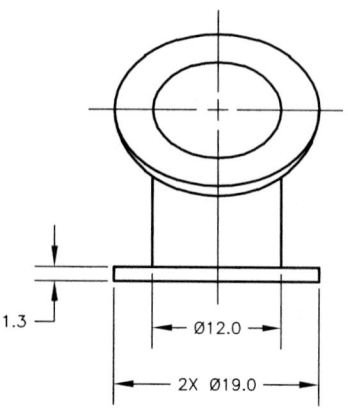
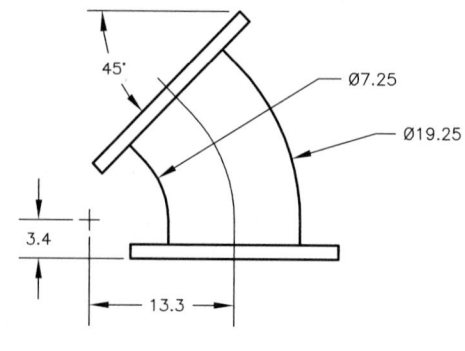

For Problems 8–13, use object snap modes and tracking to draw the objects shown. Do not draw dimensions. Save the drawing as P7-*(problem number).*

8.

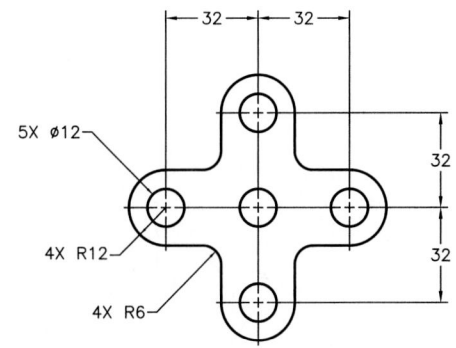

9.

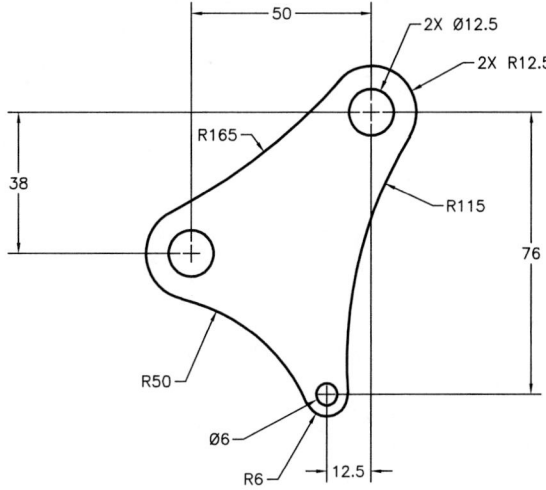

10.

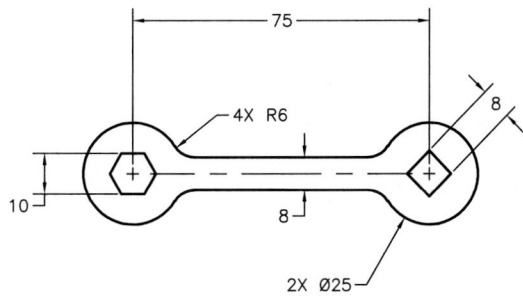

11.

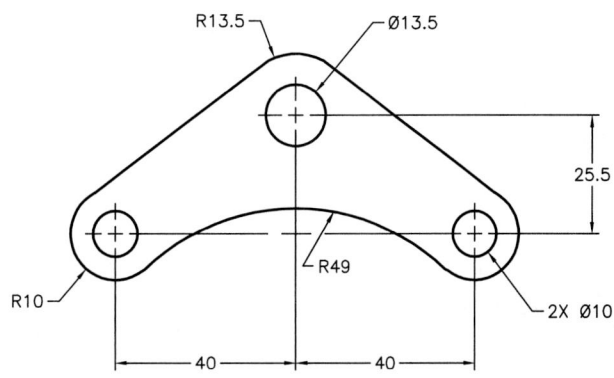

12.

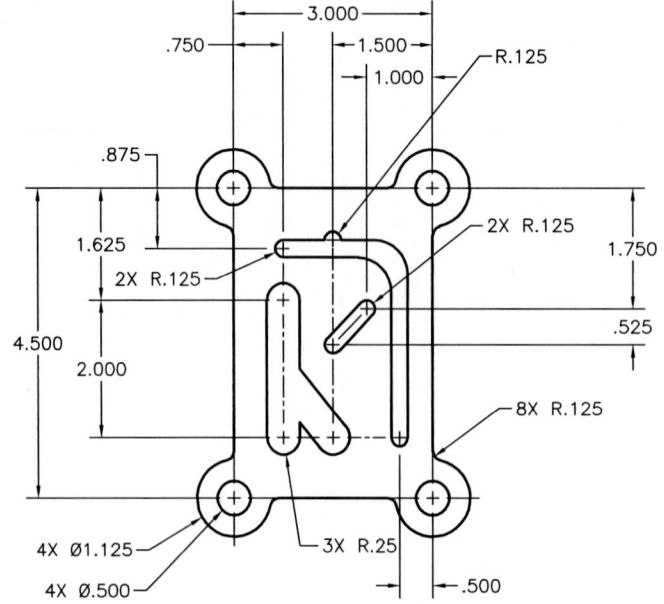

13.

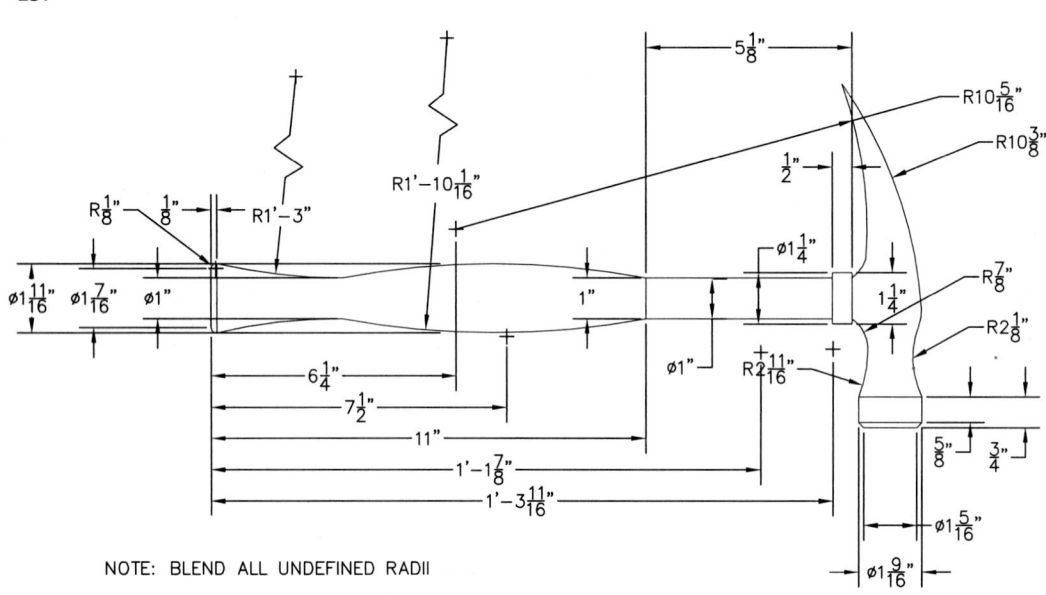

NOTE: BLEND ALL UNDEFINED RADII

Geometric Constructions

Learning Objectives

After completing this chapter, you will be able to do the following:

✓ Use the **OFFSET** command to draw parallel lines and curves.
✓ Divide existing objects into equal lengths using the **DIVIDE** command.
✓ Use the **MEASURE** command to set designated increments on an existing object.
✓ Create orthographic multiview drawings.
✓ Adjust UCS settings to construct auxiliary views.
✓ Use construction lines to assist in drawing orthographic views and auxiliary views.

This chapter explains how to create parallel offset copies, divide objects, and place point objects. These skills, and the other geometry-creating skills you have acquired, are applied in the creation of multiview drawings.

Using Offset to Draw Parallel Lines and Curves

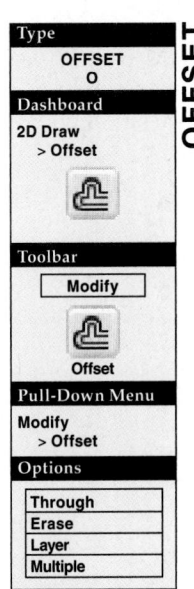

The **OFFSET** command is used to draw concentric circles, concentric arcs, concentric curves, parallel polylines, and parallel lines. This command is accessed by picking the **Offset** button in the **Modify** toolbar or the **2D Draw** control panel of the **Dashboard**, picking **Modify > Offset**, or typing O or OFFSET.

Specifying a Distance to Offset

The simplest way to use the **OFFSET** command is to enter an offset value at the Specify offset distance or [Through/Erase/Layer] <*current*>: prompt. The last offset distance used is the default and is shown in brackets. For example, if you want to draw two parallel circles a distance of .1 unit apart, use the following command sequence. See **Figure 8-1.**

Command: **O** *or* **OFFSET**↵
Current settings: Erase source=*current* Layer=*current* OFFSETGAPTYPE=*current*
Specify offset distance or [Through/Erase/Layer] <*current*>: **.1**↵
Select object to offset or [Exit/Undo] <*current*>: *(pick the object)*
Specify point on side to offset or [Exit/Multiple/Undo] <*current*>: *(pick the side of the object on which the offset will be drawn)*
Select object to offset or [Exit/Undo] <*current*>: *(select another object or press* [Enter]*)*
Command:

The side panel contains:
Type
OFFSET
O
Dashboard
2D Draw
> Offset
Toolbar
Modify
Offset
Pull-Down Menu
Modify
> Offset
Options
Through
Erase
Layer
Multiple

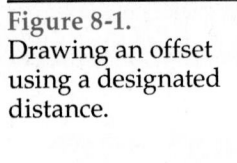

Figure 8-1.
Drawing an offset using a designated distance.

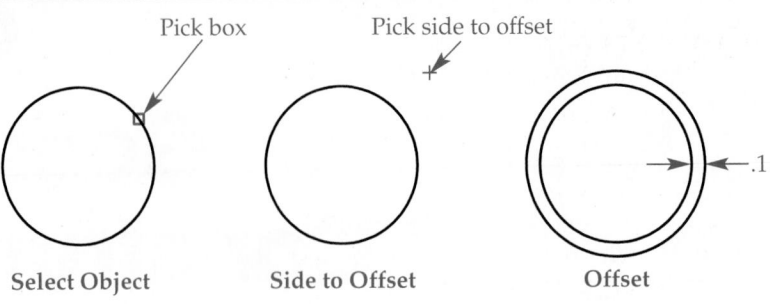

Pick box

Pick side to offset

.1

Select Object

Side to Offset

Offset

If you do not know the offset value, but two reference points exist in the drawing area, you can pick a first point and then a second point instead of typing in an offset value. The distance between these two points is used as the offset value.

When the Select object to offset or [Exit/Undo] <*current*>: prompt first appears, the cursor turns into a pick box. After the object is picked, the cursor turns back into crosshairs. No other selection option (such as window or crossing) works with the **OFFSET** command.

The other option is to pick a point through which the offset is drawn. Type T, as follows, to produce the results shown in **Figure 8-2**:

> Command: **O** *or* **OFFSET**↵
> Current settings: Erase source=*current* Layer=*current* OFFSETGAPTYPE=*current*
> Specify offset distance or [Through/Erase/Layer] <*current*>: **T**↵
> Select object to offset or [Exit/Undo] <*current*>: *(pick the object)*
> Specify through point or [Exit/Multiple/Undo] <*current*>: *(pick the point through which the offset will be drawn)*
> Select object to offset or [Exit/Undo] <*current*>: ↵
> Command:

Object snap modes can be used to assist in specifying the offset distance. For example, suppose you have a circle and a line and want to draw a concentric circle tangent to the line. Refer to **Figure 8-3** and the following command sequence:

> Command: **O** *or* **OFFSET**↵
> Current settings: Erase source=*current* Layer=*current* OFFSETGAPTYPE=*current*
> Specify offset distance or [Through/Erase/Layer] <*current*>: **QUA**↵
> of *(pick the existing circle)*
> Specify second point: **PER**↵
> to *(pick the existing line)*
> Select object to offset or [Exit/Undo] <*current*>: *(pick the existing circle)*
> Specify point on side to offset or [Exit/Multiple/Undo] <*current*>: *(pick between the circle and line)*
> Select object to offset or [Exit/Undo] <*current*>: ↵
> Command:

Figure 8-2.
Drawing an offset through a given point.

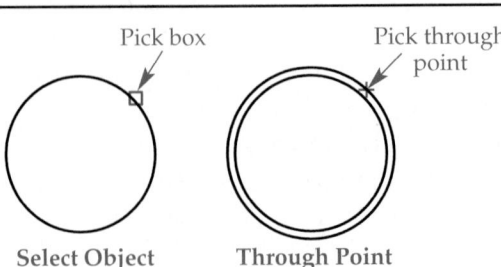

Pick box

Pick through point

Select Object

Through Point

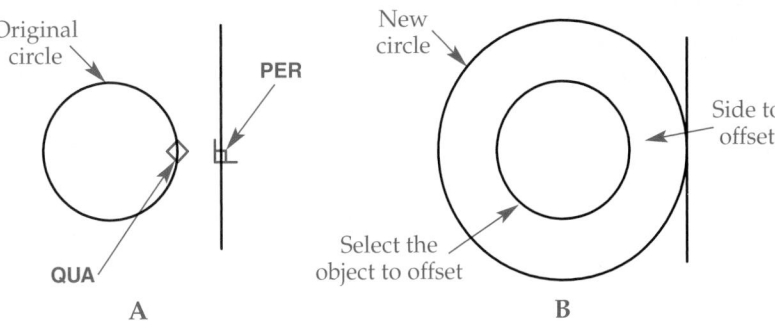

Figure 8-3.
Using **OFFSET** to draw a concentric circle tangent to a line.

Original circle

PER

New circle

Side to offset

Select the object to offset

QUA

A

B

Erasing the Original Object

When an object is being offset, you may want to remove the original object. Instead of offsetting the object and then erasing the source object, you can erase the source object when it is offset. After initiating the **OFFSET** command, select **Erase** and **Yes** from the shortcut menu to erase the source object. The **Yes** option remains as the default until it is changed to **No**. Be sure to change this option back to **No** if you do not want the source offset object to be erased the next time the **OFFSET** command is used.

Changing the Layer of the Offset Object

The **Layer** option allows you to have the offset object placed on the current layer. For example, if the offset source object resides on the Electrical layer and the offset object needs to be placed on the Lighting layer, this can be done during the command if Lighting is the current layer by following this command sequence:

    Command: O or OFFSET↵
    Current settings: Erase source=current Layer=current OFFSETGAPTYPE=current
    Specify offset distance or [Through/Erase/Layer] <current>: L↵
    Enter layer option for offset objects [Current/Source] <current>: C↵
    Specify offset distance or [Through/Erase/Layer] <current>:

When **Current** is specified, the offset object is placed on the current layer. To have the offset object remain on the same layer as the offset source object, use the **Source** option.

Offsetting Multiple Times

After the object to offset has been selected, the **Multiple** option can be used to offset an object more than once with the same distance between the objects without having to reselect the object to offset. Initiate the **OFFSET** command, specify the offset distance, and pick the source object. You can then select **Multiple** and begin picking to specify the offset direction. See **Figure 8-4.** Whenever the **Undo** option is available, it can be used to undo the last offset without exiting the command. Using the **Exit** option by typing E or Exit, pressing [Enter], or right-clicking exits the **OFFSET** command.

Exercise 8-1

Complete the exercise on the Student CD.

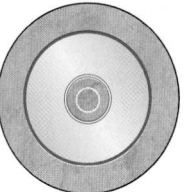

Figure 8-4.
The **Multiple** option can be use to create multiple offsets with the same distance, without picking the source object again.

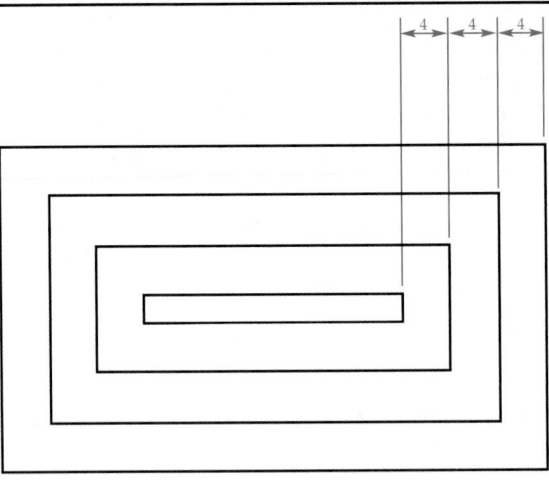

Drawing Points

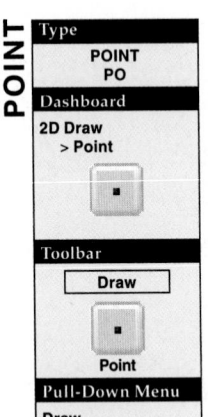

Points are useful for identifying specific locations on a drawing and, as you will see in the next section, for marking positions on objects. You can draw points anywhere on the screen using the **POINT** command. To access this command, pick the **Point** button from the **Draw** toolbar or from the **2D Draw** control panel in the **Dashboard**, type PO or POINT, or select **Draw > Point** and one of the options. You can pick or type coordinates to place the points.

If you need to place only a single point object, use the keyboard command or select the **Single Point** option from the **Point** cascading menu. If you need to draw multiple points, use the **Point** button on the **Draw** toolbar or the **Multiple Point** option from the **Point** cascading menu. Press [Esc] to exit the command.

Setting Point Style

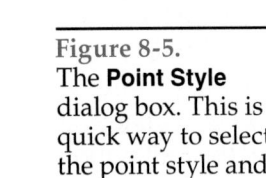

The style and size of points are set using the **Point Style** dialog box. See Figure 8-5. This dialog box is accessed by selecting **Format > Point Style...** or by typing DDPTYPE.

The **Point Style** dialog box contains twenty different point styles. The current point style is highlighted. To change the style, simply pick the graphic image of the desired style.

Figure 8-5.
The **Point Style** dialog box. This is a quick way to select the point style and change the point size.

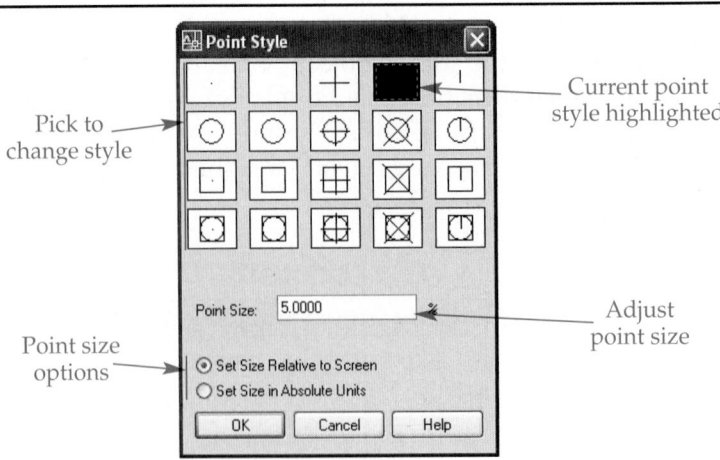

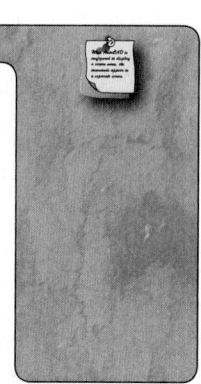

NOTE

The point style is stored in the **PDMODE** system variable. This variable can be changed at the Command: prompt. The **PDMODE** values of the point styles shown in the top row of the **Point Style** dialog box are 0 through 4, from left to right. These are the basic point styles. Add a circle (second row in dialog box) by adding 32 to the basic **PDMODE** value. Add 64 to draw a square (third row), and add 96 to draw a circle and square (bottom row). For example, a point display of an X inside a circle has a **PDMODE** value of 35. This is the sum of the X value of 3 and the circle value of 32.

Set the point size by entering a value in the **Point Size:** text box of the **Point Style** dialog box. Pick the **Set Size Relative to Screen** option button if you want the point size to change in relation to different screen magnifications. Picking the **Set Size in Absolute Units** option button makes the points appear the same size no matter what screen magnification is used. The effects of these options are shown in **Figure 8-6.**

NOTE

The point size and relative/absolute settings can also be modified by changing the **PDSIZE** (point display size) system variable. Positive **PDSIZE** values change size in relation to different display options (relative to screen). Negative **PDSIZE** values make the points appear the same size no matter how much you zoom the drawing (absolute units).

Exercise 8-2
Complete the exercise on the Student CD.

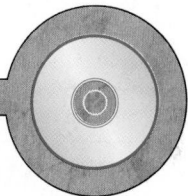

Figure 8-6.
Points sized with the **Set Size Relative to Screen** setting change size as the drawing is zoomed. Points sized with the **Set Size in Absolute Units** setting remain a constant size.

Size Setting	Original Point Size	2X Zoom	0.5 Zoom
Relative to Screen	⊠	⊠	⊠
Absolute Units	⊠	⊠	⊠

Dividing an Object

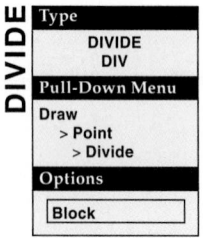

DIVIDE

Type
DIVIDE
DIV

Pull-Down Menu
Draw
> Point
> Divide

Options
Block

A line, circle, arc, or polyline can be divided into an equal number of segments using the **DIVIDE** command. To start the **DIVIDE** command, select **Draw** > **Point** > **Divide** or type DIV or DIVIDE. The **DIVIDE** command does not break an object into multiple parts. It places point objects or blocks at the locations where the breaks would occur if the object were actually divided into multiple segments.

Suppose you have drawn a line and want to divide it into seven equal parts. Enter the **DIVIDE** command, select the object to divide, and then enter the number of segments. See **Figure 8-7**.

The **Block** option of the **DIVIDE** command allows you to place a block at each division point. To initiate the **Block** option, type B at the Enter the number of segments or [Block]: prompt. AutoCAD asks if the block is to be aligned with the object. A *block* is a previously drawn symbol or shape. Blocks are discussed in detail in Chapter 23 of this text.

block: A previously drawn symbol or shape.

After the number of segments is given, the object is divided with points. By default, however, points are displayed as dots, which may not show very well. Change the point style to make the points more visible.

Figure 8-7.
Using the **DIVIDE** command. Note that the default marks (points) have been changed to Xs.

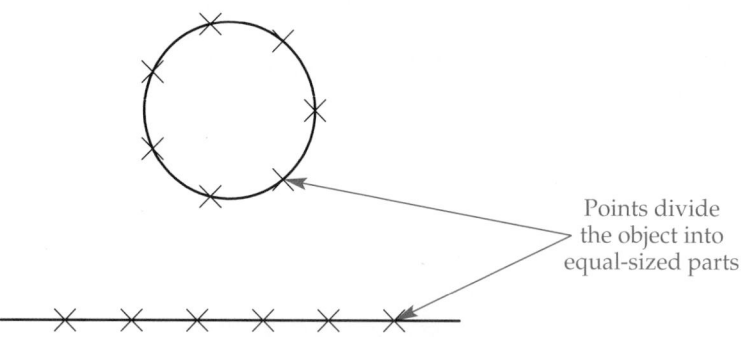

Points divide the object into equal-sized parts

Marking an Object at Specified Distances

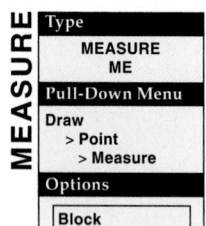

MEASURE

Type
MEASURE
ME

Pull-Down Menu
Draw
> Point
> Measure

Options
Block

Unlike the **DIVIDE** command, in which an object is divided into a specified number of parts, the **MEASURE** command places marks a specified distance apart. To activate the **MEASURE** command, pick **Draw** > **Point** > **Measure** from the pull-down menu or type ME or MEASURE. Pick the object and type in the distance. The line shown in **Figure 8-8** is measured with .75 unit segments.

Measuring begins at the end closest to where the object is picked. All increments are equal to the specified segment length, except the last segment, which may be shorter. The point style determines the type of marks placed on the object, just as it does with the **DIVIDE** command. Blocks can be inserted at the given distances using the **Block** option of the **MEASURE** command.

Exercise 8-3
Complete the exercise on the Student CD.

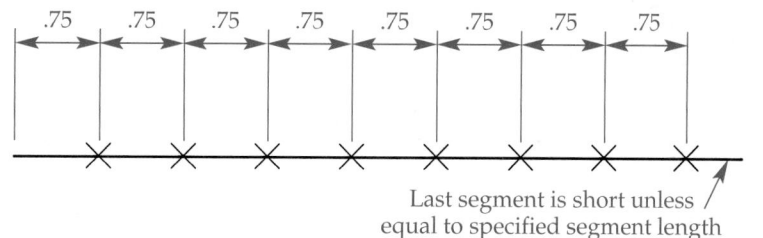

Figure 8-8.
Using the **MEASURE** command. Notice that the last segment may be shorter than the others, depending on the total length of the object.

.75 .75 .75 .75 .75 .75 .75 .75

Last segment is short unless / equal to specified segment length

Orthographic Multiview Drawings

Each field of drafting has its own method to present views of a product. Architectural drafting uses plan views, exterior elevations, and sections. In electronics drafting, symbols are placed in a schematic diagram to show a circuit layout. In civil drafting, contour lines are used to show the topography of land. Mechanical drafting uses *multiview drawings*.

Multiview drawings are based on the standard ASME Y14.3M, *Multiview and Sectional View Drawings*. The views of a multiview drawing are created through orthographic projection. *Orthographic projection* involves projecting object features onto an imaginary plane called a *projection plane*. The imaginary projection plane is placed parallel to the object. Thus, the line of sight is perpendicular to the object. This results in views that appear two-dimensional. See **Figure 8-9.**

Six two-dimensional views show all sides of an object. The six views are the front, right side, left side, top, bottom, and rear. The views are placed in a standard arrangement so others can read the drawing. The front view is the central, or most important, view. Other views are placed around the front view. See **Figure 8-10.** Notice in this figure that the horizontal and vertical edges illustrated in the front view are aligned with the corresponding edges in the other views. You will create the other views from the front view by using the object snapping and tracking features covered in Chapter 7.

Very few products require all six views. The number of views needed depends on the complexity of the object. Use only enough views to completely describe the object. Drawing too many views is time-consuming and can clutter the drawing. In some cases, a single view may be enough to describe the object. The object shown in **Figure 8-11** needs only two views. These two views completely describe the width, height, depth, and features of the object.

multiview drawings: Presentation of views of drawings created through orthographic projection.

orthographic projection: Projecting object features onto an imaginary plane.

projection plane: The imaginary projection plane that is parallel to the object.

Figure 8-9.
Obtaining a front view with orthographic projection.

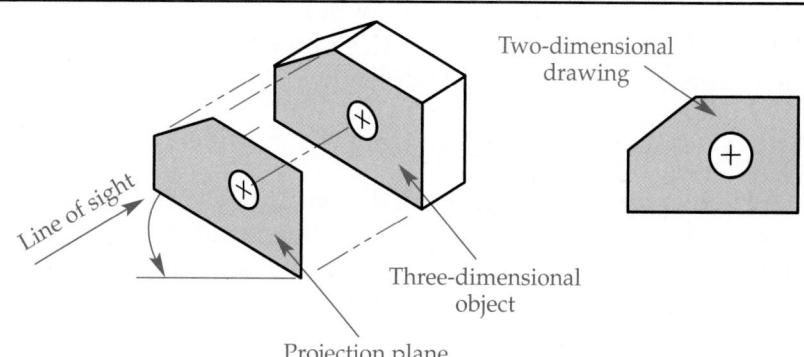

Line of sight

Two-dimensional drawing

Three-dimensional object

Projection plane

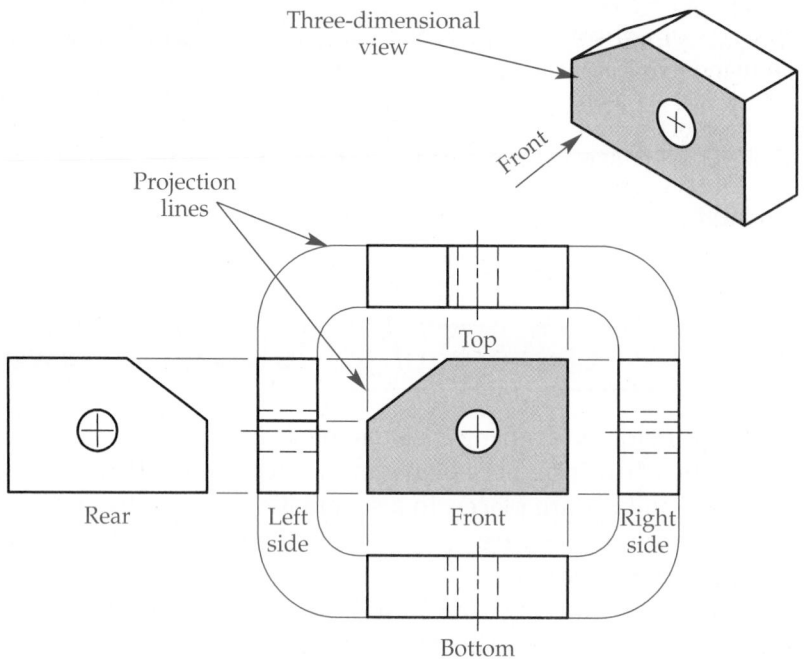

Figure 8-10.
Arrangement of the six orthographic views.

Three-dimensional view

Front

Projection lines

Top

Rear

Left side

Front

Right side

Bottom

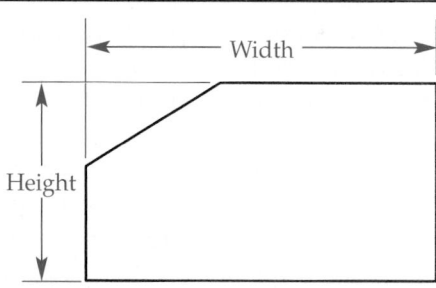
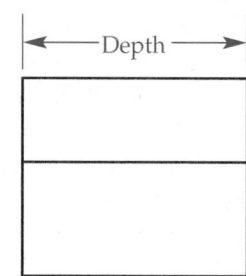

Figure 8-11.
The views you choose to describe the object should show all height, width, and depth dimensions.

Width

Depth

Height

Selecting the Front View

The front view is usually the most descriptive view. The following attributes should be considered when selecting the front view:
- ✓ Most descriptive
- ✓ Most natural position
- ✓ Most stable position
- ✓ Provides the longest dimension
- ✓ Contains the least number of hidden features

Additional views are selected relative to the front view. Remember to choose only the views needed to completely describe the object's features.

Showing Hidden Features

Hidden features are parts of the object not visible in the view at which you are looking. A visible edge appears as a solid line. A hidden edge is shown with a hidden line. Hidden lines were discussed in Chapter 5. Notice in **Figure 8-12** how hidden features are shown as hidden lines. Hidden lines are thin to provide contrast to object lines.

Exercise 8-4
Complete the exercise on the Student CD.

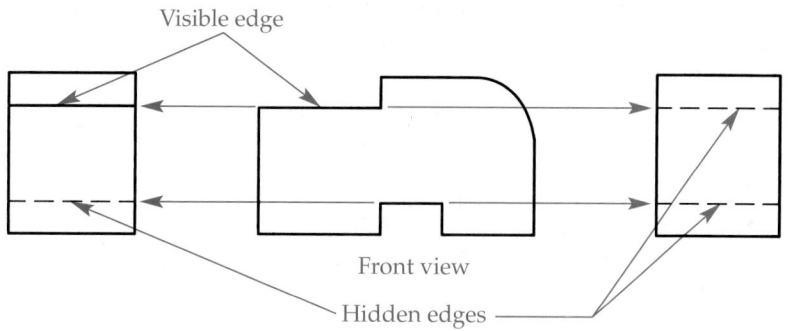

Figure 8-12.
Hidden features are shown with hidden lines.

Visible edge

Front view

Hidden edges

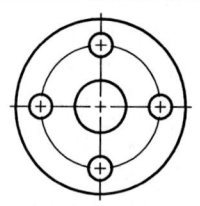

Figure 8-13.
A one-view drawing of a gasket. The thickness is given in a note.

NOTE: THICKNESS 1.5mm

One-View Drawings

In some instances, an object can be fully described using one view. A thin part, such as a gasket, can be drawn with one view. See **Figure 8-13.** The thickness is given as a note in the drawing or in the title block.

Showing Symmetry and Circle Centers

The centerlines of symmetrical objects and the centers of circles are shown with centerlines. For example, in one view of a cylinder, the axis is drawn as a centerline. In the other view, centerlines cross to show the center in the circular view. See **Figure 8-14.** The only place the small centerline dashes should cross is at the center of a circle.

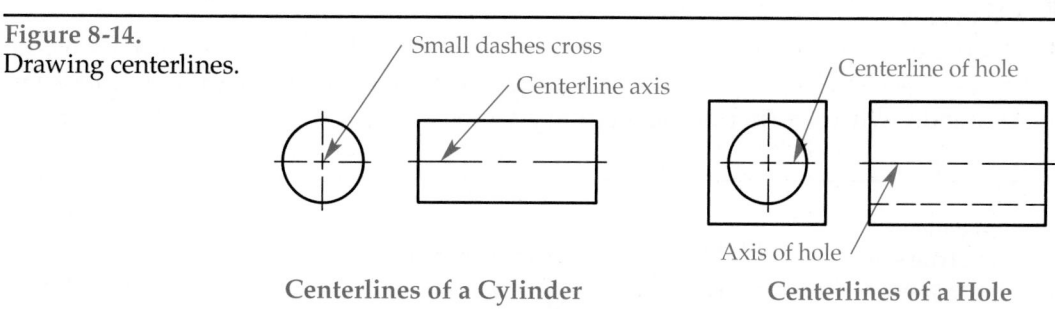

Figure 8-14.
Drawing centerlines.

Small dashes cross

Centerline axis

Centerline of hole

Axis of hole

Centerlines of a Cylinder

Centerlines of a Hole

Drawing Auxiliary Views

In most cases, an object can be completely described using a combination of one or more of the six standard views. Sometimes, however, the multiview layout is not enough to properly identify some object surfaces. It may then be necessary to draw an auxiliary view.

An *auxiliary view* is typically needed when a surface on the object is at an angle to the line of sight in all of the standard views. This slanted surface is *foreshortened* in a standard view, meaning it is shorter than the true size and shape of the surface. To show this surface in true size, an auxiliary view is needed. Foreshortened dimensions are not recommended.

auxiliary view:
View needed when a surface on an object is at an angle to the three principal projection planes.

foreshortened:
Shorter than the true size and shape of the surface.

An auxiliary view is drawn by projecting lines perpendicular (90°) to a slanted surface. Usually, one projection line remains on the drawing. It connects the auxiliary view to the view where the slanted surface appears as a line. The resulting auxiliary view shows the surface in true size and shape. For most applications, the auxiliary view needs only to show the slanted surface, not the entire object. This is called a *partial auxiliary view* and is shown in Figure 8-15.

partial auxiliary view: An auxiliary view that shows only a single surface of an object, rather than the entire object.

In some situations, there may not be enough room on the drawing to project directly from the slanted surface. The auxiliary view is then placed elsewhere. See Figure 8-16. A viewing-plane line is drawn next to the view where the slanted surface appears as a line. The *viewing-plane line* is drawn with a thick dashed or phantom line in accordance with ASME Y14.2M. It is terminated with bold arrowheads that point toward the slanted surface.

viewing-plane line: Line identifying the viewing direction of a related view.

Each end of the viewing-plane line is labeled with a letter. The letters relate the viewing-plane line with the proper auxiliary view. A title such as "VIEW A-A" is placed under the auxiliary view. When more than one auxiliary view is drawn, labels continue with B-B through Z-Z (if necessary). The letters *I*, *O*, and *Q* are not used because they may be confused with numbers. An auxiliary view drawn away from the standard view retains the same angle as if it is projected directly.

Using the User Coordinate System for Auxiliary Views

All the features on your drawing originate from the *world coordinate system (WCS)*. This system includes the X, Y, and Z coordinate values measured from the origin (0,0,0). The WCS is fixed. A *user coordinate system (UCS)*, on the other hand, can be moved to any orientation. User coordinate systems are discussed in detail in *AutoCAD and Its Applications—Advanced*.

world coordinate system (WCS): X, Y, and Z coordinate values measured from the origin (0,0,0).

user coordinate system (UCS): A coordinate system with a user-defined origin location and axes rotation.

In general, a UCS allows you to set your own coordinate origin. The WCS 0,0,0 origin has been in the lower-left corner of the screen for the drawings you have done so far. In many cases, this is fine, but when drawing an auxiliary view, it is best to have the measurements originate from a corner of the view. This, in turn, makes all auxiliary view features and the coordinate display true, as measured from the corner of the view. This method makes it easier to locate and later dimension the auxiliary view features.

Figure 8-17 shows an example of aligning the UCS to the auxiliary view. Draw the principal views, such as the front, top, and right side. Move the UCS origin to a location that coincides with a corner of the auxiliary view.

Figure 8-15.
Auxiliary views show the true size and shape of an inclined surface.

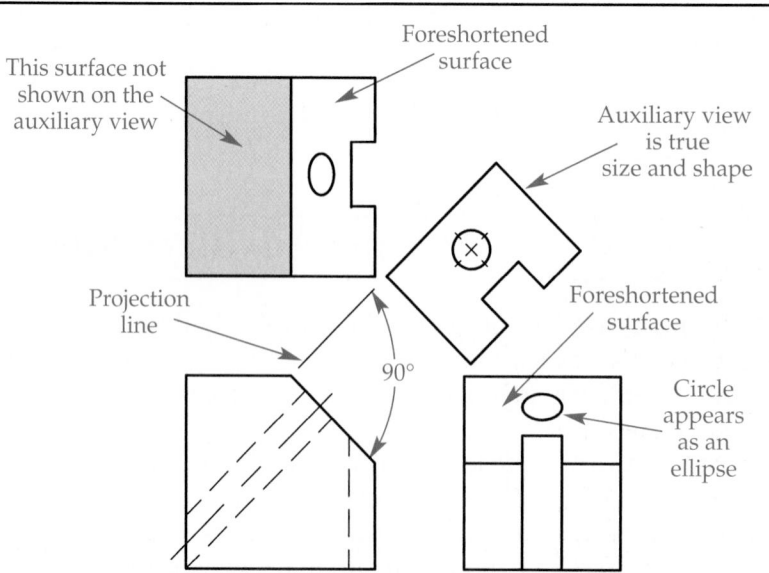

Figure 8-16.
Identifying an auxiliary view with a viewing-plane line. If there is not enough room, the view can be moved to a different location.

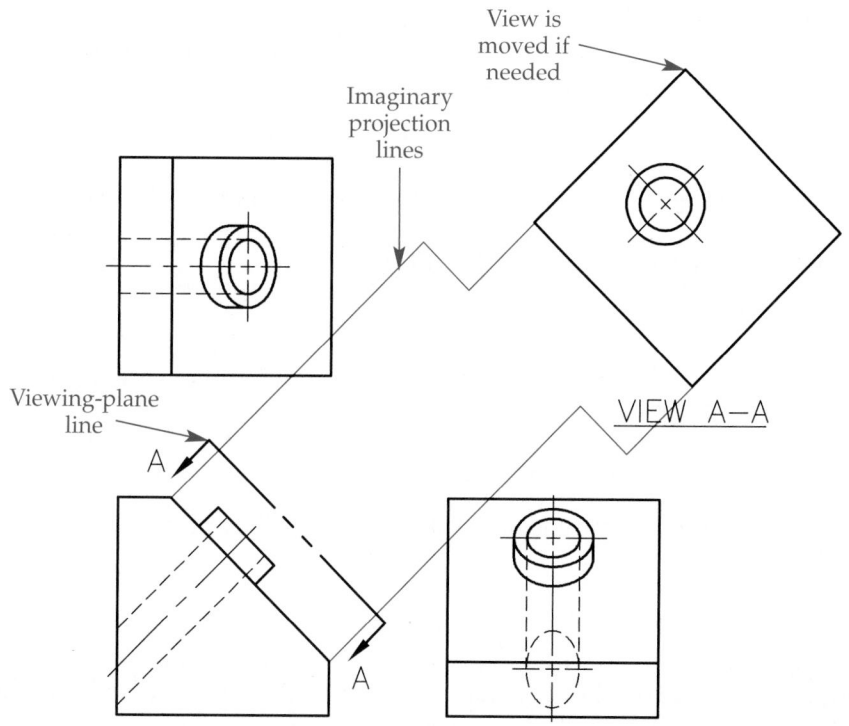

Figure 8-17.
Relocating the origin and rotating the Z axis of the UCS system. A—Rotating the UCS to align with the auxiliary view angle. B—The UCS icon is displayed at the current UCS origin at the corner of the auxiliary view.

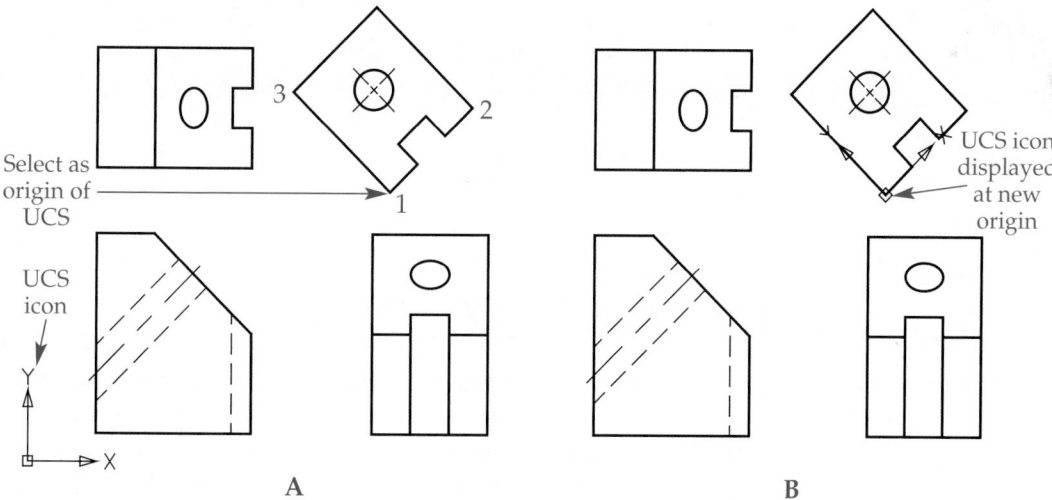

A   B

To move the UCS origin, type UCS, select the **3 Point** button on the **UCS** toolbar, or select **Tools** > **New UCS** > **3 Point**. The command sequence is as follows:

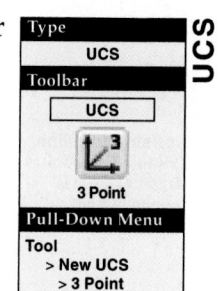

> Command: **UCS.**⌐
> Current ucs name: *current*
> Enter an option [New/Move/orthoGraphic/Prev/Restore/Save/Del/Apply/?/World] <World>: **N.**⌐
> Specify origin of new UCS or [ZAxis/3point/OBject/Face/View/X/Y/Z] <0,0,0>: **3.**⌐
> Specify new origin point <0,0,0>: *(select Point A, as shown in Figure 8-17)*
> Specify point on positive portion of X-axis *<current>*: *(select Point B)*
> Specify point on positive-Y portion of the UCS XY plane *<current>*: *(select Point C)*
> Command:

The icon is rotated and moved, as shown in **Figure 8-17B.** If you want the UCS displayed in the lower-left corner of the drawing area, select **Tools > Named UCS...** from the pull-down menu. This displays the **UCS** dialog box. In the **Settings** tab, uncheck the **Display at UCS origin point** check box.

Before you begin drawing the auxiliary view, use the **Save** option of the **UCS** command to name and save the new UCS:

Command: **UCS.⏎**
Current ucs name: *current*
Enter an option [New/Move/orthoGraphic/Prev/Restore/Save/Del/Apply/?/World]
    <World>: **S.⏎**
Enter name to save current UCS or [?]: **AUX.⏎**
Command:

Now, proceed by drawing the auxiliary view. When you have finished, select the **World UCS** button from the **UCS** toolbar or enter the **UCS** command and use the default **World** option to reset the UCS back to the WCS origin:

Command: **UCS.⏎**
Current ucs name: AUX
Enter an option [New/Move/orthoGraphic/Prev/Restore/Save/Del/Apply/?/World]
    <World>: ⏎
Command:

PROFESSIONAL TIP

Polar tracking is another method that can be used to draw auxiliary views. It can be used in place of or in addition to the UCS method described in this section. Polar tracking was covered in Chapter 7.

Exercise 8-5

Complete the exercise on the Student CD.

Construction Lines and Rays

The tracking vectors and alignment paths you used in the previous sections are efficient methods of creating geometry because these types of lines appear only when they are needed. Sometimes, you may want the lines to stay visible while you continue to create geometry. This is when you want to use construction lines (**XLINE**) and rays (**RAY**). Both commands can be used for similar purposes. However, the **XLINE** command has more options and flexibility than the **RAY** command.

Using the Xline Command

construction line (xline): A line in AutoCAD that is infinite in both directions.

A *construction line*, or *xline*, is a line of infinite length used to help build accurate geometry. Although these lines are infinite, they do not change the drawing extents. This means they have no effect on zooming operations.

Construction lines can be modified by moving, copying, trimming, and other editing operations. Editing commands such as **TRIM** or **FILLET** change the object type.

AutoCAD and Its Applications—Basics

For example, if one end of a construction line is trimmed off, it becomes a ray. A *ray* is considered semi-infinite because it is infinite in one direction only. If the infinite end of a ray is trimmed off, it becomes a line object.

Construction lines and rays are drawn on the current layer and plot the same as other objects. This may cause conflict with other lines on that layer. A good way to handle this problem is to set up a special layer just for construction lines.

The **XLINE** command can be accessed by picking the **Construction Line** button on the **Draw** toolbar or from the **2D Draw** control panel of the **Dashboard**, picking **Draw > Construction Line** in the pull-down menu, or typing XL or XLINE. You can specify two points through which the construction line passes. The first point of a construction line is called the *root point*. After you pick the first point, you can select as many points as you would like. Xlines are created between every point and the root point.

Figure 8-18 shows how construction lines can be used to help project features between views. After picking the first point, right-click the drawing area to see the following **XLINE** options in the shortcut menu:

- **Hor.** Draws a horizontal construction line through a single specified point.
- **Ver.** Draws a vertical construction line through a specified point.
- **Ang.** Draws a construction line at a specified angle through a selected point. The default lets you specify an angle and then pick a point through which the construction line is to be drawn. This works well if you know the angle. You can also pick two points in the drawing to describe the angle. The **Reference** option allows you to use the angle of an existing line object as a reference angle for construction lines. This option is useful when you do not know the angle of the construction line, but you know the angle between an existing object and the construction line. **Figure 8-19** shows the **Ang** option used to draw construction lines establishing the location of an auxiliary view.
- **Bisect.** This option draws a construction line that bisects a specified angle. This is a convenient tool for use in some geometric constructions, as shown in **Figure 8-20**.
- **Offset.** This **XLINE** option draws a construction line a specified distance from a selected line object. You have the option of specifying an offset distance or using the **Through** option to pick a point through which to draw the construction line.

ray: Line that is infinite in one direction only.

Type
XLINE
XL

Dashboard
2D Draw
> Construction Line

Toolbar
Draw

Construction Line

Pull-Down Menu
Draw
> Construction Line

Options
| Hor |
| Ver |
| Ang |
| Bisect |
| Offset |

XLINE

root point: The first point of a construction line.

Figure 8-18.
Creating horizontal construction lines using two points and the **Hor** option.

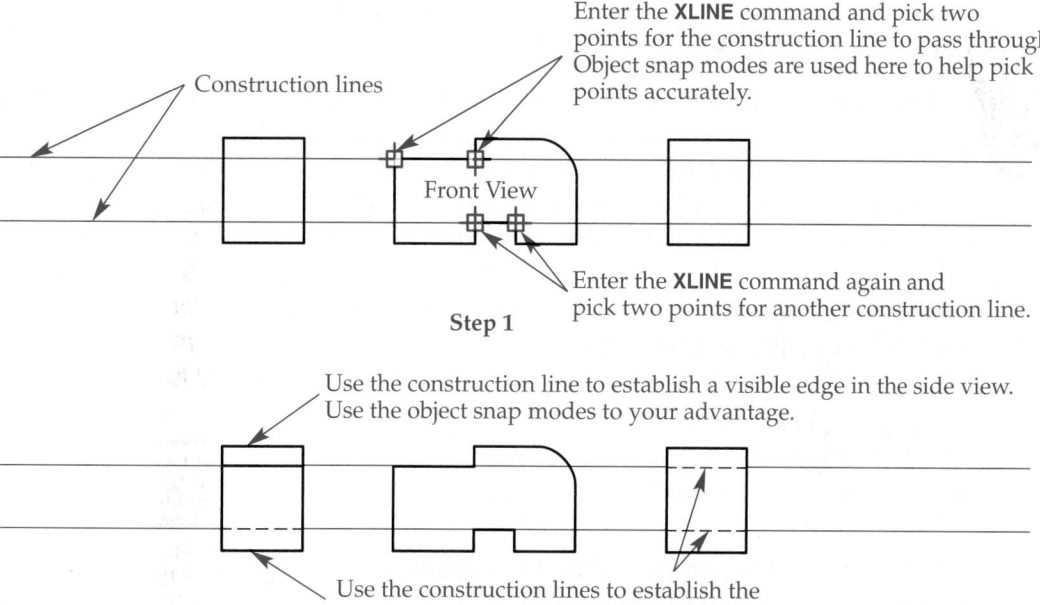

Figure 8-19.
Using the **XLINE**
command **Ang**
option.

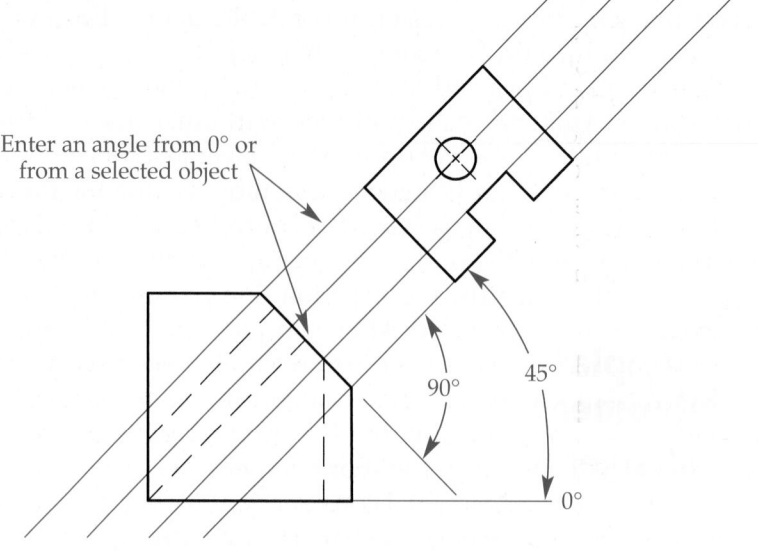

Enter an angle from 0° or
from a selected object

90°

45°

0°

Figure 8-20.
Using the **XLINE**
command **Bisect**
option.

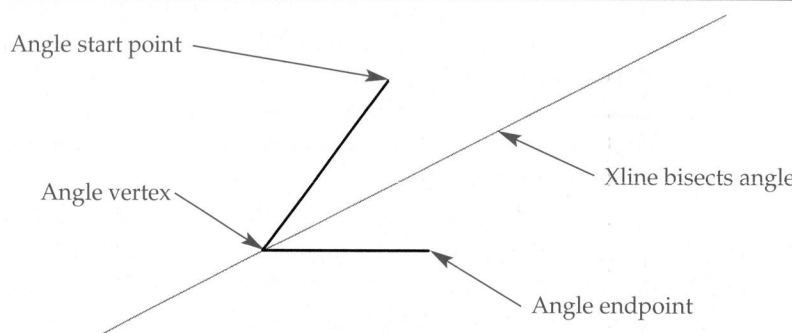

Angle start point

Angle vertex

Xline bisects angle

Angle endpoint

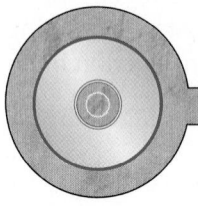

Exercise 8-6
Complete the exercise on the Student CD.

Using the Ray Command

The **RAY** command is limited, compared to the **XLINE** command. The **RAY** command allows you to specify the point of origin and a point through which the ray passes. In this manner, the **RAY** command works much like the default option of the **XLINE** command. The ray, however, extends beyond only the second pick point. The **XLINE** command results in a construction line that extends both directions from the pick points.

The **RAY** command can be accessed by picking **Draw > Ray** or by typing RAY. The **RAY** command sequence is as follows:

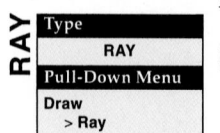

Command: **RAY**↵
Specify start point: (*pick a point*)
Specify through point: (*pick a second point*)
Specify through point: (*draw more construction lines or press* [Enter])
Command:

Both the **RAY** command and the **XLINE** command allow the creation of multiple objects. You must press [Enter] to end the command.

Editing Construction Lines and Rays

The construction lines you create using the **XLINE** and **RAY** commands can be edited and modified using standard editing commands. These commands are introduced in Chapter 11 and Chapter 12. The construction lines will change into a new object type when infinite ends are trimmed off. An xline trimmed on one side becomes a ray, and an xline trimmed on both ends becomes a normal line object. A ray that has its infinite end trimmed also becomes a line object. Therefore, in many cases, your construction lines can be modified to become part of the actual drawing. This approach can save a significant amount of time in many drawings.

Template Development

Chapter 8

Many drafters rely on points created by the **POINT, DIVIDE**, and **MEASURE** commands to construct geometry accurately. Point styles vary according to personal preference, but you can add your preferred style to your drawing templates. Refer to the Student CD for detailed instructions to add your preferred point style to your mechanical, architectural, and civil drawing.

Chapter Test

Answer the following questions. Write your answers on a separate sheet of paper or complete the electronic chapter test on the Student CD.

1. List two ways to establish an offset distance using the **OFFSET** command.
2. What option of the **OFFSET** command is used to remove the source offset object?
3. How do you draw a single point, and how do you draw multiple points?
4. How do you access the **Point Style** dialog box?
5. How do you change the point size in the **Point Style** dialog box?
6. Give the command needed to divide a line into 24 equal parts.
7. If you use the **DIVIDE** command and nothing appears to happen, what should you do?
8. What is the difference between the **DIVIDE** and **MEASURE** commands?
9. Provide at least four guidelines for selecting the front view of an orthographic multiview drawing.
10. When can a part be shown with only one view?
11. When is an auxiliary view needed, and what does an auxiliary view show?
12. What is the angle of projection from the slanted surface into the auxiliary view?
13. Name the AutoCAD command that allows you to draw construction lines.
14. Why is it a good idea to put construction lines on their own layer?
15. Name the option that can be used to bisect an angle with a construction line.
16. What is the difference between the construction lines drawn with the command identified in Question 13 and rays drawn with the **RAY** command?

Drawing Problems

Load AutoCAD for each of the following problems, and use one of your templates or start a new drawing using your own variables.

1. Use the **OFFSET** command to draw the elevation of the desk shown. Do not draw dimensions. Save the drawing as P8-1.

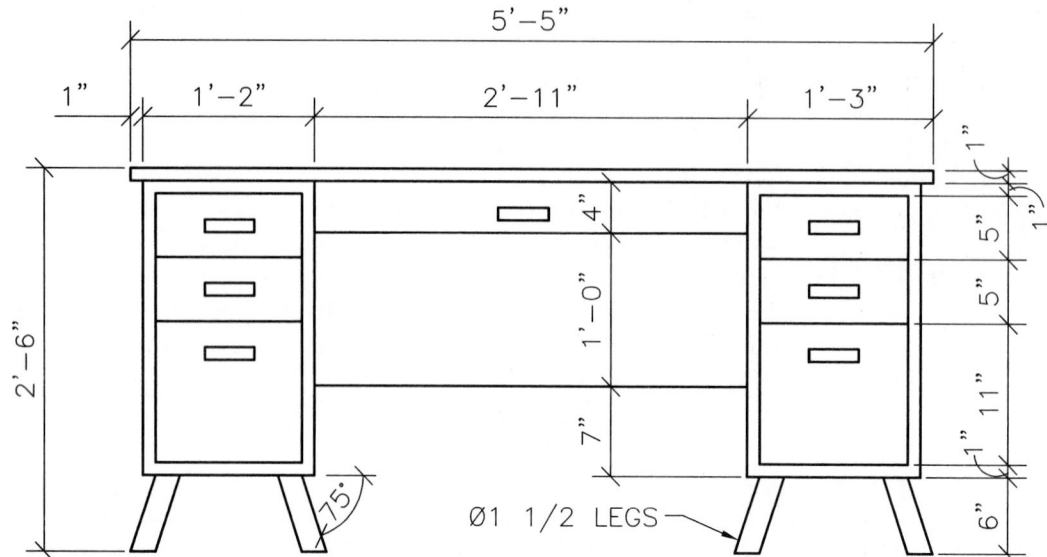

2. Draw the front and side views of this offset support. Use object snap modes and tracking. Do not draw the dimensions. Save your drawing as P8-2.

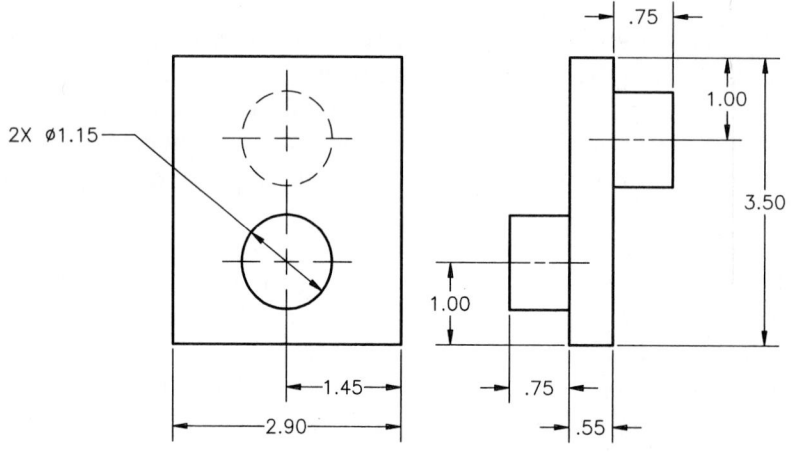

3. Draw the top and front views of this hitch bracket. Use object snap modes and tracking. Do not draw the dimensions. Save your drawing as P8-3.

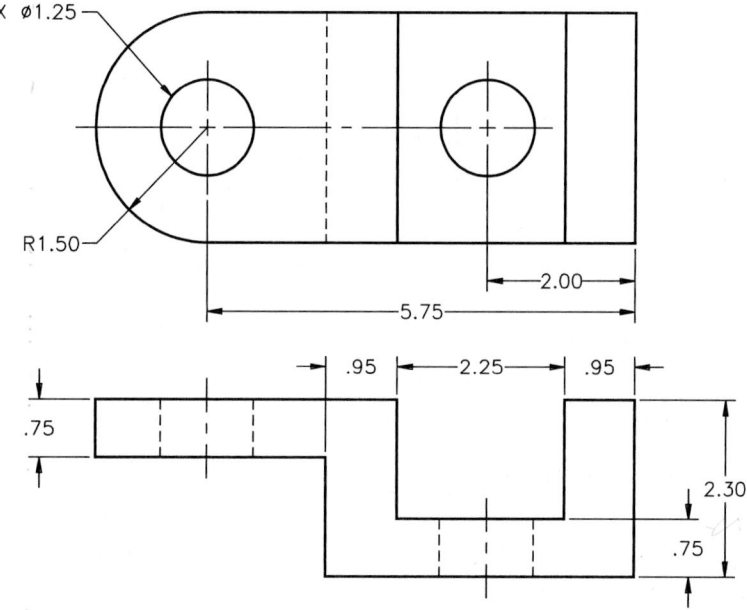

4. Draw this aluminum spacer. Use object snap modes and tracking. Do not draw the dimensions. Save the drawing as P8-4.

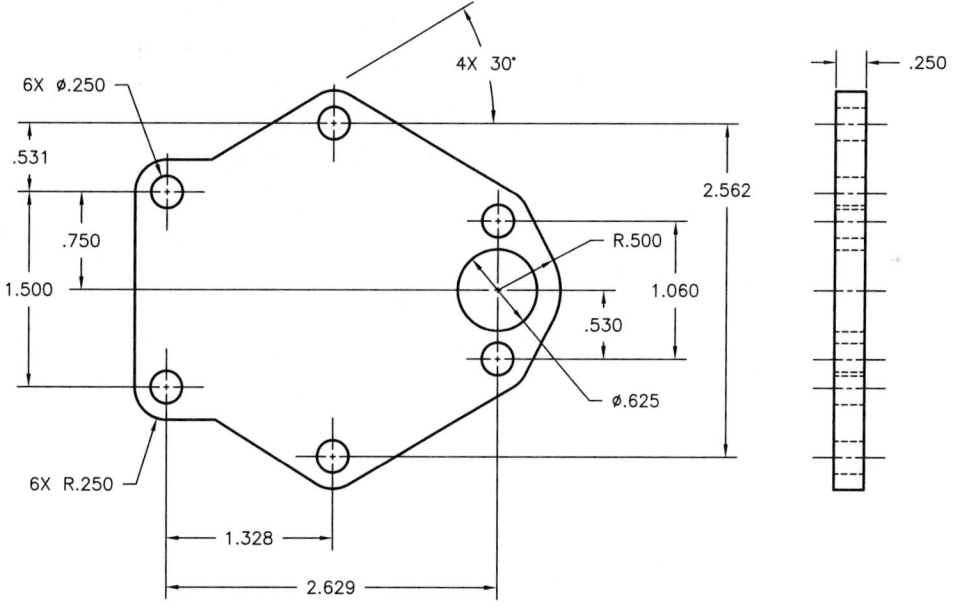

5. Draw this spring using the **OFFSET** command for material thickness. Do not draw the dimensions. Save the drawing as P8-5.

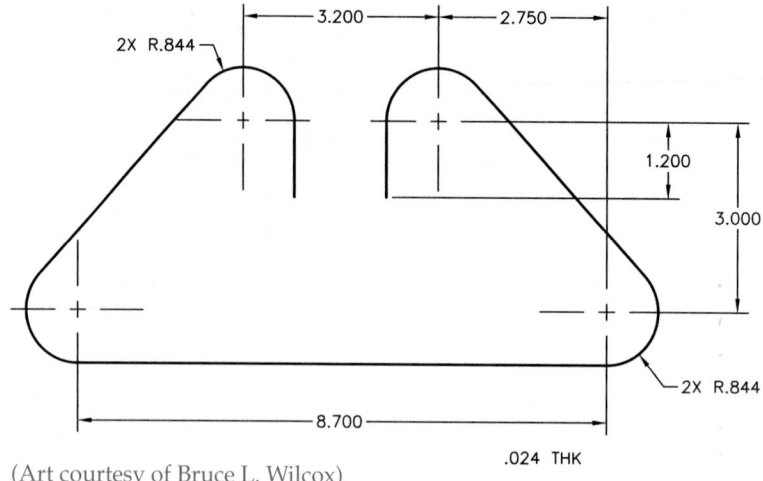

(Art courtesy of Bruce L. Wilcox)

6. Draw this gasket. Do not draw the dimensions. Save the drawing as P8-6.

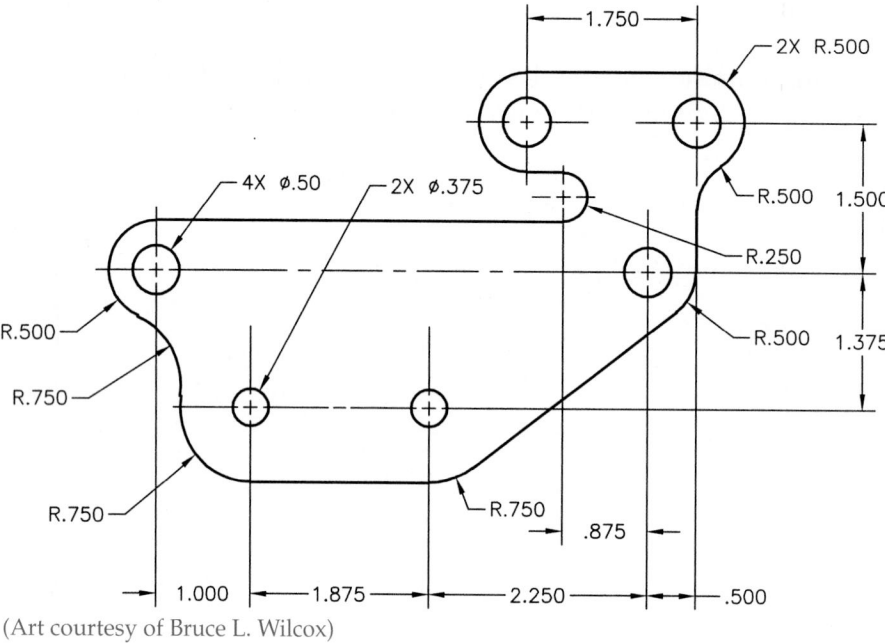

(Art courtesy of Bruce L. Wilcox)

7. Draw this sheet metal chassis. Do not draw the dimensions. Use object snap tracking and polar tracking to your advantage. Save the drawing as P8-7.

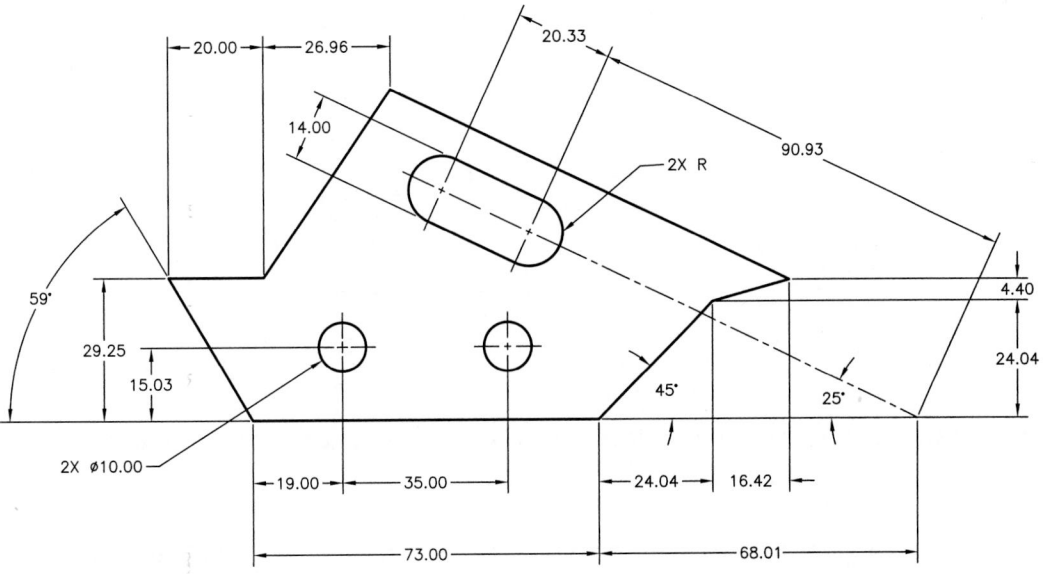

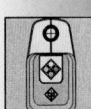

(Art courtesy of Bruce L. Wilcox)

8. Draw this cup. Do not draw the dimensions. Save the drawing as P8-8.

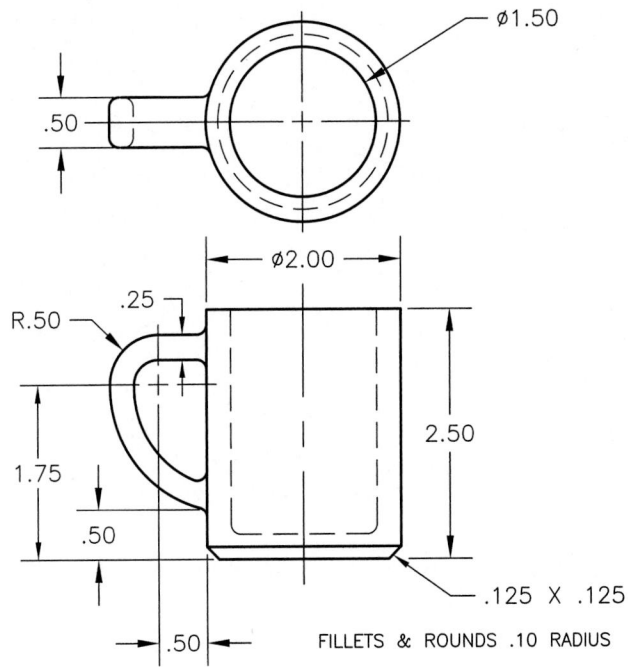

9. Draw this bushing. Do not draw the dimensions. Save the drawing as **P8-9**.

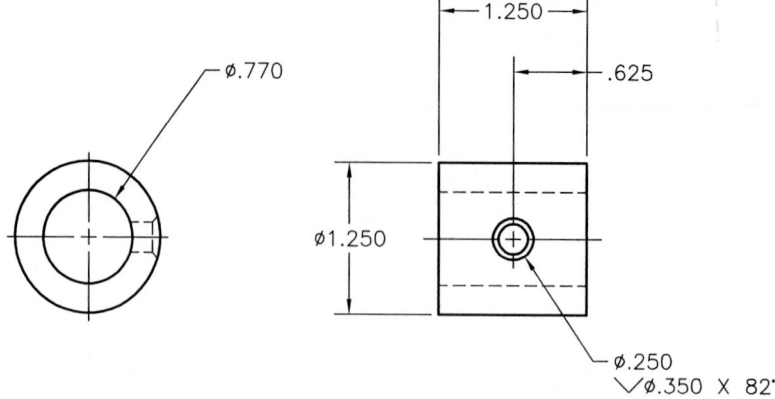

10. Draw this wrench. Do not draw the dimensions. Save the drawing as **P8-10**.

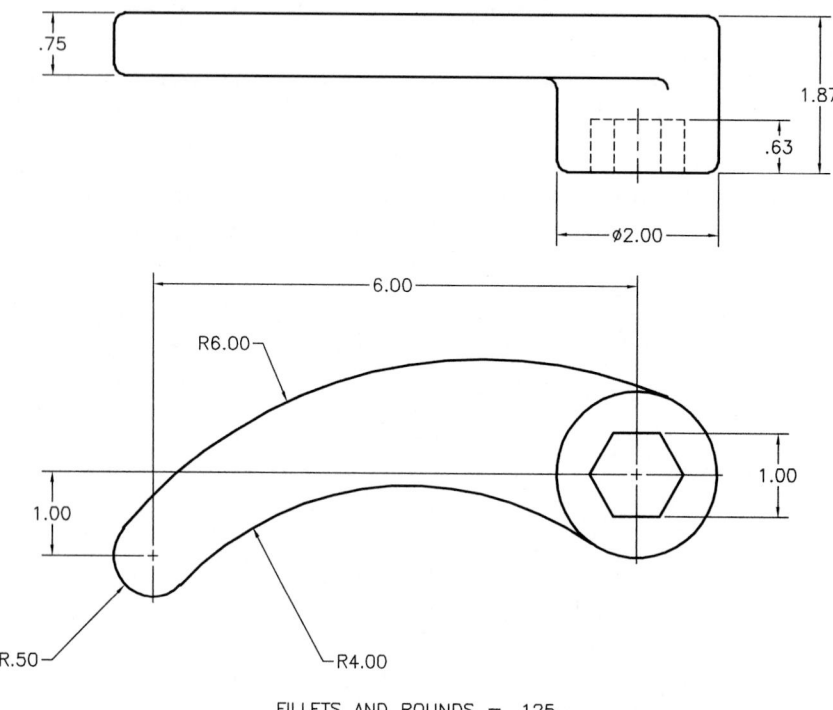

FILLETS AND ROUNDS = .125

11. Draw this support. Do not draw the dimensions. Save the drawing as **P8-11**.

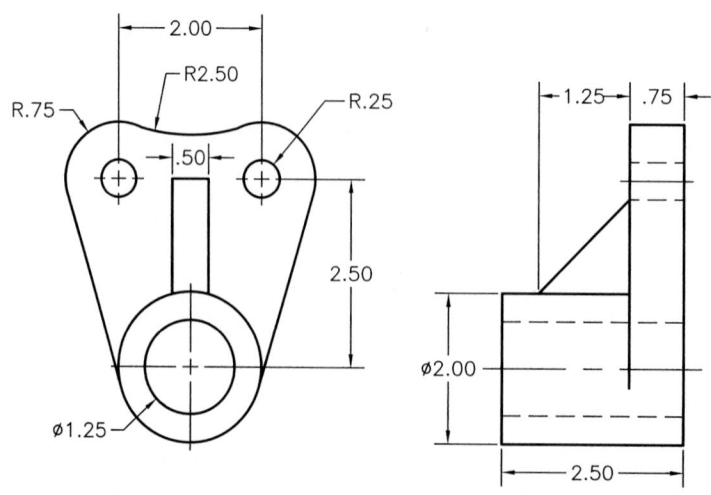

In Problems 12 through 17, draw the views needed to completely describe the objects. Use object snap modes, AutoTrack modes, and offsets as needed. Do not dimension. Save the drawings as P8-(problem number).

12.

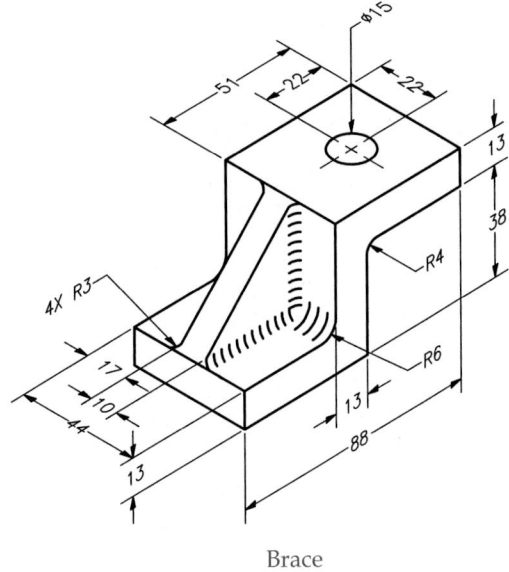

Brace

13.

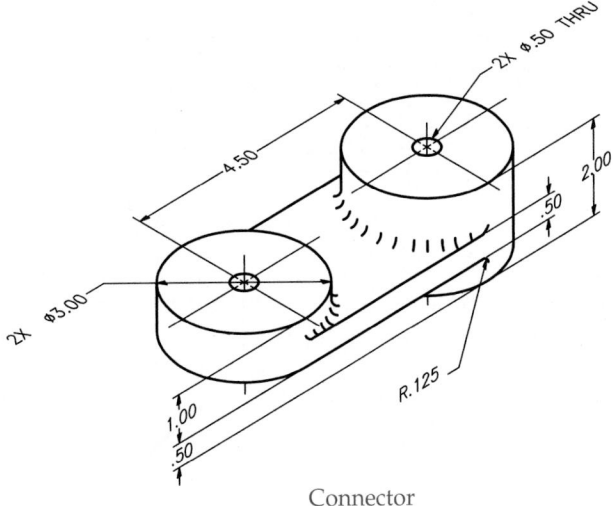

Connector

14.

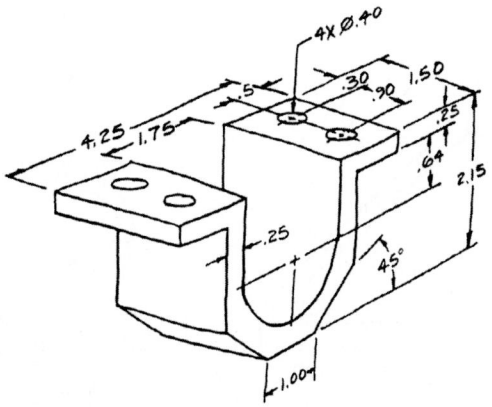

Journal Bracket (Engineer's Rough Sketch)

15.

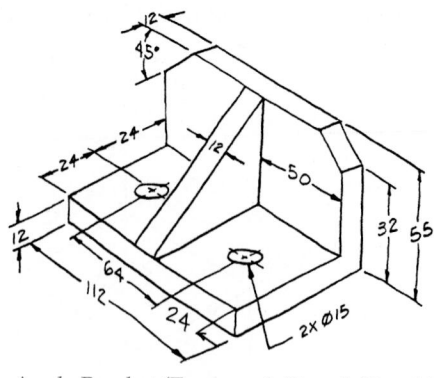

Angle Bracket (Engineer's Rough Sketch)
(Metric)

16.

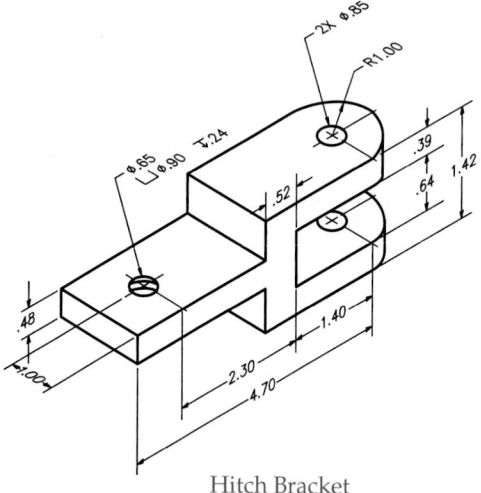

Hitch Bracket

17. Draw the views of this pillow block, including the auxiliary view. Do not draw the dimensions. Save your drawing as P8-17.

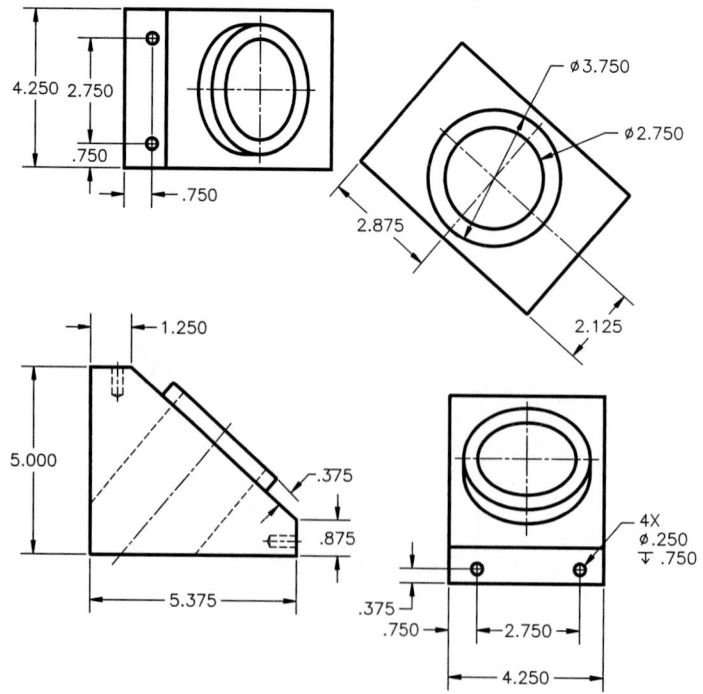

Placing Text on Drawings

Learning Objectives

After completing this chapter, you will be able to do the following:

✓ Describe and use proper text standards.
✓ Calculate drawing scale and text height.
✓ Create text styles.
✓ Make multiple lines of text with the **MTEXT** command.
✓ Use the **TEXT** command to create single-line text.
✓ Insert fields into text.
✓ Edit existing text.
✓ Check your spelling.
✓ Search for and replace material automatically.

Information on a drawing that cannot be described using objects and symbols is added using letters, numbers, words, and notes. In manual drafting, letters and numbers on drawings have traditionally been added by hand lettering. This is a slow, time-consuming task. Computer-aided drafting programs significantly reduce the tedious nature of adding notes to a drawing. In computer-aided drafting, lettering is referred to as *text*. Lettering with AutoCAD is fast and produces text that is consistent and easy to read . This chapter shows how text can be added to drawings and explains standards for proper text presentation based on ASME Y14.2M, *Line Conventions and Lettering*.

text: Lettering on a CAD drawing.

Text Standards

Industry and company standards dictate how text appears on a drawing. The ASME Y14.2M lettering standard recommends several text heights based on the particular function of the text on the drawing. The height of most text, such as dimensions and notes, is .12″ (3 mm). Taller text, used for titles and unique applications, is .24″ (6 mm) high. Many companies, especially those who produce architectural and civil drawings, depart from the ASME standard and use a minimum text height of .125″ (3 mm) and a text height of between .188″ and .25″ (5 mm to 6.5 mm) .25″ for taller text. Some companies specify a .188″, or 5/32″ (5 mm), lettering height for standard text. Regardless of the text height, all text should be consistent and easy to read.

Figure 9-1.
Vertical and inclined text.

ABC.. abc.. 123..
ABC.. abc.. 123..

Vertical text is standard on engineering drawings, although inclined text may be used depending on company preference. See **Figure 9-1.** The recommended slant for inclined text is 68° from horizontal. Text on a drawing is normally uppercase, but lowercase letters are used in some instances. Typically, the same style of text is used throughout a drawing, but in some cases, such as text on maps, a combination of text styles is used.

Numbers in dimensions and notes are the same height as standard text. When fractions are used in dimensions, the fraction bar should be placed horizontally between the numerator and denominator. AutoCAD provides methods for stacking text. However, many notes placed on drawings have fractions displayed with a diagonal (/) fraction bar. A dash or space is usually placed between the whole number and the fraction. Examples of text for numbers and fractions in different unit formats are shown in **Figure 9-2.**

Figure 9-2.
Examples of text for different unit formats.

Decimal Inch	Fractional Inch			Millimeter		
2.750 .25	$2\frac{3}{4}$	2–3/4	2 3/4	2.5	3	0.7

Text Composition

Composition refers to the spacing, layout, and appearance of the text. With manual lettering, it is necessary to space letters freehand. Spacing is performed automatically with computer-generated text.

AutoCAD text commands provide great control over the layout and appearance of text. Text can be laid out horizontally, as is typically the case when adding notes, or drawn at any angle according to specific requirements. AutoCAD automatically sets lines of text apart at an equal distance. This helps maintain the identity of individual notes.

Drawing Scale and Text Height

Ideally, you should determine drawing scale, scale factors, and text heights before you begin a drawing. These items are best incorporated as settings within your template drawing files, but they can be changed as needed. The scale factor of a drawing is important because this value is used to make sure the text is shown on-screen and plotted at the proper height. To help understand the concept of drawing scale, look at the portion of a floor plan shown in **Figure 9-3.** Everything drawn in model space is drawn at full scale. This means that the bathtub, for example, is actually drawn 5′

Figure 9-3.
An example of a portion of a floor plan drawn at full scale in model space. If text is drawn at full scale, as shown in A, the text is very small compared to the large objects. The text must be scaled, as shown in B, in order to be seen and plotted correctly.

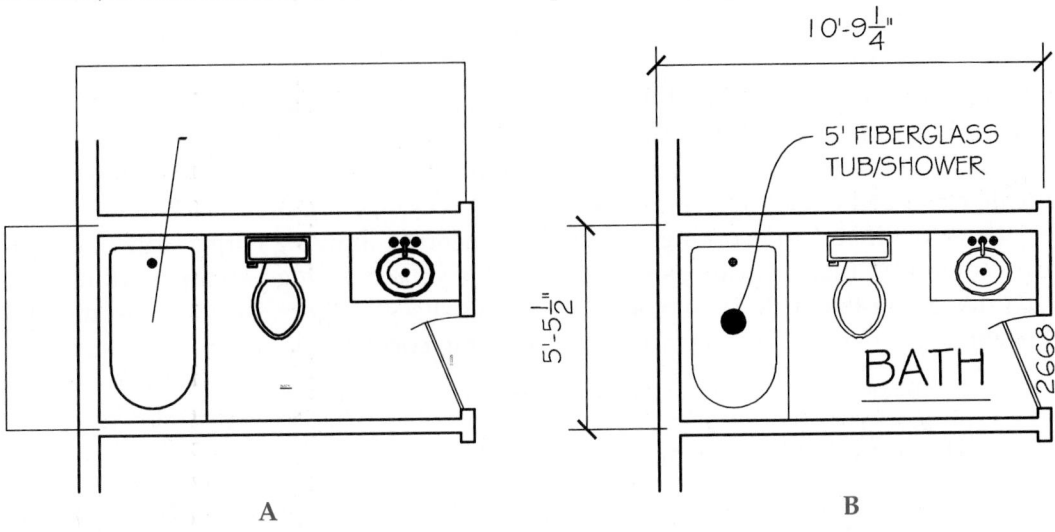

long. However, at this scale, text size becomes an issue, because text that is drawn at full scale (1/8″ high) is extremely small compared to the other full-scale objects, as shown in **Figure 9-3A**. As a result, you must adjust the height of the text according to the drawing scale. In **Figure 9-3B**, the text has been scaled properly. You can calculate the scale factor manually and apply it to the text height, or you can allow AutoCAD to calculate it by using annotative text.

Scaling Text Manually

To manually adjust the height of text according to a specific drawing scale, you must calculate the drawing scale factor. The scale factor is multiplied by the desired plotted text height to get the model space text height.

Calculating the scale factor

The scale factor is always a reciprocal of the drawing scale. For example, if you wish to plot a drawing at a scale of 1/2″ = 1″, calculate the scale factor as follows:

```
1/2″ = 1″
.5″ = 1″
1/.5 = 2
The scale factor is 2.
```

An architectural drawing that is to be plotted at a scale of 1/4″ = 1′-0″ has a scale factor calculated as follows:

```
1/4″ = 1′-0″
.25″ = 12″
12/.25 = 48
The scale factor is 48.
```

The scale factor of a civil engineering drawing that has a scale of 1″ = 60′ is calculated as follows:

```
1″ = 60′
1″ = (60 × 12)″
720/1 = 720
The scale factor is 720.
```

If your drawing is in millimeters with a scale of 1:1, the drawing can be converted to inches with the formula 1″ = 25.4 mm. Therefore, the scale factor is 25.4. When the metric drawing scale is 1:2, the scale factor for converting to inches is 1″ = 25.4 × 2, or 1″ = 50.8. The scale factor is 50.8.

Calculating text height

After you have determined the scale factor, you should calculate the height of the AutoCAD text. In a drawing with a scale of 1″ = 1″, the scale factor equals 1. Therefore, the text height in the drawing will be 1/8″ high, because the text height multiplied by a scale factor of 1 equals 1/8″ high text.

However, if you are working on a civil engineering drawing with a scale of 1″ = 60′, text drawn 1/8″ high appears as a dot. Remember, the drawing you are working on is 720 times larger than it is when plotted at the proper scale. Therefore, you must multiply the text height by the 720 scale factor to have text in correct proportion on the screen:

> text height × scale factor = model space scaled text height
> .125″ × 720 = 90″
> The proper text height in model space is 90″.

An architectural drawing with a scale of 1/4″ = 1′-0″ has a scale factor of 48. Text that is to be 1/8″ high when printed should be drawn 6″ high (1/8″ × 48 = 6″).

Annotative Text

Annotative text is scaled by AutoCAD according to the *annotation scale* you select, which is the same as the drawing scale. This eliminates the need for you to calculate the scale factor. When an annotation scale is selected, AutoCAD determines the scale factor and applies it automatically to annotative text, as well as any other annotative object. For example, if you manually scale 1/8″ high text for a drawing with a scale of 1/4″ = 1′-0″, or a scale factor of 48, you must draw the text using a *text height* of 6″ (1/8″ × 48 = 6″) in model space. When placing annotative text, using this example, you set an annotation scale of 1/4″ = 1′-0″. Then you draw the text using a *paper text height* of 1/8″ in model space. The 1/8″ high text is scaled to 6″ automatically because of the preset 1/4″ = 1′-0″ annotation scale.

Annotative text offers several advantages over manually scaled text, including the ability to control text scale based on annotation scale, not scale factor. Using annotative text is especially effective when drawing scale changes or when objects viewed at different scales are placed on a single sheet.

PROFESSIONAL TIP

If you anticipate preparing scaled drawings, you should become familiar with annotative text and use it instead of traditional manual scaling. However, scale factor does influence other non-annotative items on a drawing and is still an important value to identify and use throughout the drawing process.

Setting annotation scale

Annotation scale should usually be set before you begin typing text so that the text height is automatically scaled. However, this is not always possible. It may be necessary to adjust the annotation scale throughout the drawing process, especially if multiple drawings with different scales are prepared on one sheet. This chapter approaches annotation scaling in model space only, using the process of selecting the desired annotation scale before typing text. When text at another scale is needed, pick the new annotation scale and then type the text.

Many additional annotative object tools are described throughout this book. Some of these tools are more appropriate when working with layout viewports, as described in Chapter 25.

The **Annotation Scale** flyout button located on the status bar is the primary tool for adjusting annotation scale. See **Figure 9-4.** Pick the desired annotation scale from the menu, remembering that the annotation scale is typically the same as the drawing scale. You can also adjust the annotation scale using the **CANNOSCALE** system variable.

Editing annotation scales

If a certain scale is not available, or if you want to change existing scales, pick the arrow next to **Annotation Scale:** in the status bar to display the list of scales and choose the **Custom...** option to access the **Edit Scale List** dialog box. This dialog box can be used to move the highlighted scale up or down in the list by picking the **Move Up** or **Move Down** button. The highlighted scale can be removed from the list by picking the **Delete** button or modified by picking the **Edit...** button. Selecting **Edit...** opens the **Edit Scale** dialog box Here you can change the name of the scale and adjust the scale by entering the paper and drawing units. For example, a scale of 1/4″ = 1′-0″ uses a paper units value of .25 or 1 and a drawing units value of 12 or 48.

Figure 9-4.
Primary annotation scale options are located on the status bar.

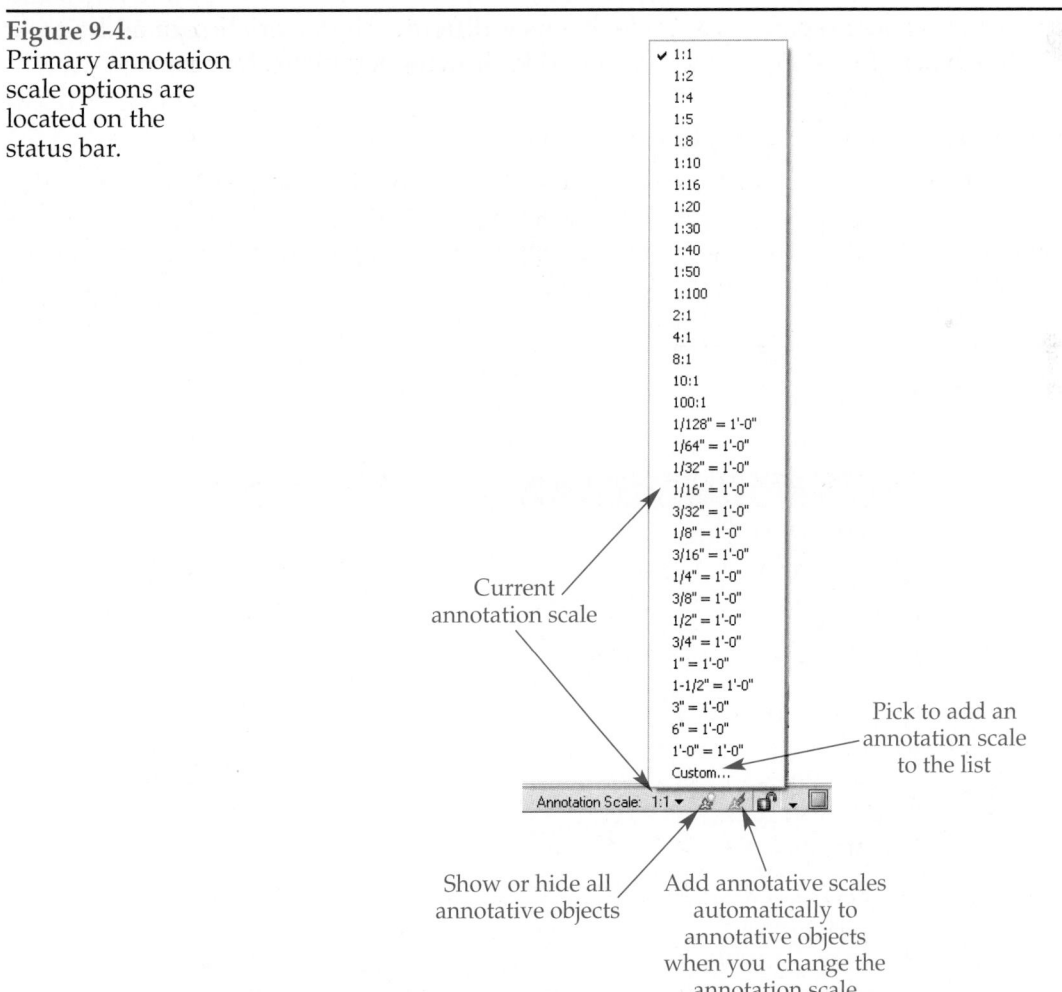

To create a new annotation scale, pick the **Add...** button to display the **Add Scale** dialog box, which functions the same as the **Edit Scale** dialog box previously described. Pick the **Reset** button to restore the default annotation scale. When the annotation scale is set current, you are ready to type annotative text that is automatically created at the correct text height according to the drawing scale.

> **NOTE**
>
> The **Edit Scale List** dialog box can also be accessed by picking **Format** > **Scale List...** from the pull-down menu.

AutoCAD Text Styles

text style: A saved collection of settings for text height, width, oblique angle, and other text effects.

AutoCAD text styles are used to set text characteristics. A *text style* defines the text height, width, oblique angle (slant), and other text effects. You may have several text styles, depending on the different characteristics needed for the text displayed in your drawing. Text characteristics can be manipulated independently of a text style. However, you should create a text style for each unique text requirement. For example, you may have a text style that is used for most applications, such as adding notes and dimensions, and a separate text style that uses different characteristics for adding text to a title block. Text styles should be added to drawing templates for repeated use.

Working with Text Styles

Text styles are created, modified, and deleted using the **Text Style** dialog box. See **Figure 9-5**. Access this dialog box by selecting the **Text Style...** button in the **Styles** toolbar or the **Text** control panel in the **Dashboard**, picking **Format** > **Text Style...** from the pull-down menu, or typing ST or STYLE.

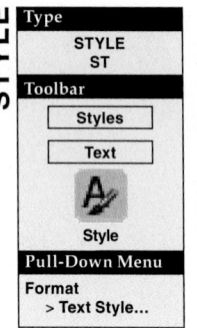

STYLE

Type
STYLE ST
Toolbar
Styles
Text
Style
Pull-Down Menu
Format > Text Style...

Figure 9-5.
The **Text Style** dialog box is used to set the characteristics of a text style.

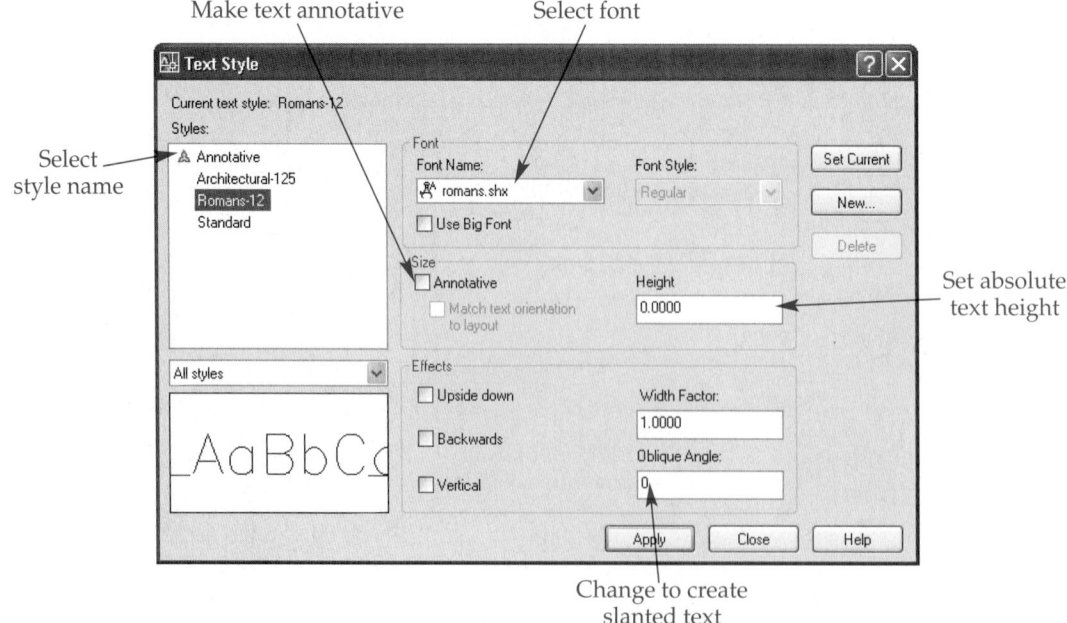

The **Styles** list box displays existing text styles. By default, Annotative and Standard text styles are available. Both use the txt font, a 0° rotation angle, a width of 1, and a 0° oblique angle. The Annotative text style is preset to create annotative text, as indicated by the icon to the left of the style name. The Standard text style does not use the annotative function.

You can make a text style current by double-clicking the style name; right-clicking the name and selecting the **Current** option; or picking the name and selecting the **Current** button. Below the **Styles** list box is a drop-down list that can be used to filter the number of text styles displayed in the **Text Style** dialog box. Pick the **All Styles** option to show all text styles in the file or pick the **Styles in use** option to show only the current style and styles used in the drawing.

Creating a New Text Style

To create a new text style, first select an existing text style from the **Styles** list box to be used as a base for formatting the new text style. Then pick the **New...** button in the **Text Style** dialog box. This opens the **New Text Style** dialog box. See **Figure 9-6.** Notice style1 is in the **Style Name** text box. You can keep a text style name like style1 or style2, but you should replace it with a more descriptive name. For example, to create a text style for mechanical drawings that uses the Romans font and characters .12″ high, you should choose a style name that you can remember, such as ROMANS-12. A text style for architectural drawings that uses a Stylus BT font and characters .125″ could be named ARCHITECTURAL-125.

It is also a good idea to record the names and details about the text styles you create and keep this information in a log for future reference. Text style names can have up to 255 characters, including letters, numbers, dashes (–), underlines (_), and dollar signs ($). You can type uppercase or lowercase letters. After entering the text style name, pick the **OK** button. The new text style is displayed in the **Styles** list box of the **Text Style** dialog box, and you are ready to adjust text style characteristics.

Setting Text Style Font

A *font* is a particular letter face design. Examples of standard AutoCAD text fonts are shown in **Figure 9-7.** The standard fonts have .shx file extensions.

font: A letter face design.

Figure 9-6.
Enter a descriptive name for the new text style in the **New Text Style** dialog box.

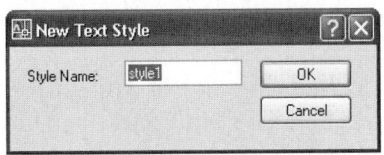

Default Style   New Style

Figure 9-7.
Standard AutoCAD fonts.

	Fast Fonts		**Simplex Fonts**
Txt	abcdABCD12345	Romans	abcdABCD12345
Monotxt	abcdABCD12345	Italic	abcdABCD12345
	Triplex Fonts		**Complex Fonts**
Romant	abcdABCD12345	Romanc	abcdABCD12345
Italict	abcdABCD12345	Italicc	abcdABCD12345

The txt font is the AutoCAD default. This font draws letters with a minimum of line segments, resulting in a rough appearance but allowing it to regenerate faster than other fonts. The Romans (roman simplex) font is smoother than txt. It closely duplicates the single-stroke lettering that has long been the standard for most drafting.

TrueType fonts are scaleable and have an outline. *Scaleable fonts* can be displayed on the screen or printed at any size and still maintain proportional letter thickness. TrueType fonts appear filled in the AutoCAD window, but the **TEXTFILL** system variable controls whether the plotted fonts are filled. The **TEXTFILL** default is 1, which draws filled fonts. A setting of 0 draws the font outlines. Examples of TrueType fonts are shown in **Figure 9-8.** The Stylus BT font is an excellent choice for the artistic appearance desired on architectural drawings.

The **Preview** area of the **Text Style** dialog box displays an example of the selected font. This is a very convenient way to see what the font looks like before using it in a new style. Text style effects such as **Backwards** and **Vertical** can also be previewed.

NOTE

Additional standard fonts, characters, and TrueType fonts can be seen by experimenting within AutoCAD or reviewing the *AutoCAD Fonts* document in the *Reference Materials* section of the Student CD.

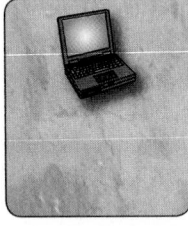

PROFESSIONAL TIP

TrueType fonts and other complex text fonts can be taxing on system resources. They can slow down display changes and increase drawing regeneration time significantly. Use these fonts only when necessary. When you must use complex fonts, set your system variables to speed-optimized settings.

The **Font** area of the **Text Style** dialog box is where you select an available font and the style of the selected font. Use the **Font Name** drop-down list to access the available fonts. All SHX fonts are identified with an AutoCAD compass icon, and the TrueType fonts have the TrueType icon. The **Font Style** drop-down list is inactive unless the selected font has options available, such as bold or italic. None of the SHX fonts have additional options, but some of the TrueType fonts do. For example, the SansSerif font has Regular, Bold, BoldOblique, and Oblique options. Each option provides the font with a different appearance.

Asian and other large format fonts are called *Big Fonts* and are activated by selecting the **Use Big Font** check box. See **Figure 9-9.** The **Big Font:** drop-down list is a supplement to define many symbols not available in normal font files.

Figure 9-8.
A few of the many TrueType fonts available.

Swiss 721		Architect's Hand Lettered	
swiss (regular)	abcdABCD12345	stylus BT	abcdABCD I 2345
swissi (italic)	abcdABCD12345		
swissb (bold)	abcdABCD1234	Vineta (shadow)	
swissbi (bold italic)	abcdABCD12345	vinet (regular)	abcdABCD12345

Figure 9-9.
When you check the **Use Big Font** check box, the **Font Style:** drop-down list changes to display a list of available Big Fonts.

The **Big Font:** drop-down list displays the available nonstandard fonts

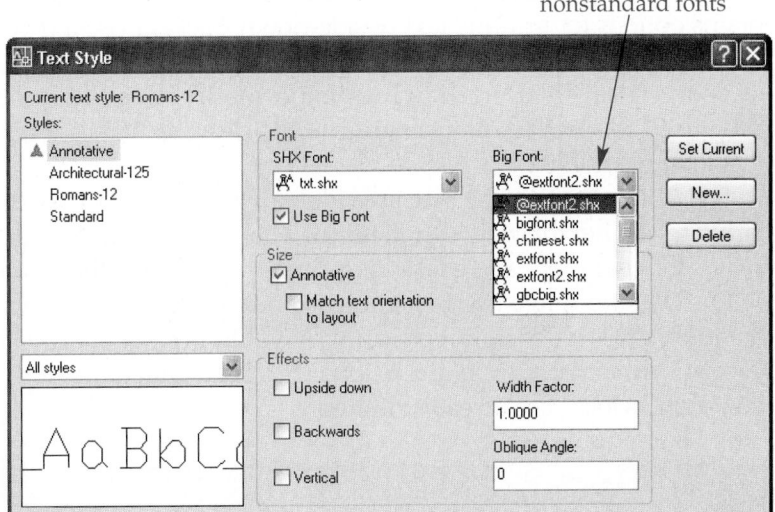

Text Style Height Options

AutoCAD 2008
NEW FEATURE

The **Size** area of the **Text Style** dialog box contains options for defining text style height. Select the **Annotative** check box to set the text style as annotative. An annotative text style adjusts the height of text according to a selected annotation scale. The following options are available when the **Annotative** check box is checked:

- **Match text orientation to layout.** Pick this check box to match the orientation of text in layout viewports with the layout orientation. Layouts are described in Chapter 25.
- **Paper Text Height.** The default paper text height is 0.0000. This setting allows you to set the text height with the **TEXT** command. If you set a value such as .125, the text height becomes fixed for this text style and you are not prompted for the text height. Setting a text height value other than zero saves time during the command process, but also eliminates your flexibility.

When the **Annotative** check box is not selected, text must be scaled manually using the drawing scale factor. The **Height** text box presets the text height. The default is 0.0000. This setting allows you to set the text height with the **TEXT** command. If you set a value, the text height becomes fixed for this text style and you are not prompted for the text height.

> **NOTE**
>
> The default text height is stored in the **TEXTSIZE** system variable. When a text style has a height other than 0, the style height overrides any default value stored in this variable.

> **PROFESSIONAL TIP**
>
> It is recommended that a text height value of 0 be used for text styles used in dimensions. Dimension styles allow you to specify a text height value for the annotation text. If you specify a text height in the text style, this value overrides the dimension text height. Dimension styles are described in Chapter 16.

Adjusting Text Style Effects

The **Effects** area of the **Text Style** dialog box is used to set the text format. It contains options for printing text upside-down, backwards, and vertically. See **Figure 9-10.** The Vertical check box is inactive for all TrueType fonts. A check in this box makes SHX font text vertical. Text on drawings is normally placed horizontally, but vertical text can be used for special effects and graphic designs. Vertical text works best when the rotation angle is 270°.

The **Width Factor** text box provides a value that defines the text character width relative to the height. A width factor of 1 is the default. A width factor greater than 1 expands the characters, and a factor less than 1 compresses the characters. See **Figure 9-11.**

The **Oblique Angle** text box allows you to set the angle at which text is slanted. The 0 default draws characters vertically. A value greater than 0 slants the characters to the right, while a negative value slants the characters to the left. See **Figure 9-12.** Some fonts, such as *italic*, are already slanted.

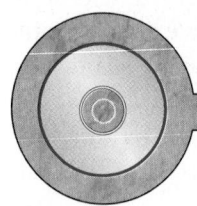

> **PROFESSIONAL TIP**
>
> Some drafting companies, especially those in structural drafting, like to slant text 15° to the right. Also, water features named on maps often use text that is slanted to the right.

Exercise 9-1
Complete the exercise on the Student CD.

Figure 9-10.
Special effects for text styles can be set in the **Effects** area of the **Text Style** dialog box.

Upside-Down Text   Backwards Text   Vertical Text

Figure 9-11.
Examples of width factor settings for text.

Width Factor	Text
1	ABCDEFGHIJKLM
.5	ABCDEFGHIJKLMNOPQRSTUVWXY
1.5	ABCDEFGHI
2	ABCDEFG

Figure 9-12.
Oblique angle
settings for text.

Obliquing Angle	Text
0	ABCDEFGHIJKLM
15	*ABCDEFGHIJKLM*
–15	ABCDEFGHIJKLM

Changing, Renaming, and Deleting Text Styles

You can change the current text style without affecting existing text objects. The changes are applied only to text added using that style.

Existing text styles can be renamed in the **Text Style** dialog box. To rename a text style, slowly double-click the name or right-click the name and select the **Rename** option.

To delete a text style, right-click the name and select the **Delete** option, or pick the style and select the **Delete** button. AutoCAD does not allow you to delete a text style that has been used to create text objects in the drawing. If you want to delete a style that is in use, change the text objects in the drawing to a different style. You cannot delete or rename the Standard style.

NOTE

If you change the font and orientation of an existing text style, all text items with that style are redrawn with the new values.

PROFESSIONAL TIP

You can use the template development applications found on the Student CD to start this process and continue your template development as you proceed. Complete, predesigned templates are also provided on the Student CD.

Quickly Setting a Text Style Current

You can set a text style current using the **Text Style** dialog box, but a faster way is to use the drop-down list located in the **Text** control panel of the **Dashboard** or the **Styles** toolbar. The name of the current text style is displayed in the box. Pick the drop-down arrow to display the text style list, as shown in **Figure 9-13**. Pick a text style name from the list to set the style current.

PROFESSIONAL TIP

You can import text styles from existing drawings using **Design-Center**. See Chapter 5 for more information about using **Design-Center** to import layers, linetypes, text styles, and other settings.

Figure 9-13.
The fastest way to
set a style current
is to use the drop-
down list on the
Dashboard.

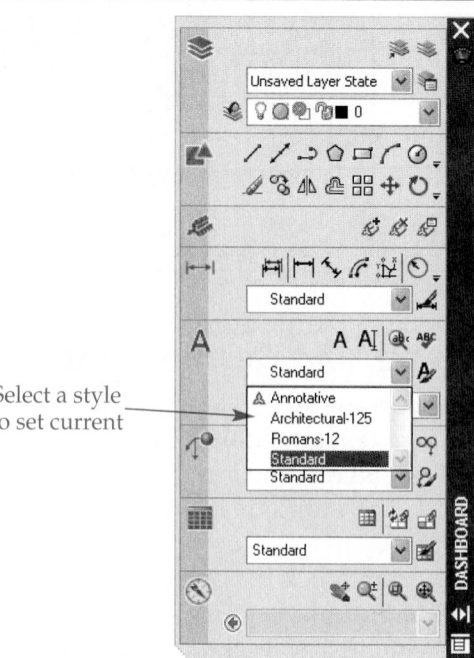

Select a style
to set current

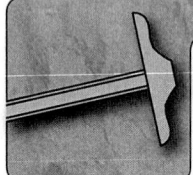

Using AutoCAD to Draw Text

AutoCAD provides two basic systems for creating text. Multiline text is created
with the **MTEXT** command and is used to prepare a single text object that may consist
of multiple lines of text, such as paragraphs or a list of general notes. Single-line text
is created with the **TEXT** command and is used to create single-line text objects. Each
command is used differently, but the options are similar.

text boundary: An
imaginary box that
sets the width for
multiline text.

Multiline Text

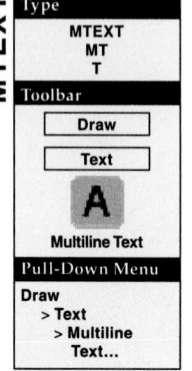

The **MTEXT** command is used to create multiline text objects. All the lines of text
are part of the same object. The **MTEXT** command is accessed by picking the **Multiline
Text** button in the **Draw** or **Text** toolbar or the **2D Draw** or **Text** control panel of the
Dashboard, picking **Draw > Text > Multiline Text...** in the pull-down menu, or typing
T, MT, or MTEXT.

When you enter the **MTEXT** command, AutoCAD asks you to specify the first and
opposite corners of the text boundary. The *text boundary* is a box within which your
text will be placed. When you pick the first corner of the text boundary, the cursor
changes to a box with grayed-out letters that represent the current text height. Move
the box to specify the desired size for your paragraph and pick the opposite corner.
See **Figure 9-14.**

Figure 9-14.
The text boundary is a box within which your text will be placed. The arrow indicates the direction of text flow.

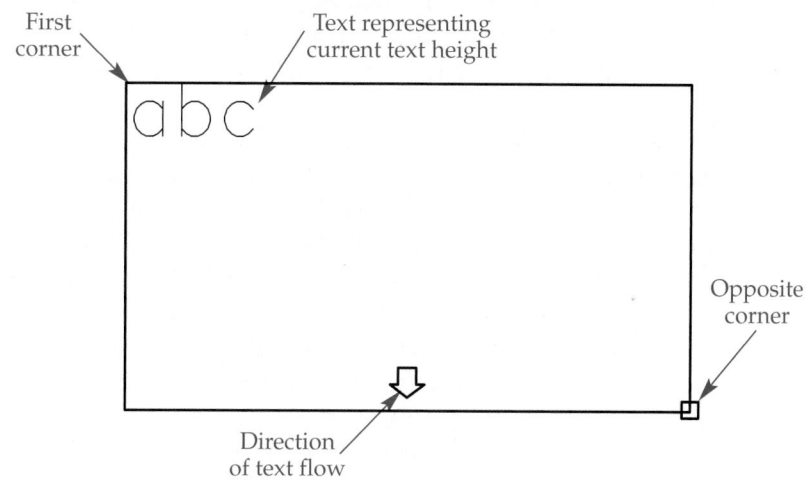

When you create the text boundary, an arrow in the boundary shows the direction of text flow. While the width of the boundary provides a limit to the width of the text paragraphs, it does not affect the possible height. The boundary height is automatically resized to fit the actual text typed. The direction of text flow indicates where the boundary will be expanded, if necessary. After you specify the text boundary, the **In-Place Text Editor** appears. See **Figure 9-15.**

Using the In-Place Text Editor

The **In-Place Text Editor** functions much like a word processor. If you have ever used a software program such as Microsoft® Word, you will find similar controls and features in the **In-Place Text Editor**. The **In-Place Text Editor** is divided into the **Text Formatting** toolbar and the *text editor*. The **Text Formatting** toolbar controls the

text editor: The part of the **In-Place Text Editor** that contains the text cursor.

Figure 9-15.
The **In-Place Text Editor** is used to create multiline text.

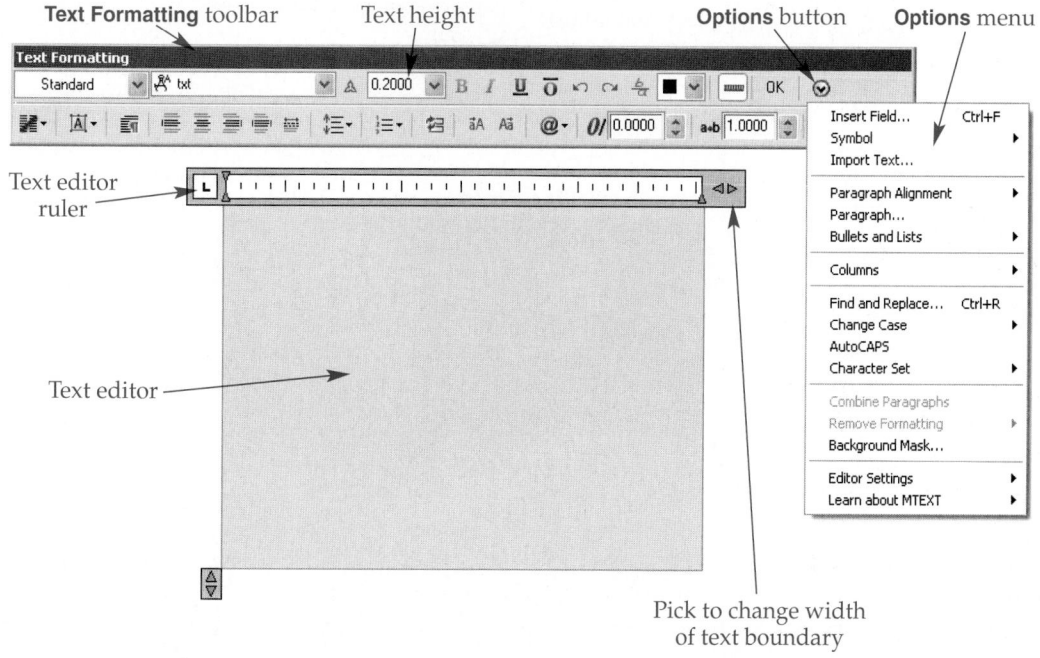

properties of text typed into the text editor. The text editor includes a ruler where indent and tab stops and an indent and tab markers are located. A cursor is displayed within the text editor at the height set in the **Text Formatting** toolbar. This is where text is typed to create a paragraph. The text editor is transparent by default so that you can see how the text you type appears on-screen in relation to other objects.

A shortcut menu can be accessed by right-clicking anywhere outside of the **Text Formatting** toolbar. The menu and its options are displayed and explained in **Figure 9-16**. An **Edit** cascading submenu is available at the top of the menu, providing **Undo**, **Redo**, and Windows Clipboard functions. The Clipboard functions allow you to cut, copy, or paste text to or from the text editor. Selecting the **Learn about MTEXT** option provides access to help-related information about multiline text. Most of the options given in the shortcut menu can also be accessed by picking the **Options** flyout button on the **Text Formatting** toolbar. All of the options listed in the **Options** flyout button menu are available in the text editor shortcut menu. Refer to **Figure 9-15**.

As you move the cursor into the editing window, it changes shape. If you have used other Windows text editors, you will recognize the familiar text cursor shape. Pointing to a character position within the text and pressing the pick button causes the cursor to be placed at the selected location. You can then begin typing or editing as needed. If you begin typing where the text cursor is initially placed, your text begins in the upper-left corner of the text boundary.

NOTE

The **In-Place Text Editor** displays the text horizontally, right-side up, and forward. Any special effects such as vertical, backwards, or upside down take effect when you pick **OK** to exit the editor.

Figure 9-16.
Display the text editor shortcut menu by right-clicking while the cursor is in the text editor.

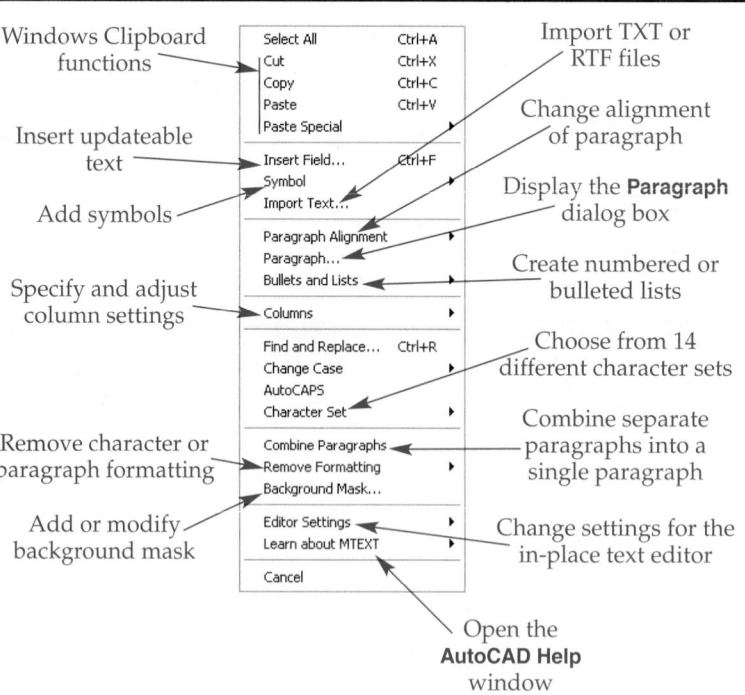

Most Windows-standard keystroke combinations work in AutoCAD's text editor. Examples include:

[Ctrl]+[C]   Copies text to the Clipboard
[Ctrl]+[V]   Pastes text from the Clipboard
[Ctrl]+[Z]   Undoes the previous action
[Home]   Moves the cursor to the start of the current line
[End]   Moves the cursor to the end of the current line

All keystrokes and functions are provided on the Student CD for your reference.

PROFESSIONAL TIP

Text can be pasted from any text-based application into the **In-Place Text Editor**. For example, you can copy text from an application such as Microsoft® Word, and then paste it into the **In-Place Text Editor**. The pasted text retains its properties. Likewise, text copied or cut from the **In-Place Text Editor** can be pasted into another text-based application.

The procedure for selecting text is the same as in standard Windows text editors. Place the cursor at one end of the desired selection, press and hold the pick button, drag the cursor until the desired text is highlighted, and release the pick button. Any editing operations you perform affect the highlighted text. Another way to highlight text is to move the cursor to the word to be highlighted and double-click. To replace the highlighted text with entirely new text, either paste the new text from the Clipboard or begin typing. The selection is erased and the new text appears in its place.

To change the width of the text editor, drag one of the arrows at the end of the paragraph ruler. You can also change the width by right-clicking the text editor ruler or the arrows at the bottom of the text editor and selecting **Set Mtext Width...** from the shortcut menu. This displays the **Set Mtext Width** dialog box, where a new width for the paragraph can be specified. To change the height of the text editor, drag the arrows at the bottom of the text editor. You can also change the height by right-clicking the ruler or the arrows at the bottom of the text editor and selecting **Set Mtext Height...** from the shortcut menu. This displays the **Set Mtext Height** dialog box, where a new height for the paragraph can be specified.

PROFESSIONAL TIP

Change the width and height of the text editor to increase or decrease the number of lines of text.

When finished typing text, pick the **OK** button in the **Text Formatting** toolbar to exit the text editor.

Exercise 9-2

Complete the exercise on the Student CD.

Basic Text Formatting Options

The features in the **Text Formatting** toolbar are shown in **Figure 9-17.** The following list describes basic **Text Formatting** toolbar features. Keep in mind as you review these features that *selected text* refers to text that you have highlighted in the text editor.

- **Style.** Provides access to existing text styles. Pick a text style to set it current, or select existing text in the text editor. Then pick a text style from the drop-down list to change the style of the selected text. A single multiline text object can use a combination of text styles.
- **Font.** Selects a text font to use for newly typed text, or changes the font of existing text. The default text font is the font selected for the current text style. Changing the font using the **Font** drop-down list overrides the font used in the current text style. A single multiline text object can use a combination of text fonts.
- **Annotative.** Makes text in the text editor annotative. If the current text style is annotative, this button is selected by default. If desired, the **Annotative** button can be used to make a portion of the multiline text object annotative.

AutoCAD 2008
NEW FEATURE

- **Size.** Used to enter or select a text height to use for newly typed text or to change the height of existing text. This overrides the current setting of the **TEXTSIZE** system variable and the text height set within the text style. A single multiline text object can use a combination of text heights. If the current text style is annotative, or you pick the **Annotative** button, the height you enter is the paper text height. If the current text style is not annotative, or you deselect the **Annotative** button, the height you enter is the text height and must be multiplied by the scale factor.
- **Bold.** Makes the selected text become bold, overriding the font style used in the current text style. This only works with some TrueType fonts. The SHX fonts do not have this capability.
- **Italic.** Makes the selected text become italic, overriding the font style used in the current text style. This only works with some TrueType fonts. The SHX style fonts do not have this capability.
- **Underline.** Underlines text.
- **Overline.** Places a line over text.

Figure 9-17.
The **Text Formatting** toolbar.

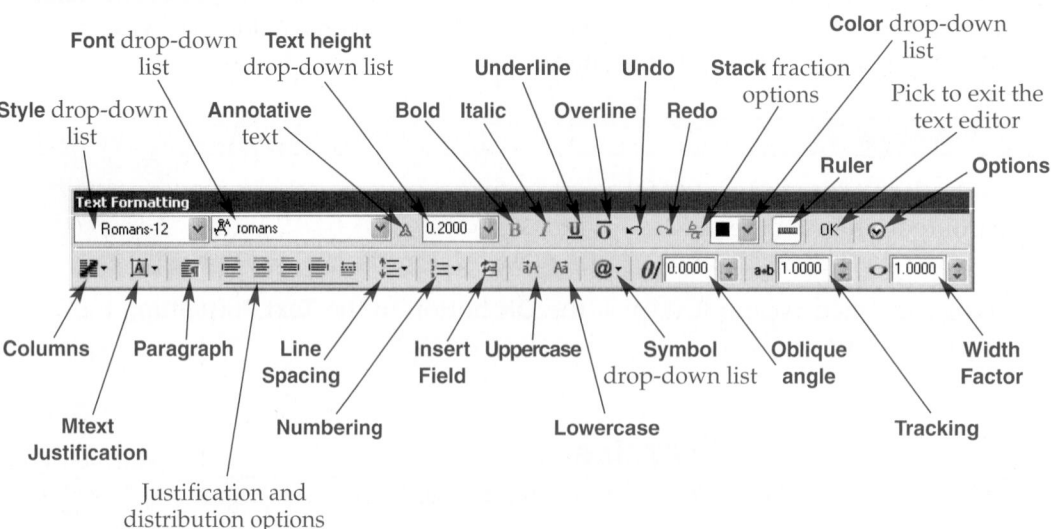

NOTE

Pick the **Bold**, **Italic**, **Underline**, or **Overline** buttons to turn on the formatting option. When text is typed, it is automatically formatted. To turn the feature off, pick the button again.

- **Undo.** Undoes the previous activity.
- **Redo.** Redoes undone operations.
- **Stack.** Stacks selected text vertically or diagonally. To use this feature for drawing a vertically stacked fraction, place a forward slash between the top and bottom items. Then select the text and pick the **Stack** button. This button is also used to unstack text that has been previously stacked. To stack items without a fraction bar, use the caret (^) character between the top and bottom items. This is called a *tolerance stack*. Typing a number sign (#) between selected numbers results in a diagonal fraction bar. See **Figure 9-18**.

  If you highlight stacked text and right-click, the shortcut menu appears with two additional options. The first option is **Unstack**, which causes the fraction to unstack. The upper and lower values are placed on a single line with the appropriate character (^, #, or /) displayed between the numbers. The second option is **Stack Properties**, which displays the **Stack Properties** dialog box. The features of this dialog box are described in **Figure 9-19**.
- **Color.** The color is set to ByLayer by default, but you can change the text color by picking one of the colors in the **Color** drop-down list. Though color should usually be defined as ByLayer, a single multiline text object can use a combination of text colors.
- **Ruler.** Turns the display of the paragraph ruler on or off.
- **Uppercase.** Changes all of the selected text to uppercase formatting.
- **Lowercase.** Picking this button changes all of the selected text to lowercase formatting.

tolerance stack: Text that is stacked without a horizontal fraction bar.

Figure 9-18.
Different types of stack characters. ASME standards recommend that the text height of stacked fraction numerals be the same as the other dimension numerals.

	Selected Text	Stacked Text
Vertical Fraction	1/2	$\frac{1}{2}$
Tolerance Stack	1^2	$\frac{1}{2}$
Diagonal Fraction	1#2	½

Figure 9-19.
The **Stack Properties** dialog box.

Top and bottom numbers in stack

Set horizontal, diagonal, or tolerance style

Select bottom, center, or top alignment

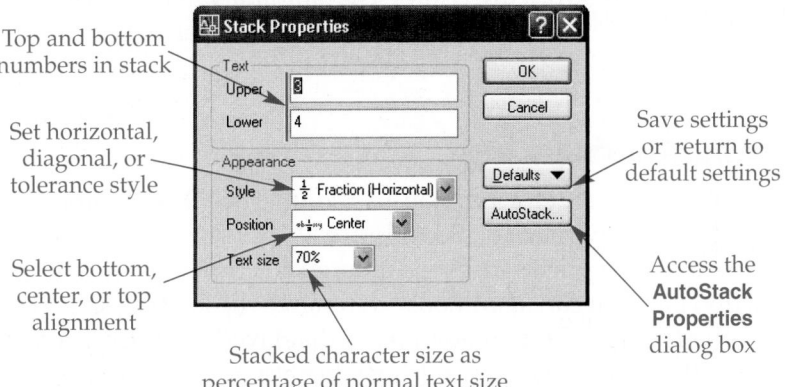

Save settings or return to default settings

Access the **AutoStack Properties** dialog box

Stacked character size as percentage of normal text size

- **Oblique Angle.** Changes the angle at which text is slanted. The default oblique angle corresponds to the oblique angle entered for the current text style. Changing the oblique angle using the **Oblique Angle** text box overrides the angle used in the current text style. A single multiline text object can use a combination of oblique angles.
- **Tracking.** Determines the amount of space between text characters. The default value is 1, which results in normal spacing. The higher the value, the more space added between characters. The lower the value, the tighter the spacing between characters. You can enter a value between 0.75 and 4.0. See Figure 9-20.
- **Ruler.** Turns the display of the paragraph ruler on or off.
- **Width Factor.** Allows you to change the text character width. The default width is the width entered for the current text style. Changing the width using the **Width Factor** text box overrides the width used in the current text style. A single multiline text object can use a combination of width factors.

Figure 9-20.
The **Tracking** option for multiline text determines the spacing between characters.

AutoCAD tracking
Normal Spacing

AutoCAD tracking
Tracking = 0.75

A u t o C A D   t r a c k i n g
Tracking = 2.0

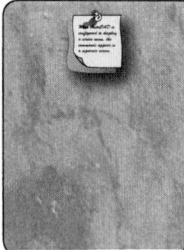
Using AutoStacking

When you enter a fraction in the **In-Place Text Editor**, the **AutoStack Properties** dialog box is displayed. See Figure 9-21. This dialog box allows you to activate AutoStacking, which causes the entered fraction to stack with a horizontal or diagonal fraction bar. You can also choose to remove the leading space between a whole number and the fraction. This dialog box is displayed each time a fraction is entered. If you decide that you do not want this dialog box to pop up each time you create a fraction, you can pick the **Don't show this dialog again; always use these settings** check box.

AutoCAD and Its Applications—Basics

Figure 9-21.
The **AutoStack Properties** dialog box.

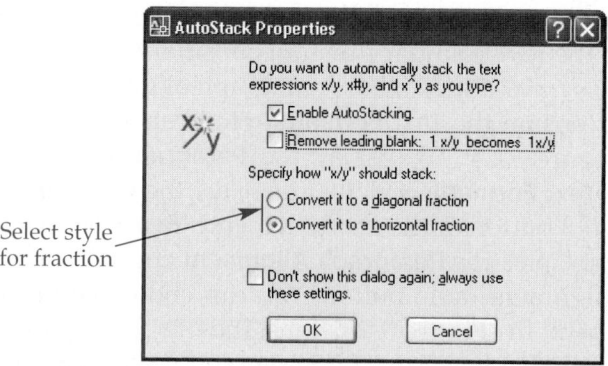

Select style
for fraction

Mtext Justification and Paragraph Settings

The term *justify* means to align the text to fit a given location. For example, left-justified text is aligned along an imaginary left border. Both the text boundary and the text within the boundary can be justified. The text boundary defines the size and location of the text editor, and the extents of the text within the text editor. The text boundary can be arranged and located according to a specific justification, while the text within the boundary can be arranged independently of the text boundary justification. This provides great flexibility when determining the location and arrangement text.

To justify the text boundary, select a justification option from the **Mtext Justification** flyout button of the **Text Formatting** toolbar, or pick a justification option from the **Mtext Justification** cascading submenu available from the **Options** flyout button or the shortcut menu. Justification also determines the direction of text flow. **Figure 9-22** displays the options for justifying the multiline text boundary vertically and horizontally.

justify: Align the margins or edges of text.

Figure 9-22.
Options for justifying the multiline text boundary.

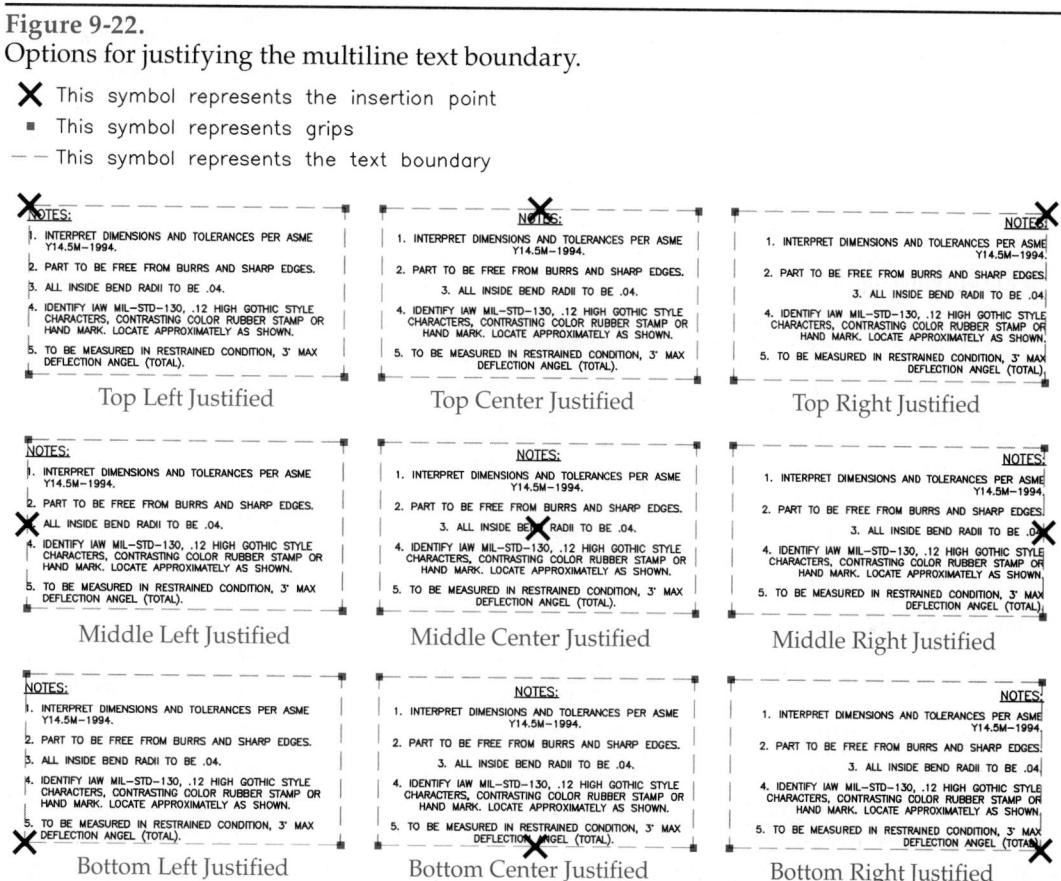

✗ This symbol represents the insertion point
■ This symbol represents grips
— — This symbol represents the text boundary

paragraph alignment: The alignment of multiline text inside the text boundary.

Justifying the text inside the text boundary is known as *paragraph alignment*. For example, when you apply a **Middle Center** text box justification, then set the paragraph alignment to **Left**, the text inside the boundary is aligned to the left edge of the text boundary, while the text boundary remains positioned according the **Middle Center** justification. See **Figure 9-23**. To adjust paragraph alignment, select one of the paragraph alignment buttons on the **Text Formatting** toolbar or access the **Paragraph** dialog box, shown in **Figure 9-24**. To display the **Paragraph** dialog box, pick the **Paragraph** button on the **Text Formatting** toolbar or select the **Paragraph** option available from the **Options** flyout button or the shortcut menu. To set paragraph alignment in the **Paragraph** dialog box, pick the **Paragraph Alignment** check box, then choose the appropriate paragraph alignment radio button. You can choose from five paragraph alignment options, as shown in **Figure 9-25**. Tabs, indents, paragraph spacing, and paragraph line spacing can also be set in the **Paragraph** dialog box. The additional paragraph settings include:

Figure 9-23.
Paragraph alignment can be adjusted independently of text boundary justification.

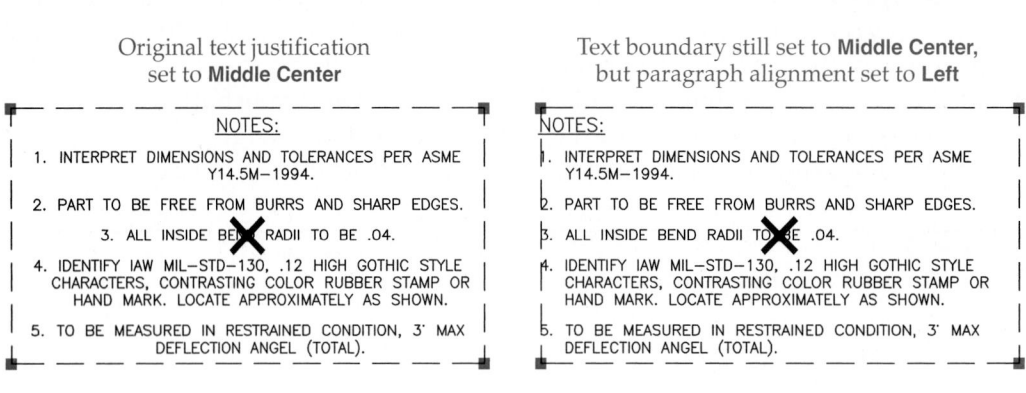

Figure 9-24.
The **Paragraph** dialog box.

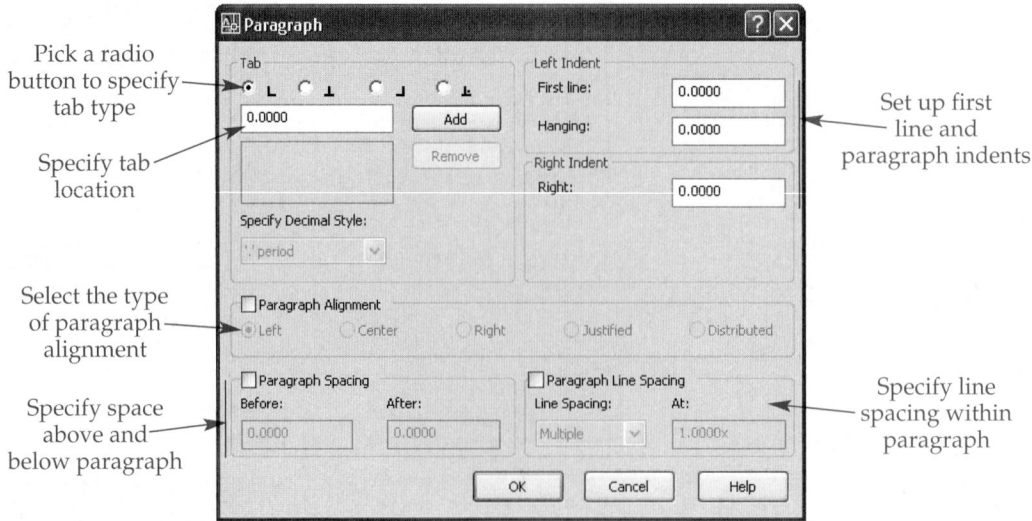

AutoCAD and Its Applications—Basics

Figure 9-25.
Paragraph alignment options for multiline text. In each of these examples, the text boundary justification is set to Top Left.

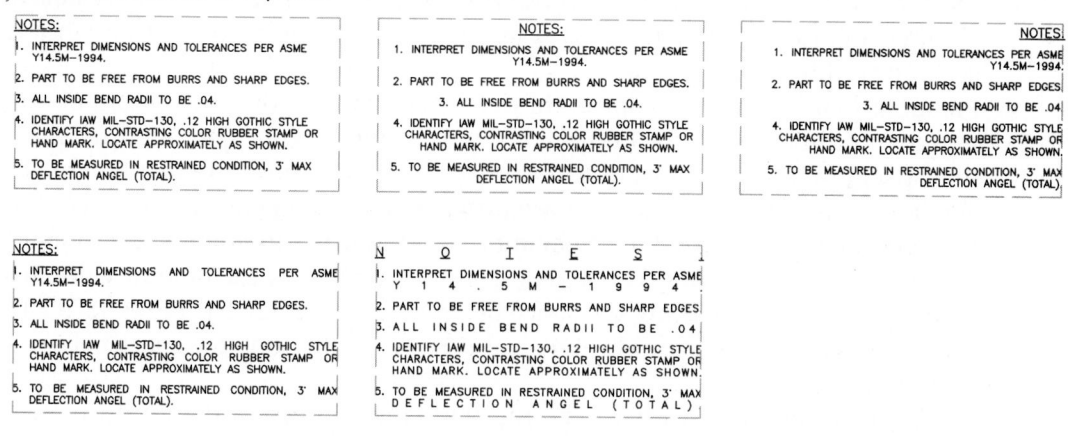

- **Tab.** Sets custom tab stops. Pick the tab type radio button, enter a value for the tab in the text box, and select the **Add** button to add it to the list and insert the tab on the ruler. **Figure 9-26** shows and briefly describes each tab option. You can add as many custom tabs as necessary. Custom tabs can also be added to the ruler by picking the tab button on the far left side of the ruler until the desired tab symbol is displayed. Then, pick a location on the ruler to insert the tab.
- **Left Indent.** Sets up the indentation for the first line of a paragraph of text as well as the remaining portion of a paragraph. Each time you start a new paragraph, the **First line** indent is used. As text wraps to the next line, the **Hanging** indent is used.
- **Right Indent.** Sets up the indentation for the right side of a paragraph. As text is typed, the **Right** indent value, not the right edge of the text boundary, determines when the text is wrapped to the next line.

Figure 9-26.
Using custom tabs to position text in the text editor. When you press the [Tab] key, the cursor moves to the tab position. The type of tab then determines text behavior.

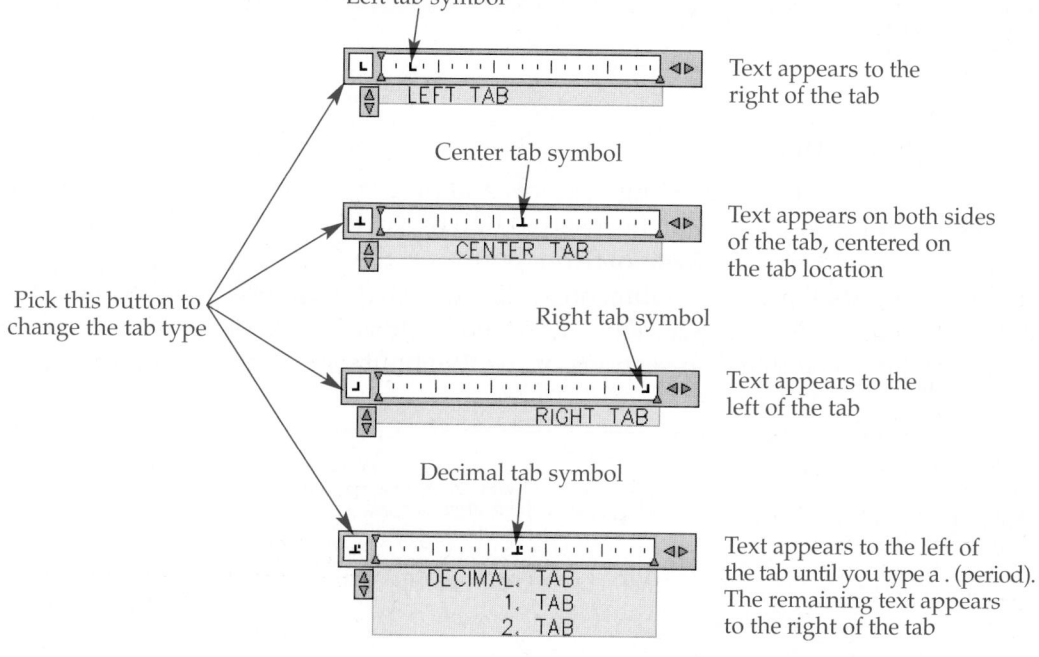

- **Paragraph Spacing.** Sets the amount of space before and after paragraphs. To set paragraph line spacing, pick the **Paragraph Spacing** check box. Then enter the spacing above a paragraph in the **Before** text box, and the spacing below a paragraph in the **After** text box. **Figure 9-27** shows examples of paragraph spacing settings.
- **Paragraph Line Spacing.** Adjusts the vertical distance from the bottom of one line of multiline text to the bottom of the next line, or *line spacing*. AutoCAD line spacing for single lines of text is equal to 1.5625 times the text height. To adjust the line spacing, pick the **Paragraph Line Spacing** check box. Select the **Multiple** option from the **Line Spacing** drop-down list to enter a multiple of the text height in the **At** text box. For example, 1.5625x is the default value for single-spaced lines, making the space between lines of .12″ high text .1875″. To double-space lines, you could enter a value of 3.125x, making the space between lines of text .375″.

To force the line spacing to be the same for all lines of the multiline text object, select the **Exactly** option from the **Line Spacing** drop-down list and enter a value in the **At** text box. If you enter an exact line spacing that is less than the text height, lines of text are stacked on top of each other.

To add spaces between lines automatically based on the height of the characters in the line, choose the **At Least** option from the **Line Spacing** drop-down list and enter a value in the **At** text box. The result is an equal spacing even between lines of text that have different heights.

NOTE

Line spacing can also be set using the **Line Spacing** flyout button on the **Text Formatting** toolbar. Select one of the available multiple options, pick the **More...** button to display the **Paragraph** dialog box, or choose the **Clear Line Spacing** option to apply an automatic spacing, similar to the **At Least** function.

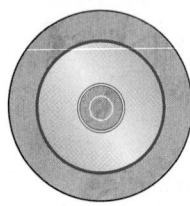

Exercise 9-3

Complete the exercise on the Student CD.

Adding Symbols

A variety of common drafting symbols and other unique characters that are not found on a typical keyboard can be inserted into the text editor. Symbol characters can be inserted by selecting the **Symbol** flyout button on the **Text Formatting** toolbar or by picking the **Symbol** cascading submenu available from the **Options** flyout button or the shortcut menu. See **Figure 9-28**. This menu allows the insertion of symbols at the text cursor location. The first two sections in the **Symbol** menu contain commonly used

Figure 9-27. Examples of paragraph spacing. Each example uses .1875″ high text and a first line left indent of .5″.

| Paragraph one typed with no paragpah spacing. Paragraph two typed with no paragraph spacing | Paragraph one typed with .25 before spacing and no after spacing. Paragraph two typed with .25 before spacing and no after spacing. | Paragraph one typed with .125 before spacing and .5 after spacing. Paragraph two typed with .125 before spacing and .5 after spacing. |

AutoCAD and Its Applications—Basics

Figure 9-28.
The **Symbol** menu options.

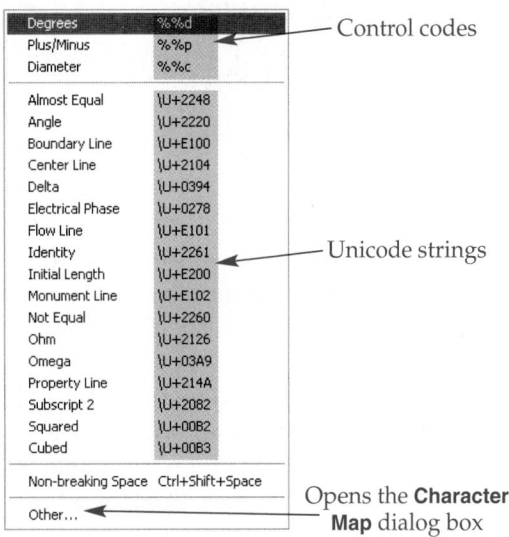

Control codes

Unicode strings

Opens the **Character Map** dialog box

symbols. The third section contains the **Non-breaking Space** option, which keeps two separate words together. Pick any of these symbols to insert them at the text cursor location and hide the **Symbol** menu. The **Other...** option opens the **Character Map** dialog box, shown in **Figure 9-29.** To use this dialog box, pick the desired symbols from the **Font:** drop-down list. The following are the steps for using a symbol or symbols:

1. Pick the desired symbol and then pick the **Select** button. The selected symbol is displayed in the **Characters to copy:** box.
2. Pick the **Copy** button to copy the selected symbol or symbols to the Clipboard.
3. Pick the **Close** button to close the dialog box.
4. In the **In-Place Text Editor**, place the text cursor where you want the symbols displayed.
5. Right-click to display the text editor shortcut menu. Pick the **Paste** option from the **Edit** cascading submenu to paste the symbol at the cursor location.

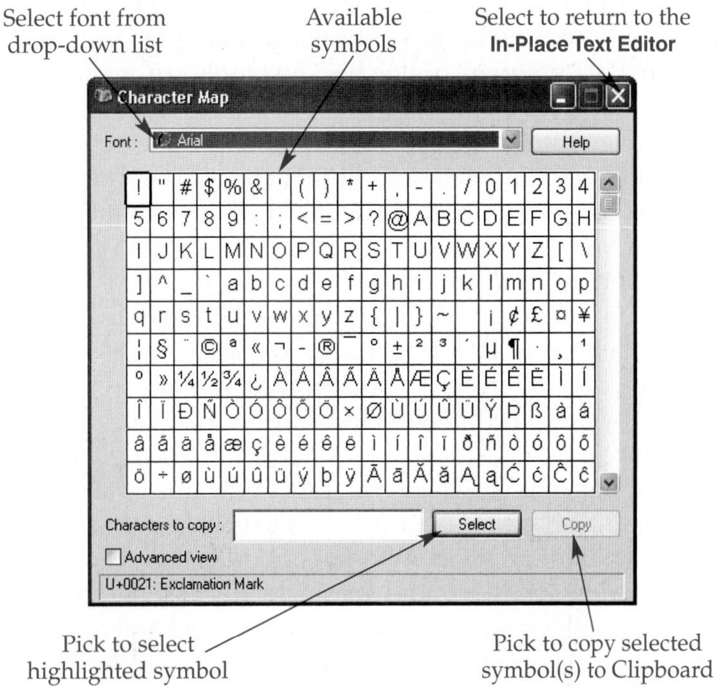

Figure 9-29.
The **Character Map** dialog box.

Select font from drop-down list

Available symbols

Select to return to the **In-Place Text Editor**

Pick to select highlighted symbol

Pick to copy selected symbol(s) to Clipboard

Importing Text

The **Import Text** option allows you to import text from an existing text file directly into the **In-Place Text Editor**. The text file can be either a standard ASCII text file (TXT) or an RTF (rich text format) file. The imported text becomes a part of the current multi-line text object.

To import text from an existing TXT or RTF file, pick **Import Text...** from the **Options** flyout button on the **Text Formatting** toolbar or right-click and choose the **Import Text...** option from the shortcut menu. The **Select File** dialog box is displayed. Select the text file to be imported and pick the **Open** button. The text is then inserted at the current cursor location.

PROFESSIONAL TIP

Text can be pasted from any text-based application into the **In-Place Text Editor**. For example, you can copy text from an application such as Microsoft® Word, and then paste it into the **In-Place Text Editor**. The pasted text retains its properties. Likewise, text copied or cut from the **In-Place Text Editor** can be pasted into another text-based application.

Creating Lists

Lists are commonly used to organize information. They provide a way to arrange related items in a logical order. They also help make lines of text more readable. General notes are usually provided in list format.

AutoCAD allows you to apply list formatting to existing text or create lists as you enter text. The numbering or lettering adjusts automatically if items are added to a list or removed. Lists can be set up to contain sublevel items. Sublevel items are designated with double numbers, letters, or bullets. Default tab settings are used unless you make settings in the **Paragraph** dialog box. List tools are available from the **Numbering** flyout button on the **Text Formatting** toolbar or the **Bullets and Lists** cascading submenu available from the **Options** flyout button or the shortcut menu. These tools are used to create numbered, bulleted, and alphabetical lists. The **Allow Bullets and Lists** option must be selected in order to create a list. This option is active by default. Unchecking this option converts any list items in the text object to plain text characters and disables the other options in the menu.

You can create an alphabetical list by choosing an option from the **Lettered** cascading submenu. Pick **Uppercase** to use uppercase lettering or choose **Lowercase** to use lowercase lettering. The **Uppercase** option is set by default. Numbered lists can be created by picking the **Numbered** option. To create a default style bulleted list, select the **Bulleted** option. This places a solid circle (the default bullet symbol) at the beginning of the line of text. When you start a new line of text, the next line is also bulleted.

Another method of creating lists is to use the **Allow Auto-list** option, which is active by default. When the **Allow Auto-list** option is turned on, AutoCAD detects characters that are used to start a list and automatically assigns the first list item. For example, if a line of text begins with a numeral or letter and a period, AutoCAD assumes that you are starting a list and formats any additional lines of text to continue the list.

To create a numbered or lettered auto-list, you must include punctuation (such as a period, parenthesis, or colon) and a tab after the number or letter that begins the first item. After you type the line of text and press the [Enter] key to start a new line, the next line uses the same formatting and the next consecutive number or letter. To end the list, press [Enter] twice. A numbered list is shown in **Figure 9-30.**

When creating a bulleted auto-list, you can use typical keyboard characters, such as a hyphen [-], tilde [~], bracket [>], or asterisk [*], at the at the beginning of a line. Another option is to insert a symbol at the beginning of a line. Then, to form the list, enter a tab and type the line of text. When you press the [Enter] key, the line is formatted as a bulleted item and the next line uses the same bullet symbol and formatting. See **Figure 9-31.**

NOTE

Picking the **Use Tab Delimiter Only** option limits unwanted list formatting by instructing AutoCAD to recognize tabs only when starting a list. If the **Use Tab Delimiter Only** option is unchecked, list formatting is applied when a space or tab follows the initial list item character.

Multiple lines of text can be converted to a list by selecting all of the lines of text and then picking a list formatting option. AutoCAD detects where the [Enter] key was used to start a new line of text and lists the lines in sequence. When you create a list in this manner, space is automatically placed after the number, letter, or symbol preceding the text. The size of the space can be adjusted by setting tabs and indents.

The following options are also available when creating lists:
- **Off.** Removes any list characters or bulleting from selected text.
- **Restart.** Renumbers or re-letters selected items in a new sequence. The numbering or lettering starts from the beginning (using 1 or A).
- **Continue.** Adds selected items to a list that exists above the currently selected item. The selected item is numbered to continue the previous list. Items below the selected item are also renumbered.

Figure 9-30.
Framing notes arranged in a numbered list.

FRAMING NOTES:
1. ALL FRAMING NOTES TO BE DFL #2 OR BETTER.
2. ALL HEATED WALLS @ HEATED LIVING AREA TO BE 2 X 6 @ 16" OC. FRAME ALL EXTERIOR NON-BEARING WALLS W/2 X 6 STUDS @ 24" OC.
3. USE 2 X 6 NAILER AT THE BOTTOM OF ALL 2-2 X 12 OR 4 X HEADERS @ EXTERIOR WALLS, BACK HEADER W/2" RIGID INSULATION.
4. BLOCK ALL WALLS OVER 10'-0" HIGH AT MID HEIGHT.

Figure 9-31.
In addition to the regular bullet symbol, other keyboard characters can be used for items in bulleted lists.

- An elevation of the beam with end views or sections
- Complete locational dimensions for holes, plates, and angles
- Length dimensions

Bulleted List with Bullet Symbols

~ Connection specifications
~ Cutouts
~ Miscellaneous notes for the fabricator

Bulleted List with Tilde Characters

Forming Columns

It is sometimes necessary to break up text into multiple sections, or columns. This is especially true when you add lengthy general notes or when information must be organized in groups. See **Figure 9-32**. Multiline text columns are created inside the text editor as a single object. This eliminates the need to create multiple text objects to form separate columns of text. AutoCAD allows you to apply column formatting to existing text or create columns as you enter text.

Column tools are available from the **Columns** flyout button on the **Text Formatting** toolbar, or the **Columns** cascading submenu available from the **Options** flyout button or the shortcut menu. By default, the **No Columns** option is selected. This forms the text boundary, or single column, described throughout this chapter. You can create one of two types of columns. *Dynamic columns* calculate the total number of columns automatically, according to the amount of text and the height and width of the columns. *Static columns* divide the text into a specified number of columns.

Dynamic columns can be created by choosing an option from the **Dynamic Columns** cascading submenu. Pick the **Auto height** option to produce columns of equal height. **Figure 9-33** shows methods for adjusting dynamic columns using **Auto height**. Increasing column width or height reduces the number of columns, and decreasing column width or height produces more columns. Pick the **Manual height** option to produce columns that can be adjusted individually for height to produce distinct groups of information. Pick and drag the arrows at the bottom of each column to adjust column height. See **Figure 9-34**.

Static columns can be created by choosing the number of columns from the **Static Columns** cascading submenu. The amount of text in static columns depends on how much text is in the text editor and the height and width of the columns. However, the selected number of columns does not change even if text does not fill or extends past a column. **Figure 9-35** shows methods for adjusting static columns. Increasing column width or height rearranges the text in the specified number of columns, but the number of static columns does not change based on column width or height.

dynamic columns: Columns calculated automatically by AutoCAD based on amount of text and column size.

static columns: Columns of a set size defined by the user.

Figure 9-32.
An example of drawing notes created as a single multiline text object, divided into three columns.

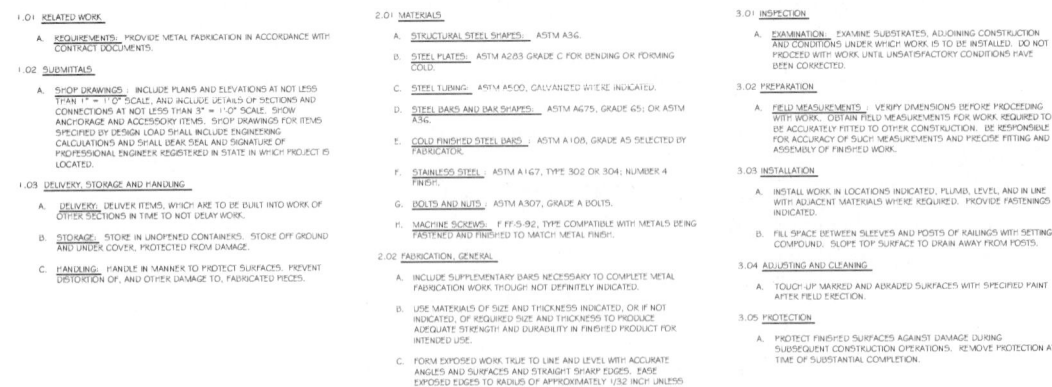

Figure 9-33.

Controlling columns using the dynamic column **Auto Height** option. Notice how column text flows from one column to the next by default.

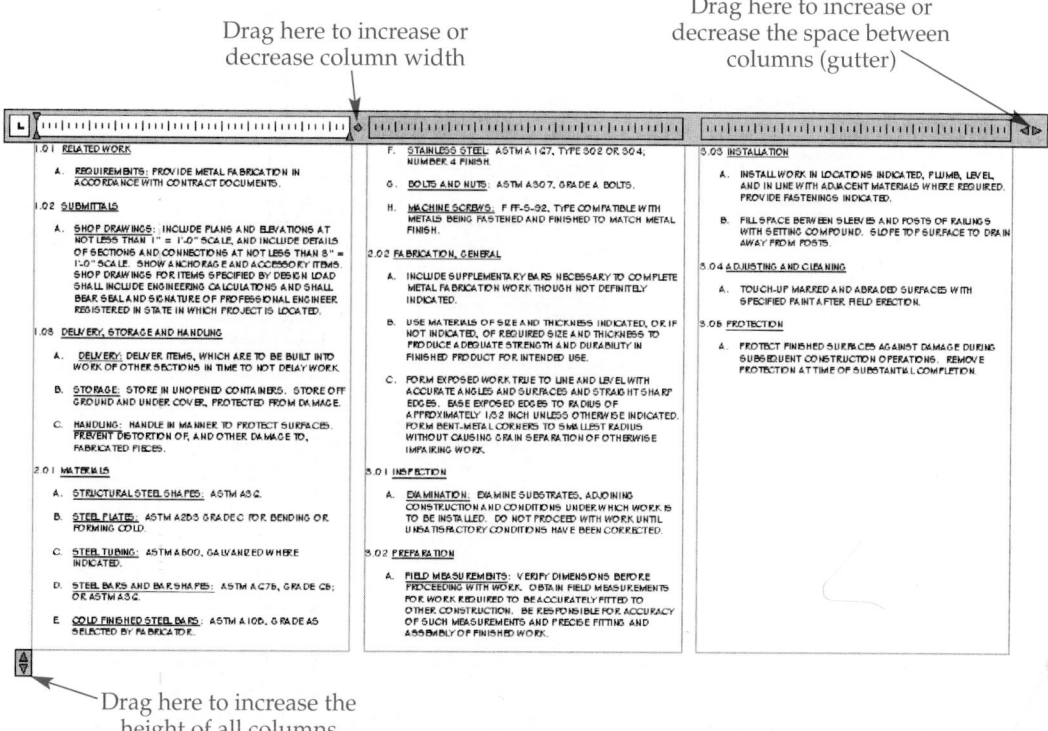

Drag here to increase or decrease column width

Drag here to increase or decrease the space between columns (gutter)

Drag here to increase the height of all columns

Figure 9-34.

Controlling the length of dynamic columns individually (manually).

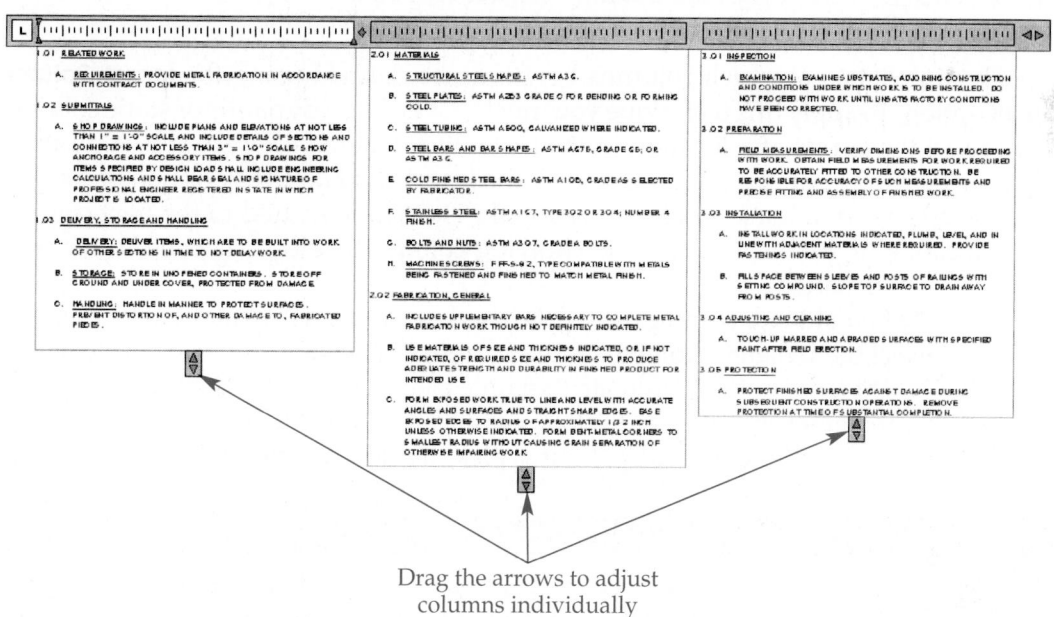

Drag the arrows to adjust columns individually

Figure 9-35.
Controlling static columns.

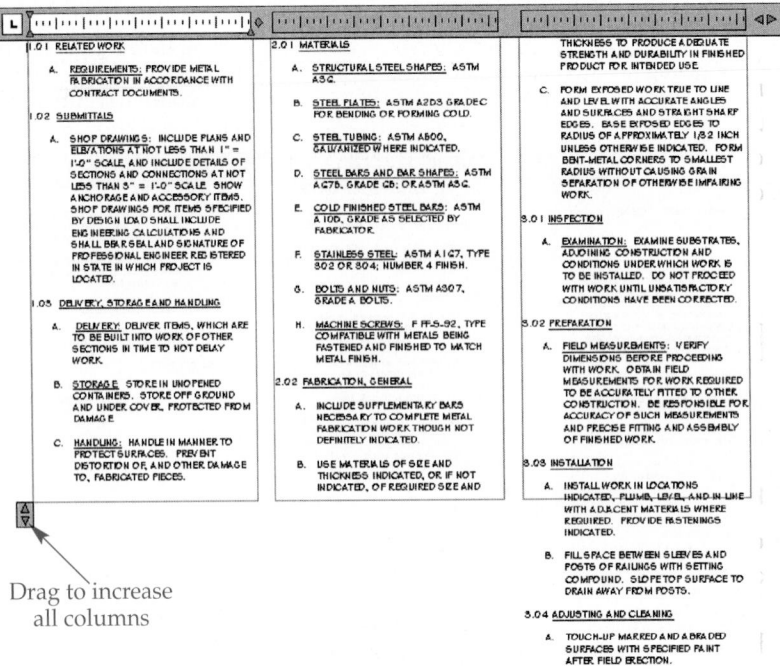

Drag to increase
all columns

NOTE

To create more than six static columns, pick the **More...** option to access the **Column Settings** dialog box and enter the number of columns in the **Column Number** text box.

The line of text at which columns begin can be defined using the **Insert Column Break** option. To apply this technique you must first define a dynamic or static column. Then place the cursor at a location in the text editor where you want the columns to start, such as the start of a paragraph. Pick the **Insert Column Break** option or use the [Alt]+[Enter] key combination to form the break. The text is shifted to the next column at the location of the break. Continue applying column breaks as needed to separate sections of information.

The **Column Settings...** dialog box can be used as an alternative method for creating columns. Select the **Dynamic Columns** radio button, followed by either the **Auto height** or **Manual height** radio button, to create dynamic columns. Choose the **Static Columns** radio button and enter the number of static columns in the **Column Number** text box to create static columns. To eliminate columns, pick the **No Columns** radio button.

NOTE

If you choose to remove columns using the **No Columns** option, any column breaks added using the **Insert Column Break** function will remain. Backspace to remove column breaks.

The following options are also available in the **Column Settings** dialog box:

- **Height.** Contains a text box that allows you to enter the height for all static or dynamic columns.
- **Width.** Sets column width and the space between columns, known as the *gutter*. Enter the column width in the **Column** text box, and the gutter width in the **Gutter** text box. The **Total** text box is only available with static columns and is used to enter the total width of the text editor, which is the sum of the width of all columns and the gutter spacing between columns.

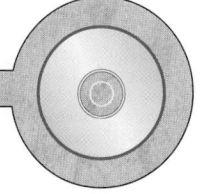

gutter: The space between columns of text.

Exercise 9-6
Complete the exercise on the Student CD.

Using a Background Mask

Sometimes text has to be placed over existing objects in a drawing, such as graphic patterns, making the text hard to read. A *background mask* can be used to hide any portion of the objects behind and around the text so that no objects obstruct the text. To mask objects behind text, select **Background Mask...** from the **Options** flyout button or the shortcut menu. This displays the **Background Mask** dialog box. See **Figure 9-36.**

background mask: A mask that hides a portion of objects behind and around text so that the text is unobstructed.

To apply the mask settings to the current multiline text object, check the **Use background mask** check box. The **Border offset factor:** text box sets how much of the underlying objects are masked out. This value, from 1 to 5, works with the text height value. If the border offset factor is set to 1, then the mask occurs directly within the boundary of the text. To offset the mask beyond the text boundary, use a value greater than 1. The formula is: border offset factor × text height = total masking distance from the bottom of the text. See **Figure 9-37.** The **Fill Color** area of the **Background Mask** dialog box allows you to apply color to the mask using the background color or a different color.

Finding and Replacing Text

AutoCAD allows you to search for text in a paragraph and replace it with a different piece of text. To display the **Find and Replace** dialog box, pick the **Find and Replace...** option from the **Options** flyout button or the shortcut menu or use the [Ctrl]+[R] key combination. See **Figure 9-38.** Enter the text you are searching for in the **Find what:** text box. Enter the text that will be substituted in the **Replace with:** text box. Then pick the **Find Next** button to highlight the next instance of the search text. You can then pick the **Replace** or the **Replace All** button to replace the highlighted text or all words that match your search criteria.

The **Match whole word only** check box is used to specify a search for a whole word, and not part of another word. For example, if **Match whole word only** is not checked, a search for the word *the* would find those letters wherever they occur—including as part of other words, such as o<u>the</u>r or wea<u>the</u>r. You can also select the **Match case** check box if you are searching for words that are case specific.

Figure 9-36.
The **Background Mask** dialog box is used to specify settings for a text mask.

Determines how much of the background is masked

Sets mask color same as background color

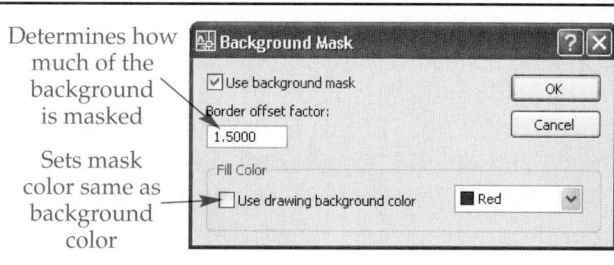

Figure 9-37.
The border offset factor determines the size of the background mask. The text in the figure is 1/8″ with different border offset factors.

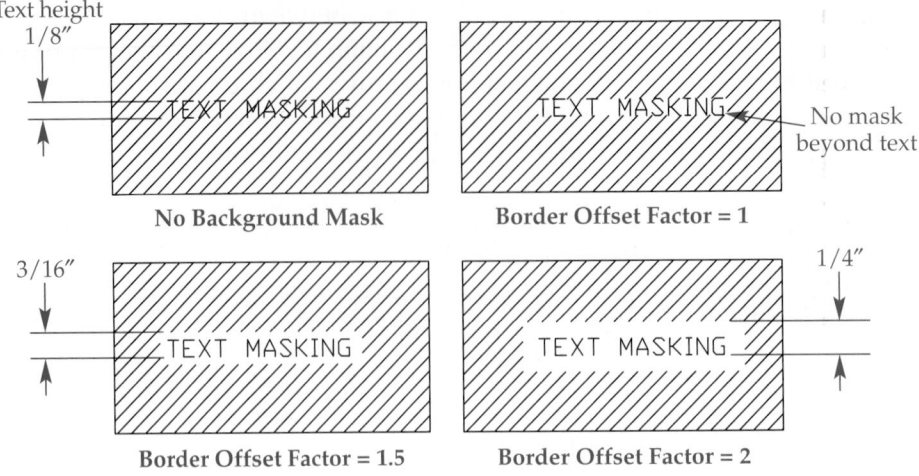

Figure 9-38.
Using the **Find and Replace** dialog box.

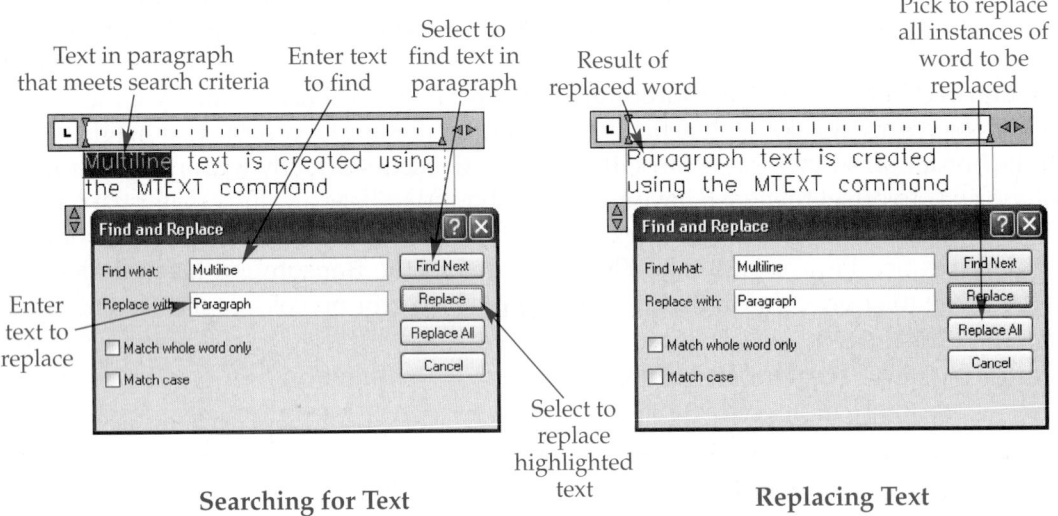

Additional Mtext Options

The following options are also available from the **Options** flyout button or the shortcut menu when using the **In-Place Text Editor**:

- **Insert Field.** Opens the **Field** dialog box, which allows you to insert text that can be updated. Fields are described later in this chapter.
- **Display Options.** Contains settings for customizing the **In-Place Text Editor** display. The **Show Toolbar** option determines whether the **Text Formatting** toolbar is displayed. Pick **Show Options** to display the second row of buttons on the **Text Formatting** toolbar. Select or deselect the **Show Ruler** option to show or hide the ruler. Choose the **Opaque Background** option to show the text editor as opaque instead of translucent. Select the **Text Highlight Color...** option to change the color of highlighted text using the **Select Color** dialog box.
- **Select All.** Selects all lines of text in the multiline text object.
- **AutoCAPS.** Turns on the [Caps Lock] on the keyboard when you open the **In-Place Text Editor**. The caps lock is turned off when you exit the text editor so text in other programs is not all uppercase.

- **Remove Formatting.** Removes formatting such as bold, italic, or underline from any highlighted text in the text editor.
- **Combine Paragraphs.** Combines highlighted text into a single paragraph.
- **Character Set.** Displays a menu of code pages. A code page provides support for character sets used in different languages. Select a code page to apply it to the selected text.

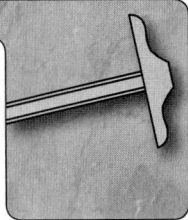

Single-Line Text

The **TEXT** command allows you to create single-line text. This means that each line of text is a single text object. The **TEXT** command is most useful for text items that require only one line of text. Whenever the text has more than one line or requires mixed fonts, sizes, colors, or other characteristics, multiline text should be used.

The **TEXT** command can be issued by picking the **Single Line Text** button in the **Text** toolbar or the **Text** control panel of the **Dashboard**, picking **Draw > Text > Single Line Text**, or typing TEXT. When you enter the **TEXT** command, the default option allows you to select a point on the screen where you want the text to begin. This point becomes the lower-left corner of the text, using default justification. Next you enter the text height. If the current text style is annotative, the height you enter is the paper text height. If the current text style is not annotative, the height you enter is the text height and must be multiplied by the scale factor.

The next prompt asks for the text's rotation angle. The default value is 0, which places the text horizontally. Other values rotate text in a counterclockwise direction. The text pivots about the starting point as shown in **Figure 9-39.**

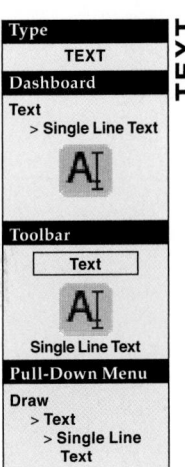

Figure 9-39.
Rotation angles for text. The start point is indicated here with a plus sign.

If the default angle orientation or direction (**ANGBASE** or **ANGDIR** system variable) is changed, the text rotation is affected.

After the text height and rotation angle are set, a text editor equal in height to the text height appears on the screen at the start point. As text is typed, the text editor increases in size to display the characters. See **Figure 9-40.** You can enter multiple lines of text by pressing [Enter] at the end of each line. The text cursor automatically moves to the start point one line below the preceding line. Press [Enter] twice to exit the command and keep what you have typed. You can cancel the command at any time by pressing the [Esc] key. This action erases any incomplete lines of text.

A number of options for the **TEXT** command are available by right-clicking to display a shortcut menu. These shortcut menu options function much like those for the **MTEXT** command. Options for accessing help files and canceling the **TEXT** command are also available from the shortcut menu

In previous releases of AutoCAD, the **DTEXT** command was used to create single-line text. This command has been replaced by the **TEXT** command. If you type DTEXT or its alias, DT, the **TEXT** command is activated.

Single-Line Text Justification

The **TEXT** command offers a variety of justification options. Left justification is the default. If you want another option, type J at the Specify start point of text [Justify/Style]: prompt or pick the **Justify** dynamic input option. When you select the **Justify** option, you can use one of several text alignment options.

When the **Align** option is selected, AutoCAD automatically adjusts the text height to fit between the start point and endpoint. The height varies according to the distance between the points and the number of characters. The **Fit** option is similar to the **Align** option, except you can select the text height. AutoCAD adjusts the letter width to fit between the two given points, while keeping text height constant. **Figure 9-41** shows the effects of the **Align** and **Fit** options.

PROFESSIONAL TIP

The **TEXT** command is not recommended for aligned text because the text height for each line is adjusted according to the width. One line may run into another.

The **Center** option allows you to select the center point for the baseline of the text. The **Middle** option allows you to center text both horizontally and vertically at a given point. The **Right** option justifies text at the lower-right corner. The letter height and rotation can also be changed when using these options. **Figure 9-42** compares the **Center, Middle,** and **Right** options.

Figure 9-40.
Entering text with the **TEXT** command.

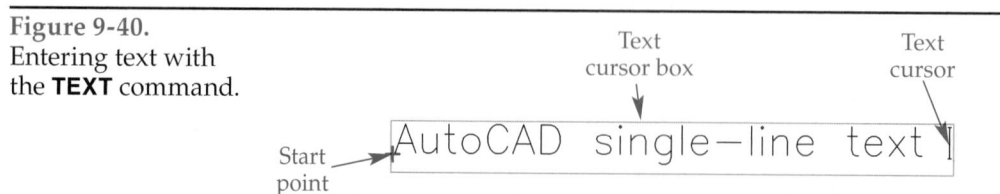

Figure 9-41.
Examples of aligned and fit text. With aligned text, the text height is adjusted. With fit text, the text width is adjusted.

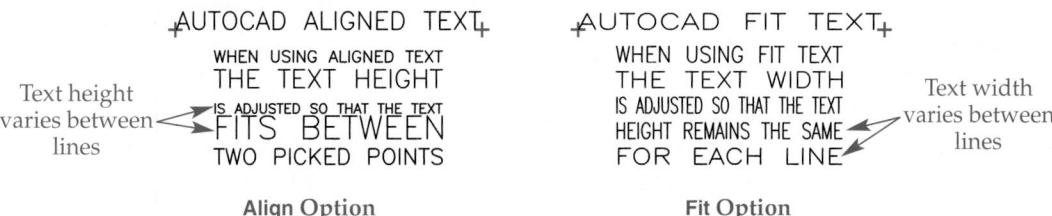

Text height varies between lines		Text width varies between lines

Align Option   Fit Option

Figure 9-42.
The **Center**, **Middle**, and **Right** text justification options.

AUTOCAD CENTERED TEXT

Center Option

AUTOCAD MIDDLE TEXT

Middle Option

AUTOCAD RIGHT—JUSTIFIED TEXT

Right Option

A number of text alignment options allow you to place text on a drawing in relation to the top, bottom, middle, left side, or right side of the text. These alignment options are shown in **Figure 9-43.** To use one of these options, type the two letters for the desired option and press [Enter].

Exercise 9-7

Complete the exercise on the Student CD.

Figure 9-43.
Using the **TL**, **TC**, **TR**, **ML**, **MC**, **MR**, **BL**, **BC**, and **BR** text alignment options. Notice what the abbreviations stand for.

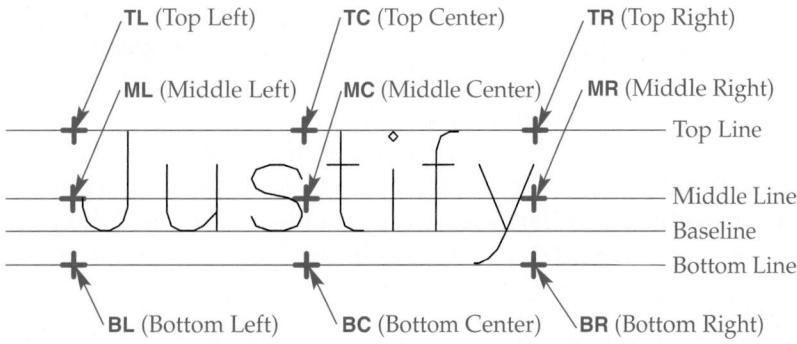

Inserting Symbols

In order to insert a symbol with the **TEXT** command, AutoCAD requires a control code. The *control code sequence* for a symbol begins with two percent signs (%%). The next character you enter represents the symbol. For example, in order to add the note ∅2.75, the control code sequence %%C2.75 is entered in the text cursor box. The common control code sequences available with the **TEXT** command are shown in **Figure 9-28**. A single percent sign can be added normally. However, when a percent sign must precede another control code sequence, %%% can be used to force a single percent sign.

Drawing Underscored or Overscored Text

Text can be underscored (underlined) or overscored with the **TEXT** command by typing a control code sequence in front of the line of text. The control code sequences are:

%%O = overscore
%%U = underscore

To create the note <u>UNDERSCORING TEXT</u>, for example, you must enter the following: %%UUNDERSCORING TEXT. A line of text may require both underscoring and overscoring. To do this, use both control code sequences. For example, the control code sequence %%O%%ULINE OF TEXT produces the note with both underscore and overscore.

The %%O and %%U control codes are toggles that turn overscoring and underscoring on and off. Type %%U preceding a word or phrase to turn underscoring on. Type %%U after the desired word or phrase to turn underscoring off. Any text following the second %%U then appears without underscoring. For example, <u>DETAIL A</u> HUB ASSEMBLY would be entered as %%UDETAIL A%%U HUB ASSEMBLY.

PROFESSIONAL TIP

Many drafters prefer to underline labels such as <u>SECTION A-A</u> or <u>DETAIL B</u>. Rather than draw line or polyline objects under the text, use **Middle** or **Center** justification modes and underscoring. The view labels are automatically underlined and centered under the views or details they identify.

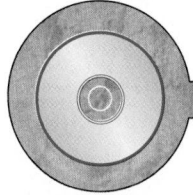

Exercise 9-8
Complete the exercise on the Student CD.

Working with Fields

A *field* is a special type of text object that can display a specific property value, setting, or characteristic. Fields can display information related to a specific object, general drawing properties, or the current user or computer system.

AutoCAD can update field information automatically. This makes fields useful tools for displaying information that may change throughout the course of a project. For example, you could insert the **Date** field into a title block. The field is then updated automatically with the current date throughout the life of the drawing file.

Inserting Fields

Fields can be inserted in both multiline and single-line text. To insert a field in multiline text, pick the **Insert Field** button from the **Text Formatting** toolbar, select the **Insert Field...** option available from the **Options** flyout button or the shortcut menu, or use the [Ctrl]+[F] key combination. To insert a field in single-line text, right-click and select **Insert Field...** from the shortcut menu while entering text on-screen. You can also insert a field without first accessing the **MTEXT** or **TEXT** commands by picking **Insert > Field...** from the pull-down menu.

Regardless of the method used, the **Field** dialog box is displayed when you select to insert a field. See **Figure 9-44.** Many preset fields can be selected from the **Field** dialog box. To make it easier to locate a specific field, they are separated into categories. When you select a category from the **Field category** drop-down list, only the fields within the category are displayed in the **Field names** list box. This makes it much easier to locate a desired field.

Pick the field category, and then pick the field to be inserted from the **Field name** list box. The selected field and its current value are displayed in the center of the **Field** dialog box. You can also select from a list of formats to determine the display of the field. The **Format** list varies, depending on the selected field.

After you select the field and format, pick the **OK** button to insert the field. The field assumes the current text style. By default, the field text has a gray background. See **Figure 9-45.** This keeps you aware that the text is actually a field, so the value displayed may change. You can deactivate the background in the **Fields** area of the **User Preferences** tab of the **Options** dialog box. See **Figure 9-46.**

Figure 9-44.
Select fields using the **Field** dialog box.

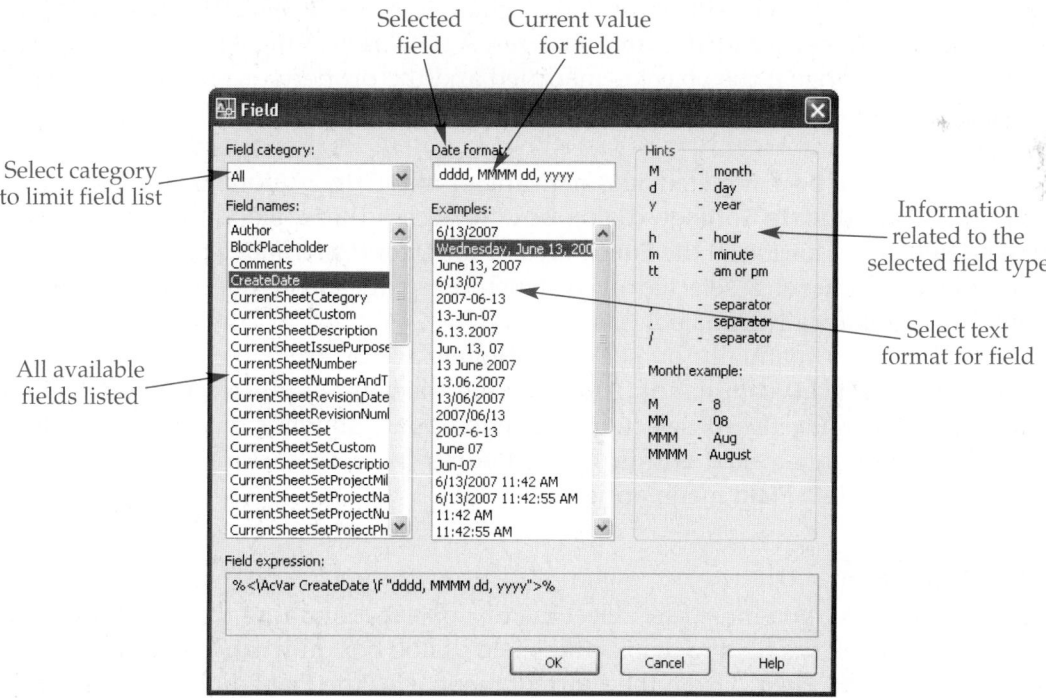

Figure 9-45.
A date and time field inserted into multiline text. The gray background identifies the text as a field.

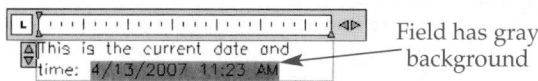

Field has gray background

Figure 9-46.
Control the background display for fields in the **User Preferences** tab of the **Options** dialog box.

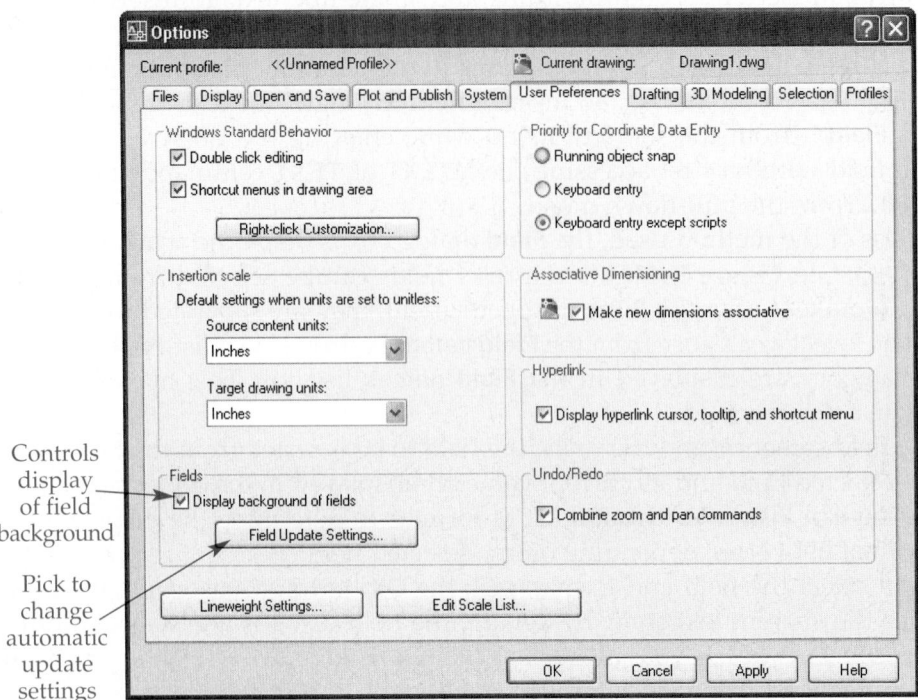

Controls display of field background

Pick to change automatic update settings

Updating Fields

After a field is inserted into a drawing, the value being displayed may change. For example, a field displaying the current date changes every date. A field displaying the file name will change if the file name changes. A field displaying the value of an object property will change if the object is modified and the property is changed. *Updating* is AutoCAD's process of checking the value of the field and changing the display if needed.

Updating can be completed automatically or manually. Automatic updating is set using the **Field Update Settings** dialog box. To access this dialog box, pick the **Field Update Settings...** button in the **Fields** area of the **User Preferences** tab of the **Options** dialog box. Whenever a selected event (such as saving or regenerating) occurs, all fields are automatically updated.

Update fields manually by selecting **Update Fields** from the **Tools** pull-down menu (**UPDATEFIELD** command). After picking the command, select the fields to be updated. You can use the **All** selection option to update all fields in a single operation. You can also update a field within the text editor by right-clicking on the field and selecting the **Update Field** menu option.

Editing Fields

To edit a field, you must first select the text object containing the field for editing. Then double-click the field to display the **Field** dialog box. You can also right-click the field and pick **Edit Field...** from the shortcut menu. Use the **Field** dialog box to modify the field settings and pick **OK** to apply the changes.

You can also convert a field to standard text. When you convert a field, the currently displayed value becomes text, the association to the field is lost, and the value no longer updates. To convert a field to text, select the text for editing, right-click the field, and pick the **Convert Field To Text** option.

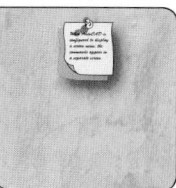

Exercise 9-9
Complete the exercise on the Student CD.

Revising Text

AutoCAD provides several methods for reentering the text editor to make changes to text content. The easiest way to reopen the text editor is to double-click a multiline or single-line text object. Double-clicking a multiline text object opens the **In-Place Text Editor**. Double-clicking a single-line text object allows you to edit the text in the text cursor box. Type the new text string or modify the text. Then pick outside of the text cursor box and press the [Enter] key to apply the changes.

Another technique to edit text entries is to use the **DDEDIT** command. This command is accessed by picking **Modify > Object > Text > Edit...** from the pull-down menu, typing ED or DDEDIT, or selecting the **Edit...** button on the **Text** toolbar. The **DDEDIT** command can also be accessed by selecting the text object, right-clicking, and selecting **Edit...** from the shortcut menu. The **DDEDIT** command is a universal text editing tool that can be used to modify the content of most text objects, including multiline and single-line text. Multiline text can also be edited using the **MTEDIT** command. This command is accessed by typing MTEDIT or by right-clicking and selecting **Mtext Edit...** from the shortcut menu.

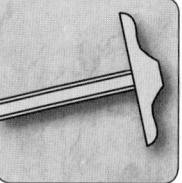

Changing Text with the Properties Palette

The **Properties** palette can be used to change text properties. To open the **Properties** palette, pick the **Properties** button on the **Standard Annotation** toolbar, select **Modify > Properties**, select **Tools > Palettes > Properties**, or type CH, MO, PROPS, or PROPERTIES. You can also open the **Properties** palette by selecting the desired text and then right-clicking and selecting **Properties** from the shortcut menu.

You can select text first and then display the **Properties** palette, or you can display the **Properties** palette and then select the text. If you display the **Properties** palette first, you may need to move the palette before you can select the text (if the palette covers the text you want to pick). Either way, the **Properties** palette opens, as shown in **Figure 9-47.**

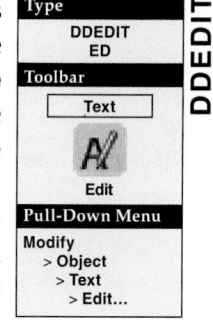

Figure 9-47.
The **Properties** palette shows the properties of the selected text. The properties of single-line text are slightly different from those of multiline text.

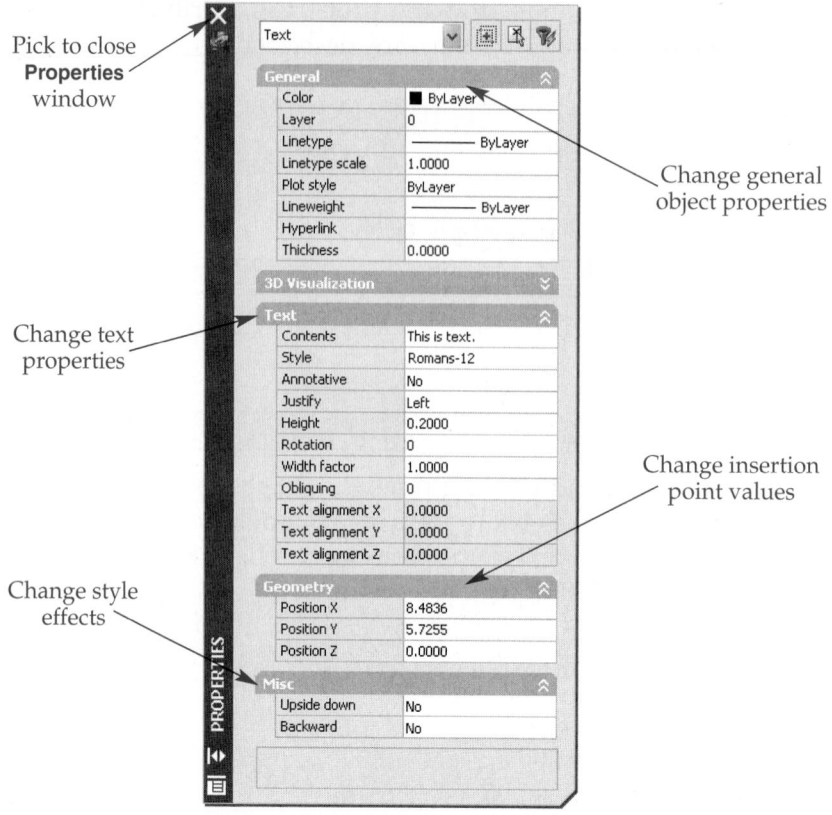

The top of the palette identifies the type of object selected. In **Figure 9-47**, Text appears in the box because a single-line text object has been selected. If multiple objects are selected, the drop-down list is used to select which object's properties are displayed. Picking a property allows you to modify its value. The text properties are divided into the following categories:

- **General.** Properties found in nearly all AutoCAD object types. The general properties include color, layer, linetype, linetype scale, plot style, lineweight, hyperlink, and thickness.
- **3D Visualization.** Properties for an object's material. This feature is used in 3D applications.
- **Text.** Contains properties such as text style and justification. The text properties available for single-line text and multiline text are identified later in this section.
- **Geometry.** The X, Y, and Z coordinate locations of the text insertion point.
- **Misc.** The Upside down and Backward properties. These properties are not listed for multiline text objects.

To change a property, pick the property or property setting with the cursor. The property setting can then be edited. For some properties, a drop-down list or dialog box can be used to select other settings. See **Figure 9-48**.

After you make the desired changes to your text, press [Enter] to apply the changes or pick the "X" in the **Properties** palette title bar to close the **Properties** palette. Then press the [Esc] key to deselect the text.

Figure 9-48.
Modifying a property using the **Properties** palette. When the **Justify** property is picked, a drop-down arrow appears next to the Left setting. Picking the arrow displays a drop-down list of options.

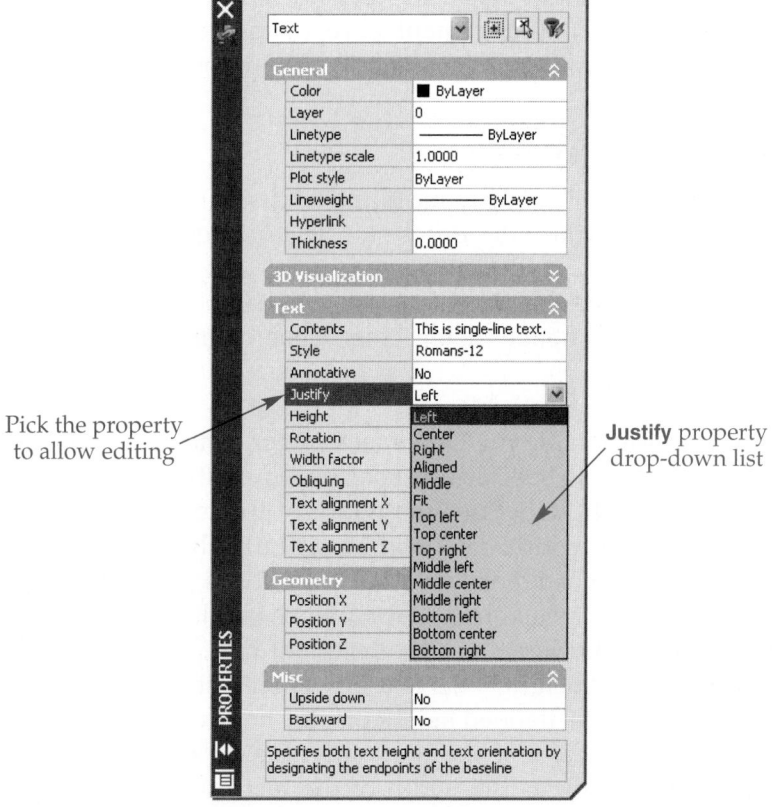

Pick the property to allow editing

Justify property drop-down list

Properties common to single-line and multiline text

The selections listed on the **Properties** palette for single-line text are different from those listed with multiline text. The following properties are available when either single-line or multiline text is selected:

- **Contents.** Displays the selected text. Changes can be made to single-line text by modifying the value in the text box. When multiline text is selected, picking the ellipses (…) button opens the **In-Place Text Editor**.
- **Style.** Use this drop-down list to select a different text style.
- **Annotative.** Makes text annotative or non-annotative.
- **Annotative scale.** Displays the annotation scale currently applied to the selected annotative object. Picking the ellipses (…) button opens the **Annotation Object Scale** dialog box. The function of this dialog box is described in Chapter 27.
- **Justify.** Provides justification options for single-line or multiline text.
- **Paper text height.** Sets paper text height. This text box is only shown if the selected text is annotative. The **Model text height** display box is provided for reference and shows the height of the text after the scale factor is applied.
- **Text height.** Sets text height for non-annotative text. This text box is only shown if the selected text is non-annotative.
- **Match orientation to layout.** Aligns the orientation of annotative text with the layout viewport. Layouts are described in Chapter 25.
- **Rotation.** Sets the text rotation value in degrees. If multiline text is selected, the entire text object is rotated. If single-line text is selected, the single line of text is rotated.

Properties for single-line text only

The properties unique to single-line text include:
- **Width factor.** Sets the text character width.
- **Obliquing.** Sets the slant angle for text characters.
- **Text alignment.** The **Text alignment X**, **Text alignment Y**, and **Text alignment Z** properties set the location of the alignment point for the text based on the justification setting.

Properties for multiline text only

The following items are unique to multiline text:
- **Direction.** Specifies the horizontal or vertical direction of the multiline text object.
- **Line space.** Redefines the line spacing options specified in the **In-Place Text Editor**. Use the **Line space factor**, **Line space distance**, and **Line space style** properties.
- **Background mask.** Sets a background for the text.
- **Paper defined width.** Use the **Line space factor**, **Line space distance**, and **Line space style** settings to specify line spacing for multiline text.
- **Paper defined width.** Redefines the width of the text boundary based on the unscaled boundary width. This text box is only shown if the selected text is annotative. The **Model defined width** display box is provided for reference and shows the width of the text boundary after the scale factor is applied.
- **Paper defined height.** Redefines the height of the text boundary based on the unscaled boundary height. This text box is only shown if the selected text is annotative. The **Model defined height** display box is provided for reference and shows the height of the text boundary after the scale factor is applied.
- **Defined width.** Redefines the width of the text boundary for non-annotative text.
- **Defined height.** Redefines the height of the text boundary for non-annotative text.
- **Columns.** Creates or modifies multiline text columns. Pick the ellipses (…) button to open the **Column Settings** dialog box.

Exercise 9-10
Complete the exercise on the Student CD.

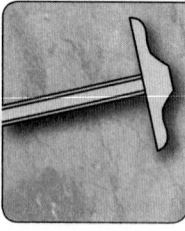

LEGACY NOTE

The **CHANGE** command can also be used to modify single-line text objects. This command is accessed by typing -CH or CHANGE. After selecting the text, you can change the text style, height, rotation angle, insertion point, object properties, and other settings on the command line.

Scaling Text

To change the height of text objects, use the **SCALETEXT** command. This command allows you to scale text objects in relation to their individual insertion points or in relation to a single base point. **SCALETEXT** is accessed by selecting the **Scale** button on the **Text** toolbar, picking **Modify > Object > Text > Scale**, or typing SCALETEXT.

The **SCALETEXT** command works with single-line and multiline text objects. You can also select both types of text objects simultaneously. The prompts for the **SCALETEXT** command are as follows:

Command: **SCALETEXT**↵
Select objects: *(select the text object(s) to be scaled)*
Enter a base point option for scaling [Existing/Left/Center/Middle/Right/TL/TC/TR/
    ML/MC/MR/BL/BC/BR] <Existing>: *(specify justification for base point)*
Specify new height or [Match object/Scale factor] *<default>*: *(specify scaling option)*
Command:

Type
SCALETEXT
Toolbar
Text
Scale
Pull-Down Menu
Modify
  >Object
    >Text
      >Scale

SCALETEXT

All the justification options except **Existing** and **Left** are shown in Figure 9-42 and Figure 9-43. Using the **Existing** option scales the text objects using their existing justification setting as the base point. Using the **Left** option scales the text objects using their lower-left point as the base point. Figure 9-49 shows text with different justification points being scaled using the **Existing** option. Notice how the text is scaled in relation to its own justification setting.

After you specify the justification to be used as the base point, AutoCAD prompts for the scaling type. The **Specify new model height** option (default) is used to type a new value for the text height of non-annotative objects. If the selected text is annotative, the value you enter is ignored. The **Paper height** option is used to type a new value for the text height of annotative objects. The value entered here is the paper text height. If the selected text is non-annotative, the value you enter is ignored. The **Match object** option allows you to pick an existing text object. The selected text object's height adopts the text height from the text object you pick. Use the **Scale factor** option to scale text objects that have different heights in relation to their current heights. For example, using a scale factor of 2 scales all the selected text objects to twice their current size.

Changing Text Justification

If you use the **Properties** palette to change the justification of a text object, the text object(s) move to adjust to the new justification point. The justification point does not move. To change the justification point without moving the text, use the **JUSTIFYTEXT** command. This command is accessed by selecting the **Justify** button on the **Text** toolbar, picking **Modify > Object > Text > Justify**, or typing JUSTIFYTEXT.

Type
JUSTIFYTEXT
Toolbar
Text
Justify
Pull-Down Menu
Modify
  >Object
    >Text
      >Justify

JUSTIFYTEXT

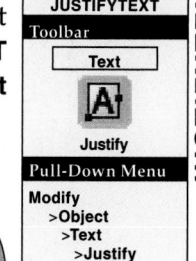

Exercise 9-11
Complete the exercise on the Student CD.

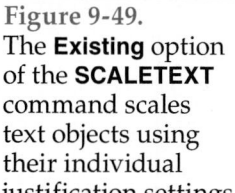

Figure 9-49.
The **Existing** option of the **SCALETEXT** command scales text objects using their individual justification settings.

+BL Justification
MC Justification
TR Justification
Original Text

+BL Justification
MC Justification
TR Justification
**Text Scaled Using
Existing Base Point Option**

Finding and Replacing Text

FIND

You were previously introduced to the **Find and Replace** option available for searching and replacing text within the **MTEXT** or **TEXT** command. If you want to find a piece of text in your drawing and replace it with an alternative piece of text in a single instance or throughout your drawing, you should use the **FIND** command.

To find a string of text in the drawing, pick the **Find** button in the **Text** toolbar or the **Text** control panel of the **Dashboard**, type FIND, pick **Edit > Find...** from the pull-down menu. AutoCAD displays the **Find and Replace** dialog box, which contains the following elements:

- **Find text string.** Specify the text string you want to find in this text box or choose one of the six most recently used strings from the drop-down list.
- **Replace with.** Specify the text string you want to replace in this text box or choose one of the most recently used strings from the drop-down list.
- **Search in.** Specify whether to search the entire drawing or only the current selection. If there is a current selection set, **Current selection** is the default value. If there is no current selection set, **Entire drawing** is the default value. Picking the **Select Objects** button closes the dialog box temporarily, allowing you to select objects in the drawing. Press [Enter] to return to the dialog box.
- **Options....** Displays the **Find and Replace Options** dialog box, in which you can define the search criteria for the text you want to find. See **Figure 9-50**.
- **Context.** Displays and highlights the currently found text string in its surrounding context. If you choose **Find Next**, AutoCAD refreshes the **Context** area and displays the next found text string in its surrounding context.
- **Find/Find Next.** Finds the text in the **Find text string** text box. Once you find the first instance of the text, the **Find** button becomes the **Find Next** button, which you can use to find the next instance.
- **Replace.** Replaces found text with the text in the **Replace with** text box.
- **Replace All.** Finds all instances of the text in the **Find text string** text box and replaces all occurrences with the text in the **Replace with** text box.
- **Select All.** Finds and selects all loaded objects containing instances of the text in the **Find text string** text box. This option is available only when you are searching the **Current selection**. When you pick this button, the dialog box closes and AutoCAD displays a message indicating the number of objects found and selected.
- **Zoom to.** Displays the area in the drawing that contains the found text.

NOTE

The find and replace strings are saved with the drawing file and may be reused.

Figure 9-50.
The **Find and Replace Options** dialog box.

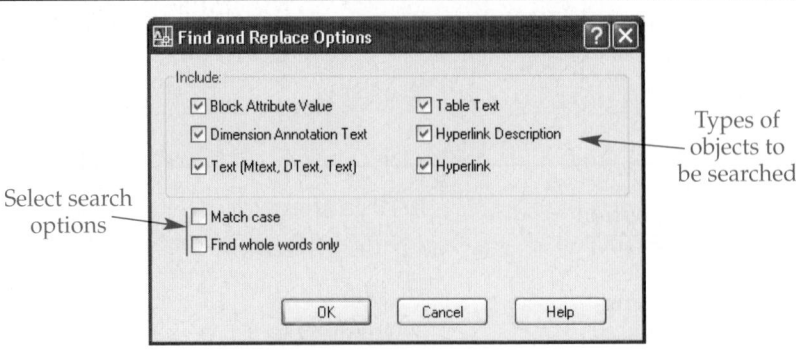

Select search options

Types of objects to be searched

Checking Your Spelling

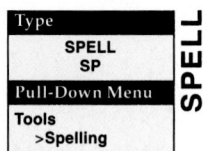

AutoCAD has a powerful and convenient tool for checking the spelling on your drawing. To check spelling, pick the **Spell Check** button in the **Text** toolbar or the **Text** control panel of the **Dashboard**, type SP or SPELL or pick **Tools > Spelling** to display the **Check Spelling** dialog box. See **Figure 9-51.** Before you check the spelling of text, you may want to adjust some of the spell checking preferences by picking the **Settings** button to access the **Check Spelling Settings** dialog box.

To check spelling, you must first identify the portion of the drawing you want to spell-check by selecting an option from the **Where to Check** drop-down list. Pick the **Entire drawing** option to check the spelling of all text objects in the drawing file, including model space and all layouts, or choose the **Current space/layout** to check spelling only of text objects in the active layout or model space, if model space is active. You can also choose to check the spelling of certain text objects by picking the **Selected objects** option. Then pick the **Select text objects** button to enter the graphics window and select all the text objects for which you want to check the spelling.

Spelling Options

After you define where to check, pick the **Start** button to begin checking text spelling. The **Check Spelling** dialog box contains the following features:

- **Main dictionary.** Selects the dictionary to use while checking the spelling of the selected text.
- **Dictionaries....** Displays the **Dictionaries** dialog box, which can be used to set the current main dictionary or access and modify custom dictionaries.
- **Current word.** Displays words that may be spelled incorrectly.
- **Suggestions.** Lists possible correct spellings for the current word. The highlighted word in the first box is AutoCAD's best guess. Following the highlighted word is a list of other choices. If there are many choices, a scroll bar is available for you to use. If you do not like the word that AutoCAD has highlighted, move the cursor to another word and pick it. The word you pick then becomes highlighted in the list and is shown in the **Suggestions** text box. If none of the words in the **Suggestions** text box or list are correct and the current word is not correct either, you can enter the correct word in the text box.
- **Ignore.** Skips the current word. In **Figure 9-51,** ASME is not a misspelled word; it just is not recognized by the dictionary. Select the **Ignore** button to proceed to the next word.

Figure 9-51.
The **Check Spelling** dialog box.

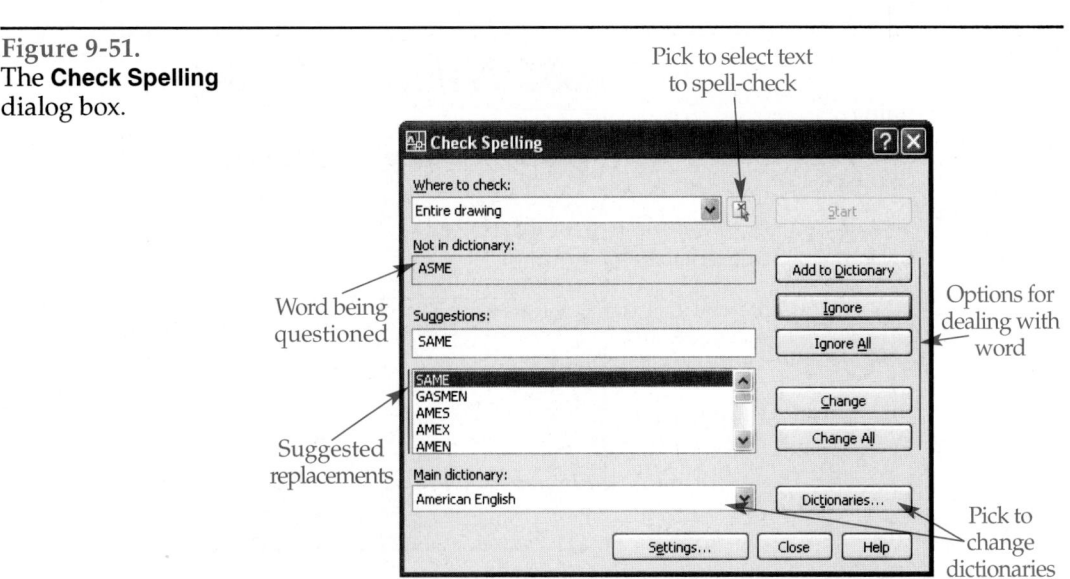

- **Ignore All.** Ignores all words that match the currently found misspelled word.
- **Change.** Replaces the current word with the word in the **Suggestions** text box.
- **Change All.** Replaces the current word with the word in the **Suggestions** text box throughout the entire selection set.
- **Add to Dictionary.** Adds the current word to the custom dictionary. You can add words with up to 63 characters.

Changing Dictionaries

AutoCAD provides 19 dictionaries for spelling, including dictionaries for several non-English languages. Pick the **Dictionaries...** button to access the **Dictionaries** dialog box. See **Figure 9-52.**

The **Main dictionary** list can be used to select one of the many language dictionaries to use as the current main dictionary. The main dictionary is protected; you cannot add definitions to it. The **Custom dictionary** list can be used to select the active custom dictionary. The default custom dictionary is sample.cus. Type a word in the **Content** text box that you either want to add or delete from the custom dictionary. For example, ASME Y14.5M is custom text used in engineering drafting. Pick the **Add** button to accept the custom word in the text box, or pick the **Delete** button to remove the word from the custom dictionary. Custom dictionary entries may be up to 63 characters in length.

You can create and manage custom dictionary by picking the **Manage Custom Dictionaries...** option from the drop-down list to access the **Manage Custom Dictionary** dialog box. Pick the **New** button to create a new custom dictionary by entering a new file name with a .cus extension. Words can be added or deleted and dictionaries can be combined using any standard text editor. If you use a word processor such as Microsoft Word, be sure to save the file as *text only*, with no special text formatting or printer codes. Add an existing custom dictionary by picking the **Add** button, and choose the **Remove** button to delete a custom dictionary from the list. Existing custom dictionaries can also be added by picking the **Import...** button from the **Custom dictionary** area.

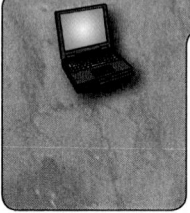

PROFESSIONAL TIP

You can create custom dictionaries for various disciplines. For example, common abbreviations and brand names for mechanical drawings might be added to a mech.cus file. A separate file named arch.cus might contain common architectural abbreviations and frequently used brand names.

Figure 9-52.
The **Change Dictionaries** dialog box.

Pick to select main dictionary

Current dictionary

Enter words to add to custom dictionary

Words defined in custom dictionary

Pick to import words from a word list or different dictionary

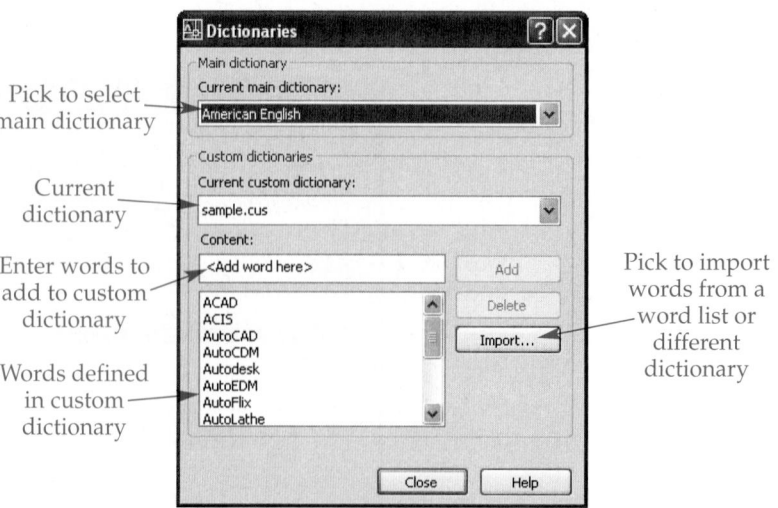

AutoCAD and Its Applications—Basics

Exercise 9-12

Complete the exercise on the Student CD.

Additional Text Tips

Text presentation is important on any drawing. It is a good idea to plan your drawing using rough sketches to allow room for text and notes. Some things to consider when designing the drawing layout include:

- ✓ Arrange text to avoid crowding.
- ✓ Place related notes in groups to make the drawing easy to read.
- ✓ Place all general notes in a common location. Locate notes in the lower-left corner or above the title block when using ASME standards. Place notes in the upper-left corner when using military standards.
- ✓ Always use the spell checker.

Express Tools
Chapter 9

The following Express Tools are related to topics described in this chapter. Refer to the Student CD for information on these tools:

Remote Text	**Text Fit**
Text Mask	**Unmask Text**
Explode Text	**Convert Text to Mtext**
Arc-Aligned Text	**Justify Text**
Rotate Text	**Enclose Text with Object**
Automatic Text Numbering	**Change Text Case**

Template Development
Chapter 9

Most drafting standards specify the style and size of text to be used on drawings. It is therefore a good idea to set up appropriate styles on your drawing templates. Refer to the Student CD for detailed instructions to add text styles to your mechanical, architectural, and civil drawing templates in compliance with ASME or related industry drafting standards.

Chapter Test

Answer the following questions. Write your answers on a separate sheet of paper or complete the electronic chapter test on the Student CD.

1. Which ASME standard contains guidelines for lettering?
2. Define *composition*.
3. Determine the AutoCAD text height for text to be plotted .188″ high using a half (1″ = 2″) scale. (Show your calculations.)
4. Determine the AutoCAD text height for text to be plotted .188″ high using a scale of 1/4″ = 1′-0″. (Show your calculations.)
5. Explain the function of annotative text and give an example.
6. What is the relationship between the drawing scale and the annotation scale for annotative text?
7. Define *text style*.
8. Outline at least five steps that are used to create a new text style with the **Text Style** dialog box.
9. Describe how to create a text style that has the name ROMANS-12_15, uses the romans.shx font, has a fixed height of .12, a text width of 1.25, and an oblique angle of 15.
10. Define *font*.
11. What system variable controls whether TrueType fonts are filled on plotted drawings?
12. What are Big Fonts?
13. How would you specify text to display vertically on the screen?
14. When setting text height in the **Text Style** dialog box, what value do you enter so text height can be altered each time the **TEXT** command is used?
15. What does a width factor of .5 do to text when compared to the default width factor of 1?
16. Explain how to make a text style current quickly.
17. Name the command that lets you create multiline text objects.
18. How does the width of the multiline text boundary affect what you type?
19. What happens if the multiline text you are entering exceeds or is not as long as the boundary length that you initially establish?
20. When typing text in the **In-Place Text Editor**, how do you remove the character located in front of the text cursor?
21. When you are in the **In-Place Text Editor**, how do you open the text editor short-cut menu?
22. How do you paste text from the Clipboard into the **In-Place Text Editor**?
23. How do you draw stacked fractions when using the **MTEXT** command?
24. What is the purpose of tracking?
25. What happens when you enter a fraction for the first time in the **In-Place Text Editor**, and what does this action allow you to do?
26. What is the difference between text boundary justification and paragraph alignment?
27. Define *line spacing*.
28. What happens when you pick the **Other...** option in the **Symbol** cascading menu of the text editor shortcut menu?
29. Explain the function of the **Allow Auto-list** option.
30. Explain how to convert multiple lines of text into a numbered list using the text editor shortcut menu.
31. Briefly discuss the difference between dynamic columns and static columns.
32. How can you insert a column break in static columns?
33. What text feature allows you to hide parts of objects behind and around text?

34. List three ways to access the **TEXT** command.
35. Give the control code sequence required to draw the following symbols when using the **TEXT** command:
    A. 30°
    B. 1.375 ± .005
    C. ∅24
    D. <u>NOT FOR CONSTRUCTION</u>
36. Briefly discuss the function and purpose of fields.
37. What is different about the on-screen display of fields compared to that of text?
38. How can you access the **Field Update Settings** dialog box?
39. Explain how to convert a field to text.
40. What appears if you double-click on multiline text?
41. Identify the command used to revise existing single-line text on the drawing by editing the text in-place.
42. Name two commands that allow you to edit multiline text.
43. Explain how to edit text in the **Properties** palette.
44. When using the **SCALETEXT** command, which base point option would you select to keep the text object's current justification point?
45. What is the difference between using the **JUSTIFYTEXT** command and using the **Properties** palette to change the justification point of a text object?
46. Name the command that allows you to find a piece of text and replace it with an alternative piece of text in a single instance or for every instance in your drawing.
47. Identify three ways to access the AutoCAD spell checker.
48. What is the purpose of the word found in the **Current word** box of the **Check Spelling** dialog box?
49. How do you change the main dictionary for use in the **Check Spelling** dialog box?
50. How do you change the **Current word** if you do not think the word that is displayed in the **Suggestions:** text box of the **Check Spelling** dialog box is the correct word, but one of the words in the list of suggestions is the correct word?

1. Start AutoCAD, start a new drawing using one of your templates, and create text styles as needed. Use the **TEXT** command to type the following information. Change the text style to represent each of the four fonts named. Use a .25 unit text height and 0° rotation angle. Save the drawing as P9-1.

   > TXT–AUTOCAD'S DEFAULT TEXT FONT, WHICH IS AVAILABLE FOR USE WHEN YOU BEGIN A DRAWING.
   > ROMANS–SMOOTHER THAN TXT FONT AND CLOSELY DUPLICATES THE SINGLE-STROKE LETTERING THAT HAS BEEN THE STANDARD FOR DRAFTING.
   > ROMANC–A MULTISTROKE DECORATIVE FONT THAT IS GOOD FOR USE IN DRAWING TITLES.
   > ITALICC–AN ORNAMENTAL FONT SLANTED TO THE RIGHT AND HAVING THE SAME LETTER DESIGN AS THE COMPLEX FONT.

2. Start AutoCAD, start a new drawing using one of your templates, and create text styles as needed. Change the options as noted in each line of text. Then use the **TEXT** command to type the text, changing the text style to represent each of the fonts named. Use a .25 unit text height. Save the drawing as P9-2.

   > TXT–EXPAND THE WIDTH BY THREE.
   > MONOTXT–SLANT TO THE LEFT –30°.
   > ROMANS–SLANT TO THE RIGHT 30°.
   > ROMAND–BACKWARDS.
   > ROMANC–VERTICAL.
   > ITALICC–UNDERSCORED AND OVERSCORED.
   > ROMANS–USE 16d NAILS @ 10″ OC.
   > ROMANT–∅32 (812.8).

3. Start AutoCAD and use the setup option of your choice. Create text styles with a .375 height with the following fonts: Arial, BankGothic Lt BT, CityBlueprint, Stylus BT, Swis721 BdOul BT, Vineta BT, and Wingdings. Use the **TEXT** command to type the complete alphabet and numbers 1–10 for the text styles. Also, type all symbols available on the keyboard and the diameter, degree, and plus/minus symbols. Save the drawing as P9-3.

4. Use the **MTEXT** command to type the following text using a text style with the Romans font and a .12 text height. The heading text height is .24. Check your spelling. Save the drawing as P9-4.

NOTES:

1.   INTERPRET DIMENSIONS AND TOLERANCES PER ASME Y14.5M−1994.
2.   REMOVE ALL BURRS AND SHARP EDGES.

CASTING NOTES UNLESS OTHERWISE SPECIFIED:
1.   .31 WALL THICKNESS.
2.   R.12 FILLETS.
3.   R.06 ROUNDS.
4.   1.5°−3.0° DRAFT.
5.   TOLERANCES:
     ± 1° ANGULAR
     ±.03 TWO PLACE DIMENSIONS.
6.   PROVIDE .12 THK MACHINING STOCK ON ALL MACHINE SURFACES.

5. Use the **MTEXT** command to type the following text using a text style with the Stylus BT font and a .125 text height. The heading text height is .188. After typing the text exactly as shown, edit the text with the following changes:
   A. Change the \ in item 7 to 1/2.
   B. Change the [in item 8 to 1.
   C. Change the 1/2 in item 8 to 3/4.
   D. Change the ^ in item 10 to a degree symbol.
   E. Check your spelling after making the changes.
   F. Save as drawing P9-5.

COMMON FRAMING NOTES:

1. ALL FRAMING LUMBER TO BE DFL #2 OR BETTER.
2. ALL HEATED WALLS @ HEATED LIVING AREAS TO BE 2 X 6 @ 24" OC.
3. ALL EXTERIOR HEADERS TO BE 2-2 X 12 UNLESS NOTED, W/ 2" RIGID INSULATION BACKING UNLESS NOTED.
4. ALL SHEAR PANELS TO BE 1/2" CDX PLY W/8d @ 4" OC @ EDGE, HDRS, & BLOCKING AND 8d @ 8" OC @ FIELD UNLESS NOTED.
5. ALL METAL CONNECTORS TO BE SIMPSON CO. OR EQUAL.
6. ALL TRUSSES TO BE 24" OC. SUBMIT TRUSS CALCS TO BUILDING DEPT. PRIOR TO ERECTION.
7. PLYWOOD ROOF SHEATHING TO BE \ STD GRADE 32/16 PLY LAID PERP TO RAFTERS. NAIL W/8d @ 6" OC @ EDGES AND 12" OC @ FIELD.
8. PROVIDE [1/2" STD GRADE T&G PLY FLOOR SHEATHING LAID PERP TO FLOOR JOISTS. NAIL W/10d @ 6" OC @ EDGES AND BLOCKING AND 12" OC @ FIELD.
9. BLOCK ALL WALLS OVER 10'-0" HIGH AT MID.
10. LET-IN BRACES TO BE 1 X 4 DIAG BRACES @ 45^ FOR ALL INTERIOR LOAD BEARING WALLS.

6. Create the window schedule shown below. Create the text using a text style with the Stylus BT font. Create a layer for the text. Draw the hexagonal symbols in the SYM column. Save the drawing as P9-6.

WINDOW SCHEDULE

SYM.	SIZE	MODEL	ROUGH OPEN	QTY.
Ⓐ	12 x 60	JOB BUILT	VERIFY	2
Ⓑ	96 x 60	W4N5 CSM.	8'-0 3/4" x 5'-0 7/8"	1
Ⓒ	48 x 60	W2N5 CSM.	4'-0 3/4" x 5'-0 7/8"	2
Ⓓ	48 x 36	W2N3 CSM.	4'-0 3/4" x 3'-6 1/2"	2
Ⓔ	42 x 42	2N3 CSM.	3'- 6 1/2" x 3'-6 1/2"	2
Ⓕ	72 x 48	G64 SLDG.	6'-0 1/2" x 4'-0 1/2"	1
Ⓖ	60 x 42	G536 SLDG.	5'-0 1/2" x 3'-6 1/2"	4
Ⓗ	48 x 42	G436 SLDG.	4'-0 1/2" x 3'-6 1/2"	1
Ⓙ	48 x 24	A41 AWN.	4'-0 1/2" x 2'-0 7/8"	3

7. Create the door schedule shown below. Create the text using a text style with the Stylus BT font. Create a layer for the text. Draw the circle symbols in the SYM column. Save the drawing as P9-7.

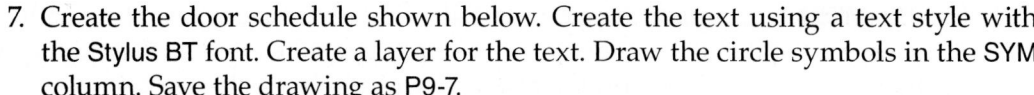

DOOR SCHEDULE

SYM.	SIZE	TYPE	QTY.
①	36 x 80	S.C. R.P. METAL INSULATED	1
②	36 x 80	S.C. FLUSH METAL INSULATED	2
③	32 x 80	S.C. SELF CLOSING	2
④	32 x 80	HOLLOW CORE	5
⑤	30 x 80	HOLLOW CORE	5
⑥	30 x 80	POCKET SLDG.	2

8. Create the interior finish schedule shown below. Create the text using a text style with the Stylus BT font. Save the drawing as P9-8.

INTERIOR FINISH SCHEDULE

ROOM	FLOOR					WALLS				CEILING		
	VINYL	CARPET	TILE	HARDWOOD	CONCRETE	PAINT	PAPER	TEXTURE	SPRAY	SMOOTH	BROCADE	PAINT
ENTRY					●							
FOYER			●			●			●			●
KITCHEN			●				●		●			●
DINING				●		●			●		●	●
FAMILY		●				●			●		●	●
LIVING		●				●	●				●	●
MSTR. BATH			●			●			●			●
BATH #2			●			●			●	●		●
MSTR. BED		●				●	●				●	●
BED #2		●				●			●		●	●
BED #3		●				●			●		●	●
UTILITY	●					●			●	●		●

9. Create the block diagram shown below. Create the text using a text style with the Romans font. Create a layer for the text. Save the drawing as P9-9.

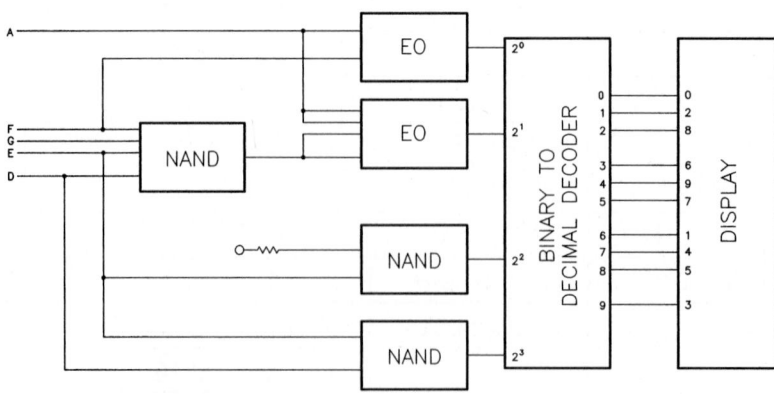

10. Create the block diagram shown below. Create the text using a text style with the Romans font. Create a layer for the text. Save the drawing as P9-10.

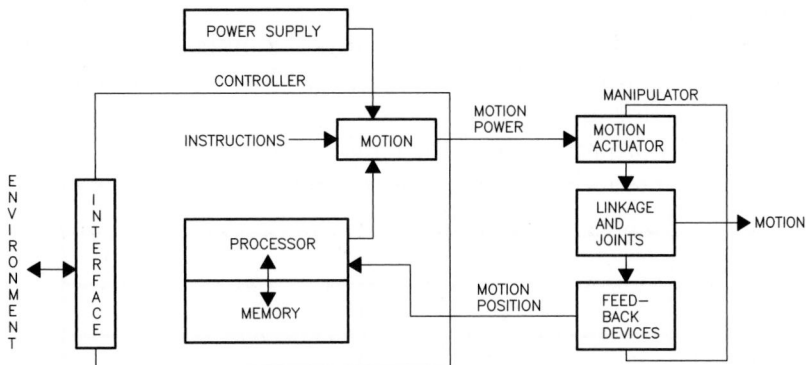

11. Open P5-4 and add text to the circuit diagram. Use a text style with the Romans font. Create a layer for the text. Save the drawing as P9-11.

12. Add title blocks, borders, and text styles to the template drawings you created in earlier chapters. Create a Border layer for the border lines and thick title block lines. Create a Title block layer for thin title block lines and text. Make three template drawings with borders and title blocks for your future drawings. Use the following guidelines:
   A. Template 1 used for A-size, 8 1/2 × 11 drawings, named TITLEA–MECH.
   B. Template 2 used for B-size, 11 × 17 drawings, named TITLEB–MECH.
   C. Template 3 used for C-size, 17 × 22 drawings, named TITLEC–MECH.
   D. Set the following values for the drawing aids:
      Units = three-place decimal
      Grid = .500
      Snap = .250
   E. Draw a border 1/2" from the drawing limits.
   F. Design a title block using created text styles. Place it in the lower-right corner of each drawing. The title block should contain the following information: Company or school name, address, date (field), drawn by, approved by, scale, title, drawing number, material, revision number. See the example below.
   G. Record the information about each template in a log.

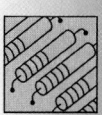

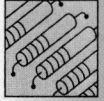

13. Start a new drawing using the C-size mechanical drawing template located on the Student CD. Draw a small parts list connected to the title block, similar to the one shown below.
   A. Enter PARTS LIST with a style containing a complex font.
   B. Enter the other information using text and the **TEXT** command.
   C. Save the drawing as TITLEC–PARTS.
   D. Record the information about the template in a log.

3	HOLDING PINS	12
2	SIDE COVERS	3
1	MAIN HOUSING	1
KEY	DESCRIPTION	QTY

PARTS LIST

UNLESS OTHERWISE SPECIFIED
ALL DIMENSIONS IN

INCHES

AND TOLERANCES FOR:

1	PLACE DIMS:	±.1
2	PLACE DIMS:	±.01
3	PLACE DIMS:	±.005
	ANGULAR:	±30'
	FRACTIONAL:	±.1/32
	FINISH:	125? in.

JANE'S DESIGN

DR: JANE	SCALE: FULL	DATE: XX–XX–XX	APPD:
MATERIAL: MILD STEEL			
NAME: XXX–XXXX			

| FIRST USED ON: | SIMILAR TO: | B | PART NO: 123–321 | REV: 0 |

14. Create an architectural template for a 17″ × 22″ or 22″ × 34″ sheet size with a title block along the right side similar to the one shown below. Use the same guidelines given for Problem 12. Save the drawing as ARCH. Record the information about the template in a log.

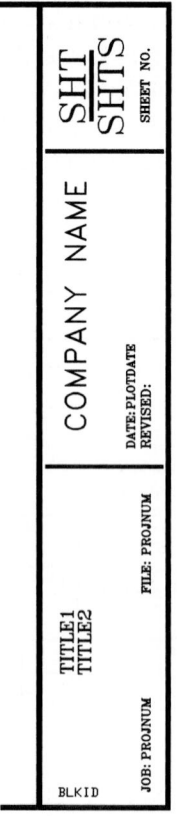

15. Draw title blocks with borders for your electrical, piping, and general drawings. Use the same guidelines provided in Problem 12. The title block can be similar to the one displayed with Problem 12, but the area for mechanical drafting tolerances is not required. Research sample title blocks to come up with your design. Save the drawings as templates named ELEC A, ELEC B, PIPE A, PIPE B, or use names related to the drawing type and sheet size.

16. Draw the AND/OR schematic shown below. Save your drawing as P9-16.

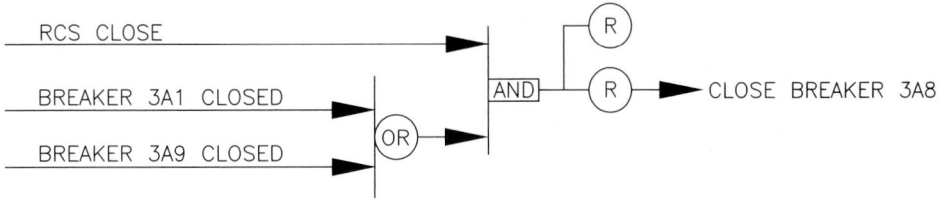

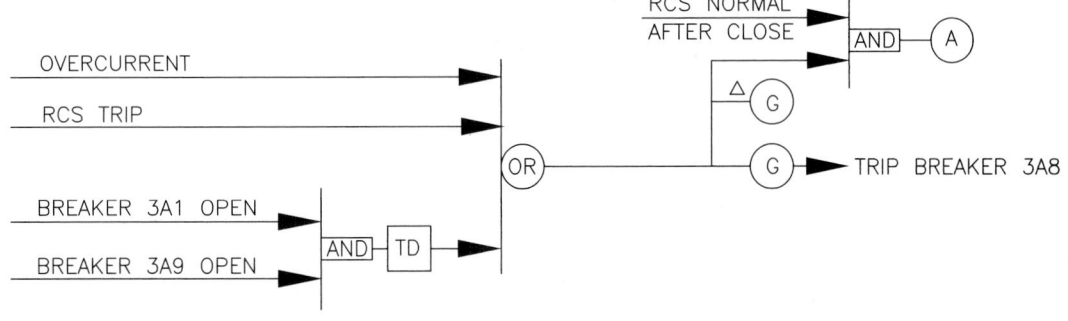

17. Draw the controller schematic shown below. Save your drawing as P9-17.

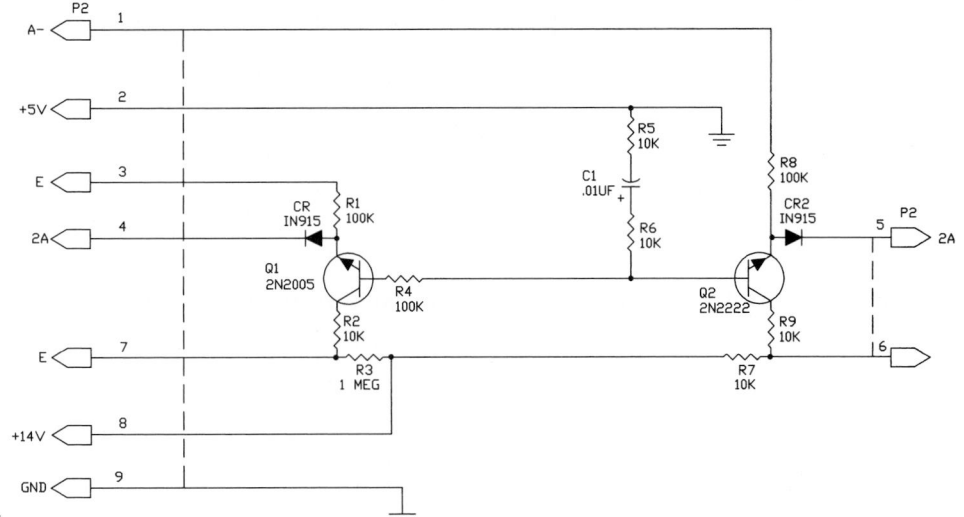

NOTES:

1. INTERPRET ELECTRICAL AND ELECTRONICS DIAGRAMS PER ANSI Y14.15.

2. UNLESS OTHERWISE SPECIFIED:

   RESISTANCE VALUES ARE IN OHMS.
   RESISTANCE TOLERANCE IS 5%.
   RESISTORS ARE 1/4 WATT.
   CAPACITANCE VALUES ARE IN MICROFARADS.
   CAPACITANCE TOLERANCE IS 10%.
   CAPACITOR VOLTAGE RATING IS 20V.
   INDUCTANCE VALUES ARE IN MICROHENRIES.

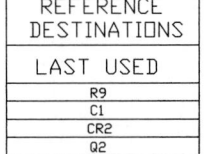

REFERENCE DESTINATIONS	
LAST USED	
R9	
C1	
CR2	
Q2	

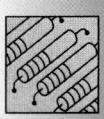

18. Draw the general caulking notes shown below. Save your drawing as P9-18.

<u>CAULKING NOTES</u>:

CAULKING REQUIREMENTS BASED ON 1992
OREGON RESIDENTIAL ENERGY CODE

1. SEAL THE EXTERIOR SHEATHING AT CORNERS,
   JOINTS, DOORS, WINDOWS, AND FOUNDATION
   SILL WITH SILICONE CAULK.
2. CAULK THE FOLLOWING OPENINGS W/
   EXPANDED FOAM, BACKER RODS, OR SIMILAR:
   • ANY SPACE BETWEEN WINDOW AND DOOR
     FRAMES
   • BETWEEN ALL EXTERIOR WALL SOLE
     PLATES AND PLY SHEATHING
   • ON TOP OF RIM JOIST PRIOR TO PLYWOOD
     FLOOR APPLICATION
   • WALL SHEATHING TO TOP PLATE
   • JOINTS BETWEEN WALL AND FOUNDATION
   • JOINTS BETWEEN WALL AND ROOF
   • JOINTS BETWEEN WALL PANELS
   • AROUND OPENINGS

19. Draw the basic organizational chart shown below. Save your drawing as P9-19.

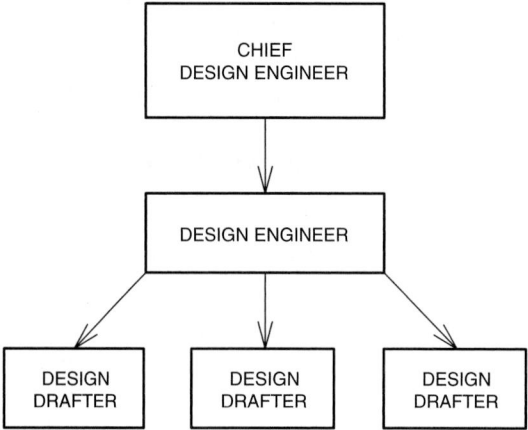

20. Draw the finish schedule shown below. Save your drawing as P9-20.

INTERIOR FINISH SCHEDULE										
ROOM	FLOOR				WALLS				CEIL		
	CARPET	VINYL	TILE	HARDWOOD	PAINT	PAPER	TEXTURE	SPRAY	SMOOTH	BROCADE	PAINT
FOYER			•		•		•		•		•
KITCHEN			•			•		•	•		•
DINING				•	•		•		•		•
FAMILY	•				•		•		•		•
LIVING	•				•		•		•		•
MAST BED	•				•		•		•		•
MAST BATH			•			•		•	•		•
BATH 2		•				•		•			•
BED 2	•				•		•		•		•
BED 3	•				•		•		•		•
UTILITY		•				•		•	•	•		•

21. Draw the flow chart shown below. Save your drawing as P9-21.

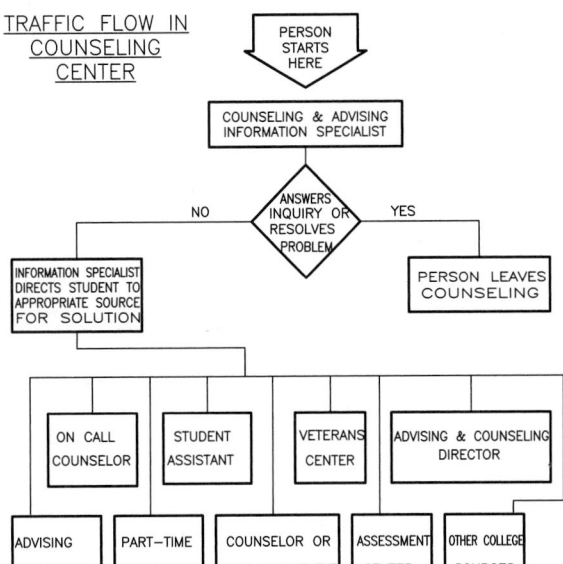

22. Draw the engineering change notice form shown below. Save your drawing as P9-22.

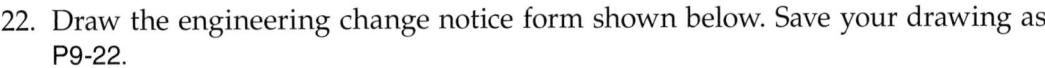

Engineering Change Notice — ECN NO.

Disposition of production stock:
A =Alter or rework U=Use in production
T=Transfer to service stock S=Scrap

Qty.	Drawing Size Part No.	R/N	Description	Change	Other Usage in Production	D/S
01						
02						
03						
04						
05						
06						
07						
08						
09						
10						
11						
12						
13						
14						
15						
16						
17						
18						

Reason:

Castings & forgings affected? ☐ Yes ☐ No	Design engineer:	Supervisor approval:	Release date:	Page

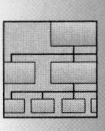

23. Draw the electrical notes shown below. Save your drawing as P9-23.

ELECTRICAL NOTES:

1. ALL GARAGE AND EXTERIOR PLUGS AND LIGHT FIXTURES TO BE ON GFCI CIRCUIT.
2. ALL KITCHEN PLUGS AND LIGHT FIXTURES TO BE ON GFCI CIRCUIT.
3. PROVIDE A SEPARATE CIRCUIT FOR MICROWAVE OVEN.
4. PROVIDE A SEPARATE CIRCUIT FOR PERSONAL COMPUTER. VERIFY LOCATION WITH OWNER.
5. VERIFY ALL ELECTRICAL LOCATIONS W/ OWNER.
6. EXTERIOR SPOTLIGHTS TO BE ON PHOTOELECTRIC CELL W/ TIMER.
7. ALL RECESSED LIGHTS IN EXTERIOR CEILINGS TO BE INSULATION COVER RATED.
8. ELECTRICAL OUTLET PLATE GASKETS SHALL BE INSULATED ON RECEPTACLE, SWITCH, AND ANY OTHER BOXES IN EXTERIOR WALL.
9. PROVIDE THERMOSTATICALLY CONTROLLED FAN IN ATTIC WITH MANUAL OVERRIDE. VERIFY LOCATION WITH OWNER.
10. ALL FANS TO VENT TO OUTSIDE AIR. ALL FAN DUCTS TO HAVE AUTOMATIC DAMPERS.
11. HOT WATER TANKS TO BE INSULATED TO R-11 MINIMUM.
12. INSULATE ALL HOT WATER LINES TO R-4 MINIMUM. PROVIDE ALTERNATE BID TO INSULATE ALL PIPES FOR NOISE CONTROL.
13. PROVIDE 6 SQ. FT. OF VENT FOR COMBUSTION AIR TO OUTSIDE AIR FOR FIREPLACE CONNECTED DIRECTLY TO FIREBOX. PROVIDE FULLY CLOSABLE AIR INLET.
14. HEATING TO BE ELECTRIC HEAT PUMP. PROVIDE BID FOR SINGLE UNIT NEAR GARAGE OR FOR A UNIT EACH FLOOR (IN ATTIC).
15. INSULATE ALL HEATING DUCTS IN UNHEATED AREAS TO R-11. ALL HVAC DUCTS TO BE SEALED AT JOINTS AND CORNERS.

24. Draw the electrical legend shown below. Save your drawing as P9-24.

ELECTRICAL LEGEND:

⏀	110 VOLT DUPLEX CONVENIENCE OUTLET
⏀ GFCI	110 VOLT GROUND FAULT CIRCUIT INTERRUPT DUPLEX OUTLET
⏀WP GFCI	110 VOLT WATERPROOF GFCI DUPLEX OUTLET
⏀	110 VOLT SPLIT WIRED OUTLET
⏀	220 VOLT OUTLET
	JUNCTION BOX
TV	CABLE TELEVISION OUTLET
	CLOCK OUTLET
	DOORBELL
$	SINGLE-POLE SWITCH
$³	THREE-WAY SWITCH
O	CEILING-MOUNTED LIGHT
	WALL-MOUNTED LIGHT
	FLUORESCENT LIGHT
⊙	CIRCULAR RECESSED LIGHT
⊡	SQUARE RECESSED LIGHT
	LIGHT, FAN COMBINATION
	LIGHT, FAN, HEAT COMBINATION
O SD	CEILING-MOUNTED SMOKE DETECTOR
SD	WALL-MOUNTED SMOKE DETECTOR

Working with Tables

Learning Objectives

After completing this chapter, you will be able to do the following:

✓ Create and modify table styles.
✓ Insert a table into a drawing.
✓ Extract data from a drawing to create a table.
✓ Edit a table.
✓ Insert formulas into table cells to perform calculations on numeric data.

A *table* consists of rows and columns that organize data to make it easier to read. Tables are commonly used in drafting to show bills of materials, door and window schedules, legends, and title block information. Review the tables and terminology shown in **Figure 10-1**. This will help you better understand tables and table information as you read this chapter.

table: An arrangement of rows and columns that organize data.

Figure 10-1.
Tables in AutoCAD can be created with the title and header rows at the top or the bottom.

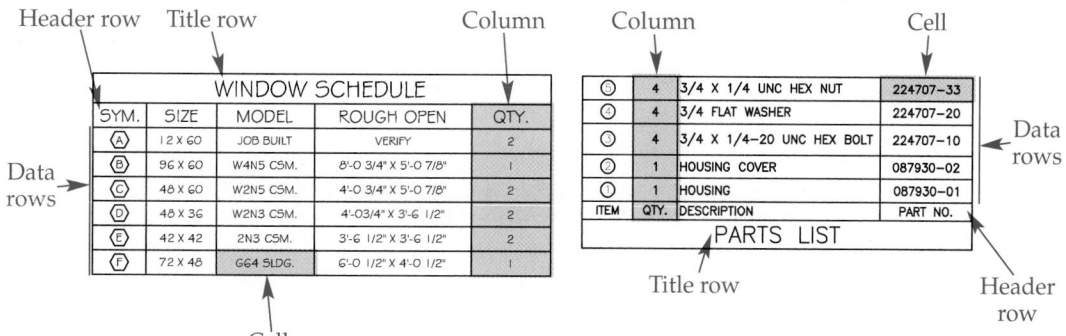

AutoCAD Table Styles

AutoCAD table styles are used to set table characteristics. A *table style* defines multiple table format settings, including direction, text appearance, and margin spacing. You may have several table styles depending on the variety of tables you create and different characteristics needed. Table format options can be adjusted independently of a table style when a table is placed or edited in the drawing. However, you should create a table style for each unique table requirement. For example, you can have one table style for creating door and window schedules, and another table style with different characteristics for adding an interior finish schedule. In mechanical drafting, you might prepare a table style for parts lists and another table style for gear data tables. Table styles should be added to drawing templates for repeated use.

Working with Table Styles

The **Table Style** dialog box allows you to create and modify table styles. To open the **Table Style** dialog box, pick the **Table Style...** button in the **Tables** control panel in the **Dashboard** or the **Styles** toolbar, select **Format** > **Table Style...**, or type TS or TABLESTYLE. The **Table Style** dialog box can also be opened from the **Insert Table** dialog box, described later in this chapter, by picking the **Launch the Table Style dialog** button. The **Table Style** dialog box is shown in **Figure 10-2**.

The **Styles** list box displays existing table styles. By default, the Standard table style is available and current. When you insert a table into the drawing, it uses the formatting settings from the current table style. To set a style current, pick it once in the **Styles** list box, and then select the **Set Current** button. A table style can also be set current by double-clicking the style in the **Styles** list box or right-clicking the style and selecting the **Set current** menu option. Below the **Styles** list box is a drop-down list that can be used to filter the number of table styles displayed in the **Table Style** dialog box. Pick the **All Styles** options to show all table styles in the file, or pick the **Styles in use** option to show only the styles used in the drawing.

Creating a New Table Style

To create a new table style, first select an existing table style from the **Styles** list box. This style is used as a basis for formatting the new table style. Then pick the **New...** button in the **Table Style** dialog box. The **Create New Table Style** dialog box is

---

Figure 10-2.
The **Table Style** dialog box.

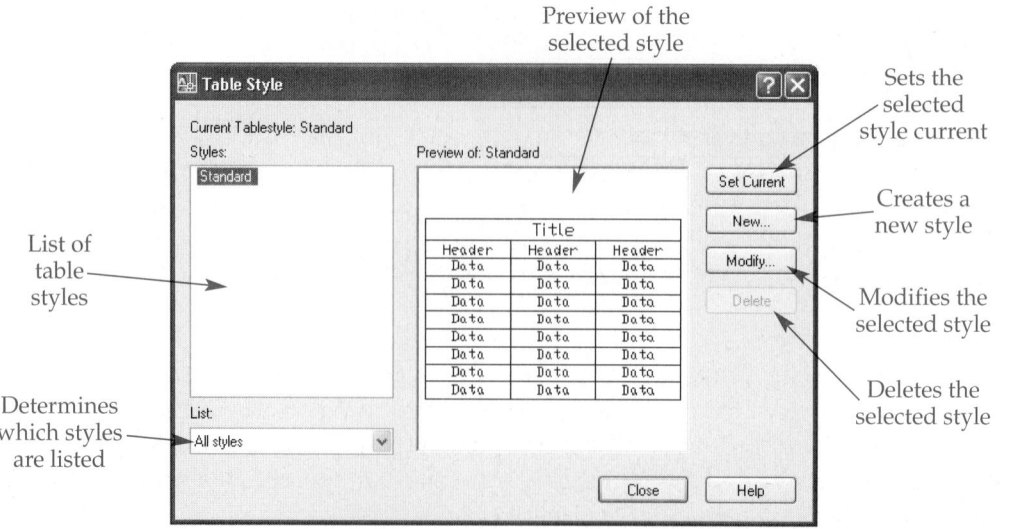

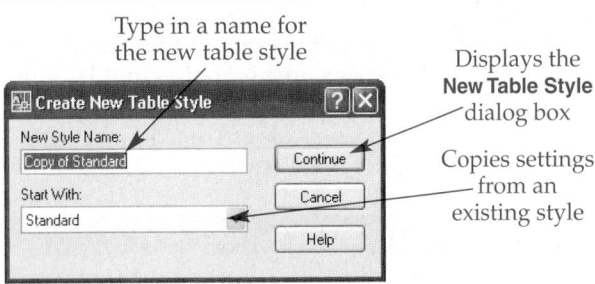

Type in a name for the new table style

Displays the **New Table Style** dialog box

Copies settings from an existing style

displayed. See **Figure 10-3**. In the **New Style Name** text box, type a name for the new table style. The new table can be based on the formatting settings from a different existing table style by selecting the name of the table style from the **Start With** drop-down list.

The default new table style name is Copy of followed by the name of the selected existing style. You can keep the default name, but you should usually enter a more descriptive name, such as Parts List, Parts List No Heading, or Door Schedule. It is also a good idea to record the names and details about the table styles you create and keep this information in a log for future reference. Table style names can have up to 255 characters, including letters, numbers, dashes (–), underlines (_), and dollar signs ($). You can type uppercase or lowercase letters. After entering the table style name, pick the **Continue** button to open the **New Table Style** dialog box and adjust table style characteristics. See **Figure 10-4**.

Formatting Table Styles

The **New Table Style** dialog box is divided into areas that are used to create starting table styles, adjust table direction, and control the display of cell content. The preview area allows you to see how the selected table style characteristics appear in a table. This is a very convenient way to see what the table will look like before it is created.

When you are finished adjusting table style properties, pick **OK** to return to the **Table Style** dialog box. Then pick the **Set Current** button to set the new style current.

NOTE

The **New Table Style** dialog box is the same as the **Modify Table Style** dialog box used to change existing table style settings. To access the **Modify Table Style** dialog box, select the style in the **Styles** list box and pick the **Modify** button.

Adjusting table direction

The **Table direction** setting in the **General** area of the **New Table Style** dialog box determines the placement of the data rows. The two options are **Down** and **Up**. When the **Down** option is selected, the data rows are placed below the title and header rows. When the **Up** option is selected, the data rows are placed above the title and header rows. The difference can be viewed in the preview window. Refer to **Figure 10-1**.

Cell style options

Three default cell styles are available in the **Cell Styles** area of the **New Table Style** dialog box: **Data**, **Header**, and **Title**. Cell styles allow data cell rows, the column header row, and the title row to have their own formatting properties. Picking a cell style from the drop-down list displays the properties for the corresponding element. In **Figure 10-4**, the **Data** cell style is selected.

Figure 10-4.
The formatting properties for a new style are specified in the **New Table Style** dialog box. The **Data** tab in the **Cell styles** area is shown in this figure.

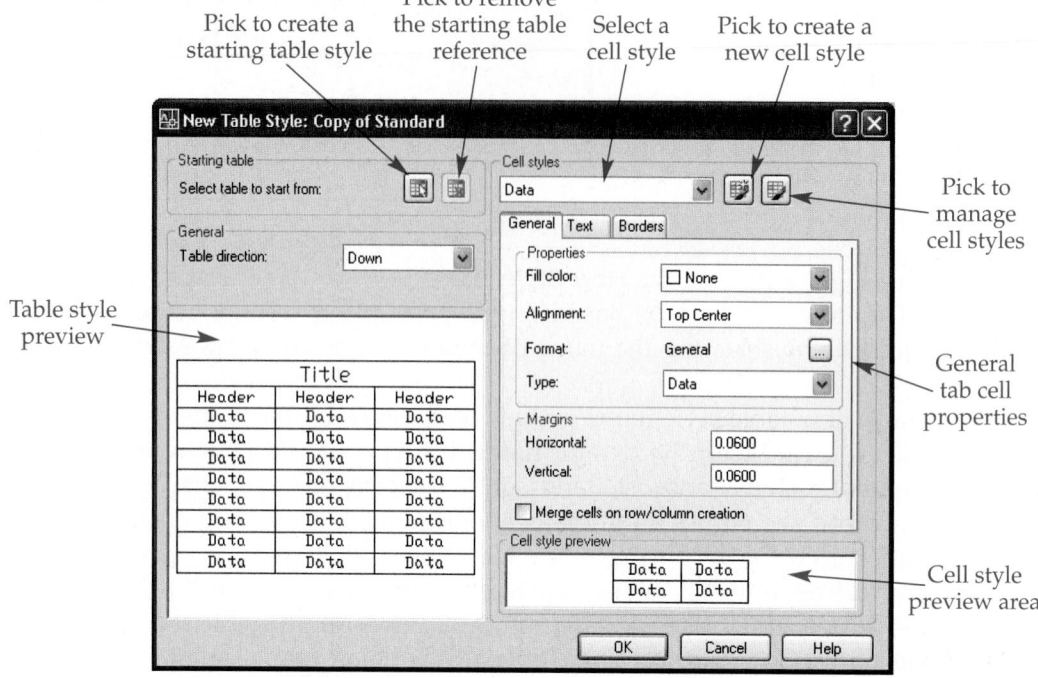

Pick to create a starting table style

Pick to remove the starting table reference

Select a cell style

Pick to create a new cell style

Table style preview

Pick to manage cell styles

General tab cell properties

Cell style preview area

Cell formatting properties are set using the **General**, **Text**, and **Borders** tabs. The options in these tabs are the same for adjusting data, header, and title cell style types. The following options are available in the **General** tab, shown in **Figure 10-4**:

*   **Fill color.** Adjusts the color used to fill cells. The default setting is None, which does not fill cells with a color. The drawing window color determines the on-screen table display. You can fill cells with color to highlight or organize table information. Pick a color from the drop-down list to fill the cells with the selected color.
*   **Alignment.** Justifies text within the cell. Pick the appropriate alignment option according to where you want text to be justified in the cell.
*   **Format.** Shows the current cell format, which is General by default. Pick the ellipsis (…) button to access the **Table Cell Format** dialog box. See **Figure 10-5**. The **Data Type** area lists options for formatting the selected table cell: **Angle**,

Figure 10-5.
Many different data types are available to format a table cell.

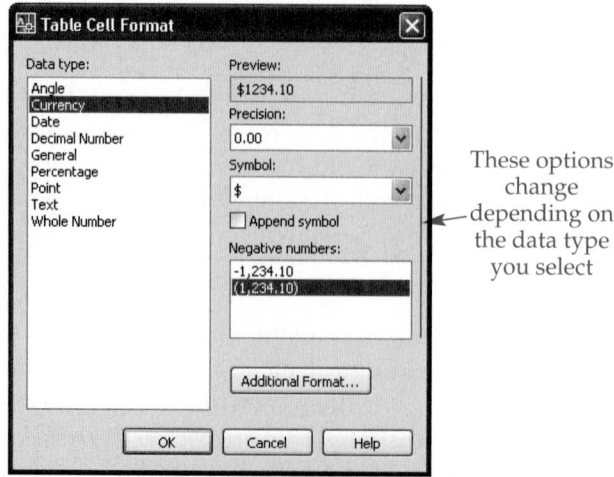

These options change depending on the data type you select

Currency, Date, Decimal Number, General, Percentage, Point, Text, and **Whole Number.** Selecting a format presents options for adjusting the format characteristics. Different options are available depending on the selected format.

- **Type.** Determines the type of data displayed in the cell. Pick **Data** from this drop-down list to define a data cell type. Choose **Label** if the cell is a label cell type, such as a column heading or the table title.
- **Margins.** Sets the spacing between the cell content and the borders. This spacing applies to text and blocks. The values in the **Horizontal** and **Vertical** text boxes determine the spacing between the content and the cell border. The default setting is .06.
- **Merge cells on row/column creation.** Pick this check box to merge the row of cells together to form a single cell. This check box is selected by default for the **Title** cell style. This provides an example of when you may want to merge cells.

The following options are available in the **Text** tab, shown in **Figure 10-6:**

- **Text style.** Displays all of the text styles that are defined in the current drawing. Select a style from the drop-down list or pick the ellipsis (**...**) button to the right of the drop-down list to open the **Text Style** dialog box to create a new text style or modify an existing text style. Text styles are described in Chapter 9.
- **Text height.** Specifies the height of the text. The default setting for data row and column header cells is 0.1800. If a text height other than 0 has been set in the text style, this setting is grayed out.
- **Text color.** Sets the color of the text.
- **Text angle.** Defines the rotation angle of text within the table cell. **Figure 10-7** shows an example of a 90° text angle applied to the **Header** cell style.

The following options are available in the **Borders** tab, shown in **Figure 10-8:**

- **Lineweight.** Assigns a unique lineweight to cell borders.

NOTE

AutoCAD displays border lineweights on-screen only if lineweights are being displayed. Pick the **LWT** button on the status bar to display lineweights.

Figure 10-6.
The **Text** tab in the **New Table Style** dialog box allows you to set text properties.

General	Text	Borders

Properties

Text style:	Standard
Text height:	0.1800
Text color:	ByBlock
Text angle:	0

Figure 10-7.
In this table, a 90° text angle has been applied to the header cell style.

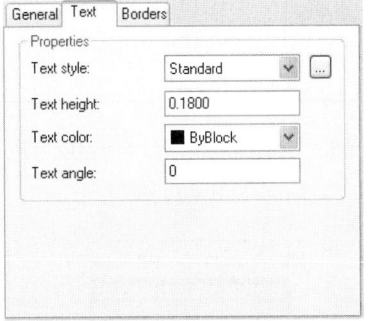

ROOM SCHEDULE

NUMBER	NAME	LENGTH	WIDTH	HEIGHT	AREA
1	BEDROOM 1	11'-0"	10'-0"	9'-0"	110 SQ. FT.
2	BEDROOM 2	10'-0"	11'-0"	9'-0"	110 SQ. FT.
3	MASTER BEDROOM	12'-0"	14'-0"	9'-0"	168 SQ. FT.
4	LIVING ROOM	12'-0"	16'-0"	9'-0"	192 SQ. FT.
5	DINING ROOM	11'-0"	12'-0"	9'-0"	132 SQ. FT.
6	KITCHEN	11'-0"	10'-0"	9'-0"	110 SQ. FT.

Figure 10-8.
The **Borders** tab in the **New Table Style** dialog box allows you to set cell border properties.

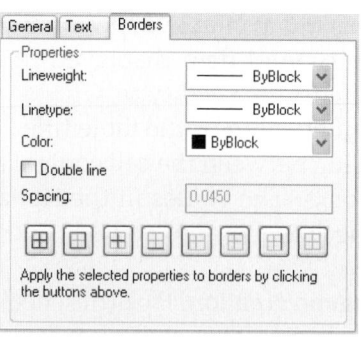

- **Linetype.** Assigns a unique linetype to cell borders. As when creating layers, you must load linetypes if they are not currently loaded in the file in order to apply them to the cell border.
- **Color.** Sets the color of the cell borders.
- **Double line.** Adds another line around the default single line border style. When this check box is selected, the **Spacing** edit box becomes available, allowing you to enter the distance between the double lines. The default double line border spacing is 0.0450.
- **Border buttons.** These buttons are used to control how the **Lineweight**, **Linetype**, **Color**, and **Double line** border properties are applied to the cell borders. From right to left, the options are: **All Borders**, **Outside Borders**, **Inside Borders**, **Bottom Border**, **Left Border**, **Top Border**, **Right Border**, and **No Borders**. Once you set the desired border properties, select or deselect these buttons according to how you want cell borders displayed. An example of each border style is shown in **Figure 10-9**.

The default **Data**, **Header**, and **Title** cell styles are all that are needed for typical table applications. However, you can further increase the flexibility and options for creating tables by developing additional cell styles. For example, you can create a cell style called Data Yellow that is the same as the **Data** cell style but fills cells with a yellow color. Then when you draw a table you can choose from either the **Data** or the Data Yellow cell style, depending on the application.

Figure 10-9.
There are several border options for table cells. The settings shown are for data rows only.

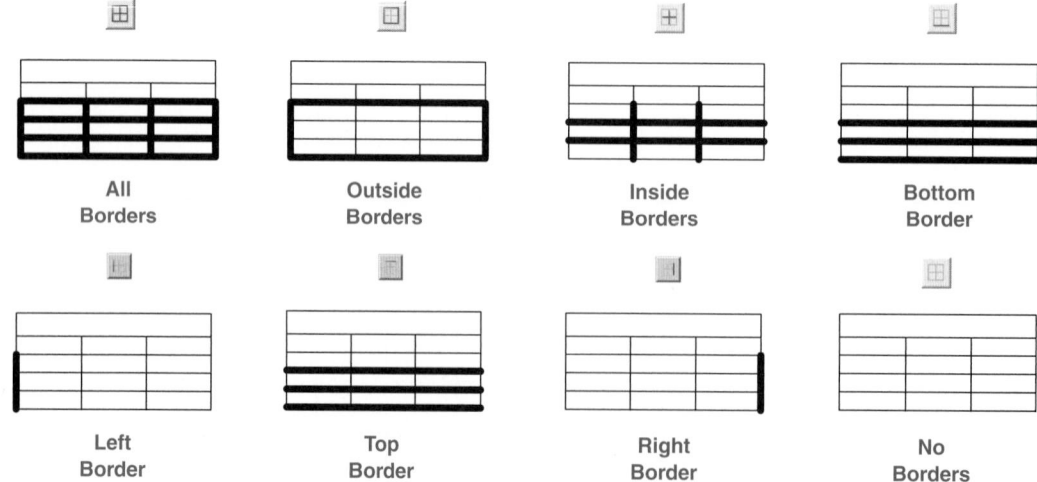

To create a new cell style, first select an existing cell style from the **Cell Styles** area drop-down list. This style will be used as a basis for formatting the new cell style. Then, pick the **Create new cell style...** button from the **Cell Styles** area, or select **Create new cell style...** from the **Cell Styles** area drop-down list. The **Create New Cell Style** dialog box is displayed. In the **New Style Name** text box, type a name for the new cell style. The new cell style can be based on the formatting settings of a different existing cell style by selecting the name of the cell style from the **Start With** drop-down list.

Cell styles can be created, renamed, and deleted using the **Manage Cell Styles** dialog box, shown in **Figure 10-10.** To access this dialog box, pick the **Manage Cell Style dialog...** button from the **Cell Styles** area, or select **Manage cell styles...** from the **Cell Styles** area drop-down list.

> **NOTE**
>
> If a cell's formatting properties have been specified in the **Text Formatting** toolbar, the table cell shortcut menu, or the **Properties** palette, these settings override the table style settings.

Developing a starting table style

One technique for creating a table is to base the new table on an existing table. This method is accomplished using a starting table style. A starting table style can be considered a table template that already contains all of the table style characteristics and the same table rows, columns, and data entries drawn in an existing table. Using a starting table style is much like copying a complete table and editing the table as needed. A starting table style can save a significant amount of time if you prepare similar tables often. For example, using a starting table style is effective if you have already created a complete door schedule, and then want to add a very similar door schedule to a new drawing project that contains most of the same doors.

Before you can create a starting table style, a table must be available for selection in the drawing. A starting table style references the characteristics of the selected reference table, including the number of columns and rows and the table direction. Other table style characteristics, such as text style, are set according to the selected base table style. As a result, it is usually most appropriate to create a new starting table style using a base table style that is the same as that used when the reference table was drawn. For example, if a door schedule was created using a table style named Door Schedule, you should base the new starting table style from the Door Schedule table style.

Figure 10-10.
The **Manage Cell Styles** dialog box is used to create new cell styles and to rename and delete existing cell styles.

Right-click to access **New, Rename,** and **Delete** options from the shortcut menu

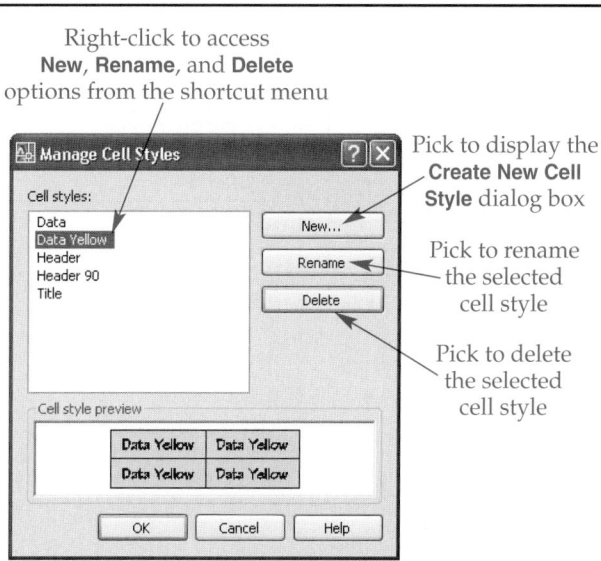

Pick to display the **Create New Cell Style** dialog box

Pick to rename the selected cell style

Pick to delete the selected cell style

To create a starting table style, pick the **Select table to start from** button in the **Starting table** area. Then pick a border line of the table you want to reference to form the starting table style. The preview will display the selected table and the table style settings of the base table style. See **Figure 10-11.** You can modify the table direction and cell style options using the **General** and **Cell Styles** areas. Pick the **Remove Table** button to remove the table reference from the table style. A table is added to a drawing using a starting table style by picking the **Start from Table style** insertion option described later in this chapter.

Exercise 10-1
Complete the exercise on the Student CD.

Changing, Renaming, and Deleting Table Styles

You can change the current table style without affecting existing tables. The changes are applied only to tables drawn using that style.

Existing table styles can be renamed in the **Table Style** dialog box. To rename a table style, slowly double-click the name or right-click the name and select the **Rename** option.

NOTE

Styles can also be renamed using the **Rename** dialog box. You can access this dialog box by selecting **Format** > **Rename...** from the pull-down menu or by typing RENAME. Select **Table styles** in the **Named Objects** list to rename the style.

Figure 10-11.
Creating a starting table style that references an existing table.

Pick to create a starting table style

Pick to remove the starting table reference

Select existing table

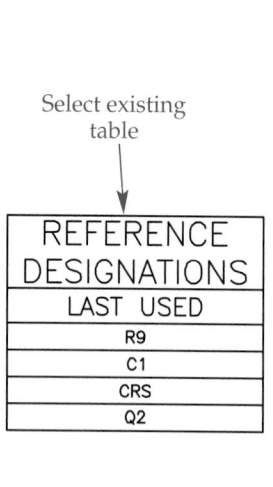

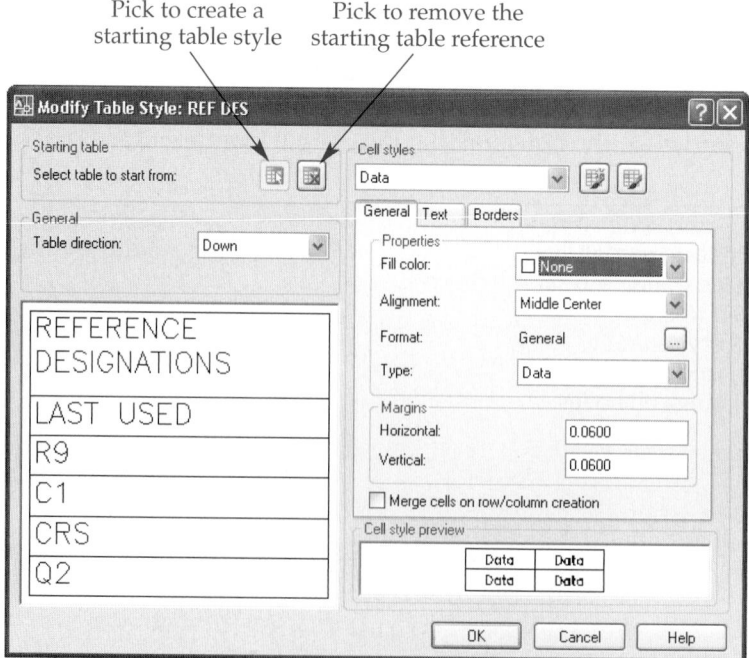

To delete a table style, right-click the name and select the **Delete** option, or pick the style and select the **Delete** button. AutoCAD will not allow you to delete a table style that has been used to create text objects in the drawing. If you want to delete the style, change the tables in the drawing to a different style. You cannot delete or rename the Standard style.

Quickly Setting a Table Style Current

You can quickly make a table style current using the **Tables** control panel of the **Dashboard** or the **Table Style** drop-down list located in the **Styles** toolbar. The name of the current table style is displayed in the box. Pick the drop-down arrow to display a table style list, as shown in **Figure 10-12**. Pick a text style name from the list, and that text style is set current.

Figure 10-12.
The **Styles** drop-down list is available on the **Dashboard** and on the **Styles** toolbar. The **Dashboard** list is shown here.

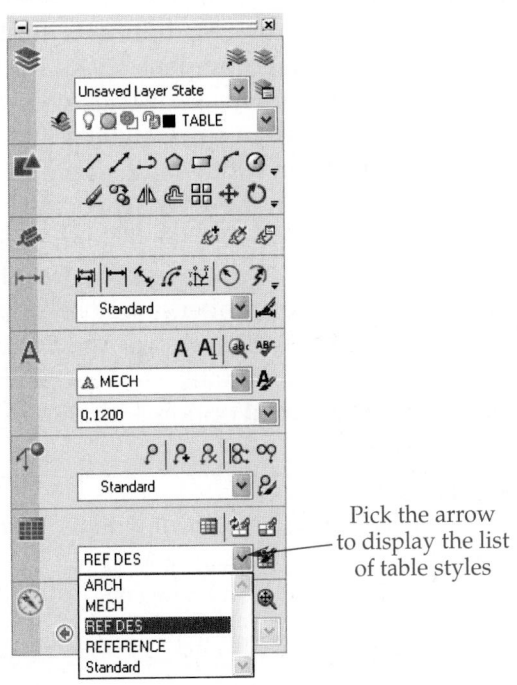

Pick the arrow to display the list of table styles

Inserting Tables

The **TABLE** command allows you to insert an empty table by specifying the number of rows and columns. After the table is inserted, text can be typed into the table cells. You can also insert blocks and fields into table cells. The **TABLE** command also provides other methods for inserting tables, such as beginning a table using a starting table style, forming a table from data that has already been created in Microsoft® Excel, and creating a table by referencing AutoCAD data.

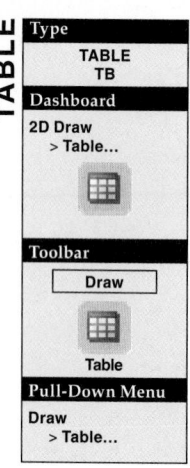

TABLE

Type

TABLE
TB

Dashboard

2D Draw
> Table...

Toolbar

Draw

Table

Pull-Down Menu

Draw
> Table...

To insert a table, pick the **Table** button in the **Tables** control panel of the **Dashboard** or in the **Draw** toolbar, pick **Draw > Table...**, or type TB or TABLE. This opens the **Insert Table** dialog box. See **Figure 10-13**.

Placing an Empty Table

An empty table is made by selecting the desired number of columns and data rows. Content is then typed in each cell, creating the table of information. Before placing a table, select a table style from the **Table Style** drop-down list, or pick the ellipsis (**...**) button to create or modify a style. The preview area shows a preview of a table with the current table style settings. The preview area does not adjust to the column and row settings, but shows table style properties such as general, text style, and border settings. You cannot use a starting table style to form an empty table.

To place an empty table, pick the **Start from empty table** radio button from the **Insert options** area. An empty table can be inserted by picking an insertion point or by windowing an area. This option is set in the **Insertion Behavior** area. When you select the **Specify insertion point** radio button, a table is created using the values in the **Column & row settings** area. Then you select a single point to place the table in the drawing. The number in the **Columns** text box determines the total number of table columns. The **Column width** value specifies the initial width of all columns. You may want to enter a width larger than necessary in the **Column width** text box and then stretch the columns to size later. The number in the **Data rows** text box determines the total number of data table rows. The **Row height** value specifies the initial height of all rows based on the number of lines typed and the table style margin settings. After you make these settings and pick the **OK** button, AutoCAD prompts you to specify the insertion point of the table. A table created with three columns and five data rows using the **Insertion point** option is shown in **Figure 10-14A**.

Figure 10-13.
The **Insert Table** dialog box, shown with the **Start from empty table** insert option selected.

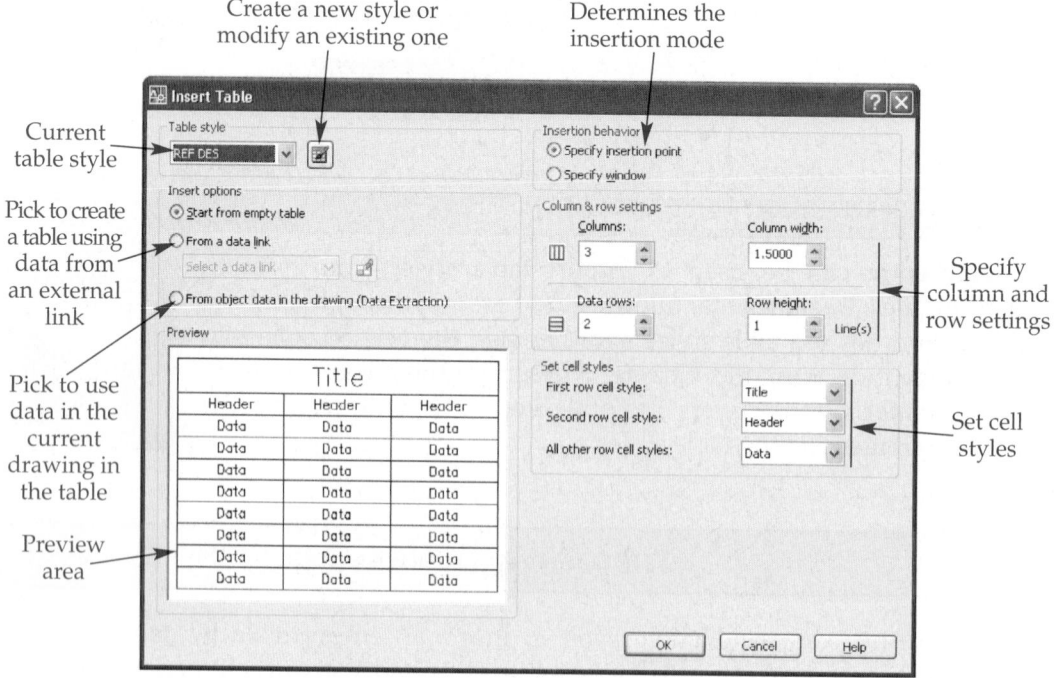

Figure 10-14.
Two ways to insert a table. A—Specifying a single insertion point. B—Windowing an area with two pick points.

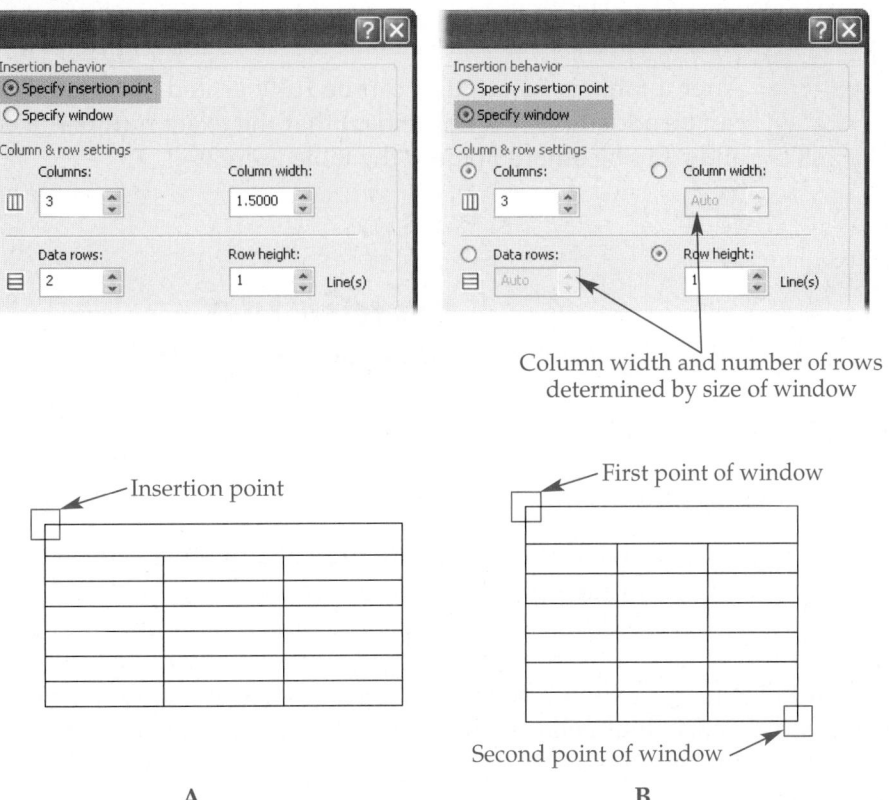

Column width and number of rows
determined by size of window

A   B

NOTE

When you use the **Specify insertion point** option to place a table, the point at which the cursor is attached to the table is based on the table style direction.

Pick the **Specify window** radio button to create a table that fits into a designated area. When the **Specify window** radio button is selected, only one column setting and one row setting are available. The radio buttons control which settings are active. If you want to set a fixed number of columns, choose the **Columns** radio button. The **Column width** setting becomes unavailable and the table width you pick determines the column width. The alternative is to set a fixed column width by selecting the **Column width** radio button. The **Columns** setting becomes unavailable and the total number of table columns is determined based on the width of the table. If you want to set a fixed number of rows, pick the **Data rows** radio button. The row height is determined by the height of the table. The other option is to set a fixed row height by selecting the **Row height** radio button. The **Data rows** setting becomes unavailable and the total number of table rows is determined based on the height of the table. After you make these settings and pick the **OK** button, AutoCAD prompts you to select the upper-left and lower-right corners for the table. The fixed **Column & row settings** values are used and the other settings are adjusted to fit the window. A table created with three columns and five data rows using the **Specify window** option is shown in **Figure 10-14B**.

The number of data rows you set in the **Insert Table** dialog box does not include the title and header rows. If you set the **Data Rows** setting to 1, for example, the table will have three rows because the top two rows are used for the table title and content headers. The default value for the row height is based on the text height and cell margin

---

settings in the current table style. For example, enter a row height of 1 if you plan to have only a single line of text occupy each cell.

NOTE

After a table is inserted, it can be fully edited. Rows and columns can be added, so it is not critical that the exact number of columns and rows be entered before the table is created.

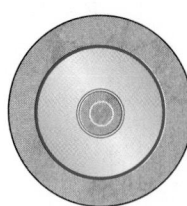

Exercise 10-2

Complete the exercise on the Student CD.

Entering Text into a Table

When a table is inserted, the **Text Formatting** toolbar appears above the table and the text cursor is placed in the top cell ready for typing. See **Figure 10-15.** The active cell is indicated by a dashed line around its border and a light gray background. The columns and rows making up the table have identifying letters and numbers. These appear in a grid along the outer border. This grid is called the *table indicator.* It is used to identify individual cells in the table. This identification system is used to assign formulas to table cells for calculation purposes. Formulas are described later in this chapter.

Before typing text in a cell, adjust the text settings in the **Text Formatting** toolbar, if needed. Holding the [Alt] key and pressing [Enter] inserts a return within the cell. When you are finished entering the text in the active cell, press the [Tab] key to move to the next cell. Holding the [Shift] key and pressing the [Tab] key moves the cursor backward (to the left or up) and makes the previous cell active. Pressing the [Enter] key makes the cell directly below the current cell active. The arrow keys on the keyboard can also be used to navigate through the cells in a table. When you are finished entering text in the table, pick the **OK** button on the **Text Formatting** toolbar or pick anywhere in the drawing area to exit the **TABLE** command. **Figure 10-16** shows a completed table.

table indicator:
The grid of letters and numbers that identifies individual cells in a table.

Figure 10-15.
The **Text Formatting** toolbar is used to add and modify text table cell text. The active cell is indicated by a blinking cursor, a dashed border, and a light gray background.

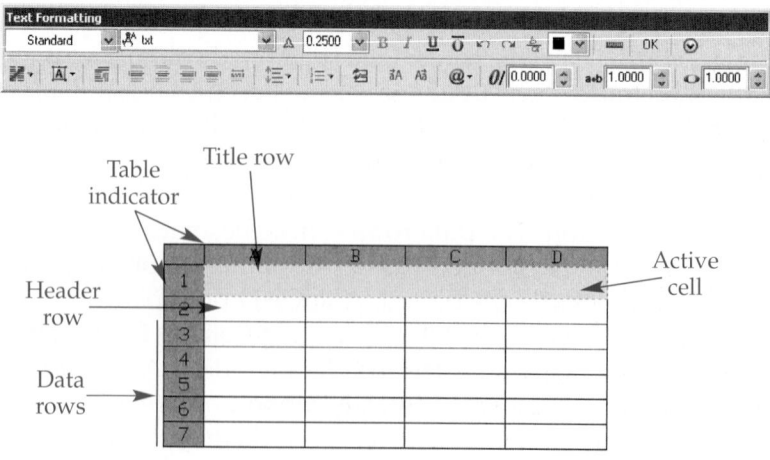

AutoCAD and Its Applications—Basics

Figure 10-16.
A completed parts list table.

Parts List		
Part Number	Part Type	Qty
100—SCR—45	Screw	18
202—BLT—32	Bolt	18
340—WSHR—06	Washer	18

NOTE

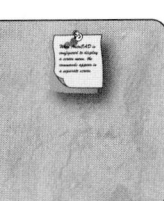

The options and settings available in the **Text Formatting** toolbar and shortcut menu function the same in table cells as they do in multiline text. Refer to Chapter 9 for more information about text formatting options.

Exercise 10-3
Complete the exercise on the Student CD.

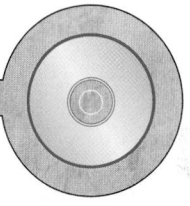

Using a Starting Table Style

If a predefined starting table style is available in your drawing, you can place a new table by referencing the starting table style. Developing a starting table style was described earlier in this chapter. To create a table by referencing a starting table style, first select a starting table style from the **Table Style** drop-down list or select the ellipsis (**...**) button to create or modify a style. When you select a starting table style, the **Start from Table Style** radio button becomes selected in the **Insert options** area. See **Figure 10-17.** The preview area shows a preview of the parent table with the current table style settings and table options.

The **Specify insertion point** insertion behavior option is the only method for inserting a table using a starting table style. However, you can add columns and rows to the table by entering or selecting values in the **Additional columns** and **Additional rows** text boxes. You can also specify which items from the parent table are included in the new table by selecting and deselecting **Table options** check boxes. For example, pick the **Data cell text** check box to create a new table that contains all the text entries added to the data cells of the parent table. After you make these settings and pick the **OK** button, AutoCAD prompts you to specify the insertion point of the table. A table created by referencing an existing starting table style with two additional rows is shown in **Figure 10-18.**

NOTE

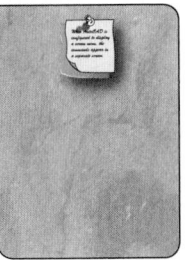

When a table is inserted using a starting table style, the **Text Formatting** toolbar appears above the table and the text cursor is placed in the top cell ready to enter new content or edit existing values. When you have finished entering text in the table, pick the **OK** button on the **Text Formatting** toolbar or pick anywhere in the drawing area to exit the **TABLE** command.

Figure 10-17.
The **Insert Table** dialog box can be used to create a new table using a starting table style.

Pick to create a new table
using a starting table style

**Start from
Table Style**
becomes
active

Preview
of parent
table

Determines
table
properties
to copy from
starting
table style

Figure 10-18.
You can create a new table quickly by referencing a starting table style.

Existing table style
used to form a starting
table style

In the new table, all
table options are retained
and two rows are added

REFERENCE DESIGNATIONS		REFERENCE DESIGNATIONS
LAST USED		LAST USED
R9		R9
C1		C1
CRS		CRS
Q2		Q2
		T4
		R6

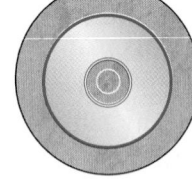

Exercise 10-4
Complete the exercise on the Student CD.

object linking:
Referencing data
from one application
to use in another.

OLE server: The
source application
in an object linking
operation.

OLE client:
The destination
application in
an object linking
operation.

linking: Maintaining
a link between two
applications so that
changes to one
application update
both.

Linking a Table to Excel Data

Existing data entered in a Microsoft® Excel spreadsheet or a CSV (comma separated) file can be used to create an AutoCAD table. This is an example of *object linking* —the process of referencing data from one application to use in another. In this case, Excel data is referenced to create an AutoCAD table. The object is the Excel data, and Excel is the source application, or *OLE server*. OLE stands for "object linking and embedding." AutoCAD is the destination application, or *OLE client*. The term *linking* means maintaining a connection between two applications so that changes to one application update both applications. In this case, Excel data is being used to create an

AutoCAD and Its Applications—Basics

AutoCAD table, allowing for changes made to the Excel spreadsheet to be updated in the AutoCAD table, while changes made to the AutoCAD table can be written back to the Excel spreadsheet.

To create a table based on an existing Excel or CSV file, pick the **From a data link** radio from the **Insert options** area of the **Insert Table** dialog box. See Figure 10-19. Next, you must establish a data link that links Excel with AutoCAD. If an existing link has already been formed, it is available from the drop-down list and can be selected for use. To create a new data link, pick the **Launch the Data Link Manager** dialog button, or choose the **Launch Data Link Manager...** option from the drop-down list. The **Select a Data Link** dialog box which is the same as the **Data Link Manager** dialog box, is displayed. See Figure 10-20.

NOTE

The **Data Link Manager** dialog box can also be accessed by picking the **Data Link Manager** button in the **Tables** control panel of the **Dashboard**, selecting **Tools** > **Data Link** > **Data Link Manager...**, or typing DATALINK.

Pick the **Create a new Excel Data link** button to display the **Enter Data Link Name** dialog box, and enter a name for the data link in the **Name** text box. See Figure 10-21. The name does not have to be the same as the source file, but it may help to use the same name. After entering a data link name, pick the **OK** button to display the **New Excel Data Link:** dialog box. See Figure 10-22. If this is the first file linked to your

---

Figure 10-19.
Choosing to create a table linked to an existing Excel or CSV file.

Select an existing link   Pick to launch the **Data Link Manager** dialog box

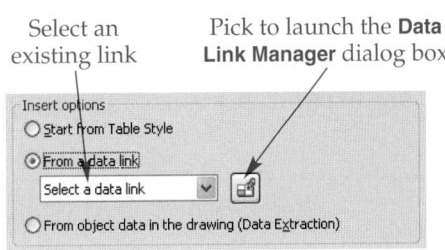

Figure 10-20.
Picking the **Launch Data Link Manager...** button displays the **Select a Data Link** dialog box.

Pick to create a new Excel data link

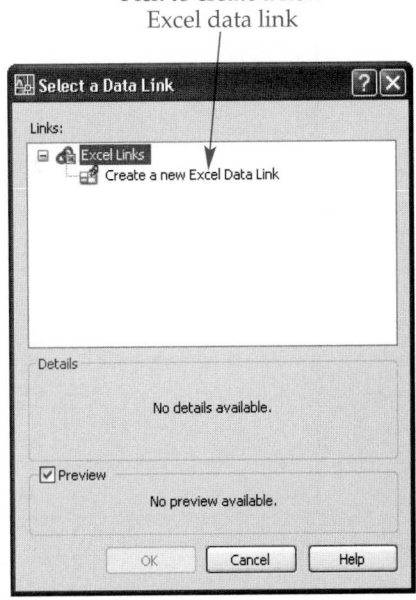

Figure 10-21.
Enter a name for
the data link in the
Name text box.

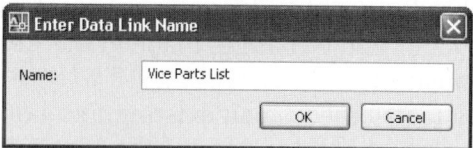

Figure 10-22.
This dialog box
allows you to
browse for a file to
link to the AutoCAD
file.

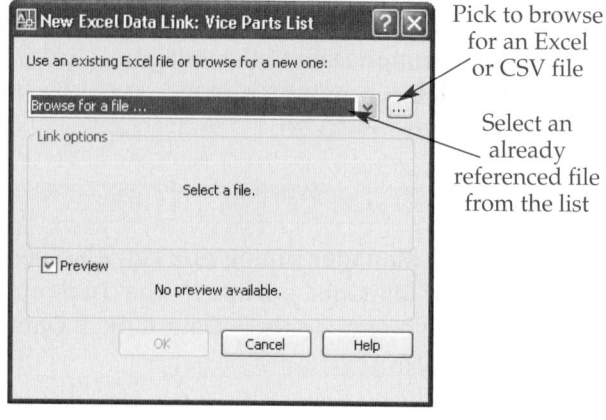

Pick to browse
for an Excel
or CSV file

Select an
already
referenced file
from the list

drawing, pick the ellipses button (…) to launch the **Save As** dialog box and browse for
an Excel or CSV file. Choose a file and pick the **Open** button to return to the **New Excel
Data Link:** dialog box. See **Figure 10-23.**

NOTE

To see the right side of the dialog box shown in **Figure 10-23,** pick
the expansion arrow at the lower right corner.

Figure 10-23.
When you select
a file to be linked,
the **New Excel Data
Link** box reappears,
showing a preview
of the contents of the
selected file.

Deselect to
hide the
preview

AutoCAD and Its Applications—Basics

When a file is selected, the **New Excel Data Link:** dialog box contains the following options:

- **Link options.** Use this area to specify how much of the selected file is linked to AutoCAD to form the table. Pick the **Link entire sheet** radio button to link a sheet selected from the **Select Excel sheet to link to** drop-down list. If a named range is available in the selected Excel file, you can choose the named range by picking the **Link to a named range** radio button and selecting the named range from the drop-down list. The third option is to pick the **Link to range** radio button and enter a range of cells in the text box. For example, entering A1:M9 selects only cells A1 through M9. Pick the **Preview** button to update the preview display according to the selected link option.

- **Cell contents.** This area defines how cell entries are converted from Excel to AutoCAD. Pick the **Convert data types to text** check box to convert all data types, such as currency or percentage, to text. Deselecting the **Convert data types to text** check box makes the **Retain formulas** check box available, allowing you to maintain existing formulas. The **Allow writing to source file** check box must be selected in order to write changes you make in the AutoCAD table back to the Excel spreadsheet.

- **Cell formatting.** Pick the **Use Excel formatting** check box to use the format settings in the Excel spreadsheet to create the AutoCAD table. When this check box is selected, you can choose to allow formatting changes made in the Excel spreadsheet to update in the AutoCAD table by selecting the **Keep table updated to Excel formatting** radio button. Pick the **Start with Excel formatting, but do not update** radio button to draw the initial table using the Excel format, but prevent formats from updating when changes are made in Excel. Deselect the **Use Excel formatting** check box to convert the format used for the Excel spreadsheet to the current table style.

  After selecting options in the **New Excel Data Link:** dialog box, pick the **OK** button to return to the **Select a Data Link** dialog box. Pick the **OK** button in the **Select a Data Link** dialog box to return to the **Insert Table** dialog box. To place the linked table, pick the **OK** button and select the table insertion point. A table and the linked Excel spreadsheet are shown in **Figure 10-24**.

NOTE

An alternative method for creating a table from Excel data is to copy the spreadsheet data from the Excel file and paste it into the drawing using the **Paste Link** function of the **Paste Special** tool. (**Edit** > **Paste Special…**). Paste the copied Excel data using the **AutoCAD Entities** option.

Exercise 10-5
Complete the exercise on the Student CD.

Extracting Table Data

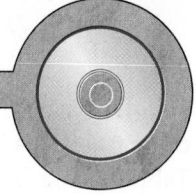
NEW FEATURE

Existing AutoCAD drawing information can be reused to create a table. This is an example of *data extraction*, which involves the process of gathering drawing content for other uses. You can extract data from most AutoCAD objects. Examples of data that can be extracted include the size and location of drawing geometry, attributes, and file properties such as Title and Author. *Attributes* are text or numerical values that can be assigned to blocks. Blocks and attributes are described fully in Chapter 22 and Chapter 25, respectively.

data extraction: The process of gathering data for a specific use or purpose.

attributes: Text or numerical values assigned to blocks.

Figure 10-24.
An example of an
Excel spreadsheet
used to create an
AutoCAD table.

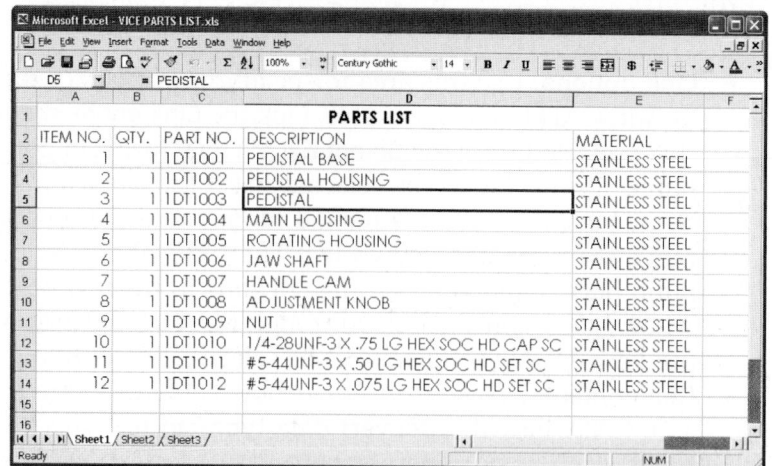

Excel Spreadsheet

PARTS LIST				
ITEM NO.	QTY.	PART NO.	DESCRIPTION	MATERIAL
1	1	1DT1001	PEDISTAL BASE	STAINLESS STEEL
2	1	1DT1002	PEDISTAL HOUSING	STAINLESS STEEL
3	1	1DT1003	PEDISTAL	STAINLESS STEEL
4	1	1DT1004	MAIN HOUSING	STAINLESS STEEL
5	1	1DT1005	ROTATING HOUSING	STAINLESS STEEL
6	1	1DT1006	JAW SHAFT	STAINLESS STEEL
7	1	1DT1007	HANDLE CAM	STAINLESS STEEL
8	1	1DT1008	ADJUSTMENT KNOB	STAINLESS STEEL
9	1	1DT1009	NUT	STAINLESS STEEL
10	1	1DT1010	1/4-28UNF-3 X .75 LG HEX SOC HD CAP SC	STAINLESS STEEL
11	1	1DT1011	#5-44UNF-3 X .50 LG HEX SOC HD SET SC	STAINLESS STEEL
12	1	1DT1012	#5-44UNF-3 X .075 LG HEX SOC HD SET SC	STAINLESS STEEL

Extracted AutoCAD Table

Using existing drawing data speeds up the process of drawing tables. The data is already available, so you can add it to a table without having to type the information. Data that is extracted to form a table is also associated with the drawing. As a result, when changes are made to the drawing data, the information in the table is updated automatically.

NOTE

In order to be extracted, data must be in the current drawing or in another drawing that you include in the data source.

To create a table that references drawing data, pick the **From object data in the drawing (Data Extraction)** radio button from the **Insert options** area of the **Insert Table** dialog box. Refer again to **Figure 10-13**. Pick the **OK** button to launch the **Data Extraction** wizard. The wizard is also available by picking the **Attribute Extraction...** button on the **Modify II** toolbar, picking **Tools > Attribute Extraction...** from the pull-down menu, or typing DATAEXTRACTION, or DX. The **Data Extraction** wizard is used to select exactly what information is extracted.

Data extraction has many applications, and multiple data extraction tools and options are available. The following information focuses on a basic example of using data extraction to develop a table. This information can be applied to a variety of similar and more advanced data extraction requirements, as described in Chapter 25. **Figure 10-25** shows an example of a basic wiring diagram. The wires are drawn as

Figure 10-25.
An example of a basic wiring diagram drawn using lines and arcs. The layer name and
length of each line and arc can be extracted to form a wire list.

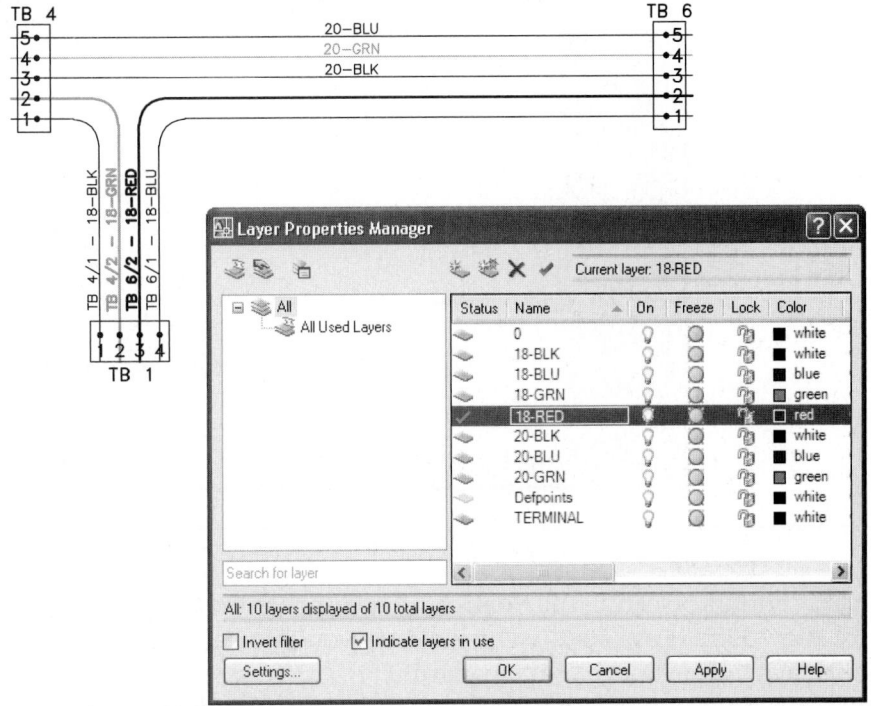

lines and arcs and are placed on an appropriate layer. The layer names identify the size
(18 and 20 gauge) and color code. Data extraction is used in this example to extract the
size, color, and length of each wire to create a wire list.

Begin page

The **Begin** page of the **Data Extraction** wizard begins the data extraction process
by creating, editing, or referencing a data extraction file. See **Figure 10-26**. To create a
new data extraction file (DXE), select the **Create a new data extraction** radio button and

Figure 10-26.
Use the **Begin** page of the **Data Extraction** wizard to create a new data extraction file,
reference a data extraction template, or edit an existing data extraction file.

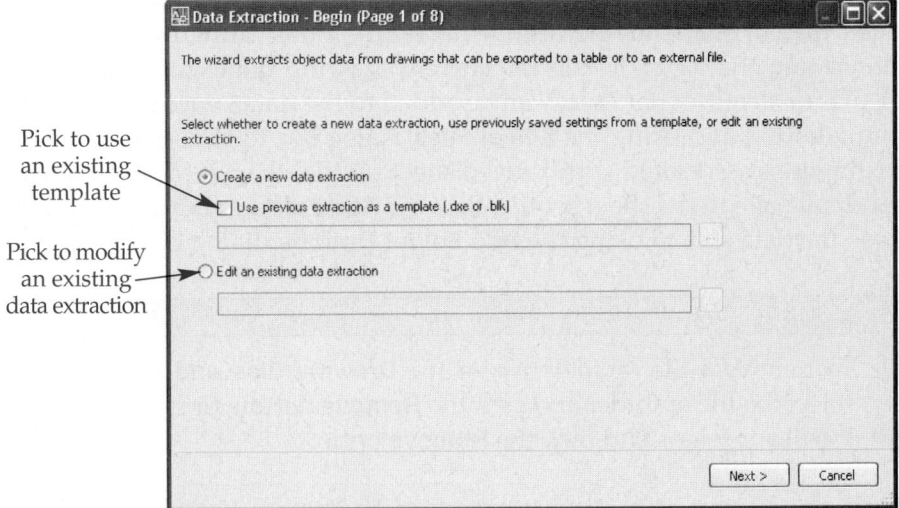

Figure 10-27.
Save the data extraction file. In this example, the new DXE file has been named **Wire List** because the data extraction will be used to draw a wire list table.

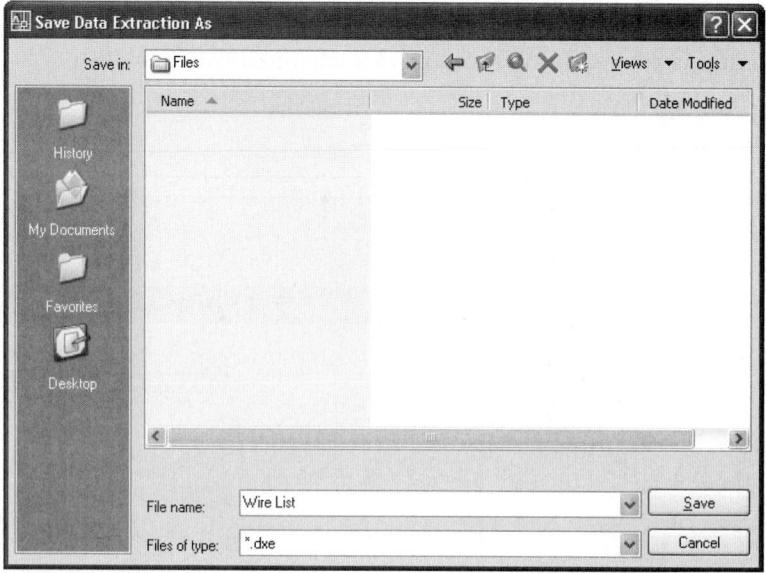

pick the **Next>** button. Selecting the **Next>** button launches the **Save Data Extraction As** dialog box, shown in **Figure 10-27**, which allows you to create a DXE file. Saving the DXE file displays the next page of the wizard.

If you want to use an existing DXE file to form a new data extraction, pick the **Create a new data extraction** radio button and the **Use previous extraction as a template (.dxe or .blk)** check box on the **Begin** page. Pick the ellipsis (…) button to open the **Open Template** dialog box and select the existing data extraction (DXE) or a template (BLK) file. Pick the **Next>** button to display the next page of the wizard.

You also have the option of modifying an existing data extraction file by picking the **Edit existing data extraction** radio button. Pick the ellipsis (…) button to open the **Select Existing Data Extraction File** dialog box and choose the DXE file to modify. Then pick the **Next>** button to display the next page of the wizard.

Define Data Source page

The next page of the wizard, **Define Data Source,** allows you to specify the drawings, sheet set, or individual objects from which the data is to be gathered. See **Figure 10-28**. Sheet sets are described in Chapter 28. The selected drawing files or objects are known as the *data source*. The **Drawing files and folders** list shows the files and folders added to the data source. Pick the **Drawings/sheet set** radio button to gather information from the current drawing and, if necessary, other drawings. Select the **Include current drawing** check box to add the current drawing file to the data source. Other drawing files or sheet set data files can be added to the data source by selecting the **Add Drawing…** button and using the **Select Files** dialog box to choose the files. To select all of the drawings associated with a saved sheet set file, change the **Files of type** option to **.dst** and navigate to the sheet set file. Pick the **Add Folder…** button to add the files in a folder to the data source using the **Add Folder Options** dialog box.

data source: The files or objects from which data is extracted.

> **NOTE**
>
> To remove a file or folder from the **Drawing files and folders** list, select the file or folder and pick the **Remove** button, or right-click on the file or folder and pick the **Remove** option.

Figure 10-28.
Select the drawing or drawings, sheet set, or objects from which to extract data. In this example, the current drawing of the wiring diagram is selected as the data source.

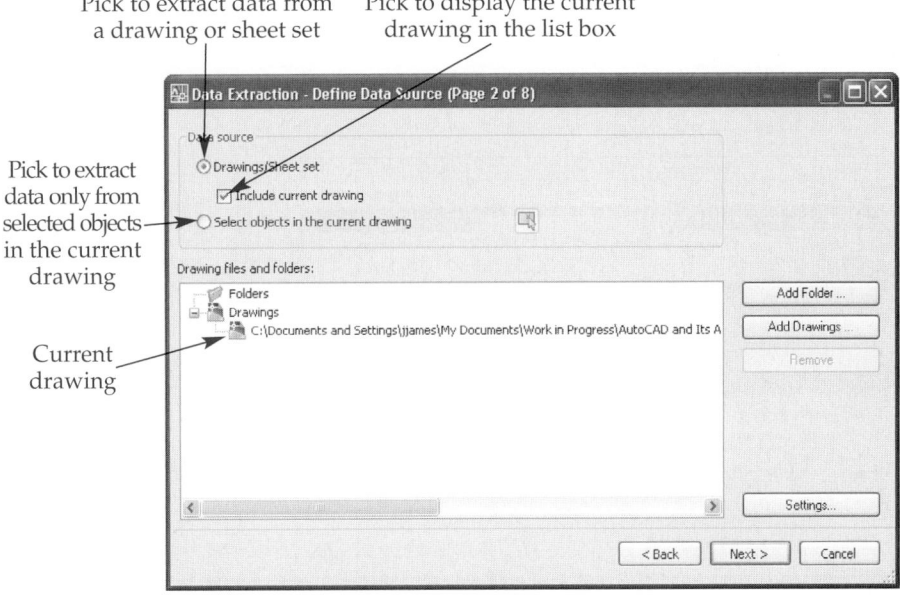

Pick to extract data from a drawing or sheet set

Pick to display the current drawing in the list box

Pick to extract data only from selected objects in the current drawing

Current drawing

Another option for gathering data is to select specific objects in the current drawing. Pick the **Select objects** radio button and then pick the **Select object in the current drawing** button. This returns you to the drawing area so that you can select the objects to be included in the data source. Objects can only be selected from the current drawing.

Picking the **Settings...** button opens the **Data Extraction—Additional Settings** dialog box. The options in this dialog box are specific to extracting information from blocks, xrefs and layouts, described in later chapters.

> **PROFESSIONAL TIP**
>
> Add multiple files or a sheet set to the data source to compile file properties such as Title, Comments, Drawing Revision, and File Name. This data can be used to draw a title block or similar type of table. Sheet sets are discussed in Chapter 28.

Select Objects page

After you have selected a data source, pick the **Next** button to display the **Select Objects** page. See **Figure 10-29.** This page lists all the data source objects. An *object* is any item added to the data source, such as drawing geometry (lines, circles and arcs), text, blocks, hatch patterns, dimensions, and tables. The wire diagram drawing contains arcs, lines, polylines, and text.

object: The data or item being linked in an object linking operation.

Use the **Select Objects** page to choose the objects that contain the data, or properties, you want to reference when creating the table. For example, only arc and line objects are selected to create the wire list, because the wires were drawn as arcs and lines, not polylines or text. Pick the check box corresponding to the objects you want to reference to create the table. Right-clicking an object in the list provides a shortcut menu that allows you to select all objects, deselect all objects, or invert the selection.

Figure 10-29.
Select the objects in the data source from which to extract properties. In this example, data will only be extracted from arcs and lines to create the wire list.

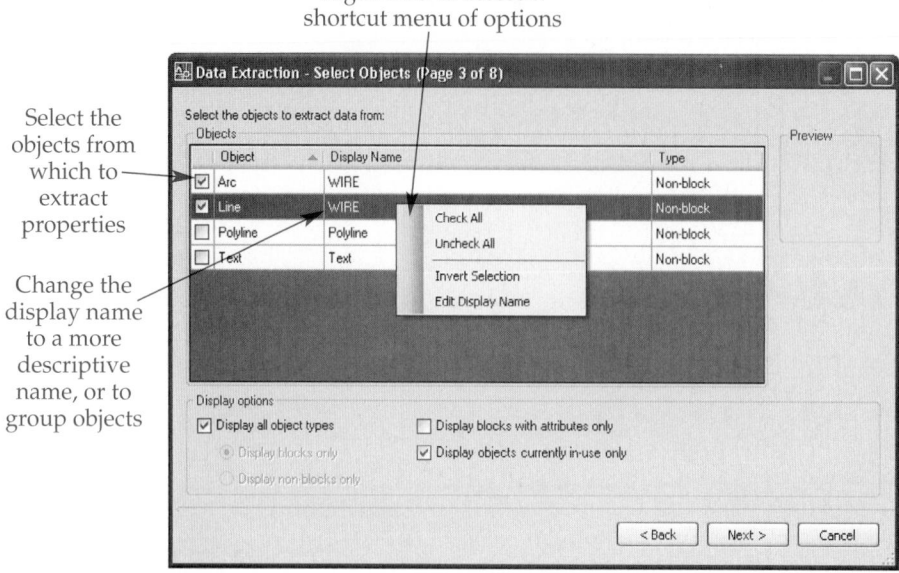

You can change the display name of an object by right-clicking and selecting **Edit Display Name** or by slowly double-clicking in the **Display Name** text box. Changing the object display name can be a critical step when you are extracting certain types of data. Using the same display name for different objects is effective for grouping data into single item. For example, **Figure 10-29** shows how the default display names Arc and Line were both renamed to WIRE. This is an important step in this example, because some of the wires are drawn with both line and arc segments. The arcs and lines must be calculated together to determine the length of each wire. Renaming arc and line objects to WIRE results in a wire list that displays the length of wires, not the length of each object (arc or line) used to create the wires. Changing the display name also provides a more descriptive name for the object.

Select Properties page

After selecting objects on the **Select Objects** page, pick the **Next** button to display the **Select Properties** page. See **Figure 10-30.** This page lists all the properties found in the selected objects and the data source files. Every object and file contains certain properties, or data. For example, a line contains length, color, linetype, and position properties.

The **Select Properties** page allows you to choose the object properties to use in creating the table. The selected properties correspond to the table columns. For example, layer and length properties are selected to create the WIRE (layer name) and LENGTH table columns. Pick the check box corresponding to the properties you want to reference to create the table. Right-clicking a property in the list provides a shortcut menu that allows you to select all objects, deselect all objects, or invert the selection. The property's display name is used as the table column header, and can also be adjusted during the next phase of data extraction.

NOTE

Reduce the number of properties shown in the list by deselecting the appropriate check boxes found in the **Category filter** area.

Figure 10-30.
Choose the properties to extract from the selected objects. In this example, only the layer and length properties are needed to create the wire list.

Select the object properties to extract →

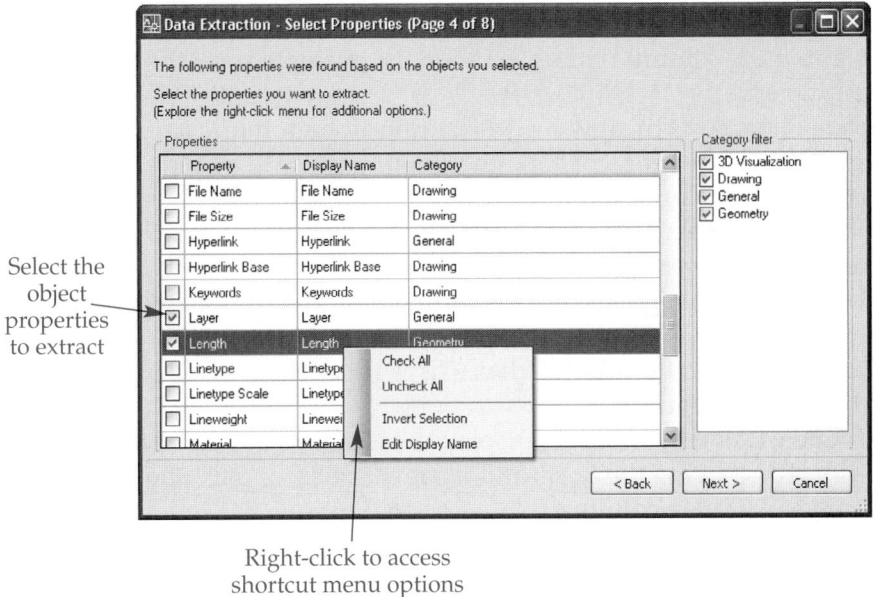

Right-click to access shortcut menu options

Refine Data page

After selecting the properties to be extracted, pick the **Next>** button to display the **Refine Data** page. See **Figure 10-31**. This page allows you to adjust table content and display characteristics before inserting the table. The results of the extraction are shown in a table format, with selected properties displayed in columns and each object in a separate row.

Figure 10-31.
Adjust table content and display characteristics before inserting the table into the drawing.

Property columns   Right-click to access shortcut menu options

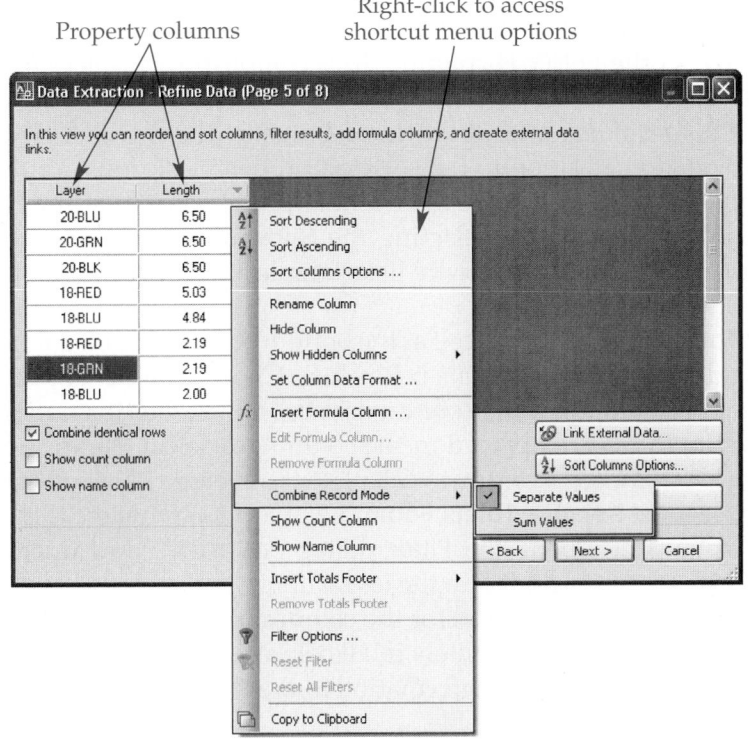

Most options can be accessed by right-clicking a column to display the shortcut menu shown in **Figure 10-31**. The options are:

- **Sort Ascending.** Sorts the rows in ascending alphanumeric order. Ascending row order can also be set by picking the heading once to display an up arrow to the right of the column name. The wire list example sorts the WIRE column in ascending order.
- **Sort Descending.** Sorts the rows in descending alphanumeric order. Descending row order can also be set by picking the heading twice to display a down arrow to the right of the column name.
- **Sort Columns Options....** Opens the **Sort Columns** dialog box, used for sorting rows.
- **Rename Column.** Renames the column heading. For the wire list example, the default Layer column name is replaced with WIRE and the Length column name is retyped in uppercase letters.
- **Hide Column.** Hides the column that was right-clicked. Hidden columns are not included in the extraction.
- **Show Hidden Columns.** Pick to display a cascading submenu that provides options for redisplaying the Count and Name columns, or pick **Show All Columns** to redisplay all hidden columns.
- **Set Column Data Format....** Pick this option to access the **Set Cell Format** dialog box. The **Data Type** area lists, in alphabetical order, options for formatting the selected table cell: **Angle**, **Currency**, **Date**, **Decimal Number**, **General**, **Percentage**, **Point**, **Text**, and **Whole Number**. Selecting a format presents options for adjusting the format characteristics. Different options are available depending on the selected format. The wire list example uses a TEXT cell format for data in the WIRE column and a DECIMAL cell format for data in the LENGTH column.
- **Insert Formula Column....** Pick this option to access the **Insert Formula Column** dialog box, which is used to add a column that uses a formula to calculate cell data. Formulas are described later in this chapter.
- **Combine Record Mode.** This cascading submenu is available only when the **Combine identical rows** check box is selected. Pick the **Separate Values** option to display a row for each unique data value. Using the wire list example, you can see in **Figure 10-31** how each different length arc or line segment is provided in a separate row in the LENGTH column. This may be appropriate for some applications, but in this example, the total length of each type of wire should be shown in the LENGTH column. To accomplish this, select the **Sum Values** option. The result is shown in **Figure 10-32**.
- **Show Count Column** and **Show Name Column.** The Count and Name columns are provided in addition to the selected property columns. You can use these columns in your table or hide them if not needed. The Count and Name columns can also be hidden by deselecting the **Show count column** and **Show name column** check boxes. For the wire list example, the Count and Name columns are not needed and are hidden.
- **Insert Totals Footer.** Adds a cell at the bottom of the selected column that calculates and displays column data cell values. Choose the **Sum** option to calculate the sum of all values in the column data cells. Pick the **Max** option to show the largest single value displayed in the column, or select **Min** to show the lowest single value. Choose **Average** to calculate the average value of the column data cells. Select the **Remove Totals Footer** menu option to delete the cell.
- **Filter Options....** Opens the **Filter** dialog box. Any rows unchecked in this dialog box are not included in the extraction.
- **Reset Filter.** Resets any filters for the column you right-clicked.
- **Reset All Filters.** Resets all filters in all columns.
- **Copy to Clipboard.** Copies information to the Windows Clipboard in the same format as displayed in the table.

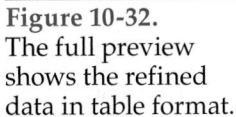

Figure 10-32.
The full preview
shows the refined
data in table format.

Pick to close the preview and
return to the **Refine Data** page

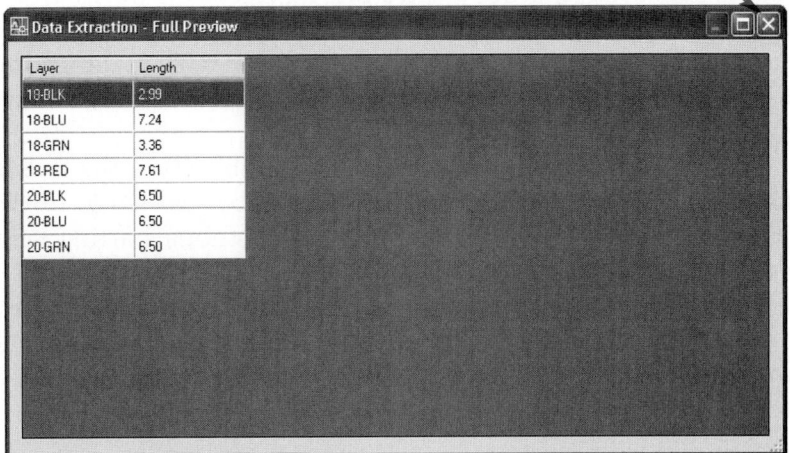

To display a preview of the data, as shown in **Figure 10-32**, pick the **Full Preview** button below the list of data. The window that opens displays the data as it will appear when extracted. Close the preview window by pressing the [Esc] key or using the Windows control button (X).

> **NOTE**
>
> Existing data entered in a Microsoft Excel spreadsheet or a CSV file can be added to the table by picking the **Link External Data...** button to access the **Link External Data** dialog box.

Choose Output page

After you have adjusted the data using the **Refine Data** page, pick the **Next** button to display the **Choose Output** page. See **Figure 10-33**. In the **Output options** area, pick whether the data is displayed as a table in the current drawing, extracted to an external file, or both. To create a table, check the **Insert data extraction table into drawing** check box.

To save the data to an external file, check the **Output data to external file (.xls .csv .mbt .txt)** check box. Then, pick the ellipsis (...) button to display the **Save As** dialog box. Specify a file name and folder for the file. The type of file to be saved is selected in the **File of type:** drop-down list. The default file formats are comma separated (CSV) and tab separated (TXT). If Microsoft Excel and Microsoft Access are installed, the XLS and MDB formats are also available. Pick the **Save** button to return to the **Choose Output** page.

Figure 10-33.
Choose whether to
create a table in the
current drawing or
save the table to an
external file.

Choose to
display a
table in the
drawing

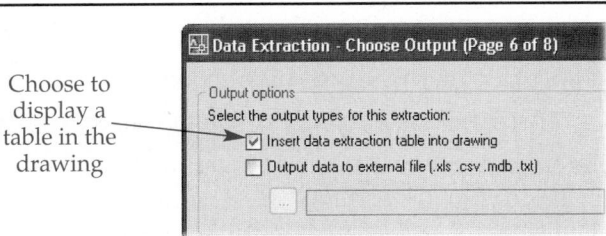

Table Style page

Pick the **Next>** button to continue with the wizard. If the **Insert data extraction table into drawing** check box in the **Choose Output** page is checked, the **Table Style** page is displayed next. See **Figure 10-34.** Select a table style from the **Table Style** drop-down list, or pick the ellipsis (...) button to create or modify a style. The preview area shows a preview of a table with the current table style settings. The preview area does not adjust to the column and row settings. It shows table style properties such as general, text style, and border settings.

If the selected table style is a starting table style, the **Use table in table style for label rows** radio button is available and can be selected to use the starting table style title and headers. If the selected table style is not a starting table style, or you do not want to use the starting table style title and headers, pick the **Manually setup table** radio button. Enter a title for the table in the **Enter a title for your table:** text box. Select a title, header, or data cell style from the drop-down lists if necessary. Pick the **Use property names as additional column headers** check box to use the column display names shown in **Refine Data** page as the table column heads.

Finish page

The last page of the **Data Extraction** wizard is the **Finish** page. See **Figure 10-35.** Pick the **Finish** button to finish the data extraction.

Output

When you pick the **Finish** button, you are prompted to specify an insertion point for the table if the **Insert data extraction table into drawing** check box was checked on the **Choose Output** page. Pick a point or enter coordinates to complete the extraction process. The wire list table example described throughout this section is shown in **Figure 10-36.**

Figure 10-34.
Choose a table style and add a title and column headers.

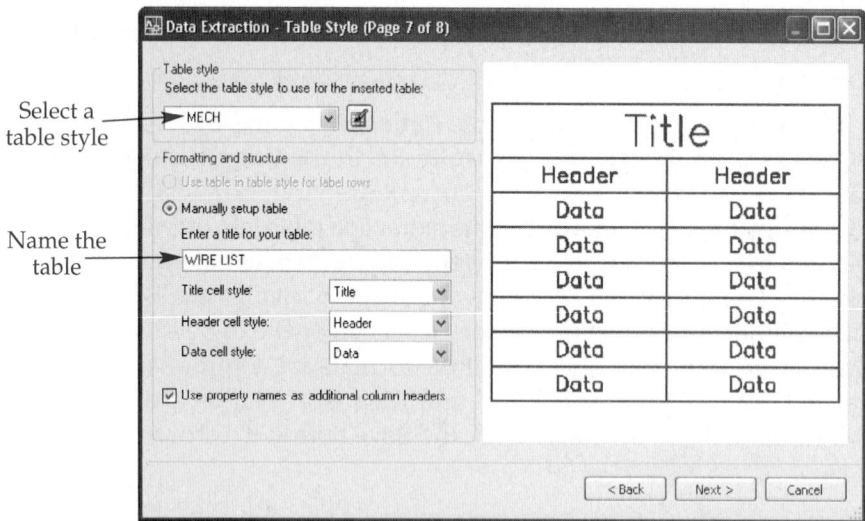

Figure 10-35.
The **Finish** page allows you to finish the procedure and insert the table or save the external file.

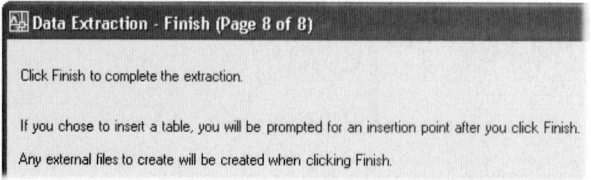

Figure 10-36.
The result of the wire list table extraction described in this section.

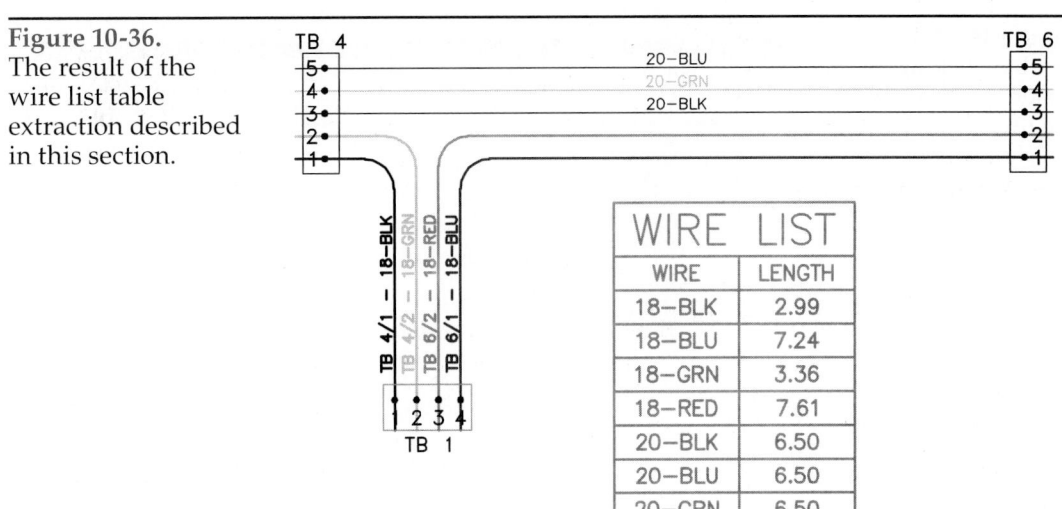

WIRE LIST	
WIRE	LENGTH
18–BLK	2.99
18–BLU	7.24
18–GRN	3.36
18–RED	7.61
20–BLK	6.50
20–BLU	6.50
20–GRN	6.50

NOTE

When you create a table using data extraction, you can update it when the data extraction file changes. A notification in the status bar tray will tell you when changes have been made. You can also update a data extraction at any time using the **DATALINKUPDATE** command.

Exercise 10-6

Complete the exercise on the Student CD.

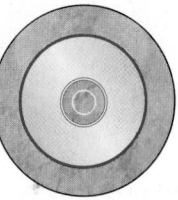

Editing Tables

AutoCAD provides several options for editing existing tables. One option is to edit the text in a table cell. For example, you may need to modify the text contents or change the text formatting, such as the font type or text height. Another option is to make changes to the table layout. These changes include adding, removing and resizing rows and columns, and wrapping table columns to break a large table into sections.

Editing Table Cell Text

You can edit the text in a table cell by double-clicking inside the cell, typing TABLEDIT and then selecting the cell, or picking inside the cell, right-clicking, and selecting **Edit Text** from the table cell shortcut menu. This makes the selected cell active and displays the **Text Formatting** toolbar above the selected cell. See **Figure 10-37**. When you are finished editing table cell text, pick the **OK** button on the **Text Formatting** toolbar or pick anywhere in the drawing area to exit the **TABLE** command.

Figure 10-37.
Double-clicking
inside a cell opens
the text formatting
function, allowing
you to make changes
to the text.

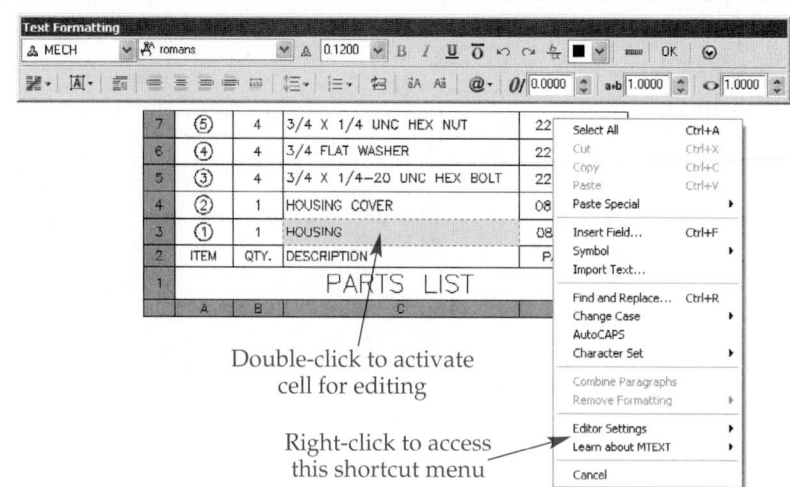

Double-click to activate
cell for editing

Right-click to access
this shortcut menu

NOTE

The options and settings available in the **Text Formatting** toolbar and right-click shortcut menu function the same when typing in table cells as when placing multiline text. Refer to Chapter 9 for more information on text formatting options.

Exercise 10-7
Complete the exercise on the Student CD.

Picking Inside a Cell to Edit Table Layout

Several table layout settings can be accessed by picking (single-clicking) inside a cell to make the selected cell active and display the **Table** toolbar above the table. See **Figure 10-38**. The **Table** toolbar contains options for adjusting table and individual cell layout. The highlighted cell includes *grips* that can be used to adjust row height and column width, as well as auto-fill function.

grips: Small boxes that appear at strategic points on an object, allowing you to edit the object directly.

NOTE

The TABLETOOLBAR system variable controls the display of the **Table** toolbar. The value is set to 1 by default to show the **Table** toolbar. Enter 0 to hide the **Table** toolbar.

While a cell is selected, you can display the shortcut menu shown in **Figure 10-38** by right-clicking anywhere in the graphics window. The first section of the shortcut menu contains the Windows Clipboard functions. These options affect the entire contents of the cell. Selecting **Recent Input** displays a list of previously entered commands. Most of the options in the shortcut menu can also be accessed from the **Table** toolbar.

AutoCAD and Its Applications—Basics

Figure 10-38.
Several table layout modification options are available when you pick inside a cell.

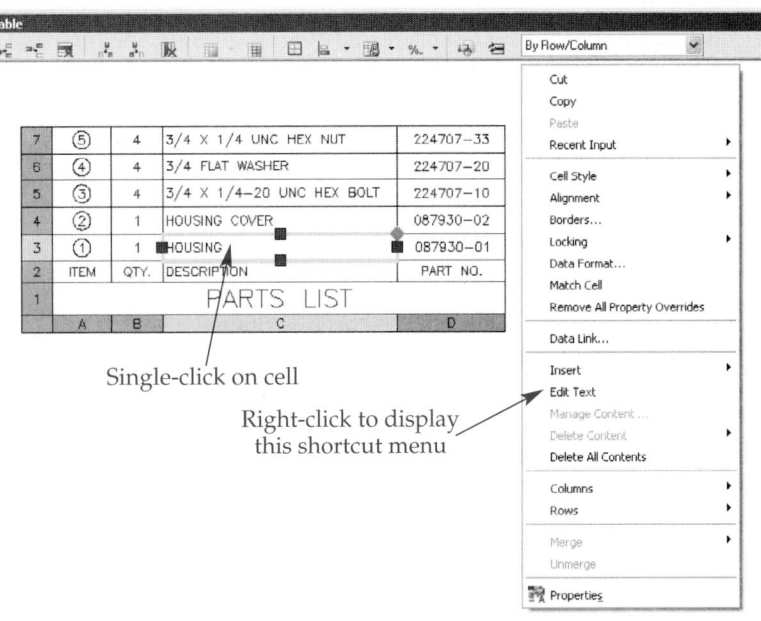

Single-click on cell

Right-click to display
this shortcut menu

AutoCAD provides several ways to select multiple cells and apply changes to all the cells at once. One option is to pick in a cell and drag the window over the other cells. When you release the pick button, all of the cells touching the window become selected. Multiple cells can also be selected by picking a cell, holding down the [Shift] key, and then picking another cell. This process selects the picked cells and all of the cells between them. You can select entire columns or rows by picking the column or row number of the table indicator. To select the entire table, pick the corner of the table indicator. See **Figure 10-39.**

NOTE

Make sure you pick completely inside of the cell. If you accidentally select one of the cell borders, the entire table becomes the selected object. Editing table layout by selecting a cell border is described later in this chapter.

Quickly copying cell content

The most effective method for copying the content of one cell to multiple cells is to use the auto-fill function. To use auto-fill, pick inside the cell that contains the content you want to copy. The auto-fill grip is a diamond-shaped grip located in a corner of the cell. See **Figure 10-40.** Select the auto-fill grip. Then you may want to adjust how auto-fill copies the cell content by right-clicking directly on the auto-fill grip and selecting one of the following options:

- **Fill Series.** Fills cells with the cell content and any format overrides that have been applied. This option automatically increases or decreases values of certain data types, such as dates, as the fill occurs. See **Figure 10-41.**
- **Fill Series Without Formatting.** Fills cells with the content of the selected cell, but does not include any format overrides that have been added.
- **Copy Cells.** Copies the content and format overrides that have been applied to the selected cell. This option creates a static cell copy that does not adjust data values. Refer to **Figure 10-41.**

Figure 10-39.
Selecting multiple cells in a table for editing. A—Using the pick and drag method. B—Picking a range of cells using the [Shift] key. C—Selecting a row, column, or the entire table.

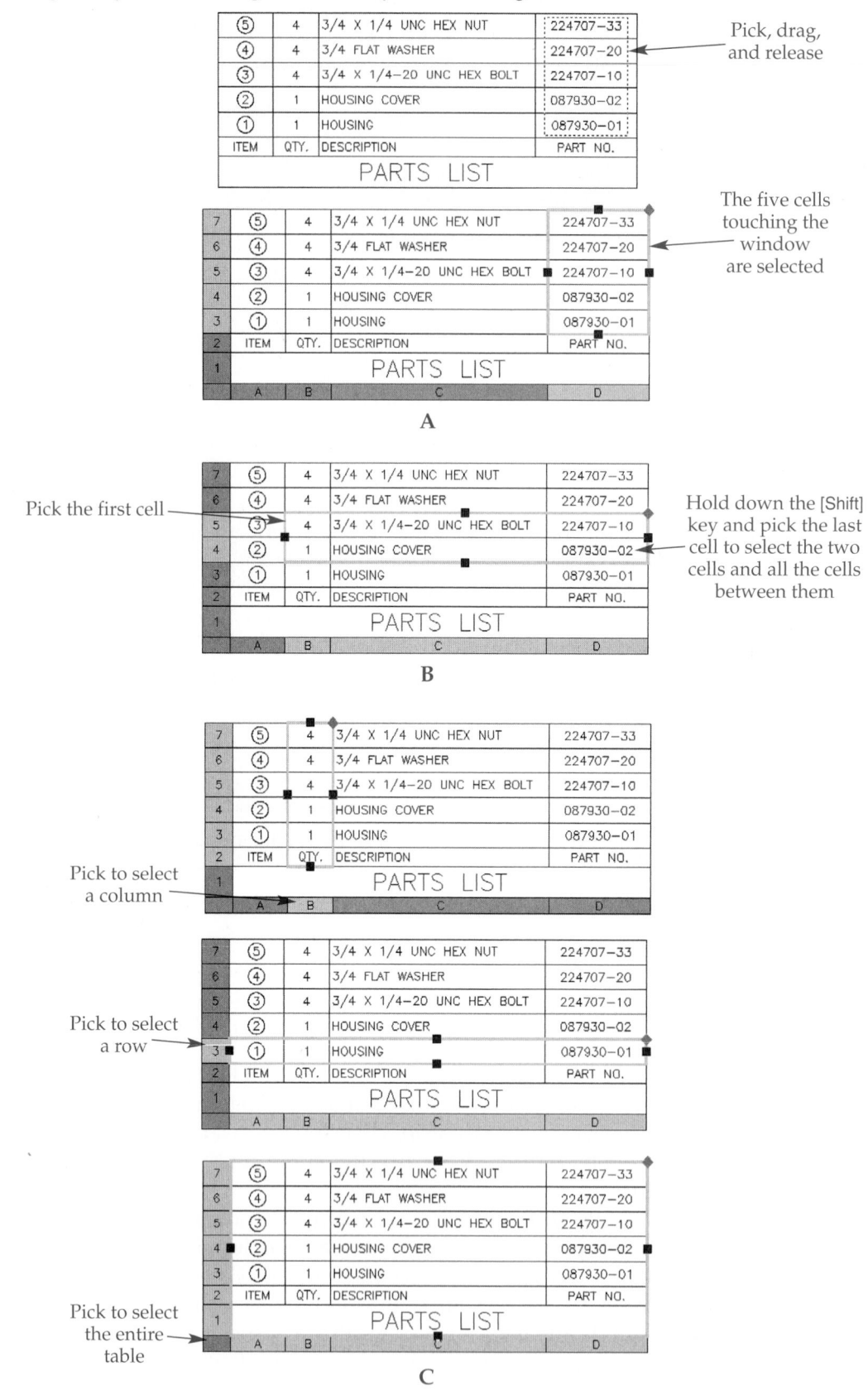

Figure 10-40.
Using the auto-fill function to copy cell content to multiple cells.

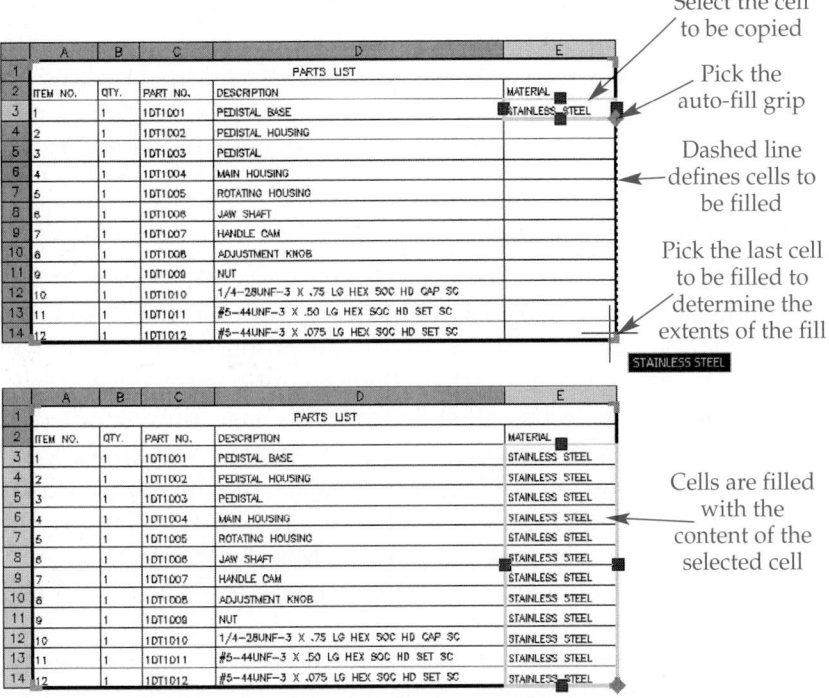

Select the cell to be copied

Pick the auto-fill grip

Dashed line defines cells to be filled

Pick the last cell to be filled to determine the extents of the fill

Cells are filled with the content of the selected cell

Figure 10-41.
Using the auto-fill options to control fill characteristics.

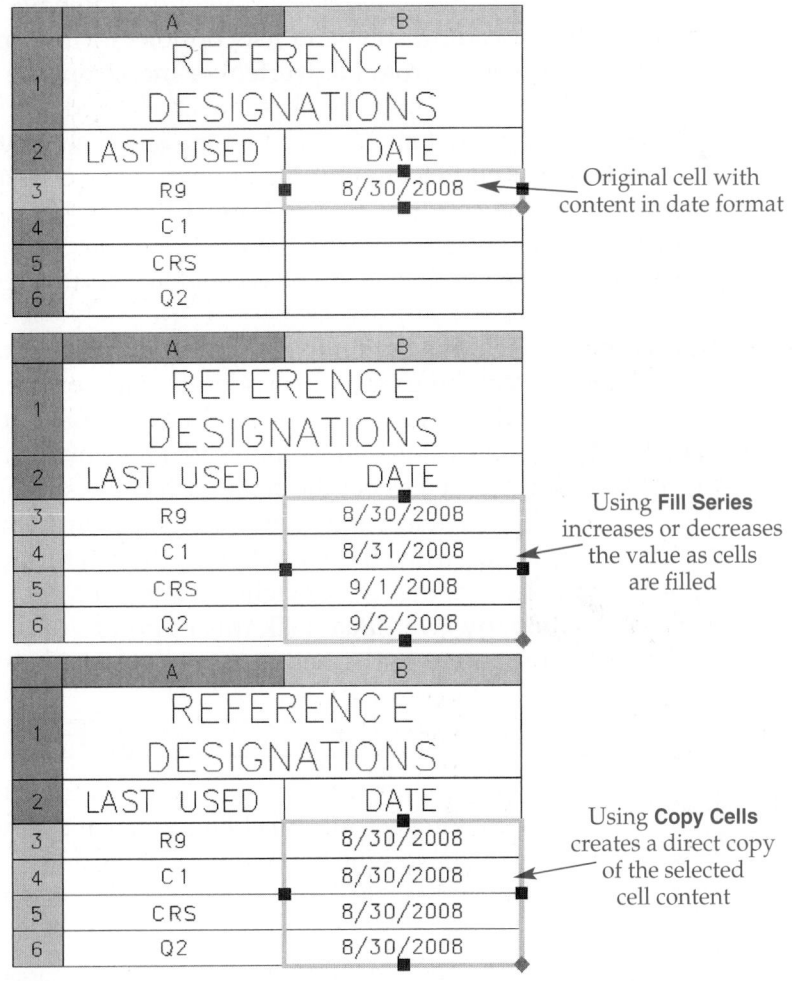

Original cell with content in date format

Using **Fill Series** increases or decreases the value as cells are filled

Using **Copy Cells** creates a direct copy of the selected cell content

- **Copy Cells Without Formatting.** Copies cells with the content of the selected cell, but does not include any format overrides that have been added.
- **Fill Formatting Only.** Fills the cells only with format overrides that have been applied to the selected cell, allowing you to enter cell content manually.

After you have chosen the appropriate fill option, move the cursor to the last cell to which you want to copy the cell content and pick inside the cell. All cells between the first and last cell you picked are filled with the content of the active cell. See **Figure 10-40.**

Modifying cell properties

Most cell properties are defined according to the table style used to create the table. However, cell properties can be overridden for individual cells or groups of cells as needed. You can override or adjust cell properties by selecting cell or cells, right-clicking, and selecting one of the following options from the shortcut menu:

- **Cell Style.** Select a cell style from this cascading submenu to override the cell style used for the active cell. If you have made changes to the active cell, you can save the changes as a new cell style that can be used for adjusting the display of other cells or applied to a table style. To save the cell properties as a new cell style, pick the **Save as New Cell Style...** option from the **Cell Style** cascading submenu, and enter a name for the style in the **Save as New Cell Style** dialog box.
- **Cell Alignment.** Select an alignment option from this cascading menu to override the justification of content within the selected cell. Cell content is located in relation to the cell borders.
- **Borders.** Pick this option to open the **Cell Border Properties** dialog box. This dialog box can be used to override cell border display properties and contains the same options found in the **Border** tab of the **Table Style** dialog box.
- **Locking.** This cascading submenu lists options for locking cells. Cells can be locked to protect them from inadvertent or inappropriate changes. The locked icon appears when you move the cursor over a locked cell. The **Unlocked** option unlocks the cell so that changes can be made to cell content and format. The **Content Locked** option locks only the content of the cell, still allowing changes to be made to the cell format. The **Format Locked** option locks only the cell format, still allowing changes to be made to the content of the cell. The **Content and Format Locked** option locks cell content and format so that no changes can be made.
- **Data Format....** Pick this option to open the **Table Cell Data Format** dialog box. This dialog box can be used to override the data format for the selected cell. This is the same dialog box available for adjusting table styles.
- **Match Cell.** The **Match Cell** option allows you to copy formatting settings from one cell to another. First select the cell that has the settings you want to copy. Then right-click and select the **Match Cell** shortcut menu option. AutoCAD prompts you to select a destination cell. Pick the cell to which you want to copy the settings. Select another cell or right-click to exit.
- **Remove All Property Overrides.** Pick this option to restore the cell or cells to their original properties as defined in the selected table style.

NOTE

The default cell properties are defined in the current table style. If you are making significant changes to cell properties, it is better to modify the table style or create a new style.

Adjusting data links

Data from a Microsoft® Excel spreadsheet or a CSV file can be added to an existing table by selecting the **Data Link...** shortcut menu option or picking **Link Cell...** button from the **Table** toolbar. The **Select a Data Link** dialog box is displayed. This is the same dialog box used to create a new table from a data link.

Data link table content is identified by brackets, and the data link icon is displayed when you move the cursor over linked data. See **Figure 10-42**. The following options are available from the **Data Links** cascading submenu of the shortcut menu:

- **Download Changes from Source File.** Updates the table to include any changes that have been made to the source file, such as the Excel spreadsheet.
- **Upload User Changes to Source File.** Updates the source file, such as the Excel spreadsheet, to include any changes that have been made to the AutoCAD table.

NOTE

The content of cells created as data links is locked by default. You must unlock the cells in order to make changes to the content. Unlocking a cell does not break the data link.

- **Edit Data Link.** Allows you to edit the data link using the **Modify Excel Data Link:** dialog box. This dialog box is the same as the **New Excel Data Link:** dialog box used to create a data link.
- **Open Data Link File.** Opens the source file, such as the Excel spreadsheet.
- **Detach Data Link.** Detaches, or breaks, the link between the AutoCAD table and the source file. Detaching a data link creates a static table that is no longer linked to the source file.

Inserting blocks

In addition to text, table cells can contain AutoCAD blocks, fields, and formulas. Blocks are useful when creating a legend, or when you want to display images of parts in a parts list table. The options for inserting a block in a table are briefly described here. For detailed information about blocks, refer to Chapter 22.

To insert a block into a table cell, select the **Block...** option from the **Insert** cascading submenu of the table cell shortcut menu, or pick the **Insert Block...** button from the **Table** toolbar. This opens the **Insert a Block in a Table Cell** dialog box. The following options are available:

- **Name.** Allows you to choose the block from a drop-down list of the blocks stored in the current drawing.
- **Browse.** Displays the **Select Drawing File** dialog box, where a drawing file can be selected and inserted into the table cell as a block.

Figure 10-42.
Data link table content is identified by brackets at all four corners of the linked data. The data link icon is displayed when you move the cursor over linked data.

Data link brackets

Data link cells are automatically locked

Data link icon

	A	B	C	D	E
1				PARTS LIST	
2	ITEM NO.	QTY.	PART NO.	DESCRIPTION	MATERIAL
3	1	1	1DT1001	PEDISTAL BASE	STAINLESS STEEL
4	2	1	1DT1002	PEDISTAL HOUSING	STAINLESS STEEL
5	3	1	1DT1003	PEDISTAL	STAINLESS STEEL
6	4	1	1DT1004	MAIN HOUSING	STAINLESS STEEL
7	5	1	1DT1005	ROTATING HOUSING	STAINLESS STEEL
8	6	1	1DT1006	JAW SHAFT	STAINLESS STEEL
9	7	1	1DT1007	HANDLE CAM	STAINLESS STEEL
10	8	1	1DT1008	ADJUSTMENT KNOB	STAINLESS STEEL
11	9	1	1DT1009	NUT	STAINLESS STEEL
12	10	1	1DT1010	1/4-28UNF-3 X .75 LG HEX SOC HD CAP SC	STAINLESS STEEL
13	11	1	1DT1011	#5-44UNF-3 X .50 LG HEX SOC HD SET SC	STAINLESS STEEL
14	12	1	1DT1012	#5-44UNF-3 X .075 LG HEX SOC HD SET SC	STAINLESS STEEL

- **AutoFit.** Scales the block automatically to fit inside the cell.
- **Scale.** Sets the block insertion scale. A value of 2 inserts the block at twice its original size. A value of .5 inserts the block at half its created size. If the **AutoFit** check box is checked, the **Scale** option is not available.
- **Rotation angle.** Rotates the block to the specified angle.
- **Overall cell alignment.** Determines the justification of the block in the cell. This setting overrides the current cell alignment setting.

> **NOTE**
>
> A cell can contain both text and blocks. Double-clicking a block in a cell opens the **Insert a Block in a Table Cell** dialog box. Double-clicking on text in a cell, or right-clicking and selecting the **Edit Text** option, opens the **Text Formatting** function.

Inserting fields

You can insert a field into a table cell by selecting the **Field...** option from the **Insert** cascading submenu of the table cell shortcut menu or by picking the **Insert Field...** button from the **Table** toolbar. This opens the **Field** dialog box. This is the same dialog box that is used to insert fields into single line and multiline text. Refer to Chapter 9 for more information on inserting and using text.

> **NOTE**
>
> Fields can also be inserted using the **Text Formatting** function.

Inserting formulas

Formulas used in table cells are inserted as fields. To insert a formula, select **Formula** from the **Insert** cascading submenu of the table cell shortcut menu to display a cascading menu with formula options. You can also access formula options from the **Insert Formula** flyout button of the **Table** toolbar. Formulas are described later in this chapter.

Adding and resizing columns and rows

Columns and rows can be added, deleted, and resized after a table is created. The following options are available from the **Columns** cascading submenu of the table cell shortcut menu:
- **Insert Left.** Adds a new column to the left of the selected cell.
- **Insert Right.** Adds a new column to the right of the selected cell.
- **Delete.** Picking this option deletes the entire column (or set of columns) containing the selected cell(s).
- **Size Equally.** Automatically sizes the selected columns to the same width. This option is only available when cells belonging to multiple columns are selected.

The following options are available from the **Rows** cascading submenu of the table cell shortcut menu:
- **Insert Above.** Adds a new row above the selected cell.
- **Insert Below.** Adds a new row below the selected cell.
- **Delete.** Deletes the row (or set of rows) containing the selected cell(s).
- **Size Equally.** Automatically sizes the selected rows to the same height. This option is only available when cells belonging to multiple rows are selected.

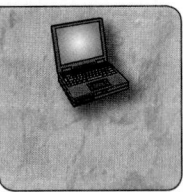

The size of the columns and rows in a table can also be adjusted using grips. Grips are the boxes located in the middle of cell border lines. To resize a column or row, select a grip and move the mouse and pick. Grips are described in detail in Chapter 12.

Merging cells

You can combine adjacent cells by merging the cells. First select multiple cells to be merged. Then pick the **Merge** option from the table cell shortcut menu, or select the **Merge cells** flyout button on the **Table** toolbar. Selecting the **All** option merges all cells into one space. The **By Row** and **By Column** options allow you to merge cells in multiple rows or columns without removing the horizontal or vertical borders. The **Unmerge Cells** option separates merged cells back into individual cells.

Editing cells using the Properties palette

Selecting the **Properties** option from the table cell shortcut menu opens the **Properties** palette, displaying the settings of the selected cell. The options that are not available in the table cell shortcut menu, the **Table** toolbar, the text formatting shortcut menu, or the **Text Formatting** toolbar are highlighted in **Figure 10-43:**

- **Row style.** Overrides the cell style of all cells in the row.
- **Column style.** Overrides the cell style of all cells in the column.
- **Cell width.** Adjusts the cell width. This also affects the other cells in the column.
- **Cell height.** Adjusts the cell height. This also affects the other cells in the row.
- **Background fill.** Changes the cell background color.
- **Horizontal cell margin.** Overrides the space between the content of the cell and the horizontal cell border lines.

Figure 10-43.
The **Properties** palette contains some options for cell settings that cannot be accessed by other means.

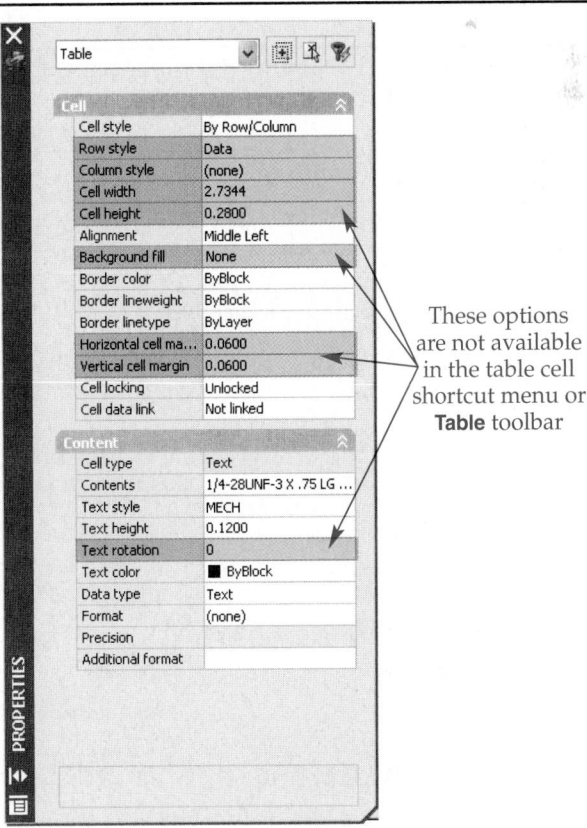

These options are not available in the table cell shortcut menu or **Table** toolbar

- **Vertical cell margin.** Overrides the space between the content of the cell and the vertical cell border lines.
- **Text rotation.** Rotates the text in the current cell.

NOTE

Selecting **Delete All Contents** menu option deletes the contents in the selected cell. This is the same as selecting a cell and pressing the [Delete] key.

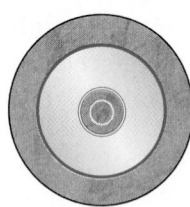

Exercise 10-8

Complete the exercise on the Student CD.

Picking a Cell Edge to Edit Table Layout

Additional methods for adjusting table layout become available when you pick the edge, or border, of a cell. This displays the table indicator grid, grips that can be used to adjust row height and column width, and the table break function. After picking a cell border, right-click anywhere in the graphics window to display the shortcut menu shown in **Figure 10-44**.

Adjusting table style

Select an existing table style from the **Table Style** cascading submenu of the shortcut menu to select a different table style for the selected table. Picking the **Set as Table in Current Table Style** option creates a starting table style based on the selected table and the current table style. This is an alterative technique for creating a starting

Figure 10-44.
Several additional table layout modification options are available when you pick any cell border.

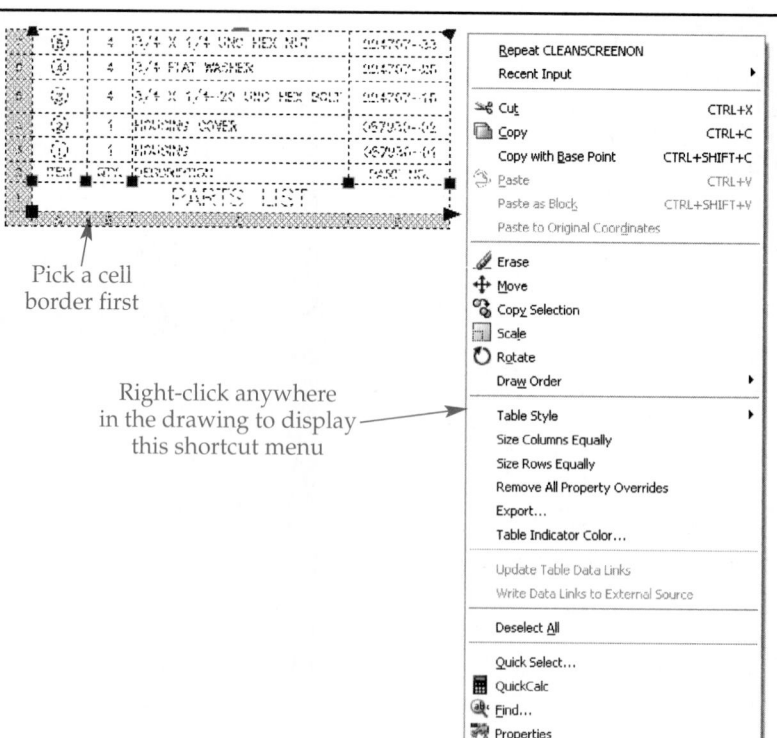

Pick a cell border first

Right-click anywhere in the drawing to display this shortcut menu

table style without opening the **Table Style** dialog box. If the selected table was drawn using a starting table style, selecting the **Set as Table in Current Table Style** redefines the starting table. To save modifications made to the table as a new table style, pick the **Save as New Table Style...** option and enter a name for the style in the **Save as New Table Style** dialog box.

NOTE

Table style and direction can also be modified using the **Table Style** and **Direction** drop-down lists available in **Table** section of the **Properties** palette when the table is selected.

Resizing columns and rows

The size of the columns and rows in a table can also be adjusted using the grips boxes shown when a table cell border is selected. Grips are the boxes and arrowheads located at the corners of columns and the table. To resize a column or row, select a grip box, move the cursor, and pick. The arrowhead grips can be used to increase or decrease row height and/or column width uniformly.

The **Size Columns Equally** option sizes all the columns in the table to the same width automatically. The total width of the table is divided evenly among the columns. The **Size Rows Equally** option sizes all the rows in the table to the same height. All rows increase in height to match the height of the tallest row in the table. The overall height and width of the table can also be adjusted by entering values in the **Table width** and **Table height** text boxes in the **Table** section of the **Properties** palette when the table is selected.

PROFESSIONAL TIP

If the height of rows is taller than desired, or if rows are no longer equal height, enter a very small value in the **Table height** text box to return all rows to the smallest height possible based on the margin spacing between cell content and cell borders.

Updating and writing data link changes

The **Update Table Data Links** and **Write Data Links to External Source** options available from the shortcut menu can be used to download and upload data link changes. Pick the **Update Table Data Links** option to update the table to reflect any changes that have been made to the source file, such as the Excel spreadsheet. This is the same function as the **Download Changes from Source File** option available when a cell is selected. Pick the **Write Data Links to External Source** option to update the source file, such as the Excel spreadsheet, to reflect any changes that have been made to the AutoCAD table. This is the same function as the **Upload User Changes to Source File** option available when a cell is selected.

Using table breaks

Long tables may need to be divided into sections in order to fit the table on a sheet. Use the table break function to break a table into separate sections while maintaining a single table object. Table breaking is accessed by picking a cell edge. The table breaking grip is located midway between the sides of the table at the top or the bottom of the table, depending on the table direction. See **Figure 10-45.**

Figure 10-45.
The procedure for breaking, or wrapping, a table into sections.

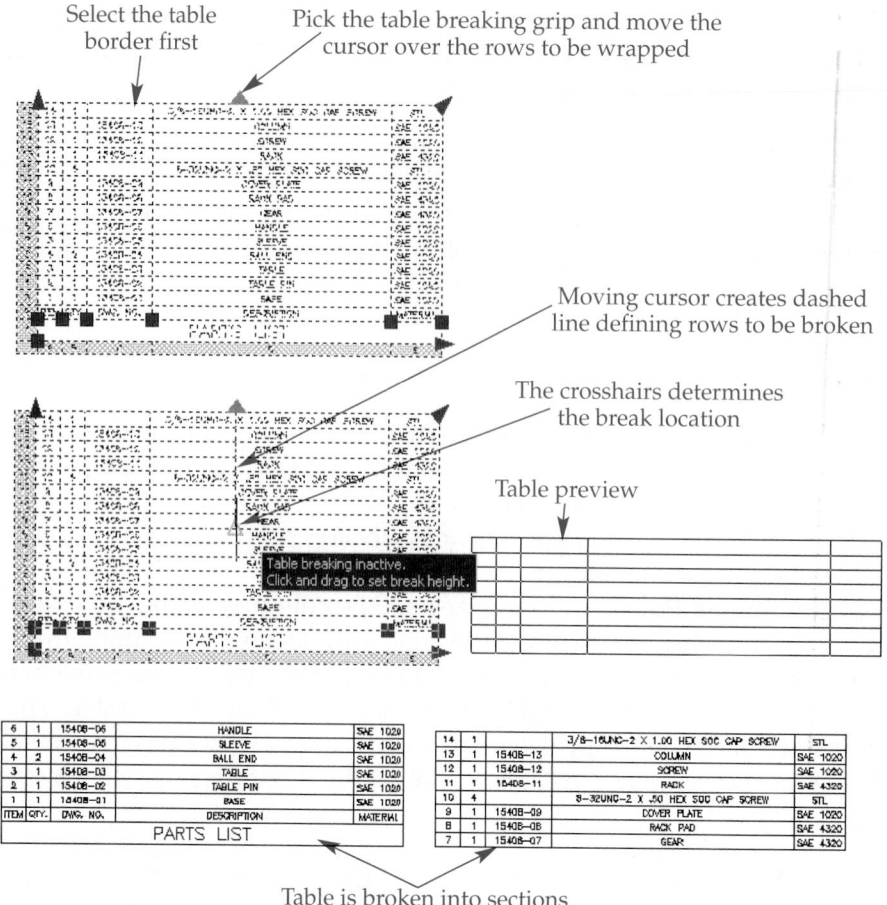

Select the table border first

Pick the table breaking grip and move the cursor over the rows to be wrapped

Moving cursor creates dashed line defining rows to be broken

The crosshairs determines the break location

Table preview

Table breaking inactive.
Click and drag to set break height.

Table is broken into sections

To break a table, first select the table breaking grip. Then move the cursor into the table to display a preview of the table sections and a dashed line with crosshairs. The crosshairs determines the location of the break. The closer to the table title and headers the crosshairs appears, the more sections are created, as reflected in the table preview. When the preview of the table looks correct, pick the location to form the table breaks.

After you add table breaks, several options become available from the **Properties** palette for adjusting the table sections. See **Figure 10-46.** These options are available from the **Table Breaks** section of the **Properties** palette:

- **Enabled.** Toggles between the broken and unbroken table display. Table breaking is enabled and displays **Yes** when the break is created. To return the table to its unbroken display, pick **No**.
- **Direction.** Defines direction of flow, or wrap, when a table is broken. Picking **Right** wraps the table to the right and is the default value; selecting **Left** wraps the table to the left; and picking **Up** wraps the table above. The table in **Figure 10-46** displays the **Left** option.
- **Repeat top labels.** Repeats cells that use a **Label** cell type at the beginning of each table section. Typically, the title cell and header cells use a **Label** cell type. Choose **Yes** to add the title and header cells to the wrapped table sections.
- **Repeat bottom labels.** Repeats cells that use a **Label** cell type at the end of each table section.
- **Manual positions.** Allows you to move table sections independently while maintaining the table as a single object. When **No** is selected, table sections move as a group.

Figure 10-46.
Use the options in the **Table Breaks** portion of the **Properties** palette to adjust the display of tables that have been divided into sections.

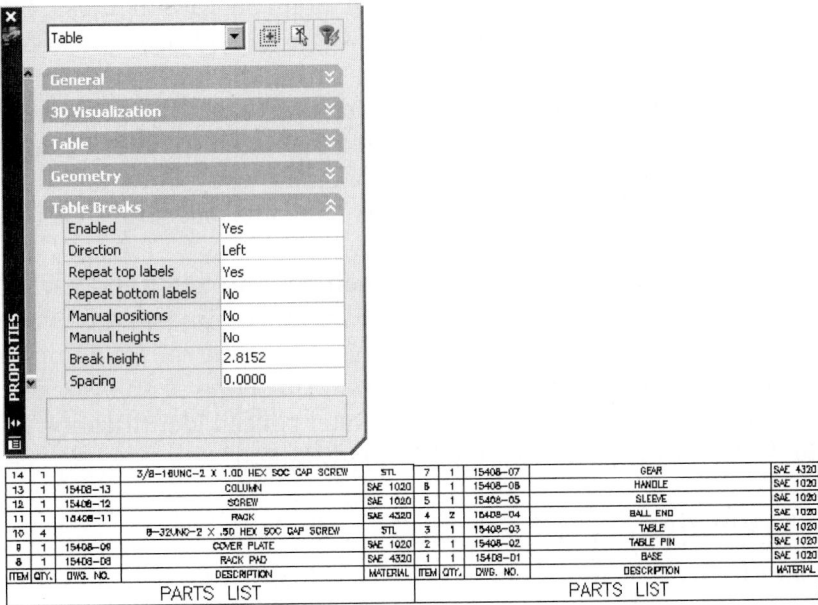

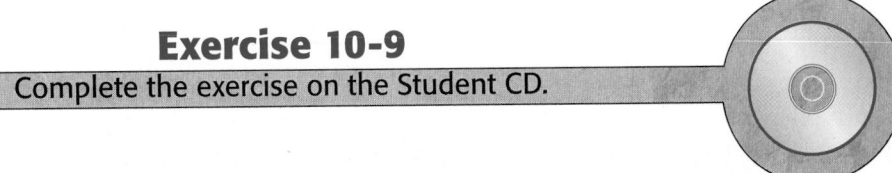

- **Manual height.** Adds a table breaking grip to each table section. This allows you to adjust the number of rows in each table section independently and add additional breaks in each section. When **No** is selected, the table breaking grip is provided at the original table section only and controls the number of breaks.
- **Break height.** Defines the height of each table section. The number of sections is calculated based on the selected height.
- **Spacing.** Defines the spacing between table sections. A value of 0 places the sections together. A table with a spacing of 0 is shown in **Figure 10-46.**

Additional table layout options

The following additional table options are available from the shortcut menu:
- **Remove All Property Overrides.** Restores the table to its original properties, defined according to the selected table style.
- **Export.** Exports the table as a CSV file.
- **Table Indicator Color....** Allows you to change the color of the table indicator shown when you pick inside a cell.

Exercise 10-9
Complete the exercise on the Student CD.

Calculating Values in Tables

It is frequently necessary to perform calculations on data in tables. For example, in a parts list, it is common to add the number of parts and show the total. In a door or window schedule, a total count of the doors or windows is commonly calculated. In a room schedule, square footage is often calculated and listed for various areas. Mathematical expressions called *formulas* can be created in tables to calculate sums and perform other computations. Formulas calculate operations based on numeric data in table cells. AutoCAD allows you to write formulas for sums, averages, counts, and other basic mathematical functions.

formulas:
Mathematical expressions that allow you to perform calculations within table cells.

Table cells are identified in formulas by their column letter and row number. As described earlier in this chapter, the table indicator grid appears when a table cell is being edited. This grid provides a numbering system for the cells. Columns are identified with letters, and rows are identified with numbers. For example, the cell located in Column A and Row 3 is identified as A3. This system of cell identification is illustrated in **Figure 10-47.** In the table shown, cell C6 is highlighted.

Creating Formulas

When you insert a formula into a cell, it evaluates values from other cells and displays the resulting value. Formulas are field objects. As with other types of fields, both the expression and the resulting value are displayed with a gray background. The value can change if values in the corresponding expression change. This enables you to update data in a table cell automatically when you update the data in other cells.

Table cells with existing numeric values are used in writing formulas. For example, you may want to add all of the values in a single column and display the total at the bottom of the column. You can define a formula that evaluates a range of continuous cells or cells that do not share a common border.

In a formula, the common symbols used for mathematical functions are entered as operators in the expression. These basic symbols are shown below:

Symbol	Function
+	Addition
−	Subtraction
*	Multiplication
/	Division
^	Exponentiation

Figure 10-47.
Table cells are identified by column letter and row number. The table indicator grid provides a reference for identifying each cell.

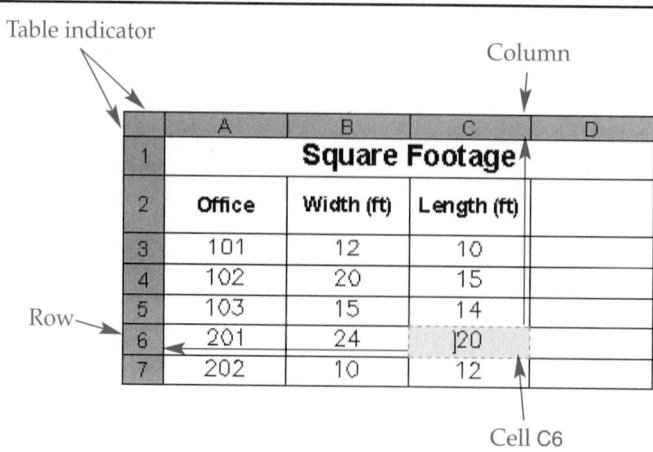

Parentheses are used to enclose expressions for table cell formulas. To perform an operation correctly, the proper syntax must be entered in the table cell. The syntax uses the following conventions:

Entry	Description
=	The equal sign is used to begin an expression. This tells AutoCAD that you want to perform a calculation.
(	An open parenthesis is used to start the expression.
)	A closing parenthesis is used to close the expression.
(*expression*)	Write the expression by typing the cells to be evaluated and the desired operator symbol(s).

A complete expression is shown below. This expression tells AutoCAD to add the value of C3 and the value of D4 and display the sum in the current cell:

=(C3+D4)

Note that when identifying a cell in an expression, you must enter the letter before the number. For example, you cannot enter 3C to designate the cell identified as C3. If you enter an incorrect expression or an expression evaluating cells without numeric data, AutoCAD displays the pound character (#) to indicate the error.

NOTE

Parentheses are not needed in all expressions, but some expressions will not be calculated without them. It is good practice to use parentheses in all expressions.

After entering an expression, press [Enter], pick outside the table, or pick **OK** on the **Table Formatting** toolbar to close the toolbar and save the changes. An example of a multiplication formula is shown in Figure 10-48. The expression =(B3*C3) is entered in cell D3. The resulting value is shown in the cell when [Enter] is pressed.

Grouped expressions can also be used in writing formulas. The expression sets are enclosed in parentheses. Two examples are shown below. The first operation multiplies the sum of E1 and F1 by E2. The second operation multiplies the sum of E1 and F1 by the sum of E2 and F2 and divides the product by G6:

=(E1+F1)*E2
=(E1+F1)*(E2+F2)/G6

Creating sum, average, and count formulas

In addition to entering basic mathematical formulas in table cells manually, you can select from one of AutoCAD's formula types. These formulas can be used to calculate the sum, average, or count of a range of cells. To access the formula options, select a cell, right-click, and then pick **Formula** from the **Insert** cascading submenu of the table cell shortcut menu to display a cascading menu with formula options. You can also access formula options from the **Insert Formula** flyout button of the **Table** toolbar. See Figure 10-49.

The **Sum** option allows you to add the values of a range of cells by specifying a selection window on screen. AutoCAD prompts you to pick the first corner of a window defining the cell range. The range you specify can include cells from several columns and rows. Pick inside the top or bottom cell that you wish to include in the calculation. Then move the cursor and pick inside the lowest or highest cell, making sure that all of the cells to be included in the formula are included in the window selection. See **Figure 10-50**. When the second point is selected, the expression is automatically entered into the cell. In the example shown, the square footage for each office is first calculated in the Sq Ft column on the right in **Figure 10-50A**. The values are then selected for a sum formula that calculates the total square footage of all of the offices, as shown in **Figure 10-50B**.

Notice in **Figure 10-50B** that the resulting expression is =Sum(D3:D7). This formula specifies that the selected cell is equal to the sum of cells D3 through D7. The colon symbol (:) is used to indicate the range of cells for the calculation.

The **Average** and **Count** options are similar to the **Sum** option. The **Average** option creates a formula that calculates the average value of the cells you select. The average is the sum of the selected cells divided by the number of cells selected. The **Count** option

Figure 10-48.
Entering a multiplication formula. A—The expression is typed in the table cell with the correct syntax. B—The resulting value is displayed after the expression is calculated.

	A	B	C	D	
1	**Square Footage**				
2	**Office**	**Width (ft)**	**Length (ft)**	**Sq Ft**	
3	101	12	10	=(B3*C3)	← Expression
4	102	20	15		
5	103	15	14		
6	201	24	20		
7	202	10	12		

A

Square Footage				
Office	**Width (ft)**	**Length (ft)**	**Sq Ft**	
101	12	10	120	← Result
102	20	15		
103	15	14		
201	24	20		
202	10	12		

B

Figure 10-49.
The **Insert** cascading menu from the shortcut menu and **Insert Formula** flyout button of the **Table** toolbar allow you to insert a formula into a cell.

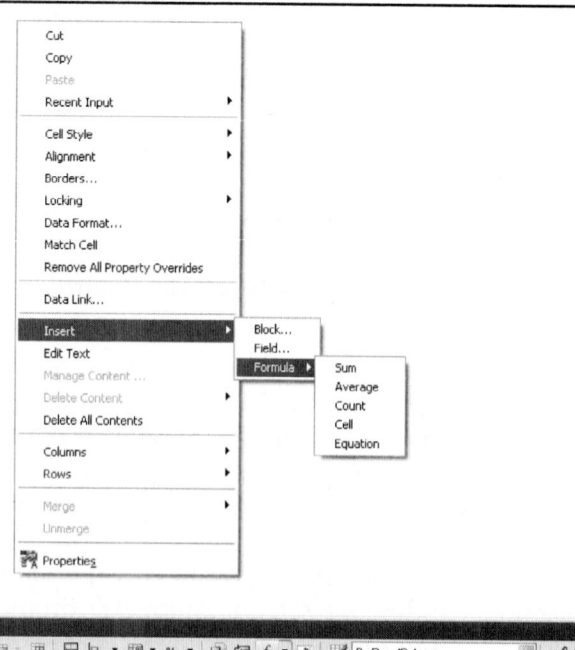

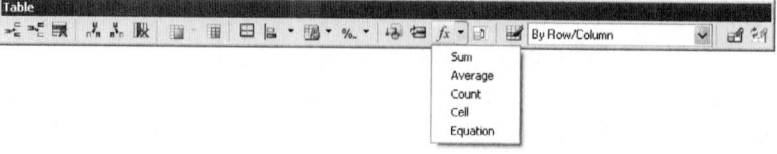

Figure 10-50.
Creating a sum
formula in a table
cell. A—Pick a cell
to hold the formula
and select a range of
cells for the formula
by windowing
around the cells.
B—After the second
point of the window
is picked, the
formula displays in
the cell.

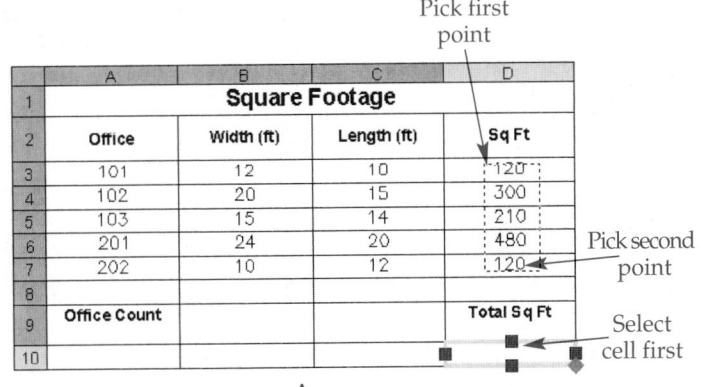

creates a formula that counts the number of selected cells. Only cells that contain a value are included in the count.

Sum, average, and count formulas can be typed directly into a cell without using the **Insert** cascading menu or **Insert Formula** flyout button. If you are calculating a value over a range of cells, use the colon symbol to designate the range. You can also write an expression that evaluates individual cells instead of a range. The cells do not have to share a common border. To write an expression using nonadjacent cells, the comma (,) is used. For example, if cells D1, D3, and D6 need to be averaged, type the following expression:

=Average(D1,D3,D6)

This formula calculates the average of the cell values for cells D1, D3, and D6.

A range of cells and individual cells can be included in the same expression. For example, if cells A1 through B10 need to be counted in addition to cells C4 and C6, enter the following expression:

=Count(A1:B10,C4,C6)

Examples of sum, average, and count formulas are shown in **Figure 10-51.**

NOTE

When using architectural units in a drawing, you can type the foot (′) and inch (″) symbols in table cells for use in values and formulas. When the foot symbol is used for a cell value, a formula in another cell automatically converts the resulting value to inches and feet.

Figure 10-51.
Sum, average, and
count formulas
and their resulting
values.

	A	B	C	D
1	Square Footage			
2	Office	Width (ft)	Length (ft)	Sq Ft
3	101	12	10	120
4	102	20	15	300
5	103	15	14	210
6	201	24	20	480
7	202	10	12	120
8				
9	Office Count	Average Sq Ft Per Room		Total Sq Ft
10	5	246.000000		1230

=Count(A3:A7) =Average(D3:D7) =Sum(D3:D7)

Other formula options

The **Insert** cascading submenu and **Insert Formula** flyout button contain additional options for writing table formulas. The **Cell** option allows you to select a table cell from a different table and insert its contents in the current cell. The cell value can then be used in a new formula. When you select the **Cell** option, AutoCAD prompts you to select the cell. The value of the selected cell is then displayed in the current cell.

The **Equation** option is used to enter an expression manually. Selecting this option places an equal sign (=) in the current cell. You can then type the expression.

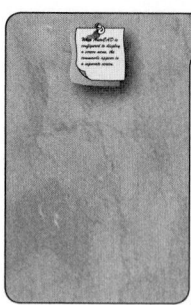

> **NOTE**
>
> You can use the **FIELD** command to insert and edit table cell formulas. Selecting **Formula** from the **Field names** list in the **Field** dialog box displays option buttons for creating sum, average, and count formulas. You can also select a cell value from a different table as a starting point. Table cells are selected on screen to define the formula. The **Formula** text box in the **Field** dialog box can be used to add to or edit the formula. Unit format options are also available.

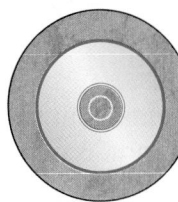

Exercise 10-10
Complete the exercise on the Student CD.

Template Development

Chapter 10

Adding a table style to your drawing templates helps ensure that your drawings have a uniform appearance and follow drafting industry standards. Refer to the Student CD for detailed instructions to add table styles to your mechanical, architectural, and civil drawing templates.

Chapter Test

Answer the following questions. Write your answers on a separate sheet of paper or complete the electronic chapter test on the Student CD.

1. What is a table?
2. Define *table style*.
3. What is the purpose of creating a table style?
4. Briefly describe the procedure for creating a table style based on an existing table style.
5. How can you quickly make a table style current?
6. By default, what two types of rows are at the top of a table when it is inserted?
7. What does the **Alignment** setting in the **New Table Style** dialog box do?
8. Which setting would you adjust in the **New Table Style** dialog box to increase the spacing between the text and the top of the cell?
9. How can creating a new table using a starting table style save time?
10. List three ways to open the **Insert Table** dialog box.
11. Describe the two ways to insert a table and explain how the methods differ.
12. By default, what toolbar opens after a table has been inserted?
13. If you are finished typing in one cell and want to move to the next cell in the same row, what two keyboard keys can you use?
14. How are table cells identified in formulas?
15. How can existing data in a Microsoft® Excel spreadsheet file be used to create an AutoCAD table?
16. Define *object linking*.
17. What AutoCAD wizard allows you to reuse data and attributes that already exists in the drawing to create a table?
18. List two ways to make a cell active for editing.
19. Explain how to insert a block into a table cell.
20. How do you insert a new row at the bottom of a table?
21. Give the table cell formula that adds the value of C3 plus the value of D4.
22. What is the function of the colon symbol (:) in the formula =Sum(D3:D7)?
23. What is the difference between a sum formula and a count formula?
24. Explain how to write a formula that calculates a function for cells that do not share common borders.
25. Give the table cell formula that averages the values of cells D1, D3, and D6.

Drawing Problems

For each of the following problems, use one of your templates or start a new drawing using your own setup option.

1. Create a parts list for a mechanical drawing with the content of your choice, or locate a drawing with a parts list and make a similar drawing. Save the drawing as P10-1.

2. Create a door and window schedule for an architectural drawing with the content of your choice, or locate a drawing with a door and window schedule and make a similar drawing. Save the drawing as P10-2.

3. Create a legend for a civil drawing with the content of your choice, or locate a drawing with a legend and make a similar drawing. Save the drawing as P10-3.

4. Create a parts list for a mechanical drawing with the content of your choice, or locate a drawing with a parts list and make a similar drawing. Save the drawing as P10-4.

5. Create the door schedule shown below. Make the measurements for the rows and columns approximately the same as in the given table. Save the drawing as P10-5.

DOOR SCHEDULE

SYM.	SIZE	TYPE	QTY.
1	36x80	S.C. RP. METAL INSULATED	1
2	36x80	S.C. FLUSH METAL INSULATED	2
3	32x80	S.C. SELF CLOSING	2
4	32x80	HOLLOW CORE	5
5	30x80	HOLLOW CORE	5
6	30x80	POCKET SLDG.	2

6. Create the window schedule shown below. Make the measurements for the rows and columns approximately the same as in the given table. Save the drawing as P10-6.

WINDOW SCHEDULE

SYM.	SIZE	MODEL	ROUGH OPEN	QTY.
A	12x60	JOB BUILT	VERIFY	2
B	96x60	W4N5 CSM.	8'-0 3/4" x 5'-0 7/8"	1
C	48x60	W2N5 CSM.	4'-0 3/4" x 5'-0 7/8"	2
D	48x36	W2N3 CSM.	4'-0 3/4" x 3'-6 1/2"	2
E	42x42	2N3 CSM.	3'-6 1/2" x 3'-6 1/2"	2
F	72x48	G64 SLDG.	6'-0 1/2" x 4'-0 1/2"	1
G	60x42	G536 SLDG.	5'-0 1/2" x 3'-6 1/2"	4
H	48x42	G436 SLDG.	4'-0 1/2" x 3'-6 1/2"	1
J	48x24	A41 AWN.	4'-0 1/2" x 2'-0 7/8"	3

7. Create the interior finish schedule shown below. Make the measurements for the rows and columns approximately the same as in the given table. Save the drawing as P10-7.

INTERIOR FINISH SCHEDULE

ROOM	FLOOR					WALLS				CEILING		
	VINYL	CARPET	TILE	HARDWOOD	CONCRETE	PAINT	PAPER	TEXTURE	SPRAY	SMOOTH	BROCADE	PAINT
ENTRY					•							
FOYER			•			•			•			•
KITCHEN			•				•			•		•
DINING				•		•			•		•	•
FAMILY		•				•			•		•	•
LIVING		•				•		•			•	•
MSTR. BATH			•			•				•		•
BATH #2			•			•			•	•		•
MSTR. BED		•				•					•	•
BED #2		•				•			•		•	•
BED #3		•				•			•		•	•
UTILITY	•					•			•	•		•

8. Create the parts list shown below. Make the measurements for the rows and columns approximately the same as in the given table. Save the drawing as P10-8.

	1	CAPS	1/2−12 UNC HEX NUT	210014−29
	1	CAPS	1/2 FLAT WASHER	320014−33
	2	CAPS	7/16 EXTERNAL SNAP RING	632043−43
	2	CAPS	1/4−20 UNC WING NUT	255010−41
	2	CAPS	3/4X1/4−20 UNC BOLT	803010−11
KEY	QTY	NAME	DESCRIPTION	PART NO.

PARTS LIST

9. Create the table shown below. Make the measurements for the rows and columns approximately the same as in the given table. Save the drawing as P10-9.

REFERENCE DESIGNATIONS

LAST USED	DATE
R9	8/30/2008
C1	8/31/2008
CRS	9/1/2008
Q2	9/2/2008

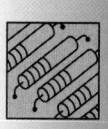

Drawing Problems – Chapter 10

10. Create the door schedule shown below. Make the measurements for the rows and columns approximately the same as in the given table. Save the drawing as P10-10.

DOOR SCHEDULE				DOOR SCHEDULE			
SYMBOL	SIZE	MODEL	QUANTITY	SYMBOL	SIZE	MODEL	QUANTITY
1	3'-0" X 6'-8"	S.C. R.P. METAL INSULATED	1	11	4'-0" X 6'-8"	BI-FOLD	1
2	3'-0" X 6'-8"	S.C.-FLUSH-METAL INSULATED	2	12	2'-0" X 6'-0"	SHATTER PROOF	1
3	2'-8" X 6'-8"	S.C.-SELF CLOSING	2	13	6'-0" X 6'-8"	WOOD FRAME-TEMP. SLDG GL.	1
4	2'-8" X 6'-8"	H.C.	5	14	9'-0" X 7'-0"	OVERHEAD GARAGE	2
5	2'-6" X 6'-8"	H.C.	3				
6	2'-6" X 6'-8"	POCKET	2				
7	2'-4" X 6'-8"	POCKET	1				
9	5'-0" X 6'-0"	BI-PASS	2				
10	3'-0" X 6'-8"	BI-FOLD	1				

Editing Using Modifying Tools

Learning Objectives

After completing this chapter, you will be able to do the following:

✓ Use the **FILLET** command to draw fillets, rounds, and other rounded corners.
✓ Draw chamfers and angled corners with the **CHAMFER** command.
✓ Remove portions of lines, circles, and arcs using the **BREAK** command.
✓ Use the **TRIM** and **EXTEND** commands to edit the length of objects.
✓ Relocate objects using the **MOVE** command.
✓ Make single and multiple copies of existing objects using the **COPY** command.
✓ Change the angular positions of objects using the **ROTATE** command.
✓ Use the **ALIGN** command to simultaneously move and rotate objects.
✓ Draw mirror images of objects using the **MIRROR** command.
✓ Create arrangements of objects using the **ARRAY** command.
✓ Change the size of objects using the **SCALE** command.
✓ Modify the length, height, and width of objects using the **STRETCH** and **LENGTHEN** commands.
✓ Combine objects using the **JOIN** command.
✓ Use selection set filters using the **Quick Select** dialog box.
✓ Create object groups using the **GROUP** command.

This chapter explains commands and methods for changing a drawing using AutoCAD's modification tools. You will learn various commands and selection set options that can be used to increase drawing efficiency. These tools are found in the **Draw** control panel of the **Dashboard**, the **Modify** toolbar, and the **Modify** pull-down menu.

NOTE

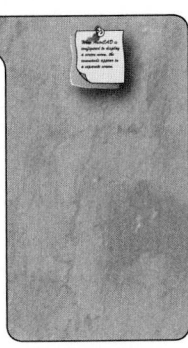

The editing commands described in this chapter include many options. When you access a command, its options can be accessed by right-clicking and selecting the option from the shortcut menu, by pressing the down arrow key with dynamic input and picking the option, or by typing the first letter of the option (typically) and pressing [Enter]. As you work through this chapter, experiment with each type of option selection method to see which is the most effective in different situations.

Drawing Rounded Corners

In mechanical drafting, an inside rounded corner is called a *fillet*. An outside rounded corner is called a *round*. AutoCAD refers to all rounded corners as fillets.

Fillets were introduced in Chapter 4 as a corner option on rectangles created with the **RECTANG** command. The **FILLET** command draws a rounded corner between intersecting and nonintersecting lines, circles, and arcs. To access the **FILLET** command, pick the **Fillet** button on the **2D Draw** control panel of the **Dashboard** or the **Modify** toolbar, select **Modify > Fillet**, or type F or FILLET. See **Figure 11-1**.

fillet: An inside rounded corner.

round: An outside rounded corner.

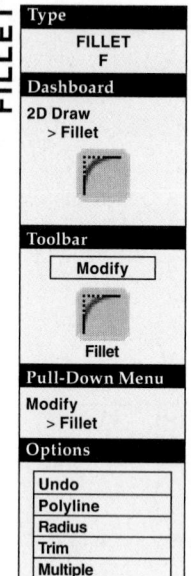

FILLET

Type
FILLET
F

Dashboard
2D Draw
> Fillet

Toolbar
Modify

Fillet

Pull-Down Menu
Modify
> Fillet

Options
Undo
Polyline
Radius
Trim
Multiple

Setting the Fillet Radius

The size of a fillet is determined by the fillet radius. You must set this value before selecting the corner to be filleted. After initiating the **FILLET** command, type R to access the **Radius** option, and enter the fillet radius dimension. You can then select the objects to be filleted.

> **NOTE**
>
> The value of the radius for fillets is stored in the **FILLETRAD** system variable. This variable is changed when you enter a new value using the **Radius** option of the **FILLET** command.

Exercise 11-1
Complete the exercise on the Student CD.

Filleting Square Corners

When the fillet radius is set to zero, you can use the **FILLET** command to join two lines. You can also create a zero-radius fillet without setting the radius to zero by holding down the [Shift] key when you pick the second line. This is a convenient way to join objects at a corner.

Rounding the Corners of a Polyline

polyline: A series of lines and arcs that constitute a single object.

Polylines are objects that can be made up of many different widths and shapes. They are described further in Chapter 13. Fillets can be drawn at all corners of a closed polyline by selecting the **Polyline** option. The current fillet radius is used with this option. See **Figure 11-2**.

Figure 11-1.
Using the **FILLET** command.

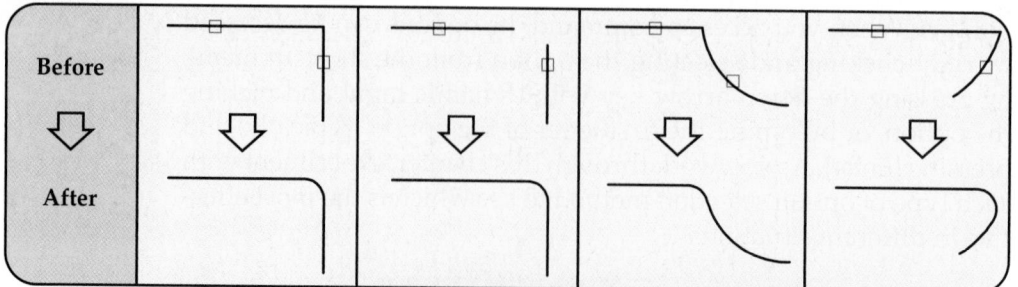

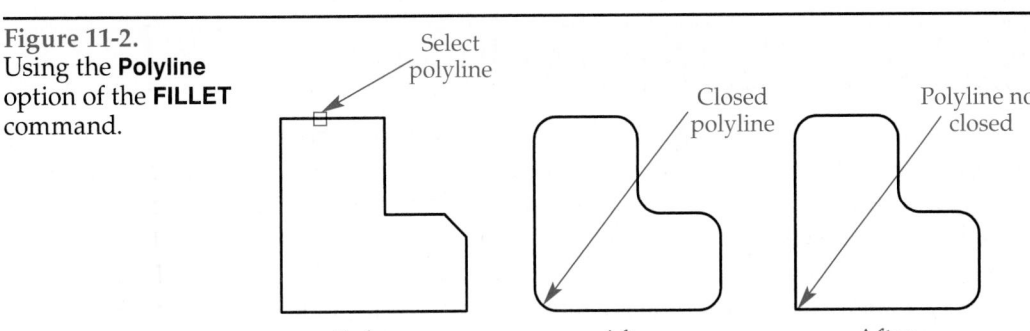

Figure 11-2.
Using the **Polyline** option of the **FILLET** command.

Select polyline

Closed polyline

Polyline not closed

Before   After   After

AutoCAD tells you how many lines were filleted. If the polyline was drawn without using the **Close** option, the beginning corner is not filleted.

Setting the Fillet Trim Mode

The **Trim** option and the **TRIMMODE** system variable control whether or not the **FILLET** command trims object segments that extend beyond the fillet radius point. When the **Trim** mode is active, objects are trimmed. When **Trim** is inactive, the filleted objects are not changed when the fillet is inserted, as shown in **Figure 11-3**.

You can also use the **TRIMMODE** system variable to set **Trim** or **No trim** by typing TRIMMODE. A setting of 1 trims the lines before chamfering, while 0 does not trim the lines.

Filleting Parallel Lines

You can also draw a fillet between parallel lines. When parallel lines are selected, a radius is placed between the two lines. With **Trim** mode active, a longer line is trimmed to match the length of a shorter line. The radius of a fillet between parallel lines is always half the distance between the two lines, regardless of the radius setting for the **FILLET** command.

Making Multiple Fillets

To make several fillets on the same object, select the **Multiple** option of the **FILLET** command. The prompt for a first object repeats. When you have made all the fillets needed, press [Enter] or [Esc]. When in **Multiple** mode, use the **Undo** option to discard the previous fillet.

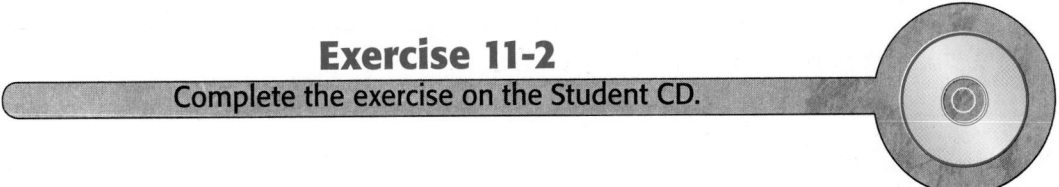

Exercise 11-2
Complete the exercise on the Student CD.

Figure 11-3.
Comparison of the **Trim** and **No trim** options of the **FILLET** command.

Before Fillet	Fillet with Trim	Fillet with No Trim

chamfer: In mechanical drafting, a small angled surface used to relieve a sharp corner.

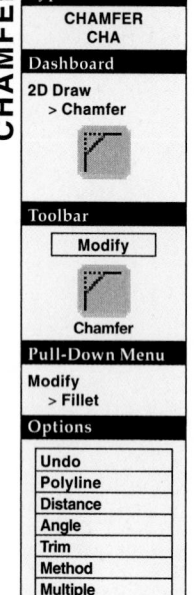

AutoCAD defines a *chamfer* as "any angled corner on the drawing." Chamfers are drawn between two lines that may or may not intersect. Chamfers can also connect polylines, xlines, and rays. A chamfer's distance from the corner determines its size. A 45° chamfer is the same distance from the corner in each direction. See Figure 11-4.

Selecting the **Chamfer** button in the **2D Draw** control panel of the **Dashboard** or the **Modify** toolbar, picking **Modify > Chamfer**, or typing CHA or CHAMFER accesses the **CHAMFER** command. The current settings are displayed for your reference. Chamfers are defined by two distances or by one distance and an angle. The defaults are zero units for the lengths and the angle. A value of .5 for both distances produces a 45° × 0.5 chamfered corner.

Setting the Chamfer Distances

The chamfer distances must be set before you can draw a chamfer. The distances you set remain in effect until changed. The chamfer distances are usually exact values, but you can pick two points to set each distance. To set the chamfer distance, initiate the **CHAMFER** command, type D, and press [Enter]. After entering each distance, select the two lines to be chamfered. AutoCAD automatically chamfers the corner. If you want to chamfer additional corners, press [Enter] to repeat the **CHAMFER** command. The results of several chamfering operations are shown in Figure 11-5.

If the specified chamfer distance is so large that the chamfered objects disappear, AutoCAD does not perform the chamfer. Instead, a message, such as Distance is too large *Invalid*, is given.

> **NOTE**
>
> For the distance method, the first and second chamfer distance values are stored in system variables. The first chamfer distance is stored in the **CHAMFERA** system variable. The second distance is stored in the **CHAMFERB** system variable.

Chamfering Square Corners

When the chamfer distances are set to zero, you can use the **CHAMFER** command to join two lines. You can also create a zero-distance chamfer without setting the distance to zero by holding the [Shift] key when you pick the second line. This is a convenient way to join objects at a corner.

Figure 11-4.
Examples of chamfers.

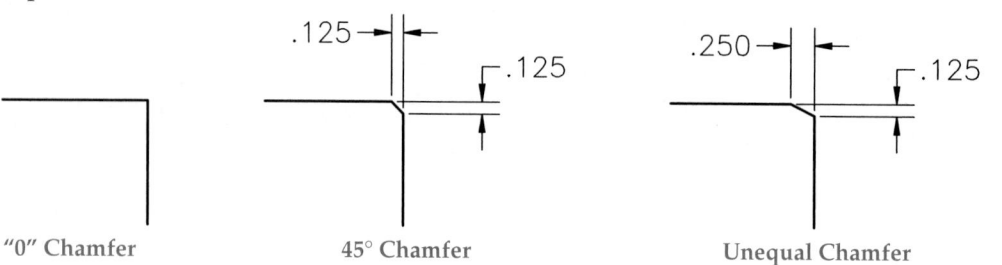

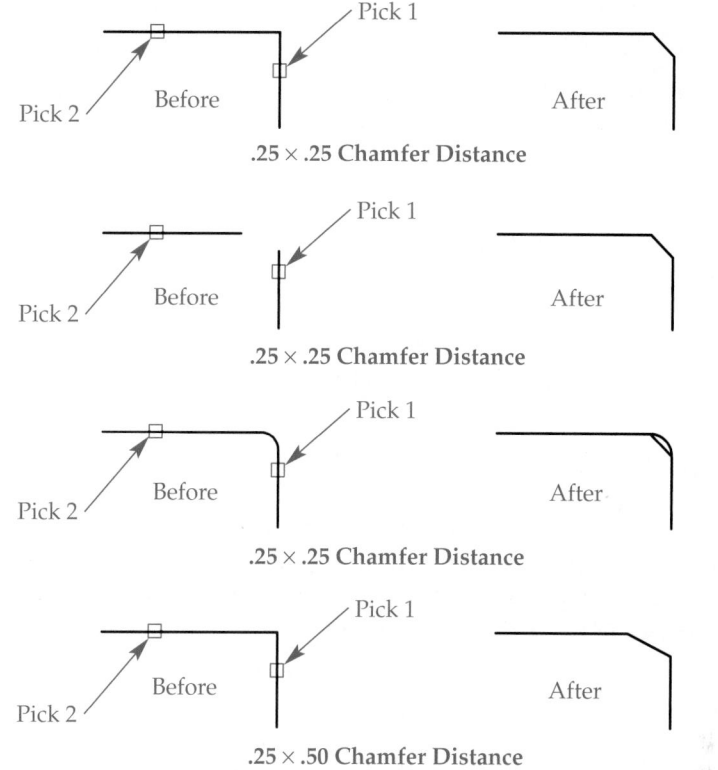

Figure 11-5.
Using the **CHAMFER** command.

Pick 1

Pick 2   Before   After

.25 × .25 Chamfer Distance

Pick 1

Pick 2   Before   After

.25 × .25 Chamfer Distance

Pick 1

Pick 2   Before   After

.25 × .25 Chamfer Distance

Pick 1

Pick 2   Before   After

.25 × .50 Chamfer Distance

Chamfering the Corners of a Polyline

All eligible corners of a closed polyline can be chamfered at one time using the **Polyline** option of the **CHAMFER** command. The term *eligible* means the chamfer distance is small enough to work on the corner. To chamfer all the corners of a polyline, select the **Polyline** option and then select the polyline. The corners of the polyline are chamfered to the distance values set. If the polyline was drawn without using the **Close** option, the beginning corner is not chamfered, as shown in **Figure 11-6**.

Setting the Chamfer Angle

Instead of setting two chamfer distances, you can set the chamfer distance for one line and set an angle to determine the chamfer to the second line. See **Figure 11-7**. To do this, start the **CHAMFER** command and use the **Angle** option. After entering the distance and angle, select the two lines to be chamfered. AutoCAD automatically chamfers the corner.

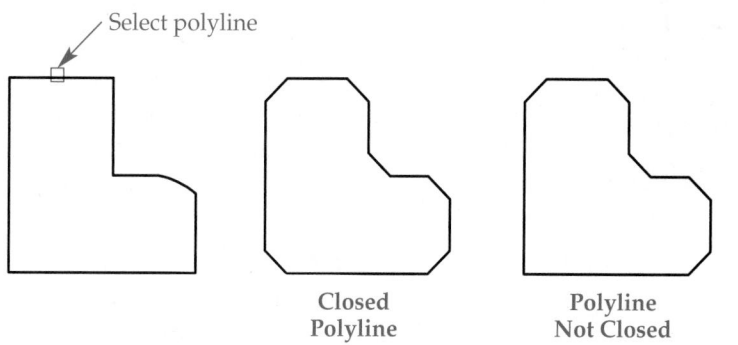

Figure 11-6.
Using the **Polyline** option of the **CHAMFER** command.

Select polyline

Closed
Polyline

Polyline
Not Closed

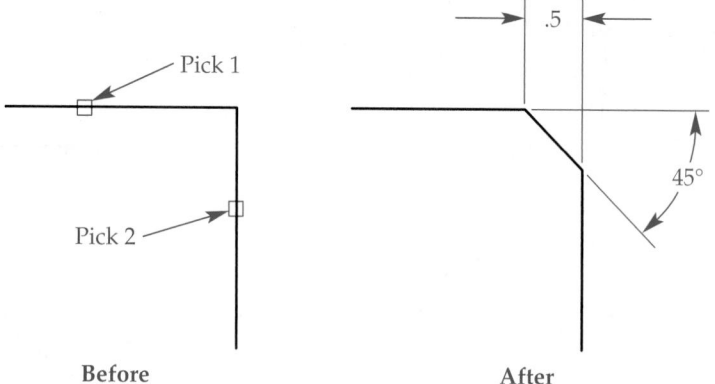

Figure 11-7.
Using the **Angle** option of the **CHAMFER** command with the chamfer length set at .5 and the angle set at 45°.

Pick 1

Pick 2

.5

45°

Before

After

NOTE

For the angle method, the chamfer distance and angle values are stored in system variables. The chamfer distance is stored in the **CHAMFERC** system variable. The angle is stored in the **CHAMFERD** system variable.

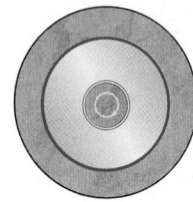

Exercise 11-3
Complete the exercise on the Student CD.

Setting the Chamfer Method

When you set chamfer distances or a distance and an angle, AutoCAD maintains the setting until you change it. You can set the values for each method without affecting the other. Use the **Method** option if you want to toggle between drawing chamfers using the **Distance** and **Angle** options.

Setting the Chamfer Trim Mode

You can have the selected lines automatically trimmed with the chamfer, or you can have the selected lines remain in the drawing after the chamfer, as shown in Figure 11-8. To set this, enter the **Trim** option, and then select either T for **Trim** or N for **No trim**.

NOTE

The **TRIMMODE** system variable affects both the **FILLET** and **CHAMFER** commands. If the **Polyline** option of either command is used with the **No trim** option active, any chamfer or fillet lines created are not part of the polyline.

When the **CHAMFER** or **FILLET** command is set to **Trim**, lines not connecting at a corner are automatically extended, and the chamfer or fillet is applied. When the **No trim** option is used, the lines are not extended, but the chamfer or fillet is drawn anyway. If you have lines drawn short of a corner and you want them to connect to the chamfer or fillet, use the **Trim** option to avoid the need to extend the lines to meet the chamfer or fillet.

AutoCAD and Its Applications—Basics

Figure 11-8.
Comparison of
the **Trim** and **No
trim** options of
the **CHAMFER**
command.

Before Chamfer	Chamfer with Trim	Chamfer with No Trim
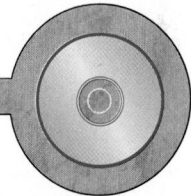		

PROFESSIONAL TIP

Objects can be chamfered even when the corners do not meet. AutoCAD extends the lines as required to generate the specified chamfer and complete the corner if **Trim** mode is on. If **Trim** mode is off, AutoCAD does not extend the lines to complete the corner.

Making Multiple Chamfers

To make several chamfers on the same object, select the **Multiple** option of the **CHAMFER** command. The prompt for a first line repeats. When you have made all the chamfers needed, press [Enter] or [Esc]. When you use the **Multiple** option, you can undo the previous chamfer by typing U for **Undo**.

Exercise 11-4
Complete the exercise on the Student CD.

Removing a Section from an Object

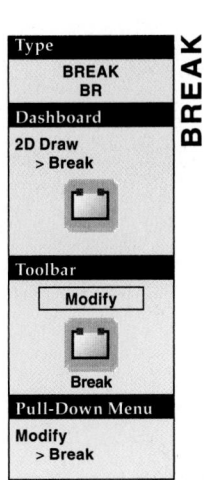

The **BREAK** command is used to remove a portion of an object. This command can also be used to divide a single object into two objects. Picking the **Break** button in the **2D Draw** control panel of the **Dashboard** or the **Modify** toolbar, picking **Modify > Break**, or typing BR or BREAK accesses the **BREAK** command.

The **BREAK** command requires you to select the object to be broken, the first break point, and the second break point. When you select the object, the point you pick is also used as the first break point by default. If you wish to select a different first break point, type F at the Specify second break point or [First point]: prompt to select the **First point** option. After both break points are specified, the part of the object between the two points is deleted. See **Figure 11-9.**

Figure 11-9.
Using the **BREAK** command to break an object. The first pick can be used to select both the object and the first break point.

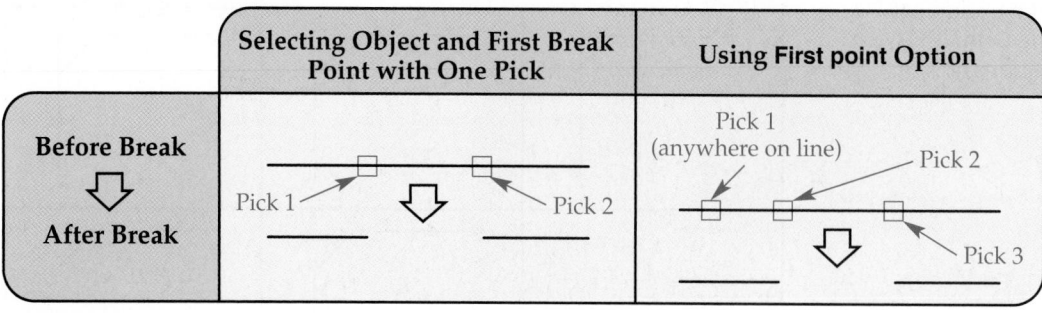

	Selecting Object and First Break Point with One Pick	Using **First point** Option
Before Break ⇩ **After Break**	Pick 1 → ⇩ ← Pick 2	Pick 1 (anywhere on line) — Pick 2 — Pick 3 ⇩

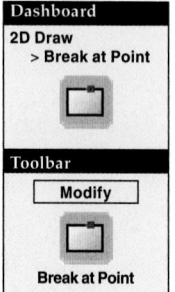

Dashboard
2D Draw
> Break at Point

Toolbar
Modify
Break at Point

If you select the same point for both the first and second break points, the **BREAK** command splits the object into two pieces without removing a portion. This can be accomplished by entering @ at the Specify second break point or [First point]: prompt. The @ symbol repeats the coordinates of the previously selected point. You can also pick the **Break at Point** button in the **2D Draw** control panel of the **Dashboard** or on the **Modify** toolbar to break an object at a single point with a single pick. Using the **BREAK** command without removing a portion of the object is shown in **Figure 11-10.**

When breaking arcs or circles, always work in a counterclockwise direction. Otherwise, you may break the portion of the arc or circle you want to keep. If you want to break off the end of a line or an arc, pick the first point on the object. Pick the second point slightly beyond the end to be cut off. See **Figure 11-11.** When you pick a second point not on the object, AutoCAD selects the point on the object nearest the point you picked.

PROFESSIONAL TIP

You may want to turn running object snaps off if they conflict with the points you are trying to pick when using the **BREAK** command. Picking the **OSNAP** button on the status bar is an easy way to deactivate the running object snaps.

Exercise 11-5
Complete the exercise on the Student CD.

Figure 11-10.
Using the **BREAK** command to break an object at a single point without removing any of the object. Select the same point as the first and second break points, or use the **Break at Point** button.

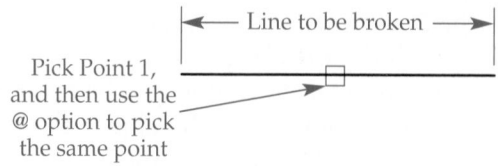

Line to be broken

Pick Point 1, and then use the @ option to pick the same point

Two lines created at break point

Break point

AutoCAD and Its Applications—Basics

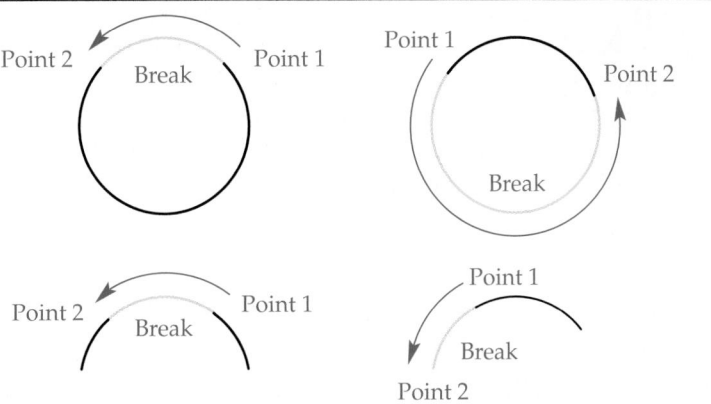

Figure 11-11.
Work counterclockwise when using the **BREAK** command on circles and arcs.

Trimming Objects

The **TRIM** command cuts lines, polylines, circles, arcs, ellipses, splines, xlines, and rays that extend beyond a desired point of intersection. To access the **TRIM** command, pick the **Trim** button in the **Draw** control panel of the **Dashboard** or the **Modify** toolbar, pick **Modify > Trim**, or type TR or TRIM.

The **TRIM** command requires you to pick a cutting edge and the object(s) to trim. The *cutting edge* can be an object such as a line, an arc, or text defining the point at which the object you are trimming will be cut. If two corners of an object overrun, select two cutting edges and two objects. Refer to **Figure 11-12** as you go through the following sequence:

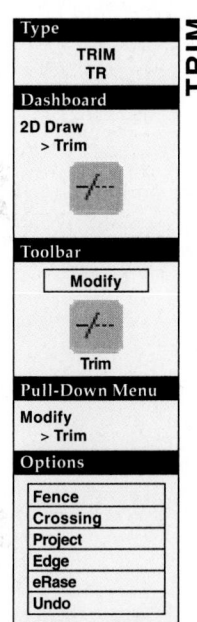

Command: **TR** *or* **TRIM**↵
Current settings: Projection=UCS, Edge=*current*
Select cutting edges …
Select objects or <select all>: *(pick the first cutting edge)*
1 found
Select objects: *(pick second cutting edge)*
1 found, 2 total
Select objects: ↵
Select object to trim or shift-select to extend or [Fence/Crossing/Project/Edge/
    eRase/Undo]: *(pick the first object to trim)*
Select object to trim or shift-select to extend or [Fence/Crossing/Project/Edge/
    eRase/Undo]: *(pick the second object to trim)*
Select object to trim or shift-select to extend or [Fence/Crossing/Project/Edge/
    eRase/Undo]: ↵
Command:

cutting edge:
The edge to which AutoCAD trims objects in a **TRIM** operation.

Figure 11-12.
Using the **TRIM** command. Note the cutting edges.

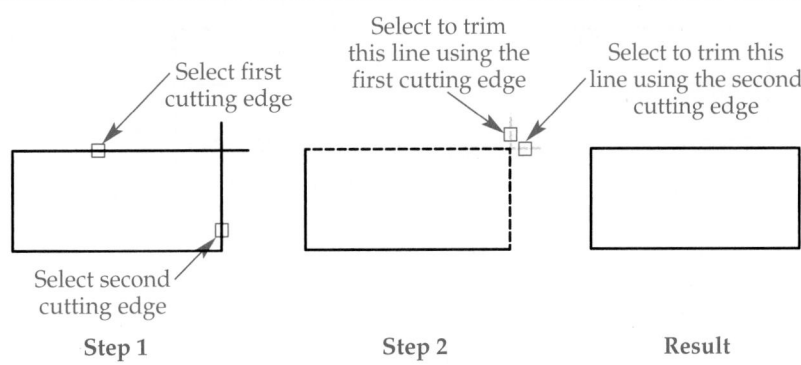

Select first cutting edge

Select to trim this line using the first cutting edge

Select to trim this line using the second cutting edge

Select second cutting edge

Step 1　　　　　　Step 2　　　　　　Result

Trimming without Selecting a Cutting Edge

You can quickly trim objects back to the nearest intersection by pressing the [Enter] key at the first Select objects or <select all>: prompt instead of picking a cutting edge. Picking an object that intersects with another object trims the selected object to the first object. If multiple objects intersect the object to be trimmed, it is trimmed back to the first intersection. After trimming an object, you can select other objects to be trimmed without having to restart the command. When you are done trimming, press the [Enter] key to exit the command.

Trim Selection Options

When multiple lines need to be trimmed, the **Fence** option can be used to draw a temporary cutting edge. Using this option is just like drawing a line. Any objects the fence line crosses are trimmed back to the cutting edge. See Figure 11-13.

The **Crossing** option allows you to select objects to be trimmed using a crossing box. This works similarly to the **Fence** option. After the objects have been selected as the cutting edges, you are prompted to specify a first corner and a second corner. Any lines crossing any of the four lines that make up the crossing window are trimmed back to the cutting edge. See Figure 11-14.

Figure 11-13.
The **Fence** option can be used to make selections around objects. In this case, the **RECTANG** command was used to create the rectangle, so the cutting edge consists of the entire rectangle.

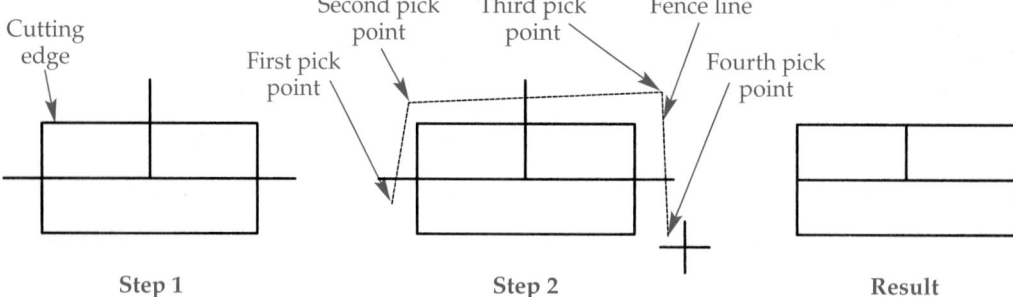

Figure 11-14.
The only objects trimmed with the **Crossing** option are those that cross the edges of the crossing window.

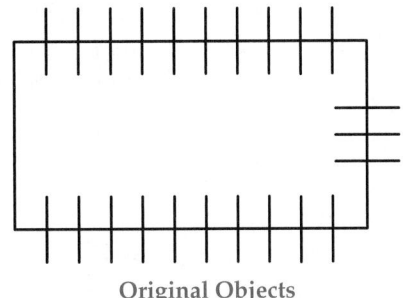

Original Objects

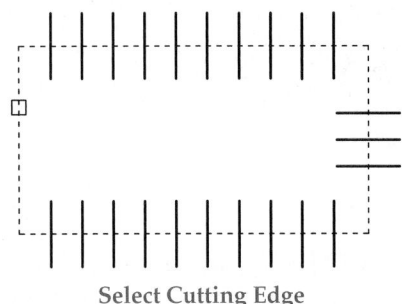

Select Cutting Edge

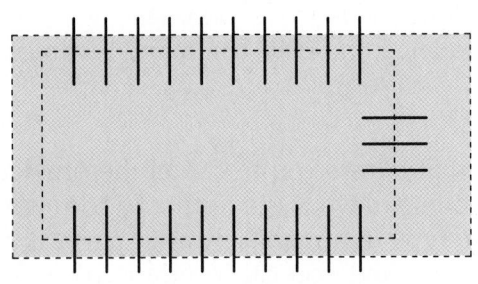

Pick Corners of Crossing Box

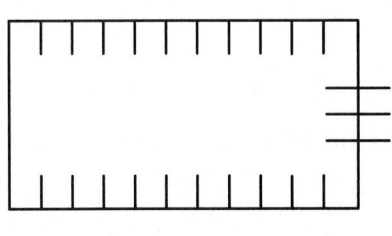

Objects Trimmed

Trimming to an Implied Intersection

An *implied intersection* is the point where two or more objects would meet if they were extended. Trimming to an implied intersection is possible using the **Edge** option of the **TRIM** command. When you enter the **Edge** option, the choices are **Extend** and **No extend**. When **Extend** is active, AutoCAD checks to see if the object selected as the cutting edge will extend to intersect the object to be trimmed. If so, the implied intersection point can be used to trim the object. This does not change the cutting edge object at all. The command sequence for setting **Extend** mode and performing the **TRIM** operation shown in **Figure 11-15** is as follows:

implied intersection: The point at which objects would meet if they were extended.

```
Command: TR or TRIM↵
Current settings: Projection=UCS, Edge=current
Select cutting edges …
Select objects or <select all>: (pick the cutting edge)
1 found
Select objects: ↵
Select object to trim or shift-select to extend or [Fence/Crossing/Project/Edge/
    eRase/Undo]: E↵
Enter an implied edge extension mode [Extend/No extend] <current>: E↵
Select object to trim or shift-select to extend or [Fence/Crossing/Project/Edge/
    eRase/Undo]: (pick the object to trim)
Select object to trim or shift-select to extend or [Fence/Crossing/Project/Edge/
    eRase/Undo]: ↵
Command:
```

The **Edge** option can also be set using the **EDGEMODE** system variable. The **EDGEMODE** settings are 1 (**Extend** mode) and 0 (**No extend** mode). This setting affects both the **TRIM** and **EXTEND** commands.

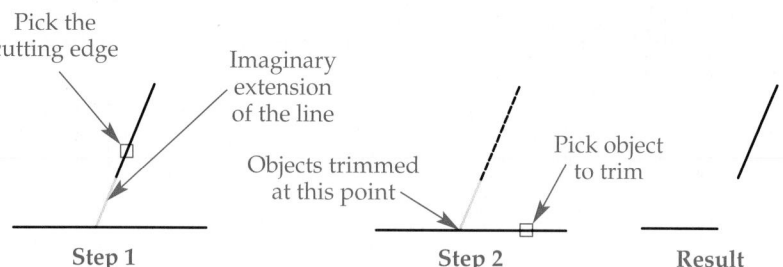

Figure 11-15.
Trimming to an implied intersection is possible when **Extend** mode is active.

Pick the cutting edge

Imaginary extension of the line

Objects trimmed at this point

Pick object to trim

Step 1 · · · · · Step 2 · · · · · Result

Using the Erase Option

While trimming objects, you may have some unneeded objects left over. Sometimes construction lines are used as trimming edges or boundaries and need to be erased after the trimming operation. While the **TRIM** command is active, the **eRase** option can be used to delete objects. After the objects are deleted, the **TRIM** command resumes.

Using the Undo Option

The **TRIM** command has an **Undo** option that allows you to cancel the previous trimming without leaving the command. This is useful when the result of a trim is not what you expected. To undo the previous trim, type U immediately after performing an unwanted trim. The trimmed portion returns, and you can continue trimming other objects.

Introduction to the Project Option

In a 3D drawing environment, some lines may not intersect, even though they appear to intersect from a certain viewpoint. In such a case, using the **Project** option of the **TRIM** command can allow trimming operations. Using AutoCAD for 3D drawing is explained in *AutoCAD and Its Applications—Advanced.*

Extending Lines

boundary edge: The edge to which objects are extended in an **EXTEND** operation.

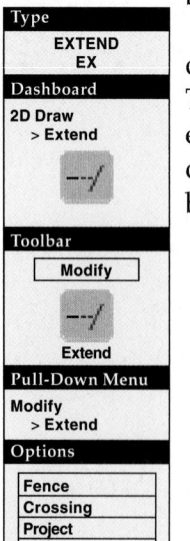

The **EXTEND** command is used to lengthen lines, elliptical arcs, rays, open polylines, and arcs to meet other objects. **EXTEND** does not work on closed polylines because an unconnected endpoint does not exist.

To use the **EXTEND** command, pick the **Extend** button in the **2D Draw** control panel of the **Dashboard** or the **Modify** toolbar, select **Modify > Extend**, or type EX or EXTEND. The command format is similar to that for **TRIM**, but you are asked to select boundary edges, as opposed to cutting edges. *Boundary edges* are objects, such as lines, arcs, or text, to which the selected objects are extended. The command sequence is shown below and illustrated in **Figure 11-16:**

Command: **EX** *or* **EXTEND**↵
Current settings: Projection=UCS, Edge=*current*
Select boundary edges …
Select objects or <select all>: *(pick the boundary edge)*
1 found
Select objects: ↵
Select object to extend or shift-select to trim or [Fence/Crossing/Project/Edge/
     Undo]: *(pick the object to extend)*
Select object to extend or shift-select to trim or [Fence/Crossing/Project/Edge/
     Undo]: ↵
Command:

AutoCAD and Its Applications—Basics

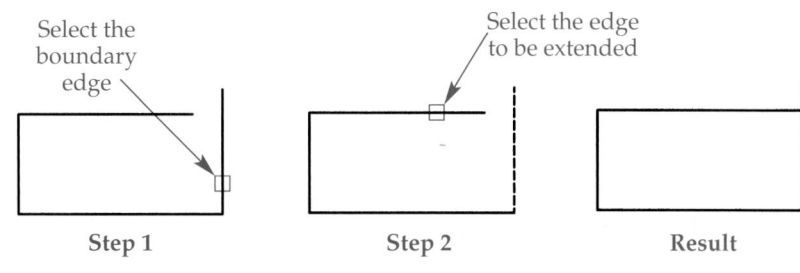

Figure 11-16.
Using the **EXTEND** command. Note the boundary edges.

Select the boundary edge

Select the edge to be extended

Step 1

Step 2

Result

If there is nothing for the selected line to meet, AutoCAD gives the message Object does not intersect an edge.

NOTE

You can access the **TRIM** command while using the **EXTEND** command. After selecting the boundary edge, hold the [Shift] key while selecting an object to trim the object at the boundary edge.

Extending without Selecting a Boundary Edge

You can quickly extend objects to the nearest object by pressing the [Enter] key at the first Select objects or <select all>: prompt, instead of picking a boundary edge. This selects all of the objects in the drawing as boundary edges. This method automatically extends objects to the nearest object in their path. If there is no object to which to extend, a message on the command line reads Object does not intersect an edge. After extending an object, you can select other objects to be extended or press the [Enter] or [Esc] key to exit the command. Figure 11-17 illustrates how to combine **EXTEND** and **TRIM**, without selecting a boundary edge, to insert a wall in a drawing.

Extend Selection Options

Multiple lines can be extended to boundary edges in the same operation by using the **Fence** option of the **EXTEND** command. After selecting F for **Fence**, you are prompted to draw a fence line. The fence line can have multiple segments. Any lines crossing the fence line are extended to the nearest boundary edge. See Figure 11-18.

Similar to the **Fence** option, the **Crossing** option selects objects to be extended using a crossing box. After selecting the boundary edges, you are prompted to specify a first corner and an opposite corner. This creates the crossing window. Any lines that cross the window lines are extended to the boundary edge. See Figure 11-19.

Figure 11-17.
To select all objects as boundary edges, press [Enter] instead of picking a boundary edge.

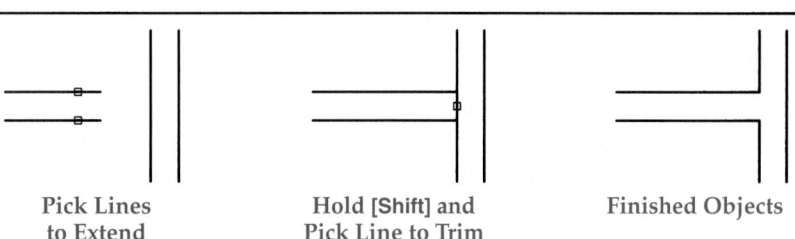

Pick Lines to Extend

Hold [Shift] and Pick Line to Trim

Finished Objects

Figure 11-18.
Multiple lines can be extended to a boundary edge by using the **Fence** option.

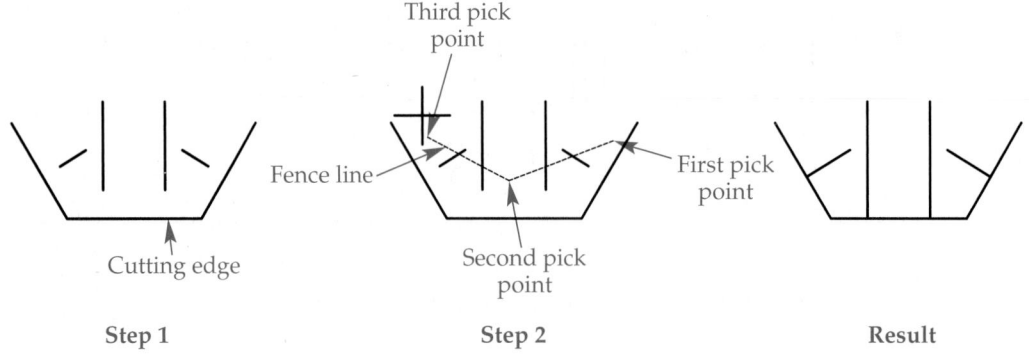

Step 1   Step 2   Result

Figure 11-19.
The only objects extended with the **Crossing** option are those that cross the edges of the selection window.

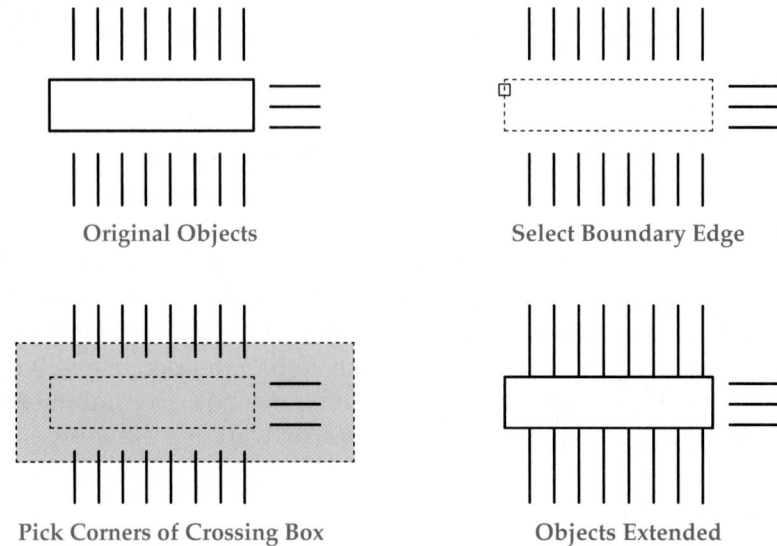

Original Objects   Select Boundary Edge

Pick Corners of Crossing Box   Objects Extended

PROFESSIONAL TIP

As with the **TRIM** command, you do not need to use the **Crossing** option to select objects using a crossing box. If you pick a point in the drawing area when selecting objects to trim, the point becomes the first corner of a crossing box. You can then select the second corner.

Extending to an Implied Intersection

You can extend an object to an implied intersection when **Extend** mode is active. **Extend** mode is set using the **Edge** option. The **Edge** option setting affects both the **TRIM** and **EXTEND** commands. When **Extend** mode is active, the boundary edge object is checked to see if it intersects an object when it is extended. If so, the implied intersection point can be used as the boundary for the object to be extended, as shown in Figure 11-20. This does not change the boundary edge object at all. The **Edge** option can also be set using the **EDGEMODE** system variable, as previously described with the **TRIM** command.

Figure 11-20.
Extending to an implied intersection with **Extend** mode.

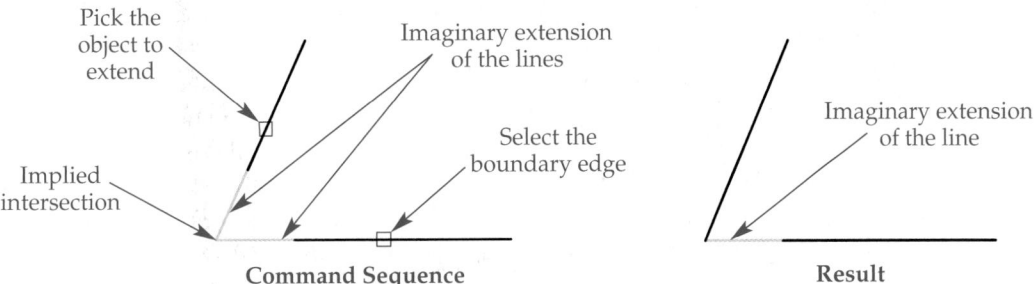

Pick the object to extend

Imaginary extension of the lines

Select the boundary edge

Implied intersection

Command Sequence

Imaginary extension of the line

Result

Using the Undo Option

The **Undo** option in the **EXTEND** command can be used to reverse the previous operation without leaving the **EXTEND** command. The command sequence is the same as described for the **TRIM** command.

The Project Option of the Extend Command

In a 3D drawing, some lines may appear to intersect in a given view, but not actually intersect. In such a case, you can use the **Project** option, as explained for the **TRIM** command.

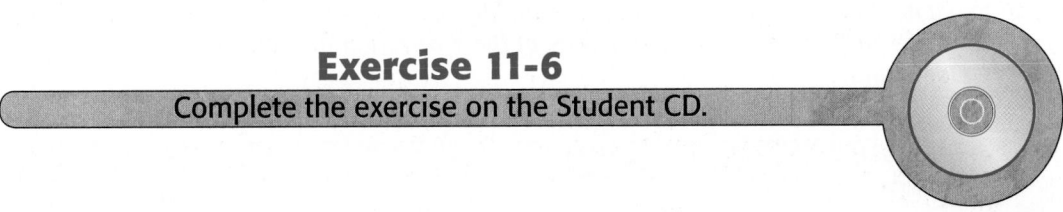

Exercise 11-6

Complete the exercise on the Student CD.

Moving Objects

In many situations, you may find that the location of a view or feature is not where you want it. This problem is easy to fix using the **MOVE** command. Picking the **Move** button in the **2D Draw** control panel of the **Dashboard** or the **Modify** toolbar, picking **Modify > Move**, or typing M or MOVE accesses the **MOVE** command.

When you enter the **MOVE** command, AutoCAD asks you to select the objects to be moved. Use any of the selection set options to select the objects. The next prompt requests the base point or displacement. The *base point* provides a reference point. Most drafters select a point on an object, the corner of a view, or the center of a circle. The next prompt asks for the second point. This is the new position. All selected entities are moved the distance from the base point to the displacement point. See Figure 11-21.

Using the First Point As Displacement

In the previous section, a base point and then a second point were selected to move an object. The object moved the specified distance and direction. You can also move the object relative to the first point. This means the coordinates you use to select the base point are automatically used as the coordinates for the direction and distance for moving the object. Follow this command sequence to do this:

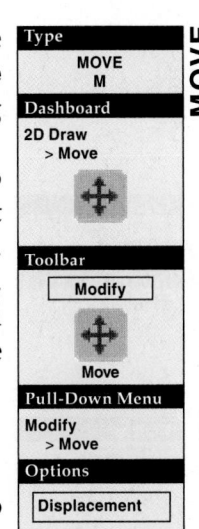

Type
MOVE
M

Dashboard
2D Draw
> Move

Toolbar
Modify
Move

Pull-Down Menu
Modify
> Move

Options
Displacement

MOVE

base point: The initial reference point AutoCAD uses when moving, copying, scaling, and stretching objects.

Figure 11-21.
Using the **MOVE**
command.

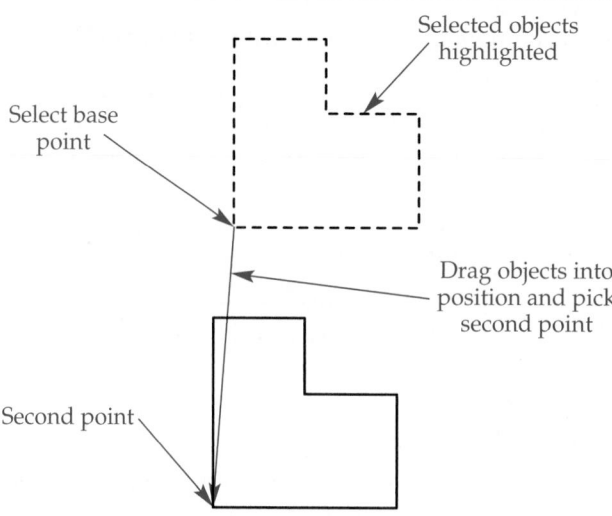

Selected objects
highlighted

Select base
point

Drag objects into
position and pick
second point

Second point

Command: **M** *or* **MOVE**.↵
Select objects: *(select the objects to move)*
n found
Select objects: ↵
Specify base point or [Displacement] <Displacement>: **2,4**↵
Specify second point or <use first point as displacement>: ↵ *(the object moves a distance and direction equal to the coordinates specified for the base point, which is 2 units in the X direction and 4 units in the Y direction in this example)*
Command:

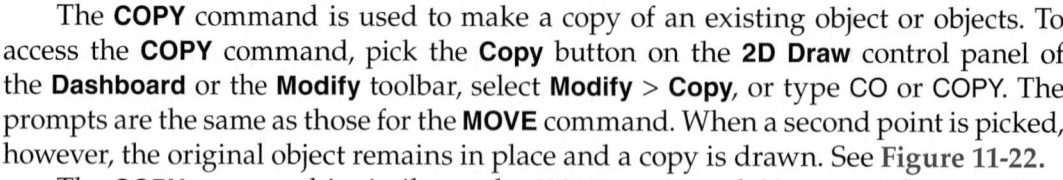

PROFESSIONAL TIP

Always use object snap modes to your best advantage with editing commands. For example, suppose you want to move an object to the center point of a circle. Use the **Center** object snap mode to select the center of the circle.

Copying Objects

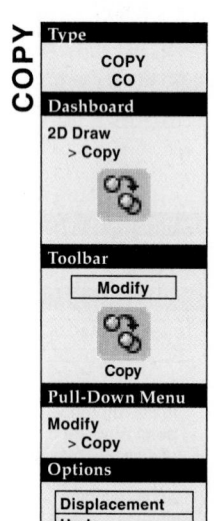

The **COPY** command is used to make a copy of an existing object or objects. To access the **COPY** command, pick the **Copy** button on the **2D Draw** control panel of the **Dashboard** or the **Modify** toolbar, select **Modify > Copy**, or type CO or COPY. The prompts are the same as those for the **MOVE** command. When a second point is picked, however, the original object remains in place and a copy is drawn. See **Figure 11-22**.

The **COPY** command is similar to the **MOVE** command. You can either specify a base point and a second point or specify a displacement. If you specify a displacement, a copy of the object is made at the specified location.

Making Multiple Copies

To make several copies of the same object, specify a point of displacement at the Specify second point of <use first point as displacement>: prompt. The prompt for a second point repeats until you end the command. When you have made all the copies needed, press [Enter] or [Esc]. The results are shown in **Figure 11-23**. To undo the previous copy, use the **Undo** option.

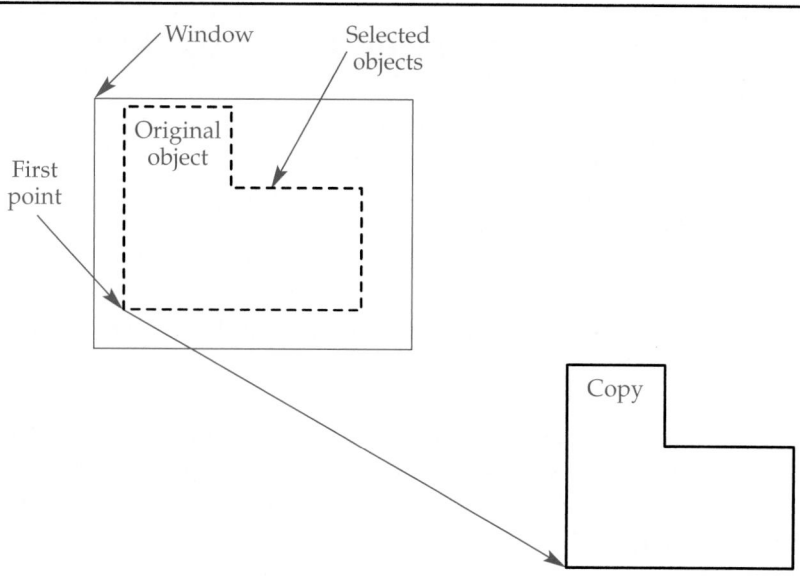

Figure 11-22.
Using the **COPY**
command.

Window

Selected
objects

Original
object

First
point

Copy

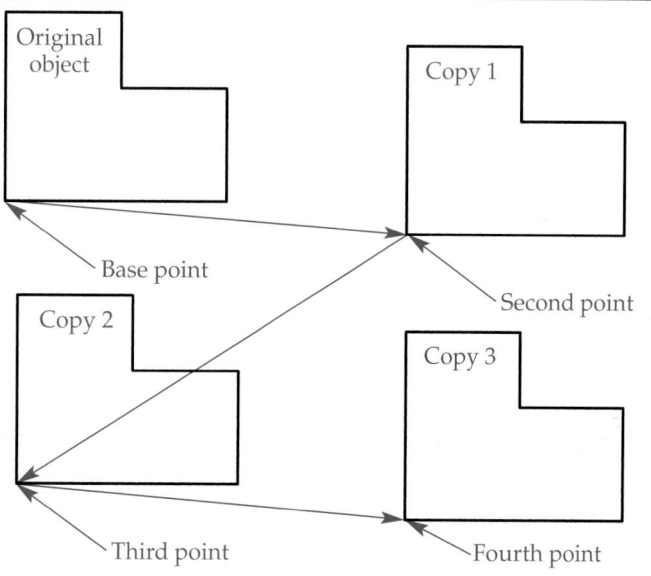

Figure 11-23.
Using the **COPY**
command to make
multiple copies.

Original
object

Copy 1

Base point

Second point

Copy 2

Copy 3

Third point

Fourth point

Making a Single Copy

The default **Multiple** copy mode allows you to make multiple copies without reselecting the **COPY** command. Set the **Single** copy mode, make a single copy of the selected objects, and exit the command after the copy is placed. To set the **Single** copy mode, enter the **mOde** option before selecting a base point or choosing the Displacement function, and select the **Single** option.

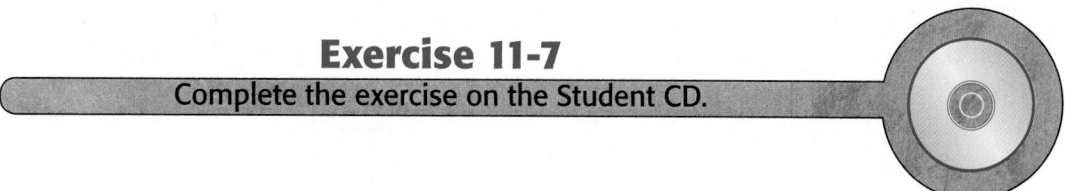

Exercise 11-7
Complete the exercise on the Student CD.

Rotating Existing Objects

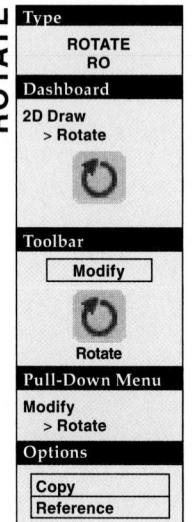

ROTATE

Type
ROTATE
RO

Dashboard
2D Draw
> Rotate

Toolbar
Modify

Rotate

Pull-Down Menu
Modify
> Rotate

Options
Copy
Reference

Design changes often require an object, feature, or view to be rotated. For example, an office furniture layout may have to be rotated for an interior design. AutoCAD allows you to revise the layout easily to obtain the final design.

To rotate selected objects, pick **Modify > Rotate** from the pull-down menu, pick the **Rotate** button on the **2D Draw** control panel of the **Dashboard** or the **Modify** toolbar, or type RO or ROTATE. Objects can be selected using any of the selection set options. After selecting the objects, pick a base point and enter a rotation angle. A negative rotation angle revolves the object clockwise. A positive rotation angle revolves the object counterclockwise. See **Figure 11-24**.

If an object is already rotated and you want a different angle, you can change the angle in two ways. Both ways involve using the **Reference** option after selecting the object for rotation. The first way is to specify the existing angle and then the new angle. See **Figure 11-25A**:

Figure 11-24.
Rotation angles.

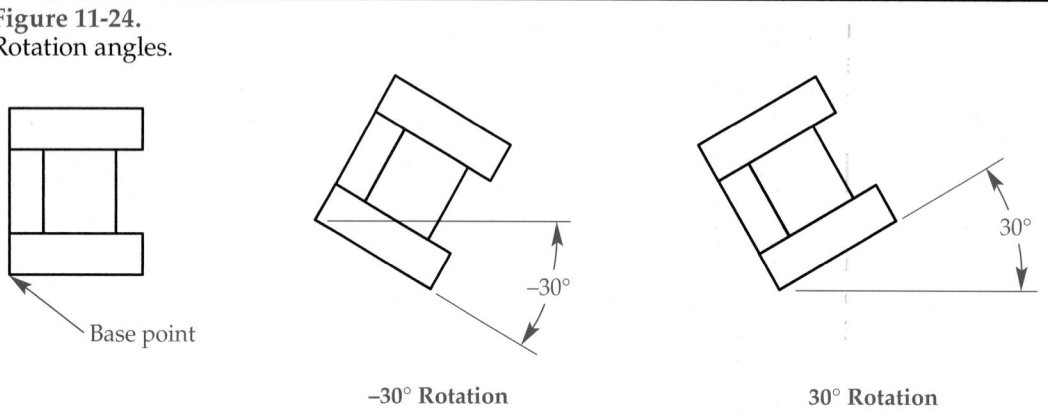

−30° Rotation   30° Rotation

Figure 11-25.
Using the **Reference** option of the **ROTATE** command. A—Entering reference angles. B—Selecting points on a reference line.

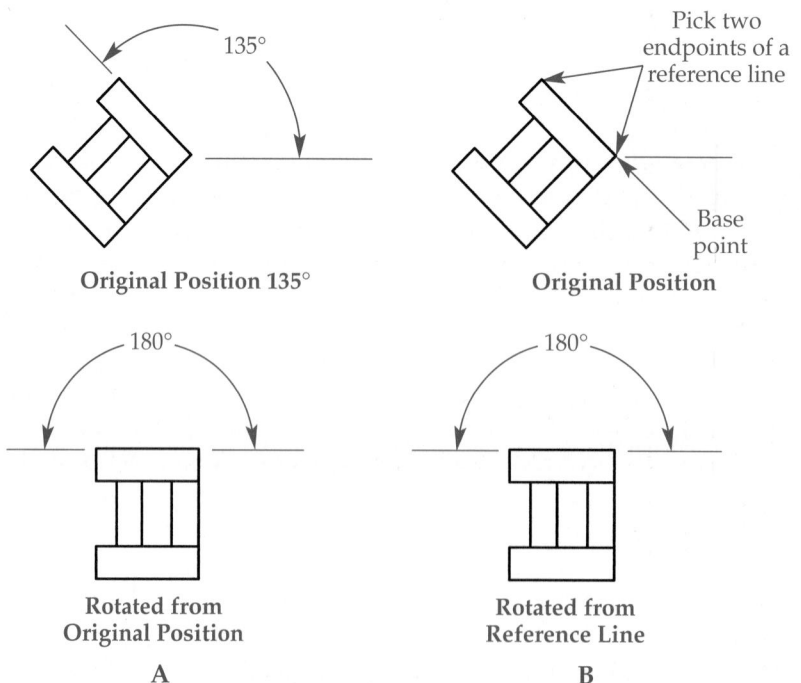

A   B

Specify rotation angle or [Copy/Reference] <current>: **R**↵
Specify the reference angle <current>: (specify a reference angle, such as 135, and
    press [Enter])
Specify the new angle or [Points] <current>: (specify a new angle, such as 180, and
    press [Enter])
Command:

The other method is to pick a reference line on the object and rotate the object in relationship to the reference line. See **Figure 11-25B**:

Specify rotation angle or [Copy/Reference] <current>: **R**↵
Specify the reference angle <current>: (pick an endpoint of a reference line that
    forms the existing angle)
Specify second point: (pick the other point of the reference line that forms the existing
    angle)
Specify the new angle or [Points] <current>: (specify a new angle, such as 180, and
    press [Enter])
Command:

An object can be copied and rotated at the same time, leaving the original object in place. This can be done by using the **Copy** option when prompted to Specify rotation angle or [Copy/Reference] <current>. After specifying the rotation angle, a new object is created and rotated, and the source object is left unchanged.

PROFESSIONAL TIP

Always use the object snap modes to your best advantage when editing. For example, suppose you want to rotate an object. It may be difficult to find an exact corner without using object snap mode. To select the base point, use the **Endpoint** or **Intersection** object snap mode.

Exercise 11-8
Complete the exercise on the Student CD.

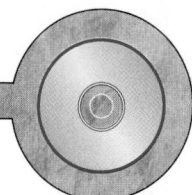

Aligning Objects

Use the **ALIGN** command when you want to move and rotate an object at the same time. **ALIGN** is a 3D command that can also be used for 2D drawings. For 2D applications, you only need two source points and two destination points. Press [Enter] when the prompt requests the third source and destination points. The *source points* define a line related to the object's original position. The *destination points* define the location of this line relative to the object's new location. See **Figure 11-26**. To access the **ALIGN** command, pick **Modify > 3D Operations > Align**, or type AL or ALIGN. The command sequence is as follows:

Command: **AL** or **ALIGN**↵
Select objects: (select the objects)
n found
Select objects: ↵
Specify first source point: (pick the first source point)

source points:
Points to define a reference line for an **ALIGN** operation.

destination points:
Points to define the new alignment of an object.

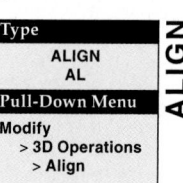

Type	
ALIGN	
AL	
Pull-Down Menu	
Modify	
> 3D Operations	
> Align	

ALIGN

Figure 11-26.
Using the **ALIGN** command to move and rotate a kitchen cabinet layout against a wall.

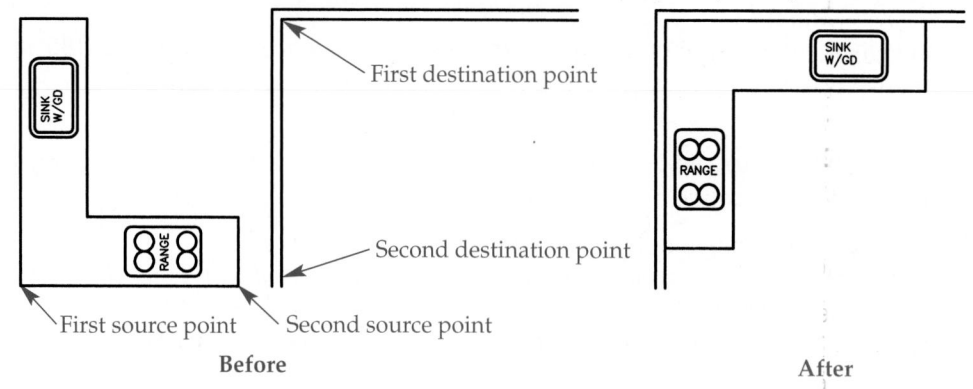

Before   After

Specify first destination point: *(pick the first destination point)*
Specify second source point: *(pick the second source point)*
Specify second destination point: *(pick the second destination point)*
Specify third source point or <continue>: ↵
Scale objects based on alignment points? [Yes/No] <N>: *(enter Y to scale the object if the distance between the source points is different from the distance between the destination points, and press [Enter])*
Command:

The last prompt allows you to change the size of the object that is being moved. Figure 11-27 illustrates this process by moving, rotating, and scaling a rectangle to match a side of a hexagon.

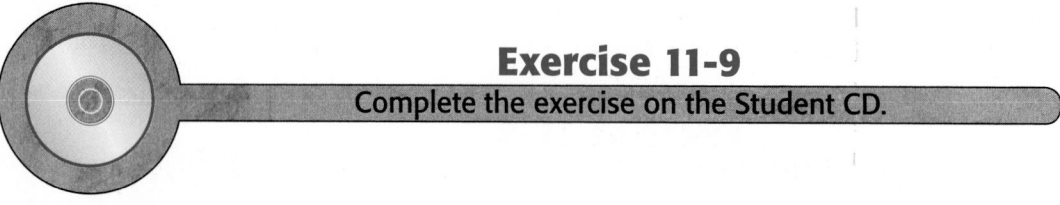

Exercise 11-9
Complete the exercise on the Student CD.

Figure 11-27.
The **Scale** option of the **ALIGN** command is used to change the size of an object while it is moved and rotated.

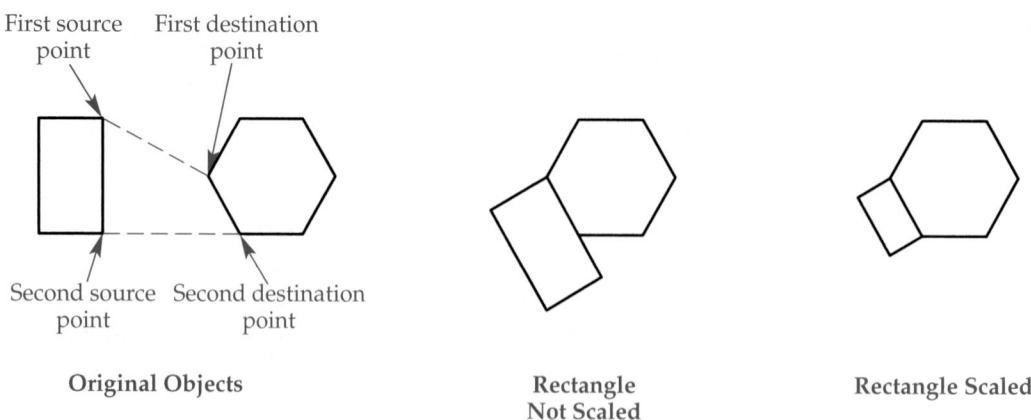

First source point   First destination point

Second source point   Second destination point

Original Objects   Rectangle Not Scaled   Rectangle Scaled

Mirroring an Object

It is often necessary to draw an object in a reflected, or mirrored, position. The **MIRROR** command performs this task. Mirroring an entire drawing is common in architectural drafting, when a client wants a plan drawn in reverse. Picking the **Mirror** button in the **2D Draw** control panel of the **Dashboard** or the **Modify** toolbar, selecting **Modify** > **Mirror**, or typing MI or MIRROR accesses the **MIRROR** command.

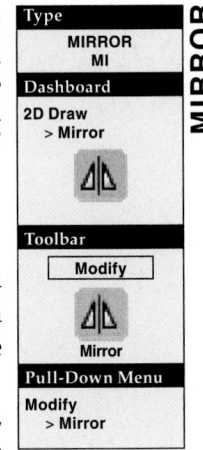

Selecting the Mirror Line

When you enter the **MIRROR** command, you select the objects to mirror and then select a mirror line. The *mirror line* is the hinge, or line of symmetry, about which objects are reflected. The objects and any space between the objects and the mirror line are reflected. See **Figure 11-28**.

The mirror line can be placed at any angle. After you pick the first endpoint, a mirrored image appears and moves with the crosshairs. When you select the second mirror line endpoint, you have the option to delete the original objects. See **Figure 11-29**.

mirror line: The line of symmetry about which objects are mirrored.

Exercise 11-10
Complete the exercise on the Student CD.

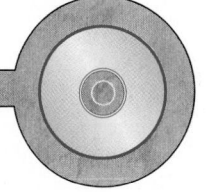

Mirroring Text

The **MIRROR** command can reverse any text associated with the selected objects. Backward text is generally not acceptable, although it is used for reverse imaging. There are two values for **MIRRTEXT**, as shown in **Figure 11-30**:
- **1.** Text is mirrored in relation to the original object.
- **0.** Prevents text from being reversed. This is the default value.

Figure 11-28.
When an object is reflected about a mirror line, the space between the object and the mirror line is also mirrored.

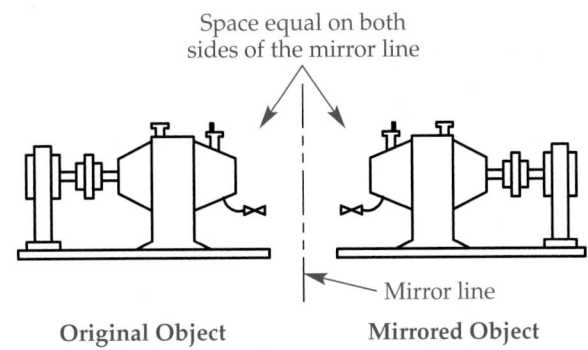

Space equal on both sides of the mirror line

Mirror line

Original Object   Mirrored Object

Figure 11-29.
The **MIRROR** command gives you the option to delete the old objects.

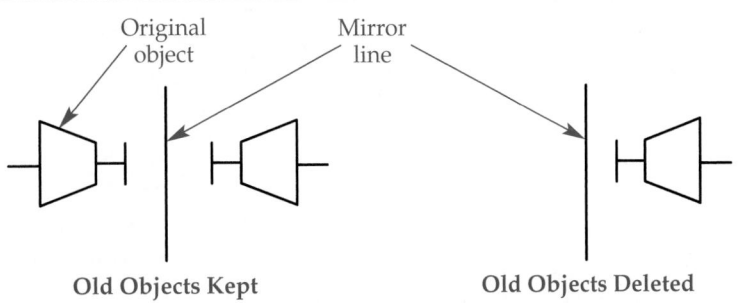

Original object   Mirror line

Old Objects Kept   Old Objects Deleted

Figure 11-30.
The **MIRRTEXT**
system variable
options.

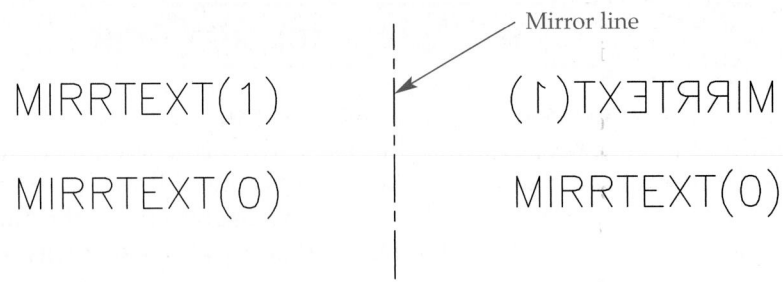

To keep the text readable, the **MIRRTEXT** system variable must be 0. This is the default value. To draw a mirror image of an existing object and reverse the text, set the **MIRRTEXT** variable to 1 by typing MIRRTEXT and entering 1. Proceed to the **MIRROR** command.

Exercise 11-11
Complete the exercise on the Student CD.

Patterning Objects with Array

Some designs require a rectangular or circular pattern of the same object. For example, office desks are often arranged in rows. Suppose your design calls for five rows, each having four desks. You can create this design by drawing one desk and copying it nineteen times. This operation, however, is time-consuming. A quicker method is to create an array.

rectangular array: A pattern made up of columns and rows of objects.

polar array: A circular pattern of objects.

There are two types of arrays: rectangular and polar. A *rectangular array* creates rows and columns of the selected items, and you must provide the spacing. A *polar array* constructs a circular arrangement. For a polar array, you must specify the number of items to array, the angle between items, and the center point of the array. Some examples are shown in **Figure 11-31.**

Figure 11-31.
Examples of arrays.

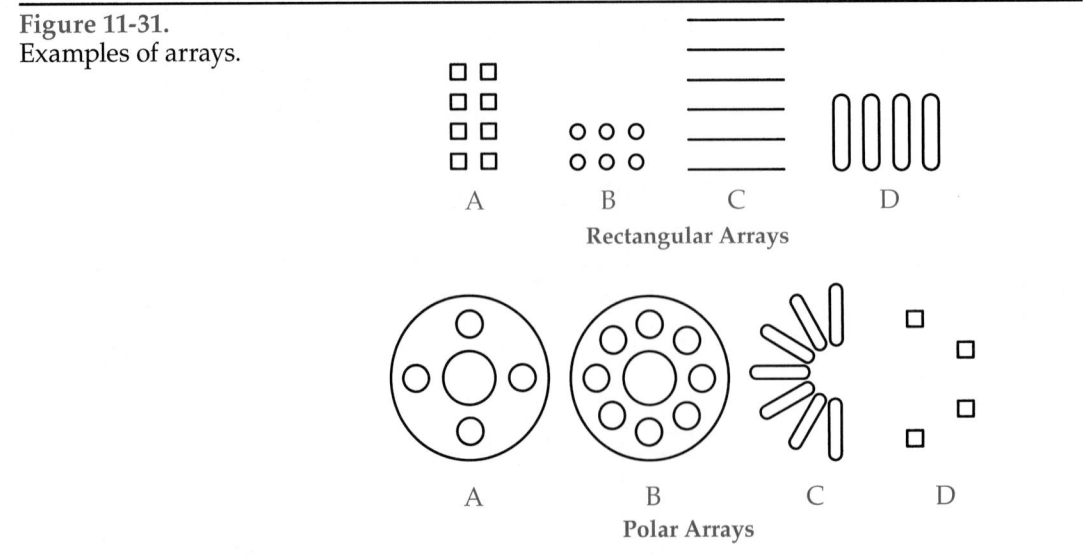

Arrays are specified using the **Array** dialog box. To access this dialog box, pick the **Array...** button in the **2D Draw** control panel of the **Dashboard** or the **Modify** toolbar, select **Modify** > **Array...** from the pull-down menu, or type AR or ARRAY. All input needed to create the array is specified in the **Array** dialog box. See **Figure 11-32.** Use the **Rectangular Array** and **Polar Array** radio buttons to specify the type of array. Pick the **Select objects** button to return to the AutoCAD window and pick the objects to be included in the array.

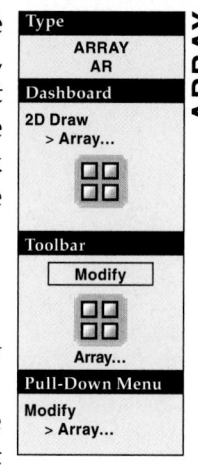

Arranging Objects in a Rectangular Pattern

A rectangular array places objects in line along the X and Y axes. You can specify a single row, a single column, or multiple rows and columns.

To create a rectangular pattern for a .5 unit square having three rows, three columns, and a .5 spacing between objects, enter 3 in the **Rows:** and **Columns:** text boxes and 1.0000 in the **Row offset:** and **Column offset:** text boxes. This is shown in **Figure 11-33.** Notice that the distances do not refer to the space between the objects, but the distances between the same point on each object.

The distances can also be entered by picking points—two methods are available. You can also use the **Pick Row Offset** and **Pick Column Offset** buttons in the **Array** dialog box to specify each distance separately. The second method uses the **Pick Both Offsets** button to specify both distances in one pick. **Figure 11-34** illustrates the **Pick**

Figure 11-32.
The **Array** dialog box options for a rectangular array.

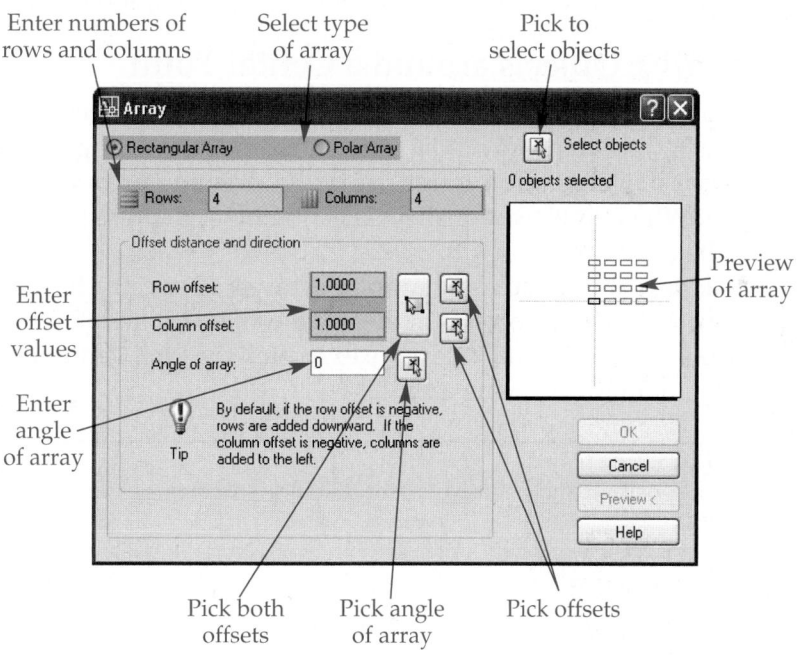

Figure 11-33.
The original object (in dashed lines) and the created rectangular array. Note how the distances between rows and columns are determined.

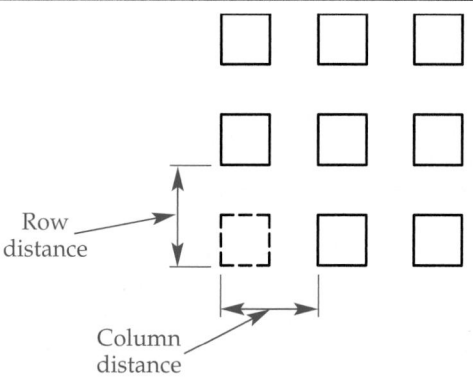

Figure 11-34.

The spacing of rows and columns in an array can be specified with a single point.

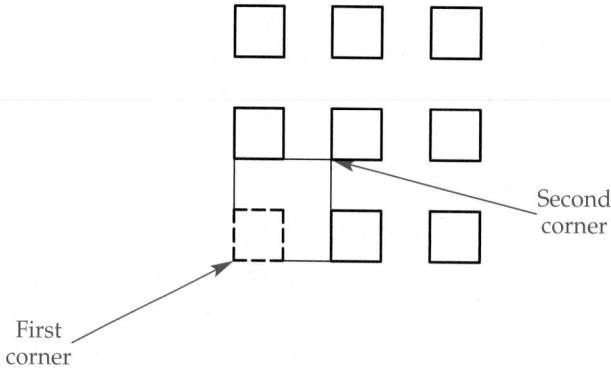

Both Offsets method. You can use any point selection method—such as object snap modes, relative coordinates, and polar coordinates—to pick the second point.

Figure 11-35 shows the four directions in which an array can grow. The direction is based on the use of positive and negative distance values for row and column offsets.

You can also create an angled rectangular array. Enter the angle in the **Angle of array:** text box or pick the **Pick Angle of Array** button to specify the angle with the crosshairs. The column and row alignments are rotated, not the objects. See **Figure 11-36.**

Arranging Objects around a Center Point

A polar array creates a circular pattern using the selected object. To create a polar array, pick the **Polar Array** radio button in the **Array** dialog box. See **Figure 11-37.** Pick the **Select objects** button to return to the drawing area and select the objects to be arrayed. When you have finished selecting objects, press [Enter] to return to the **Array** dialog box.

The next step in creating a polar array is to specify the center point. This is the point about which the objects in the array will be rotated. Enter the coordinates for the center point in the **X:** and **Y:** text boxes or pick the **Pick Center Point** button to select the center point in the drawing area.

Figure 11-35.

The use of positive and negative offset distances determines the direction in which an array will grow.

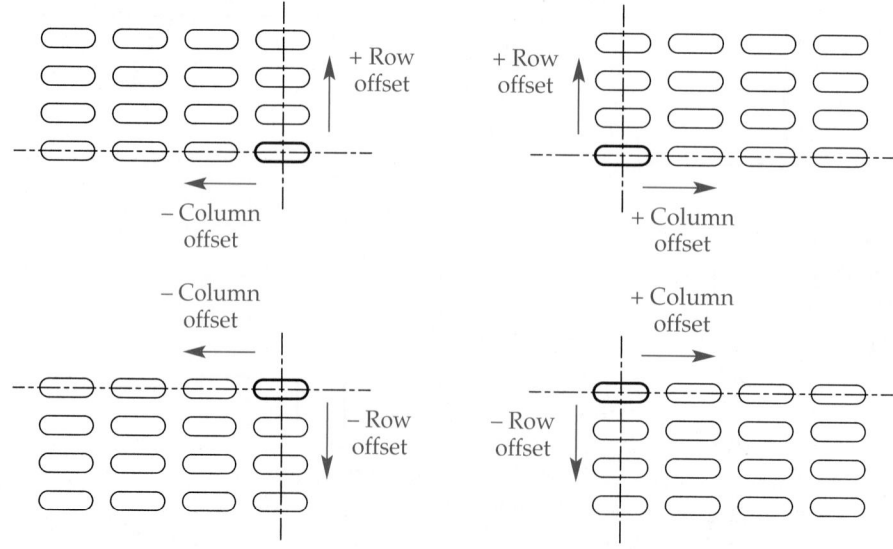

Figure 11-36.
Rectangular arrays can be arranged using the **Angle of array:** setting.

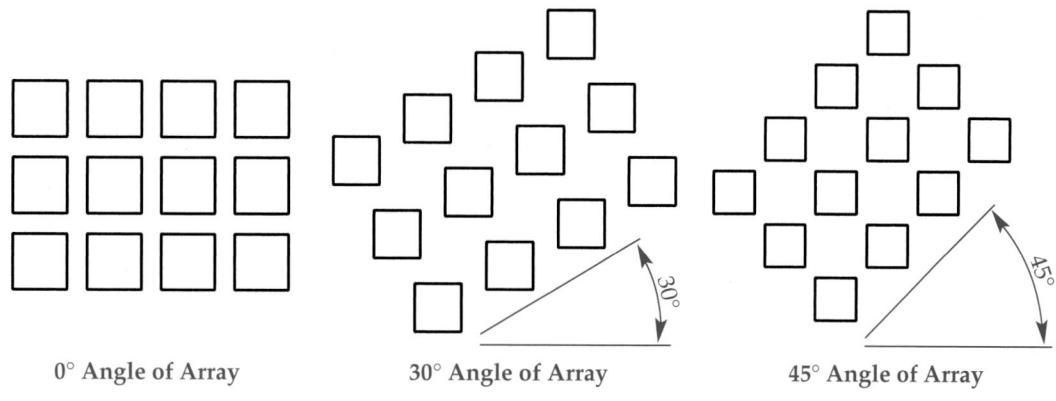

Figure 11-36.
Rectangular arrays can be arranged using the **Angle of array:** setting.

0° Angle of Array   30° Angle of Array   45° Angle of Array

Figure 11-37.
The **Array** dialog box options for a polar array.

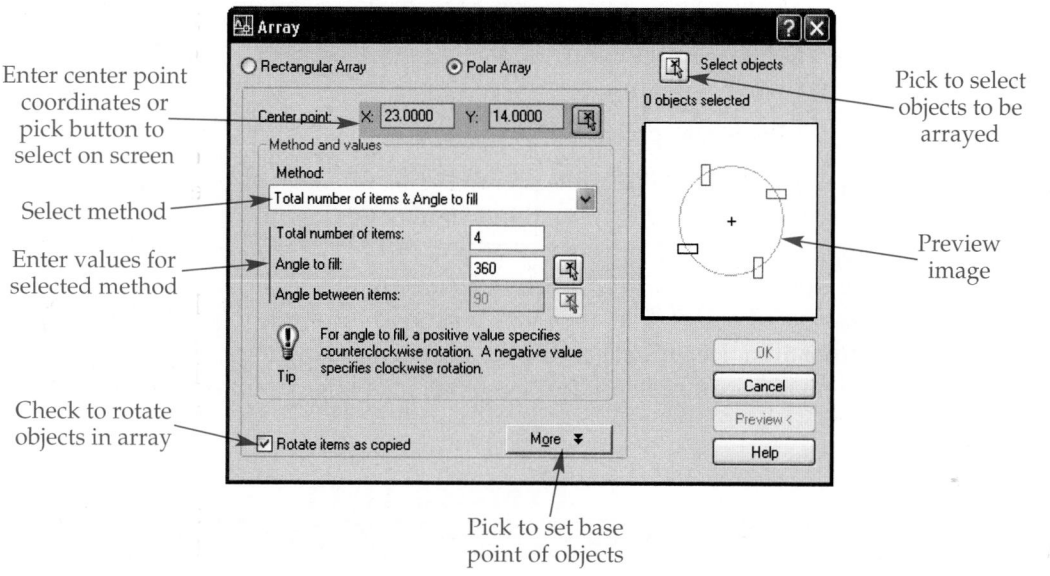

Enter center point coordinates or pick button to select on screen

Select method

Enter values for selected method

Check to rotate objects in array

Pick to select objects to be arrayed

Preview image

Pick to set base point of objects

After selecting the center point, you must specify the type of polar array to be created using the **Method:** drop-down list. The selected method determines which settings in the dialog box are available. Three methods are available:

- Total number of items & Angle to fill
- Total number of items & Angle between items
- Angle to fill & Angle between items

The **Total number of items:** setting is the total number of objects to be in the array, including the originally selected object. If you do not know how many items will be in the array, use the Angle to fill & Angle between items method. The **Angle to fill:** setting can be positive or negative. To array the object in a counterclockwise direction, enter a positive angle. To array the object in a clockwise direction, enter a negative angle. Enter 360 to create a complete circular array. The **Angle between items:** setting specifies the angular distance between adjacent objects in the array. For example, if you are creating a circular pattern of five items spaced 18° apart, enter 5 in the **Total number of items:** text box and 18 in the **Angle between items:** text box.

You can have the objects rotated as they are copied around the center point by checking the **Rotate items as copied** check box. This keeps the same face of each object pointing toward the center point. If objects are not rotated as they are copied, they remain in the same orientation as the original object. See Figure 11-38.

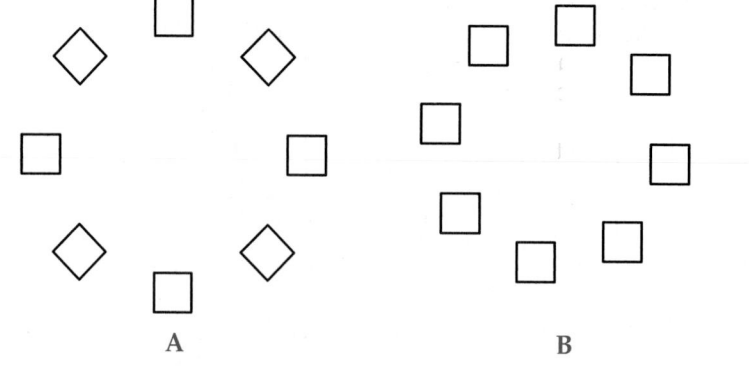

Figure 11-38.
Rotating objects in a polar array. A—The square is rotated as it is arrayed. B—The square is not rotated as it is arrayed.

A   B

When AutoCAD creates a polar array, the base point of the object is rotated and remains at a constant distance from the center point. The default base point varies for different types of objects, as shown in the following table:

Object Type	Default Base Point
Arc, circle, ellipse	Center
Rectangle, polygon	First corner
Line, polyline, donut	Start point
Block, text	Insertion point

If the default base point does not produce the desired array, you can select a different base point for the selected object. Pick the **More** button in the **Array** dialog box to display the **Object base point** area. Deactivate the **Set to object's default** check box. Enter a new base point in the text boxes or pick the button to select a base point on screen.

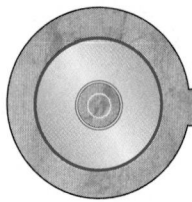

Exercise 11-12
Complete the exercise on the Student CD.

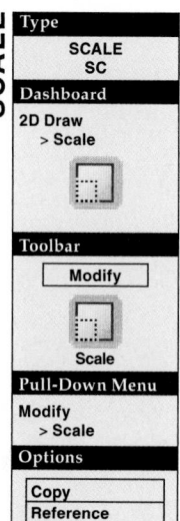

Type

SCALE
SC

Dashboard

2D Draw
> Scale

Toolbar

Modify

Scale

Pull-Down Menu

Modify
> Scale

Options

Copy
Reference

Changing the Size of an Object

A convenient editing command that saves hours of drafting time is the **SCALE** command. This command lets you change the size of a single object or an entire drawing. The **SCALE** command enlarges or reduces the entire object proportionately. If associative dimensioning is used, the dimensions also change to reflect the new size. This is described in Chapter 17.

To scale objects, pick the **Scale** button in the **2D Draw** control panel of the **Dashboard** or the **Modify** toolbar, pick **Modify > Scale**, or type SC or SCALE. Pick a base point—the point the selected objects move away from or toward during the scale operation. The next step is to specify the scale factor. Enter a number to indicate the amount of enlargement or reduction. For example, if you want to double the scale, type 2 at the Specify scale factor or [Copy/Reference] <*current*>: prompt, as shown in **Figure 11-39**. The chart in **Figure 11-40** shows sample scale factors.

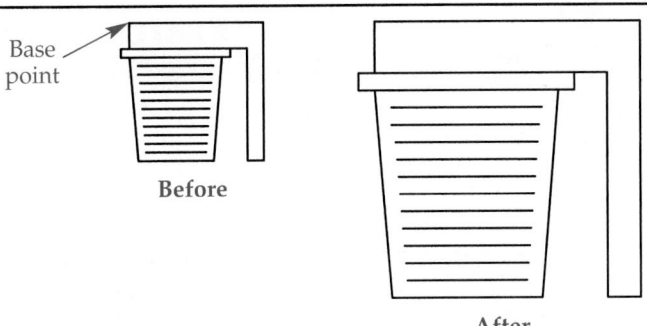

Figure 11-39.
Using the **SCALE** command. The base point does not move, but every other point in the object does.

Base point

Before

After

Figure 11-40.
Scale factors and the resulting sizes.

Scale Factor	Resulting Size
10	10 times bigger
5	5 times bigger
2	2 times bigger
1	Equal to existing size
.75	3/4 of original size
.50	1/2 of original size
.25	1/4 of original size

Creating a Copy while Scaling

If an object needs to be copied and then scaled, these changes can be made at the same time in the **SCALE** command. The **Copy** option of the **SCALE** command copies the selected object and scales it, leaving the original object unchanged.

Using the Reference Option

An object can also be scaled by specifying a new size in relation to an existing dimension. For example, suppose you have a shaft that is 2.50″ long, and you want to make it 3.00″ long. To do so, use the **Reference** option, as shown in **Figure 11-41**:

Specify scale factor or [Copy/Reference] <*current*>: **R**↵
Specify reference length <*current*>: **2.5**↵
Specify new length or [Points] <*current*>: **3**↵
Command:

NOTE

The **SCALE** command changes all dimensions of an object proportionately. If you want to change only the width or length of an object, use the **STRETCH** or **LENGTHEN** command.

Figure 11-41.
Using the **Reference** option of the **SCALE** command.

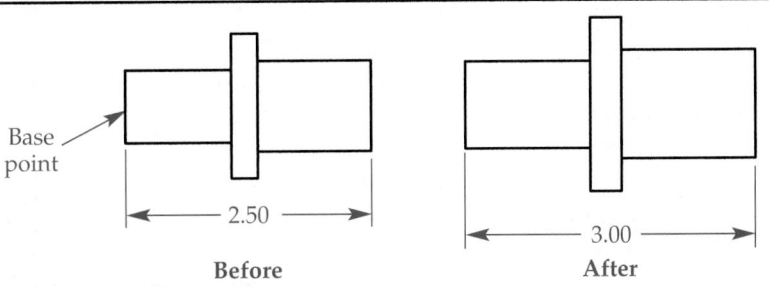

Base point

2.50

Before

3.00

After

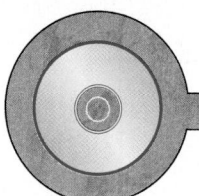

Exercise 11-13
Complete the exercise on the Student CD.

Stretching an Object

Unlike the **SCALE** command, which changes the length and width of an object proportionately, the **STRETCH** command changes only one dimension of an object. It is common to increase the length of a part while leaving the diameter or width the same. In architectural design, room sizes may be stretched to increase the square footage.

To access the **STRETCH** command, pick the **Stretch** button in **2D Draw** control panel of the **Dashboard** or the **Modify** toolbar, pick **Modify > Stretch**, or type S or STRETCH. Use a crossing window or a crossing polygon to select only the objects that will be stretched, as shown in **Figure 11-42**. If you select the entire object, the **STRETCH** command works like the **MOVE** command.

After selecting the objects to be stretched, you are asked to pick the base point. This is the point from which the object will be stretched. Pick a position for the base point. As you move the crosshairs, the object is stretched or compressed. When the displayed object is stretched to the desired position, pick a point to accept the stretch.

Using the Displacement Option

The **Displacement** option works the same with the **STRETCH** command as with the **MOVE** and **COPY** commands. After selecting the objects to be stretched, enter a displacement, as shown in the following sequence:

Specify base point or [Displacement] <Displacement>: **2,3**↵
Specify second point or <use first point as displacement>: ↵
Command:

When you press [Enter] at the Specify second point or <use first point as displacement>: prompt, the object is automatically stretched as you specified with the X and Y coordinates. In this case, the object is stretched 2 units in the X direction and 3 units in the Y direction.

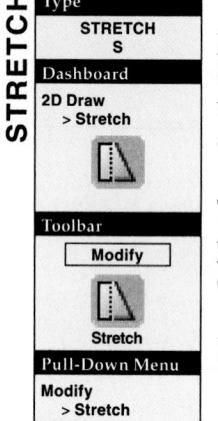

STRETCH

Type
STRETCH
S

Dashboard
2D Draw
> Stretch

Toolbar
Modify

Stretch

Pull-Down Menu
Modify
> Stretch

Figure 11-42.
Using the **STRETCH** command.

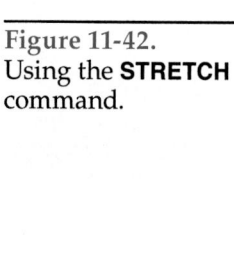

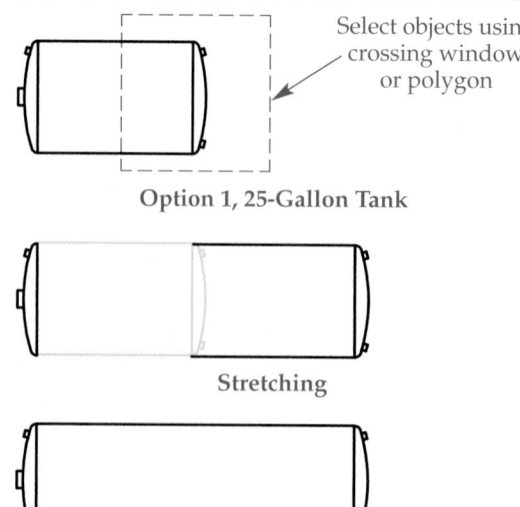

Select objects using crossing window or polygon

Option 1, 25-Gallon Tank

Stretching

Option 2, 50-Gallon Tank

It may not be common to have objects lined up in a convenient manner for using the crossing box selection method with the **STRETCH** command. You should consider using the crossing polygon selection method to make selecting the objects easier. If the stretched object is not what you expected, cancel the command with the [Esc] key. The **STRETCH** command and other editing commands described in this chapter work well with Ortho mode or polar tracking activated.

Exercise 11-14

Complete the exercise on the Student CD.

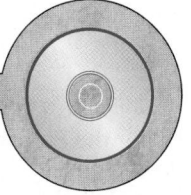

Changing the Length of an Object

The **LENGTHEN** command can be used to change the length of objects and the included angle of an arc. Only one object can be lengthened at a time. The **LENGTHEN** command does not affect closed objects. For example, you can lengthen a line, a polyline, an arc, an elliptical arc, or a spline, but you cannot lengthen a closed polygon or circle.

To access the **LENGTHEN** command, pick **Modify > Lengthen** or type LEN or LENGTHEN. When you select an object, AutoCAD gives you the current length if the object is linear, or the included angle if the object is an arc. The **LENGTHEN** command has four options:

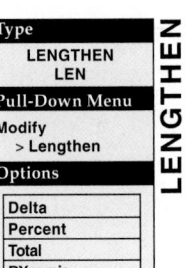

Type
LENGTHEN
LEN
Pull-Down Menu
Modify
> Lengthen
Options
Delta
Percent
Total
DYnamic

LENGTHEN

- **DElta.** The **DElta** option allows you to specify a positive or negative change in length, measured from the endpoint of the selected object. The lengthening or shortening happens closest to the selection point and changes the length by the amount entered. See **Figure 11-43.** The **DElta** option has an **Angle** suboption that lets you change the included angle of an arc by a specified angle. See **Figure 11-44.**
- **Percent.** The **Percent** option allows you to change the length of an object or the angle of an arc by a specified percentage. The original length is considered to be 100 percent. You can make the object shorter by specifying less than 100 percent or longer by specifying more than 100 percent. See **Figure 11-45.**

Figure 11-43.
Using the **DElta** option of the **LENGTHEN** command with values of .75 and –.75.

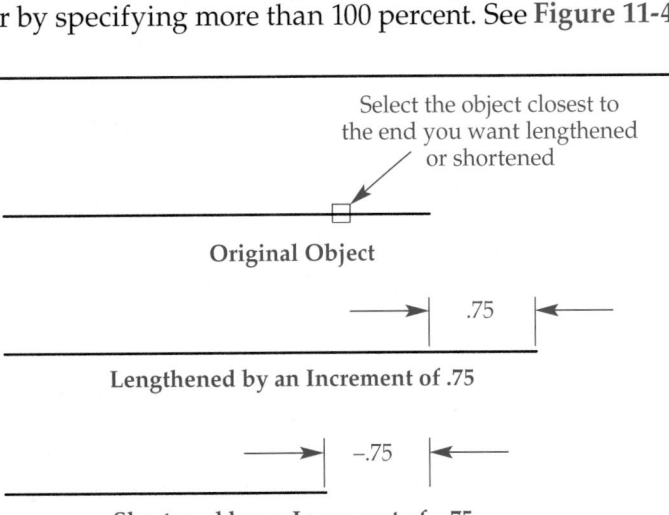

Select the object closest to the end you want lengthened or shortened

Original Object

.75

Lengthened by an Increment of .75

–.75

Shortened by an Increment of –.75

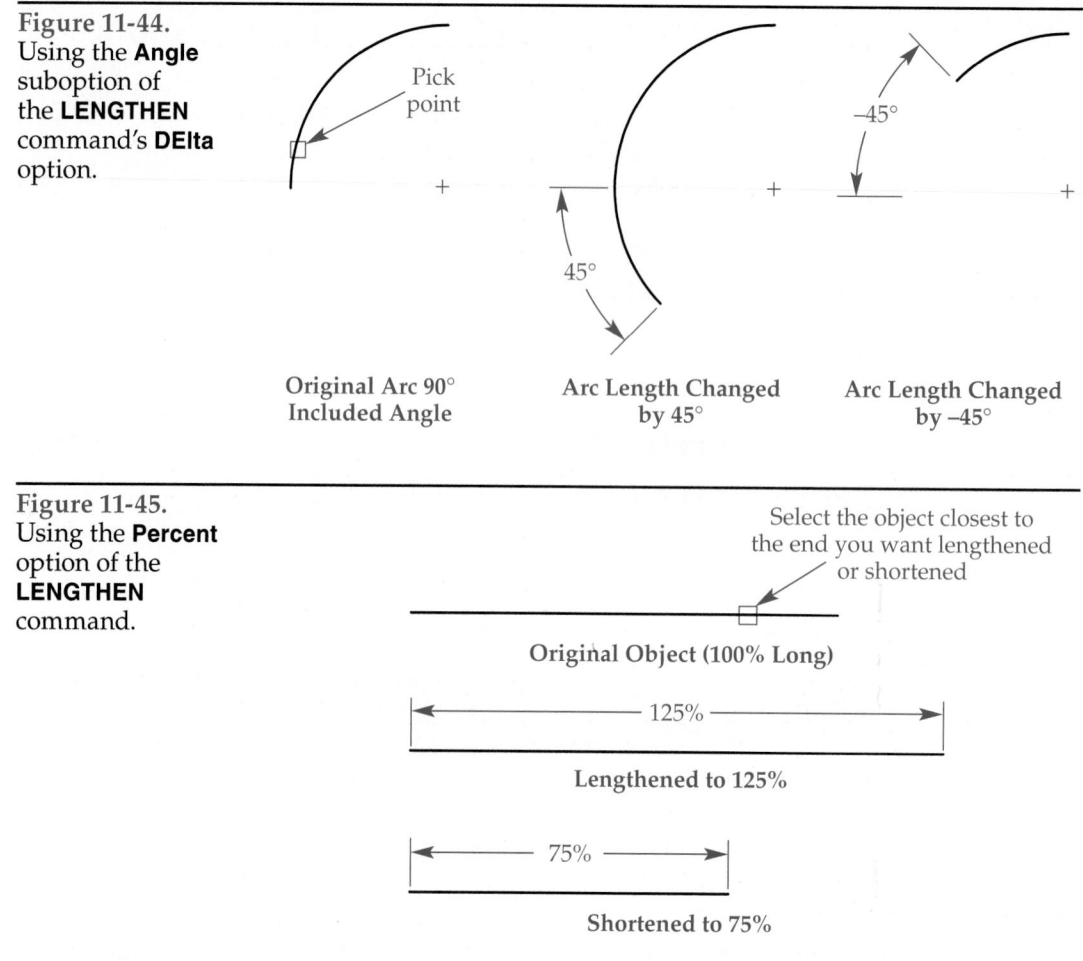

Figure 11-44.
Using the **Angle** suboption of the **LENGTHEN** command's **DElta** option.

Pick point

45°

−45°

Original Arc 90°
Included Angle

Arc Length Changed
by 45°

Arc Length Changed
by −45°

Figure 11-45.
Using the **Percent** option of the **LENGTHEN** command.

Select the object closest to
the end you want lengthened
or shortened

Original Object (100% Long)

125%

Lengthened to 125%

75%

Shortened to 75%

- **Total.** The **Total** option allows you to set the total length or angle to the value you specify. You do not have to select the object before entering one of the options, but doing so lets you know the current length and, if it is an arc, the angle of the object. See **Figure 11-46.**
- **DYnamic.** This option lets you drag the endpoint of the object to the desired length or angle using the crosshairs. See **Figure 11-47.** It is helpful to have the grid and snap set to usable increments when using this option.

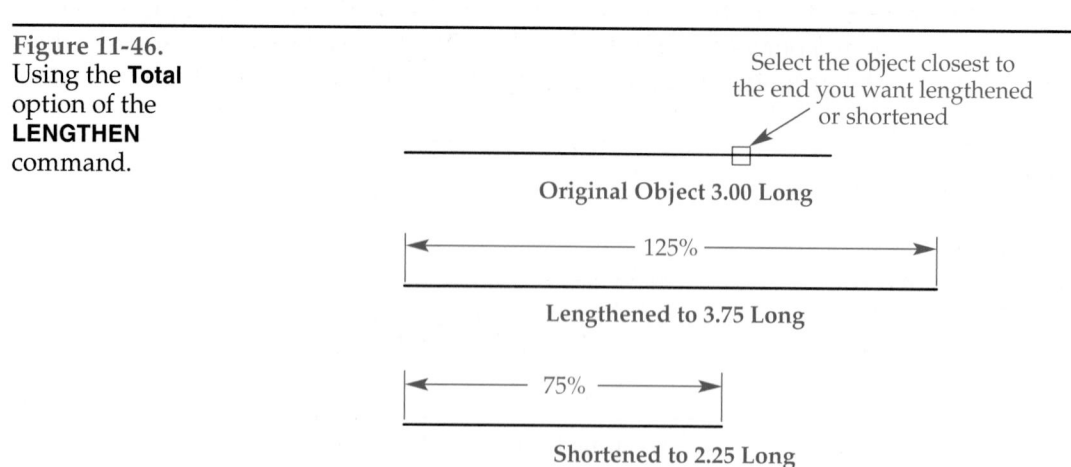

Figure 11-46.
Using the **Total** option of the **LENGTHEN** command.

Select the object closest to
the end you want lengthened
or shortened

Original Object 3.00 Long

125%

Lengthened to 3.75 Long

75%

Shortened to 2.25 Long

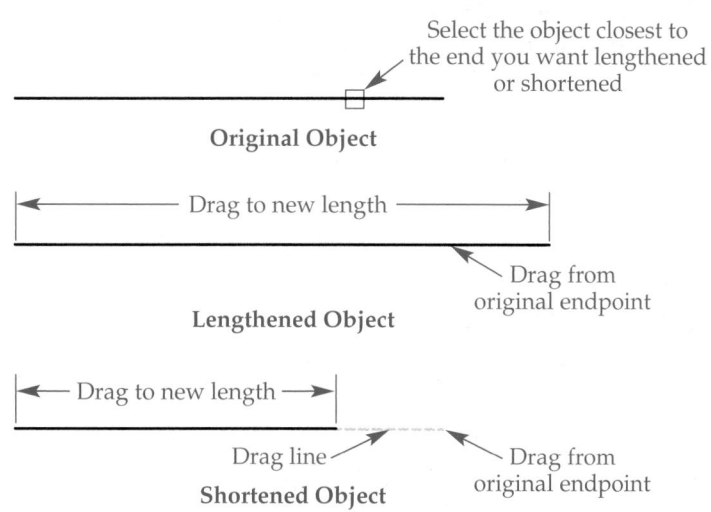

Figure 11-47.
Using the **DYnamic** option of the **LENGTHEN** command.

Select the object closest to the end you want lengthened or shortened

Original Object

Drag to new length

Lengthened Object

Drag from original endpoint

Drag to new length

Drag line

Shortened Object

Drag from original endpoint

NOTE

Only lines and arcs can be lengthened dynamically. A spline's length can only be decreased. Splines are described in Chapter 14.

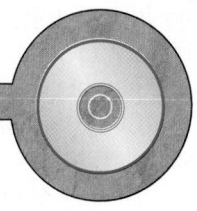

Exercise 11-15
Complete the exercise on the Student CD.

Joining Objects Together

It is common to have unneeded objects in a drawing after working on the drawing for a while. After using some commands that edit objects, the result often is multiple objects that should be one object. These multiple objects make the drawing file size larger and the drawing more cumbersome.

The **JOIN** command can join certain objects together to make one object. To access this command, pick the **Join** button in the **2D Draw** control panel of the **Dashboard** or the **Modify** toolbar, select **Modify** > **Join**, or type J or JOIN. This command can be used on lines, polylines, splines, arcs, and elliptical arcs. Only objects of the same type can be joined together. For example, a line can be joined to another line, but a line cannot be joined to a polyline. Also, joined objects must be in the same plane.

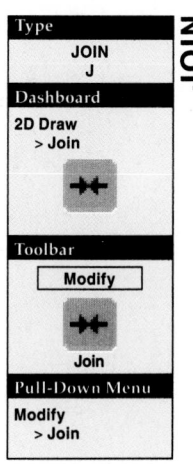

Joining Lines

Each type of object has different rules for joining. To join lines, the lines must be collinear. The lines can be touching, have gaps between them, or be overlapping. See Figure 11-48.

Joining Polylines and Splines

To join polylines together, the polylines must have a common endpoint. No gaps can exist between the segments, and they cannot overlap. See Figure 11-49. The rules for joining splines together are the same as for polylines. The spline objects must share a common endpoint.

Figure 11-48.
Lines must be collinear to be joined, but there can be gaps and overlaps between the lines.

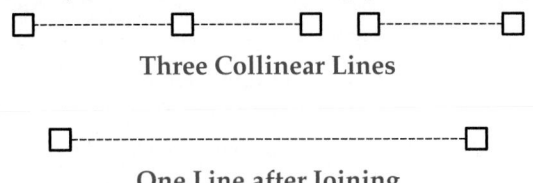

Three Collinear Lines

One Line after Joining

Figure 11-49.
Only polylines that share an endpoint can be joined.

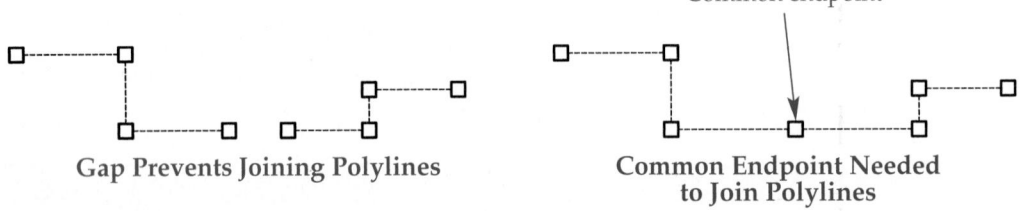

Gap Prevents Joining Polylines

Common endpoint

Common Endpoint Needed
to Join Polylines

Joining Arcs and Elliptical Arcs

Arcs that share the same center point and reside on the same circular path can be joined together. The arcs can be overlapping or have a gap between them. In Figure 11-50, two arcs with a gap have been joined together. When there is more than one gap between two arcs to be joined, using the **JOIN** command may close a gap other than the one you desired. When closing gaps in arcs, make sure to pick the arcs in a counterclockwise direction.

Elliptical arcs can be joined together using the same rules as the arc. The elliptical arcs must reside on the same elliptical path. They can, however, overlap or have gaps between them.

Both arcs and elliptical arcs can be closed using the **JOIN** command. When you use the **cLose** option on an arc, it becomes a circle. Using this option on an elliptical arc creates an ellipse.

Figure 11-50.
Arcs can have a gap or be overlapping, as shown on the left, but they must share the same circular path. On the right, the two arcs are shown after they have been joined.

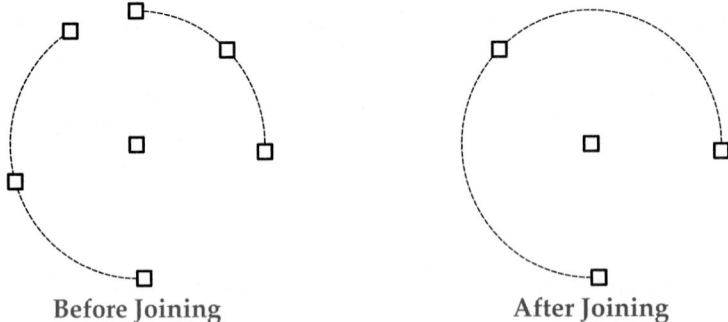

Before Joining

After Joining

Creating Selection Sets

When creating complex drawings, you often need to perform the same editing operation on many objects. For example, assume you have designed a complex metal part with more than 40 holes for 1/8" bolts. A design change occurs, and you are notified that 3/16" bolts will be used instead of 1/8" bolts. Therefore, the hole size will also change. You could select and modify each circle individually, but it would be more efficient to create a selection set of all the circles and then modify them simultaneously.

AutoCAD provides two methods of creating selection sets: the **Quick Select** dialog box and the **Object Selection Filter** dialog box. The **Quick Select** dialog box is used to create simple selection sets by specifying object types and property values for selection. The **Object Selection Filter** dialog box provides additional selection criteria and allows you to save selection sets.

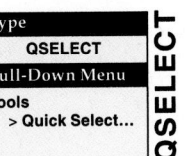

NOTE

The following section describes the **Quick Select** dialog box. This is the more common of the two tools for creating selection sets, since it is easier to access and use. The **Object Selection Filter** dialog box does provide some additional options, including the capability of saving selection set filters. Refer to the *Object Selection Filters* document in the *Supplemental Material* section of the Student CD for more information on this advanced tool.

Using Quick Select to Create Selection Sets

With the **Quick Select** dialog box, you can quickly create a selection set based on the filtering criteria you specify. To access this dialog box, pick **Tools > Quick Select...** from the pull-down menu, type QSELECT, or right-click in the drawing area and choose **Quick Select...** from the shortcut menu. See **Figure 11-51.** You can also open the **Quick Select** dialog box by picking the **Quick Select** button if the **Properties** palette is open.

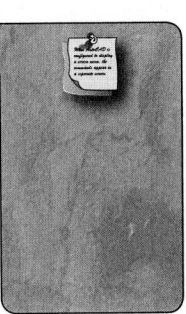

Type	
QSELECT	QSELECT
Pull-Down Menu	
Tools	
> Quick Select...	

A selection set can be defined in several ways using the **Quick Select** dialog box:

- Pick the **Select objects** button and select the objects on screen.
- Specify an object type (such as text, line, or circle) to be selected throughout the drawing.
- Specify a property (such as a color or layer) that objects must possess in order to be selected.

Once the selection criteria are defined, you can use the radio buttons in the **How to apply:** area to include or exclude the defined objects.

Look at **Figure 11-52** as you follow this example that uses the **Quick Select** command:

1. Select **Tools > Quick Select...** to open the **Quick Select** dialog box.
2. In the **Apply to:** drop-down list, select **Entire drawing**. If you access the **Quick Select** dialog box after a selection set is defined, there is also a **Current selection** option that allows you to create a subset of the existing set.
3. In the **Object type:** drop-down list, select **Multiple**. This will allow you to select any object type. The drop-down list contains all the object types in the drawing.
4. In the **Properties:** list, select **Color**. The items in the **Properties:** list vary depending on what is specified in the **Object type:** drop-down list.
5. In the **Operator:** drop-down list, select **= Equals**.

Figure 11-51.
Selection sets can be defined in the **Quick Select** dialog box.

Select specific object type or multiple

Pick to select objects with pick box

Specify operator to be used to define selected objects using property value

Value for selected property

Determines if objects defined above are selected or not selected

Check if adding items to an existing selection set

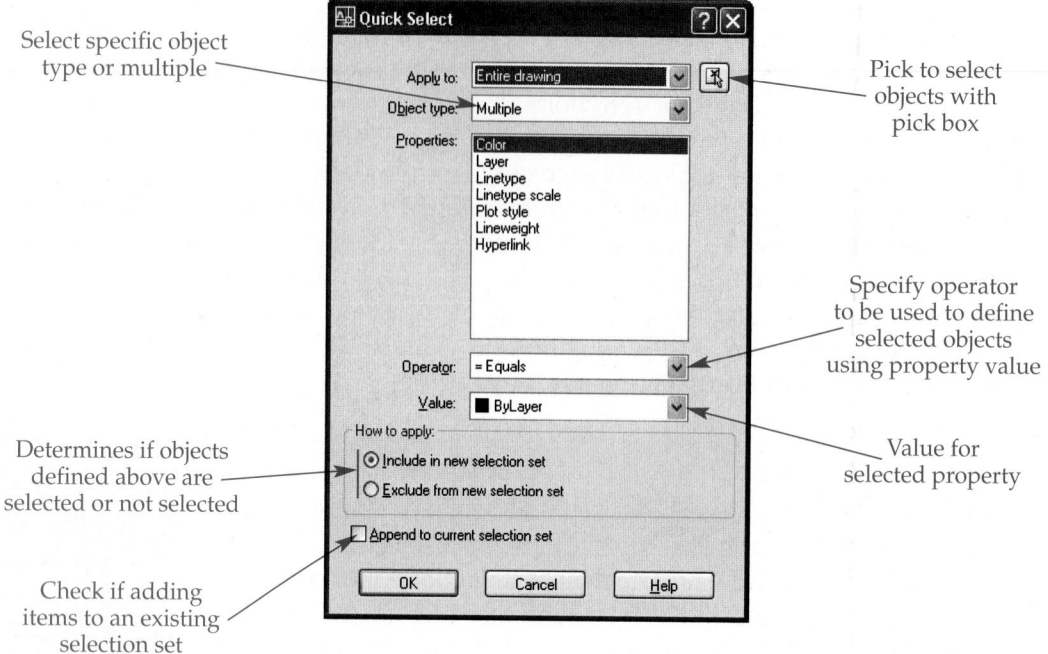

Figure 11-52.
Creating selection sets with the **Quick Select** dialog box. A—Objects in drawing. B—Selection set containing objects with the display color specified. C—Circle object added to initial selection set.

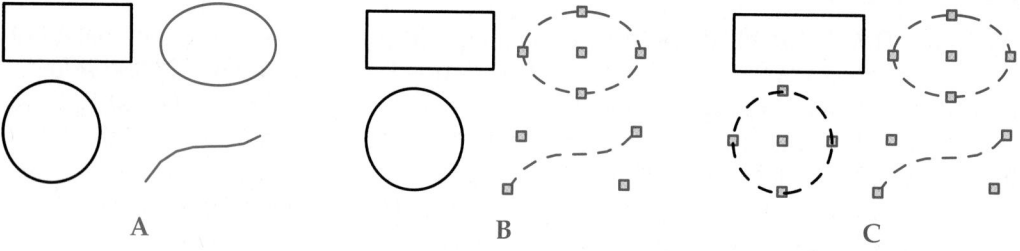

A   B   C

6. The **Value:** drop-down list contains values corresponding to the entry in the **Properties:** drop-down list. In this case, color values are listed. Select the color of the right-hand objects in **Figure 11-52A**.

7. Under the **How to apply:** area, pick the **Include in new selection set** radio button.

8. Pick the **OK** button.

AutoCAD selects all objects with the color specified in the **Value:** drop-down list, as shown in **Figure 11-52B**.

Once a set of objects has been selected, the **Quick Select** dialog box can be used to refine the selection set. Use the **Exclude from new selection set** option to exclude objects or use the **Append to current selection set** option to add objects. The following procedure refines the selection set created above to include any circles in the drawing that have a black color.

1. While the initial set of objects is selected, right-click in the drawing area and select **Quick Select...** from the shortcut menu to open the **Quick Select** dialog box.

2. Check the **Append to current selection set** check box at the bottom of the dialog box. AutoCAD automatically selects the **Entire drawing** option in the **Apply to:** drop-down list.

3. Select **Circle** in the **Object type:** drop-down list, **Color** in the **Properties:** drop-down list, **= Equals** in the **Operator:** drop-down list, and **Black** (or **ByLayer**, as appropriate) in the **Value:** drop-down list.
4. In the **How to apply:** area, pick the **Include in new selection set** radio button.
5. Pick the **OK** button. The selection now appears as shown in **Figure 11-52C**.

Creating Object Groups

A *group* is a named selection set. Groups are saved with the drawing and therefore exist throughout multiple drawing sessions. Objects can be members of more than one group, and groups can be nested. A *nested group* is a group defined inside of, or as a subset of, another group. By default, selecting one object in a group causes the entire group to be selected. Nesting can be used to place smaller groups into larger groups for easier editing.

An object existing in multiple groups creates an interesting situation. For example, if a line and an arc are grouped, and the arc is then grouped with a circle, moving the first group moves the line and arc, and moving the second group moves the arc and circle. Groups can be deactivated in the **Selection** tab of the **Options** dialog box, with the **Object grouping** check box in the **Selection Modes** area.

Typing G or GROUP accesses the **Object Grouping** dialog box, in which groups can be defined and modified. See **Figure 11-53**. The **Object Grouping** dialog box consists of many elements. The text box displays the **Group Name** and lists whether or not the group is selectable. If a group is selectable, picking any object in it selects the entire group. Making a group nonselectable allows individual objects within the group to be edited.

The **Group Identification** area has several components:
- **Find Name.** This button displays a dialog list of all groups with which an object is associated. When you pick this button, a Pick a member of a group prompt appears. When you pick an object, the **Group Member List** dialog box lists any groups with which the object is associated.
- **Highlight.** This button allows a group name to be specified and then highlights all its members in the drawing editor. This allows you to see the parts of the drawing identified as members of that group. Pick the **Continue** button or press [Enter] to return to the **Object Grouping** dialog box.

group: A named selection set.

nested group: A group that exists within another group.

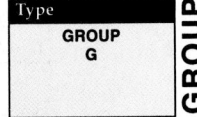

Figure 11-53.
The various elements of the **Object Grouping** dialog box.

Currently defined groups

Options for creating a new group

Group identification

Options for changing a group

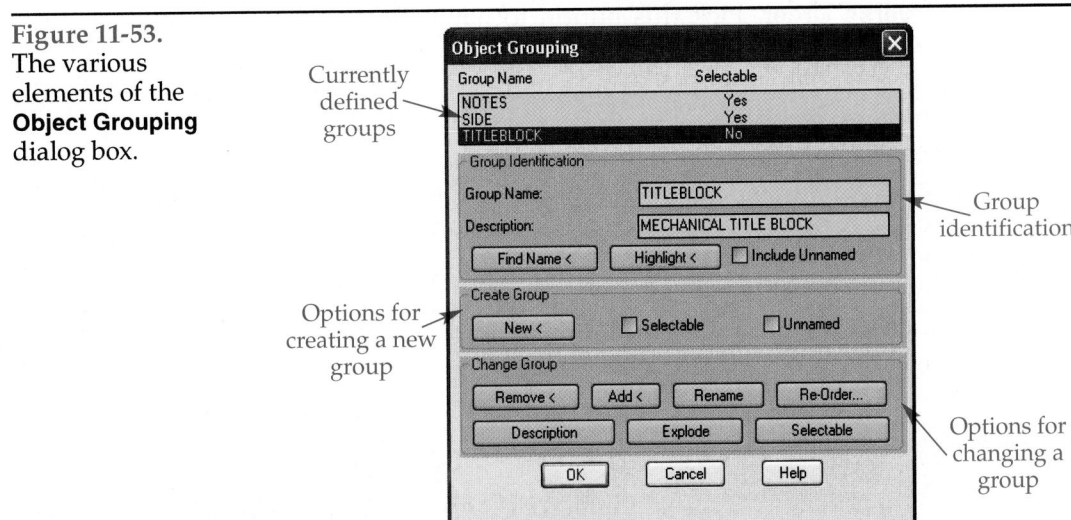

- **Include Unnamed.** This check box causes unnamed groups to be listed with named groups. Unnamed groups are given a default name by AutoCAD in the format of *A*x*, where *x* is an integer value that increases with each new group, such as *A6. Unnamed groups can be named later using the **Rename** option.

The **Create Group** area contains the options for creating a new group:
- **New.** This button creates a new group from the selected objects using the name entered in the **Group Name:** text box. AutoCAD issues a Select objects for grouping: Select objects: prompt after you enter a new name in the **Group Name:** text box.
- **Selectable.** A check in this box sets the initial status of the **Selectable** value as Yes for the new group. This is indicated in the **Selectable** list described earlier. No check here specifies No in the **Selectable** list. This can be changed later.
- **Unnamed.** This indicates whether or not the new group will be named. If this box is checked, AutoCAD assigns its own default name as detailed previously.

The **Change Group** area of the **Object Grouping** dialog box shows the options for changing a group:
- **Remove.** Pick this button to remove objects from a group definition.
- **Add.** This button allows objects to be added to a group definition.
- **Rename.** Pick this button to change the name of an existing group, including unnamed groups.
- **Re-Order.** Objects are numbered in the order they are selected when defining the group. The first object is numbered 0, not 1. This button allows objects to be reordered within the group. For example, if a group contains a set of instructions, you can reorder the instructions to create tool paths. The **Order Group** dialog box is displayed when you pick this button. The elements of this dialog box are briefly described as follows:
  - **Group Name.** Displays the name of the selected group.
  - **Description.** Displays the description for the selected group.
  - **Remove from position (0-*n*).** Position number of the object to reorder, where *n* is one less than the total number of objects found in the group. You place the desired order in the text boxes to the right of this feature and the next two features.
  - **Enter new position number for the object (0-*n*).** Position to which the object is being moved, where *n* is one less than the total number of objects found in the group.
  - **Number of objects (1-*n*).** Displays the number of objects or the range to reorder, where *n* is the total number of objects found in the group.
  - **Reverse Order.** Pick this button to have the order of all members in the group reversed.
- **Description.** Updates the group with the new description entered in the **Description:** text box.
- **Explode.** Pick this button to delete the selected group definition, but not the group's objects. The group name is removed, and the original group is exploded. Copies of the group become unnamed groups. By selecting the **Include Unnamed** check box, these unnamed groups are displayed and can then be exploded, if needed.
- **Selectable.** Toggles the selectable value of a group. This is where you can change the value in the **Selectable** list.

Exercise 11-16
Complete the exercise on the Student CD.

Express Tools
Chapter 11

The following Express Tools are related to topics described in this chapter. Refer to "Chapter 11: Express Selection" in the Express Tools area on the Student CD for information on these tools:

Get Selection Set

Fast Select

Chapter Test

Answer the following questions. Write your answers on a separate sheet of paper or complete the electronic chapter test on the Student CD.

1. How is the size of a fillet specified?
2. Explain how to set the radius of a fillet to .50.
3. Name the system variable used to preset the fillet radius.
4. Which option of the **CHAMFER** command would you use to specify a .125 × .125 chamfer?
5. What is the purpose of the **mEthod** option in the **CHAMFER** command?
6. Describe the difference between the **Trim** and **No trim** options when using the **CHAMFER** and **FILLET** commands.
7. How can you split an object in two without removing a portion?
8. In what direction should you pick points to break a portion out of a circle or an arc?
9. Name the command that trims an object to a cutting edge.
10. The **EXTEND** command is the opposite of the _____ command.
11. Name the command associated with boundary edges.
12. Name the option in the **TRIM** and **EXTEND** commands allowing you to trim or extend to an implied intersection.
13. List two locations drafters normally choose as the base point when using the **MOVE** or **COPY** commands.
14. Define the term *displacement*, as it relates to the **MOVE** and **COPY** commands.
15. Explain the difference between the **MOVE** and **COPY** commands.
16. Briefly explain how to make several copies of the same object.
17. How would you go about rotating an object 45° clockwise?
18. Name the command that can be used to move and rotate an object simultaneously.
19. What command allows you to draw a reverse image of an existing object?
20. What is the difference between polar and rectangular arrays?
21. What four values should you know before you create a rectangular array?
22. Suppose an object is 1.5" (38 mm) wide and you want to create a rectangular array with .75" (19 mm) spacing between objects. What should you specify for the distance between columns?
23. How do you specify a clockwise polar array rotation?
24. What values should you know before you create a polar array?
25. What command would you use to reduce the size of an entire drawing by one-half?
26. Which control panel of the **Dashboard** contains the **MOVE, COPY, TRIM, EXTEND,** and **STRETCH** commands?
27. How do you cancel the **STRETCH** command?
28. Identify the **LENGTHEN** command option corresponding to each of the following descriptions:
    A. Allows a positive or negative change in length from the endpoint.
    B. Changes a length or an arc angle by a percentage of the total.
    C. Sets the total length or angle to the value specified.
    D. Drags the endpoint of the object to the desired length or angle.

29. What command can be used to combine two collinear lines into a single line object?

30. Give the keyboard shortcuts for the following commands:
    A. **CHAMFER**
    B. **FILLET**
    C. **BREAK**
    D. **TRIM**
    E. **EXTEND**
    F. **MOVE**
    G. **COPY**
    H. **MIRROR**
    I. **ROTATE**
    J. **ALIGN**
    K. **ARRAY**
    L. **SCALE**
    M. **LENGTHEN**

31. What is a selection set?

32. Identify four ways to open the **Quick Select** dialog box.

33. Define *group*.

34. How do you access the **Object Grouping** dialog box?

35. Describe how you create a new group.

Drawing Problems

Use your templates as appropriate for each of the following problems. Start a new drawing for each problem, unless indicated otherwise.

1. Draw Object A using the **LINE** and **ARC** commands. Make sure the corners overrun and the arc is centered on the lines, but does not touch the lines. Use the **TRIM**, **EXTEND**, and **MOVE** commands to make Object B. Save the drawing as P11-1.

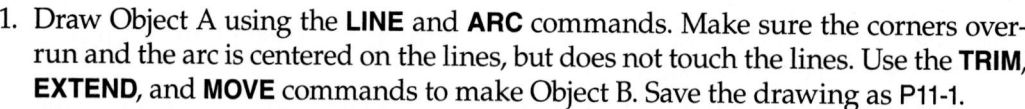

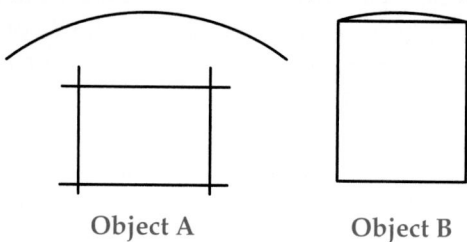

Object A   Object B

2. Open drawing P11-1 for further editing (Object A). Using the **STRETCH** command, change the shape to create Object B. Make a copy of Object B. Change the copy to represent Object C. Save the drawing as P11-2.

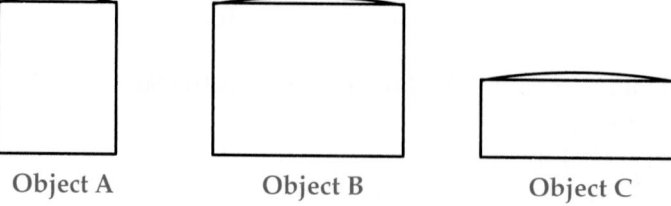

Object A   Object B   Object C

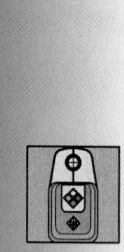

3. Refer to Figure 11-42 in this chapter. Draw and make three copies of the object shown in Option 1. Stretch the first copy to twice its length, as shown in Option 2. Stretch the second copy to twice its height. Double the size of the third copy using the **SCALE** command. Save the drawing as P11-3.

4. Draw Objects A, B, and C at the sizes shown below, but do not include the dimensions. Move Objects A, B, and C to new positions. Select a corner of Object A and the centers of Objects B and C as the base points. Save the drawing as P11-4.

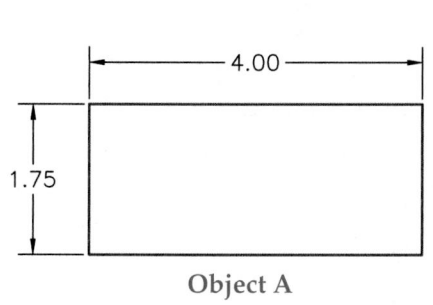
Object A

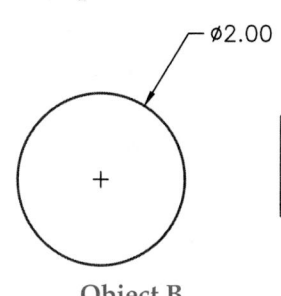
Object B

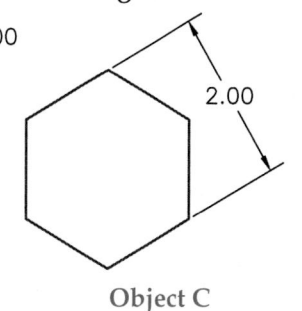
Object C

5. Draw Objects A, B, and C, shown in Problem 11-4, on the left side of the screen. Make a copy of Object A two units to the right. Make four copies of Object B three units to the right, center to center. Make three copies of Object C three units to the right, center to center. Save the drawing as P11-5.

6. Draw the object shown using the **ELLIPSE**, **COPY**, and **LINE** commands. Use the **BREAK** or **TRIM** command when drawing and editing the lower ellipse. Save the drawing as P11-6.

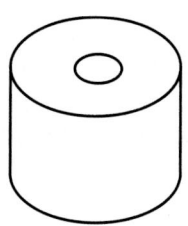

7. Open drawing P11-6 for further editing. Shorten the height of the object using the **STRETCH** command, as shown below. Next, add to the object as indicated. Save the drawing as P11-7.

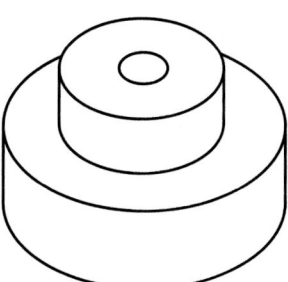

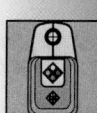

8. You have been given an engineer's sketches and notes to construct a drawing of a sprocket. Create a front and side view of the sprocket using the **ARRAY** command. Place the drawing on one of your templates. Do not add dimensions. Save the drawing as P11-8.

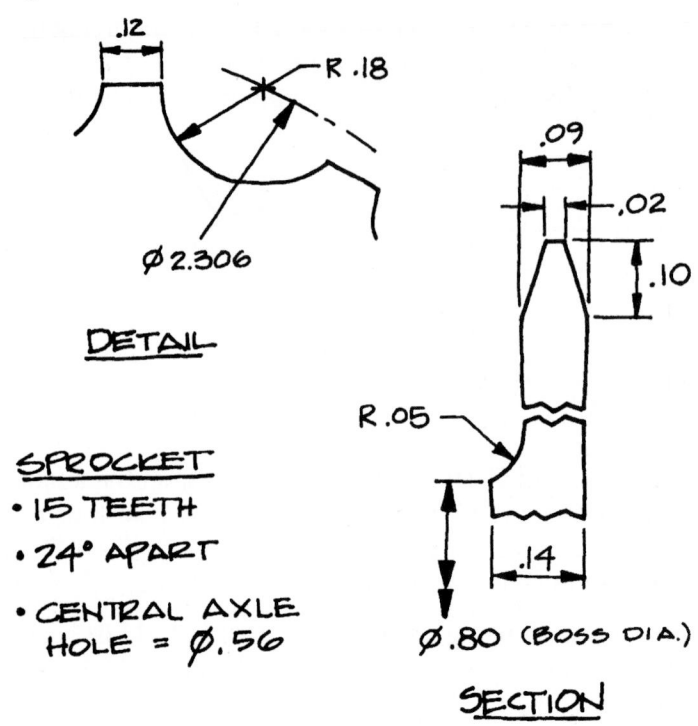

DETAIL

SPROCKET
- 15 TEETH
- 24° APART
- CENTRAL AXLE HOLE = Ø.56

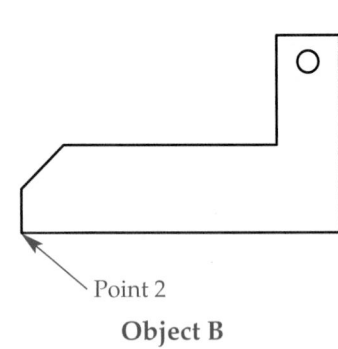

SECTION

9. Draw Object A without dimensions. Use the **CHAMFER** and **FILLET** commands to your best advantage. Draw a mirror image as Object B. Now, remove the original view and move the new view so that Point 2 is at the original Point 1 location. Save the drawing as P11-9.

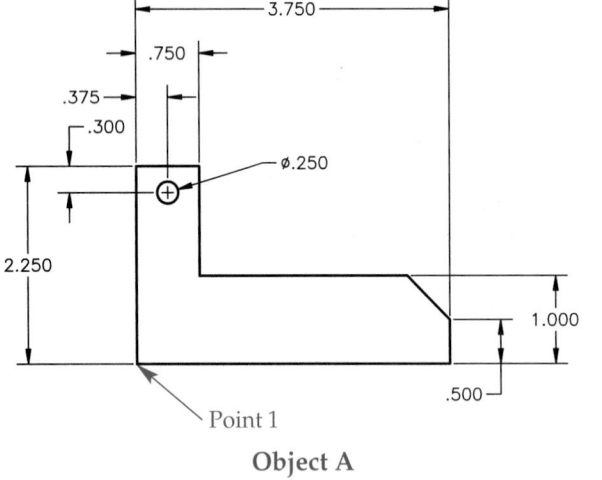

Point 1

Object A

Point 2

Object B

10. Draw the object shown below without dimensions. The object is symmetrical; therefore, draw only one half. Mirror the other half into place. Use the **CHAMFER** and **FILLET** commands to your best advantage. All fillets and rounds are .125. Use the **JOIN** command where necessary. Save the drawing as P11-10.

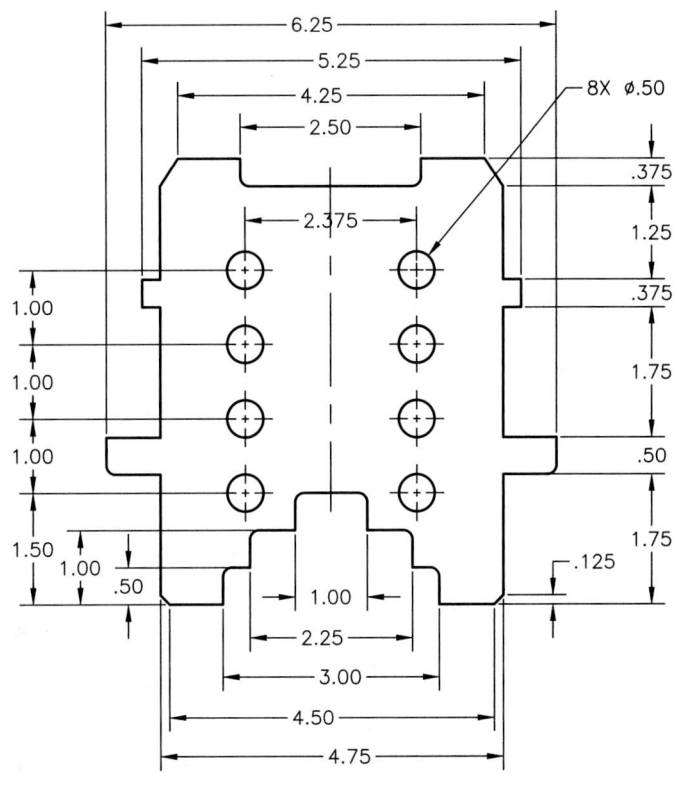

11. Use the **TRIM** and **OFFSET** commands to assist you in drawing this object. Do not draw centerlines or dimensions. Save the completed drawing as P11-11.

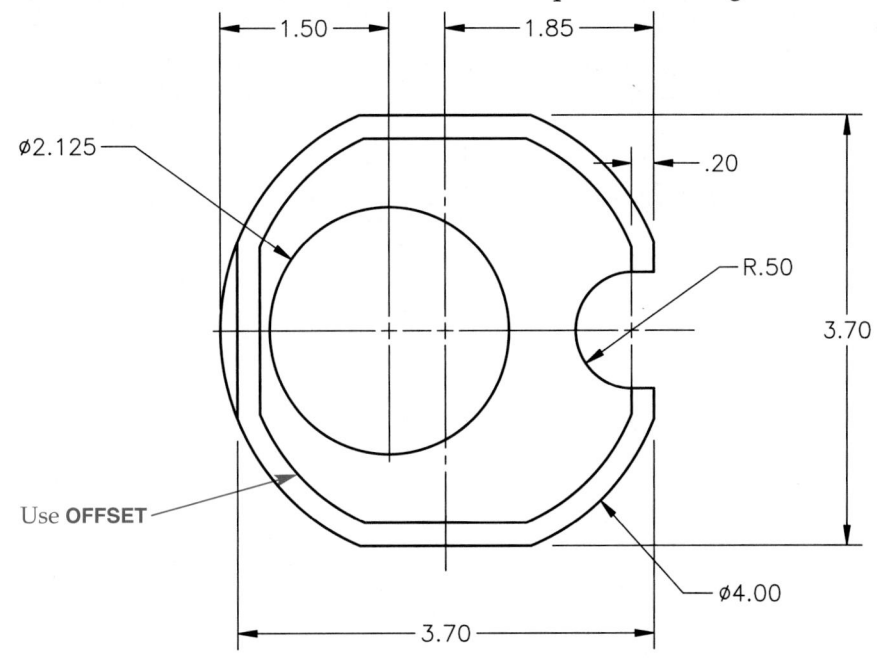

12. Draw the object shown below without dimensions. Mirror the right half into place. Use the **CHAMFER** and **FILLET** commands to your best advantage. Save the drawing as P11-12.

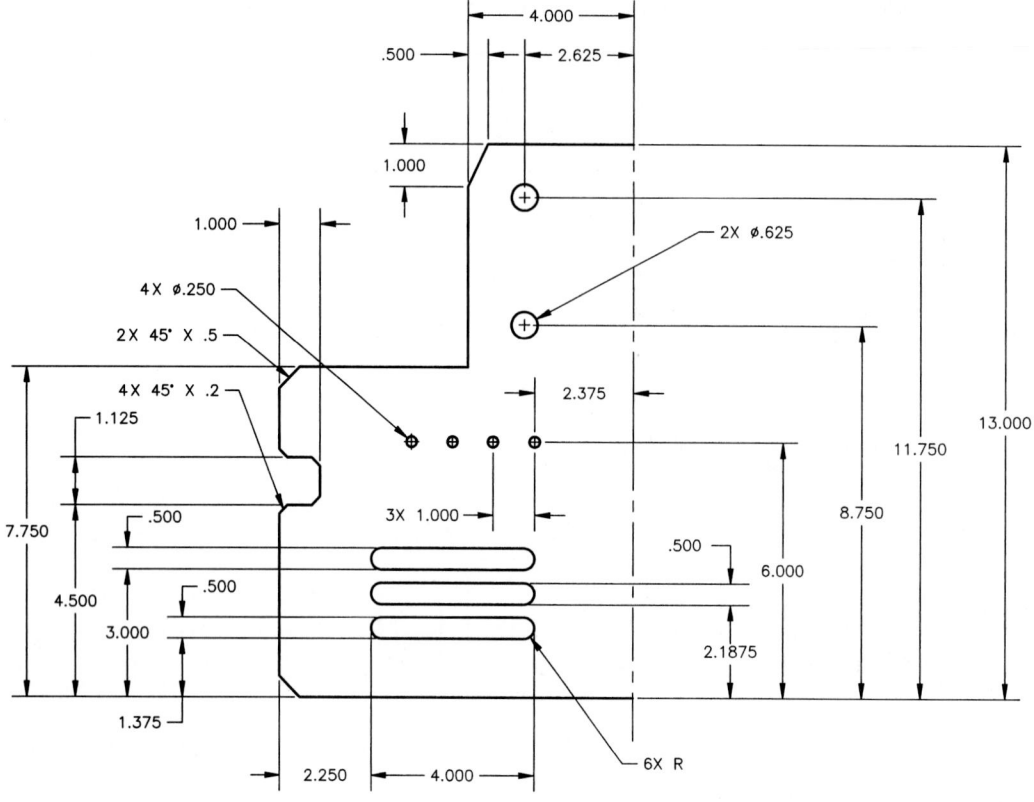

13. Redraw the objects shown below. Mirror the drawing, but make sure the text remains readable. Delete the original image during the mirroring process. Save the drawing as P11-13.

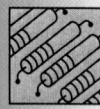

2b1

TRANSFER

5a2 4a1 8a1

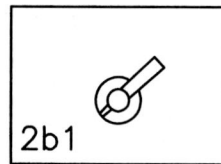

LTS. HTRS. FANS

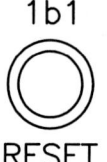

2b1

1b1

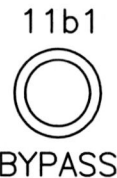

RESET

11b1

BYPASS

14. Draw the following object views using the dimensions given. Use **ARRAY** to construct the hole and tooth arrangements. Use one of your templates for the drawing. Do not add dimensions. Save the drawing as P11-14.

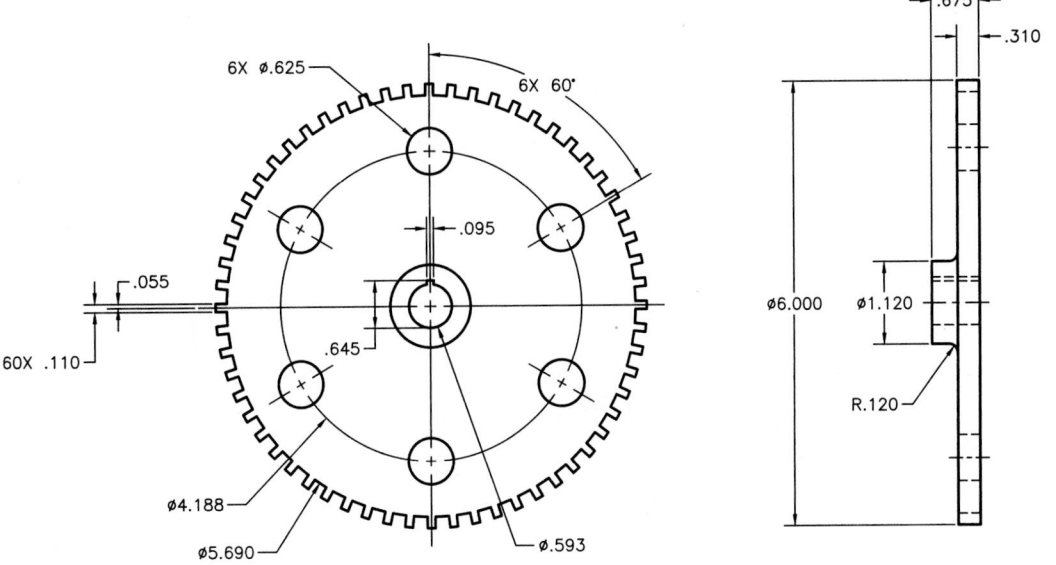

15. Draw the following object without dimensions. Use the **TRIMMODE** setting to your advantage. Save the drawing as P11-15.

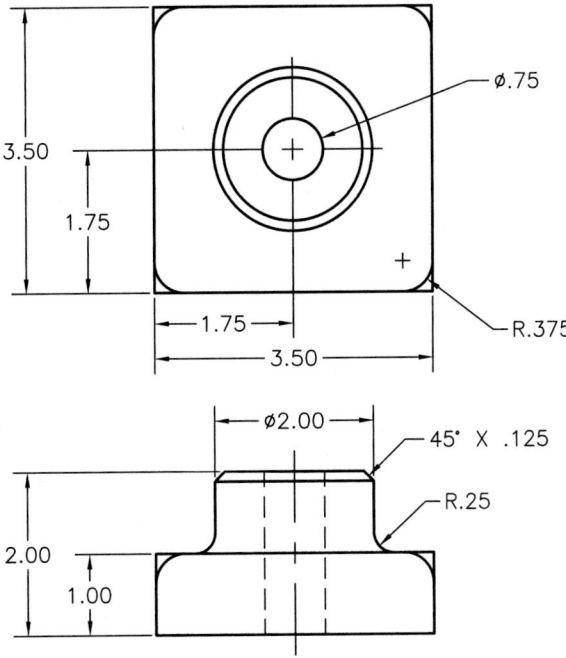

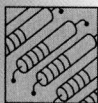

16. Draw the objects shown below. Use the **GROUP** command to name each of the objects with the names below them. Use the object groups to draw the one-line electrical diagram shown below. Use the **Explode** option to edit the symbols at 1 and 2 in the diagram, as shown. Save the drawing as P11-16.

Switch   Regulator   Ground-switch   Ground-overcurrent   Fuse

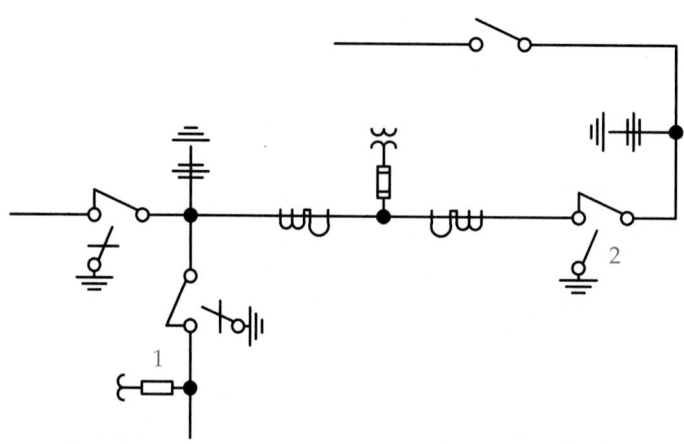

17. Draw the following bracket. Do not include dimensions in your drawing. Use the **FILLET** command where appropriate. Save the drawing as P11-17.

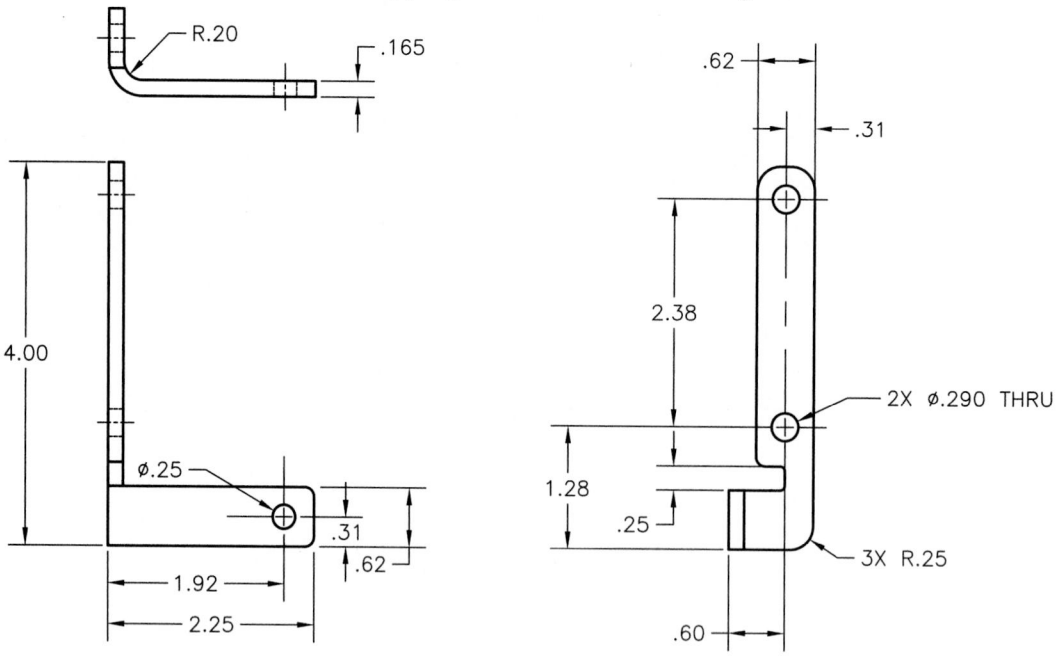

ALL FILLETS AND ROUNDS R.06

18. Draw this refrigeration system schematic. Save the drawing as P11-18.

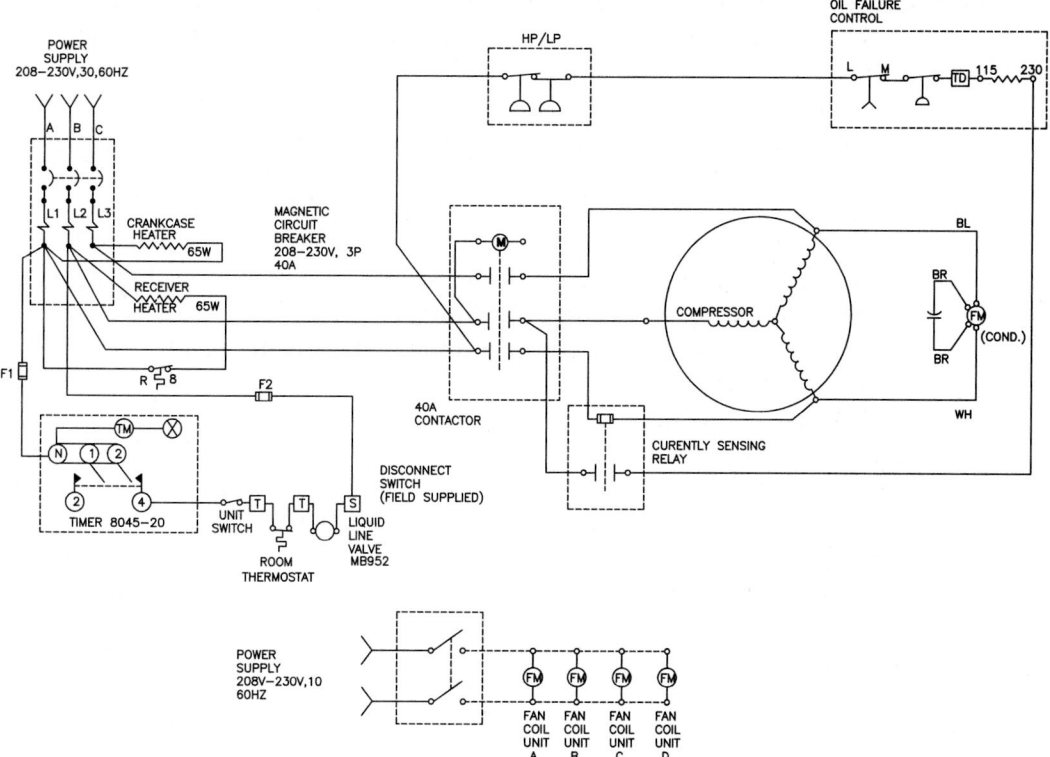

19. Draw this timer schematic. Save the drawing as P11-19.

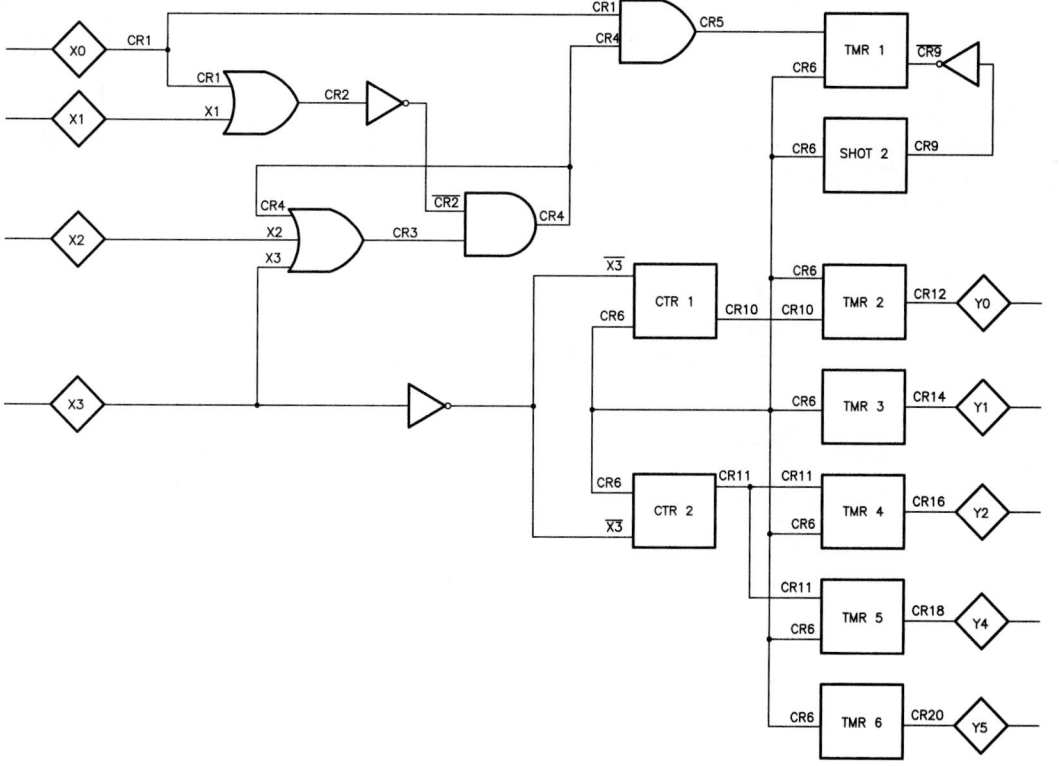

20. The following structural sketch shows a steel column arrangement on a concrete floor slab for a new building. The *I*-shaped symbols represent the steel columns. The columns are arranged in "bay lines" and "column lines." The column lines are numbered *1*, *2*, and *3*. The bay lines are labeled *A* through *G*. The width of a bay is 24'-0". Line balloons, or tags, identify the bay and column lines. Draw the arrangement, using **ARRAY** for the steel column symbols and the tags. Do not dimension the drawing. The following guidelines will help you:

A. Begin a new drawing or use an architectural template.
B. Select architectural units and set up the drawing to print on a 36 × 24 sheet size. Determine the scale required for the floor plan to fit on this sheet size and specify the drawing limits accordingly.
C. Draw the steel column symbol to the dimensions given.
D. Set the grid spacing at 2'-0" (24").
E. Set the snap spacing at 12".
F. Draw all other objects.
G. Place text inside the balloon tags. Set the running object snap mode to **Center** and justify the text to **Middle**. Make the text height 6".
H. Place a title block on the drawing.
I. Save the drawing as P11-20.

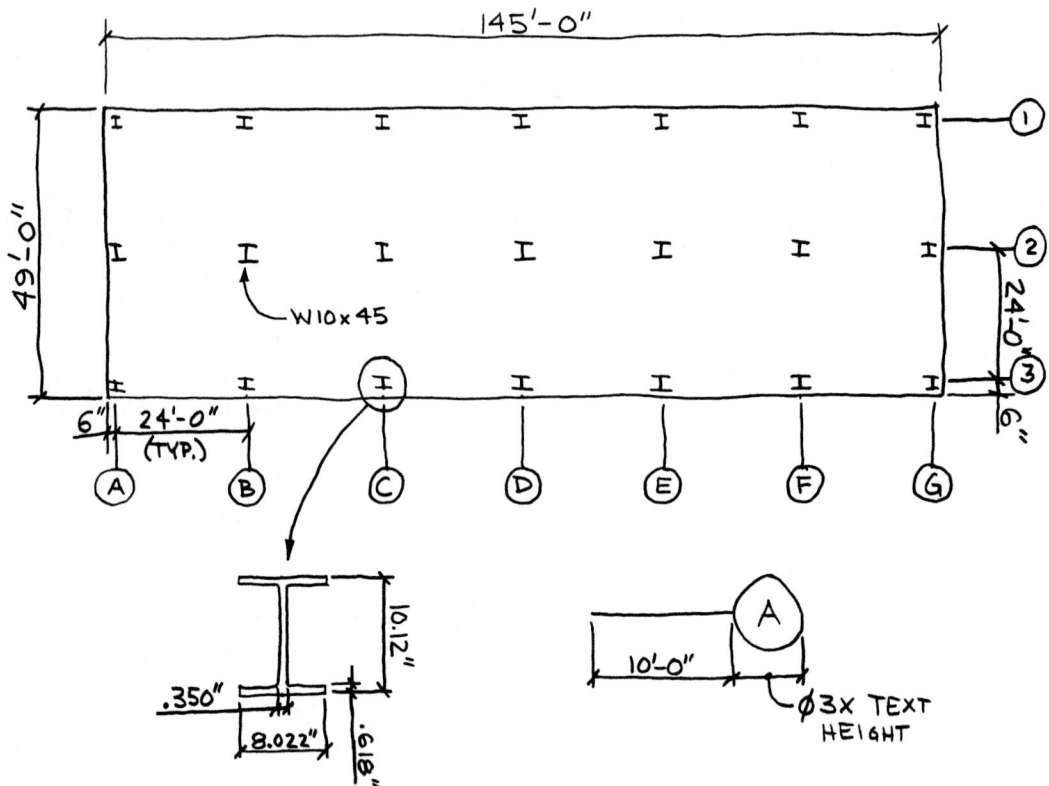

21. The sketch shown below is a proposed office layout of desks and chairs. One desk is shown with the layout of a chair, keyboard, monitor, and tower-mounted computer (drawn with dotted lines). All of the desk workstations should have the same configuration. The exact sizes and locations of the doors and windows are not important for this problem. Use the following guidelines to complete this problem:

A. Begin a new drawing.
B. Choose architectural units.
C. Set up the drawing to print on a C-size sheet, and be sure to create the drawing in model space.
D. Use the appropriate drawing and editing commands to complete this problem quickly and efficiently.
E. Draw the desk and computer hardware to the dimensions given.
F. Do not dimension the drawing.
G. Save the drawing as P11-21.

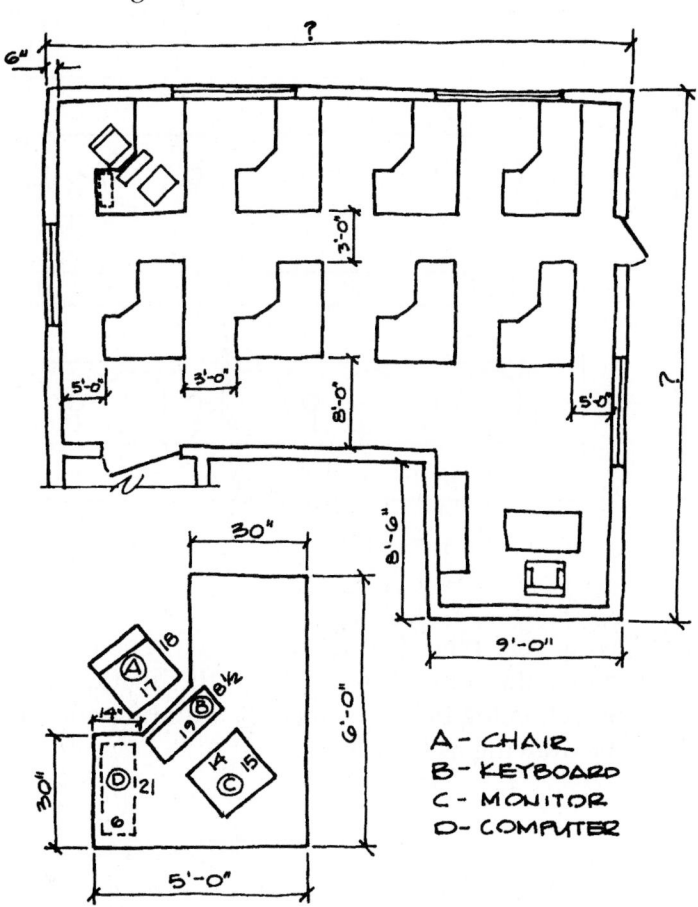

A - CHAIR
B - KEYBOARD
C - MONITOR
D - COMPUTER

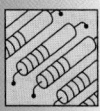

22. Use tracking and object snaps to draw the object shown below based on these instructions:
    A. Draw the outline of the object first, followed by the ten ⌀.500 holes (A).
    B. The holes labeled B are located vertically halfway between the centers of the holes labeled A. They have a diameter one-quarter the size of the holes labeled A.
    C. The holes labeled C are located vertically halfway between the holes labeled A and B. Their diameter is three-quarters of the diameter of the holes labeled B.
    D. The holes labeled D are located horizontally halfway between the centers of the holes labeled A. These holes have the same diameter as the holes labeled B.
    E. Draw the rectangles around the circles as shown.
    F. Do not draw dimensions, notes, or labels.
    G. Use the **Quick Select** dialog box to erase all circles less than ⌀.500.
    H. Save the drawing as P11-22.

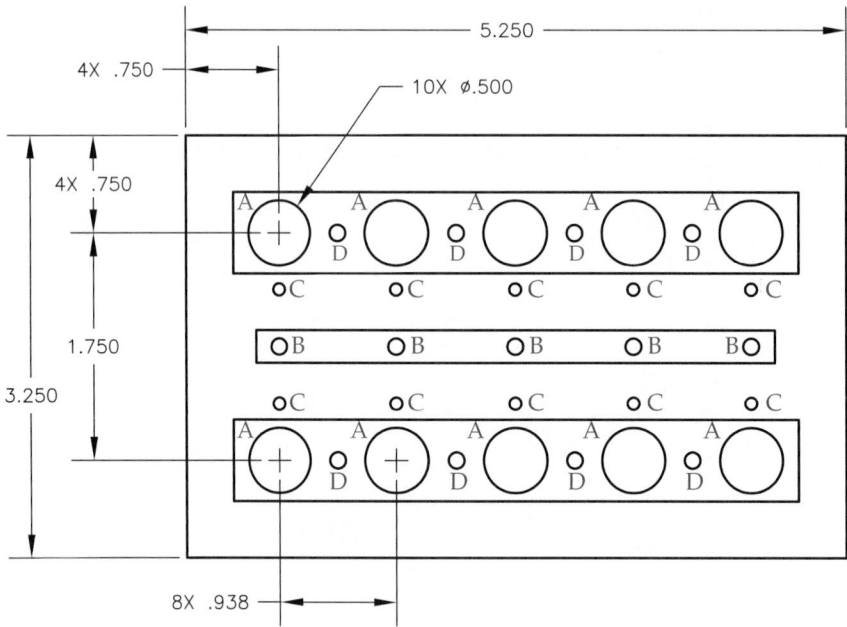

23. Draw the following roof plan. Do not dimension. Then, use the **Quick Select** dialog box to change the color of the roof and the linetype to CENTER. Finally, use the **Quick Select** dialog box to change the building outline to a continuous linetype. Save the drawing as P11-23.

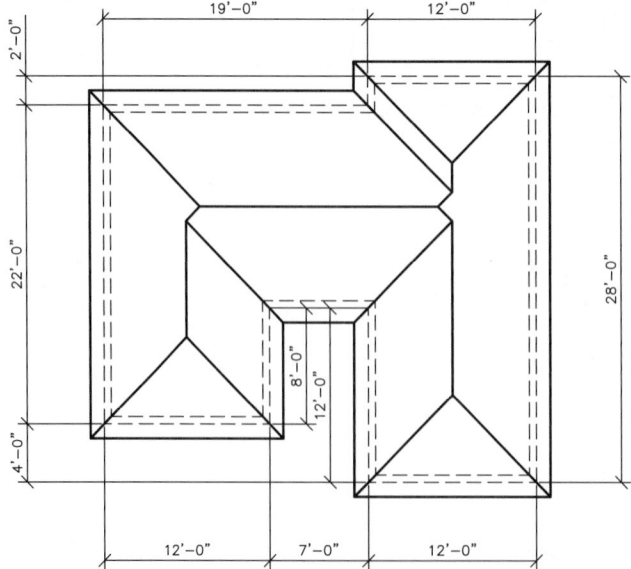

24. Draw the portion of the gasket shown on the left. Do not include dimensions. Use the **MIRROR** command to complete the gasket as shown on the right. Save the drawing as P11-24.

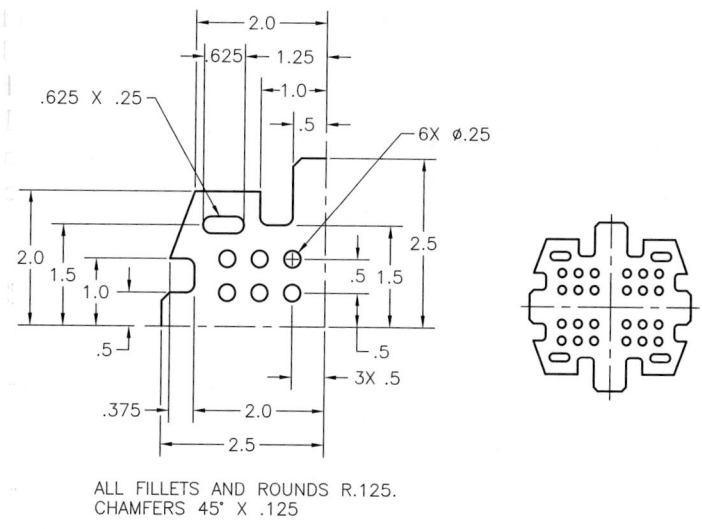

ALL FILLETS AND ROUNDS R.125.
CHAMFERS 45° X .125

25. Draw the padded bench. Do not dimension. Use the **COPY** and **ARRAY** commands as needed. Save the drawing as P11-25.

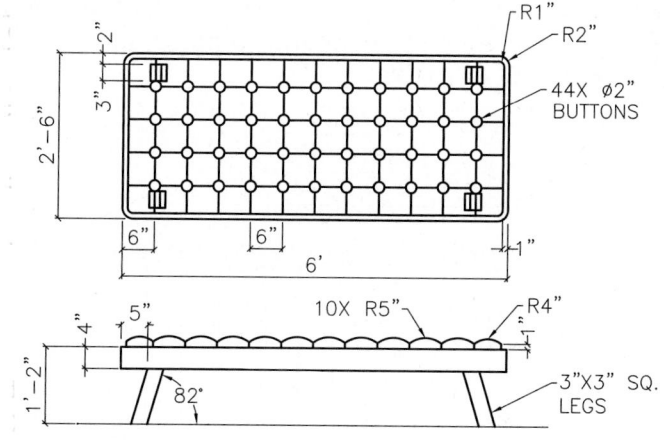

26. Draw the handwheel shown below. Do not dimension. Use the **ARRAY** command to draw the spokes. Save the drawing as P11-26.

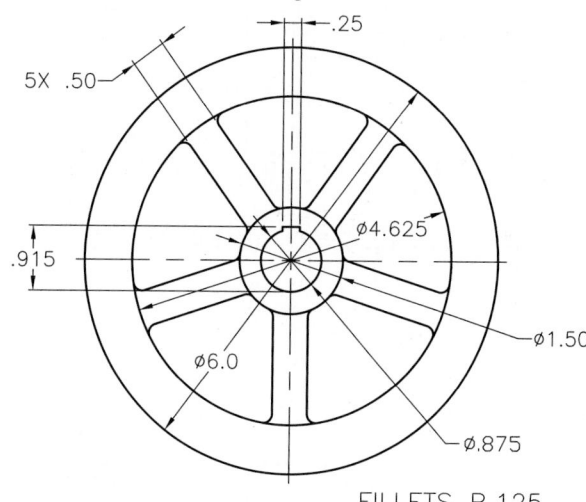

FILLETS R.125

Drawing Problems - Chapter 11

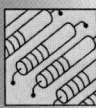

27. Draw the control diagram. Draw one branch (including text) and use the **COPY** command to your advantage. Use text editing commands as needed. Save the drawing as P11-27. (Design and drawing by EC Company, Portland, Oregon)

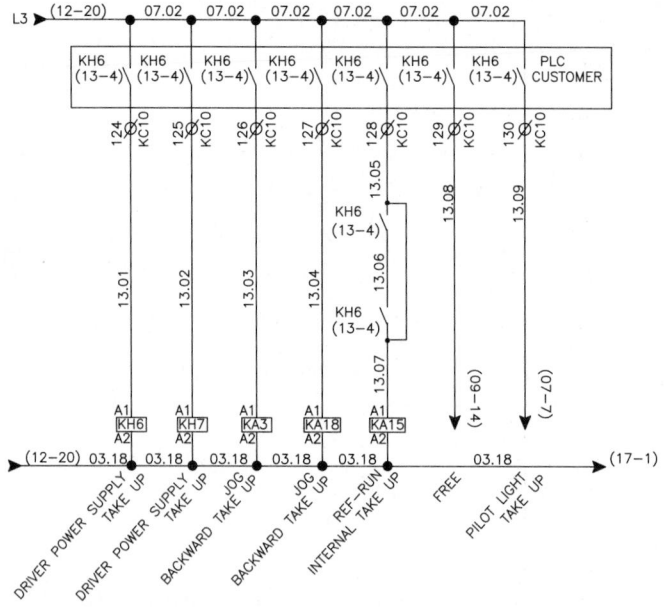

28. Draw the front elevation of this house. Create the features proportional to the given drawing. Use the **ARRAY** command to place the siding and porch rails evenly. Save the drawing as P11-28.

Drawing Problems - Chapter 11

CHAPTER 12

Editing Using Grips and Properties

Learning Objectives

After completing this chapter, you will be able to do the following:

✓ Use grips to stretch, copy, move, rotate, scale, and mirror objects.
✓ Use the noun/verb selection method to edit objects.
✓ Edit objects using the **Properties** palette.
✓ Override layer properties.
✓ Use the **MATCHPROP** command to match object properties.
✓ Edit between drawings.
✓ Use the **Revision Cloud** tool to mark up drawings.

In Chapters 3, 4, and 11, you learned how to use commands that let you perform a variety of drawing and editing activities with AutoCAD. These editing commands give you a great deal of flexibility and increase productivity. Typically, when using tools such as **ERASE**, **MOVE**, and **COPY,** you enter a command first and then select the object to be edited. This chapter takes editing a step further, however, by allowing you to select an object first and then perform editing operations.

AutoCAD Grips

In AutoCAD, *grips* are small boxes that appear at strategic points on an object when you select the object while no command is active. For example, the grips appear at the endpoints and midpoint of a straight line and at the center and quadrant points of a circle. **Figure 12-1** shows the locations of grips on several different types of objects.

To activate the grips for editing, select an object without first entering a command. Then pick any of the displayed grips to perform **STRETCH**, **COPY**, **MOVE**, **ROTATE**, **SCALE**, or **MIRROR** operations. When grips are activated, a pick box is located at the intersection of the screen crosshairs.

You can control grip settings in the **Selection** tab of the **Options** dialog box. To open the **Options** dialog box, pick **Tools > Options...** from the pull-down menu or right-click in the drawing area and select **Options...** from the shortcut menu. You can access the **Selection** tab of the **Options** dialog box directly by typing GR or DDGRIPS. The **Selection** tab of the **Options** dialog box is shown in **Figure 12-2**.

grips: Small boxes that appear at strategic points on an object, allowing you to edit the object's size and other properties.

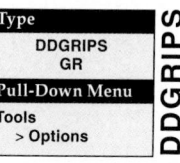

Type	
	DDGRIPS
	GR
Pull-Down Menu	
Tools	
> Options	

DDGRIPS

Figure 12-1.
Grips are placed at strategic locations on objects.

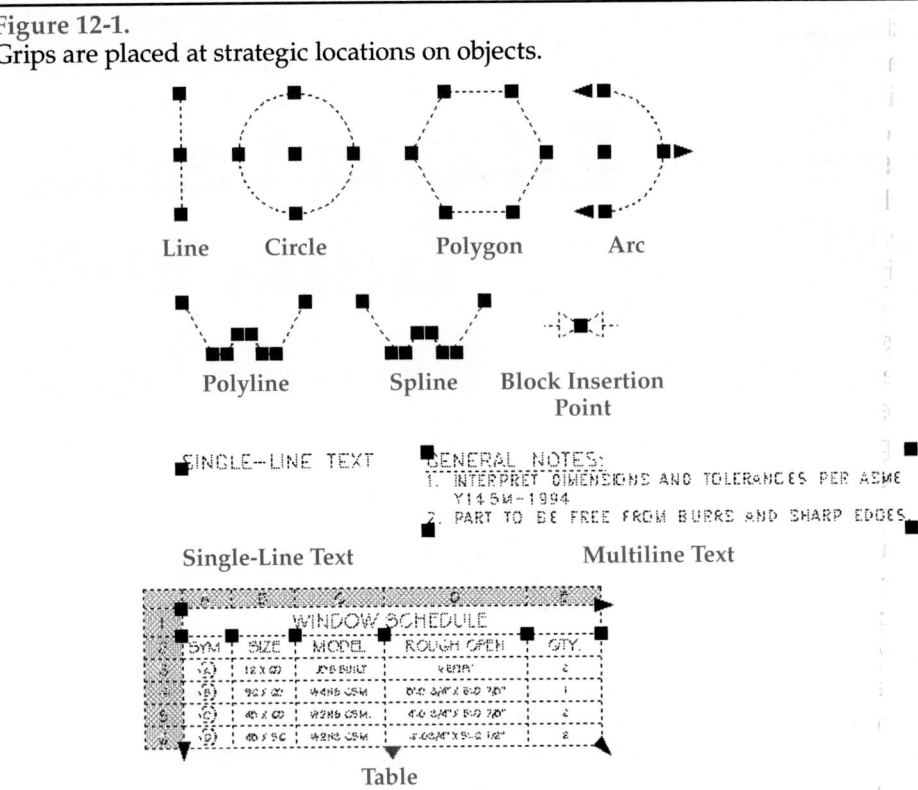

Figure 12-2.
The **Selection** tab of the **Options** dialog box contains grip control settings.

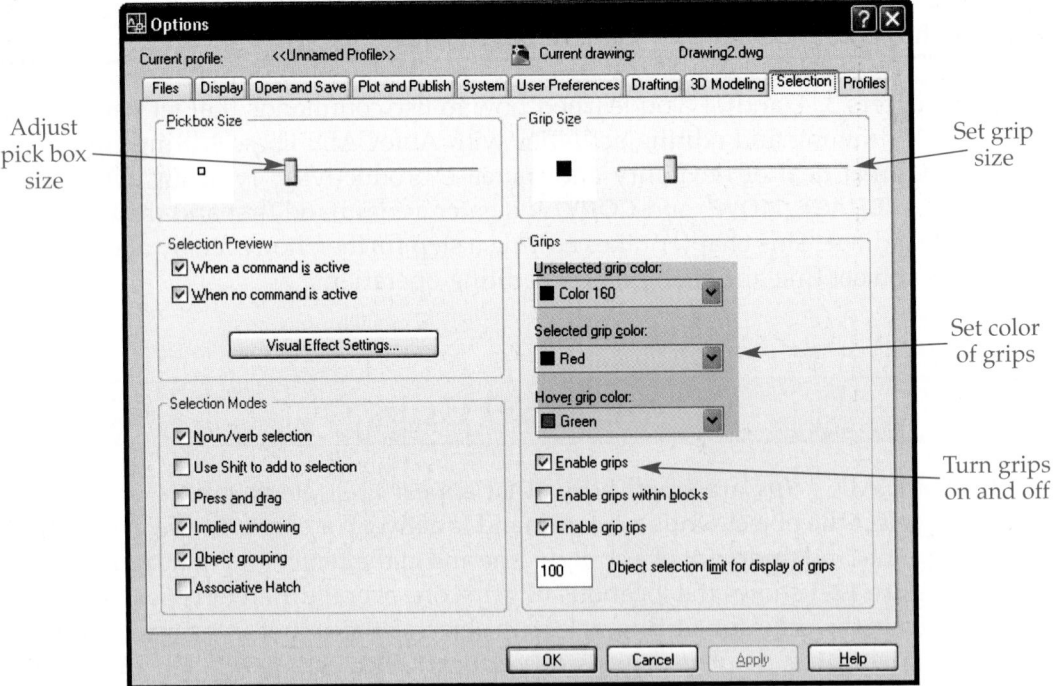

The **Pickbox Size** scroll bar lets you adjust the size of the pick box. The sample in the preview area gets smaller or larger as you move the scroll bar. Stop when you have the desired size. The pick box size is also controlled by the **PICKBOX** system variable, in which the desired size is set in pixels.

The **Grip Size** scroll bar in the **Selection** tab of the **Options** dialog box lets you graphically change the size of the grip box. The sample in the image tile gets smaller or larger as you move the scroll bar. Change the grip size to whatever works best for your drawing. Very small grip boxes may be difficult to pick. The grips may overlap, however, if they are too large. The grip size can be given a numerical value using the **GRIPSIZE** system variable. To change the default setting of 5, enter GRIPSIZE and type a desired size in pixels.

The three color drop-down lists allow you to change the color of grips. The grips displayed when you first pick an object are referred to as *unselected grips* because you have not yet picked them to perform an operation. An unselected grip is a filled-in square box the color of the **Unselected grip color:** setting. Unselected grips are Blue by default and are considered *warm grips*.

After you pick a grip, it is called a *selected grip*. A selected grip appears as a filled-in square box of the color specified by the **Selected grip color:** setting. Selected grips are Red by default and are considered *hot*. If more than one object is selected (has warm grips), what you do with the hot grips affects all of the selected objects. Objects having warm and hot grips are highlighted and are part of the current selection set.

You can remove highlighted objects from a selection set by holding down the [Shift] key and picking the objects to be removed. The [Shift] key can also be used to add or remove hot grips. If you want to make a second grip hot, hold the [Shift] key down while selecting both the first and second grip. To add more grips to the hot grip selection set, continue to hold the [Shift] key down and select the other grips. With the [Shift] key held down, selecting a hot (red) grip returns it to the warm (blue) stage. **Figure 12-3** shows two circles being modified simultaneously using hot grips. Moving the crosshairs over a warm grip and pausing changes the color of the grip to the **Hover grip color:** setting specified in the **Selection** tab of the **Options** dialog box. By default, this color is Green. This is useful when multiple grips are close together. Pausing over the warm grip and letting it change color ensures that you select the correct grip.

You can also control grip color with the **GRIPCOLOR**, **GRIPHOT**, and **GRIPHOVER** system variables. **GRIPCOLOR** controls the color of warm grips, **GRIPHOT** regulates the color of hot grips, and **GRIPHOVER** sets the hover grip color. When you enter one of these variables, set the color number as desired.

unselected grips: Grips that have not yet been picked to perform an operation.

warm grips: An adjective to describe unselected grips.

selected grip: A grip that has been selected to perform an operation.

hot: An adjective to describe selected grips.

Figure 12-3.
You can modify multiple objects by using the [Shift] key to select grips to make them hot.

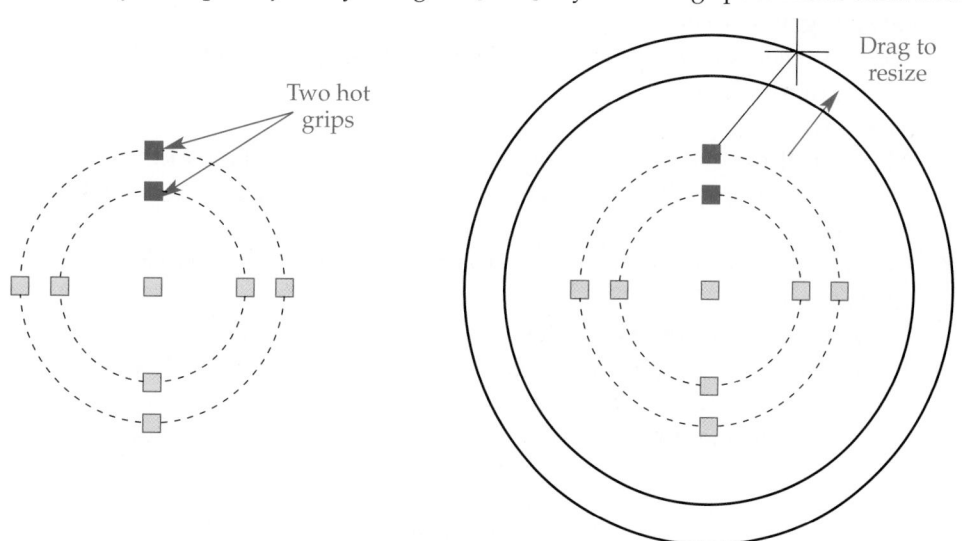

Notice the three check boxes in the **Grips** area. Pick the **Enable grips** check box to turn grips on or off. This setting can also be set using the **GRIPS** system variable.

block: A special, user-defined symbol designed to be used multiple times.

Pick the **Enable grips within blocks** check box to have grips displayed on every subobject of a block. A *block* is a special symbol designed to be used multiple times. Blocks are described in detail in Chapter 22. When this check box is off, the grip location for a block is at the insertion point, as shown in **Figure 12-1**. Grips in blocks can also be controlled with the **GRIPBLOCK** system variable.

When the **Enable grip tips** box is checked, a tip relating to the selected object displays. This option only works on custom objects that support grip tips. Standard AutoCAD objects do not have grip tips. The **GRIPTIPS** system variable also controls this option.

Using Grips

To activate grips, move the pick box to the desired object and pick. The object is highlighted, and the warm grips are displayed. To select a grip, move the pick box to the desired grip and pick it. Notice that the crosshairs snap to a grip. When you pick a grip, the command line shows the following prompt:

```
** STRETCH **
Specify stretch point or [Base point/Copy/Undo/eXit]:
```

This activates the **STRETCH** command. All you have to do is move the cursor to make the selected object stretch, as shown in **Figure 12-4**. If you pick the middle grip of a line or an arc, the center grip of a circle, or the insertion point grip of a block, single-line text, multiline text, or table, the object moves. These are the other options:

- **Base point.** Type B and press [Enter] to select a base point other than the hot grip.
- **Copy.** Type C and press [Enter] to make one or more copies of the selected object.
- **Undo.** Type U and press [Enter] to undo the previous operation.
- **eXit.** Type X and press [Enter] to exit the command. The hot grip is gone, but the warm grips remain. You can also use the [Esc] key to cancel the command. Pressing [Esc] twice removes the selected and unselected grips.

You can pick objects individually or use a window or crossing box. **Figure 12-5** shows two methods to stretch features of an object. Step 1 in **Figure 12-5A** stretches the first corner, and Step 2 stretches the second corner. Alternatively, you can combine the two operations by holding down the [Shift] key as you pick the two grips, as shown in **Figure 12-5B**. Here are some general rules and guidelines that can help make grips work for you:

- ✓ Be sure grips are enabled.
- ✓ Pick an object or group of objects to activate grips. Objects in the selection set are highlighted.
- ✓ Pick a warm grip to make it hot.
- ✓ Make multiple grips hot by holding the [Shift] key while picking warm grips.
- ✓ If more than one object has hot grips, they are all affected by the editing commands.
- ✓ Change grips from hot to warm by holding down the [Shift] key and picking them.
- ✓ Return objects to the selection set by picking them again.
- ✓ Remove all hot grips from the selection set by pressing the [Esc] key to cancel. Cancel again to remove all grips from the selection set. You can also right-click and select **Deselect All** from the shortcut menu to remove all grips.

Figure 12-4.
Using the automatic **STRETCH** command. Note the selected grip.

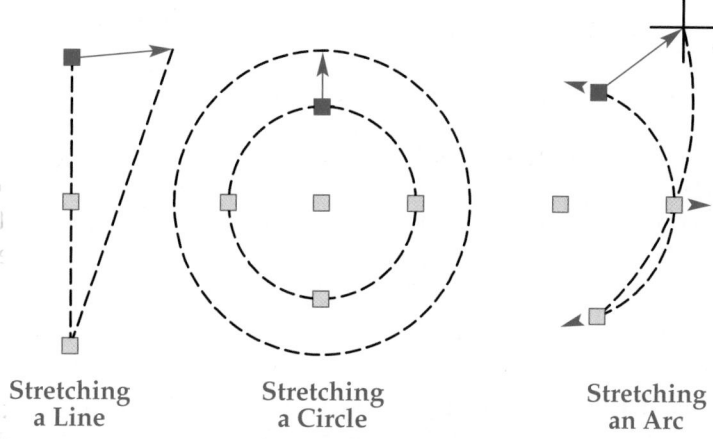

Stretching a Line

Stretching a Circle

Stretching an Arc

Figure 12-5.
Stretching an object. A—Select corners to stretch individually. B—Select several hot grips by holding down the [Shift] key.

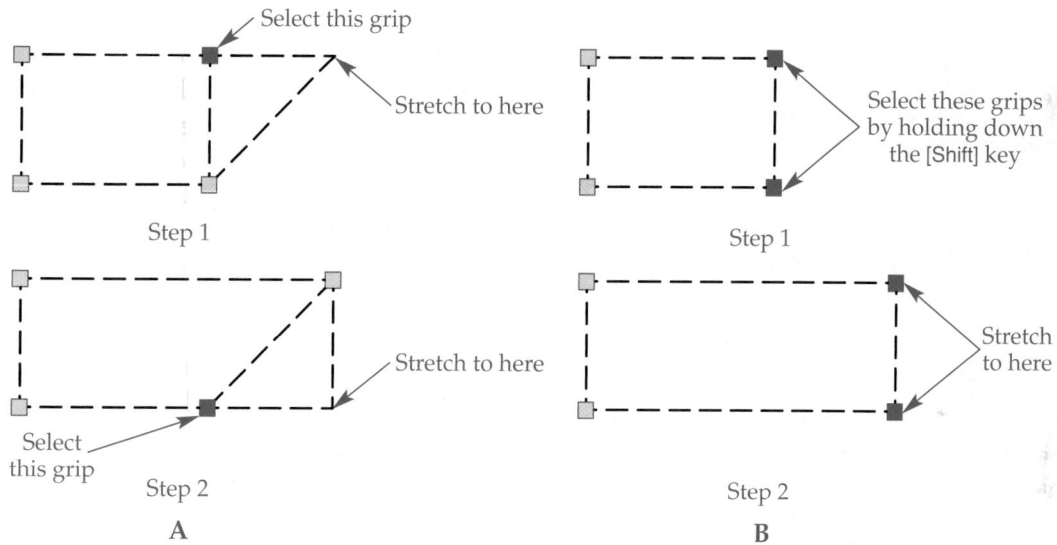

Select this grip

Stretch to here

Step 1

Stretch to here

Select this grip

Step 2

A

Select these grips by holding down the [Shift] key

Step 1

Stretch to here

Step 2

B

PROFESSIONAL TIP

When editing with grips, you can enter coordinates to help improve your accuracy. Remember that any of the coordinate entry methods work.

Exercise 12-1

Complete the exercise on the Student CD.

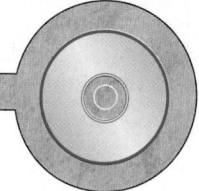

You can also use the **MOVE**, **ROTATE**, **SCALE**, and **MIRROR** commands with grips to edit objects. All you have to do is pick the object and select one of the grips. When you see the ** STRETCH ** Specify stretch point or [Base point/Copy/Undo/eXit]: prompt, press [Enter] to cycle through the command options:

```
** STRETCH **
Specify stretch point or [Base point/Copy/Undo/eXit]: ↵
** MOVE **
Specify move point or [Base point/Copy/Undo/eXit]: ↵
** ROTATE **
Specify rotation angle or [Base point/Copy/Undo/Reference/eXit]: ↵
** SCALE **
Specify scale factor or [Base point/Copy/Undo/Reference/eXit]: ↵
** MIRROR **
Specify second point or [Base point/Copy/Undo/eXit]: ↵
** STRETCH **
Specify stretch point or [Base point/Copy/Undo/eXit]:
```

As an alternative to cycling through the command options, you can enter the first two characters of the desired command from the keyboard. Type MO for **MOVE**, MI for **MIRROR**, RO for **ROTATE**, SC for **SCALE**, and ST for **STRETCH**.

AutoCAD also allows you to right-click to access a grips shortcut menu, as shown in **Figure 12-6.** This menu is only available after a hot grip has been activated. The shortcut menu allows you to access the five grip editing options without using the keyboard.

PROFESSIONAL TIP

Many of the conventional AutoCAD editing operations can be performed when warm grips are displayed on-screen. For example, the **ERASE** command can be used to clear the screen of all objects displayed with warm grips by first picking the objects and then selecting the **ERASE** command. This technique is available if **Noun/verb selection** is enabled (**Selection Modes** are of the **Selection** tab in the **Options** dialog box).

Moving an Object

To move an object with grips, select the object, pick a grip to use as the base point, and then press [Enter] to cycle through the commands until you get to this prompt:

```
** MOVE **
Specify move point or [Base point/Copy/Undo/eXit]:
```

The selected grip becomes the base point. Move the object to a new point by picking the new location. You may want to use object snap mode or coordinates to place it in a new location. See **Figure 12-7.** If you accidentally pick the wrong grip or want to have a base point other than the selected grip, type B and press [Enter] for the **Base point** option. Pick a new base point.

Figure 12-6.
The grips shortcut menu appears when a grip is selected and you right-click.

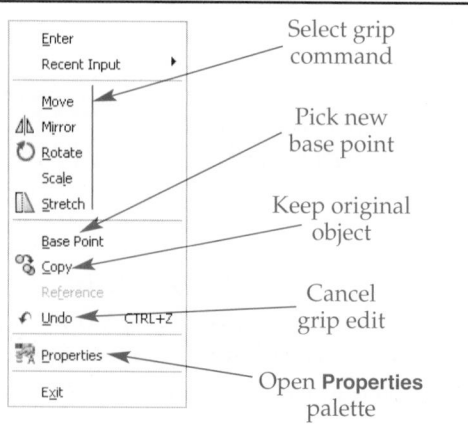

Figure 12-7.
When you specify
the **MOVE** command,
the selected grip
becomes the base
point for the move.

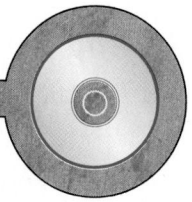

Pick a grip to be
a base point

Step 1

Move the rectangle
to this point

Step 2

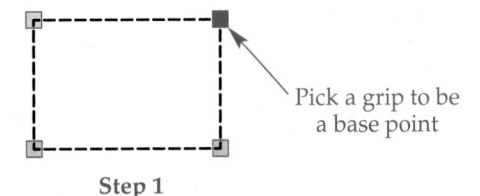

Exercise 12-2
Complete the exercise on the Student CD.

Copying an Object

The **Copy** option is included in each of the editing commands. When you use the **STRETCH** command, the **Copy** option allows you to make multiple copies of the object you are stretching. The **Copy** option in the **MOVE** command is the true form of the **COPY** command.

The **Copy** option works similarly in each of the editing commands. Try it with each to see what happens. You can also access the **Copy** option directly by picking the right mouse button to open the grips shortcut menu.

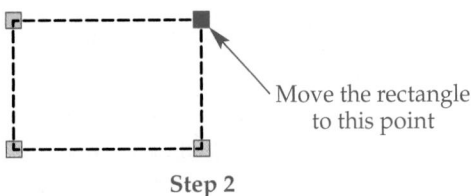

Exercise 12-3
Complete the exercise on the Student CD.

Rotating an Object

To rotate an object using grips, select the object, pick a grip to use as the base point, and press [Enter] until you see this prompt:

** ROTATE **
Specify rotation angle or [Base point/Copy/Undo/Reference/eXit]:

Then move your pointing device to rotate the object. Pick the desired rotation point or enter a rotation angle at the prompt.

The **Reference** option may be used when the object is already rotated at a known angle and you want to rotate it to a new angle. Type R and press [Enter] to use this option. The reference angle is the current angle, and the new angle is the desired angle. Figure 12-8 shows the **ROTATE** options.

Exercise 12-4
Complete the exercise on the Student CD.

Figure 12-8.
The rotation angle and **Reference** options of the **ROTATE** command.

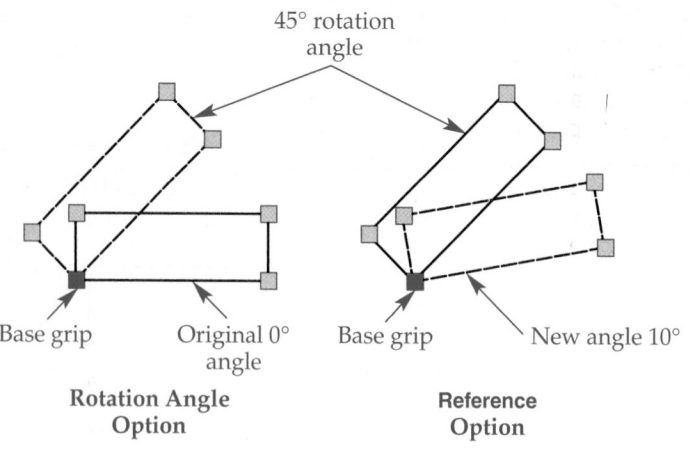

45° rotation angle

Base grip   Original 0° angle

Rotation Angle Option

Base grip   New angle 10°

Reference Option

Scaling an Object

To scale an object with grips, cycle through the editing options until this prompt appears:

```
** SCALE **
Specify scale factor or [Base point/Copy/Undo/Reference/eXit]:
```

Drag with the crosshairs and pick when the object is the desired size. You can also enter a scale factor to increase or decrease the scale of the original object. If you know a current length and a desired length, you can use the **Reference** option. The selected base point remains in the same place when the object is scaled. **Figure 12-9** shows the two **SCALE** options.

Exercise 12-5
Complete the exercise on the Student CD.

Mirroring an Object

When you mirror an object using grips, the selected grip becomes the first point of the mirror line. Press [Enter] to cycle through the editing commands until this prompt appears:

```
** MIRROR **
Specify second point or [Base point/Copy/Undo/eXit]:
```

Figure 12-9.
When using the **SCALE** command with grips, you can enter a scale factor or use the **Reference** option.

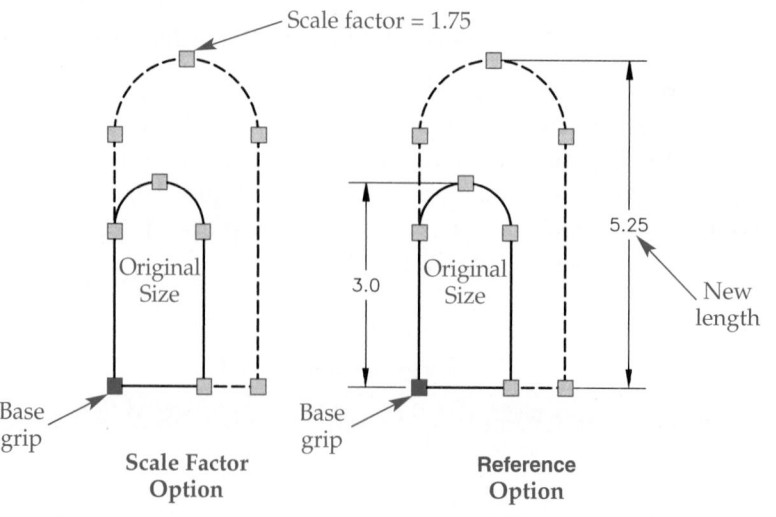

Scale factor = 1.75

Original Size

Base grip

Scale Factor Option

3.0   Original Size

5.25   New length

Base grip

Reference Option

Figure 12-10.
When you use grips to access the **MIRROR** command, the selected grip becomes the first point of the mirror line, and the original object is automatically deleted.

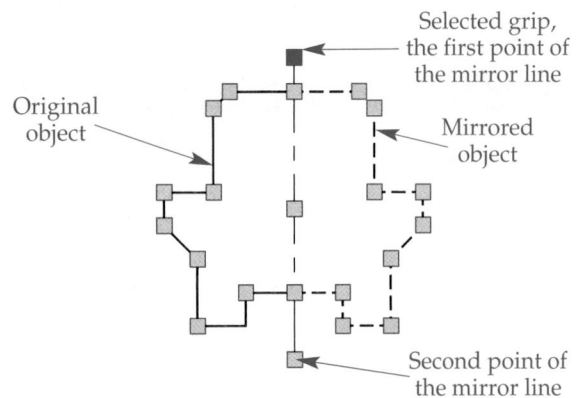

Selected grip, the first point of the mirror line

Original object

Mirrored object

Second point of the mirror line

Use the **Base point** option to reselect the first point of the mirror line. Pick another grip or any point on the screen as the second point of the mirror line. See **Figure 12-10.** Unlike the standard **MIRROR** command, the grips version of the **MIRROR** command does not give you the option to delete the old objects. The old objects are deleted automatically. If you want to keep the original object while mirroring, use the **Copy** option in the **MIRROR** command.

Exercise 12-6

Complete the exercise on the Student CD.

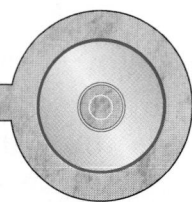

Selection Options for Editing

In Chapters 3 and 11, you were introduced to editing using modify tools. Modify tools allows you to enter a command first and then select the object to be edited. You can also enable settings so you select the objects first and then enter the command. The editing features described in this chapter use grips and related editing commands to edit an object by selecting it before you enter a command.

The **Selection Modes** area of the **Selection** tab in the **Options** dialog box allows you to control the way you use editing commands. See **Figure 12-11.** Select or deselect the following options, based on your own preferences:

- **Noun/verb selection.** The process of selecting objects first and then entering a command is referred to as *noun/verb selection*. The pick box is displayed at the screen crosshairs. A "✓" in this check box means the noun/verb method is active. The **PICKFIRST** system variable can also be used to set **Noun/verb selection**. Remove the "✓" from the **Noun/verb selection** check box to enter the command before selecting the objects. This is known as *verb/noun selection*.

noun/verb selection: Performing tasks in AutoCAD by selecting the object(s) before entering a command.

verb/noun selection: Performing tasks in AutoCAD by entering a command before selecting objects.

NOTE

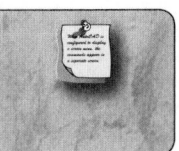

Some editing commands, such as **FILLET**, **CHAMFER**, **DIVIDE**, **MEASURE**, **OFFSET**, **EXTEND**, **TRIM**, and **BREAK**, require that you enter the command before you select the object.

Figure 12-11.
The **Selection Modes** area of the **Selection** tab in the **Options** dialog box.

Adjust
pick box
size

Default
selection
modes

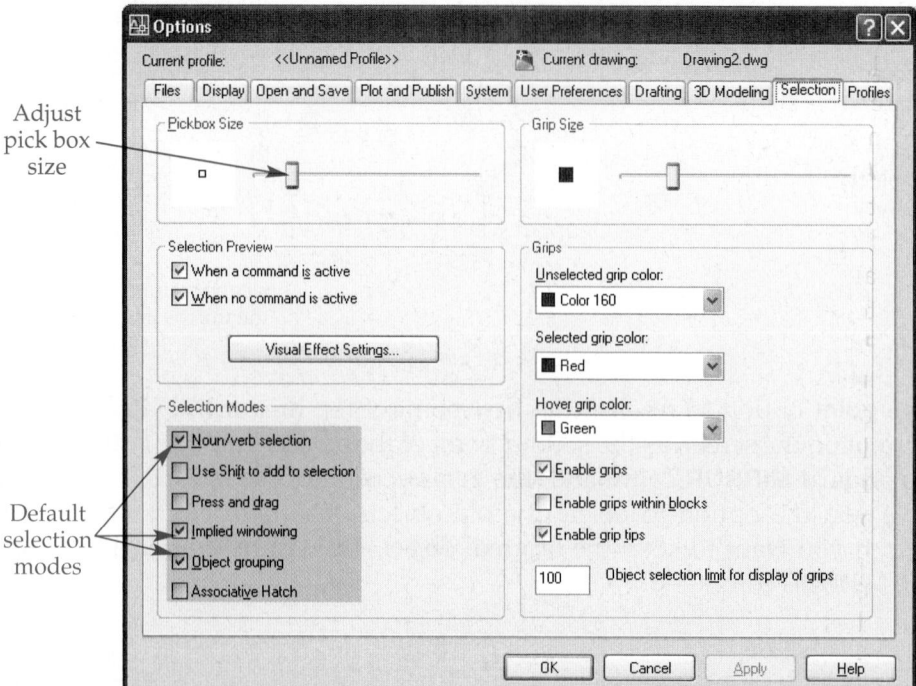

- **Use Shift to add to selection.** When this check box is off, every object or group of objects you select is highlighted and added to the selection set. If you pick this check box, it changes the way AutoCAD accepts objects you pick. For example, if you pick an object, it is highlighted and added to the selection set. If you pick another object, however, it is highlighted, and the first one is removed from the selection set. This means you can only select one object by picking or one group of objects with a selection window. If you want to add more items to the selection set, you must hold down the [Shift] key as you pick them. Turning off the **PICKADD** system variable does the same thing as turning on this feature.
- **Press and drag.** This is the same as turning on the **PICKDRAG** system variable. With **Press and drag** on, you create a selection window by picking the first corner and moving the cursor while holding down the pick button. Release the pick button when you have the desired selection window. By default, this option is off. This means you need to pick both the first and second corners of the desired selection window.
- **Implied windowing.** By default, this option is on. This means you can automatically create a window box by picking the first point and moving the cursor to the right to pick the second point, or you can make a crossing box by picking the first point and moving the cursor to the left to pick the second point. This is the same as turning on the **PICKAUTO** system variable.
- **Object grouping.** This option controls whether AutoCAD recognizes grouped objects as single objects. When it is off, the individual elements of a group can be selected for separate editing without having to explode the group first.
- **Associative Hatch.** The default is off, which means, if an associative hatch is moved, the hatch boundary does not move with it. Select this toggle if you want the boundary of an associative hatch to move when you move the hatch pattern. It is a good idea to have this on for most applications. Hatches and hatch boundaries are fully explained in Chapter 20.

PROPERTIES

Type
PROPERTIES
PROPS
CH
MO
[Ctrl]+[1]
Toolbar
Standard Annotation

Properties
Pull-Down Menu
Modify
> Properties

Using the Properties Palette

As you have seen in previous chapters, object properties can be edited using the **Properties** palette. The **Properties** palette was first introduced in Chapter 1 and is described where it applies throughout this text.

To edit an object using the **Properties** palette, pick the **Properties** button from the **Standard Annotation** toolbar; pick **Tools** > **Palettes** > **Properties**; pick **Modify** > **Properties**; or type MO, CH, PROPS, or PROPERTIES. You can also toggle the **Properties** palette on and off using the [Ctrl]+[1] key combination. If an object has already been selected, you can access the **Properties** palette by right-clicking and selecting **Properties** from the shortcut menu. You can also double-click many objects to select the object and open the **Properties** palette automatically.

The **Properties** palette is shown in **Figure 12-12.** It can be docked in the drawing area, just as a toolbar can be docked. You can enter commands and continue to work in AutoCAD while the **Properties** palette is displayed. To close the palette, pick the **X** in the top-left corner, pick the **Properties** button on the **Modify** toolbar, or use the [Ctrl]+[1] key combination.

When you access the **Properties** palette without first selecting an object, No selection can be seen in the top drop-down list. This means AutoCAD does not have any objects selected to modify. The five categories—**General**, **3D Visualization**, **Plot style**, **View**, and **Misc**—list the current settings for the drawing.

Underneath each category is a list of object properties. For example, in **Figure 12-12,** the current color of the selected line is ByLayer. To change a property, pick the property or its current value. While the property is highlighted, use one of the following methods to set the new value:

- A drop-down arrow with a list of values.
- A pick point button, which allows you to pick a new coordinate location.
- A text box that opens when you select certain properties, such as the radius of an arc. Entering a new value in this box allows you to change the radius.

Figure 12-12.
The **Properties** palette can be used to modify the properties of an object.

Type of object selected

Category

Properties within category (pick to modify)

Quick Select button

Select Objects button

Pick to toggle **PICKADD** variable

Current property settings (pick to modify)

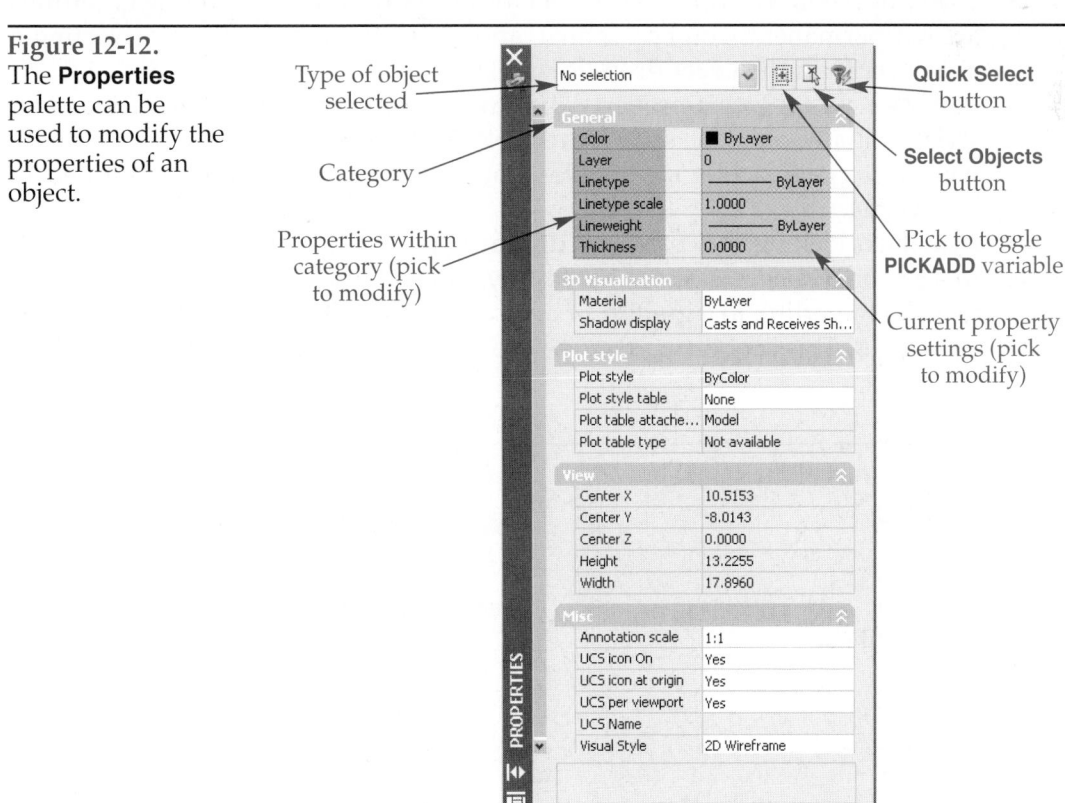

After you have selected a property to be modified, a description of what that property does is shown at the bottom of the dialog box.

The upper-right portion of the **Properties** palette contains three buttons. Pick the **Quick Select** button to access the **Quick Select** dialog box, where you can create object selection sets. This dialog box is described in Chapter 11. Picking the **Select Objects** button deselects the currently selected objects and changes the crosshairs to a pick box. The third button toggles the value of the **PICKADD** system variable, which determines whether you need to hold the [Shift] key when adding objects to a selection set.

In order to modify an object using the **Properties** palette, the palette must be open and an object must be selected. For example, if a circle and a line are drawn and you need to modify the circle, either double-click the circle or pick the circle to make the grips appear and then use one of the methods to open the **Properties** palette. The **Properties** palette displays the categories that can be modified for the circle.

When multiple objects are selected, you can use the **Properties** palette to modify all of the objects, or you can pick only one of the selected objects to be modified. The drop-down list displays the types of objects selected. See **Figure 12-13**. Select All (*n*) to change the properties of all selected objects. Only properties shared by all selected objects are displayed when All (*n*) is selected. To modify only one type of object, select the appropriate object type.

When all the changes to the object have been made, press the [Esc] button on the keyboard to clear the grips and remove the object from the **Properties** palette. The object is now displayed in the drawing window with the desired changes.

General Properties

All objects have a **General** category in the **Properties** palette. Refer to **Figure 12-12**. The **General** category allows you to modify properties such as color, layer, linetype, linetype scale, plot style, lineweight, and thickness. A description of some of the properties in the **General** category follows. Other general properties are described later in this chapter.

- **Layer.** You should always draw objects on an appropriate layer, but layer settings are not permanent. You can change an object's layer if needed by selecting a new layer from the **Layer** drop-down list.
- **Plot style.** Picking this property displays a drop-down list with various plot styles. Initially, only one style is available: ByColor. To create a list of plot styles, you must create a plot style table. Plotting and plot styles are described in Chapter 24.
- **Hyperlink.** Picking this property displays an **...** (ellipsis) button. By selecting this button, you can access the **Insert Hyperlink** dialog box. Use this dialog box to add a hyperlink to a graphic or a description or URL address to an object.
- **Thickness.** This property allows you to change the thickness of a 3D object in a text box.

Figure 12-13.
The **Properties** palette with three objects selected. You can edit the objects individually or all together by selecting All (3).

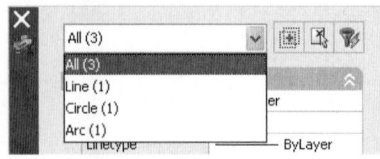

Geometry Properties

One of the most common **Properties** palette categories is **Geometry.** See **Figure 12-14.** Although most objects have a **Geometry** category, the properties within the category vary depending on the type of object. Typically, three properties allow you to change the absolute coordinates for the object by specifying the X, Y, and Z coordinates. When you pick one of these properties, a pick button is displayed. The button allows you to pick a point in the drawing for the new location. In addition to choosing a point with the pick button, you can change the value of the coordinate in a text box or use the calculator button to calculate a new location.

An example of the properties displayed when a circle is selected is shown in **Figure 12-15.** The **Geometry** category displays the current location of the center of the

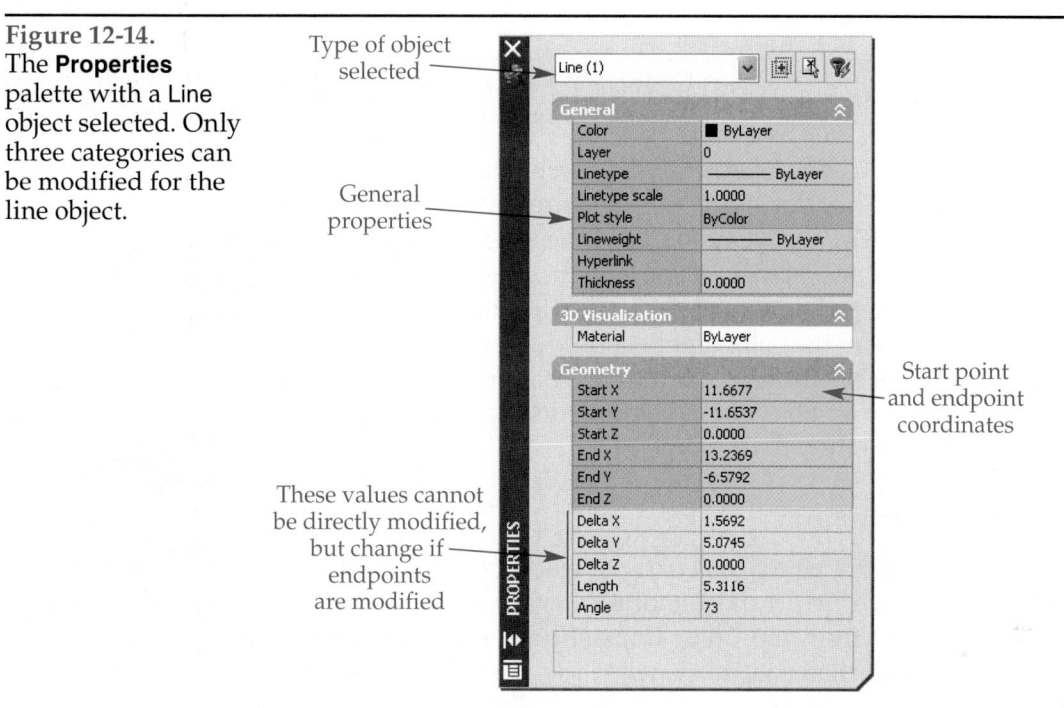

Figure 12-14.
The **Properties** palette with a Line object selected. Only three categories can be modified for the line object.

Type of object selected

General properties

Start point and endpoint coordinates

These values cannot be directly modified, but change if endpoints are modified

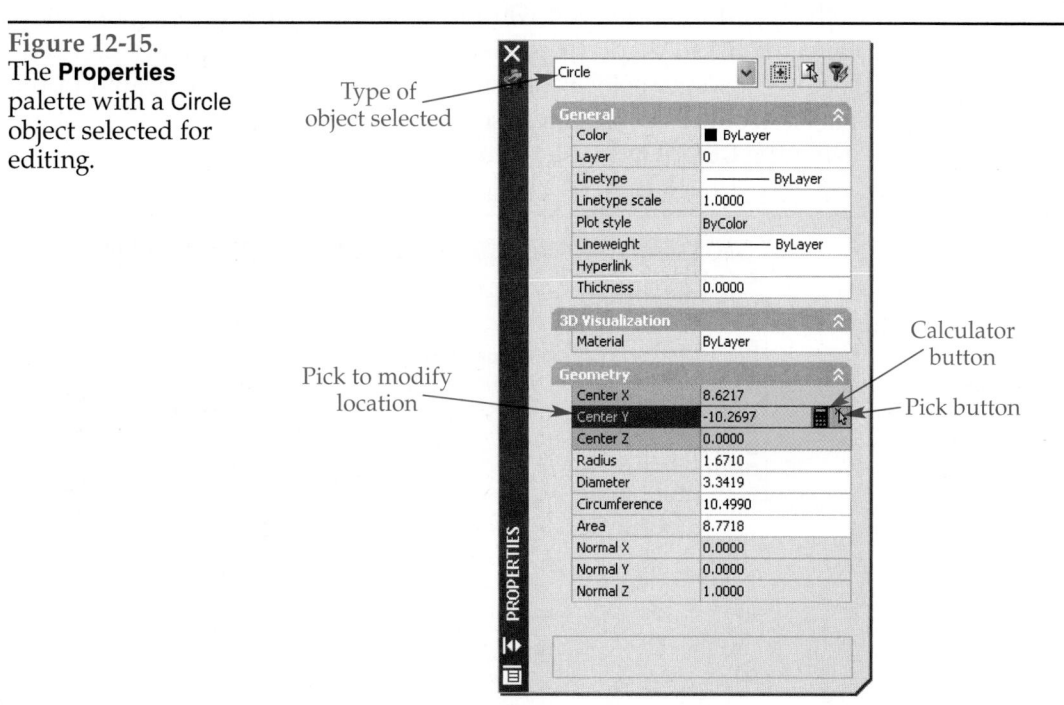

Figure 12-15.
The **Properties** palette with a Circle object selected for editing.

Type of object selected

Pick to modify location

Calculator button

Pick button

circle by showing three properties: **Center X**, **Center Y**, and **Center Z**. To choose a new center location for the circle, select the appropriate property. Pick a new point or type or calculate the coordinate values. Other properties can also be modified for the circle, such as the radius, diameter, circumference, and area. By changing any of these values, you are modifying the size of the circle.

Exercise 12-7
Complete the exercise on the Student CD.

Overriding Layer Properties

When you create a layer, you also establish a color, linetype, and lineweight to go with the layer. These property settings are used when the color, linetype, and lineweight are specified as ByLayer. This is the most common method for managing these settings. Sometimes, however, you may need objects to reside on a specific layer but have color, linetype, or lineweight properties that are different than the layer settings. In such a situation, the color, linetype, and lineweight can be set to an ***absolute value***, and current layer settings are ignored. The term *absolute*, as used here and in future content, refers to an object being assigned specific properties that are not reliant on a layer or block for their definitions.

absolute value: In property settings, a value set directly instead of being referenced by layer.

Overriding Color

An absolute value for the current object color can be set by selecting a color from **Color** drop-down list in the **General** category of the **Properties** palette. A color can also be selected from the **Color Control** drop-down list of the **Properties** toolbar or the **Object Properties** control panel of the **Dashboard**. See **Figure 12-16.** The default ByLayer setting is recommended for most applications. To change this setting, pick another color from the list. If the color you want is not on the list, you can pick **Select Color** at the bottom of the list to display the **Select Color** dialog box, or you can type COL or COLOR. Once an absolute color is specified, all new objects are drawn in the specified color, regardless of the current layer settings. Another way to set the current object color is by using the **CECOLOR** system variable.

Figure 12-16.
You can set an absolute color for an object using the **Color Control** drop-down list.

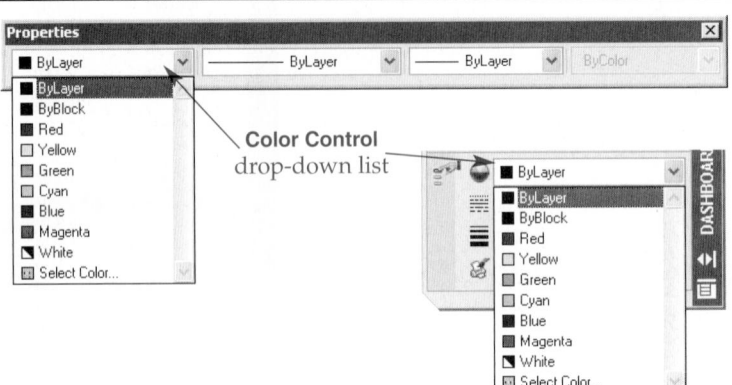

Overriding Linetype

An absolute value for the current object linetype can be set by selecting a linetype from the **Linetype** drop-down list in the **General** category of the **Properties** palette. You can also select a linetype from the **Linetype Control** drop-down list from the **Properties** toolbar or the **Object Properties** control panel of the **Dashboard**. See **Figure 12-17.** If the linetype you want has not been loaded into the current drawing yet, it does not appear in the listing. You can select **Other...** from the list to display the **Linetype Manager** and load new linetypes. You can also adjust the **CELTYPE** system variable, which controls the current object linetype.

Overriding Lineweight

An absolute value for the current object lineweight can be set by selecting a lineweight from the **Lineweight** drop-down list in the **General** category of the **Properties** palette. A lineweight can also be selected from the **Lineweight Control** drop-down list from the **Properties** toolbar or the **Object Properties** control panel of the **Dashboard**. See **Figure 12-18.** You can also adjust the **CELWEIGHT** system variable, which controls the current object linetype.

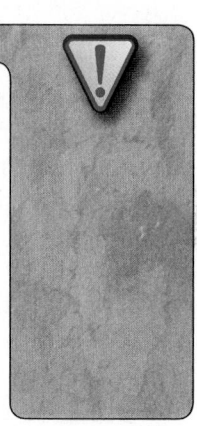

CAUTION

Colors, linetypes, and lineweights are usually set as ByLayer. ByLayer is known as a *logical color*, while red, for instance, is known as an *explicit color*. If an object uses ByLayer as its color, its color is displayed as the color assigned to the layer on which the object resides. Explicit properties, however, override logical properties. Therefore, if an object's color is set explicitly to red, it appears red regardless of the layer on which it resides. It is a common mistake for AutoCAD users to set object property override settings to some value other than ByLayer and then wonder why new objects do not use the color of the current layer!

logical color: A color that is layer-dependent.

explicit color: A color that remains the same regardless of the color setting for the layer on which an object resides.

Figure 12-17.
You can set an absolute linetype for objects using the **Linetype Control** drop-down list.

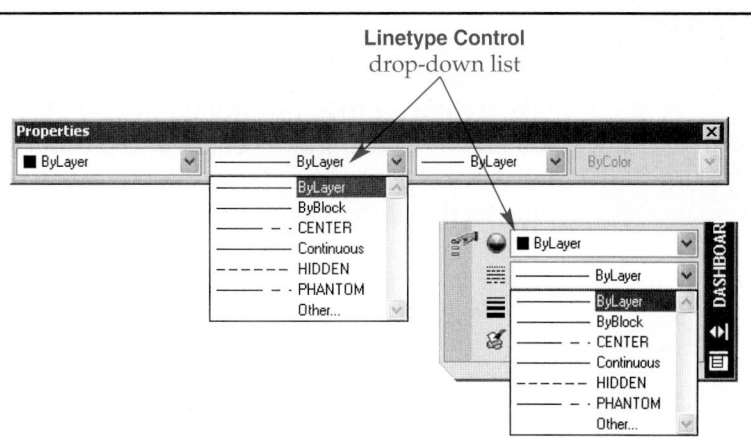

Figure 12-18.
You can set an
absolute lineweight
for objects using the
Lineweight Control
drop-down list.

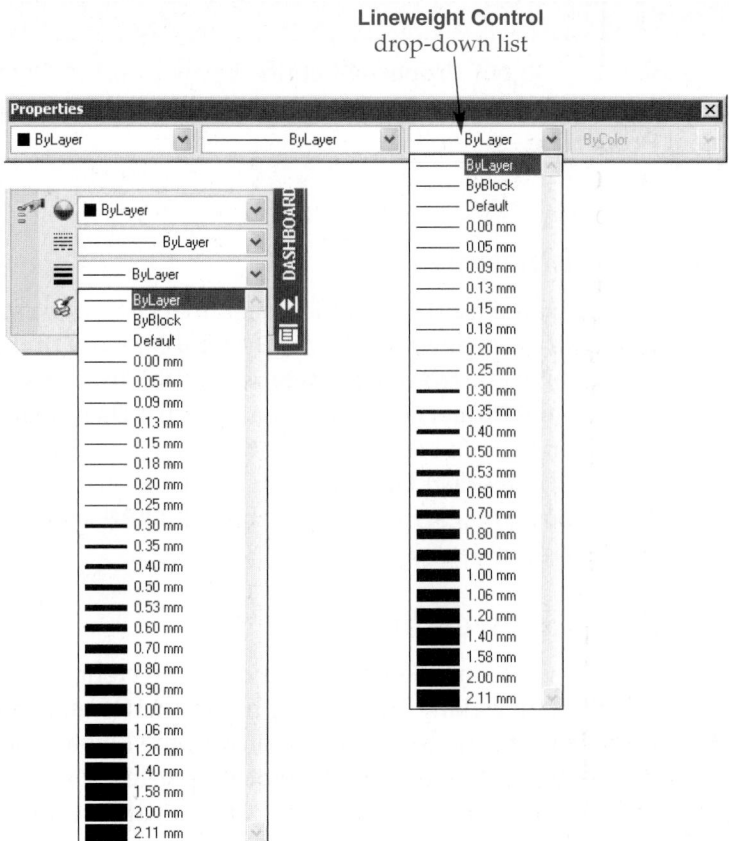

Lineweight Control
drop-down list

Setting Individual Object Linetype Scale

When you select a line object to modify, a **Linetype scale** property is listed in the **General** category of the **Properties** palette. You can change the linetype scale of the object by entering a new value in this field. A value less than 1.0 makes the dashes and spaces smaller than those in the global setting, while a value greater than 1.0 makes the dashes and spaces larger than those in the global setting. Using this information, you can experiment with different linetype scales until you achieve the desired results. Be careful when changing linetype scales to avoid making your drawing look odd, with a variety of line formats.

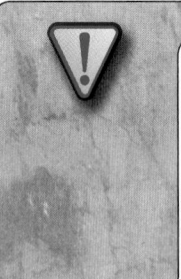

CAUTION

For most applications, linetype scale should be set globally so that the linetype scale of all objects is constant. Adjusting the linetype scale of individual objects can create nonstandard drawings and make it difficult to adjust linetype scale globally. Use the **LTSCALE** variable to make a global change to the linetype scale. The default global linetype scale factor is 1.0000. Any line with dashes initially assumes this factor.

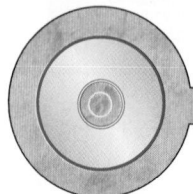

Exercise 12-8
Complete the exercise on the Student CD.

Matching Properties

The **MATCHPROP** command allows you to copy properties from one object to one or more objects. This can be done in the same drawing or between drawings. To access the **MATCHPROP** command, select the **Match Properties** button from the **Standard Annotation** toolbar; select **Modify > Match Properties**; or enter MA, MATCHPROP, or PAINTER.

When you first access the **MATCHPROP** command, AutoCAD prompts you for the source object. The source object is the object with the properties you would like to copy to another object or series of objects. After you have selected the source object, AutoCAD displays the properties it will paint to the destination object. The next prompt allows you to pick the objects you want to receive the properties of the source object. If you want the properties painted to all objects in the drawing, type ALL at this prompt.

To change the properties to be painted, access the **Settings** option by typing S and pressing [Enter]. The **Property Settings** dialog box appears, showing the types of properties that can be painted. See **Figure 12-19**. The following describes the major areas of the **Property Settings** dialog box:

- **Basic Properties.** This area lists the general properties of the selected object. If you do not want a specific property to be copied, deselect the appropriate check box. All active properties will be transferred to the destination objects.
- **Special Properties.** In addition to general properties, you can also paint over dimension styles, text styles, and hatch patterns. These properties are replaced in the destination object if these check boxes are active.

For example, if you want to paint only the color property and text style of one text object to another text object, uncheck all boxes except the **Color** and **Text** property check boxes.

Type
MATCHPROP
MA
PAINTER

Toolbar
Standard Annotation
Match Properties

Pull-Down Menu
Modify
> Match
Properties

MATCHPROP

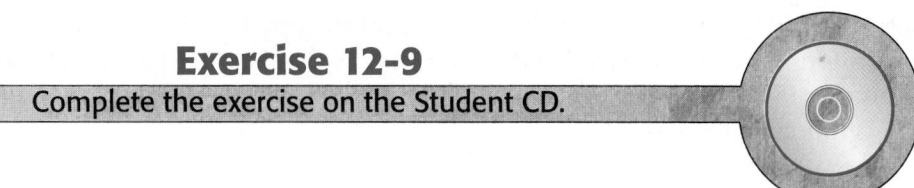

Exercise 12-9
Complete the exercise on the Student CD.

Figure 12-19.
The **Property Settings** dialog box for the **MATCHPROP** command. Select the properties to paint onto a new object.

Properties to be painted to other objects

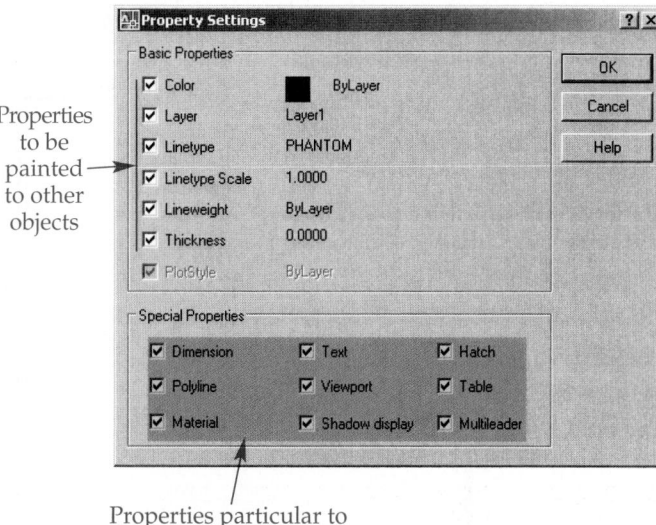

Properties particular to specific objects

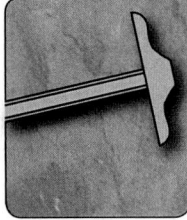

LEGACY NOTE

The **CHANGE** and **CHPROP** commands can also be used to modify some object properties. The **CHANGE** command also provides a stretch option. Using **CHANGE** and **CHPROP** are typically less efficient than using the **Properties** palette, **Object Properties** control panel on the **Dashboard**, **Properties** toolbar, and grip editing.

Editing between Drawings

One of the advantages of AutoCAD is the capability of editing in more than one drawing at a time. This allows you to copy objects from one drawing to another drawing. You can also refer to another drawing to obtain information, such as a distance, while working in a different drawing.

To see how this works, open drawing EX12-8, and then open drawing EX12-7. Two drawings have now been opened in AutoCAD. Pick **Window** > **Tile Horizontally**. This "tiles" the two open drawings. See **Figure 12-20**.

PROFESSIONAL TIP

Use the **Partial Open** option in the **OPEN** command to partially open existing drawings to be used as source objects for copying or property matching. **Partial Open** is described in Chapter 2.

copy and paste: A Windows function that allows an object to be copied and then pasted in another location or file.

The Windows *copy and paste* function is used to copy an object from one drawing to another. To use this feature in AutoCAD, the object you intend to copy must be selected with grips. For example, if you want to copy the circle from drawing EX12-8 to drawing EX12-7, first select the circle. Then right-click to display the shortcut menu shown in **Figure 12-21**. The shortcut menu has two options that allow you to copy to the Windows Clipboard:

Figure 12-20.
Multiple drawings can be tiled to make editing easier.

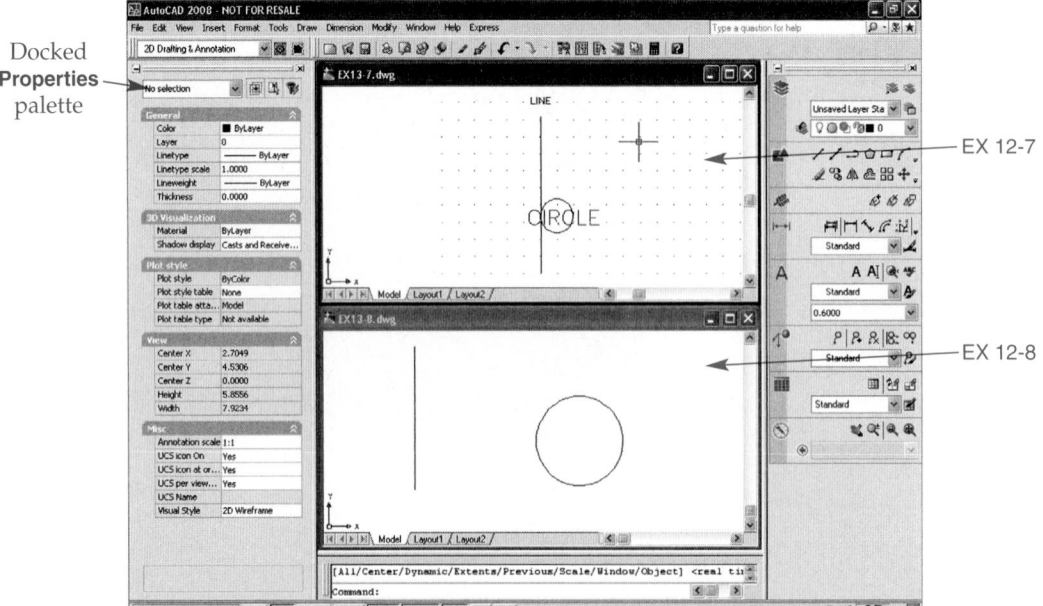

Figure 12-21.
Two copy options
appear on the
shortcut menu.

Copy
options

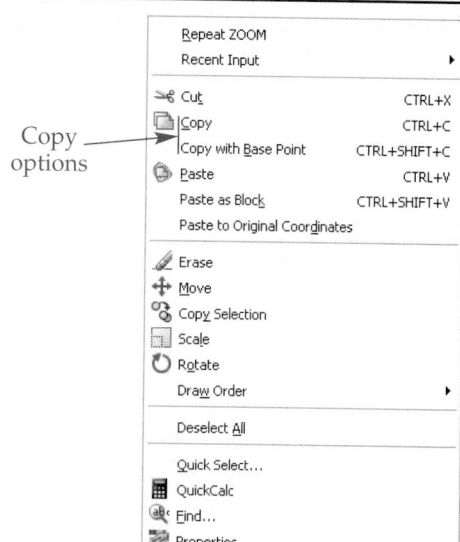

- **Copy.** This option copies selected objects from AutoCAD onto the Windows Clipboard to be used in another application or AutoCAD drawing.
- **Copy with Base Point.** This option also copies the selected objects to the Clipboard, but it allows you to specify a base point to position the copied object when it is pasted. When you use this option, AutoCAD prompts you to select a base point. Select a logical base point, such as a corner or center point of the object.

After you have selected one of the two copy options, make the second drawing active by picking in it. Right-click to display the shortcut menu shown in **Figure 12-22**. Notice that the copy options remain available, but three paste options are now available below the copy options. The paste options are only available if there is something on the Clipboard. The three options are:

- **Paste.** This option pastes any information on the Clipboard into the current drawing. If the **Copy with Base Point** option was used to place objects in the Clipboard, the objects being pasted are attached to the crosshairs at the specified base point.
- **Paste as Block.** This option "joins" all objects on the Clipboard when they are pasted into the drawing. The pasted objects act like a block in that they are single objects grouped together to form one object. Blocks are covered in Chapter 22. Use the **EXPLODE** command to break up the block so that the objects act individually again.

Figure 12-22.
Choose one of the
three paste options
from the shortcut
menu.

Paste
options

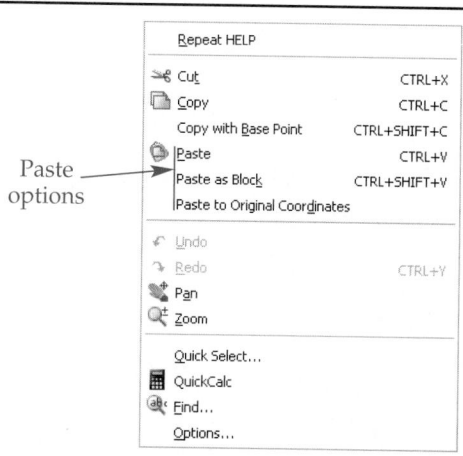

- **Paste to Original Coordinates.** This option pastes the objects from the Clipboard to the same coordinates at which they were located in the original drawing.

Exercise 12-10
Complete the exercise on the Student CD.

Creating a Revision Cloud

revision cloud:
A polyline of sequential arcs used to form a cloud shape around changes in a drawing.

A *revision cloud* is a polyline of sequential arcs forming a cloud-shaped object. **Figure 12-23** shows a cloud with a leader and note attached. Revision clouds are typically used by people who review drawings and mark notes and changes. The revision cloud points the drafter to a specific portion of the drawing that may need to be edited.

To create a revision cloud, pick a starting location, move the crosshairs to shape the cloud, and then move the crosshairs toward the beginning of the cloud. AutoCAD automatically closes the cloud and ends the command. This command can be entered by picking the **Revision Cloud** button from the **2D Draw** control panel on the **Dashboard** or the **Draw** toolbar, by selecting **Draw > Revision Cloud**, or by typing REVCLOUD. The following prompt is displayed when you enter the **REVCLOUD** command:

REVCLOUD

| Type |
| **REVCLOUD** |
| Dashboard |
| **2D Draw** > Revision Cloud |
| Toolbar |
| **Draw** |
| Revision Cloud |
| Pull-Down Menu |
| **Draw** > Revision Cloud |

Figure 12-23.
A revision cloud can be used to identify areas of a drawing that have been modified.

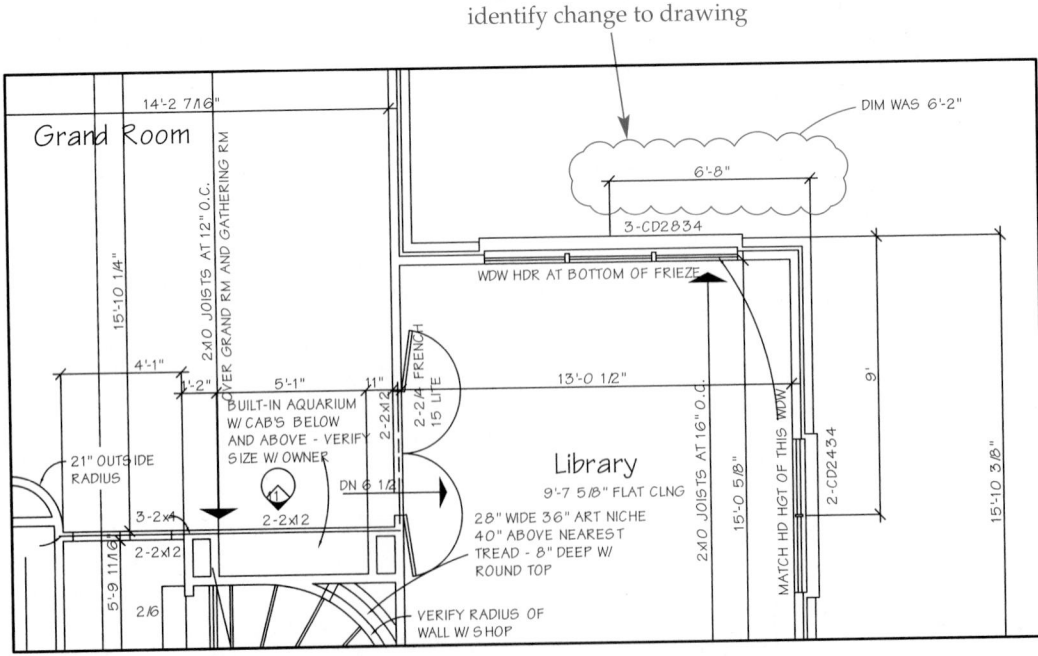

Command: **REVCLOUD**↵
Minimum arc length: *current*   Maximum arc length: *current*   Style: *current*
Specify start point or [Arc length/Object/Style] <*current option*>:

To begin drawing the revision cloud, pick a start point in the drawing. After picking the start point, the prompt tells you to guide the crosshairs along the cloud path. Move the crosshairs around the objects to be enclosed, until you come close to the start point. AutoCAD then closes the cloud automatically.

The size of the arcs can be set by entering the **Arc length** option. This value measures the length of an arc from its start point to its end point. You can change the arc length to any desired value. Upon entering the **Arc length** option, you are prompted for the following:

Specify start point or [Arc length/Object/Style] <*current option*>: **A**↵
Specify minimum length of arc <*current size*>: (*enter a minimum arc length*)
Specify maximum length of arc <*current size*>: (*enter a maximum arc length*)
Specify start point or [Arc length/Object/Style] <*current option*>: (*pick a start point for the cloud*)

Specifying different minimum and maximum values causes the revision cloud to have an uneven, hand-drawn look.

Circles, closed polylines, ellipses, polygons, and rectangles can be converted to revision clouds by selecting the **Object** option. The command sequence follows:

Specify start point or [Arc length/Object/Style] <*current option*>: **O**↵
Select object: (*pick the object to convert to a revision cloud*)
Reverse direction [Yes/No] <*default*>: (*enter* N, *or enter* Y *to reverse the cloud arcs*)
Revision cloud finished.
Command:

The **Style** option of the **Revision Cloud** tool offers two different style choices: **Normal** and **Calligraphy**. The default style is **Normal**, in which the arcs are a consistent width. With the **Calligraphy** style, the start and end widths of the individual arcs are different, creating a more stylish revision cloud. See **Figure 12-24.** To change the revision cloud style, the command sequence is as follows:

Specify start point or [Arc length/Object/Style] <*current option*>: **S**↵
Select arc style [Normal/Calligraphy] <*current*>: **C**↵
Arc style = Calligraphy
Specify start point or [Arc length/Object/Style] <*current option*>: (*pick a start point for the cloud*)
Guide crosshairs along cloud path… (*move the crosshairs around the objects to be enclosed, until you come close to the start point*)
Revision cloud finished.
Command:

Exercise 12-11
Complete the exercise on the Student CD.

Figure 12-24.
Revision clouds can be created in two different styles: the **Normal** style and the **Calligraphy** style.

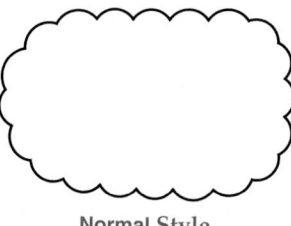

Normal Style

Calligraphy Style

Chapter Test

Answer the following questions. Write your answers on a separate sheet of paper or complete the electronic chapter test on the Student CD.

1. Name the editing commands that can be accessed automatically using grips.
2. Identify two ways to access the **Selection** tab of the **Options** dialog box.
3. What is the purpose of the **Selection** tab of the **Options** dialog box?
4. Explain two ways to change the pick box size.
5. Name the three system variables that control the color of grips.
6. How do you turn grips on and off?
7. What is the purpose of the **Base Point** option in the grips shortcut menu?
8. Explain the function of the **Undo** option in the grips shortcut menu.
9. What happens when you choose the **Exit** option from the grips shortcut menu?
10. When grips are active, how do you cycle through the available commands?
11. How do you access the grips shortcut menu?
12. When grip editing, which option of the **ROTATE** command would you use to rotate an object from an existing 60° angle to a new 25° angle?
13. What scale factor would you use to scale an object to become three-quarters of its original size?
14. Name the system variable that allows you to set noun/verb selection.
15. Explain the difference between noun/verb selection and verb/noun selection.
16. What does **Use Shift to add to selection** mean?
17. Describe how the **Press and drag** option works.
18. Name the system variable used to turn on the **Press and drag** option.
19. Name the system variable that turns on the **Implied windowing** option.
20. Identify at least two ways to access the the **Properties** palette.
21. Explain how you would change the radius of a circle from 1.375 to 1.875 using the **Properties** palette.
22. How can you change the color of an object using the **Properties** palette?
23. How can you change the linetype of an object using the **Properties** palette?
24. What does it mean when color, linetype, and lineweight are specified as ByLayer?
25. What command is used to change the properties of objects to match the properties of a different object?
26. Briefly discuss how the Windows copy and paste function works to copy an object from one drawing to another.
27. Name the option that joins a group of objects as a block when they are pasted.
28. When you use the option described in Question 27, how do you separate the objects back into individual objects?
29. What is the purpose of a revision cloud?
30. How do you close a revision cloud?

Drawing Problems

Use templates as appropriate for each of the following problems. Use grips and the associated editing commands or other editing techniques described in this chapter.

1. Draw the objects labeled A, below, and then use the **STRETCH** command to make them look like the objects labeled B. Do not include dimensions. Save the drawing as P12-1.

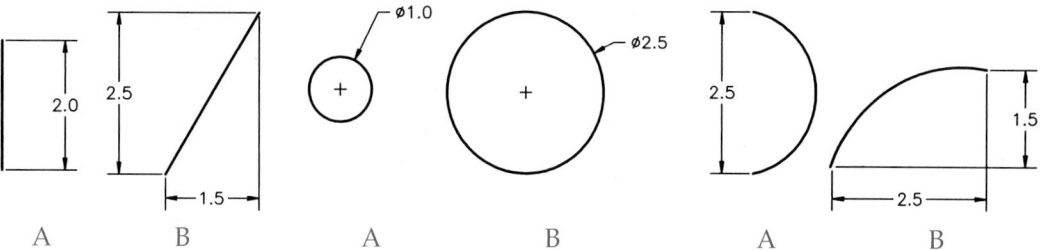

2. Draw the object labeled A. Using the **Copy** option of the **MOVE** command, copy the object to the position labeled B. Edit Object A so it resembles Object C. Edit Object B so it looks like Object D. Do not include dimensions. Save the drawing as P12-2.

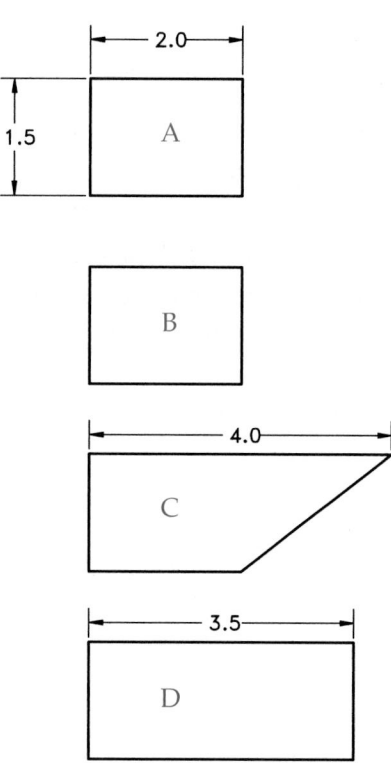

3. Draw the object labeled A. Copy the object, without rotating it, to a position below, as indicated by the dashed lines. Rotate the object 45°. Copy the rotated object labeled B to a position below, as indicated by the dashed lines. Use the **Reference** option to rotate the object labeled C to 25°, as shown. Do not include dimensions. Save the drawing as P12-3.

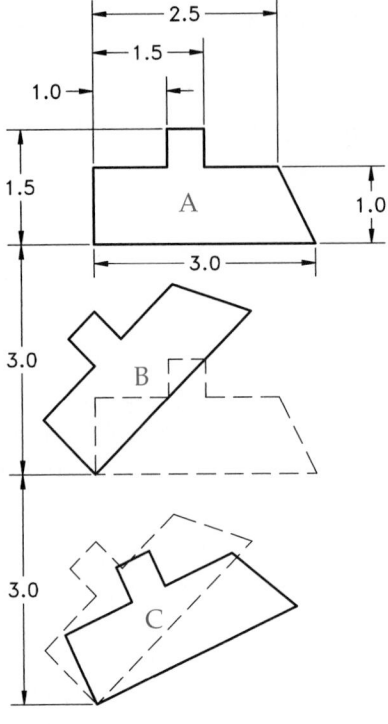

4. Draw the individual objects (vertical line, horizontal line, circle, arc, and C shape) in A, below, using the dimensions given. Use grips and the editing commands to create the object shown in B. Do not include dimensions. Save the drawing as P12-4.

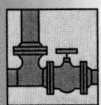

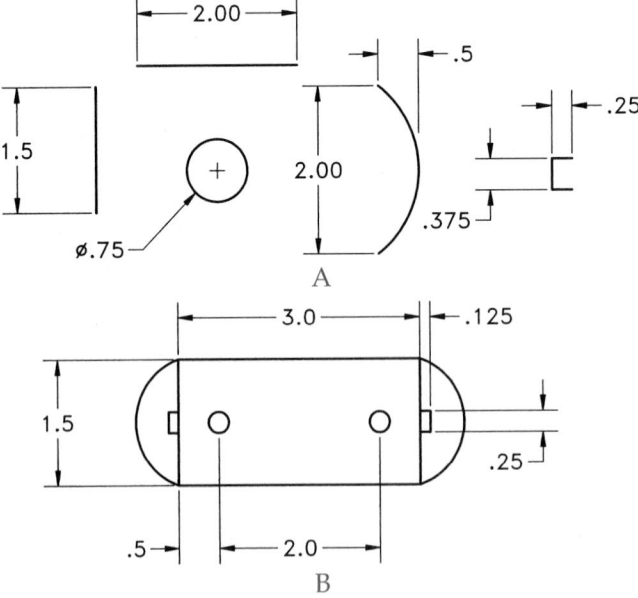

5. Use the completed drawing from Problem 12-4. Erase everything except the completed object and move it to a position similar to A, below. Copy the object two times to positions B and C. Use the automatic **SCALE** command to scale the object in position B to 50 percent of its original size. Use the **Reference** option of the **SCALE** command to enlarge the object in position C from the existing 3.0 length to a 4.5 length, as shown in C. Do not include dimensions. Save as P12-5.

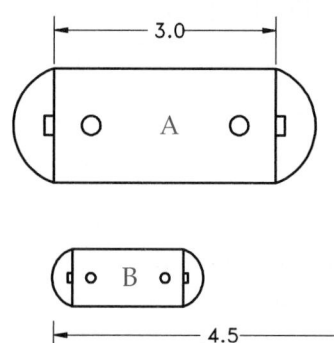

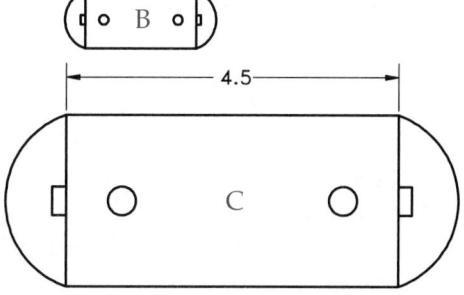

6. Draw the dimensioned partial object shown in A. Do not include dimensions. Mirror the drawing to complete the four quadrants, as shown in B. Change the color of the horizontal and vertical parting lines to Red and the linetype to CENTER. Save the drawing as P12-6.

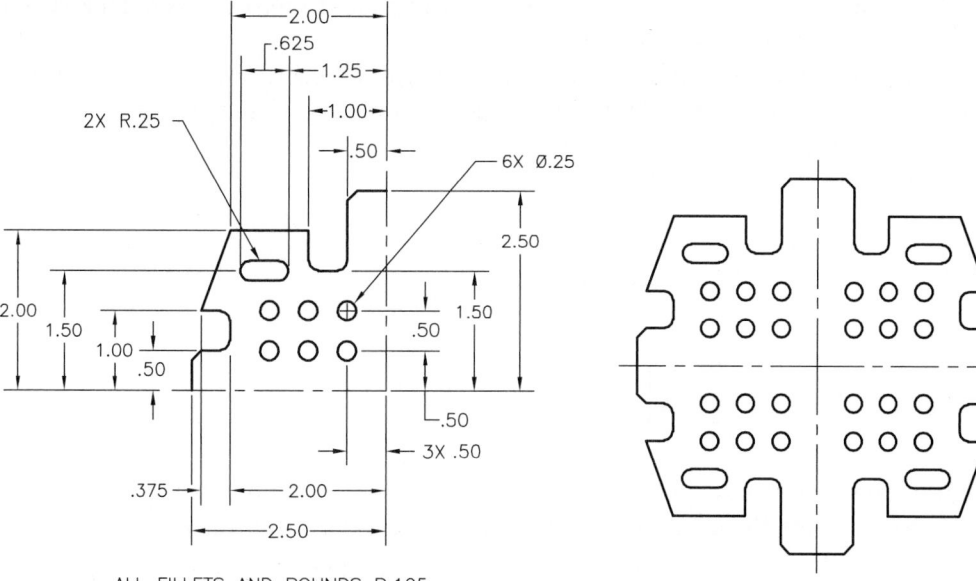

ALL FILLETS AND ROUNDS R.125.
CHAMFERS 45° X .125

7. Load the final drawing you created in Problem 12-6. Use the **Properties** palette to change the diameters of the circles from .25 to .125. Change the linetype of the slots to PHANTOM. Be sure the linetype scale allows the linetypes to be displayed. Save the drawing as P12-7.

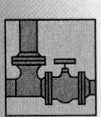

8. Use the editing commands described in this chapter to assist you in drawing the following object. Draw the object within the boundaries of the given dimensions. All other dimensions are flexible. Do not include dimensions in the drawing. Save the drawing as P12-8.

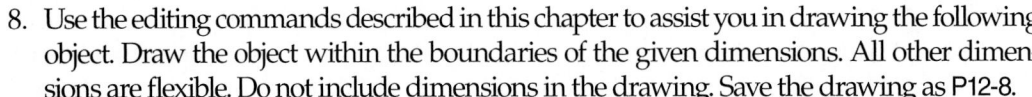

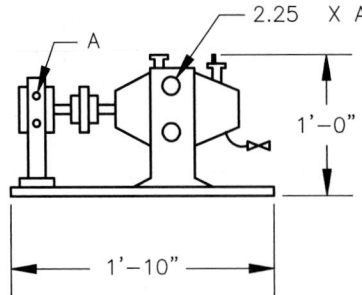

9. Draw the following object within the boundaries of the given dimensions. All other dimensions are flexible. Do not include dimensions. After drawing the object, create a page for a vendor catalog, as follows:

- All labels should be ROMAND text, centered directly below the view. Use a text height of .125″.
- Label the drawing ONE-GALLON TANK WITH HORIZONTAL VALVE.
- Keep the valve the same scale as the original drawing in each copy.
- Copy the original tank to a new location and scale it so it is 2 times its original size. Rotate the valve 45°. Label this tank TWO-GALLON TANK WITH 45° VALVE.
- Copy the original tank to another location and scale it to 2.5 times the size of the original. Rotate the valve 90°. Label this tank TWO-AND-ONE-HALF GALLON TANK WITH 90° VALVE.
- Copy the two-gallon tank to a new position and scale it so it is 2 times this size. Rotate the valve to 22°30′. Label this tank FOUR-GALLON TANK WITH 22°30′ VALVE.
- Left-justify this note at the bottom of the page: Combinations of tank size and valve orientation are available upon request.
- Use the **Properties** palette to change all tank labels to ROMANC, .25″ high.
- Change the note at the bottom of the sheet to ROMANS, centered on the sheet, using uppercase letters.
- Save the drawing as P12-9.

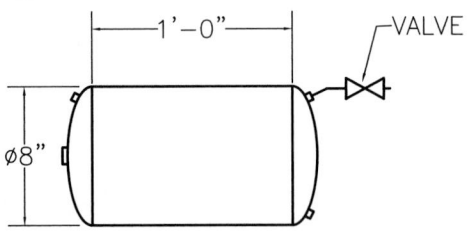

10. Draw the gasket half shown below. Do not include dimensions. Mirror the drawing to complete the other half of the gasket. Save the drawing as P12-10.

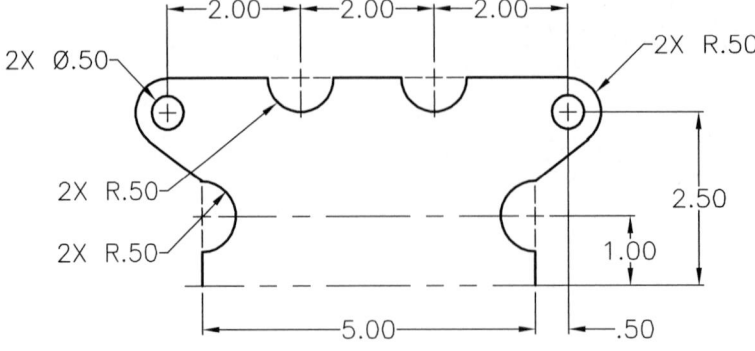

Drawing Problems - Chapter 12

CHAPTER 13

Obtaining Drawing Information

Learning Objectives

After completing this chapter, you will be able to do the following:

✓ Use the **AREA** command to calculate the area of an object by adding and subtracting objects.
✓ Display object properties in a drawing using fields.
✓ List data related to a single point, an object, a group of objects, or an entire drawing.
✓ Find the distance between two points.
✓ Identify a point location.
✓ Determine the amount of time spent in a drawing session.
✓ Determine the status of drawing parameters.
✓ Perform basic and advanced mathematical calculations using the **QuickCalc** calculator.
✓ Convert units using the **QuickCalc** calculator.

When working on a drawing, you may need to ask AutoCAD for information about the drawing, such as object distances and areas. You can also ask AutoCAD to tell you how much time you have spent on a drawing. The commands to do this include **AREA**, **DBLIST** (database list), **DIST** (distance), **ID** (identification), **LIST**, **STATUS**, and **TIME**.

These commands are accessed from the **Tools** > **Inquiry** cascading menu. You can also access these commands from the **Inquiry** toolbar. See **Figure 13-1.** To display this toolbar, right-click on any visible toolbar and select **Inquiry** from the shortcut menu.

> **NOTE**
>
> The **Region/Mass Properties** button and pull-down menu entry provide data related to the properties of a 2D region or 3D solid. This topic is discussed in *AutoCAD and Its Applications—Advanced*.

Figure 13-1.
The inquiry commands are grouped on the **Inquiry** toolbar and in the **Inquiry** cascading menu in the **Tools** pull-down menu.

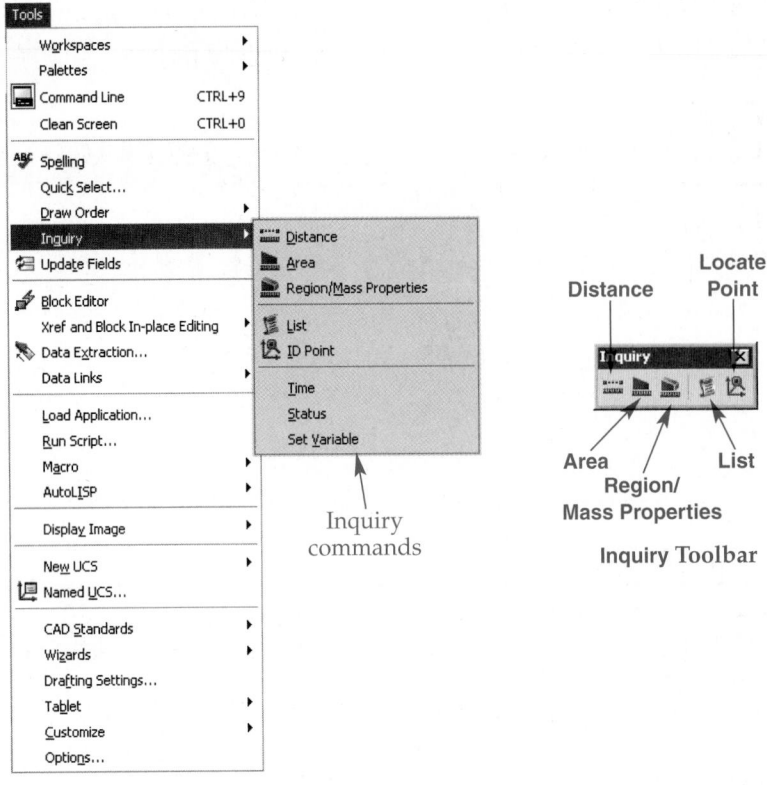

Inquiry Cascading Menu

Inquiry Toolbar

Finding the Area of Shapes and Objects

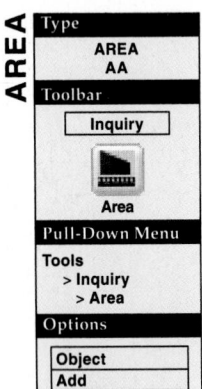

AREA

Type
AREA
AA

Toolbar
Inquiry

Area

Pull-Down Menu
Tools
> Inquiry
> Area

Options
Object
Add
Subtract

The most basic function of the **AREA** command is to find the area of any object, circle, polygon, polyline, or spline. The command sequence to find the area of a circle is:

Command: **AA** *or* **AREA**↵
Specify first corner point or [Object/Add/Subtract]: **O**↵
Select objects: *(pick the circle)*
Area = *n.nnnn*, Circumference = *n.nnnn*
Command:

The two numeric values represented by *n.nnnn* indicate the area and circumference of the circle. The second value returned by the **AREA** command varies, depending on the type of object selected, as shown in the following table:

Object	Value returned
Line	Selected value does not have an area (no value given)
Polyline	Length or Perimeter
Circle	Circumference
Spline	Length or Perimeter
Rectangle	Perimeter

Shapes drawn with polylines do not need to be closed for AutoCAD to calculate
their areas. AutoCAD calculates the area as if a line segment connects the first and last
points. To find the area of a shape created with the **LINE** command, pick all the vertices
of that shape. This is the default mode of the **AREA** command. Setting a running
object snap mode, such as **Endpoint** or **Intersection**, helps you pick the vertices. See
Figure 13-2.

> Command: **AREA**↵
> Specify first corner point or [Object/Add/Subtract]: *(pick point 1)*
> Specify next corner point or press ENTER for total: *(pick point 2)*
> Specify next corner point or press ENTER for total: *(continue picking points until all*
> *corners of the object have been selected, and then press* [Enter])
> Area = *n.nnnn*, Perimeter = *n.nnnn*
> Command:

Using the **Add** option of the **AREA** command, you can pick multiple objects or
areas. As you add objects or areas, a running total of the area is automatically calculated. The **Subtract** option allows you to remove objects or areas from the selection set.
Once either of these options is entered, the **AREA** command remains in effect until
canceled.

The next example shows how to use these two options in the same operation.
Refer to **Figure 13-3** as you go through the following command sequence:

> Command: **AREA**↵
> Specify first corner point or [Object/Add/Subtract]: **A**↵
> Specify first corner point or [Object/Subtract]: **O**↵
> (ADD mode) Select objects: *(pick the polyline)*
> Area = 13.7854, Perimeter = 20.1416
> Total area = 13.7854
> (ADD mode) Select objects: ↵
> Specify first corner point or [Object/Subtract]: **S**↵
> Specify first corner point or [Object/Add]: **O**↵
> (SUBTRACT mode) Select objects: *(pick the first circle)*
> Area = 0.7854, Circumference = 3.1416
> Total area = 13.0000
> (SUBTRACT mode) Select objects: *(pick the second circle)*
> Area = 0.7854, Circumference = 3.1416
> Total area = 12.2146
> (SUBTRACT mode) Select objects: ↵
> Specify first corner point or [Object/Add]: ↵
> Command:

Figure 13-2.
Pick all vertices to
find the area of an
object drawn with
the **LINE** command.

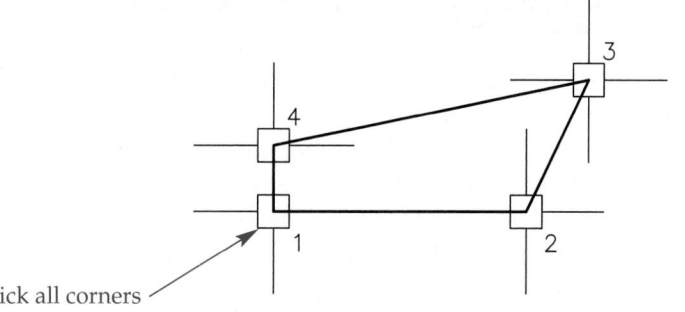

Pick all corners

Figure 13-3.
To calculate the area of an object drawn with the **PLINE** command, first select the outer boundary of the object using the **Add** option of the **AREA** command. Select the inner boundaries (the circles) using the **Subtract** option of the **AREA** command. This will calculate the area of the object.

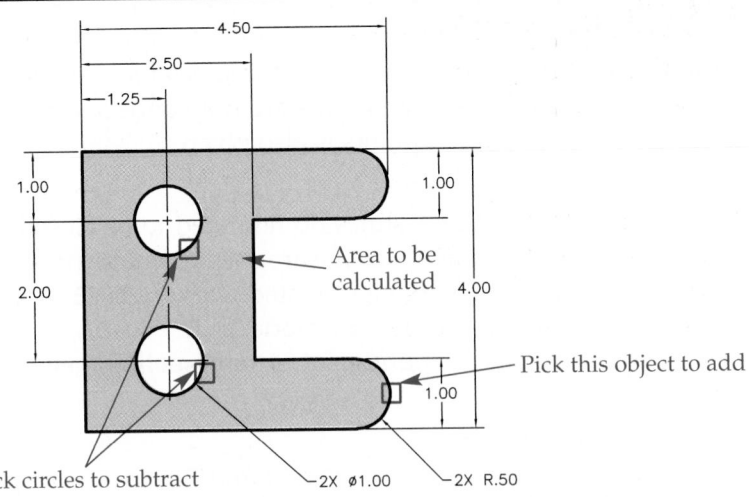

The total area of the object in **Figure 13-3** after subtracting the areas of the two holes is 12.2146. An area value and a perimeter or circumference value are given for each object as it is selected. These values are not affected by the adding or subtracting functions.

Notice in the previous command sequence that, when you are finished adding objects and wish to subtract, you must press [Enter] at the (ADD mode) Select objects: prompt. You can also right-click and type S to enter **Subtract** mode. If you have finished subtracting and wish to add, you must press [Enter] at the (SUBTRACT mode) Select objects: prompt or right-click and type A to enter **Add** mode.

PROFESSIONAL TIP

Calculating area, circumference, and perimeter values of shapes drawn with the **LINE** command can be time-consuming. You must pick each vertex on the object. If you need to calculate areas, it is best to create lines and arcs with the **PLINE** or **SPLINE** command. Use the **Object** option of the **AREA** command when adding or subtracting objects.

Exercise 13-1
Complete the exercise on the Student CD.

Displaying Information with Fields

field: Text object that displays a property, setting, or value for an object, drawing, or computer system.

You can list some object properties and drawing information using fields. A *field* is a text object that displays a set property, setting, or value for an object, a drawing, or a computer system. If the value of the field setting changes, the text is updated automatically to reflect the change. Fields were introduced in Chapter 9. Each object type, such as a line, circle, or polyline, has different properties that can be displayed in a field. For example, using fields, you can place text next to a circle listing its area and circumference.

Figure 13-4.
Pick the Object field to add a property for a specific object to a field. Pick the **Select object** button to select the object.

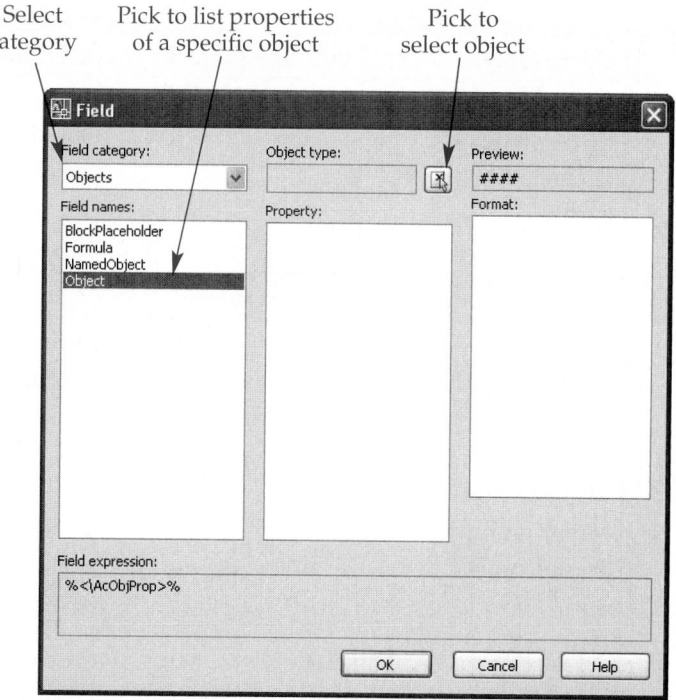

To display an object property value using a field, access the **Field** dialog box by selecting **Insert** > **Field...** from the pull-down menu. In the **Field** dialog box, pick Objects from the **Field category:** drop-down list, and then pick Object in the **Field names:** list box. See **Figure 13-4.** Pick the **Select object** button to return to the drawing window and pick the object.

When you select the object, the **Field** dialog box reappears with the available properties listed. See **Figure 13-5.** Pick the property, select the format, and pick **OK** to have the field inserted in the text object. Once the field is created, whenever the object is

Figure 13-5.
After you pick the object, properties specific to the object type are listed. Pick the property and format for the field.

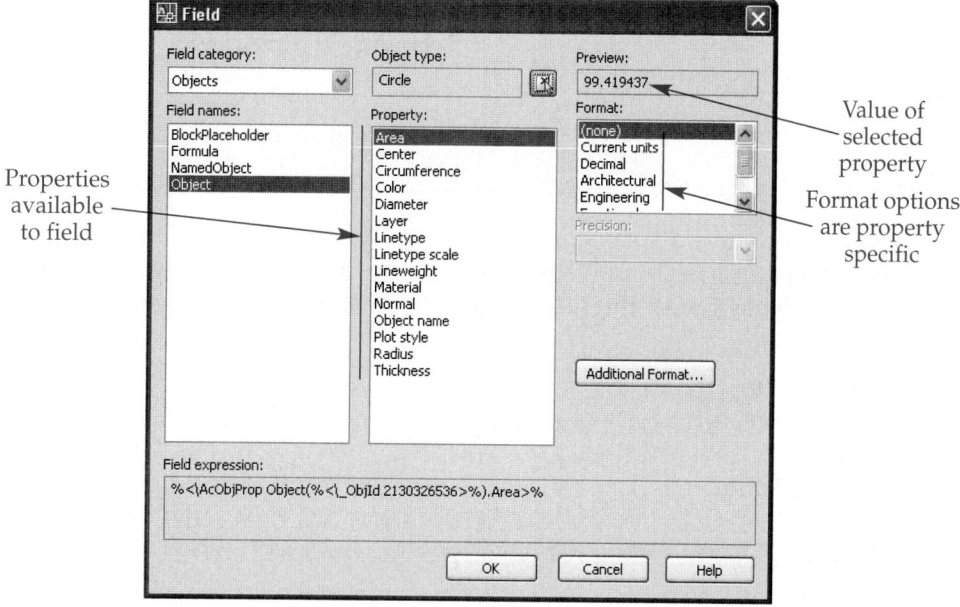

Figure 13-6.
This table is a partial listing of inquiry properties available for various object types.

Object Properties Available for Display in Fields			
Line Object	**Circle Object**	**Polyline Object**	**Rectangle Object**
Length Angle Delta Start End	Area Circumference Diameter Radius Center	Area Length	Area Length
Arc Object	**Ellipse Object**	**Spline Object**	**Region Object**
Area Arc length Radius Center Total angle Start End Start angle End angle	Area Center Major axis Minor axis Major radius Minor radius Radius ratio Start End Start angle End angle	Area Degree Start tangent End tangent	Area Perimeter

modified, the value displayed in the field automatically updates. In addition to object property settings such as layer, linetype, lineweight, and plot style, many inquiry properties can be included in a field. The table in **Figure 13-6** lists some of the inquiry data that can be displayed in fields for various object types.

Exercise 13-2
Complete the exercise on the Student CD.

Listing Drawing Data

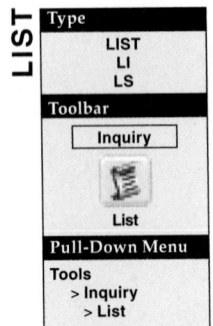

LIST

Type
> LIST
> LI
> LS

Toolbar
Inquiry

List

Pull-Down Menu
Tools
> Inquiry
> List

The **LIST** command displays data about any AutoCAD object. Line lengths, circle and arc locations and radii, polyline widths, and object layers are just a few of the items you can identify with the **LIST** command. You can select several objects to list. The command sequence is:

Command: **LI**, **LS**, *or* **LIST**↵
Select objects: *(pick one or more objects using any selection method)*
n found
Select objects:

When you press [Enter], the data for each object you picked is displayed in the text window. The following data is given for a line:

```
LINE Layer:   "layer name"
              Space: Model or Paper space
     Handle = nn
from point,   X= nn.nnnn      Y= nn.nnnn     Z=  0.0000
to point,     X= nn.nnnn      Y= nn.nnnn     Z= 0.0000
Length = nn.nnnn,    Angle in XY Plane = nnn
Delta X = nn.nnnn,   Delta Y = nn.nnnn, Delta Z = 0.0000
```

The Delta X and Delta Y values indicate the horizontal and vertical distances between the *from point* and *to point* of the line. These two values, along with the length and angle, provide you with four measurements for a single line. An example of the data and measurements provided for two-dimensional lines is shown in **Figure 13-7**. If a line is three-dimensional, the **LIST** command displays an additional line of information:

```
3D Length = nn.nnnn,  Angle from XY Plane = nnn
```

The **LIST** command can also be used to determine information about text and multiline text. The information listed for text, multiline text, circles, and splines is:

```
TEXT          Layer:  "layer name"
          Space: Model or Paper space
          Layout: Only in Paper space
     Handle = nn
     Style = "name"
     Annotative: Yes or No
     Font file = name
     start point,   X= n.nnnn        Y= n.nnnn       Z= 0.0000
     height         n.nnnn
     text    text contents
     rotation       angle    n
     width scale factor      n.nnnn
     obliquing      angle    n
     generation     normal
     MTEXT         Layer:  "layer name"
           Space: Model or Paper space
     Handle = nn
     Location:      X= n.nnnn        Y= n.nnnn       Z= 0.0000
     Width:  n.nnnn
     Normal:X= n.nnnn       Y= n.nnnn       Z= 0.0000
     Rotation:      n
     Text style:    "style name"
     Annotative: Yes or No
     Text height:   n.nnnn
```

Figure 13-7.
The various data and measurements of a line provided by the **LIST** command.

A = XY location
B = XY location
C = length
D = delta X
E = delta Y
F = angle

```
Line spacing:        Multiple (n.nnnnnnx      =         n.nnnn)
Attachment:          corner of multiline text insertion point
Flow direction:      direction text is read based on language
Contents:            multiline text contents
   CIRCLE            Layer:  "layer name"
   Space:            Model or Paper space
   Handle = nn
center point, X= n.nnnn Y= n.nnnn          Z= 0.0000
radius  n.nnnn
circumference     n.nnnn
area  n.nnnn
   SPLINE           Layer:  "layer name"
   Space:           Model or Paper space
   Handle = nn
   Length:          n.nnnn
   Order:           n
   Properties:   Planar, Non-Rational, Non-Periodic
   Parametric Range:    Start    n.nnnn
                    End    n.nnnn
   Number of control points:      n
   Control Points:          X = n.nnnn,     Y= n.nnnn,     Z = 0.0000
        (the XYZ of all control points are listed)
   Number of fit points:  n
   User Data:    Fit Points
        X = n.nnnn,      Y = n.nnnn,     Z = 0.0000
        (the XYZ of all fit points are listed)
   Fit point tolerance:     n.nnnn
```

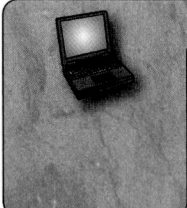

PROFESSIONAL TIP

The **LIST** command is the most powerful inquiry command in AutoCAD. It provides all the information you need to know about an object. Also, the **LIST** command reports the area and perimeter of polylines so you do not need to use the **AREA** command. The **LIST** command also reports an object's color and linetype, unless both are BYLAYER.

Listing Drawing Data for All Objects

The **DBLIST** (database list) command lists all data for every object in the current drawing. This command is initiated by typing DBLIST. The information is provided in the same format used by the **LIST** command. As soon as you enter the **DBLIST** command, the information begins to scroll up the screen in the text window. The scrolling stops when a complete page (or screen) is filled with database information. Press [Enter] to scroll to the end of the next page. Use the scroll buttons to move forward and backward through the listing. If you find the data you need, press the [Esc] key to exit the **DBLIST** command. You can hide the text window by pressing the [F2] function key.

Finding the Distance between Two Points

The **DIST** (distance) command is used to find the distance between two points. As with the **AREA** command, you should use object snap modes to accurately pick locations. The **DIST** command provides the distance between the points and the angle of the line from the positive X axis. It also gives delta X, Y, and Z dimensions. To access the **DIST** command, pick the **Distance** button in the **Inquiry** toolbar, select **Tools** > **Inquiry** > **Distance**, or type DI or DIST. The button and pull-down selections issue the command transparently and can be used within other commands.

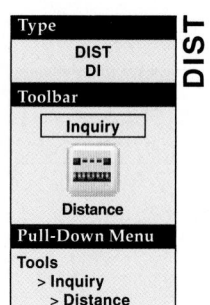

Type
DIST
DI
Toolbar
Inquiry
Distance
Pull-Down Menu
Tools
> Inquiry
> Distance

DIST

> Command: **DI** or **DIST**↵
> Specify first point: *(select point)*
> Specify second point: *(select point)*
> Distance = *n.nnnn*,   Angle in XY Plane = *n*, Angle from XY Plane = *n*
> Delta X = *n.nnnn*,   Delta Y = *n.nnnn*,   Delta Z = 0.0000
> Command:

Identifying Point Locations

The **ID** command displays the coordinate location of a single point in the drawing. This command can be used to find the coordinates of a line endpoint or the center of a circle. Simply pick the point to be identified when the Specify point: prompt appears. Use the object snap modes for accuracy.

Type
ID
Toolbar
Inquiry
Locate Point
Pull-Down Menu
Tools
> Inquiry
> ID Point

ID

> Command: **ID**↵
> Specify point: *(select the point)*
> X = *n.nnnn*   Y = *n.nnnn*   Z = 0.0000
> Command:

In conjunction with "blip" mode, the **ID** command can help you identify where a coordinate is on the screen. A *blip* is a small cross that is displayed when a point is picked on the screen. Suppose you want to see where the point 8.75,6.44 is located. Enter these numbers at the Specify point: prompt. AutoCAD responds by placing a blip at that exact location. In order to use this feature, you must turn the **BLIPMODE** system variable on.

blip: Small cross that may be displayed when a point is picked on the screen.

> Command: **BLIPMODE**↵
> Enter mode [ON/OFF] <*current*>: **ON**↵
> Command: **ID**↵
> Specify point: **8.75,6.44**↵
>   X = 8.7500   Y = 6.4400   Z = 0.0000
> Command:

Exercise 13-3

Complete the exercise on the Student CD.

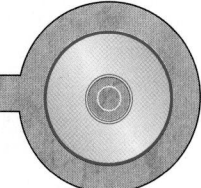

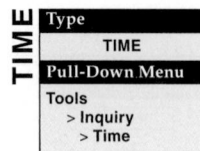
Checking the Time

Type

TIME

Pull-Down Menu

Tools
> Inquiry
> Time

The **TIME** command allows you to display the current time, time related to your drawing, and time related to the current drawing session. The following is an example of the information displayed in the text window when the **TIME** command is entered:

```
Command: TIME↵
Current time:    Monday, February 13, 2007      13:39:22:210 PM
Times for this drawing:
  Created:       Saturday, February 11, 2007    10:24:48:130 AM
  Last updated: Saturday, February 11, 2007     14:36:23:460 PM
  Total editing time:     0 days 01:23:57:930
  Elapsed timer (on):     0 days 00:35:28:650
  Next automatic save in:      0 days 01:35:26:680
Enter option [Display/ON/OFF/Reset]:
```

You should keep a few things in mind when you check the text window display after issuing the **TIME** command. First, the drawing creation time starts when you begin a new drawing, not when a new drawing is first saved. Second, the **SAVE** command affects the Last updated: time. If you exit AutoCAD and do not save the drawing, however, all time in that session is discarded. Finally, you can time a specific drawing task by using the **Reset** option of the **TIME** command to reset the elapsed timer.

When the **TIME** command is issued, the times shown in the text window are static. This means that none of the times are being updated. You can request an update by using the **Display** option at the following prompt:

Enter option [Display/ON/OFF/Reset]:

When you enter the drawing area, the timer is on by default. If you want to stop the timer, simply enter OFF at the Enter option [Display/ON/OFF/Reset]: prompt. If the timer is off, enter ON to start it again.

NOTE

The Windows operating system maintains the date and time settings for the computer. You can change these settings in the Windows Control Panel. To access the Control Panel, pick Settings and then Control Panel from the start menu.

Exercise 13-4

Complete the exercise on the Student CD.

Determining the Drawing Status

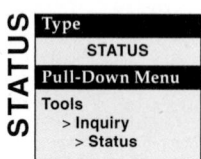

STATUS

Type

STATUS

Pull-Down Menu

Tools
> Inquiry
> Status

While working on a drawing, you may forget some of the drawing parameters, such as the limits, grid spacing, or snap values. All the information about a drawing can be displayed using the **STATUS** command. Access this command by typing STATUS or selecting **Tools** > **Inquiry** > **Status**. The drawing information is displayed in the text window. See **Figure 13-8.**

Figure 13-8.
The drawing information listed by the **STATUS** command is shown in the text window.

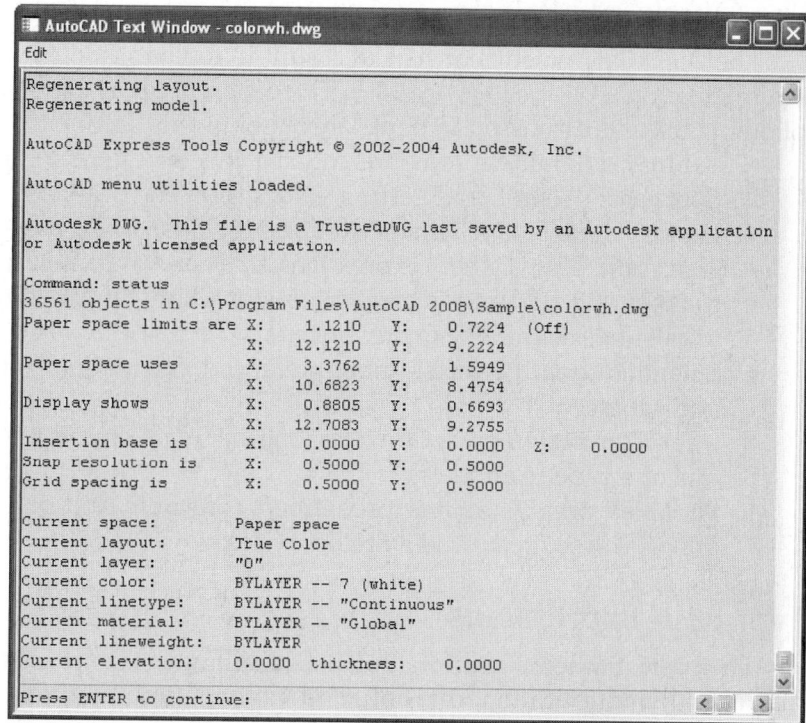

The number of objects in a drawing refers to the total number of objects—both erased and existing. Free dwg disk (C:) space: represents the space left on the drive containing your drawing file. Drawing aid settings are shown, along with the current settings for layer, linetype, and color. These topics are discussed in later chapters of this textbook. When you have finished reviewing the information, press [F2] to close the text window. You can also switch to the graphics window without closing the text window by picking anywhere inside the graphics window or using the Windows [Alt]+[Tab] feature.

NOTE

Another way to move between the graphics window and the text window is to use the AutoCAD commands **GRAPHSCR** and **TEXTSCR**. Typing TEXTSCR displays the text window. Typing GRAPHSCR closes the text window. You can also open the text window by selecting **View > Display > Text Window**.

Using QuickCalc

AutoCAD commands require precise input. Often, the input is variable and based on objects or locations within a drawing. **QuickCalc** is a palette that contains a basic calculator, a scientific calculator, a units converter, and a variables feature.

When you are professionally drafting, most days will find you grabbing for your handheld calculator. You may be working from a sketch with missing dimensions, you may need to calculate a distance or angle, or some dimensions may need to be double-checked. **QuickCalc** can be used to do these things and much more. **QuickCalc** can be used like a basic calculator or it can be used while drafting, by passing values to the command line while a command is active. **QuickCalc** is a palette that can be opened by picking the **QuickCalc** button in the **Standard Annotation** toolbar, picking **Tools > Palettes > QuickCalc**, typing QC or QUICKCALC, or using the [Ctrl]+[8] key combination.

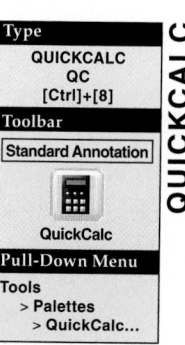

Type
QUICKCALC
QC
[Ctrl]+[8]

Toolbar
Standard Annotation

QuickCalc

Pull-Down Menu
Tools
> Palettes
> QuickCalc...

QUICKCALC

The QuickCalc Palette

The **QuickCalc** palette consists of a built-in toolbar, calculation and history areas, and calculation tools. See **Figure 13-9**. The different areas are briefly explained in the following list and discussed in depth throughout this section.

- **Toolbar.** Contains commands for clearing the calculator, passing values to the Command: prompt, and getting values from the drawing.
- **History area.** Stores a history of the previously used expressions.
- **Input box.** This is where expressions are typed or passed from the other tools.
- **Number Pad.** Serves as a basic calculator where numbers and symbols are used to calculate arithmetic expressions.
- **Scientific area.** Performs more advanced calculations, such as trigonometry and geometry.
- **Units Conversion area.** Converts length, area, volume, and angular units from one unit type to another.
- **Variables area.** Contains predefined constants and functions variables and allows you to create and store new ones.

Typing in Expressions

The basic mathematical functions used in numeric expressions include addition, subtraction, multiplication, division, and exponential notation. Parentheses are used to group symbols and values into sets. The symbols used for the basic mathematical operators are shown in the following table:

Symbol	Function	Example
+	Addition	3+26
–	Subtraction	270–15.3
*	Multiplication	4*156
/	Division	256/16
^	Exponent	22.6^3
( )	Grouped expressions	2*(16+2^3)

Figure 13-9.
All the areas of the **QuickCalc** window can be used to do calculations.

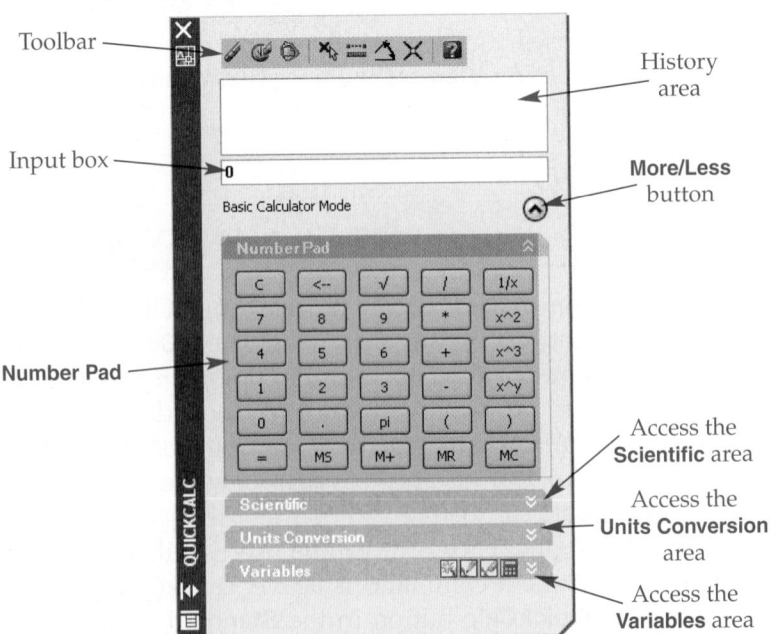

Expressions can be typed directly into the input box using the number pad and symbols on the keyboard. After typing the expression, press [Enter] to have the expression evaluated. The result displays in the input box and the expression is moved to the history area. **Figure 13-10** displays the **QuickCalc** palette after calculating 96.27 + 23.58. The following are examples of expressions that can be entered in the input box:

268+182↵
450

49.2–19.8↵
29.4

49*12↵
588

15/4.5↵
3.333

6^4↵
1296

NOTE

If you move the cursor outside of the **QuickCalc** palette, the drawing area automatically becomes active. To make **QuickCalc** active, pick anywhere inside the **QuickCalc** palette.

Grouped expressions can be entered by using parentheses to break up the expressions that need to be calculated separately. For example, to calculate the result of 6 + 2 and then to multiply the result by 4, enter (6+2)*4. If the parentheses are not added, the result will be wrong.

If you make a mistake in the input box, you do not need to clear the input box and start over again. Use the left and right arrow keyboard keys to move through the field. Right-clicking in the input box displays the shortcut options for copying and pasting text.

Figure 13-10.
A—Type expressions into the input box.
B—After typing the expression, press the [Enter] key to have the expression evaluated. The expression and result are stored in the history area.

A

Result —

Expression and result

More/Less button

B

When you are using only the input box of **QuickCalc**, you can hide the additional sections to save valuable drawing space. To do this, pick the **More/Less** button below the input box. See **Figure 13-10.** When the **QuickCalc** palette displays all of the areas, the button is an up arrow and its tooltip reads **Less**. To display the areas after they have been hidden, pick the button again.

Clearing the Input and History Areas

After pressing the [Enter] key to evaluate an expression, you can type a new expression without having to clear the last result. AutoCAD automatically starts a new expression. The input box can be cleared manually when needed by either placing the cursor in the input box and using the [Backspace] or [Delete] key from the keyboard, or by picking the **Clear** button from the **QuickCalc** toolbar. The history area can also be cleared by picking the **Clear History** button. See **Figure 13-11.**

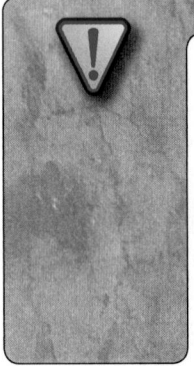

CAUTION

If you enter an expression that cannot be evaluated, AutoCAD displays an **Error in Expression** dialog box. Pick the **OK** button, correct the error, and try it again.

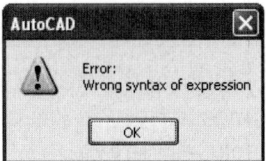

Using the Number Pad

Expressions can also be entered by picking the numbers and symbols with the cursor in the **Number Pad**. Picking a number or symbol places that item into the input box. The **Number Pad** offers some options that are not available from the keyboard. These options are displayed in **Figure 13-12.**

Advanced Calculations

Trigonometry functions, some geometry functions, and exponential functions can be found in the **Scientific** area of **QuickCalc**. See **Figure 13-13.** To use one of the expressions, type a value in the input box, pick the appropriate expression button, and press [Enter]. When you pick the expression button, the input box value is displayed in

Figure 13-11.
The input box and history areas can be cleared using the buttons on the **QuickCalc** toolbar.

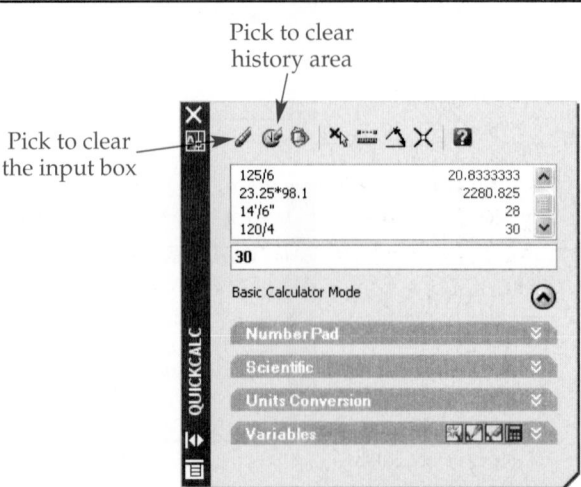

Figure 13-12.
The basic **Number Pad** area contains additional options that cannot be accessed using the keyboard.

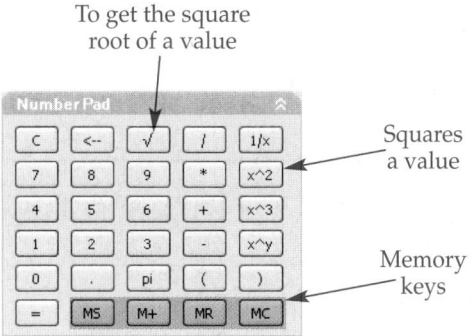

To get the square
root of a value

Squares
a value

Memory
keys

Figure 13-13.
The **Scientific** expressions available in **QuickCalc**.

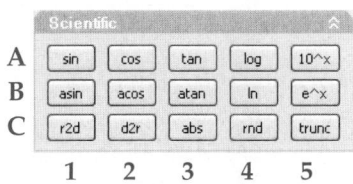

	1	2	3	4	5
A	Sine	Cosine	Tangent	Base–10 Log	Base–10 Exponent
B	Arcsine	Arccosine	Arctangent	Natural Log	Natural Exponent
C	Convert Radians to Degrees	Convert Degrees to Radians	Absolute Value	Round	Truncate

parentheses after the expression. For example, to get the *sine* of 14, clear the input box, type 14 in the input box, and pick the **sin** button. The input box now reads sin(14). Press the [Enter] key to get the result.

> **NOTE**
>
> The expression button can be picked first, but it puts a default value of 0 in parentheses. You can then place the cursor in the input box to type a different number in the parentheses if needed.

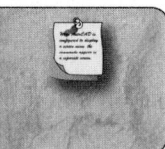

Converting Units

The **Units Conversion** area allows you to convert one unit type to another. The unit types available are **Length, Area, Volume**, and **Angular**. To use the unit converter to convert 23 centimeters to inches, pick in the **Units type** field to display the drop-down list. See **Figure 13-14.** Pick the drop-down list button to display the different unit types and select Length. Activate the **Convert from** field and select Centimeters from the drop-down list. Activate the **Convert to** field and select Inches from the drop-down list. Type 23 in the **Value to convert** field and press the [Enter]. The **Converted value** field now displays the converted units.

The converted value can be passed to the input box to use in an expression by picking the **Return Conversion to Calculator Input Area** button. See **Figure 13-15.** If the button is not visible, pick once on the converted units in the **Converted value** field.

Figure 13-14.
Picking the current unit type activates the field and displays the drop-down list button.

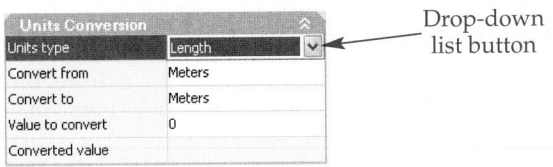

Drop-down list button

Figure 13-15.
After a value has been converted, it can be passed to the input box.

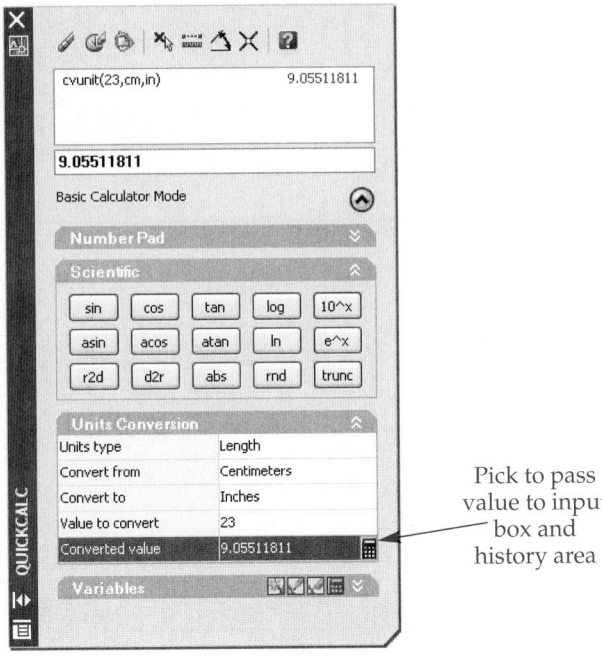

Pick to pass value to input box and history area

Using Variables

variable: Text item that represents another value that can be accessed later as needed.

If you use an expression or value frequently, you can save it as a *variable* so you do not have to type it every time. The **Variables** area of **QuickCalc** includes two types of predefined variables: **Constants** and **Functions**. A *constant* is an expression or value that stays the same—remains constant. A *function* is an expression that asks for user input to get values that can be passed to the expression.

constant: Expression or value that stays the same.

In the **Variables** area, variables can be created, edited, deleted, and passed to the input box. See **Figure 13-16.** The tool buttons contain the following functions:

function: Expression that asks for user input to get values that can be passed to the expression.

- **New Variable.** Opens the **Variable Definition** dialog box, where a new variable can be created.
- **Edit Variable.** Opens the **Variable Definition** dialog box with the information for the selected variable. If no variable is selected, this button is grayed out.
- **Delete.** Deletes the selected variable.
- **Return Variable to Input Area.** Passes the selected variable to the input box. The variable can also be passed to the input box by double-clicking the variable name.

These commands can also be accessed by right-clicking in the **Variable** area to display the shortcut menu. The following two additional options are available:

- **New Category.** Creates a new category for saving variables.
- **Rename.** Allows you to rename the selected variable. This also can be accessed by selecting the variable, pausing, and then selecting it again.

Creating a new variable

To create a new variable, select the **New Variable...** button or right-click and select **New Variable...** from the shortcut menu. This opens the **Variable Definition** dialog box shown in **Figure 13-17.** Type a name for the variable in the **Name:** field. Select a group for the variable to reside in the **Group with:** field. In the **Value or expression:** field, type

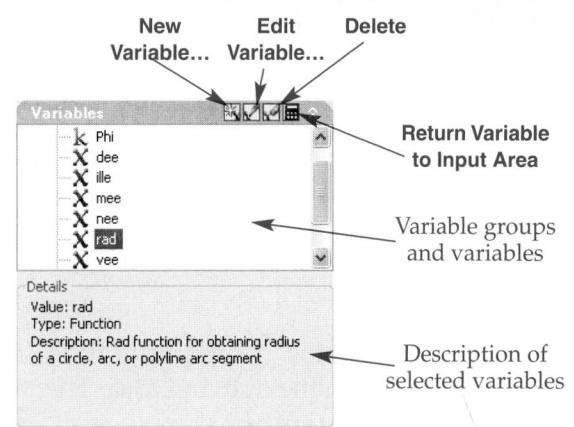

Figure 13-16.
The **Variables** area of **QuickCalc** allows you to store values and expressions for later use.

New Variable... Edit Variable... Delete

Return Variable to Input Area

Variable groups and variables

Description of selected variables

Figure 13-17.
A new variable is defined in the **Variable Definition** dialog box.

the value or the expression for the variable. Give a description for the variable in the **Description** field. Pick the **OK** button to save the variable and display it in the **Variables** area.

PROFESSIONAL TIP

The predefined variables and their functions are explained in the AutoCAD help file. To view these, pick the **Help** button on the **Standard Annotation** toolbar to open the **AutoCAD Help** window. Pick the **Search** tab, type QUICKCALC, and then pick the **Search** button. In the results, pick on **QUICKCALC (Quick Reference)** calculator to view the page. On the **Quick Reference** tab of the page, pick the **Variables Area** link and then scroll down to the bottom of the page.

Getting and passing values from the AutoCAD window

Values can be passed from the input box to be used with commands, and values can be obtained from the AutoCAD drawing and passed to the input box using commands on the **QuickCalc** toolbar. See **Figure 13-18.** The commands include.

- **Paste value to command line.** Places the current input box value on the Command: prompt. This button is typically used while a command is active.

Figure 13-18.
Values can be passed
from **QuickCalc** to
AutoCAD, and they
can be retrieved
from AutoCAD and
passed to **QuickCalc**.

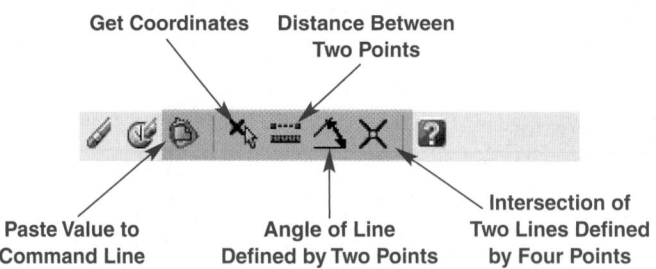

- **Get Coordinates.** Temporarily hides the **QuickCalc** palette so a point can be selected from the drawing area. The X,Y,Z coordinates of the selected point are placed in the input box.
- **Distance Between Two Points.** Temporarily hides the **QuickCalc** palette so two points can be selected from the drawing area. The distance between the two selected points is placed in the input box.
- **Angle of Line Defined by Two Points.** Allows you to select two points on a line. The angle of the line is calculated and placed in the input box.
- **Intersection of Two Lines Defined by Four Points.** Allows you to find the intersection of two lines by picking points on the two lines. The X,Y,Z coordinates of the intersection is placed in the input box.

Using QuickCalc with Commands

While drafting, you may need to calculate an unknown distance or angle before you can draw an object. **QuickCalc** can help with these calculations. To use **QuickCalc** during a command, start the command and, when prompted for the value that needs to be calculated, pick the **QuickCalc** button from the **Standard Annotation** toolbar or enter 'QC or 'QUICKCALC. The **QuickCalc** window opens in command mode. See **Figure 13-19.** Use the necessary tools to evaluate an expression and then pick the **Apply** button to pass the value back to the command. The following procedure draws a line a distance of 14′8″ + 26′3″ horizontally from the selected point:

> Command: **LINE**↵
> Specify first point: *(pick a point)*
> Specify next point or [Undo]: *(with polar tracking on, drag the mouse to the right of the first selected point so the line is at 0°)* '**QC**↵

Figure 13-19.
When **QuickCalc**
is opened during
a command, the
active command is
displayed and the
Apply and **Close**
buttons are available
at the bottom of the
window.

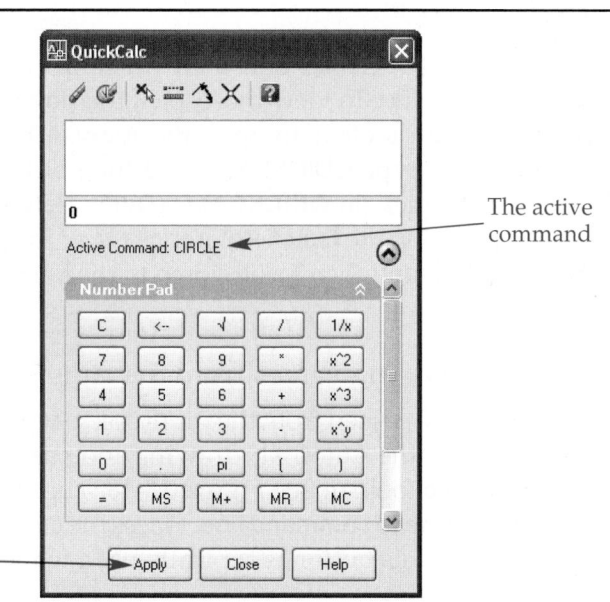

The active command

Pick to pass value back to command

In the input box of the **QuickCalc** palette enter 14'8" + 26'3" and press [Enter]. The result is 40'11". Pick the **Apply** button and this value is passed as the distance for the Y coordinate. Press [Enter] and the line is drawn.

QuickCalc can also be used in the middle of a command to do calculations without passing the result back to the command. To prevent the result from being passed back to the command, pick the **Close** button.

PROFESSIONAL TIP

The unit you use in **QuickCalc** must match the drawing units. In the preceding example, architectural units are used. The drawing units must be architectural. If needed, use the **Drawing Units** dialog box to change the drawing units to Architectural.

Using QuickCalc with Object Properties

QuickCalc can also be used to calculate expressions for an object in the **Properties** palette. When the **Properties** palette is open, picking a field that contains a numeric value displays the calculator icon. In **Figure 13-20,** a circle is selected, and the **Radius** field in the **Properties** palette is active. Picking the calculator icon opens the **QuickCalc** palette in property calculation mode. Expressions and values can be used in the same manner as when using **QuickCalc** in the middle of a command. When the expression has been evaluated in the input box, pick the **Apply** button to pass the value to the property field in the **Properties** palette. The object automatically updates based on the new value.

Additional QuickCalc Options

The history area contains some settings and features that can only be accessed from the shortcut menu. This menu is displayed when you right-click anywhere in the history area. See **Figure 13-21.** The following options are available:
- **Expression Font Color.** Allows you to change the color of the expression font.
- **Value Font Color.** Allows you to change the color of the value font.
- **Copy.** Copies the expression and value to the Windows clipboard.
- **Append Expression to Input Area.** Passes the expression to the input box.
- **Append Value to Input Area.** Passes the value to the input box.
- **Clear History.** Clears the history area.
- **Paste to Command Line.** Passes the value to the Command: prompt.

Figure 13-20.
The calculator icon is displayed after selecting a numeric field in the **Properties** window.

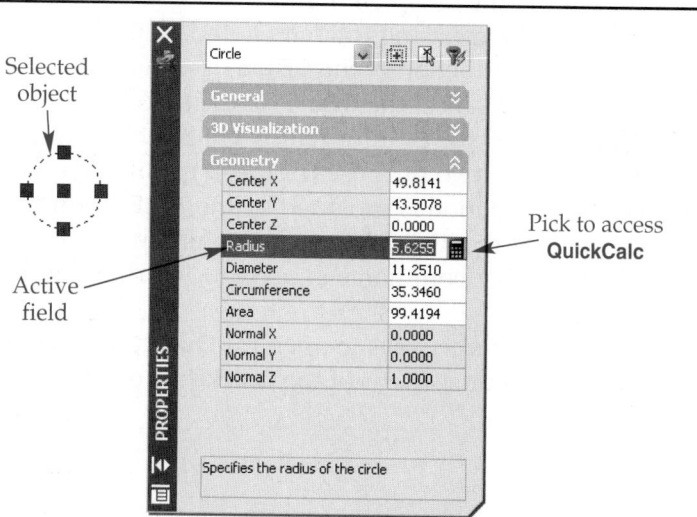

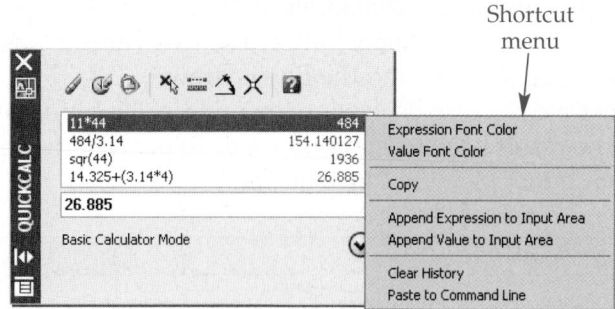

As with other palettes, picking the **Properties** button on the **QuickCalc** palette displays the **Properties** menu. The options allow you to change the settings for the palette's appearance, including its ability to be docked, hidden, or made transparent. The settings for these properties are discussed in Chapter 1.

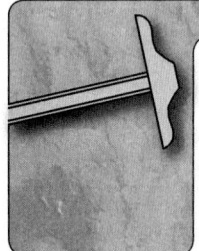

LEGACY NOTE

AutoCAD also includes an older **CAL** command that activates a command line calculator. This calculator allows you to perform math calculations and extract and use the information in your drawings. For additional information about this calculator, refer to the *Geometry Calculator* document in the *Supplemental Materials* section of the Student CD.

Chapter Test

Answer the following questions. Write your answers on a separate sheet of paper or complete the electronic chapter test on the Student CD.

1. What information is provided by the **AREA** command?
2. To add the areas of several objects when using the **AREA** command, when do you select the **Add** option?
3. Explain how picking a polyline when using the **AREA** command is different from picking an object drawn with the **LINE** command.
4. A(n) _____ is a text object that displays a set property, setting, or value for an object.
5. For what is the **LIST** command used?
6. Describe the meanings of delta X and delta Y.
7. What is the function of the **DBLIST** command?
8. How do you cancel the **DBLIST** command?
9. What three types of information are provided by the **DIST** command?
10. What are the two purposes of the **ID** command?
11. What information is provided by the **TIME** command?
12. When does the drawing creation time start?
13. What inquiry command is used to list drawing aid settings for your current drawing?
14. List at least three ways to open the **QuickCalc** palette.
15. Name the four sections of the **QuickCalc** palette.

16. Give the proper symbol to use for the following math functions:
    A. Addition
    B. Subtraction
    C. Multiplication
    D. Division
    E. Exponent
    F. Grouped expressions
17. Under which section of the **QuickCalc** palette can the square root function be found?
18. Under which section of the **QuickCalc** palette can the arccosine function be found?
19. When using one of the scientific functions, which should you do first: pick the scientific function button or type in the value to be used in the input box?
20. Name the four types of units that can be converted using **QuickCalc**.
21. A(n) _____ is a text item that represents another value that can be accessed later as needed.
22. Which tool button is used to pass the value in the input box to the command line?
23. Name the three ways to start **QuickCalc** while in the middle of a command.
24. When using **QuickCalc** in the middle of a command, how do you pass the value to the command line?
25. When the **Properties** palette is open, what do you need to do first to see the calculator icon, so **QuickCalc** can be used?

Drawing Problems

*Use **QuickCalc** to calculate the result of the following equations.*

1. 27.375 + 15.875
2. 16.0625 − 7.1250
3. 5 × 17′-8″
4. 48′-0″ ÷ 16
5. (12.625 + 3.063) + (18.250 − 4.375) − (2.625 − 1.188)
6. 7.25^2
7. Show the calculation and answer that would be used with the **LINE** command to make an 8″ line .006 in./in. longer in a pattern to allow for shrinkage in the final casting. Show only the expression and answer.
8. Solve for the deflection of a structural member. The formula is written as $PL^3/48EI$, where P = pounds of force, L = length of beam, E = Modulus of Elasticity, and I = moment of inertia. The values to be used are P = 4000 lbs, L = 240″, and E = 1,000,000 lbs/in². The value for I is the result of the beam (Width × $Height^3$)/12, where Width = 6.75″ and Height = 13.5″.
9. Convert 4.625″ to millimeters.
10. Convert 26 mm to inches.
11. Convert 65 miles to kilometers.
12. Convert 5 gallons to liters.
13. Calculate the coordinate located at 4,4,0 + 3<30.
14. Calculate the coordinate located at (3 + 5,1 + 1.25,0) + (2.375,1.625,0).
15. Find the square root of 360.
16. Calculate 3.25 squared.

Given the following right triangle, make the required trigonometry calculations.

17. Length of side c (hypotenuse).
18. Sine of angle *A*.
19. Sine of angle *B*.
20. Cosine of angle *A*.
21. Tangent of angle *A*.
22. Tangent of angle *B*.

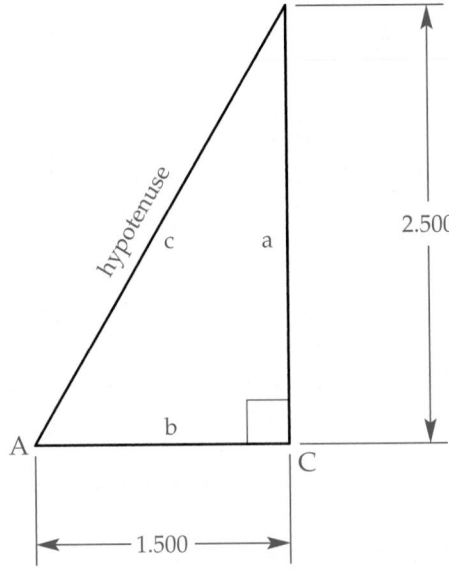

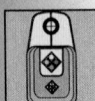

23. Draw the object shown below using the dimensions given. Check the time when you start the drawing. Draw all the features using the **PLINE** and **CIRCLE** commands. Use the **Object, Add,** and **Subtract** options of the **AREA** command to calculate the following measurements:

A. The area and perimeter of Object A.
B. The area and perimeter of area B. The slot ends are full radius.
C. The area and circumference of one of the circles.
D. The area of Object A, minus the area of Object B.
E. The area of Object A, minus the areas of the other three features.

Enter the **TIME** command and note the editing time spent on your drawing. Save the drawing as P13-23.

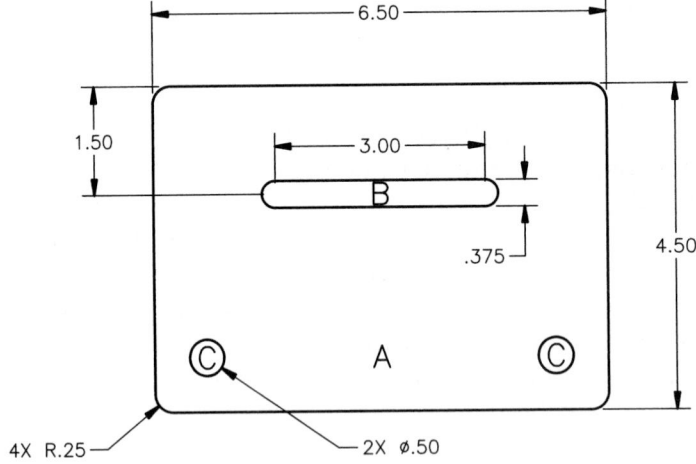

24. Draw the deck shown below using the **PLINE** command. Using the **POLYGON** command, draw the hexagon. Use the following guidelines to complete this problem:
    A. Specify architectural units for your drawing. Use 1/2″ fractions and decimal degrees. Leave the remaining settings for the drawing units at the default values.
    B. Set the limits to 100′,80′ and use the **All** option of the **ZOOM** command.
    C. Set the grid spacing to 2′ and the snap spacing to 1′.
    D. Calculate the measurements listed below.
        a. The area and perimeter of Object A.
        b. The area and perimeter of Object B.
        c. The area of Object A, minus the area of Object B.
        d. The distance between Point C and Point D.
        e. The distance between Point E and Point C.
        f. The coordinates of Points C, D, and F.
    E. Enter the **DBLIST** command and check the information listed for your drawing.
    F. Enter the **TIME** command and note the total editing time spent on your drawing.
    G. Save the drawing as P13-24.

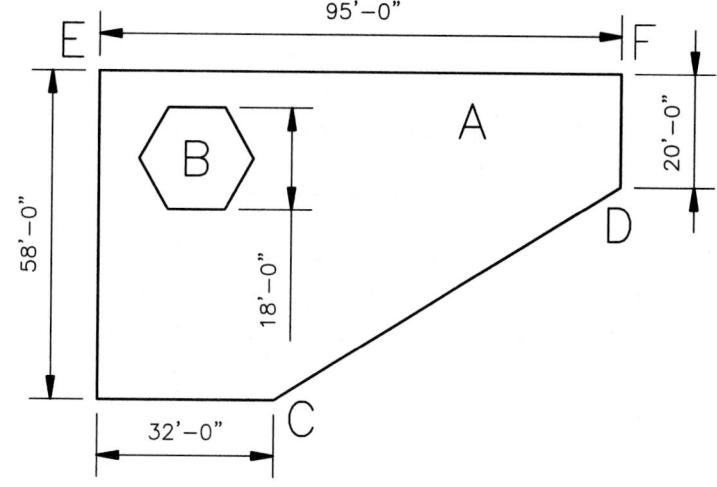

Drawing Problems - Chapter 13

25. The drawing below is a view of the gable end of a house. Draw the house using the dimensions given, and draw the windows as single lines only (the location of the windows is not important). The spacing between each of the second-floor windows is 3″. The width of this end of the house is 16′-6″. The length of the roof is 40′. You may want to use the **PLINE** command to assist in creating specific shapes in this drawing, except as noted above. Save the drawing as P13-25. Calculate the following:

A. The total area of the roof.
B. The diagonal distance from one corner of the roof to the other.
C. The area of the first-floor window.
D. The total area of all second-floor windows, including the 3″ spaces between each of them.
E. Siding will cover the house. What is the total area of siding for this end?

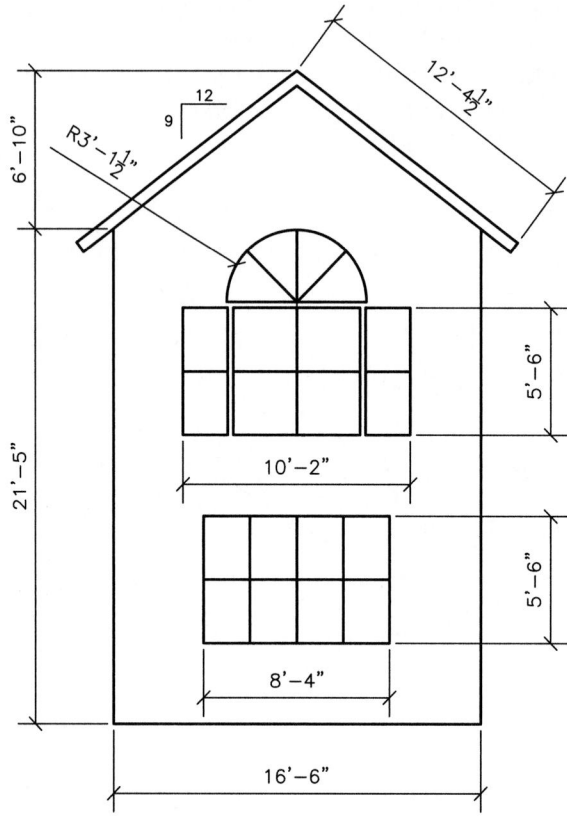

26. The drawing shown below is a side view of a pyramid. The pyramid has four sides. Create an auxiliary view showing the true size of a pyramid face. Save the drawing as P13-26. Using inquiry techniques, calculate the following:
    A. The area of one side.
    B. The perimeter of one side.
    C. The area of all four sides.
    D. The area of the base.
    E. The true length (distance) from the midpoint of the base on one side to the apex.

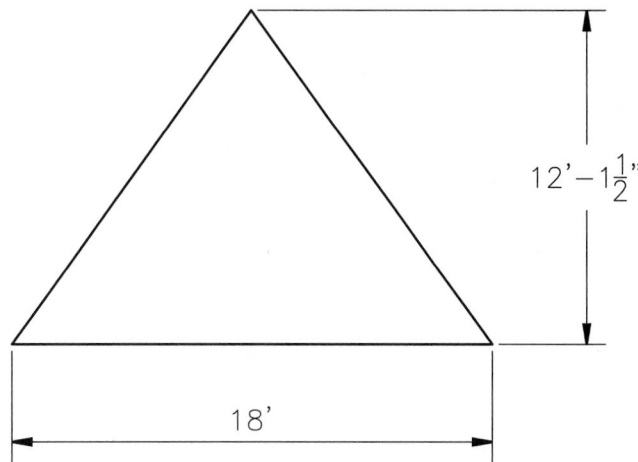

$12'-1\frac{1}{2}"$

$18'$

27. Draw the property plat shown below. Label property line bearings and distances only if required by your instructor. Calculate the area of the property plat in square feet and convert to acres. Save the drawing as P13-27.

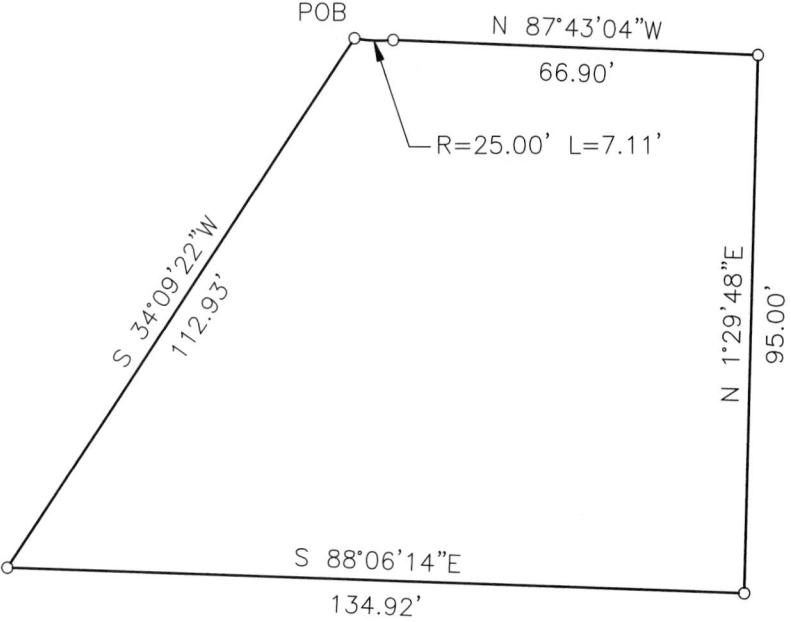

POB

N 87°43'04"W
66.90'

R=25.00' L=7.11'

S 34°09'22"W
112.93'

N 1°29'48"E
95.00'

S 88°06'14"E
134.92'

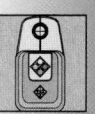

28. Draw the subdivision plat shown below. Label the drawing as shown. Calculate the acreage of each lot and record each value as a label inside the corresponding lot (for example, .249 AC). Save the drawing as P13-28.

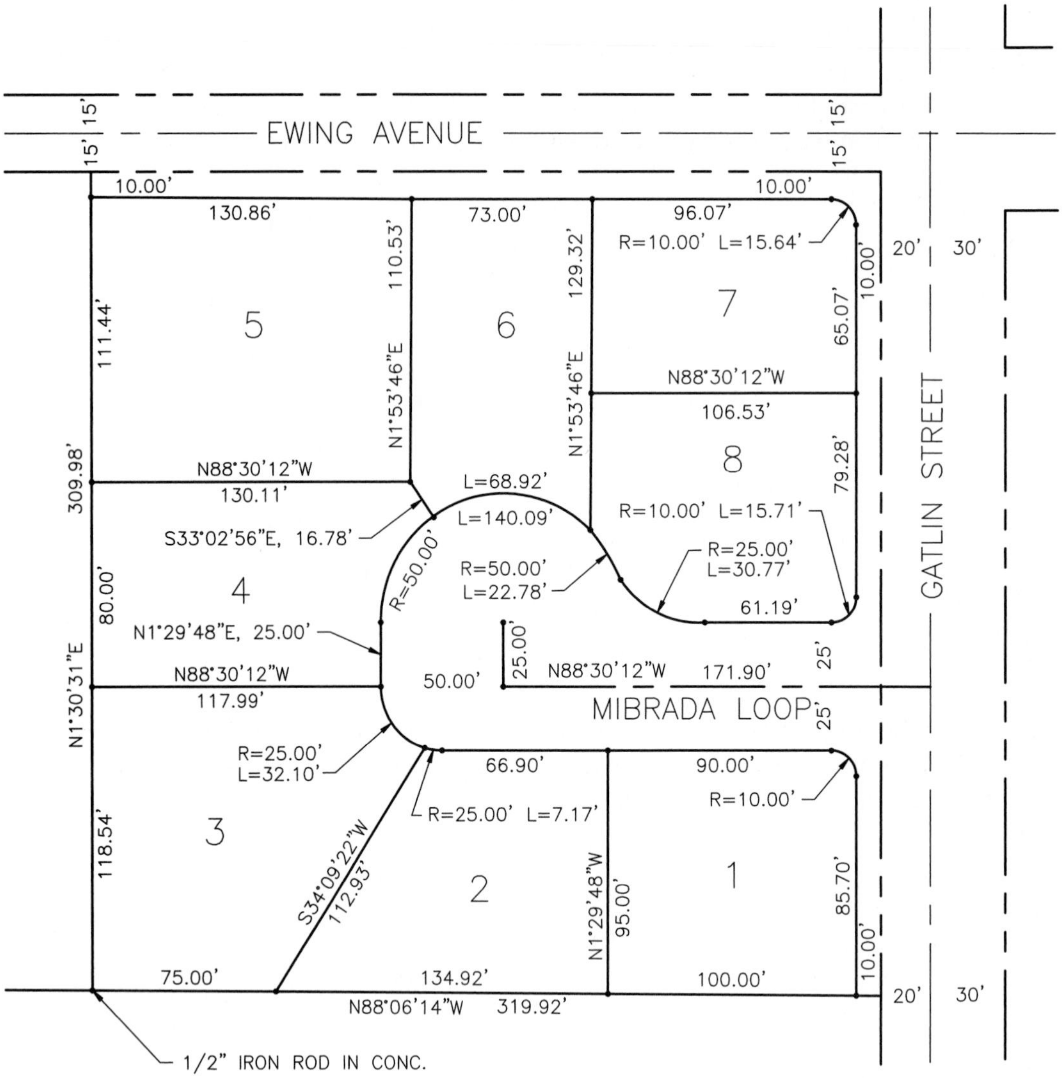

EWING AVENUE

15' 15'

10.00'

130.86'

111.44'

5

309.98'

N88°30'12"W
130.11'

S33°02'56"E, 16.78'

80.00'

4

N1°29'48"E, 25.00'

N88°30'12"W
117.99'

N1°30'31"E

R=25.00'
L=32.10'

118.54'

3

S34°09'22"W
112.93'

75.00'

N88°06'14"W 319.92'

1/2" IRON ROD IN CONC.

N1°53'46"E 110.53'

73.00'

6

N1°53'46"E 129.32'

L=68.92'
L=140.09'

R=50.00'

R=50.00'
L=22.78'

50.00'

25.00'

N88°30'12"W

66.90'

R=25.00' L=7.17'

2

N1°29'48"W 95.00'

134.92'

10.00'

96.07'
R=10.00' L=15.64'

7

65.07'

N88°30'12"W
106.53'

8

R=10.00' L=15.71'

R=25.00'
L=30.77'

61.19'

79.28'

10.00'

20' 30'

GATLIN STREET

171.90'

MIBRADA LOOP

25'

25'

90.00'
R=10.00'

1

85.70'

100.00'

10.00'

20' 30'

Learning Objectives

After completing this chapter, you will be able to do the following:

✓ Use the **PLINE** command to draw straight and curved polylines.
✓ Compare the results of turning the **FILL** mode on and off.
✓ Edit existing polylines with the **PEDIT** command.
✓ Describe the function of each **PEDIT** command option.
✓ Use the **EXPLODE** command to change polylines into individual line and arc segments.
✓ Create a polyline boundary.

The term *polyline* is composed of the word parts *poly-* and *line*. *Poly-* means "many." A ***polyline*** is a single object made up of one or more line and/or arc segments. Each line segment can vary in width. Polylines are drawn with the **PLINE** command and its various options. The **PLINE** command can be used to draw a variety of special shapes, including thick and tapered lines and polyline arcs. This chapter explains how to use the **PLINE** command to draw polylines and the **PEDIT** command to edit polylines.

polyline: A single object made up of one or more line and/or arc segments.

Introduction to Polylines

The **PLINE** command is used to draw polylines and any related objects made up of line segments. Polylines have many advantages over normal lines:

- They can be used to draw a single object comprised of arcs and straight lines of varying thicknesses.
- They can be drawn as thick or tapered lines.
- Polylines provide much more flexibility than lines.
- They can be used with any linetype.
- Polylines can be edited using specialized editing features.
- The area and perimeter of polylines can be determined easily.

Type
PLINE
PL

Dashboard
2D Draw
> Polyline

Toolbar
Draw
Polyline

Pull-Down Menu
Draw
> Polyline

Options
Arc
Halfwidth
Length
Undo
Width

Drawing Polylines

The function of the **PLINE** command is similar to the function of the **LINE** command. However, **PLINE** offers additional command options. Also, all segments of a polyline are treated as a single object. To draw a polyline, you can pick the **Polyline** button on the **2D Draw** control panel of the **Dashboard** or the **Draw** toolbar, pick **Draw** > **Polyline**, or type PL or PLINE.

A line width of 0.0000 produces a polyline of minimum width. If this is acceptable, select the endpoint of the line segment. If you draw additional line segments, the endpoint of the first line segment automatically becomes the starting point of the next line segment. When you are finished drawing line segments, press [Enter] or [Esc] to end the **PLINE** command.

Setting the Polyline Width

To change the width of a line segment, enter the **PLINE** command, select the first point, and use the **Width** option. When the **Width** option is selected, AutoCAD prompts you to specify the starting and ending widths of the line. The starting width value becomes the default setting for the ending width. Therefore, to draw a line segment with one width, press [Enter] at the second prompt. To create a tapered line segment, enter different values for the starting and ending widths. After the widths are specified, the rubberband line from the first point reflects the width settings. **Figure 14-1** shows a 4″ long polyline with starting and ending widths of .25″. Notice that the starting and ending points of the line are located at the center of the line segment's width.

Drawing a Tapered Polyline

By entering different starting and ending width values, you can draw a tapered polyline. In the example shown in **Figure 14-2**, the starting width is .25 unit, and the ending width is .5 unit. One special use of a tapered polyline is the creation of arrowheads. To draw an arrowhead, use the **Width** option of the **PLINE** command, specify 0 as the starting width, and then use any desired ending width.

Using the Halfwidth Option

The **Halfwidth** option of the **PLINE** command allows you to specify the width of the polyline from the center to one side. After picking the first point of the polyline, enter the **Halfwidth** option. Specify starting and ending values. Notice that the polyline in **Figure 14-3** is twice as wide as the polyline in **Figure 14-2**, even though the same values are entered.

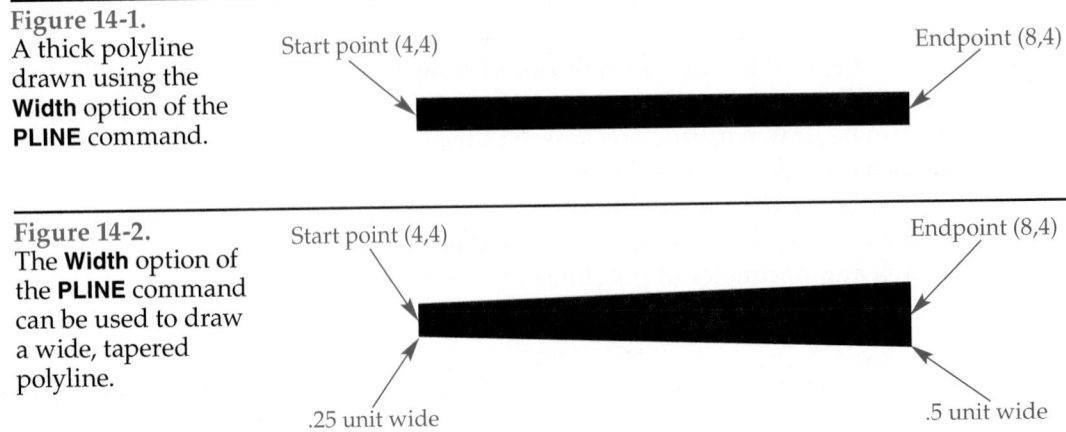

Figure 14-1.
A thick polyline drawn using the **Width** option of the **PLINE** command.

Start point (4,4)   Endpoint (8,4)

Figure 14-2.
The **Width** option of the **PLINE** command can be used to draw a wide, tapered polyline.

Start point (4,4)   Endpoint (8,4)

.25 unit wide   .5 unit wide

Specifying a New Center Point

When a polyline arc is drawn as a continuation of a polyline segment, the center point of the arc is calculated automatically. You may want to pick a new center point if the polyline arc does not continue from another object or if the center point AutoCAD calculated is not suitable. The **CEnter** suboption allows you to specify a new center point for the arc. When you pick the center point, the arc's radius is set as the distance from the center point to the starting point. You can then choose from three methods to complete the polyline arc:

- Pick the endpoint of the arc
- Use the **Angle** option to specify the included angle
- Use the **Length** option to specify the chord length of the arc

Using the Direction Suboption

The **Direction** suboption alters the bearing of the arc. By default, a polyline arc is created tangent to the last polyline, arc, or line drawn. The **Direction** suboption is used to change this and can also be entered when you are drawing an unconnected polyline arc. It functions much like the **Direction** option of the **ARC** command.

After selecting the **Direction** suboption of the **PLINE Arc** option, specify the tangent direction for the start point of the arc. You can enter a numeric angle value, or you can pick a point to define the angle relative to the start point.

Drawing a Polyline Arc by Radius

Polyline arcs can be drawn by giving the arc's radius. Enter the **Radius** suboption of the **PLINE Arc** option, specify the radius, and then specify the second endpoint for the arc.

Specifying a Three-Point Polyline Arc

A three-point polyline arc can be drawn using the **Second pt** suboption. After entering the **Second pt** suboption, AutoCAD prompts you to pick the second point and endpoint of the arc.

Using the Close Suboption

The **CLose** suboption saves drafting time by automatically adding the last segment to close a polygonal shape. Using this suboption of the **PLINE Arc** option closes the shape with a polyline arc segment, rather than a straight line segment. See Figure 14-6. CL is entered at the prompt line to distinguish this option from the **CEnter** suboption.

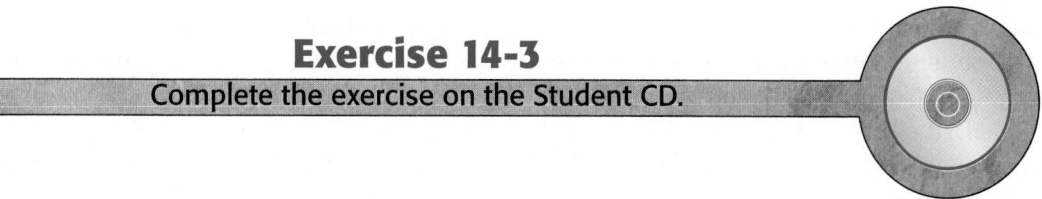

Exercise 14-3
Complete the exercise on the Student CD.

Figure 14-6.
Using the **CLose** suboption to close a polygonal shape.

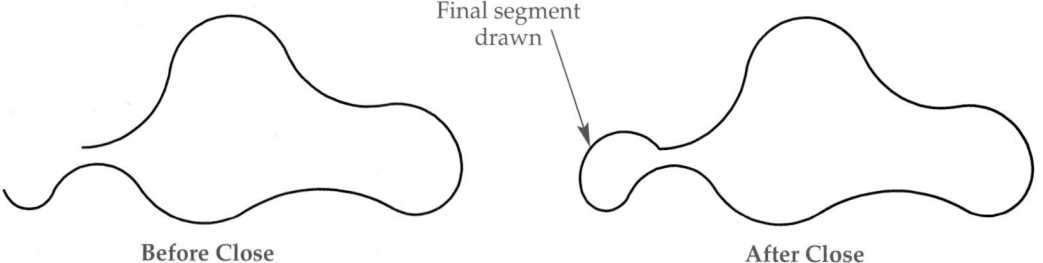

Final segment drawn

Before Close   After Close

Filling Polylines and Traces

In the description of the **PLINE** command earlier in this chapter, the results were shown as if the objects were solid, or filled in. You can display polylines as filled objects or as an outline only. See **Figure 14-7**. These functions are controlled by the **Apply solid fill** setting in the **Display performance** area of the **Display** tab in the **Options** dialog box. This setting can also be changed by typing FILL or FILLMODE.

PROFESSIONAL TIP

When a drawing contains many wide polylines, it is best to turn solid fills off. This saves time when redrawing, regenerating, or plotting a check copy of the drawing. Activate solid fills for the final plotting.

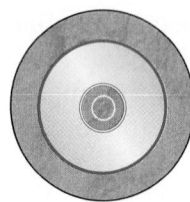

Exercise 14-4

Complete the exercise on the Student CD.

Figure 14-7.
Examples of the **FILL** mode on and off.

FILL Mode On

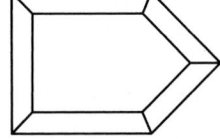

FILL Mode Off

Revising Polylines

Polylines are drawn as multiple segments. A single polyline can be drawn as a straight segment joined to an arc segment and completed with another straight segment. Even though you have drawn separate segments, AutoCAD puts them all together. The result is one polyline treated as a single object. When editing a polyline, you must either edit it as one object or divide it into its individual segments. These changes are made with the **PEDIT** and **EXPLODE** commands. The **EXPLODE** command is described later in this chapter.

The **PEDIT** command is accessed by picking the **Edit Polyline** button on the **Modify II** toolbar, selecting **Modify > Object > Polyline**, or typing PE or PEDIT. You can also select a polyline, right-click in the drawing area, and choose **Polyline Edit** from the shortcut menu.

When selecting a wide polyline, you must pick the edge of a polyline segment rather than in the center. If you want to edit more than one polyline, type M before selecting to access the **Multiple** option. If the object you select is a line or arc object, AutoCAD issues a prompt that gives you the option to turn it into a polyline. The command then continues normally. Its options are explained later in this chapter.

You can set AutoCAD to turn lines and arcs into polylines automatically without displaying the prompt. The value of the **PEDITACCEPT** system variable controls this feature. When it is set to 0, AutoCAD issues a prompt when a line or an arc is selected.

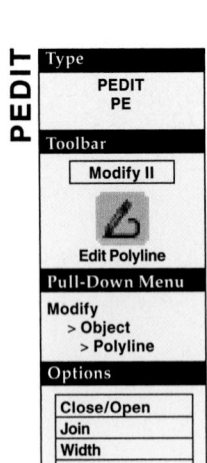

PEDIT

Type
PEDIT
PE

Toolbar
Modify II

Edit Polyline

Pull-Down Menu
Modify
> Object
> Polyline

Options
Close/Open
Join
Width
Edit vertex
Fit
Spline
Decurve
Ltype Gen
Undo

When the system variable is set to 1, AutoCAD automatically turns the selected lines and arcs into polylines. The command then continues normally.

Circles drawn with the **CIRCLE** command cannot be changed to polylines for editing purposes. Polyline circles can be created by using the **Arc** option of the **PLINE** command and drawing two 180° arcs or by using the **DONUT** command.

PROFESSIONAL TIP

A group of connected lines and arcs can be turned into a continuous polyline using the **Join** option of the **PEDIT** command. This option is described later in this chapter.

Revising a Polyline As One Unit

A polyline can be edited as a single object, or it can be divided into individual segments. The segments can then be revised individually. This section describes the options for changing the entire polyline. There is no default option for the **PEDIT** command; you must select one of the options.

Opening and Closing a Polyline

You may decide to close an open polyline or open a closed polyline. These functions are performed with the **Open** and **Close** options of the **PEDIT** command. Open and closed polylines are shown in **Figure 14-8**.

The **Open** option is only available if the polyline was closed using the **Close** option of the **PLINE** command. It is not displayed if the polyline was closed by drawing the final segment manually. Instead, the **Close** option is displayed. If you select an open polyline, the **Close** option is displayed instead of the **Open** option. Enter this option to close the polyline.

Joining Polylines to Other Objects

Connected polylines, lines, and arcs can be joined to create a single polyline. This is done with the **Join** option of the **PEDIT** command. The **Join** option works only if the polyline and other existing objects meet *exactly*. They cannot cross, nor can there be any spaces or breaks between the objects. See **Figure 14-9**.

Select each object to be joined or group the objects with one of the selection set options. The original polyline can be included in the selection set, but it does not need to be. See **Figure 14-10**. If you select lines and arcs to join, AutoCAD automatically converts these objects to polylines, regardless of the **PEDITACCEPT** setting.

PROFESSIONAL TIP

Once items have been joined into a continuous polyline, the polyline can be closed using the **Close** option of the **PEDIT** command.

Figure 14-8.
Open and closed polylines.

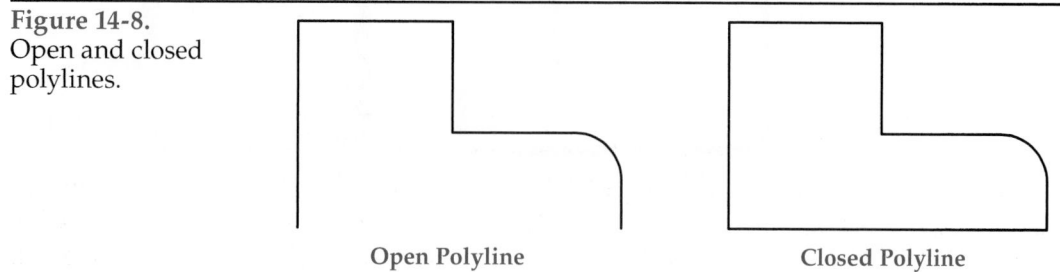

Open Polyline   Closed Polyline

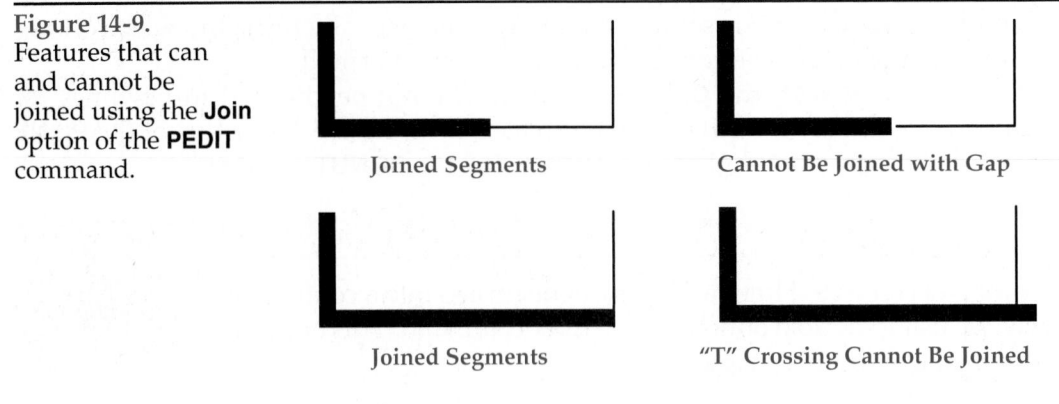

Figure 14-9.
Features that can and cannot be joined using the **Join** option of the **PEDIT** command.

Joined Segments

Cannot Be Joined with Gap

Joined Segments

"T" Crossing Cannot Be Joined

Figure 14-10.
Joining a polyline to other connected lines and arcs.

Window other lines

Select polyline

Changing the Width of a Polyline

The **Width** option of the **PEDIT** command allows you to assign a new width to a polyline. The width of the original polyline can be constant, or it can vary. *All* segments will be changed, however, to the constant width you specify. An unedited polyline and the same polyline after using the **Width** option of the **PEDIT** command are shown in Figure 14-11. The width of donuts can be changed using this procedure as well.

Exercise 14-5
Complete the exercise on the Student CD.

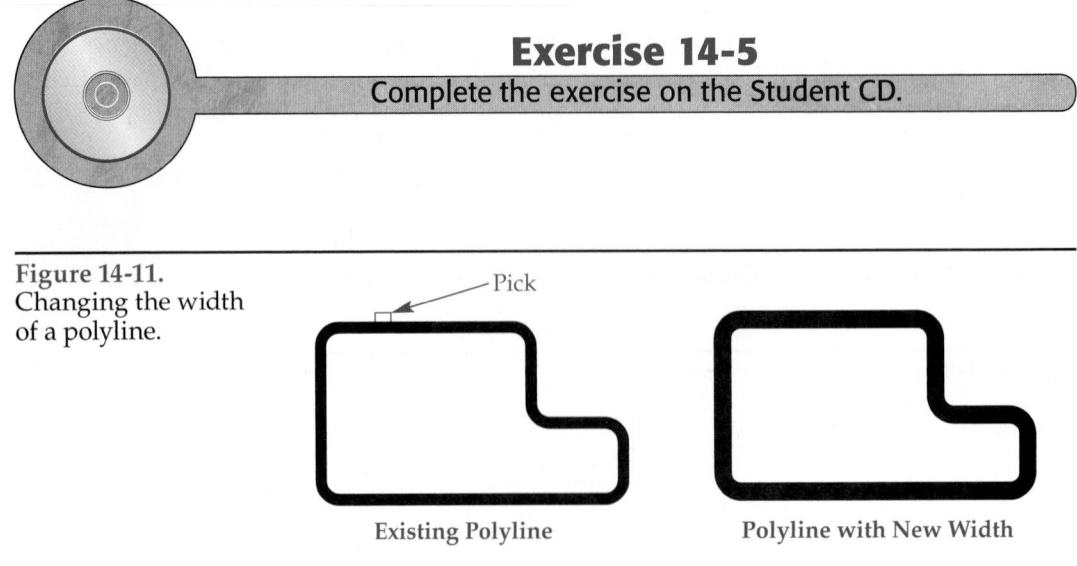

Figure 14-11.
Changing the width of a polyline.

Pick

Existing Polyline

Polyline with New Width

Editing a Polyline Vertex or Point of Tangency

The **Edit vertex** option of the **PEDIT** command is used to edit polyline vertices and points of tangency. This option is not available if you have selected multiple polylines for editing. A *polyline vertex* is the point at which straight polyline segments meet, and a *point of tangency* is the point at which a polyline arc meets another polyline arc or a straight polyline segment. When you enter the **Edit vertex** option, an "X" marker appears on the screen at the first polyline vertex or point of tangency. The **Edit vertex** option contains the following suboptions:

- **Next.** Moves the "X" marker to the next vertex or point of tangency on the polyline.
- **Previous.** Moves the "X" marker to the previous vertex or point of tangency on the polyline.
- **Break.** Breaks the polyline between two vertices or points of tangency.
- **Insert.** Adds a new polyline vertex at a selected point.
- **Move.** Moves a polyline vertex to a new location.
- **Regen.** Generates the revised version of the polyline.
- **Straighten.** Straightens a polyline arc segment or multiple segments between two points.
- **Tangent.** Specifies a tangent direction for curve-fitting with the **Fit** option of the **PEDIT** command.
- **Width.** Changes the width of a polyline segment.
- **eXit.** Returns to the **PEDIT** command prompt.

> **polyline vertex:**
> The point at which two straight polyline segments meet.
>
> **point of tangency:**
> The point at which a polyline arc meets another polyline arc or a straight polyline segment.

Only the current point identified by the "X" marker is affected by editing functions. In **Figure 14-12,** the marker is moved clockwise through the points using the **Next** option and counterclockwise using the **Previous** option. If you edit the vertices of a polyline and nothing appears to happen, use the **Regen** option to regenerate the polyline.

Making breaks in a polyline

You can break a polyline into two separate polylines with the **Break** option of the **PEDIT Edit vertex** option. Once the **Edit vertex** option is entered, use the **Next** or **Previous** option to move the "X" marker to the first vertex where the polyline is to be broken. Enter the **Break** option. A marker is placed at the first break point. After moving to the second vertex of the break, enter the **Go** option.

The **Go** option instructs AutoCAD to remove the portion of the polyline between the two points. You can also break the polyline without removing a segment by specifying **Go** without moving to a second vertex. The results of the following command sequence are illustrated in **Figure 14-13.** The polyline was drawn clockwise.

Figure 14-12.
Using the **Next** and **Previous** vertex editing options to specify polyline vertices. Note the different positions of the "X" marker.

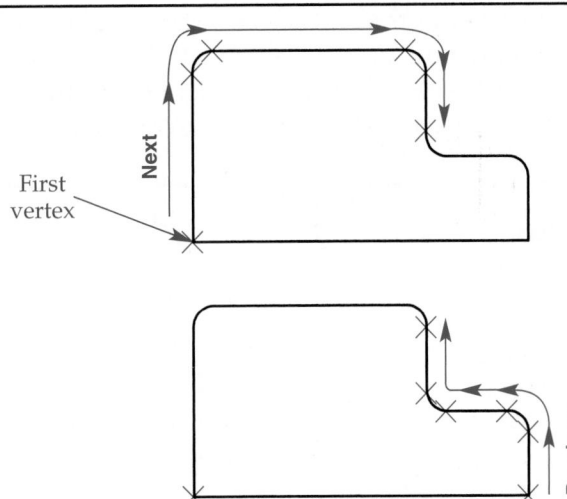

First vertex

Next

Previous

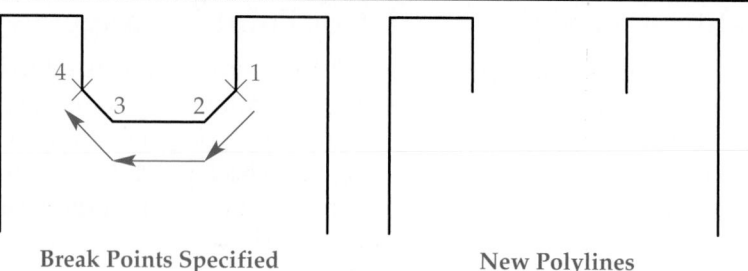

Figure 14-13.
Using the **Break** vertex editing option to break a polyline and remove a portion.

Break Points Specified   New Polylines

Enter a vertex editing option
[Next/Previous/Break/Insert/Move/Regen/Straighten/Tangent/Width/eXit] <N>: *(use* **Next** *to move to Point 1)*
Enter a vertex editing option
[Next/Previous/Break/Insert/Move/Regen/Straighten/Tangent/Width/eXit] <N>: **B.↵** *(specifies Point 1)*
Enter an option [Next/Previous/Go/eXit] <N>: **P.↵** *(specifies Point 2)*
Enter an option [Next/Previous/Go/eXit] <P>: ↵ *(specifies Point 3)*
Enter an option [Next/Previous/Go/eXit] <P>: ↵ *(specifies Point 4)*
Enter an option [Next/Previous/Go/eXit] <P>: **G.↵** *(breaks the polyline between Points 1 and 4)*
Enter a vertex editing option
[Next/Previous/Break/Insert/Move/Regen/Straighten/Tangent/Width/eXit] <P>:

Inserting a new vertex in a polyline

A new vertex can be added to a polyline using the **Insert** vertex editing option. The new vertex can be inserted on an existing polyline segment, but does not need to be. First, use the **Next** or **Previous** option to locate the vertex next to where you want the new vertex. Select the **Insert** option and pick the new vertex location. See **Figure 14-14**.

Moving a polyline vertex

The **Move** vertex editing option enables you to move a polyline vertex to a new location. The "X" marker must first be placed on the vertex you want to move. Enter the **Move** option and specify the new vertex location. See **Figure 14-15**.

Straightening polyline segments or arcs

The **Straighten** vertex editing option allows you to straighten polyline segments or arcs between two points. Position the "X" marker at one end of the polyline segment to be straightened and enter the **Straighten** option. The **Straighten** option has four suboptions: **Next**, **Previous**, **Go**, and **Exit**. Use the **Next** and **Previous** options to position the "X" marker at the end of the segment to be straightened. Then enter the **Go** option to straighten the polyline segment. If the "X" marker is not moved before G is entered, AutoCAD straightens the segment from the marked point to the next vertex. This provides a quick way to straighten an arc. See **Figure 14-16**.

Figure 14-14.
Using the **Insert** vertex editing option to add a new vertex to a polyline.

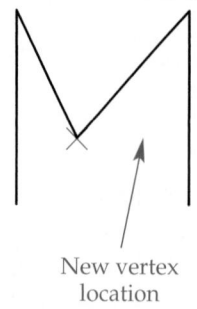

New vertex location

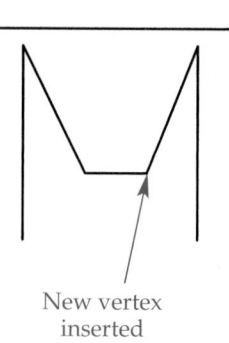

New vertex inserted

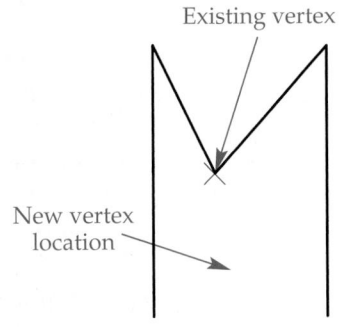
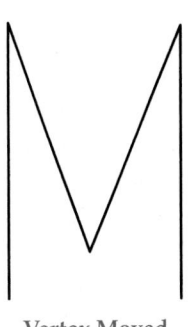

Figure 14-15.
Using the **Move** vertex editing option to move a polyline vertex to a new location.

Existing vertex

New vertex location

Vertex Moved

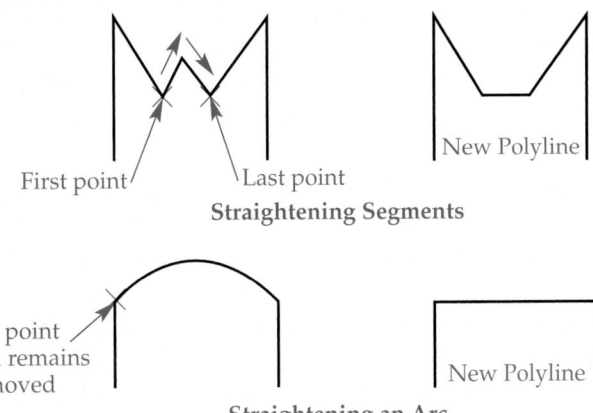

Figure 14-16.
The **Straighten** vertex editing option is used to straighten polyline segments and arcs.

First point

Last point

New Polyline

Straightening Segments

First point marked remains unmoved

New Polyline

Straightening an Arc

Changing polyline segment widths

The **Width** vertex editing option is used to change the starting and ending widths of an individual polyline segment. To change a segment width, move the "X" marker to the beginning vertex of the segment to be altered. Enter the **Width** option and specify the new width.

The default starting width value is the current width of the segment to be changed. The default ending width value is the same as the revised starting width. If nothing appears to happen to the segment when you specify the ending width and press [Enter], enter the **Regen** option to have AutoCAD draw the revised polyline. See Figure 14-17.

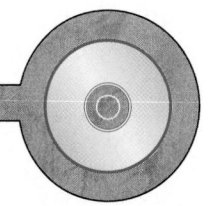

Exercise 14-6
Complete the exercise on the Student CD.

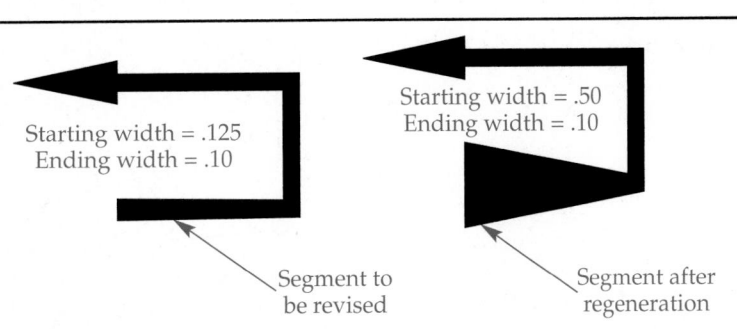

Figure 14-17.
Changing the width of a polyline segment with the **Width** vertex editing option. Use the **Regen** option to display the change.

Starting width = .125
Ending width = .10

Starting width = .50
Ending width = .10

Segment to be revised

Segment after regeneration

Fitting a Curve to a Polyline

curve fitting:
Converting a
polyline into a series
of smooth curves.

fit curve: A curve
that passes through
all of its control
points.

In some situations, you may need to convert a polyline into a series of smooth curves. One example of this is a graph. A graph may show a series of plotted points as a smooth curve rather than straight segments. This process is called *curve fitting* and is accomplished using the **Fit** option and the **Tangent** vertex editing option of the **PEDIT** command. The **Fit** option creates a *fit curve* by constructing pairs of arcs that pass through control points. You can specify the control points, or you can use the vertices of the polyline.

Prior to curve fitting, each vertex can be given a tangent direction. AutoCAD then fits the curve based on the tangent directions you set. You do not, however, need to enter tangent directions. Specifying tangent directions is a way to edit vertices when the **Fit** option of the **PEDIT** command does not produce the best results.

The **Tangent** vertex editing option is used to edit tangent directions. After entering the **PEDIT** command and the **Edit vertex** option, move the "X" marker to the first vertex to be changed. Enter the **Tangent** option and enter a tangent direction in degrees or pick a point in the expected direction. An arrow placed at the vertex then indicates the direction you chose.

Continue by moving the marker to each vertex you want to change, entering the **Tangent** option for each vertex, and selecting a tangent direction. When the tangent directions have been specified for all vertices to be changed, enter the **Fit** option of the **PEDIT** command to create the curve.

You can also enter the **PEDIT** command, select a polyline, and then enter the **Fit** option without adjusting tangencies, if desired. The polyline shown in **Figure 14-18** was made into a smooth curve using the **Fit** option. If the resulting curve does not look like what you had anticipated, enter the **Edit vertex** option. Make changes using the various vertex editing options, as necessary.

Using the Spline Option

When you edit a polyline with the **Fit** option of the **PEDIT** command, the resulting curve passes through each of the polyline's vertices. The **Spline** option of the **PEDIT** command also smoothes the corners of a straight-segment polyline. This option, however, produces different results. It creates a *spline curve* that passes through the first and last control points or vertices only. The curve *pulls* toward the other vertices, but does not necessarily pass through them. The results of using the **Fit** and **Spline** options on a polyline are illustrated in **Figure 14-19**.

spline curve: A
curve that passes
through the first and
last control points
and is influenced
by the other control
points.

cubic curve: A
very smooth curve
created by the
PEDIT Spline option
when **SPLINETYPE**
is set at 6.

quadratic curve: A
curve created by the
PEDIT Spline option
when **SPLINETYPE**
is set at 5.

The **Spline** option creates a curve that approximates a true B-spline. You can choose between two types of calculations to create the curve—cubic and quadratic. A *cubic curve* is extremely smooth. A *quadratic curve* is not as smooth as a cubic curve, but it is smoother than a curve produced with the **Fit** option. Like a cubic curve, a

Figure 14-18.
Using the **Fit** option of the **PEDIT** command to turn a polyline into a smooth curve.

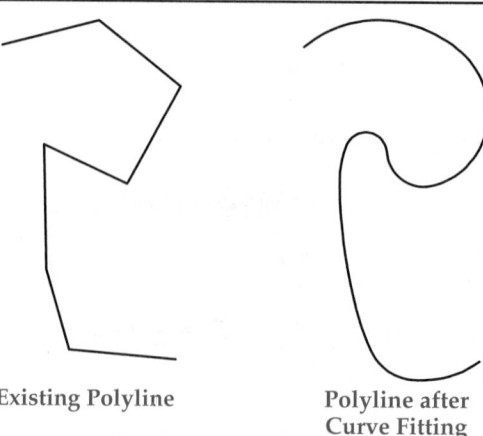

Existing Polyline   Polyline after
                         Curve Fitting

Figure 14-19.
A comparison of polylines edited with the **Fit** and **Spline** options of the **PEDIT** command.

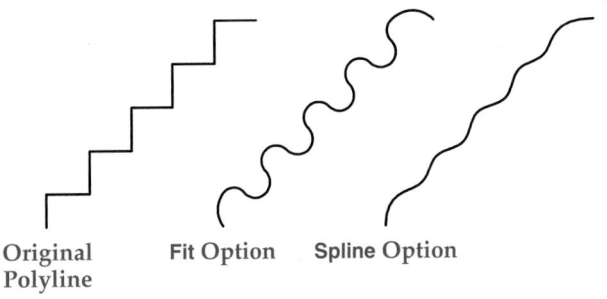

Original Polyline   Fit Option   Spline Option

quadratic curve passes through the first and last control points. The remainder of the curve is tangent to the polyline segments between the intermediate control points, as shown in **Figure 14-20.**

The **SPLINETYPE** system variable determines whether AutoCAD draws cubic or quadratic curves. The default setting is 6. At this setting, a cubic curve is drawn when using the **Spline** option of the **PEDIT** command. If the **SPLINETYPE** system variable is set to 5, a quadratic curve is generated. The only valid values for **SPLINETYPE** are 5 and 6.

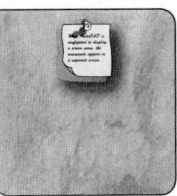

NOTE

Both the **Fit** option and the **Spline** option of the **PEDIT** command create approximations of a B-spline curve. To create a true B-spline curve, use AutoCAD's **SPLINE** command instead. The **SPLINE** command is described in Chapter 15.

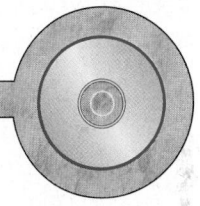

Exercise 14-7
Complete the exercise on the Student CD.

The **SPLINESEGS** system variable controls the number of line segments used to construct spline curves. It can be set by typing SPLINESEGS or by entering a value in the **Segments in a polyline curve** text box in the **Display resolution** area of the **Display** tab of the **Options** dialog box. The **SPLINESEGS** default value is 8, which creates a

Figure 14-20.
A comparison of curves drawn with the **Fit** and **Spline** options of the **PEDIT** command. The **SPLINETYPE** system variable controls whether a quadratic or cubic curve is drawn with the **Spline** option.

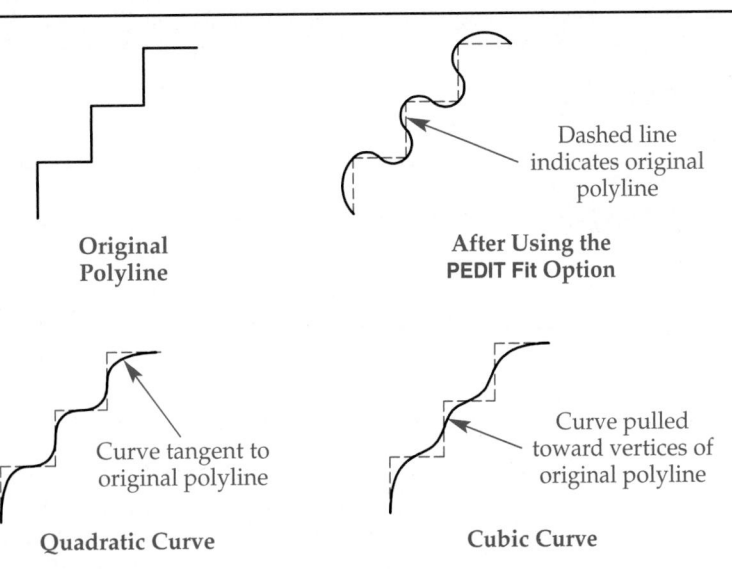

Original Polyline

Dashed line indicates original polyline

After Using the PEDIT Fit Option

Curve tangent to original polyline

Quadratic Curve

Curve pulled toward vertices of original polyline

Cubic Curve

Figure 14-21.
A comparison of curves drawn with different settings for the **SPLINESEGS** system variable.

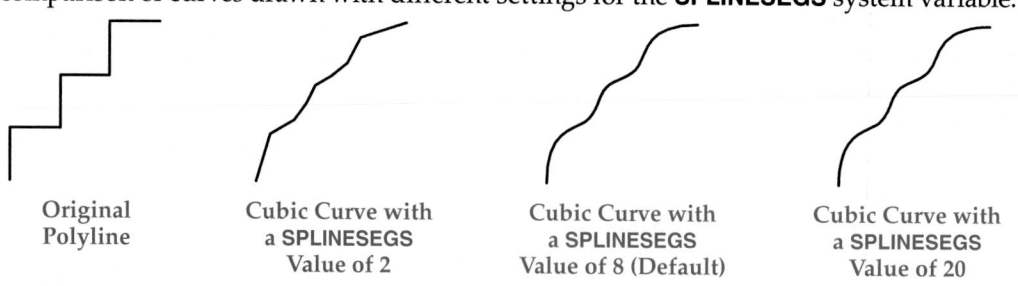

Original
Polyline

Cubic Curve with
a **SPLINESEGS**
Value of 2

Cubic Curve with
a **SPLINESEGS**
Value of 8 (Default)

Cubic Curve with
a **SPLINESEGS**
Value of 20

fairly smooth spline curve with moderate regeneration time. If you decrease the value, the resulting spline curve is less smooth. The resulting spline curve is smoother if you increase the value, but the regeneration time and drawing file size increase. The relationship between **SPLINESEGS** values and spline curves is shown in Figure 14-21.

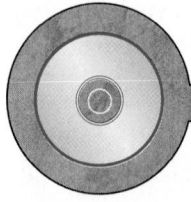

Exercise 14-8
Complete the exercise on the Student CD.

Straightening All Segments of a Polyline

The **Decurve** option of the **PEDIT** command returns a polyline edited with the **Fit** or **Spline** options to its original form. The information entered for tangent directions is kept, however, for future reference. You can also use the **Decurve** option to straighten the curved segments of a polyline. See Figure 14-22.

PROFESSIONAL TIP

If you make a mistake while editing a polyline, remember that the **PEDIT** command includes an **Undo** option. Using the **Undo** option more than once allows you to step backward through each operation.

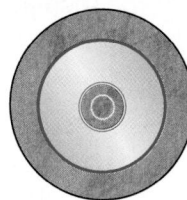

Exercise 14-9
Complete the exercise on the Student CD.

Figure 14-22.
The **Decurve** option of the **PEDIT** command is used to straighten the curved segments of a polyline.

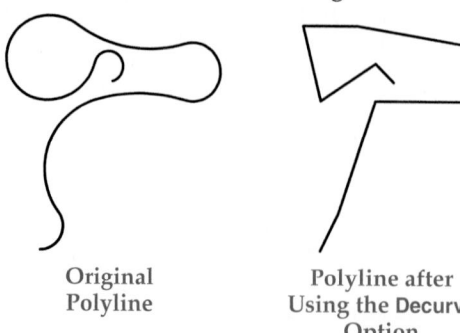

Original
Polyline

Polyline after
Using the **Decurve**
Option

Changing the Appearance of Polyline Linetypes

The **Ltype gen** (linetype generation) option of the **PEDIT** command determines how linetypes other than Continuous appear in relation to the vertices of a polyline. For example, when a Center linetype is used and the **Ltype gen** option is disabled, the polyline has a long dash at each vertex. When the **Ltype gen** option is activated, the polyline is generated with a constant pattern in relation to the polyline as a whole. The difference between having the **Ltype gen** option off and on is illustrated in Figure 14-23.

You can also change the **Ltype gen** option setting for new polylines with the **PLINEGEN** system variable. This variable must be set before the polyline is drawn. Changing the setting does not affect existing polylines. The settings for the **PLINEGEN** system variable are 0 (off) and 1 (on).

Figure 14-23.
A comparison of polylines and splined polylines with the **Ltype gen** option of the **PEDIT** command on and off.

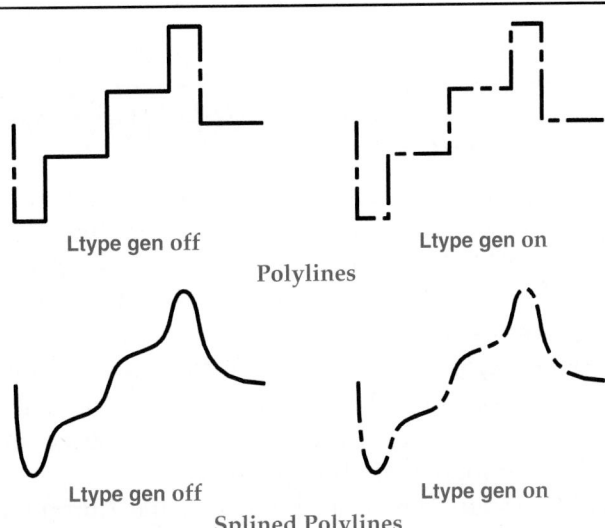

Ltype gen off   Ltype gen on

Polylines

Ltype gen off   Ltype gen on

Splined Polylines

Exploding a Polyline

The **EXPLODE** command allows you to change a polyline into a series of individual lines and arcs. You can then edit each segment individually. The resulting segments are not, however, polylines. When a wide polyline is exploded, the width is lost and the resulting line or arc is redrawn along the centerline of the original polyline. See Figure 14-24.

Figure 14-24.
Exploding a wide polyline causes it to lose width information.

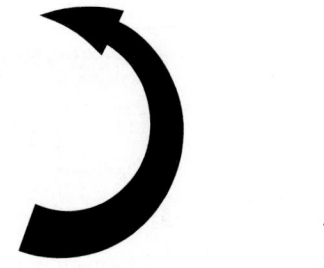

Original Polyline   Exploded Polyline

EXPLODE

Type
EXPLODE
X
Dashboard
2D Draw
> Explode

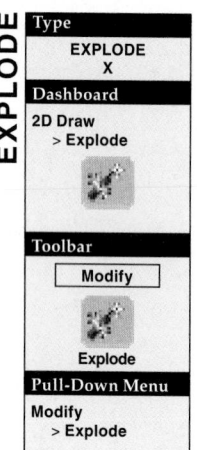

Toolbar
Modify

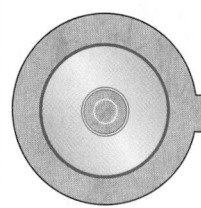

Explode
Pull-Down Menu
Modify
> Explode

To explode an object, pick the **Explode** button on the **2D Draw** control panel of the **Dashboard** or the **Modify** toolbar, select **Modify > Explode**, or type X or EXPLODE. AutoCAD asks you to select the objects to be exploded.

The **EXPLODE** command removes all width characteristics and tangency information. If you explode a wide polyline, AutoCAD reminds you of this fact. Using the **UNDO** command restores the polyline.

Exercise 14-10
Complete the exercise on the Student CD.

Creating a Polyline Boundary

BOUNDARY

Type
BOUNDARY
BO
Pull-Down Menu
Draw
> Boundary...

When you draw an object with the **LINE** command, each line segment is a single object. You can create a polyline boundary from line segments that form a closed area using the **BOUNDARY** command. To do so, pick **Draw > Boundary...** from the pull-down menu or type BO or BOUNDARY. This displays the **Boundary Creation** dialog box. See **Figure 14-25**.

The **Object type:** drop-down list contains two options—**Polyline** and **Region**. The **Polyline** option is the default and creates a polyline around the area. If you select **Region**, AutoCAD creates a *region* that can be used for area calculations, shading, extruding a solid model, or other purposes.

region: A closed 2D area that can have physical properties such as centroids and products of inertia.

In the **Boundary set** drop-down list, the **Current viewport** setting is active. A *boundary set* is the portion or area of the drawing that AutoCAD evaluates when defining a boundary. The **Current viewport** option defines the boundary set from everything visible in the current viewport, even if it is not in the current display. The **New** button, located to the right of the drop-down list, allows you to define a boundary set. When you pick this button, the **Boundary Creation** dialog box closes and the Select objects: prompt appears. You can then select the objects you want to use to create a boundary set. After you are done, press [Enter]. The **Boundary Creation** dialog box returns with **Existing set** active in the **Boundary set** drop-down list. This means the boundary set is defined from the objects you selected.

boundary set: The part of the drawing AutoCAD evaluates to define a boundary.

The **Island detection** setting specifies whether objects within the boundary are used as boundary objects. Closed areas inside a boundary are called *islands*. See **Figure 14-26**. When **Island detection** is checked, islands within a boundary will be detected and turned into separate boundaries.

island: A closed area inside a boundary.

Figure 14-25.
The **Boundary Creation** dialog box.

Pick to create a polyline or region boundary

Check to include automatic island detection

Select the boundary set

Select the type of boundary object

Pick to define a new boundary set

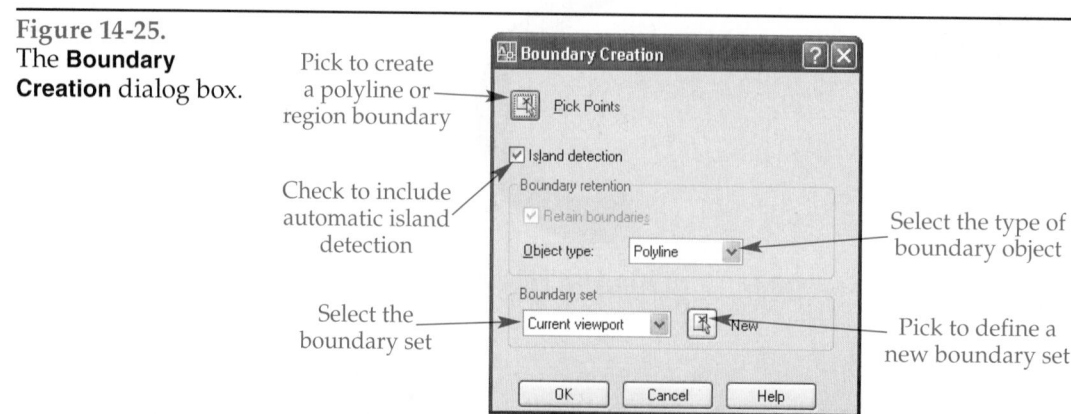

Figure 14-26.
When you define a boundary set, you can include or exclude islands.

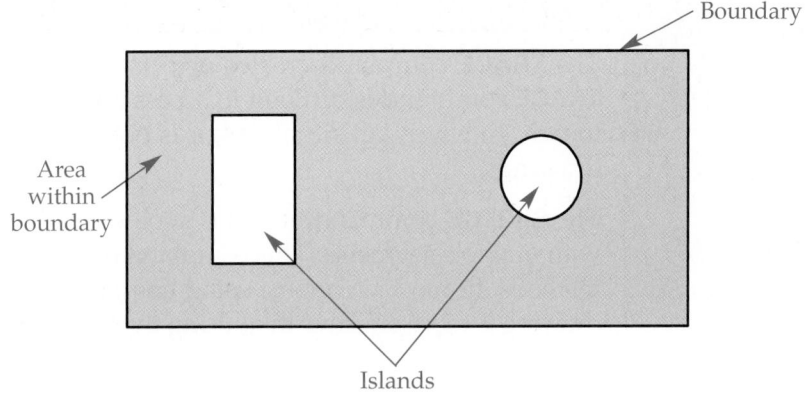

The only other active feature in the **Boundary Creation** dialog box is the **Pick Points** button, which is located in the upper-left corner. When you pick this button, the **Boundary Creation** dialog box closes and the Pick internal point: prompt appears. If the point you pick is inside a closed polygon, the boundary is highlighted, as shown in **Figure 14-27.** The **Boundary Definition Error** alert box appears if the point you pick is not within a closed polygon. Pick **OK** and try again.

Unlike an object created with the **Join** option of the **PEDIT** command, a polyline boundary created with the **BOUNDARY** command does not replace the original objects from which it was created. The polyline traces over the defining objects with a polyline. The separate objects still exist underneath the newly created boundary. To avoid duplicate geometry, move the boundary to another location on the screen, erase the original defining objects, and then move the boundary back to its original position.

PROFESSIONAL TIP

Area calculations can be simplified by using the **BOUNDARY** command or joining objects with the **Join** option of the **PEDIT** command before issuing the **AREA** command. Use the **Object** option of the **AREA** command to perform the area calculation. The **AREA** command is covered in Chapter 13. If you want to retain the original separate objects, explode the polyline after the area calculation if you used the **Join** option of the **PEDIT** command. Erase the polyline boundary after the calculation if you used the **BOUNDARY** command.

Figure 14-27.
When you select a point inside a closed polygon, the boundary is highlighted.

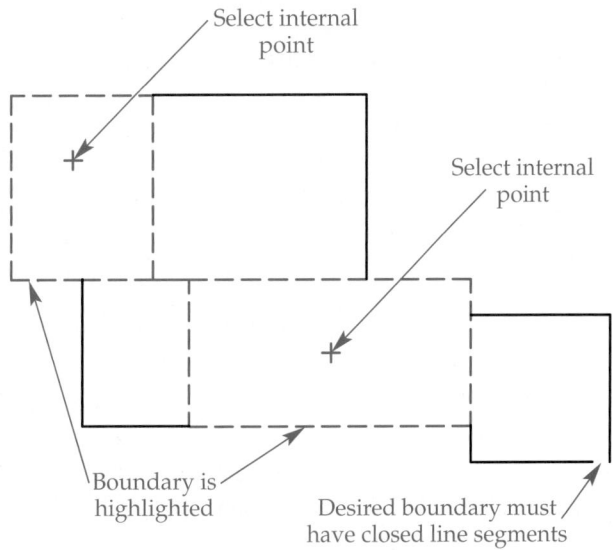

Chapter Test

Answer the following questions. Write your answers on a separate sheet of paper or complete the electronic chapter test on the Student CD.

1. How do you draw a filled arrow using the **PLINE** command?
2. Which **PLINE** command option allows you to specify the width from the center to one side?
3. What is an advantage of leaving solid fills turned off?
4. Which system variable controls the automatic conversion of lines and arcs to polylines when they are selected within the **PEDIT** command?
5. Which two **PEDIT** command options allow you to open a closed polyline and close an open polyline?
6. Name the command required to turn three connected lines into a single polyline.
7. When you enter the **Edit vertex** option of the **PEDIT** command, where does AutoCAD place the "X" marker?
8. How do you move the "X" marker to edit a different polyline vertex?

*For Questions 9 through 15, name the **Edit vertex** option of the **PEDIT** command that relates to the definition given.*

9. Moves the "X" marker to the next position.
10. Moves a polyline vertex to a new location.
11. Breaks a polyline at a point or between two points.
12. Generates the revised version of a polyline.
13. Specifies a tangent direction.
14. Adds a new polyline vertex.
15. Returns to the **PEDIT** command prompt.

16. Which **PEDIT** command option and suboption allow you to change the starting and ending widths of a polyline?
17. Why might it appear that nothing happens when you change the starting and ending widths of a polyline?
18. Name the **PEDIT** command option and the **Edit vertex** suboption used for curve fitting.
19. Can you use the **Fit** option of the **PEDIT** command without using the **Tangent** vertex editing suboption first? Explain.
20. Explain the difference between a fit curve and a spline curve.
21. Compare a quadratic curve, cubic curve, and fit curve.
22. Describe the appearance of a quadratic curve.
23. Which **SPLINETYPE** setting allows you to draw a cubic curve?

24. Which **SPLINETYPE** system variable setting allows you to draw a quadratic curve?
25. Name the system variable that can be set to adjust the smoothness of a spline curve.
26. Name the pull-down menu selections used to access the polyline editing options.
27. Explain how you can adjust the way polyline linetypes are generated using the **PEDIT** command.
28. Name the system variable that allows you to alter the way polyline linetypes are generated.
29. Which command removes all width characteristics and tangency information from a polyline?
30. Name the command used to create a polyline boundary.

Drawing Problems

1. Use the **PLINE** command to draw the following object with a .032 line width. Do not draw dimensions. Save the drawing as P14-1.

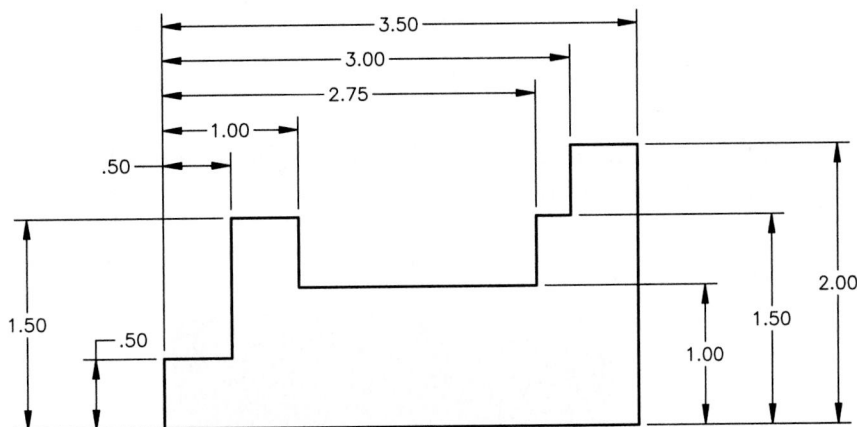
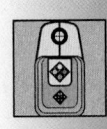

2. Use the **PLINE** command to draw the following object with a .032 line width. Do not draw dimensions. Save the drawing as P14-2.

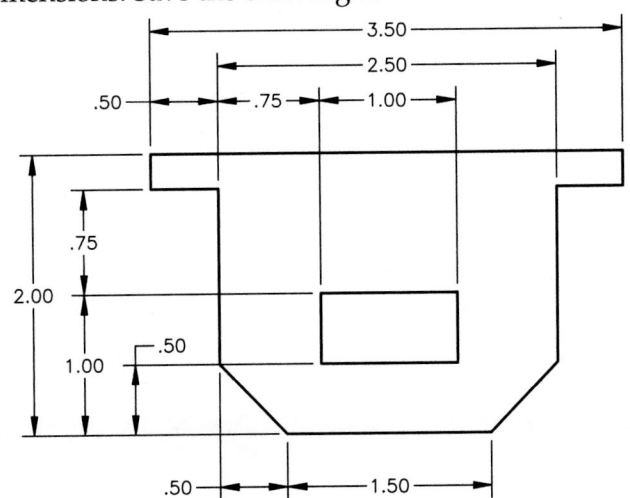

3. Use the **PLINE** command to draw the following object with a .032 line width. Do not draw dimensions.
   A. Deactivate solid fills and use the **REGEN** command, and reactivate solid fills and reissue the **REGEN** command.
   B. Observe the difference with solid fills enabled.
   C. Save the drawing as P14-3.

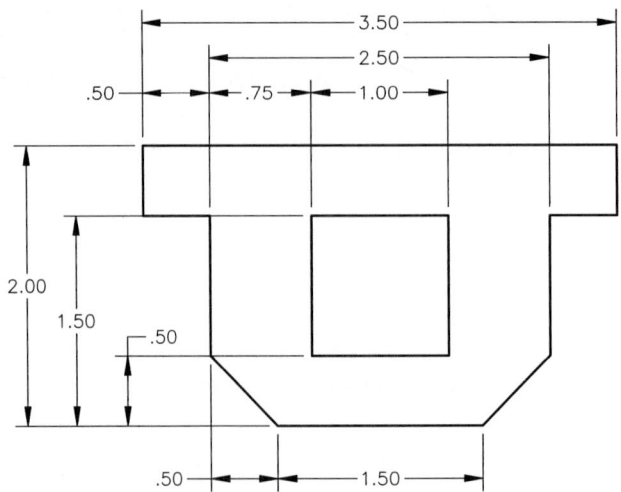

4. Use the **PLINE** command to draw the filled rectangle shown below. Do not draw dimensions. Save the drawing as P14-4.

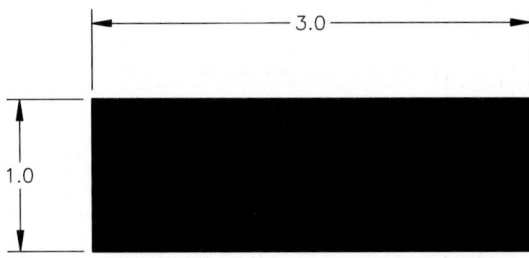

5. Draw the objects shown below. Do not draw dimensions. Save the drawing as P14-5.

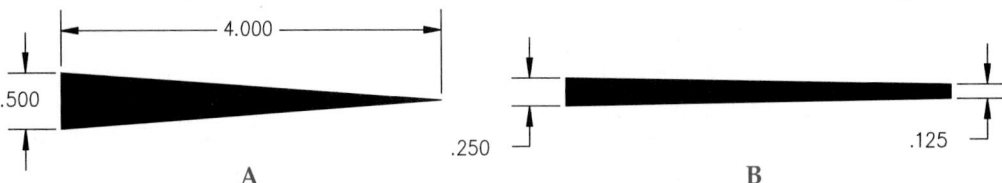

6. Draw the object shown below. Do not draw dimensions. Set decimal units; .25 grid spacing; .0625 snap spacing; and limits of 11,8.5. Save the drawing as P14-6.

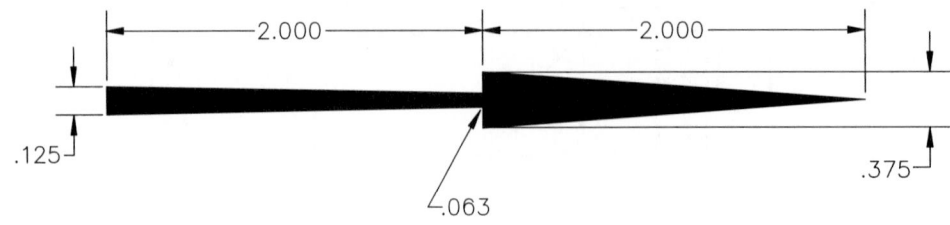

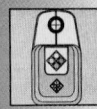

7. Open P9-10 and add the arrowheads. Draw one arrowhead using the **PLINE** command, and then use the necessary editing commands to place the rest. Refer to the original problem. Save the drawing as P14-7.

8. Draw the flow chart shown below. Use polylines to draw the connecting lines, arrows, and diamonds. Use AutoCAD's grid and snap to locate points. Save the drawing as P14-8.

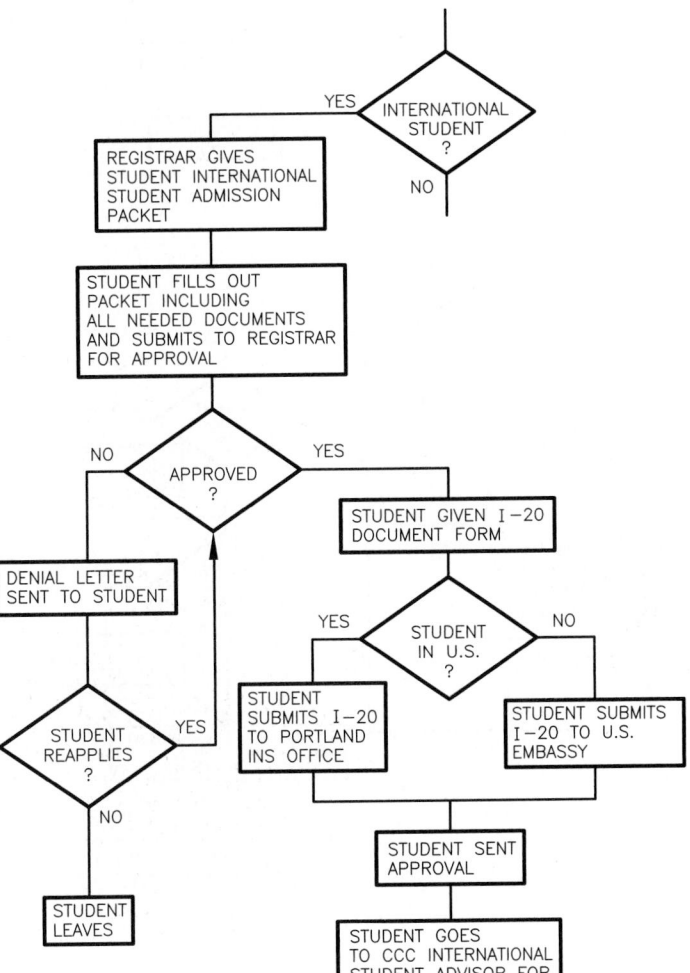

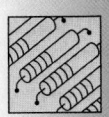
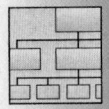

9. Draw the flow chart shown below. Use polylines to draw the connecting lines, arrows, and diamonds. Use AutoCAD's grid and snap to locate points. Save the drawing as P14-9.

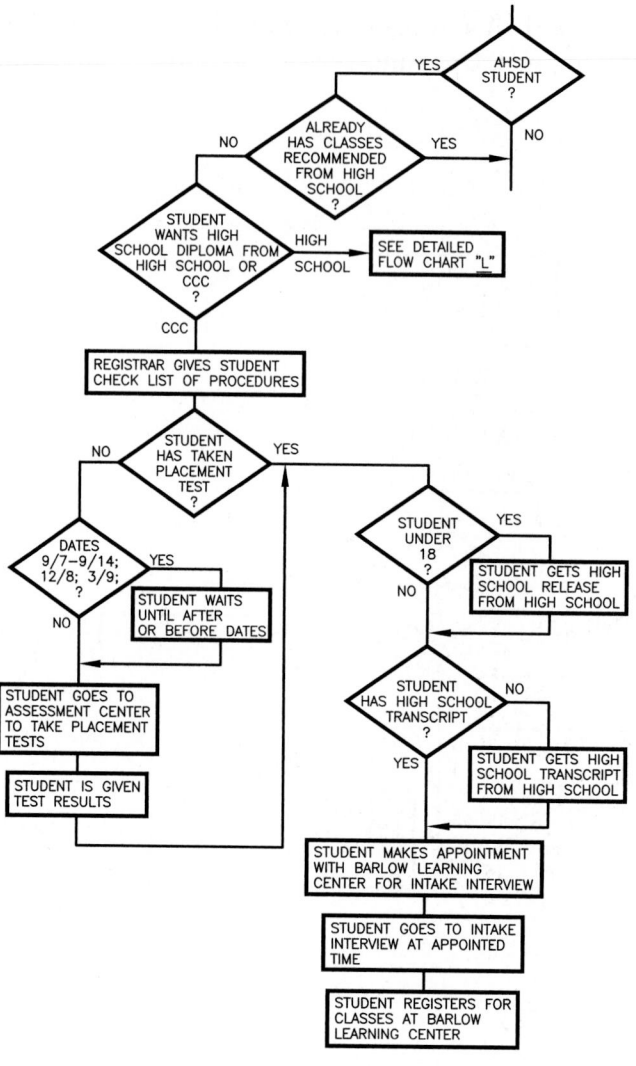

10. Draw the single polyline shown below. Use the **Arc**, **Width**, and **Close** options of the **PLINE** command to complete the shape. Set the polyline width to 0, except at the points indicated. Save the drawing as P14-10.

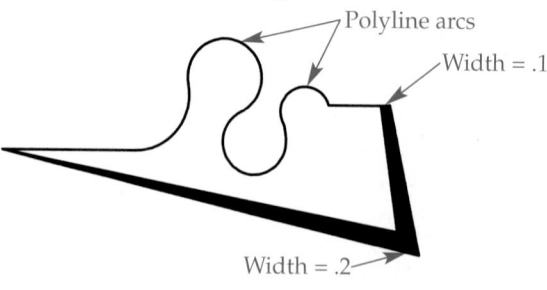

11. Draw the two curved arrows shown below using the **Arc** and **Width** options of the **PLINE** command. The arrowheads should have a starting width of 1.4 and an ending width of 0. The body of each arrow should have a beginning width of .8 and an ending width of .4. Save the drawing as P14-11.

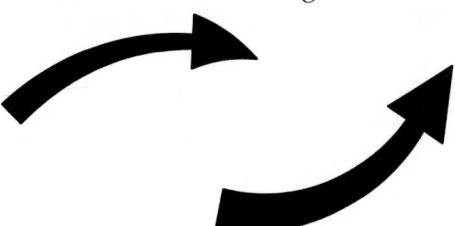

12. Open drawing P14-10 and make a copy of the original object to edit. Use the **PEDIT** command to change the object drawn into a rectangle. Use the **Decurve** and **Width** options and the **Straighten**, **Insert**, and **Move** vertex editing options of the **PEDIT** command. Save the completed drawing as P14-12.

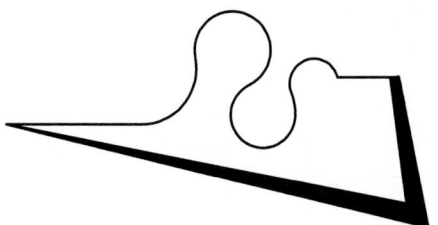

13. Open drawing P14-11 and make the following changes. Save the drawing as P14-13.
    A. Combine the two polylines using the **Join** option of the **PEDIT** command.
    B. Change the beginning width of the left arrow to 1.0 and the ending width to .2.
    C. Draw a polyline .062 wide, similar to Line A, as shown.

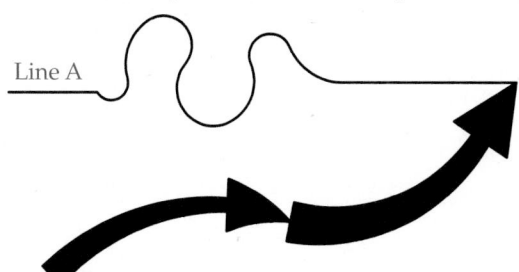

Line A

14. Draw a polyline .032 wide, using the following absolute coordinates.

Point	Coordinates	Point	Coordinates	Point	Coordinates
1	1,1	5	3,3	9	5,5
2	2,1	6	4,3	10	6,5
3	2,2	7	4,4	11	6,6
4	3,2	8	5,4	12	7,6

Copy the polyline three times so there are four polylines. Use the **Fit** option of the **PEDIT** command to smooth the first copy. Use the **Spline** option of the **PEDIT** command to turn the second copy into a quadratic curve. Make the third copy into a cubic curve. Use the **Decurve** option of the **PEDIT** command to return one of the three copies to its original form. Save the drawing as P14-14.

15. Use the **PLINE** command to draw a patio plan similar to the one shown in Example A below. Draw the house walls 6″ wide. Copy the drawing three times and use the **PEDIT** command to create the remaining designs shown. Use the **Fit** option for Example B, a quadratic spline for Example C, and a cubic spline for Example D. Change the **SPLINETYPE** system variable as required. Save the drawing as P14-15.

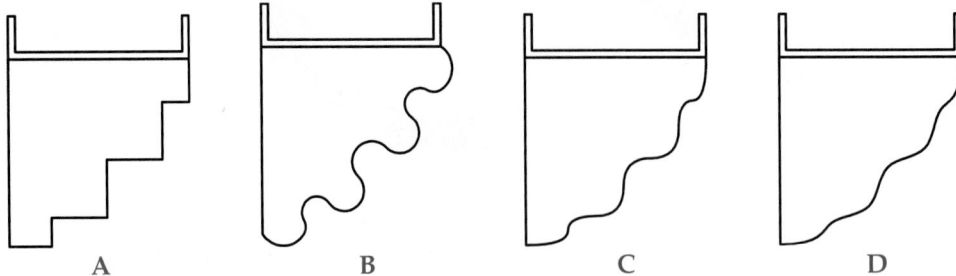

A   B   C   D

16. Open drawing P14-15 and create four new patio designs. This time, use grips to edit the polylines and create designs similar to Examples A, B, C, and D below. Save the drawing as P14-16.

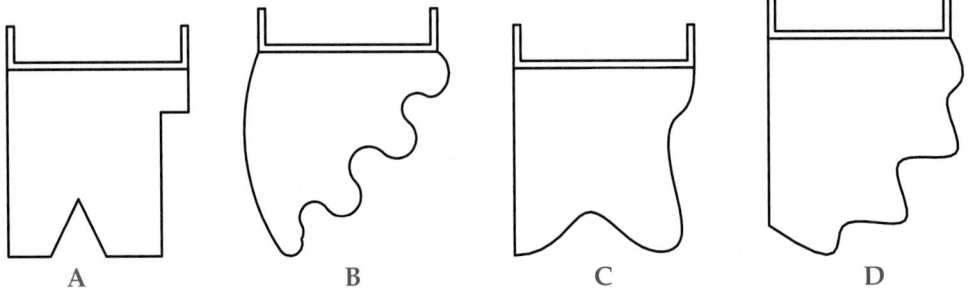

A   B   C   D

Drawing Problems - Chapter 14

CHAPTER 15

Multilines and Splines

Learning Objectives

After completing this chapter, you will be able to do the following:

✓ Use the **MLINE** command to draw multilines.
✓ Create your own multiline styles with the **MLSTYLE** command.
✓ Edit multiline intersections, corners, and vertices.
✓ Draw and edit spline curves.

This chapter explores drawing and editing AutoCAD multilines and splines. *Multilines* are combinations of parallel lines consisting of up to 16 individual lines called *elements*. You can offset the elements as needed to create a pattern for any field of drafting, such as architectural, schematic, or mechanical. Multilines are drawn using the **MLINE** command and its options and are modified using the **MLEDIT** command.

A *spline* is a special type of nonuniform curved line. The **SPLINE** command is used to create true splines. Splines can be edited using the **SPLINEDIT** command.

> **multiline:** A single object consisting of up to 16 parallel line elements.
>
> **elements:** The individual lines that make up a multiline.
>
> **spline:** A special type of nonuniform curved line.

Drawing Multilines

The **MLINE** command is used to draw multilines. To access the **MLINE** command, pick **Draw > Multiline** or type ML or MLINE. The prompts and options for the **MLINE** command are similar to those for the **LINE** command. You can use the **Close** option at the last prompt to close a polygon. Enter U during the command sequence to undo the previously drawn multiline segment.

A multiline configuration, or style, can be set using the **MLSTYLE** command. The default AutoCAD multiline style has two elements and is called STANDARD and consists of two parallel lines. If you pick on one line to display grips, you can see that the entered coordinates correspond to both lines. Multiline styles are described later in this chapter.

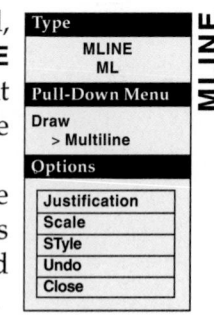

Type	
MLINE	
ML	
Pull-Down Menu	
Draw	
> Multiline	
Options	
Justification	
Scale	
STyle	
Undo	
Close	

MLINE

Multiline Justification

Multiline justification determines how the line elements are offset from the definition points provided. *Definition points* are the points you pick or coordinates you enter when drawing multilines. The justification is based on counterclockwise movement and can be specified only once during a single **MLINE** command sequence. The **Justification** options are **Top** (default), **Zero**, and **Bottom**.

> **definition points:** The points you pick or coordinates you enter to specify multilines.

To change the justification, type J at the first prompt displayed after entering the **MLINE** command. Enter the first letter of the desired justification format (T, Z, or B). The results of the three different **Justification** options using identical point entries are shown in **Figure 15-1**. Observe each orientation as you go through the following command sequence:

Command: **ML** *or* **MLINE**.↵
Current settings: Justification = *current*, Scale = *current*, Style = *current*
Specify start point or [Justification/Scale/STyle]: **J**↵
Enter justification type [Top/Zero/Bottom] <*current*>: *(type T, Z, or B, and press* [Enter])
Current settings: Justification = *specified value*, Scale = *current*, Style = *current*
Specify start point or [Justification/Scale/STyle]: **2,2**↵
Specify next point: **6,2**↵
Specify next point or [Undo]: **6,6**↵
Specify next point or [Close/Undo]: **2,6**↵
Specify next point or [Close/Undo]: **C**↵
Command:

The current multiline justification setting is stored in the **CMLJUST** system variable. You can change the setting by entering 0 for the **Top** option, 1 for the **Zero** option, or 2 for the **Bottom** option.

PROFESSIONAL TIP

As shown in **Figure 15-1**, the multiline **Justification** options control the direction of the offsets for elements of the current style. The multiline segments in these examples are drawn in a counterclockwise direction. Unexpected results can sometimes occur when you use the **MLINE** command, depending on the justification and drawing direction.

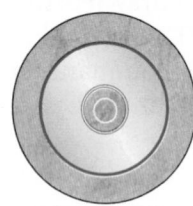

Exercise 15-1
Complete the exercise on the Student CD.

Adjusting the Multiline Scale

The **Scale** option of the **MLINE** command is a multiplier applied to the offset distance specified in the multiline style. The multiplier is stored in the **CMLSCALE** system variable. The example in the previous section used a default scale setting of 1. With this setting, the distance between multiline elements is equal to 1 times the

---

Figure 15-1.
Multilines drawn using each of the three justification options. The definition points (represented by plus symbols) are picked in a counterclockwise rotation.

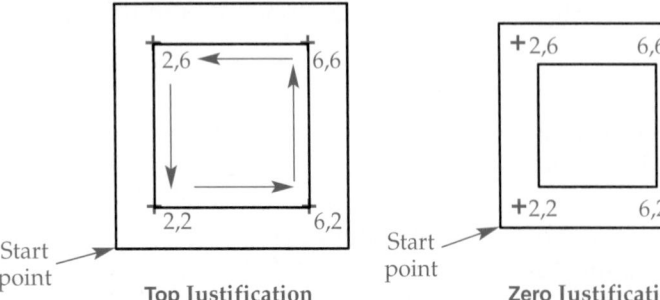
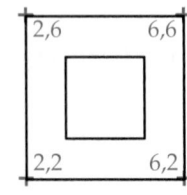

offset distance. For example, if the offset distance is .5, the distance between multiline elements is .5 when the multiline scale is 1. If the multiline scale is specified as 2, however, the distance between multiline elements is 1 (.5 × 2). Multilines drawn with different scale settings are shown in Figure 15-2.

Exercise 15-2
Complete the exercise on the Student CD.

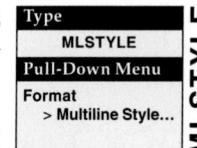

Creating Multiline Styles

Multiline styles are defined using the **Multiline Style** dialog box. The current style is stored in the **CMLSTYLE** system variable. The **Multiline Style** dialog box can be accessed by picking **Format** > **Multiline Style...** from the pull-down menu or by typing MLSTYLE.

The **Multiline Style** dialog box allows you to define, edit, and save multiline styles. See Figure 15-3. You can save styles to an external file so they can be used in other drawings. The **Preview of:** area in the lower part of the **Multiline Style** dialog box displays a representation of the selected multiline style.

Type	
	MLSTYLE
Pull-Down Menu	
Format	
	> **Multiline Style...**

MLSTYLE

Figure 15-2.
Multiline scale settings.

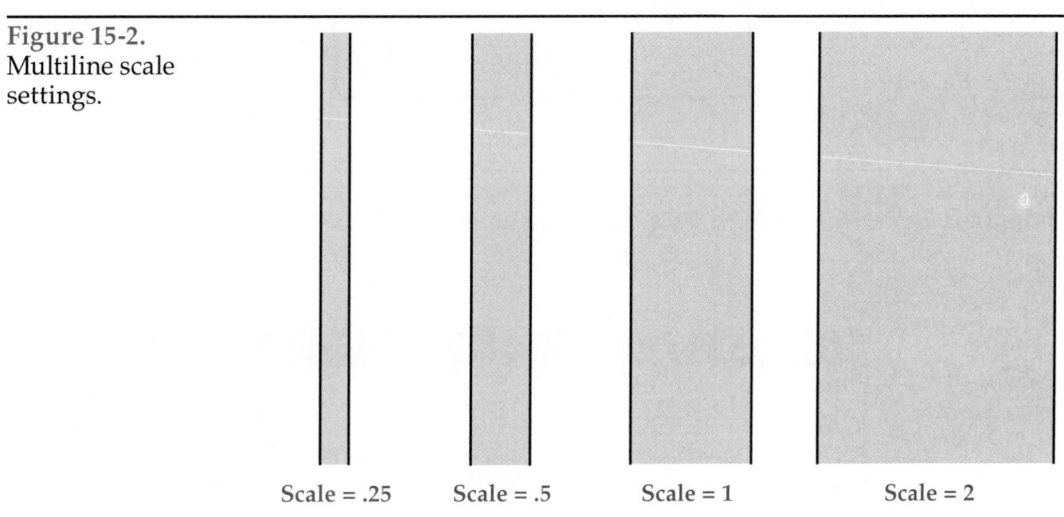

Scale = .25   Scale = .5   Scale = 1   Scale = 2

Figure 15-3.
The **Multiline Style** dialog box is used to define, edit, and save multiline styles.

List of available styles

Description of selected style

Preview of selected style

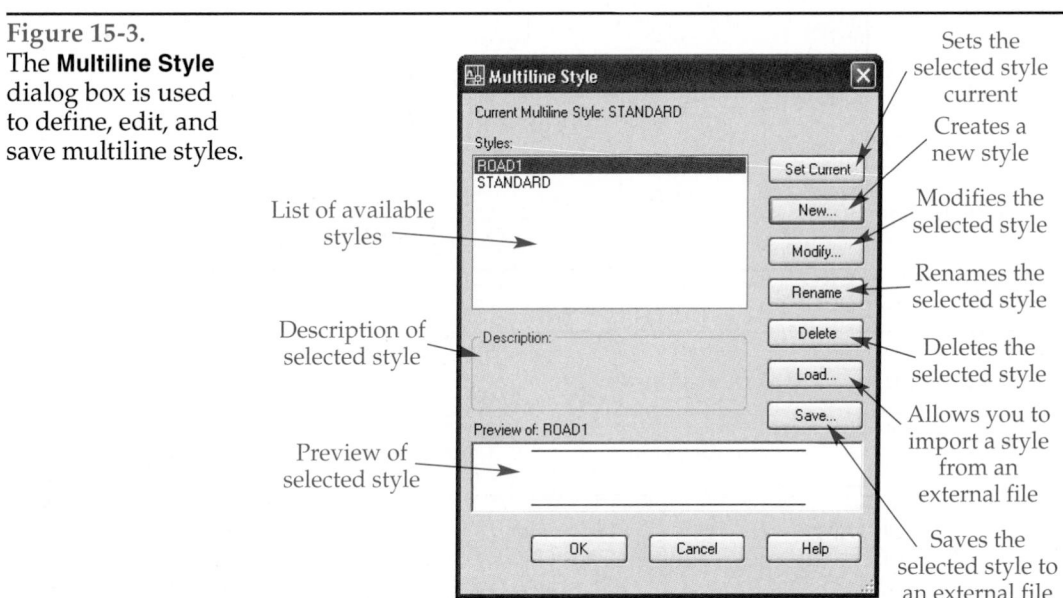

Sets the selected style current

Creates a new style

Modifies the selected style

Renames the selected style

Deletes the selected style

Allows you to import a style from an external file

Saves the selected style to an external file

Picking the **New...** button in the **Multiline Style** dialog box displays the **Create New Multiline Style** dialog box shown in **Figure 15-4**. In the **New Style Name:** text box, enter a name for the new multiline style. The properties from an existing style can be used for the new style by selecting it from the **Start With:** drop-down list.

After a name has been entered, the **Continue** button becomes active. Picking this button opens the **New Multiline Style** dialog box. The options in this dialog box define the appearance of the multiline. See **Figure 15-5**. The **Description:** field is optional, but it can be used to enter a brief description of the multiline style.

Using the caps, fill, and joints settings

caps: Short lines connecting the start points and endpoints of multiline elements.

The settings in the **Caps** area control the placement of caps on multilines. *Caps* are lines connecting the corresponding vertices of the start points or endpoints of the multiline elements. Using the check boxes, you can set caps at the start points, endpoints, or both. Several examples of different cap options are shown in **Figure 15-6**.

Figure 15-4.
To create a new multiline style, specify a name and existing multiline style settings in the **Create New Multiline Style** dialog box.

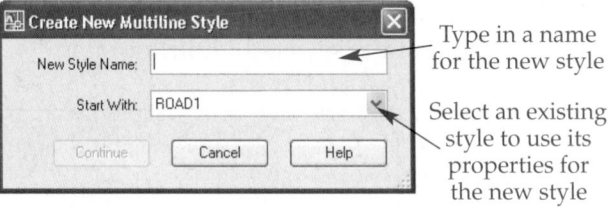

Type in a name for the new style

Select an existing style to use its properties for the new style

---

Figure 15-5.
The options in the **New Multiline Style** dialog box control all the settings for a multiline.

Description of the style

Caps area controls multiline capping

Determines the fill setting for the multiline style

Option for displaying joints

Elements area sets the lines and their properties

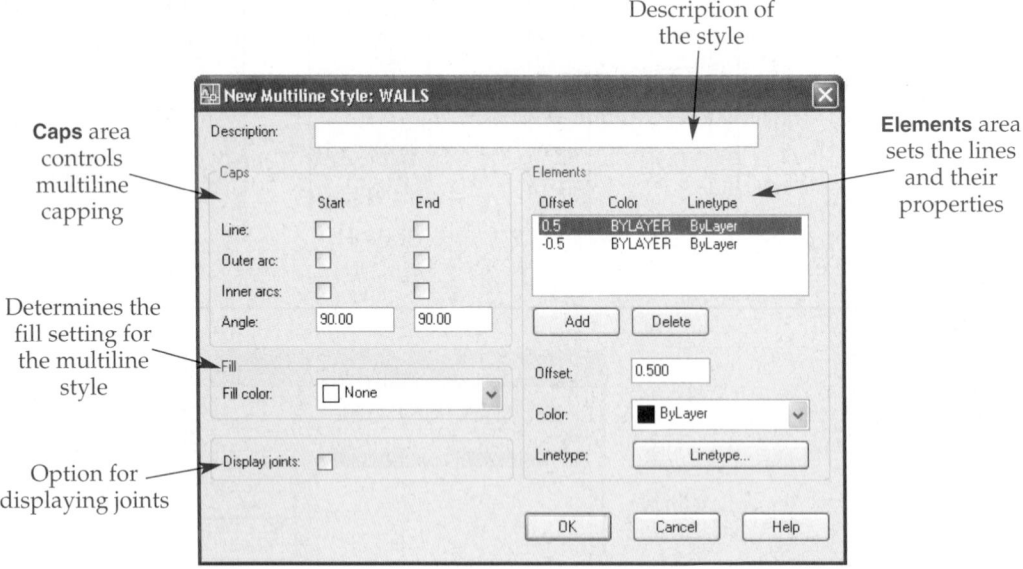

Figure 15-6.
Various cap options used with multilines.

Caps Off	Line Caps On	Outer Arcs On	Inner Arcs On

90° Angle Caps Off	45° Angle Caps Off	45° Angle Line Caps On

AutoCAD and Its Applications—Basics

The caps can be drawn as straight lines or arcs. Arcs can be set to connect the ends of the outermost elements only, pairs of inner elements, or both the outer and inner elements. The multiline style must contain at least two multiline elements for outer arcs to be drawn. Arcs are drawn tangent to the elements they connect. You can also change the angle of the caps relative to the direction of the multiline elements. To do this, enter values in the **Angle:** text boxes. There is a text box for the start points and another for the endpoints.

The **Fill color:** setting in the **Fill** area allows you to create a solid multiline. When the **Fill color:** setting is set to **None**, there is no fill. To specify the fill color, select a color from the **Fill color:** drop-down list. Multilines drawn with and without fills are shown in **Figure 15-7**.

When **Display joints:** is checked, joints are displayed on the multiline. *Joints* are lines connecting the vertices of adjacent multiline elements. They are also referred to as *miters*. Multilines drawn with and without joints are shown in **Figure 15-8**.

joints (miters): Lines connecting the vertices of adjacent multiline elements.

Setting the element properties

The **Elements** area allows you to add or delete more elements (lines) from the multiline style and specify the properties of each element. The options in this area change properties including linetype, color, and offset. After you have set the properties, pick **OK** to apply them to the new multiline style. The new style is then added to the **Multiline Style** dialog box.

Changing the Multiline Style

You can specify the current multiline style by using the **STyle** option of the **MLINE** command. To use a saved multiline style, enter ST to access the **STyle** option, and then enter the style name. Before you can access a new multiline style, however, you must create and save it using the **Multiline Style** dialog box.

If you forget the name of the desired multiline style, you can enter ? at the Enter mline style name or [?]: prompt. The text window opens, listing the currently loaded multiline styles. See **Figure 15-9**. Type the name of the style you want to use.

If you try to specify a multiline style that is not loaded, the **Load multiline style from file** dialog box is displayed. You can look for the desired multiline style in the acad.mln file library, or you can pick the **Tools** button and then **Find...** to open the **Find:** dialog box.

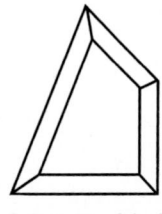

Exercise 15-3
Complete the exercise on the Student CD.

Figure 15-7.
The multiline
Fill color: setting
allows you to draw
multilines with a
solid fill pattern.

Fill Setting On   Fill Setting Off

Figure 15-8.
Multilines can be
drawn with or
without displayed
joints.

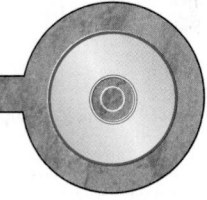

Joints Enabled   Joints Disabled

Figure 15-9.
A list of loaded multiline styles can be displayed in the text window.

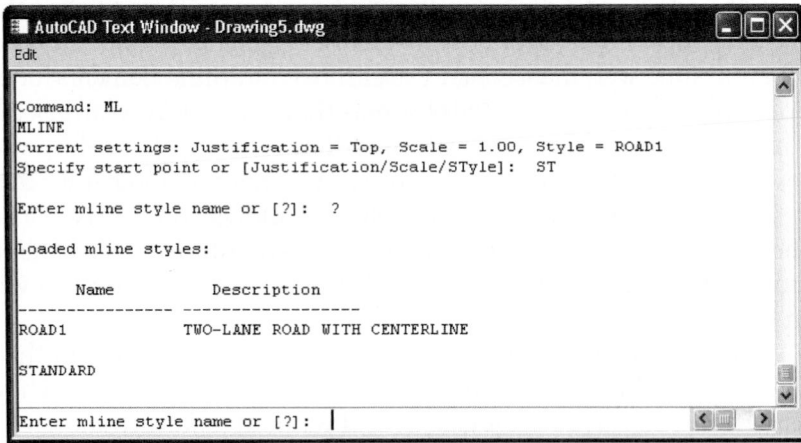

```
AutoCAD Text Window - Drawing5.dwg
Edit

Command: ML
MLINE
Current settings: Justification = Top, Scale = 1.00, Style = ROAD1
Specify start point or [Justification/Scale/STyle]:  ST

Enter mline style name or [?]:   ?

Loaded mline styles:

      Name              Description
---------------   ------------------
ROAD1             TWO-LANE ROAD WITH CENTERLINE

STANDARD

Enter mline style name or [?]:  |
```

Editing Multilines

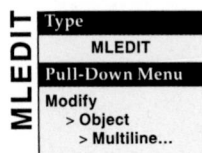

Type
MLEDIT
Pull-Down Menu
Modify
> Object
> Multiline...

The **MLEDIT** command permits limited editing operations for multiline objects. To display the **Multilines Edit Tools** dialog box, pick **Modify** > **Object** > **Multiline...** from the pull-down menu or type MLEDIT. See **Figure 15-10**. This dialog box contains four columns. Each column contains three buttons of related command options. The image on each button gives you an example of what to expect when using the editing option.

When you pick a button, the dialog box closes and AutoCAD prompts you to continue with the command. The command options are described in the following sections.

Editing Intersections

The first (left) column in the **Multilines Edit Tools** dialog box displays three different types of multiline intersections. Picking a button allows you to create the type of intersection shown. The effects of the buttons in the first column are shown in **Figure 15-11** and described below.

- **Closed Cross.** When you use this option, the first multiline you select is called the *background*, and the second multiline is called the *foreground*. A closed cross intersection is created by trimming the background, while the foreground remains unchanged. The trimming is apparent, not actual. The line visibility of the background multiline is changed, but it is still a single multiline.

background: The first multiline you select to create a closed cross intersection.

foreground: The second multiline you select to create a closed cross intersection.

Figure 15-10.
The **Multilines Edit Tools** dialog box has twelve different options for editing multilines.

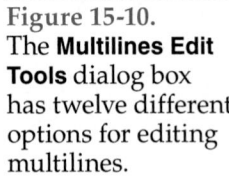

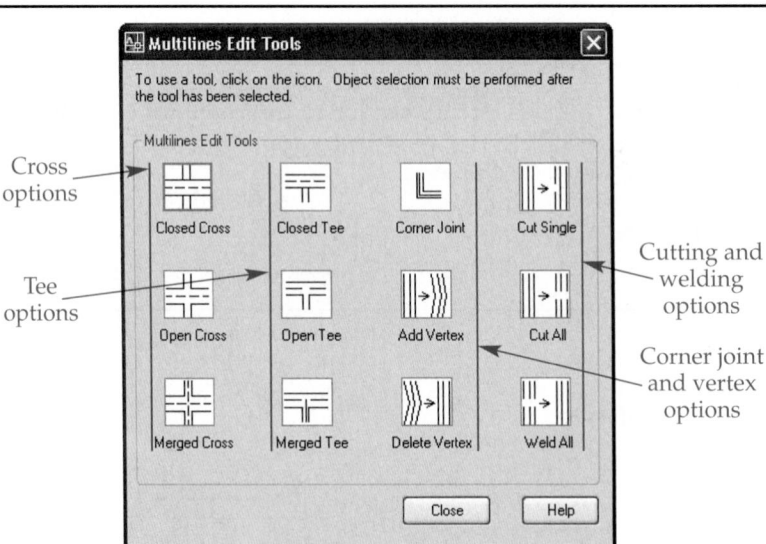

Figure 15-11.
Creating closed
cross, open cross,
and merged cross
intersections
with the **MLEDIT**
command.

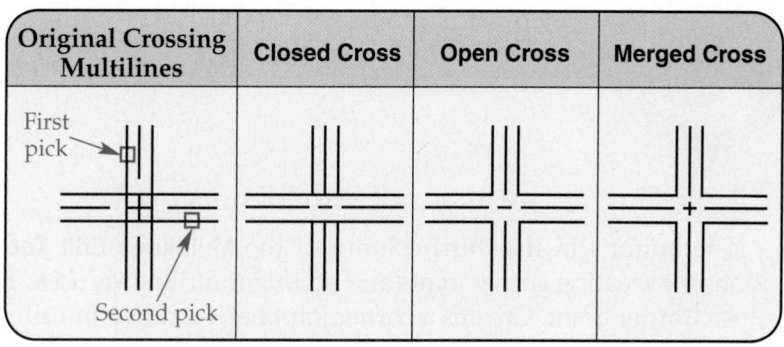

Original Crossing Multilines	Closed Cross	Open Cross	Merged Cross

- **Open Cross.** Select the **Open Cross** button to trim all the elements of the first multiline and only the outer elements of the second multiline. The command sequence is the same as that used for the **Closed Cross** option.
- **Merged Cross.** The **Merged Cross** button allows you to trim the outer elements of both multilines. The inner elements are not changed.

Exercise 15-4
Complete the exercise on the Student CD.

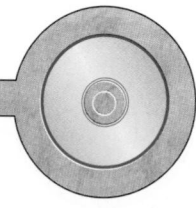

Editing Tees

The buttons in the second column of the **Multilines Edit Tools** dialog box are used to edit multiline tees. The results of using the tee options are illustrated in **Figure 15-12.** The three options are:

- **Closed Tee.** Trims or extends the first selected multiline to its intersection with the second multiline.
- **Open Tee.** Trims the elements where a trimmed or extended multiline intersects with another multiline. The first pick specifies the multiline to trim or extend, and the second pick specifies the intersecting multiline. The intersecting multiline is trimmed and left open where the two multilines join.
- **Merged Tee.** Trims the intersecting multiline after the first multiline is trimmed or extended. The inner elements, however, are joined. This creates an open appearance with the outer elements, while merging the inner elements.

Figure 15-12.
Using the tee
options of the
MLEDIT command to
edit multiline tees.

Original Multilines	Closed Tee	Open Tee	Merged Tee

Exercise 15-5
Complete the exercise on the Student CD.

Editing Corner Joints and Multiline Vertices

The buttons in the third column of the **Multilines Edit Tools** dialog box provide options for creating corner joints and editing multiline vertices. The three options are:

- **Corner Joint.** Creates a corner joint between two multilines. The first multiline is trimmed or extended to its intersection with the second multiline, as shown in **Figure 15-13.**
- **Add Vertex.** Adds a vertex to an existing multiline at the location you pick. See **Figure 15-14.** The command sequence differs slightly from the sequences used with the other **MLEDIT** options. After you select the **Add Vertex** option, AutoCAD prompts you to pick a location for the vertex.
- **Delete Vertex.** Removes a vertex from an existing multiline. The vertex closest to the location you pick is deleted. See **Figure 15-14.** The command sequence is the same as for the **Add Vertex** option.

Exercise 15-6
Complete the exercise on the Student CD.

Figure 15-13.
A corner joint can be created between two multilines using the **Corner Joint** option of the **MLEDIT** command.

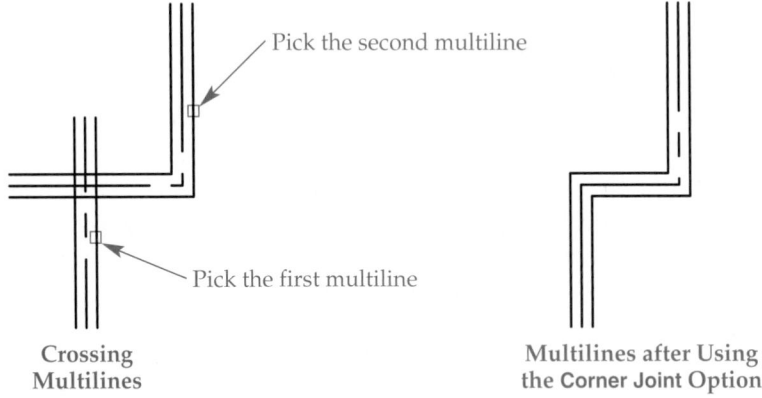

Pick the second multiline

Pick the first multiline

Crossing
Multilines

Multilines after Using
the Corner Joint Option

Figure 15-14.
The **Add Vertex** and **Delete Vertex** options of the **MLEDIT** command are used to edit multiline vertices.

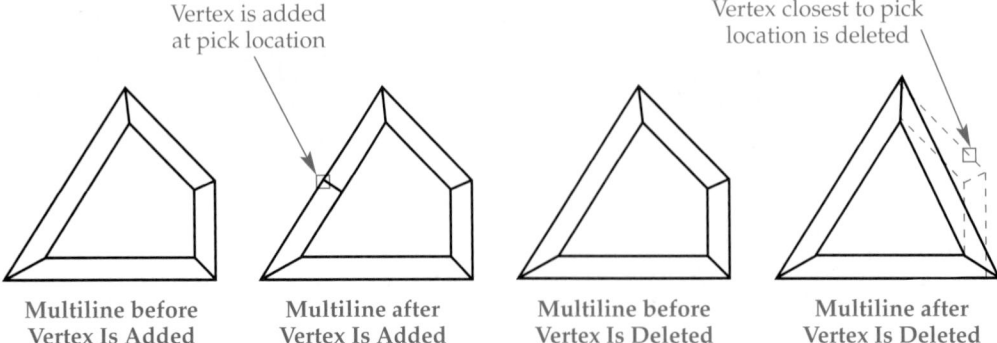

Vertex is added
at pick location

Vertex closest to pick
location is deleted

Multiline before
Vertex Is Added

Multiline after
Vertex Is Added

Multiline before
Vertex Is Deleted

Multiline after
Vertex Is Deleted

Figure 15-15.
The **MLEDIT** cutting options allow you to cut single multiline elements or entire multilines between two specified points.

Original Multiline	Cut Single	Cut All

Pick points

Cutting and Welding Multilines

The fourth column of buttons in the **Multilines Edit Tools** dialog box is used for *cutting* a portion out of a single multiline element or the entire multiline. The spaces between multiline elements can also be connected. AutoCAD refers to the connecting operation as *welding*. The **MLEDIT** cutting and welding options are:

- **Cut Single.** Cuts a single multiline element between two specified points, as shown in **Figure 15-15.** Cutting affects only the visibility of elements and does not separate a multiline object. The multiline is still a single object. After you select the **Cut Single** option, AutoCAD prompts you to pick the cutting points.
- **Cut All.** Cuts all elements of a multiline between specified points. See **Figure 15-15.** The multiline is still a single object, even though it appears to be separated.
- **Weld All.** Repairs all cuts in a multiline. Select the **Weld All** button and select a point on each side of the cut multiline. The multiline is restored to its precut condition.

cutting: The process deleting a portion of a multiline element or an entire multiline.

welding: The process of connecting the spaces between multiline elements.

PROFESSIONAL TIP

Multiline objects can be converted to individual line segments with the **EXPLODE** command. This command is explained in Chapters 14 and 23.

Exercise 15-7
Complete the exercise on the Student CD.

---

nonuniform rational B-spline (NURBS) curve: A true (mathematically correct) spline.

Drawing Splines

The **SPLINE** command is used to create a special type of curve called a *nonuniform rational B-spline (NURBS) curve.* A NURBS curve is considered to be a true spline. A spline created by fitting a spline curve to a polyline is merely a linear approximation of a true spline and is not as accurate. An additional advantage of spline objects over smoothed polylines is that splines use less disk space. To access the **SPLINE** command, pick the **Spline** button on the **2D Draw** control panel of the **Dashboard** or the **Draw** toolbar, pick **Draw > Spline**, or type SPL or SPLINE. A spline is created by specifying the control points using any standard coordinate entry method.

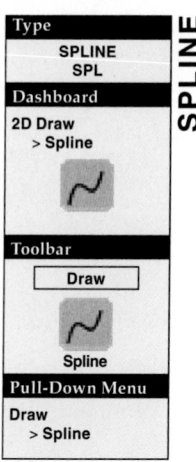

Type	
SPLINE	
SPL	

Dashboard
2D Draw
> Spline

Toolbar
Draw

Spline

Pull-Down Menu
Draw
> Spline

SPLINE

```
Command: SPL or SPLINE↵
Specify first point or [Object]: 2,2↵
Specify next point: 4,4↵
Specify next point or [Close/Fit tolerance] <start tangent>: 6,2↵
Specify next point or [Close/Fit tolerance] <start tangent>: ↵
Specify start tangent: ↵
Specify end tangent: ↵
Command:
```

After you have specified all the necessary points along the spline, press [Enter] to end the point specification process and to allow the start tangency and end tangency to be entered. Specifying the tangents changes the direction in which the spline curve begins and ends. Pressing [Enter] at these prompts accepts the default direction, as calculated by AutoCAD, for the specified curve. The results of the previous command sequence are shown in **Figure 15-16**.

NOTE

If you specify only two points for a spline curve and accept Auto-CAD's default start and end tangents, an object that looks like a line is created, but the object is a spline.

Drawing Closed Splines

The **Close** option of the **SPLINE** command enables you to draw closed splines. See **Figure 15-17**. After closing a spline, you are prompted to specify a tangent direction for the start point or endpoint of the spline. Pressing [Enter] accepts the default calculated by AutoCAD.

Figure 15-16.
A spline drawn with the **SPLINE** command. AutoCAD's default start and end tangents were used for this spline.

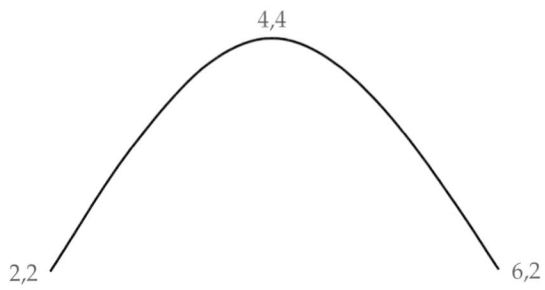

Figure 15-17.
Using the **Close** option of the **SPLINE** command with AutoCAD default tangents to draw a closed spline. Compare this spline to the object shown in **Figure 15-16**.

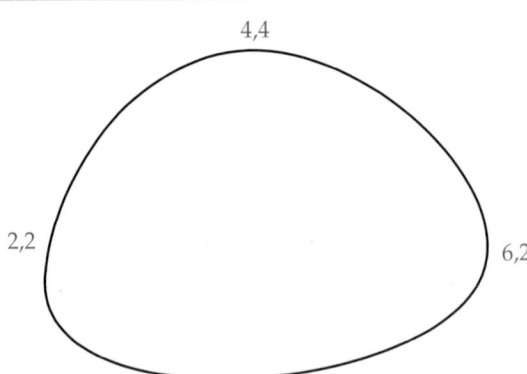

Altering the Fit Tolerance Specifications

When drawing splines, you can achieve different results by altering the specifications used with the **Fit tolerance** option. The outcomes of different settings vary depending on the configuration of the individual spline object. The setting specifies a tolerance within which the spline curve falls as it passes through the control points.

Specifying the Start and End Tangents

The previous **SPLINE** command examples used AutoCAD's default start and end tangents. You can set start and end tangent directions by entering values at the prompts that appear after you pick the points of the spline. The tangency is based on the tangent direction of the selected point. The results of using the horizontal and vertical tangent directions using Ortho mode are shown in **Figure 15-18**.

Converting a Spline-Fitted Polyline to a Spline

A spline-fitted polyline object can be converted to a spline object using the **Object** option of the **SPLINE** command. This option works for both 2D and 3D polylines.

Exercise 15-8
Complete the exercise on the Student CD.

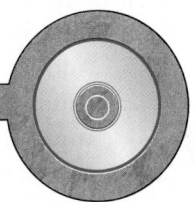

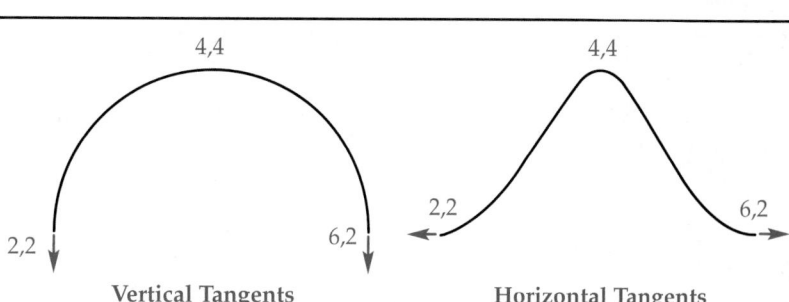

Figure 15-18. These splines were drawn through the same points, but they have different start and end tangent directions. The arrows indicate the tangent directions.

Vertical Tangents Horizontal Tangents

Editing Splines

fit points: Spline control points.

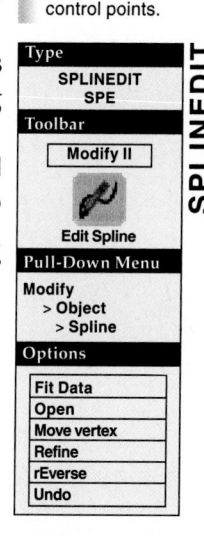

The **SPLINEDIT** command allows you to edit spline objects. Several editing options are available. You can add, move, or delete control points to alter the shape of an existing curve. You can also open or close a spline and change the start and end tangents.

To access the **SPLINEDIT** command, pick the **Edit Spline** button on the **Modify II** toolbar, pick **Modify > Object > Spline**, or type SPE or SPLINEDIT. You are prompted to select the spline to be edited. When you pick a spline, the control points are identified by grips, as shown in **Figure 15-19**. You must then select one of the six **SPLINEDIT** options. These are described in the following sections.

Editing Fit Data

The **Fit data** option of the **SPLINEDIT** command allows spline control points to be edited. Spline control points are called *fit points*. The **Fit data** option has several suboptions:

Figure 15-19.
The control points
for a spline are
displayed as grips.

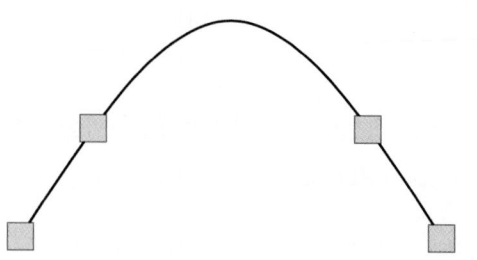

Command: **SPE** *or* **SPLINEDIT**↵
Select spline: *(pick a spline)*
Enter an option [Fit data/Close/Move vertex/Refine/rEverse/Undo]: **F**↵
Enter a fit data option
[Add/Close/Delete/Move/Purge/Tangents/toLerance/eXit] <eXit>:

Each of the **Fit data** suboptions is explained next. See **Figure 15-20** for examples of using these options.

- **Add.** This suboption adds new fit points to a spline definition. A new fit point can be located by picking a point or entering coordinates. Fit points appear as unselected grips. When a fit point is selected, it becomes highlighted along with the next fit point on the spline. You can then add a fit point between the two highlighted points. If the endpoint of the spline is selected, only the endpoint

Figure 15-20.
Examples of using
the **Fit data** options
of the **SPLINEDIT**
command to edit
a spline. Compare
the original spline
to each of the edited
objects.

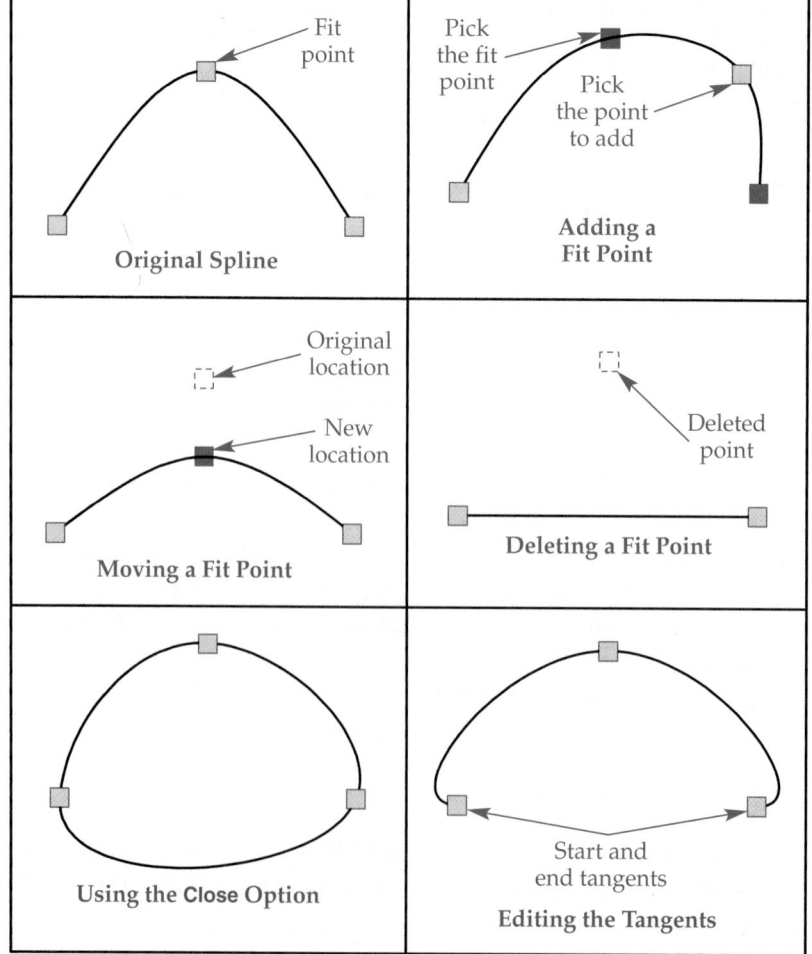

becomes highlighted. If the start point of the spline is selected, you are asked whether you want the new fit point inserted before or after the existing one. Respond by entering A or B accordingly. When a fit point is added, the spline curve is refit through the added point.

The **Add** suboption functions in a running mode. This means you can continue to add points as needed. By pressing [Enter] at a Specify new point <exit>: prompt, you can select other existing fit points to add points anywhere on the spline.

- **Close/Open.** If the selected spline is open, the **Close** suboption is displayed. If the spline is closed, the **Open** suboption is displayed. These options allow you to open a closed spline or close an open spline.
- **Delete.** The **Delete** suboption deletes fit points as needed. At least two fit points, however, must remain. Like the **Add** suboption, the **Delete** suboption operates in a running mode, allowing as many deletions as needed. The spline is recurved through the remaining fit points.
- **Move.** This suboption allows fit points to be moved as necessary. When you enter the **Move** suboption, the start point of the spline is highlighted. You can specify a different location by picking a new point. You can also specify other fit points to move. The options are explained as follows:
  - **Specify new location.** Allows you to move the currently highlighted point to a specified location.
  - **Next.** Highlights the next fit point. This option is activated by pressing [Enter].
  - **Previous.** Highlights the previous fit point.
  - **Select point.** Allows you to pick a different fit point to move.
  - **eXit.** Returns you to the **Fit data** option prompt.
- **Purge.** This suboption lets you remove fit point data from a spline. After using this option, the resulting spline is not as easy to edit. In very large drawings in which many complex splines have been created, such as Geographical Information Systems (GIS) drawings, purging fit point data reduces the file size by simplifying the spline definitions. After a spline is purged, the **Fit data** option is no longer displayed by the **SPLINEDIT** command for the purged spline.
- **Tangents.** This suboption allows you to edit the start and end tangents for an open spline and the start tangent for a closed spline. The tangency is based on the direction of the selected point. You can also use the **System default** option to set the tangency values to the AutoCAD defaults.
- **toLerance.** Fit tolerance values can be adjusted using this suboption. The results are immediate, so the fit tolerance can be adjusted as necessary to produce different results.
- **eXit.** Entering this suboption returns you to the **SPLINEDIT** command option prompt.

Opening or Closing a Spline

The **Open** and **Close** options of the **SPLINEDIT** command are alternately displayed, depending on the current status of the spline object being edited. If the spline is open, the **Close** option is displayed. The **Open** option is displayed if the spline is closed.

Moving a Vertex

The **Move vertex** option of the **SPLINEDIT** command allows you to move the fit points of a spline. When you access this option, you can specify a new location for a selected fit point. The options displayed are identical to those used with the **Move** suboption of the **Fit data** option. You can pick a new location for the highlighted fit point, or you can enter a suboption. The **Move vertex** suboptions are explained below:

- **Specify new location.** Moves the currently highlighted point to a specified location.
- **Next.** Highlights the next fit point.

- **Previous.** Highlights the previous fit point.
- **Select point.** Picks a different fit point to move, rather than cycling through points with the **Next** or **Previous** suboptions.
- **eXit.** Returns to the **SPLINEDIT** prompt.

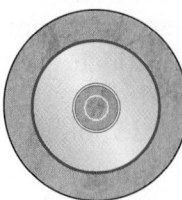

Exercise 15-9
Complete the exercise on the Student CD.

Smoothing or Reshaping a Section of the Spline

The **Refine** option of the **SPLINEDIT** command allows fine-tuning of the spline curve. Fit points can be added to help smooth or reshape a section of the spline. When you use this option, the fit point data is removed from the spline. The following refining options are available:

- **Add control point.** Specifies new fit points on a spline as needed.
- **Elevate order.** Causes more control points to appear on the curve for greater control. The *order* of a spline is the degree of the spline polynomial + 1. In simple terms, it is the degree of refinement of the spline. For example, a cubic spline has an order of 4. In **Figure 15-21**, the order of the spline is elevated from 4 to 6. The order setting can be from 4 to 26, but it cannot be adjusted downward. For example, if the order is set to 24, the only remaining settings are 25 and 26.
- **Weight.** Changes the weight of a control point. When all control points have the same weight, they exert the same amount of pull on the spline. When a weight value is reduced for a control point, the spline is not pulled as close to the point as before. Likewise, when a weight value is increased, the control point exerts more pull on the spline. See **Figure 15-21**. The default setting of 1.0000 can be adjusted to a higher or lower value. The weight setting must be positive. The control point selection suboptions of the **Weight** option are the same as those used with the **Move vertex** option of the **SPLINEDIT** command. You can specify a new weight for the highlighted control point using the **Enter new weight** option.

order: In a spline, the degree of the spline polynomial + 1.

Figure 15-21.
The effects of elevating the order of a spline and increasing the weight of an individual control point.

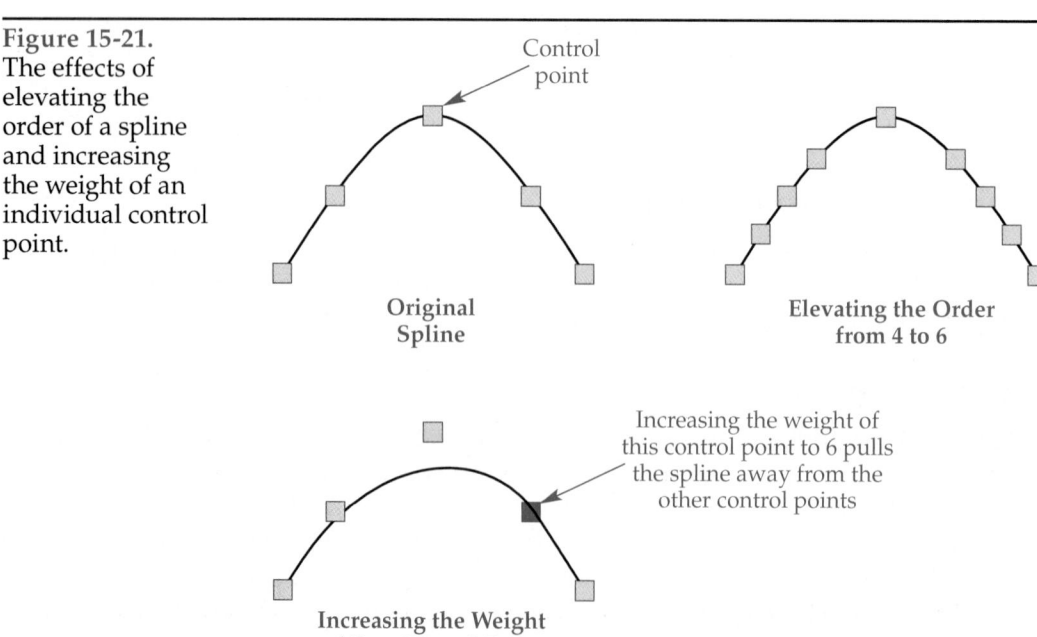

AutoCAD and Its Applications—Basics

Reversing the Order of Spline Control Points

The **rEverse** option of the **SPLINEDIT** command allows you to reverse the listed order of the spline control points. This makes the previous start point the new endpoint and the previous endpoint the new start point. Using this option affects the various control point selection options.

Undoing Splinedit Changes

The **Undo** option of the **SPLINEDIT** command undoes the previous change made to the spline. You can use this option to undo changes back to the beginning of the current **SPLINEDIT** command sequence.

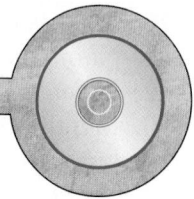

Exercise 15-10
Complete the exercise on the Student CD.

Chapter Test

Answer the following questions. Write your answers on a separate sheet of paper or complete the electronic chapter test on the Student CD.

1. Give the command and entries needed to draw a multiline with zero justification and the saved style ROAD1.
   A. Command: _____
   B. Current settings: Justification = *current*, Scale = *current*, Style = *current*
      Specify start point or [Justification/Scale/STyle]: _____
   C. Enter mline style name or [?]: _____
   D. Current settings: Justification = *current*, Scale = *current*, Style = ROAD1
      Specify start point or [Justification/Scale/STyle]: _____
   E. Enter justification type [Top/Zero/Bottom] <*current*>: _____
   F. Current settings: Justification = Zero, Scale = *current*, Style = ROAD1
      Specify start point or [Justification/Scale/STyle]: _____
   G. Specify next point: _____
   H. Specify next point or [Undo]: _____
2. Name the **MLINE** command option that establishes how the resulting lines are offset based on the definition points provided.
3. Name the system variable that controls the multiplier value for the offset distances specified with the **MLINE** command.
4. How do you access the **Multiline Style** dialog box?
5. Define *caps*.
6. Define *joints*.
7. What is displayed when you enter the **MLEDIT** command?
8. How do you access one of the **MLEDIT** options?
9. List the three options used for editing multiline intersections with the **MLEDIT** command.
10. Name the **MLEDIT** option in which the intersecting multiline is trimmed and left open after the first multiline is trimmed or extended to its intersection with the intersecting multiline.
11. Name the **MLEDIT** option that allows you to remove a vertex from an existing multiline.
12. Name the **MLEDIT** option that lets you remove a portion from an individual multiline element.

13. Name the **MLEDIT** option that removes all the elements of a multiline between two specified points.
14. Name the **MLEDIT** option that repairs all cuts in a multiline between two selected points.
15. Name the command that can be used to create a true spline.
16. How do you accept the AutoCAD defaults for the start and end tangents of a spline?
17. Name the **SPLINE** command option that allows you to turn a spline-fitted polyline into a true spline.
18. Name the command that allows you to edit splines.
19. What is the purpose of the **Add** suboption of the **Fit data** option of the **SPLINEDIT** command?
20. What is the minimum number of fit points for a spline?
21. Name the **SPLINEDIT** option that allows you to move the fit points in a spline.
22. What is the purpose of the **Refine** option of the **SPLINEDIT** command?
23. Identify the **Refine** suboption of the **SPLINEDIT** command that lets you increase, but not decrease, the number of control points appearing on a spline curve.
24. Name the **Refine** suboption of the **SPLINEDIT** command that controls the pull exerted by a control point on a spline.
25. How many operations can you undo inside the **SPLINEDIT** command with the **Undo** option?

Drawing Problems

Start a new drawing for each of the following problems. Specify your own units, limits, and other settings to suit each problem.

1. Draw the objects shown using the **MLINE** command. Use the justification options indicated with each illustration. Set the limits to 11,8.5; grid spacing to .50; snap spacing to .25; and the offset for the multiline elements to .125. Do not add text or dimensions. Save the drawing as P15-1.

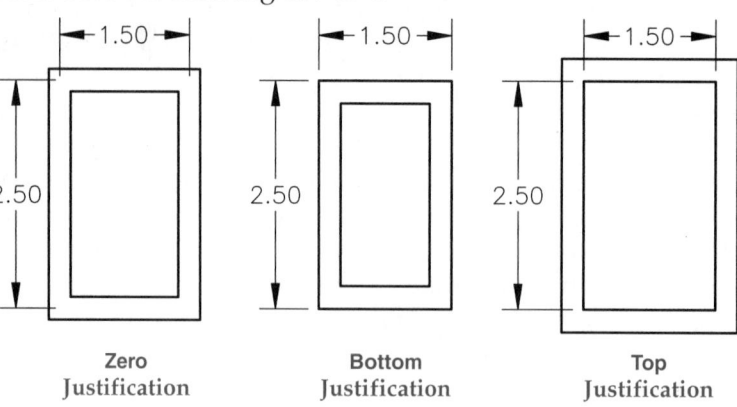

| Zero | Bottom | Top |
| Justification | Justification | Justification |

2. Draw the partial floor plan using the multiline commands. Carefully observe how the dimensions correlate with the multiline elements to determine your justification settings. Also, use the appropriate cap and multiline editing options. Use architectural units. Set the limits to 88",68"; grid spacing to 24"; and snap spacing to 12". Make all walls 6" thick. Do not add dimensions. Save the drawing as P15-2.

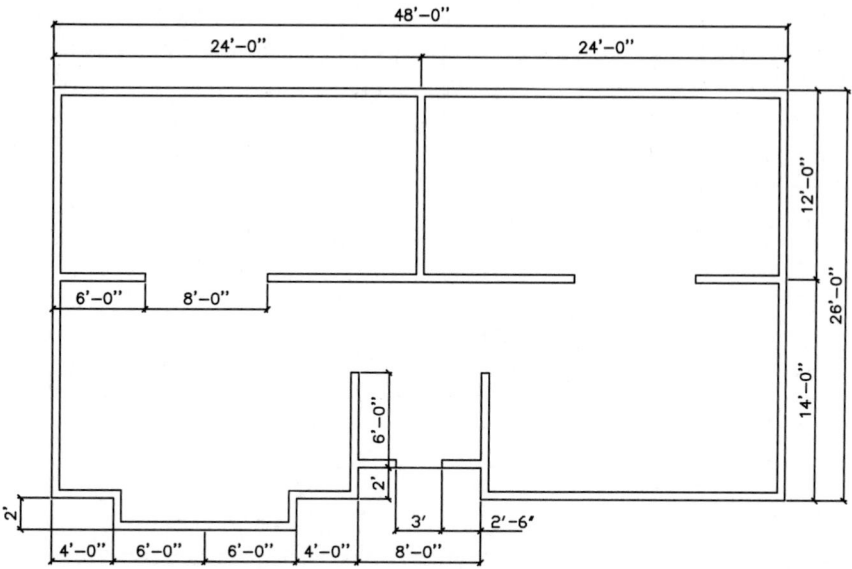

3. Draw the proposed subdivision map using the multiline commands. The roads are 30' wide. Use a centerline linetype for the center of each road. Adjust the linetype scale as needed. Do not include dimensions. Save the drawing as P15-3.

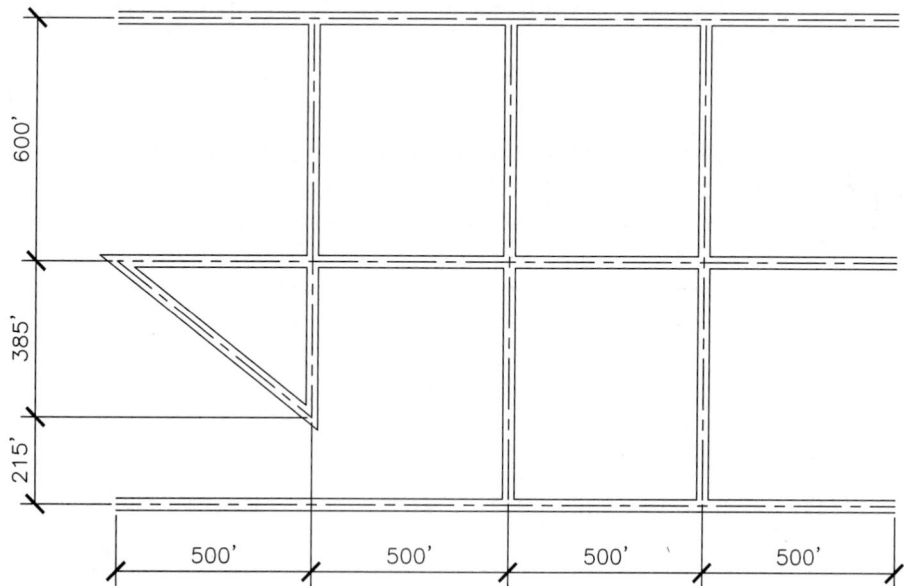

4. Draw the partial floor plan using multilines for the walls. Do not dimension the floor plan. Save the drawing as P15-4.

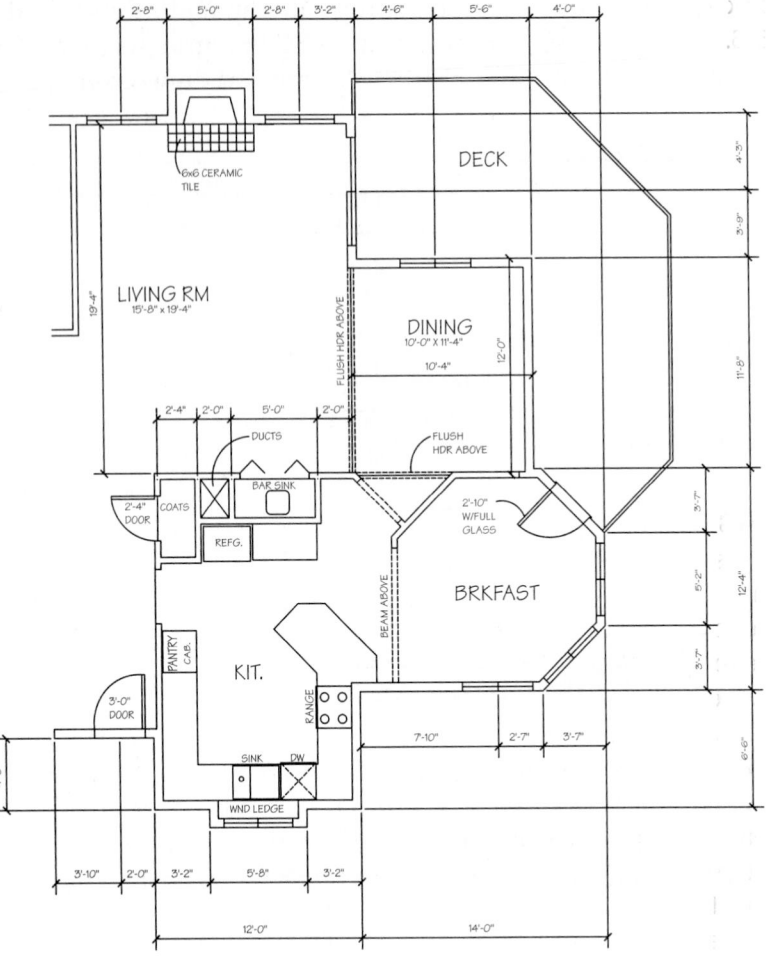

5. Draw the proposed electrical circuit using the multiline commands. Establish a line offset proportional to the given layout. Use a phantom linetype for the center of each run. Do not draw the grid, which is provided as a drawing aid. Save the drawing as P15-5.

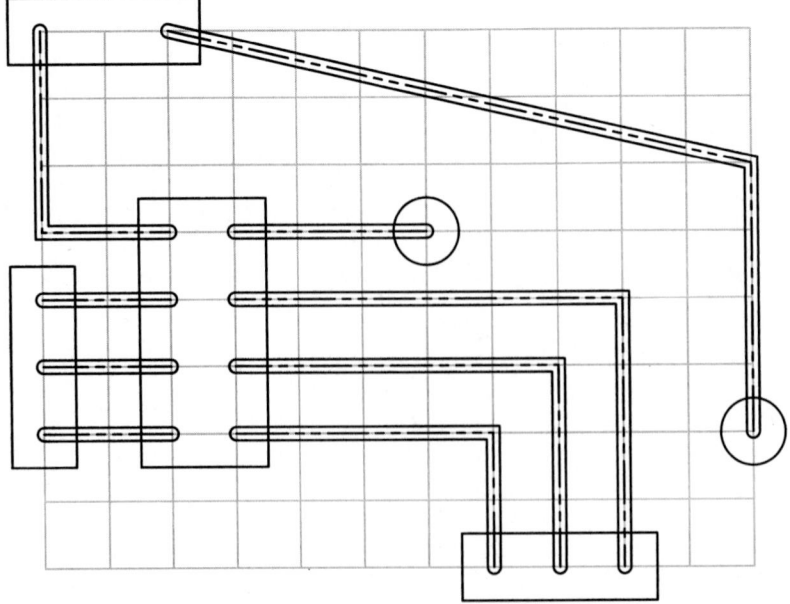

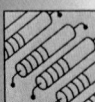

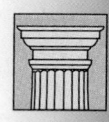

6. Use **SPLINE** and other commands, such as **ELLIPSE**, **MIRROR**, and **OFFSET**, to design an architectural door knocker similar to the one shown. Use an appropriate text command and font to place your initials in the center. Save the drawing as P15-6.

7. Use the **SPLINE** command to draw the curve for the cam displacement diagram below. Use the following guidelines and the given drawing to complete this problem:
   A. The total rise equals 2.000.
   B. The total displacement can be any length.
   C. Divide the total displacement into 30° increments.
   D. Draw a half circle divided into 6 equal parts on one end.
   E. Draw a horizontal line from each division of the half circle to the other end of the diagram.
   F. Draw the displacement curve with the **SPLINE** command by picking points where the horizontal and vertical lines cross.
   G. Label the displacement increments along the horizontal scale as shown. Save the drawing as P15-7.

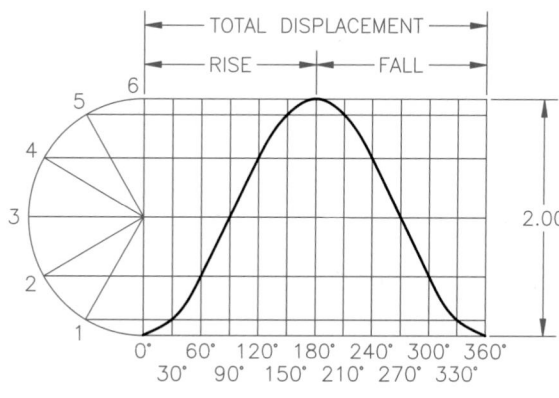

8. Draw a spline similar to the original spline shown below. Copy the spline seven times to create a layout similar to the one given. Perform the **SPLINEDIT** operations identified under each of the seven copies. Save the drawing as P15-8.

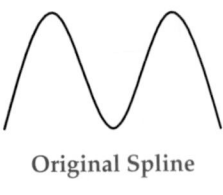

Original Spline

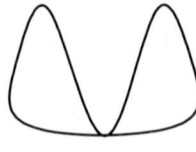

Close

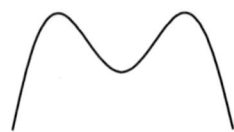

Move a Control Point

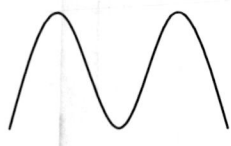

Elevate the Order to 10

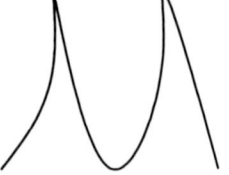

Add Two Control Points

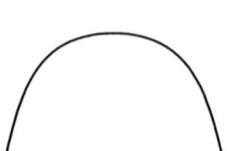

Delete a Control Point

Edit the Tangents

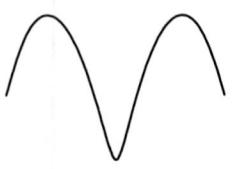

Increase the Weight of a Control Point to 4

Dimension Styles and Linear Dimensioning

Learning Objectives

After completing this chapter, you will be able to do the following:

✓ Use AutoCAD dimensioning commands to dimension objects to ASME and other drafting standards.
✓ Create and use dimension styles.
✓ Place general notes on drawings.
✓ Add linear and angular dimensions to a drawing.
✓ Insert common drafting symbols within dimension text.
✓ Draw datum and chain dimensions.
✓ Add dimensions for multiple items using the **QDIM** command.

Dimensions are placed on a drawing to describe the size, shape, and location of features on an object or structure. A dimension may consist of numerical values, lines, symbols, and notes. Typical AutoCAD dimensioning features and applications are shown in **Figure 16-1.**

AutoCAD's dimensioning functions provide you with unlimited flexibility. Dimension styles allow you to control the height, width, style, and spacing of the individual components of a dimension. Dimension commands allow you to dimension linear distances, circles, and arcs. You can also add specific notes using leaders.

When you dimension objects with AutoCAD, the objects are automatically measured exactly as you have drawn them. This makes it important for you to draw original objects and features accurately. Use object snap modes to your best advantage when dimensioning.

This textbook covers the comprehensive elements of AutoCAD dimensioning in five chapters. This chapter covers fundamental standards and practices for linear dimensioning. Chapter 17 covers techniques for dimensioning features, as well as alternate dimensioning practices. Chapter 18 covers editing procedures for dimensions. Chapter 19 covers dimensioning applications with tolerances. Chapter 20 introduces geometric dimensioning and tolerancing practices.

dimensions:
Descriptions of the size, shape, and location of features on an object or structure.

Figure 16-1.
Dimensions describe size and location. Follow accepted conventions when dimensioning.

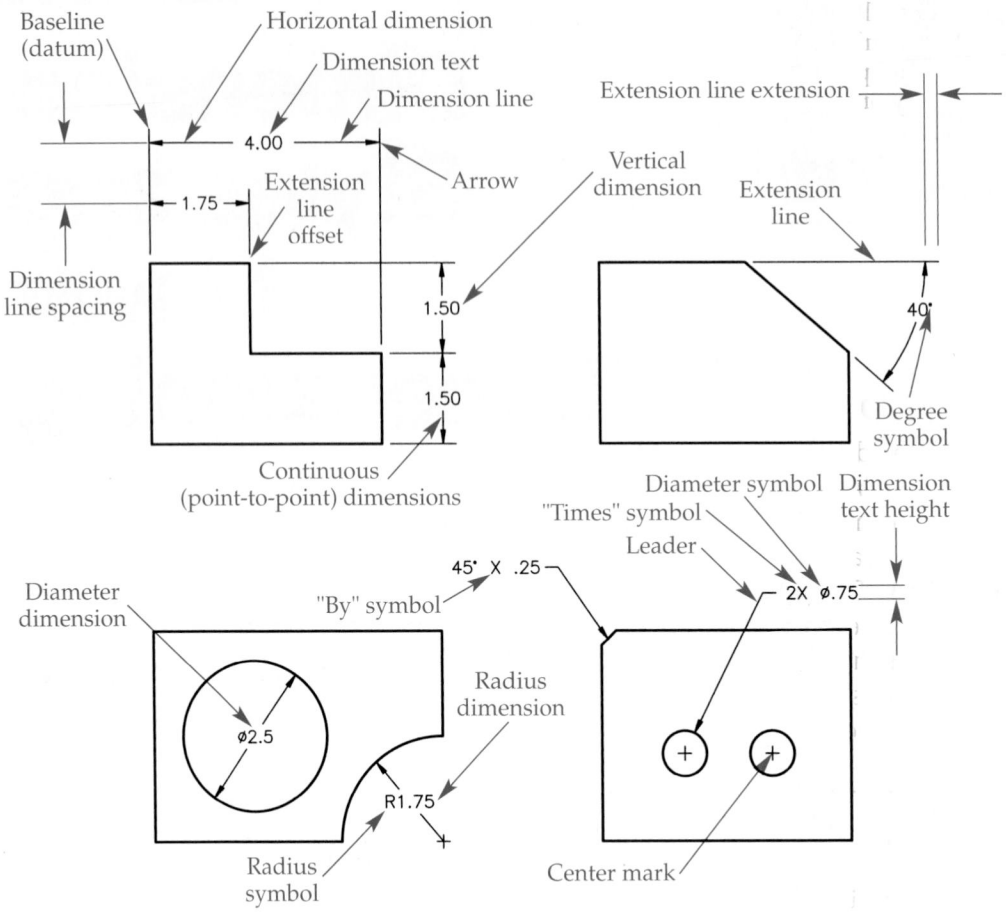

Dimension Standards

Dimensions communicate information about the drawing. Each drafting field, such as mechanical, architectural, civil, and electronics, uses a different type of dimensioning technique. It is important for a drafter to place dimensions in accordance with industry and company standards. The standard emphasized in this text is ASME Y14.5M-1994, *Dimensioning and Tolerancing*. The *M* in Y14.5M means the standard is written with metric numeric values for dimensions. ASME Y14.5M-1994 is published by the American Society of Mechanical Engineers (ASME). This text describes the correct application of both inch and metric dimensioning.

Unidirectional Dimensioning

Unidirectional dimensioning is typically used in the mechanical drafting field. The term *unidirectional* means "in one direction." In **unidirectional dimensioning**, all dimension numbers and notes are placed horizontally on the drawing. The dimensions are read from the bottom of the sheet.

Unidirectional dimensions normally have arrowheads on the ends of dimension lines. The dimension number is usually centered in a break near the center of the dimension line. See **Figure 16-2.**

unidirectional dimensioning: A dimensioning system in which all dimensions and numbers are placed horizontally on the drawing.

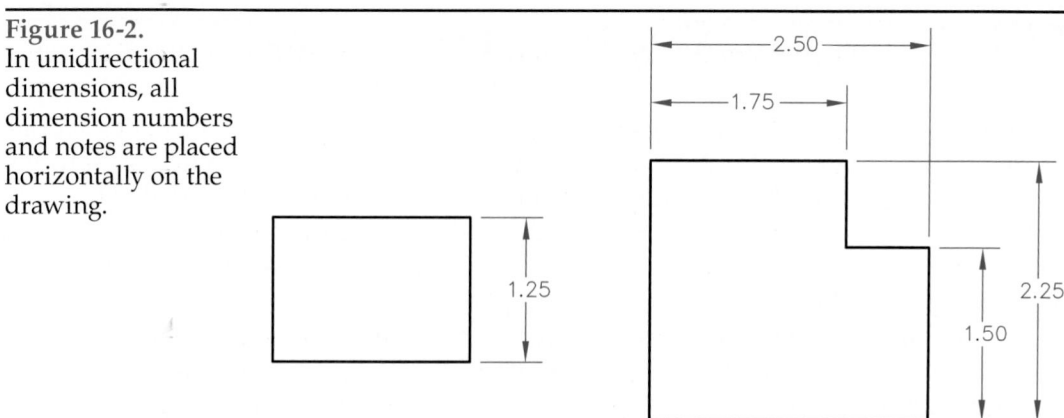

Figure 16-2.
In unidirectional dimensions, all dimension numbers and notes are placed horizontally on the drawing.

Aligned Dimensioning

Aligned dimensions are typically placed on architectural and structural drawings. In *aligned dimensioning*, the dimension numbers are lined up with the dimension lines. The dimension text for horizontal dimensions reads horizontally. Dimension text for vertical dimensions is placed so it reads from the right side of the sheet. See **Figure 16-3**. Text for dimensions placed at an angle reads at the same angle as the dimension line. Notes are usually placed so they read horizontally.

When using the aligned system, terminate dimension lines with tick marks, dots, or arrowheads. In architectural drafting, the dimension number is generally placed above the dimension line and tick marks are used as terminators. See **Figure 16-4**.

aligned dimensioning: A dimension system in which the dimension numbers line up with the dimension lines.

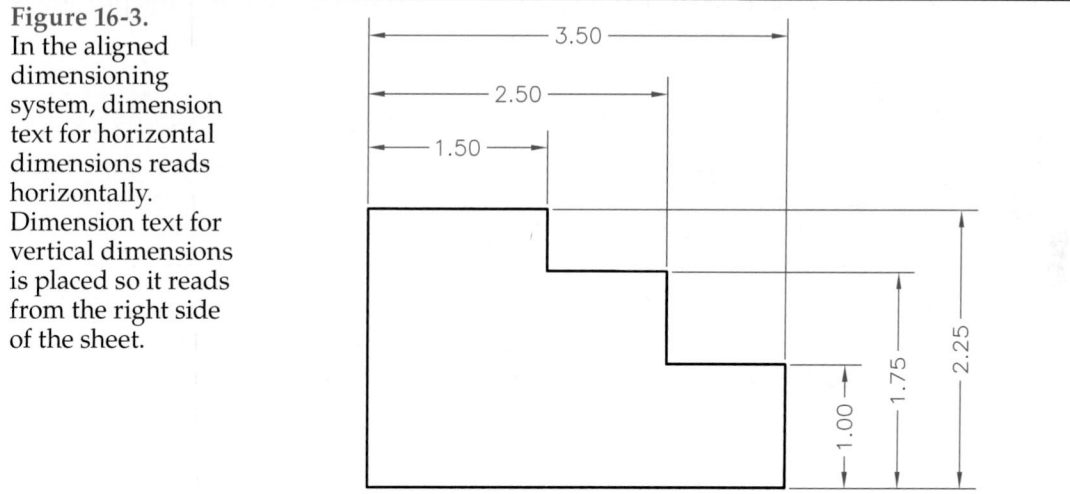

Figure 16-3.
In the aligned dimensioning system, dimension text for horizontal dimensions reads horizontally. Dimension text for vertical dimensions is placed so it reads from the right side of the sheet.

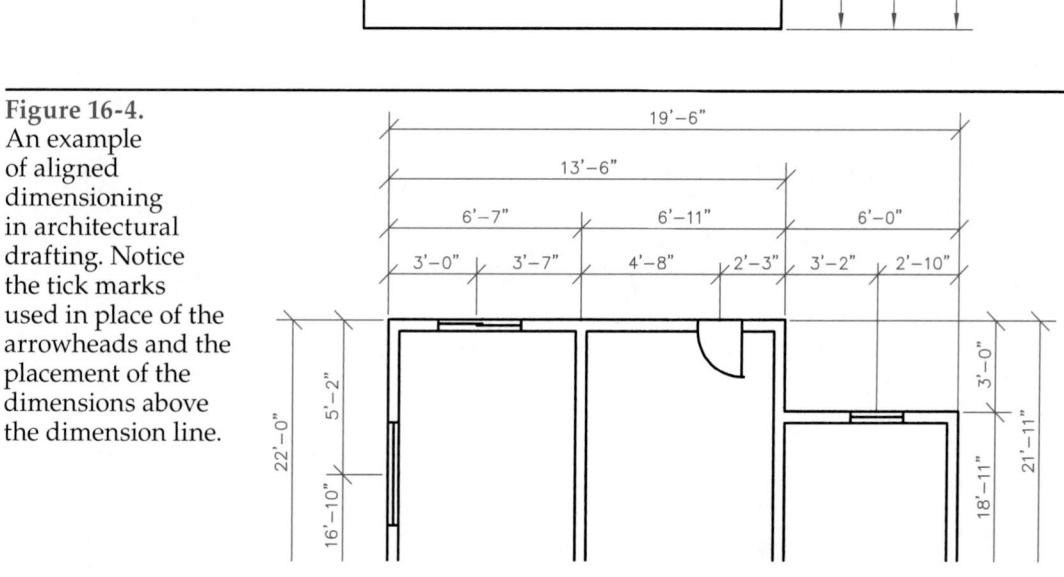

Figure 16-4.
An example of aligned dimensioning in architectural drafting. Notice the tick marks used in place of the arrowheads and the placement of the dimensions above the dimension line.

Ideally, drawing scale, scale factors, and size of dimension characteristics should be determined before beginning a drawing. They are best incorporated as settings within your template drawing files, but they can be changed as needed. The scale factor of a drawing is important because this value is used to make sure dimension characteristics, such as the height of dimension text, is shown on-screen and plotted at the proper size. To help understand the concept of drawing scale, look at the portion of a floor plan shown in **Figure 16-5**. Everything drawn in model space is drawn at full-scale. This means that the bathtub, for example, is actually drawn 5′ long. However, this becomes an issue when adding dimensions, because dimension characteristics are drawn at full scale. For example, 1/8″ dimension text is extremely small compared to the other full-scale objects, as shown in **Figure 16-5A**. To display the text properly, you must adjust the size of dimension characteristics according to the drawing scale, as shown in **Figure 16-5B**. This involves finding the scale factor. The scale factor can be calculated manually and applied to a dimension style, or it can be adjusted by AutoCAD using annotative functionality.

Scaling Dimensions Manually

To adjust the size of dimension features manually according to a specific drawing scale, you must first calculate the drawing scale factor. The scale factor is then multiplied by the desired plotted dimension size to get the model space dimension size. This calculation can be applied to each dimension automatically by entering the scale factor in the **Fit** tab of the **New** (or **Modify**) **Dimension Style** dialog box. This process is described later in this chapter.

> **NOTE**
>
> Refer to Chapter 9 for information on determining the drawing scale factor.

Figure 16-5.
An example of a portion of a floor plan drawn at full scale in model space. If dimensions are drawn at full scale, as shown in A, the dimensions are very small compared to the large objects. The dimensions must be scaled, as shown in B, in order to be seen and plotted correctly.

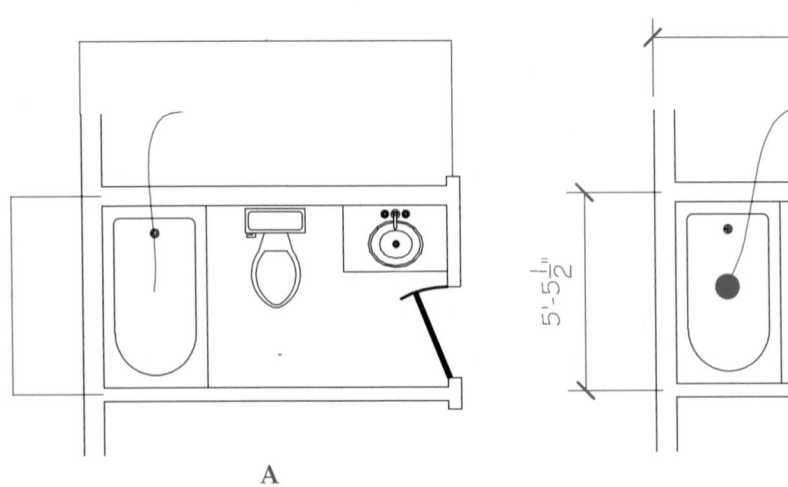

A

B

Annotative Dimensions

AutoCAD scales annotative dimensions according to the annotation scale you select, which is the same as the drawing scale, eliminating the need for you to calculate the scale factor. When you select an annotation scale, AutoCAD determines the scale factor and automatically applies it to annotative dimensions or annotative objects. For example, if you scale dimensions manually at a drawing scale of 1/4″ = 1′-0″, or a scale factor of 48, you must enter 48 in the **Fit** tab of the **New** (or **Modify**) **Dimension Style** dialog box. If you place annotative dimensions, using this example, you set an annotation scale of 1/4″ = 1′-0″. Then, when annotative dimensions are added, AutoCAD scales them automatically according to the 1/4″ = 1′-0″ annotation scale.

Annotative dimensions offer several advantages over manually scaled dimensions, including the ability to control the scale of dimension features based on annotation scale, not scale factor. Using annotative dimensions is especially effective when objects viewed at different scales are placed on a single sheet, and when drawing scale changes.

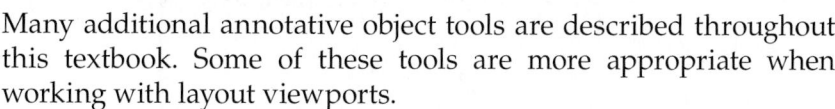

PROFESSIONAL TIP

If you anticipate preparing scaled drawings, you should become familiar with annotative dimensions and use them instead of traditional manual scaling. However, scale factor does influence other non-annotative items on a drawing and is still an important value to identify and use throughout the drawing process.

Setting annotation scale

Annotation scale should be set before you begin adding dimensions, so that the dimension characteristics are automatically scaled. However, this is not always possible. It may be necessary to adjust the annotation scale throughout the drawing process, especially if multiple drawings at different scales are prepared on one sheet. This chapter approaches annotation scaling in model space only, by first selecting the desired annotation scale and then placing dimensions. When dimensions at another scale are to be added, pick the new annotation scale, and then place the dimension.

NOTE

Many additional annotative object tools are described throughout this textbook. Some of these tools are more appropriate when working with layout viewports.

The **Annotation Scale** flyout button located on the status bar is the primary tool for adjusting annotation scale. See **Figure 16-6**. Pick the desired annotation scale, which is typically the same as the drawing scale, from the menu. If a certain scale is not available, choose the **Custom...** option to access the **Edit Scale List** dialog box. See **Figure 16-7**.

NOTE

The **CANNOSCALE** system variable can also be used to set the annotation scale.

Figure 16-6.
Annotation scale
options can be found
on the status bar.

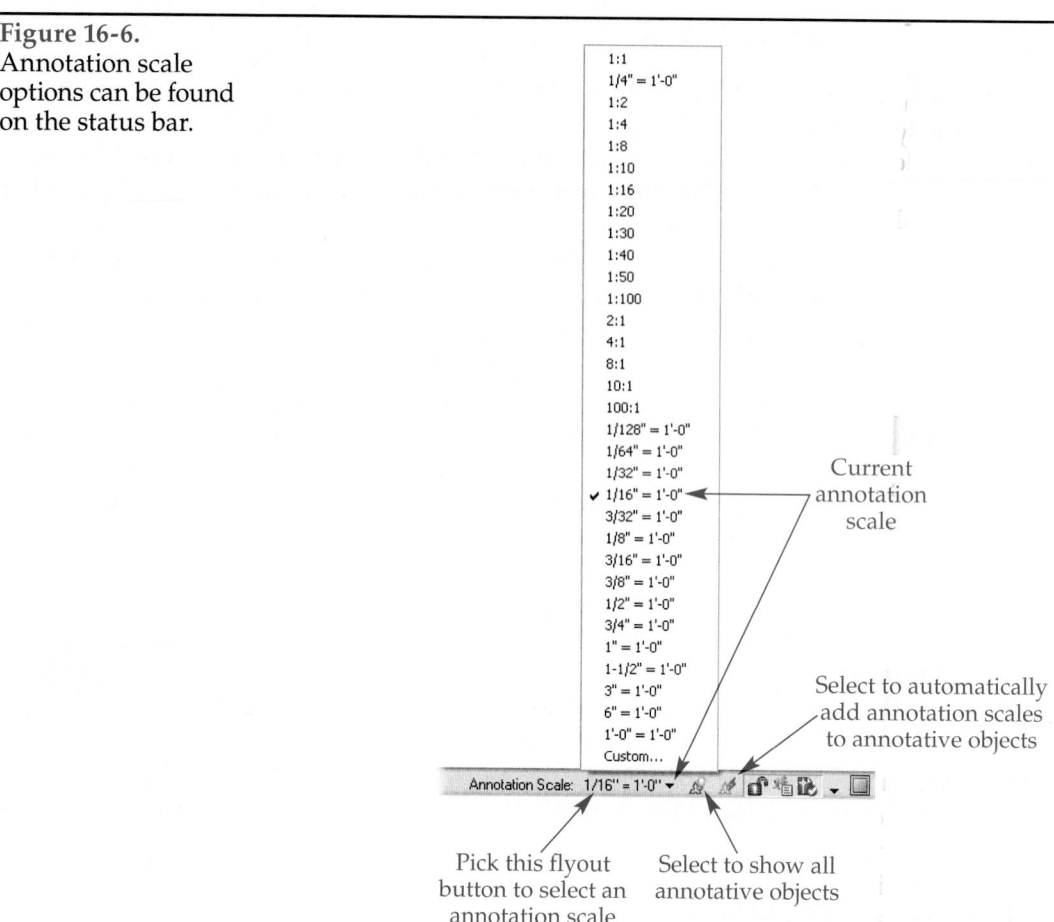

Current
annotation
scale

Select to automatically
add annotation scales
to annotative objects

Pick this flyout
button to select an
annotation scale

Select to show all
annotative objects

Figure 16-7.
The **Edit Scale List**
dialog box is used to
modify the display
of the annotation
scale list and to add
annotation scales.

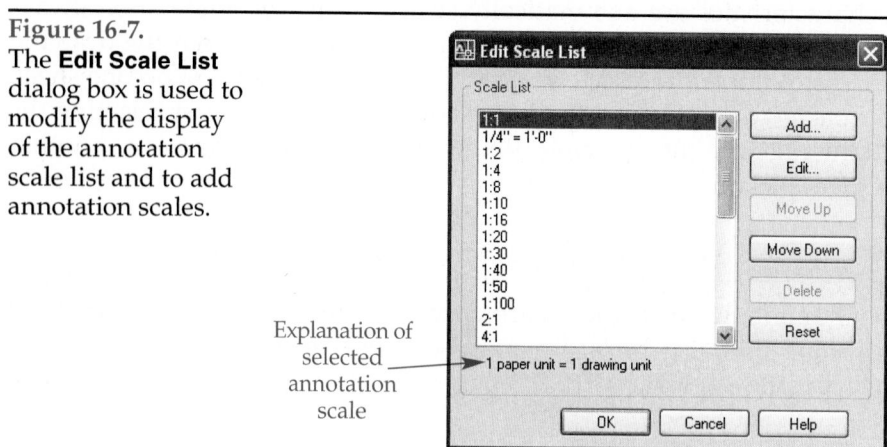

Explanation of
selected
annotation
scale

In the **Edit Scale List** dialog box, you can move the highlighted scale up or down in the list by picking the **Move Up** or **Move Down** button. To remove the highlighted scale from the list, pick the **Delete** button, or to modify it, pick the **Edit...** button. Selecting **Edit...** opens the **Edit Scale** dialog box, as shown in **Figure 16-8.** Here you can change the name of the scale and adjust the scale by entering the paper and drawing units. For example, a scale of 1/4″ = 1′-0″ uses a paper units value of .25 or 1 and a drawing units value of 12 or 48. To create a new annotation scale, pick the **Add...** button in the **Edit Scale List** dialog box to display the **Add Scale** dialog box, which functions the same as the **Edit Scale** dialog box previously described. Pick the **Reset** button to restore the default annotation scale. Once the annotation scale is set current, you are ready to place dimensions that are created at the correct size automatically according to the drawing scale.

Figure 16-8.
The **Edit Scale** dialog box can be used to modify the name and scale of the selected annotation scale.

Change the scale's name →

Change the scale's values →

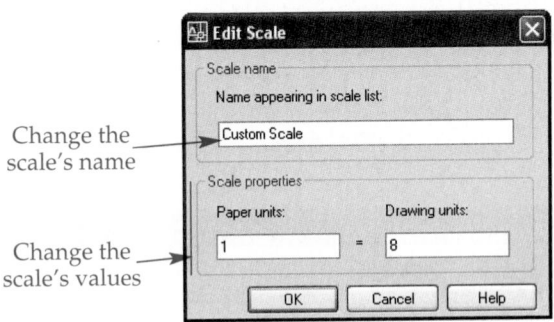

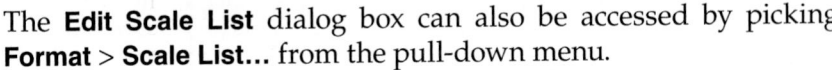

NOTE

The **Edit Scale List** dialog box can also be accessed by picking **Format** > **Scale List...** from the pull-down menu.

AutoCAD Dimension Styles

The appearance of dimensions, from the size and the style of the text to the color of the dimension line, is controlled by many different settings. *Dimension styles* are saved configurations of these settings.

A dimension style is created by changing the dimension settings as needed to achieve the desired appearance for the drafting application. For example, a dimension style used for mechanical drafting probably has the Romans text font placed in a break in the dimension line, and the dimension lines are probably terminated with arrowheads. Refer to **Figure 16-2**. The dimension style for architectural drafting may use the CityBlueprint or Stylus BT text font placed above the dimension line, and dimension lines may be terminated with slashes. Refer to **Figure 16-4**.

You might think of dimension styles as the dimensioning standards you use. Dimension styles are usually established for a specific type of drafting field or application. You can customize dimension styles to correspond to drafting standards such as ASME/ANSI, International Organization for Standardization (ISO), military (MIL), architectural, structural, or civil standards, or your own school or company standards.

Some drawings only require a single dimension style because of AutoCAD's ability to control all dimension characteristics using one dimension style. However, you may have multiple dimension styles depending on the variety of dimensions displayed in your drawing and different characteristics used. Dimension characteristics can be overridden for individual dimensions. However, you should generally create a dimension style for each unique dimensioning requirement. Dimension styles should be added to drawing templates for repeated use.

> **dimension styles:** Saved configurations of settings for the appearance of dimensions.

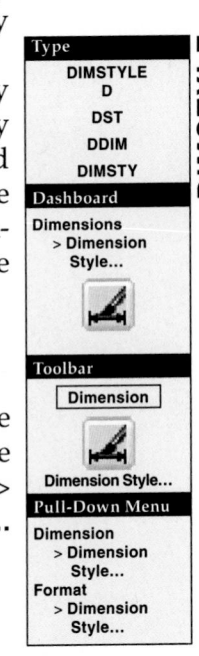

Working with Dimension Styles

Dimension styles are created using the **Dimension Style Manager** dialog box. See **Figure 16-9**. This dialog box is accessed by picking the **Dimension Style...** button on the **Dimension** toolbar or the **Dimension** control panel in the **Dashboard**, selecting **Format** > **Dimension Style...** in the pull-down menu, or selecting **Dimension** > **Dimension Style...** in the pull-down menu. You can also type D, DST, DDIM, DIMSTY, or DIMSTYLE.

Figure 16-9.
The **Dimension Style Manager** dialog box. The non-annotative dimension style Standard and the annotative dimension style Annotative are available by default.

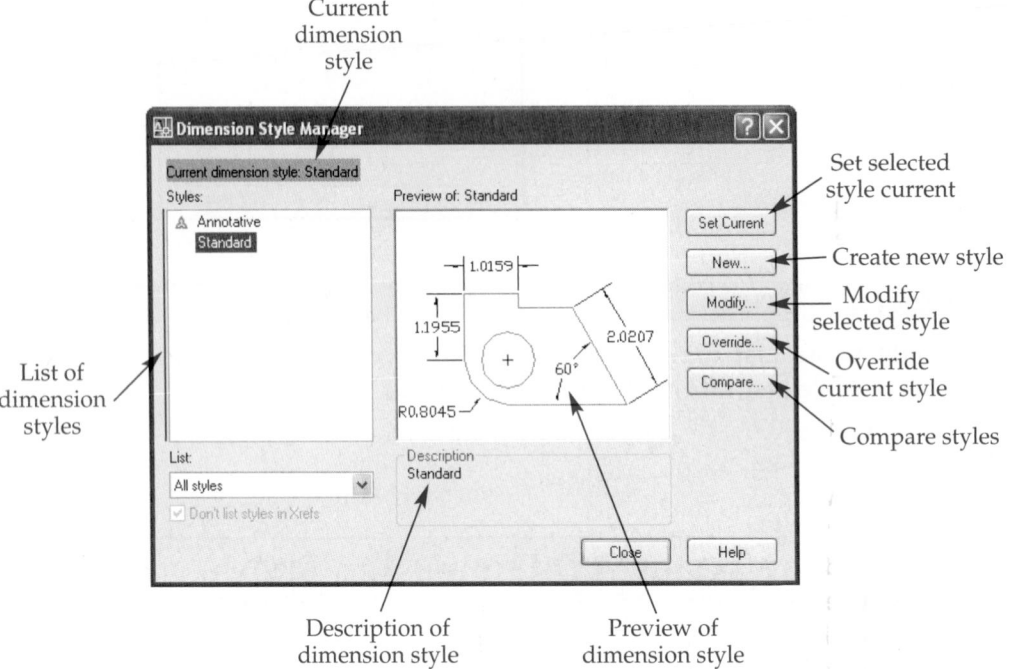

Current dimension style

Set selected style current

Create new style

Modify selected style

Override current style

Compare styles

List of dimension styles

Description of dimension style

Preview of dimension style

The current dimension style, which is initially a non-annotative style named Standard, is noted at the top of the **Dimension Style Manager** dialog box. An annotative dimension style named Annotative is also available. The **Styles:** box displays the dimension styles found within the current drawing. You can make a dimension style current by double-clicking the style name; right-clicking on the name and selecting the **Set current** option; or picking the name and selecting the **Current** button. When a dimension style is current, all new dimensions are created in that style. Existing dimensions are not affected by a change to the current style.

The selection in the **List:** drop-down list controls whether all styles or only the styles in use are displayed in the **Styles:** box. If there are external reference drawings (xrefs) within the current drawing, the **Don't list styles in Xrefs** box can be checked to eliminate xref-dependent dimension styles from the **Styles:** box. This is often valuable because xref dimension styles cannot be set current, and they cannot be used to create new dimensions. External references are described in Chapter 28.

The **Description** area and **Preview of:** image provide information about the selected dimension style. If you change any of the AutoCAD default dimension settings without first creating a new dimension style, the changes are automatically stored in a dimension style override.

Creating a New Dimension Style

To create a new dimension style, first select an existing dimension style from the **Styles** list box that will be used as a base for formatting the new dimension style. Then pick the **New...** button in the **Dimension Style Manager**. This opens the **Create New Dimension Style** dialog box. See **Figure 16-10.** The following options are available in this dialog box:

- **New Style Name.** Contains the name of the new style. Give your new dimension style a descriptive name, such as Architectural or Mechanical.
- **Start With.** Saves time by basing the settings for a new style on an existing dimension style.

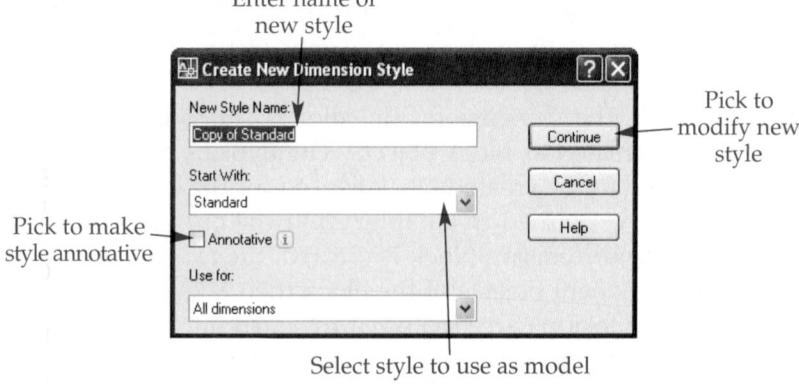

- **Annotative.** Makes the dimension style annotative. The dimension style can also be made annotative by selecting the **Annotative** check box in the **Fit** tab of the **New** (or **Modify**) **Dimension Style** dialog box.
- **Use for.** Specifies the dimensions to which the new style will be applied. The choices are **All dimensions**, **Linear dimensions**, **Angular dimensions**, **Radius dimensions**, **Diameter dimensions**, **Ordinate dimensions**, and **Leaders and Tolerances**. Use the **All dimensions** option to create a new dimension style. If you select one of the other options, you create a "substyle" of the dimension style specified in the **Start With:** text box.
- **Continue.** Accesses the **New Dimension Style** dialog box so that you can adjust dimension style characteristics.

The **New Dimension Style** dialog box is shown in **Figure 16-11.** The **Lines**, **Symbols and Arrows**, **Text**, **Fit**, **Primary Units**, **Alternate Units**, and **Tolerances** tabs access the settings used for changing the way dimensions are displayed. These tabs are described in the next sections. After completing the information in all tabs, pick the **OK** button to return to the **Dimension Style Manager** dialog box.

Figure 16-11.
The **Lines** tab of the **New Dimension Style** dialog box.

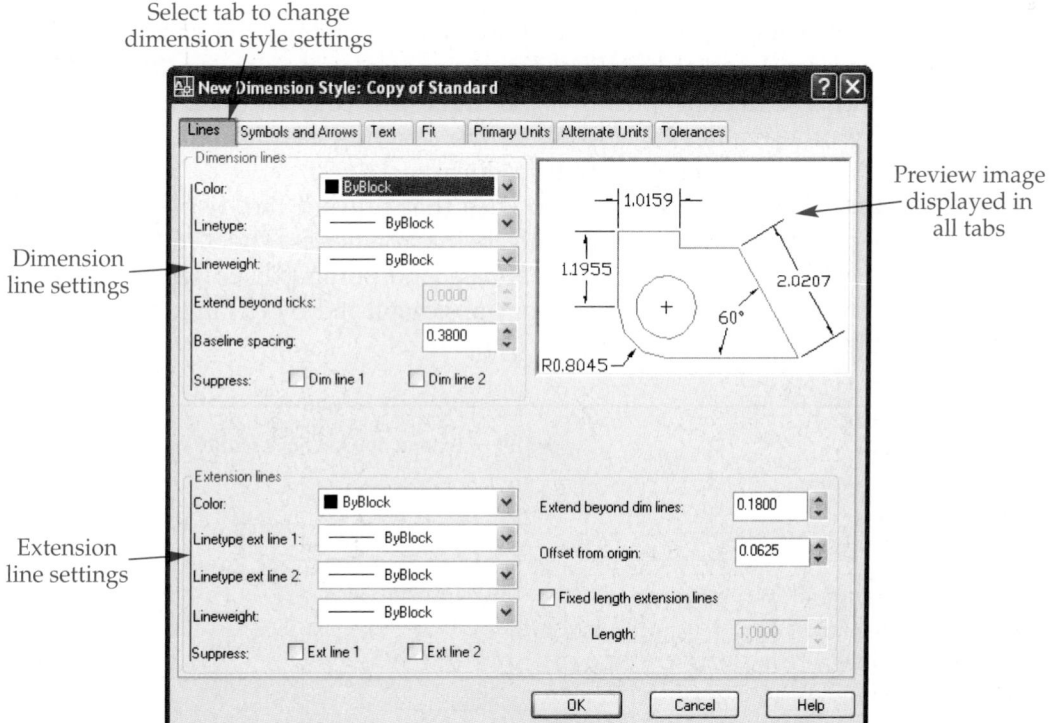

Using the Lines Tab

The **Lines** tab of the **New** (or **Modify**) **Dimension Style** dialog box controls all settings for the display of the dimension and extension lines. See **Figure 16-11**. The **Dimension lines** area is used to change the format of the dimension line with the following settings:

- **Color.** By default, the dimension line color is set to ByBlock. All associative dimensions are created as block objects. The ByBlock color setting means that the color assigned to the created block is used for the component objects of the block. Blocks are explained in Chapter 23. If the current entity color is set to ByLayer when the dimension block is created, then it comes in with a ByLayer setting. The component objects of the block then take on the color of the layer on which the dimensions are created. If the current object color is an absolute color, then the component objects of the block take on that specific color regardless of the layer on which the dimension was created.

- **Linetype.** By default, the dimension line linetype is set to ByBlock. To change the dimension style, select the drop-down list button. The currently loaded linetypes are available from the list. To use one of these, select it from the list. To use a linetype not in the list, pick the **Other...** option to open the **Select Linetype** dialog box. Linetypes are described in Chapter 5.

- **Lineweight.** By default, the dimension line lineweight is set to ByBlock. If the current object lineweight is set to ByLayer when the dimension block is created, then it comes in with a ByLayer setting. The component objects of the block then take on the lineweight of the layer on which the dimensions are created. If the current object lineweight is an absolute lineweight, the component objects of the block take on that specific lineweight regardless of the layer on which the dimension was created.

- **Extend beyond ticks.** This text box is inactive unless you are using tick marks instead of arrowheads. Architectural tick marks or oblique arrowheads are often used for dimensions on architectural drawings. In this style of dimensioning, the dimension lines often cross extension lines. The extension represents how far the dimension line extends beyond the extension line. See **Figure 16-12**. The 0.00 default is used to draw dimensions that do not extend past the extension lines.

- **Baseline spacing.** This text box allows you to change the spacing between the dimension lines of baseline dimensions created with the **DIMBASELINE** command. The default spacing is .38 units, which is too close for most drawings. Try other values to help make the drawing easy to read. **Figure 16-13** shows the default dimension line spacing.

- **Suppress.** This option has two toggles that prevent the display of the first, second, or both dimension lines and their arrowheads. The **Dim line 1** and **Dim line 2** check boxes refer to the first and second points picked when the dimension is created. Both dimension lines are displayed by default. The results of using these options are shown in **Figure 16-14**.

Figure 16-12.
Using the **Extend beyond ticks** setting to allow the dimension line to extend past the extension line. With the default value of 0, the dimension line does not extend.

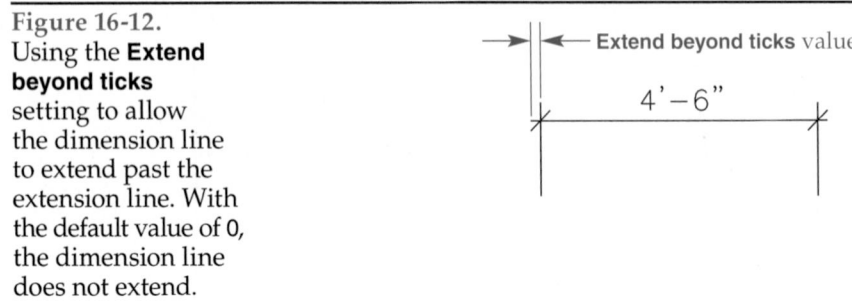

Figure 16-13.
The **Baseline spacing** setting controls the spacing between dimension lines.

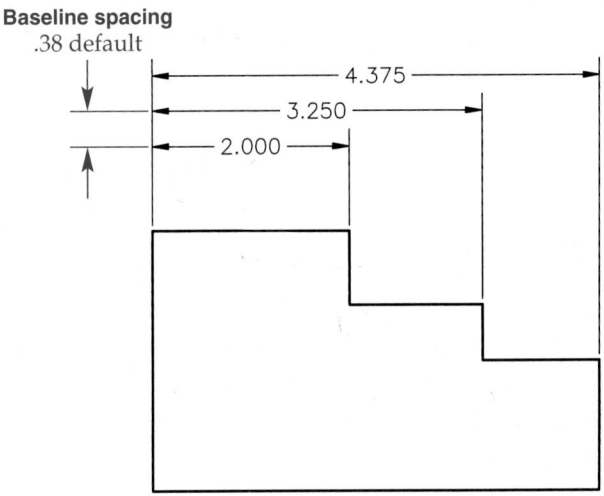

Figure 16-14.
Using the **Dim line 1** and **Dim line 2** dimensioning settings. "Off" is equivalent to an unchecked **Suppress** check box in the **Lines** tab.

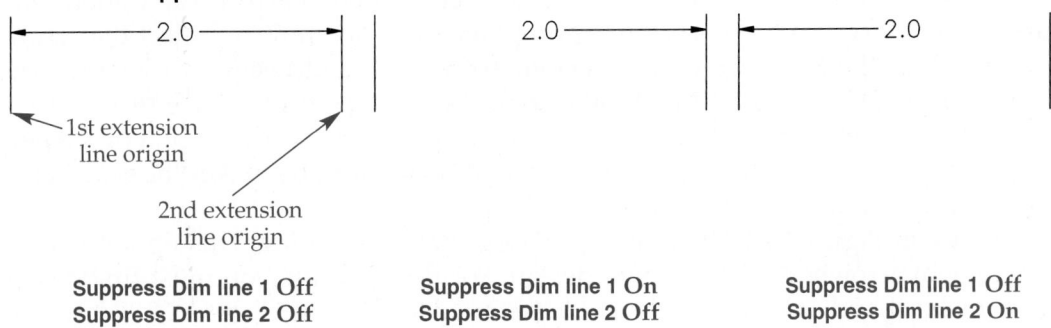

The **Extension lines** area of the **Lines** tab is used to change the format of the extension lines with the following dimension settings:

- **Color.** Controls the extension line color. The default value is ByBlock.
- **Linetype ext line 1.** Specifies the linetype to be used for the first extension line. The first extension line is determined by the first point picked when the dimension is created.
- **Linetype ext line 2.** Determines the linetype of the second extension line.
- **Lineweight.** Controls the lineweight of the extension lines.
- **Extend beyond dim lines.** Sets the distance the extension line runs past the last dimension line. See **Figure 16-15.** The default value is .18; an extension line extension of .125 is common on most drawings.
- **Offset from origin.** Changes the distance between the object and the beginning of the extension line. See **Figure 16-15.** Most applications require this small offset. The default is .0625. When an extension line meets a centerline, use a setting of 0.0 to prevent a gap.
- **Fixed length extension lines.** Sets a given length for extension lines. When this option is checked, the **Length** text box becomes active. The value in this text box is used to set a restricted length for the extension lines. The length is measured from the dimension line toward the extension line origin.
- **Length.** Sets a fixed length for extension lines. This option is activated when the **Fixed length extension lines** option is turned on.

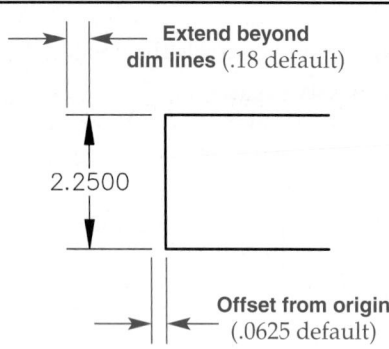

Figure 16-15.
The extension line extension and the extension line offset settings.

Extend beyond
dim lines (.18 default)

2.2500

Offset from origin
(.0625 default)

- **Suppress.** Suppresses the first, second, or both extension lines using the **Ext line 1** and **Ext line 2** check boxes. Extension lines are displayed by default. An extension line might be suppressed, for example, if it coincides with an object line. See **Figure 16-16.**

Using the Symbols and Arrows Tab

The settings in the **Symbols and Arrows** tab are used to control the appearance of arrowheads, center marks, and other symbol components of dimensions. See **Figure 16-17.** The **Arrowheads** area provides several different arrowhead options and controls the arrowhead size. Use the appropriate drop-down list to select the arrowhead used for the **First** arrowhead, **Second** arrowhead, and **Leader** arrowhead. The default arrowhead is closed filled; other options are shown in **Figure 16-18.** Check your drafting standards and then select the appropriate arrowhead. If you pick a new arrowhead in the **First:** drop-down list, AutoCAD automatically makes the same selection for the **Second:** drop-down list.

Notice in **Figure 16-18** there is no example of a user arrow. This option is used to access an arrowhead of your own design. For this to work, you must first design an arrowhead and save it as a block. Blocks are described in Chapter 23. When you pick **User Arrow...** in an **Arrowheads** drop-down list, the **Select Custom Arrow Block** dialog box is displayed. Type the name of your custom arrow block in the **Select from Drawing Blocks:** text box or pick a block from the drop-down list and then pick **OK** to specify the arrow for the style.

When you select the oblique or architectural tick arrowhead, the **Extend beyond ticks:** text box in the **Lines** tab is activated. This allows you to enter a value for a dimension line projection beyond the extension line. The default value is zero, but some architectural companies like to project the dimension line past the extension line. Refer to **Figure 16-12.**

The **Arrow size:** text box allows you to change the size of arrowheads. The default value is .18. An arrowhead size of .125″ is common on mechanical drawings. **Figure 16-19** shows the arrowhead size value.

The **Center marks** area of the **Symbols and Arrows** tab allows you to select the way center marks are placed in circles and arcs. The options are:
- **None.** Provides for no center marks to be placed in circles and arcs.
- **Mark.** Places center marks without centerlines.
- **Line.** Places center marks and centerlines.

Figure 16-16.
Suppressing extension lines.

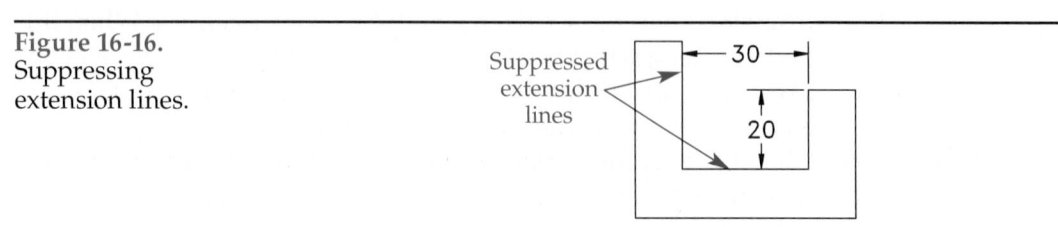

Suppressed extension lines

30

20

Figure 16-17.
The **Symbols and Arrows** tab of the **New Dimension Style** dialog box.

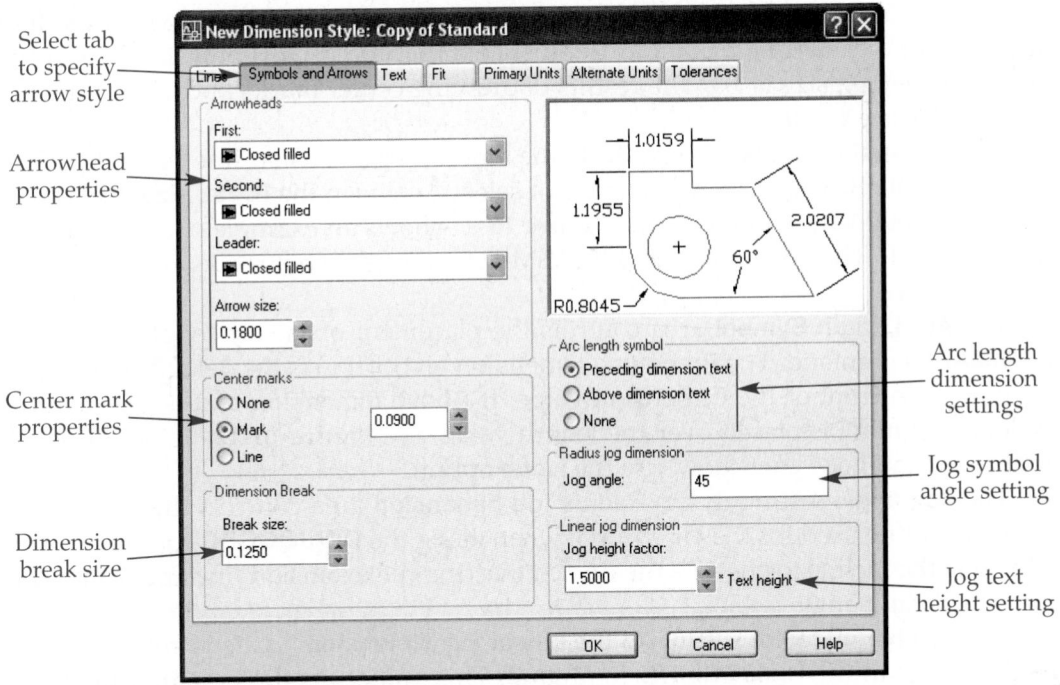

Figure 16-18.
Examples of dimensions drawn using the options found in the **Arrowheads** drop-down lists.

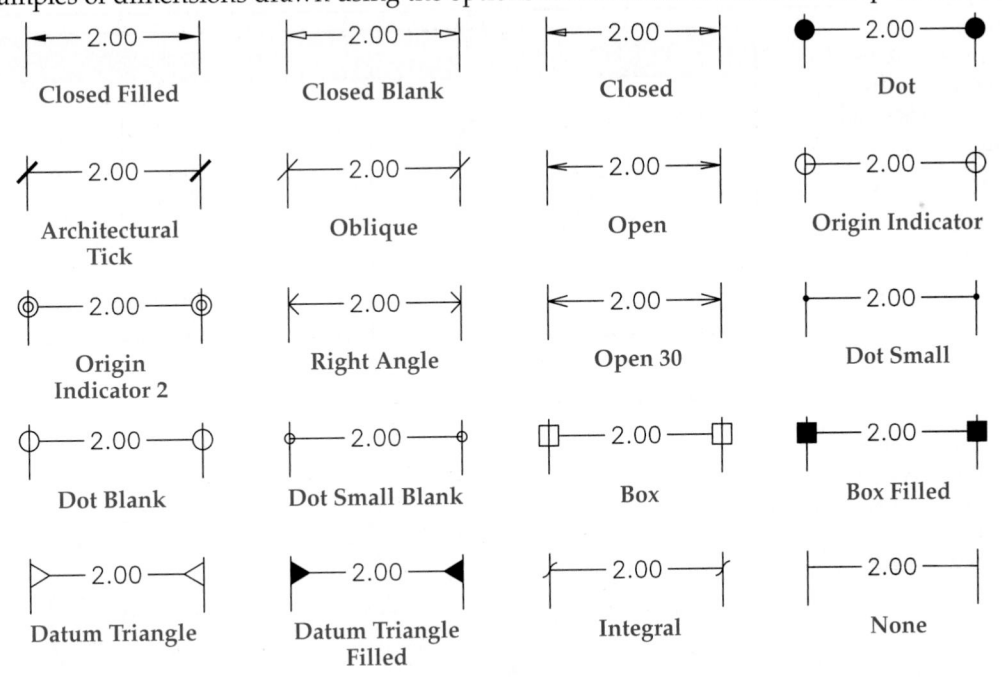

Figure 16-19.
The default arrow size is .18. ASME standards specify an arrowhead size of .125″.

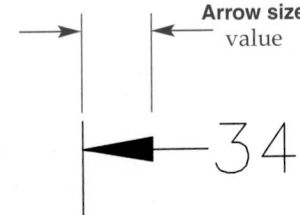

After selecting either the **Mark** or **Line** option, you can place center marks on circles and arcs by using the **DIMCENTER** command. The **Size:** text box in the **Center marks** area is used to change the size of the center mark and centerline. The size defines half the length of a centerline dash and the distance that the centerline extends past the object. The default size is .09. The results of drawing center marks and centerlines are shown in **Figure 16-20.**

The **Dimension Break** area controls the amount of extension line removed when you use the **DIMBREAK** command. Enter or select a value in the **Break size:** text box to specify the total length of the break. **Figure 16-21** shows an example of a 3 mm extension line break. The default size is .125. ASME standards do not recommend breaking extension lines.

The **Arc Length Symbol** area controls the placement of the arc length symbol in the **DIMARC** command. The **Preceding dimension text** option is the default. This places the symbol in front of the dimension value. If **Above dimension text** is selected, the arc length symbol is placed over the length value. See **Figure 16-22.** To suppress the symbol so that it does not show, use the **None** option.

The **Jog angle** setting in the **Radius jog dimension** area controls the appearance of the break line used for the jog symbol when using the **DIMJOGGED** command. This value sets the incline formed by the line connecting the extension line and dimension line. The default angle is 45°.

The **Jog height factor** setting in the **Linear jog dimension** area controls the size of break symbol in the **DIMJOGLINE** command. This value sets the height of the break symbol based on a multiple of the text height. For example, the default value of 1.5 creates a break symbol that is .18" tall if the text height is .12". The default angle is 45°.

Figure 16-20.
Arcs and circles displayed with center marks and centerlines.

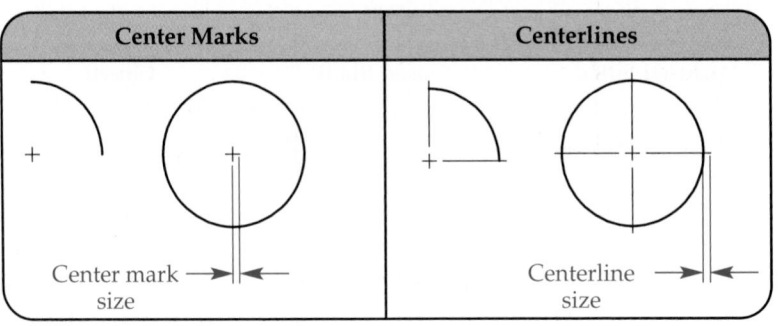

Figure 16-21.
Use the **Break size** setting to specify the length of the break created using the **DIMBREAK** command.

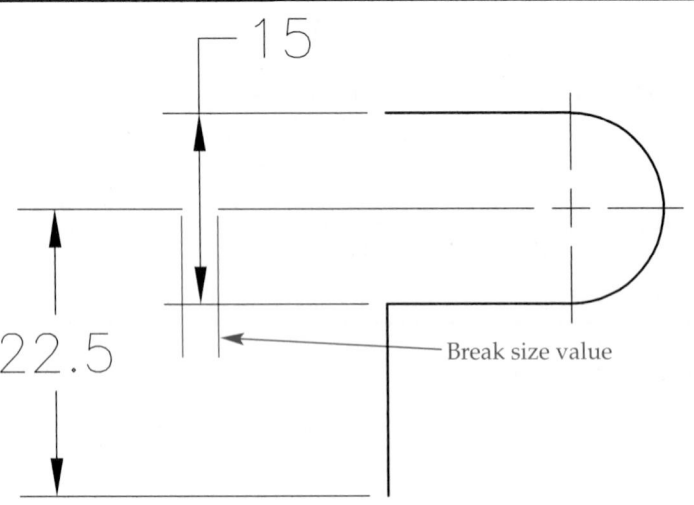

AutoCAD and Its Applications—Basics

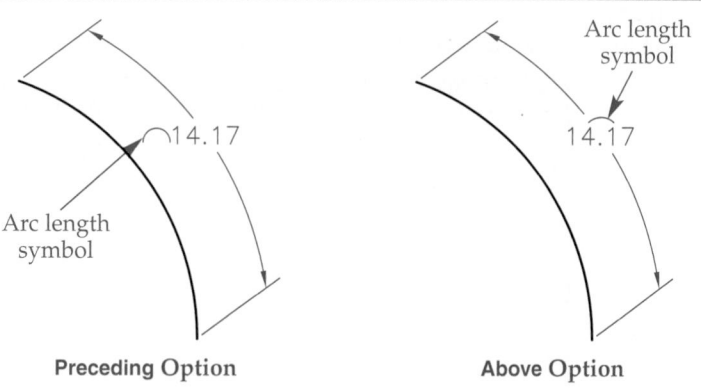

Figure 16-22.
The arc length symbol can be placed in front of or above the arc dimension text.

Arc length symbol

⌒14.17

Arc length symbol

14.17

Preceding Option

Above Option

NOTE

The values of dimension style settings are stored in AutoCAD system variables called *dimension variables*. For example, the center mark type setting in the **Center marks** area of the **Symbols and Arrows** tab is stored in the **DIMCEN** dimension variable. A change to a dimension style setting changes the current value of the corresponding dimension variable.

Changing the values of dimension variables by entering the variable name on the command line is not a recommended method for setting or changing dimension style settings. Changes made in this manner can introduce inconsistencies with other dimensions. Changes to dimensions are best made by redefining styles or performing style overrides. Dimension variables have limited practical uses, and are more likely to be used in advanced applications such as scripting and customizing. For a listing of the dimension variables in AutoCAD, see the *Reference Materials* section on the Student CD.

dimension variables: System variables that store the values of dimension style settings.

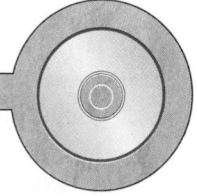

Exercise 16-1
Complete the exercise on the Student CD.

Using the Text Tab

Changes can be made to dimension text by picking the **Text** tab in the **New** (or **Modify**) **Dimension Style** dialog box. See **Figure 16-23**.

The **Text appearance** area is used to set the dimension text style, color, height, and frame. The options in this area are:

- **Text style.** The dimension text style uses the Standard text style by default. Text styles must be loaded in the current drawing before they are available for use in dimension text. Pick the desired text style from the drop-down list.
- **Text color.** The dimension color default is ByBlock. Use the drop-down list to select a color for the text. If the color is not in the drop-down list, pick **Select Color...** to select a color from the **Select Color** dialog box.

Figure 16-23.
The **Text** tab of the **Modify Dimension Style** dialog box.

Select tab to set up dimension text

Set appearance of the text

Set location of text relative to dimension line

Set alignment of text relative to dimension line

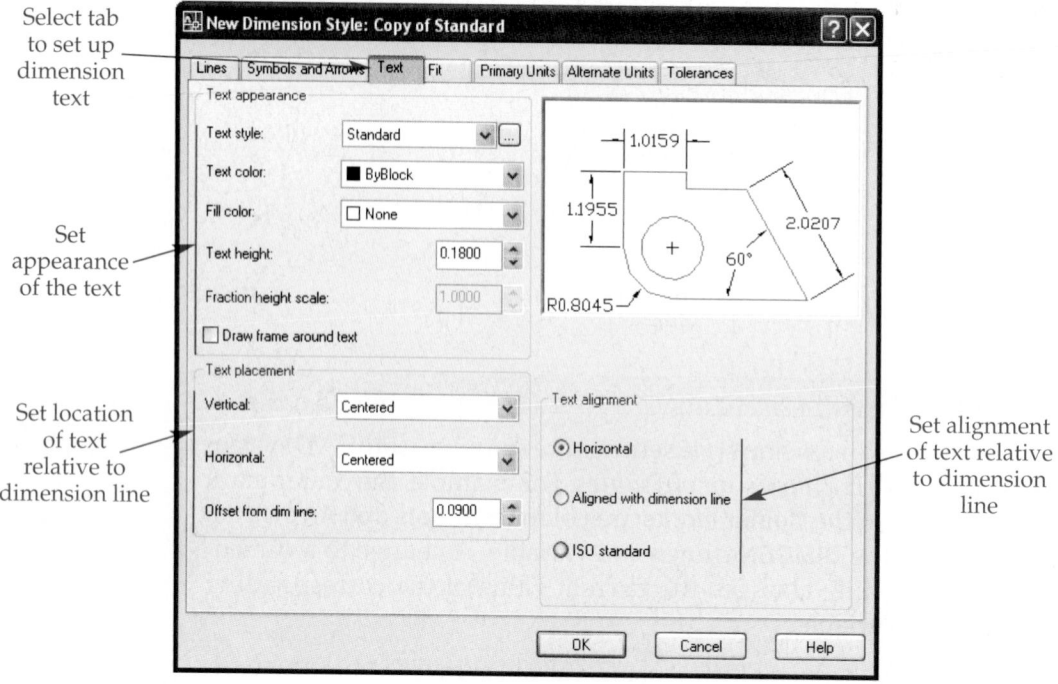

- **Text height.** Dimension text height is commonly the same as the text height for items found on the rest of the drawing except for titles, which are larger. The default dimension text height is .18, which is an acceptable standard. Many companies use a text height of .125. The ASME standard recommends text height between .12 and .18. The text height for titles and labels is usually between .18 and .24.
- **Fraction height scale.** This setting controls the height of fractions for architectural and fractional unit dimensions. The value in this box is multiplied by the text height value to determine the height of the fraction. A value of 1.0 creates fractions that are the same text height as regular (nonfractional) text, which is the normally accepted standard. A value less than 1.0 makes the fraction smaller than the regular text height.
- **Draw frame around text.** If checked, AutoCAD draws a rectangle around the text. The distance between the text and the frame is determined by the setting for the **Offset from dim line** value, which is explained later in this section.

The **Text placement** area of the **Text** tab is used to place the text relative to the dimension line. See **Figure 16-24.** The preview image changes to represent the selections you make. The **Vertical:** drop-down list has the following options for the vertical justification:

- **Centered.** Places dimension text centered in a gap provided in the dimension line. This is the dimensioning practice most commonly used in mechanical drafting and many other fields. This option is the default.
- **Above.** Places the dimension text horizontally and above horizontal dimension lines. For vertical and angled dimension lines, the text is placed in a gap provided in the dimension line. This option is generally used for architectural drafting and building construction. Architectural drafting commonly uses aligned dimensioning, in which the dimension text is aligned with the dimension lines and all text reads from either the bottom or the right side of the sheet.
- **Outside.** Places the dimension text outside the dimension line and either above or below a horizontal dimension line or to the right or left of a vertical dimension line. The direction you move the cursor determines the above/below and left/right placement.

Figure 16-24.
Dimension text justification options. A—Vertical justification options, with the horizontal Centered justification. B—Horizontal justification options, with the vertical Centered justification.

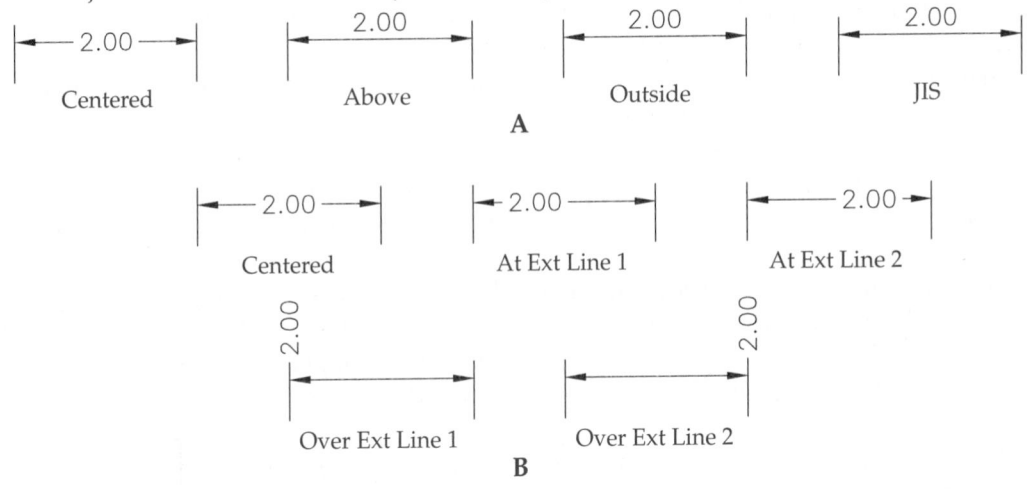

- **JIS.** Aligns the text according to the Japanese Industrial Standards.

In addition to the vertical placement of the dimension text, you can control the horizontal placement. The **Horizontal:** drop-down list has the following options for the horizontal justification:

- **Centered.** Places dimension text centered between the extension lines. This option is the AutoCAD default.
- **At Ext Line 1.** Locates the text next to the extension line placed first.
- **At Ext Line 2.** Locates the text next to the extension line placed second.
- **Over Ext Line 1.** Places the text aligned with and over the first extension line. This practice is not commonly used.
- **Over Ext Line 2.** Places the text aligned with and over the second extension line. This practice is also not commonly used.

The **Offset from dim line:** text box sets the gap between the dimension line and the dimension text. This setting also controls the distance between the leader shoulder and the text, and the space between the basic dimension box and the text. Basic dimensions are used in geometric tolerancing and are explained in Chapter 20. The default gap is .09. The gap should be set to half the text height. **Figure 16-25** shows the gap in linear and leader dimensions.

The **Text alignment** area of the **Text** tab allows you to control the alignment of dimension text. This area is used when you want to draw unidirectional dimensions or aligned dimensions. The **Horizontal** option draws the unidirectional dimensions commonly used for mechanical manufacturing drafting applications. The **Aligned with dimension line** option creates aligned dimensions, which are typically used for architectural dimensioning. The **ISO Standard** option creates aligned dimensions when the text falls between the extension lines and horizontal dimensions when the text falls outside the extension lines.

Figure 16-25.
The gap (offset) for text used in a linear dimension and a leader dimension.

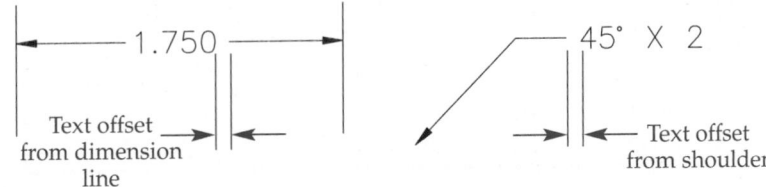

Using the Fit Tab

The **Fit** tab in the **New** (or **Modify**) **Dimension Style** dialog box is used to establish the way in which dimension text and arrowheads are placed on the drawing. The **Fit** tab is shown in **Figure 16-26** with default settings.

The **Fit options** area of the **Fit** tab controls how text and arrows should behave if they do not fit between the two extension lines. These effects are most obvious on dimensions when space is limited. Watch the preview image change as you try each of the following options. This should help you understand how each option acts. Notice that these options are radio buttons, which means only one option can be active at any given time:

- **Either text or arrows (best fit).** This is the default setting and allows AutoCAD to place text and dimension lines with arrowheads inside extension lines if space is available. Dimension lines with arrowheads are placed outside of extension lines if space is limited. Everything is placed outside of extension lines if there is not enough space between extension lines.
- **Arrows.** The text, dimension line, and arrowheads are placed inside the extension lines if there is enough space. The text is placed outside if there is enough space for only the arrowheads and dimension line inside the extension lines. Everything is placed outside if there is not enough room for anything inside.
- **Text.** The text, dimension line, and arrowheads are placed inside the extension lines if there is enough space for everything. If there is enough space for only the text inside the extension lines, then the dimension lines and arrowheads are placed outside. Everything is placed outside if there is not enough room for the text inside.
- **Both text and arrows.** When this option is used, AutoCAD places the text, dimension line, and arrowheads inside the extension lines if there is enough space, or places everything outside the extension lines if there is not enough space.
- **Always keep text between ext lines.** This option always places the dimension text between the extension lines. This may cause problems when there is limited space between extension lines.

Figure 16-26.
The **Fit** tab of the **Modify Dimension Style** dialog box.

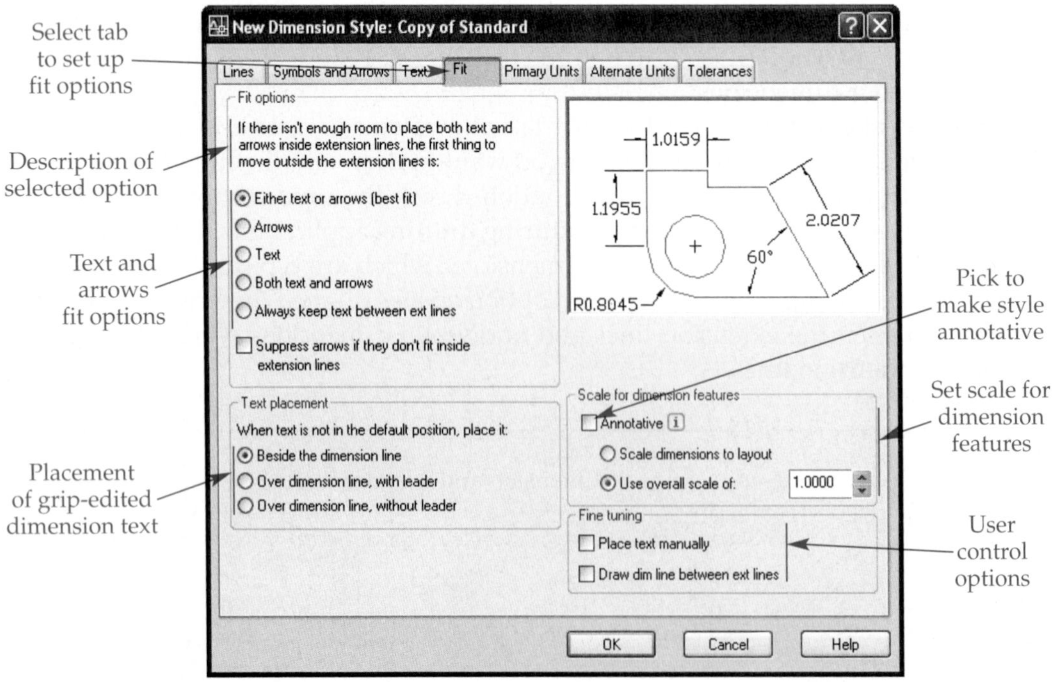

- **Suppress arrows if they don't fit inside extension lines.** This option removes the arrowheads if they do not fit inside the extension lines. Use this option with caution because it can create dimensions that violate standards.

Sometimes it becomes necessary to move the dimension text from its default position. The text can be moved by grip editing the text portion of the dimension. The options in the **Text placement** area of the **Fit** tab instruct AutoCAD how to handle these grip-editing situations. The following options are available:

- **Beside the dimension line.** When the dimension text is grip edited and moved, the text is constrained to move with the dimension line and can only be placed within the same plane as the dimension line.
- **Over dimension line, with leader.** When the dimension text is grip edited and moved, the text can be moved in any direction away from the dimension line. A leader line is created that connects the text to the dimension line.
- **Over dimension line, without leader.** When the dimension text is grip edited and moved, the text can be moved in any direction away from the dimension line without a connecting leader.

PROFESSIONAL TIP

To return the dimension text to its default position, select the dimension, right-click to display the shortcut menu, and select **Dim Text position > Home text**.

The **Scale for dimension features** area of the **Fit** tab is used to set the scale factor for all dimension features in the drawing. To create annotative dimensions, make the dimension style annotative by selecting the **Annotative** check box. The **Annotative** check box is already selected if you are modifying the default Annotative dimension style or if you pick the **Annotative** check box in the **Create New Dimension Style** dialog box.

Select the **Scale dimensions to layout** radio button if you are dimensioning in a floating viewport in a layout (paper space) tab. You must add dimensions to the model in a floating viewport in order for this option to function. Scaling dimensions to the layout allows the overall scale to adjust according to the active floating viewport by setting the overall scale equal to the viewport scale factor.

Pick the **Use overall scale of** radio button to enter the drawing scale factor used to adjust the size of dimension features according to a specific drawing scale. The scale factor is multiplied by the desired plotted dimension size to get the model space dimension size. For example, if the height of the dimensioning text is set to .12 and the value for the overall scale is set to 2, for a half scale drawing, then the dimension text can be measured within the drawing to be .24 units ($2 \times .12$). If the drawing is plotted with a plot scale of 1:2 (half), the size of the dimension text on the paper measures .12 units.

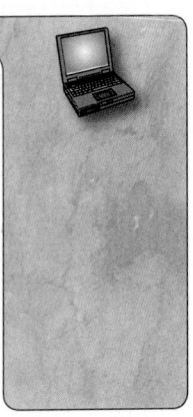

PROFESSIONAL TIP

Dimensions can be drawn in either model space or layout (paper) space. Model space dimensions must be scaled by the drawing scale factor to achieve the correct feature sizes, such as text height and arrow size. Associative paper space dimensions automatically adjust to model modifications and do not need to be scaled. Also, if you dimension in paper space, you can dimension the model differently in two viewports. However, paper space dimensions are not visible when you are working in model space, so you must be careful not to move a model space object into a paper space dimension. Avoid using nonassociative paper space dimensions.

The **Fine tuning** area of the **Fit** tab provides you with maximum flexibility in controlling where you want to place dimension text. The **Place text manually** option gives you control over text placement and dimension line length outside extension lines. You can place the text where you want it, such as to the side within the extension lines, or outside of the extension lines.

The **Draw dim line between ext lines** option forces AutoCAD to place the dimension line inside the extension lines, even when the text and arrowheads are outside. The default application is with the dimension line and arrowheads outside the extension lines. See **Figure 16-27**. Forcing the dimension line inside the extension lines is not an ASME standard, but it is preferred by some companies.

PROFESSIONAL TIP

When dimensioning mechanical drawings, it is common to have **Place text manually** turned on, centered horizontal and vertical justification, and horizontal text alignment.

For architectural drafting, it is typical to have **Place text manually** turned on, **Draw dim line between ext lines** turned on, centered horizontal justification, above vertical justification, and text aligned with dimension lines.

Exercise 16-2
Complete the exercise on the Student CD.

Using the Primary Units Tab

The **Primary Units** tab of the **New** (or **Modify**) **Dimension Style** dialog box is used to set units for linear and angular dimensions. The **Linear dimensions** area is used to specify settings for linear dimensions. See **Figure 16-28**. This area has the following options:

- **Unit format.** Sets the type of units for dimension text. The default selection is **Decimal** units. Definitions and examples of the different types of units are provided in Chapter 2.
- **Precision.** This drop-down list allows you to decide how many zeros follow the decimal place when decimal-related units are selected. The default is 0.0000; the 0.00 and 0.000 settings are also common in mechanical drafting. When fractional units are selected, the precision values specify the smallest desired fractional denominator. The default is 1/16″, but you can choose other options ranging from 1/256″ to 1/2″; 0″ displays no fractional values. A variety of dimension precisions may be found on the same drawing.

Figure 16-27.
The effects of the **Draw dim line between ext lines** option of the **Fine tuning** area of the **Fit** tab.

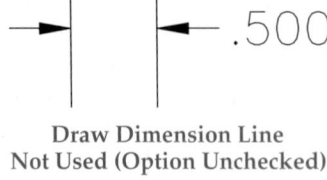

Draw Dimension Line
Not Used (Option Unchecked)

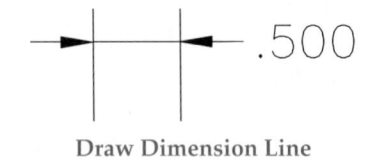

Draw Dimension Line
Enabled (Option Checked)

Figure 16-28.
The **Primary Units** tab of the **Modify Dimension Style** dialog box.

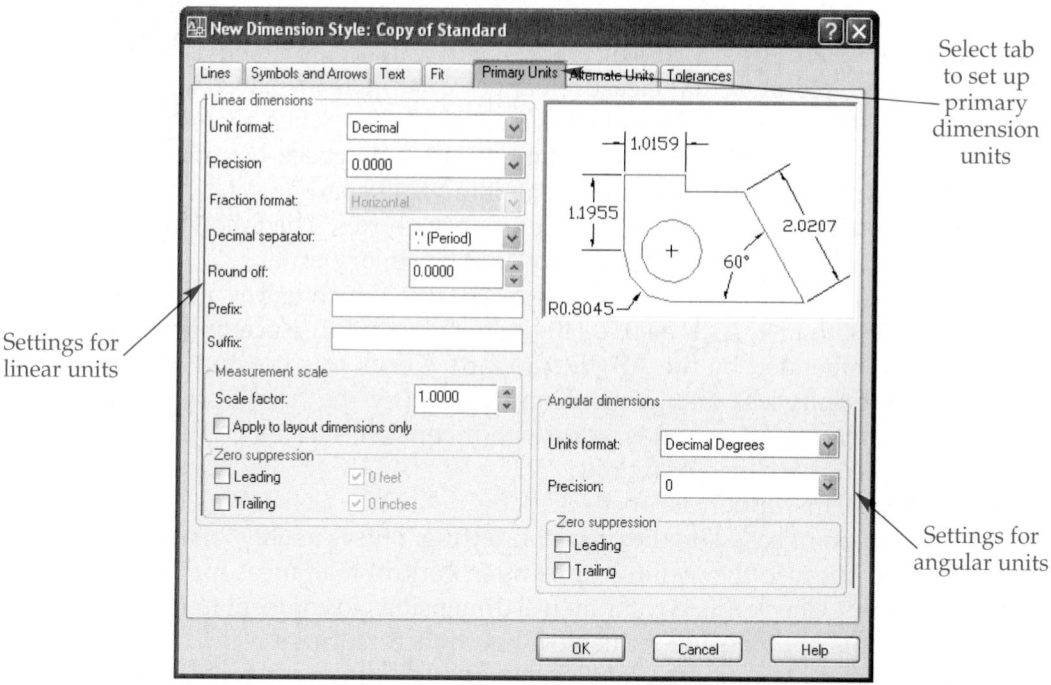

Select tab to set up primary dimension units

Settings for linear units

Settings for angular units

- **Fraction format.** The options for controlling the display of fractions are **Diagonal**, **Horizontal**, and **Not Stacked**. The **Fraction format** option is only available if the unit format is **Architectural** or **Fractional**.
- **Decimal separator.** Decimal numbers may use commas, periods, or spaces as separators. The '.' **(Period)** option is the default. The **Decimal separator** option is not available if the unit format is **Architectural** or **Fractional**.
- **Round off.** This text box specifies the accuracy of rounding for dimension numbers. The default is zero, which means that no rounding takes place and all dimensions are placed exactly as measured. If you enter a value of .1, all dimensions are rounded to the closest .1 unit. For example, an actual measurement of 1.188 is rounded to 1.2.
- **Prefix.** *Prefixes* are special notes or applications placed in front of the dimension text. A typical prefix might be SR3.5 where SR means spherical radius. When a prefix is used on a diameter or radius dimension, the prefix replaces the ∅ or R symbol.
- **Suffix.** *Suffixes* are special notes or applications placed after the dimension text. A typical suffix might be 3.5 MAX, where MAX is the abbreviation for maximum. The abbreviation in can also be used when one or more inch dimensions are placed on a metric dimensioned drawing. Conversely, a suffix of mm can be used on one or more millimeter dimensions placed on an inch drawing.

prefixes: Special notes or applications placed in front of the dimension text.

suffixes: Special notes or applications placed after the dimension text.

PROFESSIONAL TIP

Usually, a prefix or suffix is not used on every dimension in the drawing. A prefix or suffix is normally a special specification and might be used in only a few cases. Because of this, you might set up a special dimension style for these applications or enter them when needed by using the **MText** or **Text** option of the related dimensioning command.

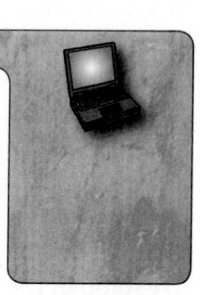

The **Measurement scale** area in the **Linear dimensions** area of the **Primary Units** tab is used to set the scale factor of linear dimensions. Set the value in the **Scale factor:** text box. If a value of 1 is set, dimension values are displayed the same as they are measured. If the setting is 2, dimension values are twice as much as the measured amount. For example, an actual measurement of 2 inches is displayed as 2 with a scale factor of 1, but the same measurement is displayed as 4 when the scale factor is 2. Placing a check in the **Apply to layout dimensions only** check box makes the linear scale factor active only for dimensions created in paper space.

The **Zero suppression** area provides four check boxes. The following options are used to suppress leading and trailing zeros in the primary units:

- **Leading.** This option is unchecked by default, which leaves a zero on decimal units less than 1, such as 0.5. This option is used to place metric dimensions as recommended by the ASME standard. Check this box to remove the 0 on decimal units less than 1, as recommended by the ASME standard for inch dimensioning. The result is a decimal dimension, such as .5. This option is not available for architectural units.
- **Trailing.** This option is unchecked by default, which leaves zeros after the decimal point based on the precision setting. This is usually off for inch dimensioning because the trailing zeros often control tolerances for manufacturing processes. Check this box for metric dimensions to conform to the ASME standard. This option is not available for architectural units.
- **0 feet.** This option is checked by default. It removes the zero in feet and inch dimensions when there are zero feet. For example, when unchecked, a dimension may read 0'-11". When checked, however, the dimension reads 11". This option is only available for architectural and engineering units.
- **0 inches.** This option is checked by default. It removes the zero when the inch part of feet and inch dimensions is less than one inch, such as 12'-7/8". If checked, the same dimension reads 12'-0 7/8". Also, this option removes the zero from a dimension with no inch value; for example, 12' is used rather than 12'-0". This option is only available for architectural and engineering units.

The **Angular dimensions** area of the **Primary Units** tab is used to set the type of angular units for dimensioning. Angular units are described in the section in Chapter 2 that explains the **Drawing Units** dialog box. (The **Drawing Units** dialog box does not control the type of units used for dimensioning.) The following settings are found in the **Angular dimensions** area:

- **Units format.** Sets the dimension units. The default setting is **Decimal Degrees**. The other options are **Degrees Minutes Seconds**, **Gradians**, and **Radians**.
- **Precision.** Sets the desired precision of the angular dimension value.

The **Zero suppression** area has check boxes for the **Leading** and **Trailing** suppression options. These options are used to keep or remove leading or trailing zeros on the angular dimension.

Using the Alternate Units Tab

The **Alternate Units** tab of the **New** (or **Modify**) **Dimension Style** dialog box is used to set alternate units. See **Figure 16-29**. *Alternate units*, or *dual dimensioning units*, have inch measurements followed by millimeters in brackets, or millimeters followed by inches in brackets. Dual dimensioning practices are no longer a recommended ASME standard. ASME recommends that drawings be dimensioned using inch or metric units only. However, alternate units can be used in many other applications.

alternate units (dual dimensioning units): Dimensions in which inch measurements are followed by millimeters in brackets, or millimeters are followed by inches in brackets.

The **Alternate Units** tab has many of the same settings found in the **Primary Units** tab. However, the **Display alternate units** check box must be checked in order to activate the settings. The **Multiplier for alt units** setting is multiplied by the primary unit to establish the value for the alternate unit. The default is 25.4 because an inch value is

Figure 16-29.
The **Alternate Units** tab of the **Modify Dimension Style** dialog box.

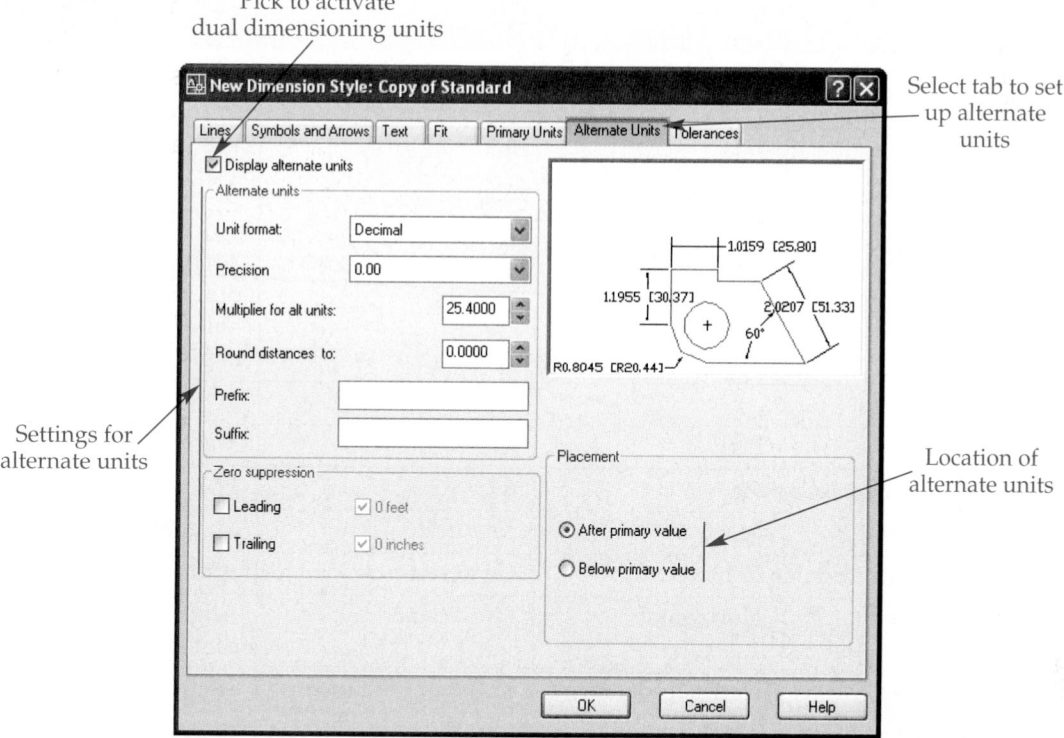

Pick to activate
dual dimensioning units

Select tab to set
up alternate
units

Settings for
alternate units

Location of
alternate units

multiplied by 25.4 to convert it to millimeters. The **Placement** area controls the location of the alternate-unit dimension. The two options are **After primary value** and **Below primary value**.

NOTE

The final tab in the **Modify Dimension Style** dialog box, **Tolerances**, is described in Chapter 19.

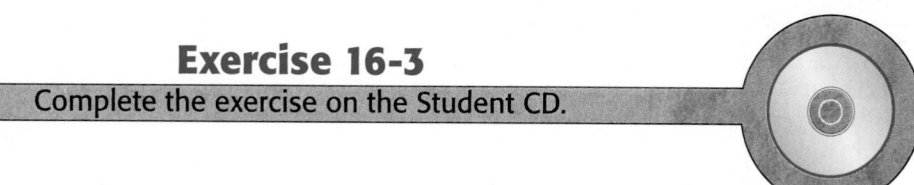

Exercise 16-3
Complete the exercise on the Student CD.

Making Your Own Dimension Styles

Creating and recording dimension styles is part of your AutoCAD management responsibility. You should carefully evaluate the items contained in the dimensions for the type of drawings you do. During this process, be sure to check school, company, or national standards carefully to verify the accuracy of your plan. Then make a list of features and values for the dimensioning settings you use based on what you have learned in this chapter. When you are ready, use the **Dimension Style Manager** dialog box options to establish dimension styles named to suit your drafting practices.

The chart in **Figure 16-30** provides possible settings for three dimension styles. One list is for mechanical manufacturing using inch measurements, another is for mechanical manufacturing using metric units, and the last is for architectural drafting applications. For settings not listed here, use the AutoCAD defaults.

Figure 16-30.
This chart shows dimension settings for typical mechanical and architectural drawings.

Setting	Mechanical (Inch)	Mechanical (Metric)	Architectural
Dimension line spacing	.50	12	1/2″
Extension line extension	.063	3	1/8″
Extension line offset	.0625	1.5	3/32″
Arrowhead options	Closed filled, closed, or open	Closed filled, closed, or open	Architectural tick, dot, closed filled, oblique, or right angle
Arrowhead size	.125	3	1/8″
Center	Line	Line	Mark
Center size	.25	6	1/4″
Text placement	Manually	Manually	Manually
Vertical justification	Centered	Centered	Above
Text alignment	Horizontal	Horizontal	Aligned with dimension line
Primary units	Decimal (default)	Decimal (default)	Architectural
Dimension precision	0.000	0.000	1/16″
Zero suppression (metric)	Leading off Trailing on	Leading off Trailing on	Leading off Trailing on
Zero suppression (inch)	Leading on Trailing off	Leading on Trailing off	Leading on Trailing off
Angles	Decimal degrees (default)	Decimal degrees (default)	Decimal degrees
Tolerances	By application	By application	None
Text style	RomanS	RomanS	Stylus BT
Text height	.12	3	1/8″
Text gap	.063	1.5	1/16″

PROFESSIONAL TIP

To save valuable drafting time, add dimension styles to your template drawings.

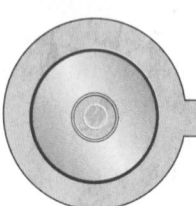

Exercise 16-4
Complete the exercise on the Student CD.

Changing Dimension Styles

You can change the current dimension style without affecting existing dimensions. The changes are applied only to dimensions added using the current style. The following options in the **Dimension Style Manager** can be used to change existing dimension styles:

- **Modify.** Selecting this button opens the **Modify Dimension Style** dialog box, which allows you to make changes to the style highlighted in the **Styles** list.
- **Override.** An *override* is a temporary change to the current style settings. Including a text prefix for just a few of the dimensions on a drawing is an example of an override. Picking this button opens the **Override Current Style** dialog box. This button is only available for the current style. Once an override is created, it is made current and is displayed as a branch, called the *child*, of the style from which it is created. The dimension style from which the child is created is called the *parent*. The override settings are lost when any other style, including the parent, is set current.
- **Compare.** Sometimes it is useful to view the details of two styles to determine their differences. When the **Compare...** button is selected, the **Compare Dimension Styles** dialog box opens. You can compare two styles by entering the name of one style in the **Compare:** drop-down list and the name of the other in the **With:** drop-down list. The differences between the selected styles are displayed in the dialog box.

override: A temporary change to the current style settings.

child: A style override.

parent: The dimension style from which a style override is created.

The **New Dimension Style**, **Modify Dimension Style**, and **Override Current Style** dialog boxes have the same tabs. These tabs are described in the previous sections.

NOTE

If you change the characteristics of an existing dimension style, all dimensions with that style are redrawn with the new values.

Renaming and Deleting Dimension Styles

Existing dimension styles can be renamed in the **Dimension Style Manager**. To rename a dimension style, slowly double-click the name or right-click the name and select the **Rename** option.

NOTE

Styles can also be renamed using the **Rename** dialog box. You can access this dialog box by selecting **Format > Rename...** from the pull-down menu or by typing RENAME. Select **Dimension styles** in the **Named Objects** list to rename the style.

To delete a dimension style, right-click the name and select the **Delete** option, or pick the style and select the **Delete** button. If you try to delete a dimension style that has been used to create dimensions in the drawing, AutoCAD gives you the following message:

Style in use, can't be deleted.

This means that there are dimensions in the drawing that reference this style. If you want to delete the style, change the dimensions in the drawing to a different style.

Quickly Setting a Dimension Style Current

You can quickly make a dimension style current by using the **Dimension Style** drop-down list located in the **Dimension** toolbar or the **Dimension** control panel of the **Dashboard**. The name of the current dimension style is displayed in the box. Pick the drop-down arrow to display a list of dimension styles. Pick a dimension style from the list to set it current.

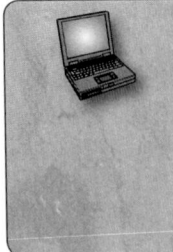

PROFESSIONAL TIP

DesignCenter can be used to import dimension styles from existing drawing files. **DesignCenter** allows you to browse through drawing files to find desired dimension styles, and then add the needed style into your current drawing file. Chapter 9 describes the process of using **DesignCenter** to reuse existing text styles. Apply the same techniques to reuse existing dimension styles.

Exercise 16-5
Complete the exercise on the Student CD.

Dimensioning Practices

Dimensioning practices often depend on product requirements, manufacturing accuracy, standards, and tradition. Dimensional information includes size dimensions, location dimensions, and notes. Two methods that identify size and location are chain and datum dimensioning. The method used depends on the accuracy needed for the product and the drafting field. Both methods are covered later in this chapter.

Size Dimensions and Notes

size dimensions: Dimensions that provide the size of physical features and include lines, notes, or dimension lines and numbers.

Size dimensions provide the size of physical features. They include lines, notes, or dimension lines and numbers. Size dimensioning practices depend on the methods used to dimension different geometric features. See Figure 16-31. A *feature* is any physical portion of a part or object, such as a surface, hole, window, or door. Dimensioning standards are used so an object designed in one place can be manufactured or built somewhere else.

feature: Any physical portion of a part or object, such as a surface, hole, window, or door.

specific notes: Notes that relate to individual or specific features on the drawing.

Specific notes and general notes are the two types of notes on a drawing. *Specific notes* relate to individual or specific features on the drawing. They are attached to the feature being dimensioned using a leader line. *General notes* apply to the entire drawing and are placed in the lower-left corner, upper-left corner, or above or next to the title block. Where they are placed depends on sheet size and industry, company, or school practice.

general notes: Notes that apply to the entire drawing and are placed in the lower-left corner, upper-left corner, or above or next to the title block.

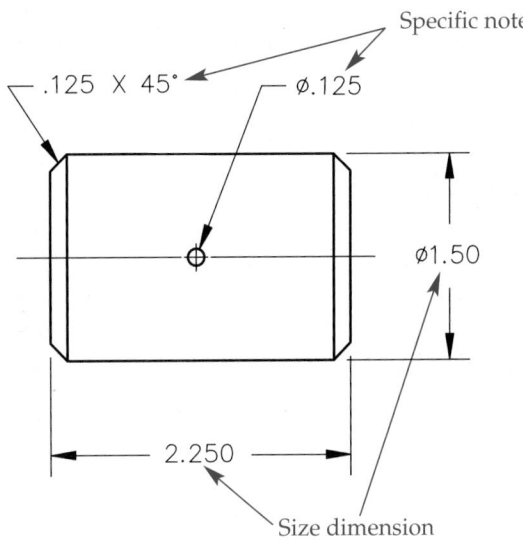

Figure 16-31.
Size dimensions and specific notes.

Specific note

.125 X 45°

Ø.125

Ø1.50

2.250

Size dimension

Location Dimensions

Location dimensions are used to locate features on an object. These dimensions do not specify the size of the feature. Holes and arcs are dimensioned to their centers in the view in which they appear circular. Rectangular features are dimensioned to their edges. See **Figure 16-32.** In architectural drafting, windows and doors are dimensioned to their centers on the floor plan.

The rectangular coordinate system and the polar coordinate system are the two basic systems used for creating location dimensions. See **Figure 16-33.** The *rectangular coordinate system* uses linear dimensions to locate features from surfaces, centerlines, or center planes. AutoCAD performs this type of dimensioning using a variety of dimensioning commands. The most frequently used linear dimensioning command is the **DIMLINEAR** command. The *polar coordinate system* uses angular dimensions to locate features from surfaces, centerlines, or center planes. Angular dimensions in the polar coordinate system are drawn using AutoCAD's **DIMANGULAR** command.

Dimensioning Features and Architectural Objects

In mechanical drafting, flat surfaces are dimensioned by giving measurements for each feature. If an overall dimension is provided, you can omit one of the dimensions. The overall dimension controls the omitted dimension. In architectural drafting, it is common to place all dimensions without omitting any of them. The idea is that all dimensions should be shown to help make construction easier. See **Figure 16-34.**

location dimensions: Dimensions used to locate features on an object without specifying the size of the feature.

rectangular coordinate system: A system for locating dimensions from surfaces, centerlines, or center planes using linear dimensions.

polar coordinate system: A coordinate system in which angular dimensions locate features from surfaces, centerlines, or center planes.

Figure 16-32.
Location dimensions are used to locate circular and rectangular features.

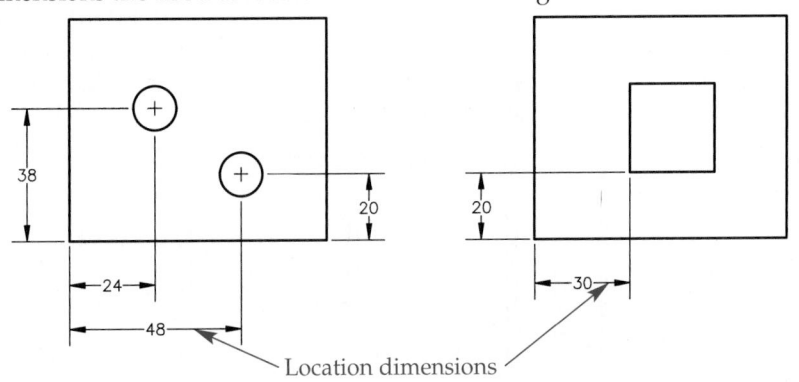

38

20

20

24

48

30

Location dimensions

Figure 16-33.
A—Rectangular coordinate location dimensions. B—Polar coordinate location dimensions.

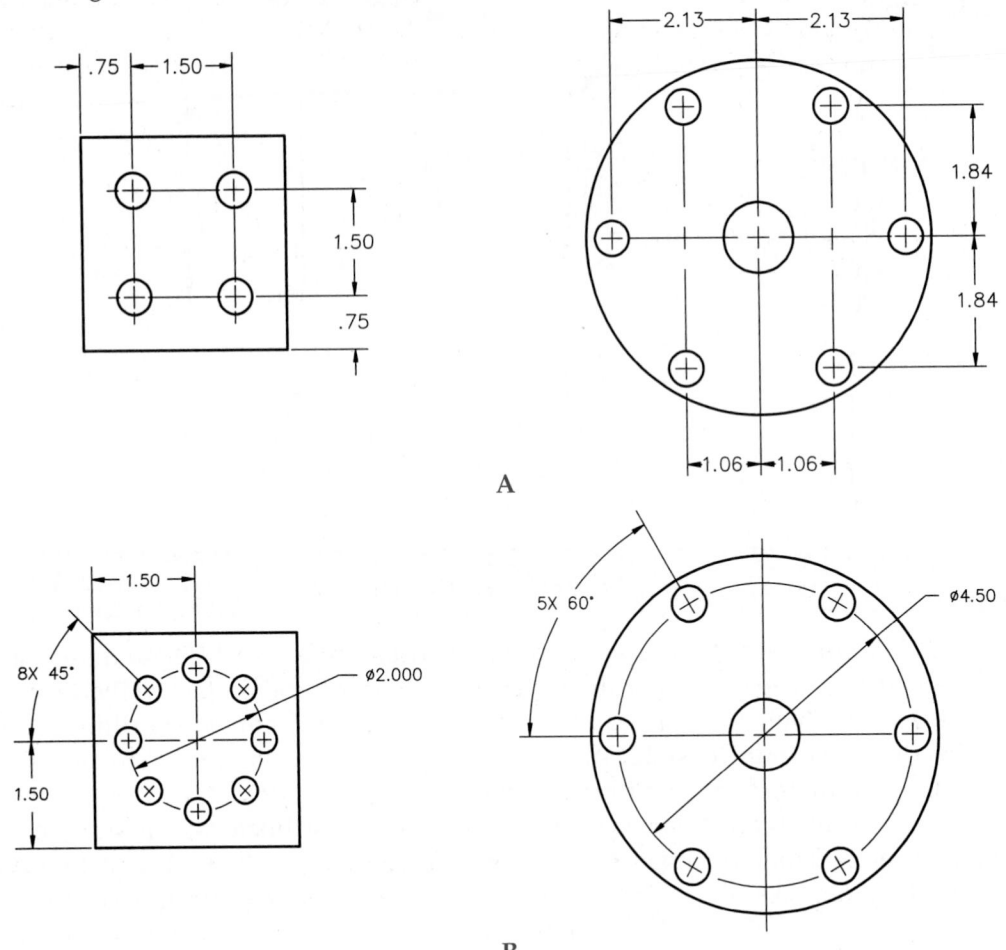

A

B

Figure 16-34.
Dimensioning
flat surfaces and
architectural
features.

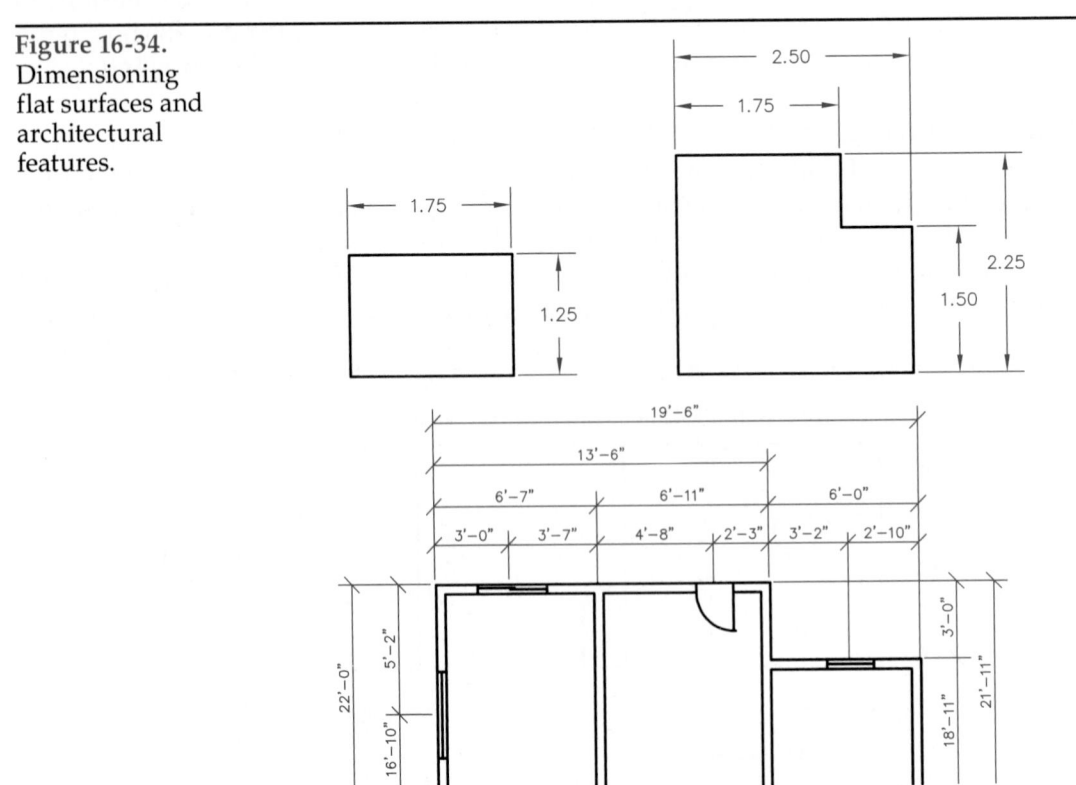

Dimensioning Cylindrical Shapes

Both the diameter and the length of a cylindrical shape can be dimensioned in the view in which the cylinder appears rectangular. See **Figure 16-35**. The diameter symbol next to the dimension indicates that the part is a cylinder. This allows the view in which the cylinder appears as a circle to be omitted.

Dimensioning Square and Rectangular Features

Square and rectangular features are usually dimensioned in the views in which the length and height are shown. The square symbol can be used preceding the dimension for the square feature. See **Figure 16-36**. The square symbol can be added to the dimension text using the **In-Place Text Editor**.

Dimensioning Cones and Regular Polygons

There are two ways to dimension a conical shape. One method is to dimension the diameters at both ends and the length. See **Figure 16-37**. Another method is to dimension the taper angle and the length. Regular polygons that have an even number of sides are dimensioned by giving the distance across the flats and the length.

Figure 16-35.
Dimensioning cylindrical shapes.

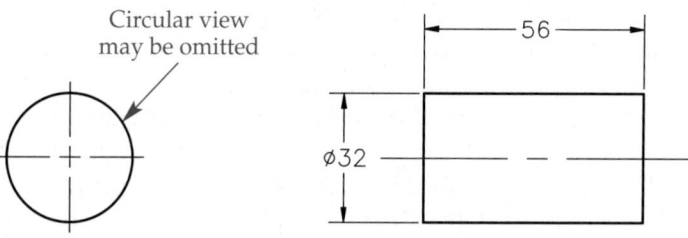

Figure 16-36.
Dimensioning square and rectangular features.

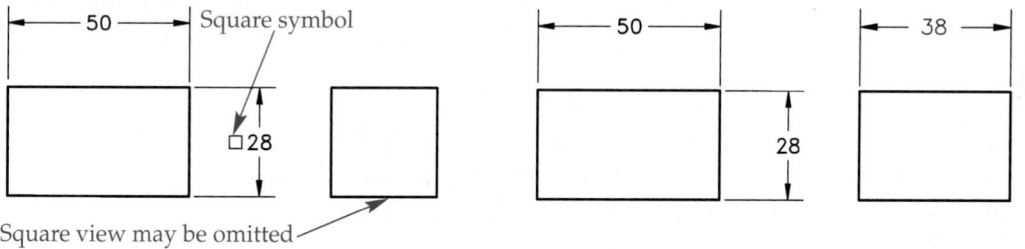

Figure 16-37.
Dimensioning cones and hexagonal cylinders.

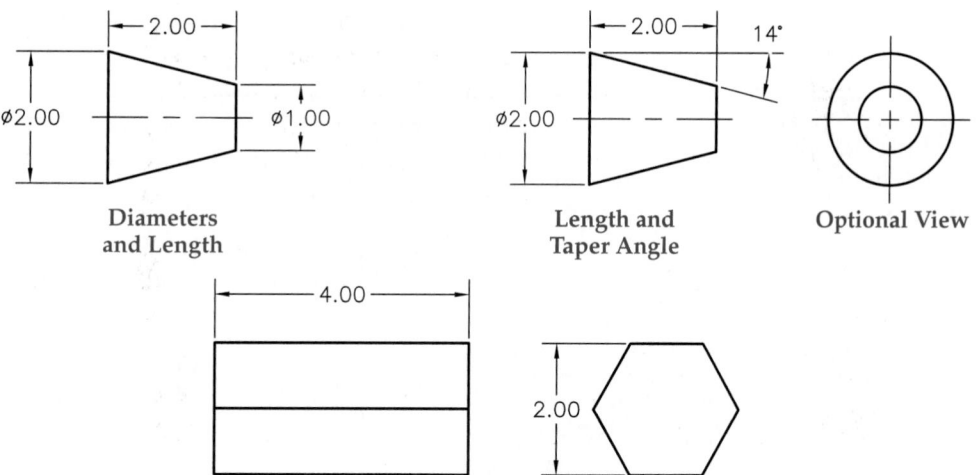

Drawing Linear Dimensions

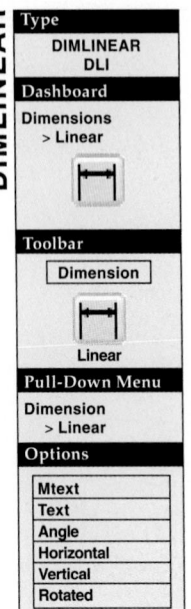

linear: Configured in a straight line.

Type
DIMLINEAR
DLI

Dashboard
Dimensions > Linear
⊢−−⊣

Toolbar
Dimension
⊢−−⊣
Linear

Pull-Down Menu
Dimension > Linear

Options
Mtext
Text
Angle
Horizontal
Vertical
Rotated

Linear means straight. In most cases, dimensions measure straight distances, such as horizontal, vertical, or slanted surfaces. The **DIMLINEAR** command allows you to measure the length of an object and place the dimension line, extension lines, dimension text, and arrowheads. To do this, pick the **Linear** button in the **Dimension** toolbar or the **Dimension** control panel in the **Dashboard**, select **Dimension > Linear** from the pull-down menu, or type DLI or DIMLINEAR.

Once the command is initiated, you are asked to pick the origin of the first extension line. Then you are asked for the origin of the second extension line. The points you pick are the extension line origins. See **Figure 16-38.** Place the crosshairs directly on the corners of the object where the extension lines begin. Use object snap modes for accuracy.

The **DIMLINEAR** command allows you to generate horizontal, vertical, or rotated dimensions. After you select the object or points of origin for dimensioning, the Specify dimension line location or [Mtext/Text/Angle/Horizontal/Vertical/Rotated] prompt appears. The options are as follows:

- **Specify dimension line location.** This is the default. Drag the dimension line to a desired location and pick. See **Figure 16-39.** This is where preliminary plan sheets and sketches help you determine proper distances to avoid crowding. The extension lines, dimension line, dimension text, and arrowheads are automatically drawn after you pick the location.

- **Mtext.** This option accesses the **In-Place Text Editor** and the **Text Formatting** toolbar. See **Figure 16-40.** Here you can provide a specific measurement or text format for the dimension. See Chapter 9 for a complete description of the **In-Place Text Editor** and the **Text Formatting** toolbar. The highlighted value represents the current dimension value. Edit the dimension text and pick **OK**. For example, the ASME standard recommends that a reference dimension be displayed enclosed in parentheses. Type open and closed parentheses around the value to create a reference dimension. If you want to change the current dimension value, pick the value and type the new value.

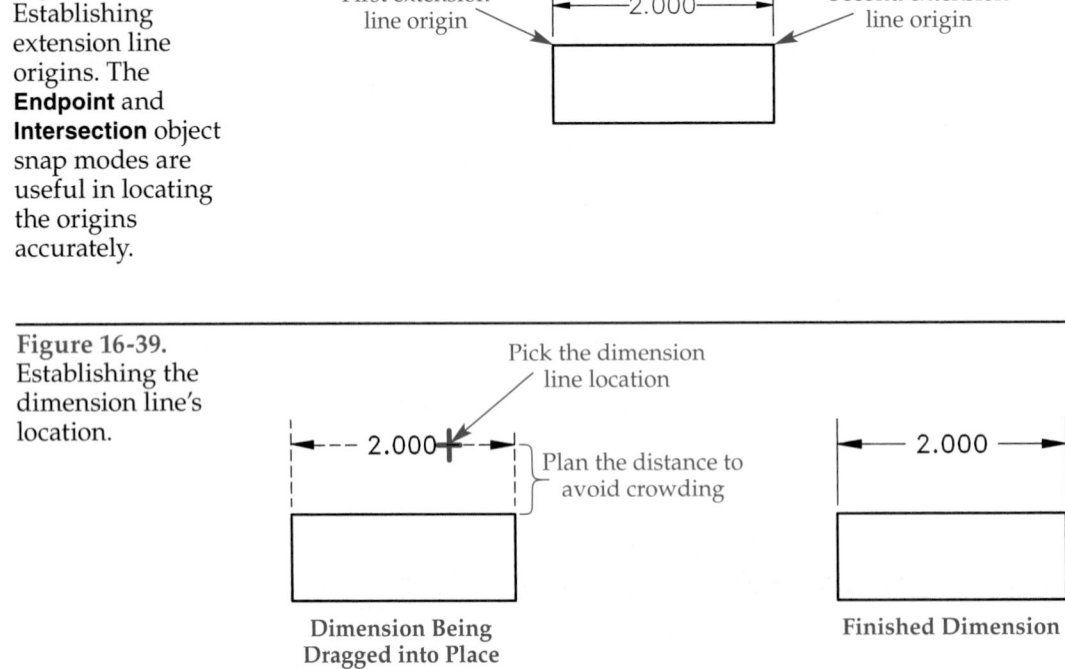

Figure 16-38. Establishing extension line origins. The **Endpoint** and **Intersection** object snap modes are useful in locating the origins accurately.

Figure 16-39. Establishing the dimension line's location.

Figure 16-40.
When you use the **Mtext** option, the **In-Place Text Editor** and **Text Formatting** toolbar appear. The value represents the dimension value AutoCAD has calculated.

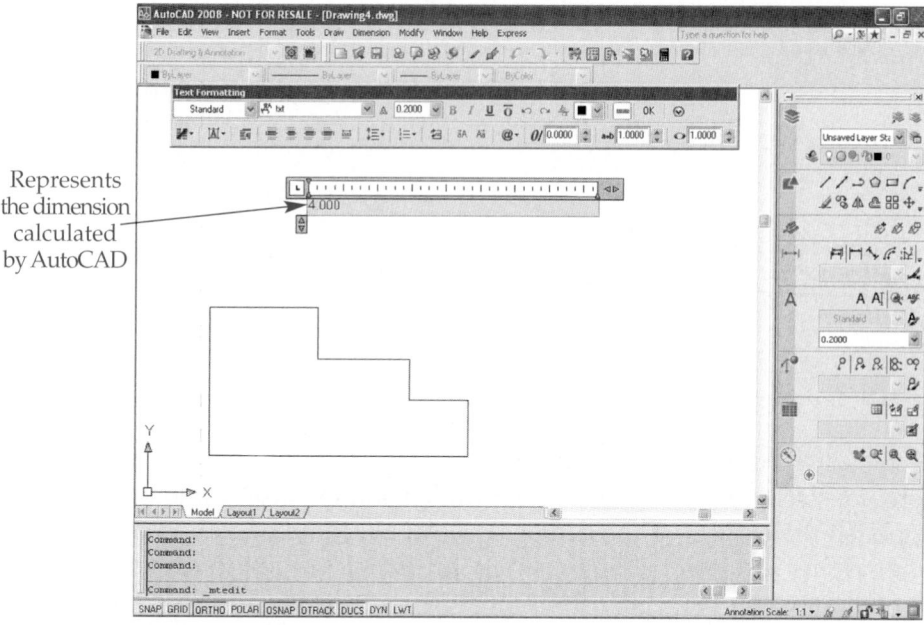

Represents the dimension calculated by AutoCAD

- **Text.** This option allows you to use the command line to change dimension text. This is convenient if you prefer to type the desired text rather than use the **In-Place Text Editor**. The **Text** and **Mtext** options both create multiline text objects. The **Text** option displays the current dimension value in brackets. Pressing [Enter] accepts the current value. If you need to modify the text, type the new text. For example, you can type parentheses around the value to create a reference dimension.

- **Angle.** This option allows you to change the dimension text angle. This option can be used to create rotated dimensions or to adjust the dimension text to a desired angle. Enter the desired angle at the Specify angle of dimension text: prompt.

- **Horizontal.** This option sets the dimension being created to a horizontal distance only. This may be helpful when dimensioning the horizontal distance of a slanted surface. The **Mtext**, **Text**, and **Angle** options are available again in case you want to change the dimension text value or angle.

- **Vertical.** This option sets the dimension being created to a vertical distance only. This may be helpful when dimensioning the vertical distance of a slanted surface. As with the **Horizontal** option, the **Mtext**, **Text**, and **Angle** options are available.

- **Rotated.** This option allows you to specify an angle for the dimension line. A practical application is dimensioning to angled surfaces and auxiliary views. This technique is different from other dimensioning commands because you are asked to provide a dimension line angle. See **Figure 16-41**. At the Specify angle of dimension line <0>: prompt, enter a value, such as 45, or pick two points on the line to be dimensioned.

Exercise 16-6

Complete the exercise on the Student CD.

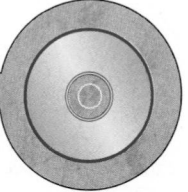

Figure 16-41.
Rotating a
dimension for an
angled view.

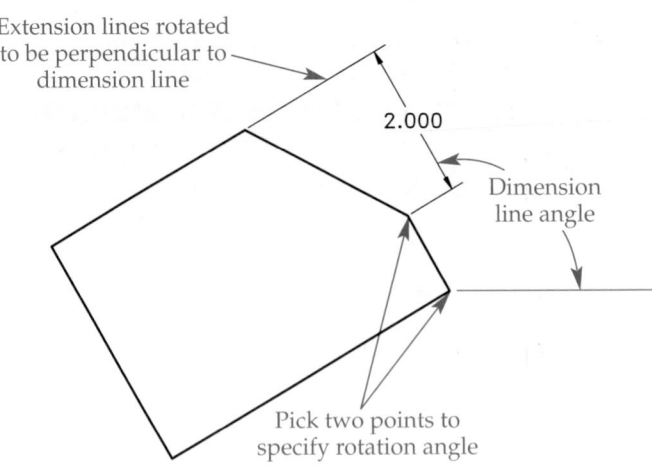

Extension lines rotated
to be perpendicular to
dimension line

2.000

Dimension
line angle

Pick two points to
specify rotation angle

Selecting an Object to Dimension

In the previous section, individual linear dimension extension line origins were picked to establish the extents of the dimension. An alternative method for defining extension line origins involves picking a single line, circle, or arc to dimension. This function also works when using the **DIMALIGNED** and **QDIM** commands, described later in this chapter. You can use this option whenever you see the Specify first extension line origin or <select object>: prompt. Press [Enter] and then pick the object being dimensioned. When you select a line or arc, AutoCAD begins the extension lines from the endpoints. If you pick a circle, the extension lines are drawn from the closest quadrant and its opposite quadrant. See **Figure 16-42.**

PROFESSIONAL TIP

Dimensioning in AutoCAD should be performed as accurately and neatly as possible. You can achieve consistently professional results by using the following guidelines:

- Always construct drawing geometry accurately. Never truncate, or round off, decimal values when entering locations, distances, or angles. For example, enter .4375 for 7/16 rather than .44.
- Set the desired precision level before beginning your dimensioning. Most drawings have varying levels of precision for specific drawing features, so select the most common precision level to start with and adjust the precision as needed for each dimension. Setting the dimension precision is explained later in this chapter.
- Always use the precision drawing aids to ensure the accuracy of dimensions. If the point being dimensioned does not coincide with a snap point or a known coordinate, use an appropriate object snap override.
- *Never* type a different dimension value from what appears in the brackets. If a dimension needs to change, revise the drawing or dimensioning settings accordingly. The ability to change the dimension in the brackets is provided by AutoCAD so a different text format can be specified for the dimension. Prefixes and suffixes can also be added to the dimension in the brackets. A typical example of a prefix might be to specify the number of times a dimension occurs, such as 4X 1.750. Other examples of this capability appear later in this chapter.

Figure 16-42.
AutoCAD can determine the extension line origins automatically if you select a line, arc, or circle.

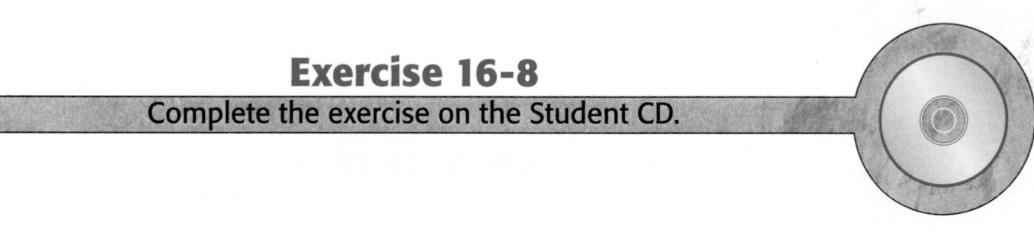

Pick an object

1.250   1.250   1.250

Exercise 16-7
Complete the exercise on the Student CD.

Dimensioning Angled Surfaces and Auxiliary Views

When you are dimensioning a surface drawn at an angle, it may be necessary to align the dimension line with the surface. For example, auxiliary views are normally placed at an angle. In order to dimension these features properly, use the **DIMALIGNED** command or the **Rotated** option of the **DIMLINEAR** command.

Using the Dimaligned Command

The **DIMALIGNED** command can be accessed by picking the **Aligned** button in the **Dimension** toolbar or the **Dimension** control panel in the **Dashboard**, picking **Dimension > Aligned** in the pull-down menu, or typing DAL or DIMALIGNED. The results of the **DIMALIGNED** command are shown in Figure 16-43. Notice the difference between the aligned dimension in this figure and the rotated dimension in Figure 16-41.

Type
DIMALIGNED
DAL
Dashboard
Dimensions > Aligned
Toolbar
Dimension
Aligned
Pull-Down Menu
Dimension > Aligned
Options
Mtext
Text
Angle

DIMALIGNED

Exercise 16-8
Complete the exercise on the Student CD.

Figure 16-43.
The **DIMALIGNED** dimensioning command allows you to place dimension lines parallel to angled features.

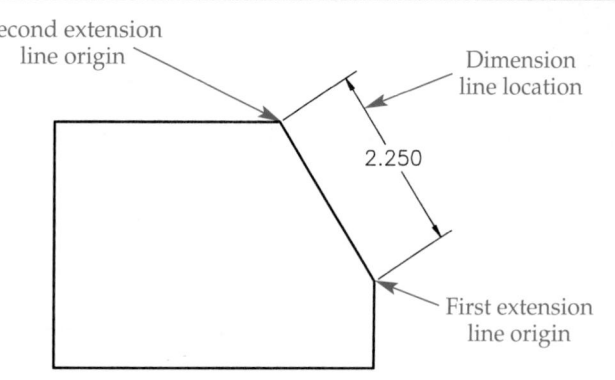

Second extension line origin

Dimension line location

2.250

First extension line origin

Dimensioning Long Objects

conventional break (break): A notation used to "cut out" part of a long object that has a constant shape to make the object fit better on the drawing sheet.

When you create a drawing of a long part that has a constant shape, the view may not fit on the desired sheet size, or may look strange compared to the rest of the drawing. To overcome this problem, a *conventional break* is used to shorten the view. For many long parts, the use of a conventional break, or *break*, is required to display views or increase the view scale without increasing the sheet size. See Figure 16-44.

Dimensions added to conventional breaks still describe the actual length of the product, in its unbroken form. Often a break symbol is added to the dimension line to indicate that the drawing view has been broken and that the feature is longer than it appears in the drawing view.

The **DIMJOGLINE** command can be used to add a break symbol to dimension lines created using the **DIMLINEAR** or **DIMALIGNED** commands. To access the **DIMJOGLINE** command, pick the **Jogged Linear** button in the **Dimension** toolbar or the **Dimension** control panel in the **Dashboard**, pick **Dimension** > **Jogged Linear** from the pull-down menu, or type DIMJOGLINE. Refer to Figure 16-44 as you go through the following command sequence:

Command: **DIMJOGLINE**↵
Select dimension to add jog or [Remove]: *(pick a linear or aligned dimension line)*
Specify jog location (or press ENTER): *(pick a point to place the break symbol)*
Command:

After you select the dimension line, pick a point to locate the center of the break symbol, or press the [Enter] key to accept the default location. The break can be moved by using grip editing after the symbol is placed, or by reusing the **DIMJOGLINE** command to select a different location. To remove the break symbol, access the **DIMJOGLINE** command and select the **Remove** option.

NOTE

A single break symbol can be added to a dimension line.

Exercise 16-9

Complete the exercise on the Student CD.

Figure 16-44.
Using the **DIMJOGLINE** command to place a dimension line break symbol.

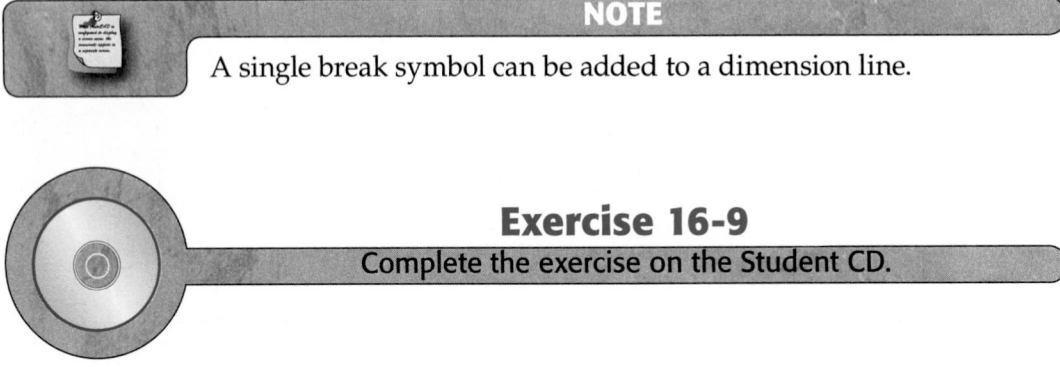

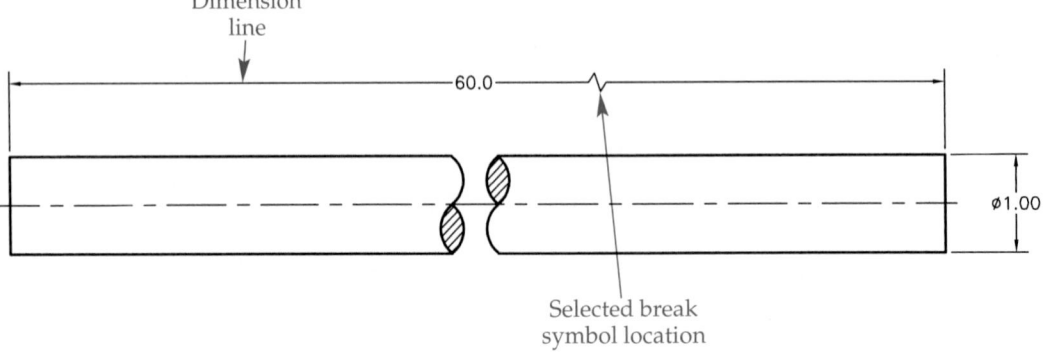

Dimensioning Angles

Coordinate and angular dimensioning are both accepted for dimensioning angles. In *coordinate dimensioning* of angles, dimensions locate the corners of the angle, as shown in **Figure 16-45**. This can be accomplished with the **DIMLINEAR** command.

Angular dimensioning locates one corner with a dimension and provides the value of the angle in degrees. See **Figure 16-46**. You can dimension the angle between any two nonparallel lines. The intersection of the lines is the angle's *vertex*. AutoCAD automatically draws extension lines if they are needed.

The **DIMANGULAR** command is used for the angular method. It is accessed by picking the **Angular** button in the **Dimension** toolbar or the **Dimension** control panel in the **Dashboard**, picking **Dimension > Angular** in the pull-down menu, or by typing DAN or DIMANGULAR. The dimension in **Figure 16-46A** was drawn with the following sequence:

> Command: **DAN** or **DIMANGULAR**↵
> Select arc, circle, line, or <specify vertex>: *(pick the first leg of the angle to be dimensioned)*
> Select second line: *(pick the second leg of the angle to be dimensioned)*
> Specify dimension arc line location or [Mtext/Text/Angle/Quadrant]: *(pick the desired location of the dimension line arc)*
> Dimension text = 30
> Command:

The last prompt asks you to pick the dimension line arc location. If there is enough space, AutoCAD places the dimension text, dimension line arc, and arrowheads inside the extension lines. If there is not enough room between extension lines for the arrowheads and text, AutoCAD automatically places the arrowheads outside and the text inside the extension lines. If space is very tight, AutoCAD may place the dimension line arc and arrowheads inside and the text outside, or place everything outside of the extension lines. See **Figure 16-47**.

coordinate dimensioning: A method of dimensioning angles in which dimensions locate the corner of the angle.

angular dimensioning: A method of dimensioning angles in which one corner of an angle is located with a dimension and the value of the angle is provided in degrees.

vertex: The point at which the two lines forming an angle meet.

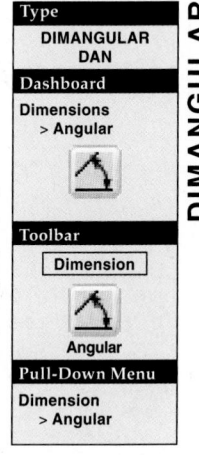

DIMANGULAR

Type
DIMANGULAR
DAN
Dashboard
Dimensions
> Angular
Toolbar
Dimension
Angular
Pull-Down Menu
Dimension
> Angular

Figure 16-45.
Coordinate dimensioning of angles.

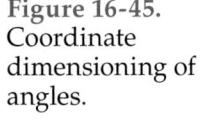
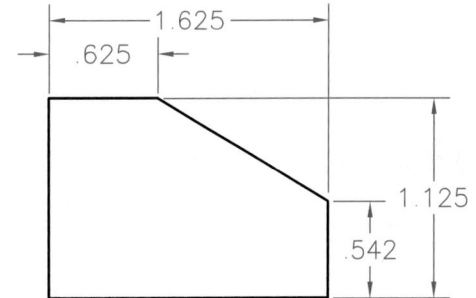

Figure 16-46.
Two examples of drawing angular dimensions.

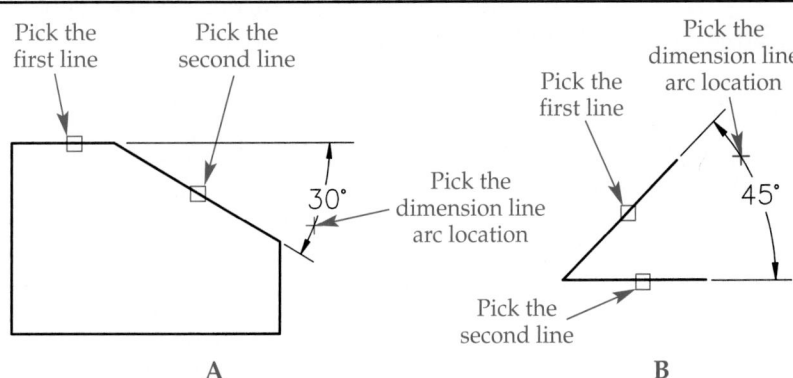

A

B

Figure 16-47.
The dimension
line arc location
determines where
the dimension line
arc, text, and arrows
are displayed.

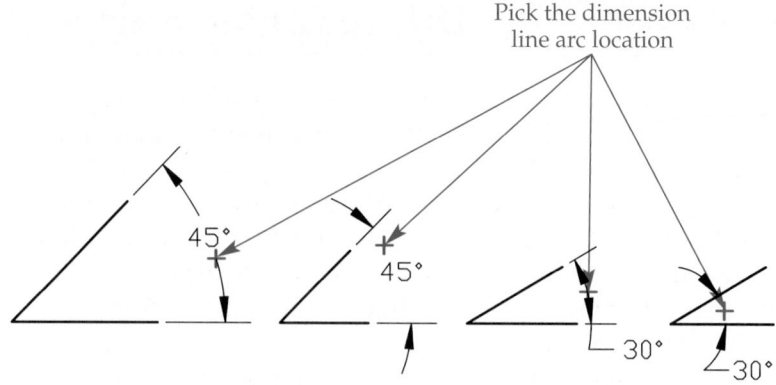

Pick the dimension
line arc location

PROFESSIONAL TIP

Four possible dimensions (two different angles) can be created with
an angular dimension. These options can be previewed by moving
the dimension to a different location, around an imaginary circle.
Use the **Quadrant** option of the **DIMANGULAR** command to isolate
a specific quadrant of the imaginary circle and force the dimension
to produce the value found in the selected quadrant.

Placing Angular Dimensions on Arcs

The **DIMANGULAR** command can be used to dimension the included angle of an
arc. The arc's center point becomes the angle vertex, and the two arc endpoints are the
origin points for the extension lines. See **Figure 16-48**.

Placing Angular Dimensions on Circles

The **DIMANGULAR** command can also be used to dimension a portion of a circle.
The circle's center point becomes the angle vertex and two picked points are the origin
points for the extension lines. See **Figure 16-49**. The point you pick on the circle is the
endpoint of the first extension line. You are then asked for the second angle endpoint,
which is the endpoint of the second extension line.

PROFESSIONAL TIP

Using angular dimensioning for circles increases the number of
possible solutions for a given dimensioning requirement, but the
actual uses are limited. One professional application is dimensioning
an angle from a quadrant point to a particular feature without having
to first draw a line to dimension. Another benefit of this option is the
ability to specify angles that exceed 180°.

Figure 16-48.
Placing angular
dimensions on arcs.

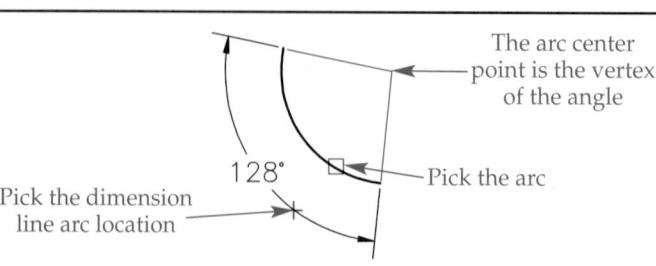

The arc center
point is the vertex
of the angle

Pick the arc

128°

Pick the dimension
line arc location

Figure 16-49.
Placing angular dimensions on circles.

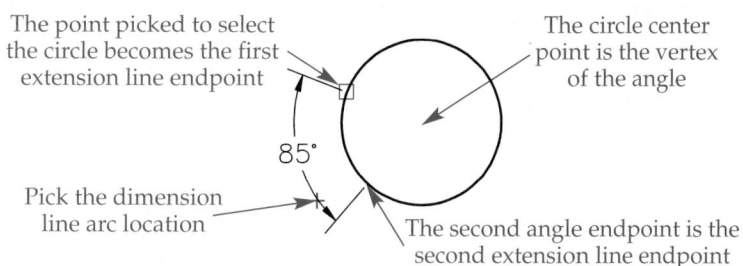

The point picked to select the circle becomes the first extension line endpoint

The circle center point is the vertex of the angle

85°

Pick the dimension line arc location

The second angle endpoint is the second extension line endpoint

Figure 16-50.
Placing angular dimensions using three points.

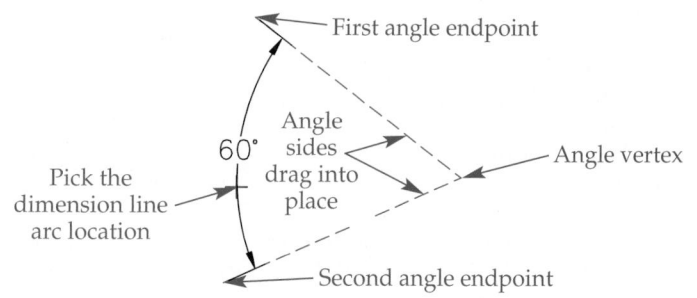

First angle endpoint

Angle sides drag into place

Angle vertex

60°

Pick the dimension line arc location

Second angle endpoint

Angular Dimensioning through Three Points

You can also establish an angular dimension through three points. The points are the angle vertex and two angle line endpoints. See **Figure 16-50**. To do this, press [Enter] after the first prompt, pick the vertex, and then pick the two endpoints. This method also dimensions angles over 180°.

Exercise 16-10
Complete the exercise on the Student CD.

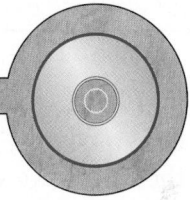

Including Symbols with Dimension Text

After you select a feature to dimension, AutoCAD responds with the measurement dimension text. In some cases, such as when you are dimensioning radii and diameters, AutoCAD automatically places the radius (R) or diameter (∅) symbol before the dimension number. However, in other cases, this is not automatic. The recommended ASME standard for a diameter dimension is to place the diameter symbol (∅) before the number. This can be done using the **Mtext** option of the dimensioning commands. When the **In-Place Text Editor** appears, place the cursor at the location where you want the symbol, such as in front of the text. Then pick **Symbol** from the **Text Formatting** toolbar or right-click to display the shortcut menu and select **Diameter** from the **Symbol** cascading menu. After you pick **OK** in the text editor, the command continues and you are asked to pick the dimension line location.

Other symbols are also available from the **Symbol** cascading menu. Another option is to use the control codes to place symbols. The **In-Place Text Editor** and drawing special symbols are covered in Chapter 9 of this text.

Another way to place symbols with dimension text is to create a dimension style that has a text style using the gdt.shx font. A text style with the gdt.shx font allows you to place commonly used dimension symbols with the lowercase letter keys. This

Figure 16-51.
Common dimensioning symbols and how to draw them. The lowercase letter displayed in parentheses with some symbol names is the keystroke for placing the symbol with the gdt.shx font and h = text height.

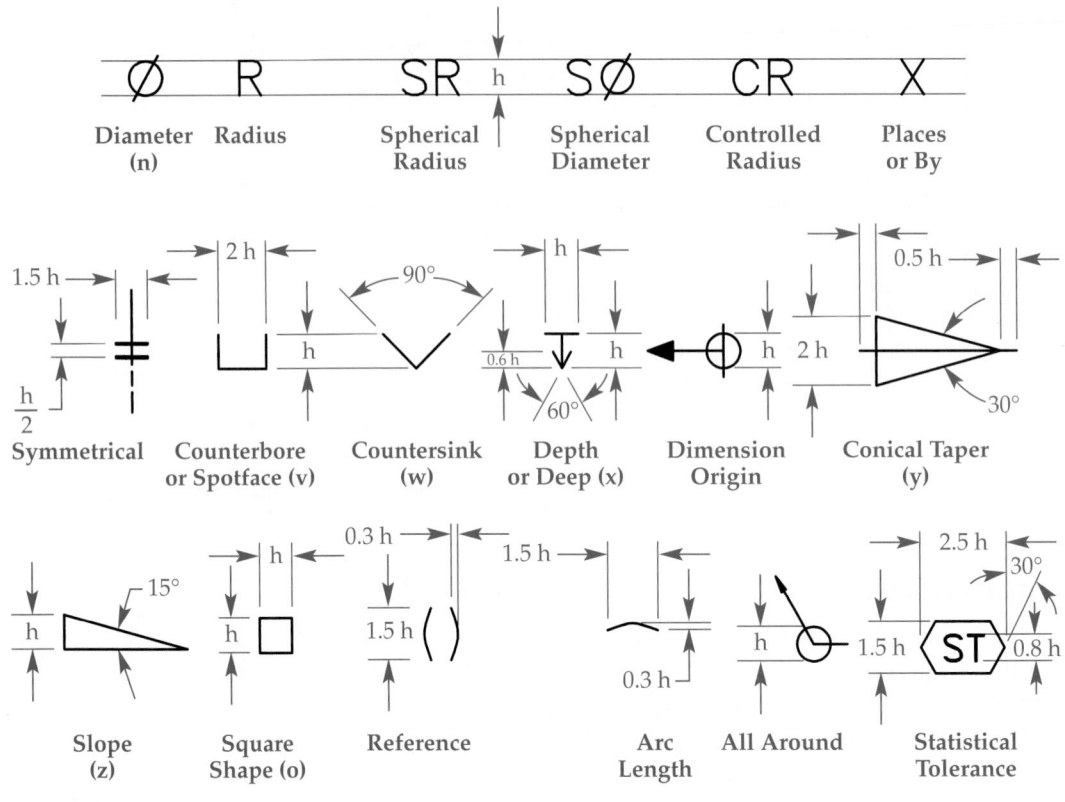

font is used for placing geometric dimensioning and tolerancing (GD&T) symbols. Often-used ASME symbols are shown in **Figure 16-51**. The letter in parentheses is the lowercase letter that you press at the keyboard to make the symbol. Additional GD&T symbols are available by pressing other keyboard keys. GD&T is covered in Chapter 20.

datum dimensioning (baseline dimensioning): A method of dimensioning in which several dimensions originate from a common surface, centerline, or center plane.

datum: Theoretically perfect surface, plane, point, or axis from which measurements can be taken.

chain dimensioning (point-to-point dimensioning): A method of dimensioning in which dimensions are placed in a line from one feature to the next.

Datum and Chain Dimensioning

With *datum dimensioning*, or *baseline dimensioning*, dimensions on an object originate from common surfaces, centerlines, or center planes. Datum dimensioning is commonly used in mechanical drafting because each dimension is independent of the others. This achieves more accuracy in manufacturing. A *datum* is a theoretically perfect surface, plane, point, or axis from which accurate measurements can be taken. **Figure 16-52** shows an object dimensioned with surface datums.

Chain dimensioning, also called *point-to-point dimensioning*, places dimensions in a line from one feature to the next. Chain dimensioning is sometimes used in mechanical drafting. However, there is less accuracy than with datum dimensioning since each dimension is dependent on other dimensions in the chain. In mechanical drafting, it is common to leave one dimension blank and provide an overall dimension. Architectural drafting uses chain dimensioning in most applications. Architectural drafting practices usually show dimensions all the way across features plus an overall dimension. **Figure 16-53** shows two examples of chain dimensioning.

Figure 16-52.
Datum dimensioning.

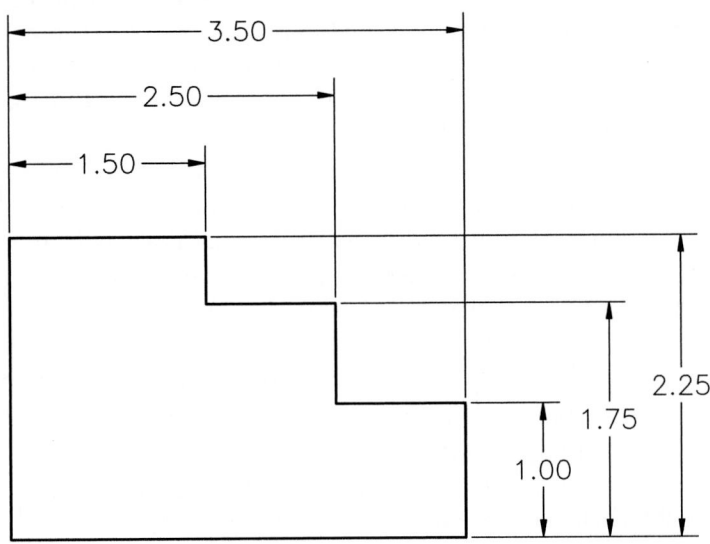

Figure 16-53.
Chain dimensioning.

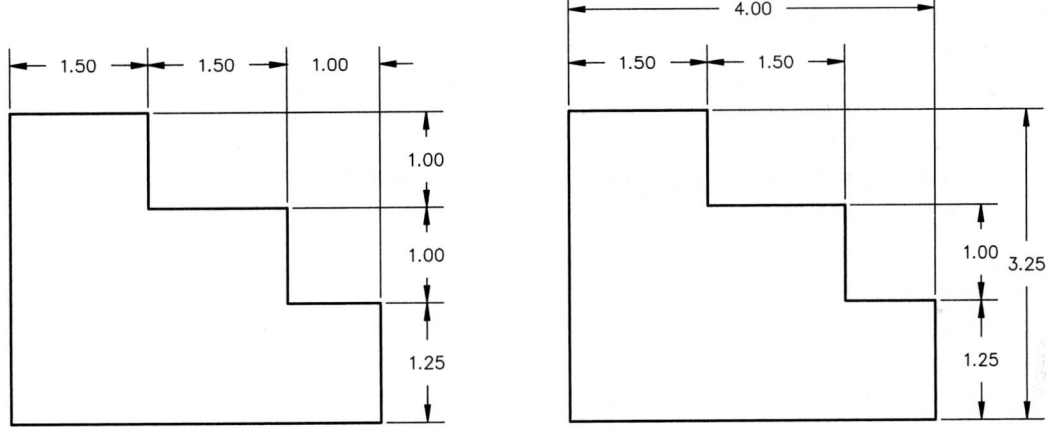

Quickly Adding Datum and Chain Dimensions

AutoCAD refers to datum dimensioning as baseline dimensioning and chain dimensioning as *continued* dimensioning. Datum dimensioning is controlled by the **DIMBASELINE** command. Chain dimensioning is controlled by the **DIMCONTINUE** command. Both of these commands allow you to select several points quickly to define a series of datum or chain dimensions, as described in the following sections. The **DIMBASELINE** and **DIMCONTINUE** commands are used in the same manner. The prompts and options are the same. Use the **Undo** option in the **DIMBASELINE** or **DIMCONTINUE** command to undo previously drawn dimensions.

continued dimensioning: A method of dimensioning in which dimensions are placed in a line from one feature to the next.

Datum Dimensions

Datum dimensions are created by picking the **Baseline** button in the **Dimension** toolbar or the **Dimension** control panel in the **Dashboard**, picking **Dimension > Baseline** in the pull-down menu, or by typing either DBA or DIMBASELINE. Baseline dimensions can be created with linear, angular, and ordinate dimensions. Ordinate dimensions are described in Chapter 17.

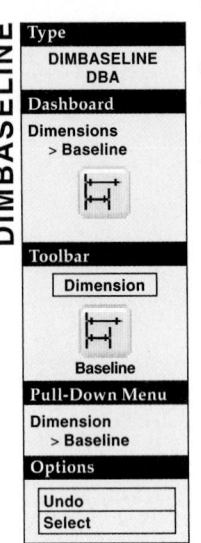

DIMBASELINE

Type
DIMBASELINE
DBA
Dashboard
Dimensions > Baseline

Toolbar
Dimension

Baseline
Pull-Down Menu
Dimension > Baseline
Options
Undo
Select

When you enter the **DIMBASELINE** command, AutoCAD asks you to specify a second extension line origin. This is because a baseline dimension is a continuation of an existing dimension. Therefore, a dimension must exist before you can use the command. AutoCAD automatically selects the most recently drawn dimension as the base dimension unless you specify a different one. As you continue to add datum dimensions, AutoCAD automatically places the extension lines, dimension lines, arrowheads, and text. For example, use the following procedure to dimension the series of horizontal baseline dimensions shown in **Figure 16-54:**

Command: **DLI** or **DIMLINEAR**↵
Specify first extension line origin or <select object>: *(pick the first extension line origin)*
Specify second extension line origin: *(pick the second extension line origin)*
Specify dimension line location or
[Mtext/Text/Angle/Horizontal/Vertical/Rotated]: *(pick the dimension line location)*
Dimension text = 2.000
Command: **DBA** or **DIMBASELINE**↵
Specify a second extension line origin or [Undo/Select] <Select>: *(pick the next second extension line origin)*
Dimension text = 3.250
Specify a second extension line origin or [Undo/Select] <Select>: *(pick the next second extension line origin)*
Dimension text = 4.375
Specify a second extension line origin or [Undo/Select] <Select>: ↵
Select base dimension: ↵
Command:

You can continue to add baseline dimensions until you press [Enter] twice to return to the Command: prompt. Notice as additional extension line origins are picked, AutoCAD automatically places the dimension text; you do not specify a location.

If you want to add datum dimensions to an existing dimension other than the most recently drawn one, use the **Select** option by pressing [Enter] at the first prompt. At the Select base dimension: prompt, pick the dimension to serve as the base. The extension line nearest the point where you select the dimension is used as the baseline point. Then select the new second extension line origins as described earlier.

Figure 16-54.
Using the
DIMBASELINE
command.
AutoCAD
automatically places
the extension lines,
dimension lines,
arrowheads, and
text.

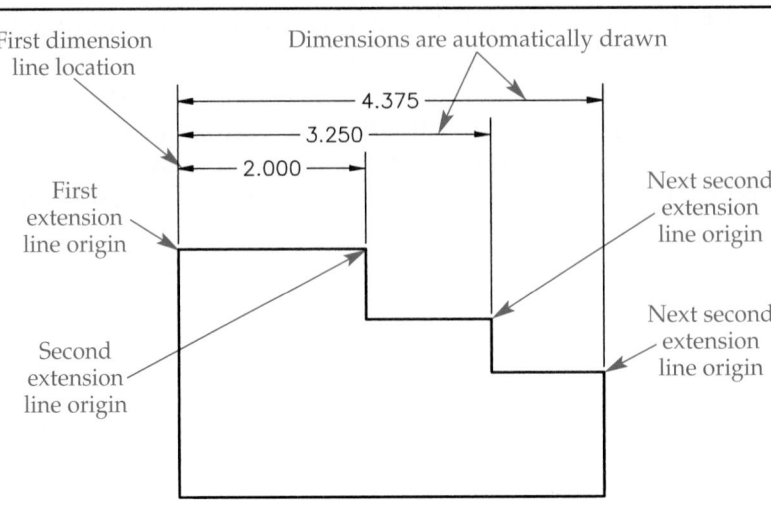

First dimension line location
Dimensions are automatically drawn
4.375
3.250
2.000
First extension line origin
Second extension line origin
Next second extension line origin
Next second extension line origin

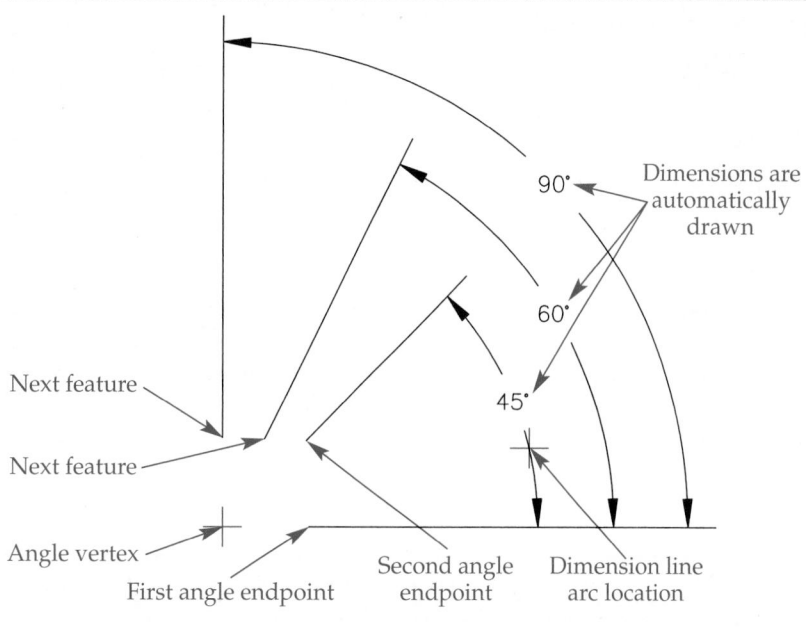

Figure 16-55.
Using the **DIMBASELINE** command to add datum dimensions to angular features.

Labels in figure: Dimensions are automatically drawn; 90°; 60°; 45°; Next feature; Next feature; Angle vertex; First angle endpoint; Second angle endpoint; Dimension line arc location

You can also draw baseline dimensions to angular features. First, draw an angular dimension. Then enter the **DIMBASELINE** command. **Figure 16-55** shows angular baseline dimensions. You can also pick an existing angular dimension other than the one most recently drawn.

Chain Dimensions

As previously mentioned, when creating chain dimensions, you will see the same prompts and options you see while creating datum dimensions. Chain dimensioning is shown in **Figure 16-56**. Chain dimensions (continued dimensions) are created by picking **Dimension** > **Continue** in the pull-down menu, picking the **Continue** button in the **Dimension** toolbar or the **Dimension** control panel in the **Dashboard**, or by typing DCO or DIMCONTINUE. Continued dimensions can be created with linear, angular, and ordinate dimensions. Ordinate dimensions are described in Chapter 17.

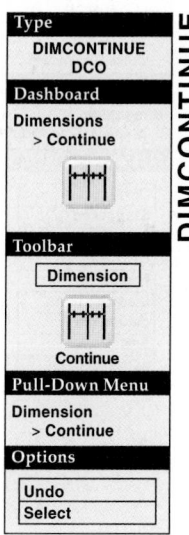

Figure 16-56.
Using the **DIMCONTINUE** command to create chain dimensions.

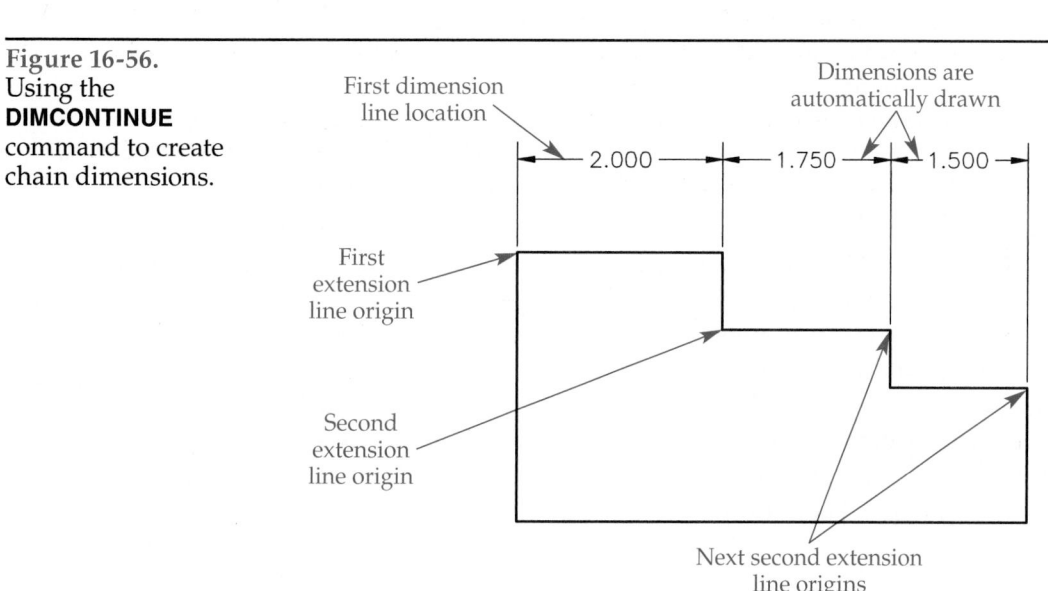

Labels in figure: First dimension line location; Dimensions are automatically drawn; 2.000; 1.750; 1.500; First extension line origin; Second extension line origin; Next second extension line origins

Exercise 16-11

Complete the exercise on the Student CD.

Using Qdim to Dimension

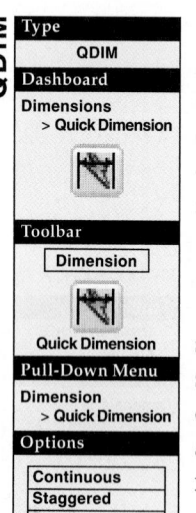

The **QDIM**, or quick dimension, command makes chain and datum dimensioning easy by eliminating the need to define the exact points being dimensioned. Often, the points that need to be selected for dimensioning are the endpoints of lines or the center points of arcs. AutoCAD automates the process of point selection in the **QDIM** command by finding those points for you. The **QDIM** command can be accessed by selecting **Dimension > Quick Dimension** from the pull-down menu, picking the **Quick Dimension** button in the **Dimension** toolbar or the **Dimension** control panel in the **Dashboard**, or typing QDIM.

The type of geometry selected affects the **QDIM** output. If a single polyline is selected, **QDIM** attempts to draw linear dimensions to every vertex of the polyline. If a single arc or circle is selected, **QDIM** draws a radius or diameter dimension. If multiple objects are selected, linear dimensions are drawn to the vertex of every line or polyline and to the center of every arc or circle. In each case, AutoCAD finds the points automatically. The command sequence is:

```
Command: QDIM↵
Associative dimension priority = Endpoint
Select geometry to dimension: (pick several lines, polylines, arcs, and/or circles)
Select geometry to dimension: ↵
Specify dimension line position, or
[Continuous/Staggered/Baseline/Ordinate/Radius/Diameter/datumPoint/Edit/seT-
    tings] <current>: (pick a position for the dimension lines)
Command:
```

Figure 16-57 shows examples of different types of objects being dimensioned with the **QDIM** command. The upper dimensions are created by selecting each object separately. The lower dimensions are created by selecting all of the objects at once.

The **Continuous** option creates chain dimensions. The **Baseline** option creates datum dimensions. The **Staggered** option creates staggered (noncontinuous) dimensions. The **Ordinate**, **Radius**, and **Diameter** options are described in Chapter 17. In Figure 16-57, the polyline labeled A was dimensioned with the **Baseline** option of the **QDIM** command. The command sequence is:

Figure 16-57.
The **QDIM** command can dimension multiple features or objects at the same time.

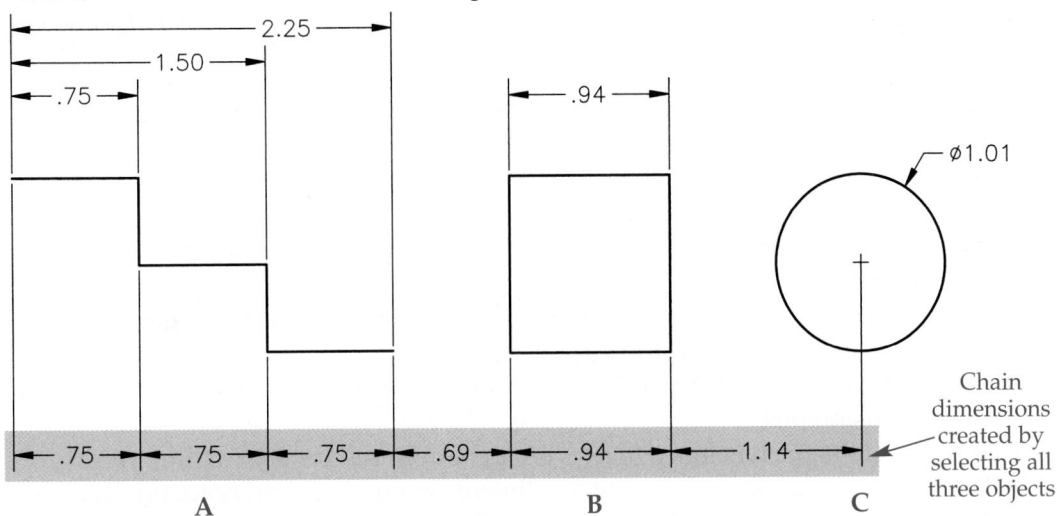

```
Command: QDIM↵
Select geometry to dimension: (pick the polyline shown in Figure 16-51A)
Specify dimension line position, or
[Continuous/Staggered/Baseline/Ordinate/Radius/Diameter/datumPoint/Edit/seTtings]
<Continuous>: B↵
Specify dimension line position, or
[Continuous/Staggered/Baseline/Ordinate/Radius/Diameter/datumPoint/Edit/seTtings]
<Baseline>: (pick a position for the dimension line)
Command:
```

The dimensions at the bottom of **Figure 16-57** were created using the **Continuous** option of the **QDIM** command and selecting all three objects.

The **datumPoint** option can be used to change the datum point for datum or chain dimensions. The **Settings** option allows you to set the object snap mode for establishing the extension line origins to **Endpoint** or **Intersection**.

The **QDIM** command can also be used as a way to edit any existing associative dimension. Editing dimensions and a description of the **Edit** option of the **QDIM** command are described in Chapter 18.

Template Development
Chapter 16

Dimensions require time and effort to set up properly. By adding them to your drawing templates, you can avoid having to repeat this process each time you begin a new drawing. Refer to the Student CD for detailed instructions to add dimension styles to your mechanical, architectural, and civil drawing templates.

Chapter Test

Answer the following questions. Write your answers on a separate sheet of paper or complete the electronic chapter test on the Student CD.

1. What does the *M* mean in the title of the standard ASME Y14.5M-1994?
2. Define *dimension style*.
3. Name the dialog box that is used to create dimension styles.
4. Identify at least three ways to access the dialog box identified in Question 3.
5. Name the dialog box tab used to control the appearance of dimension lines and extension lines.
6. Name at least four arrowhead types that are available in the **Symbols and Arrows** tab for common use on architectural drawings.
7. Name the dialog box tab used to control the dimensioning settings that display the dimension text.
8. What has to happen before a text style can be accessed for use in dimension text?
9. What is the recommended height for dimension numbers and notes on drawings?
10. Name the area in the **Modify Dimension Style** dialog box in which vertical justification of text can be set.
11. Name the dialog box tab used to control dimensioning settings that adjust the location of dimension lines, dimension text, arrowheads, and leader lines.
12. How do you quickly set a dimension style current?
13. Define the term *general notes*.
14. Name the **DIMLINEAR** option that opens the **In-Place Text Editor** for changing the dimension text.
15. Name the two dimensioning commands that provide linear dimensions for angled surfaces.
16. Name the command used to dimension angles in degrees.
17. Give two examples of symbols that are automatically placed with dimensions.
18. AutoCAD refers to datum dimensioning as _____ dimensioning.
19. AutoCAD refers to chain dimensioning as _____ dimensioning.
20. What is the keyboard shortcut (command alias) for the **DIMBASELINE** command?
21. How do you place a datum dimension from the origin of the previously drawn dimension?
22. How do you place a datum dimension from the origin of a dimension that was drawn during a previous drawing session?
23. Which command other than **DIMBASELINE** can be used to create baseline dimensions?
24. Which type of dimensions are created when you select multiple objects in the **QDIM** command?
25. Name at least three modes of dimensioning available through the **QDIM** command.

Drawing Problems

Use one of your templates for each problem. Set limits, units, dimension styles, and other parameters as needed. Use the following general guidelines.

A. Use dimension styles that match the type of drawing as described in this chapter.
B. Use object snap modes to your best advantage.
C. Apply dimensions accurately using ASME or other related industry/architectural standards. Dimensions are in inches, or feet and inches, unless otherwise specified.
D. Set separate layers for dimensions and other features.
E. For mechanical drawings, place the following general notes 1/2" from the lower-left corner:

> NOTES:
> 1. INTERPRET DIMENSIONS AND TOLERANCES PER ASME Y14.5M-1994.
> 2. REMOVE ALL BURRS AND SHARP EDGES.
> 3. UNLESS OTHERWISE SPECIFIED, ALL DIMENSIONS ARE IN INCHES (or MILLIMETERS as applicable).

1. Create the views of a shaft and dimension as shown. Save the drawing as **P16-1**.

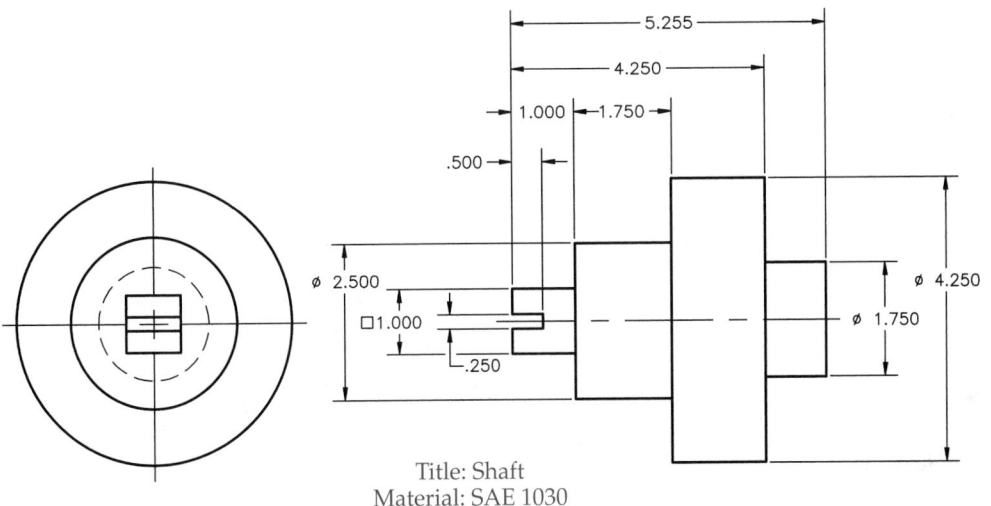

Title: Shaft
Material: SAE 1030

2. Open P3-3 and finish the drawing by adding the dimensions. Save the drawing as **P16-2**.

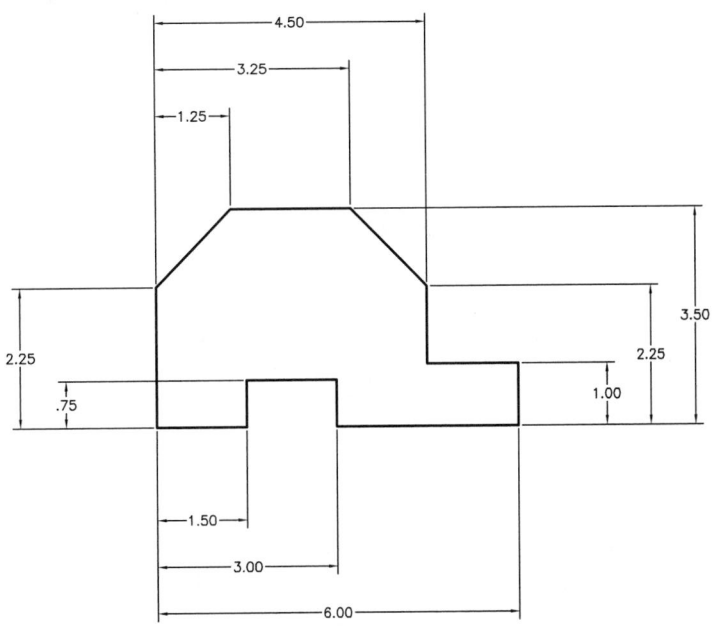

3. Open a new drawing using a mechanical template and save it as P16-3. Then open P3-4 and copy one instance of Object A and Object B to the new drawing. Dimension the two objects. Save the drawing.

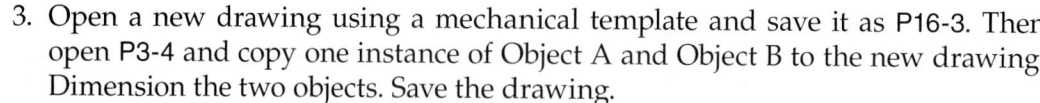

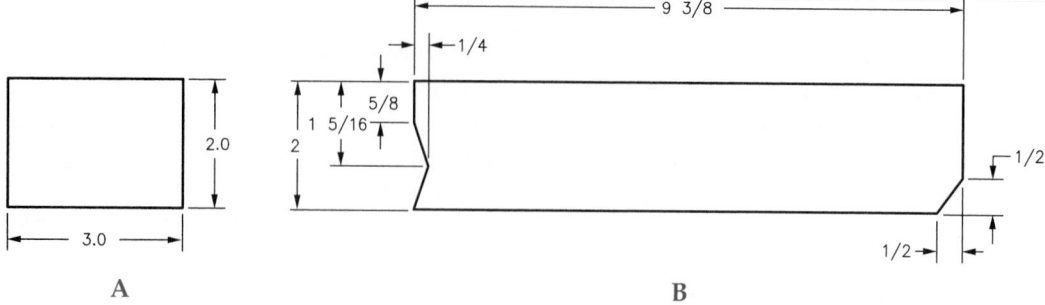

A   B

4. Open P3-5 and finish the drawing by adding the dimensions. Use datum dimensioning. Save the drawing as P16-4.

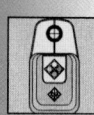

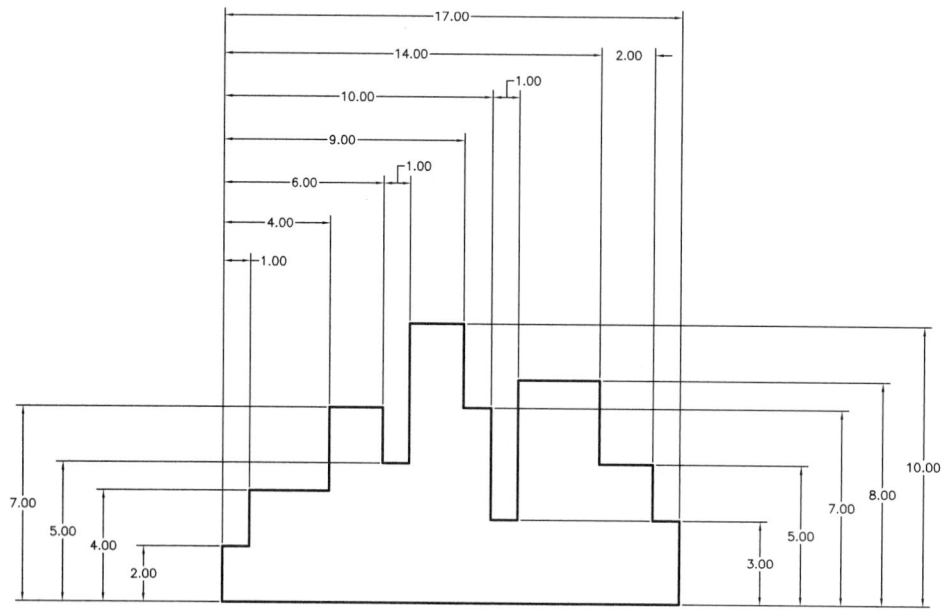

5. Open P3-7 and finish the drawing by dimensioning both objects. Save the drawing as P16-5.

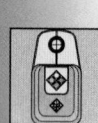

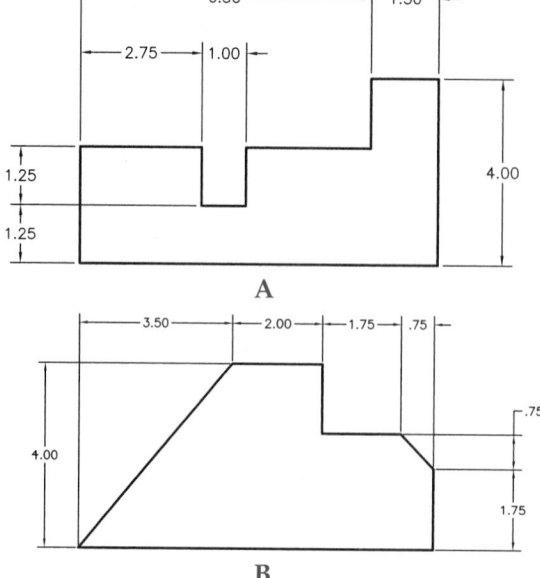

A

B

6. Open a new drawing using an architectural template. Draw the elevation of the desk and dimension as shown. Save the drawing as P16-6.

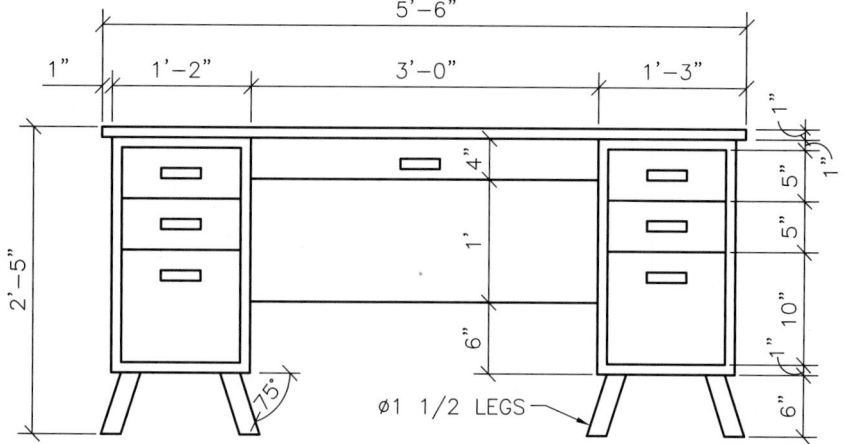

7. Open P3-8 and finish the drawing by adding dimensions. Save the drawing as P16-7.

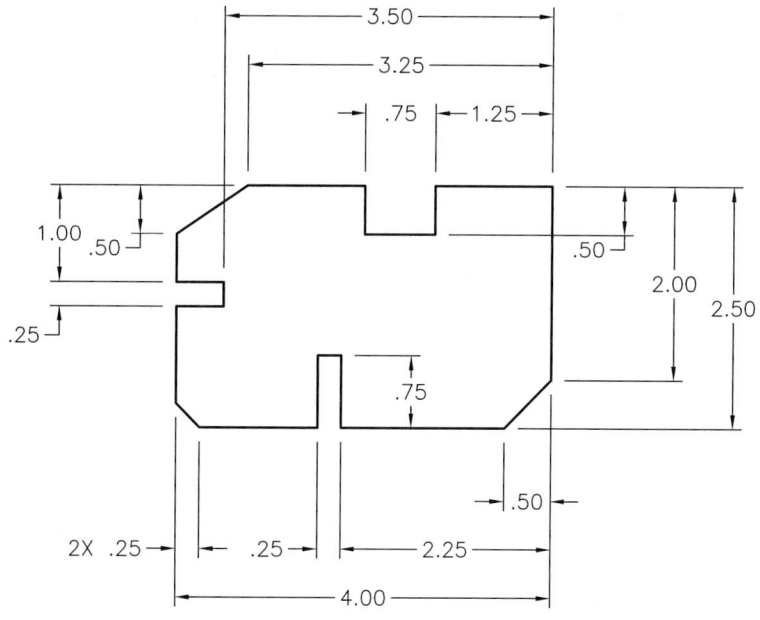

8. Open P3-9 and finish the drawing by adding dimensions. Note that this is a metric drawing. Save the drawing as P16-8.

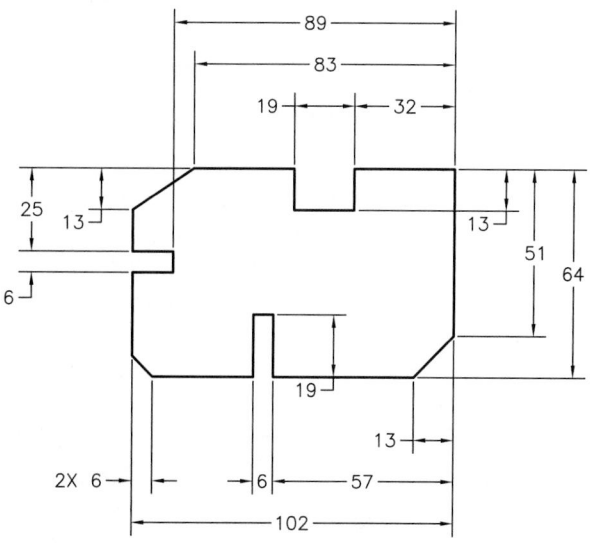

9. Open P3-10 and finish the drawing by adding dimensions. Save the drawing as P16-9.

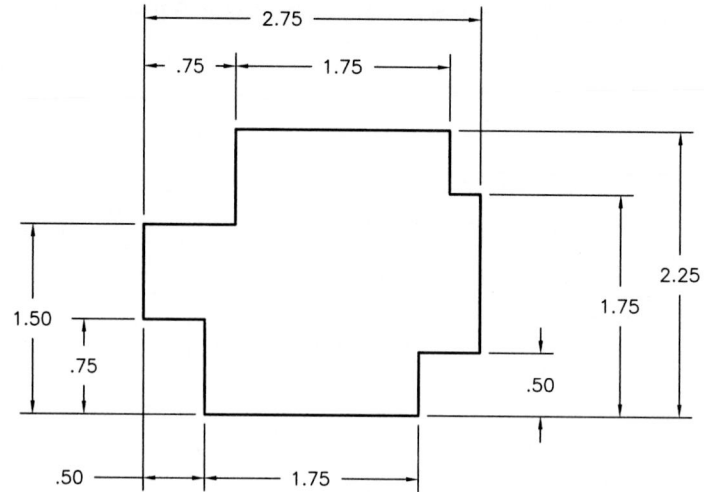

10. Open P3-11 and finish the drawing by adding dimensions. Save the drawing as P16-10.

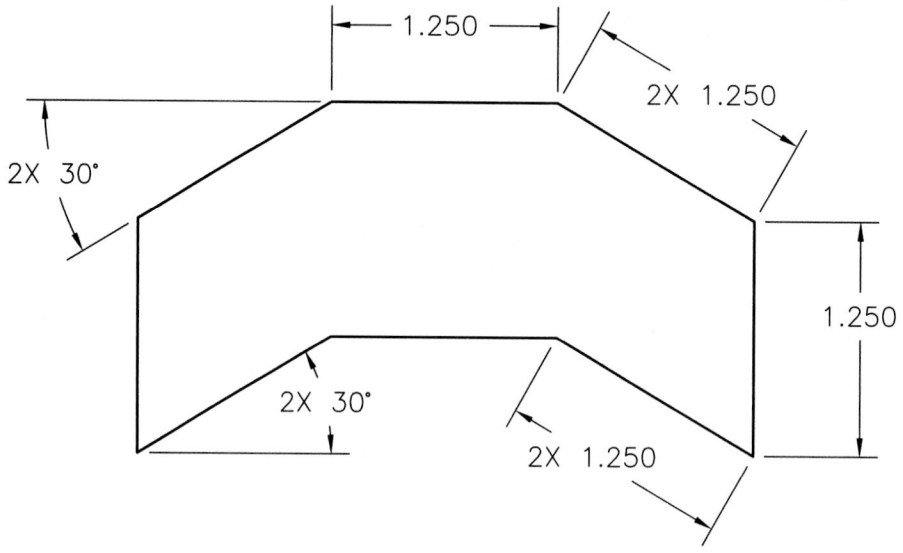

11. Open P3-12 and finish the drawing by adding dimensions. Save the drawing as P16-11.

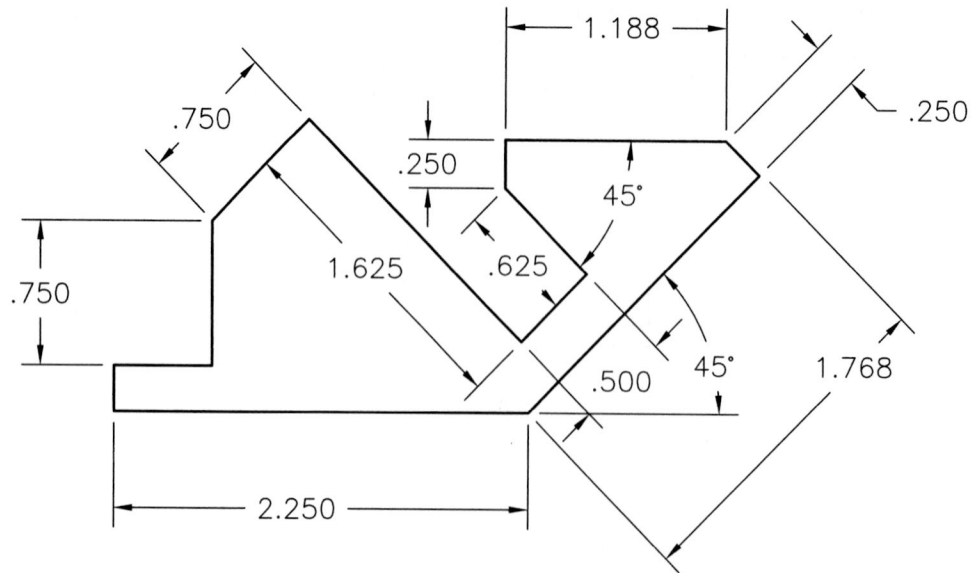

12. Open a new drawing using an architectural template. Create the partial floor plan shown below and dimension as shown. Save the drawing as P16-12.

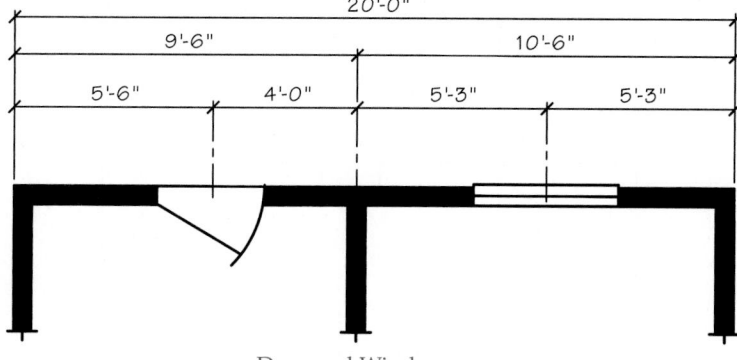

Door and Window

13. Open a new drawing using an architectural template. Create the partial floor plan and dimension as shown. Save the drawing as P16-13.

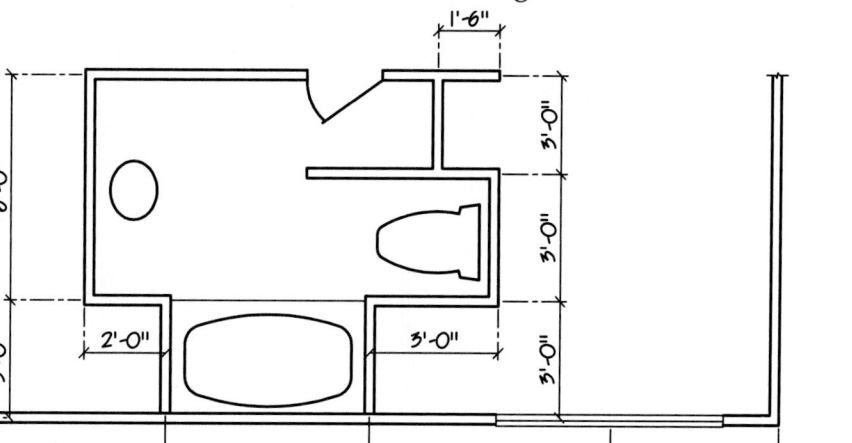

Bathroom Area

14. Open a new drawing using a mechanical template. Create the object and dimension as shown. Save the drawing as P16-14.

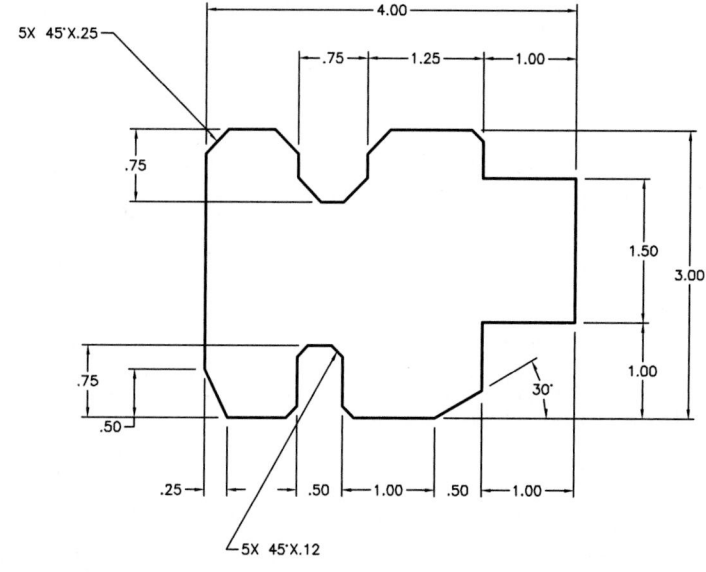

15. Open a new drawing using a mechanical template. Create the object and dimension as shown. Save the drawing as P16-15.

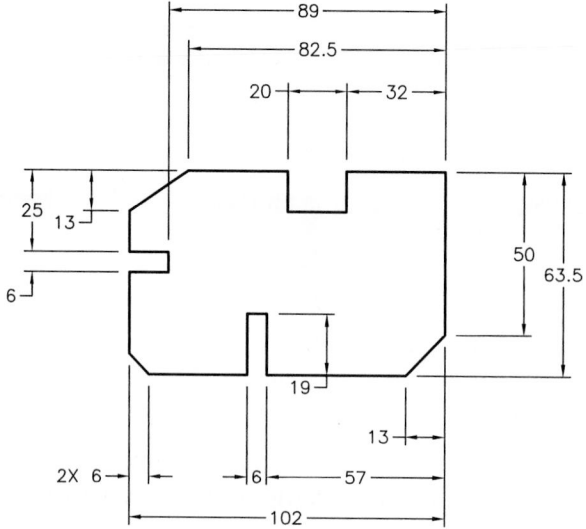

16. Draw this floor plan. Size the windows and doors to your own specifications. Save the drawing as P16-16.

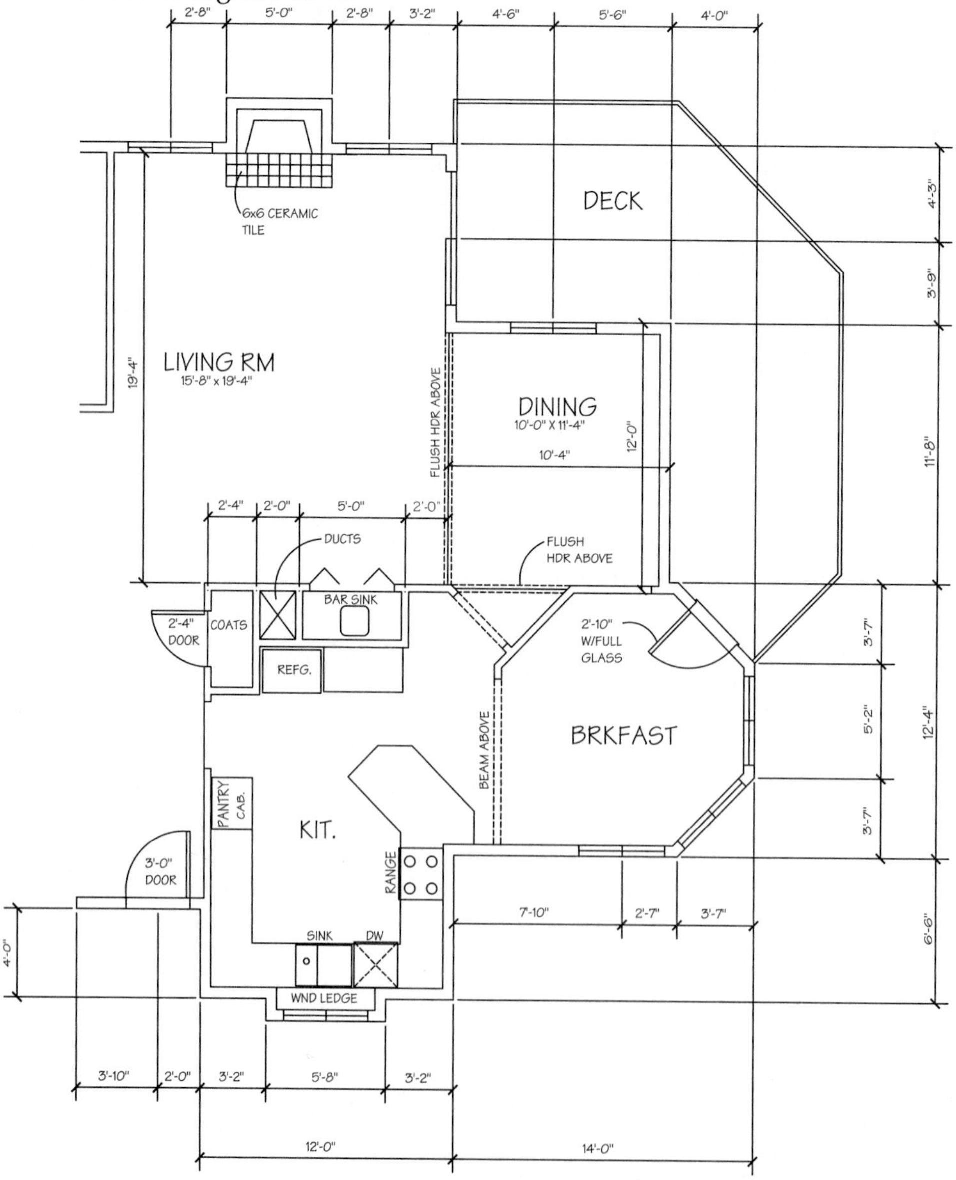

Dimensioning Features and Alternate Practices

Learning Objectives

After completing this chapter, you will be able to do the following:

✓ Add diameter and radius dimensions to a drawing.
✓ Create and use multileader styles.
✓ Use the **MLEADER** command to draw specific notes with linked leader lines.
✓ Prepare thread symbols and notes.
✓ Dimension objects with arrowless tabular dimensions.

Most objects or parts to be manufactured contain holes, slots, or other features. The size and location of these features must be described for manufacturing. This chapter describes dimensioning practices for object features and also introduces alternate dimensioning practices that are becoming common in mechanical drawings.

Dimensioning Circles

Circles are normally dimensioned by giving the diameter. The ASME standard for dimensioning arcs is to give the radius. However, AutoCAD allows you to dimension either a circle or an arc with a diameter dimension. Diameter dimensions are produced by picking the **Diameter** button in the **Dimension** toolbar or the **Dimension** control panel in the **Dashboard**, picking **Dimension > Diameter** in the pull-down menu, or typing DDI or DIMDIAMETER. You are then prompted to select the arc or circle.

When you select the arc or circle, a leader line and diameter dimension value attach to the crosshairs. You can drag the leader to any desired location and length. Pick the location and length to place the dimension. The resulting leader points to the center of the circle or arc just as recommended by the ASME standard. See **Figure 17-1.**

The **DIMDIAMETER** command also has the **Mtext**, **Text**, and **Angle** options that were introduced earlier. Use the **Mtext** or **Text** option if you want to change the text value or the **Angle** option if you want to change the angle of the text.

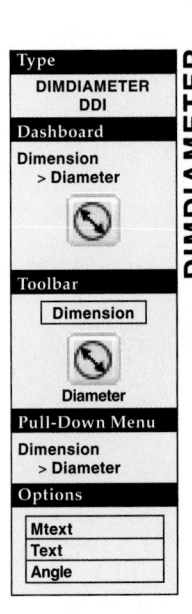

DIMDIAMETER	
Type	DIMDIAMETER DDI
Dashboard	Dimension > Diameter
Toolbar	Dimension / Diameter
Pull-Down Menu	Dimension > Diameter
Options	Mtext / Text / Angle

Exercise 17-1

Complete the exercise on the Student CD.

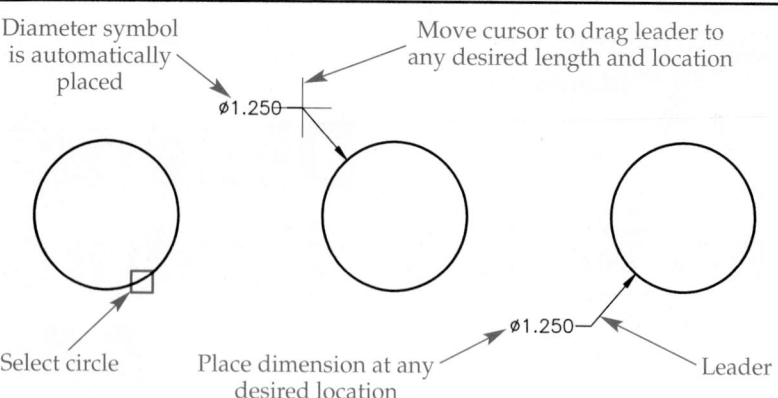

Figure 17-1.
Using the
DIMDIAMETER
command.

Diameter symbol is automatically placed

Move cursor to drag leader to any desired length and location

Ø1.250

Select circle

Place dimension at any desired location

Ø1.250

Leader

Dimensioning Holes

Holes are dimensioned in the view in which they appear as circles. Give location dimensions to the center and a leader showing the diameter. Leader lines can be drawn using the **DIMDIAMETER** command, as previously described. The center mark type and size are controlled in the dimension style. Multiple holes of the same size can be noted with one hole dimension by preceding the dimension with the number of occurrences followed by X. In **Figure 17-2**, the 2X Ø.50 dimension is an example of this practice. Use the **Mtext** or **Text** option to create this dimension. The **Angle** option can be used to change the angle of the text numbers, but this is not commonly done.

PROFESSIONAL TIP

The ASME standard recommends a small space between the object and the extension line. This happens when the **Offset from origin** setting in the dimension style is set to its default or some other desired positive value. This is very useful *except* when you are dimensioning to centerlines for the location of holes. When you pick the endpoint of the centerline, a positive value leaves a space between the centerline and the beginning of the extension line. This is not a preferred practice. Change the **Offset from origin** setting to 0 to remove the gap. Be sure to change back to the positive setting when dimensioning other objects.

Figure 17-2.
Dimensioning holes.

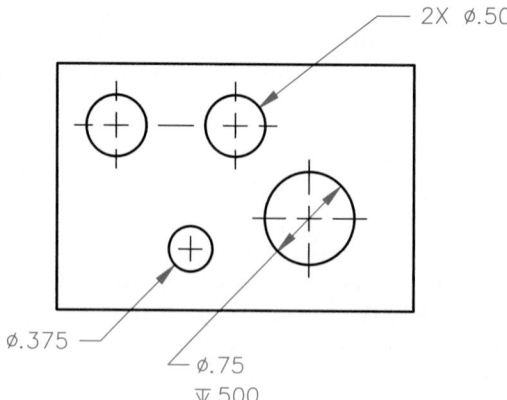

2X Ø.50

Ø.375

Ø.75
▽.500

Dimensioning for Manufacturing Processes

A *counterbore* is a larger-diameter hole machined at one end of a smaller hole. It provides a place for the head of a bolt. A *spotface* is similar to a counterbore except that it is not as deep. The spotface provides a smooth, recessed surface for a washer. A *countersink* is a cone-shaped recess at one end of a hole. It provides a mating surface for a screw head of the same shape. Notes for these features are provided in drawings using symbols. First, locate the centers in the circular view. Then place a leader providing machining information in a note. See Figure 17-3.

Symbols for these types of applications can be customized as blocks, as described in Chapter 23. These symbols can also be drawn by creating a dimension style with a text style using the gdt.shx font, as explained in Chapter 16.

The **DIMDIAMETER** command allows you to use multiline text to create the dimension. Additional text can be added by editing the dimension text, since it is actually a multiline text object.

counterbore: A larger-diameter hole machined at one end of a smaller hole that provides a place for the head of a bolt.

spotface: A larger-diameter hole machined at one end of a smaller hole that provides a smooth, recessed surface for a washer; similar to a counterbore, except not as deep.

countersink: A cone-shaped recess at one end of a hole that provides a mating surface for a screw head of the same shape.

PROFESSIONAL TIP

After creating any dimension, you can edit the dimension text directly using the **Properties** palette. Editing dimensions is covered in Chapter 18.

Dimensioning Repetitive Features

Repetitive features refer to many features having the same shape and size. When this occurs, the number of repetitions is followed by an X, a space, and the size dimension. The dimension is then connected to the feature with a leader. See Figure 17-4.

repetitive features: Many features having the same shape and size.

Exercise 17-2
Complete the exercise on the Student CD.

Figure 17-3. Dimension notes for machining processes. The symbols can be inserted as blocks or with lowercase letters when the gdt.shx font is used.

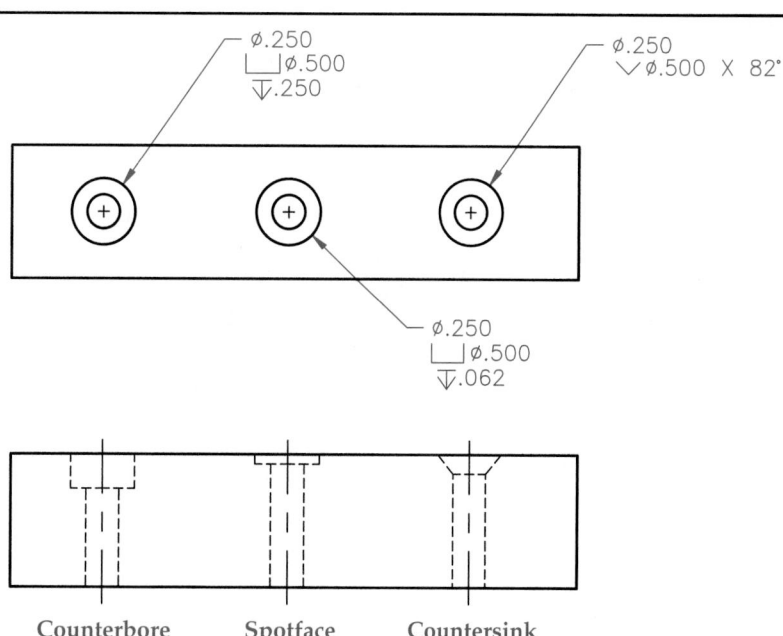

Figure 17-4.
Dimensioning repetitive features (shown in color).

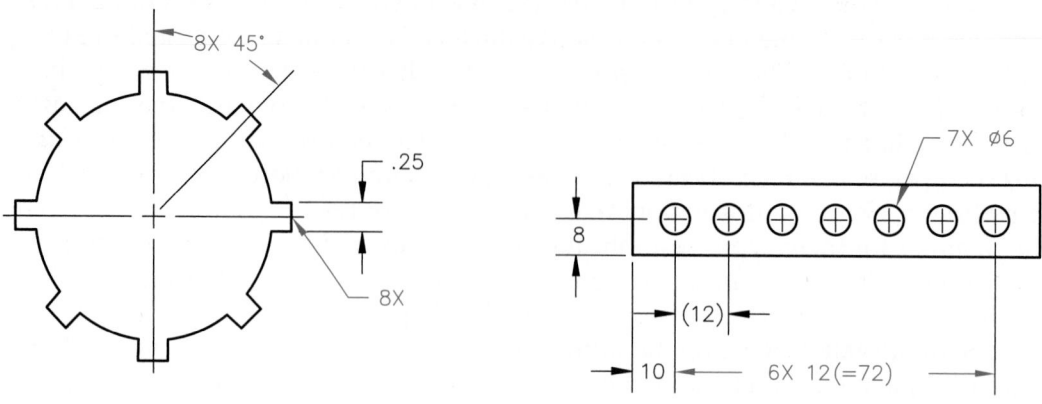

Dimensioning Arcs

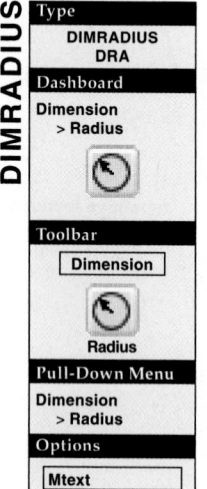

The standard for dimensioning arcs is a radius dimension. A radius dimension is placed with the **DIMRADIUS** command. Access this command by picking the **Radius** button on the **Dimension** toolbar or the **Dimension** control panel in the **Dashboard**, picking **Dimension > Radius** in the pull-down menu, or typing either DRA or DIMRADIUS.

When you pick the desired arc or circle to dimension, a leader line and radius dimension value become attached to the crosshairs. You can drag the leader to any desired location and length. Pick the location and length to place the dimension. The resulting leader points to the center of the arc or circle as recommended by the ASME standard. See **Figure 17-5.**

As with the previously described dimensioning commands, you can use the **Mtext** or **Text** option to change the dimension text. You can also use the **Angle** option to change the angle of the text value.

Figure 17-5.
Using the **DIMRADIUS** command to dimension arcs.

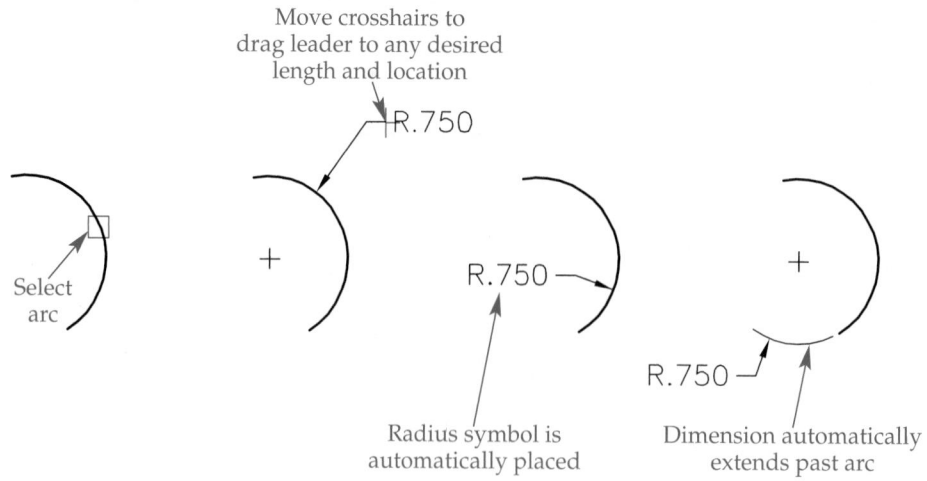

Dimensioning Arc Length

The length of an arc can be dimensioned using the **DIMARC** command. The length measures the distance along the arc segment. To access the **DIMARC** command, pick the **Arc Length** button on the **Dimension** toolbar or the **Dimension** control panel in the **Dashboard**, pick **Dimension** > **Arc Length** from the pull-down menu, or type DAR or DIMARC.

When you select the arc to be dimensioned, the arc length symbol and dimension value become attached to the cursor. By default, the symbol is placed before the text. To place the dimension, move the text to the desired location and pick. The ASME standard recommends placing the symbol over the text, as shown in **Figure 17-6**. The **Modify Dimension Style** dialog box controls the symbol placements.

Before placing the dimension, you can change the dimension text with the **Mtext** or **Text** option, or you can use the **Angle** option to change the angle of the text. Use the **Partial** option if you do not want to dimension the length of the entire arc. Entering this option prompts you to select a first point on the arc and a second point. The length between these two points is dimensioned. When the arc is greater than 90°, the **Leader** option is also available. This allows you to add a leader pointing to the arc being dimensioned.

DIMARC	
Type	DIMARC DAR
Dashboard	Dimension > Arc Length
Toolbar	Dimension / Arc Length
Pull-Down Menu	Dimension > Arc Length
Options	Mtext / Text / Angle / Partial / Leader

Dimensioning Large Circles and Arcs

When a circle or arc is so large that its center point cannot be displayed on the layout, the **DIMJOGGED** command can be used. This command allows you to draw a radius dimension by selecting a center point origin and placing a break symbol on the dimension line. To access the **DIMJOGGED** command, pick the **Jogged** button in the **Dimension** toolbar or the **Dimension** control panel in the **Dashboard**, pick **Dimension** > **Jogged** from the pull-down menu, or type JOG or DIMJOGGED. Refer to **Figure 17-7** as you go through the following command sequence:

> Command: **JOG** *or* **DIMJOGGED**↵
> Select arc or circle: *(pick the arc or circle)*
> Specify center location override: *(pick a point for the origin of the center location)*
> Specify dimension line location or [Mtext/Text/Angle]: *(pick to place the dimension line)*
> Specify jog location: *(pick a point to place the break symbol)*
> Command:

DIMJOGGED	
Type	DIMJOGGED JOG
Dashboard	Dimension > Jogged
Toolbar	Dimension / Jogged
Pull-Down Menu	Dimension > Jogged
Options	Mtext / Text / Angle

After you specify the dimension line location, pick a point to locate the center of the break symbol. The different components of the dimension can be moved by using grip editing after the dimension is placed.

Dimensioning Fillets and Rounds

Small inside arcs are called *fillets*. Small arcs on outside corners are called *rounds*. Fillets are designed to strengthen inside corners. Rounds are used to relieve sharp corners. Fillets and rounds can be dimensioned individually as arcs, using the **DIMRADIUS** command, or in a general note. See **Figure 17-8**. On mechanical drawings, it is common to include a general note such as ALL FILLETS AND ROUNDS R.125 UNLESS OTHERWISE SPECIFIED on the drawing.

fillets: Small inside arcs.

rounds: Small arcs on outside corners.

Figure 17-6.
Using the **DIMARC** command to dimension the length of an arc.

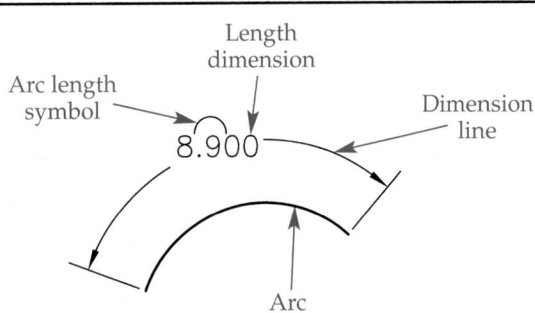

Figure 17-7.
Using the **DIMJOGGED** command to place a radius dimension for a large arc.

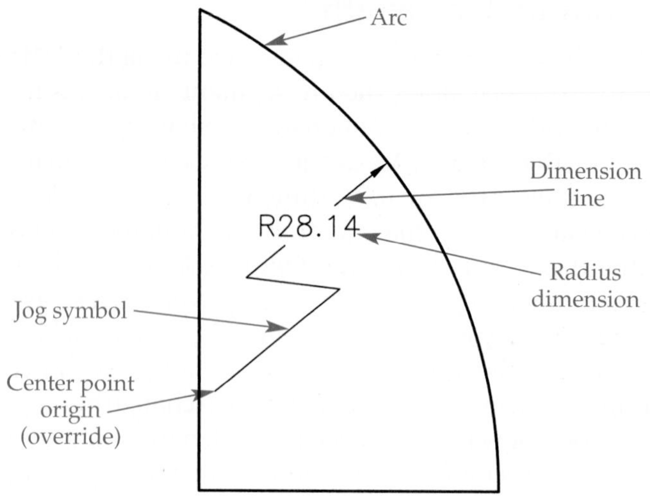

Arc

Dimension line

R28.14

Radius dimension

Jog symbol

Center point origin (override)

Figure 17-8.
Dimensioning fillets and rounds.

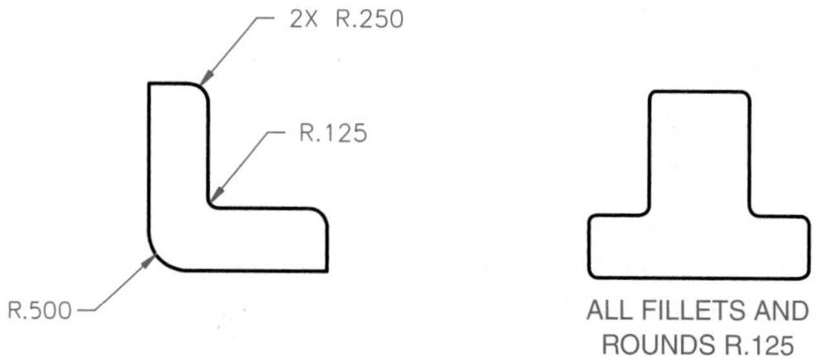

2X R.250

R.125

R.500

ALL FILLETS AND ROUNDS R.125

Exercise 17-3

Complete the exercise on the Student CD.

Dimensioning Curves

When possible, curves are dimensioned as arcs. When they are not in the shape of a constant-radius arc, they should be dimensioned to points along the curve using the **DIMLINEAR** command. See Figure 17-9.

Figure 17-9.
Dimensioning curves that do not have a constant radius.

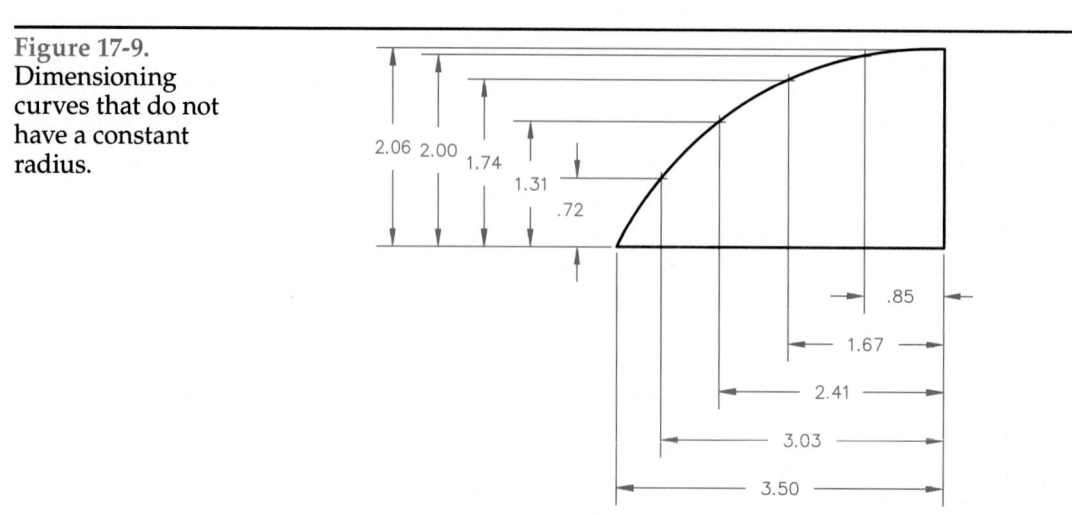

2.06 2.00 1.74 1.31 .72

.85

1.67

2.41

3.03

3.50

Drawing Center Dashes or Centerlines

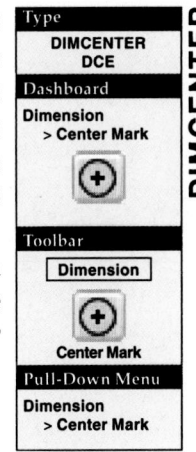

When small circles or arcs are dimensioned, the **DIMDIAMETER** and **DIMRADIUS** commands leave center dashes. If the dimension of a large circle crosses through the center, the dashes are left out. However, you can add center dashes and centerlines manually with the **DIMCENTER** command. This command is accessed by picking the **Center Mark** button in the **Dimension** toolbar or the **Dimension** control panel in the **Dashboard**, picking **Dimension > Center Mark** in the pull-down menu, or typing DCE or DIMCENTER.

Once the command is entered, you are prompted to pick an arc or circle. When you pick the circle or arc, the center marks appear. The size of the center marks and the length that the centerlines extend outside the circle or arc is controlled by the **Center marks** area in the **Symbols and Arrows** tab of the **Modify Dimension Style** dialog box.

Leader Lines

The **DIMDIAMETER** and **DIMRADIUS** commands automatically place leaders on the drawing. AutoCAD multileaders allow you to begin and end a leader line where you desire. You can also place single or multiple lines of text and symbols with the leader. Multileaders are ideal for:

- Adding specific notes to a drawing.
- Staggering a leader line to go around other drawing features. Staggering leader lines is not a recommended ASME standard.
- Drawing multiple leaders. Drawing two or more leaders from one note is not a recommended ASME standard.
- Making custom leader lines.
- Drawing curved leaders for architectural applications.
- Aligning and combining specific notes.

The **MLEADER** command is used to create leader lines and related notes. This command provides you with the flexibility to add a variety of leader lines and place annotations and symbols with the leader. An *annotation* is text on a drawing, such as a note or dimension. Multileader line characteristics, such as leader format, annotation style, and the arrowhead size, are controlled by multileader styles. Multiple-segment leaders can also be created, and separate leaders can be aligned and grouped. Adding and removing multiple leader lines and aligning leaders is described in Chapter 18.

annotation: Text on a drawing, such as a note or dimension.

Multileader Styles

NEW FEATURE

The appearance of leaders created using multileader commands, from the size and the style of the text to the color of the leader line, is controlled by several different settings. *Multileader styles* are saved configurations of these settings.

A multileader style is created by changing the multileader settings as needed to achieve the desired appearance for your drafting application. This process is very similar to developing a dimension style. In mechanical drafting, properly drawn leaders have one straight segment extending from the feature to a horizontal *shoulder* that is 1/8″–1/4″ (3 mm–6 mm) long. While most other fields also use straight leaders, AutoCAD provides the option of drawing curved leaders, which are commonly used in architectural drafting. See Figure 17-10.

multileader styles: Saved configurations for the appearance of leaders.

shoulder: A short horizontal line usually added to the end of straight leader lines.

Figure 17-10.
Multileader styles control the display of leaders created using the **MLEADER** command. This example shows the difference between an architectural and mechanical style leader.

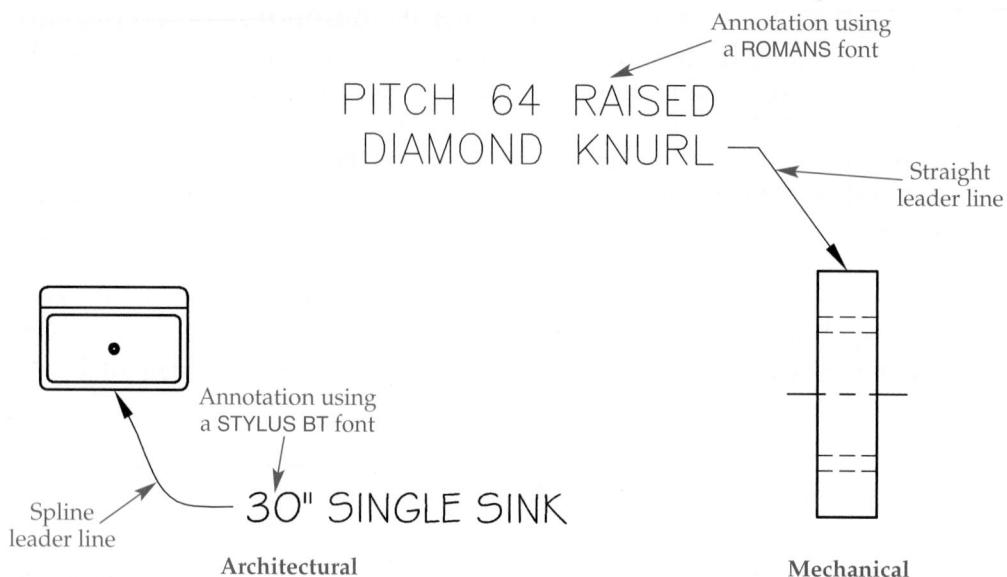

Annotation using
a ROMANS font

PITCH 64 RAISED
DIAMOND KNURL

Straight
leader line

Annotation using
a STYLUS BT font

30" SINGLE SINK

Spline
leader line

Architectural

Mechanical

Working with Multileader Styles

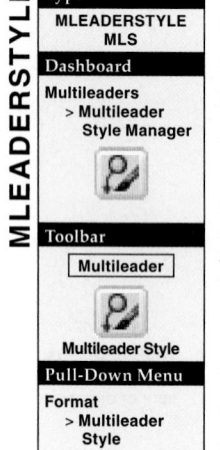

Type
**MLEADERSTYLE
MLS**

Dashboard
**Multileaders
> Multileader
Style Manager**

Toolbar
Multileader

Multileader Style

Pull-Down Menu
**Format
> Multileader
Style**

MLEADERSTYLE

Multileader styles are created using the **Multileader Style Manager** dialog box. See **Figure 17-11.** This dialog box is accessed by picking the **Multileader Style** button from the **Multileader** toolbar or the **Multileader Style Manager** button from the **Multileaders** control panel in the **Dashboard**, by selecting **Format** > **Multileader Style** in the pull-down menu, or by typing MLS or MLEADERSTYLE.

The current multileader style, Standard by default, is noted at the top of the **Multileader Style Manager** dialog box. The **Styles:** box displays the multileader styles defined in the current drawing. All new multileaders are created in the current style, but existing multileaders are not affected. The selection in the **List:** drop-down list controls whether all styles or only the styles in use are displayed in the **Styles:** box.

The **Preview of:** image displays the characteristics of the selected multileader style. If you change any of the AutoCAD default multileader settings without first creating a new multileader style, the changes are automatically stored in a multileader style override.

Figure 17-11.
The **Multileader Style Manager** dialog box. The Standard multileader style is the AutoCAD default.

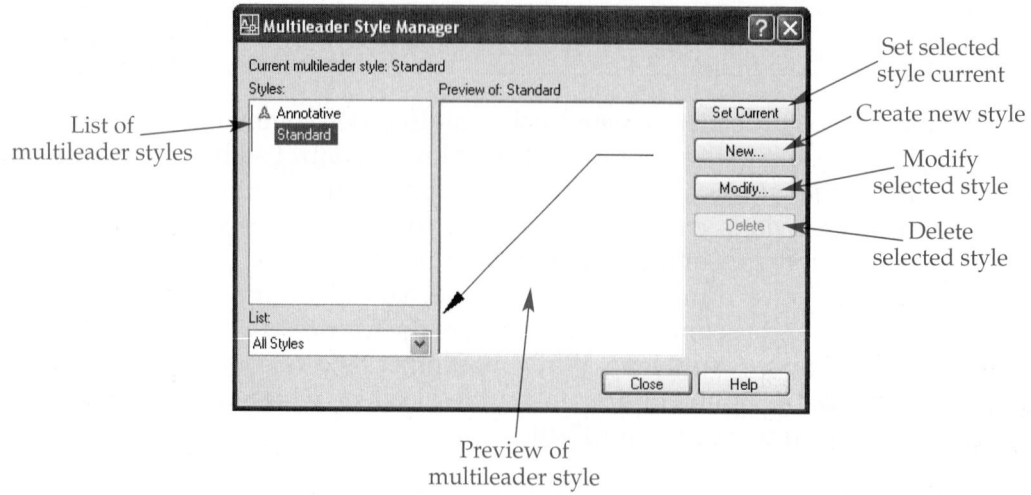

List of
multileader styles

Set selected
style current

Create new style

Modify
selected style

Delete
selected style

Preview of
multileader style

Figure 17-12.
The **Create New Multileader Style** dialog box.

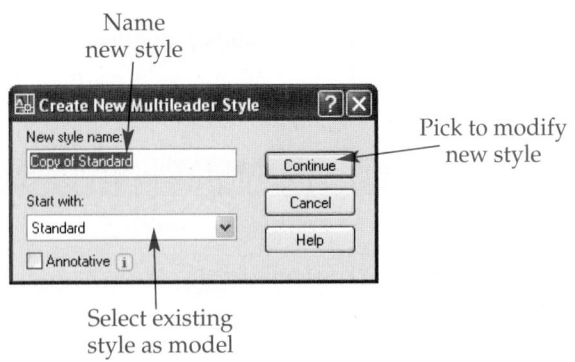

Name new style

Pick to modify new style

Select existing style as model

Creating a New Multileader Style

To create a new multileader style, first select an existing multileader style from the **Styles** list box to be used as a base for formatting the new multileader style. Then pick the **New...** button in the **Multileader Style Manager**. This opens the **Create New Multileader Style** dialog box. See **Figure 17-12.** The following options are available in this dialog box:

- **New Style Name.** Give the new multileader style a descriptive name, such as Architectural, Mechanical, Straight, or Spline.
- **Start With.** This option helps you save time by basing the settings for a new style on an existing multileader style.
- **Annotative.** Pick this check box to make the multileader style annotative. The multileader style can also be made annotative later by selecting the **Annotative** check box in the **Leader Structure** tab of the **Modify Multileader Style** dialog box.

Once you have made your selections, pick the **Continue** button. This will open the **Modify Multileader Style** dialog box, where you can adjust the multileader style's characteristics.

The **Modify Multileader Style** dialog box is shown in **Figure 17-13.** The **Leader Format**, **Leader Structure**, and **Content** tabs access the settings used for changing the way multileaders are displayed. These tabs are described in the next sections. After completing the information in all tabs, pick the **OK** button to return to the **Multileader Style Manager** dialog box.

Leader Format Settings

The **Leader Format** tab of the **Modify Multileader Style** dialog box, shown in **Figure 17-13,** controls leader line display settings. The **General** area contains the following settings:

- **Type.** Specifies the leader line shape. The **Straight** option produces leaders with straight-line segments. The **Spline** option produces curved leader lines. The spline leader is commonly used in architectural drafting. **Figure 17-10** shows examples of straight and spline leader lines. Pick the **None** option to create a multileader style that does not use a leader line, but can be associated with other multileaders using **MLEADERALIGN** and **MLEADERCOLLECT** commands.
- **Color.** Specifies the color of the multileader. Multileader color options are the same as those available for dimension styles.
- **Linetype.** Specifies the multileader linetype. Multileader linetype options are the same as those available for dimension styles.
- **Lineweight.** Specifies the multileader lineweight. Multileader lineweight options are the same as those available for dimension styles.

The **Arrowhead** area of the **Leader Format** tab provides several different arrowhead options and controls the arrowhead size. Select the arrowhead style from the **Symbol** drop-down list. The arrowhead symbol options are the same as those for dimension

Figure 17-13.
The **Leader Format** tab of the **Modify Multileader Style** dialog box.

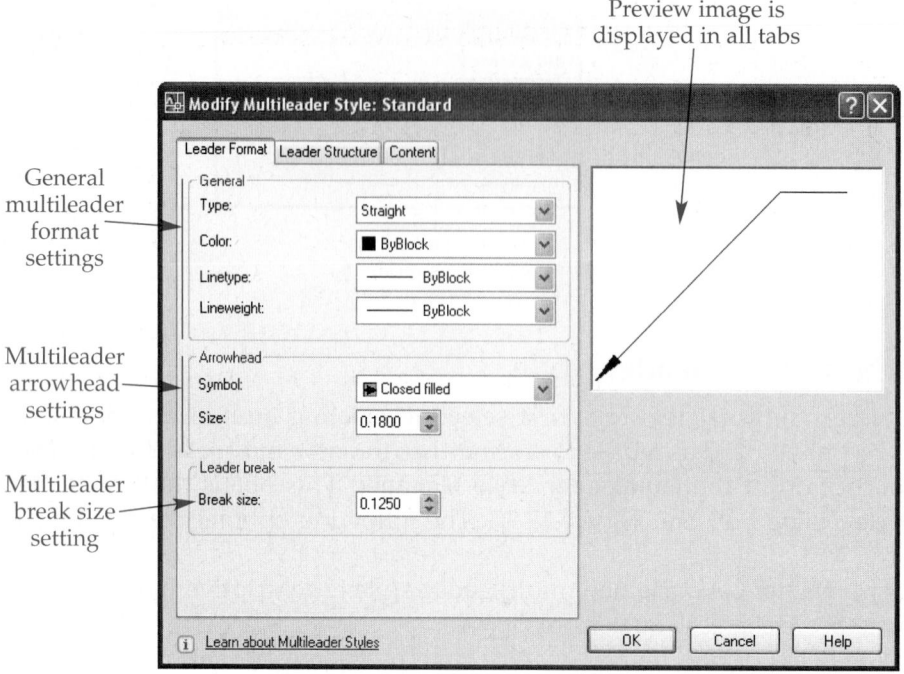

Preview image is displayed in all tabs

General multileader format settings

Multileader arrowhead settings

Multileader break size setting

arrowheads. The **Size:** text box allows you to change the size of the leader arrowhead. The default value is .18. An arrowhead size of .125″ (3mm) is used on most drawings.

The **Leader Break** area controls the amount of leader line removed by the **DIMBREAK** command. Enter or select a value in the **Break size:** text box to specify the total length of the break. The default size is .125. ASME standards do not recommend breaking leader lines.

Leader Structure Settings

The **Leader Structure** tab of the **Modify Multileader Style** dialog box is shown in **Figure 17-14.** The **Constraints** area of the **Leader Structure** tab restricts the number of points requested when a multileader is drawn and defines the leader angle. Pick the **Maximum leader points** check box to set the maximum number of vertices on the leader line. After the maximum number is reached, the multileader is automatically formed. To use fewer than the maximum number of points, press the [Enter] key at the Specify next point: prompt. Deselect the **Maximum leader points** check box to allow an unlimited number of vertices.

The first two segments of the leader line can be restricted to certain angles using the **First segment angle** and **Second segment angle** check boxes. Deselect the check boxes to draw leader lines at any angle. Select the check boxes and pick a value from the drop-down list to restrict the angle of the leader segment according to the selected value. The **Ortho** mode setting overrides the angle constraints, so it is advisable to turn **Ortho** mode off while using this command.

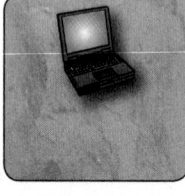

PROFESSIONAL TIP

The ASME standard for leaders recommends that leader lines not have angles less than 15° or greater than 75° from horizontal. Use the **First segment angle** and **Second segment angle** settings to help maintain these standards.

AutoCAD and Its Applications—Basics

Figure 17-14.
The **Leader Structure** tab of the **Modify Multileader Style** dialog box.

Apply limits to leader lines

Specify shoulder options

Set up the multiline scale

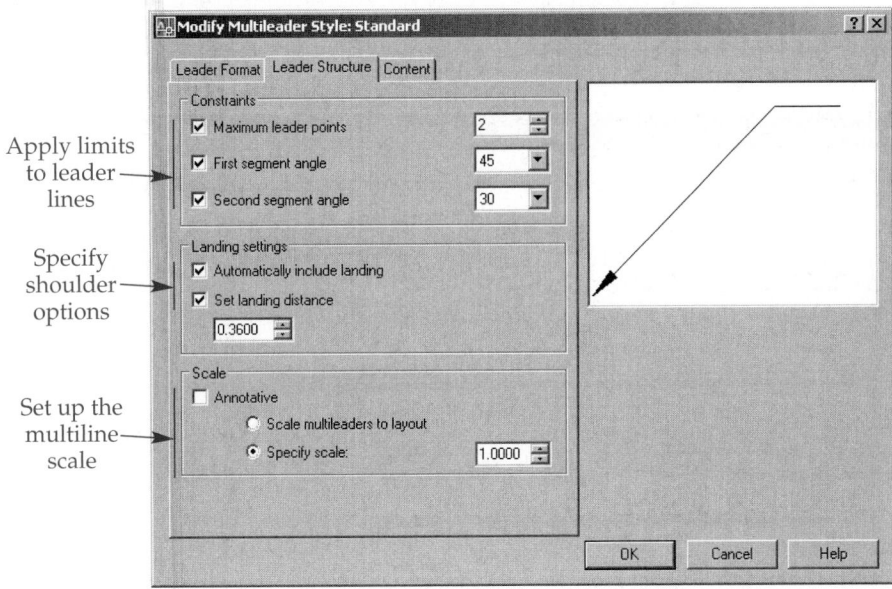

AutoCAD refers to a leader shoulder as a *landing*. The **Landing settings** area of the **Leader Structure** tab controls the display and size of the shoulder and is only available with straight multileader styles. Select the **Automatically include landing** check box to display a shoulder automatically when the second point of a leader line has been selected. This is the preferred method of creating straight leader lines. Deselect the check box to create leaders without shoulders, or to draw the shoulders manually as the third leader point. When the **Automatically include landing** check box is selected, the **Set landing distance** check box becomes available for selection. Pick the **Set landing distance** check box to define a specific shoulder length, typically 1/8"–1/4" (3 mm–6 mm), in the text box. Deselect the text box to be prompted for the shoulder length when you place a multileader.

The **Scale** area of the **Leader Structure** tab is used to set the scale factor for all multileaders in the drawing. To create annotative multileaders, first make the multileader style annotative by selecting the **Annotative** check box. If you picked the **Annotative** check box in the **Create New Multileader Style** dialog box, the **Annotative** check box will already be selected here.

Select the **Scale dimensions to layout** radio button if you are adding multileaders in a floating viewport in paper space. You must add multileaders to the model in a floating viewport in order for this option to function. Scaling multileaders to the layout allows the overall scale to adjust according to the active floating viewport by setting the overall scale equal to the viewport scale factor. Pick the **Use overall scale of** radio button to enter the drawing scale factor that will be used to adjust the size of multileaders according to a specific drawing scale. The scale factor is multiplied by the plotted dimension size to get the model space dimension size.

Content Settings

The **Content** tab of the **Modify Multileader Style** dialog box, shown in Figure 17-15, controls the display of text or a block with the leader line. Use the **Multileader type:** drop-down list to select the type of object to be inserted and attached to the end of the leader line or shoulder. The options include **Mtext**, **Block**, and **None**. See Figure 17-16.

landing: AutoCAD's term for a leader shoulder.

Figure 17-15.
The **Content** tab of the **Modify Multileader Style** dialog box with the **Mtext** multileader type selected.

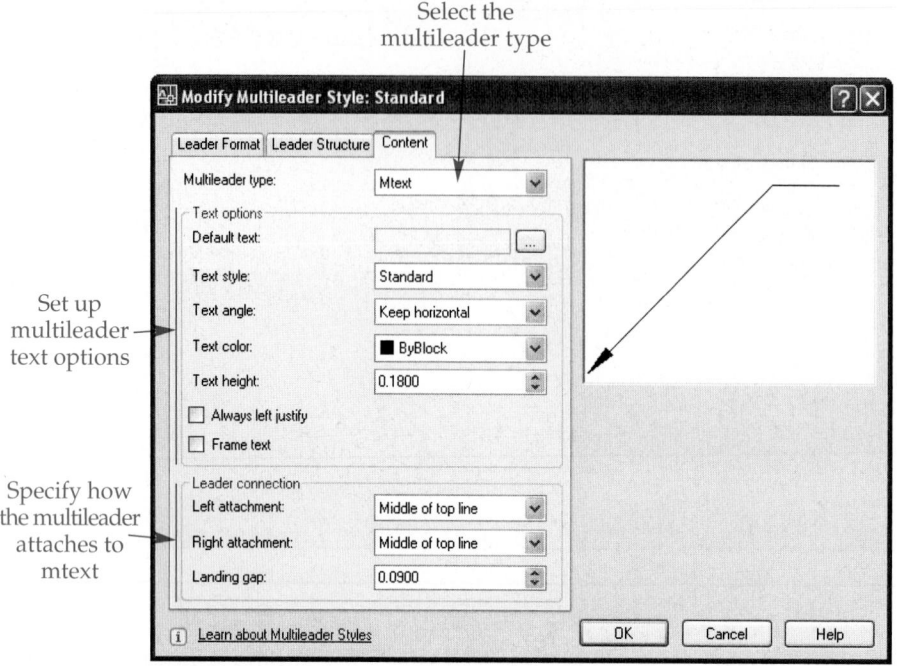

Figure 17-16.
Examples of each multileader content type.

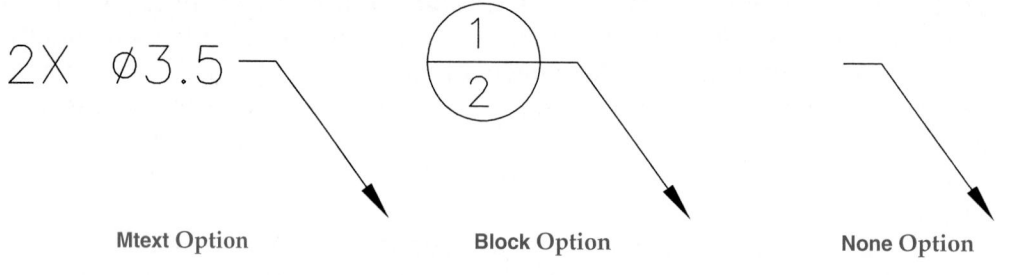

Attaching Mtext

Pick the **Mtext** option from the **Multileader type:** drop-down list to attach a multiline text object to the leader. The **Mtext** option is selected in **Figure 17-15.** The **Text options** area of the **Content** tab is displayed when **Mtext** is selected as the content type. The following options are available:

- **Default text.** This option allows you to use the same text automatically for all multileaders. This is useful when the same note or symbol is required in many places throughout a drawing. Pick the ellipses (...) button to return to the graphics screen and use the **In-Place Text Editor** to enter text that will be used each time the leader is drawn. Pick the **OK** button to return to the **Modify Multileader Style** dialog box.
- **Text style.** Multileaders use the Standard text style by default. Text styles must be defined or loaded in the current drawing before they are available for use in multileader text.
- **Text angle.** Select an option from this drop-down list to control the angle at which text is placed in reference to the angle of the leader line or shoulder. **Figure 17-17** shows the effects of each text angle option when applied to the same multileader.

Figure 17-17.
Text angle options available for mtext.

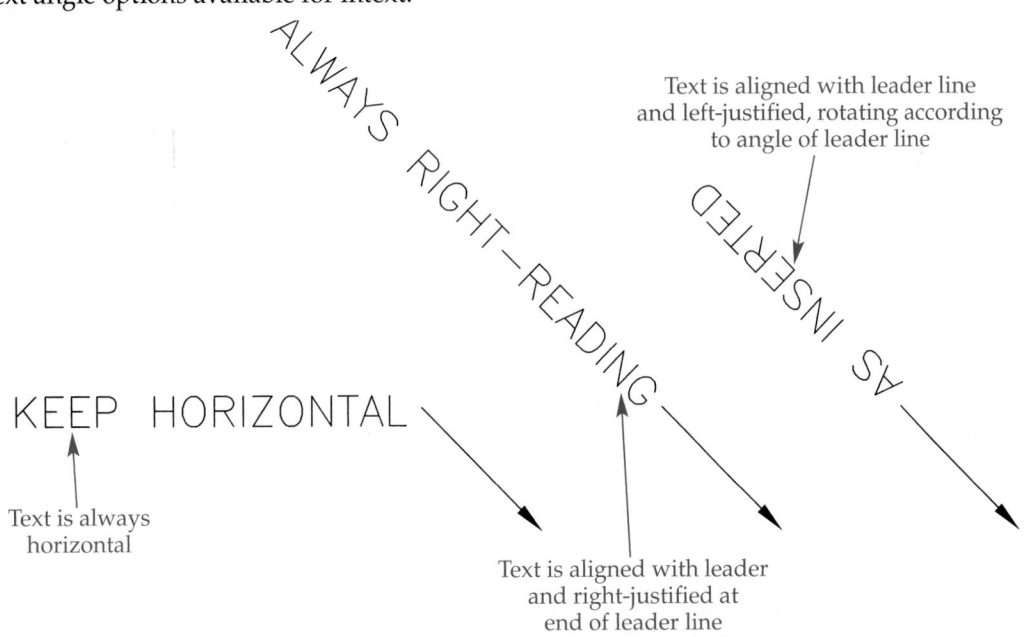

- **Text color.** Use the drop-down list to select a color for the text. If the color is not in the drop-down list, pick **Select Color...** to select a color from the **Select Color** dialog box. The multileader text color default is ByBlock.
- **Text height.** Set the multileader text height by entering the desired value. Multileader text height is usually the same as dimension text height.
- **Always left justify.** This option forces the multiline text to be left-justified, regardless of the direction of the leader line.
- **Frame text.** This option creates a box around the multiline text box. The default properties of the frame are controlled by the settings of the current multileader style.

The **Leader connection** area of the **Content** tab is also displayed when the **Mtext** option is selected. This area contains options that determine how the mtext object is positioned relative to the endpoint of the leader line shoulder. Use the **Left attachment:** drop-down list to define where multiple lines of text are positioned when the leader is on the left side of the text. Use the **Right attachment:** drop-down list to define where multiple lines of text are positioned when the leader is on the right side of the text. These options are shown in **Figure 17-18.** The **Underline bottom line** option causes a

Figure 17-18.
Placement of mtext is controlled by the options in the **Content** tab of the **Modify Multileader Style** dialog box. The shaded examples are the recommended ASME standards.

	Top of Top Line	Middle of Top Line	Middle of Multiline Text	Middle of Bottom Line	Bottom of Bottom Line
Text on Left Side	⌀.250 ⊔⌀.500 ▽.062	⌀.250 ⊔⌀.500 ▽.062	⌀.250 ⊔⌀.500 ▽.062	⌀.250 ⊔⌀.500 ▽.062	⌀.250 ⊔⌀.500 ▽.062
Text on Right Side	⌀.250 ⊔⌀.500 ▽.062	⌀.250 ⊔⌀.500 ▽.062	⌀.250 ⊔⌀.500 ▽.062	⌀.250 ⊔⌀.500 ▽.062	⌀.250 ⊔⌀.500 ▽.062

line to be drawn along the bottom of the multiline text box. The **Underline all text** option underlines each line of leader text. The **Leading gap** text box is used to specify the space between the leader line or shoulder and the text. The default is .09, but .063 is standard.

Common drafting practice is to use the **Middle of bottom line** option for left-sided text and the **Middle of top line** option for right-sided text. These are the default settings.

Inserting a symbol

block: A symbol that was previously created and saved.

Pick the **Block** option from the **Multileader type:** drop-down list to insert a specified block at the end of the leader. A *block* is a symbol that was previously created and saved for future use. Multiple-use symbols are explained in detail in Chapter 23. The **Block** area of the **Content** tab is displayed when the **Block** option is selected. See **Figure 17-19**.

A variety of block symbols that contain attributes are available by default from the **Source block:** drop-down list. You also have the option of using your own saved block by picking the **User Block...** option. The **Select Custom Content Block** dialog box is displayed when you pick the **User Block...** option. Pick a block from the **Select from Drawing Blocks:** drop-down list and then pick **OK**.

Use the **Attachment:** drop-down list to select how the block is attached to the leader line. Pick the **Insertion point** option to attach the block to the leader according to the block insertion point, or base point. Choose the **Center extents** option to attach the block directly to the leader, aligned to the block's center, even if the block insertion point is not on the block itself. See **Figure 17-20**.

The block color default is ByBlock. Use the **Color** drop-down list to select a color for the block. If the color is not in the drop-down list, pick **Select Color...** to select a color from the **Select Color** dialog box.

Figure 17-19.
The **Content** tab of the **Modify Multileader Style** dialog box with the **Block** multileader type selected.

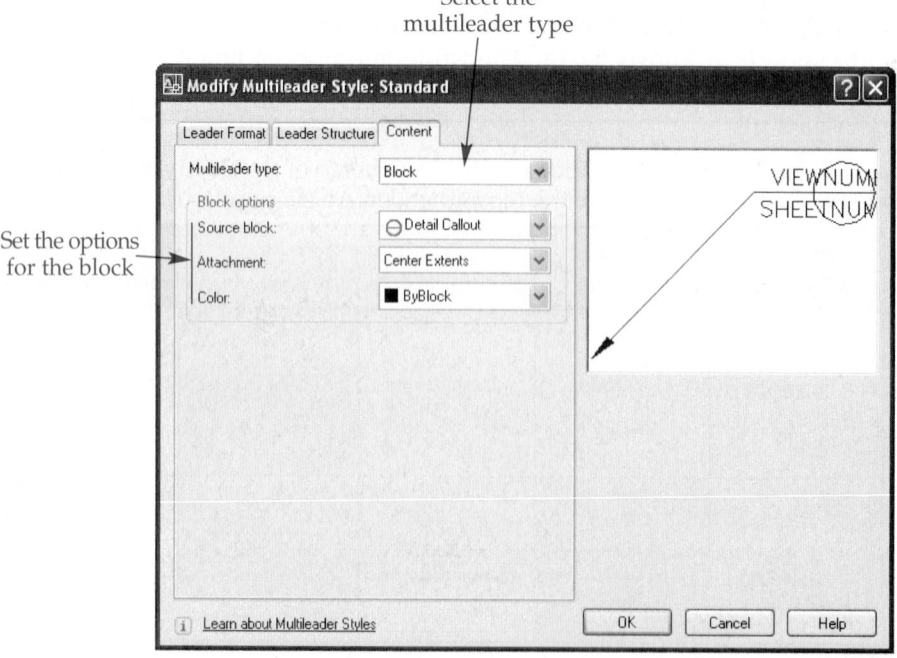

Figure 17-20.
Adjusting multileader block attachment.

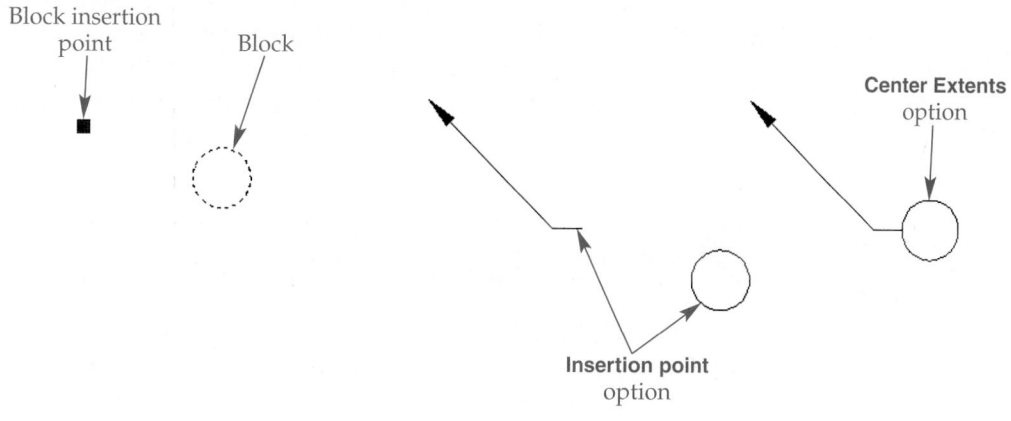

Using no content

Select the **None** option from the **Multileader type:** drop-down list to end the leader with no annotation of any kind. The **None** option can be used whenever there is a need to create only a leader, without text or a symbol attached to the leader line or shoulder.

> **NOTE**
>
> Leaders can be added to existing multileaders using the **Add Leader** tool. This eliminates the need to create a separate multileader style that uses the **None** multileader type for most applications.

Exercise 17-4
Complete the exercise on the Student CD.

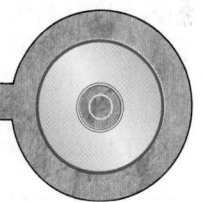

Modifying Multileader Styles

You can change the current multileader style without affecting existing multileaders. The changes are applied only to multileaders added using the current style. Select the **Modify** button to reopen the **Modify Multileader Style** dialog box, which allows you to make changes to the style highlighted in the **Styles** list.

You can rename existing multileader styles in the **Multileader Style Manager**. Either slowly pick the style name twice or right-click the name and select the **Rename** option. To delete a multileader style, right-click on the name and select the **Delete** option, or pick the style and select the **Delete** button. If you try to delete a multileader style that has been used to create leaders in the drawing, AutoCAD gives you the following message:

> Style in use, can't be deleted.

This means either this is the current style, or there are multileaders in the drawing that reference this style. If you want to delete the style, make a different style current, or change the leaders in the drawing to a different style.

Quickly Setting a Multileader Style Current

You can quickly make a multileader style current using the **Multileader Style** drop-down list located in the **Multileader** toolbar or the **Multileader** control panel of the **Dashboard**. The name of the current multileader style is displayed in the box. Pick the drop-down arrow to display a multileader style list. Pick a multileader style from the list to set it current.

Drawing Multileaders

Leaders are drawn using the **MLEADER** command. Once multileaders are added, additional tools are available for adding and removing multiple leader lines, arranging multiple leaders, and combining leader content.

Once you develop a multileader style and make the style current, you are ready to insert a leader using the **MLEADER** command. The **MLEADER** command is accessed by picking the **Multileader** button in the **Multileader** toolbar or the **Multileaders** control panel of the **Dashboard**, by selecting **Dimension** > **Multileader** in the pull-down menu, or by typing MLEADER or MLD.

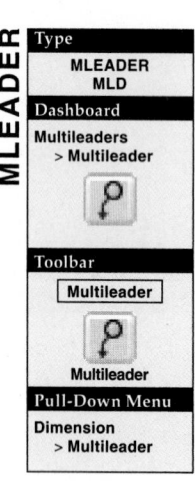

Type
MLEADER
MLD
Dashboard
Multileaders
> Multileader

Toolbar
Multileader

Multileader
Pull-Down Menu
Dimension
> Multileader

Inserting a Multileader

How you place a leader depends on the multileader style settings you select. In general, there are three methods for inserting a multileader, depending on what portion of the leader is selected first. Review the components of a leader, shown in Figure 17-21, before reading the options for creating a multileader.

The first option for inserting a leader is **Specify leader arrowhead location**. To use this option, first select the location where the arrowhead points. Then choose where the leader ends and the shoulder begins. If the **Mtext** option is active, enter leader text.

The second method uses the **leader Landing first** option. To use this technique, first select where the leader ends and the shoulder begins. Then choose the location where the arrowhead points. If the **Mtext** option is active, enter leader text.

The third method involves picking the **Content first** option. To use this technique, first define the leader content. If the **MText** option is active, type text using the **In-Place Text Editor**. Then you can select the location where the arrowhead points.

Figure 17-21.
Examples of leaders created using the **MLEADER** command. The architectural example uses a spline leader line and three leader points. The mechanical example uses a straight leader line and two leader points.

Architectural

Mechanical

Select **Options** to access a list of options that can be used to override the current multileader style characteristics. These options are the same as those found in the **Modify Multileader Style** dialog box.

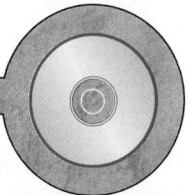

Exercise 17-5
Complete the exercise on the Student CD.

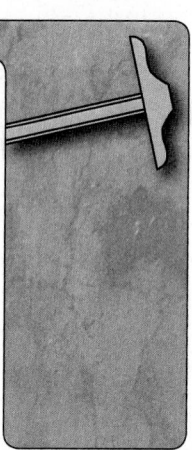

Dimensioning Chamfers

A *chamfer* is an angled surface used to relieve sharp corners. The ends of bolts are commonly chamfered to allow them to engage the threaded hole more easily. Chamfers of 45° are dimensioned either with a leader giving the angle and linear dimension, or with two linear dimensions. This can be accomplished using the **MLEADER** command. See **Figure 17-22.**

chamfer: An angled surface used to relieve sharp corners.

Chamfers other than 45° must have either the angle and a linear dimension or two linear dimensions placed on the view. See **Figure 17-23.** The **DIMLINEAR** and **DIMANGULAR** commands are used for this purpose.

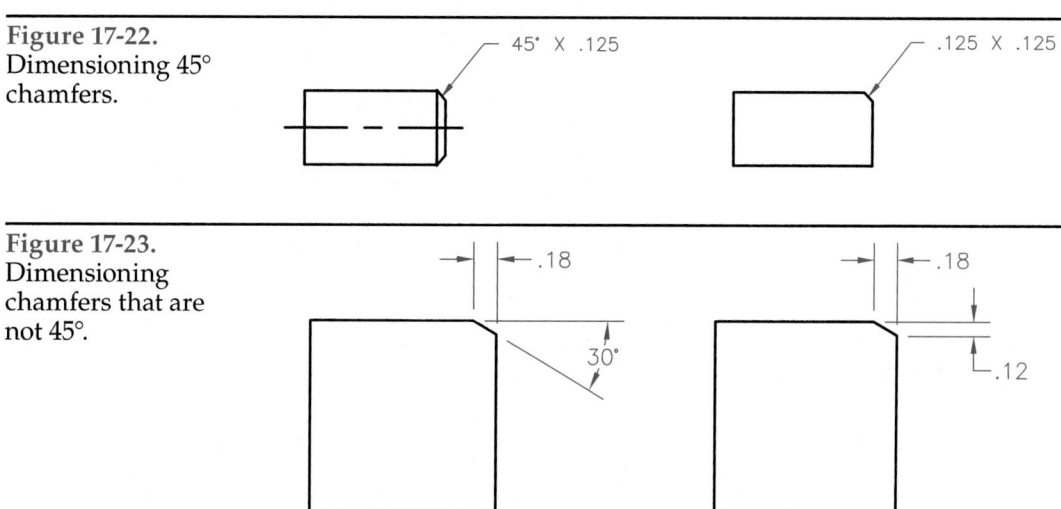

Figure 17-22.
Dimensioning 45°
chamfers.

Figure 17-23.
Dimensioning
chamfers that are
not 45°.

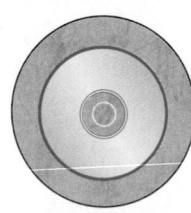

Exercise 17-6
Complete the exercise on the Student CD.

Thread Drawings and Notes

The parts of a screw thread are shown in **Figure 17-24**. Threads are commonly shown on a drawing with a simplified representation. Thread depth is shown with a hidden line. This method is used for both external and internal threads. See **Figure 17-25**. A chamfer is often placed on the external thread. This makes it easier to engage the mating thread.

The objects show the reader that a thread exists, but the thread note gives exact specifications. The thread note is typically connected to the thread with a leader. See **Figure 17-26**. The most common thread forms are the Unified and metric screw threads. The thread note for Unified screw threads must be specified in the following format:

       3/4-   **10UNC -**   **2A**
       (1)   (2) (3)   (4) (5)

(1) Major diameter of thread. Given as a fraction or number.
(2) Number of threads per inch.
(3) Thread series. UNC = Unified National Coarse. UNF = Unified National Fine.
(4) Class of fit. 1 = large tolerance. 2 = general purpose tolerance. 3 = tight tolerance.
(5) Thread type. A = external thread. B = internal thread.

The thread note for metric threads is specified in the following format:

       M   **14 X 2**
       (1) (2) (3)

(1) M = metric thread.
(2) Major diameter in millimeters.
(3) Pitch in millimeters.

There are too many Unified and metric screw threads to describe in detail here. Refer to the *Machinery's Handbook*, available from Goodheart-Willcox Publisher, or a comprehensive drafting text for more information.

Figure 17-24.
Parts of a screw thread.

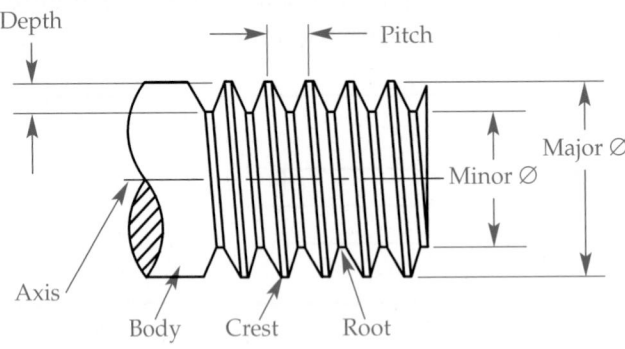

Figure 17-25.
Simplified thread representations.

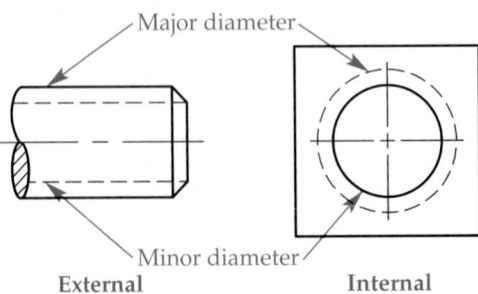

Figure 17-26.
Displaying the
thread note with a
leader.

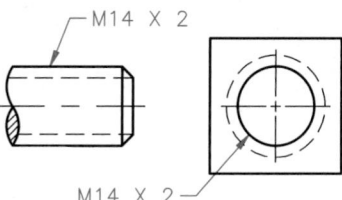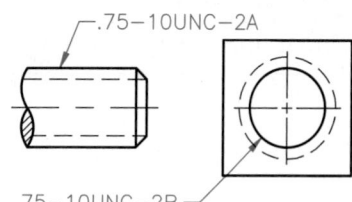

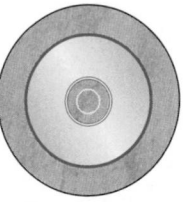

Exercise 17-7
Complete the exercise on the Student CD.

Alternate Dimensioning Practices

It is becoming common to omit dimension lines in industries in which computer-controlled machining processes are used. Arrowless, tabular, and chart dimensioning are three types of dimensioning that omit dimension lines.

Arrowless Dimensioning

Arrowless dimensioning is becoming popular in mechanical drafting. It is also used in electronics drafting, especially for chassis layout. This type of dimensioning has only extension lines and text. Dimension lines and arrowheads are omitted. The dimension text is aligned with the extension lines. Each dimension represents a measurement originating from a common point. This starting, or 0, dimension is typically known as a *datum*, or baseline. Holes or other features are labeled with identification letters. Sizes for these features are given in a table placed on the drawing. See **Figure 17-27**.

Tabular Dimensioning

Tabular dimensioning is a form of arrowless dimensioning in which dimensions to features are shown in a table. Each feature is labeled with a letter or number that correlates to the table. The table gives the location of features from the X and Y axes. It also provides the depth of features from a Z axis, when appropriate. See **Figure 17-28**.

arrowless dimensioning (ordinate dimensioning): Type of dimensioning that includes only extension lines and text.

datum: The 0 dimension from which all measurements are made in arrowless dimensioning.

tabular dimensioning: A form of arrowless dimensioning in which dimensions are shown in a table.

Figure 17-27.
Arrowless
dimensioning.

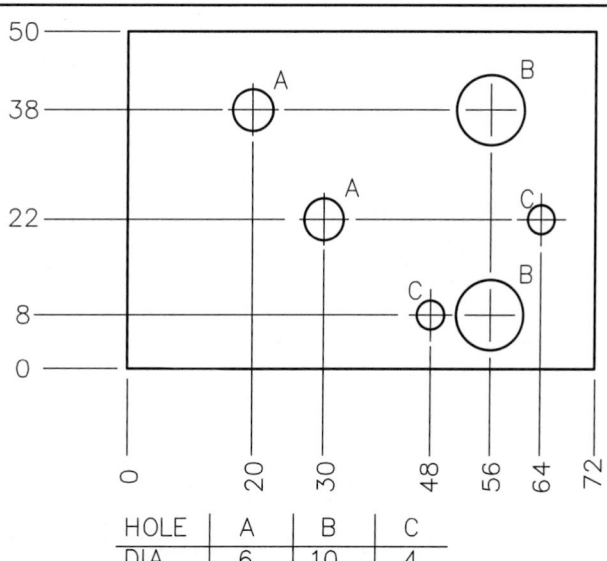

HOLE	A	B	C
DIA.	6	10	4

Figure 17-28.
Tabular dimensioning. (Doug Major)

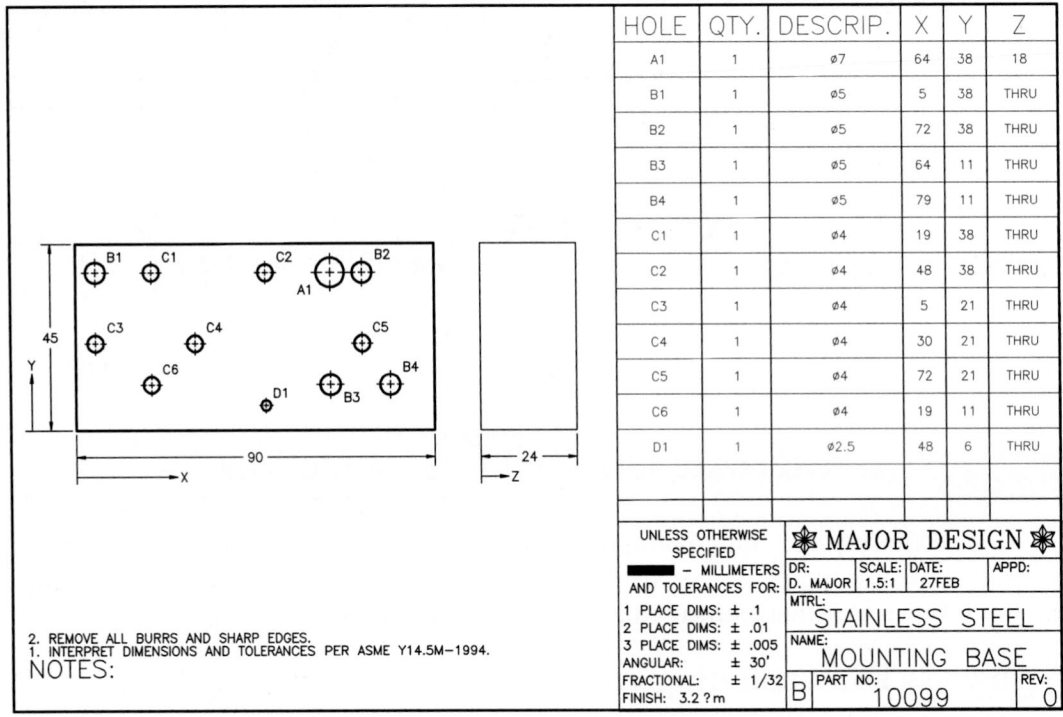

HOLE	QTY.	DESCRIP.	X	Y	Z
A1	1	⌀7	64	38	18
B1	1	⌀5	5	38	THRU
B2	1	⌀5	72	38	THRU
B3	1	⌀5	64	11	THRU
B4	1	⌀5	79	11	THRU
C1	1	⌀4	19	38	THRU
C2	1	⌀4	48	38	THRU
C3	1	⌀4	5	21	THRU
C4	1	⌀4	30	21	THRU
C5	1	⌀4	72	21	THRU
C6	1	⌀4	19	11	THRU
D1	1	⌀2.5	48	6	THRU

UNLESS OTHERWISE SPECIFIED
■ – MILLIMETERS AND TOLERANCES FOR:
1 PLACE DIMS: ± .1
2 PLACE DIMS: ± .01
3 PLACE DIMS: ± .005
ANGULAR: ± 30'
FRACTIONAL: ± 1/32
FINISH: 3.2 ?m

❋ MAJOR DESIGN ❋
DR: D. MAJOR | SCALE: 1.5:1 | DATE: 27FEB | APPD:
MTRL: STAINLESS STEEL
NAME: MOUNTING BASE
B | PART NO: 10099 | REV: 0

2. REMOVE ALL BURRS AND SHARP EDGES.
1. INTERPRET DIMENSIONS AND TOLERANCES PER ASME Y14.5M–1994.
NOTES:

Chart Dimensioning

Chart dimensioning may take the form of unidirectional, aligned, arrowless, or tabular dimensioning. It provides flexibility when dimensions change as requirements of the product change. The views of the product are drawn and variable dimensions are shown with letters. The letters correlate to a chart in which the different options (possible dimensions) are given. See **Figure 17-29**.

WCS and UCS

The origin (0,0,0 coordinate) of the world coordinate system (WCS) has been in the lower-left corner of the screen for the drawings you have already completed. In most cases, this is fine. However, when using arrowless dimensioning on a drawing, it is best to have the dimensions originate from a primary datum, which is often a corner of the object. Depending on how the object is drawn, this point may or may not align with the WCS origin.

Figure 17-29.
Chart dimensioning.

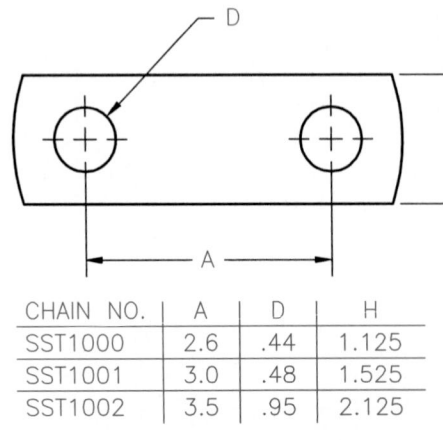

CHAIN NO.	A	D	H
SST1000	2.6	.44	1.125
SST1001	3.0	.48	1.525
SST1002	3.5	.95	2.125

NOTE:
OVERALL LENGTH IS 1.5 X A
END RADII ARE .9 X A

The WCS is fixed; a user coordinate system (UCS), on the other hand, can be moved to any orientation desired. User coordinate systems are described in detail in *AutoCAD and Its Applications—Advanced*. As a general practice, a UCS allows you to set your own coordinate system.

Arrowless dimensions are drawn in AutoCAD with the **DIMORDINATE** command, which is described in the next section. Measurements made with this command originate from the current UCS origin. By default, this is the 0,0 origin. You can move the UCS origin to the corner of an object or an appropriate datum feature by selecting **Tools** > **Move UCS**. You are then prompted to specify a new origin point. Use an object snap mode to select the corner of the object or the appropriate datum feature. See Figure 17-30.

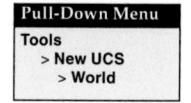

When you have finished drawing arrowless dimensions from a datum, you can leave the UCS origin at the datum or move it back to the WCS origin. To return to the WCS, select **Tools** > **New UCS** > **World**.

Drawing Arrowless Dimensions

AutoCAD refers to arrowless dimensioning as *ordinate dimensioning*. Ordinate dimensions are drawn using the **DIMORDINATE** command, which is accessed by picking the **Ordinate** button from the **Dimension** toolbar or the **Dimension** control panel on the **Dashboard**, by picking **Dimension** > **Ordinate** in the **Dimension** pull-down menu, or by typing DOR or DIMORDINATE. When using this command, AutoCAD automatically places an extension line and a dimension at the location you pick. The dimension is measured as an X or Y coordinate distance.

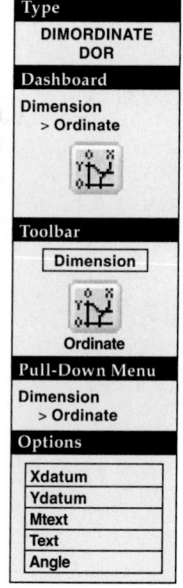

Since you are working in the XY plane, it is often best to have **Ortho** mode on. Also, if the drawing includes circles, use the **DIMCENTER** command to place center marks in the circles, as shown in Figure 17-31. This makes the drawing conform to ASME standards and provides something to pick when you dimension the circle locations.

Figure 17-30.
Move the UCS origin to the appropriate datum location.

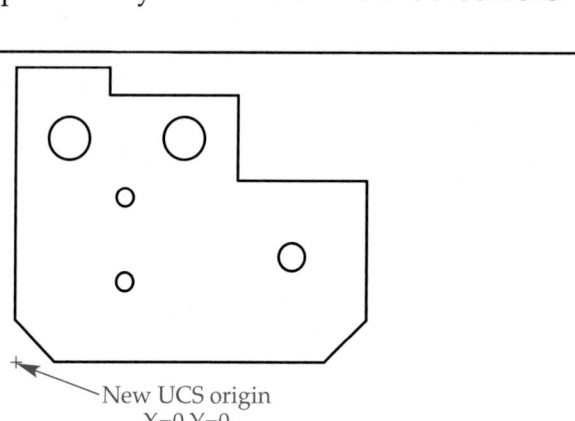

Figure 17-31.
Add center marks to circles in the drawing.

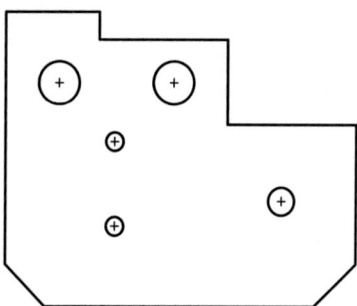

Now you are ready to start placing the ordinate dimensions. Enter the **DIMORDINATE** command. When the Specify feature location: prompt appears, move the crosshairs to the point or feature to be dimensioned. If the feature is the corner of the object, pick the corner. If the feature is a circle, pick the end of the center mark. This leaves the required space between the center mark and the extension line. Zoom in if needed and use the object snap modes. The next prompt asks for the leader endpoint. This actually refers to the extension line endpoint, so pick the endpoint of the extension line.

If the X axis or Y axis distance between the feature and the extension line endpoint is large, the default axis used for the dimension by AutoCAD may not be the desired axis. When this happens, use the **Xdatum** or **Ydatum** option to specify the axis from which the dimension originates. The **Mtext**, **Text**, and **Angle** options are identical to the options available with other dimensioning commands. Pick the leader endpoint to complete the command.

Figure 17-32A shows the ordinate dimensions placed on the object. Notice that the dimension text is aligned with the extension lines. Aligned dimensioning is standard with ordinate dimensioning. Finally, complete the drawing by adding any missing lines, such as centerlines or fold lines. Identify the holes with letters and create a correlated dimensioning table. See **Figure 17-32B**.

Figure 17-32.
A—Placing ordinate dimensions.
B—Completing the drawing.

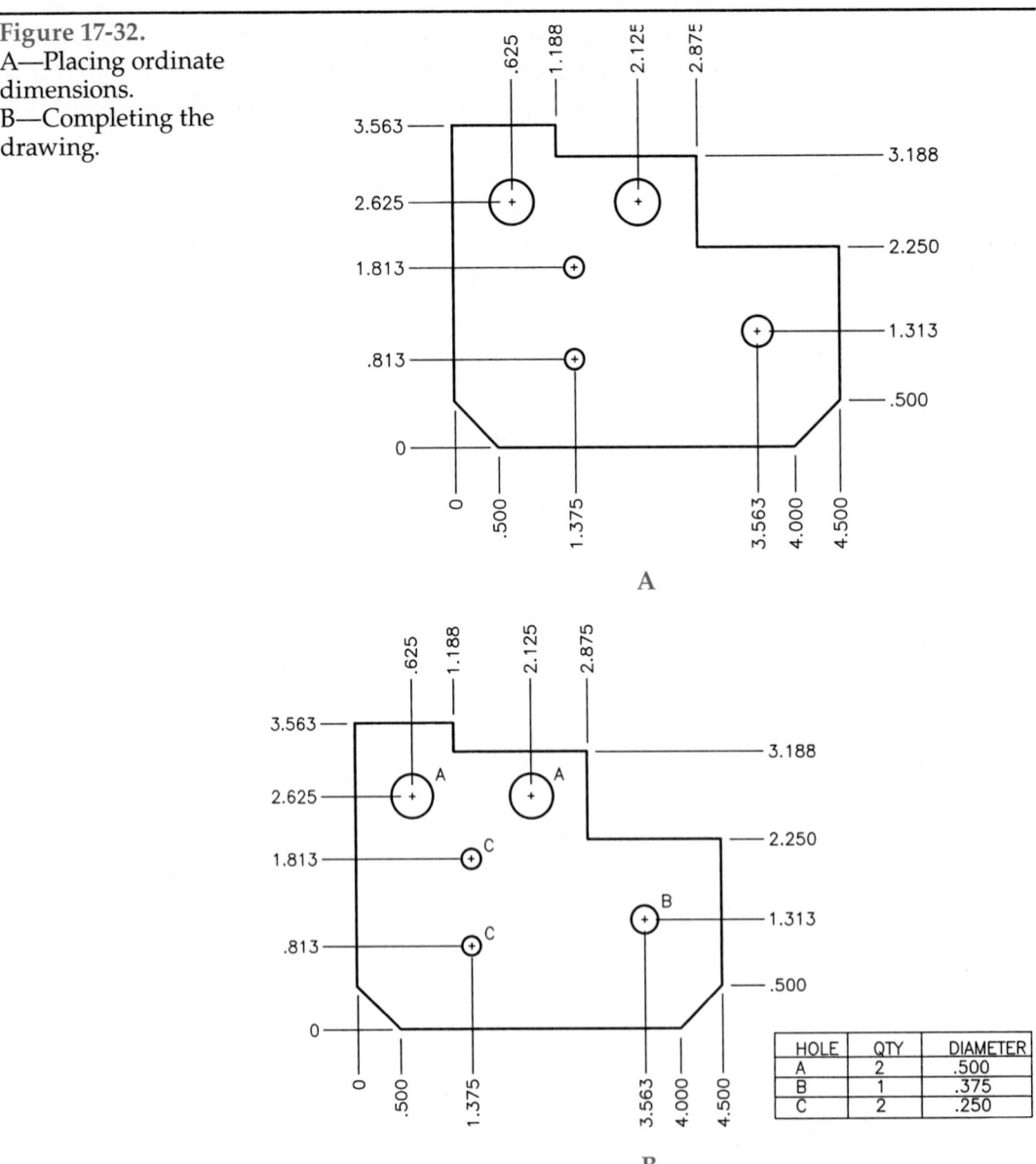

Most ordinate dimensioning tasks work best with **Ortho** mode on. However, when the extension line is too close to an adjacent dimension, it is best to stagger the extension line as shown in the following illustration. With **Ortho** mode off, the extension line is automatically staggered when you pick the offset second extension line point, as shown here.

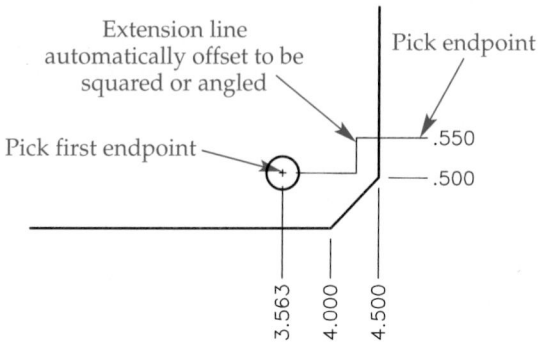
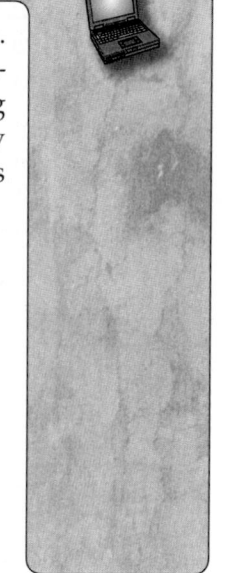
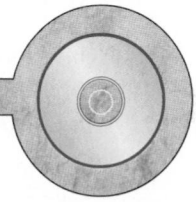

Exercise 17-8
Complete the exercise on the Student CD.

Dimensions can also be created in dimensioning mode. To access dimensioning mode, type DIM. The Command: prompt becomes the Dim: prompt and you can enter dimensioning commands. To exit dimensioning mode, press the [Esc] key and the Command: prompt is displayed.

This method was common in earlier releases of AutoCAD, but it has become an inefficient method of command entry. Some dimensioning commands, such as **MLEADER** and **QDIM**, cannot be accessed from the Dim: prompt.

Template Development

Chapter 17

Like dimension styles, multileaders require a considerable effort to set up properly. By adding them to your drawing templates, you can avoid having to repeat this process each time you begin a new drawing. Refer to the Student CD for detailed instructions to add multileader styles to your mechanical, architectural, and civil drawing templates.

Chapter Test

Answer the following questions. Write your answers on a separate sheet of paper or complete the electronic chapter test on the Student CD.

1. The command used to provide diameter dimensions for circles is _____.
2. The command used to provide radius dimensions for arcs is _____.
3. Define the term *annotation*.
4. How do you make a multileader style current?
5. Describe the three different ways you can place a multileader.
6. Identify the elements of this Unified screw thread note: 1/2-13UNC-2B.
   A. 1/2
   B. 13
   C. UNC
   D. 2
   E. B
7. Identify the elements of this metric screw thread note: M 14 X 2.
   A. M
   B. 14
   C. 2
8. Define the term *arrowless dimensioning*.
9. What is the importance of the user coordinate system (UCS) when drawing arrowless dimensions?
10. AutoCAD refers to arrowless dimensioning as _____ dimensioning.

Drawing Problems

Use one of your templates for each problem. Set limits, units, dimension styles, and other parameters as needed. Use the following general guidelines.

A. Use dimension styles and multileader styles that match the type of drawing as described in this chapter and Chapter 16.
B. Use object snap modes to your best advantage.
C. Apply dimensions accurately using ASME or other related industry/architectural standards. Dimensions are in inches, or feet and inches, unless otherwise specified.
D. Set separate layers for dimensions and other features.
E. For mechanical drawings, place the following general notes 1/2" from the lower-left corner:

> NOTES:
> 1. INTERPRET DIMENSIONS AND TOLERANCES PER ASME Y14.5M-1994.
> 2. REMOVE ALL BURRS AND SHARP EDGES.
> 3. UNLESS OTHERWISE SPECIFIED, ALL DIMENSIONS ARE IN INCHES (or MILLIMETERS as applicable).

1.

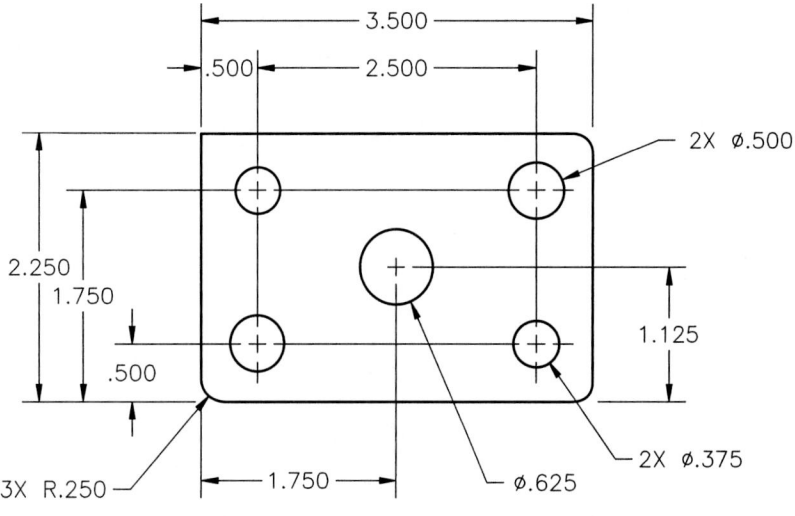

Title: Gasket

2.

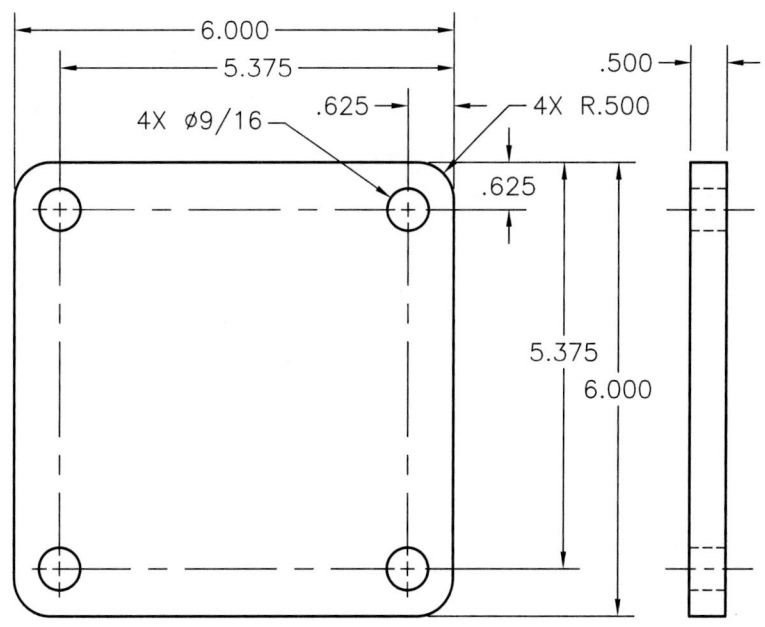

Title: Mounting Plate
Material: Mild Steel

3.

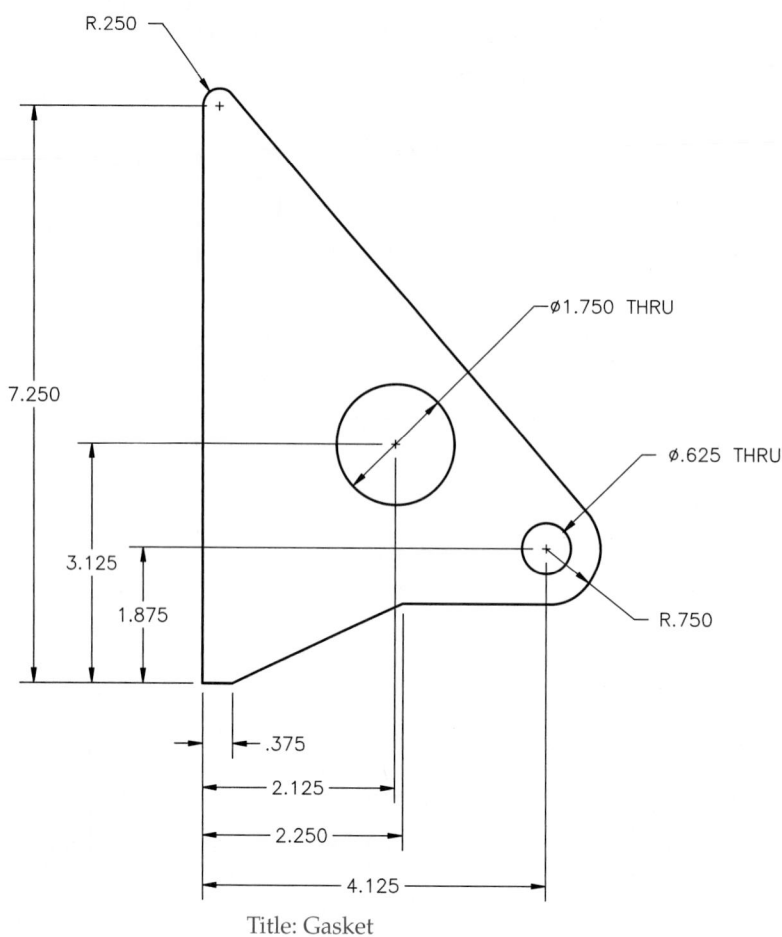

Title: Gasket
Material: .062 Brass

4.

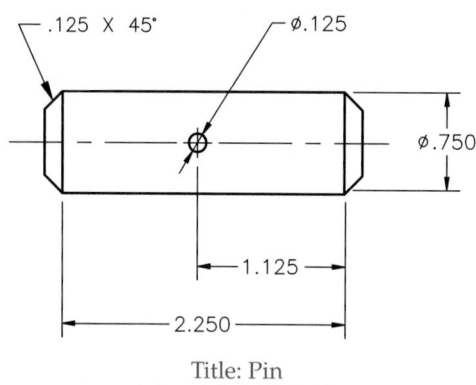

Title: Pin
Material: SAE 4320

5.

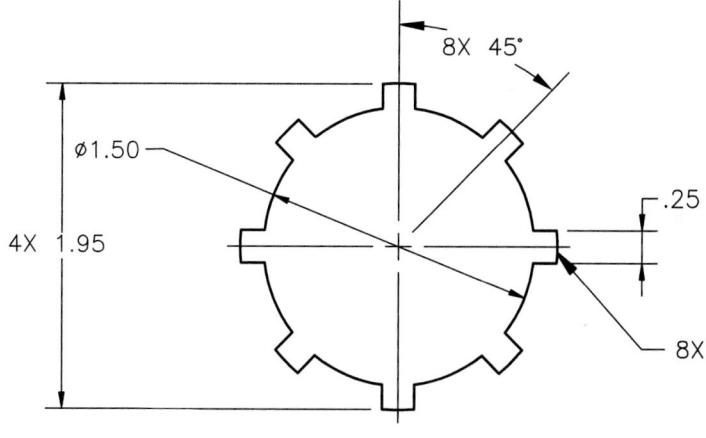

Title: Spline
Material: MS .125 THK

6.

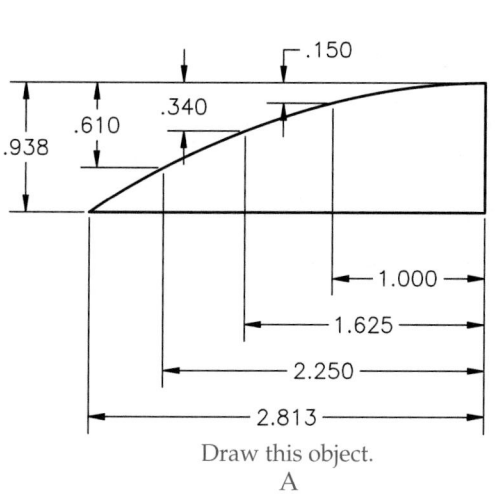

Draw this object.
A

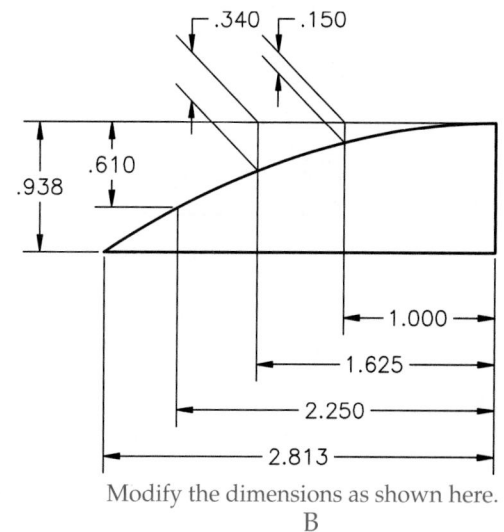

Modify the dimensions as shown here.
B

Title: Shim

Drawing Problems - Chapter 17

7.

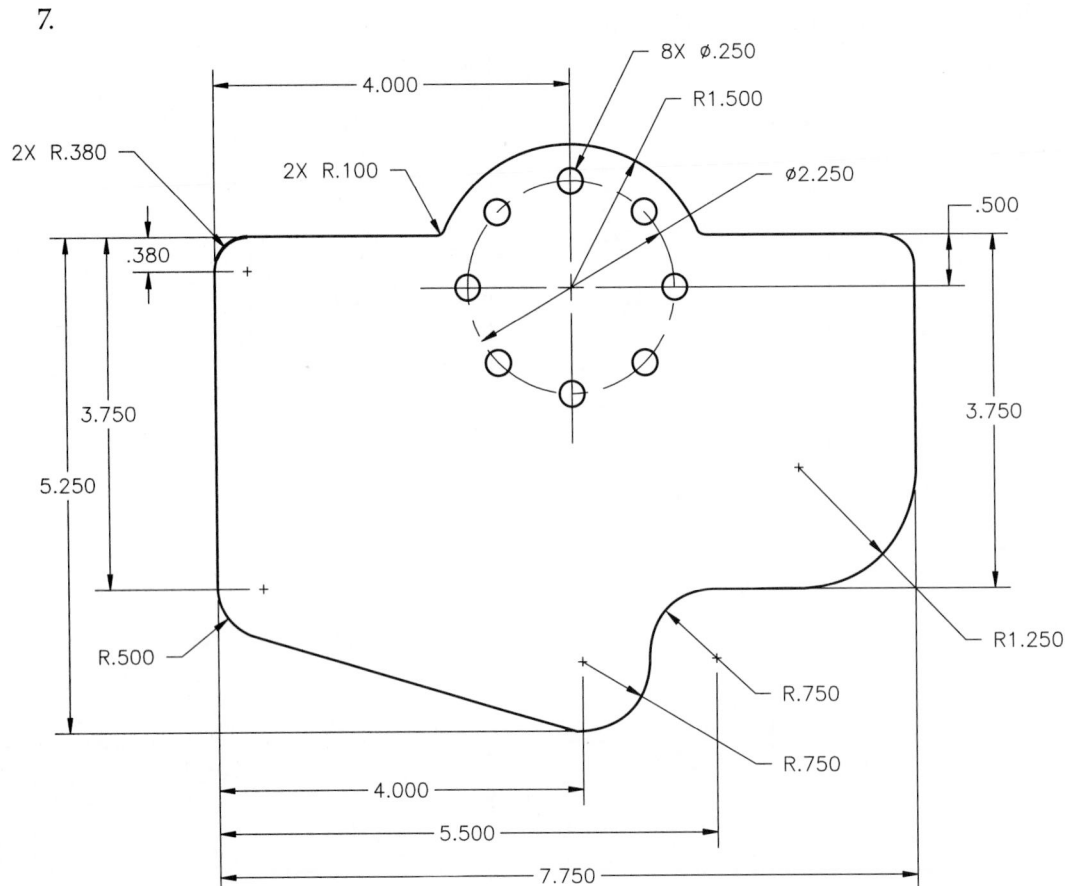

Title: Gasket
Material: 00 Phosphor Bronze

8.

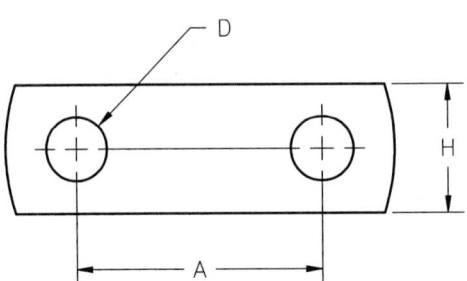

CHAIN NO.	A	D	H
SST1000	2.6	.44	1.125
SST1001	3.0	.48	1.525
SST1002	3.5	.95	2.125

Note:
Overall Length is 1.5XA
end radii are .9XA

Title: Chain Link
Material: Steel

9. Convert the given drawing to a drawing with the holes located using arrowless dimensioning based on the X and Y coordinates given in the table. Place a table above your title block with Hole (identification), Quantity, Description, and Depth (Z axis).

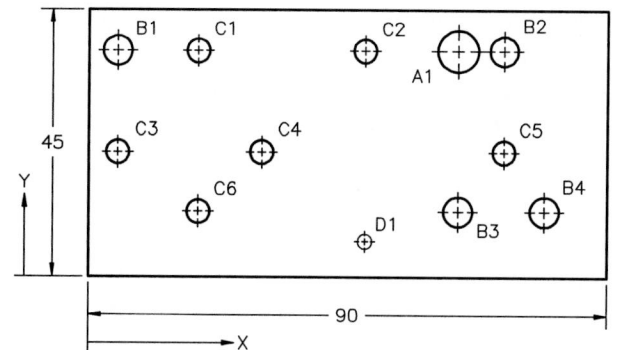

HOLE	QTY	DESC	X	Y	Z
A1	1	ø7	64	38	18
B1	1	ø5	5	38	THRU
B2	1	ø5	72	38	THRU
B3	1	ø5	64	11	THRU
B4	1	ø5	79	11	THRU
C1	1	ø4	19	38	THRU
C2	1	ø4	48	38	THRU
C3	1	ø4	5	21	THRU
C4	1	ø4	30	21	THRU
C5	1	ø4	72	21	THRU
C6	1	ø4	19	11	THRU
D1	1	ø2.5	48	6	THRU

Title: Base
Material: Bronze

10.

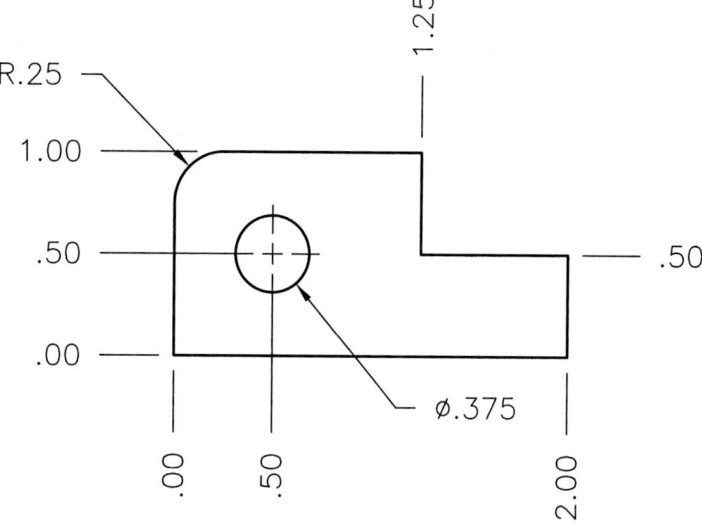

11.

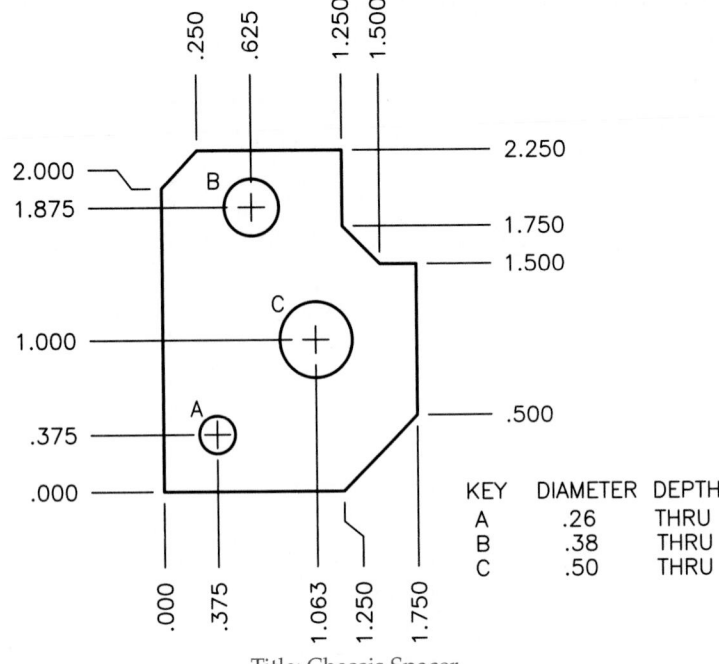

KEY	DIAMETER	DEPTH
A	.26	THRU
B	.38	THRU
C	.50	THRU

Title: Chassis Spacer
Material: .008 Aluminum

12.

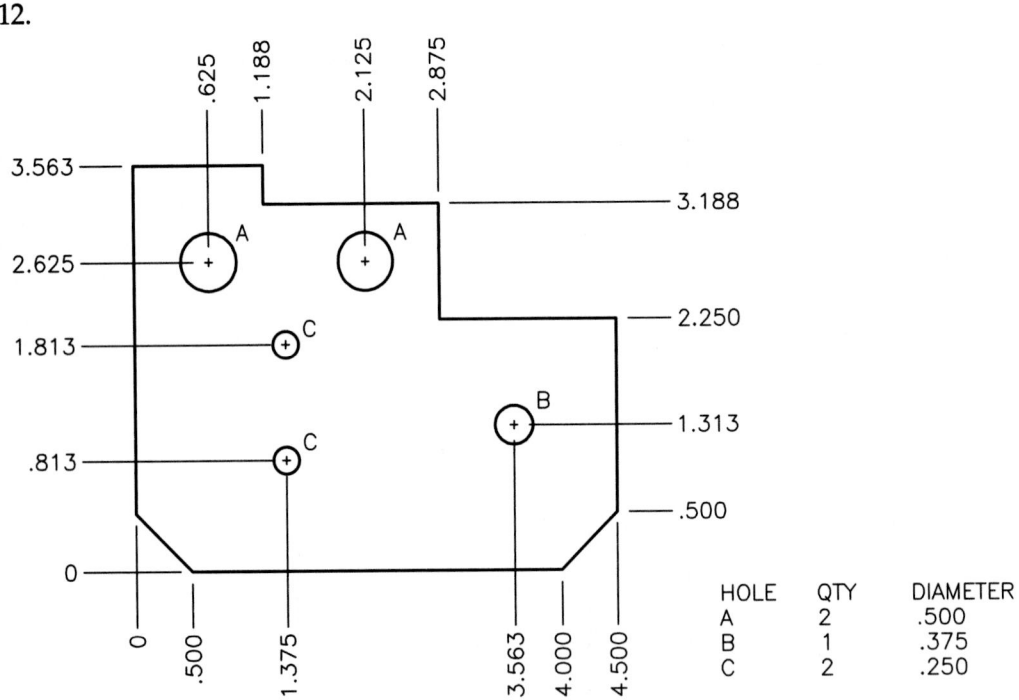

HOLE	QTY	DIAMETER
A	2	.500
B	1	.375
C	2	.250

Title: Chassis
Material: Aluminum .100 THK

13.

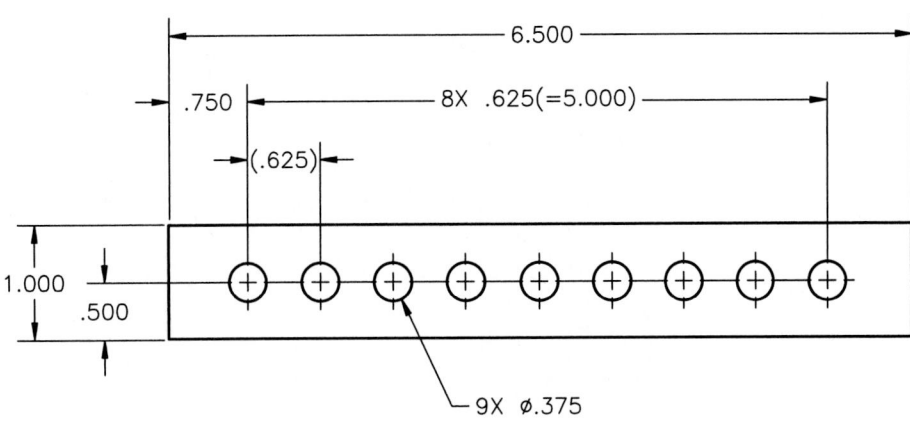

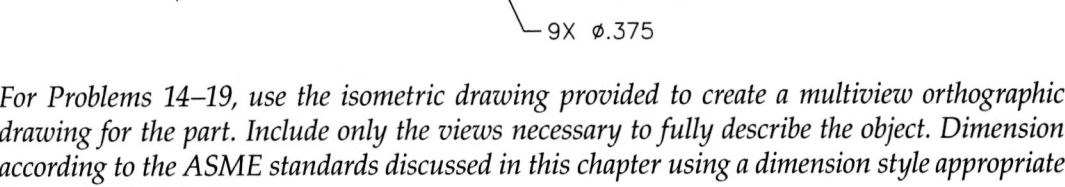

For Problems 14–19, use the isometric drawing provided to create a multiview orthographic drawing for the part. Include only the views necessary to fully describe the object. Dimension according to the ASME standards discussed in this chapter using a dimension style appropriate for mechanical drafting.

14.

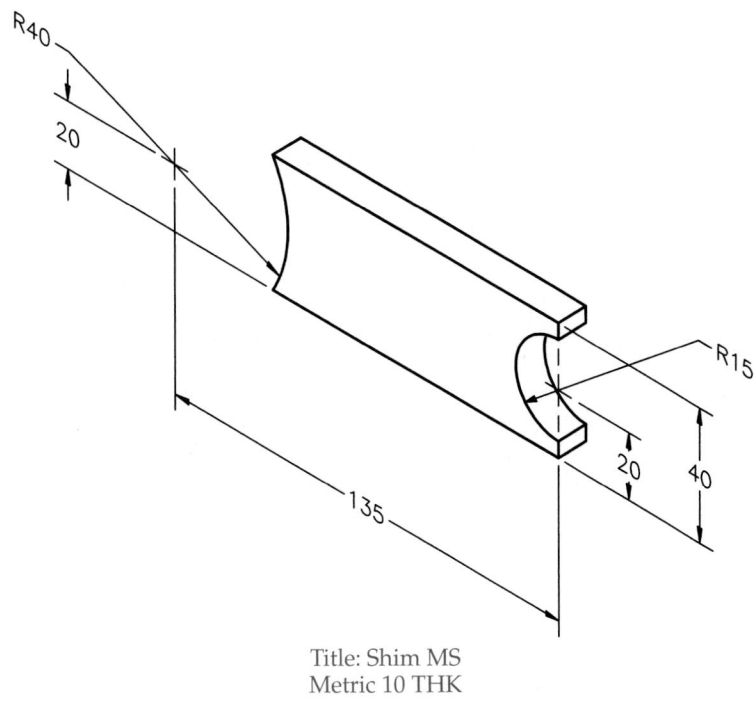

Title: Shim MS
Metric 10 THK

15. Half of the object is removed for clarity. The entire object should be drawn.

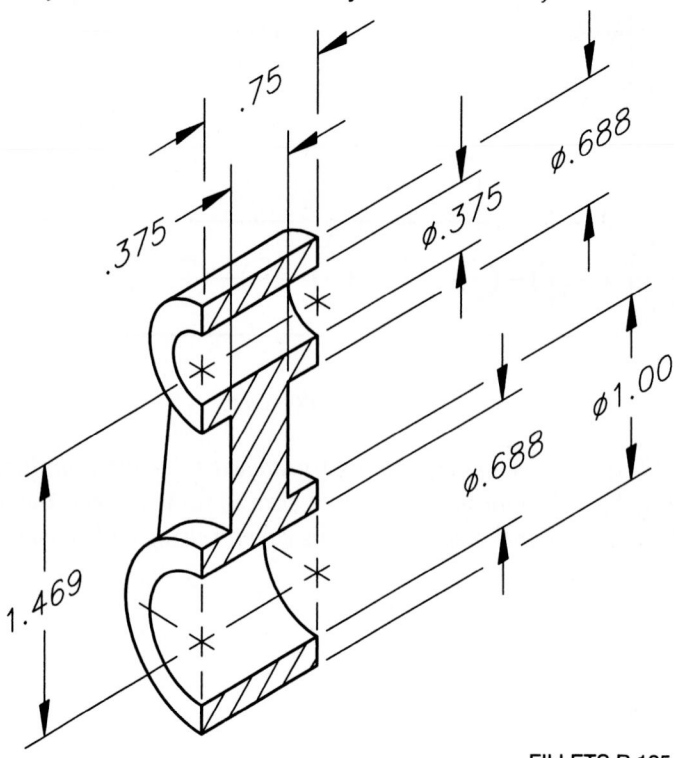

FILLETS R.125

Title: Shaft Support
Material: Cast Iron (CI)

16. Half of the object is removed for clarity. The entire object should be drawn.

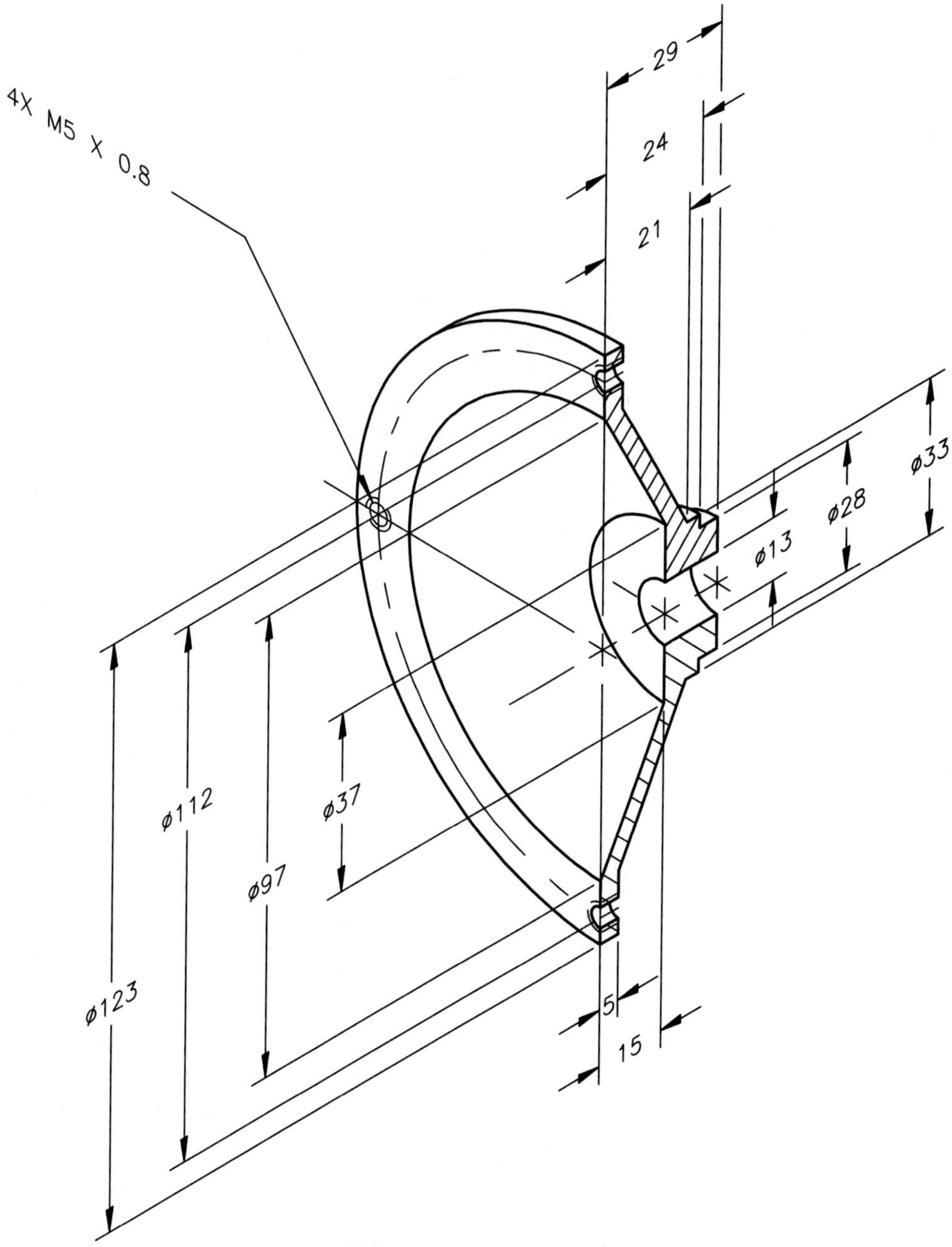

4X M5 X 0.8

29

24

21

ø33

ø28

ø13

ø112

ø97

ø37

ø123

5

15

Title: Transmission Cover
Material: Cast Iron (CI)
Metric

17.

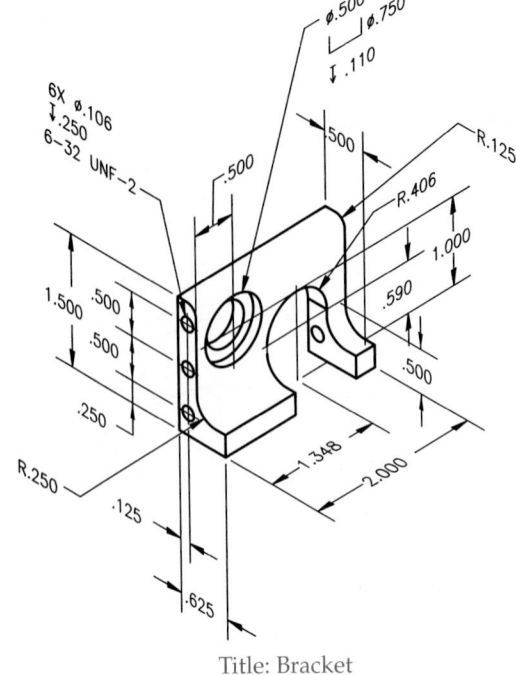

Title: Bracket
Material: SAE4320

18.

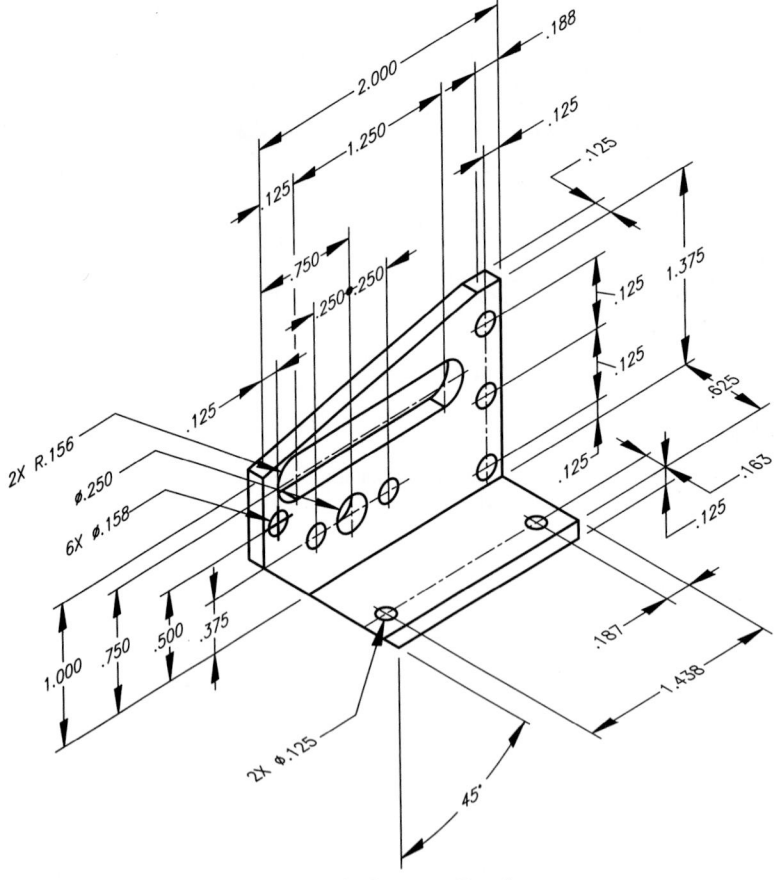

Title: Right Support Bracket
Material: Aluminum

19.

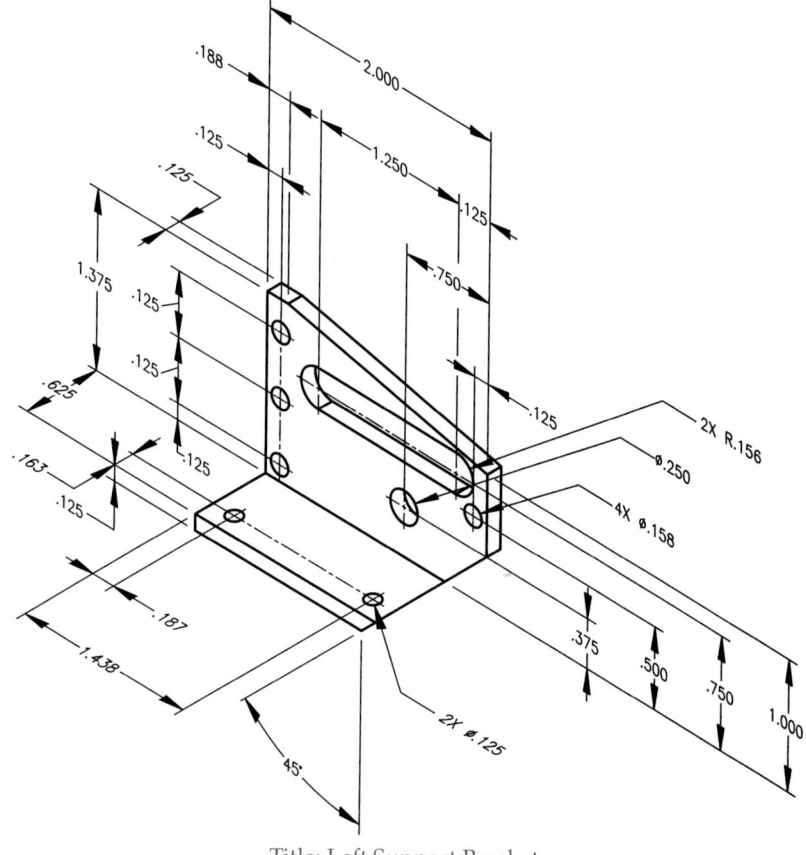

Title: Left Support Bracket
Material: Aluminum

20.

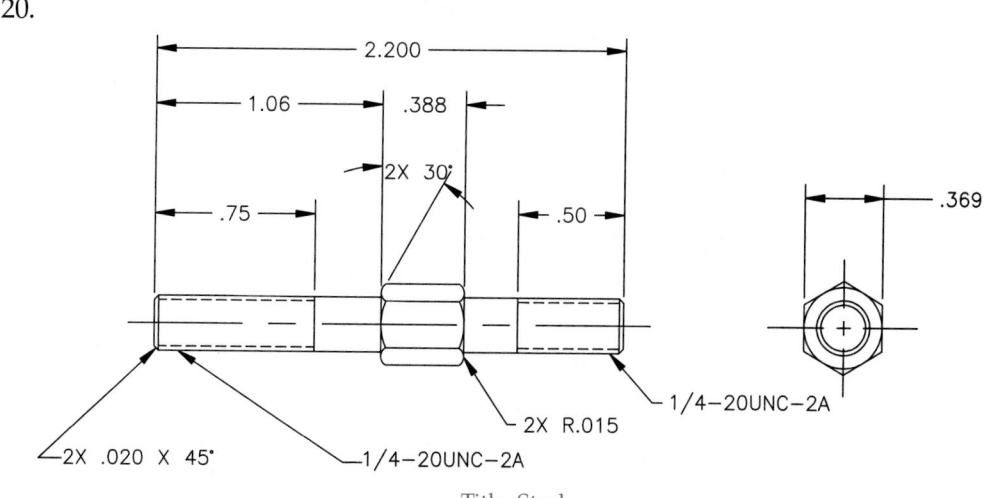

Title: Stud
Material: Stainless Steel

21.

HOLE LAYOUT

KEY	SIZE	DEPTH	NO. REQD
A	⌀.250	THRU	6
B	⌀.125	THRU	4
C	⌀.375	THRU	4
D	R.125	THRU	2

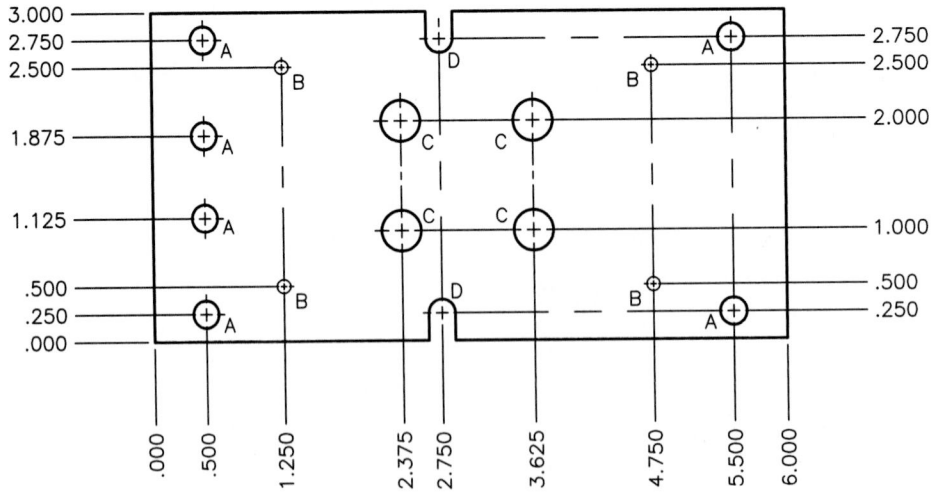

Title: Chassis Base (datum dimensioning)
Material: 12 gage Aluminum

22.

HOLE LAYOUT

KEY	SIZE	DEPTH	NO. REQD
A	⌀.250	THRU	6
B	⌀.125	THRU	4
C	⌀.375	THRU	4
D	R.125	THRU	2

Title: Chassis Base (arrowless dimensioning)
Material: 12 gage Aluminum

23.

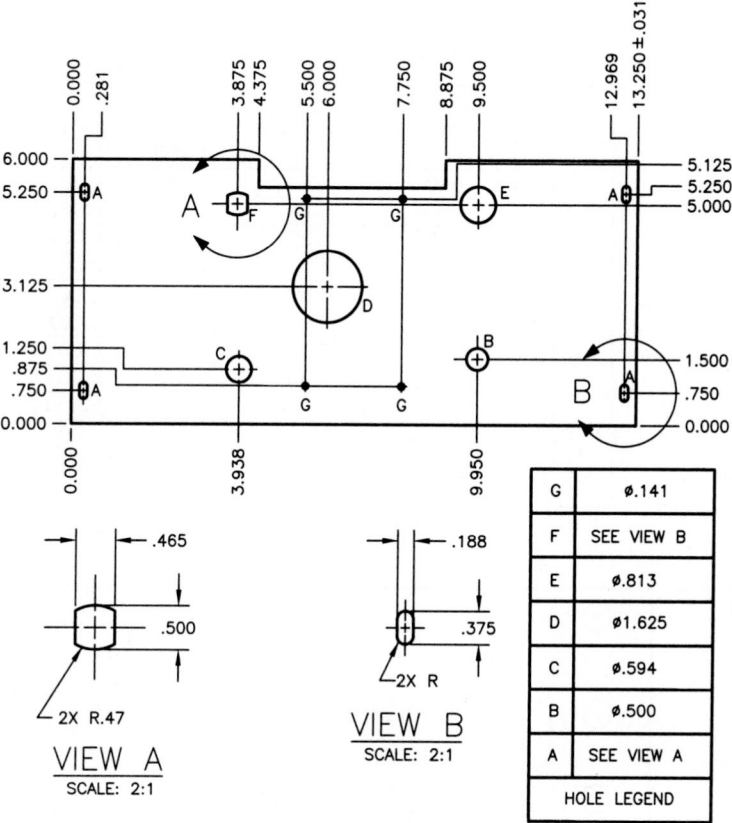

G	ø.141	
F	SEE VIEW B	
E	ø.813	
D	ø1.625	
C	ø.594	
B	ø.500	
A	SEE VIEW A	
HOLE LEGEND		

VIEW A
SCALE: 2:1

VIEW B
SCALE: 2:1

2X R.47

2X R

24.

KEY	X	Y	SIZE	TOL
A1	.500	2.750	⌀.250	±.002
A2	.500	1.875	⌀.250	±.002
A3	.500	1.125	⌀.250	±.002
A4	.500	.250	⌀.250	±.002
A5	5.500	2.750	⌀.250	±.002
A6	5.500	.250	⌀.250	±.002
B1	1.250	2.500	⌀.125	±.001
B2	1.250	.500	⌀.125	±.001
B3	4.750	2.500	⌀.125	±.001
B4	4.750	.500	⌀.125	±.001
C1	2.375	2.000	⌀.375	±.005
C2	2.375	1.000	⌀.375	±.005
C3	3.625	2.000	⌀.375	±.005
C4	3.625	1.000	⌀.375	±.005
D1	2.750	2.750	R.125	±.002
D2	2.750	.250	R.125	±.002

HOLE LAYOUT

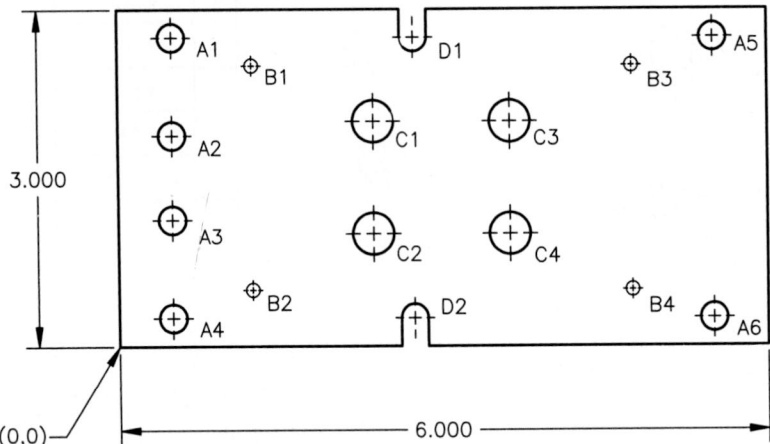

Title: Chassis Base (arrowless tabular dimensioning)
Material: 12 gage Aluminum

25.

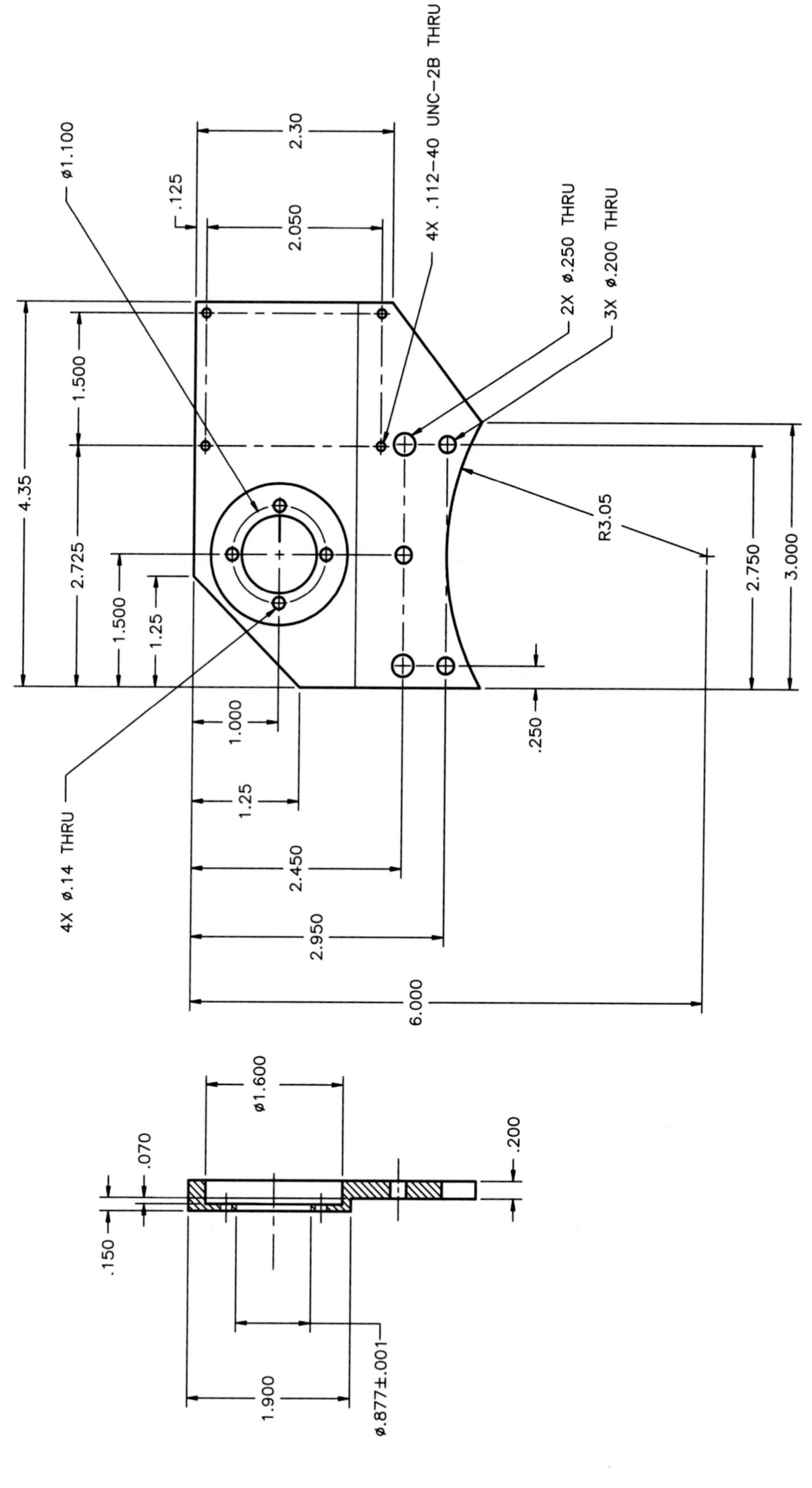

⌀1.100
.125
2.30
2.050
4X .112-40 UNC-2B THRU
2X ⌀.250 THRU
3X ⌀.200 THRU
4.35
1.500
2.725
1.500
1.25
R3.05
2.750
3.000
.250
1.000
1.25
2.450
2.950
6.000
4X ⌀.14 THRU
⌀1.600
.070
.150
.200
1.900
⌀.877±.001

Title: Bracket
Material: SAE 1040

26.

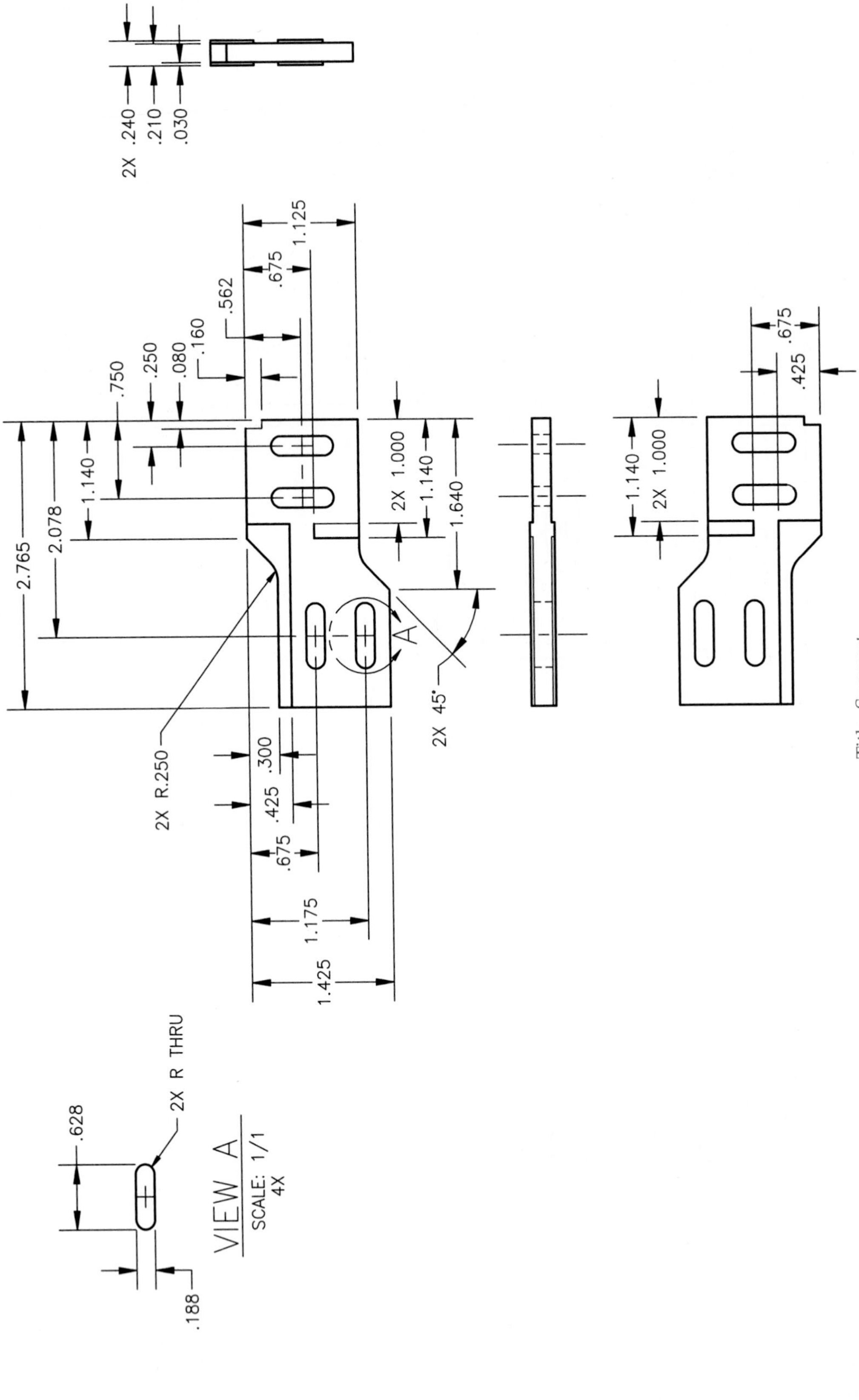

2X .240
.210
.030

1.125
.675
.562
.250
.080
.160
.750
1.140
2.078
2.765

2X 1.000
1.140
1.640

2X 45°

2X R.250

.425 .300
.675
1.175
1.425

.675
.425
1.140
2X 1.000

.628

2X R THRU

.188

VIEW A
SCALE: 1/1
4X

Title: Support
Material: Aluminum

CHAPTER 18

Editing Dimensions

Learning Objectives

After completing this chapter, you will be able to do the following:
- ✓ Make changes to and control the appearance of existing dimensions.
- ✓ Update a dimension to reflect the current dimension style.
- ✓ Use the **Properties** palette to edit individual dimension properties.
- ✓ Edit individual elements of associative dimensions.
- ✓ Change dimension line spacing and alignment.
- ✓ Break dimension, extension, and leader lines.
- ✓ Create inspection dimensions.
- ✓ Edit existing multileaders.

The tools used to edit dimensions vary from simple erasing techniques to object editing commands. You may find it necessary to edit the placement of dimension text, a text value, or the settings in a dimension style. When an object with associative dimensions is edited, the dimensions are automatically updated to reflect the changes. This chapter provides you with a variety of useful techniques for editing dimensions.

Erasing Dimensions

The **ERASE** command was introduced earlier in this text. Among the many selection options used with this command are **Last**, **Previous**, **Window**, **Crossing**, **WPolygon**, **CPolygon**, and **Fence**.

Erasing existing features such as large groups of dimensions often becomes difficult. For example, the objects may be very close to other parts of the drawing. When many objects are present, it is usually time-consuming to erase each one individually. When this situation occurs, the **Crossing**, **CPolygon**, and **Fence** object selection options are useful. A comparison of using the **Window** and **Crossing** selection options with the **ERASE** command on a group of dimensions is shown in **Figure 18-1**. For a review of these techniques, refer to Chapter 3.

Figure 18-1.
Using the **Window** and **Crossing** object selection options to erase dimensions.

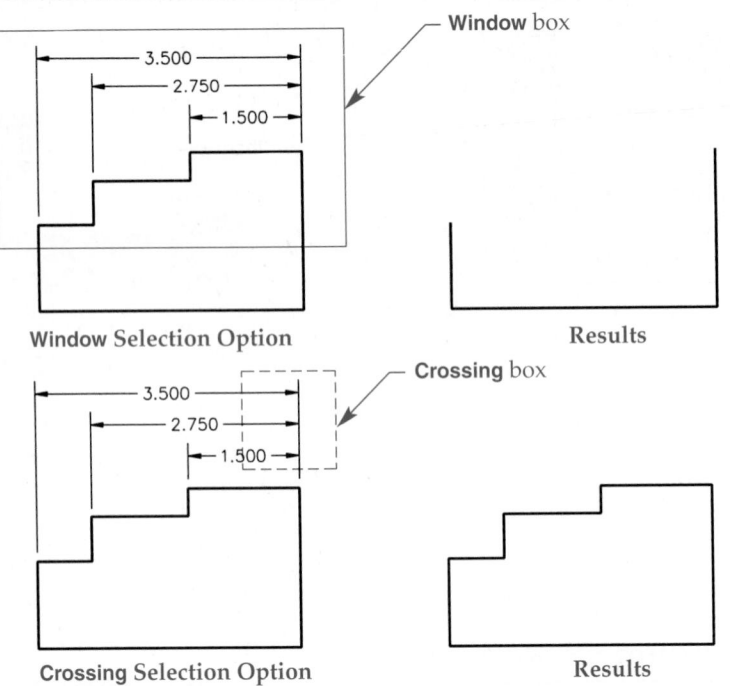

Window Selection Option

Results

Crossing Selection Option

Results

PROFESSIONAL TIP

Dimensions are treated as block objects in AutoCAD. After erasing dimensions, use the **PURGE** command to purge the erased dimension blocks. The **PURGE** command is described in Chapter 23.

Editing Dimension Text Values

The **DDEDIT** command can be used to edit existing dimension text. You can add a prefix or suffix to the text, or edit the dimension text format. This is useful when you wish to alter dimension text without creating a new dimension. For example, a linear dimension does not automatically place a diameter symbol with the text value, yet you need a diameter symbol to dimension linear diameters. Using the **DDEDIT** command is one way to place this symbol on the dimension after the dimension has been placed in the drawing.

You can access the **DDEDIT** command by picking **Modify > Object > Text > Edit...** from the pull-down menu, picking the **Edit...** button from the **Text** toolbar, or typing ED or DDEDIT. When this command is issued, the Select an annotation object or [Undo]: prompt is displayed.

After you select a dimension to edit, the dimension value is highlighted and the **Text Formatting** toolbar is displayed. See Figure 18-2. The dimension value is highlighted in blue in a text window. In this selection mode, the cursor is placed at the beginning of the text string, so you can add a symbol in front of the value without moving the cursor. You can move to the end of the value by pressing the right arrow key on the keyboard. Picking once on the dimension value highlights the value in the text window. The entire dimension value is selected, and typing new text replaces the existing text.

DDEDIT

Type
DDEDIT
ED

Toolbar
Text

Edit...

Pull-Down Menu
Modify
> Object
> Text
> Edit...

AutoCAD and Its Applications—Basics

Figure 18-2.
The **DDEDIT**
command allows
you to edit
dimension text
using a text window
and the **Text
Formatting** toolbar.

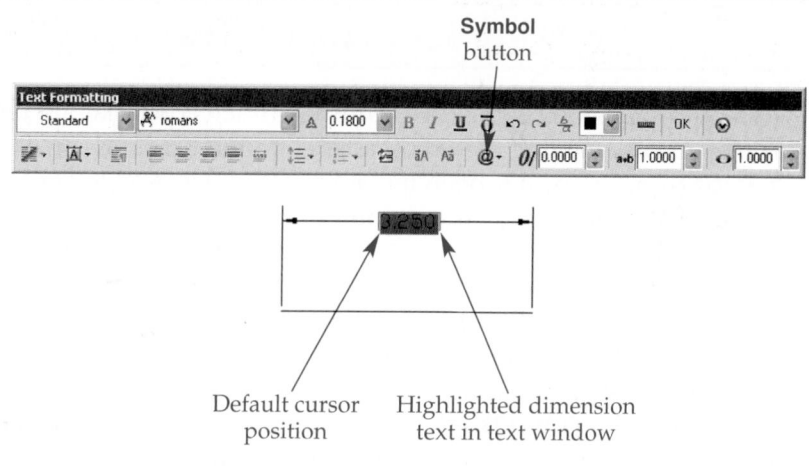

Default cursor
position

Highlighted dimension
text in text window

To add a diameter symbol to the text, place the cursor at the position where you want to add the symbol and then select the **Symbol** button from the **Text Formatting** toolbar. Then select **Diameter** from the **Symbol** menu. You can also right-click and select **Diameter** from the **Symbol** cascading menu. This adds the diameter symbol to the text object. Pick the **OK** button on the **Text Formatting** toolbar to close the text window and exit the command. The result of changing an existing dimension in this manner is shown in **Figure 18-3**.

When using the **DDEDIT** command to edit dimension text, remember that the value is initially highlighted in blue. Any text that you type is added to the existing text. If you pick on the text, the entire text string is selected and the highlight color changes. Any text that you type replaces the entire string. You can change back to the initial selection mode by picking to the left of the text value or pressing the left arrow key on the keyboard. You can also pick to the right of the text value or press the right arrow key on the keyboard. The highlight color turns back to blue, indicating that the dimension value is not discarded, but that the new text or symbol is added to it.

PROFESSIONAL TIP

You can replace the highlighted text representing the dimension value with numeric values. However, if the dimension is subsequently stretched, trimmed, or extended, the dimension text value will not change. Therefore, leave the default value intact whenever possible.

Exercise 18-1
Complete the exercise on the Student CD.

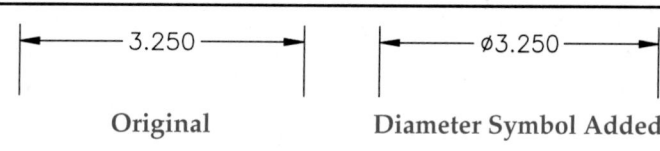

Figure 18-3.
Using the **DDEDIT**
command to add
a diameter symbol
to an existing
dimension.

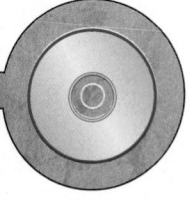

├──── 3.250 ────┤   ├──── ⌀3.250 ────┤

Original   Diameter Symbol Added

Editing Dimension Text Placement

Good dimensioning practice requires dimensions that are clear and easy to read. This may involve moving the text of adjacent dimensions. As an example, in **Figure 18-4**, one of the dimensions has been moved to a new location to separate the text elements. The **DIMTEDIT** command allows you to change the placement and orientation of an existing associative dimension text value. An *associative dimension* is one in which all elements of the dimension (including the dimension line, extension lines, arrowheads, and text) are connected to the object being dimensioned. Thus, if the object is modified, the dimension updates automatically. Associative dimensioning is controlled by the **DIMASSOC** system variable and is active by default.

To access the **DIMTEDIT** command, pick the **Dimension Text Edit** button on the **Dimension** toolbar, type DIMTEDIT, or pick **Dimension > Align Text** and one of the options from the pull-down menu. After entering the command, select the dimension to be altered.

If the dimension is associative, the text of the selected dimension automatically drags with the screen cursor. This allows you to relocate the text with your pointing device. If you pick a point, AutoCAD automatically moves the text and reestablishes the break in the dimension line. You can also select from the options offered at the Specify new location for dimension text or [Left/Right/Center/Home/Angle]: prompt.

- **Left.** Moves horizontal text to the left and vertical text down.
- **Right.** Moves horizontal text to the right and vertical text up.
- **Center.** Centers the dimension text on the dimension line.
- **Home.** Moves relocated text back to its original position.
- **Angle.** Allows you to place dimension text at an angle. When you enter the **Angle** option, you are asked to specify a rotation angle. The text is then rotated about its middle point.

The result after using each of the **DIMTEDIT** command options is shown in **Figure 18-5**.

associative dimension: Dimension in which all elements are connected to the object being dimensioned; updates when the associated object is changed.

DIMTEDIT

Type
DIMTEDIT
Toolbar
Dimension
Dimension Text Edit
Pull-Down Menu
Dimension > Align Text
Options
Left
Right
Center
Home
Angle

PROFESSIONAL TIP

If you wish to relocate existing dimension text, using grips is the quickest way to adjust the text position. This method requires only picks and no command entry. Pick the dimension, pick the dimension text grip, and drag the text to the new location.

Figure 18-4.
Using the **DIMTEDIT** command to stagger dimension text.

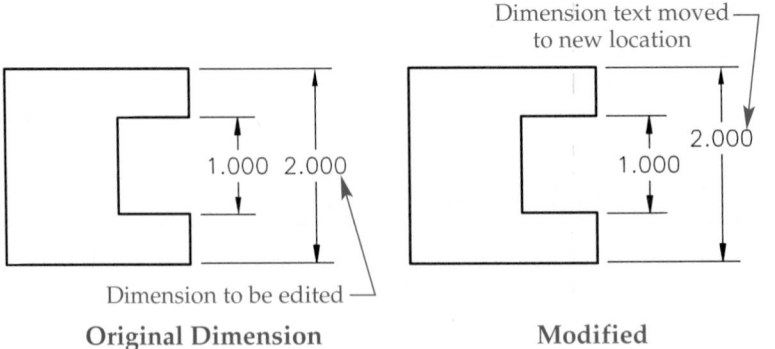

Dimension text moved to new location

Dimension to be edited

Original Dimension   Modified

Figure 18-5.
A comparison of the
DIMTEDIT command
options.

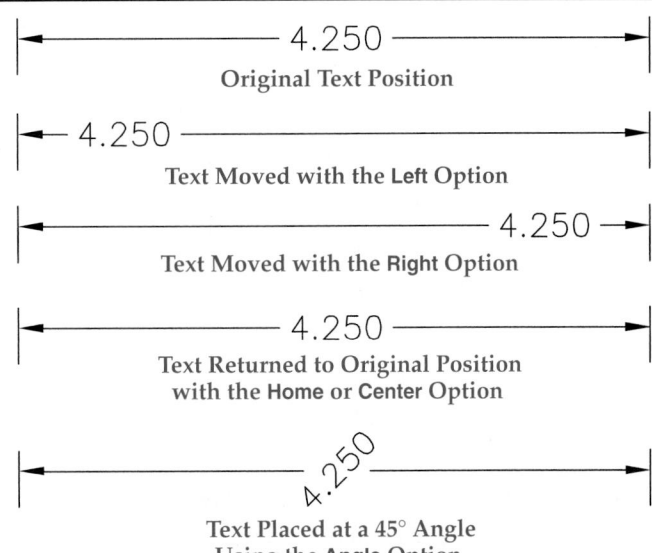

Original Text Position

Text Moved with the **Left** Option

Text Moved with the **Right** Option

Text Returned to Original Position
with the **Home** or **Center** Option

Text Placed at a 45° Angle
Using the **Angle** Option

NOTE

When you are creating new dimensions, dimension text can be placed more easily by activating the **Place text manually** check box in the **Fit** tab of the **New** (or **Modify**) **Dimension Style** dialog box. This option allows you to locate the text as desired without using automatic horizontal justification.

Using the Dimedit Command

The **DIMEDIT** command can also be used to edit the placement and orientation of an existing associative dimension. Most of the command options are similar to those available with other dimension editing commands. However, the **Oblique** option is unique to the **DIMEDIT** command and allows you to change the angle of the extension lines of an existing dimension.

To access the **DIMEDIT** command, pick the **Dimension Edit** button on the **Dimension** toolbar, pick **Dimension > Oblique** to enter the oblique option of the **DIMEDIT** command, or type DIMEDIT. After entering the command, select the dimension to be altered. Then, select from the options offered at the Enter type of dimension editing [Home/New/Rotate/Oblique]: prompt.

- **Home.** This option functions the same as the **Home** option available with the **DIMTEDIT** command, and can be used to move relocated or rotated dimension text back to its original position.
- **New.** This option is very similar to editing dimension text values using the **DDEDIT** command. When you enter the **New** option, the **In-Place Text Editor** is displayed with a 0.0000 (depending on the precision) value highlighted. The highlighted 0.0000 value represents the associated dimension value. Replace or add to the 0.0000 value. Then, pick the **OK** button and select the dimension to make the change.
- **Rotate.** This option functions the same as the **Angle** option available with the **DIMTEDIT** command. When you enter the **Rotated** option, you are asked to specify a rotation angle. Then select the dimension to be rotated and press [ENTER]. The text is then rotated about its middle point.

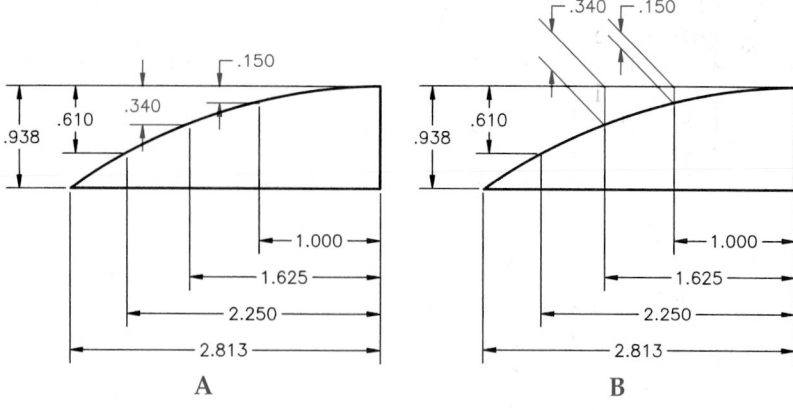

Figure 18-6.
Drawing dimensions with oblique extension lines.

A

B

- **Oblique.** The curve shown in **Figure 18-6A** is dimensioned using the normal practice, but in some cases, space may be limited and oblique extension lines are used. First, dimension the object using the **DIMLINEAR** command as appropriate, even if dimensions are crowded or overlap. See **Figure 18-6A.**

  The .150 and .340 dimensions are to be placed at an oblique angle above the view. To do this, enter the **Oblique** option and pick the dimensions to be redrawn at an oblique angle. In this case, the .150 and .340 dimensions are selected. Next, you are asked for the obliquing angle. Careful planning is needed to make sure the correct obliquing angle is entered. Obliquing angles originate from 0° East and revolve counterclockwise. In the example shown in **Figure 18-6B,** the obliquing angle for the extension lines is 135°.

NOTE

The **Oblique** option of the **DIMEDIT** command can also be used to dimension oblique and isometric drawings.

Using Shortcut Menu Options

If you select a dimension and right-click, a shortcut menu is displayed. See **Figure 18-7.** The shortcut menu contains the following dimension-specific options:

- **Dim Text position.** The options in this cascading menu automatically move the dimension text.
- **Precision.** The options in this cascading menu allow you to adjust the number of decimal places displayed in a dimension text value.
- **Dim Style.** This cascading menu allows you to create a new dimension style based on the properties of the selected dimension. You can also change the dimension style of the dimension.
- **Flip Arrow.** This option allows you to flip the direction of a dimension arrowhead to the opposite side of the extension line or object that it is touching. For example, if the arrowheads and the dimension value are crowded inside the extension lines, the arrowheads can be flipped to the outside of the extension lines quickly to make the dimension easier to read. When this option is used with a dimension that has a first and second arrowhead, only one of the arrowheads is flipped at a time. This allows you to control the arrowheads independently. The arrowhead that is flipped is determined by which arrowhead is closer to the point picked when you select the dimension (not the right-click point).

Figure 18-7.
Select a dimension and then right-click to access this shortcut menu.

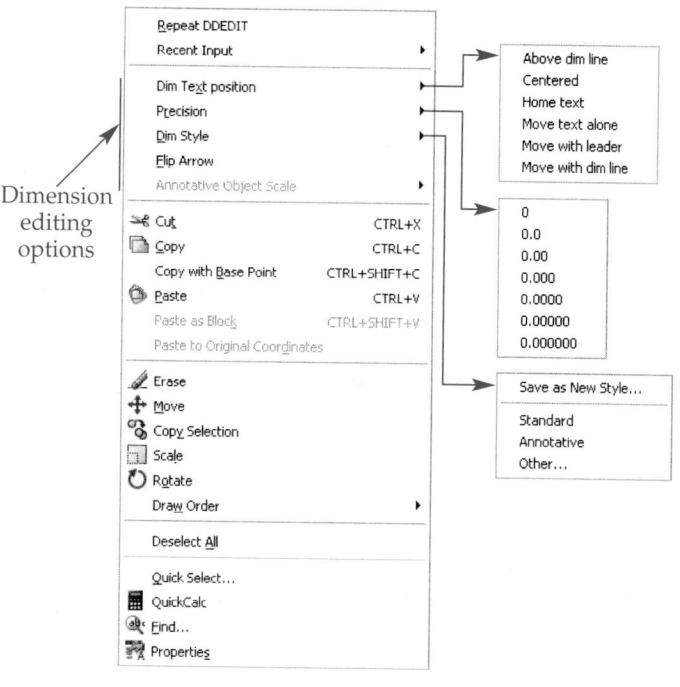

Dimension editing options

Exercise 18-2

Complete the exercise on the Student CD.

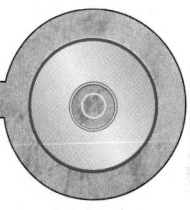

Editing Dimensions with the Qdim Command

The **QDIM** command can be used to place a new dimension in a drawing. This was described in Chapter 16. The **QDIM** command can also be used to perform several dimension editing operations. You can change the arrangement of existing dimensions, add a dimension, or remove an existing dimension. The **QDIM** command can be accessed by picking the **Quick Dimension** button from the **Dimension** control panel of the **Dashboard** or the **Dimension** toolbar, picking **Dimension > Quick Dimension**, or typing QDIM.

The **Continuous** option allows you to change a selected group of dimensions to chain dimensions. In chain, or continuous, dimensioning the dimensions are placed next to each other in a line, or end to end. This is described in Chapter 16. An example of continuous dimensioning is shown in **Figure 18-8A.**

The **Baseline** option allows you to create a series of baseline dimensions from existing dimensions. In baseline dimensioning, all dimensions originate from common features. Baseline dimensions are shown in **Figure 18-8B.** In this example, the **Baseline** option has been used to change the dimensioning arrangement from continuous to baseline.

The **Edit** option allows you to add dimensions to, or remove dimensions from, a selected group and then automatically reorder the group. You can use the **Add** suboption of the **Edit** option to add a dimension. The **Remove** suboption is used to remove a dimension. The command sequence to add the dimension shown in **Figure 18-8** to the baseline dimensions is:

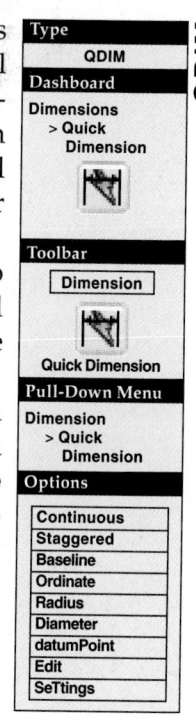

Figure 18-8.
The **QDIM** command can be used to change existing dimension arrangements and add or remove dimensions.

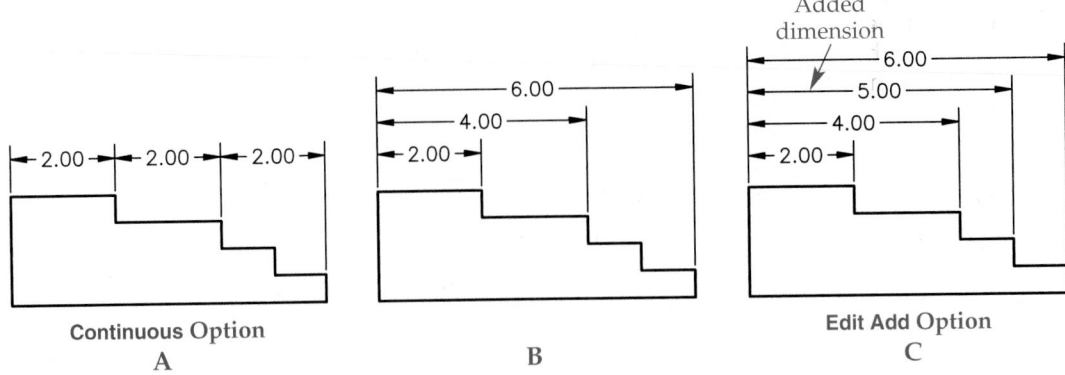

Continuous Option
A

B

Edit Add Option
C

```
Command: QDIM↵
Associative dimensions priority = Endpoint
Select geometry to dimension: (select all dimensions in the group to change)
Select geometry to dimension: ↵
Specify dimension line position, or
[Continuous/Staggered/Baseline/Ordinate/Radius/Diameter/datumPoint/Edit/
    seTtings] <Baseline>: E↵
Indicate dimension point to remove, or [Add/eXit] <eXit>: A↵
Indicate dimension point to add, or [Remove/eXit] <eXit>: (pick the location or feature
    for which the dimension is to be added)
One dimension point added.
Indicate dimension point to add, or [Remove/eXit] <eXit>: ↵
Specify dimension line position, or
[Continuous/Staggered/Baseline/Ordinate/Radius/Diameter/datumPoint/Edit/
    seTtings] <Baseline>: (pick a location for the baseline dimension arrangement)
```

The dimensions are automatically realigned after you pick a location for the arrangement. You do not have to pick all of the dimensions in the group. However, if you do not pick the entire group, you must select the location carefully. The spacing for the edited dimension and the dimensions in the group that were not selected may not be consistent.

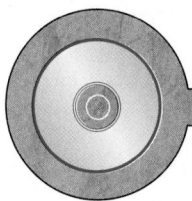

Exercise 18-3
Complete the exercise on the Student CD.

Changing the Dimension Style

Chapter 16 describes the process of making changes to an existing dimension style using the **Modify Dimension Style** dialog box. When you make changes to a dimension style, any dimensions drawn using the dimension style automatically adjust according to the new dimension style settings.

If your drawing contains a number of dimension styles, you may need to change the style of an existing dimension to a different style. A dimension's style can be changed using any of the following methods:

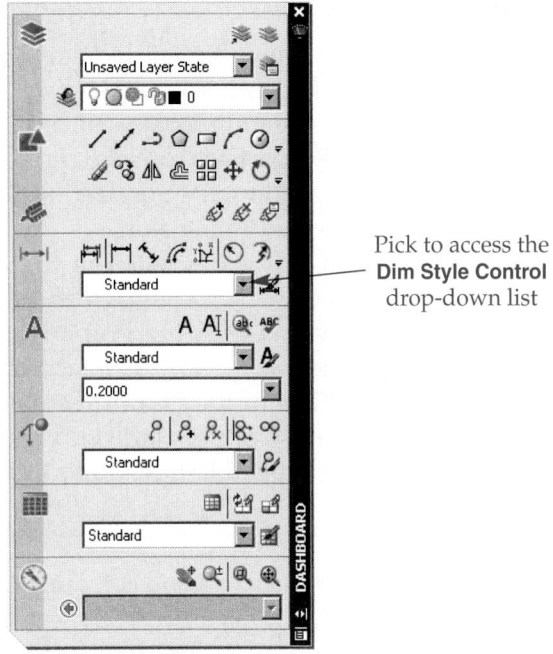

Figure 18-9.
The **Dim Style Control** drop-down list on the **Dashboard** can be used to change the style of an existing dimension.

Pick to access the **Dim Style Control** drop-down list

- **Dim Style cascading menu in the shortcut menu.** Select the dimension and right-click to display the shortcut menu. Select a new dimension style from the cascading menu.
- **Dim Style Control drop-down list in the Dimension control panel of the Dashboard or the Dimension toolbar.** Select the dimension and select the new dimension style from this drop-down list. See **Figure 18-9**.
- **Dim Style Control drop-down list in the Styles toolbar.** Select the dimension and select the new dimension style from this drop-down list.
- **Properties palette.** Select a new dimension style in the **Misc** category. Refer to Chapter 12 for a discussion on how to change settings in the **Properties** palette.
- **Update option.** The **Update** dimension command changes the style of the selected dimension to the current dimension style. This command can be accessed by picking the **Dimension Update** button from the **Dimension** control panel of the **Dashboard** or the **Dimension** toolbar or by selecting **Dimension > Update**.

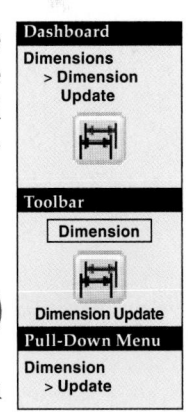

Dashboard
Dimensions
> Dimension Update

Toolbar
Dimension

Dimension Update
Pull-Down Menu
Dimension
> Update

Overriding Existing Dimension Style Settings

Generally, it is appropriate to have one or more dimension styles set to perform specific tasks that relate to your dimensioning practices. However, in some situations, a few dimensions require settings that are not covered by your basic styles. These situations may be too few and far between to warrant creating a new style. For example, assume you have the value for **Offset from origin** set at .063, which conforms to ASME standards. However, three dimensions in your final drawing require a 0 **Offset from origin** setting. For these dimensions, you can perform a *dimension style override* and temporarily alter the settings for the dimension style without actually modifying the style.

dimension style override: A temporary alteration of settings for the dimension style that does not actually modify the style.

Dimension Style Overrides for Existing Dimensions

<table>
<tr><td>

Type

PROPERTIES
PROPS
CH
MO
[Ctrl]+[1]

Toolbar

Standard Annotation

Properties

Pull-Down Menu

Modify
>Properties

</td></tr>
</table>

To override the dimension style of an existing dimension, first select the dimension. Then open the **Properties** palette by picking the **Properties** button on the **Standard Annotation** toolbar, selecting **Modify** > **Properties** from the pull-down menu, selecting **Tools** > **Palettes** > **Properties** from the pull-down menu, or typing PROPERTIES. You can also right-click in the viewport and select **Properties** from the shortcut menu or double-click the selected dimension.

The dimension properties listed in the **Properties** palette are broken down into eight categories. See **Figure 18-10**. To change an existing property or value, access the proper category and pick the property to highlight it. You can then change the corresponding value.

The changes made in the **Properties** palette are overrides to the dimension style for the selected dimension. The changes do not alter the original dimension style. Also, the changes are not applied to new dimensions.

Figure 18-10.
The **Properties** palette can be used to edit dimension properties and create a dimension style override.

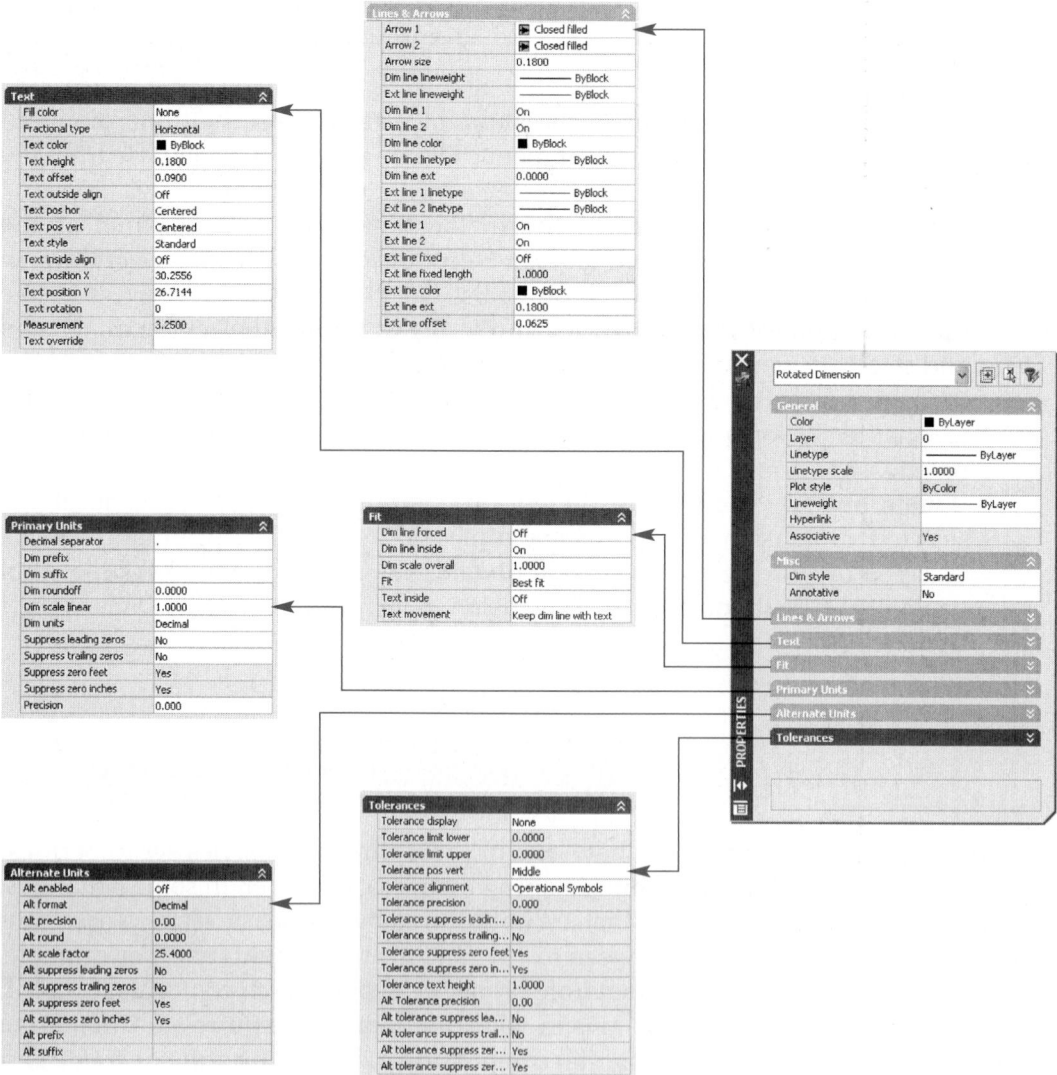

Dimension Style Overrides for New Dimensions

To override the dimension style for dimensions you are about to draw, open the **Dimension Style Manager**. Then select the dimension style that you are going to override from the **Styles** list. Pick the **Override...** button to display the **Override Current Style** dialog box. This dialog box has the same features as the **New** (or **Modify**) **Dimension Style** dialog box. Make any changes to the style and pick the **OK** button. The style you overrode now has a branch under it labeled **<style overrides>**, which is set as the current style. Close the **Dimension Style Manager** and draw the needed dimensions.

To clear the overrides, return to the **Dimension Style Manager** and set any other style current. However, this discards the overrides. If you want to incorporate the overrides into the style that was overridden, right-click on the **<style overrides>** name and select **Save to current style** from the shortcut menu. To save the changes to a new style, pick the **New...** button. Then select **<style overrides>** in the **Start With** drop-down list in the **Create New Dimension Style** dialog box. In the **New Dimension Style** dialog box, simply pick **OK** to save the overrides as a new style.

PROFESSIONAL TIP

Carefully evaluate the dimensioning requirements in a drawing before performing a style override. It may be better to create a new style. For example, if a number of the dimensions in the current drawing require the same overrides, generating a new dimension style is a good idea. If only one or two dimensions need the same changes, performing an override may be more productive.

Exercise 18-4
Complete the exercise on the Student CD.

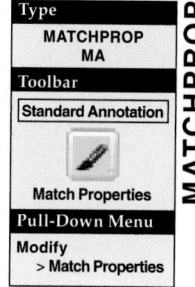

Using the Matchprop Command

The dimension editing methods presented in this chapter have focused on updating individual dimension properties and changing dimensions to a different dimension style. You can also edit dimensions by matching the properties of one dimension to another. The **MATCHPROP** command allows you to select the properties of one dimension and apply those properties to one or more existing dimensions.

The **MATCHPROP** command can be accessed by picking the **Match Properties** button on the **Standard Annotation** toolbar, selecting **Modify > Match Properties**, or typing MA or MATCHPROP. Pick the source dimension that has the desired properties and then pick the dimensions that will change. Press [Enter] and all of the destination dimensions are updated to reflect the properties of the source dimension. This command is covered more completely in Chapter 12.

For the **MATCHPROP** command to work with dimensions, the **Dimension** setting must be active. You can check this after you have selected the source object. When the Current active settings: prompt line appears, Dim should appear with the other settings. If this setting does not appear when you are prompted to select a destination object, type S for the **Settings** option. This displays the **Property Settings** dialog box. Activate the **Dimension** check box in the **Special Properties** area and pick **OK**. Then select the destination dimensions.

Type	
MATCHPROP MA	**MATCHPROP**
Toolbar	
Standard Annotation	
Match Properties	
Pull-Down Menu	
Modify > Match Properties	

Exercise 18-5

Complete the exercise on the Student CD.

Editing Associative Dimensions

As described earlier in this chapter, an associative dimension is made up of a group of individual elements that are treated as a single object. When an associative dimension is selected for editing, the entire group of elements is highlighted. If you use the **ERASE** command, for example, you can pick the dimension as a single object and erase all of its elements at once.

One benefit of associative dimensioning is that it permits existing dimensions to be updated as an object is edited. This means that when a dimensioned object is edited, the dimension value automatically changes to match the edit. The automatic update is only applied if you accepted the default text value during the original dimension placement. This provides you with an important advantage when editing an associatively dimensioned drawing. Any changes to objects are automatically transferred to the dimensions.

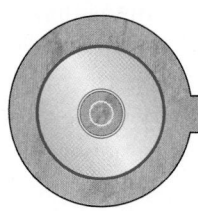

NOTE

You can determine whether a dimension is associative by selecting the dimension, displaying the **Properties** palette, and verifying the **Associative** property value in the **General** area.

Associative dimensioning is controlled by the **DIMASSOC** dimension variable. To set associative dimensioning, you can also open the **Options** dialog box and select the **User Preferences** tab. Then check or uncheck the **Make new dimensions associative** option in the **Associative Dimensioning** area.

The three settings for the **DIMASSOC** dimension variable are 0, 1, and 2. A setting of 0 turns off associative dimensioning. In this case, elements of the dimension are created separately, as if the dimension is exploded. The dimension is not updated when the object is edited. With a setting of 1, the components that make up a dimension are grouped together, but the dimension is not associated with an object. If you edit the object, you also have to edit the dimension.

If **DIMASSOC** is set to 2, the components that make up a dimension are grouped and the dimension is associated with the object. If the object is stretched, trimmed, or extended, the dimension updates automatically. See **Figure 18-11.** An associative dimension also updates when you use grips or the **MOVE**, **MIRROR**, **ROTATE**, or **SCALE** commands.

In the **Options** dialog box, checking the **Make new dimensions associative** check box sets **DIMASSOC** to 2. If you uncheck the check box, the **DIMASSOC** value is changed to a previous value other than 2 (either 1 or 0).

Figure 18-11.
The original drawing was created with associative dimensions. The drawing was revised to change the rectangle dimensions and the circle diameter. The dimensions automatically updated to the new object geometry.

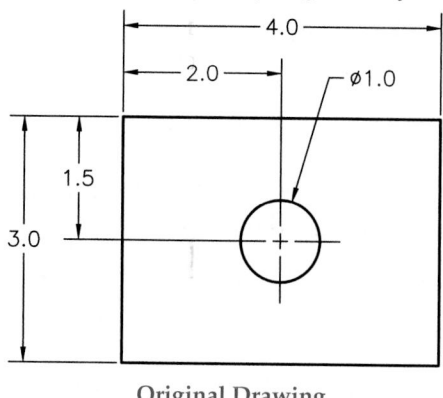

Original Drawing

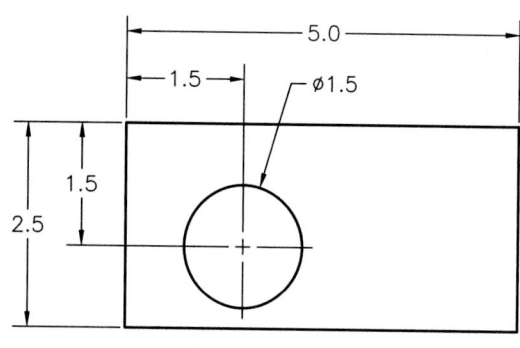

Revised Drawing

NOTE

Associative dimensions created in paper space but attached to model space objects also automatically update when the object is edited.

Nonassociative dimensions can be converted to associative dimensions using the **DIMREASSOCIATE** command. To access this command, select **Dimension > Reassociate Dimensions** or type DRE or DIMREASSOCIATE. You are prompted to select the dimensions to be associated. After you select the dimensions, an X marker appears at the first extension line endpoint. Select the point on an object with which to associate this extension line. Then select the associated point for the second extension line.

Use the **Next** option to advance to the next definition point. You can also use the **Select object** option to select an object with which to associate the dimension. The extension line endpoints are then automatically associated with the object endpoints.

To disassociate a dimension from an object, type DDA or DISASSOCIATE and then select the dimension. The dimension objects are still grouped together, but the dimension will not be associated with an object.

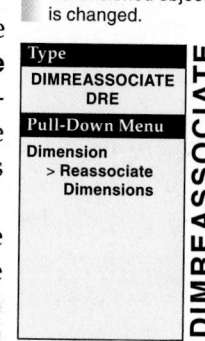

Type
DIMREASSOCIATE
DRE
Pull-Down Menu
Dimension
> Reassociate
Dimensions

DIMREASSOCIATE

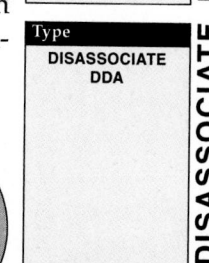

Type
DISASSOCIATE
DDA

DISASSOCIATE

Exercise 18-6
Complete the exercise on the Student CD.

Type
EXPLODE
X
Dashboard
2D Draw
> Explode

Toolbar
Modify

Explode
Pull-Down Menu
Modify
> Explode

EXPLODE

Exploding an Associative Dimension

As previously described, the component parts of an associative dimension cannot be edited separately. An associative dimension is treated as one object even though it consists of extension lines, a dimension line, arrowheads, and text. At times, you may find it necessary to edit the individual parts. To do this, you must first explode the dimension using the **EXPLODE** command.

PROFESSIONAL TIP

One way to edit individual dimension properties without removing the associative dimensioning feature is to use the **Properties** palette to create a dimension style override.

Dimension Definition Points

definition points (defpoints): The points used to specify the dimension location and the center point of the dimension text.

When you draw an associative dimension, the points used to specify the dimension location and the center point of the dimension text are called the *definition points*, or *defpoints*. When a dimension location is redefined, the revised position is based on the definition points. The definition points are located on the Defpoints layer. This layer is automatically created by AutoCAD. The definition points are displayed with the dimension.

Normally, the Defpoints layer does not plot. The definition points are plotted only if the Defpoints layer is renamed and the layer is set to plot. The definition points are displayed when the dimensioning layer is on, even if the Defpoints layer is turned off.

If you select an object for editing and wish to include the dimensions in the edit, you must include the definition points of the dimension in the selection set. If you need to snap to a definition point only, use the **Node** object snap.

Using the Dimspace Command

The amount of space between a drawing feature and the first dimension line, and between dimension lines, varies depending on the drawing and industry or company standard. ASME standards recommend a minimum spacing of .375" (10mm) from a drawing feature to the first dimension line and a minimum spacing of .25" (6mm) between dimension lines. A minimum spacing of 3/8" is common for architectural drawings.

Typically, the spacing between dimension lines is equal, and chain dimensions are aligned. See **Figure 18-12.** As a result, it is important to determine the correct location and spacing of dimension lines. However, dimension line spacing and alignment can be adjusted after dimensions are added. This is a common requirement when there is a need to increase or decrease the space between dimension lines, such as when the scale of the drawing changes or when dimensions are spaced unequally, or misaligned.

The **STRETCH** and **DIMTEDIT** commands or grips can be used to adjust the location and alignment of dimension lines individually. You must determine the exact location or amount of stretch applied to each dimension line before using these tools. An alternative method is to use the **DIMSPACE** command, which can be used to adjust the space equally between dimension lines or align dimension lines. To access the **DIMSPACE** command, pick the **Dimspace** button in the **Dimension** toolbar or the **Dimension** control panel of the **Dashboard**, select **Dimension > Dimension Space** in the pull-down menu, or type DIMSPACE.

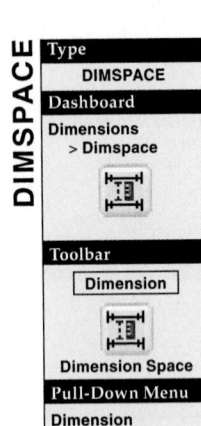

DIMSPACE

Type
DIMSPACE

Dashboard
Dimensions > Dimspace

Toolbar
Dimension

Dimension Space

Pull-Down Menu
Dimension > Dimension Space

Figure 18-12.
Correct drafting practice requires dimension lines to be equally spaced and aligned for readability.

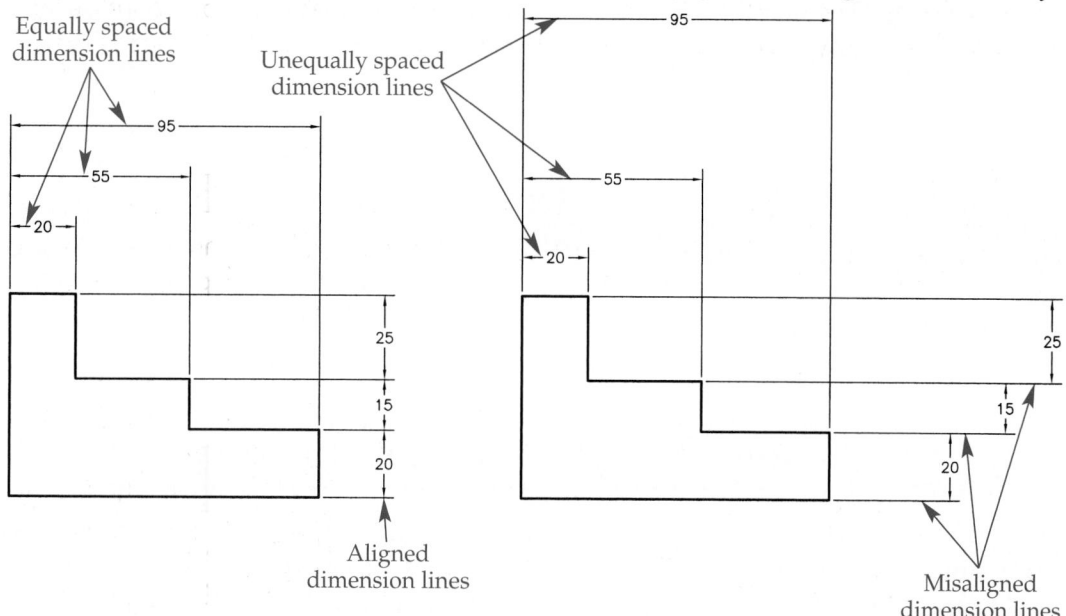

When you access the **DIMSPACE** command, you are prompted to select the base dimension. The *base dimension* is the dimension line that will remain in the same location. The other dimension lines are spaced to or aligned with the selected base dimension. Once you select the base dimension, you are prompted to pick the dimensions to space. Select each dimension to space or align and press [Enter]. The Enter value or [Auto]: prompt appears. Enter a space value to space the dimension lines equally according to the value. For example, enter .5 to space the selected dimension lines .5″ apart. Enter a value of 0 to align the dimensions. See **Figure 18-13.** Use the **Auto** option to space dimension lines using a value that is twice the height of the dimension text.

base dimension: The dimension line with which other dimension lines are spaced or aligned.

Figure 18-13.
Using the **DIMSPACE** command to space and align dimension lines correctly.

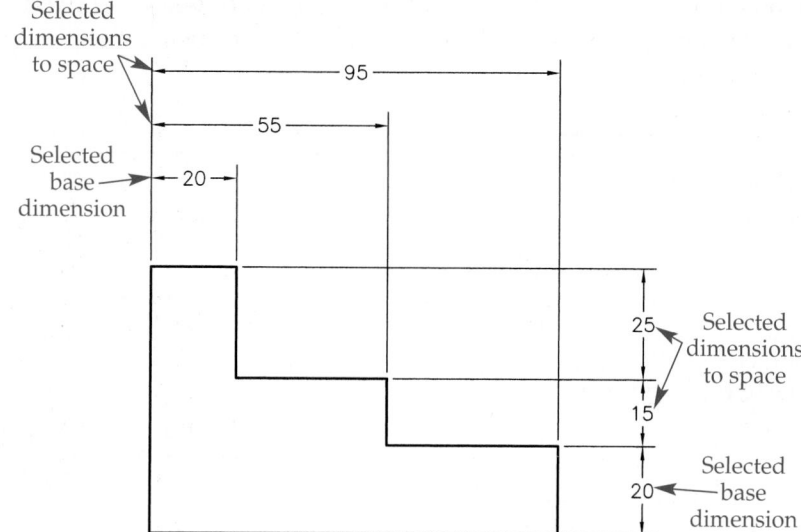

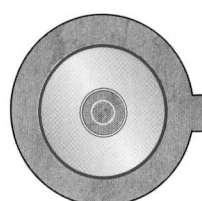

Exercise 18-7

Complete the exercise on the Student CD.

Using the Dimbreak Command

DIMBREAK

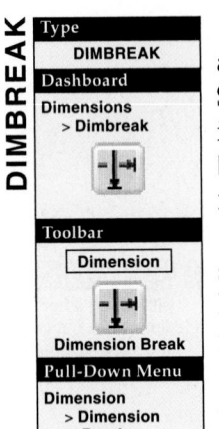

Type
DIMBREAK

Dashboard
Dimensions > Dimbreak

Toolbar
Dimension
Dimension Break

Pull-Down Menu
Dimension > Dimension Break

Drafting standards state that when dimension, extension, or leader lines cross a drawing feature or another dimension, the line is not broken at the intersection. See Figure 18-14. However, the **DIMBREAK** command can be used to create breaks if desired. To access the **DIMBREAK** command, pick the **DIMBREAK** button in the **Dimension** toolbar or the **Dimension** control panel of the **Dashboard**, select **Dimension** > **Dimension Break** in the pull-down menu, or type DIMBREAK.

When you enter the **DIMBREAK** command, you are prompted to select the dimension to break. This is the dimension that contains the dimension, extension, or leader line that you want to break across an object. Another option is to use **Multiple** to select more than one dimension. If you pick a single dimension to break, the Select object to break dimension or [Auto/Restore/Manual]: prompt is displayed. If you use the **Multiple** option to select multiple dimensions, you must press [Enter] after the dimensions are selected to display the Enter and option [Break/Restore]: prompt. The following options are available when you pick a single dimension:

- **Auto.** Breaks the dimension, extension, or leader line at the selected object. The size of the break is defined by the **Dimension Break** setting of the current dimension style. You can pick additional objects if necessary to break the dimension at other locations. See Figure 18-15. This option is set by default.
- **Manual.** Allows you to define the size of the break by selecting two points along the dimension, extension, or leader line, instead of using the break size set in the current dimension style.

Figure 18-14.
Drafting standards state that when dimension, extension, or leader lines cross a drawing feature or another dimension, the line is not broken at the intersection.

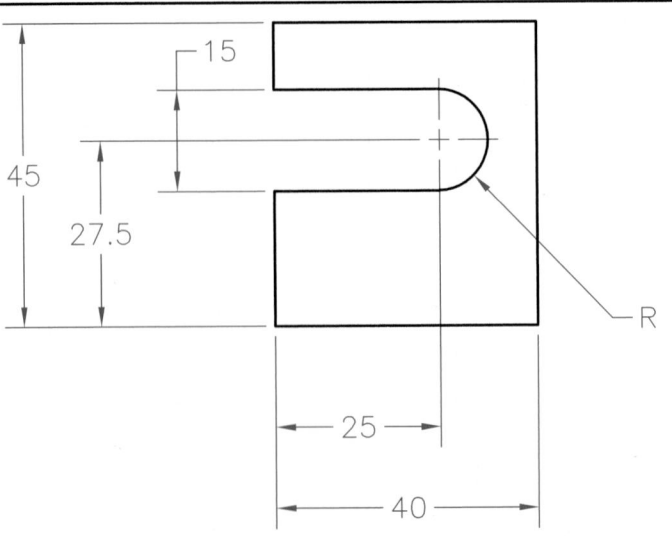

Figure 18-15.
Use the **DIMBREAK** command to break dimension, extension, or leader lines when they cross an object. This example violates ASME standards and is for reference only. Extension and leader lines do not break over object lines, but drafters commonly prefer to break an extension line when it crosses a dimension line.

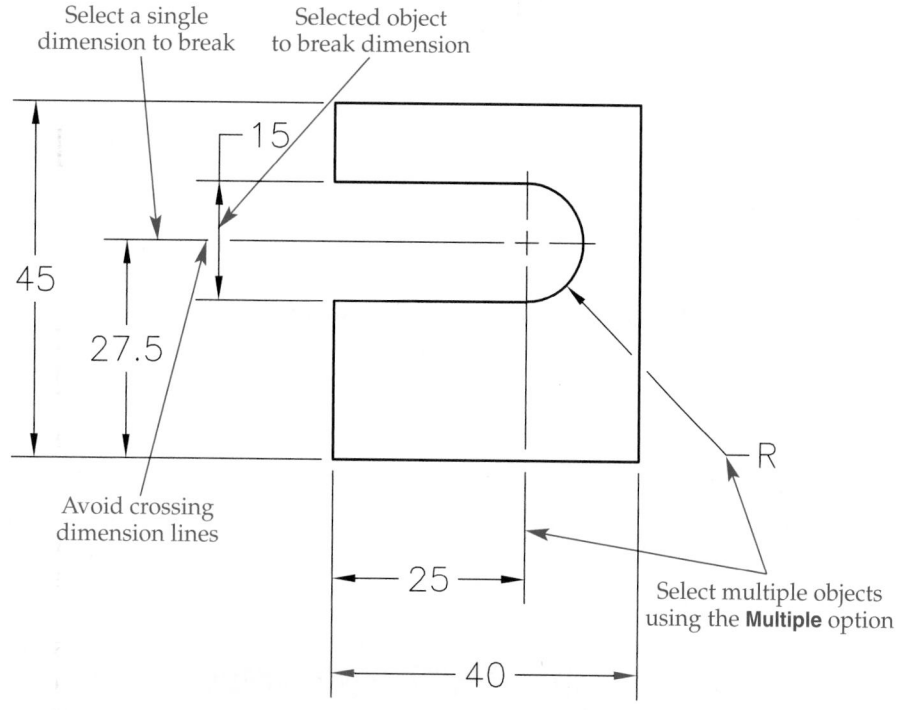

Select a single dimension to break

Selected object to break dimension

15

45

27.5

Avoid crossing dimension lines

R

25

Select multiple objects using the **Multiple** option

40

- **Restore.** Removes an existing break created using the **DIMBREAK** command.

When you use the **Multiple** option to select multiple dimensions, the **Break** and **Restore** options are available. Select the **Break** option to break the selected dimension, extension, or leader lines everywhere they intersect another object. See **Figure 18-15.** Use the **Restore** option to remove any existing breaks that have been added to the selected dimensions using the **DIMBREAK** command.

Exercise 18-8
Complete the exercise on the Student CD.

Creating Inspection Dimensions

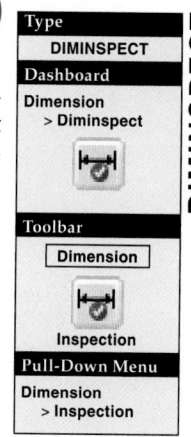

Inspections and tests often occur throughout the design and manufacturing of a product. These tests are usually done to ensure the correct size and location of product features. In some cases, size and location dimensions include information about how frequently the dimension should be tested for consistency and tolerance during the manufacturing of a product. See **Figure 18-16.** This information can be added to most existing dimensions using the **DIMINSPECT** command.

To access the **DIMINSPECT** command, pick the **Diminspect** button in the **Dimension** toolbar or the **Dimension** control panel of the **Dashboard**, select **Dimension > Inspection** in the pull-down menu, or type DIMINSPECT. This displays the **Inspection Dimension** dialog box shown in **Figure 18-17.**

Figure 18-16.
An example of an inspection dimension added to a part drawing. This example shows an angular shape with a label, dimension, and inspection rate frame.

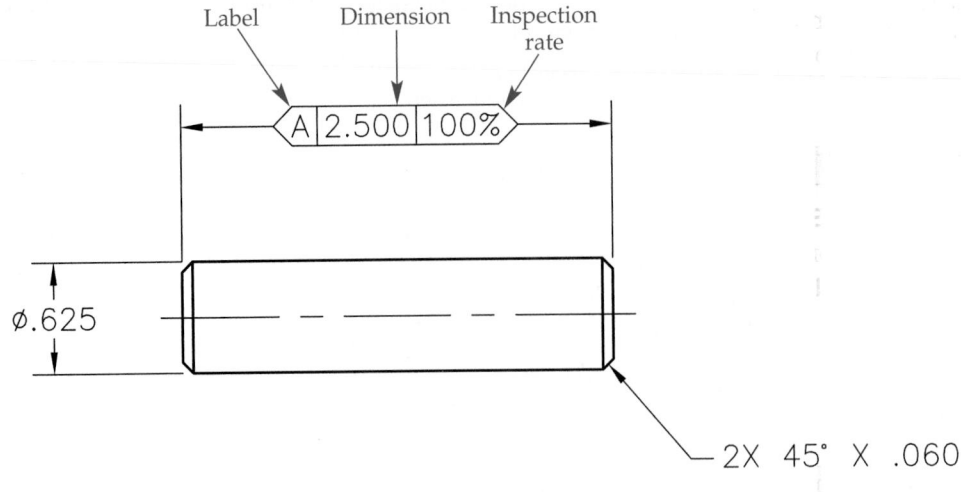

Figure 18-17.
The **Inspection Dimension** dialog box is used to add inspection information to existing dimensions.

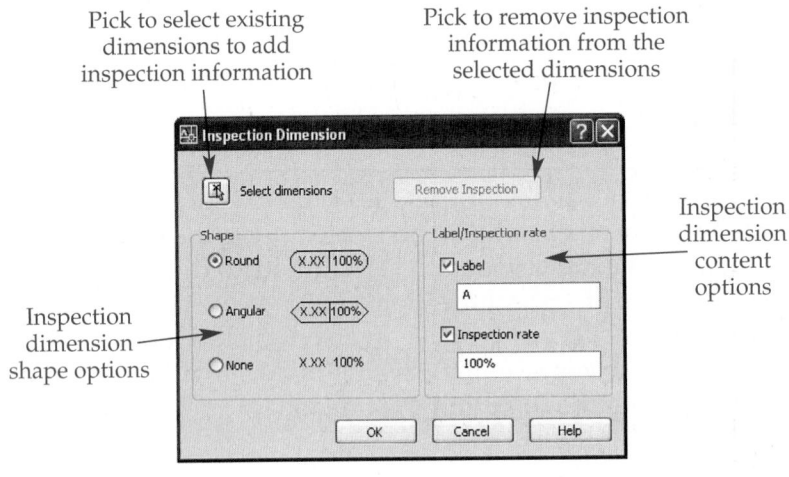

To create an inspection dimension, pick the **Select dimensions** button and choose the dimensions to which you want to add inspection information. You can select multiple dimensions, though the same inspection specifications will be added to each. Next, define the shape of the inspection dimension frame by picking the appropriate radio button in the **Shape** area. The inspection dimension contains the inspection label, the dimension value, and the inspection rate. Frames around the values are omitted when the **None** shape option is selected.

To include a label, pick the **Label** check box and type the label in the text box. The label is located on the left side of the inspection dimension and identifies the specific dimension. The inspection dimension shown in **Figure 18-16** is labeled A. The dimension frame houses the dimension value specified when the dimension is created. The length of the part shown in **Figure 18-16** is 2.500 and was created using the **DIMLINEAR** command. The **Inspection rate** check box is selected by default and allows you to describe how often the dimension should be tested by entering a value in the text box. The inspection rate for the dimension shown in **Figure 18-16** is 100%. This rate can have different meanings depending on the application. In this example, the inspection rate of 100% means that the length of the part must be checked for tolerance every time the part is added to an assembly.

To remove an inspection dimension, first access the **DIMINSPECT** command. Then, pick the **Select dimensions** button in the **Inspection Dimension** dialog box and choose the dimensions that contain the inspection information you want to remove. Press [Enter] to return to the **Inspection Dimension** dialog box, and pick the **Remove Inspection** button to return the dimension to its condition prior to adding the inspection content.

NOTE

The **-DIMINSPECT** command can be used to add and remove inspection dimensions using the Command: prompt or dynamic input instead of the **Inspection Dimension** dialog box.

Exercise 18-9
Complete the exercise on the Student CD.

Editing Multileaders

Multileaders can also be edited. Tools exist to add leader lines to or remove them from existing multileaders. The **MLEADERALIGN** command allows you to space and align leaders in an easy-to-read pattern. The **MLEADERCOLLECT** command allows separate multileaders to be grouped together using a single leader line.

Adding and Removing Multiple Leader Lines

Additional leader lines can be added to an existing multileader using the **Add Leader** tool. Multiple leaders are not a recommended ASME standard, but they are used for some applications, such as welding symbols. See **Figure 18-18.** To access the **Add Leader** tool, pick the **Add Leader** button in the **Multileader** toolbar or the **Multileader** control panel of the **Dashboard**, select **Modify > Object > Multileader > Add Leader** in the pull-down menu.

Once you access the **Add Leader** tool, pick the existing multileader to which you want to add a leader line. Then select the location for the additional leader line arrowhead. You can place as many additional leader lines as needed without accessing the tool again. When you are finished, press [Enter] or [Esc] to draw the leader lines and exit the tool.

When a leader line is added to a multileader using the **Add Leader** tool, all the leader lines become one object. Use the **Remove Leader** tool to remove unneeded multiple leader lines. To access the **Remove Leader** tool, pick the **Remove Leader** button in the **Multileader** toolbar or the **Multileader** control panel of the **Dashboard**, select **Modify > Object > Multileader > Remove Leader** in the pull-down menu. Then, pick the existing leader lines you want to remove and press [Enter] or [Esc] to delete the selected leader lines.

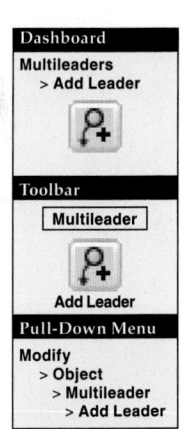

NOTE

The **MLEADEREDIT** command can be used to add and remove multileader lines.

Figure 18-18.
Applications of multiple leader lines. A—Do not use multiple leader lines in mechanical applications. B—Multiple leader lines are often used in welding applications.

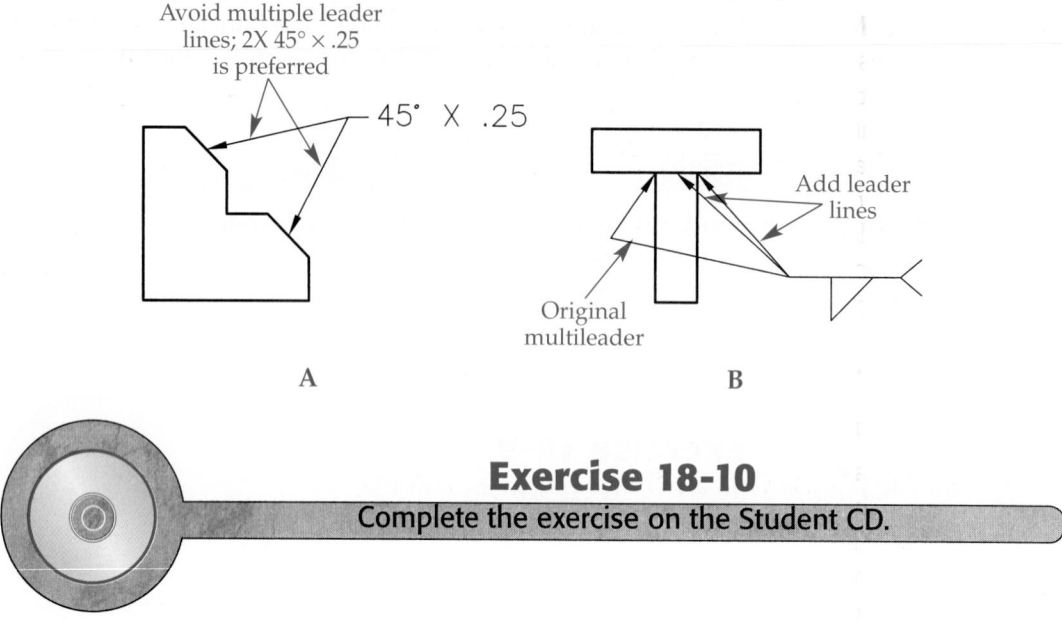

A

B

Exercise 18-10
Complete the exercise on the Student CD.

Aligning Multileaders

Another advantage to using multileaders is the ability to space and align leaders in an easy-to-read pattern. It is important to determine the correct location and spacing of leaders while adding the leaders. However, leader spacing and alignment can be adjusted after leaders are added. This is a common requirement when there is a need to increase or decrease the space between leader lines, such as when the scale of the drawing changes, when leaders are spaced unequally, or when leaders are misaligned. See **Figure 18-19**.

Figure 18-19.
Leaders that are equally spaced and aligned improve drawing readability.

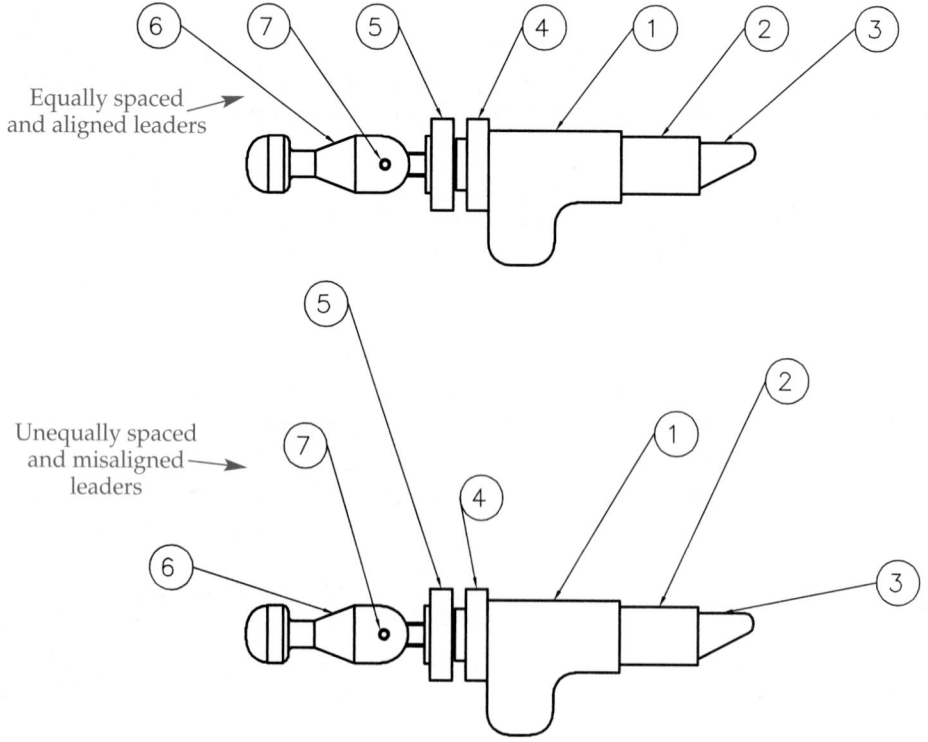

The **STRETCH** command or grips can be used to adjust the location and alignment of leaders individually. You must determine the exact location of or amount of stretch applied to each leader before using these tools. An alternative method is to use the **MLEADERALIGN** command, which can be used to align and adjust the space between leaders. To access the **MLEADERALIGN** command, pick the **Align Multileaders** button in the **Multileader** toolbar or the **Multileader** control panel of the **Dashboard**, select **Modify > Object > Multileader > Align** in the pull-down menu, or type MLEADERALIGN.

When you access the **MLEADERALIGN** command, you are prompted to select the leaders you want to space and align. You can use this command to adjust the location of a single leader in reference to another leader, but for most applications, several leaders are selected. Select each leader to space or align and press [Enter]. The default multileader alignment is set to **Use current spacing**. When you are prompted to select the multileader to align to, select the **Options** option to change the multileader alignment. The following sections describe each option.

Type
MLEADERALIGN

Dashboard
Multileaders > Align Multileaders

Toolbar
Multileader

Align Multileaders

Pull-Down Menu
Modify
  > Object
    > Multileader
      > Align

MLEADERALIGN

Using the distribute option

Pick the **Distribute** option to align and distribute, or divide, the selected leaders equally between two points. When you select the **Distribute** option, you are prompted to specify the first point. The first point you pick identifies the location of one of the leaders and determines the beginning of area from which the rest of the selected leaders are distributed. After you select the first point, you are prompted to specify the second point. The second point you pick identifies the location of each additional leader. The leaders are aligned with the first point and are equally divided among the distance between the first and second points. See **Figure 18-20**.

Making leader segments parallel

Pick the **make leader segments Parallel** option to make all the selected leader lines parallel to one of the selected leader lines. When you select the **make leader segments Parallel** option, you are prompted to select the multileader to align to. This is an existing leader that you want to keep in the same location and at the same angle. All other leaders will become parallel to this selection. The length of each leader line, except for the leader aligned to, increases or decreases in order to become parallel with the first leader. See **Figure 18-21**.

Figure 18-20.
Using the **Distribute** option to align and equally space leaders. In this example, horizontally aligned points are used.

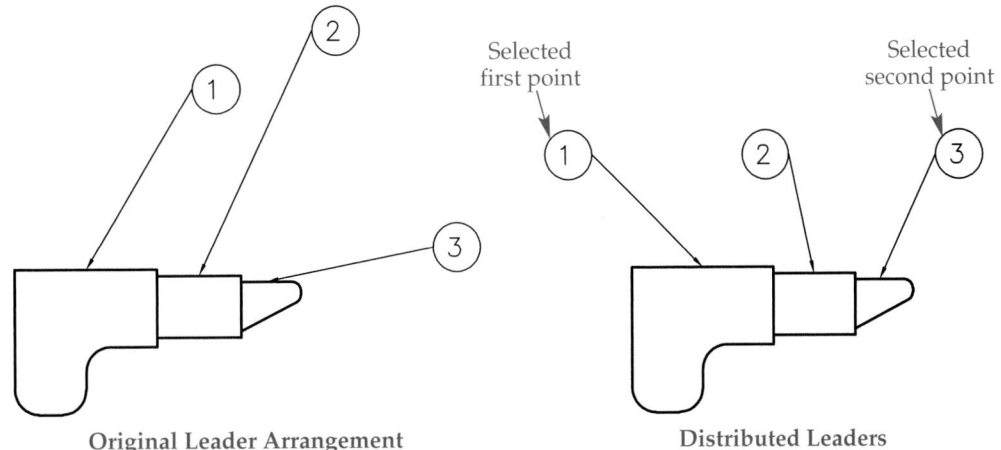

Original Leader Arrangement   Distributed Leaders

Figure 18-21.
Using the **make leader segments Parallel** option to make leader lines parallel to each other.

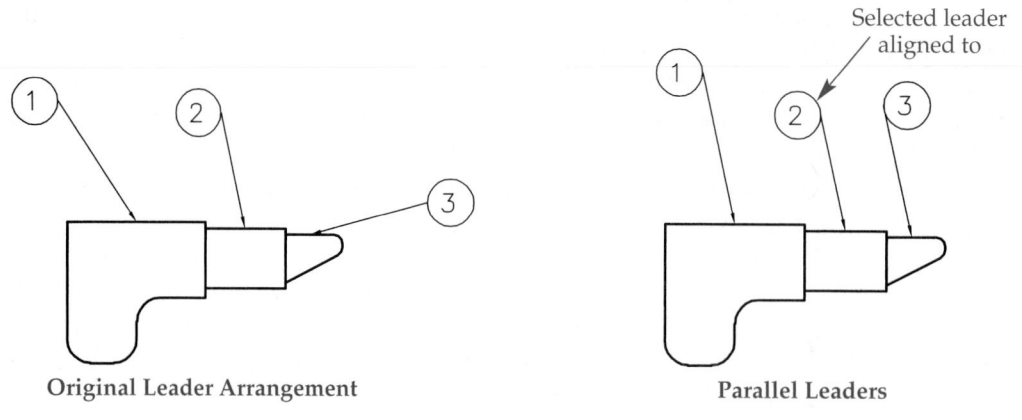

Original Leader Arrangement

Parallel Leaders

Specify the leader spacing

Pick the **Specify spacing** option to align and equally space the selected leaders according to distance between each leader. The spacing is the distance, or clear space, between the extents of each leader's content. After you enter the spacing, you are prompted to select the multileader to align to. This is an existing leader you want to keep in the same location and at the same angle. All other leaders are aligned with and spaced from this selection. Finally, specify the direction of the leader arrangement by entering or picking a point. See **Figure 18-22.**

Using the current leader spacing

Pick the **Use current spacing** option to align and space the selected leaders equally according to the distance between one of the selected leaders and the next closest leader. When you select the **Use current spacing** option, you are prompted to select the multileader to align to. This is an existing leader you want to keep in the same location and at the same angle. All other leaders will be aligned with and spaced from this selection. Next, specify the direction of the leader arrangement by entering or picking a point. See **Figure 18-23.**

Figure 18-22.
Using the **Specify spacing** option to align and equally space leaders.

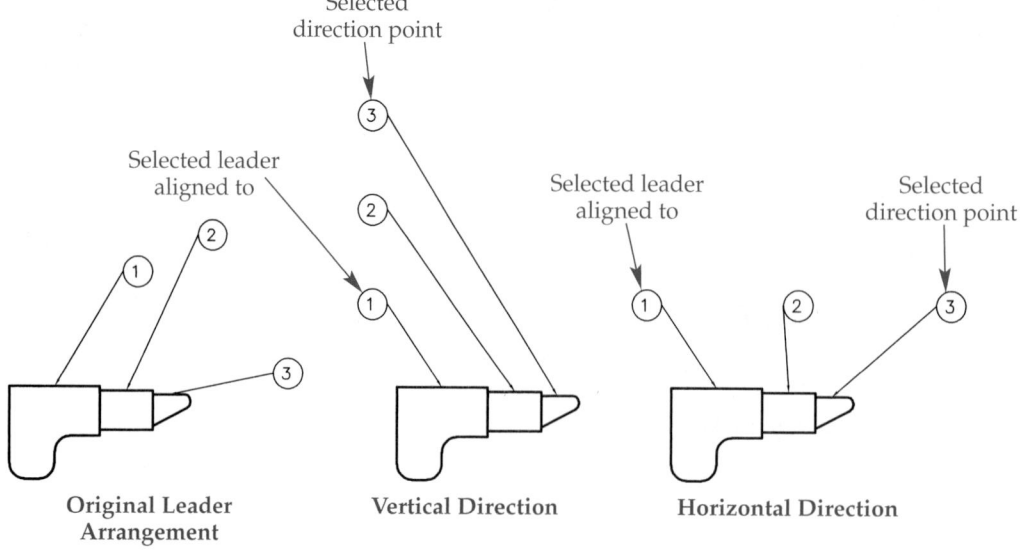

Original Leader
Arrangement

Vertical Direction

Horizontal Direction

Figure 18-23.
Using the **Use current spacing** option to align and equally space leaders.

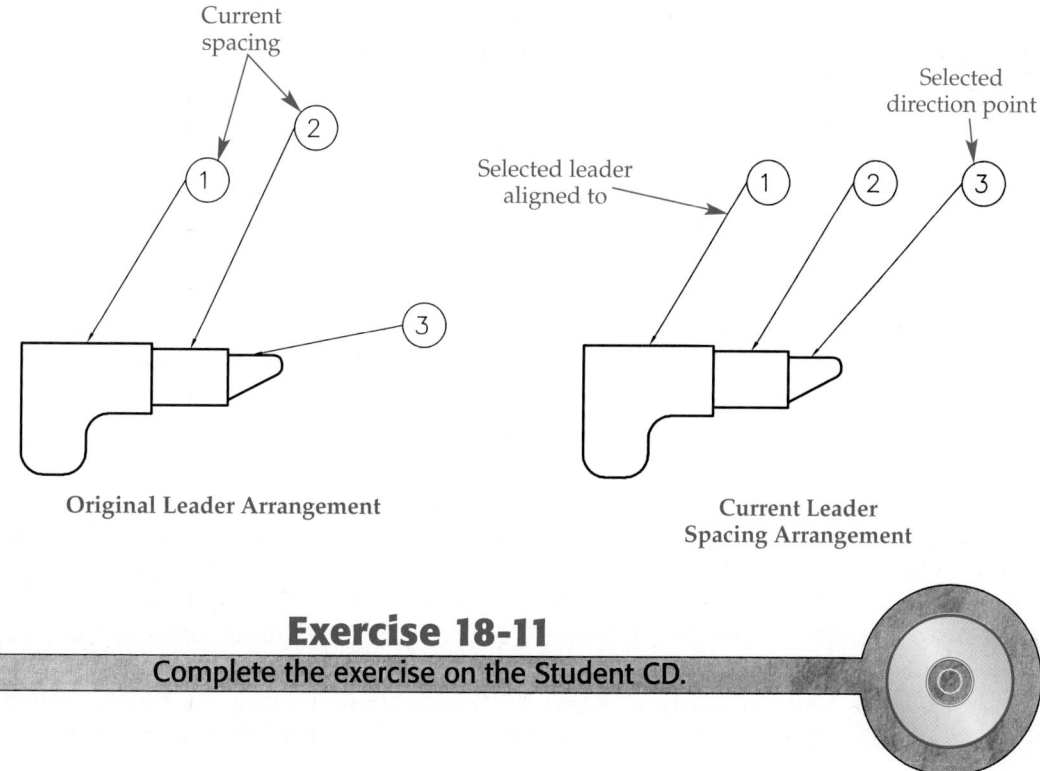

Original Leader Arrangement

Current Leader
Spacing Arrangement

Exercise 18-11
Complete the exercise on the Student CD.

Grouping Multileaders

Separate multileaders created using a **Block** multileader content style can be grouped together using a single leader line. This practice is common when adding balloons to assembly drawings. *Balloons* are circles connected to the related part with a leader line. A number or letter is normally placed inside the balloon to identify the part and correlate the part to a parts list or bill of materials. Balloons may be grouped together for closely related clusters of assembly components, such as a bolt, washer, and nut. *Grouped balloons* share the same leader, which is typically connected to the most obviously displayed component, such as the bolt mentioned in the previous example. See **Figure 18-24.**

balloons: Circles that contain identification information and are connected to a part with a leader line.

grouped balloons: Balloons that share the same leader.

Figure 18-24.
Grouped balloons can be used for closely related features.

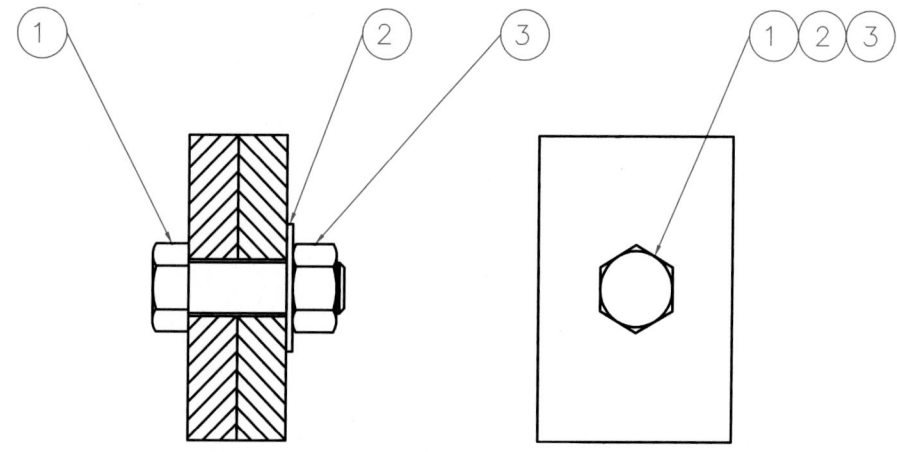

Use the **MLEADERCOLLECT** command to group multiple existing leaders together using a single leader line. To access the **MLEADERCOLLECT** command, pick the **Collect Multileaders** button in the **Multileader** toolbar or the **Multileader** control panel of the **Dashboard**, select **Modify** > **Object** > **Multileader** > **Collect** in the pull-down menu, or type MLEADERCOLLECT.

When you access the **MLEADERCOLLECT** command, you are prompted to select the leaders you want to space and align. The order in which you select the leaders determines how the leaders are grouped. Select leaders in a sequential order, ending with the leader that has the leader line you want to keep. The following options, shown in Figure 18-25, become available after the leaders have been selected:

- **Horizontal.** Aligns the grouped leader content horizontally. Pick a point to locate the grouped leader.
- **Vertical.** Aligns the grouped leader content vertically. Pick a point to locate the grouped leader.
- **Wrap.** Wraps the grouped leader content to additional lines as needed when the number of items exceeds a specified width or quantity. Enter the width at the Specify width prompt, or use the **Number** option to enter a quantity not to exceed before the grouped leaders are wrapped. Then pick a point to locate the grouped leader.

NOTE

Only symbols attached to leaders created using the **Block** content style option can be grouped using the **MLEADERCOLLECT** command.

Figure 18-25.
Examples of options for grouping leaders using the **MLEADERCOLLECT** command.

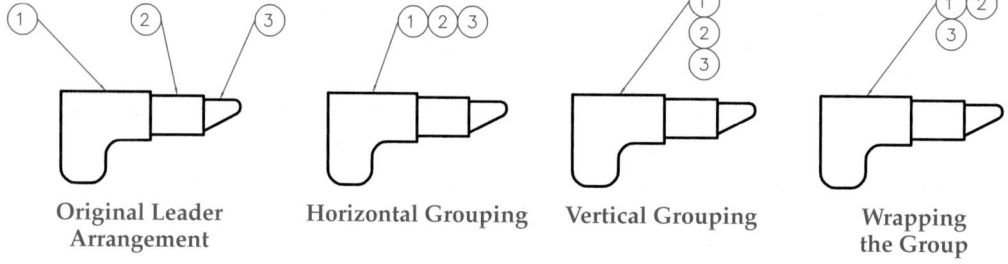

Original Leader Arrangement   Horizontal Grouping   Vertical Grouping   Wrapping the Group

Chapter Test

Answer the following questions. Write your answers on a separate sheet of paper or complete the electronic chapter test on the Student CD.

1. Name three object selection options that can be used to erase a group of dimensions surrounding an object without erasing any part of the object.
2. Explain how to add a diameter symbol to a dimension text value using the **DDEDIT** command.
3. Name the command that allows you to control the placement and orientation of an existing associative dimension text value.
4. Which four command options related to dimension editing are available in the shortcut menu accessed when a dimension is selected?
5. Which command and option can you use to add a new baseline dimension to an existing set of baseline dimensions?
6. Name three methods of changing the dimension style of a dimension.
7. How does the **Dimension Update** command affect selected dimensions?
8. When you use the **Properties** palette to edit a dimension, what is the effect on the dimension style?
9. How do you access the **Property Settings** dialog box?
10. Define *associative dimension*.
11. Why is it important to have associative dimensions for editing objects?
12. Which **Options** dialog box setting controls associative dimensioning?
13. Describe the differences among the dimensions created using the three **DIMASSOC** settings.
14. Which command is used to convert nonassociative dimensions to associative dimensions?
15. Which command is used to convert associative dimensions to nonassociative dimensions?
16. What are definition points?
17. Identify an alternate method to the **STRETCH** and **DIMTEDIT** commands or grips that can be used to adjust the space equally between dimension lines or to align dimension lines.
18. What two options are available when you use the **Multiple** option of the **DIMBREAK** command?
19. What command is used to add information about how frequently the dimension should be tested for consistency and tolerance during the manufacturing of a product?
20. Identify the four options available to change the multileader alignment.

Drawing Problems

1. Open P16-1 and edit as follows.
   A. Erase the front (circular) view.
   B. Stretch the vertical dimensions to provide more space between dimension lines. Be sure the space you create is the same between all vertical dimensions.
   C. Stagger the existing vertical dimension text numbers if they are not staggered as shown in the original problem.
   D. Erase the 1.750 horizontal dimension and then stretch the 5.255 and 4.250 dimensions to make room for a new datum dimension from the baseline to where the 1.750 dimension was located. This should result in a new baseline dimension that equals 2.750. Be sure all horizontal dimension lines are equally spaced.
   E. Save the drawing as P18-1.

2. Open P17-1 and edit as follows.
   A. Stretch the total length from 3.500 to 4.000, leaving the holes the same distance from the edges.
   B. Fillet the upper-left corner. Modify the 3X R.250 dimension accordingly.
   C. Save the drawing as P18-2.

3. Open P17-4 and edit as follows.
   A. Use the existing drawing as the model and make four copies.
   B. Leave the original drawing as it is and edit the other four pins in the following manner, keeping the ∅.125 hole exactly in the center of each pin.
   C. Give one pin a total length of 1.500.
   D. Create the next pin with a total length of 2.000.
   E. Edit the third pin to a length of 2.500.
   F. Change the last pin to a length of 3.000.
   G. Organize the pins on your drawing in a vertical row ranging in length from the smallest to the largest. You may need to change the drawing limits.
   H. Save the drawing as P18-3.

4. Open P17-5 and edit as follows.
   A. Modify the spline to have twelve projections, rather than eight.
   B. Change the angular dimension, linear dimension, and 8X dimension to reflect the modification.
   C. Save the drawing as P18-4.

5. Open P17-13 and edit as follows.
   A. Stretch the total length from 6.500 to 7.750.
   B. Add two more holes that continue the equally spaced pattern of .625 apart.
   C. Change the 8X .625(=5.00) dimension to read 10X .625(=6.250).
   D. Save the drawing as P18-5.

6. Open P16-15 and edit as follows.
   A. Make the bathroom 8'-0" wide by stretching the walls and vanity that are currently 6'-0" wide to 8'-0". Do this without increasing the size of the water closet compartment. Provide two equally spaced oval sinks where there is currently one.
   B. Save the drawing as P18-6.

7. Open P17-22 and edit as follows.
   A. Lengthen the part .250 on each side for a new overall dimension of 6.500.
   B. Change the width of the part from 3.000 to 3.500 by widening an equal amount on each side.
   C. Save the drawing as P18-7.

8. Open P17-20 and edit as follows.
   A. Shorten the .75 thread on the left side to .50.
   B. Shorten the .388 hexagon length to .300.
   C. Save the drawing as P18-8.

CHAPTER 19

Dimensioning with Tolerances

Learning Objectives

After completing this chapter, you will be able to do the following:

✓ Define and use dimensioning and tolerancing terminology.
✓ Identify different types of tolerance dimensions.
✓ Create dimension styles with specified tolerance settings.

Chapter 16 introduced the creation of dimension styles and explained how to set the specifications for dimension geometry, fit format, primary units, alternate units, and text. This chapter describes the basics of tolerancing and explains how to prepare dimensions with tolerances for mechanical manufacturing drawings.

Dimensioning Conventions

Dimension styles help standardize drawings within a company or industry. Dimensioning for mechanical drafting usually uses the following AutoCAD settings, depending on company practices.

Lines and Arrows

The following conventions apply to most mechanical drawings. These settings are usually incorporated into appropriate dimensions styles that are, in turn, included in drawing templates.

- The minimum dimension line spacing for baseline dimensioning is .375 (10 mm). A value of .5 (12 mm) or .75 (19 mm) is usually more appropriate.
- The extension line extension is .125 (3 mm), and the extension line offset is .063 (1.5 mm).
- Arrowheads are usually closed filled, but closed blank, closed, or open arrowheads are sometimes used.
- A small dot is used on a leader pointing to a surface.
- The centerline option is used for center marks for circles and located arcs. Fillets and rounds generally have no center marks.

Fit Format

fit format: The arrangement of dimension text and arrowheads on a drawing.

As you may recall, *fit format* refers to the arrangement of dimension text and arrowheads on a drawing. AutoCAD provides several options for fit format. Keep the following points in mind when you set up the fit format for a drawing or template:

- The manually defined format is convenient for flexible text placement.
- The best-fit option for text and arrows is common, but other format options work better for some applications.
- Horizontal and vertical justifications are usually in centered format.
- Text placement is normally inside and outside horizontal for unidirectional dimensioning.

Primary Units, Text, and Tolerances

Although exact settings are often dictated by company policy or the intended use of a drawing, the following guidelines apply to most mechanical drawings:

- Objects are dimensioned in inches or millimeters.
- The primary units are typically decimal, with the number of decimal places controlled by the feature tolerance.
- Using alternate units for dual dimensioning is not a recommended ASME practice.
- The text is usually placed using the romans.shx font, a height of .12 (3 mm), and a gap of .063 (1.5 mm).
- The tolerance method depends on the application.

Tolerancing Fundamentals

tolerance: Total amount a specific dimension is permitted to vary.

A *tolerance* is the total amount a specific dimension is permitted to vary. Tolerances are not given to values identified as reference, maximum, minimum, or stock sizes. A tolerance may be applied directly to the dimension, indicated by a general note, or identified in the drawing title block. See **Figure 19-1.**

Figure 19-1.
Tolerances can be specified on the dimension, in a general note, or in the drawing title block.

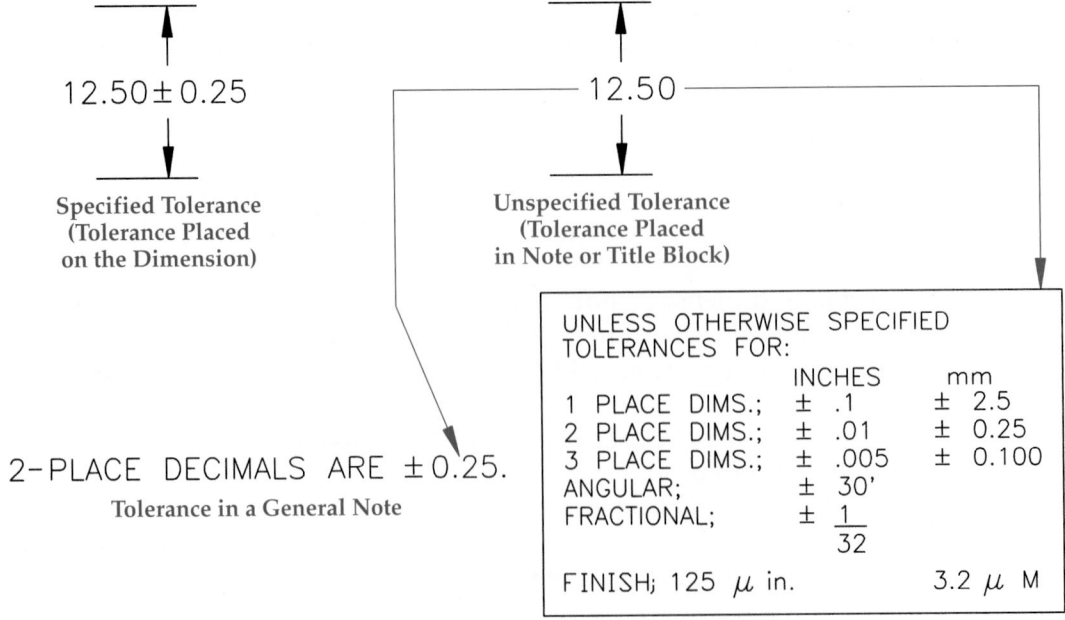

	INCHES	mm
1 PLACE DIMS.;	± .1	± 2.5
2 PLACE DIMS.;	± .01	± 0.25
3 PLACE DIMS.;	± .005	± 0.100
ANGULAR;	± 30'	
FRACTIONAL;	± $\frac{1}{32}$	
FINISH; 125 μ in.		3.2 μ M

Tolerances in a Title Block

The *limits* of a dimension are the largest and smallest numerical values the feature can be. In Figure 19-2, the dimension stated as 12.50±0.25 is in a style known as *plus-minus dimensioning*. The tolerance of this dimension is the difference between the maximum and minimum limits. This tolerance style can be used when the variance is the same in the positive and negative directions. In this case, the upper limit is 12.75 (12.50 + 0.25), and the lower limit is 12.25 (12.50 − 0.25). To find the tolerance, subtract the lower limit from the upper limit. The tolerance is .50.

The specified dimension is the part of the dimension from which the limits are calculated. In Figure 19-2, the specified dimension of the feature shown is 12.50. A tolerance on a drawing may be calculated and shown using *limits dimensioning*. In this style, the specified dimension is not shown. Many schools and companies prefer this method because the limits are given and calculations are not required.

A *bilateral tolerance* permits different variance in the positive and negative directions from the specified dimension. An *equal bilateral tolerance* has the same variance in both directions. In an *unequal bilateral tolerance*, the variance from the specified dimension is not the same in both directions. See Figure 19-3. A *unilateral tolerance* permits a variance in only one direction from the specified dimension. See Figure 19-4.

limits: The largest and smallest numerical values the feature can be.

plus-minus dimensioning: , tolerance style in which the positive and negative variance is equal and is preceded by a ± symbol.

limits dimensioning: Method in which the limits are given and calculations are not required.

bilateral tolerance: A tolerance style that permits variance in both the positive and negative directions from the specified dimension.

equal bilateral tolerance: A tolerance that has the same variance in both directions.

unequal bilateral tolerance: A tolerance in which variance from the specified dimension is not the same in both directions.

unilateral tolerance: Permits an increase or a decrease in only one direction from the specified dimension.

Figure 19-2.
Examples of plus-minus dimensioning and limits dimensioning.

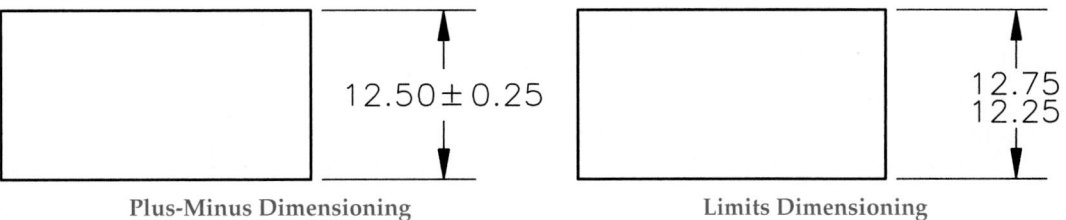

12.50±0.25

12.75
12.25

Plus-Minus Dimensioning   Limits Dimensioning

Figure 19-3.
Examples of bilateral tolerances.

$$24^{+0.08}_{-0.20} \qquad .750^{+.002}_{-.003}$$

Metric   Inch

Unequal Bilateral Tolerance

$$24\pm 0.1 \qquad .750\pm .005$$

Metric   Inch

Equal Bilateral Tolerance

Figure 19-4.
The variance of a unilateral tolerance is in only one direction from the specified dimension.

$$24^{\ 0}_{-0.2} \qquad .625^{+.000}_{-.004}$$

$$24^{+0.2}_{\ 0} \qquad .625^{+.004}_{-.000}$$

Metric   Inch

Assigning Decimal Places

The ASME Y14.5M *Dimensioning and Tolerancing* standard has separate recommendations for the display of decimal places in inch and metric dimensions. Examples of decimal dimension values in inches and metric units are shown in **Figure 19-3** and **Figure 19-4**.

Inch Dimensioning

General rules for displaying dimensions in drawings dimensioned in decimal inches include.

- A specified inch dimension is expressed to the same number of decimal places as its tolerance. Zeros are added to the right of the decimal point if needed. For example, the inch dimension .250±.005 has an additional zero added to the .25 to match the three-decimal tolerance. Similarly, the dimensions 2.000±.005 and 2.500±.005 both have zeros added to match the tolerance.
- Both values in a plus-minus tolerance for an inch dimension have the same number of decimal places. Zeros are added to fill in where needed. For example:

$$\begin{array}{ccc} +.005 & & +.005 \\ -.010 & not & -.01 \end{array}$$

Metric Dimensioning

General rules for displaying dimensions in drawings dimensioned using metric units include.

- The decimal point and zeros are omitted from the dimension when the metric dimension is a whole number. For example, the metric dimension 12 has no decimal point followed by a zero. This rule is true unless tolerance values are displayed.
- When a metric dimension includes a decimal portion, the last digit to the right of the decimal point is not followed by a zero. For example, the metric dimension 12.5 has no zero to the right of the 5. This rule is true unless tolerance values are displayed.
- Both values in a bilateral tolerance for a metric dimension have the same number of decimal places. Zeros are added to fill in where needed.
- Zeros are not added after the specified dimension to match the tolerance. For example, both 24±0.25 and 24.5±0.25 are correct. Some companies prefer to add zeros after the specified dimension to match the tolerance, however, in which case 24.00±0.25 and 24.50±0.25 are both correct.

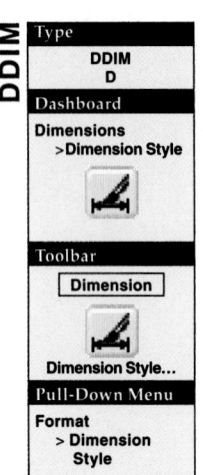

DDIM

Type
DDIM
D

Dashboard

Dimensions
> Dimension Style

Toolbar

Dimension

Dimension Style...

Pull-Down Menu

Format
> Dimension
Style

Setting Primary Units

As described in Chapter 16, a dimension style can be created with specific formatting, justification, and text settings. The **Dimension Style Manager** dialog box is used both to create and to modify dimension styles. See **Figure 19-5**. To modify a dimension style, highlight the style you want to modify and pick the **Modify...** button to access the **Modify Dimension Style** dialog box. The **Primary Units** tab is used to set the type of units and precision of the dimension. See **Figure 19-6**.

Figure 19-5.
The **Dimension Style Manager** dialog box.

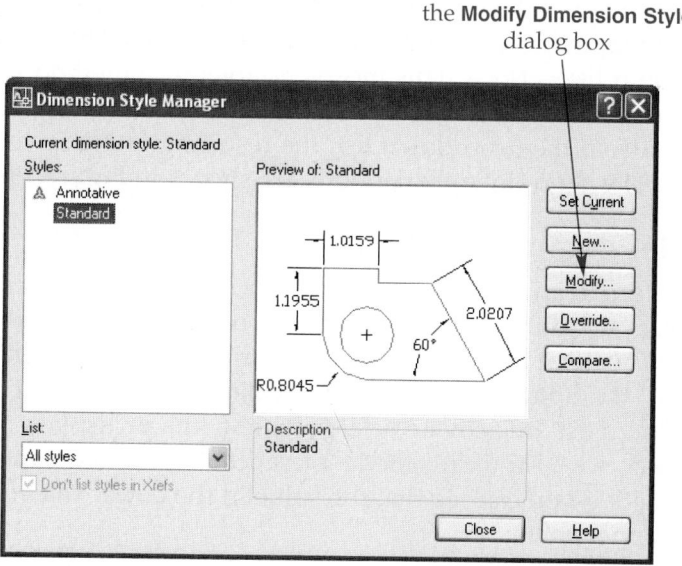

Pick to access
the **Modify Dimension Style**
dialog box

Figure 19-6.
Settings for the unit format and precision of linear dimensions are located in the **Primary Units** tab.

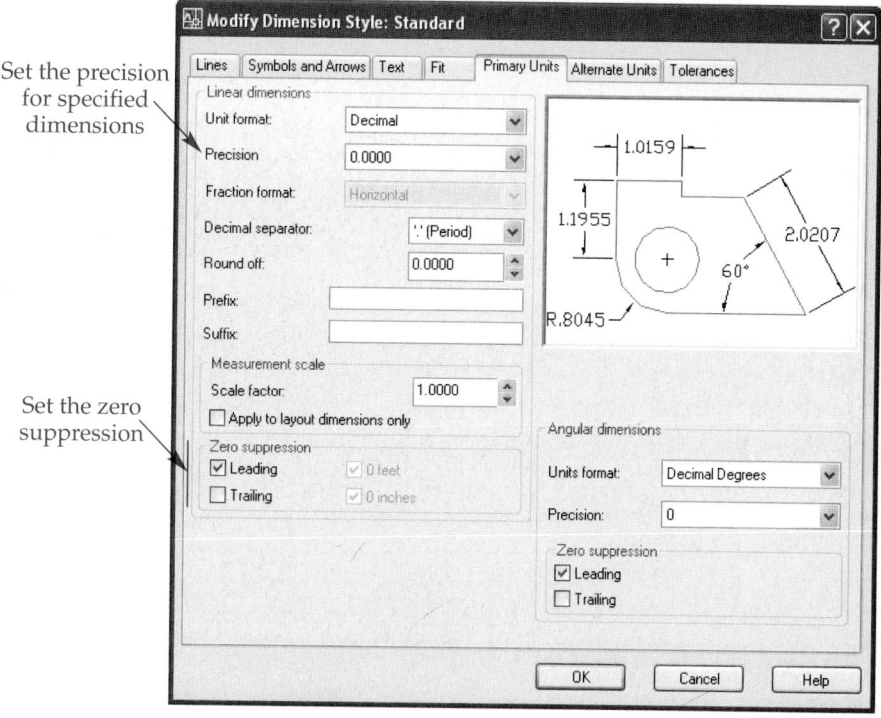

Set the precision
for specified
dimensions

Set the zero
suppression

In the **Linear dimensions** area of the **Primary Units** tab, the **Precision** drop-down list allows you to specify the number of zeros displayed after the decimal point of the specified dimension. The ASME standard recommends that the precision for the dimension and the tolerance be the same for inch dimensions, but it may be different for metric values, as previously described.

The **Zero suppression** settings were explained in Chapter 16. For metric dimensions, the **Leading** options should be off, and the **Trailing** options should be on. For inch dimensions, the **Leading** options should be on, and the **Trailing** options should be off.

The **Tolerances** tab of the **New** (or **Modify**) **Dimension Style** dialog box is used to apply a tolerance method to your drawing. See **Figure 19-7**. The default option in the **Method:** drop-down list is None. This means no tolerance method is used with your dimensions. As a result, most of the options in this area are disabled. If you pick a tolerance method from the drop-down list, the resulting image in the tab reflects the method selected. The drop-down list options are shown in **Figure 19-8**.

Symmetrical Tolerance Method

symmetrical tolerance: AutoCAD's term for an equal bilateral tolerance.

AutoCAD refers to an equal bilateral tolerance as a *symmetrical tolerance*. The **Symmetrical** tolerance dimensioning option is used to draw dimension text that displays an equal bilateral tolerance in the plus-minus format. When the **Symmetrical** option is selected, the **Upper value:** text box, **Scaling for height:** text box, and **Vertical position:** drop-down list are activated. The preview image displays an equal bilateral tolerance. See **Figure 19-9**. You can enter a tolerance value in the **Upper value:** text box. Although it is inactive, you can see that the value in the **Lower value:** text box matches the value in the **Upper value:** text box.

Figure 19-7.
The **Tolerances** tab contains formatting settings for tolerance dimensions.

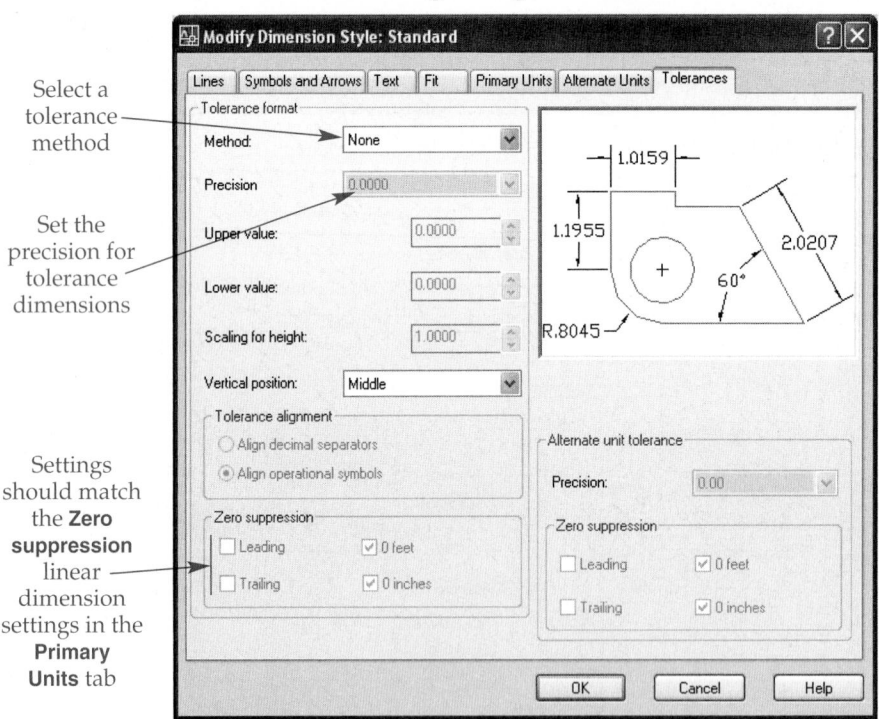

Select a tolerance method

Set the precision for tolerance dimensions

Settings should match the **Zero suppression** linear dimension settings in the **Primary Units** tab

---

Figure 19-8.
A tolerance dimensioning method can be selected from the options in the **Method:** drop-down list, located in the **Tolerance format** area of the **Tolerances** tab.

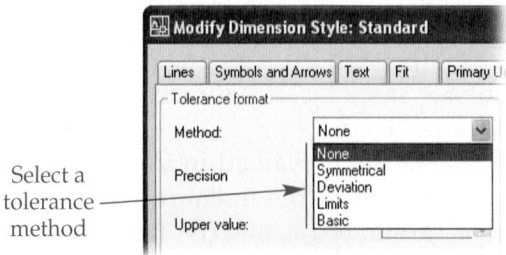

Select a tolerance method

Figure 19-9.
Setting the **Symmetrical** tolerance method option current, with an equal bilateral tolerance value of .005.

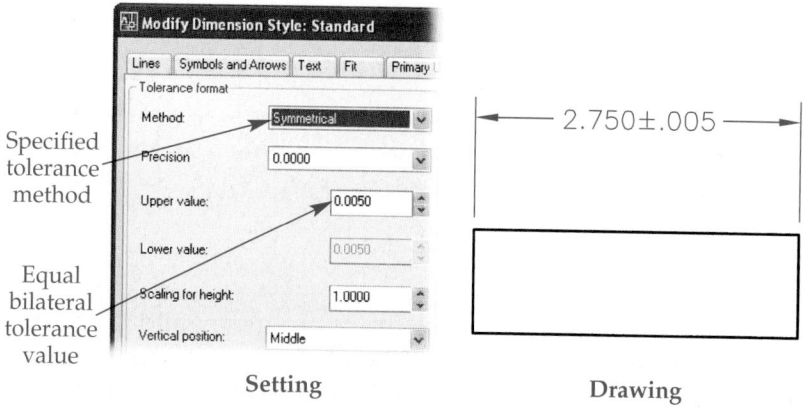

Specified tolerance method

Equal bilateral tolerance value

Setting   Drawing

Exercise 19-1
Complete the exercise on the Student CD.

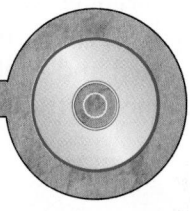

Deviation Tolerance Method

AutoCAD refers to an unequal bilateral tolerance as a ***deviation tolerance***. This means the tolerance deviates (departs) from the specified dimension with two different values. The deviation tolerance method can be set by selecting **Deviation** in the **Method:** drop-down list of the **Tolerances** tab. After selecting this option, the **Upper value:** and **Lower value:** text boxes are activated so you can enter the desired upper and lower tolerance values. See **Figure 19-10**. The preview image in the tab changes to match a representation of an unequal bilateral tolerance.

The deviation option can also be used to draw a unilateral tolerance by entering 0 for either the **Upper value:** or **Lower value:** setting. If you are using inch units, AutoCAD includes the plus or minus sign before the zero tolerance. When metric units are used, the sign is omitted for the zero tolerance. See **Figure 19-11**.

deviation tolerance:
AutoCAD's term for an unequal bilateral tolerance.

Exercise 19-2
Complete the exercise on the Student CD.

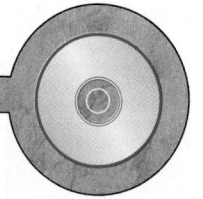

Figure 19-10.
Setting the **Deviation** tolerance method option current, with unequal bilateral tolerance values.

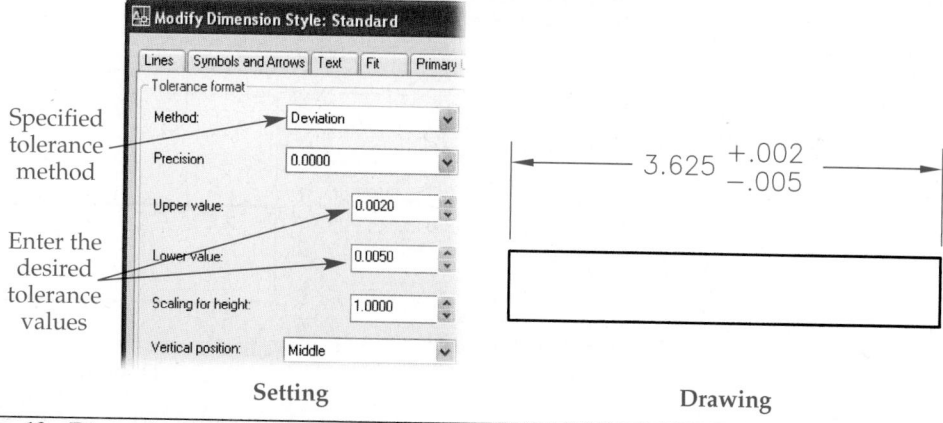

Specified tolerance method

Enter the desired tolerance values

Setting   Drawing

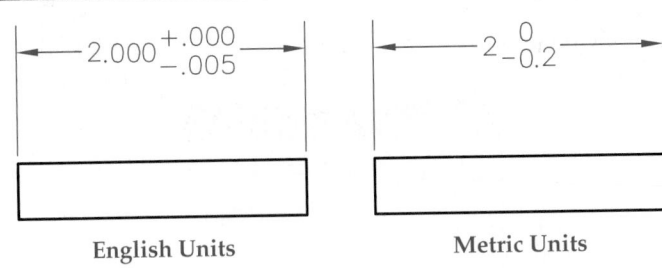

Figure 19-11.
When a unilateral tolerance is specified, AutoCAD automatically places the plus or minus symbol in front of the zero tolerance, if English units are used. The symbol is omitted with metric units.

English Units   Metric Units

Limits Tolerance Method

In limits dimensioning, the tolerance limits are given, and no calculations from the specified dimension are required (unlike plus-minus dimensioning). The limits tolerance method can be set by picking **Limits** in the **Method:** drop-down list in the **Tolerances** tab. When this option is set, the **Upper value:** and **Lower value:** text boxes are activated. You can then enter the desired upper and lower tolerance values that are added and subtracted from the specified dimension. The values you enter can be the same or different. See **Figure 19-12**.

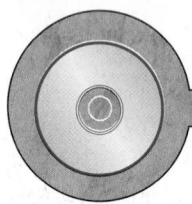

Exercise 19-3
Complete the exercise on the Student CD.

Basic Tolerance Method

basic dimension: A theoretically perfect dimension.

The basic tolerance method is used to draw basic dimensions. A *basic dimension* is a theoretically perfect dimension and is used in geometric dimensioning and tolerancing, which is covered in Chapter 20. The basic tolerance method can be set by picking **Basic** in the **Method:** drop-down list in the **Tolerances** tab. With this setting, the **Upper value:** and **Lower value:** options in the **Tolerance format** area are disabled because a basic dimension has no tolerance. A basic dimension is distinguished from other dimensions by a rectangle placed around the dimension number, as shown in **Figure 19-13**.

> **NOTE**
>
> Picking the **Draw frame around text** check box in the **Text** tab of the **New** (or **Modify**) **Dimension Style** dialog box also activates the basic tolerance method.

Figure 19-12.
Selecting the limits tolerance method and setting limit values.

Specified tolerance method

Enter the desired tolerance values

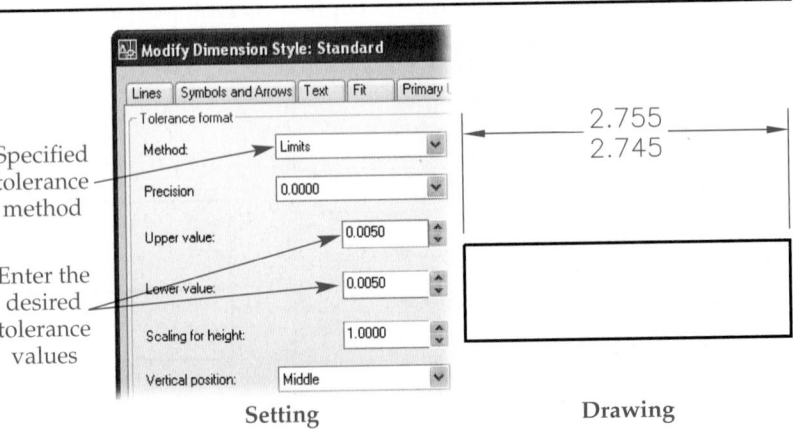

Setting   Drawing

AutoCAD and Its Applications—Basics

Figure 19-13.
The basic tolerance method is used for basic dimensioning. The dimension text for a basic dimension is placed inside a rectangle.

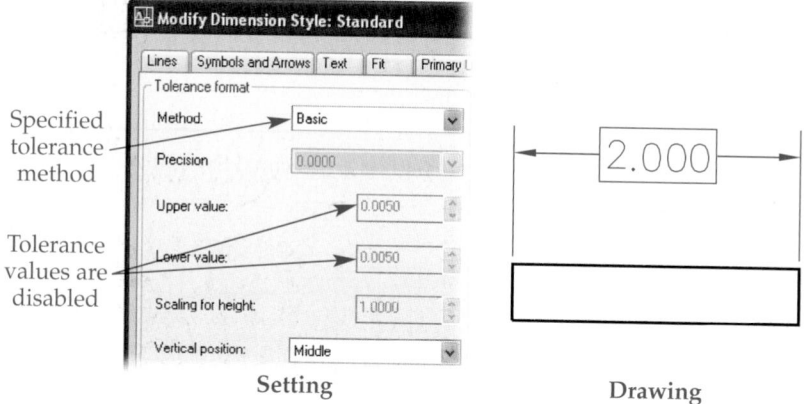

Specified tolerance method

Tolerance values are disabled

Setting   Drawing

Tolerance Precision and Zero Suppression

After a tolerance method is specified in the **Method:** drop-down list of the **Tolerances** tab, you can set the precision of the tolerance. By default, when you set the primary unit precision on the **Primary Units** tab, AutoCAD automatically makes the tolerance precision in the **Tolerances** tab the same unit precision. If the setting does not reflect the level of precision you want, change it using the **Precision** drop-down list in the **Tolerance format** area.

As is the case with the precision settings, a tolerance method must be selected before the **Zero suppression** tolerance format options can be specified. The suppression settings for linear dimensions in the **Tolerances** tab should be the same as the **Zero suppression** tolerance format settings in the **Primary Units** tab. AutoCAD does not automatically match the tolerance setting to the primary units setting.

Tolerance Justification

Using the options in the **Vertical position:** drop-down list in the **Tolerance format** area of the **Tolerances** tab, you can control the alignment, or justification, of deviation tolerance dimensions. The **Middle** option centers the tolerance with the specified dimension and is the default. This is also the recommended ASME practice. The other justification options are **Top** and **Bottom**. Deviation tolerance dimensions displaying each of the justification options are shown in Figure 19-14.

The options in the **Tolerance alignment** area become available for selection when you use a deviation or limits tolerance method. The selected option controls the left and right tolerance justification. When using a deviation tolerance method, pick the **Align decimal separators** radio button to vertically align the upper and lower tolerance value decimal points. Select the **Align operational symbols** radio button to vertically align the upper and lower tolerance plus and minus symbols. See Figure 19-15. When

Figure 19-14.
Examples of the tolerance justification options for deviation tolerance dimensions.

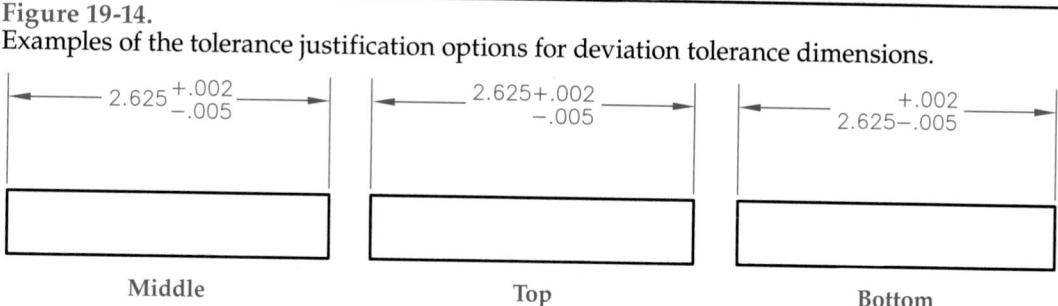

Middle   Top   Bottom

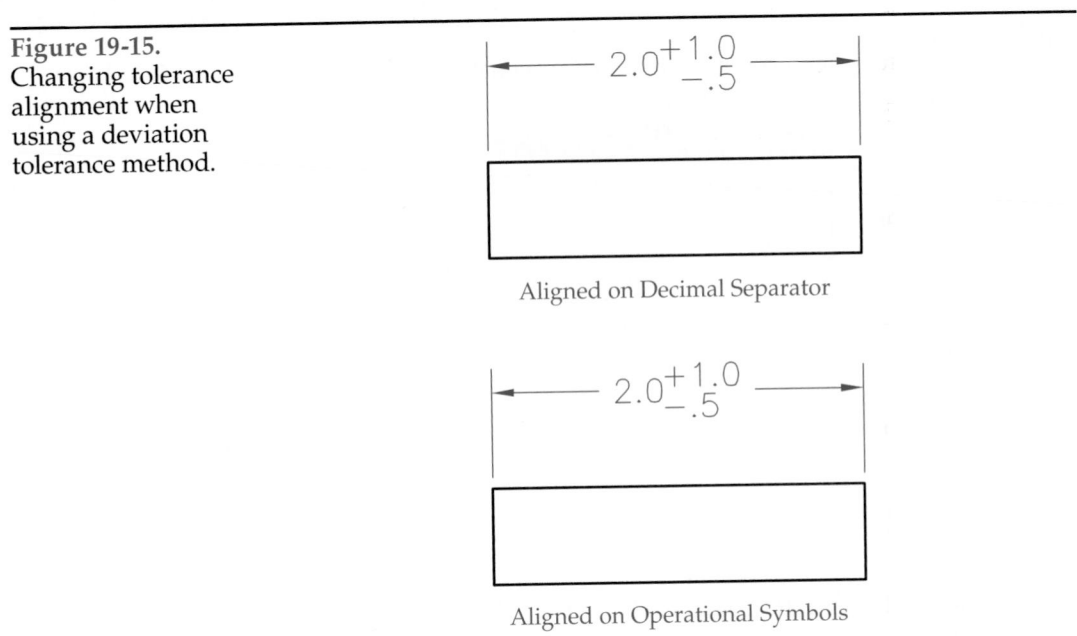

Aligned on Decimal Separator

Aligned on Operational Symbols

using the limits tolerance method, pick the **Align decimal separators** radio button to vertically align the upper and lower limit decimal points. Select the **Align operational symbols** radio button to left-justify the upper and lower limits. See **Figure 19-16.**

Tolerance Height

You can set the text height of the tolerance dimension in relation to the text height of the specified dimension using the **Scaling for height:** text box in the **Tolerance format** area of the **Tolerances** tab. The default of 1.0000 makes the tolerance dimension text the same height as the specified dimension text. This is the recommended ASME standard. If you want the tolerance dimension height to be three-quarters as high as the specified dimension height, type .75 in the **Scaling for height:** text box. Some companies prefer this practice to keep the tolerance part of the dimension from taking up additional space. Examples of tolerance dimensions with different text heights are shown in **Figure 19-17.**

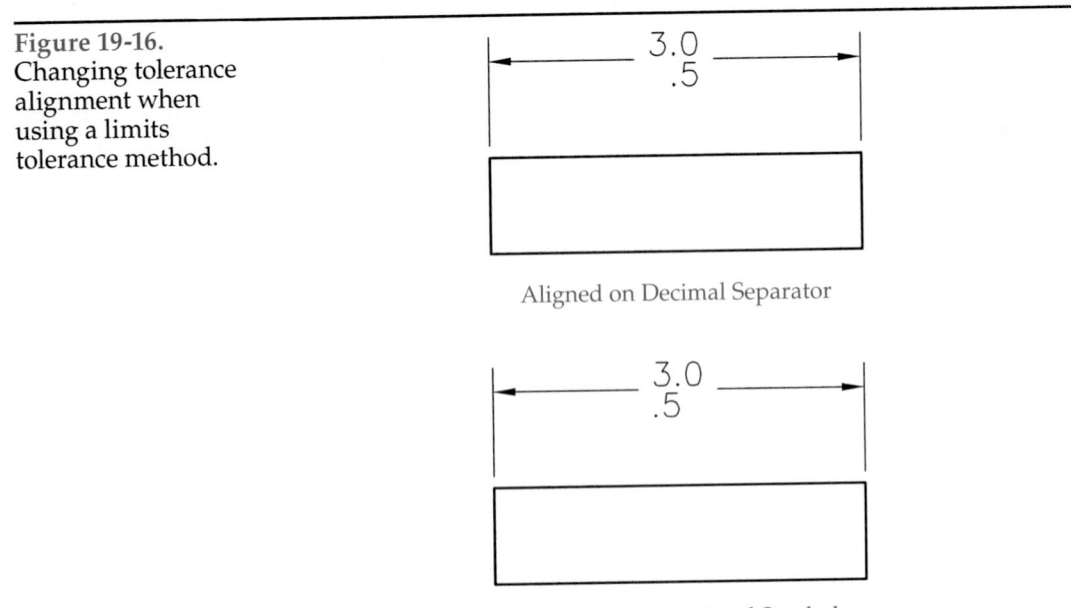

Figure 19-16.
Changing tolerance
alignment when
using a limits
tolerance method.

Aligned on Decimal Separator

Aligned on Operational Symbols

AutoCAD and Its Applications—Basics

Figure 19-17.
Using different scale settings for the text height of tolerance dimensions.

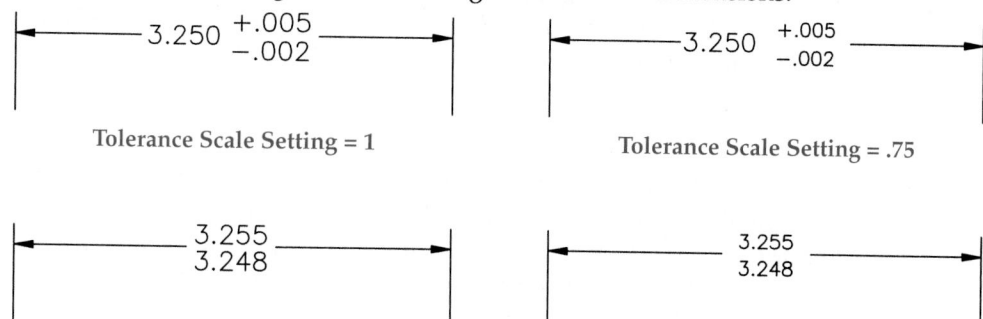

Tolerance Scale Setting = 1   Tolerance Scale Setting = .75

Tolerance Scale Setting = 1   Tolerance Scale Setting = .75

Tolerance Method Review

✓ Each tolerance method option you pick is represented by an image preview in the **Modify Dimension Style** dialog box.

✓ Choose a tolerance method based on the characteristics of the tolerance. If the upper and lower variance is equal, you can choose the **Symmetrical** option to create an equal bilateral tolerance. If the upper and lower variance differs, use the **Deviation** option. Use the **Limits** option to show only the minimum and maximum allowed values.

✓ Specify the decimal precision for the primary units and tolerances according to the ASME guidelines for inch-based or metric drawings.

✓ When drawing inch tolerance dimensions, you should activate the **Leading** check box in the **Zero suppression** area of the **Tolerances** tab. The same option should be activated for linear dimensions in the **Primary Units** tab. You can then properly draw inch tolerance dimensions without placing the zero before the decimal point, as recommended by ASME standards. These settings allow you to draw a tolerance dimension such as .625±.005.

✓ When drawing metric tolerance dimensions, deactivate the **Leading** check box in the **Zero suppression** area of the **Tolerances** tab. Deactivate the same option for linear dimensions in the **Primary Units** tab. This allows you to place a metric tolerance dimension with the zero before the decimal point, as recommended by ASME standards, for example, a dimension such as 12±0.2.

Exercise 19-4
Complete the exercise on the Student CD.

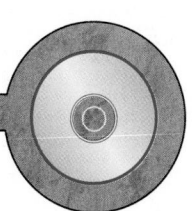

Chapter Test

Answer the following questions. Write your answers on a separate sheet of paper or complete the electronic chapter test on the Student CD.

1. Define the term *tolerance*.
2. What are the limits of the tolerance dimension 3.625±.005?
3. Give an example of an equal bilateral tolerance in inches and in metric units.
4. Give an example of an unequal bilateral tolerance in inches and in metric units.
5. Give an example of a unilateral tolerance in inches and in metric units.
6. Which dialog box is used to create dimension styles? How is it accessed?
7. How do you open the **Tolerances** tab?
8. How do you set the number of zeros displayed after the decimal point for a tolerance dimension?
9. Which **Zero suppression** settings should be specified for linear and tolerance dimensions when using metric units?
10. Which **Zero suppression** settings should be specified for linear and tolerance dimensions when using inch units?
11. What happens to the preview image in the **Tolerances** tab when a tolerance method option is picked from the **Method:** drop-down list?
12. What is the purpose of the **Symmetrical** tolerance method option?
13. What is the purpose of the **Deviation** tolerance method option?
14. What is the purpose of the **Limits** tolerance method option?
15. Name the tolerance dimension justification option recommended by the ASME standards.
16. Explain the results of setting the **Scaling for height:** option to 1 in the **Tolerances** tab.
17. What setting would you use for the **Scaling for height:** option if you wanted the tolerance dimension height to be three-quarters of the specified dimension height?

Drawing Problems

Set the limits, units, dimension style options, and other parameters as needed for the following problems. Use the guidelines given below.

A. Draw and dimension the necessary views for the following drawings to exact size. These problems are presented in 3D. Draw the proper 2D views for each.

B. Apply dimensions accurately using ASME standards. Create dimension styles that suit the specific needs of each drawing. For example, save different dimension styles for metric and inch dimensions.

C. Create separate layers for the views and dimensions.

D. Plot the drawings with 0.6 mm object lines and 0.3 mm thin lines.

E. Place the following general notes in the lower-left corner of each drawing.

   3. UNLESS OTHERWISE SPECIFIED, ALL DIMENSIONS ARE IN MILLIMETERS.
   (or INCHES, *as applicable)*
   2. REMOVE ALL BURRS AND SHARP EDGES.
   1. INTERPRET PER ASME Y14.5M-1994.
   NOTES:

F. Save the drawings as P19-1 through P19-7.

1.

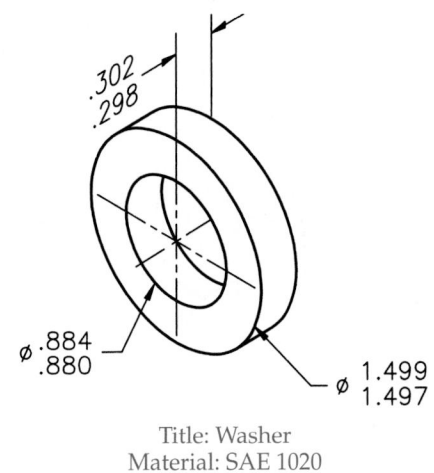

Title: Washer
Material: SAE 1020
Inch

2.

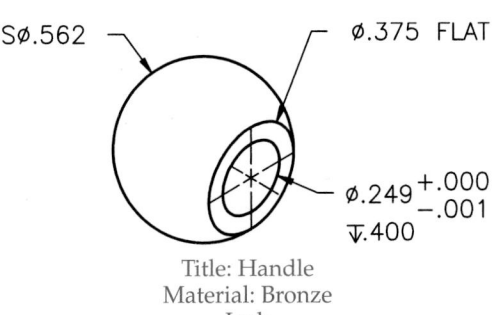

Title: Handle
Material: Bronze
Inch

3.

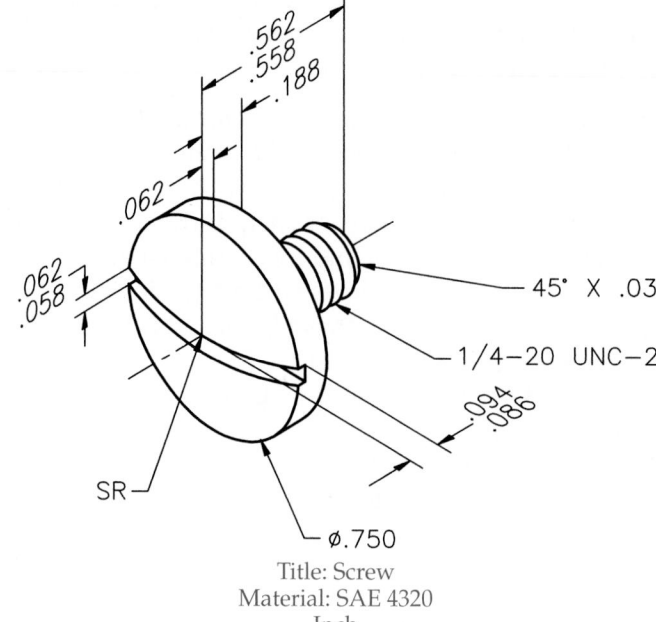

.562
.558
.188
.062
.062
.058
45° X .03
1/4−20 UNC−2
.094
.086
SR
ø.750

Title: Screw
Material: SAE 4320
Inch

4.

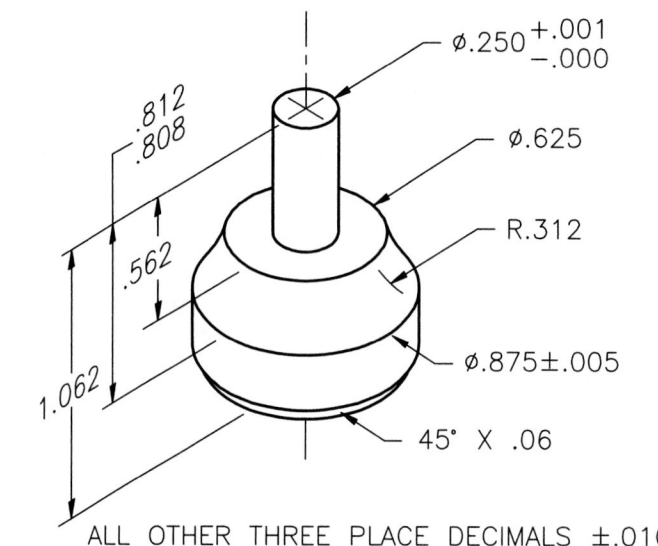

ø.250 +.001 −.000
.812
.808
ø.625
.562
R.312
1.062
ø.875±.005
45° X .06

ALL OTHER THREE PLACE DECIMALS ±.010

Title: Pin
Material: Mild Steel
Inch

5. This object is shown as a section for clarity. Do not draw a section.

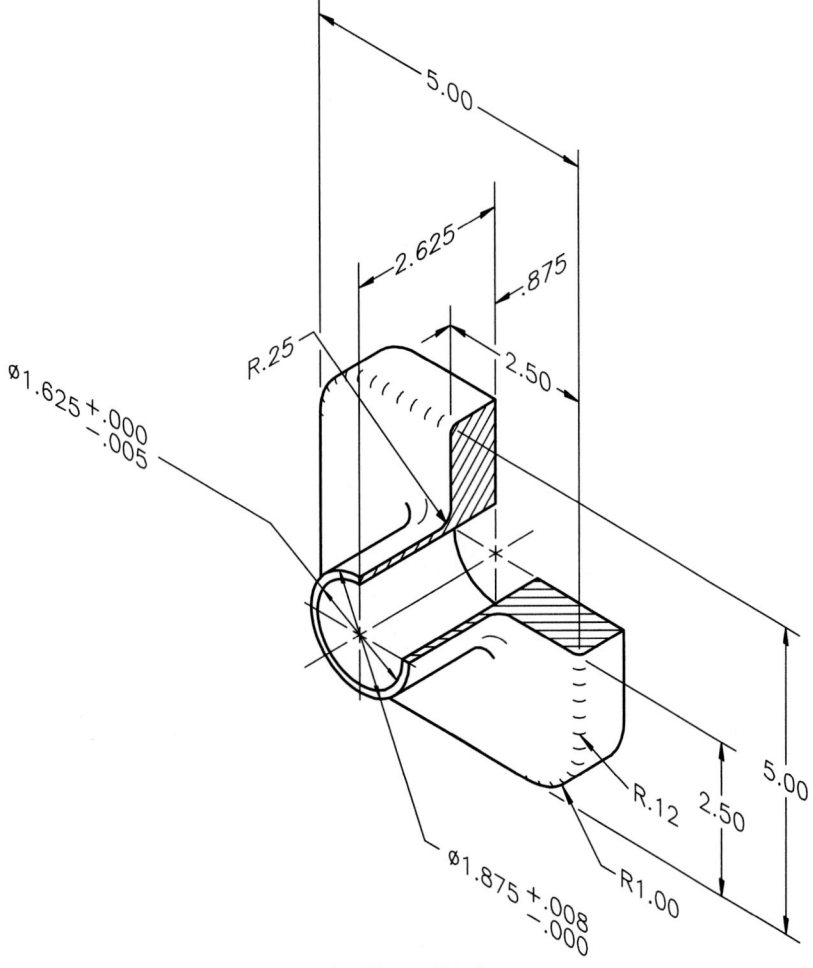

Title: Thrust Washer
Material: SAE 5150
Inch

6.

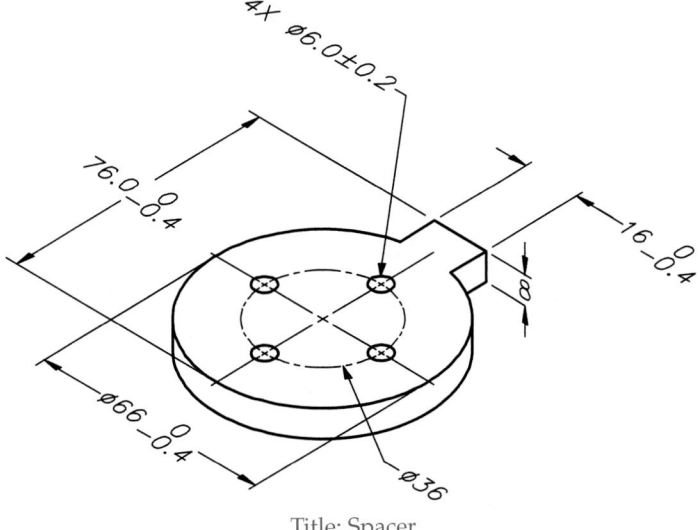

Title: Spacer
Material: Cold Rolled Steel
Metric

7.

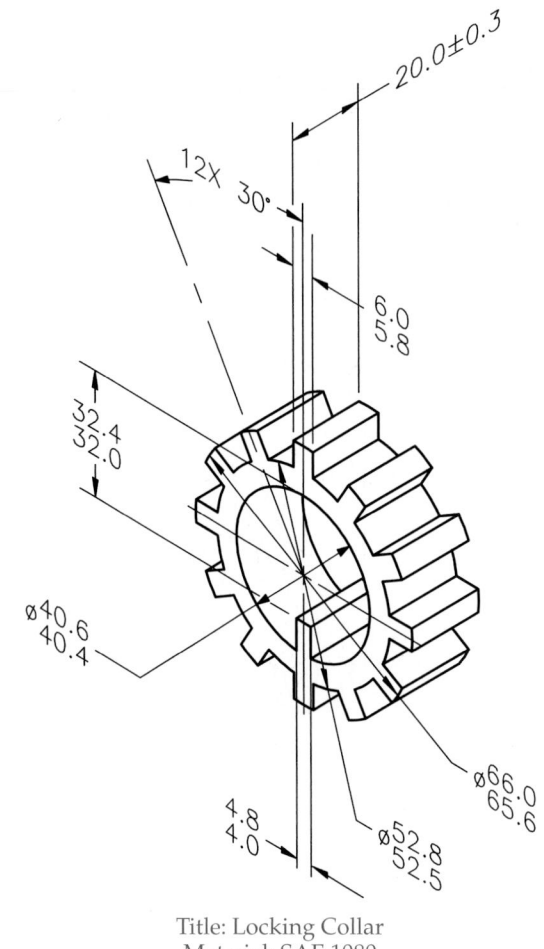

Title: Locking Collar
Material: SAE 1080
Metric

8. Draw the vise clamp shown below. Save the drawing as P19-8.

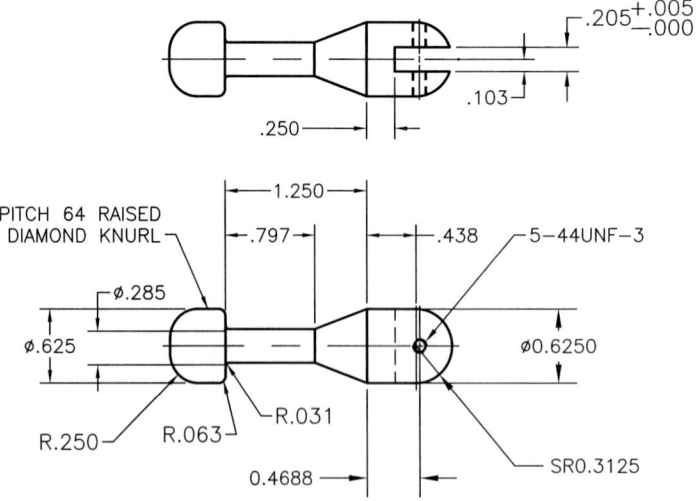

CHAPTER 20

Geometric Dimensioning and Tolerancing

Learning Objectives

After completing this chapter, you will be able to do the following:

✓ Identify symbols used in geometric dimensioning and tolerancing (GD&T).
✓ Use the **TOLERANCE** and **QLEADER** commands to create geometric tolerancing symbols.
✓ Draw and edit feature control frames.
✓ Draw and edit datum feature symbols.
✓ Place basic dimensions on a drawing.

This chapter is an introduction to geometric dimensioning and tolerancing (GD&T) principles, as adopted by the American National Standards Institute (ANSI) and published by the American Society of Mechanical Engineers (ASME) for engineering and related document practices. The standard is ASME Y14.5M-1994, *Dimensioning and Tolerancing*. *Geometric tolerancing* is a general term that refers to tolerances used to control the form, profile, orientation, runout, and location of features on an object.

The drafting applications covered in this chapter use the AutoCAD geometric tolerancing capabilities and additional recommendations to comply with the ASME Y14.5M-1994 standard. This chapter is only an introduction to GD&T. For complete coverage of GD&T, refer to *Geometric Dimensioning and Tolerancing*, published by Goodheart-Willcox Co., Inc. Before beginning this chapter, it is recommended that you have a solid understanding of dimensioning and tolerancing standards and AutoCAD applications, as presented in Chapters 16, 17, 18, and 19 of this textbook. This chapter divides dimensioning and geometric tolerancing symbols into five basic types:

geometric tolerancing: Tolerances used to control the form, profile, orientation, runout, and location of features on an object.

- Dimensioning symbols
- Geometric characteristic symbols
- Material condition symbols
- Feature control frames
- Datum feature symbols

When you draw GD&T symbols, it is recommended that you place them on a dimensioning layer so the symbols and text can be plotted as lines that have the same thickness as extension and dimension lines (.01″ or 0.3 mm). The suggested text font is romans.shx. These practices correspond with the standard ASME Y14.2M-1992, *Line Conventions and Lettering*.

Dimensioning Symbols

symbols: Graphic representations of specific information that would be difficult and time-consuming to duplicate in note form.

Symbols represent specific information that would be difficult and time-consuming to duplicate in note form. They must be clearly drawn to the required size and shape so they communicate the desired information uniformly. ASME Y14.5M recommends symbols because the language of symbols is international; they are read the same way in any country. In an international economy, it is important to have effective communication on engineering drawings. Symbols make this communication process uniform. ASME Y14.5M also states that the adoption of dimensioning symbols does not prevent the use of equivalent terms or abbreviations in situations where symbols are considered inappropriate.

The use of symbols aids in clarity and drawing presentation and reduces the time required to create a drawing. Creating and using AutoCAD symbols is covered later in this chapter and in Chapter 23. A sample group of recommended dimensioning symbols is shown in Figure 20-1.

Geometric Characteristic Symbols

geometric characteristic symbols: Symbols that are used to provide specific controls related to the form or features of an object.

In GD&T, symbols are used to provide specific controls related to the form of an object, orientation of features, outlines of features, relationship of features to an axis, or location of features. These symbols are known as *geometric characteristic symbols*. Geometric characteristic symbols are separated into five types: form, profile, location, orientation, and runout. See Figure 20-2.

Figure 20-1.
Dimensioning symbols recommended by ASME Y14.5M-1994. (h = text height)

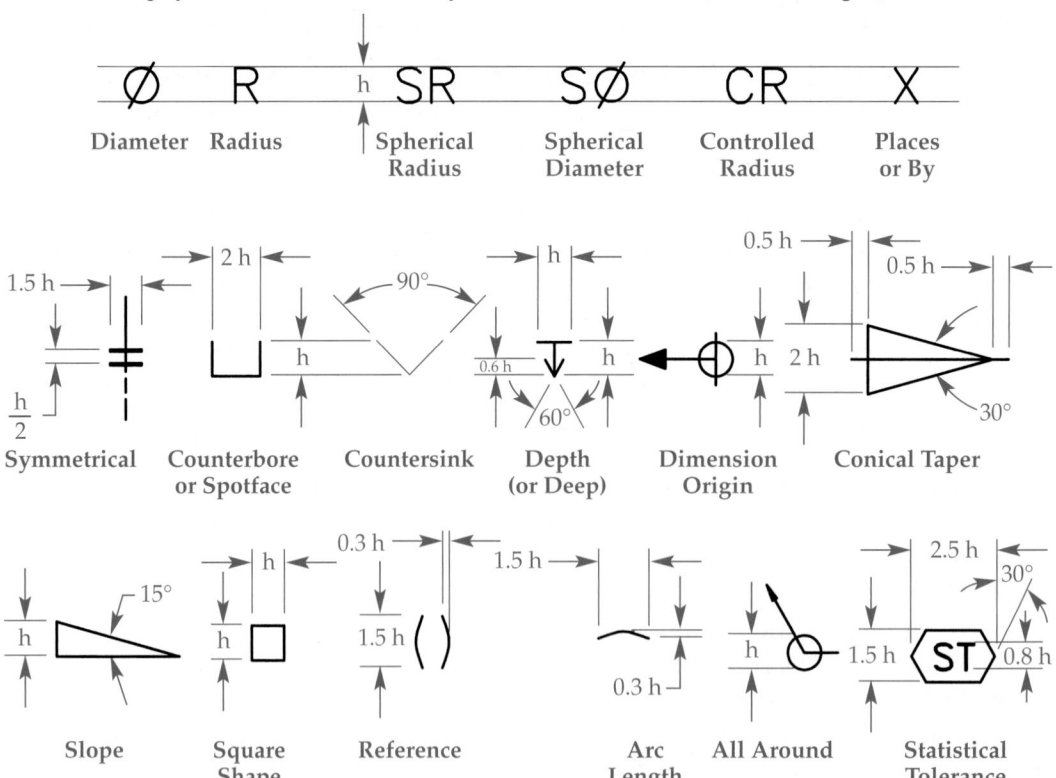

Figure 20-2.
Geometric
characteristic
symbols
recommended by
ASME Y14.5M-1994.

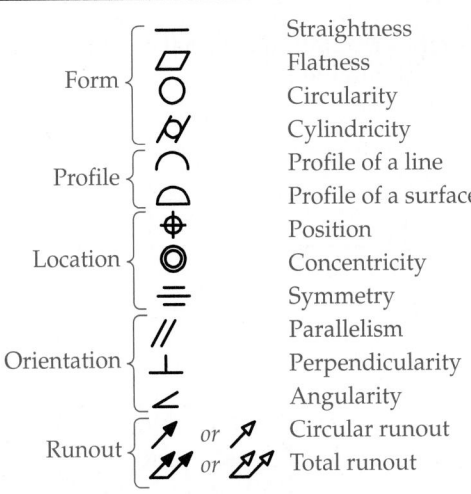

Form	Straightness
	Flatness
	Circularity
	Cylindricity
Profile	Profile of a line
	Profile of a surface
Location	Position
	Concentricity
	Symmetry
Orientation	Parallelism
	Perpendicularity
	Angularity
Runout	Circular runout
	Total runout

Material Condition Symbols

Material condition symbols are often referred to as *modifying symbols* because they modify the geometric tolerance in relation to the produced size or location of the feature. These symbols are only used in geometric dimensioning applications. The symbols used to indicate maximum material condition (MMC) or least material condition (LMC) are shown in **Figure 20-3**.

Maximum material condition (MMC) control

If the material condition control is *maximum material condition (MMC)*, the symbol for MMC must be placed in the feature control frame. See **Figure 20-4**. When this application is used, the specified geometric tolerance is held at the MMC produced size. See the table in **Figure 20-4**. The term *produced size*, when used here, means the actual size of the feature when measured after manufacture. As the produced size varies from MMC, the geometric tolerance increases, equal to the change. The maximum geometric tolerance is at the LMC produced size.

Least material condition (LMC) control

If the material condition control is *least material condition (LMC)*, the symbol for LMC must be placed in the feature control frame. When this application is used, the specified geometric tolerance is held at the LMC produced size. As the produced size varies from LMC, the geometric tolerance increases, equal to the change. The maximum geometric tolerance is at the MMC produced size.

Surface control, regardless of feature size (RFS)

When no material condition symbol follows the geometric tolerance in a feature control frame, regardless of feature size (RFS) is assumed as the material condition. *Regardless of feature size (RFS)* means the geometric tolerances remain the same, regardless of the actual produced size.

material condition symbols (modifying symbols): Symbols used to modify the geometric tolerance in relation to the produced size or location of the feature.

maximum material condition (MMC): The maximum allowable produced size.

produced size: The actual size of the feature when measured after manufacture.

least material condition (LMC): The minimum allowable produced size.

regardless of feature size (RFS): The geometric tolerances remain the same, regardless of the actual produced size.

Figure 20-3.
Material condition
symbols. In ASME
Y14.5M-1994, there
is no symbol for
regardless of feature
size (RFS), since RFS
is assumed unless
otherwise specified.
(h = text height)

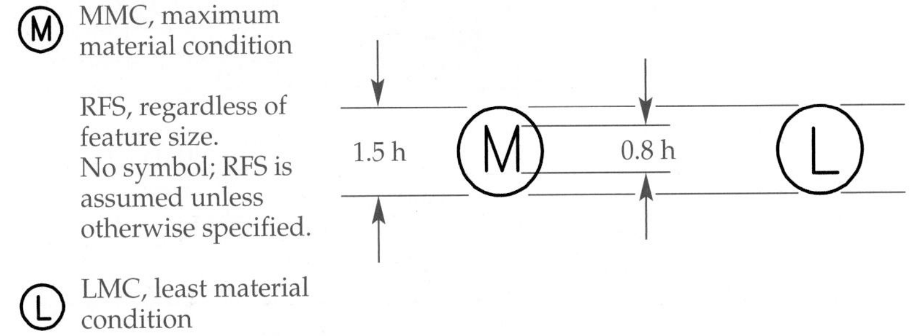

Ⓜ MMC, maximum material condition

RFS, regardless of feature size. No symbol; RFS is assumed unless otherwise specified.

Ⓛ LMC, least material condition

1.5 h   Ⓜ   0.8 h   Ⓛ

Figure 20-4.
The drawing specifies maximum material condition (MMC) applied to a feature. The symbol for MMC is shown highlighted.

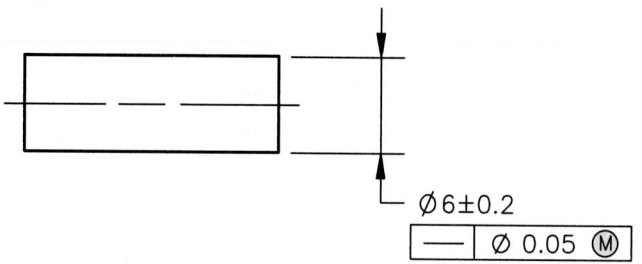

	Possible produced sizes	Maximum out-of-straightness
MMC	6.20	0.05
	6.10	0.15
	6.00	0.25
	5.90	0.35
LMC	5.80	0.45

surface control:
A feature control frame that is connected to a feature surface with a leader or an extension line.

perfect form:
The object cannot exceed a true geometric form boundary established at MMC.

When a feature control frame is connected to a feature surface with a leader or an extension line, it is referred to as *surface control*. See Figure 20-5. The geometric characteristic symbol shown is straightness, but the format is the same for any characteristic.

Look at the table in Figure 20-5 and notice that the possible sizes range from 6.20 (MMC) to 5.80 (LMC). With surface control, perfect form is required at MMC. *Perfect form* means the object cannot exceed a true geometric form boundary established at MMC. The geometric tolerance at MMC is zero, as shown in the chart. As the produced size varies from MMC in the chart, the geometric tolerance increases, until it equals the amount specified in the feature control frame.

Figure 20-5.
The drawing specifies surface control, regardless of feature size (RFS). The actual meaning of the geometric tolerance is shown in the table.

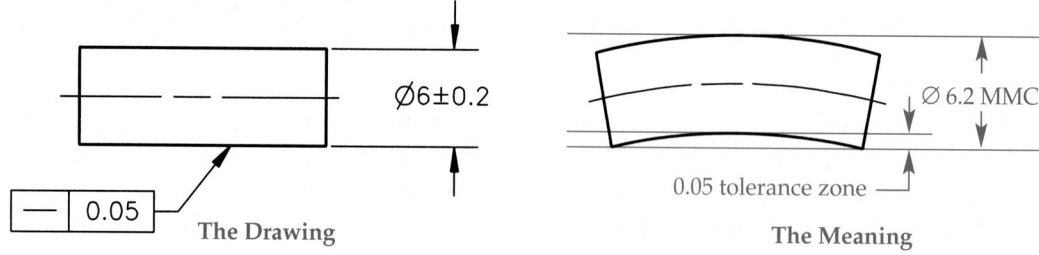

The Drawing

The Meaning

	Possible produced sizes	Maximum out-of-straightness
MMC	6.20	* 0
	6.10	0.05
	6.00	0.05
	5.90	0.05
LMC	5.80	0.05

* Perfect form required

Figure 20-6.
The drawing specifies axis control, regardless of feature size (RFS). The actual meaning of the geometric tolerance is shown in the table.

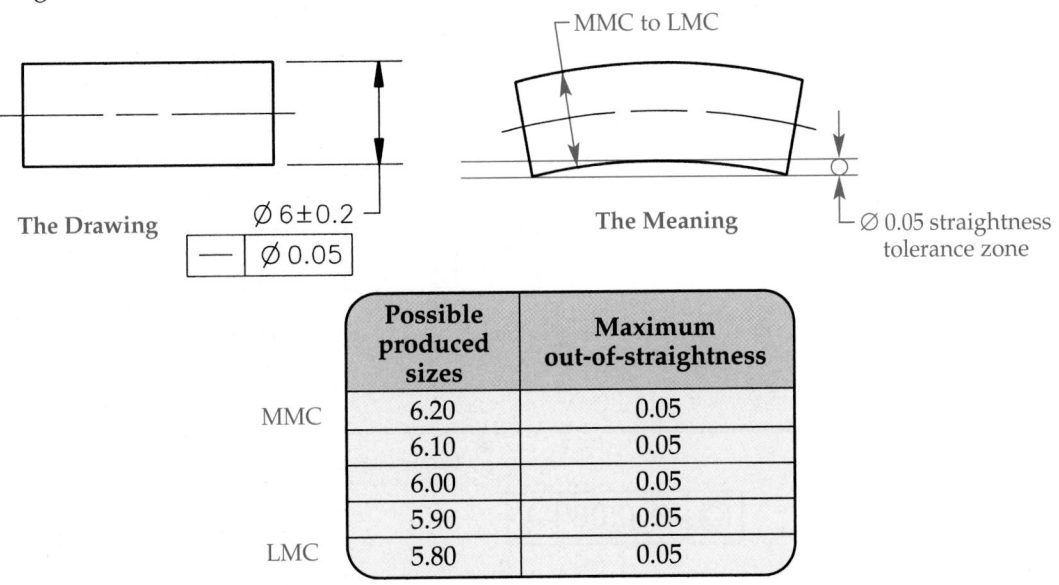

	Possible produced sizes	Maximum out-of-straightness
MMC	6.20	0.05
	6.10	0.05
	6.00	0.05
	5.90	0.05
LMC	5.80	0.05

Axis control, regardless of feature size

Axis control is indicated when the feature control frame is shown with a diameter dimension. See **Figure 20-6.** Regardless of feature size (RFS) is assumed. With axis control, perfect form is not required at MMC. Therefore, the specified geometric tolerance stays the same at every produced size. See the table in **Figure 20-6.**

Feature Control Frames

The geometric characteristic, geometric tolerance, material condition, and datum reference (if any) for an individual feature are specified by means of a feature control frame. The *feature control frame* is divided into compartments. The geometric characteristic symbol is placed in the first compartment, followed by the geometric tolerance. Where applicable, the geometric tolerance is preceded by the diameter symbol, which describes the shape of the tolerance zone, and is followed by a material condition symbol (if other than RFS). See **Figure 20-7.**

When a geometric tolerance is related to one or more datums, the datum reference letters are placed in compartments following the geometric tolerance. *Datums* are theoretically perfect surfaces, planes, points, or axes. When two datums are referenced, the datum reference letters are separated by a dash and placed in a single compartment after the geometric tolerance. A *multiple datum reference* is established by two datum features, such as an axis established by two datum diameters. Several feature control frames with datum references are shown in **Figure 20-8.**

Elements in a feature control frame are displayed in a specific order. See **Figure 20-9.** Notice that the datum reference letters can be followed by a material condition symbol where applicable.

axis control: A control that specifies how far out-of-true an axis can be; indicated when the feature control frame is shown with a diameter dimension.

feature control frame: The rectangular frame that contains the geometric characteristic, geometric tolerance, material condition, and datum reference (if any) for an individual feature.

datums: Theoretically perfect surfaces, planes, points, or axes.

multiple datum reference: Established by two datum features.

Figure 20-7.
Feature control
frames contain
the geometric
characteristic
symbol, geometric
tolerance, and
diameter symbol
(as applicable). Note
that the geometric
tolerance is
expressed as a total,
not a plus-minus
value.

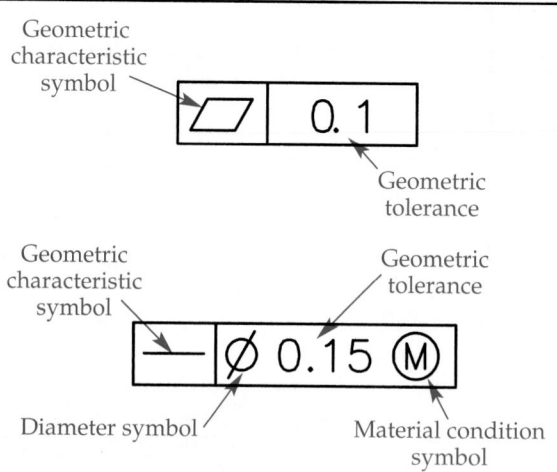

Figure 20-8.
Examples of datum
references indicated
in feature control
frames.

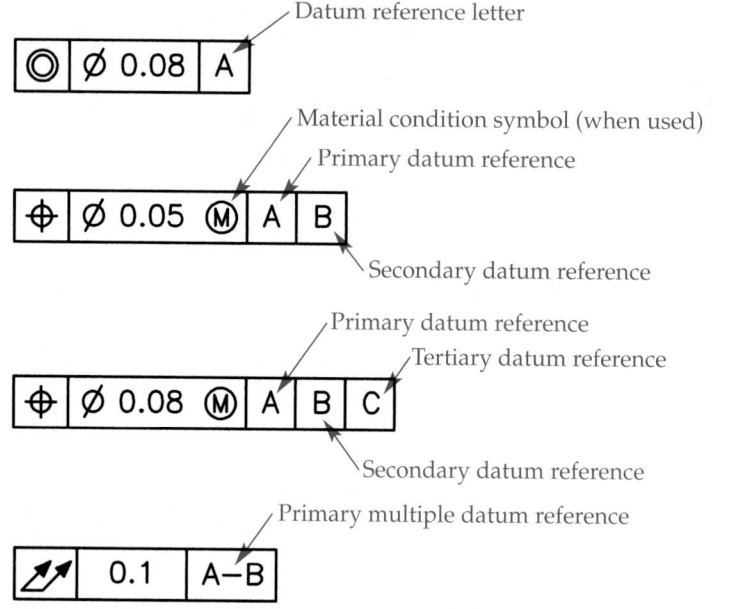

Figure 20-9.
The order of
elements in a feature
control frame.
(h = text height)

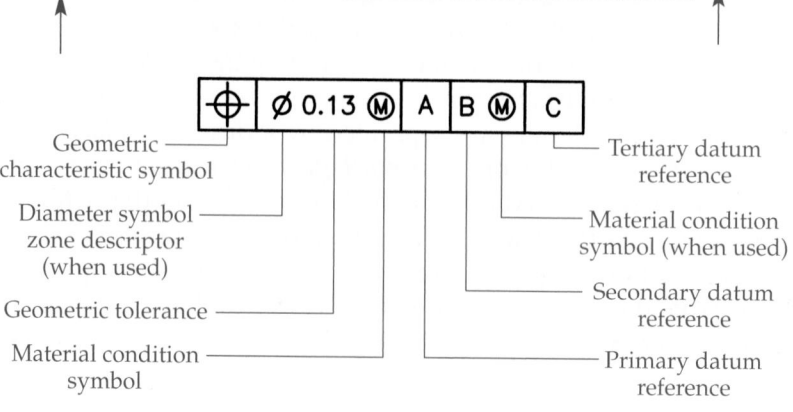

Basic Dimensions

A *basic dimension* is a theoretically perfect dimension. Basic dimensions are used to describe the theoretically exact size, profile, orientation, and location of a feature. These dimensions provide the basis from which permissible variations are established by tolerances on other dimensions, in notes, or in feature control frames. In simple terms, a basic dimension tells you where the geometric tolerance zone or datum target is located. The *geometric tolerance zone* is the zone within which the produced size must fall to be within the tolerance specifications. A *datum target* is a specific point, line, or area used to establish a datum.

Basic dimensions are shown on a drawing with a rectangle placed around the dimension text, as shown in **Figure 20-10.** A general note can also be used to identify basic dimensions in some applications. For example, the note UNTOLERANCED DIMENSIONS LOCATING TRUE POSITION ARE BASIC indicates the use of basic dimensions. The basic dimension rectangle is a signal to the reader to look for a geometric tolerance in a feature control frame related to the features being dimensioned.

Figure 20-10. Basic dimensions are identified with a rectangle drawn around the text. (h = text height)

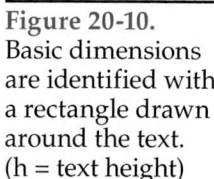
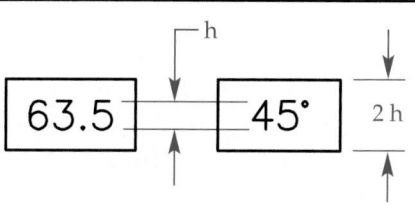
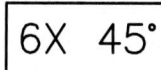
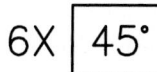

The number of times or places may be applied to a basic dimension by placement inside or outside of the basic dimension symbol.

Additional Symbols

Other symbols commonly used in GD&T are shown in **Figure 20-11.** These symbols include:

- **Free state symbol.** Describes the distortion of a part after the removal of forces applied during manufacture. The free state symbol is placed in the feature control frame after the geometric tolerance and the material condition (if any), if the feature must meet the tolerance specified while in free state.
- **Tangent plane symbol.** Placed after the geometric tolerance in the feature control frame when it is necessary to control a feature surface by contacting points of tangency.
- **Projected tolerance zone symbol.** Placed in the feature control frame to inform the reader that the geometric tolerance zone is projected away from the primary datum.
- **Between symbol.** Used with profile geometric tolerances to identify where the profile tolerance is applied.

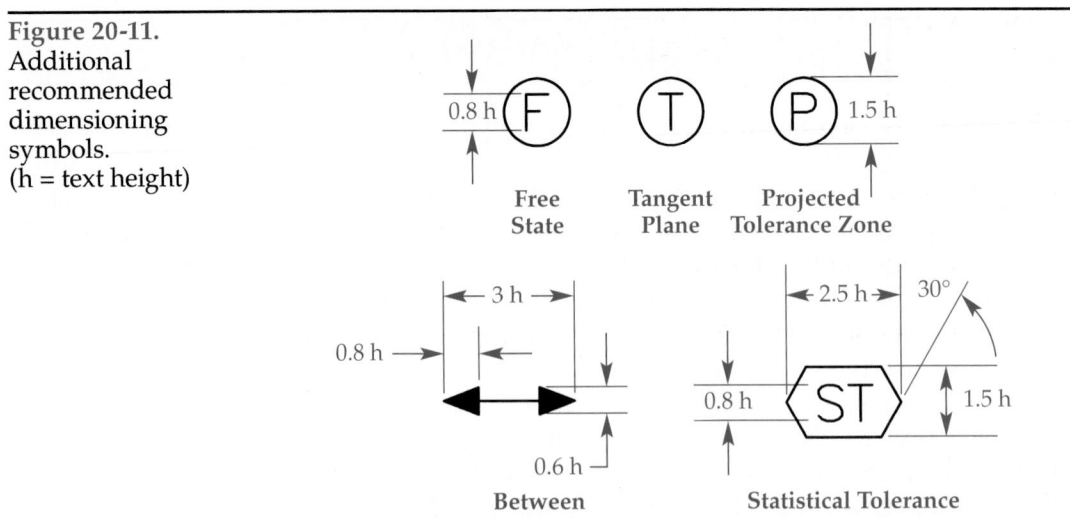

Figure 20-11.
Additional recommended dimensioning symbols.
(h = text height)

Free State   Tangent Plane   Projected Tolerance Zone

Between   Statistical Tolerance

- **Statistical tolerance symbol.** Indicates that a tolerance is based on statistical tolerancing. *Statistical tolerancing* is the assignment of tolerances to related dimensions based on the requirements of statistical process control. *Statistical process control (SPC)* is a method of monitoring and adjusting a manufacturing process based on statistical signals. The statistical tolerancing symbol is placed after the dimension or geometric tolerance that requires SPC. See **Figure 20-12.** When the feature can be manufactured by either SPC or conventional means, both the statistical tolerance with the statistical tolerance symbol and the conventional tolerance must be shown. An appropriate general note should accompany the drawing. Either of the two following notes is acceptable:
  - FEATURES IDENTIFIED AS STATISTICAL TOLERANCED SHALL BE PRODUCED WITH STATISTICAL PROCESS CONTROL.
  - FEATURES IDENTIFIED AS STATISTICAL TOLERANCED SHALL BE PRODUCED WITH STATISTICAL PROCESS CONTROL OR THE MORE RESTRICTIVE ARITHMETIC LIMITS.

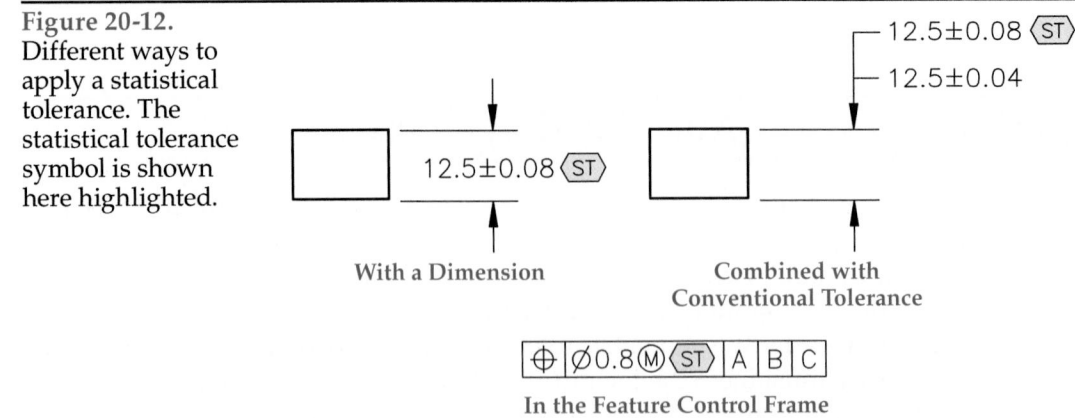

Figure 20-12.
Different ways to apply a statistical tolerance. The statistical tolerance symbol is shown here highlighted.

12.5±0.08 〈ST〉
12.5±0.04

12.5±0.08 〈ST〉

With a Dimension

Combined with Conventional Tolerance

⊕ ⌀0.8 Ⓜ 〈ST〉 A B C

In the Feature Control Frame

Datum Feature Symbols

As previously described, datums refer to theoretically perfect surfaces, planes, points, or axes. In this introduction to datum-related symbols, the datum is assumed. In GD&T, the datums are identified with a *datum feature symbol*.

Each datum feature requiring identification must have its own identification letter. Any letter of the alphabet can be used to identify a datum, except *I, O,* or *Q.* These letters can be confused with the numbers *1* or *0.* When the number of datums on a drawing exceeds 23, double letters are used, starting with *AA* through *AZ* and then continuing with *BA* through *BZ.* Datum feature symbols can be repeated only as necessary for clarity.

Figure 20-13 shows examples of datum feature symbols recommended by ASME Y14.5M-1994. The leader line tipped with a datum terminator is used to connect the datum feature to the datum identification. When a surface is used to establish a datum plane on a part, the datum feature symbol is placed on the edge view of the surface or on an extension line in the view where the surface appears as a line. See Figure 20-14.

When the datum is an axis, the datum feature symbol can be placed on the drawing using one of the following methods. See Figure 20-15.
- The symbol can be placed on the outside surface of a cylindrical feature.
- The symbol can be centered on the opposite side of the dimension line arrowhead.
- The symbol can replace the dimension line and arrowhead when the dimension line is placed outside the extension lines.
- The symbol can be placed on a leader line shoulder.
- The symbol can be placed below and attached to the center of a feature control frame.

Elements on a rectangular symmetrical part or feature can be located and dimensioned in relationship to a datum center plane. Datum center plane symbols are shown in Figure 20-16.

datum feature symbol: Symbols used to identify datums in a feature control frame.

Figure 20-13.
The datum feature symbol, based on ASME Y14.5M-1994.
(h = text height)

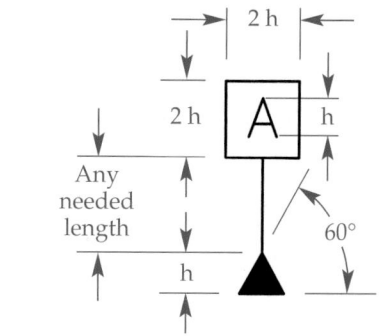

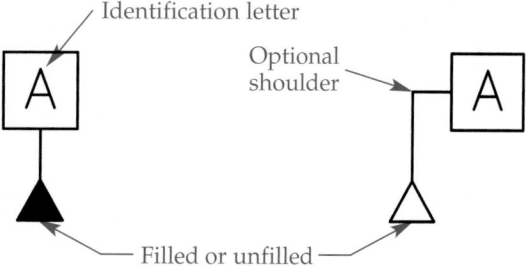

Figure 20-14.
Datum feature symbols used to identify datum planes.

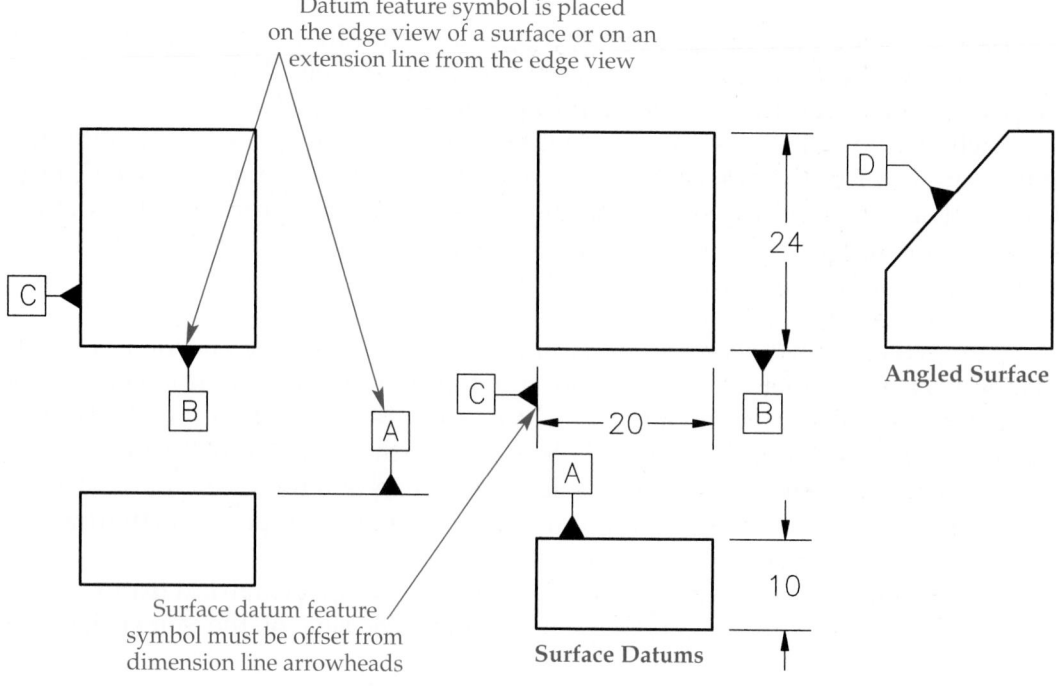

Figure 20-15.
Different methods of using the datum feature symbol to represent a datum axis.

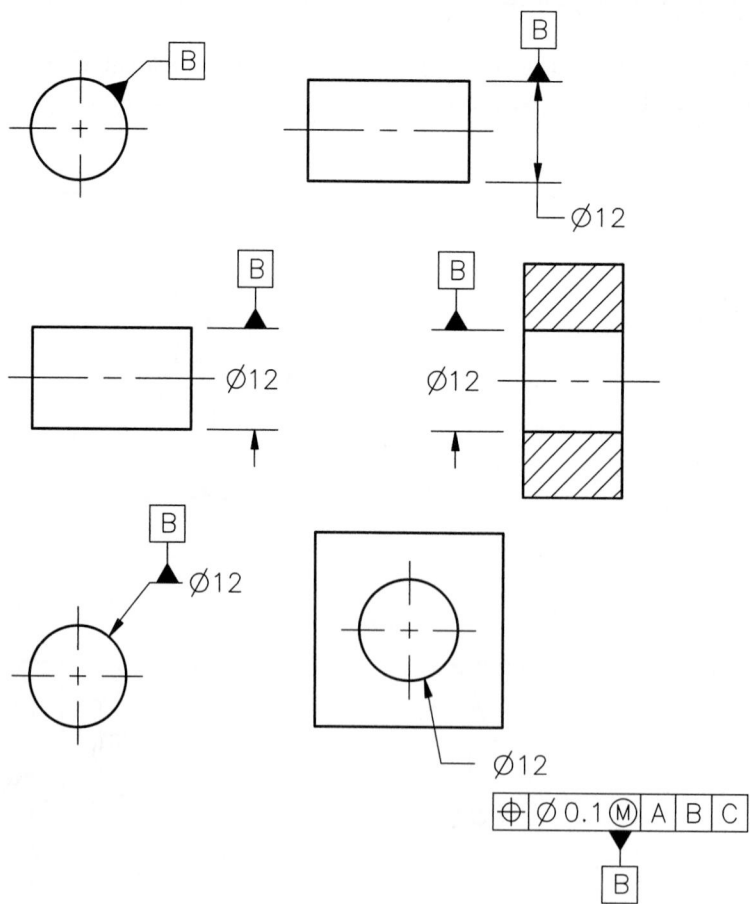

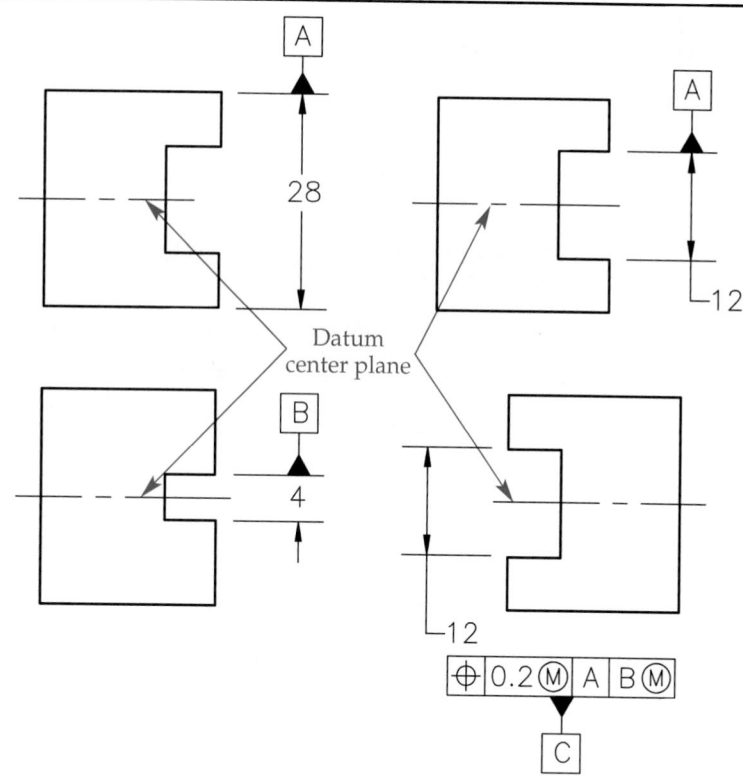

Figure 20-16.
Placing datum center plane symbols. Axis and center plane datum feature symbols must align with, or replace, the dimension line arrowhead, or the datum feature symbol must be placed on the feature, leader shoulder, or feature control frame.

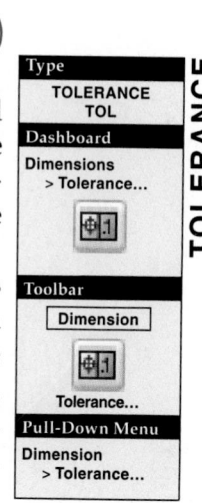

GD&T with AutoCAD

AutoCAD provides you with the ability to add certain GD&T symbols to your drawings using the **TOLERANCE**, **QLEADER**, and **MLEADER** commands. The **TOLERANCE** command launches the **Geometric Tolerance** dialog box, which is the primary method for adding feature control frames and datum target symbols.

GD&T symbols can also be connected to a leader using a combination of the **TOLERANCE** and **MLEADER** commands. The **MLEADER** command has replaced the **QLEADER** command as the primary method for placing leaders. However, the **QLEADER** command continues to provide a quick and effective option for producing GD&T symbols that are automatically attached to a leader. These commands are described in the following sections.

Using the Tolerance Command

The **TOLERANCE** command provides tools for creating feature control frames and datum target symbols. To access this command, pick the **Tolerance...** button on the **Dimension** toolbar or the **Dimension** control panel in the **Dashboard**, pick **Dimension > Tolerance...** from the pull-down menu, or type TOL or TOLERANCE. This displays the **Geometric Tolerance** dialog box. See **Figure 20-17.**

The **Geometric Tolerance** dialog box is divided into areas containing compartments that relate to the components found in a feature control frame. The compartments in the two **Tolerance** and three **Datum** areas allow you to specify geometric tolerance and datum reference values. Each area contains two levels that can be used to create a feature control frame. The first, or upper, level is used to make a single feature control frame. The lower level is used to create a double feature control frame. The dialog box

Figure 20-17.
The **Geometric Tolerance** dialog box is used to draw geometric dimensioning and tolerancing (GD&T) symbols and feature control frames to desired specifications.

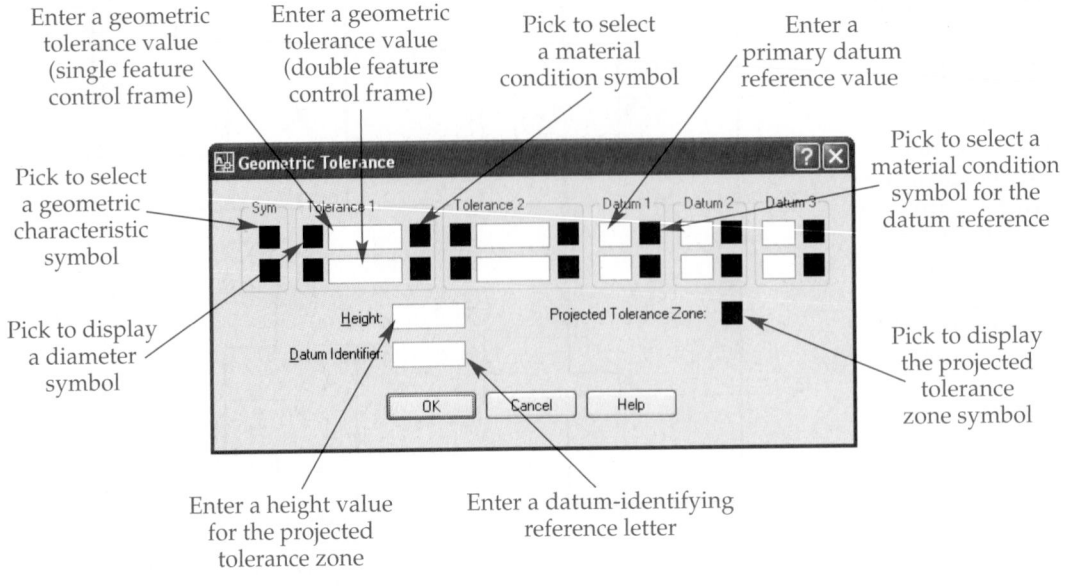

also provides options for displaying a diameter symbol and a modifying symbol. In addition, the **Geometric Tolerance** dialog box allows you to display a projected tolerance zone symbol and value and part of the datum feature symbol.

Selecting a Geometric Characteristic Symbol

Geometric characteristic symbols can be accessed in the **Sym** area located at the far left of the **Geometric Tolerance** dialog box. This area has two boxes that can be used to display one or two geometric characteristic symbols. Remember that the corresponding text boxes along the upper row in each area are used for a single feature control frame. The text boxes in the lower row are used to create a double feature control frame.

Picking one of the boxes in the **Sym** area opens the **Symbol** dialog box. See **Figure 20-18**. Pick a symbol to display it in the **Sym** box you selected. After making a selection, the **Geometric Tolerance** dialog box returns. You can pick the same box again to select a different symbol, if you wish. To remove a previously selected symbol, pick the blank image in the lower-right corner of the **Symbol** dialog box.

Tolerance 1 Area

The **Tolerance 1** area of the **Geometric Tolerance** dialog box allows you to enter the first geometric tolerance value used in the feature control frame. If you are drawing a single feature control frame, enter the desired value in the upper text box. If you are drawing a double feature control frame, also enter a value in the lower text box. Double feature control frames are described later in this chapter. You can add a diameter symbol by picking the box to the left of the text box. Pick the diameter box again to remove the diameter symbol.

The box to the right of the text box is used to place a material condition symbol. When you pick this box, the **Material Condition** dialog box appears. See **Figure 20-19**. Pick the desired symbol to display it in the box you selected. To remove a material condition symbol, pick the blank tile in the **Material Condition** image tile menu. The RFS symbol in **Figure 20-19** was used in ANSI Y14.5M-1982. The symbol is not used in ASME Y14.5M-1994 because RFS is assumed unless otherwise specified.

Figure 20-18.
The **Symbol** dialog box is used to select a geometric characteristic symbol for use in a feature control frame.

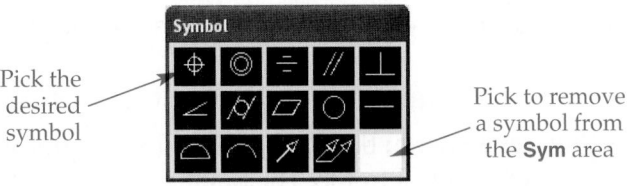

Pick the desired symbol

Pick to remove a symbol from the **Sym** area

Figure 20-19.
The **Material Condition** dialog box. Pick the desired material condition symbol for the geometric tolerance and datum reference. Notice that the symbol for regardless of feature size (RFS) is available. This symbol is not used in ASME Y14.5M-1994, but you may need it when editing older drawings.

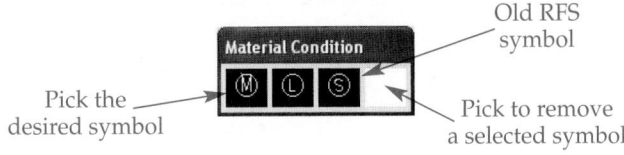

Old RFS symbol

Pick the desired symbol

Pick to remove a selected symbol

In Figure 20-20, a position symbol is shown in the **Sym** image tile, and 0.5 is entered as the tolerance value in the upper text box in the **Tolerance 1** area. The tolerance value is preceded by a diameter symbol and followed by an MMC symbol. Remember that a zero precedes metric decimals, but not inch decimals.

Tolerance 2 Area

The **Tolerance 2** area of the **Geometric Tolerance** dialog box is used for the addition of a second geometric tolerance to the feature control frame. This is not a common application, but it may be used in some cases where there are restrictions placed on the geometric tolerance specified in the first compartment. For example, a second geometric tolerance value of 0.8 MAX means that the specification given in the first compartment is maintained, but it cannot exceed 0.8.

Datum Areas

The **Datum 1** area of the **Geometric Tolerance** dialog box is used to establish the information needed for the primary datum reference compartment. Like the **Tolerance** areas, this area offers two levels of text boxes to create single or double feature control frames. You can also specify a material condition symbol for the datum reference by

Figure 20-20.
The **Geometric Tolerance** dialog box with a diameter symbol, geometric tolerance value, and maximum material condition (MMC) symbol added to the **Tolerance 1** area.

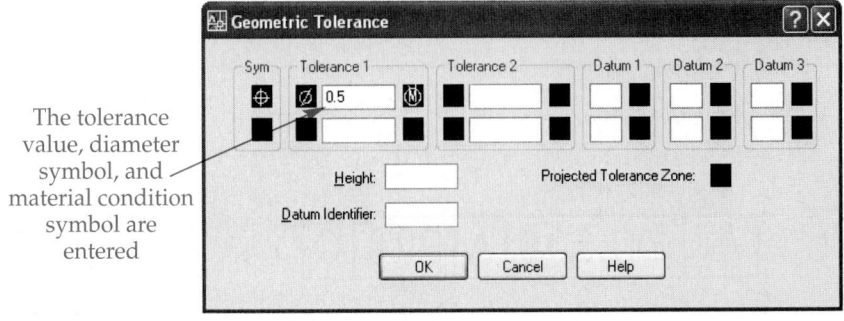

The tolerance value, diameter symbol, and material condition symbol are entered

picking the box to the right of the corresponding text box to open the **Material Condition** dialog box. The **Datum 2** and **Datum 3** areas are used to specify the secondary and tertiary datum reference information. Refer to Figure 20-9 to see how the datum reference and related material condition symbols are placed in the feature control frame.

Projected Tolerance Zone Box and Height Text Box

The **Projected Tolerance Zone:** box can be picked to display a projected tolerance zone symbol in the feature control frame. The **Height:** text box specifies the height of a projected tolerance zone. The projected tolerance zone symbol and the height value are used together when a projected tolerance zone is applied to the drawing. The use of a projected tolerance zone in a drawing is described later in this chapter.

Datum Identifier Text Box

The **Datum Identifier:** text box is used to enter a datum-identifying reference letter to be used as part of the datum feature symbol. An uppercase letter should be entered.

Completing the Command

After you have entered all the desired information in the **Geometric Tolerance** dialog box, pick **OK** and pick a point to place the tolerance in the drawing. The feature control frame for the given example is shown in Figure 20-21.

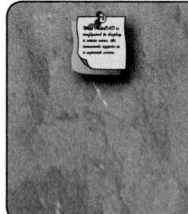

NOTE

The height of the feature control frame is automatically set to twice the height of the text. Text on engineering drawings is generally drawn at a height of .12″ (3 mm), which makes the feature control frame height .24″ (6 mm). This complies with the ASME Y14.5M standard.

Figure 20-21.
In this example, primary, secondary, and tertiary datum reference values have been added and are shown highlighted, along with the geometric tolerance value. The feature control frame created by the values specified in the dialog box is shown.

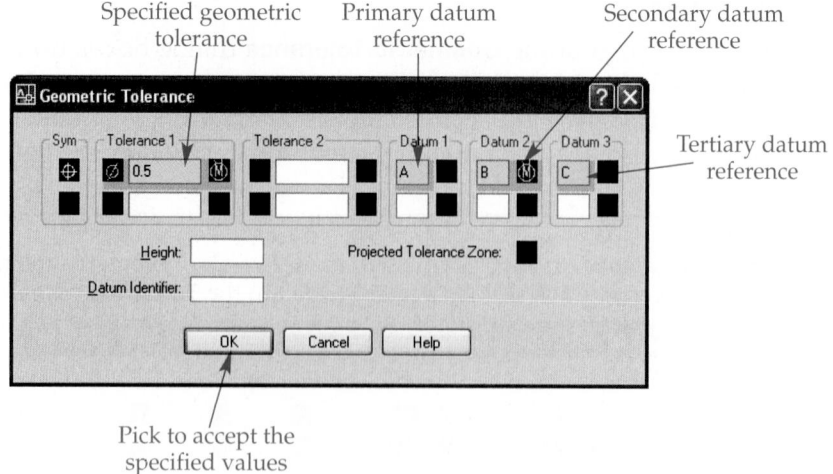

Feature Control Frame

Attaching Feature Control Frames to Leaders

In many cases, leader lines are connected to feature control frames in order to identify toleranced features. The **QLEADER** command allows you to draw leader lines and access the **Geometric Tolerance** dialog box used to create feature control frames in one operation. This is the most effective technique for creating a feature control frame that is automatically attached and associated with a leader. However, other GD&T symbols, such as datum feature symbols are more effectively created using different methods. These options are described later in this chapter.

Using the Mleader Command

The **MLEADER** command is used to create leaders, without providing an option to create a feature control frame at the same time. As a result, you are required to draw the leader separately using **MLEADER** command and the feature control frame using the **TOLERANCE** command. Apply the **None** multileader content type when using this method. The leader can be drawn before or after the symbol. See Figure 20-22.

Using the Qleader Command

The **QLEADER** command provides you with the ability to place a leader and attach a feature control frame in one operation. Some of the leader line characteristics, such as the arrowhead size, are controlled by the dimension style settings. Other features, such as the leader format and annotation style, are controlled by the **Settings** option in the **QLEADER** command.

Figure 20-22.
Use the **MLEADER** command to create a leader before drawing the feature control frame using the **TOLERANCE** command, or add the leader to an existing feature control frame.

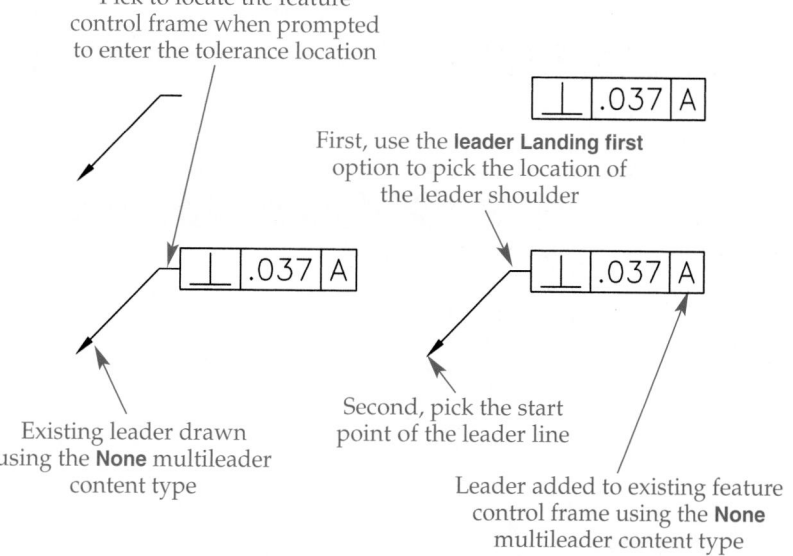

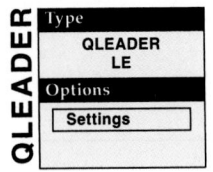

Type

QLEADER
LE

Options

Settings

The **QLEADER** command can be accessed by typing LE or QLEADER. When you enter this command, use the **Settings** option to open the **Leader Settings** dialog box. See Figure 20-23. Select the **Annotation** tab if it is not displayed. Then pick the **Tolerance** radio button to display the **Geometric Tolerance** dialog box for creation of a feature control frame after the leader line is drawn.

Next, select the **Leader Line & Arrow** tab of the **Leader Settings** dialog box. Pick the **Straight** radio button to create a leader with straight-line segments. When adding a feature control frame to a leader line, you should set the maximum number of vertices in the **Maximum** text box of the **Number of Points** area to 2. When you set the maximum number of leader points to 2, you select the start and endpoints of the leader line. Then the **QLEADER** command stops drawing the leader, automatically places the leader shoulder, and displays the **Geometric Tolerance** dialog box.

The **Arrowhead** area of the **Leader Line & Arrow** tab uses the default value assigned to leaders within the current dimension style. To change the appearance of the arrowhead, pick the drop-down list and select a terminator from the full range of choices. Changing the **Arrowhead** setting creates a dimension style override.

The first two segments of the leader line can be restricted to certain angles. These angles are set in the **Angle Constraints** area of the **Leader Line & Arrow** tab. The options for each segment are **Any angle**, **Horizontal**, **90°**, **45°**, **30°**, and **15°**. The **Ortho** mode setting overrides the angle constraints, so it is advisable to turn **Ortho** mode off while using this command.

Pick the **OK** button to exit the **Leader Settings** dialog box. When asked to specify the first leader point, pick the leader start point. Now, pick the next leader point. If the maximum number of leader points is set to 2, the **Geometric Tolerance** dialog box is displayed. Otherwise, press [Enter] to end the leader line and display the **Geometric Tolerance** dialog box. Specify the desired settings and values for the feature control frame. Pick the **OK** button. The feature control frame is connected to the leader line in your drawing, as shown in Figure 20-24.

LEGACY NOTE

The **LEADER** command can also be used to draw GD&T symbols that are automatically attached to leaders. However, this command does not provide the same convenience and ability to comply with drafting standards as the **QLEADER** command.

Exercise 20-2
Complete the exercise on the Student CD.

Figure 20-23.
The **Leader Settings** dialog box. Activate the **Tolerance** radio button when placing a feature control frame with the **QLEADER** command.

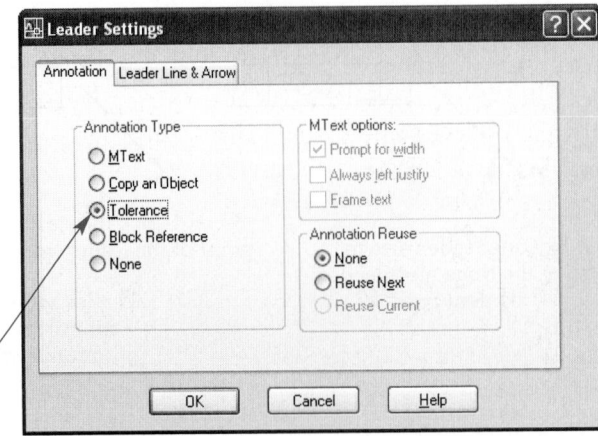

Tolerance option activated

AutoCAD and Its Applications—Basics

Figure 20-24.
When you complete the **QLEADER** command, the feature control frame is connected to the leader line.

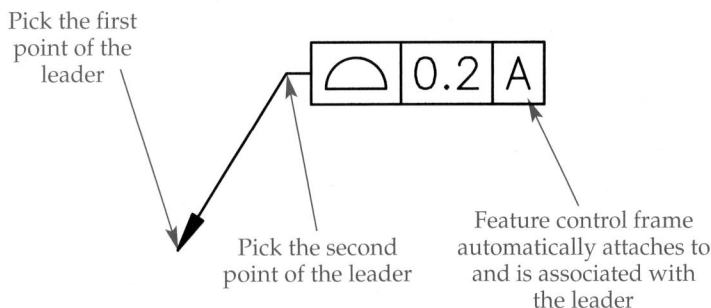

Pick the first point of the leader

Pick the second point of the leader

Feature control frame automatically attaches to and is associated with the leader

Introduction to Projected Tolerance Zones

In some situations where positional tolerance is used entirely in out-of-squareness, it may be necessary to control perpendicularity and position next to the part. The use of a *projected tolerance zone* is recommended when variations in perpendicularity of threaded or press-fit holes may cause the fastener to interfere with the mating part. A projected tolerance zone is usually specified for a fixed fastener, such as the threaded hole for a bolt or the press-fit hole for a pin. The length of a projected tolerance zone can be specified as the distance the fastener extends into the mating part, the thickness of the part, or the height of a press-fit stud.

The normal positional tolerance extends through the thickness of the part. This application, however, can cause an interference between the location of a thread or press-fit object and its mating part. This is because the actual angle of a threaded hole controls the attitude of the fixed fastener. No clearance is available to provide flexibility. For this reason, the projected tolerance zone is established at true position and extends away from the primary datum at the threaded feature. The projected tolerance zone provides a larger tolerance because it is projected away from the primary datum, rather than within the thread. A projected tolerance is also easier to inspect than the tolerance applied to the pitch diameter of the thread. This is because a thread gauge with a post projecting above the threaded hole can easily be used to verify the projected tolerance zone with a coordinate measuring machine (CMM).

projected tolerance zone: A tolerance zone established at true position and extending away from the primary datum; used when variations in perpendicularity of threaded or press-fit holes may cause the fastener to interfere with the mating part.

Representing a Projected Tolerance Zone

One method for displaying the projected tolerance zone is to place the projected tolerance zone symbol and height in the feature control frame after the geometric tolerance and related material condition symbol. The related thread specification is then connected to the section view of the thread symbol. With this method, the projected tolerance zone is assumed to extend away from the threaded hole at the primary datum. See **Figure 20-25.**

To provide additional clarification, the projected tolerance zone can be shown using a chain line in the view where the related datum appears as an edge and the minimum height of the projection is dimensioned. See **Figure 20-26.** The projected tolerance zone symbol is shown alone in the feature control frame after the geometric tolerance and material condition symbol (if any). The meaning is the same as previously described.

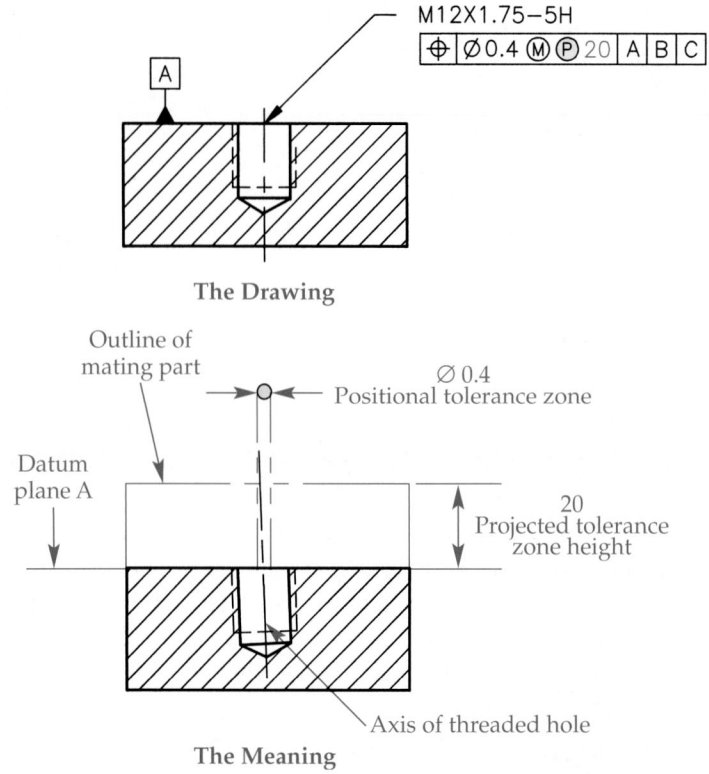

Figure 20-25.
A projected tolerance zone representation with the length of the projected tolerance zone given in the feature control frame. The projected tolerance zone symbol is shown highlighted.

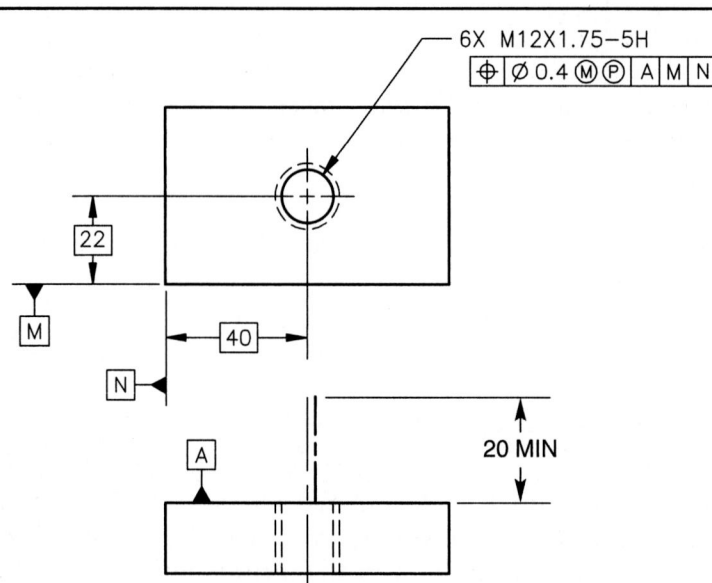

Figure 20-26.
A projected tolerance zone representation with the length of the projected tolerance zone shown with a chain line and a minimum dimension in the adjacent view.

Drawing the Projected Tolerance Zone

AutoCAD specifies projected tolerance zones according to the 1982 standard. When following this standard, enter the desired geometric tolerance, diameter symbol, material condition symbol, and datum reference in the **Geometric Tolerance** dialog box, as previously described. Pick the **Projected Tolerance Zone:** box to display the projected tolerance zone symbol and enter the height in the **Height:** text box. See **Figure 20-27.** Place the feature control frame in the desired location in the drawing. Notice that AutoCAD displays the projected tolerance zone height in a separate compartment below the feature control frame, in accordance with ANSI Y14.5M-1982.

Figure 20-27.
To add projected tolerance zone specifications to the feature control frame, enter the projected tolerance zone height and symbol in the **Geometric Tolerance** dialog box.

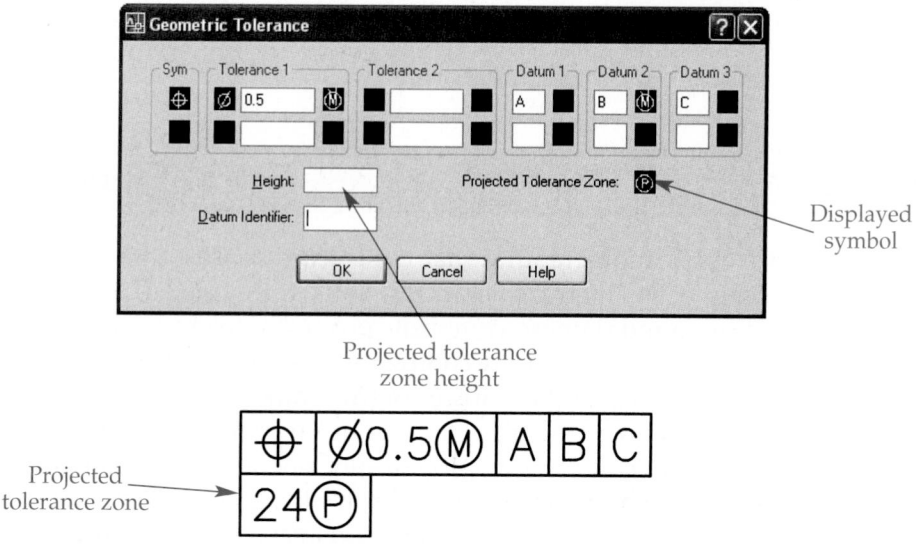

Projected tolerance zone height

Displayed symbol

Projected tolerance zone →

Feature Control Frame

To specify a projected tolerance zone according to the 1994 standard, create a feature control frame with any modifier letters and the letter P after the tolerance value. The height of the projected tolerance zone is typed after the P. Leave one space between each letter and the height value. See **Figure 20-28.** Then use the **CIRCLE** command to draw a circle around the modifier and the letter P. You can use the **GROUP** command to group the feature control frame and circles so they can be selected as a single object.

Figure 20-28.
Specifying a projected tolerance zone in accordance with ASME Y14.5M-1994.

Type letters for modifier and projected tolerance zone

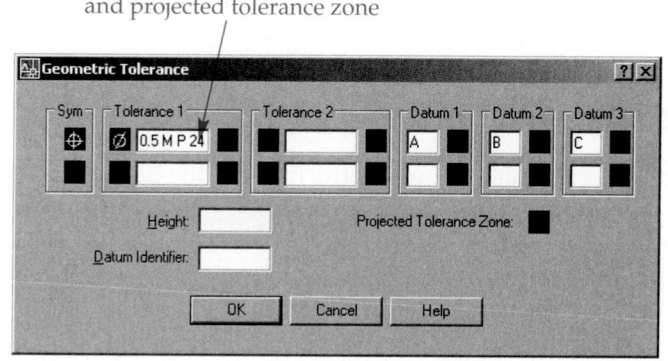

Modifier

Circles are drawn manually

Projected tolerance zone symbol

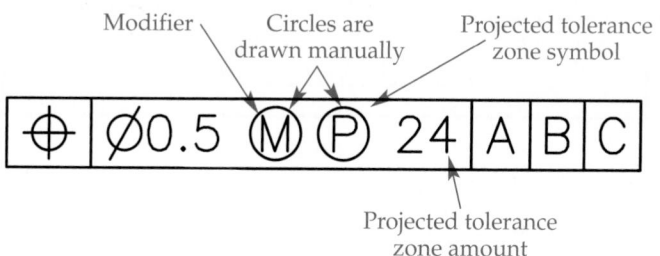

Projected tolerance zone amount

Feature Control Frame

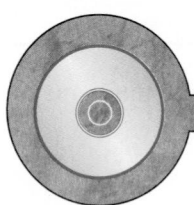

Exercise 20-3
Complete the exercise on the Student CD.

Drawing a Double Feature Control Frame

Several GD&T applications require that the feature control frame be doubled in height, with two sets of geometric tolerancing values provided. These applications include unit straightness and flatness, composite positional tolerance, and coaxial positional tolerance. To draw a double feature control frame, use the **TOLERANCE** command to create the desired first level of the feature control frame in the **Geometric Tolerance** dialog box as previously described. You can also use the **QLEADER** command, if you are connecting the feature control frame to a leader line. Next, pick the lower box in the **Sym** area. When the **Symbol** dialog box is displayed again, pick another geometric characteristic symbol. This results in two symbols displayed in the **Sym** area. Continue specifying the needed information in the lower-level **Tolerance** and **Datum** compartments. Sample entries for a double feature control frame are shown in Figure 20-29.

If the symbols in the two **Sym** boxes are the same, the double feature control frame is drawn with one geometric characteristic symbol displayed in a single compartment. This is called a *composite frame*. Some situations require the same geometric characteristic symbol twice, one in the upper frame and another in the lower frame. These are two single-segment feature control frames. To create this type, draw two separate feature control frames and group them. If you are drawing a double feature control frame with different geometric characteristic symbols for a combination control, the feature control frame must have two separate compartments. See Figure 20-30.

composite frame: Used when the double feature control frame is drawn with one geometric characteristic symbol displayed in a single compartment.

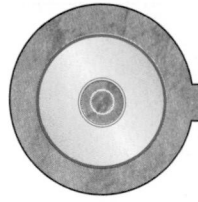

Exercise 20-4
Complete the exercise on the Student CD.

Figure 20-29.
Specifying information for a double feature control frame in the **Geometric Tolerance** dialog box.

Pick to select a second geometric characteristic symbol

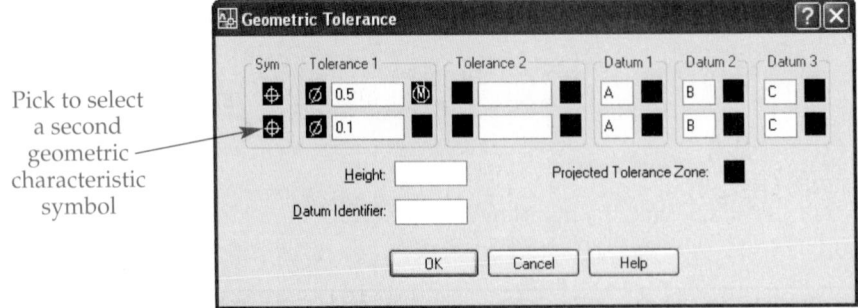

Figure 20-30.
If the same geometric characteristic symbol is entered in both **Symbol** boxes of the **Geometric Tolerance** dialog box, only one symbol is shown in the first compartment of the feature control frame. Create two separate feature control frames to display the same symbol in both frames. If two different symbols are used, they are displayed in separate compartments.

⊕	Ø0.5Ⓜ	A	B	C
	Ø0.1Ⓜ	A	B	

Same Symbol for Both Control Frames

⊕	Ø0.5Ⓜ	A	B	C
⊕	Ø0.3Ⓜ	A	B	

Create Separate Single Control Frames to Repeat Symbol

∥	0.5	A
⊥	0.1	B

Double Feature Control Frame with Different Symbols

Drawing Datum Feature Symbols

As described earlier in this chapter, datums in a drawing are identified by datum feature symbols. You can draw datum feature symbols using the **TOLERANCE** and **QLEADER** commands. However, usually you must use a combination of **TOLERANCE** and **MLEADER** or **QLEADER** commands to draw an appropriate datum feature symbol. The method used to draw a datum feature symbol depends on the feature the symbol identifies. When you use the **Geometric Tolerance** dialog box to specify a datum feature symbol, enter the datum reference letter in the **Datum Identifier:** text box. See Figure 20-31.

Options for Drawing Datum Feature Symbols

The datum feature symbols shown in Figure 20-32 can be drawn using the **TOLERANCE** and **MLEADER** or **QLEADER** commands. One option is to use the **TOLERANCE** command first to place the datum identifier and then add a leader that connects the feature to the identifier. The other option is to draw a leader first and then use the **TOLERANCE** command to add the datum identifier. This usually requires you to move the datum identifier to the correct location using object snaps. Both methods are shown in Figure 20-33.

When using the **MLEADER** command to add the leader, create a separate multi-leader style that uses a **Datum triangle filled** arrowhead symbol, set the maximum leader points to 2, do not include a landing, and use the **None** multileader content type.

Figure 20-31.
Using the **Geometric Tolerance** dialog box to enter a datum-identifying reference letter. This letter is used to create the datum feature symbol.

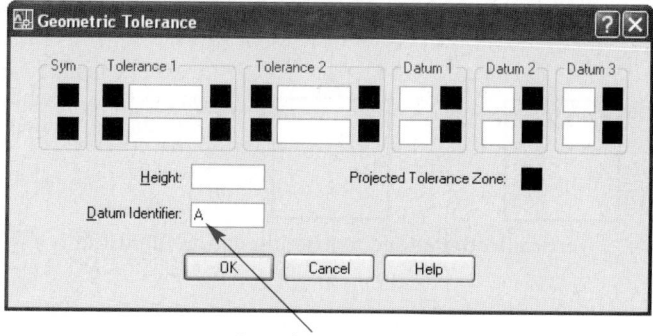

Specified datum reference letter

Figure 20-32.
Examples of datum feature symbols created using a combination of **TOLERANCE** and **MLEADER** or **QLEADER** commands.

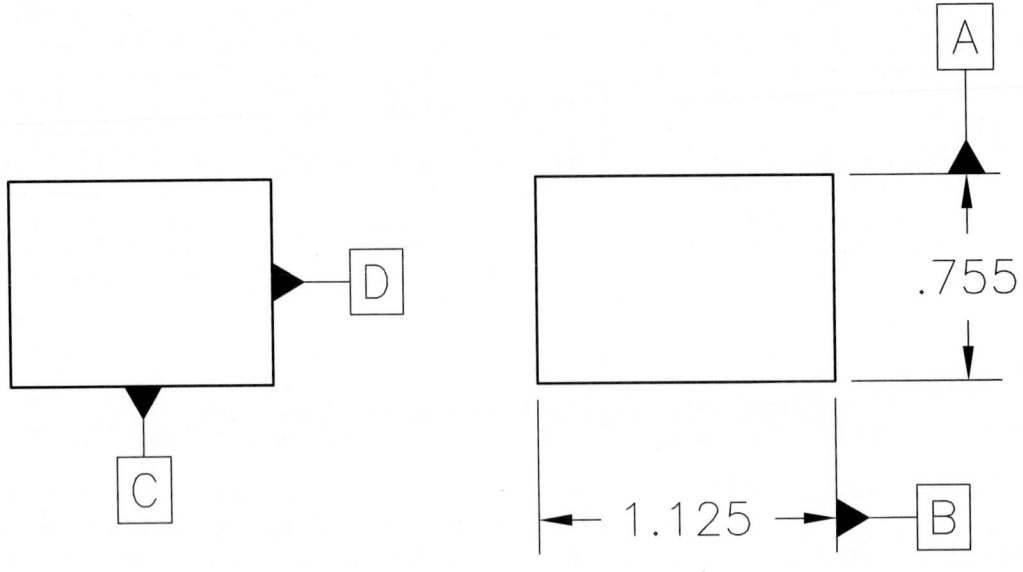

Figure 20-33.
Use the **MLEADER** or **QLEADER** commands to add a leader before a feature control frame is drawn using the **TOLERANCE** command, or add the leader to an existing feature control frame.

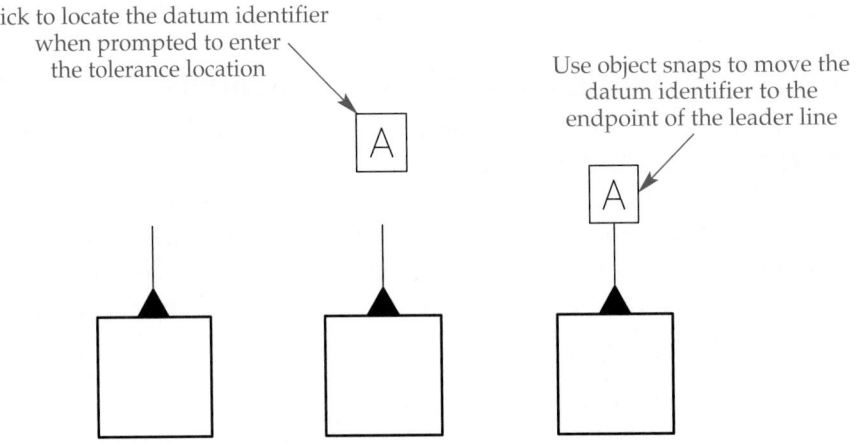

Pick to locate the datum identifier when prompted to enter the tolerance location

Use object snaps to move the datum identifier to the endpoint of the leader line

Datum identifier added to existing (vertical) leader

First, pick the start point of the leader line

Second, use the object snaps to locate the endpoint of the leader line

Vertical leader added to existing datum identifier

When using the **QLEADER** command to add the leader, create a dimension style that uses the **Datum triangle filled** leader, use the **None** annotation type, and set the maximum leader points to 2.

Adding Datum Feature Symbols to Angled Surfaces

You must follow specific steps in order to add a datum feature symbol to an angled surface, as shown in **Figure 20-34.** One option is to use the **QLEADER** command. Before adding the leader, create a dimension style that uses the **Datum triangle filled** leader. Enter the **QLEADER** command and use the **Settings** option to open the **Leader Settings** dialog box. Select the **Annotation** tab if it is not displayed. Then pick the **Tolerance** radio button. Select the **Leader Line & Arrow** tab of the **Leader Settings** dialog box and pick the **Straight** radio button. When adding a datum feature to a leader line, you should set the maximum number of vertices in the **Maximum** text box of the **Number of Points** area to 3. This allows you to construct the leader shoulder manually. If you let AutoCAD form the leader shoulder automatically, it will shift the angle of the leader line.

Select the **OK** button to exit the **Leader Settings** dialog box. Pick the leader start point and then the next leader point. The second point must create a line segment that is perpendicular to the angled surface. Pick the third point to define the length of the leader shoulder. If the maximum number of leader points was set to 3, the **Geometric Tolerance** dialog box is displayed. Otherwise, press [Enter] to end the leader line and display the **Geometric Tolerance** dialog box. Specify a value in the **Datum identifier** text box, and pick the **OK** button.

Figure 20-34.
Use the **Tolerance** annotation option of the **QLEADER** command to add a datum feature symbol to an angled surface.

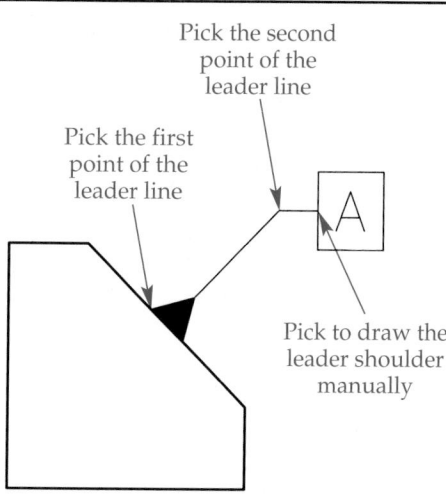

Pick the second point of the leader line

Pick the first point of the leader line

Pick to draw the leader shoulder manually

Exercise 20-5
Complete the exercise on the Student CD.

Drawing Basic Dimensions

A basic dimension is shown in Figure 20-35. Basic dimensions can be drawn automatically by setting a basic tolerance in the **Tolerances** tab of the **Modify Dimension Style** dialog box, as described in Chapter 19. It is recommended that you establish a separate dimension style for basic dimensions because not all of the dimensions on a drawing will be basic.

The height of the basic dimension rectangle is twice the height of the text, as shown in Figure 20-10. Text on engineering drawings is generally drawn at a height of .12" (3 mm), which makes the basic dimension rectangle height .24" (6 mm). As a result, the distance from the text to the basic dimension rectangle should be equal to half the text height. For example, if the height of the drawing text is .12", the space between the text and the basic dimension rectangle should be .06" to result in a .24" high frame. The distance from the text to the basic dimension rectangle is controlled by the **Offset from dim line:** setting in the **Text** tab of the **New** (or **Modify**) **Dimension Style** dialog box. The setting also controls the gap between the dimension line and the dimension text for linear dimensions.

NOTE

Picking the **Draw frame around text** check box in the **Text** tab of the **New** (or **Modify**) **Dimension Style** dialog box also activates the basic tolerance method.

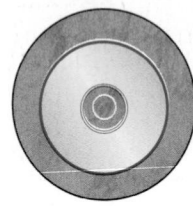

Exercise 20-6
Complete the exercise on the Student CD.

Figure 20-35.
A basic dimension.

3.250

Editing Feature Control Frames

A feature control frame acts as one object. When you pick any location on the frame, the entire object is selected. You can edit feature control frames using AutoCAD editing commands such as **ERASE**, **COPY**, **MOVE**, **ROTATE**, and **SCALE**. The **STRETCH** command only allows you to move a feature control frame. This effect is similar to the results of using the **STRETCH** command with text objects.

You can edit the values inside a feature control frame using the **DDEDIT** command. To access the command, select **Modify > Object > Text > Edit...** from the pull-down menu, or type ED or DDEDIT. When you enter this command and select the desired frame, the **Geometric Tolerance** dialog box is displayed with all the current values. After you make the desired changes, pick **OK** to update the feature control frame.

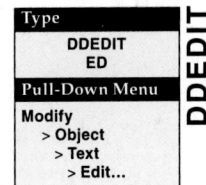

You can also use the **DDEDIT** command to edit basic dimensions. When you select a basic dimension for editing, the **In-Place Text Editor** is displayed. You can then edit the basic dimension as you would any other dimension.

NOTE

If you double-click on a dimension object, AutoCAD opens the **Properties** palette.

Sample GD&T Applications

This chapter is intended to give you a general overview of GD&T applications and basic instructions on how to draw GD&T symbols using AutoCAD. If you are in the manufacturing industry, you may have considerable use for GD&T. The support information presented in this chapter may be a review, or it may inspire you to learn more about this topic. The drawings in **Figure 20-36** are intended to show you some common GD&T applications using the dimensioning and geometric characteristic symbols available in AutoCAD.

Figure 20-36.
Examples of typical geometric dimensioning and tolerancing (GD&T) applications using various dimensioning and geometric characteristic symbols.

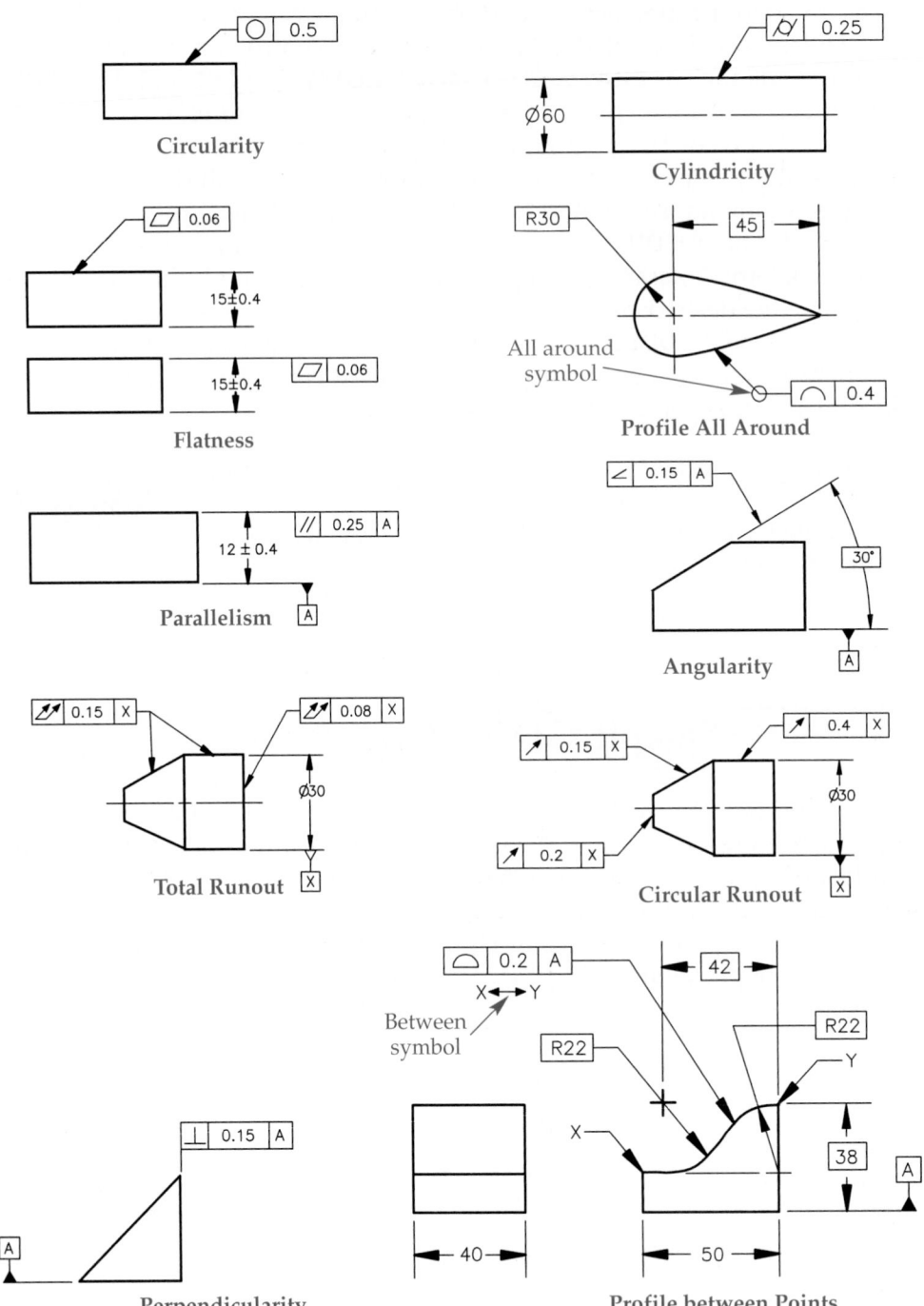

Chapter Test

Answer the following questions. Write your answers on a separate sheet of paper or complete the electronic chapter test on the Student CD.

1. Name the current standard for dimensioning and tolerancing adopted by the American National Standards Institute (ANSI) and published by the American Society of Mechanical Engineers (ASME).
2. Identify each of the following geometric characteristic symbols:

A.	⏤	H.	◎
B.	⏥	I.	⌯
C.	○	J.	//
D.	⌭	K.	⊥
E.	⌒	L.	∠
F.	⌓	M.	↗
G.	⌖	N.	⌰

3. Identify the parts of the feature control frame shown below.

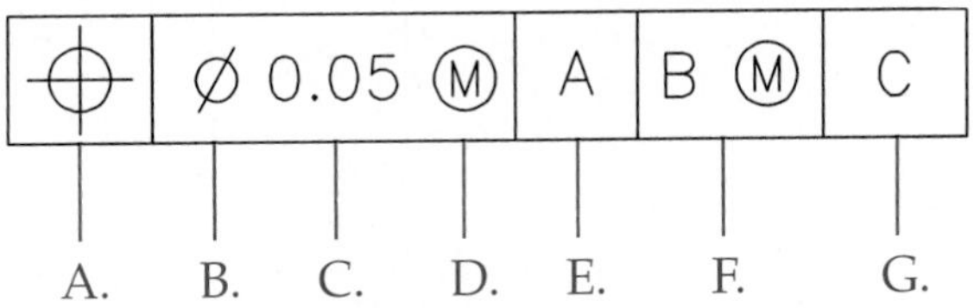

4. Name three commands that can be used to add GD&T symbols to your drawing.
5. Identify the dialog box containing settings used to create a feature control frame.
6. How do you access the **Symbol** dialog box, in which a geometric characteristic symbol can be selected?
7. How do you remove a geometric characteristic symbol from one of the image tiles in the **Sym** area of the **Geometric Tolerance** dialog box?
8. Identify the command that provides you with the ability to place a leader and attach a feature control frame in one operation.
9. Describe the procedure used to draw a feature control frame connected to a leader line.
10. Describe how to place a projected tolerance zone symbol and height value with the feature control frame, based on ANSI Y14.5M-1982.
11. Explain how to create a double feature control frame.
12. Which AutoCAD setting allows you to draw basic dimensions? How is it accessed?
13. Identify the AutoCAD setting controlling the space between the text in a feature control frame and the surrounding frame.
14. Describe how to draw a datum feature symbol without an attached feature control frame. How do you add a leader line with a filled datum triangle to the symbol?
15. Name the command that can be used to edit the existing values in a feature control frame.

Drawing Problems

Create dimension styles that will assist you with the following problems. Draw fully dimensioned multiview drawings. The required number of views depends on the problem and is to be determined by you. Apply geometric tolerancing as described in this chapter. Modify the available AutoCAD drawing applications to comply with ASME Y14.5M-1994 standards. The problems are presented in accordance with ASME Y14.5M-1994.

1. Open drawing **P18-5**. Edit the drawing by adding the geometric tolerancing applications shown below. Untoleranced dimensions are ±.02 for two-place decimal precision and ±.005 for three-place decimal precision. If you did not draw P18-5, start a new drawing and draw the problem now. The problem is shown as a cutaway for clarity. You do not need to draw a section. Save the drawing as **P20-1**.

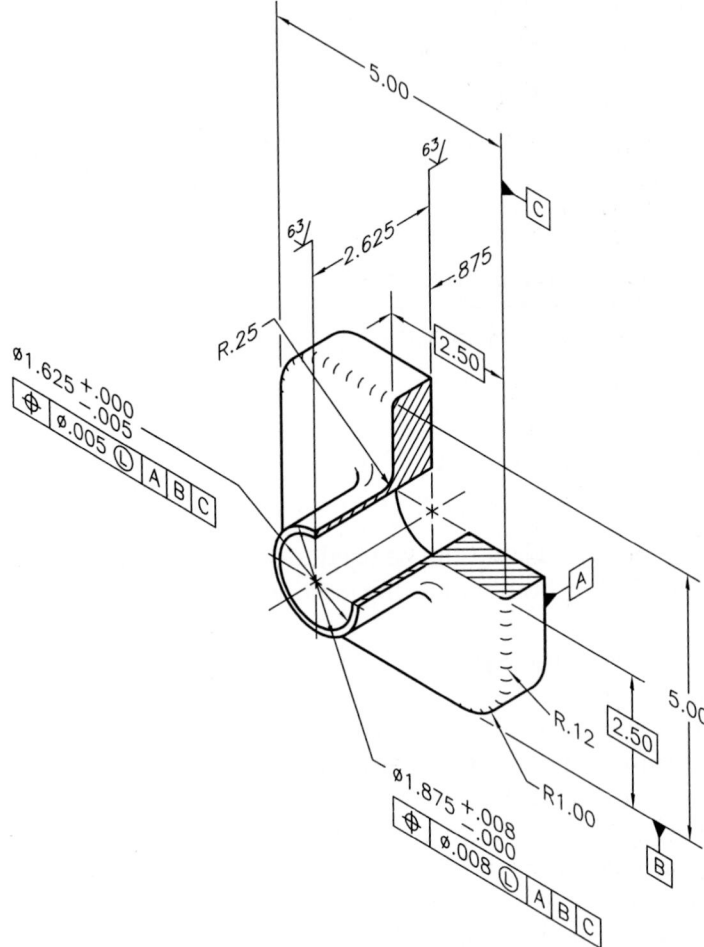

2. Open drawing P18-6. Edit the drawing by adding the geometric tolerancing applications shown below. Untoleranced dimensions are ±0.5. If you did not draw P20-6, start a new drawing and draw the problem now. Save the drawing as P20-2.

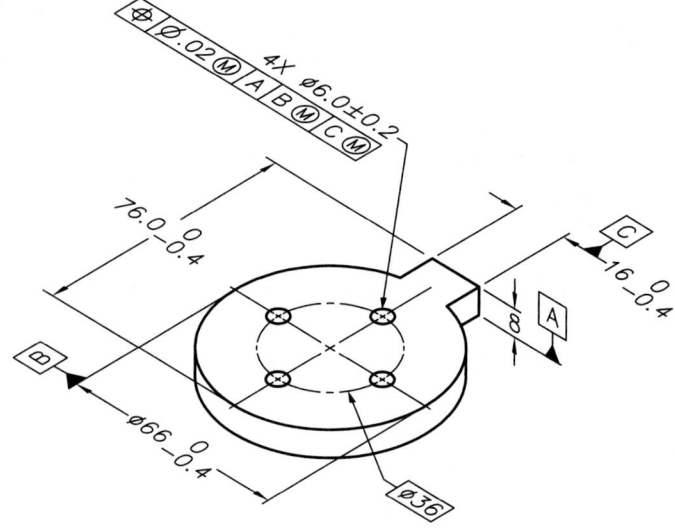

3. Open drawing P20-7. Edit the drawing by adding the geometric tolerancing applications shown below. If you did not draw P18-7, start a new drawing and draw the problem now. Save the drawing as P20-3.

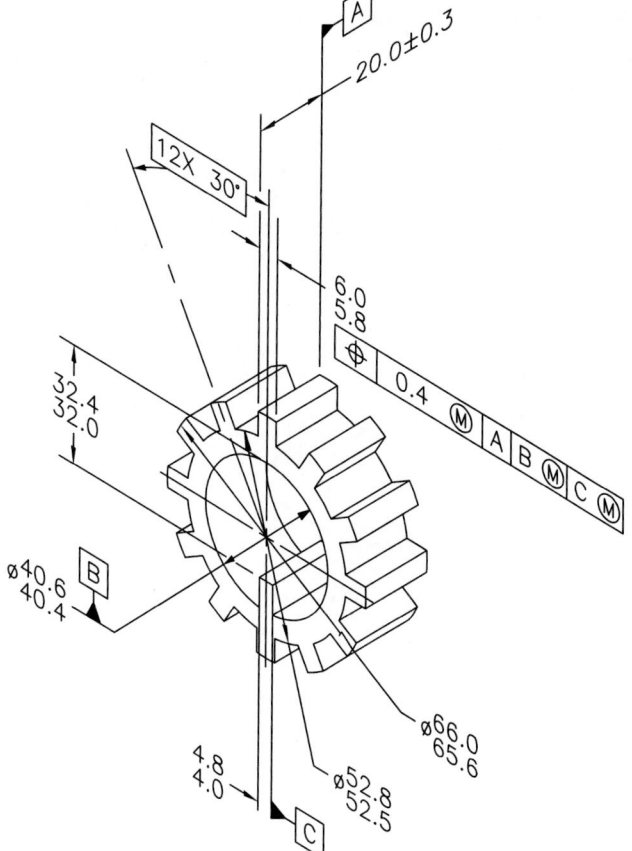

4. Draw the following object as previously instructed. Untoleranced dimensions are ±0.3. Save the drawing as P20-4.

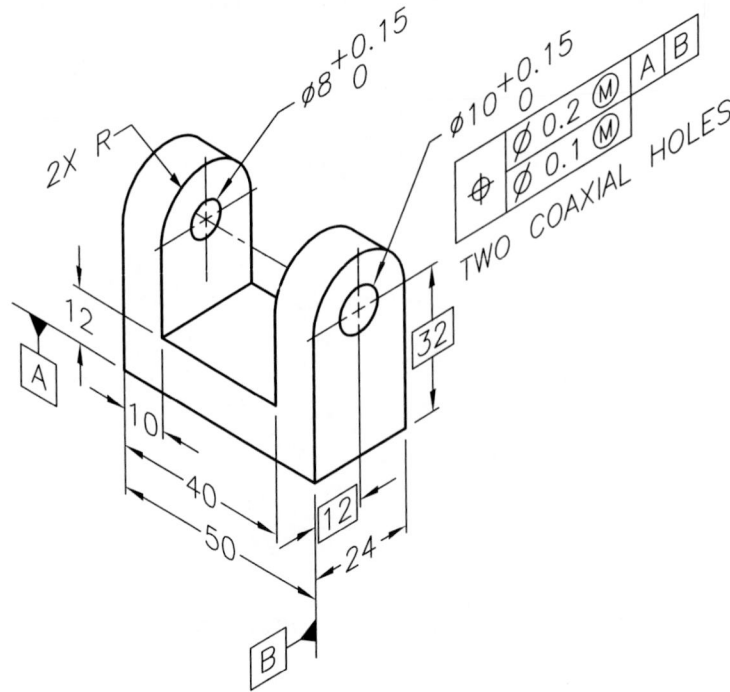

5. Draw the following object as previously instructed. The problem is shown with a full section for clarity. You do not need to draw a section. Untoleranced dimensions are ±.010. Save the drawing as P20-5.

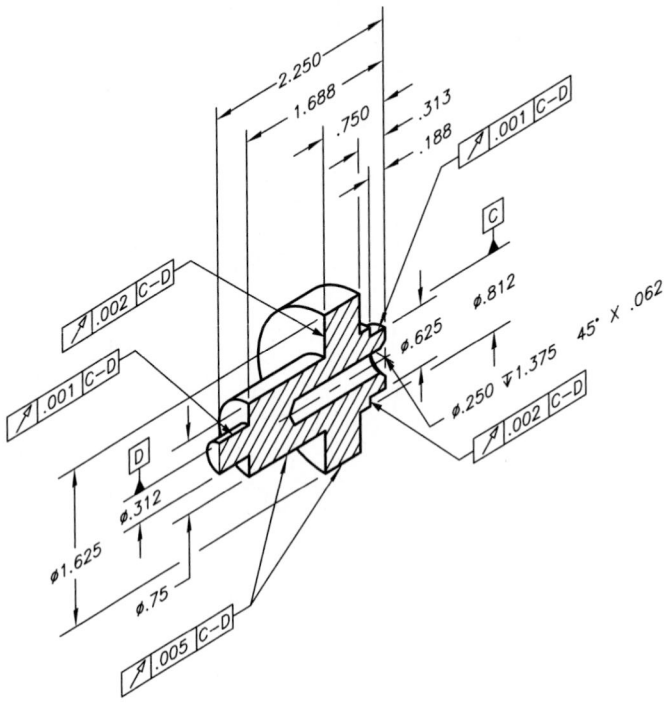

6. Open drawing P17-25. Edit the drawing by adding the geometric tolerancing applications shown below. If you did not draw P16-29, start a new drawing and draw the problem now. Save the drawing as P20-6.

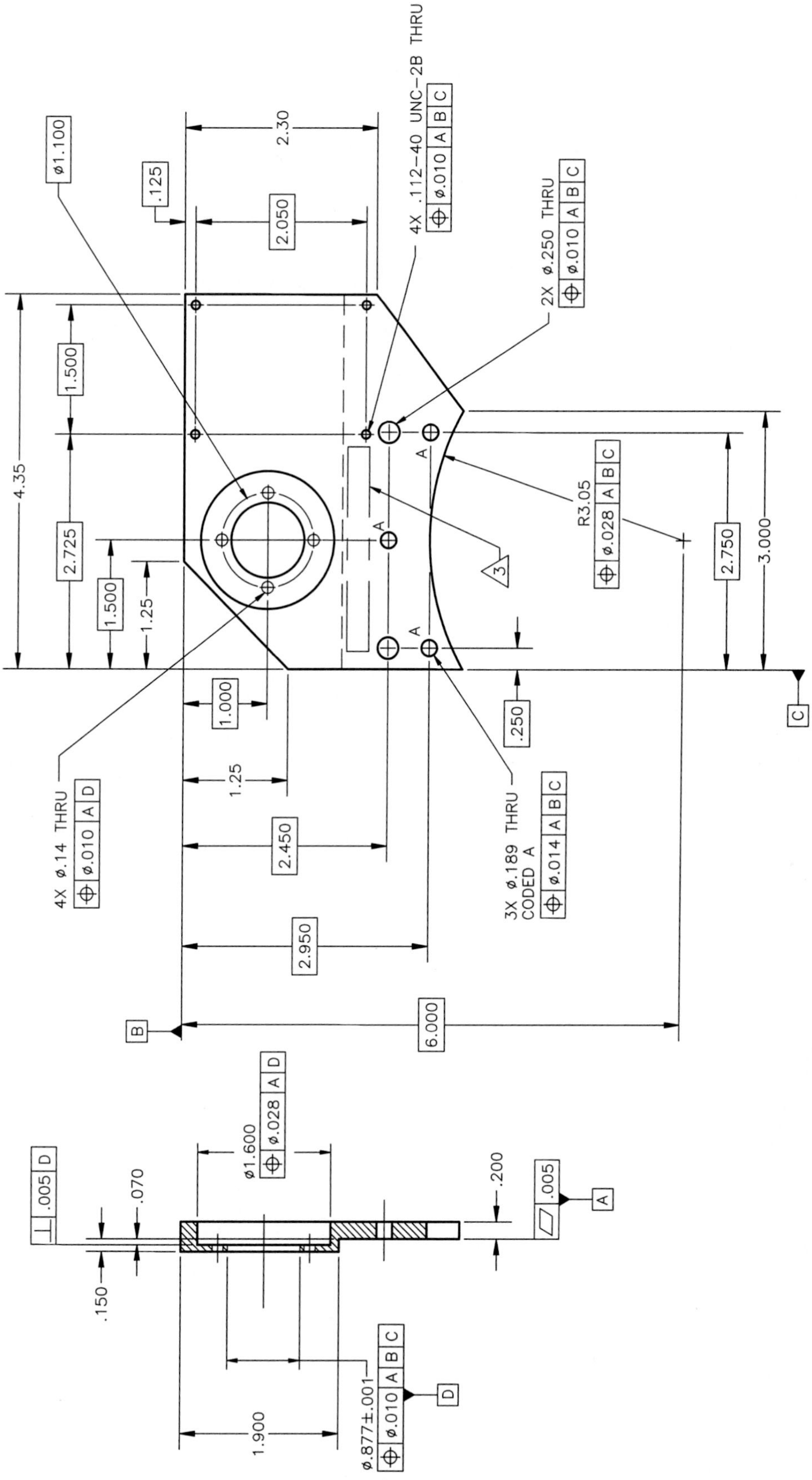

7. Draw the following object as previously instructed. The problem is shown with a half section for clarity. You do not need to draw a section. Untoleranced dimensions are ±.010. Save the drawing as P20-7.

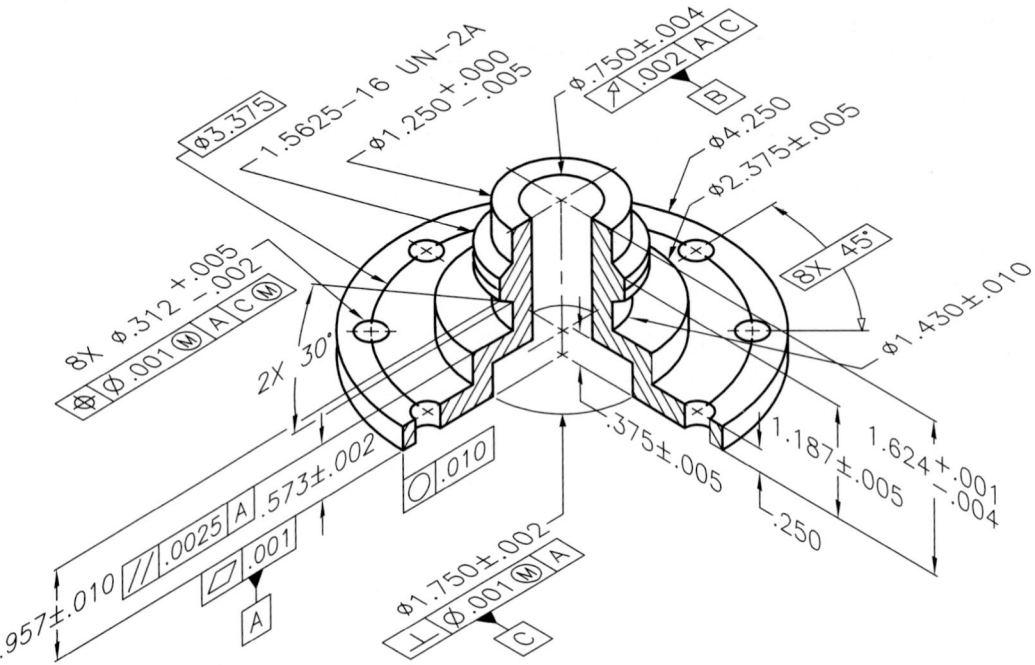

Section Views and Graphic Patterns

Learning Objectives

After completing this chapter, you will be able to do the following:

✓ Identify sectioning techniques.
✓ Draw section material using the **BHATCH** and **SOLID** commands.
✓ Insert hatch patterns into drawings using **DesignCenter** and tool palettes.
✓ Edit existing hatch patterns with the **HATCHEDIT** command.
✓ Draw objects containing solid fills.

Many drawings use repetitive symbols or objects to describe specific information. For example, the front elevation of the house shown in **Figure 21-1** contains patterns of lines that create graphic representations of siding, brick, and roof materials. The patterned arrangement of the objects of a symbol is known as a *graphic pattern*.

AutoCAD includes commands, such as **BHATCH** and **SOLID**, that can be used to draw graphic patterns quickly. One of the most common graphic patterns is a group of section lines added to a section view.

graphic pattern:
The patterned arrangement of the objects in a symbol.

Figure 21-1.
Graphic patterns are used to describe patterns of information on a drawing, such as the siding, brick, and roof materials added to the front elevation of a house.

Introduction to Section Views

In mechanical drafting, internal features in drawings appear as hidden lines. It is poor practice to dimension to hidden lines, but these features must be dimensioned. Therefore, section views are used to clarify the hidden features.

section view: A view that shows internal features as if a portion of the object has been cut away.

A *section view* shows internal features as if a portion of the object has been cut away. Section views are used in conjunction with multiview drawings to completely describe the exterior and interior features of an object.

When sections are drawn, a *cutting-plane line* is placed in one of the views to show where the cut was made. The cutting plane is the *saw* that cuts through the object to expose internal features. The cutting-plane line is drawn with a thick dashed or phantom line in accordance with ASME Y14.2M, *Line Conventions and Lettering*. The arrows on the cutting-plane line indicate the line of sight when looking at the section view.

cutting-plane line: The line that cuts through the object to expose internal features.

Cutting-plane lines are often labeled with letters that relate to the proper section view. A title, such as SECTION A-A, is placed under the view. When more than one section view is drawn, labels continue with B-B through Z-Z. The letters *I*, *O*, and *Q* are not used because they may be confused with numbers.

Labeling section views is necessary for drawings with multiple sections. When only one section view is present and its location is obvious, a label is not needed. Section lines are used in the section view to show where material has been cut away. See **Figure 21-2**.

Sectioning is also used in other drafting fields, such as architectural and structural drafting. Cross sections through buildings show the construction methods and materials. See **Figure 21-3**. The cutting-plane lines used in these fields are often composed of letter and number symbols. This helps coordinate the large number of sections found in a set of architectural drawings.

Figure 21-2.
A three-view multiview drawing with a full section view.

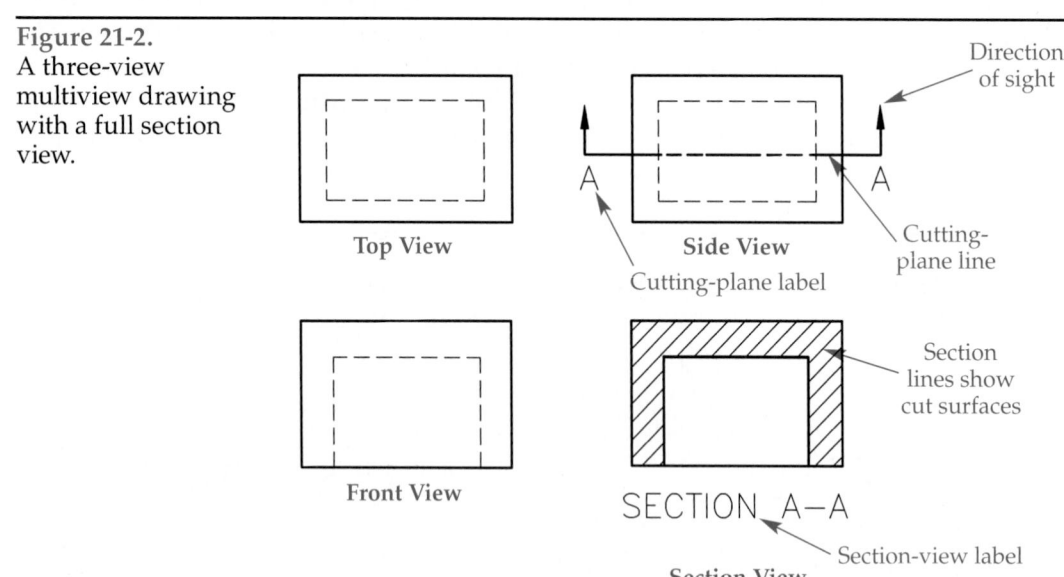

Top View

Side View

Front View

Direction of sight

Cutting-plane label

Cutting-plane line

Section lines show cut surfaces

SECTION A—A

Section-view label

Section View

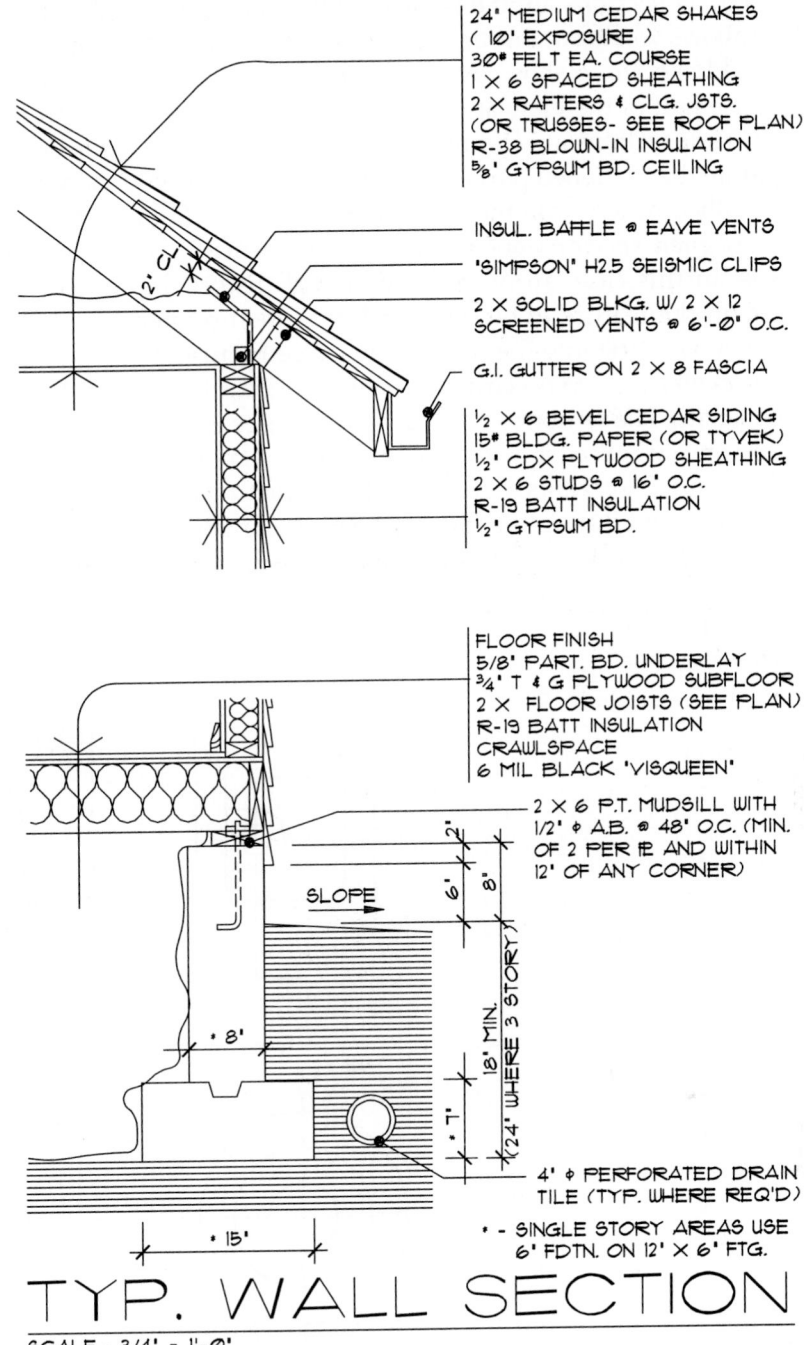

Figure 21-3. An architectural section view. (Alan Mascord Design Associates)

24' MEDIUM CEDAR SHAKES (10' EXPOSURE)
30# FELT EA. COURSE
1 X 6 SPACED SHEATHING
2 X RAFTERS & CLG. JSTS. (OR TRUSSES- SEE ROOF PLAN)
R-38 BLOWN-IN INSULATION
5/8' GYPSUM BD. CEILING

INSUL. BAFFLE @ EAVE VENTS
'SIMPSON' H2.5 SEISMIC CLIPS
2 X SOLID BLKG. W/ 2 X 12 SCREENED VENTS @ 6'-0' O.C.
G.I. GUTTER ON 2 X 8 FASCIA
1/2 X 6 BEVEL CEDAR SIDING
15# BLDG. PAPER (OR TYVEK)
1/2' CDX PLYWOOD SHEATHING
2 X 6 STUDS @ 16' O.C.
R-19 BATT INSULATION
1/2' GYPSUM BD.

FLOOR FINISH
5/8' PART. BD. UNDERLAY
3/4' T & G PLYWOOD SUBFLOOR
2 X FLOOR JOISTS (SEE PLAN)
R-19 BATT INSULATION
CRAWLSPACE
6 MIL BLACK 'VISQUEEN'

SLOPE

2 X 6 P.T. MUDSILL WITH 1/2' Ø A.B. @ 48' O.C. (MIN. OF 2 PER PC AND WITHIN 12' OF ANY CORNER)

18' MIN. ('24' WHERE 3 STORY)

4' Ø PERFORATED DRAIN TILE (TYP. WHERE REQ'D)

• - SINGLE STORY AREAS USE 6' FDTN. ON 12' X 6' FTG.

TYP. WALL SECTION

SCALE : 3/4' = 1'-0'

Types of Sections

Many types of sections are available for the drafter to use. The section used depends on the detail to be sectioned. For example, one object may require the section be taken completely through the object. Another may only need to remove a small portion to expose the interior features.

Full sections remove half the object. Refer to **Figure 21-2**. In this type of section, the cutting plane passes completely through the object along the center plane, as shown by the cutting-plane line.

full sections: Sections in which half the object is removed.

Offset sections are the same as full sections, except the cutting plane is staggered. This allows you to cut through features that are not in a straight line. See **Figure 21-4.**

Half sections show one-quarter of the object removed. The term *half* is used because half of the view appears in section and the other half is shown as an exterior view. Half sections are commonly used on symmetrical objects. A centerline is used to separate the sectioned part of the view from the unsectioned portion. Hidden lines are normally omitted from the unsectioned side. See **Figure 21-5.**

Aligned sections are used when a feature is out of alignment with the center plane. In this case, an offset section will distort the image. The cutting plane cuts through the feature to be sectioned. It is then rotated to align with the center plane before projecting into the section view. See **Figure 21-6.**

Revolved sections clarify the contour of objects that have the same shape throughout their length. The section may be revolved in place within the object, or part of the view may be broken away. See **Figure 21-7.** This type of section makes dimensioning easier.

Removed sections serve much the same function as revolved sections. The section view is removed from the regular view. A cutting-plane line shows where the section has been taken. When multiple removed sections are taken, the cutting-plane lines

Figure 21-4.
An offset section.

Figure 21-5.
A half section.

Figure 21-6.
An aligned section.

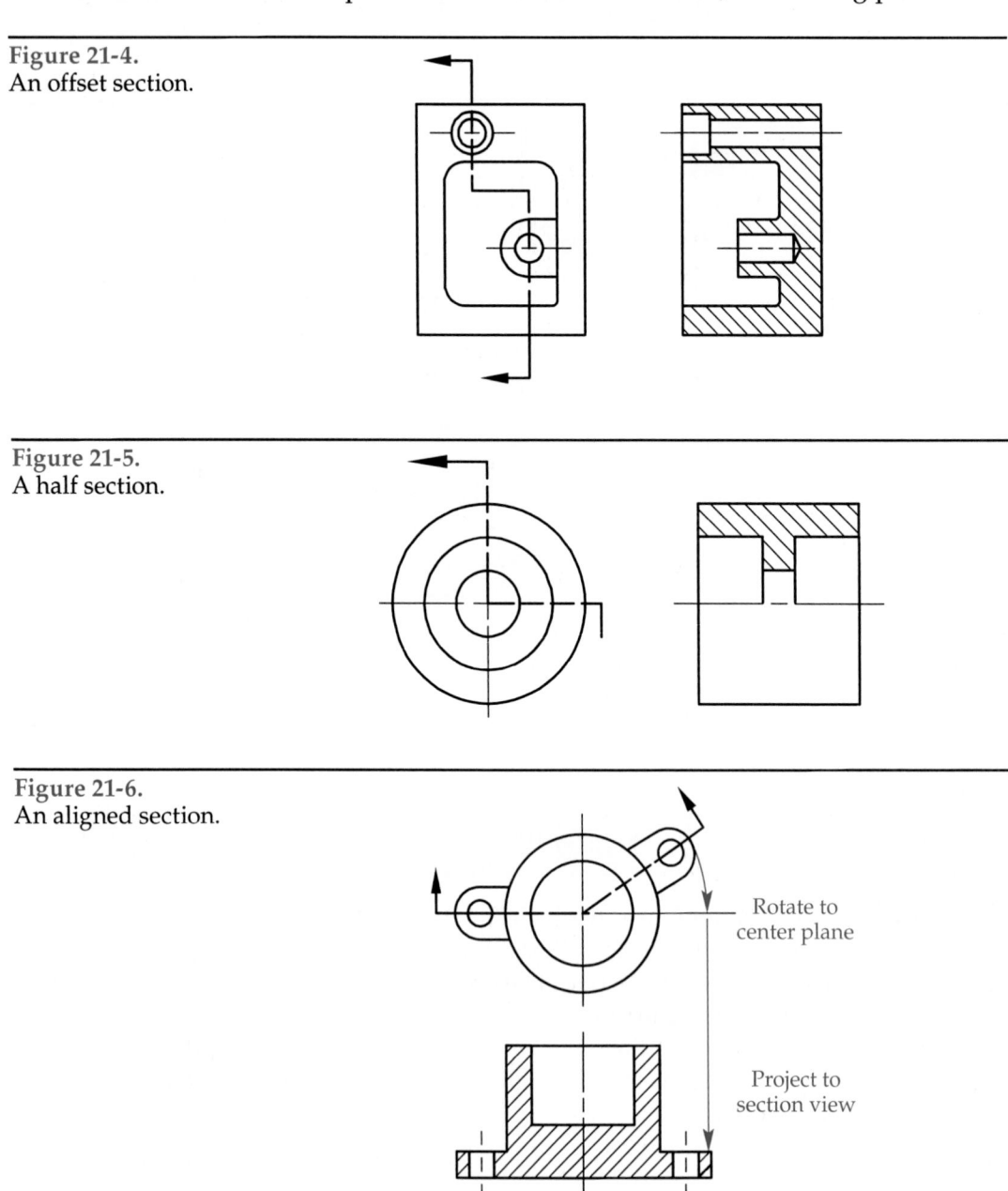

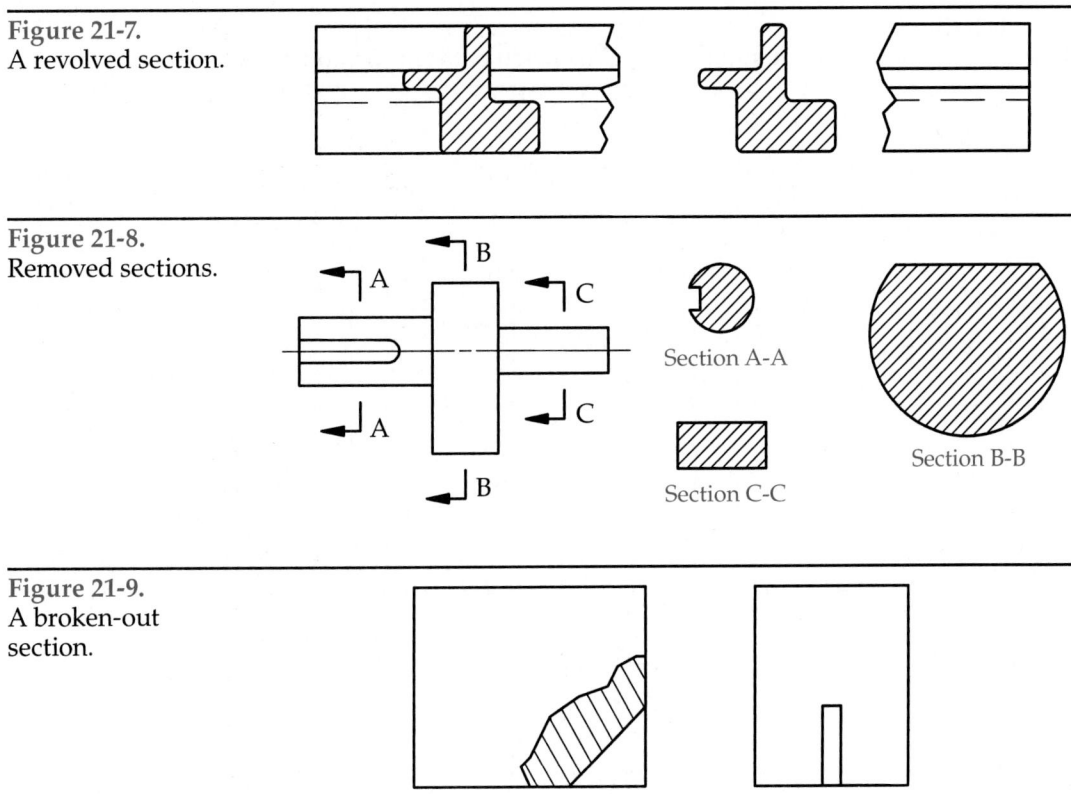

Figure 21-7.
A revolved section.

Figure 21-8.
Removed sections.

Section A-A

Section C-C

Section B-B

Figure 21-9.
A broken-out
section.

and related views are labeled. Drawing only the ends of the cutting-plane lines simplifies the views. See **Figure 21-8**.

Broken-out sections show only a small portion of the object removed. This type of section is used to clarify a hidden feature. See **Figure 21-9**.

broken-out sections: Sections that show only a small portion of the object removed.

Section Line Symbols

Section line symbols are placed in the section view to show where material has been cut away. A sampling of standard AutoCAD hatch patterns is shown in **Figure 21-10**. The following rules govern section line symbol usage:

- Section lines are placed at 45° unless another angle is required to satisfy the next two rules.
- Section lines should not be drawn parallel or perpendicular to any other adjacent lines on the drawing.
- Section lines should not cross object lines.
- Avoid section lines placed at angles greater than 75° or less than 15° from horizontal.

Section lines may be drawn using different patterns to represent the specific type of material. Equally spaced section lines represent a general application. This is adequate in most situations. Additional patterns are not necessary if the type of material is clearly indicated in the title block. Different section line material symbols are needed when connected parts of different materials are sectioned.

hatch patterns: AutoCAD's standard section line symbols.

AutoCAD provides standard section line symbols. These are referred to as *hatch patterns*. These symbols are defined in the acad.pat file. The AutoCAD pattern labeled ANSI31 is the general section line symbol and is the default pattern in a new drawing. It is also used when representing cast iron in a section. The ANSI32 symbol is used for sectioning steel. When you change to a different hatch pattern, the new pattern becomes the default in the current drawing until it is changed.

Figure 21-10.

Examples of some of the standard AutoCAD hatch patterns. (Autodesk, Inc.)

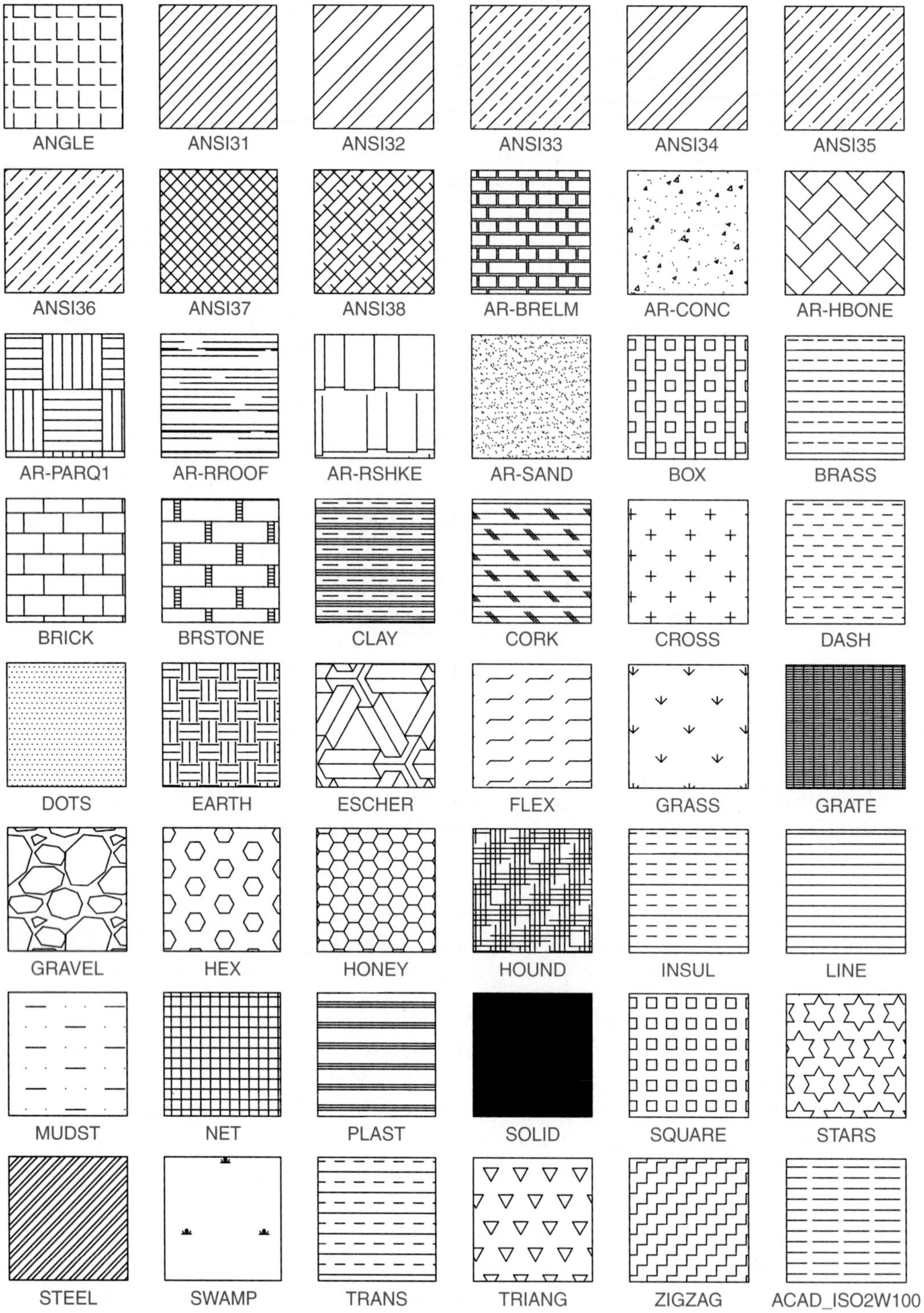

When very thin objects are sectioned, the material may be completely blackened or shaded to clarify features. To do this, use AutoCAD's Solid hatch pattern. The ASME Y14.2M standard recommends that very thin sections be drawn without section lines or solid fill.

AutoCAD and Its Applications—Basics

Drawing Hatch Patterns Using the Bhatch Command

AutoCAD hatch patterns are not limited to sectioning. They can be used as artistic patterns in a graphic layout for an advertisement or promotion. They might also be added as shading on a technical illustration or an architectural elevation, as shown in **Figure 21-1**.

The **BHATCH** command simplifies the hatching process by automatically hatching any enclosed area. Hatch patterns are selected and applied using the **Hatch and Gradient** dialog box. Access this dialog box with the **BHATCH** command by picking the **Hatch** button on the **2D Draw** control panel in the **Dashboard** or the **Draw** toolbar, by picking **Draw > Hatch...** in the pull-down menu, or by typing H or BHATCH.

The **Hatch and Gradient** dialog box is divided into **Hatch** and **Gradient** tabs. The **Hatch** tab is separated into different areas that control the hatch settings. See **Figure 21-11**.

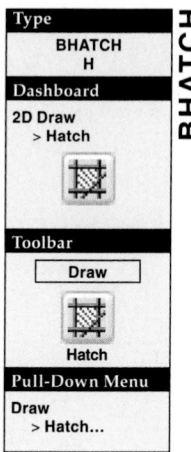

Type
BHATCH
H
Dashboard
2D Draw > Hatch
Toolbar
Draw
Hatch
Pull-Down Menu
Draw > Hatch...

Selecting a Hatch Pattern

The hatch pattern is selected in the **Type and pattern** area on the **Hatch** tab of the **Hatch and Gradient** dialog box. The following categories of hatch patterns are available in the **Type:** drop-down list:

- **Predefined.** Contains predefined AutoCAD patterns stored in the acad.pat and acadiso.pat files.
- **User defined.** Creates a pattern of lines based on the current linetype in your drawing. You can control the angle and spacing of the lines.

Figure 21-11.
The **Hatch** tab of the **Hatch and Gradient** dialog box.

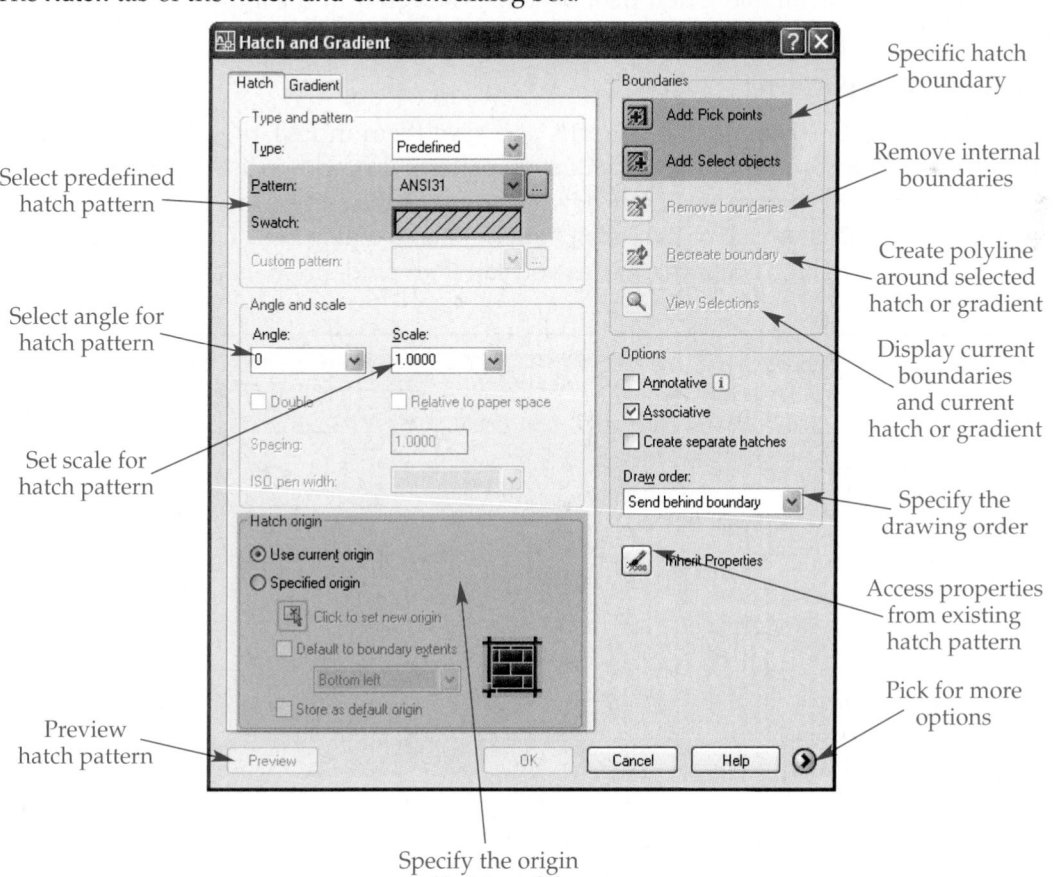

Select predefined hatch pattern

Select angle for hatch pattern

Set scale for hatch pattern

Preview hatch pattern

Specify the origin of hatch or fill

Specific hatch boundary

Remove internal boundaries

Create polyline around selected hatch or gradient

Display current boundaries and current hatch or gradient

Specify the drawing order

Access properties from existing hatch pattern

Pick for more options

- **Custom.** Allows you to specify a pattern defined in any custom PAT file that you have added to the AutoCAD search path. (To use the patterns in the supplied acad.pat and acadiso.pat files, choose Predefined.)

Predefined hatch patterns

AutoCAD has many predefined hatch patterns. To select a predefined hatch pattern, select **Predefined** in the **Type:** drop-down list and then select the predefined pattern. You can select the pattern from the **Pattern:** drop-down list, or you can pick the ellipsis (**...**) button next to the **Pattern:** drop-down arrow to display the **Hatch Pattern Palette** dialog box. See **Figure 21-12.**

The **Hatch Pattern Palette** dialog box provides sample images of the predefined hatch patterns. The hatch patterns are divided among the four tabs: **ANSI, ISO, Other Predefined**, and **Custom.** Select the desired pattern from the appropriate tab and pick the **OK** button to return to the **Hatch and Gradient** dialog box. The selected pattern is displayed in the **Swatch:** preview box and listed in the **Pattern:** text box. You can also access the **Hatch Pattern Palette** dialog box by picking the image displayed in the **Swatch:** preview box.

You can control the angle and scale of any predefined pattern using the **Angle:** and **Scale:** drop-down lists located in the **Angle and scale** area. For predefined ISO patterns, you can also control the ISO pen width using the **ISO pen width:** drop-down list.

User defined hatch patterns

A user defined hatch pattern is a pattern of lines drawn using the current linetype. The angle for the pattern relative to the X axis is set in the **Angle:** text box, and the spacing between the lines is set in the **Spacing:** text box. Both of these options are located in the **Angle and scale** area of the **Hatch and Gradient** dialog box.

You can also specify double hatch lines by selecting the **Double** check box. This check box is only available when User defined is selected in the **Type:** drop-down list. Figure 21-13 shows examples of user defined hatch patterns.

Custom hatch patterns

You can create custom hatch patterns and save them in PAT files. When you select Custom in the **Type:** drop-down list, the **Custom pattern:** drop-down list is enabled. You can select a custom pattern from this drop-down list, or pick the ellipsis (**...**) button to select the pattern from the **Custom** tab of the **Hatch Pattern Palette** dialog box. You can set the angle and scale of custom hatch patterns, just as you can with predefined hatch patterns.

Figure 21-12.
The **Hatch Pattern Palette** dialog box can be used to select a predefined or custom hatch pattern.

Select a tab to see other patterns

Select icon for desired hatch pattern

Pick to return to **Hatch and Gradient** dialog box

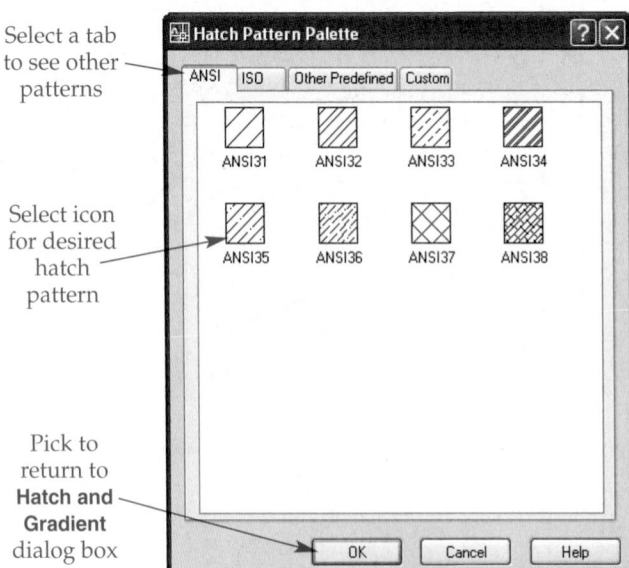

Figure 21-13.
Examples of user defined hatch patterns with different hatch angles and spacing.

Angle	0°	45°	0°	45°
Spacing	.125	.125	.250	.250
Single Hatch				
Double Hatch				

Setting the Hatch Pattern Scale

Predefined and custom hatch patterns can be scaled by entering a value in the **Scale:** text box. The drop-down list contains common scales in .25 increments. The scales in this list start with .25 and progress to a scale of 2, although you can type any scale in the text box.

The pattern scale default is 1. If the drawn pattern is too small or too large, enter a new scale. **Figure 21-14** shows examples of different scales.

PROFESSIONAL TIP

Use a smaller hatch scale for small objects and a larger hatch scale for larger objects. This makes your section lines look appropriate for the drawing scale. Often you must use your best judgment when selecting a hatch scale.

It is important to consider the scale factor of a drawing when selecting the hatch pattern scale. You must enter an appropriate hatch scale in order to make sure the hatch pattern is shown on-screen and plotted at the proper size. To understand the concept of hatch scale, look at the section view shown in **Figure 21-15**. In this example, the section line spacing should be the same distance apart regardless of drawing scale. The section lines on the drawing displayed at a scale of 1:1 are shown correctly. The section lines drawn using the same hatch scale are too close when the drawing is displayed at a scale of 1:2, and are too far apart when the drawing is displayed at a scale of 2:1. To overcome this issue, you must adjust the hatch pattern scale according to the drawing scale. This involves finding the scale factor. The scale factor can be calculated manually and applied to hatch pattern scale, or it can be adjusted by AutoCAD using annotative functionality.

Figure 21-14.
Hatch pattern scale factors.

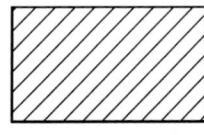
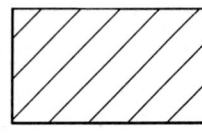
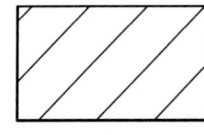

Scale = 1   Scale = 2   Scale = 3

Figure 21-15.
The hatch pattern scale may appear incorrect as the drawing scale changes.

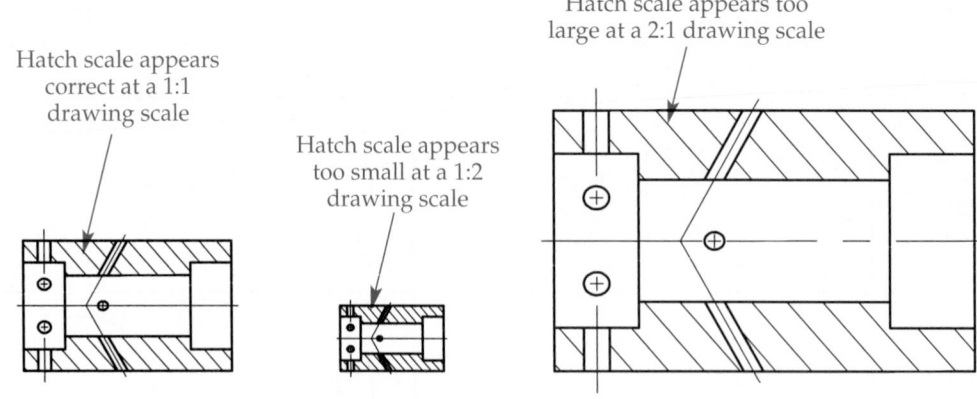

Hatch scale appears correct at a 1:1 drawing scale

Hatch scale appears too small at a 1:2 drawing scale

Hatch scale appears too large at a 2:1 drawing scale

Scaling hatch patterns manually

To manually adjust hatch scale according to a specific drawing scale, you must calculate the drawing scale factor. Then multiply the scale factor by the desired plotted hatch scale to get the model space hatch scale. Enter this value in the **Scale:** text box. **Figure 21-16** shows examples of adjusting hatch scale according to drawing scale.

Annotative hatch patterns

Pick the **Annotative** check box in the **Options** area to make the hatch pattern annotative. Annotative hatch patterns are scaled by AutoCAD according to the annotation scale you select, which is the same as the drawing scale, eliminating the need for you to calculate the scale factor and multiply the scale factor by the hatch scale. When an annotation scale is selected from the **Annotation Scale** flyout button located on the status bar, the scale factor is determined by AutoCAD and is automatically applied to annotative hatch patterns, or any annotative object. The result is a hatch pattern that is displayed at the proper scale regardless of the drawing scale, much like the example shown in **Figure 21-16**, but without having to change the hatch scale between different drawing scales. For example, if you enter a value in the **Scale:** text box that

Figure 21-16.
The hatch pattern scale may require adjusting, depending on the drawing scale.

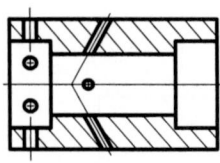 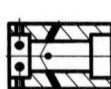 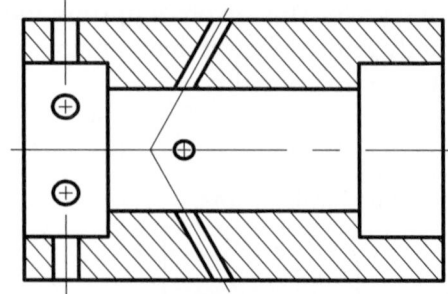

Drawing Scale: 1:1
Drawing Scale Factor: 1
Hatch Scale: 1

Drawing Scale: 1:2
Drawing Scale Factor: 2
Hatch Scale: 2

Drawing Scale: 2:1
Drawing Scale Factor: .5
Hatch Scale: .5

is appropriate for an annotation scale of 1/4″ = 1′-0″, and then change the annotation scale to 1″ = 1′-0″, the displayed scale of the hatch pattern relative to the drawing scale does not change. It looks the same on the 1/4″ = 1′-0″ scale drawing as it does on the 1″ = 1′-0″ scale drawing.

NOTE

When displayed in a floating viewport, annotative hatch patterns remain planar to the layout, even if the drawing view is rotated, using 3D view commands, or twisted into a position that is nonplanar to the layout, using the **TWist** option of the **DVIEW** command. See Chapter 25 for more information about floating viewports.

Scaling hatch patterns relative to paper space

The **Relative to paper space** check box in the **Angle and scale** area is used to scale the hatch pattern relative to the scale of the active viewport. You must enter a floating layout viewport in order to select the **Relative to paper space** check box. The hatch scale automatically adjusts according to the viewport scale. For example, a floating viewport scale set to 4:1 uses a scale factor of .25 (1 ÷ 4 = .25). If you enter a hatch scale of 1, the hatch scale is automatically drawn at a scale of .25 (1 × .25 = .25).

Setting the Hatch Origin Point

When creating hatch patterns, you may sometimes want lines on the hatch pattern to line up with an existing object. This could be the case when using one of the brick hatch patterns, for example. By default, the current UCS origin point is used as the defining point for how the hatch pattern is created and how it repeats itself. The pattern of a hatch can be started in a different location by specifying a custom origin point.

In the **Hatch origin** area of the **Hatch and Gradient** dialog box, the default setting is **Use current origin**. This refers to the current UCS origin. To specify a different origin point, select **Specified origin**. See **Figure 21-17**. When this option is selected, the other settings become available. Picking the **Click to set new origin** button temporarily hides the **Hatch and Gradient** dialog box so a different origin can be selected in the drawing area. For example, if you want a hatch pattern to start in the lower-left corner of a rectangle, use the **Endpoint** object snap to select the corner of the rectangle. In **Figure 21-18A**, the **Use current origin** setting is used. In **Figure 21-18B**, notice how it seems that the hatch pattern starts perfectly from the lower-left corner of the rectangle. This is because this corner was picked to be the origin point. After you select a point for the origin, the **Hatch and Gradient** dialog box is displayed again.

The hatch origin point can be aligned with specific points on the hatch boundary. To use this setting, check the **Default to boundary extents** box. When this is checked, the drop-down list below it becomes available. The options in the drop-down list are **Bottom left**, **Bottom right**, **Top right**, **Top left**, and **Center**. The hatch origin is defined at the selected point on the boundary.

Figure 21-17.
The **Specified origin** setting in the **Hatch origin** area of the **Hatch** tab activates the other hatch origin settings.

Pick to specify a different origin point

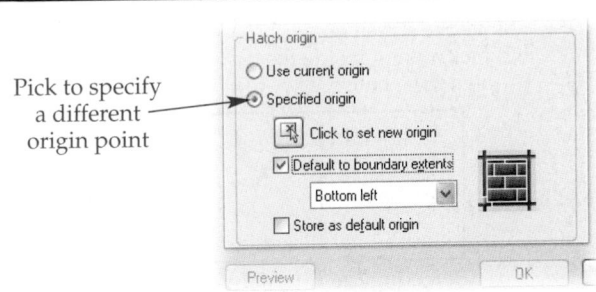

Figure 21-18.
A—The **Use current origin** setting is used. B—The **Specified origin** option is selected and the **Click to set new origin** button is used to select the lower-left corner of the rectangle.

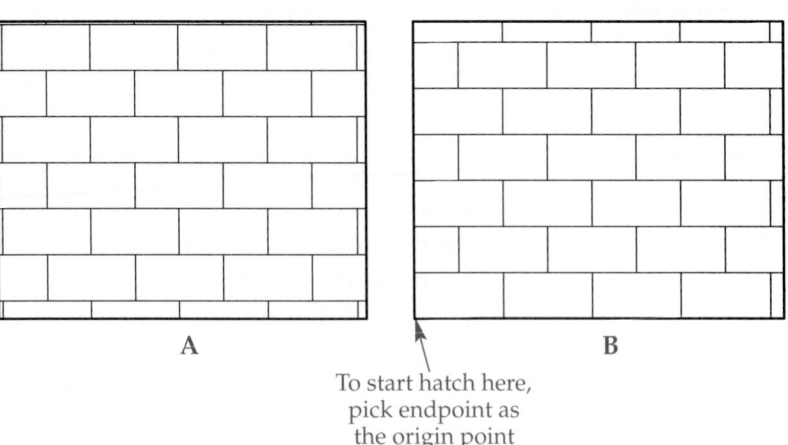

A   B

To start hatch here,
pick endpoint as
the origin point

The custom origin point can be saved by checking **Store as default origin**. The X and Y coordinates are saved to the **HPORIGIN** system variable. This new origin point is then used as the default for new hatch patterns.

Selecting Areas to Be Hatched

Areas to be hatched can be selected by one of two methods: picking points or selecting objects. Both of these selection methods are accessed by picking a button in the **Boundaries** area of the **Hatch and Gradient** dialog box.

Using the **Add: Pick points** button is the easiest method of defining an area to be hatched. When you pick the button, the drawing returns. Pick a point within the region to be hatched, and AutoCAD automatically defines the boundary around the selected point. More than one internal point can be selected. When you are finished selecting points, press [Enter] to return to the **Hatch and Gradient** dialog box. Then pick the **OK** button to apply the hatch. See **Figure 21-19.**

NOTE

At the Select internal point: prompt, you can type U or UNDO to undo the last selection, in case you picked the wrong area. You can also undo the hatch pattern by typing U after the pattern is drawn. However, to save time, you can preview the hatch before applying it.

Use the **Add: Select objects** button to define the hatch boundary if you have items that you want to hatch by picking the object, rather than picking inside the object. See **Figure 21-20.** These items can be circles, polygons, or closed polylines. This method works especially well if the object to be hatched is crossed by other objects, such as the graph lines that cross the bars in **Figure 21-21.** Picking a point inside the bar results

Figure 21-19.
Defining the hatch boundary by picking a point.

Move the screen cursor and pick a point inside the area to be hatched

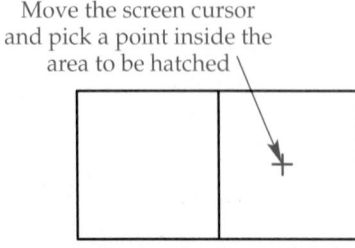

Selecting the Internal Point   The Results

Figure 21-20.
Selecting objects to be hatched.

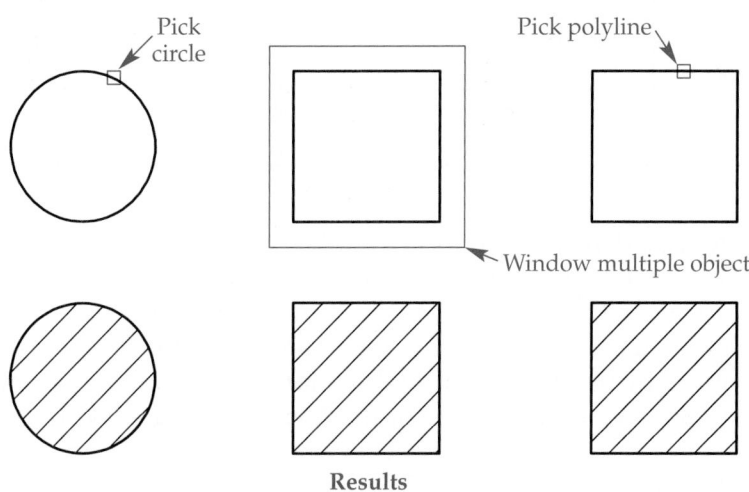

Figure 21-21.
A—Applying a hatch pattern to objects that cross each other using the **Add: Pick points** button.
B—Applying a hatch pattern to a closed polygon using the **Add: Select objects** button.

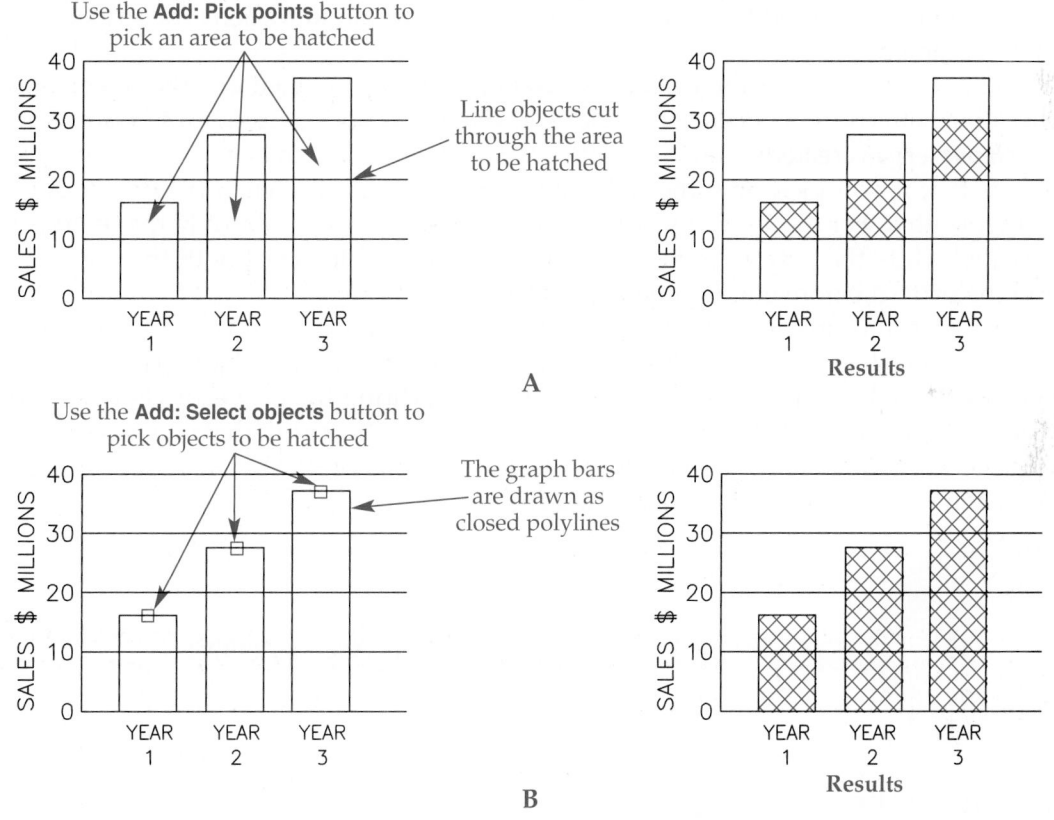

in the hatch displayed in **Figure 21-21A.** You can pick inside each individual area of each bar, but this can be time-consuming. If the bars were drawn using a closed polyline, all you have to do is use the **Add: Select objects** button to pick each bar. See **Figure 21-21B.**

The **Add: Select objects** button can also be used to pick an object inside an area to be hatched to exclude it from the hatch pattern. An example of this is the text shown inside the hatch area in **Figure 21-22.**

Figure 21-22.
Using the **Add: Select objects** button to exclude an object from the hatch pattern.

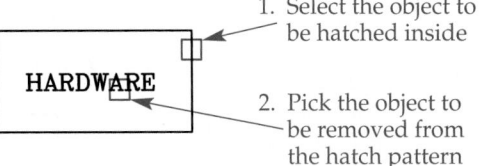

1. Select the object to be hatched inside

2. Pick the object to be removed from the hatch pattern

Results

The **Remove boundaries** button is active after either points or objects have been selected. Picking this button returns you to the drawing screen and allows you to select objects to remove their boundaries from the hatch area. Once the objects have been selected, press [Enter] to display the **Hatch and Gradient** dialog box. Boundaries can also be removed by using the **remove Boundaries** option at the Command: prompt while using the **Add: Pick points** button or the **Add: Select objects** button.

Specifying the Hatch Pattern Composition

The **BHATCH** command creates associative hatch patterns by default, but it can be set to create nonassociative patterns. *Associative hatch patterns* update automatically when the boundary is edited. If the boundary is stretched, scaled, or otherwise edited, the new area automatically fills with the original hatch pattern. Associative hatch patterns can be edited using the **HATCHEDIT** command, which is described later in this chapter.

The **Options** area of the **Hatch and Gradient** dialog box contains the **Associative** check box. This option is selected by default. When it is not selected, a *nonassociative hatch pattern* is created. A nonassociative hatch is independent of its boundaries. This means that if you pick only the hatch boundary to edit, the hatch pattern does not change with it. For example, if you pick a hatch boundary to scale, only the boundary is scaled while the pattern remains the same. You need to select both the boundary and the pattern before editing if you want to modify both.

To create multiple hatch patterns, multiple areas and objects can be selected during a single procedure. By default, these hatch patterns are a single object. This means if you select one hatch pattern, they are all selected. Editing the properties of one of the hatch patterns edits all of them. This may not always be the result that you want. When you check the **Create separate hatches** check box in the **Options** area before applying the hatch patterns, individual hatch patterns are created for each boundary.

associative hatch patterns: Patterns that update automatically when the boundary is edited.

nonassociative hatch pattern: A pattern that does not automatically update when the boundary is changed.

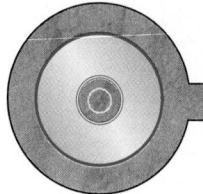

Exercise 21-1
Complete the exercise on the Student CD.

Defining the Drawing Order

A hatch pattern can be displayed in front of or behind other objects when it is placed in the drawing. The **Draw order** options in the **Options** area of the **Hatch and Gradient** dialog box control the order of display when the hatch pattern overlaps another object. The following options are available in the **Draw order** drop-down list:

- **Send behind boundary.** The hatch pattern appears behind the boundary that defines the hatch pattern area. This is the default option.
- **Bring in front of boundary.** The hatch pattern appears on top of the boundary that defines the hatch pattern area.
- **Do not assign.** No drawing order setting is assigned to the hatch pattern.

- **Send to back.** The hatch pattern is sent behind all other objects in the drawing. Any objects that are in the hatching area appear as if they are on top of the hatch pattern.
- **Bring to front.** The hatch pattern is in front, or on top of, all other objects in the drawing. Any objects that are in the hatching area appear as if they are behind the hatch pattern.

If the draw order setting needs to be changed after the hatch pattern is created, use the **DRAWORDER** command. You can also select the hatch pattern, right-click, and then select the appropriate shortcut menu option from the **Draw Order** cascading menu.

Selecting an Existing Pattern

You can specify the hatch pattern by selecting an identical hatch pattern from the drawing. Picking the **Inherit Properties** button allows you to select a previously drawn hatch pattern and use it for the current hatch pattern settings. The prompts look like this:

Select associative hatch object: *(pick the desired hatch pattern)*
Inherited Properties: Name *<hatch name>*, Scale *<hatch scale>*, Angle *<hatch angle>*
Select internal point: *(pick a point inside the new area to be hatched)*

After picking the internal point desired, press [Enter] to return to the **Hatch and Gradient** dialog box. The dialog box displays the settings of the selected pattern. At the Select internal points or [Select objects/remove Boundaries]: prompt, typing S for the **Select objects** option allows you to select additional objects for the hatch pattern. Type B for the **remove Boundaries** option to remove objects from the current selection set being hatched.

Previewing the Hatch

Before applying a hatch pattern to the selected area, you can use preview tools to be sure the hatch pattern and hatch boundary settings are correct. The following buttons, which are found in the **Hatch and Gradient** dialog box, can be used to preview the boundary and hatch pattern:

- **View Selections button (Boundaries area).** You can instruct AutoCAD to let you see the boundaries of selected objects. The **View Selections** button is available after you pick objects to be hatched. Pick this button to display the drawing with the hatch boundaries highlighted. When you are finished, press [Enter] or right-click to return to the **Hatch and Gradient** dialog box.
- **Preview button.** Pick the **Preview** button if you want to look at the hatch pattern before you apply it to the drawing. This allows you to see if any changes need to be made before the hatch is drawn. When you use this option, AutoCAD temporarily places the hatch pattern on your drawing. You can press [Enter] or right-click to accept the results. If you want to make changes after previewing the hatch, press [Esc] to return to the **Hatch and Gradient** dialog box. Change the hatch pattern, scale, or rotation angle as needed and preview the hatch again. When you are satisfied with the preview of the hatch, pick the **OK** button in the **Hatch and Gradient** dialog box to apply it to the drawing.

Hatching Objects with Islands

Boundaries inside another boundary are known as *islands*. AutoCAD can either ignore these internal boundary objects and hatch through them or consider them as islands and hatch around them. See **Figure 21-23**.

islands: Boundaries inside another boundary.

When you use the **Add: Pick points** button to hatch an internal area, islands are left unhatched by default, as shown in **Figure 21-23B**. However, if you want islands to be hatched, use the **remove Boundaries** option or pick the **Remove boundaries** button in the **Hatch and Gradient** dialog box after selecting the internal point. The drawing window returns with the following prompts:

Figure 21-23.
A—Original objects. B—Using the **Add: Pick points** button to hatch an internal area leaves islands unhatched. C—After picking an internal point, use the **Remove boundaries** button and pick the islands. This allows the islands to be hatched.

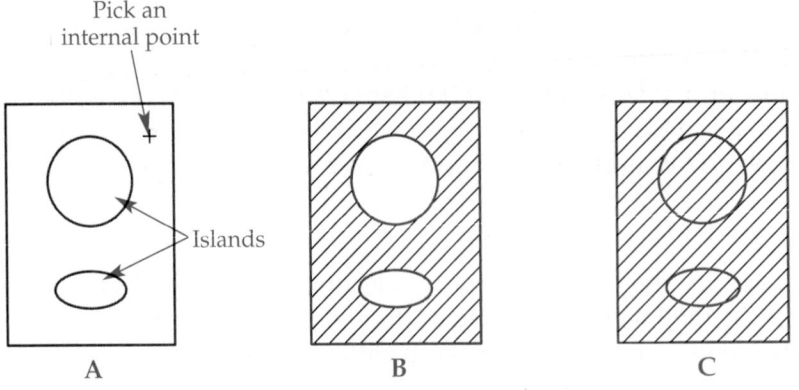

Select objects or [Add boundaries]: *(pick the islands to remove)*
Select objects or [Add boundaries//Undo]: ↵

Select the islands to remove and press [Enter] to return to the dialog box. The island objects are now hatched. See **Figure 21-23C**.

The island detection style and method is set in the **Islands** area of the **Hatch and Gradient** dialog box. By default, this area is hidden. Expand the dialog box to show this area by picking the **More Options** button in the lower-right corner of the dialog box. Refer to **Figure 21-11**. This area of the **Hatch and Gradient** dialog box can be hidden again by picking the **Less Options** button in the lower-right corner. The **Islands** area is shown in **Figure 21-24**. If no islands exist, specifying an island detection style has no effect.

Three options allow you to choose the features to be hatched. These options are illustrated by the images in the dialog box. The three options are:

- **Normal.** Hatches inward from the outer boundary. If AutoCAD encounters an island, it turns off hatching until it encounters another island. Then the hatching is reactivated. Every other closed boundary is hatched with this option.
- **Outer.** Hatches inward from the outer boundary. AutoCAD turns hatching off when it encounters an island and does not turn it back on. AutoCAD hatches only the outermost level of the structure and leaves the internal structure blank.
- **Ignore.** Ignores all islands and hatches everything within the selected boundary.

PROFESSIONAL TIP

Pick the **Outer** island display style to ensure islands are not unintentionally hatched.

Improving Boundary Hatching Speed

In most situations, boundary hatching works with satisfactory speed. Normally, AutoCAD evaluates the entire drawing visible on screen to establish the boundary. This process can take some time on a large drawing.

You can improve the hatching speed and resolve other problems using options in the expanded **Hatch and Gradient** dialog box. See **Figure 21-25**. The drop-down list in the **Boundary set** area specifies what is evaluated when hatching. The default setting is Current viewport. If you want to limit what AutoCAD evaluates when hatching, you can define the boundary area so the **BHATCH** command only considers a specified

AutoCAD and Its Applications—Basics

Figure 21-24.
The **Islands** area of the **Hatch and Gradient** dialog box is displayed by picking the **Less Options** button.

Island detection style

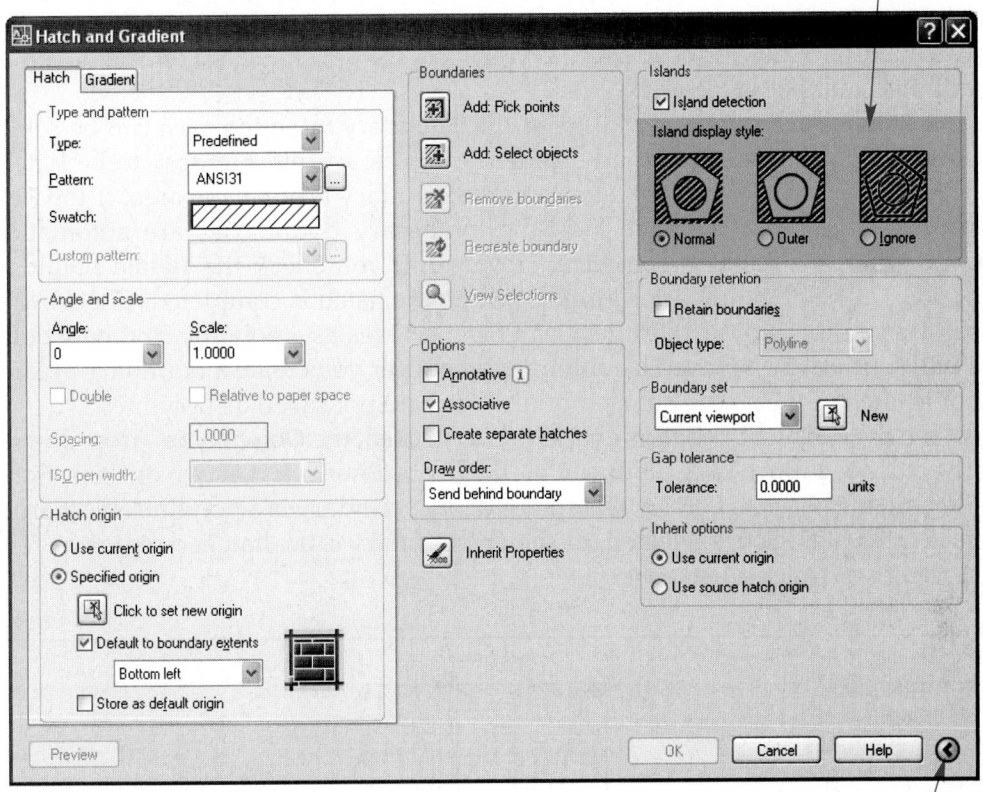

Pick to hide right column of dialog box

Figure 21-25.
The **Boundary retention** and **Boundary set** areas of the **Hatch and Gradient** dialog box provide options to improve hatching efficiency.

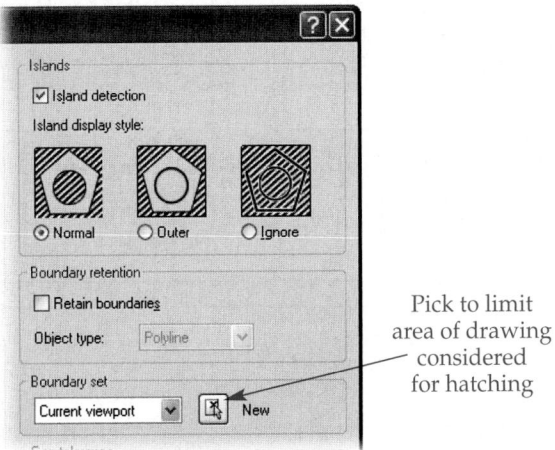

Pick to limit area of drawing considered for hatching

portion of the drawing. To do this, pick the **New** button. At the Select objects: prompt, use a window to select the features of the object to be hatched. This is demonstrated in **Figure 21-26**.

After you select the object(s), the **Hatch and Gradient** dialog box returns. Notice in the **Boundary set** area that the drop-down list now displays Existing set, as shown in **Figure 21-27**. The drawing with the new hatch pattern applied is shown in **Figure 21-28**. You can make as many boundary sets as you wish. However, the last one made remains current until another is created.

The **Retain boundaries** check box in the **Boundary retention** area can be selected as soon as a boundary set is made. When you pick an internal area to be hatched, AutoCAD automatically creates a temporary boundary around the area. If the **Retain boundaries** check box is unchecked, the temporary boundaries are automatically removed when the hatch is complete. However, if you check the **Retain boundaries** check box, the hatch boundaries are kept when the hatch is completed. Checking this box allows you to keep the boundary of a hatched area as a polyline, and new boundaries will continue to be saved as polylines whenever you create a boundary area. The default is unchecked, so the hatched boundaries are not saved as polylines.

When the **Retain boundaries** check box is checked, the **Object type:** drop-down list is activated. See **Figure 21-29**. Notice that the drop-down list has two options: Polyline (the default) and Region. If Polyline is selected, the boundary is a polyline object around the hatch area. If Region is selected, the hatch boundary is the hatched region. A *region* is a closed two-dimensional area.

region: A closed two-dimensional area.

Figure 21-26.
The boundary set limits the area that AutoCAD evaluates during a hatching operation.

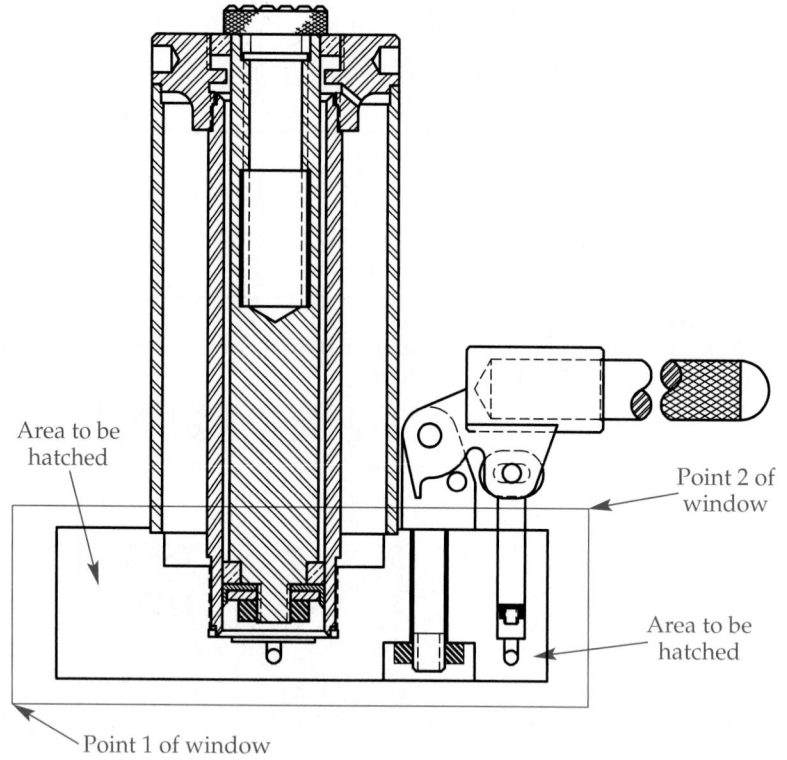

Area to be hatched

Point 2 of window

Area to be hatched

Point 1 of window

Figure 21-27.
When the drop-down list in the **Boundary set** area displays Existing set, AutoCAD only evaluates objects within the boundary for the hatch.

Figure 21-28.
Results of hatching
the drawing in
Figure 21-26 after
selecting a boundary
set.

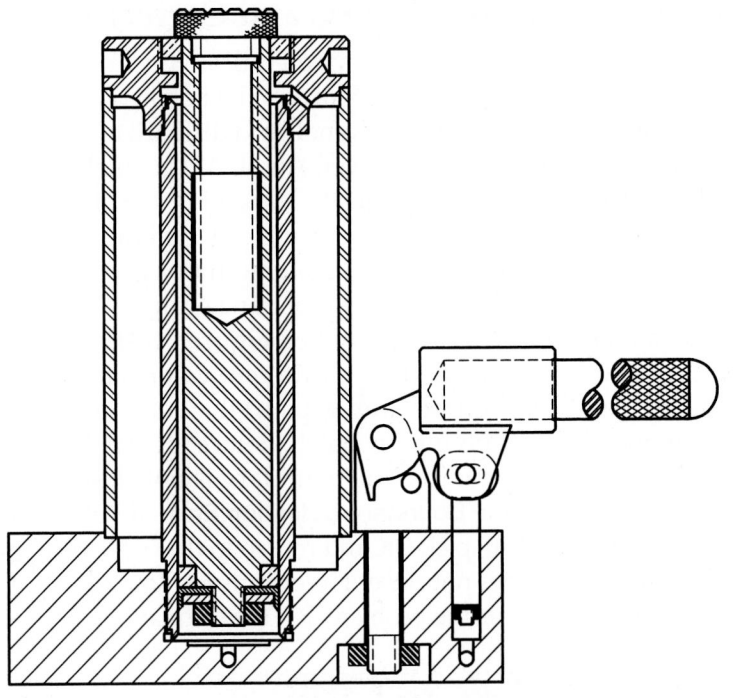

Figure 21-29.
A boundary can be
saved as either a
polyline or a region.
These options are
only available if the
Retain boundaries
option is checked.

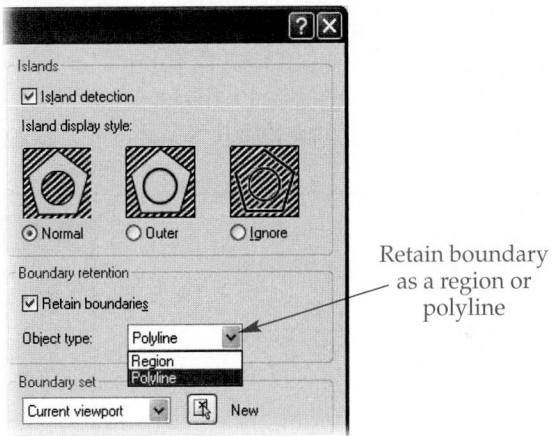

Retain boundary
as a region or
polyline

PROFESSIONAL TIP

A number of techniques can help you save time when hatching,
especially with large and complex drawings. These include:
- Zoom in on the area to be hatched to make it easier for you to
  define the boundary. When you zoom into an area to be hatched,
  the hatch process is much faster because AutoCAD does not have
  to search the entire drawing to find the hatch boundaries.
- Preview the hatch before you apply it. This allows you to make
  last-minute adjustments easily.
- Turn off layers that contain lines or text that might interfere with
  your ability to define hatch boundaries accurately.
- Create boundary sets of small areas within a complex drawing to
  help save time.

Hatching Unenclosed Areas and Correcting Boundary Errors

The **BHATCH** command works well unless you have an error in the hatch boundary or pick a point outside a boundary area to be hatched. The most common error is a gap in the boundary. This can be very small and difficult to detect, and it happens when you do not close the geometry. However, AutoCAD is quick to let you know by displaying the **Boundary Definition Error** alert box. See Figure 21-30. This alert notifies you that the area cannot be hatched unless you close the boundary or specify a gap tolerance value. The *gap tolerance* controls the amount of gap allowed between segments of a boundary when hatching. The gap tolerance can be set in the **Gap Tolerance** area of the **Hatch and Gradient** dialog box. See Figure 21-31. The value in the **Tolerance:** text box is set to 0 by default. Setting a different value allows you to hatch an unenclosed boundary. AutoCAD ignores any gaps in the boundary equal to or smaller than the gap tolerance when applying the hatch. Before the hatch is generated, AutoCAD issues a warning to remind you that the boundary is not closed.

If you encounter the **Boundary Definition Error** alert box and decide you want to find and correct the problem, pick **OK** and return to the drawing. Figure 21-32 shows an object in which the corner does not close. The error is too small to see on the screen, but using the **ZOOM** command reveals the problem. Fix the error and use the **BHATCH** command again.

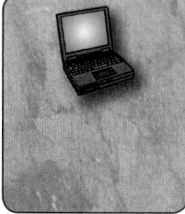

PROFESSIONAL TIP

When creating an associative hatch, it is best to specify only one internal point per hatch block placement. If you specify more than one internal point in the same operation, AutoCAD creates one hatch object from all points picked. This can cause unexpected results when trying to edit what appears to be a separate hatch object.

Figure 21-30.
The **Boundary Definition Error** alert box is displayed if problems occur in your hatching operation.

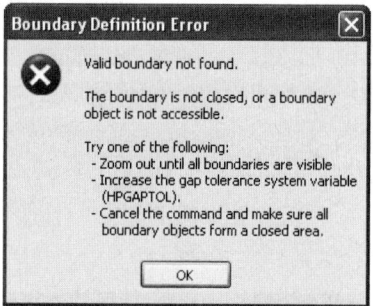

Figure 21-31.
The **Tolerance** setting controls whether hatching can be applied to open boundaries.

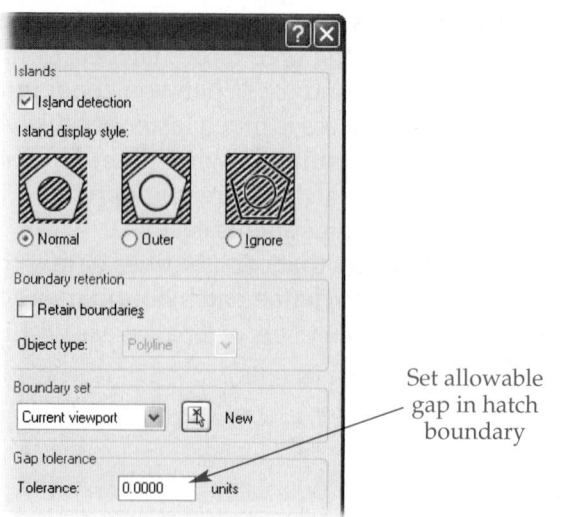

Set allowable gap in hatch boundary

Figure 21-32.
Using the **ZOOM** command to find the source of a hatching error.

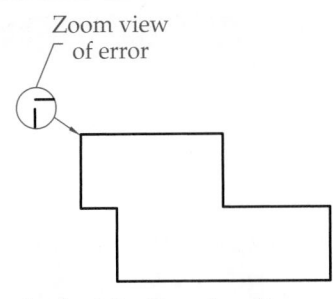

Zoom view of error

Look at the Boundary Error

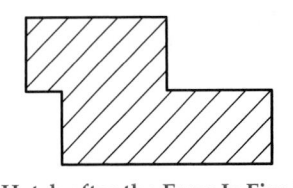

Hatch after the Error Is Fixed

Defining Inherit Options

The **Inherit Properties** button allows you to use the settings from an existing hatch pattern in the drawing by selecting it. This button was described earlier in this chapter. When this button is used, the **Inherit options** area in the **Hatch and Gradient** dialog box controls the hatch origin. See **Figure 21-33**.

The default option is **Use current origin**. When this option is selected, the hatch being created uses the origin point setting specified in the **Hatch origin** area on the **Hatch** tab in the **Hatch and Gradient** dialog box. Selecting the **Use source hatch origin** option causes the hatch being created to use the origin point of the hatch that was selected with the **Inherit Properties** button.

Creating Solid Hatch Patterns

As described earlier in this chapter, solid hatches can be created with the Solid predefined hatch pattern. See **Figure 21-34**. This pattern can be accessed from the **Pattern:** drop-down list in the **Hatch and Gradient** dialog box or the **Other Predefined** tab in the **Hatch Pattern Palette** dialog box. The pattern can be assigned a color. However, the hatching options used with other predefined hatches are not available. This is a quick way to fill a closed object solid.

More advanced types of fills can be applied to closed objects using the gradient fill hatching options available with the **BHATCH** command. A *gradient fill* is a shading transition between the tones of one color or two separate colors. Gradient fills can be used to simulate color-shaded objects. Nine different gradient fill patterns are available. They are accessed in the **Gradient** tab of the **Hatch and Gradient** dialog box. See **Figure 21-35**.

Figure 21-33.
The **Inherit options** area of the **Hatch and Gradient** dialog box is displayed by picking the **More Options** button.

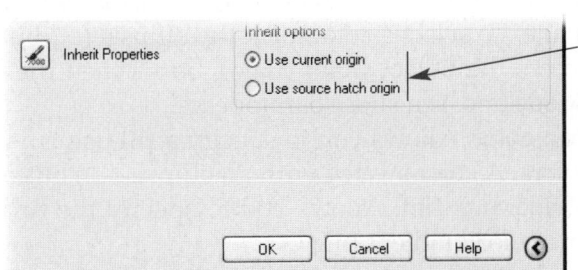

Set hatch origin for inherited hatches

Figure 21-34.
Using the Solid hatch pattern to make a basic solid hatch object.

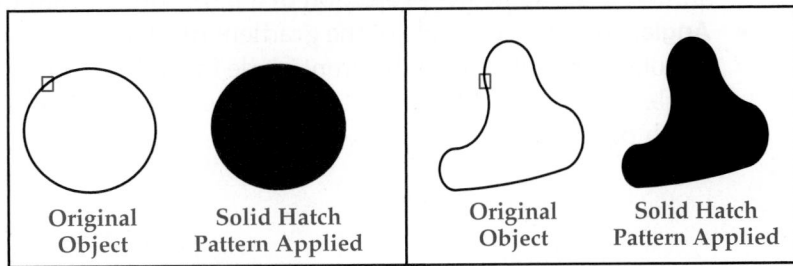

Original Object | Solid Hatch Pattern Applied | Original Object | Solid Hatch Pattern Applied

Figure 21-35.
The **Gradient** tab of the **Hatch and Gradient** dialog box contains options for creating gradient fill hatch patterns.

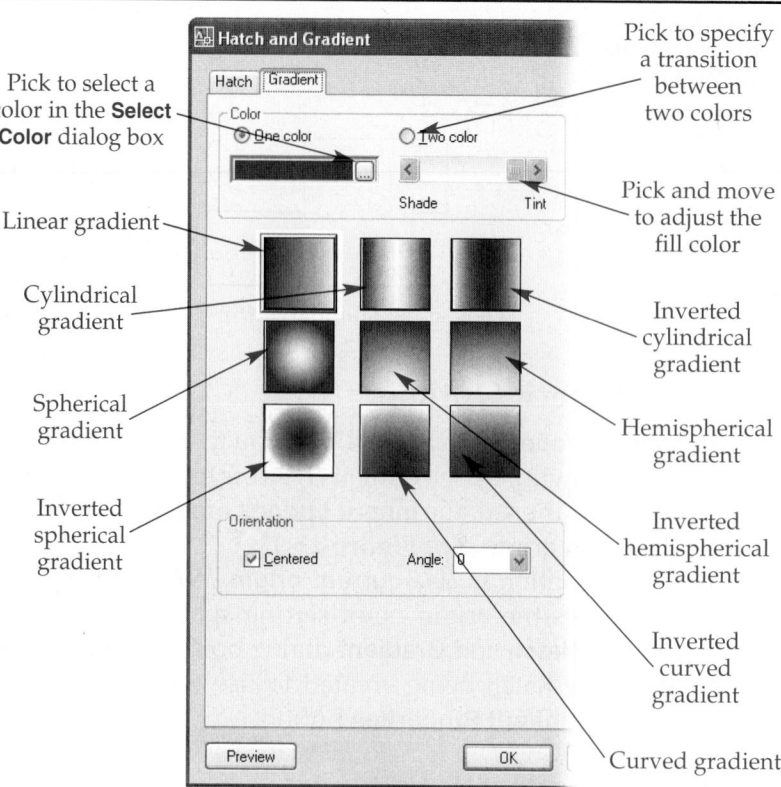

Pick to select a color in the **Select Color** dialog box

Pick to specify a transition between two colors

Linear gradient

Cylindrical gradient

Pick and move to adjust the fill color

Inverted cylindrical gradient

Spherical gradient

Hemispherical gradient

Inverted spherical gradient

Inverted hemispherical gradient

Inverted curved gradient

Curved gradient

The fills are based on linear sweep, spherical, radial, and curved shading. They create the appearance of a lit surface with a gradual transition from an area of highlight to a filled area. When two colors are used, a transition from light to dark between the colors is simulated.

As with other types of hatch patterns, gradient fills are associative when applied by default. They can also be edited in the same way as other hatch patterns with the **HATCHEDIT** command.

The options in the **Gradient** tab of the **Hatch and Gradient** dialog box include settings for one or two fill colors, gradient configuration, and fill angle. The options are:

- **One color.** Specifies a fill that has a smooth transition between the darker shades and lighter tints of one color. This is the default option. A *shade* is a specific color mixed with gray or black. A *tint* is a specific color mixed with white. To select a color, pick the ellipsis (**...**) button next to the color swatch to access the **Select Color** dialog box. When the **One color** option is active, the **Shade** and **Tint** slider bar appears.

- **Two color.** Allows you to specify a fill using a smooth transition between two colors. A color swatch with an ellipsis (**...**) button is displayed for each color.

- **Shade and Tint.** Allows you to specify the tint or shade of a color used for a one-color gradient fill.

- **Centered.** Specifies the gradient configuration. Picking the check box applies a symmetrical configuration. If this option is not selected, the gradient fill is shifted to simulate the projection of a light source from the left of the object.

- **Angle.** Specifies the angle of the gradient fill. The default angle is 0°. The fill can be rotated by selecting a different angle from the drop-down list. The specified angle is relative to the current UCS and is independent of the angle setting for hatch patterns.

shade: A specific color mixed with gray or black.

tint: A specific color mixed with white.

AutoCAD and Its Applications—Basics

Using DesignCenter to Insert Hatch Patterns

Hatch patterns can be readily located and previewed before they are inserted using **DesignCenter**. To insert a hatch pattern into the current drawing, you can use a drag-and-drop operation. To access **DesignCenter**, pick the **DesignCenter** button on the **Standard Annotation** toolbar, select **Tools** > **Palettes** > **DesignCenter**, type ADC or ADCENTER, or use the [Ctrl]+[2] key combination. To drag and drop a hatch pattern from **DesignCenter**, you need to select a PAT file. Once the PAT file is selected, the hatch patterns it contains are displayed in the preview pane. See **Figure 21-36**.

NOTE

AutoCAD includes two PAT files: acad.pat and acadiso.pat. Both are AutoCAD support files located in the Documents and Settings folder path set by the AutoCAD Support File Search Path. To verify the location of AutoCAD support files, access the **Files** tab in the **Options** dialog box and check the path listed under the Support File Search Path.

Pick a hatch pattern in the preview palette to display a preview of the pattern. Use one of the following three methods to transfer a hatch pattern from **DesignCenter** into the active drawing:

- **Drag and drop.** Pick the hatch pattern from **DesignCenter** and hold down the mouse button. When you move the cursor into the active drawing, a hatch pattern symbol is displayed under the cursor, as shown in **Figure 21-37A**. Place the cursor in the area to be hatched and release the pick button. The hatch is applied automatically. See **Figure 21-37B**.
- **Hatch and Gradient dialog box.** Right-click a hatch pattern in **DesignCenter** and select **BHATCH...** from the shortcut menu to access the **Hatch and Gradient** dialog box. The selected hatch pattern is displayed automatically.

Figure 21-36.
Pick a PAT file in **DesignCenter** to display the available hatch patterns in the preview palette.

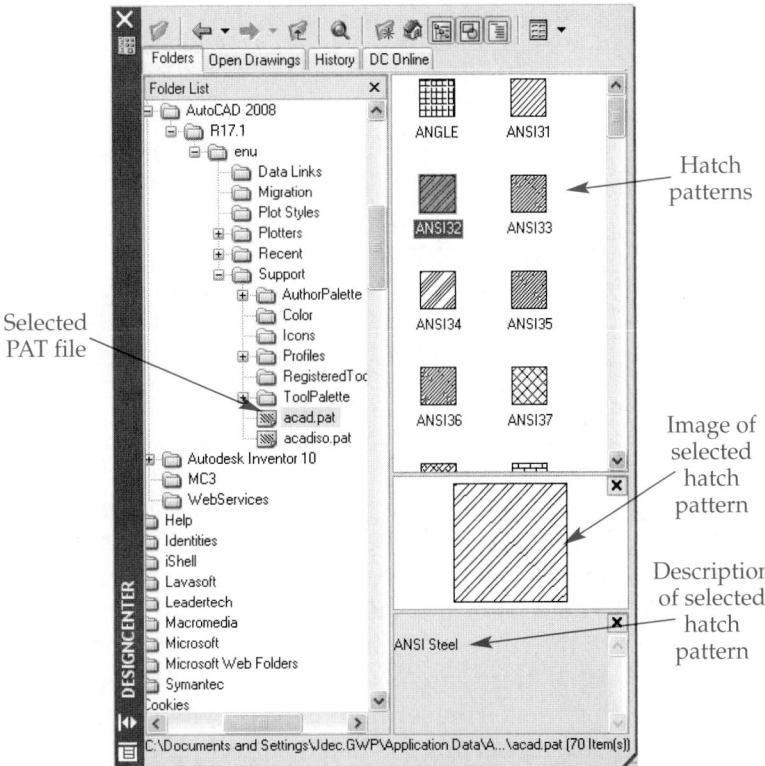

Figure 21-37.
When a hatch pattern is selected in the preview pane, a preview image appears. A—The hatch pattern symbol appears under the cursor during the drag-and-drop and paste operations. B—Pick a point to apply the hatch pattern.

Selected hatch pattern

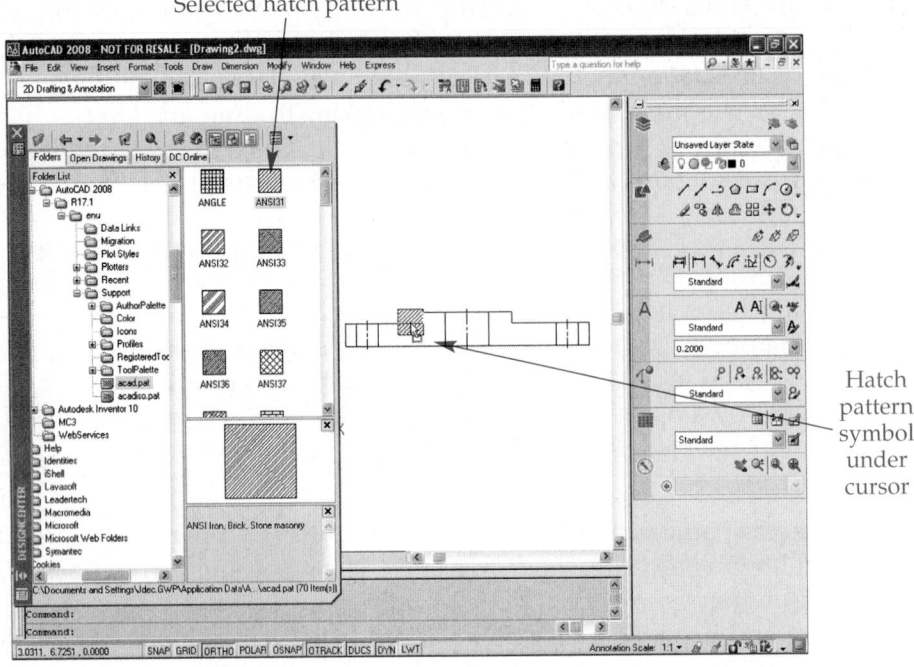

Hatch pattern symbol under cursor

A

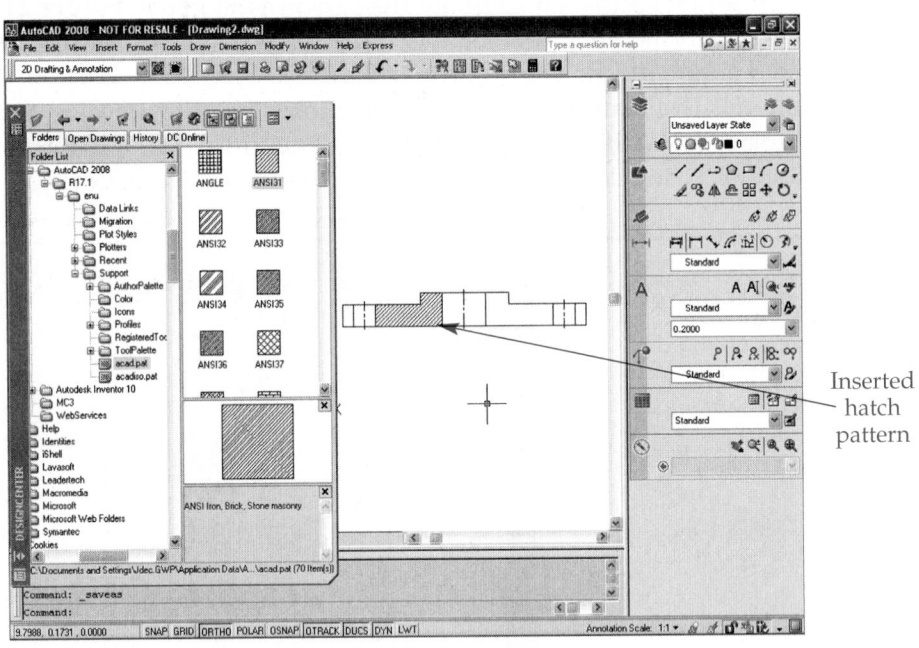

Inserted hatch pattern

B

- **Copy and paste.** Hatch patterns can also be inserted using a copy and paste operation. Right-click the hatch pattern in **DesignCenter** and pick **Copy** from the shortcut menu. Move the cursor into the active drawing, right-click, and select **Paste** from the shortcut menu. The hatch pattern symbol is displayed beneath the cursor. Pick in the area to be hatched to apply the hatch pattern.

When hatch patterns are inserted from **DesignCenter**, the angle, scale, and island detection settings match the settings of the previous hatch pattern. If you wish to change these settings after inserting the hatch pattern, use the **HATCHEDIT** command.

Exercise 21-2

Complete the exercise on the Student CD.

Using Tool Palettes

The **Tool Palettes** window provides a number of ways to manage frequently used blocks, hatch patterns, and other types of objects, such as gradients, images, tables, and external reference files. This section describes the various features in the **Tool Palettes** window.

To open the **Tool Palettes** window, pick the **Tool Palettes** button on the **Standard Annotation** toolbar, select **Tools > Palettes > Tool Palettes**, type TP or TOOLPALETTES, or use the [Ctrl]+[3] key combination. The **Tool Palettes** window is shown in **Figure 21-38**.

Figure 21-38.
The **Tool Palettes** window can be used to access and insert hatch patterns.

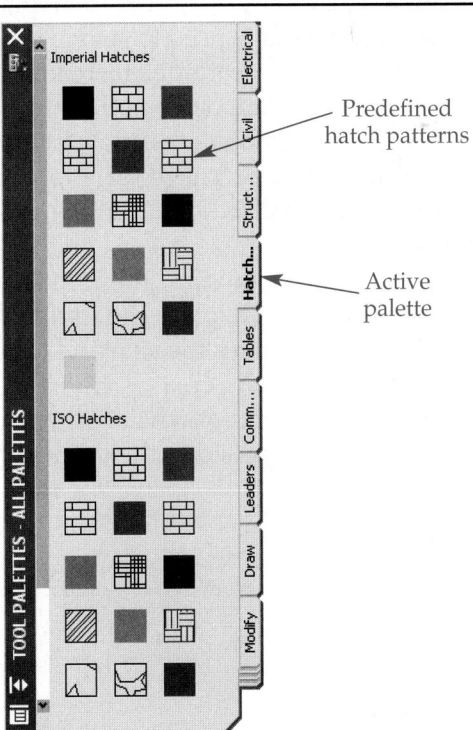

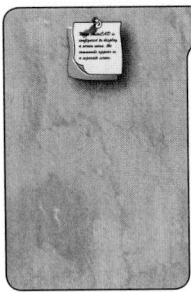
Locating and Viewing Content

Each tool palette in the **Tool Palettes** window has its own tab. You can navigate through the tools, or content in each palette in a number of ways. You can also choose viewing options to display the content in different ways.

To view the content in a tool palette, pick the related tab to open it. If the **Tool Palettes** window contains more palettes than can be displayed on-screen, pick on the edge of the lowest tab to display a selection menu listing the palette tabs. Locate the name of the tab to access the related tool palette.

The tool palette can be navigated using one of two scroll methods. If all of the content of a selected tool palette does not fit in the window, the remainder can be viewed by using the scroll bar or the scroll hand. The scroll hand appears when the cursor is placed in an empty area in the tool palette. Picking and dragging scrolls the tool palette up and down.

By default, the tools in each palette are represented by icons. The appearance of the tools can be adjusted to suit user preference. To access the viewing options in a tool palette, right-click in the tool area to display the shortcut menu. See **Figure 21-39**. The **View Options…** listing is used to set viewing options. The options in the lower areas of the menu are used to create, delete, rename, and rearrange tool palettes. These options and the **Paste** option are described in the sections that follow.

Picking **View Options…** displays the **View Options** dialog box. See **Figure 21-40**. The size of the preview image for a tool can be adjusted by moving the **Image size:** slider. The **View style:** radio button options control how the content is displayed. The three options are:

- **Icon only.** Displays just the icon (a preview image).
- **Icon with text.** Displays the icon and the name of the tool.
- **List view.** Displays the icon and the name of each tool in the palette in a single-column format.

In the **Apply to:** drop-down list, you can specify how the view settings are assigned. The settings can be applied to the current palette only or to all palettes.

Figure 21-39.
Viewing options for each tool palette can be accessed by right-clicking in the tool palette to display the shortcut menu.

AutoCAD and Its Applications—Basics

Figure 21-40.
Settings in the **View Options** dialog box control how the content is displayed in each tool palette.

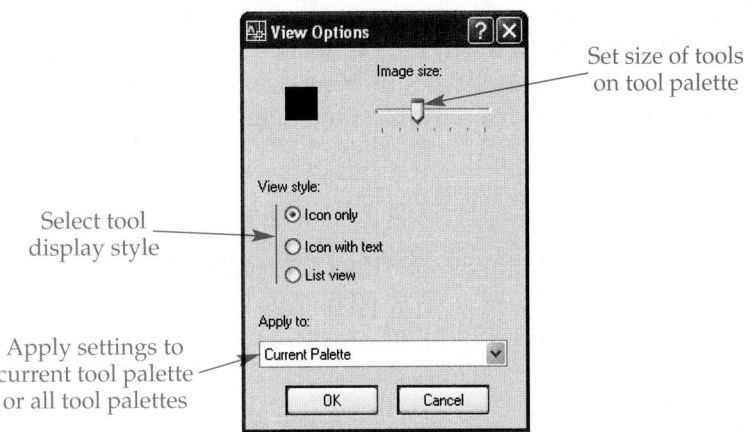

Set size of tools on tool palette

Select tool display style

Apply settings to current tool palette or all tool palettes

NOTE

An image can be used in place of the default tool icon by right-clicking a tool icon in the tool palette and selecting the **Specify image...** shortcut menu option. To return the icon to the original display, right-click on the icon and select the **Remove specified image** shortcut menu option.

Insert Hatch Patterns Using Tool Palettes

Inserting hatch patterns with the **Tool Palettes** window is similar to inserting them with **DesignCenter**. As with **DesignCenter**, a pattern can be previewed in a tool palette before it is applied.

To drag and drop a hatch pattern from the **Tool Palettes** window, access the tool palette in which the pattern resides. Then, either pick the pattern and drag the image into the drawing while holding down the mouse button, or place the cursor over the hatch pattern image and pick once. When you move the cursor into the drawing area, the hatch pattern is attached to the crosshairs. The location where the crosshairs and the hatch pattern are connected is defined by the insertion point of the hatch pattern. Drag the pattern image to the desired boundary area and pick.

After the hatch pattern is inserted, you can make modifications with the **HATCHEDIT** command. Hatch editing is described later in this chapter.

Adding Hatch Patterns to a Tool Palette

Hatch patterns and gradient fills can be added to tool palettes using a drag-and-drop procedure. The pattern must be in the current drawing or defined in an AutoCAD hatch pattern file. If you are adding a hatch pattern or gradient fill to a tool palette from the current drawing, first open the desired palette in the **Tool Palettes** window. Select the hatch pattern or gradient object in the drawing to highlight it. Then pick anywhere on the hatch pattern or gradient (do not select the grip) and drag it onto the tool palette.

As previously mentioned, the predefined hatch patterns provided with AutoCAD are stored in the acad.pat and acadiso.pat files. If you want to add a predefined pattern to a tool palette, one of the files must be located in **DesignCenter**. By default, these files are AutoCAD support files stored in the Support File Search Path folder. This path location can be determined by accessing the **Files** tab in the **Options** dialog box and identifying the path listed under Support File Search Path. Once a hatch pattern file is located, its contents can be displayed in the **Content** area of **DesignCenter**. You can then add one or more hatch patterns to a tool palette.

To create a palette that contains all of the hatch patterns in a single PAT file, right-click the hatch pattern file in the **Folder List** area and select **Create Tool Palette of Hatch Patterns** from the shortcut menu. To add an individual hatch pattern to a palette, drag and drop the pattern from the **Content** area into the desired palette.

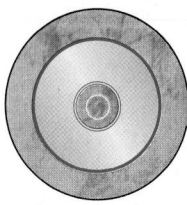

Exercise 21-3
Complete the exercise on the Student CD.

Editing Hatch Patterns

You can edit hatch boundaries and hatch patterns with grips and editing commands such as **ERASE, COPY, MOVE, ROTATE, SCALE,** and **TRIM.** If a hatch pattern is associative, whatever you do to the hatch boundary is automatically done to the associated hatch pattern. As explained earlier, a hatch pattern is associative if the **Associative** option in the **Options** area of the **Hatch and Gradient** dialog box is active.

A convenient way to edit a hatch pattern is to use the **HATCHEDIT** command. You can access this command by picking **Modify > Object > Hatch...** from the pull-down menu, picking the **Edit Hatch** button on the **Modify II** toolbar, or typing HE or HATCHEDIT. You can also double-click the hatch pattern you wish to edit.

When you select a hatch pattern or patterns to edit, the **Hatch Edit** dialog box is displayed. See **Figure 21-41.** The **Hatch Edit** dialog box has the same features as the **Hatch and Gradient** dialog box, except the **Recreate boundary** button in the **Boundaries** area is available.

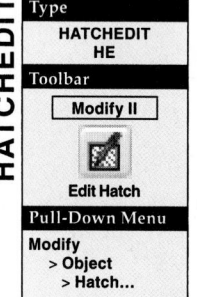

Figure 21-41.
The **Hatch Edit**
dialog box is used to
edit hatch patterns.
Notice that only the
options related to
hatch characteristics
are available.

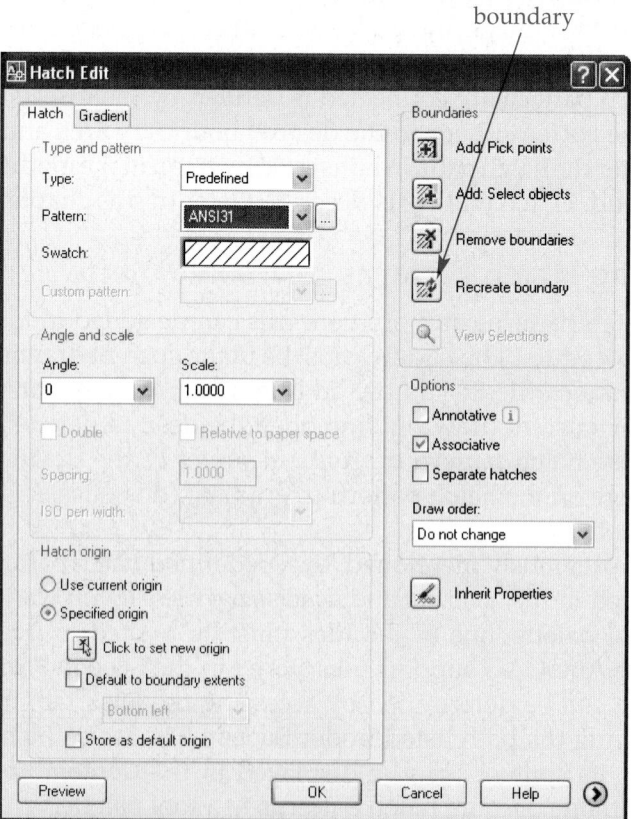

The **Recreate boundary** button can be used to create a new boundary for the hatch pattern. It basically redraws a new boundary on top of the existing boundary. If the current boundary is made up of several different lines, this command can be used to draw the boundary very quickly in one object. When you pick the **Recreate boundary** button, the **Hatch Edit** dialog box is temporarily hidden. Then decide if the boundary type will be a region or a polyline. The next query asks if you want the hatch pattern to be associated with the new boundary. The **Hatch Edit** dialog box then displays again.

The other features work just like they do in the **Hatch and Gradient** dialog box. You can change the pattern type, scale, or angle; remove the associative qualities; or set the inherit properties of an existing hatch pattern. You can also preview the edited hatch before applying it to your drawing.

PROFESSIONAL TIP

The **MATCHPROP** command can be used to inherit the properties of an existing hatch pattern and apply it to the hatch pattern you wish to edit. This command applies existing hatch patterns to objects in the current drawing file or to objects in other drawing files that are open in AutoCAD.

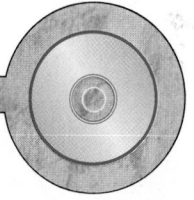

Exercise 21-4
Complete the exercise on the Student CD.

Editing Associative Hatch Patterns

When you edit an object with an associative hatch pattern, the hatch pattern changes to match the edit. For example, when the object in **Figure 21-42A** is stretched, the hatch pattern matches the new object. When the island in **Figure 21-42B** is erased, the hatch pattern is automatically revised to fill the area where the island was located. As long as the original boundary is being edited, the associative hatch will update.

Figure 21-42.
Editing objects with associative hatch patterns. The hatch pattern changes to match the edit.

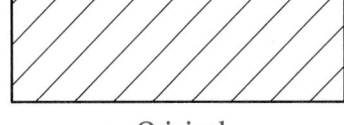
Original

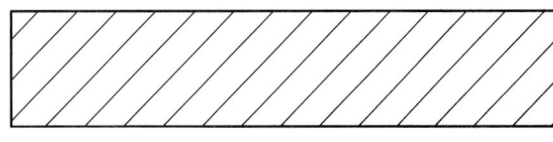
Object Stretched

A

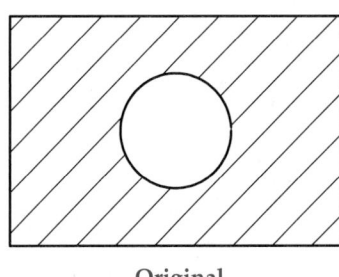
Original

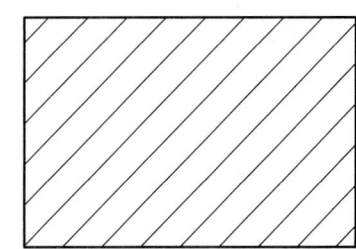
Circle Erased

B

Figure 21-43.
Objects can be added to a hatch pattern boundary after the pattern is created.

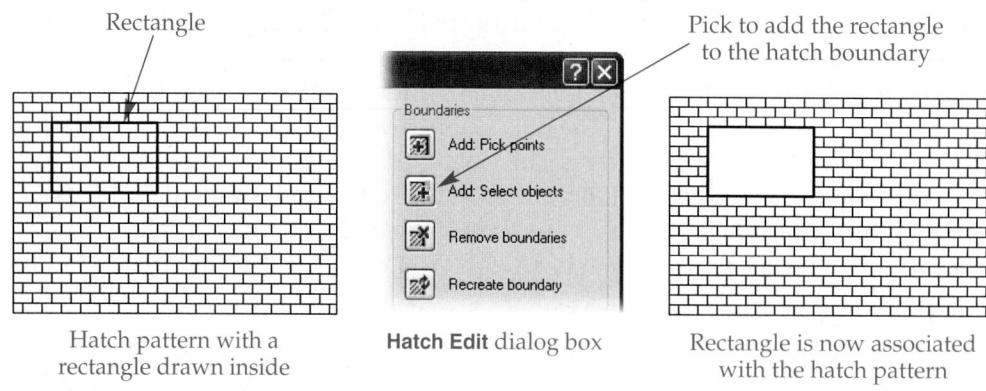

Hatch pattern with a rectangle drawn inside

Hatch Edit dialog box

Rectangle is now associated with the hatch pattern

Drawing a new object and associating it with an existing hatch pattern creates a new island. See **Figure 21-43.** In this example, a rectangle has been drawn and needs to be added to the hatch boundary to create an island. After a rectangle is drawn, double-click the hatch pattern to open the **Hatch Edit** dialog box. Picking the **Add: Select objects** button hides the dialog box and allows you to pick the rectangle. Press [Enter] and the **OK** button to finish. The rectangle is now an associated island.

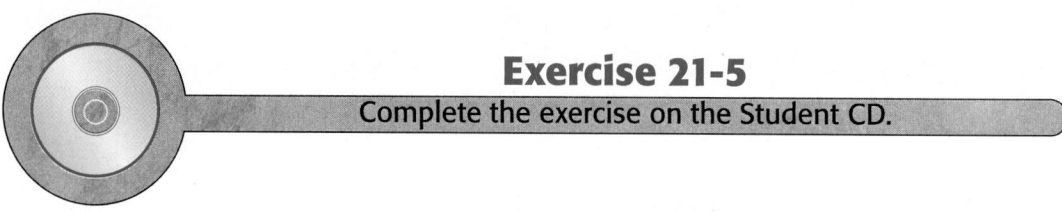

Exercise 21-5
Complete the exercise on the Student CD.

Drawing Objects with Solid Fills

In previous chapters, you learned that polylines, trace segments, and donuts may be filled in solid when **FILL** mode is on. When **FILL** mode is off, these objects are drawn as outlines only. The **SOLID** command works in much the same manner except that it fills objects or shapes that are already drawn and fills areas defined by picking points.

The **SOLID** command is accessed by picking **Draw > Modeling > Meshes > 2D Solid** or typing SO or SOLID. You are then prompted to select points. If the object to fill solid is rectangular, pick the corners in the numbered sequence shown in **Figure 21-44.**

Notice that AutoCAD prompts you for another third point after the first four. This prompt allows you to fill in additional parts of the same object, if needed. AutoCAD assumes that the third and fourth points of the previous solid are now points one and two for the next solid. The subsequent points you select fill in the object in a triangular fashion. Continue picking points, or press [Enter] to stop. See **Figure 21-45.**

Figure 21-44.
Using the **SOLID** command. Select the points in the order shown.

Figure 21-45.
The **SOLID** command allows you to enter a second "third point" (Point 5 here) after you enter the fourth point.

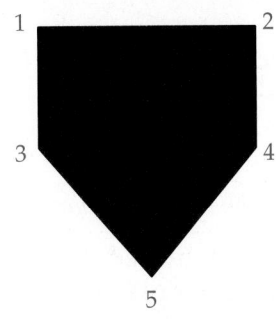

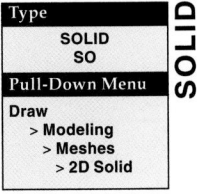

Different types of solid arrangements can be drawn by altering the pick sequence. See Figure 21-46. Also, the **SOLID** command can be used to draw filled shapes without prior use of the **LINE**, **PLINE**, or **RECTANG** commands, by picking the points. Consider using various object snap modes when picking the points of existing geometry.

PROFESSIONAL TIP

Keep in mind that many solids and dense hatches require extensive time to regenerate. On a complex drawing, create filled solids and hatching on a separate layer and keep the layer frozen until you are ready to plot the drawing. Many solids and dense hatch patterns also adversely affect plot time. Save plotting time by making check plots with **FILL** mode off.

Exercise 21-6
Complete the exercise on the Student CD.

Figure 21-46.
Using different pick sequences with the **SOLID** command results in different solid patterns.

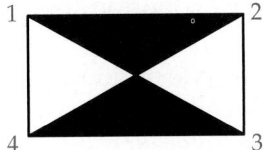 

Express Tools
Chapter 21

The following Express Tools are related to topics described in this chapter. Refer to "Chapter 21: Super Hatch" in the Express Tools area on the Student CD for information on this tool:

Super Hatch

Chapter Test

Answer the following questions. Write your answers on a separate sheet of paper or complete the electronic chapter test on the Student CD.

For Questions 1–6, name the type of section identified in each of the following statements:

1. Half of the object is removed; the cutting-plane line generally cuts completely through along the center plane.
2. The cutting-plane line cuts through one-quarter of the object; used primarily on symmetrical objects.
3. The cutting-plane line is staggered through features that do not lie in a straight line.
4. The section is turned in place to clarify the contour of the object.
5. The section is rotated and located away from the object. The location of the section is normally identified with a cutting-plane line.
6. A small portion of the view is removed to clarify an internal feature.
7. AutoCAD's standard section line symbols are called _____.
8. Which AutoCAD hatch pattern is used as a general section line symbol?
9. Identify two ways to select a predefined hatch pattern in the **Hatch and Gradient** dialog box.
10. Explain the purpose and function of the ellipsis (**...**) buttons in the **Hatch and Gradient** dialog box.
11. How do you change the hatch angle in the **Hatch and Gradient** dialog box?
12. Explain how to set a hatch scale in the **Hatch and Gradient** dialog box.
13. If you use the **Add: Pick points** button inside the **Hatch and Gradient** dialog box to hatch an area, how do you hatch around an island inside the area to be hatched?
14. Describe the fundamental difference between using the **Add: Pick points** and the **Add: Select objects** buttons in the **Hatch and Gradient** dialog box.
15. How do you hatch an object with text inside without hatching the text?
16. Define *associative hatch pattern*.
17. What is the result of stretching an object that is hatched with an associative hatch pattern?
18. Explain how to use an existing hatch pattern on a drawing as the pattern for your next hatch.
19. Describe the purpose of the **Preview** button found in the **Hatch and Gradient** dialog box.
20. Explain the three island detection style options.
21. How do you limit AutoCAD hatch evaluation to a specific area of the drawing?
22. What is the purpose of the **Gap Tolerance** setting in the **Hatch and Gradient** dialog box?
23. What are gradient fill hatch patterns? How are they created with the **BHATCH** command?
24. Name the two files that contain hatch patterns that can be copied from **DesignCenter**.
25. Explain how to use drag and drop to insert a hatch pattern from **DesignCenter** into an active drawing.
26. Explain two ways to use drag and drop for inserting a hatch pattern from a tool palette into the drawing.

27. Name the command that may be used to edit existing associative hatch patterns.
28. How does the **Hatch Edit** dialog box compare to the **Hatch and Gradient** dialog box?
29. What happens if you erase an island inside an associative hatch pattern?
30. In addition to the **BHATCH** command, what command can be used to fill an object with a solid color?

Drawing Problems

For Problems 1–4, use the following guidelines:

A. Use an appropriate template with a mechanical drawing title block.
B. Create separate layers for views, dimensions, and section lines.
C. Place the following general notes 1/2″ from the lower-left corner.
   NOTES:
   1. INTERPRET DIMENSIONS AND TOLERANCES PER ASME Y14.5M-1994
   2. REMOVE ALL BURRS AND SHARP EDGES

1. Draw and dimension the given views. Save the drawing as P21-1.

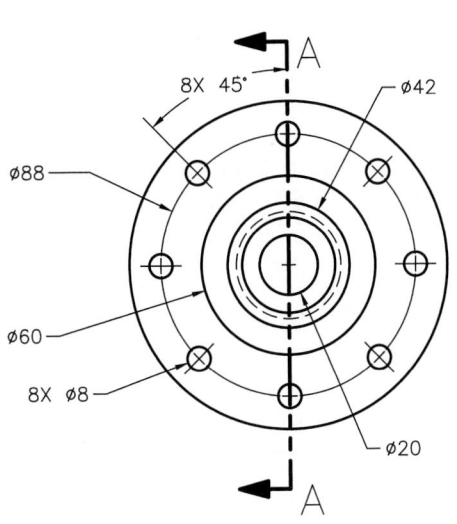

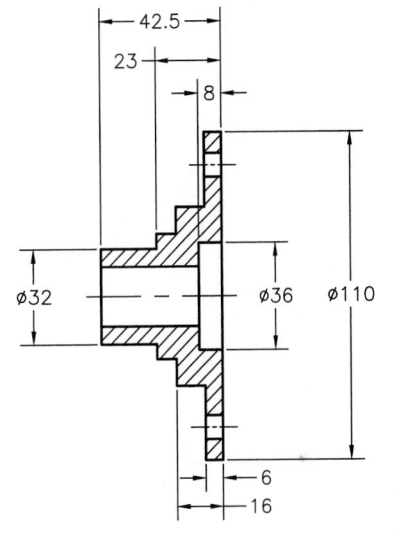

SECTION A–A

Name: Hub
Material: Cast Iron

2. Draw and dimension the given views. Add the following notes: OIL QUENCH 40-45C, CASE HARDEN .020 DEEP, and 59-60 ROCKWELL C SCALE. Save the drawing as P21-2.

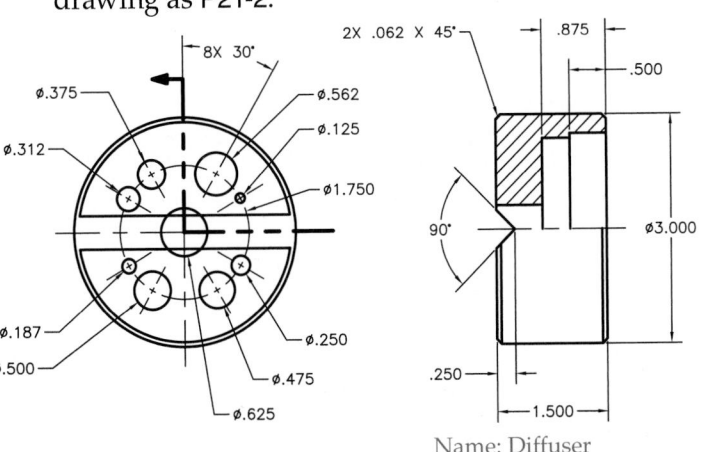

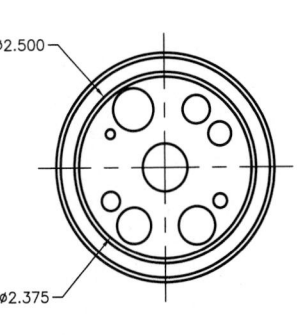

Name: Diffuser
Material: AISI 1018

3. Given the engineer's rough sketch, draw and dimension the given views, including the aligned section shown on the right. Add the following notes: FINISH ALL OVER 1.63 mm UNLESS OTHERWISE SPECIFIED and ALL DIMENSIONS ARE IN MILLIMETERS. Save the drawing as P21-3.

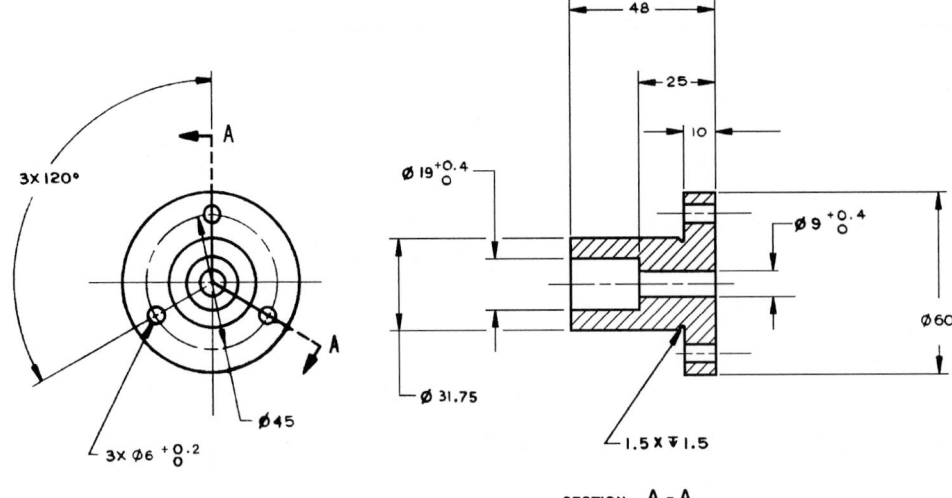

Name: Bushing
Material: SAE 1030

4. Draw and dimension these views, which include aligned and broken-out sections. Add the following notes: FINISH ALL OVER 1.63 mm UNLESS OTHERWISE SPECIFIED and ALL DIMENSIONS ARE IN MILLIMETERS. Save the drawing as P21-4.

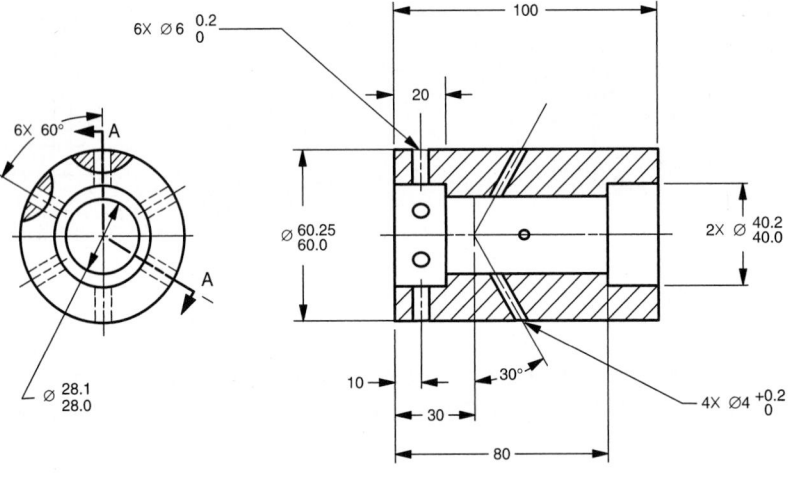

Name: Nozzle
Material: Phosphor Bronze

Drawing Problems - Chapter 21

5. Draw and dimension the views of the chain guide as shown. Save the drawing as P21-5.

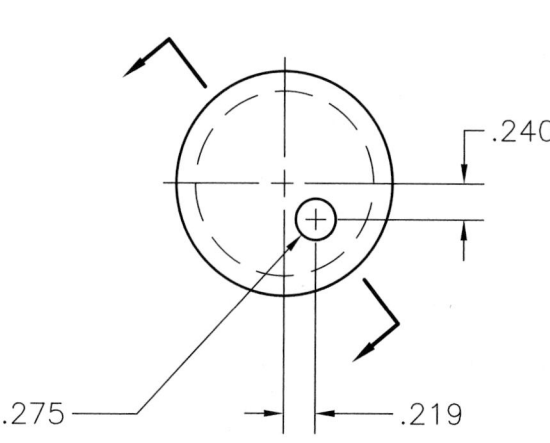

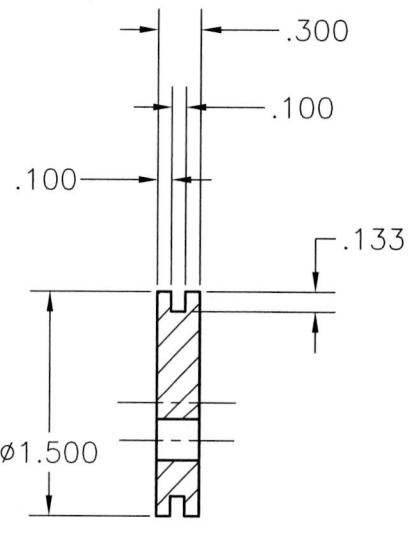

6. Draw and dimension the views of the sleeve and notes as shown. Save the drawing as P21-6.

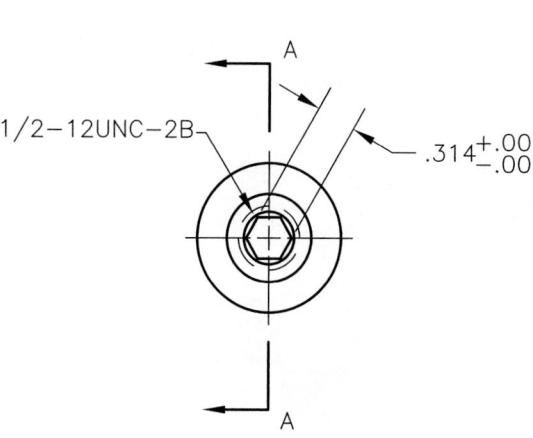

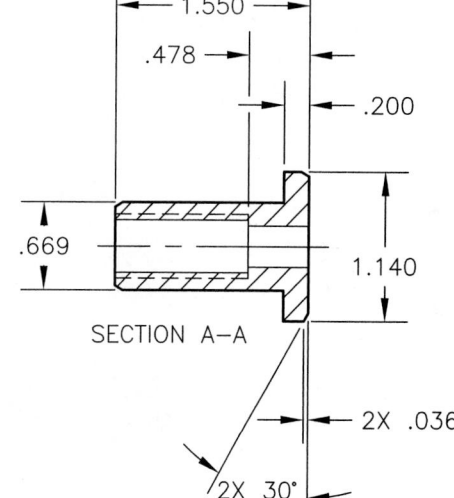

4. PAINT ACE GLOSS BLACK ALL OVER.
3. CASE HARDEN 45–50 ROCKWELL
2. REMOVE ALL BURRS AND SHARP
   EDGES.
1. INTERPRET ALL DIMENSIONS AND
   TOLERANCES PER ASME
   Y14.5M–1994.

Drawing Problems – Chapter 21

7. Draw and dimension the views of the toe hook as shown. Save the drawing as P21-7.

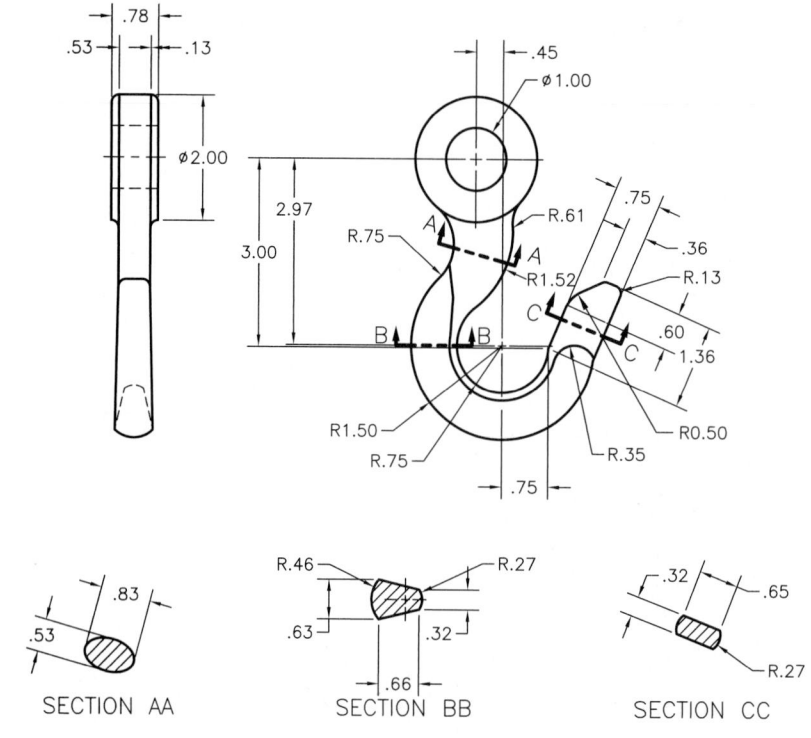

Draw the following problems using commands described in this chapter and in previous chapters. Use an appropriate template for each problem. Use text styles that correlate with the problem content. Place dimensions and notes when needed. Make your drawings proportional to the given problems when dimensions are not given. Save each of the drawings as **P21-**(problem number).

8.

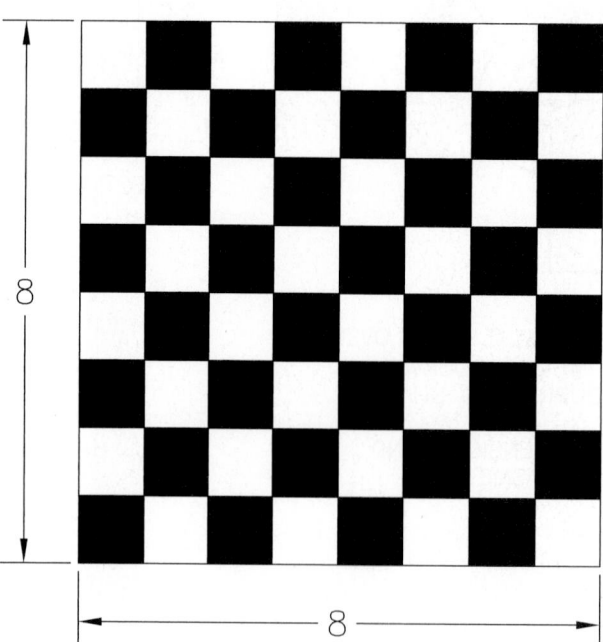

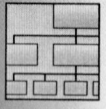

9.

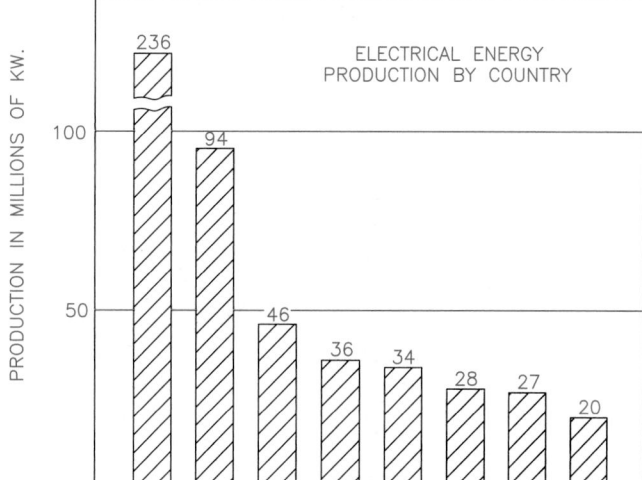

10.

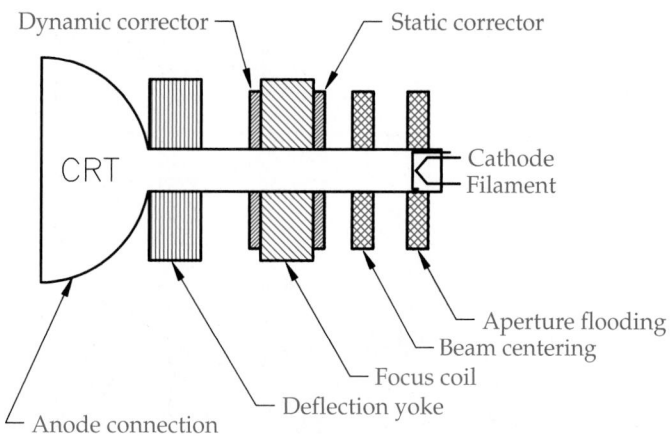

11.

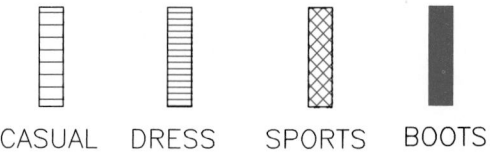

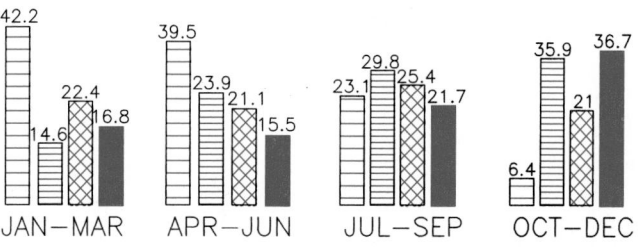

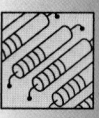

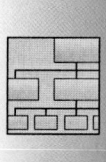

Drawing Problems - Chapter 21

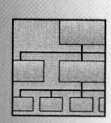

12.

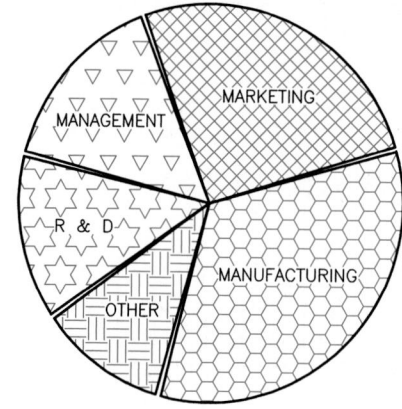

DIAL TECHNOLOGIES
EXPENSE BUDGET
FISCAL YEAR

13.

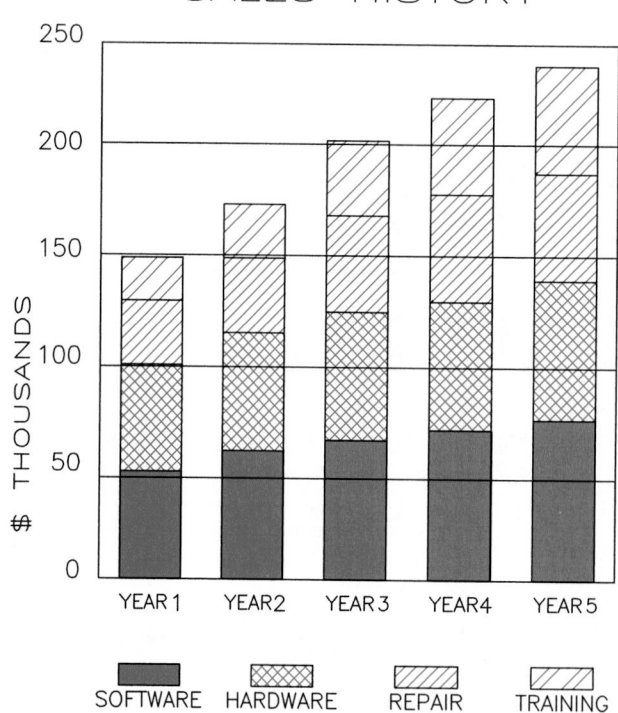

SALES HISTORY

14.

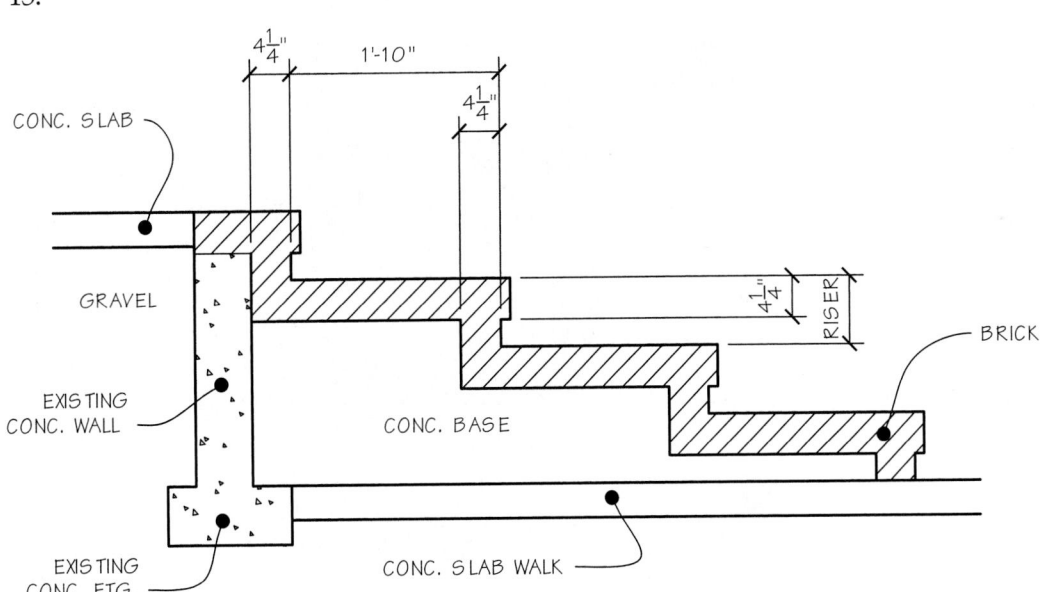

1" R-5 FOAM SHEATHING

WALL AT GARAGE

SLOPE GRADE AWAY FROM FOUNDATION @ 5" IN FIRST 10'-10" (TYP)

8" MIN.

DEPTH AS REQD BY CODE OR LOCAL FROST LINE 2' MINIMUM

#5 DOWELS @ 4'-0" O.C.

16" x 8" FTG. W/ (2)#5 CONT.

FILL TOP 2 COURSES W/ GROUT AT BOLTS

1/2" EXPANSION JOINT

4" CONC. SLAB W/ 6X6 10/10 WWM

W/ 1/2" DIA. ANCHOR BOLTS AT 4' O.C. EMBEDDED PER LOCAL CODE

6 MIL VAPOR BARRIER

4" SAND CUSHION OR CRUSHED STONE

#5 AT 4' O.C. FILL BLKS SOLID W/ CONC. AT VERT. #5

8" C-90 CONC. BLK. (# OF COURSES DETERMINED BY FROST LINE)

15.

4 1/4"   1'-10"   4 1/4"

CONC. SLAB

GRAVEL

EXISTING CONC. WALL

EXISTING CONC. FTG.

CONC. BASE

CONC. SLAB WALK

4 1/4" RISER

BRICK

16.

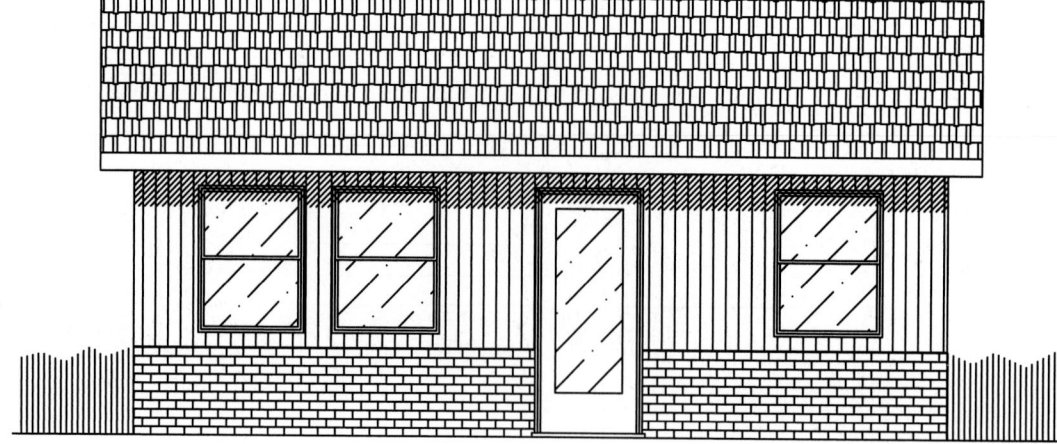

17.

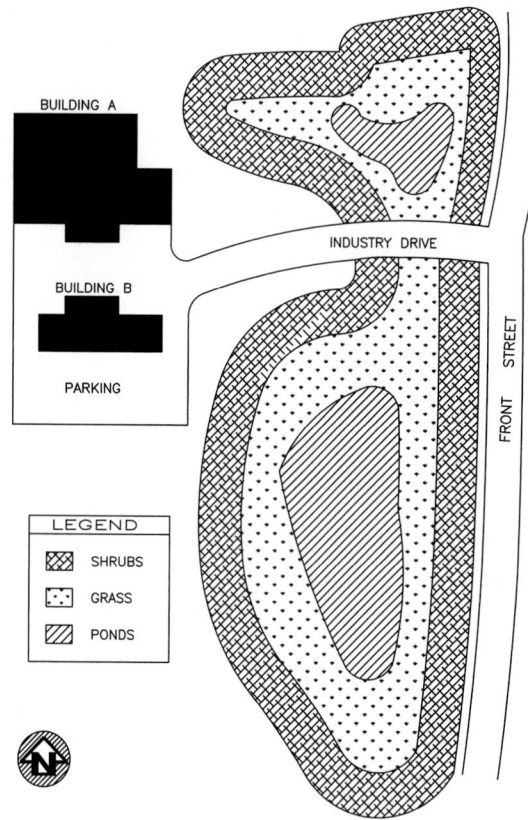

18.

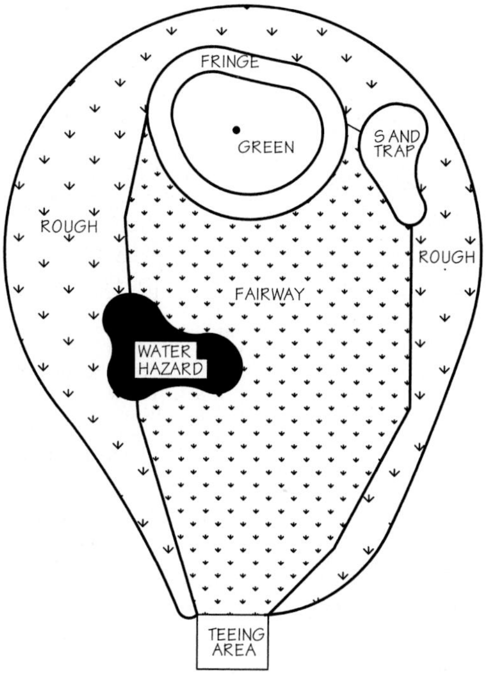
FRINGE
GREEN
SAND TRAP
ROUGH
ROUGH
FAIRWAY
WATER HAZARD
TEEING AREA

19.

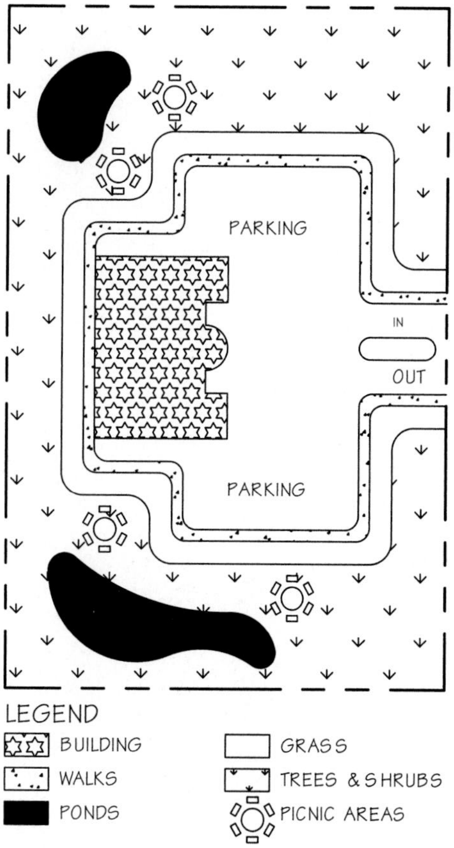
PARKING
IN
OUT
PARKING
LEGEND
BUILDING
WALKS
PONDS
GRASS
TREES & SHRUBS
PICNIC AREAS

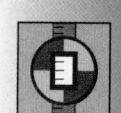

20.

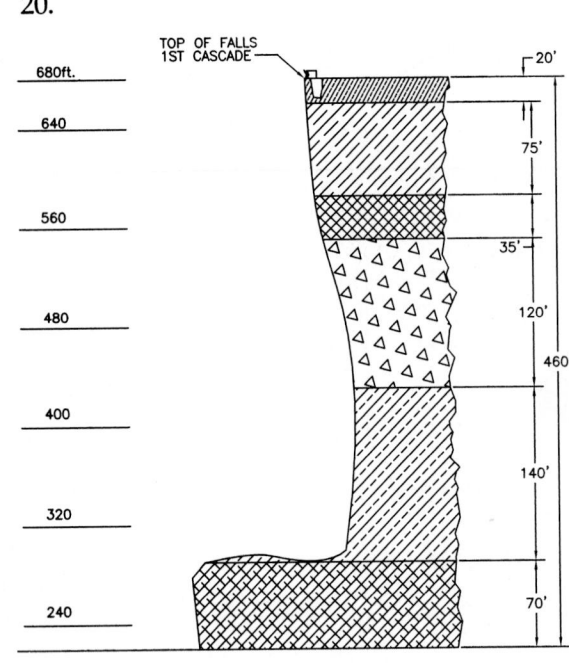

TOP OF FALLS
1ST CASCADE

680ft.
640
560
480
400
320
240

20'
75'
35'
120'
460'
140'
70'

SCALE 1:480

30' 10'   40'   120'
40' 20' 0'   80'

PROFILE OF MULTNOMAH FALLS
&
GEOLOGIC INFORMATION

20' COLLONADE OF AN 80-FOOT THICK FLOW, NOTCHED BY MULTNOMAH CREEK.

75' PILLOW LAVA

35' A GLASSY FLOW, WITH WELL-FORMED ENTABLATURE AND COLLONADE.

120' CONSISTING OF TWO TIERS OF HACKLY-JOINTED BASALT, WITH NO COLLONADE.

140' ENTABLATURE WITH THIN COLUMNS, TOPPED BY A VESICULAR ZONE.

70' OF ENTABLATURE BENEATH THE LOWER FALLS.

BRIEF DESCRIPTION OF TERMS.
COLONNADE: THE LOWER PORTION OF A LAVA FLOW OF COLUMNAR-JOINTED BASALT.
ENTABLATURE: THE UPPER MASSIVE OF A LAVA FLOW OF HACKLY-JOINTED BASALT.

* INFORMATION TAKEN FROM:
"THE MAGNIFICENT GATEWAY"
   AUTHOR: JOHN ELIOT ALLEN
   PAGES: 89-91

CHAPTER 22

Basic Pictorial Drawings

Learning Objectives

After completing this chapter, you will be able to do the following:

✓ Describe the nature of isometric and oblique views.
✓ Set up an isometric grid.
✓ Construct isometric objects.
✓ Create isometric text styles.
✓ Demonstrate isometric and oblique dimensioning techniques.

Being able to visualize and draw three-dimensional shapes is a skill that every drafter, designer, and engineer should possess. This is especially important in 3D modeling. However, there is a distinct difference between drawing a view that *looks* three-dimensional and creating a *true* 3D model.

A 3D model can be rotated on the display screen and viewed from any angle. The computer calculates the points, lines, and surfaces of the objects in space. For information on 3D modeling, see *AutoCAD and Its Applications—Advanced*. The focus of this chapter is creating views that *look* three-dimensional using some special AutoCAD functions and two-dimensional coordinates and objects.

Pictorial Drawing Overview

The word *pictorial* means "like a picture." It refers to any form of 2D drawing that illustrates height, width, and depth. Several forms of pictorial drawings are used in industry today. The least realistic is oblique. However, this is the simplest type. The most realistic, but also the most complex, is perspective. Isometric drawing falls midway between the two as far as realism and complexity are concerned.

pictorial: A drawing that is similar to a picture.

Oblique Drawings

An *oblique drawing* shows objects with one or more parallel faces having true shape and size. A scale is selected for the orthographic, or front, faces. Then an angle for the depth (receding axis) is chosen. The three types of oblique drawings are cavalier, cabinet, and general. See **Figure 22-1.** These vary in the scale of the receding axis. The receding axis is drawn at full scale for a cavalier view and at half scale for a cabinet view. The general oblique is normally drawn with a 3/4 scale for the receding axis.

oblique drawing: A drawing that shows objects with one or more parallel faces having true shape and size.

Figure 22-1.
The scale of the receding axis differs in the three types of oblique drawings.

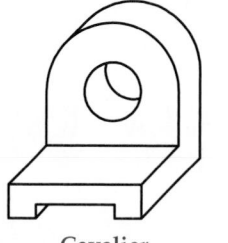  

Cavalier	Cabinet	General

Axonometric Drawings

The general term for drawings that display three dimensions on a two-dimensional surface such as a drawing sheet is *axonometric drawings*. The three types of axonometric drawings are isometric, dimetric, and trimetric.

Isometric drawings are more realistic than oblique drawings. The entire object appears as if it is tilted toward the viewer. The word *isometric* means "equal measure." This equal measure refers to the angle between the three axes (120°) after the object has been tilted. The tilt angle is 35°16′. This is shown in **Figure 22-2**. The 120° angle corresponds to an angle of 30° from horizontal. In the construction of isometric drawings, lines that are parallel in the orthogonal views must be parallel in the isometric view.

The most appealing aspect of isometric drawing is that all three axis lines can be measured using the same scale. This saves time, while still producing a pleasing pictorial of the object.

Dimetric and trimetric drawings are closely related to isometric drawing. These forms of pictorial drawing differ from isometric in the scales used to measure the three axes. *Dimetric* drawing uses two different scales and *trimetric* uses three scales. Using different scales is an attempt to create *foreshortening*. This means the lengths of the sides appear to recede. The relationship between isometric, dimetric, and trimetric drawings is illustrated in **Figure 22-3**.

Perspective Drawing

The most realistic form of pictorial drawing is a *perspective drawing*. The eye naturally sees objects in perspective. Look down a long hall and notice that the wall and floor lines seem to converge in the distance at an imaginary point. That point is called the *vanishing point*. The most common types of perspective drawing are one-point and two-point perspectives. These forms of pictorial drawing are often used in architecture. They are also used in the automotive and aircraft industries. Examples of one-point and two-point perspectives are shown in **Figure 22-4**. A perspective of a true 3D model can be produced in AutoCAD using the **3DORBIT** command. See *AutoCAD and Its Applications—Advanced* for complete coverage of **3DORBIT**.

Figure 22-2.
An object is tilted 35°16′ to achieve an isometric view having 120° between the three axes. Notice the highlighted face in each view.

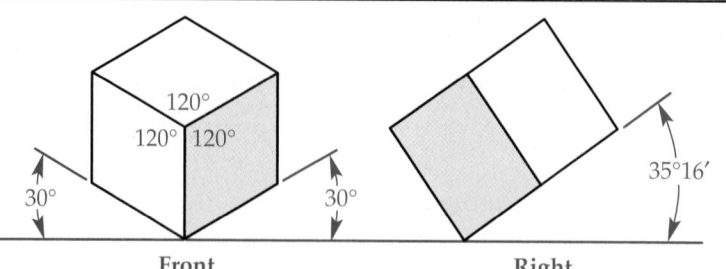

Figure 22-3.
Isometric, dimetric, and trimetric drawings differ in the scales used to draw the three axes. In the isometric shown here, all three sides are drawn at full scale, or 1. You can see how the dimetric and trimetric scales vary.

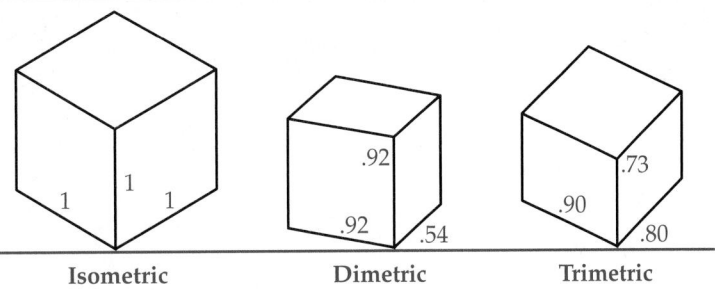

Figure 22-4.
An example of one-point perspective and two-point perspective.

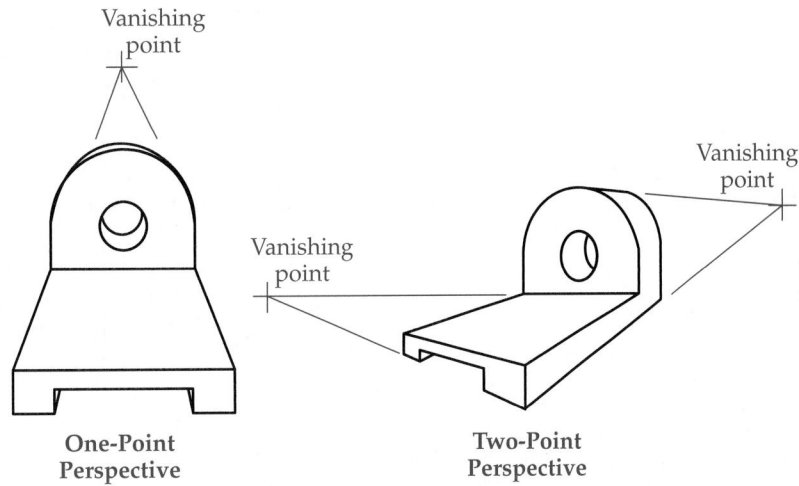

Isometric Drawing

The most common method of pictorial drawing used in industry is isometric. Isometric drawings provide a single view showing three sides that can be measured using the same scale. An isometric view has no perspective and may appear somewhat distorted. Two of the isometric axes are drawn at 30° to horizontal, while the third is drawn at 90°. See **Figure 22-5.**

The three axes shown in **Figure 22-5** represent the width, height, and depth of the object. Lines that appear horizontal in an orthographic view are placed at a 30° angle. Lines that are vertical in an orthographic view are placed vertically. These lines are parallel to the axes. Any line parallel to an axis can be measured and is called an *isometric line.* Lines that are not parallel to the axes are called *nonisometric lines* and cannot be measured. Note the two nonisometric lines in **Figure 22-5.**

Circles appear as ellipses in an isometric drawing. Circular features shown on isometric objects must be oriented properly or they appear distorted. The correct orientation of isometric circles on the three principal planes is shown in **Figure 22-6.** The small diameter (minor axis) of the ellipse must always align on the axis of the circular feature. Notice that the centerline axes of the holes in **Figure 22-6** are parallel to one of the isometric planes.

A basic rule to remember about isometric drawing is that lines that are parallel in an orthogonal view must be parallel in the isometric view. AutoCAD's **ISOPLANE** feature makes that task, and the positioning of ellipses, easy.

isometric line: Any line that is parallel to an axis in an isometric drawing.

nonisometric lines: Lines that are not parallel to the axes in an isometric drawing.

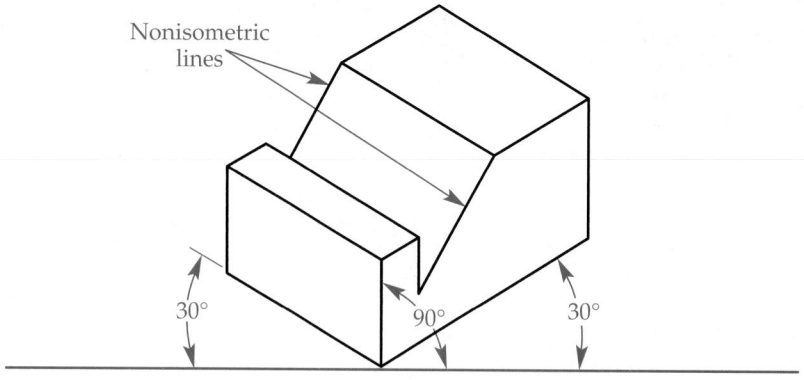

Figure 22-5.
Layout of the isometric axes.

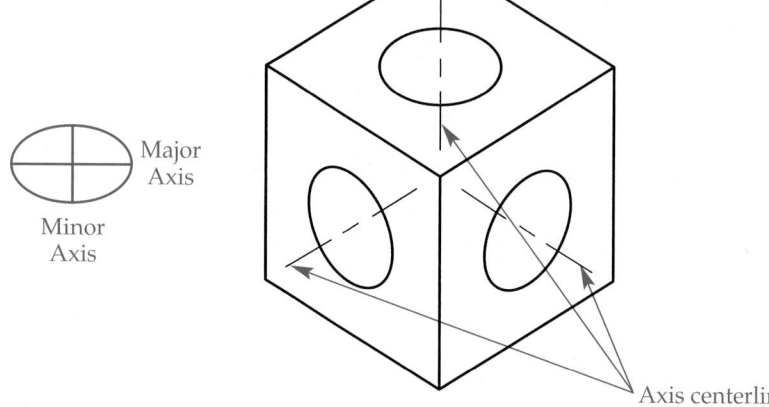

Figure 22-6.
Proper isometric circle (ellipse) orientation on isometric planes. The minor axis always aligns with the axis centerline.

PROFESSIONAL TIP

If you are ever in doubt about the proper orientation of an ellipse in an isometric drawing, remember that the minor axis of the ellipse must always be aligned on the centerline axis of the circular feature. This is shown clearly in **Figure 22-6.**

Settings for Isometric Drawing

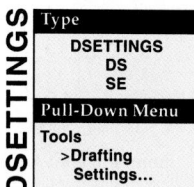

You can quickly set your isometric variables in the **Snap and Grid** tab of the **Drafting Settings** dialog box. See **Figure 22-7.** To access this dialog box, enter DS, SE, or DSETTINGS, or select **Tools** > **Drafting Settings...** from the pull-down menu. This dialog box can also be accessed by right-clicking the **SNAP** or **GRID** status bar button and then selecting **Settings...** from the shortcut menu.

To activate the isometric snap grid, pick the **Isometric snap** radio button in the **Snap type** area. Notice that the **Snap X spacing** and **Grid X spacing** text boxes are now grayed out. Since X spacing relates to horizontal measurements, it is not used in the isometric mode. You can only set the Y spacing for grid and snap in isometric. Be sure to check the **Snap On (F9)** and **Grid On (F7)** check boxes if you want **Snap** and **Grid** modes to be activated. Pick the **OK** button to display the grid dots on the screen in an isometric orientation, as shown in **Figure 22-8.** If the grid dots are not visible, turn the grid on. You may also need to zoom in or out to display the grid.

Figure 22-7.
The **Drafting Settings** dialog box allows you to make settings needed for isometric drawing.

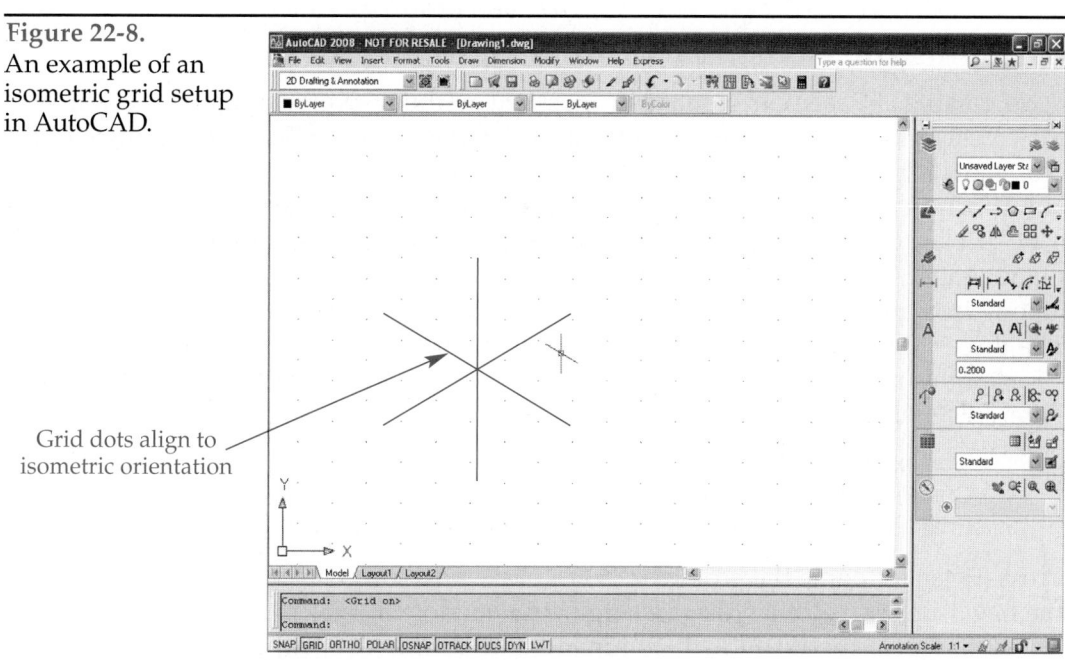

Pick to activate isometric snap grid

Figure 22-8.
An example of an isometric grid setup in AutoCAD.

Grid dots align to isometric orientation

Notice that the crosshairs appear angled. This aids you in drawing lines at the proper isometric angles. Try drawing a four-sided surface using the **LINE** command. Draw the surface so it appears to be the left side of a box in an isometric layout. See **Figure 22-9.** To draw nonparallel surfaces, you can change the angle of the crosshairs to make your task easier, as discussed in the next section.

To turn off the **Isometric Snap** mode, pick the **Rectangular snap** radio button in the **Snap type** area. The **Isometric Snap** mode is turned off and you are returned to the drawing area when you pick the **OK** button.

NOTE

You can also set the **Isometric Snap** mode by typing SNAP or SN, selecting the **Style** option, and then typing I to select **Isometric**.

Figure 22-9.
A four-sided object drawn with the **LINE** command can be used as the left side of an isometric box.

Draw the left side of an isometric box

Changing the Isometric Crosshairs Orientation

Drawing an isometric shape is possible without ever changing the angle of the crosshairs. However, the drawing process is easier and quicker if the angle of the crosshairs aligns with the isometric axes.

Whenever the isometric snap style is enabled, simply press the [F5] key or the [Ctrl]+[E] key combination to change the crosshairs immediately to the next isometric plane. AutoCAD refers to the isometric positions or planes as *isoplanes*. As you change among isoplanes, the current isoplane is displayed on the prompt line as a reference. The three crosshairs orientations and their angular values are shown in Figure 22-10.

Another method to toggle the crosshairs position is to use the **ISOPLANE** command. Enter ISOPLANE as follows.

> Command: **ISOPLANE**↵
> Current isoplane: *current*
> Enter isometric plane setting [Left/Top/Right] <*current*>: ↵

Press [Enter] to toggle the crosshairs to the next position. The command line displays the new isoplane setting. You can toggle immediately to the next position by pressing [Enter] to repeat the **ISOPLANE** command and pressing [Enter] again. To specify the plane of orientation, type the first letter of that position. The **ISOPLANE** command can also be used transparently.

The crosshairs are always in one of the isoplane positions when **Isometric Snap** mode is in effect. An exception occurs during a display or editing command when a multiple selection set method, such as a window, is used. In these cases, the crosshairs

isoplanes: The three isometric positions or planes.

Figure 22-10.
You can toggle among the three isometric crosshairs positions using the [F5] function key, the [Ctrl]+[E] key combination, or the **ISOPLANE** command.

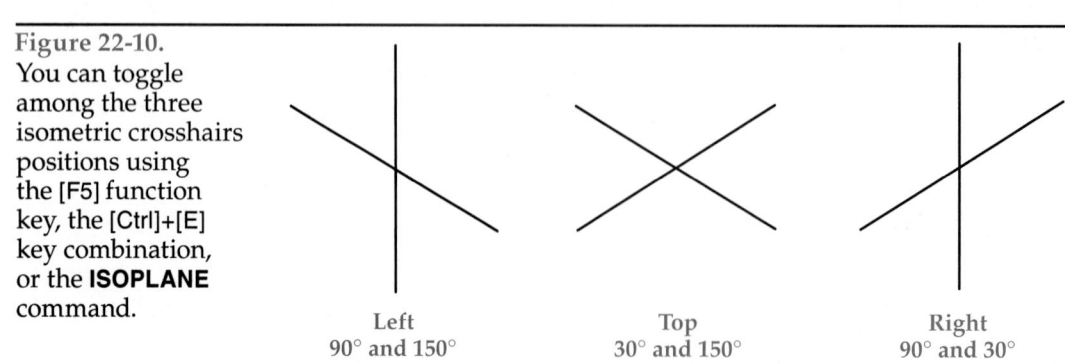

Left	Top	Right
90° and 150°	30° and 150°	90° and 30°

change to the normal vertical and horizontal positions. At the completion of the display or editing command, the crosshairs revert to their former isoplane orientation.

PROFESSIONAL TIP

The quickest way to change the isoplane is to press the [F5] function key or press the [Ctrl]+[E] key combination.

Exercise 22-1
Complete the exercise on the Student CD.

Isometric Ellipses

Placing an isometric ellipse on an object is easy with AutoCAD because of the **Isocircle** option of the **ELLIPSE** command. An ellipse is positioned automatically on the current isoplane. To use the **ELLIPSE** command, first make sure you are in **Isometric Snap** mode. Then, pick the **Ellipse** button from the **2D Draw** control panel of the **Dashboard** or from the **Draw** toolbar, select **Draw > Ellipse > Axis, End**, or type EL or ELLIPSE. Once the **ELLIPSE** command is initiated, type I for the **Isocircle** option. Once you select the **Isocircle** option, pick the center point and then set the radius or diameter. Note that the **Isocircle** option only appears when you are in **Isometric Snap** mode.

Always check the isoplane position before placing an ellipse (isocircle) on your drawing. You can dynamically view the three positions that an ellipse can take. Initiate the **ELLIPSE** command, enter the **Isocircle** option, pick a center point, and press [F5] to toggle the crosshairs orientation. See Figure 22-11. The ellipse rotates each time you toggle the crosshairs.

The isometric ellipse (isocircle) is a true ellipse. If selected, grips are displayed at the center and four quadrant points. See Figure 22-12. However, do not use grips to resize or otherwise adjust an isometric ellipse. As soon as you resize an isometric ellipse in this manner, its angular value is changed and it is no longer isometric. You can use the center grip to move the ellipse. Also, if you rotate an isometric ellipse while **Ortho** mode is on, it will not appear in a proper isometric plane. You *can* rotate an isometric ellipse from one isometric plane to another, but you must enter a value of 120°.

Figure 22-11.
The orientation of an isometric ellipse is determined by the current isometric plane.

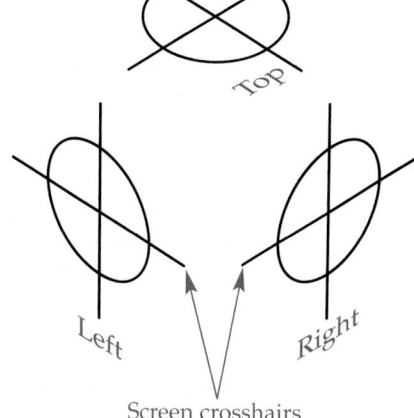

Figure 22-12.
An isometric ellipse
has grips at its four
quadrant points and
center.

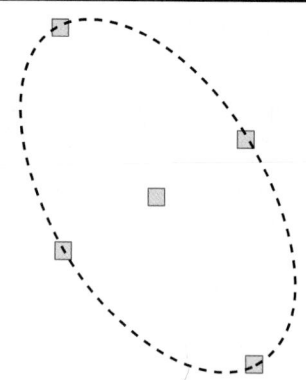

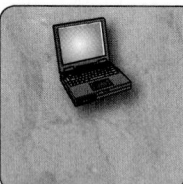

PROFESSIONAL TIP

Prior to drawing isometric ellipses, it is good practice to place a marker at the ellipse center point. A good technique is to draw a point at the center using an easily visible point style. This is especially useful if the ellipse does not fall on grid or snap points.

Exercise 22-2

Complete the exercise on the Student CD.

Constructing Isometric Arcs

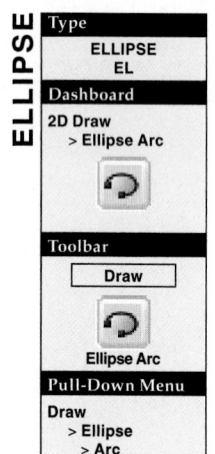

ELLIPSE

Type
ELLIPSE
EL

Dashboard
2D Draw
> Ellipse Arc

Toolbar
Draw

Ellipse Arc

Pull-Down Menu
Draw
> Ellipse
> Arc

The **ELLIPSE** command can also be used to draw an isometric arc of any included angle. To construct an isometric arc, use the **Arc** option of the **ELLIPSE** command while in isometric mode. To access the **Arc** option, pick the **Ellipse Arc** button from the **2D Draw** control panel of the **Dashboard** or from the **Draw** toolbar, type EL or ELLIPSE followed by A for the **Arc** option, or select **Draw** > **Ellipse** > **Arc**. Once the **Arc** option is initiated, the following prompts appear:

Specify axis endpoint of elliptical arc or [Center/Isocircle]: I↵
Specify center of isocircle: (*pick the center of the arc*)
Specify radius of isocircle or [Diameter]: (*pick the radius or type a value and press* [Enter])
Specify start angle or [Parameter]: (*pick a start angle or type a value and press* [Enter])
Specify end angle or [Parameter/Included angle]: (*pick an end angle or type an included angle value and press* [Enter])
Command:

A common application of isometric arcs is drawing fillets and rounds. Once a round is created in isometric, the edge (corner) of the object sits back from its original, unfilleted position. See Figure 22-13A. You can draw the complete object first and then trim away the excess after locating the fillets. You can also draw the isometric arcs and then the connecting lines. Either way, the center point of the ellipse is a critical feature and should be located first. The left-hand arc in Figure 22-13A was drawn first and copied to the back position. Use Ortho mode to help quickly draw 90° arcs.

The next step is to move the original edge to its new position, which is tangent to the isometric arcs. You can do this by snapping the endpoint of the line to the quadrant point of the arc. See Figure 22-13B. Notice the grips on the line and on the arc. The endpoint of the line is snapped to the quadrant grip on the arc. The final step is to trim away the excess lines and arc segment. The completed feature is shown in Figure 22-13C.

AutoCAD and Its Applications—Basics

Figure 22-13.
Fillets and rounds can be drawn with the **Arc** option of the **ELLIPSE** command. A broken line is used to represent an edge that is viewed straight on.

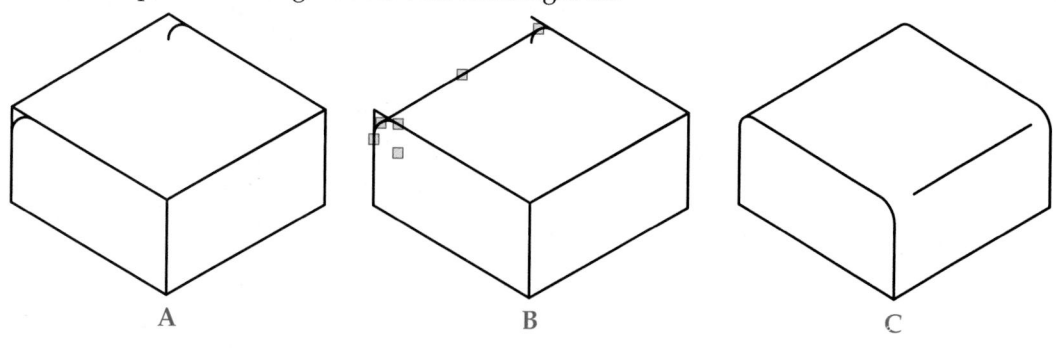

A   B   C

Rounded edges, when viewed straight on, cannot be shown as complete-edge lines that extend to the ends of the object. Instead, a good technique to use is a broken line in the original location of the edge. This is clearly shown on the right-hand edge in Figure 22-13C.

Exercise 22-3
Complete the exercise on the Student CD.

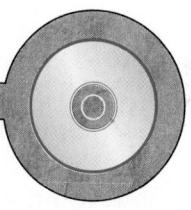

Creating Isometric Text Styles

Text placed in an isometric drawing should appear to be parallel to one of the isometric planes. Text should align with the plane to which it applies. Text may be located on the object or positioned away from it as a note. Drafters and artists occasionally neglect this aspect of pictorial drawing and it shows on the final product.

Properly placing text on an isometric drawing involves creating new text styles. Figure 22-14 illustrates possible orientations of text on an isometric drawing. These examples were created using only two text styles. The text styles have an obliquing angle of either 30° or –30°. The labels in Figure 22-14 refer to the chart below. The angle in the figure indicates the rotation angle entered when using one of the text commands. For example, ISO-2 90 means that the ISO-2 style was used and the text was rotated 90°. This technique can be applied to any font.

Name	Font	Obliquing Angle
ISO-1	Romans	30°
ISO-2	Romans	–30°

Exercise 22-4
Complete the exercise on the Student CD.

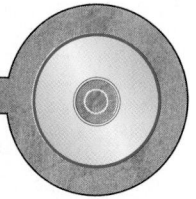

Figure 22-14.
Isometric text applications. The text shown here indicates which style and angle were used.

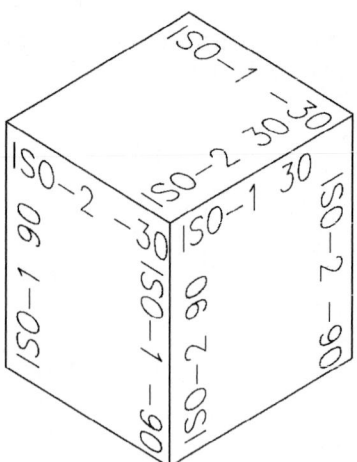

Isometric Dimensioning

An important aspect of dimensioning in isometric is to place dimension lines, text, and arrowheads on the proper plane. Remember these guidelines:

✓ Extension lines should always extend in the plane being dimensioned.
✓ The heel of the arrowhead should always be parallel to the extension line.
✓ Strokes of the text that would normally be vertical should always be parallel with the extension lines or dimension lines.

These techniques are shown on the dimensioned isometric part in **Figure 22-15.** AutoCAD does not automatically dimension isometric objects. You must first create isometric arrowheads and text styles. Then, manually draw the dimension lines and text as they should appear in each of the three isometric planes. This is time-consuming when compared to dimensioning normal 2D drawings.

You have already learned how to create isometric text styles. These can be set up in an isometric template drawing if you draw isometrics often. Examples of arrows for the three isometric planes are shown in **Figure 22-16.**

Figure 22-15.
A dimensioned isometric part. Note the text and arrowhead orientation in relation to the extension lines.

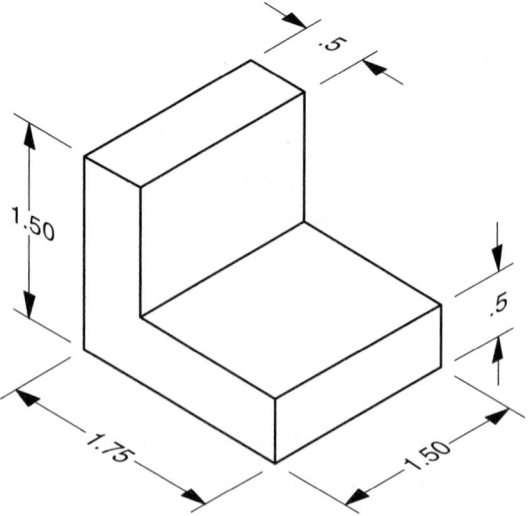

AutoCAD and Its Applications—Basics

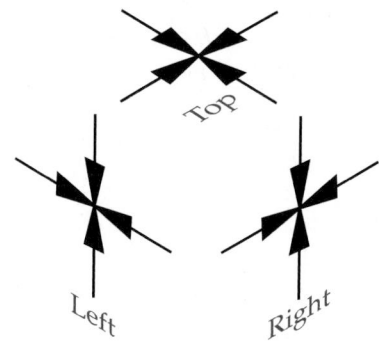

Figure 22-16.
Examples of arrowheads in each of the three isometric planes.

Isometric Arrowheads

You can draw isometric arrowheads and fill them in with a solid hatch pattern, or you can use the **SOLID** command to create a filled arrowhead. A variable-width polyline cannot be used because the heel of the arrowhead will not be parallel to the extension lines.

Every arrowhead does not need to be drawn individually. First, draw two isometric axes, as shown in **Figure 22-17A**. Then, draw one arrowhead like the one shown in **Figure 22-17B**. Use the **MIRROR** command to create additional arrows. As you create new arrows, move them to their proper plane.

You can save each arrowhead as a block in your isometric template or prototype. Use block names that are easy to remember. Blocks are discussed in Chapter 23.

Oblique Dimensioning

AutoCAD has a way to dimension isometric and oblique lines semiautomatically. First, draw the dimensions using any of the linear dimensioning commands. The object in **Figure 22-18A** was dimensioned using the **DIMALIGNED** and **DIMLINEAR** commands. Then, use the **Oblique** option of the **DIMEDIT** command to rotate the extension lines. See **Figure 22-18B**.

To access the **Oblique** option, type DED or DIMEDIT and then type O for **Oblique**. You can also select **Dimension > Oblique**. When prompted, select the dimension and enter the obliquing angle.

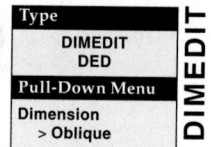

This technique creates suitable dimensions for an isometric drawing and is quicker than the method previously discussed. However, this method does not rotate the arrows to align the arrowhead heels with the extension lines. It also does not draw the dimension text aligned in the plane of the dimension. Therefore, this method does not produce technically correct dimensions.

Figure 22-17.
Creating isometric arrowheads.
A—Draw the two isometric axes for arrowhead placement. B—Draw the first arrowhead on one of the axis lines. Then mirror the arrowhead to create the others.

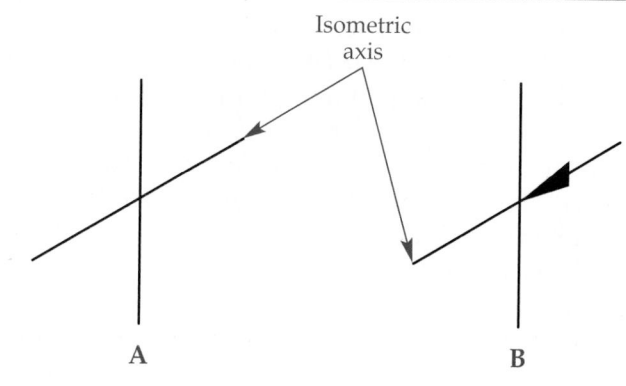

Figure 22-18.
Using the **Oblique** option of the **DIMEDIT** command, you can create semiautomatic isometric dimensions by editing existing dimensions.

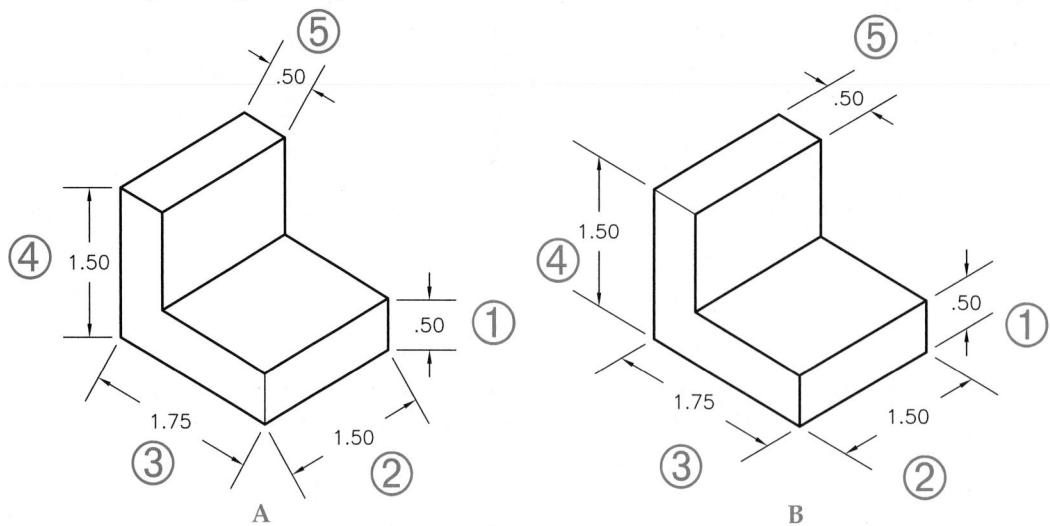

Dimension	Obliquing Angle
1	30°
2	–30°
3	30°
4	–30°
5	30°

Chapter Test

Answer the following questions. Write your answers on a separate sheet of paper or complete the electronic chapter test on the Student CD.

1. The simplest form of pictorial drawing is _____.
2. How does isometric drawing differ from oblique drawing?
3. How do dimetric and trimetric drawings differ from isometric drawings?
4. The most realistic form of pictorial drawing is _____.
5. Which command allows you to access the **Drafting Settings** dialog box?
6. What must be set in the **Drafting Settings** dialog box to turn on **Isometric Snap** mode and set a snap spacing of .2?
7. What function does the **ISOPLANE** command perform?
8. Name the command and option used to draw an isometric circle.
9. What factor determines the orientation of an isometric ellipse?
10. Where are grips located on a circle drawn in isometric?
11. Can grips be used to resize an isometric circle correctly? Explain your answer.
12. How are isometric arcs drawn?
13. Which text style setting allows you to create text that can be used on an isometric drawing?
14. What technique does AutoCAD provide for dimensioning isometric objects?

Drawing Problems

Create an isometric template drawing. Items that should be set in the template include grid spacing, snap spacing, ortho setting, and text size. Save the template as isoproto.dwt. *Use the template to construct the isometric drawings in Problems 1–10. Save the drawing problems as* P22-*(problem number).*

1.

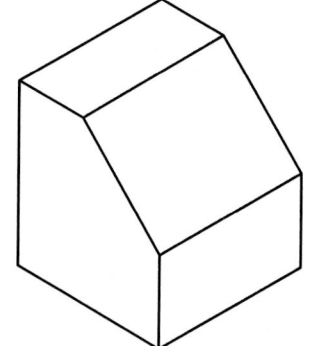

2.

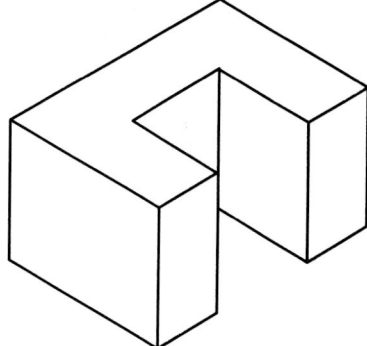

3.

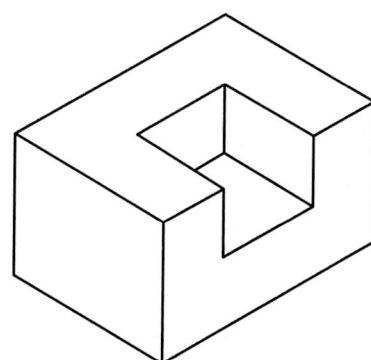

4.

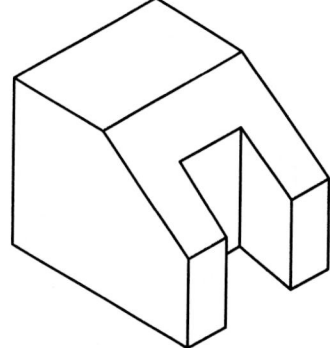

5.

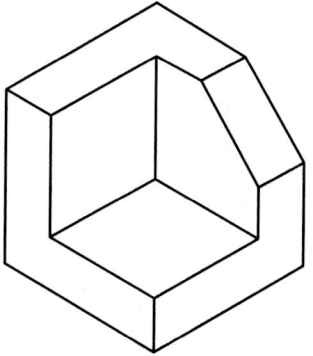

6.

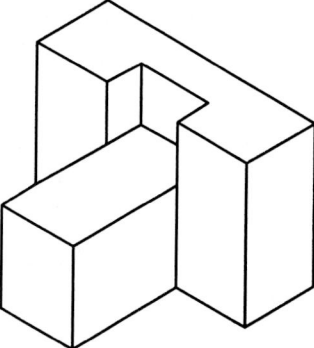

7.

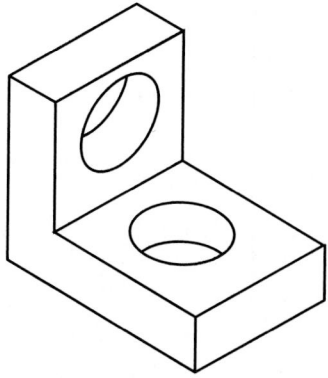

8.

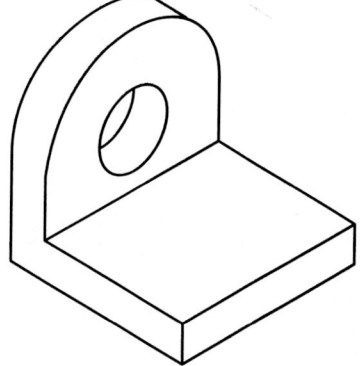

9.

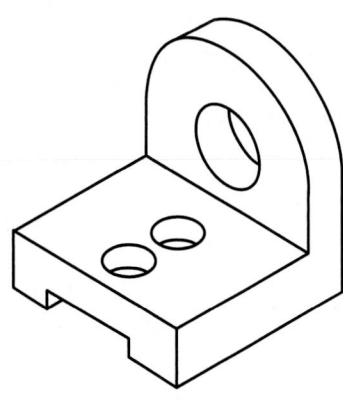

10.

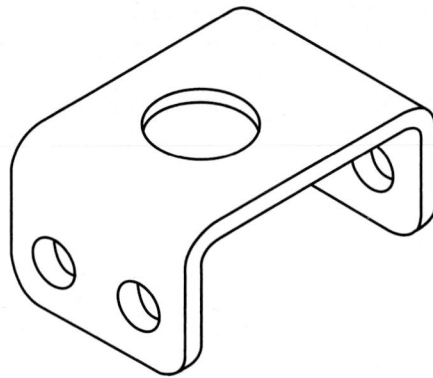

For Problems 11–14, create isometric drawings using the views shown. Measure the drawings to obtain the dimensions.

11.

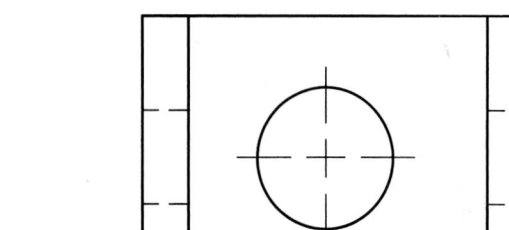
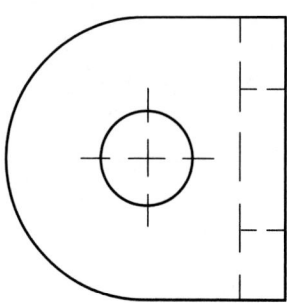

12.

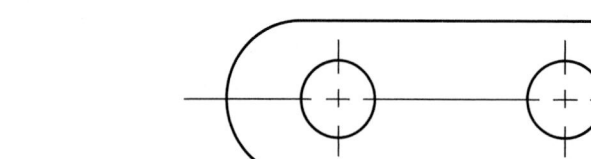

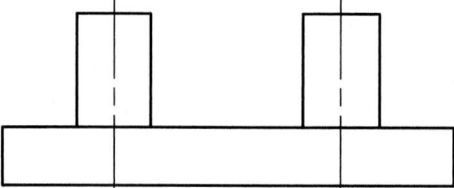

13.

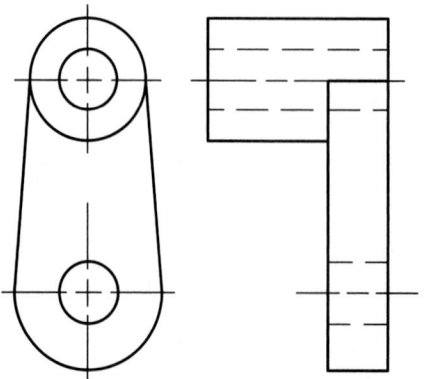

14.

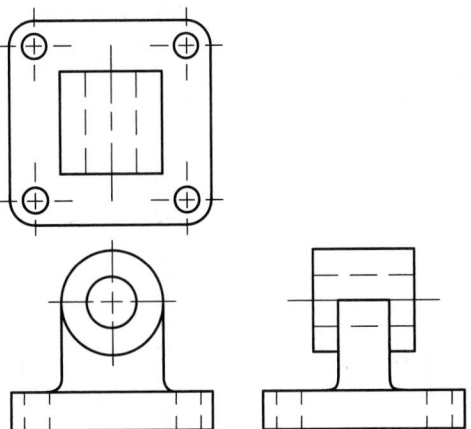

15. Construct a set of isometric arrowheads to use when dimensioning isometric drawings. Load your isometric template drawing. Create arrowheads for each of the three isometric planes. Name them with the first letter indicating the plane: T for top, L for left, and R for right. Also, number them clockwise from the top. See the example below for the right isometric plane. Do not include the labels in your drawing. Save the template again when finished.

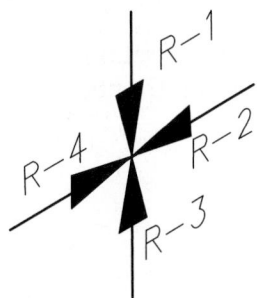

16. Create a set of isometric text styles like those shown in **Figure 22-14.** Load your template drawing and make a complete set in one font. Make additional sets in other fonts if you wish. Enter a text height of 0 so that you can specify the height when placing the text. Save the template when finished.

17. Begin a new drawing using your isometric template. Select one of the following problems from this chapter and dimension it: Problem 5, 7, 8, or 9. When adding dimensions, be sure to use the proper arrowhead and text style for the plane on which you are working. Save the drawing as P22-17.

18. Create an isometric drawing of the switch plate shown below. Select a view that best displays the features of the object. Do not include dimensions. Save the drawing as P22-18.

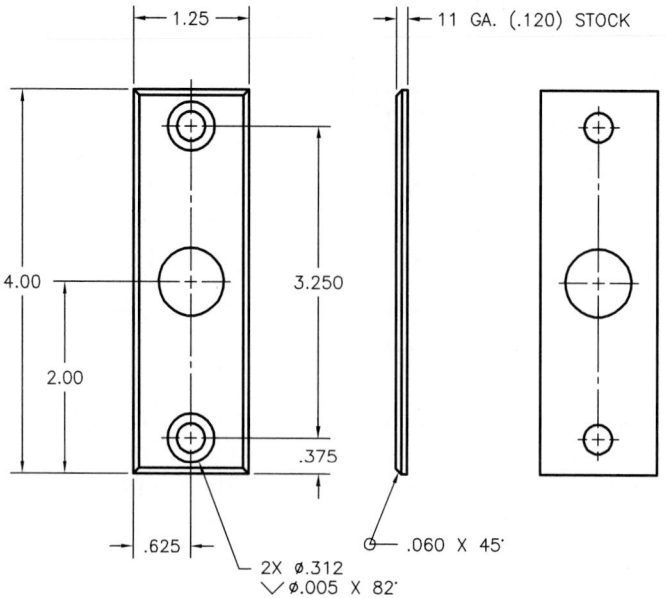

19. Create an isometric drawing of the retainer shown below. Select a view that best displays the features of the object. Do not include dimensions. Save the drawing as P22-19.

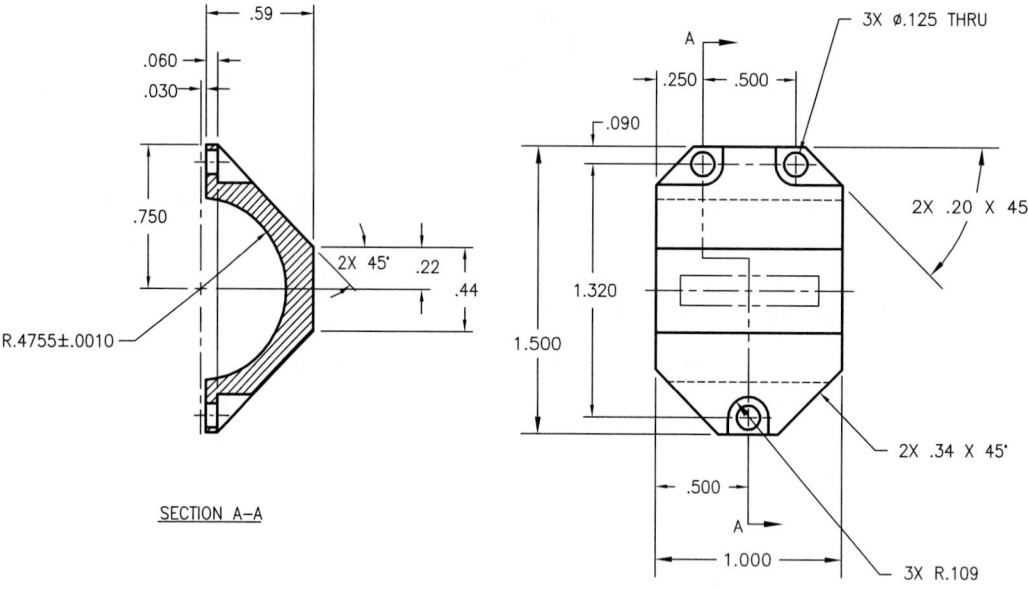

CHAPTER 23

Creating Symbols for Multiple Use

Learning Objectives

After completing this chapter, you will be able to do the following:
- ✓ Create and save blocks.
- ✓ Insert blocks into a drawing.
- ✓ Edit a block and update it in a drawing.
- ✓ Create blocks as drawing files.
- ✓ Construct and use a symbol library of blocks.
- ✓ Purge blocks from a drawing file.

One of the greatest benefits of AutoCAD is its ability to store symbols for future use. These symbols, or *blocks*, can be inserted into a drawing, scaled, and rotated in one operation. If a block is edited, drawings containing the block can be updated to include the new version. This chapter describes the construction and management of blocks, wblocks, and symbol libraries.

block: A user-created symbol that has been saved and stored in a drawing for future use.

Introduction to Blocks

AutoCAD provides two types of block definitions. A block created with the **BLOCK** command is stored within a drawing as a *block definition*. The block can be inserted into the drawing in which it was defined as many times as needed. A *wblock* created with the **WBLOCK** command is saved as a separate drawing file and can be inserted as many times as needed into *any* drawing. Both types of blocks can be scaled and rotated as they are inserted to meet the drawing requirements, and both types can be shared between drawings. Blocks can be copied between drawings using **DesignCenter** or tool palettes, and wblocks can be inserted into drawings using **DesignCenter**, tool palettes, and the **INSERT** command.

When a drawing is inserted or referenced into another (current) drawing, it becomes part of the drawing on screen, but its content is not added to the current drawing file. Any named objects, such as blocks and layers, are referred to as *dependent symbols*. AutoCAD automatically updates dependent symbols in a drawing the next time the drawing is opened.

block definition: Information about a block that is stored within the drawing file.

wblock: A block definition that is saved as a separate drawing file.

dependent symbols: Named objects in a drawing that has been inserted or referenced into another drawing.

Constructing Blocks

A block can be any shape, group of objects, symbol, view, or drawing. Before constructing a block, review the drawing you are working on. This is where a sketch of your drawing can be useful. Look for any shapes, components, notes, and assemblies that are used more than once. These features can be drawn once and then saved as blocks for multiple use.

Selecting a Layer

Before you begin drawing block components, you should identify the appropriate layer on which to create the objects. It is critical that you understand how layers and object properties are applied when you create and insert blocks.

When you draw block objects, you can use one of two methods for layer placement. The first method is to draw all block objects on the 0 layer. If the objects used for a block are originally created on the 0 layer, the block assumes, or inherits, the properties of the layer on which it is inserted. This is the preferred method of block creation and usage. If the objects have been drawn on a different layer, place all the objects on layer 0 before using the **BLOCK** command.

The second method for using layers is to create block objects using a layer or layers other than the 0 layer. If the objects for the block are originally created on a layer other than the 0 layer, the objects belong to the layer on which the block is inserted, but they retain the properties of the layer or layers on which the objects were created. This method can often cause confusion because a group of objects (a block) belongs to one layer, but has the properties of a different layer. As a result, you should usually draw objects for a block on the 0 layer.

To create a block that maintains a specific color and linetype regardless of the layer it is to be used on, set the absolute color and linetype before drawing the objects. If the block should assume the current color and linetype when it is inserted into a drawing, set the current object color and linetype to ByBlock.

To set the color to ByBlock, pick **ByBlock** in the **Color Control** drop-down list of the **Properties** toolbar or the **Object Properties** control panel of the **Dashboard**, or pick the **ByBlock** button in the **Select Color** dialog box. See **Figure 23-1**.

To set the linetype to ByBlock, pick **ByBlock** in the **Linetype Control** drop-down list of the **Properties** toolbar or the **Object Properties** control panel of the **Dashboard**, or set ByBlock current using the **Linetype Manager** dialog box. See **Figure 23-2**.

When the current color and linetype are both set to ByBlock, you can create blocks. A block created with these settings assumes the current color and linetype when it is inserted into a drawing, regardless of the current layer setting.

Figure 23-1.
After picking **Format** > **Color...** from the pull-down menu to display the **Select Color** dialog box, pick the **ByBlock** button to have the block assume the current color when it is inserted into a drawing.

Pick to change the color to ByBlock

Current color setting

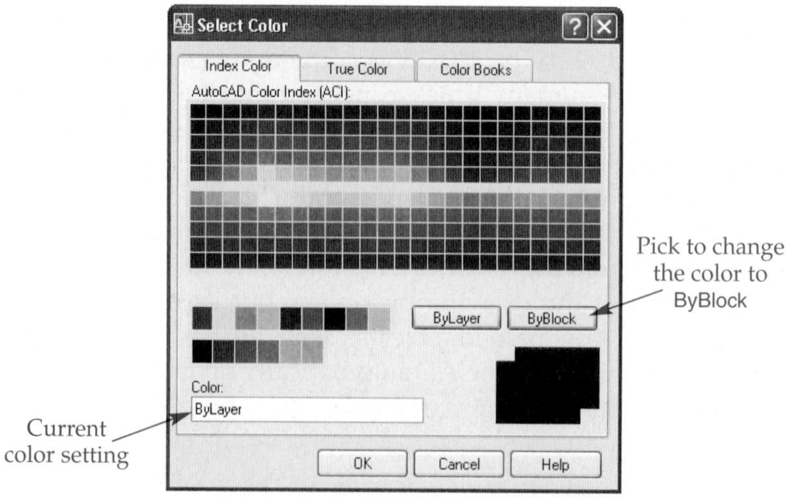

Figure 23-2.
To set the ByBlock linetype current, pick ByBlock in the **Linetype** list of the **Linetype Manager** dialog box and then pick the **Current** button.

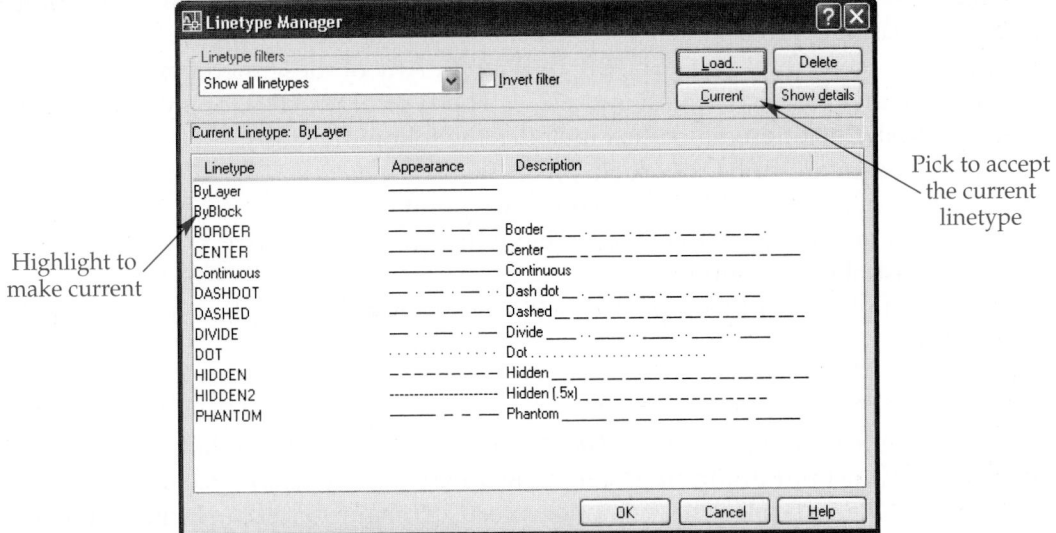

Highlight to make current

Pick to accept the current linetype

Drawing the Block Components

Draw a block as you would any other drawing geometry. When you finish drawing the object, determine the best location to use as an *insertion base point*. When you insert the block into a drawing, the insertion base point attaches to the crosshairs for placement. Several examples of commonly used blocks are shown in **Figure 23-3** with their insertion points highlighted.

insertion base point: The point on a block that attaches to the crosshairs for insertion into the drawing.

PROFESSIONAL TIP

Multiple features that are identical except for scale can be created from a single block. In these cases, the base block should be drawn to fit inside a one-unit square. It does not matter if the object is measured in feet, inches, or millimeters. This makes it easy to scale the symbol later when you insert it into a drawing.

Figure 23-3.
Common drafting symbols and their insertion points for placement on drawings. The insertion points are shown here as colored dots.

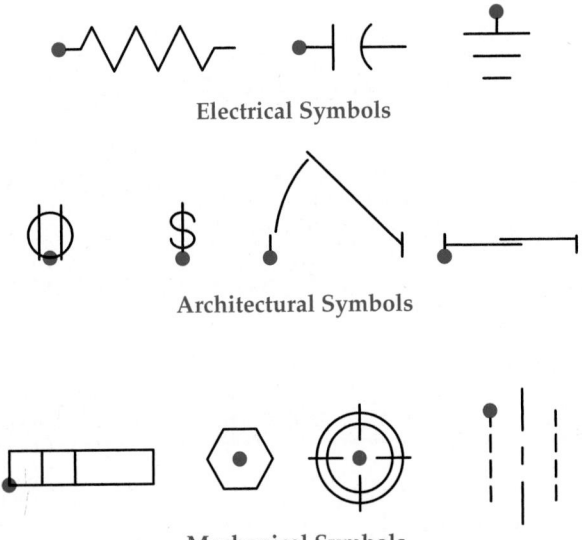

Electrical Symbols

Architectural Symbols

Mechanical Symbols

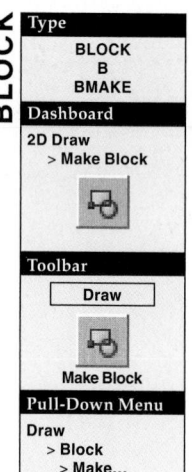

Creating Blocks

When you draw a shape or symbol, you have not yet created a block. To save your object as a block, pick the **Make Block** button on the **Draw** toolbar or the **Block Attributes** or **Draw** control panels of the **Dashboard**, pick **Draw > Block > Make...** from the pull-down menu, or type B, BLOCK, or BMAKE. Any of these methods displays the **Block Definition** dialog box. See **Figure 23-4**. The typical process for creating a block using the **Block Definition** dialog box includes the following steps:

1. Name and describe the block.
2. Enter or select the block insertion base point.
3. Select existing drawing objects that will make up the block.
4. Adjust block definition options.
5. Pick the **OK** button to exit the **Block Definition** dialog box and create the block.

Naming and describing the block

Enter a name for the block in the **Name:** text box of the **Block Definition** dialog box. For example, a vacuum pump might be named PUMP or a certain size door might be named DOOR_3068. The block name cannot exceed 255 characters. It can include numbers, letters, and spaces, as well as the dollar sign ($), hyphen (-), and underscore (_).

A block name is often descriptive enough to identify the correct block. However, you can enter a textual description of the block in the **Description:** text box to help identify the block for easy reference. For example, the PUMP block might include the description This is a vacuum pump symbol, or the DOOR_3068 block might include the description This is 3' wide by 6'-8" tall interior single-swing door.

Defining the block insertion base point

The **Base point** area of the **Block Definition** dialog box is used to define the block insertion base point. You can enter the coordinates for the insertion base point by typing values in the **X:**, **Y:**, and **Z:** text boxes, or you can select the insertion base point directly from the drawing.

Figure 23-4.
Blocks are created using the **Block Definition** dialog box.

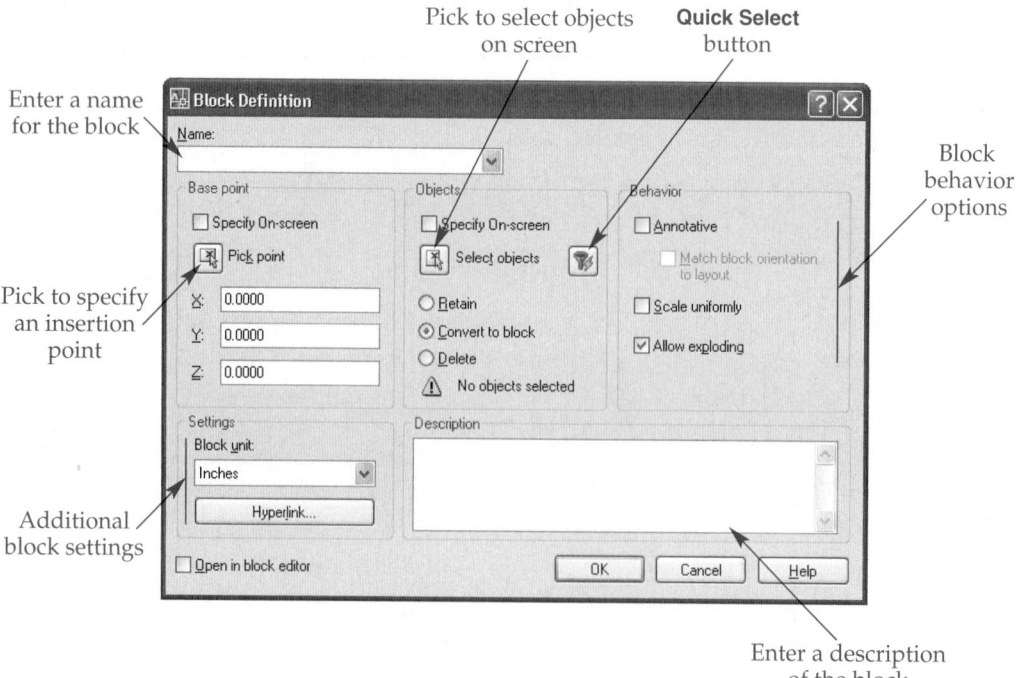

AutoCAD and Its Applications—Basics

Choose the **Pick point** button to return to the drawing and select an insertion base point. The **Block Definition** dialog box reappears once the insertion base point is selected. An alternative technique is to choose the **Specify On-screen** check box. When selected, this option allows you to pick an insertion base point from the drawing after you pick the **OK** button to exit the **Block Definition** dialog box. This method can save time by picking the insertion base point without using the **Pick point** button and reentering the **Block Definition** dialog box.

Selecting block objects

The **Objects** area of the **Block Definition** dialog box contains options for selected objects for the block definition. Pick the **Select objects** button to return to the drawing and select objects that will make up the block. Press [Enter] when you are finished to redisplay the **Block Definition** dialog box. The number of selected objects is shown in the **Objects** area and an image of the selection is displayed next to the **Name** drop-down list. If you want to create a selection set, use the **Quick Select** button to define a filter for your selection set. The **Quick Select** dialog box is described in Chapter 11.

An alternative method for selecting objects is to choose the **Specify On-screen** check box. When selected, this option allows you to pick objects from the drawing after you pick the **OK** button to exit the **Block Definition** dialog box. This method can save time by selecting objects without using the **Select objects** button and reentering the **Block Definition** dialog box.

The **Objects** area is also used to specify whether to retain, convert, or delete the selected objects. If you want to keep the selected objects in the current drawing (in their original state), pick the **Retain** radio button. If you want to replace the selected objects with the block you are creating, pick the **Convert to block** radio button. If you want to remove the selected objects after the block is defined, pick the **Delete** radio button.

PROFESSIONAL TIP

If you select the **Delete** option and then decide that you want to keep the original geometry in the drawing after you have defined the block, enter the **OOPS** command. This returns the original objects to the screen and keeps the block definition, whereas using the **UNDO** command removes the block definition from the drawing.

Block scale settings

To make the block annotative, pick the **Annotative** check box in the **Behavior** area. AutoCAD scales blocks that you define as annotative according to the annotation scale you select, which is the same as the drawing scale, eliminating the need for you to calculate the scale factor. Block scaling options are further described later in this chapter.

When you select the **Annotative** check box, the **Match block orientation to layout** check box becomes available. Pick this check box to keep annotative blocks planar to the layout in a floating viewport, even if the drawing view is rotated, as it might be if you rotate the UCS. Selecting this option also prohibits you from using the **ROTATE** command to rotate a block.

If the **Scale uniformly** check box in the **Behavior** area is checked, you do not have the option of specifying different X and Y scale factors when the block is inserted into a drawing.

Additional block definition settings

The **Block Definition** dialog box contains several additional block definition options:

- **Allow exploding.** If this check box in the **Behavior** area is checked, the block can be exploded. If the box is not checked, the block cannot be exploded either when it is inserted or after it is inserted in the drawing.
- **Block unit.** Select a unit type from this drop-down list in the **Settings** area to specify the insertion units of the block.
- **Hyperlink....** Pick this button to access the **Insert Hyperlink** dialog box to insert a hyperlink in the block.
- **Open in block editor.** If this check box is checked, the new block is immediately opened in the **Block Definition Editor** after the block is created. The **Block Definition Editor** is described later in this chapter.

NOTE

To verify that the block was saved properly, reopen the **Block Definition** dialog box. Pick the **Name:** drop-down list button to display a list of all blocks in the current drawing. The block names are organized in numerical and alphabetical order.

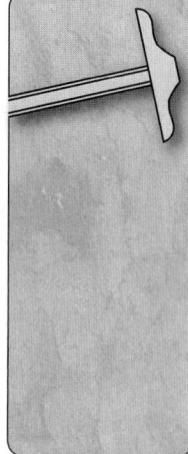

LEGACY NOTE

The **-BLOCK** command provides the same options found in the **Block Definition** dialog box, presented as prompts on the command line. To display a list of all block names, type ?, press [Enter], and press [Enter] again. Block information is then displayed in the **AutoCAD Text Window**. The listing reports each block name, as well as the different types of blocks and the number of each type in the drawing. The first entry in the block listing is that of *defined* blocks. *User blocks* are those created by you. *External references* are drawings referenced with the **XREF** command. External references are described in Chapter 28. Blocks that reside in a referenced drawing are called *dependent blocks*. *Unnamed blocks* are objects such as associative and nonassociative dimensions.

user blocks: Blocks created and saved by the user of the AutoCAD software.

external references: External drawings that appear on-screen for reference when you use the XREF command.

dependent blocks: Blocks that reside in a referenced drawing.

unnamed blocks: Blocks that AutoCAD considers "anonymous," such as associative dimensions.

nesting: Creating a block that includes other blocks.

PROFESSIONAL TIP

Blocks can be used to create other blocks. Suppose you design a complex part or view that will be used repeatedly. You can insert existing blocks into the view and then save the entire object as a block. This is called *nesting*, where blocks contain other blocks. The top-level block must be given a name that is different from any nested block. Proper planning and knowledge of all existing blocks can speed up the drawing process and the creation of complex parts.

Exercise 23-1
Complete the exercise on the Student CD.

AutoCAD and Its Applications—Basics

Using Blocks in a Drawing

Once a block has been created, it is easy to insert it into a drawing. First, determine the proper size and rotation angle for the block. Blocks are normally inserted on specific layers, so set the proper layer *before* inserting the block. Once a block has been inserted into a drawing, it is referred to as a ***block reference***.

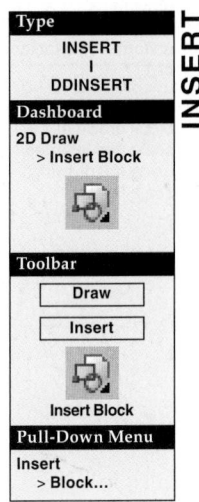

block reference: A specific instance of a block inserted into a drawing.

Inserting Blocks Using the Insert Command

Blocks and wblocks are placed in a drawing with the **INSERT** command. Pick the **Insert Block** button on the **2D Draw** control panel of the **Dashboard** or the **Draw** or **Insert** toolbar, pick **Insert > Block...** from the pull-down menu, or type I, INSERT, or DDINSERT. This opens the **Insert** dialog box, as shown in **Figure 23-5**.

Selecting the block to insert

Pick the **Name:** drop-down list button to show the blocks defined in the current drawing. Then select the name of the block you wish to insert. You can also type the name of the block in the **Name:** text box. Once the desired block has been specified, you must specify the insertion location, scale, and rotation angle. You can also specify whether to explode the block while inserting it. Pick the **Browse...** button to display the **Select Drawing File** dialog box in which you can select a drawing file (wblock) for insertion into the current drawing.

Defining the block insertion point

The **Insertion point** area of the **Insert** dialog box contains options for specifying where the block is to be inserted. If the **Specify On-screen** check box is selected, the block is inserted dynamically when you pick **OK** and you must pick an insertion point on screen. If you wish to insert the block using absolute coordinates, disable the check box and enter the coordinates in the **X:**, **Y:**, and **Z:** text boxes.

Scaling blocks

The **Scale** area of the **Insert** dialog box allows you to specify scale values for the block in relation to the X, Y, and Z axes. By default, the **Specify On-screen** check box is inactive. If the check box is inactive, you can enter scale values in the **X:**, **Y:**, and **Z:** text boxes. If you want to be prompted for the scale when inserting the block, select the **Specify On-screen** check box.

If you activate the **Uniform Scale** check box, you can specify a scale value for the X axis. The same value is then used for the Y and Z axes when the block is inserted.

Figure 23-5.
The **Insert** dialog box allows you to select and prepare a block for insertion. Select the block you wish to insert from the drop-down list or enter the block name in the **Name:** text box.

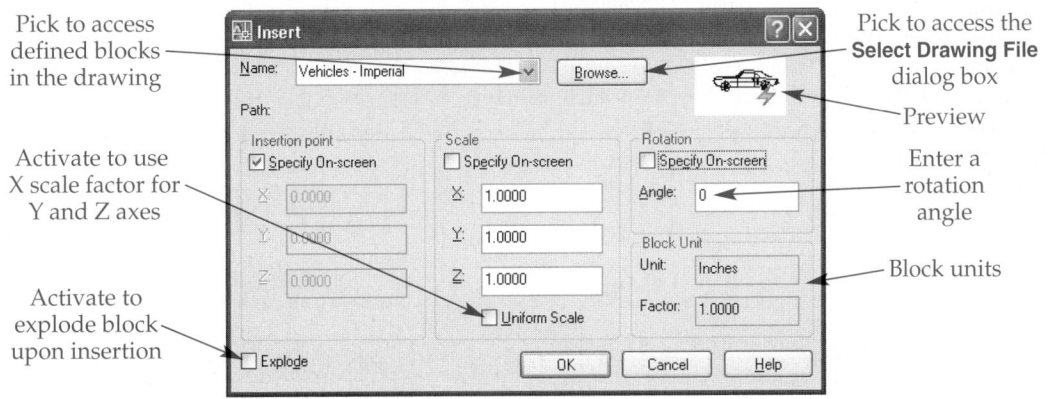

If the block was created with the **Scale uniformly** check box checked in the **Block Definition** dialog box, only the **X** value is active. The Y and Z coordinates also use this value so the block stays uniform.

It is possible to create a mirror image of a block by entering a negative value for the scale factor. For example, entering –1 for both the X scale factor and the Y scale factor mirrors the block to the opposite quadrant of the original orientation specified and retains the original size. Different mirroring techniques are shown in **Figure 23-6**. The insertion point is indicated by a dot.

A block that is scaled during insertion can be classified as a real block, schematic block, or unit block. A *real block* is one that is drawn at a one-to-one scale. It is then inserted into the drawing using 1 for both the X and Y scale factors. Examples of real blocks could include a bolt, a bathtub, a pipe fitting, or the car shown in **Figure 23-7A**.

real block: A block drawn at a 1:1 scale and inserted with a uniform scale factor of 1.

A *schematic block* is a block that is originally drawn at a one-to-one scale. It is then inserted using the drawing scale factor for both the X and Y scale values. Examples of schematic blocks could include notes, detail bubbles, or section symbols. See **Figure 23-7B**. Annotative blocks are typically classified as schematic blocks. When you insert an annotative schematic block, AutoCAD automatically determines the block scale based on the annotation scale. When you insert a non-annotative schematic block, you must specify the scale factor.

schematic block: A block drawn at a 1:1 scale and inserted using the drawing scale factor.

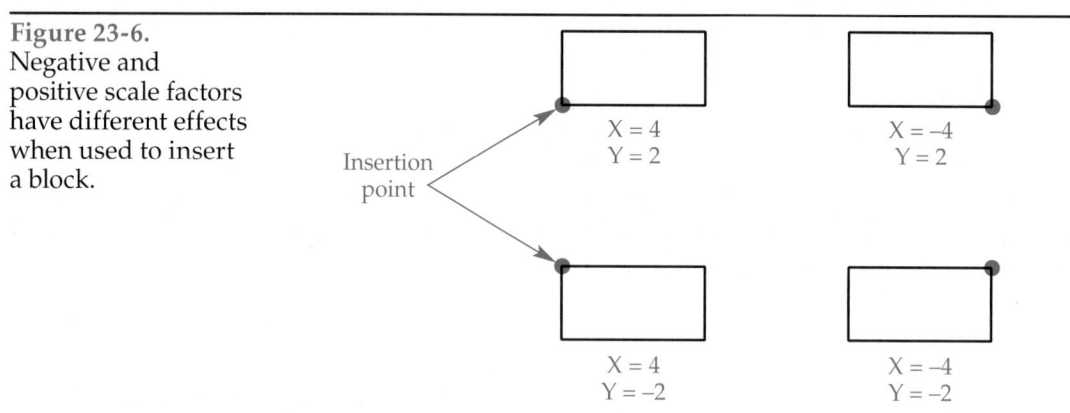

Figure 23-6.
Negative and positive scale factors have different effects when used to insert a block.

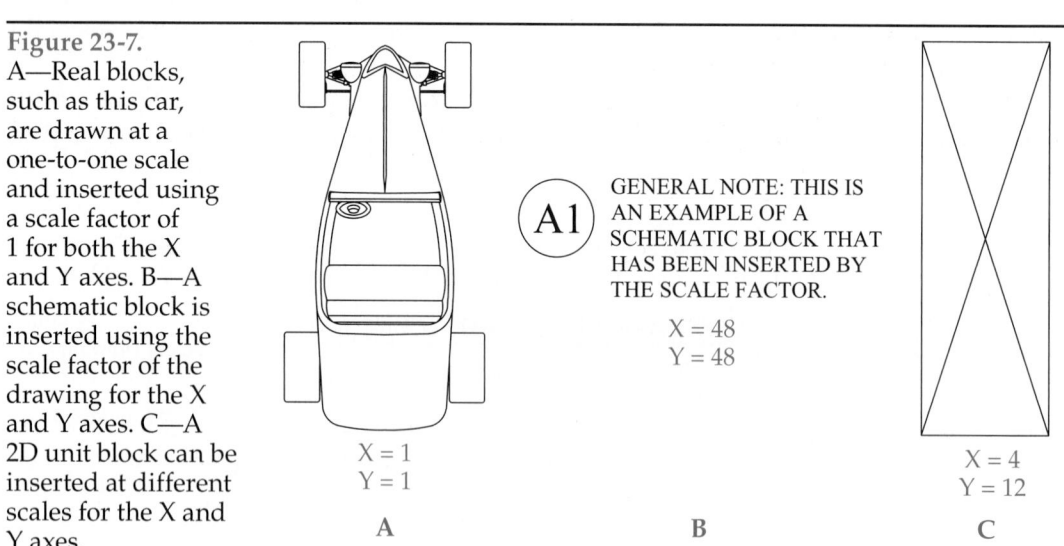

Figure 23-7.
A—Real blocks, such as this car, are drawn at a one-to-one scale and inserted using a scale factor of 1 for both the X and Y axes. B—A schematic block is inserted using the scale factor of the drawing for the X and Y axes. C—A 2D unit block can be inserted at different scales for the X and Y axes.

AutoCAD and Its Applications—Basics

For most applications, annotative blocks should be inserted at a scale of 1 in order for the annotation scale to be applied correctly. Entering a scale other than 1 adjusts the scale of the block by multiplying the scale value by the annotative scale factor.

A *unit block* is also originally drawn at a one-to-one scale. There are three different types of unit blocks. One example of a *1D unit block* is a 1-unit (1″, for example) line object that is turned into a block. A *2D unit block* is any blocked object that can fit inside a 1-unit × 1-unit (1″ × 1″ for example) square. A *3D unit block* is any blocked object that can fit inside a 1-unit (1″ for example) cube. To use a unit block, insert the block and determine the individual scale factors for each axis. For example, a 1D unit block could be inserted at a scale of 4, which would turn the line into a 4″ line, when using inch units. A 2D unit block could be assigned different scale factors for the X and Y axes, such as 4 for the X axis and 12 for the Y axis, to create the 4″ × 12″ beam shown in **Figure 23-7C**. A 3D unit block could be inserted at different scales for the X, Y, and Z axes.

unit block: A 1D, 2D, or 3D block drawn to fit in a 1-unit, 1-unit-square, or 1-unit-cubed area so that it can be scaled easily.

1D unit block: A 1-unit, one-dimensional object, such as a straight line segment, that has been saved as a block.

2D unit block: A 2D object that fits into a 1-unit × 1-unit square and has been saved as a block.

3D unit block: A 3D object that fits into a 1-unit × 1-unit × 1-unit cube and has been saved as a block.

Rotating blocks

The **Rotation** area of the **Insert** dialog box allows you to insert the block at a specified angle. By default, the **Specify On-screen** check box is inactive and the block is inserted at an angle of zero. If you want to use a different angle, enter a value in the **Angle:** text box. If you want to be prompted for the rotation angle when you insert the block, check the **Specify On-screen** check box.

Blocks defined using the **Match block orientation to layout** option cannot be rotated.

A block's rotation angle can be based on the current UCS. If you want to insert a block at a specific angle based on the current UCS or an existing UCS, be sure the proper UCS is active. Then insert the block and use a rotation angle of zero. If you decide to change the UCS later, any inserted blocks retain their original angle.

Additional block insertion items

The **Insert** dialog box contains the following additional items:
- **Explode check box.** When a block is created, it is saved as a single object, no matter how many objects were used to create the block. Activate the **Explode** check box if you wish to explode the block into its original objects for editing purposes. If you explode the block on insertion, it assumes its original properties, such as its original layer, color, and linetype. If **Allow exploding** was unchecked when the block was created, the **Explode** check box in the **Insert** dialog box is inactive.
- **Block Unit area.** This area displays information about the selected block. The **Unit:** text box indicates the units for the block. This is the value of the **INSUNIT** system variable. The **Factor:** text box indicates the scale factor based on the **INSUNIT** system variable. These text boxes are read-only.

Working with specify on-screen prompts

When you pick the **OK** button, prompts appear for any values defined as **Specify On-screen** in the **Insert** dialog box. If you are specifying the insertion point on-screen, the following prompt appears:

> Specify insertion point or [Basepoint/Scale/X/Y/Z/Rotate/PScale/PX/PY/PZ/ PRotate]: *(pick the point to insert the block)*

If you select one of the options, the new value overrides any setting in the **Insert** dialog box. The options allow you to specify a different base point, enter a value for the overall scale, enter independent scale factors for the X, Y, and Z axes, enter a rotation angle, and preview the scale of the X, Y, and Z axes or the rotation angle before entering actual values. The following prompt appears if you are specifying the X scale factor on screen:

> Enter X scale factor, specify opposite corner, or [Corner/XYZ] <1>: *(pick a point or enter a value for the scale)*

Moving the cursor dynamically scales the block as it is dragged. If you want to scale the block visually, pick a point when the object appears to be at the correct size. You can also use the **Corner** option to scale the block dynamically.

If you enter an X scale factor or press [Enter] to accept the default scale value, you are then prompted with the following:

> Enter Y scale factor <use X scale factor>: *(enter a value or press* [Enter] *to accept the same scale specified for the X axis)*

The X and Y scale factors allow you to stretch or compress the block to suit your needs. See **Figure 23-8**. This is why it is a good idea to draw blocks to fit inside a one-unit square. It makes the block easy to scale because you can enter the exact number of units for the X and Y dimensions. If you want the block to be three units long and two units high, respond with the following:

> Enter X scale factor, specify opposite corner, or [Corner/XYZ] <1>: **3**↵
> Enter Y scale factor <use X scale factor>: **2**↵

The insertion base point that was specified when the block was created may not always be the best point when inserting the block. Instead of inserting the block and then moving it, you can use the **Basepoint** option to specify a different base point before inserting the block. To use this option, type B for **Basepoint** when prompted to specify the insertion point. The block is then temporarily placed on the screen. When you pick the new desired base point for the block, the block is reattached to the cross-hairs at that point. A message appears indicating that the command is resuming and you are prompted to specify the insertion point.

Exercise 23-2
Complete the exercise on the Student CD.

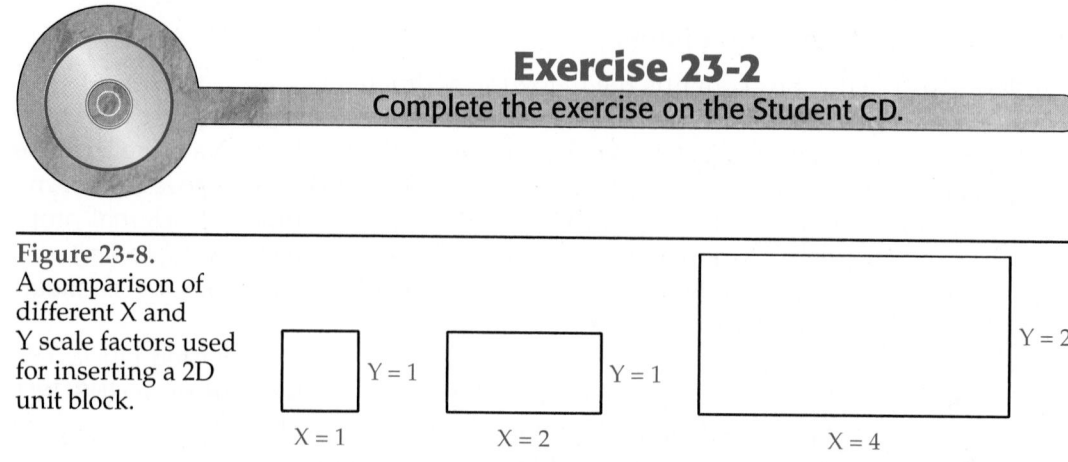

Figure 23-8.
A comparison of different X and Y scale factors used for inserting a 2D unit block.

Y = 1   X = 1   **A**

Y = 1   X = 2   **B**

Y = 2   X = 4   **C**

Inserting Multiple Arranged Copies of a Block

The features of the **INSERT** and **ARRAY** commands are combined using the **MINSERT** (multiple insert) command. This method of inserting and arraying blocks saves time and disk space. Type MINSERT to access the **MINSERT** command.

An example of an application using the **MINSERT** command is the arrangement of desks on a drawing. Suppose you want to draw the layout shown in **Figure 23-9**. First, specify architectural units and set the limits to 30′,22′. Draw a 4′ × 3′ rectangle and save it as a block named DESK. The arrangement is to be three rows and four columns. Make the horizontal spacing between desks 2′, and the vertical spacing 4′. Use the following command sequence:

> Command: **MINSERT**↵
> Enter block name or [?]: *<current>*: **DESK**↵
> Units: Inches   Conversion: 0′-1″
> Specify insertion point or [Basepoint/Scale/X/Y/Z/Rotate/PScale/PX/PY/PZ/
>   PRotate]: *(pick a point)*
> Enter X scale factor, specify opposite corner, or [Corner/XYZ] <1>: ↵
> Enter Y scale factor <use X scale factor>: ↵
> Specify rotation angle <0>: ↵
> Enter number of rows (- - -) <1>: **3**↵
> Enter number of columns (|||) <1>: **4**↵
> Enter distance between rows or specify unit cell (- - -): **7′**↵
> Specify distance between columns (|||): **6′**↵

The complete pattern takes on the characteristics of a block, except that an array created with the **MINSERT** command cannot be exploded. Since the array cannot be exploded, you must use the **Properties** palette to modify the number of rows and columns, change the spacing between objects, or change the layer, color, or linetype properties. If the initial block is rotated, all arrayed objects are also rotated about their insertion points. If the arrayed objects are rotated about the insertion point while using the **MINSERT** command, all objects are aligned on that point.

PROFESSIONAL TIP

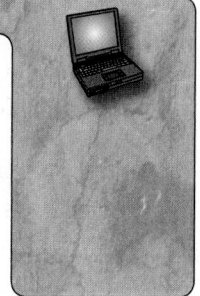

As an alternative to the previous example, if you were working with different desk sizes, a 2D unit block may serve your purposes better than an exact size block. To create a 5′ × 3′-6″ (60″ × 42″) desk, for example, insert a one-unit-square block using either the **INSERT** or **MINSERT** command, and enter the following for the X and Y scale factors:

> Enter X scale factor, specify opposite corner, or [Corner/XYZ] <1>: **60**↵
> Enter Y scale factor <use X scale factor>: **42**↵

Figure 23-9.
Creating an arrangement of desks using the **MINSERT** command.

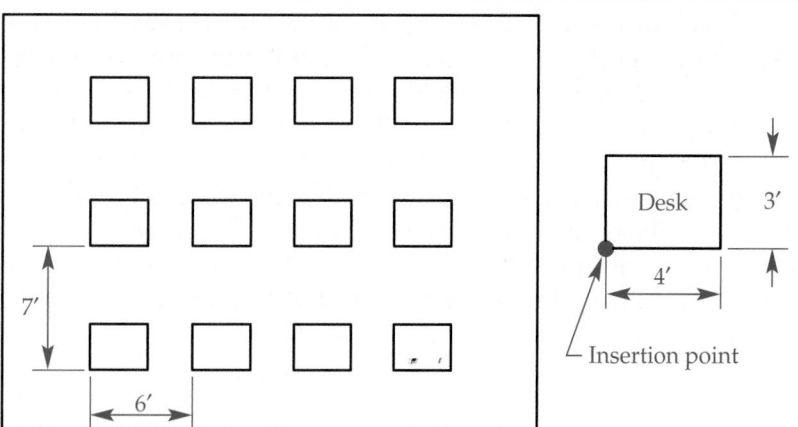

Exercise 23-3
Complete the exercise on the Student CD.

Inserting Entire Drawings

The **INSERT** command can also be used to insert an entire drawing file into the current drawing. To do so, type INSERT and pick the **Browse...** button in the **Insert** dialog box to access the **Select Drawing File** dialog box. You can then select a drawing file to insert, as described earlier in this chapter.

When one drawing is inserted into another, the inserted drawing becomes a block reference. As a block, it may be moved to a new location with a single pick. The drawing is inserted on the current layer, but it does not inherit the color, linetype, or thickness properties of that layer. You can explode the inserted drawing back to its original objects if desired. Once exploded, the drawing objects revert to their original layers. A drawing that is inserted brings any existing block definitions, layers, linetypes, text styles, and dimension styles into the current drawing.

By default, every drawing has an insertion base point of 0,0,0 when you insert it into another drawing. If you want to change the insertion base point of the drawing, use the **BASE** command. Pick **Draw > Block > Base** or type BASE, and select a new insertion base point. Save the drawing before inserting it into another drawing.

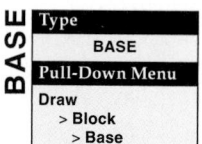

BASE

Type
    BASE
Pull-Down Menu
Draw
  > Block
    > Base

PROFESSIONAL TIP

It is common practice in industry to refer to other drawings to check features or dimensions while working on a drawing. When you need to reference another drawing, you can insert it into your current drawing with the **INSERT** command. When you are finished checking the features or dimensions you need, use the **UNDO** command to undo the **INSERT** operation or erase the inserted drawing.

Exercise 23-4
Complete the exercise on the Student CD.

Creating a Block from a Drawing File

You can create a block from any existing drawing. This allows you to avoid redrawing the object as a block, thus saving time. Remember, if something has already been drawn, try to use it as a block rather than redrawing it.

For example, to define a block named BOLT from an existing drawing file named fastener.dwg, enter the **INSERT** command and use the **Browse...** button to select the fastener.dwg file. The selected file is displayed in the **Name:** text box. Use this text box to change the name from fastener to BOLT and pick **OK**. You can then insert the file into the drawing or press the [Esc] key to exit the command. A block named BOLT has now been created from the file and can be used as desired.

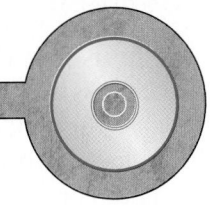

Using DesignCenter to Insert Blocks

DesignCenter can be used to drag and drop blocks or entire drawings into your current drawing. You can also use **DesignCenter** to browse through existing drawings for blocks, show images of blocks and drawings, and display other information about saved blocks or files.

To access **DesignCenter**, pick the **DesignCenter** button on the **Standard Annotation** toolbar, pick **Tools** > **Palettes** > **DesignCenter**, type ADC or ADCENTER, or use the [Ctrl]+[2] key combination. When **DesignCenter** opens, it displays the content that was selected the last time it was open.

The **Folders** tab shows the hierarchy of files and folders on your computer, including network drives. Navigating in the tree view is similar to using Windows Explorer. The **Open Drawings** tab displays all of the drawing files open in the current AutoCAD session. The **History** tab displays the files most recently accessed in **DesignCenter**. The **DC Online** tab gives you access to drawing content that can be downloaded from the Internet. See Figure 23-10.

To view the blocks defined in a drawing, select the **Blocks** branch in the tree view or double-click on the **Blocks** icon in the content area. Once you have found the desired block, you can use a drag-and-drop operation or the **Insert** dialog box to insert it into the current drawing.

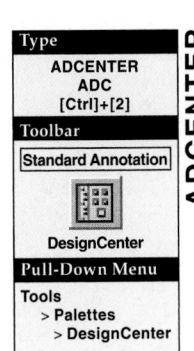

Figure 23-10.
DesignCenter Online provides many sources for blocks and other drawing content.

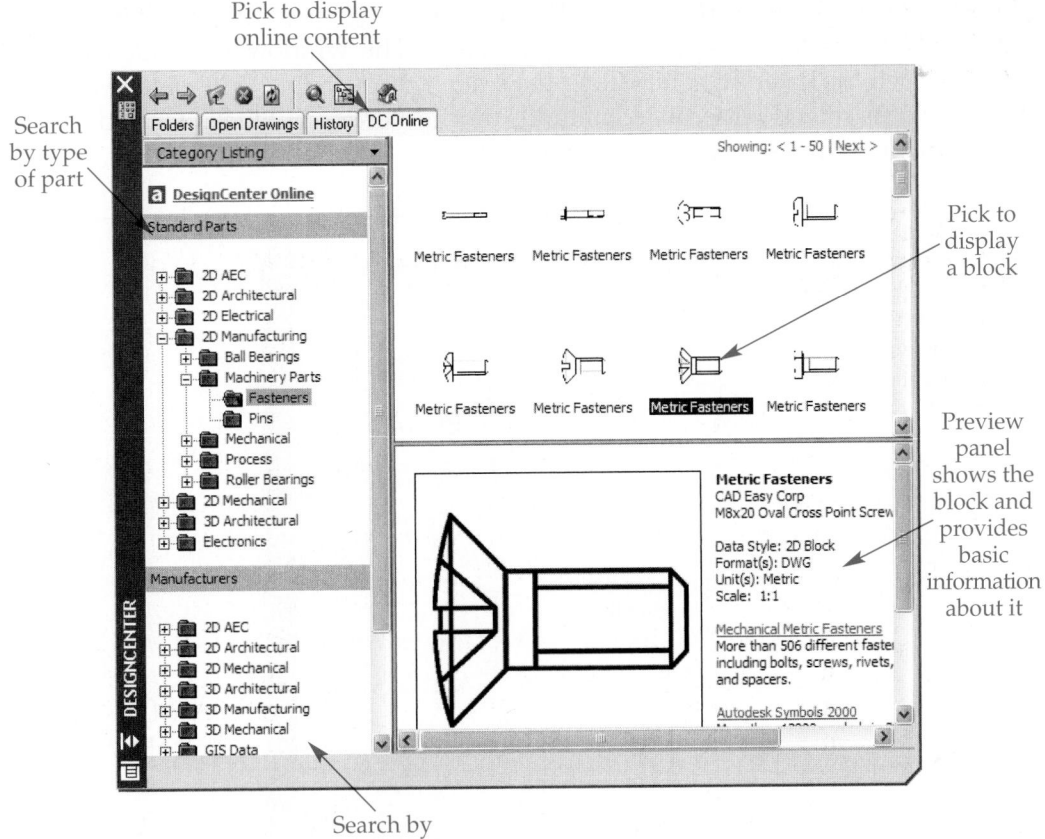

To use the drag-and-drop method, move the cursor over the block in the content area, press and hold down the pick button, and drag the cursor to the drawing editor. Release the pick button to insert the block into the drawing where the cursor is located. The block is inserted based on the type of block units specified when the block was created. For example, if the original block was a 1 × 1 square and the block units were specified as feet when the block was created, then the block will be a 12″ × 12″ square when it is inserted from **DesignCenter**.

To use the **Insert** dialog box to insert a block from **DesignCenter**, right-click the block icon in the content. Select **Insert Block...** from the shortcut menu to activate the **INSERT** command. This allows you to scale, rotate, or explode the block during insertion.

To insert an entire drawing using **DesignCenter**, select the folder in the tree view that contains the drawing. Any drawings in the selected folder appear in the content area. Drag and drop the desired drawing into the current drawing. You can also right-click a drawing icon in the content area and select **Insert as Block...** from the shortcut menu.

PROFESSIONAL TIP

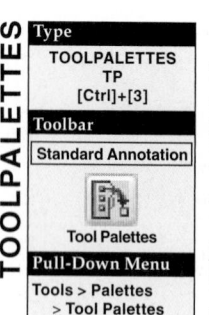

In addition to blocks and drawings, **DesignCenter** can be used to insert dimension styles, layers, layouts, linetypes, table styles, text styles, and external references.

Using Tool Palettes to Insert Blocks

TOOLPALETTES
Type
TOOLPALETTES
TP
[Ctrl]+[3]
Toolbar
Standard Annotation
[icon]
Tool Palettes
Pull-Down Menu
Tools > Palettes
> Tool Palettes

The **Tool Palettes** window provides another quick way to access blocks for insertion into a drawing. This feature is similar to **DesignCenter** in that blocks can be previewed before inserting them. To open the **Tool Palettes** window, pick the **Tool Palettes Window** button on the **Standard Annotation** toolbar, pick **Tools > Palettes > Tool Palettes**, type TP or TOOLPALETTES, or use the [Ctrl]+[3] key combination. The **Tool Palettes** window is shown in **Figure 23-11**. The window is divided into *tool palettes*, each indicated by a tab along the side of the window. Tool palettes are used to store blocks, hatch patterns, commands, and other tools. Blocks located in a tool palette are known as *block insertion tools*.

tool palettes: Collections of related blocks, hatches, commands, and other tools arranged in a visual palette format for quick selection.

block insertion tools: Blocks located on a tool palette.

Figure 23-11.
The **Tool Palettes** window. Blocks may be inserted into the current drawing from a selected tab.

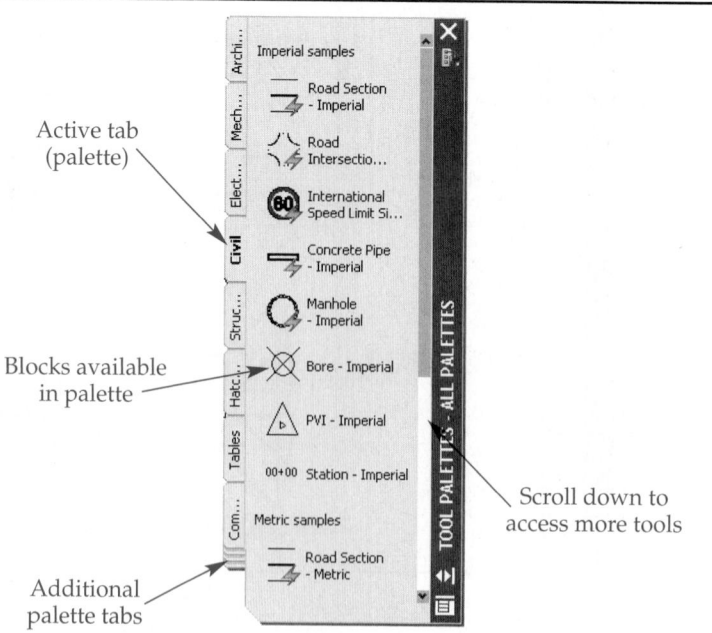

Active tab (palette)

Blocks available in palette

Additional palette tabs

Scroll down to access more tools

AutoCAD and Its Applications—Basics

To insert a block from the **Tool Palettes** window, select the tool palette tab in which the block resides and locate the block. Use the scroll bar on the side of the window to move up or down in the tool palette, if needed. When you locate the block, place the cursor over the block icon. If the block contains a description, the description appears next to the cursor. You can use the drag-and-drop method to insert the block, or you can pick once on the block icon. Then move the cursor into the drawing area and pick again to place the block. With either method, the block is attached to the crosshairs once the cursor is moved into the drawing area. The block is connected to the crosshairs at the insertion point of the block.

When inserting a block with the "pick-pick" method, you can access scaling and rotation options for the block on the command line before picking an insertion point. Enter S to scale the block along the XYZ axes or R to specify a rotation angle for the block. Blocks inserted from tool palettes are automatically scaled based on a ratio of the current drawing scale to the scale used in the original block definition.

Exercise 23-6

Complete the exercise on the Student CD.

Adding blocks to tool palettes

AutoCAD provides several default palettes that contain block insertion tools. You can also create your own tool palettes and assign block insertion tools to them. To create a new, blank tool palette, right-click the title bar of the **Tool Palettes** window or a blank area of a tool palette. Select **New Tool Palette** from the shortcut menu. The new tool palette is added and a text box appears with the default name highlighted. Enter a name for the palette and press [Enter]. Choose a name that identifies the contents of the palette.

One of two methods can be used to add block insertion tools to a new or existing palette. If the blocks are located in a file on the hard drive, you can use **DesignCenter** to locate the file and then drag the blocks onto the tool palette. If the blocks you want to add are displayed in the current drawing, you can drag and drop them into the desired palette.

Using DesignCenter to create a palette of blocks

DesignCenter can be used to create a new palette that contains block insertion tools for all of the blocks within a single drawing file. To accomplish this task, navigate to the drawing in **DesignCenter** and right-click the drawing file name in the **Folders** tab. Then, select **Create Tool Palette** from the shortcut menu. See **Figure 23-12**. In the example shown, a new palette is created from the Analog Integrated Circuits drawing file. The resulting palette contains block insertion tools for all of the blocks within the file and has the same name as the file. A palette can also be created in this manner by expanding the contents of a drawing file in the **Folder List** area and right-clicking on the **Blocks** item in either the **Folder List** area or the content area. When the shortcut menu appears, select **Create Tool Palette**.

DesignCenter can also be used to add individual block insertion tools to a tool palette from selected blocks in a drawing file. To use this technique, first navigate to and expand the drawing file in the **Folder List** of the **Folders** tab. Select the **Blocks** branch to display the blocks within the drawing in the content area. Then open the **Tool Palettes** window and display the tool palette into which you want to place the block insertion tools. Finally, drag each block from the content area of **DesignCenter** and drop it onto the tool palette. To create a new palette containing a block insertion

Figure 23-12.
Right-clicking a drawing name in **DesignCenter** and selecting **Create Tool Palette** creates a new tool palette with the name of the drawing file. All of the blocks defined in the drawing become block insertion tools in the palette.

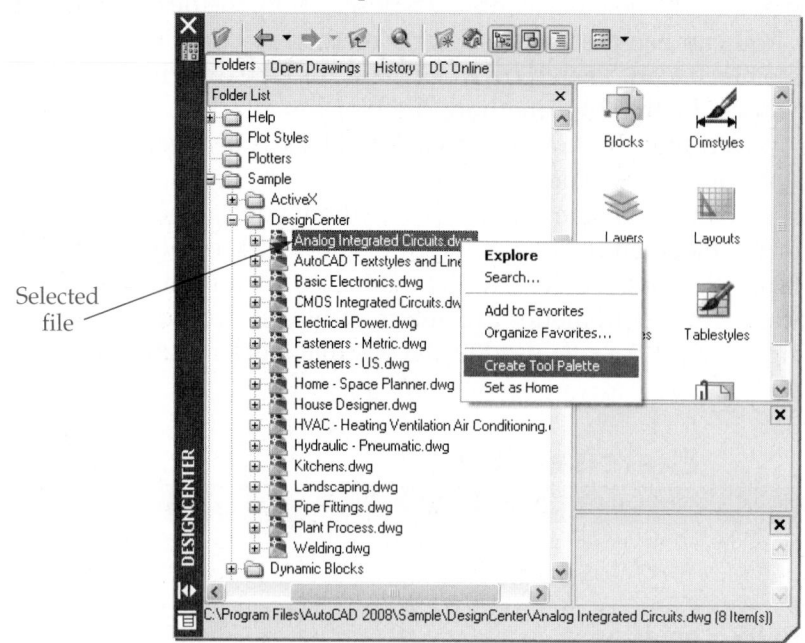

Selected file

tool for a single block, right-click on the block in the content area of **DesignCenter** and select **Create Tool Palette** from the shortcut menu. AutoCAD prompts you for a new name for the palette.

Another option is to use **DesignCenter** to add a block insertion tool of an entire drawing file to a tool palette. To apply this method, first navigate to the folder that contains the drawing file. Then, select the file in the content area, drag it to the tool palette, and drop it onto the palette. When the new tool is used to insert the drawing file into a drawing, the inserted drawing becomes a block within the current drawing.

You can also use **DesignCenter** to create a single tool palette that contains block insertion tools for all of the blocks within all of the drawing files in a folder. To accomplish this task, first navigate to the folder in the **Folder List** area of **DesignCenter**. Right-click the folder and select **Create Tool Palette of Blocks** from the shortcut menu. A new palette is created in the **Tool Palettes** window with the same name as the folder. This palette contains block insertion tools for all of the blocks in all of the drawings in the selected folder.

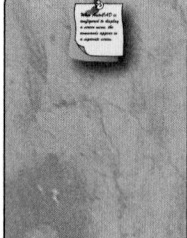

NOTE

A block that has been added to a tool palette as a block insertion tool is directly linked to the drawing file in which the block resides. If the block has been modified in the source file, inserting it from a tool palette inserts the updated block. Blocks that were added to a drawing before changes were made to the block insertion tool can be updated by right-clicking the block insertion tool in the tool palette and selecting the **Redefine** shortcut menu option.

Creating a palette of blocks from blocks in the current drawing

A block in the current drawing can be added to a tool palette as a block insertion tool. Open the **Tool Palettes** window and select the tool palette in which the block insertion tool is to be located. Next, pick the block once in the drawing to display grips. The **PICKFIRST** system variable must be set to 1. Then, pick and hold on the block anywhere *except* on a grip, drag it onto the tool palette, and drop the block. Do not pick the grip of the block for this step. If you pick the block grip, AutoCAD thinks you are trying to move the block in the drawing area.

> **NOTE**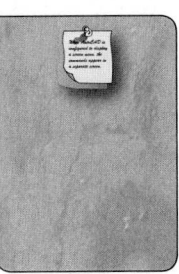
>
> Tool palettes can be used to store many different types of drawing content and tools, such as AutoCAD drawing and editing commands, custom commands, and AutoLISP routines. Examples of command tools are provided in the **Command Tools** tool palette. For detailed information about tool palette customization, refer to *AutoCAD and Its Applications—Advanced*.

Exercise 23-7
Complete the exercise on the Student CD.

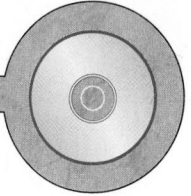

Changing Block Properties

If you insert a block on the wrong layer or if you want to change the color or linetype properties of the block, you can use the **Properties** palette to modify it. When you select the block to modify, its properties are listed. See **Figure 23-13.** Notice that Block Reference is specified in the drop-down list.

Figure 23-13.
The **Properties** palette allows you to change the layer, color, linetype, and other properties of a block.

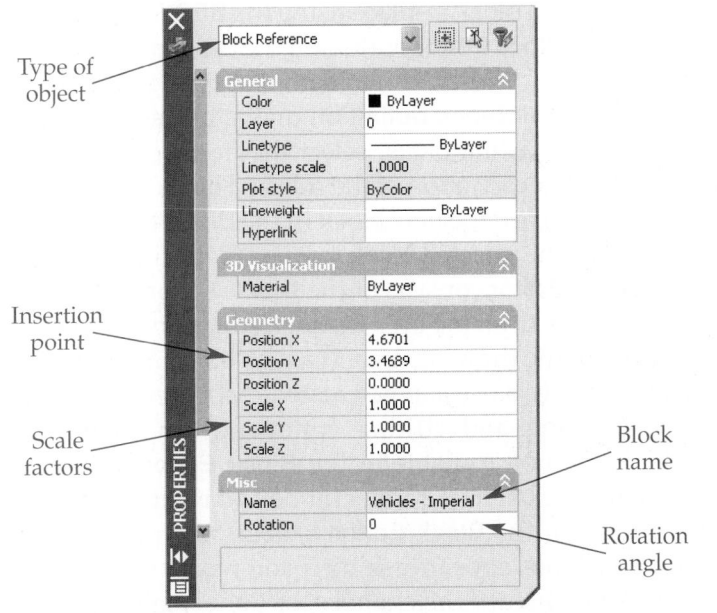

To modify the layer of the selected block, pick **Layer** in the **General** category of the **Properties** palette. A drop-down arrow appears, allowing you to access the layer you want to use for the block. Once the new layer has been selected, pick the close button (**X**) at the upper-right corner of the **Properties** palette to close the window. The block is now changed to the specified layer.

You may also want to change the color or linetype of a block. This can be done if the block was originally created on layer 0 and the color/linetype properties were set up as ByLayer. If the block was originally created on layer 0, it assumes the color and linetype of the current layer when it is inserted. If it was created on another layer, it retains its original color and linetype.

If you wish to change the color or linetype of an inserted block, you can access the **Properties** palette and select the corresponding property in the **General** section after selecting the block. Select the desired color or linetype from the corresponding drop-down list.

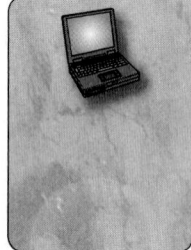

PROFESSIONAL TIP

If you want to change the properties of several blocks, you can use the **Quick Select** dialog box to create a selection set of block reference objects. After you have selected the blocks, change the properties using the **Properties** palette, **Object Properties** toolbar, or the **Object Properties** control panel of the **Dashboard**. The **Quick Select** dialog box is discussed in Chapter 11.

Editing Blocks

A block inserted in a drawing is edited as if it were a single object. That is, it can be moved, rotated, copied, and mirrored. However, the separate objects within the block cannot be modified directly. In order to modify the block, you must either use the **Block Editor** or explode the block. These methods are described in the following sections.

Using the Block Editor

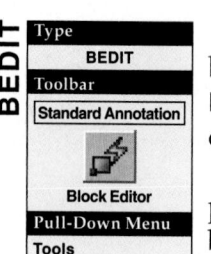

BEDIT
Type
BEDIT
Toolbar
Standard Annotation
Block Editor
Pull-Down Menu
Tools
>Block Editor

You can edit a block in-place using the **BEDIT** command. This command is accessed by picking the **Block Editor** button on the **Standard Annotation** toolbar, picking **Tools > Block Editor** from the pull-down menu, or typing BEDIT. When you activate the **BEDIT** command, the **Edit Block Definition** dialog box appears. See **Figure 23-14**.

To edit an existing block, select the name of the block from the list of blocks. A preview and the description of the selected block are shown. You can create a new block by typing a name for the new block in the **Block to create or edit** field. Then pick the **OK** button to open the selected block (or new block) in the **Block Editor**. See **Figure 23-15**.

The **Block Editor** consists of the **Block Editor** toolbar, the **Block Authoring Palettes** window, and the drawing area in block edit mode. If a block was selected for editing, it is displayed in the drawing area. If a new block name was entered, the drawing area is empty so the new block can be created. All other objects in the drawing are hidden.

Use drawing and editing commands to create or modify the block. Some commands are not available in the **Block Editor**. When you finish editing, close the **Block Editor**. To exit block editing mode and return to the drawing, pick the **Close Block Editor** button on the **Block Editor** toolbar or type BCLOSE. If changes have not been saved, a dialog box appears asking if you wish to save the changes. Pick **Yes** to save the changes, **No** to discard the changes, or **Cancel** to return to block editing mode.

Figure 23-14.
The **Edit Block Definition** dialog box.

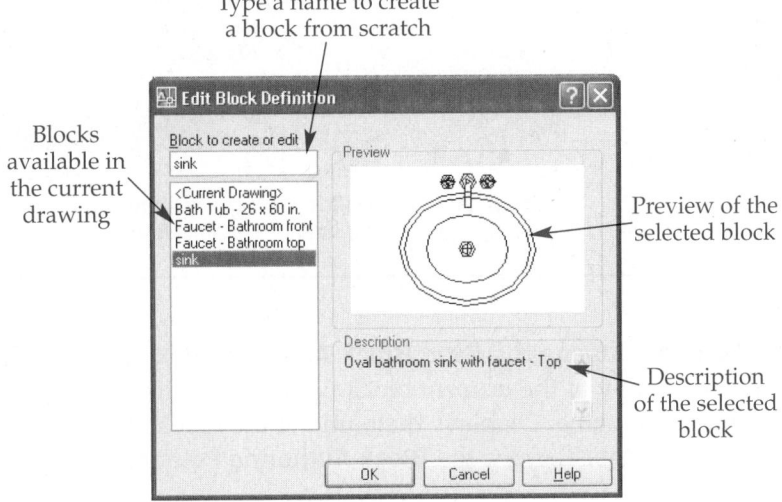

Type a name to create
a block from scratch

Blocks
available in
the current
drawing

Preview of the
selected block

Description
of the selected
block

Figure 23-15.
In block editing mode, the **Block Editor** toolbar and the **Block Authoring Palettes** window are available.

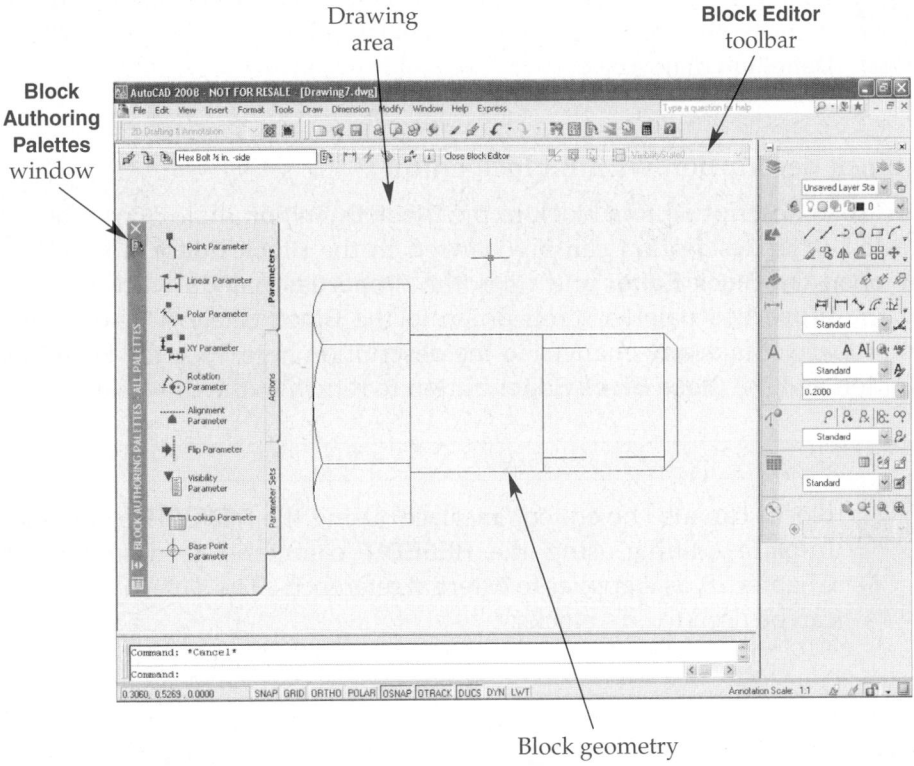

Drawing
area

Block Editor
toolbar

Block
Authoring
Palettes
window

Block geometry

The commands in the **Block Editor** toolbar are used to create blocks and block geometry. Refer to **Figure 23-16.** The buttons on the toolbar include:

- **Edit or Create Block Definition.** Opens the **Edit Block Definition** dialog box, which is the same dialog box displayed when entering block editing mode. You can select a different block to edit or specify the name of a new one to create from scratch.
- **Save Block Definition.** Saves the changes and updates the block.

Figure 23-16.
The **Block Editor** toolbar is displayed in the **Block Editor**.

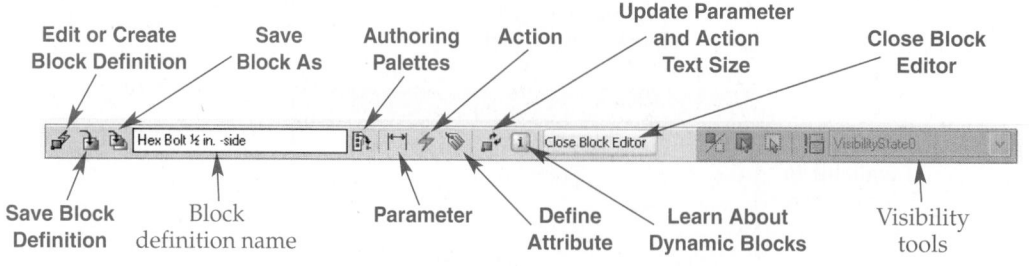

- **Save Block As.** Opens the **Save Block As** dialog box. This dialog box allows you to save a copy of the current block under a different name.
- **Block definition name.** Displays the name of the block currently being edited.
- **Authoring Palettes.** Toggles the **Block Authoring Palettes** window off and on.

PROFESSIONAL TIP

A block can be opened directly in the **Block Editor** by right-clicking the block in the drawing and selecting **Block Editor** from the shortcut menu. A block can also be opened directly in the **Block Editor** when it is created by checking the **Open in block editor** check box in the **Block Definition** dialog box.

Adding a block description within block editor

You can add a description to a block in the **Block Definition** dialog box when the block is created. This description can be changed in the **Block Editor**. To modify a description, open the **Block Editor** and open the **Properties** palette with no objects selected. In the **Properties** palette, scroll down to the **Block** category and find the **Description** property. Make any changes to the description here. Pick the **Save Block Definition** button and the **Close Block Editor** button to return to the drawing.

NOTE

Blocks can also be edited "in-place" using the **REFEDIT** command. In-place editing using the **REFEDIT** command is described in Chapter 28, as it applies to external references. The same techniques can be used to edit blocks.

Exercise 23-8
Complete the exercise on the Student CD.

Exploding a Block

As previously described, you can explode a block as it is inserted using the **Insert** dialog box. This is useful when you want to edit the individual objects of the block. You can also use the **EXPLODE** command after the block is inserted to break it apart into its individual objects.

The **EXPLODE** command can be used to break apart any existing block, poly-line, or dimension. To access this command, pick the **Explode** button on the **2D Draw** control panel of the **Dashboard** or the **Modify** toolbar, pick **Modify > Explode**, or type X or EXPLODE. Then select the objects to explode. When you have finished selecting objects, press [Enter] to explode them.

When a block is exploded, its component objects can be edited individually. To see if the **EXPLODE** command worked properly, select any object that was formerly part of the block. Only that object should be highlighted. If so, the block was exploded properly.

NOTE

The block cannot be exploded if a block was created with **Allow exploding** unchecked in the **Block Definition** dialog box. If you try to use the **EXPLODE** command on a block like this, the message 1 could not be exploded appears on the command line.

Redefining Existing Blocks

As you have seen, one way to edit a block is to use the **BEDIT** command. Once the block is modified and the changes saved, all instances of that block in the drawing are also updated. You can also redefine a block using the **EXPLODE** and **BLOCK** commands together. To redefine an existing block, follow this procedure:

1. Insert the block to be redefined anywhere in your drawing.
2. Make sure you know where the insertion point of the block is located.
3. Explode the block using the **EXPLODE** command.
4. Edit the components of the block as needed.
5. Recreate the block definition using the **BLOCK** command.
6. Give the block the same name and insertion point as it originally had.
7. Select the objects to be included in the block.
8. Pick **OK** in the **Block Definition** dialog box to save the block. When a message from AutoCAD appears asking if you want to redefine the block, pick **Yes**.
9. When the **BLOCK** command is complete, all insertions of the block are updated.

A common mistake is to forget to use the **EXPLODE** command before redefining the block. When you try to create the block again with the same name, an alert box indicating the block references itself is displayed. This means you are trying to create a block that already exists. When you press the **OK** button, the alert box disappears and the **Block Definition** dialog box is redisplayed. Press the **Cancel** button, explode the block to be redefined, and try again.

Understanding the Circular Reference Error

As described in the previous example, when you try to redefine a block that already exists using the same name, a *circular reference error* occurs. AutoCAD informs you that the block references itself or that it has not been modified. The concept of a block referencing itself may be a little difficult to grasp at first without fully understanding how AutoCAD works with blocks. A block can be composed of any objects, including other blocks. When you use the **BLOCK** command to incorporate an existing block into a new block, AutoCAD makes a list of all the objects that compose the new block. This means AutoCAD refers to any existing block definitions that are selected to be part of the new block. If you select an instance, or reference, of the block being redefined as a component object for the new definition, a problem occurs. You are trying to redefine a block name using a previous version of the block with the same name. In other words, the new block refers to a block of the same name, or references itself.

circular reference error: An error that occurs when a block definition references itself.

For example, assume you create a block named BOX that is composed of four line objects in the shape of a square. You insert the block and then decide it needs to be changed; a small circle must be added in the lower-left corner of the square. If the original BOX block is exploded, all that is left are the four line objects. After drawing the required circle, you can enter the **BLOCK** command and recreate a block named BOX by selecting the four lines and the circle as the component objects. Redefining a block destroys the old definition and creates a new one. Any blocks with the same name are redefined with the updated changes. Make sure you want to redefine the block before agreeing to do so. Otherwise, give the block a new name. The correct way to redefine a block is shown in **Figure 23-17A**.

Alternately, suppose you do not explode the block, but still draw the circle and try to redefine the block. When you select the BOX block *and* the circle, a new block named BOX would now be a block reference of the BOX block with a circle. The old block definition of BOX has not been destroyed, but a new definition has been attempted. Thus, AutoCAD is trying to define a new block named BOX by using an instance of the BOX block, creating a circular reference. Refer to **Figure 23-17B**.

Changing Block Properties to ByLayer

If you override the properties of an object, such as by changing the color from ByLayer to Blue, you can change the properties of the object back to ByLayer using the **Properties** palette, **Object Properties** toolbar, or the **Object Properties** control panel of the **Dashboard**. Another method is to use the **SETBYLAYER** command to reset object properties to ByLayer. This command is especially useful for setting the properties of blocks back to ByLayer.

If block component properties, such as color and linetype, were originally set to values other than ByLayer, the objects belong to the selected layer, but they retain the properties of the layer on which the objects were created. To solve this problem you can edit the blocks using one of the methods described in this chapter. The edit would include setting all the object properties to ByBlock. The **SETBYLAYER** command accomplishes the same task without editing the block.

Access the **SETBYLAYER** command by picking **Modify** > **Change to ByLayer** in the pull-down menu or typing SETBYLAYER. The Select objects or [Settings]: prompt is displayed. Enter the **Settings** option to display the **SetByLayer Settings** dialog box. See **Figure 23-18.** Select the check boxes that correspond to the object properties that you want to convert to ByLayer. Pick **OK** to exit the **SetByLayer Settings** dialog box.

Figure 23-17.
A—The correct procedure for redefining a block. B—Redefining a block that has not first been exploded creates an invalid circular reference.

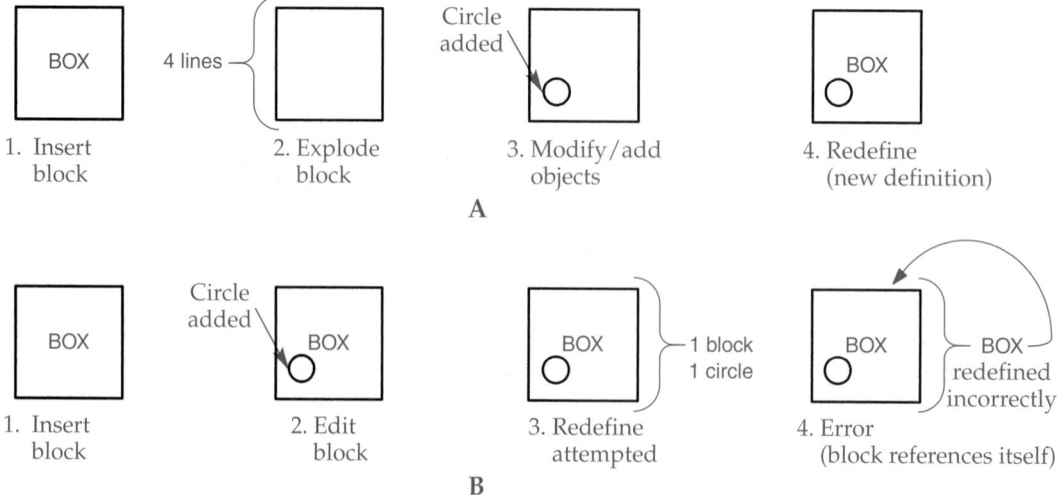

Figure 23-18.
Use the **SetByLayer Settings** dialog box to choose the properties that will be set to ByLayer.

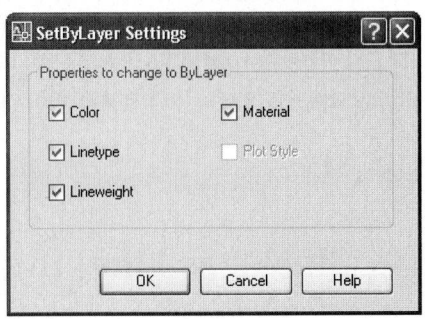

Next, select the objects whose properties you want to set to ByLayer. When you have finished selecting objects, press [Enter] to display the Change ByBlock to ByLayer? prompt. Select the **Yes** option to change all object properties currently set to ByBlock to ByLayer. Pick the **No** option to change all object properties currently set to values other than ByBlock to ByLayer. AutoCAD then asks if you want to include blocks. If the selected object is a block, choosing **Yes** converts the properties of all references of the same block in the drawing to ByLayer. If you pick **No**, only the properties of the selected block will be set to ByLayer. All other references of the same block remain unchanged.

> **NOTE**
>
> The **SETBYLAYERMODE** system variable can be used to adjust the same options found in the **SetByLayer Settings** dialog box. Refer to AutoCAD's *Command Reference* for the integer settings that control these options.

Renaming Blocks

Blocks can be renamed using the **RENAME** command. Access this command by picking **Format > Rename...** in the pull-down menu or typing REN or RENAME. This displays the **Rename** dialog box. See **Figure 23-19.**

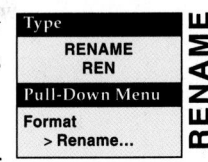

Type
RENAME
REN
Pull-Down Menu
Format
> Rename...

RENAME

Figure 23-19.
The **Rename** dialog box allows you to change the name of blocks and other named objects.

Select type of objects to rename

Select block to rename

New block name

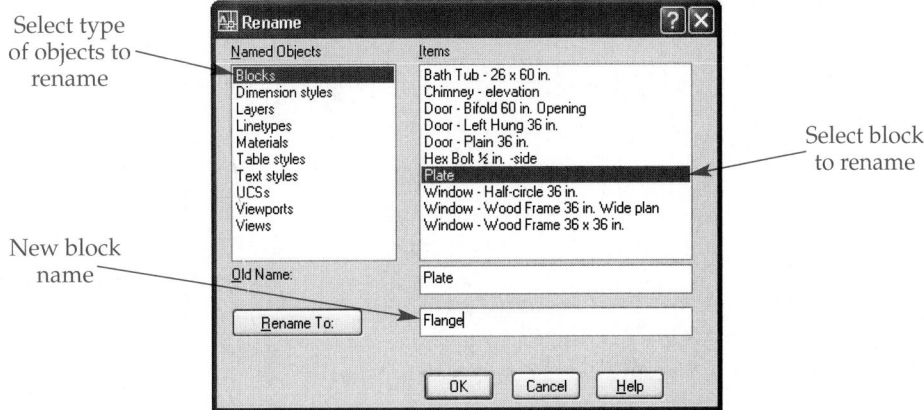

To change the name of the CIRCLE block to HOLE, select Blocks from the **Named Objects** list. A list of block names defined in the current drawing appears in the **Items** list. Highlight CIRCLE in the list. When this name appears in the **Old Name:** text box, type the new block name HOLE in the **Rename To:** text box. When you pick the **Rename To:** button, the new block name appears in the **Items** list. Pick **OK** to exit the **Rename** dialog box.

Creating Blocks as Drawing Files

Blocks created with the **BLOCK** command are stored in the drawing in which they are made. The **WBLOCK** (write block) command allows you to create a drawing (DWG) file from a block. You can also use the **WBLOCK** command to create a global block from any object. It does not have to be previously saved as a block. The resulting drawing file can then be inserted as a block into any drawing.

There are several ways to use the **WBLOCK** command. To see how the first method works, open drawing EX23-1.dwg. You will convert the CIRCLE block in this drawing to a permanent block by making it into a separate drawing file. The first step is to open the **Write Block** dialog box by typing WBLOCK. This dialog box is similar to the **Block Definition** dialog box. See Figure 23-20.

In the **Source** area, pick the **Block:** radio button and select the CIRCLE block from the drop-down list. In the **Destination** area, specify the name and location for the wblock in the **File name and path:** text box. By default, the new drawing file has the same name as the block. This is shown with the folder path in the **File name and path:** text box in Figure 23-20. Picking the ellipsis (...) button next to the text box displays the **Browse for Drawing File** dialog box. Navigate to the folder where you want to save the file, confirm the name of the file in the **File name:** text box, and pick the **Save** button. The **Write Block** dialog box is redisplayed with the path and file name shown in the **File name and path:** text box. Next, select the type of units that **DesignCenter** will use to insert the block in the **Insert units:** drop-down list. This is also located in the **Destination** area. When you are finished, pick **OK**. The block is saved as a wblock in the folder you specified. Now, you can use the **INSERT** command in any drawing to insert the CIRCLE block.

Figure 23-20.
Using the **Write Block** dialog box to create a wblock from an existing block.

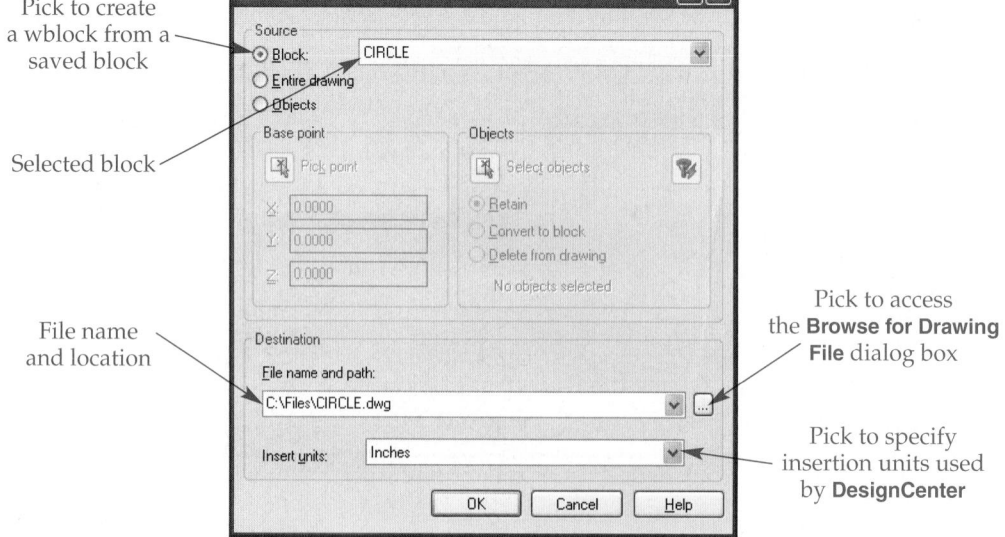

Creating a New Wblock

Suppose you want to create a wblock from a shape you have just drawn, but you have not yet made a block. The following sequence is used to save a selected object as a drawing file. Refer to **Figure 23-21.**

First, enter the **WBLOCK** command and select the **Objects** radio button in the **Write Block** dialog box. (It is active by default.) Next, pick the **Select objects** button. The dialog box is hidden to allow you to select the objects to be saved to the drawing file. Press [Enter] when you are finished selecting objects to redisplay the **Write Block** dialog box.

Next, pick the **Pick point** button to select the insertion point. Again, the dialog box is hidden to allow you to select an insertion point. After you pick a point, the dialog box is redisplayed. You can also enter coordinates of the insertion point in the **X:, Y:,** and **Z:** text boxes instead of picking a point on-screen. Also, specify a path and file name for the block in the **File name and path:** text box. Finally, select the type of units that **DesignCenter** will use to insert the block in the **Insert units:** drop-down list. Pick the **OK** button to create the wblock.

This sequence is the same as that used with the **BLOCK** command. However, the wblock is saved to disk as a drawing file, *not* as a block in the current drawing. Be sure to specify the correct file path in the **File name and path:** text box when using the **Write Block** dialog box. A drawing file named desk that is to be saved in the blocks folder on the C: hard drive, for example, would be saved as C:\blocks\desk.

Storing a Drawing as a Wblock

An entire drawing can also be stored as a wblock. To do this, pick the **Entire drawing** radio button in the **Write Block** dialog box. Specify the name and location to save the wblock using the **File name and path:** text box. Select the type of units **DesignCenter** will use to insert the block in the **Insert units:** drop-down list. Pick **OK** when you are finished.

In this case, the whole drawing is saved to disk as if you had used the **SAVE** command. However, all unused blocks are deleted from the drawing. If the drawing contains any unused blocks, this method may reduce the size of a drawing considerably.

Figure 23-21.
Using the **Write Block** dialog box to create a wblock from selected objects without first defining a block.

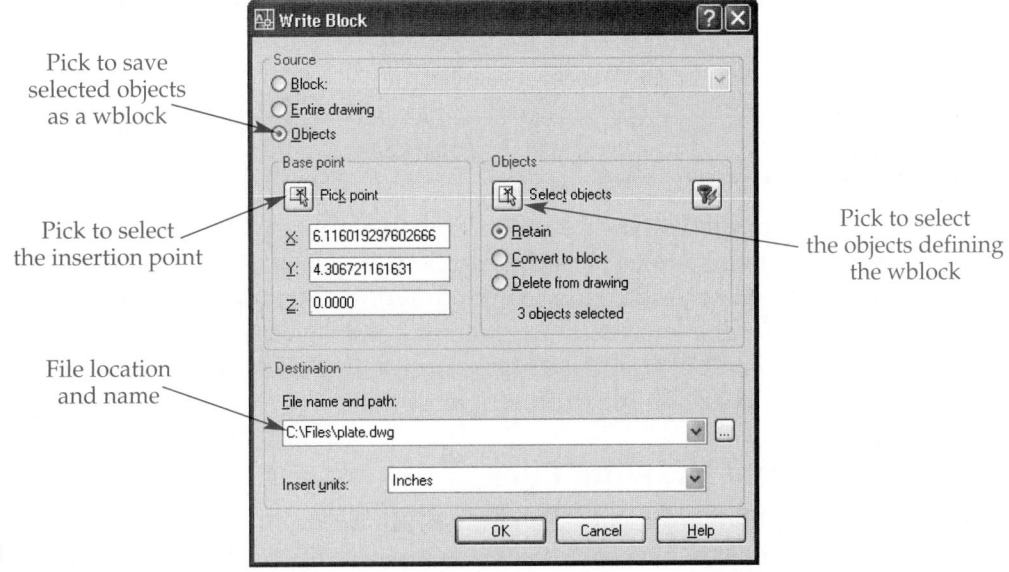

Using the **Entire drawing** wblock option is a good way to remove unused named objects to reduce the file size. Use this routine when you have completed a drawing and decide the unused blocks, layers, styles, and other unused objects are no longer needed. The **PURGE** command can also be used to remove any unused objects. The **PURGE** command is described later in this chapter.

Exercise 23-9

Complete the exercise on the Student CD.

Revising an Inserted Drawing

You may find that you need to revise a drawing file that has been used in other drawings. If this happens, you can quickly update any drawing in which the revised drawing is used. For example, if a drawing file named pump was modified after being used several times in a drawing, enter the **INSERT** command and access the original drawing file with the **Select Drawing File** dialog box. Then activate the **Specify On-screen** check box in the **Insertion point** area and pick **OK**. When a message from AutoCAD appears and asks if you want to redefine the block, pick **Yes**. All of the pump references are automatically updated. Next, press the [Esc] key. By canceling the command, no new insertions of the pump drawing are made.

If you work on projects in which inserted drawings may be revised, it may be more productive to use reference drawings instead of inserted drawing files. Reference drawings are used with the **XREF** command, which is described in Chapter 28. All referenced drawings are automatically updated when a drawing file that contains the externally referenced material is loaded into AutoCAD.

Symbol Libraries

symbol library: A collection of related blocks, shapes, views, symbols, or other content used repeatedly in drawings.

As you become proficient with AutoCAD, you will want to start constructing symbol libraries. A *symbol library* is a collection of related blocks, shapes, views, symbols, and other content used repeatedly in drawings. Arranging a storage system for frequently used symbols increases productivity and saves time. First, you need to establish how the symbols are stored (as blocks or drawing files) and determine where they will be stored for insertion into different drawings.

Blocks vs. Separate Drawing Files

The two basic options for creating a symbol library are to save all of the blocks within a single drawing or to save each block to a separate file (wblock). If you decide to have one drawing that contains all of the blocks, each person in the office or classroom must have access to that drawing. This is often done by creating the blocks in a template file or a separate drawing file. If individual drawing files (wblocks) are used, each student or employee must have access to the files.

Creating a Symbol Library

Once you have created a set of related block definitions, you can arrange the blocks in a symbol library. Each block should be identified with a name and insertion point location. Whether the symbols are being stored in a single drawing file or as individual files, several guidelines can be used to create the symbol library:

- Assign one person to create the symbols for each specialty.
- Follow school or company standards for blocks and symbols.
- When saving multiple blocks in a drawing file, save one group of symbols per drawing file. When using wblocks, give the drawing files meaningful names so they can be assigned to separate folders on the hard drive. For example, you may want to create several different symbol libraries based on the following types of symbols: electronic, electrical, piping, mechanical, structural, architectural, landscaping, and mapping.
- Print a hard copy of the symbol library. Include a representation of each symbol, its insertion point, where it is located, and any other necessary information. A sample is shown in **Figure 23-22**. Provide all users of the symbols with a copy of the listing.
- If a network is not in use, place the symbol library file(s) on each workstation in the classroom or office.
- Keep backup copies of all files in a secure place.
- When symbols are revised, update all files containing the edited symbols.
- Inform all users of any changes to saved symbols.

Storing Symbol Drawings

The local or network hard drive is one of the best places to store a symbol library. It is easy to access, quick, and more convenient to use than portable media. Recordable CDs or other removable media can be used for backup purposes if a network drive with an automatic backup function is not available. In the absence of a network or modem, removable media can also be used to transport files from one workstation to another.

Figure 23-22.
A printed copy of piping flow diagram blocks stored in a symbol library. The colored dots indicate insertion points and are not part of the block.

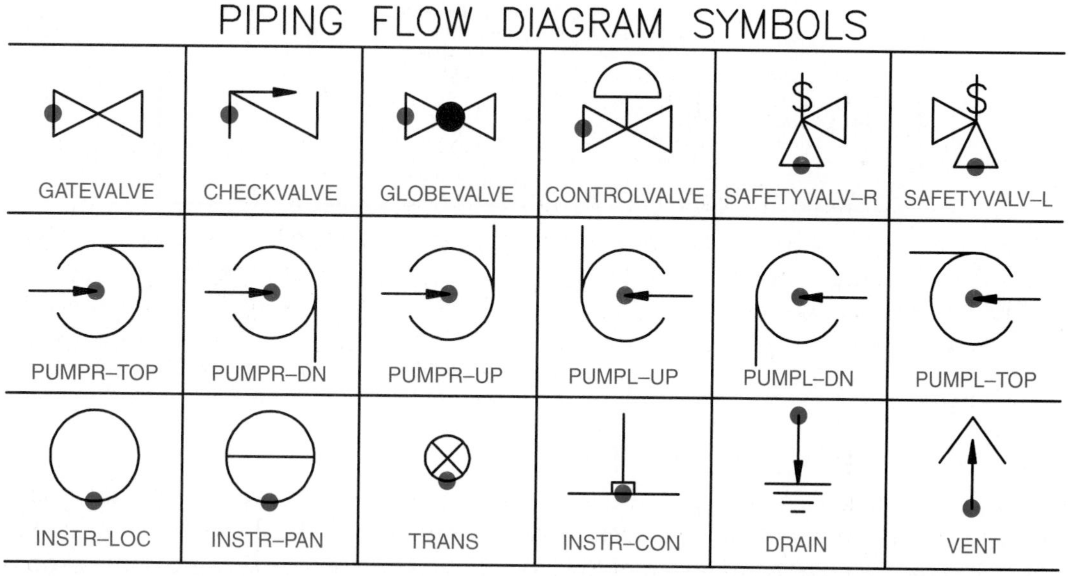

PIPING FLOW DIAGRAM SYMBOLS

GATEVALVE	CHECKVALVE	GLOBEVALVE	CONTROLVALVE	SAFETYVALV–R	SAFETYVALV–L
PUMPR–TOP	PUMPR–DN	PUMPR–UP	PUMPL–UP	PUMPL–DN	PUMPL–TOP
INSTR–LOC	INSTR–PAN	TRANS	INSTR–CON	DRAIN	VENT

There are several methods of storing symbols on the hard drive. Symbols can be saved as wblocks and organized within folders. It is recommended to store symbols outside of the AutoCAD folder. This will keep the system folder uncluttered and allow you to differentiate which folders and files were originally installed with AutoCAD. A good idea is to create a \Blocks folder for storing your blocks, as shown in **Figure 23-23**.

If multiple symbols are saved within a drawing, they can be inserted using **DesignCenter** or the **Tool Palettes** window. When using this system, several drawing files may be used to group similar symbols. For example, electrical symbols can be saved in a drawing named electrical.dwg and piping symbols can be saved in a drawing named piping.dwg. Limit the symbols in a drawing to a reasonable number so the symbols can be found relatively easily. If there are too many blocks in a drawing, it may be difficult to locate the desired symbol.

Drawing files saved on the hard drive should be arranged in a logical manner. The following guidelines apply:

- All workstations in the classroom or office should have folders with the same names.
- One person should be assigned to update and copy symbol libraries to all workstations.
- Drawing files should be copied onto each workstation from a master CD or network drive.
- The master and backup versions of the symbol libraries should be kept in separate locations.

Figure 23-23.
An efficient way to store blocks saved as drawing files is to set up a Blocks folder containing folders for each type of block on the hard drive.

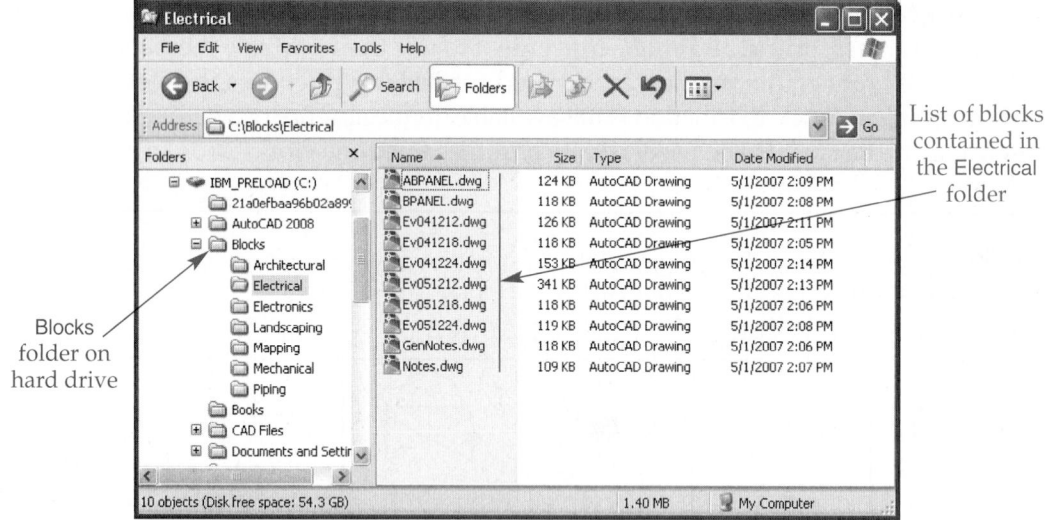

Purging Named Objects

A block is one example of a named object. In many drawing sessions, not all of the named objects defined within a drawing are used. For example, your drawing may contain several layers, text styles, and blocks that are not used. Since these objects increase the drawing file size, it is good practice to delete or *purge* the unused objects from the drawing. The **PURGE** command is used to do this.

purge: Delete unused named objects from a drawing file.

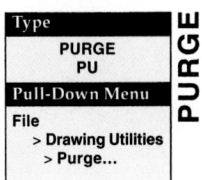

To access the **PURGE** command, pick **File > Drawing Utilities > Purge...** from the pull-down menu or type PU or PURGE. The **Purge** dialog box is displayed, as shown in **Figure 23-24.** Select the appropriate radio button at the top of the dialog box to view content that can be purged or to view content that cannot be purged.

Before purging, select the **Confirm each item to be purged** check box to have an opportunity to review each item before it is deleted. If you wish to purge nested items, check the **Purge nested items** check box.

If you want to purge only some items, use the tree view to locate and highlight the items, and then pick the **Purge** button. If you want to purge all unused items, pick the **Purge All** button. Purging may cause other named objects to become unreferenced. Thus, you may need to purge more than once to completely purge the drawing of unused named objects.

Figure 23-24.
The **Purge** dialog box.

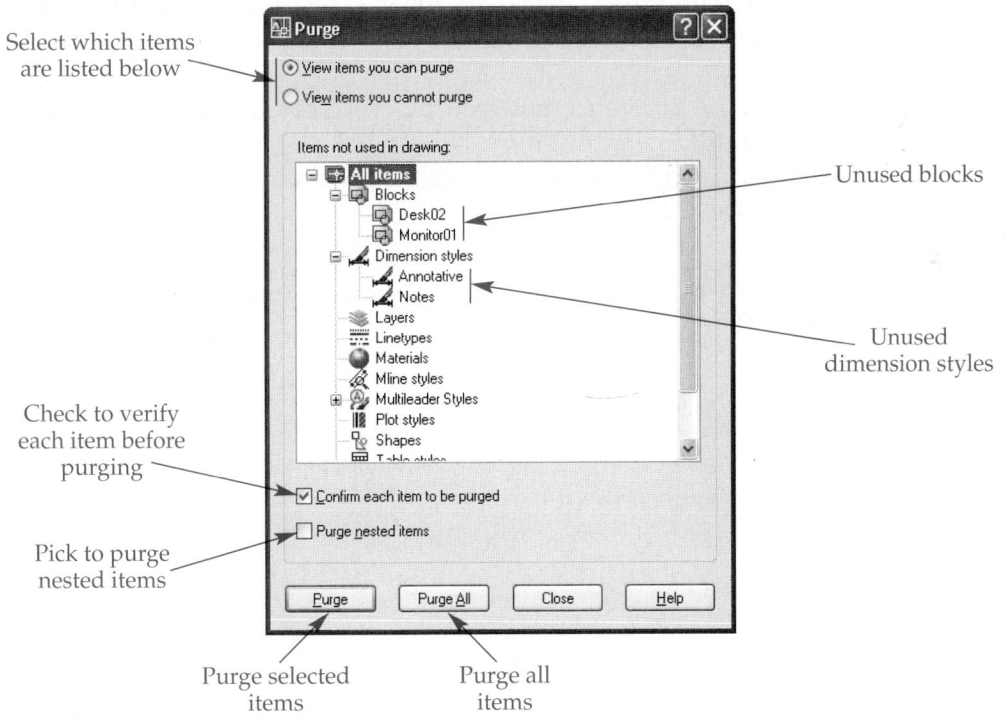

Chapter Test

Answer the following questions. Write your answers on a separate sheet of paper or complete the electronic chapter test on the Student CD.

1. Which color and linetype settings should you use if you want a block to assume the current color and linetype when it is inserted into a drawing?
2. Why would you draw blocks on layer 0?
3. What properties do blocks drawn on a layer other than layer 0 assume when inserted?
4. A block name cannot exceed _____ characters.
5. Define the term *nesting* in relation to blocks.
6. What are two ways to access a listing of all blocks in the current drawing?
7. How do you preset block insertion variables using the **Insert** dialog box?
8. Describe the effect of entering negative scale factors when inserting a block.
9. When should a block be drawn to fit inside a one-unit square, and what type of block is this called when it is inserted?
10. Name a limitation of an array pattern created with the **MINSERT** command.
11. What is the purpose of the **BASE** command?
12. Identify two ways to add block insertion tools to tool palettes.
13. How can you create a new tool palette that contains block insertion tools for all of the blocks in a drawing file?
14. Identify the command that allows you to break an inserted block into its individual objects for editing purposes.
15. Suppose you have found that a block was incorrectly drawn. Unfortunately, you have already inserted the block 30 times. How can you edit all of the blocks quickly?
16. What is the primary difference between blocks created with the **BLOCK** and **WBLOCK** commands?
17. Explain two ways to remove all unused blocks from a drawing.
18. Define *symbol library.*
19. Name an advantage of having a symbol library of blocks in a single drawing, rather than using wblocks.
20. What is the purpose of the **PURGE** command?

Drawing Problems

1. Create a symbol library for one of the drafting disciplines listed below and save it as a template or drawing file. Then, after checking with your instructor, draw a problem using the library. If you save the symbol library as a template, start the problem with the template. If you save it as a drawing file, start a new drawing and insert the symbol library into it. Specialty areas you might create symbols for include:
   - Mechanical (machine features, fasteners, tolerance symbols)
   - Architectural (doors, windows, fixtures)
   - Structural (steel shapes, bolts, standard footings)
   - Industrial piping (fittings, valves)
   - Piping flow diagrams (tanks, valves, pumps)
   - Electrical schematics (resistors, capacitors, switches)
   - Electrical one-line (transformers, switches)
   - Electronics (IC chips, test points, components)
   - Logic diagrams (AND gates, NAND gates, buffers)
   - Mapping, civil (survey markers, piping)
   - Geometric tolerancing (feature control frames)

   Save the drawing as P23-1 or choose an appropriate file name, such as ARCH-PRO or ELEC-PRO.

2. Display the symbol library created in Problem 1 on-screen and print a hard copy. Put the printed copy in your notebook as a reference.

3. Open P11-20 from Chapter 11. The sketch for this drawing is shown below. Erase all copies of the symbols that were made, leaving the original objects intact. These include the steel column symbols and the bay and column line tags. Then, do the following:
   A. Make blocks of the steel column symbol and the tag symbols.
   B. Use the **MINSERT** command or the **ARRAY** command to place the symbols in the drawing.
   C. Dimension the drawing as shown in the sketch.
   D. Save the drawing as P23-3.

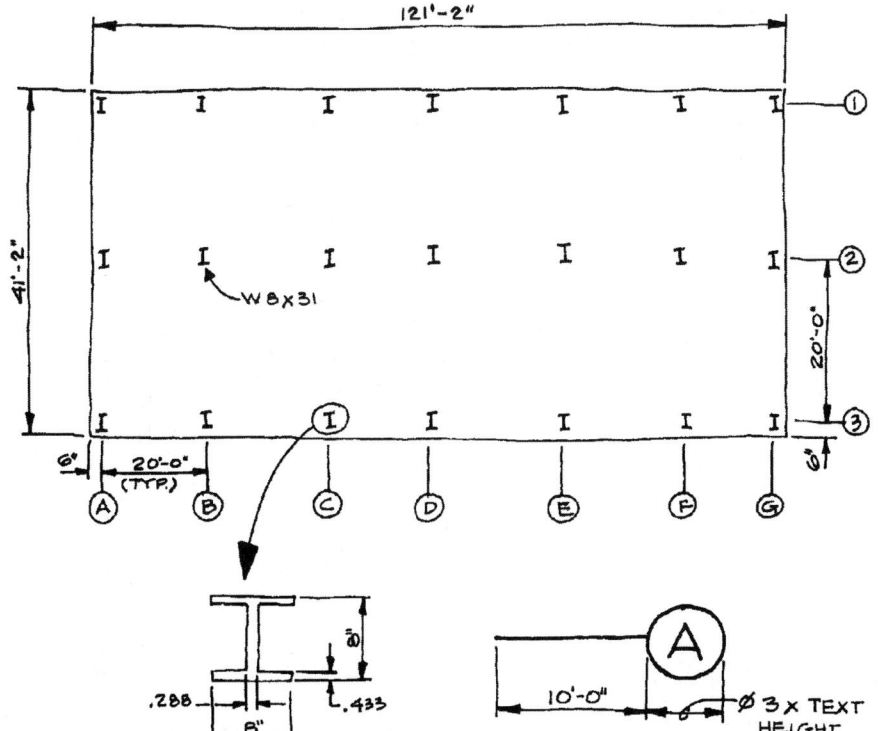

Problems 4–6 represent a variety of diagrams created using symbols as blocks. Create each drawing as shown (the drawings are not drawn to scale). The symbols should first be created as blocks or wblocks and then saved in a symbol library using one of the methods described in this chapter. Place a border and title block on each drawing. Save the drawings as P23-4, P23-5, and so on.

4.

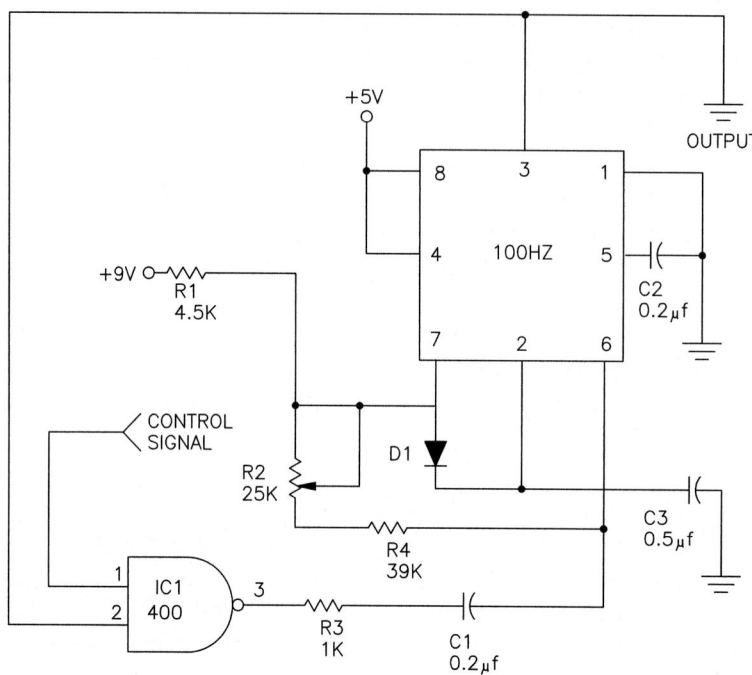

Integrated Circuit for Clock

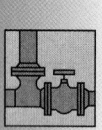

5.

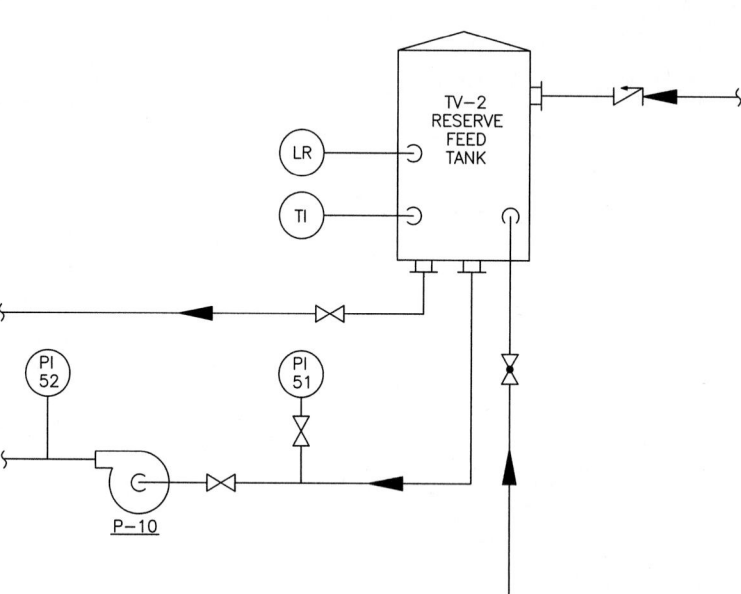

Piping Flow Diagram

AutoCAD and Its Applications—Basics

6.

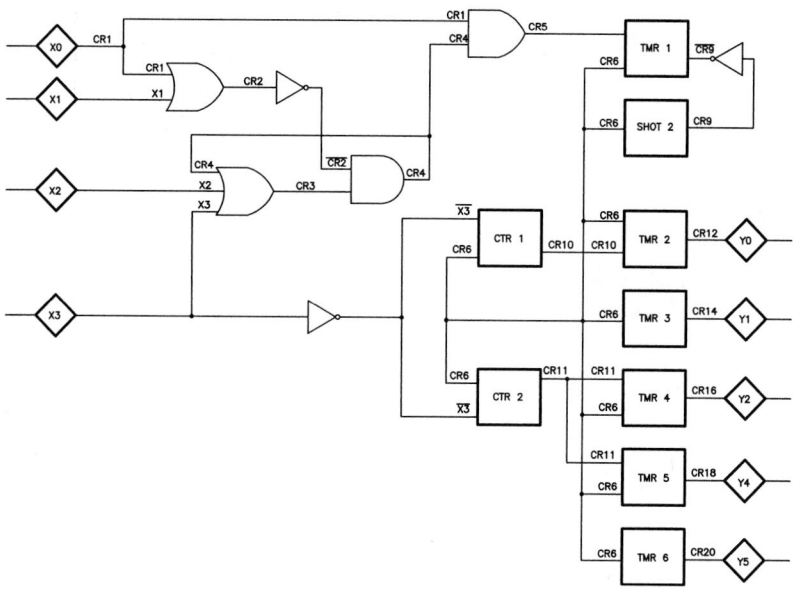

Logic Diagram of Marking System

7. Open P11-21 from Chapter 11. The sketch for this drawing is shown below. Erase all of the desk workstations except one. Then do the following:
   A. Create a block of the workstation.
   B. Insert the block into the drawing using the **MINSERT** command.
   C. Dimension one of the workstations as shown in the sketch.
   D. Save the drawing as P23-7.

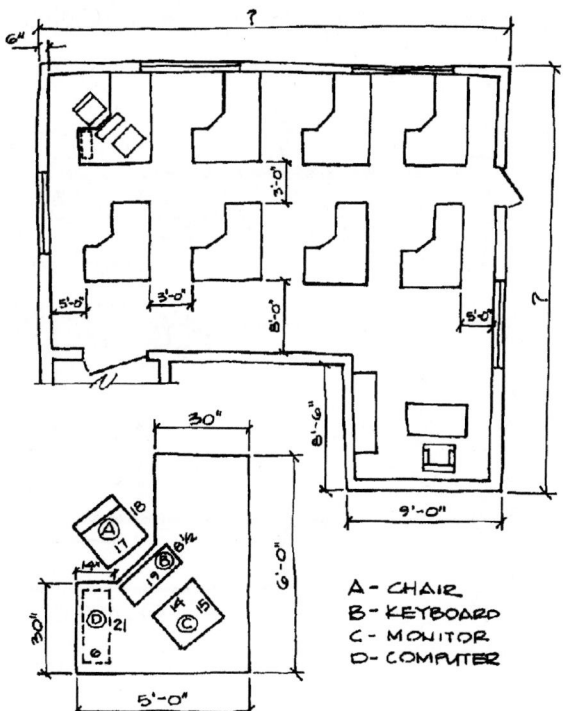

A - CHAIR
B - KEYBOARD
C - MONITOR
D - COMPUTER

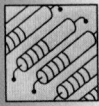

Problems 8–12 are presented as engineering sketches. They are schematic drawings created using symbols and are not drawn to scale. The symbols should first be drawn as blocks and then saved in a symbol library. Place a border and title block on each of the drawings.

8. The rough sketch shown below is a logic diagram of a portion of a computer's internal components. Create the drawing on a C-size sheet. Save the drawing as P23-8.

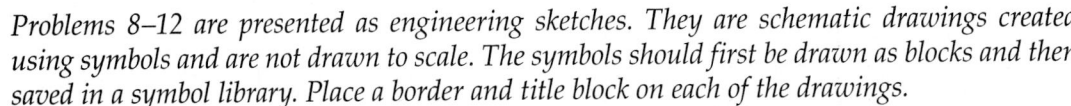

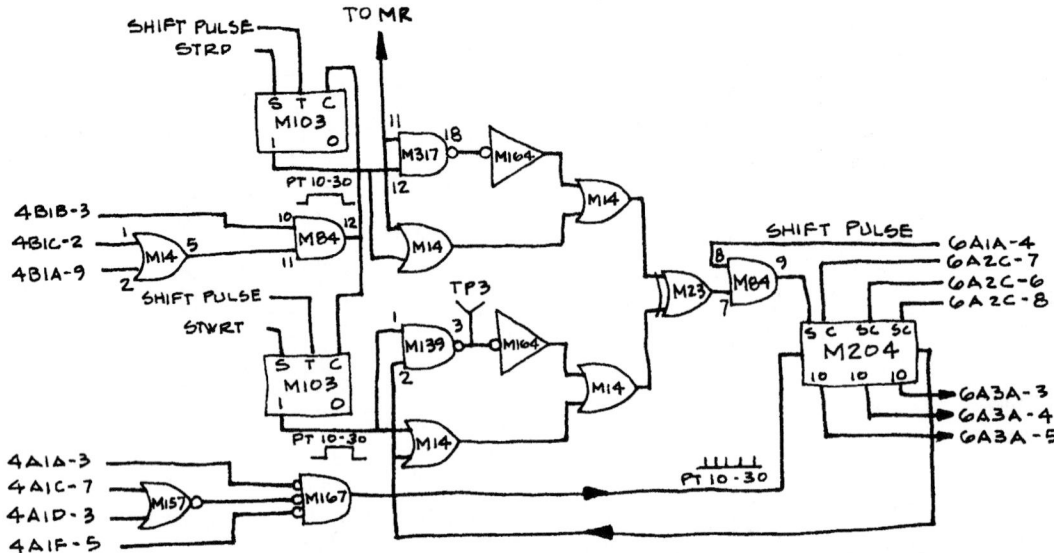

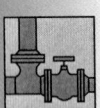

9. The rough sketch shown below is a piping flow diagram of a cooling water system. Create the drawing on a B-size sheet. Look closely at this drawing before you begin. Using blocks and the correct editing commands, it may be easier to complete than you think. Draw the thick flow lines with polylines. Save the drawing as P23-9.

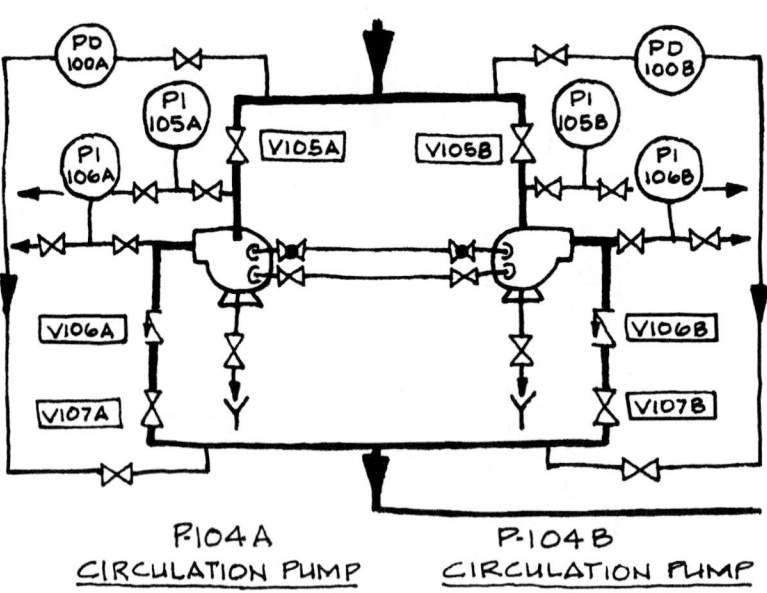

AutoCAD and Its Applications—Basics

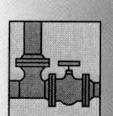

10. The rough sketch shown below is the general arrangement of a basement floor plan for a new building. The engineer has shown one example of each type of equipment. Use the following instructions to complete the drawing:

    A. Create the drawing on a C-size sheet.
    B. All text should be 1/8″ high, except the text for the bay and column line tags, which should be 3/16″ high. The line balloons for the bay and column lines should be twice the diameter of the text height.
    C. The column and bay line steel symbols represent wide-flange structural shapes and should be 8″ wide × 12″ high.
    D. The PUMP and CHILLER installations (except PUMP #4 and PUMP #5) should be drawn per the dimensions given for PUMP #1 and CHILLER #1. Use the dimensions shown for the other PUMP units.
    E. TANK #2 and PUMP #5 (P-5) should be drawn per the dimensions given for TANK #1 and PUMP #4.
    F. Tanks T-3, T-4, T-5, and T-6 are all the same size and are aligned 12′ from column line A.
    G. Plan this drawing carefully and create as many blocks as necessary to increase your productivity. Dimension the drawing as shown, and provide location dimensions for all equipment not shown in the engineer's sketch.
    H. Save the drawing as P23-10.

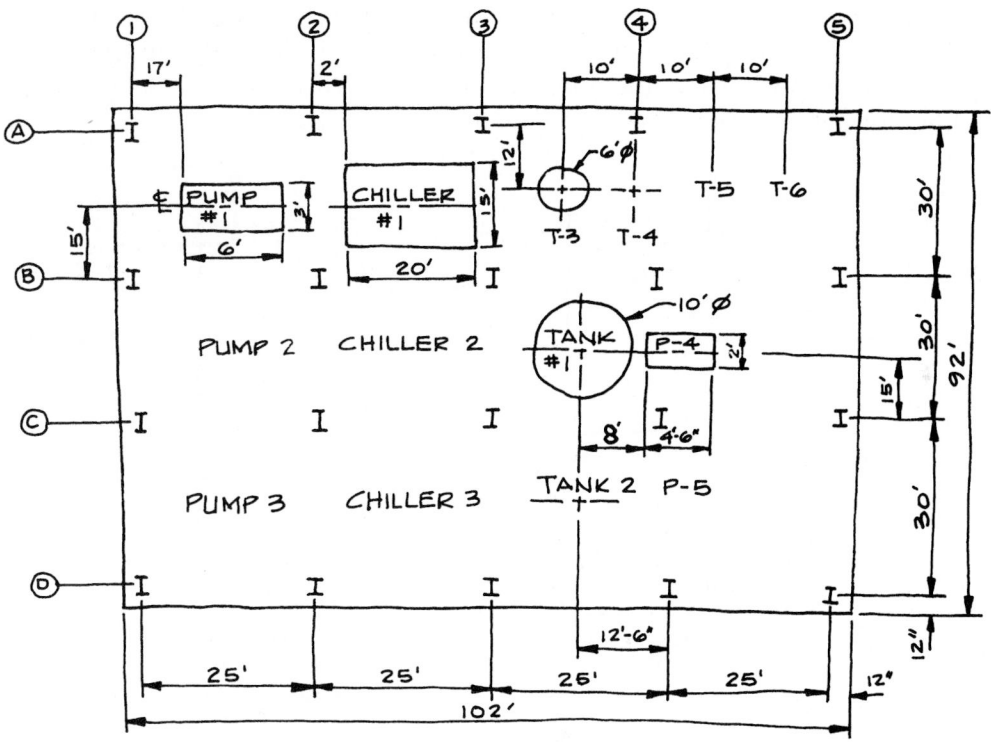

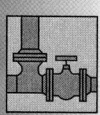

11. The rough sketch saved as P23-10 must be revised. The engineer has provided you with a sketch of the necessary revisions. It is up to you to alter the drawing as quickly and efficiently as possible. The dimensions shown on the sketch below *do not* need to be added to the drawing; they are provided for construction purposes only. Revise P23-10 so that all chillers and the four tanks reflect the changes. Save the drawing as P23-11.

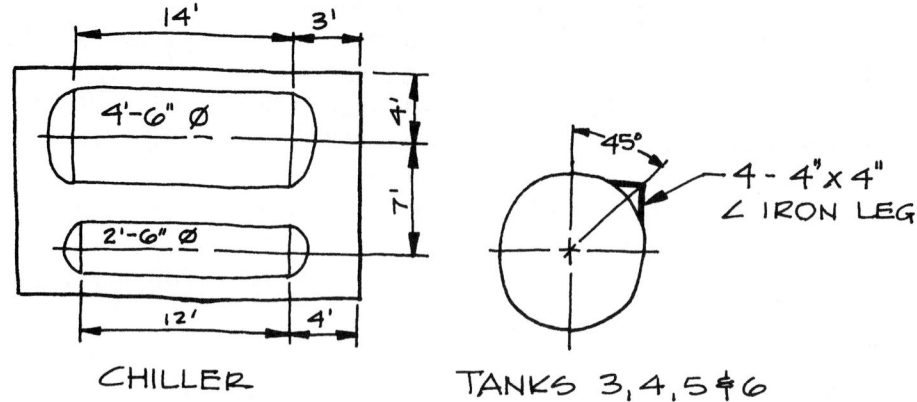

12. The rough sketch of a piping flow diagram shown below is part of an industrial effluent treatment system. Draw it on a C-size sheet. Eliminate as many bends in the flow lines as possible. Place arrowheads at all flow line intersections and bends. The flow lines should not run through any valves or equipment. Use polylines for the thick flow lines. Save the drawing as P23-12.

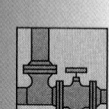

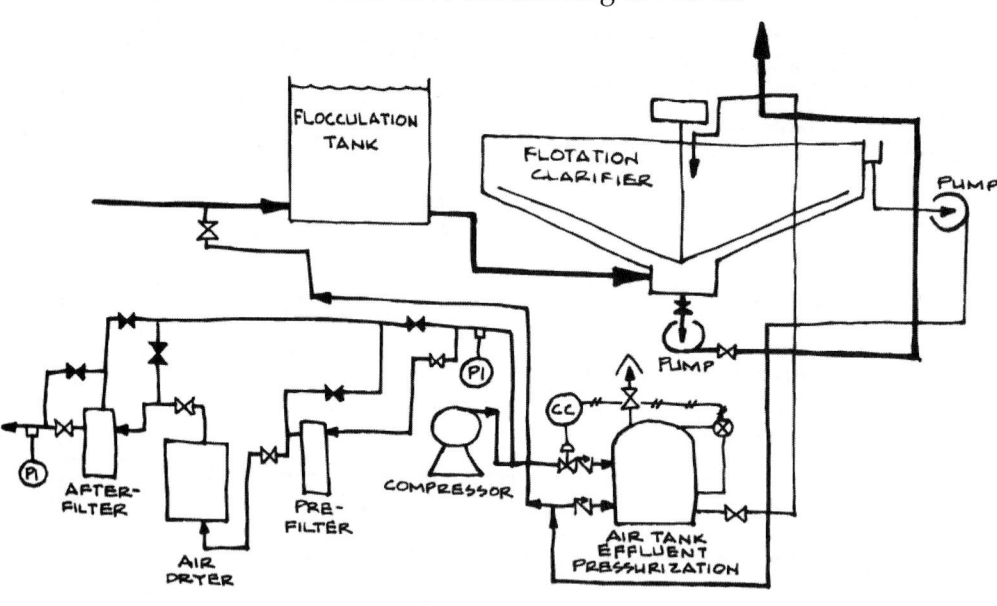

13. Draw the digital logic circuit shown. Create each type of component in the circuit as a block. Save the drawing as P23-13.

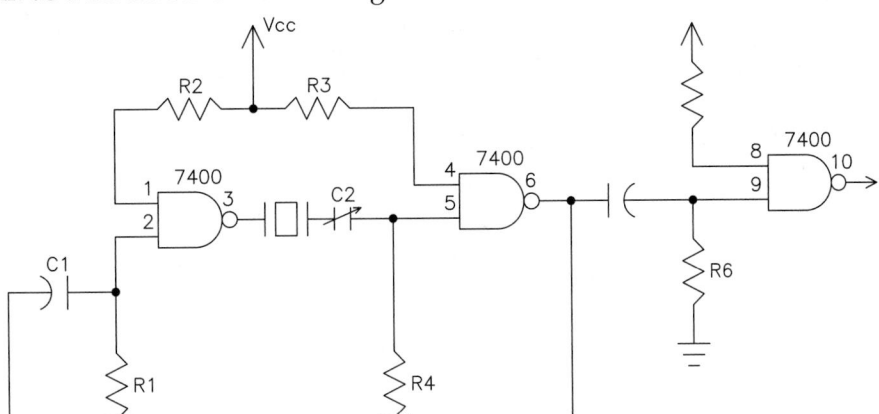

14. Open P23-13. Modify the NAND gates to become XNOR gates, as shown below, by modifying the block definition. Save the drawing as P23-14.

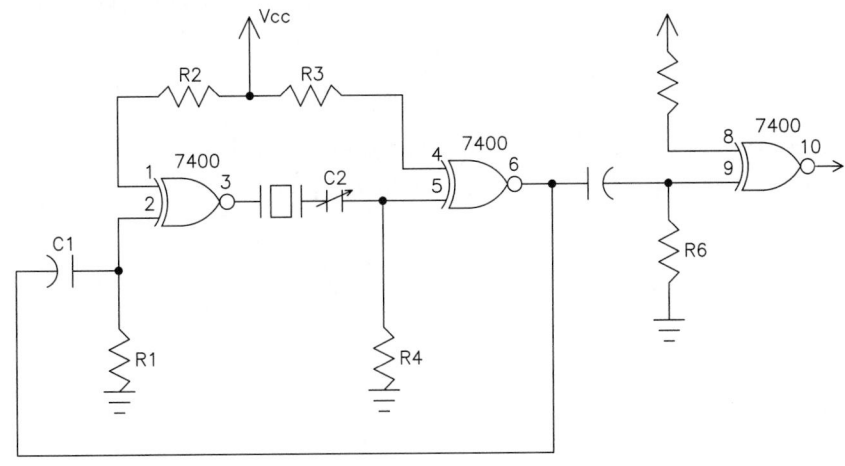

15. Create computer, plotter, and printer/copier blocks and then draw the network diagram. Save the drawing as P23-15.

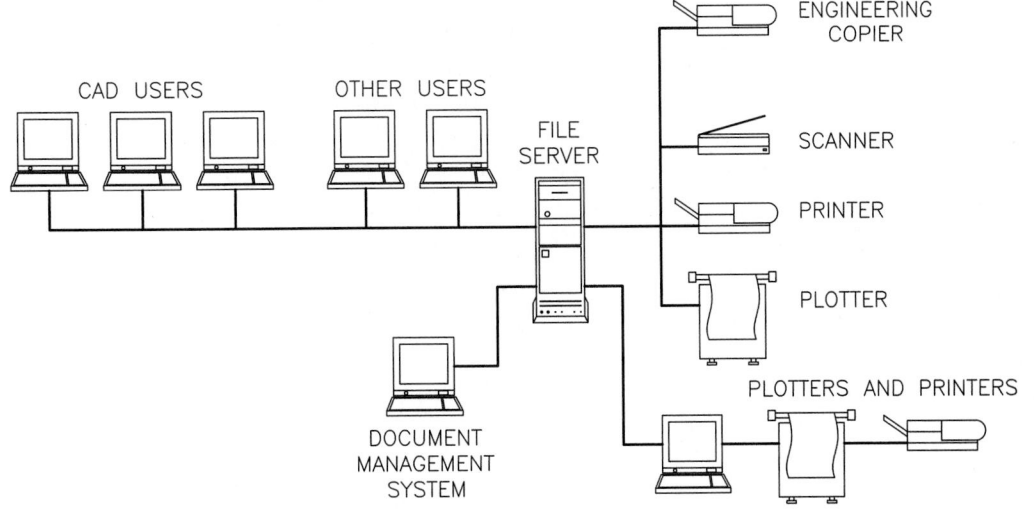

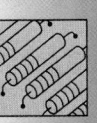

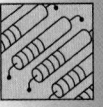

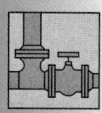

16. Draw the piping diagram shown, creating blocks for each type of fitting. Save the drawing as P23-16.

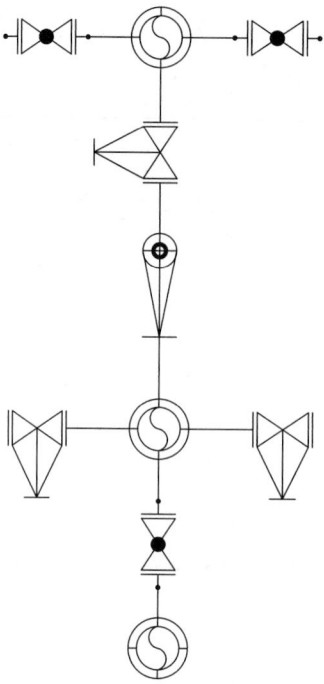

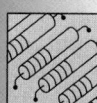

17. Create component blocks based on the dimensions shown. Then use the blocks to draw the schematic below. Save the drawing as P23-17.

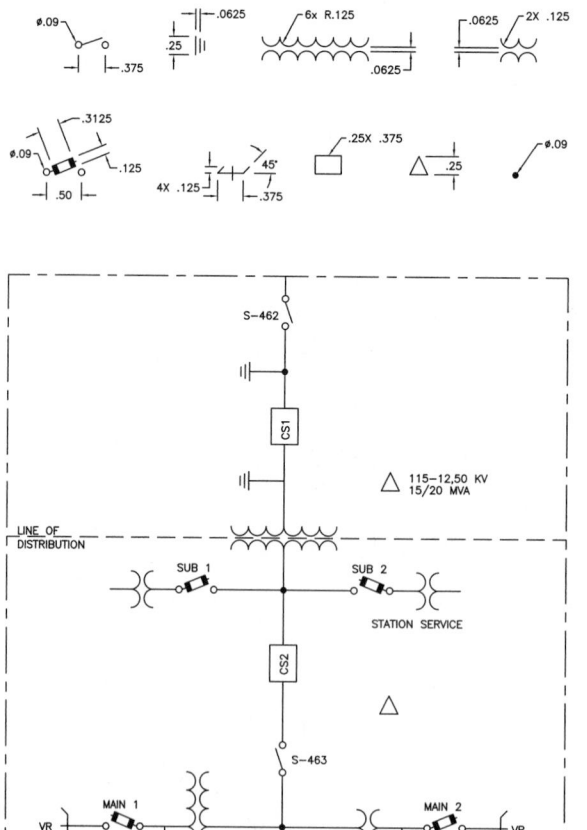

Drawing Problems - Chapter 23

Creating Dynamic Blocks

Learning Objectives

After completing this chapter, you will be able to do the following:

✓ Use AutoCAD's **Block Editor** to create dynamic blocks.
✓ List the parameters and actions that can be used to create a dynamic block.
✓ Insert parameters into blocks.
✓ Assign actions to parameters.
✓ Insert and use dynamic blocks.
✓ Use parameter sets.
✓ Modify parameters and actions.

Symbol libraries can contain hundreds or even thousands of blocks. The more blocks you have, the more time it takes to manage and work with them. In addition, many blocks may resemble several other blocks with only slight variances. For example, you may need to create a block of a bolt that is 1″ long. If the same style of bolt is also available in three other lengths, then three additional blocks may be created. An alternative is to create a single dynamic block that can be adjusted according to each unique bolt length. This chapter describes how to create and use dynamic blocks.

Introduction to Parameters and Actions

A *dynamic block* is a normal block in which parameters and actions have been assigned to objects within the block. This allows special modifications to be performed on a single block while it is in the drawing without affecting other instances of the same block.

To create a dynamic block, a *parameter* is inserted into the block and then an *action* is assigned to the parameter. Each parameter contains custom properties for objects within the block that specify the positions, distances, and angles of the block's geometry. An action controls how the block's geometry can be modified in the drawing. Once a parameter and action have been inserted into a block and the block has been saved, the block is considered a dynamic block.

A dynamic block is modified by selecting it in the drawing to display the *parameter grips*, which can then be selected to modify the block. **Figure 24-1** shows an example of a bolt that has been created as a dynamic block. The shaft objects of the bolt block have been assigned a linear parameter with a stretch action. The linear

dynamic block: A block to which parameters and actions have been assigned.

parameter: A value that defines custom properties such as positions, distances, and angles for objects in a dynamic block.

action: A definition that controls how the parameters of a dynamic block behave.

parameter grips: Special grips that allow you to change the parameters of a dynamic block.

Figure 24-1.
A linear parameter and stretch action have been assigned to the shaft objects in this block of a bolt. A—Selecting the block displays the linear grips. B—Selecting a linear grip and dragging it stretches the shaft of the bolt.

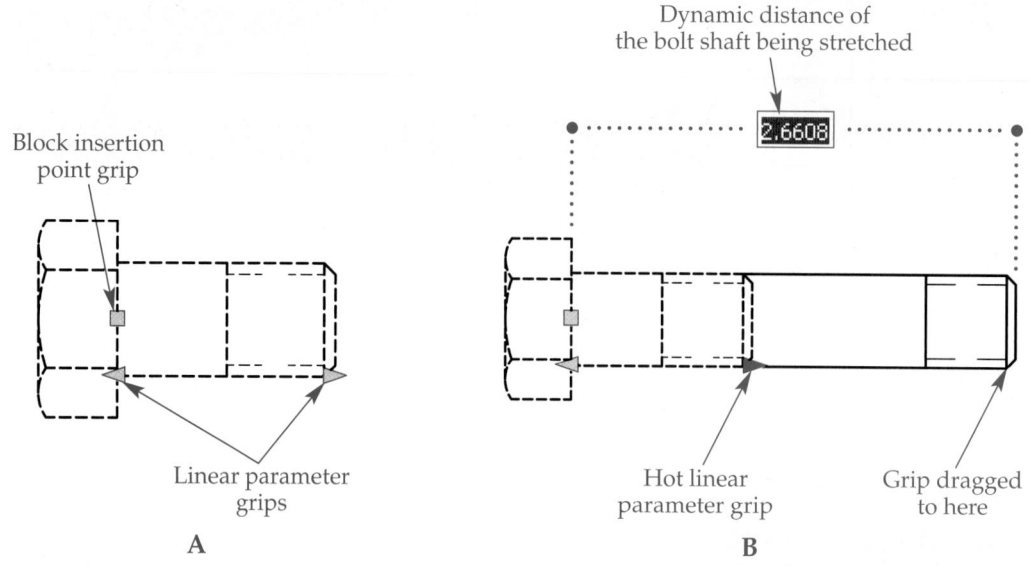

Dynamic distance of the bolt shaft being stretched

2.6608

Block insertion point grip

Linear parameter grips

Hot linear parameter grip

Grip dragged to here

A

B

parameter grips are shown in **Figure 24-1A.** To increase the length of the bolt, the right-hand linear parameter grip is selected and dragged to the right. See **Figure 24-1B.** The modification affects only this instance of the bolt block. Other references to the same block in the drawing are *not* updated. In this way, dynamic blocks can be used so only one block is inserted into the drawing, but multiple variations of the symbol can appear in the drawing.

The different types of parameters and actions can be seen in the **Block Authoring Palettes** window by selecting the appropriate tab. The **Parameters** tab and **Actions** tab are shown in **Figure 24-2.** Only certain actions can be assigned to a given parameter.

Figure 24-2.
The available parameters and actions can be accessed from the **Block Authoring Palettes** window.

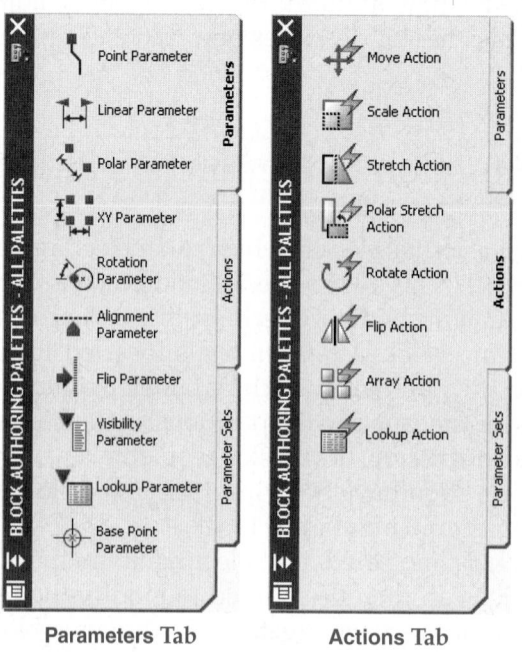

Parameters Tab

Actions Tab

The following chart lists parameters and the actions that can be assigned to them.

Parameter	Actions That Can Be Associated
alignment	none
base point	none
flip	flip
linear	move, scale, stretch, and array
lookup	lookup
point	move and stretch
polar	move, scale, stretch, polar stretch, and array
rotation	rotate
visibility	none
XY	move, scale, stretch, and array

Adding Dynamic Properties with the Block Editor

Dynamic properties can be assigned to an existing block in the drawing by using the **Block Editor**. To edit a block in the **Block Editor**, pick the **Block Editor** button on the **Standard** toolbar, pick **Tools** > **Block Editor**, type BEDIT, or double-click on a block in the drawing. The **Edit Block Definition** dialog box appears with a list of blocks. See **Figure 24-3**.

To edit an existing block, select the name of the block from the list of blocks. A preview and the description of the selected block are shown. A new block can be created by typing a name for the new block in the **Block to create or edit** field. Pick the **OK** button to open the selected block (or new block) in the **Block Editor**. Refer to **Figure 22-15**.

Tools available from the **Block Editor** toolbar and the **Block Authoring Palettes** window are used to create dynamic blocks. Some commands are not available in the **Block Editor**. When you finish editing, close the **Block Editor** and return to the drawing by picking the **Close Block Editor** button on the **Block Editor** toolbar or by typing BCLOSE. If changes have not been saved, a dialog box appears asking if you wish to save the changes. Pick **Yes** to save the changes, **No** to discard the changes, or **Cancel** to return to block editing mode.

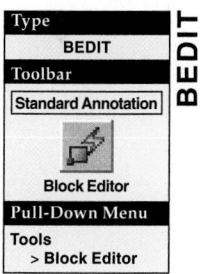

Type
BEDIT
Toolbar
Standard Annotation
Block Editor
Pull-Down Menu
Tools
> Block Editor

Figure 24-3.
The **Edit Block Definition** dialog box.

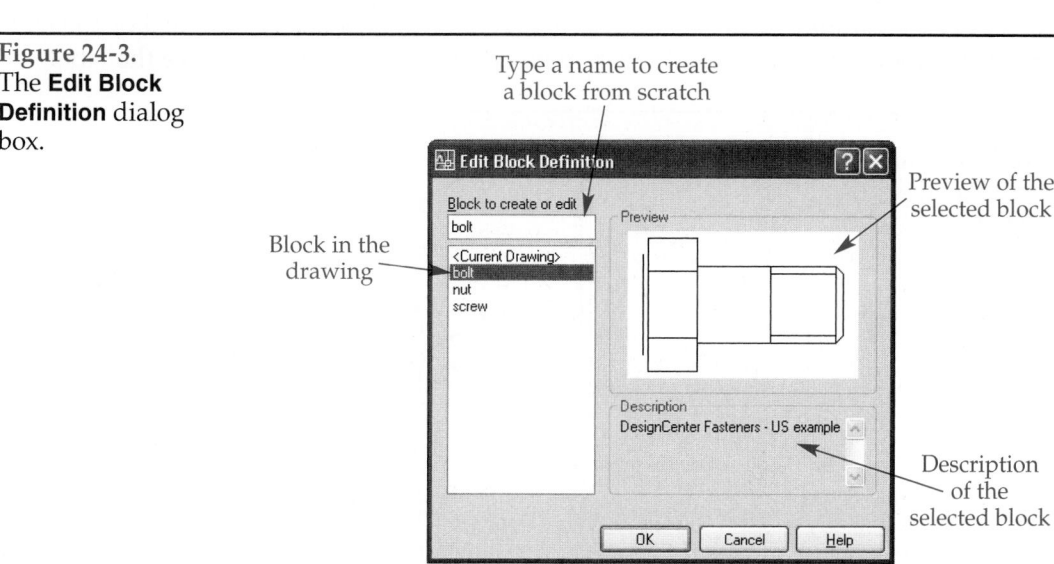

Type a name to create a block from scratch

Preview of the selected block

Block in the drawing

Description of the selected block

NOTE

Refer to Chapter 23 for more information about basic **Block Editor** options.

Adding Point Parameters

point parameter:
A parameter that defines an XY coordinate location in the drawing.

A *point parameter* defines an XY coordinate location in the drawing and can be used with the move and stretch actions. For example, suppose a block of a door includes a door tag as part of the block. A point parameter with a move action can be assigned to the door tag so the tag can be moved independently of the door after the block is inserted into the drawing.

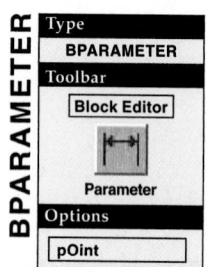

To insert a point parameter, pick the **Parameter** button on the **Block Editor** toolbar or type BPARAMETER. Then select the **pOint** option. You can also enter this directly by selecting **Point Parameter** from the **Parameters** tab in the **Block Authoring Palettes** window. The following prompt appears on the command line. Refer to **Figure 24-4** while working through the command sequence.

Specify parameter location or [Name/Label/Chain/Description/Palette]: *(pick the center of the door tag)*
Specify label location: *(drag the label to the side of the door tag and pick)*
Command:

The parameter location defines the grip point and the X and Y coordinates. This is the parameter grip that appears when the block is selected in the drawing. Selecting the parameter grip and moving it carries out the action that is assigned to the parameter. In this example, it is not essential that the center of the door tag be selected as the parameter location, but it makes more sense to put it there. If the parameter location is selected off the object, it may not be clear what the grip is for when the block is selected. If you want to move the parameter location after it has been inserted, you can select the grip in the **Block Editor** and move it.

parameter label: A label that indicates the purpose of a parameter.

The *parameter label* is like a note that indicates the purpose of the parameter. All parameters have a label. It appears only in block editing mode. By default, the label for a point parameter is POSITION. However, this can be changed to a more descriptive label. You can change the parameter label text when you create the parameter by using the **Label** option before specifying the parameter location. After the parameter is created, you can change the label text in the **Properties** palette. You can also move the label after the parameter has been inserted. To do this, select the label text or the label line to highlight the label, select the grip next to the label text, and move the label.

Figure 24-4.
A point parameter consists of the grip location and a label.

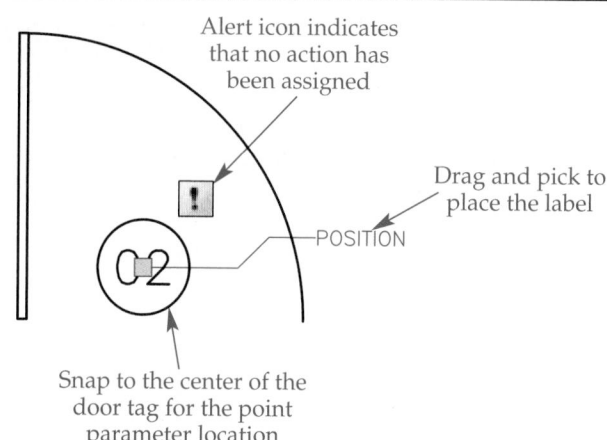

Before you specify the parameter location, the following options are available. These options can also be modified in the **Properties** palette after the label has been inserted.

- **Name.** Allows you to specify a name for the parameter.
- **Label.** Allows you to specify the text for the parameter label. The label is the text that appears next to the parameter.
- **Chain.** Determines whether the parameter can be affected by a chain action. Chain actions are described in more detail later in this chapter.
- **Description.** Allows you to type a description for the parameter. This is longer than the name or label and is used to explain more fully the purpose of the parameter. The description you enter displays as a tooltip when the dynamic block is used.
- **Palette.** Determines whether the label text is displayed in the **Properties** palette when the block is selected in the drawing.

Exercise 24-1

Complete the exercise on the Student CD.

Assigning a Move Action to a Point Parameter

After inserting a point parameter, a move or stretch action needs to be assigned to the parameter to make the block dynamic. The yellow alert icon shown in **Figure 24-4** indicates that no action has been assigned to the parameter. An action can be assigned to a parameter by picking the **Action** button on the **Block Editor** toolbar, typing BACTION, selecting the action from the **Actions** tab of the **Block Authoring Palette** window, or double-clicking any part of the parameter.

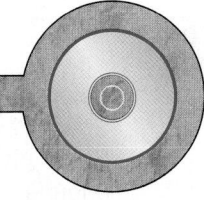

The sequence of prompts will be slightly different depending on the method used to access the action. If you pick the **Action** button from the **Block Editor** toolbar or type BACTION, the prompts are:

Select parameter: *(pick the parameter)*
Enter action type [Move/sTretch]: *(specify the action)*
Specify selection set for action
Select objects: *(select the objects to be modified by the action; this prompt differs depending on which type of action is selected)*
Select objects: ⏎
Specify action location or [Multiplier/Offset]: *(pick a point near the parameter label to place the action icon)*
Command:

If you select the action from the **Block Authoring Palette** window, the Enter action type [Move/sTretch]: prompt is not displayed. If you double-click the parameter, the Select parameter: prompt is not displayed.

For the door example, select **Move Action** from the **Block Authoring Palette** window to assign a move action to the point parameter. Refer to **Figure 24-5** while following this command sequence:

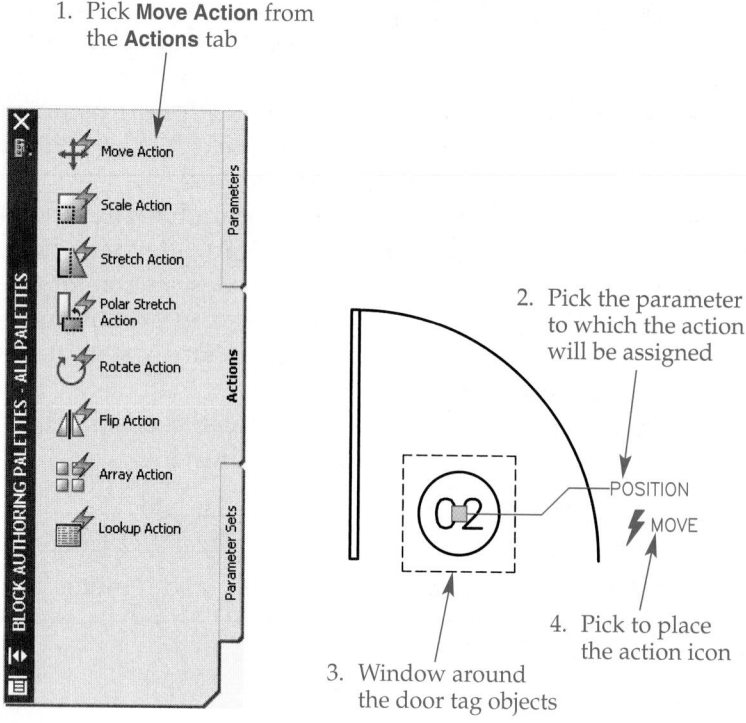

Figure 24-5.
Assigning a move action to a point parameter.

1. Pick **Move Action** from the **Actions** tab

2. Pick the parameter to which the action will be assigned

3. Window around the door tag objects

4. Pick to place the action icon

Select parameter: *(pick the parameter)*
Specify selection set for action
Select objects: *(window around the door tag objects)*
n found
Select objects: ↵
Specify action location or [Multiplier/Offset]: *(pick a point near the parameter label to place the action icon)*
Command:

When prompted to select objects, select all of the objects to be associated with this action. You can pick objects individually or by using a window/crossing selection. In this example, the objects that make up the door tag need to be selected.

The dynamic block is now ready to be saved and used. To save the block, pick the **Save Block Definition** button on the **Block Editor** toolbar or type BSAVE. An AutoCAD alert appears stating that saving the edits to the block updates any block references in the drawing. Pick the **Yes** button to save the edits. To exit the **Block Editor**, pick the **Close Block Editor** button on the **Block Editor** toolbar or type BCLOSE.

BSAVE

Type
   BSAVE
Toolbar
   Block Editor

Save Block Definition

PROFESSIONAL TIP

In most cases, when you select objects to include with an action, you should also select the parameter with which the action will be associated. If the parameter is not selected, the parameter grip will not be part of the action. Thus, the parameter grip may be left behind when a move, rotate, or stretch action is used.

Using a Move Action Dynamically

Once a dynamic block contains the appropriate parameters and actions and has been saved, the block is ready for use. In **Figure 24-6**, the door block is selected in the drawing. The point parameter grip is displayed as a light blue square and is shown in

Figure 24-6.
When the block is selected to display grips, the point parameter grip is shown as a light blue square.

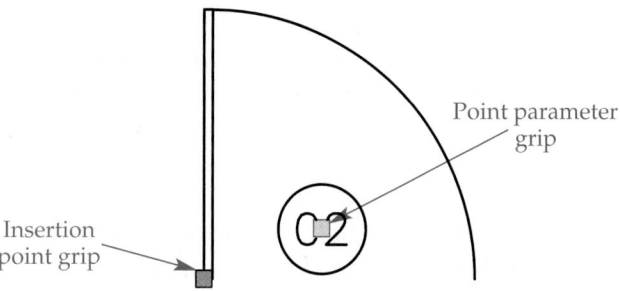

the center of the door tag. The insertion point that was specified when the block was created is displayed as a darker blue square surrounded by a dark line. It is shown in the lower-left corner of the block.

To move the objects composing the door tag within the block, select the block to display grips and select the point parameter grip to make it active. Drag the door tag objects to a new location. See **Figure 24-7A**. Pick a point in the drawing area to specify a new location for the door tag. See **Figure 24-7B**.

Being able to move part of a block can be very helpful. In the case of the door block example, there may be areas in the drawing where other objects pass through the door tag when the tag is in its default location. Being able to move the tag quickly, while maintaining the block definition, results in a drawing that is much cleaner and easier to read. If a normal block is used, the block must be exploded before the door tag objects can be moved. Once exploded, the objects are no longer associated with the block definition.

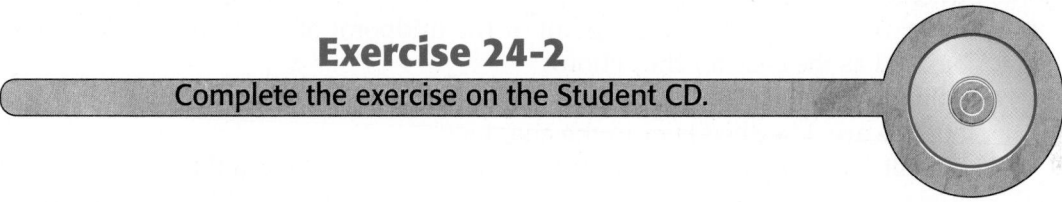

Exercise 24-2
Complete the exercise on the Student CD.

Figure 24-7.
Dynamically moving an action assigned to a point parameter. A—Select the point parameter grip and move it. B—The door tag is at a new location, but it is still part of the block.

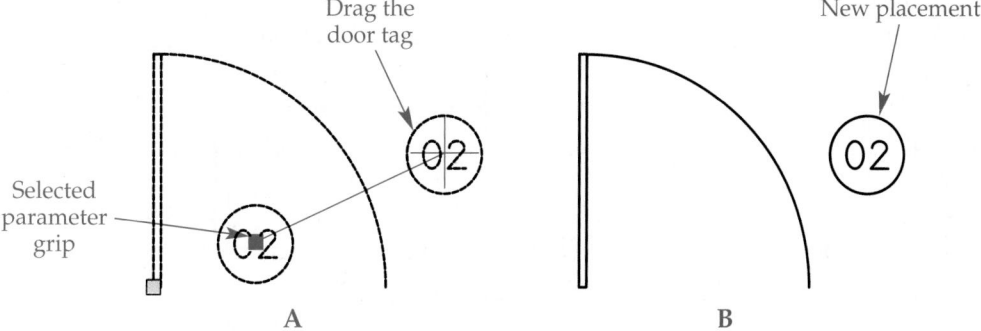

Adding Linear Parameters

linear parameter:
A parameter that creates a measurement reference between two points.

A *linear parameter* establishes a measurement reference between two points. Inserting a linear parameter into a block is like creating a linear dimension in a drawing. A move, scale, stretch, or array action can be assigned to a linear parameter. The objects that are included in the action selection set can then be modified within the block.

For example, a block of a bolt can contain a linear parameter. A stretch action can be assigned to the parameter so that the bolt shaft can be lengthened in a drawing. A second linear parameter and stretch action can be assigned to the bolt head to control its diameter.

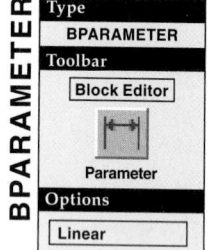

BPARAMETER

Type
BPARAMETER
Toolbar
Block Editor
Parameter
Options
Linear

To insert a linear parameter, pick the **Parameter** button on the **Block Editor** toolbar or type BPARAMETER. Then select the **Linear** option. You can also enter this directly by selecting **Linear Parameter** from the **Parameters** tab in the **Block Authoring Palettes** window. For the bolt example, use the **Label** option to name the linear parameter SHAFT LENGTH and then assign the parameter to the bolt shaft. Refer to **Figure 24-8**.

Specify start point or [Name/Label/Chain/Description/Base/Palette/Value set]:
LABEL↵
Enter distance property label: <*current*> **SHAFT LENGTH**↵
Specify start point or [Name/Label/Chain/Description/Base/Palette/Value set]: *(pick the endpoint of the lower edge of the shaft that is connected to the bolt head)*
Specify endpoint: *(using the extension object snap, pick the point where the edge of the shaft would meet the end if extended)*
Specify label location: *(drag the label away from the bolt and pick)*
Command:

Notice that the linear parameter has the same **Name**, **Label**, **Chain**, **Description**, and **Palette** options available when placing a point parameter. However, two additional options are available:

- **Base.** Allows either the start point or the midpoint of the linear parameter to be used as the base for the action.
- **Value set.** Allows specific values to be defined for the action. Both of these options are described later in the chapter.

By default, a linear parameter has two parameter grips—one at the first pick point and another at the second pick point. These are the grips that will be selected in the drawing to carry out the action that is assigned to the parameter.

Figure 24-8.
Defining a linear parameter.

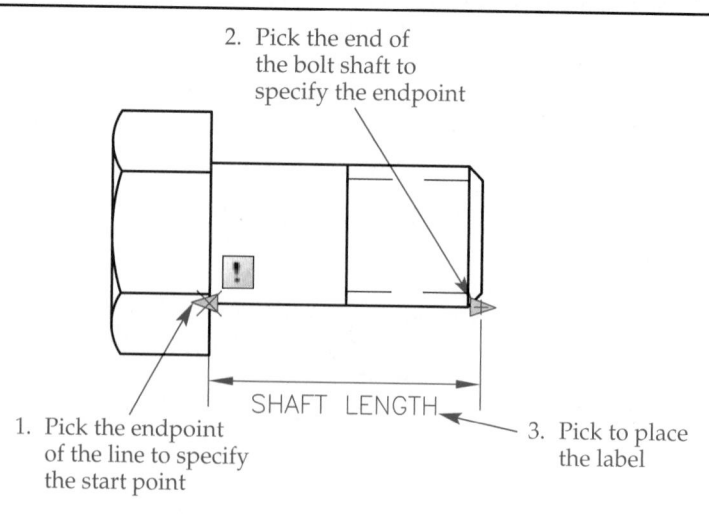

2. Pick the end of the bolt shaft to specify the endpoint

1. Pick the endpoint of the line to specify the start point

SHAFT LENGTH

3. Pick to place the label

Assigning a Stretch Action to a Linear Parameter

A stretch action can be assigned to the linear parameter. For the following command sequence, the **Action** button was picked from the **Block Editor** toolbar. Refer to **Figure 24-9**.

Select parameter: *(pick the parameter)*
Enter action type [Array/Move/Scale/sTretch]: **STRETCH.**↵
Specify parameter point to associate with action or enter [sTart point/Second point]
    <current>: *(move the cursor close to the parameter point that this action will be associated with; a red snap marker appears at the parameter point; pick to select the point)*
Specify first corner of stretch frame or [CPolygon]: *(pick a point to the upper-right of the end of the bolt shaft; see **Figure 24-9A**)*
Specify opposite corner: *(pick a point near the lower-middle of the shaft making sure that all the shaft objects are selected; see **Figure 24-9A**)*
Specify objects to stretch
Select objects: *(pick near the first point of the stretch frame; see **Figure 24-9B**)*
Specify opposite corner: *(pick near the second point of the stretch frame; see **Figure 24-9B**)*
n found
Select objects: ↵
Specify action location or [Multiplier/Offset]: *(pick a point near the parameter to place the stretch action icon; see **Figure 24-9C**)*
Command:

When a parameter has more than one parameter grip, as in the case of the linear parameter, AutoCAD needs to know the grip (parameter point) to which the action is associated. The parameter point can be selected with the cursor. Use the **sTart point** option to select the first point that was picked when creating the linear parameter or use the **Second point** option to select the second point.

Figure 24-9.
Assigning a stretch action to a linear parameter.
A—Specify the parameter, parameter grip, and stretch frame.
B—Use a crossing window to specify the objects that will be affected by the stretch action.
C—Pick near the parameter point to place the action icon.

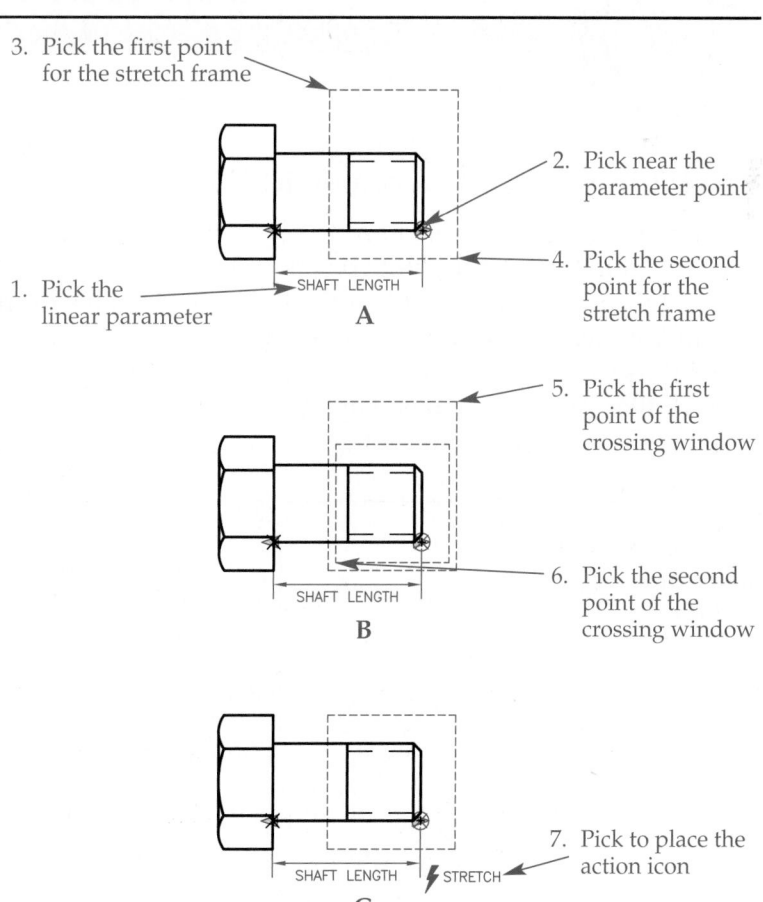

3. Pick the first point for the stretch frame
2. Pick near the parameter point
1. Pick the linear parameter
4. Pick the second point for the stretch frame
A

5. Pick the first point of the crossing window
6. Pick the second point of the crossing window
B

7. Pick to place the action icon
C

To save the changes to the block, pick the **Save Block Definition** button from the **Block Editor** toolbar or type BSAVE. You can now exit block editing mode. The block is ready to be used dynamically.

Using a Stretch Action Dynamically

After inserting the block, select it to display grips. The linear parameter grips are displayed as light blue arrows on screen. In the bolt example shown in Figure 24-10, the stretch action is assigned to the grip at the far end of the bolt shaft. The block is inserted with its default shaft length. To increase the length, select the parameter grip at the end of the shaft and drag it to the new length. If dynamic input is enabled, the distance of the shaft is dynamically updated in the distance field as you stretch the shaft. You can specify an exact length by entering a value in the distance field and pressing the [Enter] key. Relative coordinates can also be specified, which is useful if dynamic input is not enabled.

PROFESSIONAL TIP

The distance field displayed when dynamic input is enabled is a special property of the linear parameter. This feature allows you to enter an exact distance or length. Therefore, to get the best results when using the linear parameter, it is important that the first and second parameter points be inserted at the correct locations. Other parameters display similar fields when dynamic input is enabled.

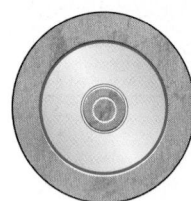

Exercise 24-3
Complete the exercise on the Student CD.

Stretching Objects Symmetrically

For parts of a block that need to stay symmetrical, the **Base** option can be used to specify a midpoint for the stretch action. This option can be specified before the first point of the linear parameter is picked or set later in the **Properties** palette.

In the following example, a linear parameter with a stretch action is assigned to the objects composing the bolt head. Refer to Figure 24-11. First, open the block in the **Block Editor**. Then pick **Linear Parameter** in the **Parameters** tab of the **Block Authoring Palette** window. Continue as follows:

Figure 24-10.
Selecting the block in the drawing displays the parameter grips.

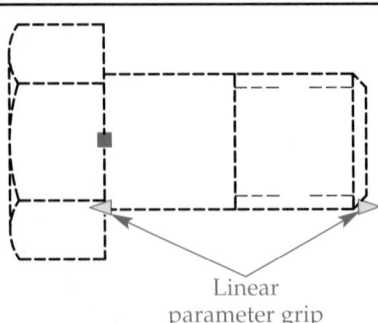

Linear
parameter grip

Figure 24-11.
The base point of a linear parameter is displayed as an X. When the **Midpoint** option is used, the base point is in the center between the two parameter grips.

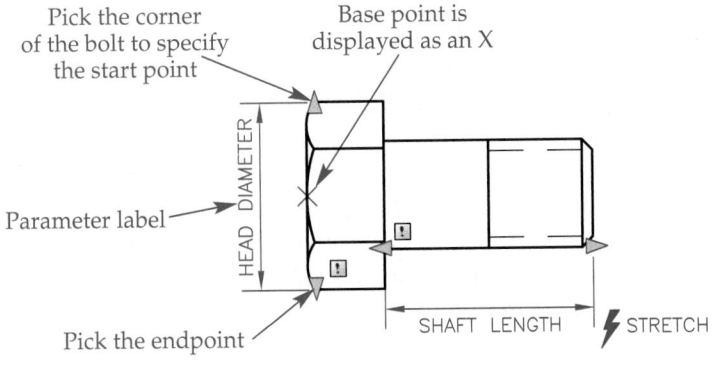

Specify start point or [Name/Label/Chain/Description/Base/Palette/Value set]: **BASE**↵
Enter base location [Startpoint/Midpoint]: <Startpoint>: **MIDPOINT**↵
Specify start point or [Name/Label/Chain/Description/Base/Palette/Value set]: **LABEL**↵
Enter distance property label <*current*>: **HEAD DIAMETER**↵
Specify start point or [Name/Label/Chain/Description/Base/Palette/Value set]: *(pick the upper-left corner of the bolt head to specify the start point; the midpoint is automatically calculated based on the start and endpoints)*
Specify endpoint: *(pick the lower-left corner of the bolt head to specify the endpoint)*
Specify label location: *(pick to the left of the bolt to place the label)*
Command:

Now a stretch action must be assigned to the parameter for each side of the bolt head. Refer to **Figure 24-12**. First, pick **Stretch Action** from the **Actions** tab of the **Block Authoring Palette** window. Then continue as follows:

Select parameter: *(pick the* HEAD DIAMETER *parameter)*
Specify parameter point to associate with action or enter [sTart point/Second point] <Second>: *(pick the upper linear parameter point; see Figure 24-12A)*
Specify first corner of stretch frame or [CPolygon]: *(pick the first corner of the stretch frame above and to the left of the bolt head)*
Specify opposite corner: *(pick just above the midpoint and within the shaft)*
Select objects: *(select the upper objects of the bolt head; see Figure 24-12B)*
Select objects: ↵

Figure 24-12.
Assigning a stretch action to one side of the bolt head. A—Create a stretch frame around the top of the bolt head. B—Use a window to select the objects to be included in the stretch.

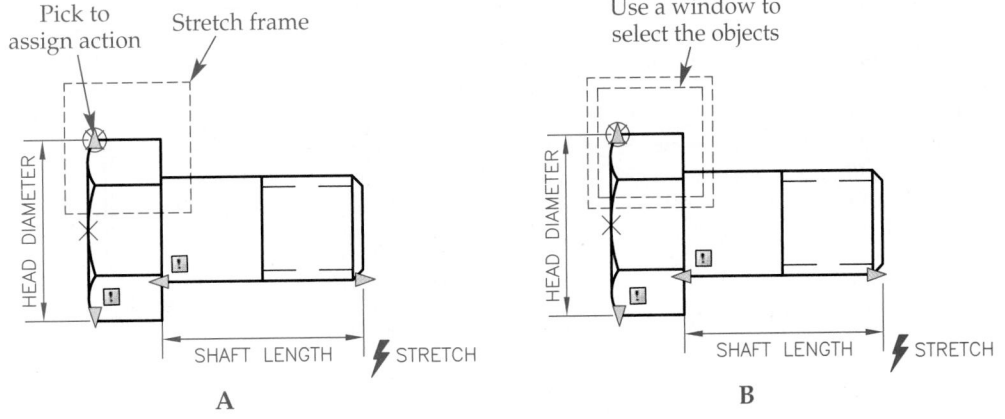

A

B

Specify action location or [Multiplier/Offset]: *(pick to place the action icon near the parameter point)*
Command:

Repeat this sequence to assign a second stretch action to the parameter. Associate it with the lower parameter point and specify the objects as the lower objects of the bolt head. Save the block and exit the **Block Editor**.

Now, dragging one of the parameter grips increases or decreases the opposite side of the bolt head the same length. Select the block in the drawing area to display grips. Select either of the grips for the HEAD DIAMETER parameter and drag the cursor. Notice how the opposite side of the bolt head is moving the same distance. See **Figure 24-13**. If dynamic input is enabled, you can specify an exact diameter for the bolt head by typing in a value in the distance field.

Assigning a Scale Action to a Linear Parameter

The scale action allows you to scale some of the objects within a block independently of the other objects. This action is similar to the **SCALE** command, which is described in Chapter 11. For example, a block of a countertop consists of the countertop and a sink. The dimensions of the countertop have to remain static, but different size sinks can go in the countertop. Instead of having a different block for each countertop/sink combination, you can create one block that includes both. A linear parameter and scale action can be assigned to the objects that make up the sink. This allows the sink to be scaled to the correct size as needed.

First, insert a linear parameter along the length of the objects composing the sink. Use the **Base** option to define the midpoint so the sink is scaled symmetrically. Refer to **Figure 24-14**.

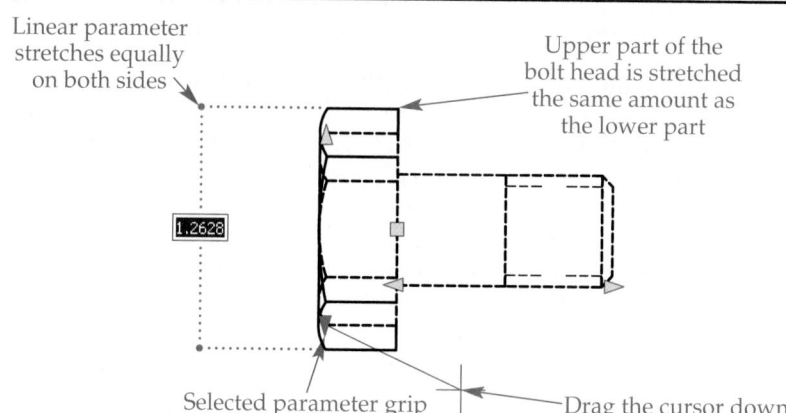

Figure 24-13.
Dynamically stretching the bolt head. Note that the head is stretched symmetrically.

Linear parameter stretches equally on both sides

Upper part of the bolt head is stretched the same amount as the lower part

1.2628

Selected parameter grip

Drag the cursor down

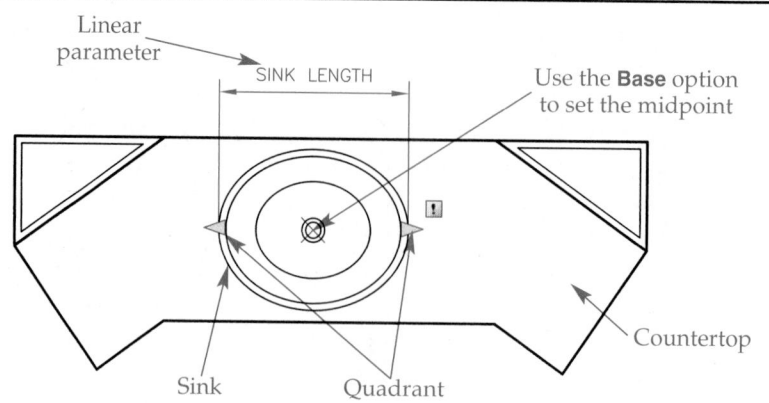

Figure 24-14.
A linear parameter is inserted into the block of a sink and countertop. The base point is specified as the center of the sink so it will stretch symmetrically.

Linear parameter

SINK LENGTH

Use the **Base** option to set the midpoint

Sink

Quadrant

Countertop

Specify start point or [Name/Label/Chain/Description/Base/Palette/Value set]: **BASE**↵
Enter base location [Startpoint/Midpoint] <Startpoint>: **MIDPOINT**↵
Specify start point or [Name/Label/Chain/Description/Base/Palette/Value set]: **LABEL**↵
Enter distance property label <Distance>: **SINK LENGTH**↵
Specify start point or [Name/Label/Chain/Description/Base/Palette/Value set]: *(pick the quadrant on one side of the sink)*
Specify endpoint: *(pick the quadrant on the opposite side of the sink)*
Specify label location: *(pick a location for the label)*
Command:

Now assign the scale action to the parameter. For the following command sequence, pick the **Action** button on the **Block Editor** toolbar. Then, continue:

Select parameter: *(pick the parameter)*
Enter action type [Array/Move/Scale/sTretch]: **SCALE**↵
Specify selection set for action
Select objects: *(select the linear parameter and all of the objects that make up the sink; use a window, crossing, or individual selections)*
n found
Select objects: ↵
Specify action location or [Base type]: **B**↵
Enter base point type [Dependent/Independent] <Dependent>: **I**↵
Specify base point location <current>: *(pick the center of the sink)*
Specify action location or [Base type]: *(pick a point near the parameter to place the scale action icon)*
Command:

When using the scale action, it is critical to scale the objects relative to the correct location (base point). If the base point is not in the correct location, undesirable results are produced. For the sink, it is important that the objects be scaled relative to the exact center of the sink. This keeps the sink centered within the countertop.

Notice in the previous command sequence that there are two options for the base point of the scale action. The default option is **Dependent**, which scales the objects relative to the base point of the associated parameter. To specify a different location, use the **Independent** option. AutoCAD prompts you to specify the base point, which is then used as the base to scale the objects.

The dynamic block is now defined. Save the block and close the **Block Editor**.

PROFESSIONAL TIP

In the previous command sequence, the **Independent** option was used to set the center of the sink as the base point for the scale action. This is needed because the base point of the linear parameter is the first pick point, not the midpoint. The midpoint was defined for the parameter so that the parameter (and its grips) are scaled about its midpoint, not its start point. The **Independent** option of the scale action is used to specify the point about which the geometry (not the parameter) is scaled.

Using a Scale Action Dynamically

After inserting the block, select it to display grips. Select either of the linear parameter grips and drag the cursor to dynamically scale the sink objects. Since the center of the sink was selected as the base point, the sink objects are scaled relative to that point. In **Figure 24-15**, the right-hand grip is selected and dragged to the right to increase the size of the sink. Pick a point to resize the sink. If dynamic input is enabled, you can also type a value in the distance field.

Chapter 24 Creating Dynamic Blocks

Figure 24-15.
Scaling the sink
dynamically. The
scale action is not
applied to the
countertop.

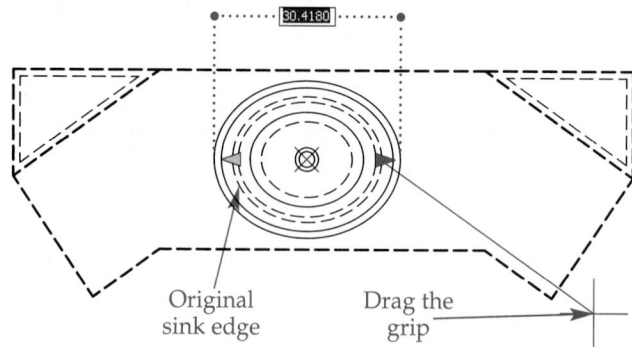

Original
sink edge

Drag the
grip

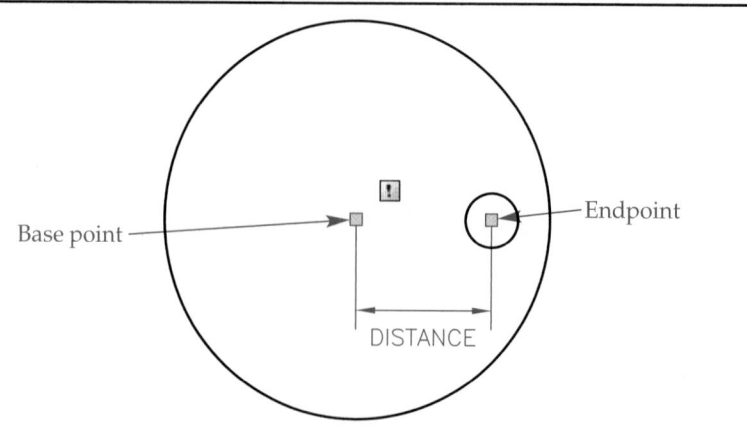

Exercise 24-4
Complete the exercise on the Student CD.

Adding Polar Parameters

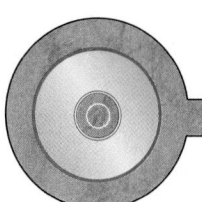

polar parameter:
A parameter that
includes both a
distance property
and an angle
property.

A *polar parameter* includes two parameter points with a distance property, such as a linear property, but also includes an angle property. The action types that can be assigned to a polar parameter are move, scale, stretch, polar stretch, and array.

For example, a block has been created that consists of a large circle containing a smaller circle. See **Figure 24-16.** A polar parameter can be inserted into the block to specify a distance and angle. Also, a move action can be assigned to the parameter that acts on the smaller circle. Then the smaller circle can be moved a specified distance and angle without affecting the larger circle.

To insert a polar parameter, pick the **Parameter** button from the **Block Editor** toolbar or type BPARAMETER. Then select the **Polar** option. You can also enter this directly by selecting **Polar Parameter** from the **Parameters** tab in the **Block Authoring Palettes** window. The following command sequence places a polar parameter in the block shown in **Figure 24-16.**

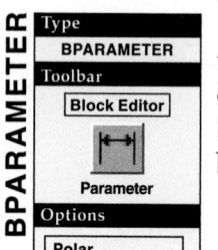

Enter parameter type
[Alignment/Base/pOint/Linear/Polar/Xy/Rotation/Flip/Visibility/looKup]: **POLAR.↵**
Specify base point or [Name/Label/Chain/Description/Palette/Value set]: *(pick the center of the large circle)*
Specify endpoint: *(pick the center of the small circle)*

Figure 24-16.
Inserting a polar
parameter.

Base point

Endpoint

DISTANCE

Specify label location: *(pick a point to place the label)*
Enter number of grips [0/1/2] <2>: ⏎
Command:

Notice that you must specify the number of grips. Now that the parameter has been assigned, an action can be associated to it.

Assigning a Move Action to a Polar Parameter

Assigning a move action to a parameter is described earlier in this chapter. For this example, the small circle is selected for the move action. In this way, the small circle can be moved independently of the large circle even though they are part of the same block object. Refer to **Figure 24-17** while following these steps:

1. Open the block in block editing mode.
2. Pick **Move Action** from the **Actions** tab of the **Block Authoring Palette** window.
3. Select the polar parameter.
4. Select the parameter point in the center of the small circle to associate the move action with this parameter grip.
5. Select the small circle as the object to be included in the move action.
6. Pick a location for the move action icon.
7. Save the block and close the **Block Editor**.

Using a Move Action Dynamically

After the block is inserted, select it to display grips. Select the parameter grip in the center of the small circle and drag it. Pick a point to place the small circle at a new location, or enter polar coordinates to move the circle an exact distance and angle. For example, to move the small circle three inches away from the center of the large circle at 45°, type @3<45 and press [Enter]. Using polar coordinates is covered in Chapter 3. If dynamic input is enabled, the distance the circle is being moved is displayed in the distance field and the angle is displayed next to the distance field. See **Figure 24-18**.

PROFESSIONAL TIP

In this example, the parameter grip for the base point can also be moved by selecting it and dragging. No action or objects are assigned to the base point grip, so only the grip itself is moved. However, this affects the distance and angle to the endpoint.

Figure 24-17.
Assigning a move action to a polar parameter.

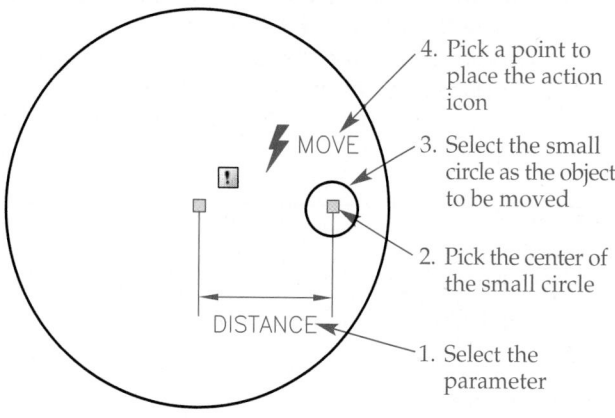

4. Pick a point to place the action icon

3. Select the small circle as the object to be moved

2. Pick the center of the small circle

1. Select the parameter

MOVE

DISTANCE

Figure 24-18.
Moving an object with a polar parameter displays the distance and the angle from the base point if dynamic input is enabled.

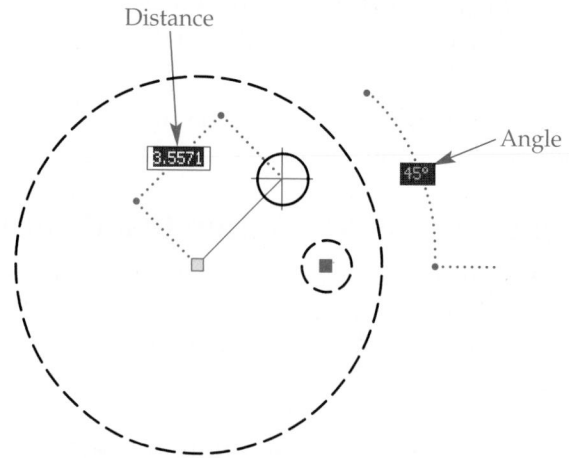

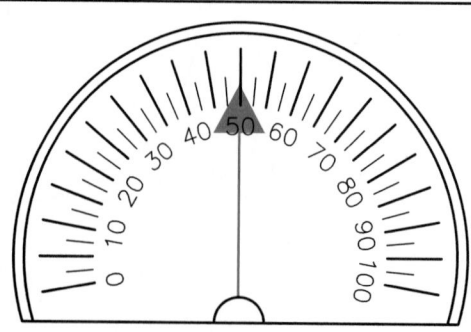

Exercise 24-5

Complete the exercise on the Student CD.

Adding Rotation Parameters

A *rotation parameter* allows objects within a block to be independently rotated. This parameter allows you to define a rotation point and beginning angle. Only a rotate action can be assigned to a rotation parameter.

For example, look at the speedometer block shown in **Figure 24-19.** The needle pointer should be able to rotate around the circumference of the dial. A rotation parameter with an associated rotation action can be used to allow this.

To insert a rotation parameter, pick the **Parameter** button on the **Block Editor** toolbar or type BPARAMETER. Then select the **Rotation** option. You can also enter this directly by selecting **Rotation Parameter** from the **Parameters** tab in the **Block Authoring Palettes** window. The following command sequence adds a rotation parameter to the speedometer block:

Specify base point or [Name/Label/Chain/Description/Palette/Value set]: *(pick the center of the needle's circular base)*
Specify radius of parameter: *(pick a point to define a circle on which the rotation parameter grip will be placed)*
Specify default rotation angle or [Base angle]: *(pick the tip of the arrow or type 90; the grip will be placed here)*
Specify label location: *(pick a point to place the label)*
Command:

Figure 24-19.
The needle can be rotated to indicate different speeds on this speedometer by assigning a rotation parameter with a rotate action to the needle.

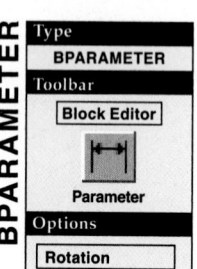

AutoCAD and Its Applications—Basics

Figure 24-20.
Inserting a rotation
parameter into the
speedometer block.

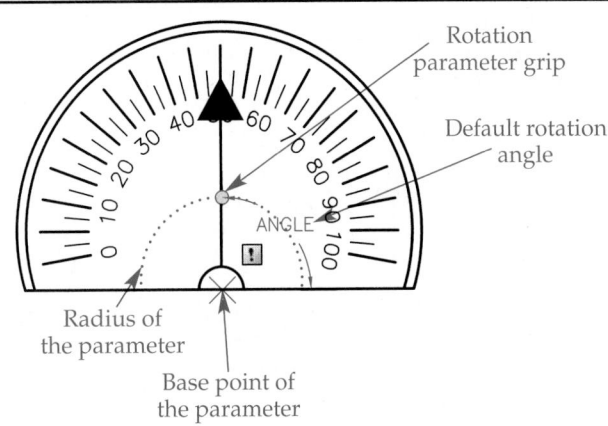

As shown in Figure 24-20, an angle of 90° places the parameter grip in line with the arrow. By default, the base angle for a drawing is at 0° to the east. The **Base angle** option allows you to specify a base angle that is different from the current drawing base angle.

Assigning a Rotate Action to a Rotation Parameter

After a rotation parameter has been inserted, a rotate action can be assigned to the parameter. This action is similar to the **ROTATE** command, which is described in Chapter 11. The rotate action allows individual objects within a block to be rotated without affecting the other objects in the block. For the following command sequence, **Rotate Action** was picked from the **Actions** tab of the **Block Authoring Palette** window:

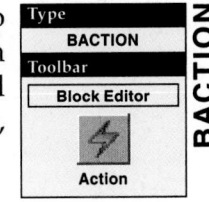

> Select parameter: (*pick the rotation parameter*)
> Specify selection set for action
> Select objects: (*select the rotation parameter and all of the objects that make up the arrow*)
> *n* found
> Select objects: ↵
> Specify action location or [Base type]: (*pick a point near the parameter to place the rotate action icon*)
> Command:

The **Base type** option can be used to define a different rotational base point. By default, the rotation point is the base point of the rotation parameter.

The dynamic block is now defined. Save the block and close the **Block Editor.**

Using a Rotate Action Dynamically

After the block is inserted, select it to display grips. See Figure 24-21A. Select the parameter grip and drag. The needle objects are rotated around the base point. Pick to rotate the objects or use relative coordinates. If dynamic input is enabled, the angle is displayed dynamically as you drag the grip. In Figure 24-21B, the needle is dragged until a value of 45° is displayed.

Exercise 24-6
Complete the exercise on the Student CD.

Figure 24-21.
A—The parameter grip is displayed when the block is selected. B—Dynamically rotating the needle.

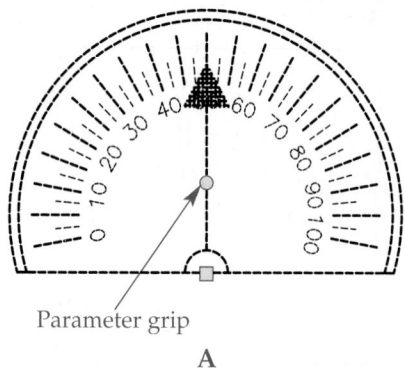
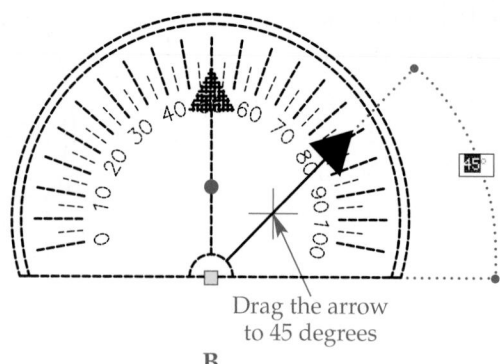

Parameter grip

Drag the arrow to 45 degrees

A   B

Adding Alignment Parameters

An *alignment parameter* allows a block to be automatically aligned with another object in the drawing. When the block is moved near another object in the drawing, the block automatically rotates to align with that object based on the angle and alignment line defined in the block. This parameter saves time by eliminating the need to determine an angle of rotation and use the **ROTATE** command on the block. An alignment parameter affects the entire block, not individual components. Therefore, no actions are assigned to this parameter.

Inserting an Alignment Parameter

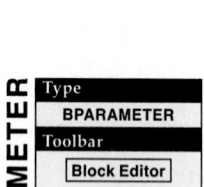

To insert an alignment parameter, pick the **Parameter** button on the **Block Editor** toolbar or type BPARAMETER. Then use the **Alignment** option. This can be entered directly by selecting **Alignment Parameter** from the **Parameters** tab in the **Block Authoring Palettes** window. Refer to valve block shown in **Figure 24-22**. By inserting an alignment parameter into the block, the gate valve can be moved near any pipe line and it will automatically rotate to align with the pipe. Continue as follows:

Specify base point of alignment or [Name]: *(pick the point in the center of the valve; this is where the parameter grip is located)*
Alignment type = *current*
Specify alignment direction or alignment type [Type] <Type>: **TYPE**↵
Enter alignment type [Perpendicular/Tangent] <*current*>: **TANGENT**↵
Specify alignment direction or alignment type [Type] <Type>: *(pick the endpoint shown in Figure 24-22)*
Command:

Figure 24-22.
Inserting an alignment parameter into the gate valve block.

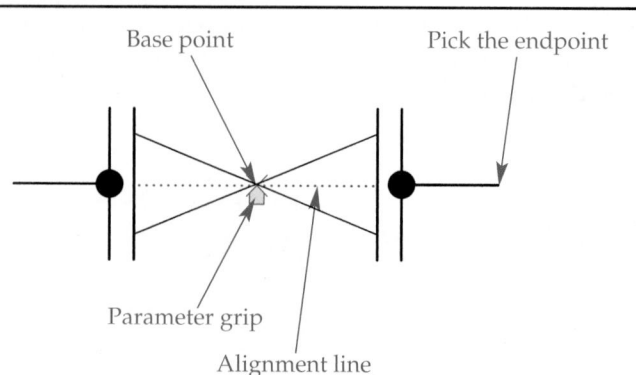

Base point

Pick the endpoint

Parameter grip

Alignment line

The base point is used as the first point in defining the angle of the alignment line. It is also where the alignment parameter grip is located. After specifying the base point, drag the pointer in the direction that is desired for the angle and pick. The angle between the first point and the second point defines the alignment line.

There are two types of alignments—perpendicular and tangent. Use the **Type** option to specify the type of alignment. These options do not affect how the block is aligned; they determine the direction of the alignment grip. When set to perpendicular, the grip points perpendicular to the alignment line. When set to tangent, the grip points tangent to the alignment line.

The parameter grip for an alignment parameter looks like a small square with a triangle on one side. See **Figure 24-22**. When the parameter has been assigned to the block, the triangle on the parameter grip points in the direction of alignment. This "arrow" points perpendicular to or tangent to the object in the drawing to which the block is being aligned.

The dynamic block is now defined. Save the block and close the **Block Editor**.

Using an Alignment Parameter Dynamically

After the block is inserted in the drawing, select it to display grips. Select the parameter grip and drag the block near another object. The block is automatically aligned to the object. The rotation is determined by the alignment path, the type of alignment, and the angle of the other object. In **Figure 24-23**, the gate valve block is dragged near the pipe line.

NOTE

When you manipulate a block with an alignment parameter, the **Nearest** object snap is temporarily turned on, if it is not already on.

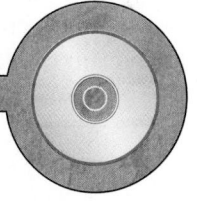

Exercise 24-7
Complete the exercise on the Student CD.

Figure 24-23.
When the gate valve block is dragged near the angled line, the block automatically aligns with the line.

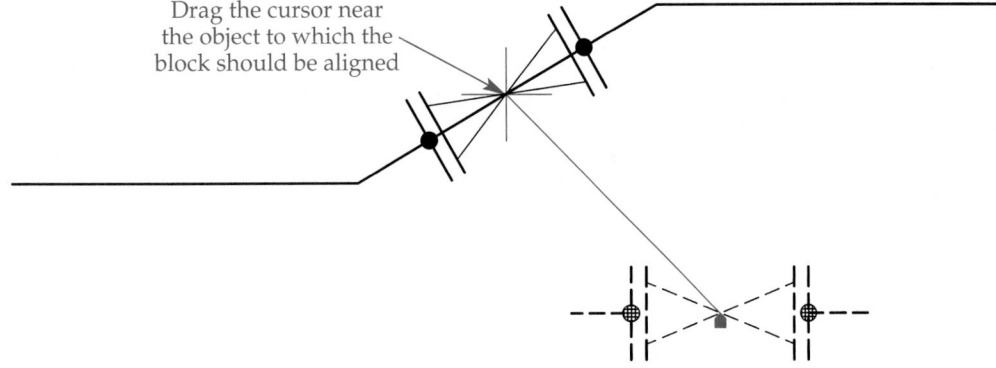

Drag the cursor near the object to which the block should be aligned

Adding Flip Parameters

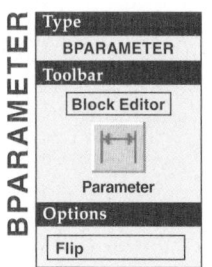

Type
BPARAMETER
Toolbar
Block Editor
Parameter
Options
Flip

BPARAMETER

Using a *flip parameter,* selected objects within a block can be mirrored by picking the parameter grip. To do this, insert a flip parameter, specify a defining line (mirror line), assign a flip action to the parameter, and select the objects to be flipped. For example, look at the block of a door shown in **Figure 24-24**. Depending on the side of the swing needed for the door, the block may need to be flipped. By inserting a flip parameter, you can easily provide both versions using a single block.

To insert a flip parameter, pick the **Parameter** button from the **Block Editor** toolbar or type BPARAMETER. Then choose the **Flip** option. You can also enter this directly by selecting **Flip Parameter** from the **Parameters** tab in the **Block Authoring Palettes** window.

Specify base point of reflection line or [Name/Label/Description/Palette]: *(pick the base point shown in **Figure 24-24A**; the parameter grip is placed here)*
Specify endpoint of reflection line: *(pick the endpoint of the swing arc, as shown in **Figure 24-24A**)*
Specify label location: *(pick a point to place the label)*
Command:

The block will be mirrored about the reflection line. However, with the line in its current position, an incorrect flip will result. Since a door is placed in a 4″ wall, the reflection line should be 2″ lower than the door. Using the **MOVE** command, select the reflection line and move it 2″ down. The label and parameter grip also move. An alternative is to construct the correct location of the reflection line before adding the flip parameter. Be sure to erase the construction objects before saving the block so the objects are not included in the block definition. In addition, you may want to move the parameter grip horizontally to the middle of the door opening. This may help in placing and flipping the block as it is inserted into the drawing. The **MOVE** command can be used to move the grip. See **Figure 24-24B**.

Assigning a Flip Action to a Flip Parameter

Type
BACTION
Toolbar
Block Editor
Action

BACTION

The objects to which a flip action applies are specified when the action is assigned to the flip parameter. The following prompt sequence defines a flip parameter:

Select parameter: *(pick the flip parameter)*
Specify selection set for action
Select objects: *(select all of the objects in the door block)*
n found
Select objects: ↵
Specify action location: *(pick a point near the parameter to place the flip action icon)*
Command:

The dynamic block is now defined. Save the block and close the **Block Editor**.

Figure 24-24.
A—Inserting a flip parameter. B—Moving the parameter so the block will correctly flip about the centerline of a wall.

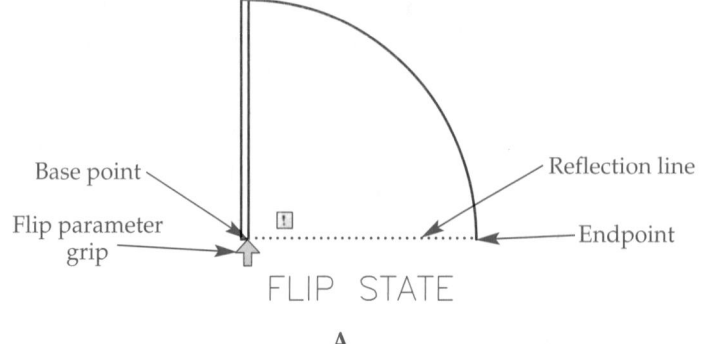
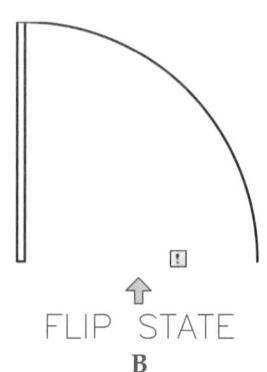

Base point
Reflection line
Flip parameter grip
Endpoint
FLIP STATE
A

FLIP STATE
B

Figure 24-25.
A—The flip parameter grip is displayed when the block is selected. B—Picking the flip parameter grip flips the block about the reflection line. Since all of the objects within the block were selected for the action, the entire block is flipped.

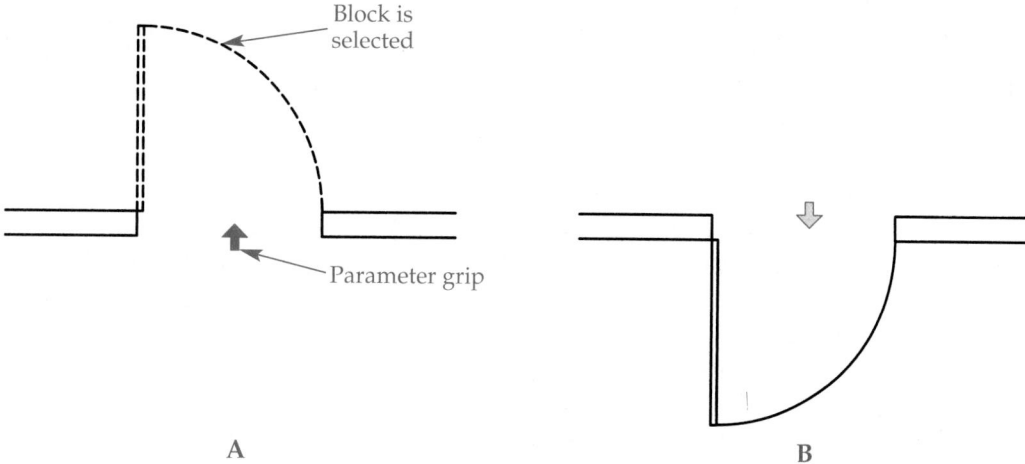

Block is selected

Parameter grip

A   B

Using a Flip Action Dynamically

After the block is inserted, select it to display grips. See Figure 24-25A. A pick on the parameter grip flips the objects to the other side of the reflection line, as shown in Figure 24-25B. Unlike other parameters and actions described to this point, dragging is not required. A single pick initiates the action.

PROFESSIONAL TIP

If the door block in Figure 24-25 has a second flip parameter inserted and action applied, the door can also be flipped from side to side. In this way, one block takes the place of four blocks to accommodate different door positions.

Exercise 24-8
Complete the exercise on the Student CD.

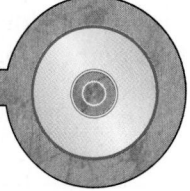

Adding XY Parameters

An *XY parameter* includes distance properties for both the X and Y directions. Four parameter grips are inserted with the XY parameter—one at each corner of a 2D box defined by the parameter. A move, scale, stretch, or array action can be assigned to an XY parameter.

To insert an XY parameter, pick the **Parameter** button on the **Block Editor** toolbar or type BPARAMETER. Then, select the **Xy** option. You can also enter this directly by selecting **XY Parameter** from the **Parameters** tab in the **Block Authoring Palettes** window.

XY parameter:
A parameter that specifies distance properties in the X and Y directions.

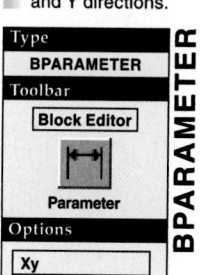

Type
BPARAMETER

Toolbar
Block Editor

Parameter

Options
Xy

BPARAMETER

Specify base point or [Name/Label/Chain/Description/Palette/Value set]: *(pick the base point)*
Specify endpoint: *(pick a point to specify the XY grip)*
Command:

The base point is the "origin" for the X and Y distances. The endpoint is where the XY grip is placed. Grips are then automatically created on the X and Y axis aligned with the base point. See **Figure 24-26.**

Assigning an Array Action to an XY Parameter

An array action allows objects within the block to be arrayed based on preset specifications. Objects in the block to which the array action is not assigned are not arrayed. For example, the block of architectural glass block shown in **Figure 24-26** can have an XY parameter and an array action applied to it. Then, by adjusting the block dynamically, you can create an architectural feature of glass blocks of any size.

To assign an array action to a parameter, pick the **Action** button from the **Block Editor** toolbar, type BACTION, select **Array Action** from the **Actions** tab of the **Block Authoring Palette** window, or double-click on any part of the parameter.

Select parameter: *(pick the parameter)*
Enter action type [Array/Move/Scale/sTretch]: **ARRAY**↵
Specify selection set for action
Select objects: *(select the objects to be included in the array)*
n found
Select objects: ↵
Enter the distance between rows or specify unit cell (- - -): *(enter a value for the distance between rows or pick two points to set the row and column values)* ↵
Enter the distance between columns (|||): *(type in a value for the distance between columns; this prompt will not appear if you selected two points to define the row and column values)* ↵
Specify action location: *(pick a point near the parameter to place the action icon)*
Command:

In the example of the glass block, be sure to allow for a grout joint when setting the row and column distance. Before assigning the action, you may want to draw a construction point offset from the block by the width of the grout joint. Then you can pick two points to define the row and column values. Be sure to erase the construction point before saving the block. Otherwise, the point will be included in the block definition.

The dynamic block is now defined. Save the block and close the **Block Editor.**

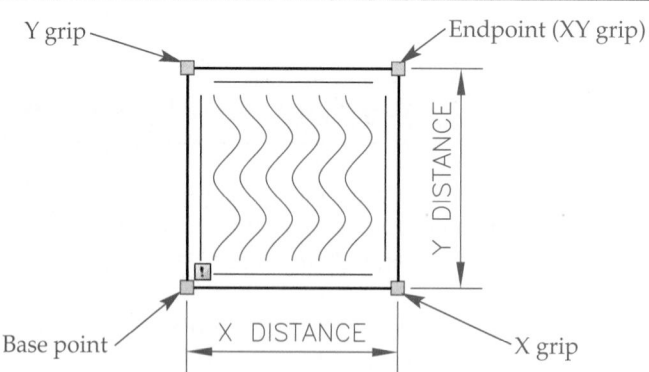

Figure 24-26. Inserting an XY parameter into a block of architectural glass block. The XY parameter consists of X and Y distance properties and four grips.

AutoCAD and Its Applications—Basics

Figure 24-27.
Dynamically creating an array of architectural glass block. The block has an XY parameter and array action. The pattern of rows and columns is created by dragging the XY parameter. Notice the grout lines between the glass blocks. By properly defining the dynamic block, these lines are added automatically.

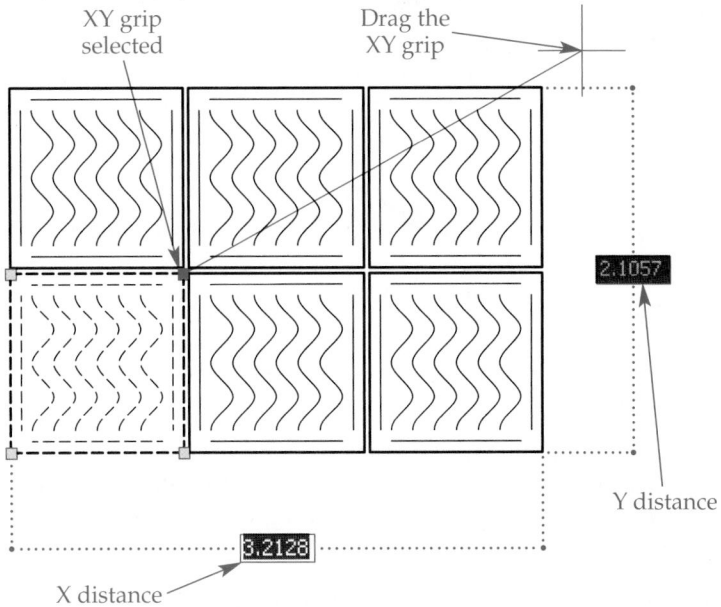

Using an Array Action Dynamically

Once the block is inserted, select it to display grips. There are four parameter grips and the block insertion point grip, which may coincide with one of the parameter grips. Selecting any of the parameter grips and dragging them arrays the objects, but the resulting array remains a single block. If dynamic input is enabled, the array dimensions are displayed as you drag the grip. In **Figure 24-27**, the block of the architectural glass block has been inserted into the drawing. By selecting a parameter grip and dragging, an array is created to fill a space. Notice that the grout lines are added because the action was properly defined.

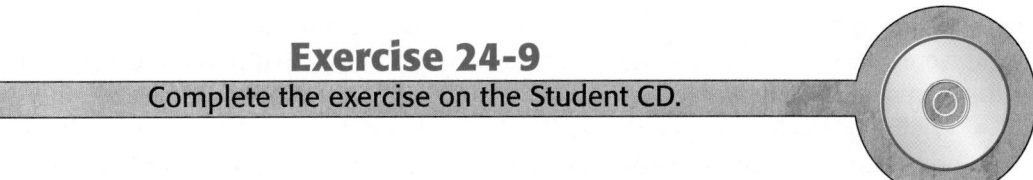

Exercise 24-9
Complete the exercise on the Student CD.

Adding Visibility Parameters

A *visibility parameter* allows different visibility states to be assigned to objects within a block. This allows for multiple views of the same block. Selecting the visibility parameter grip on a block displays a list of the visibility states (views) created for the block. Selecting one of the views changes the block to that view. No action is associated with a visibility parameter.

An example of a visibility parameter is shown in **Figure 24-28**. The four different valves shown in **Figure 24-28A** are created from a single block. When the block is defined, all of the objects representing the different variations need to be drawn. Draw the objects in reference to, or on top of, the other objects within the block. See **Figure 24-28B**. Then assign a visibility parameter and define the visibility states.

visibility parameter: A parameter that allows different views to be assigned to objects within a block.

Figure 24-28.
A—All four of these different valves can be created from one block by using a visibility parameter. B—All of the objects composing all four valves are shown together.

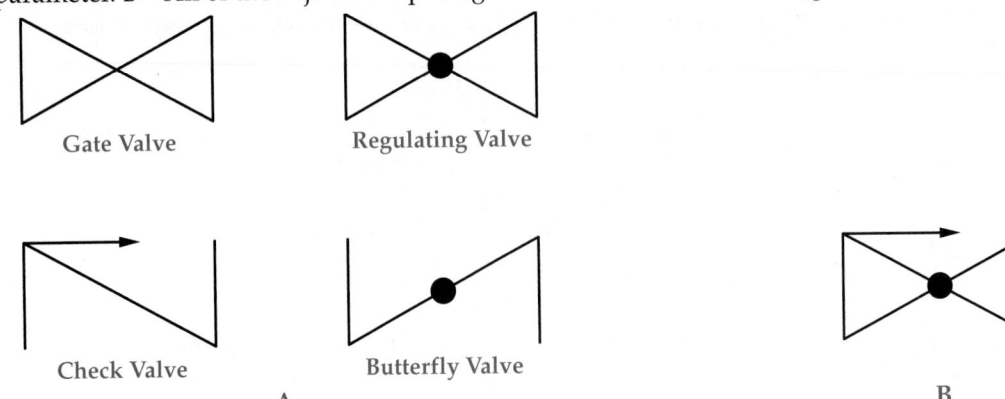

Gate Valve

Regulating Valve

Check Valve

Butterfly Valve

A

B

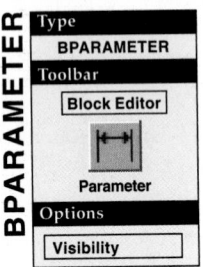

To insert a visibility parameter, pick the **Parameter** button on the **Block Editor** toolbar or type BPARAMETER. Then choose the **Visibility** option. This can also be entered directly by selecting **Visibility Parameter** from the **Parameters** tab in the **Block Authoring Palettes** window.

> Specify parameter location or [Name/Label/Description/Palette]: *(pick a point to place the visibility grip)*
> Enter number of grips [0/1] <1>: ↵
> Command:

The parameter grip is placed at the point you pick for the parameter location. Picking this grip in the drawing displays the visibility states. A visibility parameter is associated with an entire block, so there is no prompt to select objects.

Creating Visibility States

Once a visibility parameter has been assigned to a block, the visibility tools on the **Block Editor** toolbar are enabled. See **Figure 24-29.** The tools for working with visibility states are located to the far right of the **Block Editor** toolbar. Remember, at lower screen resolutions, these tools may be hidden from view. Either change to a higher screen resolution or use the clean screen option ([Ctrl]+[0]) to allow the tools to be displayed. The tools are:

- **Visibility Mode.** Toggles the visibility mode on and off. When on, the objects that are currently invisible are displayed as semitransparent. When off, only the visible objects are shown. The visibility mode can also be toggled on and off by typing BVMODE.

Figure 24-29.
The visibility tools are found on the right-hand end of the **Block Editor** toolbar. You may need to use the "clean screen" option ([Ctrl]+[0]) to allow the tools to be displayed.

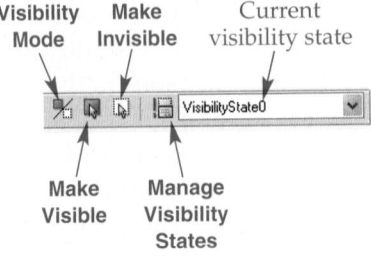

Visibility Mode

Make Invisible

Current visibility state

Make Visible

Manage Visibility States

- **Make Visible.** Prompts you to select objects to be made visible. Invisible objects are temporarily displayed as semitransparent so they can be selected.
- **Make Invisible.** Prompts you to select objects to be made invisible.
- **Manage Visibility States.** Opens the **Visibility States** dialog box, as shown in **Figure 24-30A.** This dialog box can also be opened by typing BVSTATE.
- **Current visibility state.** Displays the current visibility state. Picking the button displays all of the visibility states that have been created for the block. Selecting one of the states in the drop-down list makes it current.

To create a visibility state, open the **Visibility States** dialog box and pick the **New...** button. This opens the **New Visibility State** dialog box. See **Figure 24-30B.** In the **Visibility state name:** text box, name the new state visibility state. For the valve block example shown in **Figure 24-28,** this may be GATE VALVE, REGULATING VALVE, CHECK VALVE, or BUTTERFLY VALVE, depending on which valve the visibility state represents. In the **Visibility options for new states** area, select the option that is appropriate for the new state.

- **Hide all existing objects in new state.** When the new visibility state is created, all of the objects in the block are invisible. This allows you to turn on (display) only the objects that you want to be visible in the visibility state.
- **Show all existing objects in new state.** When the new visibility state is created, all of the objects in the block are visible. This allows you to turn off (hide) any objects that you want to be invisible for the state.
- **Leave visibility of existing objects unchanged in new state.** When the new visibility state is created, only the currently visible objects are displayed.

When you have entered a name and selected the appropriate option, pick the **OK** button in the **New Visibility State** dialog box to create the new visibility state. The new state is added to the list in the **Visibility States** dialog box and made current, as indicated by the check mark next to the name. Pick the **OK** button in the **Visibility States** dialog box to return to block editing mode.

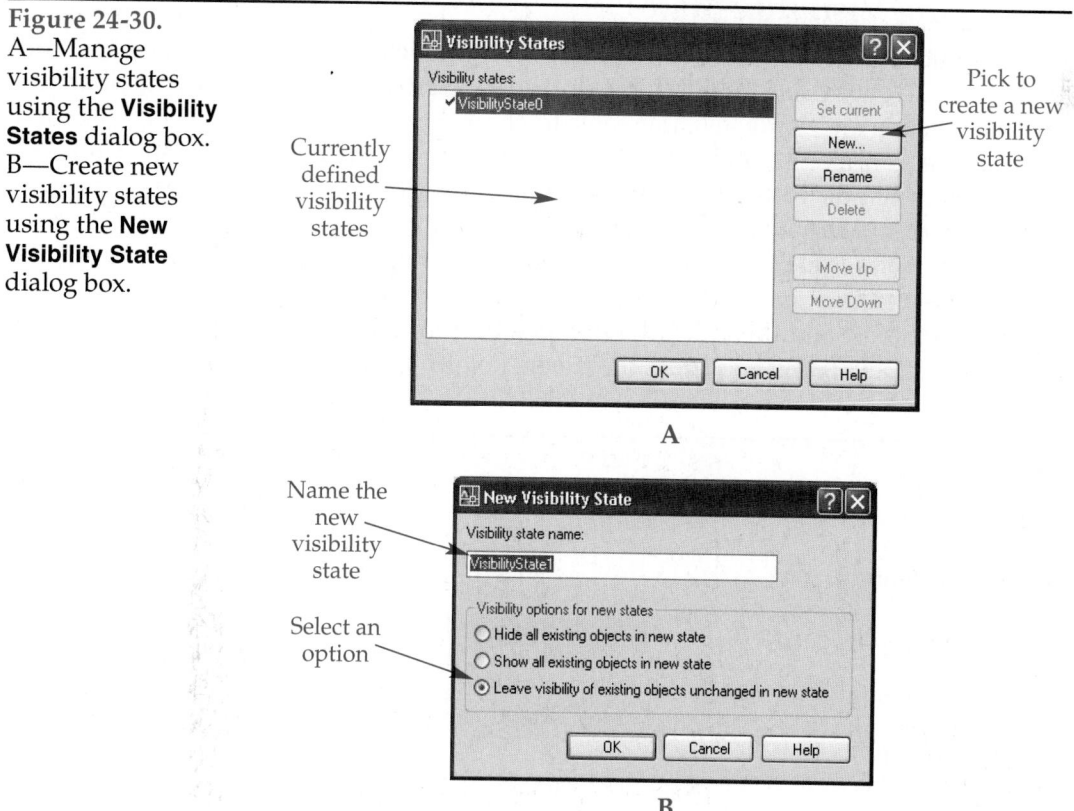

Figure 24-30.
A—Manage visibility states using the **Visibility States** dialog box.
B—Create new visibility states using the **New Visibility State** dialog box.

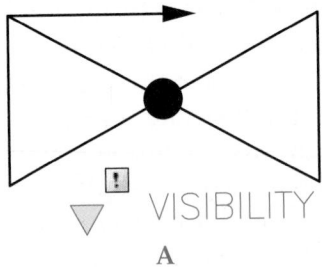
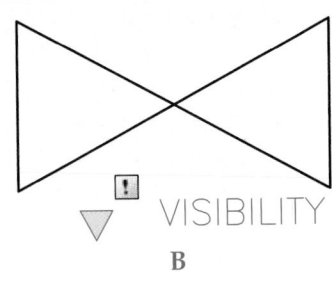

Figure 24-31.
A—The VALVE block with all of the objects visible.
B—The VALVE block after the arrow and filled circle are hidden (made invisible) to create the GATE VALVE visibility state.

Now, using the **Make Visible** and **Make Invisible** tools, display only the objects that should be visible in the state. For example, to make a visibility state to depict the gate valve shown in Figure 24-28A from the valve block shown in Figure 24-31A, use the **Make Invisible** command to turn off the filled circle and the arrow. See Figure 24-31B. The changes are automatically saved to the visibility state.

Repeat this process to create additional visibility states for the block. For the valve block, a total of four visibility states are needed. When all the visibility states have been created, save the block and close the **Block Editor**.

Using a Visibility Parameter Dynamically

Once the block is inserted, select it to display grips. The visibility grip appears as a horizontal line with a triangle below it. See Figure 24-32A. Selecting the grip displays a shortcut menu that contains the visibility states created for the block. The current visibility state has a check mark next to its name. To switch to a different view of the block, select the name of the visibility state in the list. See Figure 24-32B.

Modifying Visibility States

Visibility states can easily be modified in the **Block Editor**. Set the state you want to modify current by selecting it in the drop-down list on the **Block Editor** toolbar. Use the **Make Visible** and **Make Invisible** tools to change the visibility of objects as needed. New objects can also be drawn in block editing mode using the normal AutoCAD drawing commands. New objects are automatically hidden in all visibility states other than the current state.

The **Visibility States** dialog box can be used to rename, delete, and rearrange the order of the visibility states in the shortcut menu. To change the name of a state, select the state in the list and then pick the **Rename** button. The name is replaced by an edit box. Type the new name and press the [Enter] key. To remove a state permanently, pick

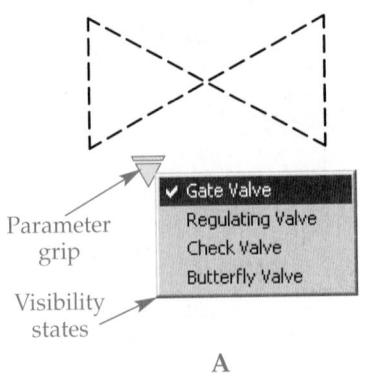
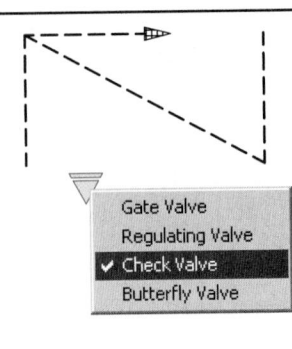

Figure 24-32.
A—Picking the visibility parameter grip displays the available visibility states shortcut menu. The current state is checked. B—Selecting a different visibility state from the shortcut menu changes the appearance of the block.

Parameter grip

Visibility states

A

B

AutoCAD and Its Applications—Basics

the **Delete** button. To reorder the states, use the **Move Up** and **Move Down** buttons. The order in which states appear in this dialog box is the same order in which they appear in the shortcut menu displayed when the grip is selected in the drawing. The state at the top of the list is the default view for the block.

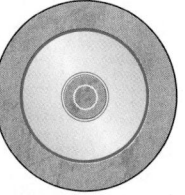

Exercise 24-10
Complete the exercise on the Student CD.

Adding Lookup Parameters

A *lookup parameter* allows custom properties created in a table to be used with existing parameter values. It is used in conjunction with a lookup action. The custom properties can then be displayed in the drawing by selecting the lookup parameter grip. A lookup action allows you to select a preset group of parameter values to carry out the actions with stored values instead of having to modify the parameter property values one by one.

A lookup parameter is similar to a visibility parameter in that it allows for multiple views of the same block. However, instead of making objects visible and invisible, a lookup parameter actually changes the objects of a block based on assigned parameters and actions.

For example, look at the blocks shown in **Figure 24-33.** These three instances are created from a single block by adjusting the rotation parameter of the middle line. The specified rotation angles are 0, 10, and 20 degrees. The length of the start and end lines automatically adjust to match the rotation of the middle line.

lookup parameter: A parameter that allows tabular properties to be used with existing parameter values.

Figure 24-33.
A lookup parameter was used to create these three views of the same block. Notice how the geometry is changed.

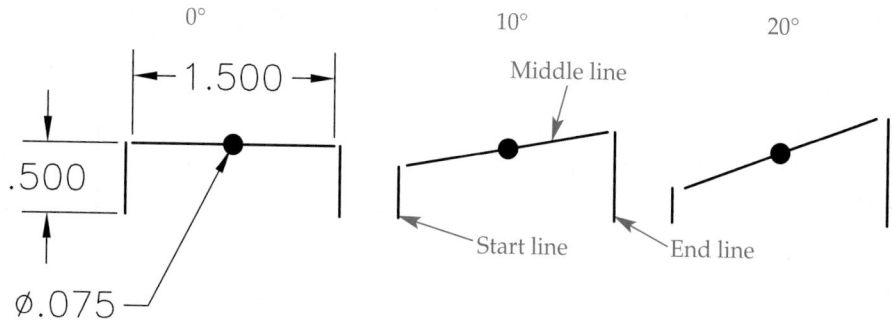

BPARAMETER

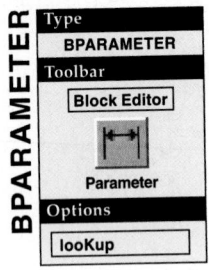

Type
BPARAMETER

Toolbar
Block Editor

Parameter

Options
looKup

To insert a lookup parameter, pick the **Parameter** button on the **Block Editor** toolbar or type BPARAMETER. Then choose the **looKup** option. This can also be entered directly by selecting **Lookup Parameter** from the **Parameters** tab in the **Block Authoring Palettes** window.

> Specify parameter location or [Name/Label/Description/Palette]: *(pick a point to place the parameter)*
> Command:

The point you pick for the parameter location is where the parameter grip is placed. Picking the grip in the drawing displays a shortcut menu that contains a list of the custom groups. A lookup parameter is associated with the entire block, so no objects are selected.

Assigning a Lookup Action to a Lookup Parameter

BACTION

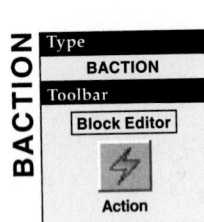

Type
BACTION

Toolbar
Block Editor

Action

To assign a lookup action to a lookup parameter, pick the **Action** button from the **Block Editor** toolbar, type BACTION, select **Lookup Action** from the **Actions** tab of the **Block Authoring Palette** window, or double-click on any part of the parameter.

> Select parameter: *(pick the lookup parameter)*
> Specify action location: *(pick a point near the parameter to place the lookup action icon)*

After specifying the action location, the **Property Lookup Table** dialog box opens. See Figure 24-34. This is where the lookup table is created, as described in the next sections.

Example Lookup Parameter Block

To help explain the lookup parameter and action, create the 0° block shown in Figure 24-33. Then insert parameters and assign actions needed so the 10° and 20° blocks can be created from the same block. Follow these steps:

1. Create the 0° block.
2. Open the block in the **Block Editor**.
3. Insert a linear parameter, label it START LINE, select the start point as the bottom of the start line, and select the endpoint as the top of the start line.

Figure 24-34.
The **Property Lookup Table** dialog box.

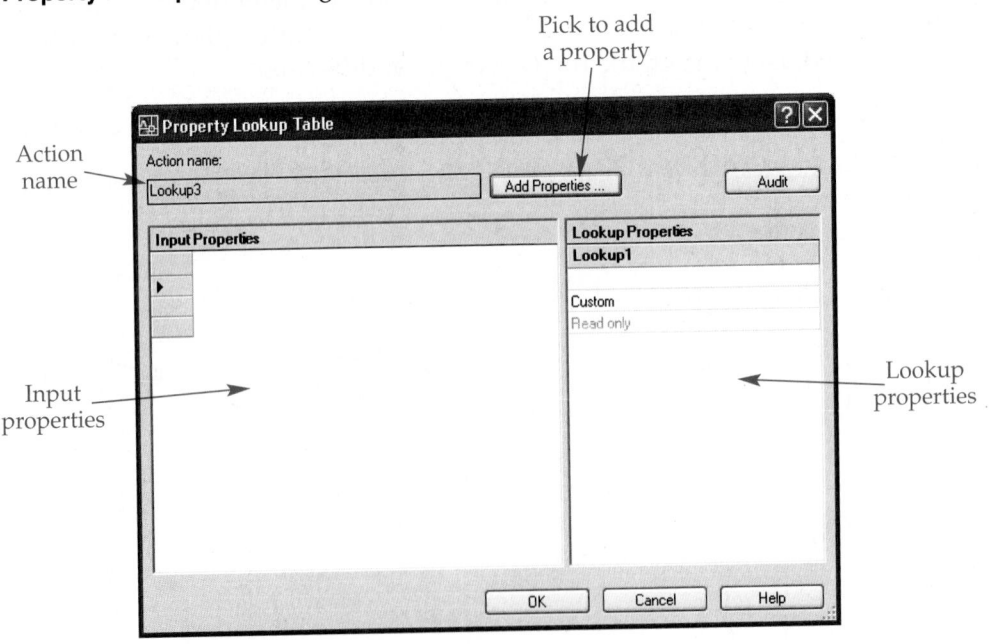

4. Assign a stretch action to the START LINE linear parameter. Associate the action with the top parameter grip, create the stretch box around the top of the start line, and select the start line as the object.
5. Insert a linear parameter, label it END LINE, select the start point as the bottom of the end line, and select the endpoint as the top of the end line.
6. Assign a stretch action to the END LINE linear parameter. Associate the action with the top parameter grip, create the stretch box around the top of the line, and select the end line as the object.
7. Insert a rotation parameter, label it MIDDLE LINE, specify the base point as the center of the circle, select the right endpoint of the middle line to set the radius, and specify the default rotation angle as 0.
8. Assign a rotate action to the MIDDLE LINE rotation parameter. Select the middle line as the object and pick the center of the circle as the rotation base point.
9. Assign a lookup parameter to the block.

The block should look similar to **Figure 24-35** in the **Block Editor**.

Creating a Lookup Table

The first step in creating a lookup table is to assign a lookup action to the lookup parameter. After you specify the action location, the **Property Lookup Table** dialog box is displayed, providing the following settings:

- **Action name: text field.** Displays the name of the lookup action associated with the table.
- **Add Properties... button.** Opens the **Add Parameter Properties** dialog box, which allows properties to be added to the table.
- **Audit button.** Checks each row (record) in the table to make sure it is unique.
- **Input Properties area.** Allows you to specify a value for parameters that have been added to the table.
- **Lookup Properties area.** Displays the name that appears in the shortcut menu when the lookup parameter grip is selected in the drawing.

To add a parameter property to the table, pick the **Add Properties...** button to open the **Add Parameter Properties** dialog box. See **Figure 24-36.** The parameters that have been assigned to the block appear in the **Parameter properties:** list. Notice that the property name is the parameter label. Only parameters containing property values are displayed in the **Parameter properties:** list. The lookup, alignment, and base point parameters do not contain property values.

The **Property type** area determines which type of property parameters are shown in the list. By default, the **Add input properties** radio button is active, which displays the available input property parameters. To display the available lookup property parameters, select the **Add lookup properties** radio button.

Figure 24-35.
The block with linear parameters and stretch actions assigned to the start and end lines and a rotation parameter and rotate action assigned to the middle line.

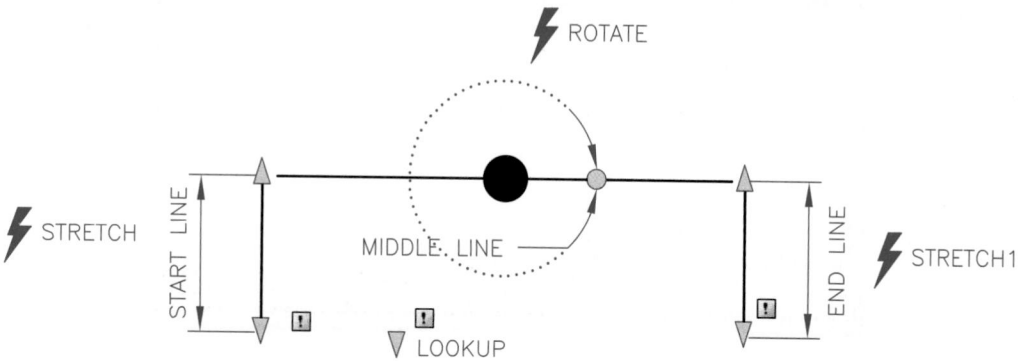

Figure 24-36.
Parameter properties are listed in the **Add Parameter Properties** dialog box.

Select a property to add

Select the type of property

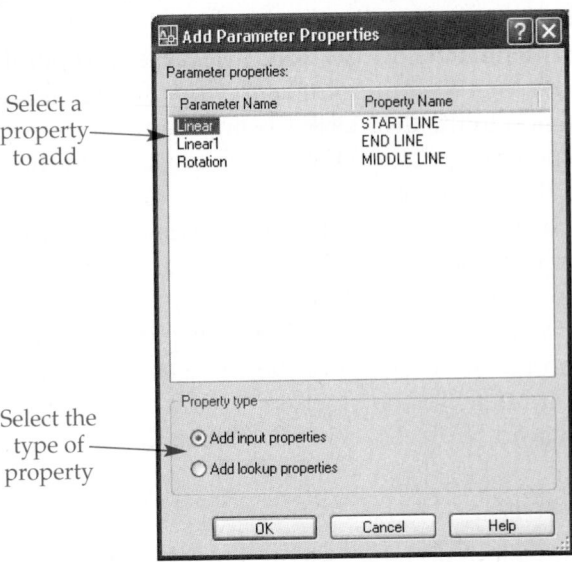

To add a parameter property to the lookup table, select the property in the **Parameter properties:** list and pick the **OK** button. A new column is then added to the **Input Properties** area of the **Property Lookup Table** dialog box. The name of the parameter property is the column header. See **Figure 24-37**. To add values for the parameter, type the value in each cell in the column. Add a custom name for each row (record) on the same row in the **Lookup** column in the **Lookup Properties** area.

For the example block, add the MIDDLE LINE, START LINE, and END LINE properties to the table. Then, complete the lookup table as shown below. Start with the MIDDLE LINE values. Press [Enter] after typing the value to add a new blank row below it. Then add the remaining values. Pick in a cell and type the value. Press [Enter], pick in a different cell, or use the tab or arrow keys to navigate through the table.

Figure 24-37.
A lookup table with multiple parameters and values added.

Parameter properties

Parameter values for the property

Custom names for the row (record)

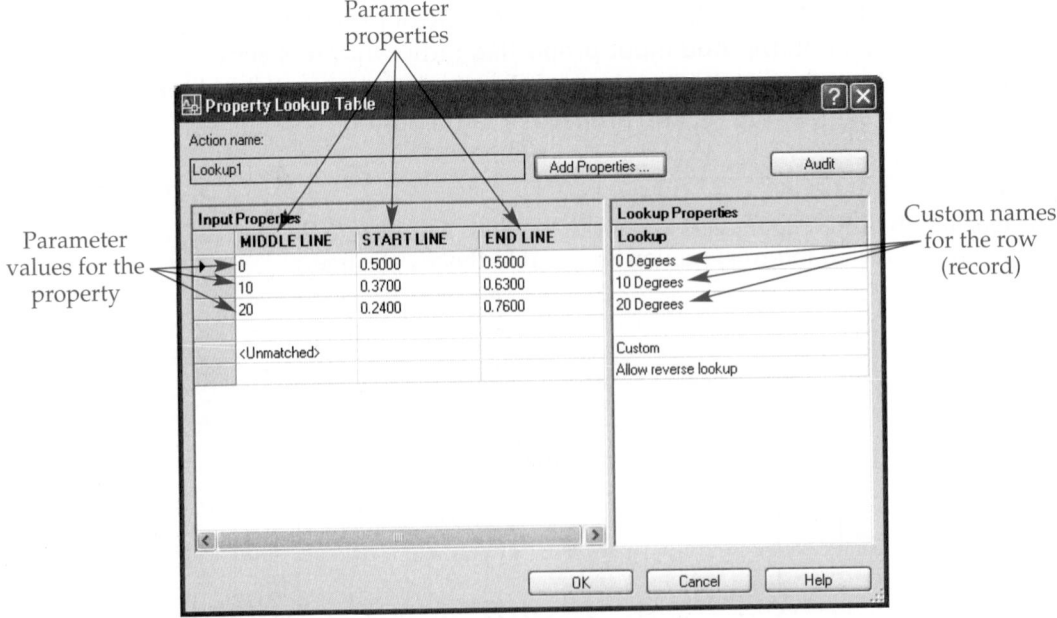

AutoCAD and Its Applications—Basics

MIDDLE LINE	START LINE	END LINE	Lookup
0	0.5000	0.5000	0 Degrees
10	0.3700	0.6300	10 Degrees
20	0.2400	0.7600	20 Degrees

The row (record) that contains the <Unmatched> value, which is named Custom in the **Lookup** column, is used when the current parameter values of the block do not match any of the records in the table. You cannot add any values to the row, but you can change the name of **Custom**.

Picking in the cell at the bottom of the **Lookup** column, which currently indicates Read only, displays a drop-down list containing two options. The default Read only setting means that the lookup parameter grip is not displayed when the block is selected in the drawing. To have the lookup parameter grip displayed, select Allow reverse lookup from the drop-down list. See Figure 24-38. This can only be selected if all names in the lookup table are unique.

After you have added all of the properties to the table and assigned values to each, pick the **Audit** button in the **Property Lookup Table** dialog box to check the table. Any errors that are found will be reported. If no errors are found, as indicated by a message box, pick the **OK** button to return to the **Block Editor**. Save the block and close the **Block Editor**.

Using a Lookup Action Dynamically

Once the block is inserted, select it to display grips. Since Allow reverse lookup was selected in the lookup table, the lookup parameter grip is displayed along with the other parameter grips. Picking the lookup parameter grip displays a shortcut menu that contains a list of the custom named lookup records. See Figure 24-39. The entries in this shortcut menu match the entries in the **Lookup** column of the **Property Lookup Table** dialog box. Picking one of the entries in the shortcut menu changes the geometry in the block based on the parameter values in the lookup table.

Other parameters assigned to the block—linear and rotation in the case of the example block—can still be changed independently. When any of the parameters is changed, the lookup parameter becomes Custom because the current parameter values do not match one of the records in the lookup table.

Figure 24-38.
The field at the bottom of the **Lookup** column determines whether the lookup parameter grip is displayed when the block is selected in the drawing.

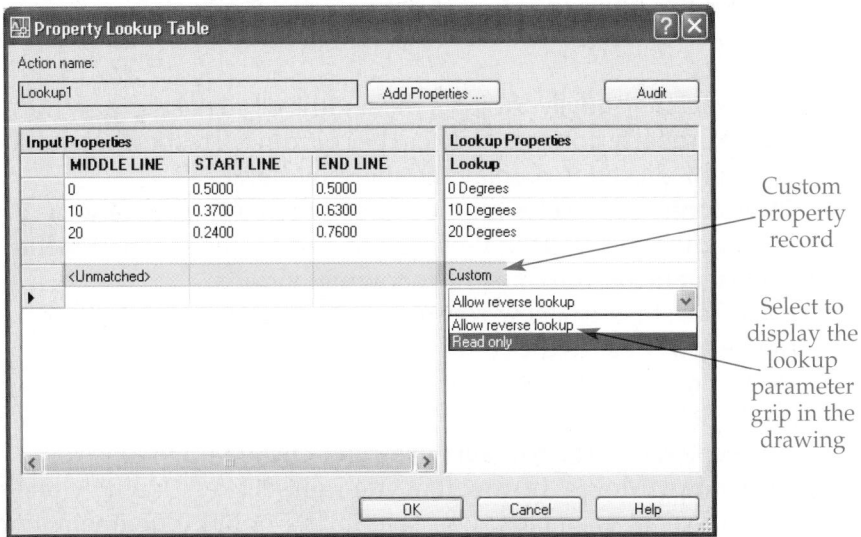

Figure 24-39.
The lookup parameter grip is displayed when the block is selected. The list of available lookup records is displayed when the lookup parameter grip is selected.

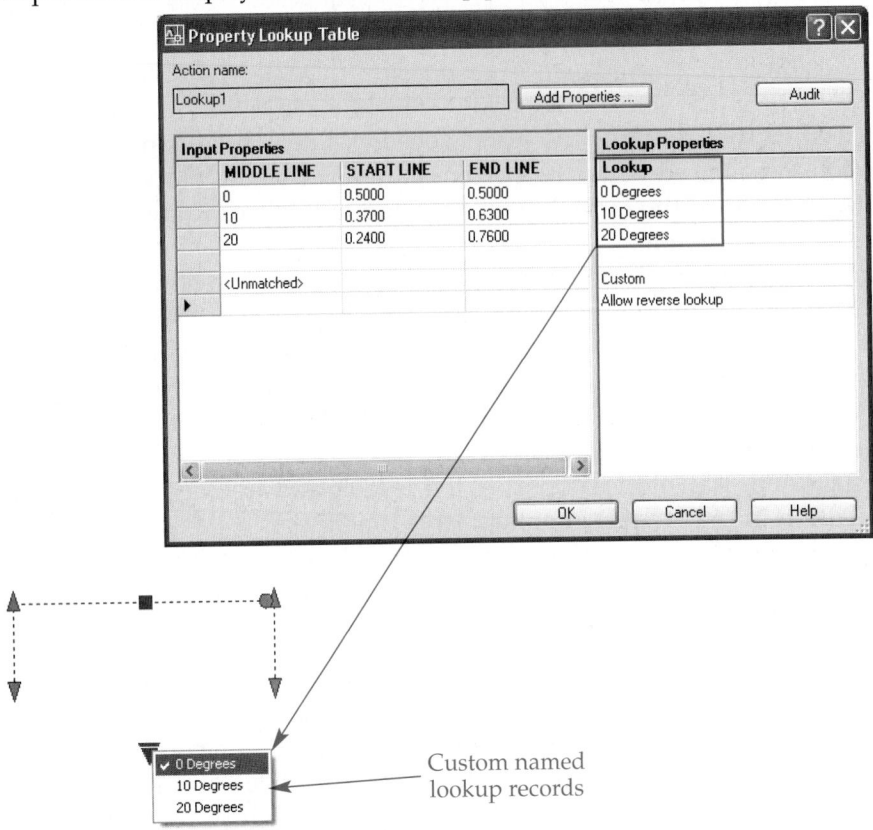

Custom named lookup records

Modifying a Lookup Table

To modify a lookup table, open the block in the **Block Editor** and double-click on the lookup action icon. The **Property Lookup Table** dialog box is opened. Edits can be made to values and properties in the same way as they were created. Additional options can be accessed by right-clicking on a column heading or on a row to display a shortcut menu. The column heading shortcut menu contains the following options:

- **Sort.** Sorts the records (rows) by the selected column's values. Picking **Sort** a second time reverses the order of the sort.
- **Maximize all headings.** Adjusts the widths of all columns to the size of the column headings.
- **Maximize all data cells.** Adjusts the widths of all columns to the values in the columns.
- **Size columns equally.** Adjusts the widths of all columns so they are equal.
- **Delete property column.** Deletes the column corresponding to the heading that you right-clicked to display the shortcut menu.
- **Clear contents.** Deletes all the values entered in the column corresponding to the heading that you right-clicked to display the shortcut menu.

The row shortcut menu contains the following options:

- **Insert row.** Inserts a new row above the row that you right-clicked.
- **Delete row.** Deletes the row that you right-clicked.
- **Clear contents.** Deletes all of the values entered in the row that you right-clicked.
- **Move up.** Moves the row that you right-clicked up by one row.
- **Move down.** Moves the row that you right-clicked down by one row.
- **Range syntax examples.** Displays in the online documentation examples of how values can be entered into a lookup table.

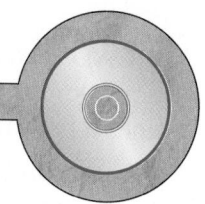

Exercise 24-11

Complete the exercise on the Student CD.

Adding Base Point Parameters

A *base point parameter* is used to define a base point for the block that is different from the base point that was specified when the block was created. To insert a base point parameter, pick the **Parameter** button from the **Block Editor** toolbar or type BPARAMETER. Then choose the **Base** option. This can also be entered directly by selecting **Base Point Parameter** from the **Parameters** tab in the **Block Authoring Palettes** window.

At the Specify parameter location: prompt, pick a point to place the base point parameter. The parameter is displayed as a circle with crosshairs. After the block has been saved, the location of the base point parameter becomes the new base point for the block.

No actions can be assigned to a base point parameter. However, the parameter can be included in the selection set for actions.

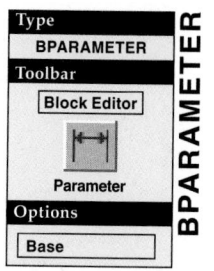

base point parameter: A parameter that defines a different base point for a block.

Adding Parameter Value Sets

A *value set* can be used to limit a parameter to certain values. This ensures that only applicable values are used when a block is dynamically modified. For example, if a window style is only available in widths of 36″, 42″, 48″, 54″, and 60″, then a value set can be created for a linear parameter to limit selection options to these sizes. Next, a stretch action can be applied to the parameter. Then, when the block is dynamically modified, the values specified in the value set are the only values that can be used for the width. See **Figure 24-40**.

A value set can be used with linear, polar, XY, and rotation parameters. The option to use a value set is available at the first prompt after selecting one of the parameters to insert:

value set: A set of allowed values for a parameter.

Specify start point or [Name/Label/Chain/Description/Base/Palette/Value set]:
    VALUE.⏎
Enter distance value set type [None/List/Increment] <None>:

Figure 24-40.
When a value set is used, tick marks appear at locations corresponding to the values in the value set. The block can only be stretched to one of these tick marks.

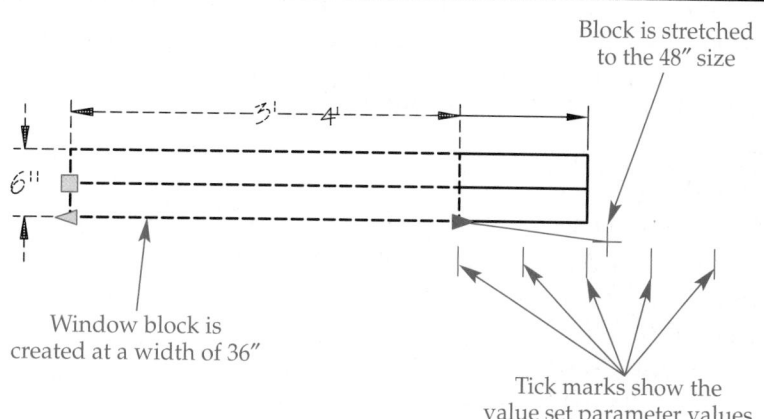

AutoCAD provides two different types of value sets—list and increment. The **List** option allows you to create a list of the possible sizes. The following command sequence defines a list value set for the available widths for the window example:

Enter distance value set type [None/List/Increment] <None>: **LIST.**↲
Enter list of distance values (separated by commas): **36,42,48,54,60** ↲ *(type all of the valid values for the parameter separated by commas)*
Specify start point or [Name/Label/Chain/Description/Base/Palette/Value set]:

Next, add the parameter as if a value set is not being used. After the parameter has been inserted and the value set has been specified, the valid values for the parameter appear as tick marks.

The **Increment** option allows you to specify an incremental value to be used by the parameter. A minimum and maximum value are also set to provide a limit for the increments. Since the width values for the window are in 6″ increments, the **Increment** option can also be used:

Specify start point or [Name/Label/Chain/Description/Base/Palette/Value set]:
  VALUE.↲
Enter distance value set type [None/List/Increment] <None>: **INCREMENT.**↲
Enter distance increment: **6.**↲
Enter minimum distance: **36.**↲
Enter maximum distance: **60.**↲
Specify start point or [Name/Label/Chain/Description/Base/Palette/Value set]:

The distance increment is the incremental value to be used. The minimum distance is the lowest value that can be used; the maximum distance is the highest value.

Using a Value Set with a Parameter

After the value set and parameter are created, an action needs to be assigned to the parameter. For the window block in **Figure 24-40**, a stretch action is assigned to the linear parameter. This allows the window to be stretched to the valid widths specified in the value set.

Once the block is inserted, select it to display grips and pick the linear parameter grip (for the window example). Tick marks appear, indicating the positions of valid values. As you drag the grip, the modified block snaps to the nearest tick mark. If dynamic input is enabled, you can also enter a value in the input field. If you type a value that is not in the value set, the nearest valid value is used.

Modifying a Value Set

To modify a value set, open the block in the **Block Editor**. Select the parameter to which the value set is assigned and open the **Properties** palette. The value set options are shown in the **Value Set** section. See **Figure 24-41.** The type of value set can be changed by selecting a different type from the **Dist type** drop-down list. The other options displayed in the **Value Set** section are based on the current type of value set. When you have finished modifying the properties, close the **Properties** palette, save the block, and exit the **Block Editor**.

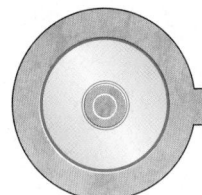

Exercise 24-12
Complete the exercise on the Student CD.

AutoCAD and Its Applications—Basics

Figure 24-41.
The value set options can be changed using the **Properties** palette.

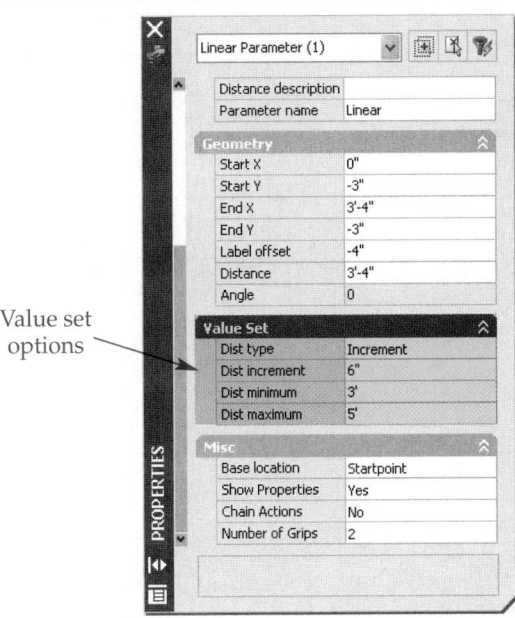

Value set options

Assigning a Chain Action to a Parameter

A *chain action* can be used to trigger a parameter's action by modifying another parameter. For example, if a table is stretched, the chairs along the table need to be arrayed to match the new table length. See **Figure 24-42**. This can be accomplished in one step by using a chain action. A chain action limits the number of edits that have to be performed by allowing one action to trigger other actions at the same time. Point, linear, polar, XY, and rotation parameters can be part of a chain action.

The option to use a chain action is available at the first prompt after selecting one of the parameters to insert:

> Specify start point or [Name/Label/Chain/Description/Base/Palette/Value set]: **CHAIN**↵
> Evaluate associated actions when parameter is edited by another action? [Yes/No] <No>:

The **Chain** option for a parameter is set to either **Yes** or **No**. The default setting is **No**, which means that the action for the parameter cannot be affected by another action. To create a chain action on a parameter, the **Chain** option must be set to **Yes**.

chain action: An action that triggers another action when a parameter is modified.

Figure 24-42.
A—A block of a table with six chairs. B—Using a chain action with a linear parameter, you can array the chairs automatically when the table is stretched.

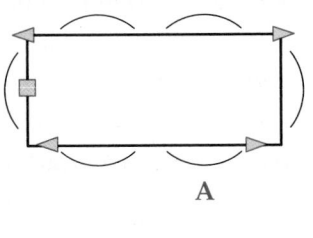

A

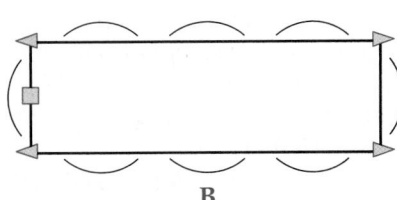

B

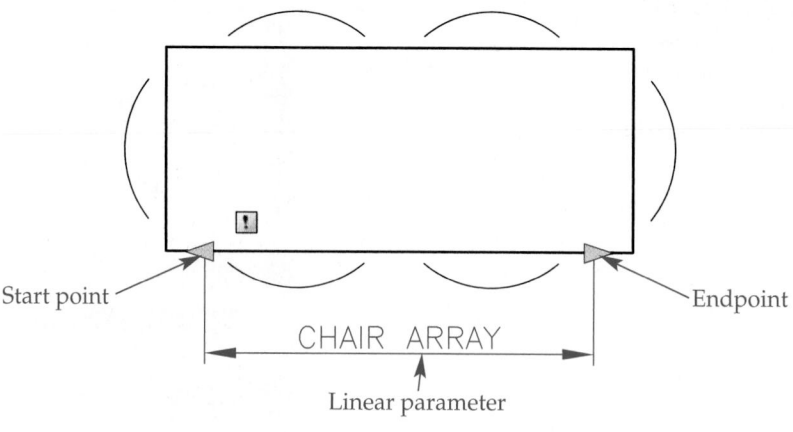

Figure 24-43.
Inserting a linear parameter to be used with an array action for the chairs.

Start point

Endpoint

CHAIR ARRAY

Linear parameter

Creating a Chain Action

Using the table and chairs example, the following sequence shows how to use a chain action to array the chairs automatically when a table is stretched. First, create a block similar to the block shown in **Figure 24-43.** Open the block in the **Block Editor,** pick **Linear Parameter** from the **Parameters** tab of the **Block Authoring Palette** window, and continue as follows.

> Specify start point or [Name/Label/Chain/Description/Base/Palette/Value set]: **CHAIN.⏎**
> Evaluate associated actions when parameter is edited by another action? [Yes/No]
>   <No>: **Y.⏎**
> Specify start point or [Name/Label/Chain/Description/Base/Palette/Value set]: **LABEL.⏎**
> Enter distance property label <Distance>: **CHAIR ARRAY.⏎**
> Specify start point or [Name/Label/Chain/Description/Base/Palette/Value set]: *(pick the start point shown in Figure 24-43)*
> Specify endpoint: *(pick the endpoint shown in Figure 24-43)*
> Specify label location: *(pick a location for the parameter label)*

Next, pick **Array Action** from the **Action** tab of the **Block Authoring Palette** window. Continue as follows.

> Select parameter: *(pick the linear parameter)*
> Select objects: *(select the chairs on the top and bottom of the table)*
> Select objects: ⏎
> Enter the distance between columns (|||): *(use objects snaps to snap to the endpoint of one of the chairs and then snap to the same endpoint on the chair next to it)*
> Specify action location: *(pick a point next to the linear parameter to place the array action icon)*

Now insert a linear parameter and stretch action for the table. Pick **Linear Parameter** from the **Parameters** tab of the **Block Authoring Palette** window and continue as follows.

> Specify start point or [Name/Label/Chain/Description/Base/Palette/Value set]:
>   **LABEL.⏎**
> Enter distance property label <Distance>: **TABLE STRETCH.⏎**
> Specify start point or [Name/Label/Chain/Description/Base/Palette/Value set]: *(pick one endpoint of the table, as shown in Figure 24-44A)*
> Specify endpoint: *(pick the opposite endpoint of the table, as shown in Figure 24-44A)*
> Specify label location: *(pick a location for the parameter label)*
> Command: **BACTION.⏎**
> Select parameter: *(pick the TABLE STRETCH parameter)*
> Enter action type [Array/Move/Scale/sTretch]: **STRETCH.⏎**
> Specify parameter point to associate with action or enter [sTart point/Second point]
>   <Start>: *(pick the endpoint parameter grip of the TABLE STRETCH parameter)*

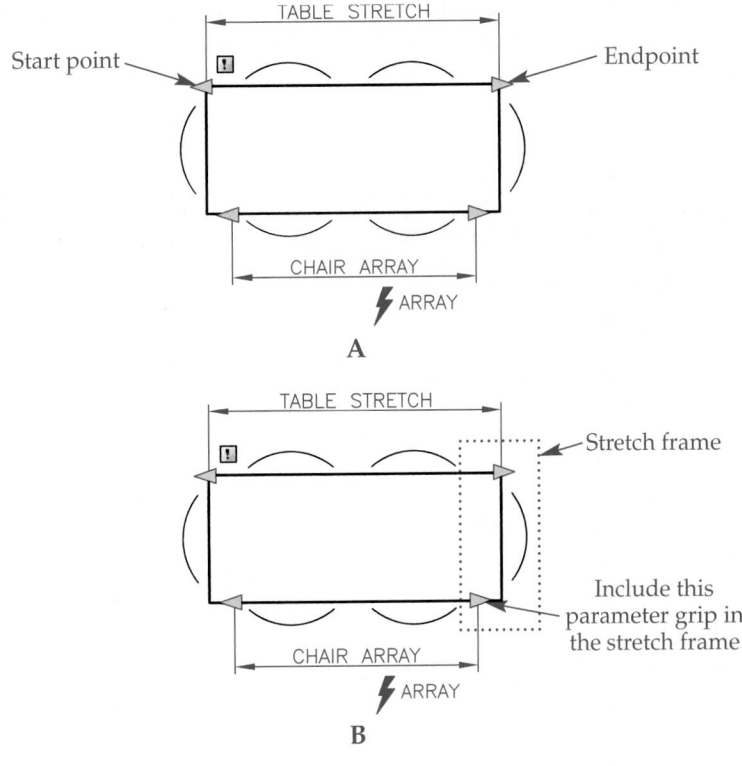

Figure 24-44.
A—Inserting a linear parameter that will be used to stretch the table. B—Assigning a stretch action to the linear parameter. When you specify the stretch frame, be sure the CHAIR ARRAY parameter grip is within the frame.

Specify first corner of stretch frame or [CPolygon]: *(include the right-hand end of the table and the right-hand parameter grip for the* CHAIR ARRAY *parameter, as shown in Figure 24-44B)*
Select objects: *(select the table, the chair at the right-hand end of the table, and the* CHAIR ARRAY *parameter)*
Select objects: ⏎
Specify action location or [Multiplier/Offset]: *(pick a location for the action icon)*
Command:

Save the block and exit the **Block Editor**.

Using a Chain Action

Insert the block and select it to display grips. Select the right TABLE STRETCH parameter grip. Drag the grip to the right to stretch the table and array the chairs. See Figure 24-45. Pick a point to create the new table length with the chairs arrayed automatically.

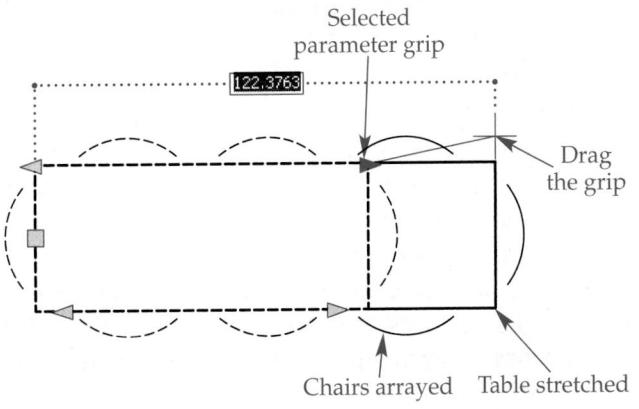

Figure 24-45.
As you drag the parameter grip, the table stretches and the chairs are arrayed.

The keys to successfully creating a chain action are to set the **Chain** option to **Yes** for the parameter that is affected automatically and to include the parameter in the object selection set when creating the action that will drive chain action.

Action Multiplier and Offset Options

When you insert a move, stretch, or polar stretch action, the following prompt appears after you select the objects to which the action applies:

Specify action location or [Multiplier/Offset]:

If you enter M for the **Multiplier** option, AutoCAD prompts you to enter a distance multiplier. The value you enter in the parameter property when you edit the parameter grip is multiplied by the value entered here. For example, if you enter 2 as the distance multiplier when creating a move action and specify a value of 4 units to move the parameter grip in the drawing, the object actually moves 8 units.

If you enter O for the **Offset** option, AutoCAD prompts you to enter an offset angle. This angle is used to increase or decrease the parameter grip angle. For example, if an offset angle value of 45 is specified when a move action is created and a parameter grip is moved at an angle of 10° in the drawing, the object actually moves to an angle of 55°.

Using Parameter Sets

The **Parameter Sets** tab of the **Block Authoring Palettes** window contains commonly used parameters and actions paired as sets. These are the same parameters and actions that are found in the **Parameters** tab and the **Actions** tab. When you choose one of the sets, you are prompted for the normal parameter settings. When you specify the parameter point, the action is automatically associated with the parameter.

The action is created without any objects associated with it, which is indicated by the yellow alert icon. If the parameter set contains an action that needs to have objects associated to it, as most do, double-click anywhere on the action icon. AutoCAD prompts you for the missing item(s). Depending on the type of action, the prompts may differ.

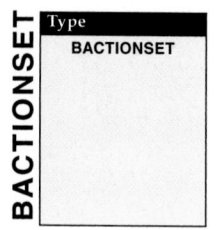

The **BACTIONSET** command can also be used to associate objects to an action. To use this command, type BACTIONSET. AutoCAD prompts you to select the action and then the objects.

Modifying Parameters and Actions

After parameters and actions have been created, their location can be edited in the **Block Editor** with grip editing and their settings can be edited using the **Properties** palette. To modify the location of a parameter grip, open the block in the **Block Editor** and select the parameter. The parameter grips and the location grip for the parameter label appear. Use normal grip editing procedures to move a grip to a different location.

All of the settings for a parameter or action can be changed in the **Properties** palette. In the **Block Editor**, open the **Properties** palette and select a parameter or action to modify. Its settings are then displayed in the **Properties** palette. The options in the **Properties** palette change depending on the type of parameter or action that is selected.

Any parameter or action can be deleted using the **ERASE** command in the **Block Editor**. Select the parameter or action when prompted by the command. A parameter or action can also be deleted by selecting it and pressing the [Delete] key.

Exercise 24-13
Complete the exercise on the Student CD.

Chapter Test

Answer the following questions. Write your answers on a separate sheet of paper or complete the electronic chapter test on the Student CD.

1. Define *dynamic block.*
2. Compare and contrast dynamic blocks and normal blocks.
3. Define *parameter.*
4. Define *action.*
5. List the parameters that can be inserted into a block.
6. Briefly describe AutoCAD's **Block Editor**.
7. What does a point parameter do? Identify the actions that can be assigned to a point parameter.
8. Describe the shape and default color of a point parameter grip.
9. What does a linear parameter do? Identify the actions that can be assigned to a linear parameter.
10. Describe the shape and default color of a linear parameter grip.
11. What does a stretch action do?
12. Compare and contrast a polar parameter and a linear parameter. Identify the actions that can be assigned to a polar parameter.
13. What does a rotation parameter do? Identify the actions that can be assigned to a rotation parameter.
14. What does an alignment parameter do? Identify the actions that can be assigned to an alignment parameter.
15. Give an example of where an alignment parameter may be used on a block.
16. What is the basic function of the flip parameter?
17. List the function of each grip of an XY parameter. Identify the actions that can be assigned to an XY parameter.
18. How are visibility states defined and used on a dynamic block?
19. Explain how a lookup parameter differs from a visibility parameter.
20. What does a base point parameter do?
21. What is a value set? Give an example of its use.
22. Name the two types of value sets.
23. Define *chain action.* Identify the parameters that can be part of a chain action.
24. Explain how the **Multiplier** and **Offset** options can be used.
25. What are parameter sets? Explain how they are used.

Drawing Problems

1. Open P23-3 from Chapter 23. Erase all copies of the steel column symbols except for the one in the lower-left corner. Insert an XY parameter into the steel column block and associate an array action with the parameter. Use the proper values for the array action so the block can be dynamically arrayed to match the drawing. Use the one dynamic block to create the rest of the steel columns in the drawing. Save the drawing as P24-1.

2. Create a block named WIRE ROLL as shown below. Do not include the dimensions. Insert a linear parameter on the entire length of the roll. Use a value set with the following values: 36″, 42″, 48″, and 54″. Assign a stretch action to the parameter and associate the action with either parameter grip. Create a stretch frame that will allow the length of the role to be stretched. Select all of the objects on one end and the length lines as the objects to be stretched. Insert the WIRE ROLL block four times into a drawing and stretch each block to use a different value set length. Save the drawing as P24-2.

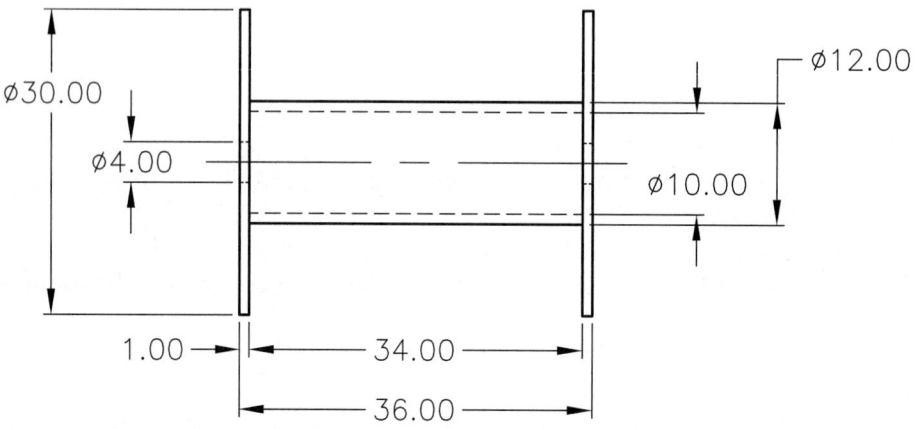

3. Create a single block that can be used to represent each of the three door blocks shown below. Name the block 30 INCH DOOR; do not include labels. Create an appropriately named visibility state for each view: 90 OPEN, 60 OPEN, and 30 OPEN. Insert the 30 INCH DOOR block into the drawing three times. Set each block to a different visibility state. Save the drawing as P24-3.

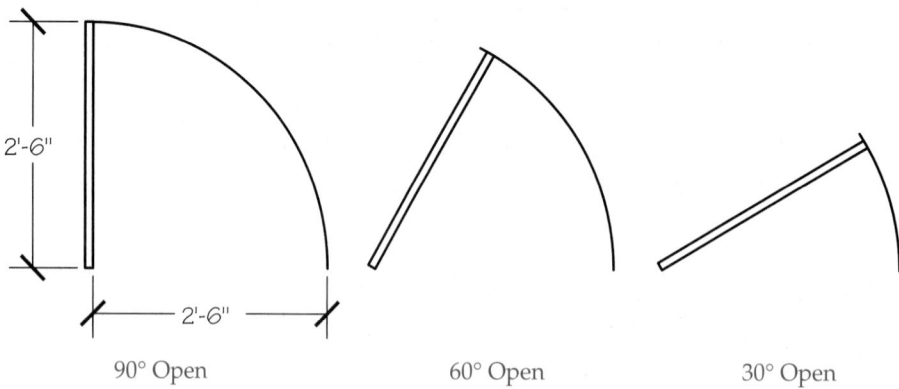

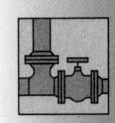

4. Create a block named 90D ELBOW as shown below on the left. Do not include the dimensions. Insert two flip parameters and two flip actions. One of the flip parameter/action combinations is to flip the elbow horizontally. The second flip parameter/action combination is to flip the elbow vertically. Use the dynamic block to create the drawing shown below on the right. Save the drawing as P24-4.

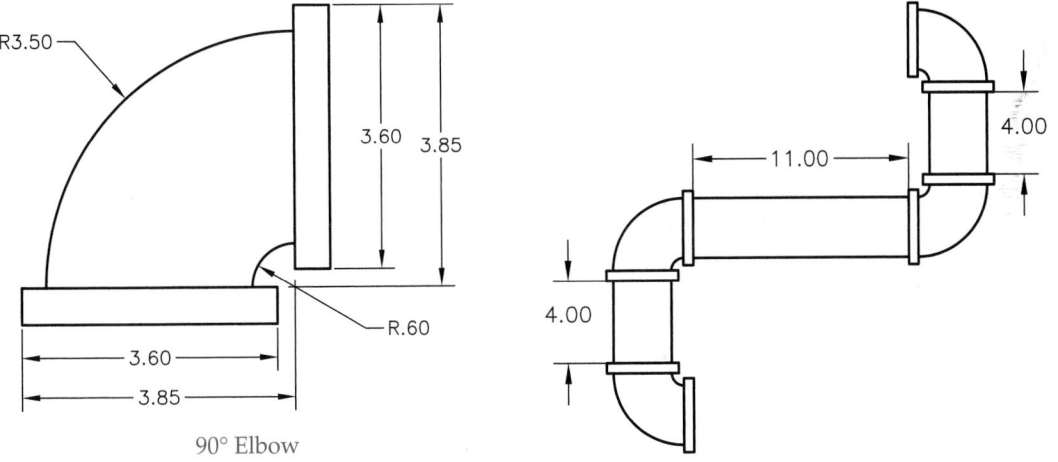

90° Elbow

5. Create a block of the 48" window shown below on the left. Do not include the dimensions. Insert an alignment parameter so the length of the window can be aligned with a wall. Then, draw the walls shown below on the right. Insert the window block as needed. Use the alignment parameter to align the window to the walls. Windows are centered on wall segments unless dimensioned. Save the drawing as P24-5.

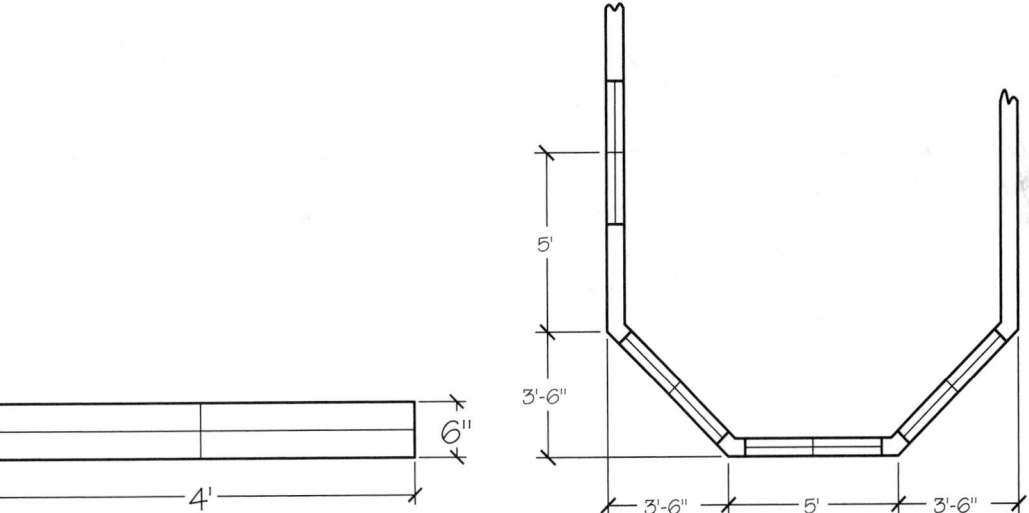

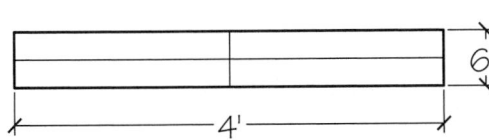

6. Create a block named FLANGE as shown below. Do not include dimensions. Insert a rotation parameter specifying the center of the flange as the base point. Assign a rotate action to the parameter, selecting the six Ø.2 circles as the objects to which the action applies. Insert the FLANGE block into the drawing twice. Use the rotation parameter to create the two configurations shown below. Save the drawing as P24-6.

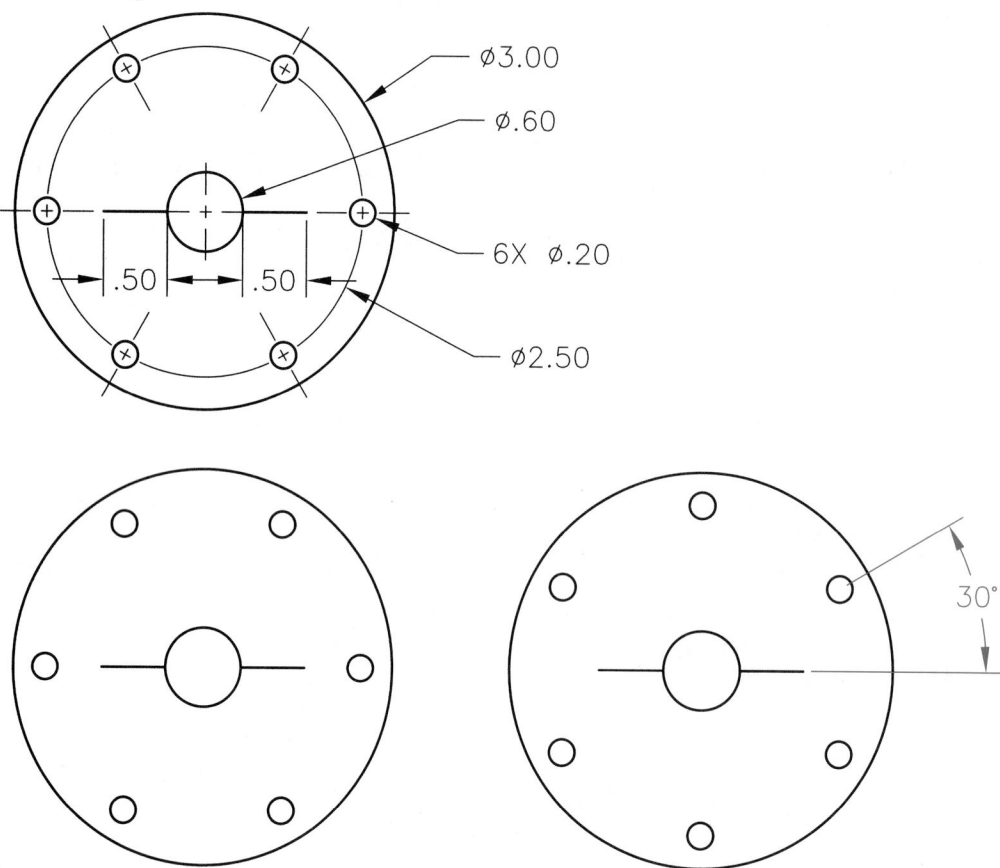

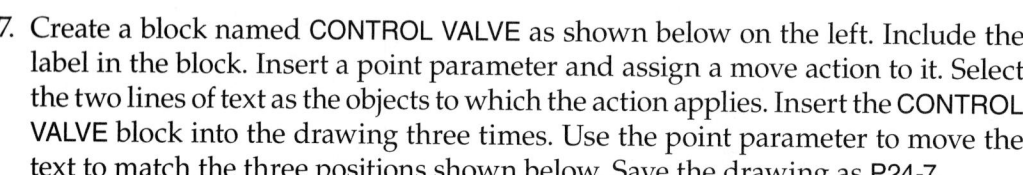

7. Create a block named CONTROL VALVE as shown below on the left. Include the label in the block. Insert a point parameter and assign a move action to it. Select the two lines of text as the objects to which the action applies. Insert the CONTROL VALVE block into the drawing three times. Use the point parameter to move the text to match the three positions shown below. Save the drawing as P24-7.

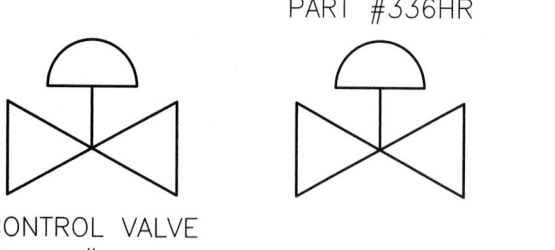

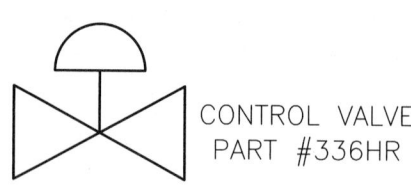

AutoCAD and Its Applications—Basics

8. Open P24-6. Save the drawing as P24-8. Open the FLANGE block in the **Block Editor** and use the **Properties** palette to give the following settings to the rotation parameter:
   A. **Angle label**—BOLT HOLES
   B. **Angle description**—ROTATION OF BOLT HOLE PATTERN
   C. **Ang type**—INCREMENT
   D. **Ang increment**—30
   E. Save the changes and exit the **Block Editor**. Save the drawing.

9. The drawing below shows a fan with an enlarged view of the motor. This fan can have one of three motors of different sizes. Create the fan as a dynamic block.
   A. Draw all the objects. Do not dimension the drawing or draw the enlarged view.
   B. Create a block named FAN consisting of the objects shown in the enlarged view.
   C. Open the block in the **Block Editor** and insert a linear parameter along the top of the motor (the 1.50″ dimension). Use a value set with the following values: 1.5, 1.75, and 2.
   D. Assign a scale action to the linear parameter. Select all of the objects that make up the motor as the objects to which the action applies. Use an independent base type and specify the base point as the lower-left corner of the motor (the implied intersection).
   E. Save the block and exit the **Block Editor**.
   F. Insert the block three times into the drawing. Use the linear parameter grip to scale the motor to the three different sizes, as shown below on the right.
   G. Save the drawing as P24-9.

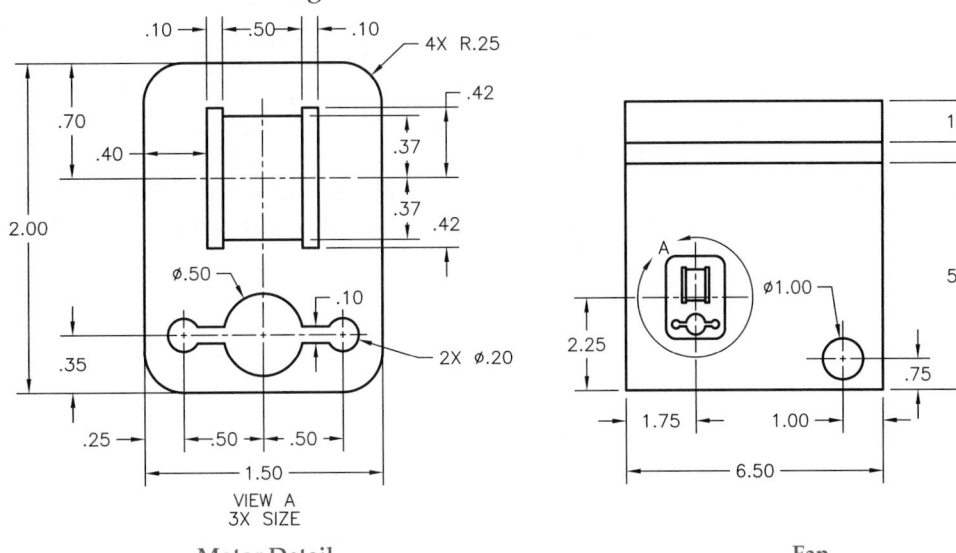

VIEW A
3X SIZE

Motor Detail

Fan

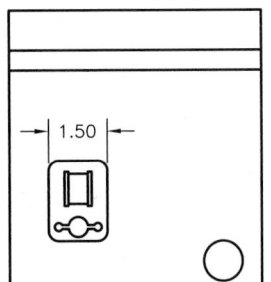
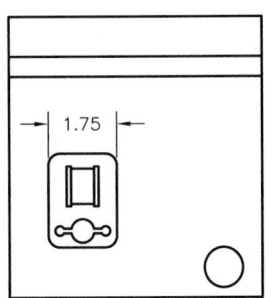
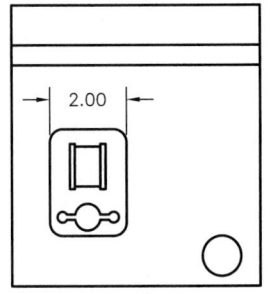

Drawing Problems - Chapter 24

10. The bolt shown in the drawing below is available in four different lengths. As the length increases, the size of the bolt head increases for added strength. Create a dynamic block that will allow the length of the shaft and the size of the bolt head to be changed in a single operation.

A. Draw the objects composing the bolt and create a block named BOLT. Do not include dimensions.

B. Insert a linear parameter along the length of the shaft from the bottom of the bolt head to the end of the shaft. Label it SHAFT LENGTH.

C. Assign a stretch action to the SHAFT LENGTH parameter. Associate the action with the parameter grip at the end of the shaft. Create a stretch frame around the end of the shaft that includes the threads. Select the end of the shaft, threads, and edges of the shaft.

D. Insert a linear parameter along the depth of the bolt head (the .3″ dimension). Label it HEAD THICKNESS.

E. Assign a scale action to the HEAD THICKNESS parameter and select the objects that compose the bolt head. Use an independent base type and specify the midpoint of the vertical line where the shaft meets the bolt head.

F. Insert a lookup parameter and then assign a lookup action to it.

G. Add the SHAFT LENGTH and the HEAD THICKNESS parameters to the lookup table. Complete the table with the following properties:

Shaft Length	Head Thickness	Lookup
1	0.3	1″ Length
1.5	0.333	1.5″ Length
2	0.366	2″ Length
2.5	0.4	2.5″ Length

H. Set the table to allow reverse lookup, save the block, and exit the **Block Editor**.

I. Insert the block four times into the drawing. Specify a different lookup property for each block.

J. Save the drawing as P24-10.

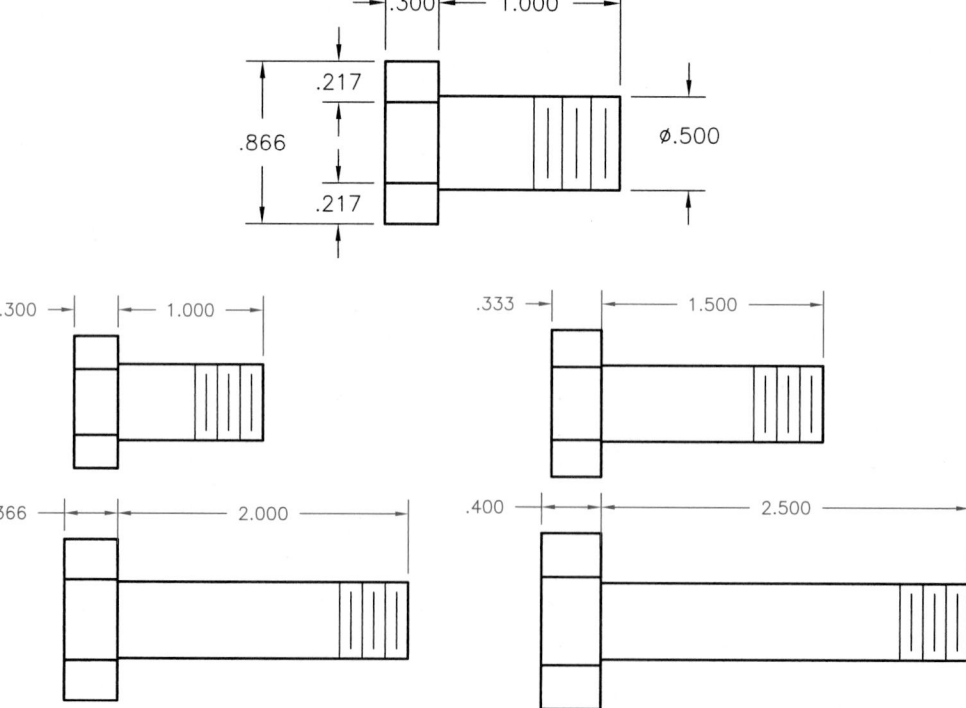

CHAPTER 25

Creating Layouts and Plotting

Learning Objectives

After completing this chapter, you will be able to do the following:

✓ Add title blocks and viewports to layouts.
✓ Create new layouts.
✓ Manage layouts.
✓ Select a plotting device and modify a plotting device configuration.
✓ Create, modify, and use plot styles and plot style tables.
✓ Select plot settings.
✓ Describe alternative plotting methods.
✓ Print or plot a drawing.
✓ Explain keys to efficient plotting.

Often, the end result of your AutoCAD work is a printed or plotted drawing. It is easier for a construction crew in the field to use a printed copy of the drawing than to use a computer to view the DWG file. Therefore, it is important for you to understand how drawings are laid out for plotting, as well as the various plotting options available in AutoCAD.

Drawings can be plotted from either model space or paper space, as described in Chapter 5. Ordinarily, however, drawings are created in model space and then are arranged or laid out for printing in paper space. This chapter describes the procedures for creating and printing layouts.

Layout Setup

A *layout* is an arrangement of objects on a sheet of paper for plotting purposes. A layout can contain many types of objects, including viewports, a title block, and various types of annotation, such as general notes, revision levels and descriptions, and a bill of materials. Assembling these items in a layout allows you to see exactly what the final plot will look like.

A single drawing can have multiple layouts. Drawings based on AutoCAD's acad.dwt drawing contain two layouts by default. These layouts are identified by the **Layout1** and **Layout2** tabs below the drawing area. Each layout tab represents a different paper space configuration.

layout: An arrangement of a drawing or model for plotting.

When you pick a layout tab for the first time, the layout is displayed using default settings primarily based on an 8.5" × 11" sheet of paper in a landscape (horizontal) orientation.

Several settings that affect the display of layouts are contained in the **Layout elements** area of the **Display** tab in the **Options** dialog box. See **Figure 25-1**. Access this dialog box by selecting **Tools** > **Options...** from the pull-down menu. Use the default settings until you are comfortable working with layouts.

Inserting a Border and Title Block

Most layouts contain a border and title block. These items are generally saved in a template file and then inserted as blocks when needed. See Chapter 23 for a complete discussion of blocks.

It is best to insert the blocks into the layout and then save it as a template file. You can then start a new drawing based on the template, and the layout with the title block is already created. To insert a title block, select **Insert** > **Block...** from the pull-down menu to access the **Insert** dialog box. Pick the **Browse...** button and select the title block drawing to be inserted. **Figure 25-2** shows an ANSI A title block inserted into a layout.

Floating Viewports

When a layout tab is selected, an image showing a preview of the final printed drawing is shown. See **Figure 25-3**. The dashed line around the edge of the paper represents the page margins. The solid lines show the outline of a *floating viewport*. By default, a single viewport is created.

floating viewports: Viewports created in paper space.

Figure 25-1.
Layout display options are found in the **Options** dialog box.

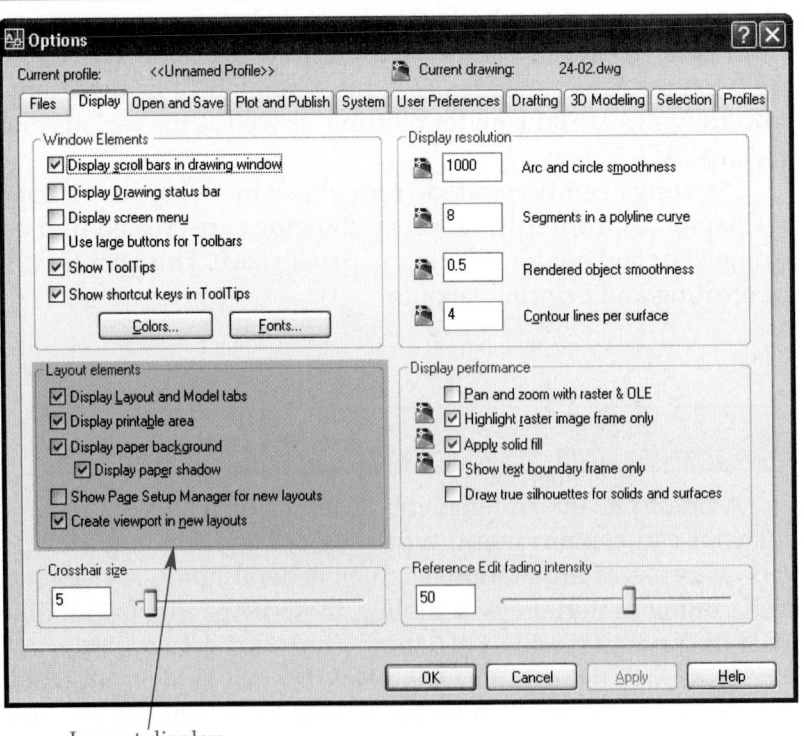

Layout display options

Figure 25-2.
An example of an ANSI A title block inserted into the layout. Note that the viewport created by default has been deleted.

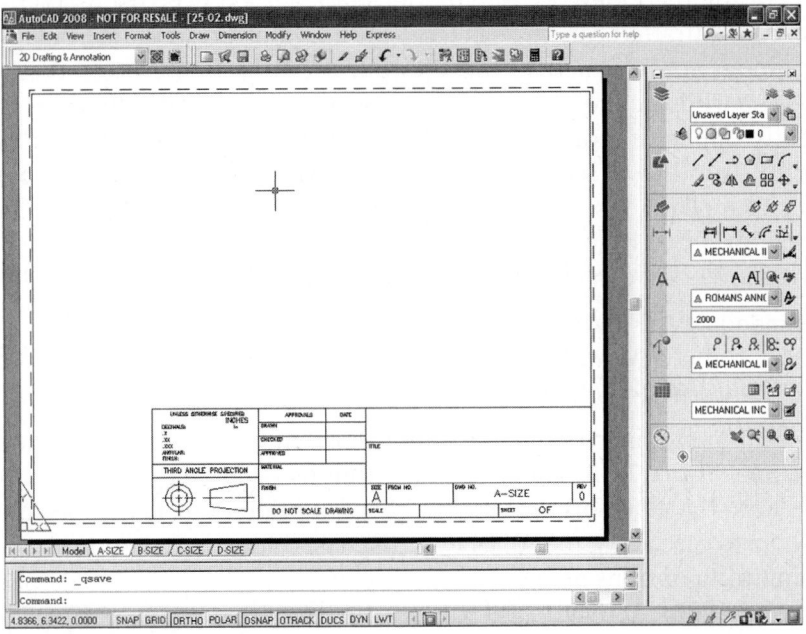

Figure 25-3.
A layout provides a preview of how the plotted drawing will appear.

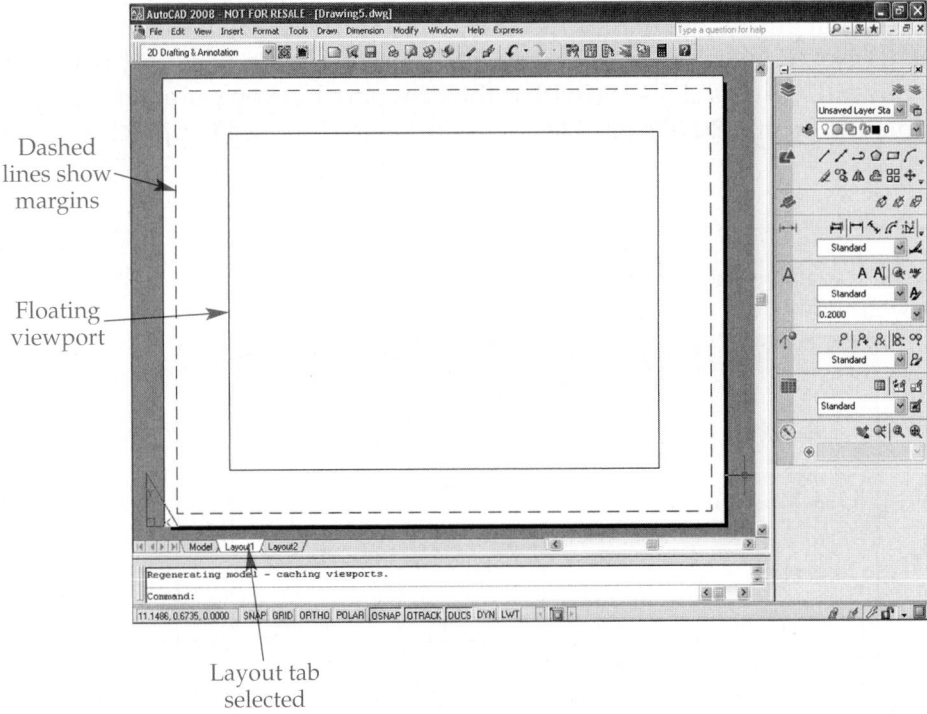

Dashed lines show margins

Floating viewport

Layout tab selected

Floating viewports are actually holes cut into the paper in the layout tab so that the model space drawing can be seen. These viewports are separate objects and can be moved around and even overlap, thus the term *floating viewports*.

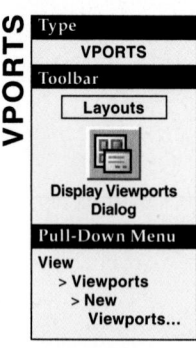

VPORTS

Type
VPORTS
Toolbar
Layouts
Display Viewports
Dialog
Pull-Down Menu
View
> Viewports
> New
Viewports...

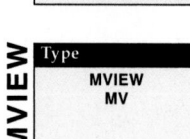

MVIEW

Type
MVIEW
MV

Creating floating viewports

The process of creating floating viewports in paper space is nearly identical to the process of creating tiled viewports in model space, which was discussed in Chapter 6. A viewport configuration can be selected from the **Viewports** dialog box.

When model space is active, the **Viewports** dialog box creates tiled viewports. When paper space is active, it creates floating viewports. The **Viewports** dialog box differs slightly depending on the current environment—model space or paper space. The **Apply to:** drop-down list found in model space becomes the **Viewport spacing:** text box in paper space. Use this setting to specify the space around the edges of the floating viewports. See Figure 25-4.

Floating viewports can also be created using the **MVIEW** command.

Command: **MV** *or* **MVIEW**⏎
Specify corner of viewport or [ON/OFF/Fit/Shadeplot/Lock/Object/Polygonal/
Restore/LAyer/2/3/4] <Fit>:

The default option is to define a rectangular floating viewport by selecting opposite corners. See Figure 25-5. The **2**, **3**, and **4** options provide preset viewport configurations similar to the **Viewports** dialog box. These options can also be selected from the **View** > **Viewports** cascading menu, as was discussed for tiled viewports.

The remaining options are:
- **ON** and **OFF.** Activate and deactivate the model space display within a viewport.
- **Fit.** Creates a single rectangular floating viewport that fills the entire printable area on the sheet.
- **Shadeplot.** Specifies how viewports in layouts appear when plotted. This option is covered in greater detail in *AutoCAD and Its Applications—Advanced.*
- **Lock.** Locks the view in one or more viewports. When a viewport is locked, you can still edit or add objects within the viewport, but you cannot use display commands such as **ZOOM** and **PAN**. This option is also used to unlock a locked viewport.

Figure 25-4.
When paper space is active, the **New Viewports** tab in the **Viewports** dialog box contains the **Viewport Spacing:** setting.

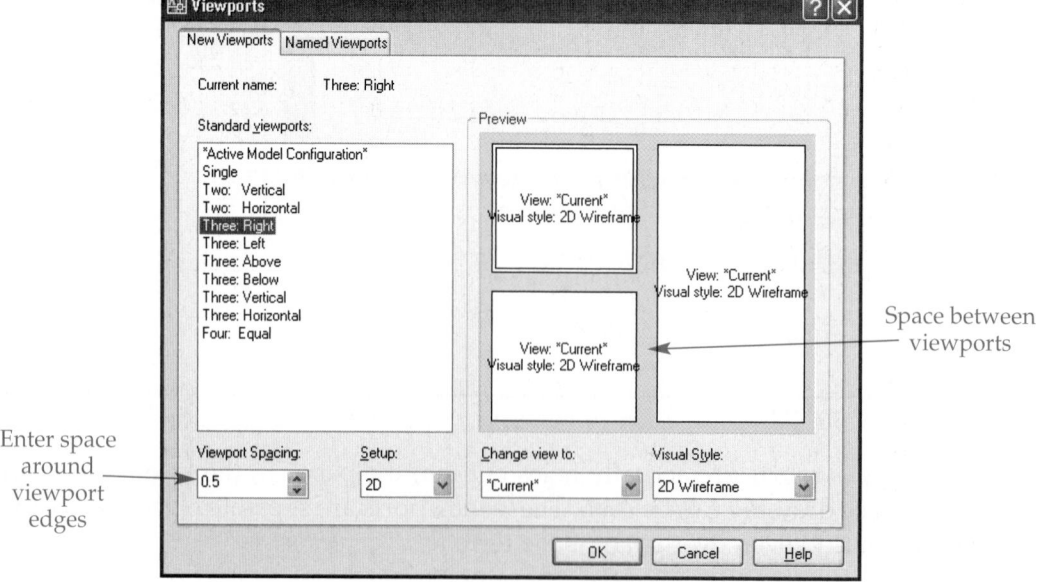

Figure 25-5.
Creating a rectangular floating viewport using the **MVIEW** command.

First corner
selected

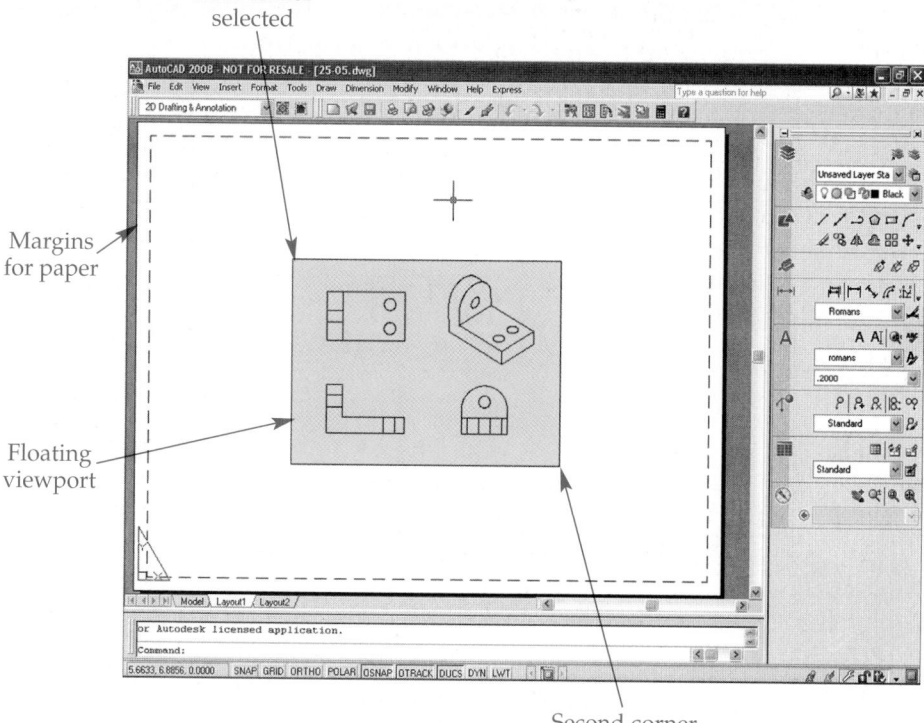

Margins
for paper

Floating
viewport

Second corner

- **Object.** Changes a closed object drawn in paper space into a floating viewport. Circles, ellipses, polygons, and other closed shapes can be used as floating viewport outlines. See **Figure 25-6.**
- **Polygonal.** Draws a floating viewport outline using a polyline. The viewport shape can be any closed shape composed of lines and arcs.
- **Restore.** Converts saved viewport configurations into individual floating viewports.
- **Layer.** Resets viewport layer property overrides.

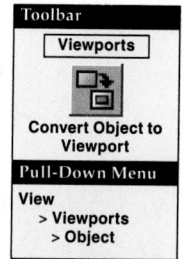

Toolbar
Viewports

Convert Object to Viewport

Pull-Down Menu
View
> Viewports
> Object

Working with floating viewports

Once the viewports are created, the display within the viewport must be set to show the correct part of the model space drawing. Using multiple viewports in a layout allows you to illustrate different aspects of the drawing. Using multiple layouts, various types of drawings can be created from a single drawing model.

Create the floating viewports after the title block has been inserted. This will allow you to position the viewports so they do not interfere with the title block. **Figure 25-7** illustrates the following procedure for establishing the display in two floating viewports:

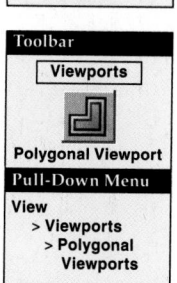

Toolbar
Viewports

Polygonal Viewport

Pull-Down Menu
View
> Viewports
> Polygonal Viewports

1. Create the first viewport using the **Viewports** dialog box. The model space drawing is typically visible in the viewport.
2. Create a second viewport.
3. Double-click in the first viewport to enter model space.
4. Use the **XP** option of the **ZOOM** command, the scale drop-down list on the **Viewports** toolbar, or the popup list on the right side of the status bar to scale the drawing within the viewport. Use realtime panning to display the area of interest in the drawing.
5. Double-click outside of the viewports to activate paper space. Use grips or the **STRETCH** command to resize the viewport.
6. Repeat steps 3-5 for the second viewport.

Figure 25-6.
Viewports can be created from closed objects. A—Draw the objects in paper space. B—Convert the objects to viewports.

Objects drawn in layout space

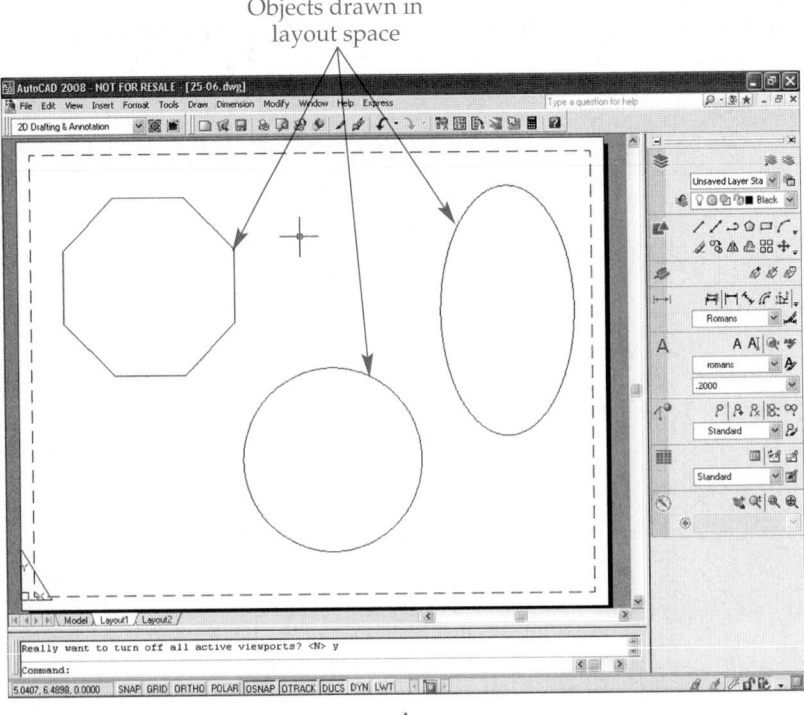

A

Objects converted to floating viewports

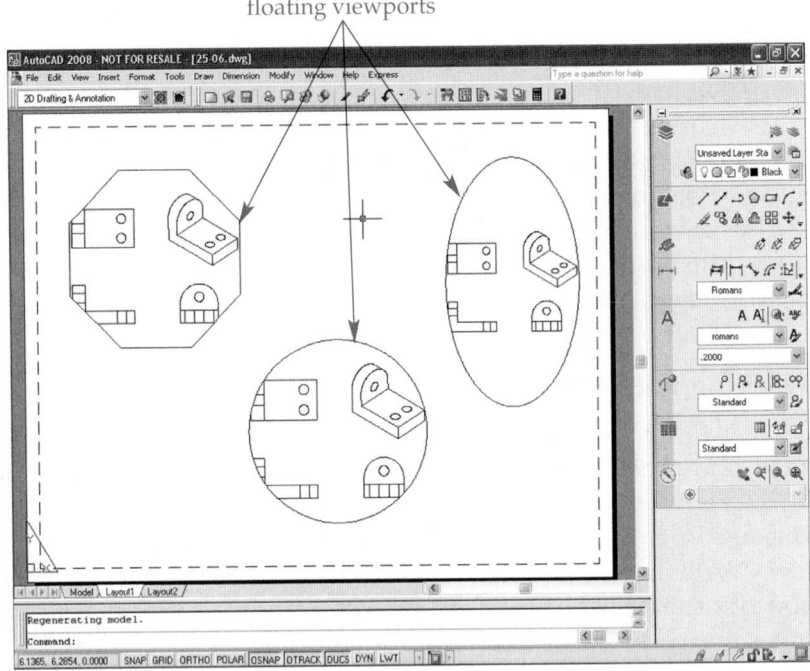

B

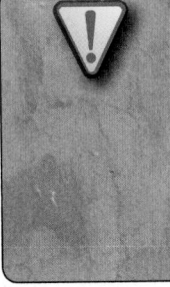

CAUTION

If you use zoom to adjust the drawing inside the viewport, the drawing may no longer be to scale. Once the area to be displayed is visible within the viewport and the viewport scale has been set using the **ZOOM XP** option, the scale drop-down list on the **Viewports** toolbar, or the popup list on the right side of the status bar, it is a good idea to lock the display of the viewport to be certain the drawing remains properly scaled inside the viewport.

AutoCAD and Its Applications—Basics

Figure 25-7.
These steps illustrate the procedure for adding viewports to a layout.

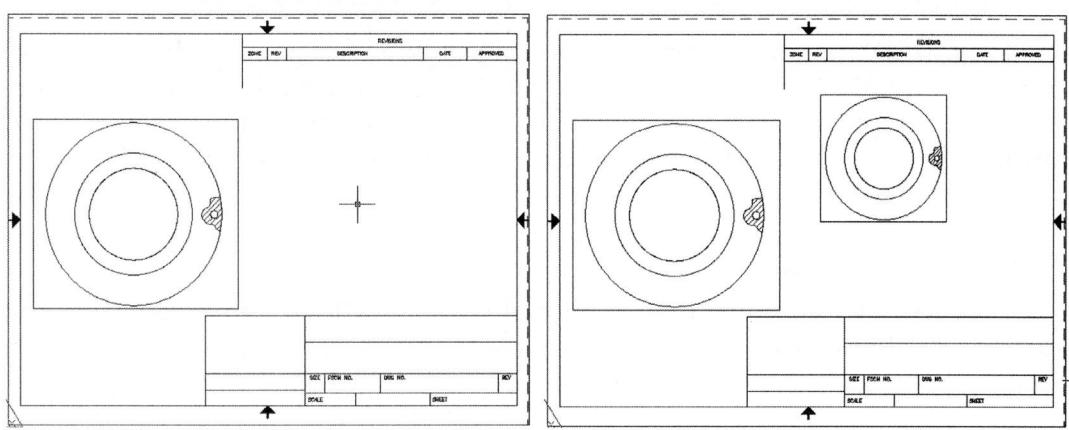

Step 1—Create viewport.　　　　　　Step 2—Create second viewport.

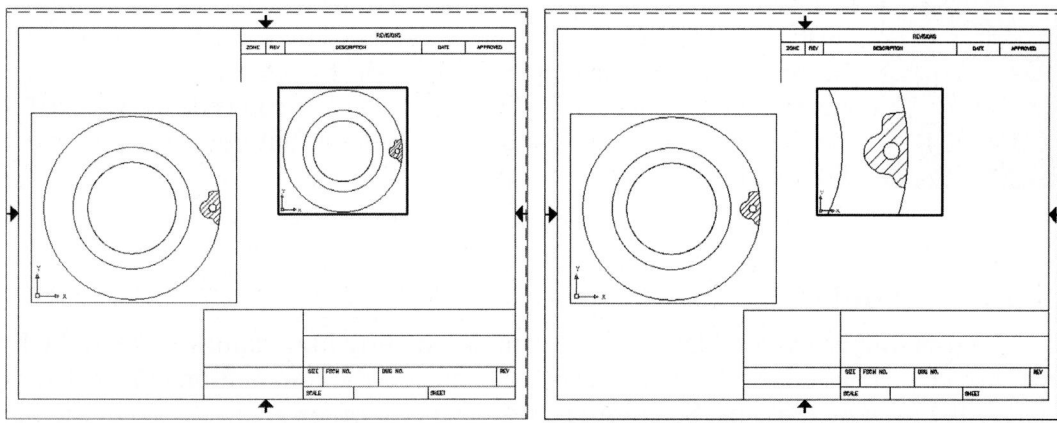

Step 3—Make second viewport active.　　Step 4—Zoom and pan display in second viewport.

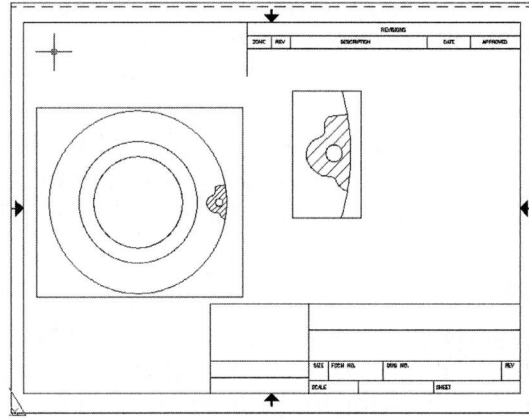

Step 5—Resize viewport.

Exercise 25-1

Complete the exercise on the Student CD.

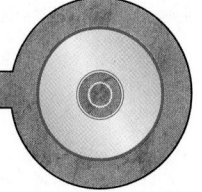

Managing Layouts

The **LAYOUT** command allows you to manage layouts. To access this command, enter LO or LAYOUT. AutoCAD prompts you to select a **LAYOUT** command option. Some of these options are also available in the **Layouts** toolbars and the **Insert** > **Layout** cascading menu. You can also position the cursor over a layout tab and right-click to display the layout shortcut menu.

Setting the Current Layout

The current layout is identified by the highlighted tab at the bottom of the drawing area. To set the current layout, pick the layout tab using the cursor. You can also use the **Set** option of the **LAYOUT** command to specify the current layout.

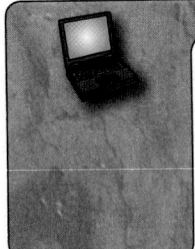

PROFESSIONAL TIP

If you are selecting options from the layout shortcut menu, you must have the appropriate layout set as current before selecting the command. For example, if you select **Delete** from the layout shortcut menu, the current layout is deleted. If you type the **LAYOUT** command, the current layout is the default, but you can specify a different layout.

Listing Layouts

If a drawing has several layouts or layouts with fairly long names, all layout tabs may not be visible. When this is the case, you can use the four buttons to the left of the tab list to view the tabs. See **Figure 25-8**. The two outer arrows display the left and right ends of the tab list. The inner arrows move the list one tab in the indicated direction. Changing the display of the tab list does not affect the current tab. You must still pick a tab to set it current. You can also use the keyboard to advance through the layouts. Hold down the [Ctrl] and press the [PageDown] key to advance through the layouts from left to right. Hold down the [Ctrl] and press the [PageUp] key to advance through the layouts from right to left.

The **?** option of the **LAYOUT** command can be used to list all layouts within the drawing. After selecting this option, you must switch to the **AutoCAD Text Window** to view the list. To do this, select **View** > **Display** > **Text Window** or use the [F2] function key.

Creating a New Layout

AutoCAD provides several methods of creating new layouts. You can create a new layout from scratch or copy it from an existing drawing or template file. Finally, you can copy a layout within the drawing to create a new layout.

Figure 25-8.
Use the arrows to scroll through the display of layout tabs.

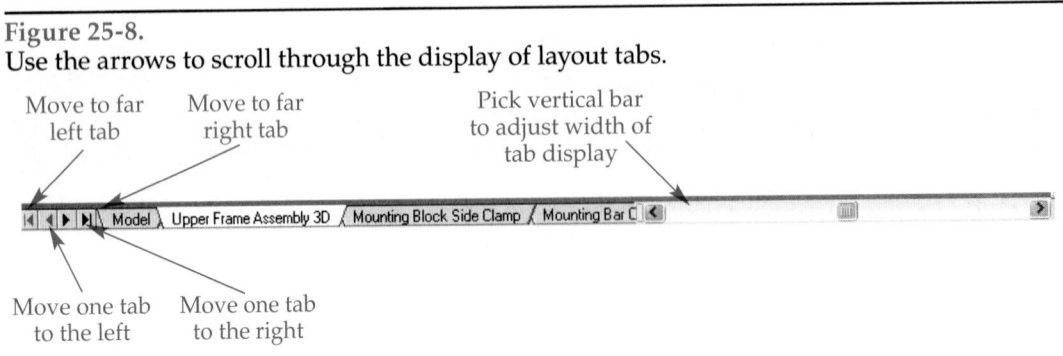

Move to far left tab

Move to far right tab

Pick vertical bar to adjust width of tab display

Move one tab to the left

Move one tab to the right

Starting from scratch

Use the **New** option of the **LAYOUT** command to create a new layout. You can also create a new layout by selecting **Insert** > **Layout** > **New Layout**, picking the **New Layout** button in the **Layouts** toolbar, or right-clicking a layout tab and selecting **New layout** from the layout shortcut menu. If you select the option from the command line, toolbar, or pull-down menu, you are prompted to enter the layout name. If you use the **New layout** option in the layout shortcut menu, the new layout is created with the default name. You can then use the **Rename** option to change the name.

Using a template

This option creates a new layout based on a layout stored in an existing drawing or template file. Select this option by selecting the **Template** option of the **LAYOUT** command, selecting **Insert** > **Layout** > **Layout from Template...** from the pull-down menu, or picking the **Layout from Template** button in the **Layouts** toolbar. You can also right-click on a layout tab and select **From template...** in the layout shortcut menu.

When you select this option, the **Select Template From File** dialog box is displayed. See **Figure 25-9A.** The Template folder in the path set by the AutoCAD Drawing Template File Location is selected by default.

Select the drawing file or template file containing the layout to be copied and pick the **Open** button. The **Insert Layout(s)** dialog box appears, as shown in **Figure 25-9B.** This dialog box lists all layouts in the selected file. Highlight the layout(s) you want to copy and pick the **OK** button.

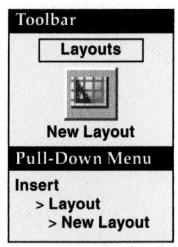

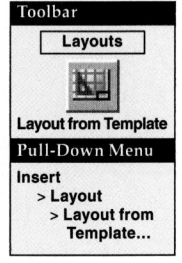

Figure 25-9.
Creating a new layout from another drawing or template. A—Select the drawing or template containing the layout. B—Highlight the layout(s) to be added to the current drawing.

Template folder opens by default

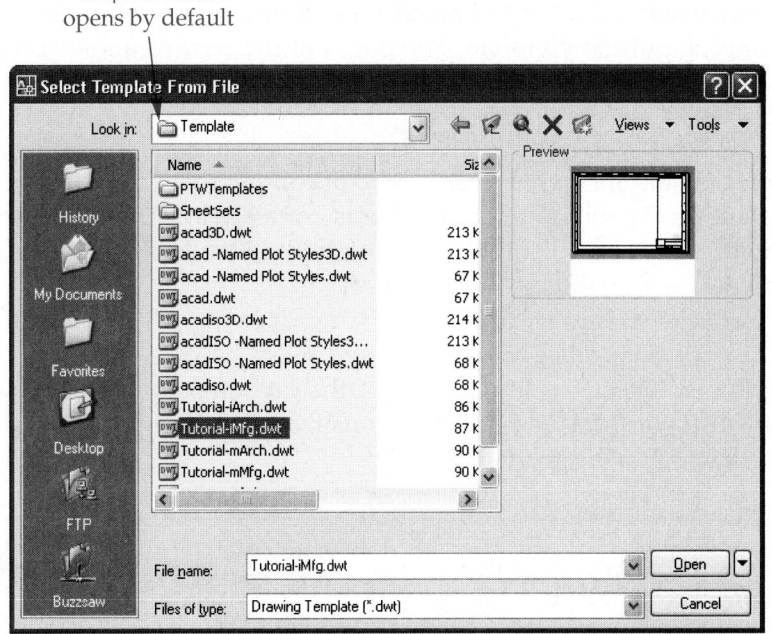

A

List of layouts in selected file

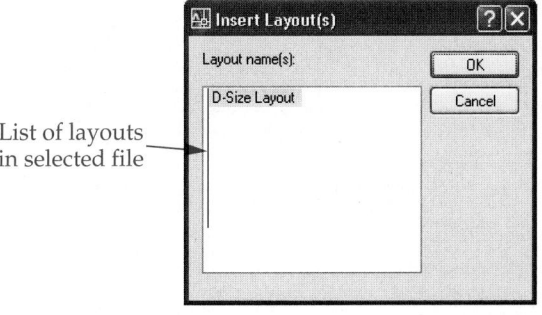

B

Copying a layout in the current drawing

You can create a new layout by copying an existing layout. If you use the **Copy** option of the **LAYOUT** command, enter the name of the layout to copy, and then enter the name for the new copy. The current layout is the default layout to copy. If you do not enter a name for the copy, AutoCAD uses the current layout name plus a number in parentheses.

You can also copy an existing layout by selecting **Move or Copy...** from the layout shortcut menu. This option provides no opportunity to change the layout to be copied; the current layout tab is copied. When you select this option, the **Move or Copy** dialog box appears. See **Figure 25-10**. Activate the **Create a copy** check box and select which layout the new layout tab should be to the left of. The default name is automatically assigned to the new layout. Use the **Rename** option to change it.

> **PROFESSIONAL TIP**
>
> Windows-standard shortcuts also work with layouts. One of the fastest ways to copy a layout is to hold down the [Ctrl] key and drag an existing layout to the right. A new layout—an exact copy of the existing layout—appears at the location indicated by the small arrow above the layout names.

Using the Create Layout wizard

You can create a new layout using the **Create Layout** wizard. To access this wizard, select **Insert** > **Layout** > **Layout Wizard** or select **Tools** > **Wizards** > **Create Layout...** from the pull-down menu. The pages of the wizard allow you to specify a title block, viewports, and many page setup values.

Copying layouts with DesignCenter

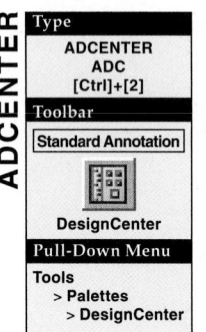

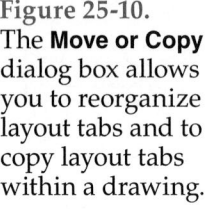

Layouts are included as a type of content that can be viewed using **DesignCenter**. To access **DesignCenter**, select **Tools** > **Palettes** > **DesignCenter** from the pull-down menu, pick the **DesignCenter** button in the **Standard** toolbar, enter ADC or ADCENTER, or use the [Ctrl]+[2] key combination.

To copy a layout from an existing drawing or template, first locate the drawing in the **DesignCenter** tree view. Then select Layouts to display the layouts within the drawing. See **Figure 25-11**. Select the layout(s) to be copied and then use the **Add Layout(s)** or **Copy** and **Paste** options from shortcut menus or drag and drop to insert the layouts in the current drawing.

Figure 25-10.
The **Move or Copy** dialog box allows you to reorganize layout tabs and to copy layout tabs within a drawing.

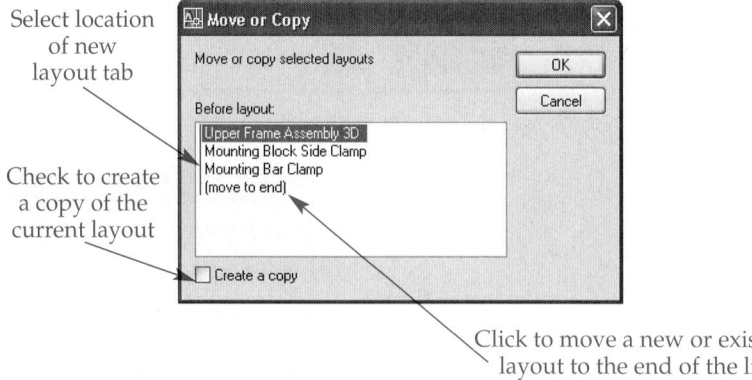

Select location of new layout tab

Check to create a copy of the current layout

Click to move a new or existing layout to the end of the list

Figure 25-11.
Layouts can be shared between drawings using **DesignCenter**.

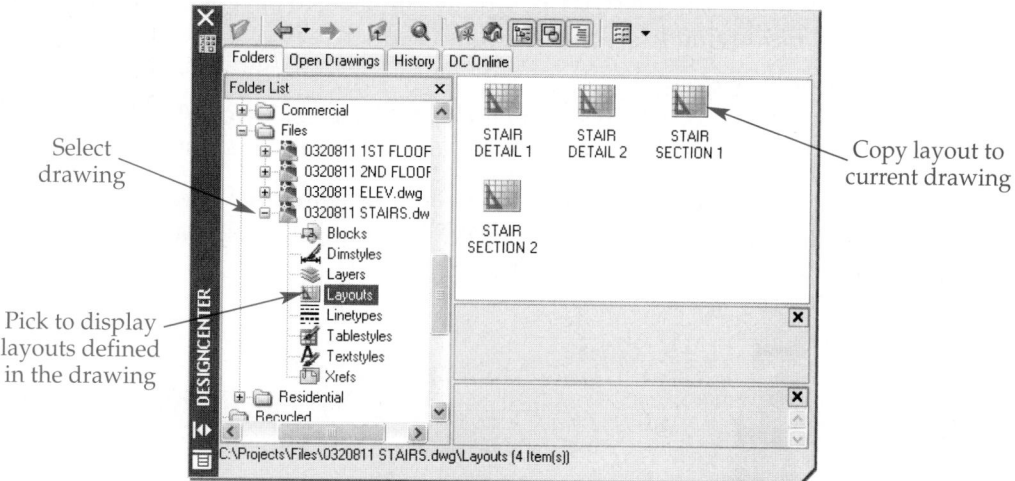

Select drawing

Pick to display layouts defined in the drawing

Copy layout to current drawing

Renaming a Layout

The name of the layout appears on its tab. Layouts created by default are named **Layout***n*, where *n* is a number. A layout created by copying another layout has the same name as the initial layout, followed by a number in parentheses. For example, the first copy of **Layout2** is named **Layout2 (2)**.

Layouts are easier to work with when they have a descriptive name. The easiest way to rename a layout is to double-click on the layout tab. The current name of the layout becomes highlighted. Type the new name to be applied to the layout and press [Enter].

Layouts can also be renamed using the **Rename** option of the **LAYOUT** command. When you select this option, AutoCAD prompts you to enter the name of the layout to be renamed. The current layout is provided as a default. When you identify the layout to be renamed, AutoCAD prompts you to enter the new layout name.

You can also rename a layout by right-clicking the layout tab and selecting **Rename** from the shortcut menu. This accesses the **Rename Layout** dialog box. If you select this option, you can rename only the current layout. Enter the new name in the text box and pick the **OK** button.

PROFESSIONAL TIP

If you are using sheet sets, you can add a layout quickly by right-clicking on a layout tab and selecting "Import Layout as Sheet…" from the shortcut menu. The drawing must be saved and the layout must be set up for the shortcut menu item to be available. Sheet sets are covered in detail in Chapter 29.

Deleting a Layout

When a layout is no longer useful, it can be deleted. You can delete a layout using the **Delete** option of the **LAYOUT** command. You can also delete the active layout by right-clicking on the layout tab and selecting **Delete** from the shortcut menu. If you select **Delete** from the layout shortcut menu, an alert box warns you that the layout will be permanently deleted. Pick the **OK** button to delete the layout.

Saving a Layout

The **Saveas** option of the **LAYOUT** command is used to save a single layout as a drawing template or drawing file. The command sequence is:

Command: **LO** *or* **LAYOUT.**↲
Enter layout option [Copy/Delete/New/Template/Rename/SAveas/Set/?] <set>: **SA.**↲
Enter layout to save to template <*current layout*>: *(enter name of layout or accept default)*

After you specify the layout to save, the **Create Drawing File** dialog box appears. You can save the layout in a DWT, DWG, or DXF file. Enter the file name and pick the **SAVE** button. The layout is now saved in the new file.

Exercise 25-2
Complete the exercise on the Student CD.

Plotting Procedure

You can create plots from model space or from the layout tabs (paper space). The general procedures for both cases are similar:
1. Create the drawing objects in model space. If you are creating a layout, create the floating viewports, title block, and other desired items in a layout tab (paper space).
2. Configure the plotting device if it is not already configured.
3. Access the **Page Setup Manager** or **Plot** dialog box and specify values for the plotting settings. Each tab can have its own settings, so each layout can produce a different plot.
4. Plot the drawing.

The following sections examine this procedure in detail.

Page Setups for Plotting

page setup: A collection of settings required to create a finished plot of a drawing.

A *page setup* contains the settings required to create a finished plot of the drawing. Most aspects of how the drawing is plotted can be established in a page setup, including printer selection, plot style (pen settings) choices, paper size and orientation, scale, and other settings that define how the model is going to appear on the final plotted output. In fact, the only difference between the **Page Setup** and **Plot** dialog boxes is that the **Page Setup** dialog box does not provide a plot preview button.

Page setup is a productivity tool that decreases the amount of time required to prepare a drawing for plotting. Each layout can have a unique page setup. Therefore, the **Page Setup Manager** dialog box is always tied to the active **Model** tab or layout tab. These settings can even be saved in the drawing file as a named page setup, which can be recalled each time the drawing is plotted.

The settings that compose the page setup are set in the **Page Setup** dialog box. This dialog box is accessed by selecting **File** > **Page Setup Manager...** from the pull-down menu, picking the **Page Setup Manager** button in the **Layouts** toolbar, entering PAGESETUP, or right-clicking on a layout tab and selecting **Page Setup Manager...** from the shortcut menu. The **Page Setup Manager** dialog box is shown in **Figure 25-12A**.

The initial dialog box of **Page Setup Manager** is divided into two areas: **Page setups** in the upper area and **Selected page setup details** below. The **Page setups** area shows a list of the available page setups on the left. On the right are buttons labeled **Set Current**, **New**, **Modify**, and **Import**.

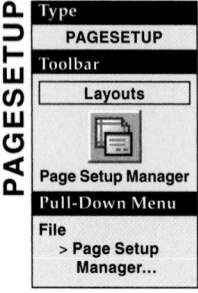

PAGESETUP

Type
PAGESETUP

Toolbar
Layouts
Page Setup Manager

Pull-Down Menu
File
> Page Setup Manager...

AutoCAD and Its Applications—Basics

Figure 25-12.
Creating a new page setup.

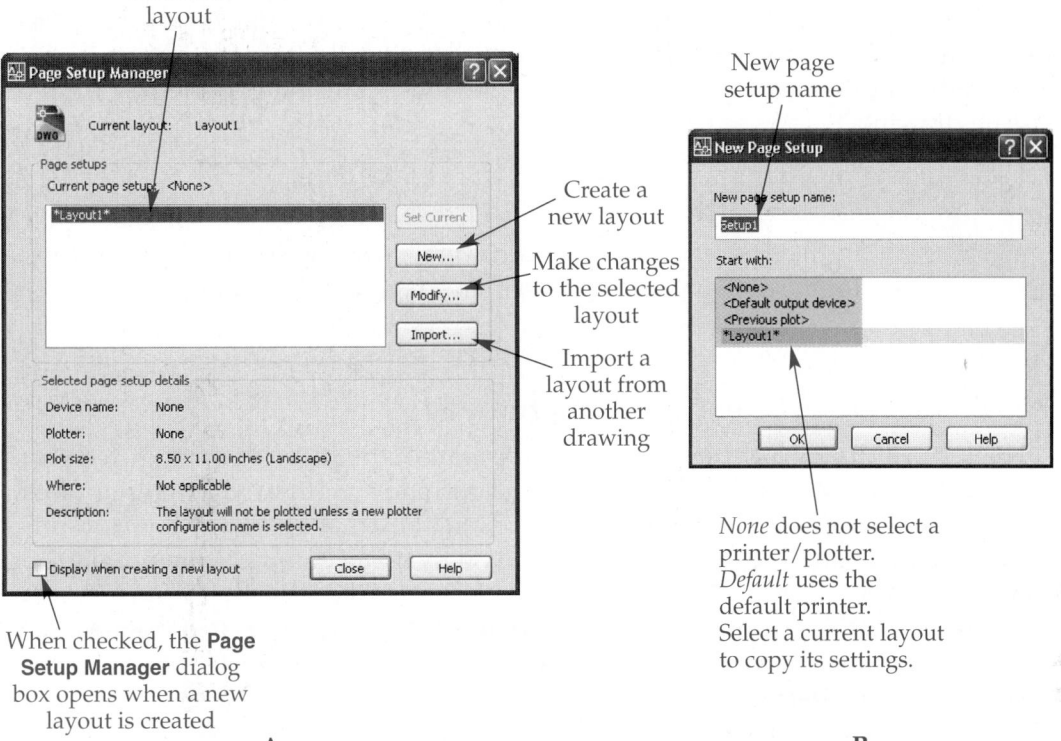

Selected layout

New page setup name

Create a new layout

Make changes to the selected layout

Import a layout from another drawing

None does not select a printer/plotter. *Default* uses the default printer. Select a current layout to copy its settings.

When checked, the **Page Setup Manager** dialog box opens when a new layout is created

A

B

Current layout or sheet set

Page setup name

C

The **Set Current** button attaches the highlighted page setup from the list of available page setups to the current layout. The **New...** button allows you to create a new page setup using the **New Page Setup** dialog box, as shown in Figure 25-12B. The **Modify...** button allows you to change the settings of an existing page setup. The **Page Setup** dialog box is displayed when you pick the **Modify...** button. See Figure 25-12C. The **Import...** button allows you to bring in previously created page setups from an existing drawing.

PROFESSIONAL TIP

In the planning stages of your work, create one or more page setups for the drawing and save them in a template drawing.

Plot Device Selection and Management

Before printing or plotting, make sure that your output device is configured properly. AutoCAD displays information about the currently configured printer or plotter in the **Printer/plotter** area of the **Page Setup** dialog box that appears when you press either the **New...** button or the **Modify...** button on the **Page Setup Manager** dialog box. See Figure 25-13.

The current device is displayed in the **Printer/plotter** area of the **Page Setup** dialog box. When additional devices are configured, you can make a different one current by picking it from the **Name:** drop-down list.

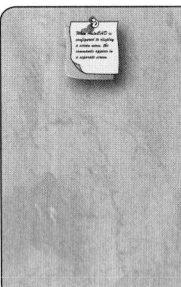

NOTE

You can add printers to the list by selecting **File > Plotter Manager...** from the pull-down menu. This executes the **PLOTTERMANAGER** command and displays the **Plotters** window. Select Add-A-Plotter Wizard to add, modify, and remove printing and plotting devices. When you install a plotter or printer using the Add-a-Plotter Wizard, AutoCAD creates a PC3 (plot configuration) file. This file contains all the settings required for the plotter to function.

Modifying the Plotter Configuration

To change the properties of the current plot device, pick the **Properties...** button in the **Printer/plotter** area. This opens the **Plotter Configuration Editor** dialog box. See Figure 25-14. Three tabs provide access to the plotting device property settings:

- **General tab.** Displays general information about the current plotter. The only item you can change is the description.

Figure 25-13.
The **Printer/plotter** area of the **Page Setup** dialog box.

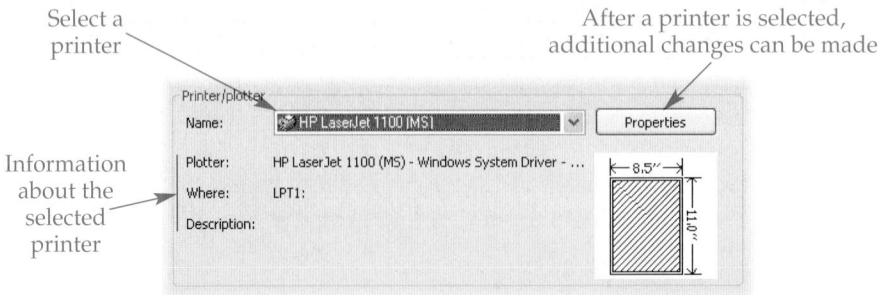

Figure 25-14.
The **Plotter Configuration Editor** dialog box. The **Device and Document Settings** tab is shown here.

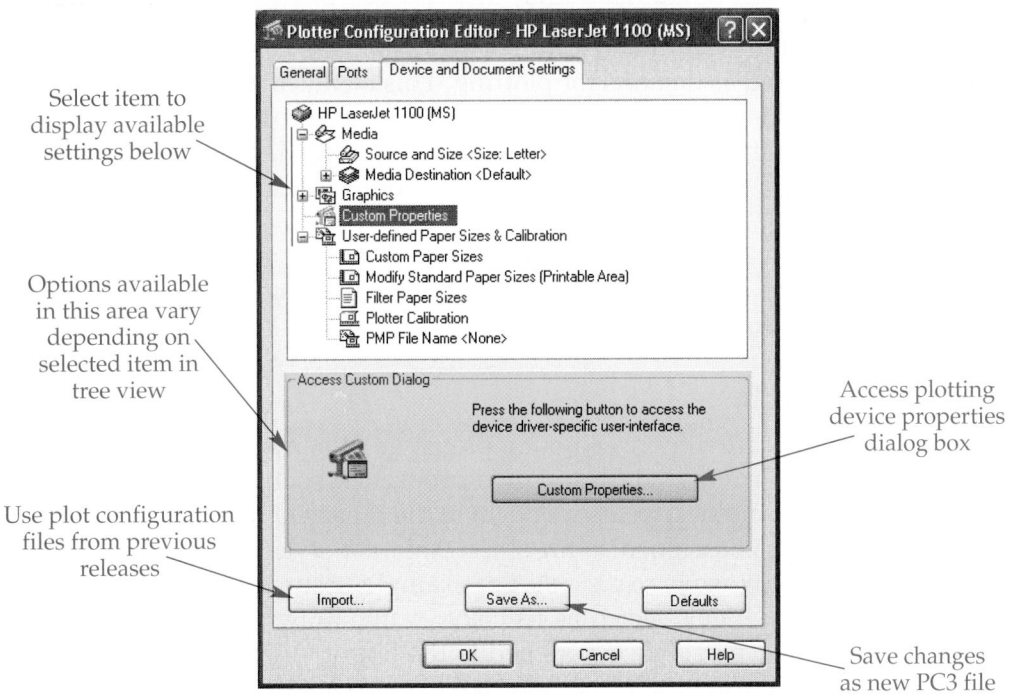

Select item to display available settings below

Options available in this area vary depending on selected item in tree view

Use plot configuration files from previous releases

Access plotting device properties dialog box

Save changes as new PC3 file

- **Ports tab.** Allows you to pick a port to send the plot to, plot to a file, or select **AutoSpool**. Using **AutoSpool**, plot files can be sent to a *plot spooler* file, which automatically plots the drawing in the background while you continue to work.

- **Device and Document Settings tab.** Displays a tree list of all the settings applicable to the current plotting device. Clicking on the desired icon enables you to modify specific settings. Items in this list that are displayed in brackets (< >) can be changed. The **Custom Properties** item is highlighted by default because it contains the properties most often changed. Pick the **Custom Properties...** button to display the properties dialog box specific to your plotter. Pick the **Save As...** button to save your changes to a PC3 file.

plot spooler: A file that manages and plots drawings automatically in the background while you work.

CAUTION

Avoid editing and saving modified PC3 files unless you have been instructed to do so. These files are critical to the proper functioning of your plotter.

Exercise 25-3
Complete the exercise on the Student CD.

Plot Styles

The properties of objects in an AutoCAD drawing, such as color, layer, linetype, and lineweight, are used as defaults for plotting. This means that all colors, linetypes, and lineweights will be plotted exactly as they appear in the drawing. You also have the ability to create multiple plots of the same drawing using different plot style tables. A *plot style table* is a named file that provides complete control over settings for plotted drawings.

plot style table:
A named file that provides complete control over plot style settings for plotted drawings.

Plot styles are a variety of settings that control, among other things, the color, thickness, linetype, line end treatment, and fill style of drawing objects. Plot styles can be assigned to any object or layer.

plot styles:
Settings that control color, thickness, linetype, line end treatment, and fill style of drawing objects in plotted drawings.

Plot Style Attributes

By default, objects are drawn without a plot style. When no plot style is applied, objects are plotted according to their assigned properties, such as color, linetype, and lineweight. The finished plot appears identical to the on-screen display.

When a plot style is assigned to an object, the plot style properties replace the object's properties *for plotting purposes only*. For example, assume a drawing has a layer named Blue, which has blue selected as its color. A line drawn on this layer appears blue on the screen. If no plot style is assigned to the line, it will plot as blue also. Now assume a plot style is created with the color red set as one of its properties. This plot style is assigned to the line. The line will now be plotted as red. However, the line still appears blue on the screen, because the plot style only takes effect when the object is plotted.

The following properties can be set in a plot style:

- **Color.** A color specified in a plot style overrides the object color in the drawing. The following options related to color can also be specified:
  - **Dithering.** *Dithering* is the mixture of dots of various colors to produce what appears to be a different color. Dithering is either enabled or disabled. It is ignored if the plotter does not support it. Dithering may create incorrect linetypes when plotting pale colors or thin lines. It is best to test dithering to see if it produces the expected results. Dithering can be used regardless of the object color selected.

dithering: The mixture of dots of various colors to produce what appears to be a different color.

  - **Convert to Grayscale.** If this option is selected, the object's colors are converted to grayscale if the plotter supports it. This option is illustrated in Figure 25-15.
  - **Use Assigned Pen Number.** This setting applies only to pen plotters. Available pens range from 1 to 32. The assigned pen number cannot be changed if the plot style color is set to Use object color, or if you are editing a plot style in a color-dependent plot style table. In these cases, the value is set to Automatic. If you enter 0 for the pen number, the field reads Automatic. AutoCAD selects a pen based on the plotter configuration.
  - **Virtual Pen Number.** Pen numbers between 1 and 255 allow non-pen plotters to simulate pen plotters using virtual pens. A 0 or Automatic setting instructs AutoCAD to assign a virtual pen from the AutoCAD Color Index (ACI).
  - **Screening.** This affects the amount of ink placed on the paper while plotting. A value of 0 produces the color white, and a value of 100 plots the color's full intensity. The effects of screening are shown in Figure 25-16.
  - **Linetype.** If you select a plot style linetype, it overrides the object's linetype when the drawing is plotted. The default value (Use object linetype) plots the object using the linetype displayed on-screen. An adaptive adjustment setting adjusts the linetype scale to keep the linetype pattern complete. This is activated by default.

Figure 25-15.
The effect of the Convert to grayscale plot style setting.

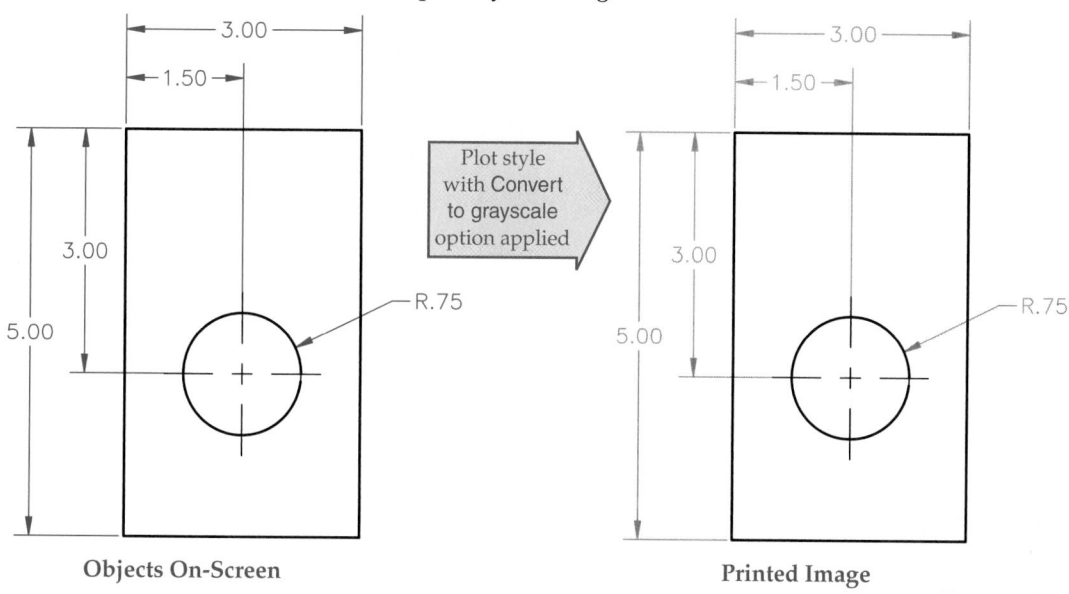

Objects On-Screen   Printed Image

Figure 25-16.
The effects of screening.

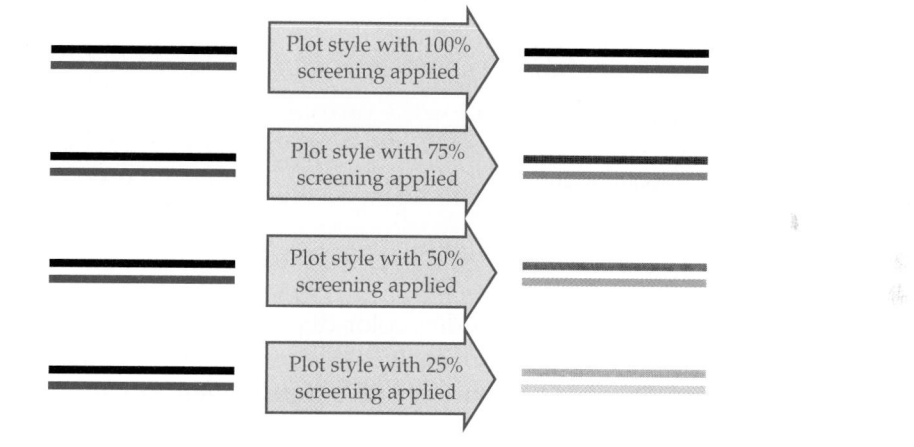

- **Lineweight.** Select a lineweight from this list if you want the plotted lineweight to override the object property in the AutoCAD drawing. The default value is Use object lineweight.
- **Line End Style.** If you select a line end style from this list, the line end style is added to the endpoints when the drawing is plotted. **Figure 25-17** illustrates the end style options. Note that the lines must be relatively thick for the end styles to be noticeable. The default setting is Use object end style.
- **Line Join Style.** If you select a line join style from this list, it overrides the object's line join style when the drawing is plotted. The default setting is Use object join style, but you can select one of the following line end styles: Miter, Bevel, Round, and Diamond.
- **Fill Style.** If you select a fill style from this list, it overrides the object's fill style when the drawing is plotted. The default setting is Use object fill style, but you can select one of the fill styles shown in **Figure 25-18**.

Figure 25-17.
Line end style options can be specified in a plot style.

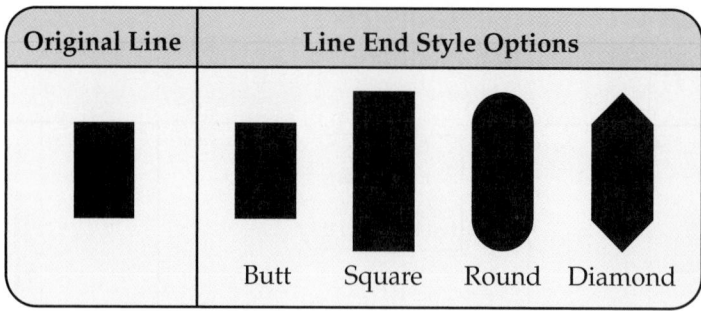

Figure 25-18.
These fill styles can be set in a plot style.

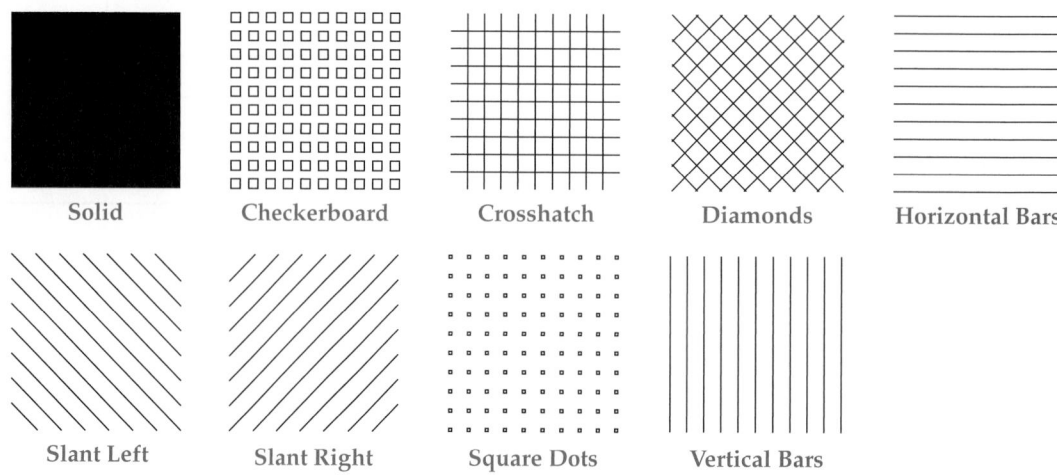

Plot Style Tables

AutoCAD has two plot style modes: color-dependent and named. You can create a *color-dependent plot style* in which each color can be assigned values for the various plotting properties. These settings are saved in a *color-dependent plot style table* file with a .ctb extension.

A *named plot style* is assigned to objects. The settings in the named plot style override the object properties when the object is plotted. *Named plot style tables* are saved in a file with an .stb extension. These tables allow you to use color properties in the drawing without having the object's color tied to its plotting characteristics. These tables are useful if, for example, you are working on a multiphase project in which different components of the drawing must be highlighted, subdued, or plotted in a specific lineweight or linetype.

AutoCAD includes several predefined plot style tables. You can also create and save your own customized tables. Plot style tables are given file names with .ctb or .stb extensions. These files are saved in the path set by the AutoCAD Plot Style Table Search Path. To verify the location of an AutoCAD plot style table, access the **Files** tab in the **Options** dialog box and check the path listed under the Plot Style Table Search Path, after expanding the **Printer Support File Path** selection.

To view the available plot style tables, select **File** > **Plot Style Manager...** from the pull-down menu or type STYLESMANAGER. The **Plot Styles** window is displayed. See **Figure 25-19.** The **Plot Styles** window displays icons for each of the saved plot style tables. There is also an icon to access the **Add Plot Style Table** wizard. You can double-click an icon to access the **Plot Style Table Editor** dialog box.

Figure 25-19.
Double-click an icon to edit a plot style table. Select the Add-A-Plot Style Table Wizard icon to create a new table.

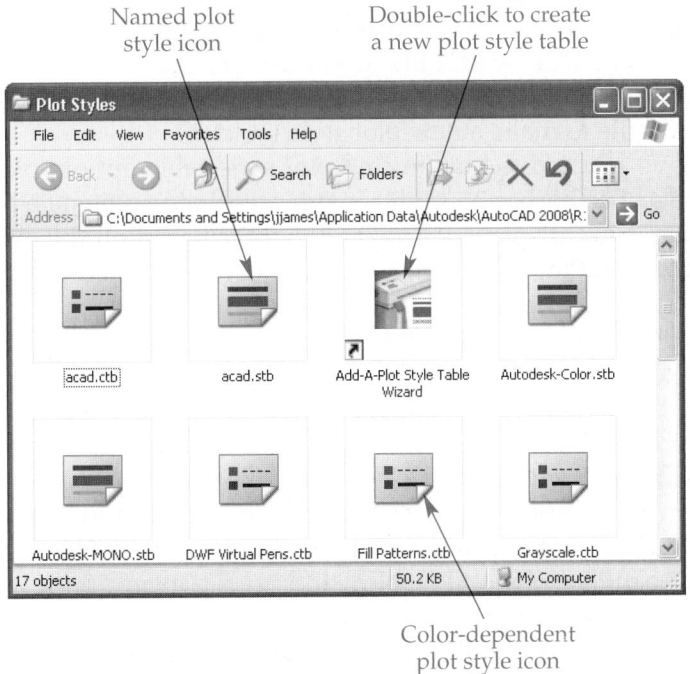

Named plot style icon

Double-click to create a new plot style table

Color-dependent plot style icon

Creating a plot style table

Create a named plot style table if you know that components of the drawing or project, such as layouts, layers, and objects, will be plotted at different times using different colors, linetypes, lineweights, or area fills.

Plot style tables are created using the **Add Plot Style Table** wizard. To access this wizard, select **Tools** > **Wizards** > **Add Plot Style Table...** from the pull-down menu. You can also select the Add-A-Plot Style Table Wizard icon in the **Plot Styles** window. The **Add Plot Style Table** wizard is displayed. Read the introductory page and pick **Next** to access the **Begin** page. See **Figure 25-20.** Four options are available:

- **Start from scratch.** Constructs a new plot style table. The **Browse File** page is skipped with this option because the new plot style table is not based on any existing settings.

Figure 25-20.
Select the basis for the plot style table in the **Begin** page of the **Add Plot Style Table** wizard.

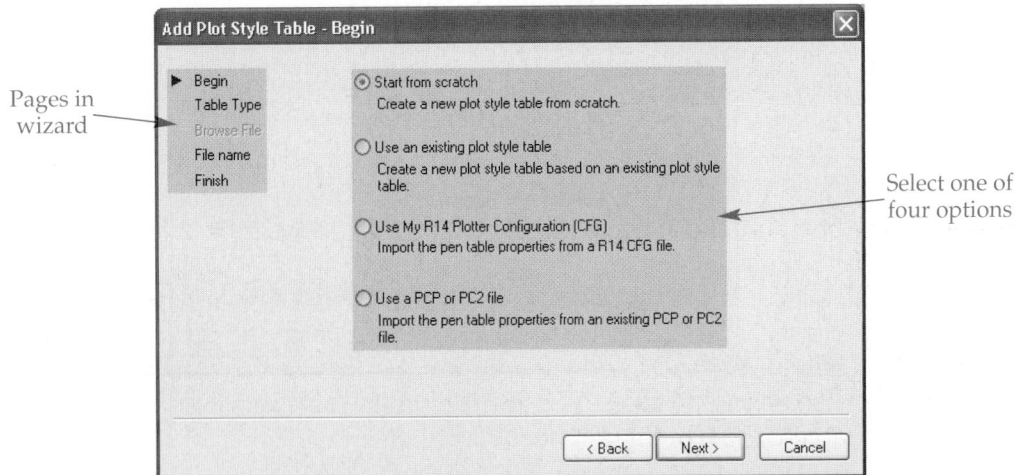

Pages in wizard

Select one of four options

- **Use an existing plot style table.** Copies an existing plot style table to be used as a template for a new one.
- **Use My R14 Plotter Configuration (CFG).** Copies the pen assignments from the acad14.cfg file to be used as a template for a new one. Use this option if you did not save either a PCP or PC2 file in Release 14.
- **Use a PCP or PC2 file.** Uses pen assignments saved previously in a Release 14 PCP or PC2 file to make a new plot style table.

After you have selected the beginning plot style table option, pick **Next** to go to the **Table Type** page. See **Figure 25-21.** If the **Use an existing plot style table** option was selected, this page is not displayed. The table type is based on the existing plot style table. Select the **Named Plot Style Table** option to use the named plot style mode, and then pick **Next**.

Select the file on which the plot style table is to be based in the **Browse File** page. This page is not displayed if the **Start from scratch** option was selected. Enter the file name in the text box or pick the **Browse...** button to display a **Select File** dialog box. The type of file you select depends on the selected beginning plot style table option. If you are using a CFG file, you must also select the plotter or printer to use.

After selecting the appropriate file, pick the **Next** button to access the **File name** page. See **Figure 25-22.** Enter a name for the new plot style table. A .ctb extension is added to color-dependent plot style tables, and an .stb extension is added to named plot style tables.

After you have entered the plot style table name, pick **Next** to display the **Finish** page. See **Figure 25-23.** Pick the check box at the bottom of the page to attach this plot style table to all new drawings by default. That is, the plot style table will be listed in the **Plot style table area** of the **Page Setup** dialog box. This check box is only available if you are creating a plot style using the mode (color-dependent or named) specified in the **Default plot style behavior for new drawings** area of the **Plot Style Table Settings** dialog box.

Pick **Finish** to create the new plot style table. The new file is saved in the folder path set by the Plot Style Table Search Path. To verify the location of this file, access the **Files** tab in the **Options** dialog box and check the path listed under the Plot Style Table Search Path after expanding the **Printer Support File Path** selection. A corresponding icon is added to the **Plot Styles** window.

Figure 25-21.
Select the plot style mode in the **Table Type** page.

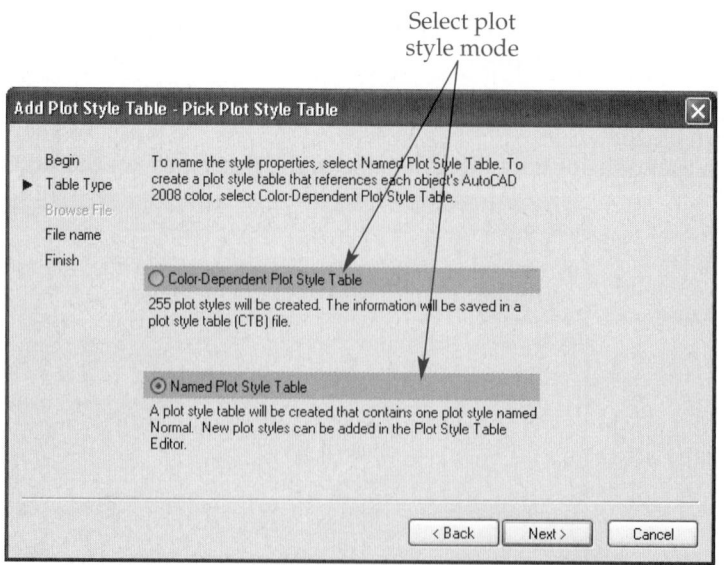

Figure 25-22.
Enter the name for the plot style table in the **File name** page.

Enter name for plot style table

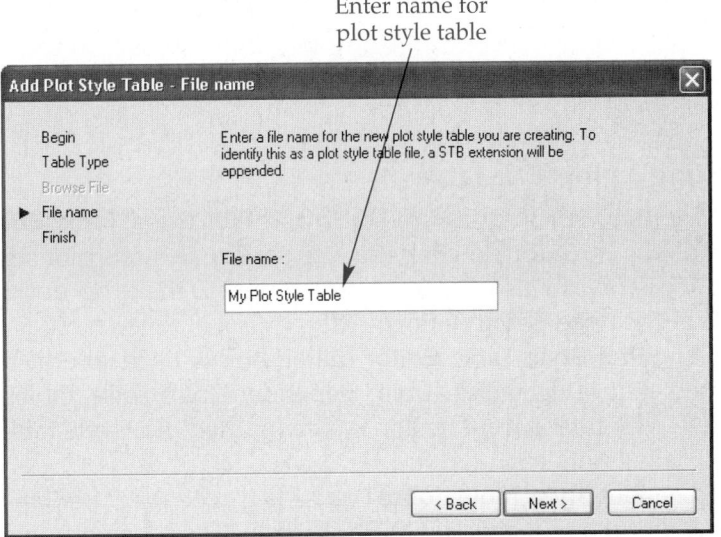

Figure 25-23.
The **Finish** page allows you to edit the new plot style table immediately and to attach the new table to all new drawings (if the plot style mode matches the setting in the **Options** dialog box).

Pick to edit plot style table

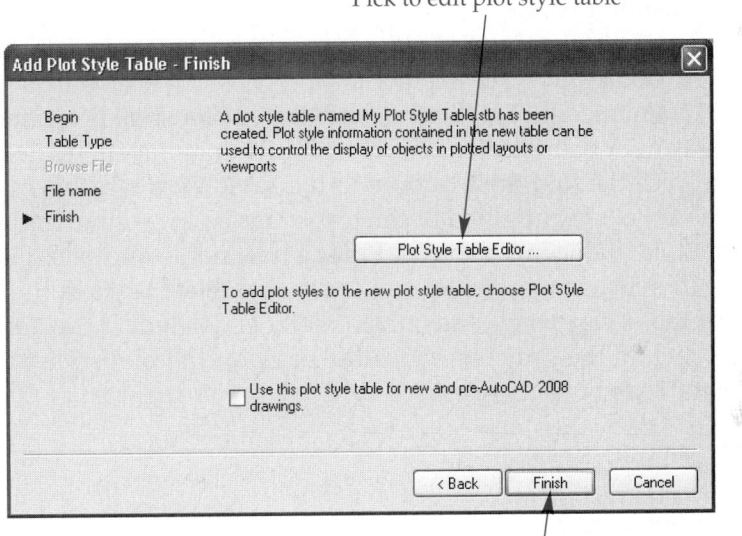

Pick to exit wizard

NOTE

The **Wizards** cascading menu contains both **Add Plot Style Table...** and **Add Color-Dependent Plot Style Table...** options. The plot style mode set for the drawing determines which option is available. The pages in these wizards are identical to the **Add Plot Style Table** wizard with the following exceptions:

- On the **Begin** page, the **Use an existing plot style table** option is not available.
- There is no **Table Type** page.
- The **Finish** page includes an option to attach the new plot style table to the current drawing.

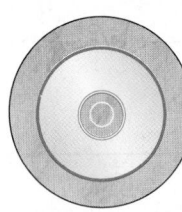

Editing a plot style table

Plot style properties are set in the **Plot Style Table Editor** dialog box. To access this dialog box, double-click the icon for the desired plot style table in the **Plot Styles** window. You can also select the button next to the drop-down list in the **Plot style table** area in the **Page Setup** dialog box.

The **Plot Style Table Editor** dialog box is used to edit both color-dependent and named plot style tables. Color-dependent plot style tables contain 255 preset plot styles—one for each ACI color. A new named plot style table contains one preset plot style called Normal.

The **Plot Style Table Editor** contains three tabs. The **General** tab contains information about the plot style table. See **Figure 25-24.** Enter a description in the text box. If the **Apply global scale factor to non-ISO linetypes and fill patterns** check box is checked, AutoCAD scales all non-ISO linetypes and fill patterns by the value entered in the **Scale factor** text box.

The **Table View** and **Form View** tabs are used to set the plot style attributes and, for named plot style tables, to create and delete plot styles. These tabs are shown in **Figure 25-25.**

In a named plot style table, the Normal plot style is created automatically. This plot style cannot be modified and is assigned to all layers by default. To create a new plot style, pick the **Add Style** button. In the **Table View** tab, this inserts a new table with the name Style *n* highlighted at the top. Enter a new name. In the **Form View** tab, the **Add Plot Style** dialog box appears. Enter a new name and pick the **OK** button.

To delete a named plot style, pick the **Delete Style** button in either tab. If the **Form View** tab is displayed, the current style is deleted. If the **Table View** tab is displayed, first pick in the gray bar above the name of the plot style to be deleted, then pick the **Delete Style** button.

Figure 25-24.
Information about a plot style table is located in the **General** tab of the **Plot Style Table Editor** dialog box.

Plot style table being edited

Enter a description for the plot style table

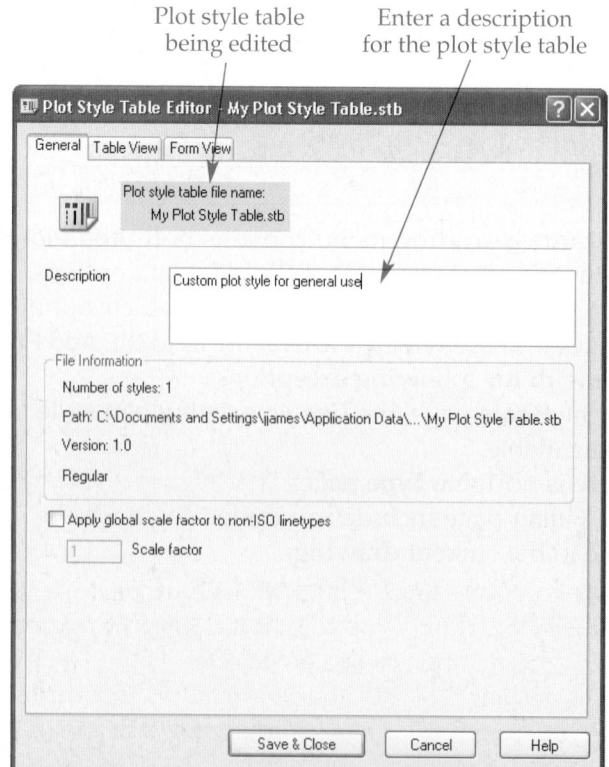

Figure 25-25.
Plot style table settings are modified in the **Plot Style Table Editor** dialog box.

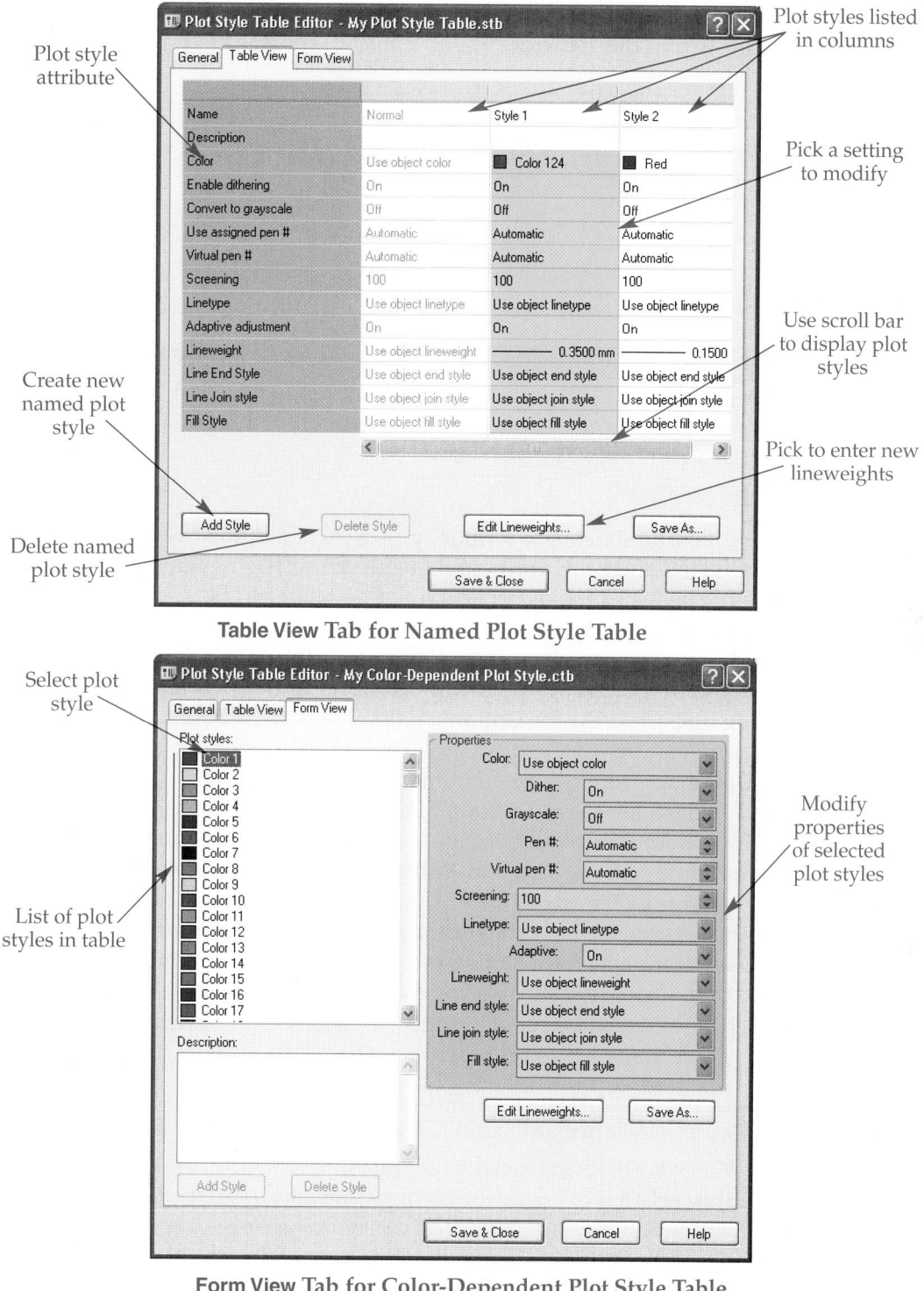

Table View Tab for Named Plot Style Table

Form View Tab for Color-Dependent Plot Style Table

To modify plot style attributes in the **Table View** tab, first use the scroll bar to display the plot style to be edited. When you pick the value to be changed, a text box or drop-down list allows you to edit it. This editing procedure is similar to changing object properties in the **Properties** palette.

The **Form View** tab lists all the attributes in a different format. To view all of the settings for a specific plot style, simply pick the plot style in the **Plot styles:** list box.

The properties of the selected plot style are listed in the **Properties** area. Modify the properties using the drop-down lists provided.

Pick the **Save As...** button to change the table name, or pick the **Save & Close** button to save the current file and exit.

NOTE

Once a plot style table is created, it can be used on new drawings and drawings created in previous releases of AutoCAD.

Exercise 25-5
Complete the exercise on the Student CD.

Applying Plot Styles

In order to assign plot styles, one or more plot style tables must be specified in the drawing. The **Model** tab and each individual layout tab can be assigned one plot style table each. Only the styles in the assigned plot style table can be applied within the layout.

The plot style mode (color-dependent or named) for a drawing is determined when the drawing is first created. The setting is found in the **Plot and Publish** tab of the **Options** dialog box. To access the **Options** dialog box, select **Tools > Options...** from the pull-down menu or enter OP or OPTIONS. You can also right-click in the drawing area and select **Options...** from the shortcut menu.

The **Plot and Publish** tab of the **Options** dialog box is shown in Figure 25-26A. To set options having to do with plot styles, pick the **Plot Style Table Settings...** button at the lower-right corner of the **Plot and Publish** tab. The **Plot Style Table Settings** dialog box is displayed in Figure 25-26B. The plot style mode for new drawings is determined by the setting in the **Default plot style behavior for new drawings** area. By default, the **Use color dependent plot styles** option is selected. When this option is selected, all new drawings are set to use color-dependent plot styles. The default plot style behavior setting can also be set using the **PSTYLEPOLICY** system variable (0 for named plot style mode and 1 for color-dependent mode).

NOTE

When you use a template to create a new drawing, the template's plot style settings override the settings you specify in the **Options** dialog box. AutoCAD's default acad.dwt template uses a color-dependent plot style table, so all new drawings created with this template will use color-dependent plot styles. To avoid this, either create and use a template that uses named plot styles or use AutoCAD's predefined acad -Named plot styles.dwt drawing template instead of acad.dwt.

The **Default plot style table** drop-down list can be used to set a default plot style table. When None is selected, objects in the new drawing are plotted based on their on-screen properties. The default plot style table is applied to the **Model** tab and layout tabs in new drawings. However, the plot style table can be changed at any time in the **Page Setup** dialog box.

Figure 25-26.
Use the **Plot and Publish** tab of the **Options** dialog box to set default plot style modes and tables for new drawings.

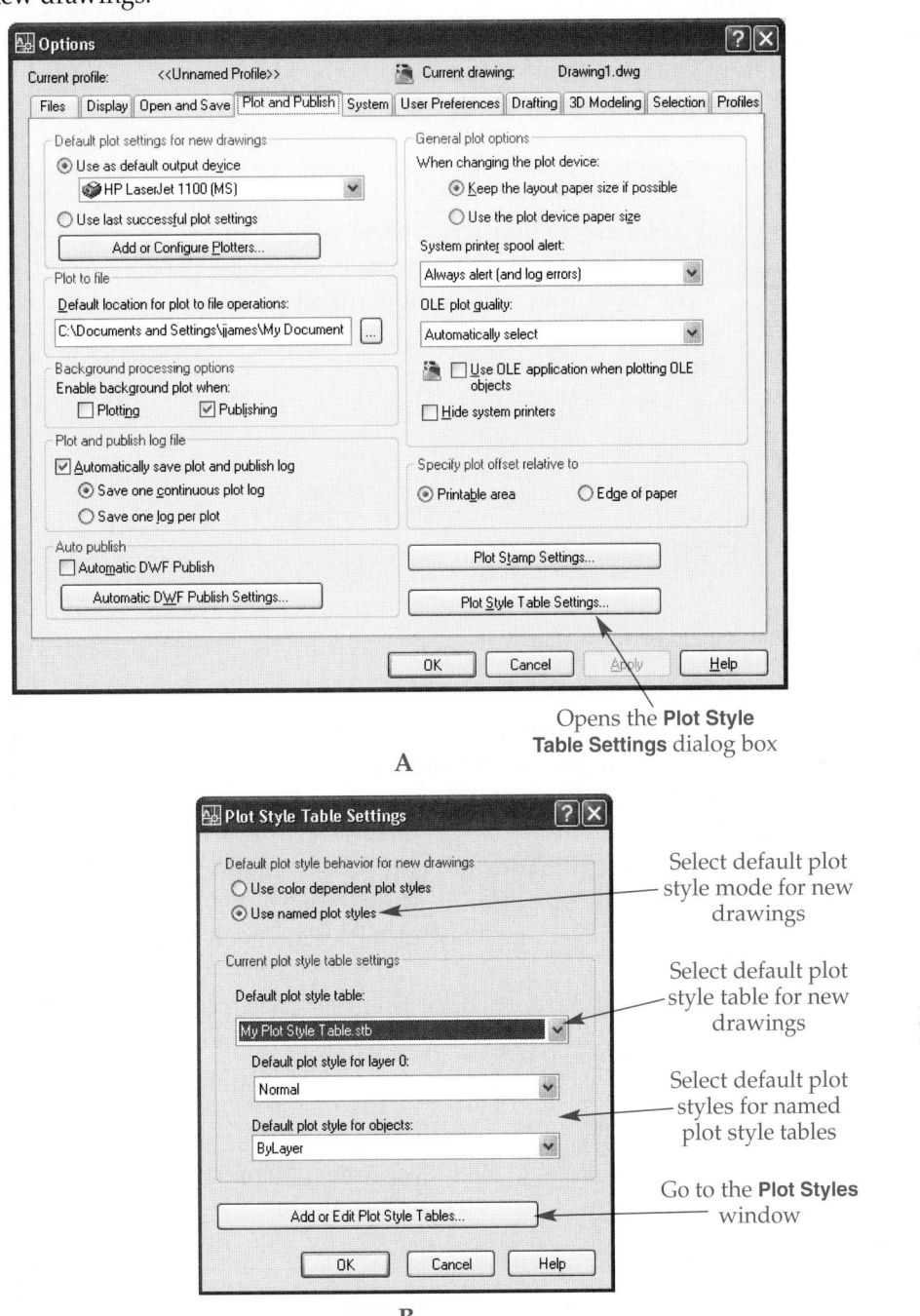

Opens the **Plot Style Table Settings** dialog box

A

Select default plot style mode for new drawings

Select default plot style table for new drawings

Select default plot styles for named plot style tables

Go to the **Plot Styles** window

B

If you select the **Use named plot styles** option, the drop-down lists below the default plot style table are activated. You can select the default plot styles for layer 0 and for objects. You can select any plot styles from the default plot style table.

The **Add or Edit Plot Style Tables...** button accesses the **Plot Styles** window. This window allows you to edit existing plot style tables and create new plot style tables.

Applying color-dependent plot styles

Color-dependent plot style tables contain 255 plot styles—one for each color available for display in AutoCAD. You cannot add or delete plot styles in a color-dependent table. When you assign a color-dependent plot style table to a layout, the property values set for the plot styles override the on-screen display values during plotting.

Color-dependent plot styles can only be applied to drawings created while the **Use color dependent plot styles** option was selected as the default plot style behavior in the **Options** dialog box. To assign a color-dependent plot style table, access the **Page Setup Manager**, select the **Modify...** button, and pick the plot style table from the **Plot style table** drop-down list of the **Page Setup** dialog box. See **Figure 25-27.** The selected plot style table is applied to the active **Model** or layout tab.

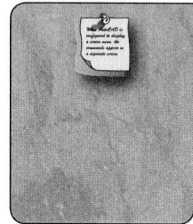

NOTE

A color-dependent plot style table cannot be attached to layers or objects because they may be composed of a variety of colors. Remember that a color-dependent plot style table should be used only when you want to show all lines of a single color plotted exactly the same color.

Exercise 25-6
Complete the exercise on the Student CD.

Applying named plot styles

In order for named plot styles to be used in a drawing, the drawing must have been created with the **Use named plot styles** option selected as the default plot style behavior in the **Options** dialog box. The drawing could also be based on a template with named plot styles.

The **Model** tab and each layout tab can have a named plot style table attached. When you select a plot style table for the **Model** tab, you are also presented the option of selecting the plot style table for all layout tabs. However, each layout tab can have a different plot style table.

Once the named plot style tables have been assigned, plot styles can be assigned to objects and layers. A plot style assigned to an object overrides a plot style assigned to a layer, just as a color or linetype assigned to an object overrides the layer setting.

Plot styles can be assigned to layers in the **Layer Properties Manager** dialog box only when the drawing was created with a named plot style. See **Figure 25-28.** To access this dialog box, pick the **Layer Properties Manager** button from the **Layers** toolbar, select **Format > Layer...** from the pull-down menu, or enter LA or LAYER.

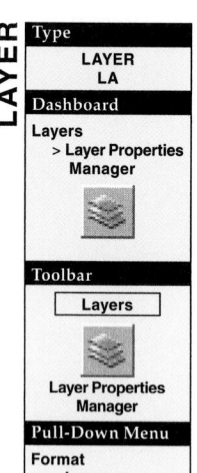

LAYER

Type
LAYER
LA
Dashboard
Layers
> Layer Properties Manager

Toolbar
Layers
Layer Properties Manager

Pull-Down Menu
Format
> Layer...

Figure 25-27.
Selecting a plot style table for a page setup.

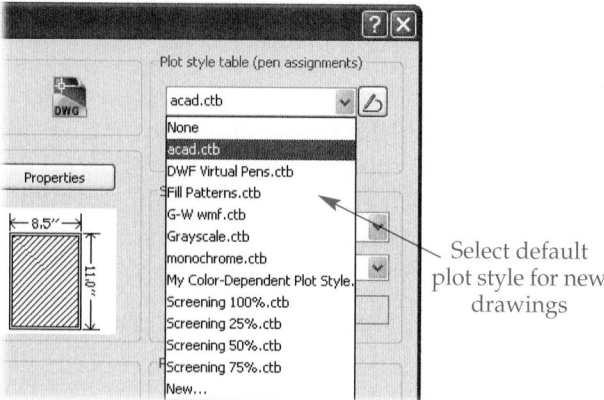

Plot style table (pen assignments)

acad.ctb

None
acad.ctb
DWF Virtual Pens.ctb
Fill Patterns.ctb
G-W wmf.ctb
Grayscale.ctb
monochrome.ctb
My Color-Dependent Plot Style.ctb
Screening 100%.ctb
Screening 25%.ctb
Screening 50%.ctb
Screening 75%.ctb
New...

Select default plot style for new drawings

Figure 25-28.
Named plot styles can be assigned to layers using the **Layer Properties Manager** dialog box.

Pick plot style name for layer
to select a different plot style

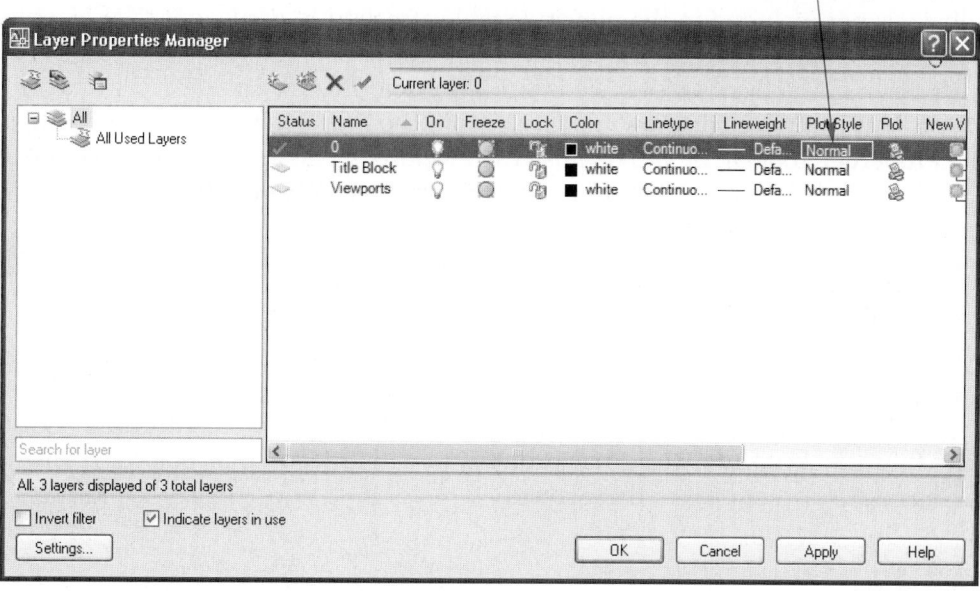

To modify the plot style, pick the current plot style listed for the layer. The **Select Plot Style** dialog box is displayed, as shown in **Figure 25-29.** This dialog box lists the plot styles available in the plot style table attached to the current tab. You can select a different plot style table from the **Active plot style table:** drop-down list. If you cannot select another plot style, the drawing was created with a color-dependent plot style. Pick the **Editor...** button to access the **Plot Style Table Editor** dialog box.

You can assign different plot styles to different views on the same layer. To assign a plot style to a specific viewport, make that viewport active. Then use the **VP Plot Style** column of the **Layer Properties Manager** dialog box to select a plot style, just as you assigned a plot style to a layer in the previous paragraph. A plot style assigned to a viewport within a layer overrides the plot style assigned to that layer under the **Plot Style** column.

Figure 25-29.
Use the **Select Plot Style** dialog box to select a plot style for a layer.

Pick plot style
for layer from list
of plot styles in
plot style table

Current plot
style table

Identifies
current
layout tab

Access **Plot Style
Table Editor**
dialog box

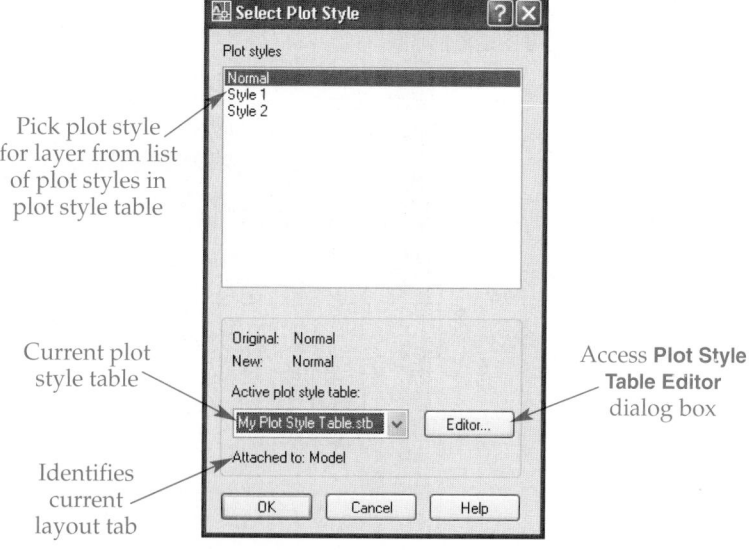

Named plot styles can also be applied to objects. When a plot style is applied to an object, the plot style remains attached to the object in all layout tabs. If the plot style attached to the object is contained in the plot style table attached to the layout tab, the object is plotted with the plot style settings. However, if the plot style assigned to the object is not included in the plot style table attached to the layout tab, the object is plotted according to its on-screen display settings.

Modifying an object's plot style is similar to modifying an object's layer, color, or linetype. You can select the new plot style from the **Plot Style Control** drop-down list in the **Properties** toolbar, or you can use the **Properties** palette to change the plot style. See **Figure 25-30**. Selecting the **Other...** option displays the **Select Plot Style** dialog box.

NOTE

Every AutoCAD object and layer is automatically assigned a plot style. If the current drawing is set to use a named plot style table, the default plot style for objects in the drawing is ByLayer. The default plot style for a layer is Normal. Objects plotted with these settings keep their original properties. This means that objects retain the properties of their layers.

Exercise 25-7

Complete the exercise on the Student CD.

Figure 25-30.
Assigning a new plot style to an object. A—Using the **Plot Style Control** drop-down list in the **Properties** toolbar. B—Using the **Properties** palette.

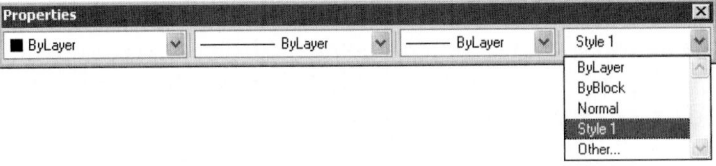

A

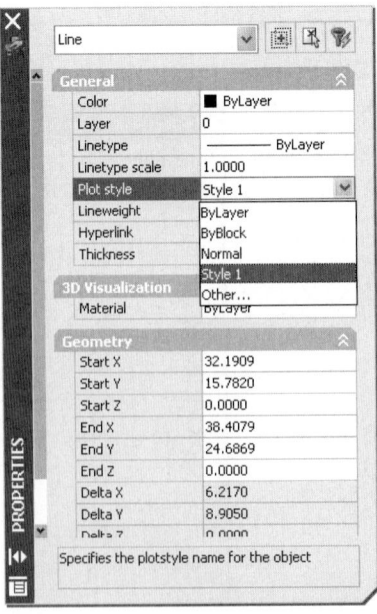

B

Viewing Plot Style Effects before You Plot

It is possible to display plot style effects on-screen to see how they will appear. To do so, pick the **Display plot styles** check box in the **Plot style table** area in the **Page Setup** dialog box. Keep in mind that these two display features can increase the time required to regenerate drawings and may decrease the performance of AutoCAD.

A quicker method is to use the print preview option in the **Plot** dialog box, as discussed later in this chapter. This displays all lineweights and plot styles exactly as they will appear on the plotted drawing.

Plot Settings

A majority of the settings that must be considered prior to plotting can be established and saved in layouts, viewports, layers, plot style tables, and template drawings. If you plan your work well, you will have to adjust few, if any, settings prior to plotting. Take a look at some of the items required for plotting, and where they can be saved.

Item	Location
Border and title block	Layout
View scales	Viewport (**Zoom XP**)
Text height	Drawing
Object color, lineweight, and end style	Layers and plot style tables
Plot device	Page setup
Plot style table	Page setup
Paper size and drawing orientation	Page setup
Plot scale, area, offset, and options	Page setup

If you prepare for plotting as soon as you begin a new drawing, the act of plotting may mean just a few clicks of your pointing device.

Selecting the desired output device and plot style table was discussed earlier in this chapter. Once these settings are complete, you can elaborate on the plot settings in the **Page Setup** dialog box of the **Page Setup Manager** or in the **Plot** dialog box. See Figure 25-31.

Paper Size, Units, and Drawing Orientation

The **Paper size** area of the **Plot** dialog box controls the paper size. Select the appropriate paper size from the drop-down list. Paper sizes are listed in inches or millimeters.

The **Drawing orientation** area of the **Plot** dialog box controls the plot rotation. You may need to select the ">" (more options) button in the lower-right corner of the **Plot** dialog box to see this area. **Portrait** orients the long side of the paper vertically and is the standard orientation for most written documents printed on 8.5 × 11 paper. **Landscape** orients the long side of the paper horizontally, and is the default for AutoCAD drawings. If you consider landscape format to be a rotation angle of 0°, the following table should help you determine how to use the **Plot upside-down button** option to achieve several rotation angles.

Figure 25-31.
The **Plot** dialog box.

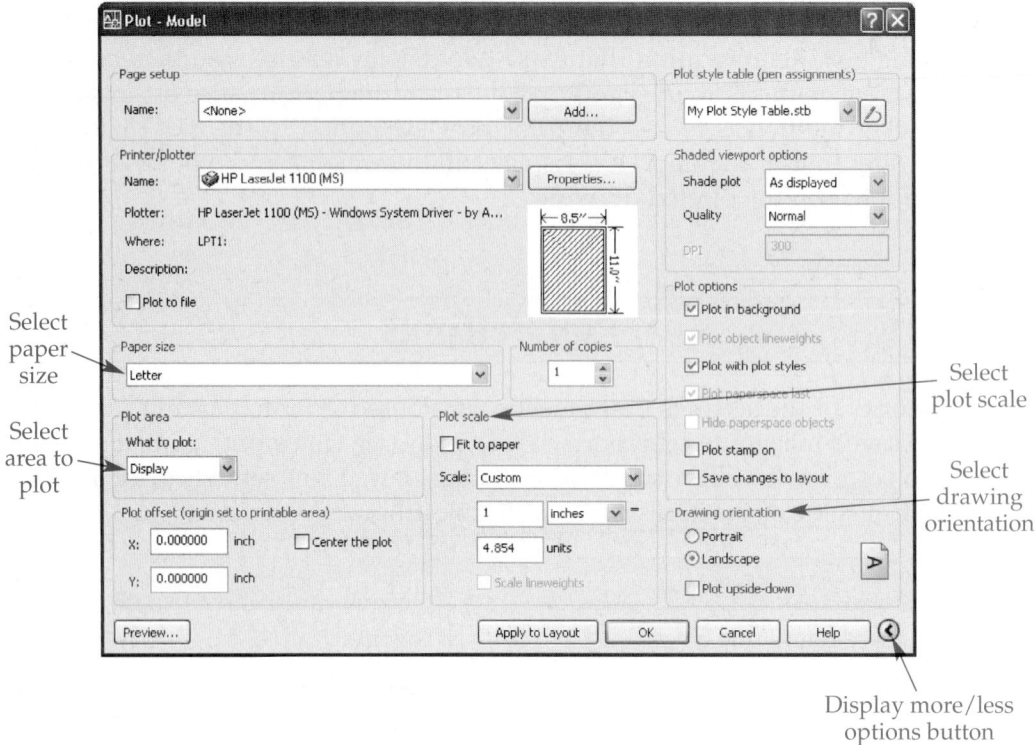

Orientation Buttons	Rotation Angle
Landscape	0°
Portrait	90°
Upside-down landscape	180°
Upside-down portrait	270°

In AutoCAD, the horizontal screen measurement relates to the long side of the paper (landscape format). However, you might create a drawing, form, or chart in portrait format. This format orients the long side of the plot vertically. AutoCAD rotates plots in 90° increments, as shown in the previous table.

Plotting Area

The **Plot area** section of the **Plot** dialog box allows you to choose the portion of the drawing to be plotted and how it is to be plotted. The options in the drop-down list are:

- **Layout/Limits.** The **Layout** option is displayed when you plot a layout. Everything inside the margins of the layout is plotted. The **Limits** option is displayed when you plot from the **Model** tab. This option plots everything inside the defined drawing limits.
- **Extents.** The **Extents** option plots only the area of the drawing in which objects are drawn. Before using this option, zoom the extents to include all drawn objects to verify exactly what will be plotted. Be aware that border lines around your drawing (such as the title block) may be clipped off if they are at the extreme edge of the screen. This often happens because you are asking the plotter to plot at the extreme edge of its active area.
- **Display.** This option plots the current screen display.

- **View.** Use this option to plot named views, which were discussed in Chapter 6. This option is not shown if no views have been saved in the drawing. Select the name of the view from the drop-down list. This option is available only when the **Model** tab is current.
- **Window.** When this option is selected, the dialog box disappears temporarily so that you can pick two opposite corners to define a window around the area to be plotted. A **Window...** button will now be displayed in the **Plot area** region. This button can be used to redefine the opposite corners of a window around the portion of the drawing to be plotted.

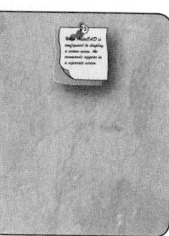

NOTE

If the window you define is too close to an object, some portion of that object may be clipped off in your plot. If this happens, simply adjust the window size the next time you plot. You can prevent these errors by using the plot preview option to see what exactly will be plotted.

Shaded Viewport Options

AutoCAD allows viewports to be plotted in shaded modes. You may need to select the ">" button in the lower-right corner of the **Plot** dialog box to see this area. The options in the **Shade plot** drop-down list pertain to 3D models and are explained in *AutoCAD and Its Applications—Advanced*. For 2D drawings, leave this setting at the default **As Displayed**. The **Quality** drop-down list provides options for setting the quality of the plot. Each predefined quality setting has a certain dots-per-inch (dpi) setting associated with it. If you choose **Custom** in the **Quality:** drop-down list, enter a value in the **DPI:** text box.

Plot Offset

The **Plot offset** area controls how far the drawing is offset from either the lower-left corner of the paper or the lower-left corner of the printable area. See **Figure 25-32**. This depends on how the **Specify plot offset relative to** area has been set in the **Publish and Plot** tab of the **Options** dialog box.

To begin plotting a drawing at the origin (either the lower-left corner of the plot media or the lower-left corner of the printable area, as described in the previous paragraph), leave the values shown in the **X:** and **Y:** text boxes at 0.00. If you want to move the drawing away from the default origin, change the required values in the text boxes. For example, to move the drawing four units to the right and three units above the plotter origin, enter 4 in the **X:** text box, and 3 in the **Y:** text box.

Figure 25-32.
The **Plot offset** area controls how far the drawing is offset from the lower-left corner of the paper.

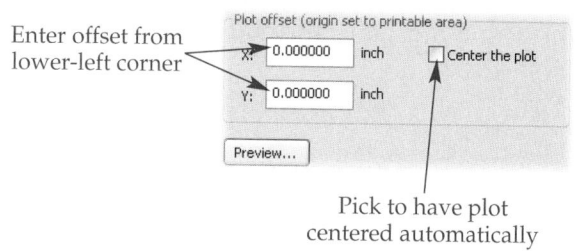

Other Plotting Options

The **Plot options** area of the **Plot** dialog box contains a list of items that can affect how, and if, objects appear on your plots, especially relating to paper space and model space objects. You may need to select the ">" button in the lower right of the **Plot** dialog box to see this area. Apply these options only when required for the plot by picking the appropriate check box. The following options are available:

- **Plot in background.** Allows you to continue working in AutoCAD while your computer processes the plot.
- **Plot object lineweights.** Plots lines having a lineweight other than 0 using the appropriate thickness. This box is checked by default.
- **Plot with plot styles.** Plots all plot styles attached to the drawing and its components.
- **Plot paperspace last.** Plots paper space objects last. (Paper space objects are plotted first by default.) Since no paper space objects are present in the **Model** tab, this option is available only when you plot from a layout tab.
- **Hide paperspace objects.** Removes hidden lines from 3D objects that have been created in paper space. This option is only available when you are plotting from a layout tab and affects only objects drawn in paper space. It does not affect any 3D objects in a viewport.
- **Plot stamp on.** Attaches a plot stamp along the edge of the plot. See the "Adding a Plot Stamp" section later in this chapter.
- **Save changes to layout.** Allows any changes made to the settings in the **Plot** dialog box to be saved to the layout as the default page setup for the layout.

Determining Drawing Scale Factors

The proper scale factor is vitally important because it ensures that text, dimension values, and dimensioning entities (such as arrowheads and tick marks) placed in model space are plotted at the proper size. The scale factor of the viewport should be established by the time you are ready to add annotation (text and dimensions) and before you plot. To obtain the correct text height, the desired plotted text height is multiplied by the scale factor. The scale factor is also used in scaling dimensions.

NOTE

Determine the viewport scale and scale factor when you begin to annotate the drawing. If you find the viewport scale factor needs to be changed after adding annotation, you may need to update dimensions and text if they were not created with the annotative property turned on. Annotative properties of text are discussed in Chapter 9.

The scale factor is always the reciprocal of the viewport scale. For example, if you wish to set a viewport in a mechanical drawing to a scale of 1/2″ = 1″, calculate the scale factor as follows:

> 1/2″ = 1″
> .5″ = 1″
> 1 ÷ .5 = 2 *(The scale factor is 2)*

For a viewport in an architectural drawing set to a scale of 1/4″ = 1′-0″, calculate the scale factor as follows:

> 1/4″ = 1′-0″
> .25″ = 12″
> 12 ÷ .25 = 48 *(The scale factor is 48)*

For a viewport in a civil engineering drawing that has been set to a scale of 1″ = 60′, calculate the scale factor as follows:

> 1″ = 60′
>
> 1″ = 60 × 12 = 720″ *(The scale factor is 720)*

Once the scale factor of the viewport has been determined, you must calculate the height of non-annotative text in model space. If text height is to be plotted at 1/8″, it should not be drawn at that height unless the text is being placed in paper space or the viewport is set to a scale of 1:1, or full scale. Remember, all geometry created in model space should be drawn at full scale.

For example, if you are working on a civil engineering drawing with a viewport set to a scale of 1″ = 60′, the scale factor equals 720. Non-annotative text drawn 1/8″ high appears as a dot within the viewport. The full-size civil engineering drawing in model space is 720 times larger than it will be when viewed and plotted with the viewport set to the proper scale. Therefore, you must multiply the text height by 720 in order to get text that appears in correct proportion within the viewport. For 1/8″ high text to appear correctly within the viewport, calculate the model space text height as follows:

> 1/8″ × 720
>
> .125 × 720 = 90 *(The proper height of the text is 90)*

Remember, scale factors and text heights should be determined before placing annotation in model space. A common practice is to have text styles with predefined text heights and dimension styles with predefined overall scale settings based on commonly used viewport scale factors for your industry, stored within your template drawing files.

Scaling the Plot

Model space geometry is created at full scale, and the drawing is scaled in a viewport on a layout to fit on the sheet size. The **Plot scale** area of the **Plot** dialog box is used to specify the plot scale. The **Scale:** drop-down list contains a selection of 34 different decimal and architectural scales, including Custom. See **Figure 25-33**. These are the same scales that are used and appear in the drop-down list on the **Viewports** toolbar or on the pop-up list on the status bar when you set the scale of the viewports. The text boxes below the predefined scales drop-down list allow you to specify the plot scale

Figure 25-33.
The **Scale:** drop-down list contains a selection of 34 different decimal and architectural scales, including Custom.

Select **Fit to paper** if scale is not a concern

Enter values here for a custom plot scale

Adjust lineweights as the plot scale changes

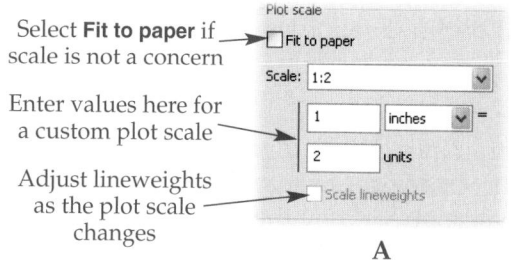

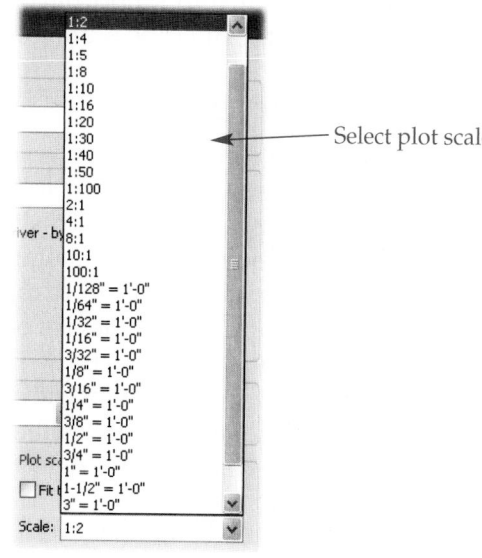

Select plot scale

A

B

as a ratio of plotted units to drawing units. An architectural drawing to be plotted at 1/4″ = 1′-0″ can be entered in the text boxes as:

$$1/4″ = 1′ \; or \; .25 = 12 \; or \; 1 = 48$$

A mechanical drawing to be plotted at a scale of 1/2″ = 1″ can be entered in the text boxes as:

$$1/2″ = 1″ \; or \; .5 = 1 \; or \; 1 = 2$$

Since the paper size is set in the page setup, and the viewports are scaled on the layouts themselves, there is rarely a need to change the scale factor in the **Plot** dialog box or the **Page Setup** dialog box to anything other than 1:1 when you print a layout. However, if you are plotting from model space, you do need to set a specific scale other than 1:1.

Pick the **Fit to paper** check box above the predefined scales drop-down list if you want AutoCAD to adjust your drawing automatically to fit on the paper. This is useful if you have a C-size pen plotter but need to plot a D-size or E-size drawing. However, keep in mind that you may have considerable blank space left on the paper, depending on the size and proportions of your drawing.

Before you plot a drawing, always check the **LTSCALE** and **PSLTSCALE** system variables. These variables control model space and paper space linetype scaling. The **LTSCALE** variable is set to a value representing the scale factor to be applied to linetypes that contain dashes and spaces. The **PSLTSCALE** variable is a toggle that can be set to either 1 or 0, "on" or "off" respectively.

When you are working in model space, set **LTSCALE** to the inverse of the scale for the viewport. For example, if the viewport scale is to be 1/48 (1/4″ = 1′-0″), **LTSCALE** should be set to 48. This way, unless you are zoomed in extremely close or extremely far out, the linetypes will be readily apparent. If the drawing is to be plotted from the **Model** tab, **LTSCALE** should remain set to this value. The **PSLTSCALE** variable setting has no effect when you are working and plotting in model space.

When you are plotting a layout, especially one with multiple viewports of two or more differing scales, the **LTSCALE** should be set to 1 and **PSLTSCALE** should be set to 1 ("on"). Setting **PSLTSCALE** to 1 allows the zoom scale factor of the viewport to control the scale factor of the linetypes. In this case, the linetypes will be displayed through the viewports at a scale factor based on the product of the viewport zoom scale factor multiplied by the **LTSCALE** setting (which should be 1). Differently scaled viewports will display and plot linetypes at the same size, relative to paper space.

When you are plotting a layout with a single viewport, or multiple viewports zoomed to the same scale, the **LTSCALE** can be set to the inverse of the zoom scale factor of the viewport(s) and the **PSLTSCALE** variable can be set to 0 ("off"). For the sake of consistency, if your school or company is using layouts, it might be a good idea to standardize on the linetype scaling method outlined in the previous paragraph.

Previewing the Plot

Depending on their size and complexity, drawings can require long plotting times. By previewing a plot before sending it to the output device, you can catch errors, saving materials and valuable plot time. This feature is controlled by the **Preview...** button at the lower-left corner of the **Plot** dialog box.

Pick the **Preview...** button to display the drawing as it will actually appear on the plotted hard copy. (A plot device other than "None" must be selected in order to activate the **Preview...** button.) The display reflects any plot style tables that have been attached to the drawing if the **Plot with plot styles** button is checked in the **Plot options** area. Displaying the preview takes the same amount of time as a drawing regeneration. Therefore, the drawing size determines how quickly the image is produced.

The drawing is displayed inside a paper outline and the Zoom cursor appears. Press and hold the pick button as you move the cursor up to enlarge and down to reduce. Right-click to display a shortcut menu that provides several display options, a **Plot** option, and an **Exit** option. The shortcut menu is handy because it allows you to examine the drawing closely before you commit to plotting. When you are finished previewing, press [Esc] or [Enter] to return to the **Plot** dialog box. You can also preview a plot by picking **File** > **Plot Preview**. This selection bypasses the **Plot** dialog box.

Before you pick **OK** in the **Plot** dialog box, check the following items:

✓ The printer or plotter is plugged in and turned on.
✓ The printer's data cable is secure.
✓ The paper and ink/toner are loaded correctly.
✓ The printer or plotter area is clear for unblocked paper movement.

Once you are satisfied with all plotter parameters and are ready to plot, pick the **OK** button to exit the **Plot** dialog box and plot the drawing. Depending on the type of plotter or printer you are using, one or more dialog boxes may be displayed, showing the drawing name and a meter showing the percentage of the file that has been regenerated and sent to the printer.

Adding a Plot Stamp

A plot stamp is specific text information included on a printed or plotted drawing. A plot stamp may include information such as the drawing name or the date and time the drawing was printed.

In the **Plot** dialog box, the **Plot stamp on** area in the **Plot options** area allows you to activate and modify the plot stamp. See **Figure 25-34**. If the **On** check box is activated, a **Plot Stamp Settings…** button appears next to the check box and a plot stamp will be printed on the drawing. You can specify the items to be included in the plot stamp by picking the **Plot Stamp Settings…** button. This accesses the **Plot Stamp** dialog box, which is shown in **Figure 25-35**.

Specify the information to be included in the plot stamp in the **Plot stamp fields** area of the **Plot Stamp** dialog box. The following items can be included:

- Drawing name
- Layout name
- Date and time
- Login name
- Device name
- Paper size
- Plot scale

You can create additional plot stamp items in the **User defined fields** dialog box, which appears when you pick the **Add/Edit** button on the **Plot Stamp** dialog box. For example, you could add a field for the client name, the project name, or the contractor who will be using the drawing.

The **Preview** area provides a preview of the location and orientation of the plot stamp. The preview does not show the actual plot stamp text.

Figure 25-34.
Activate the plot stamp in the **Plot options** area of the **Plot** dialog box. Pick the **Plot Stamp Settings…** button to access the **Plot Stamp** dialog box.

Plot options
☑ Plot in background
☑ Plot object lineweights
☑ Plot with plot styles
☑ Plot paperspace last
☐ Hide paperspace objects
☑ Plot stamp on
☐ Save changes to layout

Turn plot stamp on or off

Specify information included in plot stamp

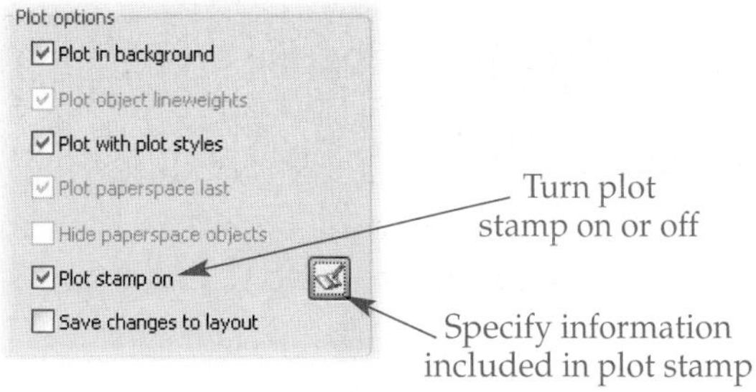

Figure 25-35.
Use the **Plot Stamp** dialog box to specify the information included in the plot stamp. You can save plot stamp settings as PSS files.

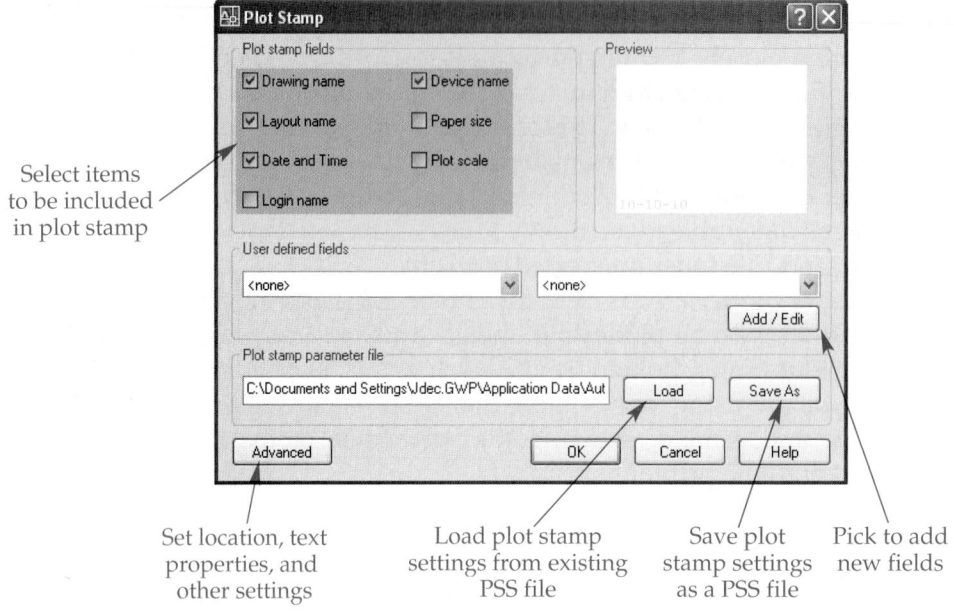

Select items to be included in plot stamp

Set location, text properties, and other settings

Load plot stamp settings from existing PSS file

Save plot stamp settings as a PSS file

Pick to add new fields

Plot stamp settings can be saved in a PSS (plot stamp parameter) file. If you load an existing PSS file, the settings saved in the file are automatically set in the **Plot Stamp** dialog box.

Additional plot stamp options are set in the **Advanced Options** dialog box. To access this dialog box, pick the **Advanced...** button in the **Plot Stamp** dialog box. The **Advanced Options** dialog box is shown in **Figure 25-36.** The following options are available:

- **Location and offset.** In this area, you can choose the placement and orientation of the plot stamp by selecting from the drop-down lists. If you want the plot stamp to print upside-down, pick the **Stamp upside-down** check box. Enter the X offset and Y offset distances in the text boxes. The offset distances are measured relative to the printable area or paper border.
- **Text properties.** Specify the text font and height. Pick the **Single line plot stamp** check box if you want the plot stamp constrained to a single line. If this check box is not checked, the plot stamp will be printed in two lines.
- **Plot stamp units.** Select the plot stamp units. The plot stamp units can be different from the drawing units.
- **Log file location.** Pick the **Create a log file** check box to create a log file of plotted items. Specify the name of the log file in the text box. Pick **Browse...** to specify the location of the log file.

NOTE

The log file settings are independent of the plot stamp settings. Thus, you can produce a log file without creating a plot stamp or have a plot stamp without producing a log file.

Figure 25-36.
Specify the plot stamp location, orientation, text font and size, and units in the **Advanced Options** dialog box.

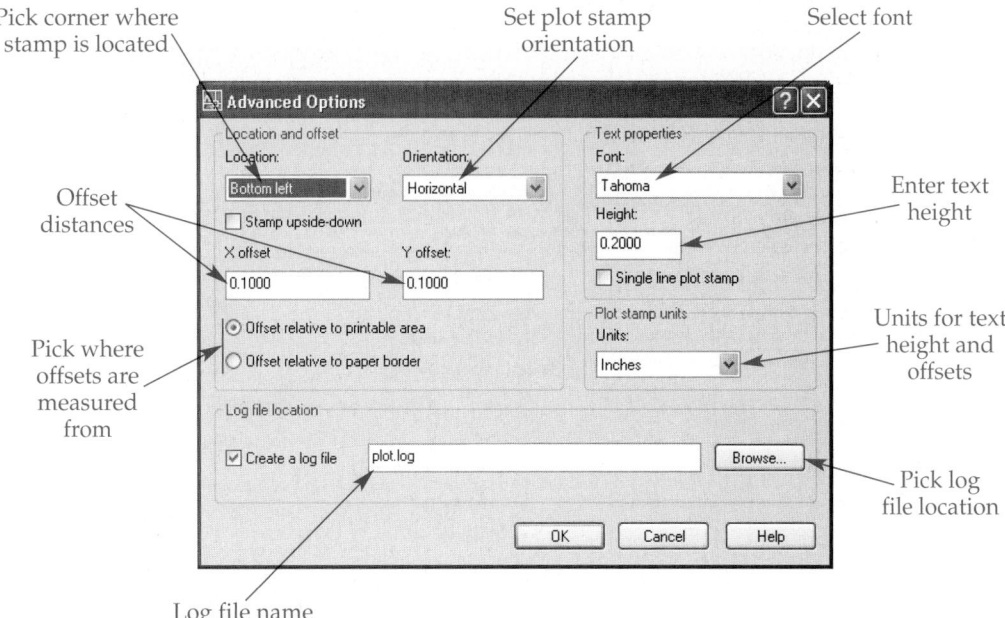

Pick corner where stamp is located

Set plot stamp orientation

Select font

Offset distances

Pick where offsets are measured from

Enter text height

Units for text height and offsets

Pick log file location

Log file name

Additional Plotting Options

The **Plot and Publish** tab of the **Options** dialog box contains general plotting settings, some of which will seldom have to be changed. See **Figure 25-37**. To access this dialog box, select **Tools** > **Options...** from the pull-down menu or enter OPTIONS or OP. The **Plot and Publish** tab provides several general plotting options. The areas are discussed briefly here.

- **Default plot settings for new drawings.** The default setting is **Use as default output device**. The device can be selected from the drop-down list. The **Use last successful plot settings** option retains the previous plot settings. Picking the **Add or Configure Plotters** button displays the **Plotters** window.
- **General plot options.** This area allows you to use either the **Keep the layout paper size if possible** option, regardless of the plotter selected, or the **Use the plot device paper size** option. If you choose to keep the layout size, AutoCAD will use the paper size specified in the **Page Setup** dialog box. If this size cannot be plotted, AutoCAD defaults to the size listed in the plotter's PC3 file.
  - **System printer spool alert.** If a port conflict occurs during plotting and a drawing is spooled to a system printer, AutoCAD can display an alert and log the error. This drop-down list gives four options for alerting and logging errors.
  - **OLE plot quality.** *OLE* is an acronym for *object linking and embedding* and refers to any text or graphic object that is imported from another software application. This drop-down list allows you to select the type of OLE objects that will be plotted.
  - **Use OLE application when plotting OLE objects.** If this check box is activated, applications used to create OLE objects are launched. This may be desirable if you wish to use the OLE software to adjust the quality of the object.
- **Auto publish.** This area allows you to save, or publish, a DWF file automatically when you save or close a drawing. A *DWF (Design Web Format)* file is a Web-compatible format. The file can be viewed using Autodesk's free application, *DWF Viewer®*. To set the options for automatically publishing drawings, select the **Automatic DWF Publish Settings** button to display the **Auto Publish Options** dialog box, as shown in **Figure 25-38**. DWF creation is discussed in more detail in *AutoCAD and Its Applications—Advanced*.

OLE (object linking and embedding): Text or graphics imported from another software application.

NEW FEATURE

DWF (Design Web Format): A Web-compatible file for publishing a drawing or set of drawings.

Figure 25-37.
The **Plot and Publish** tab of the **Options** dialog box contains general plotting settings.

General plotting options

Select default plotter option

Access **Plotters** window

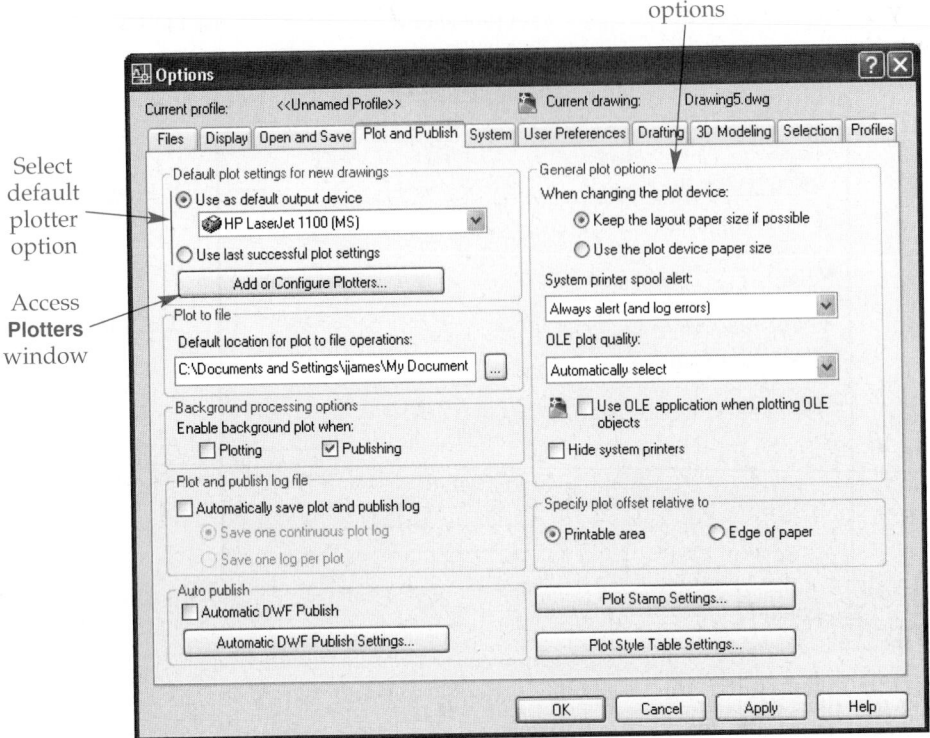

Figure 25-38.
The **Auto Publish Options** dialog box provides significant control over the format and content of DWF files.

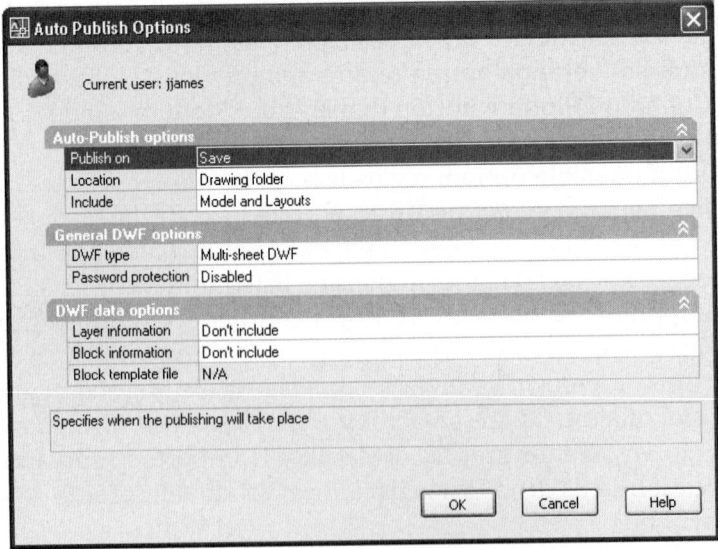

Alternative Plotting

Typically, the end result of executing the plotting procedures is a paper drawing, also known as a hard copy. Largely because of the growth of the Internet, many drawings are being exchanged as electronic files instead of paper drawings. AutoCAD can generate two types of electronic files: design web format (DWF) and plot (PLT). The DWF file may be e-mailed, uploaded to the Internet, or posted on a company's internal Web site. The other electronic file, PLT, is eventually sent to a printer or plotter. The most common reason for creating this file instead of plotting directly to paper is to save time. PLT files can be created during the workday and sent to the plotter at night, when the plotter is not busy. Sometimes the PLT files are sent to a plot spooler so the computer is not waiting for the plotter to finish.

Using Publish to Create a DWF File

In addition to creating a DWF file automatically by selecting this option in the **Options** dialog box, you can create a DWF file from the **Publish** dialog box. You can also send the drawings to a plotter from the **Publish** dialog box. You can access this dialog box by picking the **Publish** button on the **Standard Annotation** toolbar, picking **File** > **Publish**, or typing PUBLISH. The listing of sheets to publish will be empty unless the **Model** or layout tabs have been initialized. If open, close the **Publish** dialog box and create some geometry and text in the **Model** view. Pick each layout tab to initialize them. Open the **Publish** dialog box again and notice the three sheets listed in the **Sheets to publish** area. It should say No errors under the status title for each sheet. See **Figure 25-39**.

The eight buttons below the **Sheets to publish** area are:
- **Preview.** Same as **Plot Preview**.
- **Add Sheets.** Adds a sheet from another drawing.
- **Remove Sheets.** Removes the selected sheet from the list.
- **Move Sheet Up.** Moves a sheet up on the list. The published sheets are viewed or plotted in the order shown in the list.
- **Move Sheet Down.** Used with the **Move Sheet Up** button to reorder the sheets for plotting.

Figure 25-39.
DWF files and paper copies can be created from the **Publish** dialog box.

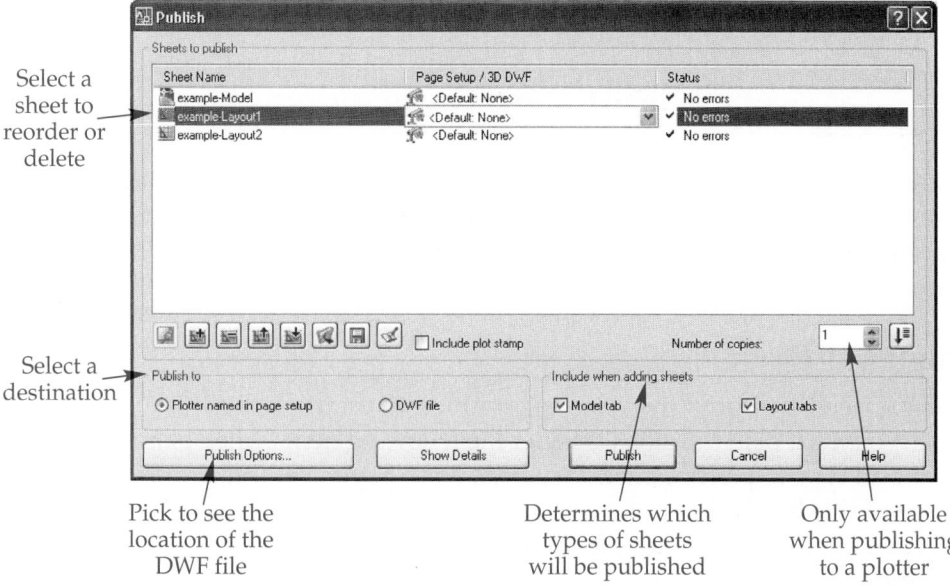

Select a sheet to reorder or delete

Select a destination

Pick to see the location of the DWF file

Determines which types of sheets will be published

Only available when publishing to a plotter

- **Load Sheet List.** Loads a previously saved list of sheets to publish.
- **Save Sheet List.** Saves the current sheet list. This button is available after the current drawing is saved.
- **Plot Stamp Settings.** Same as the **Plot Stamp Settings** in the **Plot** dialog box.

Below these buttons is the **Publish to** area, containing two destinations. The first, **Plotter named in page setup**, sends each sheet directly to the plotter designated in its page setup. Each sheet plots using the page setup named in the **Sheets to Publish** area. The second, **DWF File**, creates a Design Web Format file. The location of this file, along with other options, can be found by picking the **Publish Options** button.

Other features to note are the **Number of copies** text box and the **Include when adding sheets** area. The number of copies applies only when the destination is a plotter and the page setup is not plotting to a file. The type of sheets, model or layout, to include when publishing is controlled in the **Include when adding sheets** area. After configuring the necessary options, pick **Publish** to create the DWF file or send the sheets to a plotter.

Creating a PLT File

The PLT file is generated from the **Plot** dialog box. All of the options that you would configure for a paper plot have to be considered when you create the PLT file. Even the plotter has to be selected for a file to be created. Open the **Plot** dialog box and prepare all of the options as you would when making a hard copy. Make sure that you have chosen a plotter. Then put a check in the **Plot to file** check box located in the **Printer/plotter** area. See **Figure 25-40.** When you pick the **OK** button, the **Browse for Plot File** dialog box appears. If necessary, you can change the file name and location before saving the file.

Figure 25-40.
PLT files are created from the **Plot** dialog box.

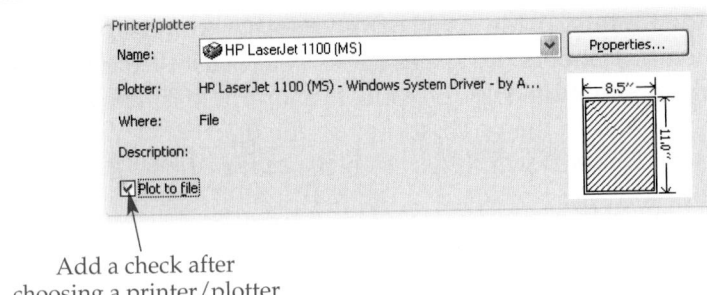

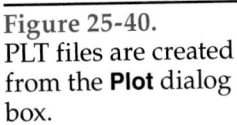
Add a check after choosing a printer/plotter

Plotting Hints

Plotting can slow down productivity in an office or a classroom if not done efficiently. Establish and follow a procedure for using the plotter, and instruct all drafters, engineers, and other plotter users of the proper operating procedures. Post these in strategic locations.

Planning Your Plots

Planning is the key word when dealing with plots. In the same way you planned the drawing, you must plan the plot. Consider the following items when planning to plot:

- ✓ Size and type of plotting media, such as bond paper, vellum, or polyester film
- ✓ Type of title block
- ✓ Location and scale of multiple views
- ✓ Origin location and scale of the drawing

- ✓ Orientation of 3D views
- ✓ Portion to be plotted: layout, view, window, display, limits, or extents

This is only a sample of decisions that should be made before you begin plotting. Usually, the plotter is the funnel that all drawings must go through before they are evaluated, approved, and sent to production or the client.

Eliminate Unnecessary Plots

The easiest way to eliminate the problems associated with plotting is to eliminate plotting. Make plots *only* when absolutely necessary. This results in time and money savings. A few additional suggestions include:

- ✓ Obtain approvals of designs while the drawings are on-screen
- ✓ Transfer files for the checker's comments
- ✓ Create a special layer with a unique color for markups. Freeze or erase this layer when finally making a plot
- ✓ Use "redlining" software that enables the checker to review the drawing and apply markups to it without using AutoCAD
- ✓ Check drawings on disk. Use a special layer for comments.
- ✓ Avoid making plots for backups. Rather, establish a reliable electronic backup procedure. This may be accomplished using CDs, DVDs, or other external storage devices.

If You Must Plot...

Industry still exists on a paper-based system. Therefore, it is important that plotters be used efficiently. This means using the plotter only for what is required. Here are a few hints for doing just that:

- ✓ Ask yourself, "Do I *really* need a plot?" If the answer is an unqualified *yes*, then proceed.
- ✓ Plan your plot!
- ✓ Pick the least busy time to make the plot.
- ✓ Select the smallest piece of paper possible.
- ✓ Use the lowest quality paper possible.
- ✓ Create sheet sets and plot these sheet sets at times when plotter or printer use is light.

Producing Quality Plots

When you must plot the highest quality drawing for reproduction, evaluation, or presentation, use the plotter in a manner that does the job right the first time. Keep these points in mind:

- ✓ Choose the device that will produce the quality of print needed. Select the right tool for the job.
- ✓ Choose the paper type and size appropriate for the project.
- ✓ If using wet ink pens, select the proper ink for your climate.
- ✓ Apply the appropriate plot style table.

Template Development Chapter 25

The layouts you use in your drawing files depend on the types of drawings you create and the paper size you use. Because layouts take time and thought to prepare, you should add commonly used layouts to your drawing templates. Refer to the Student CD for detailed instructions to set up appropriate layouts for your mechanical, architectural, and civil drawing templates.

Chapter Test

Answer the following questions. Write your answers on a separate sheet of paper or complete the electronic chapter test on the Student CD.

1. What is a layout?
2. How do you create floating viewports in a layout?
3. When working in a layout tab, how do you activate a viewport in order to zoom or pan the viewport display?
4. If all layout tabs are not visible on screen, how do you select a tab that is not currently visible?
5. List three methods used to create a new layout tab.
6. How can you rename a layout?
7. To what types of files can a layout be saved?
8. Define *page setup*.
9. How do you add a printer to the **Printer/plotter** area of the **Plot** dialog box?
10. What is a plot style table?
11. Name the two plot style modes and the file extensions assigned to their plot style tables.
12. How do you access the **Plot Styles** window?
13. How do you create a new plot style table?
14. When you create a new color-dependent plot style table, how many plot styles does it contain?
15. List two ways to access the **Plot Style Table Editor**.
16. When you create a new named plot style table, how many plot styles does it contain?
17. What determines the plot style mode for a drawing?
18. Explain how you can specify a plot style table to be attached to all new drawings by default.
19. How does a color-dependent plot style table attached to a layout affect the plotting of the layout?
20. Which plot style mode allows you to attach plot styles to layers and objects?
21. Explain how to assign a plot style to a layer.
22. Name two methods of assigning a plot style to an object.
23. What setting is used to have the effect of plot styles displayed in a layout?
24. Identify the two types of paper orientation.
25. Calculate the scale factors for viewports with the following scales:
    A. 1/4″ = 1″
    B. 1/8″ = 1′-0″
    C. 1″ = 30′
26. What do you enter to specify a plot scale of 1/4″ = 1′-0″?
27. What system variable controls paper space linetype scaling?
28. Explain how to zoom while viewing a plot preview.
29. How do you save a plot file named PLOT1 to a specific folder?
30. Explain why you should plan your plots.

For Questions 31-35, specify if the statement is true or false.

31. Plot styles can be added to and deleted from color-dependent plot style tables.
32. Plot styles can be added to and deleted from named plot style tables.
33. The plot style mode of a drawing cannot be changed.
34. A plot style assigned to a layer will override a plot style assigned to an object on the layer when the drawing is plotted.
35. If a drawing has multiple layouts, all layouts must use the same plot style table.

Drawing Problems

Note: The templates on the Student CD provide layout and plot setups. The problems in this chapter provide additional practice in developing layouts and may overlap or duplicate those templates.

1. Open P8-1. Create a layout tab named **A Size**. Modify the page setup for this layout tab using the following parameters:
   - **Plotter:** None
   - **Paper size:** ANSI A (8.5 x 11)
   - **What to plot:** Layout
   - **Scale:** 1:1
   - **Plot style table:** None
   - **Paper orientation:** Landscape

   Center the model within the viewport and set the scale of the viewport to 1:1, then lock the viewport. Place the viewport on a layer called **Viewports**. Save the drawing as P25-1.

2. Open P8-2. Do everything as called out in Problem 1, except set the paper orientation to **Portrait**, and set the scale of the viewport to 1:2. Save the drawing as P25-2.

3. Open P8-6. Create two layout tabs, one named **B Size** and the other named **C Size**. Modify the page setups for each tab as in the first two problems, except use **ANSI B (11 x 17)** and **ANSI C (17 x 22)** paper sizes on the appropriate tabs. Resize the viewports to fill the paper more appropriately. Center the model within the viewport on each layout and select an appropriate scale for the viewport so the model is displayed on the paper at an acceptable size. Save the drawing as P25-3.

4. Start a new drawing using the acad.dwt template. Create a plot style table named Black35mm.cbt that will plot all colors in the AutoCAD drawing in black ink on the paper, with a lineweight of 0.35 mm. (Hint: To make the same change to a property of all the plot styles, select the first plot style in the list, in this case Color 1, then scroll to the end of the list, hold down the shift key and select the last plot style in the list, in this case Color 255).

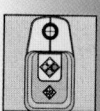

5. Start a new drawing using the acad -Named Plot Styles.dwt template. Create a plot style table named BlackShades.stb. Create the following plot styles:
   - Black100% with color set to black, all other properties to their default values
   - Black50% with color set to black, screening set to 50, all other properties to their default values
   - Black25% with color set to black, screening set to 25, all other properties to their default values

   Save the drawing as P25-5.

6. Create a template file for mechanical or machine parts using the following guidelines:
   A. Use the acad -Named Plot Styles.dwt template to begin the new template.
   B. Set linear unit measurement to a precision of four decimal places, and angular unit precision to two decimal places.
   C. Set the limits in model space to 0,0 for the lower-left corner, and 44,34 for the upper-right corner; **ZOOM All**.
   D. Set **LTSCALE** to .5, **PSLTSCALE** to 1, and **LWDEFAULT** to 30.
   E. Use the named plot style table called BlackShades.stb, created in the previous exercise.
   F. Create the following layer scheme:

Name	Color	Linetype	Lineweight	Plot Style
Annotation	Red	Continuous	Default	Black100
Border	Blue	Continuous	1.00 mm	Black100
Center	Yellow	Center	Default	Black100
Construction	252	Continuous	Default	Black100
CuttingPlane	Blue	Phantom	0.80 mm	Black100
Dimension	Red	Continuous	Default	Black100
Hidden	Cyan	Hidden	Default	Black100
Object	Green	Continuous	0.70 mm	Black100
Phantom	Magenta	Phantom	Default	Black100
SectionLine	White	Continuous	Default	Black100
Viewports	253	Continuous	Default	Black100
Xrefs	White	Continuous	Default	Black50

   G. Create six page setups as follows. Change the printer name to a printer configured for your system.

Name	Printer	Paper size	What to plot	Scale	Plot style table	Paper orientation
Check Plot	None	ANSI B (11 x 17)	Window	Fit to paper	BlackShades.stb	Landscape
A Size – Vertical	None	ANSI A (8.5 x 11)	Layout	1:1	BlackShades.stb	Portrait
A Size – Horizontal	None	ANSI A (8.5 x 11)	Layout	1:1	BlackShades.stb	Landscape
B Size	None	ANSI B (11 x 17)	Layout	1:1	BlackShades.stb	Landscape
C Size	None	ANSI C (17 x 22)	Layout	1:1	BlackShades.stb	Landscape
D Size	None	ANSI D (22 x 34)	Layout	1:1	BlackShades.stb	Landscape
E Size	None	ANSI E (34 x 44)	Layout	1:1	BlackShades.stb	Landscape

   H. Create six layouts named **A Size – H**, **A Size – V**, **B Size**, **C Size**, **D Size**, and **E Size**.
   I. Assign the appropriate page setup to each of the layout tabs, and assign the **Check Plot** page setup to the **Model** tab.
   J. Make the **Border** layer current. On each layout, draw a polyline border just inside the plottable area of the paper.
   K. Use grips to resize the viewports on each layout so the viewport edges are just inside the edges of the drawn border. Double-click inside each viewport and **ZOOM All**. Also be sure each viewport is on the Viewports layer.
   L. Save the file as a template file named MECH-IMPERIAL.dwt.

7. Start a new drawing using the MECH-IMPERIAL.dwt template created in the previous exercise.
   A. Rename each of the page setups as follows (to rename an item, click the title once in the **Page Setup Manager**, then click it again, being careful not to double-click it):
      A Size - Vertical = ISO A4 - Vertical
      A Size - Horizontal = ISO A4 - Horizontal
      B Size = ISO A3
      C Size = ISO A2
      D Size = ISO A1
      E Size = ISO A0
   B. Rename each of the layout tabs to match the names of the page setups in part A.
   C. Assign the newly renamed page setups to the layout tabs, respectively.
   D. Use grips to resize the borders and viewports appropriately.
   E. Set the limits in model space to 0,0 for the lower-left corner and 1189,841 for the upper-right corner; **ZOOM All**.
   F. Double-click inside each viewport and **ZOOM All**. Also be sure each viewport is on the Viewports layer.
   G. Set **LTSCALE** to 12.7.
   H. Save the file as MECH-METRIC.dwt.

8. Open P25-8 from the student CD supplied with the text. Create a layout, plot style, and page setup so it can be plotted as follows: Using color-dependent plot styles, have the equipment (shown in color in the diagram) plot with a lineweight of 0.8 mm and 80% screening on an A size sheet oriented horizontally. Plotted text height should be 1/8". Plot in paper space at 1:1. Save the drawing as P25-8.

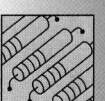

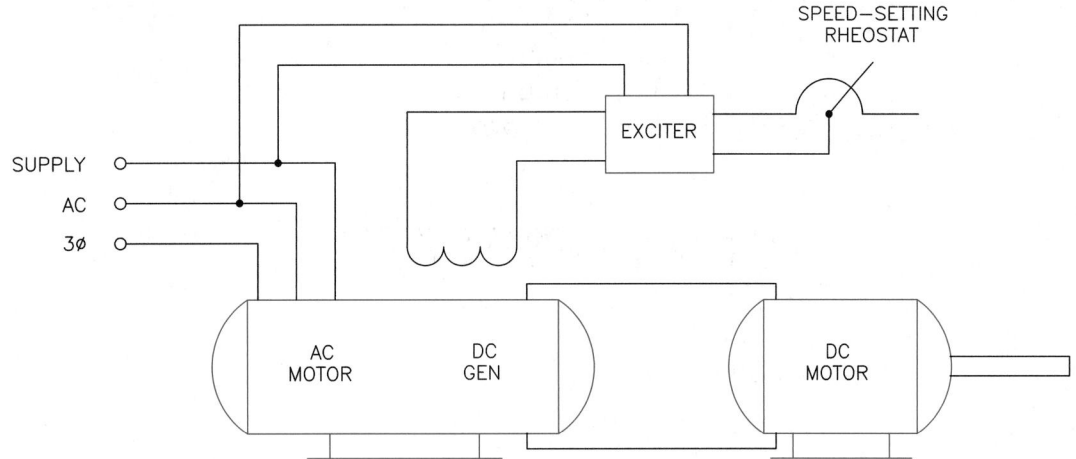

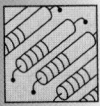

9. Open P25-9 from the student CD supplied with the text. Create four layouts with the names and displays as follows:

    A. The **Entire Schematic** layout plots the entire schematic on a B-size sheet.

    B. The **3 Wire Control** layout plots only the 3 Wire Control diagram on an A-size sheet, horizontally oriented.

    C. The **Motor** layout plots the motor symbol and connections in the lower center of the schematic on an A-size sheet, oriented vertically.

    D. The **Schematic** layout plots schematic without the 3 Wire Control and motor components on an A-size sheet, oriented horizontally.

Set up the layouts so they can be plotted with a text height of 1/8″. Plot in paper space at a scale of 1:1. Save the drawing as P25-9.

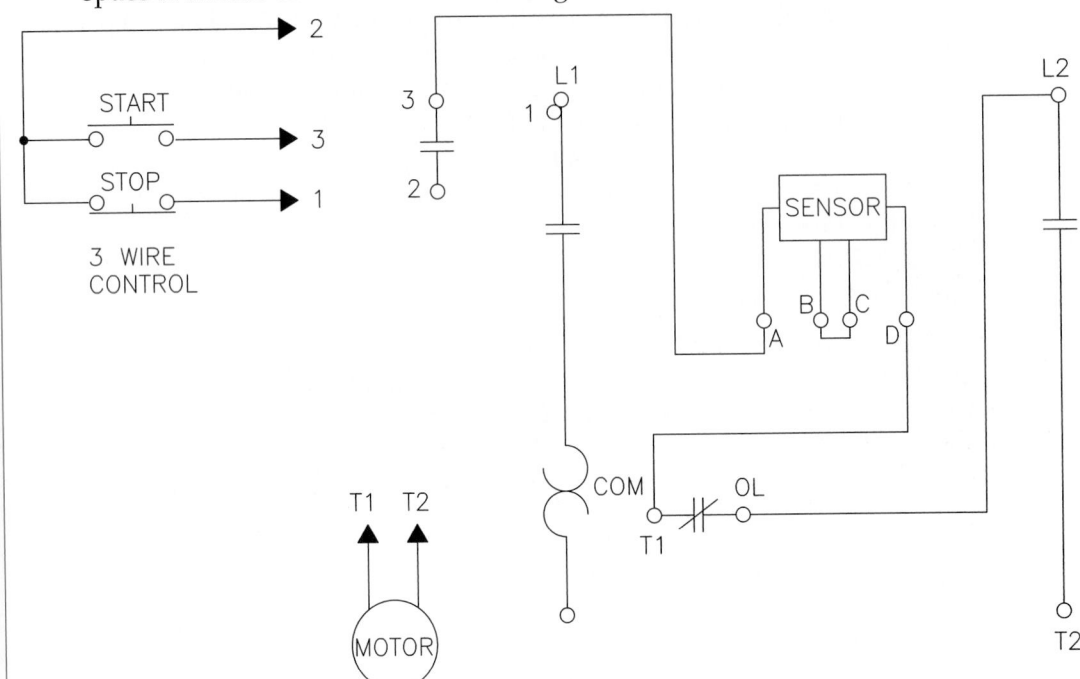

Drawing Problems - Chapter 25

Using Attributes

Learning Objectives

After completing this chapter, you will be able to do the following:

✓ Assign attributes to blocks.
✓ Edit attributes defined for existing blocks.
✓ Create title blocks, revision blocks, and parts lists.
✓ Extract attribute values to create a bill of materials.
✓ Create a table from attribute information.

Blocks become more useful when written information is provided with them. It is even more helpful to be able to assign information to a block and make it either visible or hidden. From this data, a list very similar to a bill of materials can be requested and printed.

Written or numerical values assigned to blocks are called *attributes*. In addition to being used as text, attribute information can be *extracted* from a drawing. Several blocks with attributes are shown in **Figure 26-1**.

attributes: Text or numerical values assigned to blocks.

extracted: Gathered from the drawing file database and displayed either in the drawing or in an external document.

Figure 26-1.
Examples of blocks with defined attributes.

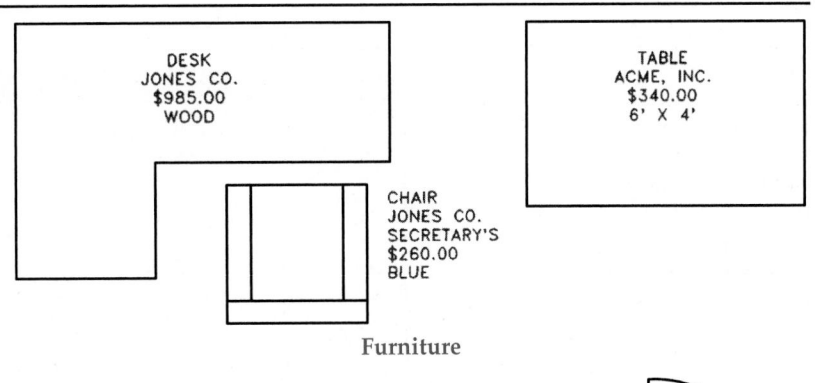

DESK
JONES CO.
$985.00
WOOD

TABLE
ACME, INC.
$340.00
6' X 4'

CHAIR
JONES CO.
SECRETARY'S
$260.00
BLUE

Furniture

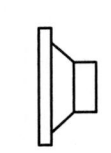
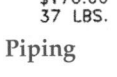

GLOBE VALVE
JAMESBURY
ø 6"
$325.00
95 LBS.

WELD NECK FLANGE
GRINNELL
ø 8"
150# PSI
$170.00
37 LBS.

90° ELBOW
TAYLOR FORGE
ø 8"
300# PSI
$146.00
48 LBS.

Piping

Attributes are created during the initial phase of block development, along with any objects to be included in the block definition. The typical process for using attributes includes the following steps:

1. Draw objects that will be used to make the block. This step is necessary only if the block will contain objects, such as the blocks shown in **Figure 26-1**.
2. Add attributes using the **Attribute Definition** dialog box.
3. Create the block by selecting the objects and attributes together.
4. Insert the block and adjust the attribute values as needed.

Once a block is inserted, attribute values can be modified using the **Enhanced Attribute Editor**, attribute definitions can be adjusted using the **Block Attribute Manager**, and block and attribute text data can be exported into other applications using data extraction.

Assigning Attributes to Blocks

Before defining attributes for a block, you must determine the text information needed for the block. In most cases, the name of the object should be the first attribute. This could be followed by other attribute items, such as the manufacturer, type, size, price, and weight. Suppose you are drawing a valve symbol for a piping flow diagram. You might want to list all of the product-related data along with the symbol. The number of attributes you can create is limited only by the project requirements.

The **ATTDEF** (attribute define) command is used to assign attributes. To access this command, pick **Draw > Block > Define Attributes...** from the pull-down menu, select the **Define Attributes...** button from the **Block Attributes** control panel of the **Dashboard**, or type ATT or ATTDEF. This displays the **Attribute Definition** dialog box. See **Figure 26-2**.

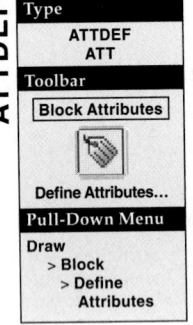

ATTDEF

Type
ATTDEF
ATT

Toolbar
Block Attributes

Define Attributes...

Pull-Down Menu
Draw
> Block
> Define
Attributes

NOTE

To display the **Block Attributes** control panel in the **Dashboard**, right-click any existing control panel, select **Control Panels**, and choose **Block Attributes** from the list.

Figure 26-2.
Attributes can be assigned to blocks using the **Attribute Definition** dialog box. The options are shown when the **Multiple lines** check box is activated.

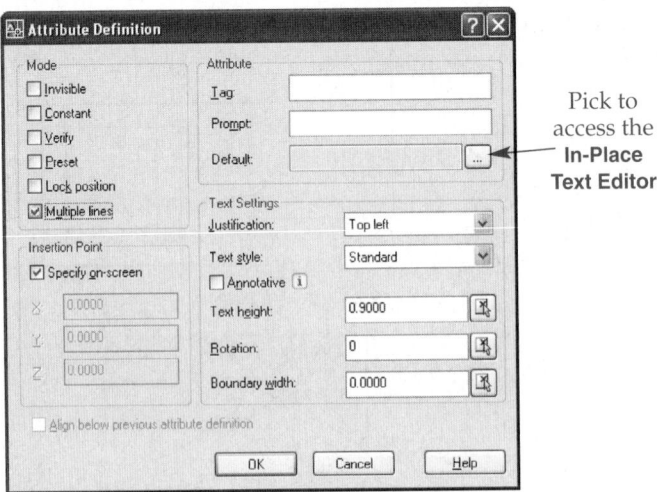

Pick to access the **In-Place Text Editor**

The **Attribute Definition** dialog box is divided into four main areas. Each area allows you to set specific aspects of an attribute.

Setting Attribute Modes

The **Mode** area of the **Attribute Definition** dialog box is used to set the attribute modes. The mode settings include:

- **Invisible.** If this check box is activated, the attribute is not displayed when the block is inserted. Otherwise, the attribute is shown with the inserted block. Select the **Invisible** option if you want to include attribute data in the block that can be referenced and extracted, but you do not want to see the information.
- **Constant.** If the value of the attribute should always be the same, activate the **Constant** check box. All insertions of the block will display the same value for the attribute; you are not prompted for a new value. Leave this check box inactive to use different attribute values for multiple insertions of the block.
- **Verify.** Activate this check box if you want a prompt to ask you whether or not the specified attribute value is correct when the block is inserted.
- **Preset.** Activate this check box to have the attribute assume preset values during block insertion. This option disables the attribute prompt. Leave this check box inactive to display the normal prompt.
- **Lock position.** Select this check box if you do not want to have the option of moving the attribute independently of the block when inserted. The **Lock position** check box is also used for an attribute that will be part of a dynamic block. This check box must be checked for the attribute to be included as part of the action selection set when assigning an action to a dynamic block. If it is unchecked, the attribute is filtered out when the action is assigned to the dynamic block. Dynamic blocks are covered in Chapter 24.
- **Multiple lines.** The **Attribute Definition** dialog box can be used to create single-line or multiple-line attributes. Pick the **Multiple lines** check box to activate options for creating a multiple-line attribute. Deselect the check box to create a single-line attribute. When the **Multiple lines** check box is selected, the **Insert Field** button changes to an ellipsis, as shown in **Figure 26-2**. Picking this button accesses the **In-Place Text Editor**, which can be used to insert multiple lines of text.

> **NOTE**
>
> The **Multiple lines** check box can be removed from the **Attribute Definition** dialog box by setting the **ATTMULTI** system variable to 0. The **ATTMULTI** system variable is set to 1 by default, allowing you to create multiple-line attributes.

Using the Attribute Area

The **Attribute** area of the **Attribute Definition** dialog box lets you assign a tag, prompt, and default value to the attribute. The entries in these text boxes can contain up to 256 characters. If the first character in an entry is a space, start the string with a backslash (\). If the first character is a backslash, begin the entry with two backslashes (\\). The attribute values you can set include:

- **Tag.** Use this text box to enter the name, or tag, of the attribute. For example, the tag for a size attribute of a valve block could be SIZE. You must enter a tag in order to create an attribute. Any characters can be used *except* spaces. All text is displayed in uppercase.

- **Prompt.** Enter a statement in this text box that AutoCAD will use to prompt you when the block is inserted. For example, if SIZE is specified as the attribute tag, What is the valve size? or Enter valve size: might be entered as the prompt. If the **Constant** attribute mode is inactive, this option is disabled. The prompts can be left blank.
- **Default.** The entry in this text box is used as a default attribute value when the block is inserted. You might decide to enter a message regarding the type of information needed, such as 10 SPACES MAX or NUMBERS ONLY. If the **Multiple lines** attribute mode is inactive, the default value can be entered directly in the text box. Use the **Insert field** button to include a field in the default value. If the **Multiple lines** attribute mode is active, the ellipsis (**...**) button is displayed. Pick this button to enter the drawing area and place multiline text. This process is very similar to adding multiline text to your drawing using the **MTEXT** command. **Figure 26-3** displays the **In-Place Text Editor** used for adding a multiple line attribute. Multiline text is covered in Chapter 9. The default value can be left blank.

> **NOTE**
>
> The abbreviated **Text Formatting** toolbar shown in **Figure 26-3** is provided by default. To display the complete **Text Formatting** toolbar, as displayed when using the **MTEXT** command, set the **ATTIPE** system variable to 1. The **ATTIPE** system variable is set to 0 by default.

Adjusting Attribute Text Settings

The **Text Options** area of the **Attribute Definition** dialog box allows you to specify the following attribute text settings. Many of these options function like the text settings for single-line and multiline text, as described in Chapter 9.

- **Justification.** Use this drop-down list to select a justification for the attribute text. The default option is Left. In single-line attributes, the text itself is justified. In the **Multiple lines** attribute mode, the text boundary is justified.
- **Text Style.** Use this drop-down list to select a text style for the attribute from the styles defined in the current drawing.
- **Annotative.** Pick this check box to make the attribute text height annotative. AutoCAD scales annotative attributes according to the annotation scale you select, which is the same as the drawing scale. This eliminates the need for you to calculate the scale factor.

Figure 26-3.
The **In-Place Text Editor** is used to define multiple-line attributes. An abbreviated version of the **Text Formatting** toolbar is provided by default.

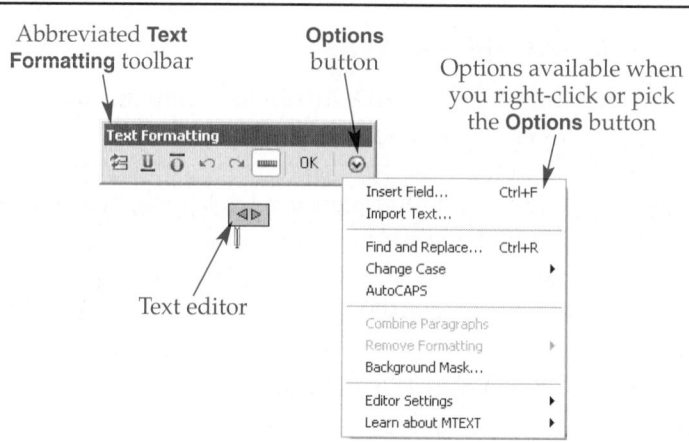

AutoCAD and Its Applications—Basics

- **Height.** Specify the height of the attribute text in this text box or pick the **Text Height** button to the right of the text box to return temporarily to the drawing area and pick two points to indicate the text height. Once the points are picked, the dialog box returns and the corresponding height is shown in the text box.
- **Rotation.** Enter an angular value in this text box to specify a rotation angle for the attribute text or pick the **Rotation** button to the right of the text box and specify a rotation by picking two points in the drawing area.
- **Boundary width.** This option is only available when the **Multiple lines** attribute mode is active. It can be used to set the text boundary width of multiple-line attributes. Enter a width for the text boundary in the **Boundary width** text box, or pick the **Boundary width** button to the right of the text box and specify a text boundary width by picking two points in the drawing area.

Defining the Attribute Insertion Point

The **Insertion Point** area of the **Attribute Definition** dialog box provides options for defining the location of the attribute. Coordinates can be entered in the text boxes if the **Specify On-screen** check box is unchecked. If the check box is checked, you must select the attribute location on-screen after picking the **OK** button to close the **Attribute Definition** dialog box.

An alternative attribute placement method involves selecting the **Align below previous attribute definition** check box. If the drawing does not contain any attributes, this check box is grayed out. If the drawing contains at least one attribute, this check box is available. Checking it places the attribute that is being created directly below the most recently created attribute using the justification of that attribute. When this check box is checked, the **Text Options** and **Insertion Point** areas become inactive. This is an effective technique for placing a group of different attributes in the same block.

Placing the Attribute

After all elements of the attribute are defined, pick **OK** to close the **Attribute Definition** dialog box. The attribute tag is then placed on-screen if coordinates are specified, or if the **Align below previous attribute definition** option is used. You are prompted to select a location if coordinates were not included in the definition. When the block is inserted, you are prompted for information based on the attribute definition. If the attribute mode is set to **Invisible**, do not be dismayed by the fact that the tag is visible; this is the only time the tag appears.

Editing Attribute Properties

The **Properties** palette provides expanded editing capabilities for attributes. To activate the **Properties** palette, pick the **Properties** button on the **Standard Annotation** toolbar; pick **Modify** > **Properties** from the pull-down menu; pick **Tools** > **Palettes** > **Properties** from the pull-down menu; type CH, MO, PROPS, or PROPERTIES; or use the [Ctrl]+[2] key combination. The attribute to be edited can also be selected while no command is active by right-clicking and selecting **Properties** from the shortcut menu.

Figure 26-4 shows the **Properties** palette with an attribute selected. You can change the color, linetype, or layer of the selected attribute in the **General** section. The attribute tag, prompt, and default value entries are listed in the **Text** section. You can select **Tag**, **Prompt**, or **Value** to change the corresponding values. If the value contains a field, it appears as normal text in the **Properties** palette. If you modify the field text, it is automatically converted to text. The **Text** section also contains options to change the attribute text settings. You can change the insertion point of the text attribute in the **Geometry** section by using the **Position** options to enter new coordinates. Additional text options are available in the **Misc** section.

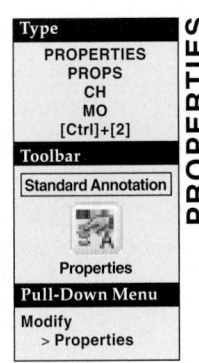

Figure 26-4.
The **Properties**
palette can be used
to modify attributes.

Selected
object to edit

Pick to change
the attribute tag

Pick to change
an attribute mode
setting

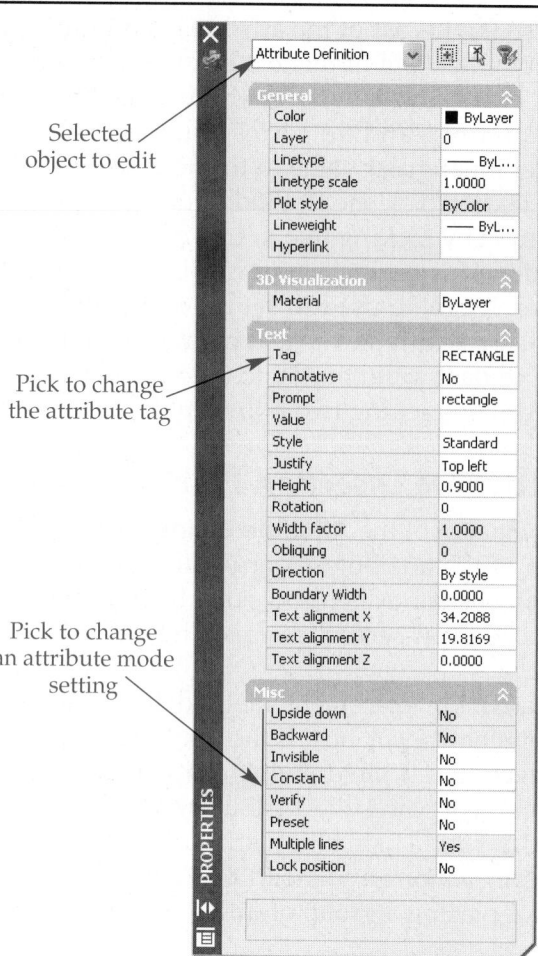

Perhaps the most powerful feature of the **Properties** palette for editing attributes is the ability to change the attribute modes that were originally defined. As described earlier, an attribute may be defined with the **Invisible**, **Constant**, **Verify**, or **Preset** modes active. These settings are located in the **Misc** section of the **Properties** palette.

Creating Blocks with Attributes

Once attributes have been created for an object, use the **BLOCK** or **WBLOCK** command to define the block. Blocks are described in Chapters 23 and 24. When creating the block, be sure to select all of the objects and attributes that go with the block. The order in which you select the attribute definitions is the order in which you are prompted or the order in which the attributes appear in the **Enter Attributes** dialog box. If you select the attribute definitions using either the **Window** or **Crossing** selection method, you will be prompted for the attribute values in the *reverse* order of creation of the attribute definitions.

When creating the block, activate the **Delete** option button in the **Block Definition** dialog box. When the block is created, the selected objects and attributes disappear. If any attributes remain on-screen, undo the command and try again, making sure all of the attributes are selected.

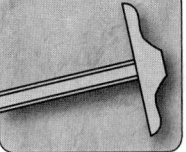
Inserting Blocks with Attributes

When you use the **INSERT** command to place a saved block containing attributes into a drawing, you are prompted for additional information after the block's insertion point, scale factors, and rotation angle are specified. The prompt statement entered with the **ATTDEF** command appears and the default attribute value is shown in brackets. If the attribute was created as a single-line attribute, you can accept the default value by pressing [Enter] or provide a new value and press [Enter]. The attribute is then displayed with the block.

If the attribute was created as a multiple-line attribute, you can accept the default value by pressing [Enter] or provide a new value. Type the first line and then press [Enter] to type the next line. Continue this process as necessary, and press [Enter] when finished. The attribute is then displayed with the block. If the attribute value includes a field, the default must be accepted to maintain the field. If the value is changed at the Command: prompt, the field is lost.

Attribute prompts are answered in a dialog box if the **ATTDIA** system variable is set to 1. After you issue the **INSERT** command and enter the insertion point, scale, and rotation angle of a block, the **Enter Attributes** dialog box appears. See **Figure 26-5**. If the attribute was created as a single-line attribute, the value is entered directly in the text box. If the attribute was created as a multiple-line attribute, the ellipsis (...) button is available for selection, allowing you to enter text using the **In-Place Text Editor**.

The **Enter Attributes** dialog box can list up to eight attributes. If the block has more than eight attributes, the next page of attributes is displayed by picking the **Next** button at the bottom of the dialog box. When you are finished entering values for the attributes, pick **OK** to close the dialog box. The inserted block then appears on-screen with any visible attributes.

Responding to attribute prompts in a dialog box has distinct advantages over answering prompts on the command line. With the dialog box, you can see at a glance whether all of the attribute values are correct. To change a value, move to the incorrect value and enter a new one. If a value includes a field, you can right-click the field to edit it or convert it to text. You can quickly move forward through the attributes and buttons in the **Enter Attributes** dialog box by using the [Tab] key. Using the [Shift]+[Tab] key combination cycles through the attributes and buttons in reverse order.

Figure 26-5.
The **Enter Attributes**
dialog box allows
you to enter or
change attribute
definitions when a
block is inserted.

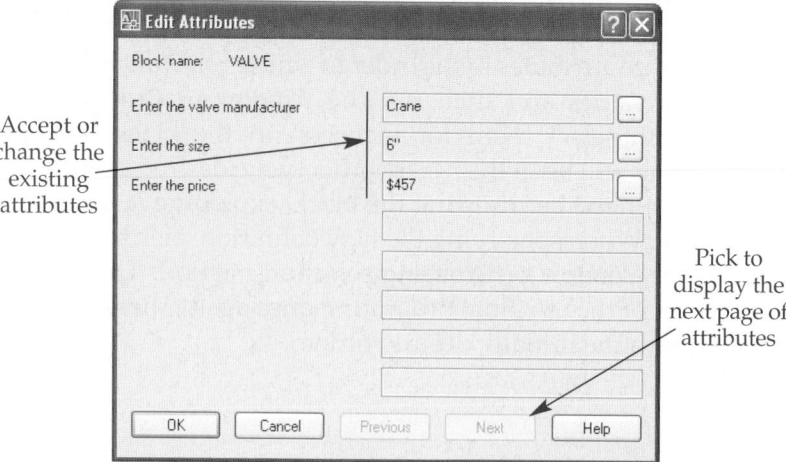

Accept or
change the
existing
attributes

Pick to
display the
next page of
attributes

PROFESSIONAL TIP

Set the **ATTDIA** system variable to 1 in your template drawings to activate the **Enter Attributes** dialog box automatically whenever a block with attributes is inserted.

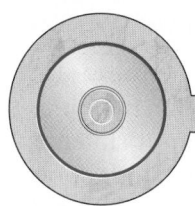

Exercise 26-1

Complete the exercise on the Student CD.

Attribute Prompt Suppression

Some drawings may use blocks with attributes that always retain their default values. In this case, there is no need to be prompted for the attribute values when inserting a block. You can turn off the attribute prompts by setting the **ATTREQ** system variable to 0.

After making this setting, try inserting the VALVE block created in Exercise 26-1. Notice that none of the attribute prompts appear. To display attribute prompts again, change the setting back to 1. The **ATTREQ** system variable setting is saved with the drawing.

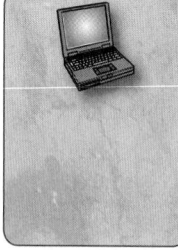

PROFESSIONAL TIP

Part of your project and drawing planning should involve the setting of system variables such as **ATTREQ**. Setting **ATTREQ** to 0 before using blocks can save time in the drawing process. Always remember to set **ATTREQ** back to 1 when you want to use the prompts instead of accepting defaults. When anticipated attribute prompts are not issued, you should check the current **ATTREQ** setting and adjust it if necessary.

Controlling the Display of Attributes

Attributes are intended to contain valuable information about the blocks in a drawing. Some attributes are used only to generate materials lists and to speed accounting. These types of attributes are not displayed on-screen or during plotting.

AutoCAD and Its Applications—Basics

To control the display of attributes on-screen, use the **ATTDISP** (attribute display) command. This command can be accessed by picking **View** > **Display** > **Attribute Display** or by typing ATTDISP. This command has three options:

- **Normal.** Displays attributes exactly as they were created. This is the default setting.
- **ON.** Displays *all* attributes, including those defined with the **Invisible** mode.
- **OFF.** Suppresses the display of *all* attributes.

PROFESSIONAL TIP

After attributes have been drawn, defined with blocks, and checked for accuracy, hide them with the **Off** option of the **ATTDISP** command. If attributes are left on, they clutter the screen and lengthen regeneration time. In a drawing in which attributes should be visible but are not, check the current setting of **ATTDISP** and adjust it if necessary.

Changing Attribute Values

You can edit attributes before they are included in a block using the **Properties** palette. However, once a block with attributes is inserted in a drawing, different commands are used to edit the inserted attributes. Inserted attribute values within a single block can be modified using the **Enhanced Attribute Editor**.

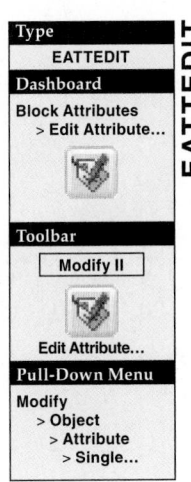

To access the **Enhanced Attribute Editor** dialog box, pick the **Edit Attribute...** button on the **Modify II** toolbar or the **Block Attributes** control panel of the **Dashboard**, select **Modify** > **Object** > **Attribute** > **Single...** from the pull-down menu, or type EATTEDIT. You are then prompted to select a block. Pick the block containing the attributes you wish to modify to display **Enhanced Attribute Editor**. See **Figure 26-6**.

The **Enhanced Attribute Editor** contains three tabs. The **Attribute** tab is displayed by default with the attributes in the selected block listed in the window. Pick the attribute to be modified. Then enter a new value for the attribute in the **Value:** text box. If the attribute was created as a multiple-line attribute, the ellipsis (...) button is available for selection, allowing you to modify text using the **In-Place Text Editor**. Pick the **Apply** button after adjusting the value. You can also edit multiple-line attribute values without accessing the **Enhanced Attribute Editor** by using the **ATTIPEDIT** command.

Figure 26-6.
Select the attribute to be modified and change its value in the **Attribute** tab of the **Enhanced Attribute Editor**.

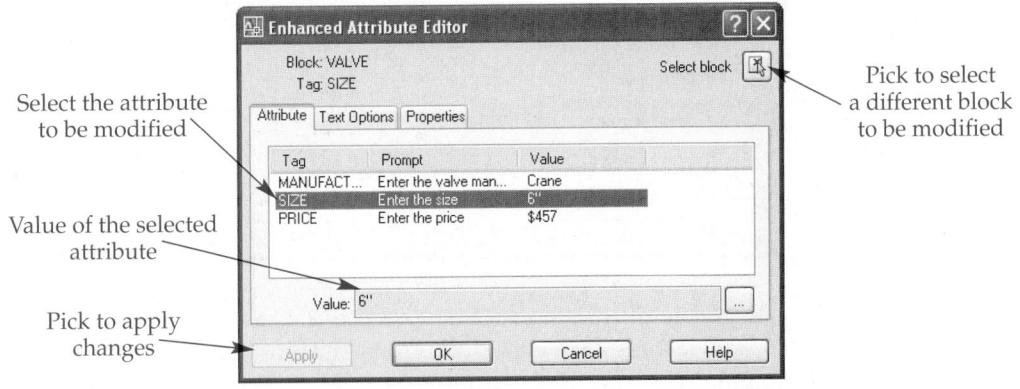

If you want to select a different block to modify, pick the **Select block** button in the dialog box. The dialog box closes temporarily to allow you to select a different block in the drawing. The dialog box is then redisplayed with the attributes for the selected block shown.

Other properties of the selected attribute can be modified using the two other tabs in the **Enhanced Attribute Editor** dialog box. The **Text Options** tab allows you to modify the text properties of the attribute. See **Figure 26-7**. The **Properties** tab contains settings for the object properties of the attribute. See **Figure 26-8**.

After editing the attribute values and properties, pick the **Apply** button to have the changes reflected on-screen. Picking the **OK** button closes the dialog box and applies any changes.

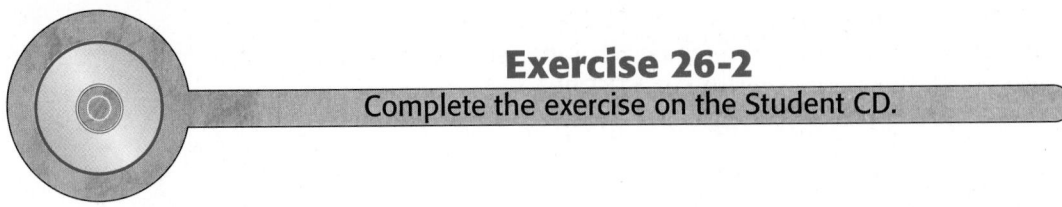

Exercise 26-2

Complete the exercise on the Student CD.

Figure 26-7.
The **Text Options** tab provides options in addition to those set in the **Attribute Definition** dialog box.

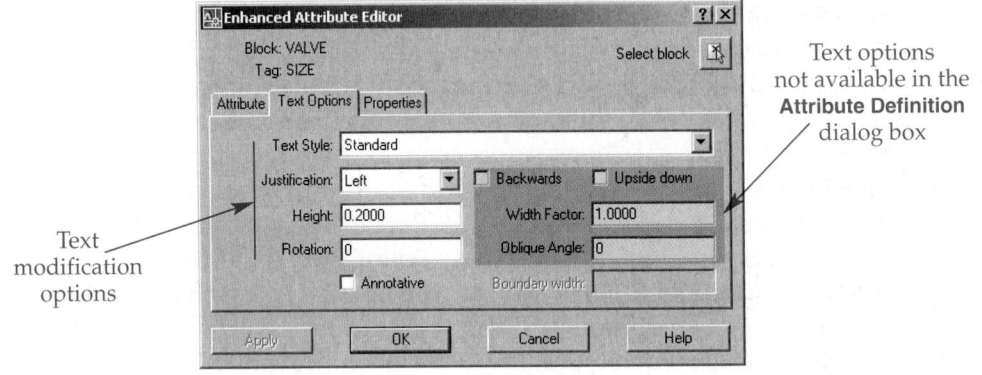

Figure 26-8.
The **Properties** tab can be used to modify an attribute's object properties.

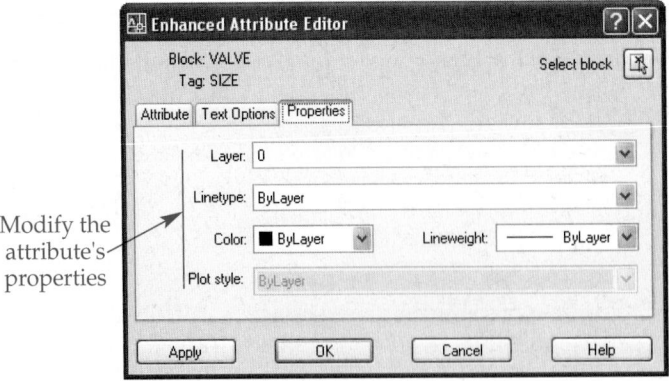

AutoCAD and Its Applications—Basics

Using the Find Command to Edit Attributes

One of the quickest ways to edit attributes is to use the **FIND** command. With no command active, right-click in the drawing area and select **Find...** from the shortcut menu. The **Find and Replace** dialog box is displayed. You can then search the entire drawing or a selected group of objects for an attribute. The **Find and Replace** dialog box is described in detail in Chapter 9.

PROFESSIONAL TIP

If you know specific attributes may need to be changed in the future, make a group out of them. Use the **GROUP** command, select all of the attributes, and give the group a name. Then, after picking the **Select objects** button in the **Find and Replace** dialog box, type G and specify the name of the group. All objects in that group are selected.

Editing Attribute Values and Properties Globally

The **Enhanced Attribute Editor** allows you to edit attribute values by selecting blocks one at a time. You can also edit several block attributes at once or edit attributes individually by answering prompts on the command line. This type of attribute editing is done with the **-ATTEDIT** command. To access this command, select **Modify > Object > Attribute > Global** or type -ATE or -ATTEDIT.

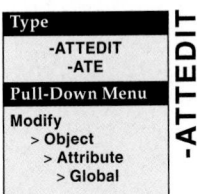

Type
-ATTEDIT
-ATE

Pull-Down Menu
Modify
> Object
> Attribute
> Global

-ATTEDIT

This prompt asks if you want to edit attributes individually. Pressing [Enter] at this prompt to accept the default Yes allows you to select any number of different block attributes for individual editing. AutoCAD lets you edit them all, one at a time, without leaving the command.

It is also possible to change the same attribute on several insertions of the same block. If you enter the **-ATTEDIT** command and respond with No, you can change specific letters, words, and values of a single attribute. This lets you change all other insertions, or instances, of the same block and is known as *global attribute editing*. For example, suppose a block with the attribute RESISTOR was inserted on a drawing in twelve locations. However, you misspelled the attribute as RESISTER. If you enter the **-ATTEDIT** command and specify No when asked whether to edit attributes individually, you can edit the attribute globally.

global attribute editing: Editing or changing all insertions, or instances, of the same block in a single operation.

Each **-ATTEDIT** editing technique allows you to determine the exact block and attribute specifications to edit. The following prompts appear after you specify individual or global editing:

> Enter block name specification <*>:
> Enter attribute tag specification <*>:
> Enter attribute value specification <*>:

To selectively edit attribute values, respond to each prompt with the correct name or value. You are then prompted to select one or more attributes. Suppose you receive the following message after entering an attribute value and selecting an attribute:

> 0 found

You picked an attribute that was not specified correctly. It is often quicker to press [Enter] at each of the three specification prompts and then pick the attribute you need to edit.

In **Figure 26-9A**, the VALVE block from Exercise 26-1 was inserted three times with the manufacturer's name specified as CRANE. Unfortunately, the name was supposed to be POWELL. To change the attribute for each insertion, enter the **-ATTEDIT** command and specify global editing. Then, press [Enter] at each of the three specification prompts and respond to the prompts that follow.

Chapter 26   Using Attributes

Figure 26-9.
Using the global editing technique with the **-ATTEDIT** command allows you to change the same attribute on several block insertions.

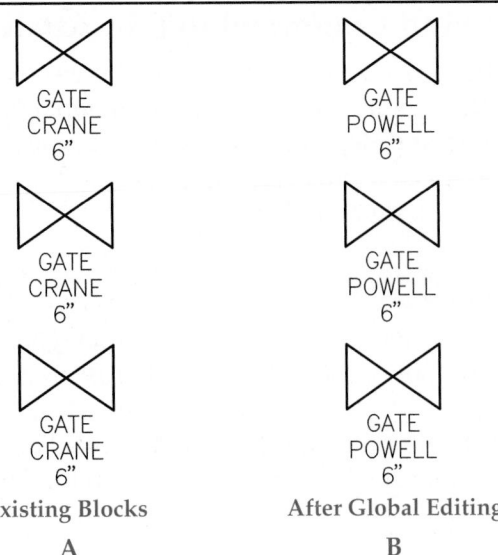

Existing Blocks   After Global Editing

A   B

Command: **-ATE** *or* **-ATTEDIT.**↵
Edit attributes one at a time? [Yes/No] <Y>: **N**↵
Performing global editing of attribute values.
Edit only attributes visible on screen? [Yes/No] <Y>: ↵
Enter block name specification <*>: ↵
Enter attribute tag specification <*>: ↵
Enter attribute value specification <*>: ↵
Select Attributes: (*pick* CRANE *on each of the* VALVE *blocks and press* [Enter] *when completed*)
3 attributes selected.
Enter string to change: **CRANE**↵
Enter new string: **POWELL**↵

After pressing [Enter], the CRANE attributes on the selected blocks are changed to the new value POWELL. See **Figure 26-9B**.

PROFESSIONAL TIP

Use care when assigning the **Constant** mode to attribute definitions. The **-ATTEDIT** command displays 0 found if you attempt to edit a block attribute with a **Constant** mode setting. Assign the **Constant** mode only to attributes you know will not change.

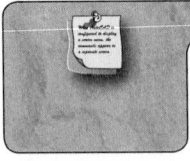

NOTE

The **-ATTEDIT** command can also be used to edit individual attribute values and properties. However, it is more efficient to use the **Enhanced Attribute Editor** for changing individual attributes.

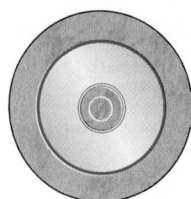

Exercise 26-3

Complete the exercise on the Student CD.

Changing Attribute Definitions

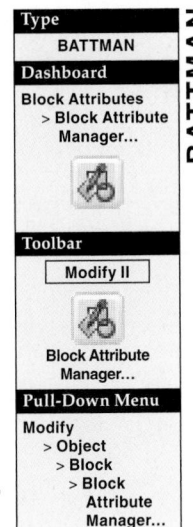
Before saving an attribute within a block, you can modify the tag, prompt, and default value using the **DDEDIT** command. However, once an attribute is saved in a block definition, you must use the **Block Attribute Manager** to change the attribute definition.

The **Block Attribute Manager** is accessed by picking the **Block Attribute Manager...** button from the **Modify II** toolbar or the **Block Attributes** control panel of the **Dashboard**, selecting **Modify > Object > Attribute > Block Attribute Manager...** from the pull-down menu, or typing BATTMAN. The **Block Attribute Manager** is shown in Figure 26-10.

The **Block Attribute Manager** lists the attributes for the selected block. To select a block, choose it from the **Block:** drop-down list or pick the **Select block** button to return to the drawing area and pick the block. By default, the tag, prompt, default value, and modes for each attribute are listed.

The attribute list reflects the order in which prompts appear when a block is inserted. To change the order, use the **Move Up** and **Move Down** buttons to change the location of the selected attribute within the list. To delete an attribute, pick the **Remove** button.

You can select the attribute properties to be listed in the **Block Attribute Manager** by picking the **Settings...** button to open the **Settings** dialog box. See Figure 26-11. Select the properties to list in the **Display in list** area. When the **Emphasize duplicate tags** check box at the bottom of the dialog box is checked, attributes with identical tags are highlighted in red. If you want the changes you make in the **Block Attribute**

Figure 26-10.
Use the **Block Attribute Manager** to change attribute definitions, delete attributes, and change the order of attribute prompts.

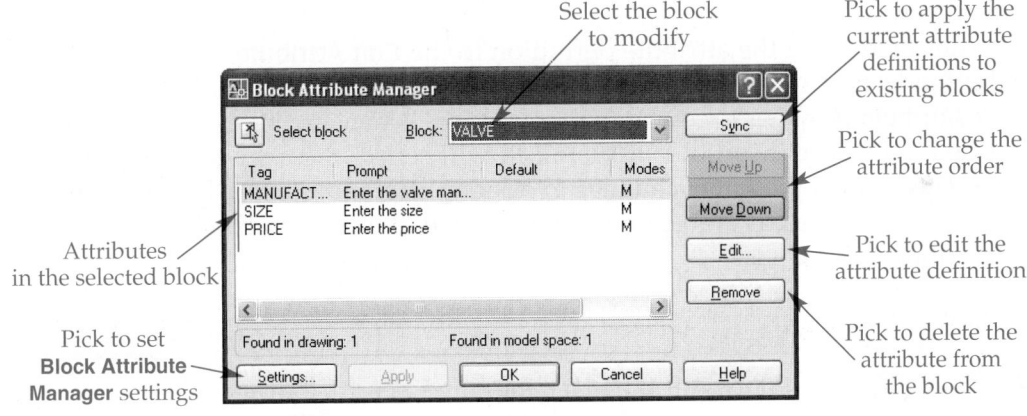

Figure 26-11.
The **Settings** dialog box controls the types of attributes displayed in the **Block Attribute Manager**.

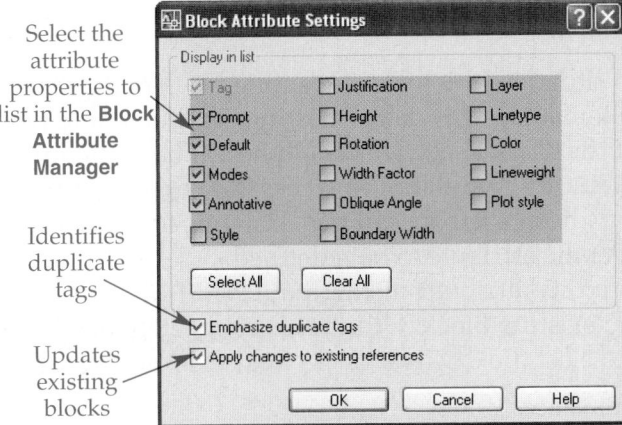

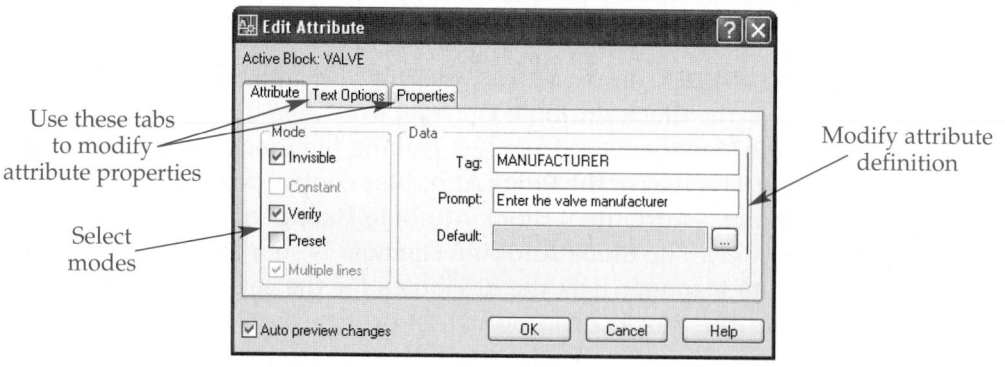

Manager applied to existing blocks, check the **Apply changes to existing references** check box. When all settings have been made in the **Settings** dialog box, pick the **OK** button to close it and return to the **Block Attribute Manager**.

To modify an attribute definition, select the attribute in the **Block Attribute Manager** and pick the **Edit...** button. The **Edit Attribute** dialog box is displayed, as shown in Figure 26-12. The **Attribute** tab of this dialog box allows you to modify the modes, tag, prompt, and default value.

The **Text Options** and **Properties** tabs of the **Edit Attribute** dialog box are identical to the tabs found in the **Enhanced Attribute Editor**. These tabs allow you to modify the object properties of the attributes. If the **Auto preview changes** check box at the bottom of the dialog box is checked, changes to attributes are displayed in the drawing area immediately.

After modifying the attribute definition in the **Edit Attribute** dialog box, pick the **OK** button to return to the **Block Attribute Manager**. Then pick the **OK** button in the **Block Attribute Manager** to return to the drawing. When attributes within a block are modified, all future insertions of the block will reflect the changes. Existing blocks are updated only if the **Apply changes to existing references** check box in the **Settings** dialog box is checked. If this option is not selected, the existing blocks retain the original attribute definitions.

> **NOTE**
>
> The **Block Attribute Manager** modifies attribute *definitions,* not attribute *values.* Attribute values can be modified with the **Enhanced Attribute Editor**.

Redefining a Block and Its Attributes

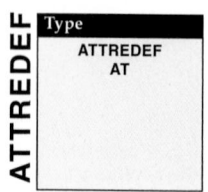

You may encounter a situation in which an existing block and its associated attributes must be revised. You may need to delete existing attributes, add new attributes, or revise the geometry of the block itself. This could be a time-consuming task, but it is made easy with the **ATTREDEF** command. To access this command, type ATTREDEF. If the command has already been used once in this drawing, you can also type AT. You are then prompted to select the attribute to be redefined.

To redefine a block and its attributes using the **ATTREDEF** command, you must first explode a copy of the existing block. Otherwise, completely new geometry must be used. If you attempt to select the existing block, this error message is displayed:

New block has no attributes.

After you explode the existing block (or draw new geometry) and modify the attributes as needed, use the **ATTREDEF** command:

> Command: **AT** *or* **ATTREDEF**↵
> Enter name of the block you wish to redefine: *(enter the block name and press* [Enter]*)*
> Select objects for new Block...
> Select objects: *(select the block geometry and all new and existing attributes; then press* [Enter]*)*
> Specify insertion base point of new Block: *(pick the insertion base point)*

When you pick the insertion point, all existing instances of the block and attributes are immediately updated. If any of the attributes were omitted from the redefined block, they are not included in the new version.

Automating Drafting Documentation

So far, you have seen that attributes are extremely powerful tools for assigning textual information to drawing symbols. However, attributes can also be used to automate any detailing or documentation task that requires a great deal of text. Such tasks include the creation of title block information, revision block data, and a parts list or list of materials.

Creating Title Blocks

After a drawing is completely developed and dimensioned, it is necessary to fill out the information used in the drawing title block. This is usually one of the more time-consuming tasks associated with drafting documentation, and it can be efficiently automated by assigning attributes. The following guidelines are suggested:

- First draw the title block format in accordance with industry or company standards. Use the correct layer(s), typically the 0 layer, and be sure to include your company or school logo in the title block. If you work in an industry that produces items for the federal government, also include the applicable Federal Supply Code for Manufacturers (FSCM) in the title block. A typical title block drawn in accordance with the ASME Y14.1 *Decimal Inch Drawing Sheet Size and Format* standard is shown in **Figure 26-13**.

> **NOTE**
>
> The FSCM is a five-digit numerical code identifier applicable to any organization that produces items used by the federal government. It also applies to government activities that are responsible for the development of certain specifications, drawings, or standards that control the design of items.

Figure 26-13.
A title block must comply with applicable standards. This title block complies with the ASME Y14.1, *Decimal Inch Drawing Sheet Size and Format* standard.

Figure 26-14.

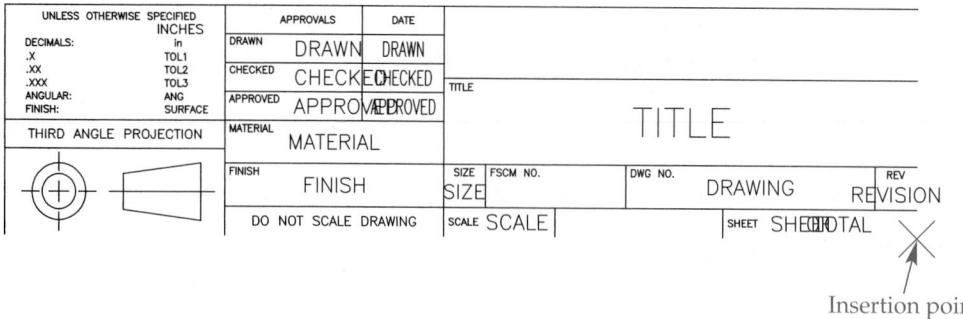

Insertion point

- Define attributes for each area of the title block. As you create the attributes, determine the appropriate text height and justification for each definition. Attributes should be defined for the drawing title, drawing number, drafter, checker, dates, drawing scale, sheet size, material, finish, revision letter, and tolerance information. See **Figure 26-14.** Include any other information that may be specific to your organization or application.
- Assign default values to the attributes wherever possible. For example, if your organization consistently specifies the same overall tolerances on drawing dimensions, the tolerance attributes can be assigned default values.

PROFESSIONAL TIP

The size of each area within the title block limits on the number of characters you can have in a line of text. You can provide a handy cue to yourself by including a reminder in the attribute. When defining an attribute in which you wish to place a reminder, include the information in the attribute prompt. For example, the prompt could read Enter drawing name (15 characters max). Each time a block or drawing containing the attribute is used, the prompt displays the reminder.

Once you have defined each attribute in the title block, you can use the **WBLOCK** command to save the drawing as a file to disk so it can be inserted into a new drawing. You can also use the **BLOCK** command to create a block of the defined attributes within the current file, which can then be saved as a template or wblock file. Both methods are acceptable and are explained in the next sections.

Regardless of the method used, attributes allow you to enter title block data quickly and accurately without the use of text commands. **Figure 26-15** shows the completed title block after insertion of the attribute block created in **Figure 26-14.** If the attributes are entered using the **Enter Attributes** dialog box, all the information can be seen at once and mistakes can be corrected quickly. Attributes can easily be edited at a later date if necessary.

Wblock method

The **WBLOCK** command saves a drawing file to disk so it can be inserted into any drawing that is currently open. Drawings used in this manner should be given descriptive names. An A-size title block, for example, could be named TITLE_A or FORMAT_A. Also, be sure to use 0,0 as the insertion point for the title block.

To use the wblock file, begin a new drawing and insert the template drawing. After you locate and scale the drawing, the attribute prompts are displayed. If the **ATTDIA** system variable is set to 1, all of the attributes can be accepted or edited in the

Figure 26-15.
The title block after insertion of the attributes. When the drawing is complete, dates and approvals can be added.

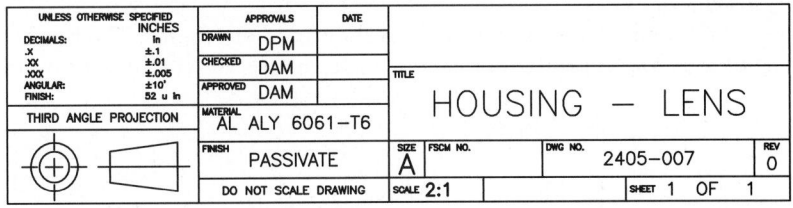

Enter Attributes dialog box. When you pick **OK** to close the dialog box, the attributes are placed in the title block. This method requires that you begin with a new drawing and know the information requested by the attribute prompts.

Block method

The **BLOCK** command uses the **Block Definition** dialog box to create a block of the defined attributes in the title block. When you select the objects for the block, be sure to select only the defined attributes. Do not select the headings of the title block areas or any of the geometry in the title block. When selecting the insertion base point, pick a corner of the title block that will be convenient to use each time the block is inserted into a drawing. The point indicated in **Figure 26-14** shows an appropriate location for the insertion base point.

Finally, activate the **Delete** option button in the **Block Definition** dialog box so the attribute definitions will be removed from the title block. When the block is inserted, the attribute values are inserted where the attribute definitions were located. You can also place the attribute definitions on a frozen layer so the original attributes will not be displayed. The current drawing now contains a block of defined attributes for use in the title block.

If you save the drawing as a template file and begin a new drawing using the template, the title block data can be entered at any time during the creation of the new drawing. To do so, issue the **INSERT** command, enter the name of the block in the **Insert** dialog box, and pick the proper insertion base point. The attribute prompts are then displayed either on the command line or in a dialog box, depending on the value of the **ATTDIA** system variable.

Creating Revision Blocks

It is almost certain that a detail drawing will require revision at some time. Typical changes that occur include design improvements and the correction of drafting errors. The first time a drawing is revised, it is usually assigned the revision letter *A*. If necessary, revision letters continue with *B* through *Y*, but the letters *I*, *O*, *Q*, *S*, *X*, and *Z* are not used because they might be confused with numbers.

Drawing layout formats include an area specifically designated to record all drawing changes. This area is normally located at the upper-right corner of the drawing sheet and is commonly called the *revision block*. The revision block provides space for the revision letter, a description of the change, the date, and approvals. These items are entered in columns. A column for the zone is only included if applicable. *Zones* are intended for larger drawings and used to help direct the print reader's attention to the correction location on the drawing. Zones are identified in the margins of a title block sheet by letters and numbers. They are used for reference purposes in the same way reference letters and numbers are used to identify a street or feature on a road map. Although A-size and B-size title blocks may include zones, they are rarely needed.

Block attributes provide a handy means of completing the necessary information in a revision block. Refer to **Figure 26-16** as you follow these steps to create a revision block:

revision block: A block that provides space for the revision letter, a description of the change, the date, and approvals.

zones: A system of letters and numbers used on large drawings to help direct the print reader's attention to the correction location on the drawing.

Figure 26-16.
The revision block consists of lines and defined attributes. The border lines must be drawn as part of the block, and the upper-left corner is used as the insertion point.

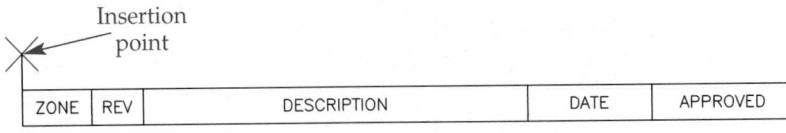

1. Create the drawing geometry for the revision block using the appropriate layer(s), typically the 0 layer.
2. Define attributes that describe the zone (optional), revision letter, description of change, date, and change approval. Use left-justified text for the change description attribute and middle-justified text for the remainder of the attributes.
3. Use the **WBLOCK** command to save the revision block and attributes as a drawing file. Use a descriptive name, such as REVBLK or REV. Keep in mind that each line of the revision block has its own border lines. Therefore, the borders must be saved with the attributes. Use the upper-left endpoint of the revision block as the insertion point.

After a drawing has been revised, insert the revision block at the correct location. If the **ATTDIA** system variable is set to 1, the attribute prompts are answered in the **Enter Attributes** dialog box. After providing the change information, pick the **OK** button and the completed revision block is automatically added to the title block sheet. See **Figure 26-17.**

Creating Parts Lists

Assembly drawings require a parts list, or list of materials, that provides information about each component of the assembly or subassembly. This information includes the quantity, FSCM (when necessary), part number, description, and item number for each component. In some organizations, the parts list is generated as a separate document, usually in an 8-1/2″ × 11″ format. In other companies, it is common practice to include the parts list on the face of the assembly drawing. If the parts list is added to the assembly drawing, it is usually placed directly above the title block, depending on industry and company standards. Whether created as a separate document or as part of the assembly drawing itself, parts lists provide another example of how attributes can be used to automate the documentation process.

Usually, the most effective way to create a parts list is to use a table. Creating and using tables is described in Chapter 10. Table data can even be linked to existing spreadsheet content, or it can be extracted from the drawing to create a separate document. Blocks and attributes can be used as an alternative to creating parts lists. Refer to **Figure 26-18** as you follow these steps for creating a parts list:

Figure 26-17.
The completed revision block after it is inserted into the drawing.

REVISION HISTORY				
ZONE	REV	DESCRIPTION	DATE	APPROVED
C3	A	ADDED .125 CHAMFER	08−12−09	

Figure 26-18.
The parts list block is drawn with defined attributes and the insertion point located at the lower-left endpoint.

ITEM
QTY
FSCM
PART
DESC
MATL
Insertion point

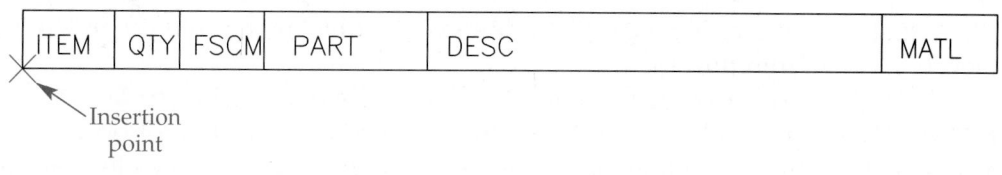

1. Create a parts list block using the appropriate drawing layer(s), typically the 0 layer.
2. Define attributes that describe the quantity, FSCM (when necessary), part number, item description, material specification, and item number for the components of an assembly drawing. Use left-justified text for the item description attribute and middle-justified text for the other attributes.
3. Use the **WBLOCK** command to save the parts list block to disk with a descriptive name, such as PL for parts list or BOM for bill of materials. You can also use the **BLOCK** command to create a block of the parts list in the current drawing. Use the lower-left endpoint of the parts list block as the insertion point, as shown in Figure 26-18.

Now, after an assembly drawing has been completed, insert the parts list block into the drawing at the correct location. If the **ATTDIA** system variable is set to 1, the attribute prompts are answered in the **Enter Attributes** dialog box. After providing the necessary information, pick the **OK** button and the completed parts list block is automatically added to the title block sheet. See Figure 26-19. Repeat the procedure as many times as required until each component of the assembly drawing is included in the parts list.

Figure 26-19.
The completed parts list block after it is inserted into the drawing.

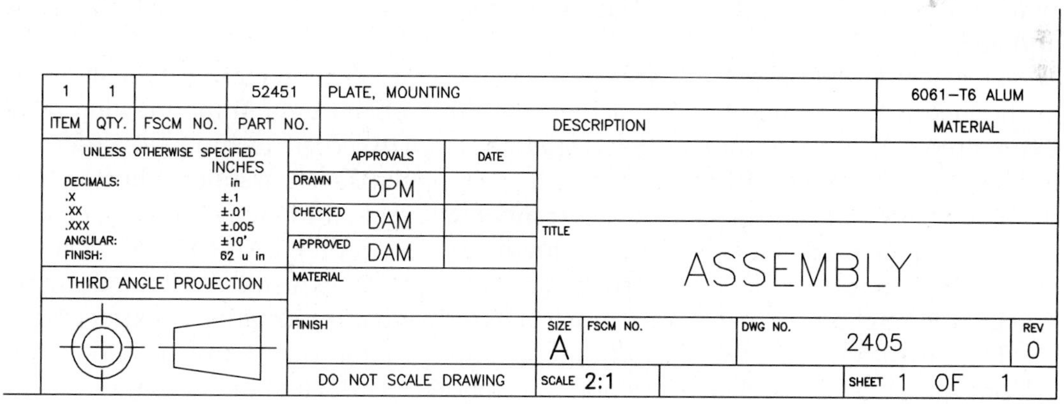

1
1
52451
PLATE, MOUNTING
6061–T6 ALUM
ITEM
QTY.
FSCM NO.
PART NO.
DESCRIPTION
MATERIAL
UNLESS OTHERWISE SPECIFIED
INCHES
in
DECIMALS:
.X ±.1
.XX ±.01
.XXX ±.005
ANGULAR: ±10'
FINISH: 62 u in
APPROVALS
DATE
DRAWN DPM
CHECKED DAM
APPROVED DAM
MATERIAL
THIRD ANGLE PROJECTION
FINISH
DO NOT SCALE DRAWING
TITLE
ASSEMBLY
SIZE A
FSCM NO.
DWG NO. 2405
REV 0
SCALE 2:1
SHEET 1 OF 1

Using Fields to Reference Attributes

You can list attributes in fields. This allows you to display the value of an attribute in a location away from the block.

To display an attribute value in a field, access the **Field** dialog box from within the **MTEXT** or **TEXT** command or by picking **Insert > Field...** from the pull-down menu. In the **Field** dialog box, pick **Objects** from the **Field category:** drop-down list and then pick **Object** in the **Field names:** list box. Next, pick the **Select object** button to return to the drawing window and select the block containing the attribute.

When you select the block, the **Field** dialog box reappears with the available properties listed. Pick the desired attribute tag to display the corresponding value in the **Preview:** box. Select the format and pick **OK** to have the field inserted in the text object.

Collecting Attribute Information

data extraction:
The process of extracting drawing content to a table or exporting it to an external file.

Existing AutoCAD drawing information, including attributes, can be reused to create a table or exported to an external file. This process is known as *data extraction*, which involves the process of extracting drawing content. In Chapter 10, you were introduced to extracting layer and object geometry to create a table. The same process can be used to extract additional drawing information. In fact, you can extract the data from most AutoCAD objects.

Attribute values and definitions can be extracted from a drawing and organized in a table or text file. This is an excellent application for data extraction, and it is useful for creating bills of materials, schedules, and parts lists. Using existing drawing data automates the process of drawing tables and listing information. Data is already available and can be added to a table or external file, without you having to type and locate the information. Extracted data is also associated with the drawing. As a result, when changes are made to the drawing data, the information in the table or text file can be updated.

DATAEXTRACTION

Type
DATAEXTRACTION
DX
EATTEXT

Dashboard
Block Attributes
> Data Extraction...

Toolbar
Modify II

Data Extraction...

Pull-Down Menu
Tools
> Data Extraction...

Data is extracted using the **Data Extraction** wizard. This wizard can be accessed in the **Insert Table** dialog box by picking the **From object data in the drawing (Data Extraction)** radio button from the **Insert options** area. This access technique is described in Chapter 10. The wizard is also available by picking the **Data Extraction...** button from the **Block Attributes** control panel in the **Dashboard** or from the **Modify II** toolbar, picking **Tools > Data Extraction...** from the pull-down menu, or typing DATAEXTRACTION, DX, or EATTEXT. In most cases, only certain types of data are extracted from the drawing. The **Data Extraction** wizard is used to select exactly what information is extracted.

Data extraction has many applications, and multiple data extraction tools and options are available for data extraction. The following information focuses on a basic example of using data extraction to develop a bill of materials. This information can be applied to a variety of similar and more advanced data extraction requirements. **Figure 26-20** shows an example of a basic landscape plan. The trees, shrubs, and plants are drawn as blocks and include attributes that specify species, height, diameter, and cost. The blocks were inserted on the appropriate TREE, SHRUB, or PLANT layer. **Figure 26-21** shows the original objects and attributes used to create the block, and each type of item created using the block. Data extraction will be used in this example to extract the species, height, diameter, cost, and quantity of each different tree, shrub, and plant to create a landscape bill of materials.

Figure 26-20.

An example of a basic landscaping plan. Tree, shrub, and plant blocks contain attributes that can be extracted to form a bill of materials.

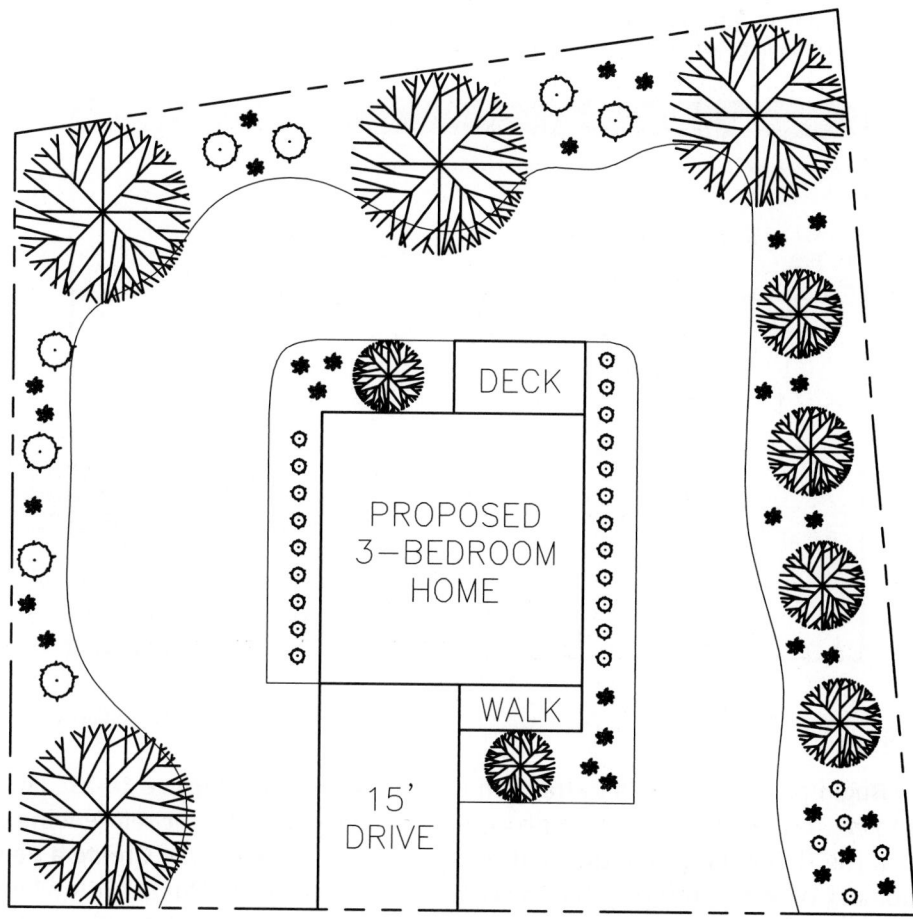

Figure 26-21.

Original object and attributes before they have been turned into blocks. The blocks are scaled and the attributes are defined when inserted. This process is used to create various trees, shrubs, and plants.

Block	Used to Create
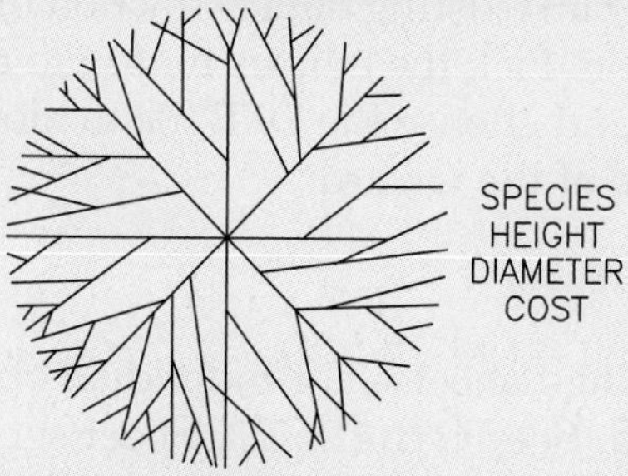 SPECIES HEIGHT DIAMETER COST	Birch trees: 30' tall, 20' diameter, $50 each Lace leaf maple trees: 5' tall, 8' diameter, $250 each Crab apple trees: 15' tall, 10' diameter, $35 each
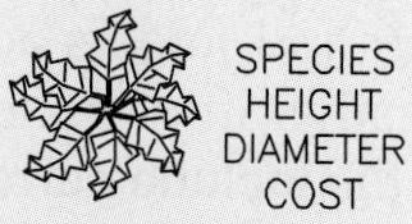 SPECIES HEIGHT DIAMETER COST	Geranium plants: 10" tall, 18" diameter, $10 each Fern plants: 18" tall, 18" diameter, $12 each
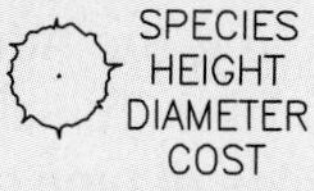 SPECIES HEIGHT DIAMETER COST	Rhododendron shrubs: 4' tall, 4' diameter, $75 each Heather shrubs: 18" tall, 18" diameter, $15 each

Figure 26-22.
Use the **Begin** page of the **Data Extraction** wizard to create a new data extraction file, reference a data extraction template, or edit an existing data extraction file.

Pick to create a new data extraction
using an existing template

Pick to create a new data extraction

Pick to modify an existing data extraction

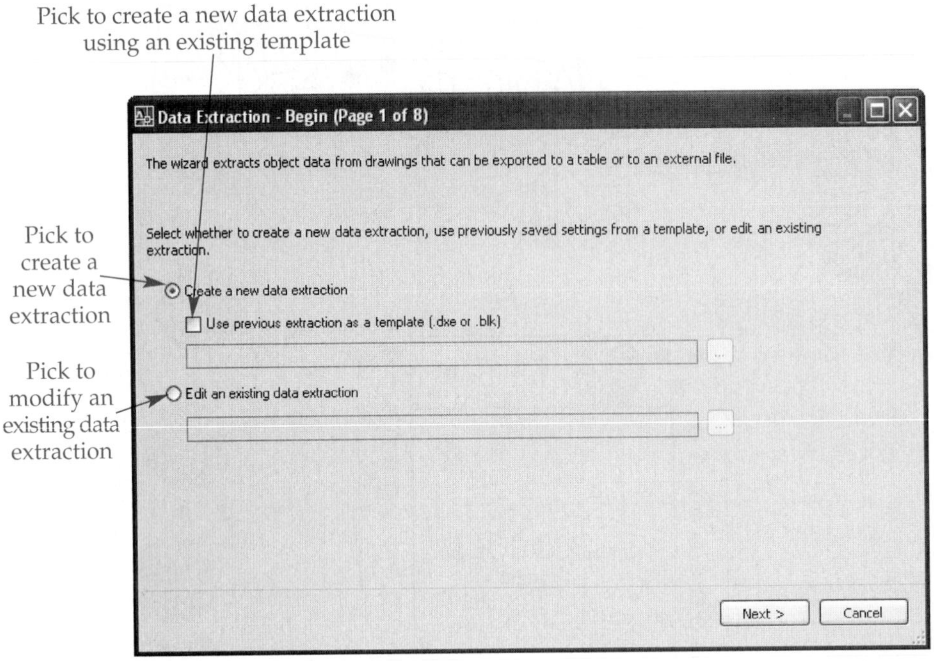

Begin Page

The **Begin** page of the **Data Extraction** wizard is shown in **Figure 26-22.** This page is used to begin the data extraction process by creating, editing, or referencing a data extraction file. To create a new data extraction file (DXE), select the **Create a new data extraction** radio button and pick the **Next>** button. Selecting the **Next>** button launches the **Save Data Extraction As** button dialog box, which allows you to create a DXE file. Saving the DXE file displays the next page of the wizard.

If you want to use an existing DXE file to form a new data extraction, pick the **Use previous extraction as a template (.dxe or .blk)** check box, available when the **Create a new data extraction** radio button is selected. Pick the ellipsis button to open the **Open Template** dialog box and select the existing data extraction template (DXE) or an attribute extraction template (BLK) file. Then pick the **Next>** button to display the next page of the wizard. You also have the option of modifying an existing data extraction file by picking the **Edit existing data extraction** radio button. Pick the ellipsis button to open the **Select Existing Data Extraction File** dialog box and choose the DXE file to modify. Then pick the **Next>** button to display the next page of the wizard.

Define Data Source Page

In the next page, **Define Data Source**, the drawings, sheet set or individual objects from which the data is to be gathered is specified. See **Figure 26-23.** Sheet sets are described in Chapter 29. The selected drawing files or objects are known as the data source. The **Drawing files and folders:** area shows the files and folders added to the data source. Pick the **Drawings/Sheet set** radio button to gather information from the current drawing and, if necessary, other drawings. Select the **Include current drawing** check box to add the current drawing file to the data source. Other drawing files or sheet set data files can be added to the data source by selecting the **Add Drawings...** button and using the **Select Files** dialog box to choose the files. To select all of the drawings associated with a saved sheet set file, change the **Files of type** option to ***.dst** and navigate to the sheet set file. Pick the **Add Folder...** button to add the files in a folder to the data source using the **Add Folder Options** dialog box.

Figure 26-23.
Use the **Define Data Source** page of the **Data Extraction** wizard to select the drawing or drawings, sheet set, or objects from which to extract data.

Pick to extract data from the current drawing, other drawing files, or sheet sets

Check to extract data from the current drawing

Pick to extract data from objects selected in the current drawing

Data Extraction - Define Data Source (Page 2 of 8)

Data source
○ Drawings/Sheet set
  ☑ Include current drawing
○ Select objects in the current drawing

Drawing files and folders:
  📁 Folders
  ⊟ 📁 Drawings
      C:\Documents and Settings\Jdec.GWP\My Documents\AutoCAD\Basics 2008\Art\Ch25\

Add Folder ...
Add Drawings ...
Remove

Settings...

< Back   Next >   Cancel

Current drawing

Another option for gathering data is to select specific objects in the current drawing. Pick the **Select objects** radio button and the **Select objects in the current drawing** button to return to the drawing area and select the objects to be included in the data source. Objects can only be selected from the current drawing.

Picking the **Settings...** button opens the **Data Extraction - Additional Settings** dialog box. The following options are available in this dialog box:

- **Extract objects from blocks.** Includes block information in the extraction.
- **Extract objects from xrefs.** Includes objects in xrefs in the extraction. Otherwise, xref content is not included.
- **Include xrefs in block count.** Causes xrefs to be counted as blocks.
- **Objects in model space.** Extracts only the objects in model space. Objects in paper space are ignored.
- **All objects in drawing.** Includes all objects in the drawing in the extraction.

PROFESSIONAL TIP

Add multiple files or a sheet set to the data source to compile file properties such as Tile, Comments, Drawing Revision, and File Name. This data can be used to draw a parts list or similar type of table.

Figure 26-24.
Use the **Select Objects** page of the **Data Extraction** wizard to select the objects found in the data source from which to extract properties.

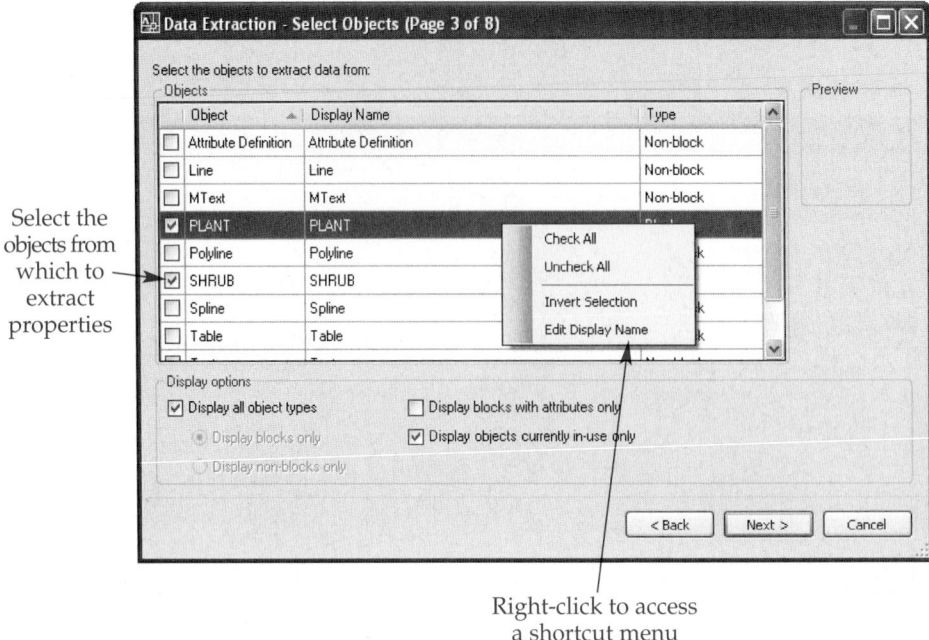

Select the objects from which to extract properties →

Right-click to access a shortcut menu

Select Objects Page

After you have selected a data source, pick the **Next** button to display the **Select Objects** page. See **Figure 26-24.** This page lists all the data source objects. In this context, an *object* is any item added to the data source, such as drawing geometry, text, blocks, hatch patterns, dimensions, and tables. The landscape plan drawing contains lines, splines, polylines, single-line and multiline text, blocks, and attribute definitions.

Use the **Select Objects** page to choose the objects that contain the data, or properties, you want to reference when creating the table. For example, only blocks are selected to create the landscape bill of materials, because the blocks contain all attribute information needed.

You can specify which objects are listed by adjusting the settings in the **Display options** area. Deselect the **Display all object types** check box to filter the display of blocks. Choose the **Display blocks only** radio button to only list blocks. Then, you can choose to list only those blocks with attributes by picking the **Display blocks with attributes only** check box. Pick the **Display non-blocks only** radio button to list all objects except blocks. Select the **Display objects currently in-use only** check box to show only the objects found in the data source.

After you adjust the display options, pick the check boxes corresponding to the objects you want to reference to create the table. Right-clicking an object in the list provides a shortcut menu that allows you to select all objects, deselect all objects, or invert the selection. See **Figure 26-24.** The display name of an object can be changed by right-clicking and selecting the **Edit Display Name** menu option, or by slowly double-clicking in the **Display Name** text box. Changing the object display name can be a critical step when extracting certain types of data. Using the same display name for different objects is effective for grouping data into a single item. Changing the display name also provides a more descriptive name for the object. For the landscape plan example, the display name is set according to the block name, which does not require modification in this example.

Figure 26-25.
Use the **Select Properties** page of the **Data Extraction** wizard to extract properties from the selected objects. Only those properties associated with the selected objects and the data source files are available.

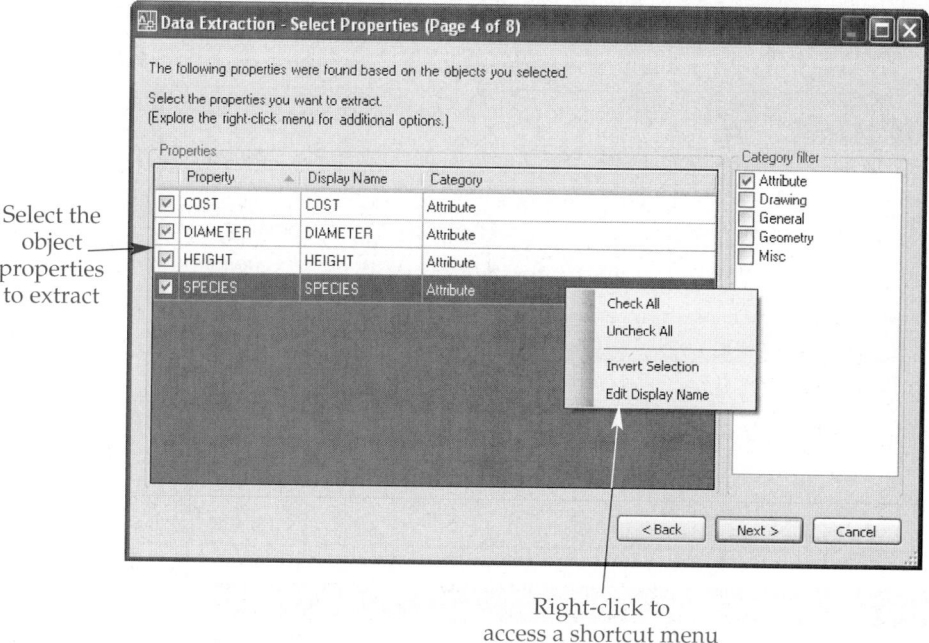

Select the object properties to extract

Right-click to access a shortcut menu

Select Properties Page

After selecting objects using the **Select Objects** page, pick the **Next** button to display the **Select Properties** page. See **Figure 26-25.** This page lists all the properties found in the selected objects and the data source files. Every object and file contains certain properties, or data. For example, the properties of a line include length, color, linetype, and position.

The **Select Properties** page is used to choose the object properties that will be used to create the table or external file. The selected properties correspond to the table or list columns. For example, the COST, DIAMETER, HEIGHT, and SPECIES attribute properties are selected to create the landscape bill of materials columns. All of the attributes that were created using the **ATTDEF** command are listed. Pick the check box corresponding to the properties you want to reference to create the table or list. Right-clicking a property in the list provides a shortcut menu that allows you to select all objects, deselect all objects, or invert the selection. See **Figure 26-25.** The display name of a property can be changed by right-clicking and selecting the **Edit Display Name** menu option. The property display name is used as the table or list column header. This can also be adjusted during the next phase of data extraction.

NOTE

If an attribute contains a field, the field is automatically converted to text during the extraction process.

PROFESSIONAL TIP

To reduce the number of properties shown in the list, deselect the appropriate check boxes in the **Category filter** area. Notice how all the category filter check boxes, except for the **Attributes** check box, have been unselected in **Figure 26-25.** This makes it very easy to select just the desired attributes.

Figure 26-26.
Use the **Refine Data** page of the **Data Extraction** wizard to adjust table or list content and display characteristics before inserting the table or creating the external file.

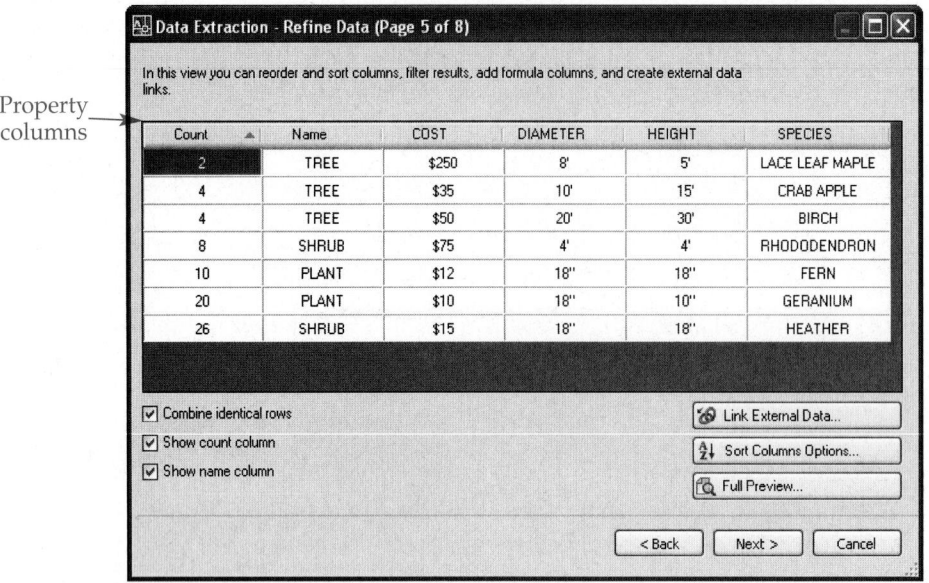

Property columns

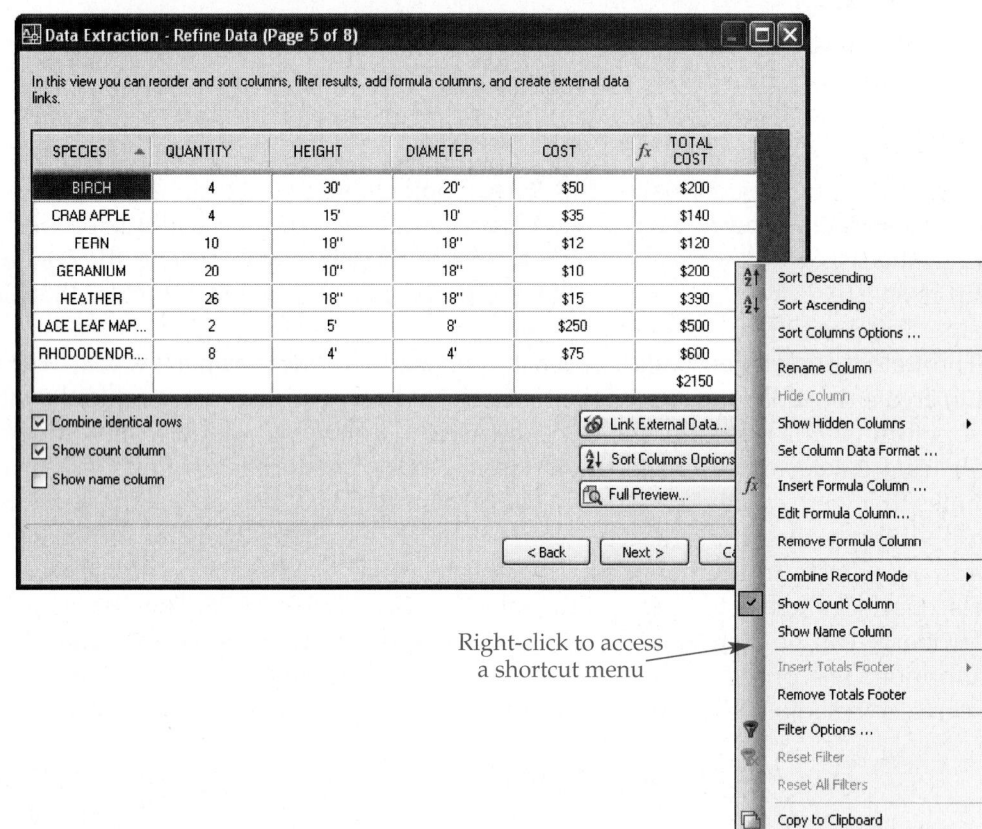

Right-click to access a shortcut menu

Refine Data Page

After selecting the properties to be extracted, pick the **Next>** button to display the **Refine Data** page. See **Figure 26-26A.** This page allows you to adjust table or list content and display characteristics before inserting the table or creating the external file. The results of the extraction are shown in a table, with the selected properties displayed in columns and each object placed in a row.

Most options can be accessed by right-clicking on a column to display the shortcut menu shown in **Figure 26-26B.** The options are:

- **Sort Ascending.** Sorts the rows in ascending alphanumeric order. Ascending row order can also be set by picking the heading once to display an up arrow to the right of the column name. The landscape bill of materials example sorts the SPECIES column in ascending order.
- **Sort Descending.** Sorts the rows in descending alphanumeric order. Descending row order can also be set by picking the heading twice to display a down arrow to the right of the column name.
- **Sort Columns Options.** Opens the **Sort Columns** dialog box, used for sorting rows. The **Sort Columns** dialog box can also be accessed by picking the **Sort Columns Options...** button.
- **Rename Column.** Renames the column heading. Type a new name and press [Enter] to rename the column. For the landscape bill of materials example, the default Count column name is replaced with QUANTITY.
- **Hide Column.** Hides the column that was right-clicked. Hidden columns are not included in the extraction. The Count and Name columns are provided in addition to the selected property columns. You can use these columns in your table or hide them if not needed. For the landscape bill of materials example, the Name column is not needed and is hidden.
- **Show Hidden Columns.** Pick to display a cascading submenu that provides options for redisplaying the Count and Name columns, or pick the **Show All Columns** to redisplay all hidden columns.
- **Set Column Data Format.** Pick this option to access the **Set Cell Format** dialog box. The **Data Type** area lists, in alphabetical order, options for formatting the selected table cell: **Angle, Currency, Date, Decimal Number, General, Percentage, Point, Text,** and **Whole Number.** Selecting a format presents options for adjusting the format characteristics. Different options are available depending on the selected format. The landscape bill of materials example uses a Text cell format for data in the SPECIES column, a Whole Number cell format for data in the QUANTITY column, a Currency cell format for data in the COST column, and a Decimal Number cell format for data in the HEIGHT and DIAMETER columns.

NOTE

A currency symbol, such as $, is added to Currency cell format column. As a result, you should *not* enter $ before the attribute value when inserting a block. Adding the $ symbol manually will not allow formulas to function.

- **Insert Formula Column...** Pick this option to access the **Insert Format Column** dialog box, which is used to add a column that uses a formula to calculate cell data. For example, the landscape bill of materials example contains a QUANTITY column and COST column. A formula column named TOTAL COST is added that uses a <QUANTITY>*<COST> formula to calculate the cost for the total number of same items. Pick **Edit Formula Column...** to edit the formula used in the column. Select **Remove Formula Column...** to delete the selected formula column. Formulas are described in Chapter 10.
- **Combine Record Mode.** This cascading submenu is only available when the **Combine identical rows** check box is selected. Pick the **Separate Values** option to display a row for each unique data value. Select the **Sum Values** option to add the data values of equal items together. This option is used in the landscape bill of materials example to total the total quantity of each type of tree, shrub, and plant.

- **Insert Totals Footer.** Adds a cell at the bottom of the selected column that calcu-lates and displays column data cell values. Choose the **Sum** option to calculate the sum of all values in the column data cells. Pick the **Max** option to show the largest single value displayed in the column, or select **Min** to show the lowest single value. Another option is to choose **Average** to calculate the average value of the column data cells. Select **Remove Totals Footer** to delete the cell. A SUM totals footer has been added to the TOTAL COST column in **Figure 26-26B**.
- **Filter Options.** Opens the **Filter** dialog box. Any rows unchecked in this dialog box are not included in the extraction.
- **Reset Filter.** Resets any filters for the column that was right-clicked.
- **Reset All Filters.** Resets all filters in all columns.
- **Copy to Clipboard.** The information is copied to the Windows Clipboard in the same format as displayed in the table.

To display a preview of the data, pick the **Full Preview** button below the list of data. The window that opens displays the data as it will appear when extracted. Close the preview window by pressing the [Esc] key or using the Windows control button (X).

NOTE

Existing data entered in a Microsoft Excel spreadsheet or a CSV file can be added to the table by picking the **Link External Data...** button to access the **Link External Data** dialog box.

Choose Output Page

After the data has been adjusted, pick the **Next>** button to display the **Choose Output** page. See **Figure 26-27**. In the **Output options** area, pick the destination of the extracted data. To create a table, check the **Insert data extraction table into drawing** check box. To save the data to an external file, check the **Output data to external file (.xls .csv .mbt .txt)** check box. Then pick the ellipsis (...) button to display the **Save As** dialog box. Specify a file name and folder for the file. Select the type of file to be saved in the **File of type:** drop-down list. The default file formats are comma-separated (CSV) and tab-separated (TXT). If Microsoft Excel and Microsoft Access are installed, the

Figure 26-27.
Use the **Choose Output** page of the **Data Extraction** wizard to determine how the data is extracted.

Choose the output

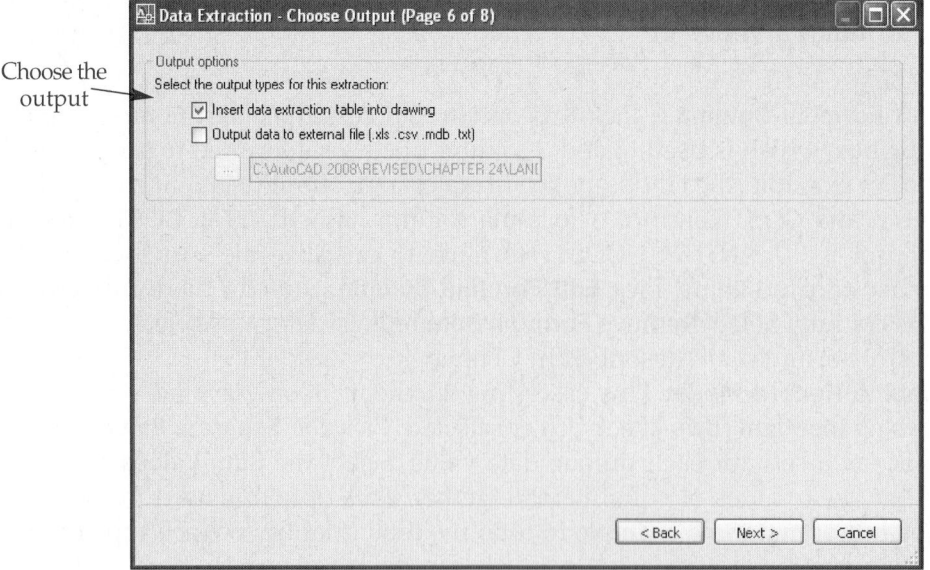

XLS and MDB formats are also available. Pick the **Save** button to return to the **Choose Output** page. The folder location and file name are displayed in the text box below the **External file** check box.

Pick the **Next>** button to continue with the wizard. If the **Insert data extraction table into drawing** check box in the **Choose Output** page is checked, the **Table Style** page is displayed next. If the **Insert data extraction table into drawing** check box is unchecked, this page is skipped and the wizard continues to the **Finish** page.

Table Style Page

The **Table Style** page is shown in **Figure 26-28.** Select a table style from the **Table Style** drop-down list, or pick the **Table Style...** button to create or modify a style. The preview area shows a preview of a table with the current table style settings. The preview area does not adjust the column and row settings, but it shows table style properties, such as general, text style, and border settings.

If the selected table style is a starting table style, the **Use table in table style for label rows** radio button is available and can be selected to use the starting table style title and headers. If the selected table style is not a starting table style, or if you do not want to use the starting table style title and headers, pick the **Manually setup table** radio button. A title for the table can be entered into the **Enter a title for your table:** text box. A unique title, header, or data cell style can be selected from the drop-down lists if necessary. Pick the **Use property names as additional column headers** check box to use the column display names shown in **Refine Data** page as the table column headers.

Finish Page

The last page of the **Data Extraction** wizard is the **Finish** page, shown in **Figure 26-29.** Pick the **Finish** button to finish the data extraction. You are prompted to specify an insertion point for the table if the **Insert data extraction table into drawing** check box was checked on the **Choose Output** page. Pick a point or enter coordinates to complete the extraction process. The landscape bill of materials example described throughout this section is shown in table format in **Figure 26-30.**

Figure 26-28.
Use the **Table Style** page of the **Data Extraction** wizard to choose a table style and add a title and column headers.

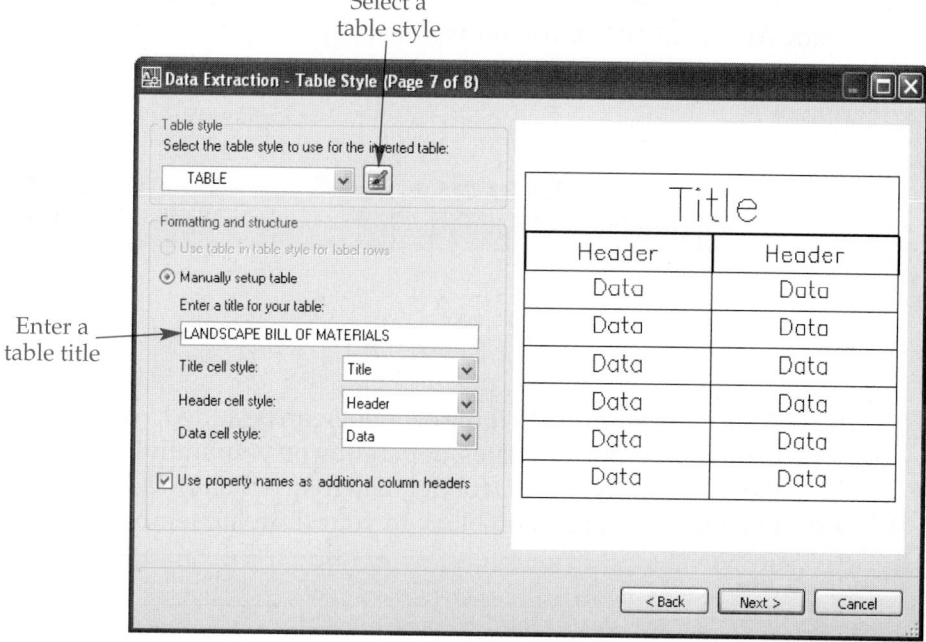

Figure 26-29.
Pick **Finish** to complete the data extraction.

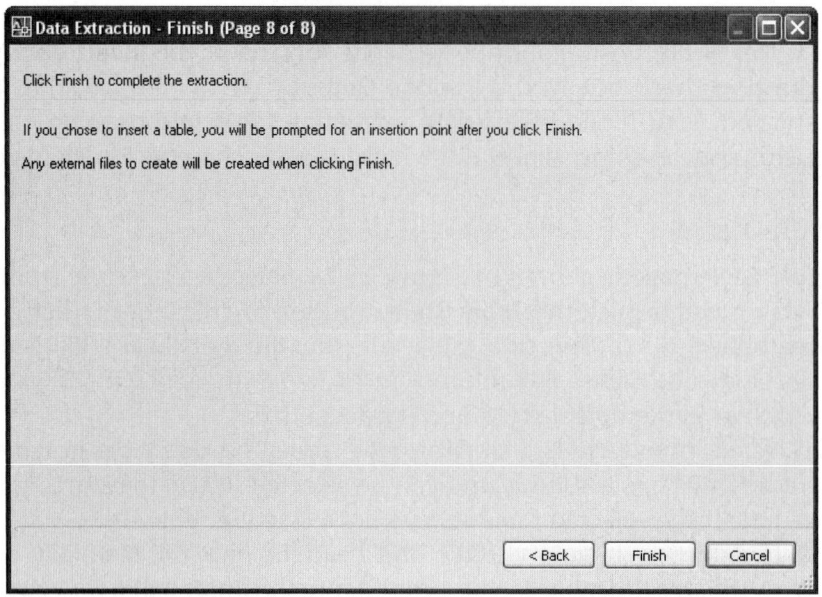

If you chose to save the data to an external file, the data can be displayed on-screen using appropriate applications, such as Windows Notepad or Microsoft Excel. See **Figure 26-30**.

NOTE

When a table is created using data extraction, it can be updated when the data extraction file is changed. You can update a data extraction at anytime using the **DATALINKUPDATE** command.

PROFESSIONAL TIP

The bill of materials listing described in this chapter is a basic list of each block's selected attributes. As you become familiar with AutoCAD, customize it to meet your needs.

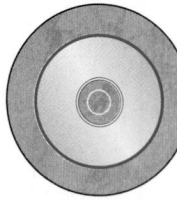

Exercise 26-4

Complete the exercise on the Student CD.

Template Development

Chapter 26

A variety of useful attribute elements can be added to the layouts in your drawing templates, depending on your individual needs. Refer to the Student CD for detailed instructions to add a border, title block, and revision block to your drawing templates.

Figure 26-30.
Examples of extracted attribute data used to create a table and saved as external files.

LANDSCAPE BILL OF MATERIALS					
SPECIES	QUANTITY	HEIGHT	DIAMETER	COST	TOTAL COST
BIRCH	4	30'	20'	$50	$200
CRAB APPLE	4	15'	10'	$35	$140
FERN	10	18"	18"	$12	$120
GERANIUM	20	10"	18"	$10	$200
HEATHER	26	18"	18"	$15	$390
LACE LEAF MAPLE	2	5'	8'	$250	$500
RHODODENDRON	8	4'	4'	$75	$600
				PROJECT COST	$2150

AutoCAD Table

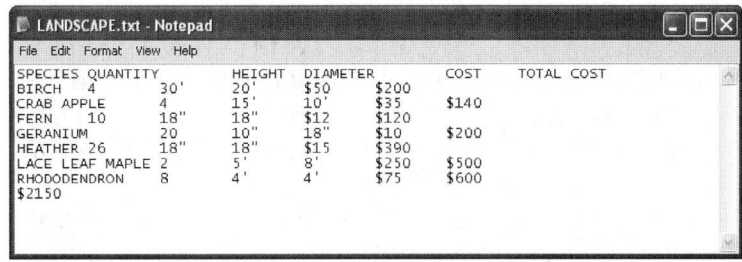

Tab-Separated File (TXT)

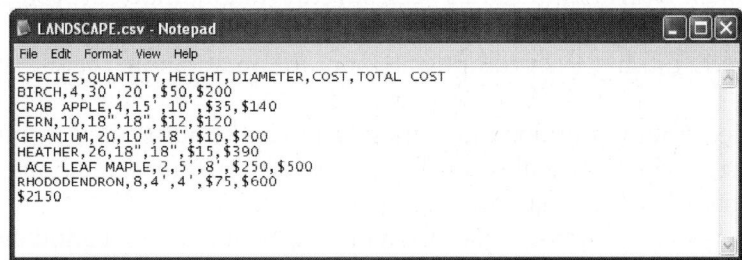

Comma-Separated File (CSV)

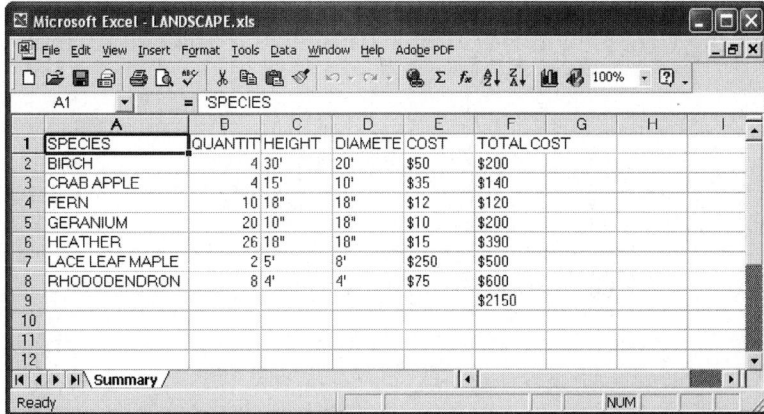

Excel File (XLS)

Chapter Test

Answer the following questions. Write your answers on a separate sheet of paper or complete the electronic chapter test on the Student CD.

1. What is an attribute?
2. Explain the purpose of the **ATTDEF** command.
3. Define the function of the following attribute modes:
   A. **Invisible**
   B. **Constant**
   C. **Verify**
   D. **Preset**
4. Which attribute information does the **ATTDEF** command request?
5. How can you change an existing attribute from visible to invisible?
6. If you select a block's attributes using the **Window** or **Crossing** selection method as the attributes are created, in what order will you be prompted for the attribute values?
7. To enter attributes using a dialog box, you must set the **ATTDIA** system variable to _____.
8. What purpose does the **ATTREQ** system variable serve?
9. List the three options for the **ATTDISP** command.
10. Explain how to change the value of an inserted attribute.
11. What is meant by *global attribute editing*?
12. Identify two ways to edit attributes before they are included within a block.
13. After a block with attributes has been saved, what method can you use to change the order of prompts when the block is inserted?
14. How do you modify the prompt statement for an attribute that is saved within a block?
15. What three detailing or documentation tasks can be automated using attributes?
16. What section of an assembly drawing provides information about each component of the assembly or subassembly?
17. What allows you to display the value of an attribute in a location away from the block?
18. List three uses for extracted block and attribute data.
19. What do you have to decide when taking the first step in extracting attributes?
20. What are the two general file formats in which extracted attribute data can be saved?

Drawing Problems

1. Start a new drawing. Draw the structural steel wide flange shape shown below using the dimensions given. Do not dimension the drawing. Create attributes for the drawing using the information given. Make a block of the drawing and name it W12 X 40. Insert the block once to test the attributes. Save the drawing as P26-1.

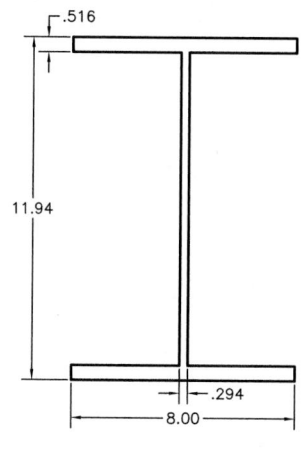

Attributes		
Steel	W12 × 40	Visible
Mfr.	Ryerson	Invisible
Price	$.30/lb	Invisible
Weight	40 lbs/ft	Invisible
Length	10′	Invisible
Code	03116WF	Invisible

2. Open the drawing from Problem 1 (P26-1) and construct the floor plan shown using the dimensions given. Dimension the drawing. Insert the block W12 X 40 six times as shown. Required attribute data are given in the chart below the drawing. Enter the appropriate information for the attributes as you are prompted. Note the steel columns labeled 3 and 6 require slightly different attribute data. You can speed the drawing process by using **ARRAY** or **COPY**. Save the drawing as P26-2.

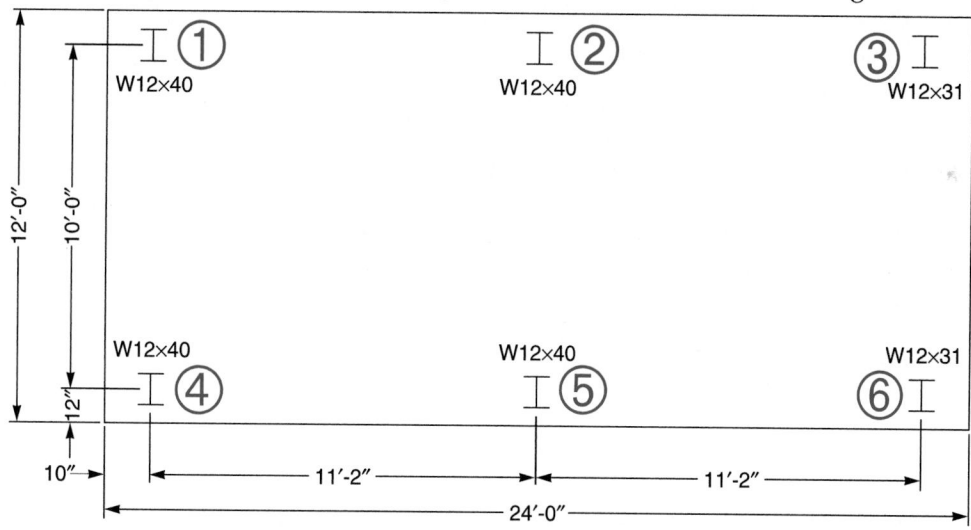

	Steel	Mfr.	Price	Weight	Length	Code
Blocks ①, ②, ④, & ⑤	W12 × 40	Ryerson	$.30/lb	40 lbs/ft	10′	03116WF
Blocks ③ & ⑥	W12 × 31	Ryerson	$.30/lb	31 lbs/ft	8.5′	03125WF

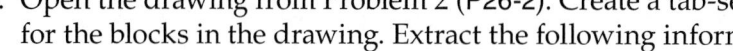

3. Open the drawing from Problem 2 (P26-2). Create a tab-separated extraction file for the blocks in the drawing. Extract the following information for each block:
   - Block name
   - Steel
   - Manufacturer
   - Price
   - Weight
   - Length
   - Code

   Save the file as P26-3.txt.

4. Select a drawing from Chapter 23 and create a bill of materials for it using the **Data Extraction** wizard. Use the comma-separated format to display the file. Display the file in Windows Notepad.

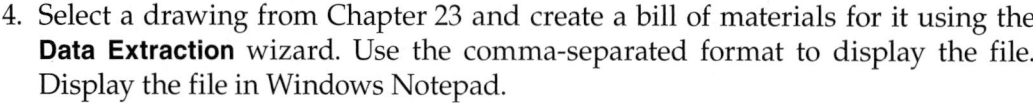

5. Create a drawing of the computer workstation layout in the classroom or office in which you are working. Provide attribute definitions for all of the items listed here.
   - Workstation ID number
   - Computer brand name
   - Model number
   - Processor chip
   - Amount of RAM
   - Hard disk capacity
   - Video graphics card brand and model
   - CD-ROM/DVD-ROM speed
   - Date purchased
   - Price
   - Vendor's phone number
   - Other data as you see fit

   Generate an extract file for all of the computers in the drawing.

6. Open one of your template drawings. Define attributes for the title block information, revision block, and parts list, as described in this chapter. Use the **WBLOCK** command to save the entire drawing to disk using 0,0 as the insertion base point. Repeat the procedure for other templates.

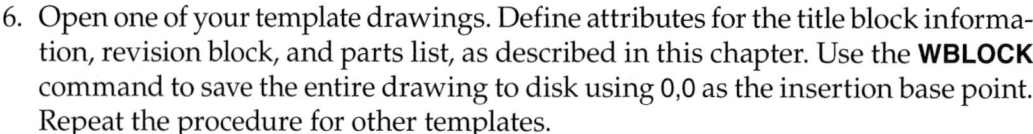

7. Open the drawing from Problem 2 (P26-2). Create a table from the block attribute data and insert it into the drawing. Save the drawing as P26-7.

CHAPTER 27

Annotative Objects

Learning Objectives

After completing this chapter, you will be able to do the following:

✓ Explain the differences between manual and annotative object scaling.
✓ Define objects as annotative.
✓ Create and use annotative objects in model space.
✓ Display annotative objects in scaled layout viewports.
✓ Adjust the scale of annotations according to a new drawing scale.
✓ Use annotative objects to help prepare multiview drawings.

Information on a drawing that cannot be described using drawing features and symbols is added using letters, numbers, words, and notes. This information is commonly referred to as *annotation*. Annotation can include objects such as the dimension lines, extension lines, and arrowheads used with dimension annotations.

annotation: Letters, numbers, words, and notes used to describe information on a drawing.

Because objects are drawn at full scale in model space, text and other objects, such as dimensions and hatches, must often be scaled so they appear on-screen and are plotted correctly relative to full-scale objects. Using AutoCAD's annotative tools automates the process of scaling these objects and provides additional flexibility for creating multiview drawings. This chapter describes the commands and options for creating and using annotative objects.

Manual vs. Annotative Object Scaling

Recall that objects should always be drawn at full scale in model space. For example, if you are drawing a small machine part and the length of a line in the drawing is 2 mm long, the line should actually be drawn 2 mm long in model space. Or, if you are drawing a building and the length of a line in the drawing is 80′ long, the line should actually be drawn 80′ long in model space.

For layout and printing purposes, most drawings must therefore be scaled to fit properly on a drawing sheet. Drawing scale is a ratio between the actual size of drawing objects and the size at which the objects are plotted on a sheet of paper. When you scale a drawing, you increase or decrease the *displayed* size of drawing objects. This is done using a floating viewport in a layout.

Figure 27-1.
The drawing features in this example are so large they must be scaled in order to fit on a standard size sheet. The annotations are scaled according to the plotted size of the drawing; otherwise they would be so small they could not be seen.

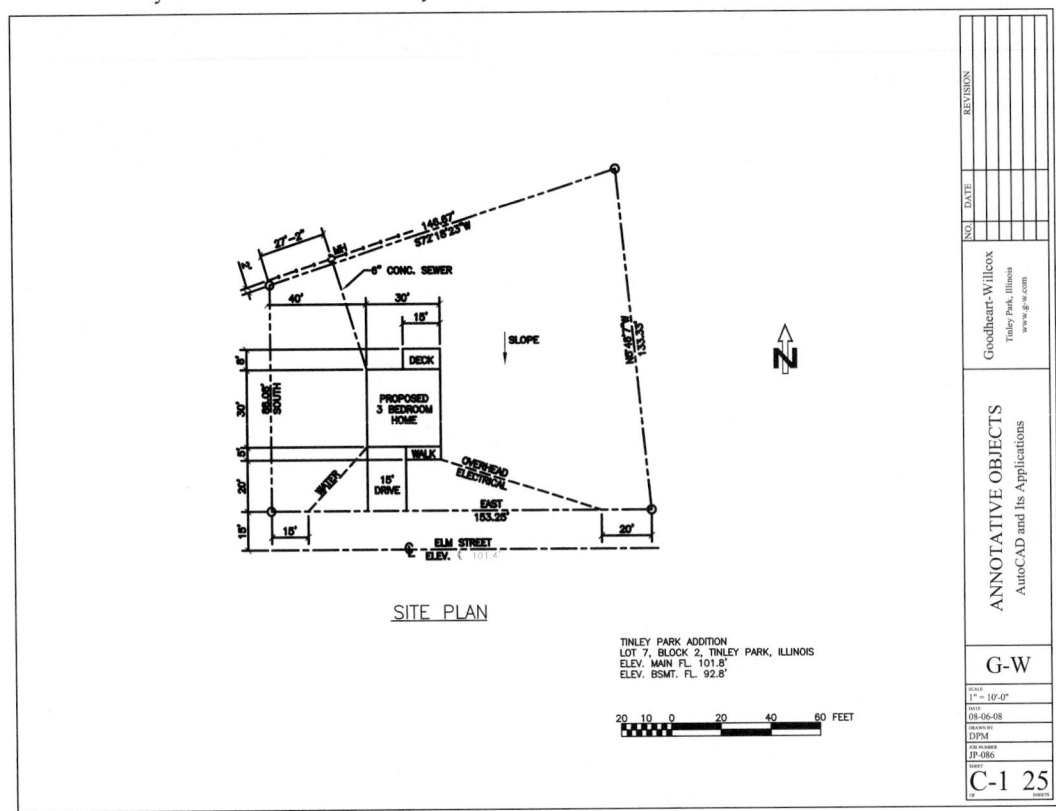

Scaling a drawing greatly affects the display of items added to drawing objects in model space, such as annotations, because these items should be the same size on a plotted sheet relative to other objects, regardless of the displayed size, or scale, of the rest of the drawing. See **Figure 27-1.**

Traditionally, annotations, hatches, and other objects are scaled manually, which means you determine the scale factor of the drawing scale and then multiply the scale factor by the plotted size of the objects. In contrast, annotative objects are scaled by AutoCAD automatically according to the annotation scale you select, which is the same as the drawing scale. This eliminates the need for you to calculate the scale factor and manually adjust the size of objects according to the drawing scale.

Defining Annotative Objects

annotative objects: AutoCAD objects that can be made to adapt automatically to the current drawing scale.

AutoCAD objects that can be made annotative are known as *annotative objects*. These objects include single-line and multiline text, dimensions, leaders and multileaders, GD&T symbols created using the **TOLERANCE** command, hatch patterns, blocks, and attributes.

Creating New Annotative Objects

The method used to define objects as annotative varies depending on the object type. To make an object annotative when you first create the object, proceed as follows:

- **Single-line and multiline text.** Defined as annotative when drawn using an annotative text style. To make a text style annotative, pick the **Annotative** check box in the **Size** area of the **Text Style** dialog box. See **Figure 27-2.** For most applications, a drawing should contain at least one annotative and one non-annotative text style.
- **Dimensions, leaders, and GD&T symbols.** If created using the **TOLERANCE** command, then defined as annotative when drawn using an annotative dimension style. To make a dimension style annotative, pick the **Annotative** check box in the **Fit** tab of the **New** (or **Modify**) **Dimension Style** dialog box. See **Figure 27-3.**

Figure 27-2.
Single-line and multiline text objects are annotative if they are drawn using an annotative text style.

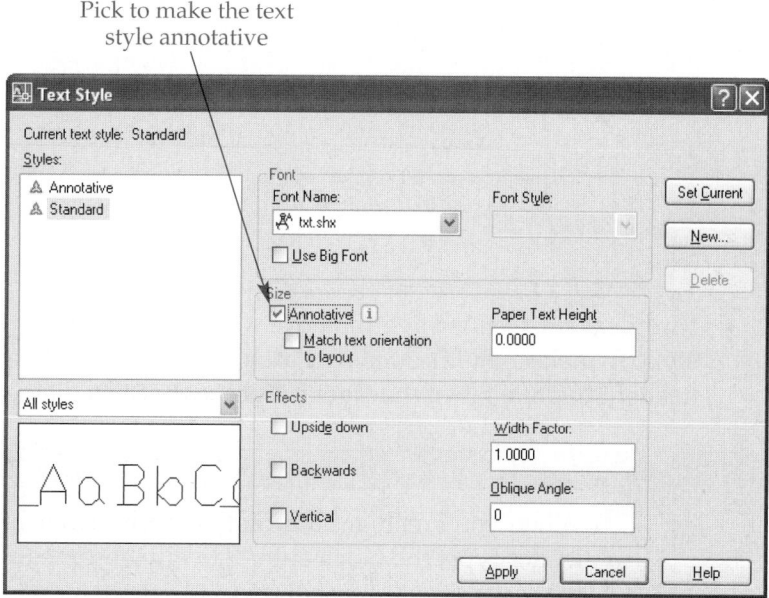

Pick to make the text style annotative

Figure 27-3.
Dimensions, leaders, and GD&T symbols created using the **TOLERANCE** command are annotative if they are drawn using an annotative dimension style.

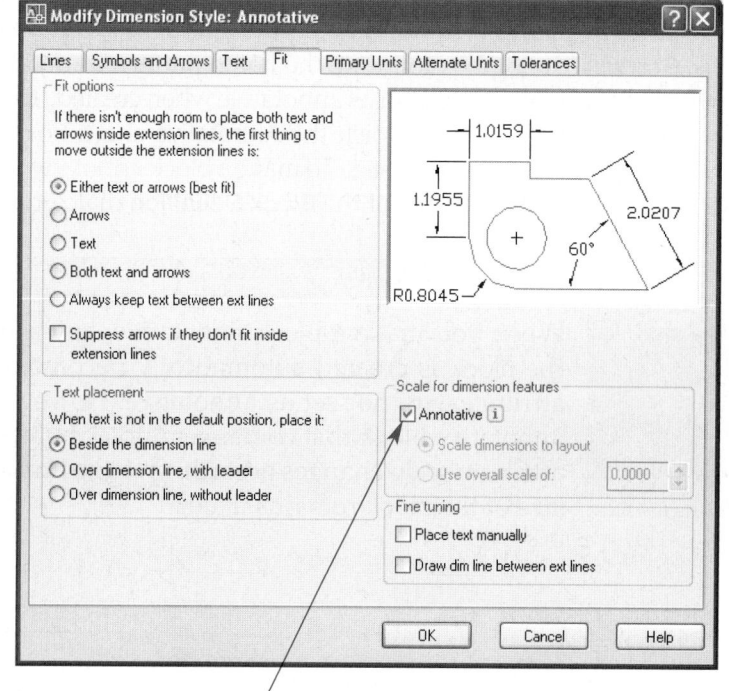

Pick to make the dimension style annotative

Figure 27-4.
Multileaders are
annotative if they
are drawn using
an annotative
multileader style.

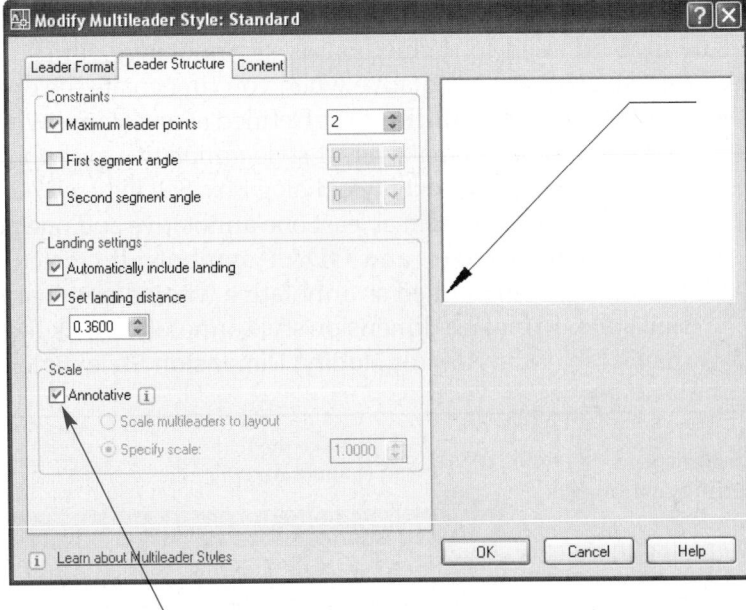

Pick to make the multileader
style annotative

- **Multileaders.** Defined as annotative when drawn using an annotative multileader style. To make a multileader style annotative, pick the **Annotative** check box in the **Leader Structure** tab of the **Modify Multileader Style** dialog box. See **Figure 27-4.**

NOTE

When you create an annotative multileader using the block multileader type, the block automatically becomes annotative, even if the block is not set as annotative.

- **Hatch pattern.** The hatch scale is set as annotative when you create the hatch pattern. Pick the **Annotative** check box in the **Options** area of the **Hatch and Gradient** dialog box to make the hatch pattern annotative. See **Figure 27-5.**
- **Blocks and attributes.** Set as annotative when created. To make attribute text height and spacing annotative, pick the **Annotative** check box in the **Attribute Definition** dialog box. See **Figure 27-6A.** To make a block annotative, pick the **Annotative** check box in the **Behavior** area of the **Block Definition** dialog box. See **Figure 27-6B.**

NOTE

When you make a block annotative, any attributes selected when the block is created automatically become annotative, even if the attributes are not set as annotative. However, if you create a nonannotative block that contains annotative attributes, the annotative attribute scale changes according to the annotation scale, while the size of the block remains fixed.

Figure 27-5.
Set the hatch pattern scale to be annotative when you create the hatch pattern.

Pick to make the hatch scale anotative

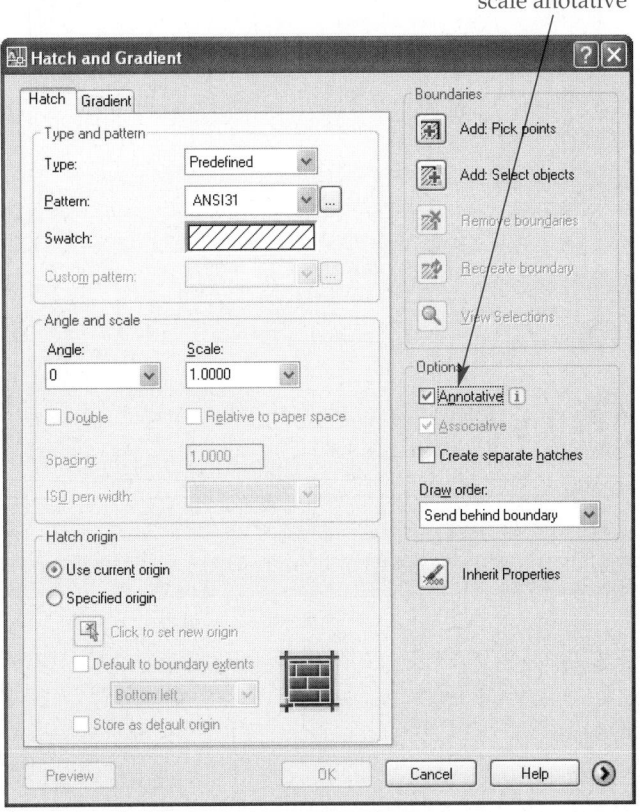

Making Existing Objects Annotative

You should specify objects as annotative when you first create them. However, any of the objects described in the previous section that were originally drawn as non-annotative can be given annotative status. The appropriate style controls the annotative status of single-line and multiline text, dimensions, leaders and multileaders, and GD&T symbols created using the **TOLERANCE** command. As a result, changing the style in which the original object was drawn to an annotative style makes the object annotative. Existing hatch patterns, blocks, and attributes must be edited or recreated in order to be defined as annotative.

Another method to make existing objects annotative is to override the non-annotative status of an object using the **Properties** palette. This technique is most effective when you want to make a limited number of objects annotative. To open the **Properties** palette, pick the **Properties** button on the **Standard Annotation** toolbar, select **Modify** > **Properties**, select **Tools** > **Palettes** > **Properties**, or type CH, MO, PROPS, or PROPERTIES. You can also open the **Properties** palette by selecting the desired annotative object and then right-clicking and selecting **Properties** from the shortcut menu.

The location of the annotative properties in the **Properties** palette varies depending on the selected object. The **Annotative** and **Annotative scale** properties are common to all annotative objects. The **Annotative** property can be used to make non-annotative objects annotative by selecting **Yes** from the drop-down list. To make annotative objects non-annotative, pick the **No** from the **Annotative** drop-down list. Additional annotative object settings found in the **Properties** palette are described later in this chapter.

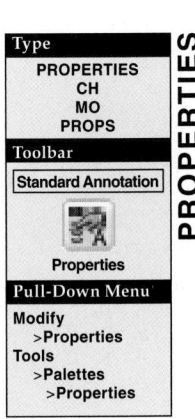

Type
PROPERTIES
CH
MO
PROPS

Toolbar
Standard Annotation

Properties

Pull-Down Menu
Modify
    >Properties
Tools
    >Palettes
        >Properties

PROPERTIES

Figure 27-6.
Blocks and attributes are set as annotative when they are created.

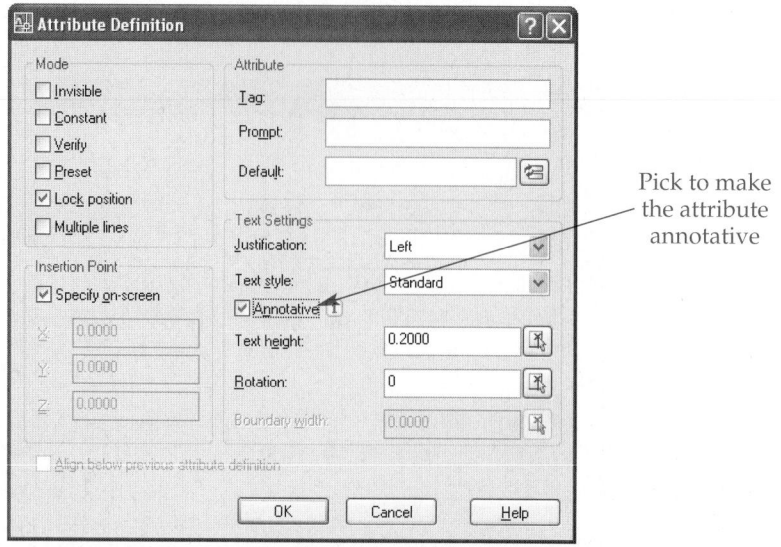

Pick to make the attribute annotative

A

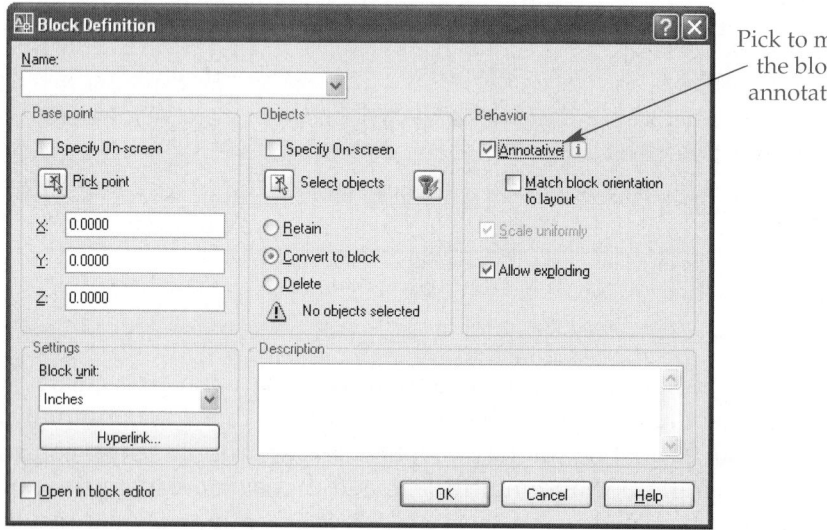

Pick to make the block annotative

B

PROFESSIONAL TIP

Use caution when overriding an object to annotative status. Annotative objects such as text should originally be drawn in or changed to an annotative text style for most applications.

NOTE

The **MATCHPROP** command can be used to select the properties of annotative objects and apply those properties to existing objects, making the objects annotative.

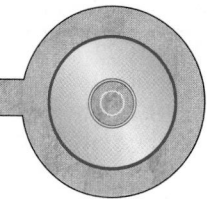

Drawing Annotative Objects

Using annotative objects reduces the need to determine the drawing scale factor. However, you must still identify the appropriate drawing scale. The drawing scale is the same as the *annotation scale*, which is used by AutoCAD to calculate the scale factor that is applied to annotative objects. Ideally, drawing scale should be determined during template development and incorporated into settings within your template files. If drawing scale is not applied to settings within your templates, you should try to identify the scale before beginning a drawing, or at least before you begin placing annotations.

annotation scale: The scale AutoCAD uses to calculate the scale factor that is applied to annotative objects.

Setting Annotation Scale

Annotation scale should be set before you begin adding annotations, so that annotations are automatically scaled. It may be necessary to adjust the annotation scale throughout the drawing process, especially if multiple drawings with different scales are prepared on one sheet or if the drawing scale changes. You should approach scaling annotations in model space by first selecting the desired annotation scale and then placing annotative objects. When annotations at another scale are to be drawn, pick the new annotation scale before placing the annotative objects.

The **Annotation Scale** flyout button, located on the status bar as shown in **Figure 27-7**, is the primary tool used for adjusting annotation scale. Pick the desired annotation scale from the menu. The **CANNOSCALE** system variable can also be used to set the annotation scale.

If a desired scale is not available from the **Annotation Scale** menu, choose the **Custom...** option to access the **Edit Scale List** dialog box. The **Edit Scale List** dialog box can also be accessed by picking **Format > Scale List...** from the pull-down menu. The **Edit Scale List** dialog box can be used to move the highlighted scale up or down in the list by picking the **Move Up** or **Move Down** button. You can remove the highlighted scale from the list by picking the **Delete** button, or you can modify it by picking the **Edit...** button. Selecting **Edit...** opens the **Edit Scale** dialog box, shown in **Figure 27-8**. Here you can change the name of the scale or adjust the scale by entering new paper and drawing units. For example, a scale of 1/4″ = 1′-0″ uses a paper units value of .25 or 1 and a drawing units value of 12 or 48. Pick the **Reset** button to restore the default annotation scale.

To create a new annotation scale, pick the **Add...** button in the **Edit Scale List** dialog box to display the **Add Scale** dialog box, which functions the same way as the **Edit Scale** dialog box previously described. Once the annotation scale is set current, you are ready to add annotative objects that are automatically created at the correct scale according to the drawing scale.

NOTE

The annotation scale can also be set in the **Properties** palette by selecting the annotation scale from the **Annotation Scale** option of the **Misc** section. This option is available when no objects are selected.

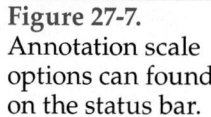

Figure 27-7.
Annotation scale
options can found
on the status bar.

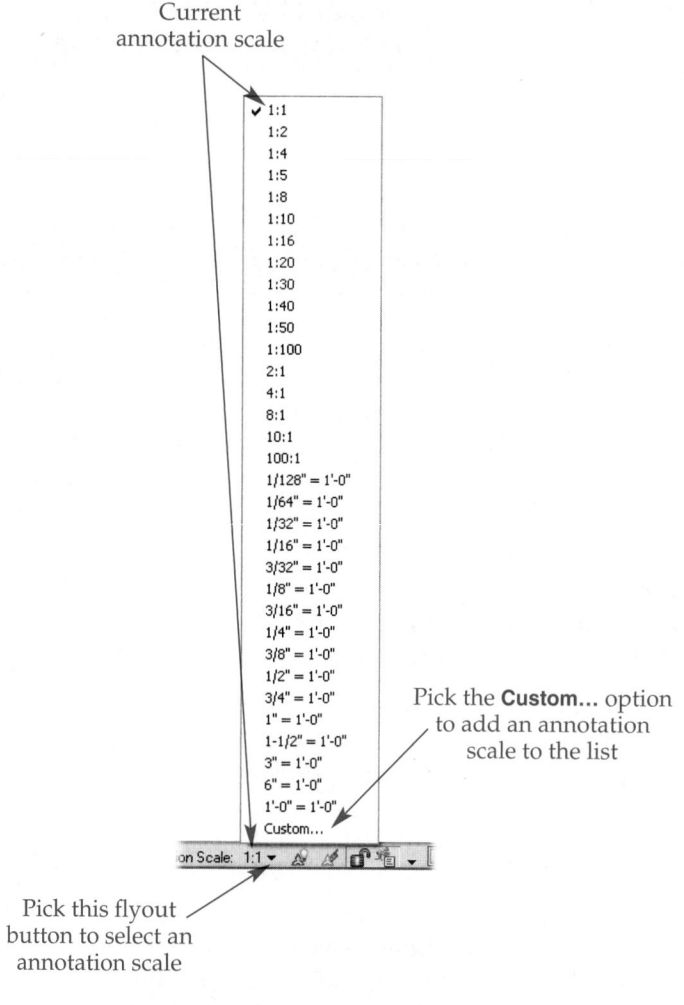

Current
annotation scale

Pick the **Custom...** option
to add an annotation
scale to the list

Pick this flyout
button to select an
annotation scale

Figure 27-8.
The **Edit Scale** dialog
box can be used to
modify the name of
a default annotation
scale, as well as the
name and scale of a
custom annotation
scale.

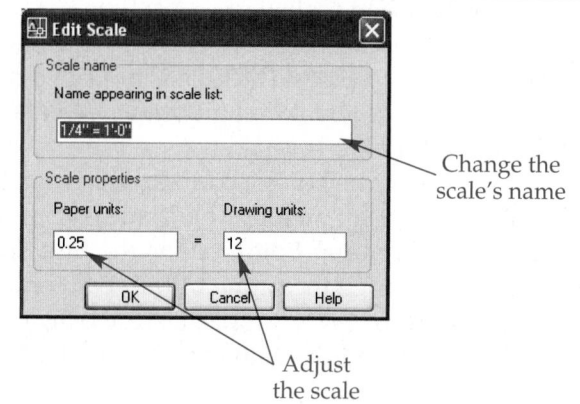

Change the
scale's name

Adjust
the scale

Using Annotative Linetype Scale

As described in Chapter 5, the **LTSCALE** system variable is used to make a global
change to the linetype scale to increase or decrease the lengths of dashes and spaces
found in some linetypes. The **LTSCALE** value usually must be modified in order for
linetypes to match standard drafting practices. The **LTSCALE** value defines the full, or
plotted, linetype scale. As a result, it is necessary to adjust the **LTSCALE** value according
to the drawing scale. This can be calculated automatically based on the current annotation scale, or it can be adjusted manually.

By default, the **MSLTSCALE** system variable is set to 1. As a result, you do not have to calculate the drawing scale factor when entering an **LTSCALE** value. For example, if you enter an **LTSCALE** value of .5 and your annotation scale is set to 1/4″ = 1′-0″, the correct linetype scale is automatically displayed (a scale factor of 48 × .5 = 24), without you having to consider the drawing scale factor. Objects appear at the correct linetype scale in both model space and paper space. You do not have to adjust the **LTSCALE** value in each environment.

If you set the **MSLTSCALE** system variable to 0, the model space **LTSCALE** value you enter is the drawing scale factor multiplied by the desired linetype scale. The **LTSCALE** value would then have to be set back to a full-scale value in paper space. Using the previous example, you would have to enter an **LTSCALE** value of 24 while working in model space and an **LTSCALE** value of .5 while working in paper space, in order for linetypes to appear at the correct scale in each environment.

PROFESSIONAL TIP

When you open a drawing in AutoCAD 2008 that was created in an earlier version of AutoCAD, the **MSLTSCALE** system variable is set to 0. Change the value to 1 to take advantage of annotative linetype scaling.

Drawing Annotative Text

Annotative text is drawn using the same commands as non-annotative text. The difference is the value you enter for text height. When creating annotative multiline text, select the **Annotative** button in the **In-Place Text Editor** and enter the paper text height in the **Size** text box, such as 1/4″. See **Figure 27-9**. The text scale, which includes spacing, width, and paragraph settings, automatically adjusts according to the current annotation scale.

When drawing annotative single-line text, after you pick the start point, you are prompted to specify the paper height, such as 1/4″. The text scale automatically adjusts according to the current annotation scale.

Figure 27-9.
Creating annotative multiline text. Multiline text could potentially contain both annotative and non-annotative text.

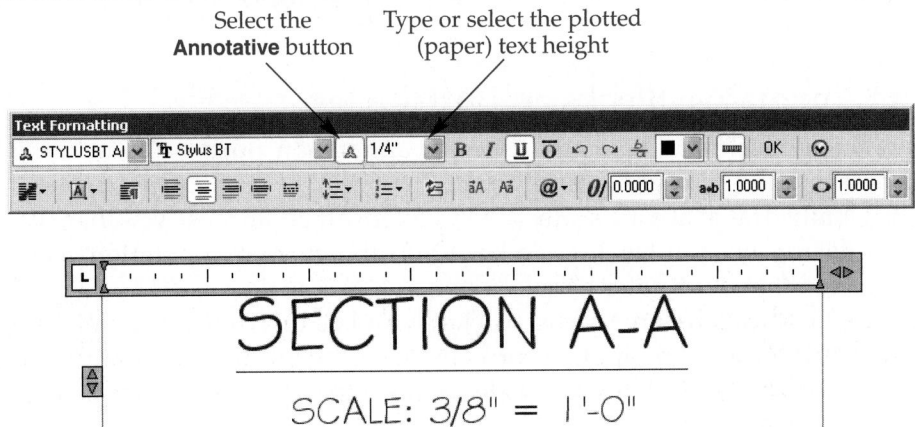

Drawing Annotative Dimensions

Annotative dimensions, leaders, GD&T symbols created using the **TOLERANCE** command, and multileaders are drawn using the same commands as non-annotative dimensions. Once you activate an annotative dimension or multileader style and select the appropriate annotation scale, the process of placing correctly scaled dimensions is automatic.

However, you must still determine the correct text location and spacing from objects, and dimension location and spacing from objects, when adding text and dimensions to scaled drawings. This involves multiplying the scale factor by the plotted spacing. For example, if your first dimension line should be 3/4″ from an object when plotted, and your drawing is scaled to 1/4″ = 1′-0″, the correct spacing in model space is 36″ from the object (a scale factor of 48 × 3/4″ = 36″).

Adding Annotative Hatch Patterns

The difference between adding annotative and non-annotative hatch patterns is the way in which the hatch scale is affected by the drawing scale. When you create annotative hatch patterns, the scale you enter in the **Scale:** text box produces the same results regardless of the annotation scale you select. For example, if you enter a value in the **Scale:** text box that is appropriate for an annotation scale of 1/4″ = 1′-0″, and then change the annotation scale to 1″ = 1′-0″, the displayed scale of the hatch pattern does not change. It looks the same on the 1/4″ = 1′-0″ scaled drawing as on the 1″ = 1′-0″ scaled drawing.

In contrast, when you create non-annotative hatch patterns, if you enter a value in the **Scale:** text box that is appropriate for a drawing scaled to 1/4″ = 1′-0″ and then change the drawing scale to 1″ = 1′-0″, the displayed scale of the hatch pattern increases. It looks four times as large on the 1″ = 1′-0″ scaled drawing as on the 1/4″ = 1′-0″ scaled drawing.

Placing Annotative Blocks and Attributes

schematic block:
A block that is originally drawn at a 1:1 scale.

Annotative blocks are typically used for annotation purposes and can be classified as schematic blocks. As described in Chapter 23, a *schematic block* is a block that is originally drawn at a 1:1 scale. When you insert an annotative schematic block, AutoCAD determines the block scale based on the current annotation scale, eliminating the need for you to enter a scale factor.

For most applications, annotative blocks should be inserted at a scale of 1 in order for the annotation scale to be applied correctly. Entering a scale other than 1 adjusts the scale of the block by multiplying the scale value by the annotative scale factor.

Exercise 27-2

Complete the exercise on the Student CD.

Displaying Annotative Objects in Layouts

Once you create drawing features and symbols, and add annotative objects to your drawing according to the appropriate annotation scale, you are ready to display and plot your drawing using a paper space layout. As described in Chapter 25, paper space represents the sheet of paper used to lay out, scale, and plot a drawing. Paper space can be accessed by picking one of the **Layout** tabs at the bottom of the drawing area, or using the **LAYOUT** command.

Scaling a Layout Viewport

A drawing is scaled in an active paper space viewport. To activate a viewport, double-click inside the viewport area, pick the **Maximize Viewport** button from the status bar, or use the **MSPACE** command. The viewport scale is the same as the drawing scale. To set the viewport scale, once the viewport is active, pick the appropriate scale from the **VP Scale** flyout button, which is located on the status bar as shown in Figure 27-10. The viewport scale can also be set using the **XP** option of the **ZOOM** command, or it can be selected from the **Viewports** toolbar.

Figure 27-10 shows an example of a drawing scaled to 3/8″ = 1′-0″. The drawing features were drawn at full scale in model space. The annotation scale in model space was then set to 3/8″ = 1′-0″, and annotative text, dimensions, multileaders, hatch patterns, and blocks were added. The annotative objects were automatically scaled according to the 3/8″ = 1′-0″ annotation scale. Notice in Figure 27-10 how the viewport scale and the annotation scale are the same, which is typical when scaling annotative objects. If you select a different annotation scale from the **Annotation Scale** flyout button, the viewport scale automatically adjusts according to the annotation scale. If you select a different viewport scale from the **VP Scale** flyout button, the annotation scale automatically adjusts according to the viewport scale. However, if you adjust the viewport scale by zooming, for example, the annotation scale does not change. The viewport scale and the annotation scale must match in order for your drawing and annotative objects to be scaled correctly.

The **Properties** palette can also be used to control viewport and annotation scale. In order to use this method, you must be in a layout tab to access the viewport properties. In the **Properties** palette, select **Standard scale** from the list, pick the drop-down arrow, and choose a viewport scale. The annotation scale can be adjusted using the **Annotation scale** option. See Figure 27-11.

Figure 27-10.
A drawing is scaled in a floating paper space viewport. Picking the **VP Scale** flyout button is one of the easiest ways to set the viewport scale.

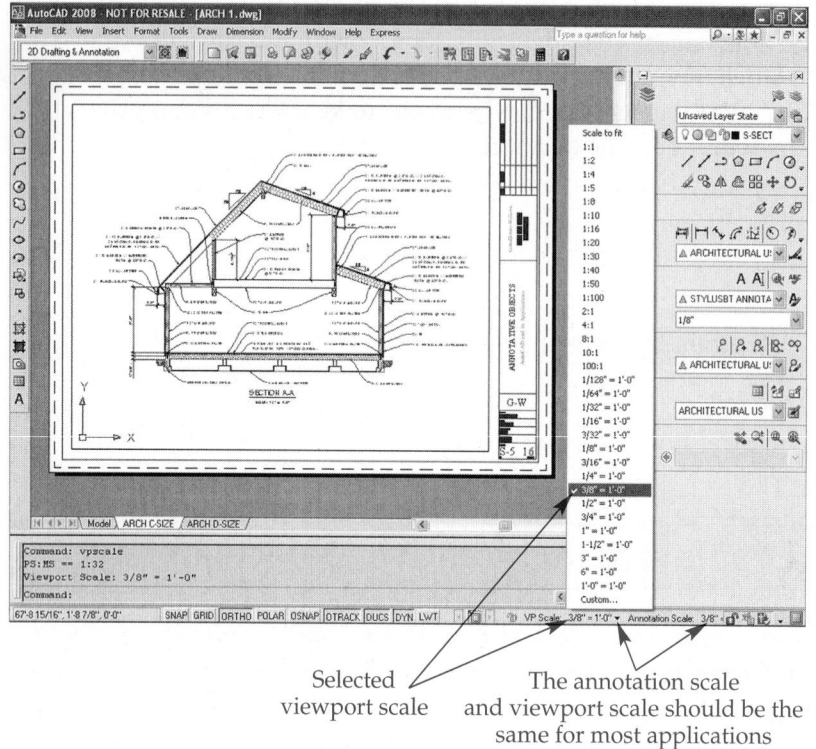

Selected
viewport scale

The annotation scale
and viewport scale should be the
same for most applications

Figure 27-11.
The **Properties** palette can also be used to set the viewport and annotation scale.

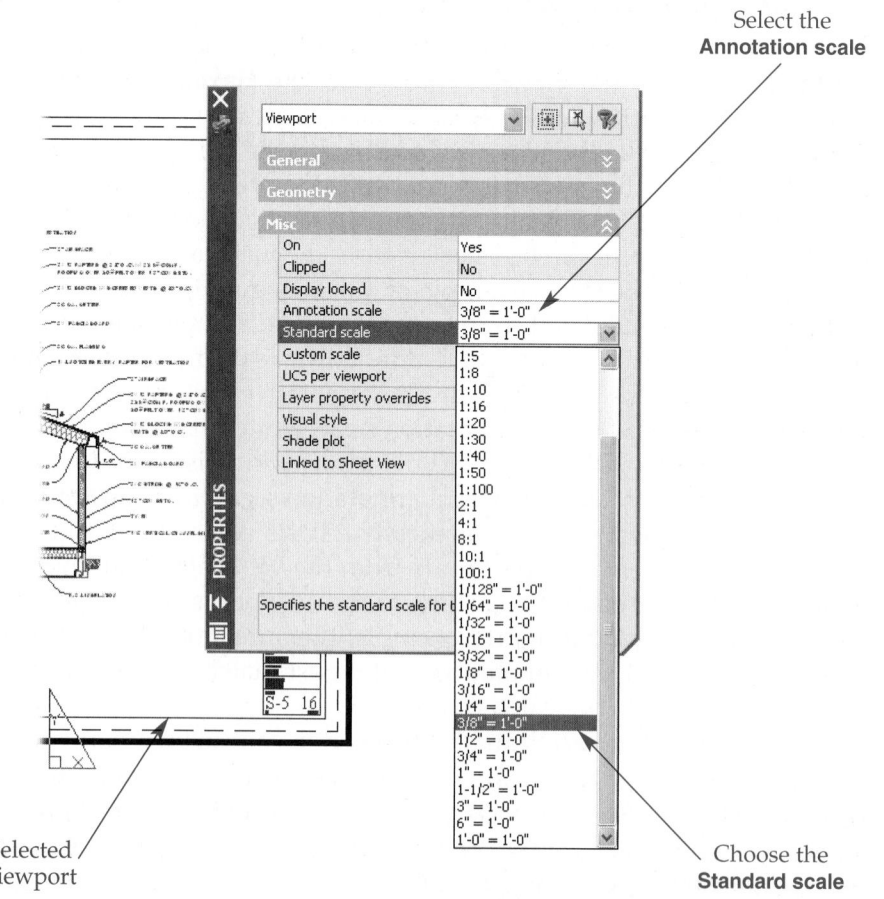

Select the
Annotation scale

Selected
viewport

Choose the
Standard scale

Lock the viewport display to avoid zooming and disassociating the viewport scale from the annotation scale. A viewport can be locked when the viewport is active or selected. To lock the viewport, select the **Lock/Unlock Viewport** button on the status bar. The viewport can also be locked in a layout tab by right-clicking the viewport and selecting **Yes** from the **Display Locked** cascading menu of the shortcut menu. Another method is to use the **Properties** palette. With the viewport selected in a layout tab, change the **Display locked** property to **Yes**.

Exercise 27-3

Complete the exercise on the Student CD.

Changing Drawing Scale

No matter how much you plan a drawing, drawing scale can change throughout the drawing process for a variety of reasons. If it is necessary to use a smaller sheet, drawing scale may need to be reduced. If drawing features are redesigned and become larger, or if additional detail must be shown on the drawing, the drawing scale may need to be increased.

Changing the drawing scale impacts the size and position of your annotations. A major advantage to using annotative objects is the ease in which annotation scale can be adjusted according to different drawing scales. When adjusting drawing scale, remember that the annotation scale is the same as the drawing scale.

You can change annotation scale in model space by selecting a new annotation scale from the **Annotation Scale** flyout button. To change the annotation scale in an active viewport in a layout, select a new annotation scale from the **Annotation Scale** flyout button, or adjust the viewport scale by selecting the drawing scale from the **VP Scale** flyout button. Again, the viewport and annotation scale should be set to the same scale for most applications.

Using the Annoupdate Command

When you create non-annotative single-line text using a non-annotative text style, and then change the style to be annotative, text drawn using the style becomes annotative. However, the properties of the annotative text remain set according to the non-annotative text style. When you create annotative text using an annotative text style, and then change the style to be non-annotative, text drawn in the style becomes non-annotative. However, the properties of the non-annotative text remain set according to the annotative style.

Use the **ANNOUPDATE** command to update text properties according to the current properties of the text style in which the text is drawn. Access the **ANNOUPDATE** command by typing ANNOUPDATE. When prompted to select objects, pick the text you want to update according to the current modified text style. After making your selections, press [Enter] to exit the command and update the text.

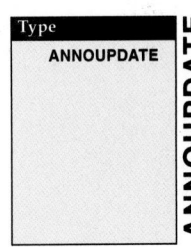

Type
ANNOUPDATE

ANNOUPDATE

Introduction to Scale Representations

So far, the content of this chapter has assumed that a drawing has been developed according to a single annotation scale. In order for the scale of annotative objects to change when the drawing scale changes, annotative objects must support the new scale. This involves assigning new annotation scales to annotative objects. If annotative

annotative object representation: Display of an annotative object at an annotation scale that the object supports.

objects do not support the new scale, the annotative object scale does not change, and can actually cause the objects to become hidden. An *annotative object representation* is the display of an annotative object according to the current annotation scale that the object supports. The following example helps to describe this concept.

Figure 27-12A shows an example of a drawing scaled to 3/8″ = 1′-0″ and placed on an architectural C-size sheet. The annotation scale in this example is set to 3/8″ = 1′-0″, so the annotative objects are automatically scaled according to a 3/8″ = 1′-0″ drawing scale. If you want to change the scale of the drawing to 1/2″ = 1′-0″, for example, to display additional detail, you must ensure that the annotative objects support a scale of 1/2″ = 1′-0″.

Figure 27-12.
A—An example of a drawing created using an annotation scale of 3/8″ = 1′-0″ on an architectural C-size sheet. The annotative objects are automatically drawn at the correct scale. B—An example of the same drawing, modified to an annotation scale of 1/2″ = 1′-0″ and placed on an architectural D-size sheet. An annotation scale of 1/2″ = 1′-0″ has been added to all the annotative objects, allowing the objects to adapt to the new scale automatically.

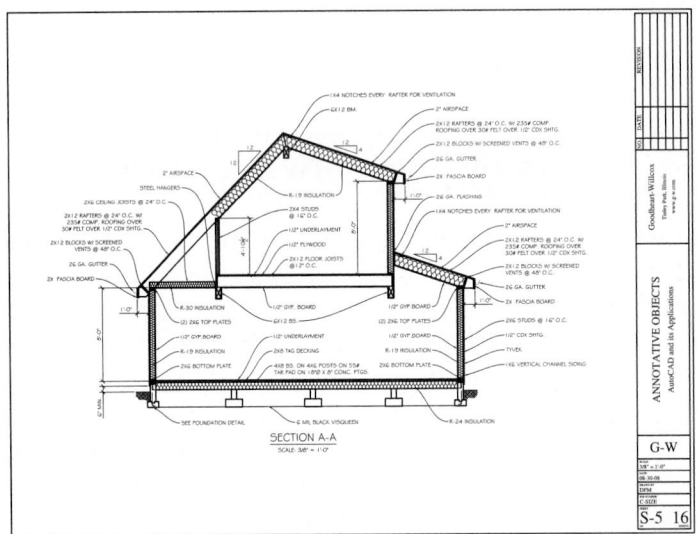

Once the annotation scale of 1/2″ = 1′-0″ is added to the annotative objects, you can change the annotation scale or the viewport scale to 1/2″ = 1′-0″ and the annotative objects are automatically scaled correctly. See **Figure 27-12B.** The annotative objects in this example support two annotation scales: 3/8″ = 1′-0″ and 1/2″ = 1′-0″. As a result, two annotative object representations can be displayed.

Understanding Annotation Visibility

Before changing the current annotation scale, you should understand its effects on annotative object visibility. If annotative objects do not support an annotation scale, the annotative object scale does not change. Additionally, annotative objects can be made to disappear when an annotation scale that the objects do not support is made current. For example, if annotative objects only support an annotation scale of 3/8″ = 1′-0″, when an annotation scale of 1/2″ = 1′-0″ is set current, the annotative object scale remains set at 3/8″ = 1′-0″, and the objects can be hidden.

Figure 27-13.
Examples of annotative objects that support single and multiple annotation scales.

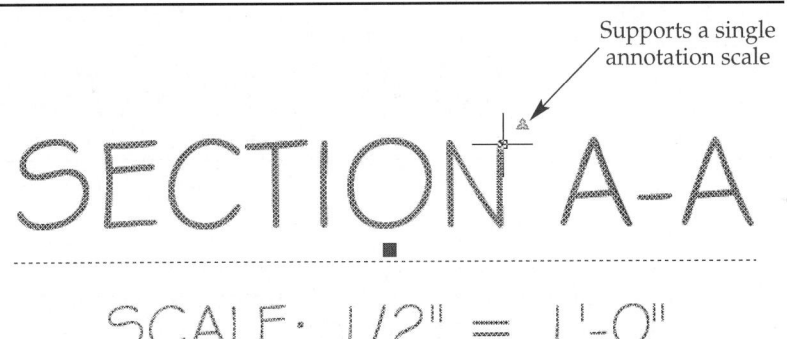

Supports a single
annotation scale

Single Annotation Scale
A

Supports multiple
annotation scales

Multiple Annotation Scales
B

Figure 27-14.
A—The annotative objects in this example only support a 3/8″ = 1′-0″ annotation scale. However, with **ANNOALLVISIBLE** turned on, all annotative objects are shown, even with the annotation scale set to 1/2″ = 1′-0″. B—The **Annotation Visibility** button on the status bar controls this feature.

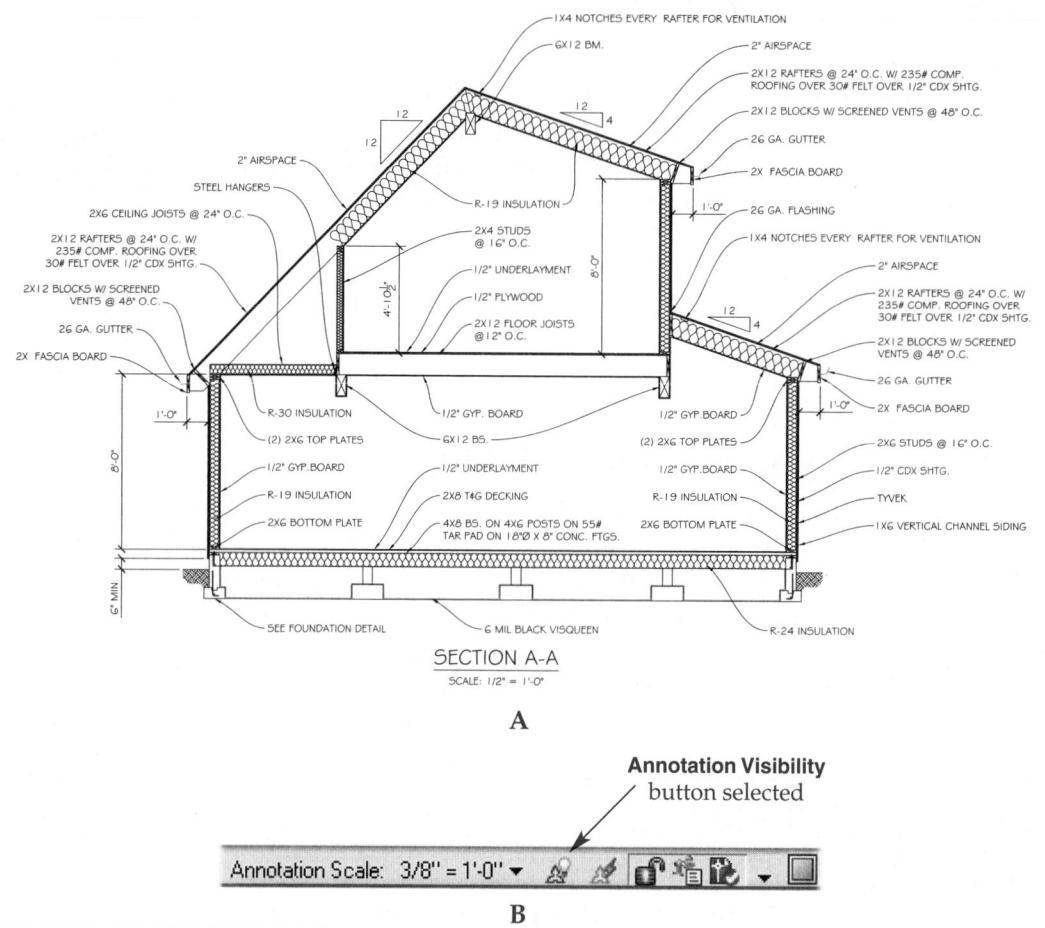

The easiest way to turn on and off annotative object visibility according to the current annotation scale is to pick the **Annotation Visibility** button on the status bar. You can also set the **ANNOALLVISIBLE** system variable to 1 or select the **Annotation Visibility** button in order to display all annotative objects, regardless of the current annotation scale. See **Figure 27-14.** This is most effective when adding and deleting annotation scales to or from annotative objects. If multiple annotation scales have been added to the annotative objects, the annotative object representation is shown, based on the current scale.

Set the **ANNOALLVISIBLE** system variable to 0 or deselect the **Annotation Visibility** button to display only the annotative objects that support the current annotation scale. When this option is used, any annotative objects that are not supported by the current annotation scale are hidden. See **Figure 27-15.** This is most effective when you want to annotate a drawing, or a portion of a drawing, using a different annotation scale and you do not want to see annotative object representations specific to a different annotation scale. Turning off the visibility of annotative objects that do not support the current annotation scale is also extremely effective when you are preparing multiview drawings because it eliminates the need to create separate layers for objects displayed at different scales. This process is described later in this chapter.

Figure 27-15.
When **ANNOALLVISIBLE** is turned off, only those annotative objects that support the current annotation scale are shown. The annotative objects in this example are not shown because they only support a 3/8″ = 1′-0″ annotation scale, and the current annotation scale is 1/2″ = 1′-0″.

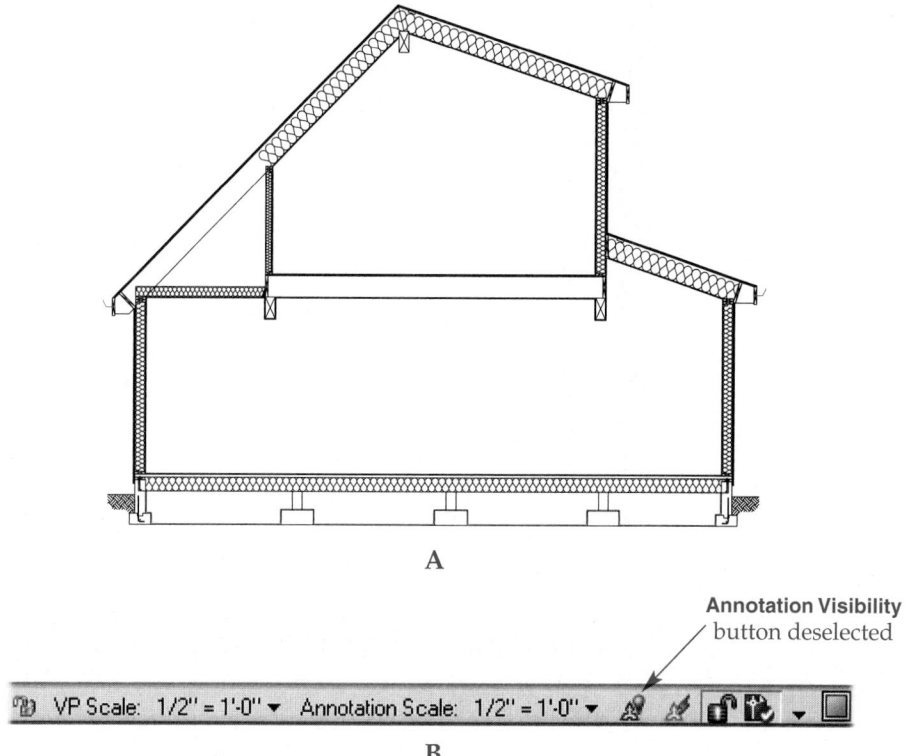

A

Annotation Visibility
button deselected

B

Adding and Deleting Annotation Scales

One method for assigning additional annotation scales to annotative objects is to add the scales to selected objects. This method can be used whenever the drawing scale changes, but it is especially effective when you only want to add annotation scales to specific objects, such as when creating multiview drawings. Examples that demonstrate this function are described later in this chapter. You can add annotation scales to selected objects using the **Properties** palette or annotation scaling tools.

If an annotation scale is no longer used, should not be displayed in a specific view, or is making it difficult to work with annotative objects, the annotation scale can be deleted from the annotative objects. When an annotation scale is deleted from annotative objects, the scale is no longer applied. You can delete annotation scales from selected objects using the **Properties** palette or annotation scaling tools.

Using the Properties palette

The **Properties** palette can be used to add annotation scales to selected annotative objects. The location of the annotative properties in the **Properties** palette varies depending on the selected object. The **Annotative scale** property displays the annotation scale currently applied to the selected annotative object, and contains an ellipsis button (...) that opens the **Annotation Object Scale** dialog box when selected. See **Figure 27-16.** The **Annotation Object Scale** dialog box can be used to define the annotative scales associated with the selected object.

The **Object Scale List** shows all of the annotation scales associated with the selected annotative object. A scale must be listed in order for the scale to be applied to the annotative object. If a different annotation scale is selected, and that scale is not displayed in the **Object Scale List**, annotative objects do not adapt to the new annotation scale, and you have the option of turning off the annotative objects' visibility. Using the previous

Figure 27-16.
The **Annotation scale** property in the **Properties** palette is one way to access the **Annotation Object Scale** dialog box, which can be used to add and delete annotation scales to and from annotative objects.

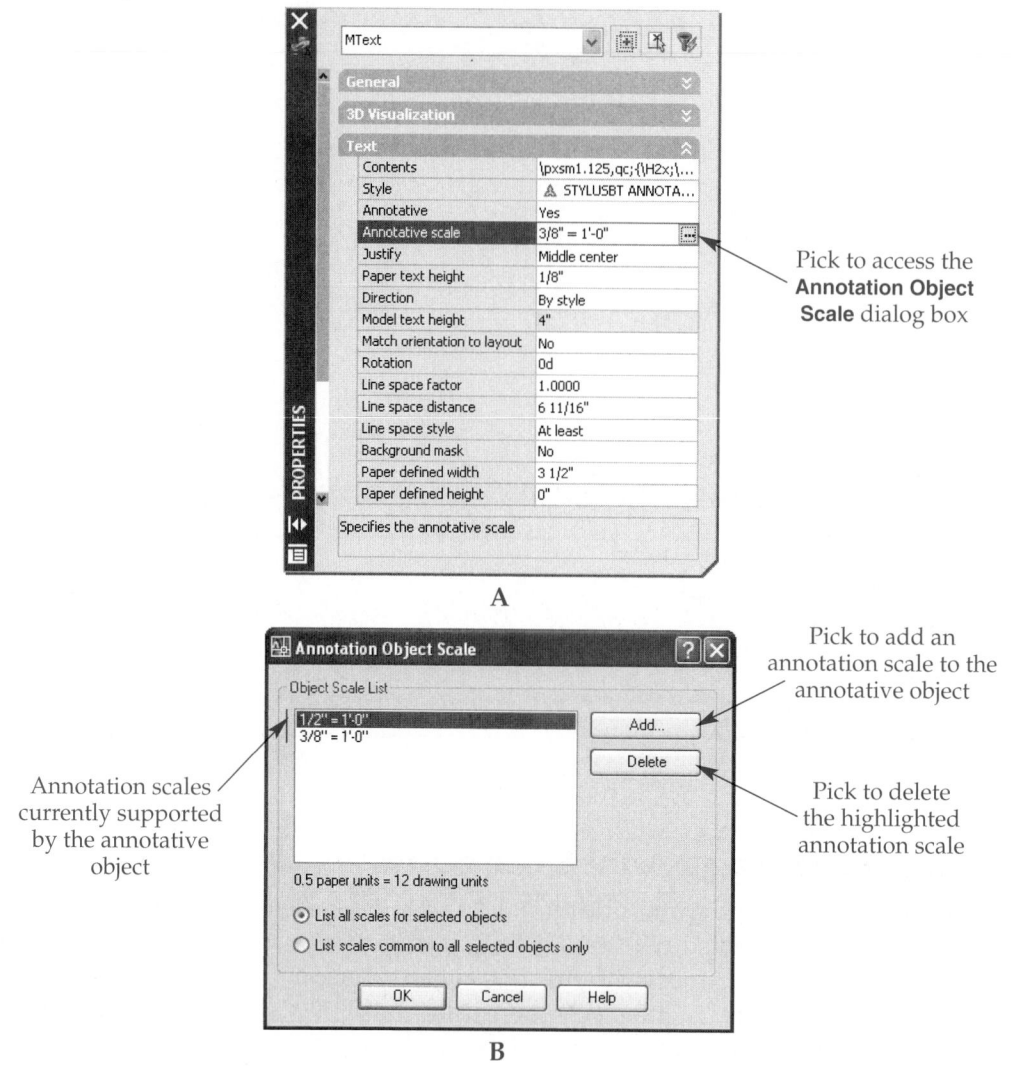

Pick to access the **Annotation Object Scale** dialog box

A

Pick to add an annotation scale to the annotative object

Annotation scales currently supported by the annotative object

Pick to delete the highlighted annotation scale

B

example, 1/2″ = 1′-0″ must be listed in the **Object Scale List** in order for the annotative objects to adapt to the new annotation scale of 1/2″ = 1′-0″.

Pick the **Add…** button to add a scale to the **Object Scale List**. This opens the **Add Scales to Object** dialog box. Highlight scales in the **Scale List** and pick the **OK** button to add the scales to the **Object Scale List**. Once a scale has been added to the **Object Scale List**, picking an annotation scale that corresponds to any of the listed scales automatically scales the selected annotative object. To remove a scale from the **Object Scale List**, highlight the scales you want to remove and pick the **Delete** button.

If multiple annotative objects have been selected, it may be helpful to display only the annotative scales that are common to the selected objects. This can be done by selecting the **List scales common to all selected objects only** radio button. To show all the annotation scales associated with any of the selected objects, even if some of the objects do not support the listed scales, pick the **List all scales for selected objects** radio button. Picking this option is helpful when you want to delete a scale that is listed but that is only applied to certain objects.

Using the Objectscale command

The **OBJECTSCALE** command can also be used to add and delete annotation scales supported by annotative objects. To access the **OBJECTSCALE** command, select an annotative object and then right-click and pick the **Add/Delete Scale...** option from the **Annotative Objects Scales** cascading menu of the shortcut menu, pick **Modify** > **Annotative Object Scale** > **Add/Delete Scales...** from the pull-down menu, or type OBJECTSCALE.

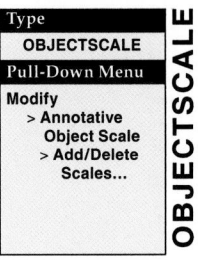

If you activate the **OBJECTSCALE** command by right-clicking objects, the **Annotation Object Scale** dialog box is displayed and annotation scales can be added to or deleted from the selected objects. If you access the command before selecting objects, all annotative objects are displayed, even those objects that do not support the current annotation scale. Select the annotative objects to or from which you want to add or remove annotation scales. Then, press [Enter] to display the **Annotation Object Scale** dialog box. Refer to the previous section for more information about the **Annotation Object Scale** dialog box.

The **-OBJECTSCALE** command accomplishes the same tasks as the **OBJECTSCALE** command, but functions using the Command: prompt instead of the **Annotation Object Scale** dialog box. This command is most effectively used to add or remove the current annotation scale to or from selected annotative objects. To use the **-OBJECTSCALE** command, first make the annotation scale you want to add or delete current. Then, if you want to add the current annotation scale to selected objects, access the **-OBJECTSCALE** command by selecting the annotative objects and then right-clicking and picking the **Add Current Scale** option from the **Annotative Objects Scales** cascading menu of the shortcut menu, pick **Modify** > **Annotative Object Scale** > **Add Current Scale**, or type -OBJECTSCALE.

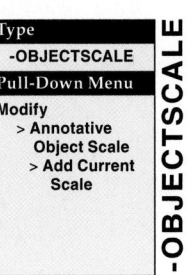

If you activate the **-OBJECTSCALE** command by right-clicking objects, the current annotation scale is added to the selected annotative objects. If you access the command before selecting objects, all annotative objects are displayed, even those objects that do not support the current annotation scale. The command sequence is as follows:

Command: **-OBJECTSCALE**⏎
Select annotative objects: *(select the objects)*
Select objects: ⏎
Enter an option [Add/Delete/?] <Add>: *(type A to add the current annotation scale to the selected annotative objects)*
Enter named scale to add or [?] <current>: ⏎
Enter named scale to add or [?]: ⏎
Command:

If you want to delete the current annotation scale from selected objects, access the **-OBJECTSCALE** command by selecting the annotative objects and then right-clicking and picking the **Delete Current Scale** option from the **Annotative Object Scales** cascading menu of the shortcut menu, pick **Modify** > **Annotative Object Scale** > **Delete Current Scale**, or type -OBJECTSCALE.

If you activate the **-OBJECTSCALE** command by right-clicking objects, the current annotation scale is deleted from the selected annotative objects. If you access the command before selecting objects, all annotative objects are displayed, even those objects that do not support the current annotation scale. The command sequence is as follows:

Command: **-OBJECTSCALE**↵
Select annotative objects: *(select the objects)*
Select objects: ↵
Enter an option [Add/Delete/?] <Delete>: *(type D to delete the current annotation scale from the selected annotative objects)*
Enter named scale to add or [?] <current>: ↵
Enter named scale to add or [?]: ↵
Command:

Automatically Adding Annotation Scales

Another technique for assigning additional annotation scales to annotative objects is to add a selected annotation scale automatically to all annotative objects in the drawing. This eliminates the need to add annotation scales to individual annotative objects and quickly produces newly scaled drawings.

The ability to add an annotation scale to all existing annotative objects is controlled by the **ANNOAUTOSCALE** system variable. You can enter 1, -1, 2, -2, 3, -3, 4, or -4 depending on the desired effect. The table in **Figure 27-17A** describes each option. Once the initial value is entered, the easiest way to toggle this system variable on and off is to pick the button on the status bar, shown in **Figure 27-17B**.

Figure 27-17.
A—Options of the **ANNOAUTOSCALE** system variable. B—Once the initial **ANNOAUTOSCALE** system variable is entered, use the button on the status bar to toggle **ANNOAUTOSCALE** on and off.

Value	Mode	Description
1	On	Adds the selected annotation scale to annotative objects, not including those drawn on a layer that is turned off, frozen, locked, or frozen in a viewport.
–1	Off	1 behavior is used when **ANNOAUTOSCALE** is turned back on.
2	On	Adds the selected annotation scale to annotative objects, not including those drawn on a layer that is turned off, frozen, or frozen in a viewport.
–2	Off	2 behavior is used when **ANNOAUTOSCALE** is turned back on.
3	On	Adds the selected annotation scale to annotative objects, not including those drawn on a layer that is locked.
–3	Off	3 behavior is used when **ANNOAUTOSCALE** is turned back on.
4	On	Adds the selected annotation scale to all annotative objects regardless of the status of the layer on which the annotative object is drawn. 4 is the AutoCAD default setting when toggled on.
–4	Off	4 behavior is used when **ANNOAUTOSCALE** is turned back on. –4 is the AutoCAD default setting when toggled off.

A

Pick to toggle the
ANNOAUTOSCALE system
variable on or off

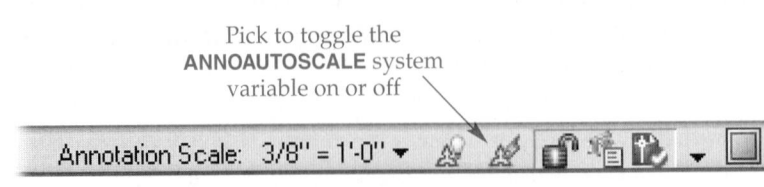

B

AutoCAD and Its Applications—Basics

Exercise 27-4

Complete the exercise on the Student CD.

Preparing Multiview Drawings

Mechanical drawings and architectural construction drawings often contain sections and details drawn at different scales. Using annotative objects offers several advantages, especially when objects in model space are viewed at different scales in layouts. Several views can be created in model space in a single file. A different annotation scale can be applied to each drawing view that contains annotative objects, reducing the need to calculate multiple drawing scale factors. Additionally, by adjusting the annotative scale representation's visibility and position, you can prepare differently scaled multiview drawings, while eliminating the need to use separate scale-specific layers and annotations.

Creating Differently Scaled Drawings

The concepts described in this chapter can be applied to developing multiview drawings, with each view using a specific scale. By adjusting the annotation scale, you can draw annotative objects at different scales while maintaining the appropriate scale of previously drawn annotative objects.

Figure 27-18A shows an example of two different drawing views, both drawn at full scale in model space. The full section in Figure 27-18A is scaled to 3/8″ = 1′-0″. To prepare this view, the annotation scale in model space is set to 3/8″ = 1′-0″, and annotative text, dimensions, multileaders, hatch patterns, and blocks are added. The annotative objects are automatically scaled according to the 3/8″ = 1′-0″ annotation scale. The stair section in this example is scaled to 1/2″ = 1′-0″. To prepare this view, the annotation scale in model space is changed from 3/8″ = 1′-0″ to 1/2″ = 1′-0″. Then annotative text, dimensions, and multileaders are added. The annotative objects are automatically scaled according to the 1/2″ = 1′-0″ annotation scale. If you look closely, you can see the different scales applied to the drawing views.

With annotation visibility on, as shown in Figure 27-18A, you can see all annotative objects, and observe the effects of using different scales. With annotation visibility off, as shown in Figure 27-18B, only annotative objects that support the current annotation scale can be seen, which is 1/2″ = 1′-0″ in this example.

The next step to creating the multiview drawing is to display and plot the drawing using multiple paper space viewports. Figure 27-19 shows an architectural D-size sheet layout with two floating viewports. One viewport is used to display the full section at a viewport scale of 3/8″ = 1′-0″. The other viewport is used to display the stair section at a viewport scale of 1/2″ = 1′-0″.

Figure 27-18.
An example of two different drawing views, drawn at full scale in model space. The full section uses an annotation scale of 3/8" = 1'-0", while the stair section uses an annotation scale of 1/2" = 1'-0".

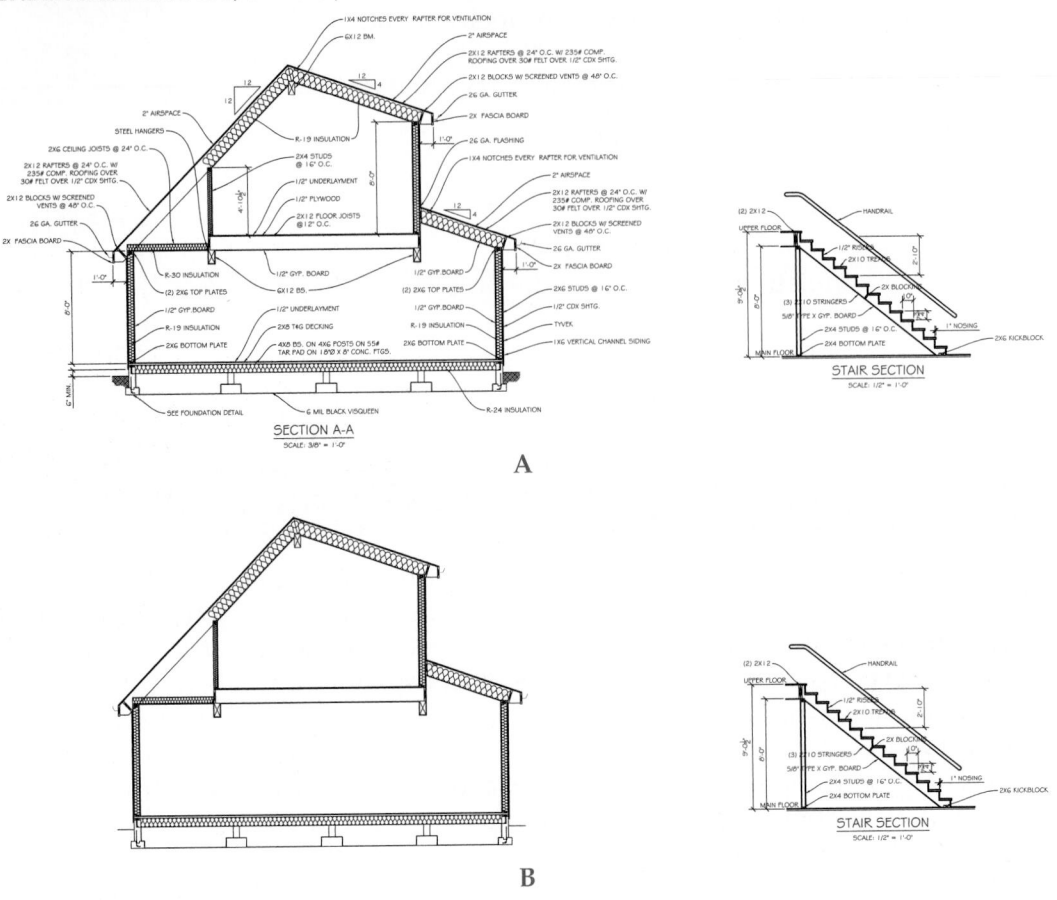

A

B

Figure 27-19.
Using viewports with different scales to create a multiview drawing.

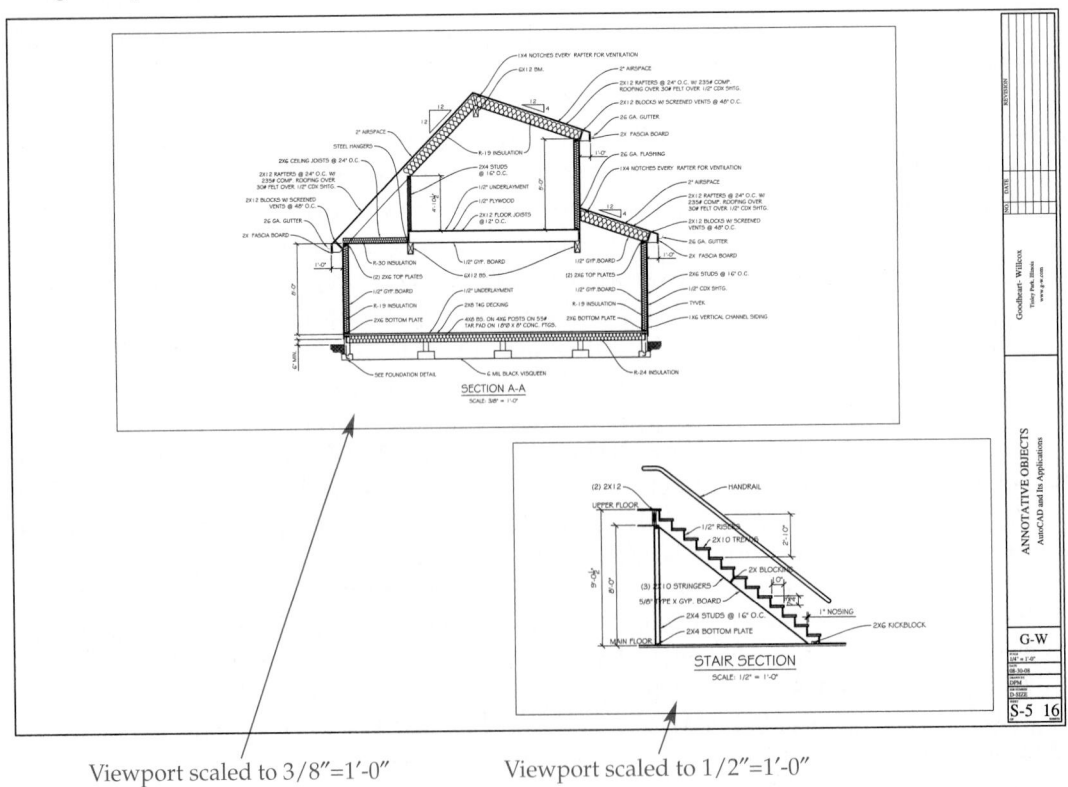

Viewport scaled to 3/8"=1'-0"

Viewport scaled to 1/2"=1'-0"

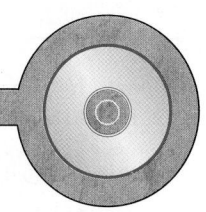

Exercise 27-5

Complete the exercise on the Student CD.

Reusing Annotative Objects

Often the same drawing features must be shown at different scales. For example, you may want to plot a drawing on a large sheet using a large scale, and also plot the same drawing on a smaller sheet using a smaller scale. Or, you may want to enlarge a portion of an existing view and add annotations to the view enlargement. Traditionally, these processes involve creating scale-specific layers and then drawing copies of annotations on the layers that are appropriate for the drawing scale. The layers that do not match the scale of the floating layout viewport can then be frozen.

Using annotative objects significantly improves the ability to reuse existing drawing features. You can use annotation visibility to hide annotative objects not supported by the current annotation scale. You can also adjust the position of scale representations according to the appropriate annotation scale. These options give you the ability to include differently scaled annotative objects on the same drawing sheet without creating copies of the objects and without using scale-specific layers.

Using invisible scale representations

As described earlier in this chapter, if annotative objects do not support an annotation scale, the annotative objects can be made to disappear when the annotation scale that the objects do not support is made current. This is a valuable technique for displaying certain items at a specific scale. Annotative object visibility is controlled by the **ANNOALLVISIBLE** system variable, and can be turned on and off by picking the **Annotation Visibility** button on the status bar.

The following example shows how adjusting the visibility of annotative objects that only support the current annotation scale can be used to create an additional view from existing drawing features. In this example, an annotation scale of 3/4″ = 1′-0″ is used to create a foundation detail. To begin constructing the foundation detail, the 3/4″ = 1′-0″ annotation scale is added to the existing earth hatch pattern so it can be shown on the full section and the foundation detail. See **Figure 27-20**. Next, with the current annotation scale set to 3/4″ = 1′-0″, annotative text, dimensions, multileaders, and hatch patterns are added to the foundation detail. See **Figure 27-21**. These objects only support the 3/4″ = 1′-0″ annotation scale, so they can be hidden on the 3/8″ = 1′-0″–scaled full section.

PROFESSIONAL TIP

If objects already support an annotation scale, but you do not want to display those annotations at the current scale, delete the annotation scale from the objects.

Adjusting scale representation position

A major benefit of using annotative objects is the ability to reuse objects for differently scaled drawing views. The previous example of adding a 3/4″ = 1′-0″ annotation scale to the earth hatch pattern highlights this concept. Additionally, the location and spacing of annotative objects on one scale are often not appropriate for another scale. To overcome this issue, you can reposition each scale representation.

In the foundation detail example, some of the existing 3/8″ = 1′-0″–scaled full section dimensions and multileaders are to be reused in the foundation detail. The

Figure 27-20.
The earth hatch pattern can be reused by adding the 3/4″ = 1′-0″ foundation detail scale to the annotative hatch pattern.

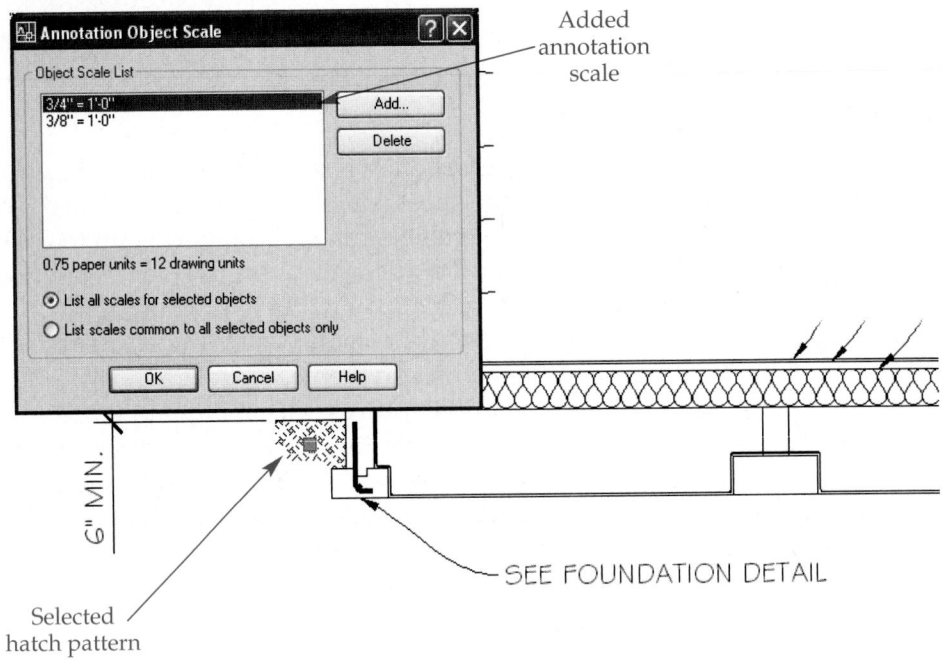

Figure 27-21.
Adding annotative text, dimensions, multileaders, and hatch patterns using a 3/4″ = 1′-0″ annotation scale.

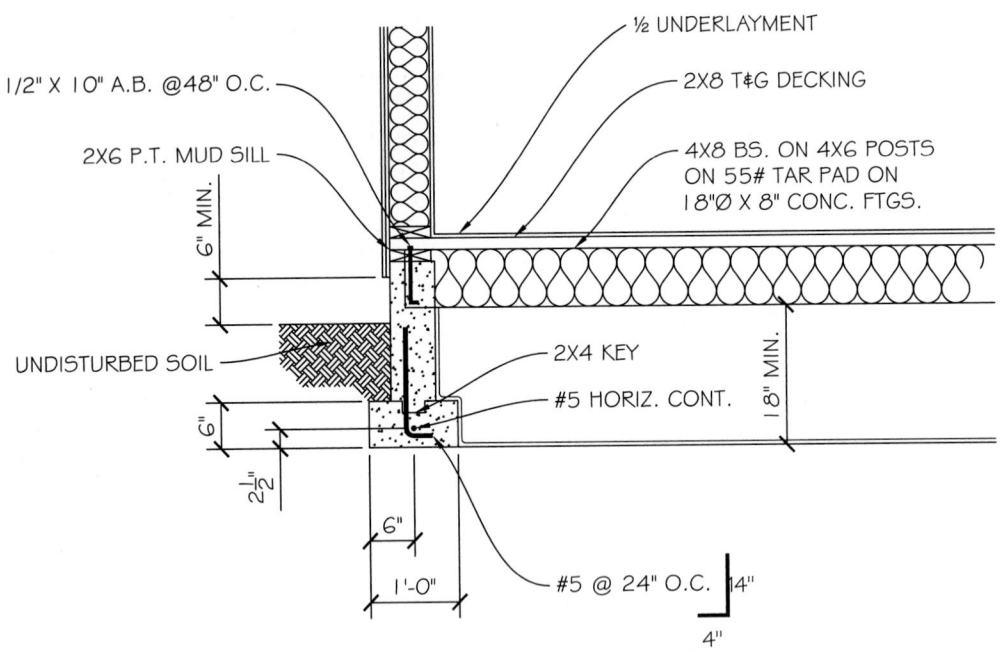

Figure 27-22.
A—Some of the existing 3/8″ = 1′-0″ scaled objects can be reused to create another drawing view. B—Adding a 3/4″ = 1′-0″ annotation scale to existing objects and setting the annotation scale to 3/4″ = 1′-0″.

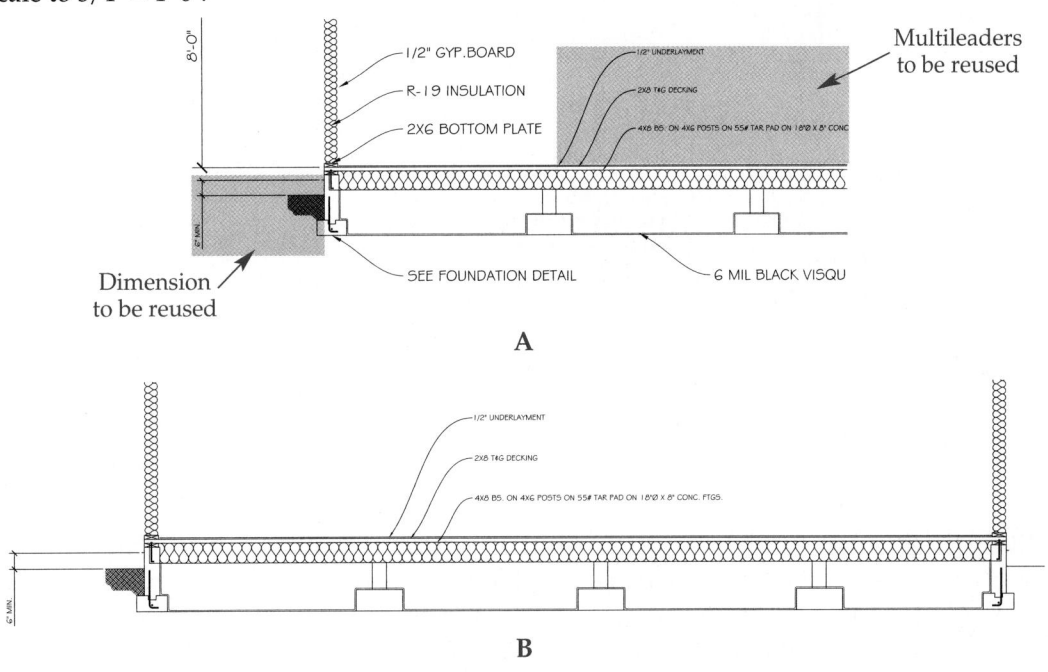

A

B

first step to reusing the annotative objects is to add a 3/4″ = 1′-0″ annotation scale to the objects. Next, with **ANNOALLVISIBLE** turned off, as shown in **Figure 27-22,** you can see the resulting position of the selected objects, which is initially the same location as the 3/8″ = 1′-0″ objects. The only difference is that now the 3/8″ = 1′-0″ objects also support a 3/4″ = 1′-0″ scale.

The position of annotation scale representations can be adjusted using grip editing methods. When you select annotative objects that support more than one annotation scale, all scale representations are shown by default. See **Figure 27-23.** Grips are attached to the scale representation that corresponds to the current annotation scale. Using grips to edit scale representations is similar to editing the object used to create the scale representation. An annotative object is a single object, but it can contain several scale representations. The difference when editing a scale representation is that you are adjusting a scaled "copy" of the object. **Figure 27-24** shows the effects of

Figure 27-23.
The position of annotation scale representations can be adjusted using grip editing techniques. When you select annotative objects that support more than one annotation scale, all scale representations are shown by default.

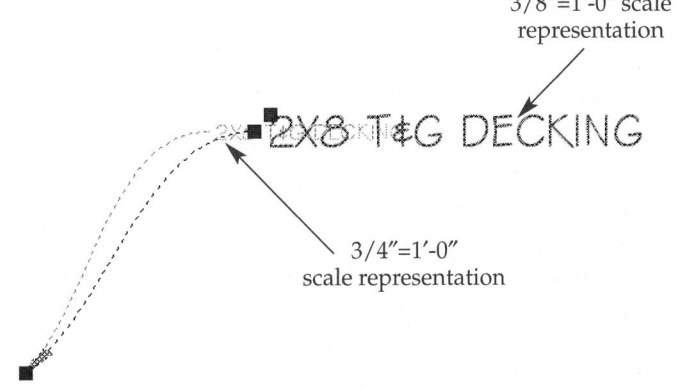

Figure 27-24.
Editing the position of scale representations is much like creating scaled copies of existing annotations.

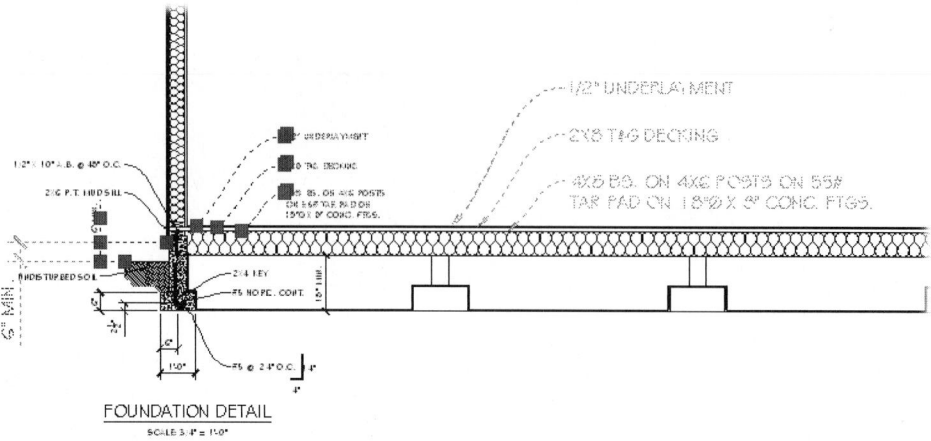

editing the position of dimension and multileader scale representations on the foundation detail. The representations are selected to help demonstrate the effects of editing scale representation position. Notice that all elements of the scale representation can be edited to produce the desired annotations at the appropriate location.

> **PROFESSIONAL TIP**
>
> Use the **DIMSPACE** and **MLEADERALIGN** commands to quickly adjust the dimension spacing and multileader alignment after the drawing scale changes.

The display of selected scale representations is controlled by the **SELECTIONANNODISPLAY** system variable, which is set to 1 by default. As a result, all scale representations are shown and appear dimmed when you pick an annotative object that supports multiple annotation scales. See **Figure 27-23.** If the selected object supports several annotation scales, the display can be confusing. Set the **SELECTIONANNODISPLAY** system variable to 0 in order to display only the scale representation that corresponds to the current annotation scale.

> **NOTE**
>
> Scale representations can only be edited individually using grip editing techniques. When modify commands are used to edit an annotative object, all scale representations are edited simultaneously.

Resetting scale representation position

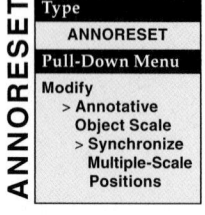

Type
ANNORESET
Pull-Down Menu
Modify > **Annotative**   **Object Scale**   > **Synchronize**   **Multiple-Scale**   **Positions**

The **ANNORESET** command can be used to change the position of all selected scale representations to the position of the scale representation that is set according to the current annotation scale. This command removes all unique scale representation positions. To access the **ANNORESET** command, select annotative objects, right-click and pick the **Synchronize Multiple-scale Positions** option from the **Annotative Object Scale** cascading menu of the shortcut menu, pick **Modify** > **Annotative Object Scale** > **Synchronize Multiple-scale Positions**, or type ANNORESET.

If you activate the **ANNORESET** command by right-clicking objects, the position of the selected objects is reset. If you access the command before selecting objects, pick the annotative objects. After making your selections, press [Enter] to exit the command and reset the scale representation positions.

Completing a Multiview Drawing

The last step to creating the multiview drawing is to display and plot the drawing using multiple paper space viewports. **Figure 27-25** shows an architectural D-size sheet layout with three floating viewports. One viewport is used to display the full section at a viewport scale of 3/8″ = 1′-0″. A second viewport is used to display the stair section at a viewport scale of 1/2″ = 1′-0″. A third viewport is used to display the foundation detail at a viewport scale of 3/4″ = 1′-0″.

PROFESSIONAL TIP

When drawings using annotative objects are saved to earlier versions of AutoCAD, scale representations can be converted to non-annotative objects, but automatically placed on unique layers. To use this function, select **Tools > Options... > Open and Save** tab > **Maintain visual fidelity for annotative objects** check box.

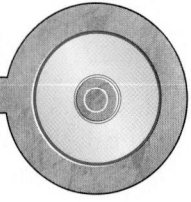

Exercise 27-6
Complete the exercise on the Student CD.

Figure 27-25.
A complete multiview drawing created using annotative objects.

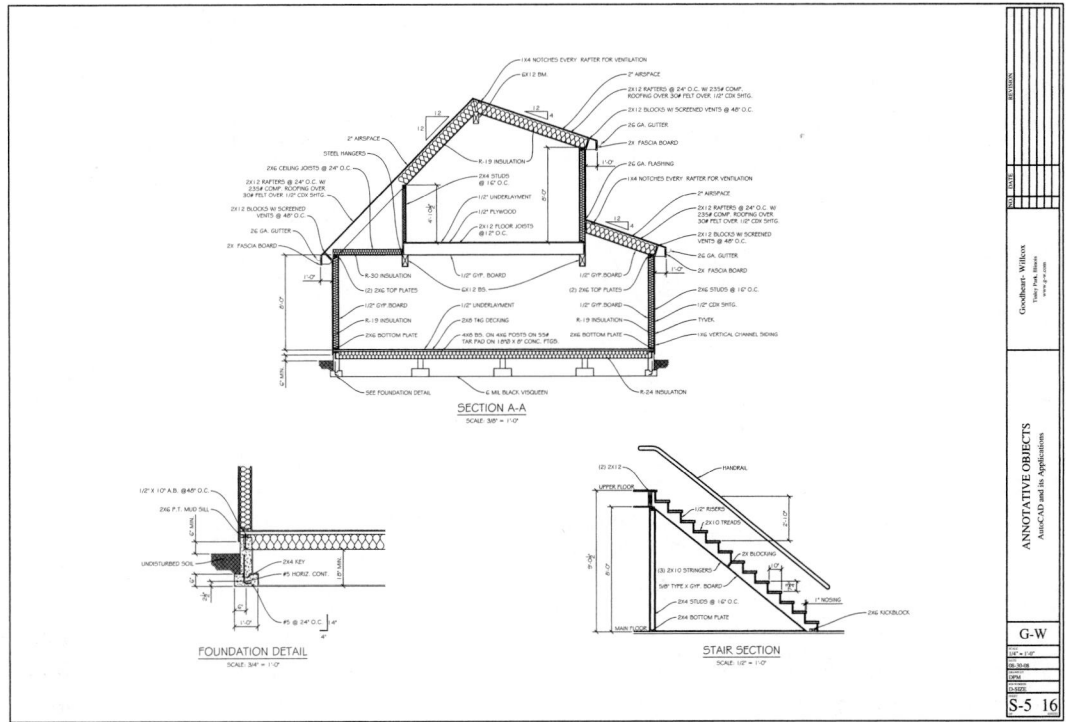

Chapter Test

Answer the following questions. Write your answers on a separate sheet of paper or complete the electronic chapter test on the Student CD.

1. Define the term *annotation*.
2. What are annotative objects? Identify at least four types of objects that can be made annotative.
3. Which **MSLTSCALE** system variable setting should you use so you do not have to calculate the drawing scale factor when entering an **LTSCALE** value?
4. How do you set the text scale, including spacing, width, and paragraph settings to adjust automatically according to the current annotation scale?
5. Calculate the correct spacing in model space if your first dimension line should be 3/4″ from an object when plotted, and your drawing is scaled to 1/4″ = 1′-0″.
6. Identify an important relationship between the viewport scale and the annotation scale.
7. Name the command used to update text properties according to the current properties of the text style on which the text is drawn.
8. What is an annotative object representation?
9. Briefly describe the result of setting the **ANNOAUTOSCALE** system variable to a value of 4.
10. Briefly discuss the effect of turning annotation visibility on and off.

Drawing Problems

1. Create the section view and side view shown. Use annotative objects to prepare a full-scale drawing of the part. Change the annotation scale to 2:1 and adjust the scale representations as needed according to the new scale. Save the drawing as P27-1.

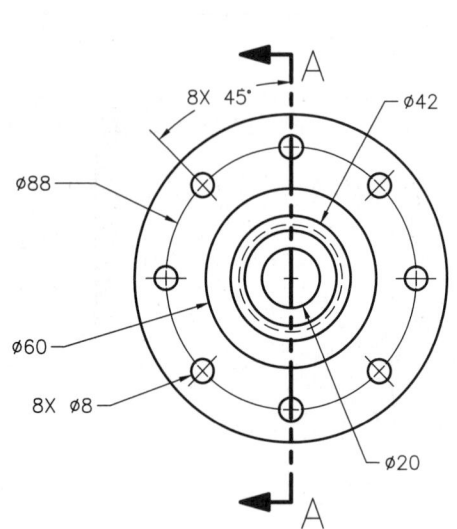

Name: Hub
Material: Cast Iron

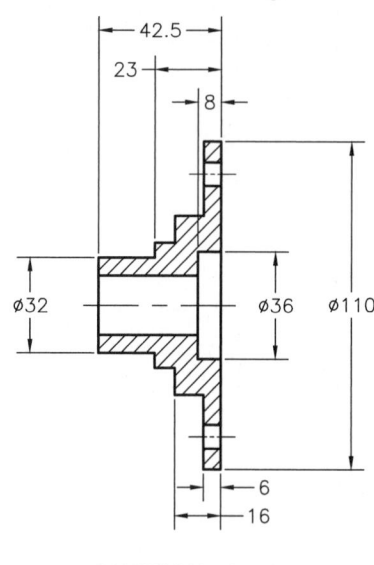

SECTION A—A

2. Create the section view and side views shown. Use annotative objects to prepare a full-scale drawing of the part. Change the annotation scale to 2:1 and adjust the scale representations as needed according to the new scale. Save the drawing as P27-2.

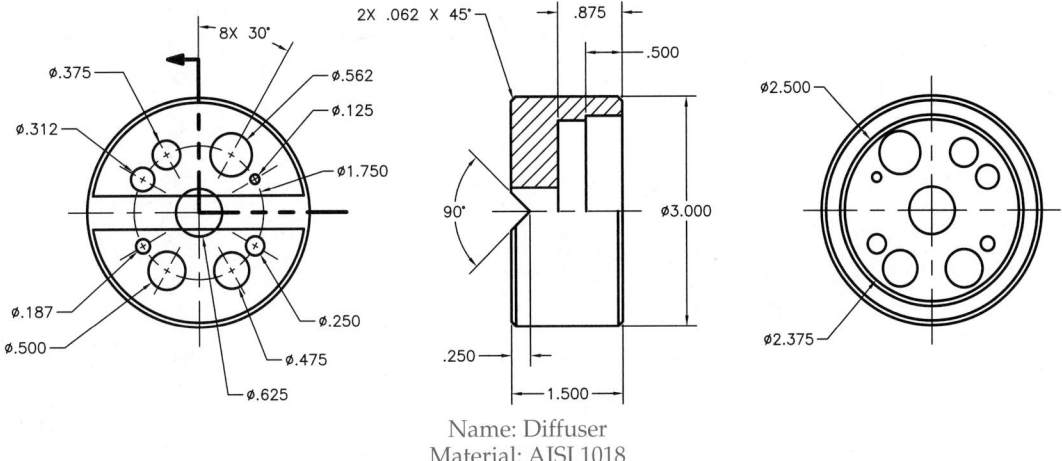

Name: Diffuser
Material: AISI 1018

3. Draw the fan shown at full scale in model space. Use annotative objects to prepare a full-scale view of the fan as shown and a view enlargement of the motor. You should not have to create a copy of the motor or develop scale specific layers. Save the drawing as P27-3.

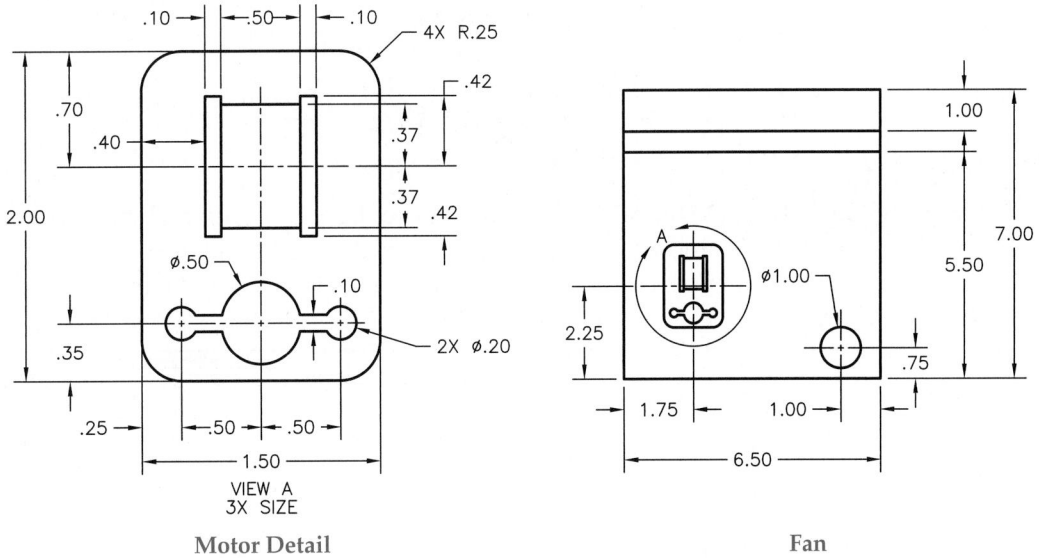

Motor Detail   Fan

4. Refer to an existing drawing that contains non-annotative objects. Convert all the non-annotative objects to annotative. Save the drawing as P27-4.

5. Refer to an existing drawing that contains non-annotative objects. Recreate the drawing using annotative objects. Save the drawing as P27-5.

6. Draw the floor plan shown at full scale in model space. Use annotative objects to prepare a 1/4″ = 1′-0″ view. Change the annotation scale to 1/8″ = 1′-0″ and adjust the scale representations as needed according to the new scale. Save the drawing as P27-6.

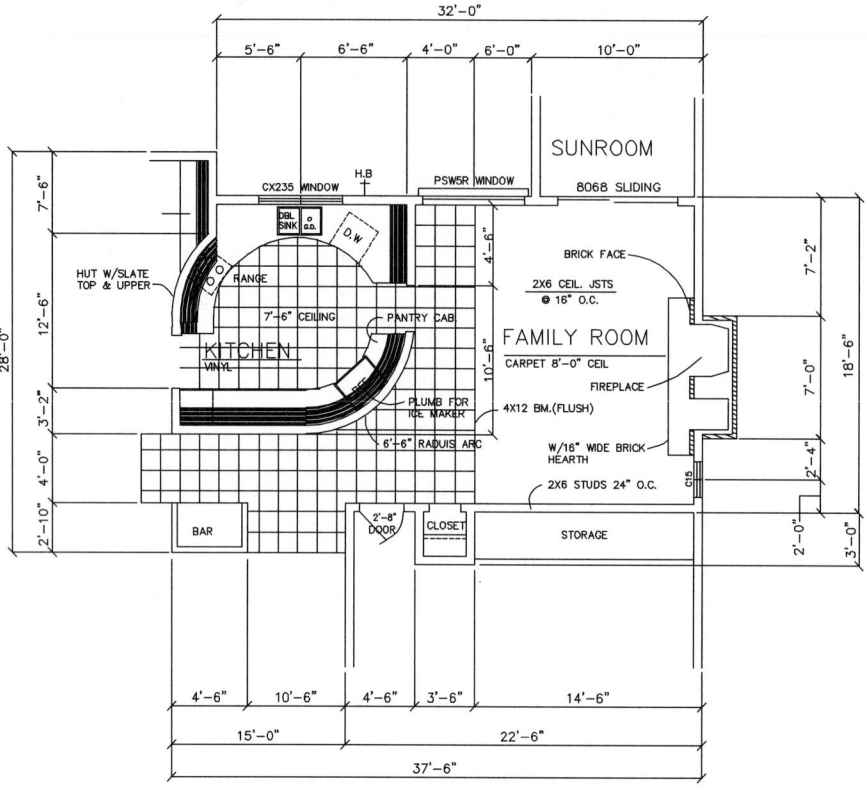

7. Draw the part show at full scale in model space. Use annotative objects to prepare a full-scale view and a view enlargement of the part as shown. You should not have to create a copy of the part or develop scale specific layers. Save the drawing as P27-7.

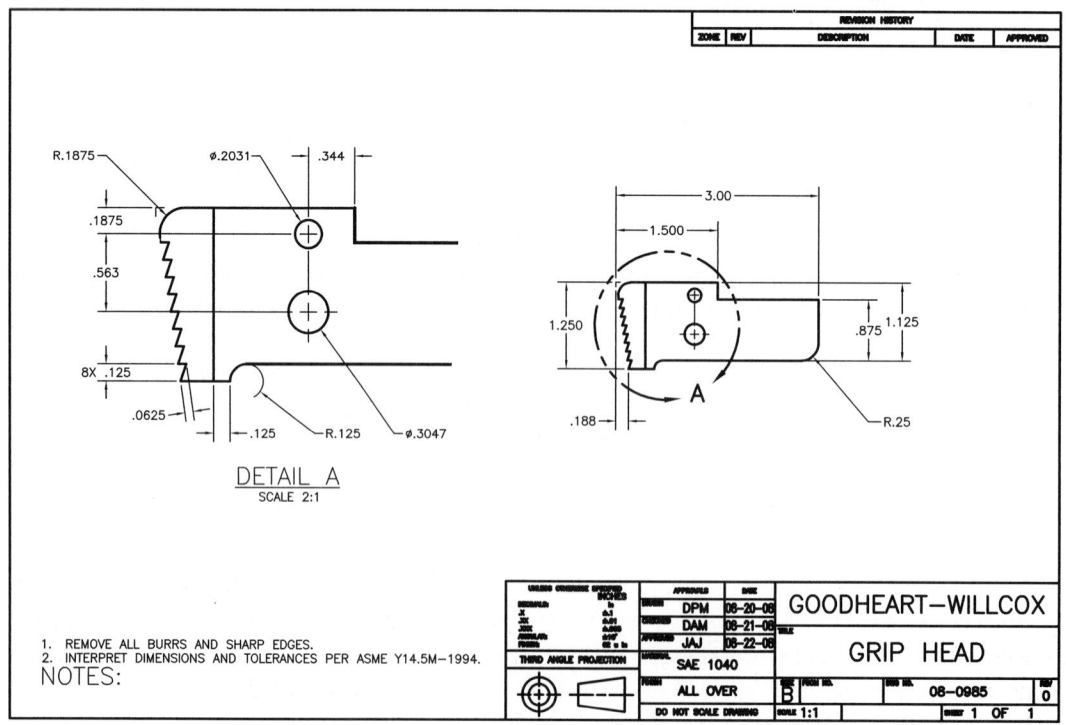

CHAPTER 28

External Reference Drawings

Learning Objectives

After completing this chapter, you will be able to do the following:

✓ Explain the function of external references.
✓ Attach an existing drawing to the current drawing.
✓ Use **DesignCenter** and tool palettes to attach external references.
✓ Bind external references and selected dependent objects to a drawing.
✓ Edit external references in the current drawing.
✓ Use external references to create a multiview layout.
✓ Control the display of layers in viewports using the **Layer Properties Manager** dialog box.

When you create multiple objects in a drawing by copying them, the drawing file grows in size because AutoCAD must maintain a complete description of the geometry of each copied object. On the other hand, when you use a block to represent multiple objects, AutoCAD maintains only one description of the block's geometry. All other instances of the block are recorded as X, Y, and Z coordinates, and AutoCAD refers to the original block definition to obtain the block's data. The size of a drawing is decreased considerably if blocks are used rather than copied objects.

AutoCAD allows you to further control the size of drawing files by using external references. An *external reference (xref)* allows you to incorporate, or reference, existing drawing, design web format, and raster image files into the current drawing without adding new file data. This procedure is excellent for applications in which existing base drawings, complex symbols, images and details are shared by several users, are used often, or can be used to develop new drawings. This chapter explains the use of external references and introduces the various applications for reference drawings.

external reference (xref): A drawing, DWF file, or raster image that has been incorporated into the current drawing by reference only.

Introduction to External References

Any machine or electrical appliance contains a variety of components that are assembled to create the final product. The final product occupies a greater amount of space and weighs more than any of the individual components. In the same way, a drawing composed of a variety of blocks, inserted drawings, and other data such as raster images, is larger than the individual files.

AutoCAD allows you to reference existing drawing (DWG), design web format (DWF), and raster image files into the *master drawing* on which you are currently working. When you externally reference a file, the file's geometry is not added to the current drawing, but it is displayed on-screen. This makes for much smaller files. It also allows several people in a class or office to reference the same file, with the assurance that any revisions to the reference file are displayed in any drawing where it is used.

In addition to reducing drawing file size, one of the greatest benefits of using xrefs is that whenever the master drawing is opened, the latest versions of the xrefs are displayed. If the original externally referenced files are modified between the time you revise the master drawing and the next time you open and plot the drawing, all revisions are automatically reflected. This is because AutoCAD reloads each xref whenever the master drawing is loaded.

The use of xrefs provides other significant advantages as well. They can be nested, and you can use as many xrefs as needed for any drawing. *Nested xrefs* are details referenced to the master drawing that are composed of smaller xrefed details. You can also attach other xrefs to the referenced file and have these newly attached xrefs automatically added to the master drawing when it is opened.

Placing External Reference Drawings

Existing drawing (DWG), design Web format (DWF), and raster image files can be referenced into the current drawing. DWF files are AutoCAD drawing files or other application files that are compressed for publication and viewing on the Web. A DWF file is usually referenced into a drawing in order to share information from the Web or from an application other than AutoCAD, though the high compression of DWF files may limit their effective use. Raster image files are referenced into a drawing whenever there is a need to add an image to a drawing, such as for a company logo in a title block. Externally referencing an image into a drawing is an excellent technique, because the large file size often associated with a raster image is not reproduced in the current drawing. External reference DWF and image files are further described in *AutoCAD and Its Applications—Advanced.*

External reference drawings can be used to:
- Construct a drawing using predrawn symbols or details (a method similar to the use of blocks).
- Develop a new drawing using an existing drawing as a pattern or source of needed drawing geometry.
- Lay out drawings composed of multiple views or details using different existing drawings. When working with sheet sets, you can use external references to arrange sheet views in paper space layouts. Sheet sets are described in Chapter 29.

Attaching an Xref Drawing to the Current Drawing

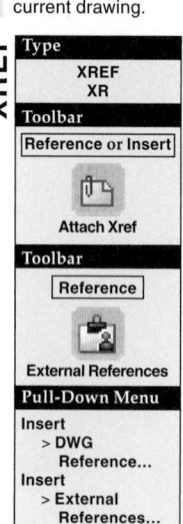
A referenced drawing that is inserted into the current drawing said to be *attached* to the drawing. To attach an external reference drawing, pick the **Attach Xref** button from either the **Reference** or **Insert** toolbar or pick **Insert > DWG Reference...** from the pull-down menu. An xref can also be attached using the **External References** palette. To access the **External References** palette, pick the **External References** button from the **Reference** toolbar, pick **Insert > External References...** from the pull-down menu, pick **Tools > Palettes > External References...** from the pull-down menu, or type XREF or XR. The **External References** palette, shown in **Figure 28-1,** is a complete external reference management tool.

Figure 28-1.
The **External References** palette provides access to all options for externally referenced files.

Pick to attach an
external reference to
the current drawing

Information about
the highlighted
file reference

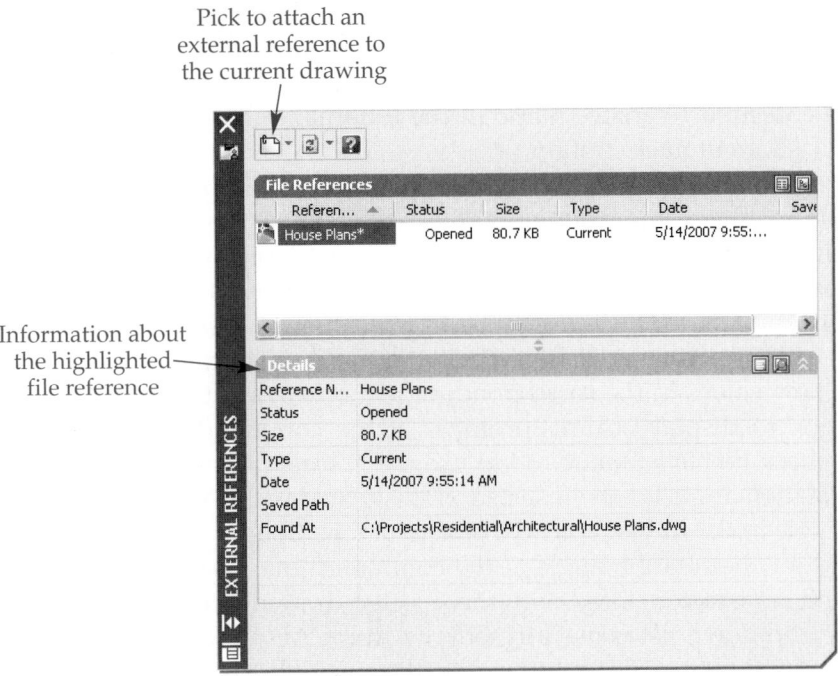

To attach an xref drawing using the **External References** palette, pick the **Attach DWG** button from the flyout, or right-click on the **File References** pane and select the **Attach DWG...** shortcut menu option. These selection techniques display the **Select Reference File** dialog box, which allows you to locate and select the drawing file to be attached. Then pick the **Open** button to display the **External Reference** dialog box. See **Figure 28-2**. This dialog box is used to indicate how and where the reference is to be placed in the current drawing. The name and path of the selected xref are shown in the upper-left corner of the dialog box. To change the drawing to be attached, pick the **Browse...** button and select the new file in the **Select Reference File** dialog box.

Figure 28-2.
The **External Reference** dialog box is used to specify how an external reference is placed in the current drawing.

Pick to access
existing xrefs

Pick to select
a new file to attach

Select path
type to save
with xref

Check to specify
values at the
command line

Activate to select
a point on-screen

Default
rotation angle

Scaling
parameters

Block unit
settings

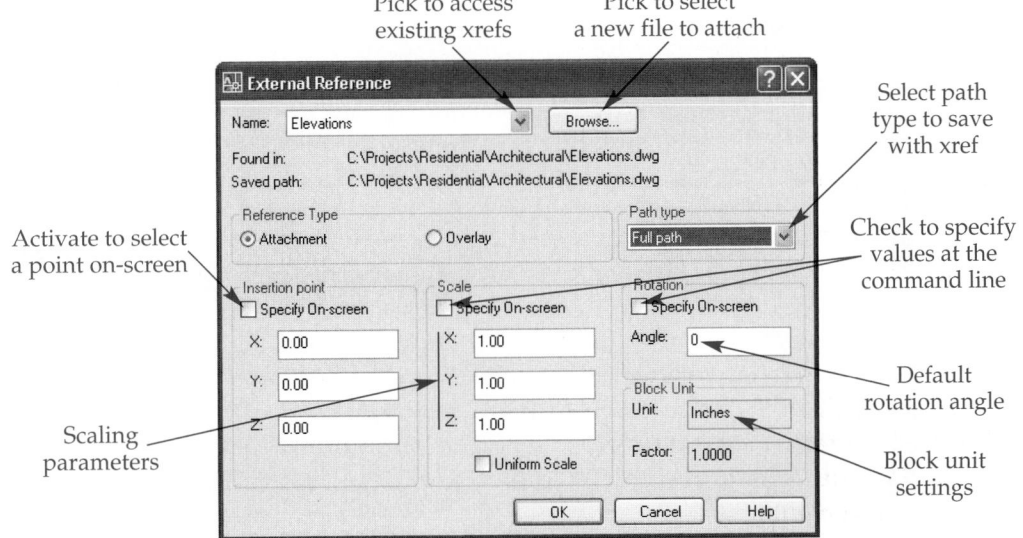

When attaching an xref, pick the default **Attachment** option in the **Reference Type** area. Working with the **Overlay** option is described later in this chapter.

If an external reference already exists in the current drawing, you can attach another copy of it by picking the **Name:** drop-down list arrow and choosing the existing drawing file you want to attach again. You can also attach an existing xref by right-clicking on the desired reference name in the **External References** palette and picking the **Attach...** shortcut menu option.

The lower portion of the **External Reference** dialog box contains the options for the xref insertion location, scaling, rotation angle, and block unit settings. The text boxes in the **Insertion point** area allow you to enter 2D or 3D coordinates for insertion of the xref if the **Specify On-screen** check box is not checked. Activate the **Specify On-screen** check box if you want to specify the insertion location on-screen. Scale factors for the xref can be set in the **Scale** area. By default, the X, Y, and Z scale factors are set to 1. You can enter new values in the corresponding text boxes or activate the **Specify On-screen** check box to display scaling prompts at the command line. Checking the **Uniform Scale** check box tells AutoCAD to use the X scale factor for the Y and Z scale factors. The rotation angle for the inserted xref is 0 by default. You can specify a different rotation angle in the **Angle:** text box, or activate the **Specify On-screen** check box to be prompted for the rotation angle at the command line. The **Block Unit** area displays the unit and scale factor stored with the selected drawing file.

The **Path type** drop-down list is used to set how AutoCAD stores the path to the xref file. This path is used to find the xref file when the master file is opened. The path is displayed in the **External References** palette, as shown in **Figure 28-3.** It also appears under the xref name in the **Saved path:** listing in the **External Reference** dialog box.

Using the full path

absolute path: A path to a file defined by the file's location on the computer system.

The **Full path** option is an *absolute path* and is active by default. When you use the **Full path** option, the xref drawing location is defined by its location on the computer system, which means that the xref drawings must be located in the same drive and folder specified in the saved path. The master drawing can be moved to any location, but the xref drawings must remain in the saved path. This option is acceptable if it is unlikely that the master and xref drawings will be copied to another computer or drive or moved to another folder.

Figure 28-3.
An xref file attached to the current drawing can be referenced with a full path, a relative path, or no path. The type of path used is displayed in the **Save Path** column in the **External References** palette.

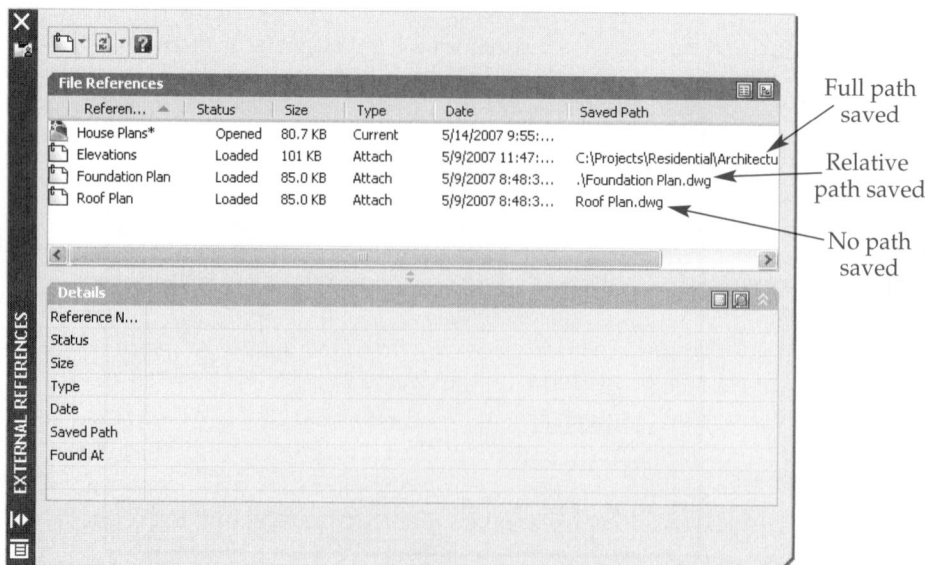

Using a relative path

If you share your drawings with a client or eventually archive the drawings, the **Relative path** option is more appropriate. This option saves a *relative path*, identifying it in relation to the master drawing file. The **Relative path** option cannot be used if the xref file is on a local or network drive other than the drive that stores the master file. If the master drawing and xref files are located in a single folder and subfolders, this folder can be copied to any location without losing the connection between files. For example, the folder can be copied from the C: drive of one computer to the D: drive of another computer, to a folder on a CD, or to an archive server. If these types of transfers are performed with the **Full path** option, you need to open the master drawing after copying and redefine the saved paths for all xref files.

relative path: A path to a file defined according to its location relative to the master drawing.

Using the No Path option

You can also choose not to save the path to the xref file. If you use the **No Path** option, the xref file can only be found and loaded if the path to the file is included in one of the Support File Search Path locations or if the xref file is in the same folder as the master file. The Support File Search Path locations are specified in the **Files** tab of the **Options** dialog box.

NOTE

AutoCAD also searches for xref files in all paths of the current project name. These paths are listed under the Project Files Search Path in the **Files** tab of the **Options** dialog box. You can create a new project as follows:

1. Pick Project Files Search Path to highlight it, and then pick the **Add...** button.
2. Enter a project name if desired.
3. Pick the plus sign icon (+), and then pick the word Empty.
4. Pick the **Browse...** button and locate the folder that is to become part of the project search path. Then pick **OK**.
5. Complete the project search path definition by entering the **PROJECTNAME** system variable and specifying the same name that is used in the **Options** dialog box.

After specifying a reference and path type for an xref in the **External Reference** dialog box, you can insert the xref into the current drawing. In the example given in **Figure 28-2**, a file named Elevations is selected for attachment. Because the **Specify On-screen** check box in the **Insertion point** area is activated, the dialog box disappears when you pick **OK**. The xref is attached to your cursor and you are prompted for the insertion point. You can use any valid point specification option, including object snap modes.

The insertion options for attaching an xref are essentially the same as those used to insert a block. Both commands function in a similar manner, but the internal workings and results are different. Remember that externally referenced files are not added to the current drawing file's database, as are inserted blocks. Therefore, using external references helps keep your drawing file size to a minimum.

PROFESSIONAL TIP

An xref is placed on the current layer when you attach it to a drawing. It is advisable to create an xref layer for each reference that you plan on using. This makes it easier to manage xrefs in your drawing because the individual layers can be frozen or thawed to change the display of different files.

Understanding Xref Drawing Paths

In the **Saved Path** list in the **External References** palette, AutoCAD uses prefixes to describe the relative paths to xref files. In **Figure 28-3**, the path to the FPlans reference file is preceded by the characters .\. The period (.) represents the folder containing the master drawing. From that folder, AutoCAD looks in the Architectural folder, where the FPlans drawing is found. A similar specification is used for the Elevation reference file in **Figure 28-4.** In this instance, the Elevation file is found in the same folder as the master drawing. The specification for the Wall reference file is preceded by the characters ..\. The double period (..) instructs AutoCAD to move up one folder level from the current location. The double period can be repeated to move up multiple folder levels. For example, the Panel reference file in **Figure 28-4** is found by moving up two folder levels from the folder of the master drawing and then opening the Symbols folder.

Figure 28-4.
Relationship between the symbols in the **Saved Path** list and file locations within the folder structure.

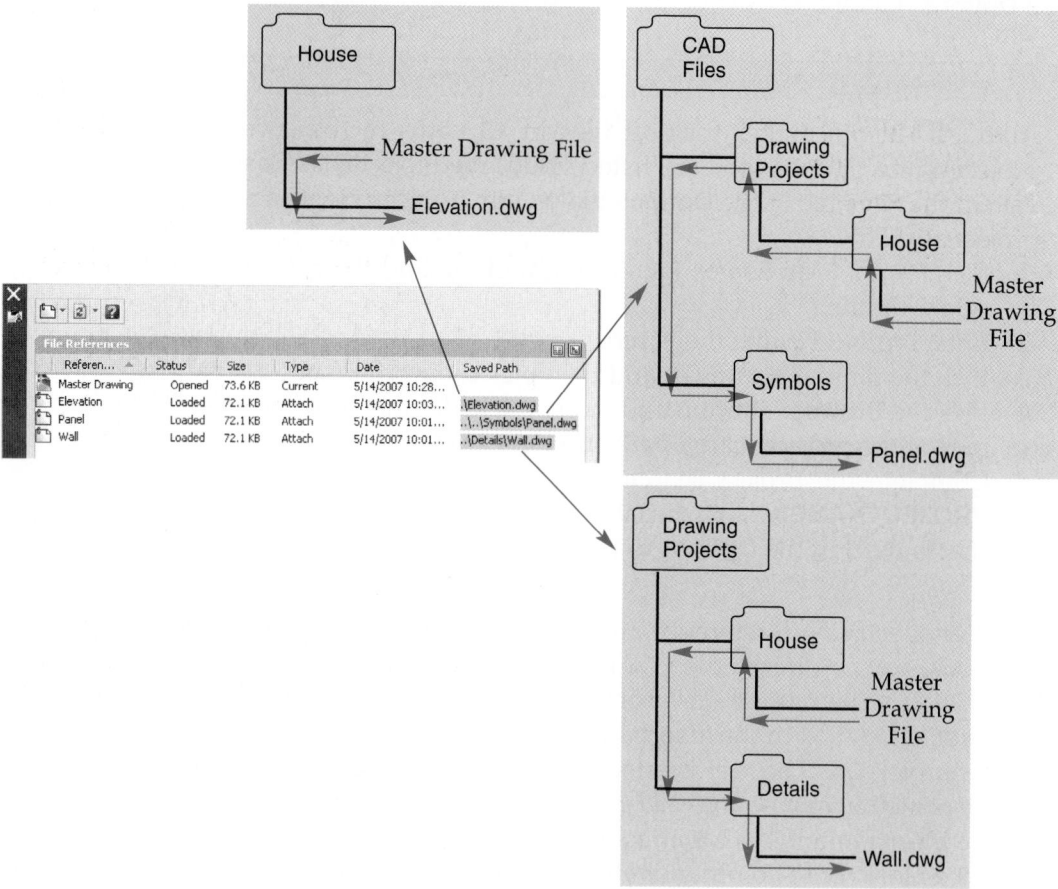

Attaching Xrefs with DesignCenter and Tool Palettes

External references can be attached to a drawing quickly using **DesignCenter** or the **Tool Palettes** window. Inserting blocks using these features is described in Chapter 23. Similar procedures are used for attaching xrefs. Use the following technique to attach an xref to the current drawing with **DesignCenter**:

1. Find the folder containing the drawing to be attached in the **Tree View** area of **DesignCenter**. Display the drawing files located in the selected folder in the **Content** area.
2. Right-click the drawing file in the **Content** area and select **Attach as Xref...** from the shortcut menu, or drag and drop the drawing into the current drawing area using the *right mouse button* and select **Attach as Xref...** from the shortcut menu.
3. Enter the appropriate values in **External Reference** dialog box and pick **OK**.

You can also attach a drawing file to the current drawing as an xref from the **Tool Palettes** window. To add an xref to a tool palette, drag an existing xref from the current drawing or an xref from the **Content** area of **DesignCenter** into the **Tool Palettes** window. The xref can then be attached to the current drawing from the palette using drag and drop.

Xref files in tool palettes are identified with an external reference icon. If a drawing file, not an xref, is added to a tool palette from the current drawing or **DesignCenter**, it is designated as a block tool. You can convert the block tool to an xref tool by right-clicking the image in the **Tool Palettes** window and selecting **Properties...** to display the **Tool Properties** dialog box. Then change the **Insert as** field status from Block to Xref using the drop-down list.

Overlaying the Current Drawing with an Xref

External reference drawings can be used to see what your drawing looks like with another drawing overlaid on it. *Overlaying* the current drawing with an external reference file allows you to view the xref temporarily without attaching it to the current drawing. To do this, pick the **Overlay** radio button in the **Reference Type** area of the **External Reference** dialog box after selecting an xref.

overlaying: Displaying a reference file temporarily without attaching it to the current drawing.

The difference between an overlaid xref and an attached xref is related to the way in which nested xrefs are handled. As mentioned earlier, nesting occurs when an externally referenced file is referenced by an xref file that has been attached to the current drawing. The xref file that is attached is known as the *parent xref*. When an xref is overlaid, any nested xrefs that it contains are displayed if those xrefs are *attached*, but not if they are *overlaid*. In other words, any nested overlays are not carried into the master drawing with the parent xref.

parent xref: An xref that contains one or more other xrefs.

Managing External References

The **External References** palette is the primary tool for managing and accessing current information about external references that have been attached to or overlaid on a drawing. The **External References** palette displays an upper **File References** pane and a lower **Details** pane. See **Figure 28-5**. The **File References** pane can be displayed in either list view or tree view. The list view display mode shown in **Figure 28-5** is active by default, and can be set by picking the **List View** button or pressing the [F3] key. The labeled columns displayed in list view include:

- **Reference Name.** Displays the current drawing file name followed by the names of all existing external references in alphabetical or chronological order. The current drawing is indicated with the standard AutoCAD drawing file icon, and xrefs appear as a sheet of paper with a paper clip.
- **Status.** Describes the current status of each xref. The xref status can be:
  - **Loaded.** The xref is attached to the drawing.
  - **Unloaded.** The xref is attached but not displayed or regenerated.
  - **Unreferenced.** The xref has nested xrefs that are not found or are unresolved. An unreferenced xref is not displayed.
  - **Not Found.** The xref file is not found in the specified search paths.
  - **Unresolved.** The xref file is missing or cannot be found.
  - **Orphaned.** The parent of the nested xref cannot be found.
- **Size.** Lists the file size for each xref.
- **Type.** Indicates whether the xref is attached or referenced as an overlay.
- **Date.** Indicates the last modification date for the file being referenced.
- **Saved Path.** Lists the path name saved with the xref. If only a file name appears here, the path has not been saved.

Figure 28-5.

The **External References** palette is used to view and manage referenced files. The **File References** pane is shown in **List View** mode and **Details** pane is shown in **Details** mode.

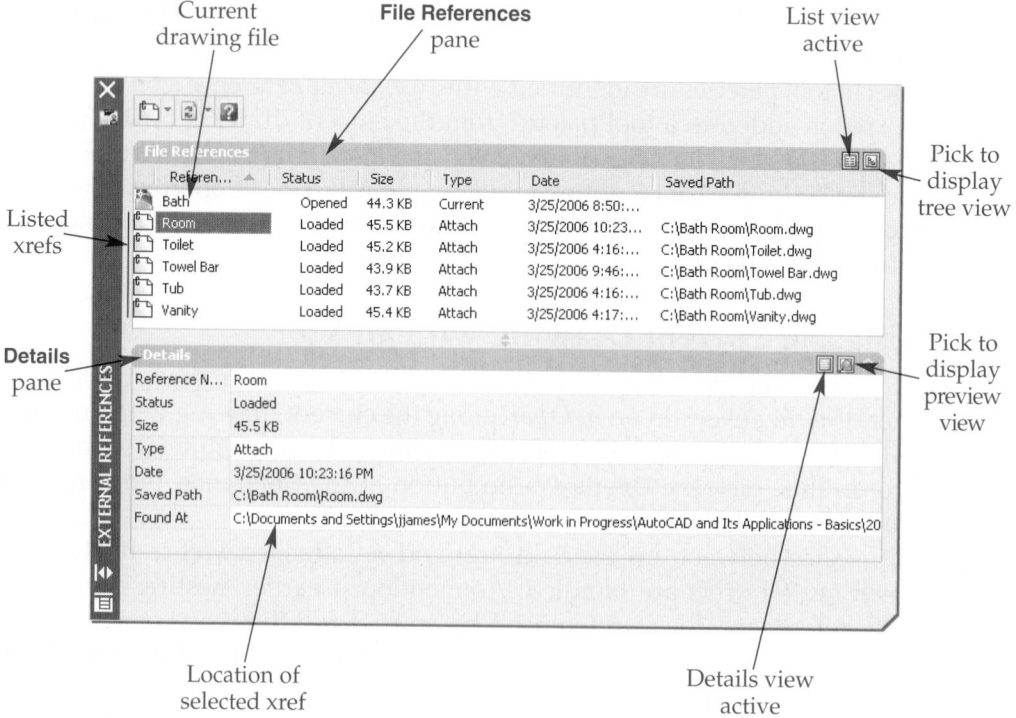

AutoCAD and Its Applications—Basics

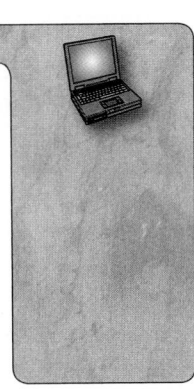

In the list view display mode, the column widths can be adjusted as necessary to view complete information. To adjust the width of a column, move the cursor to the edge of the button at the top of the column until the cursor changes to a horizontal resizing cursor. Press and hold the left mouse button and drag the column to the desired width. The column width adjustments you make are used for subsequent displays of the dialog box. If the columns extend beyond the width of the dialog box window, a horizontal scroll bar appears at the bottom of the list.

To see a list of externally referenced files in the **File References** pane, and to show nesting levels, pick the **Tree View** button or press the [F4] key. See **Figure 28-6.** Nesting levels are shown in a format that is similar to the arrangement of folders. The xref icon can take on different appearances, depending on the current status of the xref. An xref whose status is unloaded or not found has a grayed-out icon. An upward arrow shown with the icon means the xref has just been reloaded, and a downward arrow means the xref has just been unloaded.

The **Details** pane can be displayed in either **Preview** mode or **Details** mode. To display an image of the xref selected in the **File References** pane, pick the **Preview** button on the **Details** pane. See **Figure 28-6.**

The **Details** mode, shown in **Figure 28-5,** is active by default and can be activated by picking the **Details** button. The information listed in the **Details** pane corresponds to the xref selected in the **File References** pane. The rows displayed while in **Detail** mode are exactly the same as the columns found in the **List view** mode of the **File References** pane. However, the **Details** pane can be used to modify the reference name by entering a new name in the **Reference Name** text box. It can also be used to adjust the reference

---

Figure 28-6.
The **File References** pane in **Tree View** mode shows nested xref levels. The **Details** pane in **Preview** mode shows a thumbnail preview of the selected xref.

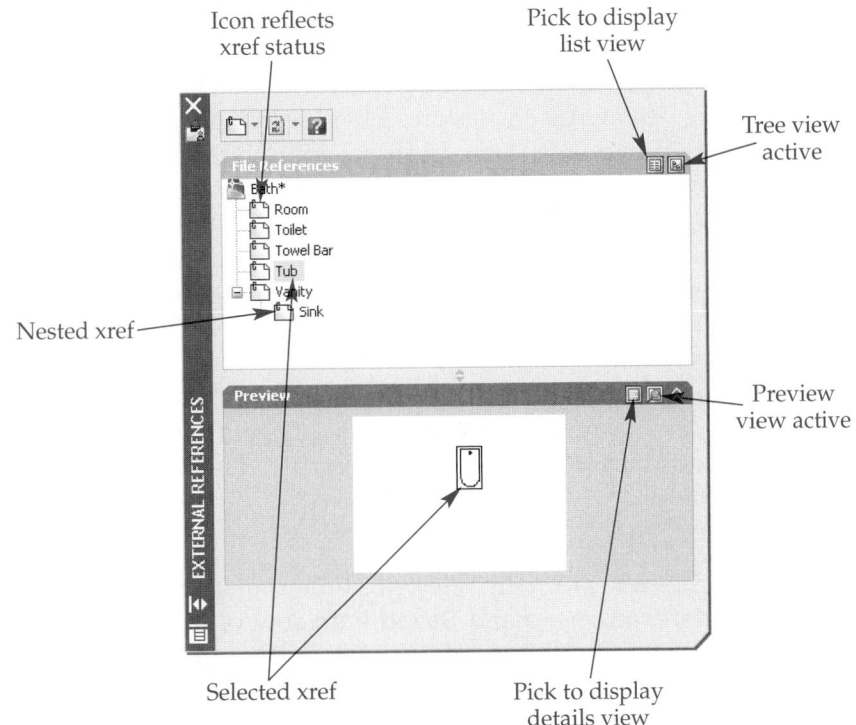

type from an attachment to an overlay or from an overlay to an attachment by picking the appropriate option from the **Type** drop-down list. In addition, the **Details** pane contains a **Found At** row that can be used to update the location of an xref path.

Detaching, Reloading, and Unloading Xrefs

detach: Remove an xref from a master drawing.

Each time you open a master drawing containing an attached xref, the xref is also loaded and appears on-screen. This attachment remains permanent until it is removed or detached. Erasing an xref does not detach it from the master drawing. To *detach* an xref, right-click the reference name in the **File References** pane of the **External References** palette and picking the **Detach** shortcut menu option. When you detach an externally referenced file, all instances of the xref and all referenced data is removed from the current drawing. All xrefs nested within the detached file are also removed.

reload: Update an xref in the master drawing file.

There may be situations in which you need to update, or *reload*, an xref file in the master drawing. For example, if an externally referenced file is edited by another user while the master drawing is open, the version on disk may be different from the version currently displayed. To update the xref, right-click the reference name in the **File References** pane of the **External References** palette and pick the **Reload** shortcut menu option, or pick the **Reload All Reference** button from the flyout to reload all unloaded xrefs. Reloading xrefs forces AutoCAD to read and display the most recently saved version of each drawing.

unload: Suppress the display of an xref without removing it from the master drawing.

When you need to temporarily remove, or suppress, an xref without actually detaching it, you can *unload* the xref. To do so, right-click on the reference name in the **File References** pane of the **External References** palette and pick the **Unload** shortcut menu option. When an xref is unloaded, it is not displayed or regenerated, and AutoCAD's performance increases. To display the xref again, right-click the reference name in the **File References** pane of the **External References** palette and pick the **Reload** shortcut menu option, or pick the **Reload All Reference** button from the flyout to reload all unloaded xrefs.

log file: An XLG file that logs the attachment, detachment, loading, and reloading of xrefs.

> **NOTE**
>
> You can instruct AutoCAD to create and maintain a *log file* of the attaching, detaching, and reloading functions used in any drawing containing xrefs by setting the **XREFCTL** system variable to 1. At this setting, AutoCAD creates an XLG file having the same name as the current drawing, and the file is saved in the same folder. Each time you load a drawing that contains xrefs, or attach, detach, or reload xrefs, AutoCAD adds information to the log file. A new heading, or title block, is added to the log file each time the related drawing file is opened. The log file provides the following information:
> - The drawing name and the date, time, and type of each xref operation.
> - The nesting level of all xrefs affected by the operation.
> - A list of xref-dependent objects affected by the operation and the names of the objects temporarily added to the drawing.

Updating the Xref Path

library path: The path AutoCAD searches by default to find an xref file, including the current folder and locations set in the **Options** dialog box.

A file path saved with an externally referenced file is displayed in the **Saved Path** column of the **File References** pane and **Saved Path** row of the **Details** pane in the **External References** palette. If an xref file is not found in the **Saved Path** location when the master drawing is opened, AutoCAD searches along the *library path*, which includes the current drawing folder and the Support File Search Path locations set in the **Files** tab of the **Options** dialog box. If a file with a matching name is found, it is resolved. In such a case, the **Saved Path** location differs from where the file was actually found. You can check this in the **External References** palette by comparing the path listed in the **Saved Path** column of the **File References** pane and **Saved Path** row of the **Details** pane with the listing in the **Found At** row of the **Details** pane. To update the **Saved Path** location, select the path in the **Found At** edit box and pick the **Browse...** button to the right of the edit box to access the **Select new path** dialog box. Use this dialog box to locate the new folder and select the desired file. Then press **Open** to update the path.

When a referenced drawing has been moved and the new location is not on the library path, its status is indicated as Not Found. To find the xref file and update the **Saved Path** location, select the path in the **Found At** edit box and pick the **Browse...** button to the right of the edit box to access the **Select new path** dialog box. Use this dialog box to locate the new folder and select the desired file. Then press **Open** to update the path.

The Manage Xrefs Icon

When changes are made to parent drawings for xrefs used in a master drawing, a notification appears in the AutoCAD status bar tray. This tray is located in the lower-right corner of the drawing window. Changes are indicated by the appearance of the **Manage Xrefs** icon, a balloon message, or both. Notifications in the status bar tray for xref changes and other system updates are controlled by options in the **Tray Settings** dialog box. This dialog box is accessed by selecting **Tray Settings...** from the status bar drop-down menu. If the **Display icons from services** check box is selected in the **Tray Settings** dialog box, the **Manage Xrefs** icon is displayed in the status bar tray when an xref is attached to the current drawing. If an xref in the current file has been modified since the file was opened, the **Manage Xrefs** icon appears with an exclamation sign over it. Picking the **Manage Xrefs** icon, or right-clicking on the **Manage Xrefs** icon and selecting the **External References...** shortcut menu option, opens the **External References** palette so the xref file can be reloaded.

When the **Display notifications from services** check box is selected in the **Tray Settings** dialog box, a balloon message notification appears with the name of the modified xref file. See **Figure 28-7A.** You can then pick on the xref file name in the balloon message to reload the file. In the example shown, a Towel Bar xref has been added to the Room parent xref drawing. The xref is then reloaded in the current drawing named Bath. See **Figure 28-7B.** Xrefs can also be reloaded by right-clicking on the **Manage Xrefs** icon and selecting **Reload DWG Xrefs** from the shortcut menu.

Clipping an Xref

In some cases it may be necessary to display only a specific portion of an external reference drawing. To accommodate this need, AutoCAD allows you to create a boundary that displays a *subregion* of an xref. All geometry occurring outside the border is invisible, while objects that are partially within the subregion appear to be trimmed at the boundary. Although clipped objects appear trimmed, the referenced file is not changed in any way. Clipping is applied to a selected instance of an xref, and not to the actual xref definition.

subregion: The displayed portion of a clipped xref.

Figure 28-7.
The **Manage Xrefs** icon in the AutoCAD status bar tray provides a notification when an xref file has been modified and saved. A—A balloon message is displayed with an exclamation point over the icon. B—Reloading the xref file updates the current drawing and changes the appearance of the icon.

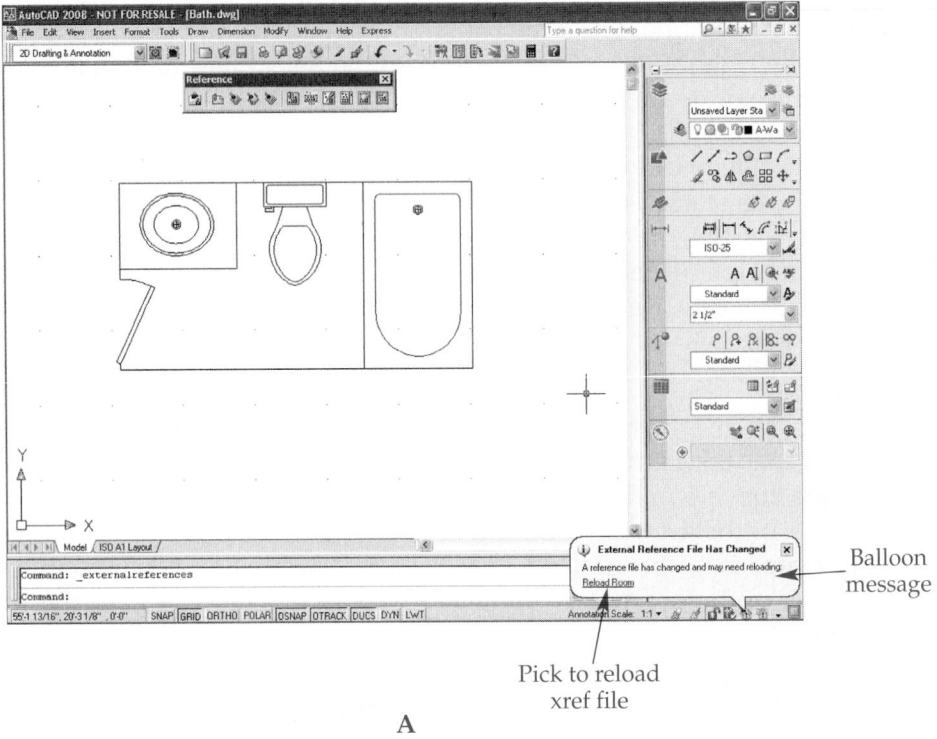

Balloon message

Pick to reload xref file

A

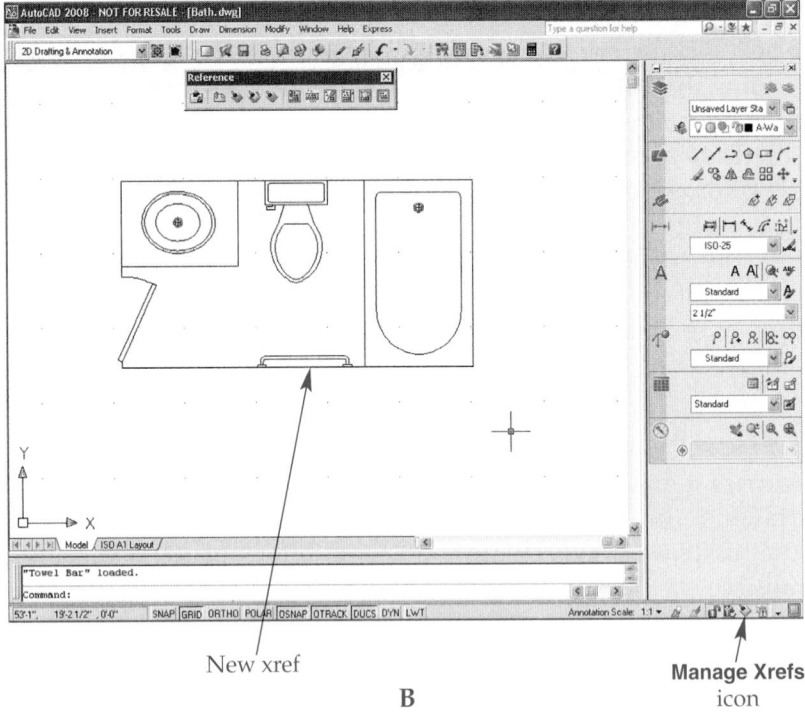

New xref

Manage Xrefs icon

B

The **XCLIP** command is used to create and modify clipping boundaries. To access the **XCLIP** command, select an object that is part of the xref file in the drawing area, then right-click and select the **Clip Xref** shortcut menu option, pick the **Clip Xref** button from the **Reference** toolbar, pick **Modify > Clip > Xref**, or type XC or XCLIP. The prompt sequence for creating a rectangular boundary for an xref is:

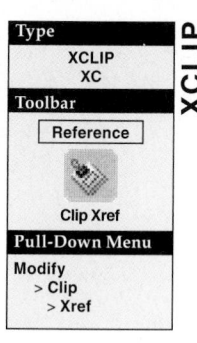

Type
XCLIP
XC

Toolbar
Reference

Clip Xref

Pull-Down Menu
Modify
> Clip
> Xref

```
Command: XC or XCLIP↵
Select objects: (select any number of xref objects)
Select objects: ↵
Enter clipping option
[ON/OFF/Clipdepth/Delete/generate Polyline/New boundary] <New>: ↵
```

The Select objects: prompt allows you to select any number of xrefs to be clipped. After selecting the xrefs, press [Enter] to accept the default **New boundary** option and select the clipping boundary. The other options of the **XCLIP** command can be used after a boundary has been defined. These options include:

- **ON** and **OFF.** Turn the clipping feature on or off as needed. Xrefs must already be clipped for these options to function.
- **Clipdepth.** Allows front and back clipping planes to be defined. The front and back clipping planes define what portion of a 3D drawing is displayed. Xrefs must already be clipped for this option to function. Clipping 3D models is described in *AutoCAD and Its Applications—Advanced*.
- **Delete.** Removes an existing clipping boundary, returning the xref to its unclipped display.
- **generate Polyline.** Creates and displays, or frames, a polyline object at the clip boundary. Xrefs must already be clipped for this option to function.

After the **New boundary** option is selected, the **XCLIP** command sequence continues as follows:

```
Specify clipping boundary:
[Select polyline/Polygonal/Rectangular/Invert clip] <Rectangular>: (press [Enter] to
    create a rectangular boundary)
Specify first corner: (pick the first corner)
Specify opposite corner: (pick the other corner)
```

An example of using the **XCLIP** command is illustrated in **Figure 28-8.** Note that the geometry outside the clipping boundary is no longer displayed after the command is completed. You can invert the portion of the selected xrefs that is clipped by picking the **Invert clip** option. By default, the portion of the xrefs outside of the clipping boundary is no longer displayed. Inverting the clip displays only the portion of the xref outside of the boundary. A clipped xref can be edited just like an unclipped xref. Additionally, the clipping boundary moves with the xref. Note also that nested xrefs are clipped according to the clipping boundary for the parent xref.

If you do not want to create a rectangular clipping boundary after selecting an xref, AutoCAD supplies two other options for defining a boundary:

- **Select polyline.** Allows you to select an existing polyline object as a boundary definition. The border can consist only of straight line segments, so any arc segments in the selected polyline are treated as straight line segments. If the polyline is not closed, the start and end points of the boundary are connected.
- **Polygonal.** Allows you to draw an irregular polygon as a boundary. This option is similar to the **WPolygon** selection option and allows a fairly flexible boundary definition.

The clipping boundary, or frame, is invisible by default. The frame can be displayed by setting the **XCLIPFRAME** system variable to 1, by picking the **Xref Frame** button from the **Reference** toolbar, or by picking **Modify > Object > External Reference > Frame.**

Figure 28-8.
A clipping boundary is used to clip selected areas of an xref. A—Using the **Rectangular** boundary selection option. B—The clipped xref.

Rectangular clipping boundary

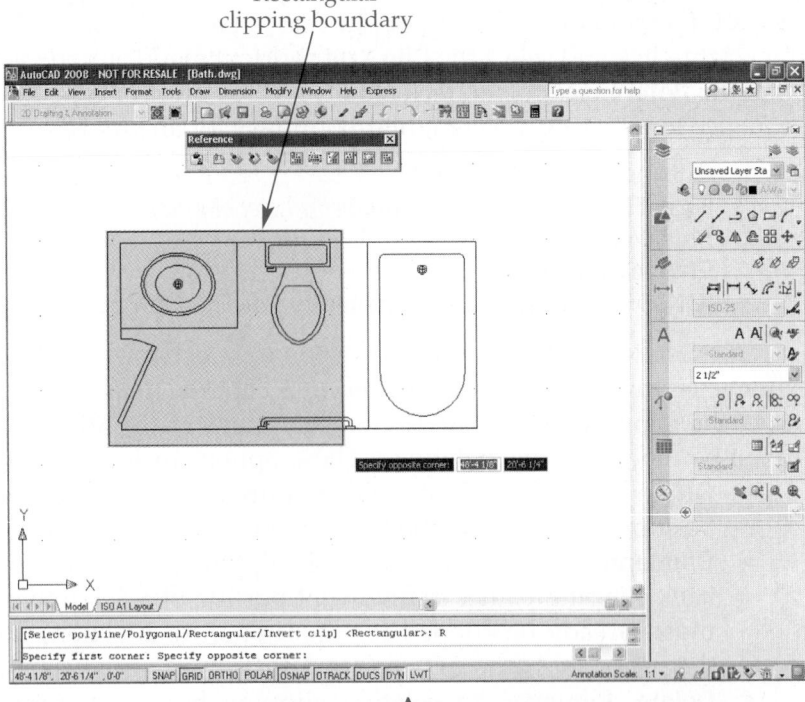

A

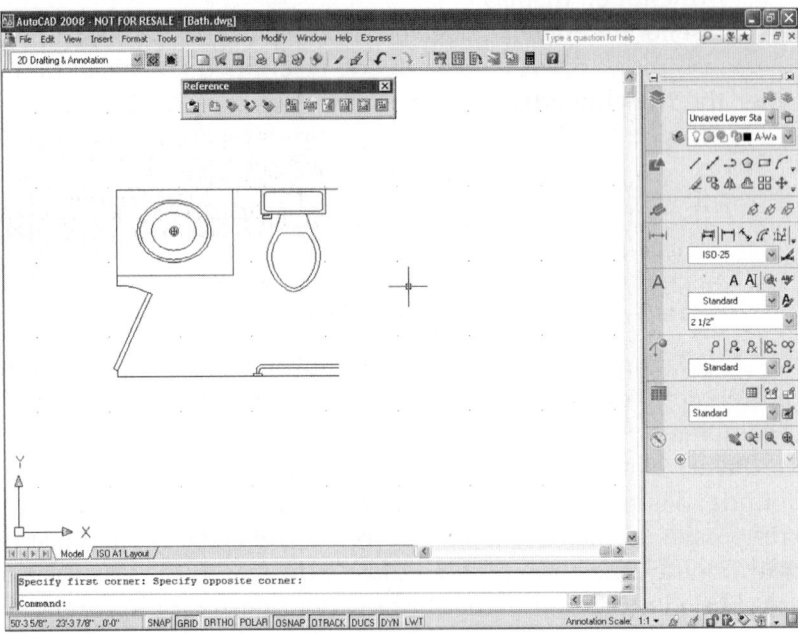

B

Using Demand Loading and Xref Editing Controls

demand loading:
Loading only the part of an xref file necessary to regenerate the master drawing.

Demand loading controls how much of an external reference file is loaded when it is attached to the master drawing. When demand loading is active, the only portion of the xref file loaded is the part necessary to regenerate the master drawing. This improves performance and saves disk space because the entire xref file is not loaded. For example, any data on frozen layers, as well as any data outside of clipping regions, is not loaded.

If a drawing will be used as an external reference, it is good practice to save the file with *spatial indexes* and *layer indexes*. These lists help improve AutoCAD's performance when you reference drawings with frozen layers and clipping boundaries. Layers that are frozen are not loaded when demand loading is enabled, and any areas outside clipping boundaries are also not loaded.

You can create spatial and layer indexes using the following procedure:
1. Access the **Save Drawing As** dialog box.
2. Pick **Options...** from the **Tools** flyout button and select the **DWG Options** tab of the **Saveas Options** dialog box.
3. Select the type of index required from the **Index type:** drop-down list.
4. Pick the **OK** button and save the drawing.

spatial index: A list of objects ordered according to their locations in 3D space.

layer index: A list of objects ordered according to the layers on which they reside.

Demand loading is enabled by default. To check or change the setting, open the **Open and Save** tab of the **Options** dialog box. The three demand loading options are found in the **Demand load Xrefs:** drop-down list in the **External References (Xrefs)** area. The options include:

- **Enabled with copy.** Turns on demand loading. Other users can edit the original drawing because AutoCAD uses a copy of the referenced drawing.
- **Enabled.** Turns on demand loading. While the drawing is being referenced, the xref file is kept open and other users cannot edit the file.
- **Disabled.** Turns off demand loading.

Two additional settings in the **Open and Save** tab of the **Options** dialog box control the effects of changes made to xref-dependent layers and in-place reference editing. The settings are controlled by check boxes in the **External References (Xrefs)** area.

- **Retain changes to Xref layers.** Allows you to keep all changes made to the properties and states of xref-dependent layers. Any changes to layers take precedence over the layer settings in the xref file. The edited properties are retained even if an xref is reloaded. This option is active by default.
- **Allow other users to Refedit current drawing.** Controls whether the current drawing can be edited in place by others while it is open and when it is referenced by another file. This option is active by default.

Binding an External Reference

An externally referenced file can be made a permanent part of the master drawing as if it had been inserted with the **INSERT** command. This is called *binding* an xref. Binding is useful when you need to send the full drawing file to another location or user, such as a plotting service or a client.

binding: Converting an xref to a permanently inserted block in the master drawing.

Layer Naming Conventions

When a drawing is referenced to the master drawing, all dependent named objects are renamed. All xref-dependent layer names are given the name of the referenced drawing, followed by the vertical bar symbol (|), and then the layer name. This naming convention enables you to quickly identify which layers belong to a specific referenced drawing. In **Figure 28-9**, the **Layer Properties Manager** dialog box shows how layer names in the master drawing are distinguished from those belonging to different xref

Figure 28-9.
Xref-dependent layer names in the master drawing are preceded by the xref drawing name and the vertical bar symbol (|).

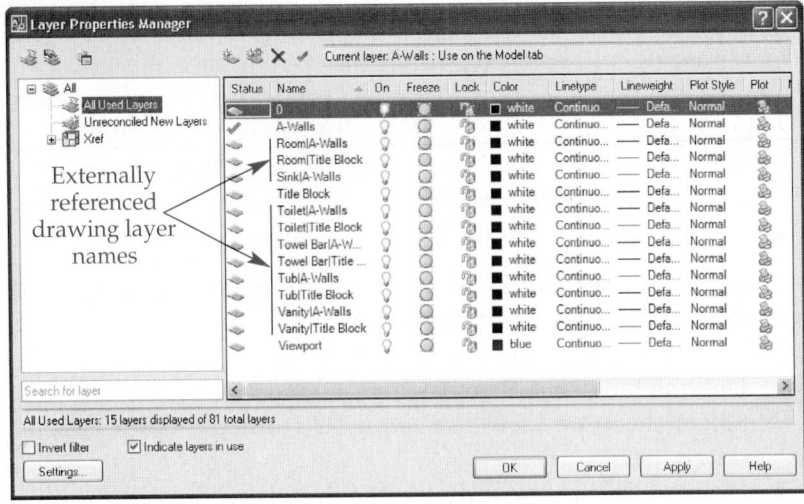

Externally referenced drawing layer names

files. For example, a layer named Notes within an externally referenced drawing file named Title comes into the master drawing as Title|Notes. This is done to distinguish the xref-dependent layer name from the same layer name in the master drawing.

When an xref file is bound to the master drawing, the dependent objects are renamed again to reflect that they have become a permanent part of the drawing. The new name assigned depends on the type of binding that is performed. To bind an xref using the **External References** palette, right-click on the reference name and pick the **Bind...** shortcut menu option. This displays the **Bind Xrefs** dialog box, which contains the **Bind** and **Insert** option buttons.

The **Insert** option brings the xref into the drawing as if you had used the **INSERT** command to place the file. All instances of the xref are converted to normal block objects. Also, the drawing is entered into the block definition table and all named objects, such as layers, blocks, and styles, are incorporated into the master drawing as named in the xref. For example, if an xref named PLATE is bound and it contains a layer named OBJECT, the xref-dependent layer PLATE|OBJECT becomes the locally defined layer OBJECT. All other xref-dependent objects are stripped of the xref name, and they assume the properties of the locally defined objects with the same name. The **Insert** binding option provides the best results for most purposes.

The **Bind** option also brings the xref in as a native part of the master drawing and converts all instances of the xref to blocks. However, the xref name is kept with the names of all dependent objects, and the vertical line in each of the names is replaced with two dollar signs with a number in between. For example, an xref layer named Title|Notes is renamed Title0Notes when the xref is bound using the **Bind** option. The number inside the dollar signs is automatically incremented if a local object definition with the same name exists. For example, if Title0Notes already exists in the drawing, the layer is renamed to Title1Notes. In this manner, unique names are created for all xref-dependent object definitions that are bound. Any of the named objects can be renamed as desired using the **RENAME** command.

Binding Dependent Objects to a Drawing

Binding an xref allows you to make all dependent objects in an xref file a permanent part of the master drawing. Dependent objects include named items such as blocks, dimension styles, layers, linetypes, and text styles. Before binding, you cannot directly use any dependent objects from a referenced drawing in the master drawing. For example, a layer that exists only in a referenced drawing cannot be made current in the master drawing. The same applies for text styles.

In some cases, you may only need to incorporate one or more specific named objects, such as a layer or block, from an xref into the master drawing, instead of binding the entire xref. If you only need selected items, it can be counterproductive to bind an entire drawing. Instead, you can use the **XBIND** command to bind only the named objects you select.

To access the **XBIND** command, pick the **Xbind** button from the **Reference** toolbar, pick **Modify** > **Object** > **External Reference** > **Bind...** from the pull-down menu, or type XB or XBIND. This displays the **Xbind** dialog box. See **Figure 28-10.** This dialog box allows you to select individual xref-dependent objects for binding.

The xrefs shown are indicated by the AutoCAD drawing file icons. To select an individually named object from a group, you must first expand the group listing by clicking on the plus sign next to the corresponding icon. To select an object for binding, highlight it and pick the **Add** button. The names of all objects selected and added are displayed in the **Definitions to Bind** list. When all desired objects have been selected, pick the **OK** button. A message displayed on the command line indicates how many objects of each type were bound.

Individual objects that are bound using the **XBIND** command are renamed in the same manner as objects that are bound using the **Bind** option in the **Bind Xrefs** dialog box. In addition to being renamed, a bound layer can also be assigned a linetype that was not previously defined in the master drawing. An automatic bind is performed, so the required linetype definition can be referenced by the new layer. A new linetype name, such as xref1$0$hidden, is created for the linetype. In similar fashion, a previously undefined block may be automatically bound to the master drawing as a result of binding nested blocks. Bound objects can be renamed using the **RENAME** command.

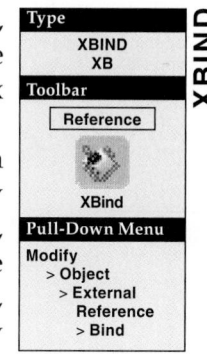

Type	
XBIND	
XB	
Toolbar	
Reference	
XBind	
Pull-Down Menu	
Modify	
> Object	
> External	
Reference	
> Bind	

Figure 28-10.
The **Xbind** dialog box is used to bind xref-dependent objects individually to the master drawing.

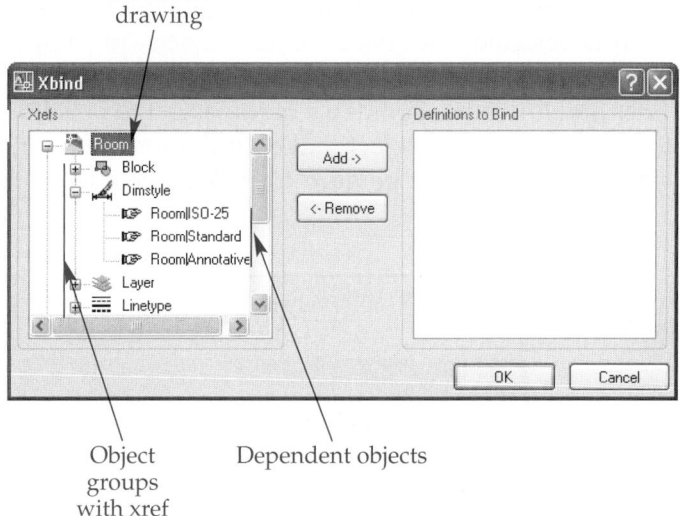

Editing External Reference Drawings

Reference drawings can be edited in place, or within the master drawing. This function, called *reference editing*, allows you to edit reference drawings without opening the original xref file. Any changes can then be saved to the original drawing from within the master drawing.

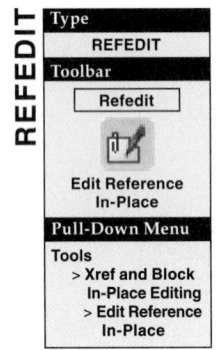

NOTE

In-place reference editing is best suited for minor revisions. Larger revisions should be done in the original drawing. Making major changes with in-place editing can decrease the performance of AutoCAD because additional disk space is required.

REFEDIT

Type
REFEDIT
Toolbar
Refedit
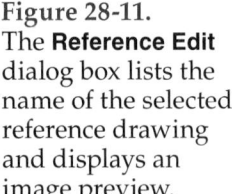
Edit Reference In-Place
Pull-Down Menu
Tools > Xref and Block In-Place Editing > Edit Reference In-Place

The **REFEDIT** command is used to edit externally referenced drawings in place. To access the **REFEDIT** command, select an object that is part of the xref file in the drawing area, then right-click and select the **Edit Xref In-place** shortcut menu option, pick the **Edit Reference In-Place** button from the **Refedit** toolbar, pick **Tools** > **Xref and Block In-Place Editing** > **Edit Reference In-Place**, or type REFEDIT.

The Select reference: prompt asks you to select a reference to edit; in this case an xref is selected. After you make a selection, the **Reference Edit** dialog box is displayed with the **Identify Reference** tab active. See **Figure 28-11.** A preview of the selected xref is shown in the **Preview** panel, and the name of the file is highlighted. In the example shown, the Room reference drawing has been selected. Notice how nested blocks, like the DOOR-RIGHT HUNG block found in the Room reference, are listed under their parent xref.

In the **Path:** area, the radio button labeled **Automatically select all nested objects** is active by default. Using this option makes all the xref objects available for editing. If you want to edit only certain xref objects, you can use the **Prompt to select nested objects** option. When this option is selected, the Select nested objects: prompt is displayed after you pick **OK**. This prompt asks you to pick objects that belong to the previously selected xref. Pick all lines and any other geometry of the object to be edited, and then press [Enter]. The nested objects that you select make up the *working set*. If multiple instances of the same xref are displayed, be sure to pick objects from the one you originally selected.

Figure 28-11.
The **Reference Edit** dialog box lists the name of the selected reference drawing and displays an image preview.

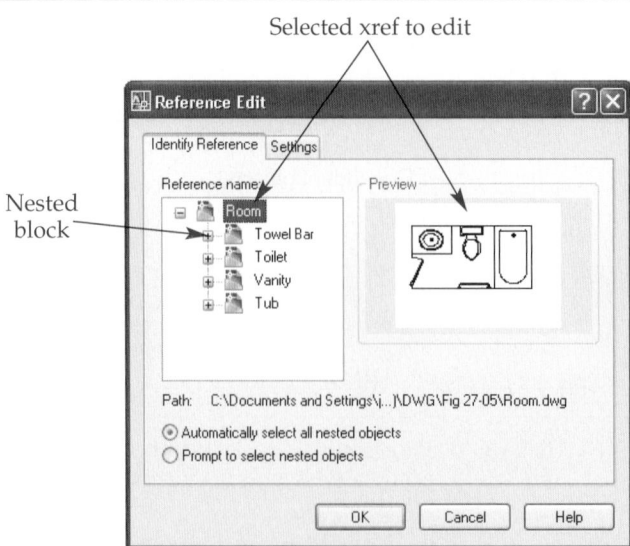

Additional options for reference editing are available in the **Settings** tab of the **Reference Edit** dialog box. The **Create unique layer, style, and block names** option controls the naming of selected layers and objects that are *extracted*, or temporarily removed from the drawing, for editing purposes. If this check box is selected, layer and object names are given the prefix n, with *n* representing an incremental number. This is similar to the renaming method used when you bind an xref.

extracted:
Temporarily removed from the drawing for editing purposes.

The **Display attribute definitions for editing** option is available only if a block object is selected in the **Identify Reference** tab of the **Reference Edit** dialog box. Checking this option allows you to edit any attribute definitions included in the reference. Attributes are covered in detail in Chapter 26.

To prevent accidental changes to objects that do not belong to the working set, you can check the **Lock objects not in working set** option. This makes all objects outside of the working set unavailable for selection in reference editing mode.

If the selected xref file contains other references, the **Reference name:** area lists all nested xrefs and blocks in tree view. In the example given, Toilet, Tub, Vanity, and Towel Bar are nested xrefs in the Room xref. If you pick the drawing file icon next to Vanity, for example, in the tree view, an image preview is displayed and the selected xref is highlighted in the graphics window. See **Figure 28-12.**

When you are finished adjusting settings, pick **OK** to begin editing the xref file and display the **Refedit** toolbar in the drawing area. This toolbar displays the name of the selected reference drawing and is left on-screen for the remainder of the reference editing session. See **Figure 28-13.** You can use the toolbar to add objects to the working set, remove objects from the working set, and save or discard changes to the original xref file.

Figure 28-12.
The **Preview** panel displays the Vanity nested xref after it is selected in the tree view.

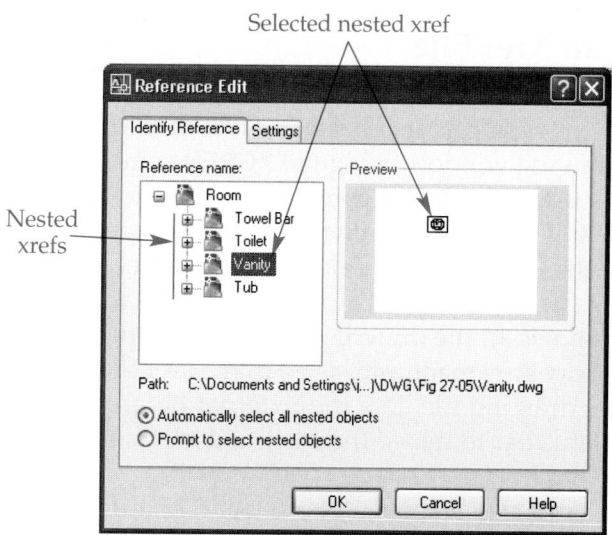

Figure 28-13.
The **Refedit** toolbar is used to perform reference editing functions.

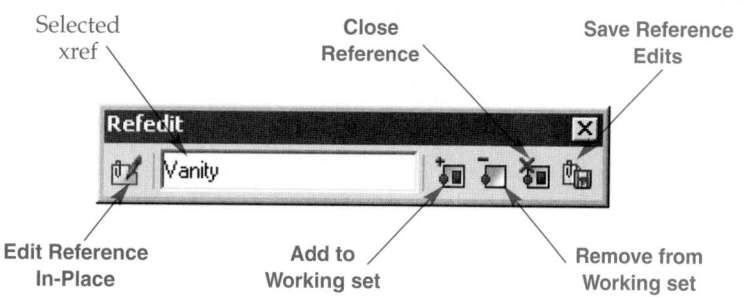

Any object that is drawn during the in-place edit is automatically added to the working set. Additional existing objects can also be added to the working set by using the **Add to Working set** button. If an object is added to the working set, it is extracted, or removed, from the host drawing. The **Remove from Working set** button allows you to remove selected objects from the working set. When a previously extracted object is removed, it is added back to the host drawing.

After you define the working set, all nonselected objects are faded, or grayed out, as shown in Figure 28-14A. The objects in the working set appear in the normal display mode. Once the working set has been defined, you can use any drawing or editing commands to alter the object. In the example given in Figure 28-14A, the vanity has been selected from the room so the sink can be redesigned and a faucet added.

Once the necessary changes have been made, pick the **Save Reference Edits** button from the **Refedit** toolbar. If you want to exit the reference editing session without saving changes, pick the **Close Reference** button. If you save changes, pick **OK** when AutoCAD asks if you want to continue with the save and redefine the xref. All instances of the xref are updated. See Figure 28-14B.

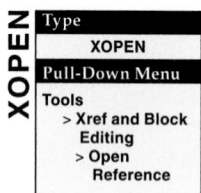

CAUTION

All reference edits made in this manner are saved back to the original drawing file and affect any master drawing that references the file when the master is opened. For this reason, it is critically important that external references be edited only with the permission of your instructor or supervisor.

Opening an Xref File

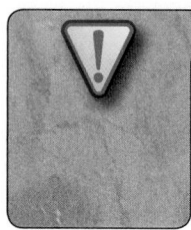

Using the **REFEDIT** command allows you to edit xref objects within the current drawing. An xref file can also be opened from within its parent drawing into a new AutoCAD drawing window using the **XOPEN** command. This is essentially the same procedure as using the **OPEN** command, but quicker. To use the **XOPEN** command, pick **Tools > Xref and Block Editing > Open Reference** or type XOPEN.

At the Select Xref: prompt, selecting any object that is a part of an xref opens the xref drawing file into a new AutoCAD drawing window. Picking the **Window** pull-down menu shows all the drawing files that are open in the AutoCAD session.

After changes are made and saved in the xref file, the xref file needs to be reloaded in the master drawing file. Use the **External References** palette or the **Manage Xrefs** icon in the status bar to reload the modified xref file. This ensures that the master file you are working in is up-to-date.

Xref files can also be opened by selecting an object that is part of the xref file in the drawing area, right-clicking, and selecting the **Open Xref** shortcut menu option. You can also open an xref in the **External References** palette by right-clicking the xref name and selecting the **Open** shortcut menu option.

Figure 28-14.
Reference editing.
A—Objects in the
drawing that are
not a part of the
working set are
grayed out during
the reference editing
session. B—All
instances of the xref
are immediately
updated after
reference editing.

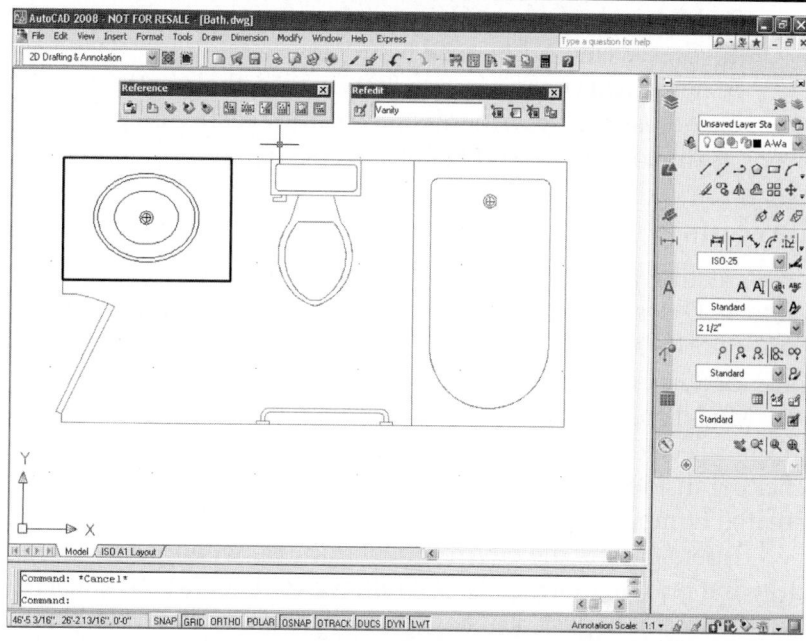

A

B

Using External References in Multiview Layouts

Mechanical drawings and architectural construction drawings often contain sections and details drawn at different scales. These sections and details can be created as separate drawing files and then attached as xrefs to a master drawing. By controlling the display of layers within multiple viewports, you can create a multiview layout.

The following general procedure is used to create a multiview layout using external references:

1. Create the drawings and details to be displayed in the multiview drawing as separate drawing files.
2. Begin a new master drawing based on a template containing a border and title block.

3. Make a layer for referenced drawings and a layer for viewports.
4. Create viewports in a layout tab.
5. Place external reference drawings in the master drawing.
6. Adjust the drawing display within each viewport according to the required drawing scale and visible layers.

Layouts

Creating a multiple viewport layout requires a basic understanding of the two AutoCAD designing environments: model space and paper space. Model space and paper space are described in Chapter 5, and a thorough explanation of layouts is provided in Chapter 25.

Model space is the environment in which you draw and design. When the **Model** tab is selected, model space is active. Model space can also be accessed by double-clicking inside a floating viewport in a layout tab. All drawings and models should be created in model space at full scale.

Paper space is the environment you use when you want to create a layout of the drawing prior to plotting. By default, paper space is active when a layout tab is selected. One powerful aspect of using paper space is that you can create a layout of several different drawings and views, each with different scales. You can even mix 2D and 3D views in the same paper space layout.

Viewports

The most important visualization aspect involved in creating a multiview layout is to imagine that the sheet of paper you are creating contains several cutouts, called *viewports*, through which you can see other drawings, or *models*. See **Figure 28-15**.

To create a multiview layout of multiple drawings, double-click inside a viewport to make it active and then reference, or insert, the drawing to be displayed.

Now, imagine that a piece of architectural C-size paper (18″ × 24″) is hanging up in front of you, and the first viewport is cut 12″ wide and 12″ high. You want to display the floor plan of a house inside the opening. If you place the full-size model of the floor plan directly behind the paper, the house will extend many feet beyond the edges of the paper, because a 40′ × 36′ floor plan is much larger than an 18″ × 24″ piece of paper. In order to place the drawing within the viewport, you must scale it. If the floor plan should be displayed inside the viewport at a scale of 1/4″ = 1′-0″, and the scale factor of 1/4″ = 1′-0″ is 48, you need to move the floor plan model away from the paper until it is

Figure 28-15.
Views of other drawings can be seen through viewports cut into paper space.

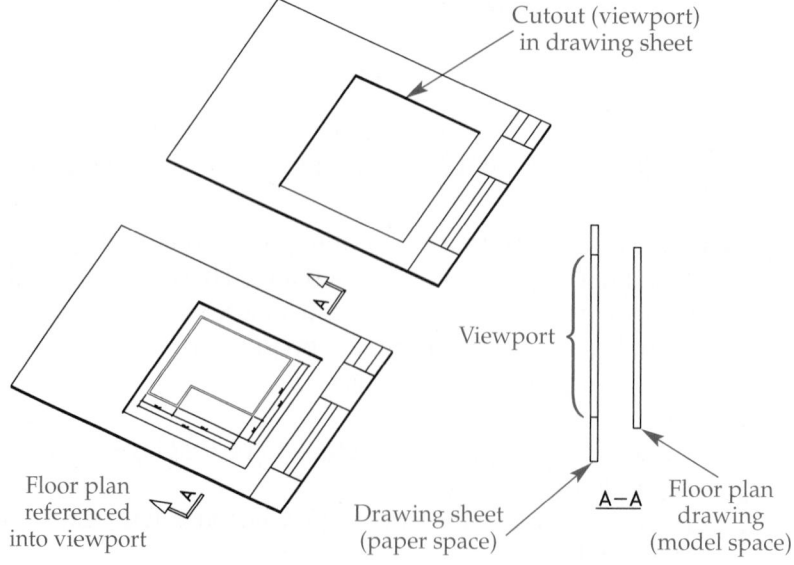

Cutout (viewport) in drawing sheet

Viewport {

Floor plan referenced into viewport

Drawing sheet (paper space)

A—A

Floor plan drawing (model space)

Figure 28-16.
A floor plan placed inside a viewport.

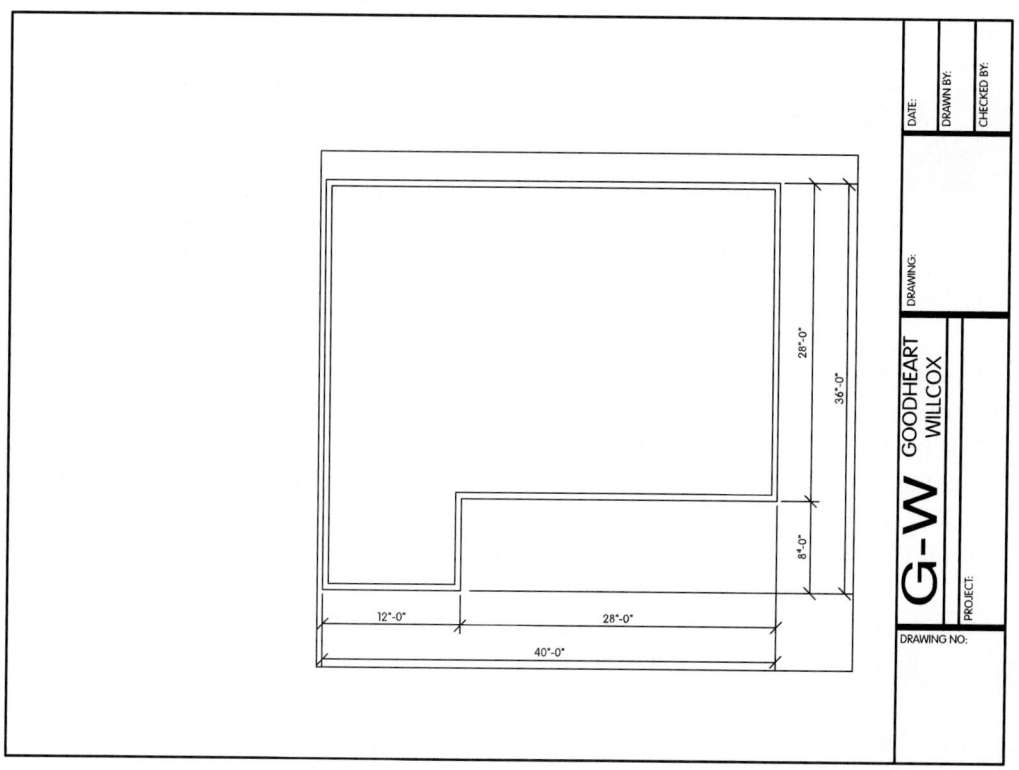

1/48 (the reciprocal of 48) the size it is now. When you do that, the entire floor plan fits inside the viewport you cut. This is accomplished with the **XP** (times paper space) option of the **ZOOM** command, which is described later in this chapter. See **Figure 28-16**.

Constructing a Multiview Drawing

Now that you have a good idea of the multiview layout process, the following example leads you through the details of the procedure. This example uses a house floor plan, a stair detail, and a footing detail. This drawing is *not* among the sample drawings furnished with AutoCAD. Instead, the drawing is based on Exercise 28-1. Complete Exercise 28-1 before working through the example.

Exercise 28-1
Complete the exercise on the Student CD.

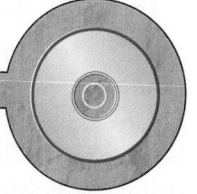

Initial Drawing Setup

The first aspect of drawing setup is to place a border and title block in the paper space, or layout, work environment. They should be the proper size for the plot you want to make according to the paper size. This can be accomplished in one of the following ways, depending on the depth of your preparation:
- Draw a border and a title block on separate layers or the same "sheet" layer
- Draw a border and insert a predrawn title block
- Insert a predrawn border and title block
- Open or insert a predrawn standard border and title block template containing all constant text and attributes for variable information

The method you use is not of primary importance for this example, but it is always best to use existing borders and title blocks, preferably in an existing template, to maximize efficiency and consistency.

clip limits: The distance from the edges of a sheet of paper that a printer can print.

To set up a multiview drawing, first display a paper space layout. Then set the units to match the type of drawing you are creating. Be sure the extents of your border and title block match the maximum active plotting area, or *clip limits*, of your plotter. This example uses a standard architectural C-size sheet (18″ × 24″) and assumes that the plotter's active area is .75″ less along the top and bottom and 1.25″ less on the sides, for a total plotting area of 16.5″ × 21.5″.

NOTE

Use the page setup options to create an appropriate layout accurately based on a specific plotter or printer and its available paper sizes. Settings selected in the **Page Setup** dialog box are immediately reflected in the selected layout. See Chapter 25 for information on the **Page Setup** dialog box.

Set up the new layout as follows (if you do not use a template):
1. Pick a layout tab.
2. Set the following in the **Drawing Units** dialog box:
   • Architectural units.
   • Units precision = 1/2″.
   • System of angle measure = Decimal degrees.
   • Angle precision = 0.
   • Direction for angle 0 = East.
   • Angles measured counterclockwise.
3. Perform a **Zoom All**.

Creating New Layers

The border and title block should be on a separate layer, so you may want to create a new layer called Border or Title and assign it a separate color. An alternative is to create a Sheet layer or a drawing-specific layer, such as A-ANNO-SHEET, on which the border and title block are placed. Be sure to make the new layer current before you draw the border and title block. If you want to use an existing border and title block, insert it now.

One of the principal functions of this example is to use existing drawings in a layout. The house floor plan, stairs, and footing drawings do not become a part of the new drawing. Instead, they are referenced to the current drawing in order to save drawing file space. Therefore, you should also create a new layer for these drawings and name it Xref. Assign the color 7 to the Xref layer. The layers of any existing drawings that you reference (xref) into your new drawing remain intact. Therefore, you do not have to create additional layers unless you want to add information to your drawing, such as general notes or other drawing objects.

The referenced drawings fit inside viewports that can be any shape. Viewports are added to the layout and can be edited like any other AutoCAD object. Create a layer called Viewport or VPRT for these objects and assign a color.

If you do not have an existing architectural C-size border and title block, you can draw a border at this time. Make the Border layer current and draw a border using the **RECTANG** command at the dimensions of 16.5″ × 21.5″. Draw a title block if you want. Your screen should look similar to **Figure 28-17.**

Creating Viewports

When you create a drawing in a layout, your screen represents a sheet of paper. The process of creating viewports is completed in a paper space layout because viewports are cut out of the paper. Now you create an opening through which you can view a referenced drawing in model space.

Methods of creating viewports in paper space are explained in Chapter 25. For this example, you can select the **Single Viewport** button in the **Viewports** toolbar to create each viewport. Be sure to set the Viewports layer current before creating the viewport. This allows the viewports to be turned off for plotting. Select two points to create a 12″ × 12″ viewport positioned as shown in **Figure 28-18.**

Placing Views in the Drawing

Use the new viewport to insert the drawing of the floor plan named Floor. Instead of using the **INSERT** command, which combines an existing drawing with the new one, use an external reference (**XREF** command) so that AutoCAD creates a reference to the Floor drawing. This allows the size of the new drawing to remain small because the Floor drawing has not been combined with it.

Figure 28-17.
The border and title block in paper space.

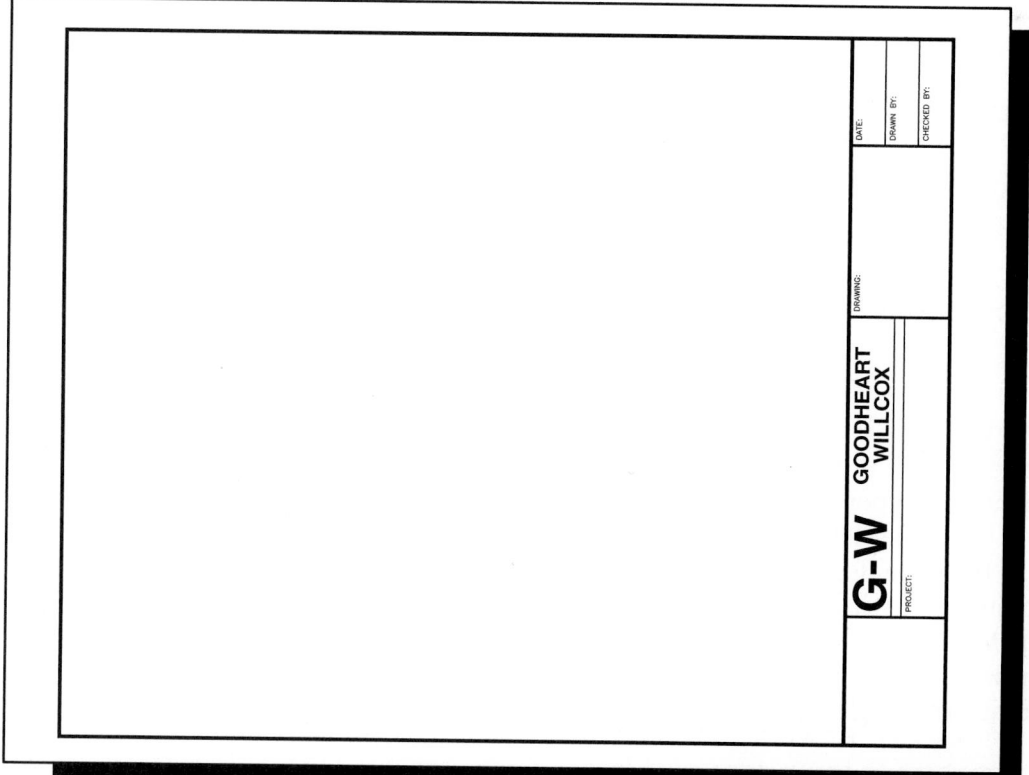

Figure 28-18.
A viewport added to the drawing in paper space.

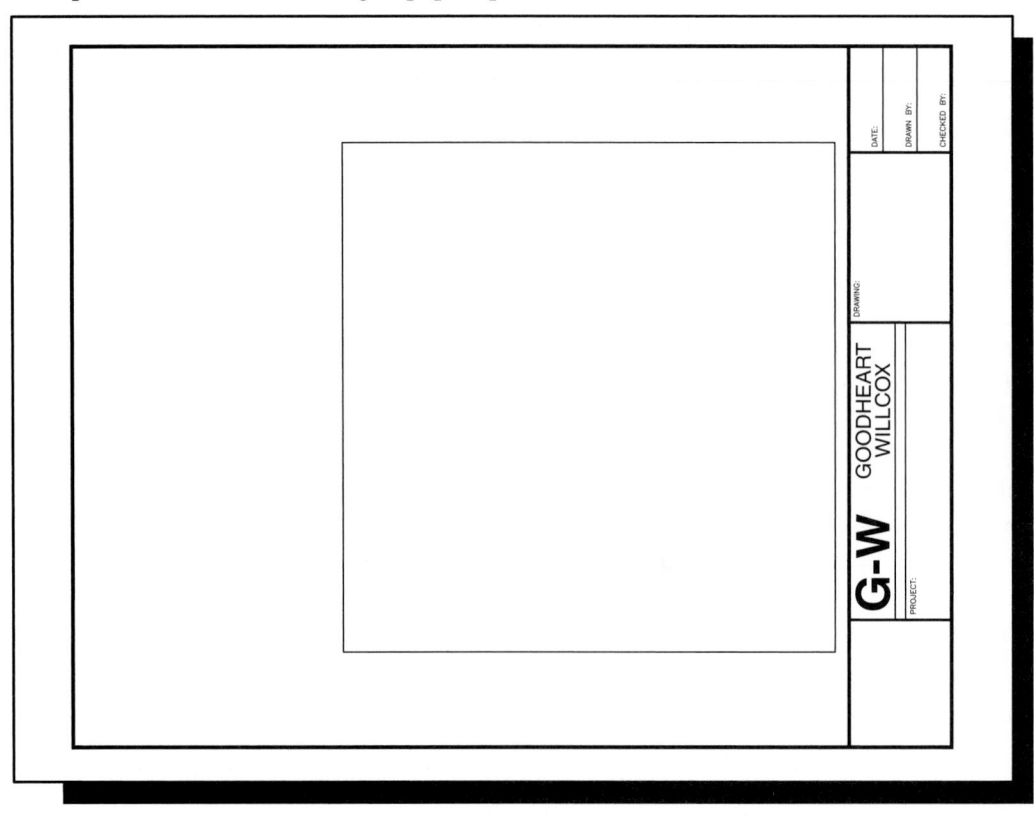

The following procedure allows you to enter model space, reference an existing drawing to the new one, and zoom the view to see the referenced drawing.

1. With the layout tab active, double-click inside the viewport to activate model space within the viewport.
2. Set the Xref layer current.
3. Pick **Insert** > **DWG Reference...** from the pull-down menu. The **Select Reference File** dialog box is displayed.
4. Select Floor.dwg in the dialog box, and pick the **OK** button. See **Figure 28-19**.

The **External Reference** dialog box is displayed. Set the insertion point to 0,0,0, the X, Y, and Z scale to 1.0, and the rotation angle to 0. Pick the **OK** button and perform a **ZOOM Extents**. Your drawing should now resemble the one shown in **Figure 28-20**.

Scaling a Drawing in a Viewport

When a drawing has been referenced and placed in a viewport, it is ready to be scaled. If you use the **Extents** option of the **ZOOM** command, the referenced drawing fills the viewport. However, the drawing is not displayed at the correct scale.

The scale factor of each view of the multiview drawing is important to remember; it is the scale used to size your drawing in the viewport. The scale factor is used in conjunction with the **XP** option of the **ZOOM** command, or it can be selected from the **Viewports** toolbar. Since the intended final scale of the floor plan on the plotted drawing is 1/4″ = 1′-0″, the scale factor is 48, or 1/48 of full size. Detailed information on determining scale factors is given in Chapter 25.

Figure 28-19.
The Floor.dwg file is selected in the **Select Reference File** dialog box.

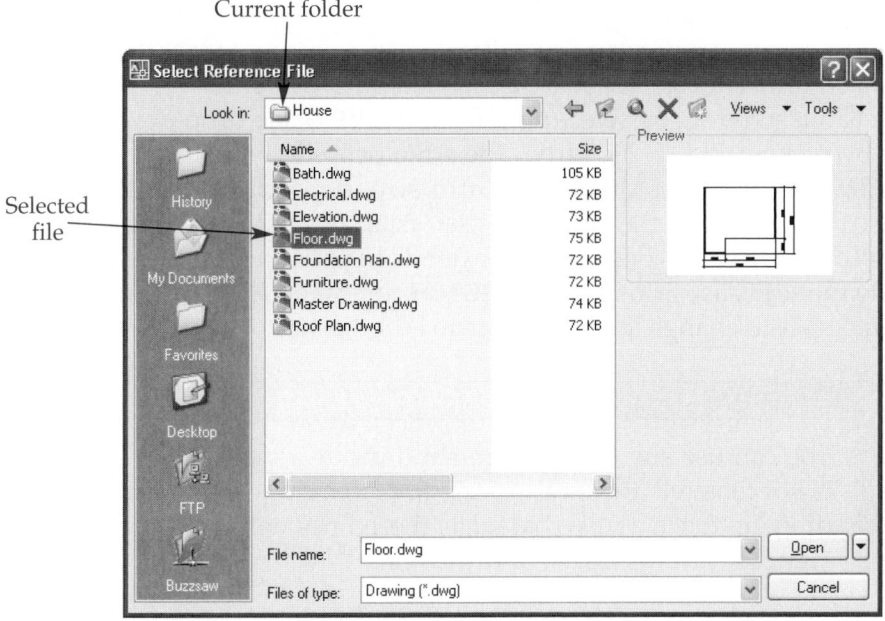

Figure 28-20.
The floor plan is referenced into the first viewport.

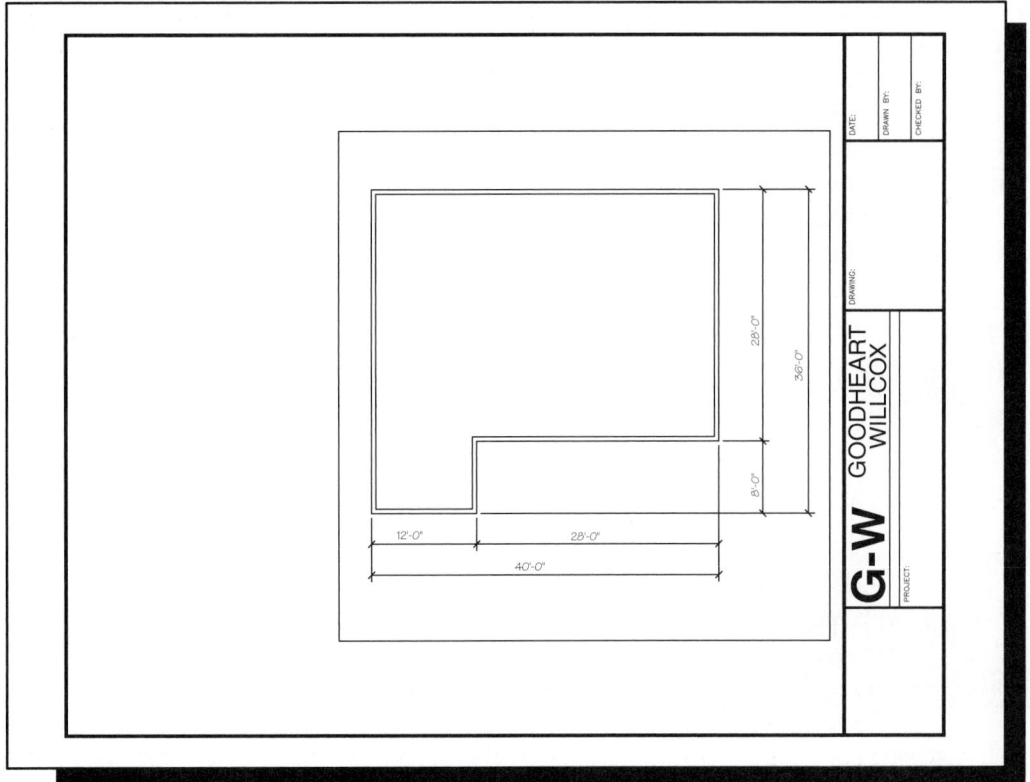

Be sure you are still in the model space environment within the viewport. Enter the following:

Command: **Z** *or* **ZOOM**↵
Specify corner of window, enter a scale factor (nX or nXP), or [All/Center/Dynamic/Extents/Previous/Scale/Window/Object] <real time>: **1/48XP**↵

The scale can also be set by selecting it from the **VP Scale** drop-down list in the status bar or by picking 1/4″ = 1′-0″ from the scale drop-down list in the **Viewports** toolbar. The drawing may not change much in size, depending on the size of the viewport. Also, keep in mind the viewport itself is an object that can be moved and stretched if needed. If part of your drawing extends beyond the edge of the viewport after you apply the scale, use grips or the **STRETCH** command to change the size of the viewport. Remember to change to paper space to edit the size of the viewport.

PROFESSIONAL TIP

You can use any display command inside a viewport. If a drawing is not centered after scaling, use **PAN** to move it around. If lines of a drawing touch a viewport edge, those lines will not be visible if the viewport layer is frozen or turned off.

Controlling Viewport Layer Visibility

If you create another viewport, the floor plan will immediately fill it. This is because a viewport is just a window through which you can view a drawing or 3D model that has been referenced to the current drawing. One way to control what is visible in addition to viewports is to freeze all layers of the Floor drawing in any new viewports that are created. Access the **Layer Properties Manager** dialog box and set all layers from the Floor xref to be frozen in new viewports by picking the icons in the New VP Freeze column. When the snowflake icon appears in this column, the layer is not displayed in any new viewports. The frozen or thawed status in the current viewport is controlled by the icons in the Current VP Freeze column.

PROFESSIONAL TIP

Use the [Shift] and [Ctrl] keys in combination with picking to select multiple layer names. When multiple layers are selected, toggling one setting makes the same new setting apply to all highlighted layer names.

NOTE

The **New VP Freeze** and **Current VP Freeze** settings in the **Layer Properties Manager** dialog box can also be set using the **VPLAYER** command at the Command: prompt.

Creating Additional Viewports

The same process used to create the viewport in the preceding section can be used to create the additional two viewports for the Stair and Footing drawings. We will create both viewports before externally referencing the additional drawing files. If you know the number, size, and location of all viewports needed on a multiview drawing, it may save time to create them all at once.

AutoCAD and Its Applications—Basics

Now that the floor plan layers are frozen in new viewports, the other two viewports can be created. Use the following procedure:

1. Double-click outside the viewport to activate paper space.
2. Set the Viewports layer current.
3. Draw a viewport to the dimensions shown in **Figure 28-21** using the **Polygonal Viewport** button in the **Viewports** toolbar.
4. Draw a third viewport 6" wide and 5" high.

The final arrangement of the three viewports is shown in **Figure 28-22.**

Now that the viewports are complete, you can begin referencing the remaining two drawings. The following procedure uses **DesignCenter** to reference the Stair drawing:

1. Set the current layer to Xref and double-click in the lower-left viewport to make model space active.
2. Activate **DesignCenter**. Locate the folder that contains the Stair.dwg file and pick it. Files contained in the selected folder are displayed in the **Content** area.
3. Right-click the Stair.dwg file and select **Attach as Xref...** from the shortcut menu to display the **External Reference** dialog box. Enter 0,0,0 for the insertion point, 1.0 for the scale, and 0 for the rotation angle.
4. Press [Ctrl]+[2] to dismiss **DesignCenter** temporarily.
5. The scale factor for the Stair drawing is 32. Use the **ZOOM** command and enter 1/32XP to scale the drawing correctly.

The drawing now appears as shown in **Figure 28-23.** Notice that the Stair drawing is shown in all three viewports. Use the **Layer Properties Manager** dialog box to freeze the stair layers in selected viewports using the following procedure:

1. Pick in the large viewport to make it active.
2. Open the **Layer Properties Manager** dialog box.
3. Select all layers that begin with the name of the referenced drawing you want to freeze in the active viewport. In this case, all layers that begin with Stair are selected.

Figure 28-21.
Draw this polygonal viewport.

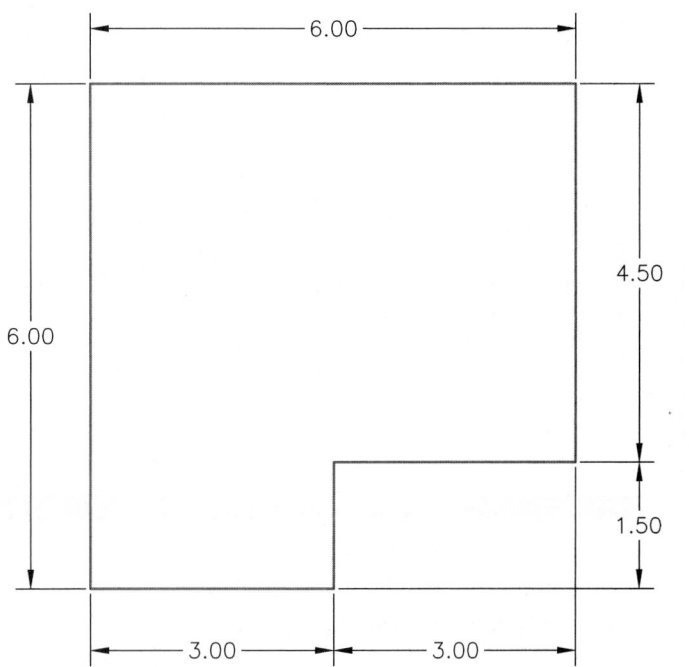

Figure 28-22.
Two additional viewports have been placed and sized in the drawing.

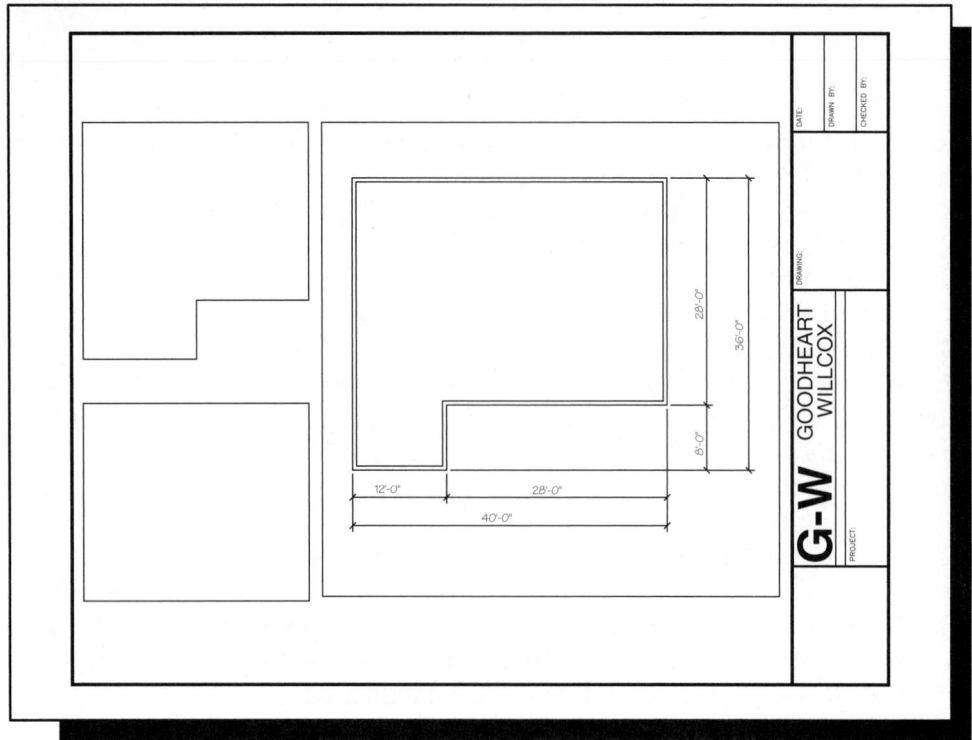

Figure 28-23.
The reference drawing Stair is displayed in all viewports. Use the **Layer Properties Manager** dialog box to restrict its visibility.

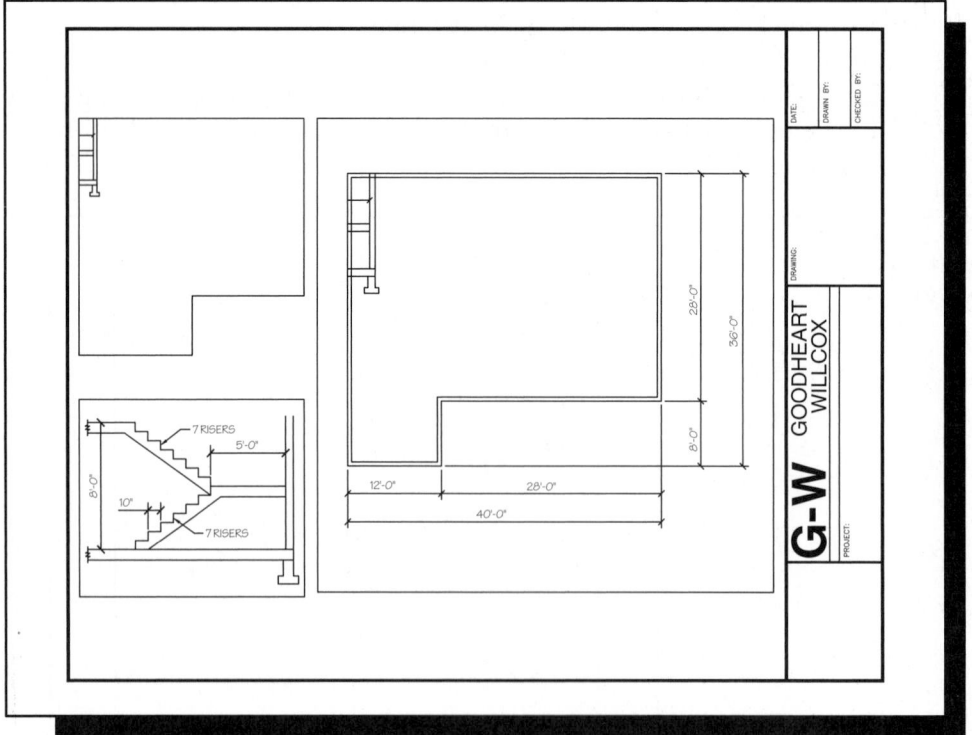

4. Pick the sun icon in the **Current VP Freeze** column of one of the selected layers. All selected icons change to a snowflake. Pick **OK**. The Stair drawing is now removed from the large viewport.

5. Repeat this procedure to freeze the stair layers in the upper-left viewport.

The final drawing can now be inserted into the last viewport. Prepare the third view by following these steps:

1. Double-click in the upper-left viewport.
2. Set the Xref layer current.
3. Attach the Footing drawing as an xref using one of the methods explained earlier in this chapter.
4. Freeze the Footing layers in the other two viewports.
5. Use the **ZOOM** command and enter 1/16XP.

The drawing should now appear as shown in **Figure 28-24**.

NOTE

Be sure to set the current layer to Xref when referencing a drawing so the inserted drawing is not placed on another layer, such as Viewports.

Adjusting Viewport Display, Size, and Location

If you need to adjust a drawing within a viewport, first be sure that model space is active. Then, pick the desired viewport to make it active, and use an appropriate display command, such as **ZOOM** or **PAN**.

The entire viewport can be moved to another location, but you must first activate paper space. Pick the viewport border to display its grips. Objects inside the viewport are not selected when picking because they are in model space. After selection, adjust the location of the viewports.

Figure 28-24.
The drawing is completed by referencing the Footing drawing.

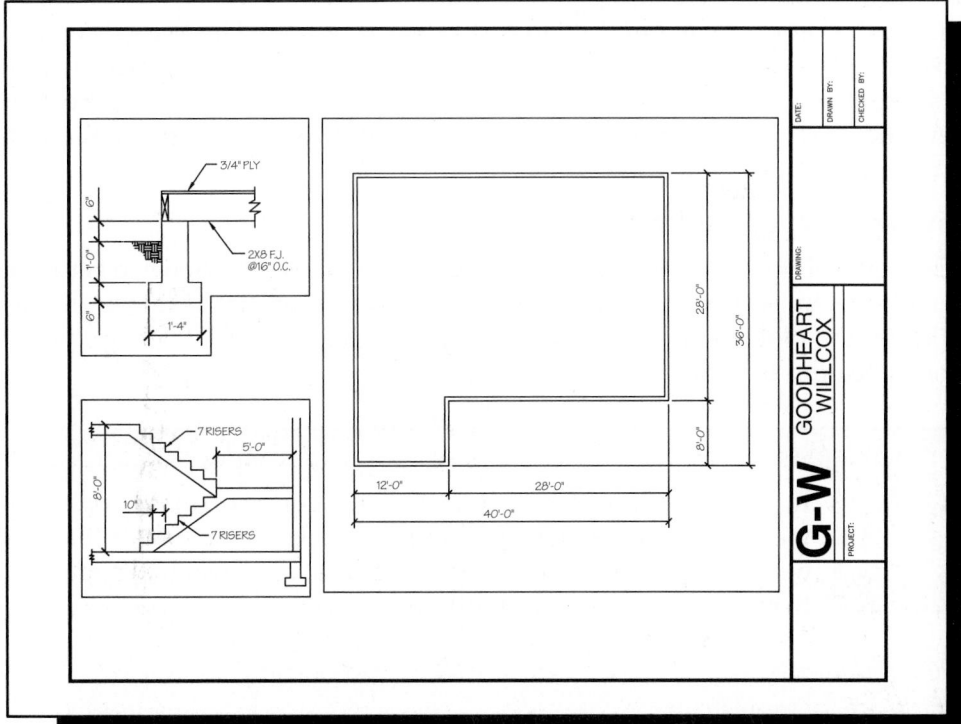

Type
VPCLIP
Toolbar
Viewports

Clip Esisting Viewport

Pull-Down Menu

Modify
> Clip
> Viewport

Changing viewport shape and size

Paper space viewport shape and size can be quickly changed using the **VPCLIP** command. To access the **VPCLIP** command, select a viewport in paper space, then right-click and select the **Viewport Clip** shortcut menu option, pick the **Clip Existing Viewport** button from the **Viewports** toolbar, pick **Modify** > **Clip** > **Viewport**, or type VPCLIP. A viewport can be clipped by either selecting an existing shape that has been drawn or drawing a new polygon. Use the following procedure to change the shape of a viewport.

1. Activate a paper space layout. Pick the **Clip Existing Viewport** button in the **Viewports** toolbar.
2. Select the outline of the viewport to be resized.
3. Select the new clipping object, such as a circle that has previously been drawn over the current viewport. The old viewport is deleted.

The **Delete** option of the **VPCLIP** command enables you to delete a viewport that was previously clipped. It prompts you to select the clipping object, which is the new shape that was drawn to clip the old viewport. When you select the viewport and press [Enter], the original viewport is redrawn and the clipped version is deleted.

Locking the viewport

Once a drawing has been scaled properly inside a viewport, it is important to avoid using a zoom again prior to plotting. AutoCAD provides a viewport locking feature that helps prevent inadvertent zooms. To lock the display in a viewport, access the **Properties** palette and select the viewport from paper space. Change the Display locked property to Yes. You can also quickly lock or unlock a floating viewport while it is active by selecting the **Lock/Unlock Viewport** button on the status bar. Repeat the procedure for all viewports you want to lock.

Adding notes and titles

There are two ways in which titles and notes can be added to a multiview drawing with referenced drawings. The first method is to add the notations to the original drawing. This is the best system to use if the titles, scale label, and notes will not change.

However, titles may change. You may want to be sure that all titles of views use the same text style, or you might want to add a special symbol. This is easily completed after the drawings are referenced. The most important thing to remember is that the paper space layout must be active to add text. Do not place text in model space. You can use new and existing text styles to add titles and notes to a drawing using the **TEXT** or **MTEXT** command. See **Figure 28-25**.

Removing viewport outlines

Viewport outlines are usually turned off for plotting purposes, as shown in **Figure 28-25**. To turn off viewports before plotting, open the **Layer Properties Manager** dialog box and click on the plot icon for the Viewports layer. A diagonal slash is placed over the symbol, indicating that the layer will not plot.

> **NOTE**
>
> If you freeze the Viewports layer and a box surrounds one of the views, you are probably still in model space. Remember that a box outlines the current viewport in model space. Switch to paper space to make the model space outline disappear.

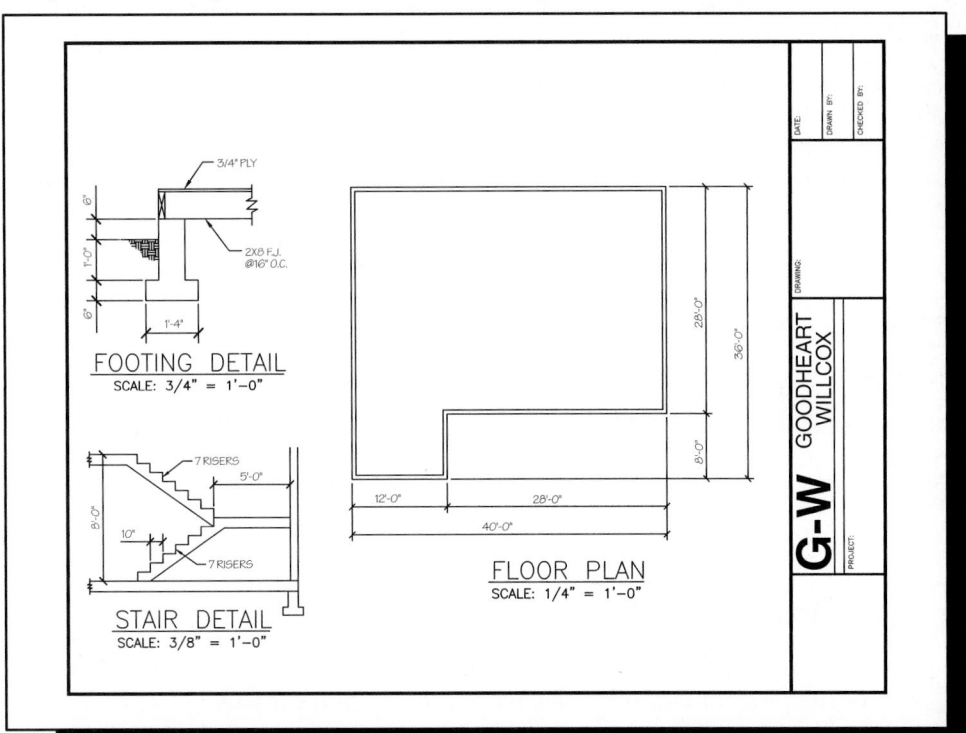

Plotting a Multiview Drawing

You have already taken care of scaling the views because you used the **XP** option of the **ZOOM** command when you referenced them. The drawing that now appears on your screen in paper space must be plotted at full scale, 1 = 1, in order for the correct viewport scales to be plotted.

The process of creating and plotting a properly scaled multiview layout will go smoothly if you planned your drawing at the start of the project. Review the following items, and keep them in mind when starting any drawing or design project—especially one that involves the creation of a multiview paper space layout.

- Determine the size of paper to be used.
- Determine the type of title block, notes, revision blocks, parts lists, etc., that will appear on the drawing.
- Prepare a quick sketch of the view layouts and their plotted scales.
- Determine the scales to be used for each viewport.
- Establish proper text styles and heights based on the drawing scale factors.
- Set the **DIMSCALE** variable using the proper scale factor when creating drawings in model space.

There is no substitute for planning a project before you begin. It may seem like an unnecessary expense of time, but it will save time later in the project, and it may help you become more productive in all your work.

You may never have to specify a scale other than full (1 = 1) when plotting. Any object or design, whether 2D or 3D, can be referenced into a border and title block drawing, scaled with **ZOOM XP**, and then plotted. Use the paper space layout procedure for all your drawings, even if they are just a single view. You will find that you need fewer border and title block template drawings, and the process will become much quicker.

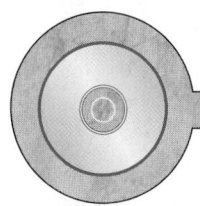

Exercise 28-2

Complete the exercise on the Student CD.

Chapter Test

Answer the following questions. Write your answers on a separate sheet of paper or complete the electronic chapter test on the Student CD.

1. What effect does the use of referenced drawings have on drawing file size?
2. When are xrefs updated in the master drawing?
3. What is a nested xref?
4. What three types of files can be referenced into an AutoCAD drawing?
5. What is the difference between an absolute path and a relative path?
6. What is the difference between an overlaid xref and an attached xref?
7. What is the purpose of the **Detach** option in the **External References** palette?
8. What could you do to suppress an xref temporarily without detaching it from the master drawing?
9. Which command allows you to display only a specific portion of an externally referenced drawing?
10. What are spatial and layer indexes, and what function do they perform?
11. Why would you want to bind a dependent object to a master drawing?
12. What does the layer name WALL0NOTES mean?
13. What command is used to edit external references in place?
14. What command allows you to open a parent xref drawing into a new AutoCAD drawing window by selecting the xref in the master drawing?
15. Indicate the command and value you would use to specify a 1/2″ = 1′-0″ scale inside a viewport.
16. How do you freeze all layers of a referenced drawing inside any new viewports?
17. What is the function of the **VPCLIP** command?
18. Do you need to be in paper space or model space in order to resize a viewport?
19. What is the purpose of locking a viewport?
20. Explain why you should plan your plots.

AutoCAD and Its Applications—Basics

Drawing Problems

1. Open one of your dimensioned drawings from Chapter 19. Construct a multi-view layout and generate a plot on C-size paper.
   A. Create four viewports of equal size, separated by 1" of empty space.
   B. Select each viewport and display a different view of the drawing.
   C. Plot the drawing and be sure to use the scale of 1:1.
   D. Save the drawing as P28-1.

2. Open one of your dimensioned drawings from Chapter 19. Construct a multi-view layout and generate a plot on C-size or B-size paper. Plot at the scale of 1:1. Save the drawing as P28-2.

3. Open one of your dimensioned drawings from Chapter 20. Construct a multi-view layout and generate a plot on C-size or B-size paper. Plot at the scale of 1:1. Save the drawing as P28-3.

4. Open one of your dimensioned drawings from Chapter 21. Construct a multi-view layout and generate a plot on C-size or B-size paper. Plot at the scale of 1:1. Save the drawing as P28-4.

Elevation section. (Steve D. Bloedel)

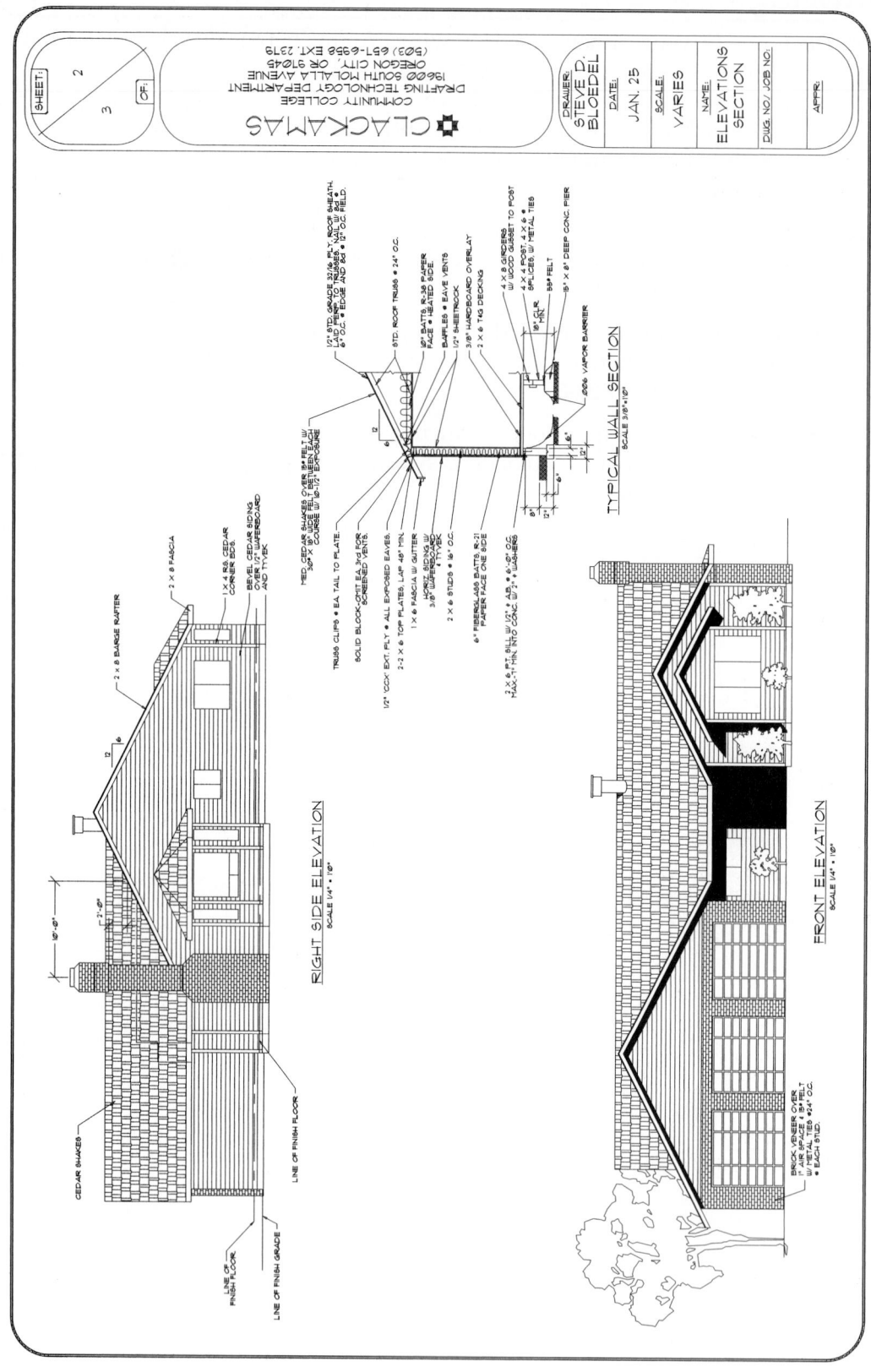

CHAPTER 29

Creating and Using Sheet Sets

Learning Objectives

After completing this chapter, you will be able to do the following:
- ✓ Identify and describe the functions of the **Sheet Set Manager**.
- ✓ Create sheet sets.
- ✓ Add sheets and sheet views to a sheet set.
- ✓ Plot or publish a set of sheets.
- ✓ Insert callout blocks and view labels into sheet views.
- ✓ Set up custom properties for a sheet set.
- ✓ Create a sheet list table.
- ✓ Archive a set of electronic files for a sheet set.

Organizing and distributing drawings during the course of a design project can involve a wide range of tasks. Drawings often need to be shared with clients and other personnel to make sure the design is accurate and any changes are incorporated. As the project is developed, a set of drawings is used to build the design. The design can be relatively simple, such as the views for a mechanical part, or complex, such as the plans for a building or new highway off-ramp. While a simple mechanical part may require only one drawing sheet for manufacturing, a 10-story office building may require a set of 100 sheets or more. Although design needs vary, the ability to organize drawings for exchange purposes is important because any project typically involves input from a number of sources. This ability becomes critical at the end of the project, when delivery of the drawings must take place in an orderly manner.

The **Sheet Set Manager** helps simplify the management of a project with multiple drawings and views. This chapter describes how to use the **Sheet Set Manager** to structure different drawing layouts into groups of files for reviewing, plotting, and publishing purposes.

Sheet Sets Overview

sheet set: A collection of drawing sheets for a project.

sheet: A printed drawing or electronic layout produced for a project.

fields: Special text objects that display values that can be updated automatically.

A *sheet set* is a collection of drawing sheets for a project. The term *sheet* refers to a drawing produced for the project. In AutoCAD, sheets are created on layout tabs in a drawing file and can have additional project-specific properties.

All of the sheets in a sheet set can use a single template. The template can contain a title block with attributes containing *fields*. The field values may include items such as project name and sheet number. Thus, if the project name changes during the course of the project, the field can be modified in the template, and the change is automatically applied to all sheets within the set. If a new sheet is inserted into a sheet set, the sheet numbers and all sheet references update automatically. This automation can save a great deal of time and improve the accuracy of the set of drawings.

Once the sheet set is complete, you can easily print, publish, and archive the entire set in a single operation. This is very efficient. For example, it is far easier to plot a sheet set containing twenty sheets than to open and plot twenty separate drawings.

Introduction to the Sheet Set Manager

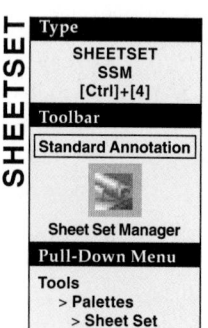

Sheet sets are created, organized, and accessed using the **Sheet Set Manager**. To open the **Sheet Set Manager**, pick the **Sheet Set Manager** button on the **Standard Annotation** toolbar, select **Tools > Palettes > Sheet Set Manager**, type SSM or SHEETSET, or use the [Ctrl]+[4] key combination. See **Figure 29-1A**. The window is divided into three tabs: **Sheet List**, **Sheet Views**, and **Model Views**. The **Sheet Set Control** drop-down list at the top of the **Sheet Set Manager** is used to open and create sheet sets. See **Figure 29-1B**. The buttons next to the drop-down list control and manage the items listed in the **Sheet Set Manager** window. These buttons vary depending on the currently selected tab. The area at the bottom of the window (labeled **Details** or **Preview**) shows a text description or preview image of a selected sheet or view.

The **Sheet Set Manager** is a palette. It can be resized, docked, and set to autohide. The **Expand/Collapse** buttons in the upper and lower portions of the **Sheet Set Manager** window can be used to hide or display the information. The **Details** and **Preview** areas can be toggled by picking the appropriate button on the title bar.

Figure 29-1.
The **Sheet Set Manager**. A—The window contains the **Sheet List**, **Sheet Views**, and **Model Views** tabs. B—The **Sheet Set Control** drop-down list contains options for creating and opening a sheet set.

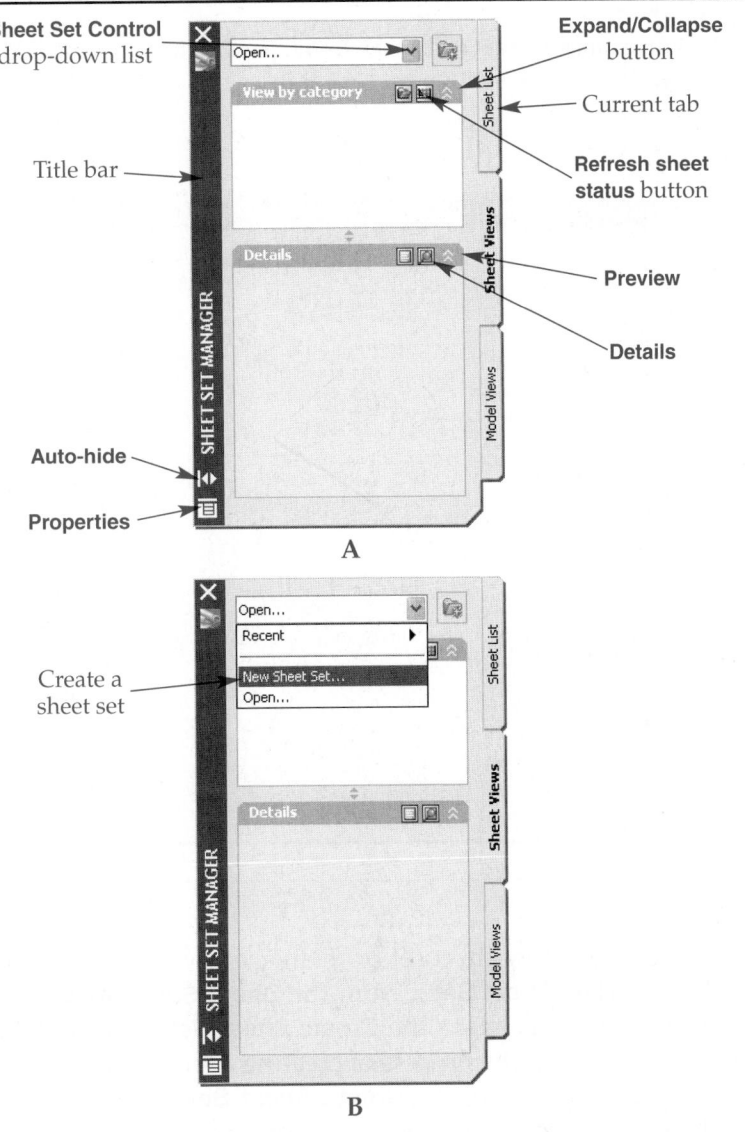

Creating Sheet Sets

Sheet sets are created with the **Create Sheet Set** wizard. This wizard can be accessed from within the **Sheet Set Manager** by picking **New Sheet Set...** from the **Sheet Set Control** drop-down list. The **Create Sheet Set** wizard can also be accessed by selecting **File** > **New Sheet Set...** from the pull-down menu. Sheet sets can be created from an example sheet set or from existing drawing files.

Creating a Sheet Set from an Example Sheet Set

When you create a new sheet using an example sheet set, you select an existing sheet set as a model, and then modify it as needed to fit the needs of the new sheet set. AutoCAD provides several example sheet sets based on different drafting disciplines. You are not limited to the examples provided—you can use any existing sheet set as an example sheet set.

Figure 29-2.
Select **An example sheet set** on the **Begin** page to use an AutoCAD sheet set or another existing sheet set as a template.

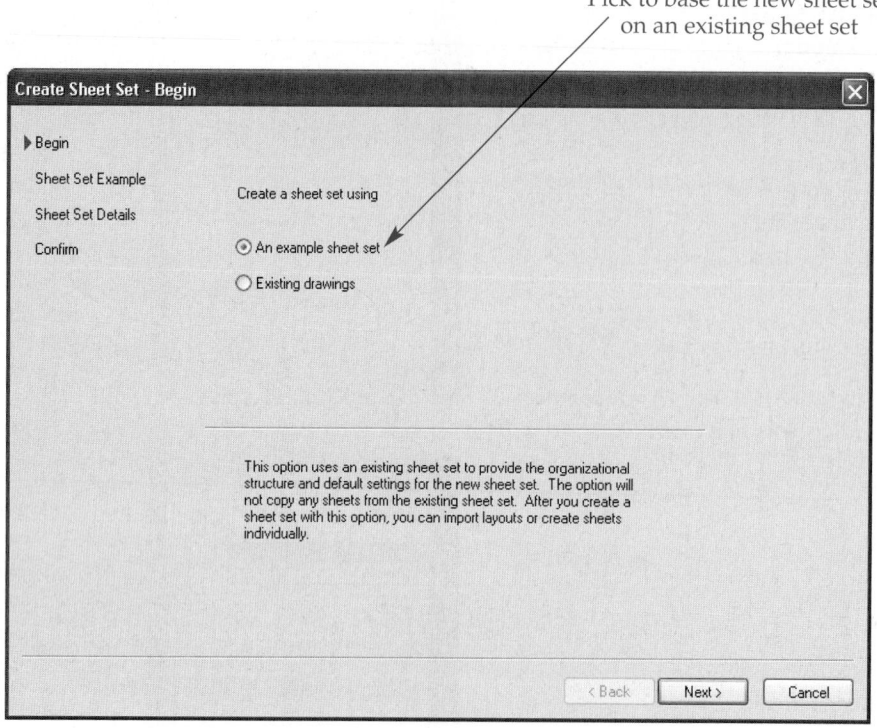

To create a new sheet set from an example sheet set, open the **Sheet Set Manager** and select **New Sheet Set...** from the **Sheet Set Control** drop-down list, as shown in **Figure 29-1B**. This opens the **Create Sheet Set** wizard. See **Figure 29-2**. This wizard steps you through the process of creating a sheet set.

The **Begin** page of the **Create Sheet Set** wizard provides two options. Pick **An example sheet set** to start your sheet set using an example sheet set. The second option, **Existing drawings**, is described in the next section. Pick the **Next** button to display the **Sheet Set Example** page. See **Figure 29-3**.

Sheet set information is saved in a DST file (sheet set data file). When you create a sheet set from an example sheet set, you are starting from an existing DST file. The list box on the **Sheet Set Example** page lists all DST files in the default Template folder. You can pick one of these sheet sets, or you can pick the **Browse to another sheet set to use as an example** radio button and then select the ellipsis (**...**) button and use the dialog box to locate a DST file in another folder.

After selecting the DST file for the example sheet set, pick the **Next** button to display the **Sheet Set Details** page. See **Figure 29-4**. This page allows you to modify the existing sheet set data and create settings for your new project.

Figure 29-3.
Use the **Sheet Set Example** page to select an example sheet set.

List of sheet sets
in Template folder

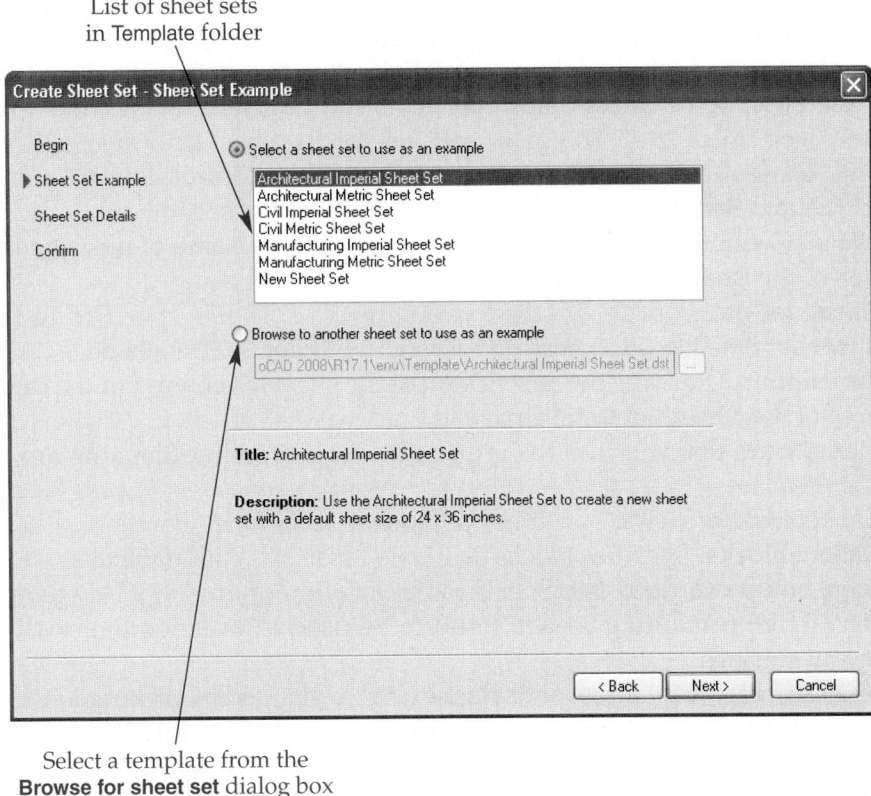

Select a template from the
Browse for sheet set dialog box

Figure 29-4.
Enter a name, description, and file path location for the new sheet set on the **Sheet Set Details** page.

Enter a name

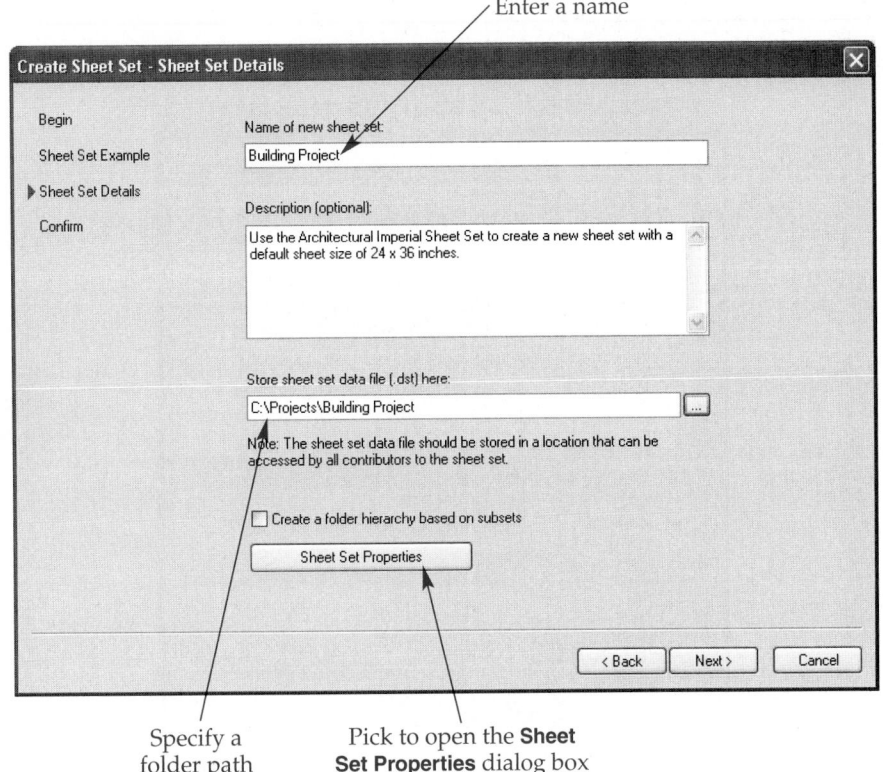

Specify a
folder path

Pick to open the **Sheet
Set Properties** dialog box

Enter the name, or title, of the sheet set in the **Name of new sheet set** text box. This is typically the project number or a short description of the project. A description for the sheet set can be entered in the **Description** area. The **Store sheet set data file (.dst) here** text box determines where the sheet set file is saved on the hard drive. Pick the ellipsis (...) button and select a folder in the dialog box to redefine the default sheet set file location. Picking the **Sheet Set Properties** button opens the **Sheet Set Properties** dialog box. See **Figure 29-5**. The main settings for the sheet set are specified in this dialog box. There are four sections: **Sheet Set**, **Project Control**, **Sheet Creation**, and **Sheet Set Custom Properties**. The settings in the **Sheet Set** section are:

- **Name.** Contains the sheet set name entered in the **Name of new sheet set** text box of the **Sheet Set Details** page.
- **Sheet set data file.** Shows the location of the DST file, specified in the **Store sheet set data file (.dst) here** text box of the **Sheet Set Details** page.
- **Description.** Contains the description of the sheet set entered in the **Description** area of the **Sheet Set Details** page.
- **Model view.** Specifies the folder(s) containing drawing files that are used for the sheet set.
- **Label block for views.** Specifies the block used to label views.
- **Callout blocks.** Specifies blocks available for use as callout blocks.
- **Page setup overrides file.** Specifies the location of an AutoCAD template file (DWT file) containing a page setup to be used to override the existing sheet layout settings.

All of these settings except **Sheet set data file** can be changed by picking in the text box to activate it. When file locations are required, the ellipsis (...) button appears. Picking this button allows you to navigate to the location you want to specify.

The properties in the **Project Control** section allow you to store and update information based on the current project. The properties in the **Sheet Creation** section determine the location for the drawing files for new sheets and the template used to create them. When a new sheet is added to a sheet set, AutoCAD creates a new drawing file based on

---

Figure 29-5.
The main properties of a sheet set are stored in the **Sheet Set Properties** dialog box.

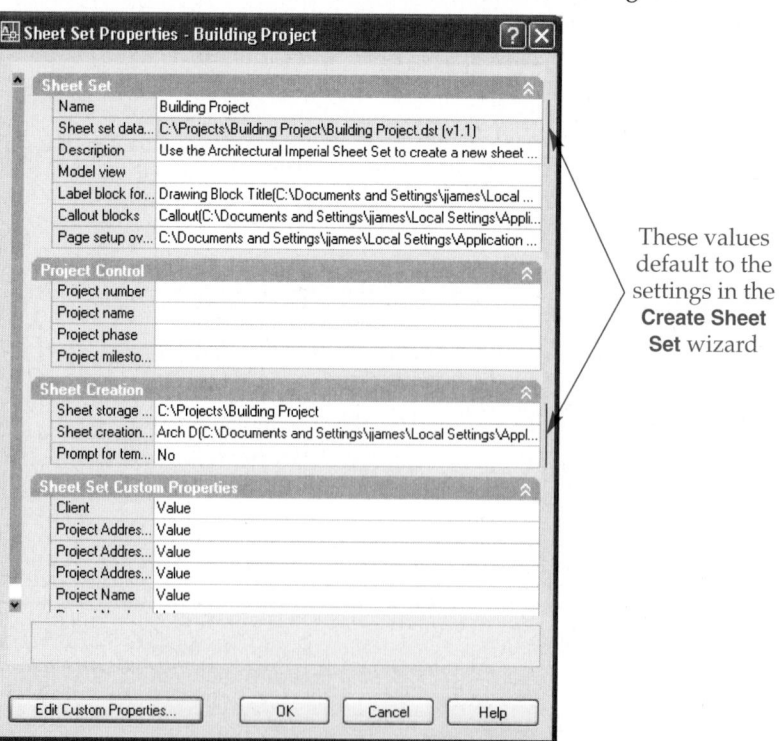

These values default to the settings in the **Create Sheet Set** wizard

the template and layout specified in the **Sheet creation template** setting. The folder path in the **Sheet storage location** field determines where the new file is saved. It is important to specify the correct location so you know where the files are being saved.

When selecting the **Sheet creation template** value, you must specify both a template file and a layout. To modify this setting, pick in the text box and then pick the ellipsis (...) button. This displays the **Select Layout as Sheet Template** dialog box. See **Figure 29-6.** All layouts in the selected template are displayed in the list box. Select the layout and then pick **OK**.

If the value in the **Prompt for template** field is set to **No**, the template layout specified in the **Sheet creation template** field is automatically used when a new sheet is created. This is the default setting. If the field value is set to **Yes**, you can select a different layout when creating a new sheet.

Information specific to the project can be set up in the **Sheet Set Custom Properties** section. This topic is described later in this chapter.

Once all the values in the **Sheet Set Properties** dialog box are set, pick **OK**. This returns you to the **Sheet Set Details** page. Pick the **Next** button to continue creating the new sheet set. The **Sheet Set Preview** area on the **Confirm** page displays all of the information associated with the sheet set. See **Figure 29-7.** In the example shown, a sheet set named Building Project has been created. This sheet set contains a number of *subsets* related to the project, such as General and Architectural. After the sheet set is created, sheets can be added to each subset.

> **subsets:** Groups of layouts based on folder hierarchy.

After reviewing the information on the **Confirm** page, pick the **Finish** button to create the sheet set. If a setting needs to be changed, use the **Back** button.

PROFESSIONAL TIP

The information in the **Sheet Set Preview** area can be copied to a word processing program to be saved or printed. To do this, highlight all of the text and then use the [Ctrl]+[C] key combination. Open a new document in the word processing program and then use the [Ctrl]+[V] key combination to paste the text into the document.

When you pick the **Finish** button, the sheet set data file is saved to the specified location. The sheet set can then be opened in the **Sheet Set Manager**. Since a sheet set is not associated with a particular drawing file, any sheet set can be opened, regardless of the open drawing file.

Figure 29-6.
An existing layout is used as a template for new sheets in a sheet set.

Pick to select a different template file

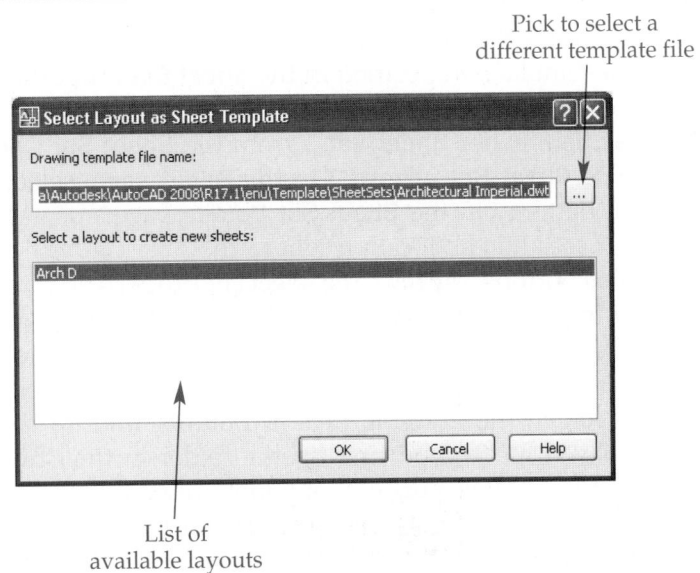

List of available layouts

Figure 29-7.
Use the **Confirm** page to preview settings before creating the sheet set.

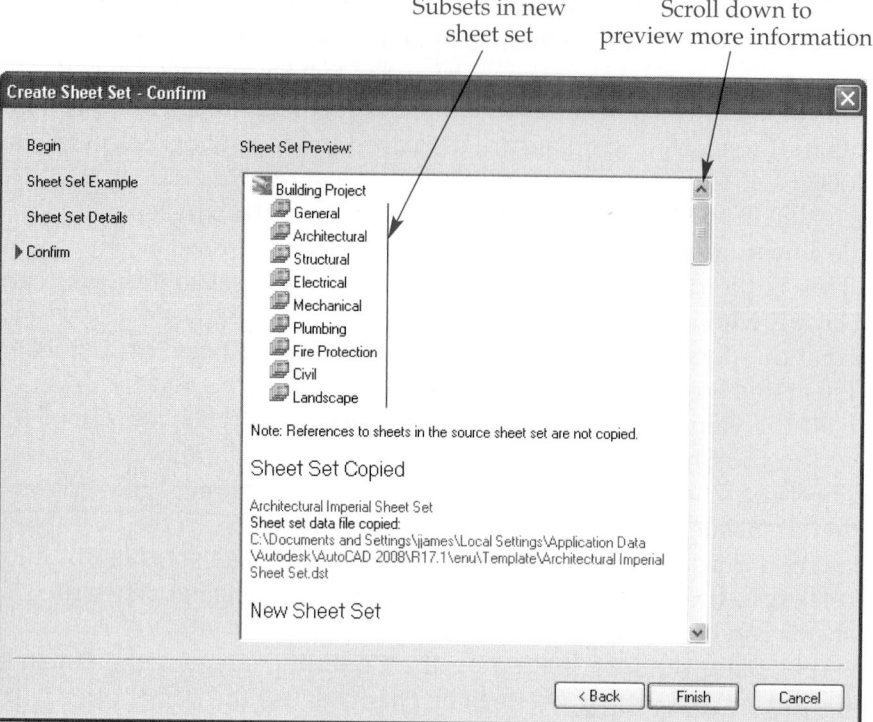

Subsets in new sheet set

Scroll down to preview more information

Exercise 29-1
Complete the exercise on the Student CD.

Creating a Sheet Set from Existing Drawing Files

You can use existing drawings to create a sheet set. Layouts are imported from the drawing files to create the sheets. Each layout in the drawings becomes a separate sheet.

When creating a sheet set in this manner, organize all files used in the project in a structured hierarchy of folders. To simplify access to the different layout tabs, it is recommended that you place only one layout in each drawing file. To ensure that all sheets have the same layout settings, you should create a sheet creation template as well. The template is specified in the **Sheet Set Properties** dialog box.

To create a new sheet set from an existing drawing project, open the **Sheet Set Manager**. Select **New Sheet Set...** from the **Sheet Set Control** drop-down list to open the **Create Sheet Set** wizard. On the **Begin** page, select **Existing drawings** and pick the **Next** button. On the **Sheet Set Details** page, specify a name and description for the sheet set and the location where the data file will be saved. Pick the **Sheet Set Properties** button to specify the sheet set properties.

Picking the **Next** button displays the **Choose Layouts** page. This page is used to specify the drawings and layouts to be added to the sheet set. Pick the **Browse...** button to select the folder(s) containing the drawing files with the desired layouts. The selected folder, the drawing files it contains, and all layouts within those drawings are displayed. When you first open a folder in the **Choose Layouts** page, all of the drawing files with layouts in that folder are added for selection. Each item has a check box next to it. The layouts that are checked are added to the new sheet set. If a layout should not be part of the new sheet set, uncheck the box next to it. In **Figure 29-8**, the

AutoCAD and Its Applications—Basics

Figure 29-8.
Existing layouts can be imported to a new sheet set from the **Choose Layouts** page.

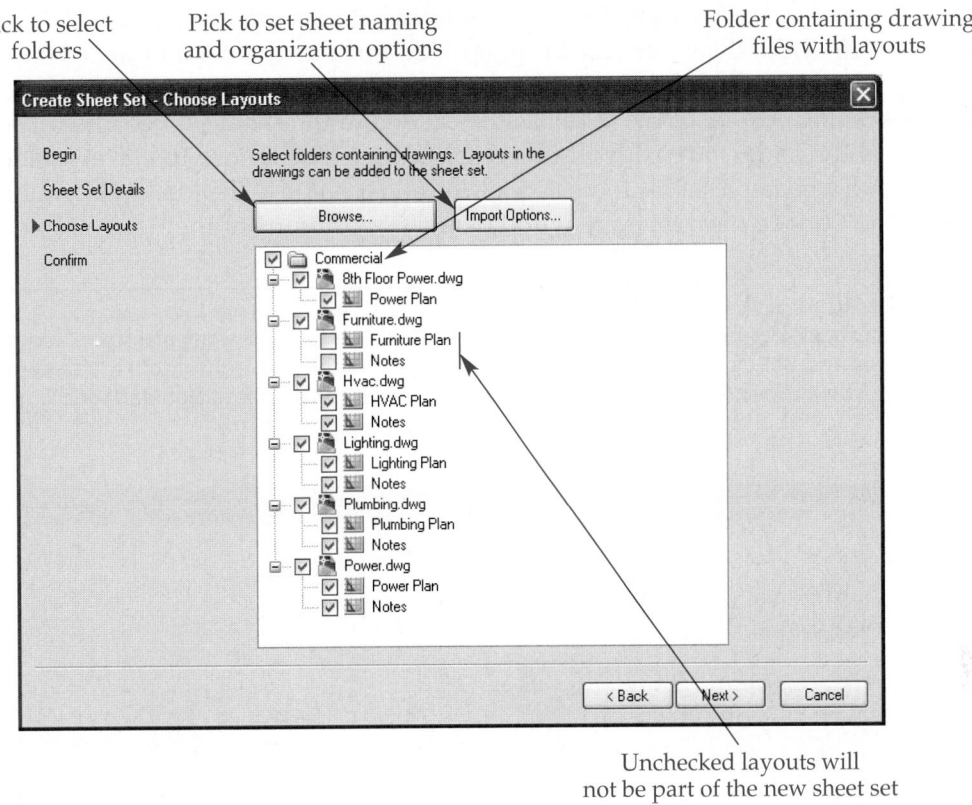

Pick to select folders

Pick to set sheet naming and organization options

Folder containing drawing files with layouts

Unchecked layouts will not be part of the new sheet set

boxes next to Furniture.dwg and its layouts have been unchecked, so they will not be included in the sheet set. Unchecking a drawing file automatically unchecks all of the layouts within it. If the folder is unchecked, all of the layouts in the drawing files are unchecked. More folders can be added to the **Choose Layouts** page by using the **Browse for Folder** dialog box.

When a sheet set is created using existing layouts, the name for a new sheet can be the same as the layout name, or it can be the drawing file name combined with the layout name. Sheet naming options can be accessed by picking the **Import Options...** button to display the **Import Options** dialog box. See **Figure 29-9.** If the **Prefix sheet titles with file name** check box is checked, the layouts that become sheets are named with the drawing file name and the name of the layout. For example, if a layout named

Figure 29-9.
Naming conventions for sheets and folder structuring options are specified in the **Import Options** dialog box.

Check to include drawing file name with layout name for new sheets

Check to create subsets from folders

Check to omit top folder name from subset structure

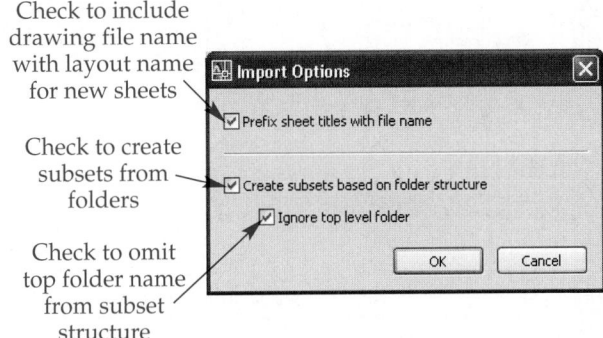

First Floor Electrical is imported from the drawing file Electrical Plan.dwg, the sheet that is created is named Electrical Plan – First Floor Electrical. To have the sheets take on only the layout name, uncheck the **Prefix sheet titles with file name** check box.

An imported sheet set can be organized so that the folders are grouped into subsets. If the **Create subsets based on folder structure** option is checked in the **Import Options** dialog box, all of the folder names added to the sheet set become subsets. The layouts in the folders are added under each subset. The **Ignore top level folder** option determines whether a subset is created for the folder name at the top level. **Figure 29-10A** shows the **Choose Layouts** page with layouts imported from the Residential folder for

---

Figure 29-10.
Creating a sheet set named Residential Project with subsets. A—Layouts are imported from the Architectural and Structural subfolders in the Residential folder. The subfolders are designated as subsets for the new sheet set. B—The subsets are shown in the **Sheet Set Manager**.

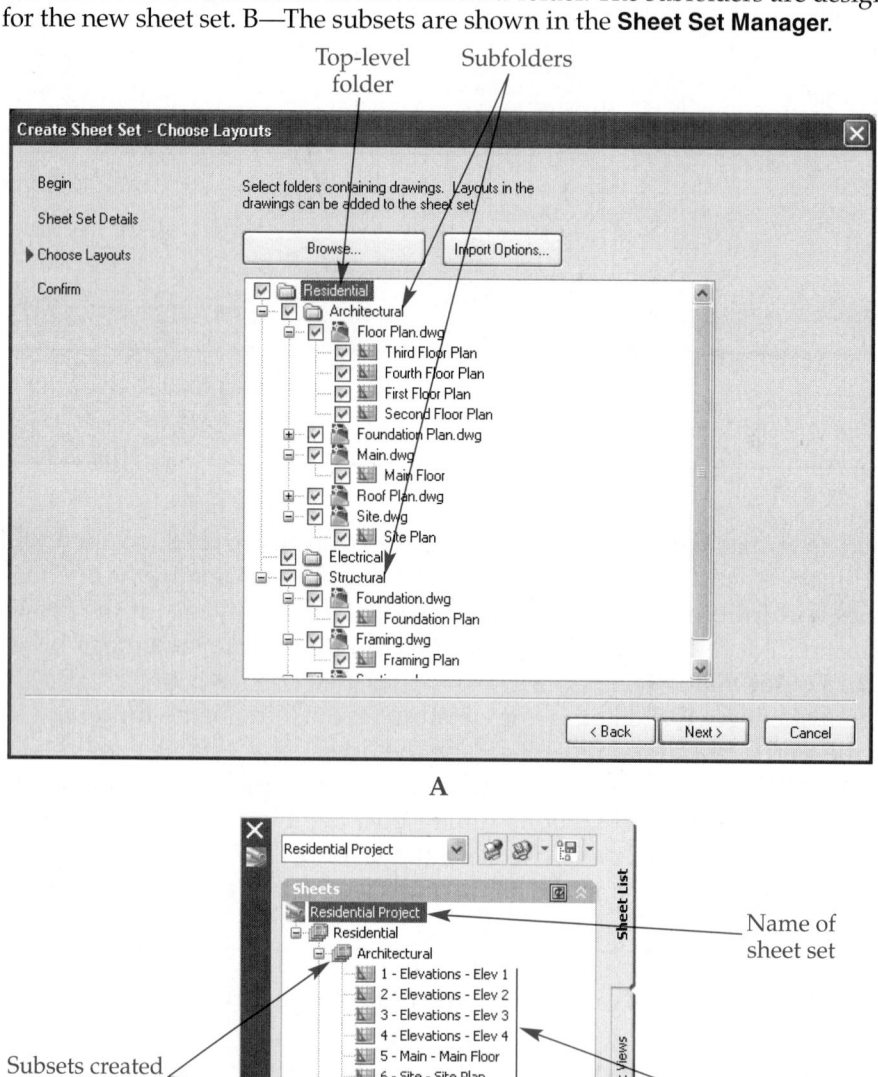

the Residential Project sheet set. This sheet set has been created with the **Create subsets based on folder structure** and **Ignore top level folder** options checked in the **Import Options** dialog box. The result of this configuration is shown in the **Sheet Set Manager** in **Figure 29-10B**. Creating subsets for sheet sets helps organize the sheets.

Notice how the sheets are named in **Figure 29-10B**. Each sheet has a number preceding its name. By default, a sheet is displayed in the **Sheet Set Manager** with its number, a dash, and then the name of the sheet.

When all folders and layouts have been selected for the new sheet set and all settings have been specified, pick the **Next** button on the **Choose Layouts** page. This displays the **Confirm** page. In the **Sheet Set Preview** area, review the sheet set properties. Pick the **Finish** button to create the new sheet set. If a setting needs to be changed, use the **Back** button.

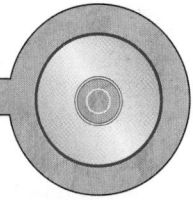

Exercise 29-2
Complete the exercise on the Student CD.

Working with Sheet Sets

Once a sheet set has been created, it can be accessed and edited in the **Sheet Set Manager**. Sheet sets are opened from the **Sheet Set Control** drop-down list. See **Figure 29-11**. The top area lists the sheet sets that have been opened in the current AutoCAD session. When AutoCAD is closed, this area is cleared. Selecting **Recent** displays a list of the most recently opened sheet sets. Selecting **Open...** displays the **Open Sheet Set** dialog box. You can then navigate to a sheet set data file (DST file) and open it in the **Sheet Set Manager**. A sheet set can also be opened by selecting **File** > **Open Sheet Set...** from the pull-down menu.

Sheets in a sheet set are managed in the **Sheet List** tab of the **Sheet Set Manager**. Sheet views are managed in the **Sheet Views** tab, and drawing files with layouts are managed in the **Model Views** tab. Almost all of the options for working with sheet sets are available from shortcut menus. Right-clicking a sheet set displays the shortcut menu shown in **Figure 29-12**. The menu options are:

Figure 29-11.
The **Sheet Set Control** drop-down list displays sheet sets that are currently open. Picking **Open...** allows you to browse for a sheet set that is not in the list.

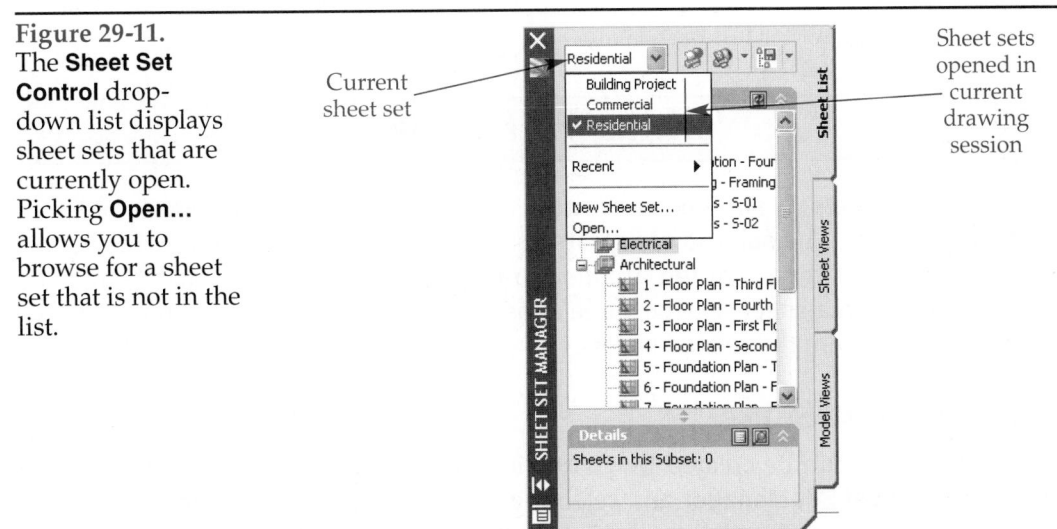

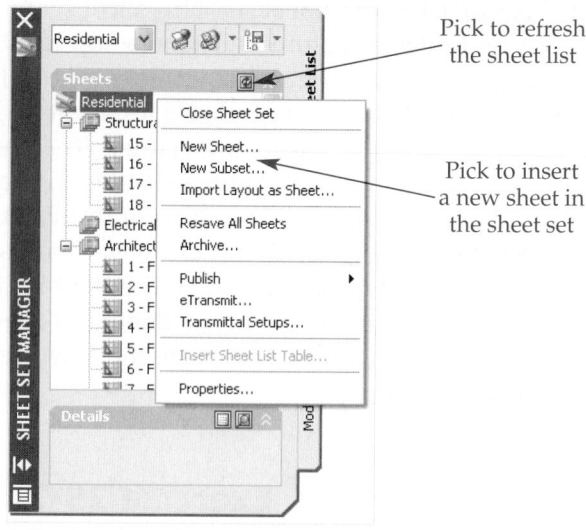

Figure 29-12.
This shortcut menu is displayed by right-clicking a sheet set name in the **Sheet List** tab.

Pick to refresh the sheet list

Pick to insert a new sheet in the sheet set

- **Close Sheet Set.** Removes the sheet set from the **Sheet Set Manager**.
- **New Sheet.** Creates a new sheet in the sheet set.
- **New Subset.** Creates a new subset in the sheet set.
- **Import Layout as Sheet.** Creates a new sheet containing an existing layout.
- **Resave All Sheets.** Updates the drawing files that are part of the current sheet set. All of the files need to be closed first. An open drawing file cannot be updated.
- **Archive.** Saves all drawing files and associated files to one location.
- **Publish.** Displays the **Publish** cascading menu of options for publishing and plotting a sheet set.
- **eTransmit.** Displays the **Create Transmittal** dialog box for use with the **eTransmit** feature. This option is very similar to the **Archive** option. It is used to package together files and associated files for Internet exchange.
- **Transmittal Setups.** Displays the **Transmittal Setups** dialog box, which is used to configure **eTransmit** settings.
- **Insert Sheet List Table.** Gathers information about all the sheets in the sheet set and inserts the data into the drawing as a table. This option is only available when a drawing file with a layout in the sheet set is open with the layout tab current.
- **Properties.** Opens the **Sheet Set Properties** dialog box.

To manually update changes to the sheet list, pick the **Refresh Sheet Status** button. See **Figure 29-12.**

Working with Subsets

Creating subsets is similar to creating subfolders under a top-level folder in Windows Explorer. The subsets are created to help manage the contents of the sheet set. For example, if there are ten architectural sheets, ten electrical sheets, and ten plumbing sheets in a sheet set, the three subsets Architectural, Electrical, and Plumbing can be created to store the related sheets.

Creating a New Subset

A new subset can be created by right-clicking the sheet set name or an existing subset in the **Sheet Set Manager** and selecting **New Subset...** from the shortcut menu. This opens the **Subset Properties** dialog box. See **Figure 29-13.** The name of the new

AutoCAD and Its Applications—Basics

Figure 29-13.
Settings for a new subset are made in the **Subset Properties** dialog box.

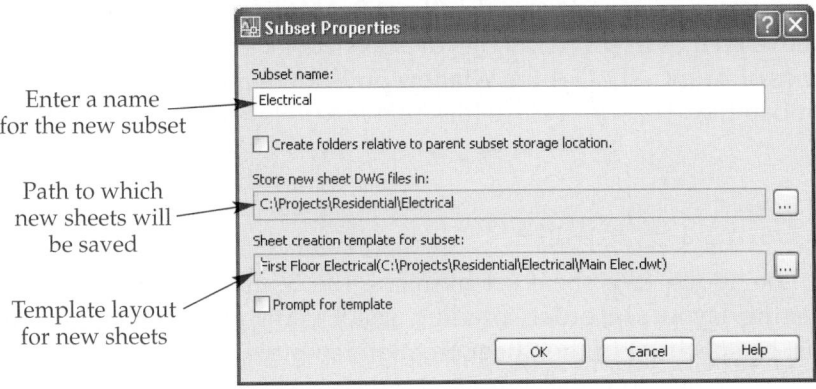

Enter a name for the new subset

Path to which new sheets will be saved

Template layout for new sheets

subset is entered in the **Subset name** text box. If a subset is being created for all of the electrical sheets in a sheet set, for example, then the subset can be named Electrical. When a new sheet is added to the subset using a template, the sheet is saved as a drawing file to the hard drive. A new folder can be created for the subset by checking **Create folders relative to parent subset storage location**. The folder structure will then mimic the subset structure. The **Store new sheet DWG files in** setting determines the path to which new sheets are saved. The default value is the location specified when the sheet set was initially created.

Each subset can also have its own template and layout for new sheets. This is specified in the **Sheet creation template for subset** setting. For example, if the electrical sheets use their own title block and notes, a template sheet with these settings should be used. Specifying the template and layout for a subset is identical to the procedure used in selecting the sheet set properties.

Modifying a Subset

After a subset has been created, its settings can be modified by right-clicking on the subset and selecting **Properties...** from the shortcut menu. This displays the **Subset Properties** dialog box. The **Rename Subset...** shortcut menu option also opens the **Subset Properties** dialog box.

A subset can be deleted by right-clicking the subset and selecting **Remove Subset** from the shortcut menu. This option is unavailable if the subset contains sheets.

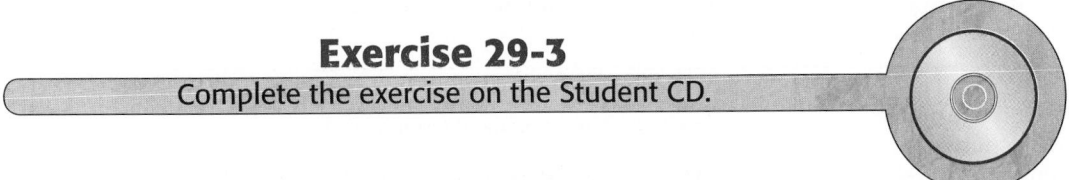

Exercise 29-3
Complete the exercise on the Student CD.

Working with Sheets

One of the most useful features of the **Sheet Set Manager** is the ability to open a sheet quickly for review or modification. You can open a sheet by double-clicking the sheet or by right-clicking the sheet and selecting **Open** from the shortcut menu. The drawing file that contains the referenced layout tab opens and the layout is set current.

Adding a Sheet Using a Template

A new sheet can be added to a sheet set by using the template layout sheet or by importing an existing layout. In order to add a sheet using the template layout sheet, a template must be specified in the **Sheet creation template** setting of the **Sheet Set** properties. To add a sheet using the template, right-click on the sheet set name or the subset where the sheet needs to be added, and then select **New Sheet...** from the shortcut menu. If a template layout is not specified, an alert appears and you are directed to pick a template layout using the **Select Layout as Sheet Template** dialog box. If a template layout was previously defined, or after selecting the template layout, the **New Sheet** dialog box is displayed. See **Figure 29-14.**

Enter the sheet number in the **Number** text box and the sheet name in the **Sheet title** text box. A new drawing file is created. The sheet title becomes the name of the layout in the drawing file. Enter the name for the file in the **File name** text box. By default, this is the sheet number and title. The **Folder path** field shows where the drawing file will be saved. This path is specified in the **Subset Properties** or **Sheet Set Properties** dialog box.

Adding an Existing Layout as a Sheet

An existing drawing layout can be added to a sheet set directly from an open drawing or using the **Sheet Set Manager**. To add an existing layout to a sheet set using the **Sheet Set Manager**, right-click on the sheet set name or the subset in which the sheet needs to be added. Then select **Import Layout as Sheet...** from the shortcut menu. This displays the **Import Layouts as Sheets** dialog box. See **Figure 29-15.** Pick the **Browse for Drawings** button to select a drawing file. The layouts from the drawing file are then listed in the list box. The **Status** field indicates whether the layout can be imported into the sheet set. If a layout is already part of a sheet set, it cannot be imported. By default, all of the layouts in the drawing are checked in the list, unless the layout is already part of a sheet set. Uncheck the box to exclude a layout from being imported as a sheet. If the **Prefix sheet titles with file name** check box is checked, the name of the file is included in the sheet title. To import the sheets, pick the **Import Checked** button.

Figure 29-14.
When you create a new sheet from a template, the sheet is defined in the **New Sheet** dialog box.

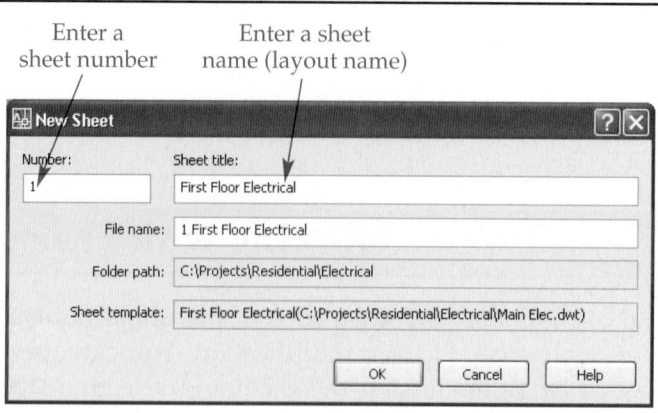

Enter a sheet number

Enter a sheet name (layout name)

AutoCAD and Its Applications—Basics

Figure 29-15.
Existing layouts can be added as sheets to a sheet set from the **Import Layouts as Sheets** dialog box.

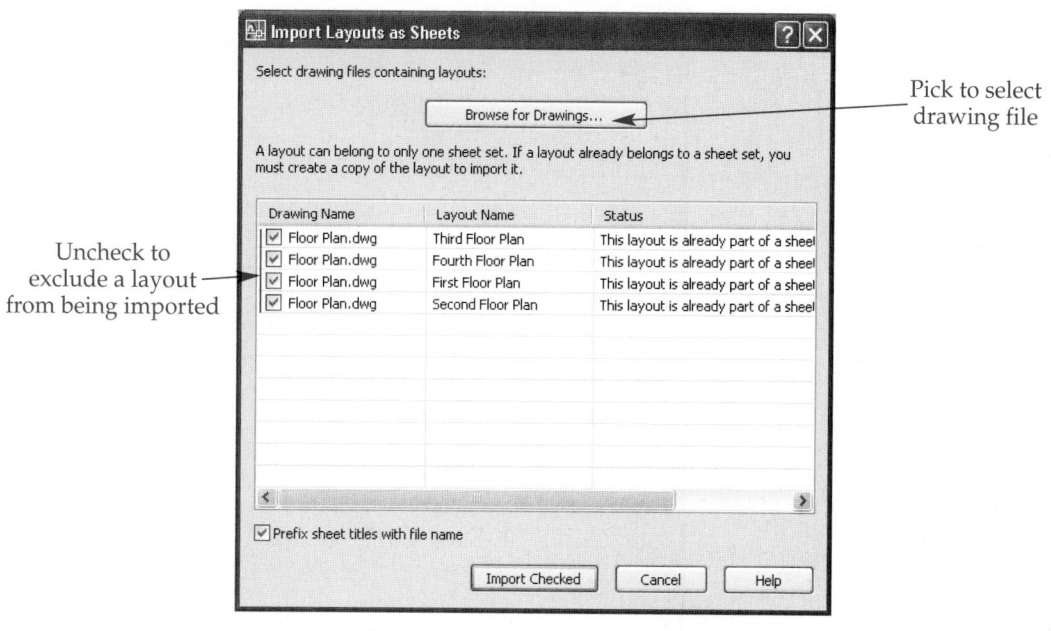

Pick to select drawing file

Uncheck to exclude a layout from being imported

To add an existing layout to a sheet set directly from an open drawing, right-click the layout you want to import and select **Import Layout as Sheet...** from the shortcut menu. This displays the **Import Layouts as Sheets** dialog box previously described, with the selected layout listed automatically.

Exercise 29-4
Complete the exercise on the Student CD.

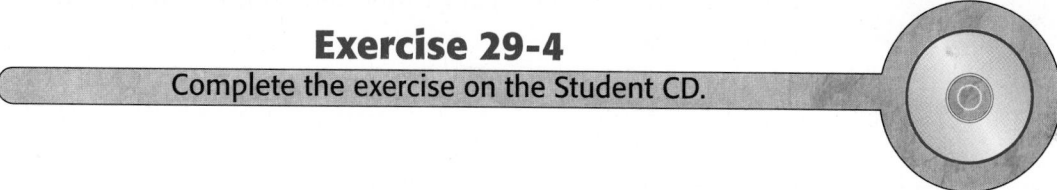

Modifying Sheet Properties

The properties of a sheet, such as the name, number, and description, can be modified by right-clicking the sheet name in the **Sheet Set Manager** to display the shortcut menu. The sheet name and number can be changed by selecting **Rename & Renumber...** from this menu. This displays the **Rename & Renumber Sheet** dialog box, which is similar to the **New Sheet** dialog box. If the sheet is one of several in a subset, picking the **Next** button moves to the next sheet in the subset.

The **Sheet Properties** dialog box also allows you to change the sheet name and number, along with the description and the publish option. To open the **Sheet Properties** dialog box, right-click the sheet name and select **Properties...** from the shortcut menu. See **Figure 29-16.** A description of the sheet can be entered in the **Description** text box. The **Include for publish** option determines whether the sheet is included when the sheet set is published or plotted. The default value is **Yes**.

The **Expected layout** and **Found layout** text boxes display the file path where the sheet was originally saved and the file path where the sheet was found. If the paths are different, you can update the **Expected layout** field by picking the ellipsis (...) button.

A sheet can be deleted from a sheet set by selecting **Remove Sheet** from the shortcut menu. This does not delete the drawing file from the hard drive; it only removes the sheet from the sheet set.

Figure 29-16.
The properties
of a sheet can be
modified in the
Sheet Properties
dialog box.

Determines whether
the sheet is published
or included in plot

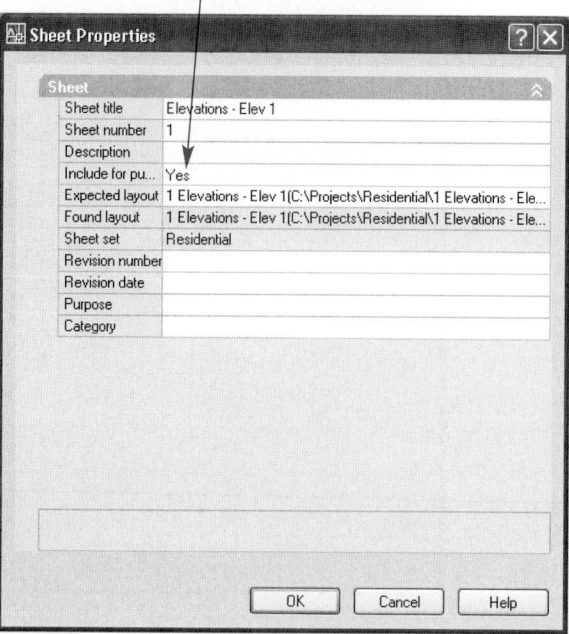

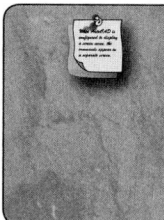

If the hard drive location of a drawing file is modified and the
drawing file has layouts that are associated with a sheet set, the
association is broken. You must reimport the layouts into the sheet
set or update the specified path to the drawing file in the **Sheet
Properties** dialog box.

Publishing a Sheet Set

publishing:
Creating electronic
files for distribution
or plotting.

In AutoCAD, *publishing* refers to the creation of electronic files for distribution
purposes or the plotting of hard copy prints. Sheet sets can be published by creating
drawing web format (DWF) files. DWF files are compressed, vector-based files that
can be viewed with the Autodesk DWF Viewer, which is installed with AutoCAD. A
sheet set can also be published by sending it to a plotter. For more information about
outputting DWF files, refer to *AutoCAD and Its Applications—Advanced.*

Using the Publish Shortcut Menu

An entire sheet set can be published to a DWF file or plotted using the options
in the **Publish** shortcut menu in the **Sheet Set Manager.** The **Publish** shortcut menu
can be accessed by picking the **Publish** button on the **Sheet Set Manager** toolbar or by
selecting **Publish** from the shortcut menu. See **Figure 29-17.**

A sheet set, a subset, or individual sheets can be selected for
publishing. Select the appropriate items using the [Shift] and [Ctrl]
keys in the **Sheet Set Manager.**

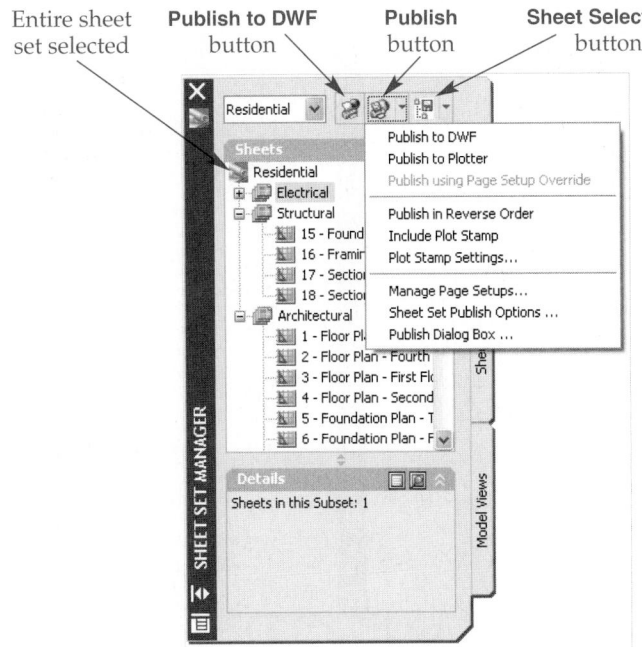

Figure 29-17.
The **Publish** shortcut menu options are used to prepare a sheet set for publishing or plotting.

The options in the **Publish** shortcut menu are:

- **Publish to DWF.** Creates a DWF file from the sheet set or the selected sheets. In the **Select DWF File** dialog box, specify a name and location for the file. The file is created with each sheet on a separate page in a multisheet file.
- **Publish to Plotter.** Plots the sheet set or selected sheets to the default plotter or printer using the plot settings from each layout.
- **Publish using Page Setup Override.** Displays the page setups that are available for use as overrides. Selecting a page setup from the list forces the sheet to use the selected page setup settings instead of the plot settings that are saved with the layout. This option is unavailable if a page setup override has not been specified for the sheet set or subset.
- **Publish in Reverse Order.** Publishes sheets in the opposite order from the order displayed in the **Sheet Set Manager**. Publishing a sheet set in reverse order is helpful when you are plotting sheets so that the last sheet is on the bottom of the stack, at the end of the entire set.
- **Include Plot Stamp.** Places the plot stamp information for the layout on the sheet when it is plotted.
- **Plot Stamp Settings.** Opens the **Plot Stamp** dialog box to specify the plot stamp settings.
- **Manage Page Setups.** Opens the **Page Setup Manager**, allowing you to create a new page setup or modify an existing one.
- **Sheet Set Publish Options.** Displays the **Sheet Set Publish Options** dialog box. This displays the available settings for creating a DWF file.
- **Publish Dialog Box.** Opens the **Publish** dialog box. All of the sheets in the current sheet set or the sheet selection are listed.

Creating Sheet Selection Sets

During the course of a project, the same set of sheets may need to be published many times. A selection of sheets can be saved so that it can be accessed again quickly for publishing. To save a sheet selection set, select the sheets to be included in the set. If you want to select all of the sheets in a subset, select the subset. Then pick the **Sheet Selections** button on the **Sheet Set Manager** toolbar and select **Create...** from the

Figure 29-18.
Sheet selection sets can be created from selected sheets or subsets in a sheet set. They are accessed from the **Sheet Selections** shortcut menu.

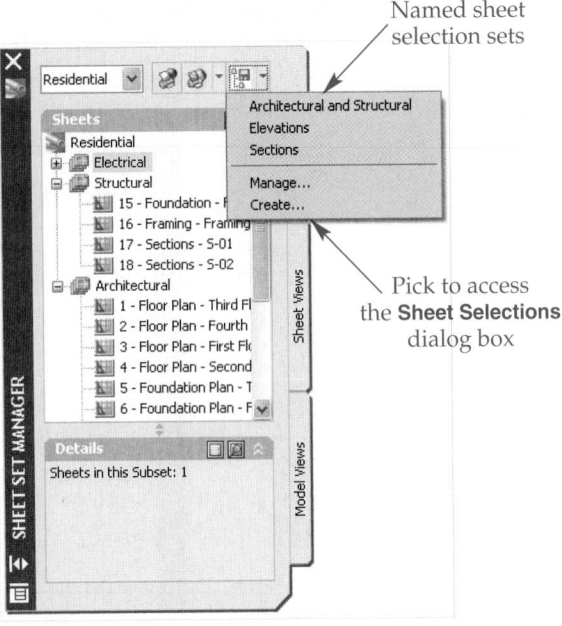

shortcut menu. In the **New Sheet Selection** dialog box, enter a name for the selection set and pick **OK**. The new selection set is then listed when you pick the **Sheet Selections** button. In Figure 29-18, three different sheet selection sets are shown. When a selection set is selected from the shortcut menu, the sheets are automatically highlighted in the **Sheet Set Manager**.

To rename or delete a sheet selection set, pick **Manage...** from the **Sheet Selections** shortcut menu. In the **Sheet Selections** dialog box, select the sheet selection set and then pick the **Rename** or **Delete** button.

Using Sheet Views

sheet view: A referenced portion of a drawing set.

Sheets can contain sheet views. A *sheet view* is any referenced portion of a drawing set, such as an elevation, a section, or a detail. Sheet views can be automatically labeled, placed on separate sheets, and referenced to each other through the use of blocks with attributes containing fields. These sheet view field values update automatically to reflect changes in sheet numbering.

The **Sheet Views** tab of the **Sheet Set Manager** is used to manage sheet views. Using this tab, views can be grouped by category and opened for viewing and editing. Special tools in the **Sheet Set Manager** can be used to identify views with numbers, labels, and callout blocks.

Adding a View Category

View categories are used to organize views in the **Sheet Views** tab. View categories are similar to the subsets created in the **Sheet List** tab. To create a new view category, make the **Sheet Views** tab current and ensure that the **View by category** button is selected. See Figure 29-19. Pick the **New View Category** button or right-click the sheet set name and select **New View Category...** from the shortcut menu. This opens the **View Category** dialog box. See Figure 29-20. In the **Category name** text box, enter a name for the category. For example, if you are going to add four elevation views to the new category, it could be named Elevations.

Figure 29-19.
View categories are created in the **Sheet Views** tab of the **Sheet Set Manager**.

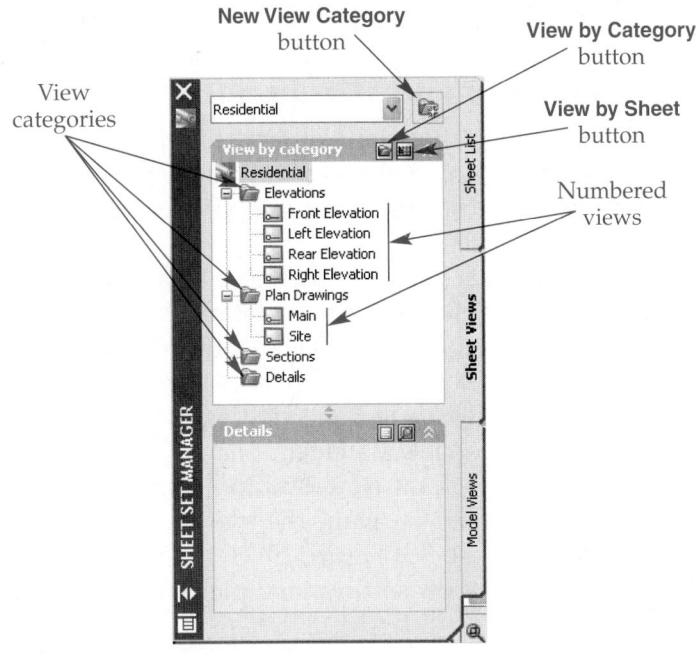

Figure 29-20.
The **View Category** dialog box is used to name the category and select callout blocks for use with views.

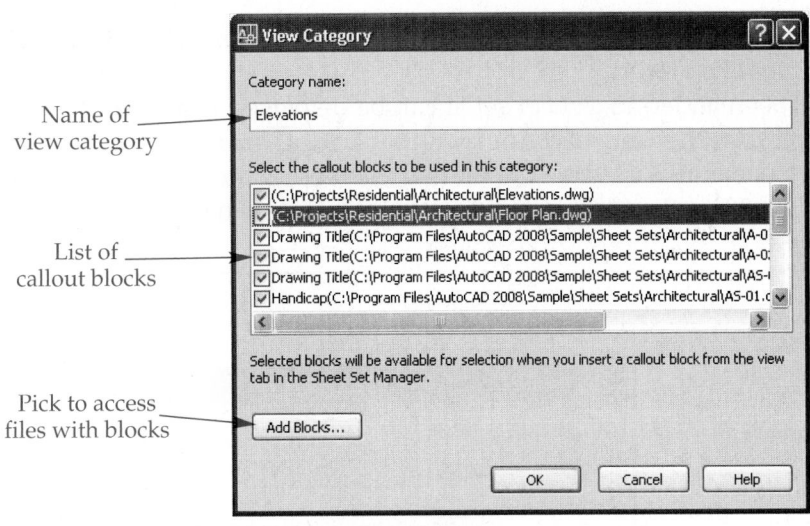

The **View Category** dialog box lists all of the available callout blocks for the current view category. Check the box next to the callout block to make it available for all of the views that are added to this category. If a block is not in the list, use the **Add Blocks...** button to select it from a drawing file. Once the necessary callout blocks are selected, pick the **OK** button to create the new category. Callout blocks are described later in this chapter.

Modifying a View Category

View category properties can be modified by right-clicking the category name in the **Sheet Set Manager** and selecting **Rename...** or **Properties...** from the shortcut menu. Selecting either of these options opens the **View Category** dialog box. The category name can be changed and different callout blocks can be added to the category.

A category can be deleted by right-clicking the category name and selecting **Remove Category** from the shortcut menu. The **Remove Category** option is unavailable if there are views under the category. The views must be removed before the category can be deleted.

Creating Sheet Views in an Existing Sheet

New views can be added to sheets and organized within sheet sets from the **Sheet Set Manager**. Use the following procedure to add a view to an existing sheet set:

1. Open the desired sheet set and add a category for the view if it has not already been created.
2. To add a view to a sheet, the sheet has to be a part of the sheet set. If the sheet has not been added to the sheet set, add it now.
3. Open the drawing file and set the layout tab current where the new view will be created.
4. Use display commands to orient the view as needed and then enter the **VIEW** command to access the **View Manager**.
5. In the **View Manager**, pick the **New...** button to open the **New View** dialog box.
6. Select the category that you want the view to be a part of from the **View category** drop-down list. See **Figure 29-21.**
7. Specify the rest of the view settings and pick **OK** to save the view.

NOTE

Refer to Chapters 6 and 25 for more information on creating your own working views and using the **View Manager**.

The newly saved view now appears in the **Sheet Set Manager** under the view category that was selected in the **New View** dialog box.

Once a view has been added to a sheet set, it can be displayed from the **Sheet Set Manager** by double-clicking the view name or by right-clicking the name and selecting **Display** from the shortcut menu. If the drawing file is already open, the view is set current. If the drawing file is not open, the file is opened so that the view can be set current.

Figure 29-21.
The **View category** drop-down list displays the available view categories for the view being defined.

Name of new view

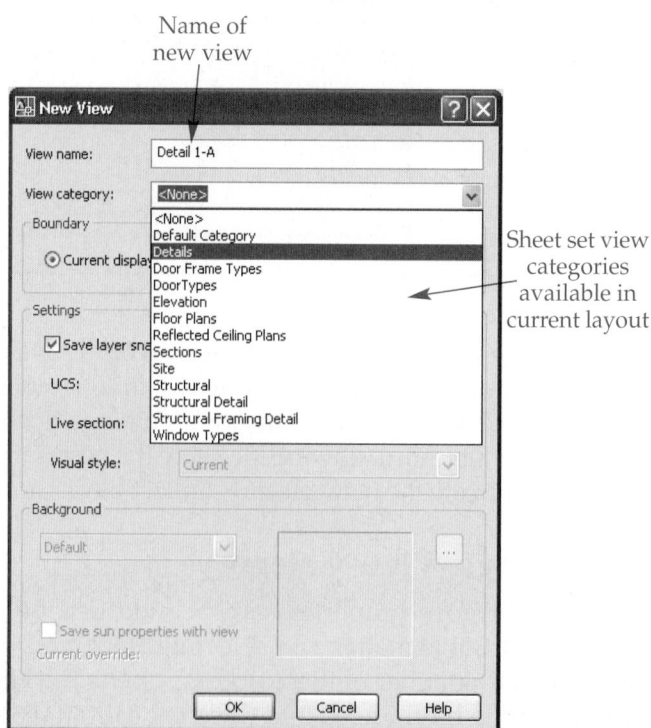

Sheet set view categories available in current layout

The view list can be displayed by category or by sheet. Refer to **Figure 29-19.** The **View by category** button displays all of the categories. The views are accessed by expanding the category and then the sheet. Picking the **View by sheet** button displays the sheet name. Expand the sheet name to display the saved views within the sheet.

Creating Sheet Views from Resource Drawings

Sheet views can be created from drawing files listed in the **Model Views** tab. The sheet view can be the entire model space drawing or a model space view. When a model space view or drawing is inserted into a sheet, the resource drawing becomes an external reference of the sheet drawing.

The **Model Views** tab is shown in **Figure 29-22.** Folders containing reference drawings are listed. To add a new folder, double-click the Add New Location entry or pick the **Add New Location** button and select a folder. You cannot select specific drawing files—you must select the folder containing the drawing. Only drawings listed in the **Model Views** tab can be inserted into a sheet to create a new sheet view. If the drawing you wish to use is not listed, you must add the folder containing the drawing to the resource drawing list.

The folder and all of the drawing files that are in it are now listed in the **Locations** list area. The model space views saved in the drawing are listed under the drawing file. The options available for a drawing file are located in the drawing file shortcut menu. To display the menu, right-click a drawing file. The options include:

- **Open.** Opens the drawing file and sets the model space tab current. Double-clicking the drawing file also opens the file.
- **Open read-only.** Opens the drawing file as read-only so that changes cannot be made to the file. This option is unavailable if the drawing file is already open.
- **Place on Sheet.** Inserts the file into the current sheet as a sheet view. AutoCAD prompts you to specify an insertion point and creates a viewport automatically in the sheet.
- **See Model Space Views.** Expands the list of model space views in the drawing. This is the same as picking the + sign next to the drawing file.
- **eTransmit.** Opens the **Create Transmittal** dialog box so the selected file and its associated files can be packaged together.

If a model space view has been saved in the drawing, it is listed under the drawing file name. You can insert the model space view as a sheet view in a sheet. To do so, right-click on the model space view name and select the **Place on Sheet** option. Pick an insertion point in the sheet.

Figure 29-22.
Sheet views can be created by inserting model space views and drawings from the **Model Views** tab.

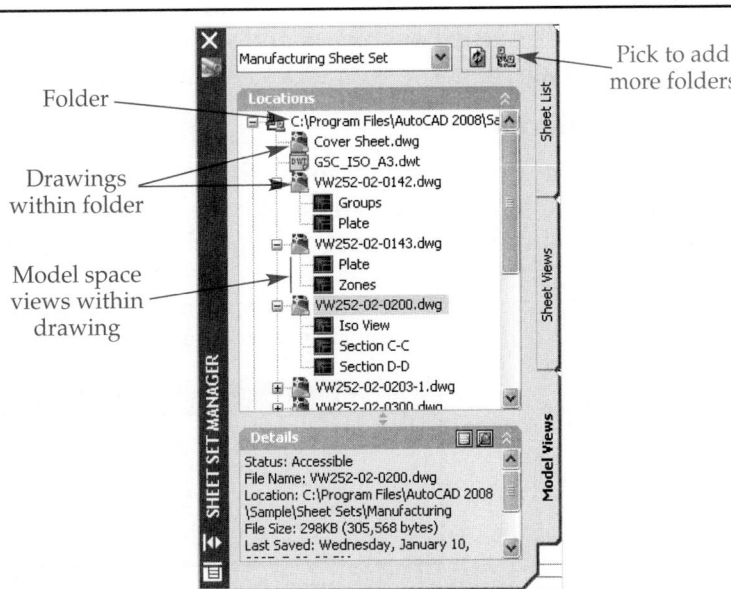

When you insert a model space view or drawing into a sheet, AutoCAD creates a viewport and an external reference to the selected drawing. AutoCAD will assign a scale for the viewport, or you can right-click before selecting the insertion point and select the scale for the sheet view. The scale is stored as the **ViewportScale** property of the **SheetView** field and is often displayed in the view label block.

When sheet views are created from resource drawings, an entry is added to the **Sheet Views**. If you insert a model space view, the view name is added to the **Sheet Views** tab. If you insert a drawing, the drawing name is added to the **Sheet Views** tab. To delete a location from a sheet set, right-click on the location and select **Remove Location** from the shortcut menu.

Naming and Numbering Sheet Views

In most projects, you will have several elevations, sections, or details. These items are typically numbered within the drawing set for easier reference. For example, the drawing set may include a foundation plan and a sheet with foundation details. On the foundation detail sheet, each detail is identified by a unique number. The foundation plan includes references to these numbers.

To change the name or number of a sheet view, right-click the sheet view name in the **Sheet Set Manager** and select **Rename & Renumber...** from the shortcut menu. The **Rename & Renumber View** dialog box is displayed. See **Figure 29-23**. Enter a number for the view in the **Number** text box. The name of the view can be modified in the **View title** text box. Picking the **Next** button moves to the next view in the view category. Pick **OK** when you are finished. The view number is displayed in front of the view name in the **Sheet Set Manager**.

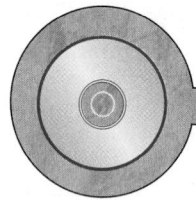

Exercise 29-5
Complete the exercise on the Student CD.

Working with Sheet View Blocks

The elevations, sections, details, and other drawings shown in sheet views are often located on one sheet and referenced on a different sheet. When using sheet views, you can insert blocks to identify the sheet view name, number, and scale on both the sheet with the sheet view and the sheet that refers to the sheet views. Typically, two types of blocks are used: callout blocks and view label blocks. Using sheet view blocks can greatly automate the process of adding drawing titles and labels.

Using callout blocks

callout block: A block inserted to indicate a reference to another sheet.

A *callout block* is used to refer to the sheet view. For example, when a section line is drawn through a building, a callout block is placed at the end of the section line. The callout block indicates the sheet or location where the section view is found and

---

Figure 29-23.
A view can be numbered in the **Rename & Renumber View** dialog box.

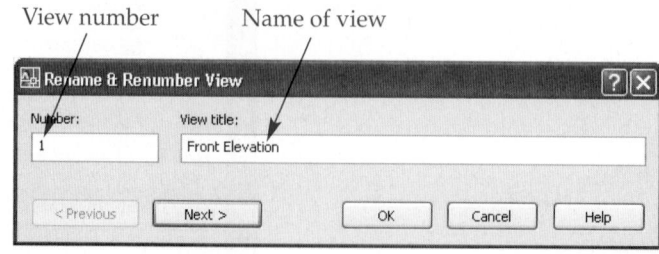

AutoCAD and Its Applications—Basics

information about the viewing direction. A callout block is also used on a foundation plan to identify an area addressed by a detail drawing. The callout block is typically located on a different sheet from the sheet view it references.

Several styles of callout blocks have been developed for use in different types of sheet views. See **Figure 29-24.** The upper value in a callout block is typically the sheet view number, and the lower value is the drawing on which the sheet view appears. In the default callout blocks, the upper value is an attribute containing the **ViewNumber** property of the **SheetView** field. See **Figure 29-25.** This lists the sheet view number specified for the sheet view. The lower value is the **SheetNumber** property of the **SheetSet** value. This lists the sheet number of the sheet containing the sheet view.

Because fields are used in the sheet view blocks, the values displayed are automatically updated if there are changes in the sheet set. For instance, if a new sheet is added in the middle of a sheet set, all subsequent sheets need to be renumbered. The sheet view block values update automatically as the sheet numbers change.

Using view label blocks

View label blocks are placed below the sheet view. The *view label block* typically includes the name and number of the section, elevation, or detail and the scale. See **Figure 29-26.** Like callout blocks, view label blocks include attributes containing fields that automatically update to reflect changes to the sheet set or sheet views. View label blocks typically include three properties of the **SheetView** fields: **ViewNumber**, **ViewTitle**, and **Viewport Scale.**

view label block: A block that contains view information such as the view name, number, and scale.

Figure 29-24.
Callout blocks provide reference information for views and sheets. A—Elements of an elevation symbol. B—Examples of commonly used callout blocks.

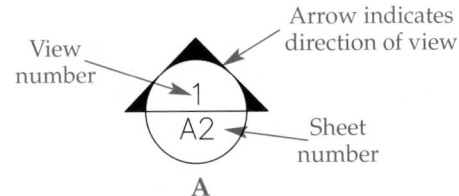

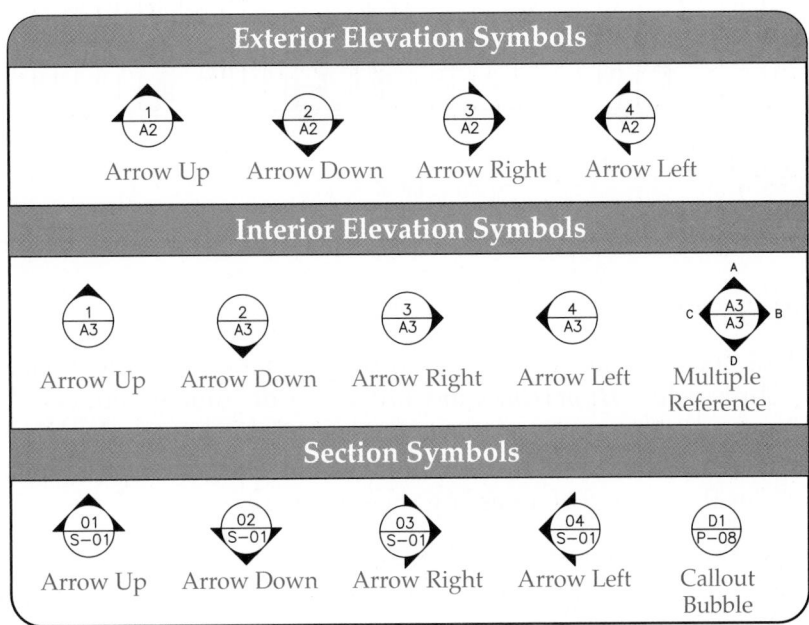

Figure 29-25.
The **ViewNumber** property displays the sheet view number. This field property is used in callout blocks.

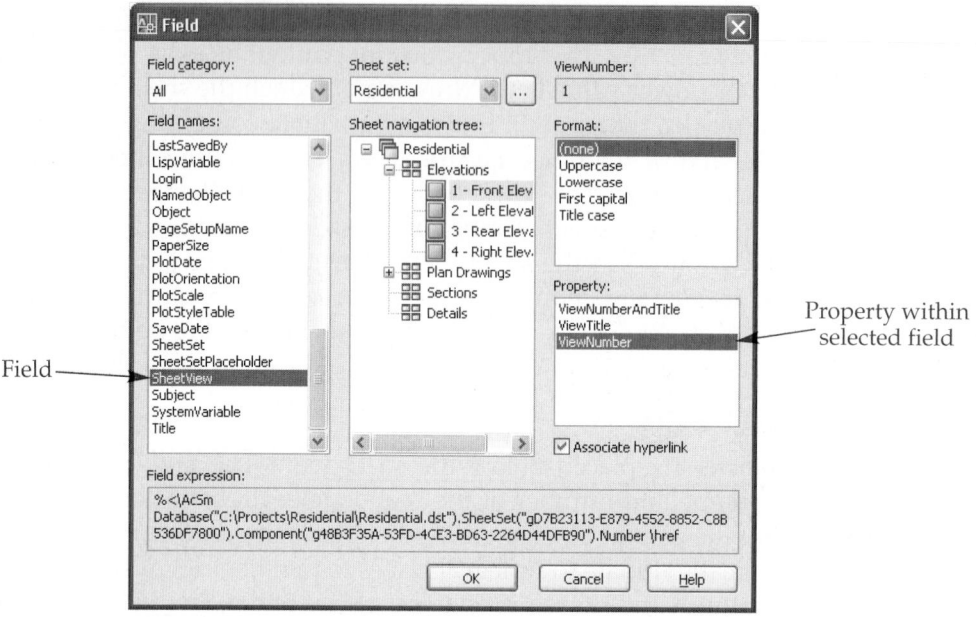

Figure 29-26.
View labels normally appear below the view on a sheet. They indicate information such as the view name, number, and scale.

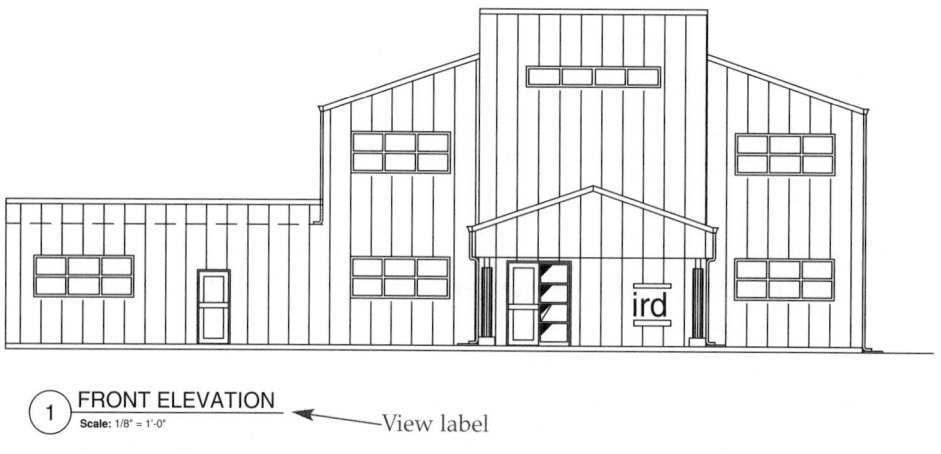

1 FRONT ELEVATION
Scale: 1/8" = 1'-0" ———View label

Using block hyperlinks

hyperlinks: Links in a document connected to related information in other documents or on the Internet.

The callout and view label blocks used in the AutoCAD sample sheet sets also include hyperlink fields. *Hyperlinks* are links in a document connected to related information in other documents or to the Internet. You can pick the hyperlink on a callout block to access the detail, section, or elevation being referenced instantly. This greatly simplifies the process of accessing sheet views.

Associating callout and view label blocks

To insert a callout or view label block from the **Sheet Set Manager**, the block first needs to be available to the sheet set in which the view is defined. These blocks are specified in the **Sheet Set Properties** dialog box. To access this dialog box, right-click the sheet set name in the **Sheet Set Manager** and select **Properties...** from the shortcut menu. The available blocks are specified in the **Callout blocks** text box and **Label block for views** text box. The name of each block is listed, followed by the path to the drawing file where the block is saved.

PROFESSIONAL TIP

A sheet set or view category can have multiple callout blocks available, but only one view label block.

To add a callout block to a sheet set, pick in the **Callout blocks** text box and then pick the ellipsis (...) button. This opens the **List of Blocks** dialog box. See **Figure 29-27.** Pick the **Add...** button to display the **Select Block** dialog box. In this dialog box, pick the ellipsis (...) button to select the drawing file that contains the block. The block can then be selected from the block list area of the **Select Block** dialog box. If the drawing file only consists of the objects that make up the drawing file, use the **Select the drawing file as a block** option. To delete a block from the block list, select it in the **List of Blocks** dialog box and pick the **Delete** button.

Specifying a view title block is similar to specifying a callout block. However, there can be only one view title block specified for the sheet set, so the **List of Blocks** dialog box is not displayed.

Each view category can be assigned its own callout blocks. This way, only the blocks that are needed for the views in a category are available. For example, a category named Section may only need a section callout bubble, while a category named Elevation may need ten different types of elevation symbols. To modify the callout blocks available for a view category, right-click the category name and select **Properties...** from the shortcut menu to open the **View Category** dialog box.

By default, the callout blocks and view title block assigned to a sheet set are displayed in the block list area. To make a block available to the view category, check the box next to the block. See **Figure 29-20.** This makes the block available to all of the views in the view category. New blocks can be added to the view category by picking the **Add Blocks...** button and accessing the **Select Block** dialog box.

Inserting callout and view label blocks

To insert a callout block into a drawing, open the sheet where the reference is to be placed. In the **Sheet Views** tab of the **Sheet Set Manager**, right-click on the sheet view name and select the block from the **Place Callout Block** cascading menu. See **Figure 29-28A.** You are then prompted to specify an insertion point for the block. The block can be scaled or rotated by using the options on the command line. When you

---

Figure 29-27.
All callout blocks available to a sheet set are listed in the **List of Blocks** dialog box.

Pick to access **Select Block** dialog box

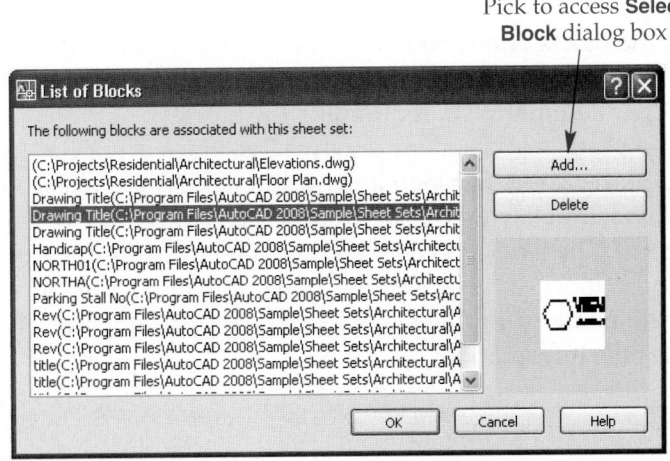

Figure 29-28.
Placing callout blocks in a view. A—Right-click the reference view name and select **Place Callout Block** to display a shortcut menu with all of the callout blocks available. B—Callout blocks are placed in the 1-Main Floor Plan view in the A-01 sheet to reference the section view named 1-Section in the A-05 sheet.

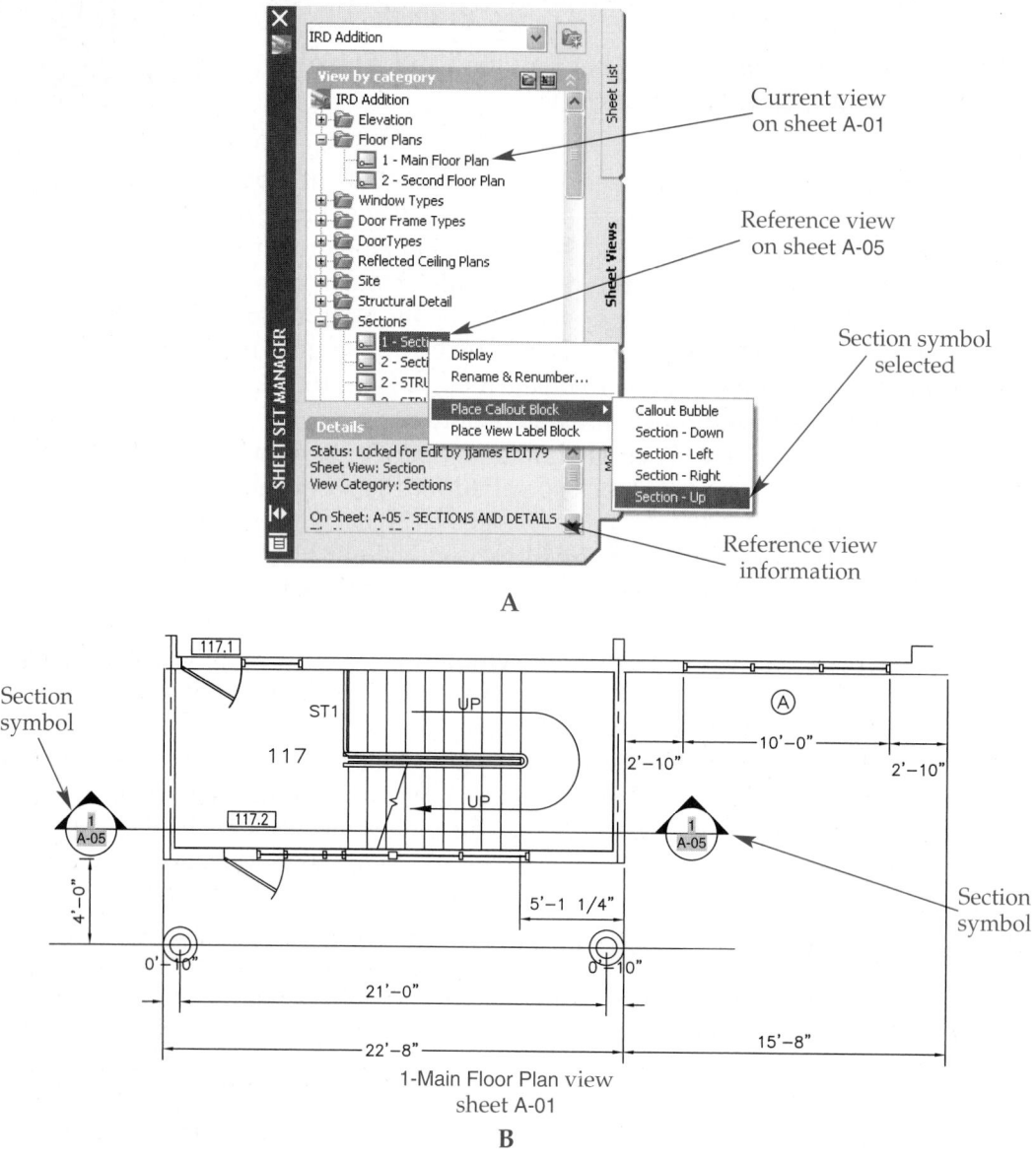

insert the block, AutoCAD gives it the same sheet view number and sheet number as the reference view and sheet. See **Figure 29-28B.** If the reference information changes, AutoCAD automatically renumbers the block.

The process of inserting a view label block is similar to that for inserting a callout block. In the **Sheet Set Manager**, right-click on the sheet view name and select **Place View Label Block** from the shortcut menu. AutoCAD prompts you to specify an insertion point. The block can be scaled or rotated using the options on the command line. When the block is inserted, the label appears with the view name and number. If the view name or number is later changed in the sheet set, AutoCAD automatically updates the information.

AutoCAD and Its Applications—Basics

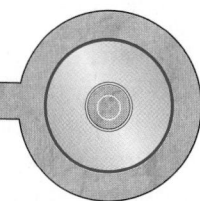

Exercise 29-6

Complete the exercise on the Student CD.

Sheet Set Fields

Information about a sheet is usually placed in the title block area of the drawing. The information may include items such as the client's name and address, the project number, the person who checked the sheet, and the date the sheet was plotted. You can create fields on sheets to display this information. A field value can change as a result of a change to the value of the field setting. Fields are valuable features for sheet sets, because text items on sheets can be set up to display up-to-date information if changes occur as the project develops.

AutoCAD provides specific field types for use with sheet sets. To create a field for a text value on a sheet, select **Insert** > **Field...** from the pull-down menu. This displays the **Field** dialog box. See **Figure 29-29**. Selecting **SheetSet** from the **Field category:** drop-down list displays a list of predefined field types in the **Field names:** list box. These fields can be inserted to display values that have been defined in the sheet, sheet view, or sheet set, such as the sheet title, number, or description. Some of the fields also have several properties. Selecting one of the field types or properties displays the related value in the **Field** dialog box.

For example, selecting the **CurrentSheetNumber** field allows you to insert a field that displays the sheet number of the current sheet. If the sheet is renumbered at a later date, the field changes to display the most current information.

Figure 29-29.

Select **SheetSet** in the **Field category:** list in the **Field** dialog box to display the many fields related to sheet sets.

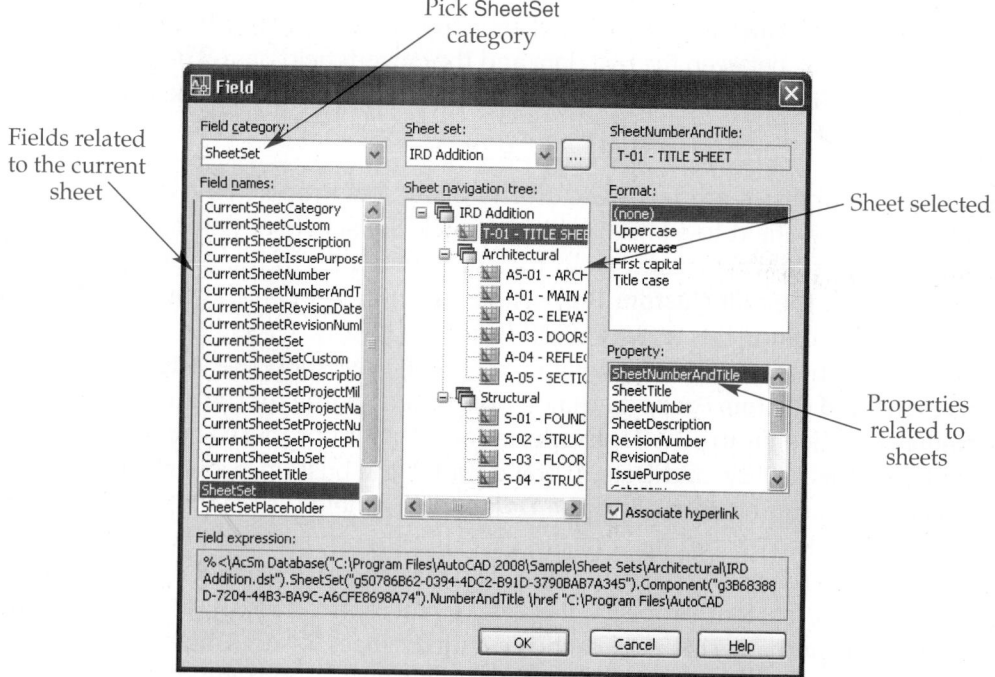

Selecting the **SheetSet** field provides options for inserting many values. When you select the **SheetSet** field, the **Sheet navigation tree** is displayed. If you select the sheet set at the top of the tree, a set of properties related to the entire set is displayed in the **Property** list box. These properties include settings that can be applied to all sheets in the set, such as project information and client information. These settings will not change from sheet to sheet, but will be the same on all sheets. When these field properties are included in the sheet set title block, all sheets display the same values.

If you select a sheet in the **Sheet navigation tree**, properties related to the individual sheet are displayed. These properties include **SheetTitle**, **SheetNumber**, **Drawn By**, and **Checked By** settings. When these field properties are included in the sheet set template title block, each sheet can display a unique value. If a new sheet is added to a sheet set, the fields automatically update.

Selecting the **SheetSetPlaceholder** field allows you to insert a field that acts as a placeholder. A *placeholder* is a temporary value for a field. Selecting a placeholder in the **Placeholder type:** list box assigns a temporary value to the associated field, such as SheetNumber. Placeholders can be used to insert temporary field values in user-defined callout blocks and view labels. When defined with attributes in a callout block, placeholders are updated to display the correct values automatically when the block is inserted onto a sheet from the **Sheet Set Manager**.

Like the **SheetSet** field, the **SheetView** field has many options. When you select the **SheetView** field, the **Sheet navigation tree** displays the view list for the sheet set. If you pick the sheet set name in the **Sheet navigation tree**, the sheet set properties are displayed. These properties are identical to those displayed with the **SheetSet** field. If you pick a sheet view name in the **Sheet navigation tree**, sheet view properties are displayed. These properties are specific to a sheet view and include **ViewTitle**, **ViewNumber**, and **ViewScale**. These field properties are used in callout and view label blocks.

> **placeholder:** A temporary value for a field.

Using Custom Properties

Selecting the **CurrentSheetCustom** or **CurrentSheetSetCustom** field allows you to insert a field that is linked to a custom property defined for a sheet or sheet set. Information about the sheet set or a specific sheet can be stored electronically with fields and custom properties. This information can then be viewed from the **Sheet Set Manager**. The data can also be inserted into the drawing using the **Field** command, which creates a link between the text data and the custom field data. The data can then be modified in the **Sheet Set Manager** and the linked data is updated in the drawing files.

Adding a custom property field

Custom properties are managed in the **Sheet Set Properties** dialog box. To add a custom property field to a sheet set, right-click the sheet set name in the **Sheet Set Manager** and select **Properties...** from the shortcut menu. In the **Sheet Set Properties** dialog box, pick the **Edit Custom Properties...** button to open the **Custom Properties** dialog box. This dialog box is shown in **Figure 29-30**.

To add a custom property field to the sheet set, pick the **Add...** button. This displays the **Add Custom Property** dialog box. Enter a name for the custom property in the **Name** field. See **Figure 29-31**. Examples of a custom property include Job Number, Client Name, Checked By, and Date. If the data for the custom property is usually the same value, this can be entered in the **Default value** field. For example, if the custom property is Checked by, and most of the sheets in this project are checked by ST, then ST could be entered as the default value. The **Owner** area has two options: **Sheet Set** and **Sheet**. If the custom property pertains to the entire project, select **Sheet Set**. If the custom property pertains to each individual sheet, select **Sheet**. When **Sheet** is selected, the custom property is available in the **Sheet Properties** dialog box and the data is attached to each individual sheet. Pick the **OK** button to add the custom property to the sheet set.

AutoCAD and Its Applications—Basics

Figure 29-30.
Information can be attached to a sheet set in the **Custom Properties** dialog box.

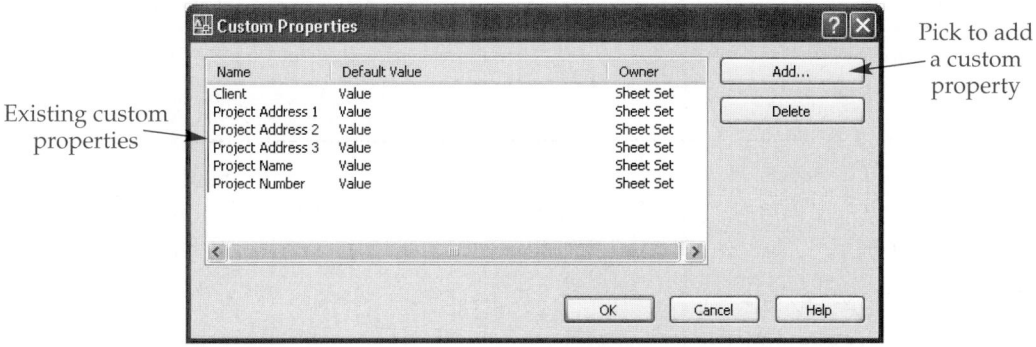

Existing custom properties

Pick to add a custom property

Figure 29-31.
Enter the information for the custom property in the **Add Custom Property** dialog box.

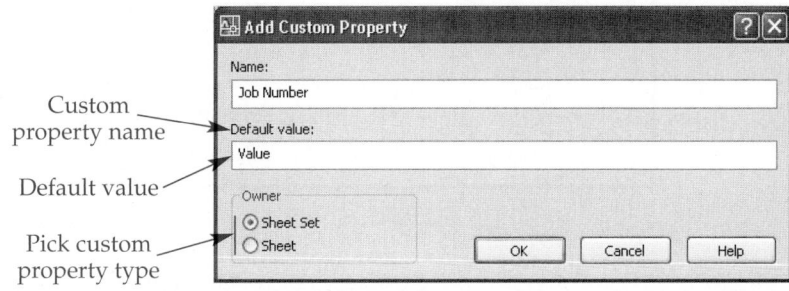

Custom property name

Default value

Pick custom property type

Entering custom property data

To modify or enter information into a custom property field for a sheet set, open the **Sheet Set Properties** dialog box and modify the value. If custom properties have been added for a sheet, the individual sheets display the custom property fields. To modify or enter information into a sheet custom property field, right-click the sheet and select **Properties...** from the shortcut menu. The custom properties are listed under the **Sheet Custom Properties** heading of the **Sheet Properties** dialog box. See **Figure 29-32.**

Deleting a custom property

If a custom property field is no longer needed, it can be deleted from the sheet set. To do this, right-click the sheet set and select **Properties...** to open the **Sheet Set Properties** dialog box. Pick the **Edit Custom Properties...** button. In the **Custom Properties** dialog box, select the custom property and pick the **Delete** button.

NOTE

If a sheet set is created from an example sheet set, any custom properties from the example sheet set are added to the new sheet set.

Exercise 29-7
Complete the exercise on the Student CD.

Figure 29-32.
Sheet set custom properties are available in the **Sheet Properties** dialog box after they have been added to the sheet set.

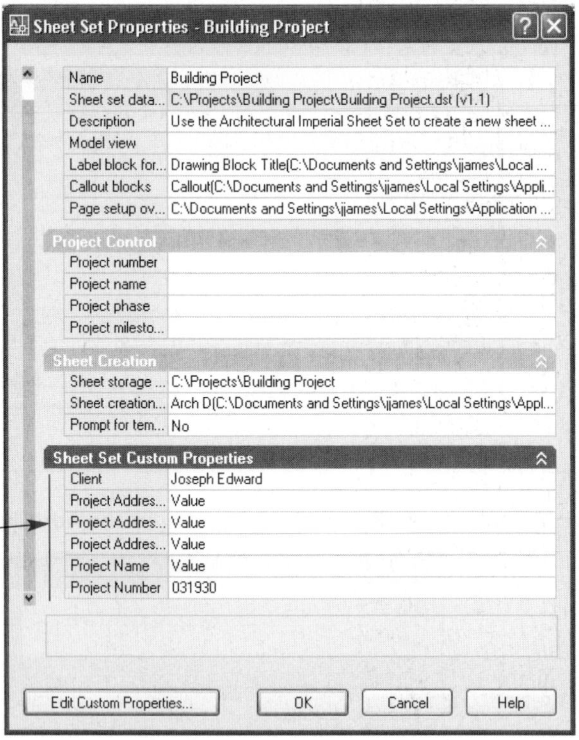

Custom properties

Creating a Sheet List Table

sheet list: A list of all the pages in a sheet set and the type of information that can be found on each sheet.

One of the first pages of a sheet set typically includes a sheet list. A *sheet list* is like the table of contents for the sheet set. It lists all of the pages in the sheet set and what type of information can be found on the sheet. The **Sheet List Table** command inserts a table object using information from the sheet properties. The information in the table is directly linked to the sheet properties, so if the sheet information is updated in the **Sheet Set Manager**, the sheet list table is updated automatically.

Inserting a Sheet List Table

A sheet list table can only be inserted into a drawing from the **Sheet Set Manager**. To insert a sheet list table, open the **Sheet Set Manager** and open the sheet where the table needs to be inserted. Right-click the sheet set name and select **Insert Sheet List Table...** from the shortcut menu. This opens the **Insert Sheet List Table** dialog box shown in **Figure 29-33**.

A preset table style for the sheet list can be selected from the **Table Style name** drop-down list. A preview of the table is displayed in the preview area. The **Show Subheader** check box determines whether the table will include a subheader row.

The information displayed in the table is set in the **Table Data Settings** area. The title for the sheet list is entered into the **Title Text** text box. The information the table contains is specified in the **Column Settings** area. Pick the **OK** button to insert the table. You are then prompted to specify the insertion point for the table. **Figure 29-34** shows a sheet list table that uses the sheet number and sheet description fields.

> **NOTE**
>
> A sheet list table can only be inserted into a layout tab of a drawing file that is a part of the sheet set. The **Insert Sheet List Table...** options are unavailable if the drawing file is not part of the sheet set or if model space is current.

Figure 29-33.
Properties for the sheet list table are set up in the **Insert Sheet List Table** dialog box.

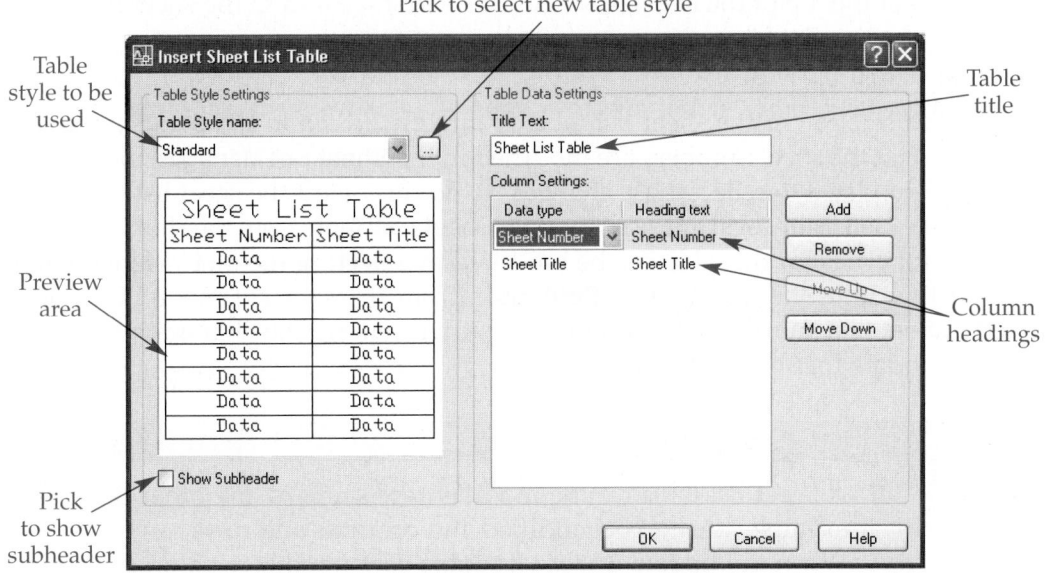

Figure 29-34.
A sheet list table displays information about each sheet in the sheet set.

Sheet Number	Sheet Description
SHEET INDEX	
T–01	SHEET INDEX, VICINITY MAP, BUILDING CODE ANALYSIS
Architectural	
AS–01	ARCHITECTURAL SITE PLAN, NOTES
A–01	MAIN FLOOR PLAN, SECOND FLOOR PLAN, WALL TYPE NOTES
A–02	EXTERIOR ELEVATIONS
A–03	DOOR & FRAME SCHEDULE, ROOM FINISH SCHEDULE, DOOR, DOOR FRAME & WINDOW TYPES
A–04	MAIN & SECOND FLOOR REFLECTED CEILING PLANS
A–05	STAIR SECTIONS AND DETAILS
Structural	
S–01	FOUNDATION PLAN, PILE SCHEDULE, PILE TYPICAL DETAIL
S–02	STRUCTURAL SECTIONS AND DETAILS
S–03	FLOOR FRAMING PLAN AND SECTIONS
S–04	STRUCTURAL SECTIONS

Modifying the Column Heading Data

A sheet list table can include various types of information from the drawing file and the sheet set. By default, the Sheet Number and Sheet Title fields are included. The sheet list table information is specified in the **Column Settings** area of the **Insert Sheet List Table** dialog box.

A new column can be added to the sheet list table by picking the **Add** button. The new column is placed under the last column in the list. To specify the data type, pick the name in the **Data type** column to activate the drop-down list. Pick the drop-down list button to display the information that can be used in the sheet list table. Select the type of data you want to include. Then type the heading for the sheet list column in the **Heading text** column. The data types that are available in the drop-down list come from sheet set properties and drawing properties. To have a different data type added to the list, you need to add a custom property to the sheet set.

To delete a data column from the list, select the data column and pick the **Remove** button. To reposition the order of the columns, use the **Move Up** and **Move Down** buttons. The column at the top of the list is inserted as the first column in the sheet list table.

Editing a Sheet List Table

The information in the sheet list table is directly linked to the data source field. For example, if the sheet numbers are modified in the **Sheet Set Manager**, the sheet list table can be updated to reflect those changes. To do this, select the sheet list table in the drawing file, then right-click and select **Update Sheet List Table** from the shortcut menu.

The properties for the table can be modified by selecting the table, right-clicking, and selecting **Edit Sheet List Table Settings...** from the shortcut menu. This opens the **Edit Sheet List Table Settings** dialog box. After making the changes, pick the **OK** button to update the sheet list table.

NOTE

A sheet list table can be modified the same as any other table. For example, text can be modified and columns and rows can be added. When the **Update Sheet List Table** command is used on the modified table, a warning dialog box is displayed stating that any manual modifications will be discarded.

Using Sheet List Table Hyperlinks

If the **Sheet Number** or **Sheet Title** columns are included in the sheet list table, hyperlinks are automatically assigned to the data. To open a sheet using a hyperlink, move the crosshairs over a sheet number or sheet title. Hold the pointing device still for a moment until the hyperlink icon and tooltip appear. The tooltip displays the message CTRL + click to follow link. Hold the [Ctrl] key on the keyboard and pick the hyperlink to open the selected sheet. This is another way to open a sheet quickly.

Exercise 29-8
Complete the exercise on the Student CD.

Archiving a Sheet Set

At different periods throughout a project, you may want to gather up all of the electronic drawing files that relate to a project and store them. This is called *archiving* the drawing set. For example, when a set of drawings in a project is presented to the client for the first time, the client will probably want to make some changes. It may be wise to archive the files for future reference, before the modifications are made.

archiving:
Gathering and storing all of the electronic drawing files related to a project.

All files in a sheet set can be archived by using the **ARCHIVE** command. This copies all of the drawing files and their related files to a single location. Related files include external references, font files, plot style table files, and template files.

Setting Up an Archive

To archive a sheet set, right-click on the sheet set name and select **Archive...** from the shortcut menu, or type ARCHIVE. The **Archive a Sheet Set** dialog box opens. See **Figure 29-35.** The **Sheets** tab displays all of the subsets and sheets in the sheet set. Check the sheets to be archived. The drawing files and their related files are listed in the **Files Tree** tab. Pick the + sign next to a file to display its related files.

A file that is not part of the sheet set can be included in the archive by picking the **Add a File** button on the **Files Tree** tab. See **Figure 29-36.** This opens the **Add File to Archive** dialog box. Any type of file can be added to the archive—the archive is not limited to AutoCAD files. You can include in the archive by typing them in the **Enter notes to include with this archive** text box. The **View Report** button lists all of the files included in the archive. This information can be saved to a text file by picking the **Save As...** button.

Figure 29-35.
The files to be archived and the archive settings are specified from the **Archive a Sheet Set** dialog box.

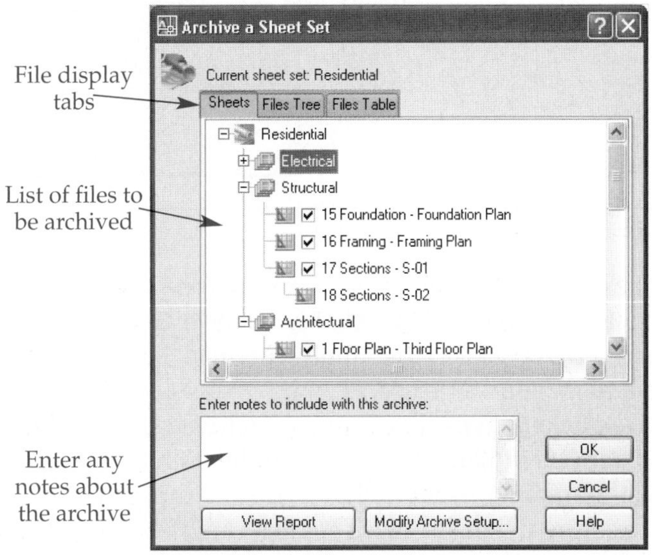

Figure 29-36.
Documents that relate to a project can be archived along with the AutoCAD files.

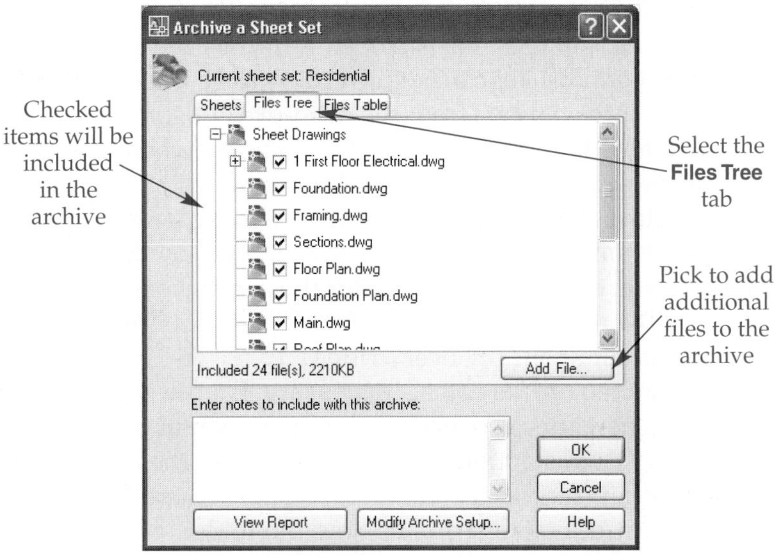

Figure 29-37.
The archive
file settings are
specified in the
**Modify Archive
Setup** dialog box.

File type
File format
File location
File name

Organization
options

Miscellaneous
options

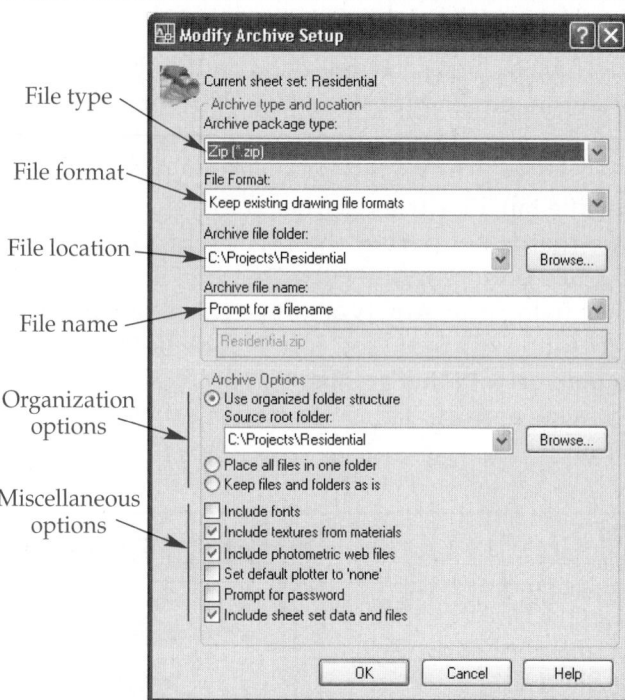

The location where the archive is saved, the type of archive that is created, and additional settings are specified in the **Modify Archive Setup** dialog box. See **Figure 29-37.** To open this dialog box, pick the **Modify Archive Setup...** button. The options in the **Archive type and location** area are:

- **Archive package type.** Files can be archived in one of three formats:
  - **Folder (set of files).** Copies all of the archived files into a single folder.
  - **Self-extracting executable (*.exe).** Compresses all of the files into a self-extracting zip (EXE) file. The files can be extracted at a later time by double-clicking on the file. A *zip file* is a file that contains one or more files that have been compressed using the Windows ZIP file format.
  - **Zip (*.zip).** Compresses all of the files into a zip file. A program that works with zip files must be used to extract the files.
- **File Format.** Files can be converted to an earlier version of AutoCAD by selecting one of the options from the drop-down list.
- **Archive file folder.** This is the location where the archive is saved. Pick the **Browse...** button to select a different location.
- **Archive file name.** The drop-down list provides naming options:
  - **Prompt for a filename.** The **Specify Zip File** dialog box is displayed so that you can specify a name for the archive package.
  - **Overwrite if necessary.** If a file with the same name already exists, that file is automatically overwritten.
  - **Increment file name if necessary.** If a file with the same name already exists, a new file is created and an incremental number is added to the file name. With this option, multiple versions of the archive package are saved.

Additional settings for the archive package are specified in the **Archive Options** area. The first option determines how the folder structure is saved. If **Use organized folder structure** is selected, the archive file duplicates the folder structure for the files. When this option is selected, the **Source root folder** setting is used to determine the root folder for files that use relative paths, such as xrefs. To archive all of the files into one single folder, use the **Place all files in one folder** option. The **Keep files and folders as is** option uses the same folder structure for all the files in the sheet set.

The other settings in the **Archive Options** area include:

- **Include fonts.** Includes all fonts used in the drawings in the archive.
- **Set default plotter to 'none'.** Disassociates the plotter name from the drawing files. This is useful if the files will be sent to someone using a different plotter.
- **Prompt for password.** Allows a password to be set for the archive. The password is then needed to open the archive package.
- **Include sheet set data and files.** Includes the sheet set data file with the archive package.

Chapter Test

Answer the following questions. Write your answers on a separate sheet of paper or complete the electronic chapter test on the Student CD.

1. What is a sheet set?
2. What does the term *sheet* refer to in relation to a sheet set and a drawing file?
3. What wizard is used to create a sheet set? What two types of ways can a new sheet set be created?
4. What file extension is applied to sheet sets?
5. What are subsets in relation to a sheet set?
6. What is the purpose of the **Create subsets based on folder structure** option in the **Import Options** dialog box?
7. Explain how to create a new subset in a sheet set and specify a template file and layout for creating new sheets in the subset.
8. List two ways to open a sheet from the **Sheet Set Manager**.
9. What is the purpose of the **Import Layouts as Sheets** dialog box?
10. How do you modify a sheet name or number?
11. Briefly explain how to publish a sheet set to a DWF file. How are the sheets organized in the resulting file?
12. How do you create a sheet selection set?
13. What are sheet views and how can they be referenced to each other within a sheet set?
14. What tab in the **Sheet Set Manager** is used to manage sheet views?
15. Briefly explain how to create a view category for a sheet set and associate callout blocks to the category.
16. Explain how to add a drawing file to a sheet set so that views in the drawing can be placed on a sheet.
17. Explain why AutoCAD callout blocks and view labels are automatically updated when changes are made to the related sheet set.
18. What information is typically provided by the upper and lower values displayed in a callout block?
19. Explain how to insert a callout block into a drawing.
20. Give three examples of fields that can be used in a sheet set.
21. What is the purpose of custom sheet set properties?
22. How do you add a custom property to a sheet set?
23. What is a sheet list table?
24. Explain how to add a column heading to a sheet list.
25. How can a table be updated to reflect changes that are made in the **Sheet Set Manager**?
26. What happens to edits made manually to a sheet list table when the **Update Sheet List Table** command is used?
27. What is the purpose of archiving a sheet set?
28. List the three packaging types available for archiving a sheet set.
29. What is a zip file?
30. How can you password-protect an archive?

Drawing Problems

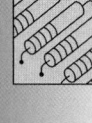

1. Create a new sheet set using the **Create Sheet Set** wizard and the **Existing drawings** option. Name the new sheet set Schematic Drawings. On the **Choose Layouts** page, pick the **Browse...** button and browse to the folder where the P25-9.dwg file from Chapter 25 is saved. Import all of the layouts from the file into the new sheet set. Continue creating the sheet set as follows:

    A. In the **Sheet Set Properties** dialog box, assign the layout named ISO A1 Layout from Tutorial-mMfg.dwt template file in the AutoCAD 2008 Template folder as the sheet creation template.

    B. Open a new drawing file using the template of your choice and create a block for a view label. Save the drawing file and then assign the block to the sheet set using the **Label block for views** setting in the **Sheet Set Properties** dialog box.

    C. Create a new view category and name it Schematics.

    D. Open the 3 Wire Control layout, create a new view, and add it to the Schematics view category. Double-click the new view name in the **Sheet Views** tab and insert the view label block you previously created. Renumber the view and save the drawing.

    E. Add a custom property to the sheet set named Checked by and set the **Owner** type to **Sheet**. Add another custom property named Client and set the **Owner** type to **Sheet Set**.

2. Create a new sheet set using the **Create Sheet Set** wizard and an example sheet set. Use the Architectural Imperial Sheet Set example sheet set. Name the new sheet set Floor Plan Drawings. Finish creating the sheet set. Under the Architectural subset, create a new sheet named Floor Plan. Number the sheet A1. In the **Model Views** tab, add a new location by browsing to the folder where the P16-16.dwg file from Chapter 16 is saved. Open the P16-16.dwg file and continue as follows:

    A. Create three model space views named Kitchen, Living Room, and Dining Room. Orient each display as needed to describe the area of the floor plan. Save and close the drawing.

    B. Open the A1-Floor Plan sheet. Create a new layer named Viewport and set it current.

    C. In the **Model Views** tab, expand the listing under the P16-16.dwg file. Right-click each view name and select **Place on Sheet**. Insert each view into the layout. Delete the default view labels inserted with the views. Double-click inside each viewport and set the viewport scale as desired.

    D. In the **Sheet Views** tab, renumber the views. Insert a new view label block under each view.

    E. Save and close the drawing.

3. Open the Floor Plan Drawings sheet set created in Problem 29-2. Create an archive of the sheet set using the self-extracting zip executable (EXE) file format.

CHAPTER

Index

AutoCAD
and Its Applications

ADVANCED

2008

by

Terence M. Shumaker
Faculty Emeritus
Former Chairperson
Drafting Technology
Autodesk Premier Training Center
Clackamas Community College, Oregon City, Oregon

David A. Madsen
Faculty Emeritus
Former Chairperson
Drafting Technology
Autodesk Premier Training Center
Clackamas Community College, Oregon City, Oregon

Director Emeritus
American Design Drafting Association

Craig P. Black
Instructor, Mechanical Design
Manager, Autodesk Premier Training Center
Fox Valley Technical College, Appleton, Wisconsin

Publisher
The Goodheart-Willcox Company, Inc.
Tinley Park, Illinois
www.g-w.com

Library of Congress Catalog Card Number 2007019739
ISBN: 978-1-59070-832-3

1 2 3 4 5 6 7 8 9 – 08 – 12 11 10 09 08 07

Library of Congress Cataloging-in-Publication Data

Shumaker, Terence M.
AutoCAD and its applications: advanced/ by Terence M.
Shumaker
p. cm.
Includes index
ISBN-13: 978-1-59070-832-3
1. AutoCAD. I. Title.
T385.S46128 2007
620'.00420285536—dc22

2007019739

Introduction

AutoCAD and Its Applications—Advanced provides complete instruction in mastering three-dimensional design and modeling using AutoCAD. This text also provides complete instruction in customizing AutoCAD and introduces programming AutoCAD. These topics are covered in an easy-to-understand sequence and progress in a way that allows you to become comfortable with the commands as your knowledge builds from one chapter to the next. In addition, *AutoCAD and Its Applications—Advanced* offers:

- Step-by-step use of AutoCAD commands.
- In-depth explanations of how and why commands function as they do.
- Extensive use of font changes to specify certain meanings. This is fully explained in the next section, Fonts Used in This Text.
- Examples and discussions of industrial practices and standards.
- Actual screen captures of AutoCAD and Windows features and functions.
- Professional tips explaining how to effectively and efficiently use AutoCAD.
- Exercises, located on the Student CD, to reinforce the chapter topics. These exercises should be completed where indicated in the text and build on previously learned material.
- Chapter tests for review of commands and key AutoCAD concepts.
- A large selection of modeling and customizing problems supplement each chapter. Problems are presented as 3D illustrations, actual plotted drawings, and engineering sketches.

With *AutoCAD and Its Applications—Advanced* you not only learn AutoCAD commands, but you also become acquainted with:

- 3D construction and layout techniques.
- Constructing models using different 3D coordinate systems.
- User coordinate systems.
- Model space viewports.
- 3D editing and display techniques.
- 3D text and dimensioning.
- Solid model construction, editing, and display.
- Modeling using sweeps and lofts.
- Model visualization and rendering.
- Customizing the AutoCAD environment.
- Customizing toolbars, pull-down menus, the **Dashboard**, and image tiles.
- The basics of AutoLISP and dialog box (DCL) programming.
- Introduction to programming using Visual Basic for Applications (VBA).

Fonts Used in This Text

Different typefaces are used throughout each chapter to define terms and identify AutoCAD commands. Important terms appear in **bold-italic face, serif** type. AutoCAD menus, commands, variables, dialog box names, and toolbar button names are printed in **bold-face, sans serif** type. File names, folder names, paths, and keyboard-entry items appear in the body of the text in Roman, sans serif type. Keyboard keys are shown inside of square brackets [ ] and appear in Roman, sans serif type. For example, [Enter] means to press the enter (return) key.

Other Text References

This text focuses on advanced AutoCAD applications. Basic AutoCAD applications are covered in *AutoCAD and Its Applications—Basics*, which is also available from Goodheart-Willcox Publisher. *AutoCAD and Its Applications* texts are also available for AutoCAD Releases 2002 through 2007. For advanced AutoCAD programming applications, refer to the texts *Visual LISP Programming* and *VBA for AutoCAD*, which are both available from Goodheart-Willcox Publisher.

Introducing the AutoCAD Commands

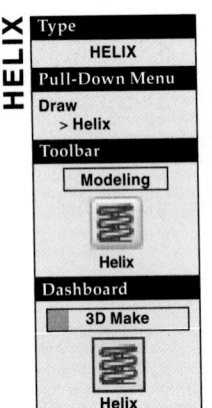

There are several ways to select AutoCAD drawing and editing commands. Selecting commands on a toolbar or from a pull-down menu is slightly different than entering them from the keyboard. All AutoCAD command-entry methods are presented in this text. When a command is introduced, these methods are illustrated in the margin next to the text reference. The example in the margin next to this paragraph illustrates the various methods of initiating the **HELIX** command to draw a helix.

Flexibility in Design

Flexibility is the keyword when using *AutoCAD and Its Applications—Advanced*. This text is an excellent training aid for both individual and classroom instruction. *AutoCAD and Its Applications—Advanced* teaches you how to apply AutoCAD to common modeling and customizing tasks. It is also an invaluable resource for any professional using AutoCAD.

When working through the text, you will see a variety of notices. These include Professional Tips, Notes, and Cautions that help you develop your AutoCAD skills.

PROFESSIONAL TIP

These ideas and suggestions are aimed at increasing your productivity and enhancing your use of AutoCAD commands and techniques.

A note alerts you to important aspects of a command function, menu, or activity that is being discussed. These aspects should be kept in mind while you are working through the text.

A caution alerts you to potential problems if instructions or commands are incorrectly used, or if an action can corrupt or alter files, folders, or storage media. If you are in doubt after reading a caution, always consult your instructor or supervisor.

AutoCAD and Its Applications—Advanced provides several ways for you to evaluate your performance. Included are:

- **Exercises.** The Student CD contains exercises for each chapter. These exercises allow you to perform tasks that reinforce the material just presented. You can work through the exercises at your own pace. However, the exercises are intended to be completed when called out in the text.
- **Chapter test.** Each chapter includes a written test at the end of the chapter. Questions require you to give the proper definition, command, option, or response to perform a certain task. You may also be asked to explain a topic or list appropriate procedures. An electronic version of the test is available on the Student CD.
- **Drawing problems.** There are a variety of drawing, design, and customizing problems at the end of each chapter. These are presented as real-world CAD drawings, 3D illustrations, and engineering sketches. The problems are designed to make you think, solve problems, use design techniques, research and use proper drawing standards, and correct errors in the drawings or engineering sketches. Graphics are used to represent the discipline to which a drawing problem applies.

These problems address mechanical drafting and design applications, such as manufactured part designs.

These problems address architectural and structural drafting and design applications, such as floor plans, furniture, and presentation drawings.

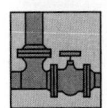

These problems address piping drafting and design applications, such as piping flow diagrams, tank drawings, and pipe layout.

These problems address a variety of general drafting, design, and customization applications. These problems should be attempted by everyone learning advanced AutoCAD techniques for the first time.

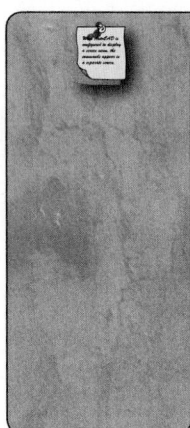

NOTE

Some problems presented in this text are given as engineering sketches. These sketches are intended to represent the kind of material from which a drafter is expected to work in a real-world situation. As such, engineering sketches often contain errors or slight inaccuracies and are most often not drawn according to proper drafting conventions and applicable standards. Errors in these problems are *intentional* to encourage you to apply appropriate techniques and standards in order to solve the problem. As in real-world applications, sketches should be considered preliminary layouts. Always question inaccuracies in sketches and designs and consult the applicable standards or other resources.

Student CD

At the back of this book is the Student CD. This CD contains the exercises and chapter test for each chapter and the appendix material. The appendix consists of:
- Appendix A Solid Modeling Tutorial
- Appendix B Legacy Customization
- Appendix C Common File Extensions
- Appendix D AutoCAD Command Aliases
- Appendix E Advanced Application Commands
- Appendix F Advanced Application System Variables
- Appendix G Basic AutoLISP Commands

As you work through each chapter, exercises on the Student CD are referenced. The exercises are intended to be completed as the references are encountered in the text. The solid modeling tutorial in Appendix A should be completed after Chapter 12. The remaining appendix material is intended as reference material.

Also included on the Student CD is the student software supplement. This contains a variety of student activities that are intended to supplement the exercises on the Student CD. These activities are referenced within the appropriate exercises and can be completed as additional practice.

About the Authors

Terence M. Shumaker is Faculty Emeritus, the former Chairperson of the Drafting Technology Department and former Director of the Autodesk Premier Training Center at Clackamas Community College. Terence taught at the community college level for over 28 years. He has professional experience in surveying, civil drafting, industrial piping, and technical illustration. He is the author of Goodheart-Willcox's *Process Pipe Drafting* and coauthor of the *AutoCAD and Its Applications* series (Releases 10 through 2007 editions) and *AutoCAD Essentials.*

David A. Madsen is Faculty Emeritus, the former Chairperson of Drafting Technology and the Autodesk Premier Training Center at Clackamas Community College and former member of the American Design and Drafting Association (ADDA) Board of Directors. David was honored by the ADDA with Director Emeritus status at the annual conference in 2005. David was an instructor and a department chair at Clackamas Community College for nearly 30 years. In addition to community college experience, David was a Drafting Technology instructor at Centennial High School in

Gresham, Oregon. David also has extensive experience in mechanical drafting, architectural design and drafting, and construction practices. He is the author of several Goodheart-Willcox drafting and design textbooks, including *Geometric Dimensioning and Tolerancing,* and coauthor of the *AutoCAD and Its Applications* series (Releases 10 through 2007 editions), *Architectural Drafting Using AutoCAD, Architectural Desktop and Its Applications, Architectural AutoCAD,* and *AutoCAD Essentials.*

Craig P. Black is an instructor of Mechanical Design and Manager of the Autodesk Premier Training Center at Fox Valley Technical College in Appleton, WI. Craig has been teaching at Fox Valley Technical College since 1990. He has served two terms on the Autodesk Training Center Executive Committee (now known as the Advisory Board) and chaired the committee in 2001. He has presented various topics at a number of Autodesk University annual training sessions, and has been contracted to teach training sessions on Autodesk products across the United States. Craig not only teaches, but also does AutoCAD customization and AutoLISP and DCL programming for area businesses and industries. Prior to his current position, Craig worked in the civil, architectural, electrical, and mechanical drafting and design disciplines.

Acknowledgments

The authors and publisher would like to thank the following individuals and companies for their assistance and contributions.

Contributing Authors

The authors wish to acknowledge the following contributors for their professional expertise in providing in-depth research and testing, technical assistance, reviews, and development of new materials.

Jeffrey Laurich for Chapters 8 and 13 through 17 and consultation on other chapters. Jeff has been an instructor at Fox Valley Technical College in Appleton, WI, since 1991. He has worked in mechanical design and drafting since 1986. Jeff has taught classes in AutoCAD, Autodesk MAP, Autodesk VIZ, and other programs. He created a certificate program at FVTC entitled Computer Rendering and Animation that utilizes the 3D capabilities of AutoCAD and Autodesk VIZ. As a side occupation, Jeff uses Autodesk 3ds max to create renderings and animations for manufacturers and architects.

Ethan Collins for Chapter 18. Ethan is a software specialist and provides technical support for Autodesk software products.

Contribution of Materials

Autodesk, Inc.
Bill Fane
CADENCE magazine
EPCM Services Ltd.
Fitzgerald, Hagan, & Hackathorn
Kunz Associates

Brief Contents

Three-Dimensional Design and Modeling

Model Visualization and Presentation

Customizing AutoCAD

Programming AutoCAD

Expanded Table of Contents

Three-Dimensional Design and Modeling

Model Visualization and Presentation

Student CD Contents

Using the Student CD

Chapter Exercises

Chapter Tests

Appendices

Appendix A Solid Modeling Tutorial
Appendix B Legacy Customization
Appendix C Common File Extensions
Appendix D AutoCAD Command Aliases
Appendix E Advanced Application Commands
Appendix F Advanced Application System Variables
Appendix G Basic AutoLISP Commands

Reference Materials

Drawing Sheet Sizes, Settings, and Scale Parameters
AutoCAD 2008 Menu Tree
Standards and Related Documents
Drafting Symbols
Standard Tables
Project and Drawing Problem Planning Sheet

Related Internet Resources

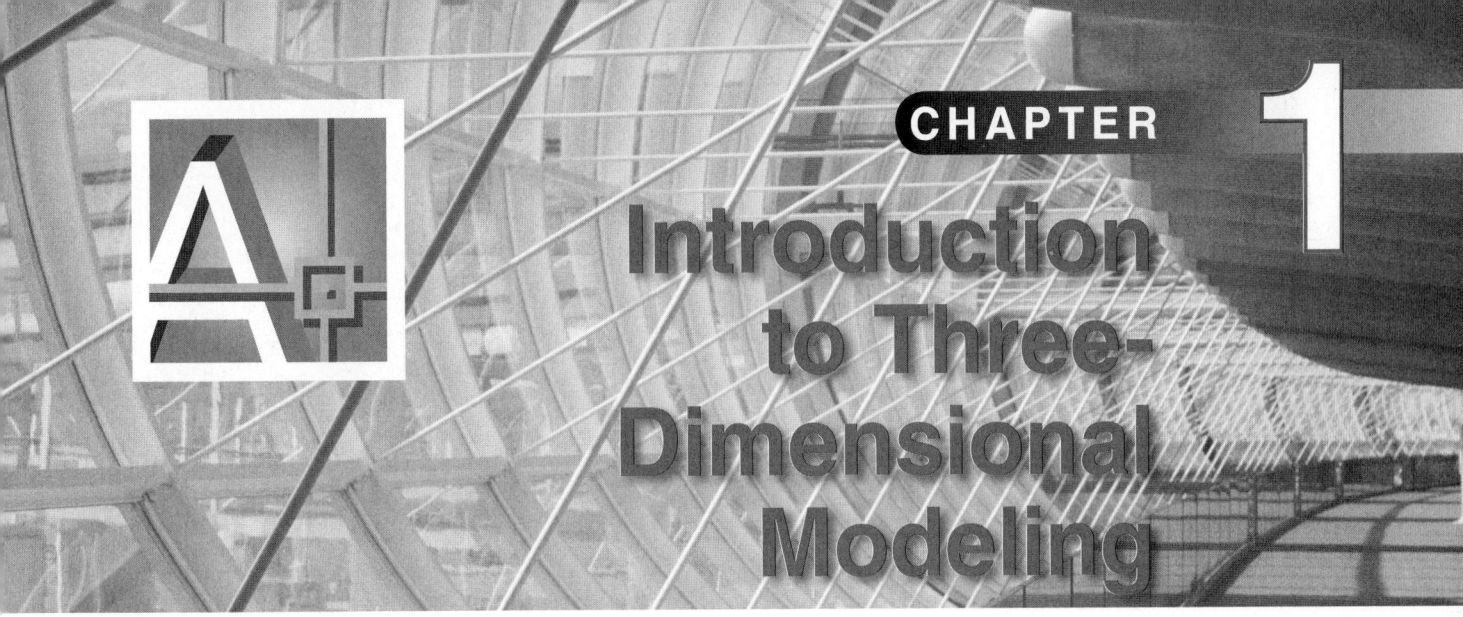

CHAPTER 1

Introduction to Three-Dimensional Modeling

Learning Objectives

After completing this chapter, you will be able to:

✓ Describe how to locate points in 3D space.
✓ Describe the right-hand rule of 3D visualization.
✓ Explain the function of the **Dashboard**.
✓ Display 3D objects from preset isometric viewpoints.
✓ Display 3D objects from any desired viewpoint.
✓ Set a visual style current.

The use of three-dimensional (3D) drawing and design as a tool is becoming more prevalent throughout industry. Companies are discovering the benefits of 3D modeling in design, visualization, testing, analysis, manufacturing, assembly, and marketing. Three-dimensional models also form the basis of computer animations, architectural walkthroughs, and virtual worlds used with virtual reality systems. Drafters who can design objects, buildings, and "worlds" in 3D are in demand for a wide variety of positions, both inside and outside of the traditional drafting and design disciplines.

The first eleven chapters of this book present a variety of techniques for drawing and designing in 3D. The skills you learn will provide you with the ability to construct any object in 3D and prepare you for entry into an exciting aspect of graphic communication.

To be effective in creating and using 3D objects, you must first have good 3D visualization skills, including the ability to see an object in three dimensions and to visualize it rotating in space. These skills can be obtained by using 3D techniques to construct objects and by trying to see two-dimensional sketches and drawings as 3D models. This chapter provides an introduction to several aspects of 3D drawing and visualization. Subsequent chapters expand on these aspects and provide a detailed examination of 3D drawing, editing, visualization, and display techniques.

Using Rectangular 3D Coordinates

In two-dimensional drawing, you see one plane defined by two dimensions. These dimensions are usually located on the X and Y axes, and what you see is the XY plane. However, in 3D drawing, another coordinate axis—the Z axis—is added. This results

Figure 1-1.
A comparison of 2D and 3D coordinate systems.

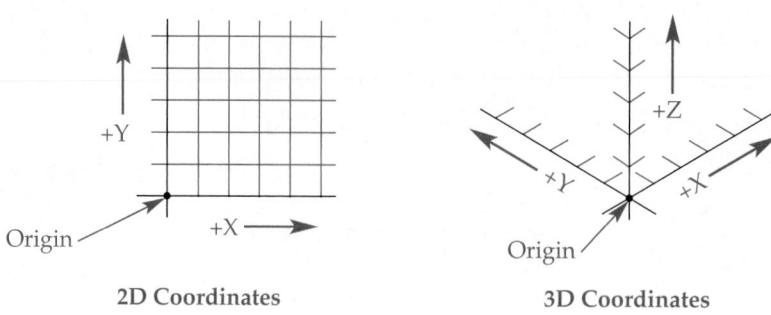

2D Coordinates   3D Coordinates

in two additional planes—the XZ plane and the YZ plane. If you are looking at a standard AutoCAD screen after AutoCAD is launched using the acad.dwt template, the positive Z axis comes directly out of the screen toward you. AutoCAD can only draw lines in 3D if it knows the X, Y, and Z coordinate values of each point on the object. For 2D drawing, only two of the three coordinates (X and Y) are needed.

Compare the 2D and 3D coordinate systems shown in **Figure 1-1**. Notice that the positive values of Z in the 3D coordinate system come up from the XY plane. Consider the surface of your computer screen as the XY plane. Anything behind the screen is negative Z and anything in front of the screen is positive Z.

The object in **Figure 1-2A** is a 2D drawing showing the top view of an object. The XY coordinate values of the origin and each point are shown. Think of the object as being drawn directly on the surface of your computer screen. However, this is actually a 3D object. When displayed in a pictorial view, the Z coordinates can be seen. Notice in **Figure 1-2B** that the first two values of each coordinate match the X and Y values of the 2D view. Three-dimensional coordinates are always expressed as (X,Y,Z). The 3D object was drawn using positive Z coordinates. Therefore, the object comes out of your computer screen. The object can also be drawn using negative Z coordinates. In this case, the object would extend behind, or into, the screen.

Study the nature of the rectangular 3D coordinate system. Be sure you understand Z values before you begin constructing 3D objects. It is especially important that you carefully visualize and plan your design when working with 3D constructions.

Figure 1-2.
A—The points making up a 2D object require only two coordinates. B—Each point of a 3D object must have an X, Y, and Z value. Notice that the first two coordinates (X and Y) are the same for each endpoint of a vertical line.

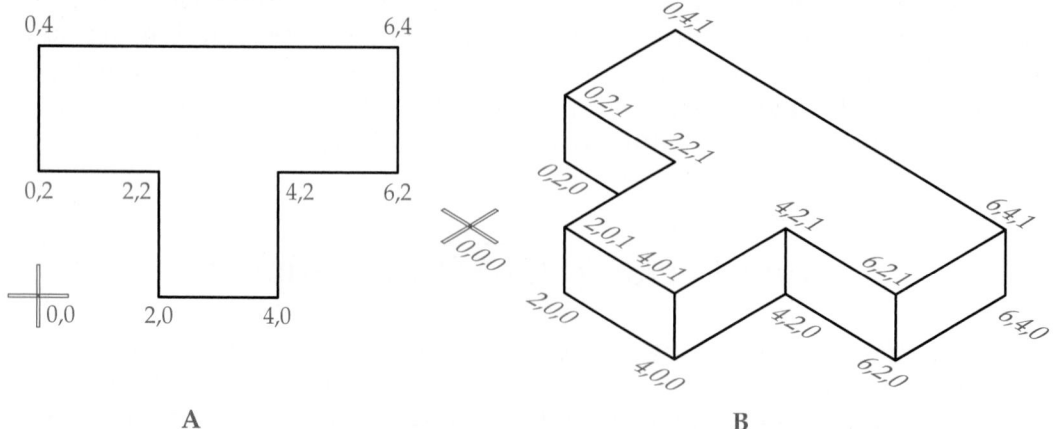

A   B

All points in three-dimensional space can be drawn using one of three coordinate entry methods—rectangular, spherical, or cylindrical. This chapter uses the rectangular coordinate entry method. Complete discussions on the spherical and cylindrical coordinate entry methods are provided in Chapter 4.

Exercise 1-1
Complete the exercise on the Student CD.

Right-Hand Rule of 3D Drawing

In order to effectively draw in 3D, you must be able to visualize objects in 3D space. The *right-hand rule* is a simple method for visualizing the 3D coordinate system. It is a representation of the positive coordinate values in the three axis directions. AutoCAD's user coordinate system (UCS) and world coordinate system (WCS) are based on this concept of visualization.

To use the right-hand rule, position the thumb, index finger, and middle finger of your right hand as shown in Figure 1-3. Although this may seem a bit unusual, it can do wonders for your understanding of the three axes. Imagine that your thumb is the X axis, your index finger is the Y axis, and your middle finger is the Z axis. Hold your hand in front of you so that your middle finger is directly pointing at you, as shown in Figure 1-3. This is the plan view of the XY plane. The positive X axis is pointing to the right and the positive Y axis is pointing up. The positive Z axis comes toward you and the origin of this system is the palm of your hand.

The concept behind the right-hand rule can be visualized even better if you are sitting at a computer and the AutoCAD graphics window is displayed. Make sure the current drawing is based on the acad.dwt template. If the UCS icon is not displayed in the lower-left corner of the screen, turn it on using the **View** pull-down menu. Now, orient your right hand as shown in Figure 1-3 and position it next to the UCS (or WCS) icon. Your index finger and thumb should point in the same directions as the Y and X axes, respectively, on the UCS icon. Your middle finger will be pointing out of the

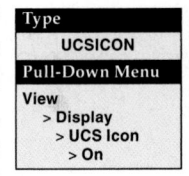

Type
UCSICON

Pull-Down Menu
View
> Display
> UCS Icon
> On

UCSICON

Figure 1-3.
Positioning your hand to use the right-hand rule to understand the relationship of the X, Y, and Z axes.

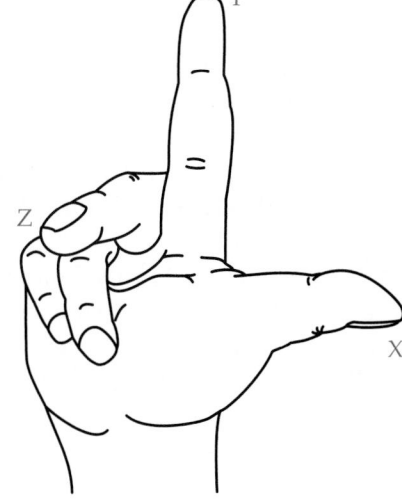

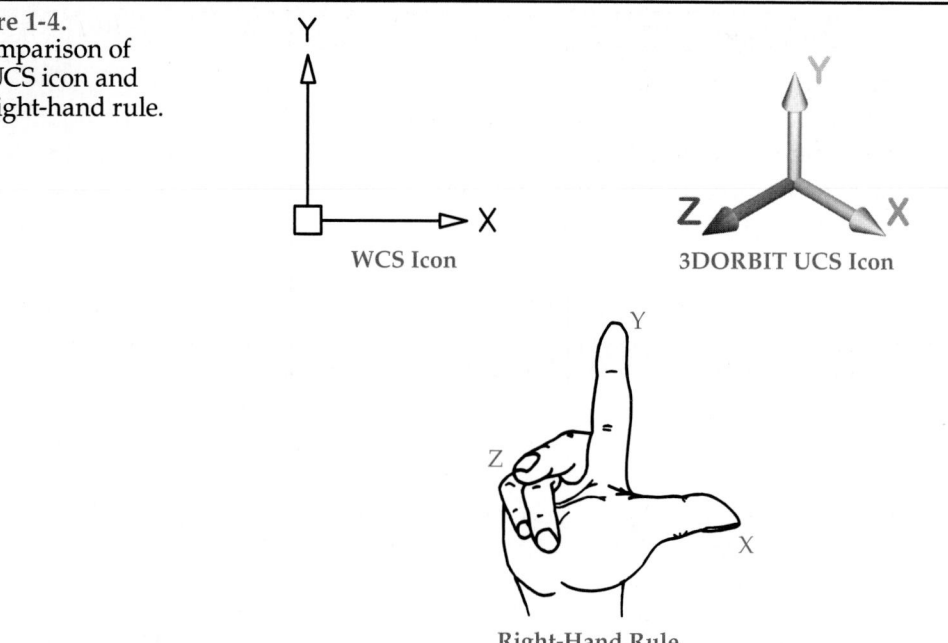

Figure 1-4.
A comparison of
the UCS icon and
the right-hand rule.

WCS Icon

3DORBIT UCS Icon

Right-Hand Rule

screen directly at you, which is the Z axis. See Figure 1-4. Notice the illustration on the right in the figure. This is the UCS icon shown when a 3D view is displayed using the **3DORBIT** command, which is discussed later in this chapter.

The right-hand rule can be used to eliminate confusion when rotating the UCS. The UCS can rotate on any of the three axes, just like a wheel rotates on an axle. Therefore, if you want to visualize how to rotate about the X axis, keep your thumb stationary and turn your hand either toward or away from you. If you wish to rotate about the Y axis, keep your index finger stationary and turn your hand to the left or right. When rotating about the Z axis, you must keep your middle finger stationary and rotate your entire arm.

If your 3D visualization skills are weak or you are having trouble visualizing different orientations of the UCS, use the right-hand rule. It is a useful technique for improving your 3D visualization skills. Rotating the UCS around one or more of the axes can become confusing if proper techniques are not used to visualize the rotation angles. A complete discussion of UCSs is provided in Chapter 4.

Basic Overview of the Interface

AutoCAD provides three working environments tailored to either 2D or 3D drawing or annotating a drawing. These environments are called workspaces and can be quickly restored. The workspace for 2D development based on the traditional AutoCAD screen layout is called AutoCAD Classic. The 2D Drafting & Annotation workspace is designed for drawing in 2D and annotating a drawing. It is similar to a streamlined version of the AutoCAD Classic layout. The workspace for 3D development is called 3D Modeling.

Workspaces can be created, customized, and saved to allow a variety of graphical user interface configurations. The principal component of the 3D Modeling workspace is the **Dashboard**, which is composed of several control panels. This section provides an overview of the 3D Modeling workspace and the layout of the **Dashboard** and its control panels.

Workspaces

A *workspace* is a drawing environment in which dockable windows, toolbars, menus, and **Dashboard** control panels are displayed for a specific task. A workspace stores not only which of these tools are visible, but also their on-screen locations. You can quickly change workspaces using the **WSCURRENT** command, **Tools** pull-down menu, or **Workspaces** toolbar, as shown in Figure 1-5. By default, the **Workspaces** toolbar is docked to the left of the **Layers** toolbar in the AutoCAD Classic workspace and to the left of the **Standard** toolbar in the 3D Modeling workspace. In the 2D Drafting & Annotation workspace, it is displayed to the left of the **Standard Annotation** toolbar. The 3D Modeling workspace is shown in Figure 1-6 with the **Tool Palettes** and **Dashboard** windows floating. By default, these are docked.

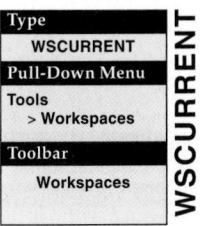

Figure 1-5.
Switching workspaces using the **Workspaces** toolbar.

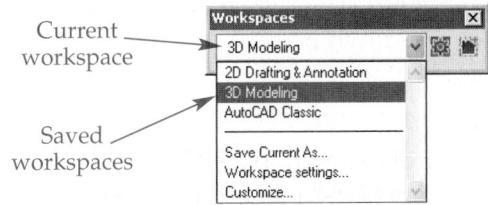

Figure 1-6.
The 3D Modeling workspace with a drawing file based on the acad3D.dwt template. The **Tool Palettes** and **Dashboard** windows have been floated.

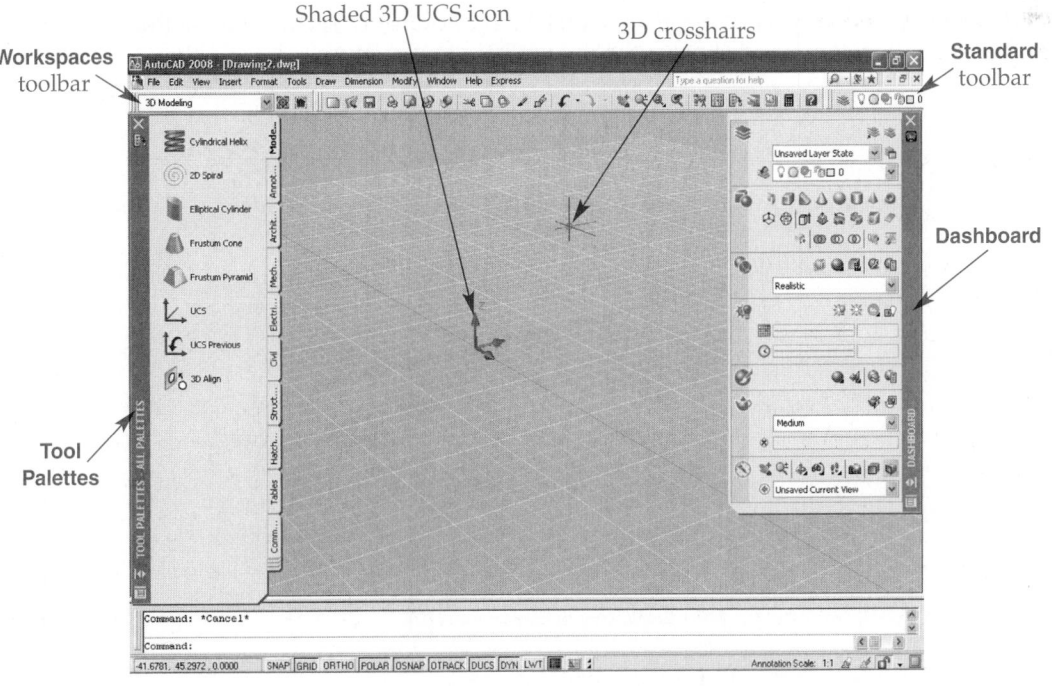

Dashboard

Working in the 3D modeling environment is efficient and intuitive with the use of the **Dashboard**. It is composed of *control panels* that enable you to work with 3D modeling, viewing, and presentation commands without using toolbars and menus. See **Figure 1-7.** Each control panel contains tools for working in 3D.

The **Dashboard** is a dockable window, or palette, that is, by default, docked on the right side of the screen. However, to increase the size of the drawing area, you may want to float the **Dashboard** by dragging it into the drawing area. Like all other palettes (dockable windows) and toolbars, the **Dashboard** can be docked on the left or right or moved to a floating position anywhere on the screen using the grab bar or title bar.

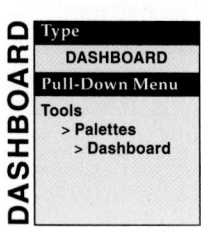

If you prefer to have the **Dashboard** floating, you may want to enable the auto-hide feature. When this feature is enabled, the **Dashboard** is reduced to just the title bar to allow more of the drawing area to be displayed. To display the full **Dashboard**, simply move the cursor over the title bar. Then, select the tool you want to use and when the cursor is moved back into the drawing area, the **Dashboard** is again reduced to the title bar. To enable the auto-hide feature, pick the **Auto-hide** button at the bottom of the **Dashboard** title bar.

You can close the **Dashboard** by picking the close control button (**X**) at the top of the title bar, or the right of the grab bar if docked. The **DASHBOARD** command can be used to display the **Dashboard**. The display of the **Dashboard** can also be toggled on and off using the **Tools** pull-down menu.

Control Panels

The seven default control panels that are displayed in the **Dashboard** in the 3D environment provide all of the functions you need to design, view, and render your 3D model. Each panel is identified by an icon in the upper-left corner of the panel. If you pause the cursor over the icon, the name of the panel is displayed. The panel can be expanded or condensed by picking this icon or by picking the maximize/minimize arrow in the

---

Figure 1-7.
The **Dashboard** is composed of control panels that provide access to 3D modeling, viewing, and presentation commands without using toolbars and menus.

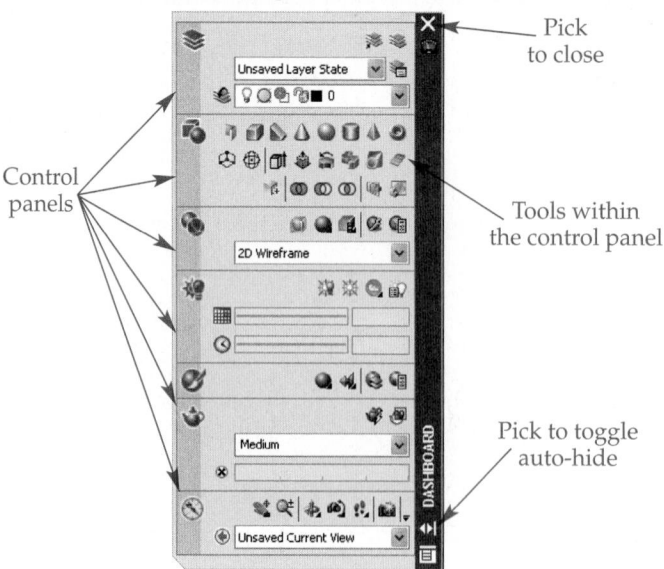

lower-left corner of the panel. See **Figure 1-8.** The maximize/minimize arrow is displayed when the cursor is over the vertical stripe on the left side of the panel. This stripe is dark gray when the panel can be expanded and orange when the panel is expanded.

You can display only those control panels that you need. Right-click anywhere on the **Dashboard** to display the shortcut menu. Select **Control panels** to display a cascading menu that contains a list of the available control panels. See **Figure 1-9.** The panels that are currently displayed in the **Dashboard** have a check mark next to their name. Select any of the checked control panels that you wish to remove from the current display. Unchecked control panels can be turned on by selecting their name.

Each control panel contains command tools. These are discussed in detail throughout the Modeling and Presentation sections of this book.

Figure 1-8.
Picking the control panel icon expands the control panel. The expanded control panel displays the minimize arrow.

Icon

Control panel name

Expanded area of the control panel

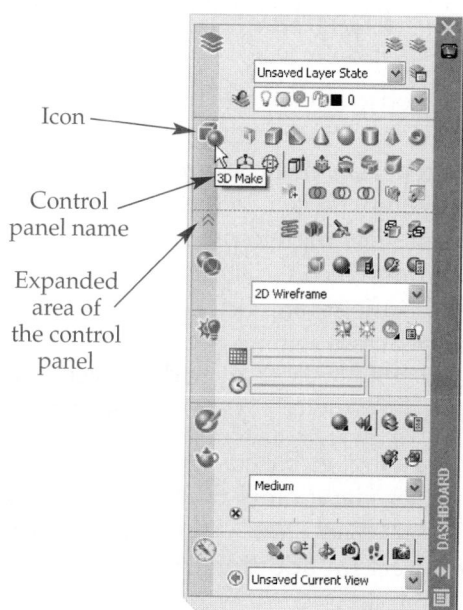

Figure 1-9.
Control panels can be displayed or hidden using the shortcut menu.

Available control panels

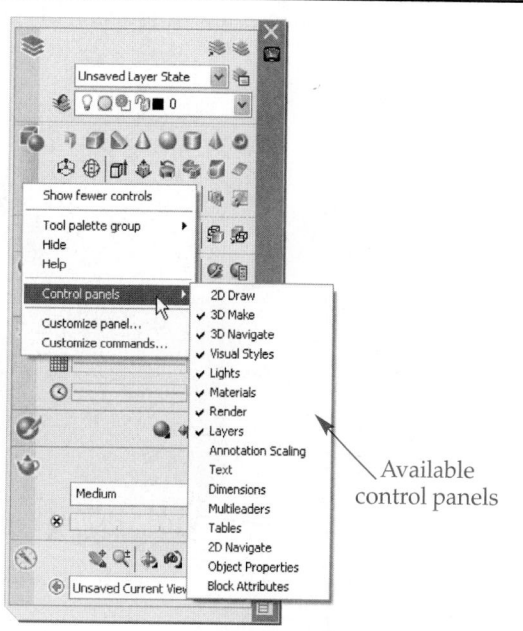

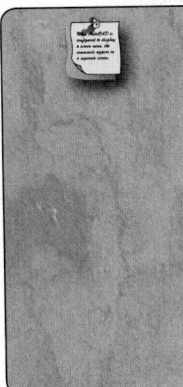

Displaying 3D Views

It does not do much good to understand how to draw in 3D space if you cannot see what you draw in three dimensions. The default view in the 2D environment based on the acad. dwt template is a plan, or top, view of the XY plane. The default view in the 3D environment based on the acad3D.dwt template is a pictorial, or 3D, view. AutoCAD provides several methods of changing your viewpoint to produce different pictorial views. The *viewpoint* is the location in space from which the object is viewed. The methods for changing your viewpoint include preset isometric and orthographic viewpoints, the **3DORBIT** command, and camera lens settings. Camera settings are discussed in detail in Chapter 15.

Isometric and Orthographic Viewpoint Presets

A 2D isometric drawing is based on angles of 120° between the three axes. AutoCAD provides preset viewpoints that allow you to view a 3D object from one of four isometric locations. See Figure 1-10. Each of these viewpoints produces an isometric view of the object. In addition, AutoCAD has presets for the six standard

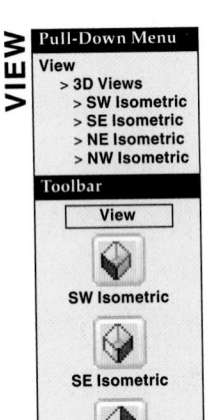

Figure 1-10.
There are four preset isometric viewpoints in AutoCAD. This illustration shows the direction from which the cube will be viewed for each of the presets. The grid represents the XY plane of the WCS.

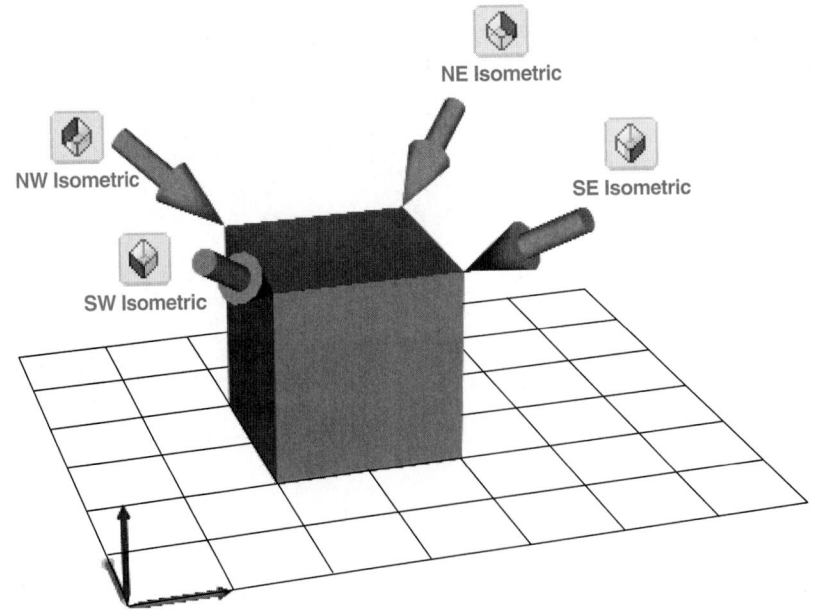

orthographic views of an object. The isometric and orthographic viewpoint presets are based on the WCS.

The four preset isometric views are southwest, southeast, northeast, and northwest. The six orthographic presets are top, bottom, left, right, front, and back. To switch your viewpoint to one of these presets, pick the drop-down list in the **3D Navigate** control panel of the **Dashboard** and select the view name. See **Figure 1-11.** You can also use the **View** pull-down menu or select the appropriate button on the **View** toolbar. This toolbar is not displayed by default.

Once you select a view, the viewpoint in the current viewport is automatically changed to display an appropriate isometric or orthographic view. Since these presets are based on the WCS, selecting a preset produces the same view of the object regardless of the current UCS.

A view that looks straight down on the current drawing plane is called a *plan view.* An important aspect of the orthographic presets is that selecting one not only changes the viewpoint, but, by default, it also changes the UCS to be plan to the orthographic view. All new objects are created on that UCS instead of the WCS (or previous UCS). Working with UCSs is explained in detail in Chapter 4. However, to change the UCS to the WCS type UCS to access the **UCS** command and then type W for the **World** option.

VIEW

Pull-Down Menu
View
> 3D Views
  > Top
  > Bottom
  > Left
  > Right
  > Front
  > Back

Toolbar
View
Top
Bottom
Left
Right
Front
Back

Dashboard
3D Navigate
> Top
> Bottom
> Left
> Right
> Front
> Back

Figure 1-11.
Selecting preset views. A—Using the **Dashboard**. B—Using the pull-down menu. C—Using the toolbar.

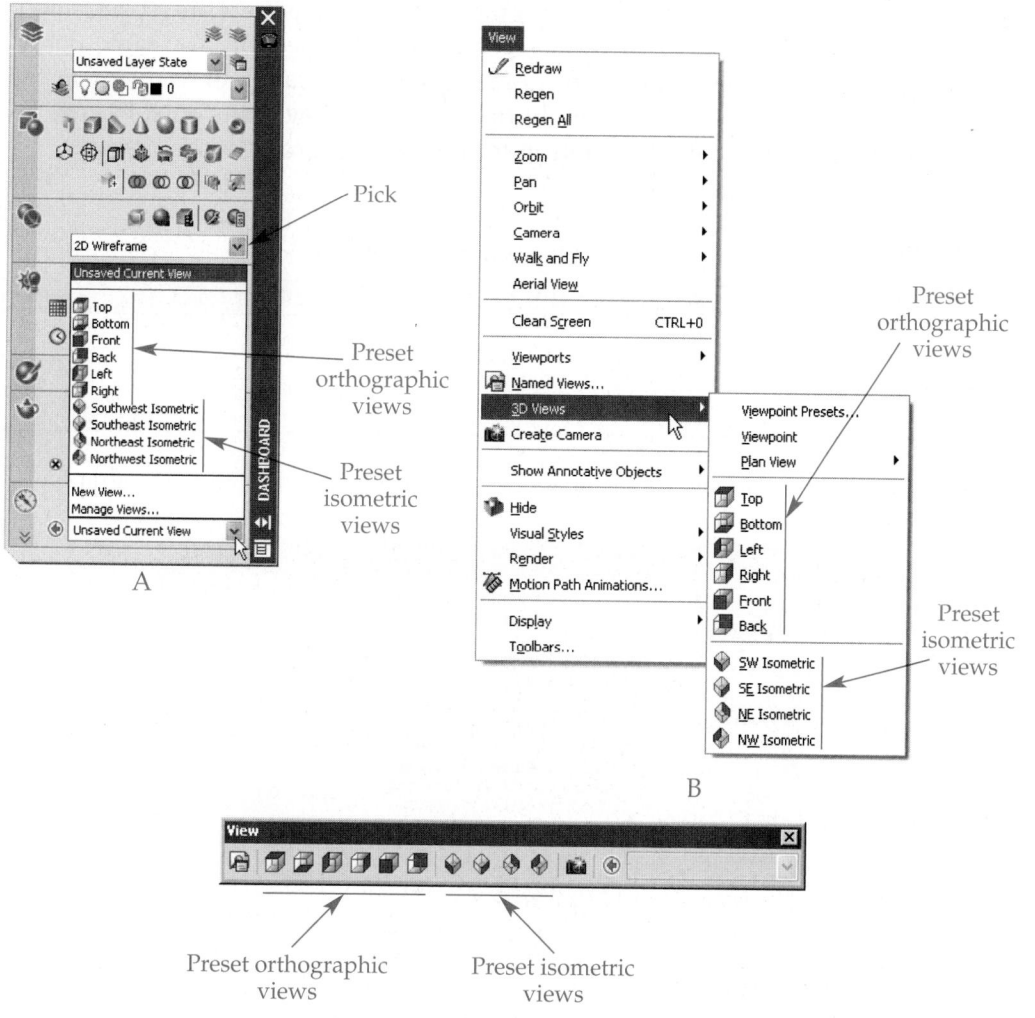

When an isometric or other 3D view is displayed, you can easily switch to a plan view of the current UCS using the **PLAN** command. Using the pull-down menus, select **View>3D Views>Plan View>World UCS**. There are also **Current UCS** and **Named UCS** options in the cascading menu. The **PLAN** command is discussed in more detail in Chapter 3.

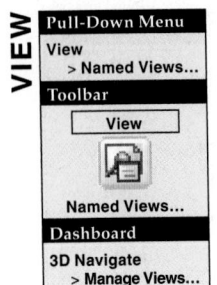

View Manager Dialog Box

The **View Manager** dialog box allows you to work with any named view, orthographic preset, or isometric preset. See **Figure 1-12.** To select a preset viewpoint, first expand the Preset Views branch in the tree on the left-hand side of the dialog box. The presets available here are the same as described above. To set a preset current, select its name in the tree and pick the **Set Current** button.

Using this dialog box, you can examine a view to determine if you like it before closing the dialog box. Select a view, such as SW Isometric, pick the **Set Current** button, and then pick the **Apply** button. You may have to move the dialog box to view the model. Use the same procedure to examine different views before you pick the **OK** button to close the dialog box.

> **NOTE**
>
> Selecting an orthographic view of a model using one of the methods described above produces a plan view, but it may not achieve the results you desire. Three-dimensional models can be displayed in AutoCAD using either parallel or perspective projection. Displaying a plan view in either projection is possible. However, a true plan view, as used in 2D orthographic projections, can only be created when the model is displayed as a parallel projection. You can quickly change the display from perspective to parallel, or vice versa, by picking the appropriate button in the **3D Navigate** control panel in the **Dashboard**. The button for the current projection is orange.

Exercise 1-2
Complete the exercise on the Student CD.

Figure 1-12.
The **View Manager** dialog box allows you to work with any named view and orthographic and isometric preset views.

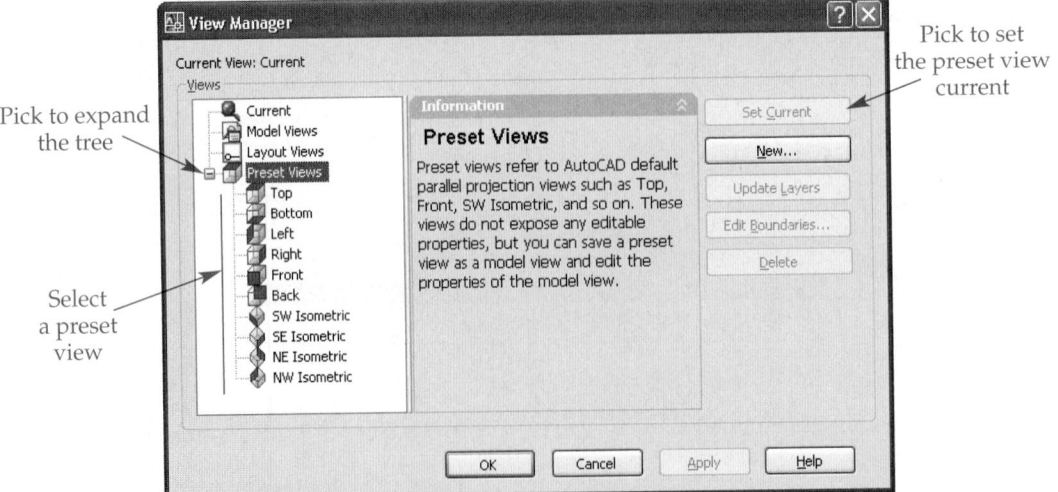

Unlimited Viewpoints

You are not limited to the preset isometric viewpoints. In fact, you can view a 3D object from an unlimited number of viewpoints. The **3DORBIT** command allows you to dynamically rotate the view of the objects to create a new viewpoint.

Notice that the cursor changes to a ball surrounded by two intersecting, circular arrows. To rotate the view, pick and hold the left mouse button. Then, drag the cursor around the drawing area. The viewpoint dynamically changes as you move the mouse. However, you are not rotating the *objects,* just the view. When you get the view you want, release the mouse button. The command remains active and you can further adjust the view. When done, right-click to display the shortcut menu. Then, select **Exit** from the menu. You can also press [Esc] to end the command.

When the command is initiated, the default orbit mode is referred to as *constrained orbit.* This means that the view can be rotated up 90°, down 90°, and horizontally 360°. You cannot display an upside-down view of the opposite side of the model.

Free orbit mode allows the model to be freely rotated in any direction without constraints. The command can be initiated in this mode using the **Orbit** toolbar, **View** pull-down menu, or the orbit flyout in the **3D Navigate** control panel in the **Dashboard**. If the command is initiated in constrained orbit, press the [2] key. In free orbit mode, a green circle appears in the middle of the current viewport. See Figure 1-13. This is called the trackball, or arcball. If you move the cursor inside of the trackball, it appears the same as in constrained orbit mode. If you move it outside of the trackball, the cursor appears as a single circle.

To change the view, pick anywhere inside of the trackball and drag the cursor. Picking outside of the trackball and dragging rotates the view about an axis extending out of the screen. Also, notice the circle handles at the four quadrants of the trackball. Picking in the right or left handle and dragging rotates the view about the vertical axis in the viewport. Picking in the top or bottom handle and dragging rotates the view about the horizontal axis in the viewport. When done, right-click to display the shortcut menu. Then, select **Exit** from the menu. You can also press [Esc] to end the command.

The **3DORBIT** command has many options. This discussion is merely an introduction to the command. The command options are covered in detail in Chapter 3.

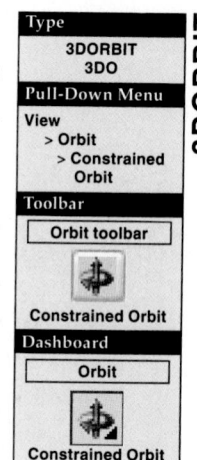

Figure 1-13.
Using the **3DORBIT** command in free orbit mode to change the viewpoint.

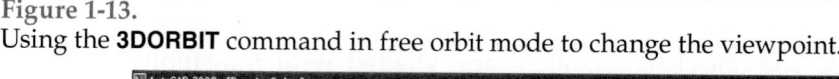

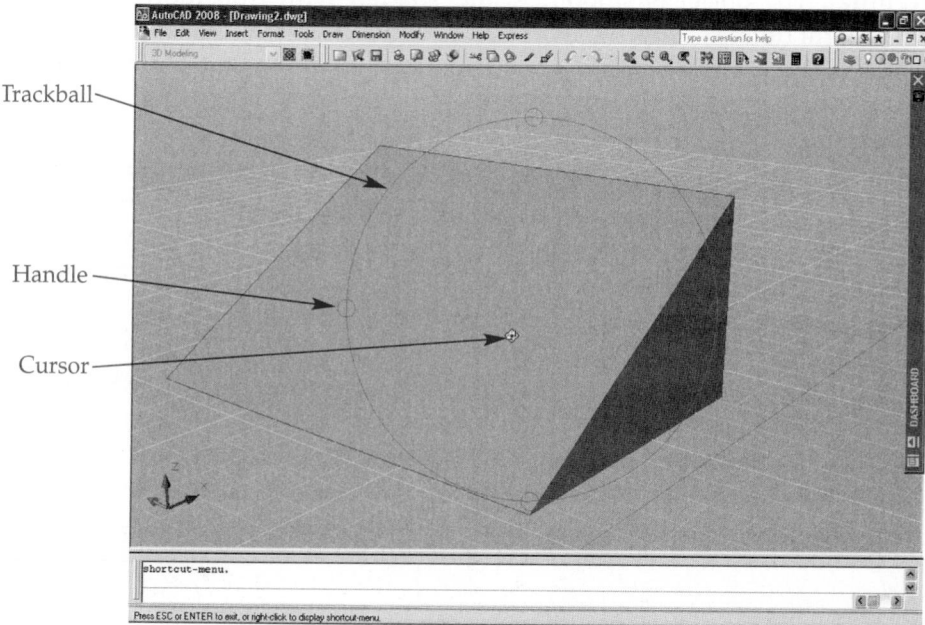

Trackball

Handle

Cursor

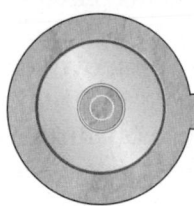

Exercise 1-3

Complete the exercise on the Student CD.

Introduction to Visual Styles

VSCURRENT

Type
VSCURRENT

Pull-Down Menu
View
> Visual Styles
> 2D Wireframe
> 3D Wireframe
> 3D Hidden
> Conceptual
> Realistic

Toolbar
Visual Styles

2D Wireframe

3D Wireframe

3D Hidden

Conceptual

Realistic

Dashboard
Visual Styles
> 2D Wireframe
> 3D Wireframe
> 3D Hidden
> Conceptual
> Realistic

A 3D model can be displayed in a variety of visual styles. A *visual style* controls the display of edges and shading in a viewport. There are five basic visual styles—2D wireframe, 3D wireframe, 3D hidden, conceptual, and realistic. A *wireframe display* shows all lines on the object, including those representing back or internal features. A *hidden display* suppresses the display of lines that would normally be hidden.

Examples of the visual styles are shown in Figure 1-14. To change styles, you can use the **VSCURRENT** command, **View** pull-down menu, **Visual Styles** toolbar, or the drop-down list in the **Visual Styles** control panel in the **Dashboard**. See Figure 1-15.

In the default 3D environment based on the acad3D.dwt template, the default display mode, or visual style, is Realistic. In this visual style, all objects appear as solids and are displayed in their assigned layer colors. Other display options are available. These options are discussed in detail in Chapter 3, but are given here as an introduction.

- **2D Wireframe.** Displays all lines of the model using assigned linetypes and lineweights. The 2D UCS icon and 2D grid are displayed, if turned on. If the **HIDE** command is used to display a hidden line view, use the **REGEN** command to redisplay the wireframe view.
- **3D Wireframe.** Displays all lines of the model. The 3D grid and the 3D UCS icon are displayed, if turned on.
- **3D Hidden.** Displays all visible lines of the model from the current viewpoint and hides all lines not visible. Objects are not shaded or colored.
- **Conceptual.** The object is smoothed and shaded with transitional colors to help highlight details.
- **Realistic.** Displays the shaded and smoothed model using assigned layer colors and materials (see Chapter 14).

NOTE

When the visual style is 2D Wireframe, you can quickly view the model with hidden lines removed by selecting **Hide** from the **View** pull-down menu or typing HIDE. The **HIDE** command can be used at any time to remove hidden lines from a wireframe display. If **HIDE** is used when the current visual style is 3D Wireframe, Conceptual, or Realistic, the 3D Hidden visual style is set current.

Exercise 1-4

Complete the exercise on the Student CD.

Figure 1-14.
The five AutoCAD default visual styles. A—2D Wireframe. B—3D Wireframe. C—3D Hidden. D—Conceptual. E—Realistic.

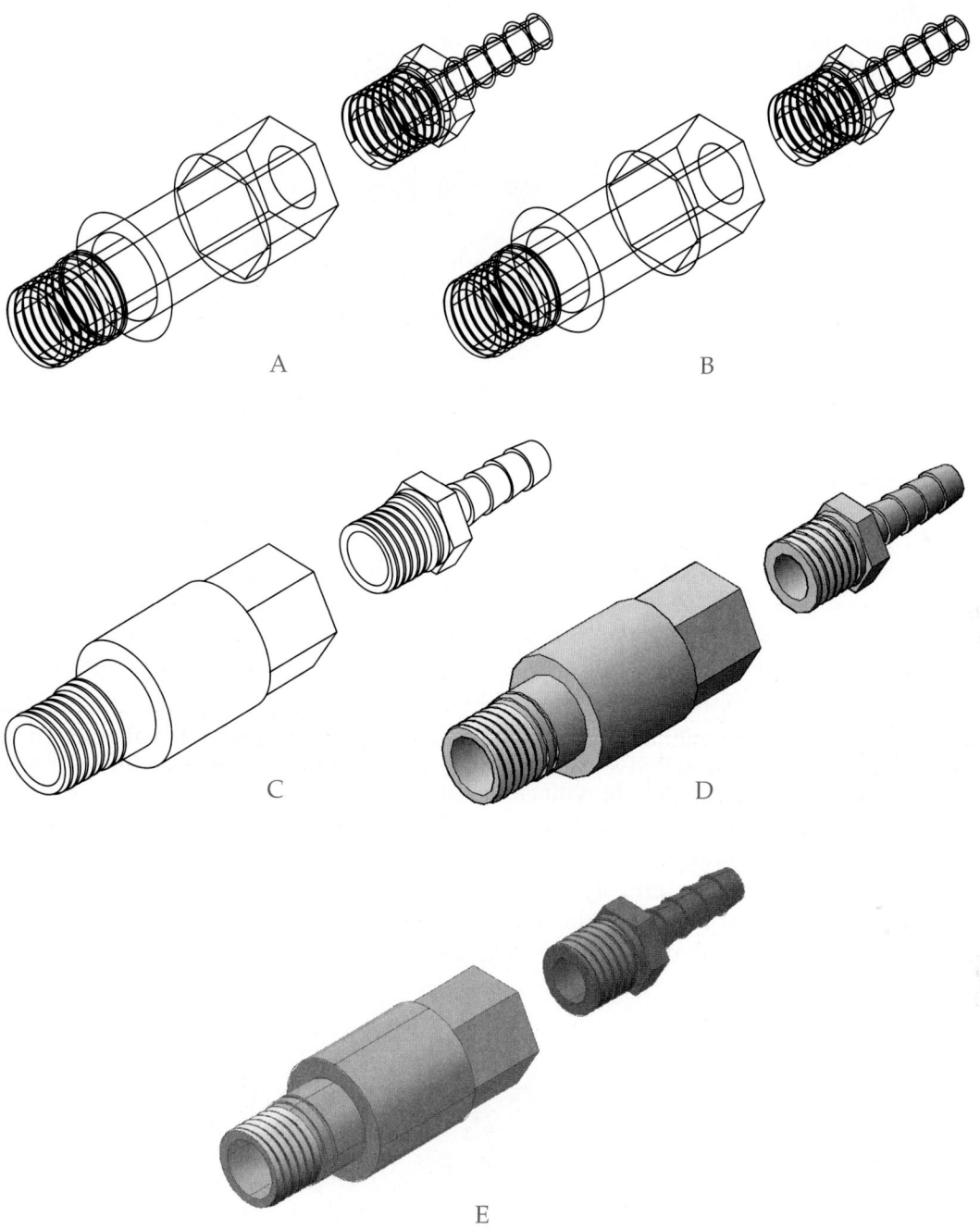

Figure 1-15.
A visual style can be set current using the drop-down list in the **Visual Style** control panel in the **Dashboard**.

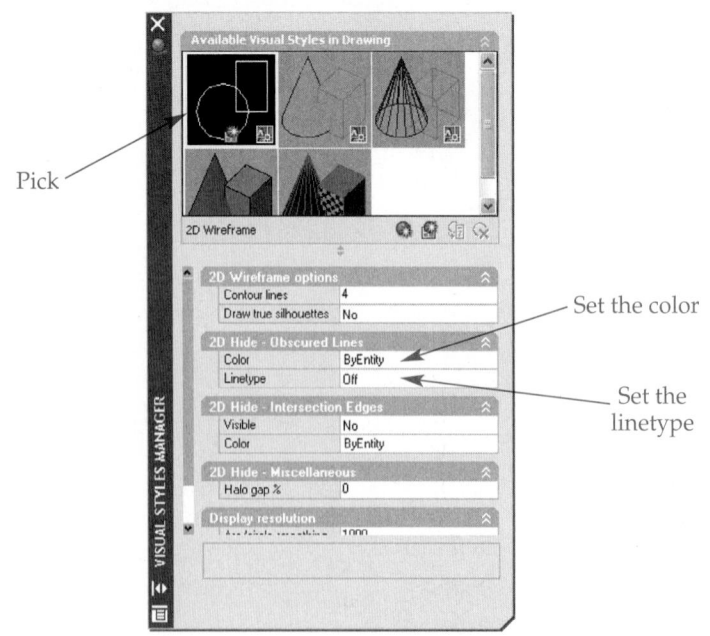

Pick to display visual styles

Pick a visual style

Hidden Line Settings

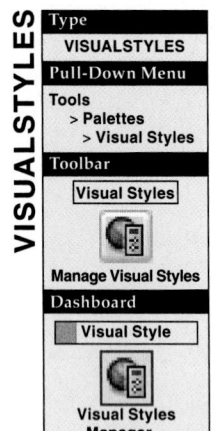

Type
VISUALSTYLES
Pull-Down Menu
Tools
> **Palettes**
> **Visual Styles**
Toolbar
Visual Styles

Manage Visual Styles
Dashboard
Visual Style

Visual Styles Manager...

By default, the **HIDE** command removes hidden lines from the display when the 2D Wireframe visual style is current. However, you can have hidden lines displayed in a different linetype and color instead of removed. To set this, open the **Visual Styles Manager** palette. See **Figure 1-16.** This can be accessed by typing the command or using the **Tools** pull-down menu, **Visual Style** control panel in the **Dashboard**, or **Visual Styles** toolbar. Using this palette, you can control all available settings for wireframe, hidden line removal, and shaded displays in AutoCAD. See Chapter 13 for a detailed discussion of this palette.

To change the hidden line style in the 2D Wireframe visual style, select the corresponding image tile at the top of the **Visual Styles Manager**. In the **2D Hide - Obscured Lines** category of the palette are drop-down lists from which you can select a linetype and color.

Figure 1-16.
The manner in which hidden lines appear in hidden displays when the **2D Wireframe** visual style is current is controlled in the **Visual Styles Manager** palette.

Pick

Set the color

Set the linetype

When the **Linetype** drop-down list is set to Off, the display of hidden lines is suppressed by the **HIDE** command. This is the default setting. When a linetype is selected from the drop-down list, hidden lines are displayed in that linetype after the **HIDE** command is used. The linetypes available in the drop-down list are not the same as the linetypes loaded into your drawing.

When a linetype is selected, you can also change the display color of the hidden lines. Simply pick a color in the **Color** drop-down list. To have the hidden lines displayed in the same color as the object, select ByEntity, which is the default. The color setting has no effect when the **Linetype** drop-down list is set to Off.

NOTE

Making changes in the **Visual Styles Manager** redefines the visual style.

3D Construction Techniques

Before constructing a 3D model, you should determine the purpose of your design. What will the model be used for—presentation, analysis, or manufacturing? This helps you determine which tools you should use to construct and display the model. Three-dimensional objects can be drawn as solids or surfaces and displayed in wireframe, hidden line removed, and shaded views.

A *wireframe object,* or model, is an object constructed of lines in 3D space. Wireframe models are hard to visualize because it is difficult to determine the angle of view and the nature of the surfaces represented by the lines. The **HIDE** command has no effect on a wireframe model because there is nothing to hide. All lines are always visible because there are no surfaces or faces between the lines. Wireframe models have very limited applications.

Surface modeling represents solid objects by creating a skin in the shape of the object. However, there is nothing inside of the object. Think of a surface model as a balloon filled with air. A surface model looks more like the real object than a wireframe and can be used for rendering. Surface models are constructed in specialized software used for applications such as civil engineering terrain modeling, automobile body design, sheet metal design and fabrication, and animation.

Like surface modeling, *solid modeling* represents the shape of objects, but also provides data related to the physical properties of the objects. Solid models can be analyzed to determine mass, volume, moments of inertia, and centroid. A solid model is not just a skin, it represents a solid object. Some third-party programs allow you to perform finite element analysis on the model. In addition, solid models can be rendered. Most 3D objects are created as solid models.

In AutoCAD, solid models can be created from primitives. *Primitives* are basic shapes used as the foundation to create complex shapes. Some of these basic shapes include boxes, cylinders, spheres, and cones. Primitives can be modified to create a finished product. See **Figure 1-17.**

Surface and solid models can be exported from AutoCAD for use in animation and rendering software, such as Autodesk 3ds max® or Autodesk VIZ®. Rendered models can be used in any number of presentation formats, including slide shows, black and white or color prints, and animation recorded to videotape, CD-ROM, or DVD. Surface and solid models can also be used to create virtual worlds for virtual reality applications.

Figure 1-17.
A—These two cylinders and the box are solid primitives. B—With a couple of quick modifications, the large cylinder becomes a shaft with a machined keyway.

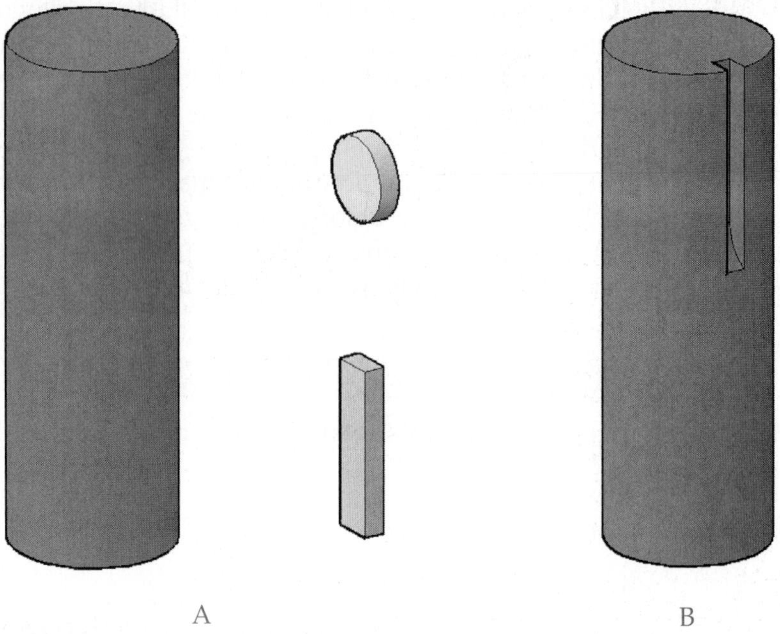

A

B

Guidelines for Working with 3D Drawings

Working in 3D, like working with 2D drawings, requires careful planning to efficiently produce the desired results. The following guidelines can be used when working in 3D.

Planning

✓ Determine the type of final drawing you need, and the manner in which it will be displayed. Then, choose the method of 3D construction that best suits your needs—wireframe, surface, or solid.

✓ When drawing objects requiring only one pictorial view, draw in isometric mode. While this is 2D, not true 3D, it is the quickest and most versatile method. Ellipses and arcs are easy to draw and work with in isometric drawings.

✓ It is best to use AutoCAD's 3D commands to construct objects and layouts that need to be viewed from different angles for design purposes.

✓ Construct only the details needed for the function of the drawing. This saves space and time, and makes visualization much easier.

✓ Use object snap modes in a pictorial view to save having to create new UCSs.

✓ Keep in mind that when the grid is displayed, the pattern appears at the current elevation and parallel to the XY plane of the current UCS.

✓ Create layers having different colors for different drawing objects. Turn them on and off as needed or freeze those not being used.

Editing

✓ Use the **Properties** window to change the color, layer, or linetype of 3D objects.

✓ Use grips to edit a solid-modeled object (see Chapter 10).

✓ Do as much editing as possible from a 3D viewpoint. It is quicker and the results are immediately seen.

Displaying

- ✓ Use the **HIDE** command and visual styles to help visualize complex drawings.
- ✓ To change views quickly, use the preset isometric views, **3DORBIT**, and **PLAN**.
- ✓ Use the **VIEW** command to create and save 3D views for quicker pictorial displays. This avoids having to repeatedly use the **3DORBIT** command.
- ✓ Freeze unwanted layers before displaying objects in 3D, and especially before using **HIDE**. AutoCAD regenerates layers that are turned off, which may cause an inaccurate hidden display to be created. Frozen layers are not regenerated.
- ✓ Before using **HIDE**, zoom in on the part of a drawing to display. This saves time in regenerating the view because only the objects that are visible are regenerated.
- ✓ You may have to slightly move objects that touch or intersect if the display removes a line you need to see or plot.

Chapter Test

Answer the following questions. Write your answers on a separate sheet of paper or complete the electronic chapter test on the Student CD.

1. What are the three coordinates needed to locate any point in 3D space?
2. In a 2D drawing, what is the value for the Z coordinate?
3. What purpose does the right-hand rule serve?
4. Which three fingers are used in the right-hand rule?
5. What is the definition of a *viewpoint?*
6. What is the function of the **Dashboard** and its control panels?
7. How do you turn the display of individual control panels on or off in the **Dashboard**?
8. How can you quickly change the display from perspective projection to parallel projection, or vice versa?
9. How many preset isometric viewpoints does AutoCAD have? List them.
10. How does changing the UCS impact using one of the preset isometric viewpoints?
11. List the six preset orthographic viewpoints.
12. When using a preset orthographic viewpoint, what happens to the UCS?
13. Which command allows you to dynamically change your viewpoint using an on-screen trackball?
14. Define *wireframe display.*
15. Define *hidden display.*
16. Define *wireframe object.*
17. Define *surface model.*
18. Define *solid model.*
19. Define *primitive.*
20. Briefly describe how to have hidden lines displayed in red when the **HIDE** command is used.

A—These four solid primitives can be used to quickly create a complex solid, called a composite solid. B—The primitives are copied, moved, rotated, and arrayed as needed. Then, the **UNION** and **SUBTRACT** commands are used to create the composite solid. The final result is a pulley on a splined shaft, shown here rendered with an anodized metal finish.

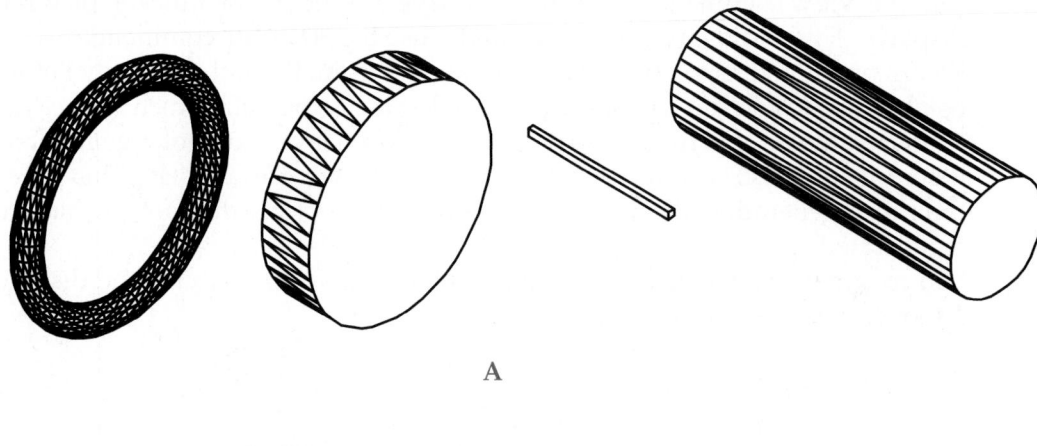

A

B

Creating Primitives and Composites

Learning Objectives

After completing this chapter, you will be able to:

✓ Construct 3D solid primitives.
✓ Explain the dynamic feedback presented when constructing solid primitives.
✓ Create complex solids using the **UNION** command.
✓ Remove portions of a solid using the **SUBTRACT** command.
✓ Create a new solid from the interference volume between two solids.
✓ Create regions.

Overview of Solid Modeling

In Chapter 1 you were introduced to the three basic forms of 3D modeling—wireframe objects, solid models, and surface models. Solid models are probably the most useful, and hence most common, type of 3D modeling. A solid model accurately and realistically represents the shape and form of a final object. In addition, a solid model contains data related to the object's volume, mass, and centroid.

Solid modeling is very flexible. You can start with solid primitives, such as a box, cone, or cylinder, and perform a variety of editing functions. You can think of creating a solid model as working with modeling clay. Starting with a basic block of clay, you can add more clay, remove clay, cut holes, round edges, etc., until you have arrived at the final shape and form of the object.

PROFESSIONAL TIP

You can use snaps on solid objects. For example, you can snap to the center of a solid sphere using the **Center** object snap. The **Endpoint** object snap can be used to select the corners of a box, apex of a cone, corners of a wedge, etc.

Constructing Solid Primitives

As you learned in Chapter 1, a primitive is a basic building block. The eight *solid primitives* in AutoCAD are a box, cone, cylinder, polysolid, pyramid, sphere, torus, and wedge. These primitives can also be used as building blocks for complex solid models. This section provides detailed information on drawing all of the solid primitives. All of the 3D modeling primitive commands can be accessed using the **3D Make** control panel in the **Dashboard**, the **Modeling** toolbar, the **Draw** pull-down menu, or by typing the name of the 3D modeling primitive. See Figure 2-1.

The information required to draw a solid primitive depends on the type of primitive being drawn. For example, to draw a solid cylinder you must provide a center point for the base, a radius or diameter of the base, and the height of the cylinder. A variety of command options are available when creating primitives, but each primitive is constructed using just a few basic dimensions. These are shown in Figure 2-2.

Certain familiar editing commands can be used on solid primitives. For example, you can fillet or chamfer the edges of a solid primitive. In addition, there are other editing commands that are specifically for use on solids. You can also perform Boolean operations on solids. These operations allow you to add one solid to another, subtract one solid from another, or create a new solid based on how two solids overlap.

Figure 2-1.
A—The **Modeling** cascading menu in the **Draw** pull-down menu. B—The **Modeling** toolbar. C—The **3D Make** control panel in the **Dashboard**.

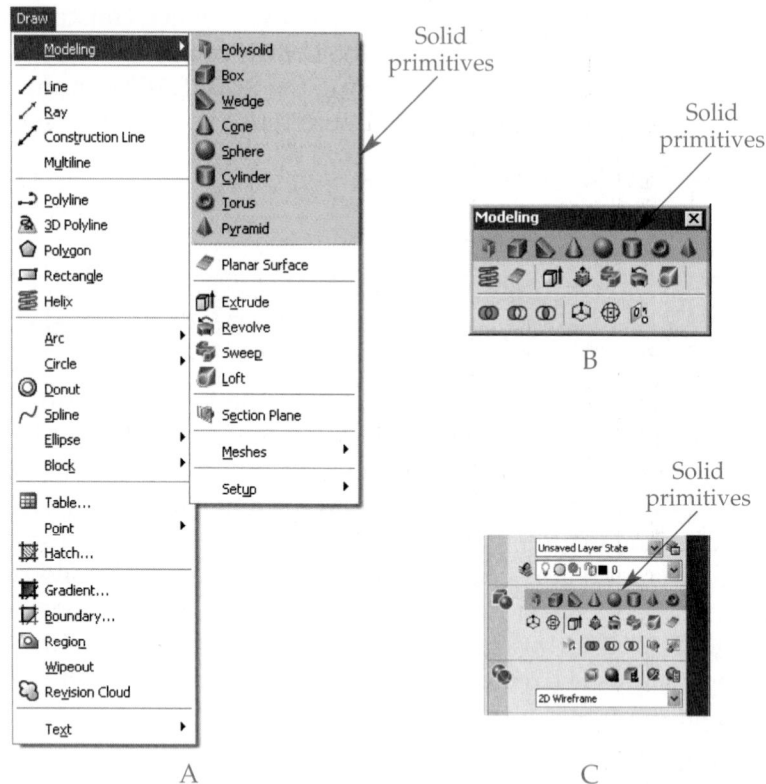

Figure 2-2.
An overview of AutoCAD's solid primitives and the dimensions required to draw them.

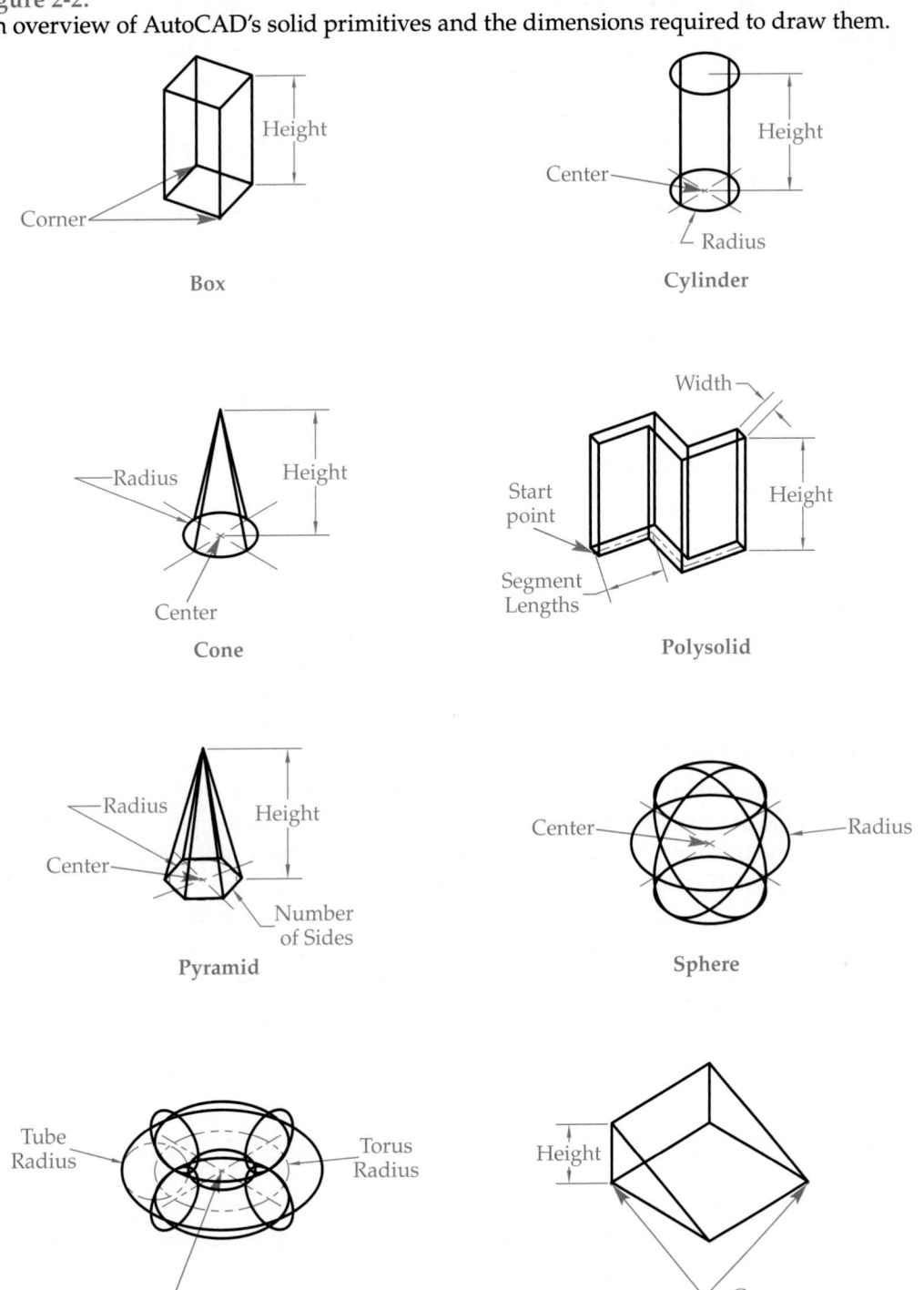

There are also *surface model primitives*: box, cone, dish, dome, mesh, pyramid, sphere, torus, and wedge. These primitives are created as polyface objects with only surface properties. They contain no volumetric data. These primitives can be created by typing 3D and then entering the primitive; typing AI_ and the name of the primitive, such as AI_BOX; or selecting **Draw>Modeling>Meshes** and the name of the mesh. For information about the surface primitives, refer to the AutoCAD online documentation. The surface modeling primitives and meshes described above are considered "legacy" commands. Their function in modeling applications is limited and they are, at best, difficult to use. Most important, the solid model editing functions in AutoCAD do not work with these surfaces. Focus your study on the use of AutoCAD's solid modeling features, which are far more productive and intuitive.

Using Dynamic Input and Dynamic Feedback

Dynamic input enables you to construct models in a "heads up" fashion with minimal eye movement around the screen. When a command is initiated, the command prompts are then displayed in the dynamic input area, which is at the lower-right corner of the crosshairs. As the pointer is moved, the dynamic input area follows it. The dynamic input area displays values of the cursor location, dimensions, command prompts, and command options (in a drop-down list). Coordinates and dimensions are displayed in boxes called *input fields*. When command options are available, a drop-down list arrow appears. Press the down arrow key on the keyboard to display the list. You can use your pointer to select the option, or press the down arrow key until a dot appears by the desired option, then press [Enter].

For example, after selecting a modeling command such as **BOX**, the first item that appears in the dynamic input area is the prompt to specify the first corner and a display of the X and Y coordinate values of the crosshairs. At this point you can use the pointer to specify the first corner or type coordinate values. Type the X value and then a comma or the [Tab] key to move to the Y value input box. This locks the typed value and any movement of the pointer will not change it.

When using dynamic input to enter coordinate values from the keyboard, it is important that you avoid pressing [Enter] until you have completed the coordinate entry. When you press [Enter], all of the displayed coordinate values are accepted and the next command prompt appears.

In addition to entering coordinate values for sizes of solid primitives, you can provide direct distance dimensions. For example, the second prompt of the **BOX** command is for the second corner of the base. When you move the pointer, two dimensional input fields appear. Also, notice that a preview of the base is shown in the drawing area. This is the *dynamic feedback* that AutoCAD provides as you create a solid primitive. See **Figure 2-3A**. If you enter a dimension at the keyboard and press the [Tab] key, the value is the length of the side. Then, press the left mouse button to set the base. But, if you enter a value followed by a comma, the dynamic input area changes to display X and Y coordinate boxes. In this case, the values entered are the X, Y, and Z coordinates of the opposite corner of the box base.

Figure 2-3.
A—Specifying the base of a box with dynamic input on. Notice the preview of the base.
B—Setting the height of a box with dynamic input on. Notice the preview of the height.

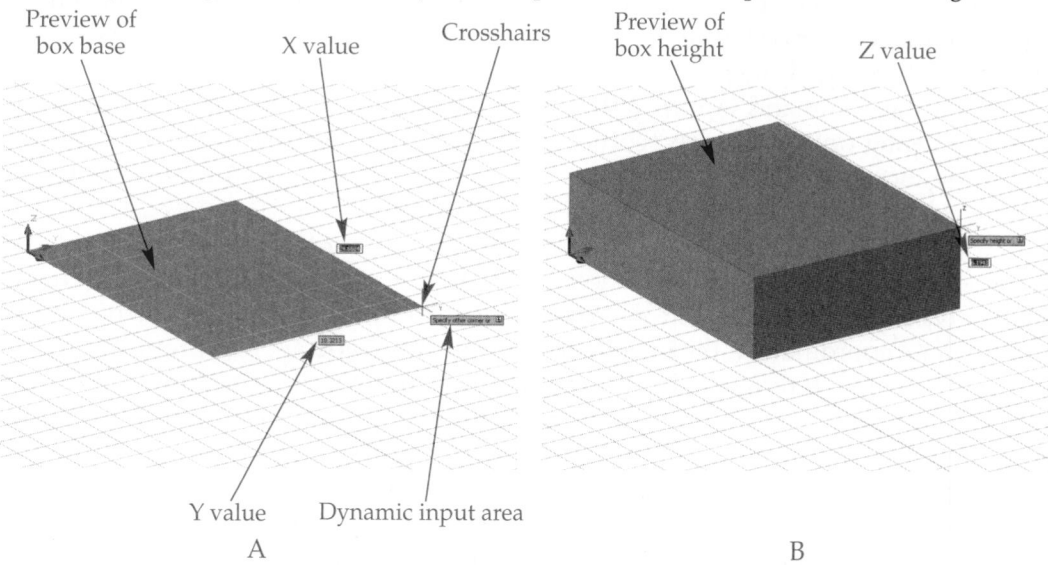

A

B

After establishing the location and size of the box base, the next prompt asks you to specify the height. Again, you can either enter a direct dimension value and press [Enter] or select the height with the pointer. See **Figure 2-3B.** AutoCAD provides dynamic feedback on the height of the box as the pointer is moved.

PROFESSIONAL TIP

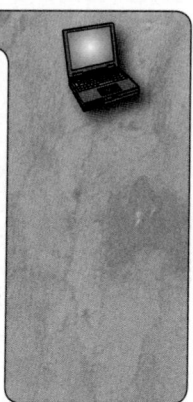

When the **BOX** command prompts you to specify the other corner, and dynamic input is on, you can provide the coordinates for the opposite corner of the box to see the shape and size of the box before completing the command. To do this, type the X coordinate value and a comma. This changes the dynamic input area from direct distance input to coordinate input. Next, type the Y value and a comma, type the Z value, and press the [Tab] key. When all three values are entered, the preview is displayed, but the command is not complete. Press the [Tab] key to cycle between the coordinate input boxes and type new values as needed. To complete the command, press the [Enter] key.

NOTE

The techniques described above can be used with any form of dynamic input. The current input field is always highlighted. You can always enter a value and use the [Tab] key to lock the input and move to the next field.

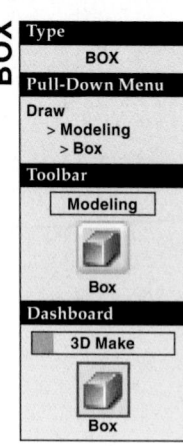

Type
BOX
Pull-Down Menu
Draw
> Modeling
> Box
Toolbar
Modeling

Box
Dashboard
3D Make

Box

Box

A *box* has six flat sides and forms square corners. It can be constructed starting from an initial corner or the center. See Figure 2-4. A cube can be constructed, as well as a box with unequal sides.

When the command is initiated, you are prompted to select the first corner or enter the **Center** option. The first corner is one corner on the base of the box. The center is the geometric center of the box, as shown in Figure 2-4. If you select the **Center** option, you are next prompted to select the center point.

After selecting the first corner or center, you are prompted to select the other corner or enter the **Cube** or **Length** option. The "other" corner is the opposite corner of the box base if you enter an XY coordinate, or the opposite corner of the box if you enter an XYZ coordinate. If the **Length** option is entered, you are first prompted for the length of one side. If dynamic input is on, you can also specify a rotation angle. After entering the length, you are prompted for the width of the box base. If the **Cube** option is selected, the length value is applied to all sides of the box.

Once the length and width of the base are established, you are prompted for the height, unless the **Cube** option was selected. Either enter the height or select the **2point** option. This option allows you to pick two points on screen to set the height. The box is created.

PROFESSIONAL TIP

If dynamic UCS is on, you can select a surface that is not parallel to the current UCS on which to locate the object. This feature is called a *dynamic UCS* and discussed in detail in Chapter 4.

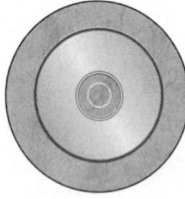

Exercise 2-1
Complete the exercise on the Student CD.

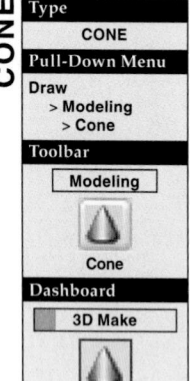

Type
CONE
Pull-Down Menu
Draw
> Modeling
> Cone
Toolbar
Modeling

Cone
Dashboard
3D Make

Cone

Cone

A *cone* has a circular or elliptical base with edges that converge at a single point. The cone may be *truncated* so the top is flat and the cone does not have an apex. See Figure 2-5. When the command is initiated, you are prompted for the center point of the cone base or to enter an option. If you pick the center, you must then set the radius of the base. To specify a diameter, enter the **Diameter** option after specifying the center.

Figure 2-4.
A—A box created using the **Cube** option.
B—A box created by selecting the center point.

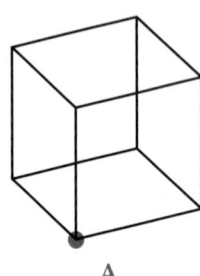

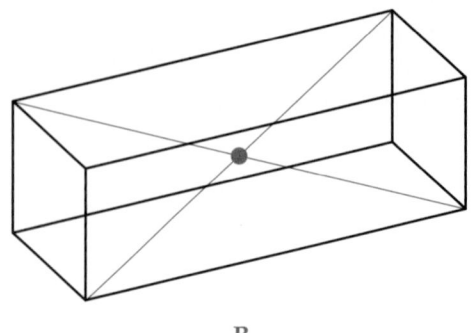

A

B

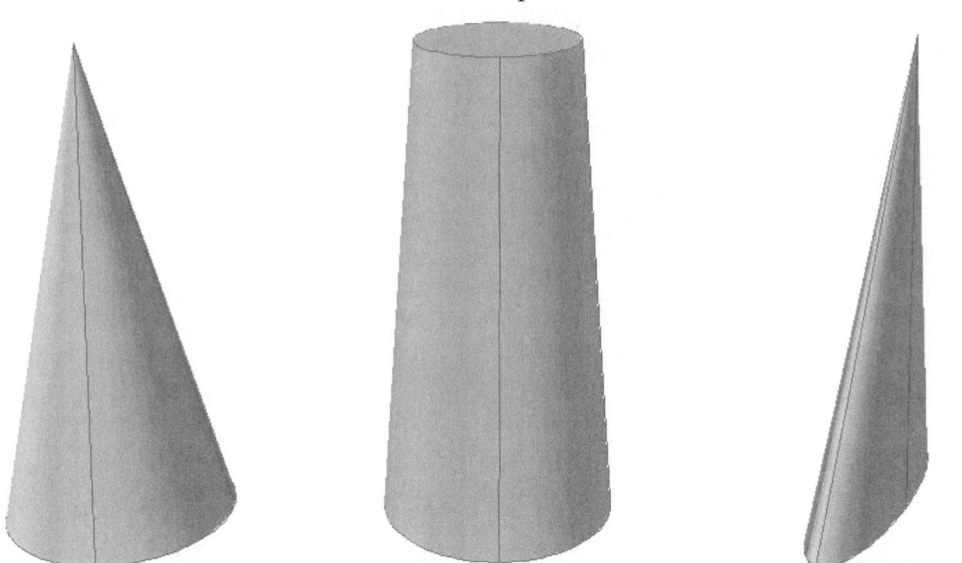

The **3P**, **2P**, and **Ttr** options are used to define a circular base using either three points on the circle, two points on the circle, or two points of tangency on the circle and a radius. The **Elliptical** option is used to create an elliptical base.

If the **Elliptical** option is entered, you are prompted to pick both endpoints of one axis and then one endpoint of the other axis. If the **Center** option is entered after the **Ellipse** option, you are asked to select the center of the ellipse and then pick an endpoint on each of the axes.

After the base is defined, you are asked to specify a height. You can enter a height or enter the **2point**, **Axis endpoint**, or **Top radius** option. The **2point** option is used to set the height by picking two points on screen. The distance between the points is the height.

The **Axis endpoint** option allows you to orient the cone at any angle, regardless of the current UCS. For example, to place a tapered cutout in the end of a block, first create a construction line. Refer to Figure 2-6. Then, locate the cone base and give a coordinate location of the apex, or axis endpoint. You can then use editing commands to subtract the cone from the box to create the tapered hole. See Chapters 10 and 11 for model editing details.

The **Top radius** option allows you to specify the radius of the top of the cone. If this option is not used, the radius is zero, which creates a pointed cone. Setting the radius to a value other than zero produces a *frustum cone,* or a cone where the top is truncated and does not come to a point.

Figure 2-6.
A—Cones can be positioned relative to other objects using the **Axis endpoint** option. B—The cone is subtracted from the box.

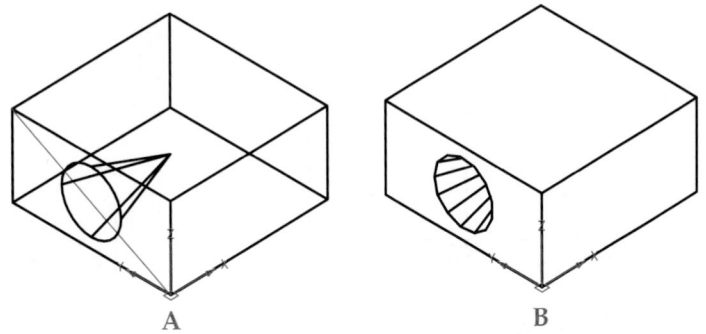

A   B

Type
CYLINDER

Pull-Down Menu

Draw
   > Modeling
     > Cylinder

Toolbar
Modeling
Cylinder

Dashboard
3D Make
Cylinder

Cylinder

A *cylinder* has a circular or elliptical base and edges that extend perpendicular to the base. See Figure 2-7. When the command is initiated, you are prompted for the center point of the cylinder base or to enter an option. If you pick the center, you must then set the radius of the base. To specify a diameter, enter the **Diameter** option after specifying the center.

The **3P**, **2P**, and **Ttr** options are used to define a circular base using either three points on the circle, two points on the circle, or two points of tangency on the circle and a radius. The **Elliptical** option is used to create an elliptical base.

If the **Elliptical** option is entered, you are prompted to pick both endpoints of one axis and then one endpoint of the other axis. If the **Center** option is entered, you are asked to select the center of the ellipse and then pick an endpoint on each of the axes.

After the base is defined, you are asked to specify a height or to enter the **2point** or **Axis endpoint** option. The **2point** option is used to set the height by picking two points on screen. The distance between the points is the height. The **Axis endpoint** option allows you to orient the cone at any angle, regardless of the current UCS, just as with a cone.

The **Axis endpoint** option is useful for placing a cylinder inside of another object to create a hole. The cylinder can then be subtracted from the other object to create a hole. Refer to Figure 2-8. If the axis endpoint does not have the same X and Y coordinates as the center of the base, the cylinder is tilted from the XY plane.

If polar tracking is on when using the **Axis endpoint** option, you can rotate the cylinder axis 90° from the current UCS Z axis, and then turn the cylinder to any preset polar increment. See Figure 2-9A. If the polar tracking vector is parallel to the Z axis of the current UCS, the tooltip displays a positive or negative Z value. See Figure 2-9B.

Figure 2-7.
A—A circular cylinder.
B—An elliptical cylinder.

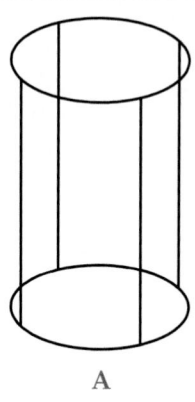
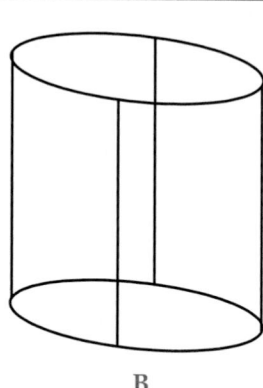

A   B

Figure 2-8.
A—A cylinder is drawn inside of another cylinder using the **Axis endpoint** option. B—The large cylinder has a hole after **SUBTRACT** is used to remove the small cylinder.

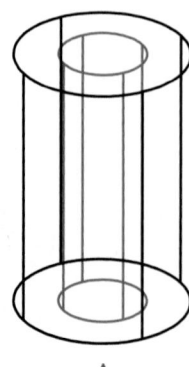
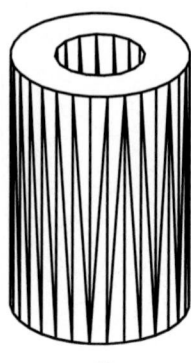

A   B

Figure 2-9.
A—If polar tracking is on, you can rotate the cylinder axis 90° from the current UCS Z axis, and then move the cylinder to any angle in the XY plane. B—If the polar tracking vector is moved parallel to the current Z axis of the UCS, the tooltip displays a positive or negative Z dimension.

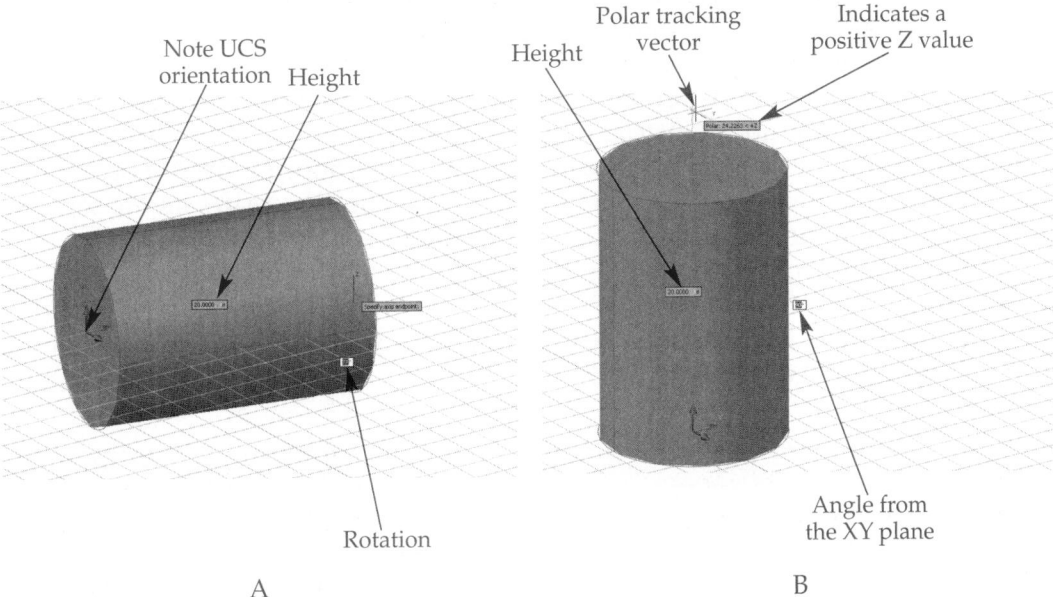

A   B

Polysolid

The *polysolid* primitive is simply a polyline that is constructed as a solid object by applying a width and height to the polyline. Many of the options used to create polylines are used with the **POLYSOLID** command. The principal difference is that a solid object is constructed using **POLYSOLID**.

When the command is initiated, you are prompted to select the first point or enter an option. By default, the width of the polysolid is equally applied to each side of the line you draw. This is center justification. Using the **Justify** option, you can set the justification to center, left, or right. The justification applies to all segments created in this command session. See **Figure 2-10.** If you select the wrong justification option, you must exit the command and begin again.

The default width is .25 units and height is four units. These values can be changed using the **Height** and **Width** options of the command. The height value is saved in the **PSOLHEIGHT** system variable. The width value is saved in the **PSOLWIDTH** system variable. Using these system variables, the default width and height can be set outside of the command.

Type
POLYSOLID
Pull-Down Menu
Draw
> Modeling
> Polysolid
Toolbar
Modeling
Polysolid
Dashboard
3D Make
Polysolid

POLYSOLID

Figure 2-10.
When you begin the **POLYSOLID** command, use the **Justify** option to select the alignment.

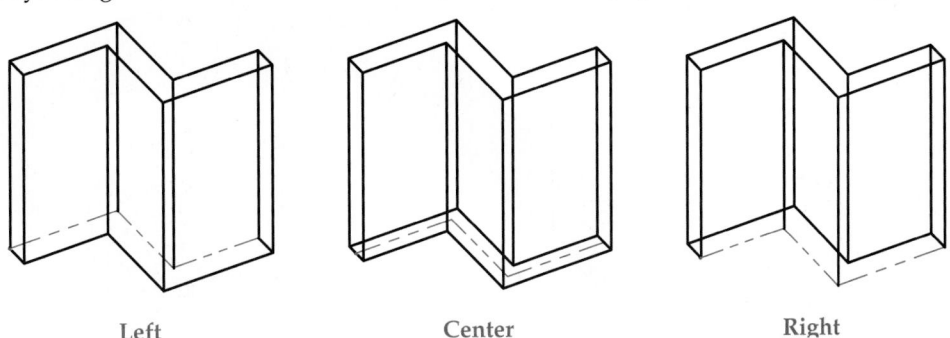

Left   Center   Right

The **Object** option allows you to convert an existing 2D object into a polysolid. AutoCAD entities such as lines, circles, arcs, polylines, polygons, and rectangles can be converted. The 2D object cannot be self intersecting. Some objects, such as 3D polylines and revision clouds, cannot be converted.

Once you have set the first point on the polysolid, pick the endpoint of the first segment. Continue adding segments as needed and press [Enter] to complete the command. After the first point is set, you can enter the **Arc** option. The current segment will then be created as an arc instead of a straight line. See Figure 2-11. Arc segments will be created until you enter the **Line** option. The suboptions for the **Arc** option are:

- **Close.** If there are two or more segments, this option creates an arc segment between the active point and the first point of the polysolid.
- **Direction.** Specifies the tangent direction for the start of the arc.
- **Line.** Returns the command to creating straight line segments.
- **Second point.** Locates the second point of a two-point arc. This is not the endpoint of the segment.

PROFESSIONAL TIP

The **Object** option of the **POLYSOLID** command is a powerful tool for converting 2D objects to 3D solids. For example, you can create a single-line wall plan using a polyline and then quickly convert it to a 3D model.

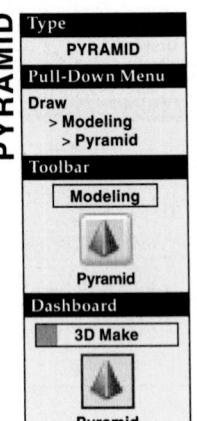

Pyramid

A *pyramid* has a base composed of straight-line segments and edges that converge at a single point. The pyramid base can be composed of three to 32 sides, much like a 2D polygon. A pyramid may be drawn with a pointed apex or as a *frustum pyramid*, which has a truncated, or flat, apex. See Figure 2-12.

Once the command is initiated, you are prompted for the center of the base or to enter an option. To set the number of sides on the base, enter the **Sides** option. Then, enter the number of sides. You are returned to the first prompt.

The base of the pyramid can be drawn by either picking the center and the radius

Figure 2-11.
The **Arc** option of the **POLYSOLID** command is used to create curved segments.

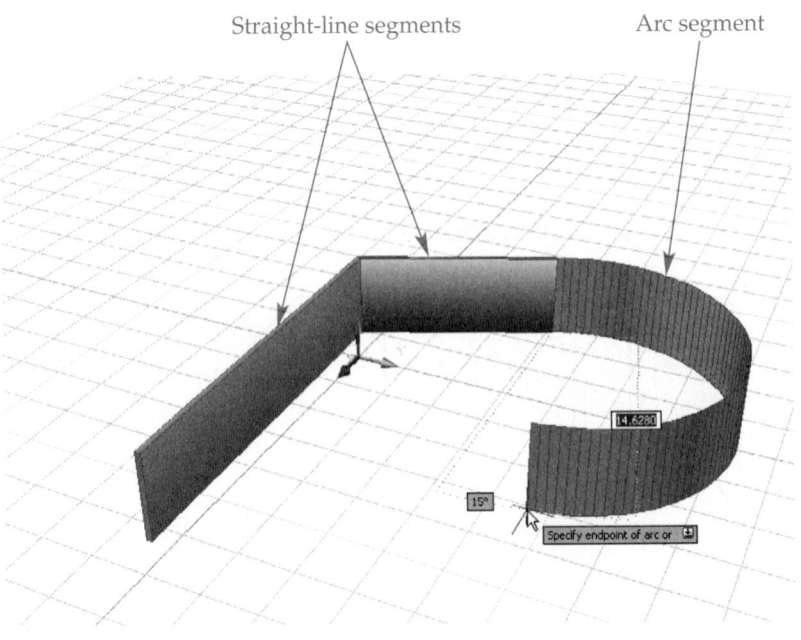

Straight-line segments

Arc segment

Figure 2-12.
A sampling of pyramids that can be constructed with the **PYRAMID** command.

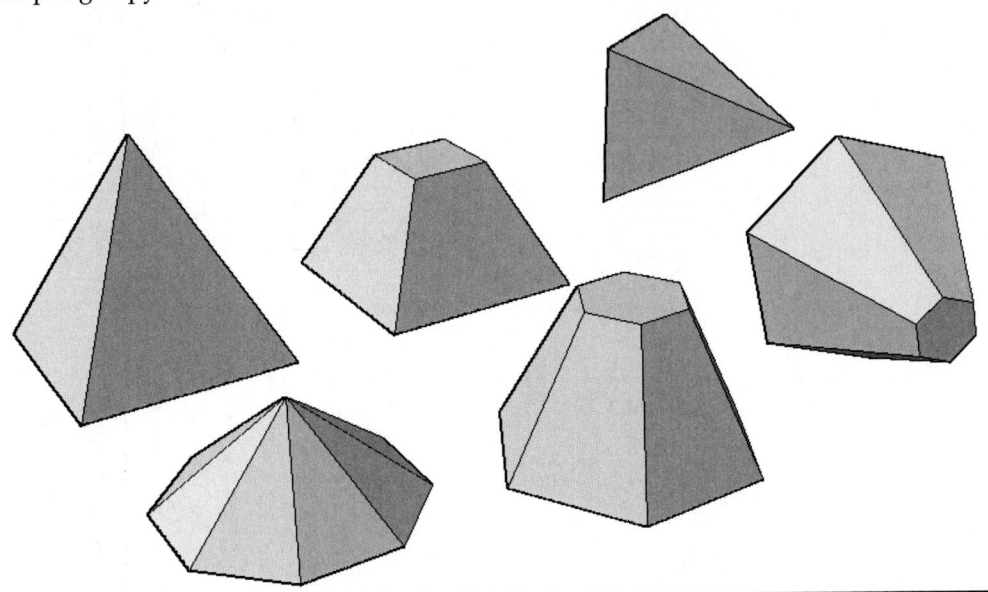

of a base circle or by picking the endpoints of one side. The default method is to pick the center. Simply specify the center and then set the radius. To pick the endpoints of one side, enter the **Edge** option. Then, pick the first endpoint of one side followed by the second endpoint. If dynamic input is on, you can also set a rotation angle for the pyramid.

If drawing the base from the center point, the polygon is circumscribed about the base circle by default. To inscribe the polygon on the base circle, enter the **Inscribed** option before setting the radius. To change back to a circumscribed polygon, enter the **Circumscribed** option before setting the radius.

After locating and sizing the base, you are prompted for the height. To create a frustum pyramid, enter the **Top radius** option. Then, set the radius of the top circle. The top will be either inscribed or circumscribed based on the base circle. You are then returned to the height prompt.

The height value can be set by entering a direct distance. You can also use the **2point** option to set the height. With this option, pick two points on screen. The distance between the two points is the height value. The **Axis endpoint** option can also be used to specify the center of the top in the same manner as a cone or cylinder.

Sphere

A *sphere* is a round, smooth object like a baseball or globe. Once the command is initiated, you are prompted for the center of the sphere or to enter an option. If you pick the center, you must then set the radius of the sphere. To specify a diameter, enter the **Diameter** option after specifying the center. The **3P**, **2P**, and **Ttr** options are used to define the sphere using either three points on the surface of the sphere, two points on the surface of the sphere, or two points of tangency on the surface of the sphere and a radius.

Spheres and other curved objects can be displayed in a number of different ways. The manner in which you choose to display these objects should be governed by the display requirements of your work. Notice in **Figure 2-13A** the lines that define the shape of the spheres in a wireframe display. These lines are called *contour lines,* also known as *tessellation lines.* The **Visual Styles Manager** can be used to set the display of contour lines and silhouettes on spheres and other curved 3D surfaces for a given visual style. See **Figure 2-14.**

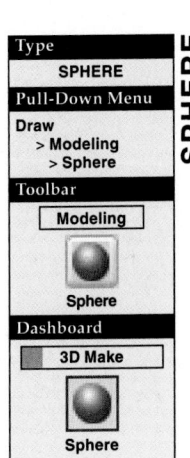

Figure 2-13.
A—The **Draw true silhouettes** setting is No and four contour lines are used. B—The **Draw true silhouettes** setting is No and 20 contour lines are used. C—The **Draw true silhouettes** setting is Yes and four contour lines are used. D—The **Draw true silhouettes** setting is Yes and the **HIDE** command is used with the 2D Wireframe visual style set current.

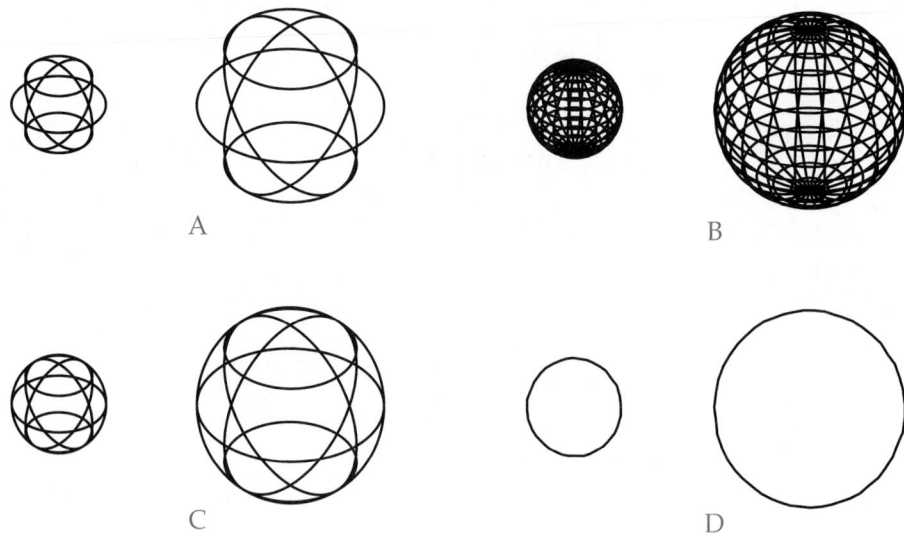

Figure 2-14.
The **2D Wireframe options** area of the **Visual Styles Manager** is used to control the display of contour lines and silhouettes on spheres and other curved 3D surfaces in a given visual style.

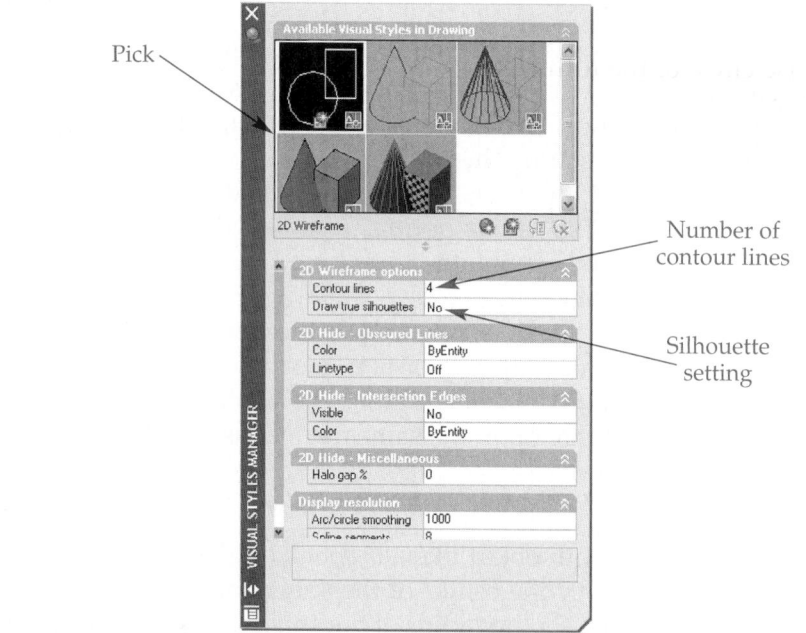

With the **Visual Styles Manager** displayed, select the 2D Wireframe image tile. The **Contour lines** setting in the **2D Wireframe options** area establishes the number of lines used to show the shape of curved objects. A similar setting appears in the 3D Wireframe, 3D Hidden, Conceptual, and Realistic visual styles if their **Edge mode** option is set to Isolines. The default value is four, but can be set to a value from zero to 2047. **Figure 2-13B** displays spheres with 20 contour lines. It is best to use a lower number during construction and preliminary displays of the model and, if needed, higher settings for more realistic visualization. The contour lines setting is also available in the **Display** tab of the **Options** dialog box or by typing ISOLINES.

The **Draw true silhouettes** setting in the **2D Wireframe options** area controls the display of silhouettes on 3D solid curved surfaces. The setting is either Yes or No. Notice the sphere silhouette in **Figures 2-13C** and **2-13D.** The **Draw true silhouettes** setting is stored in the **DISPSILH** system variable.

PROFESSIONAL TIP

The **Visual Style** control panel in the **Dashboard** can also be used to change the contour lines and silhouettes without changing the visual style definition. This is discussed in Chapter 3.

Torus

A basic *torus* is a cylinder bent into a circle, similar to a doughnut or inner tube. There are three types of tori. See **Figure 2-15.** A torus with a tube diameter that touches itself has no center hole. This is the second type of torus and is called *self intersecting.* To create a self-intersecting torus, the tube radius must be greater than the torus radius. The third type of torus looks like a football. It is drawn by entering a negative torus radius and a positive tube diameter of greater value, i.e. –1 and 1.1.

Once the command is initiated, you are prompted for the center of the torus or to enter an option. If you pick the center, you must then set the radius of the torus. To specify a diameter, enter the **Diameter** option after specifying the center. This defines a base circle that is the centerline of the tube. The **3P**, **2P**, and **Ttr** options are used to define the base circle of the torus using either three points, two points, or two points of tangency and a radius.

Once the base circle of the torus is defined, you are prompted for the tube radius or to enter an option. The tube radius defines the cross-sectional circle of the tube. To specify a diameter of the cross-sectional circle, enter the **Diameter** option. You can also use the **2point** option to pick two points on screen that define the diameter of the cross-sectional circle.

Figure 2-15.
The three types of tori are shown as wireframes and with hidden lines removed.

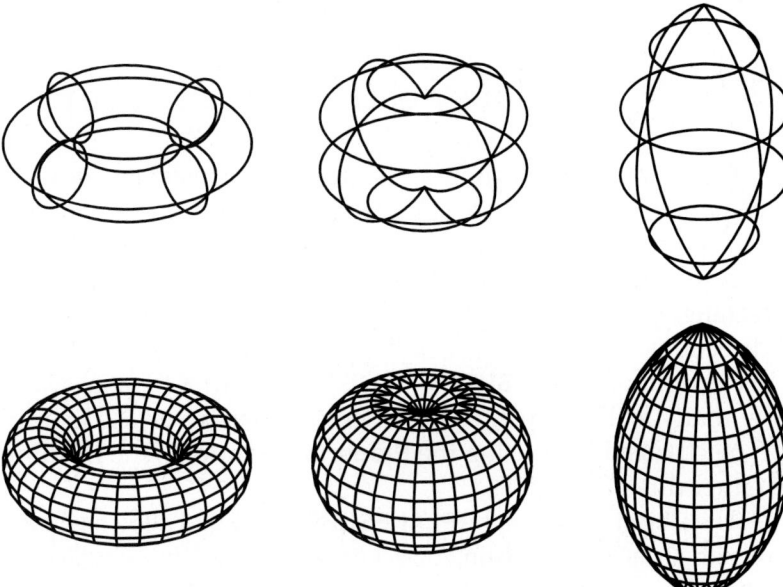

WEDGE

Type
WEDGE
WE

Pull-Down Menu
Draw
> Modeling
> Wedge

Toolbar
Modeling

Wedge

Dashboard
3D Make

Wedge

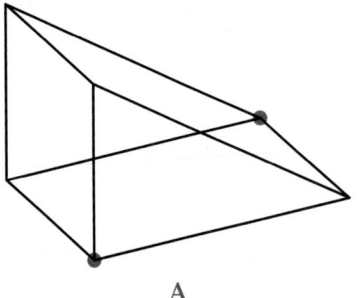 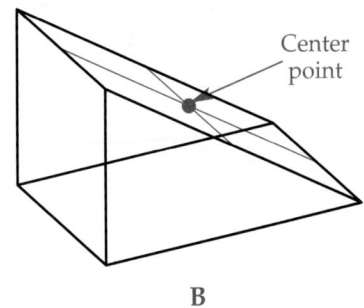

Figure 2-16.
A—A wedge drawn by picking corners and specifying a height. B—A wedge drawn using the **Center** option. Notice the location of the center.

Center point

A   B

Wedge

A *wedge* has five sides, four of which are at right angles and the fifth at an angle other than 90°. See **Figure 2-16.** Once the command is initiated, you are prompted to select the first corner of the base or to enter an option. By default, a wedge is constructed by picking diagonal corners of the base and setting a height. To pick the center point, enter the **Center** option. The center point of a wedge is the middle of the angled surface. You must then pick a point to set the width and length before entering a height. If dynamic input is on, you can also set a rotation angle for the wedge.

After specifying the first corner or the center, you can enter the length, width, and height instead of picking a second corner. When prompted for the second corner, enter the **Length** option and specify the length. You are then prompted for the width. After the width is entered, you are prompted for the height.

To create a wedge with equal length, width, and height, enter the **Cube** option when prompted for the second corner. Then, enter a length. The same value is automatically used for the width and height. Polar tracking is a good feature to use with this option.

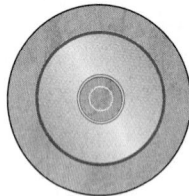

Exercise 2-2
Complete the exercise on the Student CD.

Constructing a Planar Surface

PLANESURF

Type
PLANESURF

Pull-Down Menu
Draw
> Modeling
> Planar Surface

Toolbar
Modeling

Planar Surface

Dashboard
3D Make

Planar Surface

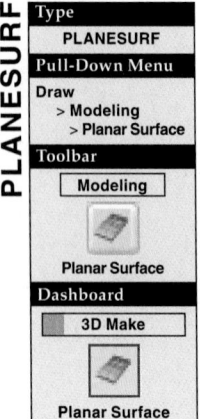

A *planar surface* primitive is an object consisting of a single plane, and is created parallel to the current XY plane. The surface that is created has zero thickness and is composed of a mesh of lines. It is created with the **PLANESURF** command. The command prompts you to specify the first corner and then the second corner of a rectangle. Once drawn, the surface is displayed as a mesh with lines in the X and Y directions. See **Figure 2-17A.** These lines are called *isolines* and do not include the object's boundary. The **SURFU** (Y axis) and **SURFV** (X axis) system variables determine how many isolines are created when the planar surface is drawn. The isoline values can be changed later using the **Properties** window. The maximum number of isolines in either direction is 200.

The **Object** option of the **PLANESURF** command allows you to convert a 2D object into a planar surface. Any existing object or objects lying in a single plane and forming a closed area can be converted to a planar surface. The objects in **Figure 2-17B** are two arcs and two lines connected at their endpoints. The resulting planar surface is shown in **Figure 2-17C.**

Figure 2-17.
A—A rectangular planar surface with four isolines in the Y direction and eight isolines in the X direction. B—These two arcs and two lines form a closed area and lie on a single plane. C—The arcs and curves are converted into a planar surface. D—The planar surface is converted into a solid.

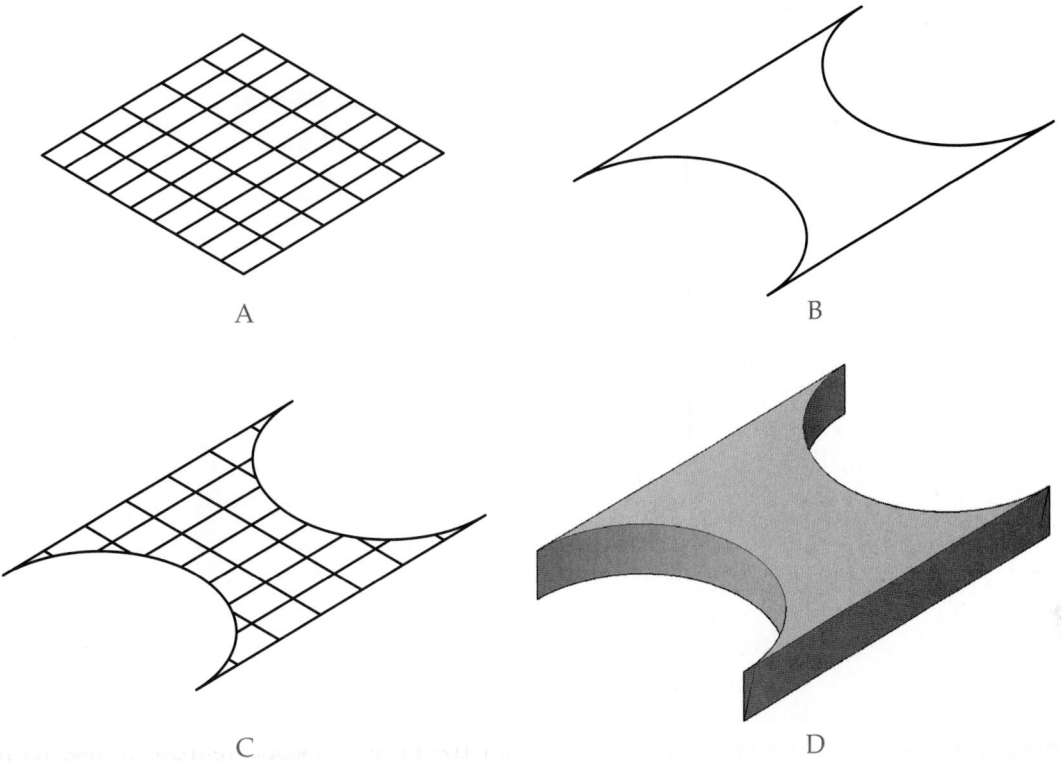

Although a planar surface is not a solid, it can be converted into a solid in a single step. For example, the object in **Figure 2-17C** is converted into a solid using the **THICKEN** command. See **Figure 2-17D**. The object that started as two arcs and two lines is now a solid model and can be manipulated and edited like any other solid. This capability enables you to create intricate planar shapes and quickly convert them to a solid for use in advanced modeling applications. Model editing procedures are discussed in detail in Chapters 7 through 11.

Creating Composite Solids

A *composite solid* is a solid model constructed of two or more solids, often primitives. Solids can be subtracted from each other, joined to form a new solid, or overlapped to create an intersection or interference. The commands used to create composite solids are found in the **3D Make** control panel in the **Dashboard**, in the **Solid Editing** cascading menu in the **Modify** pull-down menu, and on the **Solid Editing** toolbar. See **Figure 2-18.**

Introduction to Booleans

There are three operations that form the basis of constructing many complex solid models. Joining two or more solids is called a *union* operation. Subtracting one solid from another is called a *subtraction* operation. Forming a solid based on the volume

Figure 2-18.
Selecting a Boolean command. A—The **Solid Editing** cascading menu in the **Modify** pull-down menu. B—The **Solid Editing** toolbar. C—The **3D Make** control panel in the **Dashboard**.

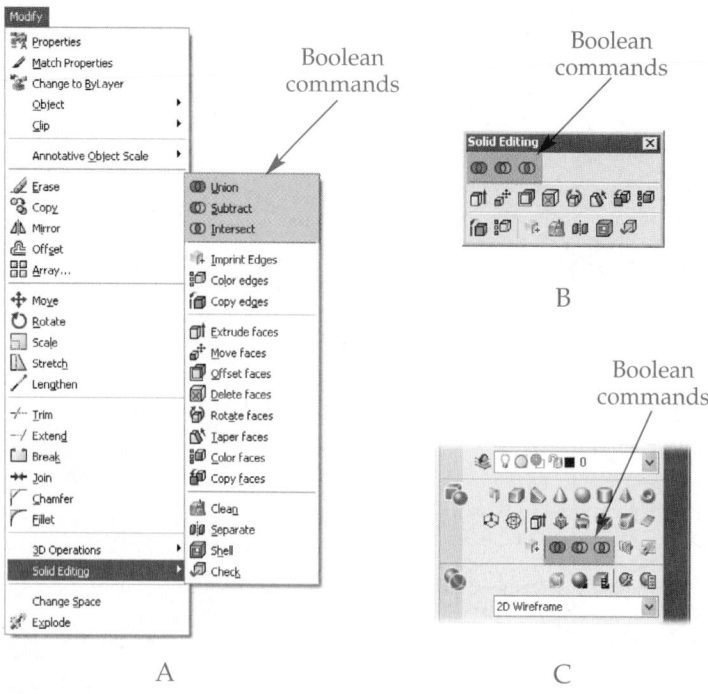

A

B

C

of overlapping solids is called an *intersection* operation. Unions, subtractions, and intersections as a group are called ***Boolean operations.*** George Boole (1815–1864) was an English mathematician who developed a system of mathematical logic where all variables have the value of either one or zero. Boole's two-value logic, or *binary algebra,* is the basis for the mathematical calculations used by computers, and specifically for those required in the construction of composite solids.

Joining Two or More Solid Objects

The **UNION** command is used to combine solid objects, **Figure 2-19.** The solids do not need to touch or intersect to form a union. Therefore, accurately locate the primitives when drawing them. After selecting the objects to join, just press [Enter] and the action is completed.

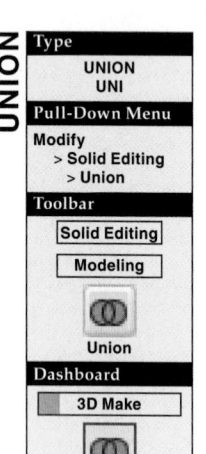

Figure 2-19.
A—The solid primitives shown here have areas of intersection and overlap. B—Composite solids after using the **UNION** command.

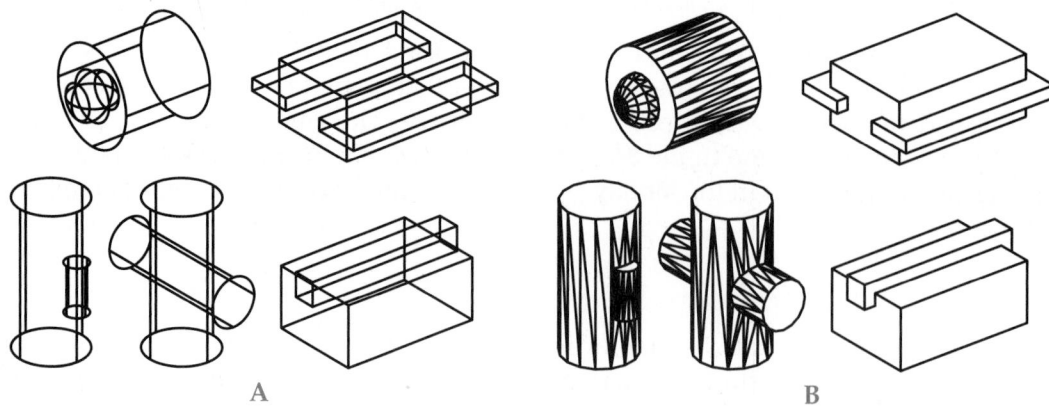

A

B

In the examples shown in Figure 2-19B, notice that lines, or edges, are shown at the new intersection points of the joined objects. This is an indication that the features are one object, not separate objects.

Subtracting Solids

The **SUBTRACT** command allows you to remove the volume of one or more solids from another solid. Several examples are shown in Figure 2-20. The first object selected in the subtraction operation is the object *from* which volume is to be subtracted. The next object is the object to be subtracted from the first. The completed object will be a new solid. If the result is the opposite of what you intended, you may have selected the objects in the wrong order. Just undo the operation and try again.

Creating New Solids from the Intersection of Solids

When solid objects intersect, the overlap forms a common volume, a space that both objects share. This shared space is called an *intersection*. An intersection (common volume) can be made into a composite solid using the **INTERSECT** command. Figure 2-21 shows several examples. A solid is formed from the common volume. The original objects are removed.

The **INTERSECT** command is also useful in 2D drawing. For example, if you need to create a complex shape that must later be used for inquiry calculations or hatching, draw the main object first. Then, draw all intersecting or overlapping objects. Next, create regions of the shapes. Finally, use **INTERSECT** to create the final shape. The resulting shape is a region and has solid properties. Regions are discussed later in this chapter.

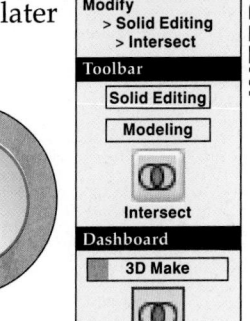

SUBTRACT

Type
SUBTRACT
SU

Pull-Down Menu
Modify
> Solid Editing
> Subtract

Toolbar
Solid Editing
Modeling
Subtract

Dashboard
3D Make
Subtract

INTERSECT

Type
INTERSECT

Pull-Down Menu
Modify
> Solid Editing
> Intersect

Toolbar
Solid Editing
Modeling
Intersect

Dashboard
3D Make
Intersect

Exercise 2-3
Complete the exercise on the Student CD.

Figure 2-20.
A—The solid primitives shown here have areas of intersection and overlap. B—Composite solids after using the **SUBTRACT** command.

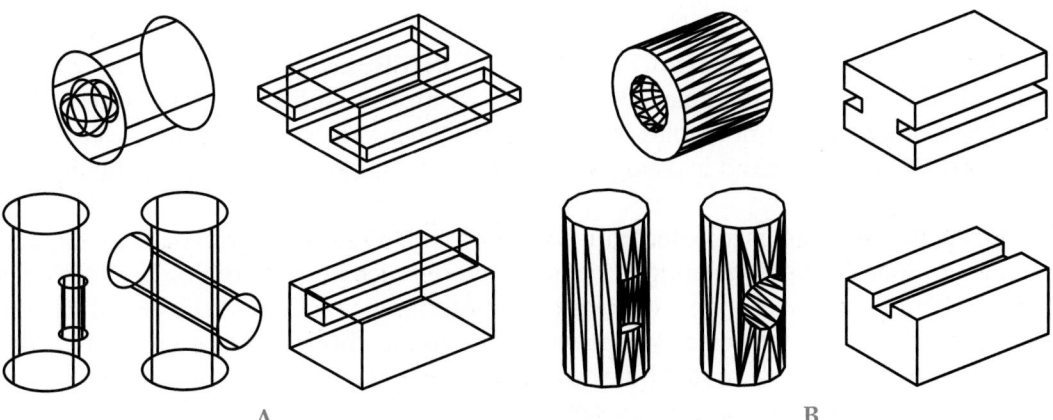

A   B

Figure 2-21.
A—The solid primitives shown here have areas of intersection and overlap. B—Composite solids after using the **INTERSECT** command.

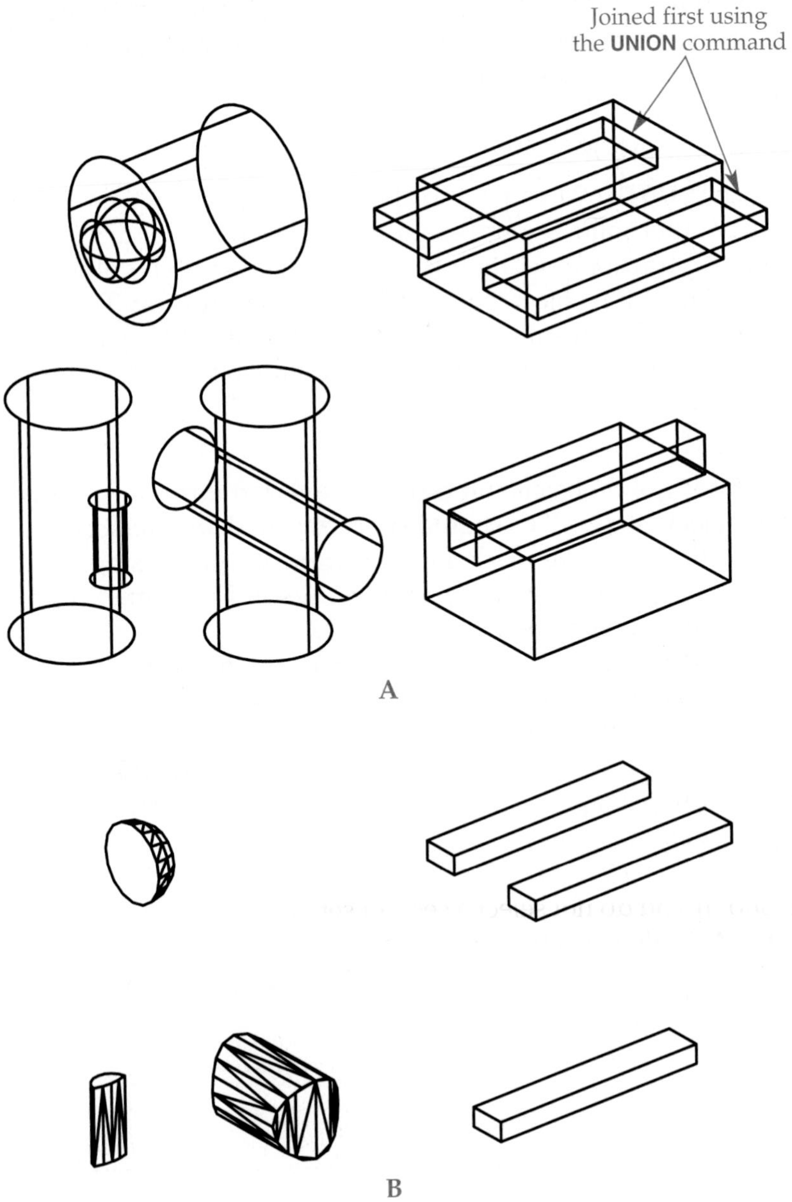

Joined first using the **UNION** command

A

B

Creating New Solids Using the Interfere Command

When you use the **SUBTRACT**, **UNION**, and **INTERSECT** commands, the original solids are deleted. They are replaced by the new composite solid. The **INTERFERE** command does not do this. A new solid is created from the interference (common volume) as if the **INTERSECT** command is used, but the original objects remain and can be deleted or retained.

Once the command is initiated, you are prompted to select the first set of solids or to enter an option. The **Settings** option opens the **Interference Settings** dialog box, which is used to change the visual style and color of the interference solid and the visual style of the viewport. The **Nested selection** option allows you to check the interference of separate solid objects within a nested block. A *nested block* is one that is composed of other blocks. When any needed options are set, select the first set of solids and press [Enter].

You are prompted to select the second set of solids or to enter an option. Entering the **Check first set** option tells AutoCAD to check the objects in the first set for interference. There is no second set when this option is used. Otherwise, select the second set of solids and press [Enter].

AutoCAD zooms in on the highlighted interference solid and displays the **Interference Checking** dialog box. See Figure 2-22. The visual style is set to a wireframe display by default and the interference solid is shaded in a color, which is red by default.

In the **Interfering objects** area of the **Interference Checking** dialog box, the number of objects selected in the first and second sets is displayed. The number of interfering pairs found in the selected objects is also displayed.

The buttons in the **Highlight** area of the dialog box are used to highlight the previous or next interference object. If the **Zoom to pair** check box is checked, AutoCAD zooms to the interference objects when the **Previous** and **Next** buttons are selected.

To the right of the **Highlight** area are three navigation buttons—**Zoom Realtime**, **Pan Realtime**, and **3D Orbit**. Selecting one of these display options temporarily hides the dialog box and activates the selected command. This allows you to navigate in the viewport. When the command is ended, the dialog box is redisplayed.

By default, the **Delete interference objects created on Close** check box is checked. This means that the object(s) created by interference is deleted. In order to retain the new solid(s), uncheck this box.

An example of interference checking and the result is shown in Figure 2-23. Notice that the original solids are intact, but new lines indicate the new solid. The new solid is retained as a separate object because the **Delete interference objects created on Close** check box was unchecked. The new solid can be moved, copied, and manipulated just like any other object. Figure 2-23C shows the new object after it has been moved and a hidden display generated.

When the **INTERFERE** command is used, AutoCAD compares the first set of solids to the second set. Any solids that are selected for both the first and second sets are automatically included as part of the first selection set and eliminated from the second. If you do not select a second set of objects or the **Check first set** option is used, AutoCAD calculates the interference between the objects in the first selection set.

Figure 2-22.
The **Interference Checking** dialog box is used to check for interference between solids. To retain the interference solid, uncheck the **Delete interference objects created on Close** check box.

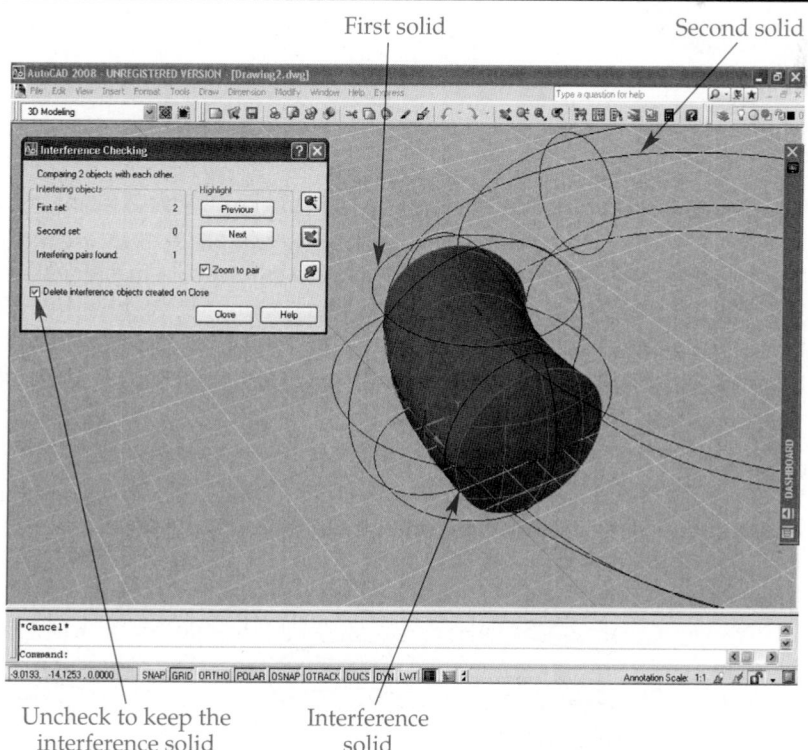

First solid

Second solid

Uncheck to keep the interference solid

Interference solid

Figure 2-23.
A—Two solids form an area of intersection. B—After using **INTERFERE**, a new solid is defined (shown here in color) and the original solids remain. C—The new solid can be moved or copied.

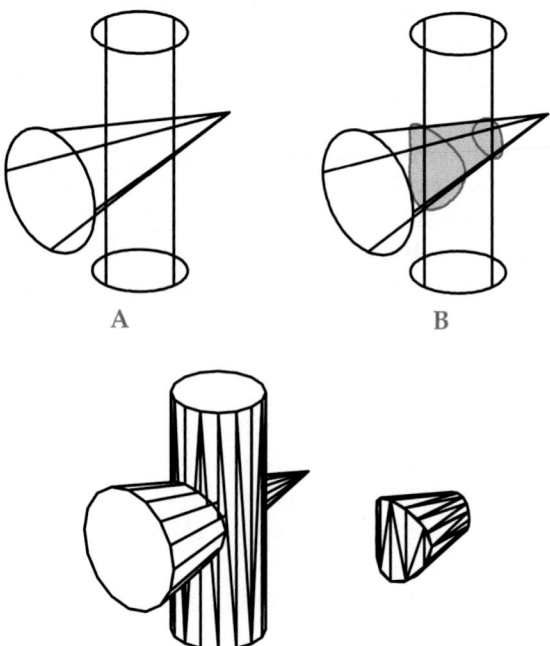

A　　　　　B

C

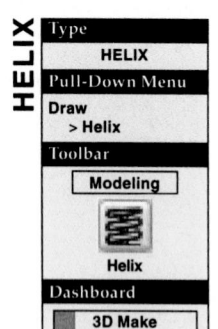

Exercise 2-4

Complete the exercise on the Student CD.

Creating a Helix

HELIX	
Type	
HELIX	
Pull-Down Menu	
Draw	
> Helix	
Toolbar	
Modeling	

Helix	
Dashboard	
3D Make	

Helix	

A *helix* is a spline in the form of a spiral and can be created as a 2D or 3D object. See Figure 2-24. It is not a solid object. However, it can be used as the path or framework for creating objects such as springs and spiral staircases.

The **3D Make** panel must be expanded in order to select the **HELIX** command. When the command is initiated, you are prompted for the center of the helix base. After picking the center, you are prompted to enter the radius of the base. If you want to specify

Figure 2-24.
Three types of helices. From left to right, equal top and bottom diameters, unequal top and bottom diameters, and unequal top and bottom diameters with the height set to zero.

the diameter, enter the **Diameter** option. After the base is defined, you are prompted for the radius of the top. You can use the **Diameter** option to enter a diameter. The top and bottom can be different sizes. Entering different sizes creates a tapered helix, if the helix is 3D. A 2D helix should have different sizes for the top and bottom.

After the top and bottom sizes are set, you are prompted to set the height or enter an option. To specify the number of turns in the helix, enter the **Turns** option. Then, enter the number of turns. The maximum is 500 and you can enter values less than one if they are greater than zero.

By default, the helix turns in a clockwise manner. To change the direction in which the helix turns, enter the **Twist** option. Then, enter CCW for counterclockwise or CW for clockwise.

The height of the helix can be set in one of three ways. First, you can enter a direct distance. To do this, type the height value or pick with the mouse to set the height. To create a 2D helix, enter a height of zero.

You can also set the height for one turn of the helix using the **Turn height** option. In this case, the total height is the number of turns multiplied by the turn height. If you provide a value for the turn height and then specify the helix height, the number of turns is automatically calculated and the helix is drawn. Conversely, if you provide values for both the turn height and number of turns, the helix height is calculated by AutoCAD.

Finally, you can pick a location for the axis endpoint using the **Axis endpoint** option. This is the same option available with a cone, cylinder, or pyramid.

As an example, a solid model of a spring can be created by constructing a helix and a circle, and then using the **SWEEP** command to sweep the circle along the helix path. See **Figure 2-25**. The **SWEEP** command is discussed in detail in Chapter 8.

First, determine the diameter of the spring wire and then draw a circle using that value. For this example, you will create two springs each with a wire diameter of .125 units, so draw two circles of that diameter, **Figure 2-26**. Their locations are not important. Next, determine the diameter of the spring and draw a corresponding helix. For this example, draw a helix anywhere on screen with a bottom diameter of one unit and a top diameter of one unit. Set the number of turns to eight and specify a height of two units. Draw another helix with the same settings, except make the top diameter .5 units.

Initiate the **SWEEP** command. You are first prompted to select the objects to sweep; pick one circle and press [Enter]. Next, you are prompted to select the sweep path. Select one of the helices. The first sweep, or spring, is completed. Repeat the procedure for the other circle and helix. The drawing is now composed of the two original, single-line helices and the two new swept solids. The circles are consumed by the **SWEEP** command.

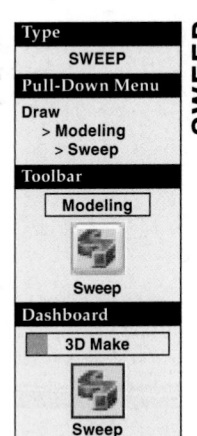

Figure 2-25.
A helix can be used as a path to create a spring.

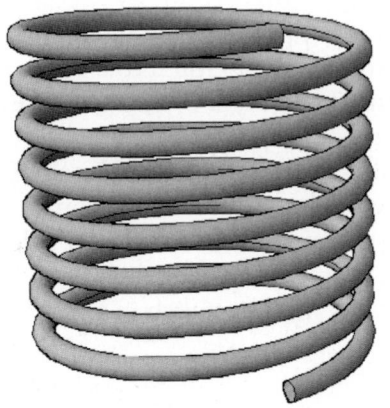
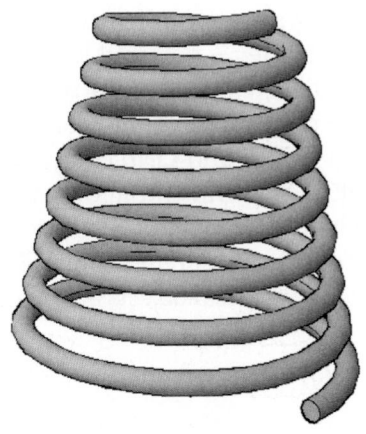

Figure 2-26.
To create a spring, first draw a circle the same diameter as the spring wire. Then, draw the helix and sweep the circle along the helix. Shown here are the two helices that are used to create the springs in Figure 2-25.

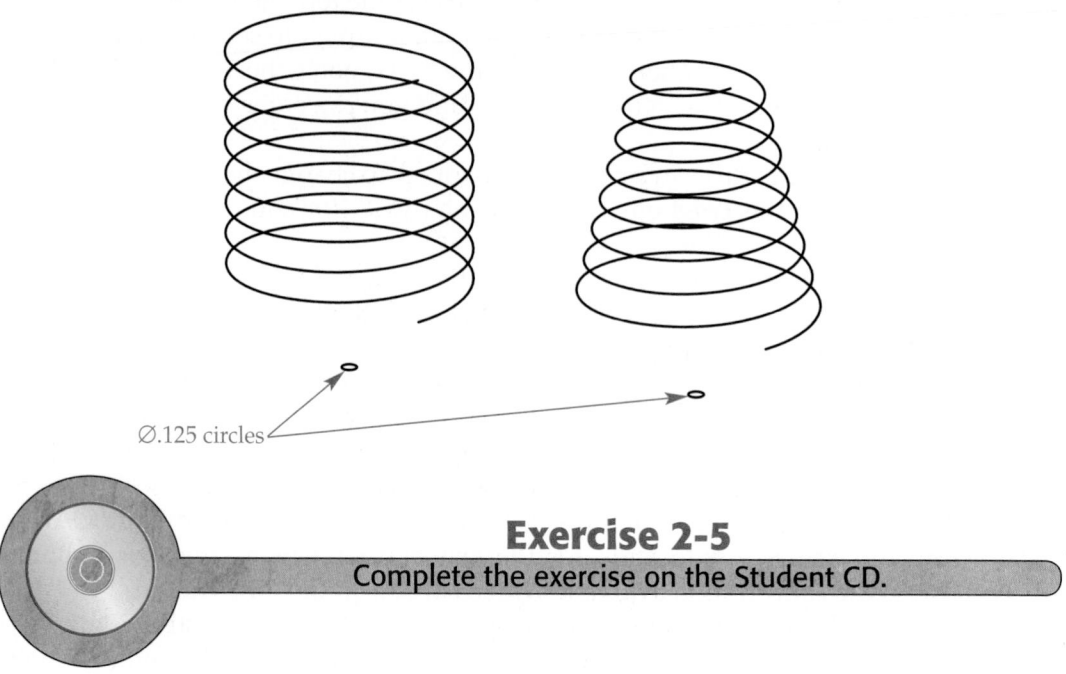

Ø.125 circles

Exercise 2-5
Complete the exercise on the Student CD.

Working with Regions

A *region* is a closed, two-dimensional solid. It is a solid model without thickness (Z value). A region can be analyzed for its mass properties. Therefore, regions are useful for 2D applications where area and boundary calculations must be quickly obtained from a drawing.

Boolean operations can be performed on regions. When regions are unioned, subtracted, or intersected, a *composite region* is created. A composite region is also called a *region model*.

A region can be quickly and easily given a thickness, or *extruded* into a 3D solid object. This means that you can convert a 2D shape into a 3D solid model in just a few steps. An application is drawing a 2D section view, converting it into a region, and extruding the region into a 3D solid model. Extruding is covered in Chapter 7.

Constructing a 2D Region Model

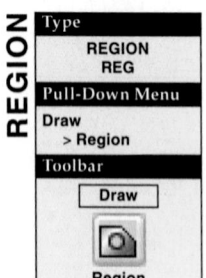

REGION

| Type |
| REGION |
| REG |
| Pull-Down Menu |
| Draw |
| > Region |
| Toolbar |
| Draw |
| Region |

The following example creates as a region the plan view of a base for a support bracket. In Chapter 7, you will learn how to extrude the region into a solid. First, start a new drawing. Next, create the profile geometry in **Figure 2-27** using the **RECTANGLE** and **CIRCLE** commands. These commands create 2D objects that can be converted into regions. The **PLINE** and **LINE** commands can also be used to create closed 2D objects.

The **REGION** command allows you to convert closed, two-dimensional objects into regions. When the command is initiated, you are prompted to select objects. Select the rectangle and four circles, and then press [Enter]. The rectangle and each circle are now separate regions and the original objects are deleted. You may need to switch to a wireframe visual

Figure 2-27.
These 2D shapes can
be made into a region.
The region can then be
made into a 3D solid.

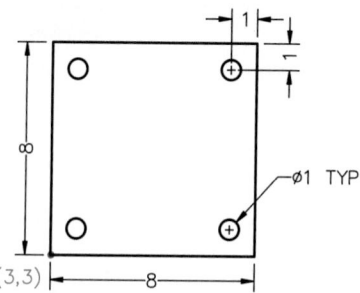

Figure 2-28.
Once the circular
regions are subtracted
from the rectangular
region, they appear as
holes. This is clear
when the Conceptual
or Realistic visual style
is set current.

style in order to see the circles. You can individually pick the regions. If you pick a circle, notice that a grip is displayed in the center, but not at the four quadrants. This is because the object is not a circle anymore. However, you can still snap to the quadrants.

In order to create the proper solid, the circle regions must be subtracted from the rectangle region. Using the **SUBTRACT** command, select the rectangle as the object to be subtracted *from*, and then all of the circles as the objects to subtract. Now, if you select the rectangle or any of the circles, you can see that a single region has been created from the five separate regions. If you set the Conceptual or Realistic visual style current, you can see that the circles are now holes in the region. See Figure 2-28.

Using the Boundary Command to Create a Region

The **BOUNDARY** command is often used to create a polyline for hatching or an inquiry. In addition, this command can be used to create a region. When the command is initiated, the **Boundary Creation** dialog box is displayed. See Figure 2-29.

Next, select **Region** from the **Object type:** drop-down list in the **Boundary retention** area of the dialog box. Also, you can refine the boundary selection method by turning island detection on or off. When the **Island detection** check box above the **Boundary retention** area is checked, island detection is on.

- **On.** When an internal point is selected in the object, AutoCAD creates separate regions of any islands that reside within the object.
- **Off.** When an internal point is selected in the object, AutoCAD ignores islands that reside within the object when creating the region.

Finally, select the **Pick Points** button. The dialog box is closed and you are prompted to select an internal point. Pick a point inside of the object that you wish to convert to a region. Press [Enter] when you are finished and the region is created. You can always check to see if an object is a polyline or region by using the **LIST** command and selecting the object.

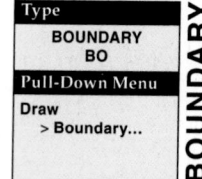

Type

BOUNDARY
BO

Pull-Down Menu

Draw
> Boundary...

BOUNDARY

Figure 2-29.
Regions can be created using the **Boundary Creation** dialog box.

Pick to select a point inside the boundary

Turn island detection on and off

Select the type of object to be created

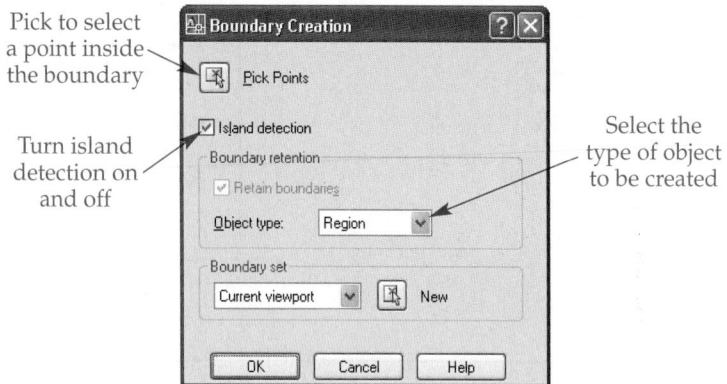

Calculating the Area of a Region

A region is not a polyline. It is an enclosed area called a *loop.* Certain values of the region, such as area, are stored as a value of the region. The **AREA** command can be used to determine the length of all sides and the area of the loop. This can be a useful advantage of using a region.

For example, suppose a parking lot is being repaved. You need to calculate the surface area of the parking lot to determine the amount of material needed. This total surface area excludes the space taken up by planting dividers, sidewalks, and light posts because you will not be paving under these items. If the parking lot and all objects inside of it are drawn as a region, the **AREA** command can give you this figure in one step using the **Object** option. If a polyline is used to draw the parking lot, all internal features must be subtracted each time the **AREA** command is used.

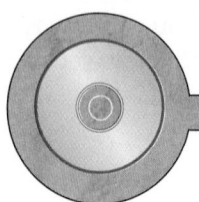

Exercise 2-6
Complete the exercise on the Student CD.

Chapter Test

Answer the following questions. Write your answers on a separate sheet of paper or complete the electronic chapter test on the Student CD.

1. What is a *solid primitive?*
2. How is a solid cube created?
3. How is an elliptical cylinder created?
4. Where is the center of a wedge located?
5. What is a *frustum pyramid?*
6. What is a *polysolid?*
7. Name at least four AutoCAD 2D entities that can be converted to a polysolid.
8. What type of entity does the **HELIX** command create, and how can it be converted into a solid model?
9. What is a *composite solid?*
10. Which type of mathematical calculations are used in the construction of solid models?
11. How are two or more solids combined to make a composite solid?
12. What is the function of the **INTERSECT** command?
13. How does the **INTERFERE** command differ from **INTERSECT** and **UNION**?
14. What is a *region?*
15. How can a 2D section view be converted to a 3D solid model?
16. What is created when regions are added to or subtracted from one another?
17. Which command allows you to remove the area of one region from another region?
18. When using the **BOUNDARY** command, what is the effect of unchecking the **Island detection** check box in the **Boundary Creation** dialog box?

Drawing Problems

Draw the objects in the following problems using the appropriate solid primitive commands and Boolean operations. Use your own measurements for objects shown without dimensions. Do not add dimensions to the models. Save the drawings as P2-(problem number). Display and plot the problems as indicated by your instructor.

1.

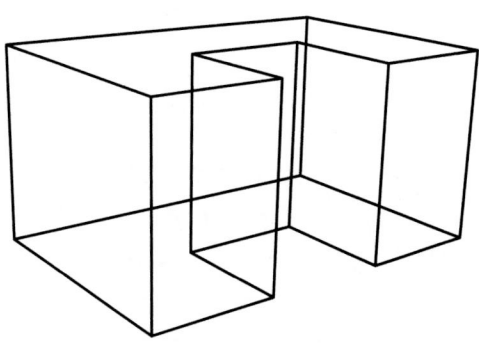

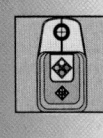
2.

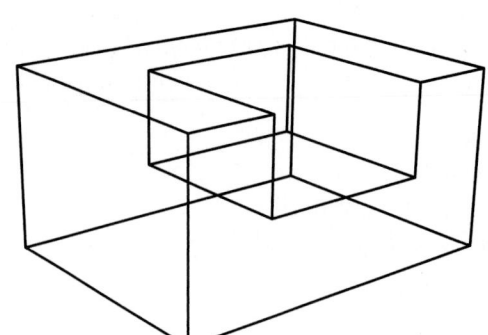

3.

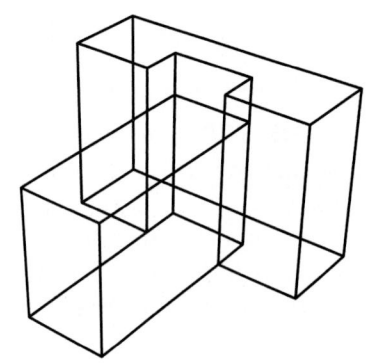

4.

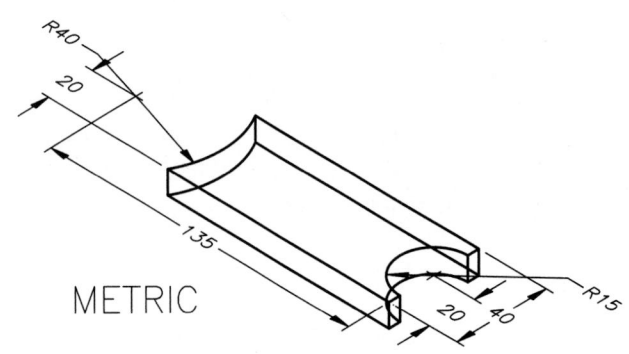

METRIC

5.

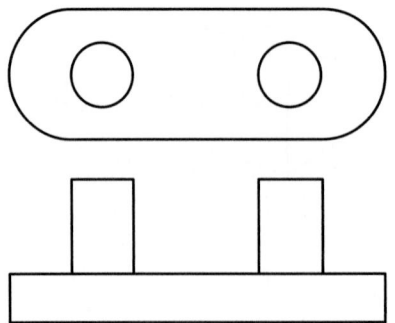

6.

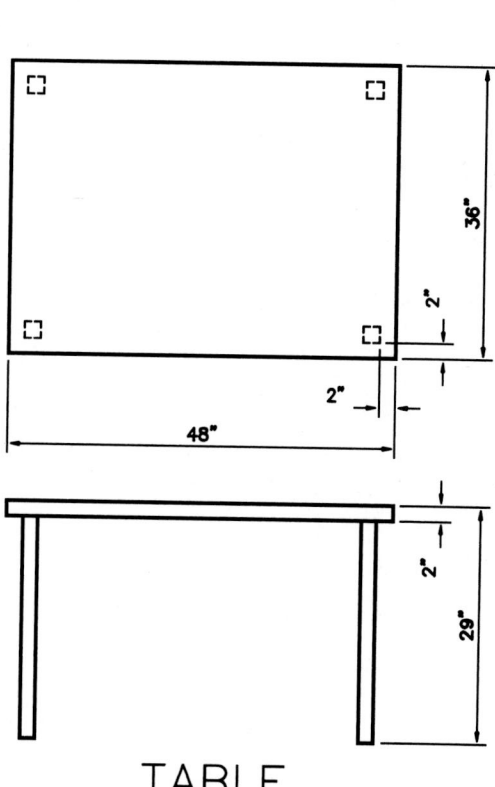

7.

8.

TABLE

9.

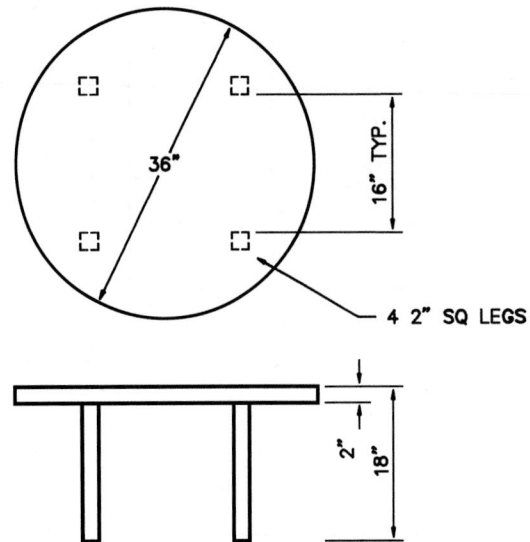

10.

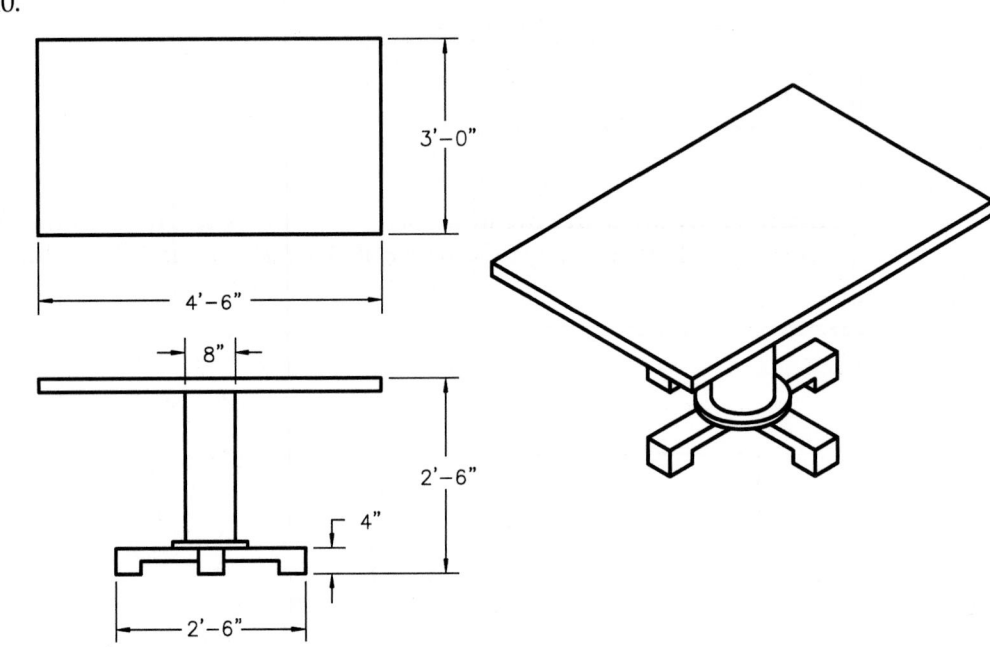

Viewing and Displaying Three-Dimensional Models

Learning Objectives

After completing this chapter, you will be able to:

✓ Use the **3DORBIT** command to dynamically rotate the display of a 3D model.
✓ Use the visual style options to create face and edge style display variations.
✓ Render a 3D model.

There are two basic ways to select a pictorial (3D) viewpoint for 3D models. These are the preset isometric viewpoints and the **3DORBIT** command. The preset isometric viewpoints are discussed in detail in Chapter 1. The **3DORBIT** command is introduced in Chapter 1 and discussed in detail in this chapter. It enables you to rotate, pan, and zoom a 3D model while the model is fully shaded. This provides a powerful design tool when working in 3D. In addition, you can display a continuously rotating model set in motion by just the movement of the mouse. This is ideal for design, demonstrations, and training.

Once a viewpoint has been selected, you can enhance the display by panning and zooming or by applying visual styles. The **Visual Style** control panel in the **Dashboard** provides a variety of ways to display a model, including wireframe, hidden line removal, and simple rendering. An introduction to visual styles is provided in Chapter 1, and additional details are discussed later in this chapter.

A more advanced rendering can be created with the **RENDER** command. It produces the most realistic image with highlights, shading, and materials, if applied. Figure 3-1 shows a 3D model of a cast iron plumbing cleanout after using **HIDE**, setting the Conceptual visual style current, and using **RENDER**. Notice how different the three displays are.

PROFESSIONAL TIP

In addition to **3DORBIT**, AutoCAD has two other commands for displaying pictorial views—**DVIEW** and **VPOINT**. The functionalities of these commands have been replaced by the more useful **3DORBIT** command.

Figure 3-1.
A—Hidden display (hidden lines removed). B—The Conceptual visual style set current.
C—Rendered with lights and materials.

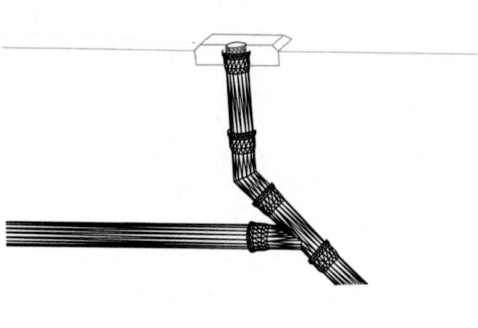

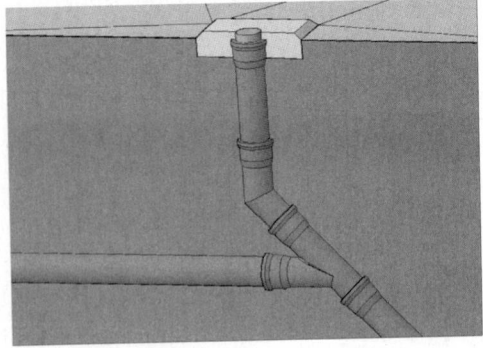

A

B

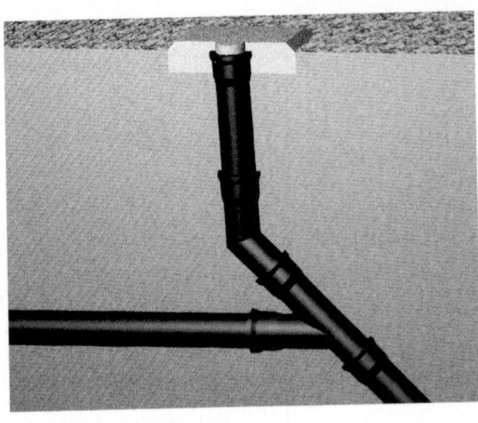

C

Plan Command Options

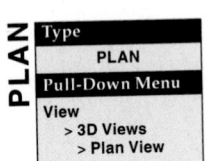

You can quickly create a plan view of any user coordinate system (UCS) or the world coordinate system (WCS) using the **PLAN** command. This command was introduced in Chapter 1. The **PLAN** command automatically performs a **ZOOM Extents**. This fills the graphics window with the plan view. The command options are:

- **Current UCS.** This creates a view of the object that is plan to the current UCS.
- **World UCS.** This creates a view of the object that is plan to the WCS. If the WCS is the current UCS, this option and the **Current UCS** option produce the same results.
- **Named UCS.** This displays a view plan to a named UCS. The preset UCSs are not considered named UCSs. This option is **Ucs** when the **PLAN** command is typed.

Dynamically Changing a 3D View

The **3DORBIT** command is a powerful and easy-to-use command for creating pictorial views of a 3D object. It allows you to dynamically rotate the view of a 3D object in real time. In addition, the model can be displayed in wireframe, hidden, or shaded display as the view is rotated. There are two basic modes for the **3DORBIT** command—constrained and free. These are discussed in the next sections.

Constrained Orbit

A *constrained orbit* means that when you press and hold the pointer button, the view can be rotated up 90°, down 90°, and horizontally 360°. You cannot display an upside-down view of the opposite side of the model. Within these constraints, the model can be freely rotated. This is the default mode when the command is typed. When the command is initiated, the constrained orbit cursor is displayed at the pointer position. See Figure 3-2.

When in constrained orbit mode, a variety of options are available from the shortcut menu. See Figure 3-3. In addition, you can select many of these options using the **3D Navigate** toolbar. These options are discussed in the following sections.

Type
3DORBIT
3DO
ORBIT

Pull-Down Menu
View
> Orbit
> Constrained
Orbit

Toolbar
Orbit
3D Navigation

Constrained Orbit

Dashboard
3D Navigate

Constrained Orbit

3DORBIT

PROFESSIONAL TIP

The constrained mode of the **3DORBIT** command can be transparently accessed from within another command or with no command active. Press and hold the [Shift] key and simultaneously press and hold the mouse wheel. Then, move the pointer to achieve a new viewpoint. If you undo the command within which **3DORBIT** was accessed, the view is returned to the previous display.

Figure 3-2.
When the **3DORBIT** command is active, the shape of the cursor indicates which function will be performed. Note the mode in which each cursor appears.

Mode	Cursor	Appearance	Description
Constrained	Two ellipses		This icon appears in constrained mode. The view can be rotated up 90°, down 90°, and horizontally 360°.
Free	Two ellipses		This icon appears when you move the cursor inside the trackball. When you pick and drag, the viewpoint can be moved in any direction—horizontally, vertically, and diagonally.
Free	Circular arrow		The circular arrow icon appears when the cursor is moved outside the trackball. When you pick and drag, the viewport is "rolled" around an axis that projects perpendicular to the screen.
Free	Horizontal ellipse		This icon appears when you move the cursor into one of the small quadrant circles on the left or right of the trackball. By picking and dragging, the viewpoint can be rotated on an axis of rotation that is vertical in the viewport.
Free	Vertical ellipse		This icon appears when you move the cursor into one of the small quadrant circles on the top or the bottom of the trackball. By picking and dragging, the viewpoint can be rotated on an axis of rotation that is horizontal in the viewport.

Figure 3-3.
The **3DORBIT** shortcut menu.

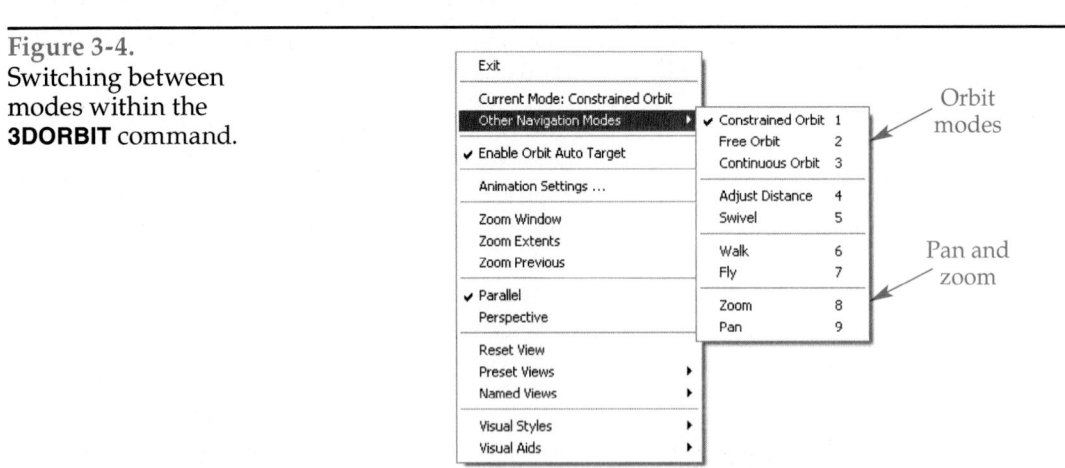

Current mode

Current projection

Free Orbit

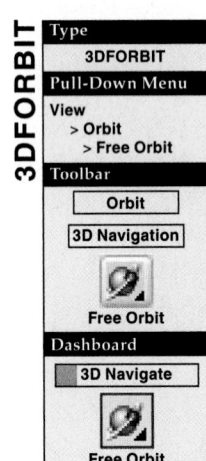

Free orbit mode allows the same movement as in constrained mode, but you can also vertically rotate the view 360°. When the command is initiated, a green circle is displayed in the middle of the current viewport. This is called the trackball, or arcball. By dragging inside or outside of the trackball, the view of the object is dynamically changed. The cursor indicates which action can be performed. Each shape is a visual cue to indicate which type of action will be performed if you pick, hold, and drag (move the pointing device). See Figure 3-2. As in the constrained orbit mode, the shortcut menu shown in Figure 3-3 is available.

Basic 3D Orbit Display Controls

Within the **3DORBIT** command, you have the ability to toggle between constrained orbit, free orbit, realtime pan, and realtime zoom. These options are available in the shortcut menu. Display the shortcut menu by right-clicking and then pick **Other Navigation Modes**. Notice that a check mark appears next to the current mode. See Figure 3-4. Also notice the numbers next to each item. The mode can be switched without displaying the shortcut menu by typing the number.

Additionally, when in orbit mode and **Enable Orbit Auto Target** is on (checked) in the shortcut menu, as shown in Figure 3-4, the viewpoint is rotated about the center of the object display. When off (unchecked), the viewpoint is rotated about the center of the viewport. In this case, the objects may be rotated out of the viewport display.

Figure 3-4.
Switching between modes within the **3DORBIT** command.

Orbit modes

Pan and zoom

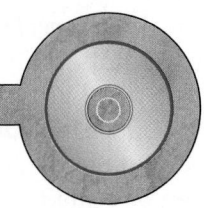

Exercise 3-1
Complete the exercise on the Student CD.

Projection and Visual Aids

Using the **3DORBIT** command, a 3D model can be displayed using a wide variety of options. These include projection methods, such as parallel and perspective; access to visual styles; and visual aids, such as a spherical compass, grid, and shaded UCS icon. These options are selected in the shortcut menu available after the **3DORBIT** command has been entered, and are described in the following sections. See **Figure 3-5**.

Projection

The projection of a pictorial view refers to how lines that recede into the background are treated. Projection of a 3D model can be either parallel or perspective. **Figure 3-6** shows the difference between a parallel and perspective projection.

In *parallel projection,* the sides of objects project parallel to each other. Axonometric views (isometric, dimetric, and trimetric) are all parallel projections.

Figure 3-5.
The **Visual Styles** and **Visual Aids** cascading menus in the **3DORBIT** shortcut menu.

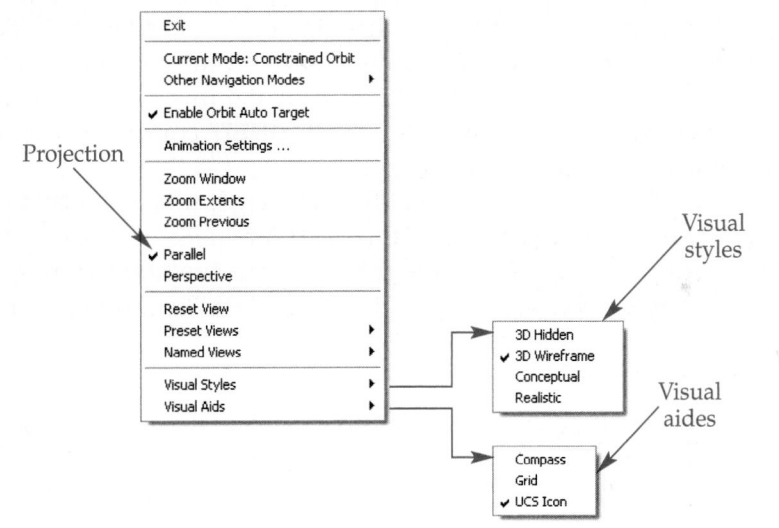

Figure 3-6.
In a parallel projection, parallel lines remain parallel. In a perspective projection, parallel lines converge to a vanishing point. Notice the three receding lines on the boxes.

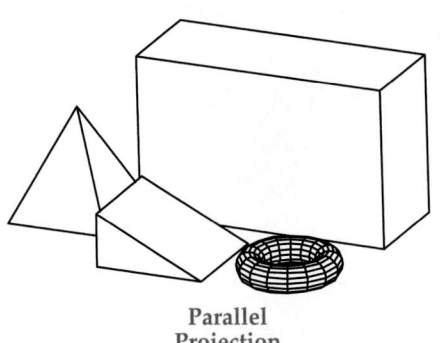

Parallel Projection

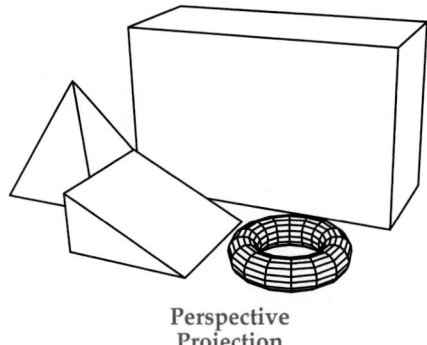

Perspective Projection

In *perspective projection,* the sides of objects project toward one or more vanishing points. In 2D drafting, it is common to represent an object in pictorial as a one- or two-point perspective, especially in architectural drafting.

Once the **3DORBIT** command is exited, the selected projection remains current. You can pan and zoom in both parallel and perspective projections. Additionally, objects can be edited in either type of projection once the **3DORBIT** command is exited.

PROFESSIONAL TIP

You can quickly change between projections at any time by picking the appropriate button in the **3D Navigate** control panel in the **Dashboard**. If the **3DORBIT** command is active, you may need to orbit the display slightly before the projection is changed.

Visual aids

Visual aids help relate the view to the UCS. There are three visual aid options in the **3DORBIT** command. The following visual aids are illustrated in **Figure 3-7.**
- **Compass.**
- **Grid.**
- **3D UCS icon.**

When the compass is on, a spherical 3D compass with the same diameter as the trackball appears. The compass has tick marks and labels indicating the X, Y, and Z axes. The compass can provide a reference for the current UCS. The **COMPASS** system variable controls this display, and is set to 0 if this item is not checked. If the compass is turned on, it remains on after the **3DORBIT** command is exited, except when the 2D Wireframe visual style is current.

The grid is displayed within the drawing limits when **Grid** is checked in the shortcut menu. If the current visual style is 2D Wireframe, the pictorial grid is displayed. The grid setting corresponds to the setting in the **Drafting Settings** dialog box. It is on by default. The setting is retained after the **3DORBIT** command is exited.

Figure 3-7.
Visual aids are available in the **3DORBIT** command that can be used to help you visualize the coordinate system.

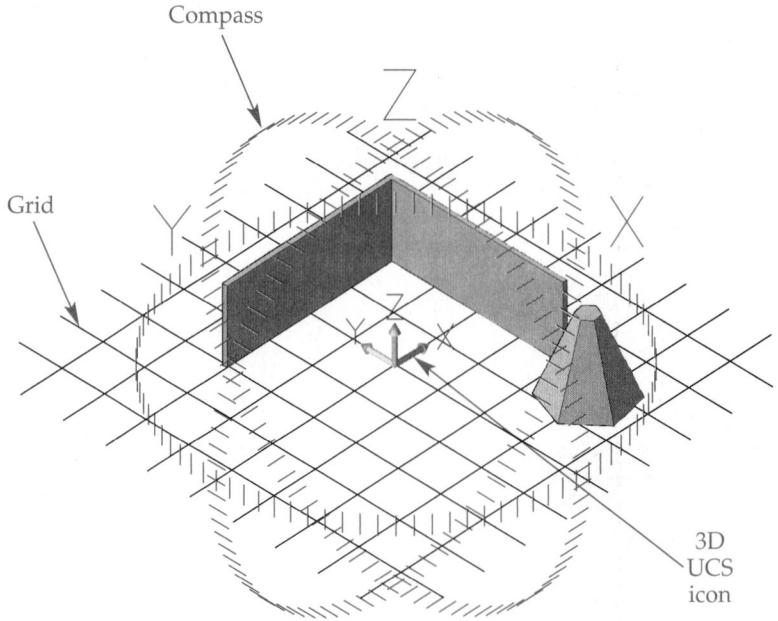

The shaded 3D UCS icon shows the orientation of the UCS. The X axis is red, Y axis is green, and Z axis is blue. When **UCS icon** is checked in the shortcut menu, the UCS icon is displayed. This is the default setting. When off (unchecked), the UCS icon is not displayed. This setting is *not* retained when the **3DORBIT** command is exited. The **UCSICON** command controls the visibility of this icon outside of the **3DORBIT** command. The 3D UCS icon is very useful and should be displayed at all times.

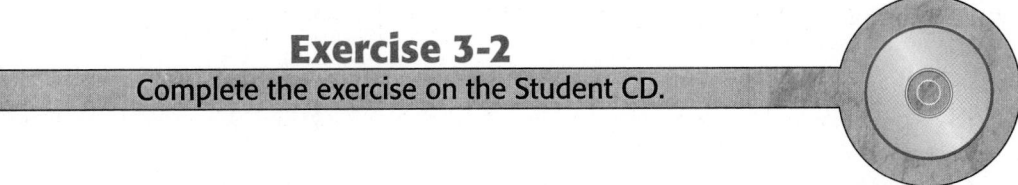

Exercise 3-2

Complete the exercise on the Student CD.

3D Orbit View Options

The **3DORBIT** command is extremely versatile because you can use a variety of established views to create a display. In addition, you can use the **3DORBIT** command to rotate the viewpoint and then reset the viewpoint to the view that was displayed prior to using the command. Three items in the 3D orbit view shortcut menu allow you to set views. See **Figure 3-8**.

- **Reset View.** Resets the view that was displayed before **3DORBIT** was invoked. The command remains active.
- **Preset Views.** Displays a list of the orthographic and isometric presets. Note: Selecting a preset orthographic view here does *not* change the UCS.
- **Named Views.** The named views in the drawing are displayed in this cascading menu.

The drop-down list in the **3D Navigation** toolbar also displays all preset and named views. See **Figure 3-9**. When the **3DORBIT** command is active, simply select a view from this list to display it. If you select one of the orthographic presets while the **3DORBIT** command is active, the UCS is not changed. However, if you select one of the orthographic presets from the drop-down list on the **3D Navigation** toolbar when the **3DORBIT** command is *not* active, the UCS *is* changed. Saved views can also be selected from the drop-down list in the toolbar when the **3DORBIT** command is not active.

Figure 3-8.
Saved and preset views can be accessed from the **3DORBIT** shortcut menu.

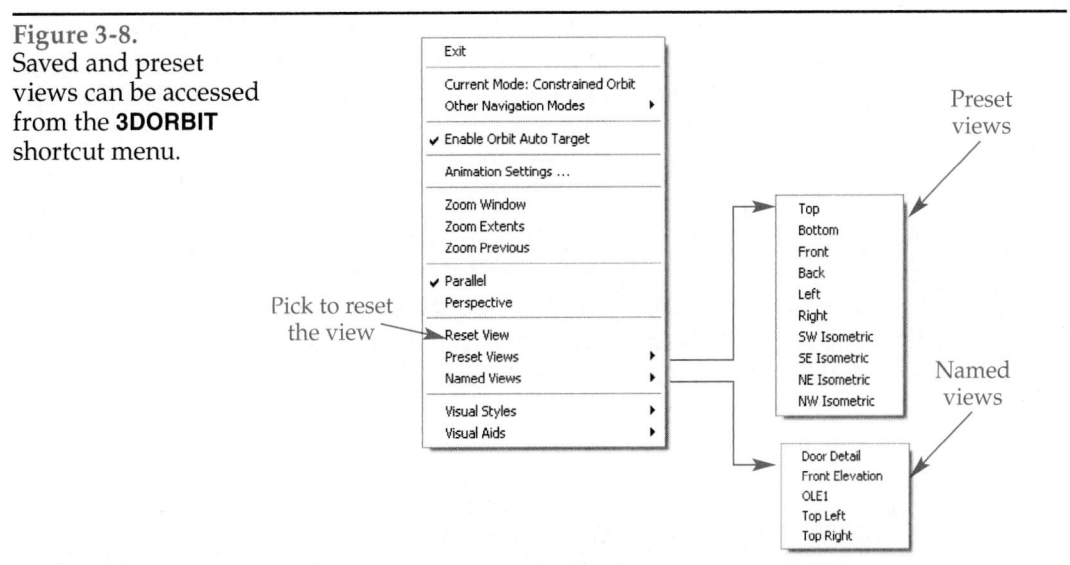

Figure 3-9.
The drop-down list in
the **3D Navigation**
toolbar displays all
preset and named views.

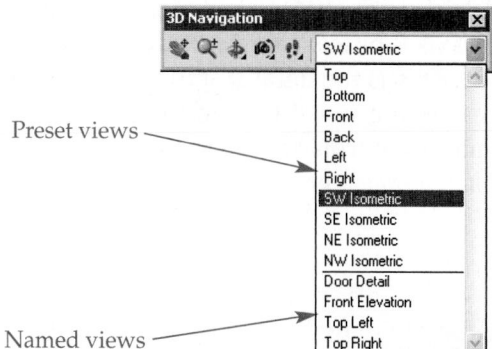

Preset views

Named views

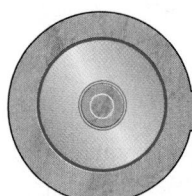

Exercise 3-3

Complete the exercise on the Student CD.

3D Orbit Camera Settings

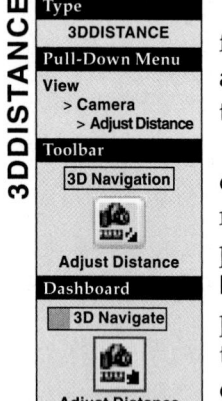

Two **3DORBIT** command options enable you to change the 3D display based on functions of a camera. The distance between camera and object can be adjusted, as well as the amount the camera is swiveled on a tripod. These options can be selected from the **3DORBIT** shortcut menu, the **3D Navigation** toolbar, or typed at the keyboard.

The distance between the viewer and the object can be set by adjusting the camera distance using the **3DDISTANCE** command. To access this command, type the command or use the **3D Navigation** toolbar, **View** pull-down menu, or **3D Navigate** control panel in the **Dashboard**. You can also select **Adjust Distance** from the **Other Navigation Modes** cascading menu in the **3DORBIT** shortcut menu. The cursor changes to arrows pointing up and down, Figure 3-10. Hold the pick button and move the cursor up to get closer to the object, or move it down to increase the camera distance from the object. Be warned, however, that this can distort the objects in the display.

In addition to adjusting the camera distance, you can also change the view by swiveling the camera. The **3DSWIVEL** command is similar to the **PAN** command except that the location from which you are viewing the objects does not change, just the direction in which you are looking. To swivel the camera, use the **3DSWIVEL** command. To access this command, type the command or use the **3D Navigation** toolbar, **View** pull-down menu, or **3D Navigate** control panel in the **Dashboard**. You can also select **Swivel** from the **Other Navigation Modes** cascading menu in the **3DORBIT** shortcut menu. The cursor changes to a camera icon, Figure 3-10. Hold the pick button and move the cursor to swivel the camera in any direction.

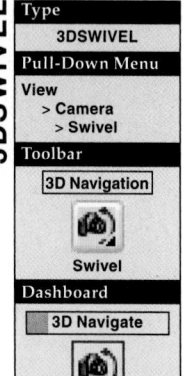

PROFESSIONAL TIP

When in the **3DDISTANCE** or **3DSWIVEL** command, you have access to the **3DORBIT** shortcut menu, even if the command was not entered from within the **3DORBIT** command.

Exercise 3-4

Complete the exercise on the Student CD.

Figure 3-10.
These cursors appear when you adjust the camera distance or swivel the camera.

Adjust
Camera
Distance

Swivel
Camera

Figure 3-11.
This is the continuous orbit cursor in the **3DCORBIT** command (or **Continuous** option of the **3DORBIT** command). Pick and hold the left mouse button. Then, move the cursor in the direction in which you want the view to rotate and release the mouse button.

Creating a Continuous 3D Orbit

The most dynamic aspect of the **3DORBIT** command is the ability to create a continuous orbit of a model. By moving your pointing device, you can set the model in motion in any direction and at any speed, depending on the power of your computer. An impressive display can be achieved using this command. To access continuous orbit mode, type the command or use the **3D Navigation** toolbar, **View** pull-down menu, or **3D Navigate** control panel in the **Dashboard**. You can also select **Continuous Orbit** from the **Other Navigation Modes** cascading menu in the **3DORBIT** shortcut menu. The continuous orbit cursor is displayed. See **Figure 3-11.** This appears slightly different than the orbit cursor.

Press and hold the pick button and move the pointer in the direction that you want the model to rotate and at the desired speed of rotation. Release the button when the pointer is moving at the appropriate speed. The model will continue to rotate until you pick the left mouse button, press [Enter] or [Esc], or right-click and pick **Exit** or another option. At any time while the model is orbiting, you can left-click and adjust the rotation angle and speed by repeating the process for starting a continuous orbit.

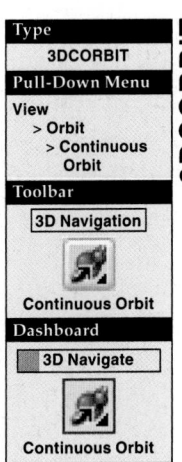

Displaying a 3D Model in Different Visual Styles

The *display* of a 3D model is how the model is presented. This does not refer to the viewing angle, but rather colors, edge display, and shading or rendering. An object can be shaded from any viewpoint. A shaded model can be edited while still keeping the object shaded. This can make it easier to see how the model is developing without having to reshade the drawing. However, when editing a shaded object, it may also be more difficult to select features.

There are four basic ways in which a model can be displayed. The first is called a *wireframe display.* This is a display in which all lines are shown. The simplest "shaded" display technique is to remove hidden lines using the **HIDE** command or the 3D Hidden visual style to create a *hidden display.* However, this is not really a "shaded" display. A *shaded display* of the model can be created by setting either the Conceptual or Realistic visual style current. The Realistic visual style is considered the most realistic *shaded* view. A more detailed shaded model, a *rendered display* of the model, can be created with the **RENDER** command. A rendering is the most realistic presentation.

Visual styles were introduced in Chapter 1. The following sections discuss AutoCAD's visual styles and introduce rendering in AutoCAD. Detailed discussions on rendering, materials, lights, and animations appear in Chapter 13 through Chapter 16.

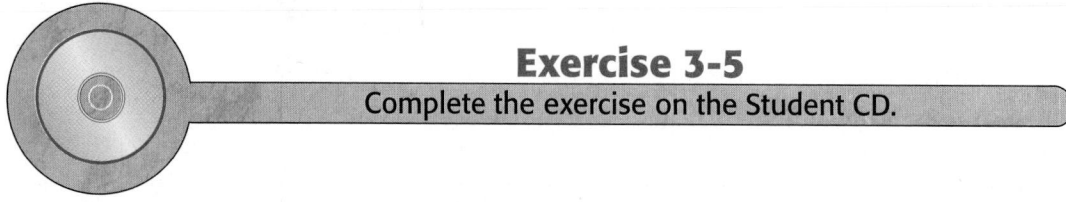

Exercise 3-5
Complete the exercise on the Student CD.

Using the Visual Styles Control Panel

A *visual style* controls the manner in which the edges and shading of a model are displayed in a viewport. The **Visual Style** control panel in the **Dashboard** provides quick and dynamic access to a variety of settings that create instant changes to the model display. See **Figure 3-12**. This section presents all of the settings available for visual styles that do not rely on the use of lights and materials. The application of lights, cameras, and materials is presented in Chapters 13 through 15.

You learned in Chapter 1 that the **Visual Styles Manager** tool palette enables you to gain access to the full range of settings available to create a visual style. On the other hand, the **Visual Style** control panel in the **Dashboard** displays a group of intuitive controls that enable you to quickly alter the display of the model on the screen without redefining the visual style. It may be easier and quicker to first use the **Visual Style** control panel to change settings when working with variations of model display. These changes provide instant visual feedback, not only while constructing a model, but also when displaying it for evaluation or presentation purposes. Then, should you wish to make detailed changes to the visual style using specific settings and values, use the **Visual Styles Manager** tool palette. A complete discussion of the **Visual Styles Manager** is provided in Chapter 13.

Visual style face settings

Three buttons above the **Visual styles** drop-down list give you the ability to change the transparency, shadows, and face colors on the model when the 3D Hidden, Conceptual, or Realistic visual style is current. If the **Visual Style** control panel is expanded, there are three buttons below the **Visual styles** drop-down list that allow you to set a face style current and control the smoothing of curved objects.

Figure 3-12.
The **Visual Style** control panel in the **Dashboard** provides access to options for setting a visual style current and modifying the properties set by a visual style.

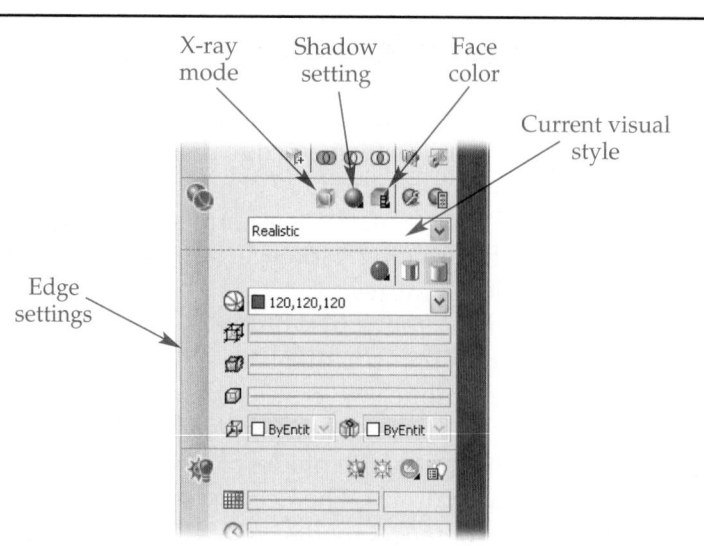

X-ray mode   Shadow setting   Face color

Current visual style

Edge settings

AutoCAD and Its Applications—Advanced

When the **X-ray mode** button is on, all faces in the viewport are transparent. This is a toggle button that is off by default. When on, the button is displayed in orange. The results of turning X-ray on and off are shown in **Figure 3-13.**

The three buttons in the shadows flyout allow you to turn shadows on and off in the viewport, and to select the type of shadow. Ground shadows are displayed on the XY plane of the WCS. In order to display full shadows in the viewport, lights must be added to the model. This is discussed in Chapters 13 and 15. Also, hardware acceleration must be enabled. Refer to the online documentation for information on enabling hardware acceleration.

A *facet* is one flat portion, or plane, of a curved surface. Curved surfaces can be displayed faceted or smooth. See **Figure 3-14.** When displayed smooth, AutoCAD applies smoothing groups to the curved surfaces, which can increase regeneration time. The **Facets** and **Smooth** buttons below the **Visual styles** drop-down list act like radio buttons. One or the other is on, but both cannot be on or off.

Face Colors. The face colors flyout contains four buttons that determine the manner in which the colors of the model faces are displayed. This flyout is located above the **Visual styles** drop-down list. The color display is based on settings in the **Visual Styles Manager** tool palette, which is discussed in Chapter 13.

When the **Regular face colors** button is selected in the flyout, face color options are not used. The faces are displayed in their assigned color. This may be ByLayer or an explicit color.

When the **Desaturate mode** button is selected in the flyout, the faces are displayed in their assigned colors. However, the colors are softened, or desaturated, and appear lighter.

Faces are displayed in shades of a specified color when the **Monochrome mode** button is selected in the flyout. The default color is white resulting in shades of gray.

Figure 3-13.
A—The **Conceptual** visual style is set current. X-ray mode is off. B—X-ray mode is turned on.
C—The **3D Hidden** visual style is set current and X-ray mode is off. D—X-ray mode is turned on.

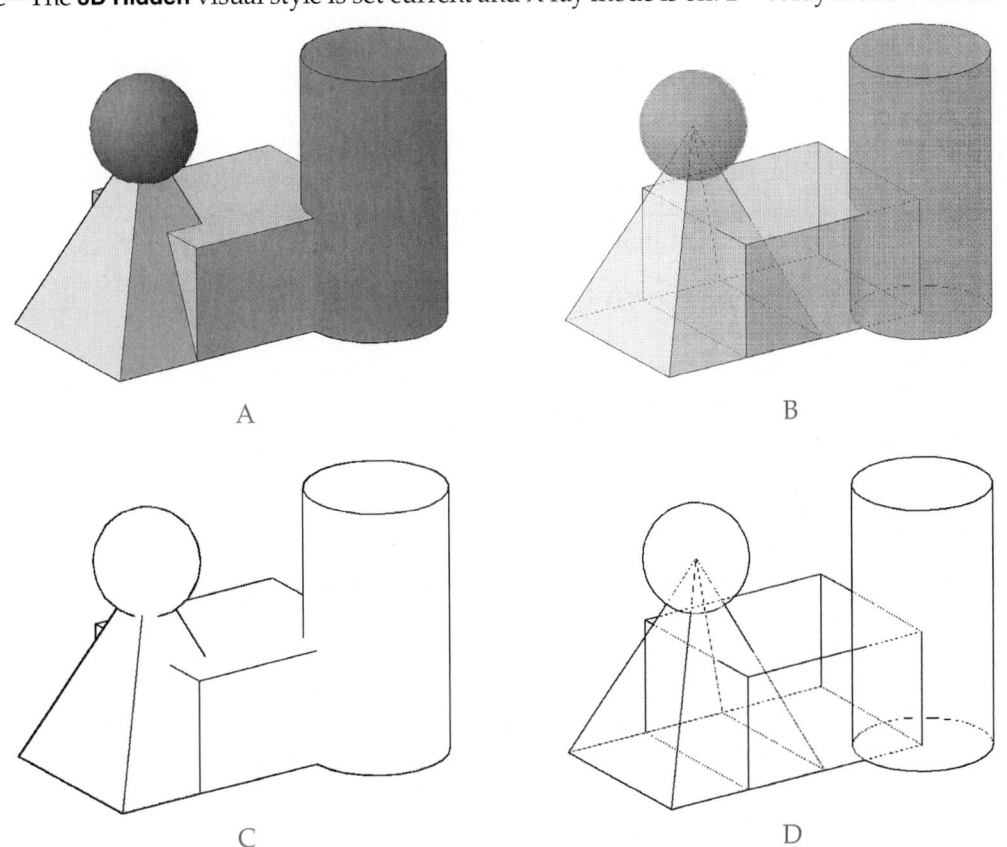

A

B

C

D

Figure 3-14.
A—The **Facets** button in the **Visual Style** control panel turns on the display of facets. B—The **Smooth** button in the **Visual Style** control panel turns the facet display off so that curved surfaces appear smooth.

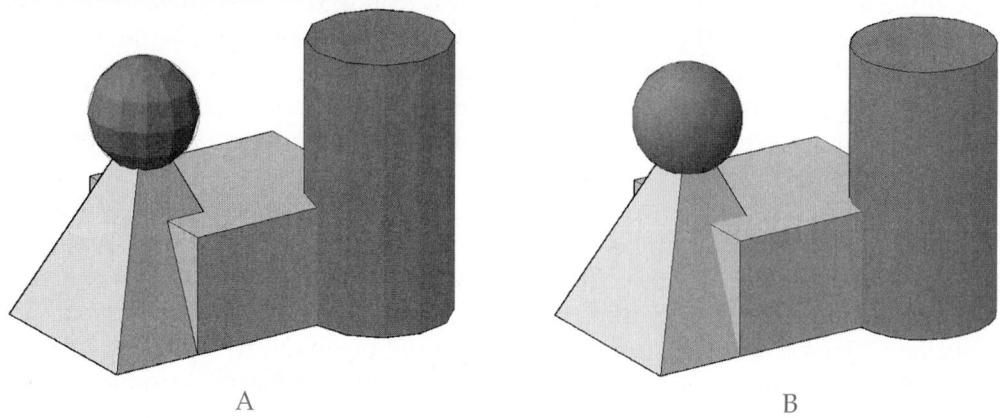

A   B

The color is controlled by the **VSMONOCOLOR** system variable.

When the **Tint mode** button is selected in the flyout, a tint is applied to the colors assigned to faces. The hue and saturation of the assigned colors is altered by applying a selected color. The color is controlled by the **VSMONOCOLOR** system variable.

Face Style. The face style flyout contains three buttons that determine the style in which the model faces are displayed. This flyout is located below the **Visual styles** drop-down list. The use of these options is shown in Figure 3-15.

- **No face style.** No colors or materials are displayed.
- **Realistic.** The default setting displays faces as realistically as possible without rendering.
- **Gooch.** Subdued colors eliminate darkness and highlights that might otherwise obscure or hide faces and details.

NOTE

Whenever you make a change to the face or edge settings, the name of the visual style in the **Visual styles** drop-down list changes to *Current*. If you select a named visual style from the drop-down list, the settings of that visual style override the settings you made.

Visual style edge settings

There are six settings at the bottom of the **Visual Style** control panel that control the appearance of both visible and obscured edges. Obscured edges are those that would normally be hidden by the object or other objects.

Edge Display. The flyout and drop-down list directly below the **Facets** and **Smooth** buttons control the lines displayed to define solids. Set the color of the lines using the drop-down list. The flyout contains three buttons:

- **No edges.** Object edges are not shown. The **Obscured edges** and **Intersection edges** options at the bottom of the control panel are disabled. This is the same as setting the **VSEDGES** system variable to 0.
- **Isolines.** Displays isolines based on the current **ISOLINES** system variable setting. The isolines are shown in the color set in the **Edge color** drop-down list next to the button. The **Obscured edges** and **Intersection edges** options at the bottom of the control panel are disabled. This is the same as setting the **VSEDGES** system variable to 1.

Figure 3-15.
A—The **Conceptual** visual style is set current, then the **No face style** button is selected in the **Visual Style** control panel. No colors or materials are displayed. B—The **Gooch** button is selected. Subdued colors eliminate darkness and highlights that might otherwise obscure or hide faces and details. This is the default setting for the **Conceptual** visual style. C—The **Realistic** button is selected. The faces are displayed as realistically as possible without rendering.

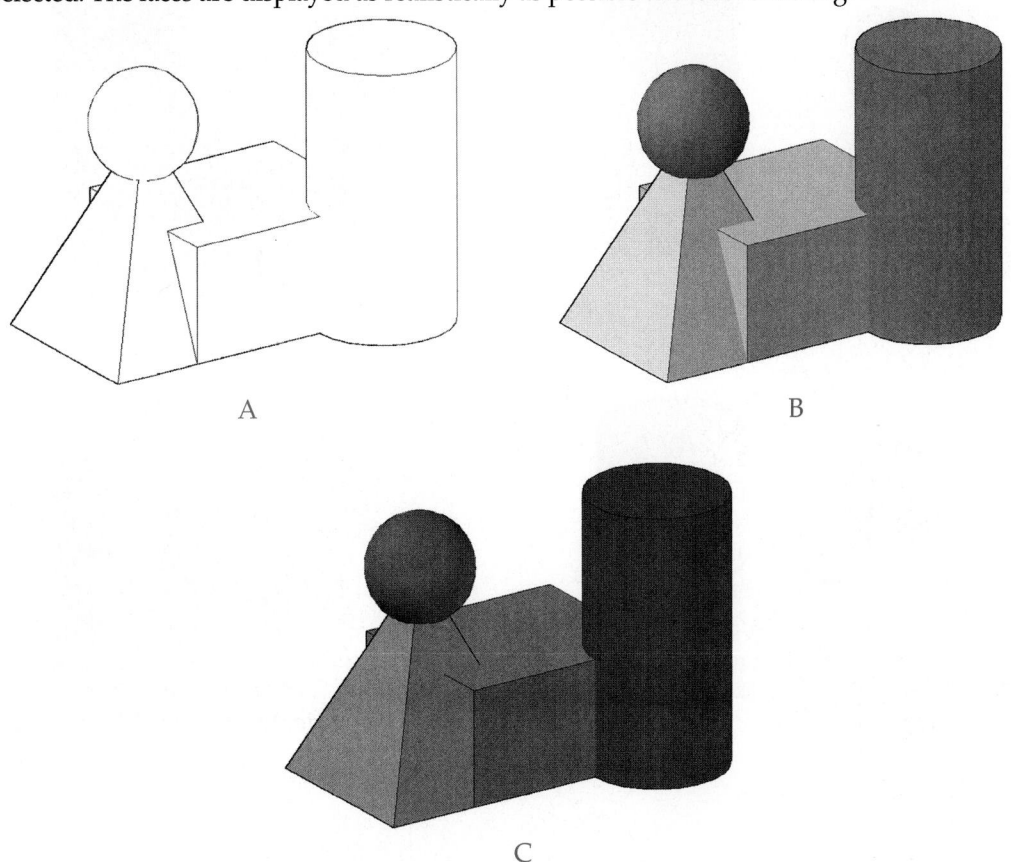

A   B

C

- **Facet edges.** Edges of 3D faces are displayed in the color selected in the **Edge color** drop-down list next to the button. The **Obscured edges** and **Intersection edges** options at the bottom of the control panel are enabled. This is the same as setting the **VSEDGES** system variable to 2.

Edge Overhang. This setting determines if straight edges extend or "overhang" beyond corners. See **Figure 3-16A.** Extended edges are used to create the look of an architectural sketch. The **Edge overhang** button is either on or off. When on, the button is displayed in orange. Use the **Edge overhang** slider bar next to the button to increase or decrease the amount of overhang. As you drag the slider, the overhang dynamically changes in the viewport. This setting is controlled by the **VSEDGEOVERHANG** system variable.

Edge Jitter. Edge jitter creates a sketch look along the entire length of edges by drawing multiple lines for the edges. See **Figure 3-16B.** The **Edge jitter** button is either on or off. When on, the button is displayed in orange. The number of lines drawn for edges can be from zero to three. This can be set using the **Edge jitter** slider next to the button or changing the **VSEDGEJITTER** system variable.

Silhouette Edges. The **Silhouette edges** button determines whether or not a highlighting line is applied to the silhouettes of objects. See **Figure 3-16C.** The button is either on or off. When on, the button is displayed in orange and the highlighting line is applied. The intersecting edges of shapes are not silhouetted. Use the **Silhouette edge width** slider bar next to the button to set the thickness of the highlighting line. This is controlled by the **VSSILHEDGES** system variable and is independent of the **DISPSILH** system variable.

Figure 3-16.
A—The model is displayed with extended edges. B—The model is displayed with edge jitter.
C—The model is displayed with the silhouette edges highlighted. D—The model is displayed
with obscured edges visible.

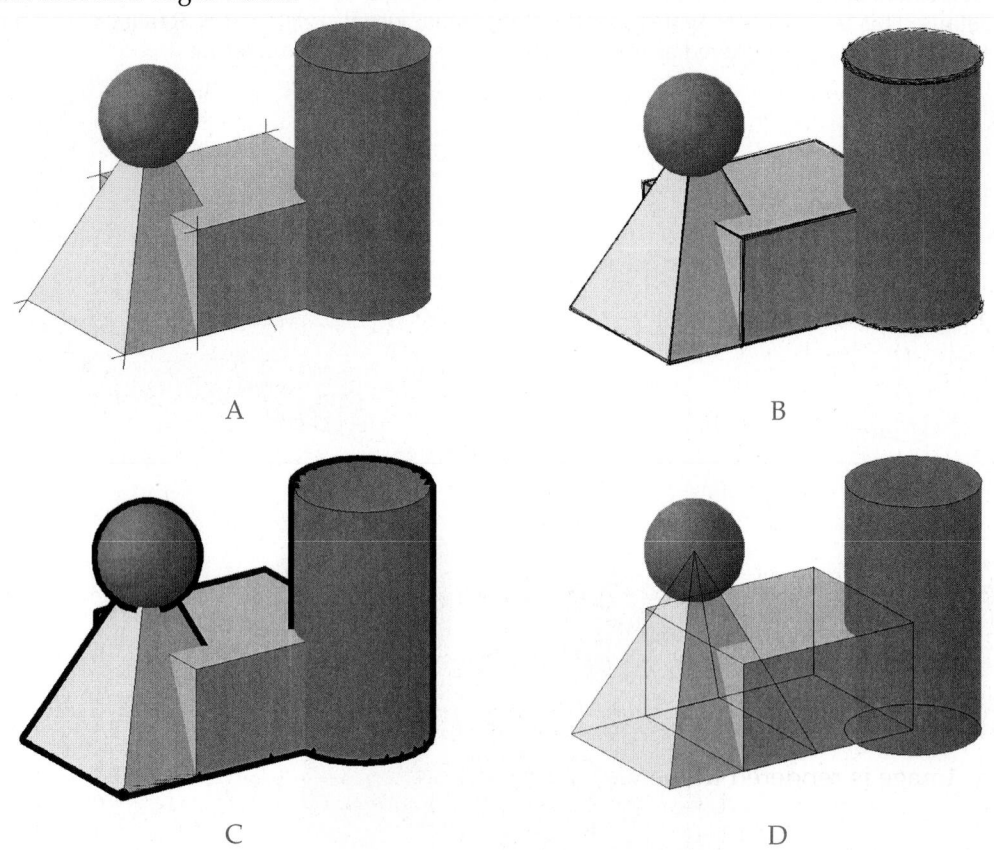

A

B

C

D

Obscured Edges. The **Obscured edges** button determines whether or not edges
that are normally hidden in the current view are displayed. The button is either on or
off. When on, the button is displayed in orange and hidden edges are displayed. See
Figure 3-16D. This setting is controlled by the **VSOBSCUREDEDGES** system variable.
Additionally, when the button is on, the edge color can be changed using the **Obscured
edge color** drop-down list next to the button.

Intersection Edges. The **Intersection edges** button determines whether or not lines
are drawn where solids overlap. The button is either on or off. When on, the button is
displayed in orange and a line is drawn at the intersection. This setting is controlled
by the **VSINTERSECTIONEDGES** system variable. Additionally, when the button is on,
the color of the intersecting edges can be changed using the **Intersection edge color**
drop-down list next to the button.

NOTE

The **ISOLINES**, **DISPSILH**, and **FACETRES** system variables are
covered in detail in Chapter 13.

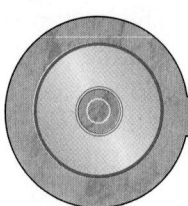

Exercise 3-6

Complete the exercise on the Student CD.

3D Orbit Visual Style Options

The **3DORBIT** shortcut menu can be used to change visual styles while the command is active. With the shortcut menu displayed, pick **Visual Styles** to display a cascading menu. This cascading menu contains four options—**3D Hidden**, **3D Wireframe**, **Conceptual**, and **Realistic**. Any user-defined visual styles are also shown in this cascading menu. Selecting a visual style here sets it current, just as using **Visual Styles** control panel in the **Dashboard** to set a visual style current. When the **3DORBIT** command is exited, the visual style is retained as the current visual style.

Rendering a Model

The **RENDER** command creates a realistic image of a model, Figure 3-17. However, rendering an image takes longer than shading an image. There are a variety of settings that you can change with the **RENDER** command that allow you to fine-tune renderings. These include lights, materials, backgrounds, fog, and preferences. Render settings are discussed in detail in Chapter 13 through Chapter 15.

When the command is initiated, the render window is displayed and the image is rendered. See Figure 3-18. The rendering that is produced is based on a variety of advanced render settings that are discussed in Chapter 13 through Chapter 15. The default render settings create an image using a single light source located behind the viewer. The light intensity is set to 1 and, if no materials are applied, the objects are rendered with a matte material that is the same color as the object display color.

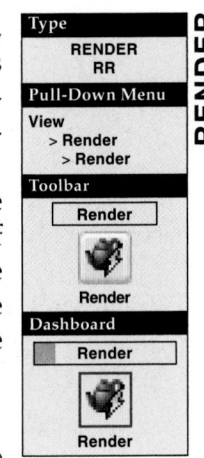

Type	
RENDER RR	**RENDER**
Pull-Down Menu	
View > Render > Render	
Toolbar	
Render	
Render	
Dashboard	
Render	
Render	

NOTE

If the image is rendered in the viewport, clean the screen using the **ZOOM, PAN, REGEN,** or **REDRAW** command. Setting the rendering destination as the viewport is discussed in Chapter 13.

Exercise 3-7
Complete the exercise on the Student CD.

Figure 3-17.
Rendering produces the most realistic display and can show shadows and materials.

Figure 3-18.
The rendered model is displayed in the render window.

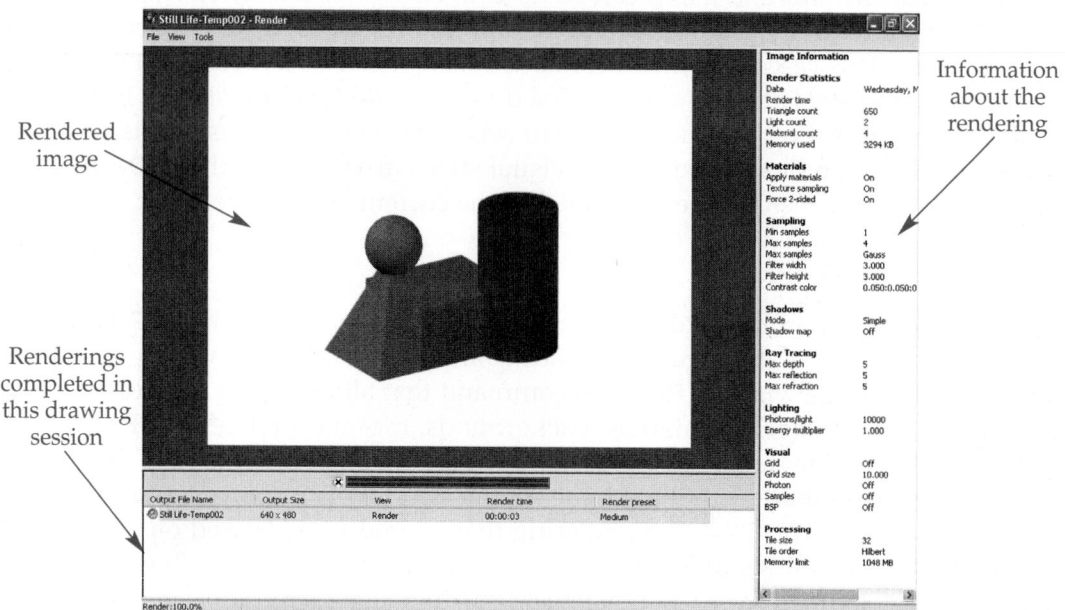

Rendered image

Information about the rendering

Renderings completed in this drawing session

Chapter Test

Answer the following questions. Write your answers on a separate sheet of paper or complete the electronic chapter test on the Student CD.

1. Which command can be used to produce a view that is parallel to the XY plane of the current UCS?
2. What are the two basic orbit modes in the **3DORBIT** command?
3. Which orbit mode allows you to rotate the view up 90°, down 90°, and horizontally 360°?
4. When the **3DFORBIT** command is active, when does the circular arrow cursor appear and what does it mean?
5. Briefly describe how to switch between orbit modes, realtime pan, and realtime zoom while the **3DORBIT** command is active.
6. Which command generates a continuous 3D orbit?
7. How do you set up a continuous orbit?
8. How can you select named views while the **3DORBIT** command is active?
9. What is the difference between *parallel projection* and *perspective projection?*
10. Which visual style is considered the highest level of shading?
11. What is the most realistic presentation?
12. Which visual style face setting produces a transparent image?
13. Which visual style edge setting produces the look of an architectural sketch?
14. How do you change the color of obscured edges in a visual style?
15. What is the function of the **RENDER** command?

Drawing Problems

1. Open one of your 3D drawings from Chapter 2. Do the following.
   A. Use the **3DORBIT** command to create a pictorial view of the drawing.
   B. While in the **3DORBIT** command, set the Conceptual visual style current.
   C. Using the **Dashboard**, display the object so that faces are shown in object colors and edges are highlighted in the color of your choice. Change the edges to different colors.
   D. Save the drawing as P03_01.

2. Open one of your 3D drawings from Chapter 2. Do the following.
   A. Display the objects in Gooch face style.
   B. Toggle the projection from parallel to perspective and turn on the grid and compass.
   C. Create four named views of different parts on the model. Redisplay these views using the **Named Views** cascading menu in the **3DORBIT** shortcut menu.
   D. Put the model into a continuous orbit.
   E. Save the drawing as P03_02.

3. Open one of your 3D drawings from Chapter 2 that was created with solid primitives. Do the following.
   A. Create three named views, each having a different viewpoint.
   B. Use a different visual style face color option in each view.
   C. Save the drawing as P03_03.

4. Open drawing P03_03 and do the following.
   A. Display one view and set obscured edges to blue.
   B. Change the edge display to isolines. What happened?
   C. Display a different view and turn facet edges on.
   D. Display intersection edges as black.
   E. Create a rendering of the object in one of the views.
   F. Save the drawing as P03_04.

Any point on a model or in 3D space can be located with X, Y, and Z coordinates.

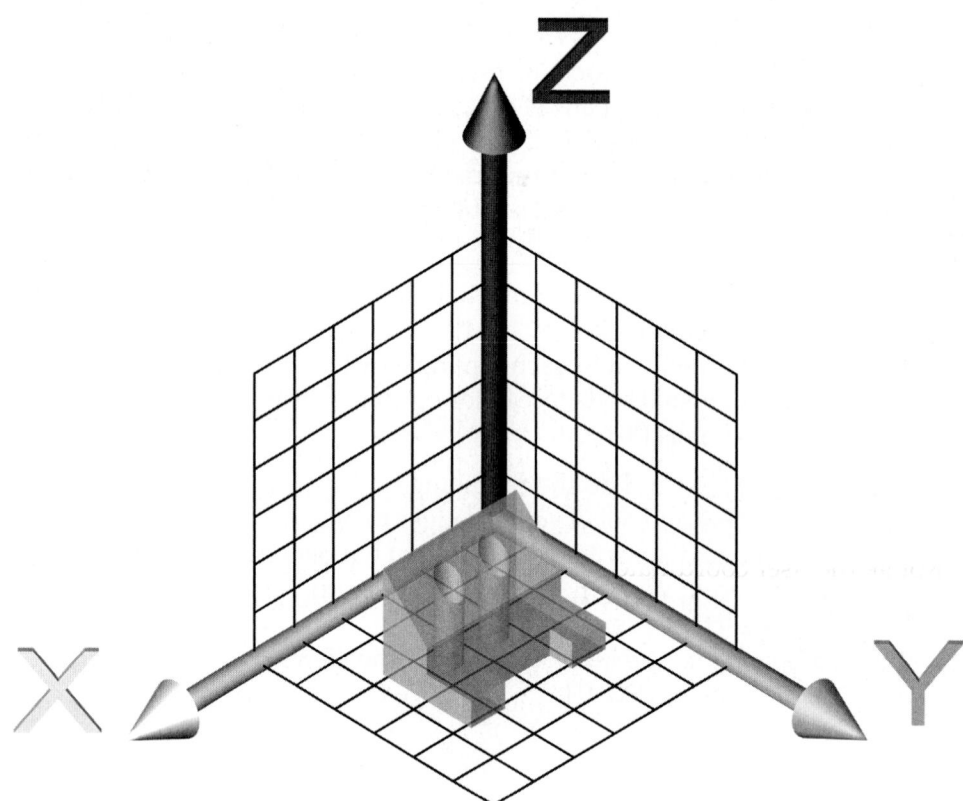

CHAPTER 4

Understanding Three-Dimensional Coordinates and User Coordinate Systems

Learning Objectives

After completing this chapter, you will be able to:

✓ Describe the rectangular, spherical, and cylindrical methods of coordinate entry.
✓ Draw 3D polylines.
✓ Describe the function of the world and user coordinate systems.
✓ Move the user coordinate system to any surface.
✓ Rotate the user coordinate system to any angle.
✓ Change the user coordinate system to match the plane of a geometric object.
✓ Use a dynamic UCS.
✓ Save and manage user coordinate systems.
✓ Restore and use named user coordinate systems.
✓ Control user coordinate system icon visibility in viewports.

As you learned in Chapter 1, any point in space can be located using X, Y, and Z coordinates. This type of coordinate entry is called *rectangular coordinates*. Rectangular coordinates are most commonly used for coordinate entry. However, there are actually three ways in which to locate a point in space. The other two methods of coordinate entry are spherical coordinates and cylindrical coordinates. These two coordinate entry methods are discussed in the following sections. In addition, this chapter introduces working with user coordinate systems (UCSs).

Introduction to Spherical Coordinates

Locating a point in 3D space with *spherical coordinates* is similar to locating a point on Earth using longitudinal and latitudinal values, with the center of Earth representing the origin. Lines of longitude connect the North and South Poles and provide an east-west measurement on Earth's surface. Lines of latitude horizontally extend around Earth and provide a north-south measurement. The origin (Earth's center) can be that of the default world coordinate system (WCS) or the current user coordinate system (UCS). See **Figure 4-1A.**

Figure 4-1.
A—Lines of longitude, representing the highlighted latitudinal segments in the illustration, run from north to south. Lines of latitude, representing the highlighted longitudinal segments, run from east to west. B—Spherical coordinates require a distance, an angle in the XY plane, and an angle from the XY plane.

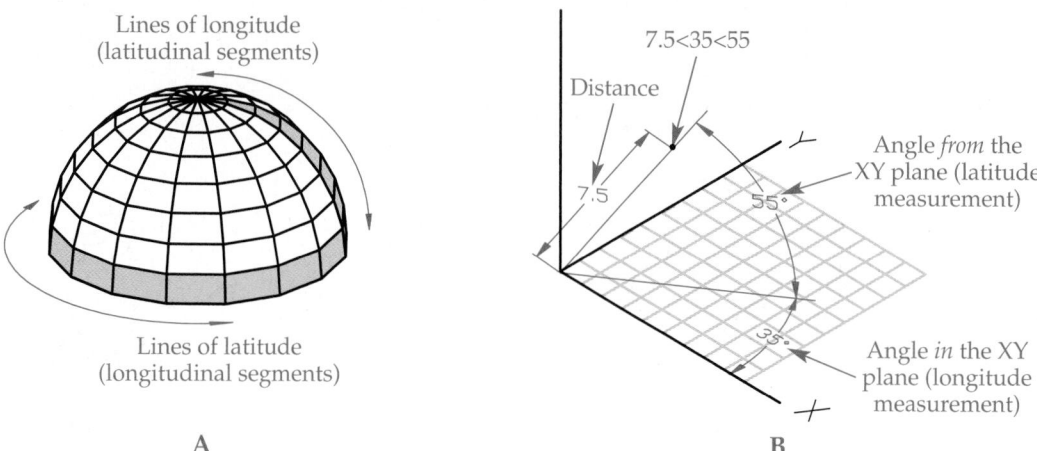

A

B

When entering spherical coordinates, the longitude measurement is expressed as the angle *in* the XY plane and the latitude measurement is expressed as the angle *from* the XY plane. See **Figure 4-1B**. A distance from the origin is also provided. The coordinates represent a measurement from the equator toward either the North or South Pole on Earth's surface. The following spherical coordinate entry is shown in **Figure 4-1B**.

7.5<35<55

This coordinate represents an absolute spherical coordinate, which is measured from the origin of the current UCS. Spherical coordinates can also be entered as relative coordinates. For example, a point drawn with the relative spherical coordinate @2<35<45 is located two units from the last point, at an angle of 35° in the XY plane, and at a 45° angle *from* the XY plane.

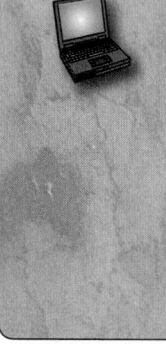

PROFESSIONAL TIP

Spherical coordinates are useful for locating features on a spherical surface. For example, they can be used to specify the location of a hole drilled into a sphere or a feature located from a specific point on a sphere. If you are working on such a spherical object, you might consider locating a UCS at the center of the sphere, then creating several different user coordinate systems rotated at different angles on the surface of the sphere. Any time a location is required, spherical coordinates can be used. Working with UCSs is introduced later in this chapter.

Using Spherical Coordinates

Spherical coordinates are well-suited for locating points on the surface of a sphere. In this section, you will draw a solid sphere and then locate a second solid sphere with its center on the surface of the first sphere.

To draw the first sphere, select the **SPHERE** command. Specify the center point as 7,5 and a radius of 1.5 units. Display a southeast isometric pictorial view of the sphere. Alternately, you can use the **3DORBIT** command to create a pictorial view. Also, set the 3D Wireframe visual style current and switch to a parallel projection. Your drawing should look similar to **Figure 4-2A.**

Since you know the radius of the sphere, but the center of the sphere is not at the origin of the current UCS (the WCS), a relative spherical coordinate will be used to draw the second sphere. The sphere you drew is a solid and, as such, you can snap to its center using object snap. Set **Center** as a running object snap and then enter the **SPHERE** command again to draw the second sphere:

> Specify center point or [3P/2P/Ttr]: **FROM**↵
> Base point: *(use the **Center** object snap to select the center of the existing sphere)*
> <Offset>: **@1.5<30<60**↵ *(1.5 is the radius of the first sphere)*
> Specify radius or [Diameter]: **.4**↵

The objects should now appear as shown in **Figure 4-2B.** The center of the new sphere is located on the surface of the original sphere. This is clear after setting the Conceptual visual style current, **Figure 4-2C.** If you want the surfaces of the spheres to be tangent, add the radius value of each sphere (1.5 + .4) and enter this value when prompted for the offset from the center of the first sphere:

> <Offset>: **@1.9<30<60**↵

Notice in **Figure 4-2B** that the polar axes of the two spheres are parallel. This is because both objects were drawn using the same UCS, which can be misleading unless you understand how objects are constructed based on the current UCS. Test this by locating a cone on the surface of the large sphere, just below the small sphere. First, display a 3D wireframe view of the objects. Then, select the **CONE** command and continue as follows.

> Specify center point of base or [3P/2P/Ttr/Elliptical]: **FROM**↵
> Base point: **CEN**↵
> of *(pick the large sphere)*
> <Offset>: **@1.5<30<30**↵
> Specify base radius or [Diameter]: **.25**↵
> Specify height or [2Point/Axis endpoint/Top radius]: **1**↵

The result of this construction with the Conceptual visual style set current is shown in **Figure 4-3.** Notice how the axis of the cone is parallel to the polar axis of the sphere. To draw the cone so that its axis projects from the center of the sphere, you will need to change the UCS. This is discussed later in this chapter.

Figure 4-2.
A—A three-unit diameter sphere shown from the southeast isometric viewpoint.
B—A .8-unit diameter sphere is drawn with its center located on the surface of the original sphere. Also, lines have been drawn between the poles of the spheres. Notice how the polar axes are parallel. C—The objects after the Conceptual visual style is set current.

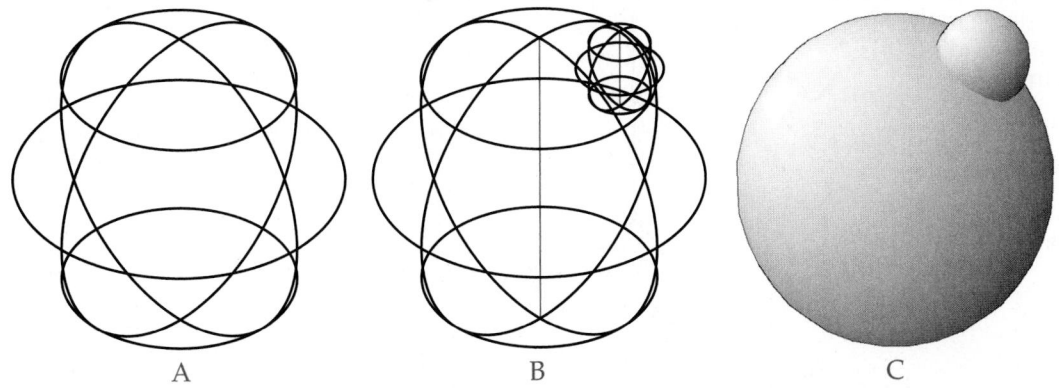

A   B   C

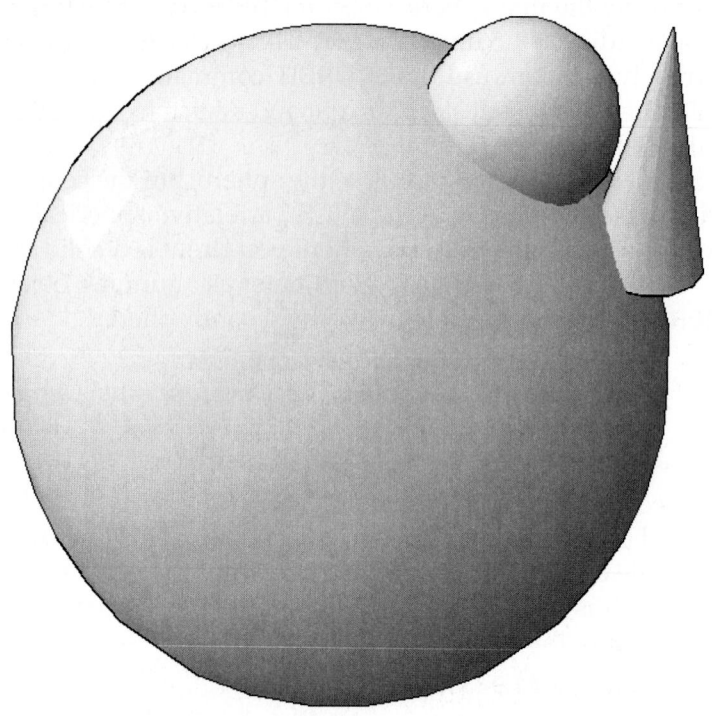

Figure 4-3.
The axis lines of objects drawn in the same user coordinate system are parallel. Notice that the cone does not project from the center of the large sphere.

Introduction to Cylindrical Coordinates

Locating a point in space with *cylindrical coordinates* is similar to locating a point on an imaginary cylinder. Cylindrical coordinates have three values. The first value represents the horizontal distance from the origin, which can be thought of as the radius of a cylinder. The second value represents the angle in the XY plane, or the rotation of the cylinder. The third value represents a vertical dimension measured up from the polar coordinate in the XY plane, or the height of the cylinder. See Figure 4-4. The absolute cylindrical coordinate shown in the figure is:

7.5<35,6

Like spherical coordinates, cylindrical coordinates can also be entered as relative coordinates. For example, a point drawn with the relative cylindrical coordinate @1.5<30,4 is located 1.5 units from the last point, at an angle of 30° in the XY plane of

Figure 4-4.
Cylindrical coordinates require a horizontal distance from the origin, an angle in the XY plane, and a Z dimension.

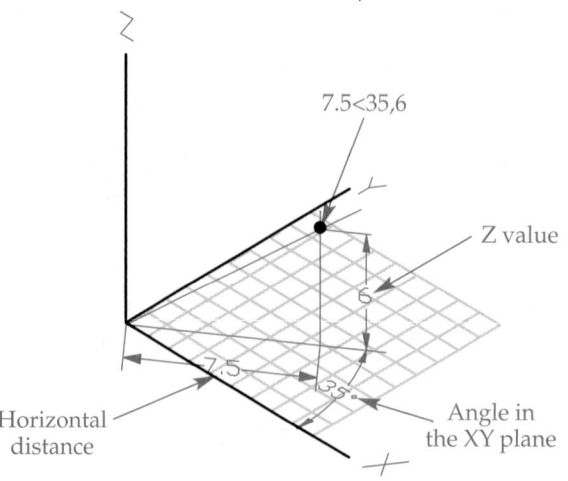

the previous point, and at a distance of four units up from the XY plane of the previous point.

Using Cylindrical Coordinates

Cylindrical coordinates work well for attaching new objects to a cylindrical shape. An example of this is specifying coordinates for a pipe that must be attached to another pipe, tank, or vessel. In **Figure 4-5,** a pipe must be attached to a 12′ diameter tank at a 30° angle from horizontal and 2′-6″ above the floor. In order to properly draw the pipe as a cylinder, you will have to change the UCS, which you will learn how to do later in this chapter. An attachment point for the pipe can be drawn using the **POINT** command and cylindrical coordinates. First, set the **PDMODE** system variable to 3. Then, enter the **POINT** command and continue:

```
Current point modes: PDMODE=3 PDSIZE=0.0000
Specify a point: FROM↵
Base point: CEN↵
of (pick the base of the cylinder)
<Offset>: @6′<30,2′6″↵ (The radius of the tank is 6′.)
```

The point can now be used as the center of the pipe (cylinder), **Figure 4-5B.** However, if you draw the pipe now, it will be parallel to the tank (large cylinder). By changing the UCS, as shown in **Figure 4-5C,** the pipe can be correctly drawn. Working with the UCS is introduced later in this chapter.

Exercise 4-1
Complete the exercise on the Student CD.

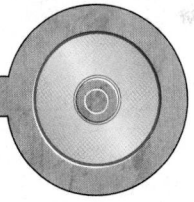

Figure 4-5.
A—A plan view of a tank shows the angle of the pipe attachment. B—A 3D view from the southeast quadrant shows the pipe attachment point located with cylindrical coordinates. C—By creating a new UCS, the pipe can be drawn as a cylinder and correctly located without editing.

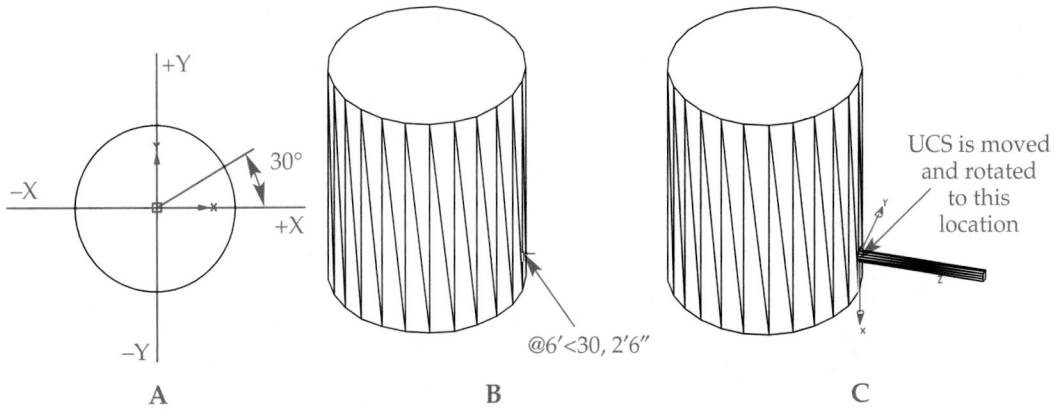

3D Polylines

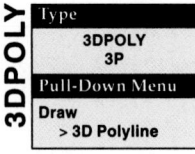

3DPOLY

Type
3DPOLY
3P

Pull-Down Menu

Draw
> 3D Polyline

A polyline drawn with the **PLINE** command is a 2D object. All segments of the polyline must be drawn parallel to the XY plane of the current UCS. A *3D polyline,* on the other hand, can be drawn in 3D space. The Z coordinate value can vary from point to point in the polyline.

The **3DPOLY** command is used to draw 3D polylines. Any form of coordinate entry is valid for drawing 3D polylines. If polar tracking is on when using the **3DPOLY** command, you can pick points in the Z direction if the polar tracking alignment path is parallel to the Z axis.

The **Close** option can be used to draw the final segment and create a closed shape. There must be at least two segments in the polyline to use the **Close** option. The **Undo** option removes the last segment without canceling the command.

The **PEDIT** command can be used to edit 3D polylines. The **PEDIT Spline** option is used to turn the 3D polyline into a B-spline curve based on the vertices of the polyline. A regular 3D polyline and the same polyline turned into a B-spline curve are shown in Figure 4-6. The **SPLFRAME** system variable controls the display of the original polyline frame and is either turned on (1) or off (0).

PROFESSIONAL TIP

A **3D Polyline** toolbar button can be placed in a custom toolbar or added to an existing toolbar. Refer to Chapter 18 for information on customizing toolbars.

Exercise 4-2
Complete the exercise on the Student CD.

Figure 4-6.
A regular 3D polyline and the B-spline curve version after using the **PEDIT** command.

Regular 3D
Polyline

A

B-spline Curve
(**SPLFRAME** On)

B

Introduction to Working with User Coordinate Systems

All points in a drawing or on an object are defined with XYZ coordinate values (rectangular coordinates) measured from the 0,0,0 origin. Since this system of coordinates is fixed and universal, AutoCAD refers to it as the *world coordinate system (WCS).* A *user coordinate system (UCS),* on the other hand, can be defined with its origin at any location and with its three axes in any orientation desired, while remaining at 90° to each other. The **UCS** command is used to change the origin, position, and rotation of the coordinate system to match the surfaces and features of an object under construction. When set up to do so, the UCS icon reflects the changes in the orientation of the UCS and placement of the origin.

The available options for creating and managing a UCS are found in the **Tools** pull-down menu and related cascading menu, on the **UCS** and **UCS II** toolbars, or by typing the **UCS** command. Two UCS selections in the **Tools** pull-down menu provide access to all UCS options. These selections are introduced here and discussed in detail later in this chapter.

- **Named UCS.** This item displays the **UCS** dialog box. The **Named UCS...** button on the **UCS II** toolbar also displays this dialog box. The three tabs in the dialog box contain a variety of UCS and UCS icon options and settings. These options and settings are described as you progress through this chapter.
- **New UCS.** This menu item displays a cascading menu containing most of the UCS command options found on the **UCS** toolbar.

Earlier in this chapter, you used spherical coordinates to locate a small sphere on the surface of a larger sphere. You also drew a cone with the center of its base on the surface of the large sphere. However, the axis of the cone, which is a line from the center of the base to the tip of the cone, is not pointing to the center of the sphere. Refer to Figure 4-3. This is because the Z axes of the large sphere and cone are parallel to the world coordinate system (WCS) Z axis. The WCS is the default coordinate system of AutoCAD.

In order for the axis of the cone to project from the sphere's center point, the UCS must be changed using the **UCS** command. Working with different UCSs is discussed in the next section. However, the following is a quick overview and describes how to draw a cone with its axis projecting from the center of the sphere.

First, draw a three-unit diameter sphere with its center at 7,5. Display the drawing from the southeast isometric preset. To help see how the UCS is changing, make sure the UCS icon is displayed at the origin of the current UCS. Select **View>Display>UCS Icon** and make sure the **On** and **Origin** entries are checked. Also, set the 3D Wireframe visual style current.

Now, the sphere is drawn and the UCS icon is displayed at the origin of the current UCS. However, the WCS is still the current user coordinate system. You are ready to start changing the UCS to meet your needs. Begin by moving the UCS origin to the center of the sphere using the **Origin** option of the **UCS** command. Notice that the UCS icon is now displayed at the center of the sphere, Figure 4-7.

Study Figure 4-8, enter the **UCS** command, and continue as follows. Keep in mind that the point you are locating—the center of the cone on the sphere's surface—is 30° from the X axis and 30° from the XY plane.

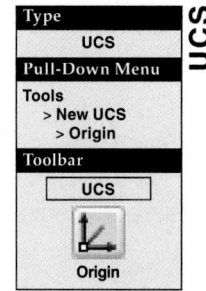

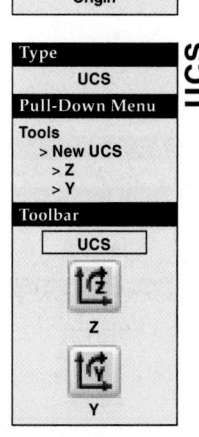

```
Current ucs name: *NO NAME*
Specify origin of UCS or [Face/NAmed/OBject/Previous/View/WorldX/Y/Z/ZAxis]
    <World>: Z↵
Specify rotation angle about Z axis <90>: 30↵ (See Figure 4-8B.)
Command: (press [Enter] or the spacebar to reissue the UCS command)
Current ucs name: *NO NAME*
Specify origin of UCS or [Face/NAmed/OBject/Previous/View/WorldX/Y/Z/ZAxis]
    <World>: Y↵
Specify rotation angle about Y axis <90>: 60↵ (See Figure 4-8D.)
```

Figure 4-7.
The UCS origin is moved to the center of the sphere.

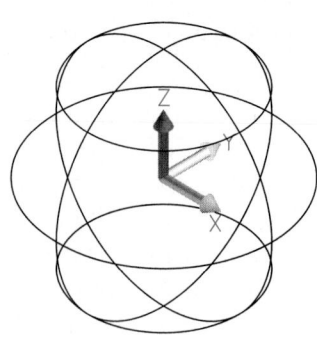

Figure 4-8.
A—The world coordinate system. B—The new UCS is rotated 30° in the XY plane about the Z axis. C—A line rotated up 30° from the XY plane represents the axis of the cone. D—The UCS is rotated 60° about the Y axis. The centerline of the cone coincides with the Z axis of this UCS.

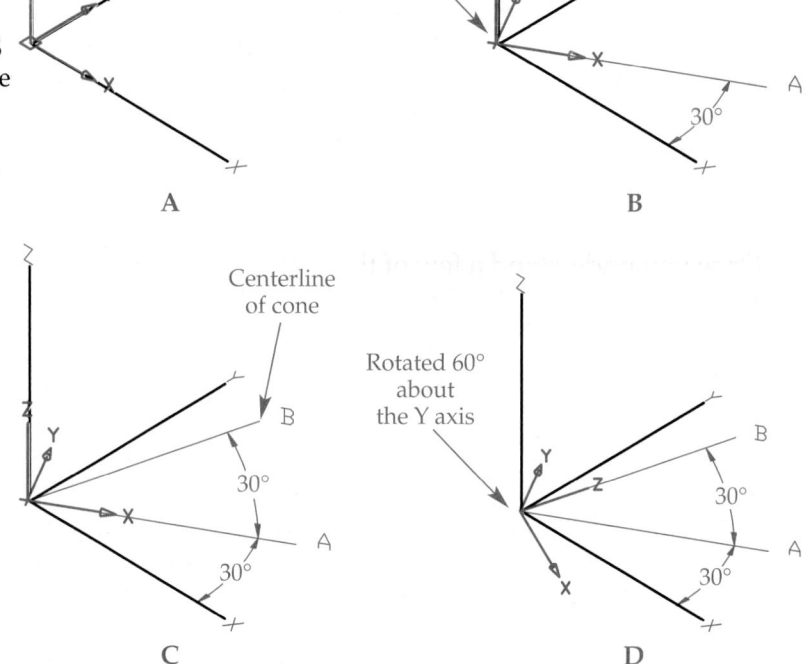

This new UCS can be used to construct a cone with its axis projecting from the center of the sphere. **Figure 4-9A** shows the new UCS located at the center of the sphere. With the UCS rotated, rectangular coordinates can be used to draw the cone. Enter the **CONE** command and specify the center as 0,0,1.5 (the radius of the sphere is 1.5 units). Enter a radius of .25 and a height of one. The completed cone is shown in **Figure 4-9B.** You can see that the axis projects from the center of the sphere. **Figure 4-9C** shows the objects after setting the Conceptual visual style current.

This same basic procedure can be used in the tank and pipe example presented earlier in this chapter. To correctly locate the pipe (cylinder), first rotate the UCS 30° about the Z axis. Then, rotate the UCS 90° about the Y axis. The Z axis of this new UCS aligns with the long axis of the pipe. Finally, use rectangular coordinates to draw the cylinder with its center at the point drawn in **Figure 4-5B.**

Once you have changed to a new UCS, you can quickly return to the WCS using the **World** option of the **UCS** command. The WCS provides a common "starting place" for creating new UCSs.

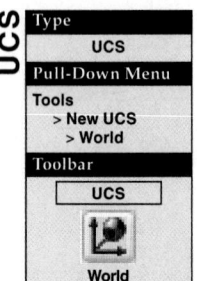

Figure 4-9.

A—A new UCS is created with the Z axis projecting from the center of the sphere. B—A cone is drawn using the new UCS. The axis of the cone projects from the center of the sphere. C—The objects after the Conceptual visual style is set current.

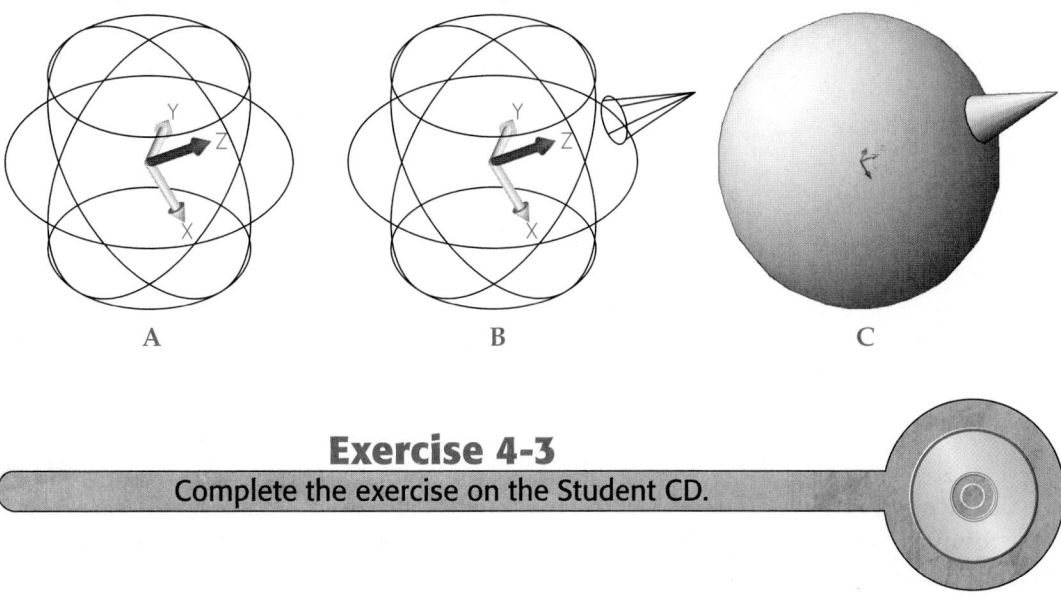

A   B   C

Exercise 4-3

Complete the exercise on the Student CD.

Working with User Coordinate Systems

Once you understand a few of the basic options of user coordinate systems, creating 3D models becomes an easy and quick process. The following sections show how to display the UCS icon, change the UCS in order to work on different surfaces of a model, and name and save a UCS. As you saw in the previous section, working with UCSs is easy.

Displaying the UCS Icon

The symbol that identifies the orientation of the coordinate system is called the *UCS icon.* When AutoCAD is first launched based on the acad3D.dwt template, the UCS icon is located at the WCS origin in the middle of viewport. The display of this symbol is controlled by the **UCSICON** command. If your drawing does not require viewports and altered coordinate systems, you may want to turn the icon off using the **OFF** option of the command. The icon disappears until you turn it on again using the **ON** option of the command. You can also turn the icon on or off and set the icon to display at the origin using the options in the **Settings** tab of the **UCS** dialog box. Refer to Figure 4-10. This dialog box is displayed by picking the **Named UCS...** button on the **UCS II** toolbar, selecting **Tools>Named UCS...**, or typing the **UCSMAN** command.

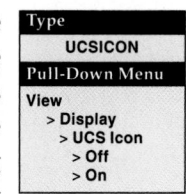

Type
UCSICON
Pull-Down Menu
View
> Display
> UCS Icon
> Off
> On

UCSICON

PROFESSIONAL TIP

It is recommended that you have the UCS icon turned on at all times when working in 3D drawings. It provides a quick indication of the current UCS.

Figure 4-10.
Setting UCS and UCS
icon options in the
UCS dialog box.

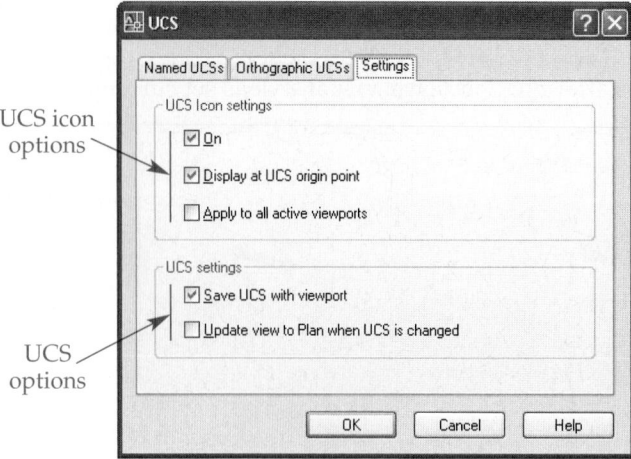

UCS icon options

UCS options

Modifying the UCS Icon

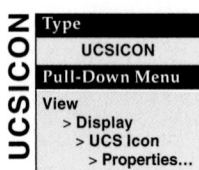

| Type |
| UCSICON |
| Pull-Down Menu |
| View |
| > Display |
| > UCS Icon |
| > Properties... |

The appearance of the wireframe UCS icon can be changed using the settings in the **UCS Icon** dialog box. See **Figure 4-11.** This dialog box is accessed using the **View** pull-down menu or the **Properties** option of the **UCSICON** command. You can modify three characteristics of the UCS icon.

- **Style.** Select either a 2D or 3D icon in the **UCS icon style** area. The 2D style was used by earlier releases of AutoCAD. If the 3D style is selected, the **Cone** and **Line width:** options are available. The line width can be one, two, or three pixels.
- **Size.** The **UCS icon size** area contains a text box and a slider. The value in the text box is the size of the UCS icon expressed as a percentage of the viewport size. Enter a new value in the text box or adjust the slider.
- **Color.** Use the drop-down lists in the **UCS icon color** area to set the color of the UCS icon. Notice that different colors can be set for model space and paper (layout) space.

NOTE

The settings in the **UCS Icon** dialog box have no effect on the shaded 3D UCS icon. This icon is displayed when the 3D Wireframe, 3D Hidden, Conceptual, or Realistic visual style is set current.

Figure 4-11.
The **UCS Icon** dialog box allows you to change the appearance of the wireframe UCS icon.

Set line thickness

Preview of settings

Set style for icon

Set size

Set icon color

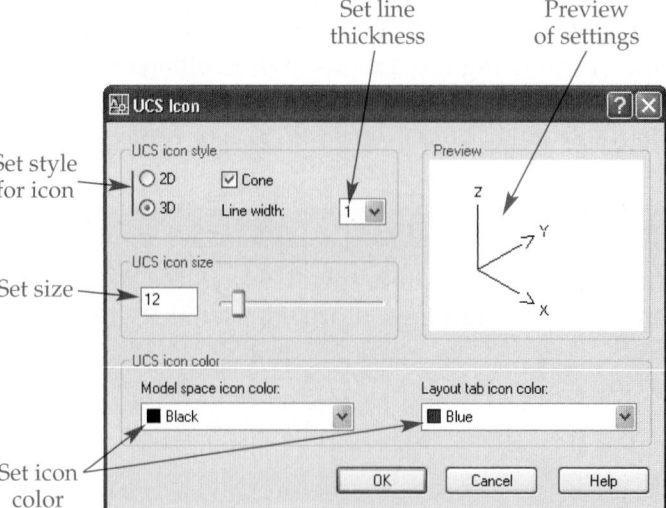

Changing the Coordinate System

To construct a three-dimensional object, you must draw shapes at many different angles. Different planes are needed to draw features on angled surfaces. To construct these features, it is easiest to rotate the UCS to match any surface on an object. The following example illustrates this process.

The object in Figure 4-12 has a cylinder on the angled surface. A solid modeling command called **EXTRUDE**, which is discussed in Chapter 7, is used to create the base of the object. The cylinder is then drawn on the angled feature. In Chapter 6, you will learn how to dimension the object as shown in Figure 4-12.

The first step in creating this model is to draw the side view of the base as a wireframe. You could determine the X, Y, and Z coordinates of each point on the side view and enter the coordinates. However, a lot of typing can be saved if all points share a Z value of 0. By rotating the UCS, you can draw the side view entering only X and Y coordinates. Start a new drawing and display the southeast isometric view. If the UCS icon is off, turn it on and display it at the origin.

Now, rotate the UCS 90° rotation about the X axis. The new UCS is parallel to the side of the object. The UCS icon is displayed at the origin of the UCS. If needed, you may want to pan the screen so the UCS icon is near the center.

Next, use the **PLINE** command to draw the outline of the side view. Refer to the coordinates shown in Figure 4-13. The **PLINE** command is used instead of the **LINE** command because a closed polyline can be extruded into a solid. Be sure to use the **Close** option to draw the final segment. A wireframe of one side of the object is created. Notice the orientation of the UCS icon.

Figure 4-12.
This object can be constructed by changing the orientation of the coordinate system.

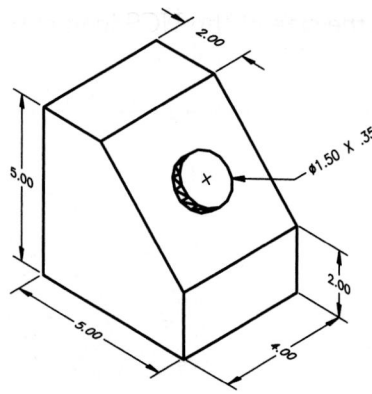

Figure 4-13.
A wireframe of one side of the base is created. Notice the orientation of the UCS.

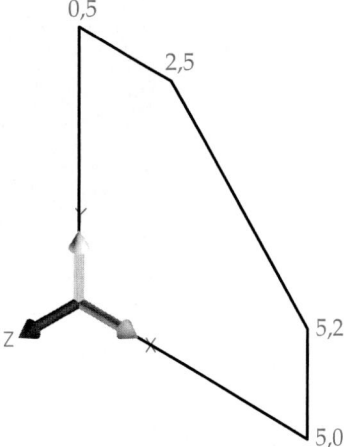

Now, the **EXTRUDE** command is used to create the base as a solid. This command is covered in detail in Chapter 7. On the same UCS used to create the wireframe side, enter the command:

Command: **EXTRUDE**⏎
Current wire frame density: ISOLINES = *current*
Select objects to extrude: *(pick the polyline)*
Select objects to extrude: ⏎
Specify height of extrusion or [Direction/Path/Taper angle]: **–4**⏎
Command:

By entering a negative value for the height of the extrusion, the resulting object extends behind (negative Z) the XY plane of the current UCS. You can also move the cursor so the preview extends below the UCS XY plane and enter positive 4. The base is created as a solid. See Figure 4-14. You may want to switch to a parallel projection, as shown in the figure.

Saving a Named UCS

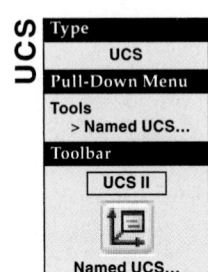

Once you have created a new UCS that may be used again, it is best to save it for future use. For example, you have created a UCS that you used to draw the wireframe of one side of the object. You can save this UCS using the **Save** option of the **UCS** command or the **UCS** dialog box.

If using the dialog box, right-click on the entry Unnamed and pick **Rename** in the shortcut menu. See Figure 4-15. You can also pick once or double-click on the highlighted name. Then, type the new name in place of Unnamed and press [Enter]. A name can have up to 255 characters. Numbers, letters, spaces, dollar signs ($), hyphens (–), and underscores (_) are valid. Use this method to save a new UCS or to rename an existing one. Now, the coordinate system is saved and can be easily recalled for future use.

Figure 4-14.
The wireframe is extruded to create the base as a solid.

Figure 4-15.
Saving a new UCS.
Select **Rename** to enter
a name and save the
Unnamed UCS.

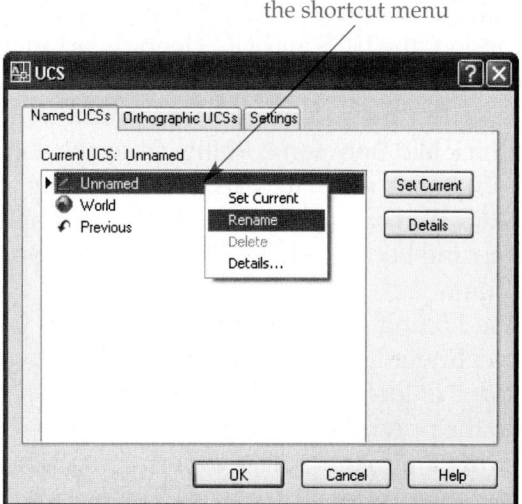

Right-click to display
the shortcut menu

PROFESSIONAL TIP

Most drawings can be created by rotating the UCS as needed without saving it. If the drawing is complex with several planes, each containing a large amount of detail, you may wish to save a UCS for each detailed face. Then, restore the proper UCS as needed. For example, when working with architectural drawings, you may wish to establish a different UCS for each floor plan and elevation view, and for roofs and walls that require detail work.

Dynamic UCS

A powerful tool for 3D modeling is the *dynamic UCS function.* A dynamic UCS is a UCS temporarily located on any existing face of a 3D model. The function is activated by picking the **DUCS** button in the status bar, pressing the [Ctrl]+[D] key combination, or setting the **UCSDETECT** system variable to 1. When the pointer is moved over a model surface, the XY plane of the UCS is aligned with that surface. This is especially useful when adding primitives or shapes to model surfaces. In addition, dynamic UCSs are useful when inserting blocks and xrefs, locating text, editing 3D geometry, editing with grips, and area calculations.

An example of using dynamic UCS is to draw the cylinder on the angled face of the object shown in Figure 4-12. First, select the **CYLINDER** command. Make sure the dynamic UCS function is on. Then, move the pointer over one of the surfaces of the object. Notice that the 3D crosshairs change when they are moved over a new surface. The red (X) and green (Y) crosshairs are flat on the face. For ease of visualizing the 3D crosshairs as they are moved across different surfaces, right-click on the **DUCS** button in the status bar and select **Display crosshair labels** to turn on the XYZ labels on the crosshairs.

As you move the pointer over the object faces, note that hidden faces are not highlighted, therefore you cannot work on those faces. If you wish to work on a hidden face you must first change the viewpoint to make that face visible.

The **CYLINDER** command is currently prompting to select a center point of the base. If you pick a point, this sets the center of the cylinder base *and* temporarily relocates the UCS so its XY plane lies on the selected face. Once the point is selected and the dynamic UCS created, the UCS icon moves to the temporary UCS. When the command is ended, the UCS and UCS icon revert to their previous locations. To locate a 1.5″ diameter cylinder in the center of the angled face, use the following procedure.

1. At the "specify center point of base" prompt, [Shift] + right-click in the drawing area and pick **Mid Between 2 Points** from the shortcut menu. See **Figure 4-16A.**
2. Use the **Endpoint** snap to pick two opposite corners of the angled face. See **Figure 4-16B.** You can also use the **Midpoint** snap and pick the midpoint of the two sides or top and bottom edges. The UCS is temporarily moved to the angled face at the pick point.
3. Specify the 1.5 unit diameter for the base.
4. Specify a cylinder height of .35 units. See **Figure 4-16C.**
5. The cylinder is located properly on the angled face and the UCS automatically returns to the previous location. See **Figure 4-16D.**

When setting a dynamic UCS, experiment with the behavior of the crosshairs as they are moved over different surfaces. The orientation of the crosshairs is related to

Figure 4-16.
Using a dynamic UCS allows you to draw a cylinder on the angled face of the object shown here without creating a new UCS. A—To set the center point of the base and select the angled face for the dynamic UCS, use the **Mid Between 2 Points** snap and select corners or midpoints of the face. B—Set the radius or diameter of the base. C—Set the height of the cylinder. D—When the command is ended, the previous UCS is restored.

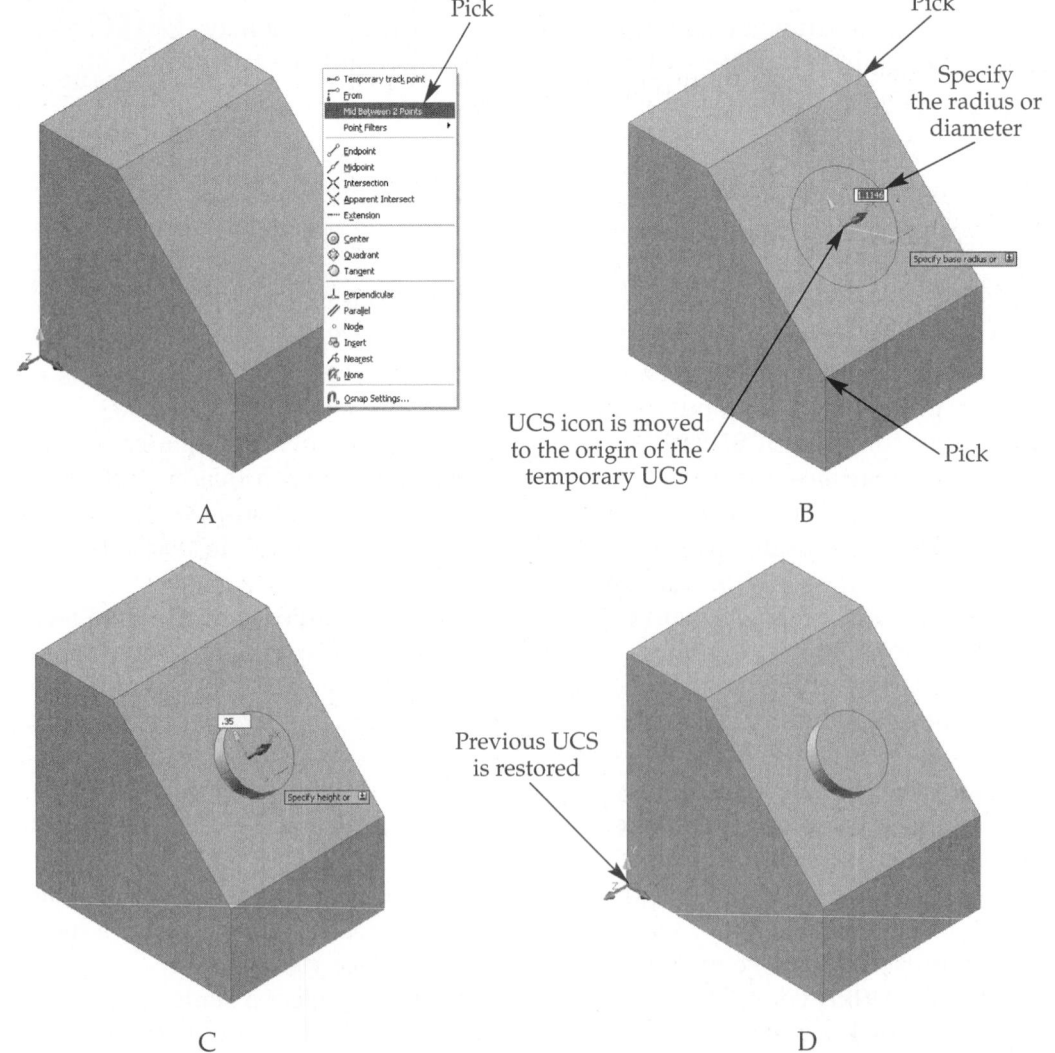

A

B

C

D

AutoCAD and Its Applications—Advanced

the edge of the face that they are moved over. Can you determine the pattern by which the crosshairs are turned? The X axis of the crosshairs is always aligned with the edge that is crossed.

Additional Ways to Change the UCS

There are other ways to change the UCS. These options include picking three points, selecting a new Z axis, and setting the UCS to an existing object. The next sections cover these options.

Selecting Three Points to Create a New UCS

The **3 Point** option of the **UCS** command can be used to change the UCS to any flat surface. This option requires that you first locate a new origin, then a point on the positive X axis, and finally a point on the XY plane that has a positive Y value. Refer to **Figure 4-17.** Use object snaps to select points that are not on the current XY plane. After you pick the third point, the point on the XY plane, the UCS icon changes its orientation to align with the angled surface of the base.

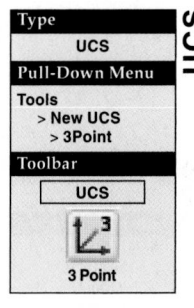

Figure 4-17.
A—A new UCS can be established by picking three points. P1 is the origin, P2 is on the positive X axis, and P3 is on the XY plane and has a positive Y value. B—The new UCS is created.

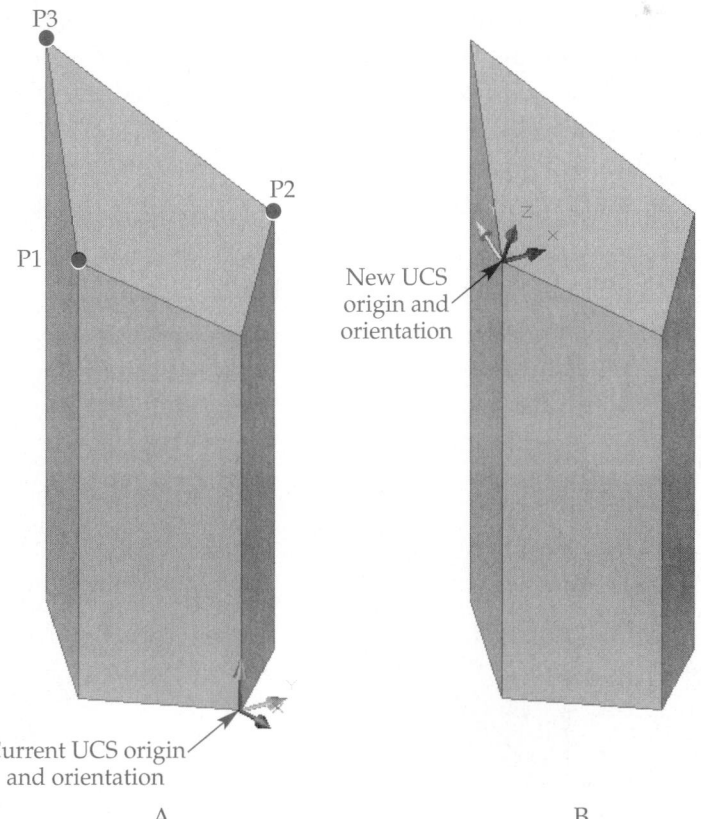

A   B

Selecting a New Z Axis

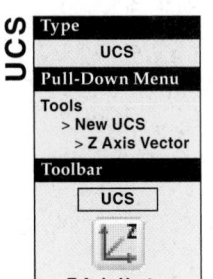

UCS

Type
UCS
Pull-Down Menu
Tools
  > New UCS
  > Z Axis Vector
Toolbar
UCS
Z Axis Vector

The **ZAxis** option of the **UCS** command allows you to select the origin point and a point on the positive Z axis. Once the new Z axis is defined, AutoCAD sets the new X and Y axes.

You will now add a cylinder to the lower face of the base created earlier. The cylinder extends into the base. Refer to the location of the UCS in **Figure 4-16D**. This is the UCS after adding the cylinder to the angled face with a dynamic UCS. The Z axis does not project perpendicular to the lower face. Therefore, a new UCS must be created on the lower-right face. Change the UCS after entering the **ZAxis** option as follows.

1. Pick the origin of the new UCS. See **Figure 4-18A**. You may have to use an object snap to select the origin.
2. Pick a point on the positive portion of the new Z axis.
3. The new UCS is established and it can be saved if necessary.

Now, use auto-tracking or object snaps to draw a ∅.5″ cylinder centered on the lower face and extending 3″ into the base. Then, subtract the cylinder from the base part to create the hole, as shown in **Figure 4-18B**.

Setting the UCS to an Existing Object

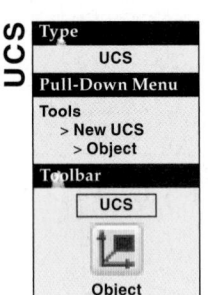

UCS

Type
UCS
Pull-Down Menu
Tools
  > New UCS
  > Object
Toolbar
UCS
Object

The **Object** option of the **UCS** command can be used to define a new UCS on an object. However, there are some objects on which this option cannot be used: 3D polylines, 3D meshes, and xlines. There are also certain rules that control the orientation of the UCS. For example, if you select a circle, the center point becomes the origin of the new UCS. The pick point on the circle determines the direction of the X axis. The Y axis is relative to X, and the UCS Z axis is the same as the Z axis of the selected object.

Look at **Figure 4-19A**. The circle shown is rotated an unknown number of degrees from the XY plane of the WCS. However, you need to create a UCS in which the circle

---

Figure 4-18.
A—Using the **ZAxis** option to establish a new UCS. B—The new UCS is used to create a cylinder, which is then subtracted from the base to create a hole.

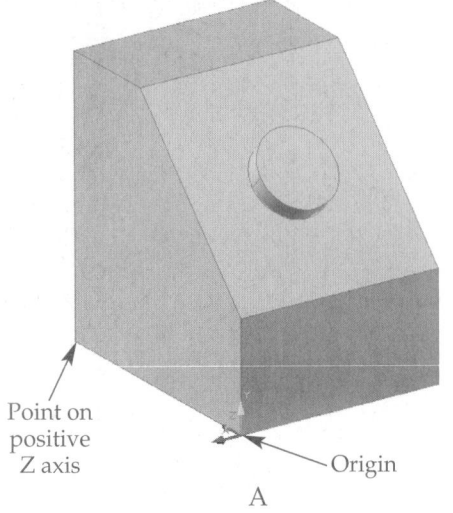

Point on positive Z axis — Origin

A

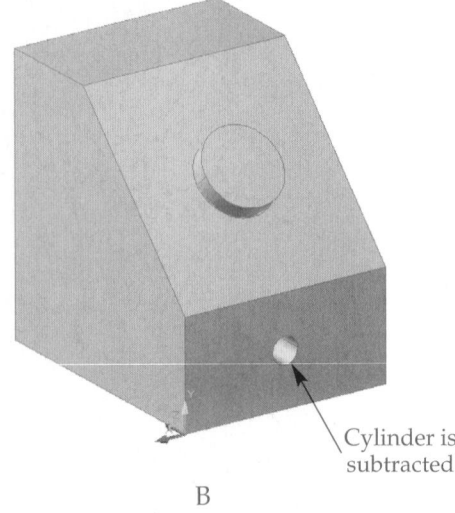

Cylinder is subtracted

B

Figure 4-19.
A—This circle is rotated off of the WCS XY plane by an unknown number of degrees. It will be used to establish a new UCS. B—The circle is on the XY plane of the new UCS. However, the X and Y axes do not align with the circle's quadrants. C—The **ZAxis** option of the **UCS** command is used to align the UCS with the quadrants of the circle.

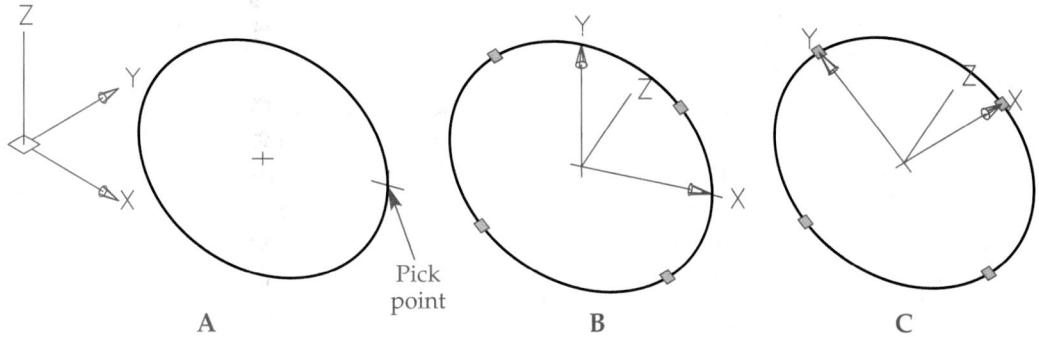

is lying on the XY plane. Select the **Object** option of the **UCS** command and then pick the circle. The UCS icon may look like the one shown in **Figure 4-19B.** Notice how the X and Y axes are not aligned with the quadrants of the cylinder base, as indicated by the grip locations. This may not be what you expected. The X axis orientation is determined by the pick point on the cylinder base. Notice how the X axis is pointing at the pick point.

To rotate the UCS in the current plane so the X and Y axes of the UCS are aligned with the quadrants of the circle, use the **ZAxis** option of the **UCS** command. Select the center of the circle as the origin and then enter the absolute coordinate 0,0,1. This uses the current Z axis location, which also forces the X and Y axes to align with the object. Refer to **Figure 4-19C.** This method may not work with all objects.

Setting the UCS to the Face of a 3D Solid

The **Face** option of the **UCS** command allows you to orient the UCS to any face on a 3D solid object. This option does not work on surface objects. Select the command and then pick a face on the solid. After you have selected a face on a 3D solid, you have the options of moving the UCS to the adjacent face or flipping the UCS 180° on the X, Y, or both axes. Use the **Next**, **Xflip**, or **Yflip** options to move or rotate the UCS as needed. Once you achieve the UCS orientation you want, press [Enter] to accept. Notice in **Figure 4-20** how many different UCS orientations can be selected for a single face.

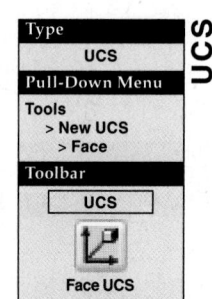

Setting the UCS Perpendicular to the Current View

You may need to add notes or labels to a 3D drawing that are plan to the current view, such as that shown in **Figure 4-21.** The **View** option of the **UCS** command makes this easy to do. Immediately after selecting the **View** option, the UCS rotates to a position so the new XY plane is perpendicular to the current line of sight. Now, anything added to the drawing is plan to the current view. The command works on the current viewport only; other viewports are unaffected.

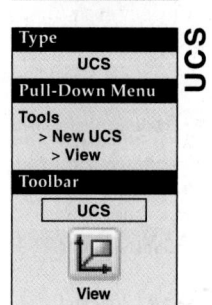

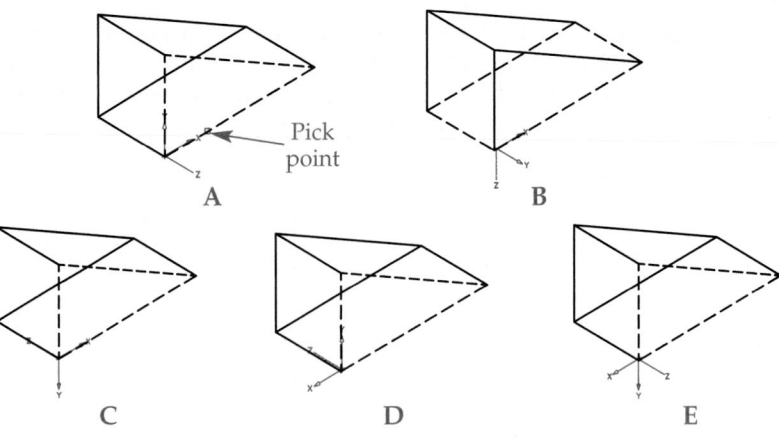

Figure 4-20.
Several different UCSs can be selected from a single pick point using the **Face** option of the **UCS** command. Given the pick point, five of the eight possibilities are shown here.

Pick point

A   B   C   D   E

Figure 4-21.
The **View** option of the **UCS** command allows you to place text plan to the current view.

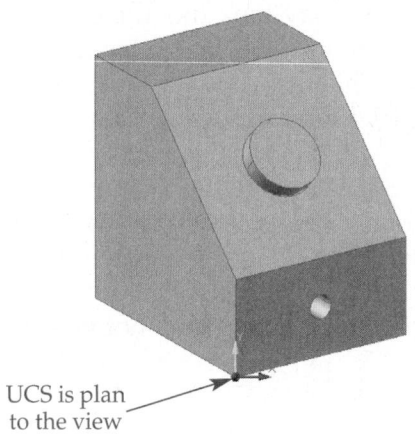

SOLID MODEL

UCS is plan to the view

Applying the Current UCS to a Viewport

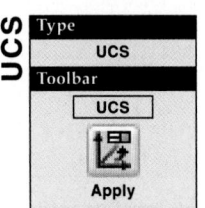

The **Apply** option of the **UCS** command allows you to apply the UCS in the current viewport to any or all model space or paper space viewports. Using the **Apply** option, you can have a different UCS displayed in every viewport, or you can apply one UCS to all viewports. With the viewport that contains the UCS to apply active, enter the **Apply** option. Then, pick a viewport to which the current UCS will be applied and press [Enter]. To apply the current UCS to all viewports, enter the **All** option.

Preset UCS Orientations

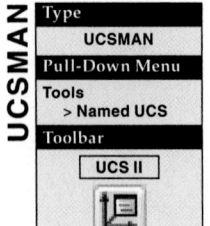

AutoCAD has six preset orthographic UCSs that match the six standard orthographic views. With the current UCS as the top view (plan), all other views are arranged as shown in Figure 4-22. These orientations can be selected in the drop-down list that appears on the **UCS II** toolbar, in the **Tools** pull-down menu, or in the **Orthographic UCSs** tab of the **UCS** dialog box.

The **Relative to:** drop-down list at the bottom of the **Orthographic UCSs** tab of the **UCS** dialog box specifies whether the orthographic UCS is relative to a named UCS or absolute to the WCS. For example, suppose you have a saved UCS named Front Corner that is rotated 30° about the Y axis of the WCS. If you set the top UCS current relative to the WCS, the new UCS is perpendicular to the WCS, Figure 4-23A. However, if the top UCS is set current relative to the named UCS Front Corner, the new UCS is also rotated from the WCS, Figure 4-23B.

Figure 4-22.
The standard orthographic UCSs coincide with the six basic orthographic views.

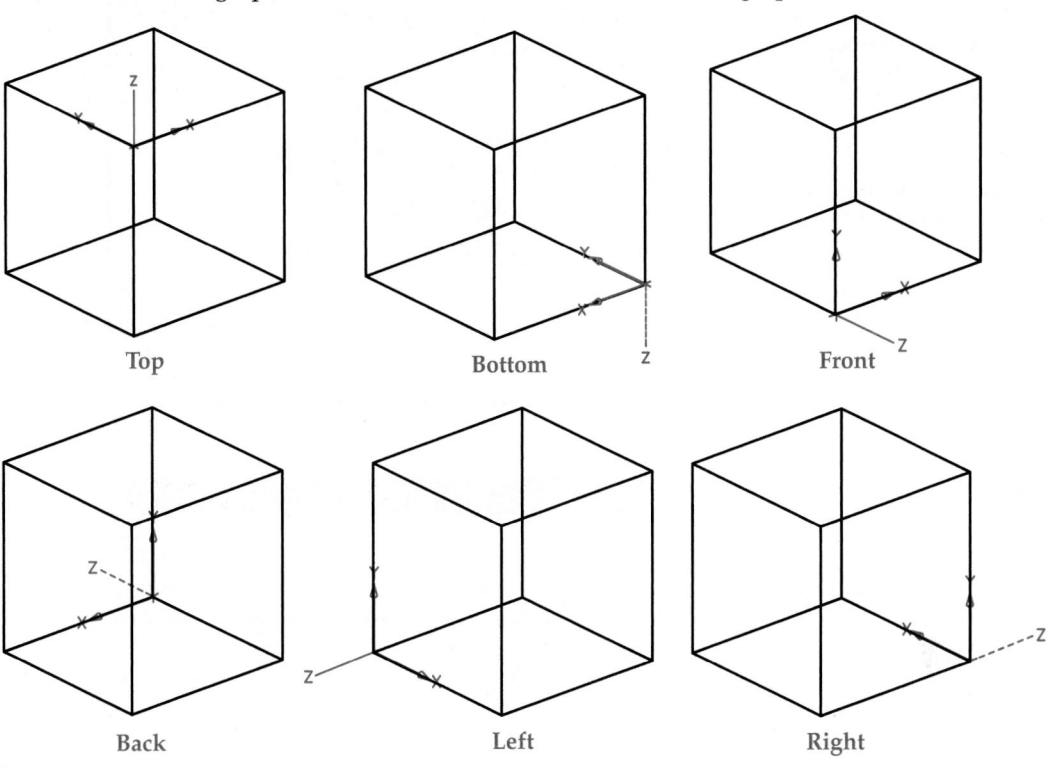

Top   Bottom   Front

Back   Left   Right

Figure 4-23.
The **Relative to:** drop-down list entry in the **Orthographic UCSs** tab of the **UCS** dialog box determines whether the orthographic UCS is based on a named UCS or the WCS. The UCS icon here represents the named UCS. A—Relative to the WCS. B—Relative to the named UCS.

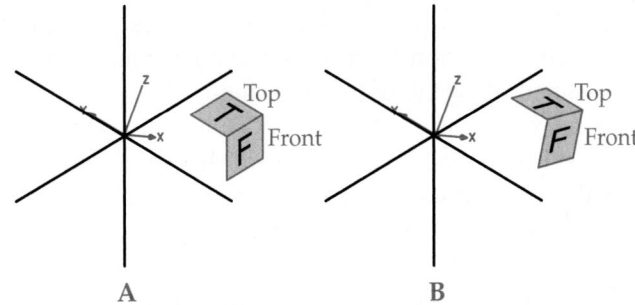

A   B

The Z value, or depth, of a preset UCS can be changed in the **Orthographic UCSs** tab of the **UCS** dialog box. First, right-click on the name of the UCS you wish to change. Then, pick **Depth** from the shortcut menu, **Figure 4-24A.** This displays the **Orthographic UCS depth** dialog box. See **Figure 4-25B.** You can either enter a new depth value or specify the new location on screen by picking the **Select new origin** button. Once the new depth has been selected, it is reflected in the preset UCS list.

PROFESSIONAL TIP

Changing the **Relative to:** setting affects *all* preset UCSs and *all* preset viewpoints! Therefore, leave this set to **World** unless absolutely necessary to change it.

Figure 4-24.
A—The Z value, or depth, of a preset UCS can be changed by right-clicking on its name and selecting **Depth**. B—Enter a new depth value or pick the **Select new origin** button to pick a new location on screen.

Right-click to display the shortcut menu

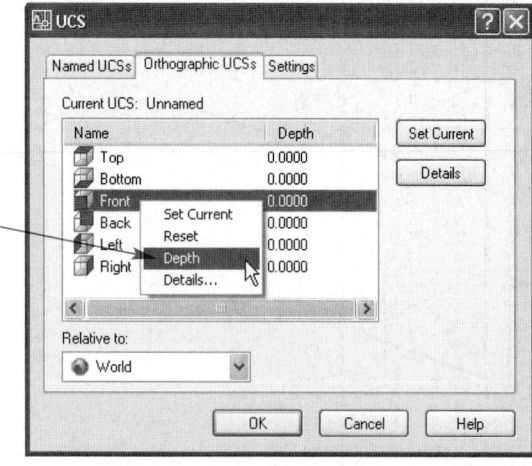

A

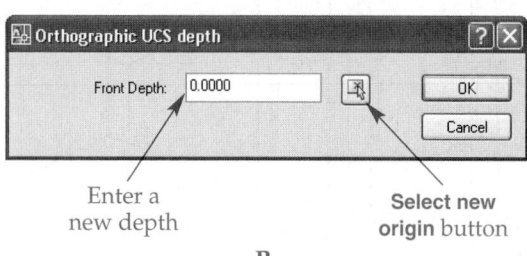

Enter a new depth

Select new origin button

B

Managing User Coordinate Systems and Displays

You can create, name, and use as many user coordinate systems as needed to construct your model or drawing. As you saw earlier, AutoCAD allows you to name (save) coordinate systems for future use. User coordinate systems can be created, renamed, set current, and deleted using the **Named UCSs** tab of the **UCS** dialog box, Figure 4-25.

The **Named UCSs** tab contains the **Current UCS:** list box. This list box contains the names of all saved coordinate systems plus World. If other coordinate systems have been used in the current drawing session, Previous appears in the list. Unnamed appears if the current coordinate system has not been named. The current UCS is indicated by a small triangle next to its name in the list. To make any of the listed coordinate systems active, highlight the name and pick the **Set Current** button.

A list of coordinate and axis values of the highlighted UCS can be displayed by picking the **Details** button. This displays the **UCS Details** dialog box shown in Figure 4-26.

If you right-click on the name of a UCS in the list in the **Named UCSs** tab, a shortcut menu is displayed. Using this menu, you can rename the UCS. Saving a UCS is discussed earlier in this chapter. You can also set the UCS current or delete it using the shortcut menu. The Unnamed UCS cannot be deleted, nor can World be deleted.

PROFESSIONAL TIP

You can manage UCSs on the command line using the **UCS** command.

Figure 4-25.
The **UCS** dialog box allows you to rename, list, delete, and set current an existing UCS.

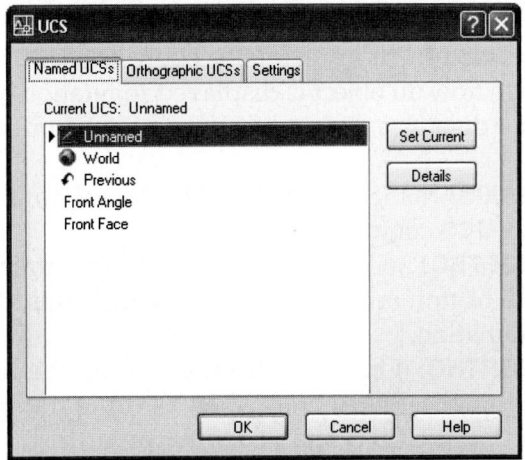

Figure 4-26.
The **UCS Details** dialog box displays the coordinate values of the selected UCS.

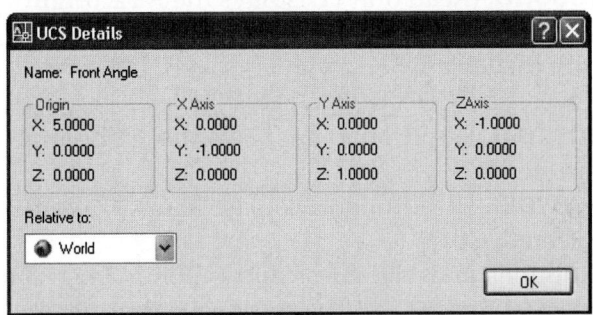

Exercise 4-4
Complete the exercise on the Student CD.

Setting an Automatic Plan Display

After changing the UCS, a plan view is often needed to give you a better feel for the XYZ directions. While you should try to draw in a pictorial view when possible as you construct a 3D object, some constructions may be much easier in a plan view. AutoCAD can be set to automatically make your view of the drawing plan to the current UCS. This is especially useful if you will be changing the UCS often, but want to work in a plan view.

The **UCSFOLLOW** system variable is used to automatically display a plan view of the current UCS. When it is set to 1, a plan view is automatically created in the current viewport when the UCS is changed. Viewports are discussed in Chapter 5. The default setting of **UCSFOLLOW** is 0 (off). After setting the variable to 1, a plan view will be automatically generated the next time the UCS is changed. The **UCSFOLLOW** variable generates the plan view only after the UCS is changed, not immediately after the variable is changed. However, if you select a different viewport, the previous viewport is set plan to the UCS if **UCSFOLLOW** has been set to 1 in that viewport. The **UCSFOLLOW** variable can be individually set for each viewport.

PROFESSIONAL TIP

To get the plan view displayed without changing the UCS, use the **PLAN** command, which is discussed in Chapter 3.

UCS Settings and Variables

As discussed in the previous section, the **UCSFOLLOW** system variable allows you to change how an object is displayed in relation to the UCS. There are also system variables that display a variety of information about the current UCS. These variables include:

- **UCSAXISANG.** (Stored value) The default rotation angle for the **X**, **Y**, or **Z** option of the **UCS** command.
- **UCSDETECT.** (On or off) Turns the dynamic UCS function on and off. The **DUCS** button on the status bar controls this variable, as does the [Ctrl]+[D] key combination.
- **UCSORTHO.** (On or off) If set to 1 (on), the related orthographic UCS setting is automatically restored when an orthographic view is restored. If turned off, the current UCS is retained when an orthographic view is restored.
- **UCSNAME.** (Read only) Displays the name of the current UCS.
- **UCSORG.** (Read only) Displays the XYZ origin value of the current UCS.
- **UCSVIEW.** (On or off) If this variable is set to 1 (on), the current UCS is saved with the view when a view is saved. Otherwise, the UCS is not saved with the view.
- **UCSXDIR.** (Read only) Displays the XYZ value of the X axis direction of the current UCS.
- **UCSYDIR.** (Read only) Displays the XYZ value of the Y axis direction of the current UCS.

UCS options and variables can also be managed in the **Settings** tab of the **UCS** dialog box. See Figure 4-10. The settings in this tab are:

- **Save UCS with viewport.** If checked, the current UCS settings are saved with the viewport and the **UCSVP** system variable is set to 1. This variable can be set for each viewport in the drawing. Viewports in which this setting is turned off, or unchecked, will always display the UCS settings of the current active viewport.
- **Update view to Plan when UCS is changed.** This setting controls the **UCSFOLLOW** variable. When checked, the variable is set to 1. When unchecked, the variable is set to 0.

Chapter Test

Answer the following questions. Write your answers on a separate sheet of paper or complete the electronic chapter test on the Student CD.

1. Explain *spherical coordinate entry.*
2. Explain *cylindrical coordinate entry.*
3. A new point is to be drawn 4.5″ from the last point. It is to be located at a 63° angle in the XY plane, and at a 35° angle from the XY plane. Write the proper spherical coordinate notation.
4. Write the proper cylindrical coordinate notation for locating a point 4. 5″ in the horizontal direction from the origin, 3.6″ along the Z axis, and at a 63° angle in the XY plane.
5. Name the command that is used to draw 3D polylines.
6. Why is the command in Question 5 needed?
7. Which command is used to change a 3D polyline into a B-spline curve?
8. How does the **SPLFRAME** system variable affect the B-spline curve created with the command in Question 7?
9. What is the *WCS?*
10. What is a *user coordinate system (UCS)?*

11. What effect does the **Origin** option of the **UCSICON** command have on the UCS icon display?
12. Describe how to rotate the UCS so that the Z axis is tilted 30° toward the WCS X axis.
13. How do you return to the WCS from any UCS?
14. Which command controls the display of the user coordinate system icon?
15. What is a *dynamic UCS* and how is one activated?
16. What is the function of the **3 Point** option of the **UCS** command?
17. How do you automatically create a display that is plan to a new UCS?
18. What do you do so that the UCS icon is displayed at the origin of the current user coordinate system?
19. How do you move the UCS along the current Z axis?
20. What is the function of the **Object** option of the **UCS** command?
21. The **Face** option of the **UCS** command can be used on which types of objects?
22. What is the function of the **Apply** option of the **UCS** command?
23. In which dialog box is the **Orthographic UCSs** tab located?
24. Which command displays the **UCS** dialog box?
25. What appears in the **Named UCSs** tab of the **UCS** dialog box if the current UCS has not been saved?

Drawing Problems

For Problems 1–4, draw each object using solid primitives and Boolean commands to create composite solids. Measure the objects directly to obtain the necessary dimensions. Plot the drawings at a 3:1 scale using display methods specified by your instructor. Save the drawings as P04_(problem number).

1.

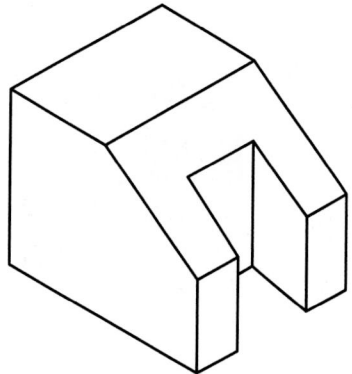

2.

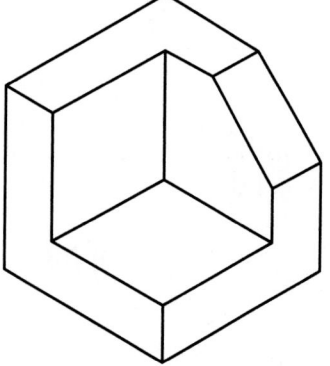

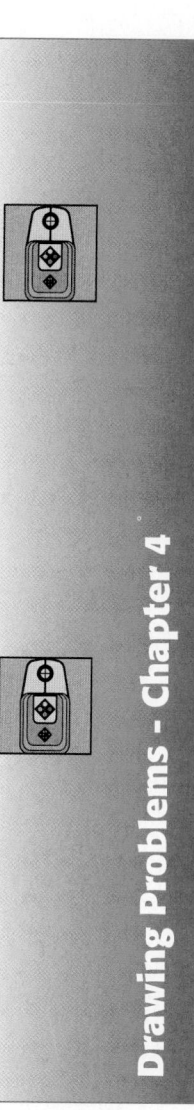

3.

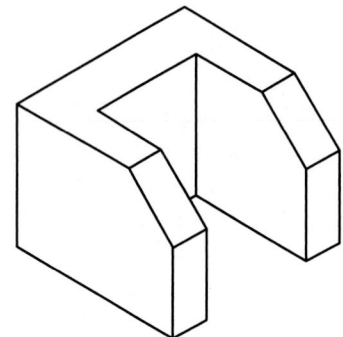

4.

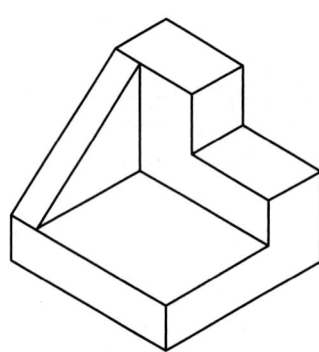

For Problems 5–7, draw each object using solid primitives and Boolean commands to create composite solids. Use the dimensions provided. Save the drawings as *P04_(problem number)*.

5.

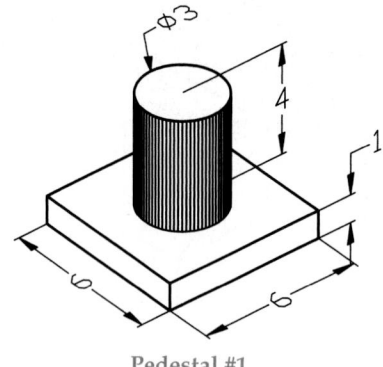

Pedestal #1

6.

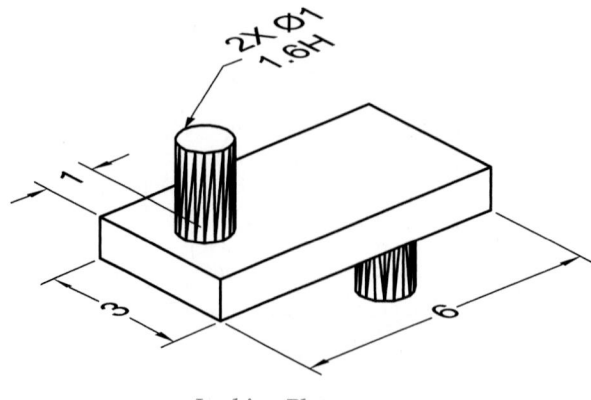

Locking Plate

7.

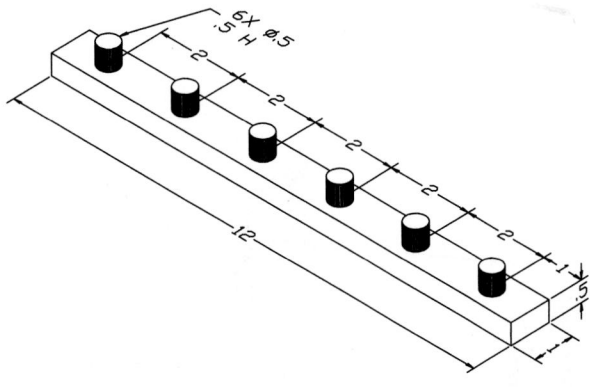

Pin Bar

8. Draw the Ø8″ pedestal shown. It is .5″ thick. The four feet are centered on a Ø7″ circle and are .5″ high. Save the drawing as P04_08.

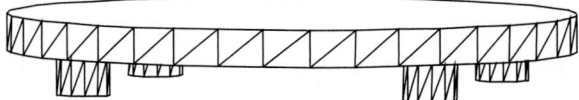

Pedestal #2

9. Four legs (cones), each 3″ high with a Ø1″ base, support this Ø10″ globe. Each leg tilts at an angle of 15° from vertical. The base is Ø12″ and .5″ thick. The bottom surface of the base is 8″ below the center of the globe. Save the drawing as P04_09.

Globe

10. The table legs (A) are 2″ square and 17″ tall. They are 2″ in from each edge. The tabletop (B) is 24″ × 36″ × 1″. Save the drawing as P04_10.

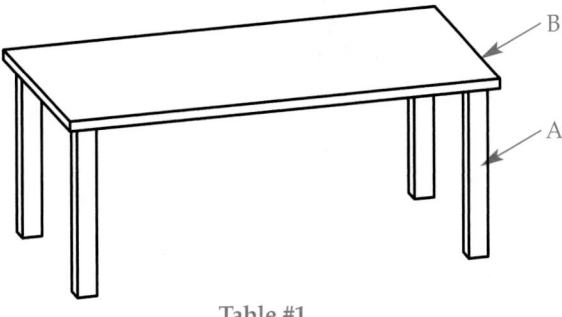

Table #1

11. The table legs (A) for the large table are Ø2" and 17" tall. The tabletop (B) is 24" × 36" × 1". The table legs (C) for the small table are Ø2" and 11" tall. The tabletop (D) is 24" × 14" × 1". All legs are 1" in from the edges of the table. Save the drawing as P04_11.

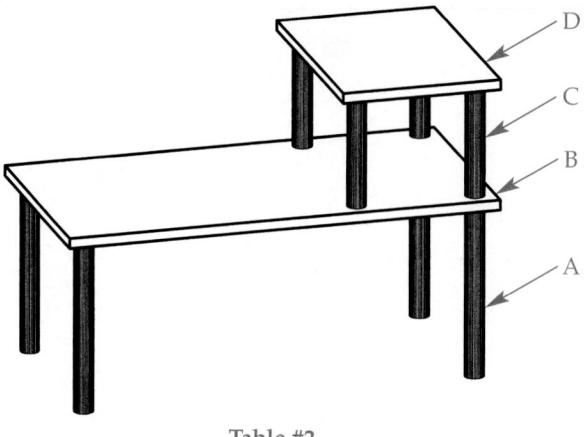

Table #2

12. The spherical objects (A) are Ø4". Object B is 6" long and Ø1.5". Save the drawing as P04_12.

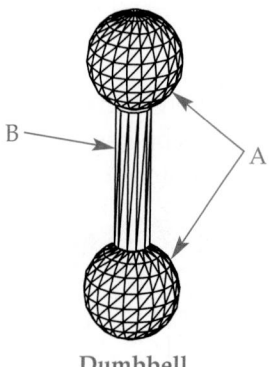

Dumbbell

13. Object A is a Ø8" cylinder that is 1" tall. Object B is a Ø5" cylinder that is 7" tall. Object C is a Ø2" cylinder that is 6" tall. Object D is a .5" × 8" × .125" box, and there are four pieces. The top surface of each piece is flush with the top surface of Object C. Object E is a Ø18" cone that is 12" tall. Create a smaller cone and hollow out Object E. Save the drawing as P04_13.

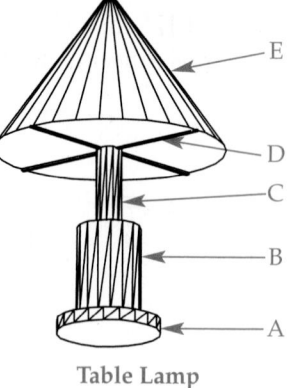

Table Lamp

14. Objects A and B are brick walls that are 5' high. The walls are two bricks thick. Research the dimensions of standard brick and draw accordingly. Wall B is 7' long and Wall A is 5' long. Lamps are placed at each end of the walls. Object C is ⌀2" and 8" tall. The center is offset from the end of the wall by a distance equal to the width of one brick. Object D is ⌀10". Save the drawing as P04_14.

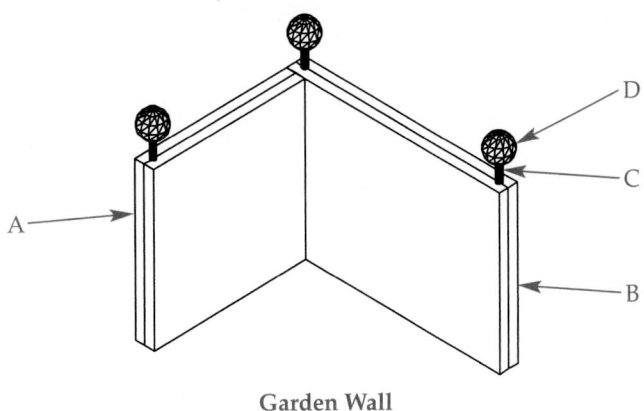

Garden Wall

15. Object A is ⌀18" and 1" tall. Object B is ⌀1.5" and 6' tall. Object C is ⌀6" and .5" tall. Object D is a ⌀10" sphere. Object E is a U-shaped bracket to support the shade (Object F). There are two items; draw them an appropriate size. Object F has a ⌀22" base and is 12" tall. Save the drawing as P04_15.

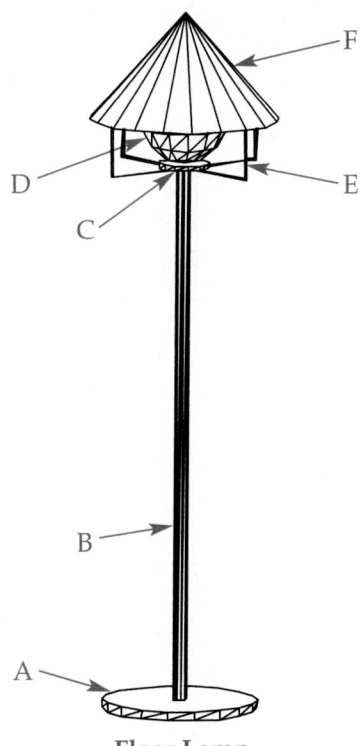

Floor Lamp

Drawing Problems - Chapter 4

16. This is a concept sketch of a desk organizer. Create a solid model using the dimensions given. Use a dynamic UCS when appropriate or create and save new UCSs as needed. Inside dimensions of compartments can vary, but the thickness between compartments should be consistent. Do not add dimensions to the drawing. Plot your drawing on a B-size sheet of paper in a visual style specified by your instructor. Save the drawing as P04_16.

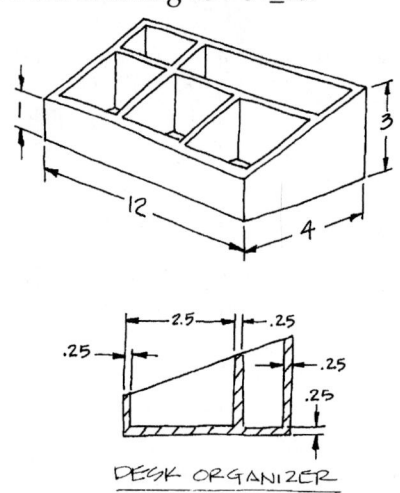

17. This is a concept sketch of a pencil holder. Create a solid model using the dimensions given. Use a dynamic UCS when appropriate or create and save new UCSs as needed. Do not add dimensions to the drawing. Plot your drawing on a B-size sheet of paper in a visual style specified by your instructor. Save the drawing as P04_17.

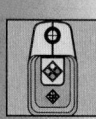

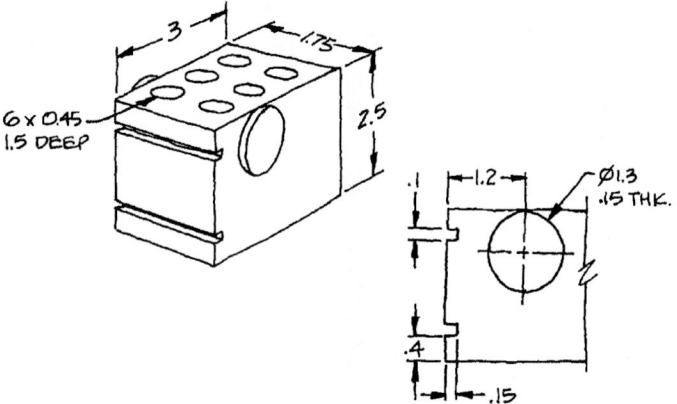

18. This is an engineering sketch of a window blind mounting bracket. Create a solid model using the dimensions given. Use a dynamic UCS when appropriate or create and save new UCSs as needed. Do not add dimensions to the drawing. Create two plots, each of a different view, on B-size paper in the visual styles specified by your instructor. Save the drawing as P04_18.

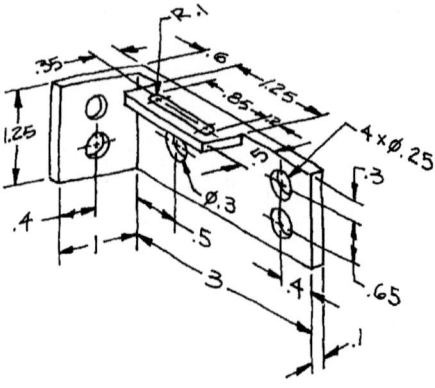

CHAPTER 5

Using Model Space Viewports

Learning Objectives

After completing this chapter, you will be able to:
- ✓ Describe the function of model space viewports.
- ✓ Create and save viewport configurations.
- ✓ Alter the current viewport configuration.
- ✓ Use multiple viewports to construct a drawing.

A variety of views can be displayed in a drawing at one time using model space viewports. This is especially useful when constructing 3D models. Using the **VPORTS** command, you can divide the drawing area into two or more smaller areas. These areas are called *viewports.* Each viewport can be configured to display a different 2D or 3D view of the model.

The *active viewport* is the viewport in which a command will be applied. Any viewport can be made active, but only one can be active at a time. As objects are added or edited, the results are shown in all viewports. A variety of viewport configurations can be saved and recalled as needed. This chapter discusses the use of viewports and shows how they can be used for 3D constructions.

Understanding Viewports

The AutoCAD drawing area can be divided into a maximum of 64 viewports. However, this is impractical due to the small size of each viewport. Four viewports are usually the maximum number practical to display at one time. The number of viewports you need depends on the model you are drawing. Each viewport can show a different view of an object. This makes it easier to construct 3D objects.

NOTE

The **MAXACTVP** (maximum active viewports) system variable sets the number of viewports that can be used at one time. The initial value is 64, which is the highest setting.

There are two types of viewports used in AutoCAD. The type of viewport created depends on whether it is defined in model space or paper space. *Model space* is the space, or mode, where the drawing is constructed. *Paper space,* or layout space, is the space where a drawing is laid out to be plotted. Viewports created in model space are called *tiled viewports.* Viewports created in paper space are called *floating viewports.*

Model space is active by default when you start AutoCAD. Model space viewports are created with the **VPORTS** command. These viewport configurations cannot be plotted because they are for display purposes only. If you plot from model space, the contents of the active viewport are plotted. Tiled viewports are not AutoCAD objects. They are referred to as *tiled* because the edges of each viewport are placed side to side, as with floor tile, and they cannot overlap.

Floating (paper space) viewports are used to lay out the views of a drawing before plotting. They are described as *floating* because they can be moved around and overlapped. Paper space viewports are objects and they can be edited. These viewports can be thought of as "windows" cut into a sheet of paper to "see into" model space. You can then insert, or *reference,* different scaled drawings (views) into these windows. For example, architectural details or sections and details of complex mechanical parts may be referenced. Detailed discussions of paper space viewports are provided in *AutoCAD and Its Applications—Basics.*

The **VPORTS** command can be used to create viewports in a paper space layout. The process is very similar to that used to create model space viewports, which is discussed next. You can also use the **MVIEW** command to create paper space viewports.

Creating Viewports

Creating model space viewports is similar to working with a multiview layout in manual drafting. In a manual multiview layout, several views are drawn on the same sheet. You can switch from one view to another simply by moving your pencil. With model space viewports, you simply pick with your pointing device in the viewport in which you wish to work. The picked viewport becomes active. Using viewports is a good way to construct 3D models because all views are updated as you draw. However, viewports are also useful when creating 2D drawings.

The project on which you are working determines the number of viewports needed. Keep in mind that the more viewports you display on your screen, the smaller each viewport. Small viewports may not be useful to you. Four different viewport configurations are shown in **Figure 5-1.** As you can see, when 16 viewports are displayed, the viewports are very small. Normally, two to four viewports are used.

A layout of one to four viewports can be quickly created by using the **Viewports** dialog box or by selecting from the options in the **Viewports** cascading menu of the **View** pull-down menu. See **Figure 5-2.** The **Viewports** dialog box is accessed by typing the **VPORTS** command. A list of preset viewport configurations is provided in the **New Viewports** tab of the dialog box, **Figure 5-3.**

There are 12 preset viewport configurations from which to choose in the **New Viewports** tab, including six different options for three-viewport configurations. See **Figure 5-4.** When you pick the name of a configuration in the **Standard viewports:** list, the viewport arrangement is displayed in the **Preview** area. After you have made a selection, you can save the configuration by entering a name in the **New name:** text box and then picking **OK** to close the dialog box. When the **Viewports** dialog box closes, the configuration is displayed on screen.

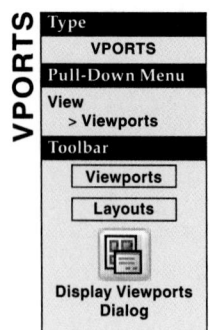

VPORTS

| Type |
| VPORTS |
| Pull-Down Menu |
| View |
| > Viewports |
| Toolbar |
| Viewports |
| Layouts |
| Display Viewports Dialog |

Figure 5-1.
A—Two vertical viewports. B—Two horizontal viewports. C—Three viewports, with the largest viewport positioned at the right. D—Sixteen viewports.

Crosshairs appear in the active viewport

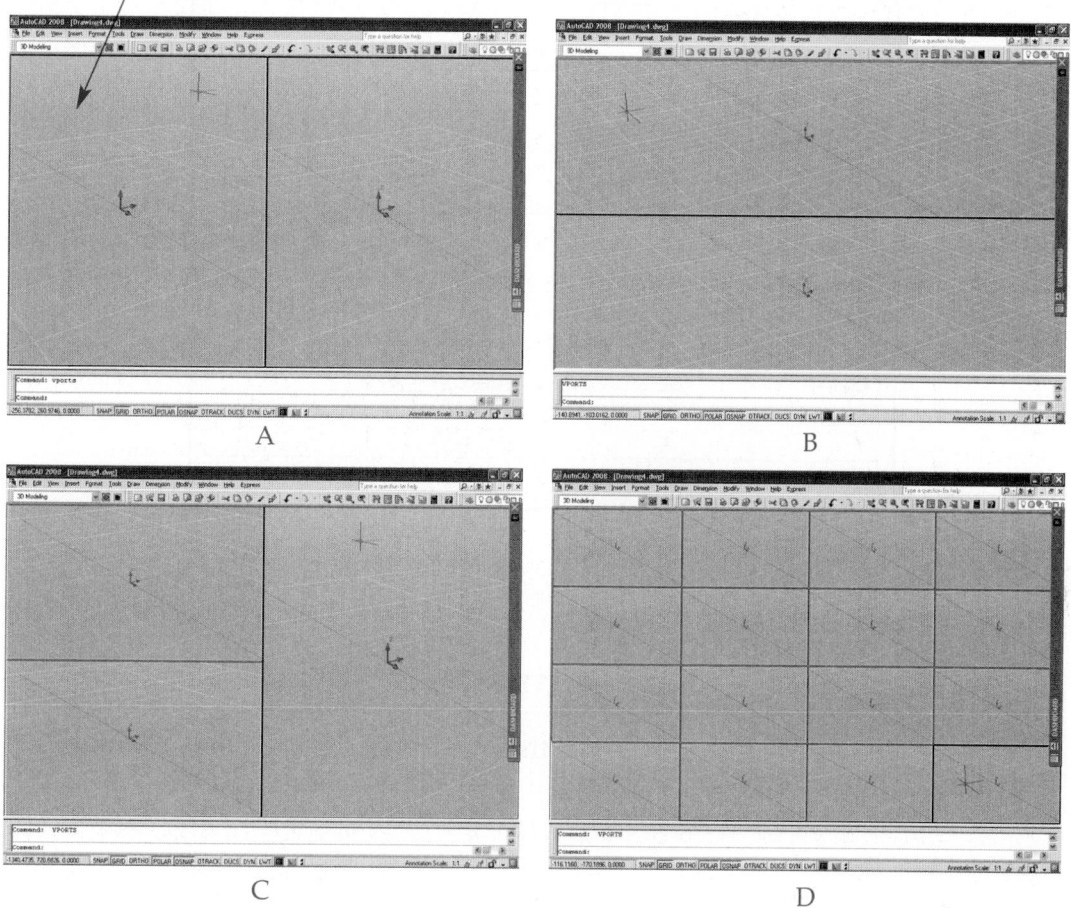

A

B

C

D

Figure 5-2.
Viewport configuration options can be selected from the **Viewports** cascading menu in the **View** pull-down menu.

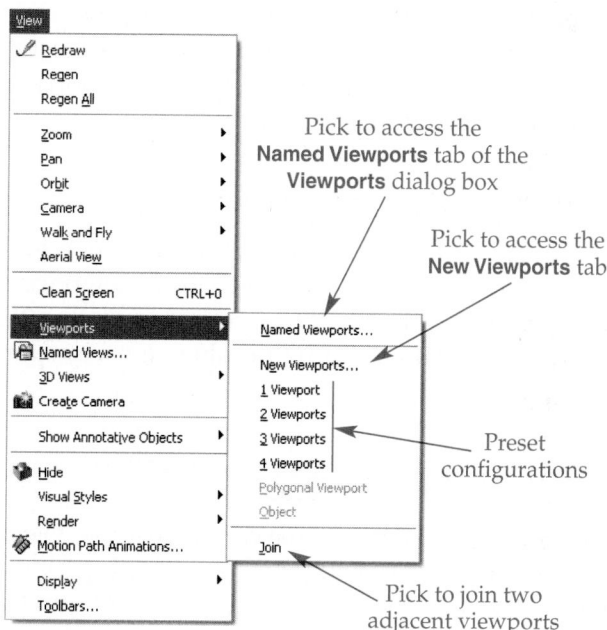

Pick to access the **Named Viewports** tab of the **Viewports** dialog box

Pick to access the **New Viewports** tab

Preset configurations

Pick to join two adjacent viewports

Figure 5-3.
Viewports are created using the **New Viewports** tab of the **Viewports** dialog box.

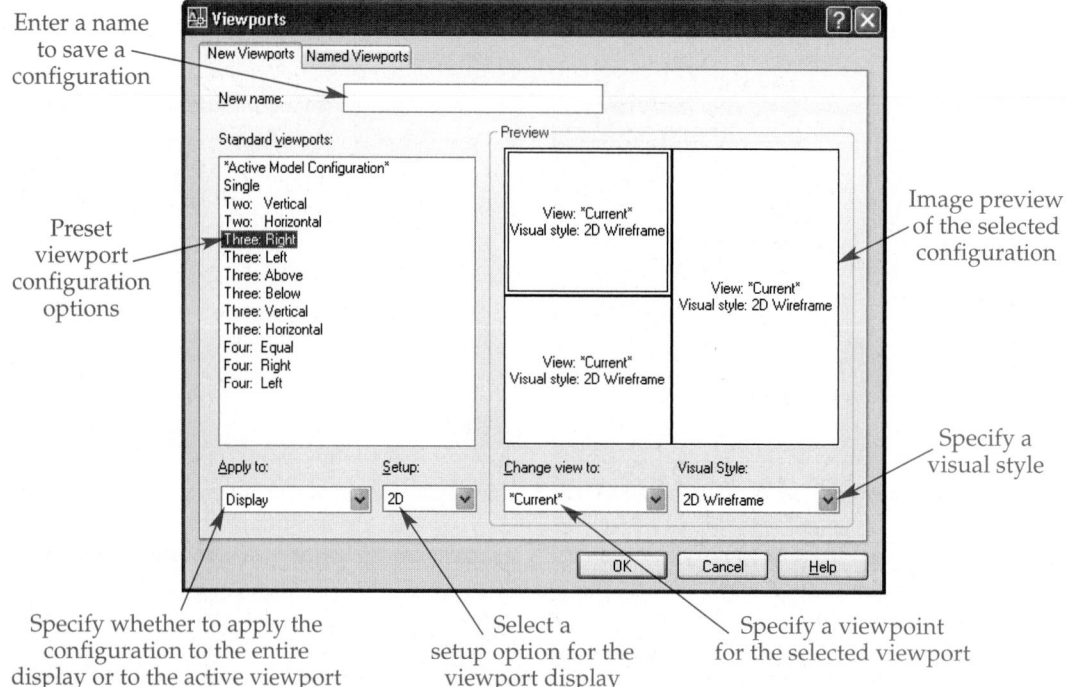

Enter a name to save a configuration

Preset viewport configuration options

Image preview of the selected configuration

Specify a visual style

Specify whether to apply the configuration to the entire display or to the active viewport

Select a setup option for the viewport display

Specify a viewpoint for the selected viewport

PROFESSIONAL TIP

Notice in **Figure 5-1** that the UCS icon is displayed in all viewports. This is an easy way to tell that several separate screens are displayed, rather than different views of the drawing.

Making a Viewport Active

After a viewport configuration has been created, a thick line surrounds the active viewport. When the screen cursor is moved inside of the active viewport, it appears as crosshairs. When moved into an inactive viewport, the screen cursor becomes an arrow.

Any viewport can be made active by moving the cursor into the desired viewport and pressing the pick button. You can also press the [Ctrl]+[R] key combination to switch viewports, or use the **CVPORT** (current viewport) system variable. Only one viewport can be active at a time.

        Command: **CVPORT↵**
        Enter new value for CVPORT <*current*>: **3↵**

The current value given is the ID number of the active viewport. The ID number is automatically assigned by AutoCAD. To change viewports with the **CVPORT** system variable, simply enter a different ID number. Using the **CVPORT** system variable is also a good way to determine the ID number of a viewport. The number 1 is not a valid viewport ID number.

PROFESSIONAL TIP

Each viewport can have its own view, viewpoint, UCS, zoom scale, limits, grid spacing, and snap setting. Specify the drawing aids in all viewports before saving the configuration. When a viewport is restored, all settings are restored as well.

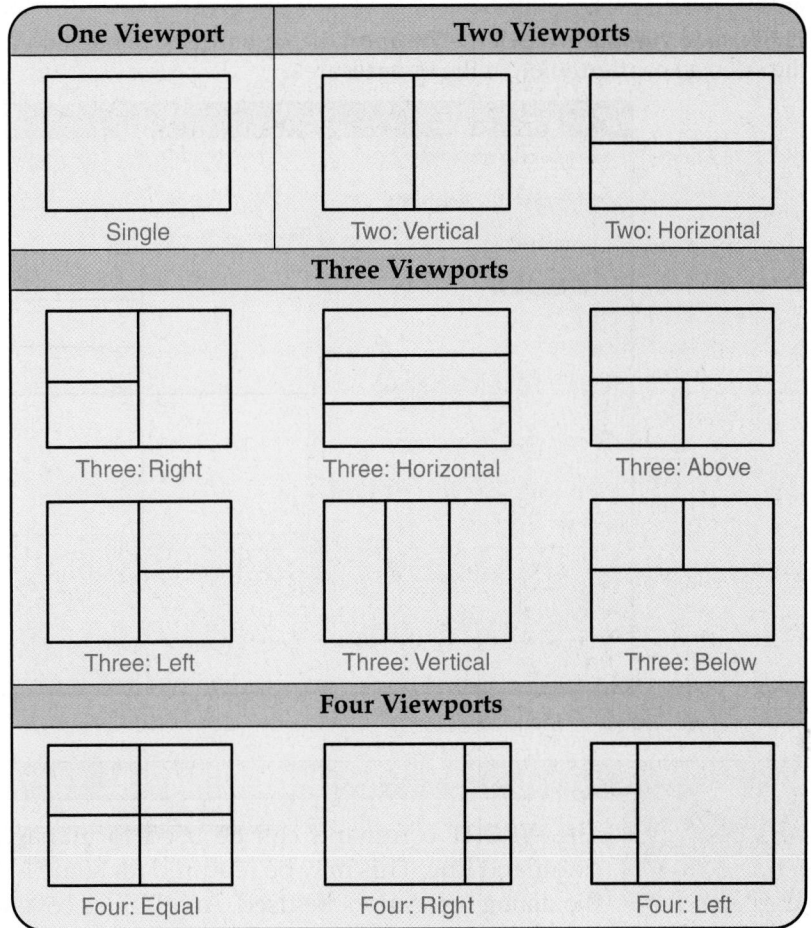

Figure 5-4.
Twelve preset tiled viewport configurations are provided in the **Viewports** dialog box.

One Viewport	Two Viewports	
Single	Two: Vertical	Two: Horizontal

Three Viewports

Three: Right	Three: Horizontal	Three: Above
Three: Left	Three: Vertical	Three: Below

Four Viewports

Four: Equal	Four: Right	Four: Left

Managing Defined Viewports

If you are working with several different viewport configurations, it is easy to restore, rename, or delete existing viewports. You can do so using the **Viewports** dialog box. To access a list of named viewports, open the dialog box and select the **Named Viewports** tab. See **Figure 5-5**. This tab can be automatically displayed by picking **Named Viewports...** from the **Viewports** cascading menu in the **View** pull-down menu. To display a viewport configuration, highlight its name in the **Named viewports:** list and then pick the **OK** button.

Assume you have saved the current viewport configuration. Now, you want to work in a specific viewport, but do not need other viewports displayed on screen. First, pick the viewport you wish to work in to make it active. Open the **Viewports** dialog box, pick the **New Viewports** tab, and then pick **Single**. The **Preview** area displays the single viewport. Pick the **OK** button to exit. The active viewport you selected is displayed on screen. To restore the original viewport configuration, redisplay the **Viewports** dialog box, pick the **Named Viewports** tab, and then select the name of the saved viewport configuration. The **Preview** area displays the selected viewport configuration. Pick the **OK** button to exit.

Viewports can also be renamed and deleted using the **Named Viewports** tab of the **Viewports** dialog box. To rename a viewport, right-click on the viewport name and pick **Rename** from the shortcut menu. You can also single-click on a highlighted name. When the name becomes highlighted text, type the new name and press [Enter]. To delete a viewport configuration, right-click on the viewport name and pick **Delete** from the shortcut menu. You can also press the [Delete] key to delete the highlighted viewport. Press **OK** to exit the dialog box.

Type	VPORTS
Pull-Down Menu	View
	> Viewports
	> Named
	Viewports...

VPORTS

Figure 5-5.
The **Named Viewports** tab of the **Viewport** dialog box lists all named viewports and displays the selected configuration in the **Preview** area.

Select a named configuration

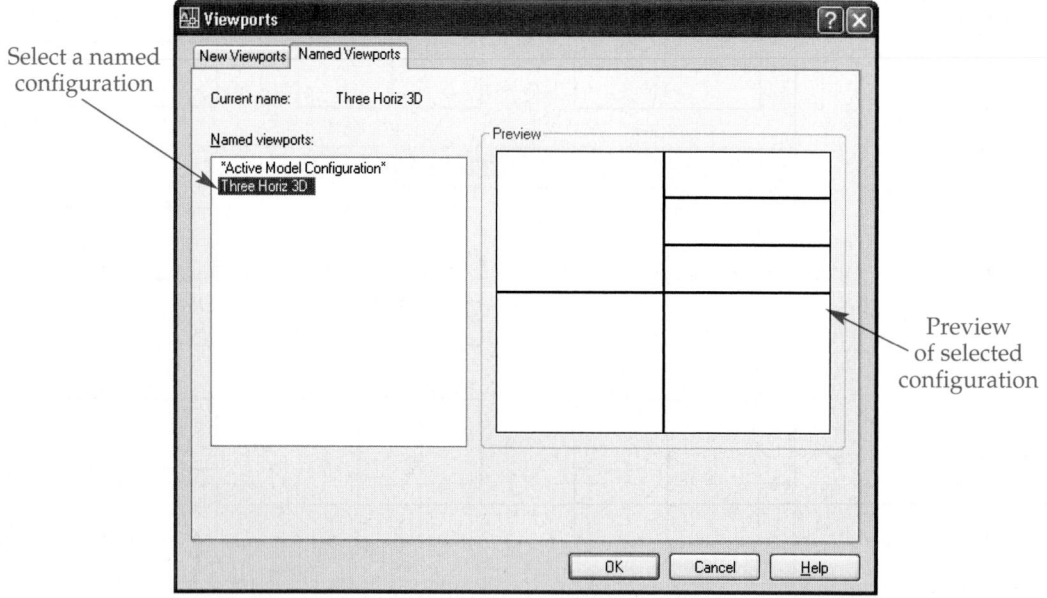

Preview of selected configuration

The **-VPORT** command can be used to manage viewports on the command line. This may be required for some LISP programs where the dialog box cannot be used. AutoLISP is covered later in this text.

Using the Viewports Toolbar

The **Viewports** toolbar, shown in **Figure 5-6,** is used with both model space and paper space viewports. As discussed earlier, the **Display Viewports Dialog** button on the toolbar displays the **Viewports** dialog box. The **Single Viewport** button allows you to create a single-viewport configuration of the active viewport. The remaining three buttons and the drop-down list apply to paper space viewports in a layout. A complete discussion of paper space viewports is given in *AutoCAD and Its Applications—Basics.*

Joining Two Viewports

You can join two adjacent viewports in an existing configuration to form a single viewport. This process is quicker than creating an entirely new configuration. However, the two viewports must form a rectangle when joined, **Figure 5-7.**

Figure 5-6.
The **Viewports** toolbar.

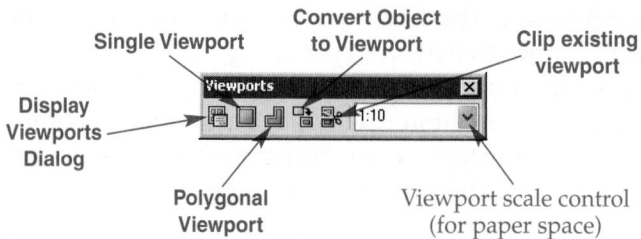

Single Viewport

Convert Object to Viewport

Clip existing viewport

Display Viewports Dialog

Polygonal Viewport

Viewport scale control (for paper space)

Figure 5-7.
Two viewports can be joined if they will form a rectangle. If the two viewports will not form a rectangle, they cannot be joined.

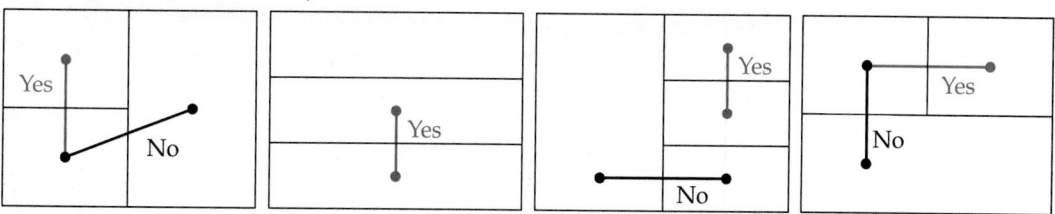

When you enter the **Join** option, AutoCAD first prompts you for the *dominant viewport.* All aspects of the dominant viewport are used in the new (joined) viewport. These aspects include the limits, grid, UCS, and snap settings.

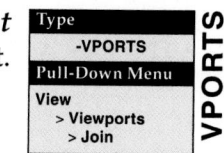

Select dominant viewport <current viewport>: *(select the viewport or press [Enter] to set the current viewport as the dominant viewport)*
Select viewport to join: *(select the other viewport)*

The two selected viewports are joined into a single viewport. If you select two viewports that do not form a rectangle, AutoCAD returns the message:

The selected viewports do not form a rectangle.

PROFESSIONAL TIP

Create only the number of viewports and viewport configurations needed to construct your drawing. Using too many viewports reduces the size of the image in each viewport and may confuse you. Also, it helps to zoom each view so that the objects fill the viewport.

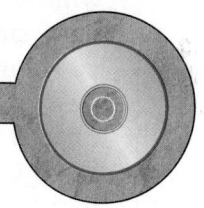

Exercise 5-1
Complete the exercise on the Student CD.

Applying Viewports to Existing Configurations and Displaying Different Views

You have total control over what is displayed in model space viewports. In addition to displaying various viewport configurations, you can divide an existing viewport into additional viewports or assign a different viewpoint to each viewport. The options for these functions are provided in the **New Viewports** tab of the **Viewports** dialog box. Refer to the options located along the bottom of the dialog box in Figure 5-3.

- **Apply to.** When a preset viewport configuration is selected from the **Standard viewports:** list, it can be applied to either the entire display or the current viewport. The previous examples have shown how to create viewports that replace the entire display. Applying a configuration to the active viewport rather than the entire display can be useful when you need to display additional viewports. For example, first create a configuration of three viewports using the Three: Right configuration option. Then, with the right (large) viewport active, open the **Viewports** dialog box again. Notice that the drop-down list under **Apply to:** is grayed out. Now, pick one of the standard configurations. This enables

New configuration is applied to the viewport

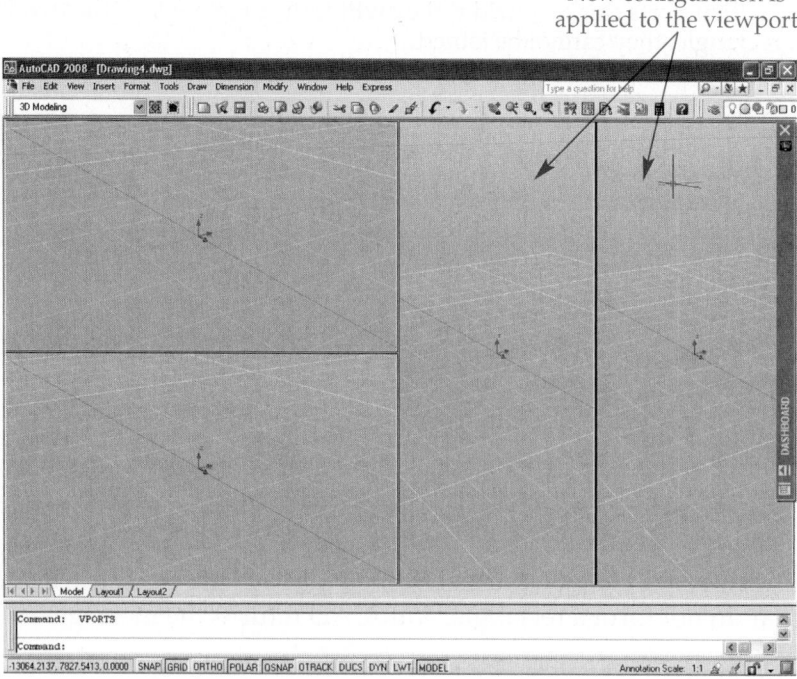

the **Apply to:** drop-down list. The default option is **Display**, which means the selected viewport configuration will replace the current display. Pick the drop-down list arrow to reveal the second option, **Current Viewport**. Pick this option and then pick the **OK** button. Notice that the selected viewport configuration has been applied to only the active (right) viewport. See **Figure 5-8**.

- **Setup.** Viewports can be set up to display views in 2D or 3D. The **2D** and **3D** options are provided in the **Setup:** drop-down list. Displaying different views while working on a drawing allows you to see the results of your work on each view, since changes are reflected in each viewport as you draw. The selected viewport **Setup:** option controls the types of views available in the **Change view to:** drop-down list.

- **Change view to.** The views that can be displayed in a selected viewport are listed in the **Change view to:** drop-down list. If the **Setup:** drop-down list is set to **2D**, the views available to be displayed are limited to the current view and any named views. If **3D** is active, the options include all of the standard orthographic and isometric views along with named views. When an orthographic or isometric view is selected for a viewport, the resulting orientation is shown in the **Preview** area. To assign a different viewpoint to a viewport, simply pick within a viewport in the **Preview** area to make it active and then pick a viewpoint from the **Change view to:** drop-down list. Important: if you set the viewport to one of the orthographic preset views, the UCS is also changed (by default) to the corresponding preset in that viewport.

- **Visual Style.** A visual style can be specified for a viewport. Pick within a viewport in the **Preview** area to make it active and then select a visual style from the **Visual Style:** drop-down list. All preset and saved visual styles are available in the drop-down list.

Exercise 5-2
Complete the exercise on the Student CD.

Drawing in Multiple Viewports

When used with 2D drawings, viewports allow you to display a view of the entire drawing, plus views showing portions of the drawing. This is similar to using the **VIEW** command, except you can have several views on screen at once. You can also adjust the zoom magnification in each viewport to suit different areas of the drawing.

Viewports are also a powerful aid when constructing 3D models. You can specify different viewpoints in each viewport and see the model take shape as you draw. A model can be quickly constructed because you can switch from one viewport to another while drawing and editing. For example, you can draw a line from a point in one viewport to a point in another viewport simply by changing viewports while inside the **LINE** command. The result is shown in each viewport.

In Chapter 4, you constructed a solid object. It was a base that had an angled surface from which a cylinder projected. See **Figure 5-9.** Now, you will construct the object using two viewports. First, create a vertical configuration of two viewports. In the **Viewports** dialog box, set the right-hand viewport to display the southeast isometric. Also, select the Conceptual visual style. Set the left-hand viewport to display the front view. Remember, this will also set the UCS to the front preset orthographic UCS in that viewport. Also, select the 2D Wireframe visual style for the left-hand viewport. Close the dialog box and make the left-hand viewport active.

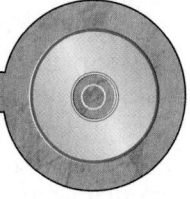

Figure 5-9.
You will construct the object from Chapter 4 using multiple viewports.

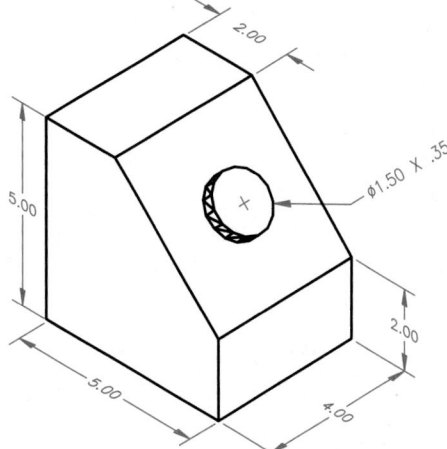

Next, draw a polyline using the coordinates shown in Figure 5-10. Be sure to use the **Close** option for the last segment. As you construct the side view, you can clearly see its true size and shape in the left-hand viewport. At the same time, you can see the construction in 3D in the right-hand viewport. Notice that each viewport has a different UCS, as indicated by the UCS icon.

The next step is to extrude the shape to create the base. The **EXTRUDE** command is used to do so, as was the case in Chapter 4. In the left-hand viewport, select the **EXTRUDE** command, pick the polyline, and enter an extrusion height of –4 units. The front face of the object is now complete, Figure 5-11.

Now, the cylinder needs to be created on the angled face. First, split the left-hand viewport into two horizontal viewports (top and bottom) using the **New Viewports** tab of the **Viewports** dialog box. Set both of the new viewports to display the current view. Pick the **OK** button to close the dialog box. Then, make the upper-left viewport current and set it up to always display a plan view of the current UCS by setting the **UCSFOLLOW** system variable to 1.

Next, create a new UCS on the angled face. Use the **3 Point** option of the **UCS** command, which was described in Chapter 4. The pick points are shown in Figure 5-11; pick them in the right-hand viewport. Notice how the view in the upper-left viewport automatically changes to a plan view of the new current UCS.

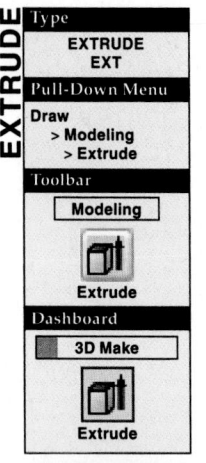

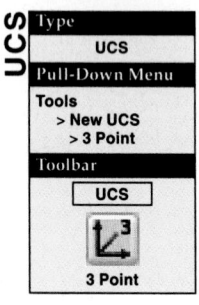

Figure 5-10.
The screen is divided into two viewports. A side view of the object appears in the left-hand viewport and a 3D view appears in the right-hand viewport. Notice the UCS icons.

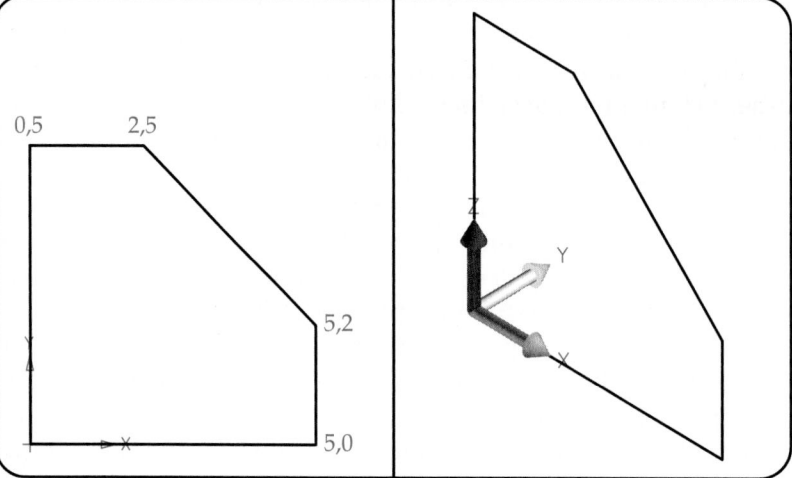

Figure 5-11.
The base of the object is now complete. A new UCS will be created based on the pick points shown here. Alternately, a dynamic UCS can be used, as shown in Chapter 4.

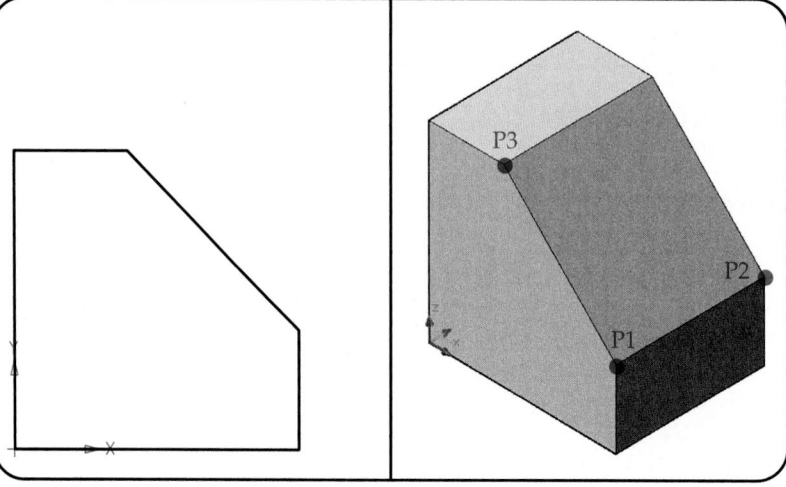

Now, set the **Midpoint** object snap and turn on object snap tracking to draw the cylinder. Work in the right-hand viewport. Acquire the midpoints of sides on the angled surface that are perpendicular to each other when specifying the center of the base. Then, enter a diameter of 1.5 units and a height of .35 units. If you are having problems acquiring points, try switching to a parallel display instead of a perspective display.

The object is now complete, Figure 5-12. Notice how the lower-left and right-hand viewports have different UCSs. Each viewport can have its own UCS. The view in the upper-left viewport is the plan view of the current UCS. If the lower-left viewport is made active, the plan view will be of the UCS in that viewport. The UCS orientation in one viewport is not affected by a change to the UCS in another viewport. If a viewport arrangement is saved with several different UCS configurations, every named UCS remains intact and is displayed when the viewport configuration is restored.

The **REGEN** command affects only the current viewport. To regenerate all viewports at the same time, use the **REGENALL** command. This command can be entered by selecting **Regen All** from the **View** pull-down menu or typing REGENALL.

The Quick Text mode is controlled by the **REGEN** command. Therefore, if you are working with text displayed with the Quick Text mode in viewports, be sure to use the **REGENALL** command in order for the text to be regenerated in all viewports.

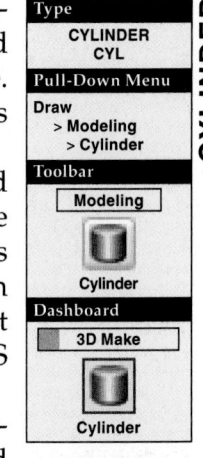

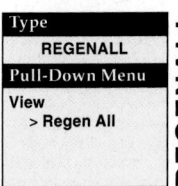

NOTE

The UCS configuration in each viewport is controlled by the **UCSVP** system variable. When **UCSVP** is set to 1 in a viewport, the UCS is independent from all other UCSs, which is the default. If **UCSVP** is set to 0 in a viewport, its UCS will change to reflect any changes to the UCS in the current viewport.

Exercise 5-3
Complete the exercise on the Student CD.

Figure 5-12.
The cylinder is drawn to complete the object. Notice the plan view in the upper-left viewport.

Plan view

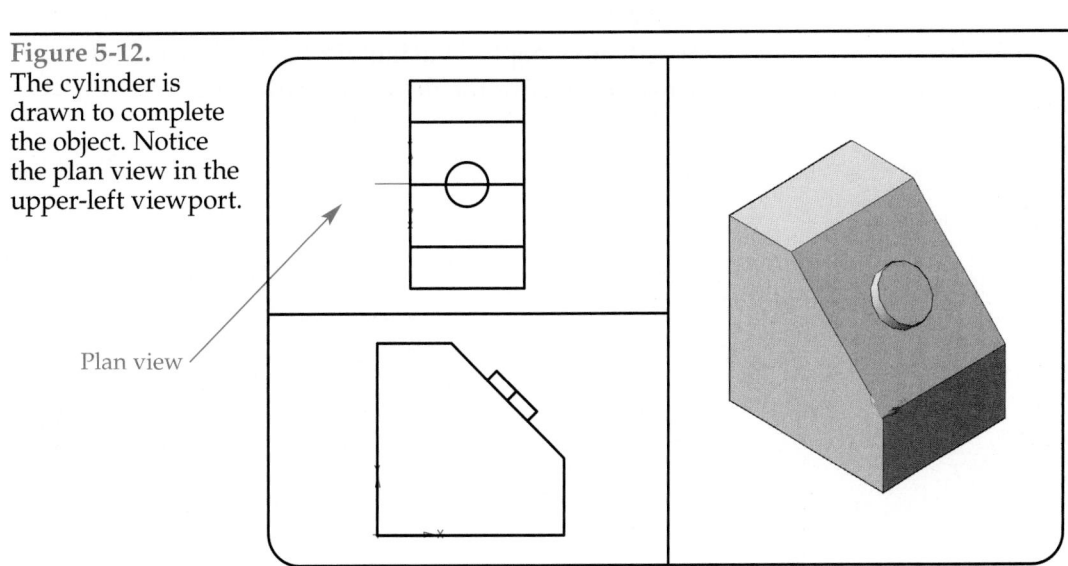

Chapter Test

Answer the following questions. Write your answers on a separate sheet of paper or complete the electronic chapter test on the Student CD.

1. What is the purpose of *viewports*?
2. How do you name a configuration of viewports?
3. What is the purpose of saving a configuration of viewports?
4. Explain the difference between *tiled* and *floating* viewports.
5. Name the system variable controlling the maximum number of viewports that can be displayed at one time.
6. How can a named viewport configuration be redisplayed on screen?
7. How can a list of named viewport configurations be displayed?
8. What relationship must two viewports have before they can be joined?
9. What is the significance of the dominant viewport when two viewports are joined?
10. When creating a new viewport configuration, how can you set a visual style in a viewport?

Drawing Problems

1. Construct seven template drawings, each with a preset viewport configuration. Use the following configurations and names. Save the templates under the same name as the viewport configuration.

Number of Viewports	Configuration	Name
2	Horizontal	TWO-H
2	Vertical	TWO-V
3	Right	THREE-R
3	Left	THREE-L
3	Above	THREE-A
3	Below	THREE-B
3	Vertical	THREE-V

2. Construct one of the problems from Chapter 3 using viewports. Use one of your template drawings from Problem 5-1. Save the drawing as P05_02.

Learning Objectives

After completing this chapter, you will be able to:
- ✓ Create text with a thickness.
- ✓ Draw text that is plan to the current view.
- ✓ Dimension a 3D drawing.

Creating Text with Thickness

A thickness can be applied to text after it is created. This is done using the **Properties** window. The thickness setting is located in the **General** section. Once a thickness is applied, the hidden lines can be removed using the **HIDE** command. **Figure 6-1** shows six different fonts as they appear with hidden lines removed after being given a thickness.

Only text created using the **TEXT** and **DTEXT** commands (text object) can be assigned thickness. Text created with the **MTEXT** command (mtext object) cannot have thickness assigned to it. In addition, only AutoCAD SHX fonts can be given thickness. AutoCAD SHP shape fonts can be compiled into SHX fonts with the **COMPILE** command. The compiled fonts can then be used to create text with thickness. Windows TrueType fonts *cannot* be used to create text with thickness.

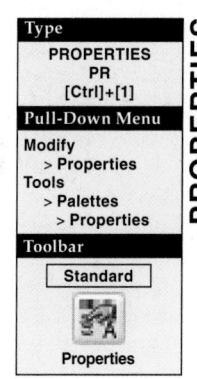

Type	
PROPERTIES PR [Ctrl]+[1]	**PROPERTIES**
Pull-Down Menu	
Modify > Properties Tools > Palettes > Properties	
Toolbar	
Standard	
Properties	

Figure 6-1.
Six different fonts with thickness after hidden lines are removed.

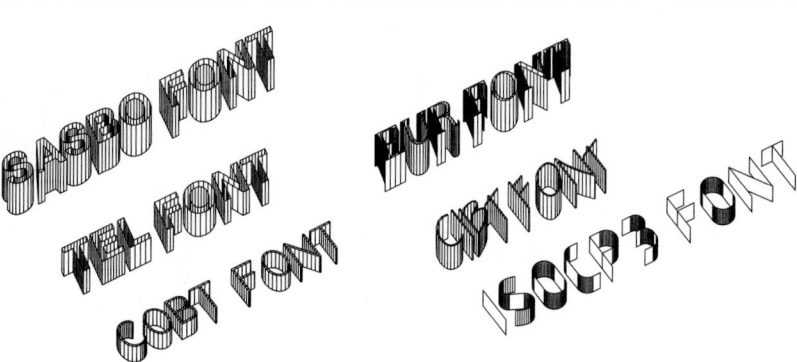

Text and the UCS

Text is created parallel to the XY plane of the UCS in which it is drawn. Therefore, if you wish to show text appearing on a specific plane, establish a new UCS on that plane before placing the text. Figure 6-2 shows several examples of text on different UCS XY planes.

Changing the Orientation of a Text Object

If text is improperly placed or created using the wrong UCS, it can be edited using grips or editing commands. Editing commands and grips are relative to the current UCS. For example, if text is drawn with the WCS current, you can use the **ROTATE** command to change the orientation of the text in the XY plane of the WCS. However, to rotate the text so it tilts up from the XY plane of the WCS, you will need to change the UCS. Rotate the UCS as needed so the Z axis of the new UCS aligns with the axis about which you want to rotate. Then, the **ROTATE** command can be used to rotate the text. The **3DROTATE** command can also be used to avoid rotating the UCS. This command is discussed in Chapter 9.

Using the UCS View Option to Create a Title

It is often necessary to create a pictorial view of an object, but with a note or title that is plan to your point of view. For example, you may need to insert the title of a 3D view. See Figure 6-3. This is done with the **View** option of the **UCS** command, which

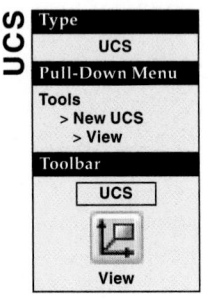

Figure 6-2.
Text located using three different UCSs.

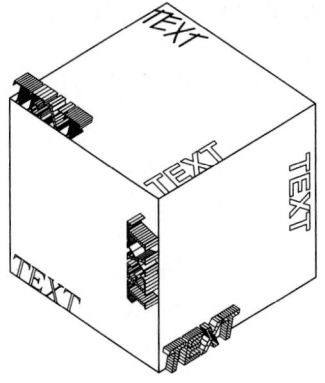

Figure 6-3.
This title (shown in color) has been correctly placed using the **View** option of the **UCS** command.

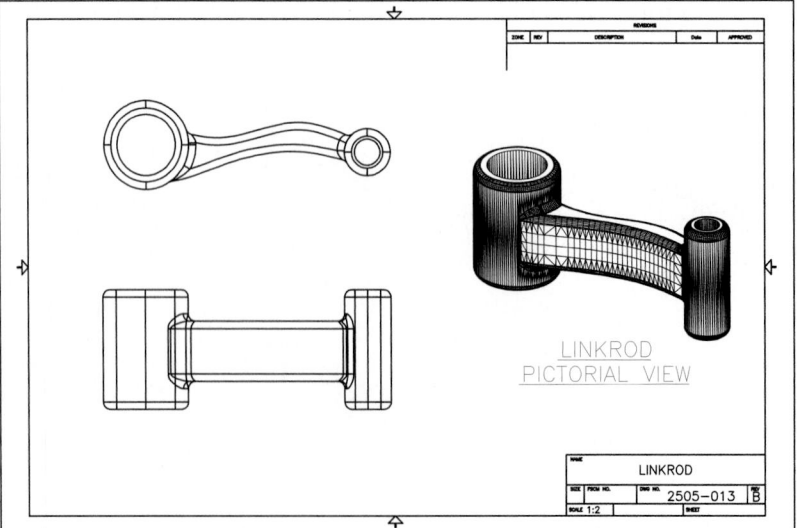

was introduced in Chapter 4. With this option, a new UCS is created perpendicular to your viewpoint. However, the view remains unchanged. Inserted text will be horizontal (or vertical) in the current view. Name and save the UCS if you will use it again.

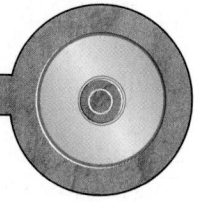

Exercise 6-1
Complete the exercise on the Student CD.

Dimensioning in 3D

Three-dimensional objects are seldom dimensioned for manufacturing, but may be used for assembly. Dimensioned 3D drawings are most often used for some sort of presentation, such as displays, illustrations, parts manuals, or training manuals. All dimensions, including those shown in 3D, must be clear and easy to read. The most important aspect of applying dimensions to a 3D object is planning. That means following a few basic guidelines.

Creating a 3D Dimensioning Template Drawing

If you often create dimensioned 3D drawings, make a template drawing containing a few 3D settings. These are outlined below.
- Create named dimension styles with appropriate text heights. See *AutoCAD and Its Applications—Basics* for detailed information on dimensioning and dimension styles.
- Establish several named user coordinate systems that match the planes on which dimensions will be placed.
- If the preset isometric viewpoints will not serve your needs, establish and save several 3D viewpoints that can be used for different objects. These viewpoints will allow you to select the display best for reading dimensions.

Placing Dimensions in the Proper Plane

The location of dimensions and the plane on which they are placed are often a matter of choice. For example, Figure 6-4 shows several options for placing a thickness dimension on an object. All of these are correct. However, several of the options

Figure 6-4.
A thickness dimension can be located in many different places. All locations shown here are acceptable.

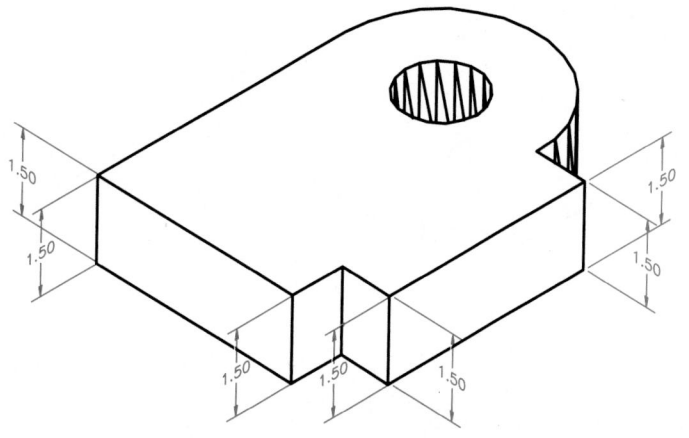

can be eliminated when other dimensions are added. This illustrates the importance of planning.

The key to good dimensioning in 3D is to avoid overlapping dimension and extension lines in different planes. A freehand sketch can help you plan this. As you lay out the 3D sketch, try to group information items together. Dimensions, notes, and item tags should be grouped so that they are easy to read and understand. This technique is called *information grouping.*

Figure 6-5A shows the object from Figure 6-4 fully dimensioned using the aligned technique. Notice that the location dimension for the hole is placed on the top surface. This avoids dimensioning to hidden points. Figure 6-5B shows the same object dimensioned using the unilateral technique.

To create dimensions that properly display, it may be necessary to modify the dimension text rotation. The dimension shown in Figure 6-6A is inverted because the positive X and Y axes are incorrectly oriented. Using the **Properties** window, change the text rotation value to 180. The dimension text is then properly displayed, Figure 6-6B. Alternately, you can rotate the UCS before drawing the dimension, but this may be more time-consuming.

Figure 6-5.
A—An example of a 3D object dimensioned using the aligned technique. B—The object dimensioned with unilateral dimensions.

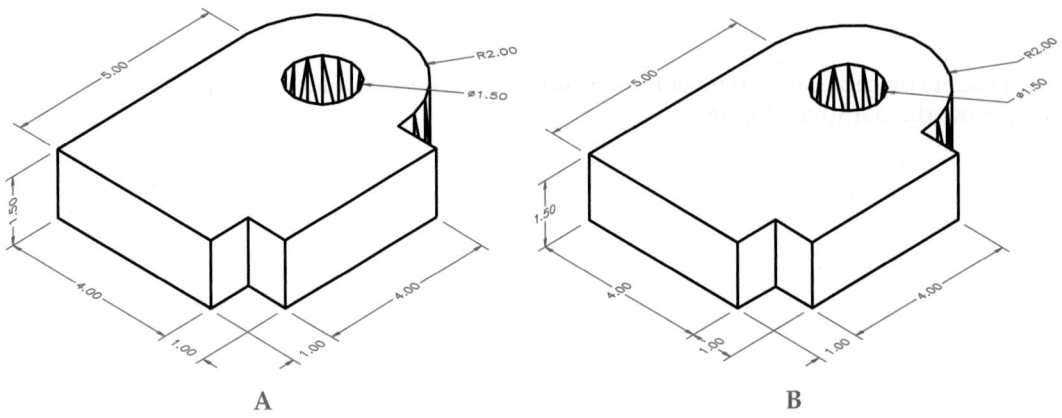

Figure 6-6.
A—This dimension text is inverted. B—The rotation value of the text is changed and the text reads correctly.

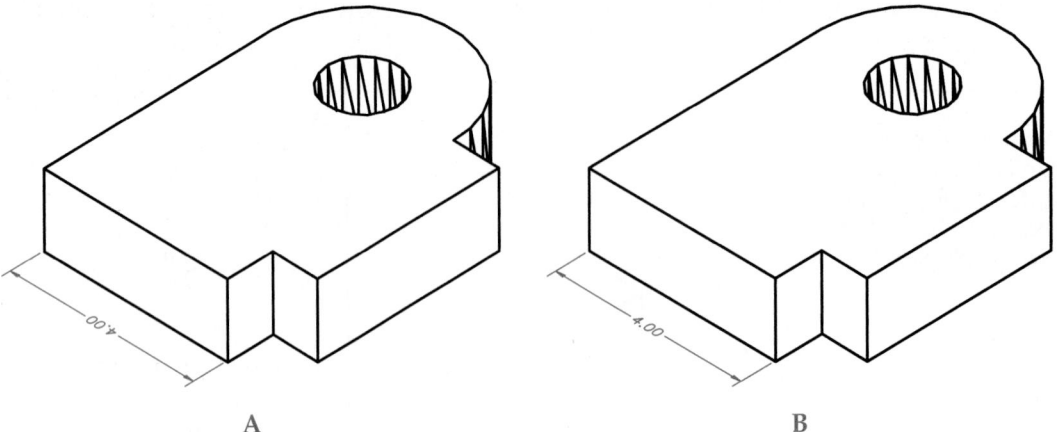

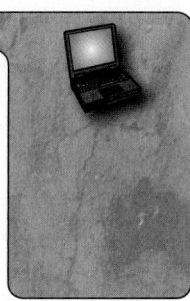

Prior to placing dimensions on a 3D drawing, you should determine the purpose of the drawing. For what will it be used? Just as dimensioning a drawing for manufacturing purposes is based on the function of the part, 3D dimensioning is based on the function of the drawing. This determines whether you use chain, datum, arrowless, architectural, or some other style of dimensioning. It also determines how completely the object is dimensioned.

Placing Leaders and Radial Dimensions in 3D

Although standards such as ASME Y14.5M should be followed when possible, the nature of 3D drawing and the requirements of the project may determine how dimensions and leaders are placed. Remember, the most important aspect of dimensioning a 3D drawing is its presentation. Is it easy to read and interpret?

Leaders and radial dimensions can be placed on or perpendicular to the plane of the feature. **Figure 6-7A** shows the placement of leaders on the plane of the top surface. **Figure 6-7B** illustrates the placement of leaders and radial dimensions on two planes that are perpendicular to the top surface of the object. Remember that text, dimensions, and leaders are always placed on the XY plane of the current UCS. Therefore, to create the layout in **Figure 6-7B** you must use more than one UCS.

Figure 6-7.
A—Leaders placed in the plane of the top surface. B—Leaders placed using two UCSs that are perpendicular to the top face.

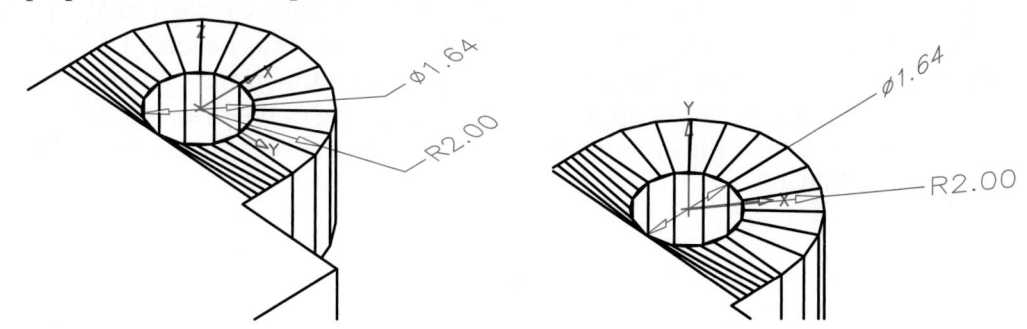

A   B

Exercise 6-2

Complete the exercise on the Student CD.

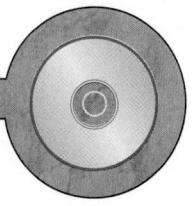

Chapter Test

Answer the following questions. Write your answers on a separate sheet of paper or complete the electronic chapter test on the Student CD.

1. How can you create 3D text with thickness?
2. If text is placed using the wrong UCS, how can it be edited to appear on the correct one?
3. How can text be horizontally placed based on your viewpoint if the object is displayed in 3D?
4. Name three items that should be a part of a 3D dimensioning template drawing.
5. What is *information grouping*?

Drawing Problems

1. This is a two-view orthographic drawing of a window valance mounting bracket. Create it as a solid model. Use solid primitives and Boolean commands as needed. Use the dimensions given. Similar holes have the same offset dimensions. Create new UCSs as needed. Display an appropriate pictorial view of the drawing. Then, add dimensions. Finally, add the material note so it is plan to the view. Plot the drawing to scale on a C-size sheet of paper. Save the drawing as P06_01.

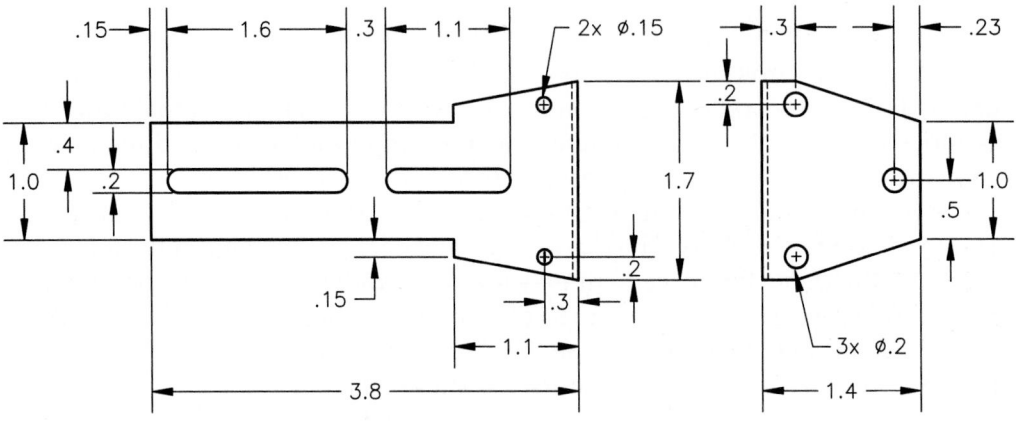

MATERIAL THICKNESS = .125"

2. This is an orthographic drawing of a light fixture bracket. Create it as a solid model. Use solid primitives and Boolean commands as needed. Use the dimensions given. Similar holes have the same offset dimensions. Create new UCSs as needed. Display an appropriate pictorial view of the drawing. Then, add dimensions. Plot the drawing to scale on a C-size sheet of paper. Save the drawing as P06_02.

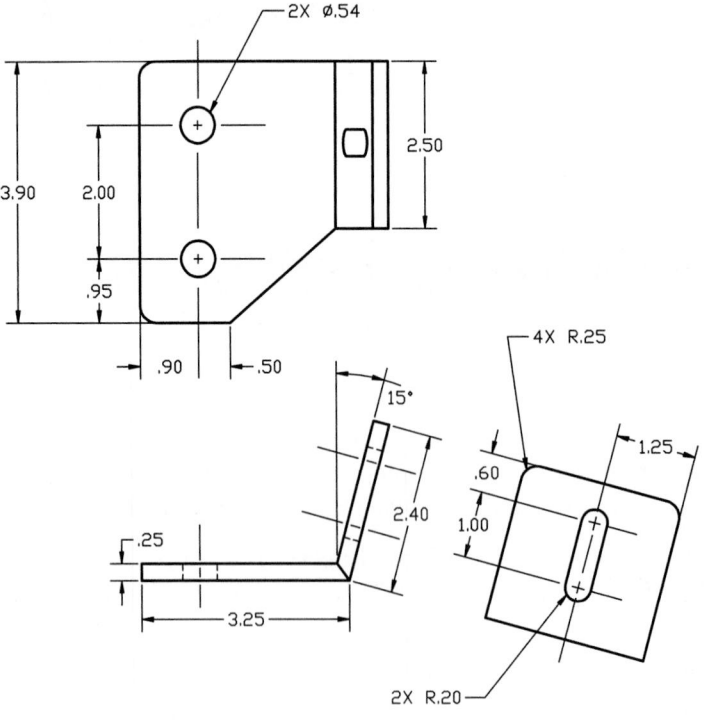

3. Create the end table as a solid model using solid primitives and Boolean commands as needed. The end result should be a single object. As a test of your object editing skills, try drawing the entire model by starting with only a single rectangle. You can copy, resize, extrude, and move objects as you create them from the single rectangle. Use the dimensions given and the following information to construct the model.

   A. Table height is 24".
   B. Top of bottom shelf is 5" off of the floor.
   C. Table legs must be located no less than 1/2" from the tabletop edge.
   D. Shelf must be no closer than .75" from the outside of table legs.
   E. Dimension the table as shown.
   F. Save the drawing as P06_03.

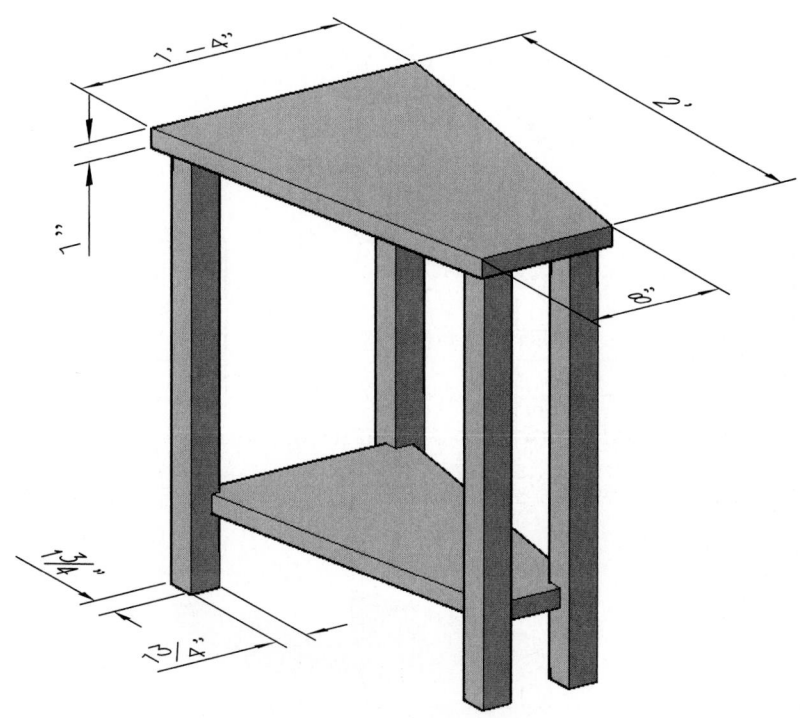

4. Shown below are the profiles of a roof gutter (for the collection of rainwater) and a gutter downspout. Draw the profiles in 3D using the dimensions shown. Use the following additional information to construct a 3D model like the one shown in the shaded view.

   A. Offset the gutter profile to create a material thickness of .025″. Be sure to close the ends to create a closed polyline so a 3D solid is created when it is extruded.
   B. Extrude the gutter profile 12″ to create a one-foot section.
   C. Relocate the downspout profile on the underside of the gutter.
   D. Construct an extrusion path for the downspout. Refer to the shaded view shown below, but use your own design.
   E. Extrude the downspout profile along the path.
   F. Dimension the end of the gutter profile in 3D.
   G. Save the drawing as P06_04.

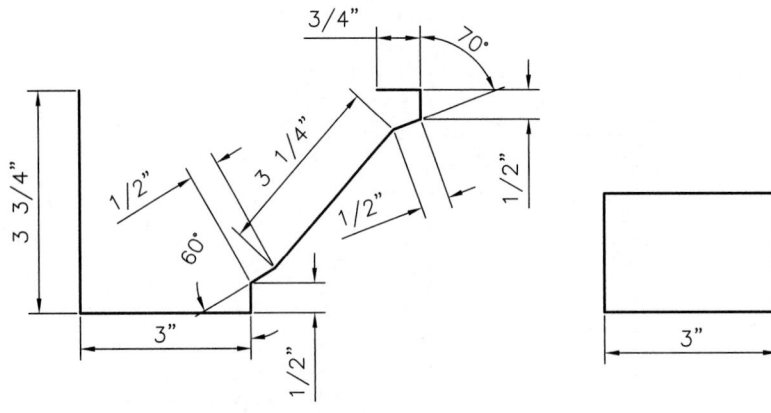

Gutter Profile Downspout Profile

A

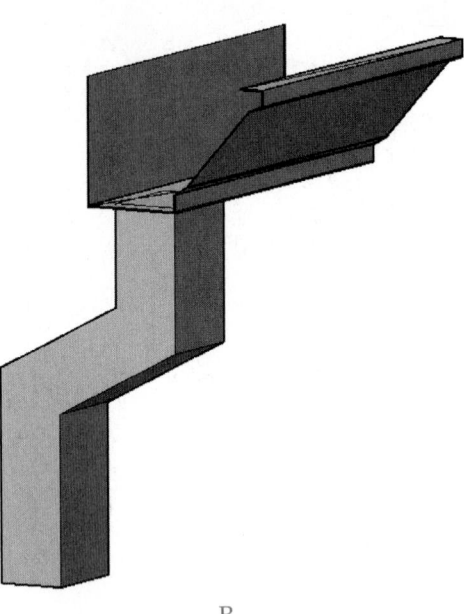

B

Problems 5–7. These problems are mechanical parts. Create a solid model of each part. Dimension each model. Place the title of each model so it is plan to the pictorial view. Plot the finished drawings on B-size paper. Save each drawing as P06_(problem number).

5.

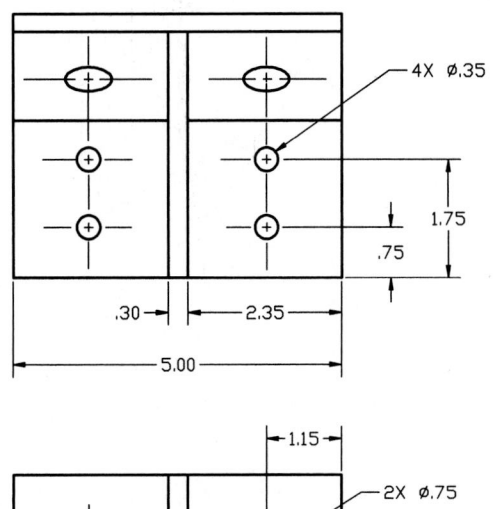

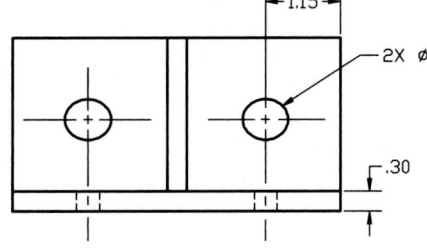

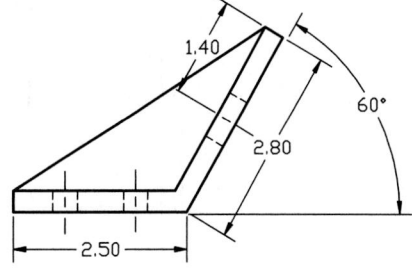

Angle Bracket

6.

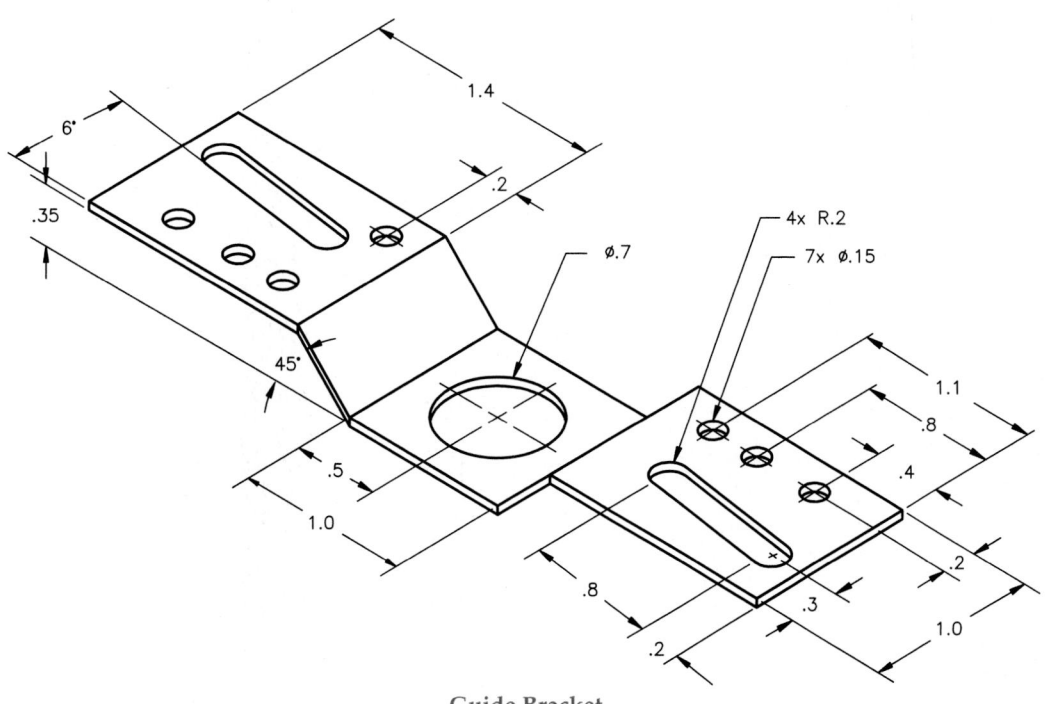

Guide Bracket

7.

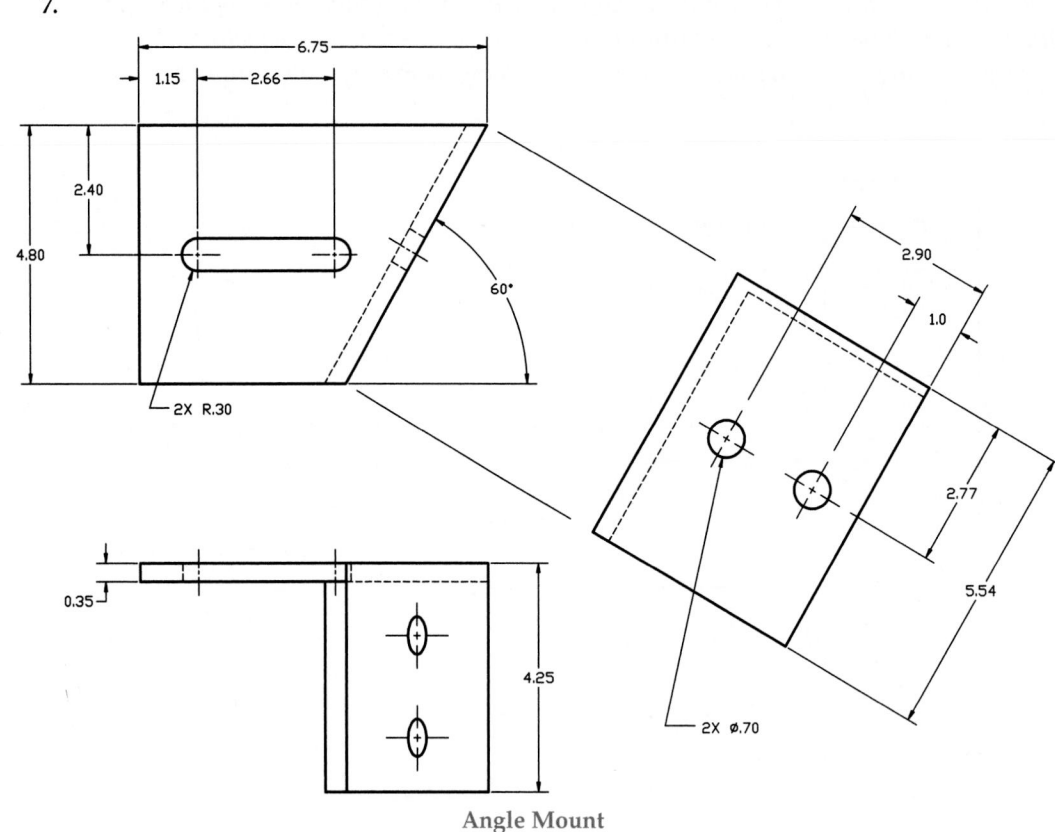

Angle Mount

CHAPTER 7

Solid Model Extrusions and Revolutions

Learning Objectives

After completing this chapter, you will be able to:

- ✓ Create solids and surfaces by extruding 2D profiles.
- ✓ Extrude planar surfaces.
- ✓ Create symmetrical 3D solids and surfaces by revolving 2D profiles.
- ✓ Revolve planar surfaces.
- ✓ Use solid extrusions and revolutions as construction tools.

Complex shapes can be created by applying a thickness to a two-dimensional profile. This is called *extruding* the shape. You have been introduced to the operation in previous chapters. Two or more profiles can be extruded to intersect. The resulting union can form a new shape by performing a Boolean operation. Symmetrical objects can be created by revolving a 2D profile about an axis to create a new solid.

Creating Solid Model Extrusions

A *solid extrusion* is a closed, two-dimensional shape that has been given thickness. The **EXTRUDE** command allows you to create extrusions from lines, arcs, elliptical arcs, 2D polylines, 2D splines, circles, ellipses, 2D solids, regions, planar surfaces, and donuts. Objects in a block cannot be extruded. Closed objects, such as circles, polygons, closed polylines, and donuts, are converted to solids when they are extruded. Open-ended objects, such as lines, arcs, polylines, elliptical arcs, and splines, are converted to a *surface extrusion* when they are extruded. Surface extrusions have no mass properties.

Extrusions can be created along a straight line or along a path curve. A taper angle can also be applied as you extrude an object. Figure 7-1 illustrates a polygon extruded into a solid.

When the **EXTRUDE** command is selected, you are prompted to select the objects to extrude. Select the objects and press [Enter]. You are then prompted for the extrusion height. The height is always applied along the Z axis of the object. A positive value extrudes above the XY plane of the object. A negative height value extrudes below the XY plane. If a pictorial view displayed, you can drag the mouse to set whether the extrusion is above or below the XY plane and then enter the height value.

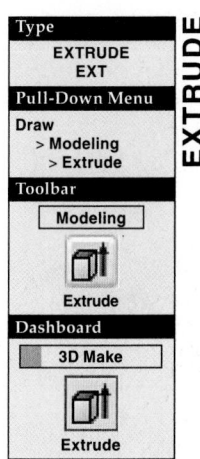

Type
EXTRUDE
EXT

Pull-Down Menu
Draw
> Modeling
> Extrude

Toolbar
Modeling
Extrude

Dashboard
3D Make
Extrude

EXTRUDE

Figure 7-1.
The **EXTRUDE**
command creates a
solid or surface by
adding thickness to
a 2D profile. A—The
initial, closed 2D
profile. B—The
extruded solid object
shown with hidden
lines removed.

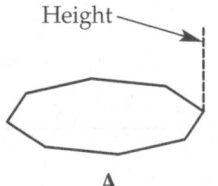 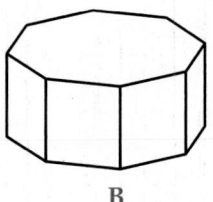

Height

A

B

Before entering a height, you can specify a taper angle. The taper angle can be any value *between* +90° and –90°. A positive angle tapers to the inside of the object from the base. A negative angle tapers to the outside of the object from the base. See **Figure 7-2.** However, the taper angle cannot result in edges that "fold into" the extruded object.

PROFESSIONAL TIP

Objects such as polylines, lines, and arcs that have a thickness can be converted to surfaces using the **CONVTOSURFACE** command. Circles and closed polylines with a thickness can be converted to solids using the **CONVTOSOLID** command.

Extrusions along a Path

A 2D shape can be extruded along a path to create a 3D solid or surface. The path can be a line, circle, arc, ellipse, polygon, polyline, or spline. Line segments and other objects can be first joined to form a polyline path. The corners of angled segments on the extruded object are mitered, while curved segments are smooth. See **Figure 7-3.**

When open objects, such as lines, arcs, polylines, elliptical arcs, and splines, are used as the profile, they are converted to a swept surface when extruded along a path. A *sweep* is a solid or surface that is created when an open or closed curve is pulled, or

Figure 7-2.
A—A positive angle
tapers to the inside of
the object from the
base. B—A negative
angle tapers to the
outside of the object.

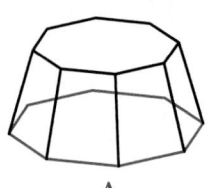 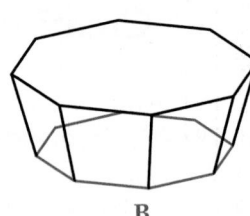

A

B

Figure 7-3.
A—Angled segments
are mitered when
extruded. B—Curves
are smoothed when
extruded.

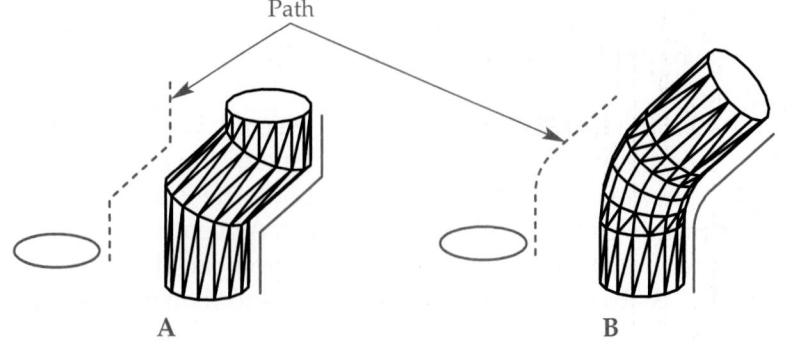

Path

A

B

swept, along a 2D or 3D path. An extrusion is really a form of a sweep. Sweeps are discussed in detail in Chapter 8.

To extrude along a path, enter the **EXTRUDE** command and select the objects to extrude. When prompted for the height of the extrusion, enter the **Path** option. If needed, first enter a taper angle. Then, pick the object to be used as the extrusion path.

Objects can also be extruded along a line at an angle to the base object, **Figure 7-4.** Notice that the plane at the end of the extruded object is parallel to the original object. Also notice that the length of the extrusion is the same as that of the path. The path does not need to be perpendicular to the object.

If the path begins perpendicular to the profile, the cross section of the resulting extrusion is perpendicular to the path, regardless if the path is a straight line, curve, or spline. See **Figure 7-5.** If the path is a spline or curve that does not begin perpendicular to the profile, the profile may not remain perpendicular to the path as it is extruded.

If one of the endpoints of the path is not on the plane of the object to be extruded, the path is temporarily moved to the center of the profile. The extrusion is then created as if the path were connected to the original object, as shown in **Figure 7-4.**

NOTE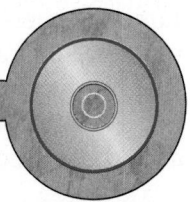

The **DELOBJ** system variable allows you to delete or retain the original extruded objects and path definitions. The settings are:

0   All original geometry and path definitions are retained.

1   Objects used for extrusion (profile curves) are deleted. This is the default.

2   All geometry used to define the extrusion, including path definitions, is deleted.

–1 You are prompted to delete objects used for the extrusion (profile curves).

–2 You are prompted to delete all geometry used to define the extrusion, including path definitions.

The **DELOBJ** system variable also affects the **REVOLVE**, **SWEEP**, and **LOFT** commands.

Exercise 7-1
Complete the exercise on the Student CD.

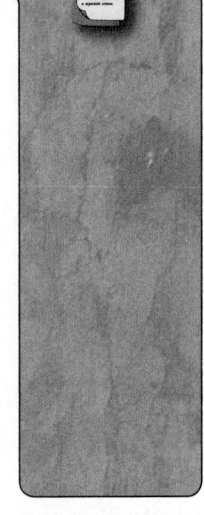

Figure 7-4.
A—An object extruded along a path. B—The end of an object extruded along an angled path is parallel to the original object.

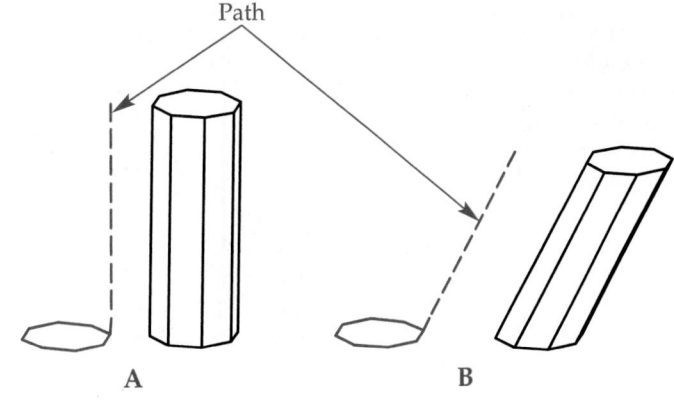

Path

A   B

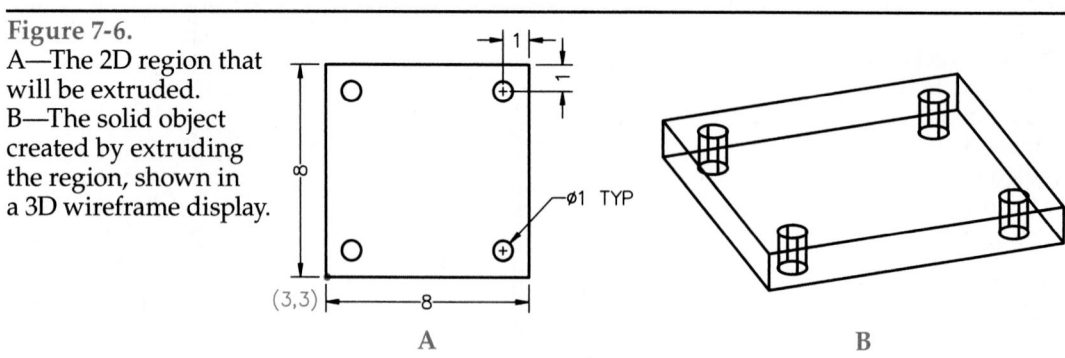

Figure 7-5.
A—Splines can be used as extrusion paths. B—The resulting extrusions.

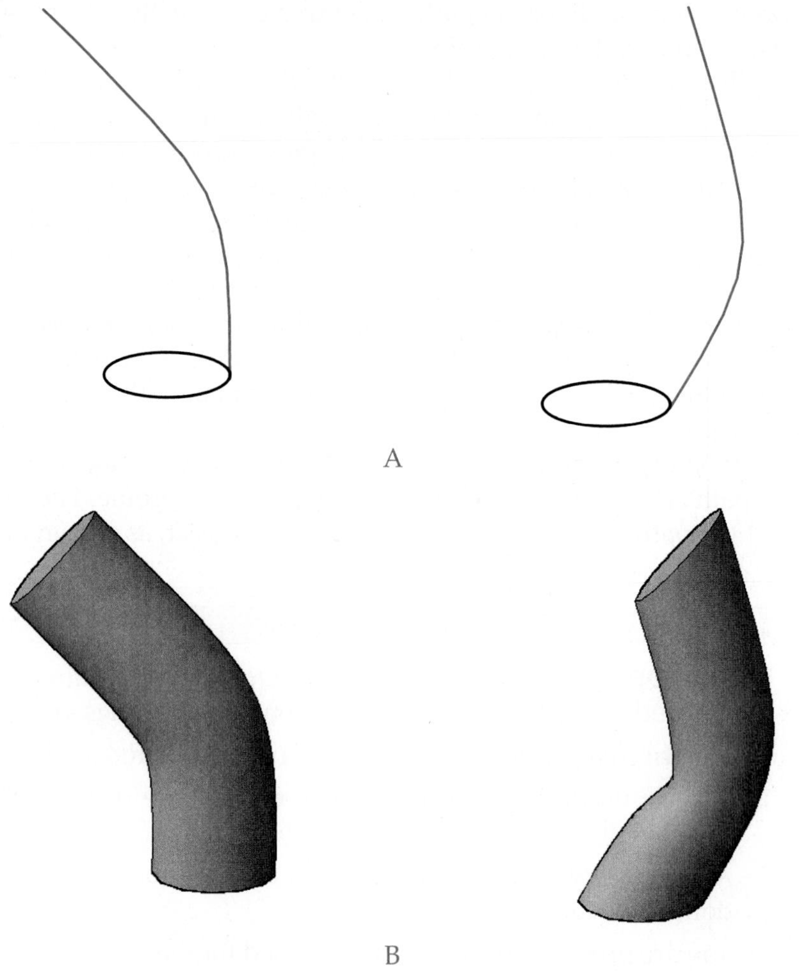

A

B

Extruding Regions

In Chapter 2, you learned how to create 2D regions. As an example, you created the top view of the base shown in **Figure 7-6A** as a region. Regions can be extruded to create 3D solids. The base you created in Chapter 2 can be extruded to create the final solid shown in **Figure 7-6B.** Any features of the region, such as holes, are extruded the same thickness as the rest of the object. If the profile was created as polylines, the holes must be separately extruded and then subtracted from the solid. Using this method, you can construct a fairly complex 2D region that includes curved profiles, holes, slots, etc. Then, a complex 3D solid can be quickly created. Additional details can then be added using editing commands or Boolean operations.

Figure 7-6.
A—The 2D region that will be extruded.
B—The solid object created by extruding the region, shown in a 3D wireframe display.

A

B

Extruding a Planar Surface

A planar surface can be extruded into a solid object in the same manner as a region. Nonplanar (curved) surfaces cannot be extruded. Whereas both surfaces and regions have no thickness, the surface is an object composed of a mesh, and the region is actually a solid that possesses mass properties. A surface can be quickly converted to a solid using the **EXTRUDE** command. Simply select the surface when prompted to select objects. The surface can be extruded in a specific direction, along a path, or at a taper angle.

Any closed object, such as a circle, rectangle, polygon, or polyline, can be converted into a surface with the **Object** option of the **PLANESURF** command. This surface can then be extruded into a 3D solid.

PROFESSIONAL TIP

You can also extrude a face on an existing solid into a new solid. When prompted to select objects, press the [Ctrl] key and pick the face to extrude. A face is a *subobject* of a solid. Subobject editing is covered in detail in Chapter 10.

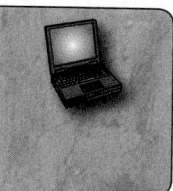

Creating Solid Model Revolutions

The **REVOLVE** command allows you to create solids and surfaces by revolving a shape about an axis. Shapes that can be revolved include lines, arcs, circles, ellipses, polygons, polylines, closed splines, regions, planar surfaces, and donuts. The selected object can be revolved at any angle up to 360°. A *solid revolution* is created when a closed shape is revolved about an axis. A *surface revolution* is created when an open shape is revolved about an axis. Surface revolutions have no mass properties.

When the command is selected, you are prompted to pick the objects to revolve. Then, you must define the axis of revolution. The default option is to pick the two endpoints of an axis of revolution. This is shown in Figure 7-7. You can also revolve about an object or the X, Y, or Z axis of the current UCS. Once the axis is defined, you are prompted to enter the angle through which the profile will be revolved. When the angle is specified, the revolution is created.

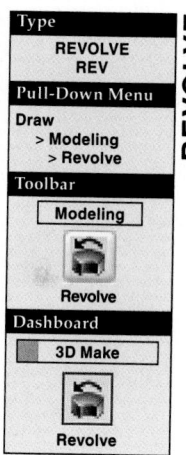

Type
REVOLVE
REV

Pull-Down Menu
Draw
> Modeling
> Revolve

Toolbar
Modeling

Revolve

Dashboard
3D Make

Revolve

REVOLVE

Figure 7-7.
Points P1 and P2 are selected as the axis of revolution for the profile.

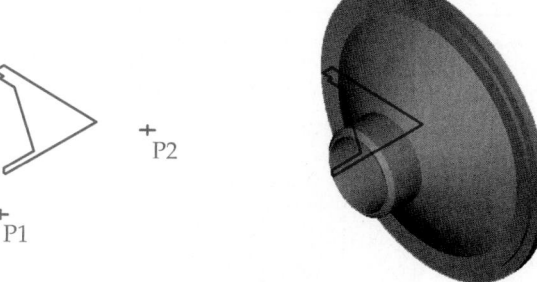

Revolving about an Axis Line Object

You can select an object, such as a line, as the axis of revolution. **Figure 7-8** shows a solid created using the **Object** option of the **REVOLVE** command. Both a full circle (360°) revolution and a 270° revolution are shown. Enter this option when prompted for the axis of revolution. Then, pick the axis object and enter the angle through which the profile will be rotated. You can use the **Start Angle** option before entering an angle of revolution. This allows you to specify the point at which the revolution starts and then the angle of revolution.

Revolving about the X, Y, or Z Axis

The X axis of the current UCS can be used as the axis of revolution by selecting the **X** option of the **REVOLVE** command. The origin of the current UCS is used as one end of the X axis line. Notice in **Figure 7-9** that two different shapes can be created from the same 2D profile by changing the UCS origin. No hole appears in the object in **Figure 7-9B** because the profile was revolved about an edge that coincides with the X axis. The Y or Z axis can also be used as the axis of revolution. See **Figure 7-10**.

Figure 7-8.
An axis of revolution can be selected using the **Object** option of the **REVOLVE** command. Here, the line is selected as the axis.

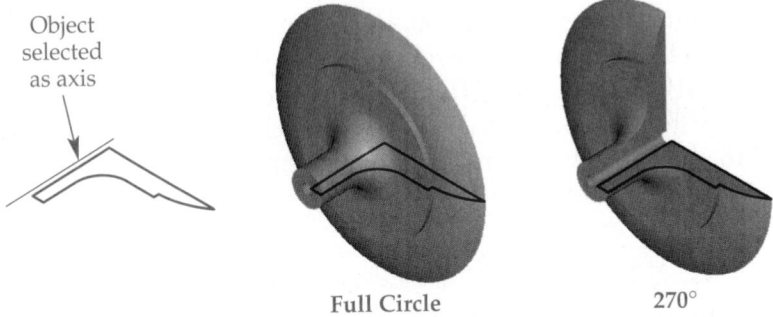

Figure 7-9.
A—A solid is created using the X axis as the axis of revolution. B—A different object is created with the same profile by changing the UCS origin.

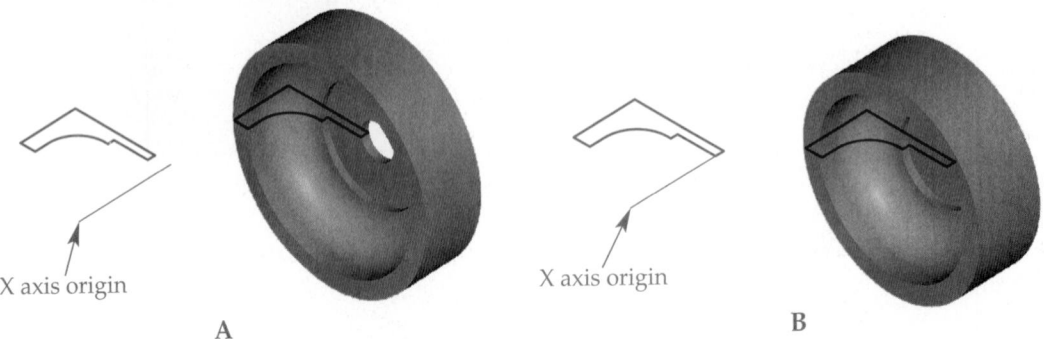

Figure 7-10.
A—A solid is created using the Y axis as the axis of revolution. B—A different object is created by changing the UCS origin.

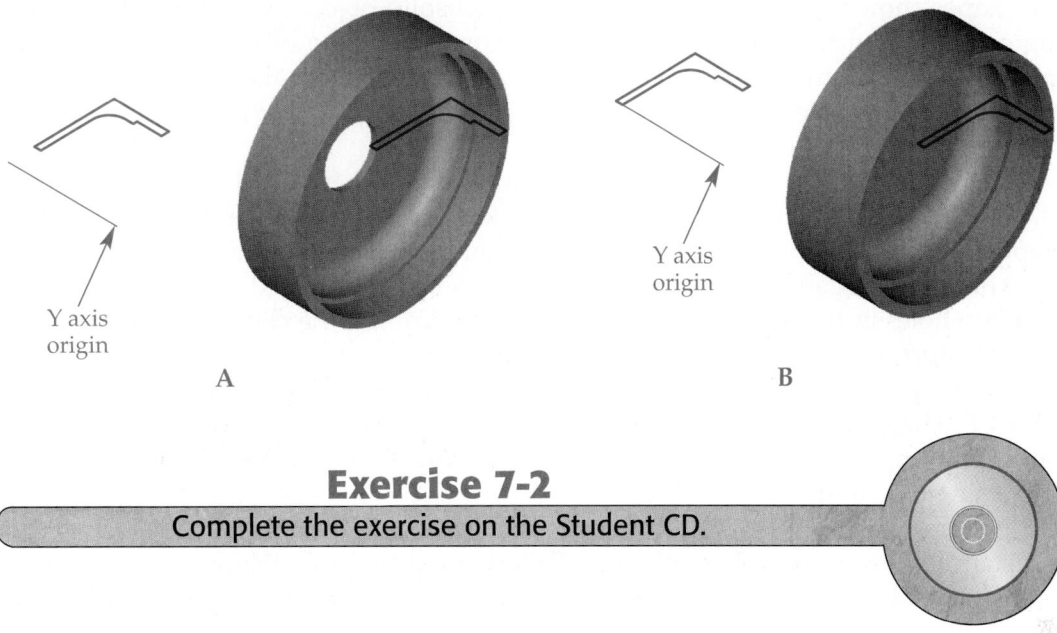

Y axis
origin

Y axis
origin

A

B

Exercise 7-2

Complete the exercise on the Student CD.

Revolving Regions

Earlier in this chapter, you learned that regions can be extruded. In this manner, holes, slots, keyways, etc., can be created. Regions can also be revolved. A complex 2D shape can be created using Boolean operations on regions. Then, the region can be revolved. One advantage of this method is it may be easier to create a region than trying to create a complex 2D profile as a single, closed polyline.

Revolving a Planar Surface

Just as a planar surface can be extruded into a solid object, it can also be revolved into a solid object. Nonplanar (curved) surfaces cannot be revolved. When the **REVOLVE** command is selected, simply pick the surface when prompted to select objects. The surface can be revolved about an axis defined by two pick points, an object, or the X, Y, or Z axis of the current UCS.

PROFESSIONAL TIP

You can also revolve a face on an existing solid into a new solid. When prompted to select objects, press the [Ctrl] key and pick the face to revolve.

Using Extrude and Revolve as Construction Tools

It is unlikely that an extrusion or revolution will result in a finished object. Rather, these operations will be used with other solid model construction methods, such as Boolean operations, to create the final object. The next sections discuss how to use **EXTRUDE** and **REVOLVE** with other construction methods to create a finished object.

Creating Features with Extrude

You can create a wide variety of features with the **EXTRUDE** command. Study the shapes shown in Figure 7-11. These detailed solid objects were created by drawing a profile and then using the **EXTRUDE** command. The objects in Figure 7-11C and Figure 7-11D must first be constructed as regions before they are extruded. For example, the five holes (circles) in Figure 7-11D must be removed from the base region using the **SUBTRACT** command.

Look at Figure 7-12. This is part of a clamping device used to hold parts on a mill table. There is a T-slot milled through the block to receive a T-bolt and one side is stair-stepped, under which parts are clamped. If you look closely at the end of the object, most of the detail can be drawn as a 2D region and then extruded. However, there are also two holes in the top of the block to allow for bolting the clamp to the mill table. These features must be added to the extruded solid.

First, change the UCS to the front preset orthographic UCS. Display a plan view of the UCS. Then, draw the profile shown in Figure 7-13 using the **PLINE** command. You can draw it in stages, if you like, and then use the **PEDIT** command to join all segments into a single polyline.

Next, use the **EXTRUDE** command to create the 3D solid. Extrude the profile a distance of −6 units with a 0° taper. This will extrude the object away from you. Display the object from the southeast isometric preset viewpoint or use the **3DORBIT**

Figure 7-11.
Detailed solids can be created by extruding the profile of an object. The profiles are shown here in color.

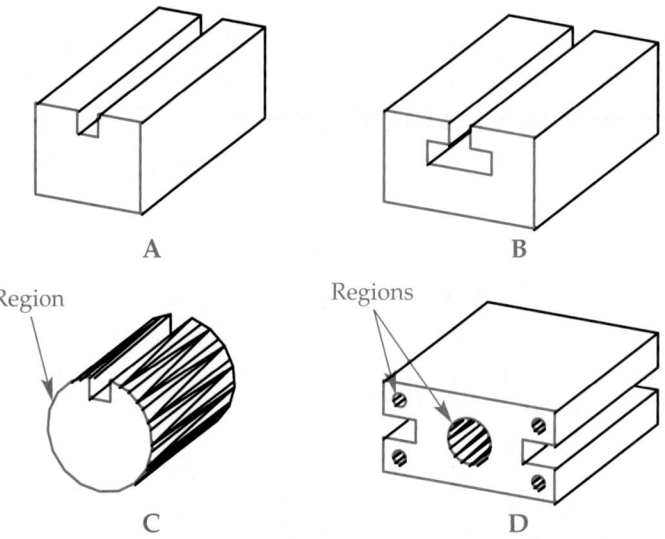

Figure 7-12.
Most of this object can be created by extruding a profile. However, the holes must be added after the extruded solid is created.

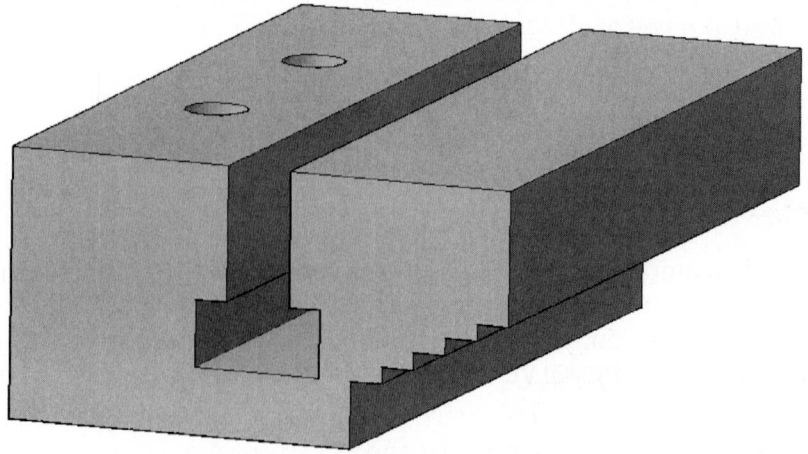

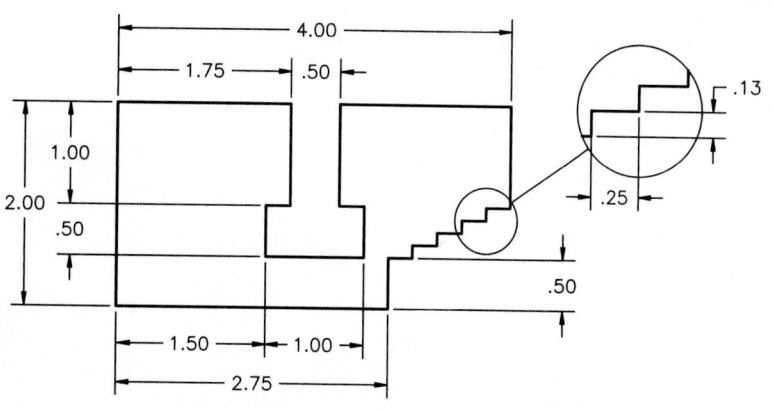

Figure 7-13.
This is the profile that will be extruded for the clamping block.

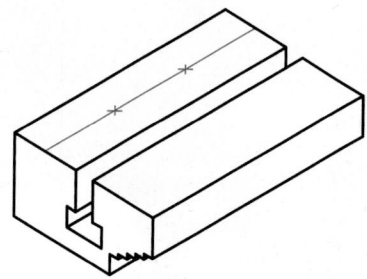

Figure 7-14.
Draw a construction line (shown here in color) and divide it into three parts.

command. The object should look similar to Figure 7-12 without the holes in the top. Set the Conceptual visual style current, if you like.

The two holes are ∅.5 units and evenly spaced on the surface through which they pass. Change to the WCS and draw a construction line from midpoint to midpoint, as shown in Figure 7-14. Then, set **PDMODE** to an appropriate value, such as 3, and use the **DIVIDE** command to divide the construction line into three parts. The two points created by the **DIVIDE** command are equally spaced on the surface and can be used to locate the two holes.

There are two ways to create a hole. You can draw a circle and extrude it or you can draw a solid cylinder. Either way, you need to subtract the cylinder to create the hole. Drawing a solid cylinder is probably easiest. When prompted for a center, use the **Node** object snap to select the point. Then, enter the diameter. Finally, enter a negative height so that the cylinder extends into the solid, or drag the cylinder down in the 3D view so it extends all of the way through the block. The actual height is not critical, as long as it extends through the block.

You can either copy the first cylinder to the second point or draw another cylinder. When both cylinders are located, use the **SUBTRACT** command to remove them from the solid. The object is now complete and should look like Figure 7-12.

Creating Features with Revolve

The **REVOLVE** command is very useful for creating symmetrical, round objects. However, many times the object you are creating is not completely symmetrical. For example, look at the camshaft in Figure 7-15. For the most part, this is a symmetrical, round object. However, the cam lobes are not symmetrical in relation to the shaft and bearings. The **REVOLVE** command can be used to create the shaft and bearings. Then, the cam lobes can be created and added.

Start a new drawing and make sure the WCS is the current UCS. Using the **PLINE** command, draw the profile shown in Figure 7-16A. This profile will be revolved through 360°, so you only need to draw half of the true plan view of the cam profile. The profile represents the shaft and three bearings.

Figure 7-15.
For the most part, this object is symmetrical about its center axis. However, the cam lobes are not symmetrical about the axis.

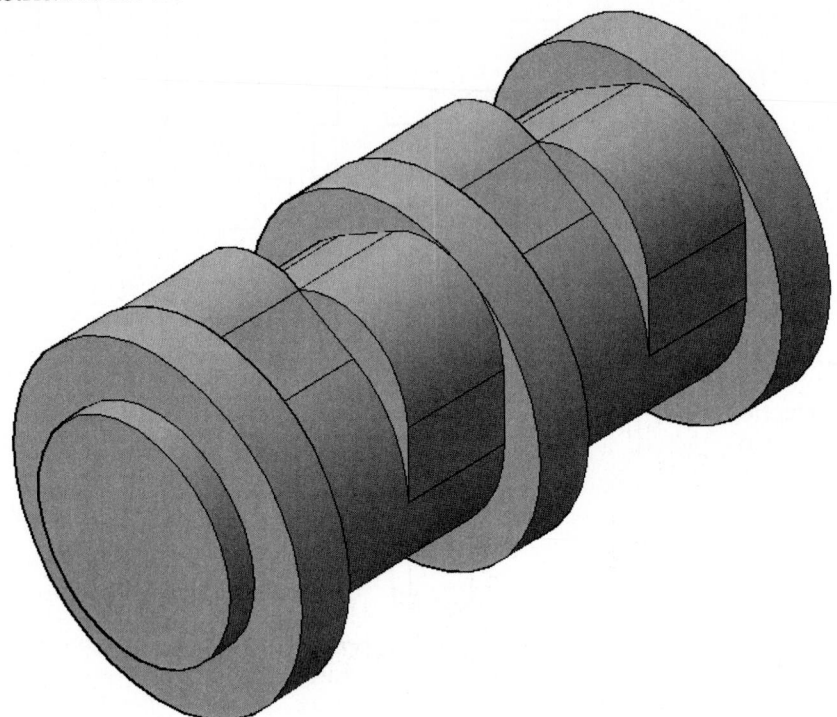

Next, display the drawing from the southwest isometric preset viewpoint. Then, use the **REVOLVE** command to create the base camshaft. Pick the endpoints shown in **Figure 7-16A** as the axis of revolution. Revolve the profile through 360°. Zoom extents and set the Conceptual visual style current to clearly see the object.

Now, you need to create one cam lobe. Change the UCS to the left orthographic preset. Then, draw a construction point in the center of the left end of the camshaft. Use the **Center** object snap and an appropriate **PDMODE** setting. Next, draw the profile shown in **Figure 7-16B**. Use the construction point you drew as the center of the large radius. You may want to create a new layer and turn off the display of the base camshaft.

Figure 7-16.
A—This profile will be revolved to create the shaft and bearings. B—This is the profile of one cam lobe, which will be extruded.

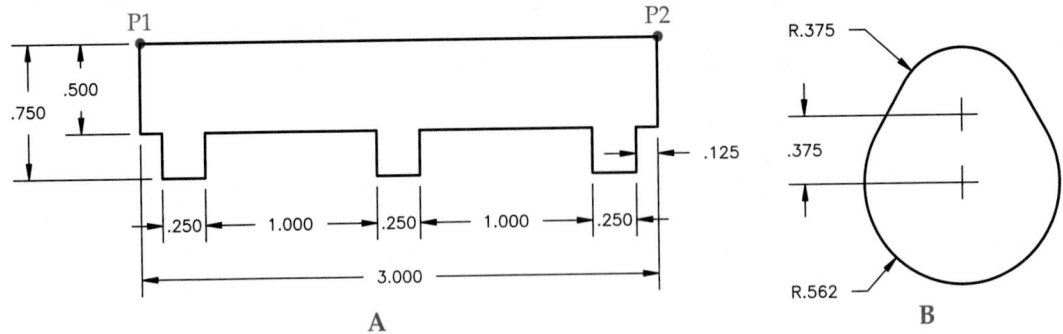

AutoCAD and Its Applications—Advanced

Once the cam lobe profile is created, use the **REGION** command to create a region. Then, use the **EXTRUDE** command to extrude the region a height of –.5 units (into the camshaft). The extrusion should have a 0° taper. If you turned off the display of the base camshaft, turn it back on now.

One cam lobe is created, but it is not in the proper position. Make sure the left UCS is current. Then, move the cam lobe –.375 units on the Z axis. This places the front surface of the cam lobe on the back surface of the first bearing. Now, make a copy of the lobe that is located –.5 units on the Z axis. Finally, copy the first two cam lobes –1.25 units on the Z axis.

You now need to rotate the four cam lobes to their correct orientations. Make sure the left UCS is still current. Then, rotate the first and third cam lobes 30°. The center of rotation should be the center of the shaft. There are many points on the shaft to which the **Center** object snap can snap; they are all acceptable. You can also use the construction point as the center of rotation. Rotate the second and fourth cam lobes –30° about the same center.

Finally, use the **UNION** command to join all objects. The final object should appear as shown in **Figure 7-15**. Use the **3DORBIT** command to view all sides of the object. You can also use the **Continuous Orbit** option to create a rotating display.

Multiple Intersecting Extrusions

Many solid objects have complex curves and profiles. These can often be constructed from the intersection of two or more extrusions. The resulting solid is a combination of only the intersecting volumes of the extrusions. The following example shows the construction of a coat hook.

1. Construct the first profile, **Figure 7-17A.**
2. Construct the second profile located on a common point with the first, **Figure 7-17B.**
3. Construct the third profile located on the common point, **Figure 7-17C.**
4. Extrude each profile the required dimension into the same area. Be careful to specify positive or negative heights for each extrusion, **Figure 7-17D** and **Figure 7-17E.**
5. Use the **INTERSECT** command to create a composite solid from the volume shared by the three extrusions, **Figure 7-17F.**

Figure 7-17.
Constructing a coat hook. A—Draw the first profile. B—Draw the second profile. C—Draw the third profile. All three profiles should have a common origin. D—Extrude each profile so that the extruded objects intersect. E—The extruded objects after the Conceptual visual style is set current. F—Use the **INTERSECT** command to create the composite solid. The final solid is shown here with the Conceptual visual style set current.

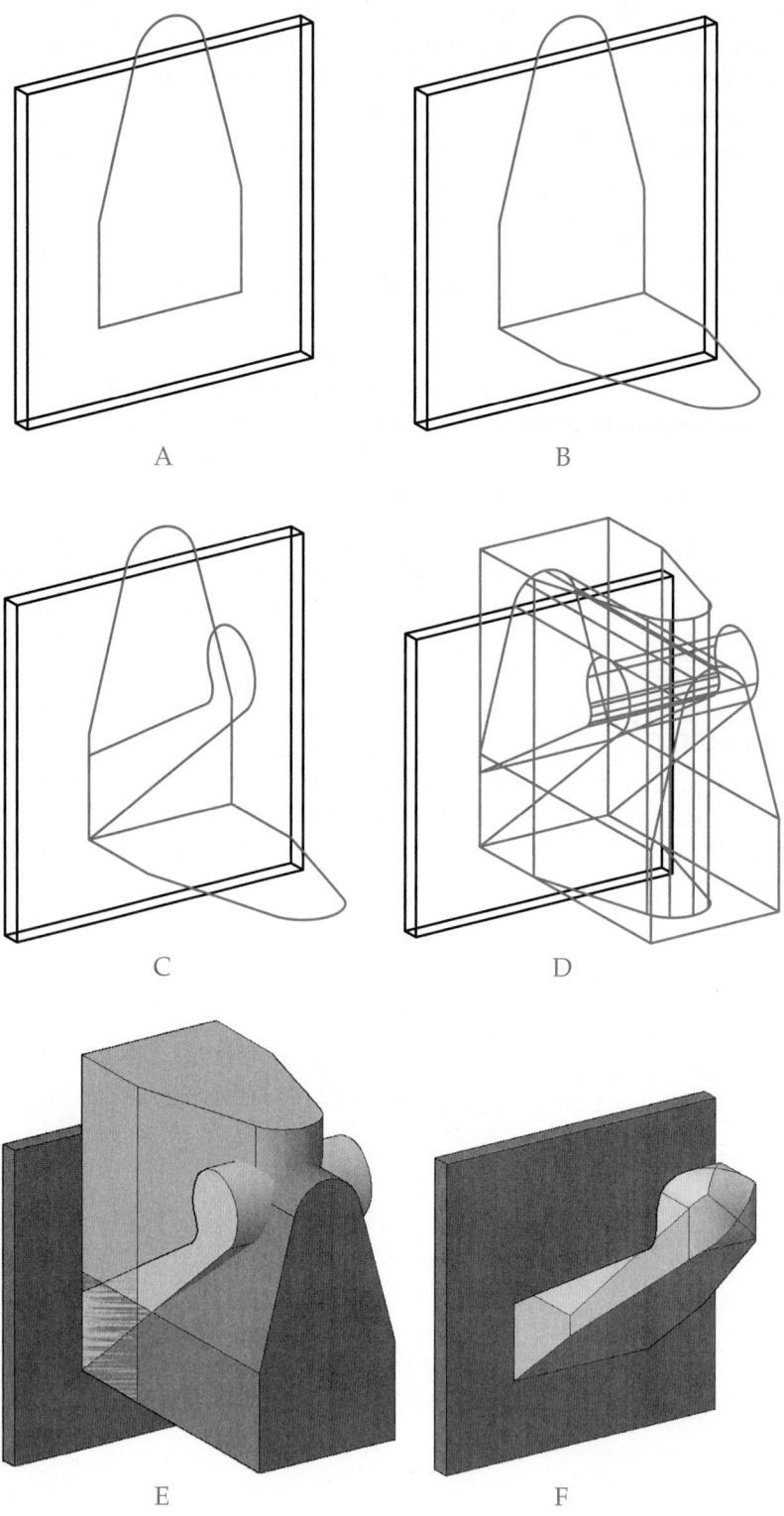

Chapter Test

Answer the following questions. Write your answers on a separate sheet of paper or complete the electronic chapter test on the Student CD.

1. What is an *extrusion?*
2. How do you create a surface extrusion?
3. Briefly describe how to create a solid extrusion.
4. Which command can be used to convert circles and closed polylines with a thickness to solids?
5. How can an extrusion be constructed to extend below the XY plane of the current UCS?
6. What is the range in which a taper angle can vary?
7. How can a curved extrusion be constructed?
8. Which system variable allows you to delete or retain the original extruded objects and path definitions?
9. How is the height of an extrusion applied in relation to the original object?
10. Which type(s) of surface(s) can be extruded?
11. What is a *surface revolution?*
12. How do you create a solid revolution?
13. What are the five different options for selecting the axis of revolution for a revolved solid?
14. How can a given profile be revolved twice (or more) about the same axis and create different shaped solids?
15. What is one advantage of revolving a region over revolving a polyline?

Drawing Problems

1. Construct a 12′ long section of wide flange structural steel with the cross section shown below. Use the dimensions given. Save the drawing as P07_01.

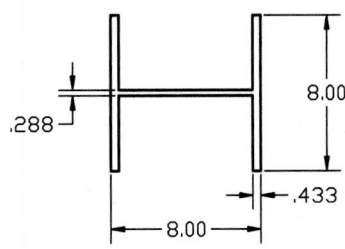

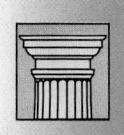

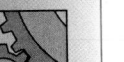

*Problems 2–7. These problems require you to use a variety of solid modeling methods to construct the objects. Use **EXTRUDE, REVOLVE**, solid primitives, new UCSs, and Boolean commands to assist in construction. Do not create section views. Save each as P07_(problem number).*

2.

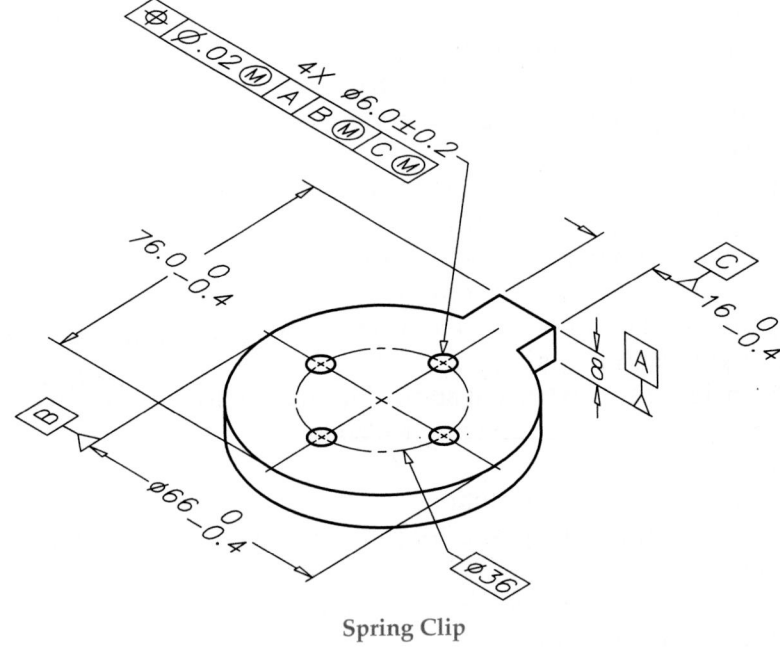

Spring Clip

3.

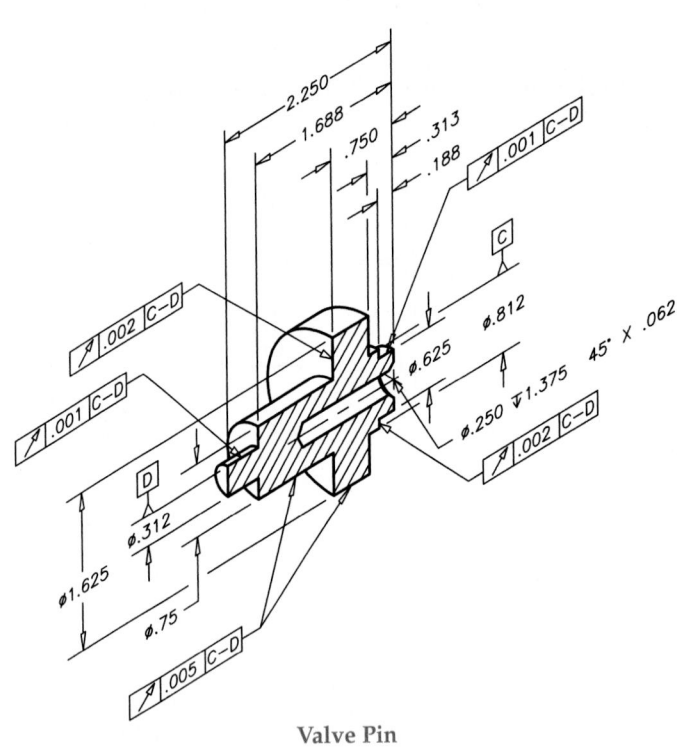

Valve Pin

AutoCAD and Its Applications—Advanced

4.

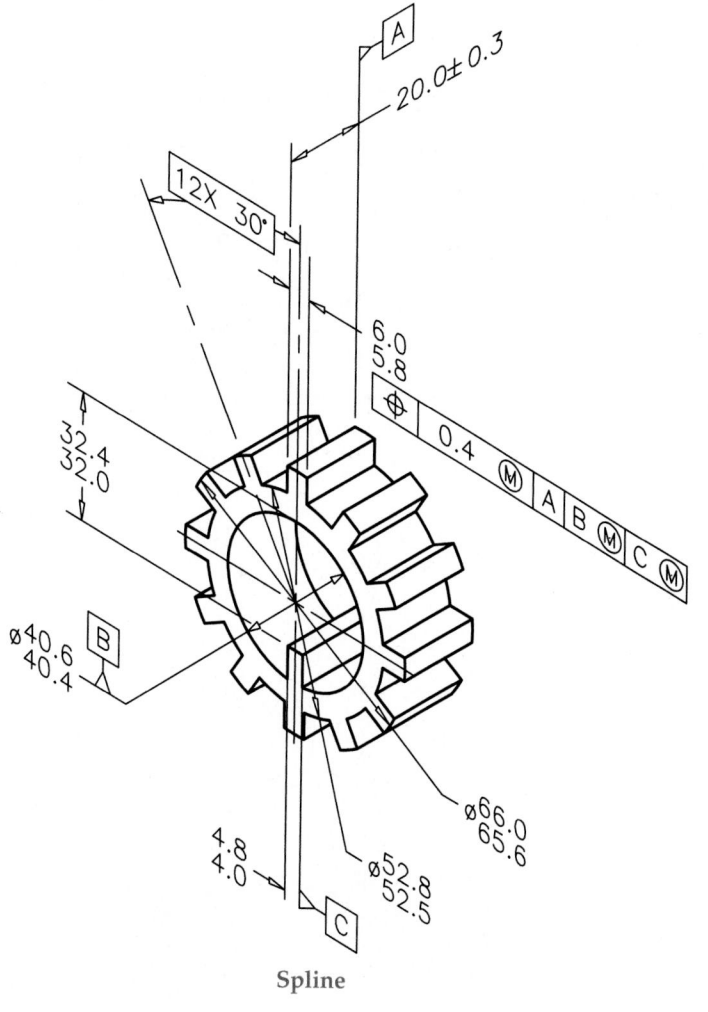

Spline

5.

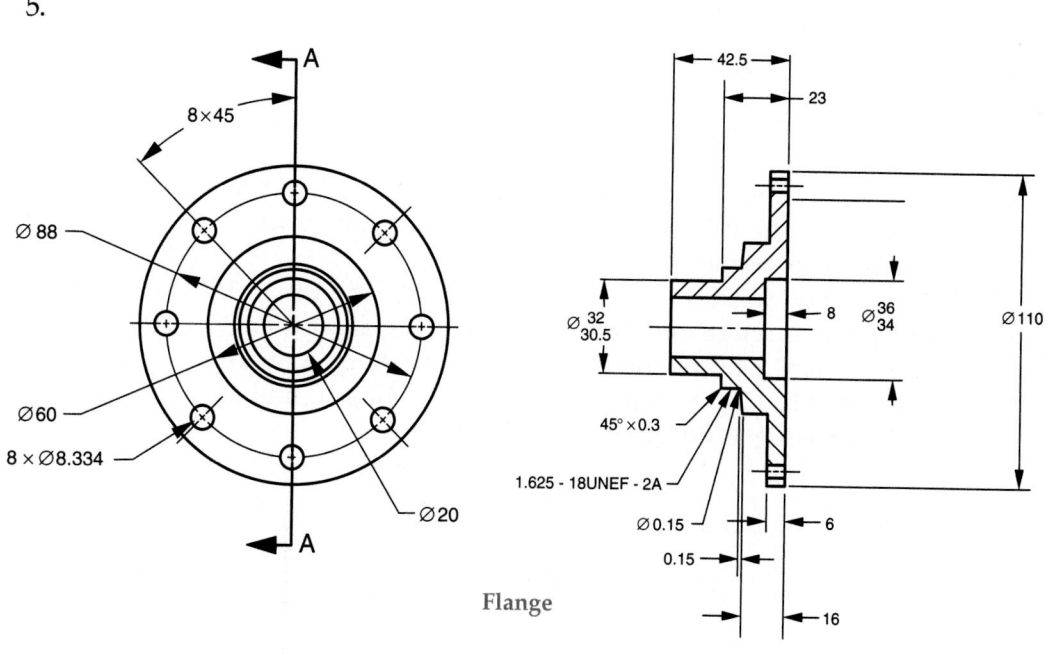

Flange

6.

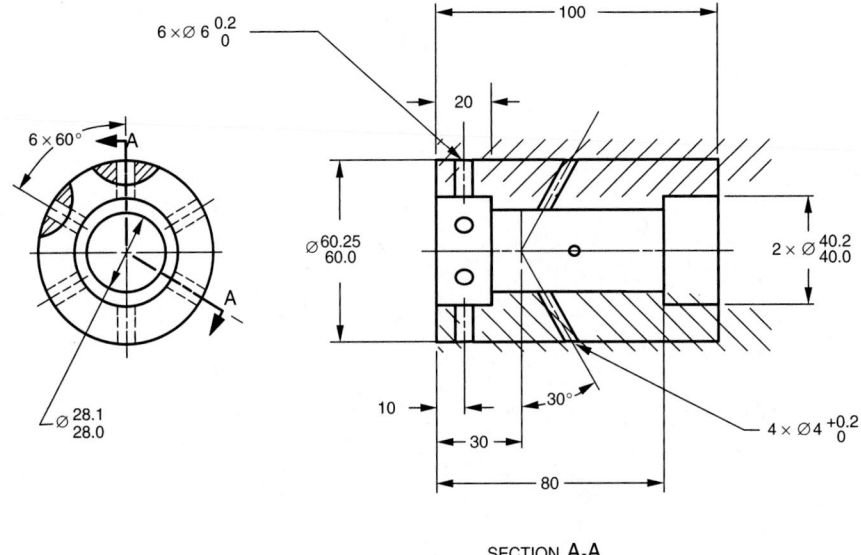

SECTION A-A

Nozzle

7.

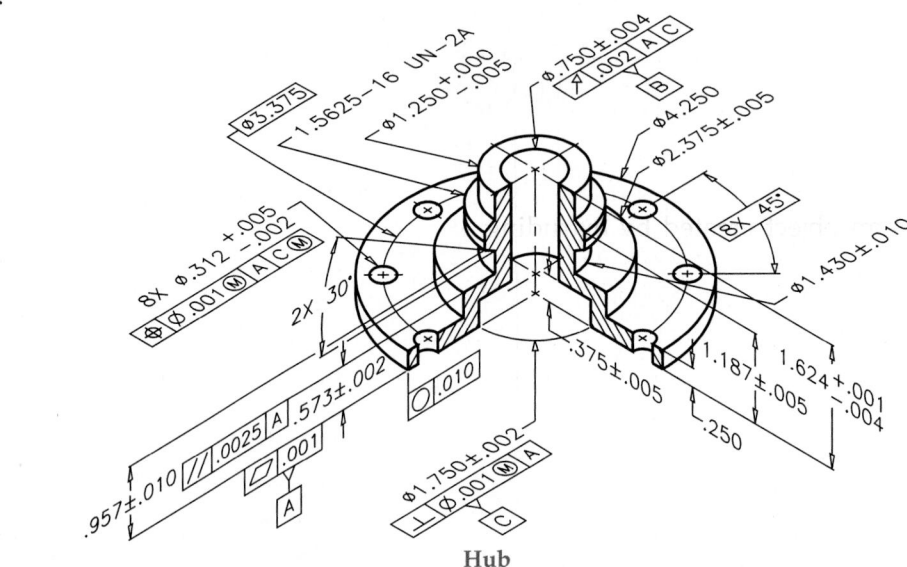

Hub

8. Construct picture frame moldings using the profiles shown below.
   A. Draw each of the closed profiles shown. Use your own dimensions for the details of the moldings.
   B. The length and width of A and B should be no larger than 1.5″ × 1″.
   C. The length and width of C and D should be no larger than 3″ × 1.5″.
   D. Construct an 8″ × 12″ picture frame using moldings A and B.
   E. Construct a 12″ × 24″ picture frame using moldings C and D.
   F. Save the drawing as P07_08.

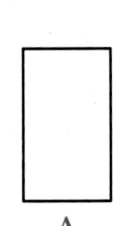

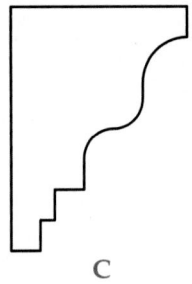

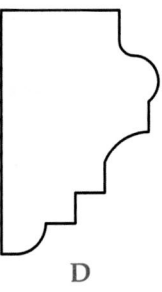

CHAPTER 8

Sweeps and Lofts

Learning Objectives

After completing this chapter, you will be able to:

✓ Sweep 2D shapes along a 2D or 3D path to create a solid or surface object.
✓ Create 3D solid or surface objects by lofting a series of cross sections.

In the previous chapter, you learned about extruded solids and surfaces. Sweeps and lofts are similar to extrusions. In fact, an extrusion is really just a type of sweep. A *sweep* is an object created by extruding a single 2D profile along a path object. Sweeping an open shape along the path results in a surface object. If a closed shape is swept, a solid object is created. A *loft* is an object created by extruding between two or more 2D profiles. The shape of the loft object blends from one cross-sectional profile to the next. The profiles can control the loft or it can be controlled by one path or multiple guide curves. As with a sweep, open shapes result in surfaces and closed shapes give you solids. Open and closed shapes cannot be used together in the same loft.

Creating Swept Surfaces and Solids

The **SWEEP** command is used to create swept surfaces and solids. The command requires at least two objects:

- 2D shape to be swept.
- 2D or 3D shape to be used as the sweep path.

The profile can be aligned with the path, you can specify the base point, a scale factor can be applied, and the profile can be twisted as it is swept. The command procedure and options are the same for both swept solids and surfaces.

Sweeping an open shape creates a surface. See Figure 8-1. The objects that can be swept to create surfaces include lines, arcs, elliptical arcs, 2D polylines, 2D splines, and traces. Sweeping a closed shape creates a solid. See Figure 8-2. The objects that can be swept to create a solid include circles, ellipses, closed 2D polylines, closed 2D splines, regions, planar surfaces, and planar faces of solids. The sweep path for either a surface or a solid can be a line, arc, circle, ellipse, elliptical arc, 2D polyline, 2D spline, 3D polyline, 3D spline, helix, or the edge of a surface or solid.

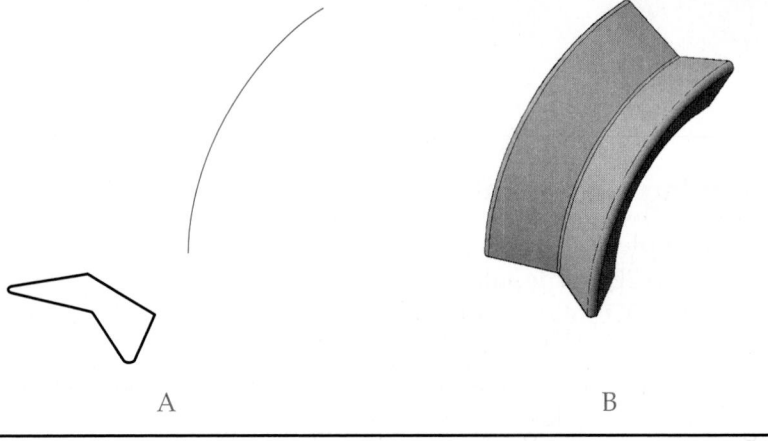

Figure 8-1.
A—This open shape will be swept along the path (shown in color). B—The resulting surface.

A   B

Figure 8-2.
A—This closed shape will be swept along the path (shown in color). B—The resulting solid.

A   B

SWEEP

Type
SWEEP

Pull-Down Menu
Draw
> Modeling
> Sweep

Toolbar
Modeling
Sweep

Dashboard
3D Make
Sweep

When the command is initiated, you are prompted to select the objects to sweep. Select the profile(s) and press [Enter]. Planar faces of solids may be selected by holding the [Ctrl] key as you select. Multiple profiles can be selected. They are swept along the same path, but separate objects are created.

Next, you are prompted to select the path. The path and profile can lie on the same plane. Select the object to be used as the sweep path and press [Enter]. To select the edge of a surface or solid as the path, press the [Ctrl] key and then select the edge. The profile is then moved to be perpendicular to the path and extruded along the path. The sweep starts at the endpoint of the path nearest to where you selected it.

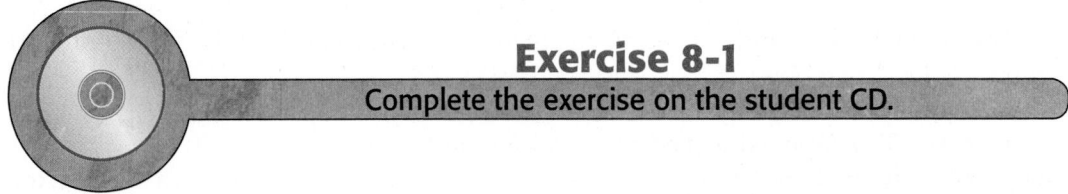

Exercise 8-1
Complete the exercise on the student CD.

Changing the Alignment of the Profile

By default, the profile is aligned perpendicular to the sweep path. However, you can create a sweep where the profile is not perpendicular to the path. See Figure 8-3. After the **SWEEP** command is initiated, select the profile and press [Enter]. Then, before selecting the path, enter the **Alignment** option. The default setting of Yes means that profile will be moved so it is perpendicular to the path. If you enter No, the profile is kept in the same position relative to the path as it is swept. The position of the 2D shape determines the alignment.

Figure 8-3.
A—The profile and path for the sweep. B—By default, the profile is aligned perpendicular to the path when swept. C—Using the **Alignment** option, the profile can be swept so it is not perpendicular to the path.

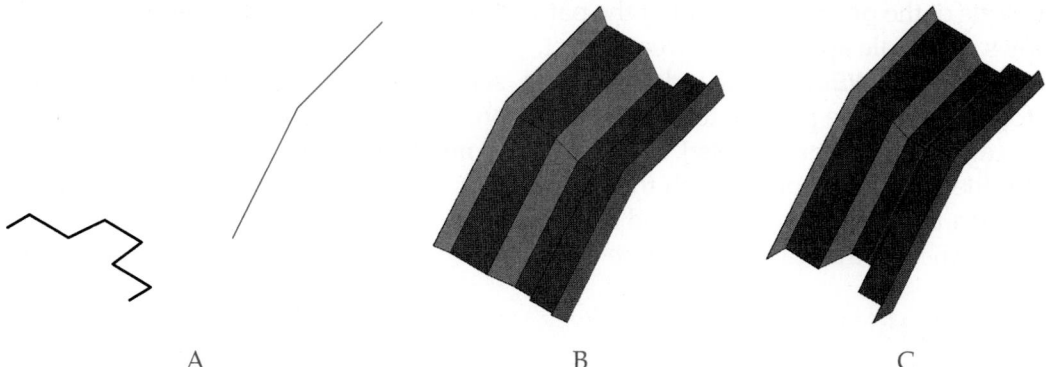

A   B   C

Changing the Base Point

The base point is the location on the shape that will be moved along the path to create the sweep. By default, if the 2D shape intersects the path, the profile is swept along the path at the point of intersection. If the 2D shape does not intersect the path, the default base point depends on the type of object being swept. When lines and arcs are swept, the default base point is their midpoint. Open polylines have a default base point at the midpoint of their total length.

The base point can be any point on the 2D shape or anywhere in the drawing. See Figure 8-4. To change the base point, use the **Base point** option of the **SWEEP** command. When the command is initiated, select the profile and press [Enter]. Then, before selecting the path, enter the **Base point** option. Next, pick the new base point. It does not have to be on an existing object. Once the new base point is selected, pick the path to create the sweep.

PROFESSIONAL TIP

If the location of the base point in relationship to the path is important, line up the shape with the path before starting the **SWEEP** command. Turn off the **Alignment** option in this situation.

Figure 8-4.
A—The profile and path for the sweep. B—The sweep is created with the default base point. C—The end of the path is selected as the base point. Notice the difference in this sweep and the one shown in B.

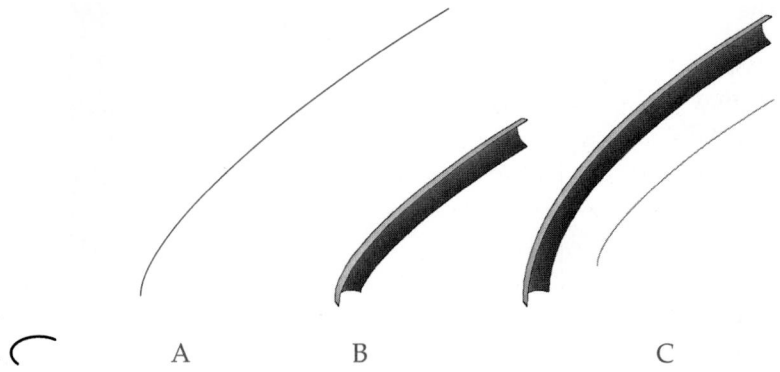

A   B   C

Scaling the Sweep Profile

By default, the size of the profile remains uniform from the beginning of the path to the end. However, using the **Scale** option of the **SWEEP** command, you can change the scale of the profile at the end of the path. This, in effect, tapers the sweep. Figure 8-5 shows a .25 scale applied to a sweep object.

Once the **SWEEP** command is initiated, select the profile and press [Enter]. Then, before selecting the path, enter the **Scale** option. You are prompted for the scale. Enter the scale value and press [Enter]. The scale value must be greater than zero. You can also enter the **Reference** option. With this option, pick two points for the first reference line and then two points for the second reference line. The difference in scale between the two distances is the scale value. Once the scale is set, pick the path to create the sweep.

Twisting the Sweep

The profile can be rotated as it is swept along the length of the path by using the **Twist** option of the **SWEEP** command. The angle that you enter indicates the rotation of the shape along the path of the sweep. The higher the number, the more twists in the sweep. Figure 8-6 shows how a simple, closed profile and a straight line can be used to create a milling tool. The profile was swept with a 270° twist.

Once the **SWEEP** command is initiated, select the profile and press [Enter]. Then, before selecting the path, enter the **Twist** option. You are prompted for the twist angle or to enter the **Bank** option.

Banking is the natural rotation of the profile on a 3D sweep path, similar to a banked curve on a racetrack. See Figure 8-7. The path must be 3D to set banking. The banking option is disabled for a 2D path, although you can go through the motions of turning it on when creating the sweep. Once you use the **Bank** option to turn banking on, it is on by default the next time the **SWEEP** command is used. To turn it off, enter a twist angle of zero (or the twist angle you wish to use). This angle becomes the default the next time the **SWEEP** command is used.

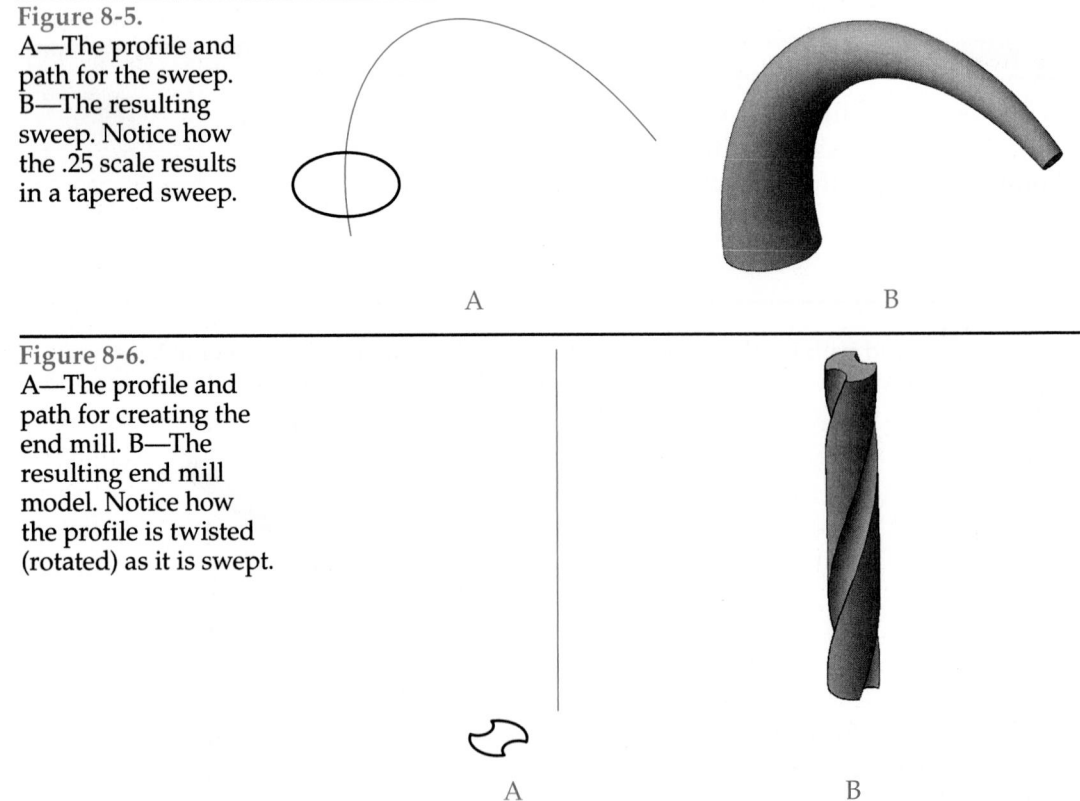

Figure 8-5.
A—The profile and path for the sweep. B—The resulting sweep. Notice how the .25 scale results in a tapered sweep.

A

B

Figure 8-6.
A—The profile and path for creating the end mill. B—The resulting end mill model. Notice how the profile is twisted (rotated) as it is swept.

A

B

Figure 8-7.
A—The profile and path for the sweep are shown in red. B—Banking is off for this sweep. When viewed from the side, you can see that the profile does not bank through the curve. Look at the upper-right corner. C—Banking is on for this sweep. Notice how the profile banks, or leans, through the curve. Compare this to B.

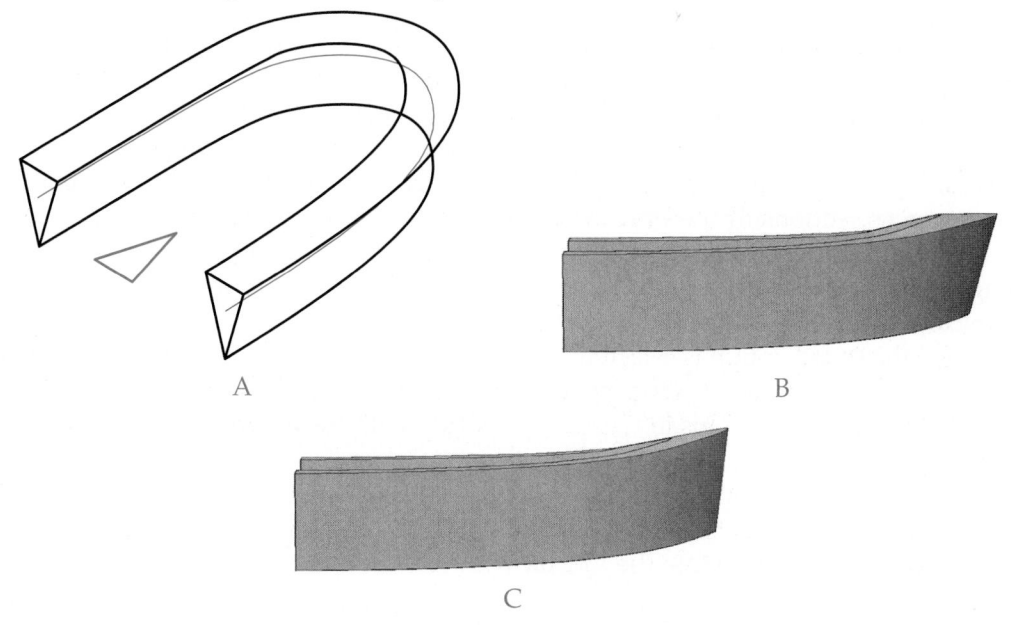

A

B

C

PROFESSIONAL TIP

The sweep options can be changed after the sweep is created using the **Properties** window. In the **Geometry** section, you will find Profile rotation (alignment), Bank (banking), Twist along path (twist angle), and Scale along path (scale) settings.

Exercise 8-2

Complete the exercise on the Student CD.

Creating Lofted Objects

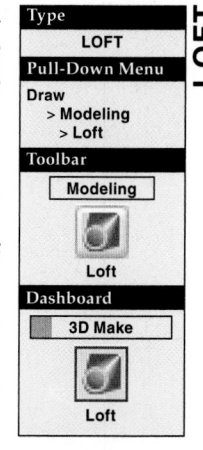

The **LOFT** command is used to create lofted surfaces and solids based on a series of cross-sectional profiles. Figure 8-8 shows an example of a loft formed from a rectangle, circle, and polygon. The loft may be guided by only the cross sections, as shown in the figure, by a path, or by guide curves. Lofting open shapes results in a surface object, while lofting closed shapes creates a solid. Open and closed shapes cannot be combined in the same loft.

Objects that can be used as cross sections include lines, circles, arcs, points, ellipses, elliptical arcs, 2D polylines, 2D splines, regions, planar faces of solids, planar surfaces, planar 3D faces, 2D solids, and traces. The loft path may be a line, circle, arc, ellipse, elliptical arc, spline, helix, or 2D or 3D polyline. Guide curves may be composed of lines, arcs, elliptical arcs, 2D or 3D splines, and 2D or 3D polylines.

Once the command is initiated, you are prompted to select the cross-sectional profiles. Pick each profile in the order in which it should appear in the loft and press [Enter]. Be sure to individually select the cross sections in the order of the loft creation. You may not get the desired loft if you randomly select them or use a window selection.

Type
LOFT
Pull-Down Menu
Draw
> Modeling
> Loft
Toolbar
Modeling
Loft
Dashboard
3D Make
Loft

LOFT

Next, you are prompted to select how the loft is to be controlled. As mentioned earlier, you can control the loft by the cross sections, a path, or guide curves. These options are discussed in the next sections.

Controlling the Loft with Cross Sections

The **Cross-sections only** option of the **LOFT** command is useful when the 2D cross sections are drawn in their proper locations in space. The command determines the transition from one cross section to the next. The cross sections are not moved by the command.

When the **Cross-sections only** option is selected, the **Loft Settings** dialog box appears, Figure 8-9. The settings in this dialog box control the transition or contour between cross sections. If the **Preview changes** check box at the bottom of the dialog box is checked, the current settings are previewed in the drawing area. As settings are changed, the preview is updated. When all settings have been made, pick the **OK** button to close the dialog box and create the loft.

When the **Ruled** option is selected in the dialog box, the loft has straight transitions between the cross sections. Sharp edges are created at each cross section. Figure 8-10 shows the same cross sections in Figure 8-8A lofted with the **Ruled** option on. Compare this to Figure 8-8B.

The **Smooth Fit** option creates a smooth transition between the cross sections. Sharp edges are only created at the first and last cross sections. This is the default setting and the one used to create the loft shown in Figure 8-8B.

Figure 8-8.
A—The three profiles will be lofted to create a solid. B—The resulting loft with the default settings.

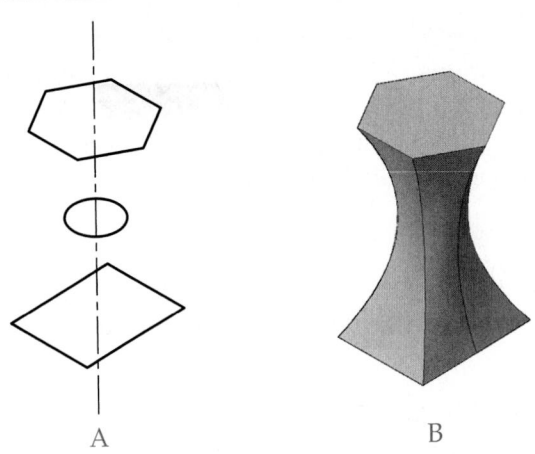

A   B

Figure 8-9.
When the loft is controlled by cross sections only, the **Loft Settings** dialog box is used to control the transition between profiles.

Select a contour setting

Check to connect the first and last cross sections

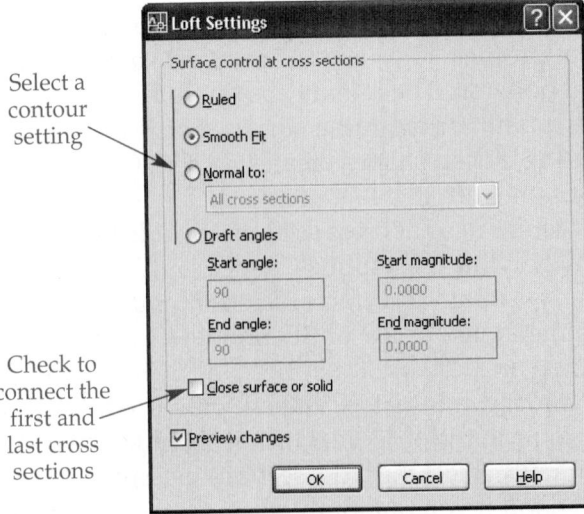

AutoCAD and Its Applications—Advanced

When the **Normal to:** option is selected in the dialog box, you can choose how the normal of the transition is treated at the cross sections. A *normal* is a vector extending perpendicular to the cross section. When the transition is normal to a cross section, it is perpendicular to the cross section. You can set the transition normal to the first cross section, last cross section, both first and last cross sections, or all cross sections. See Figure 8-11. Select the normal setting in the drop-down list. You will have to experiment with these settings to get the desired loft shape.

The **Draft Angle** option allows you to add a taper to the beginning and end of the loft. A *draft angle* is a slight taper added to a part that allows the part to be removed from a mold. Plastic or metal parts are sometimes formed in a two-part mold. In order to remove the parts, a slight angle is designed into the parts on the inside and outside surfaces to make removing the part from the mold easier.

Figure 8-10.
The profiles in Figure 8-8A are lofted with the **Ruled** option on in the **Loft Settings** dialog box. Compare this to Figure 8-8B.

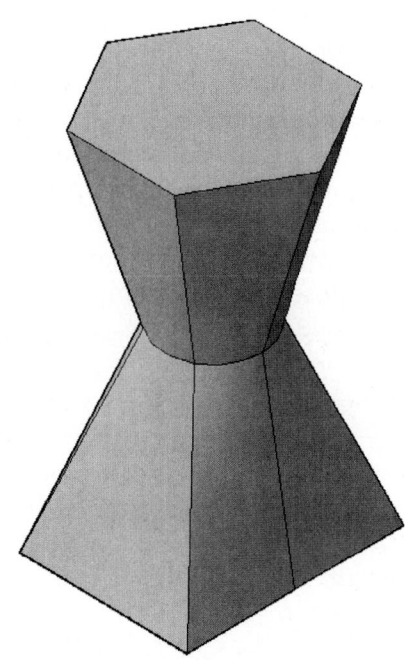

Figure 8-11.
The profiles in Figure 8-8A are lofted with the **Normal to:** option on in the **Loft Settings** dialog box. Cross sections were selected from bottom to top. Compare these results with Figure 8-8B and Figure 8-10. A—**Start cross section**. B—**End cross section**. C—**Start and End cross sections**. D—**All cross sections**.

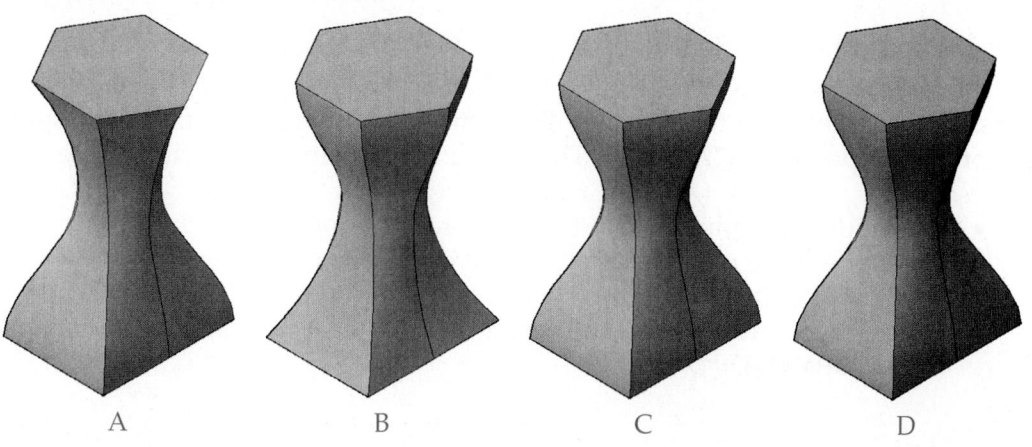

A   B   C   D

Figure 8-12.
When setting the draft angle, you can set the angle and the magnitude. A—Draft angle of 90° and a magnitude of zero. B—Draft angle of 30° and a magnitude of 180. C—Draft angle of 60° and a magnitude of 180.

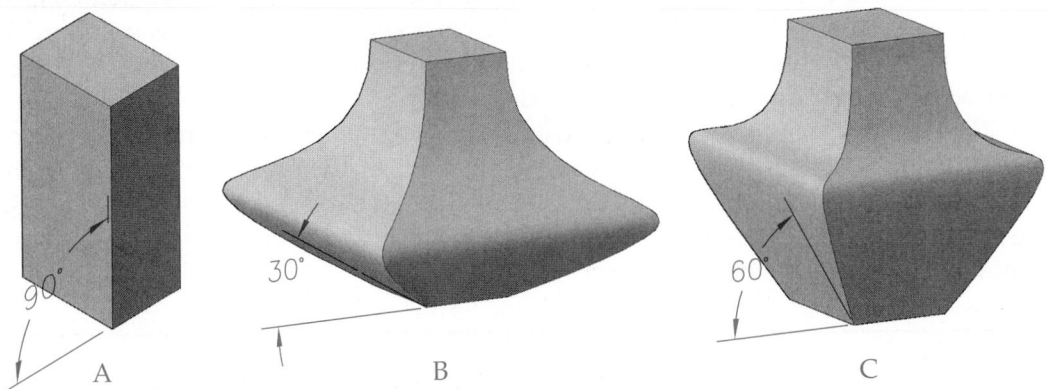

When setting the draft angle, you can set the angle and the magnitude. See Figure 8-12. The default draft angle is 90°, which means the transition is perpendicular to the cross section. The magnitude represents the relative distance from the cross section in the same direction as the draft angle before the transition starts to curve toward the next cross section. The maximum magnitude value varies depending on the loft. You may have to experiment with different magnitude and angle settings to get the desired loft shape.

The **Close surface or solid** option is used to connect the last cross section to the first cross section. This option "closes" the loft, similar to the **Close** option of the **LINE** or **PLINE** command. See Figure 8-13.

PROFESSIONAL TIP

The settings in the **Loft Settings** dialog box are retained as the default, so get in the habit of checking them each time you create a loft. The **LOFTNORMALS** system variable controls which surface control radio button is current.

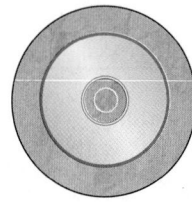

Exercise 8-3
Complete the exercise on the Student CD.

Controlling the Loft with Guide Curves

Guide curves are lines that control the shape of the transition between cross sections. They do not have to be *curves*. They can be lines, arcs, elliptical arcs, splines (2D or 3D), or polylines (2D or 3D). There are four rules to follow when using guide curves:

- The guide curve must start on the first cross section.
- The guide curve must end on the last cross section.
- The guide curve must intersect all other cross sections.
- The surface control in the **Loft Settings** dialog box must be set to **Smooth Fit** (**LOFTNORMALS** = 1).

Figure 8-13.
A—These profiles will be used to create a sealing ring. They should be selected in a counterclockwise direction starting with the first cross section. B—The resulting loft with the default settings. Notice the gap between the first and last cross sections. C—By checking the **Close surface or solid** check box in the **Loft Settings** dialog box, the loft continues from the last cross section to the first cross section.

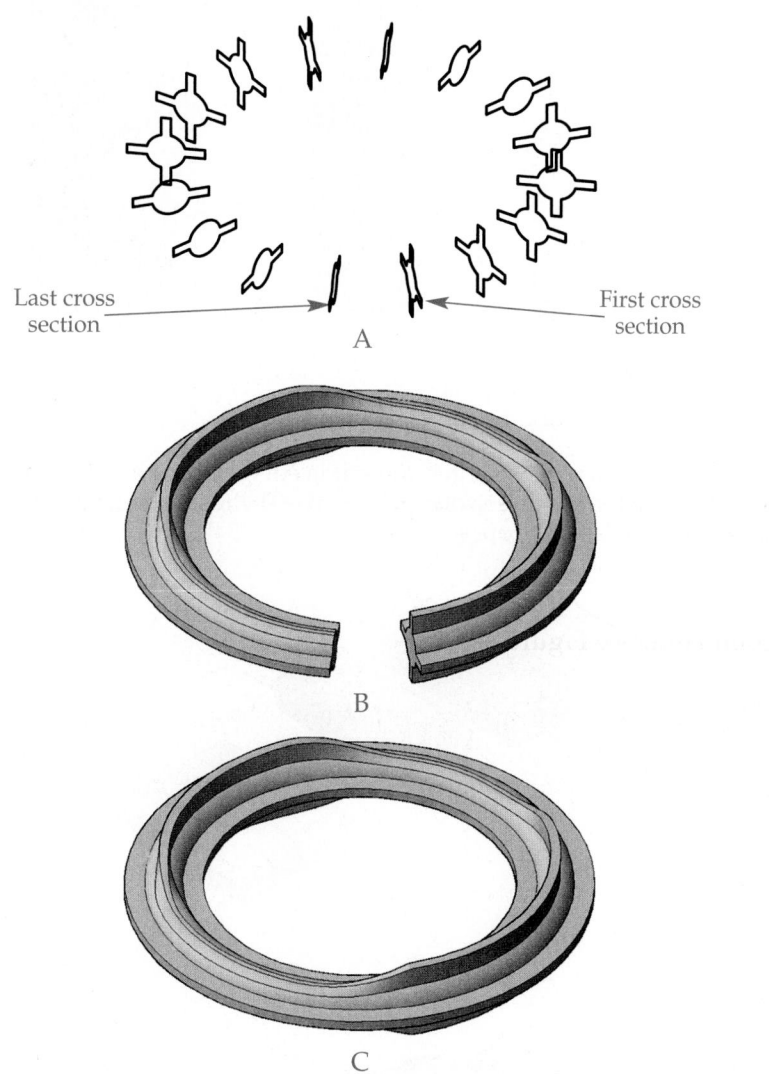

Last cross section   First cross section

A

B

C

When the **Guides** option is entered, you are prompted to select the guide curves. Select all of the guide curves and press [Enter]. The loft is created. The order in which guide curves are selected is not important.

For example, Figure 8-14A shows two circles that will be lofted. If the **Cross-sections only** option is used, a cylinder is created, Figure 8-14B. However, if the **Guides** option is used and the two guide curves shown in Figure 8-14A are selected, one side of the cylinder is deformed similar to a handle or grip. See Figure 8-14C.

Lofting is used to create open contour shapes such as fenders, automobile interior parts, fabrics, and other ergonomic consumer products. Figure 8-15 shows the use of open 2D splines in the construction of a fabric covering. Notice how each cross section is intersected by the guide curve. There is a cross section at the beginning of the guide curve and one at the end. These conditions fulfill the rules outlined earlier.

Figure 8-14.
A—These two circles will be lofted. The lines shown in color will be used as guide curves.
B—When the circles are lofted using the **Cross-sections only** option, a cylinder is created.
C—When the **Guides** option is used and the guide curves shown in A are selected, the resulting loft is shaped like a handle or grip.

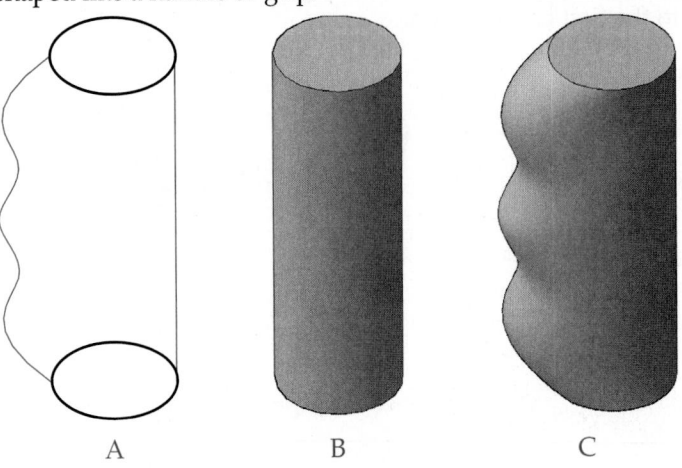

Figure 8-15.
A—The open profiles shown in black and the guide curve shown in color will be used to create a fabric covering for the three solid objects. B—The resulting fabric covering. This is a surface because the profiles were open.

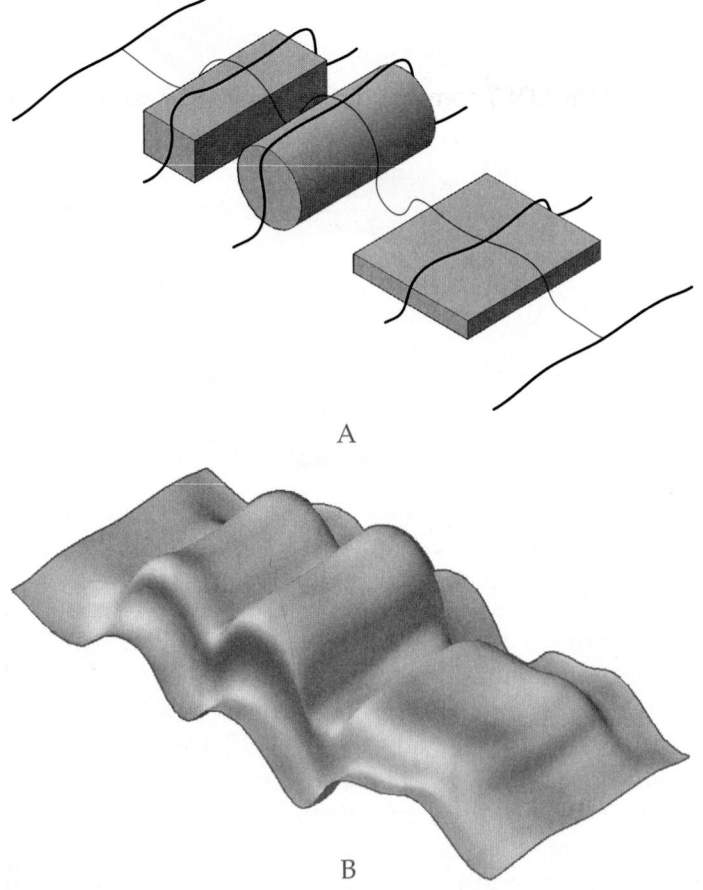

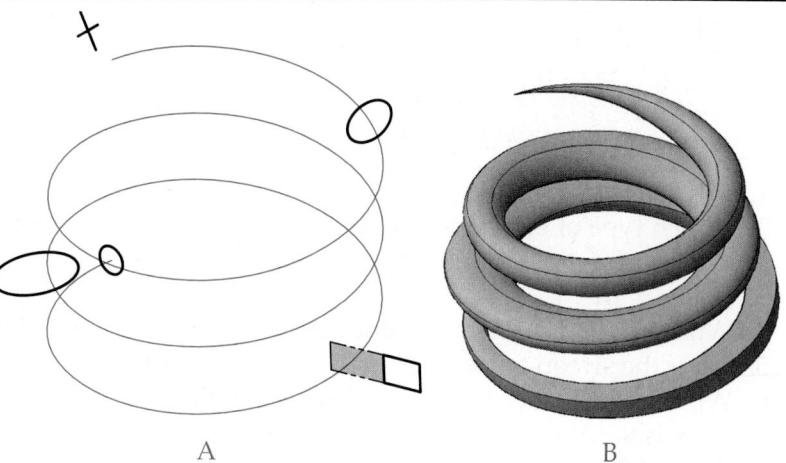

Figure 8-16.
A—The profiles shown in black will be lofted along the path shown in color. Notice how the rectangular profile is not intersected by the path, but the path does intersect the plane on which the rectangle lies. B—The resulting loft.

A   B

CAUTION

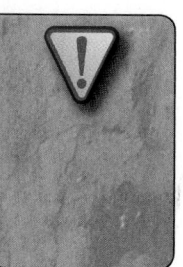

Guide curves only work well when the surface control is set to **Smooth Fit** (**LOFTNORMALS** = 1). Remember, the settings in the **Loft Settings** dialog box are retained after the previous **LOFT** command. If you get an error message when using guide curves that says The selected entities are not valid, make sure **LOFTNORMALS** is set to 1 and try it again.

Controlling the Loft with a Path

The **Path** option of the **LOFT** command places the cross sections along a single path. The path must intersect the planes on which each of the cross sections lie. However, the path does *not* have to physically touch the edge of each cross section, as is required of guide curves. When the **Path** option is entered, you are prompted to select the path. Once the path is picked, the loft is created. The cross sections remain in their original positions.

Figure 8-16 shows how 2D shapes can be positioned at various points on a path to create a loft. The rectangular shape does not cross the path. However, as long as the path intersects the plane of the rectangle, which it does, the shape will be included in the loft definition. The last shape at the top of the helix is a point object, causing the loft to taper.

PROFESSIONAL TIP

The **LOFT** command does not allow self-intersecting lofts to be created. Unfortunately, the error message you receive only states: The selected entities are not valid. If you see this message, look for areas where the path may be closing in on itself.

Exercise 8-4
Complete the exercise on the Student CD.

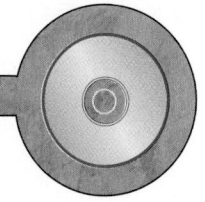

Chapter Test

Answer the following questions. Write your answers on a separate sheet of paper or complete the electronic chapter test on the Student CD.

1. What is a *loft?*
2. Which type of 2D shape results in a solid object when swept or lofted?
3. When using the **SWEEP** command, on which endpoint of the path does the sweep start?
4. What is the purpose of the **Base Point** option of the **SWEEP** command?
5. After the sweep or loft is created, how can the creation options be changed?
6. Which objects may be used as a sweep path?
7. How is the alignment of a sweep set to be perpendicular to the start of the path?
8. Which **SWEEP** command option is used to taper the sweep?
9. What is the difference between the **Ruled** and **Smooth Fit** options in the **LOFT** command?
10. What does the **Bank** option of the **LOFT** command do?
11. Where is the check box that will close the loft, similar to a polyline, and what is its name?
12. Which five objects may be used as guide curves in a loft?
13. What are the four rules that must be followed when using guide curves?
14. When using the **Path** option of the **LOFT** command, what must the path intersect?
15. How can a loft be created so it tapers to a point at its end?

Drawing Problems

1. Create the lamp shade shown below. Create two separate loft objects for the top and the bottom. Then, union the two pieces. Finally, scale a copy and hollow out the lamp shade. Save the drawing as P08_01.

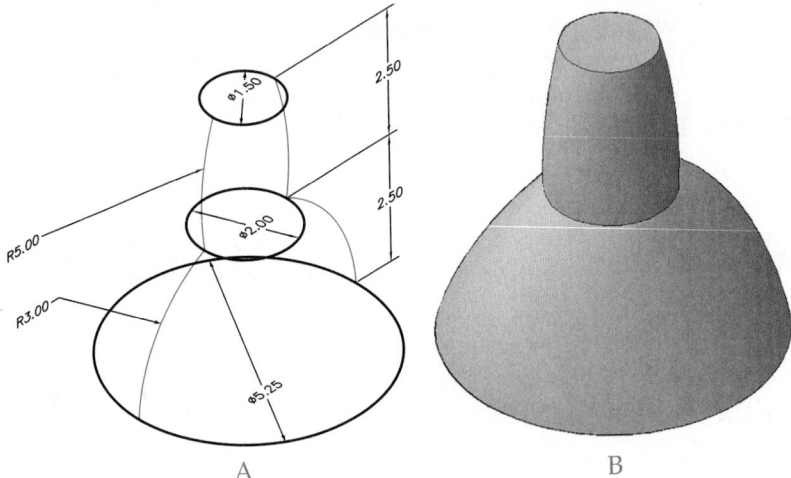

AutoCAD and Its Applications—Advanced

2. Create the two shampoo bottles shown below. One design uses cross sections only, the other uses a guide curve. Each bottle is made up of two loft objects. Join the pieces so each bottle is one solid. Save the drawing as P08_02.

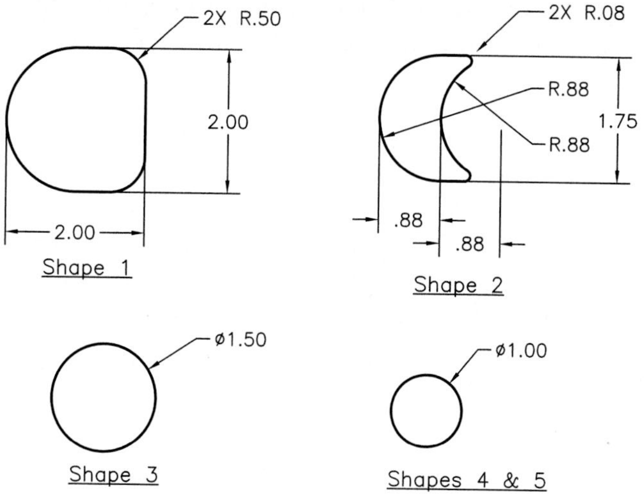

2X R.50

2.00

2.00

Shape 1

2X R.08

R.88

1.75

R.88

.88

.88

Shape 2

Ø1.50

Shape 3

Ø1.00

Shapes 4 & 5

A

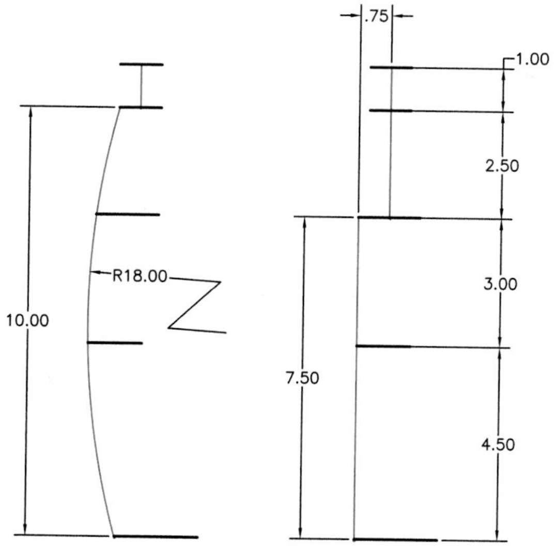

.75

1.00

2.50

3.00

R18.00

10.00

7.50

4.50

B

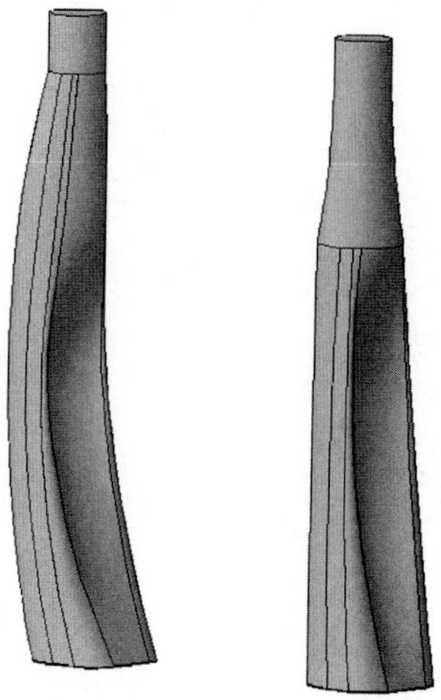

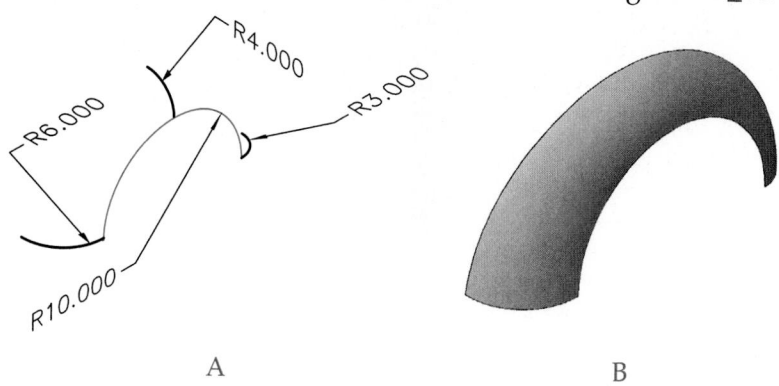

C

3. Create the automobile fender shown below as a loft. Use either the **Guide** or **Path** option and the line shown in color. Save the drawing as P08_03.

R4.000

R6.000

R3.000

R10.000

A

B

4. Draw the C-Clamp shown below as a loft. Use the shapes (A, B, C, and D) as the cross sections and the polyline (in color) as the guide curve. Add Ø1 unit cylinders to the ends. Make one cylinder .125H and the other 1.125H. The cylinders should be centered on profile D and located at the ends of the loft as shown. Make a Ø.625 hole through the larger cylinder. Save the drawing as P08_04.

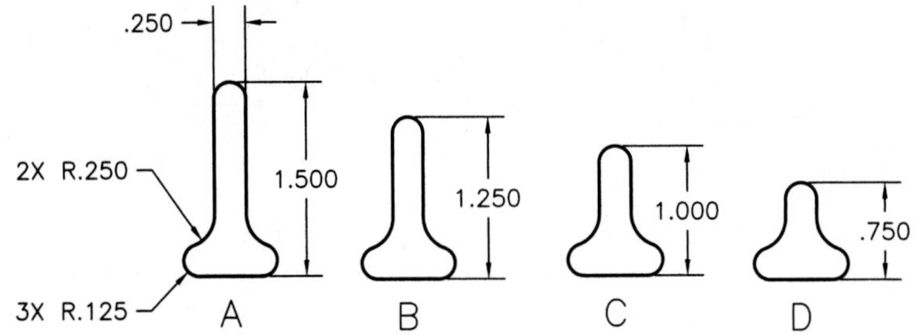

.250

2X R.250

1.500

1.250

1.000

.750

3X R.125

A

B

C

D

Cross Sections

A

B

A

B

B

5.327

B

R.500

R.500

B

2.250

100°

2.866

R.194

D

C

D

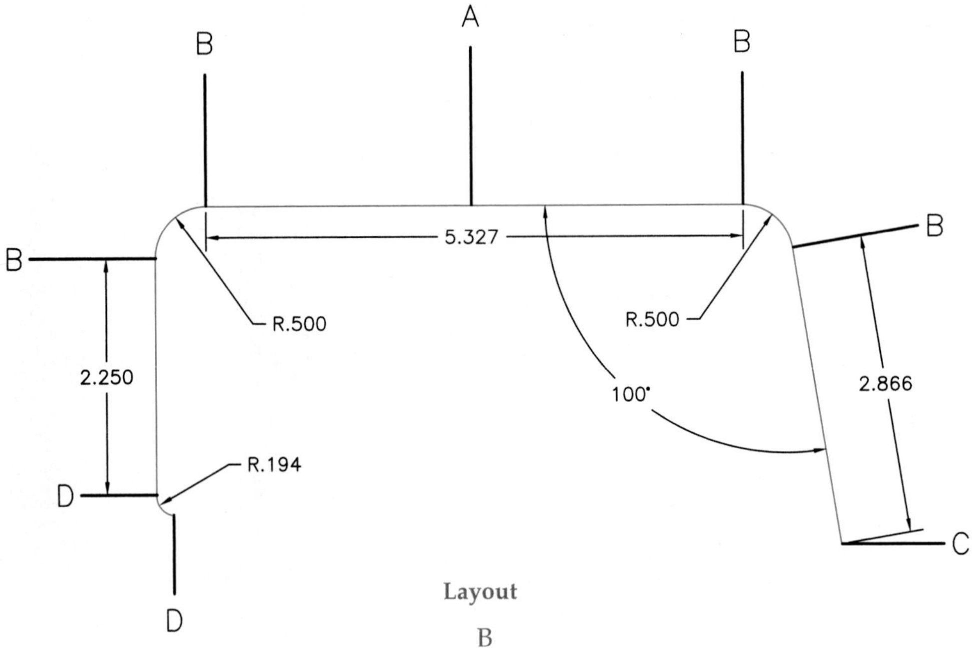

Layout

B

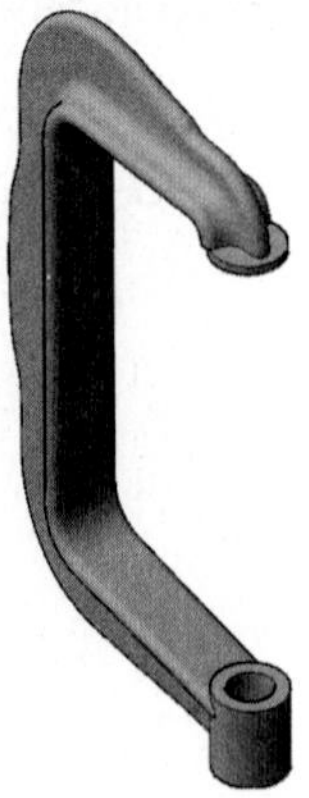

C

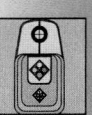

5. In this exercise you will draw a racetrack for toy cars by sweeping a 2D shape along a polyline path.

   A. Draw the polyline path shown with the coordinates given. Turn it into a spline.

   B. Draw the 2D profile shown using the dimensions given. Turn it into a region or a polyline.

   C. Use the **SWEEP** command to create the racetrack, as shown in the shaded view.

   D. You may have to use the **Properties** window to adjust the sweep after it is drawn.

   E. Save the drawing as P08_05.

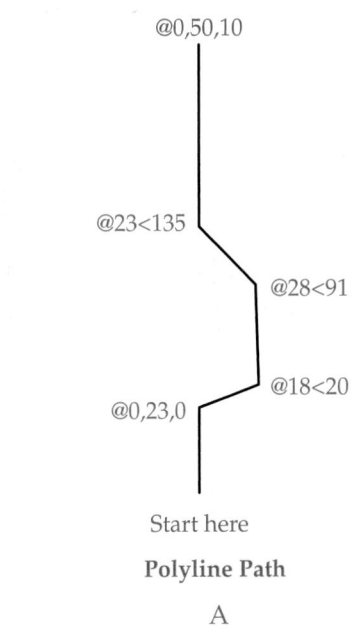

Polyline Path

A

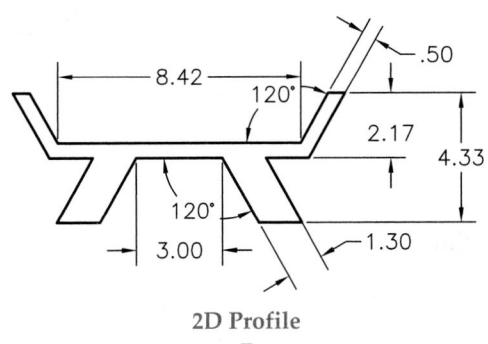

2D Profile

B

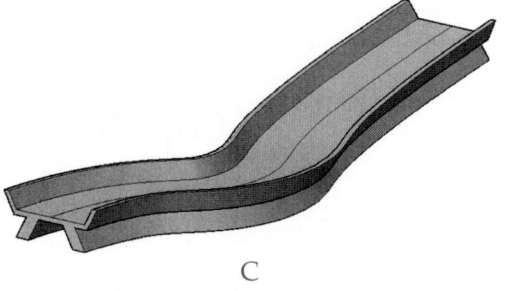

C

Drawing Problems – Chapter 8

6. In this exercise, you will cut a UNC thread in a cylinder by sweeping a 2D shape around a helix and subtracting it.
   A. Draw a ∅.25 cylinder that is 1.00 in height.
   B. Draw the thread cutter profile shown below. The long edge of the cutter should be aligned with the vertical edge of the cylinder.
   C. Draw a helix centered on the cylinder with base and top radii of .125, turn height of .050, and a total height of 1.000.
   D. Sweep the 2D shape along the helix. Then, subtract the resulting solid from the cylinder. Refer to the shaded view shown below.
   E. If time allows, create another cutter profile to cut a .0313 × 45° chamfer on the end of the thread. Use a circle as a sweep path or revolve the profile about the center of the cylinder.
   F. Save the drawing as P08_06.

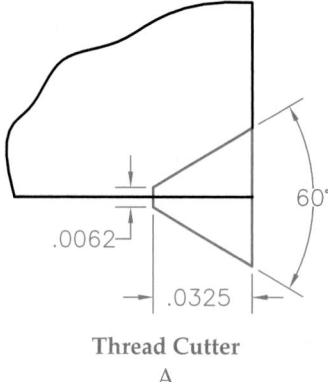

Thread Cutter
A

B

Creating and Working with Solid Model Details

Learning Objectives

After completing this chapter, you will be able to:
- ✓ Change properties on solids.
- ✓ Align objects.
- ✓ Rotate objects in three dimensions.
- ✓ Mirror objects in three dimensions.
- ✓ Create 3D arrays.
- ✓ Fillet solid objects.
- ✓ Chamfer solid objects.
- ✓ Thicken a surface into a solid.
- ✓ Convert planar objects into surfaces.
- ✓ Slice a solid using various methods.
- ✓ Construct details on solid models.
- ✓ Remove features from solid models.

Changing Properties

Properties of 3D objects can be modified using the **Properties** window, which is thoroughly discussed in *AutoCAD and Its Applications—Basics*. This window is accessed by using the **Standard** toolbar, **Modify** pull-down menu, [Ctrl]+[1] key combination, or by typing the command. You can also double-click on a solid object or select the solid, right-click, and pick **Properties** from the shortcut menu.

The **Properties** window lists the properties of the currently selected object. For example, Figure 9-1 lists the properties of a selected solid sphere. AutoCAD offers some parametric solid modeling options. A *parametric solid modeling program* allows you to change the parameters, such as a sphere's diameter, in the **Properties** window. You can also change the sphere's position, linetype, linetype scale, color, layer, lineweight, and visual settings. The categories and properties available in the **Properties** window depend on the selected object.

To modify an object property, select the property. Then, enter a new value in the right-hand column. The drawing is updated to reflect the changes. You can leave the **Properties** window open as you continue with your work.

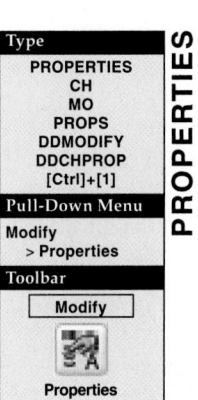

PROPERTIES

Type
PROPERTIES
CH
MO
PROPS
DDMODIFY
DDCHPROP
[Ctrl]+[1]

Pull-Down Menu

Modify
> Properties

Toolbar

Modify

Properties

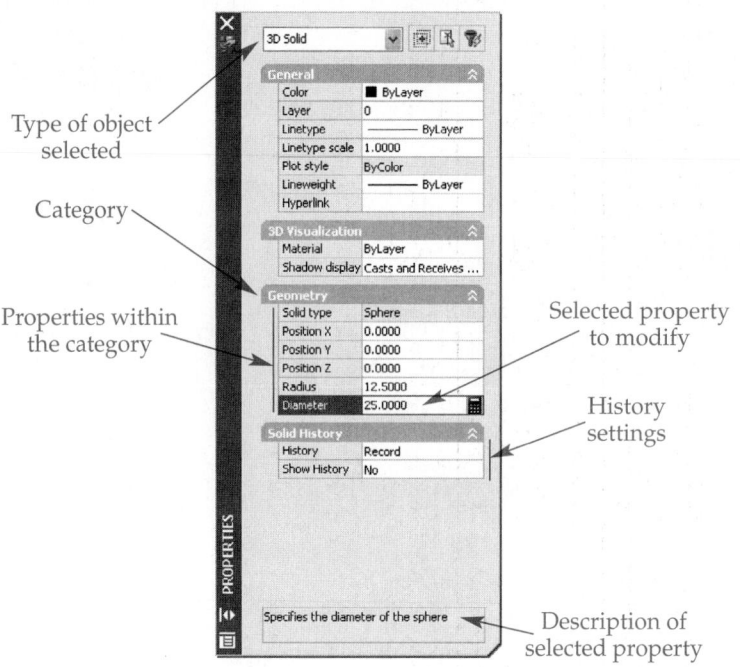

Figure 9-1.
The **Properties** window can be used to change many of the properties of a solid.

Type of object selected

Category

Properties within the category

Selected property to modify

History settings

Description of selected property

Solid Model History

AutoCAD can automatically record a history of a composite solid model's construction. The control of the history setting is found in the **Solid History** category of the **Properties** window. By default, the History property in the **Properties** window is set to Record, which means that the history will be saved. See **Figure 9-1.** It is generally a good idea to have the history recorded. Then, at any time, you can graphically display all of the geometry that was used to create the model.

If the **SOLIDHIST** system variable is set to a value of 1, all new solids have their History property set to Record. This is the default. If the system variable is set to 0, all new solids have their History property set to None (no recording). With either setting of the system variable, the **Properties** window can be used to change the setting for individual solids.

To view the graphic history of the composite solid, set the Show History property in the **Properties** window to Yes. All of the geometry used to construct the model is displayed. If the **SHOWHIST** system variable is set to 0, the Show History property is set to No for all solids and cannot be changed. If this system variable is set to 2, the Show History property is set to Yes for all solids and cannot be changed. A **SHOWHIST** setting of 1 allows the Show History property to be individually set for each solid.

An example of showing the history on a composite solid is provided in **Figure 9-2.** The object appears in its current edited format in **Figure 9-2A.** The Conceptual visual style is set current and the Show History property is set to No. In **Figure 9-2B,** the Show History property is set to Yes. Isolines have also been turned on. You can see the geometry that was used in the Boolean subtraction operations. Using subobject editing techniques, the individual geometry can be selected and edited. Subobject editing is discussed in detail in Chapter 10.

NOTE

If the Solid History property is set to Yes to display the components of the composite solid, as seen in **Figure 9-2,** the components will appear when the drawing is plotted. Be sure to set the Show History property to No before you print or plot.

Figure 9-2.
A—The object appears in its current edited format with Show History property turned off.
B—The Show History property is set to Yes and the display of isolines has been turned on.

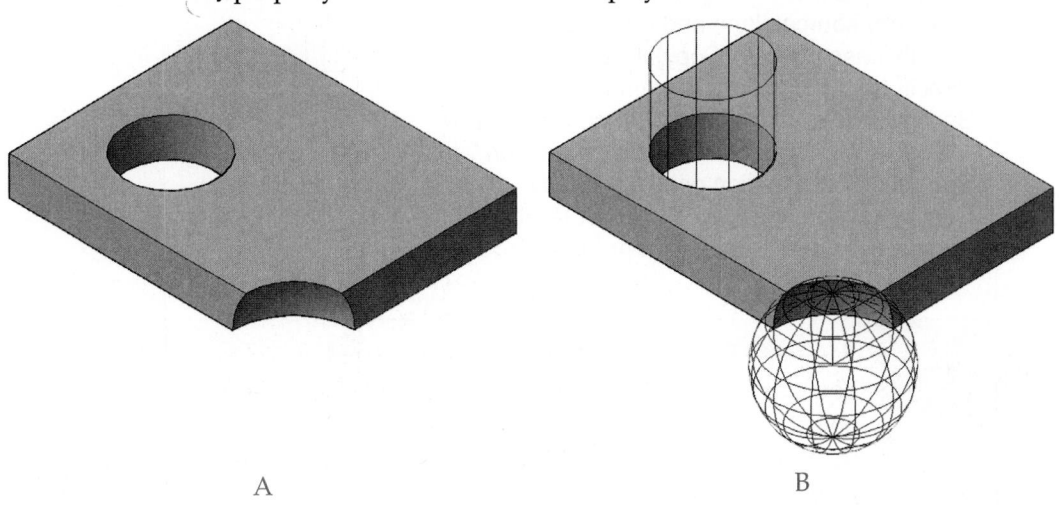

A   B

Aligning Objects in 3D

AutoCAD provides two different methods with which to move and rotate objects in a single command. This is called *aligning* objects. The simplest method is to align 3D objects by picking source points on the first object and then picking destination points on the object to which the first one is to be aligned. This is accomplished with the **3DALIGN** command, which allows you to both relocate and rotate the object. The second, and much more versatile, method allows you to not only move and rotate an object, but also to scale the object being aligned. This is possible with the **ALIGN** command.

Move and Rotate Objects in 3D Space

The basic function of moving and rotating an object relative to a second object or set of points is done with the **3DALIGN** command. It allows you to reorient an object in 3D space. Using this command, you can correct errors of 3D construction and quickly manipulate 3D objects. The **3DALIGN** command requires existing points (source) and the new location of those existing points (destination).

Type
3DALIGN
Pull-Down Menu
Modify
> 3D Operations
> 3D Align

3DALIGN

For example, refer to Figure 9-3. The wedge in Figure 9-3A is aligned in its new position in Figure 9-3B as follows. Set the **Intersection** or **Endpoint** running object snap to make point selection easier. Refer to the figure for the pick points.

Figure 9-3.
The **3DALIGN** command can be used to properly orient 3D objects. A—Before aligning. Note the pick points. B—After aligning.

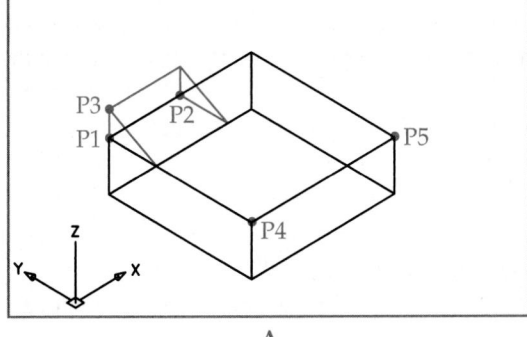
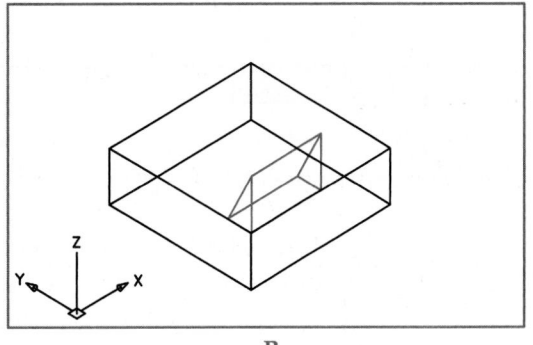

A   B

Select objects: *(pick the wedge)*
1 found
Select objects: ↵
 Specify source plane and orientation...
Specify base point or [Copy]: *(pick P1)*
Specify second point or [Continue] <C>: *(pick P2)*
Specify third point or [Continue] <C>: *(pick P3)*
 Specify destination plane and orientation...
Specify first destination point: *(pick P4)*
Specify second destination point or [eXit] <X>: *(pick P5)*
Specify third destination point or [eXit] <X>: ↵

PROFESSIONAL TIP

You can also use the **3DALIGN** command to copy, instead of move an object and realign it at the same time. Just select the **Copy** option at the Specify base point or [Copy]: prompt. Then, continue selecting the points as shown above.

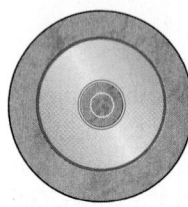

Exercise 9-1

Complete the exercise on the Student CD.

Move, Rotate, and Scale Objects in 3D Space

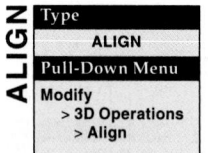

Type
ALIGN
Pull-Down Menu
Modify
> 3D Operations
> Align

The **ALIGN** command has the same functions of the **3DALIGN** command, but adds the ability to scale an object. Refer to **Figure 9-4**. The 90° bend must be rotated and scaled to fit onto the end of the HVAC assembly. Two source points and two destination points are required, **Figure 9-4A**. Then, you can choose to scale the object.

Select objects: *(pick the 90° bend)*
1 found
Select objects: ↵
Specify first source point: *(pick P1)*
Specify first destination point: *(pick P2; a line is drawn between the two points)*
Specify second source point: *(pick P3)*
Specify second destination point: *(pick P4; a line is drawn between the two points)*
Specify third source point or <continue>: ↵
Scale objects based on alignment points? [Yes/No] <N>: **Y**↵

The 90° bend is aligned and scaled to meet the existing ductwork object. See **Figure 9-4B**. You can also align using three source and three destination points. However, when doing so, you cannot scale the object.

PROFESSIONAL TIP

Before using 3D editing commands, set running object snaps to enhance your accuracy and speed.

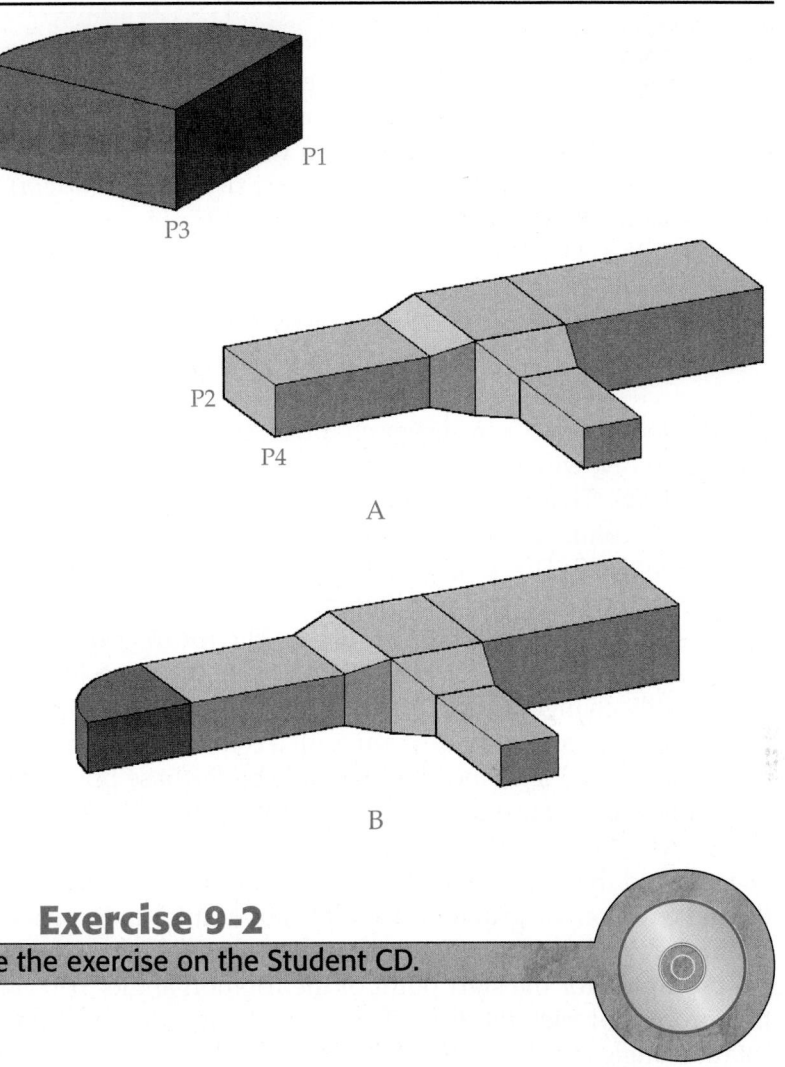

Figure 9-4.
Using the **ALIGN** command. A—Two source points and two destination points are required. Notice how the bend is not at the proper scale. B—You can choose to scale the object during the operation. Notice how the aligned bend is also properly scaled.

A

B

Exercise 9-2

Complete the exercise on the Student CD.

3D Moving

The **3DMOVE** command allows you to quickly move an object along any axis or plane of the current UCS. When the command is initiated, you are prompted to select the objects to move. After selecting the objects, press [Enter]. The *move grip tool* is displayed, attached to the cursor. The move grip tool is a tripod that appears similar to the shaded UCS icon. Pick a location to place the tool at the base of the move.

If you move the pointer over the X, Y, or Z axis of the grip tool, the axis changes to yellow. To restrict movement along that axis, pick the axis. If you move the pointer over one of the right angles at the origin of the tool, the corresponding two axes turn yellow. Pick to restrict the movement to that plane. You can complete the movement by either picking a new point or by direct distance entry.

By default, when a solid is selected with no command active, the move grip tool is displayed on the object. You can relocate the grip tool by selecting the grip at the tool's origin. Then, move the tool to a new location and pick. If the **DUCS** (dynamic UCS) button is on, you can also realign the tool.

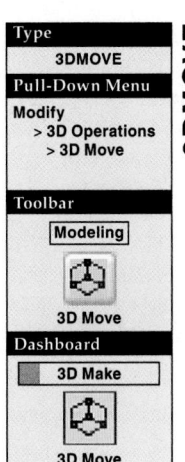

Type
3DMOVE
Pull-Down Menu
Modify
> 3D Operations
> 3D Move

Toolbar
Modeling
3D Move

Dashboard
3D Make
3D Move

3DMOVE

If the **GTAUTO** system variable is set to 1, the move grip tool is displayed when a solid is selected with no command active. If the **GTLOCATION** system variable is set to 0, the grip tool is placed on the UCS icon (not necessarily the UCS *origin*). Both of these settings are the defaults.

3D Rotating

As you have seen in earlier chapters, the **ROTATE** command can be used to rotate 3D objects. However, the command can only rotate objects in the XY plane of the current UCS. This is why you had to change UCSs to properly rotate objects. The **3DROTATE** command, on the other hand, can rotate objects on any axis regardless of the current UCS. This is an extremely powerful editing and design tool.

When the command is initiated, you are prompted to select the objects to rotate. After selecting the objects, press [Enter]. The *rotate grip tool* is displayed, attached to the cursor. See **Figure 9-5.** If the 2D Wireframe visual style is current, the visual style is temporarily changed to the 3D Wireframe because the grip tool is not displayed in 2D mode. The grip tool provides you with a dynamic, graphic representation of the three axes of rotation. Pick a location that is to be the base point of the rotation.

Now, you can use the grip tool to rotate the objects about the tool's local X, Y, or Z axis. As you hover the cursor over one of the three circles in the grip tool, a vector is displayed that represents the axis of rotation. To rotate about the tool's X axis, pick the red circle on the grip tool. To rotate about the Y axis, pick the green circle. To rotate about the Z axis, pick the blue circle. Once you select a circle, it turns yellow and you are prompted for the start point of the rotation angle. You can enter a direct angle at this prompt or pick the first of two points defining the angle of rotation. When the rotation angle is defined, the object is rotated about the selected axis.

3DROTATE

Type
3DROTATE

Pull-Down Menu
Modify
> 3D Operations
> 3D Rotate

Toolbar
Modeling

3D Rotate

Dashboard
3D Make

3D Rotate

Figure 9-5.
This is the rotate grip tool. The three axes of rotation are represented by the circles. The origin of the rotation is where you place the center grip.

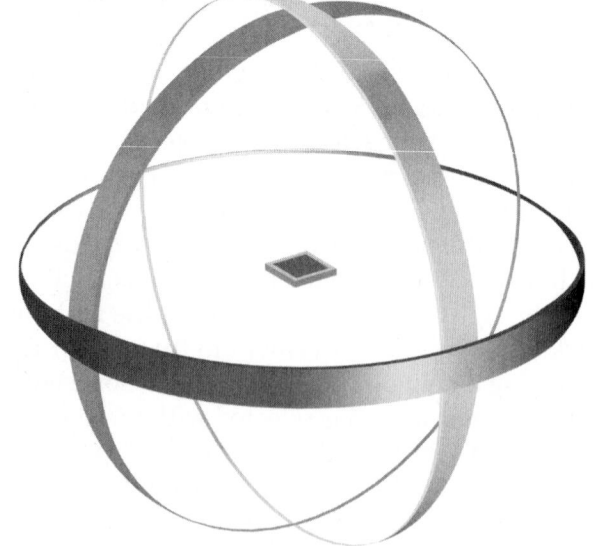

The following example rotates the bend in the HVAC assembly shown in **Figure 9-6A**. Set the **Midpoint** object snap and turn on object tracking. Then, select the command and continue:

Current positive angle in UCS: ANGDIR=*(current)* ANGBASE=*(current)*
Select objects: *(pick the bend)*
1 found
Select objects: ↵
Specify base point: *(acquire the midpoint of the vertical and horizontal edges, then pick to place the grip tool in the middle of the rectangular face)*
Pick a rotation axis: *(pick the green circle)*
Specify angle start point: **180.**↵

Note that the rotate grip tool remains visible through the base point and the angle of rotation selections. The rotated object is shown in **Figure 9-6B**.

If you need to rotate an object on an axis that is not parallel to the current X, Y, or Z, use a dynamic UCS with the **3DROTATE** command. Chapter 4 discussed the benefits of using a dynamic UCS when creating objects that need to be parallel to a surface other than the XY plane. With the object selected for rotation and the dynamic UCS option active (pick the **DUCS** button on the status bar), move the rotate grip tool over a face of the object. The grip tool aligns itself with the surface so that the Z axis is perpendicular to the face. Carefully place the grip tool over the point of rotation using object snaps. Make sure that the tool is correctly positioned before picking to locate it. Then, enter an angle or use polar tracking to rotate the object around the Z axis.

Figure 9-6.
A—Use object tracking or object snaps to place the grip tool in the middle of the rectangular face. Then, select the axis of rotation. B—The completed rotation.

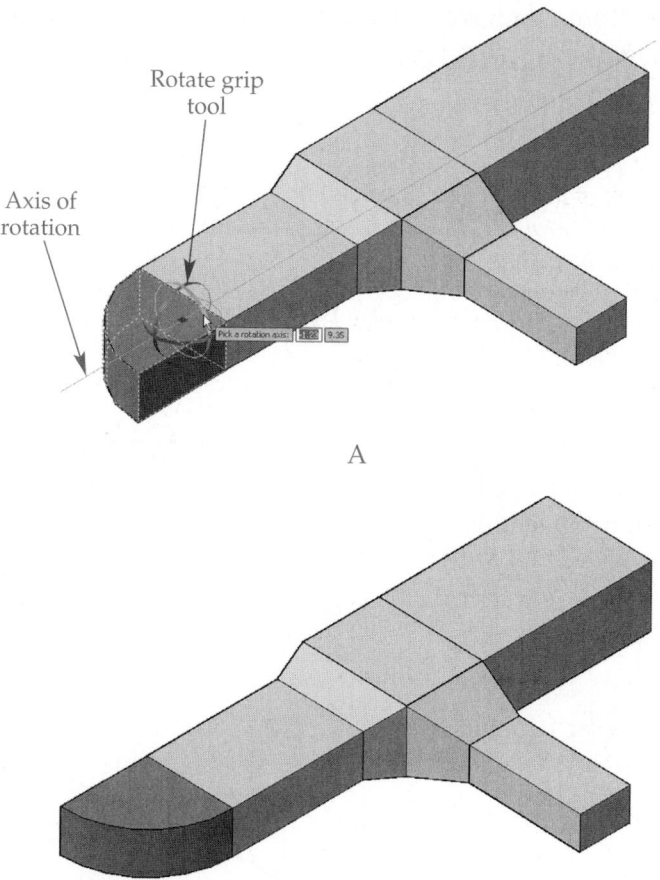

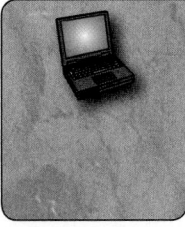

By default, the move grip tool is displayed when an object is selected with no command active. To toggle between the move grip tool and the rotate grip tool, select the grip at the tool's origin and press the space bar. Then, pick a location for the tool's origin. You can toggle back to the move grip tool using the same procedure.

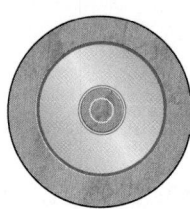

Exercise 9-3

Complete the exercise on the Student CD.

3D Mirroring

MIRROR3D

Type
MIRROR3D
3DMIRROR

Pull-Down Menu
Modify
> 3D Operations
> 3D Mirror

The **MIRROR** command can be used to rotate 3D objects. However, like the **ROTATE** command, the **MIRROR** command can only mirror objects in the XY plane of the current UCS. Often, to properly mirror objects with this command, you have to change UCSs. The **MIRROR3D** command, on the other hand, allows you to mirror objects about any plane regardless of the current UCS.

The default option of the command is to define a mirror plane by picking three points on that plane, Figure 9-7A. Object snap modes should be used to accurately define the mirror plane. To mirror the wedge in Figure 9-7A, set the **Midpoint** running object snap, select the command, and use the following sequence. The resulting drawing is shown in Figure 9-7B.

> Select objects: *(pick the wedge)*
> 1 found
> Select objects: ↵
> Specify first point of mirror plane (3 points) or
> [Object/Last/Zaxis/View/XY/YZ/ZX/3points] <3points>: *(pick P1, which is the midpoint of the box's top edge)*
> Specify second point on mirror plane: *(pick P2)*
> Specify third point on mirror plane: *(pick P3)*
> Delete source objects? [Yes/No] <N>: ↵

Figure 9-7.
The **MIRROR3D** command allows you to mirror objects about any plane regardless of the current UCS. A—The mirror plane defined by the three pick points is shown here in color. Point P1 is the midpoint of the top edge of the base. B—A copy of the original is mirrored.

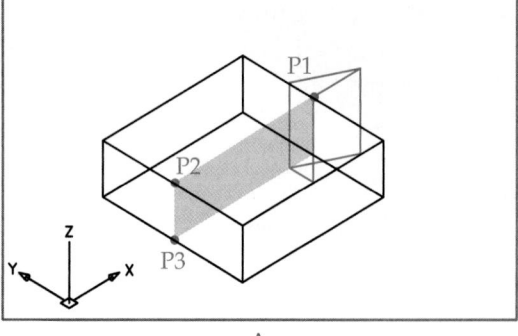

A

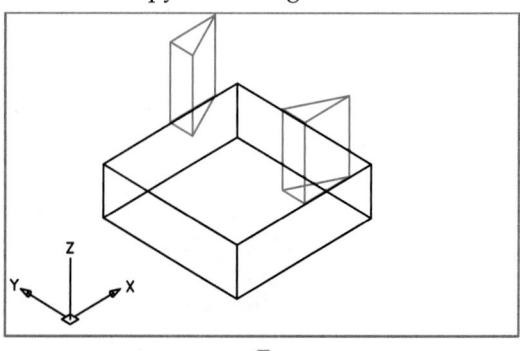

B

There are several different ways to define a mirror plane with the **MIRROR3D** command. These are:

- **Object.** The plane of the selected circle, arc, or 2D polyline segment is used as the mirror plane.
- **Last.** Uses the last mirror plane defined.
- **Zaxis.** Defines the plane with a pick point on the mirror plane and a point on the Z axis of the mirror plane.
- **View.** The viewing direction of the current viewpoint is aligned with a selected point to define the plane.
- **XY/YZ/ZX.** The mirror plane is placed in one of the three basic planes of the current UCS and passes through a selected point.
- **3points.** Allows you to pick three points to define the mirror plane.

PROFESSIONAL TIP

The **3D Mirror** button can be placed on a custom or existing toolbar. Refer to Chapter 19 for information on customizing toolbars.

Exercise 9-4

Complete the exercise on the Student CD.

Creating 3D Arrays

The **ARRAY** command can be used to create either a rectangular or polar array of a 3D object on the XY plane of the current UCS. You probably used this command to complete some of the problems in previous chapters. The **3DARRAY** command allows you to array an object in 3D space. There are two types of 3D arrays—rectangular and polar.

Rectangular 3D Arrays

In a *rectangular 3D array,* as with a rectangular 2D array, you must enter the number of rows and columns. However, you must also specify the number of *levels,* which represents the third (Z) dimension. The command sequence is similar to that used with the 2D array command, with two additional prompts.

An example of where a rectangular 3D array may be created is the layout of structural steel columns on multiple floors of a commercial building. In Figure 9-8A, you can see two concrete floor slabs of a building and a single steel column. It is now a simple matter of arraying the steel column in rows, columns, and levels.

To draw a rectangular 3D array, select the **3DARRAY** command. Pick the object to array and press [Enter]. Then, specify the **Rectangular** option:

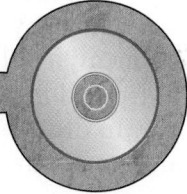

```
Enter the type of array [Rectangular/Polar] <R>: R↵
Enter the number of rows (- - -) <1>: 3↵
Enter the number of columns (¦¦¦) <1>: 5↵
Enter the number of levels (…) <1>: 2↵
Specify the distance between rows (- - -): 10'↵
Specify the distance between columns (¦¦¦): 10'↵
Specify the distance between levels (…): 12'8↵
```

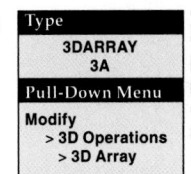

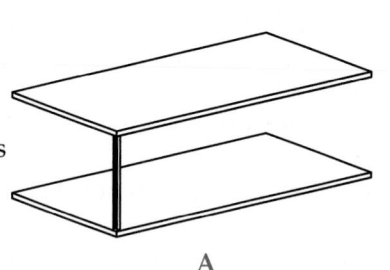

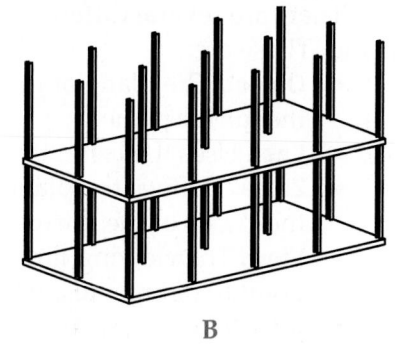

Figure 9-8.
A—Two floors and one steel column are drawn. B—A rectangular 3D array is used to place all of the required steel columns on both floors at the same time.

A   B

The result is shown in Figure 9-8B. Constructions like this can be quickly assembled for multiple levels using the **3DARRAY** command only once.

Polar 3D Arrays

A *polar 3D array* is similar to a polar 2D array. However, the axis of rotation in a 2D polar array is parallel to the Z axis of the current UCS. In a 3D polar array, you can define a centerline axis of rotation that is not parallel to the Z axis of the current UCS. You can array an object in a UCS different from the current one. Unlike a rectangular 3D array, a polar 3D array does not allow you to create levels of the object. The object is arrayed in a plane defined by the object and the selected centerline (Z) axis.

To draw a polar 3D array, select the **3DARRAY** command. Pick the object to array and press [Enter]. Then, specify the **Polar** option:

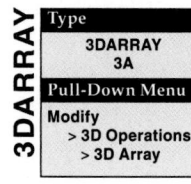

Type
3DARRAY
3A

Pull-Down Menu
Modify
> **3D Operations**
> **3D Array**

Enter the type of array [Rectangular/Polar] <R>: **P**⏎

For example, the four mounting flanges on the lower part of the duct in Figure 9-9A must be placed on the opposite end. However, notice the orientation of the UCS. First, copy one flange and rotate it to the proper orientation. Then, use the **3DARRAY** command as follows. Make sure ortho is on.

Select objects: (select the copied flange)
1 found
Select objects: ⏎
Enter the type of array [Rectangular/Polar] <R>: **P**⏎
Enter the number of items in the array: **4**⏎
Specify the angle to fill (+=ccw, −=cw) <360>: ⏎
Rotate arrayed objects? [Yes/No] <Y>: ⏎
Specify center point of array: **CEN**⏎
of: (pick the center of the upper duct opening)
Specify second point on axis of rotation: (move the cursor so the ortho line projects out of the center of the duct opening and pick)

The completed 3D polar array is shown in Figure 9-9B. If additional levels of a polar array are needed, they can be created by copying the array just created.

PROFESSIONAL TIP

A **3D Array** button can be placed on a custom or existing toolbar. Refer to Chapter 19 for information on customizing toolbars.

Figure 9-9.
A—A ductwork elbow with four flanges in place. Copies of these flanges need to be located on the opposite end. Start by creating one copy as shown. B—The flanges are properly oriented without changing the UCS by creating a 3D polar array.

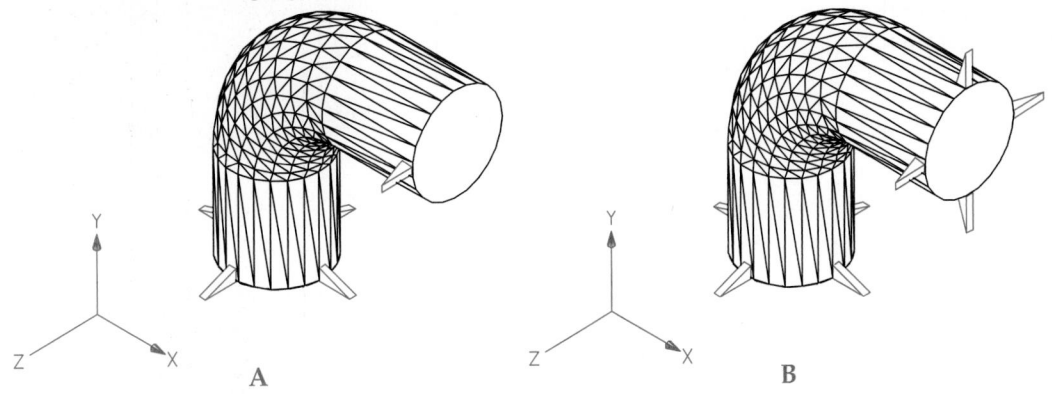

A   B

Exercise 9-5

Complete the exercise on the Student CD.

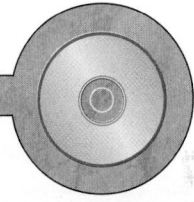

Filleting Solid Objects

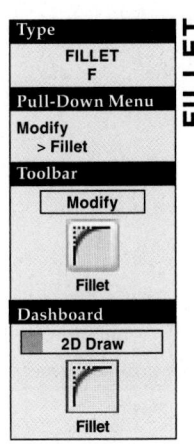

Type
FILLET
F

FILLET

Pull-Down Menu
Modify
  > Fillet

Toolbar
  Modify

Fillet

Dashboard
  2D Draw

Fillet

A *fillet* is a rounded interior edge on an object, such as a box. A *round* is a rounded exterior edge. The **FILLET** command is used to create both fillets and rounds. Before a fillet or round is created at an intersection, the solid objects that intersect need to be joined using the **UNION** command. Then, use the **FILLET** command. See Figure 9-10. Since the object being filleted is actually a single solid and not two objects, only one edge is selected. In the following sequence, the fillet radius is set at .25, then the fillet is created. First, select the **FILLET** command and then continue as follows.

> Current settings: Mode = *current*, Radius = *current*
> Select first object or [Undo/Polyline/Radius/Trim/Multiple]: **R**↵
> Specify fillet radius <*current*>: **.25**↵
> Select first object or [Undo/Polyline/Radius/Trim/Multiple]: *(pick edge to be filleted or rounded)*
> Enter fillet radius <.25>: ↵
> Select an edge or [Chain/Radius]: ↵ *(this fillets the selected edge, but you can also select other edges at this point)*
> 1 edge(s) selected for fillet.

Examples of fillets and rounds are shown in Figure 9-11.

Figure 9-10.
A—Pick the edge where two unioned solids intersect to create a fillet. B—The fillet after rendering.

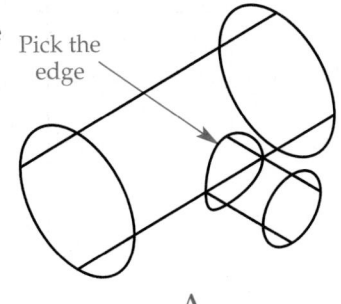

Pick the edge

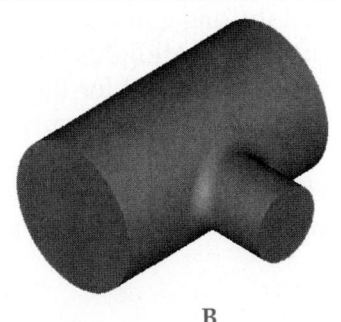

A   B

Figure 9-11.
Examples of fillets and rounds. The wireframe displays show the objects before the **FILLET** command is used.

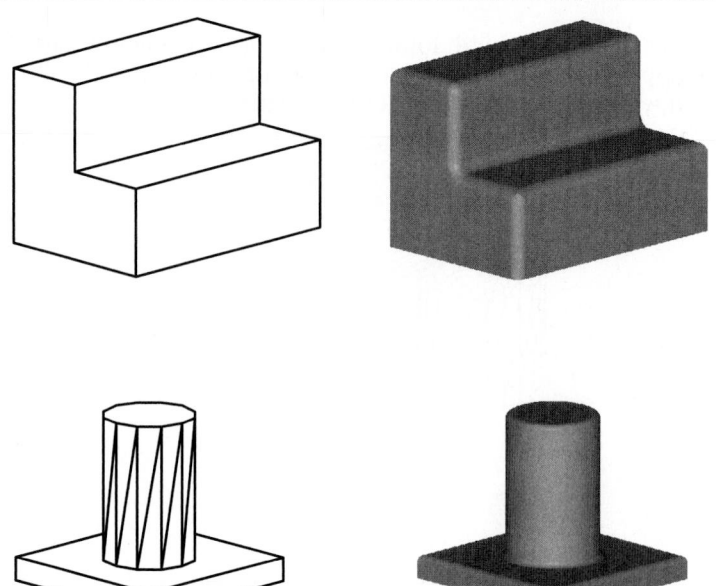

PROFESSIONAL TIP

You can construct and edit solid models while the object is displayed in a shaded view. If your computer has sufficient speed and power, it is often much easier to visualize the model in a 3D view with the Conceptual or Realistic visual style set current. This enables you to view the model realistically. If an edit or construction does not look right, just undo and try again.

Chamfering Solid Objects

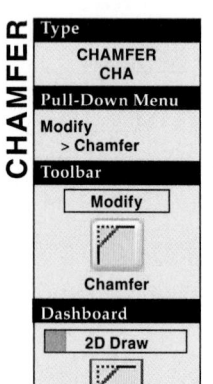

A *chamfer* is a small square edge on the edges of an object. To create a chamfer on a 3D solid, use the **CHAMFER** command. Just as when chamfering a 2D line, there are two chamfer distances. Therefore, you must specify which surfaces correspond to the first and second distances. The detail to which the chamfer is applied must be constructed before chamfering. For example, if you are chamfering a hole, the object (cylinder) must first be subtracted to create the hole. If you are chamfering an intersection, the two objects must first be unioned.

After you enter the command, you must pick the edge you want to chamfer. The edge is actually the intersection of two surfaces of the solid. One of the two surfaces is highlighted when you select the edge. The highlighted surface is associated with the first chamfer distance. This surface is called the *base surface.* If the highlighted surface is not the one you want as the base surface, enter N at the [Next/OK] prompt and press [Enter]. This highlights the next surface. An edge is created by two surfaces. Therefore, when you enter N for the next surface, AutoCAD cycles through only two surfaces. When the proper base surface is highlighted, press [Enter].

Chamfering a hole is shown in **Figure 9-12A.** The end of the cylinder in **Figure 9-12B** is chamfered by first picking one of the vertical isolines, then picking the top edge. The following command sequence is illustrated in **Figure 9-12A.**

Figure 9-12.
A—A hole is chamfered by picking the top surface, then the edge of the hole. B—The end of a cylinder is chamfered by first picking the side, then the end. Both ends can be chamfered at the same time, as shown here.

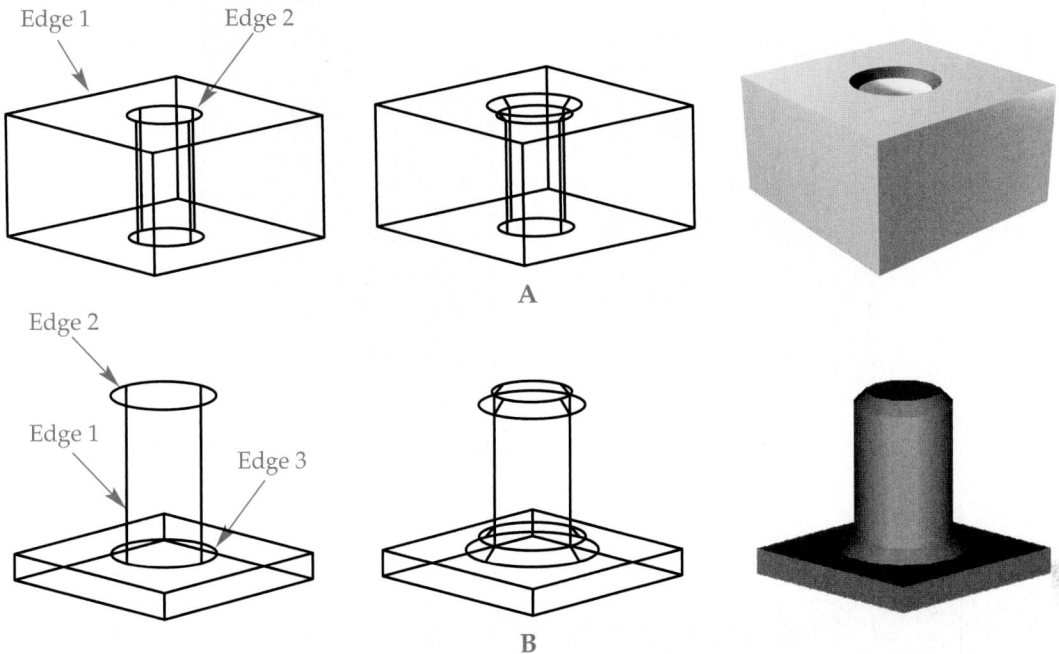

(TRIM mode) Current chamfer Dist1 = *current*, Dist2 = *current*
Select first line or [Undo/Polyline/Distance/Angle/Trim/mEthod/Multiple]: *(pick Edge 1)*
Base surface selection...
(if the side surface is highlighted, change to the top surface as follows)
Enter surface selection option [Next/OK (current)] <OK>: **N**↵
(the top surface should be highlighted)
Enter surface selection option [Next/OK (current)] <OK>: ↵
Specify base surface chamfer distance <*current*>: **.125**↵
Specify other surface chamfer distance <*current*>: **.125**↵
Select an edge or [Loop]: *(pick Edge 2, the edge of the hole)*
Select an edge or [Loop]: ↵

PROFESSIONAL TIP

If you improperly create a fillet or chamfer, it is best to undo and try again as opposed to trying to fix it with editing methods. Faces and edges can be edited using the **SOLIDEDIT** command. Grips can also be used to edit solids. These procedures are discussed in Chapter 10, and the **SOLIDEDIT** command is discussed in Chapter 11.

Exercise 9-6
Complete the exercise on the Student CD.

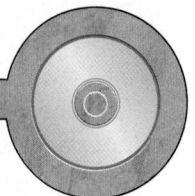

Figure 9-13.
A—This surface will be thickened into a solid. B—The thickened surface is a 3D solid.

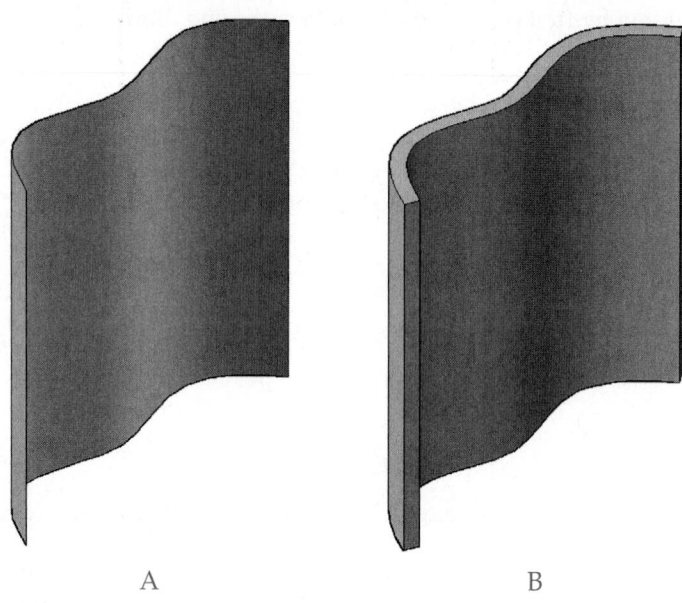

A B

Thickening a Surface into a Solid

A surface has no thickness. The value of the **THICKNESS** command does not affect the thickness of a planar surface, unlike for entities such as lines, polylines, polygons, and circles. But, a surface can be quickly converted to a 3D solid using the **THICKEN** command.

To add thickness to a surface, select the command. Then, pick the surface(s) to thicken and press [Enter]. You are then prompted for the thickness. Enter a thickness value or pick two points on screen to specify the thickness. See **Figure 9-13.**

By default, the original surface object is deleted when the 3D solid is created with **THICKEN**. This is controlled by the **DELOBJ** system variable. To preserve the original surface, change the **DELOBJ** value to zero.

Converting to Surfaces

AutoCAD provides a great deal of flexibility in converting and transforming objects. For example, a simple line can be quickly turned into a 3D solid in just a few steps. Refer to **Figure 9-14.**

1. Use the **Properties** window to give the line a thickness. Notice that the object is still a line object, as indicated in the drop-down list at the top of the **Properties** window.
2. Select the **CONVTOSURFACE** command.
3. Pick the thickened line. Its property type is now listed in the **Properties** window as a surface extrusion.
4. Use the **THICKEN** command to give the surface a thickness. Its property type is now a 3D solid.

In this process, the **CONVTOSURFACE** and **THICKEN** commands were instrumental in creating a 3D solid from a line. Other objects that can be converted to surfaces using the **CONVTOSURFACE** command are 2D solids, arcs with thickness, open polylines with a thickness and no width, regions, and planar 3D faces.

Figure 9-14.
The stages of converting a line into a solid. First, draw the line. Next, give the line thickness using the **Properties** window. Then, convert the line to a surface using the **CONVTOSURFACE** command. Finally, use the **THICKEN** command to give the surface a thickness.

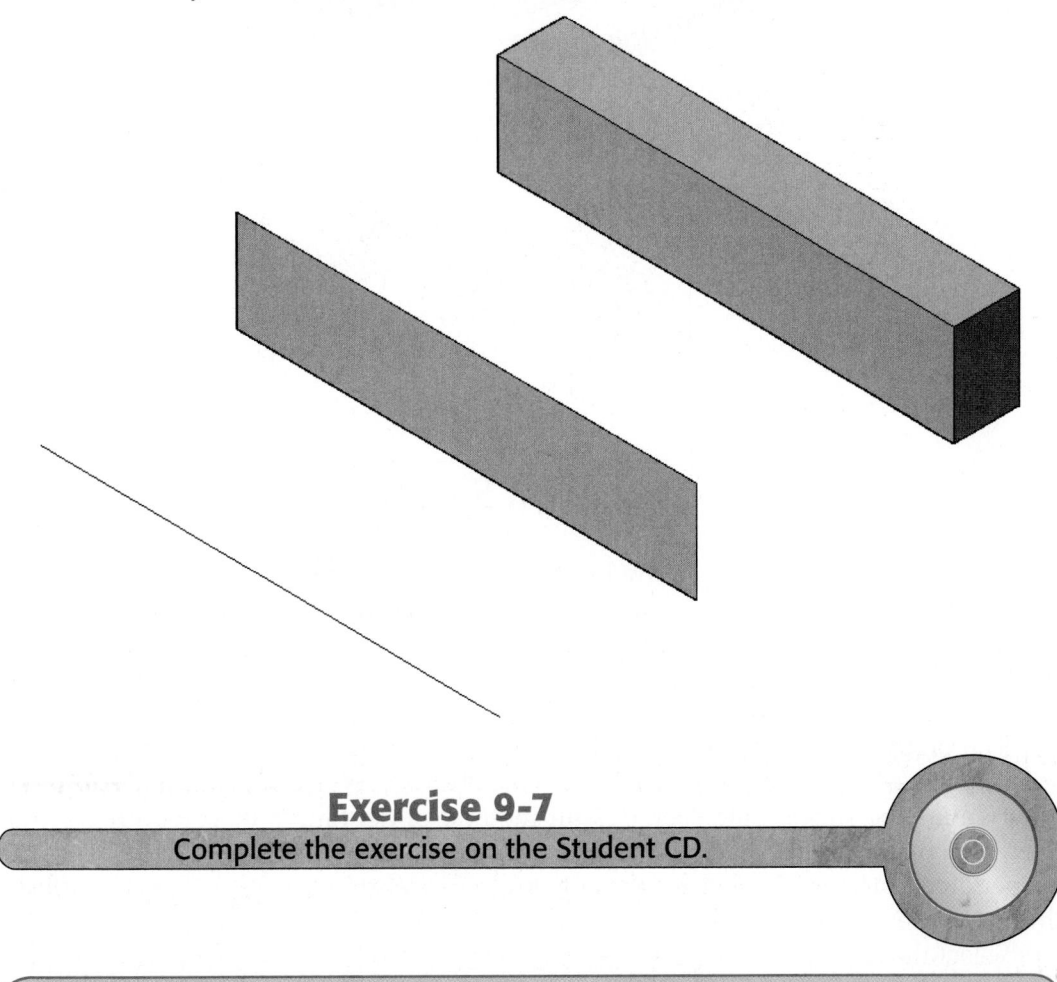

Exercise 9-7
Complete the exercise on the Student CD.

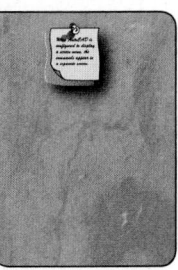

Converting to Solids

Additional flexibility in creating solids is provided by the **CONVTOSOLID** command. This command allows you to directly convert certain, closed objects into solids. You can convert:

- Circles with thickness.
- Wide, uniform-width polylines with thickness. This includes polygons and rectangles.
- Closed, zero-width polylines with thickness. This includes polygons, rectangles, and closed revision clouds.

First, select the command. Then, select the objects to convert and press [Enter]. The objects are instantly converted with no additional input required. Figure 9-15 shows the three different objects before and after conversion to a solid.

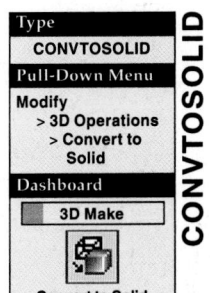

Type
CONVTOSOLID
Pull-Down Menu
Modify
> 3D Operations
> Convert to
Solid
Dashboard
3D Make
Convert to Solid

CONVTOSOLID

NOTE

If an object that appears to be a closed polyline with a thickness does not convert to a solid and the command line displays the message Cannot convert an open curve, the polyline was not closed using the **Close** option of the **PLINE** command. Use the **PEDIT** or **PROPERTIES** command to close the polyline and use the **CONVTOSOLID** command again.

Figure 9-15.
A—From left to right, two polylines and a circle that will be converted into solids. B—The resulting solids.

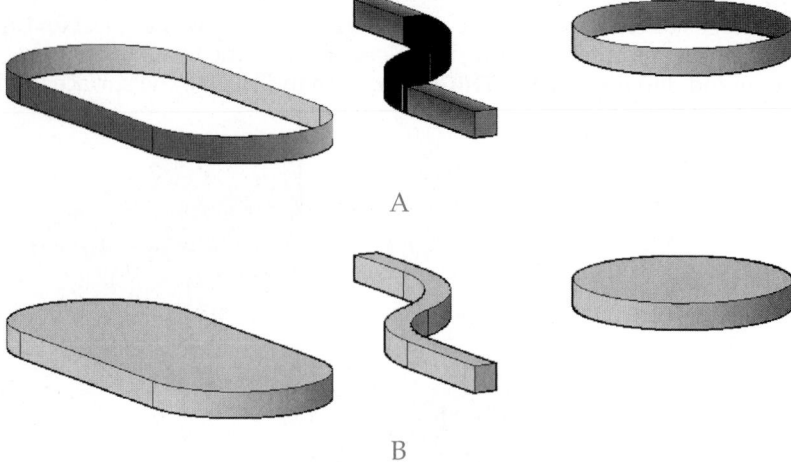

A

B

Slicing a Solid

A 3D solid can be sliced at any location by using existing objects such as circles, arcs, ellipses, 2D polylines, 2D splines, or surfaces. Additionally, you can specify a slicing line by picking two points, or specify a slicing plane by picking three points. After slicing the solid, you can choose to retain either or both sides of the model. The slices can then be used for model construction or display and presentation purposes.

The **SLICE** command is used to slice solids. When the command is initiated, you are asked to select the solids to be sliced. Select the objects and press [Enter]. Next, you must define the slicing path. The default method of defining a path requires you to specify two points on a slicing plane. The plane passes through the two points and is perpendicular to the XY plane of the current UCS. Refer to **Figure 9-16** as you follow this sequence:

1. Select the command and pick the object to be sliced
2. Pick the start point of the slicing plane. See **Figure 9-16A.**
3. Pick the second point on the slicing plane.

SLICE

Type
SLICE
SL

Pull-Down Menu
Modify
> 3D Operations
> Slice

Dashboard
3D Make

Slice

Figure 9-16.
Slicing a solid by picking two points. A—Select two points on the cutting plane. The plane passes through these points and is perpendicular to the XY plane of the current UCS. B—The sliced solid.

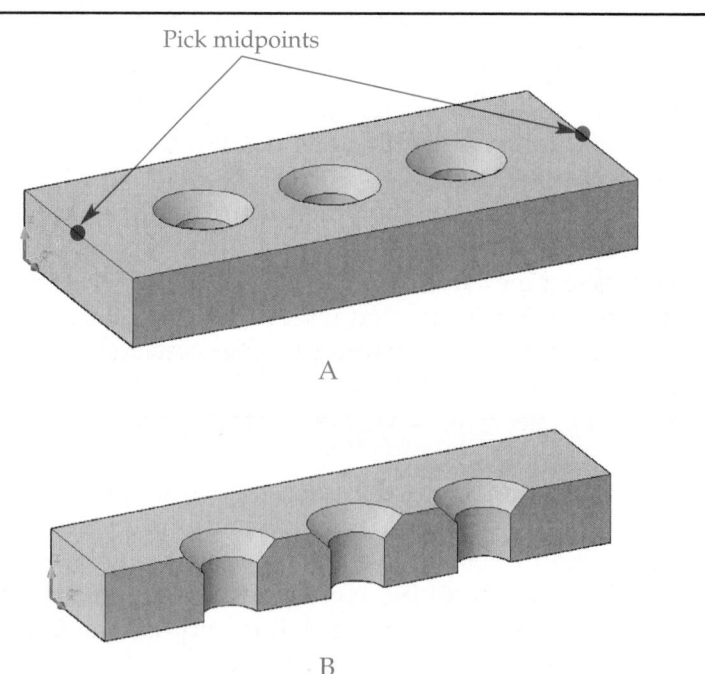

Pick midpoints

A

B

4. You are prompted to specify a point on the desired side to keep. Select anywhere on the back half of the object. The point does not have to be *on* the object. It must simply be on the side of the cutting plane that you want to keep.

5. The object is sliced and the front half is deleted. See Figure 9-16B.

When prompted to select the side to keep, you can press [Enter] to keep both sides. If both sides are retained, two separate 3D solids are created. Each solid can then be manipulated for construction, design, presentation, or animation purposes.

There are several additional options for specifying a slicing path. These options are listed here and described in the following sections.

- **Planar Object**
- **Surface**
- **Zaxis**
- **View**
- **XY**
- **YZ**
- **ZX**
- **3points**

NOTE

Once the **SLICE** command has been used, the history of the solid to that point is removed. If a history of the work is important, then save a copy of the file or place a copy of the object on a frozen layer prior to performing the slice.

Planar Object

A second method to create a slice through a 3D solid is to use an existing planar object. Planar objects include circles, arcs, ellipses, 2D polylines, and 2D splines. See Figure 9-17A. The plane on which the planar object lies must intersect the object to be sliced. The current UCS has no effect on this option.

Be sure that the object has been moved to the location of the slice. Then, select the **SLICE** command, pick the object to slice, and press [Enter]. Next, select the **Planar Object** option and select the slicing path object (the circle, in this case). Finally, specify which side is to be retained. See Figure 9-17B. Again, if both sides are kept, they are separate objects and can be individually manipulated.

Surface

A surface object can be used as the slicing path. The surface can be planar or non-planar (curved). This method can be used to quickly create a mating die. For example, refer to Figure 9-18. First, draw the required surface. The surface should exactly match the stamped part that will be manufactured, Figure 9-18A. Then, draw a box that encompasses the surface. Next, select the **SLICE** command, pick the box, and press [Enter]. Then, enter the **Surface** option and select the surface. You may need to do this in a wireframe display. Finally, when prompted to select the side to keep, press [Enter] to keep both sides. The two halves of the die can now be moved and rotated as needed, Figure 9-18B.

Figure 9-17.
Slicing a solid with a planar object. A—The circle is drawn at the proper orientation and in the correct location. B—The completed slice.

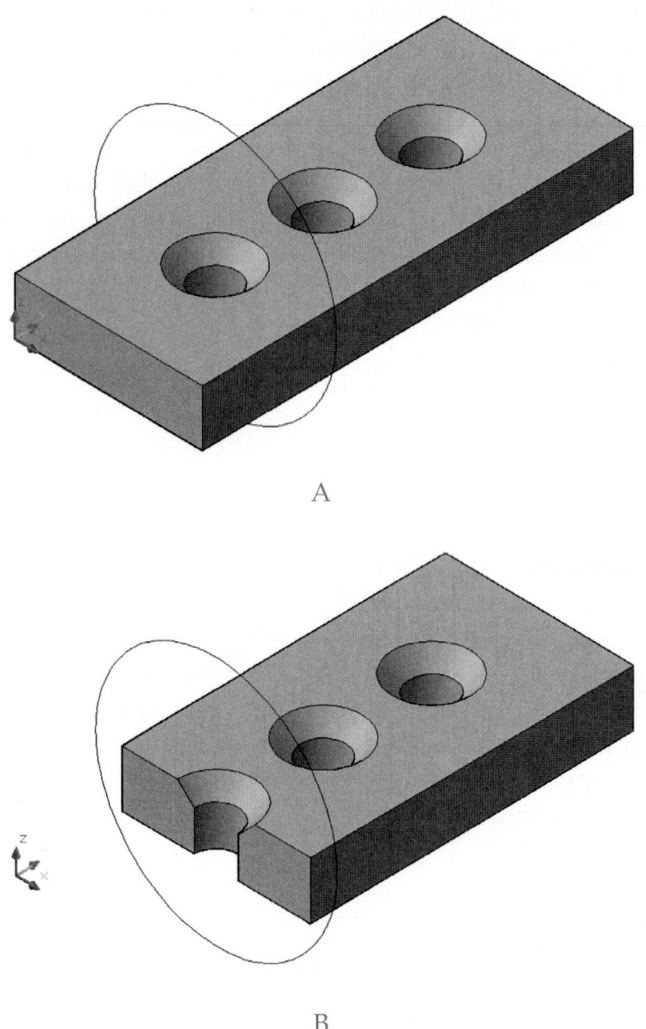

A

B

Figure 9-18.
Slicing a solid with a surface. A—Draw the surface and locate it within the solid to be sliced. The solid is represented here by the wireframe. B—The completed slice with both sides retained. The top can now be moved and rotated as shown here.

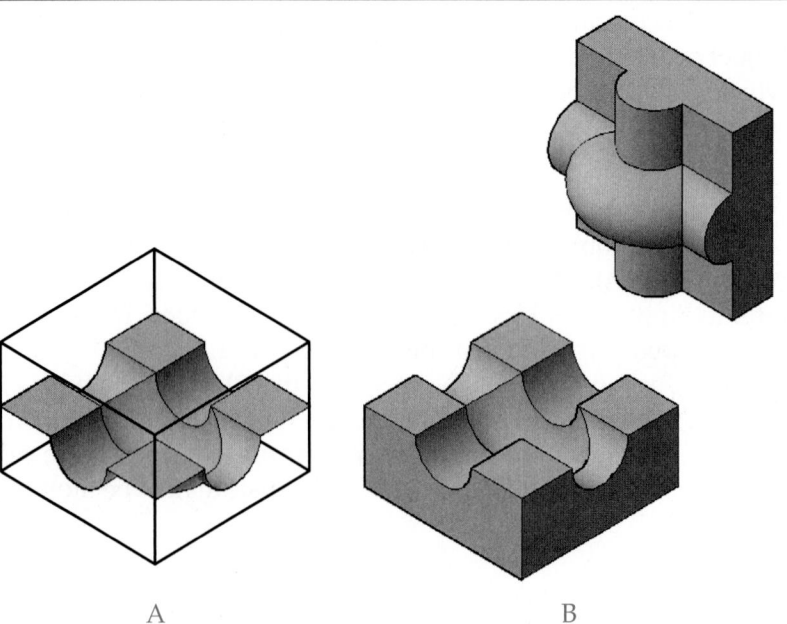

A

B

Z Axis

You can specify one point on the cutting plane and one point on the Z axis of the plane. See **Figure 9-19.** This allows you to have a cutting plane that is not parallel to the current UCS XY plane. First, select the **SLICE** command, pick the object to slice, and press [Enter]. Next, enter the **Zaxis** option. Then, pick a point on the XY plane of the cutting plane followed by a point on the Z axis of the cutting plane. Finally, pick the side of the object to keep.

View

A cutting plane can be established that is aligned with the viewing plane of the current viewport. The cutting plane passes through a point you select, which sets the depth along the Z axis of the current viewing plane. First, select the **SLICE** command, pick the object to slice, and press [Enter]. Next, enter the **View** option. Then, pick a point in the viewport to define the location of the cutting plane on the Z axis of the viewing plane. Use object snaps to select a point on an object. The cutting plane passes through this point and is parallel to the viewing plane. Finally, pick the side of the object to keep.

XY, YZ, and ZX

You can slice an object using a cutting plane that is parallel to any of the three primary planes of the current UCS. See **Figure 9-20.** The cutting plane passes through the point you select and is aligned with the primary plane of the current UCS that you specify. First, select the **SLICE** command, pick the object to slice, and press [Enter].

Figure 9-19.
Slicing a solid using the **Z axis** option. A—Pick one point on the cutting plane and a second point on the Z axis of the cutting plane. B—The resulting slice.

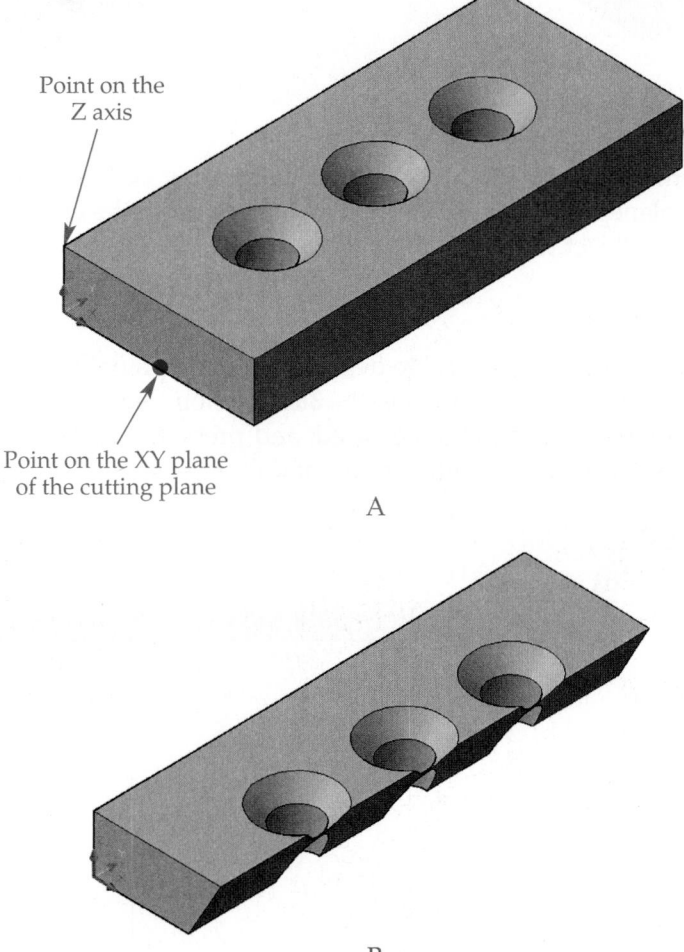

Point on the Z axis

Point on the XY plane of the cutting plane

A

B

Figure 9-20.
Slicing a solid using the **XY**, **YZ**, and **ZX** options. A—The object before slicing. The UCS origin is in the center of the first hole and at the midpoint of the height. B—The resulting slice using the **XY** option. C—The resulting slice using the **YZ** option. D—The resulting slice using the **ZX** option.

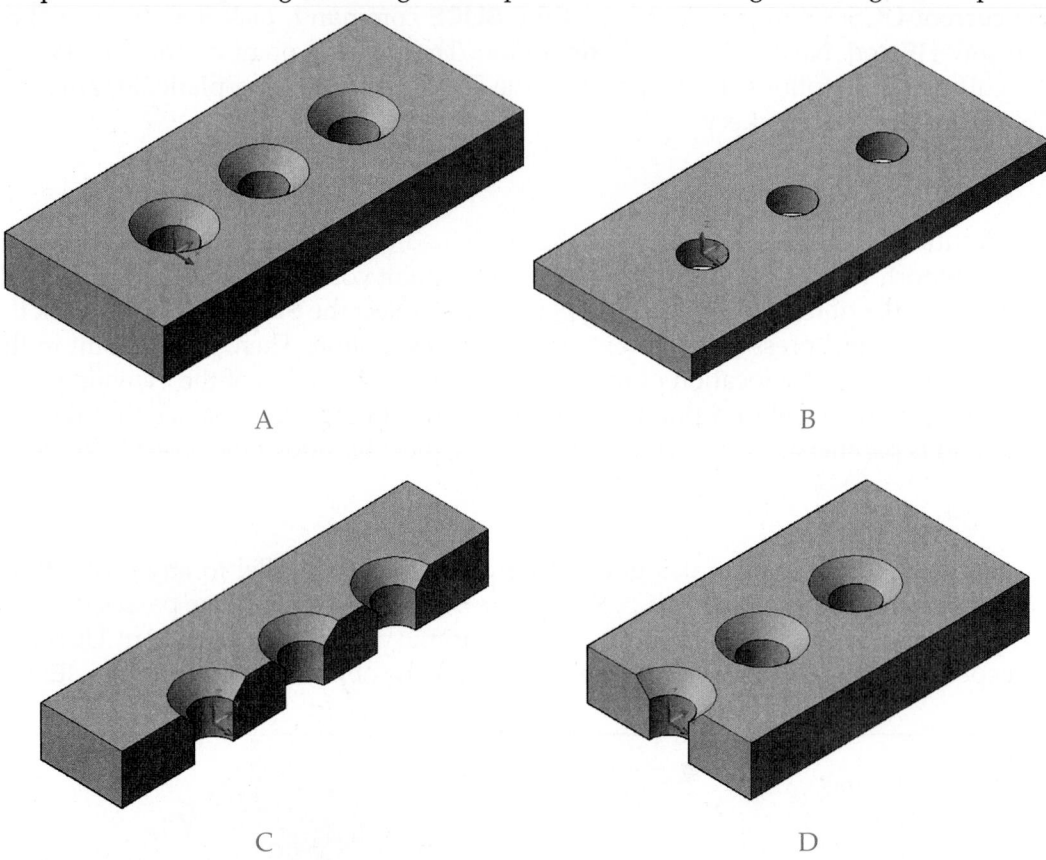

A

B

C

D

Next, enter the **XY**, **YZ**, or **ZX** option, depending on the primary plane to which the cutting plane will be parallel. Then, pick a point on the cutting plane. Finally, pick the side of the object to keep.

Three Points

Three points can be used to define the cutting plane. This allows the cutting plane to be aligned at any angle, similar to the **Zaxis** option. See Figure 9-21. First, select the **SLICE** command, pick the object to be sliced, and press [Enter]. Then, enter the **3points** option. Pick three points on the cutting plane and then select the side of the object to keep.

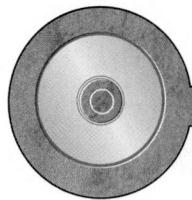

Exercise 9-8
Complete the exercise on the Student CD.

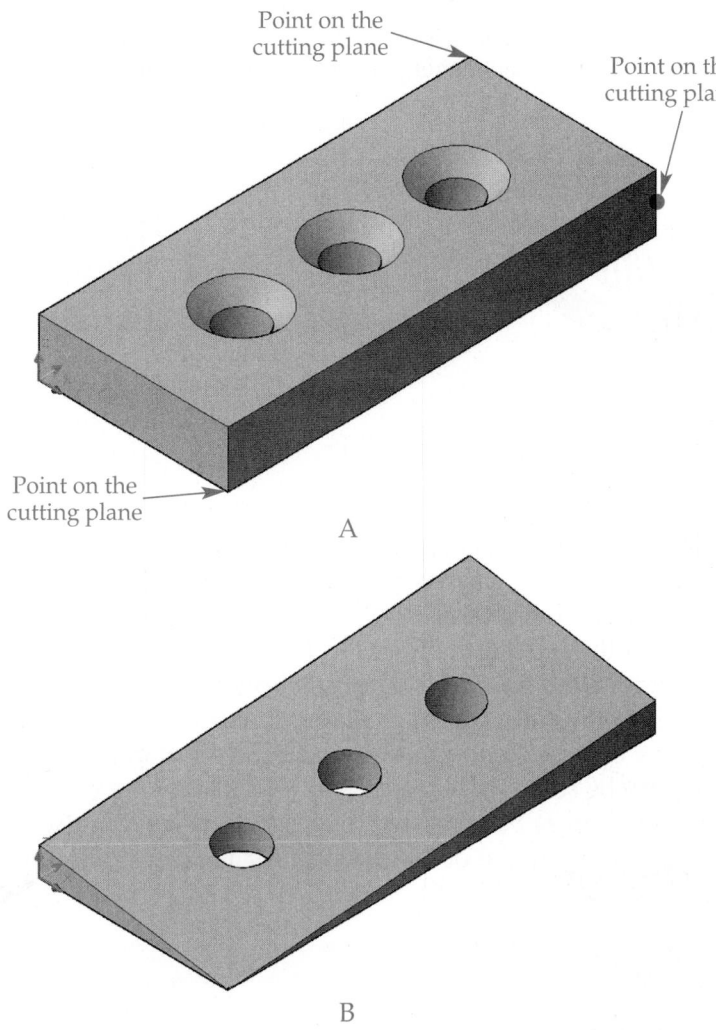

Figure 9-21.
Slicing a solid using the **3points** option. A—Specify three points to define the cutting plane. B—The resulting slice.

Point on the cutting plane

Point on the cutting plane

Point on the cutting plane

A

B

Removing Details and Features

Sometimes, it may be necessary to remove a detail that has been constructed. For example, suppose you placed a R.5 fillet on an object based on an engineering sketch. Then, the design is changed to a R.25 fillet. The **UNDO** command can only be used in the current drawing session. Also, even if the command can be used, you may have to step back through several other commands to undo the fillet. In another example, suppose an object has a bolt hole that is no longer needed. You will need to remove this feature.

In Chapter 2, solid modeling was described as working with modeling clay. If you think in these terms, you can remove features by adding "clay" to the object. Then, the new "clay" can be molded as needed.

For example, look at the object in **Figure 9-22A.** There are R.5 rounds (fillets) on the top surface of the base. However, these should be R.25 rounds. You cannot simply place the new fillets on the object. You must first add material to create a square edge. Then, the new fillets can be added.

1. Draw a solid box with the same dimensions as the base without the rounds. Center the new box on the base.
2. Use the **UNION** command to add the new box to the object. This, in effect, removes the rounds.
3. Use the **FILLET** command to place the R.25 rounds on the top edge of the base, **Figure 9-22B.**

Figure 9-22.
Removing fillets. A—The original object. B—A new base is added and the new fillets are created. C—The hole no longer passes through the object. D—The corrected object.

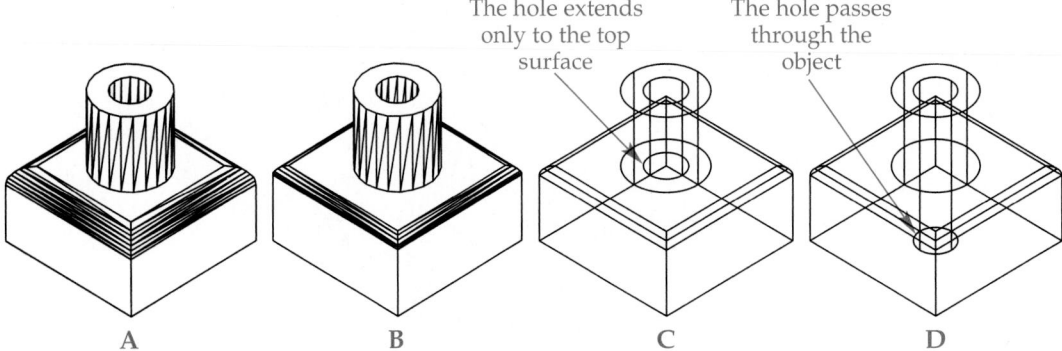

The rounds have now, in effect, been changed from R.5 to R.25. However, there is an unseen problem. Display the object in wireframe. Notice how the hole no longer passes through the object, Figure 9-22C. To correct this problem, draw a solid cylinder of the same dimensions as the hole and centered in the hole. Then, subtract the cylinder from the object. The hole now passes through the object, Figure 9-22D.

This technique of adding material can be used to remove any internal feature and some external features, such as fillets (rounds). Other external features, such as a boss, can be removed by drawing a solid over the top of the feature. The feature to be removed must be completely enclosed by the new solid. Then, subtract the new solid from the original object. Be sure to "redrill" holes and other internal features as needed.

PROFESSIONAL TIP

There are several other methods for editing solids. These are covered in detail in Chapters 10 and 11. The above procedure can be simplified with these editing methods.

Constructing Details and Features on Solid Models

A variety of machining, structural, and architectural details can be created using some basic solid modeling techniques. The features discussed in the next sections are just a few of the possibilities.

Counterbore and Spotface

A *counterbore* is a recess machined into a part, centered on a hole, that allows the head of a fastener to rest below the surface. Create a counterbore as follows.
1. Draw a cylinder representing the diameter of the hole, Figure 9-23A.
2. Draw a second cylinder that is the diameter of the counterbore and center it at the top of the first cylinder. Move the second cylinder so it extends below the surface of the object to the depth of the counterbore, Figure 9-23B.
3. Subtract the two cylinders from the base object, Figure 9-23C.

A *spotface* is similar to a counterbore, but is not as deep. See Figure 9-24. It provides a flat surface for full contact of a washer or underside of a bolt head. Construct it in the same way as a counterbore.

Figure 9-23.
Constructing a counterbore. A—Draw a cylinder to represent a hole. B—Draw a second cylinder to represent the counterbore. C—Subtract the two cylinders from the base object.

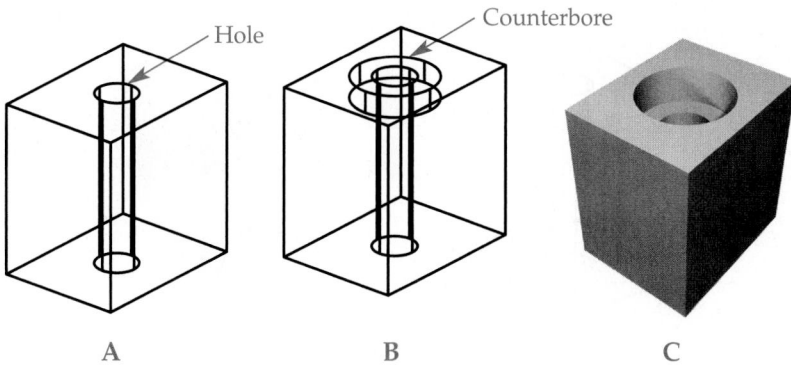

Countersink

A *countersink* is like a counterbore with angled sides. The sides allow a flat head machine screw or wood screw to sit flush with the surface of an object. A countersink can be drawn in one of two ways. You can draw an inverted cone centered on a hole and subtract it from the base, or you can chamfer the top edge of a hole. Chamfering is the quickest method.

1. Draw a cylinder representing the diameter of the hole, Figure 9-25A.
2. Subtract the cylinder from the base object.
3. Select the **CHAMFER** command.
4. Select the top edge of the base object.
5. Enter the chamfer distance(s).
6. Pick the top edge of the hole, Figure 9-25B.

Boss

A *boss* serves the same function as a spotface. However, it is an area raised above the surface of an object. Draw a boss as follows.

1. Draw a cylinder representing the diameter of the hole. Extend it above the base object higher than the boss is to be, Figure 9-26A.
2. Draw a second cylinder the diameter of the boss. Place the base of this cylinder above the top surface of the base object a distance equal to the height of the boss. Give the cylinder a negative height value so that it extends inside of the base object, Figure 9-26B.

Figure 9-24.
Constructing a spotface. A—The bottom of the second, larger-diameter cylinder should be located at the exact dept of the spotface. However, the height may extend above the surface of the base. Then, subtract the two cylinders from the base. B—The finished solid.

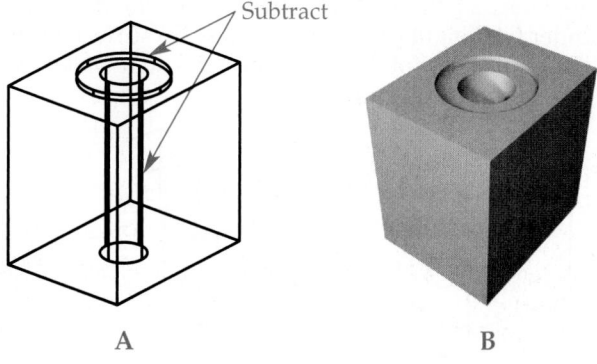

Figure 9-25.
Constructing a countersink. A—Subtract the cylinder from the base to create the hole.
B—Chamfer the top of the hole to create a countersink.

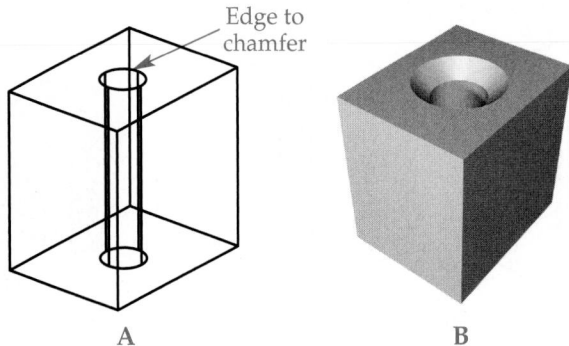

Edge to chamfer

A   B

3. Union the base object and the second cylinder (boss). Subtract the hole from the unioned object, Figure 9-26C.
4. Fillet the intersection of the boss with the base object, Figure 9-26D.

O-Ring Groove

An *O-ring* is a circular seal that resembles a torus. It sits inside of a groove constructed so that at least half of the O-ring is above the surface. An *O-ring groove* can be constructed by placing the center of a circle on the outside surface of a cylinder. Then, revolve the circle around the cylinder. Finally, subtract the revolved solid from the cylinder.

1. Construct the cylinder to the required dimensions, Figure 9-27A.
2. Rotate the UCS on the X axis (or appropriate axis).
3. Draw a circle with a center point on the surface of the cylinder, Figure 9-27B.
4. Revolve the circle 360° about the center of the cylinder, Figure 9-27C.
5. Subtract the revolved object from the cylinder, Figure 9-27D.

Architectural Molding

Architectural molding details can be quickly constructed using extrusions. First, construct the profile of the molding as a closed shape, Figure 9-28A. Then, extrude the profile the desired length, Figure 9-28B.

Corner intersections of molding can be quickly created by extruding the same shape in two different directions, and then joining the two objects. First, draw the molding profile. Then, copy and rotate the profile to orient the Z axis in the desired direction, Figure 9-29A. Next, extrude the two profiles the desired lengths, Figure 9-29B. Finally, union the two extrusions to create the mitered corner molding, Figure 9-29C.

Figure 9-26.
Constructing a boss. A—Draw a cylinder for the hole so it extends above the surface of the object. B—Draw a cylinder the height of the boss on the top surface of the object. C—Union the large cylinder to the base. Then, subtract the small cylinder (hole) from the unioned objects. D—Fillet the edge to form the boss.

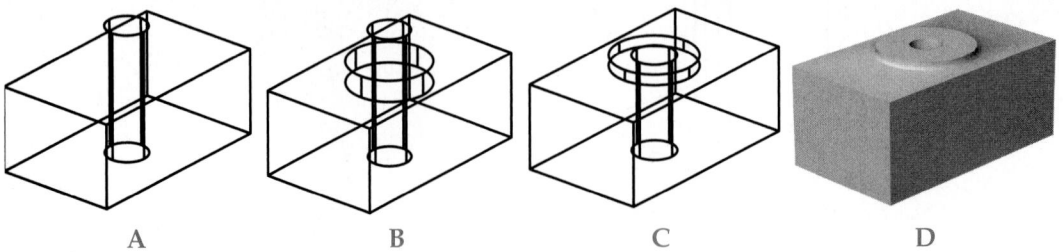

A   B   C   D

Figure 9-27.
Constructing an O-ring groove. A—Construct a cylinder; this one has a round placed on one end. B—Draw a circle centered on the surface of the cylinder. C—Revolve the circle 360° about the center of the cylinder. D—Subtract the revolved object from the cylinder. E—The completed O-ring groove.

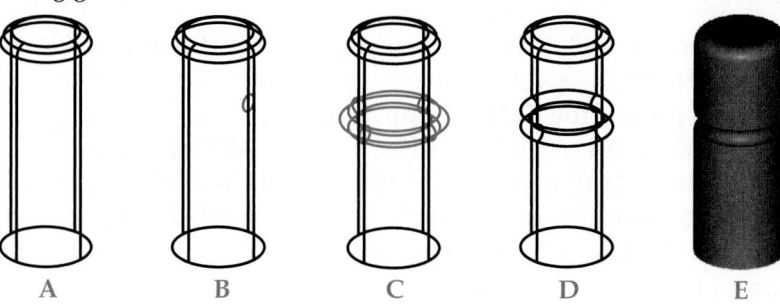

Figure 9-28.
A—The molding profile. B—The profile extruded to the desired length.

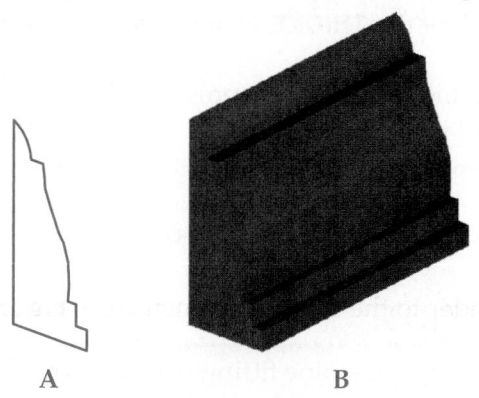

Figure 9-29.
Constructing corner molding. A—Copy and rotate the molding profile. B—Extrude the profiles to the desired lengths. C—Union the two extrusions to create the mitered corner. Note: The view has been rotated. D—The completed corner.

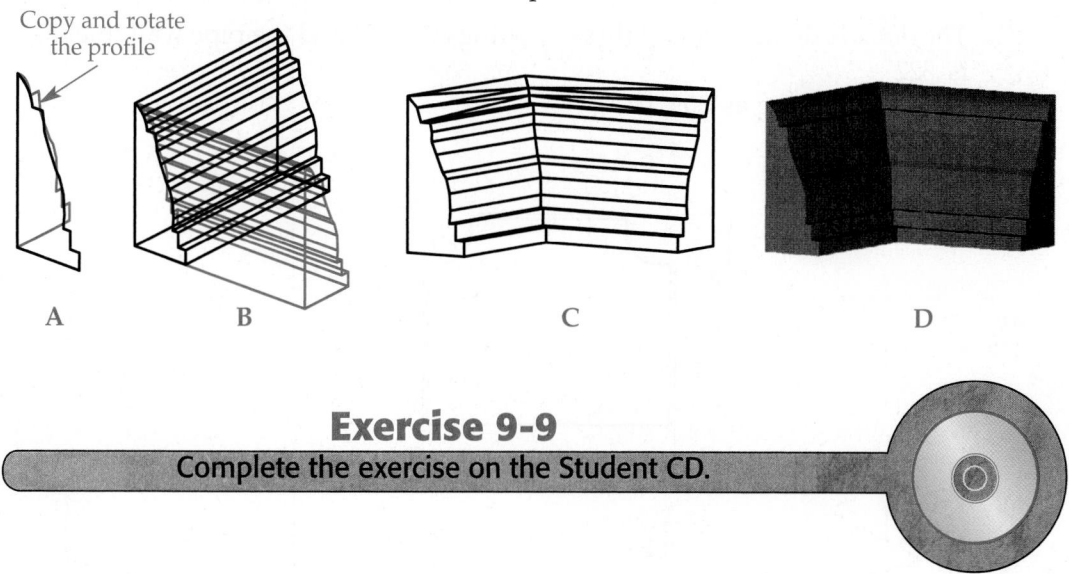

Exercise 9-9
Complete the exercise on the Student CD.

Chapter Test

Answer the following questions. Write your answers on a separate sheet of paper or complete the electronic chapter test on the Student CD.

1. Which properties of a solid can be changed in the **Properties** window?
2. What does the History property control?
3. What is the purpose of the **ALIGN** command?
4. How does the **3DALIGN** command differ from the **ALIGN** command?
5. How does the **3DROTATE** command differ from the **ROTATE** command?
6. How does the **MIRROR3D** command differ from the **MIRROR** command?
7. Which command allows you to create a rectangular array by defining rows, columns, and levels?
8. How does a 3D polar array differ from a 2D polar array?
9. How many levels can a 3D polar array have?
10. Which command is used to fillet a solid object?
11. Which command is used to chamfer a solid object?
12. What is the purpose of the **THICKEN** command, and which type of object does it create?
13. Which system variable allows you to preserve the original object when the **THICKEN** command is used?
14. List four objects that can be converted to surfaces using the **CONVTOSURFACE** command.
15. Briefly describe the function of the **SLICE** command.

Drawing Problems

1. Construct an 8″ diameter tee pipe fitting using the dimensions shown below. Hint: Extrude and union two solid cylinders before subtracting the cylinders for the inside diameters.
    A. Use **EXTRUDE** to create two sections of pipe at 90° to each other, then **UNION** the two pieces together.
    B. Use **FILLET** and **CHAMFER** to finish the object. The chamfer distance is .25″ × .25″.
    C. The outside diameter of all three openings is 8.63″ and the pipe wall thickness is .322″.
    D. Save the drawing as P09_01.

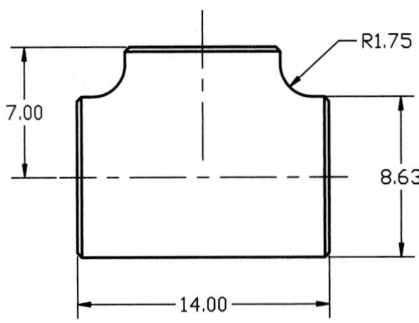

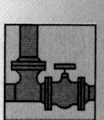

2. Construct an 8″ diameter, 90° elbow pipe fitting using the dimensions shown below.
   A. Use **EXTRUDE** or **SWEEP** to create the elbow.
   B. Chamfer the object. The chamfer distance is .25″ × .25″. Note: You cannot use the **CHAMFER** command.
   C. The outside diameter is 8.63″ and the pipe wall thickness is .322″.
   D. Save the drawing as P09_02.

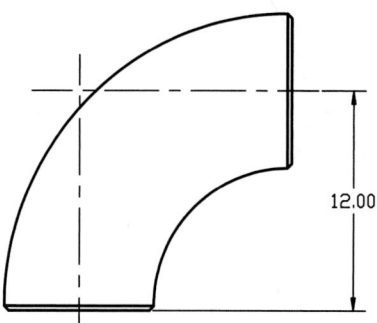

*Problems 3–6. These problems require you to use a variety of solid modeling functions to construct the objects. Use all of the solid modeling and editing commands you have learned so far to assist in construction. Use a dynamic UCS when practical, and create new UCSs as needed. Use **SOLIDHIST** and **SHOWHIST** to record and view the steps used to create the solid models. Create copies of the completed models and split them as required to show the internal features visible in the section views. Save each drawing as P09_(problem number).*

3.

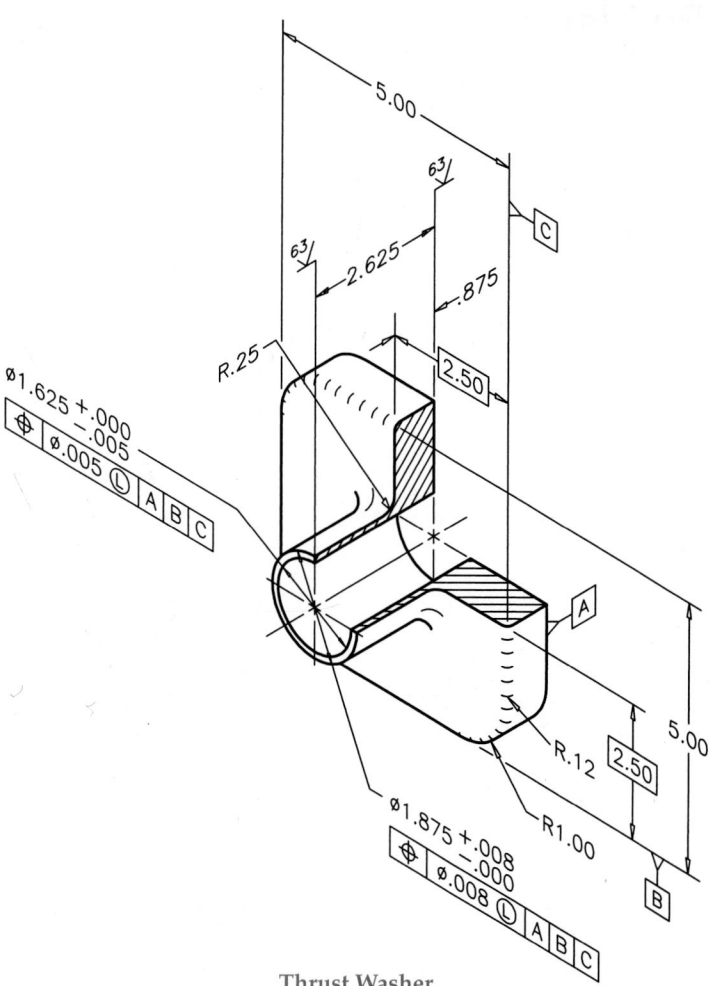

Thrust Washer

4.

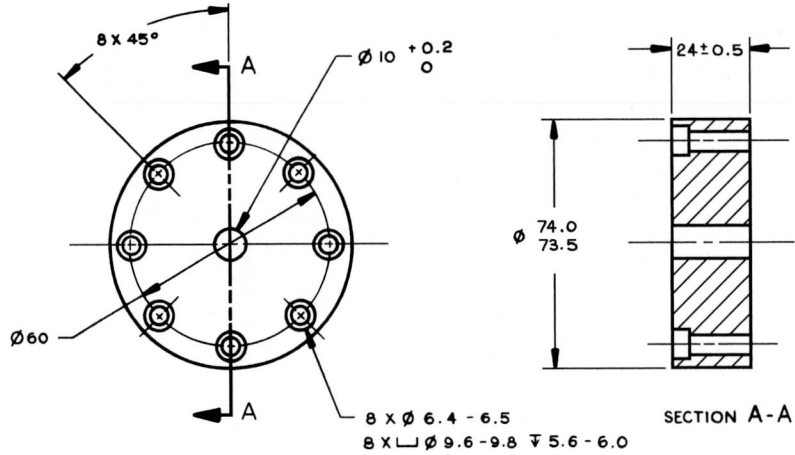

Collar

5.

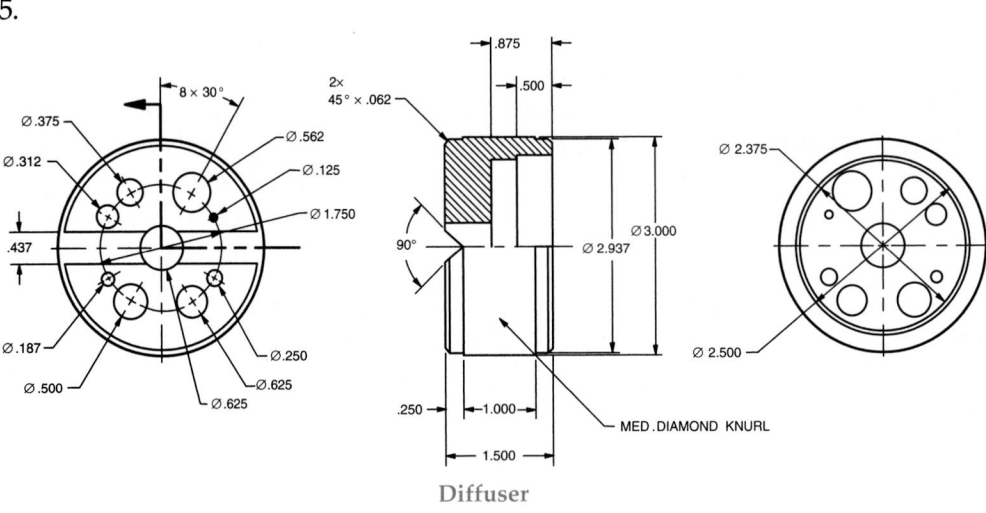

Diffuser

6.

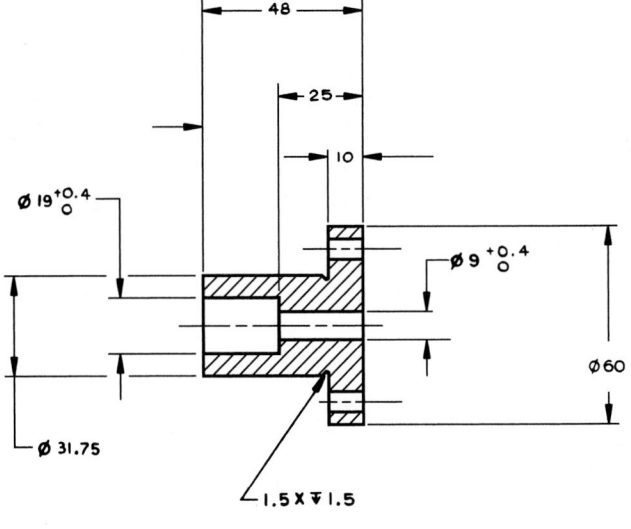

SECTION A-A

Bushing

AutoCAD and Its Applications—Advanced

CHAPTER 10

Subobject Editing

Learning Objectives

After completing this chapter, you will be able to:

✓ Select subobjects (faces, edges, and vertices).
✓ Edit solids using grips.
✓ Edit face subobjects.
✓ Edit edge subobjects.
✓ Edit vertex subobjects.
✓ Extrude a closed boundary using the **PRESSPULL** command.
✓ Extract a wireframe from a 3D solid using the **XEDGES** command.

Grip Editing

There are three basic types of 3D solids in AutoCAD. The commands **BOX**, **WEDGE**, **CYLINDER**, **SPHERE**, etc., create 3D solid *primitives*. *Sweeps* are 2D profiles given thickness by the **EXTRUDE**, **REVOLVE**, **SWEEP**, and **LOFT** commands to create a 3D solid. Finally, 3D solid *composites* are created by a Boolean operation or by using the **SOLIDEDIT** command. The **SOLIDEDIT** command is discussed in Chapter 11.

There are two types of grips—base and parameter—that may be associated with a solid object. These grips provide an intuitive means of modifying solids. Base grips are square and parameter grips are typically arrows. The editing that can be performed with these grips are discussed in the next sections.

Primitives

The 3D solid primitives (box, wedge, pyramid, cylinder, cone, sphere, and torus) all have basically the same grips. However, not all grips are available on all primitives. All primitives have a base grip at the centroid of the base. This grip functions like a standard grip in 2D work. It can be used to stretch, move, rotate, scale, or mirror the solid.

Boxes, wedges, and pyramids have square base grips at the corners that allow the size of the base to be changed. See **Figure 10-1.** Select one of these grips, move the cursor, and select a new point. The object dynamically changes in the viewport as you move the grip. You can also type the new coordinate location for the grip and press

Figure 10-1.
Boxes, wedges, and pyramids have square base grips at the corners and parameter grips on the sides of the base and center of the top face, edge, or vertex.

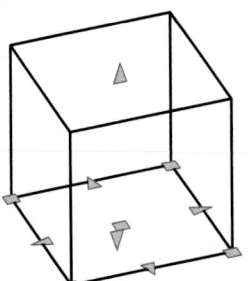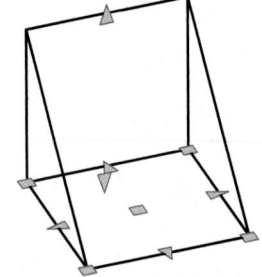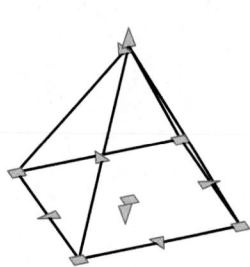

[Enter]. If ortho is off, the length and width can be changed at the same time by dragging the grip, except in the case of a pyramid. The parameter grips on the base allow the length or width to be changed. Additionally, the height of these objects can be changed using parameter grips. Each object has one parameter grip for changing the height of the apex and one for changing the height of the plane on which the base sits. A pyramid also has a parameter grip at the apex for changing the radius of the top.

Cylinders, cones, and spheres have four parameter grips for changing the radius of the base, or the cross section in the case of a sphere. See Figure 10-2. Cylinders and cones also have parameter grips for changing the height of the apex and the height of the plane on which the base sits. Additionally, a cone has a parameter grip at the apex for changing the radius of the top.

A torus has a parameter grip located at the center of the tube. See Figure 10-3. This grip is used to change the radius of the torus. There is also a parameter grip at each quadrant of the tube. These are used to change the radius of the tube.

Figure 10-2.
Cylinders, cones, and spheres have four parameter grips for changing their radius. Cylinders and cones have parameter grips for changing their height. Cones also have a parameter grip for changing the radius of the top.

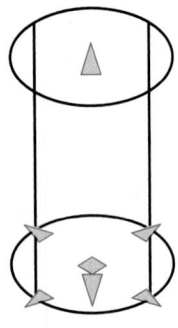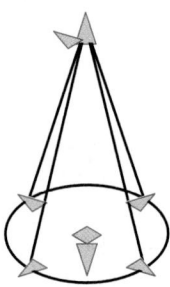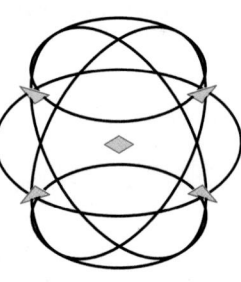

Figure 10-3.
A torus has a parameter grip located at the center of the tube for changing the radius of the torus. There are also parameter grips for changing the radius of the tube.

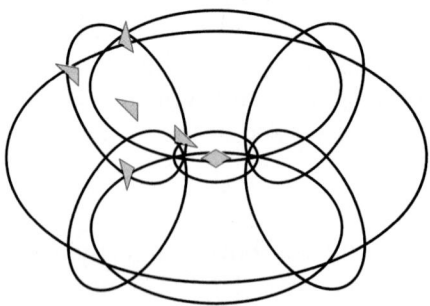

Figure 10-4.
A polysolid has a base
grip at each corner of
the starting face of the
solid and one at the
endpoint of each
segment.

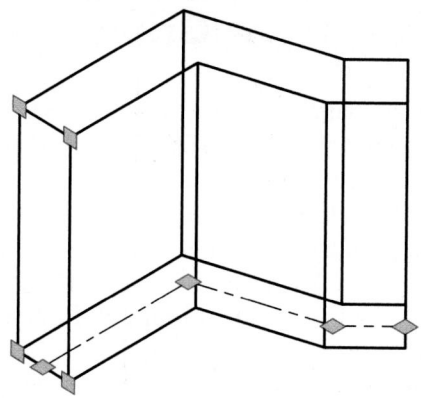

A polysolid does not have parameter grips. Instead, a base grip appears at each corner of the starting face of the solid. See Figure 10-4. Use these grips to change the cross-sectional shape of the polysolid. The corners do not need to remain square. Base grips also appear at the endpoint of each segment centerline. Use these to change the location of each segment's endpoints.

Swept Solids

Extrusions, revolutions, sweeps, and lofts are considered swept solids. Swept solids typically have base grips located at the vertices of the 2D profiles. These can be used to change the size of the profile, and thus the solid. Other grips that appear include:

- A parameter grip appears on the upper face of extrusions for changing the height.
- A base grip appears on the axis of revolved solids for changing the location of the axis in relation to the profile.
- Base grips appear on the vertices of the path of sweeps for changing the shape of the path.

Composite Solids

The Boolean commands (**UNION**, **SUBTRACT**, and **INTERSECT**) create composite solids. Solids that have been modified using any of the options of the **SOLIDEDIT** command also become composite solids. The solid may still look like a primitive, sweep, loft, etc., but it is a composite. The grips available with the previous objects are no longer available, unless performing subobject editing on a composite created with a Boolean command (discussed later in this chapter). Composite solids have a base grip located at the centroid of the base surface. This grip can be used to stretch, move, rotate, scale, or mirror the solid.

NOTE

When performing grip editing on a solid, AutoCAD must be able to "solve" the end result. If it cannot, the edit is not applied.

Using Grips with Surfaces

Surfaces can be edited using grips in the same manner as discussed with solids. A planar surface created with **PLANESURF** can be moved, rotated, scaled, and mirrored, but not stretched. Base grips are located at each corner.

As you learned in Chapter 7, a variety of AutoCAD objects can be extruded to create a surface. Three of these objects—arc, line, and polyline—are shown extruded into surfaces in Figure 10-5. Notice the location and type of grips on the surface extrusions. Base grips are located on the original profile that was extruded to make the surface. These grips enable you to alter the shape of the surface. A parameter grip located on the top of the surface is used to change the height of the extrusion.

Surfaces that have been extruded, or swept, along a path can also be edited with grips. Also, the grips located on the path allow you to change the shape of the surface extrusion. See Figure 10-6.

Figure 10-5.
Surfaces extruded from an arc, line, and polyline. Notice the grips.

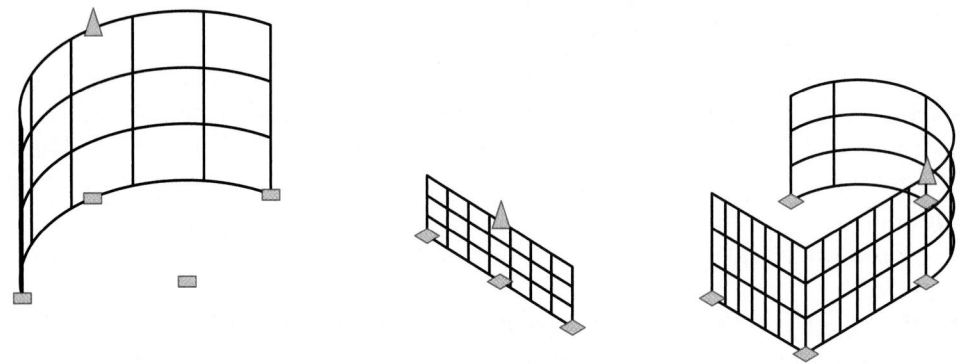

Figure 10-6.
A—Grips can be used to modify the path on this swept surface. B—The swept surface after grip editing.

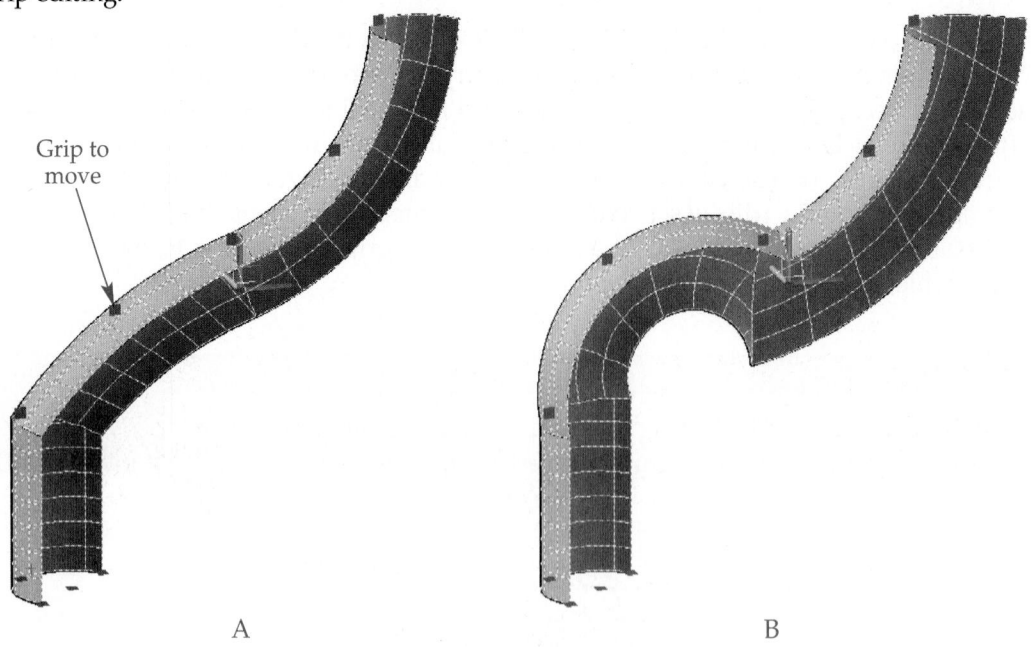

Grip to move

A   B

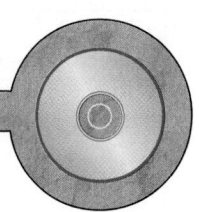

Exercise 10-1
Complete the exercise on the Student CD.

Overview of Subobject Editing

AutoCAD solid primitives, such as cylinders, wedges, and boxes, are composed of three types of subobjects: faces, edges, and vertices. In addition, the objects that are used with Boolean commands to create a composite solid are considered subobjects, if the history is recorded. The primitive subobjects can be edited. See **Figure 10-7**. Once selected, the primitive subobjects can even be deleted from the composite solid. **Figure 10-8** illustrates the difference between a composite solid model, the solid primitives used to construct it, and an individual subobject of one of the primitives.

Subobjects can be easily edited using grips, which provide an intuitive and flexible method of solid model design. For example, suppose you need to rotate a face subobject in the current XY plane. You can select the subobject, pick its base grip, and then cycle through the editing functions to **ROTATE**. You can also use the **ROTATE** command on the selected subobject.

Figure 10-7.
A—Selecting a subobject solid primitive within a composite solid displays its grips.
B—The grips on the primitive can be used to edit the primitive.

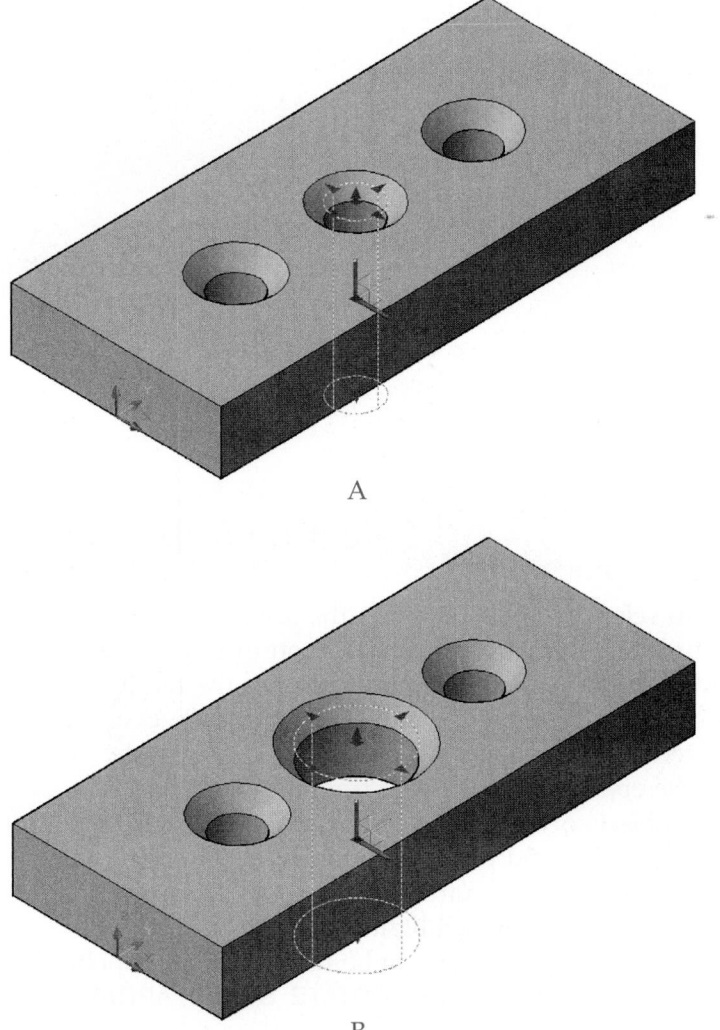

Figure 10-8.
A—The composite solid model is selected. Notice the single base grip. B—The wedge primitive subobject has been selected. Notice the grips associated with the primitive. C—An edge subobject within the primitive subobject is selected for editing.

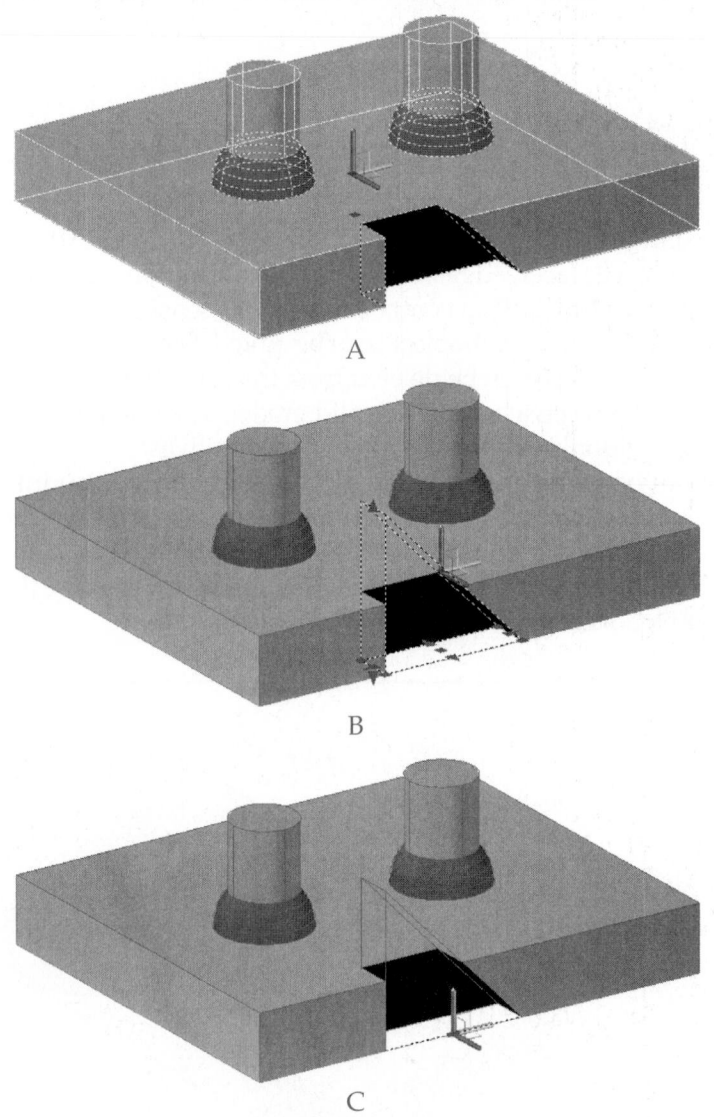

A

B

C

Selecting Subobjects

To select a subobject, press the [Ctrl] key and pick the subobject. You can select multiple subobjects and subobjects on multiple objects. To select a subobject that is hidden in the current view, first display the model as a wireframe. After creating a selection set, select a grip and edit the subobject as needed. Multiple objects can be selected in this manner. To deselect objects, press the [Shift]+[Ctrl] key combination and pick the objects to be removed from the selection set.

If objects or subobjects are overlapping, press the [Ctrl] key and the spacebar to turn on cycling and pick the subobject. Then, release the spacebar, continue holding the [Ctrl] key, and pick until the subobject you need is highlighted. Press [Enter] or the spacebar to select the highlighted subobject.

The [Ctrl] key method can be used to select subobjects for use with editing commands such as **MOVE**, **COPY**, **ROTATE**, **SCALE**, **ARRAY**, and **ERASE**. Some commands, like **ARRAY**, **STRETCH**, and **MIRROR**, are applied to the entire solid. Other operations may not be applied at all, depending on which type of subobject is selected. You can also use the **Properties** window to change the color of edge and face subobjects or the material assigned to a face. The color of a subobject primitive can also be changed, but not the color of its subobjects.

CAUTION

Using the **SOLIDEDIT** command (discussed in Chapter 11) removes the history from a composite solid. Therefore, the original objects—the subobjects—are no longer available for subobject editing. However, you may still be able to perform some subobject edits, such as moving the original objects.

Face Subobject Editing

Faces of 3D solids can be modified using commands such as **MOVE, ROTATE**, and **SCALE**, or by using grips and grip tools. To select a face on a 3D solid, press the [Ctrl] key and pick within the boundary of the face. Do not pick the edge of the face. Face grips are circular and located in the center of the face, as shown in **Figure 10-9**. In the case of a sphere, the grip is located in the center of the sphere since there is only one face. The same is true of the curved face on a cylinder or cone.

By default, the history is recorded for all solid primitives and composites. If you select a primitive or a primitive subobject within a composite solid, all of the grips associated with that primitive are displayed. See **Figure 10-10A**. If you edit a 3D solid primitive face, the history of the primitive is deleted and the object becomes a composite solid. Then, when the object is selected, a single base grip is displayed. See **Figure 10-10B**.

While pressing the [Ctrl] key and selecting a face, you may pick faces that you do not want to edit. Depending on your viewpoint and current visual style, it may be difficult to select the face you want. Additionally, it may be almost impossible to deselect faces you do not need. Use [Shift]+mouse wheel button to activate the transparent **3DORBIT** command and change your viewpoint.

NOTE

The recorded history of a solid composite can also be displayed by selecting the solid, opening the **Properties** window, and changing the Show History property in the **Solid History** category to Yes.

Figure 10-9.
Face grips are located in the center of face subobjects.

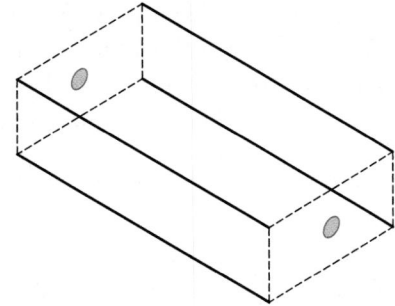
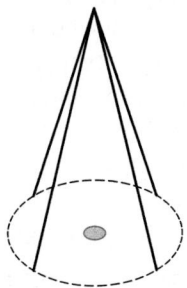

Figure 10-10.
A—This primitive is selected for editing. Notice the grips associated with the primitive.
B—If the primitive is edited, the history of that primitive is deleted and a single base grip is displayed.

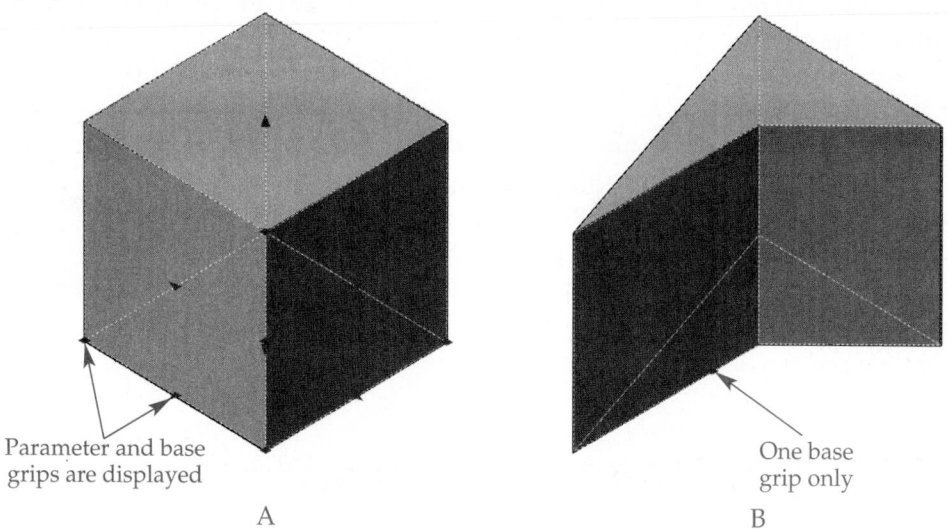

Parameter and base grips are displayed

One base grip only

A

B

Moving Faces

When a face of a 3D solid is moved, all adjacent faces are dragged and stretched with it. The shape of the original 3D primitive or solid determines the manner in which the face can be moved and how adjacent faces react. A face can be moved using the **MOVE** command, **3DMOVE** command, move grip tool, or by dragging the face's base grip. When moving a face, use the grip tool, polar tracking, or direct distance entry. Otherwise, the results may appear correct in the view in which the edit is made, but, when the view is changed, the actual result may not be what you wanted. See Figure 10-11.

The move grip tool is displayed by default (**GTAUTO** = 1) when the face is selected. This tool is discussed in detail in Chapter 9. To use the move grip tool, move the pointer over the X, Y, or Z axis of the grip tool; the axis changes to yellow. To restrict movement along that axis, pick the axis. If you move the pointer over one of the right angles at the origin of the tool, the corresponding two axes turn yellow. Pick to restrict the movement to that plane. You can complete the movement by either picking a new point or by direct distance entry.

There are a few options to achieve different results when dynamically moving a face. The [Ctrl] key is used to access these options. First, select the face. See Figure 10-12A. Then, pick the face grip or grip tool and press and release the [Ctrl] key to cycle through the options.

If the [Ctrl] key is not pressed, the moved face maintains its size, shape, and orientation. The shape and plane of adjacent faces are changed. See Figure 10-12B. Pressing the [Ctrl] key three times resets the function, as if the [Ctrl] key had not been pressed.

If the [Ctrl] key is pressed once, the moved face maintains its shape and orientation. However, its size is modified because the planes of adjacent faces are maintained. See Figure 10-12C. Adjacent faces are not subdivided.

If the [Ctrl] key is pressed twice, the moved face maintains its size, shape, and orientation. However, adjacent faces are subdivided into triangular faces, if needed.

Figure 10-11.
A—The original solid primitives. B—The box and wedge are dynamically edited without using exact coordinates or distances. C—When the viewpoint is changed, you can see that dynamic editing has produced unexpected results.

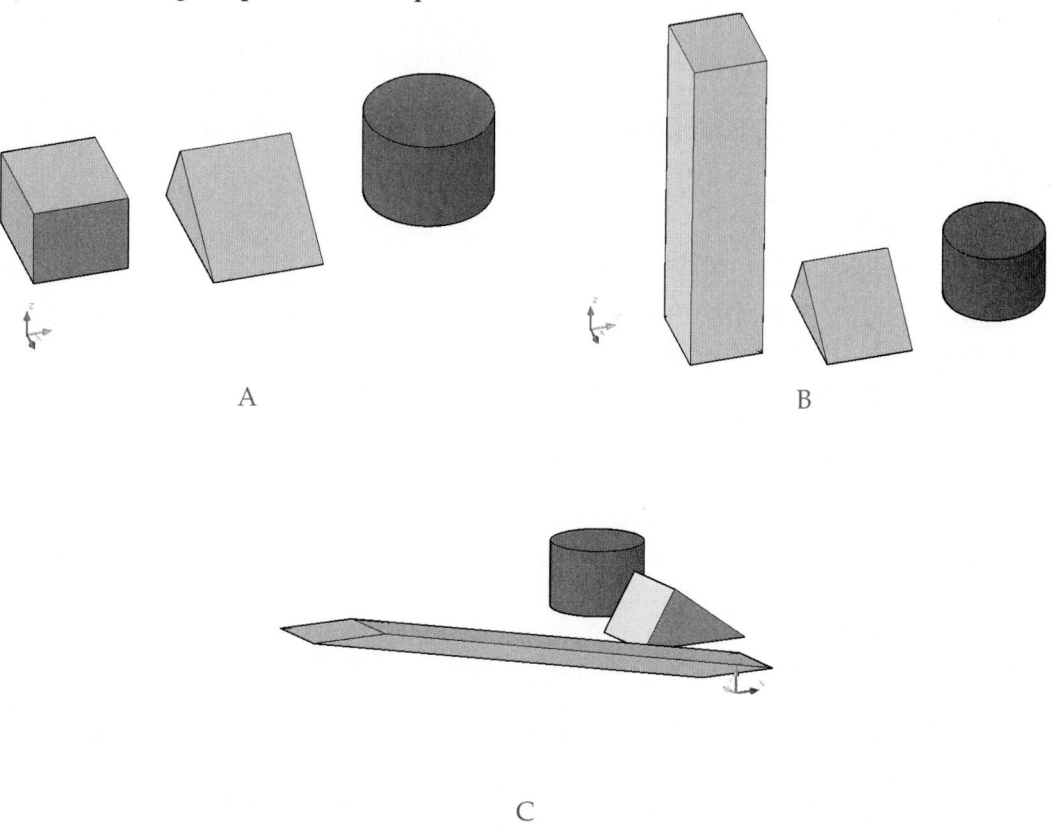

Figure 10-12.
A—The original solid primitive. B—Without pressing the [Ctrl] key, the face maintains its shape and orientation. C—Pressing the [Ctrl] key once keeps the adjacent faces in their original planes, but alters the modified face.

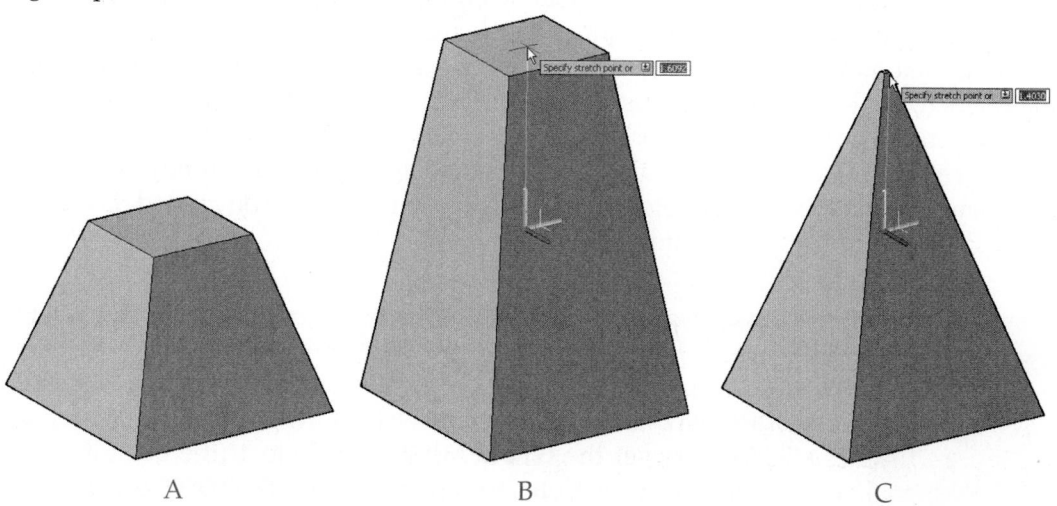

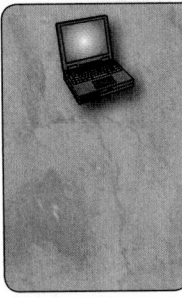
Rotating Faces

Before rotating any primitive or subobject you must know in which plane the rotation is to occur. The **ROTATE** command permits a rotation in the current XY plane. But, you can get around this limitation by using the **3DROTATE** command. This command allows you to select a rotation plane by means of the rotate grip tool. This tool is discussed in detail in Chapter 9. When a subobject is selected, you cannot use the spacebar to switch to the rotate grip tool from the move grip tool. The rotate grip tool must be placed using the **3DROTATE** command.

The rotate grip tool provides a dynamic, graphic representation of the three axes of rotation. To rotate about the tool's X axis, pick the red circle on the grip tool. To rotate about the Y axis, pick the green circle. To rotate about the Z axis, pick the blue circle. Once you select a circle, it turns yellow and you are prompted for the start point of the rotation angle. You can enter a direct angle at this prompt or pick the first of two points defining the angle of rotation. When the rotation angle is defined, the face is rotated about the selected axis.

For example, in **Figure 10-13A**, the top face is selected and the rotate grip tool is placed on a corner of the face. After picking the rotation axis on the grip tool, specify the angle start point and then the angle end point. Notice in **Figure 10-13B** that dynamic input is used to enter an exact angle value of –15. The result is shown in **Figure 10-13C**.

There are a few options to achieve different results when dynamically rotating a face. The [Ctrl] key is used to access these options. Pressing the [Ctrl] key while rotating a face affects adjacent faces in the same manner as discussed in moving faces. **Figure 10-14A** shows a rotation without pressing [Ctrl]. The shape and size of the face being rotated is maintained, while the adjacent faces change. **Figure 10-14B** shows a rotation after pressing [Ctrl] once. The shape and size of the face being rotated changes, while the plane and shape of adjacent faces are maintained. Pressing the [Ctrl] key a second time maintains the shape and orientation of the selected face, but triangular faces may be created on adjacent faces. Pressing [Ctrl] key a third time resets the function.

Figure 10-13.
Using the rotate grip tool to rotate a face. A—The top face is selected and the grip tool is placed on a base point of the face. B—The axis of rotation and a starting point for the angle are selected. C—The completed rotation.

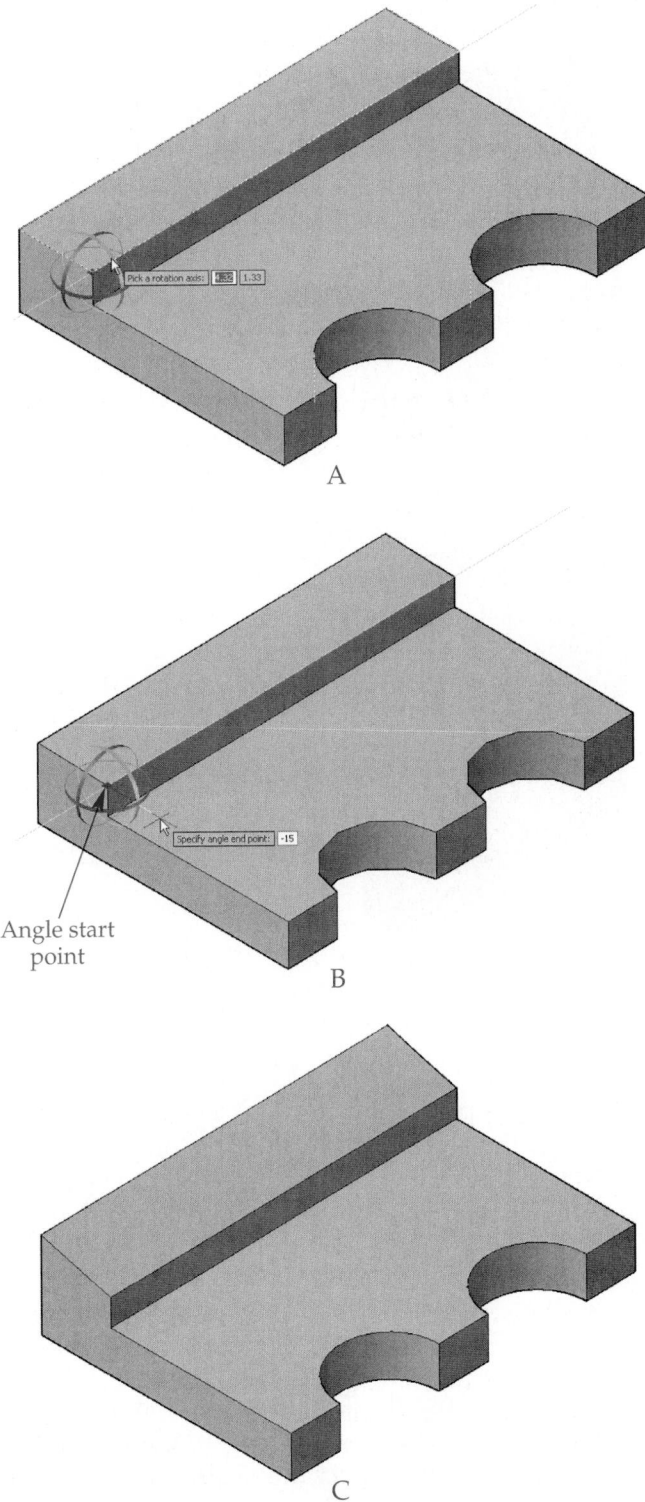

Angle start point

A

B

C

Figure 10-14.
A—Rotating a face without pressing the [Ctrl] key. The large, top face on the object shown in Figure 10-13A has been selected for rotation. B—Pressing the [Ctrl] key once keeps the adjacent faces in their original planes. The shape and size of the face being rotated changes.

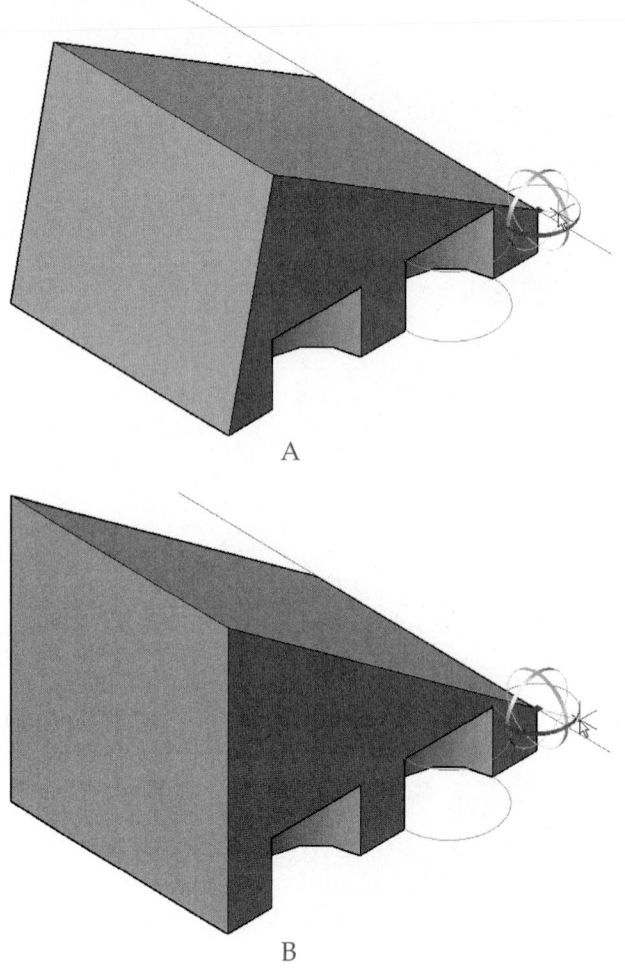

A

B

Scaling Faces

Scaling a face is a simple procedure. First, select the face to be scaled. Then, dynamically pick to change the scale or use a scale factor. See **Figure 10-15.** Pressing the [Ctrl] key has no effect on the scaling process, except to turn it off or on, if the base point is on the same plane as the face. However, if the base point is not on the same plane as the selected face, then pressing the [Ctrl] key has the same effect as for the other face-editing operations.

Coloring Faces

To change the color of a face, use the [Ctrl] key selection method to select the face. Next, open the **Properties** window. See **Figure 10-16.** In the **General** category, pick the drop-down list for the Color property. Select the desired color, or pick Select Color... and choose a color from the **Select Color** dialog box. To change the material applied to the face, pick the drop-down list for the Material property in the **3D Visualization** category. Select a material from the list. A material must be loaded into the drawing to be available in this drop-down list. Materials are discussed in detail in Chapter 14.

Figure 10-15.
Scaling a face. A—The original solid. B—The dark face is scaled down. C—The dark face is scaled up.

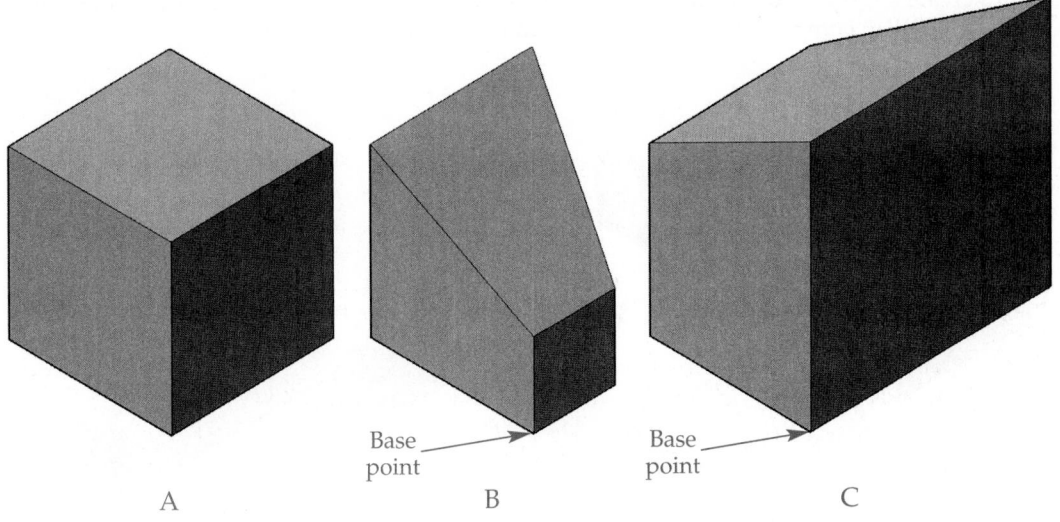

Base point

Base point

A   B   C

Figure 10-16.
Changing the color of a face or the material assigned to it.

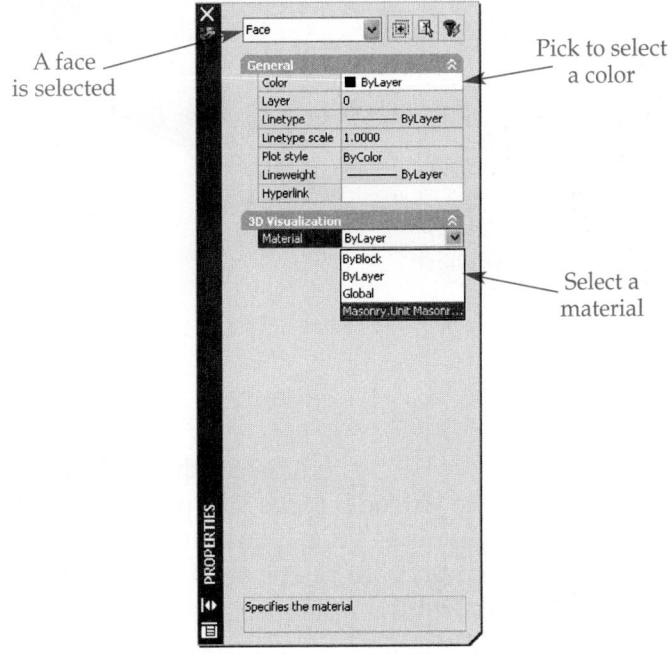

A face is selected

Pick to select a color

Select a material

Extruding a Solid Face

Planar faces on 3D solids can be extruded into new solids. Refer to the HVAC duct assembly shown in **Figure 10-17A**. A new, reduced trunk needs to be created on the left end of the assembly. This requires two pieces: a reducer and the trunk.

First, select the **EXTRUDE** command. At the "select objects" prompt, press the [Ctrl] key and pick the face subobject to be extruded. Next, since this is a reduced trunk, specify a taper angle. Enter the **Taper angle** option and specify the angle. In this case, a 15° angle is used. Finally, specify the extrusion height. The height of the reducer is 12". See **Figure 10-17B**.

Figure 10-17.
A—A new, reduced trunk needs to be created on the left end of the HVAC assembly. The face shown in color will be extruded. B—The **Taper angle** option of the **EXTRUDE** command is used to create the reducer. The face shown in color will be extruded to create the extension. C—The **EXTRUDE** command is used to create an extension from the reducer.

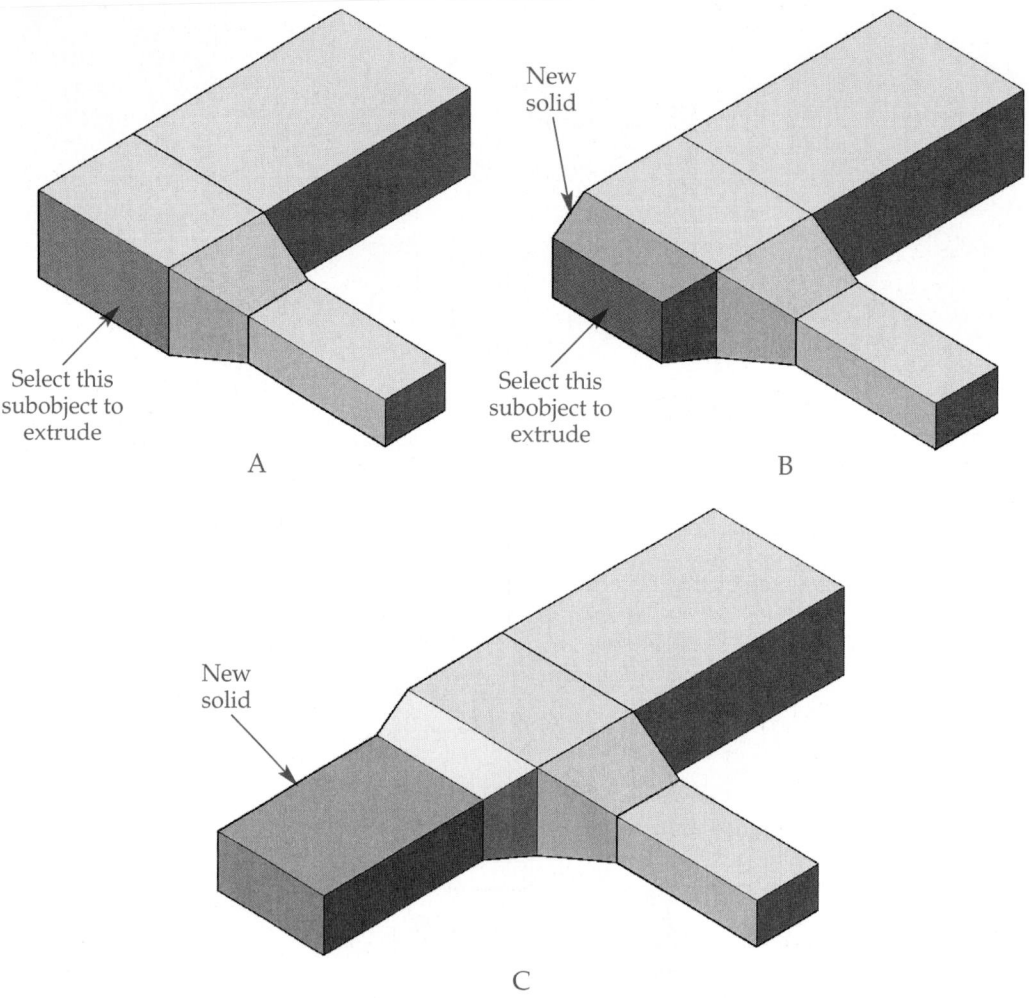

New
solid

Select this
subobject to
extrude

Select this
subobject to
extrude

A

B

New
solid

C

Now, the new trunk needs to be created. Select the **EXTRUDE** command. Press the [Ctrl] key and pick the face to extrude. Since this piece is not tapered, enter the extrusion height, which in this case is 44″. See Figure 10-17C. The two new pieces are separate solid objects. If the assembly is to be one solid, use the **UNION** command and join the two new solids to the assembly.

Revolving a Solid Face

Planar faces on 3D solids can be revolved in the same manner as other AutoCAD objects to create new solids. Refer to Figure 10-18A. The face on the left end of the HVAC duct created in the last section needs to be revolved to create a 90° bend. First, select the **REVOLVE** command. At the "select objects" prompt, press the [Ctrl] key and pick the face subobject to be revolved.

Next, the axis of revolution needs to be specified. You can pick the two endpoints of the vertical edge, but you can also pick the edge subobject. Enter the **Object** option of the command, press the [Ctrl] key, and select the edge subobject.

Finally, the 90° angle of revolution needs to be specified. Figure 10-18B shows the face revolved into a new solid. The bend is a new, separate solid. If necessary, use the **UNION** command to join the bend to the assembly.

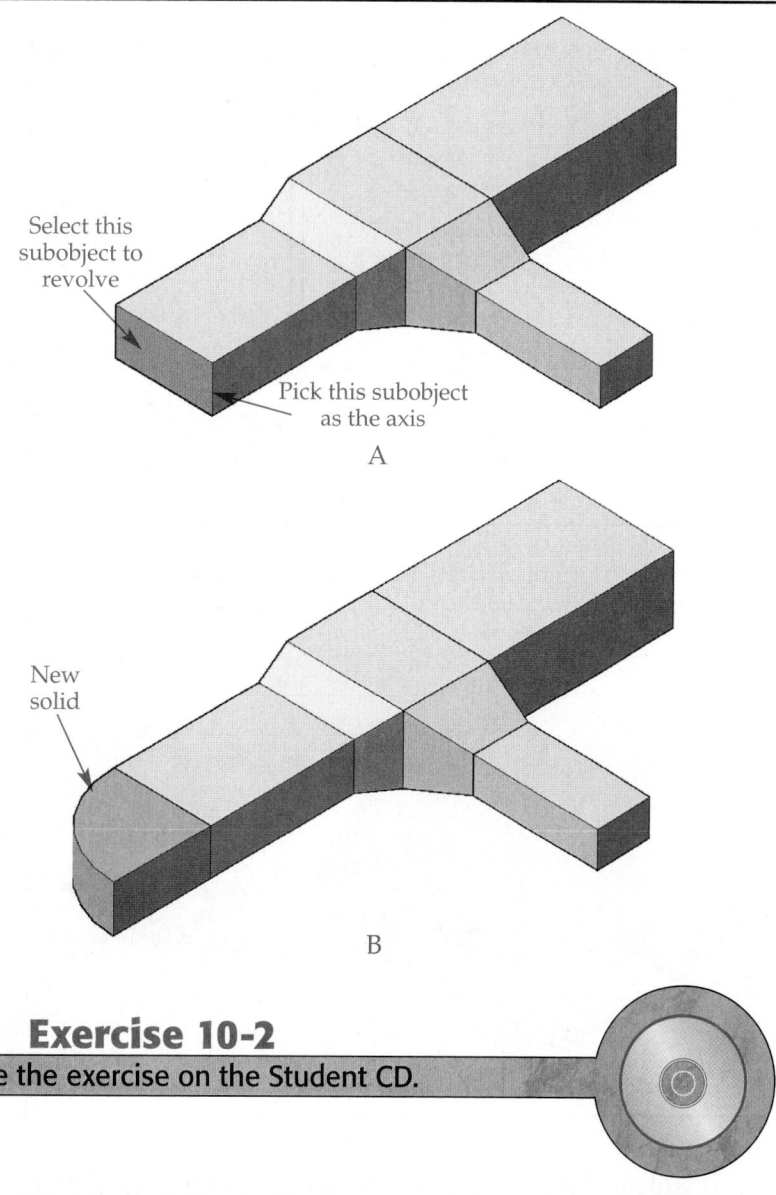

Figure 10-18.
A—The face on the left end of the HVAC duct (shown in color) needs to be revolved to create a 90° bend. B—Use the **REVOLVE** command and pick the face subobject to be revolved.

Select this subobject to revolve

Pick this subobject as the axis

A

New solid

B

Exercise 10-2
Complete the exercise on the Student CD.

Edge Subobject Editing

Individual edges of a solid can be edited using grips and grip tools in the same manner as faces. To select an edge subobject, press the [Ctrl] key and pick the edge. Grips on linear edges are rectangular and appear in the middle of the edge, **Figure 10-19.** In addition to solid edges, the edges of regions can be altered using **MOVE**, **ROTATE**, and **SCALE**, but grips are not displayed on regions as they are on solid subobjects.

Remember, editing subobjects of a primitive removes the primitive's history. This should always be a consideration if it is important to preserve the solid primitives that were used to construct a 3D solid model. Instead of editing the primitive subobjects at their subobject level, it may be better to add or remove material with a Boolean operation, thus preserving the solid's history.

Moving Edges

To move an edge, select it using the [Ctrl] key, as previously discussed. By default (**GTAUTO** = 1), the move grip tool appears. See **Figure 10-20A.** Select the appropriate axis handle and dynamically move the edge or use direct distance entry, **Figure 10-20B.** The move grip tool remains active until the [Esc] key is pressed.

Figure 10-19.
Edge grips are rectangular and displayed in the middle of the edge.

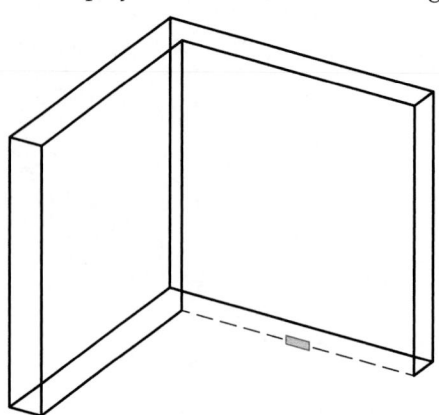

Figure 10-20.
A—Select the edge subobject to be moved. B—The edge is moved. Notice how the size of the primitive used to subtract the cutout is not affected.

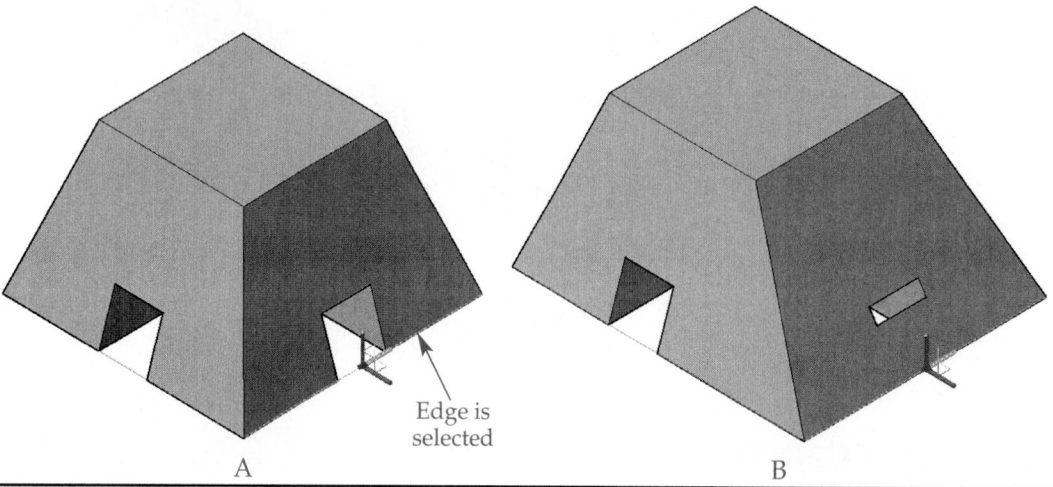

Edge is
selected

A   B

If you pick the edge grip to turn it hot, the move grip tool (if displayed) is bypassed. This places you in the standard grip editing mode. You can stretch, move, rotate, scale, and mirror the edge. In this case, the **STRETCH** function works the same as the move grip tool, but less reliably. You must be careful to use either ortho, polar tracking, or direct distance entry, but the possibility for error still exists.

There are a few options to achieve different results when dynamically moving an edge. The [Ctrl] key is used to access these options. First, select the edge. Then, pick the edge grip or grip tool and press and release the [Ctrl] key to cycle through the options.

If the [Ctrl] key is not pressed, the moved edge maintains its length and orientation. However, the shape and planes of adjacent faces are changed. See Figure 10-21A. If the [Ctrl] key is pressed three times, the function is reset, as if the [Ctrl] key had not been pressed.

If the [Ctrl] key is pressed once, the moved edge maintains its orientation, but its length is modified. This is because the planes and orientation of adjacent faces are maintained. See Figure 10-21B.

If the [Ctrl] key is pressed twice, the moved edge maintains its length and orientation. But, if the move alters the planes of adjacent faces, those faces may become *nonplanar*. In other words, the face may now be located on two or more planes. If this happens, adjacent faces are divided into triangles, Figure 10-21C. This is visible when the object in Figure 10-21C is displayed in two more orthographic views. See Figure 10-22.

Figure 10-21.
Moving an edge. A—If the [Ctrl] key is not pressed, the edge maintains its length and orientation, but the shape and planes of adjacent faces are changed. B—If the [Ctrl] key is pressed once, the moved edge maintains its orientation, but its length is modified because the planes of adjacent faces are maintained. C—If the [Ctrl] key is pressed twice, the adjacent faces may be triangulated.

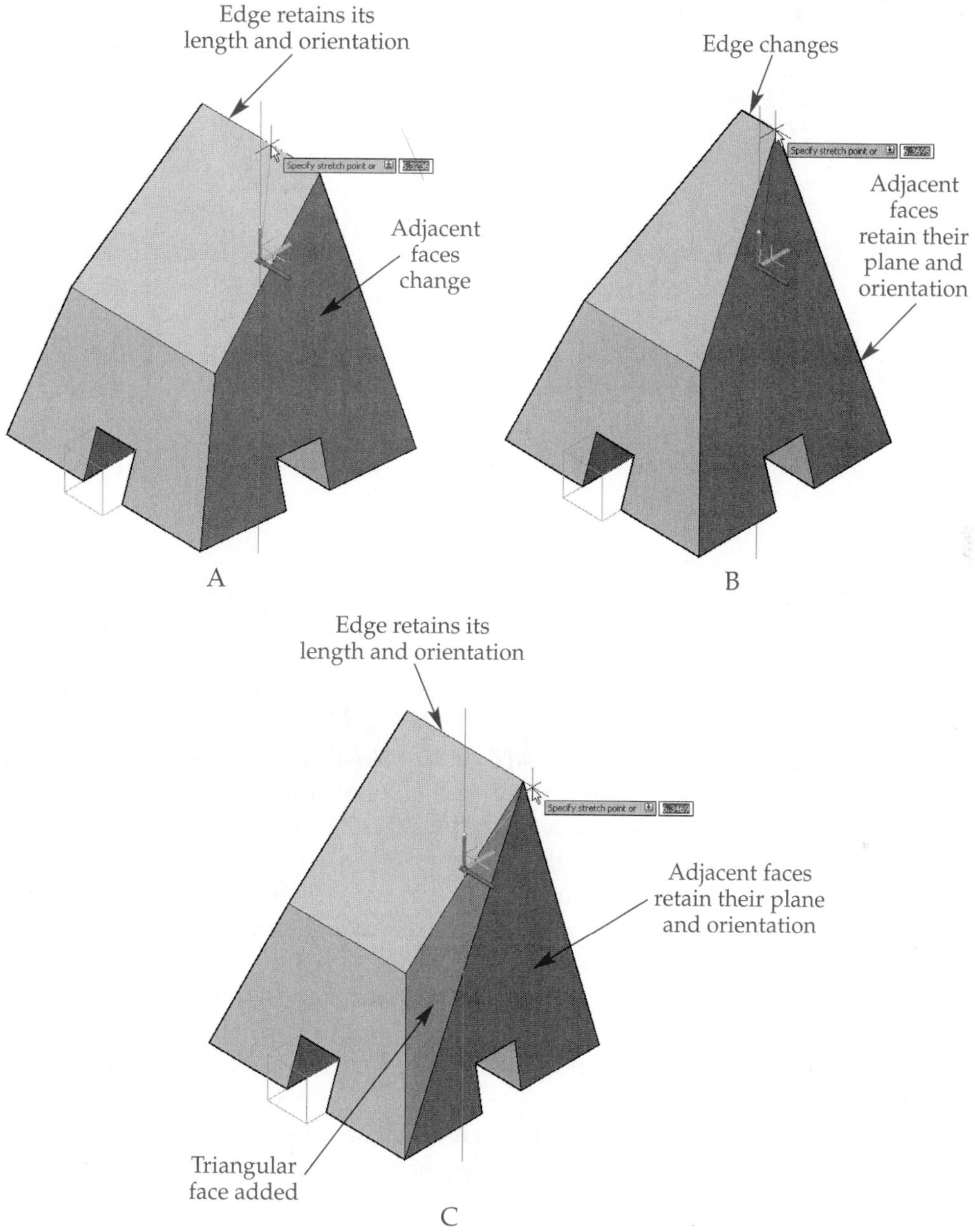

Edge retains its
length and orientation

Adjacent
faces
change

A

Edge changes

Adjacent
faces
retain their
plane and
orientation

B

Edge retains its
length and orientation

Adjacent faces
retain their plane
and orientation

Triangular
face added

C

PROFESSIONAL TIP

You can quickly enter the **MOVE**, **ROTATE**, or **SCALE** command for a subobject by selecting the subobject, right-clicking, and picking the command from the shortcut menu.

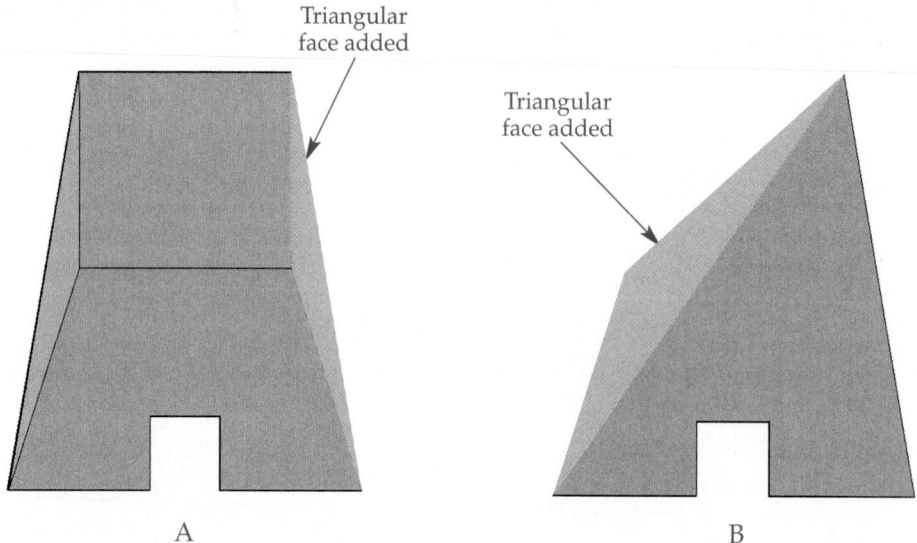

Triangular
face added

Triangular
face added

A   B

Rotating Edges

Before you select an edge to rotate, do a little planning. Since there are a wide variety of edge rotation options, it will save time if you first decide on the location of the base point about which the edge will rotate. Next, determine the direction and angle of rotation. Based on these criteria, choose the option that will accomplish the task the quickest.

To rotate an edge, enter the **ROTATE** or **3DROTATE** command. Then, pick the edge using the [Ctrl] key. Select a base point and then enter the rotation. You can also select the edge, pick the edge grip, and cycle to the **ROTATE** mode.

Edges are best rotated using the rotate grip tool. It provides a graphic visualization of the axis of rotation. If you select a dynamic UCS while using the **3DROTATE** command, you have a variety of rotation axes to use because the grip tool can be located on all planes adjacent to the selected edge.

There are a few options to achieve different results when dynamically rotating an edge. The [Ctrl] key is used to access these options. First, select the edge. Then, pick the edge grip or grip tool and press and release the [Ctrl] key to cycle through the options.

Pressing the [Ctrl] key while rotating a face affects adjacent faces in the same manner as discussed in moving faces. If the [Ctrl] key is not pressed, the rotated edge maintains its length but the shape and planes of adjacent faces are changed. See **Figure 10-23A**. If the [Ctrl] key is pressed once, the length of the rotated edge is modified because the planes of adjacent faces are maintained. See **Figure 10-23B**. If the [Ctrl] key is pressed twice, the rotated edge maintains its length, but if the rotation causes faces to become nonplanar, the adjacent faces may be triangulated. See **Figure 10-23C**. Pressing the [Ctrl] key a third time resets the function.

Scaling Edges

Only linear (straight-line) edges can be scaled. Circular edges, such as the ends of cylinders, can be modified using grips or the **SOLIDEDIT** command. These tools can be used to change the diameter or establish taper angles. See Chapter 11 for a complete discussion of the **SOLIDEDIT** command.

Figure 10-23.
Rotating an edge. A—The [Ctrl] key is not pressed. B—The [Ctrl] key is pressed once. Notice the top edge of the dark face. C—The [Ctrl] key is pressed twice.

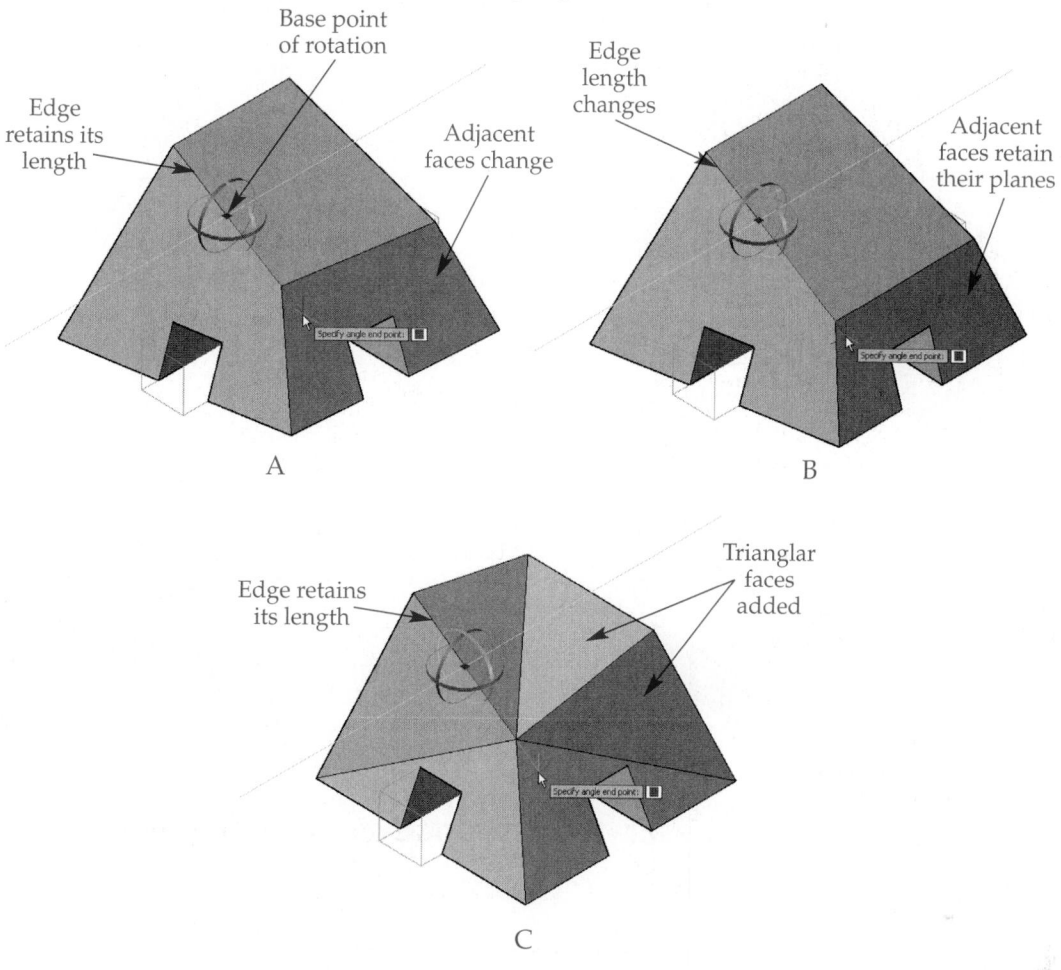

To scale a linear edge, enter the **SCALE** command. Select the edge using the [Ctrl] key. Pick a base point for the operation and enter a scale factor. You can also select the edge, pick the edge grip, and cycle to the **SCALE** mode.

The direction of the scaled edge is related to the base point you select. The base point remains stationary, while the vertices in either direction are scaled. If you enter the **SCALE** command, you are prompted for the base point. If you select the edge grip, the grip becomes the base point. The differences in opposite end and midpoint scaling of an edge are shown in **Figure 10-24.**

There are a few options to achieve different results when dynamically scaling an edge. The [Ctrl] key is used to access these options. First, select the edge. Then, pick the edge grip or enter the **SCALE** command and press and release the [Ctrl] key to cycle through the options.

If the [Ctrl] key is not pressed, the edge is scaled. The shape and planes of adjacent faces are changed to match the scaled edge. See **Figure 10-25A.**

If the [Ctrl] key is pressed once, the edge is, in effect, not scaled. This is because the planes of adjacent faces are maintained.

If the [Ctrl] key is pressed twice, the edge is scaled, as are edges attached to the modified edge. However, if the scaling causes faces to become nonplanar, they may be triangulated. See **Figure 10-25B.**

Figure 10-24.
The differences in opposite end and midpoint scaling of an edge. A—The original object.
B—The edge is scaled down with a base point on the left corner. C—The edge is scaled down
to the same scale factor, but the base point is on the right corner. D—The edge is scaled down
to the same scaled factor with the base point at the middle of the edge.

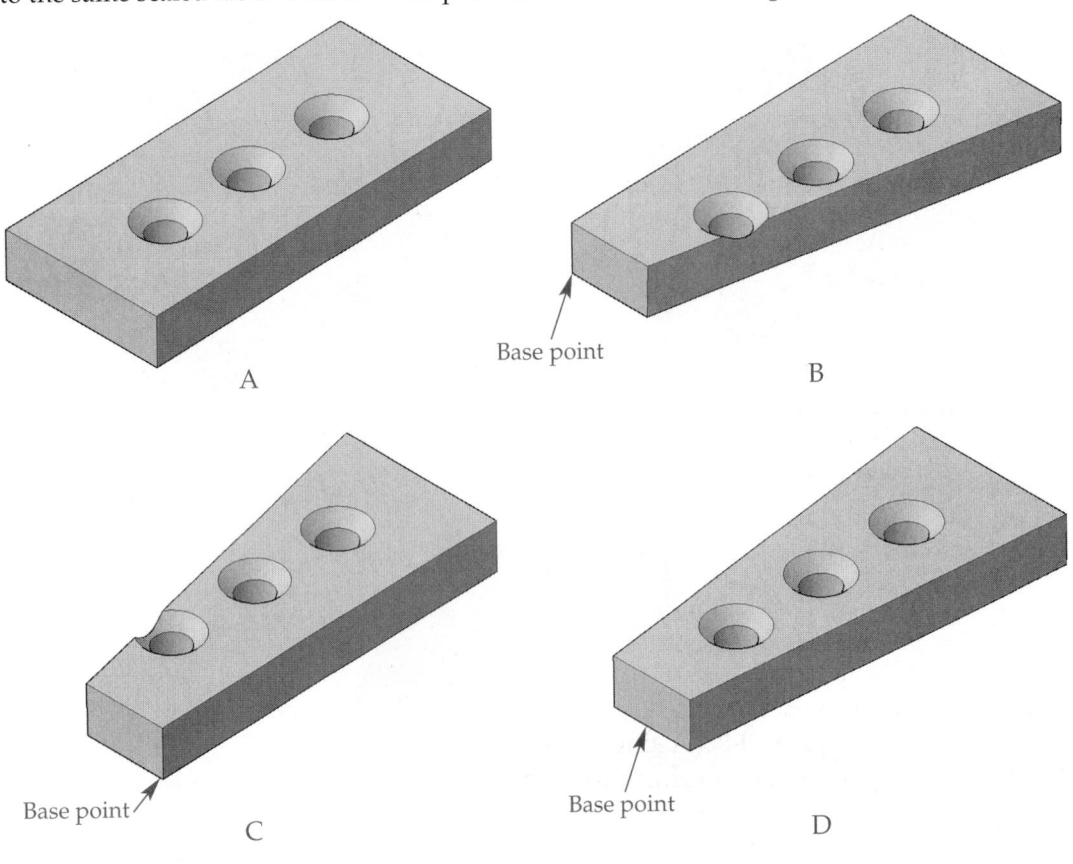

Figure 10-25.
Scaling the front edge with the base point in the middle of the edge. The original object is
shown in Figure 10-24A. A—If the [Ctrl] key is not pressed, the edge is scaled and the shape
and planes of adjacent faces are changed. B—If the [Ctrl] key is pressed twice, the edge
is scaled as are edges attached to it. If the scaling causes faces to become nonplanar, the
adjacent faces may be triangulated.

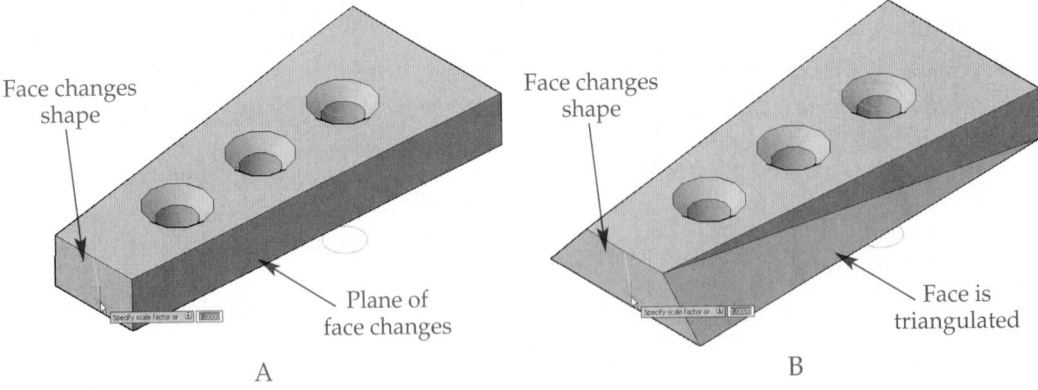

Coloring Edges

To change the color of an edge, use the [Ctrl] key selection method to select the edge. Next, open the **Properties** window. In the palette **General** category, pick the drop-down list for the Color property. Select the desired color, or pick Select Color... and choose a color from the **Select Color** dialog box. Edges cannot have materials assigned to them.

Deleting Edges

Edges can be deleted in certain situations. In order for an edge to be deleted, it must completely divide two faces that lie on the same plane. If this condition is met, the **ERASE** command or the [Delete] key can be used to remove the edge. The two faces become a single face.

Exercise 10-3
Complete the exercise on the Student CD.

Vertex Subobject Editing

The modification of a single vertex involves moving the vertex and stretching all edges and planar faces attached to it. Vertex grips are circular and located on the vertex, as shown in Figure 10-26. A single vertex cannot be rotated or scaled, but you can select multiple vertices and perform rotating and scaling edits. When editing multiple vertices in this manner you are, in effect, editing edges.

As with other subobject editing functions performed on a 3D solid primitive, the solid's history is removed when a vertex is modified. The solid can no longer be edited using the primitive grips; only a single base grip is displayed. Further editing of the solid must be with the **SOLIDEDIT** command, discussed in Chapter 11, or through subobject editing.

Moving Vertices

To move a vertex, select it using the [Ctrl] key method. By default (**GTAUTO** = 1), the move grip tool is displayed. You can use the move grip tool, the **MOVE** command, or standard grip editing modes to move the vertex. If the [Ctrl] key is not pressed while dynamically moving a vertex, adjacent faces are triangulated by the move. Pressing the [Ctrl] key once allows the vertex to be moved without triangulating adjacent faces, but the faces may change shape. In some cases, AutoCAD may deem it necessary to triangulate faces. See Figure 10-27.

Figure 10-26.
Vertex grips are circular and placed on the vertex.

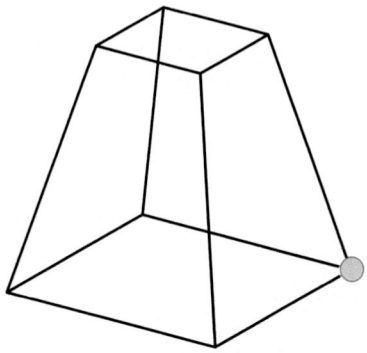

Figure 10-27.
Moving a vertex. A—The original object. B—Without pressing the [Ctrl] key, adjacent faces are triangulated. C—Pressing the [Ctrl] key once moves the vertex and changes some of the adjacent faces.

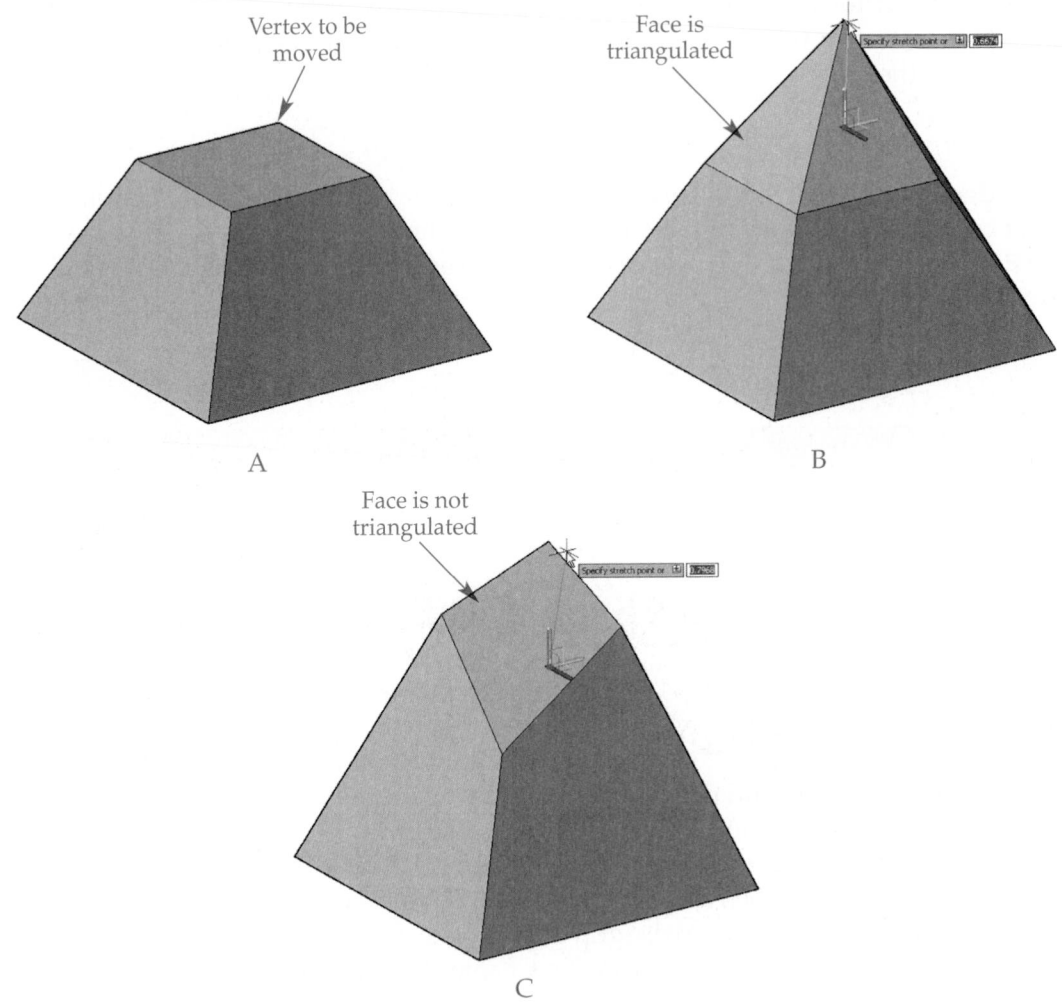

Vertex to be moved

Face is triangulated

A

B

Face is not triangulated

C

PROFESSIONAL TIP

If you are dragging a vertex and faces become triangulated, you can transparently change your viewpoint to see the effect of the triangulation. Press and hold the [Shift] key. At the same time, press and hold the mouse wheel. Now, move the mouse to change the viewpoint. This is a transparent instance of the **3DORBIT** command.

Rotating Vertices

As previously stated, a single vertex cannot be rotated or scaled, but two or more vertices can be. Since two vertices define a line, or edge, any edit is an edge modification. However, the process is slightly different than the edge modifications described earlier in this chapter.

To rotate an edge by selecting its endpoints, press the [Ctrl] key and select each vertex. See Figure 10-28A. You may need to use the [Ctrl]+space bar option to turn on cycling. Notice that grips appear at each selected vertex, but the edges between the vertices are not highlighted.

Figure 10-28.
To rotate or scale vertices, multiple vertices must be selected. In effect, the edges are modified. A—Vertices are selected to be rotated. B—The rotate grip tool is placed at the base of rotation and the rotation axis is selected. C—The vertices are rotated.

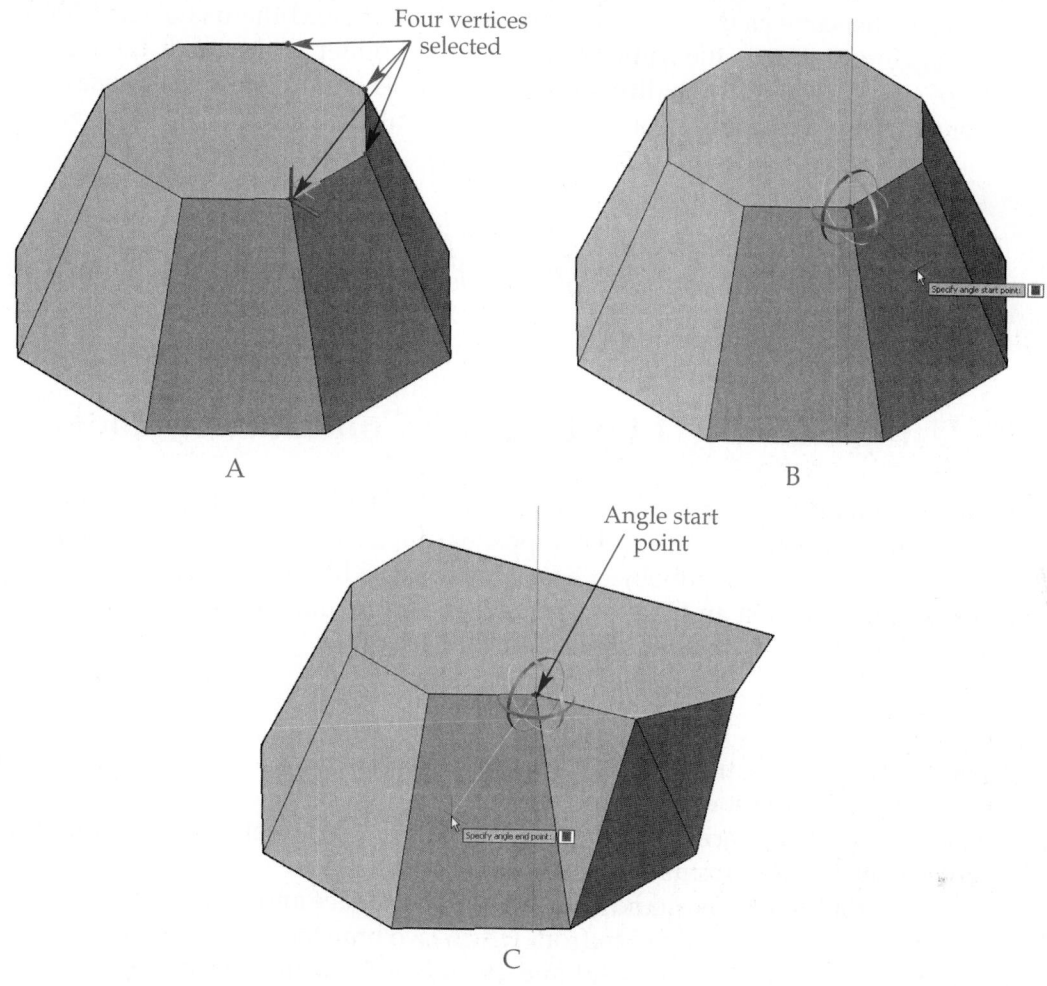

The **ROTATE** command can now be used to rotate the vertices (if **PICKFIRST** is set to 1). However, a more efficient method for rotating vertices is to use the **3DROTATE** command. The combination of the rotate grip tool and the UCS icon enable you to graphically view the rotation plane. Once the command is initiated, pick a location for the rotate grip tool, which is the base of rotation. See **Figure 10-28B**. Then, select the axis of revolution. Finally, pick the angle start point and enter the rotation. See **Figure 10-28C**.

If the [Ctrl] key is not pressed while dynamically rotating the vertices, the area of the selected vertices does not change and adjacent faces are triangulated. This is because the edges of the adjacent faces are attached to the selected vertices, so their edge length changes as the selected edge is rotated. If the [Ctrl] key is pressed once, the adjacent faces are not triangulated unless necessary, but the faces may change shape.

NOTE

If the selected edge does not dynamically rotate at the "angle end point" prompt, then the desired rotation is not possible.

Scaling Vertices

As mentioned earlier, it is not possible to scale a single vertex. However, two or more vertices can be selected for scaling. This, in effect, scales edges. The selection methods are the same as discussed for rotating vertices, and the use of the [Ctrl] key while dragging produces the same effects. As the pointer is dragged, the dynamic display of scaled edges may be difficult to visualize. Therefore, it is best to use a scale factor or the **Reference** option to achieve properly scaled edges.

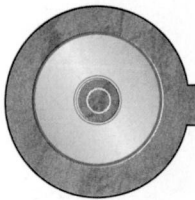

Exercise 10-4
Complete the exercise on the Student CD.

Using Subobject Editing as a Construction Tool

This section provides an example of how subobject editing can be used to not only make changes to existing solids and composites, but as a powerful construction tool. Some of the procedures of subobject editing, such as editing faces, edges, and vertices, are used to construct an HVAC assembly. The entire model is constructed from a single, solid cube. This is the only primitive you will draw.

Editing Faces

1. Begin by setting the units to Architectural and drawing a 24″ × 24″ cube. Display the model from the southeast isometric viewpoint.
2. Select the left-hand face and move it 60″ to the left. Also, select the front face and move it out 12″. This forms the first duct. See Figure 10-29.
3. Using the **EXTRUDE** command, select the left-hand face and extrude it 36″ to create a new solid. This is a T junction from which two branches will extend.
4. Select the front face of new solid and extrude it 28″ with a taper angle of 10° to create a new solid that is a reducer.

Figure 10-29.
The left-hand face of the cube is moved 60″. The front face is then moved 12″.

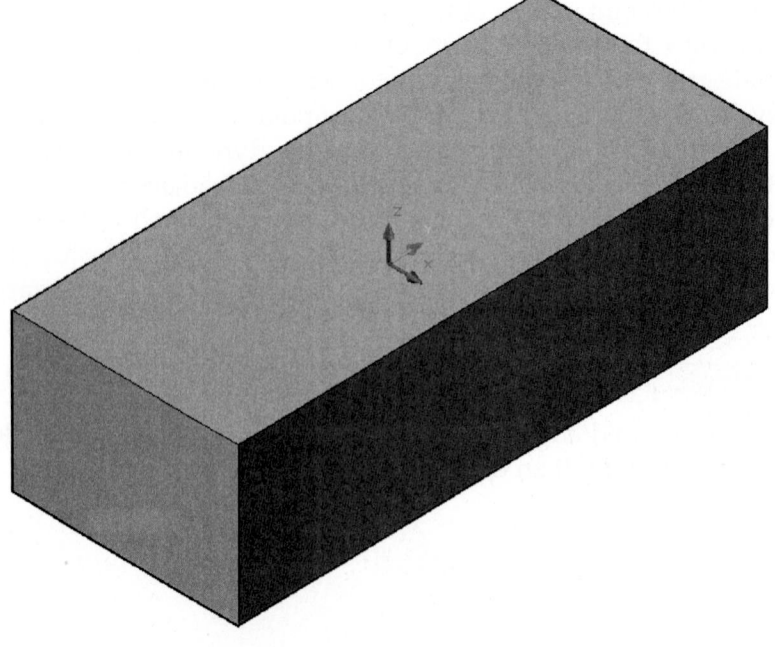

Figure 10-30.
Two reducers are created by extruding faces from the T junction.

5. Select the left-hand face of the T junction and extrude it 20″ with a taper angle of 10° to create a new solid that is a second reducer. See **Figure 10-30**.
6. Select the left-hand face of the 20″ reducer and move it 3 17/32″ along the positive Z axis. This places the top surface of the reducer level with the trunk of the duct. Next, extrude the left-hand face of this reducer 60″ into a new solid.
7. Use the **REVOLVE** command to turn the left-hand face of the 60″ extension into a new solid that is a 90° bend. Your drawing should now look like **Figure 10-31**.

Editing Edges and Vertices

1. The bottom surface of the 28″ reducer must be level with the bottom of the T junction and main trunk. Select the bottom edge of the reducer's front face and move it down 4 15/16″.
2. Select the two top vertices on the 28″ reducer's front face and move them down (negative Z) 6″.
3. Select the front, rectangular face of the 90° bend and extrude it 72″ into a new solid.

Figure 10-31.
The left end of the 60″ extrusion is revolved 90° to create an elbow.

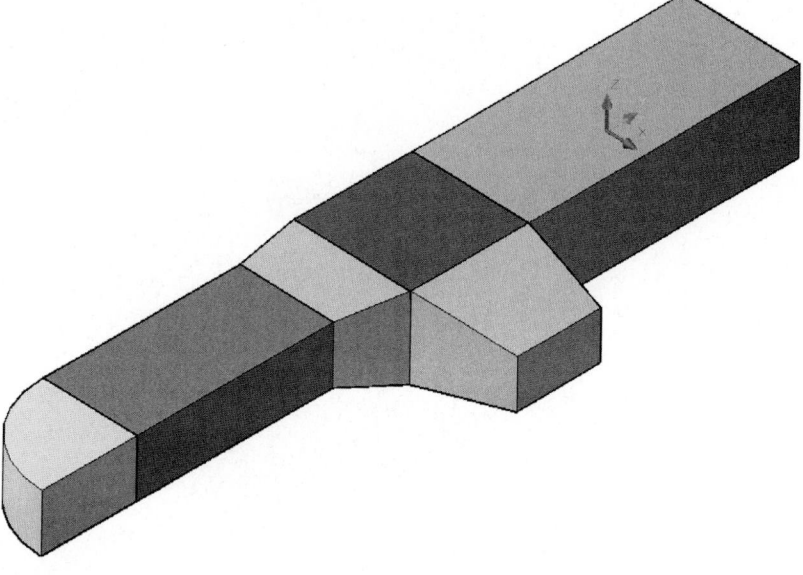

4. Select the front face of the 28″ reducer and extrude it 108″ into a new solid.
5. Select the front face of the new solid created in Step 4 and extrude it 26″ to create a new solid that will be a T junction.
6. Extrude the left-hand face of the T junction 20″. See Figure 10-32.
7. Move the top edge of the 20″ extrusion created in Step 6 down 4″.
8. Move each vertical edge of the 20″ extrusion 6″ toward the center of the duct.
9. Mirror a copy of the 20″ extrusion to the opposite side of the T junction. The completed drawing should look like Figure 10-33.

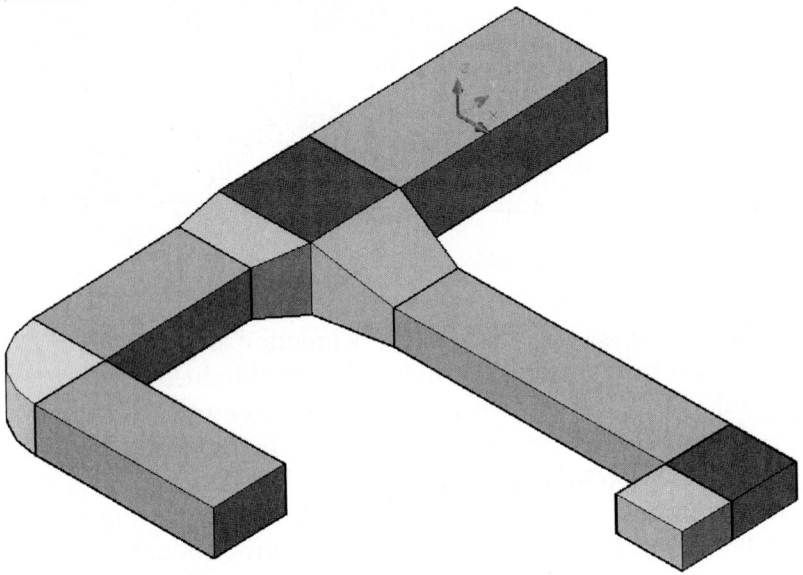

Figure 10-32.
The face of the revolved elbow is extruded 72″. The face of the right branch is extruded 108″. The right duct is then extruded 26″, and the left face of that extrusion is extruded by 20″.

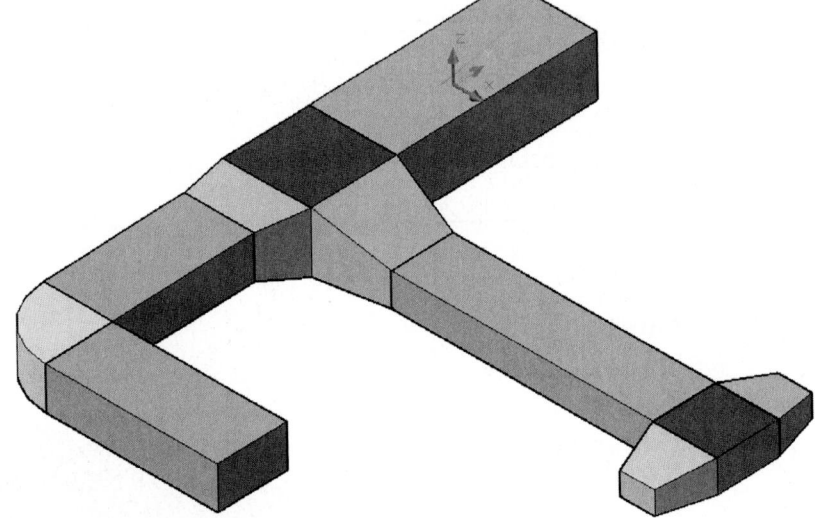

Figure 10-33.
The reducer is mirrored to create the final assembly.

Other Solid Editing Tools

There are other tools that can be used in solid model editing. As you will learn in Chapter 11, the **SOLIDEDIT** tool can be used to edit faces, edges, and vertices much like subobject editing. In addition, you can extrude a closed boundary with the **PRESSPULL** command, extract a wireframe from a solid using the **XEDGES** command, and explode a solid. The **PRESSPULL** and **XEDGES** commands and exploding a solid are discussed in the next sections.

Presspull

The **PRESSPULL** command allows any closed boundary to be extruded. The boundary can be a flat surface, a closed polyline, a circle, or a region. The extrusion is always applied perpendicular to the plane of the boundary, but can be in the positive or negative direction. When applied to the face of a solid, it is very similar to the **Extrude Face** option of the **SOLIDEDIT** command, though dynamic feedback is provided for the extrusion with **PRESSPULL**.

Once the command is initiated, you are prompted to pick inside of the bounded areas to extrude. Move the pointer inside of a boundary and pick. Then, drag the boundary to a new location and pick or, if dynamic input is on, enter the distance to extrude the face. See Figure 10-34.

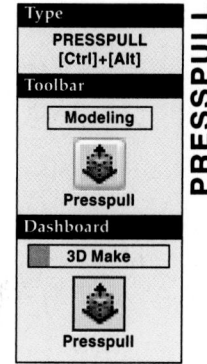

| Type |
| PRESSPULL |
| [Ctrl]+[Alt] |
| Toolbar |
| Modeling |
| Presspull |
| Dashboard |
| 3D Make |
| Presspull |

PRESSPULL

NOTE

The entire boundary must be visible on the screen, or the loop will not be found.

Extracting a Wireframe

The **XEDGES** command creates copies of, or extracts, all of the edges on a selected solid. Once the command is initiated, you are prompted to select objects. Select one or more solids and press [Enter]. The edges are extracted and placed on top of the existing edges. See Figure 10-35. The new objects are created on the current layer.

Straight edges and the curved edges where cylindrical surfaces intersect with flat or other cylindrical surfaces are the only edges extracted. Spheres and tori have no edges that can be extracted. The round bases of cylinders and cones are the only edges of those objects that will be extracted.

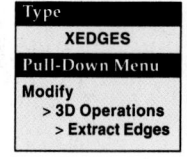

| Type |
| XEDGES |
| Pull-Down Menu |
| Modify |
| > 3D Operations |
| > Extract Edges |

XEDGES

Figure 10-34.
Using the **PRESSPULL** command. A—Pick inside of a boundary (shown in color) and drag the boundary to a new location. B—The completed operation.

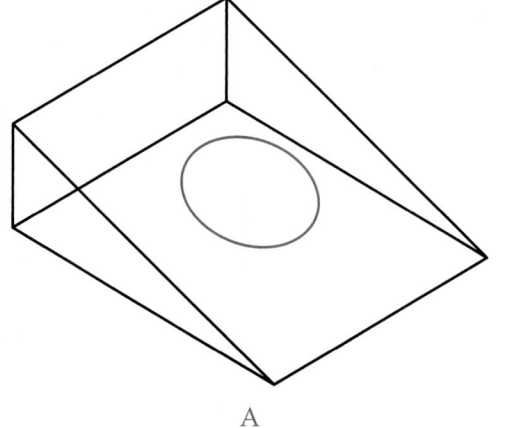

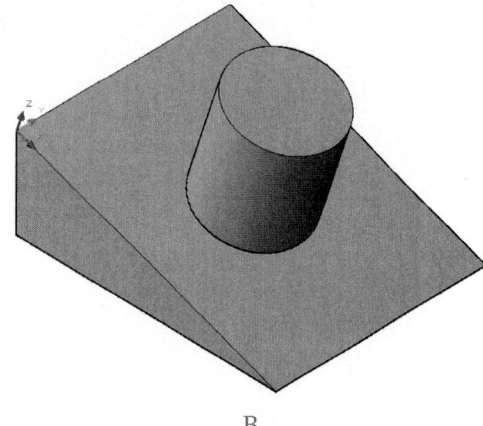

A

B

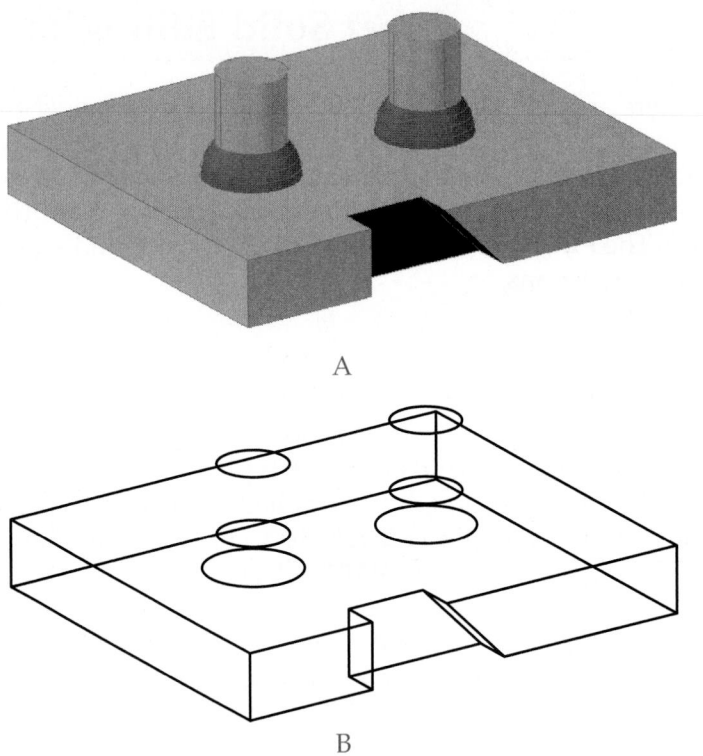

Figure 10-35.
Extracting edges with the **XEDGES** command.
A—The original object.
B—The extracted wireframe (edges).

A

B

Exploding a Solid

A solid can be exploded. This turns the solid into surfaces and/or regions. Flat surfaces on the solid are turned into regions. Curved surfaces on the solid are turned into surfaces. To explode a solid, select the **EXPLODE** command. Then, pick the solid(s) to explode and press [Enter].

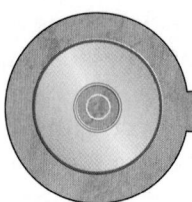

Exercise 10-5
Complete the exercise on the Student CD.

Chapter Test

Answer the following questions. Write your answers on a separate sheet of paper or complete the electronic chapter test on the Student CD.

1. How is a subobject selected?
2. How is a subobject deselected?
3. When moving a face on a solid primitive, how can you accurately control the axis of movement?
4. How can you change the results of moving a face while dragging it?
5. Describe a major difference of function between the **ROTATE** and **3DROTATE** commands.
6. Which variable enables you to use the **3DROTATE** command in a 3D view even if you select the **ROTATE** command?
7. How does the location and shape of an edge grip differ from a face grip?
8. What is the most efficient tool to use when rotating an edge, and how is it displayed?
9. What is the only type of edge that can be scaled?
10. What is the only editing function that can be done to a single vertex?
11. How are two or more vertices selected for editing?
12. What is the function of the **PRESSPULL** command?
13. On which objects can the **PRESSPULL** command be used?
14. What is the purpose of the **XEDGES** command?
15. When a solid object is exploded, which type of object is created?

Drawing Problems

1. Draw the bookcase shown below using the dimensions given. The final result should be a single solid object. Then, use grip and subobject editing procedures to edit the object as follows.
   A. Change the width of the bookcase to 3′.
   B. Change the height of the bookcase by eliminating the top section. The resulting height should be 3′-2″.
   C. Save the drawing as P10_01.

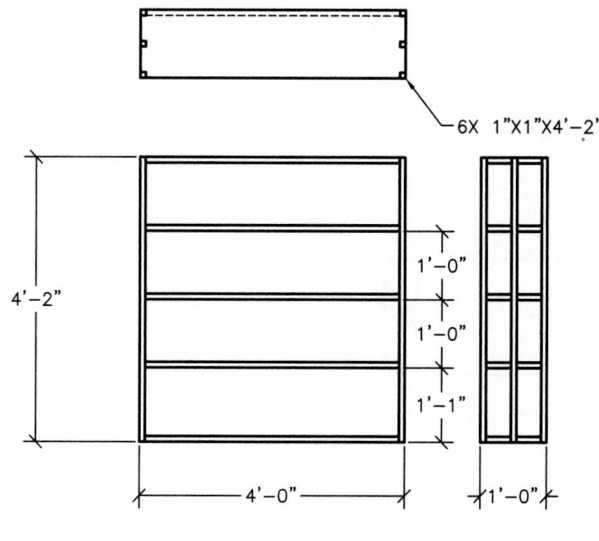

ALL WOOD THICKNESS IS 1″

2. Open problem P10_01. Save it as P10_02. Use primitive and subobject editing procedures to create the following edit.
   A. Change the depth of the top of the bookcase to 6-1/2".
   B. Change the depth of the bottom of the bookcase to 24".
   C. Reduce the height of the front uprights so they are flush with the top surface of the next lower shelf.
   D. Extend the front of the second lowest shelf to match the front of the bottom. Add two uprights at the front corners between the bottom and this shelf.
   E. Save the drawing.

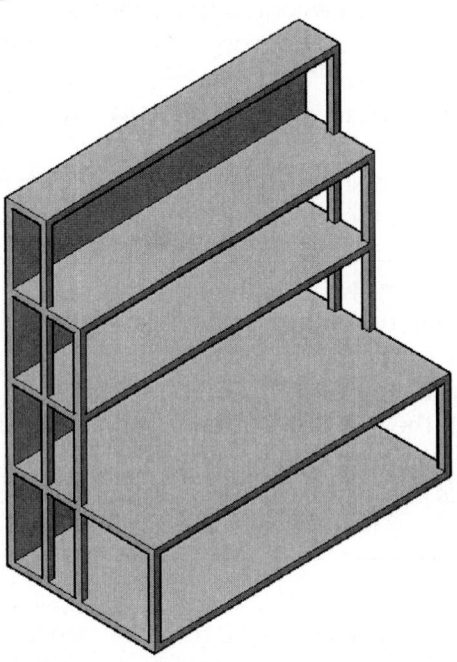

3. Draw the mounting bracket shown below. Then, use primitive and subobject editing procedures to create the following edit.

   A. Change the 3.00" dimension to 3.50".
   B. Change the 2.50" dimension in the front view to 2.75".
   C. Change the location of the slot in the auxiliary view from .60" to .70", and change the length of the slot to 1.15".
   D. Change the width of each foot in the top view from 2.00" to 1.50". The overall dimension (5.00") should not change.
   E. Change the angle of the bend from 15° to 45°.
   F. Save the drawing as P10_03.

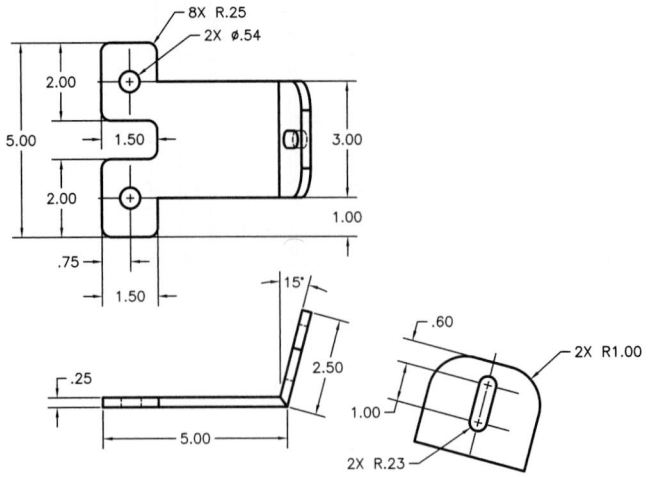

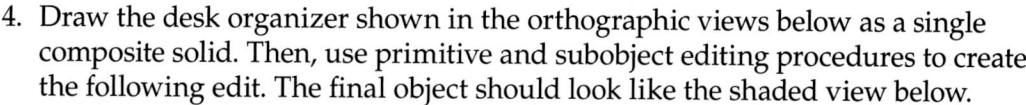

4. Draw the desk organizer shown in the orthographic views below as a single composite solid. Then, use primitive and subobject editing procedures to create the following edit. The final object should look like the shaded view below.
   A. Change the 3″ height to 3.25″.
   B. Change the 2″ height to 1.85″.
   C. Increase the thickness of the long compartment divider to .5″. The increase in thickness should be applied evenly along the centerline of the divider. Locate three evenly spaced, ∅5/16″ × 1.5″ holes in this divider.
   D. Angle the top face of the rear compartments by 30°. The height of the rear of the organizer should be approximately 4. 5″ and all corners on the bottom of the organizer should remain square.
   E. Save the drawing as P10_04.

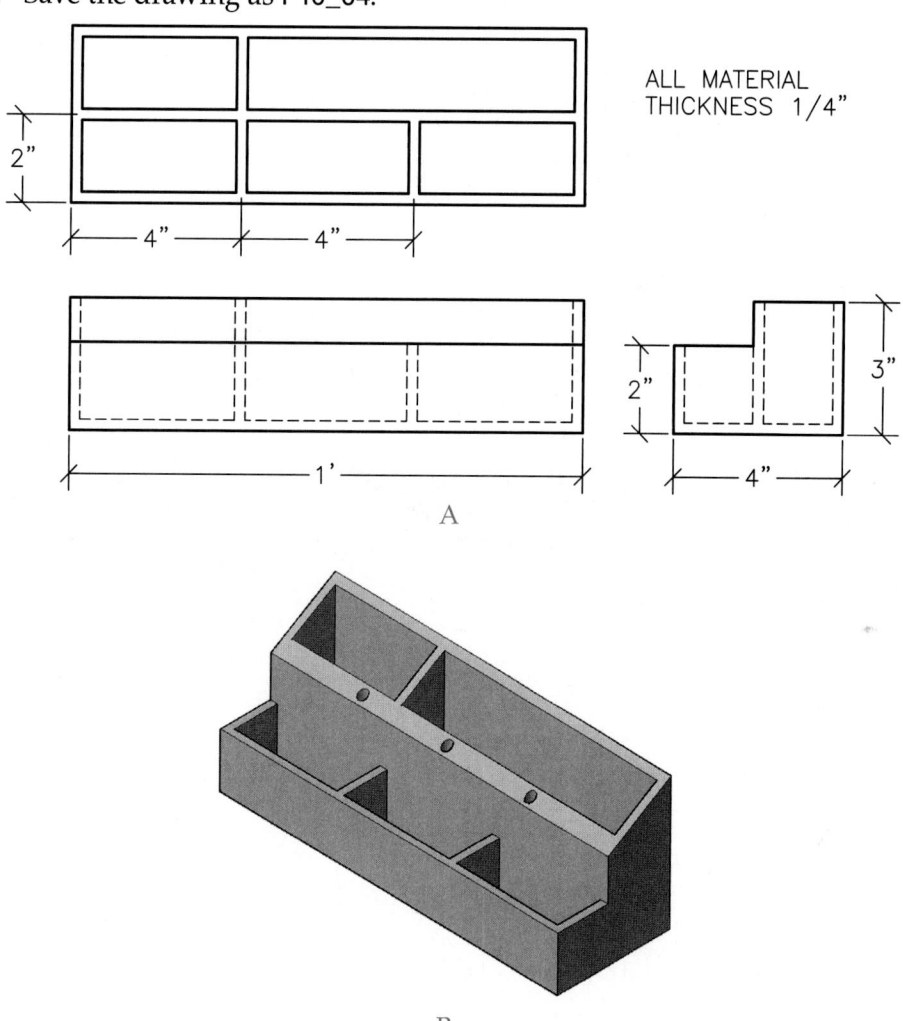

A

B

5. Draw the pencil holder shown below. Then, use primitive and subobject editing procedures to create the following edit.
   A. Change the depth of the base to 4.000". The base should be rectangular, not square, and the grooves should become shorter.
   B. Change the height of the top groove from .250" to .125".
   C. Change the diameter of two holes from ∅.450" to ∅.625".
   D. Change the diameter of the other two holes from ∅.450" to ∅1.000".
   E. Rotate the top face 15° away from the side with the grooves. The planes of the adjoining faces should not change. Refer to the shaded view shown below.
   F. Save the drawing as P10_05.

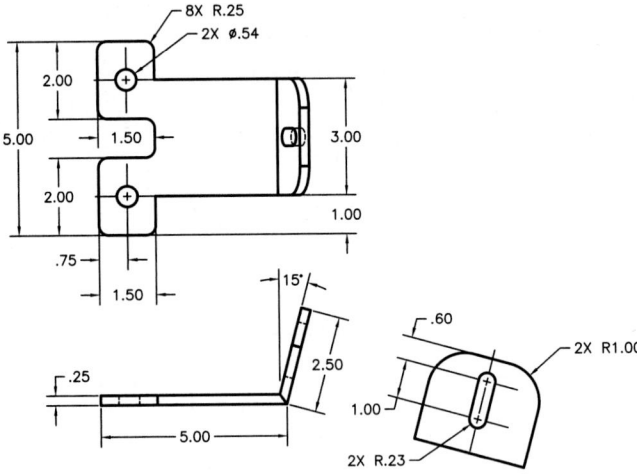

AutoCAD and Its Applications—Advanced

Solid Model Editing

Learning Objectives

After completing this chapter, you will be able to:
- ✓ Change the shape and configuration of solid object faces.
- ✓ Copy and change the color of solid object edges and faces.
- ✓ Break apart a composite solid composed of physically separate entities.
- ✓ Use the **SOLIDEDIT** command to construct and edit a solid model.

AutoCAD provides expanded capabilities for editing solid models. As you saw in the previous chapter, grips can be used to edit a solid model. Also, the subobjects that make up a solid, such as faces, edges, and endpoints, can be edited. Additionally, a single command, **SOLIDEDIT**, enables you to edit faces, edges, or the entire body of the solid.

Overview of the SOLIDEDIT Command

The **SOLIDEDIT** command allows you to edit the faces, edges, and body of a solid. Many of the subobject editing functions can also be performed with the **SOLIDEDIT** command. The features of the **SOLIDEDIT** command can be accessed in the **Modify** pull-down menu, on the **Solid Editing** toolbar, or by typing SOLIDEDIT. See **Figure 11-1**.

When the **SOLIDEDIT** command is typed, you are first asked to select the component of the solid with which you wish to work. Specify either **Face**, **Edge**, or **Body**. The editing options for the selected component are then displayed. The editing function is directly entered when the option is selected from the pull-down menu or toolbar.

The following sections provide an overview of the solid model editing features of the **SOLIDEDIT** command. Each option is explained and the results of each are shown. A tutorial later in the chapter illustrates how these options can be used to construct a model.

Figure 11-1.
Accessing the **SOLIDEDIT** command options.

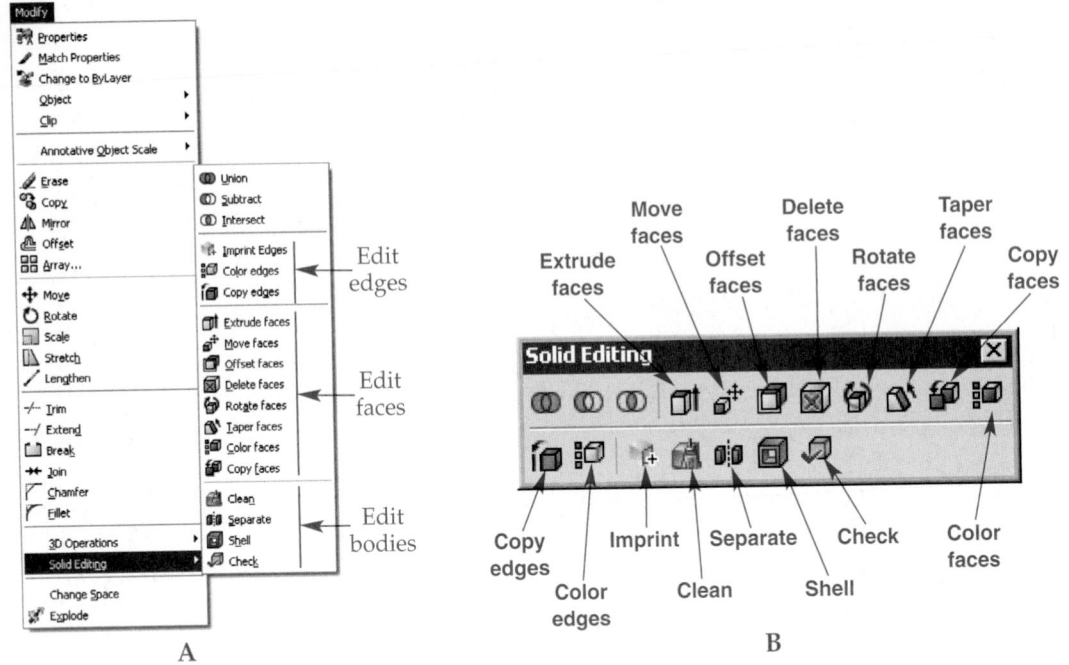

A

B

Face Editing

The basic components of a solid are its faces and the greatest number of **SOLIDEDIT** options are for editing faces. All eight face editing options ask you to select faces. It is important to make sure you select the correct part of the model for editing. Remember the following three steps when using any of the face editing options.

1. First, select a face to edit. If you pick an edge, AutoCAD selects the two faces that share the edge. If this happens, use the **Remove** option to deselect the unwanted face. A more intuitive approach is to select the open space of the face as if you were touching the side of a part. AutoCAD highlights only that face.
2. Adjust the selection set at the Select faces or [Undo/Remove/ALL]: prompt. The following options are available.
   - **Undo.** Removes the previous selected face(s) from the selection set.
   - **Remove.** Allows you to select faces to remove from the selection set.
   - **ALL.** Adds all faces on the model to the selection set. This is only available after selecting at least one face. It can also be used to remove all faces if **Remove** is current.

- **Add.** Allows you to add faces to the selection set. This is only available when **Remove** is current.
3. Press [Enter] to continue with face editing.

Extruding Faces

An extruded face is moved, or stretched, in a selected direction. The extrusion can be straight or have a taper. To extrude a face, select the command and pick the **Face>Extrude** option. You are then prompted to select the face(s) to extrude. Nonplanar (curved) faces cannot be extruded. As you pick faces, the prompt verifies the number of faces selected. For example, when an edge is selected, the prompt reads 2 faces found. When done selecting faces, press [Enter] to continue.

Next, the height of the extrusion needs to be specified. A positive value adds material to the solid, while a negative value subtracts material from the solid. A taper can also be given.

> Specify height of extrusion or [Path]: *(enter height)*
> Specify angle of taper for extrusion <0>: *(enter an angle or accept the default)*
> Solid validation started.
> Solid validation completed.
> Enter a face editing option
> [Extrude/Move/Rotate/Offset/Taper/Delete/Copy/coLor/mAterial/Undo/eXit] <eXit>: **X**↵
> Solids editing automatic checking: SOLIDCHECK=1
> Enter a solids editing option [Face/Edge/Body/Undo/eXit] <eXit>: **X**↵

Figure 11-2 shows an original solid object and the result of extruding the top face with a 0° taper angle and a 30° taper angle. It also shows the original solid object with two adjacent faces extruded with 15° taper angles.

Figure 11-2.
Extruding faces on an object. A—The original object. B—The top face is extruded with a 0° taper angle. C—The top face of the original extruded with a 30° taper angle. D—The top and right-hand faces of the original are extruded with 15° taper angles.

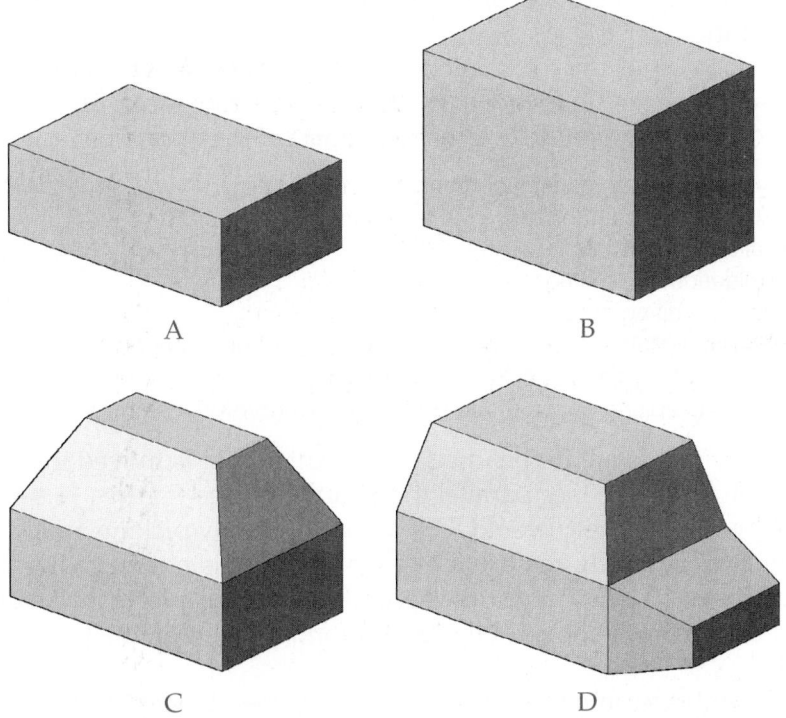

A   B

C   D

Figure 11-3.
The path of extrusion can be a line, circle, arc, ellipse, elliptical arc, polyline, or spline. Here, the paths are shown in color.

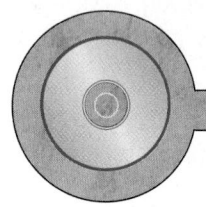

In addition to extruding a surface perpendicular to itself, the extruded face can follow a path. Select the **Path** option at the Specify height of extrusion or [Path]: prompt. The path of extrusion can be a line, circle, arc, ellipse, elliptical arc, polyline, or spline. The extrusion height is the exact length of the path. See **Figure 11-3.**

Exercise 11-1
Complete the exercise on the Student CD.

Moving Faces

The **Move Faces** option moves a face in the specified direction and lengthens or shortens the solid object. A solid model feature (such as a hole) that has been subtracted from an object to create a composite solid can be moved with this option. Object snaps may interfere with the operation of this option, so they may need to be toggled off during the operation.

To move a face, select the command and pick the **Face>Move** option. You are then prompted to select the face(s) to move. When done selecting faces, press [Enter] to continue. Next, you are prompted to select a base point of the operation:

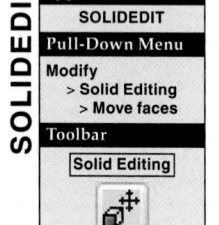

SOLIDEDIT

| Type |
| SOLIDEDIT |
| Pull-Down Menu |
| Modify |
| > Solid Editing |
| > Move faces |
| Toolbar |
| Solid Editing |
| Move faces |

Specify a base point or displacement: *(pick a base point)*
Specify a second point of displacement: *(pick a second point or enter coordinates)*
Solid validation started.
Solid validation completed.
Enter a face editing option
[Extrude/Move/Rotate/Offset/Taper/Delete/Copy/coLor/mAterial/Undo/eXit] <eXit>: **X**↵
Solids editing automatic checking: SOLIDCHECK=1
Enter a solids editing option [Face/Edge/Body/Undo/eXit] <eXit>: **X**↵

When adjacent faces are perpendicular, the edited face is moved in a direction so the new position keeps the face parallel to the original. See **Figures 11-4A** and **11-4B.** Faces that are normal to the current UCS can be moved by picking a new location or entering a direct distance. If you are moving a face that is not normal to the current UCS, you can enter coordinates for the second point of displacement, but it may be easier to first use the **Face** option of the **UCS** command to align the UCS with the face to be moved.

When adjacent faces join at angles other than perpendicular (90°), the moved face will be relocated as stated above, but only if the movement is less than the dimensional

AutoCAD and Its Applications—Advanced

Figure 11-4.
A—The hole will be moved using the **Move** option of the **SOLIDEDIT** command. B—The hole is moved. C—When the angled face is moved, a portion of it is altered to be coplanar with the vertical face. D—If the angled face is moved more, it becomes completely coplanar to the vertical face. This is a new, single face.

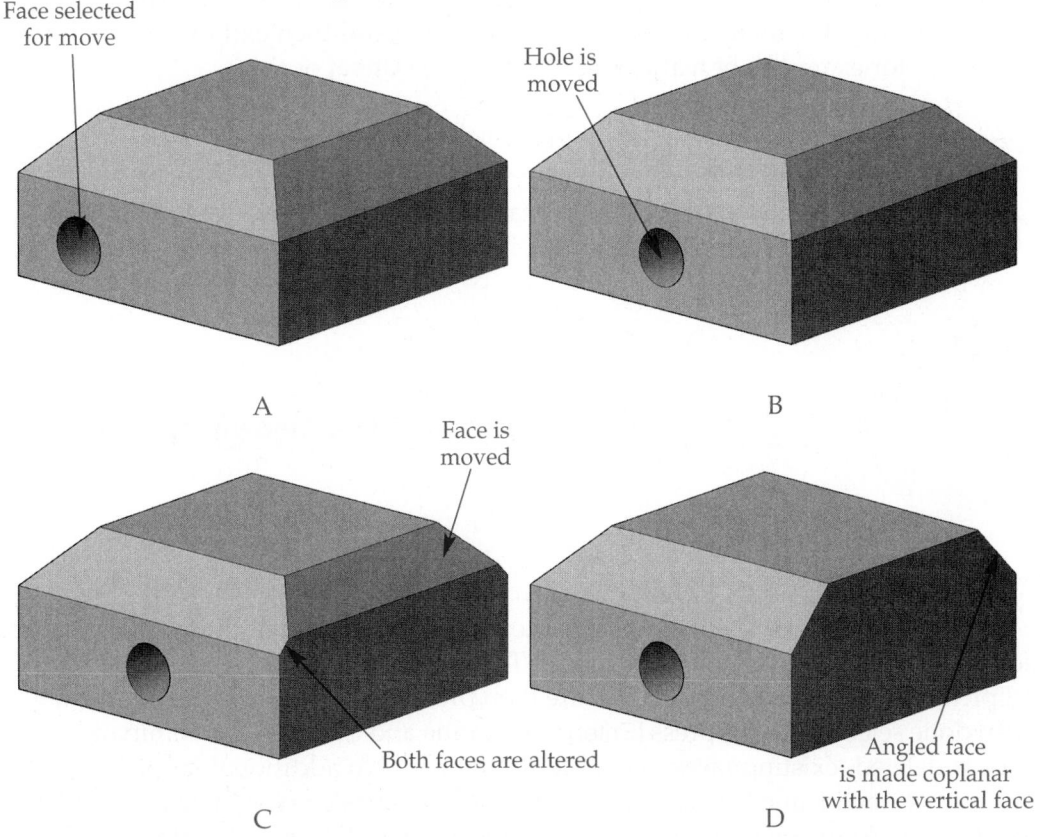

Face selected for move

Hole is moved

A

B

Face is moved

Both faces are altered

Angled face is made coplanar with the vertical face

C

D

offset of the two faces. For example, in **Figure 11-4B** the top edge of the angled face is in .5″ from the vertical face. If the angled face is moved outward a distance of less than .5″, it is altered as shown in **Figure 11-4C.** A portion of the angled face becomes coplanar with the vertical face. If the angled face is moved outward a distance greater than .5″, it is altered so that it forms a single plane with the adjacent face. What has actually happened is that the angled face is moved beyond the adjacent face, while remaining parallel to its original position. Thus, in effect, it has disappeared because the adjacent, vertical face cannot be altered. See **Figure 11-4D.** In this example, the angled face was moved .75″ using relative coordinates. The new vertical face that is created can now be moved.

Exercise 11-2

Complete the exercise on the Student CD.

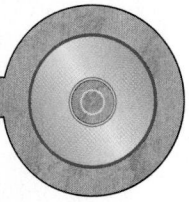

Offsetting Faces

The **Offset** option may seem the same as the **Extrude** option because it moves faces by a specified distance or through a specified point. Unlike the **OFFSET** command in AutoCAD, this option moves all selected faces a specified distance. It is most useful when you wish to change the size of features such as slots, holes, grooves, and notches in solid parts. A positive offset distance increases the size or volume of the solid (adds material), a negative distance decreases the size or volume of the solid (removes material). Therefore, if you wish to make the width of a slot wider, provide a negative offset distance to decrease the size of the solid. Direct distance entry for the offset distance is always taken as a positive value, so negative values must be entered using the keyboard.

To offset a face, select the command and pick the **Face>Offset** option. You are then prompted to select the face(s) to offset. When done selecting faces, press [Enter] to continue. Next, enter the offset distance and press [Enter] and then exit the command. See **Figure 11-5** for examples of features edited with the **Offset** option.

SOLIDEDIT

Type
SOLIDEDIT
Pull-Down Menu
Modify
> Solid Editing
> Offset faces
Toolbar
Solid Editing

Offset faces

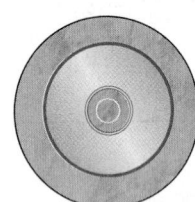

PROFESSIONAL TIP

Nonplanar (curved) faces cannot be extruded, but can be offset. Using the **Offset** option, you can, in effect, "extrude" a nonplanar face.

Exercise 11-3
Complete the exercise on the Student CD.

Deleting Faces

SOLIDEDIT

Type
SOLIDEDIT
Pull-Down Menu
Modify
> Solid Editing
> Delete faces
Toolbar
Solid Editing
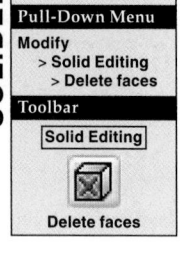
Delete faces

The **Delete** option deletes selected faces. This is a quick way to remove features such as chamfers, fillets, holes, and slots. To delete a solid face, select the command and pick the **Face>Delete** option. You are then prompted to select the face(s) to delete. When done selecting faces, press [Enter] to continue and then exit the command. When a face is deleted, existing faces extend to fill the gap. No additional faces are created. For instance, the inclined surface of a wedge cannot be deleted as there are no existing faces that can be extended to fill the gap. When the face that is a chamfered or filleted edge is deleted, the adjacent edges are extended to fill the gap. See **Figure 11-6**.

Figure 11-5.
Offsetting faces. A—The original objects. The hole is selected to offset. The interior of the L is also selected to offset. B—A positive offset distance increases the size or volume of the solid. C—A negative offset distance decreases the size or volume of the solid.

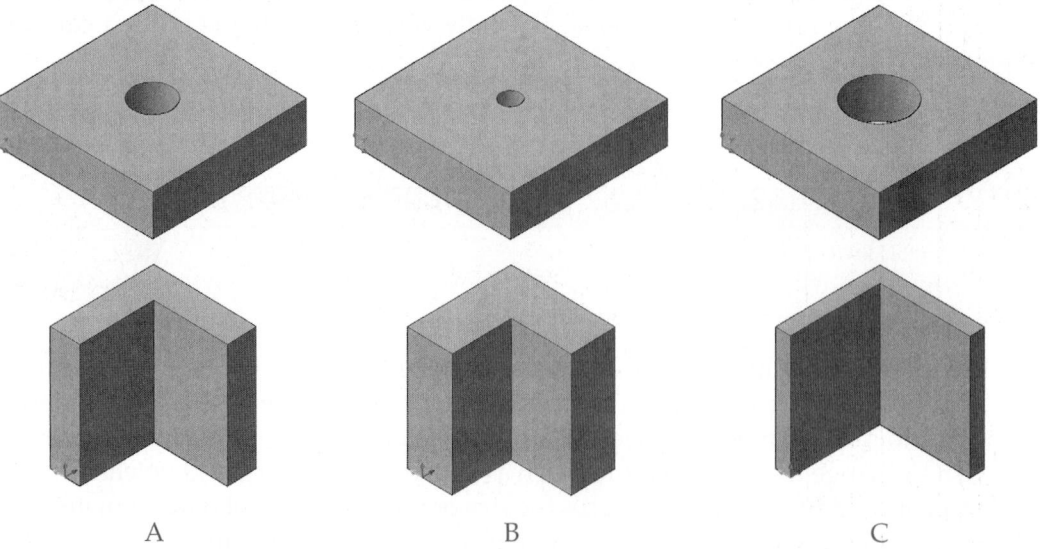

A   B   C

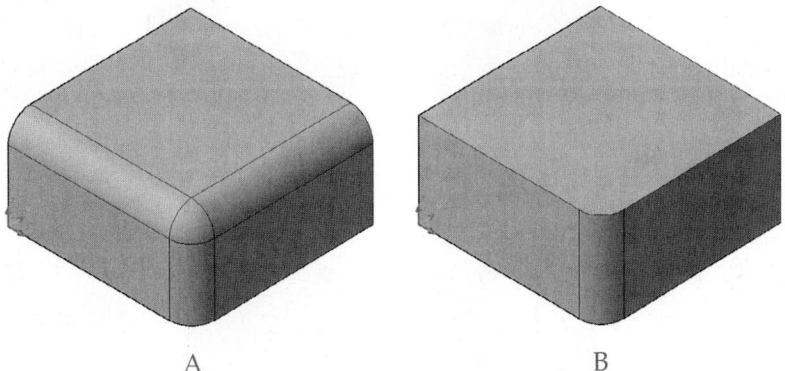

A   B

Rotating Faces

The **Rotate** option rotates a face about a selected axis. To rotate a solid face, select the command and pick the **Face>Rotate** option. You are then prompted to select the face(s) to rotate. When done selecting faces, press [Enter] to continue. There are several methods by which a face can be rotated.

The **2points** option is the default. Pick two points to define the "hinge" about which the face will rotate. Then, provide the rotation angle and exit the command.

The **Axis by object** option allows you to use an existing object to define the axis of rotation. You can select the following objects. After selecting an object, enter the angle of rotation and exit the command.

- **Line.** The selected line becomes the axis of rotation.
- **Circle, arc, or ellipse.** The Z axis of the object becomes the axis of rotation. This Z axis is a line that passes through the center of the circle, arc, or ellipse and is perpendicular to the plane on which the 2D object lies.
- **Polyline or spline.** A line connecting the polyline or spline's start point and endpoint becomes the axis of rotation.

When you select the **View** option, the axis of rotation is perpendicular to the current view, with the positive direction coming out of the screen. This axis is identical to the Z axis when the **UCS** command **View** option is used. Next, enter the angle of rotation and exit the command.

The **Xaxis**, **Yaxis**, and **Zaxis** options prompt you to select a point. Either the X, Y, or Z axis that passes through that point is used as the axis of rotation. Then, enter the angle of rotation and exit the command.

Figure 11-7 provides several examples of rotated faces. Notice how the first and second pick points determine the direction of positive and negative rotation angles.

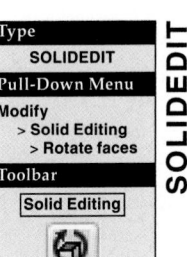

Type
SOLIDEDIT
Pull-Down Menu
Modify
> Solid Editing
> Rotate faces
Toolbar
Solid Editing
Rotate faces

SOLIDEDIT

NOTE

A positive rotation angle moves the face in a clockwise direction looking from the first pick point to the second. Conversely, a negative angle rotates the face counterclockwise. If the rotated face will intersect or otherwise interfere with other faces, an error message indicates that the operation failed or that no solution was calculated. In this case, you may wish to try a negative angle if you previously entered a positive one. In addition, you can try selecting the opposite edge of the face as the axis of rotation.

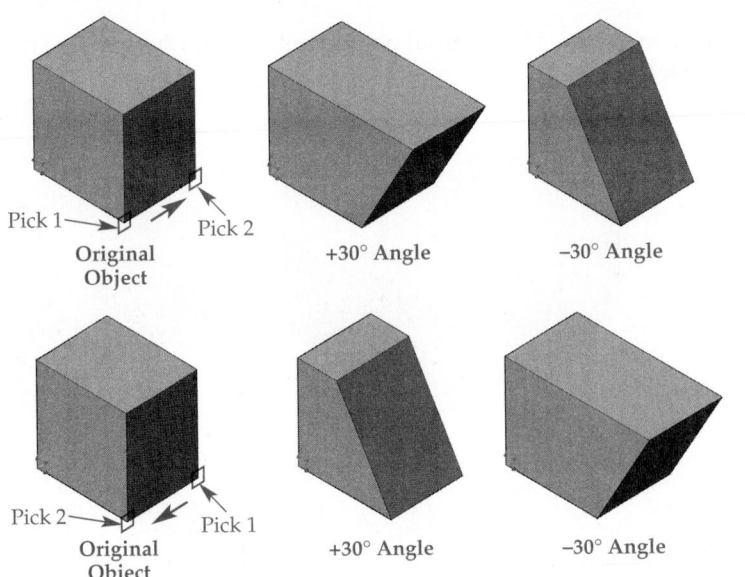

Figure 11-7.
When rotating faces, the first and second pick points determine the direction of positive and negative rotation angles.

Pick 1 — Pick 2
Original Object   +30° Angle   −30° Angle

Pick 2 — Pick 1
Original Object   +30° Angle   −30° Angle

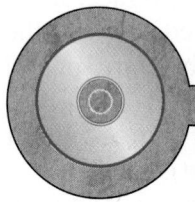

Exercise 11-4
Complete the exercise on the Student CD.

Tapering Faces

Type
SOLIDEDIT
Pull-Down Menu
Modify
> Solid Editing
> Taper faces
Toolbar
Solid Editing

Taper faces

The **Taper** option tapers a face at the specified angle, from the first pick point to the second. To taper a solid face, select the command and pick the **Face**>**Taper** option. You are then prompted to select the face(s) to taper. When done selecting faces, press [Enter] to continue:

Specify the base point: (*pick the base point*)
Specify another point along the axis of tapering: (*pick a point along the taper axis*)
Specify the taper angle: (*enter a taper value*)

Tapers work differently depending on whether the faces being tapered describe the outer boundaries of the solid, a cavity, or a removed portion of the solid. A positive taper angle always removes material. A negative taper angle always adds material. For example, if a positive taper angle is entered for a solid cylinder, the selected object is tapered in on itself from the base point along the axis of tapering, thus removing material. A negative angle tapers the object out away from itself to increase its size along the axis of tapering, thus adding material. See Figure 11-8.

On the other hand, if the faces of a feature such as a slot or hole are tapered, a positive taper angle increases the size of the feature along the axis of tapering. For example, if a round hole is tapered using a positive taper angle, its diameter increases from the base point along the axis of tapering, thus removing material from the solid. Conversely, if the same round hole is tapered using a negative taper angle, its diameter decreases from the base point along the axis of tapering, thus adding material to the solid. Figure 11-9 shows some examples of this function.

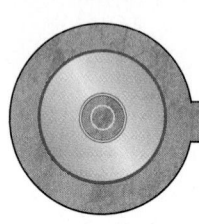

Exercise 11-5
Complete the exercise on the Student CD.

Figure 11-8.
Tapering faces.
A—The original
objects. The dark face
of the box and the
circumference of the
cylinder are selected.
B—Positive taper
angle. C—Negative
taper angle.

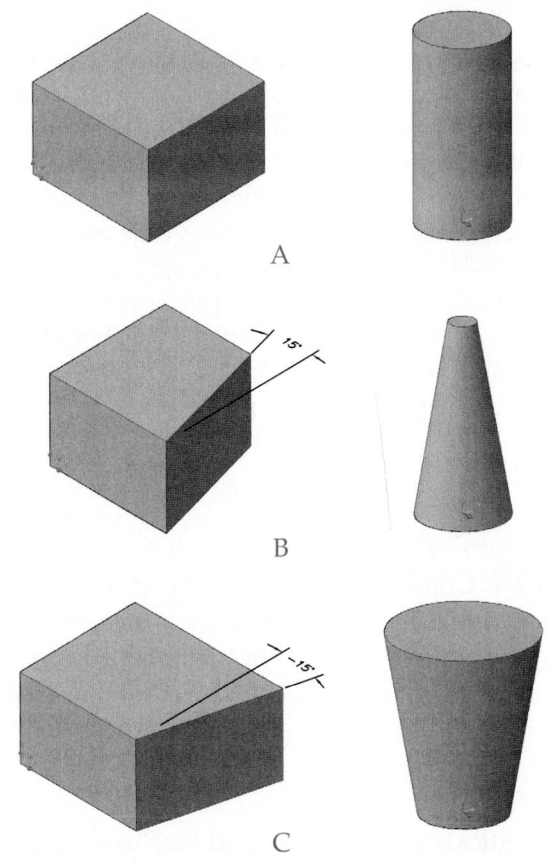

A

B

C

Figure 11-9.
If a hole or slot is
tapered using a
positive taper angle,
its diameter or width
increases from the
base point along the
axis of tapering, thus
removing material
from the solid. A
negative taper angle
increases the volume
of the solid.

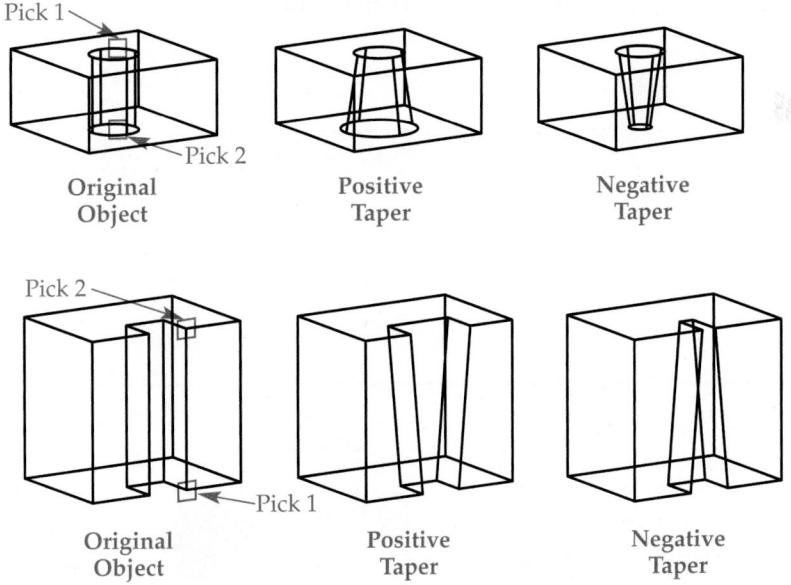

Original
Object

Positive
Taper

Negative
Taper

Original
Object

Positive
Taper

Negative
Taper

Copying Faces

Type
SOLIDEDIT
Pull-Down Menu
Modify
> Solid Editing
> Copy faces
Toolbar
Solid Editing

Copy faces

The **Copy** option copies a face to the location or coordinates given. The copied face is not part of the original solid model. It is actually a region, which can later be extruded, revolved, swept, etc., into a solid. This may be useful when you wish to construct a mating part in an assembly that has the same features on the mating faces or the same outline. This option is quick to use because you can pick a base point on the face, then enter a single direct distance value for the displacement. Be sure an appropriate UCS is set if you wish to use direct distance entry.

To copy a solid face, select the command and pick the **Face>Copy** option. You are then prompted to select the face(s) to copy. When done selecting faces, press [Enter] to continue. You are prompted for a base point for the copy. Pick this point and then pick a second point of displacement or press [Enter] to use the first point as a displacement. See **Figure 11-10** for examples of copied faces.

PROFESSIONAL TIP

Copied faces can also be useful for creating additional views. For example, you can copy a face to create a separate plan view with dimensions and notes. A copied face can also be enlarged to show details and to provide additional notation for design or assembly.

Coloring Faces

Type
SOLIDEDIT
Pull-Down Menu
Modify
> Solid Editing
> Color faces
Toolbar
Solid Editing

Color faces

You can quickly change a selected face to a different color using the **Color** option. Select the command and pick the **Face>Color** option. You are then prompted to select the face(s) to color. When done selecting faces, press [Enter] to continue. Next, choose the desired color from the **Select Color** dialog box that is displayed. Remember, the color of the object (or face) determines the shaded color.

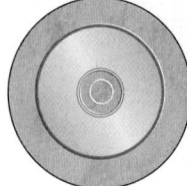

Exercise 11-6
Complete the exercise on the Student CD.

Figure 11-10.
A face can be quickly copied by picking a base point on the face and then entering a direct distance value for the displacement.

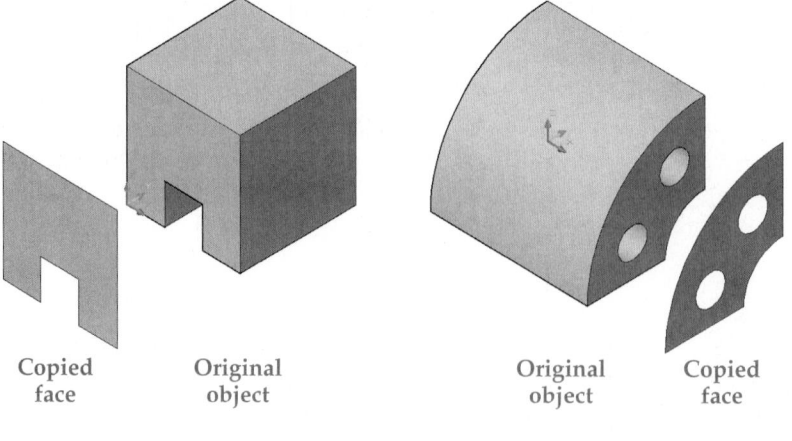

Copied face   Original object   Original object   Copied face

A   B

Edge Editing

Edges can be edited in only two ways. They can be copied from the solid. Also, the color of an edge can be changed.

Copying an edge is similar to copying a face. To copy a solid edge, select the command and pick the **Edge>Copy** option. You are then prompted to select the edge(s) to copy. When done selecting edges, press [Enter] to continue. You are prompted for a base point for the copy. Pick this point and then pick a second point of displacement or press [Enter] to use the first point as a displacement. The edge is copied as a line, arc, circle, ellipse, or spline.

To color a solid edge, select the command and pick the **Edge>Color** option. You are then prompted to select the edge(s) to color. When done selecting edges, press [Enter] to continue. Next, choose the desired color from the **Select Color** dialog box that is displayed and pick the **OK** button. The edges are now displayed with the new color. You may need to set a wireframe or hidden visual style current to see the change.

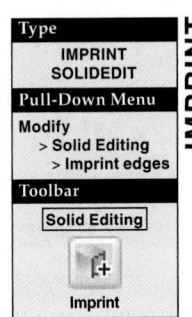

Type
SOLIDEDIT
Pull-Down Menu
Modify
> Solid Editing
> Copy edges
Toolbar
Solid Editing
Copy edges

SOLIDEDIT

Type
SOLIDEDIT
Pull-Down Menu
Modify
> Solid Editing
> Color edges
Toolbar
Solid Editing
Color edges

SOLIDEDIT

Body Editing

The body editing options of the **SOLIDEDIT** command perform editing operations on the entire body of the solid model. The body options are **Imprint**, **Separate**, **Shell**, **Clean**, and **Check**. The next sections cover these body editing options.

Imprint

Arcs, circles, lines, 2D and 3D polylines, ellipses, splines, regions, bodies, and 3D solids can be imprinted onto a solid, if the object intersects the solid. The imprint becomes a face on the surface based on the overlap between the two intersecting objects. Once the imprint has been made, the new face can be modified.

To imprint an object on a solid, select the command and pick the **Body>Imprint** option. If IMPRINT is typed, the option is directly entered. Once the option is activated, you are prompted to select the solid. This is the object on which the other objects will be imprinted. Then, select the objects to be imprinted. You have the option of deleting the source objects. The imprinted face can then be modified using face editing options. Figure 11-11 illustrates objects imprinted onto, and then extruded into, a solid model.

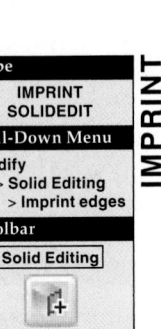

Type
IMPRINT
SOLIDEDIT
Pull-Down Menu
Modify
> Solid Editing
> Imprint edges
Toolbar
Solid Editing
Imprint

IMPRINT

NOTE

Remember that objects are drawn on the XY plane of the current UCS unless you enter a specific Z value. Therefore, before you draw an object to be imprinted onto a solid model, be sure you have set an appropriate UCS for proper placement of the object by using a dynamic UCS or the **UCS** command. Alternately, you can draw the object on the XY plane and then move the object onto the solid object.

Separate

The **Separate** option separates two objects that are both a part of a single solid composite, but appear as separate physical entities. This can happen when modifying solids using the Boolean commands. The **Separate** option may be seldom used, but it has a specific purpose. If you select a solid model and an object physically separate

---

Figure 11-11.
Imprinted objects form new faces that can be extruded into the solid. A—A solid box with three objects on the plane of the top face. B—The objects are imprinted, then the new faces are extruded through the solid.

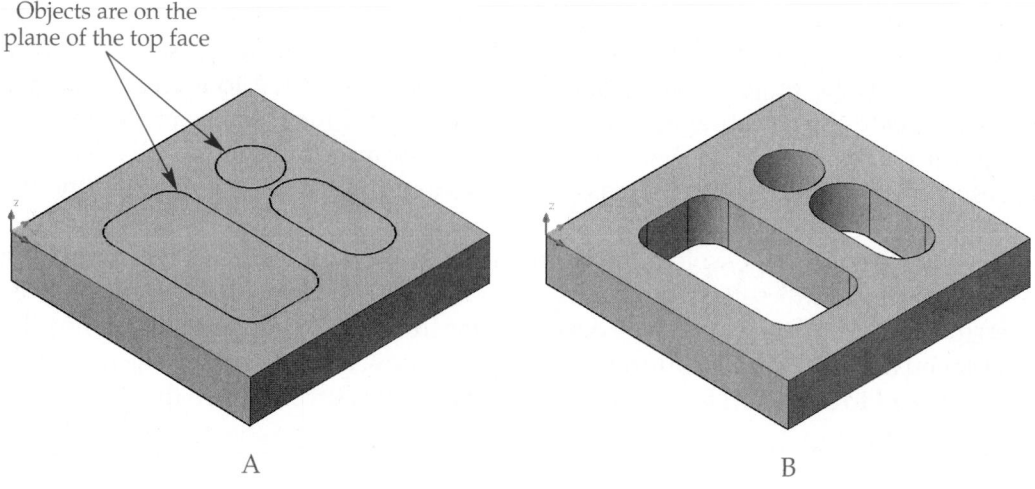

Objects are on the plane of the top face

A

B

Figure 11-12.
A—After the cylinder is subtracted from the box, the remaining solid is considered one solid. B—Use the **Separate** option to turn this single solid into two solids.

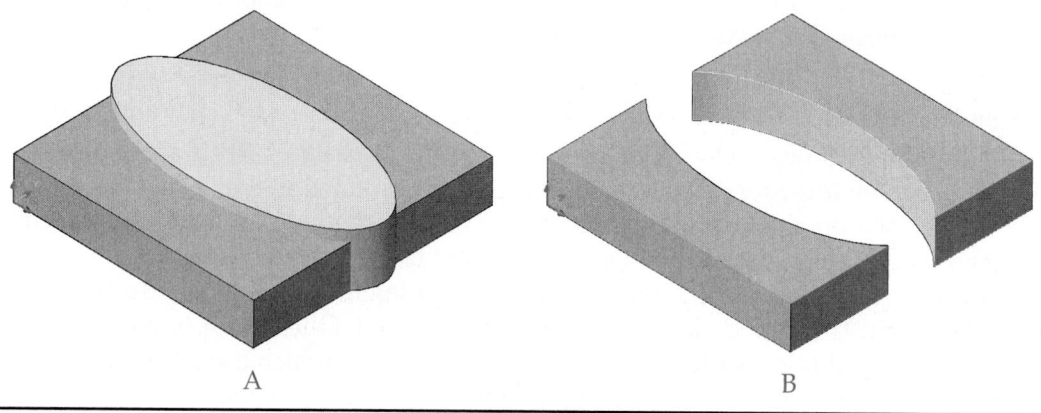

A

B

SOLIDEDIT

Type
SOLIDEDIT
Pull-Down Menu
Modify
> Solid Editing
> Separate
Toolbar
Solid Editing
Separate

from the model is highlighted, the two objects are parts of the same composite solid. If you wish to work with them as individual solids, they must first be separated.

To separate a solid body, select the command and pick the **Body>Separate** option. You are then prompted to select a 3D solid. After you pick the solid, it is automatically separated. No other actions are required and you can exit the command. However, if you select a solid in which the parts are physically joined, AutoCAD indicates this by prompting The selected solid does not have multiple lumps. A "lump" is a physically separate solid entity. In order to separate a solid, it must be composed of multiple lumps. See **Figure 11-12.**

SOLIDEDIT

Type
SOLIDEDIT
Pull-Down Menu
Modify
> Solid Editing
> Shell
Toolbar
Solid Editing
Shell

Shell

A *shell* is a solid that has been "hollowed out." The **Shell** option creates a shell of the selected object using a specified offset distance, or thickness. To create a shell of a solid body, select the command and pick the **Body>Shell** option. You are prompted to select the solid. Only one solid can be selected.

After selecting the solid, you have the opportunity to remove faces. If you do not remove any faces, the new solid object will appear identical to the old solid object when shaded or rendered. The thickness of the shell will not be visible. If you wish to create a hollow object with an opening, select the face to be removed (the opening).

After selecting the object and specifying any faces to be removed, you are prompted to enter the shell offset distance. This is the thickness of the shell. A positive shell offset distance creates a shell on the inside of the solid body. A negative shell offset distance creates a shell on the outside of the solid body. See Figure 11-13. If you shell a solid that contains internal features, such as holes, grooves, and slots, a shell of the specified thickness is placed around those features. This is shown in Figure 11-14.

Exercise 11-7
Complete the exercise on the Student CD.

PROFESSIONAL TIP

The **Shell** option of the **SOLIDEDIT** command is very useful in applications such as solid modeling of metal castings or injection-molded plastic parts.

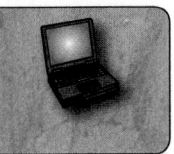

Clean

The **Clean** option removes all unused objects and shared surfaces. Imprinted objects are not removed. Select the command and pick the **Body>Clean** option. Then, pick the solid to be cleaned. No further input is required. You can exit the command.

Check

The **Check** option simply determines if the selected object is a valid 3D solid. If a true 3D solid is selected, AutoCAD displays the prompt This object is a valid ShapeManager solid., and you can exit the command. If the object selected is not a 3D solid, the prompt reads A 3D solid must be selected., and you are prompted to select a 3D solid. To access the **Check** option, select the command and pick the **Body>Check** option. Then, select the object to check.

Type
SOLIDEDIT
Pull-Down Menu
Modify
> Solid Editing
> Clean
Toolbar
Solid Editing
Clean

SOLIDEDIT

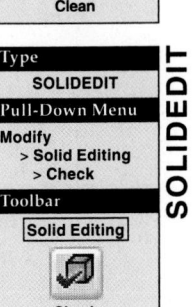

Type
SOLIDEDIT
Pull-Down Menu
Modify
> Solid Editing
> Check
Toolbar
Solid Editing
Check

SOLIDEDIT

Figure 11-13.
A—The right-front, bottom, and left-back faces (marked here by gray lines) are removed from the shell operation. B—The resulting object after the shell operation.

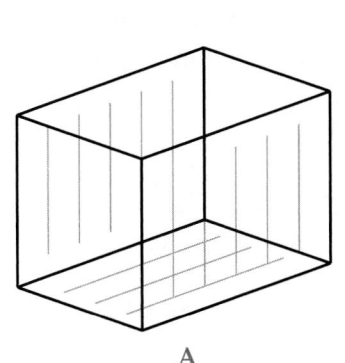

A

B

Figure 11-14.
If you shell a solid that contains internal features, such as holes, grooves, and slots, a shell of the specified thickness is also placed around those features. A—Solid object with holes subtracted. B—Wireframe display after shelling with a negative offset. C—The Conceptual visual style is set current.

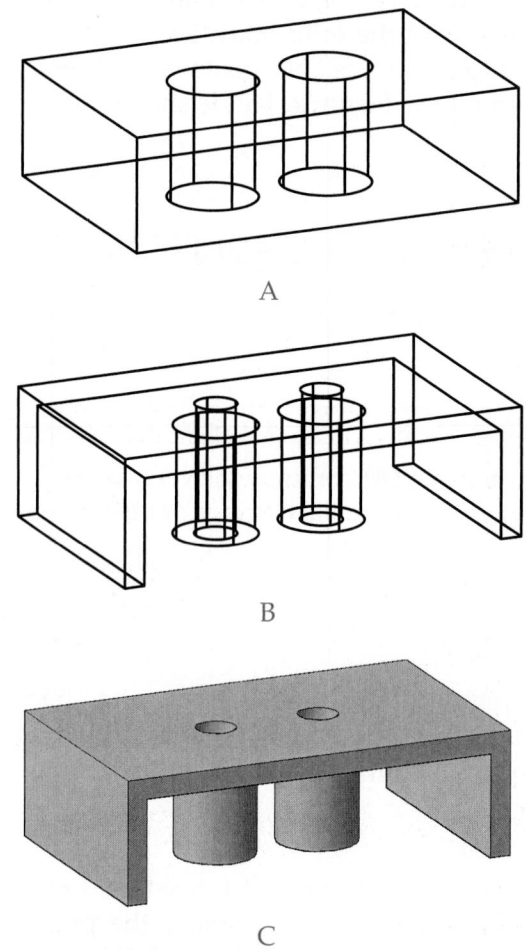

A

B

C

Using SOLIDEDIT as a Construction Tool

This section provides an example of how the **SOLIDEDIT** command options can be used not only to edit, but also to construct a solid model. This makes it easy to design and construct a model without selecting a variety of commands. It also gives you the option of undoing a single editing operation or an entire editing session without ever exiting the command.

In the following example, **SOLIDEDIT** command options are used to imprint shapes onto the model body and then extrude those shapes into the body to create countersunk holes. Then, the model size is adjusted and an angle and taper are applied to one end. Finally, one end of the model is copied to construct a mating part.

Creating Shape Imprints on a Model

The basic shape of the solid model in this tutorial is drawn as a solid box, then shape imprints are added to it. Throughout this exercise, you may wish to change the UCS to assist in the construction of the part.

1. Draw a solid box using the dimensions shown in **Figure 11-15.**
2. Set the 3D Wireframe visual style current.

Figure 11-15.
The initial setup for
the model.

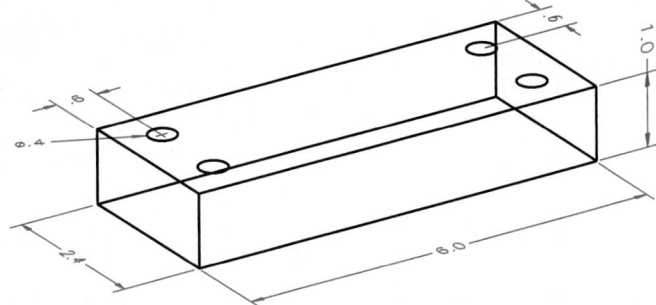

3. On the top surface of the box, locate a single ∅.4 circle using the dimensions given. Then, copy or array the circle to the other three corners as shown in the figure.
4. Use the **Imprint** option to imprint the circles onto the solid box. Delete the source objects.

Extruding Imprints to Create Features

The imprinted 2D shapes can now be extruded to create new 3D solid features on the model. Use the **Extrude Faces** option to extrude all four imprinted circles.

1. When you select the edge of the first circle, all features on that face are highlighted, but only the circle you picked and the top face have actually been selected. If you pick inside the circle, only the circle is selected and highlighted. In either case, be sure to also pick the remaining three circles.
2. Remove the top face of the box from the selection set, if needed.
3. The depth of the extrusion is .16 units. Remember to enter –.16 for the extrusion height since the holes remove material. The angle of taper for extrusion should be 35°. Your model should look like **Figure 11-16A**.
4. Extrude the small diameter of the four tapered holes so they intersect the bottom of the solid body. Select the holes by picking the small diameter circles. Instead of calculating the distance from the bottom of the chamfer to the bottom surface, you can simply enter a value that is greater than this distance, such as the original thickness of the object. Again, since the goal is to remove material, use a negative value for the height of the extrusion. There is no taper angle. Your model should now look like **Figure 11-16B**.

Moving Faces to Change Model Size

The next step is to use the **Move Faces** option to decrease the length and thickness of the solid body.

1. Select either end face and the two holes nearest to it. Be sure to select the holes *and* the countersinks. Move the two holes and end face two units toward the other end, thus changing the object length to four units.
2. Select the bottom face and move it .5 units up toward the top face, thus changing the thickness to .5 units. See **Figure 11-17**.

Figure 11-16.
A—The imprinted circles are extruded with a taper angle of 35°. B—Holes are created by further extrusion with a taper angle of 0°.

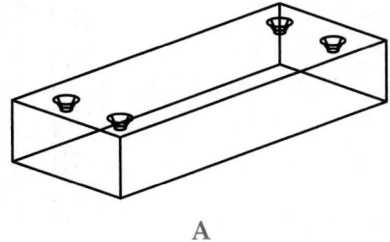

A

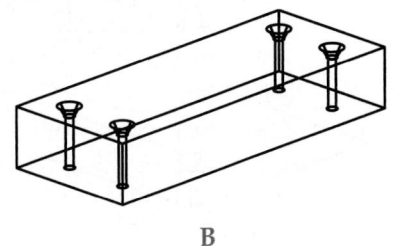

B

Figure 11-17.
The length of the object is shortened and the height is reduced.

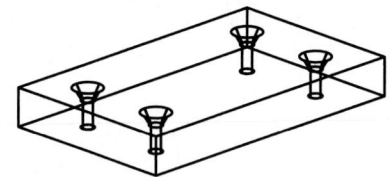

Offsetting a Feature to Change Its Size

Now, the **Offset Faces** option is used to increase the diameter of the four holes and to adjust a rectangular slot that will be added to the solid.

1. Using **Offset Faces**, select the four small hole diameters. Be sure to remove from the selection set any other faces that may be selected.
2. Enter an offset distance of –.05. This increases the hole diameter and decreases the solid volume. Exit the **SOLIDEDIT** command.
3. Select the **RECTANG** command. Set the fillet radius to .4 and draw a 2 × 1.6 rectangle centered on the top face of the solid. See **Figure 11-18A.**
4. Imprint the rectangle on the solid. Delete the source object.
5. Extrude the rectangle completely through the solid (.5 units). Remember to remove from the selection set any other faces that may be selected.
6. Offset the rectangle using an offset distance of .2 units. You will need to select all edges on the rectangle. This decreases the size of the rectangular opening and increases the solid volume. Your drawing should appear as shown in **Figure 11-18B.**

Tapering Faces

One side of the part is to be angled. The **Taper Faces** option is used to taper the left end of the solid.

1. Using **Taper Faces**, pick the face at the left end of the solid.
2. Pick Point 1 in **Figure 11-19** as the base point and Point 2 as the second point along the axis of tapering.
3. Enter a value of –10 for the taper angle. This moves the upper-left end away from the solid, creating a tapered end.

Rotating Faces

Next, use the **Rotate Faces** option to rotate the tapered end of the object. The top edge of the face will be rotated away from the holes, adding volume to the solid.

1. Using **Rotate Faces**, pick the face at the left end of the solid.
2. Pick Point 1 in **Figure 11-19** as the first axis point and Point 2 as the second point.
3. Enter a value of –30 for the rotation angle. This rotates the top edge of the tapered end away from the solid. See **Figure 11-20.**

Figure 11-18.
A—The diameter of the holes is increased and a rectangle is imprinted on the top surface.
B—The rectangle is extruded to create a slot.

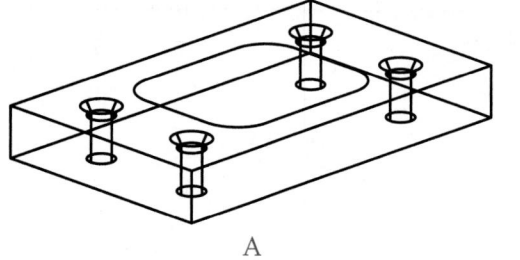

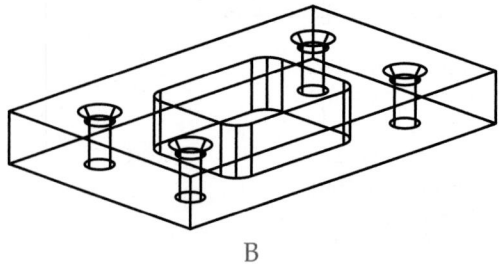

A

B

Figure 11-19.
The left end of the object is tapered. Notice the pick points. These points are also used when selecting an axis of rotation.

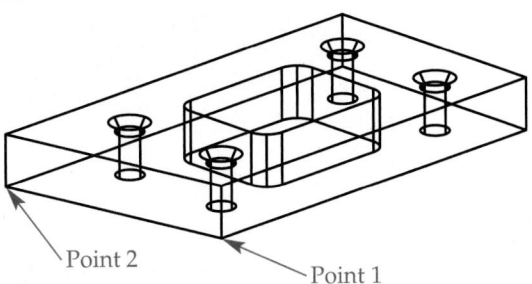

Point 2

Point 1

Figure 11-20.
The tapered end of the object is modified by rotating the face.

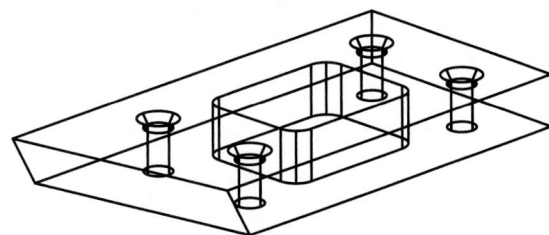

Copying Faces

A mating part will now be created. This is done by first copying the face on the tapered end of the part.

1. Using the **Copy Faces** option, pick the angled face on the left end of the solid.
2. Pick one of the corners as a base point and copy the face one unit to the left. This face can now be used to create a new solid. See **Figure 11-21A.**
3. Draw a line four units in length on the negative X axis from the lower-right corner of the copied face. Use the **EXTRUDE** command on the copied face to create a new solid. Select the **Path** option and use the line as the extrusion path. See **Figure 11-21B.** If you do not use the **Path** option, the extrusion is projected perpendicular to the face.

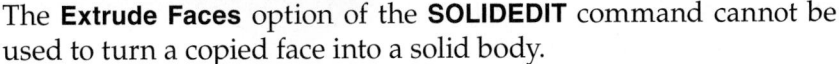

NOTE

The **Extrude Faces** option of the **SOLIDEDIT** command cannot be used to turn a copied face into a solid body.

Creating a Shell

The bottom surface of the original solid will now be shelled out. Keep in mind that features such as the four holes and the rectangular slot will not be cut off by the shell. Instead, a shell will be placed around these features. This becomes clear when the operation is performed.

1. Select the **Shell** option and pick the original solid.
2. Remove the lower-left and lower-right edges of the solid. See **Figure 11-22A.** This removes the two side faces and the bottom face.
3. Enter a shell offset distance of .15 units. The shell is created and should appear similar to **Figure 11-22A.**
4. Use the **3DORBIT** command to view the solid from the bottom. Also, set the Conceptual visual style current. Your model should look like the one shown in **Figure 11-22B.**

Figure 11-21.
Creating a mating part. A—The angled face is copied. B—The copied face is extruded into a solid.

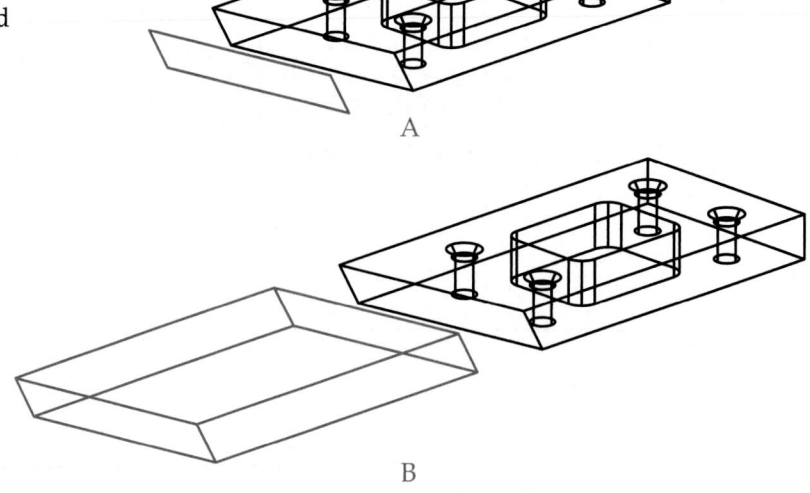

A

B

Figure 11-22.
A—The shelled object. B—The viewpoint is changed and the Conceptual visual style is set current.

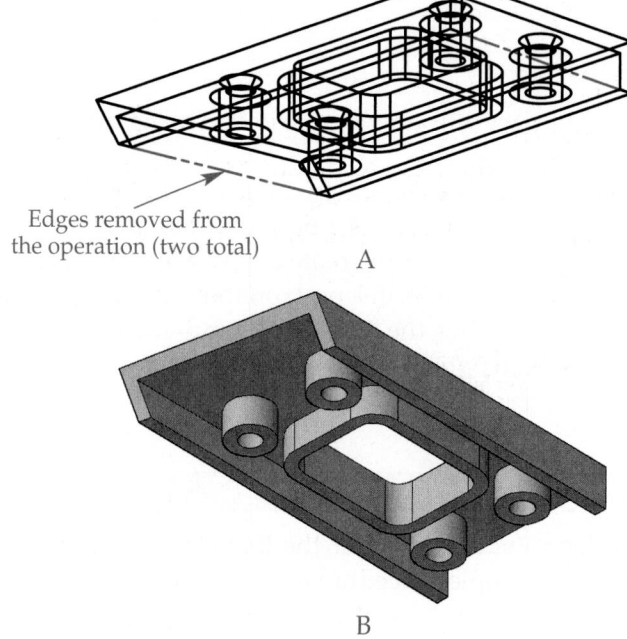

Edges removed from the operation (two total)

A

B

Chapter Test

Answer the following questions. Write your answers on a separate sheet of paper or complete the electronic chapter test on the Student CD.

1. What are the three components of a solid model?
2. When using the **SOLIDEDIT** command, how many faces are highlighted if you pick an edge?
3. How do you deselect a face that is part of the selection set?
4. How can you select a single face?
5. Which two operations can the **Extrude Faces** option perform?
6. How does the shape and length of an object selected as the path of an extrusion affect the final extrusion?
7. What is one of the most useful aspects of the **Offset Faces** option?

8. How do positive and negative offset distance values affect the volume of the solid?
9. How is a single object, such as a cylinder, affected by entering a positive taper angle when using the **Taper Faces** option?
10. When a shape is imprinted onto a solid body, which component of the solid does the imprinted object become and how can it be used?
11. In which situation would you use the **Separate** option?
12. How does the **Shell** option affect a solid that contains internal features such as holes, grooves, and slots?
13. How can you determine if an object is a valid 3D solid?

Drawing Problems

1. Complete the tutorial presented in this chapter. Then, perform the following additional edits to the original solid.
   A. Lengthen the right end of the solid by .5 units.
   B. Taper the right end of the solid with the same taper angle used on the left end, but taper it in the opposite direction.
   C. Fillet the two long, top edges of the solid using a fillet radius of .2 units.
   D. Rotate the face at the right end of the solid with the same rotation angle used on the left end, but rotate it in the opposite direction.
   E. Save the drawing as P11_01.

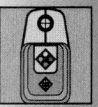

2. Construct the solid part shown below using as many **SOLIDEDIT** options as possible. After completing the object, make the following modifications.
   A. Lengthen the 1.250" diameter feature by .250".
   B. Change the .750" diameter hole to .625" diameter.
   C. Change the thickness of the .250" thick flange to .375" (toward the bottom).
   D. Extrude the end of the 1.250" diameter feature .250" with a 15° taper inward.
   E. Save the drawing as P11_02.

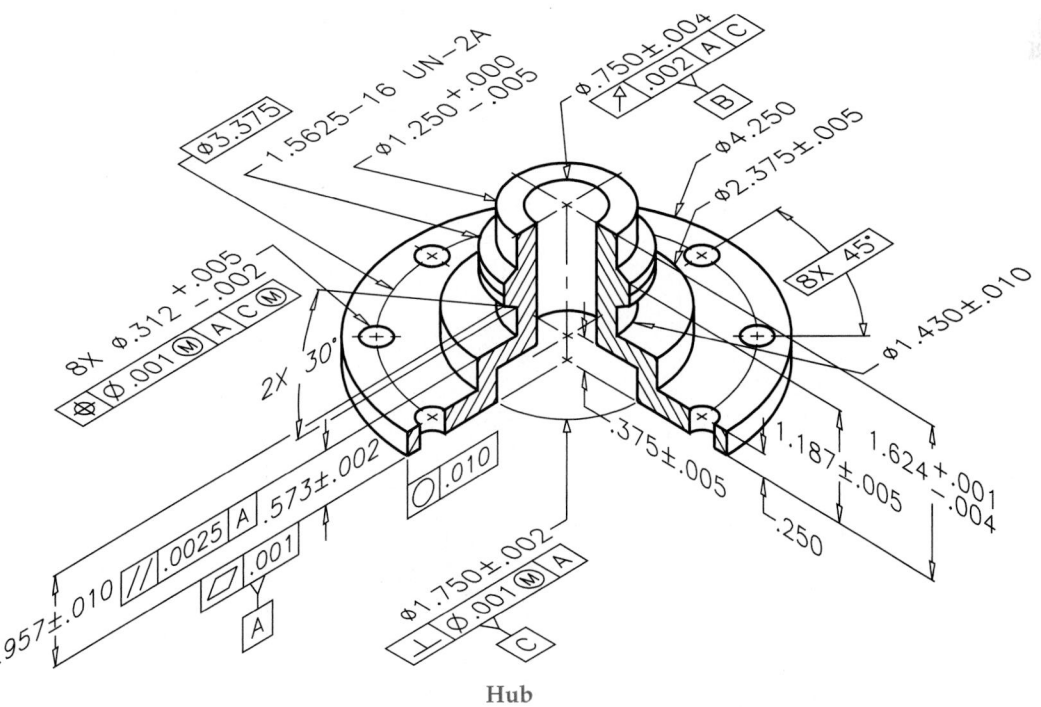

Hub

3. Construct the solid part shown below. Then, perform the following edits on the solid using the **SOLIDEDIT** command.
   A. Change the diameter of the hole to 35.6/35.4.
   B. Add a 5° taper to each inner side of each tooth (the bottom of each tooth should be wider while the top remains the same).
   C. Change the width of the 4.8/4.0 key to 5.8/5.0.
   D. Save the drawing as P11_03.

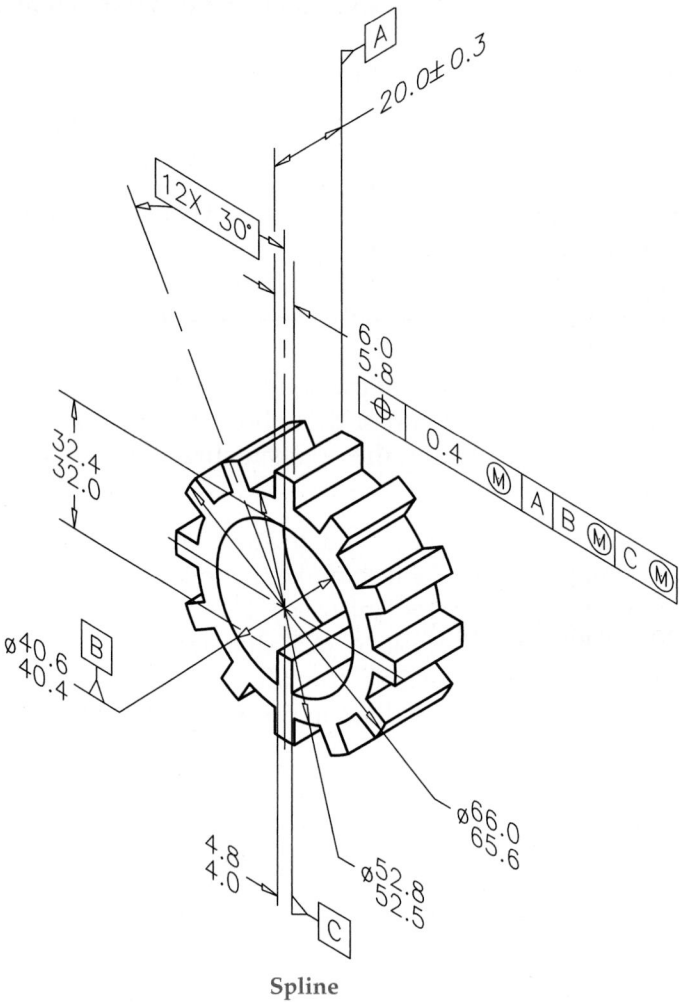

Spline

4. Construct the solid part shown below using as many **SOLIDEDIT** options as possible. Then, perform the following edits on the solid.
   A. Change the depth of the counterbore to 10 mm.
   B. Change the color of all internal surfaces to red.
   C. Save the drawing as P11_04.

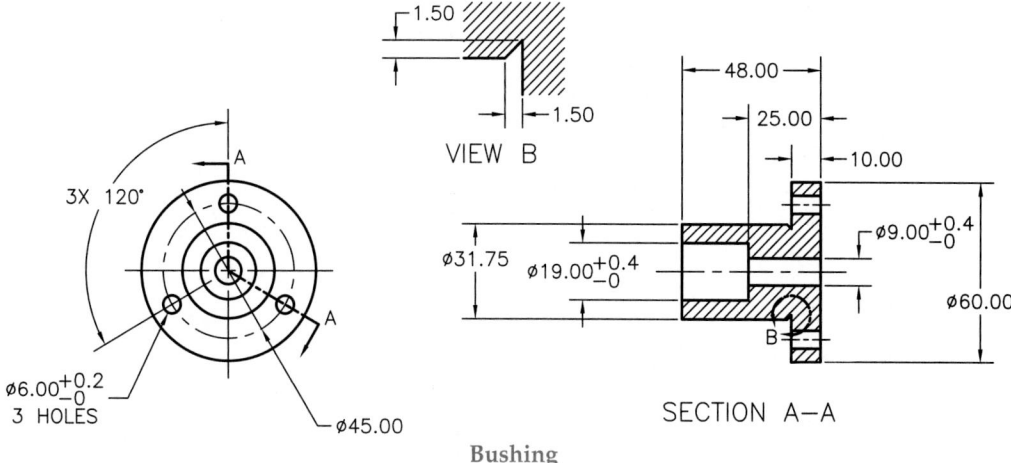

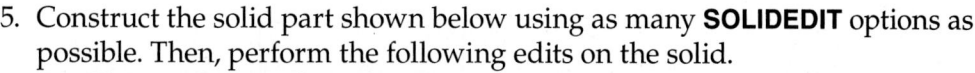

Bushing

5. Construct the solid part shown below using as many **SOLIDEDIT** options as possible. Then, perform the following edits on the solid.
   A. Change the 2.625″ height to 2.325″.
   B. Change the 1.625″ internal diameter to 1.425″.
   C. Taper the outside faces of the .875″ high base at a 5° angle away from the part. Hint: The base cannot be directly tapered.
   D. Save the drawing as P11_05.

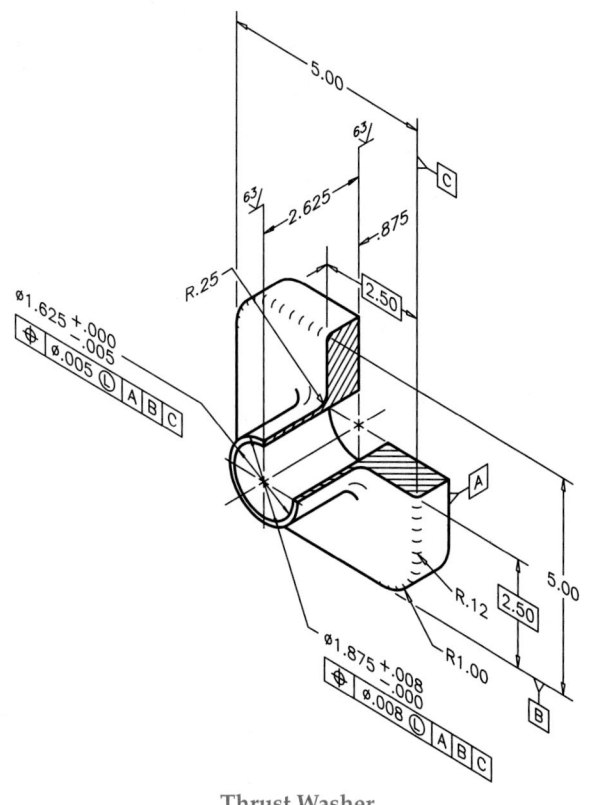

Thrust Washer

Chapter 11   Solid Model Editing

6. Construct the solid part shown below using as many **SOLIDEDIT** options as possible. Then, change the dimensions on the model as follows. Save the drawing as P11_06.

Existing	New
100	106
80	82
Ø60	Ø94
Ø40	Ø42
30°	35°

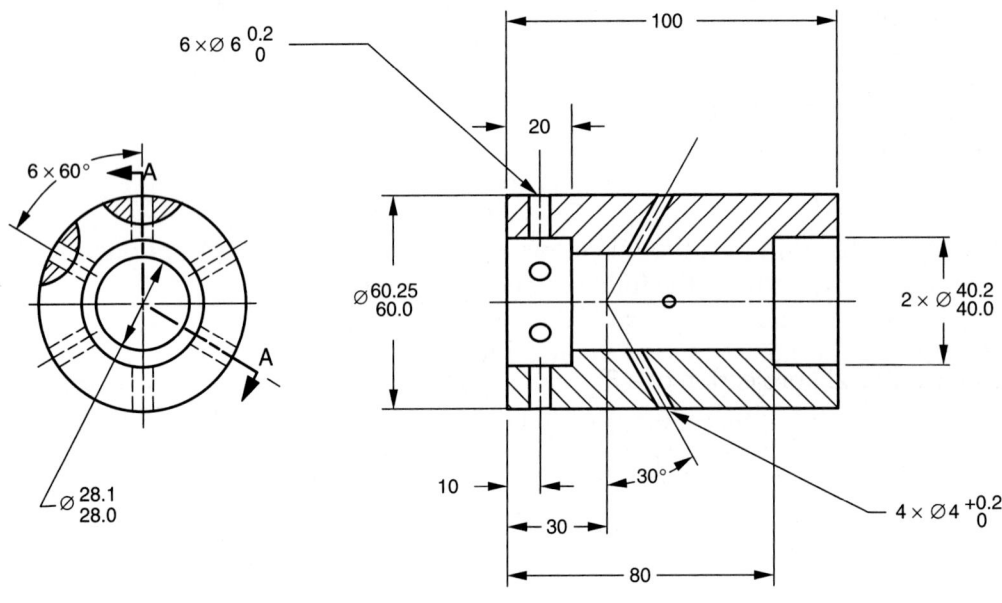

SECTION A-A

Nozzle

CHAPTER 12

Solid Model Display and Analysis

Learning Objectives

After completing this chapter, you will be able to:
- ✓ Construct a 3D section plane through a solid model.
- ✓ Adjust the size and location of section planes.
- ✓ Create a dynamic section of a 3D solid model.
- ✓ Construct 2D and 3D section blocks.
- ✓ Create a flat, 2D projection of a 3D solid model.
- ✓ Create a multiview layout of a solid model using **SOLVIEW** and **SOLDRAW**.
- ✓ Construct a profile of a solid using **SOLPROF**.
- ✓ Perform an analysis of a solid model.
- ✓ Export and import solid model data.

Certain aspects of a solid model's appearance are controlled by the **ISOLINES**, **DISPSILH**, and **FACETRES** system variables. The **ISOLINES** system variable controls the number of lines used to define solids in wireframe displays. This was introduced in Chapter 3. The **FACETRES** system variable controls the number of lines used to define solids in hidden and shaded displays. The **DISPSILH** system variable is used to display a silhouette.

Internal features of the model can be shown using the **SECTIONPLANE** command. This command can create 2D and 3D section views on an object. The **FLATSHOT** command creates a 2D projection of the current view. This chapter also looks at how sections can be combined with 2D projections created with the **SOLVIEW** and **SOLDRAW** commands to create a drawing layout for plotting. This chapter also covers how a profile of a solid can be created using the **SOLPROF** command.

Controlling Solid Model Display

AutoCAD solid models can be displayed as wireframes, with hidden lines removed, shaded, or rendered. A wireframe is the default display when a drawing is started based on the acad.dwt template and is the quickest to display. The hidden, shaded, and rendered displays require a longer regeneration time. When a drawing is started based on the acad3D.dwt template, the default display is the Realistic visual style, which is a shaded display.

Isolines

The appearance of a solid model in a wireframe display is controlled by the **ISOLINES** system variable. *Isolines* represent the edges and curved surfaces of a solid model. This setting does *not* affect the final shaded or rendered object. However, if the Edge mode property for the visual style is set to Isolines, isolines are displayed when the visual style is set current. The default **ISOLINES** value is four. It can have a value from zero to 2047. All solid objects in the drawing are affected by changes to the **ISOLINES** value, as are all visual styles with their Edge mode property set to Isolines. Figure 12-1 illustrates the difference between **ISOLINES** settings of four and 12.

The setting of the **ISOLINES** system variable can be changed in the **Visual Styles Manager** palette by changing the Number of lines property in the **Edge Settings** category. See Figure 12-2A. The Edge mode property must be set to Isolines to display the Number of lines property. The **ISOLINES** setting can also be changed in the **Contour lines per**

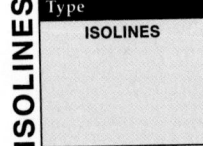

Figure 12-1.
Isolines define curved surfaces. A—**ISOLINES** = 4. B—**ISOLINES** = 12.

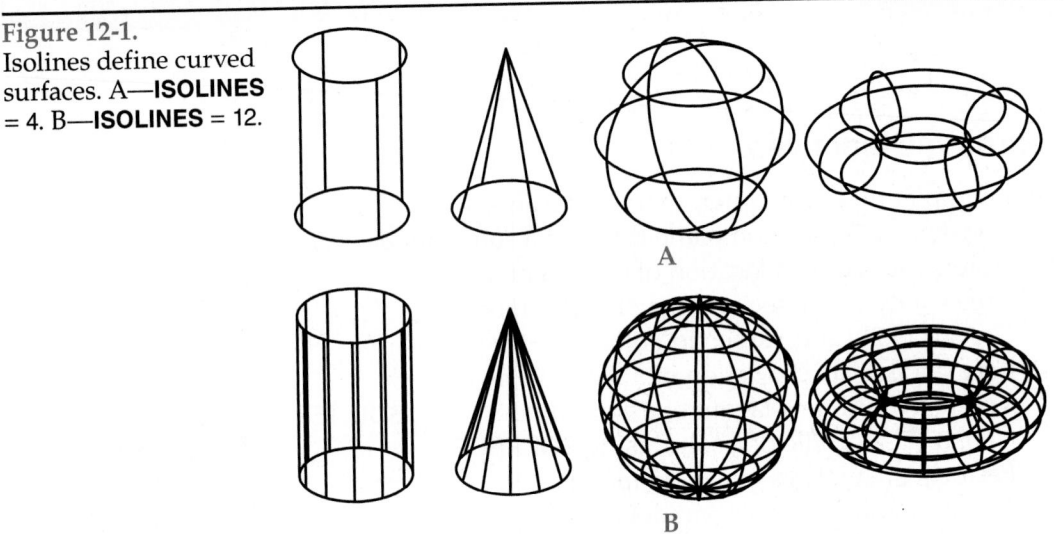

Figure 12-2.
A—The **ISOLINES** and **DISPSILH** values can be set in the **Visual Styles Manager**.
B—The **ISOLINES**, **FACETRES**, and **DISPSILH** values can be set in the **Options** dialog box.

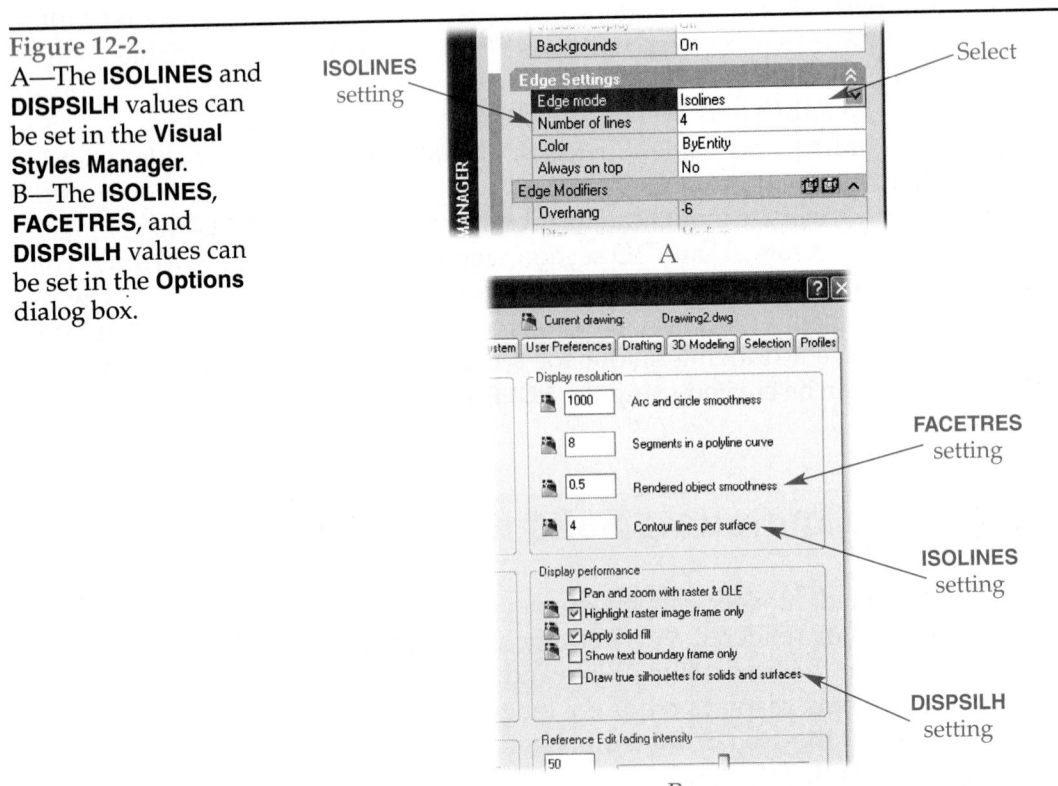

AutoCAD and Its Applications—Advanced

surface text box found in the **Display resolution** area of the **Display** tab in the **Options** dialog box, or by typing ISOLINES and then entering a new value. See Figure 12-2B.

Creating a Display Silhouette

When the Edge mode property of a visual style is set to Facet Edges, objects are defined by *tessellation lines.* The **Facets** and **Smooth** buttons in the **Visual Style** control panel also control the Edge mode setting. The number of tessellation lines is controlled by the **FACETRES** system variable, which is discussed in the next section.

A model can also appear smooth with only a silhouette displayed. This is controlled by the **DISPSILH** (display silhouette) system variable. The **DISPSILH** system variable has two values, 0 (off) and 1 (on). The setting can be changed by typing DISPSILH and entering a new value. You can also set the variable using the **Draw true silhouettes for solids and surfaces** check box in the **Display performance** area of the **Display** tab in the **Options** dialog box. Refer to Figure 12-2B. Figure 12-3 shows solids with **DISPSILH** set to 1 after setting the 2D Wireframe visual style current and then using **HIDE**.

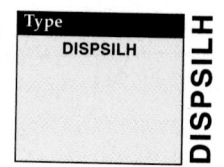

Controlling Surface Smoothness

The smoothness of curved surfaces in hidden, shaded, and rendered displays is controlled by the **FACETRES** system variable. This variable determines the number of polygon faces applied to the solid model. The value can range from .01 to 10.0 and the default value is .5. This system variable can be changed by typing FACETRES or by changing the **Rendered object smoothness** setting in the **Display resolution** area in the **Options** dialog box. Refer to Figure 12-2B. Figure 12-4 shows the effect of two different **FACETRES** settings.

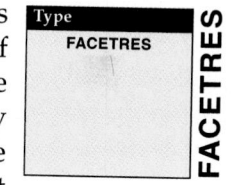

CAUTION

Avoid setting **FACETRES** any higher than necessary. Trying to plot even one solid object with a high **FACETRES** setting can overload system resources and take considerable time. Always use the lowest setting that will produce the results required by the project.

Exercise 12-1
Complete the exercise on the Student CD.

Figure 12-3.
Hidden solids appear as smooth objects with no facets when **DISPSILH** is set to 1, the 2D Wireframe visual style is set current, and the **HIDE** command is used.

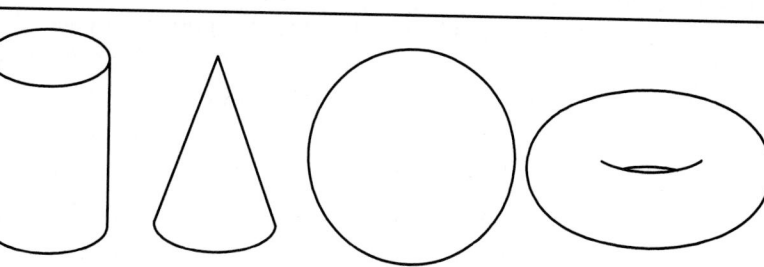

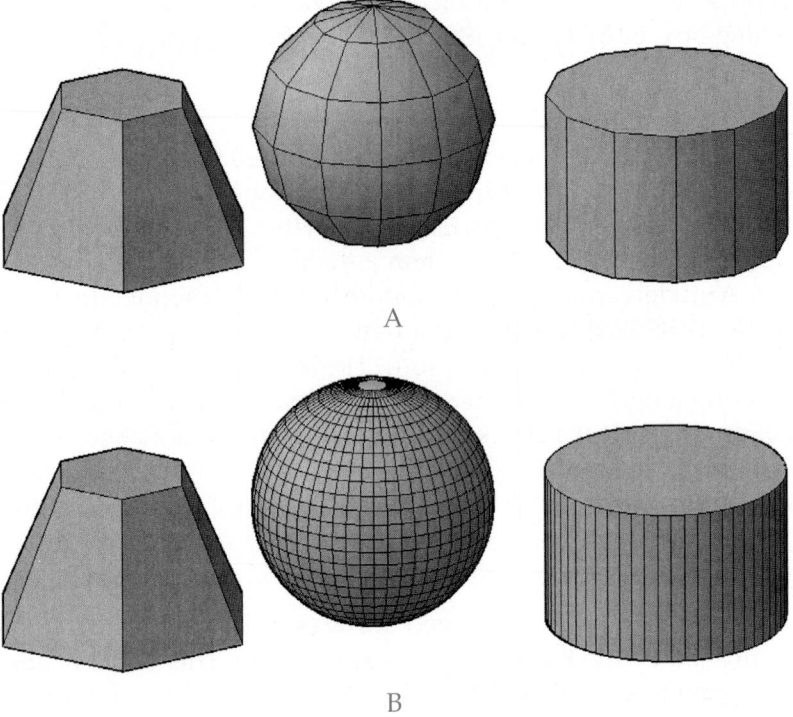

Figure 12-4.
A—The **FACETRES** setting is .5 and the Conceptual visual style set current. B—The **FACETRES** setting is 5.0 and the Conceptual visual style is set current.

A

B

Creating Section Planes

SECTIONPLANE

Type
SECTIONPLANE

Pull-Down Menu
Draw
> Modeling
> Section Plane

Dashboard
3D Make
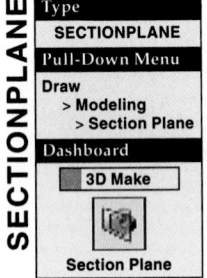
Section Plane

The **SECTIONPLANE** command offers a powerful visualization and display tool. It enables you to construct a section plane, known as an AutoCAD *section object*, that can then be used as a plane to cut through a 3D model. Once the section object is drawn, it can be moved to any location, jogs can be added to it, and it can be rendered "live" so that internal features and sectioned material are dynamically visible as the cutting plane is moved. A variety of section settings allow you to customize the appearance of section features. Additionally, you can generate 2D sections/elevations or 3D sections that can be inserted into the drawing as a block. Once the command is initiated, you are prompted to select a face, the first point on the section object, or to enter an option.

Pick a Face to Construct a Section Plane

The simplest way to create a section plane is to pick a flat face on the 3D object. Once the command is initiated, move the pointer until the face you wish to select is highlighted, then pick it. A transparent section object is placed on the face you selected and the model is cut at the plane. See Figure 12-5. The section plane can now be moved to create a section anywhere along the 3D model.

Pick Two Points to Construct a Section Plane

A second method for defining a section plane is to pick two points through which the section object passes. The section object is perpendicular to the XY plane of the current UCS. When the command is initiated, pick the first point. See P1 in Figure 12-6. As you move the pointer, notice that the section plane rotates about the first point. Next, pick the second point (P2) to define a line that cuts through the model. After the second point is picked, the section object is created. The section plane extends just beyond the edges of the model.

Figure 12-5.
Creating a section object on a face. A—The object before the face is selected. B—The section object is created.

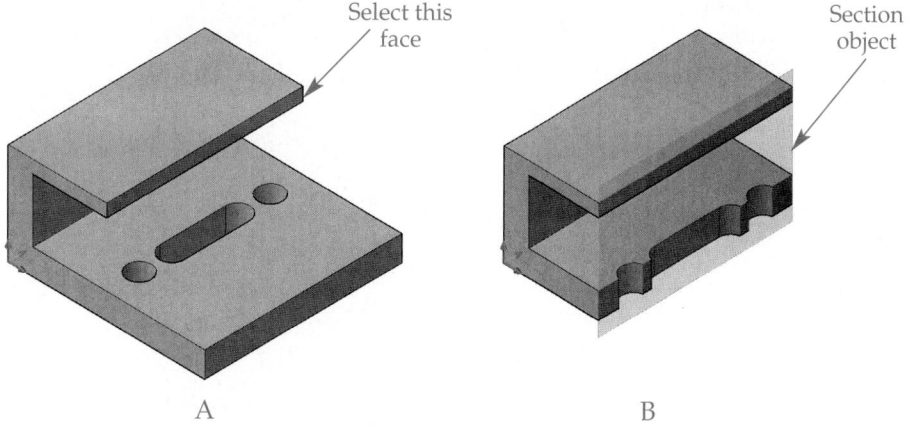

Select this face

Section object

A   B

Figure 12-6.
Creating a section object by selecting two points.

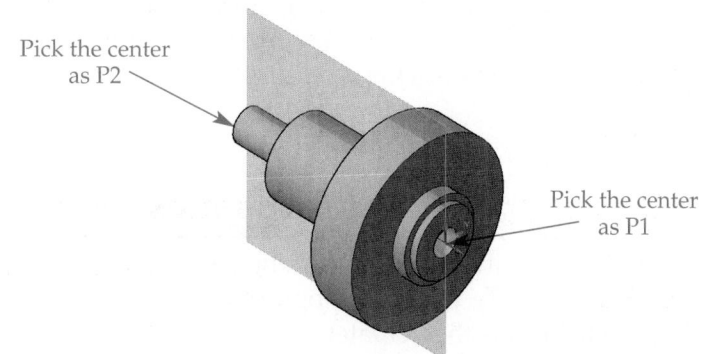

Pick the center as P2

Pick the center as P1

NOTE

When the section object is created by picking two points, notice that the model is not automatically cut as it is when a face is selected. This is because *live sectioning* is not turned on when picking two points, but is turned on when picking a face. To turn live sectioning on or off, select the section object, right-click, and select **Activate live sectioning** from the shortcut menu. Live sectioning is discussed later in this chapter.

Pick Multiple Points to Construct a Section Plane

The previous method accepts only two points to construct a single section plane. Using the **Draw section** option, you can specify multiple points in order to create section plane *jogs*. In engineering drawing terminology, a section object drawn in this manner can represent an *offset* or *aligned* section plane.

Once the command is initiated, select the **Draw section** option. Pick the start point, using object snaps if necessary. See **Figure 12-7**. Continue picking points as needed. After picking the last point to define the section plane, press [Enter]. You are then prompted to specify a point in the direction of the section view. This point is on the opposite side of the section object as the viewer. Pick a point on the model using object snaps if necessary. The section plane is created.

Notice in **Figure 12-7** that the pick points created a section object that does not

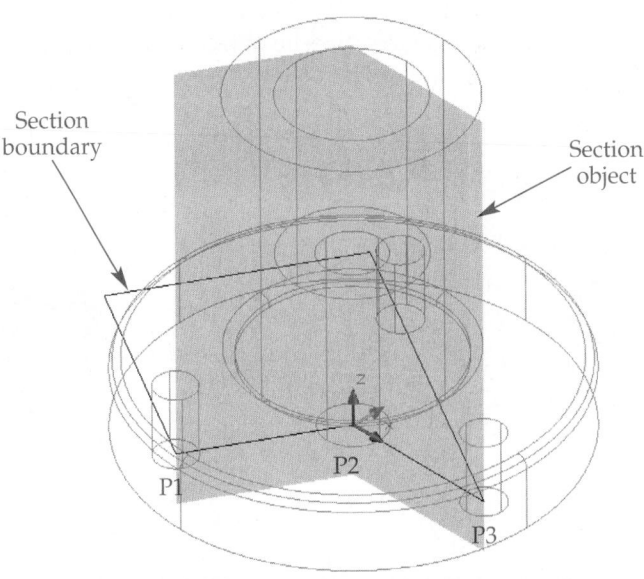

Figure 12-7.
Using the **Draw** option of the **SECTIONPLANE** command to create a section object with multiple segments.

Section boundary

Section object

extend beyond the boundary of the model. Also, the command "squares up" the section boundary to create a closed profile. Using section object grips, the section plane can be easily edited to include the entire solid. This is discussed in detail later in this chapter.

Create Orthographic Section Planes

The **Orthographic** option enables you to quickly place a section plane through the front, back, top, bottom, left, or right side of the object. See Figure 12-8. The origin is the center point of all objects in the model. Once the command is initiated, select the **Orthographic** option. Then, specify which orthographic plane you want to use as the section plane. The section object is then created.

You may encounter a situation in which there is more than one solid on the screen, and you want to use the **Orthographic** option on just one object. In this case, create a new layer, move objects you do not want to section to this layer, and then freeze the layer. The section object will be created based on the object that is visible.

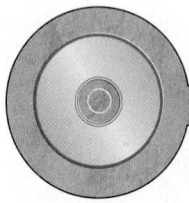

Exercise 12-2
Complete the exercise on the Student CD.

Editing and Using Section Planes

A wide range of section object editing and display options are available. However, there is no menu or toolbar access to these procedures. Instead, you must first select the section object, then right-click to display the shortcut menu. From this menu, you can access all of the display and editing functions that apply to the section object.

Section Object States

There are three possible states for the section object created by the **SECTIONPLANE** command—section plane, section boundary, and section volume. See Figure 12-9. Depending on which state is active, the section object will produce different results on the solid(s). The section object can be changed from one state to another.

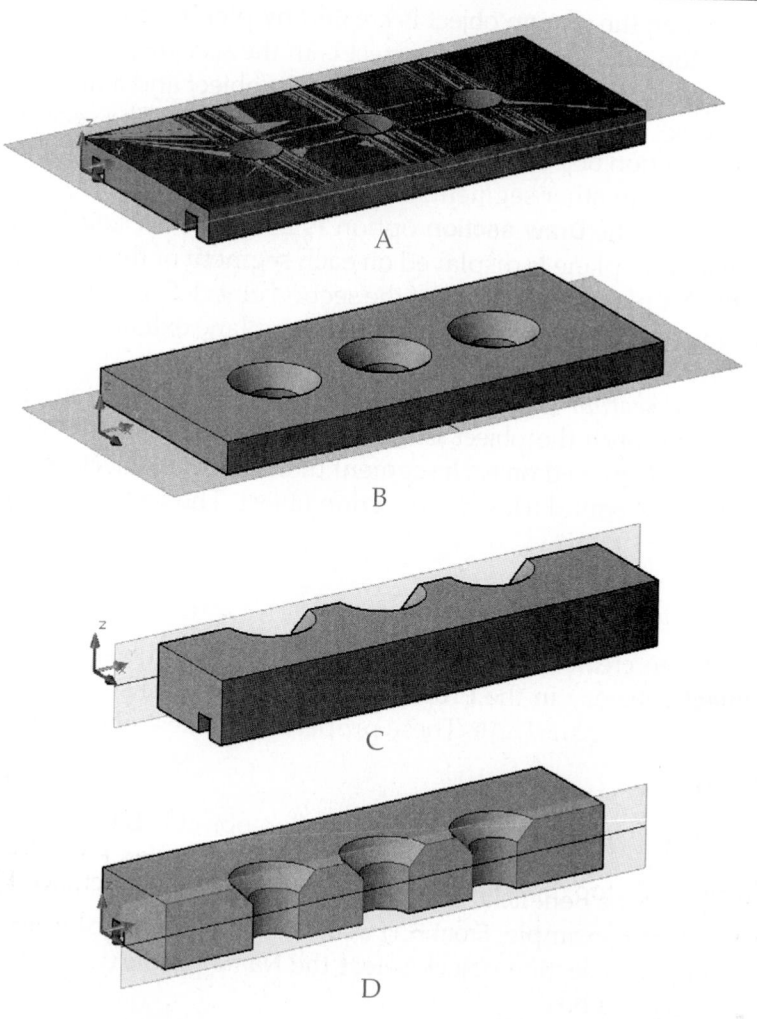

Figure 12-8.
Examples of orthographic **SECTIONPLANE** options. A—Top. B—Bottom. C—Left. D—Right.

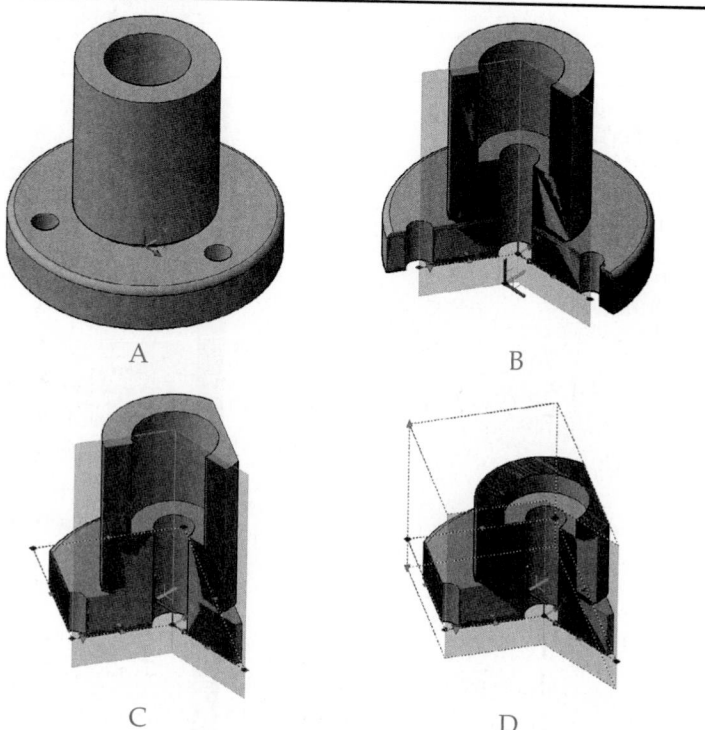

Figure 12-9.
Section object states.
A—The original object.
B—Section plane.
C—Section boundary.
D—Section volume.

When the section object is created by picking a face, picking two points, or using the **Orthographic** option, the object is in the *section plane state.* A transparent plane is displayed on each segment of the section object and a line connects the pick points (or the edges of the section object). See **Figure 12-9B.** The section plane extends infinitely in the section object's Z direction and along the direction of the object segment (unless connected to other segments).

When the **Draw section** option is used, the *section boundary state* is applied. A transparent plane is displayed on each segment of the section object. A 2D box extends to the XY plane boundaries of the section object. See **Figure 12-9C.** The sectioned object fits inside of this "footprint." The section plane extends infinitely in the section object's Z direction.

The *section volume state* is not created. The section object must be switched to this state once the object is created, as described in the next section. A transparent plane is displayed on each segment of the section object. In addition, a 3D box extends to the XYZ boundaries of the section object. The sectioned object fits inside of this box. See **Figure 12-9D.**

Section Object Properties

Once created, the properties of the section object can be changed. The **Section Object** category in the **Properties** window contains properties specific to the section object. See **Figure 12-10.** These properties are described in the next sections.

Name

The default name of the first section object is Section Plane(1). Subsequent section planes are sequentially numbered, such as Section Plane(2), Section Plane(3), and so on. It may be beneficial to rename section objects so the name is representative of the section. For example, Front Half Section is much more descriptive than Section Plane(1). To rename a section object, select the Name property. Then, type a new name in the property text box.

Figure 12-10.
The properties of a section object can be changed in the **Properties** window.

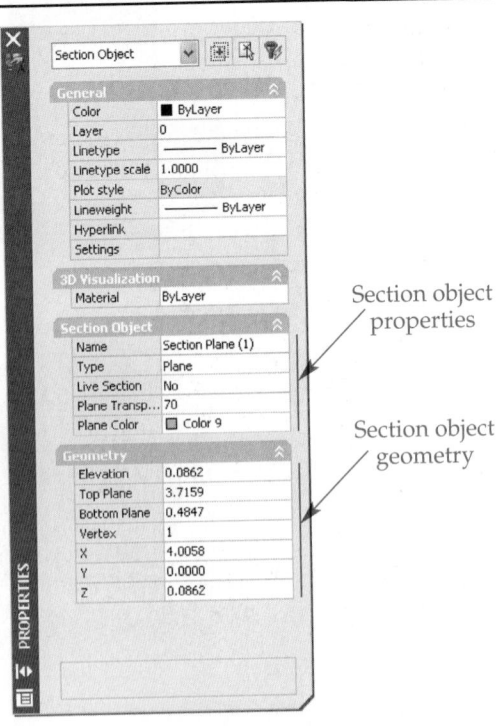

Section object properties

Section object geometry

Type

As discussed earlier, the section object is in one of three states. The three states are section plane, section boundary, and section volume. To change the state of the section object, select the Type property. Then, pick the state in the drop-down list.

Live section

Live sectioning is a tool that enables you to dynamically view the internal features of a solid, surface, or region as the section object is moved. This tool is discussed later in the chapter. To turn live sectioning on or off, select the Live Section property. Then, pick either Yes (on) or No (off) in the drop-down list.

Plane transparency

The Plane Transparency property determines the opacity of the plane for the section object. The property value can range from 1 to 100. The lower the value, the more opaque the section plane object. See Figure 12-11.

Plane color

The plane of the section object can be set to any color available in the **Select Color** dialog box. To change the color, select the Plane Color property and then select a color from the drop-down list. To choose a color in the **Select Color** dialog box, pick the Select Color... entry in the drop-down list. This property only affects the plane of the section object, not the lines defining the boundary, volume, or section line. The color of these lines is controlled by the Color property in the **General** category.

Editing the Section Object

When the translucent planes of a section object or the lines representing the section object state is picked, grips are displayed. The specific grips displayed are related to the current section object state. Refer to Figure 12-9. The types of grips are:

- Base grip.
- Menu grip.
- Direction grip.
- Second grip.
- Arrow grips.
- Segment end grips.

Base grip

The *base grip* appears at the first point picked when defining the section object. See Figure 12-12. It is the grip about which the section object can be rotated and scaled. The section object can also be moved using this grip.

Figure 12-11.
A—The Plane Transparency property of the section plane object is set to 1 (or 1% transparent). B—The Plane Transparency property of the section plane object is set to 85 (or 85% transparent).

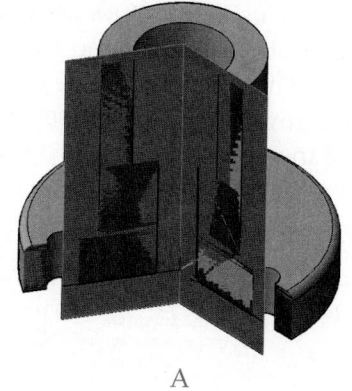
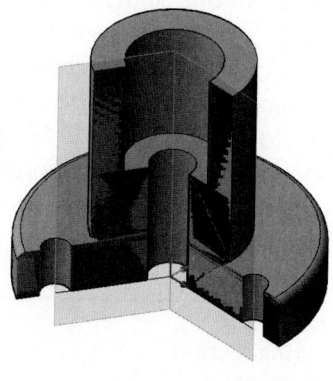

A   B

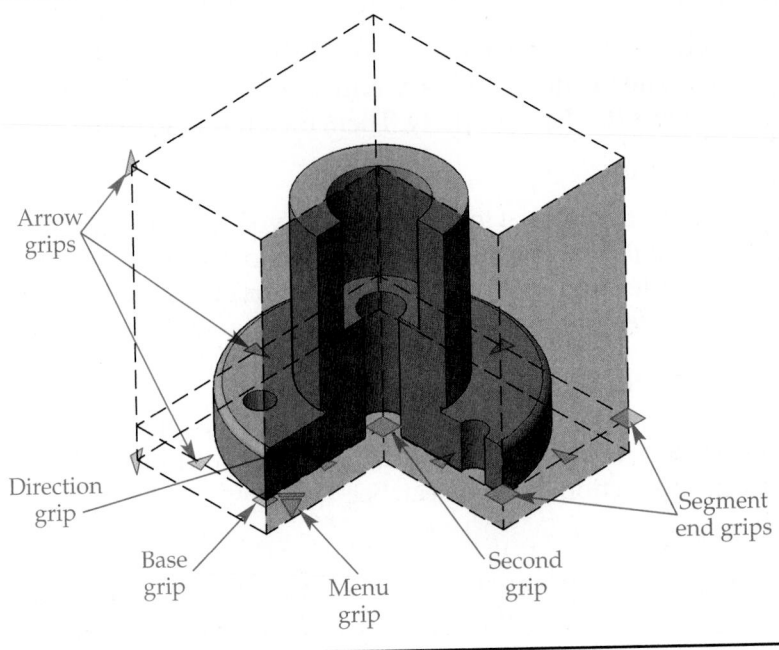

Figure 12-12.
The types of grips displayed on a section object.

Arrow grips

Direction grip

Base grip

Menu grip

Second grip

Segment end grips

Menu grip

The *menu grip* is always next to the base grip. Refer to Figure 12-12. Picking this grip displays the section state menu. See Figure 12-13. To switch the section object between states, pick the grip and then select the state from the menu.

Direction grip

The *direction grip* indicates the direction in which the section will be viewed. Refer to Figure 12-12. Pick the grip to rotate the view 180°. The direction grip also shows the direction of the live section. Live sectioning is discussed later in this chapter.

Second grip

The *second grip* appears at the second point picked when defining the section object. See Figure 12-12. The section object can be rotated and stretched about the base grip using the second grip.

Arrow grips

Arrow grips are located on all of the lines that represent the section plane, boundary, and volume. Refer to Figure 12-12. These grips are used to lengthen or shorten the section plane object segments, or the height of the section volume. The arrow grips at the top and bottom of the boundary box are used to change the height. Regardless of where the pointer is moved, the section object only extends in the segment's current plane. Changing the length of one segment of the section plane does not affect other segments.

In Figure 12-7, you saw an example of using the **Draw section** option to create a section object. The way in which the section object was created resulted in the section plane not extending beyond the solid object. This can quickly be corrected using the arrow grips. Notice in Figure 12-14 that the arrow grip is being used to extend the left side of the section plane past the boundary of the solid model. This allows any subsequent section views to display the entire object rather than just a portion of it. The right side of the section plane can be extended in the same manner using the opposite arrow grip.

Figure 12-13.
Changing section object states.

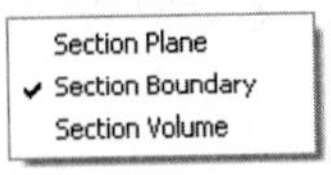

Section Plane
✔ Section Boundary
Section Volume

AutoCAD and Its Applications—Advanced

Figure 12-14.
A—The arrow grip is being used to extend the left side of the section plane past the boundary of the solid model. B—The edited section object. The right side can be corrected in the same manner.

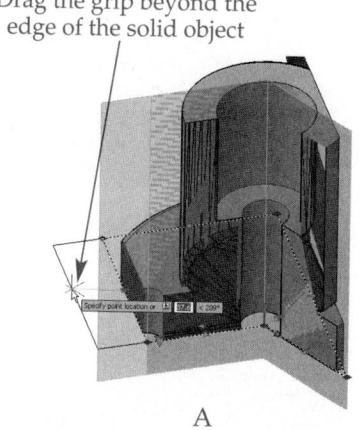

Drag the grip beyond the edge of the solid object

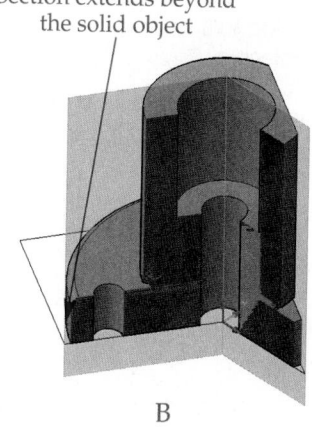

Section extends beyond the solid object

A

B

The arrow grips located on the line segments of the section plane move the position of the section plane. As a segment of the section plane is moved, it maintains its angular relationship and connection to any adjacent section plane.

Segment end grips

The *segment end grips* are located at the end of each line segment defining the section object state. Refer to **Figure 12-12.** The number of displayed segmented end grips depends on whether the section object is in the section plane, section boundary, or section volume state. These grips provide access to the standard grip editing options of stretch, move, copy, rotate, scale, and mirror. If the rotate option is used, the section plane is rotated about the selected segment end grip. Moving a segment end grip can change the angle between section plane segments.

Adding Jogs to a Section

You can quickly add a jog, or offset, to an existing section object. First, select the section object. Then, right-click to display the shortcut menu and select **Add jog to section**. You can also enter the **JOGSECTION** command. You are then prompted:

> Specify a point on the section line to add jog:

Select a point directly on the section line. If any object snap is active, the **Nearest** object snap is temporarily turned on to ensure you pick the line. Once you pick, the jog is automatically added perpendicular to the line segment. See **Figure 12-15A.**

It is not critical that you pick the exact location on the line where you want the jog to occur. Remember, grips allow you to easily adjust the section plane location later. Notice in **Figure 12-15B** that the second jog barely cuts through the first hole. The intention is to run the section plane through the middle of the hole. To fix this, drag the arrow grip so the section plane segment is in the desired location, **Figure 12-15C.**

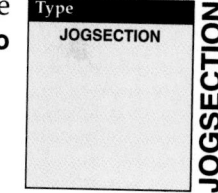

Type
JOGSECTION

JOGSECTION

PROFESSIONAL TIP

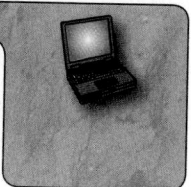

If the section plane is not properly located, you can quickly change it. Simply pick the section object and right-click to display the shortcut menu. Then, select **Move**, **Scale**, or **Rotate** from the shortcut menu. Finally, adjust the section object location as needed.

Figure 12-15.
Adding a jog to a
section object.
A—Pick a point on
the section line to add
a jog. B—The jog is
added, but it is not in
the proper location.
C—Using the arrow
grip, the jog has been
moved to the proper
location.

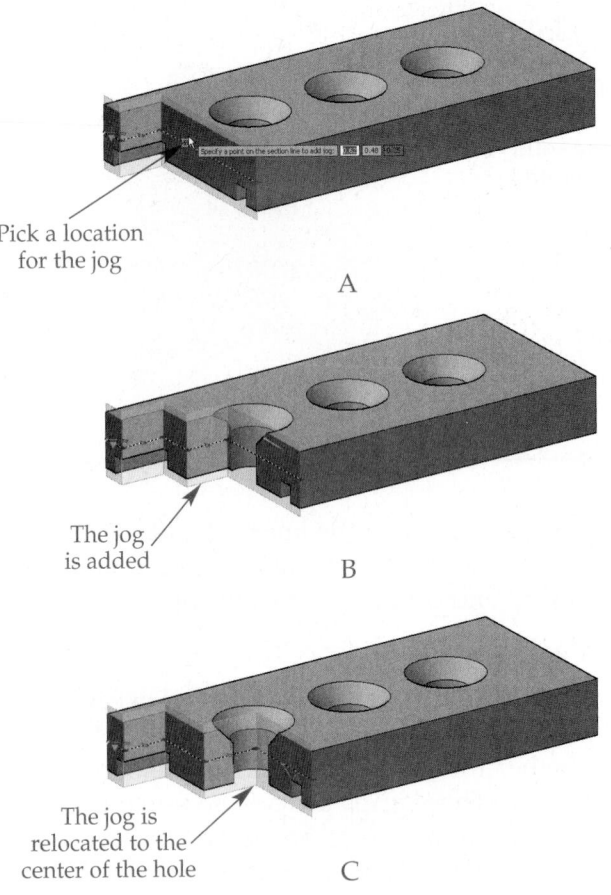

Pick a location
for the jog

A

The jog
is added

B

The jog is
relocated to the
center of the hole

C

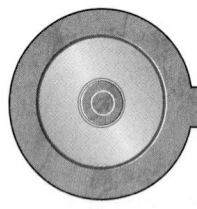

Exercise 12-3
Complete the exercise on the Student CD.

Live Sectioning

Live sectioning is a tool that enables you to view the internal features of 3D solids, surfaces, and regions that are cut by the section plane of the section object. The view is dynamically updated as the section object is moved. This tool is used for visualization of internal features and for establishing section locations from which 2D and 3D section views can be created. Live sectioning is either on or off.

As you have seen, if a face is selected as the section plane, live sectioning is automatically turned on. However, when picking two points or using the **Draw** option of the **SECTIONPLANE** command, live sectioning is off. Live sectioning can be turned on and off for individual section objects, but only one section object can be "live" at any given time. To turn live sectioning on or off, select the section object. Then, right-click to display the shortcut menu and pick **Activate live sectioning**. See Figure 12-16. A check mark appears next to the menu item when live sectioning is on. You can also enter the **LIVESECTION** command and select the section object to toggle the on/off setting. When live sectioning is turned on, the material behind the viewing direction of the section plane is removed. The cross section of the 3D object is shown in gray and the internal shape of the 3D object is visible.

A wide variety of options allow you to change the appearance of not only the live sectioning display, but also of 2D and 3D section blocks that can be created from the sectioned display. These settings are found in the **Section Settings** dialog box. See Figure 12-17. To open this dialog box, select the section object, right-click, and pick **Live section settings...** in the shortcut menu.

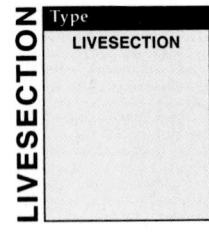

Type

LIVESECTION

LIVESECTION

Figure 12-16.
Live sectioning can be turned on for any section state by selecting the section object, right-clicking to display the shortcut menu, and picking **Activate live sectioning**.

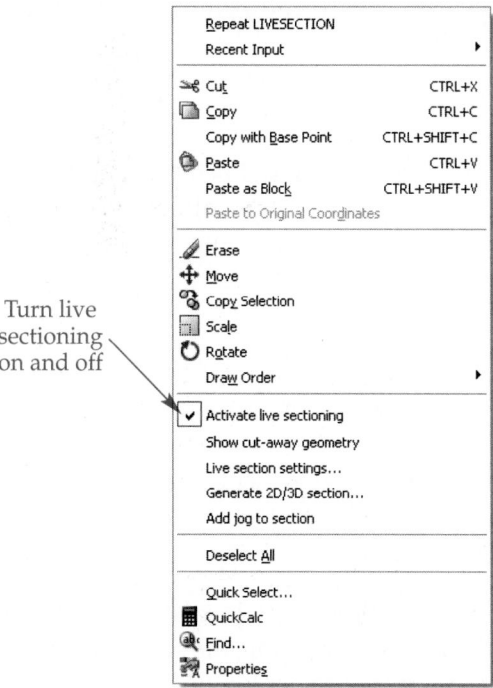

Turn live sectioning on and off

Figure 12-17.
Section settings. A—For a 2D block. B—For a 3D block. C—For live sectioning.

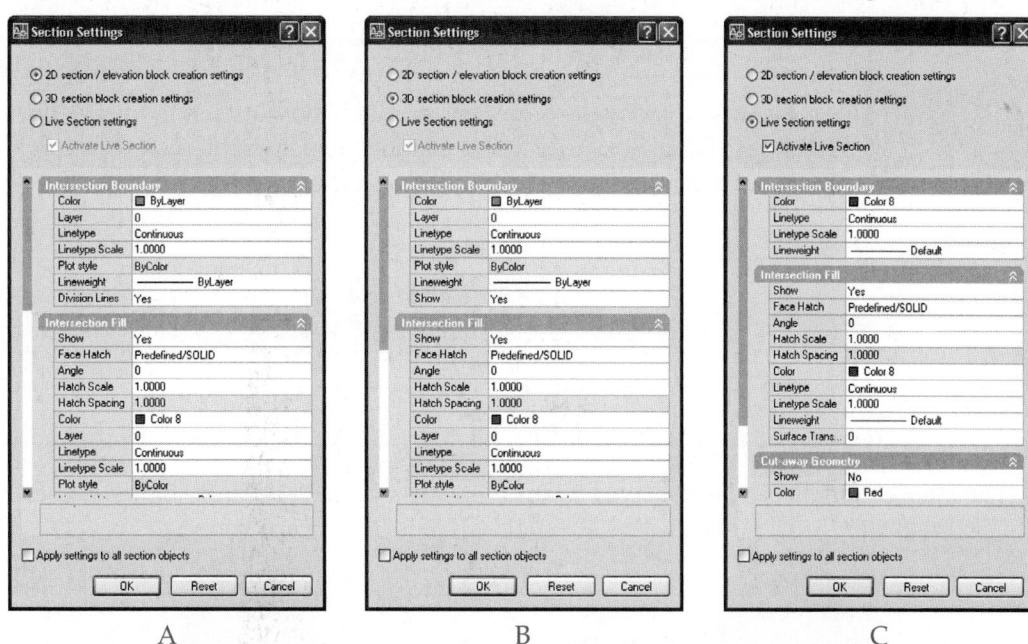

    A   B   C

  To change the settings for live sectioning, pick the **Live section settings** radio button at the top of the **Section Settings** dialog box. The categories displayed in the dialog box contain properties related to live sectioning. Settings for 2D and 3D sections and elevations are discussed later in this chapter.

  The three categories for live sectioning are **Intersection Boundary**, **Intersection Fill**, and **Cut-Away Geometry**. To display a brief description of any property, select the property in the **Section Settings** dialog box. The description is displayed at the bottom of the dialog box.

Intersection boundary

The intersection boundary is where the model is intersected by the section object. It is represented by line segments. You can set the color, linetype, linetype scale, and lineweight of the intersection boundary lines. Any linetype loaded into AutoCAD can be used.

Intersection fill

The intersection fill is the material visible on the model surface where the section object cuts. It is displayed as a solid fill, by default. Any hatch pattern available in AutoCAD can be used as the intersection fill. The angle, hatch scale, and hatch spacing can be set. In addition, the linetype, linetype scale, and lineweight can be changed. The fill pattern can even be set to be transparent.

Cutaway geometry

The cutaway geometry is the part of the model removed by the live sectioning. By default, this geometry is not displayed. Changing the Show property to Yes displays the geometry. See **Figure 12-18.** You can set the color, linetype, and linetype scale of the lines representing the cutaway geometry. In addition, the Face Transparency and Edge Transparency properties allow you to create a see-through effect, as seen in **Figure 12-19.** Each of these two properties is set to 50 by default.

PROFESSIONAL TIP

You can also display the cutaway geometry without using the **Section Settings** dialog box. Select the section object, right-click, and pick **Show cut-away geometry** in the shortcut menu.

Exercise 12-4
Complete the exercise on the Student CD.

Figure 12-18.
A—The intersection fill can be displayed as a hatch pattern in any specified color. B—The cutaway geometry is displayed.

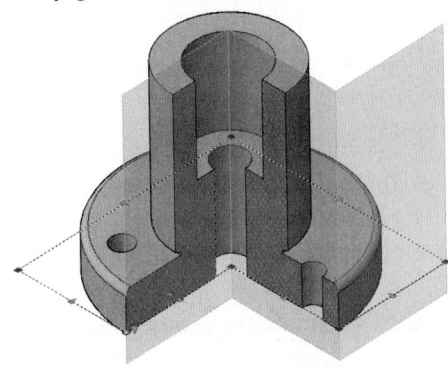

A   B

Figure 12-19.
The cutaway geometry
is displayed with 100%
transparent faces and
solid black lines.

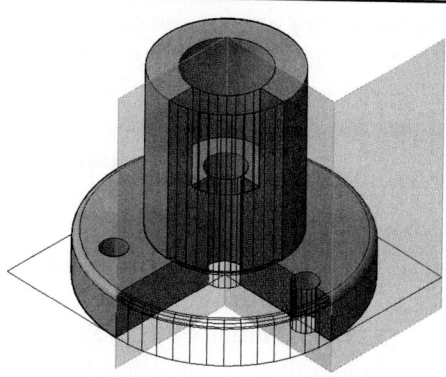

Generating 2D and 3D Sections and Elevations

The **SECTIONPLANE** command provides a fast and efficient method of creating sections. The sections can be either 2D or 3D. Not only can the sections be displayed on the current drawing, they can also be exported as a file that can then be used in any other drawing or document for display, technical drawing, or manufacturing purposes.

Creating sections

To create a section, select the section object, right-click, and pick **Generate 2D/3D section...** from the shortcut menu. The **Generate Section/Elevation** dialog box is displayed. See Figure 12-20. To expand the dialog box, pick the **Show details** button. In this dialog box, you can specify whether the section will be 2D or 3D, select what is included in the section, and specify a destination for the section.

To create a 2D section, pick the **2D Section/Elevation** radio button in the **2D/3D** area of the dialog box. A 2D section is projected onto the section plane, but is placed flat on the XY plane of the current UCS. To create a 3D section, pick the **3D Section** radio button. A 3D section is placed so its surfaces are parallel to the corresponding cut surfaces on the 3D object.

Figure 12-20.
The expanded
**Generate Section/
Elevation** dialog box.

Pick 2D or 3D

Select objects
to include

Select where
the section will
be placed

Pick to expand
or collapse the
dialog box

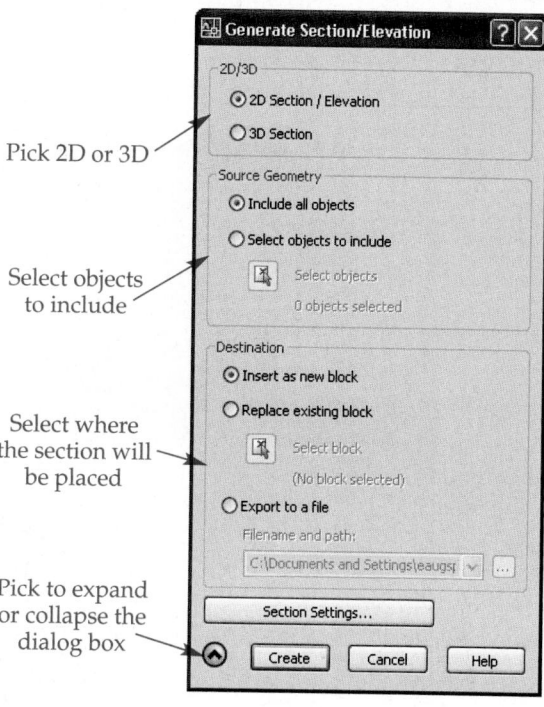

In the **Source Geometry** area of the dialog box, you can specify which geometry is included in the section. Picking the **Include all objects** radio button includes all 3D solids, surfaces, and regions in the section. To limit the section to certain objects, pick the **Select objects to include** radio button. Then, pick the **Select objects** button, select the objects on-screen, and press [Enter]. The number of selected objects is then displayed in the dialog box.

The **Destination** area of the dialog box is where you specify how the section will be placed. To place the section into the current drawing, pick the **Insert as new block** radio button. To update an existing section block, pick the **Replace existing block** radio button. Then, pick the **Select block** button, select the block on-screen, and press [Enter]. You will need to do this if the section object is changed. To save the section to a file for use in other drawings, pick the **Export to a file** radio button. Then, enter a path and file name in the text box.

Once all settings have been made, pick the **Create** button. The section is attached to the cursor and can be placed like a regular block. See **Figure 12-21.** Additionally, the options available are the same as if a regular block is being inserted. Once the block is inserted it can be moved, rotated, and scaled as needed.

Section settings

The **Section Settings…** button at the bottom of the **Generate Section/Elevation** dialog box opens the **Section Settings** dialog box discussed earlier. Using this dialog box, you can adjust all of the properties associated with the type of section being created. Depending on whether the **2D Section** or **3D Section** radio button is selected in the **Generate Section/Elevation** dialog box, the appropriate categories and properties are displayed in the **Section Settings** dialog box. Refer to **Figure 12-17.**

The categories discussed earlier related to the **Live Section Settings** radio button are available, although not all of the properties are displayed. Also, two additional categories are displayed for 2D and 3D sections:

- **Background Lines.** Available for 2D and 3D sections.
- **Curved Tangency Lines.** Only available for 2D sections.

Examples of 2D and 3D sections inserted as blocks in the drawing are shown in **Figure 12-22.** Notice how properties can be set to show cutaway geometry in a different color, and to change the section pattern, color, and linetype scale.

Figure 12-21.
Inserting a 2D section block.

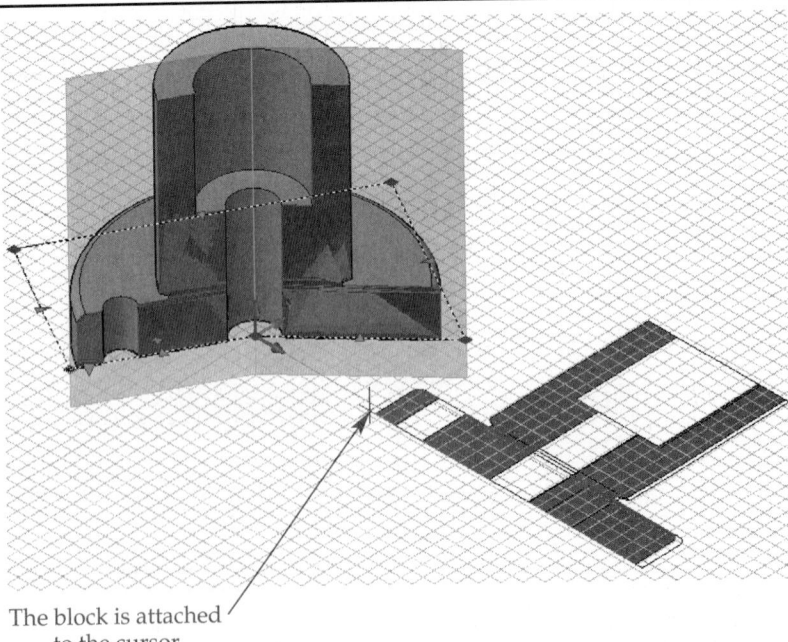

The block is attached to the cursor

Figure 12-22.
A—The section object is created. B—A 2D section block is inserted into the drawing and the view is made plan to the block. C—A 3D section block is inserted into the drawing. Notice how the hatch pattern is displayed. D—The 3D section block is updated and now the cutaway geometry is displayed.

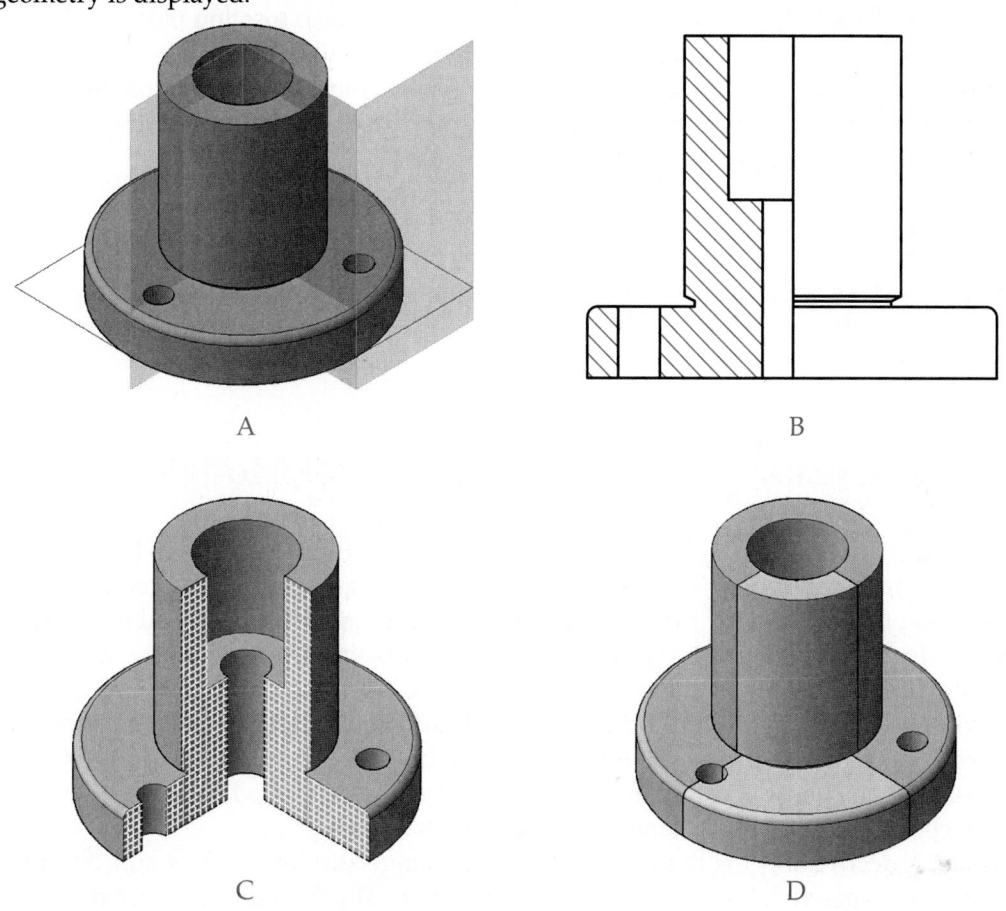

Background Lines. The properties in the **Background Lines** category provide control over the appearance of all lines that are not on the section plane. You can choose to have visible background lines, hidden background lines, or both displayed. They can be emphasized with color, linetype, or lineweight. These settings are applied to both visible and hidden background lines.

Curve Tangency Lines. The properties in the **Curved Tangency Lines** category apply to lines of tangency behind the section plane. For example, the object shown in Figure 12-22 has a round on the top of the base. This results in a line of tangency behind the section plane where the round meets the vertical edge. You can have these lines displayed or suppressed. In general, lines of tangency are not shown in a section view. If you choose to display these lines, you can set the color, layer, linetype, linetype scale, and lineweight of the lines.

NOTE

When a 3D section is created, you must turn off live sectioning to see the complete sectioned object in the block. With live sectioning on, only the cut surfaces appear in the block.

Updating the section view

Once the section view is created, it is not automatically updated if the section object is changed. To update the section view, select the section object (not the block), right-click, and pick **Generate 2D/3D section…** from the shortcut menu. Then, in the **Destination** area of the **Generate Section/Elevation** dialog box, pick the **Replace existing block** radio button. If necessary, pick the **Select block** button and select the section block in the drawing. If you want to change the appearance of the section view, pick the **Section Settings…** button and adjust the properties as needed. Finally, pick the **Create** button in the **Generate Section/Elevation** dialog box to update the section block.

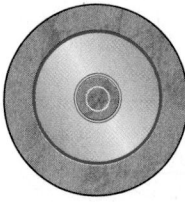

Exercise 12-5
Complete the exercise on the Student CD.

Creating a Flat Display of a 3D Model

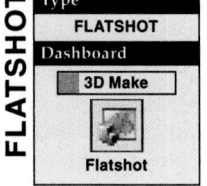

The **FLATSHOT** command creates a flat projection of the 3D objects in the drawing from the current viewpoint. The view that is created is composed of 2D geometry and is projected onto the XY plane of the current UCS. This capability is useful for creating technical documents in which pictorial views of 3D objects are required.

Once the command is initiated, the **Flatshot** dialog box is displayed. See Figure 12-23. The options in this dialog box are similar to those found in the **Section Settings** dialog box. However, the display properties of foreground and obscured lines is limited to color and linetype. You can choose whether or not obscured lines are displayed in the flat view. You can also choose whether or not tangential edges are included.

Select a destination for the flat view. Then, change the foreground and obscured lines settings as needed. Finally, pick the **Create** button. The flat view is inserted into the drawing as a block. Therefore, all of the ensuing prompts are those of a block insertion.

Figure 12-23.
The **Flatshot** dialog box.

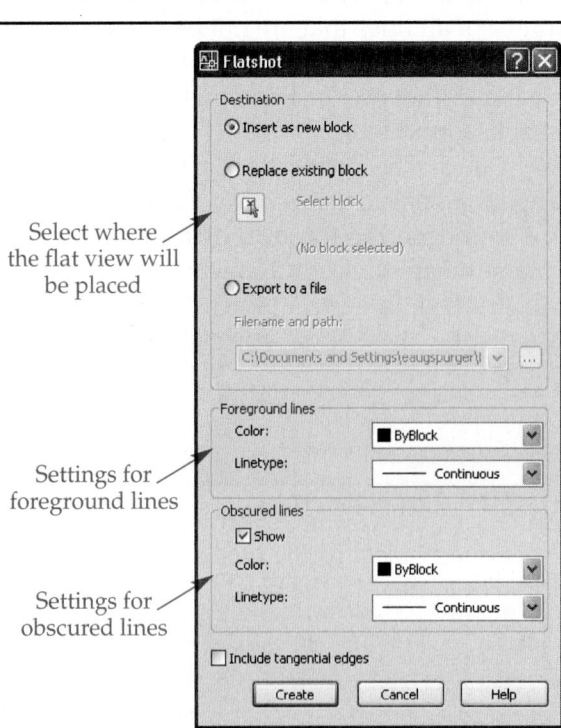

Select where the flat view will be placed

Settings for foreground lines

Settings for obscured lines

Figure 12-24.
A—The 3D view from which a flat view will be generated. B—The inserted flat view. The viewpoint is plan to the block.

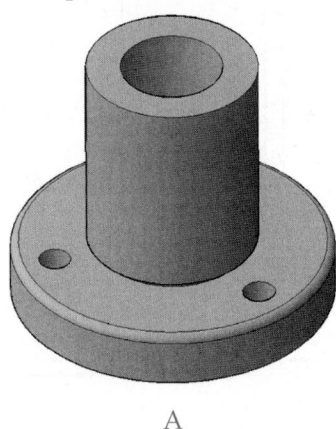
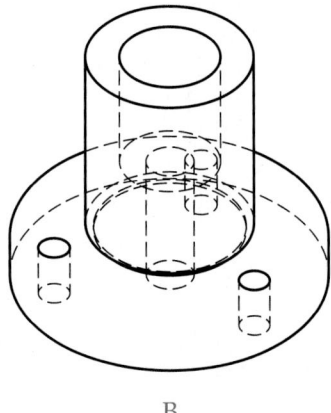

A   B

Use the **PLAN** command to obtain a plan view of the current UCS. Since the flat view is a block, it can be edited using the **BEDIT** command. Figure 12-24 shows a pictorial view of a 3D object and a plan view of the resulting flat view. To update the flat view to one from a different viewpoint, repeat the command and select the **Replace existing block** radio button in the **Destination** area of the dialog box.

PROFESSIONAL TIP

If the intention is to create a block to be used for a technical document, it may be best to export the flat view block to a file. It can then be later inserted into a new AutoCAD drawing, and/or copied into a document file.

Exercise 12-6
Complete the exercise on the Student CD.

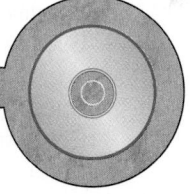

Creating and Using Multiview Layouts

Once a solid model has been constructed, it is easy to create a multiview layout using the **SOLVIEW** command. This command allows you to create a layout containing orthographic, section, and auxiliary views. The **SOLDRAW** command can then be used to complete profile and section views. **SOLDRAW** must be used after **SOLVIEW**. The **SOLPROF** command can be used to create a profile of the solid in the current view.

Creating Views with SOLVIEW

The **SOLVIEW** command is used to create new floating viewports and to establish the display within those viewports. Therefore, you may want to delete the default viewport in the paper space tab before using the **SOLVIEW** command.

First restore the WCS. This will help avoid any confusion. Then, display a plan view. See Figure 12-25. It helps to have additional user coordinate systems created prior to using **SOLVIEW**. This allows you to construct orthographic views based on a specific named UCS.

Figure 12-25.
Before using **SOLVIEW**,
display a plan view of
the WCS.

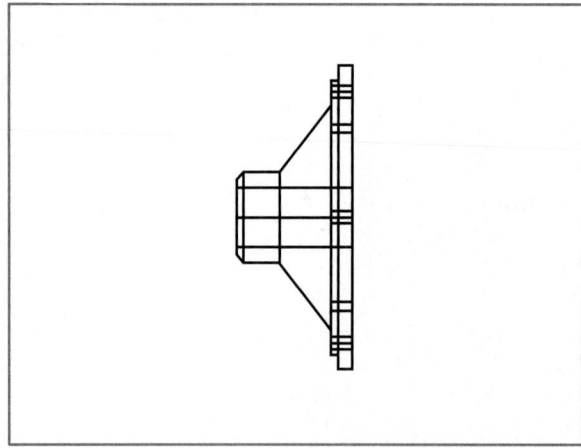

Before using the **SOLVIEW** command, visualize which view is going to be the top view (or plan view) and how you would like the model rotated in relationship to the layout. With this in mind, look at the current UCS icon and make sure that the X axis is pointing to the "right" and the Y axis is pointing "up" in your imagined layout. If this is not the case, then you must restore the WCS, rotate the current UCS, or restore a saved UCS to correctly align the axes. Then, when you enter the **SOLVIEW** command in the layout, you can simply select the current UCS and you will be creating the top or plan view of your model.

When you enter the **SOLVIEW** command while in model space, AutoCAD automatically switches to paper space (layout space). Next, create an initial view from which other views can project. This is normally the top or front. In the following example, the top view is constructed first by using the plan view of a UCS named Leftside.

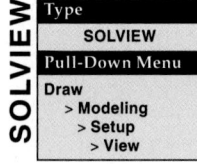

Enter an option [Ucs/Ortho/Auxiliary/Section]: **U**↵
Enter an option [Named/World/?/Current] <Current>: **N**↵
Enter name of UCS to restore: **LEFTSIDE**↵
Enter view scale <1.0>: **.5**↵
Specify view center: *(pick a location in the layout for the center of the view)*
Specify view center <specify viewport>: ↵
Specify first corner of viewport: *(pick the first corner of a paper space viewport outside of the object)*
Specify opposite corner of viewport: *(pick the opposite corner of the viewport)*
Enter view name: **TOPVIEW**↵ *(the left of the object in AutoCAD is the top of the part)*
Enter an option [Ucs/Ortho/Auxiliary/Section]: *(leave the command active at this time)*

You must provide a name for the view. The result is shown in **Figure 12-26.**

Figure 12-26.
The initial view
created with the **Ucs**
option of **SOLVIEW**.

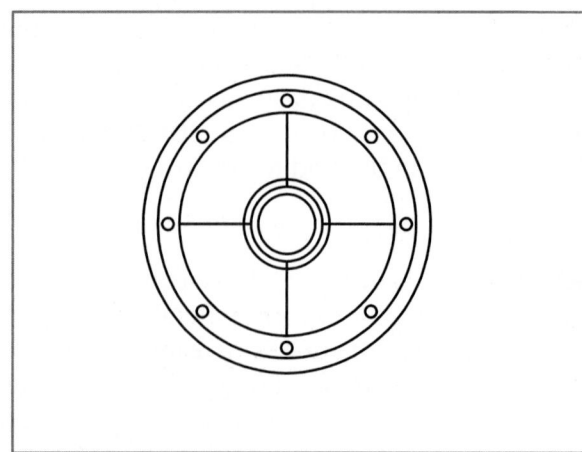

AutoCAD and Its Applications—Advanced

The **SOLVIEW** command remains active until you press the [Enter] or [Esc] key. If you exit **SOLVIEW**, you can still return to the drawing and create additional orthographic viewports. With the command active, continue and create a section view to the right of the top view:

Enter an option [Ucs/Ortho/Auxiliary/Section]: **S**↵
Specify first point of cutting plane: *(pick the quadrant at Point 1 in Figure 12-27)*
Specify second point of cutting plane: *(pick the quadrant at Point 2)*
Specify side to view from: *(pick Point 3)*
Enter view scale <0.5>: ↵
Specify view center: *(pick the center of the new section view)*
Specify view center <specify viewport>: ↵ *(this prompt remains active until [Enter] is pressed to allow you to adjust the view location if necessary)*
Specify first corner of viewport: *(pick one corner of the viewport)*
Specify opposite corner of viewport: *(pick the opposite corner of the viewport)*
Enter view name: **SECTION**↵
Enter an option [Ucs/Ortho/Auxiliary/Section]: ↵

Notice in **Figure 12-27** that the new view is shown in the current visual style and not as a section. This is normal. **SOLVIEW** is used to create the views. The **SOLDRAW** command draws the section lines. **SOLDRAW** is discussed later in this chapter.

A standard orthographic view can be created using the **Ortho** option of **SOLVIEW**. This is illustrated in the following example. The new orthographic view is shown in **Figure 12-28**.

Figure 12-27.
The section view created with **SOLVIEW** (shown on the right) does not show projection lines. The pick points are shown on the left.

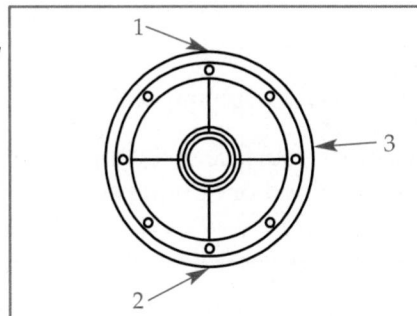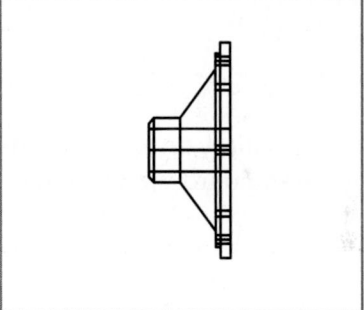

Figure 12-28.
An orthographic front view is created with the **Ortho** option of **SOLVIEW**. This is the view shown at the lower left.

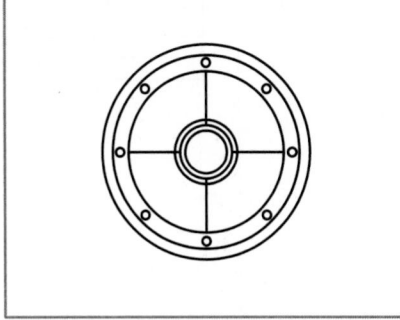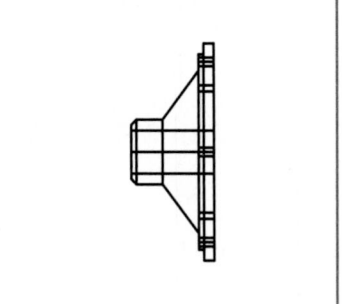

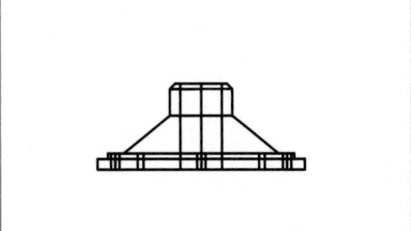

Enter an option [Ucs/Ortho/Auxiliary/Section]: **O**↵
Specify side of viewport to project: *(pick the bottom edge of the left viewport)*
Specify view center: *(pick the center of the new view)*
Specify view center <specify viewport>: ↵
Specify first corner of viewport: *(pick one corner of the viewport)*
Specify opposite corner of viewport: *(pick the opposite corner of the viewport)*
Enter view name: **FRONTVIEW**↵

The **SOLVIEW** command creates new layers that are used by **SOLDRAW** when profiles and sections are created. The layers are used for the placement of visible, hidden, dimension, and section lines. Each layer is named as the name of the view with a three letter tag, as shown in the following table. The use of these layers is discussed in the next section.

Layer Name	Object
View name-**VIS**	Visible lines
View name-**HID**	Hidden lines
View name-**DIM**	Dimension lines
View name-**HAT**	Hatch patterns (sections)

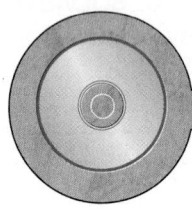

Exercise 12-7
Complete the exercise on the Student CD.

Creating Auxiliary Views with SOLVIEW

Auxiliary views are used to display a surface of an object that is not parallel to any of the standard views. It may be an inclined or oblique surface. Refer to **Figure 12-29**.

Figure 12-29.
An auxiliary view (shown in color) is created from the inclined plane in the front view.

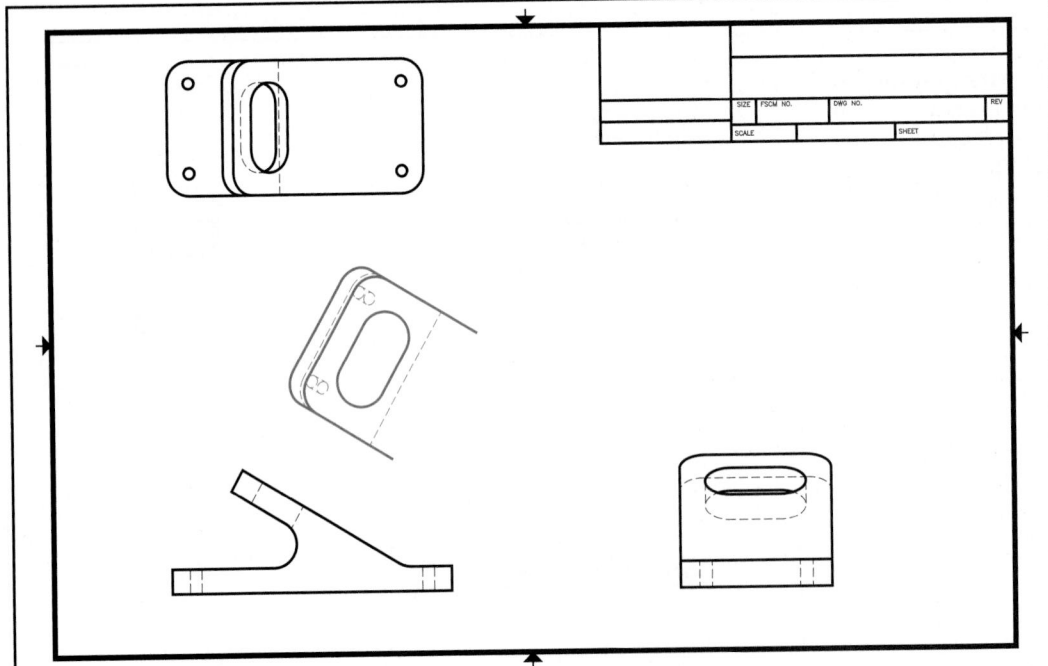

AutoCAD and Its Applications—Advanced

Sometimes these views are necessary to show or dimension a feature that is not being displayed in true size in any other view. The slot in the inclined surface in Figure 12-29 is not shown in true size in any of the standard views.

The auxiliary view is taken from one of the other views where the inclined surface is shown as an edge. The auxiliary view will be projected perpendicular to this surface. The auxiliary view is created by picking two points on the surface in the front view and another point to indicate the line of sight.

> Enter an option [Ucs/Ortho/Auxiliary/Section]: **A**↵
> Specify first point of inclined plane: (*using object snaps, pick a point on one end of the inclined surface*)
> Specify second point of inclined plane: (*pick a point on the other end of the inclined surface*)
> Specify side to view from: (*pick a point on the side of the surface from which you want to view it*)
> Specify the view center: <specify viewport>↵
> Specify first corner of viewport: (*pick one corner of the viewport*)
> Specify opposite corner of viewport: (*pick the opposite corner of the viewport*)
> Enter view name: **AUXILIARYVIEW**↵

Auxiliary views are often incomplete views, so it is acceptable to cut off portions of the view that are not necessary when you specify the corners of the viewport.

PROFESSIONAL TIP

When creating an auxiliary view, you may want to move other viewports that may be in the way to make room for the view.

Creating Finished Views with SOLDRAW

The **SOLVIEW** command saves information specific to each viewport when a new view is created. This information is used by the **SOLDRAW** command to construct a finished profile or section view. **SOLDRAW** first deletes any information currently on the *view name*-VIS, *view name*-HID, and *view name*-HAT layers for the selected view. Visible, hidden, and section lines are automatically placed on the appropriate layer. Therefore, you should avoid placing objects on any layer other than the *view name*-DIM layer.

The **SOLDRAW** command automatically creates a profile or section in the selected viewport. If you select a viewport that was created using the **Section** option of **SOLVIEW**, the **SOLDRAW** command uses the current values of the **HPNAME**, **HPSCALE**, and **HPANG** system variables to construct the section. These three variables control the angle, scale factor, and name of the hatch pattern.

If a view is selected that was not created as a section in **SOLVIEW**, the **SOLDRAW** command constructs a profile view. All new visible and hidden lines are placed on the *view name*-VIS or *view name*-HID layer. All existing objects on those layers are deleted.

Once the command is initiated, you are prompted to select objects. Pick the border of the viewport(s) for which you want the profile or section generated. When all viewports are selected, press [Enter] and the profiles and sections are created.

After the profile construction is completed, lines that should be a hidden linetype are still visible (solid). This is because the linetype set for the *view name*-HID layer is Continuous. Change the linetype for the layer to Hidden and the drawing should appear as shown in Figure 12-30, depending on the current visual style and hatch settings. You may also want to change other layer properties such as color, lineweight, and plot style.

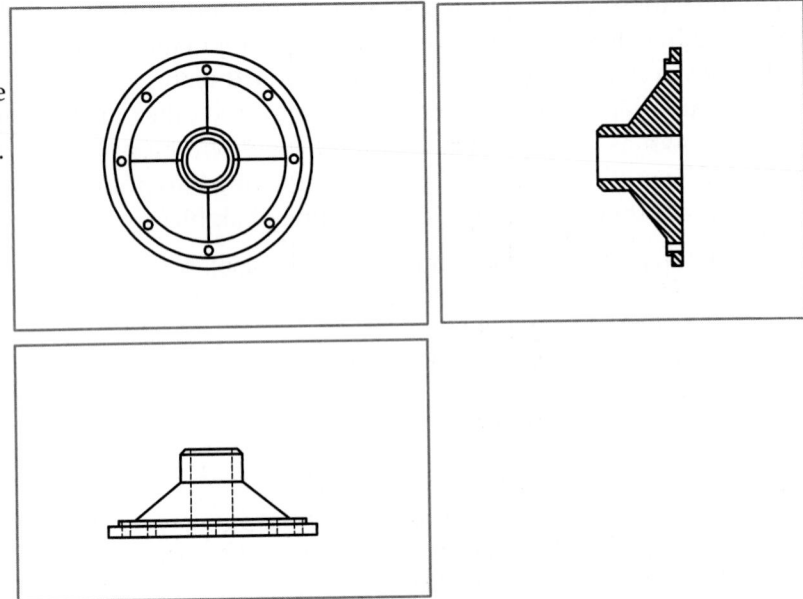

Figure 12-30.
The new front profile view shows hidden lines after the linetype is set to Hidden for the FRONTVIEW-HID layer.

Revising the 3D Model

If changes are needed after theses views are created, the best practice is to modify the original 3D solid. However, the views created with **SOLVIEW** and **SOLDRAW** will not immediately reflect changes. To update the views, simply start the **SOLDRAW** command, select the viewports, and press [Enter]. The views are then updated with the changes.

When you go to model space to edit the solid, you may find it difficult to work on the original model. The 2D views created with **SOLDRAW** are projected on the top, bottom, left, and right, and sometimes within the model itself. It may be a good idea to set up a layer filter to temporarily freeze these layers while making changes. Remember to thaw the layers before updating the viewports with **SOLDRAW**.

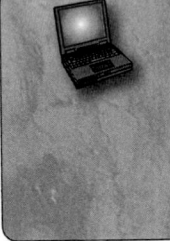

PROFESSIONAL TIP

If you wish to dimension views created with **SOLVIEW** and **SOLDRAW**, use the view-specific DIM layers. These layers are created for that purpose and are only visible in one view. **SOLDRAW** does not delete information on the DIM layers when it constructs a view. If you prefer to dimension in paper space, use a layer other than the DIM layers created by **SOLVIEW**.

Adding a 3D View in Paper Space to the Drawing Layout

If you want to add a paper space viewport that contains a 3D (pictorial) view of the solid, use the **MVIEW** or **VPORTS** command. Create a single viewport by picking the corners. The object will appear in the viewport. Next, use the **3DORBIT** command or a preset isometric viewpoint to achieve the desired 3D view. Pan and zoom as necessary. Change to the parallel or perspective projection if needed. You can also use the **Visual Style** control panel in the **Dashboard** to adjust the display of the 3D viewport. The visual style set current for this viewport does not affect the displays in the other viewports. See **Figure 12-31.**

Figure 12-31.
Create a 3D viewport with the **MVIEW** command. You can hide the lines in the viewport, as shown at the lower right. To plot the viewport as a hidden display, use the **MVIEW Shadeplot** option and set it to Hidden.

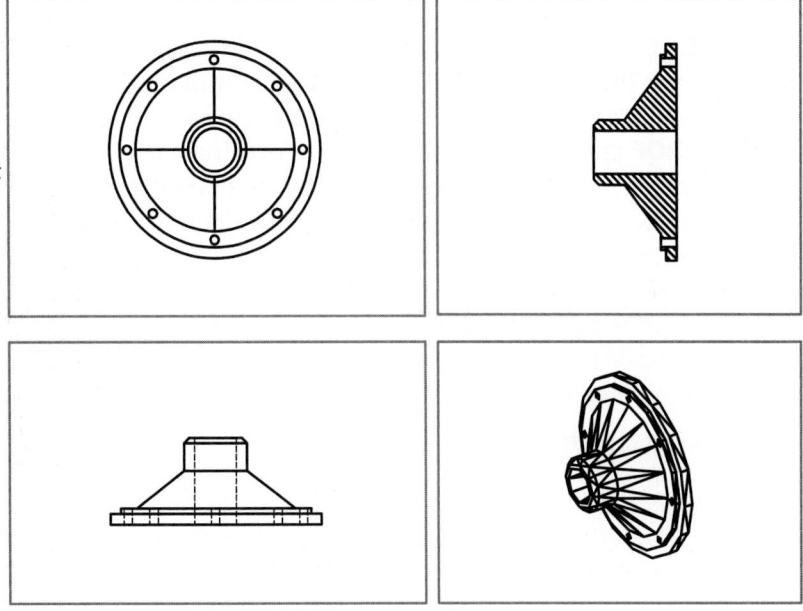

In order to have the hidden display correctly plotted, use the **MVIEW Shadeplot** option on the 3D viewport. Enter the command and select the **Shadeplot** option. Then, set the option to **Hidden**. If you have a hidden display shown in the viewport, you can also select **As displayed**. Then, pick the viewport when prompted to select objects.

Alternately, you can select the viewport and use the **Properties** window to set the Shade plot property to As Displayed or Hidden. Any visual style display of the viewport can also be plotted in this manner by setting **MVIEW Shadeplot** to **As Displayed** (when the view is shaded) or **Rendered**.

Tips

Remember the following points when working with **SOLVIEW** and **SOLDRAW**.
- Use **SOLVIEW** first and then **SOLDRAW**.
- Do not draw on the *view name*-HID and *view name*-VIS layers.
- Place dimensions for each view on the *view name*-DIM layer for that specific view.
- After using **SOLVIEW**, use **SOLDRAW** on all viewports in order to create hidden lines or section views.
- Change the linetype on the *view name*-HID layer to Hidden and adjust other layer properties as needed.
- Create 3D viewports with the **MVIEW** or **VPORTS** command and **3DORBIT** or a preset isometric view. Remove hidden lines when plotting with the **MVIEW Shadeplot** option set to **Hidden**.
- Plot the drawing in layout (paper) space at the scale of 1:1.

Exercise 12-8
Complete the exercise on the Student CD.

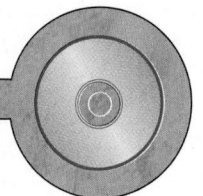

Creating a Profile with SOLPROF

SOLPROF

Type
SOLPROF
Pull-Down Menu
Draw
> Modeling
> Setup
> Profile

The **SOLPROF** command creates a profile view from a 3D solid model. This is similar to the **Profile** option of the **SOLVIEW** command. However, **SOLPROF** is limited to creating a profile view of the solid for the current view only.

SOLPROF creates a block of all lines forming the profile of the object. It also creates a block of the hidden lines of the object. The original 3D object is retained. Each of these blocks is placed on a new layer with the name of PH-*view handle* and PV-*view handle*. A ***view handle*** is a name composed of numbers and letters that is automatically given to a viewport by AutoCAD. For example, if the view handle for the current viewport is 2C9, the **SOLPROF** command creates the layers PH-2C9 and PV-2C9.

You must be in layout (paper) space and have a model space viewport active to use the command. Once the command is initiated, you are prompted to select objects:

> Select objects: *(pick the solid)*
> 1 found
> Select objects: ↵
> Display hidden profile lines on separate layer? [Yes/No] <Y>: ↵
> Project profile lines onto a plane? [Yes/No] <Y>: ↵

If you answer yes to this prompt, the 3D profile lines are projected to a 2D plane and converted to 2D objects. This produces a cleaner profile.

> Delete tangential edges? [Yes/No] <Y>: ↵

Answering yes to this prompt produces a proper 2D view by eliminating lines that would normally appear at tangent points of arcs and lines. The original object and the profile created with **SOLPROF** are shown in **Figure 12-32.**

NOTE

When plotting views created with **SOLPROF**, hidden lines may not be displayed unless you freeze the layer that contains the original 3D object.

Figure 12-32.
A—The original solid.
B—A profile created with **SOLPROF**.

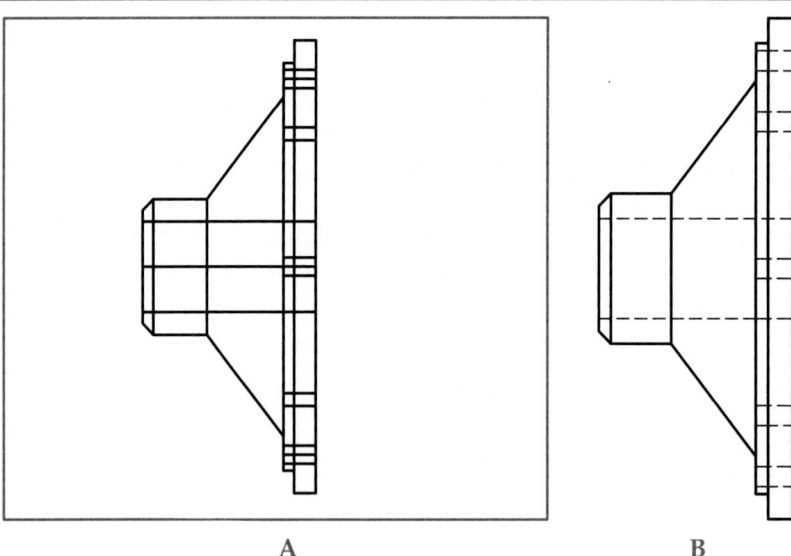

A   B

Solid Model Analysis

The **MASSPROP** command allows you to analyze a solid model for its physical properties. The data obtained from **MASSPROP** can be retained for reference by saving the data to a file. The default file name is the drawing name. The file is an ASCII text file with a .mpr (mass properties) extension. The analysis can be used for third party applications to produce finite element analysis, material lists, or other testing studies.

Type	
MASSPROP	
Pull-Down Menu	
Tools	
> Inquiry	
> Region/Mass	
Properties	

MASSPROP

Once the command is initiated, you are prompted to select objects. Pick the objects for which you want the mass properties displayed and press [Enter]. AutoCAD analyzes the model and displays the results in the AutoCAD text window. See **Figure 12-33**. The following properties are listed.

- **Mass.** A measure of the inertia of a solid. In other words, the more mass an object has, the more inertia it has. Note: Mass is *not* a unit of measurement of inertia.
- **Volume.** The amount of 3D space the solid occupies.
- **Bounding box.** The dimensions of a 3D box that fully encloses the solid.
- **Centroid.** A point in 3D space that represents the geometric center of the mass.
- **Moments of inertia.** A solid's resistance when rotating about a given axis.
- **Products of inertia.** A solid's resistance when rotating about two axes at a time.
- **Radii of gyration.** Similar to moments of inertia. Specified as a radius about an axis.
- **Principal moments and X-Y-Z directions about a centroid.** The axes about which the moments of inertia are the highest and lowest.

PROFESSIONAL TIP

Advanced applications of solid model design and analysis are possible with Autodesk Inventor® software. This product allows you to create parametric designs and assign a wide variety of materials to the solid model.

Figure 12-33.
The **MASSPROP** command displays a list of solid properties in the AutoCAD text window.

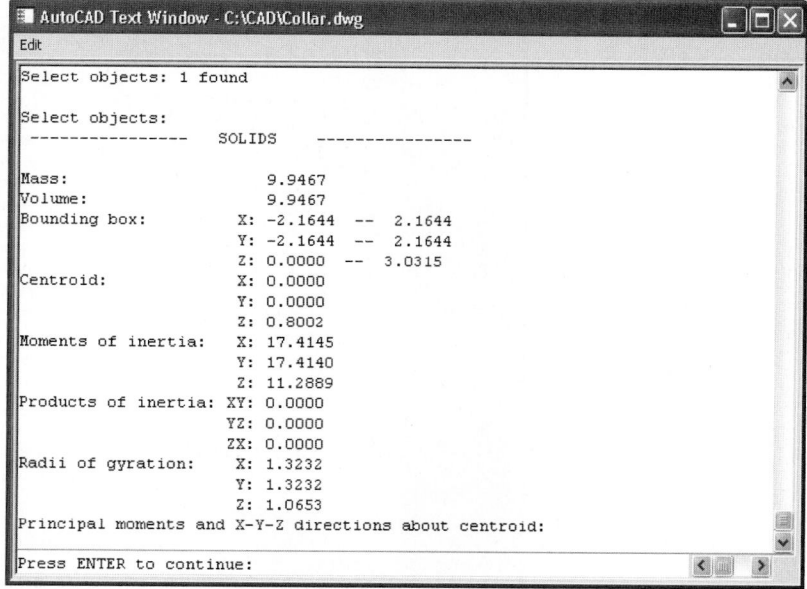

AutoCAD drawing files can be converted to files that can be used for testing and analysis. Use the **ACISOUT** command or **Export Data** dialog box to create a file with a .sat extension. These files can be imported into AutoCAD with the **ACISIN** or **IMPORT** command.

Solids can also be exported for use with stereolithography software. These files have a .stl extension. Use the **STLOUT** command or the **Export Data** dialog box to create STL files.

Importing and Exporting Solid Model Files

Type	
ACISOUT	
EXPORT	
Pull-Down Menu	
File	
> Export...	

A solid model is frequently used with analysis and testing software or in the manufacture of a part. The **ACISOUT** and **EXPORT** commands allow you to create a type of file that can be used for these purposes. Once the **ACISOUT** command is initiated, you are prompted to select objects. After selecting objects and pressing [Enter], a standard save dialog box is displayed. See **Figure 12-34.** When using the **EXPORT** command, the standard save dialog box appears first. After entering a file name and selecting a file type (SAT), you are then prompted to select objects.

Type	
ACISIN	
IMPORT	
Pull-Down Menu	
Insert	
> ACIS File...	

An SAT file can be imported into AutoCAD and automatically converted into a drawing file using the **ACISIN** and **IMPORT** commands. Once either command is initiated, a standard open dialog box appears. Change the file type to SAT, locate the file, and pick the **Open** button.

Stereolithography Files

Stereolithography is a technology that creates plastic, prototype 3D models using a computer-generated solid model, a laser, and a vat of liquid polymer. This technology is also called *rapid prototyping* or *3D printing.* A prototype 3D model can be designed and formed in a short amount of time without using standard manufacturing processes.

Most software used to create a stereolithograph can read STL files. AutoCAD can export a drawing file to the STL format, but *cannot* import STL files. Also, the solid model must be positioned in the current UCS in such a way so the entire object has positive XYZ coordinates.

Type	
STLOUT	
EXPORT	
Pull-Down Menu	
File	
> Export...	

The **STLOUT** and **EXPORT** commands can be used to create an STL file. Once the **STLOUT** command is initiated, you are prompted to select an object. You can only

Figure 12-34.
Exporting an ACIS file.

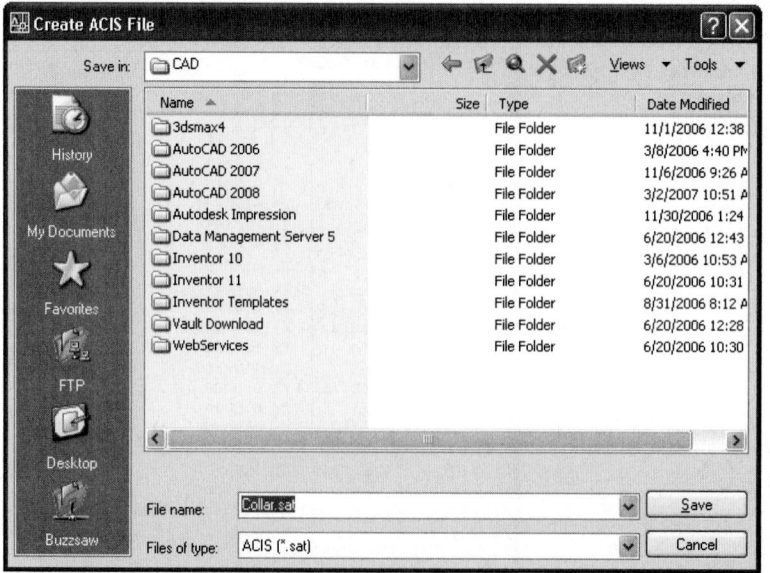

select a single object to be exported. You are then asked if you want to create a binary STL file. If you answer no to the prompt, an ASCII file is created. Keep in mind that a binary STL file may be as much as five times smaller than the same file in ASCII format. After you choose the type of file, a standard save dialog box is displayed. Type the file name in the **File name:** edit box and pick **Save** or press [Enter].

Once the **EXPORT** command is initiated, the standard save dialog box appears. Name the file and select the STL file type. Once the dialog box is closed, you are prompted to select an object. After you select the object and press [Enter], the file is created. You are not given the option of selecting a binary or ASCII format for the file.

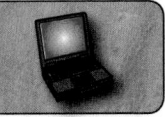

PROFESSIONAL TIP

The **FACETRES** setting affects the "resolution" of the solid in an exported STL file and, thus, the final stereolithograph.

Exercise 12-9
Complete the exercise on the Student CD.

Chapter Test

Answer the following questions. Write your answers on a separate sheet of paper or complete the electronic chapter test on the Student CD.

1. What does the **SECTIONPLANE** command create?
2. How is the **Face** option of the **SECTIONPLANE** command used?
3. Which option of the **SECTIONPLANE** command is used to create sections with jogs?
4. When a section object is created by picking a face or two points, or using the **Orthographic** option of the **SECTIONPLANE** command, which section object state is established?
5. Which section object grips are used to accomplish the following tasks?
   A. Change the section object state.
   B. Lengthen or shorten the section object segment.
   C. Rotate the section view 180°.
6. How is live sectioning turned on or off?
7. Which category in the **Section Settings** dialog box provides control over the material that is removed by the section object?
8. What are the two types of section view blocks that can be created from a section object?
9. Which command is used to create a flat view of the objects projected from the current viewpoint?
10. Which command should be used first, **SOLDRAW** or **SOLVIEW**?
11. Which option of the **SOLVIEW** command is used to create an orthographic view?
12. Name the layer(s) that the **SOLVIEW** command automatically create(s).
13. Which layer(s) in Question 12 should you avoid drawing on?
14. Which command can automatically complete a section view using the current settings of **HPNAME**, **HPSCALE**, and **HPANG**?
15. Which command creates a profile view from a 3D model?
16. What is the function of the **MASSPROP** command?

17. What is the extension of the ASCII file that can be created by **MASSPROP**?
18. What is a *centroid?*
19. Which commands export and import solid models?
20. Which type of file has an .stl extension?

Drawing Problems

1. Open one of your solid model problems from a previous chapter and do the following.
   A. Use the **Face** option of the **SECTIONPLANE** command to create a section object.
   B. Alter the section so that the section plane object cuts through features of the model.
   C. Change the section settings to display an ANSI hatch pattern.
   D. Save the drawing as P12_01.
2. Open one of your solid model problems from a previous chapter and do the following.
   A. Construct a section through the model using the **Draw** option of the **SECTIONPLANE** command. Cut through as many features as possible.
   B. Display cutaway geometry with a 50% transparency.
   C. Display section lines using an appropriate hatch pattern.
   D. Generate a 3D section block that displays the cutaway geometry in a color of your choice.
   E. Create a layout with a viewport for the 3D block displayed at half the size of the original model.
   F. Save the drawing as P12_02.
3. Open one of your solid model problems from a previous chapter and do the following.
   A. Create a multiview layout of the model. One of the views should be a section view. Use a total of three 2D views.
   B. Use **SOLVIEW** and **SOLDRAW** to create the views. Be sure that section lines and hidden lines are displayed properly.
   C. Create a fourth viewport that contains a 3D view of the solid. Place the label PICTORIAL VIEW within the viewport.
   D. Plot the drawing so the 3D view is displayed with hidden lines removed.
   E. Save the drawing as P12_03.
4. Open one of your solid model problems from a previous chapter and do the following.
   A. Display the model in a plan view.
   B. Use **SOLPROF** to create a profile view. Wblock the profile view to a file named P12_04PLN.
   C. Display the original model in a 3D view.
   D. Use **SECTION** to construct a front-view section of the model. Delete the original 3D solid.
   E. Display the section as a plan view.
   F. Insert the wblock P12_04PLN above the section view. Adjust the views so that they align properly.
   G. Save the drawing as P12_04.

5. Choose five solid model problems from previous chapters and copy them to a new folder. Then, do the following.
   A. Open the first drawing. Export it as an SAT file.
   B. Do the same for the remaining four files.
   C. Compare the sizes of the SAT files with the DWG files. Compare the combined sizes of both types of files.
   D. Begin a new drawing and import one of the SAT files.
6. Draw the object shown below as a solid model. Do not dimension the object. Then, do the following.
   A. Construct a section object that creates a full section along the centerline of the hole.
   B. Generate a 2D section and display it on the drawing at half the size of the original. Specify section settings as desired.
   C. Generate a 3D section and display it on the drawing at half the size of the original. Do not display cutaway geometry. Specify section settings as desired.
   D. Activate live sectioning. Do not view the cutaway geometry.
   E. On the original solid model, display the intersection fill as an ANSI hatch pattern.
   F. Save the drawing as P12_06.

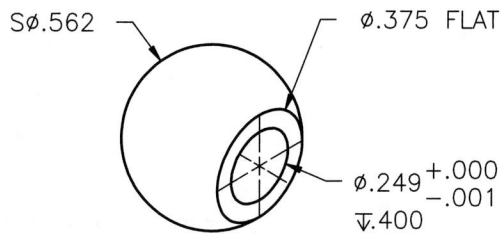

7. Draw the object shown below as a solid model. Only half of the object is shown. Do not dimension the object. Then, do the following.
   A. Construct a section plane that creates a full section, as shown.
   B. Display the intersection fill as an ANSI hatch pattern.
   C. Activate live sectioning and view the cutaway geometry with a high level of transparency.
   D. Save the drawing as P12_07.

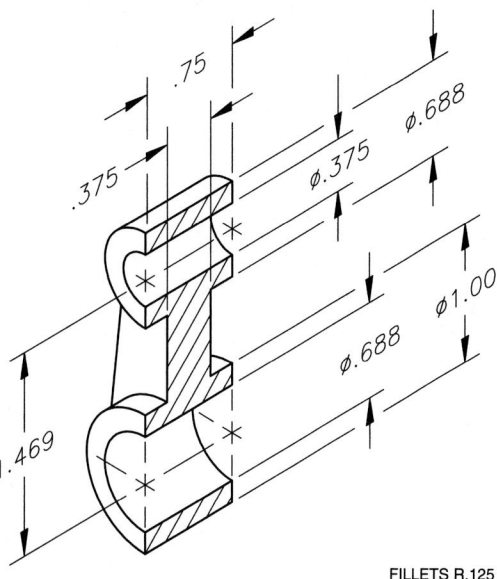

FILLETS R.125

Drawing Problems - Chapter 12

8. Draw the object as a solid model. Only half of the object is shown. Do not dimension the object. Then, do the following.
   A. Construct a section plane that creates a half section.
   B. Display the intersection fill as an ANSI hatch pattern.
   C. Activate live sectioning and view the cutaway geometry with a low level of transparency.
   D. Generate a 3D section and save it as a block.
   E. Use **SOLVIEW** to create a two-view orthographic layout. Use an appropriate scale to plot on a B-size sheet.
   F. Create a third floating viewport and insert the 3D section block scaled to half the size of the drawing.
   G. Save the drawing as P12_08.

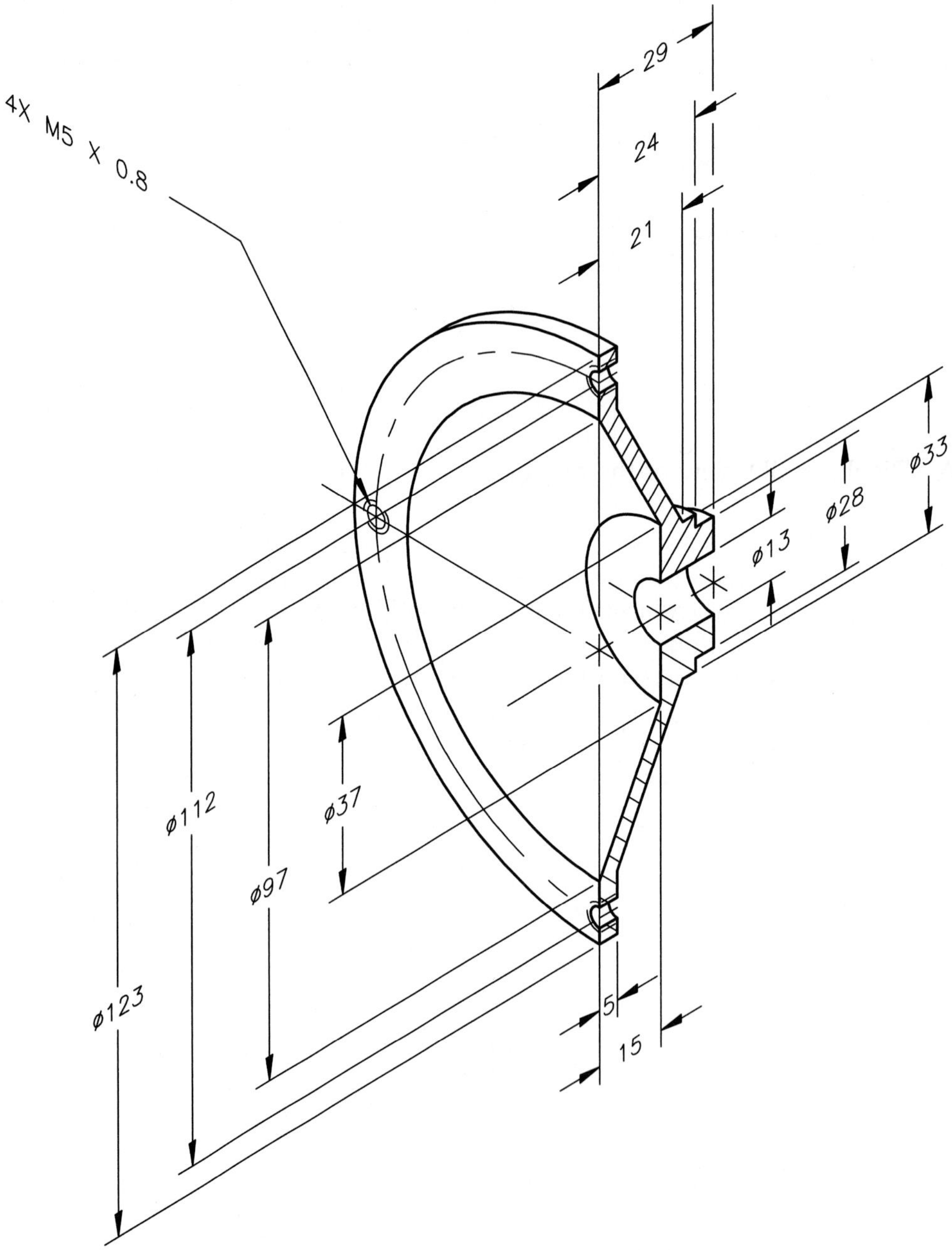

9. Draw the object shown below as a solid model. Use your own dimensions. Then, do the following.
   A. Construct a section plane that creates an offset section. The section should pass through the center of two holes in the base and through the large central hole.
   B. Display the intersection fill as an ANSI hatch pattern.
   C. Activate live sectioning and view the cutaway geometry with a low level of transparency in the color red.
   D. Generate a 3D section of the sectioned solid model and save it as a block.
   E. Use **SOLVIEW** to create a two-view orthographic layout. One view should be a half section. Use an appropriate scale to plot on a B-size sheet.
   F. Create a third floating viewport and insert the 3D section block scaled to half the size of the drawing.
   G. Save the drawing as P12_09.

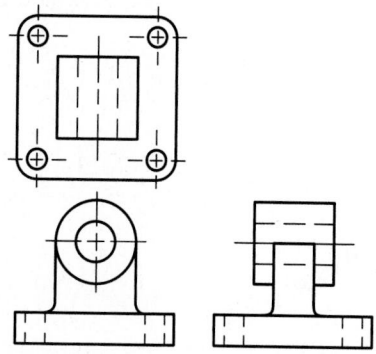

10. Draw the object shown below as a solid model. Do not dimension the object. Then, do the following.
   A. Display a 3D view of the model, generate a flat view, and save it as a block named P12_10_ FLATSHOT.
   B. Construct a section plane that creates a half section.
   C. Display the intersection fill as an ANSI hatch pattern.
   D. Activate live sectioning and view the cutaway geometry with a low level of transparency in the color red.
   E. Alter the section plane to create the section shown below.
   F. Generate a 3D section and save it as a block.
   G. Use **SOLVIEW** to create a two-view orthographic layout. One view should be a full section. Use an appropriate scale to plot on an A-size sheet.
   H. Create a third floating viewport and insert the 3D section block scaled to half the size of the drawing.
   I. Create a fourth viewport and insert the P12_10_FLATSHOT block scaled to half the size of the drawing.
   K. Save the drawing as P12_10.

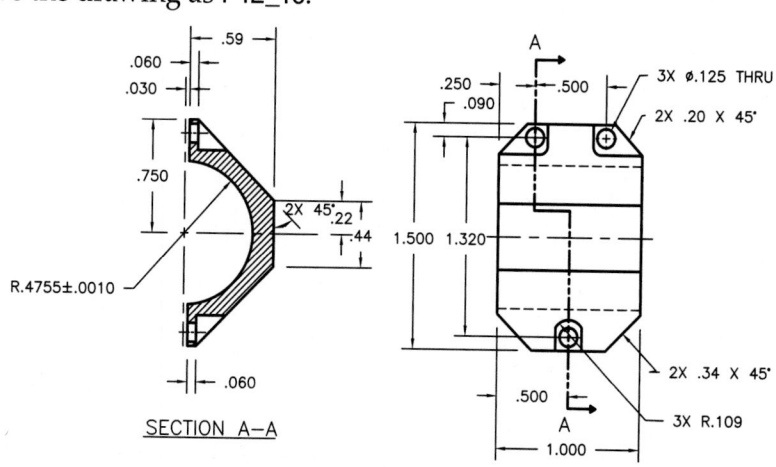

Once your model is created, you can add materials and lighting. Then, you can render the scene. Here, a model of an office building has been rendered. This model can be further refined by adding entourage such as trees, bushes, cars, people, and other buildings.

CHAPTER 13

Visual Style Settings and Basic Rendering

Learning Objectives

After completing this chapter, you will be able to:
- ✓ Describe the **Visual Style Manager**.
- ✓ Change the settings for visual styles.
- ✓ Create custom visual styles.
- ✓ Export visual styles to a tool palette.
- ✓ Render a scene using sunlight.
- ✓ Save a rendered image from the **Render** window.

In Chapter 1, you were introduced to the default visual styles. In Chapter 3, you learned how to use the **Dashboard** to adjust several settings related to how the visual style represents objects. The **Visual Styles** control panel in the **Dashboard** provides a way to quickly and easily change the appearance of the scene. In this chapter, you will learn about other visual style settings that are not available in the **Dashboard** and how to redefine the visual style. You will also learn how to create your own visual style. Finally, this chapter introduces adding lights to a model and rendering the scene.

Overview of the Visual Styles Manager

The **Visual Styles Manager** window provides access to all of the visual style settings. This window is a floating palette similar to the **Properties** window. See Figure 13-1. Changes made in the **Visual Styles Manager** redefine the visual style.

At the top of the **Visual Styles Manager** are image tiles for the defined visual styles. See Figure 13-2. The default visual styles are 2D Wireframe, 3D Hidden, 3D Wireframe, Conceptual, and Realistic. User-defined visual styles also appear as image tiles. The image on the image tile is a preview of the visual style settings. Selecting an image tile provides access to the properties of the visual style in the palette below. The name of the currently selected visual style appears below the image tiles and the corresponding image tile is surrounded by a yellow border.

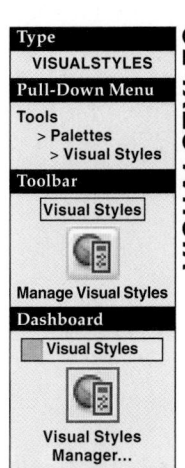

Type	
VISUALSTYLES	
Pull-Down Menu	
Tools	
> Palettes	
> Visual Styles	
Toolbar	
Visual Styles	
🖼️	
Manage Visual Styles	
Dashboard	
Visual Styles	
🖼️	
Visual Styles Manager...	

VISUALSTYLES

Figure 13-1.
The **Visual Styles Manager**.

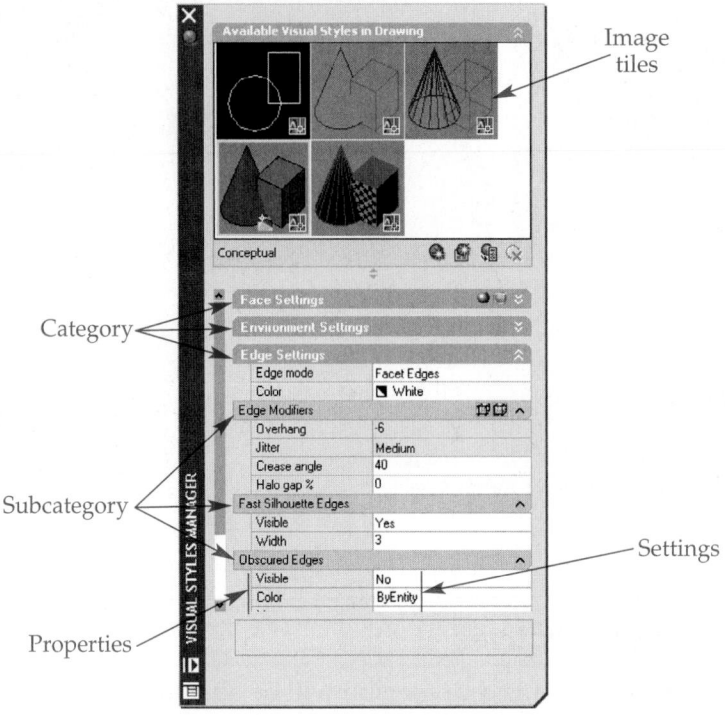

Image tiles

Category

Subcategory

Settings

Properties

Figure 13-2.
The image tiles correspond to the visual styles. The image on the image tile is a preview of the visual style's settings.

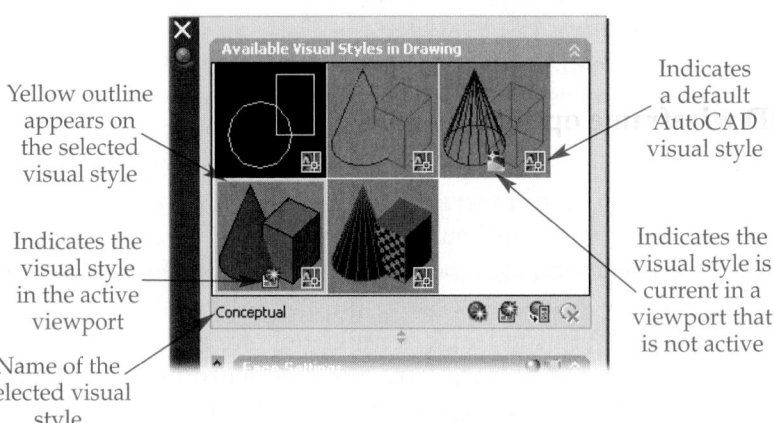

Yellow outline appears on the selected visual style

Indicates the visual style in the active viewport

Name of the selected visual style

Indicates a default AutoCAD visual style

Indicates the visual style is current in a viewport that is not active

To set a different visual style current using the **Visual Styles Manager**, double-click on the image tile. You can also select the image tile and pick the **Apply Selected Visual Style to Current Viewport** button immediately below the image tiles. An icon containing a white star is displayed in the image tile of the visual style that is current in the active viewport, as shown in Figure 13-2. A drawing icon appears in the image tile if the visual style is current in a viewport that is not active. The AutoCAD icon appears in the image tiles of the default visual styles.

Exercise 13-1
Complete the exercise on the Student CD.

As you saw in Chapter 3, the **Visual Style** control panel in the **Dashboard** provides several settings for altering the visual style. These settings are also available in the **Visual Styles Manager**. In addition, there are settings in the **Visual Styles Manager** that are not available in the **Dashboard**. The next sections discuss settings available in the **Visual Styles Manager** for the default visual styles. Remember, changing any setting in the **Visual Styles Manager** redefines the visual style. Changes made in the **Dashboard** are temporary.

2D Wireframe

When the 2D Wireframe visual style is set current, lines and curves are used to show the edges of 3D objects. Assigned linetypes and lineweights are displayed. All edges are visible as if the object is constructed of pieces of wire soldered together at the intersections (thus, the name *wireframe*). Either the 2D or 3D wireframe UCS icon is displayed and the 2D grid is displayed, if it is turned on. OLE objects will display normally. In addition, the drawing window display changes to the 2D Model Space context and parallel projection. For the 2D Wireframe visual style, the **Visual Styles Manager** displays the following categories. See Figure 13-3.
- **2D Wireframe Options**
- **2D Hide—Obscured Lines**
- **2D Hide—Intersection Edges**
- **2D Hide—Miscellaneous**
- **Display Resolution**

2D wireframe options

The Contour lines property controls the **ISOLINES** system variable. Isolines are the lines used to define curved surfaces on solid objects when displayed in a wireframe view. The setting is 4 by default and can range from 0 to 2047. Isolines are suppressed when the **HIDE** command is used with the 2D Wireframe visual style set current.

The Draw true silhouettes property controls the **DISPSILH** system variable. This determines whether or not silhouette edges are shown on curved surfaces. It is set to Off by default, which is equivalent to a **DISPSILH** setting of 0. This property is different from the **Silhouette edges** setting in the **Visual Style** control panel in the **Dashboard**.

Figure 13-3.
The categories and properties available for the 2D Wireframe visual style.

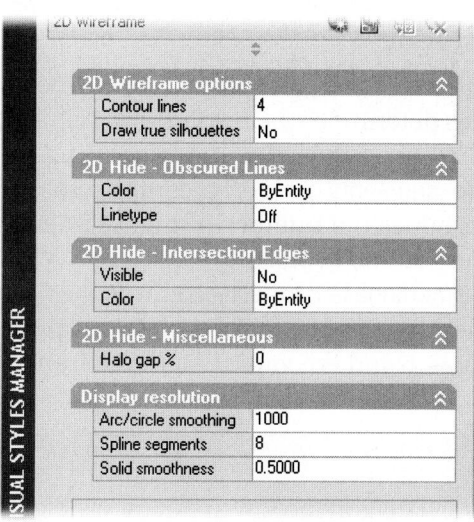

2D hide—obscured lines

The Color property in this category controls the **OBSCUREDCOLOR** system variable. This property determines the color of obscured lines. The default setting is ByEntity. This means that, when displayed, obscured lines are shown in the same color as the object.

The Linetype property controls the **OBSCUREDLTYPE** system variable. This property determines whether or not obscured lines are displayed and in which linetype they are displayed. The default setting is Off, which means that obscured lines are not displayed when the **HIDE** command is used. The available linetypes are: Solid, Dashed, Dotted, Short Dash, Medium Dash, Long Dash, Double Short Dash, Double Medium Dash, Double Long Dash, Medium Long Dash, and Sparse Dot.

NOTE

The above linetypes are not the same as the linetypes loaded into the **Linetype Manager** dialog box. They are independent of zoom levels, which means the dash size will stay the same when zooming in and out.

2D hide—intersection edges

This category is used to toggle the display of polylines at the intersection of 3D surfaces and set the color of the lines. The Visible property controls the **INTERSECTIONDISPLAY** system variable. This property determines whether or not polylines are displayed at the intersection of non-unioned 3D surfaces. The default setting is Off, which means that polylines are not displayed when the **HIDE** command is used.

The Color property in this category controls the **INTERSECTIONCOLOR** system variable. This property determines the color of the polylines displayed at intersection edges. By default, the setting is ByEntity. This means that, when displayed, the polylines at intersection edges are shown in the same color as the object.

2D hide—miscellaneous

The Halo Gap % property controls the **HALOGAP** system variable. This property determines the gap that is displayed where one object partially obscures another (between the foreground edge and where the background edge starts to show). The default setting is 0 and the value can range from 0 to 100. The value refers to a percentage of one unit. The gap is not affected by the zoom level.

Display resolution

The Arc/circle smoothing property controls the zoom percentage set by the **VIEWRES** command. This determines the resolution of circles and arcs. The value can range from 1 to 20,000. The higher the value, the higher the resolution of circles and arcs.

The Spline segments property controls the **SPLINESEGS** system variable. This property determines the number of line segments in a spline-fit polyline. The value can range from −32,768 to 32,767.

The Solid smoothness property controls the **FACETRES** system variable. This property determines the number of polygon faces applied to curved surfaces on solids. The default setting is .5 and the value can range from .01 to 10.0.

NOTE

Polygon faces will not be visible if the Draw true silhouettes property is set to On. However, a higher setting for the Solid smoothness property will make curved edges smoother.

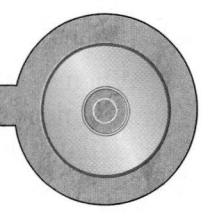

3D Hidden

The 3D Hidden visual style removes obscured lines from your view and makes 3D objects appear solid. The previous projection is retained and that context is set current. The benefit of using 3D Hidden is that you get sufficient 3D display, but it does not push the graphics system too hard. Objects are not shaded or colored. This is very useful when working on complex drawings and/or using a slow computer. For the 3D Hidden visual style, the **Visual Styles Manager** displays the following categories. See **Figure 13-4.**

- **Face Settings**
- **Environment Settings**
- **Edge Settings**

These categories are shared with the 3D Wireframe, Conceptual, and Realistic visual styles. They are discussed later in this chapter.

3D Wireframe

The 3D Wireframe visual style is similar to the 2D Wireframe visual style. All edges are visible and the shaded UCS icon is displayed. The previous projection is retained and that context is set current. When working in 3D, a wireframe view is sometimes necessary to select objects normally hidden from your view. While a 3D view can be displayed with the 2D Wireframe visual style, setting the 3D Wireframe current automatically displays grid lines and the shaded UCS icon (if they are turned on). For the 3D Wireframe visual style, the **Visual Styles Manager** displays the following categories. See **Figure 13-4.**

- **Face Settings**
- **Environment Settings**
- **Edge Settings**

These categories are shared with the 3D Hidden, Conceptual, and Realistic visual styles. They are discussed later in this chapter.

Figure 13-4.
The categories and properties available for the 3D Wireframe, 3D Hidden, Conceptual, and Realistic visual styles.

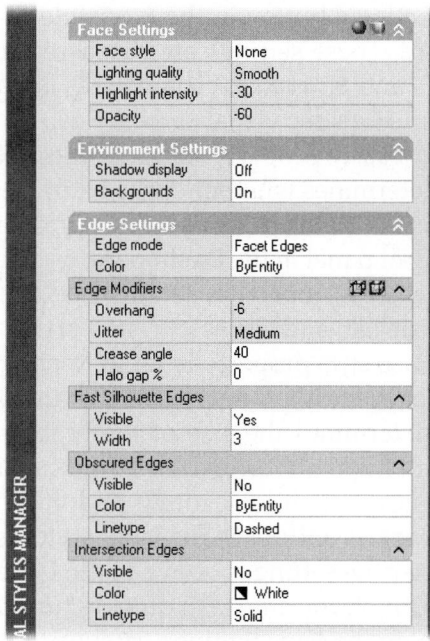

Conceptual

When the Conceptual visual style is set current, objects are smoothed and shaded. The shading is a transition from cool to warm colors. The transitional colors help highlight details. The previous projection is retained and that context is set current. For the Conceptual visual style, the **Visual Styles Manager** displays the following categories. See Figure 13-4.

- **Face Settings**
- **Environment Settings**
- **Edge Settings**

These categories are shared with the 3D Wireframe, 3D Hidden, and Realistic visual styles. They are discussed later in this chapter.

Realistic

As with the Conceptual visual style, the objects have smoothing and shading applied to them. In addition, if materials are applied to the objects, the materials are displayed. The previous projection is retained and that context is set current. This visual style is good for a final look at the scene before rendering. For the Realistic visual style, the **Visual Styles Manager** displays the following categories. See Figure 13-4.

- **Face Settings**
- **Environment Settings**
- **Edge Settings**

These settings are shared with the 3D Wireframe, 3D Hidden, and Conceptual visual styles. They are discussed in the next section.

Settings for 3D Wireframe, 3D Hidden, Conceptual, and Realistic Visual Styles

The 3D Wireframe, 3D Hidden, Conceptual, and Realistic visual styles share similar categories and settings in the **Visual Styles Manager**. The visual styles have **Face Settings**, **Environmental Settings**, and **Edge Settings** categories. These categories and the properties available in them are discussed in the next sections.

Face settings

The Face style property controls the **VSFACESTYLE** system variable. This is also the same as selecting a button in the face style flyout in the **Visual Style** control panel in the **Dashboard**. These settings are discussed in Chapter 3. The default setting for the 3D Wireframe and 3D Hidden visual styles is None, for the Conceptual visual style is Gooch, and for the Realistic visual style is Real.

The Lighting quality property controls the **VSLIGHTINGQUALITY** system variable. This property determines whether curved surfaces are displayed smooth or as a series of flat faces. This is also the same as selecting either the **Smooth** or **Facets** button in the **Visual Style** control panel in the **Dashboard**, as discussed in Chapter 3. No effect is produced if the Face style property is set to None. The default setting for the 3D Wireframe, 3D Hidden, Conceptual, and Realistic visual styles is Smooth. This property cannot be changed if the Face style property is set to None.

The Highlight intensity property controls the **VSFACEHIGHLIGHT** system variable. This property determines the size of the highlight on faces to which no material is assigned. A small highlight on an object makes it look smooth and hard. A large highlight on an object makes it look rough or soft. The initial value for the 3D Wireframe, 3D Hidden, Conceptual, and Realistic visual styles is –30, the value can range from –100 to 100. The higher the setting is above 0, the larger the highlight. Settings below 0 set the value, but turn off the effect. To quickly turn the effect on or off, pick the **Highlight intensity** button on the **Face Settings** category title bar. See Figure 13-5. This changes

Figure 13-5.
The Face Settings
category for the 3D
Wireframe, 3D Hidden,
Conceptual, and
Realistic visual styles.

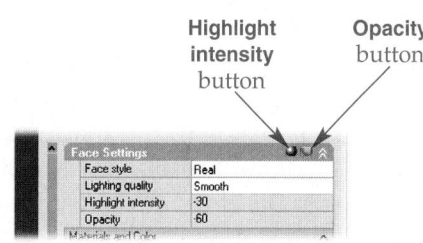

the value from negative to positive, or vice versa. This property cannot be changed if the Face style property is set to None.

The Opacity property controls the **VSFACEOPACITY** system variable. This property determines how transparent or opaque faces are in the viewport. The default setting for the 3D Wireframe, 3D Hidden, Conceptual, and Realistic visual styles is –60. The value can range from –100 to 100. When the setting is 0, the faces are completely transparent. When the setting is 100, the faces are completely opaque. Settings below 0 set the value, but turn off the effect. To quickly turn the effect on or off, pick the **Opacity** button on the **Face Settings** category title bar. See Figure 13-5. This changes the value from negative to positive, or vice versa. This property cannot be changed if the Face style property is set to None.

The **Materials and Color** subcategory is only displayed when the **Face style** property is set to Real or Gooch. There are three properties in this subcategory—Material display, Face color mode, and Monochrome color or Tint color (depending on the Face color mode setting).

The Material display property controls the **VSMATERIALMODE** system variable. The default setting for the 3D Wireframe, 3D Hidden, Conceptual, and Realistic visual styles is Off. This means that objects display in their assigned color. When the setting is changed to Materials, the objects display the color of the material, but not the textures. When the setting is changed to Materials and textures, full materials are displayed.

The Face color mode property controls the **VSFACECOLORMODE** system variable. This property determines how color is applied to the faces of an object. It is the same as picking a button in the face colors flyout in the **Visual Style** control panel in the **Dashboard**. The choices are:

- Normal. The object color is applied to faces.
- Monochrome. One color is applied to all faces. This also displays and enables the Monochrome color property.
- Tint. A combination of the object color and a specified color is applied to faces. This also displays and enables the Tint Color property. The Tint property only works when the Material display property is set to Materials.
- Desaturate. The object color is applied to faces, but the saturation of the color is reduced by 30%. The Desaturate property only works when the Material display property is set to Off.

The Monochrome color and Tint Color properties control the **VSMONOCOLOR** system variable. This system variable determines the color that is applied when the Face color mode property is set to Monochrome or Tint.

CAUTION

Displaying materials and textures on 3D objects in a complex drawing will slow system performance. Set the Face color mode property to Materials and textures only when it is absolutely necessary.

Environment settings

The Shadow display property controls the **VSSHADOWS** system variable. This property controls if and how shadows are cast when the visual style is set current. It is the same as picking a button in the shadows flyout in the **Visual Style** control panel in the **Dashboard**. The default setting for the 3D Wireframe, 3D Hidden, Conceptual, and Realistic visual styles is Off. If the property is set to Ground Shadow, objects cast shadows on the ground, but not onto other objects. The "ground" is the XY plane of the WCS. The Full Shadow setting only works if lights have been placed in the scene and hardware acceleration is enabled.

The Backgrounds property controls the **VSBACKGROUNDS** system variable. This property determines whether or not the preselected background is displayed in the viewport. The default setting for the 3D Wireframe, 3D Hidden, Conceptual, and Realistic visual styles is On. Backgrounds can only be assigned to a view when a named view is created. After the view is created, restore the view to display the background.

Edge settings

The Edge mode property controls the **VSEDGES** system variable. This property determines how edges on solid objects are represented when the visual style is set current. This is the same as picking a button in the edge display flyout in the **Visual Style** control panel in the **Dashboard**. The default for the 3D Wireframe and Realistic visual styles is Isolines. This means that isolines are displayed. The default for the 3D Hidden and Conceptual visual styles is Facet Edges. This means that faceted edges are displayed. Setting this property to None turns off isolines and facets and displays no edges. If the Face style property is set to None, this property cannot be set to None.

The Color property controls the **VSEDGECOLOR** system variable. This property determines the color of all edges on objects in the drawing. It is disabled when the Edge mode property is set to None.

The Number of lines and Always on top properties are displayed when the Edge mode property is set to Isolines. The Number of lines property controls the **ISOLINES** system variable. The Always on top property controls the **VSISOONTOP** system variable. This property determines if isolines are displayed when the model is shaded or hidden. The default for the 3D Wireframe, 3D Hidden, Conceptual, and Realistic visual styles is No. When set to Yes, edges are always displayed.

Edge Modifiers. This subcategory is not displayed if the Edge mode property is set to None. The Overhang property controls the **VSEDGEOVERHANG** system variable. This property can be used to create a hand-sketched appearance by extending the ends of edges. See Figure 13-6A. In order to make changes to this property, the **Overhanging edges** button must be on in the **Edge Modifiers** subcategory title bar. See Figure 13-7. The **Edge overhang** button in the **Visual Style** control panel in the **Dashboard** can also be turned on. The value for this property can range from −100 to 100, which is the number of pixels. The higher the setting, the longer the overhang. A negative value sets the overhang length, but turns off the property. Picking either button makes the value positive and applies the effect.

The Jitter property controls the **VSEDGEJITTER** system variable. Jitter makes edges of objects look as if they were sketched with a pencil. See Figure 13-6B. In order to make changes to this property, the **Jitter edges** button must be on in the **Edge Modifiers** subcategory title bar. See Figure 13-7. The **Edge jitter** button in the **Visual Style** control panel in the **Dashboard** can also be turned on. There are four settings from which to choose: Off, Low, Medium, and High. The number of sketched lines increases at each higher setting.

When the Edge mode property is set to Facet Edges, the Crease angle and Halo gap % properties are displayed in the **Edge Modifiers** subcategory. The Crease angle property controls the **VSEDGESMOOTH** system variable. This property determines how facet edges within a face are displayed based on the angle between adjacent faces. It does

Figure 13-6.
A—Overhanging edges have been turned on for this visual style. B—Edge jitter has been turned on for this visual style.

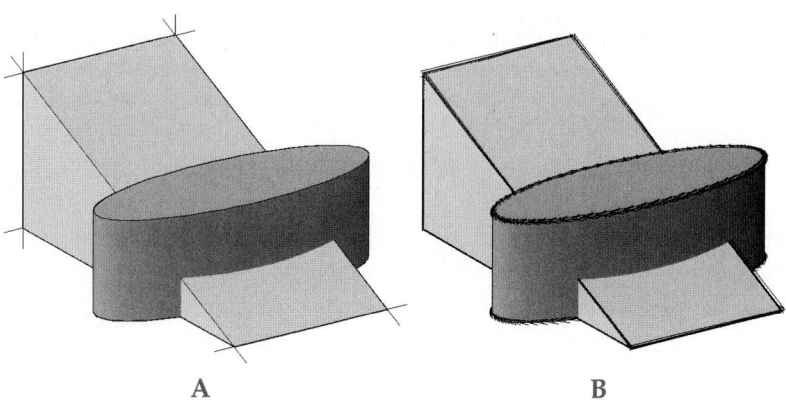

A

B

Figure 13-7.
The **Edge Modifiers** subcategory for the 3D Wireframe, 3D Hidden, Conceptual, and Realistic visual styles.

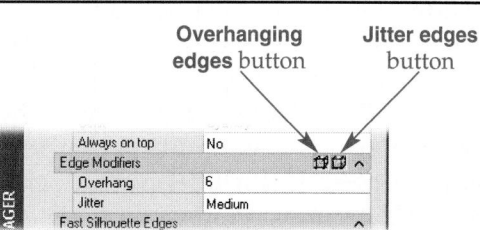

not affect edges between faces. See **Figure 13-8.** The value can range from 0 to 180, which is the number of degrees between edges below which a line is displayed. The Halo gap % property is the same as discussed earlier in the 2D Hide—Miscellaneous section.

Fast Silhouette Edges. This subcategory is available for all of the Edge mode settings. The Visible property controls the **VSSILHEDGES** system variable. It determines whether or not silhouette edges are displayed around the outside edges of all objects. The default for the 3D Wireframe and Realistic visual styles is No. The default for the 3D Hidden and Conceptual visual styles is Yes. This is the same as turning on the **Silhouette edges** button in the **Visual Style** control panel in the **Dashboard**. The Width property controls the **VSSILHWIDTH** system variable. This property determines the width of silhouette lines. It is measured in pixels and the value can range from 1 to 25. Changing this property is the same as adjusting the **Silhouette edge width** slider in the **Visual Style** control panel.

Obscured Edges. This subcategory is only available when the Edge mode property is set to Facet edges. The Visible property controls the **VSOBSCUREDEDGES** system variable. This property determines whether or not obscured edges are displayed in a hidden or shaded view. See **Figure 13-9.** The Color property controls the **VSOBSCUREDCOLOR** system variable. The Linetype property controls the **VSOBSCUREDLTYPE** system

Figure 13-8.
A—The Crease angle property is set to 0. Notice the edges between facets within each face.
B—The Crease angle property is set to 10. The edges are no longer displayed.

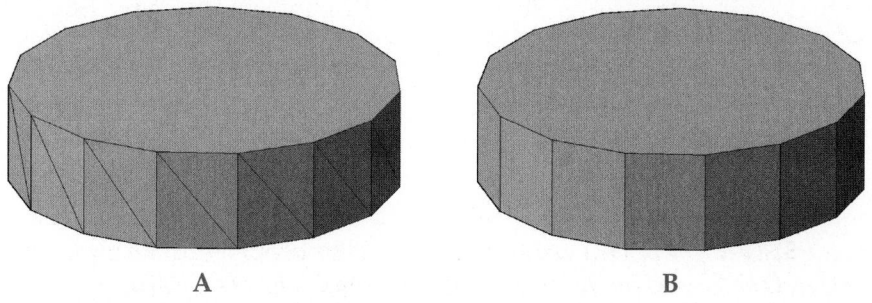

A

B

Figure 13-9.
A—Obscured lines are not shown. B—The Visible property is set to Yes and obscured lines are shown.

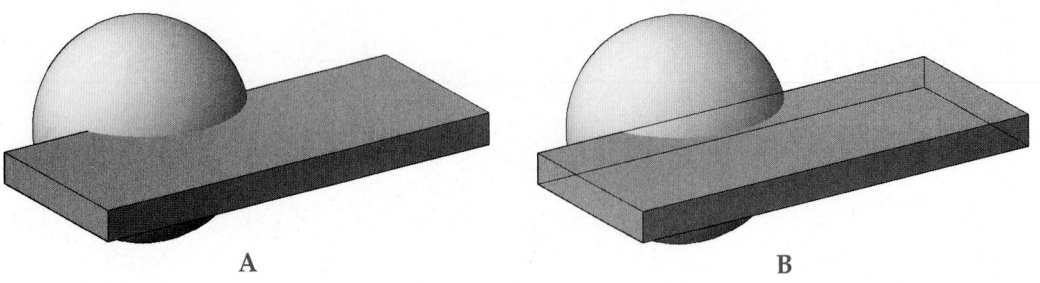

A

B

variable. These properties function the same as those discussed earlier in this chapter in the 2D Hide—Obscured Lines section.

Intersection Edges. This subcategory is only available when the Edge mode property is set to Facet edges. The Visible property controls the **VSINTERSECTIONEDGES** system variable. This property determines whether or not lines are displayed where one 3D object intersects another 3D object. See **Figure 13-10.** The Color property controls the **VSINTERSECTIONCOLOR** system variable. The Linetype property controls the **VSINTERSECTIONLTYPE** system variable. These properties function the same as those discussed earlier in this chapter in the 2D Hide—Intersection Edges section.

PROFESSIONAL TIP

Setting the intersection edges Color property to a color that contrasts with the objects in your model is a good way to quickly check for interference between 3D objects.

Figure 13-10.
A—A line does not appear where these two objects intersect. B—The Visible property is set to Yes and a line appears at the intersection.

Intersection is displayed

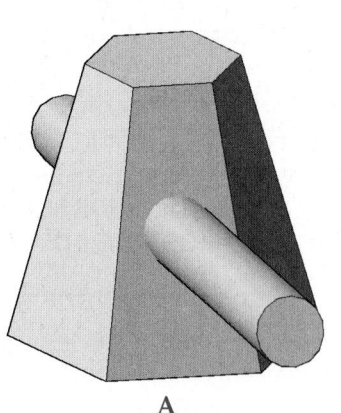

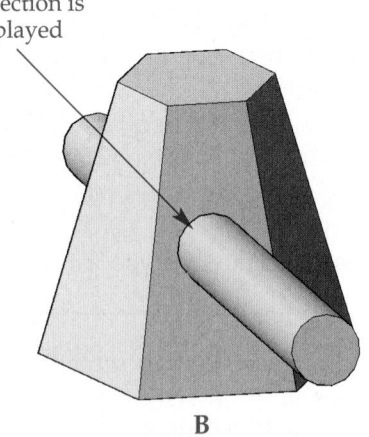

A

B

Figure 13-11.
Creating a new visual
style.

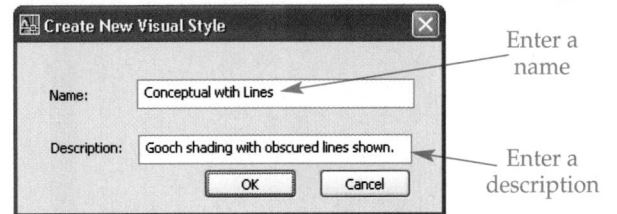

Enter a
name

Enter a
description

Creating Your Own Visual Style

As you saw in the previous sections, you can customize the default AutoCAD visual styles. However, you may also want to create a number of different visual styles to quickly change the display of the scene. Custom visual styles are easy to create.

To create a custom visual style, open the **Visual Style Manager**. Then, pick the **Create New Visual Style** button below the image tiles. You can also right-click in the image tile area and select **Create New Visual Style...** from the shortcut menu. In the **Create New Visual Style** dialog box that appears, type a name for the new style and give it a description. See Figure 13-11. Then, pick the **OK** button to create the new visual style.

An image tile is created for the new visual style. The name and description of the visual style appear as help text when the cursor is over the image tile. Select the image tile to display the default properties for the new visual style. Then, change the settings as needed to meet your requirements.

Custom visual styles are only saved in the current drawing. They are not automatically available in other drawings. To use the new visual styles in any drawing, they must be exported to a tool palette. This is discussed in the next section.

PROFESSIONAL TIP

To return one of AutoCAD's visual styles to its default settings, right-click on the image tile in the **Visual Styles Manager** and select **Restore to default** from the shortcut menu.

Exercise 13-3
Complete the exercise on the Student CD.

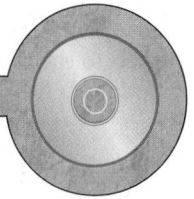

Steps for Exporting Visual Styles to a Tool Palette

To have custom visual styles available in other drawings, export them to a tool palette. Use the following procedure.

1. Create and customize a visual style as described in the previous section.
2. Open the **Tool Palettes** window by selecting **Tools>Palettes>Tool Palettes** in the pull-down menu.
3. Right-click on the **Tool Palettes** title bar and pick **New Palette** from the shortcut menu.
4. Type the name of the new palette, such as My Visual Styles, in the text box that appears. See Figure 13-12.
5. The new palette is added and active. You are ready to export your custom visual styles into it.

Figure 13-12.
Creating a new tool palette on which to place visual style tools.

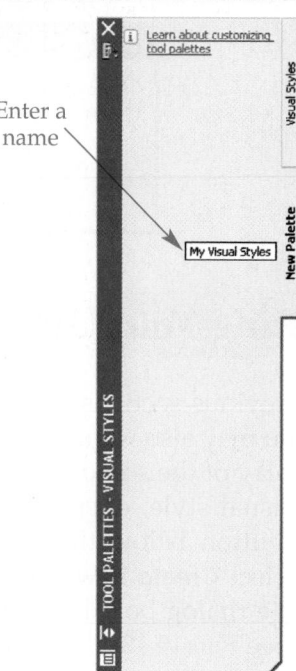

Enter a name

6. Select the image tile of the visual style in the **Visual Styles Manager**. Remember, a yellow border appears around the selected image tile.
7. Pick the **Export the Selected Visual Style to the Tool Palette** button below the image tiles. You can also right-click on the image tile and select **Export to Active Tool Palette** from the shortcut menu.

A new tool now appears in the palette with the same image, name, and description as the visual style in the **Visual Styles Manager**. See Figure 13-13. Selecting the tool applies the visual style to the current viewport. You can also right-click on the tool to display a shortcut menu. Using this menu, you can apply the visual style to the current viewport, all viewports, or add the visual style to the current drawing. The shortcut menu also allows you to rename the tool, access the properties of the visual style, and delete the visual style from the palette.

Figure 13-13.
A visual style has been copied to the tool palette as a tool.

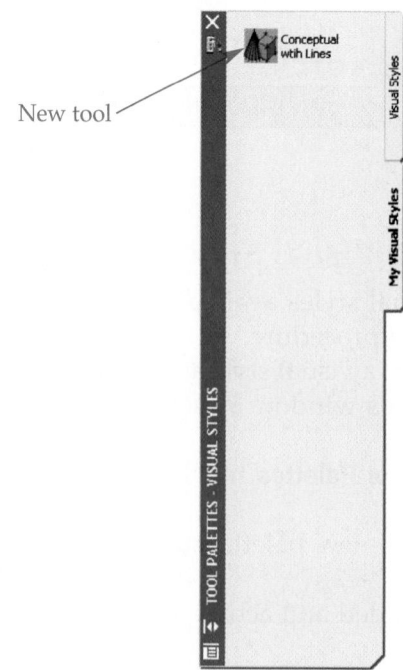

New tool

AutoCAD and Its Applications—Advanced

Exercise 13-4
Complete the exercise on the Student CD.

Deleting Visual Styles from the Visual Styles Manager

Custom visual styles can be deleted from the **Visual Styles Manager**. Pick the image tile of the visual style you want to delete. Then, pick the **Delete the Selected Visual Style** button below the image tiles. You can also right-click on the image tile and select **Delete** from the shortcut menu. You are *not* warned about the deletion. The default AutoCAD visual styles cannot be deleted, nor can a visual style that is currently in use.

Plotting Visual Styles

A visual style not only affects the on-screen display, it also affects plots. To plot objects with a specific visual style, use the following guidelines.

Plotting a Visual Style from Model Space

There are two basic methods for plotting from model space. The method you use depends strictly on your preference.

Method 1. Open the **Plot** dialog box and expand it by picking the **More Options** (>) button. Then, select the desired display from the **Shade plot** drop-down list in the **Shaded viewport options** area. Finally, plot the drawing.

Method 2. Set the desired visual style current. Then, open the **Plot** dialog box. Select **As displayed** from the **Shade plot** drop-down list in the **Shaded viewport options** area. Finally, plot the drawing.

Plotting a Visual Style from Paper Space

When plotting from paper space, the shade plot properties of the viewport(s) govern how the viewport is plotted. The viewport(s) can be set to plot visual styles in three different ways.

Method 1. Use the **Visual Styles** suboption of the **Shadeplot** option of the **MVIEW** command. When prompted to select objects, pick the border of the viewport. Do not pick the objects in the viewport.

Method 2. Use the **Properties** window to set the Shade plot property of the viewport. To do this, select the viewport in paper space and open the **Properties** window. Pick the Shade plot property in the **Misc** category and change the setting to the desired option.

Method 3. Select the viewport in paper space and right-click to display the shortcut menu. Pick **Shade plot** to display the cascading menu. Then, select the appropriate visual style.

The visual style of the viewport may also be selected when you create a viewport configuration in the **Viewports** dialog box (**VPORTS** command). Select the viewport in the **Preview** area of the dialog box. Then, pick the visual style desired from the **Visual Style**: drop-down list at the bottom of the dialog box. The **VPORTS** command can be used in model space or paper (layout) space.

Introduction to Rendering

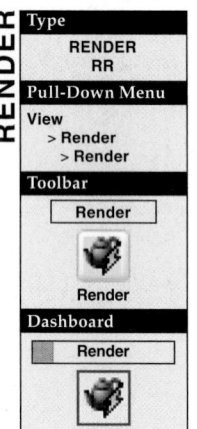

RENDER

| Type |
| RENDER |
| RR |
| Pull-Down Menu |
| View |
| > Render |
| > Render |
| Toolbar |
| Render |
| Render |
| Dashboard |
| Render |
| Render |

Visual styles provide a way to plot your 3D scene to paper or a file, but control over the appearance is limited to the visual style settings. In Chapter 3, you were briefly introduced to the **RENDER** command. The **RENDER** command offers complete control over the scene and, with its features, you can create photorealistic images. In this chapter, you will be introduced to AutoCAD's rendering and lighting tools. Materials are discussed in later chapters along with more advanced rendering and lighting features.

When you render a scene, you are making a realistic image of your design that can be printed, displayed on a web page, or used in a presentation. To create an attractive rendering, you have to figure out what view you want to display, where the lights should be placed, what types of materials need to be applied to the 3D objects, and the kind of output that is needed. This section shows you how to create a quick rendering of your scene.

Introduction to Lights

Lights provide the illumination to a scene and are essential for rendering. There are three types of lighting in AutoCAD—default lighting, sunlight, and user-created lighting. AutoCAD automatically creates two default light sources in every scene. These lights ensure that all surfaces on the model are illuminated and visible. The types of lighting are discussed in more detail in Chapter 15.

A scene can be rendered with the default lights, but the results are usually not adequate to produce a photorealistic image. See **Figure 13-14.** The appearance is very artificial and no shadows are created. Shadows anchor objects to the scene and make them look real. See **Figure 13-15.** Without shadows, objects appear to float in space. Because the default lights do not cast shadows, other lights must be added to the scene and set to cast shadows. When a light is added to a scene, the default lights must be turned off. The first time you add a light, you receive a warning to this effect (unless the warning has been disabled).

Figure 13-14.
A scene rendered with the default AutoCAD lighting.

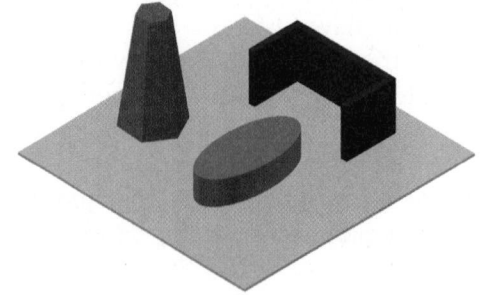

Figure 13-15.
A light has been added and set to cast shadows. Compare this rendering with Figure 13-14.

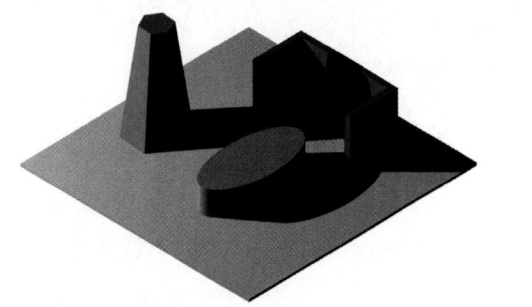

Figure 13-16.
The **Light** control panel in the **Dashboard**.

Orange indicates default lighting is off

Date setting

Sunlight is on

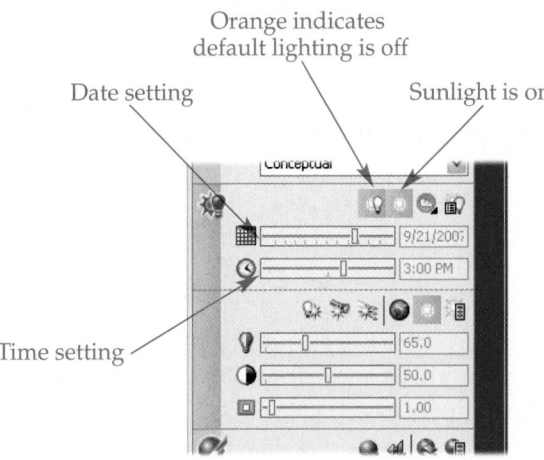

Time setting

In this section, you will learn how to add sunlight to the scene. Chapter 15 provides detailed information on lighting. Sunlight is produced by an automated distant light. Sunlight can be turned on by picking the **Sun Status** button in the **Light** control panel in the **Dashboard**. The button is orange when on. See **Figure 13-16.** Turning the **Sun Status** button on also turns on the **Viewport Lighting Mode:**, if it is off. This is simply a toggle between the default lights and user-defined light sources.

If the current visual style is set to display full shadows, you should now see shadows in the scene, provided there are areas to receive shadows. Remember, hardware acceleration must be enabled to display full shadows.

The **Date** and **Time** sliders are active when sunlight is turned on. You can drag the sliders to adjust the date and time. The current date and time are displayed to the right of the sliders. As you drag the sliders, the shadows in the scene change to reflect the settings.

Rendering the Scene

The **Render** control panel in the **Dashboard** is shown in **Figure 13-17.** There are two buttons located in this control panel to initiate a rendering. If you pick the **Render** button, the **Render** window appears (by default) and AutoCAD immediately starts rendering the viewport. You will see the rendered tiles appear in the image pane as they are calculated. The **Render** window is explained more in the next section.

If you pick the **Render cropped region** button, you are prompted to pick two points in the viewport, similar to performing a window selection. The selected area is rendered in the viewport. Rendering a cropped area is often used to test areas of the scene for possible problems before performing the final rendering.

Figure 13-17.
The **Render** control panel in the **Dashboard**.

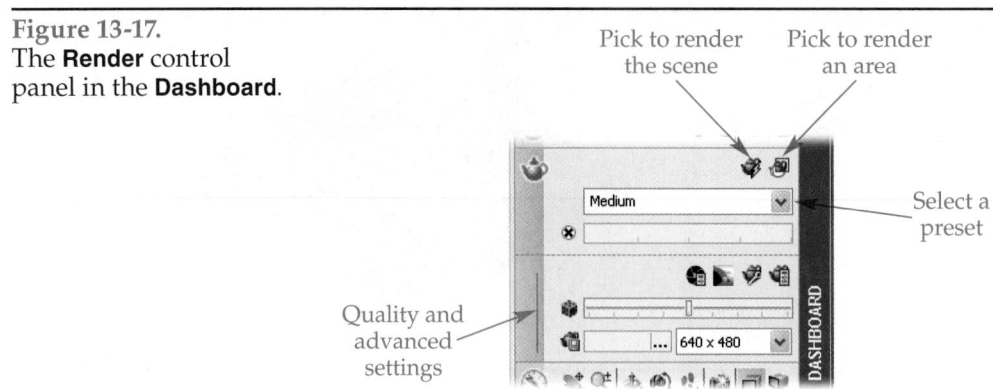

Pick to render the scene

Pick to render an area

Select a preset

Quality and advanced settings

Below the render buttons is the **Select Render Preset** drop-down list. This list gives you a selection of rendering presets based on image quality. The choices are:
- Draft
- Low
- Medium
- High
- Presentation

The Draft entry produces the lowest-quality rendering. The Presentation entry produces the highest-quality rendering. The better the quality, the longer it takes to complete the rendering process.

PROFESSIONAL TIP

Rendering a complex drawing may take a very long time and you do not want to repeat it because of some small error. It is important to make sure that everything in the scene is perfect before the final rendering. By rendering a cropped region and using lower-quality renderings, you can verify the appearance of any questionable areas without performing a full rendering.

Introduction to the Render Window

The **Render** window is composed of three main areas. See **Figure 13-18.** The image pane is where the rendering appears. The statistics pane shows the current rendering settings. The history pane shows a list of all of the images rendered from the drawing, with the most recent at the top.

You can zoom into the image in the image pane for detailed inspection. Use the mouse scroll wheel or the **Zoom +** and **Zoom −** entries in the **Render** window **Tools** pull-down menu. In the **File** pull-down menu of the **Render** window, select **Save** to save the image selected in the history pane to an image file. The symbol in front of the image in the history pane changes to a folder with a red check mark on it. The **Save Copy…** option in the **Render** window **File** pull-down menu creates a copy of the image without modifying the original in the history pane.

NOTE

Advanced rendering is discussed in Chapter 16.

Figure 13-18.
The **Render** window.

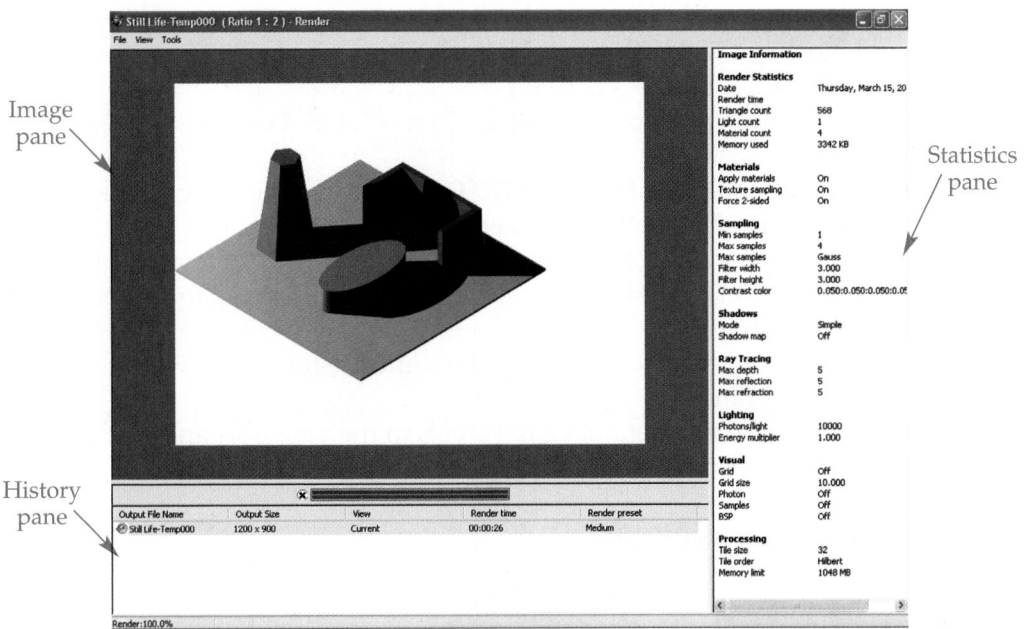

Image pane

Statistics pane

History pane

Exercise 13-5

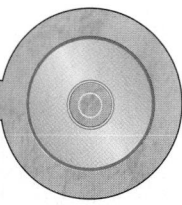

Complete the exercise on the Student CD.

Chapter Test

Answer the following questions. Write your answers on a separate sheet of paper or complete the electronic chapter test on the Student CD.

1. What is the **Visual Styles Manager**?
2. Name the five default AutoCAD visual styles that can be edited in the **Visual Styles Manager**.
3. Describe the difference between setting the Lighting quality property to Smooth and Faceted.
4. What does the Desaturate setting of the Face color mode property do?
5. What has to be added to a scene before full shadows are displayed?
6. If you want to make your scene look hand sketched, but the Overhang and Jitter properties are not available, what other setting(s) do you have to change?
7. How do you set a visual style to display silhouette edges?
8. List the four settings for the Jitter property.
9. What is an *intersection edge?*
10. How do you make your own visual styles available in other drawings?
11. Which visual styles cannot be deleted?
12. How can you turn on sunlight?
13. Explain the function of **Render Cropped Region** button in the **Render** control panel in the **Dashboard**.
14. Name the three main areas of the **Render** window.
15. How can you save a rendered image in the **Render** window?

Drawing Problems

1. In this problem, you will construct a living room scene using some simple shapes and blocks available through **DesignCenter**.

   A. Draw a 12′ × 12′ × 1″ box.

   B. Draw two boxes to represent walls, 12′ × 4″ × 8′. Position them as shown below.

   C. Open **DesignCenter** and select the **DC Online** tab. In the category listing area, expand the Standard Parts>3D Architectural tree.

   D. Find 3D blocks for the following objects, drag and drop them into the scene, and position them as shown: sofa, table, end table, lamp, plant, entertainment center, and chair.

   E. The blocks do not have to be exactly the same as shown below and may need to be scaled up or down.

   F. Apply each of the five default visual styles to the viewport and plot each. Use the As Displayed option in the **Plot** dialog box. Note the differences in each one.

   G. Save the drawing as P13_01.

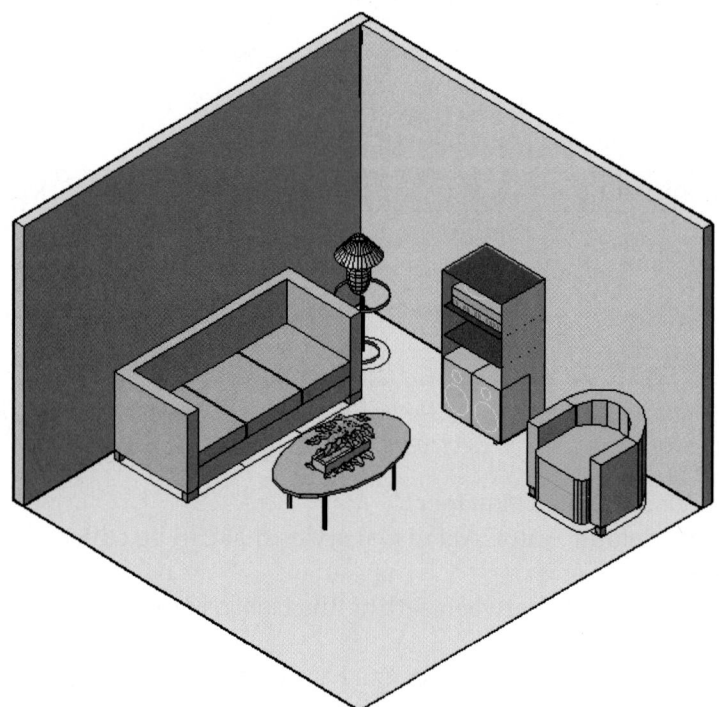

2. In this problem, you will create a new visual style to display the scene as if it is hand sketched.
   A. Open drawing P13_01.
   B. Create a new visual style named Hand Sketched with a description of Displays objects as sketched.
   C. Change the overhang and jitter settings to make the scene look as shown below.
   D. Change any other settings you like.
   E. Plot the scene. Select the new visual style in the **Shade plot** drop-down list.
   F. Export the new visual style to a tool palette so that it can be used in other drawings.
   G. Save the drawing as P13_02.

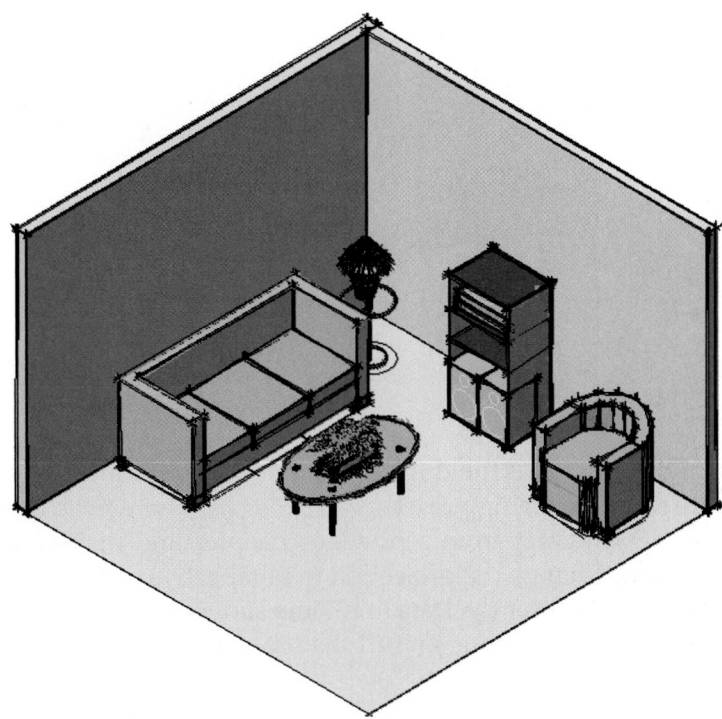

3. In this problem, you will create a realistic looking image of the car fender that you created in Chapter 8.
   A. Open drawing P08_03.
   B. Freeze any layers needed so that only the fender is displayed. Display the fender in the color you want it to be.
   C. Draw a planar surface to represent the ground.
   D. Set the Realistic visual style current. Then, turn on the highlight intensity and full shadows. Also, set the Edge Mode property to None.
   E. Turn on the sun. Adjust the **Date** and **Time** sliders to make the shadows look as shown.
   F. Render the scene and save it as a JPEG image. Name the file P13_03.jpg.
   G. Save the drawing as P13_03.

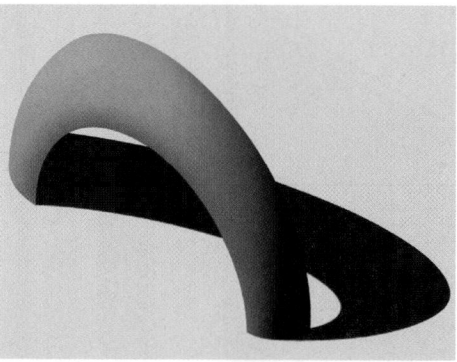

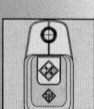

4. This problem demonstrates the differences in rendering time and image quality of the five different rendering presets.
   A. Open any 3D drawing from a previous chapter and display an appropriate isometric view. Change the projection to perspective, if it is not already.
   B. Turn on the sun and set the **Date** and **Time** sliders to place the shadows where you want them. Tip: Turning on full shadows allows you to locate the shadows without rendering.
   C. Render the scene once for each rendering preset: Draft, Low, Medium, High, and Presentation.
   D. In the history pane of the **Render** window, note the differences between the rendering time for each rendering.
   E. Save each image with a corresponding name: P13_04_Draft.jpg, P13_04_Low.jpg, P13_04_Medium.jpg, P13_04_High.jpg, and P13_04_Presentation.jpg.
   F. Save the drawing as P13_04.

CHAPTER 14

Materials in AutoCAD

Learning Objectives

After completing this chapter, you will be able to:
- ✓ Attach materials to the objects in a drawing.
- ✓ Change the properties of existing materials.
- ✓ Create new materials.

A *material* is simply an image stretched over an object to make it appear as though the object is made out of wood, marble, glass, brick, or various other materials. AutoCAD provides an assortment of materials that can be used in your drawings to create a realistic scene. The materials are grouped into categories to make them easier to find.

Materials are easy to attach. They can be dragged and dropped onto the objects, they can be attached to all selected objects, and they can even be attached based on the object's layer. Once the material is attached, you can adjust how the material is *mapped* to the object. If the current visual style is set to display materials in the viewport, you can immediately see the effects on the object. The properties of a material can also be changed to make it look shinier, softer, smoother, rougher, and so on. When you finally render the scene, you will see the full effect of the materials.

Material Library

The *material library* is the location where all materials are stored. AutoCAD uses tool palettes as a material library. The **Materials** tool palette group contains eight palettes:

- **Concrete**
- **Doors and Windows**
- **Fabric**
- **Finishes**
- **Flooring**
- **Masonry**
- **Metals**
- **Woods and Plastics**

To display only the palettes in the **Materials** group, right-click on the title bar of the **Tool Palettes** window and select **Materials** from the shortcut menu, Figure 14-1. Each palette contains several material tools. See **Figure 14-2.** Each material is displayed

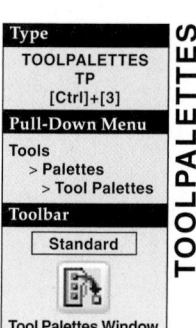

Type
TOOLPALETTES
TP
[Ctrl]+[3]
Pull-Down Menu
Tools
> Palettes
> Tool Palettes
Toolbar
Standard
Tool Palettes Window

TOOLPALETTES

Figure 14-1.
Displaying only the tool palettes in the **Materials** group. Notice that the material library has also been installed.

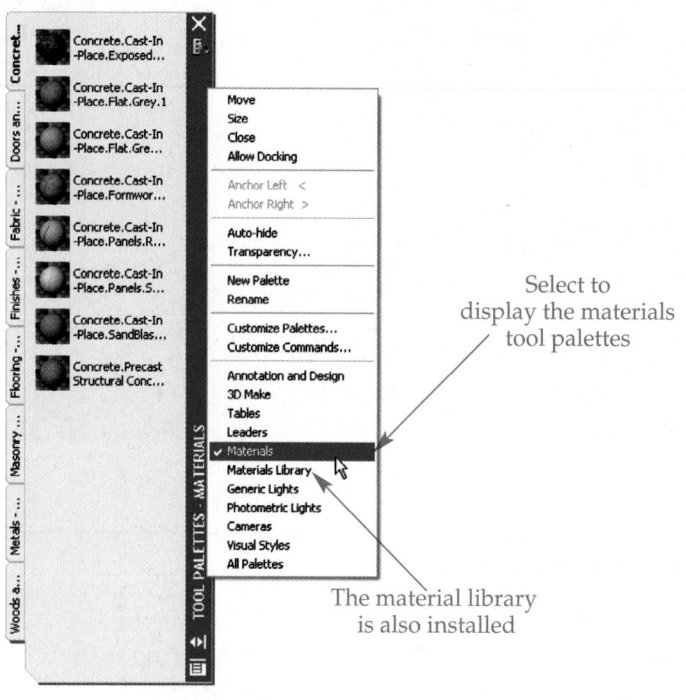

Select to display the materials tool palettes

The material library is also installed

in the palette as a sphere on a checkered background. The background is used to make the transparent materials, such as glass, more visible. The material name is, by default, shown to the right of the sphere. You may want to increase the width of the **Tool Palettes** window to see the complete name of each material. Tool palette options, such as display options, are covered in detail in Chapter 22.

The properties of the individual materials can be accessed by right-clicking on the tool in the palette and picking **Properties...** from the shortcut menu. In the **Tool**

Figure 14-2.
Selected tool palettes in the **Materials** group. A—**Doors and Windows**. B—**Flooring**. C—**Masonry**. D—**Woods and Plastics**.

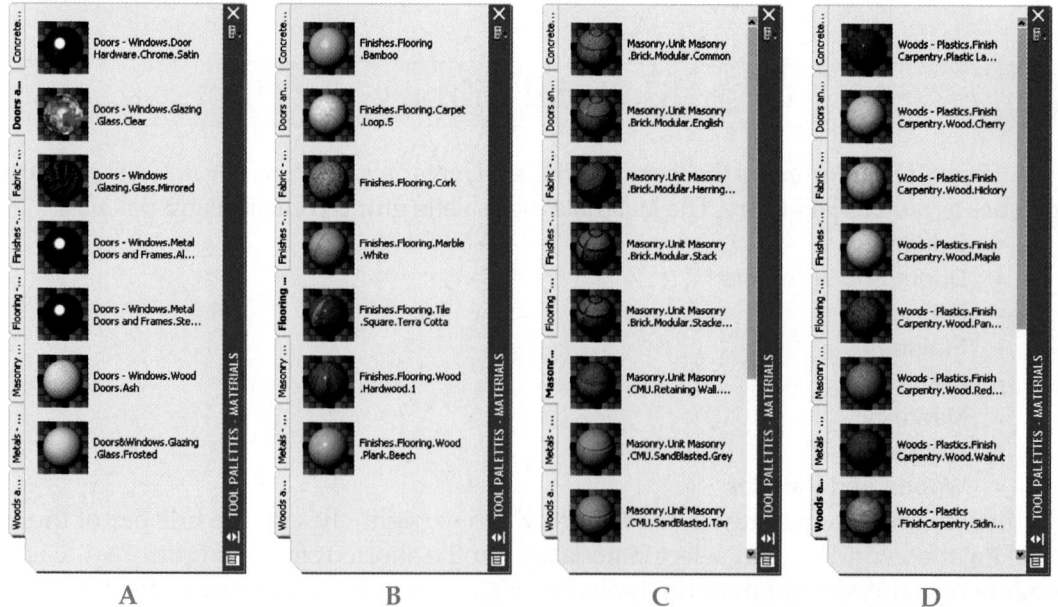

A   B   C   D

Properties dialog box that is displayed, you can change the name, description of the material, and material properties. See Figure 14-3. The **Tool Properties** dialog box is discussed in more detail in Chapter 22. Changes made to the material in this dialog box only affect the material tool. To apply these changes to objects in the current scene, the material must be reattached to the objects. The features in the material editor in the **Tool Properties** dialog box are identical to those found in the **Materials** window, which is discussed later in this chapter.

PROFESSIONAL TIP

The "typical" installation of AutoCAD includes approximately 100 materials. However, approximately 400 materials are available if you choose to install the material library. If you did not choose that option during installation of AutoCAD, you can use the installation CD to add the full material library. For information describing how to do this, select **Help>Help** or press [F1] to display the online documentation. Then, in the contents tab, select the **Installation and Licensing Guides** topic. Browse the topic for information on installing the material library.

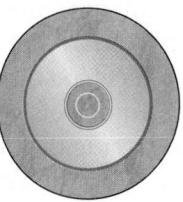

Exercise 14-1
Complete the exercise on the Student CD.

Figure 14-3.
The properties of a material tool.

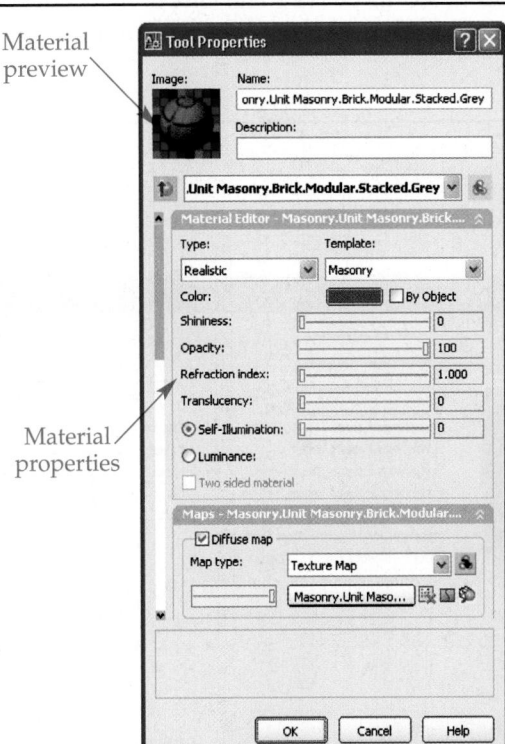

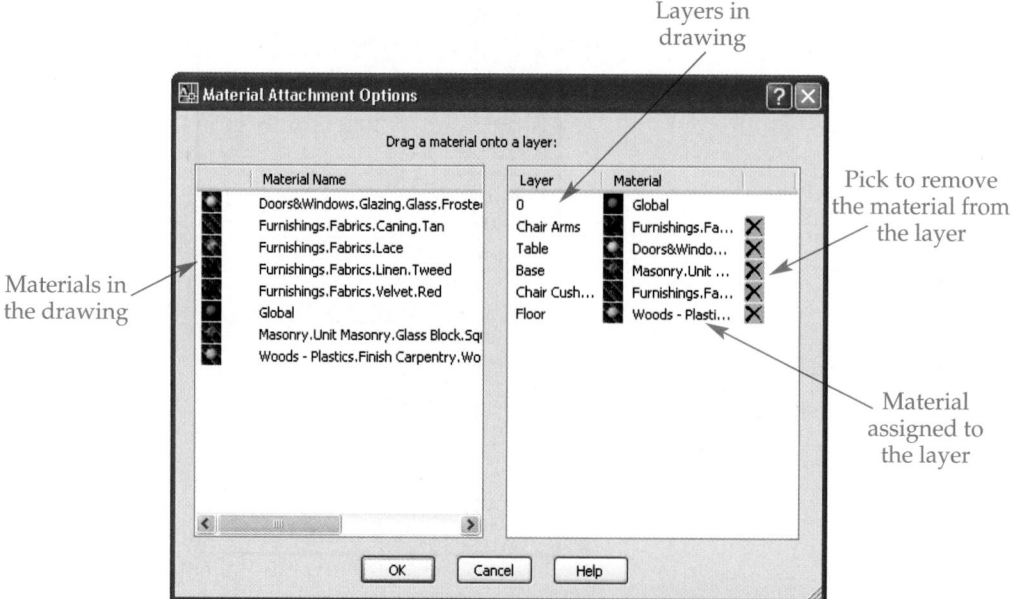

Applying and Removing Materials

To attach a material to an object in the drawing, pick once on the material image or name in the tool palette. As the cursor is moved into the drawing area, a paint brush icon appears next to the cursor. Pick the object to which you want the material applied. You can also drag the material from the tool palette and drop it onto an object. To apply a material only to a face on an object, hold the [Ctrl] key and pick the face. To apply a different material to an object, simply select the new material in the tool palette and pick the object again.

If you use the tool palette to assign a material that has already been loaded into the drawing, an AutoCAD alert appears warning of a material name conflict. AutoCAD needs to know how to handle the duplicate material. If you pick the **Create a copy** button, the material is added to the drawing as Copy of *material name* (or Copy 1 of *material name*, Copy 2 of *material name*, and so on). Picking the **Overwrite** button replaces the material in the drawing with the one you are attempting to attach. This is probably the best option in most cases, but any changes made to the existing material in the drawing are lost. The **Cancel** button allows you to cancel the operation. To avoid this naming conflict situation, use the **Materials** window to apply to other objects any materials already existing in the drawing. The **Materials** window is discussed later.

You can use the **MATERIALATTACH** command to assign materials to the layers in your drawing. Once a material is assigned to a layer, any object on that layer is displayed in that material, as long as the object's material property is set to ByLayer. When objects are created in AutoCAD, the default "material" assigned to them is ByLayer. If your objects are organized on layers, this is the easiest way to attach materials. You can override the layer material by applying a material to individual objects.

Figure 14-4 shows the **Material Attachment Options** dialog box displayed by the **MATERIALATTACH** command. The list on the left side of the dialog box shows the materials loaded into the drawing. The right side of the dialog box shows the layers in the drawing and the material attached to each layer. When no material is attached to a layer, the material is listed as Global. The Global material is a "blank" material in every drawing. To attach a material to a layer, drag the material from the list on the left and

MATERIALATTACH

Type
MATERIALATTACH
Dashboard
Materials
Attach By Layer...

Figure 14-4.
Attaching materials to layers.

Figure 14-5.
Removing a material from an object. A—The material is assigned. B—The material is removed.

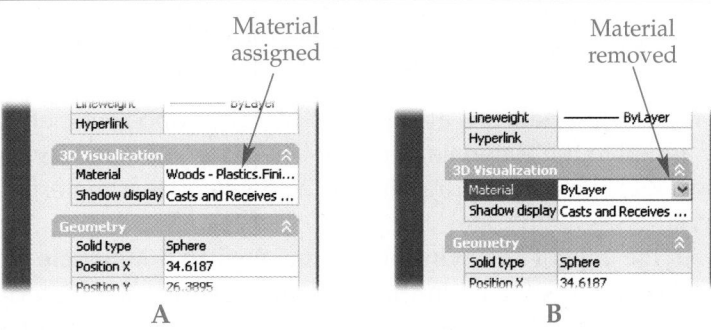

A

B

drop it onto the layer name on the right. To remove a material from a layer, pick the **X** button next to the material name on the right side of the dialog box. When all settings have been made, pick the **OK** button to close the dialog box.

The easiest way to remove a material is with the **Properties** window. To remove a material from an object or subobject, simply change the Material property in the **3D Visualization** category to Global. If a material has not been assigned to the object's layer, the property can also be set to ByLayer. See **Figure 14-5.**

PROFESSIONAL TIP

A material can be applied to an object by dragging the material from the tool palette and dropping it onto the object. Also, a material can be loaded into the drawing without attaching it to an object by picking the material tool once in the tool palette and pressing [Enter]. This makes the material available in the drawing.

Exercise 14-2
Complete the exercise on the Student CD.

Material Display Options

As you learned in the previous chapter, visual styles control how materials are displayed in the viewport. The Material display property of a visual style can be set to display materials and textures, materials only, or neither materials nor textures. The **Materials** control panel in the **Dashboard** has three buttons in a flyout that correspond to, but override, this property setting:

- **Materials and Textures Off.** Objects are displayed in their assigned colors.
- **Materials On/Textures Off.** Objects are displayed in the basic color of the material, but no other material details are displayed.
- **Materials and Textures On.** Objects are displayed with all material properties visible.

Materials Window

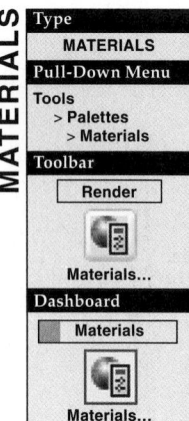

Type
MATERIALS
Pull-Down Menu
Tools
> Palettes
> Materials
Toolbar
Render
Materials...
Dashboard
Materials
Materials...

When materials are attached to objects, subobjects, or layers, they are automatically added to the **Materials** window. The **Materials** window contains all of the materials loaded into the current drawing. It also provides a material editor for modifying the materials. See **Figure 14-6.**

At the top of the window is the **Available Materials in Drawing** pane. Samples (swatches) are displayed in this pane representing the materials that have been loaded into the drawing. A drawing icon in the lower-right corner of a swatch indicates that the material is currently in use in the drawing. In addition to the loaded materials, the default AutoCAD material Global appears in the list of swatches. The swatch outlined in yellow is the currently selected material. Its properties are displayed in the material editor. The material editor consists of several panes, including the **Material Editor**, **Maps**, **Advanced Lighting Override**, **Material Scaling & Tiling**, and **Material Offset & Preview** panes.

Swatch Options

Above the material swatches, at the right-hand end of the **Available Materials in Drawing** title bar, there is a square button. This is the **Toggle Display Mode** button, which toggles the swatch area between the display of multiple materials to a single material. See **Figure 14-7.** The single-swatch display mode provides a much better view of the details of the selected material. Arrow buttons on either side of the single material swatch allow you to select the next or previous material swatch. Immediately below the swatches are several buttons:

- **Swatch Geometry**
- **Checkered Underlay**

Figure 14-6.
The **Materials** window provides swatches of the materials in the drawing and a material editor for modifying material properties.

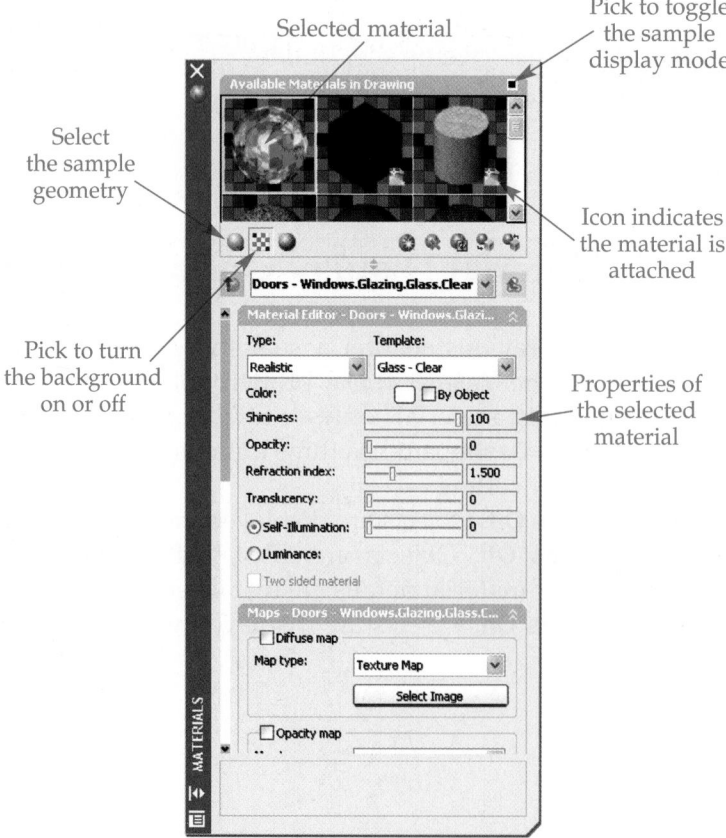

Selected material

Pick to toggle the sample display mode

Select the sample geometry

Icon indicates the material is attached

Pick to turn the background on or off

Properties of the selected material

- **Preview Swatch Lighting Model**
- **Create New Material**
- **Purge from Drawing**
- **Indicate Materials in Use**
- **Apply Material to Objects**
- **Remove Materials from Selected Objects**

The sample geometry in the swatch can be displayed as a sphere, box, or cylinder. Pick the **Swatch Geometry** flyout and select the geometry to display in the swatch. This allows you to preview the material on an object of a similar shape to the object on which the material will be used.

The **Checkered Underlay** button toggles the background in the swatch from checkered to black. The checkered underlayment is needed for transparent, semitransparent, and dark-colored materials. These materials may not be visible on a black background. The checkered underlayment also allows you to view the refraction quality of a transparent material.

The **Preview Swatch Lighting Model** determines how lighting is applied to the geometry in the sample. You can choose between single and dual lighting sources. Pick the **Single Light** button in the flyout to have one light illuminate the geometry from the upper-left side. Pick the **Back Light** button in the flyout to add a second light behind the geometry on the lower-right side.

To create a new, blank material, pick the **Create New Material** button. The **Create New Material** dialog box is displayed. Enter a name and description for the material and pick the **OK** button to close the dialog box. The new material is displayed as a new swatch and has the same properties as the Global material. Changing properties is discussed later.

If a material is not attached to an object or layer in the drawing, it can be removed from the drawing. To purge the material, select the swatch and pick the **Purge from Drawing** button. A drawing icon appearing at the corner of a material swatch indicates that the material is attached to an object or layer and cannot be purged.

When a material is applied to an object and the **Materials** window is open, the drawing icon indicating an attached material is not automatically added to the material swatch. Pick the **Indicate Materials in Use** button to update the material swatches to show which materials are attached.

Any material shown in the **Materials** window can be attached to objects in the drawing. Select the material swatch and pick the **Apply Material to Objects** button. If any objects are selected when the button is picked, and **PICKFIRST** is set to 1, the material is applied to the objects. Otherwise, you are prompted to selected objects.

Figure 14-7.
The material swatches in the **Materials** window can be displayed in different sizes. A—The medium setting. B—The full setting.

Pick to toggle the display mode

Pick to display the previous material

Pick to display the next material

A

B

You learned earlier that you can remove a material from an object by setting its Material property to Global. Picking the **Remove Materials from Selected Objects** button allows you to set an object's Material property to ByLayer. If no material is assigned to the object's layer, this in effect removes the material from the object. However, if a material is assigned to the object's layer, the object is displayed in that material.

PROFESSIONAL TIP

A material can be assigned to an object by dragging and dropping from the **Materials** window. Select the material swatch in the **Materials** window, drag the swatch into the drawing, and drop it onto the object to which you want the material attached. If you are attaching the material to a subobject, press the [Ctrl] key before dropping the material.

Swatch Shortcut Menu

Right-clicking in the swatch display area displays a shortcut menu. See Figure 14-8. This shortcut menu provides some options that are not available anywhere else:

- **Select Objects with Material.** This selects all objects in the drawing that have the current material attached to them. This option only selects objects that have the material attached *explicitly.* In other words, if the material is attached to an object's layer and the object's Material property is set to ByLayer, this option will *not* select the object.
- **Edit Name and Description.** Displays a dialog box in which the name and description of the material can be changed.
- **Export to Active Tool Palette.** Exports the selected material to the current tool palette, as long as the palette is not read only. Tool palettes are discussed in detail in Chapter 22.
- **Copy and Paste options.** These two options allow you to copy the selected material and paste it back into the swatch area as a new material with the same properties. These options are very useful when creating a group of similar materials.
- **Size.** Displays a cascading menu with options for the display size of the material swatches—**Small**, **Medium**, **Large**, and **Full**.

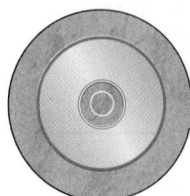

Exercise 14-3
Complete the exercise on the Student CD.

Figure 14-8.
The shortcut menu displayed by right-clicking in the swatch display area of the **Materials** window.

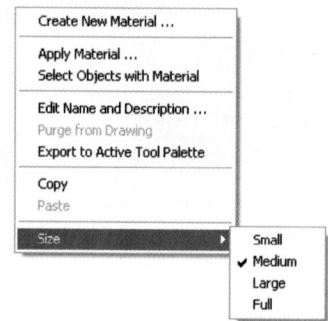

Creating and Modifying Materials

Before creating and modifying materials, it is important to know your way around the **Materials** window. There are six panes in the **Materials** window:

- **Available Materials in Drawing**
- **Material Editor**
- **Maps**
- **Advanced Lighting Override**
- **Material Scaling & Tiling**
- **Material Offset & Preview**

The **Available Materials in Drawing** pane, discussed in the previous section, contains the material preview swatches and related buttons. Depending on the material, some or all of the other five panes will be displayed.

Below the **Available Materials in Drawing** pane and above the **Material Editor** pane are three controls for working with nested maps. See **Figure 14-9A**. Maps are discussed later in this chapter. The drop-down list contains the *mapping tree*. The name in bold at the top of the list is the name of the current level of navigation. See **Figure 14-9B**. Picking one of the other levels on the tree navigates to that level. The name of that level is moved to the top of the drop-down and displayed in bold. The panes displayed in the **Materials** window are only those containing property settings for the currently selected level.

The button to the right of the drop-down list is **Up One Level to Parent Map**. Picking this button navigates up one step in the mapping tree. On the left side of the drop-down list is the **Home to Material Settings** button. Picking this button navigates to the top level of the mapping tree, or the top of the material definition, no matter where you are in the mapping tree.

Creating New Materials

The basic properties of the material selected in the **Materials** window are displayed in the **Material Editor** pane. Additional properties are displayed in the other panes in the **Materials** window. Every material created in AutoCAD is based on a template. The specific properties that are available in the various panes are determined by the template on which the material is based. Templates are discussed in the next section.

To create a new material, open the **Materials** window. Then, pick the **Create New Material** button below the material swatches or right-click on a swatch and select **Create New Material...** from the shortcut menu. In the **Create New Material** dialog box

---

Figure 14-9.
Navigating the material mapping tree. A—The top level. Note the navigation tools. B—The mapping tree is displayed in the drop-down list. The name of the current level is displayed in bold.

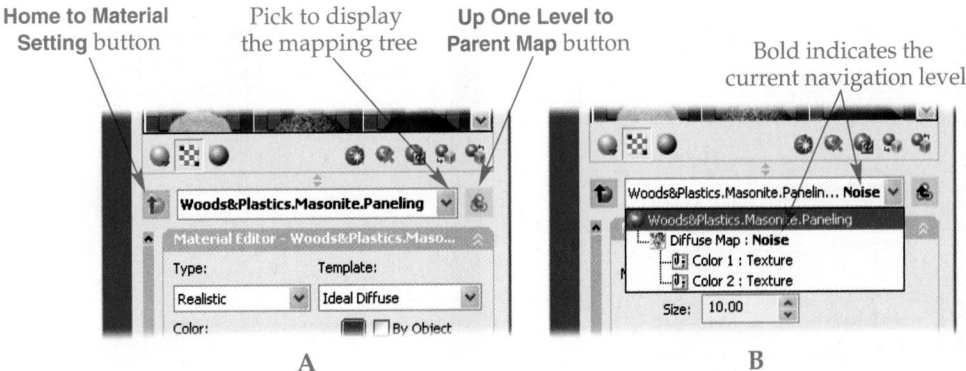

Figure 14-10.
Creating a new
material.

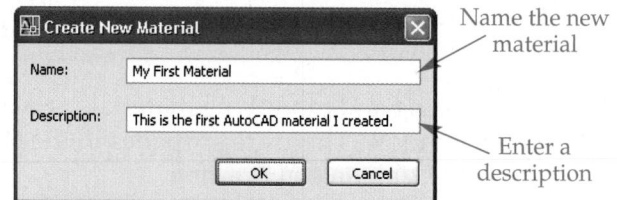

Name the new
material

Enter a
description

> **CAUTION**
>
> Do not modify the properties of the materials that come with
> AutoCAD. It may be difficult to return them to their initial settings
> without reinstalling the material library. If you want to modify one of
> these materials, first make a copy and then edit the copied material.

that appears, name the material and provide a description, Figure 14-10. The material
is automatically selected in the **Materials** window and ready to be modified. To modify
an existing material, simply select the material swatch and it is ready to be modified.

Types and Templates

A material can be one of four material types—realistic, realistic metal, advanced,
or advanced metal. The *material type* determines the basic properties available for
the material. It is set in the **Type:** drop-down list at the upper-left corner of the **Material
Editor** pane. See Figure 14-11A.

In addition to a material type, you can select a material template. A *material template*
provides you with a starting point for creating your own materials. It has settings already
established that can be easily modified to give you the appearance that you are looking for.
To select a template, pick it in the **Template:** drop-down list at the upper-right corner of the
Material Editor pane, Figure 14-11B. Material templates are only available for the realistic
and realistic metal material types. Each has its own set of templates. The advanced and
advanced metal material types do not have the **Template:** drop-down list.

Figure 14-11.
Selecting a material type and a template on which to base the new material. A—Selecting the
material type. B—Selecting a template.

Pick to select
a material type

Pick to select a
material template

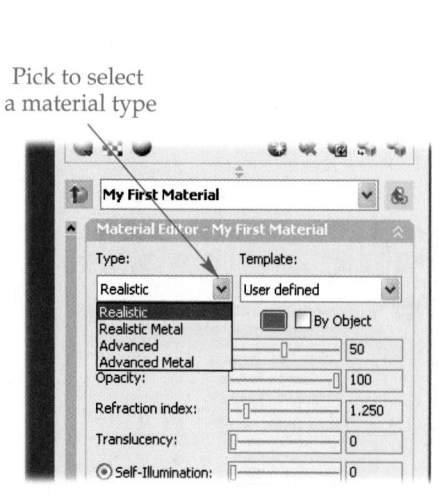

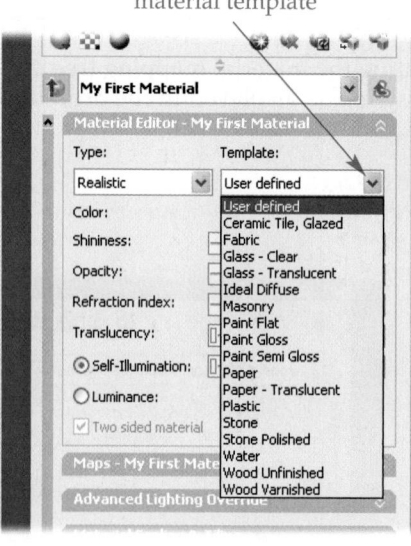

A

B

The realistic or realistic metal material type are a good starting point if you are new to material creation. Each provides basic material properties. Realistic materials are based on the physical qualities of the material: color, shininess, opacity, refraction, translucency, self illumination, and luminance. If a template other than User defined is selected, some of these properties have preset settings applied to them. This gives you a starting point to create your own fabric, glass, metal, and various other materials.

When you get comfortable with creating basic materials, the two advanced material types—advanced and advanced metal—offer more material properties to provide additional control over the material appearance. The main difference between a realistic material type and an advanced material type is the addition of ambient, diffuse, and specular color settings and a reflection property.

Color

There are three possible color settings: diffuse, ambient, and specular. All three properties are available with the advanced material types, but only diffuse is available with the realistic material types. For the advanced material types, the three color properties can be independently controlled or locked together. To lock colors, pick the lock icon next to the color swatches. See **Figure 14-12.** When locked, the diffuse color is always the dominant color. Checking the **By Object** check box turns off the color swatch. The color reverts to the object color (ByLayer, for example). To set the color, pick the color swatch to display the **Select Color** dialog box, **Figure 14-13.** Then, select a color and pick the **OK** button to close the dialog box.

The *diffuse color* is the color of the object in lighted areas, or the perceived color of the material. See **Figure 14-14.** It is the predominant color you see when you look at the object. Set this color first. The other two colors are typically based on the diffuse color.

The *ambient color* is the color of the object where light does not directly provide illumination. It can be thought of as the color of an object in shadows. In nature, shadows cast by an object typically contain some of the ambient color.

Figure 14-12.
The ambient and diffuse colors are locked. The diffuse and specular colors are not locked.

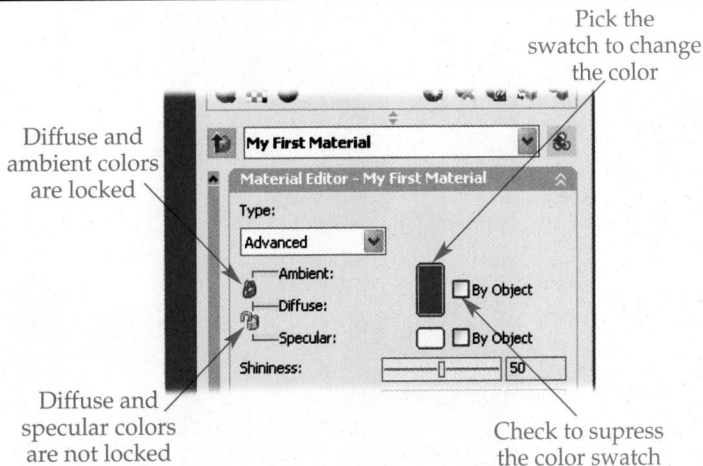

Figure 14-13.
Setting a color for a material property.

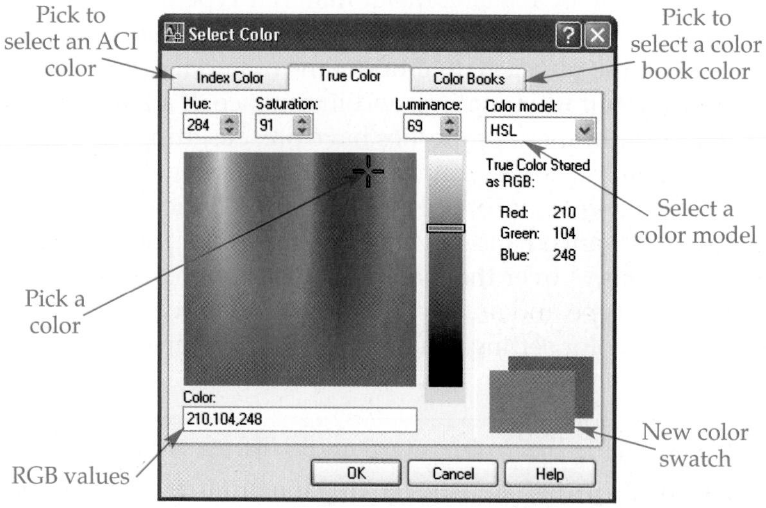

Pick to select an ACI color

Pick to select a color book color

Select a color model

New color swatch

RGB values

Pick a color

The *specular color* is the color of the highlight (the shiny spot). It is typically white or a light color. The amount of specular color shown is determined by the shininess of the material and the intensity of lighting in the scene.

PROFESSIONAL TIP

Specular highlights can be seen everywhere. Look around you right now at edges and inclined surfaces. The diffuse color of the surface typically has little to do with the color of the highlight. The color of the light source usually determines the predominant highlight color. The majority of highlights are white or near white because most light sources are white or nearly white. However, highlights in the interior of a home may have a yellow cast to them because incandescent light-bulbs generally cast yellow light. Outside with a clear sky and bright sun, highlights may have a slight blue cast. These small details are what make a scene realistic.

Figure 14-14.
The three colors of a material are illustrated here.

Diffuse color

Specular color

Ambient color

Shininess

Shininess is a measure of the surface roughness. Smooth surfaces are very shiny and have a small, hard highlight. These surfaces reflect in one direction most of the light that hits the surface. Rough surfaces tend to diffuse, or break up, light as it is reflected. Therefore, these surfaces do not appear very shiny and have a large, soft highlight. See **Figure 14-15.** To set the shininess, drag the **Shininess:** slider left to decrease the value or right to increase the value. As you drag the slider, the value appears in a tooltip next to the cursor. You can also enter a value in the text box at the right-hand end of the slider.

Opacity

Opacity is a measure of a material's transparency, or how "see through" the material is. **Figure 14-16** shows an example of using transparent materials to show the internal workings of a mechanical assembly. To change the opacity value, drag the **Opacity:** slider to the left to make the material more transparent or right to make it more opaque. You can also enter a value in the text box at the right-hand end of the slider. A value of 100 creates an opaque material. Lower values create semitransparent materials. Realistic and advanced material types have an opacity property.

Figure 14-15.
Three different shininess settings are illustrated here.

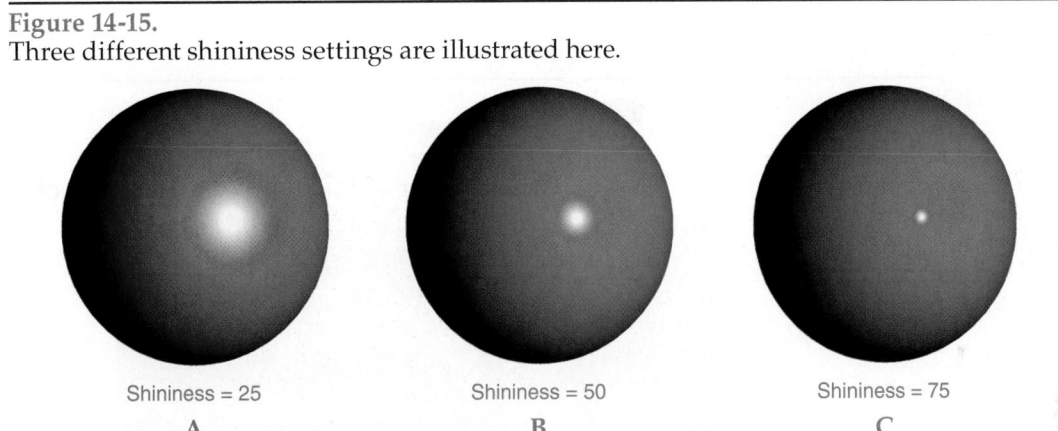

Shininess = 25
A

Shininess = 50
B

Shininess = 75
C

Figure 14-16.
The material used for the housing on this mechanism has an opacity setting of five.

Reflection

The *reflection* is a mirror image of the other objects in the scene. See **Figure 14-17.** Only the advanced and advanced metal material types have a reflection property. To make a material reflective, drag the **Reflection:** slider. Dragging the slider to the right increases the reflectivity of the material and to the left decreases reflectivity. You can also enter a value in the text box at the right-hand end of the slider.

Refraction Index

The *refraction index,* also know as the index of refraction (IOR), is a measure of how much light is bent (refracted) as it passes through transparent or semitranspar- ent materials. The refraction index is what causes objects to appear distorted when viewed through a bottle or glass of water. See **Figure 14-18.** The higher the refraction index value, the more light is bent as it passes through the material. To set the value, drag the **Refraction index:** slider to the right to increase the value or left to decrease the value. As you drag the slider, the value appears in as a tooltip next to the cursor. You can also enter a value in the text box at the right-hand end of the slider. A value of 1.000 is the refraction index of a vacuum. The value of water is 1.3333 and glass is around 1.500. Generally, the refraction index is not set much above 1.700 and is usu- ally somewhere between 1.000 and 1.500. Realistic and advanced material types have a refraction index property.

Figure 14-17.
The effect of increasing reflectivity. A—The reflection value of the material on the box is zero. B—The reflection value is increased to 100.

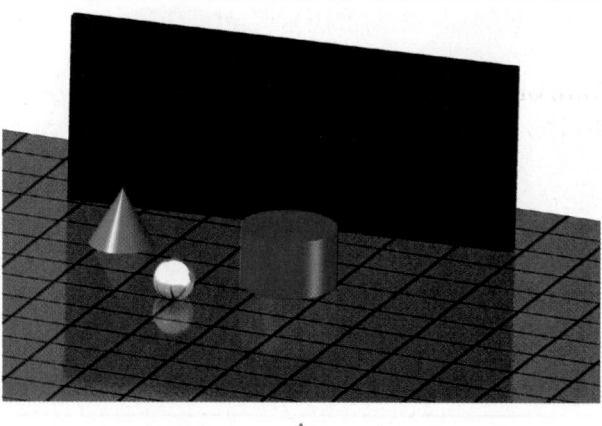

A

B

Figure 14-18.
The effect of refraction. A—The transparent material on the sphere has a refraction index of zero. B—When the refraction index is increased, the cylinder behind the sphere is distorted as light is refracted by the material.

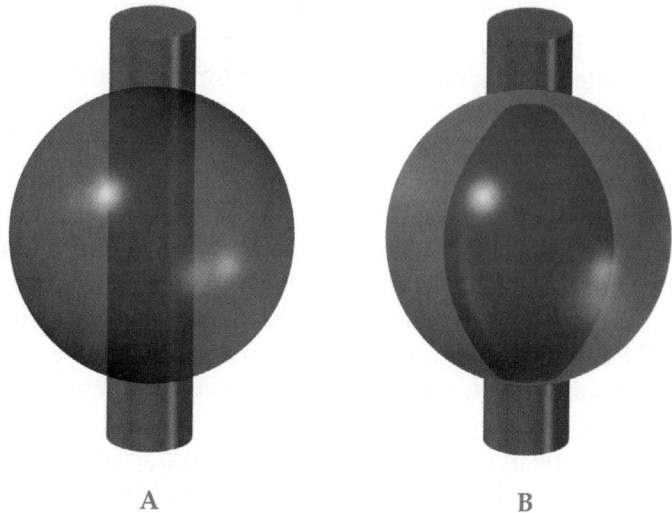

A   B

Translucency

Translucency is a quality of transparent and semitransparent materials that causes light to be diffused (scattered) as it passes through the material. See **Figure 14-19.** This makes any object with the material applied to it appear as if it is being illuminated from within, or glowing. The thicker the material, the more pronounced the effect. In AutoCAD, the translucency setting affects transparent, semitransparent, and opaque materials. With a higher setting, light appears to travel through an object lighting the opposite side. To change the translucency value, drag the **Translucency:** slider to the right to increase the value or left to decrease the value. You can also enter a value in the text box at the right-hand end of the slider. Realistic and advanced material types have a translucency property.

Figure 14-19.
The effect of translucency. A—The glass material has a translucency setting of zero. B—When the translucency setting is increased, light is diffused within the material. In this case, since the glass is thin, the effect is not as "glowing" as it would be for a thicker material.

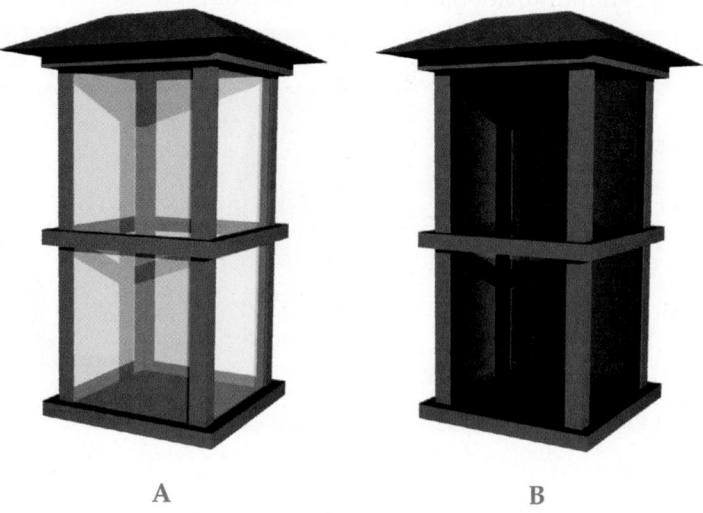

A   B

Self Illumination and Luminance

Self illumination is an effect of a material producing illumination. See **Figure 14-20.** For example, the surface of a neon tube glows. However, in AutoCAD, a material with self illumination will not actually add illumination to a scene. All four material types have a self illumination property.

Luminance is defined as the value of light reflected off a surface. For realistic and realistic metal material types, you have the choice of using either self illumination or luminance. They both have a similar affect on the material. To use self illumination, pick the **Self-Illumination:** radio button. To use luminance, pick the **Luminance:** radio button.

To set the self illumination value, drag the **Self-Illumination:** slider to the right to increase the value or left to decrease the value. You can also enter a value in the text box at the right-hand end of the slider. Valid values for self illumination are from 1 to 100.

Luminance is expressed in candelas per square meter (cd/m^2). For example, $1\ cd/m^2$ is the equivalent of 1 candela of light radiating from a surface that is 1 square meter. To set luminance, enter a value in the text box that is displayed when the **Luminance:** radio button is picked. You may want to use luminance if the maximum self illumination setting of 100 is not making the material bright enough for you. A luminance setting of 1500 cd/m^2 is about the same as a self illumination setting of 100. Luminance can be set as high as 100 million cd/m^2.

Material Maps

Below the **Material Editor** pane in the **Materials** window is the **Maps** pane. A *texture map* is simply an image applied to a material property. This type of map is known as a *2D map* because it is applied to the surface of an object and does not extend into it. On the other hand, a *procedural map* is mathematically generated based on the colors and values you select. This type of map is known as a *3D map* because it extends through the object. A material that has a map applied to at least one of its properties is called a *mapped material.*

Maps

There are eight types of maps that can be applied to material properties: texture, checker, marble, noise, speckle, tiles, waves, and wood. Each map has unique settings. A material can have separate diffuse, reflection, opacity, and bump maps, as discussed later in this chapter.

Figure 14-20.
The effect of self illumination/luminance. A—The globe of this lightbulb does not have any self illumination. B—Self illumination is applied to the globe material.

A

B

Figure 14-21.
A material with a texture map. A—The background object's material does not have any maps applied. B—A texture map has been applied to the diffuse color component of the background object's material.

A   B

Texture Map. A texture map is an image file, such as a digital photograph, that is applied to one of the material's properties. **Figure 14-21** shows a box object with an image of a forest applied to the diffuse color of the material attached to it. To specify a texture map, first select Texture Map in the drop-down list in the appropriate area of the **Maps** pane. Then, pick the **Select Image** button in the same area. The **Select Image File** dialog box is displayed, which is a standard open dialog box. Browse to the folder where the image file is saved, select the file, and pick the **Open** button.

The "select image" button is now labeled with the file name of the image file. Also, a slider is displayed to the left of the button. See **Figure 14-22.** The slider is used to set the percentage of the image file that is applied to the property. At 100% (fully right), all of the image is applied to the pro   perty. At 50% (in the middle), the image appears to be 50% transparent, which is applied to the property. All of the map types have this slider for adjusting the amount of the map that is applied to the property.

The image settings are controlled by picking the **Click for Texture Map settings** button to the right of the **Map type:** drop-down list. Three additional buttons are also displayed to the right of the "select image" button. These are used to adjust and delete the map from the property. These buttons are available for all map types and are discussed later in the section Adjusting Material Maps.

Checker. A *checker map* creates a two-color checkerboard pattern. By default, the colors are black and white, but different colors or images can be used as well. This map type can be used for checkerboard pattern floor materials. However, by changing various properties, you can simulate many different effects and use the map for other materials.

Figure 14-22.
Use the slider to adjust the percentage of the texture map that is contributed to the property. All properties that can be mapped have this slider once a map is applied.

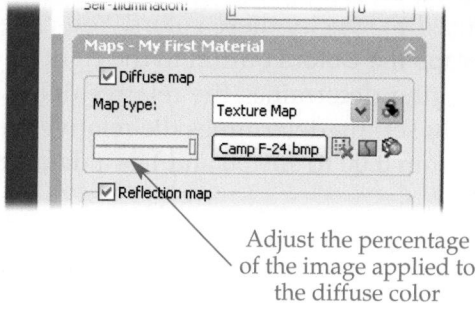

Adjust the percentage
of the image applied to
the diffuse color

Figure 14-23.
The map-level properties of a checker map.

Pick to swap the color definition

Enter a value to soften the edges

Select a map type

Pick to set the color

My First Material | Diffuse - **Checker**

Checker - My First Material

Color 1

Map type: Solid Color

Color:

Color 2

Map type: Solid Color

Color:

Soften:

0.00

Scaling & Tiling

To specify a checker map, first select Checker in the drop-down list in the appropriate area of the **Maps** pane. Then, pick the **Click for Checker settings** button next to the **Map type:** drop-down list to navigate to the checker map level of the mapping tree. The **Checker** pane is now displayed in the **Materials** window. See **Figure 14-23.** In this pane, the two colors that make up the checker pattern are defined. By default, they are both solid colors. Pick on the color swatch to change the color. To swap the color definitions, pick the **Swaps the Colors** button in the middle of the pane. You are not limited to solid colors. All of the map types are listed in the **Map type:** drop-down list, along with Solid. For example, you can add a texture map to the Color 1 definition and a noise map to the Color 2 definition. The possibilities are endless.

The **Soften:** setting is used to blur the edges between the checkers. To change the setting, enter a value in the text box or use the up and down arrows. A value of 0.00 creates sharp edges between the checkers. The maximum setting is 5.00 and produces edges that are very blurred.

PROFESSIONAL TIP

Remember to use the **Up One Level to Parent Map, Home to Material Settings** button, and the drop-down list below the material samples to navigate through the mapping tree.

Marble. A *marble map* is a procedural map generated based on the colors and values you select. To specify a marble map, first select Marble in the drop-down list in the appropriate area of the **Maps** pane. To set the marble properties, pick the **Click for Marble settings** button next to the **Map type:** drop-down list to navigate to the marble map level of the mapping tree. The **Marble** pane is now displayed in the **Materials** window. See **Figure 14-24.**

A marble map is based on two colors—stone and vein. The two color swatches in the **Marble** pane are used to specify these colors. You can swap the vein and stone colors by picking the **Swaps the Colors** button to the right of the swatches.

The **Vein spacing:** setting determines the relative distance between each vein in the marble. The **Vein width:** setting determines the relative width of each vein. Each of these settings can range from 0.00 to 100.00 and has a default of 1.00.

Figure 14-24.
The map-level
properties of a marble
map.

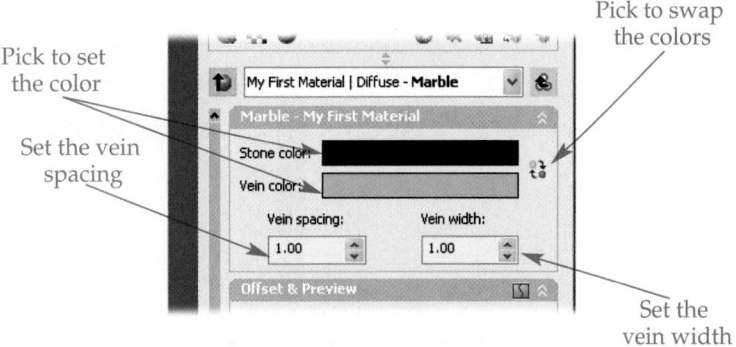

Pick to set
the color

Pick to swap
the colors

Set the vein
spacing

Set the
vein width

NOTE

The mathematical calculations that create the marble map are based on the world coordinate system. If you move or rotate the object, a different vein result is produced.

Noise. A *noise map* is a random pattern of two colors used to create an uneven appearance on the material. It is most often used to simulate materials such as concrete, soil, asphalt, grass, and so on. To specify a noise map, first select Noise in the drop-down list in the appropriate area of the **Maps** pane. To set the noise properties, pick the **Click for Noise settings** button next to the **Map type:** drop-down list to navigate to the noise map level of the mapping tree. The **Noise** pane is now displayed in the **Materials** window. See Figure 14-25.

First, you need to select the type of noise. The options in the **Noise Type:** drop-down list are:

- **Regular.** This is "plain" noise and is useful for most applications.
- **Fractal.** This creates the noise pattern using a fractal algorithm. When this is selected, the **Level:** control in the **Noise Threshold** area of the pane is enabled.
- **Turbulence.** This is similar to fractal, except that it creates fault lines.

Figure 14-25.
The map-level
properties of a
noise map.

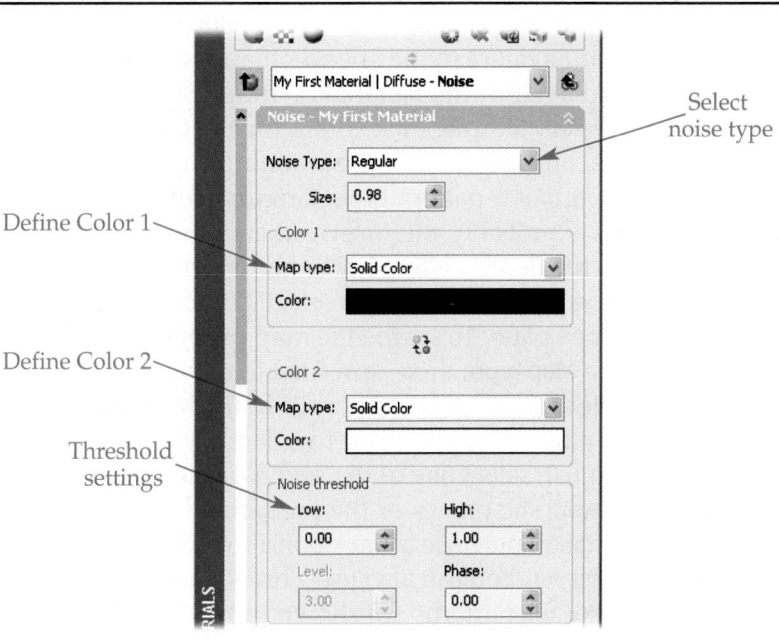

Select
noise type

Define Color 1

Define Color 2

Threshold
settings

Figure 14-26.
The map-level properties of a speckle map.

Set the colors

Set the size

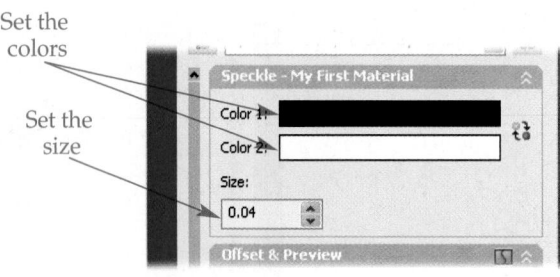

The **Size:** setting below the **Noise Type:** drop-down list controls the size scale of the noise. The larger the value, the larger the size of the noise. The default value is 1.00 and the value can range from 0.00 to 10 billion.

The Color 1 and Color 2 definitions control the color of the pattern of noise. To change the color, pick the color swatch. You can also select a map for the color definition using the **Map type:** drop-down list. To swap the color definitions, pick the **Swaps the Map Types** button.

The settings in the **Noise Threshold** area of the **Noise** pane are used to fine-tune the noise effect. The settings in this area are:

- **Low.** The closer this setting is to 1.00, the more dominate Color 1 is. The default setting is 0.00 and it can range from 0.00 to 1.00.
- **High.** The closer this setting is to 0.00, the more dominate Color 2 is. The default setting is 1.00 and it can range from 0.00 to 1.00.
- **Level.** Sets the energy amount for fractal and turbulence. Lower values make the fractal noise appear blurry and the turbulence lines more defined. The default setting is 3.00 and it can range from 0.00 upward.
- **Phase.** Randomly changes the noise pattern with each value. This allows you to have materials with the same noise map settings look slightly different.

Speckle. A *speckle map* is a random pattern of dots based on two colors. This map is great for textured walls, sand, granite, and so on. To specify a speckle map, first select Speckle in the drop-down list in the appropriate area of the **Maps** pane. To set the speckle map properties, pick the **Click for Speckle settings** button next to the **Map type:** drop-down list to navigate to the speckle map level of the mapping tree. The **Speckle** pane is now displayed in the **Materials** window. See **Figure 14-26.** The settings for a speckle map are very simple. Pick colors for the Color 1 and Color 2 definitions. You cannot use maps, only colors. The **Size:** setting controls the size of the speckles.

Tiles. A *tile map* is a pattern of rectangular colored blocks surrounded by colored grout lines. This is probably the most versatile map in the whole collection. Tiles are used to simulate tile floors, ceiling grids, hardwood floors, and many different types of brick walls. To specify a tile map, first select Tiles in the drop-down list in the appropriate area of the **Maps** pane. To set the tile map properties, pick the **Click for Tiles settings** button next to the **Map type:** drop-down list to navigate to the tile map level of the mapping tree. The **Tiles** pane is now displayed in the **Materials** window. See **Figure 14-27.**

In the **Tiles** pane, first you need to select the pattern for the map. In the **Pattern type:** drop-down list, select one of the seven predefined tile patterns or Custom Pattern to create your own. The names of the predefined patterns bring to mind brick walls. For example, a mason may use a stack bond to build a brick wall. However, remember these are only *patterns.* You can also use a brick pattern to create tile floors and acoustic ceiling panels. The tile patterns are shown in **Figure 14-28.**

The **Random seed:** setting below the **Pattern type:** drop-down list is used to create a random color variation in the tiles. Ceramic tile floors, for example, look more realistic

Figure 14-27.
The map-level
properties of a tile
map.

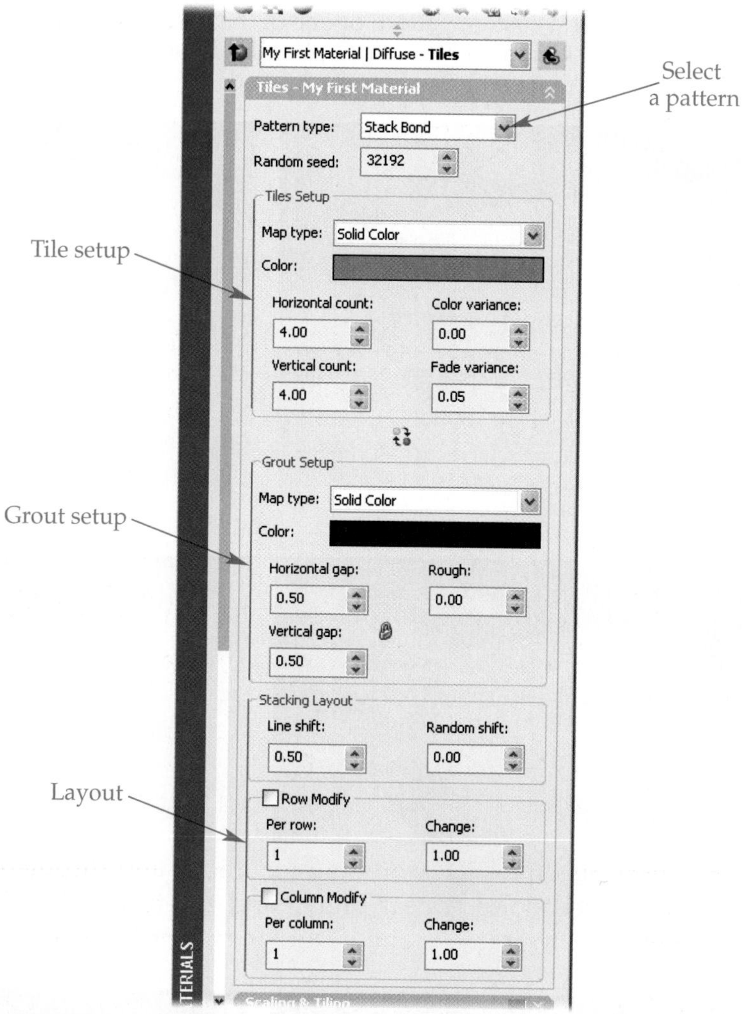

Select
a pattern

Tile setup

Grout setup

Layout

if each tile is slightly different in color. This variation is automatically applied, but entering a different random seed changes the pattern.

A tile pattern is really made up of tiles and grout. The **Tiles** pane contains **Tiles Setup** and **Grout Setup** areas in which these elements are defined. Each area has a drop-down list for selecting a map type and, if the map type is Solid Color, a color swatch for setting the color. The number and size of the tiles is controlled by the **Horizontal count:** and **Vertical count:** settings in the **Tiles Setup** area. The **Color variance:** setting in the **Tiles Setup** area can be used to slightly alter the color of each tile to create a more realistic appearance. The **Fade variance:** setting in the **Tiles Setup** area is used to slightly fade the color of each tile. You will have to experiment with the color variance and fading to create the look you need. The grout setup is mainly just controlling size of the grout with the **Horizontal gap:** and **Vertical gap:** settings. Most of the time, these values will be the same and they can be locked together with the lock button. In some cases, such as for a hardwood floor material, you will have to differently scale the pattern on the horizontal and vertical axes to make the gap thicker in one direction.

The settings in the **Stacking Layout** area are only available when Custom Tile is selected in the **Pattern type:** drop-down list. The value in the **Line shift:** text box changes the location of the vertical grout lines in every other row to create an alternate pattern of tiles. The default value is 0.50 and the range is from 0.00 to 100.00. The value in the **Random shift:** text box randomly moves the same lines. This works nicely for hardwood floor materials. Default value is 0.00 and the range is 0.00 to 100.00.

Figure 14-28.
A tile map can have a custom pattern or one of the predefined patterns shown here. A—
Running bond. B—Common Flemish. C—English bond. D—Half running bond. E—Stack
bond. F—Fine running bond. G—Fine stack bond.

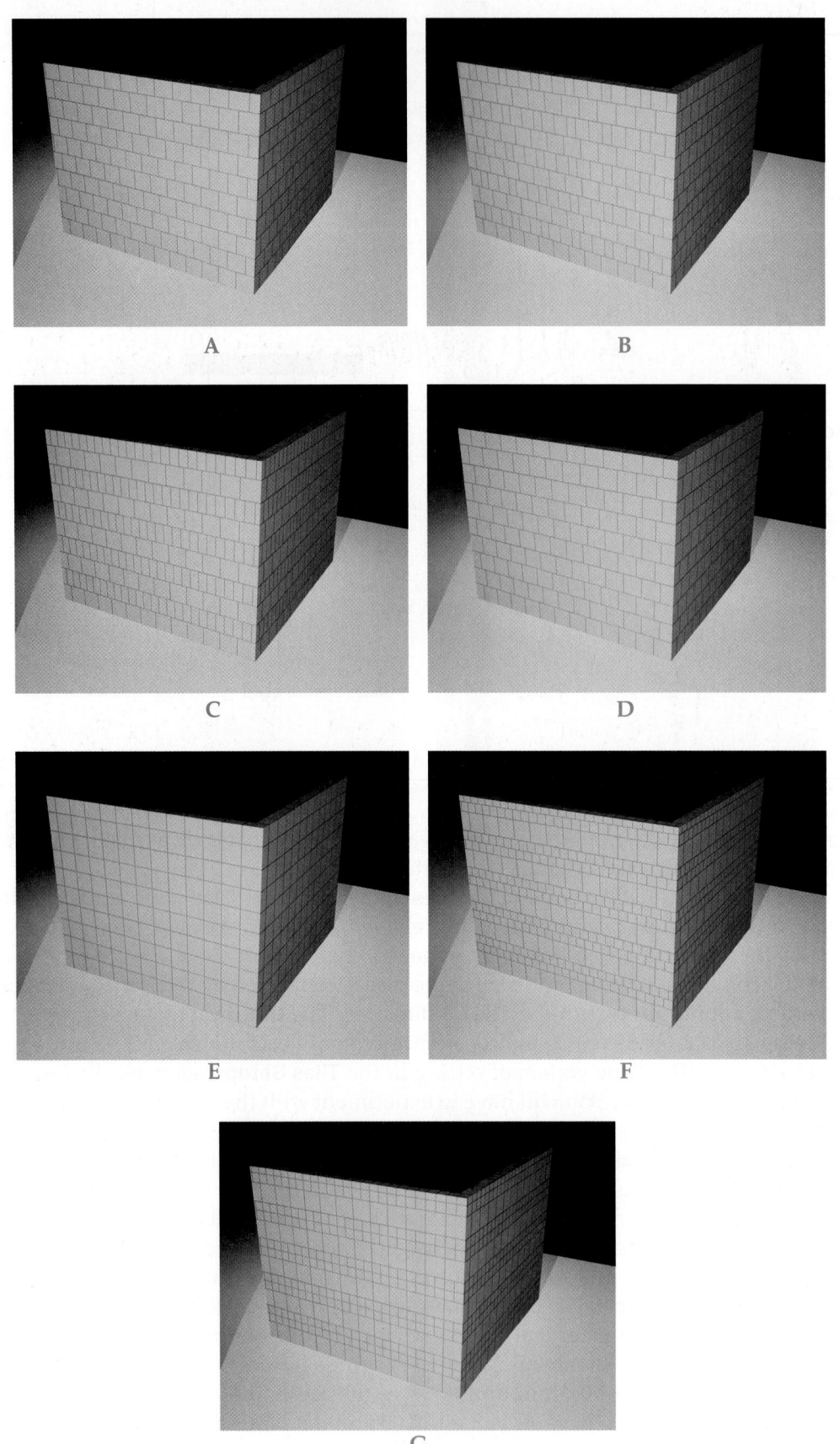

Figure 14-29.
The map-level
properties for a wave
map.

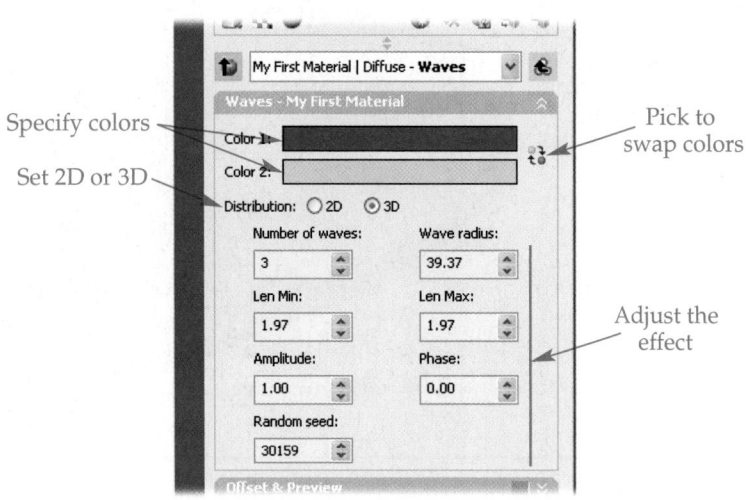

Specify colors

Set 2D or 3D

Pick to swap colors

Adjust the effect

The settings in the **Row Modify** and **Column Modify** areas are available with all tile pattern types, but may be disabled by default. To enable the settings, check the check box by the area name. The settings in these areas allow you to change the number of grout lines in the horizontal and vertical directions to create your own pattern. The **Per row:** and **Per column:** settings determine which rows and columns will be changed. When set to 0, no changes take place in the row or column. When set to 1, every row or column will be changed. When set to 2, every other row or column will be changed, and so on. The value must be a whole number. The setting in the **Change:** text box controls the size of the tiles in the row or column. A setting of 1 means that the tiles remain their original size. A setting of 0.50 makes the tiles one-half of their original size, a setting of 2 makes the tiles twice their original size, and so on. A setting of 0.00, in effect, completely turns off the row or column and the underlying color (usually black) shows through.

Waves. A *wave map* creates a pattern of concentric circles. Imagine dropping two or three stones into a pool of water and watching the ripples intersect with each other. A number of wave centers are randomly generated and a pattern created by the overlapping waves is the result. As the name implies, the wave map is usually used to simulate water. To specify a wave map, first select Waves in the drop-down list in the appropriate area of the **Maps** pane. To set the wave map properties, pick the **Click for Waves settings** button next to the **Map type:** drop-down list to navigate to the wave map level of the mapping tree. The **Waves** pane is now displayed in the **Materials** window. See **Figure 14-29.**

In the **Waves** pane, first specify the two colors that will be used in the pattern. Maps cannot be used for the color definitions. To set a color, pick on the swatch and choose a color in the **Select Color** dialog box.

Below the color swatches are two radio buttons next to the **Distribution:** label. The radio button that is selected determines how the wave centers are distributed on the object. Picking the **3D** radio button means that the wave centers are randomly distributed over the surface of an imaginary sphere. This distribution affects all sides of an object. On the other hand, picking the **2D** radio button means that the wave centers are distributed on the XY plane. This is much better for nearly flat surfaces, such as the surface of a pond or lake.

The remaining settings in the **Waves** pane define the pattern of waves. The value in the **Number of waves:** text box is the number of wave centers that are generating the waves. The **Wave radius:** value is the radius of the circle or sphere from which the waves originate. The **Len Min:** and **Len Max:** settings define the minimum and maximum interval for each wave. The value in the **Amplitude:** text box can be thought of

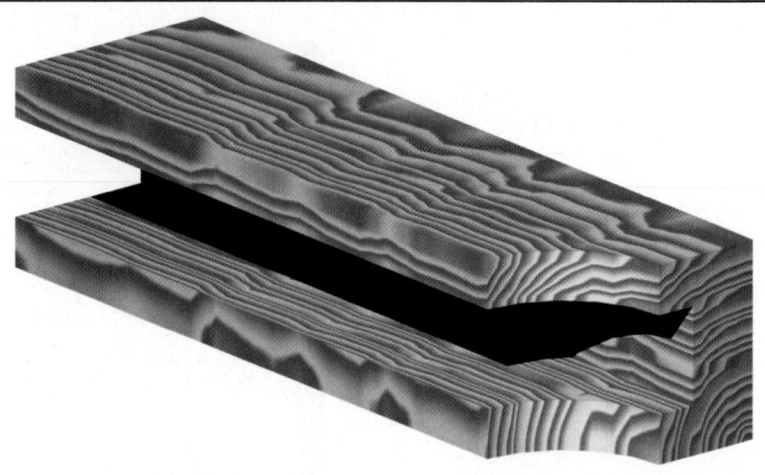

Figure 14-30.
A wood map is a procedural, or 3D, map. This type of map passes through the entire object to which it is applied.

as the "power" of the wave. The default is 1.00, but the value can range from 0.00 to 10000.00. A value less than 1.00 makes Color 1 more dominant. For a value greater than 1.00, Color 2 is more dominant. The **Phase:** text box is used to shift the pattern and the **Random seed:** text box is used to redistribute the wave centers.

PROFESSIONAL TIP

To see how your changes affect the map, check the **Auto-regen** check box in the **Offset & Preview** pane. This will automatically update the preview in that pane when you change a setting. You can also change the swatch geometry to a cube, sphere, or cylinder. Some maps, like a wave map, are easier to understand when displayed on a cube.

Wood. A *wood map* is a procedural map that generates a wood grain based on the colors and values you select. See **Figure 14-30.** To specify a wood map, first select Wood in the drop-down list in the appropriate area of the **Maps** pane. To set the wood map properties, pick the **Click for Wood settings** button next to the **Map type:** drop-down list to navigate to the wave map level of the mapping tree. The **Wood** pane is now displayed in the **Materials** window. See **Figure 14-31.**

A wood map is based on two colors. The two color swatches in the **Wood** pane are used to specify these colors, usually one dark and one light color. You can swap the two colors by picking the **Swaps the Colors** button to the right of the swatches. The **Radial noise:** setting determines the waviness of the wood's rings. The rings are found by cutting a tree crosswise. The **Axial noise:** setting determines the waviness of the length of the wood. The **Grain thickness:** setting determines the relative width of the grain.

Figure 14-31.
The map-level properties of a wood map.

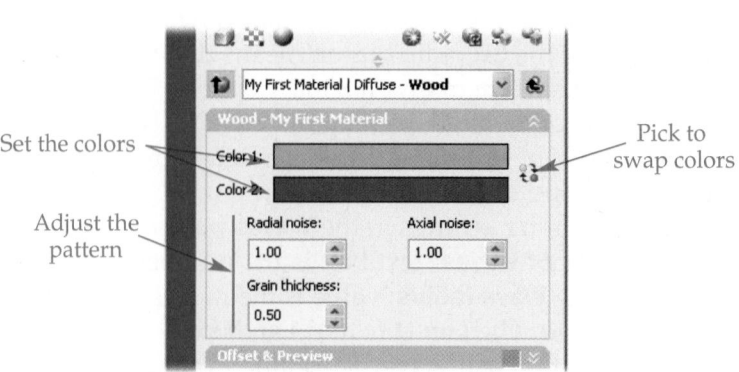

　　　　　　　　　　　　　　　　　　　AutoCAD and Its Applications—Advanced

The mathematical calculations that create the wood map are based on the world coordinate system. If you move or rotate the object, a different grain pattern is produced.

Diffuse map

A *diffuse map* is applied to the diffuse color property of a material. See Figure 14-32. This is assigned in the **Maps** pane, which is displayed at the top of the material mapping tree. The **Diffuse map** check box in the pane toggles the specified diffuse map off and on. When unchecked, the object color defined in the **Material Editor** pane controls the color of the object. If no map is specified, the toggle has no affect.

To assign a diffuse map, select the type of map to apply using the **Map type:** drop-down list in the **Diffuse map** area of the **Maps** pane. Then, define the map as described earlier. Once the map is defined, return to the top of the material mapping tree. In the **Diffuse map** area of the **Maps** pane, use the slider to adjust how much of the map is applied to the diffuse color.

Exercise 14-4
Complete the exercise on the Student CD.

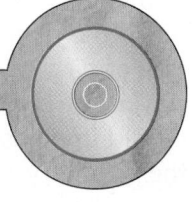

Reflection map

The advanced and advanced metal material types have a reflection property. A *reflection map* is applied to this property. This is often done for shiny materials in outdoor scenes. An image of clouds or blue sky is applied as a reflection map because the sky is not modeled. A reflection map is assigned in the **Maps** pane, which is displayed at the top of the material mapping tree. The **Reflection map** check box in the pane toggles the specified reflection map off and on.

To assign a reflection map, select the type of map to apply using the **Map type:** drop-down list in the **Reflection map** area of the **Maps** pane. Then, define the map as described earlier. Once the map is defined, return to the top of the material mapping tree. In the **Reflection map** area of the **Maps** pane, use the slider to adjust how much of the map is applied to the reflection property.

Figure 14-32.
A—The diffuse color property of the material applied to this box has no map. B—A texture map is applied to the diffuse color property of the material.

Opacity map

An *opacity map* is applied to the opacity property of a material to make an object appear transparent in different areas. Without an opacity map, the opacity property is equally applied to the object. Black areas of the map are transparent, white areas are opaque, and gray areas are semitransparent. See **Figure 14-33.** If a color appears in the map, the grayscale values of the colors are used to calculate transparency. An opacity map is assigned in the **Maps** pane, which is displayed at the top of the material mapping tree. The **Opacity map** check box in the pane toggles the specified opacity map off and on.

To assign an opacity map, select the type of map to apply using the **Map type:** drop-down list in the **Opacity map** area of the **Maps** pane. Then, define the map as described earlier. Once the map is defined, return to the top of the material mapping tree. In the **Opacity map** area of the **Maps** pane, use the slider to adjust how much of the map is applied to the opacity property.

Bump map

A *bump map* is a map applied to the material to make some areas of the material appear raised and other areas depressed. The black, white, and grayscale values of the map are used to determine raised and depressed areas. Dark areas of the map make the material surface appear depressed and light areas make the material surface appear unchanged. For example, to show the texture of a brick wall, you could physically model the grooves into the wall. This would take a lot of time to model and would immensely increase the rendering time because of the increased complexity of the geometry. Using a bump map is an easier and more efficient way to accomplish the same task. **Figure 14-34** shows a bump map used to represent an embossed stamp on a metal case. A bump map is assigned in the **Maps** pane, which is displayed at the top of the material mapping tree. The **Bump map** check box in the pane toggles the specified bump map off and on.

To assign a bump map, select the type of map to apply using the **Map type:** drop-down list in the **Bump map** area of the **Maps** pane. Then, define the map as described earlier. Once the map is defined, return to the top of the material mapping tree. In the **Bump map** area of the **Maps** pane, use the slider to adjust how much of the map is applied to the bump property.

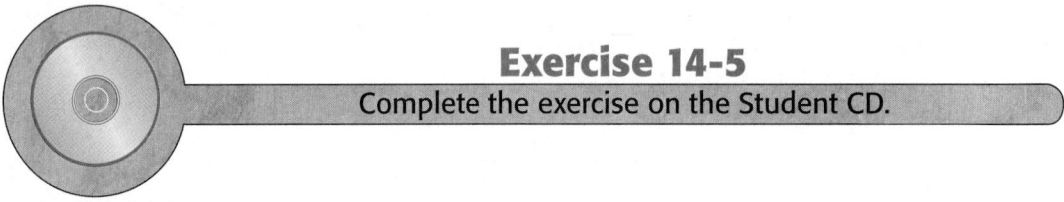

Exercise 14-5
Complete the exercise on the Student CD.

Figure 14-33.
The effect of an opacity map. A—This black and white image will be used as the opacity map. B—The material on the plane is completely opaque. C—When the opacity map is applied to the material, the dark areas of the map produce transparent areas on the object.

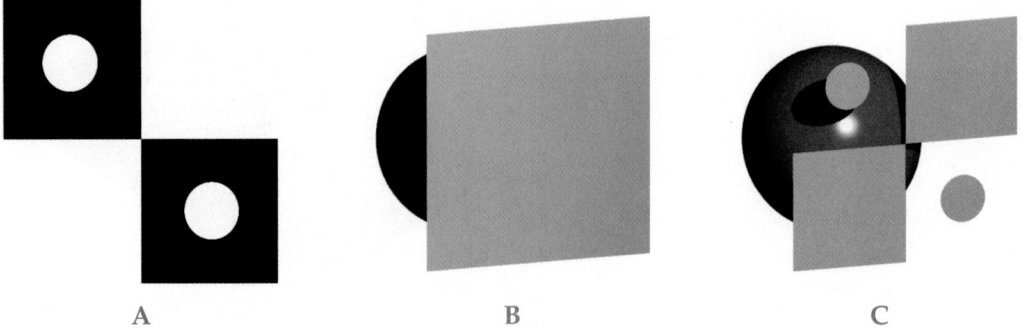

A   B   C

Figure 14-34.
The effect of a bump map. A—This image will be used as the bump map. B—When applied to the material, the bump map simulates louvers stamped into the metal case.

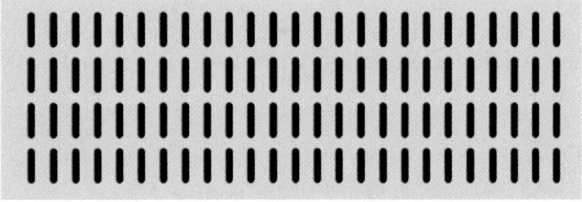

A

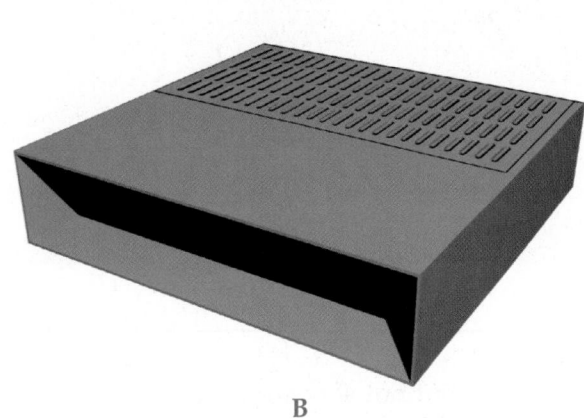

B

Adjusting Material Maps

Simply applying a map to a material rarely results in a realistic scene when the scene is rendered. The maps often need to be adjusted to produce the desired results. Maps can be adjusted at the material level or at the object level. A combination of these two adjustments is usually required to produce a photorealistic rendering.

Material-Level Adjustments

Whenever a map is applied to the diffuse, reflection, opacity, or bump property, three buttons are displayed in the corresponding area in the **Maps** pane below the **Map type:** drop-down list. See **Figure 14-35.** To remove the map from the material property, simply pick the **Delete map information from material** button. A warning may appear indicating that subtextures will also be deleted. Once the map is removed, the three buttons and the slider are removed from the area. If a texture map was removed, the "select image" button is again labeled **Select Image**, which indicates that there is no map attached to the property.

The middle button below the **Map type:** drop-down list is used to synchronize or unsynchronize the map channels within the same material definition. For example, to make a realistic tile floor, tile map is applied as a diffuse map. Another tile map is also used as a bump map to make the grout look recessed. If the scaling is changed

Figure 14-35.
The controls for a map. Once applied to a property, all maps display these controls.

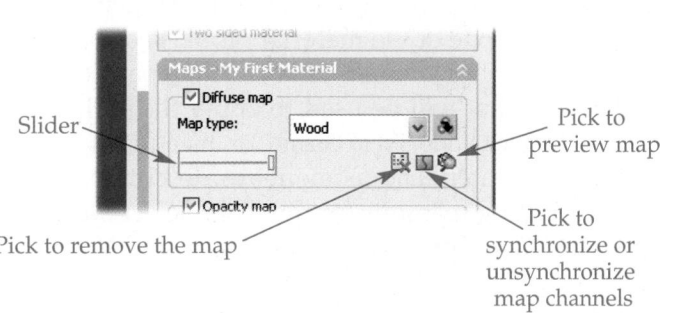

Slider

Pick to remove the map

Pick to preview map

Pick to synchronize or unsynchronize map channels

Figure 14-36.
A—This material has diffuse color and bump maps. B—If the bump map is not synchronized with the material, it will not align with the grout lines if scaled.

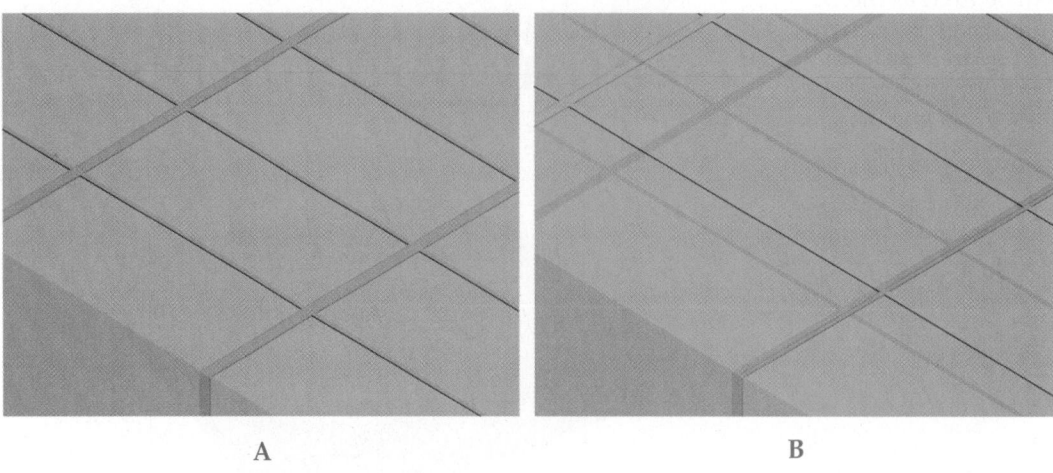

A   B

for the bump map, but not synchronized, the grout colors and indentations will not match. The synchronize button ensures that all of these settings are the same. Maps are synchronized by default. When synchronized, the button appears closed. When unsynchronized, the button appears open. When the button is picked to turn off synchronization, a warning message is displayed indicating that the other properties will be unaffected. It is recommended that you leave the synchronize feature on.

The right-hand button below the **Map type:** drop-down list opens the **Map Preview** dialog box. This dialog box displays the map channel in a larger, 2D view. This dialog box remains open until you close it. Checking the **Auto-update** check box forces the image to automatically update when a change is made to the map. If it is unchecked, the image is not updated until you manually update by picking the **Update** button in the same dialog box.

The **Material Scaling & Tiling** and **Material Offset & Preview** panes in the **Materials** window allow adjustments to be made that affect how the map image fits on the material. See **Figure 14-37.** Settings made in these panes impact all objects in the drawing that have this material applied to them. Each property map has similar panes at the map level in the mapping tree. These are named **Scaling & Tiling** and **Offset & Preview** and contains the same controls. Notice the title bars of the panes at the map level have synchronize buttons, which are the same buttons found in the **Maps** pane at the top of the material mapping tree. If unsynchronized, the settings in the **Scaling & Tiling** and **Offset & Preview** panes at the map level affect only the map. The settings in the **Material Scaling & Tiling** and **Material Offset & Preview** panes at the top of the material mapping tree are applied to all maps in the material definition.

Scaling and tiling

The map-level **Scaling & Tiling** pane is only available for texture maps (2D maps): texture map, checker, and tiles. By the same token, the **Material Scaling & Tiling** pane is only displayed if one of the material properties has a texture map.

At the top of the **Material Scaling & Tiling** pane (or map-level **Scaling & Tiling** pane), select the units that will be used to apply the scaling. In the **Scale units:** drop-down list, you can select None, Fit to Gizmo, or a standard unit of measure. The gizmo is used for object-level material adjustments, as described in the next section.

After selecting the units for the scale, select the type of tiling for the U and V axes using the left-hand drop-down lists. The U and V axes are similar to the X and Y axes

Figure 14-37.
Making map adjustments to the material. A—The **Material Scaling & Tiling** pane (or map-level **Scaling & Tiling** pane) is available for texture (2D) maps. B—The **Material Offset & Preview** pane (or map-level **Offset & Preview** pane) is available for all maps.

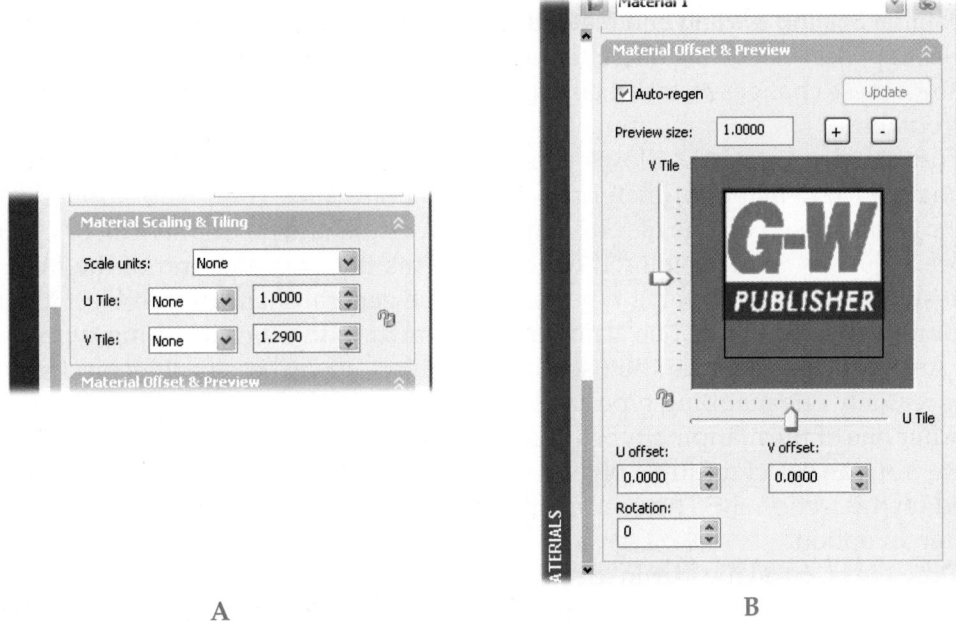

A   B

in a 2D drawing, but are relative to the map image. You can select no tiling, tiling, or mirroring. No tiling means the map will not be repeated. Mirror tiling means the map is repeated, but each tile is a mirror image of its neighbor. Finally, enter the scale on the U and V axes using the right-hand text boxes. The value is the number of times the map fits within a one-unit square (defined by the selected units). The aspect ratio can be locked using the lock button to the right of the text boxes.

Offset and preview

At the top of the **Material Offset & Preview** pane (or map-level **Offset & Preview** pane) there is the **Auto-regen** check box. With this checked, the image automatically updates when changes are made. If it is not checked, you must pick the **Update** button to see the changes.

The value in the **Preview size:** text box is a zoom factor for the preview image. If the image is not properly displaying in the preview window, use this to zoom in or out. You can also use the **Zoom the preview in** (the + button) and the **Zoom the preview out** (the – button) to zoom in and out.

The **V Tile** and **U Tile** sliders change the scale of the map. As the slider is moved, the corresponding text box value in the **Material Scaling & Tiling** pane changes. These sliders are not displayed if a real-world unit is selected in the **Scale units:** drop-down list in the **Material Scaling & Tiling** pane.

The **U Offset:** and **V Offset:** text boxes at the bottom of the **Material Offset & Preview** pane set the location of the map image within the material. The offsets can also be changed by picking and dragging the image in the preview pane.

The value in the **Rotation:** text box determines the rotation of the map about the W axis. The W axis is similar to the Z axis, but is local to the image. When spherical or cylindrical mapping is applied to an object, this setting has no effect. Object-level mapping is discussed in the next section.

Object-Level Adjustments

Material mapping refers to specifying how a mapped material is applied to an object. When a mapped material is attached to an object, a default set of mapping coordinates, or simply *default mapping,* is used to apply the map to the object. Many times, the **Material Scaling & Tiling** and **Material Offset & Preview** panes (or the corresponding map-level panes) can be used to alter how the map is applied to the default mapping. But, since these changes affect all objects to which the material is applied, this may not be acceptable.

Fortunately, AutoCAD allows you to adjust mapping at the object level for texture-mapped (2D-mapped) materials. The **MATERIALMAP** command applies a grip tool, or *gizmo,* based on one of four mapping types: planar, box, spherical, or cylindrical. See **Figure 14-38.** The colored edge represents the start and end of the map. For best results, select the mapping type based on the general shape of the object to which mapping is applied. Do not be afraid to experiment with other mapping types, however. Any mapping type can be used on any object, regardless of the object's shape. However, only one mapping type can be applied to an object at any given time.

After one of the mapping types is selected, you are prompted to select the faces or objects. You can select multiple objects or faces. After making a selection, the gizmo is placed on the section set. The command remains active for you to adjust the mapping or enter an option.

Drag the grips on the gizmo to stretch or scale the material. The effects of editing a diffuse color map are dynamically displayed if the current visual style is set to display materials and textures. Otherwise, exit the command and render the scene to see the effect of the edit. To readjust the mapping, select the same mapping type and pick the object again. The gizmo is displayed in the same location as before.

The **Move** and **Rotate** options of the command toggle between the move and rotate grip tools. Using the grip tools, you can move and rotate the map on the object. The **Reset** option of the command restores the default mapping to the object. The **Switch mapping mode** option allows you to change between the four types of mapping.

If the command is typed, there is an additional option. The **Copy mapping to** option is a quick and easy way to apply the changes made to the current object to other objects in the scene. Enter this option and then select the objects to which the current mapping will be copied. This option is also available if the **Switch mapping mode** option is entered.

For example, look at **Figure 14-39A.** The grain on the stair risers is running vertical when it should run horizontal. First, apply a planar map to the bottom riser. Next, rotate the mapping 90°, **Figure 14-39B.** Finally, use the **Copy mapping to** option to copy the mapping to the other risers, **Figure 14-39C.**

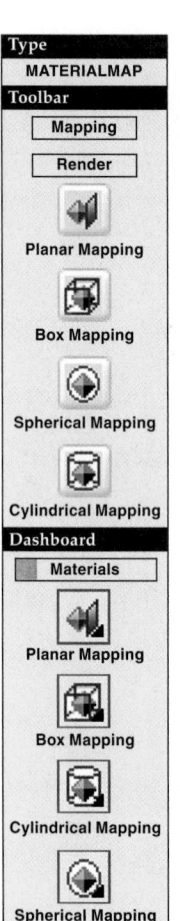

Figure 14-38.
These are the four material map gizmos. From left to right, planar, box, spherical, and cylindrical. The colored edge represents the start and end of the map.

 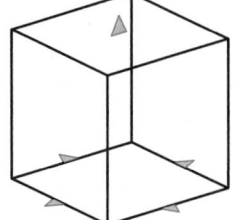 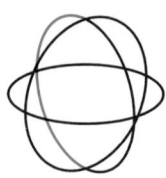 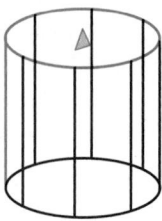

If you are using a bump, reflection, or opacity map and need to adjust it at the object level, apply the same map as a diffuse color map. Also, set the visual style to display materials and textures. Then, adjust the object mapping as needed. The edits are dynamically displayed in the viewport. When the image is in the correct location, remove the diffuse color map from the material.

Exercise 14-6

Complete the exercise on the Student CD.

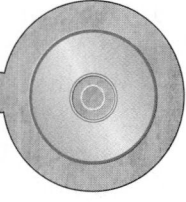

Figure 14-39.
Correcting material mapping. A—The grain on the risers runs vertical instead of horizontal. B—Rotating the map with the rotate gizmo. C—The corrected rendering. (Model courtesy of Arcways, Inc., Neenah, WI)

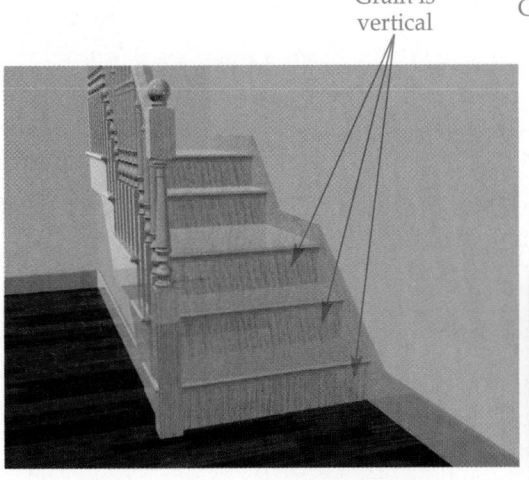
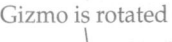
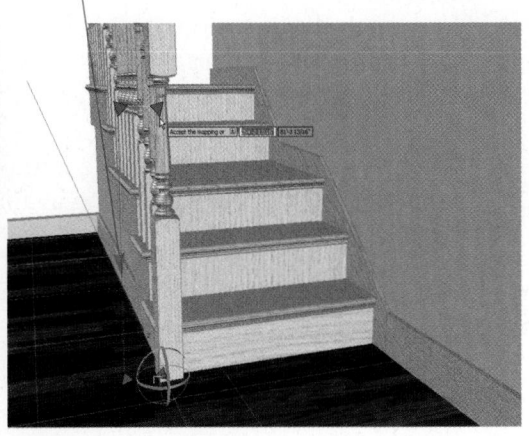

A   B

C

Chapter Test

Answer the following questions. Write your answers on a separate sheet of paper or complete the electronic chapter test on the Student CD.

1. Define *material*.
2. Define *material library*.
3. Why do the materials in the tool palettes and **Material** window have a checkered background?
4. Describe how to attach a material using a tool palette.
5. How can materials be attached to layers?
6. By default, which material is attached to newly created objects?
7. Which material is used as the base material for creating new materials?
8. Name the three material display options for a visual style that can also be set using the **Dashboard**.
9. How do you know if a material in the **Materials** window is being used in the drawing?
10. How can the name and description of an existing material be changed?
11. Name the four basic material types.
12. What are the templates available for the realistic metal material type?
13. To create a reflective material, which material type(s) can be used?
14. What are the three material color settings? Explain each.
15. Describe the difference between a transparent material and a translucent material.
16. How much illumination does a self-illuminated material add to a scene?
17. How is a marble material created?
18. Explain how black and white areas of an opacity map affect the transparency of a material.
19. Which objects do changes made in the **Material Offset & Preview** pane affect?
20. Name the four types of mapping available for adjusting texture maps at the object level.

Drawing Problems

1. In this problem, you will create a scene with basic 3D objects, attach materials to the objects, and adjust the settings of the materials.

    A. Start a new drawing and set the units to architectural.

    B. Draw a 15′ × 15′ planar surface to represent the floor.

    C. Draw two boxes to represent two walls. Make the boxes 15′ × 4″ × 9′. Position them to form a 90° corner. Alternately, you can draw a polysolid of the same dimensions.

    D. Draw a R2′ × 5′H cone in the center of the room.

    E. Open the **Tool Palettes** window, display the **Materials** palette group, and display the **Flooring** tool palette. Attach the material Finishes.Flooring.Tile.Square. Terra Cotta to the floor.

    F. Using the **Finishes** material tool palette, attach the material Finishes.Plaster. Stucco.Troweled.White to the wall.

    G. Using the same material tool palette, attach the material Finishes.Wall Covering. Stripes.Vertical.Blue-Grey to the cone.

    H. Turn on the sun and adjust the time to create good shadows. Refer to Chapter 13 for an introduction to sun settings.

    I. Render the scene. Save the rendering as P14_01.jpg.

    J. Save the drawing as P14_01.

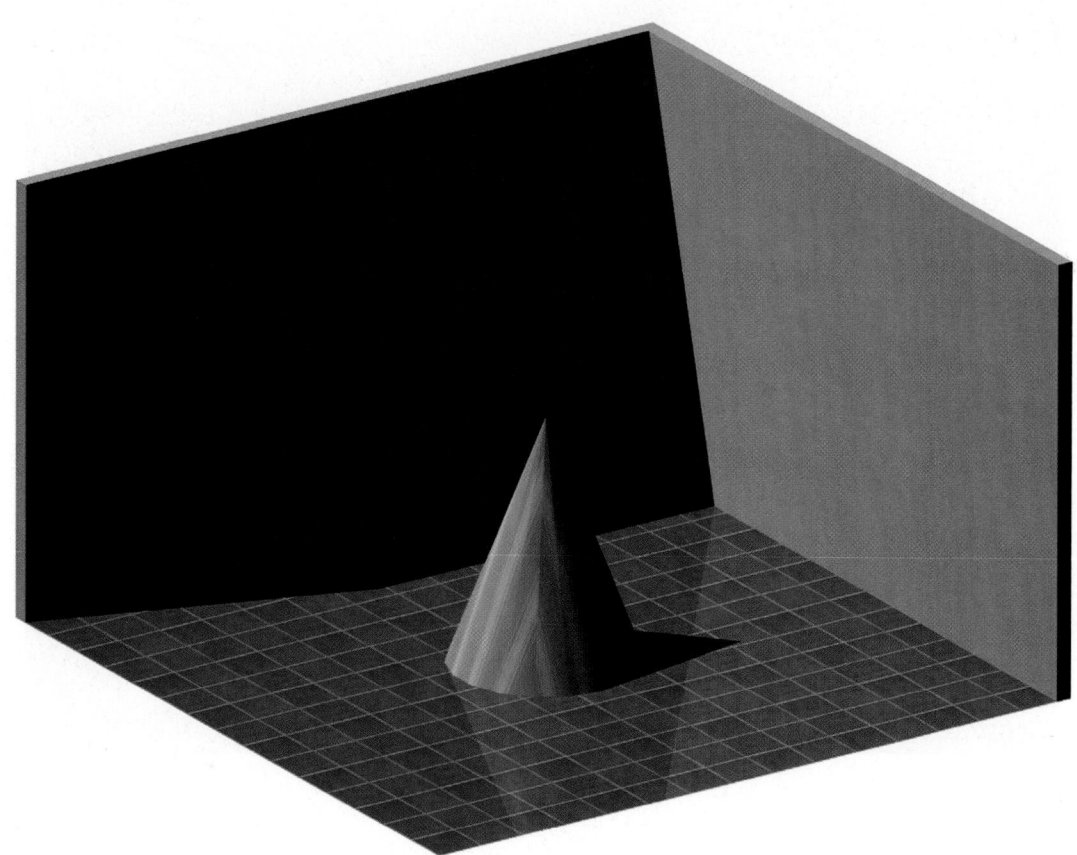

2. In this problem, you will attach materials to the objects in an existing drawing and render the scene.
   A. Open the drawing P13_01 from Chapter 13. If you did not complete this problem, do so now. Save the drawing P14_02.
   B. Open the **Tool Palettes** window and display the **Materials** palette group.
   C. Attach the materials of your choice to the objects in the scene. Do not be restricted by the names of the materials. For example, a concrete material may be suitable for foliage or even carpet with a simple color change. Be creative.
   D. If the items in the scene were inserted using the **DC Online** tab in **DesignCenter**, they may be blocks with nested layers. Instead of exploding the blocks, use the **MATERIALATTACH** command and attach materials to the layers on which the nested objects reside.
   E. Turn on the sun and adjust the time to create good shadows. Refer to Chapter 13 for an introduction to sun settings.
   F. Render the scene. Save the rendering as P14_02.jpg.
   G. Save the drawing.

3. In this problem, you will create custom wood and marble materials.
   A. Start a new drawing and save it as P14_03.
   B. Draw two 5 × 5 × 5 boxes and position them near each other. Using other primitives, cut notches and holes in the boxes. The boxes will be used to test the custom materials.
   C. In the **Materials** window, create two new materials. Name one Wood-*your initials* and Marble-*your initials*.
   D. Attach the wood material to one of the boxes and the marble material to the other box.
   E. Render the scene and make note of the wood grain and marble veins.
   F. Use the **Wood** and **Marble** panes in the material editor to change the properties of the materials.
   G. Render the scene again and make note of the changes. Using the **Render cropped region** button in the **Render** control panel in the **Dashboard** can save time when testing material changes.
   H. When you are satisfied with the materials, save the rendering as P14_03.
   I. Save the drawing.

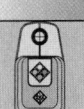

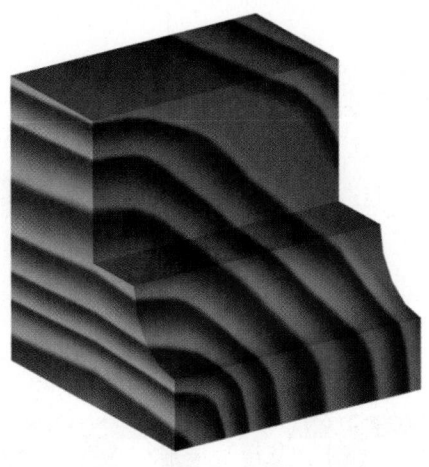

4. In this problem, you will create a bitmap and use it as opacity and bump maps.
   A. Draw a rectangle with an array of smaller rectangles inside of it, as shown below. Sizes are not important and the pattern can be varied if you like.
   B. Display a plan view of the rectangles. Then, copy all of the objects to the Windows clipboard by pressing [Ctrl]+[C] and selecting the objects.
   C. Launch Windows Paint. Then, paste the objects into the blank file. Notice how the AutoCAD background outside of the large rectangle is also included.
   D. Use the Paint select tool (rectangle) to draw a window around the large rectangle created in AutoCAD and the smaller rectangles within it. Copy this to the Windows clipboard by pressing [Ctrl]+[C].
   E. Close Paint without saving. Start a new Paint file and paste the image from the clipboard into the blank file. Now, the unwanted AutoCAD background is no longer displayed. If needed, change the small rectangles to black and the lattice to white using the Paint tools. The colors should be the reverse of what is shown below. Then, save the image file as P14_04.bmp and close Paint.
   F. In AutoCAD, draw a solid box of any size.
   G. Using the **Materials** window, create a new material.
   H. Assign the P14_04.bmp image file you just created as an opacity map. Adjust the map so that it is scaled to fit to the object.
   I. Render the scene and note the effect.
   J. Turn off the opacity map.
   K. Assign the P14_04.bmp image file as a bump map. Adjust the map so that it is scaled to fit to the object.
   L. Render the scene and note the effect.
   M. Save the drawing as P14_04.

Lighting

Learning Objectives

After completing this chapter, you will be able to:

- ✓ Describe the types of lighting in AutoCAD.
- ✓ List the user-created lights available in AutoCAD.
- ✓ Change the properties of lights.
- ✓ Generate and modify shadows.
- ✓ Add a background to your scene and control its appearance.

In Chapter 13, you were introduced to lighting. You learned how to adjust lighting by turning off the default lights and adding sunlight. In this chapter, you will learn all about the lights available in AutoCAD. You will learn lighting tips and tricks to help make the scene look its best.

Types of Lights

Ambient light is like natural light just before sunrise. It is the same intensity everywhere. All faces of the object receive the same amount of ambient light. Ambient light cannot create highlights, nor can it be concentrated in one area. AutoCAD does not have an ambient light setting. Instead, it relies on indirect illumination, which is discussed in Chapter 16.

A *point light* is like a lightbulb. Light rays from a point light shine out in all directions. A point light can create highlights. The intensity of a point light falls off, or weakens, over distance. Other programs, such as Autodesk VIZ® or Autodesk 3ds max®, may call these lights *omni lights*. A *target point light* is the same as a standard point light except that a target is specified. The illumination of the target point light is directed toward the target.

A *distant light* is a directed light source with parallel light rays. This acts much like the Sun. Rays from a distant light strike all objects in your model on the same side and with the same intensity. The direction and intensity of a distant light can be changed.

A *spotlight* is like a distant light, but it projects in a cone shape. Its light rays are not parallel. A spotlight is placed closer to the object than a distant light. Spotlights have a hotspot and a falloff. The light from a standard spotlight is directed toward a target. A *free spotlight* is the same as a standard spotlight, but without a target.

A *weblight* is a directed light that represents real-world distribution of light. The illumination is based on photometric data that can be entered for each light. The light from a standard weblight is directed toward a target. A *free weblight* is the same as a standard weblight, but without a target point.

Properties of Lights

There are several factors that affect how a light illuminates an object. These include the angle of incidence, reflectivity of the object's surface, and the distance that the light is from the object. In addition, the ability to cast shadows is a property of light. Shadows are discussed in detail later in this chapter.

Angle of Incidence

AutoCAD renders the faces of a model based on the angle at which light rays strike the faces. This angle is called the *angle of incidence.* See Figure 15-1. A face that is perpendicular to light rays receives the most light. As the angle of incidence decreases, the amount of light striking the face also decreases.

Reflectivity

The angle at which light rays are reflected off of a surface is called the *angle of reflection.* The angle of reflection is always equal to the angle of incidence. Refer to Figure 15-1.

The "brightness" of light reflected from an object is actually the number of light rays that reach your eyes. A surface that reflects a bright light, such as a mirror, is reflecting most of the light rays that strike it. The amount of reflection you see is called the *highlight.* The highlight is determined by the angle of the viewpoint relative to the angle of incidence. Refer to Figure 15-1.

The surface quality of the object affects how light is reflected. A smooth surface has a high specular factor. The *specular factor* indicates the number of light rays that have the same angle of reflection. Surfaces that are not smooth have a low specular factor. These surfaces are called *matte.* Matte surfaces *diffuse,* or "spread out," the light as it strikes the surface. This means that few of the light rays have the same angle of reflection. Figure 15-2 illustrates the difference between matte and high specular

Figure 15-1.
The amount of reflection, or highlight, you see depends on the angle from which you view the object.

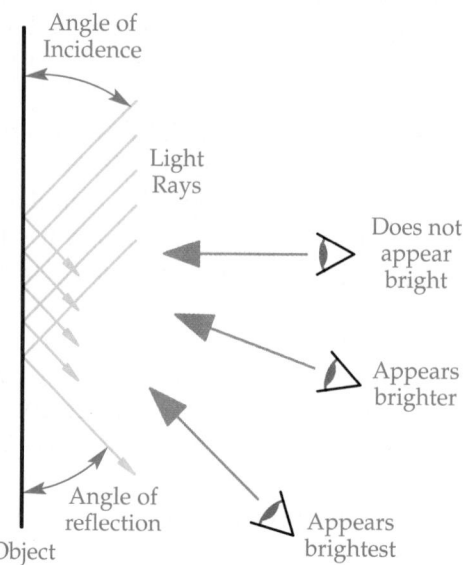

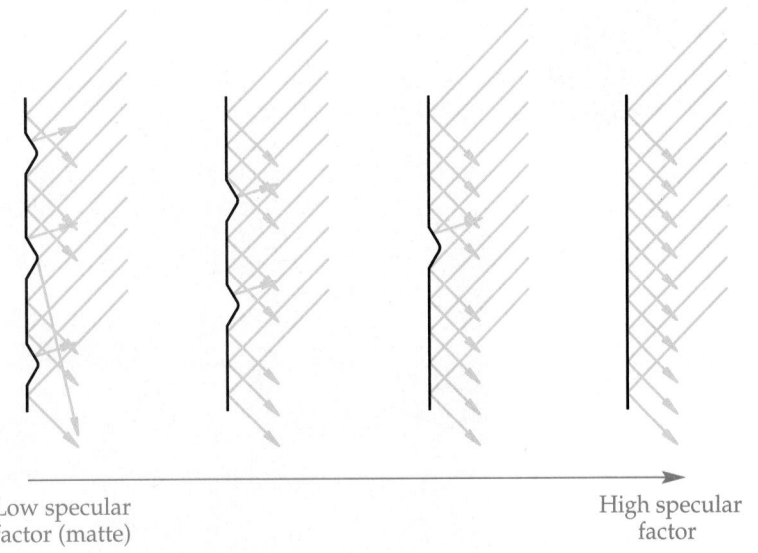

Figure 15-2.
Matte surfaces produce diffuse light. This is also referred to as having a low specular factor. Shiny surfaces evenly reflect light and have a high specular factor.

Low specular factor (matte)

High specular factor

finishes. Surfaces can also vary in *roughness.* Roughness is a measure of the polish on a surface. This also affects how diffused the reflected light is.

Hotspot and Falloff

A spotlight produces a cone of light. The *hotspot* is the central portion of the cone, where the light is brightest. See **Figure 15-3.** The *falloff* is the outer portion of the cone, where the light begins to blend to shadow. The hotspot and falloff of a spotlight are not affected by the distance the light is from an object. Spotlights are the only lights with hotspot and falloff properties.

Attenuation

The farther an object is from a point light or spotlight, the less light will reach the object. See **Figure 15-4.** The intensity of light decreases over distance. This decrease is called *attenuation.* All lights in AutoCAD, except distant lights, have some kind of

Figure 15-3.
The hotspot of a spotlight is the area that receives the most light. The smaller cone is the hotspot. The falloff receives light, but less than the hotspot. The larger cone is the falloff.

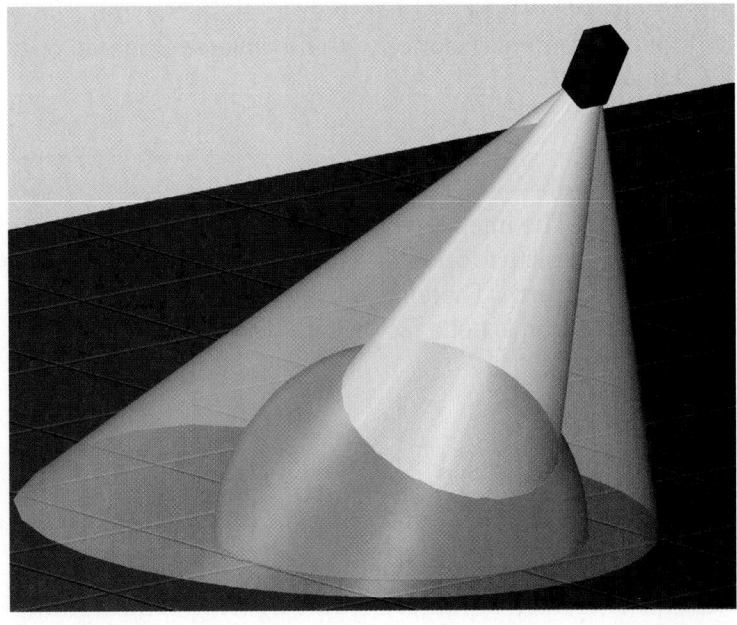

Figure 15-4.
Attenuation is the intensity of light decreasing over distance. Attenuation has been turned on in this scene.

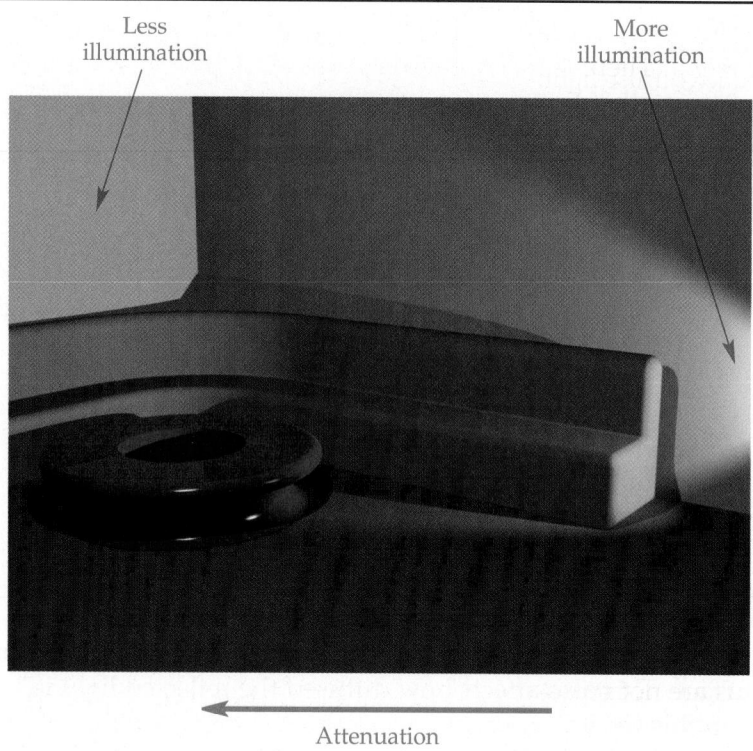

Less illumination

More illumination

Attenuation

attenuation. Often, attenuation is called *falloff* or *decay*. However, do not confuse this with the falloff of a spotlight, which is the outer edge of the cone of illumination. The following attenuation settings are available in AutoCAD.

*   **None.** Applies the same light intensity regardless of distance. In other words, no attenuation is calculated.
*   **Inverse Linear.** The illumination of an object decreases in inverse proportion to the distance. For example, if an object is two units from the light, it receives 1/2 of the full light. If the object is four units away, it receives 1/4 of the full light.
*   **Inverse Squared.** The illumination of an object decreases in inverse proportion to the square of the distance. For example, if an object is two units from the light, it receives $(1/2)^2$, or 1/4, of the full light. If the object is four units away, it receives $(1/4)^2$, or 1/16, of the full light. As you can see, attenuation is greater for each unit of distance with the **Inverse Squared** option than with the **Inverse Linear** option.

PROFESSIONAL TIP

The intensity of the Sun's rays does not diminish from one point on Earth to another. They are weakened by the angle at which they strike Earth. Therefore, since distant lights are similar to the Sun, attenuation is not a factor with distant lights.

AutoCAD Lights

AutoCAD has three types of lighting: default lighting, sunlight and sky illumination, and user-created lighting. *Default lighting* is the lighting automatically available in the scene. It is composed of two light sources that evenly illuminate all surfaces. As the viewpoint is changed, the light sources follow to maintain an even illumination of the scene. There is no control over default lighting and it must be shut off whenever one of the other types of lighting is used.

As you saw in Chapter 13, *sunlight* may be added to any scene. AutoCAD uses a distant light to simulate the parallel rays of the Sun. The date and time of day can be adjusted to create different sunlight illumination. *Sky illumination* may also be added with sunlight to simulate light bouncing off of objects in the scene and particles in the atmosphere. This helps create a more-natural feel.

User-created lighting results when you add AutoCAD light objects to the drawing. There are four types of user-created lights: distant light, weblight, point light, and spotlight. See **Figure 15-5.** A distant light is a directed light source with parallel light rays. A weblight is a directional light containing light intensity (photometric) data information. A point light is like a lightbulb with light rays shining out in all directions. A spotlight is like a distant light, but it projects light in a cone shape instead of having parallel light rays.

When created, point lights, weblights, and spotlights are represented by *light glyphs,* or icons, in the drawing. To suppress the display of light glyphs, pick the **Light glyphs** button in the expanded area of the **Light** control panel of the **Dashboard**. The button is orange when light glyphs are displayed. The default lights, sun, and distant lights are not represented by glyphs.

In this section, you will learn how to add lights. You will also learn how to adjust the various properties of sunlight and AutoCAD light objects. The tools for working with lights can be accessed using the command line, **View** pull-down menu, **Lights** toolbar, **Generic Lights** tool palette, the tool palettes in the **Photometric Lights** tool palette group, and **Lights** control panel in the **Dashboard**. See **Figure 15-6.**

So that you will never work with a completely dark scene, default lighting is applied in the viewport and to the rendering if no other lights are added. In order for your lights to be applied, you must switch between default lighting and user lighting. To do this, pick the **Viewport lighting mode:** button in the **Lights** control panel in the **Dashboard**. This button toggles the lighting between default lighting and whatever lights are available in the scene. When default lighting is on, the button is gray. When sunlight or user-created lighting is on, the button is orange. If you elected to do so, AutoCAD will automatically shut off default lighting when sunlight is turned on or a user-created light is added to the scene.

Lighting Units

There are three types of lighting units available in AutoCAD: standard (generic), international (SI), and US customary (American). Generic lighting is the type of lighting that was used in AutoCAD prior to AutoCAD 2008. This lighting provides very nice results, but the settings are not based on any real measurements. International or

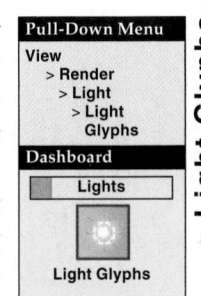

Figure 15-5.
AutoCAD has three types of user-created lights: distant, point, and spotlights.

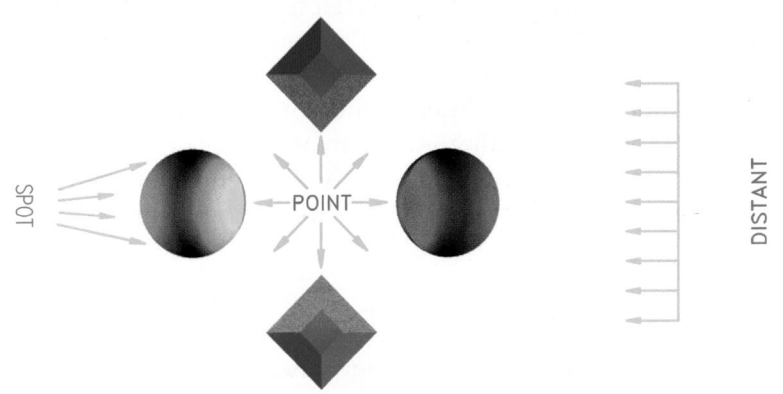

Figure 15-6.
The tools for adding and controlling lights. A—**Generic Lights** tool palette. B—The four tool palettes in the **Photometric Lights** tool palette group. C—**Lights** toolbar. D—**Light** control panel in the **Dashboard**.

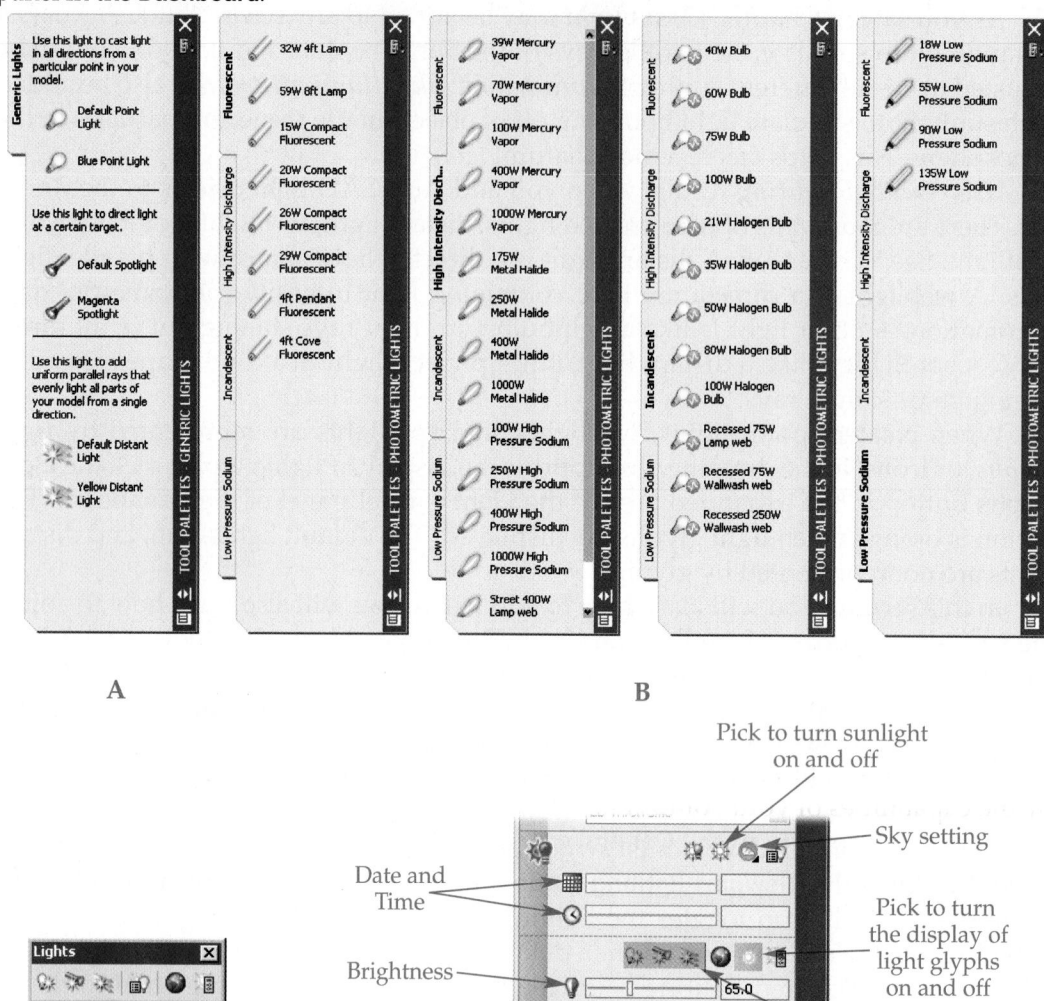

A

B

C

D

US customary lighting is called photometric lighting. *Photometric lighting* is physically correct and attenuates at the square of the distance from the source. For more accuracy, photometric data files can be imported from lighting manufacturers.

The **LIGHTINGUNITS** system variable sets which type of lighting is used. A setting of 0 means that standard (generic) lighting is used. This is the default setting for the system variable. However, for more realistic lighting, it is recommended that photometric lighting be used. Enter a value of 1 and international lighting units are used. This is photometric lighting. A setting of 2 turns on US customary lighting units. This is also photometric lighting. The only difference between a setting of 1 and 2 is that international units are *lux* and US customary units are *foot-candles*.

Sunlight

To turn sunlight on or off, pick the **Sun Status:** button in the **Light** control panel in the **Dashboard**. This button is orange when sunlight is on. Sunlight can also be turned on or off in the **Sun Properties** window, which is discussed later. Sunlight is not represented by a light glyph. The date, time, and geographic location can be set. These properties determine how the scene is illuminated by the sun.

To change the current date, pick the **Date** slider and drag it left or right. As you drag the slider, the date appears in a tooltip. The text box to the right of the slider also changes to reflect the new date. The text box can be used to type a new date.

The time is changed in the same manner as the date. Drag the **Time** slider left or right. As you drag the slider, the time appears in a tooltip. The text box to the right of the slider changes to reflect the new time and can be used to enter a time.

The location of the scene is changed in the **Geographic Location** dialog box. See Figure 15-7. The **GEOGRAPHICLOCATION** command opens this dialog box. To set the location, enter the longitude and latitude. It may be easier to pick a location on the map or select a city from the **Nearest City:** drop-down list. The direction of North in the drawing is also set using this dialog box. This is measured as an angle in the WCS XY plane.

The properties of the sun are set in the **Sun Properties** window, Figure 15-8. The **SUNPROPERTIES** command opens this dialog box. The Sun can be turned on or off using the dialog box. The date, time, and time zone can also be changed in the dialog box. These settings are the same as previously discussed. There are other properties of the sun that are only available in the **Sun Properties** window. This window contains several categories, which are discussed in the next sections.

General

The Intensity Factor property in the **General** category determines the brightness of the sun. Setting this property to zero, in effect, turns off sunlight. Increasing the property makes the sunlight brighter. The maximum value for the property is determined by the capabilities of your computer.

The Color property in the **General** category is used to set the color of the sun. By default, sunlight is white (true color 255, 255, 255). To change the color, pick the drop-down list and choose a new color. If you pick the Select Color... entry, the **Select Color** dialog box is displayed for selecting a color. Sunlight can be changed to any color, but be aware that changing the color of the light may drastically alter the appearance of

---

Type
GEOGRAPHICLOCATION
Pull-Down Menu
View
> Render
> Light
> Geographic Location...
Toolbar
Lights
Geographic Location...
Dashboard
Lights
Geographic Location

GEOGRAPHICLOCATION

Type
SUNPROPERTIES
Pull-Down Menu
View
> Render
> Light
> Sun Properties
Toolbar
Lights
Sun Properties
Dashboard
Lights
Edit the Sun

SUNPROPERTIES

Figure 15-7.
The **Geographic Location** dialog box. The geographic location may be specified by typing the latitude and longitude or simply picking a location on the map.

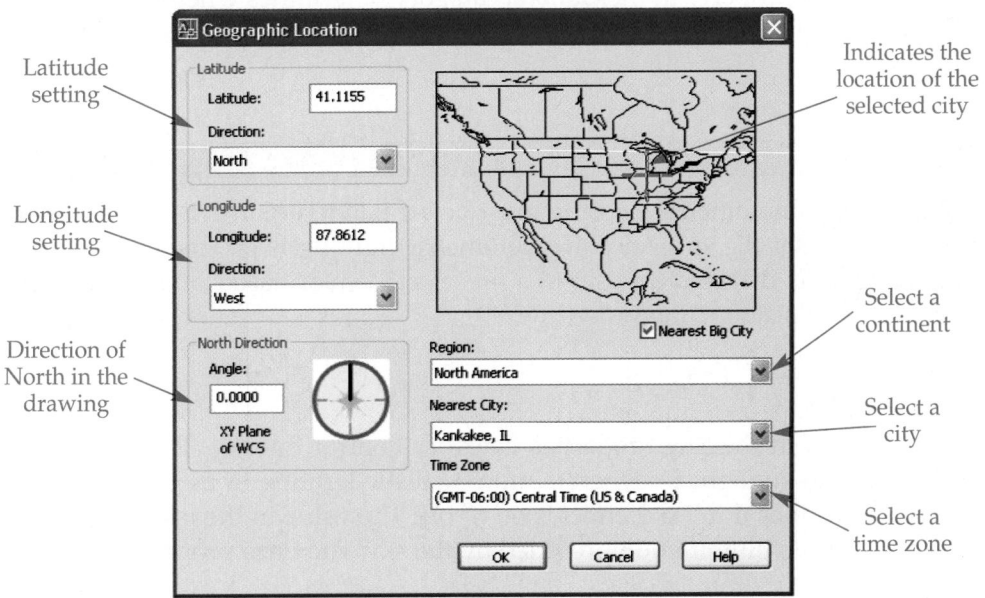

Latitude setting

Longitude setting

Direction of North in the drawing

Indicates the location of the selected city

Select a continent

Select a city

Select a time zone

Figure 15-8.
The **Sun Properties** window.

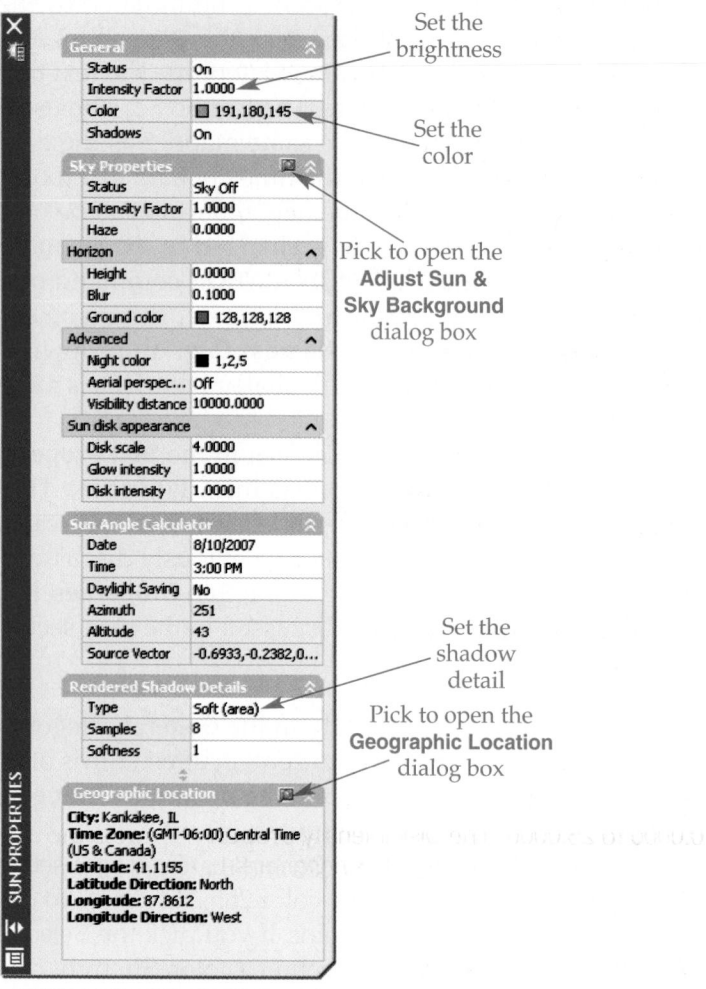

Set the
brightness

Set the
color

Pick to open the
**Adjust Sun &
Sky Background**
dialog box

Set the
shadow
detail

Pick to open the
Geographic Location
dialog box

a scene. This is especially true if materials are attached to objects in the drawing. The color of sunlight is often set to a very light blue for an outdoor scene to help convey a bright blue sky.

The Shadows property in the **General** category determines whether or not the sun casts shadows. The property is either on or off. Shadows are discussed in detail later in this chapter.

NOTE

Photometric lighting must be off (**LIGHTINGUNITS** = 0) in order to set the sun color. If photometric lighting is on, the Color property is disabled and set to a preselected color based on the geographic location, date, and time.

Sky properties

The settings in the **Sky Properties** category control the sky. The sky is used in conjunction with sunlight to generate more-realistic lighting in the scene. The Status property determines if the sky effect is on or off. The value in the Intensity property is a multiplier for the illumination provided by the sky. The Haze property controls how the sky illumination is diffused. The value can range from 0.0000–15.0000. The preset sun color is affected by this value.

Notice the button in the title bar of the **Sky Properties** category. Picking this button opens the **Adjust Sun & Sky Background** dialog box. This dialog box contains the same settings found in the **Sun Properties** window, but includes a preview of the sun disk.

The settings in the **Horizon** subcategory control what the horizon looks like and where it is located. Changing the Height property moves the horizon up or down. The default value is 0.0000. The Blur property determines how much the horizon is blurred between the ground and the sky. The range for this value is from 0.0000 to 10.0000 with a default of 0.1000. The Ground color property controls the color of the ground. The default color is true color 128,128,128, which is a medium gray.

The settings in the **Advanced** subcategory allow you to control some of the more artistic settings of your scene. The Night color property sets the color of the night sky. This is only visible if sky illumination is turned on. The Aerial perspective property determines whether or not aerial perspective is applied. This is a way of simulating distance between the camera and the sky/background. The setting is either on or off. The Visibility Distance property sets the distance from the camera at which haze obscures 10% of the objects in the background. This is a very useful tool for creating the illusion of depth in a scene. The default value is 10000.0000, but it can range from 0.0000 to whatever is needed.

Normally, lights do not appear in the rendered scene at all, only the illumination provided by the lights. The settings in the **Sun disk appearance** subcategory control what the sun looks like in the sky, or on the background. The **Disk scale** property sets the size of the sun, or solar disk, as it appears on the background. The default value is 4.0000 with the range of values being from 0.0000 to 25.0000. The Glow intensity value determines the size of the glowing halo around the sun in the sky. Default value is 1.0000 and can range from 0.0000 to 25.0000. The Disk intensity property controls the brightness of the sun on the background. The default value is 1.0000 and the range of values is from 0.0000 to 25.0000.

Sun angle calculator

The settings in the **Sun Angle Calculator** category determine the angle of the sun in relationship to the XY plane. The Date and Time properties are discussed earlier and can be controlled from the **Lights** control panel in the **Dashboard**. This category in the **Sun Properties** window also includes the Daylight saving property. This property is used to turn daylight saving on or off. The Azimuth, Altitude, and Source vector properties display the current settings, but are read only in the **Sun Properties** window. These values are automatically calculated by the settings in the **Geographic Location** dialog box.

Rendered shadow details

The Type property in the **Rendered Shadow Details** category determines the type of shadow cast by the sun, if shadows are cast. When the property is set to Sharp, raytraced shadows are cast. These shadows have sharp edges. Raytracing produces accurate shadows, but rendering may take longer. When the property is set to either Soft (mapped) or Soft (area), shadow-mapped shadows are cast. This type of shadow has soft edges. Shadow-mapped shadows may be calculated quicker than raytraced shadows, but the resulting shadows are less precise. In addition, soft shadows do not work with transparent surfaces like windows. When the Type property is set to Soft (mapped), two additional settings are available in the category:

- Map Size. This property determines the number of subdivisions, or samples, used to create the shadow. By default, shadow maps are 256 × 256 pixels in size. If shadows look grainy, increasing this setting will make them look better.
- Softness. This property determines the sharpness of the shadow's edge. The value ranges from 1 to 10. The higher the value, the softer (less sharp) the edge of the shadow.

When the Type property is set to Soft (area), the two additional settings are:

- Samples. This property sets the number of samples used on the solar disk. The value can be from 0.0000 to 1000.0000.
- Softness. This property determines the sharpness of the shadow's edge, as described above.

When the Type property is set to Sharp, the other settings are read only and not applied.

NOTE

With photometric lighting on (**LIGHTINGUNITS** = 1 or 2), only the Soft (area) selection is available in the Type property drop-down list.

Geographic location

The **Geographic Location** category at the bottom of the **Sun Properties** window displays the current geographic location settings. Changes cannot be made here, but picking the **Launch Geographic Location** button in the category's title bar opens the **Geographic Location** dialog box, which is described earlier.

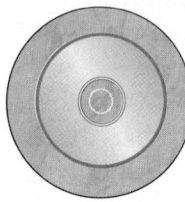

Exercise 15-1
Complete the exercise on the Student CD.

Distant Lights

Distant lights are user-created lights that have parallel light rays. See **Figure 15-9.** When a distant light is created, the location from where the light is originating must be specified along with the direction of the light rays. Distant lights are not represented in the drawing by light glyphs. Distant lights are often used to create even, uniform, overhead illumination, such as you would encounter in an office situation. The distance of the objects in the scene to the distant light has no effect on the intensity of the illumination. Distant lights do not attenuate. A distant light can also be used to simulate sunlight without having to set up a time and location. However, the light must be manually moved to change the illuminating effect.

The **DISTANTLIGHT** or **LIGHT** command is used to create a distant light. You are first prompted to specify the direction from which the light is originating or to enter the **Vector** option. If you pick a point, it is the location of the light. Next, you are prompted to specify the direction to which the light is pointing. This is simply the location where the light is aimed.

If you enter the **Vector** option instead of picking a "from" point, you must type the endpoint coordinates (in WCS units) of the direction vector. The light will point from the WCS origin to the entered endpoint.

After the light location and direction are determined, several other options are available. You can name the light, set the intensity, turn the light on or off, determine if and how shadows are cast, and set the light color. See **Figure 15-10.**

AutoCAD provides a default name for new distant lights based on the type of light and a sequential number, such as Distantlight1, Distantlight2, and so on. It is a good idea to provide a meaningful name for light. This is especially true if there are other lights in the scene. To rename a light, enter the **Name** option. Then, type the name of the light and press [Enter].

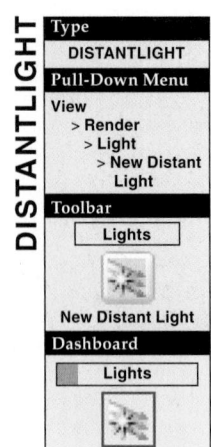

DISTANTLIGHT

Type
DISTANTLIGHT

Pull-Down Menu
View
> Render
> Light
> New Distant Light

Toolbar
Lights

New Distant Light

Dashboard
Lights

Create a distant light

Figure 15-9.
This example shows the use of a distant light to simulate sunlight shining through a window. Notice how the edges of the shadows of the grill are parallel.

Figure 15-10.
After a light has been placed, several additional options are available.

Enter an option to change
Name
Intensity
Status
shadoW
Color
● eXit

To set the brightness of the light, enter the **Intensity** option. Then, type a value and press [Enter]. The default value is 1.00. Setting the value to 0.00, in effect, turns off the light. The maximum value depends on the capabilities of your computer. This option is called **Intensity Factor** if photometric lighting is enabled.

When a light is created, it is on. To turn the light off, enter the **Status** option. Then, change the setting to **Off**.

The **Photometry** option is available when photometric lighting is active. It controls the luminous qualities of visible light sources. Once you enter the **Photometry** options, you can select one of three settings:

- **Intensity**. This is the power of the light source and can be entered as candelas (cd), luminous flux (lx), or foot-candles (fc).
- **Color**. This is the color of the light source and can be changed by typing in a name (to get a list of color names, enter ?) or by the Kelvin temperature value (k).
- **Exit**. Exits the command option.

The **Shadow** option is used to determine if and how shadows are cast by the distant light. To turn off shadow casting, enter the option and select the **Off** setting. The **Sharp** setting creates raytraced shadows. The **Softmapped** setting casts shadow-mapped shadows. Shadows are discussed later in this chapter.

By default, new distant lights cast white light (true color 255, 255, 255). To change the color of the light, enter the **Color** option. This option is called **Filter Color** if photometric lighting is enabled. To specify a new true color, simply specify the values and press [Enter]. To specify a color based on hue, saturation, and luminance (HSL), enter the **Hsl** option and specify the values. To enter an AutoCAD color index (ACI) number, enter the **Index color** option and specify the ACI number. To specify a color book color, enter the **Color Book** option and then specify the name of the color book followed by the name of the color.

Once all settings for the distant light have been made, use the **Exit** option to end the command and create the light. Do not press [Esc] to end the command. Doing so actually cancels the command and the light is not created.

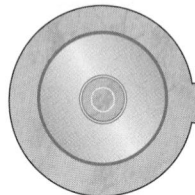

NOTE

If you attempt to create a distant light with photometric lighting on (**LIGHTINGUNITS** = 1 or 2), you will receive a warning to the effect that photometric distant lights may overexpose the scene. Also, the **Create a distant light** button in the **Dashboard** is disabled. Enter the command by typing, selecting it in the pull-down menu, or using the toolbar.

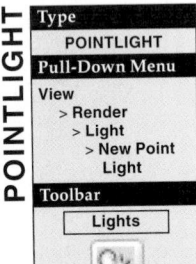

Exercise 15-2

Complete the exercise on the Student CD.

Point Lights

Point lights are user-created lights that have light rays projecting in all directions. See **Figure 15-11**. When a point light is created, its location must be specified. Since point lights illuminate in all directions, there is no "to" location for a point light. A light glyph represents point lights in the drawing. See **Figure 15-12**. Point lights can be set to attenuate. In this case, the distance of the objects in the scene to the point light affects the intensity of the illumination.

The **POINTLIGHT** or **LIGHT** command is used to create a point light. You are first prompted to specify the location of the point light. Once the location is established, several options for the light are available. You can name the light, set the intensity,

POINTLIGHT

Type
POINTLIGHT
Pull-Down Menu
View
> Render
> Light
> New Point Light
Toolbar
Lights
New Point Light
Dashboard
Lights
Create a point light

Figure 15-11.
A—A point light is placed inside of the lamp fixture. Notice how the light projects in all directions. B—When shadow casting is turned on for the light, the lampshade blocks the light from illuminating objects below the shade.

A

B

Figure 15-12.
This is the light glyph for a point light.

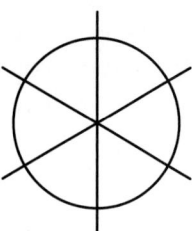

turn the light on or off, adjust the photometry settings, determine if and how shadows are cast, set the attenuation, and set the light color. The **Name**, **Intensity** (or **Intensity Factor**), **Status**, **Photometry**, **Shadow**, and **Color** (or **Filter Color**) options work the same as the corresponding options for a distant light.

The **Attenuation** option is used to set attenuation for the point light. When this option is selected, five more options are available:

- **Attenuation Type**
- **Use Limits**
- **Attenuation Start Limit**
- **Attenuation End Limit**
- **Exit**

The **Exit** option returns you to the previous prompt.

The **Attenuation Type** option is used to turn attenuation on and off and to set the type of attenuation. To turn attenuation off, select the option and then enter **None**. To turn attenuation on, select the option and then enter either **Inverse Linear** or **Inverse Squared**. Attenuation is discussed in detail earlier in this chapter.

The **Use Limits** option determines if the attenuation of the light has a beginning and an end. When this option is set to **Off**, attenuation starts at the light and ends when the illumination reaches zero. When set to **On**, attenuation begins at the starting limit and ends at the ending limit.

To set the starting point for attenuation, enter the **Attenuation Start Limit** option. Then, specify the distance from the point light where attenuation will begin. The full intensity of the light provides illumination up to this point. From this point to the attenuation end limit, the light falls off.

To set the point where the illumination attenuates to zero, enter the **Attenuation End Limit** option. Then, specify the distance from the point light where the illumination is zero. Beyond this point, AutoCAD does not calculate the effect of the light.

Target Point Lights

The target point light is like a regular point light except that the command starts by asking for a *source* location and a *target* location. The rest of the options are the same. You can type TARGETPOINT to access this command or pick the **Targetpoint** option in the **LIGHT** command.

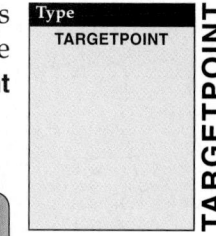

> **CAUTION**
>
> It is important to set attenuation limits. If there is no end limit for the light, AutoCAD may calculate the illumination beyond the boundary of the scene, even if there is nothing there to see. To speed processing time, tell AutoCAD where illumination stops for point and spotlights.

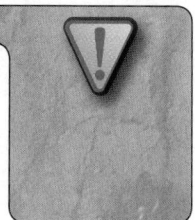

A point light may be used as an incandescent lightbulb, such as in a table lamp. Most of these lightbulbs cast a yellow light. In these cases, you may want to change the color of the light to a light yellow. Other colors can be used to give the impression of heat or colored lights.

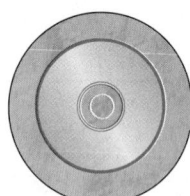

Exercise 15-3
Complete the exercise on the Student CD.

Spotlights

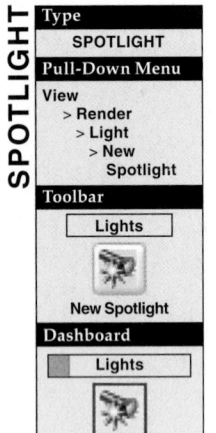
Spotlights are user-created lights that have light rays projecting in a cone shape in one direction. See **Figure 15-13**. When a spotlight is created, the location from where the light is originating must be specified along with the direction in which the light rays travel. A light glyph represents spotlights in the drawing. See **Figure 15-14**. Spotlights can be set to attenuate. In this case, the distance of the objects in the scene to the spotlight affects the intensity of the illumination.

The **SPOTLIGHT** or **LIGHT** command is used to create a spotlight. You are first prompted to specify the location of the light. This is from where the light rays will originate. Next, you are prompted for the target location. This is simply the location where the light is aimed.

Once the location and target are established, several options for the light are available. Spotlights and point lights have similar settings. You can change the name, intensity, status, photometry settings, shadow, attenuation, and color. The **Name**, **Intensity** (or **Intensity Factor**), **Status**, **Photometry**, **Shadow**, and **Color** (or **Filter Color**) options work the same as the corresponding options for a point light. However, a spotlight also has hotspot and falloff settings.

The *hotspot* is the inner cone of illumination for a spotlight. Refer to **Figure 15-15**. This is measured in degrees. To set the hotspot, enter the **Hotspot** option and then specify the number of degrees for the hotspot.

Figure 15-13.
Three spotlights are used to simulate recessed ceiling lights. Notice how the light from each spotlight projects in a cone.

Figure 15-14.
This is the light glyph
for a spotlight.

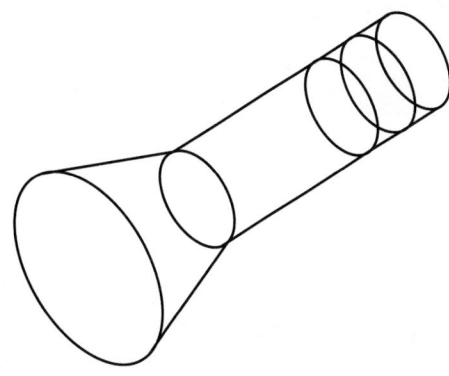

Figure 15-15.
Hotspot and falloff for
a spotlight are angular
measurements.

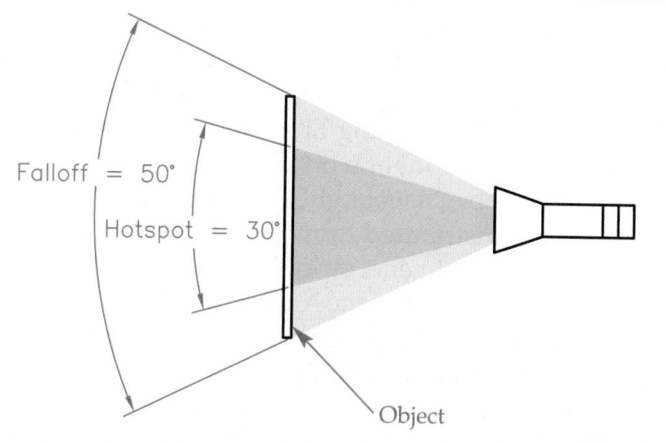

Falloff = 50°

Hotspot = 30°

Object

The *falloff,* not to be confused with attenuation, is the outer cone of illumination for a spotlight. Like the hotspot, it is measured in degrees. The falloff value must be greater than or equal to the hotspot value. It cannot be less than the hotspot value. In practice, the falloff value is often much greater than the hotspot value. To set the falloff, enter the **Falloff** option and then specify the number of degrees for the falloff.

Once the light is created and you select it in the viewport, grips are displayed. If you hover the cursor over a grip, a tooltip is displayed indicating what the grip will modify. You can use grips to change the location of the spotlight and its target, the hotspot, and the falloff.

Free Spotlight

A free spotlight is like a standard spotlight except that you do not specify a target, only the light location. The rest of the options are the same. You can type FREESPOT to access this command, or pick the **Freespot** option in the **LIGHT** command. When created, a free spotlight points down the Z axis (from positive to negative) of the current UCS. A free spotlight may be easier to control than a standard spotlight because you do not have to worry about the target point. If you want to change the angle or position of the light, use the **3DMOVE** and **ROTATE3D** commands.

Type
FREESPOT

FREESPOT

PROFESSIONAL TIP

The best way to see how colored lights affect your model is to experiment. Remember, you can render selected areas of the scene. This allows you to see how light intensity and color change objects without performing a full render.

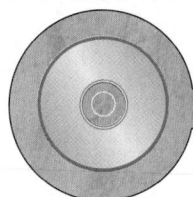

Web Light

A photometric weblight is really just a targeted point light. The difference is that a weblight provides a far more precise representation of the light. Real-world lights appear to evenly illuminate from their source, but, in reality, the shape of the light, the material used in its manufacture, and other factors make all lights distribute their energy in different ways. These data are provided by light manufacturers in the form of light distribution data. Light distribution data can be loaded into the **Photometric Web** subcategory of the **General** category in the **Properties** window when the light is selected. Select the Web file property, then pick the browse button (...) and select an IES file. IES stands for Illuminating Engineering Society. AutoCAD's online documentation has additional information on IES files.

Think of the web of a weblight as a spherical cage surrounding the light source. If the light is evenly distributed from its source, the cage is a true sphere. In actuality, a light may emit more light energy in the X direction than in the Z direction. In this case, the cage bulges out further in the X direction. The position of this bulge may be important to the illumination of the scene and you may need to rotate the web to apply more or less light in one direction or another.

To add a weblight to the scene, you can type WEBLIGHT or pick the **Web** option in the **LIGHT** command. You are prompted for source and target locations. The **Name**, **Intensity Factor**, **Status**, **Photometry**, **Shadow**, and **Filter Color** options work the same as the corresponding options for the previously discussed lights. However, weblights have an additional **Web** option. When this option is activated, these options are presented:

- **File.** Allows you to select an IES file.
- **X.** Rotates the web around the X axis.
- **Y.** Rotates the web around the Y axis.
- **Z.** Rotates the web around the Z axis.
- **Exit.** Exits the **Web** option.

Point and spotlights can be converted to weblights, and vice versa, using the **Properties** window. Simply select an existing light and open the **Properties** window. In the **General** category, the Type property determines whether the light is a point light, spotlight, or weblight. Select the type in the drop-down list. Using the **Properties** window with lights is discussed in detail later in this chapter.

Free Web Light

A free weblight is the same as a standard weblight except that there is no target. Only the source location is specified when placing the light. To change the location and direction of the light, use the **ROTATE3D** and **3DMOVE** commands.

NOTE

To create either standard or free weblights, photometric lighting must be enabled (**LIGHTINGUNITS** = 1 or 2).

Photometric Lights Tool Palette Group

Photometric lights may be easily added to the drawing using the tool palettes in the **Photometric Lights** tool palette group. Refer to Figure 15-6. This palette group contains four palettes: **Fluorescent**, **High Intensity Discharge**, **Incandescent**, and **Low Pressure Sodium**. Lights created with these tools have preset properties for **Intensity Factor**, **Shadow**, and **Filter Color**. The glyph for the long fluorescent lights has a yellow line passing through its center indicating the direction of the light. The high intensity discharge and low-pressure sodium lights are point lights. The incandescent lights are free spotlights.

Lights in Model and Properties Windows

The **Lights in Model** window is extremely useful for controlling the lights in your scene, Figure 15-16. Used in conjunction with the **Properties** window, you can manage and edit all of the lights in a scene.

Light list

The **LIGHTLIST** command displays the **Lights in Model** window. All user-created lights in the scene are displayed in the list. To modify the properties of a light, either double-click on the light name or right-click on it and select **Properties** from the shortcut menu. This opens the **Properties** window. See Figure 15-17. If the **Properties** window is already open, you can simply select a light in the **Lights in Model** window. You can select more than one light by pressing the [Ctrl] key and selecting the names in the **Lights in Model** window. This allows you to change all of their settings at the same time. This is an excellent way to make the lighting in your scene uniform or to control a series of lights with a single edit.

A light can be deleted from the scene using the **Lights in Model** window. To do so, simply right-click on the name of the light and select **Delete Light** from the shortcut menu. The light is removed from the drawing. Using the **UNDO** command restores the light.

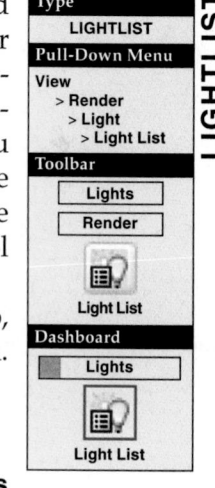

Properties window

The **Photometric Properties** subcategory of the **General** category in the **Properties** window has special settings for photometric lights. The Lamp intensity property determines the brightness of the light. The value may be expressed in candelas (cd), lumens (lm), or illuminance (lux) values. When you select the Lamp intensity property, a button

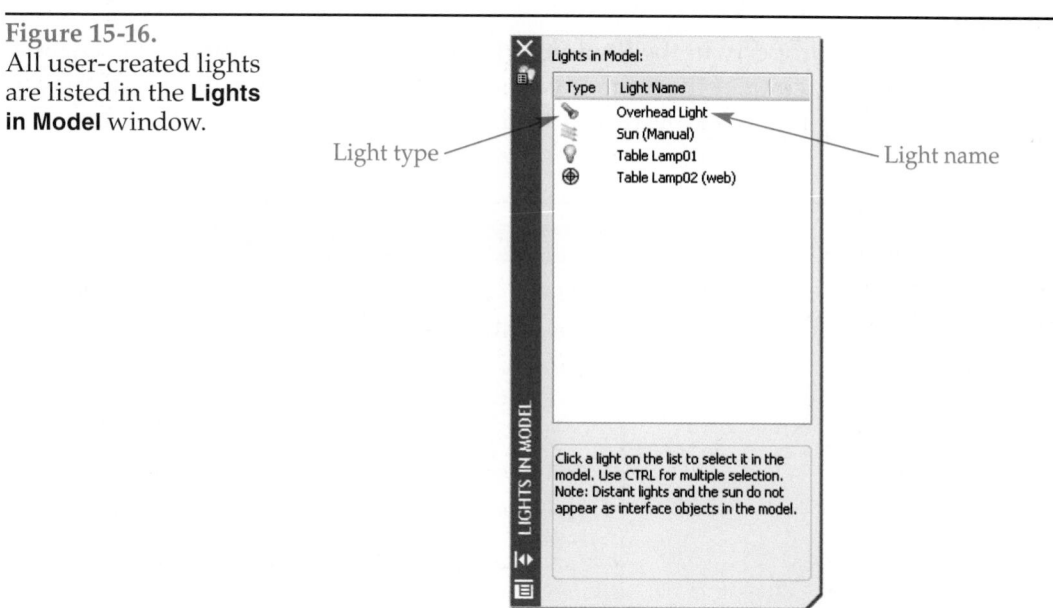

Figure 15-16.
All user-created lights are listed in the **Lights in Model** window.

Light type

Light name

Figure 15-17.
The **Properties** window with a weblight selected.

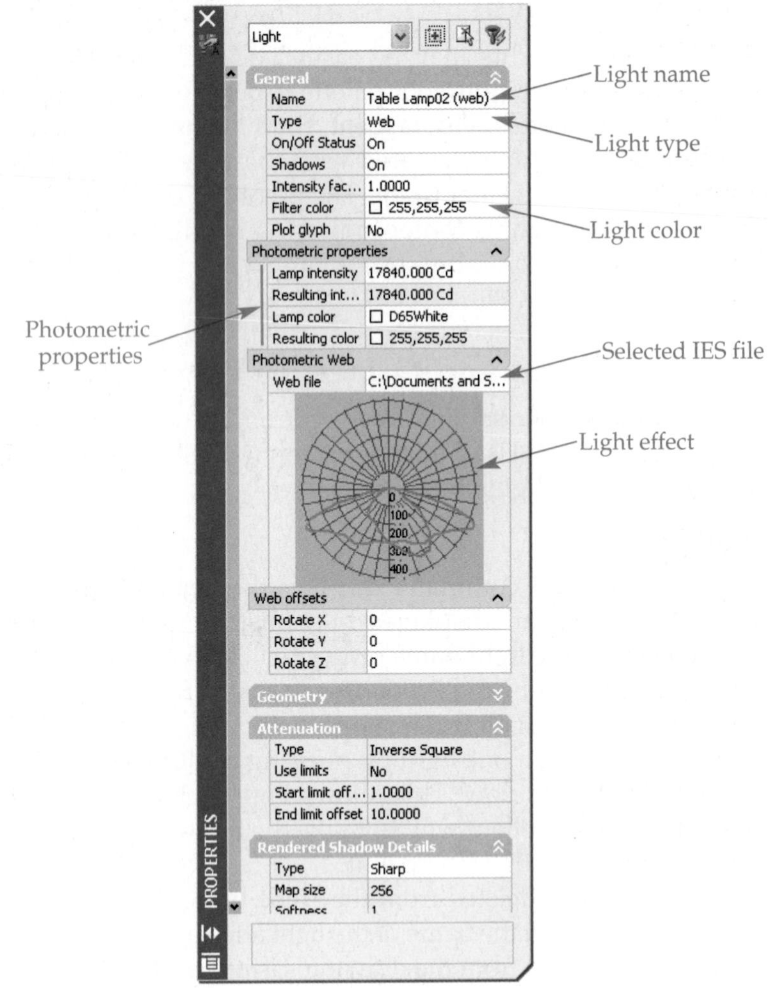

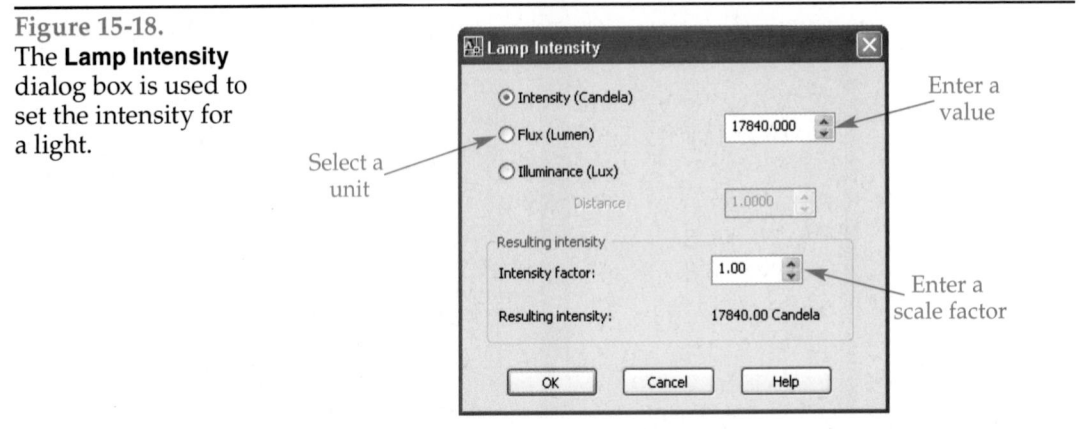

Light name

Light type

Light color

Photometric properties

Selected IES file

Light effect

is displayed to the right of the value. Picking this button opens the **Lamp Intensity** dialog box, Figure 15-18. In this dialog box, you can change the illumination units and set the intensity (Lamp intensity property). You can also set an intensity scale factor. This is multiplied by the Lamp intensity property to obtain the actual illumination supplied by the light. The read-only Resulting intensity property in the **Properties** window displays the result.

The Lamp color property in the **Photometric Properties** subcategory in the **General** category controls the color of the light. If you select the property, a button is displayed to the right of the value. Picking this button opens the **Lamp Color** dialog box. See

Figure 15-18.
The **Lamp Intensity** dialog box is used to set the intensity for a light.

Select a unit

Enter a value

Enter a scale factor

Figure 15-19.
The **Lamp Color** dialog
box is used to set the
color for the light and
a filter color, if needed.

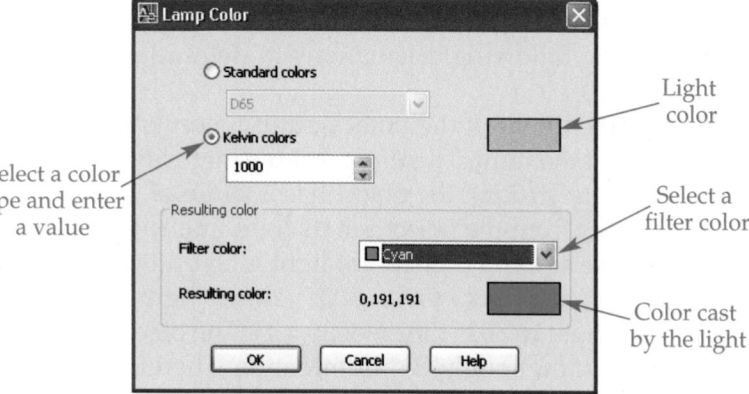

Select a color
type and enter
a value

Light
color

Select a
filter color

Color cast
by the light

Figure 15-19. This dialog gives you the option to control the color of the light by either standard spectra colors or Kelvin colors. The color selected in the **Filter color:** drop-down list is applied to the color of the light. The **Resulting color:** swatch displays the color cast by the light once the filter color is applied. If the filter color is white (255,255,255), then the light color is the color cast by the light.

The **Photometric Web** subcategory in the **General** category is where you can specify an IES file for the light. Select the Web file property, then pick the browse button (...) and select the IES file. Once the file is selected, its location is displayed in the Web file property. The effect of the data is shown in a graph at the bottom of the **Photometric Web** subcategory. Refer to **Figure 15-17.**

The **Web offsets** subcategory in the **General** category allows you to rotate the web around the X, Y, and Z axes. This is discussed earlier in the Web Light section.

In the **Geometry** category, you can change the X, Y, and Z coordinates of the light. You can also change the X, Y, and Z coordinates of the light's target. If the light is not targeted, the Target X, Target Y, and Target Z properties are not displayed. To change the light from targeted to free, and vice versa, select Yes or No in the Targeted property drop-down list.

The properties in the **Attenuation** category are the same as those discussed earlier in this chapter in the Point Lights section. In order to change these properties in the **Properties** window, photometric lighting must be off (**LIGHTINGUNITS** = 0).

The last category in the **Properties** window is **Rendered Shadow Details**. The properties in this category are used to control shadows. Shadows are discussed later in this chapter.

PROFESSIONAL TIP

It is important to give your lights names that make them easy to identify in a list. If you accept the default names for lights, they will be called Pointlight1, Spotlight5, Distantlight7, Weblight2, etc., making them difficult to identify. Use the **Name** option when creating the light or, after the light is created, the **Properties** window to change the name of the light.

Determining Proper Light Intensity

The object nearest to a point light or spotlight should receive the full illumination, or full intensity, of the light. Full intensity of any light that has an attenuation property is a value of one. Remember, attenuation is calculated using either the inverse linear or inverse square method. Therefore, you must calculate the appropriate intensity.

For example, suppose you have drawn an object and placed a point light and a spotlight. The point light is 55 units from the object. The spotlight is 43 units from the object. Use the following calculations to determine the correct intensity settings for the lights.

- **Inverse linear.** If the point light is 55 units from the object, the object receives 1/55 of the light. Therefore, set the intensity of the point light to 55 so the light intensity striking the object has a value of 1 (55/55 = 1). Since the spotlight is 43 units from the object, set its light intensity to 43 (43/43 = 1).
- **Inverse square.** If the point light is 55 units from the object, the object receives $(1/55)^2$, or 1/3025 (55^2 = 3025), of the light. Therefore, set the intensity of the point light to 3025 (3025/3025 = 1). The object receives $(1/43)^2$, or 1/1849 (43^2 = 1849), of the spotlight's illumination. Therefore, set the intensity of the spotlight to 1849 (1849/1849 = 1).

However, it should be noted that these settings are merely a starting point. You will likely spend some time adjusting lighting to produce the desired results. In some cases, it may take longer to light the scene than it did to create it.

PROFESSIONAL TIP

If you render a scene and the image appears black, all of the lights may have been turned off or have their intensity set to zero. A scene with no lights placed in it will be rendered with default lighting.

Shadows

Shadows are critical to the realism of a rendered 3D model. A model without shadows appears obviously fake. On the other hand, a model with realistic materials and shadows may be hard to recognize as computer generated. In AutoCAD, the sun, distant lights, point lights, spotlights, and weblights all can cast shadows. AutoCAD's default lighting does not cast shadows. There are two types of shadows that AutoCAD can create: shadow mapped and raytrace. The **Advanced Rendering Settings** window provides settings for controlling the creation of shadows when rendering. This window and its options are discussed in the next chapter.

The options for creating shadows are the same for all lights. The options can be set when the light is created or adjusted later using the **Properties** window. In the case of sunlight, the **Sun Properties** window is used to set the options.

Shadow-Mapped Shadow Settings

A *shadow-mapped shadow* is a bitmap generated by AutoCAD. A shadow map has soft edges that can be adjusted. Creating shadow-mapped shadows is the only way to produce a soft-edge shadow. However, shadow maps do not transmit object color from transparent objects onto the surfaces behind the object. **Figure 15-20** shows the difference between shadow-mapped shadows and raytraced shadows.

To specify shadow-mapped shadows and set the quality, or resolution, of the shadow, select the light and open the **Properties** window (or **Sun Properties** window). Use the **Lights in Model** window to select a distant light and open the **Properties** window for it. At the bottom of the window list is the **Rendered Shadow Details** category, **Figure 15-21.** To specify shadow-mapped shadows, set the Type property to Soft (shadow mapped).

Figure 15-20.
The shadow from the object in the foreground is a shadow-mapped shadow. The shadow from the object in the background is a raytraced shadow.

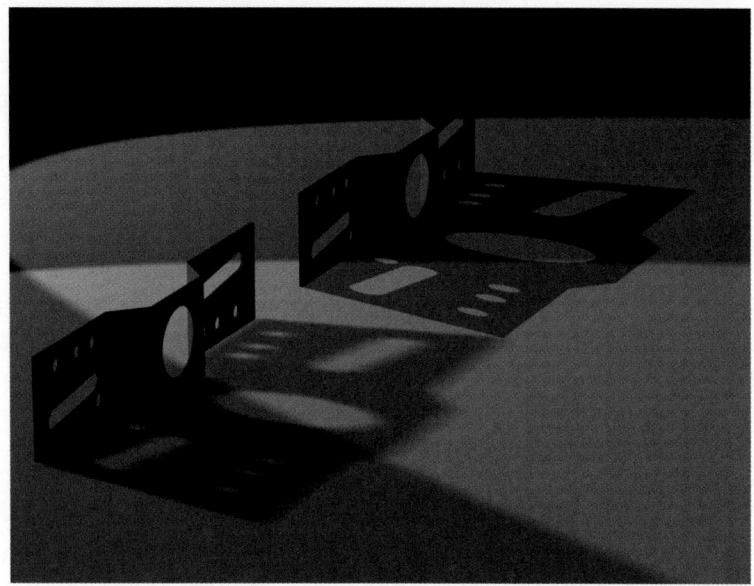

The Map size property determines the quality of the shadow. The value is the number of samples used to create the shadow. The higher the setting, the better quality of the generated shadow. However, the higher the setting, the longer it will take to render.

The value of the Softness property determines how soft the edge of the shadow is. The higher the value, the softer or blurrier the edge of the shadow. A low value can produce a very hard edge. The value can range from 1 to 5.

A variation of shadow-mapped shadows is created when the Type property to Soft (sampled). This type of shadow map must be used with photometric lighting (**LIGHTINGUNITS** = 1 or 2). In this case, different properties are displayed. The Samples property determines the number of "rays" used to generate the shadows. However, this is not considered raytracing. The Visible in rendering property determines whether the shape of the light is rendered. The Shape property sets the shape of the light. For spotlights, the shape can be either rectangular or circular (disk). For point and web-lights, the shape can be linear, rectangular, circular (disk) cylindrical, and spherical. The remaining properties are based on the selected shape and are used to define the size of the shape.

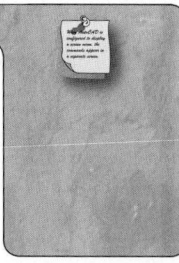

> **NOTE**
>
> For standard shadow-mapped shadows to be created, the Shadow Map property in the **Advanced Render Settings** window must be set to On. However, for the photometric shadow maps—the Soft (sampled) setting—the Shadow Map property does not affect the shadow generation. Advanced render settings are covered in the next chapter.

Figure 15-21.
The **Rendered Shadow Details** category in the **Properties** window.

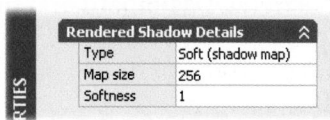

Raytrace Shadow Settings

A *raytrace shadow* is created by beams, or rays, from the light source. These rays trace the path of light as they strike objects to create a shadow. In addition, rays can pass through transparent objects, such as green glass, and project color onto surfaces behind the object. Raytrace shadows have a well-defined edge. They cannot be adjusted to produce a soft edge. Raytrace shadows can be used with standard and photometric lighting.

All lights set to cast shadows, except those set for shadow-mapped shadows, cast raytraced shadows. To switch from shadow-mapped shadows to raytrace shadows, select the light object and open the **Properties** window. In the **Rendered Shadow Details** category, set the Type property to Sharp. The other properties are disabled because they only apply to shadow-mapped shadows.

PROFESSIONAL TIP

Turning on shadow casting will increase rendering time because of the calculations that AutoCAD has to perform. It is difficult to determine if raytraced or shadow-mapped shadows will be quicker to render because every scene is different and there are many variables that come into play. You will have to experiment with your scene to determine the acceptable level of shadow detail versus rendering time.

Adding a Background

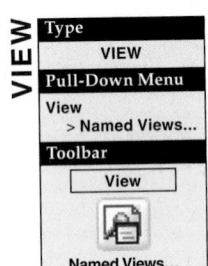

VIEW

Type	
VIEW	
Pull-Down Menu	
View	
> Named Views...	
Toolbar	
View	
Named Views...	

A *background* is the backdrop for your 3D model. The background can be a solid color, a gradient of colors, a bitmap file, the sun and sky, or the current AutoCAD drawing background color. By default, the background is the drawing background color.

To change the background for your drawing, you must first create a named view with the **VIEW** command. In the **View Manager** dialog box, pick the **New...** button to display the **New View** dialog box. See **Figure 15-22**. Near the bottom of this dialog is the **Background** area. The drop-down list in this area is used to specify the type of background. The choices are: Default, Solid, Gradient, Image, and Sun & Sky. The Default setting uses the current AutoCAD viewport color. Photometric lighting must be on (**LIGHTINGUNITS** = 1 or 2) for Sun & Sky to appear in the drop-down list.

PROFESSIONAL TIP

Before you create the named view, establish the viewpoint from which you want to see the final rendering. Set the perspective projection current, if desired. These settings are saved with the view and the drop-down list on the **View** toolbar or in the **3D Navigate** control panel in the **Dashboard** and make it very easy to recall the view.

Solid Backgrounds

If you select Solid in the drop-down list, the **Background** dialog box is displayed. The Type: drop-down list in this dialog box is automatically set to Solid and the default color is displayed in the **Preview** area. See **Figure 15-23**. In the **Solid options** area of

Figure 15-22.
Creating a new view and changing the default background.

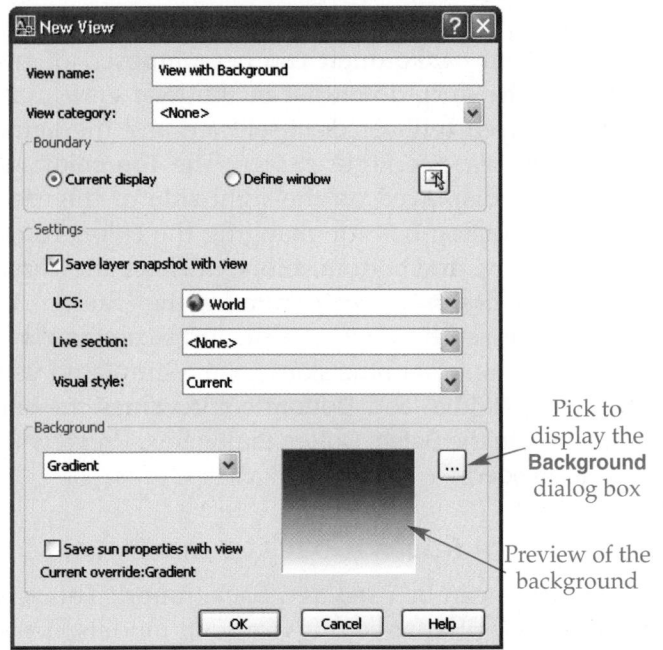

Pick to display the **Background** dialog box

Preview of the background

the dialog box, pick the horizontal **Color:** bar to open the **Select Color** dialog box. Then, select the background color that you desire. When the **Select Color** dialog box is closed, the color you picked is displayed in the **Preview** area of the **Background** dialog box. Close the **Background** dialog box, save the view, set the new view current, and close the **View Manager** dialog box.

NOTE

Make sure to do a test rendering with the background color you selected. The final result may look quite different than your expectations.

Figure 15-23.
Creating a solid background.

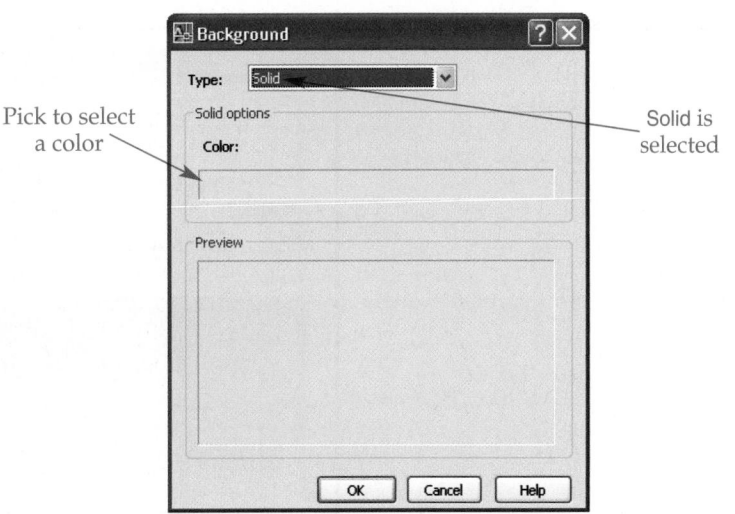

Pick to select a color

Solid is selected

Gradient Backgrounds

A gradient background can be composed of two or three colors. If you select Gradient in the drop-down list in the **New View** dialog box, the **Background** dialog box is displayed with Gradient selected and the default gradient colors displayed in the **Preview** area. See **Figure 15-24.** The **Top color:**, **Middle color:**, and **Bottom color:** swatches are displayed on the right side of the area. Selecting a swatch opens the **Select Color** dialog box for changing the color. To create a two-color gradient composed of the top and bottom colors, uncheck the **Three Color** check box. The **Rotation:** text box provides the option of rotating the gradient. Close the **Background** dialog box, save the view, set the view current, and close the **View Manager** dialog box.

Convincing, clear blue skies can be simulated using the **Gradient** option. Initially, set the **Top**, **Middle**, and **Bottom** color values the same. Then, change the lightness (luminance) in the **Select Colors** dialog box. Preview the background and make adjustments as needed.

Using an Image as a Background

An image can be used as a background. This technique can be used to produce realistic or imaginative settings for your models. If you select Image in the drop-down list in the **New View** dialog box, the **Background** dialog box is displayed with Image selected and a blank image displayed in the **Preview** area. See **Figure 15-25.** If you know the name and path of the image file, this can be typed in the text box. To locate the image file, pick the **Browse...** button to display a standard open dialog box. These image file types may be used for the background: TGA, BMP, PNG, JFIF (JPEG), TIFF, GIF, and PCX.

Once the image file is selected, it must be adjusted. The **Preview** area of the **Background** dialog box shows the image with a preview of a drawing sheet. This drawing sheet indicates how the image is going to be positioned in the view. Pick the **Adjust Image...** button to open the **Adjust Background Image** dialog box. See **Figure 15-26.**

In the **Image position:** drop-down list, pick how the image is applied to the viewport. The Center option centers the image in the view without changing its aspect ratio or scale. The Stretch option centers the image and stretches or shrinks it to fill the entire view. This is one way to plot an image file from AutoCAD. The Tile option keeps the image at its original size and shape, but moves it to the upper-left corner and duplicates it, if needed, to fill the view.

Figure 15-24.
Creating a gradient background.

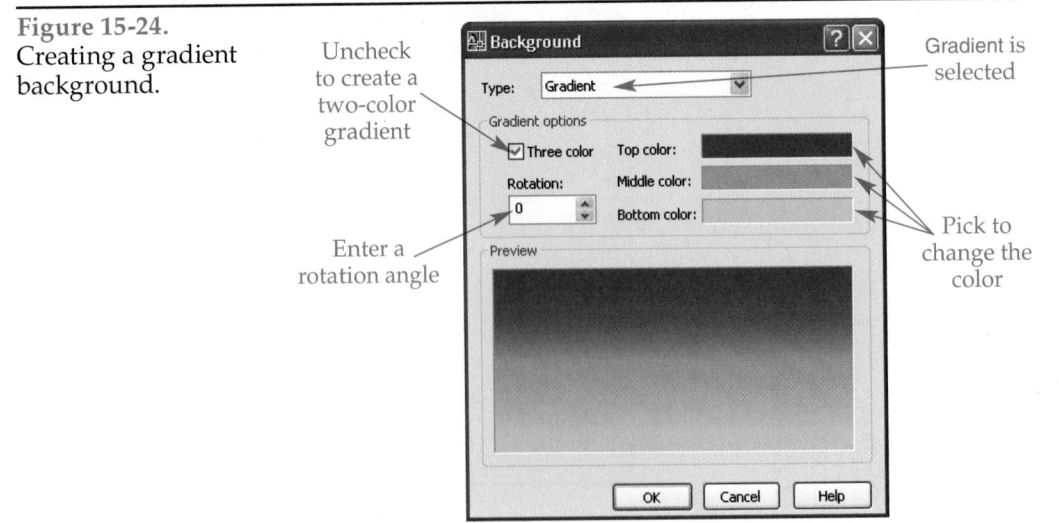

Uncheck to create a two-color gradient

Enter a rotation angle

Gradient is selected

Pick to change the color

Figure 15-25.
Setting an image as
the background.

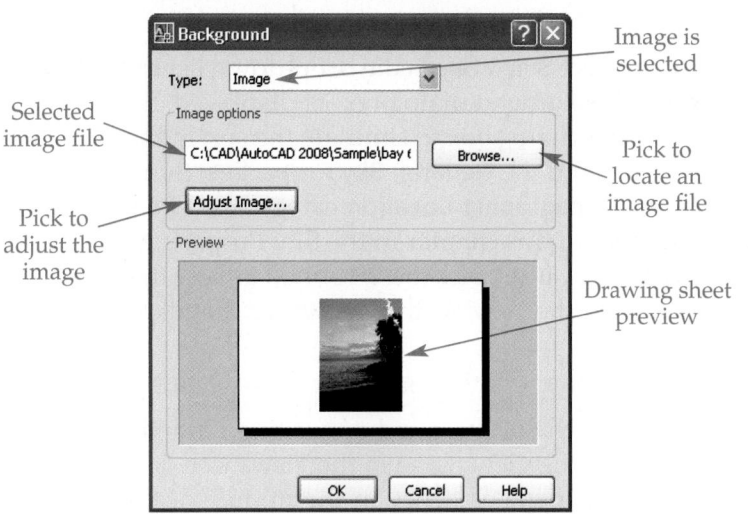

Selected
image file

Pick to
adjust the
image

Image is
selected

Pick to
locate an
image file

Drawing sheet
preview

Figure 15-26.
Adjusting the
background image.

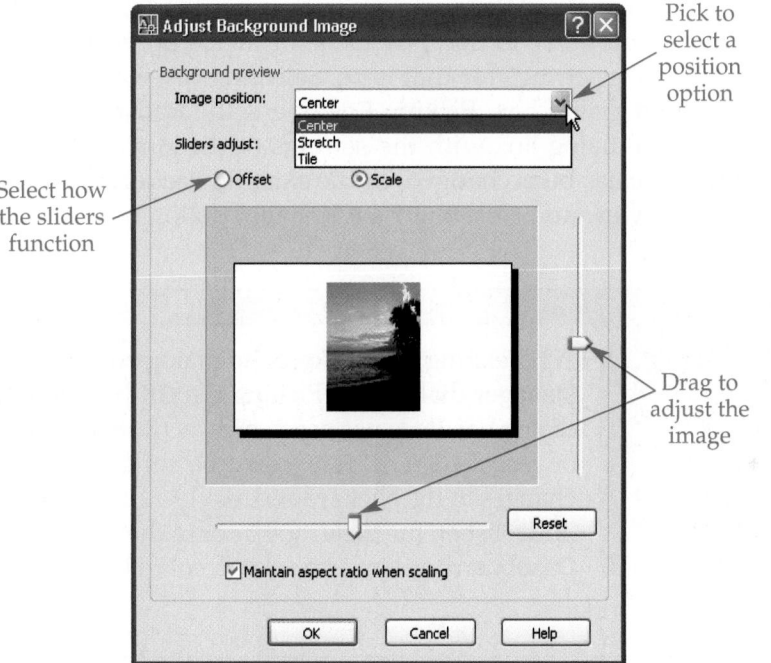

Pick to
select a
position
option

Select how
the sliders
function

Drag to
adjust the
image

After the image is positioned, use the sliders to adjust it further. The sliders are disabled if Stretch is selected in the **Image position:** drop-down list. The slider function is based on which radio button is picked above the image:

- **Offset.** The sliders move the image in the X or Y direction.
- **Scale.** The sliders scale the image in the X or Y direction. This may distort the image if it is scaled too much in one direction. To prevent distortion, check the **Maintain aspect ratio when scaling** check box at the bottom.

The **Reset** button is located at the bottom of the **Adjust Background Image** dialog box. Picking this button returns the scale and offset settings back to their original values.

Once the image is adjusted, pick the **OK** button to close the **Adjust Background Image** dialog box. Then, close the **Background** dialog box, save the view, set the view current, and close the **View Manager** dialog box.

Sun and Sky

If you select Sun & Sky in the drop-down list in the **New View** dialog box, the **Adjust Sun & Sky Background** dialog box is displayed. See **Figure 15-27.** AutoCAD uses the settings in this dialog box to simulate the sun in the sky. This dialog box has a preview tile at the top and the **General, Sky Properties, Sun Angle Calculator, Rendered Shadow Details**, and **Geographic Location** categories. The settings in these categories are discussed earlier in this chapter in the Sky Properties section.

Once the sky is set, pick the **OK** button to close the **Adjust Sun & Sky Background** dialog box. Then, save the view, set the view current, and close the **View Manager** dialog box.

Changing the Background on an Existing View

To change the background of existing named views, open the **View Manager** dialog box. Select the view name in the **Views** tree on the left-hand side of the dialog box. Then, in the **General** category in the middle of the dialog box, select the Background override property. See **Figure 15-28.** Next, pick the drop-down list for the property and select the type of background you want applied: None, Solid, Gradient, Image, Sun & Sky, and Edit. Picking None sets the background to the AutoCAD default background. Setting the property to Solid, Gradient, or Image opens the **Background** dialog where you can make settings for that type. Selecting Sun & Sky opens the **Adjust Sun & Sky Background** dialog box. Picking Edit opens the **Background** or the **Adjust Sun & Sky Background** dialog box with the settings of the current background. Once the background type has been changed, or the existing background edited, pick the **OK** button to save the view and close the **View Manager** dialog box.

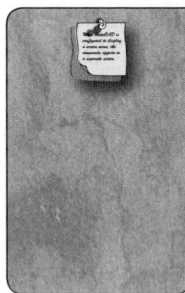

NOTE

After exiting the **Background** dialog box, you are returned to the **View Manager** dialog box. Picking the **OK** button to exit the **View Manager** dialog box does not necessarily activate the view that you just created or modified. The view must be set current to see the effects of the changes to the background. A view can be set current using the drop-down list on the **View** toolbar or in the **3D Navigate** control panel in the **Dashboard**, or it can be set current in the **View Manager** dialog box.

Figure 15-27.
The **Adjust Sun & Sky Background** dialog box contains settings for the sun and sky illumination.

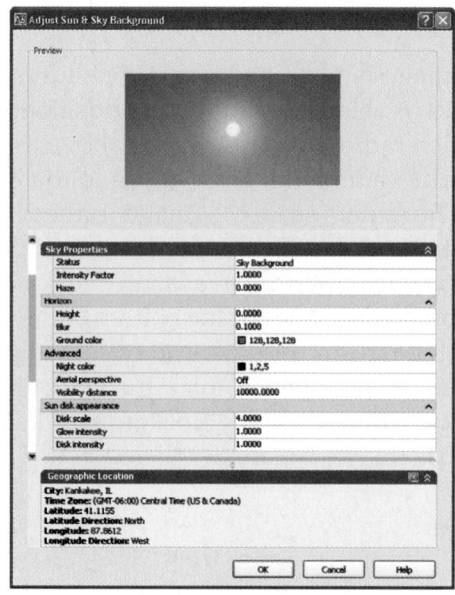

Figure 15-28.
Changing the background of an existing, named view.

Select the view

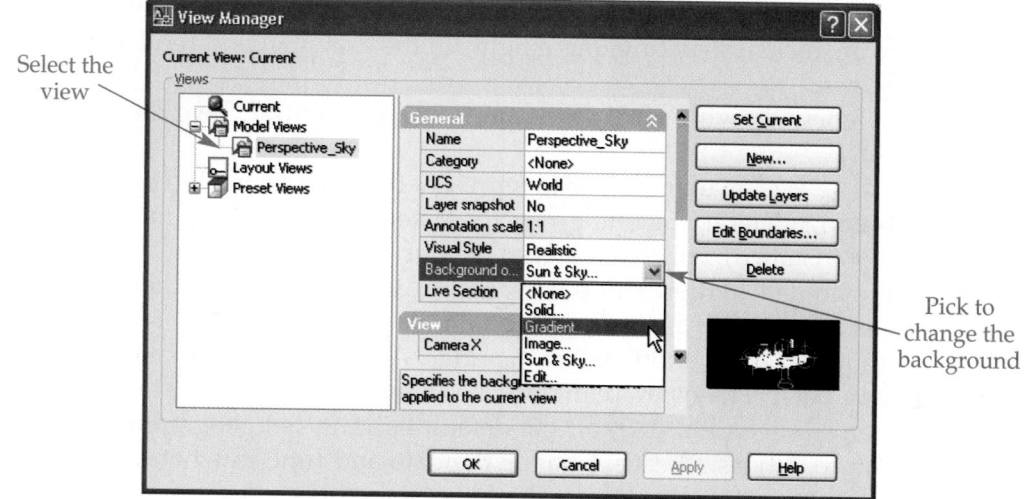

Pick to change the background

Exercise 15-5
Complete the exercise on the Student CD.

Chapter Test

Answer the following questions. Write your answers on a separate sheet of paper or complete the electronic chapter test on the Student CD.

1. Compare and contrast *ambient light, distant lights, point lights, spotlights,* and *weblights.*
2. Define *angle of incidence.*
3. Define *angle of reflection.*
4. A smooth surface has a(n) _____ specular factor.
5. Describe *hotspot* and *falloff.* Which lights have these properties?
6. What is *attenuation?*
7. What are the three types of lighting in AutoCAD?
8. What are the four types of light objects in AutoCAD?
9. What are light glyphs and which lights have them?
10. List the types of shadows that can be created in AutoCAD. Which type(s) can have soft edges?
11. Which type of shadow must be created for light to pass through transparent objects?
12. What must be created before a background can be added to a scene?
13. What are the four types of backgrounds in AutoCAD, other than the default background?

Drawing Problems

1. In this problem, you will draw some basic 3D shapes to create a building similar to an ancient structure, place lights in the drawing, and render the scene with shadows.

   A. Begin a new drawing and set the units to architectural. Save the drawing as P15_01.

   B. Draw a 32′ × 22′ planar surface to represent the floor. Using the tool palettes in the **Materials Library** palette group (or **Materials** group if the material library was not installed), attach a material of your choice to the floor.

   C. Draw cylinders to represent pillars. Make each ∅2′ × 15′ tall. There are ten pillars per side. Attach a suitable material to the pillars.

   D. The roof is 32′ × 22′ and 5′ tall at the ridge. Attach an appropriate material.

   E. Create a perspective viewpoint looking into the building.

   F. Turn on sunlight and turn off the default lighting. Set geographic location of the sun to Athens, Greece. Change the date and time to whatever you wish. Make sure the sun is set to cast shadows.

   G. Render the scene.

   H. Save the drawing.

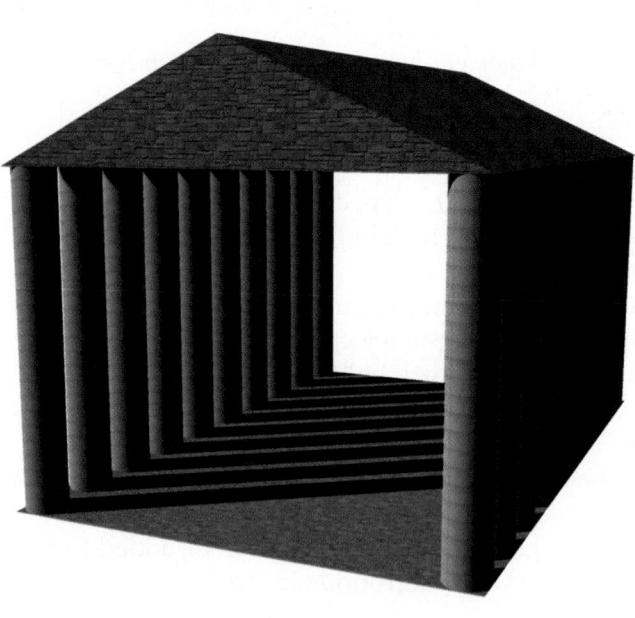

2. Using the drawing from problem 1, you will experiment with different lighting types.

   A. Open drawing P15_01 and save it as P15_02.

   B. Turn off the sun.

   C. Place three point lights inside of the building. Evenly space the lights along the centerline of the ceiling. Adjust the light intensity so that the interior is not washed out. Set the color of the middle light to white. Set the color of the outside lights to red or blue. Render the scene.

   D. Turn off the point lights.

   E. Place two spotlights, one pointing from the front corner to the rear corner and the other pointing between the pillars on the left side of the building. Target them at the floor. Render the scene. Adjust the intensity, hotspot, and falloff as needed.

   F. Turn the point lights back on and render the scene with all six lights active. Adjust the light intensities again if the rendering is too washed out with light.

   G. Save the drawing.

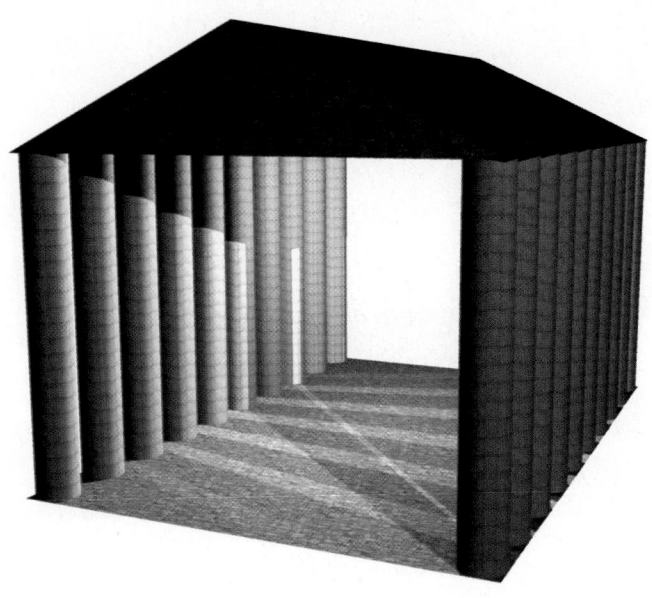

Chapter 15 Lighting

3. Using a previously created mechanical model, you will apply materials and lights to make it ready for presentation.
   A. Open drawing P07_05 created in Chapter 7. Save it as P15_03.
   B. Draw a planar surface below the flange to represent a tabletop.
   C. Using the tool palettes, attach an appropriate material, such as a wood or tile material, to the plane.
   D. Create a new material based on the Advanced material type. Attach a diffuse color map from the "all users" AutoCAD folder. There are several metal texture maps located in the \Textures folder. Apply a low reflection value to the material.
   E. Place two spotlights in the drawing and target them at the flange from different angles. Adjust their hotspot, falloff, and intensity to get the proper lighting.
   F. Create a perspective view of the scene. Then, render the scene.
   G. Save the drawing.

4. The building shown below will be used to study passive solar heating at different times of the year. Model the building using the overall dimensions given. Use your own dimensions for everything else. The side with the windows should be facing South (–Y in AutoCAD).
  A. Set the geographical location to a city in the northern hemisphere.
  B. Set the date to midsummer and the time to noon.
  C. Turn on sunlight and the default lighting off.
  D. Render the scene and note the location of the shadows inside the building.
  E. Change the date to late winter, render the scene again, and note the new location of the shadows. You can easily switch between the rendered images in the **Render** window by selecting each rendering in the **History** pane (this is discussed more in the next chapter).
  F. Observing the changes in the shadow locations, what design changes can be made to maximize sun exposure in the cold winter months? What design changes can be made to minimize sun exposure in the heat of summer?
  G. Change the geographical location to somewhere closer to the equator. Then, render the scene in summer and follow. How do the shadows compare to those in your location?
  H. Save the drawing as P15_04.

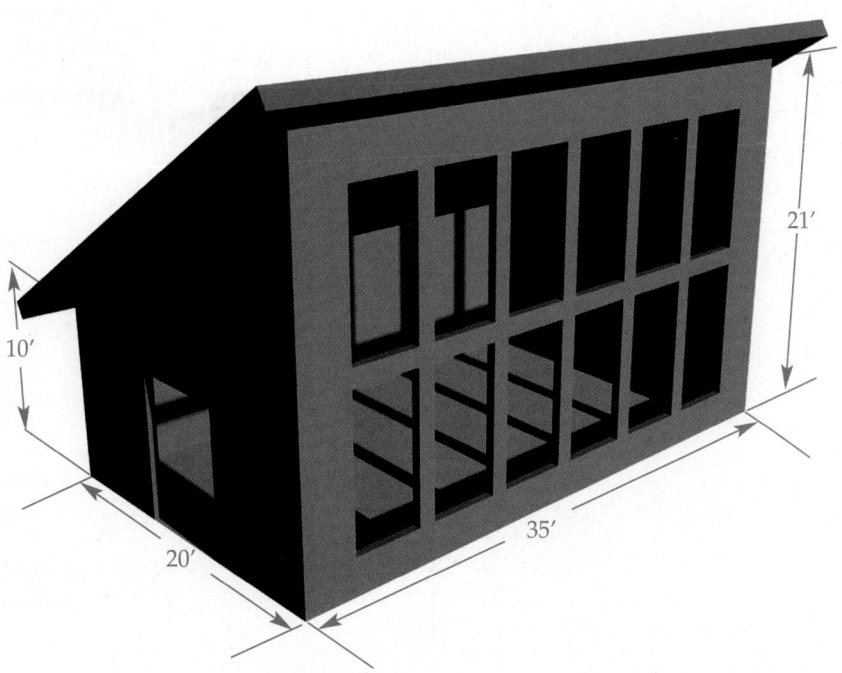

5. In this problem, you will be adding lights to a model and controlling their properties to create a pleasing scene. Model the courtyard shown below. The overall dimensions are 15′ × 16′ × 4′ (wall height). Use your own dimensions for everything else. Add lights as follows.

   A. Turn on the sun and turn off the default lighting. Set the time to late in the day so that the sun is close to the horizon.

   B. In the **Sky Properties** category of the **Sun Properties** window, select Sky Background and Illumination for the Status property.

   C. Add a point light at the center of each sphere.

   D. Attach the Doors & Windows.Glazing.Glass.Frosted material to the spheres.

   E. Create a fill light above to illuminate the scene. This can be a point or spotlight.

   F. Render the scene using the low preset to see the lighting effects.

   G. Adjust the sun properties to create the look that you want.

   H. Adjust the properties of the point lights and any other lights in the scene. You may have to increase the intensity of the lights quite a bit to illuminate the scene properly.

   I. When the scene is illuminated the way you want it, render the scene using medium or high preset.

   J. Save the drawing as P15_05.

Learning Objectives

After completing this chapter, you will be able to:

- ✓ Make advanced rendering settings.
- ✓ Set the resolution for a rendering.
- ✓ Save a rendering to an image file.
- ✓ Add fog/depth cueing to a scene.

In Chapter 13, you learned how to create a view of your scene that is more realistic than a visual style. In that chapter, you used AutoCAD's sunlight feature to create a simple rendering with mostly default settings. However, in this chapter you will learn about the advanced rendering features that allow you to create photorealistic renderings. You will learn all of the features related to rendering in AutoCAD. You will learn how to make your renderings look their best while conserving rendering time.

Render Window

By default, a drawing is rendered in the **Render** window, unless you are rendering a cropped area. This window allows you to inspect the rendering, save it to a file, compare it with previous renderings, and take note of the statistics. See **Figure 16-1**. There are three main areas of the **Render** window—the image, history, and statistics panes.

Image Pane

As AutoCAD processes the scene, the image begins to appear in the image pane in its final form. There may be as many as four phases that the rendering goes through as it is being processed:

- **Translation.** Processes the drawing information and determines light intensity, shadow placement, colors, and so on. This phase is always completed.
- **Photon emission.** *Photon emission* is a technique for calculating indirect illumination that traces photons emitted by the light source until they come to rest on a diffuse surface. It determines which areas will be illuminated by indirect, or bounced, light. The photon emission phase may or may not be processed, depending on settings in the **Advanced Render Settings** window.

Figure 16-1.
The **Render** window.

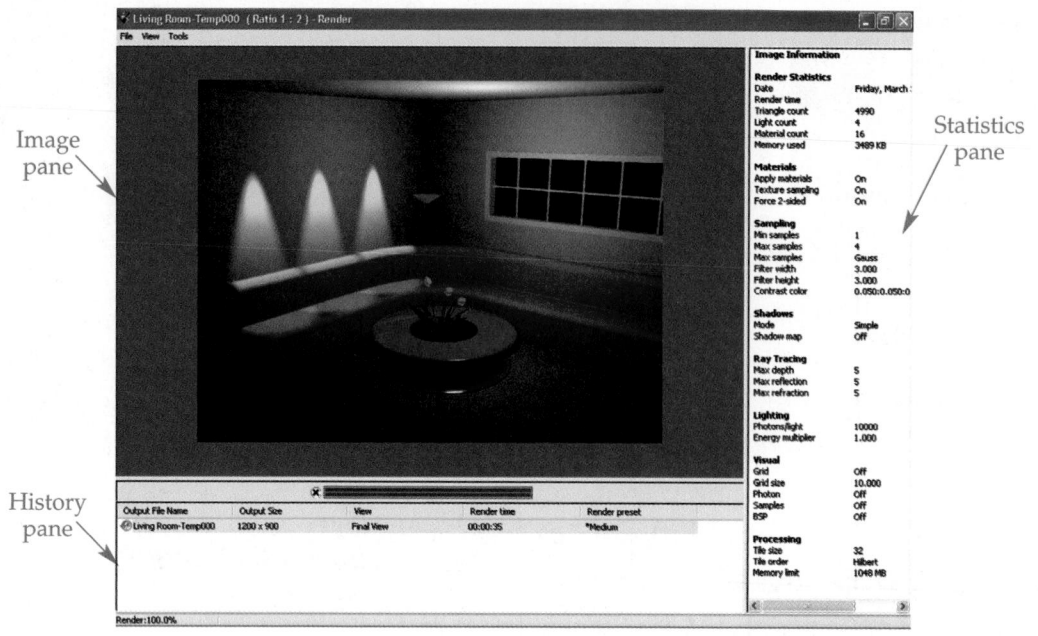

- **Final gather.** *Final gather* increases the number of rays used to calculate global illumination (GI). This phase will be processed if it is turned on in the **Advanced Render Settings** window.
- **Render.** Converts the data into an image. This phase is always completed.

Immediately below the image pane is the progress meter/status bar. The top bar displays the progress of the current phase and the bottom bar indicates the progress of the entire rendering. Also, at the very bottom of the **Render** window, below the history pane, the status of the phase is shown with its percentage complete. You can also hover the cursor over the progress meter/status bar during the rendering and a tooltip displays the percentage of completion for the current process and the overall render. The rendering can be cancelled at any time by pressing the [Esc] key or picking the **X** button to the left of the progress meter.

As discussed in Chapter 13, you can zoom the rendering in and out to inspect it. You can also save it to an image file using the **File** pull-down menu in the **Render** window.

History Pane

The history pane contains a list of all of the renderings that were created in this drawing since it was created, not just in this drawing session. The items in this list are called *history entries.* There are two types of history entries:

- **Normal.** The entry is saved to file. A link is maintained to that file. If the drawing is saved, closed, and reopened, you can pick the entry to view the rendering in the image pane.
- **Temporary.** The entry is available in the current drawing session, but is not saved to a file. If the drawing is closed, the image is lost. The name of the entry in the Output File Name column ends with -Temp$x$.

Right-clicking on an entry in the history pane displays a shortcut menu. The options in this menu can be used to save the image, render the image again, and manage the entry. The options in the shortcut menu are:

- **Render Again.** Renders the scene again using the same settings. A new entry is not added to the history pane.
- **Save.** Saves the rendered image to a file using a standard save dialog box. This turns the entry from a temporary entry into a normal entry.
- **Save Copy.** Saves the rendered image to a new file without changing the current entry.
- **Make Render Settings Current.** Sets all of the rendering settings of the entry as the current rendering settings in the drawing. This allows you to render the current scene using the settings of the entry.
- **Remove From the List.** Deletes the entry from the history pane, but any image files saved from the entry remain.
- **Delete Output File.** Deletes the image file created by saving the entry. The entry remains in the history pane, and any image files that were created as copies are retained.

Statistics Pane

The statistics pane shows the details of the rendering that is selected in the history pane. By selecting renderings in the history pane, you can see in the image pane which version provides the best result. Then, you can use the statistics pane to view the settings. The information under the Render Statistics heading (date, render time, etc.) is added when the render is completed. The rest of the information reflects the settings in the **Advanced Rendering Settings** dialog box and the **Render Preset** dialog box at the time the rendering was created.

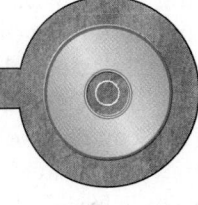

Exercise 16-1
Complete the exercise on the Student CD.

Advanced Render Settings

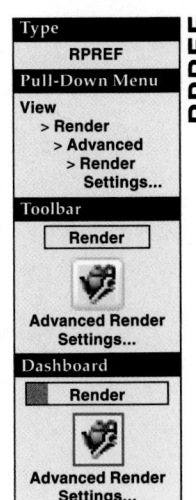

Type
RPREF
Pull-Down Menu
View
> Render
> Advanced
> Render
Settings...
Toolbar
Render
Advanced Render Settings...
Dashboard
Render
Advanced Render Settings...

RPREF

The quickest and easiest way to control the quality of a rendering is with render presets. AutoCAD provides five standard render presets: Draft, Low, Medium, High, and Presentation. The Draft preset provides the lowest-quality rendering. Each preset above Draft changes the advanced render settings to gradually improve the rendering quality, peaking with the Presentation preset. However, as the quality is improved, the rendering time increases. The presets can be selected in the **Render** control panel in the **Dashboard** or from the drop-down list at the top of the **Advanced Render Settings** window. Creating and using your own render presets is covered later in this chapter.

The **Advanced Render Settings** window provides settings that give you complete control over how a rendering is created. The **RPREF** command opens the window. There are five main categories in this window: **General**, **Ray Tracing**, **Indirect Illumination**, **Diagnostic**, and **Processing**. These categories are explained in the next sections.

General

The **General** category provides properties for controlling the rendering destination, materials, sampling, and shadows, **Figure 16-2.** It contains four subcategories: **Render Context**, **Materials**, **Sampling**, and **Shadows**.

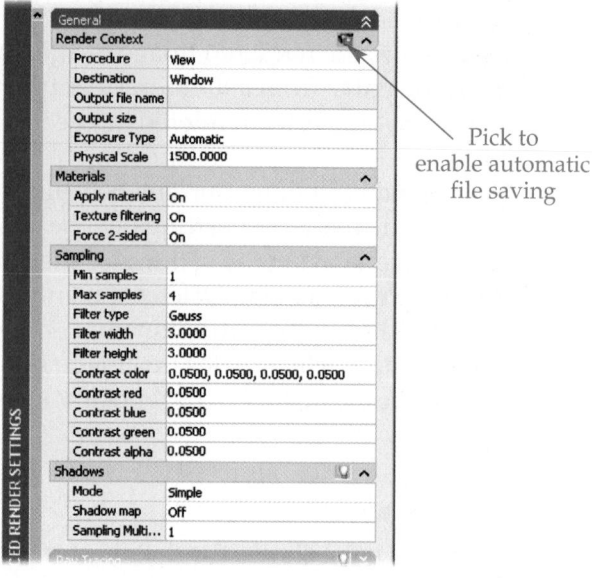

Pick to
enable automatic
file saving

Render context

The **Render Context** subcategory contains general properties that control the rendering. The Procedure property determines what will be rendered. The settings are View, Crop, and Selected. View is the default and renders whatever you see in the drawing window. Crop allows you to specify an area of the scene to render. This is very useful when you want to do a test render, but do not want to wait for the whole scene. The Selected setting allows you to pick which objects to render.

The Destination property determines where the rendered scene will be displayed. You can choose to have the rendering placed in the viewport or **Render** window.

If the save button in the subcategory title bar is picked, the Output File Name property is enabled. This property sets the name and location of the file to which the rendering will automatically be saved.

The Output Size property sets the resolution, measured in pixels × pixels, for the rendered image. You can select standard resolutions or pick Specify Output Size... for a custom resolution. In the **Output Size** dialog box that is displayed when Specify Output Size... is selected, you can enter any resolution that you want. See Figure 16-3. If you want to prevent the image from stretching, make sure the **Lock image aspect** button is selected so that the height and width remain proportional. When you change the resolution, it is stored with the drawing.

Figure 16-3.
Setting a custom
resolution.

Enter a
custom size

Preset sizes

The Exposure Type property can be set to Automatic or Logarithmic. When set to Automatic, the entire image is sampled and some of the dim lighting effects are enhanced to make them more visible. When set to Logarithmic, the brightness and contrast are used to map physical values to RGB values. This is better for scenes with high dynamic ranges.

Exposure control needs a scale to work with and, if you are using non-physical lights (**LIGHTINGUNITS** set to 0), the Physical Scale property provides a scale. Standard lights have an Intensity Factor property that is multiplied by the Physical Scale value to determine the actual brightness of the light. The default value is 1500. In other words, a point light with an Intensity Factor value of 2 has an actual lamp intensity of 3000 candelas when the Physical Scale property is set to 1500.

Materials

The properties in the **Materials** subcategory determine how materials are handled in the rendering. The Apply Materials property controls whether or not materials attached to objects are rendered. The property can be set to Yes or No. If set to No, objects are rendered in their own colors. The Texture Filtering property determines whether or not antialiasing is applied to texture maps when rendered. Antialiasing is a way of reducing "jaggies" in the rendered image. The Force 2-sided property determines if AutoCAD renders both sides of all faces. This can fix problems where objects disappear in a rendering, but will increase rendering time.

Sampling

Sampling is a technique that tests the scene color at each pixel and then determines what the final color should be. This is most important in transition areas, such as edges of objects or shadows. Increasing the sampling will smooth out the jagged edges and incorrect coloring, but increase rendering time. You may also notice thicker lines.

The Min samples and Max samples properties set the minimum and maximum number of samples computed per pixel. A value of 1 means one sample per pixel. A value of 1/4 means one sample for every four pixels. The Filter type property determines how the samples are brought together to determine the pixel value:

- Box. Quickest method; combines samples evenly and gives them equal weight.
- Triangle. Weights the samples based on a pyramid with samples in the center of the filter area receiving the most weight.
- Gauss. Weights the samples based on a bell curve with samples in the center of the filter area receiving the most weight.
- Mitchell. Most accurate. Weights samples based on a curve centered on the filter area, like Gauss; however, this curve is steeper.
- Lanczos. Weights samples based on a curve centered on the filter area, like Mitchell, but it diminishes the weight of samples at the edge of the filter area.

The Filter width and Filter height properties determine the size of the filter area. A larger filter area softens the image, but increases rendering time.

The Contrast color, Contrast red, Contrast blue, Contrast green, and Contrast alpha properties specify the threshold value of the colors involved in sampling. If a sample differs from the sample next to it by more than this color, AutoCAD takes more than one sample per pixel up to the Max samples property. Values can be from 0.0 (black) to 1.0 (fully saturated). Increasing the value can reduce the amount of sampling and, therefore, speed up the rendering. However, it may also reduce the quality of the image.

Shadows

The properties in the **Shadows** subcategory control how the renderer handles shadows generated by the lights in the scene. The Mode property controls a shader function that calculates light effects. There are three modes that determine how shading is calculated:

- Simple. Shaders are randomly created.
- Sorted. Shaders are called in order from the object to the light.
- Segment. Shaders are called in order from the volume shaders to the segments of the light rays between the object and the light.

The Shadow Map property determines whether shadow-mapped or raytrace shadows are created. When this property is set to On, shadow-mapped shadows are generated. When it is set to Off, raytraced shadows are created.

The Sampling Multiplier property limits shadow sampling for area lights. The values are preset for the rendering presets: Draft = 0, Low = 1/4, Medium = 1/2, High = 1, and Presentation = 1. However, these values can be changed. This is the same principal that is described in the Sampling section, but instead of sampling pixels for object color, it is sampling for shadows.

Ray Tracing

The **Ray Tracing** category provides properties for controlling how the rendered image is shaded, **Figure 16-4.** *Raytracing* is a method of calculating reflections, refractions, and shadows by tracing the path of the light rays from the light sources. This is more accurate at producing shadows than shadow mapping, but it takes more time and the shadow edge is always sharp. To enable raytracing, pick the button in the category's title bar. If this is off, there will be no raytracing and the properties are disabled.

The Max reflections property is the maximum number of times that a ray can be reflected. The Max refractions property is the maximum number of times that a ray can be refracted. The Max depth property is the maximum number of reflections and refractions. If this property is set to 5 and the Max reflections property is set to 3, then the Max refractions property can be set no higher than 2. A good way to figure out the required maximum depth is to imagine a light ray traveling through transparent objects or bouncing off of reflective objects in your scene. Count how many surfaces the object must contact and that is the maximum depth.

Indirect Illumination

Indirect illumination is a method in AutoCAD that simulates natural bounced light. If indirect illumination is turned off and light does not directly strike an object, the object is dark. Without indirect illumination enabled, other lights must be added to the scene to simulate indirect illumination. The properties in the **Indirect Illumination** category allow you to create a natural-looking scene. There are three subcategories in the **Indirect Illumination** category: **Global Illumination**, **Final Gather**, and **Light Properties**. See **Figure 16-5.**

Figure 16-4.
The **Ray Tracing** category of the **Advanced Rendering Settings** window.

Pick to enable raytracing

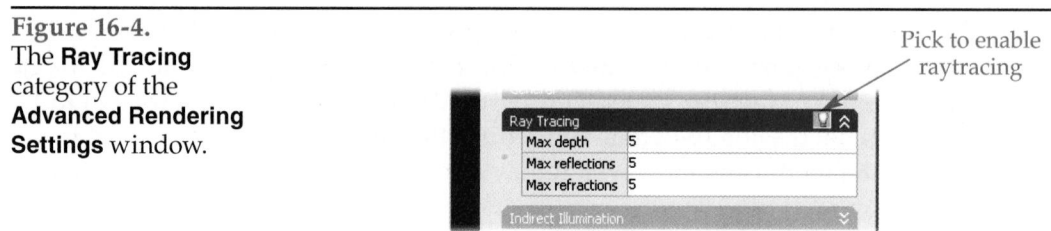

AutoCAD and Its Applications—Advanced

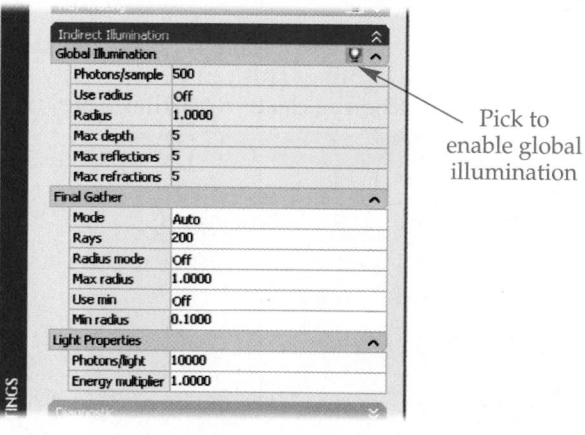

Pick to enable global illumination

Global illumination

Global illumination (GI) is indirect illumination. Bounced light is simulated by generating photon maps on surfaces in the scene. These maps are created by tracing photons from the light source. Photons bounce around the scene from one object to the next until they finally strike a diffuse surface. When a photon strikes a surface, it is stored in the photon map. To enable global illumination, pick the button in the subcategory's title bar. If this button is off, there will be no indirect illumination.

The Photons/sample property sets the number of photons used to generate the photon map. The higher the value, the less noise global illumination produces. However, rendering time is longer and the image is blurrier.

The Use radius property determines whether the photons are a default radius or a user-specified radius. When the property is set to On, the Radius property sets the size of the photon. When set to Off, the radius of each photon is 1/10th of the scene's radius.

The Max reflections property is the maximum number of times that a photon can be reflected. The Max refractions property is the maximum number of times that a photon can be refracted. The Max depth property is the maximum number of reflections and refractions. If this property is set to 5 and the Max reflections property is set to 3, then the Max refractions property can be set no higher than 2.

Final gather

The settings in the **Global Illumination** subcategory may result in dark and light areas in the scene. *Final gathering* increases the number of rays in the rendering and cleans up these artifacts. It will also greatly increase rendering time. Final gathering works the best with scenes that contain overall diffuse lighting. See **Figure 16-6.** The Mode property for final gathering can be set to:
- On. Turns on global illumination for final gathering.
- Off. Turns off global illumination for final gathering.
- Auto. Global illumination is turned on or off based on the sky light status. This is the default setting.

The Rays property sets the number of rays used to calculate indirect illumination. The higher the value, the better the result, but the longer the scene takes to render.

The Radius mode property determines how the Max radius property is applied during final gathering. There are three possible settings:
- On. The Max radius value is used for final gathering and it is measured in world units.
- Off. The radius of each area processed by final gathering is 10% of the maximum model radius.
- View. The Max radius value is used for final gathering, but it is measured in pixels instead of world units.

Figure 16-6.
A—This scene has a single point light. B—Global illumination is turned on. Notice the unevenness of the lighting. This can be especially seen on the sofa and in the corner of the walls. C—Final gathering cleans up artifacts and provides a more even illumination.

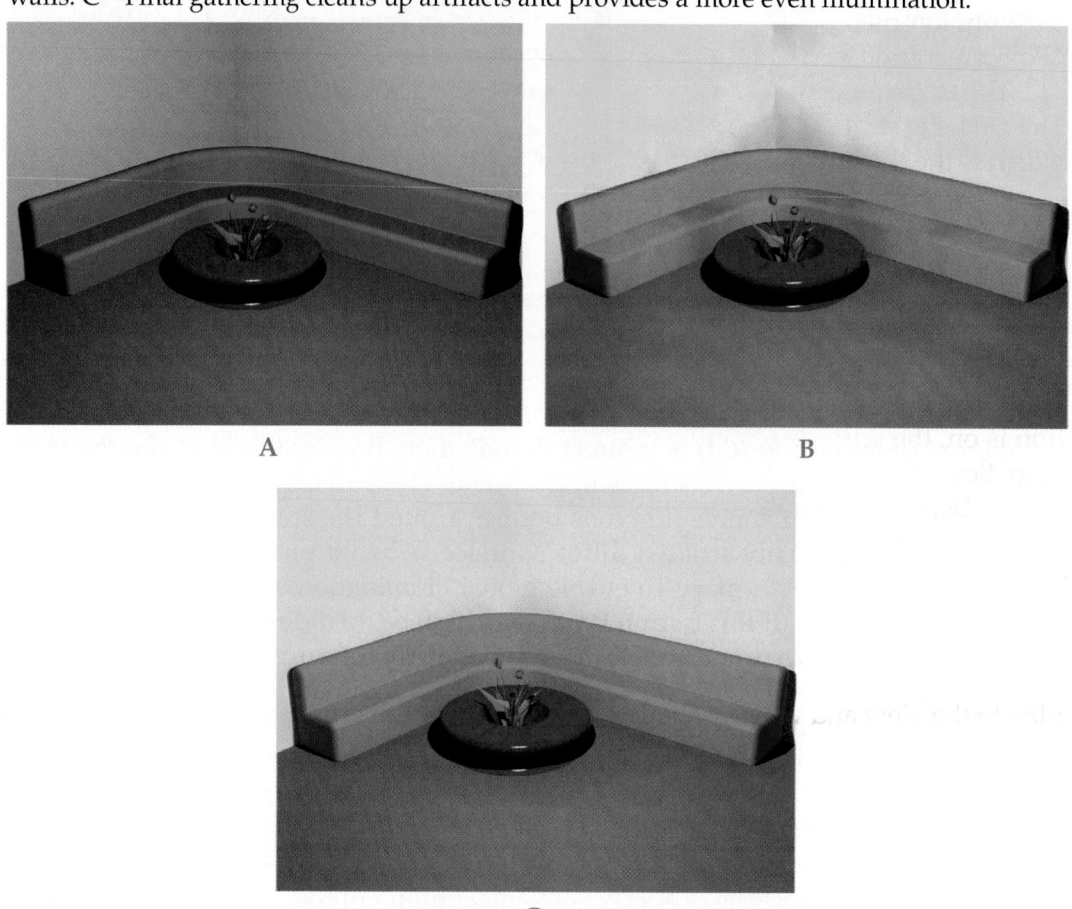

A

B

C

The Max radius property determines the maximum radius of each area processed during final gathering. The lower this value, the higher the quality of the rendering because a larger number of smaller areas is processed. However, rendering time is higher.

The Use min property determines whether or not the Min radius property is applied for final gathering. The Min radius property sets the minimum radius of the processed areas. Increasing this improves quality, but increases rendering time.

Light properties

The properties in the **Light Properties** subcategory control how the lights in the scene are applied when calculating indirect illumination. The Photons/light property sets the number of photons emitted by each light. Increasing this number makes each light cast more photons and improves the rendering quality. The Energy multiplier property determines how much light energy is used in global illumination. The default value of 1.0000 does not increase or decrease the light energy. Values less than the default decrease the light energy. Values greater than the default increase the light energy.

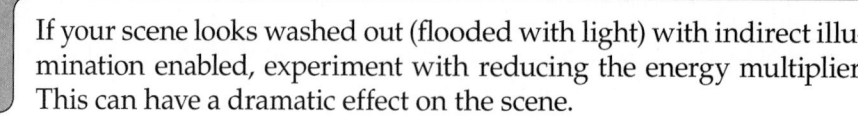

PROFESSIONAL TIP

If your scene looks washed out (flooded with light) with indirect illumination enabled, experiment with reducing the energy multiplier. This can have a dramatic effect on the scene.

Diagnostic

The properties in the **Diagnostic** category control tools to help you understand why the rendering produced the results it did, **Figure 16-7.** The scene can be rendered with photon maps, grids, and irradiance shown. These tools can help you diagnose and correct problems.

The Grid property determines if a coordinate grid is shown in the rendered image. The Grid size property sets the size of the grid. When the Grid property is set to Off, which is the default, the grid is not shown. There are three other settings:

- Object. A colored grid displays local coordinates (UVW). Each object has its own set of local coordinates.
- World. World coordinates (XYZ) are displayed in a colored grid, **Figure 16-8A.**
- Camera. Coordinates of a UCS corresponding to the camera or current view are displayed in a colored grid, **Figure 16-8B.**

The Photon property controls whether or not the effect of a photon map is shown in the rendering. When the property is set to Density or Irradiance and global illumination is on, the scene is rendered and overlaid with an image representing the photon map. See **Figure 16-9.**

- Density. Shows the photon map projected onto the scene. Higher-density areas are red and lower-density areas are the cooler colors.
- Irradiance. Similar to density, but the photons are shaded based on their irradiance value. Maximum irradiance is red and lower irradiance values are shown in the cooler colors.

The Samples property can be set to On or Off. When set to On, a grid is rendered plan to the view and varying shades of gray and white are displayed in the scene. This tool is another way to evaluate the lighting in the scene.

The BSP property determines whether or not the effects of *binary space partitioning (BSP)* are shown. BSP is a raytrace acceleration method. When rendering, if you

Figure 16-7.
The **Diagnostic** category of the **Advanced Rendering Settings** window.

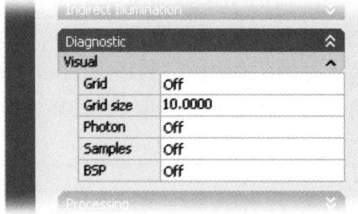

Figure 16-8.
Applying a grid to the rendering. A—The Grid property is set to World. B—The Grid property is set to Camera.

A   B

receive a message about large depth or size values or the rendering is very slow, this tool may help you locate the problem.

- Depth. The depth of the raytrace tree is displayed. Top faces are displayed in bright red. The deeper the faces are in the tree, the cooler the colors in which they are displayed, **Figure 16-10A**.
- Size. The size of the leaves in the raytrace tree are displayed. Different colors are used to identify different leaf sizes, **Figure 16-10B**.

Processing

The properties in the **Processing** category control how the final render processing takes place, **Figure 16-11**. The Tile size property controls the size of the tiles into which total image is subdivided. The larger the tile size, the fewer tiles that have to be rendered and the fewer times the image has to update. Larger tiles usually mean a

Figure 16-10.
Showing the effects of binary space partitioning. A—The BSP property is set to Depth. B—The BSP property is set to Size.

A

B

Figure 16-11.
The **Processing** category of the **Advanced Rendering Settings** window.

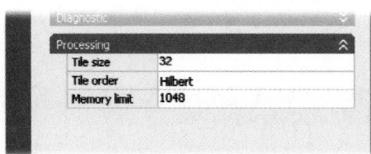

shorter rendering time. The Tile order property controls the order in which the tiles are rendered:

- Hilbert. The "cost" of switching to the next tile determines which tile is rendered next.
- Spiral. The rendering begins with the tiles in the center of the image and then spirals outward.
- Left to Right. The tiles are rendered from bottom to top and left to right in columns.
- Right to Left. The tiles are rendered from bottom to top and right to left in columns.
- Top to Bottom. The tiles are rendered from right to left and top to bottom in rows.
- Bottom to Top. The tiles are rendered from right to left and bottom to top in rows.

The Memory limit property specifies the maximum memory allocated for the rendering process. When this limit is reached, some objects may be removed from rendering.

Exercise 16-2
Complete the exercise on the Student CD.

Render Presets

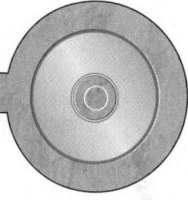

Once settings have been established that create a rendering with the desired results, the settings can be saved to a custom render preset. The **Render Presets** dialog box is used to create custom render presets, **Figure 16-12.** The **RENDERPRESETS** command opens this dialog box. You can also select Manage Render Presets... in the drop-down list at the top of the **Advanced Render Settings** window or in the **Render** control panel in the **Dashboard**.

The left side of the dialog box displays a tree that contains the standard render presets and any custom render presets. In the middle of the dialog box are all of the properties for the selected render preset. These are the same properties available in the **Advanced Render Settings** window. On the right side of the dialog box are three buttons that allow you to make a preset current, make a copy of a preset, or delete a preset.

The easiest way to create a custom preset is to start with a standard render preset and modify the properties until the desired result is produced. This preset will be indicated as the current preset in the **Render Presets** dialog box, but there will be an asterisk (*) in front of its name. The asterisk indicates that the preset has been changed from its original settings. Next, pick the **Create Copy** button in the **Render Presets**

Figure 16-12.
The **Render Presets Manager** dialog box.

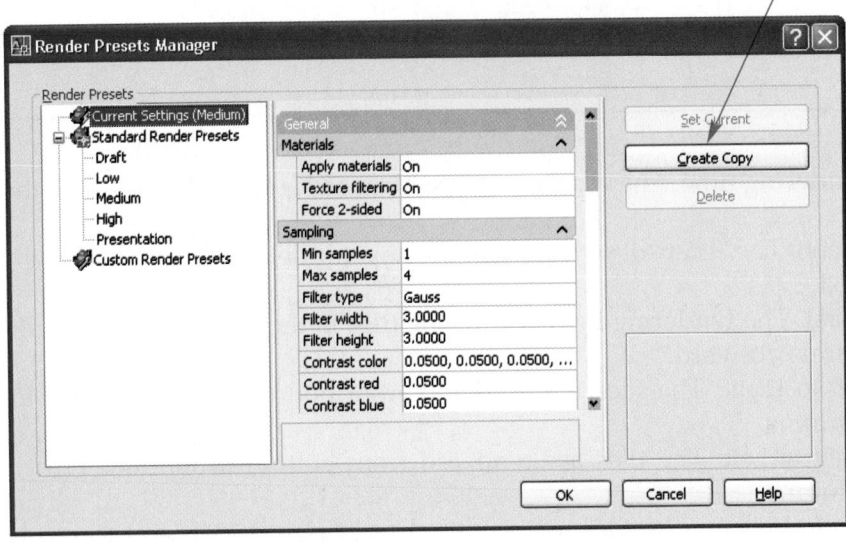

Pick to create a copy with the current settings

dialog box to make a copy. In the **Copy Render Preset** dialog box that appears, name the new render preset, provide a description, and pick the **OK** button. The new preset is saved in the Custom Render Presets branch of the tree.

Render Exposure

The **RENDEREXPOSURE** command displays the **Adjust Rendered Exposure** dialog box. See **Figure 16-13.** In this dialog box, you can globally adjust the brightness, contrast, midtones, and exterior daylight of the scene. In order to use this command, the Exposure Type property in the **General** category of the **Advanced Render Settings** window must be set to Logarithmic.

The **Preview** area in the **Adjust Rendered Exposure** dialog box displays the rendered scene with the changes you make in the dialog box so you can see how the scene will be altered. This saves the step of rerendering the scene. Change the settings until the preview looks correct and then close the dialog box. The properties in this dialog box are:

- **Brightness.** Controls the brightness of the colors. The default value is 65.0000 and it can range from 0.0000 to 200.0000. Increasing the value increases how light the colors in the scene appear.
- **Contrast.** Controls the contrast of the colors in the scene. The default value is 100.0000 and it can range from 0.0000 to 100.0000. Increasing the value increases the difference between similar colors, in effect increasing the brightness of the scene.
- **Mid tones.** Controls the midtone values of the colors. The midtones colors are neither light nor dark. The default value is 1.0000 and it can range from 0.0000 to 20.0000.
- **Exterior Daylight.** Sets the exposure for scenes illuminate with sunlight. It is either on, off, or automatic. The default setting is Auto.
- **Process Background.** Specifies whether or not the background is processed by exposure control when the scene is rendered. It is either on or off. The default setting is On.

To force the preview to update, pick the small X to the left of the rendering progress bars below the preview. The preview is updated with the current settings.

Figure 16-13.
Using the **RENDEREXPOSURE** command to adjust the rendering.

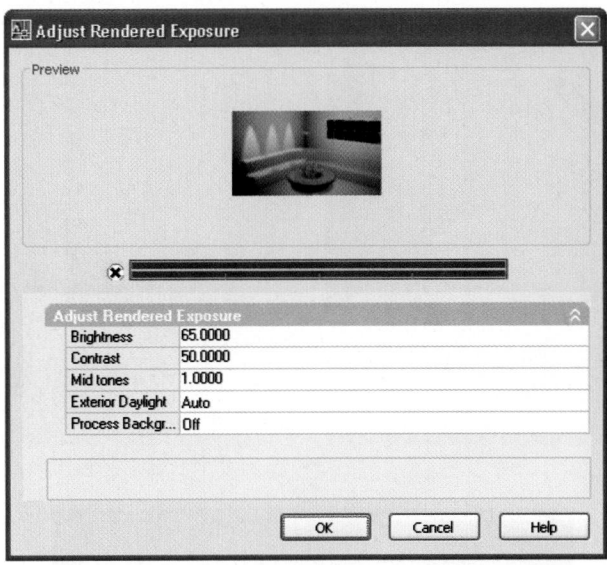

Render Environment

The render environment allows for the addition of fog or depth cueing to the scene. *Fog* and *depth cueing* in AutoCAD are actually ways of using color to visually represent the distance between the camera (viewer) and objects in the model. See Figure 16-14. This is similar to looking at an object from a distance and seeing that the object is a little obscured from haze in the air. The only difference between fog and depth cueing is the color. Fog uses white or another light color and depth cueing generally uses black. The **Render Environment** dialog box is used to add fog/depth cueing, Figure 16-15.

Creating a Camera

Before adding fog/depth cueing, a camera must be created that shows the view you want. Then, start the **3DCLIP** command and adjust the back clipping plane to where you want the effect to end. Only the back clipping plane needs to be active. The fog/depth cueing references this plane and the camera location.

Creating a camera and adjusting clipping planes is discussed in detail in Chapter 17. However, to create a camera and turn on the clipping plane(s), first select the command. Then, pick a location for the camera followed by the location for its target. Next, enter the **Clipping** option. Turn on the front clipping plane, if desired, and enter the offset distance. Then, turn on the back clipping plane and enter the offset distance. Finally, end the command (do not press [Esc]).

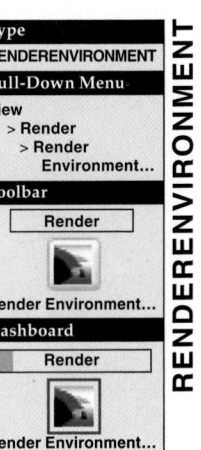

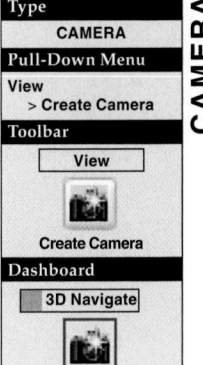

PROFESSIONAL TIP

A camera is automatically created when a view is saved as a named view. This is another good reason to save your views.

Figure 16-14.
A—This scene has no fog/depth cueing applied. B—The scene has white fog applied (including the background). C—The scene has black depth cueing applied (including the background).

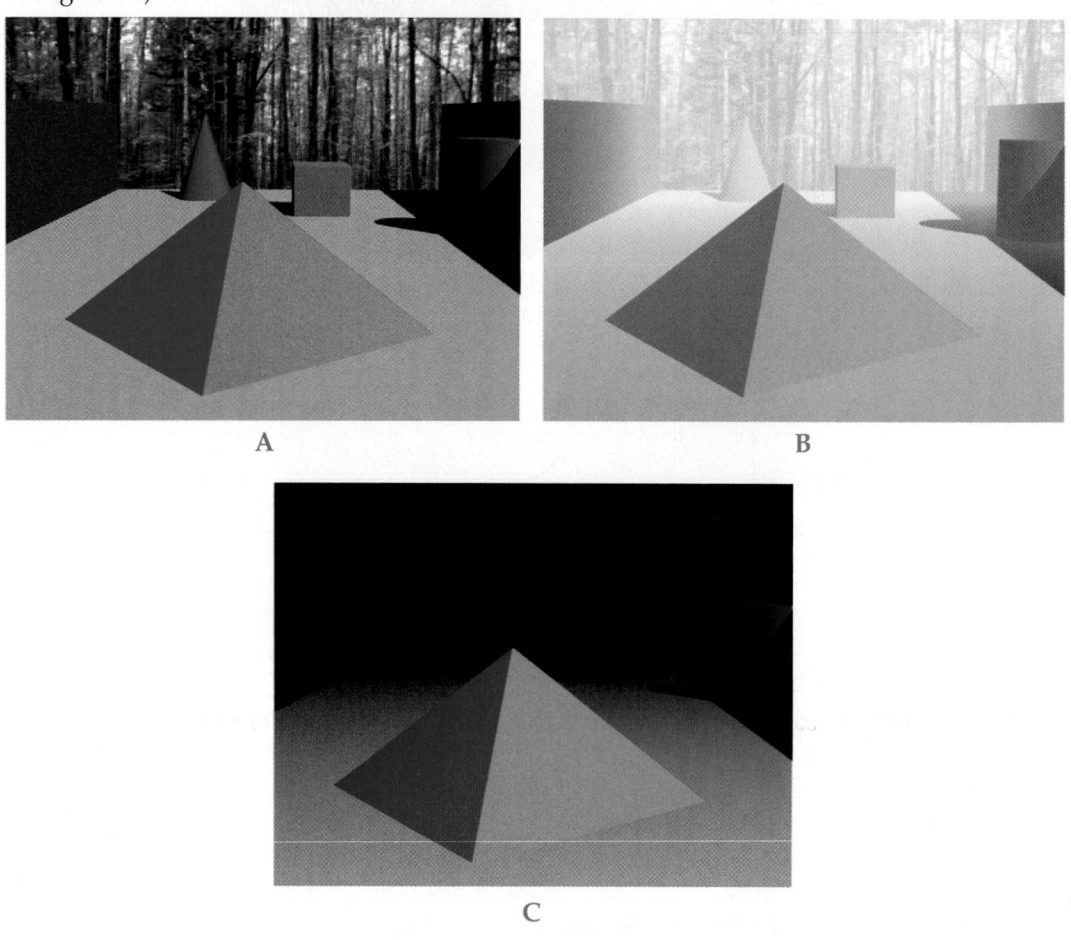

A

B

C

Figure 16-15.
The **Render Environment** dialog box is used to add fog/depth cueing to the scene.

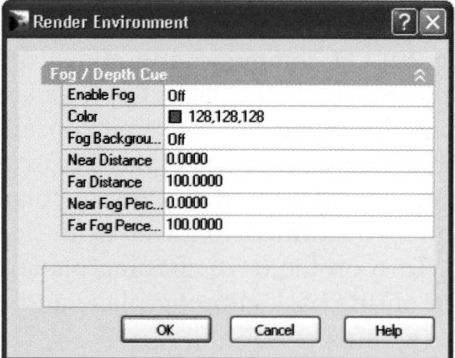

Adding Fog

Once a camera is created, open the **Render Environment** dialog box. To turn on fog/depth cueing, set the Enable Fog property to On. To set the color of the effect, select the Color property. Then, choose a color in the drop-down list. The Select Color... entry displays the **Select Color** dialog box. The Fog Background property determines whether or not the background is affected by the fog/depth cueing just like everything else.

The Near Distance property sets where the fog/depth cueing begins. This is a distance from the camera. The value can be from 0.0000 to 100.0000, which is a percentage of the total distance between the camera and the back clipping plane. The back clipping plane is where the target is located. The Far Distance property sets where the fog ends. This is also a distance from the camera. The value is also a percentage of the total distance from the camera to the back clipping plane and can be from 0.0000 to 100.0000. In other words, 100% ends at the back clipping plane.

The Near Fog Percentage property determines the opacity of the fog at its starting location. A value of 100 means the fog is 100% opaque. The near percentage is usually set to 0, or 0% opaque. The Far Fog Percentage property determines the opacity of the fog at its ending location. The fog/depth cueing will increase in opacity from the near distance to the far distance starting with the near fog percentage and ending with the far fog percentage.

Exercise 16-3

Complete the exercise on the Student CD.

Chapter Test

Answer the following questions. Write your answers on a separate sheet of paper or complete the electronic chapter test on the Student CD.

1. Describe the three panes of the **Render** window.
2. What are the three possible destinations for render output?
3. What is *sampling* and what do the properties in the **Sampling** subcategory in the **Advanced Render Settings** window control?
4. Raytracing calculates shadows, _____, and _____.
5. How does global illumination simulate bounced light?
6. What is the benefit of final gathering?
7. For what is the Energy multiplier property in the **List Properties** subcategory in the **Advanced Render Settings** window used?
8. For what are the properties in the **Diagnostic** category of the **Advanced Render Settings** window used?
9. Describe how to create a custom render preset.
10. What is *fog/depth cueing?*
11. What do you need to set up before adding fog/depth cueing?
12. What is the name of the dialog box in which fog/depth cueing is added to a scene?

Drawing Problems

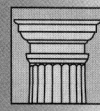

1. Using the drawing from problem 2 in Chapter 15, you will experiment with advanced render settings.
   A. Open drawing P15_02 and save it as P16_01.
   B. Make sure all of the lights are active and render the scene to the **Render** window using the Medium or High render preset.
   C. In the **Advanced Render Settings** window, enable global illumination. Then, render the scene again.
   D. Enable final gathering and render the scene again. This time it will probably take much longer to render.
   E. Which rendering has the best quality?
   F. Which setting impacted render time the most?
   G. Save the last image as P16_01.jpg.
   H. Save the drawing.

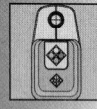

2. In this problem, you will set up fog/depth cueing.
   A. Start a new drawing and save it as P16_02.
   B. Draw a planar surface that is 50 units × 20 units.
   C. Randomly place various objects (cones, boxes, spheres, etc.) on the plane. Assign a different color or material to each object.
   D. Create a viewpoint that is almost at ground level looking down the length of the plane. Try to get as many objects in the view as possible. Save this as a named view and add a background of some type.
   E. Add a distant light source. Position it and adjust its intensity so that interesting shadows are created in the scene, but the objects are sufficiently illuminated.
   F. With the **3DCLIP** command, set up clipping planes with the back clipping plane at the far end of the plane. Make sure the back clipping plane is on.
   G. In the **Render Environment** dialog box, turn on fog and set the color to black. The far distance should be 100 and the percentage should be around 75.
   H. Render the scene.
   I. Change the fog color to white and render the scene again.
   J. Set the fog to affect the background and render the scene again.
   K. Save the image as P16_02.jpg.
   L. Save the drawing.

3. In this problem, you will experiment with the **RENDEREXPOSURE** command and final gathering. Open P15_05 created in Chapter 15 and save it as P16_03. If you did not complete this problem, do so now.

A. Open the **Advanced Render Settings** window. In the **General** category, set the Exposure Type property to Logarithmic.

B. In the **Indirect Illumination** category, change the Mode property in the **Final Gather** subcategory to Off.

C. Render the scene and note the appearance.

D. Use the **RENDEREXPOSURE** command to display the **Adjust Rendered Exposure** dialog box. Note the appearance of the preview image.

E. Change the brightness setting to 80 and note how the preview changes.

F. Pick the **OK** button to close the **Adjust Rendered Exposure** dialog and render the scene again. Does the rendered scene match the preview in the **Adjust Rendered Exposure** dialog box?

G. Turn on final gathering (Mode property = On) and open the **Adjust Rendered Exposure** dialog box. How does the preview look different? Why?

H. Adjust the brightness setting to get the exposure that you want in the preview. Then, close the dialog box and render the scene again.

I. Experiment with the other settings in the **Adjust Rendered Exposure** dialog until you get the scene the way you want it.

J. Render the scene one last time and save the image as a file called P16_03.jpg.

K. Save the drawing.

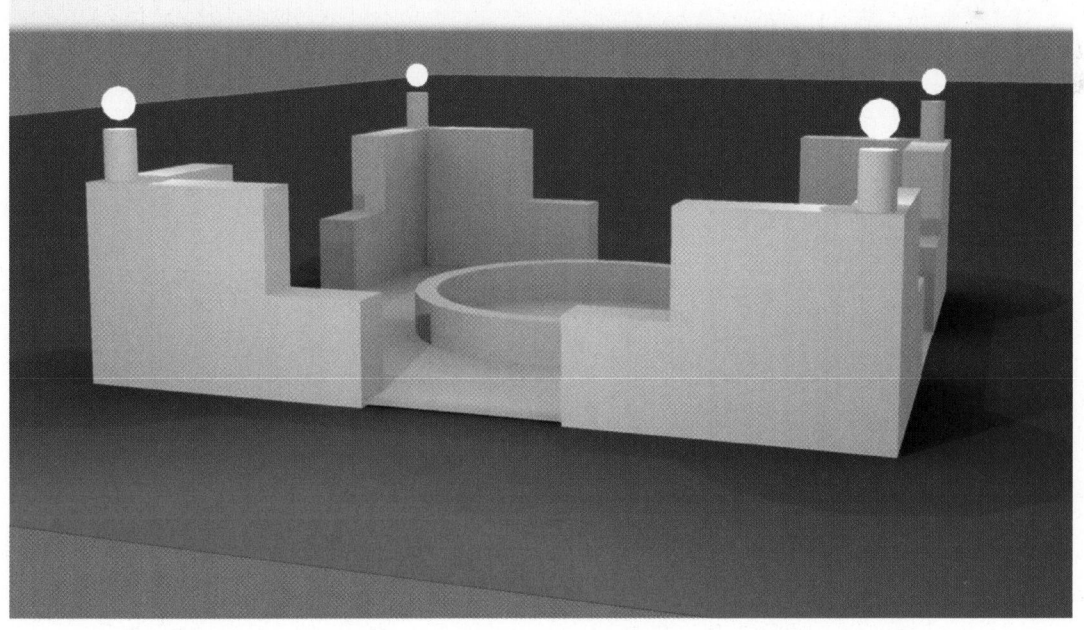

4. Using the same drawing from problem 16-3, you will perform diagnostics to determine the effects of the lights on the final rendering.
   A. Open drawing P16_03 and save it as P16_04.
   B. In the **Advanced Render Settings** window, select the Medium rendering preset. In the **Indirect Illumination** category, turn off final gathering (Mode property = Off).
   C. In the **Diagnostic** category of the **Advanced Render Settings** window, set the Grid property to Object. Render the scene.
   D. In the **Diagnostic** category of the **Advanced Render Settings** window, set the Grid property to World. Render the scene.
   E. In the **Diagnostic** category of the **Advanced Render Settings** window, set the Grid property to Camera. Render the scene.
   F. Describe the differences and explain why this is helpful in analyzing a scene.
   G. In the **Indirect Illumination** category of the **Advanced Render Settings** window, turn on global illumination. In the **Diagnostic** category, turn off the grid and set the Photon property to Density.
   H. Render the scene. Describe the effect and what can be learned from it.
   I. Set the Photon property to Irradiance and render the scene. What does this effect tell about the lighting in the scene?
   J. Which diagnostic worked the best and why?
   K. Save the drawing.

CHAPTER 17

Cameras, Walkthroughs, and Flybys

Learning Objectives

After completing this chapter, you will be able to:

✓ Create a camera to define a static 3D view.
✓ Activate and adjust front and back clipping planes.
✓ Record a walkthrough of a 3D model to a movie file.
✓ Record a flyby of a 3D model to a movie file.
✓ Create walkthroughs and flybys by following a path.
✓ Control the viewpoint, speed, and quality of the animation.

Once you have a 3D design complete, or even while still in the conceptual phase of design, you may want to take a stroll through the model and have a look around. You may also want to strap on some wings and fly over and around the model to see it from above. A *walkthrough animation* shows a scene as a person would view it walking through the scene. Walkthroughs often show the interior of a building. However, walkthroughs can be created for exterior scenes as well. A *flyby animation* is similar to a walkthrough, except that the person is not bound by gravity. In other words, the scene is viewed as a bird would see it flying through the scene. Flybys often show the exterior of a building.

The **3DWALK** command is used to create a walkthrough by recording views as a camera "walks" through the scene. The **3DFLY** command is very similar, but the movement of the camera is not limited to a single Z value. A path can also be drawn and the camera linked to the path. This chapter discusses these commands and other methods needed to create the animation you need. In addition, creating and using cameras is discussed.

Creating Cameras

Cameras are used in AutoCAD to store a viewpoint and easily recall it later when needed for viewing or rendering the scene. After the camera is established, you can zoom, pan, and orbit as needed, and then come back to the camera view. It is not necessary to create a camera before using the **3DWALK**, **3DFLY**, and **ANIPATH** commands (discussed later) because these commands create their own cameras.

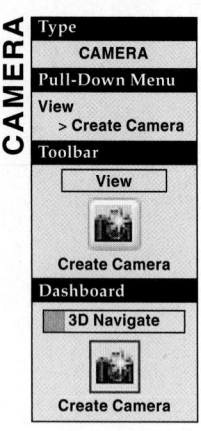

CAMERA

Type
CAMERA
Pull-Down Menu
View
> Create Camera
Toolbar
View
Create Camera
Dashboard
3D Navigate
Create Camera

The **CAMERA** command allows you to add a camera to the scene. Cameras are normally placed in the plan view of the scene to make it easy for you to pick where you want to "stand" and where you want to "look." Once the command is selected, you are first prompted to specify the camera location. A camera glyph is placed in the scene at the camera location, **Figure 17-1.** Next, you must specify the target location. As you move the cursor before picking the target location, a pyramid-shaped field of view indicates what will be seen in the view. Once you select the target location, the command remains active for you to select an option:

Enter an option [?/Name/LOcation/Height/Target/LEns/Clipping/View/eXit]<eXit>:

The list, or **?**, option allows you to list the cameras in the drawing. Type an asterisk (*) to show all of the cameras in the drawing. You can also enter a name or part of a name and an asterisk. For example, entering HOUSE* will list all of the cameras whose name begins with HOUSE, such as HOUSE_SW, HOUSE_SE, and HOUSE_PLAN.

The **Name** option allows you to change the name of the camera as you create it. If you do not rename the camera, it is given a default, sequential name, such as Camera1, Camera2, Camera3, and so on. It is always a good idea to provide meaningful names for cameras. Names such as Living Room_SW, Corner, or Hallway_Looking East leave no doubt as to what the camera shows. If you choose not to rename the camera at this point, it can be renamed later using the **Properties** window.

The **Location** option allows you to change the placement of the camera. Enter the option and then specify the new location. You can enter coordinates or pick a location in the drawing.

The **Height** option allows you to change the vertical location of the camera. Enter the option and then enter the height of the camera. The value you enter is the number of units from the current XY plane.

The **Target** option allows you to change the placement of the camera target. Enter the option and then specify the new location. You can enter coordinates or pick a location in the drawing.

The **Lens** option allows you to change the focal length of the camera lens. If you change the lens focal length, you are really changing the field of view, or the area of the drawing that the camera covers. The lower the lens focal length, the wider the field of view angle. The focal length is measured in millimeters.

The **Clipping** option is used to turn the front and back clipping planes on or off. These planes are used to limit what is shown in the camera view. Clipping planes are discussed later in this chapter.

The **View** option is used to change the current view to that shown by the camera. This option has two choices—**Yes** or **No**. If you select Yes, the active viewport switches to the camera view and the **CAMERA** command ends. If you select **No**, the previous prompt returns.

Figure 17-1.
A camera is represented by a glyph. When the camera is selected, the field of view (shown in color) and grips are displayed.

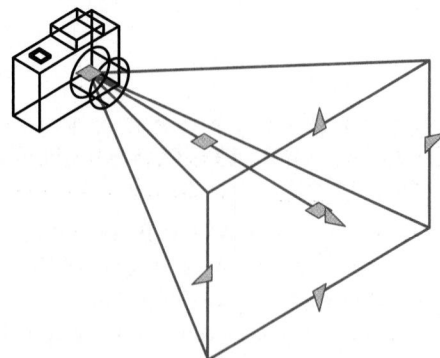

Once you have made all settings, press [Enter] or select the **Exit** option to end the command. The view (camera) is listed with the other saved views in the drop-down list in the **3D Navigate** control panel in the **Dashboard** or on the **3D Navigation** toolbar. It is also listed under the Model Views branch in the **View Manager** dialog box. Selecting the view makes it the current view in the active viewport.

Camera System Variables

The **CAMERADISPLAY** system variable controls the visibility of camera glyphs. When set to 1, which is the default, camera glyphs are displayed. When set to 0, camera glyphs are not displayed. Creating a camera automatically sets the variable to 1.

When creating a camera, if you pick the camera and target locations without using object snaps, you may assume that the camera and target are located on the XY plane (Z coordinate of 0) of the current UCS. This may or may not be true. The **CAMERAHEIGHT** system variable determines the default height of the camera if a Z coordinate is not provided. It is a good idea to set this variable to a typical eye height before placing cameras. There is no corresponding system variable for the target because the target is usually placed by snapping to an object of interest. If X and Y coordinates are entered for the target location, but a Z coordinate is not provided, the Z value is automatically 0.

Camera Tool Palette

The **Camera** tool palette provides a quick way to add a camera, but the default tools do not allow for the options described earlier. The **Normal Camera** tool creates a camera with a 50 mm focal length. This camera simulates normal human vision. The **Wide-angle Camera** tool creates a camera with a 35 mm focal length. This type of view is commonly used for scenery or interior views where it is important to show as much as possible with minimal distortion. The **Extreme Wide-angle Camera** tool creates a camera with a 6 mm focal length. This camera produces a fish-eye view, which is very distorted and mainly useful for special effects.

When using the **Properties** window to modify one of these cameras, there is no Field of view or Lens length property. Instead, you can adjust the height and width of the 3D box.

Changing the Camera View

Once the camera is placed, it is easy to manipulate. If you select a camera, the **Camera Preview** window is displayed by default. This window shows the view through the camera, **Figure 17-2.** The view in the window can be displayed in the 3D Hidden, 3D Wireframe, Conceptual, Realistic, or any other named visual style. Select the visual style in the drop-down list in the window. If the **Display this window when editing a camera** check box at the bottom of the window is unchecked, the window is not displayed the next time a camera is selected. The next time the drawing is opened, this setting is restored (checked).

Figure 17-2.
The **Camera Preview**
window is displayed,
by default, when a
camera is selected.

When a camera is selected, grips are displayed. Refer to **Figure 17-1.** If you hover the cursor over a grip, a tooltip appears indicating what the grip will alter. Picking the base grip on the camera allows you to reposition the camera in the scene. If the **Camera Preview** window is open, watch the preview as you move the camera to help guide you. Selecting the grip on the target allows the target to be repositioned. Again, use the preview in the **Camera Preview** window as a guide. The grip at the midpoint between the camera and target can be used to reposition the camera and target at the same time. If you pick and move one of the arrow grips on the end of the field of view, the lens focal length and field of view are changed.

The **Properties** window can also be used to change the camera settings. In the **Camera** category, you can change the location of the camera and target, the lens focal length, the field of view, and the roll angle. You can also set the camera glyph to plot by changing the Plot property to Yes. In the **Clipping** category, you can adjust the clipping planes. Clipping planes are discussed in the next section.

Camera Clipping Planes

Clipping planes allow you to suppress objects in the foreground or background of your scene. Picture these clipping planes as flat, 2D objects perpendicular to the line of sight that can be moved closer to or farther from the viewer. Only the objects between the front and back clipping planes, and within the field of view, are seen in the camera view. This is helpful for eliminating walls, roofs, or any other clutter that may take away from the focus of the scene. Also, as mentioned in Chapter 16, the back clipping plane should be enabled when applying fog/depth cueing using the **Render Environment** dialog box. Clipping planes can be set while creating the camera or later using the **Properties** window.

To set the clipping planes while creating the camera, enter the **Clipping** option. You are prompted:

Enable the front clipping plane? [Yes/No] <No>:

To enable the front clipping plane, enter YES. You are then asked to specify the offset from the target plane. This is described next. Once you enter the offset, or if you answer **No**, you are prompted:

Enable the back clipping plane? [Yes/No] <No>:

To enable the back clipping plane, enter YES and then specify the offset from the target plane.

The *target plane* is the 2D plane that is perpendicular to the line of sight and passing through the target point. Offsets for both front and back clipping planes are from this plane. Positive values place the clipping planes between the camera and the target

Figure 17-3.
Adjusting the clipping planes for a camera.

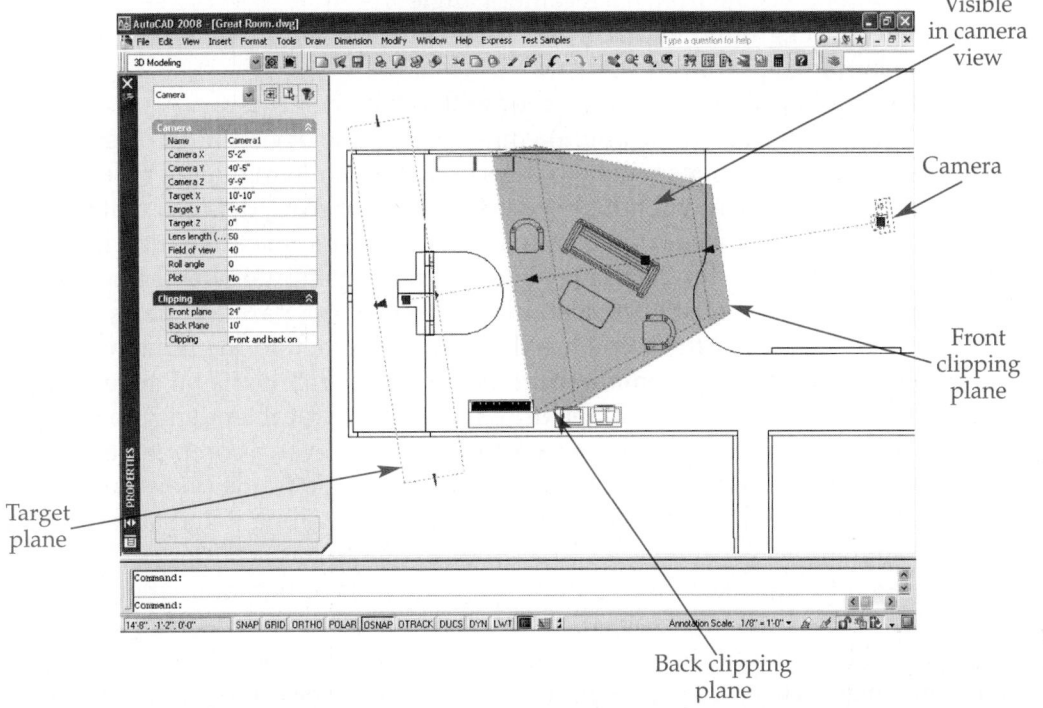

plane. Negative values place the planes on the opposite side of the target plane from the camera. You can place the clipping planes anywhere in the scene from the camera location to infinity. You cannot, however, place the back clipping plane in front of the front clipping plane.

The best way to adjust clipping planes is using the **Properties** window. Create the camera and then display a plan view of the camera and target (an approximate plan view is okay). Select the camera and open the **Properties** window. In the **Clipping** category, select the Clipping property. In the property drop-down list, select Front on, Back on, or Front and back on to turn on the appropriate clipping plane(s). Notice that the clipping planes are visible in the viewport, **Figure 17-3.** Next, enter offset values for the Front plane and Back plane properties, as appropriate. By displaying a plan view of the camera and target, you can see where the clipping planes are located and visualize their effect on the scene. If the **Camera Preview** window is open, the clipping is reflected in the preview.

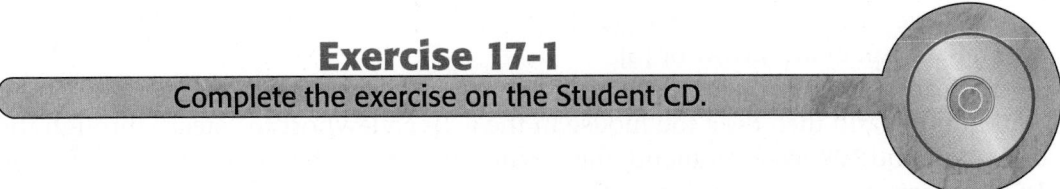

Exercise 17-1
Complete the exercise on the Student CD.

Animation Preparation

The tools presented in this chapter make it easy to lay out a path, plan camera angles, and record the movement of the camera. The resulting animation can be directly output to a number of movie file types that can be shared with others. However, there are some decisions to make first.

It is important to exactly plan out what you want to see in the animation. Think like a movie director and plan the "shots." Ask these questions:

- What will be visible from each camera angle?
- Is there a background in place?
- Is the lighting appropriate?
- Will a simple walkthrough suffice, or will a flyby be necessary?
- How close is the viewer (camera) going to be to the objects in the scene?

The answers to these questions will help determine the modeling detail required. Do not model anything that will not be seen. Also, do not place detailed materials on objects that are not the focus of the animation. Processing the animation may take a long time. Unnecessary detail may bog down the computer. In addition, walkthroughs and flybys must be created in perspective, not parallel, views.

The "visual quality" of the scene has the biggest impact on the time involved in rendering the animation. An animation can be rendered in any visual style or using any render preset that is available in the drawing. It is a natural tendency to render at the highest level to make the animation look the best. However, a computer animation has a playback rate of 30 frames per second (fps). If a single frame (view) takes three minutes to render using the Presentation render preset, how long will it take to render a 30 second animation? An animation 30 seconds in length has 900 frames (30 fps × 30 seconds). If each frame takes three minutes to render, the entire animation will take 2700 minutes, or 45 hours, to render.

Are you willing to wait two or three days for a 30 second movie? How about your boss or your client? There are trade-offs and concessions to be made. Perform test renderings on static views and note the rendering time. Then, decide on the acceptable level of quality versus rendering time and move ahead with it.

Walking and Flying

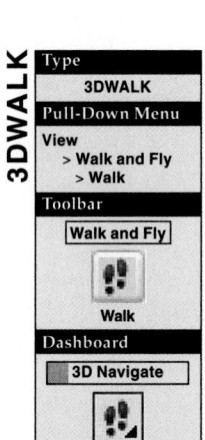

The process for creating a walkthrough or a flyby is the same. First, the command is initiated. Then, the movement is defined and recorded. Finally, the recorded movement is saved to an animation file.

When using the **3DWALK** and **3DFLY** commands, you can move through the scene using the arrow keys or the [W], [A], [S], and [D] keys on the keyboard to control your movements. Once either command is initiated, a dialog box appears that explains the key movements. See **Figure 17-4.** To continue with the command, pick the **Close** button. To redisplay this dialog box while the command is active, press the [Tab] key.

- **Move forward.** Up arrow or [W].
- **Move left.** Left arrow or [A].
- **Move right.** Right arrow or [D].
- **Back up.** Down arrow or [S].

You can also navigate through the scene using the mouse. Press and hold the left mouse button and then drag the mouse in the active viewport to "steer" through the scene. With the **3DWALK** command, the camera remains at the same Z value. With the **3DFLY** command, the Z position of the camera can change. The steps for creating a walkthrough or flyby are provided at the end of this section.

Position Locator

When the **3DWALK** or **3DFLY** command is initiated, the **Position Locator** window appears. See **Figure 17-5.** This window shows a plan view of the scene. The purpose of this window is to provide an overview of the scene, in plan, while you develop the animation. It does not need to be displayed to create an animation and can be closed if it takes up too much space or slows down the rendering.

Figure 17-4.
This dialog box shows
the keys that can be
used to navigate
through an animation.

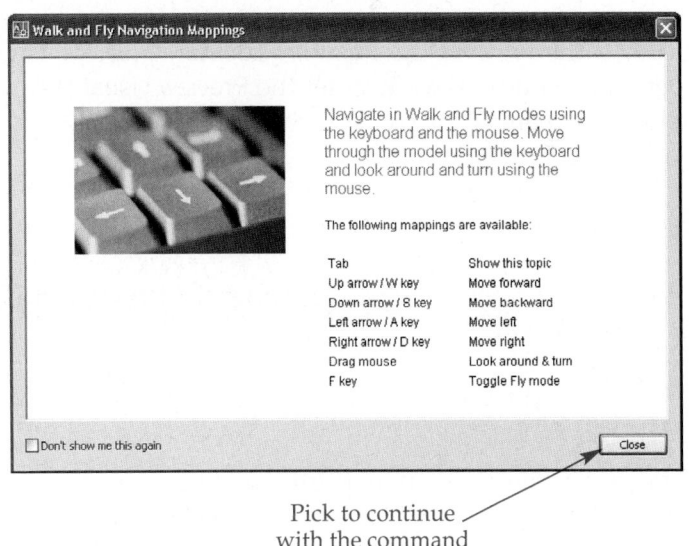

Pick to continue
with the command

Figure 17-5.
The **Position Locator**
window.

Target
indicator

Field of
view

Position
indicator

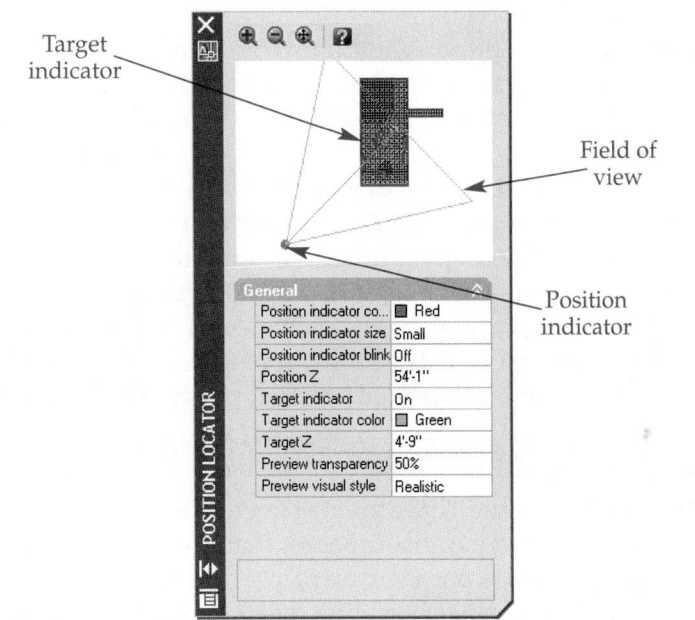

Position and target indicators appear in the plan view to show the location of the camera and its target. The green triangular shape displays the field of view. The *field of view* is the area within the camera's "vision." The field of view indicator is only displayed when the target indicator is displayed. By default, the position indicator is red. The target indicator is green by default. These properties can be changed in the **General** category at the bottom of the **Position Locator** window.

You can reposition the camera and the target in the plan view simply by picking and dragging either indicator. The effect of the change is visible in the active viewport. Moving the position and target indicators closer together reduces the field of view. Picking the field of view lines and dragging moves the position and target indicators at the same time.

In addition to changing the color of the position and target indicators, the properties in the **General** category can be used to modify the display in the **Position Locator** window. The Position indicator size property determines if the indicators are displayed small, medium, or large. If the Position indicator blink property is set to On, the indicators flash on and off in the preview. The Preview visual style property sets the visual style for the preview. This setting does not affect the current viewport or the animation. The

Preview transparency property is set to 50% by default, but can be changed to whatever you want. If the view in the **Position Locator** window is obscured by something (a roof, perhaps), you may want to set the Preview visual style property to 3D Hidden and the Preview transparency property to 80 or 90 percent. This will make the objects under the roof visible.

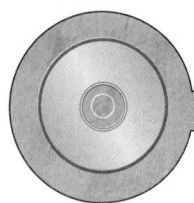

Exercise 17-2
Complete the exercise on the Student CD.

Walk and Fly Settings

WALKFLYSETTINGS

Type
WALKFLYSETTINGS

Pull-Down Menu
View
> Walk and Fly
> Walk and Fly
Settings

Toolbar
Walk and Fly

Walk and Fly
Settings...

Dashboard
3D Navigate

Walk and Fly
Settings

General settings for walkthroughs and flybys are made in the **Walk and Fly Settings** dialog box. See **Figure 17-6**. Open this dialog box by picking the **Walk and Fly Settings** button in the **3D Navigate** control panel in the **Dashboard** (in the **Walk** flyout). It can also be displayed by picking the **Walk and Fly Settings...** button in the **3D Modeling** tab of the **Options** dialog box.

The three radio buttons at the top of the dialog box are used to determine when the dialog box shown in **Figure 17-4** is displayed. The check box determines if the **Position Locator** window is automatically displayed when the **3DWALK** or **3DFLY** command is entered.

The text boxes in **Current Drawing Settings** area determine the size of each step and the number of steps per second. The **Walk/fly step size:** setting controls the **STEPSIZE** system variable. This is the number of units that the camera moves in one step. The **Steps per second:** setting controls the **STEPSPERSEC** system variable. This is the number of steps the camera takes each second. Together, these two settings determine how fast the camera moves in the animation. Both settings can also be made in the expanded area of the **3D Navigate** control panel in the **Dashboard**.

PROFESSIONAL TIP

You will have to experiment with step size and steps per second values to make an animation that is easy to watch. Start with low numbers and work your way up. Fast movements are disorienting and make the viewer feel like they are missing something. The viewer should be able to take their time and get a good look at your design.

To get a feel for the proper speed for a walkthrough, pay attention to the next movie or TV show that you watch. When the director wants you to get a good look at the setting for the scene, the camera very slowly pans around the room. To emphasize distance, the camera slowly zooms in to a target object or person.

3D Navigate Control Panel

The **3D Navigate** control panel in the **Dashboard** contains all of the tools for creating a walkthrough or flyby. See **Figure 17-7**. If the **Dashboard** is not visible, display it by typing DASHBOARD. The expanded portion of the **3D Navigate** control panel contains tools specific to creating and controlling walkthroughs and flybys.

Camera tools

The **Lens Length** and **Field of View** slider and text boxes control how much of the scene is seen by the camera. The *lens length* refers to the focal length of the camera lens. The higher the number, the closer you are to the subject. The range is from

Figure 17-6.
General settings for
the walkthrough or
flyby are made in the
Walk and Fly Settings
dialog box.

Check to
automatically
display the
Position Locator
window

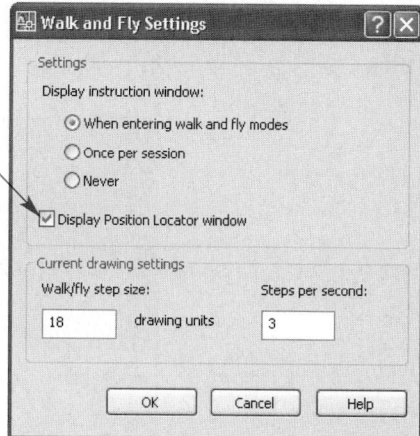

Figure 17-7.
The **3D Navigate**
control panel in the
Dashboard.

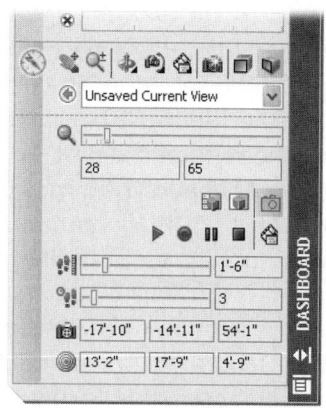

1 to 100000; 50 is a good starting point. The field of view is directly related to the lens length and changes along with it. The higher the number, the wider the angle of the view. The settings can be changed using either the slider or the text boxes.

The **Multiple Viewports** and **Single Viewport** buttons toggle between a single-viewport configuration and a multiple-viewport configuration. Whichever multiple-viewport configuration was last set current using the **VPORTS** command is restored by picking the **Multiple Viewports** button. Picking the **Single Viewport** button displays a single-viewport configuration of the active viewport. Using multiple viewports are a good idea when setting up walkthroughs and flybys. Use one of the preset 3D viewport configurations or set up your own to show the scene from different angles. The **Multiple Viewports** and **Single Viewport** buttons are a very convenient way to switch back and forth.

In Chapter 15, you learned that point and spotlights are represented in viewports by light glyphs. Cameras are also represented by glyphs. The **Display Cameras** button toggles the display of camera glyphs on and off. The button is orange when camera glyphs are displayed.

At the bottom of the expanded **3D Navigate** control panel are text boxes for the camera and target positions. These text boxes can be used to change the X, Y, and Z coordinates for the camera or target. It is usually easier to change the X and Y locations in the **Position Locator** window, but the Z coordinate cannot be set there. The Z coordinate determines eye level.

Animation tools

After the animation is recorded and saved, picking the **Play Animation** button opens the **Animation Preview** dialog box in which the animation is played, Figure 17-8. The controls in this dialog box can be used to rewind, pause, and play the animation.

Figure 17-8.
The animation is
played in the **Animation
Preview** dialog box.

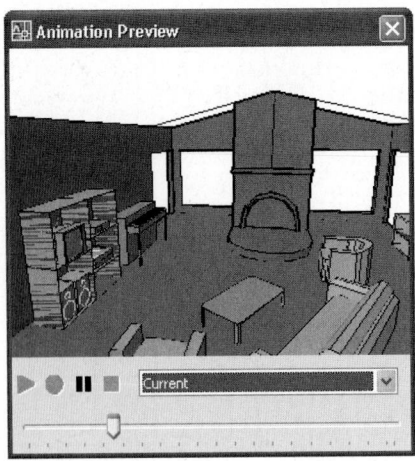

The slider can be dragged to preview part of the animation or move to a specific frame. The visual style can also be set using the drop-down list. If the animation is created using a render preset, the file must be played in Windows Media Player or another media player to view the rendered detail.

The **Start Recording Animation** button is used to initiate recording of camera movement. When the **3DWALK** or **3DFLY** command is active, the button is red until recording is initiated. Then, it turns gray until the pause or stop button is picked. Make sure that you are ready to start moving when you pick the **Start Recording Animation** button because record starts as soon as the button is picked.

Picking the **Pause Recording Animation** button temporarily stops recording. This allows you to make adjustments to the view without recording the adjustment. When you are ready to begin recording again, pick the record button to resume.

Picking the **Save Animation** button stops recording and opens the **Save As** dialog box. Name the animation file, navigate to a location, and pick the **Save** button.

Picking the **Animation Settings** button opens the **Animation Settings** dialog box. The next section describes this dialog box in detail.

CAUTION

While the **3DWALK** or **3DFLY** command is active and the record button is on (gray), you are creating an animation. If you move the camera in the **Position Locator** window and start re-recording the animation to correct a problem, but do not first exit the current **3DWALK** or **3DFLY** command session, you are adding another segment to the animation you just previewed. To start over, exit the current command session first.

Exercise 17-3
Complete the exercise on the Student CD.

Animation settings

The **Animation Settings** dialog box may contain the most important settings pertaining to walkthroughs and flybys. See **Figure 17-9.** These animation settings determine how good the animation looks, how long it is going to take to complete, and

Figure 17-9.

Figure 17-9.
The **Animation Settings** dialog box contains important settings pertaining to walkthroughs and flybys.

Select a visual style or render preset

Animation Settings

Settings

Visual style:
Conceptual

Resolution:
320 x 240

Set the resolution

Frame rate (FPS):
30

Format:
WMV

Set the frame rate

Select the output file type

OK   Cancel   Help

how big the file will be. The dialog box is displayed by picking the **Animation Settings** button in the **3D Navigate** control panel in the **Dashboard** or the **Animation Settings...** in the **Save As** dialog box displayed when saving an animation.

The **Visual Style:** drop-down list is used to set the shading level in the animation. The name of this drop-down list is a little misleading because visual styles and render presets are available. The higher the shading or rendering level selected in this drop-down list, the longer the rendering will take to process and the bigger the file will be. If you have numerous lights casting shadows, detailed materials, and global illumination and final gathering enabled, settle in for a long wait. A simple, straight-ahead walkthrough of 10 or 15 feet can easily result in 300 frames of animation. If each frame takes about five seconds to render, that equals 1500 seconds, or 25 minutes, to create an animation file that is only 10 seconds long.

The **Frame Rate (FPS):** text box sets the number of frames per second for the playback. In other words, this sets the speed of the animation playback. The default is 30 fps, which is a common playback rate.

The **Resolution:** drop-down list offers standard choices of resolution, from 160 × 120 to 1024 × 768. These are measured in pixels × pixels. Remember, higher resolutions mean longer processing times and larger file sizes.

The **Format:** drop-down list is used to select the output file type. The file type must be set in this dialog box. It cannot be changed in the **Save As** dialog box. The choices of output file type are:
- **WMV.** The standard movie file format for Windows Media Player.
- **AVI.** Audio-Video Interleaved is the Windows standard for movie files.
- **MOV.** QuickTime® Movie is the standard file format for Apple® movie files.
- **MPG.** Moving Picture Experts Group (MPEG) is another very common movie file format.

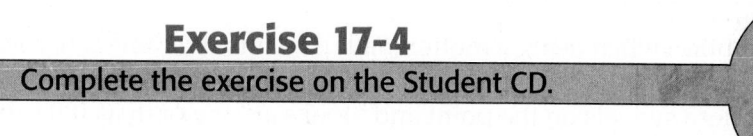

Exercise 17-4
Complete the exercise on the Student CD.

Steps to Create a Walkthrough or Flyby

1. Plan your animation: where you are moving from and to, what you are going to be looking at, and what will be the focal point of the scene.
2. Set up a multiple viewport configuration of three or four viewports.
3. In one of the viewports, create or restore a named view with the appropriate starting viewpoint. Make sure a background is set up, if desired.

Figure 17-10.
The **Creating Video**
dialog box is displayed
as AutoCAD generates
the animation.

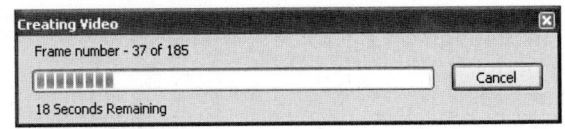

4. Start the **3DWALK** or **3DFLY** command and note in the **Position Locator** window the location of the camera and target, and the field of view. Adjust these in the expanded area of the **3D Navigate** control panel in the **Dashboard**, if necessary.
5. Open the **Animation Settings** dialog box and set up the desired shading, frame rate, resolution, and output file format.
6. Position your fingers over the navigation keys on the keyboard.
7. Pick the **Start Recording Animation** button.
8. Start navigating through the view. Try to keep the movements as smooth as possible. Any jerks and shakes will be visible in the animation.
9. When you are done, stop moving forward and then pick the stop (**Save Animation**) button. In the **Save As** dialog box, name and save the file.
10. The **Creating Video** dialog box is displayed as AutoCAD processes the frames, Figure 17-10.
11. When the **Creating Video** dialog is automatically closed, the animation file is saved and you can take a look at it. Pick the **Play Animation** button and watch the animation in the **Animation Preview** window. You can also locate the file using Windows Explorer. Then, double-click on the file to play the animation in Media Player (or whichever program is associated with the file type).
12. Exit the command. If you are not satisfied with the results and want to try it again, make sure to exit the command before you make another attempt at the walkthrough or flyby.

Motion Path Animation

You may have found it hard to create smooth motion using the keyboard and mouse. Fortunately, AutoCAD provides an easy way to create a nice, smooth animated walkthrough or flyby. This is done through the use of a motion path. A *motion path* is simply a line along which the camera, target, or both travel during the animation.

One method of using a motion path is to link the camera and target to a single path. The camera and its line of sight then follows the path much like a train follows tracks. See Figure 17-11.

Another option when using a motion path is to link the camera to a single point in the scene and the target to a path. For example, the target can be set to follow a circle or arc. The camera swivels on the point and "looks at" the path as if it is being rotated on a tripod. See Figure 17-12.

A third way to use a motion path is to have the camera follow a path, but have the target locked onto a stationary point. This is similar to riding in a vehicle and watching an object of interest on the side of the road. As the vehicle moves, your gaze remains fixed on the object. See Figure 17-13.

The fourth method of using a motion path is to have both the camera and target follow separate paths. Picture yourself walking into an unfamiliar room. As you walk into the center of the room, your gaze sweeps left and right across the room. In this case, the camera (you) follows a straight line path and the target (your gaze) follows an arc from one side of the room to the other.

Figure 17-11.
A—The camera and target are linked to the same path (shown in color). B—The camera looks straight ahead as it moves along the path.

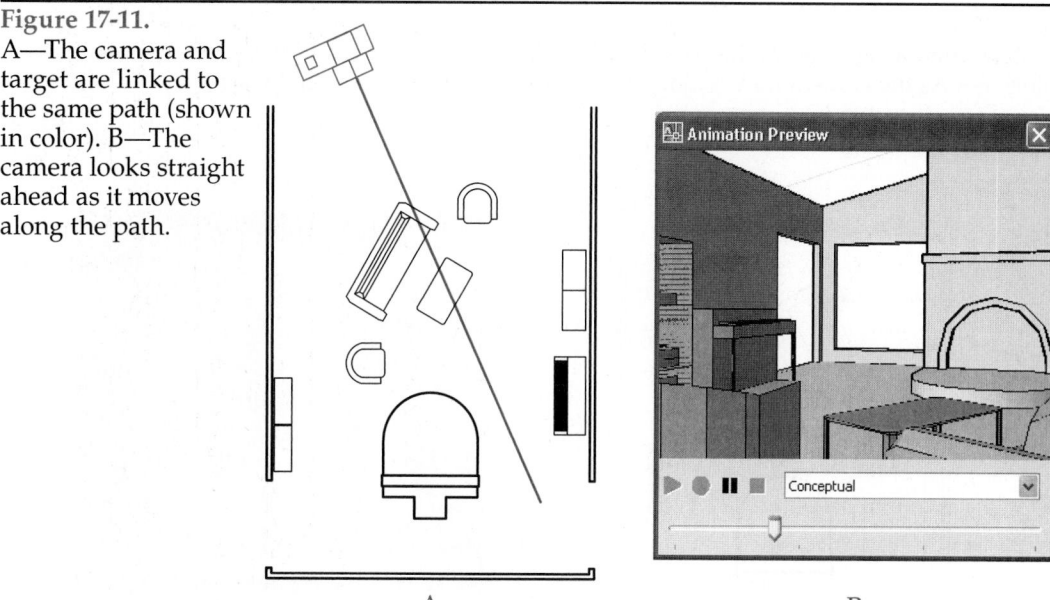

A   B

Figure 17-12.
A—The camera is linked to a point so it remains stationary. The target is linked to the circle.
B—The camera view rotates around the room as if the camera is on a swivel tripod.

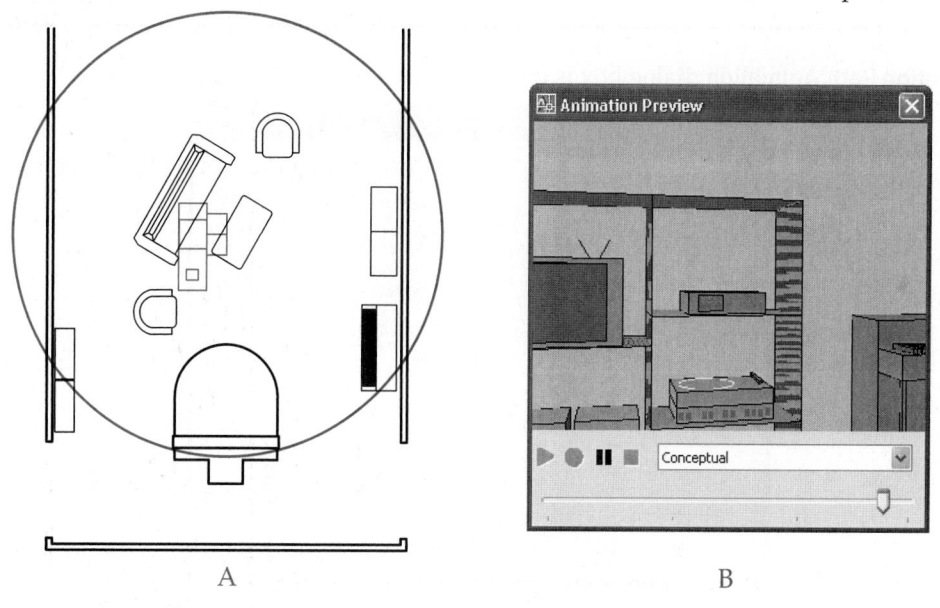

A   B

The **ANIPATH** command is used to assign motion paths. The command opens the **Motion Path Animation** dialog box. See **Figure 17-14.** This dialog box has three main areas: **Camera**, **Target**, and **Animation Settings**. These areas are described in detail in the next sections. The steps for creating a motion path animation are provided at the end of this section.

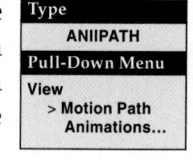

Type
ANIIPATH
Pull-Down Menu
View
  > Motion Path
    Animations...

ANIPATH

NOTE

Selecting a motion path automatically creates a camera. You cannot add a motion path to an existing camera.

Figure 17-13.
A—The camera is linked to the spline path and the target is linked to the point (shown in color). B—As the camera moves along the path, it always looks at the point.

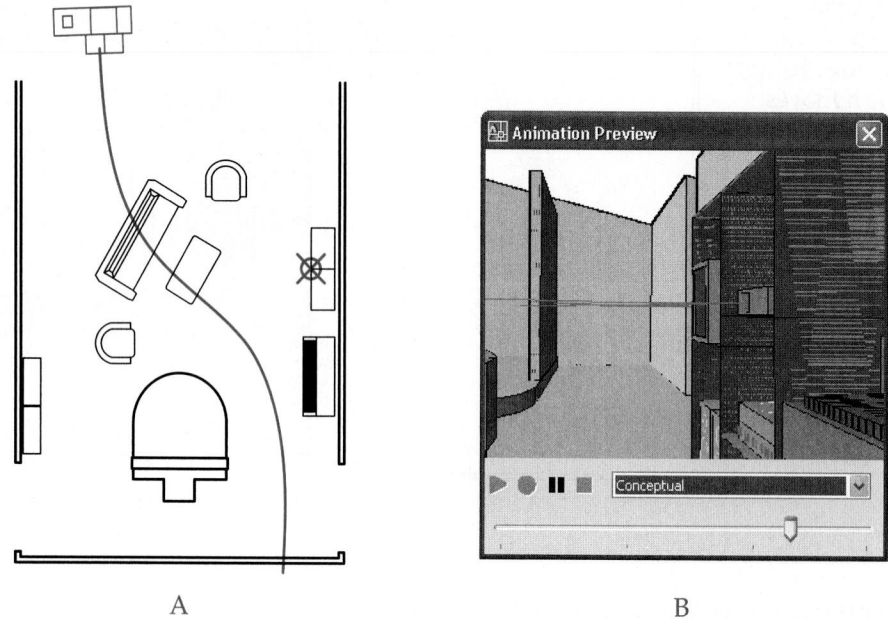

A

B

Figure 17-14.
The **Motion Path Animation** dialog box is used to create an animation that follows a path.

Camera path setting

Target path setting

Animation settings

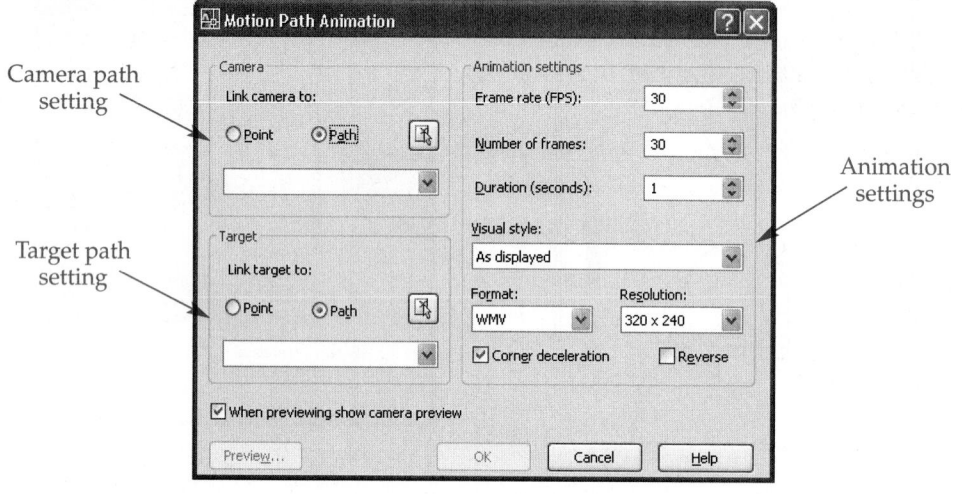

Camera Area

The camera can be linked to a path or a point. To select a path, pick the **Path** radio button and then pick the **Select Path** button. The dialog box is temporarily closed for you to select the path in the drawing. The path may be a line, arc, circle, ellipse, elliptical arc, polyline, 3D polyline, spline, or helix, but it must be drawn before the **ANIPATH** command is used. Splines are nice for motion paths because they are smooth and have gradual curves. The camera moves from the first point on the path to the last point on the path, so create paths with this in mind.

To select a stationary point, pick the **Point** radio button. Then, select the **Pick Point** button. When the dialog box is hidden, specify the location in the drawing. You can use object snaps or enter coordinates. It may be a good idea to have a point drawn and use object snaps to select the point.

The camera must be linked to either a path or a point. If neither is selected, the command cannot be completed. If you want the camera to remain stationary as the target moves, select the **Point** radio button and then pick the stationary point in the drawing.

Once a point or path has been selected, it is added to the drop-down list. All named motion paths and selected motion points in the drawing appear in this list. Instead of using the **Select Path** or **Pick Point** button, you can select the path or point in this drop-down list.

Target Area

The target is the location where the camera points. Like the camera, the target can be linked to a point or a path. To link the target to a path, select the **Path** radio button. Then, pick the **Select Path** button and select the path in the drawing. If the camera is linked to a point, the target must be linked to a path. If the camera is set to follow a path, then you actually have three choices for the target. It can be linked to a path, point, or nothing. To link the target to a point, pick the **Point** radio button. Then, select the **Pick Point** button to select the point in the drawing. The None option, which is selected in the drop-down list, means that the camera will look straight ahead down the path as it moves.

Animation Settings Area

Most of the settings in this area have the same effect as the corresponding settings in the **Animation Settings** dialog box. However, there are four settings unique to the **Motion Path Animation** dialog box.

The **Number of frames:** text box is used to set the total number of frames in the animation. Remember, a computer has a playback rate of 30 fps. Therefore, if the frame rate is set to 30, set the number of frames to 450 to create an animation that is 15 seconds long ($30 \times 15 = 450$).

The value in the **Duration (seconds):** text box is the total time of the animation. This value is automatically calculated based on the frame rate and number of frames. However, you can enter a duration value. Doing so will automatically change the number of frames based on the frame rate.

By default, the **Corner deceleration** check box is checked. This slows down the movement of the camera and target as they reach corners and curves on the path. If this is unchecked, the camera and target move at the same speed along the entire path, creating very jerky motion on curves and at corners. It is natural to decelerate on curves.

The **Reverse** check box simply switches the starting and ending points of the animation. If the camera (or target) travels from the first endpoint to the second endpoint, checking this check box makes the camera (or target) travel from the second endpoint to the first.

Previewing and Completing the Animation

To preview the animation, pick the **Preview...** button at the bottom of the **Motion Path Animation** dialog box. The camera glyph moves along the path in all viewports. If the **When previewing show camera preview** check box is checked, the **Animation Preview** window is also displayed and shows the animation.

To finish the animation, pick the **OK** button in the **Motion Path Animation** dialog box. The **Save As** dialog box is displayed. Name the file and specify the location. If you need to change the file type, pick the **Animation settings...** button to open the **Animation Settings** dialog box. Change the file type, close the dialog box, and continue with the save.

Steps to Create a Motion Path Animation

1. Plan your animation: where you are moving from and to, what you are going to be looking at, and what will be the focal point of the scene.
2. Draw the paths and points to which the camera and target will be linked. Draw the path in the direction the camera should travel (first point to last point). Do not draw any sharp corners on the paths and make sure that the Z value (height) is correct.
3. Start the **ANIPATH** command.
4. Pick the camera path or point.
5. Pick the target path or point (or None).
6. Adjust fps, number of frames, and duration to set the length and speed of the animation.
7. Select a visual style, the file format, and the resolution.
8. Preview the animation. Adjust settings, if needed.
9. Save the animation to a file.

Exercise 17-5
Complete the exercise on the Student CD.

Chapter Test

Answer the following questions. Write your answers on a separate sheet of paper or complete the electronic chapter test on the Student CD.

1. Which system variable controls the display of camera glyphs?
2. Name the three camera tools available on the **Camera** tool palette and explain the differences between them.
3. When is the **Camera Preview** window displayed, by default?
4. From where is the offset distance for the camera clipping planes measured?
5. What is the difference between the **3DWALK** and **3DFLY** commands?
6. How do you "steer" your movement when creating a walkthrough or flyby animation?
7. What is the *field of view?*
8. What is the purpose of the **Position Indicator** window?
9. In the **Walk and Fly Settings** dialog box, which settings combine to control the speed of the animation?
10. How do you start recording a walkthrough or flyby?
11. What must be done before correcting a motion error in a walkthrough or flyby?
12. What are the four file formats to which an animation may be saved in AutoCAD?
13. Motion path animation involves linking a camera or target to _____ or _____.
14. Which types of objects may be used as a motion path?
15. If None is selected as the target "path," what does the camera do in the animation?
16. Explain *corner deceleration.*

Drawing Problems

1. In this problem, you will create and manipulate a camera in a drawing from a previous chapter.

    A. Open drawing P16_02 from Chapter 16 and save it as P17_01.

    B. Create at least two viewports and display a plan view in one of them.

    C. Use the **CAMERA** command to create a camera looking at the objects from the southwest quadrant. Change the camera settings as needed to display a pleasing view of the scene.

    D. Name the camera SW View.

    E. Turn on both the front and back clipping planes. Adjust them to eliminate one object in the front and one object in the back.

    F. Open the **Camera** tool palette and create three more cameras with those tools looking at the scene from various locations. Change their names to Normal, Wide-angle, and Fish-eye to match the type of camera.

    G. Save the drawing.

2. In this problem, you will draw some basic 3D shapes to represent equipment in a small workshop. Then, you will create an animated walkthrough.

    A. Start a new drawing and set the units to architectural. Save it as P17_02.

    B. Draw a planar surface that is 15′ × 30′.

    C. Draw three 9′ tall walls enclosing the two long sides and one short side.

    D. Use boxes and a cylinder to represent equipment. Refer to the illustration shown below. Use your own dimensions.

    E. Use the **3DWALK** command to create an animation of walking into the workshop. Turn and look at the shelves at the end of the animation.

    F. Set the visual style to Conceptual and the resolution to 640 × 480.

    G. Save the animation to a file named P17_02.avi (or the format of your choice).

    H. Save the drawing.

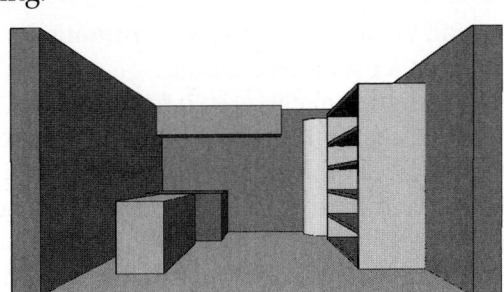

3. In this problem, you will create a motion path animation for the workshop drawn in Problem 17-2.
   A. Open drawing P17_02 and save it as P17_03.
   B. Draw a line and an arc similar to those shown in color below. The dimensions are not important.
   C. Move both objects so they are 4′ off of the floor.
   D. Using the **ANIPATH** command, link the camera to the line and the target to the arc. Set the resolution to 640 × 480.
   E. Preview the animation. Adjust the animation settings as necessary. You may need to slow down the animation quite a bit. How do you do this?
   F. Save the animation as a file named P17_03.wmv (or the file format of your choice).
   G. Save the drawing.

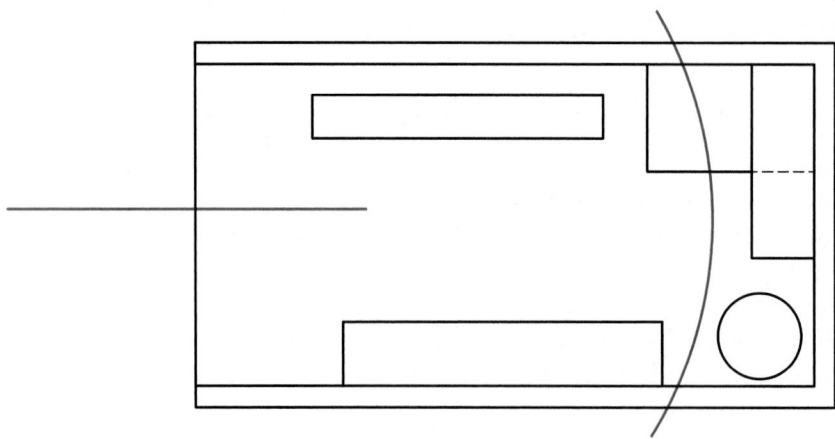

4. In this problem, you will create a motion path animation for presentation of a mechanical drawing from a previous chapter.
   A. Open drawing P15_03 and save it as P17_04.
   B. Draw a circle centered on the flange with a radius of 300.
   C. Move the circle 200 units in the Z direction.
   D. Using the **ANIPATH** command, link the camera to the circle and the target to the center of the flange.
   E. Preview the animation and adjust the animation settings as necessary. Due to the materials in the scene, the preview may play slowly, depending on the capabilities of your computer.
   F. Select a visual style that your computer can handle. Set the resolution to 320 × 240.
   G. Save the animation to a file named P17_04.avi (or the file format of your choice).
   H. Save the drawing.

5. In this problem, you will create a flyby of the building that you created in Chapter 15.
   A. Open drawing P15_01 and save it as P17_05.
   B. Create a perspective view of the scene that shows the building from slightly above it. Save the view.
   C. Start the **3DFLY** command. Practice with the movement keys to make sure you know how to fly around the temple. Then, cancel the command.
   D. Restore the starting view and select the **3DFLY** command.
   E. Record the flyby and save the animation as P17_05.wmv (or the file format of your choice).
   F. Save the drawing.

CHAPTER 18

Using Raster, Vector, and Web Graphics

Learning Objectives

After completing this chapter, you will be able to:

✓ Compare raster and vector files.
✓ Import and export raster files using AutoCAD.
✓ Import and export vector files using AutoCAD.
✓ Set image commands to manipulate inserted raster files.
✓ Create DWF files.
✓ Create PDF files.

One of the important aspects of drawing in AutoCAD is the ability to share information. Generally, this means sharing drawing data and geometry between CAD software, either other AutoCAD workstations or workstations using a different software. AutoCAD creates drawing data files in a format known as a *vector* file. However, you can also share your work, as images, with photo editing and desktop publishing software. In Chapter 13 through Chapter 17, you learned how to create realistic scenes and render them to files. A scene rendered to a file is a *raster* image. However, raster images used in AutoCAD do not have to be created in AutoCAD. They may also come from digital photographs, scanned images, or Internet sources. This chapter introduces using AutoCAD to work with raster and vector graphics files. This includes importing, exporting, and setting various parameters.

Introduction to Raster and Vector Graphics

In the world of electronic imaging, there are two basic types of files—raster and vector. AutoCAD drawings are called vector graphics. A *vector* is an object defined by XYZ coordinates. In other words, AutoCAD stores the mathematical definition of an object. *Pixels* (picture elements) are the "dots" or "bits" in the monitor that make up the display screen. When drawing vector objects in AutoCAD, your monitor uses pixels to create a representation of the object on the monitor. However, there is no relationship between the physical pixels in your monitor and a vector object. Pixels simply show the object at the current zoom percentage. Some common vector files are DWG, DXF, AI, and EPS.

Many illustrations created with drawing, painting, and presentation software are saved as raster files. A *raster file* creates a picture or image file using the location and color of the screen pixels. In other words, a raster file is made up of "dots." Raster files are usually called *bitmaps.* There are several types of raster files used for presentation graphics and desktop publishing. Some common raster file types include TIFF, JPEG, and GIF.

Working with Raster Files

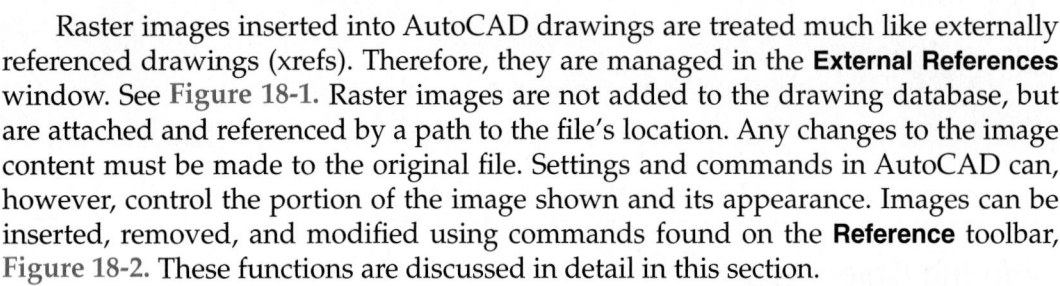

Raster images inserted into AutoCAD drawings are treated much like externally referenced drawings (xrefs). Therefore, they are managed in the **External References** window. See **Figure 18-1.** Raster images are not added to the drawing database, but are attached and referenced by a path to the file's location. Any changes to the image content must be made to the original file. Settings and commands in AutoCAD can, however, control the portion of the image shown and its appearance. Images can be inserted, removed, and modified using commands found on the **Reference** toolbar, **Figure 18-2.** These functions are discussed in detail in this section.

At the top of the **External References** window is a drop-down list containing buttons for attaching drawings (DWG), image files, DWF files, and DGN files. The **File References** area lists all files currently attached to the drawing, whether they are drawings, images, DXF files, or DGN files. Right-clicking on an entry displays a shortcut menu that allows you to unload, reload, and detach the files. At the bottom of the window is the **Details** or **Preview** pane. The buttons in the title bar are used to toggle between the **Details** pane and the **Preview** pane. The **Details** pane displays information about the file selected in the **File References** area. The **Preview** pane shows a preview of the selected file.

Figure 18-1.
The **External References** window is used to manage attached images. A—Displayed with a list and details. B—Displayed with a tree and a preview.

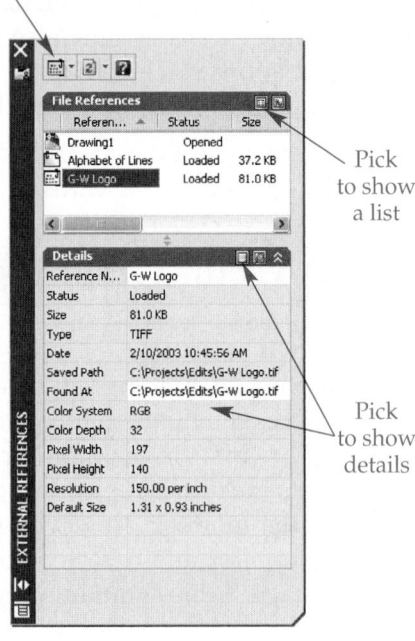

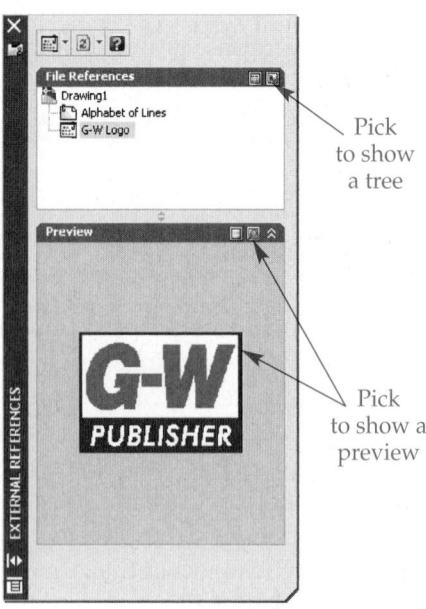

A   B

Figure 18-2.
The **Reference** toolbar
contains buttons for
the "image family"
of commands.

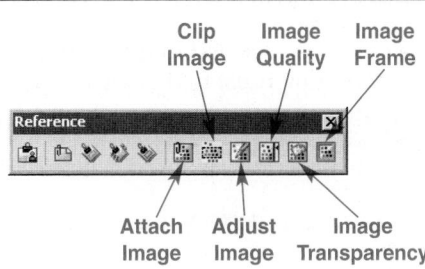

There are many different types of raster files. Some raster files used in industry today are:

- **Tagged Image File Format (TIFF).** A file format developed by Aldus Corporation and Microsoft Corporation. This is one of the most commonly used image file types.
- **Joint Photographic Experts Group (JPEG).** A highly compressed graphics image file. This type of file is very common on websites. Also known as a JPG file.
- **Graphics Interchange Format (GIF).** A file format developed to allow the exchange of graphic images over an online computer service, such as the Internet. This type of file is sometimes found on websites, often animated.
- **Personal Computer Exchange (PCX).** A file format developed by Z-Soft Corporation. This type of file has certain applications, but is not used much anymore.
- **Bitmap (BMP).** A file format developed by Microsoft Corporation. Like PCX, there are certain applications for this type of file. However, overall, this file type is not used much anymore.

Other raster file types can also be imported into AutoCAD. If you have a raster image that cannot be directly imported, you will need to first import the file into a paint or draw program. Then, export the image in a format that AutoCAD can read.

Inserting Raster Images

The **IMAGEATTACH** command is used to attach an image file to a drawing. When the command is selected, the **Select Image File** dialog box is displayed, Figure 18-3. Pick the **Files of type:** drop-down list to display all of the raster file types that can be used. If a folder contains a wide variety of raster files, you can quickly narrow your search by picking one of the file types in this list. Then, select the raster file and pick **Open**. This displays the **Image** dialog box, Figure 18-4.

The image name and path to the image file are displayed at the top of the **Image** dialog box. Also displayed is the path that will be saved in the drawing. You can choose to save the full path, a relative path, or no path. The type of path is selected in the **Path type** drop-down list.

A *full path* specifies the complete location of the image file, such as c:\images\building.tif. If the image file is moved from this location, AutoCAD cannot find it.

A *relative path* specifies the location of the image file based on the location of the drawing file. For example, the path .\images tells AutoCAD that the image file is located in a subfolder (named images) of the folder where the drawing is located. The entry ..\images tells AutoCAD to look for the file by moving up one folder from where the drawing is stored and then in the subfolder \images. The entry ..\..\images tells AutoCAD to move up two folders and then look in the subfolder \images. The current drawing must be saved in order to specify a relative path.

The *no path* option tells AutoCAD that the image is located in the same folder as the drawing. If the image file is not found in that folder, AutoCAD looks in the path

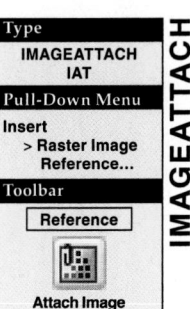

Type
IMAGEATTACH
IAT
Pull-Down Menu
Insert
> Raster Image
Reference...
Toolbar
Reference
Attach Image

IMAGEATTACH

Figure 18-3.
Select the image file to be attached to the drawing in the **Select Image File** dialog box. Pick the **Files of type:** drop-down list to display the raster file types that can be used.

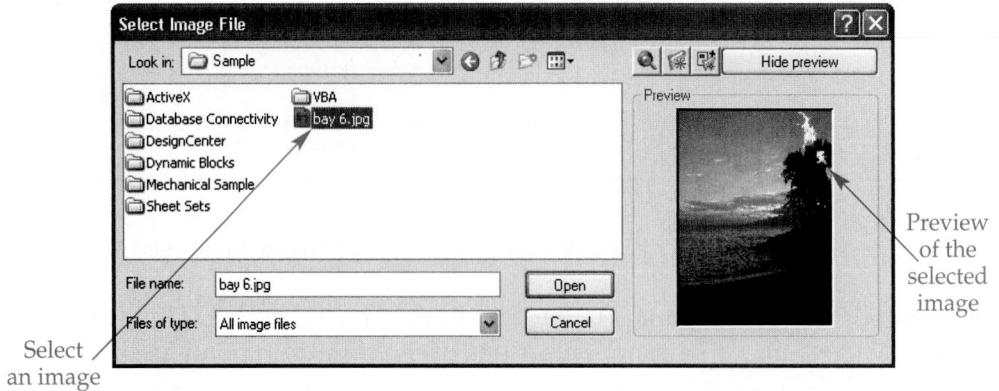

Select an image

Preview of the selected image

specified by the **PROJECTNAME** system variable, then in the **Support Files Search Path** defined in the **Files** tab of the **Options** dialog box.

You can preset image parameters (insertion point, scale, and rotation) or choose to specify them on-screen. You can view image resolution information in the **Image** dialog box by picking the **Details** button. See Figure 18-4. When the **OK** button is picked and the image placed, it is displayed in the drawing area. See Figure 18-5.

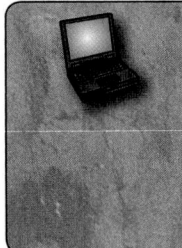

PROFESSIONAL TIP

If you are working on a project that uses xrefs and attached images, adding a "project subfolder" below the folder where the drawings are stored may be beneficial. Then, use relative paths when inserting images or xrefs. This allows all related files for a project to be found by AutoCAD, even if the folder structure is moved to a different drive or "root" folder.

Managing Attached Images

As stated earlier, the **External References** window is used to control the raster images inserted into a drawing. The **Details** area at the bottom of the window displays for the image selected in the **File References** area the image name, its status (loaded or unloaded), file size, type, date the image was last saved, and the saved path. Refer to Figure 18-1.

Right-clicking on the image name in the **File References** area displays a shortcut menu containing options to help you manage the image. The five options are:

- **Open.** This opens the image in the program associated with the file type of the image. For example, if Microsoft Photo Editor is associated with the TIFF file type, the TIFF image is displayed in this program.
- **Attach.** This opens the **Image** dialog box, discussed in the previous section, for attaching an additional image to the drawing.
- **Unload.** Unloads the selected image, but retains its path information. The Status column displays Unloaded if this option is selected. Display the list view to see the columns. An unloaded image is displayed as a frame until reloaded.
- **Reload.** Reloads the selected image file.
- **Detach.** Removes, or detaches, the selected image file from the drawing.

Figure 18-4.
The image name and path are displayed in the **Image** dialog box. Be sure to select the type of path to use. The dialog box expands to include the **Image Information** area when the **Details>>** button is picked.

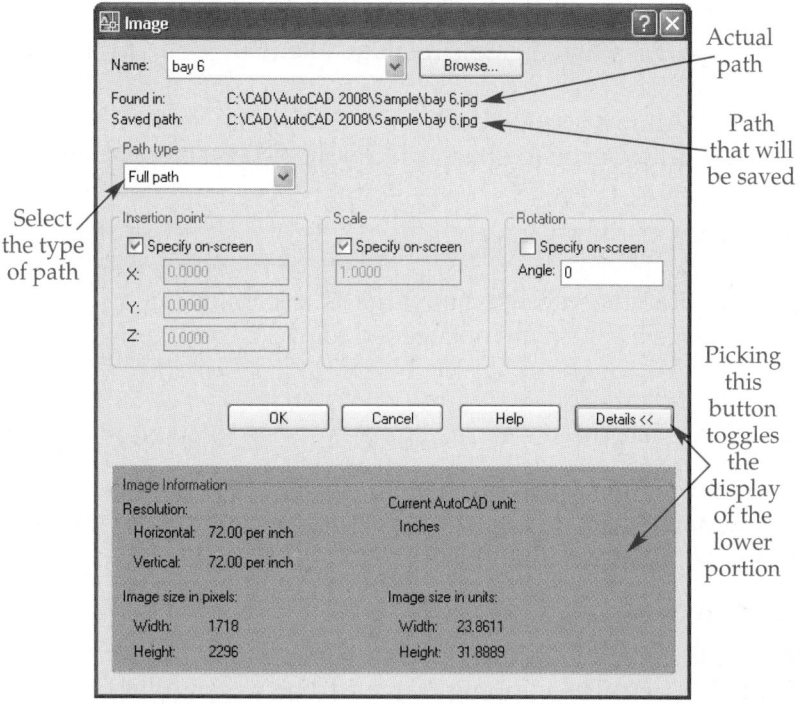

Figure 18-5.
The raster image attached to an AutoCAD drawing.

Right-clicking in **File References** area, but not on a file name, displays a different shortcut menu. This shortcut menu contains six options:

- **Reload All References.** Reloads any files attached to the current drawing.
- **Select All.** Selects all of the files listed in the **File References** area.
- **Attach DWG.** Allows you to attach other drawings as xrefs.
- **Attach Image.** Displays the **Select Image File** dialog box for attaching another raster image.
- **Attach DWF.** Allows you to attach a DWF file as an xref.
- **Attach DGN.** Allows you to attach a DGN file (Microstation drawing) as an xref.

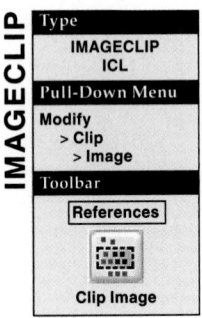

IMAGECLIP

| Type |
| IMAGECLIP |
| ICL |
| Pull-Down Menu |
| Modify |
| > Clip |
| > Image |
| Toolbar |
| References |
| Clip Image |

Controlling Image File Displays

Once an image is attached to the current drawing, its display can be adjusted if needed. The commands used to adjust images can be accessed on the **Reference** toolbar or in the **Modify** pull-down menu, **Figure 18-6.**

Clipping an image

The **IMAGECLIP** command allows you to trim away a portion of the image that does not need to be seen. The clipping frame can be rectangular or polygonal. Once the command is selected, you are prompted to pick the image to clip. Then, to create a rectangular clipping frame, continue:

```
Enter image clipping option [ON/OFF/Delete/New boundary] <New>: N↵
Enter clipping type [Polygonal/Rectangular] <Rectangular>: R↵
Specify first corner point: (pick the first corner of the clipping boundary)
Specify opposite corner point: (pick the second corner)
```

Figure 18-6.
Commands used to control image files are found in the **Modify** pull-down menu.

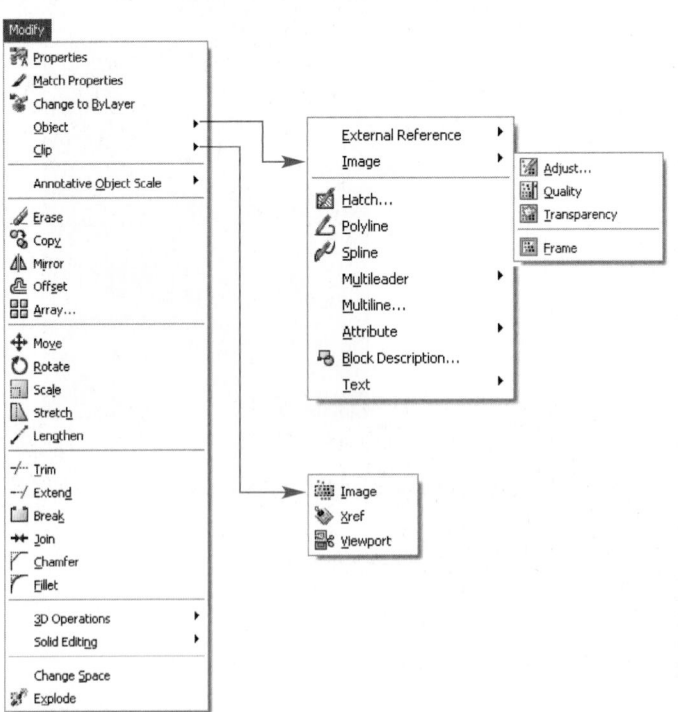

The image outside of the rectangular frame is hidden.

The **Polygonal** option allows you to construct a clipping frame composed of three or more points. Select the command, pick the image to clip, and continue:

```
Enter image clipping option [ON/OFF/Delete/New boundary] <New>: N↵
Enter clipping type [Polygonal/Rectangular] <Rectangular>: P↵
Specify first point: (pick first point to be used for the clipping boundary)
Specify next point or [Undo]: (pick second point)
Specify next point or [Undo]: (pick third point)
Specify next point or [Close/Undo]: (pick additional points as needed)
Specify next point or [Close/Undo]: ↵
```

Figure 18-7 shows the results of using the **Rectangular** and **Polygonal** options of the **IMAGECLIP** command on a raster image. Three additional options of **IMAGECLIP** allow you to work with the display of the clipped image.

- **ON.** Turns the clipping frame on to display only the clipped area.
- **OFF.** Turns off the clipping frame to display the entire original image and frame.
- **Delete.** Deletes the clipping frame and displays the entire original image.

> **NOTE**
>
> You can pick an unclipped image frame to display the grips for editing. The grips are attached to the image itself. If one grip is stretched, it affects the entire image by proportionally enlarging or reducing it. On the other hand, if you select a clipped image for grip editing, the grips are attached to the clipping frame. Stretching the clipping frame does not change the size or shape of the image, but alters the frame and retains the size of the image.

Adjusting an image

The **IMAGEADJUST** command provides control over the brightness, contrast, and fade of the image. These adjustments are made in the **Image Adjust** dialog box, **Figure 18-8**. Once the command is selected, you are prompted to pick an image. If you want the same settings applied to multiple images, you can pick them all at the same time. When done picking objects, press [Enter] to display the dialog box.

Values can be changed by typing in the text boxes or by using the slider bars. The preview tile dynamically changes as the sliders are moved. Picking the **Reset** button returns all values to their defaults.

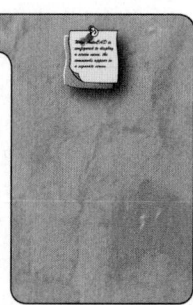

| Type |
| IMAGEADJUST |
| IAD |
| Pull-Down Menu |
| Modify |
| > Object |
| > Image |
| > Adjust... |
| Toolbar |
| Reference |

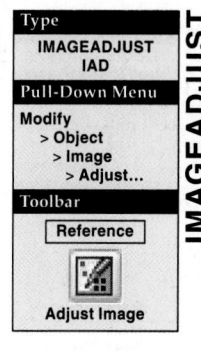

Adjust Image

IMAGEADJUST

Figure 18-7.
A—A rectangular image clip. B—A polygonal image clip. The path is shown here in color for illustration.

Polygonal path

A

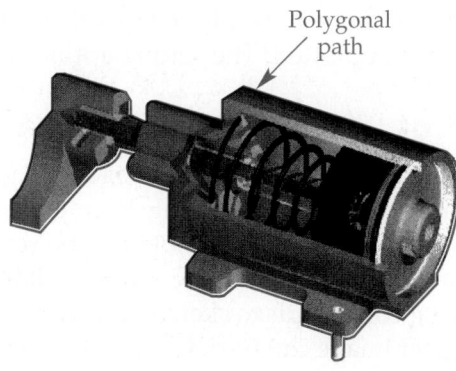

B

Figure 18-8.
In the **Image Adjust** dialog box, brightness, contrast, and fade values can be numerically entered or set using the slider bars.

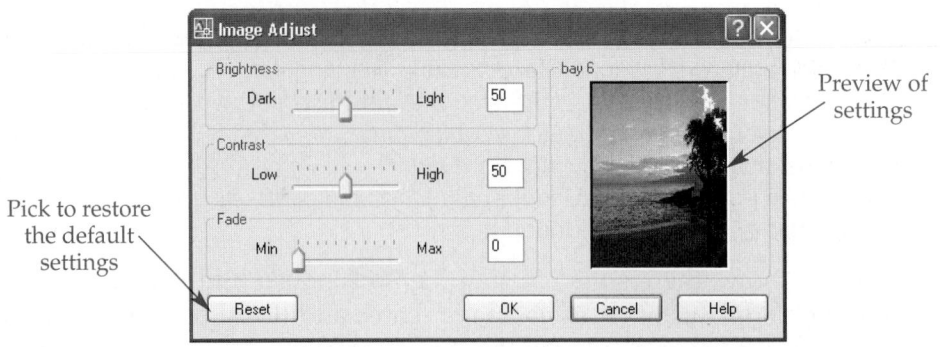

Pick to restore the default settings

Preview of settings

- **Brightness.** Controls pixel whiteness and indirectly affects the contrast. Values can range from 0 to 100, with 50 as the default value. Higher values increase the brightness.
- **Contrast.** Controls the contrast of the image, or how close each pixel is moved toward its primary or secondary color. Values can range from 0 to 100, with 50 as the default value. Higher values increase the contrast.
- **Fade.** Controls the fading of the image, or how close the image is to the background color. Values can range from 0 to 100, with 0 as the default value. Higher values increase the fading.

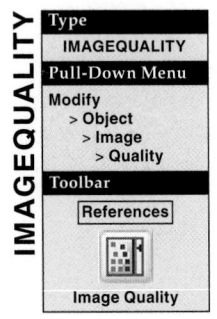

The **IMAGEQUALITY** command provides two options: **High** and **Draft**. The high quality setting produces the best image display, but requires more time to regenerate. If you are working with several images in a drawing, it is best to set the **Draft** option current. The image displayed is lower quality, but requires less time to display. The setting applies to all images in the drawing.

Transparency

Some raster images have transparent background pixels. The **TRANSPARENCY** command controls the display of these pixels. If **TRANSPARENCY** is on, the drawing will show through the image background. Images are inserted with this feature turned off. The setting applies to individual images. Multiple images can be selected at the same time. Remember, only images containing transparent pixels are affected.

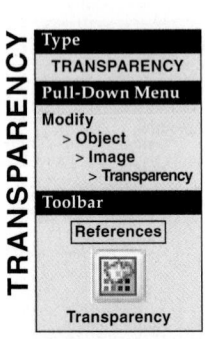

Image frame

The **IMAGEFRAME** command controls the appearance of frames around all images in the current drawing. When attaching (inserting) images, AutoCAD places a frame around the image in the current layer color and linetype. There are three settings for the **IMAGEFRAME** command. A setting of 0 turns off the display of the frame and the frame is not plotted. The default setting of 1 turns on the display of the frame and allows the frame to be plotted. A setting of 2 turns on the display of the frame, but the frame is not plotted. The setting applies to all images in the drawing.

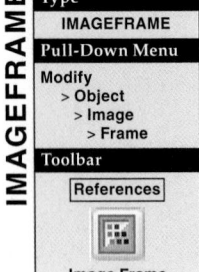

Uses of Raster Files in AutoCAD

One use of raster images is as a background for sketching or tracing. For example, you may need a line drawing of an image that is only available as a continuous tone (print) photograph. The photo can be scanned, which produces a raster image. After importing the raster image with the **IMAGEATTACH** command, use the appropriate drawing commands to sketch or trace the image. After the object is sketched, the original raster image can be deleted, frozen, or unloaded, leaving the tracing. You can then add other elements to the tracing to create a full drawing. See **Figure 18-9.**

AutoCAD and Its Applications—Advanced

Figure 18-9.
Using a raster image as a model for a drawing. A—The imported raster image. B—Use AutoCAD commands to trace the image. Then, either delete the image or freeze its layer. C—The completed drawing plotted on a title block.

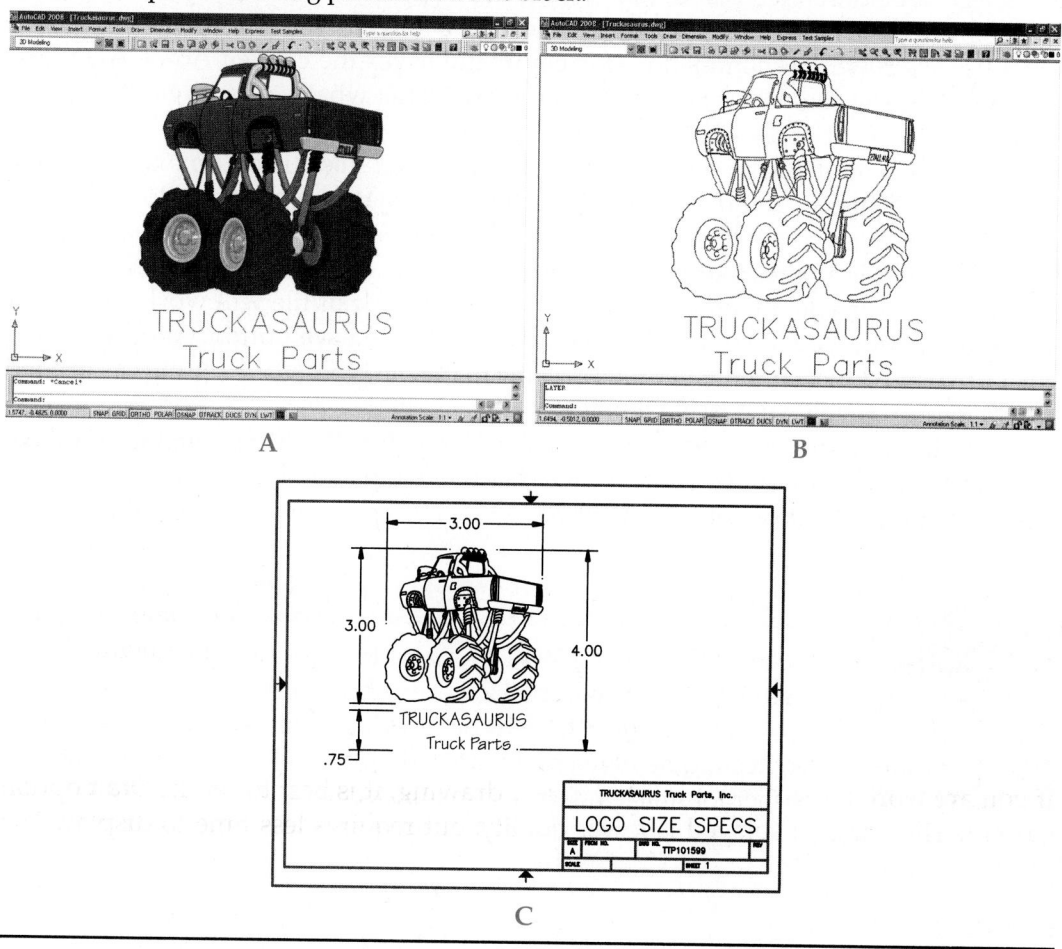

Raster files can be combined with AutoCAD drawing and modeling features in many ways to complete or complement the design. For example, company watermarks or logos can be easily added to title blocks, style sheets, and company drawing standards. Drawings that require designs, labels, and a variety of text fonts can be created using raster files in conjunction with the wide variety of TrueType fonts available with AutoCAD. Archived manual drawings can also be scanned, brought into AutoCAD, and then traced to create a CAD drawing.

You can add features to complement raster files. For example, you can import a raster file, dimension or annotate it, and even add special shapes to it. Then, export it as the same type of file. Now, you can use the revised file in the original software in which it was created. As with any creative process, let your imagination and the job requirements determine how you use this capability of AutoCAD.

Exercise 18-1
Complete the exercise on the Student CD.

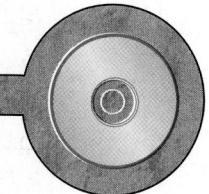

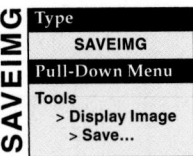

SAVEIMG

Type
SAVEIMG
Pull-Down Menu
Tools
> Display Image
> Save...

Exporting a Drawing to a Raster File

You can save a rendering to a raster file. This is discussed in Chapter 16. However, 2D objects are not rendered and, therefore, do not appear in the file. If you want what is displayed in the current viewport, including 2D objects, saved as a raster file, you must use the **SAVEIMG** command. This command saves the current AutoCAD viewport as an image file. What you see in the viewport is what you will get in the file, including the effect of the current visual style.

Once the command is selected, the **Render Output File** dialog box is displayed, Figure 18-10. This is a standard save dialog box. The **Files of type:** drop-down list displays the file types to which the image can be saved. Select the file type based on the type required for a particular process, application, job, or client. The best thing to do is ask whomever you are creating the file for which type of file will work best. After selecting the file type, give the file a name and pick the **Save** button. Another dialog box is displayed that contains settings specific to the file type. Make settings as needed and close this dialog box to save the file.

A BMP file can also be created using the **EXPORT** or **BMPOUT** command. In this manner, you can select individual objects that will be included in the image. You can also save shaded images with this method.

PROFESSIONAL TIP

You can use the **SAVEIMG** command to save a rendering that was rendered to the viewport. However, the result is a low-resolution image. Most images that will be in print, such as in a magazine or book, need to be high resolution. Check with the magazine or book publisher for image resolution requirements.

Figure 18-10.
The **Render Output File** dialog box is displayed when the **SAVEIMG** command is selected. The **Files of type:** drop-down list shows the file types available. After picking the **Save** button, another dialog box appears with settings specific to the selected file type.

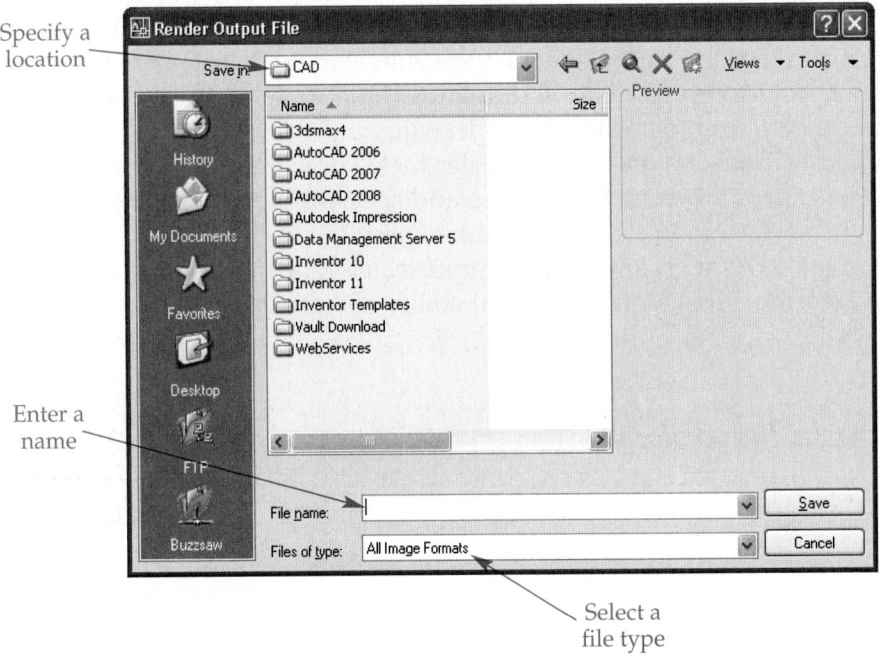

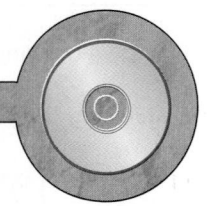

Working with Vector Files

A vector file contains objects defined by XYZ coordinates. AutoCAD's native file format (DWG) is a vector file. You can also work with other vector file types. These types include DXF, WMF, SAT, EPS, STL, and DXX. The two most commonly used types, DXF and WMF, are covered in the next sections.

Exporting and Importing DXF Files

DXF is a generic file type that defines AutoCAD geometry in an ASCII text file. Other programs that recognize the DXF format can then "read" this file. The DXF file format retains the mathematical definitions of AutoCAD objects in vector form. The DXF objects imported into other vector programs, or opened in AutoCAD, can be edited as needed.

Exporting DXF files

The **DXFOUT** command is used to save a DXF file. Once the command is selected, the **Save Drawing As** dialog box is displayed. See Figure 18-11. Select the DXF file type from the **Files of type:** drop-down list. Name the file and specify a location where you want to save it. Notice that you can select different versions of DXF. This is to ensure that the file you save is "backward compatible." For example, if you are sharing the file with somebody using AutoCAD 2000, save the DXF as that version to ensure AutoCAD 2000 can read the file.

Since this is a "save as" operation, the current drawing is saved as a DXF file. If you continue to work on the drawing, you are working on the DXF version, *not* the DWG version. In order to work on the original drawing, you must open the DWG file. However, if you continue to work on the drawing in DXF form and attempt to save or close the drawing, the **Save Drawing As** dialog box is displayed. You can save the drawing as a DWG or replace the DXF file previously saved. If you save the drawing as a DXF file, you are also informed that the drawing is not a DWG and given the opportunity to save it in that format.

When a DXF file is saved, all geometry in the drawing is saved, regardless of the current zoom percentage or selected objects. However, the current zoom percentage is saved in the DXF file. As explained later, this differs from the WMF format.

The DXF file format saves any surfaced or solid 3D objects as 3D geometry. When a DXF file containing 3D geometry is opened, the surfaced or solid 3D geometry remains intact. In addition, the current visual style is saved in the DXF file.

NOTE

Not all programs that can import DXF files are capable of correctly "reading" 3D objects or the visual style.

Figure 18-11.
The **Save Drawing As** dialog box is used to save a DXF file.

Select a location

Name the file

Select the DXF version

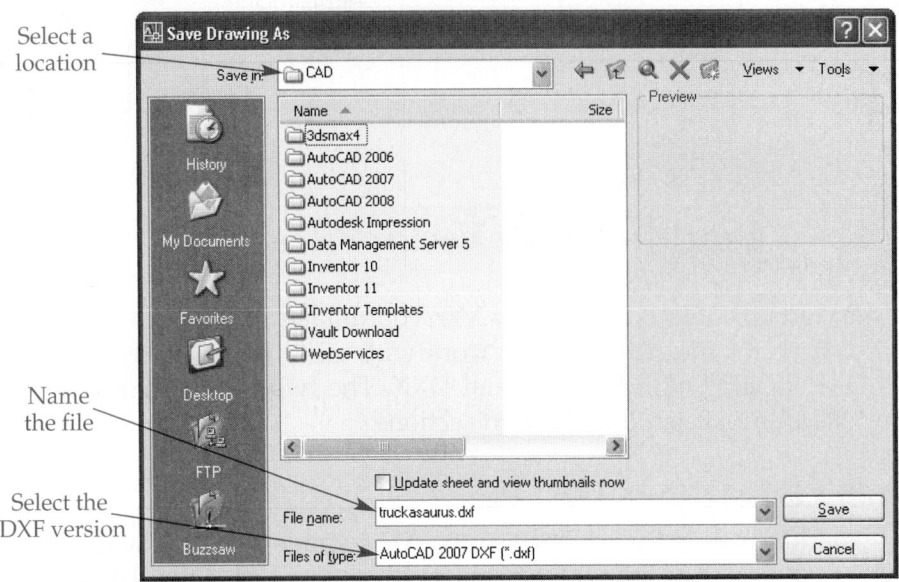

Importing DXF files

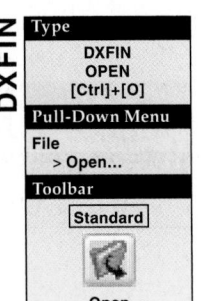

To open a DXF file, use the **DXFIN** command. Once the command is selected, the **Select File** dialog box is displayed, **Figure 18-12.** Select DXF (*.dxf) from the **Files of type:** drop-down list. Then, select the DXF file you want to open. Notice that there is no preview when the file is selected. AutoCAD does not support previews for the DXF file type. Finally, pick the **Open** button.

The DXF file is opened in a new document window. To place a DXF file into the *current* drawing, insert it as a block. If you do not want it inserted as a block, open the file (**DXFIN**), copy it to the clipboard ([Ctrl]+[C]), and paste ([Ctrl]+[V]) it into the current drawing.

> **NOTE**
>
> If you open a DXF file and try to save it, the **Save Drawing As** dialog box appears. You can save it as DXF, overwriting the existing file, or under a new name or as another file type.

Exporting and Importing Windows Metafiles

The Windows metafile (WMF) file format is often used to exchange data with desktop publishing programs. It is a vector format that can save wireframe and hidden displays. Shaded and rendered images cannot be saved. Also, perspective views are saved in parallel projection.

A WMF file cannot retain the definition of all AutoCAD object types. For example, circles are translated to line segments. Also, a WMF file does *not* save three-dimensional data. The view in the current viewport is projected onto the viewing plane and saved as a two-dimensional projection.

Figure 18-12.
The **Select File** dialog box is used to import a DXF file.

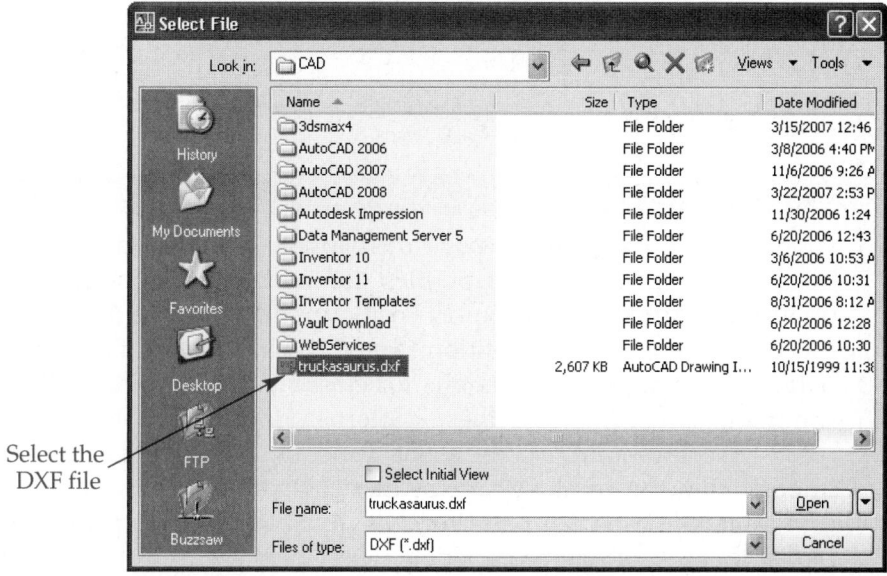

Select the DXF file

Exporting WMF files

The **WMFOUT** command is used to create a WMF file. When the command is selected, the **Create WMF File** or **Export Data** dialog box is displayed. These are standard save dialog boxes. Select Metafile (*.wmf) in the **Files of type:** drop-down list. After specifying the file name and folder location in either dialog box and picking the **Save** button, you must select the objects to place in the file. Press [Enter] when all of the objects are selected and the WMF file is saved.

Only the portions of selected objects that are visible on-screen are written into the file. If part of a selected object is not visible on screen, that part is "clipped." Also, the current view resolution affects the appearance of a Windows metafile. For example, when **VIEWRES** is set low, circles in your AutoCAD drawing may look like polygons in the WMF file. When saved to a Windows metafile, the objects are polygons (line segments) rather than circles.

Type
WMFOUT
EXPORT
EXP

Pull-Down Menu
File
> Export...

WMFOUT

Importing WMF files

Use the **WMFIN** command to import a Windows metafile into a drawing. When the command is selected, the **Import WMF** or **Import File** dialog box is displayed. Select Metafile (*.wmf) in the **Files of type:** drop-down list, then select a file.

A Windows metafile is imported as a block consisting of all of the objects in the file. You can explode the block if you need to edit the objects within it. If an object is not filled, it is created as a polyline when brought into AutoCAD. This includes arcs and circles. Objects composed of several closed polylines to represent fills are created from solid fill objects, as if created using the **SOLID** command with the **FILL** system variable off.

There are two settings used to control the appearance of Windows metafiles imported into AutoCAD. Type WMFOPTS to display the **WMF In Options** dialog box, **Figure 18-13.** You can also pick the **Options...** button in the **Tools** drop-down menu in the "import" dialog box. The dialog box contains the following two check boxes.

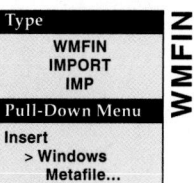

Type
WMFIN
IMPORT
IMP

Pull-Down Menu
Insert
> Windows
   Metafile...

WMFIN

- **Wire Frame (No Fills).** When checked, filled areas are imported only as outlines. Otherwise, filled areas are imported as filled objects (when **FILL** is on).
- **Wide Lines.** When this option is checked, the relative line widths of lines and borders from the WMF file are maintained. Otherwise, they are imported using a zero width.

Figure 18-13.
Setting options for
imported WMF files.

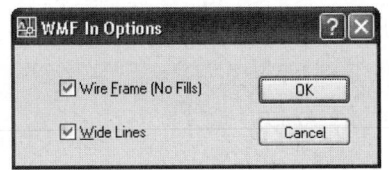

PROFESSIONAL TIP

PostScript is a copyrighted page description language developed by Adobe Systems. PostScript files are widely used in desktop publishing. AutoCAD can export PostScript files with the **PSOUT** or **EXPORT** commands. In addition, AutoCAD has several PostScript patterns that can be used as fills for closed polylines. The **PSFILL** command is used to add these patterns. However, professionals rarely use AutoCAD's PostScript functions. AutoCAD cannot import, view, or print PostScript files. In addition, any drawing that contains PostScript patterns (fills) must be sent to a printer or plotter that is PostScript compatible. These printers are not common outside of the graphics industry.

Exercise 18-3

Complete the exercise on the Student CD.

Design Web Format (DWF) Files

You can save an AutoCAD drawing as a *Design Web Format (DWF)* file. A DWF file is a highly compressed, vector file that can be viewed using the Autodesk DWF Viewer or Volo View program. In addition, when either of these programs is installed in conjunction with Microsoft Internet Explorer 5.01 or later, you can view DWF files on the web. The Autodesk DWF Viewer program is installed when AutoCAD is installed.

A DWF file is created using the **PLOT** command. The AutoCAD documentation refers to this as the "ePlot" feature. First, open the **Plot** dialog box. In the **Printer/plotter** area, select DWF6 ePlot.pc3 from the **Name:** drop-down list, Figure 18-14. The DWF6 ePlot.pc3 configuration is designed to create files that will be viewed, downloaded, and plotted. There are two other PC3 options that are used with the **PUBLISHTOWEB** command and one used to create Portable Document Format (PDF) files.

There are several settings for a DWF file that affect the final output. After the ePlot configuration is selected, pick the **Properties...** button in the **Printer/plotter** area. In the **Plotter Configuration Editor** dialog box that is displayed, select Custom Properties in the tree on the **Device and Document Settings** tab, Figure 18-15A. Then, pick the **Custom Properties...** button to display the **DWF Properties** dialog box, Figure 18-15B.

The two "resolution" areas in the **DWF Properties** dialog box have settings that control the accuracy of the resulting DWF file. A medium resolution is best in most cases. A DWF file created with high resolution may be too large for practical electronic transmission. A lower resolution will create a smaller DWF file. Small files make for easy electronic transmission. However, the resulting DWF file may not display as accurately

Figure 18-14.
When plotting to a DWF file, the DWF ePlot.pc3 configuration is optimized for plotting and viewing.

Select the DWF option

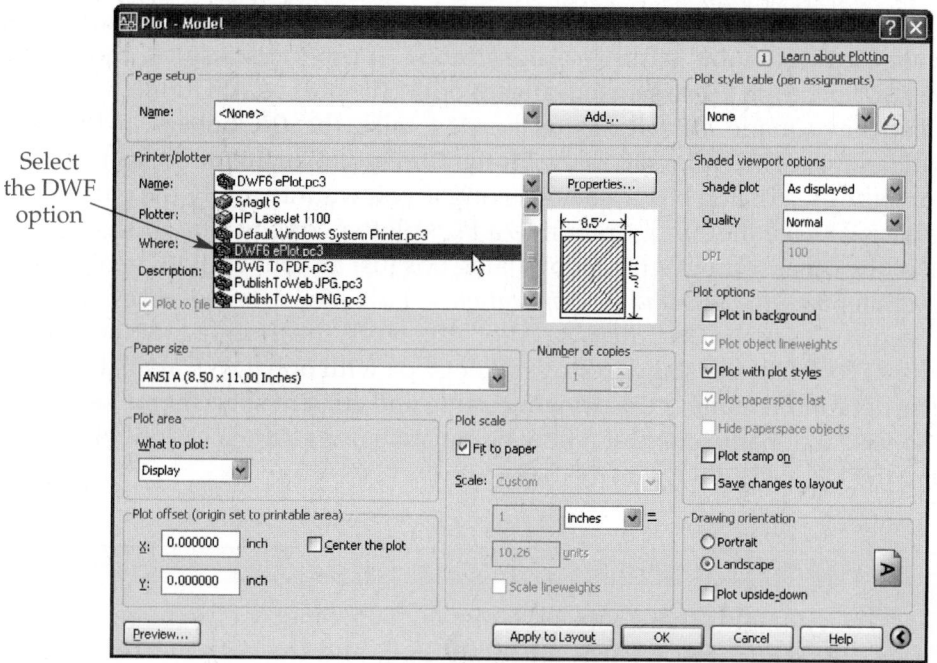

Figure 18-15.
A—Setting up custom properties for a DWF file. B—The **DWF Properties** dialog box.

Pick to adjust settings

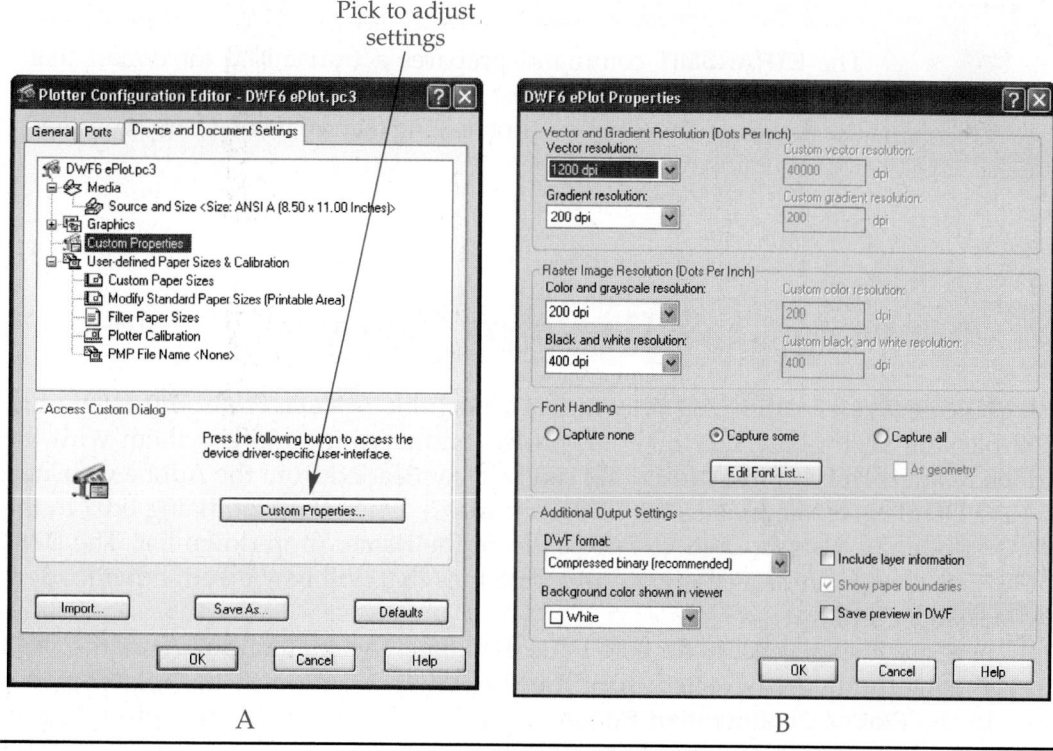

A

B

as one created at a higher resolution. You can separately set a maximum resolution for vector graphics, gradients, color/grayscale images, and black and white images.

There are two options in the **DWF format:** drop-down list in the **Additional Output Settings** area. Along with resolution, this setting determines the file size. The **Compressed Binary (recommended)** option is the default selection. It produces a small, binary file. The **Zipped ASCII encoded 2D stream (advanced)** option creates an ASCII file.

Once you have made all settings as needed, pick the **OK** button in the **DWF Properties** dialog box. Then, pick **OK** in the **Plotter Configuration Editor**. If changes were made to the settings, a dialog box appears asking if you want to apply the changes on a one-time basis or save the configuration to a PC3 plotter configuration file.

Use all of the other settings in the **Plot** dialog box just as you would when plotting a hard copy. Refer to *AutoCAD and Its Applications—Basics* for detailed information on plotting. When you pick the **OK** button to "plot" the DWF, the **Browse for Plot File** dialog box is displayed. This is a standard save dialog box with only DWF available as the file type. The default filename is the drawing name and current space name separated by a hyphen. Use that name or enter a new name, navigate to the location where you want to save the DWF file, and pick the **Save** button.

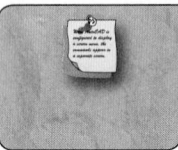

NOTE

Commands that control the display of geometry on screen, such as **VIEWRES**, **FACETRES**, and **DISPSILH**, and the current visual style affect the resulting DWF file.

PROFESSIONAL TIP

The **ETRANSMIT** command prepares a transmittal for e-mail that contains font files, plot styles, table files, and xrefs associated with the drawing. This can be a time-saving feature if you share drawings that contain xrefs.

Adobe® Portable Document Format (PDF) Files

You can save an AutoCAD drawing as a *Portable Document Format (PDF)* file. PDF files are vector-base files, like DWF files, and anyone can view them with the Adobe Reader. This is a free utility that can be downloaded from the Adobe website.

A PDF file is created using the **PLOT** command. Open the **Plot** dialog box. In the **Printer/plotter** area, select DWG To PDF.pc3 from the **Name:** drop-down list. The DWG To PDF.pc3 configuration is designed to create files that will be viewed, downloaded, and possibly plotted.

There are several settings for a PDF file that affect the final output. After the DWG To PDF configuration is selected, pick the **Properties...** button in the **Printer/plotter** area. In the **Plotter Configuration Editor** dialog box that is displayed, select Custom Properties in the tree on the **Device and Document Settings** tab. Then, pick the **Custom Properties...** button to display the **PDF Properties** dialog box, Figure 18-16.

The two "resolution" areas in the **PDF Properties** dialog box have settings that control the accuracy of the resulting PDF file. A medium resolution is best in most

Figure 18-16.
Setting up custom properties for a PDF file in the **PDF Properties** dialog box.

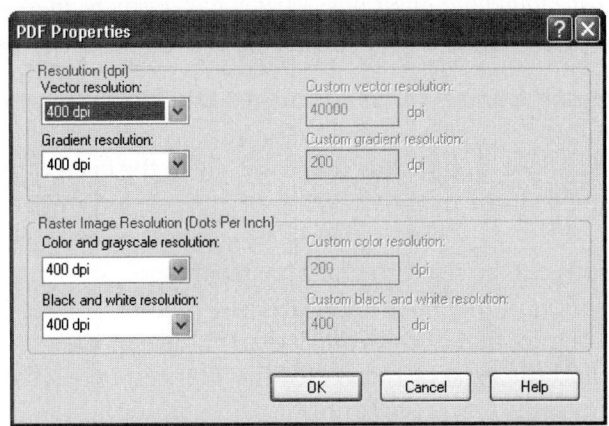

Figure 18-17.
A comparison of low resolution and high resolution PDF files. A—The lines in the low-resolution file have jaggies. B—The lines in the high-resolution file are cleaner.

cases. A PDF file created with high resolution may be too large for practical electronic transmission. A lower resolution will create a smaller PDF file. Small files make for easy electronic transmission. However, the resulting PDF file may not display as accurately as one created at a higher resolution. You can separately set a maximum resolution for vector graphics, gradients, color/grayscale images, and black and white images. See **Figure 18-17** for a comparison of resolution settings in a plotted PDF file. The file size increases as the resolution increases.

Once you have made all settings as needed, pick the **OK** button in the **PDF Properties** dialog box. Then, pick **OK** in the **Plotter Configuration Editor**. If changes were made to the settings, a dialog box appears asking if you want to apply the changes on a one-time basis or save the configuration to a PC3 plotter configuration file.

Use all of the other settings in the **Plot** dialog box just as you would when plotting a hard copy. Refer to *AutoCAD and Its Applications—Basics* for detailed information on plotting. When you pick the **OK** button to "plot" the PDF, the **Browse for Plot File** dialog box is displayed. This is a standard save dialog box with only PDF available as the file type. The default filename is the drawing name and current space name separated by a hyphen. Use that name or enter a new name, navigate to the location where you want to save the DWF file, and pick the **Save** button.

Chapter Test

Answer the following questions. Write your answers on a separate sheet of paper or complete the electronic chapter test on the Student CD.

1. Name four common formats of raster images that can be imported into AutoCAD.
2. Which command allows you to attach a raster file to the current AutoCAD drawing?
3. What is the display status in the drawing of an inserted image that has been unloaded?
4. Which two shapes can be used to clip a raster image?
5. What is the function of the **IMAGEADJUST** command?
6. Name two commands that allow you to export bitmap files.
7. Give the name and file type of the vector file that can be exchanged between object-based programs (object definitions are retained).
8. Name the commands that allow you to import and export the file type in question 7.
9. How are three-dimensional objects treated when exported to a WMF file?
10. How can a DXF be inserted into the *current* drawing?

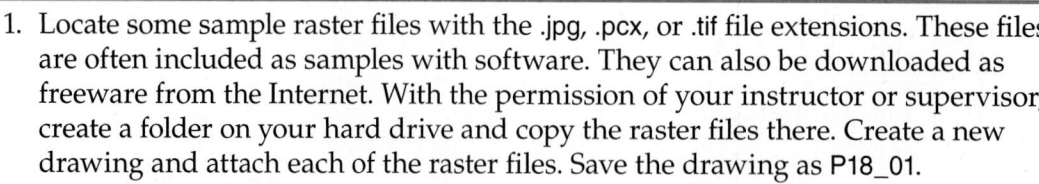

Drawing Problems

1. Locate some sample raster files with the .jpg, .pcx, or .tif file extensions. These files are often included as samples with software. They can also be downloaded as freeware from the Internet. With the permission of your instructor or supervisor, create a folder on your hard drive and copy the raster files there. Create a new drawing and attach each of the raster files. Save the drawing as P18_01.
2. Choose a small raster file and attach it to a new AutoCAD drawing.
   A. Insert the image so it fills the entire screen.
   B. Undo and insert the image again using a scale factor that fills half the screen with the image.
   C. Stretch the original object using grips, then experiment with different clipping boundaries. Stretch the image after it has been clipped and observe the result.
   D. Create a layer named Raster. Create a second layer named Object. Give each layer the color of your choice. Set the current layer to Raster.
   E. Import the same image next to the previous one at the same scale factor.
   F. Set the current layer to Object and use any AutoCAD drawing commands to trace the outline of the second raster image.
   G. Unload the raster image or freeze the Raster layer.
   H. Save the drawing as P18_02.
3. For this problem, you will import several raster files into AutoCAD. Then, you will trace the object in each file and save it as a block or wblock to be used on other drawings.
   A. Find several raster files that contain simple objects, shapes, or figures that you might use in other drawings.
   B. Create a template drawing containing Object and Raster layers.
   C. Import each raster file into AutoCAD on the Raster layer using the appropriate command. Set the Object layer current and trace the shape or objects using AutoCAD drawing commands.
   D. Detach the raster information, keeping only the traced lines of the object.
   E. Save the object as a block or wblock using an appropriate file-naming system.
   F. After all blocks have been created, insert each one into a single drawing and label each with its name. Include a path if necessary.
   G. Save the drawing as P18_03.
   H. Print or plot the final drawing.

Drawing Problems - Chapter 18

4. In this problem, you will create a memo outlining your progress on a flange.
   A. Open drawing P15_03 from Chapter 15 and save it as P18_04.
   B. Set the 3D Hidden visual style current.
   C. Set the background color to white.
   D. Use the **SAVEIMG** command and save the scene as a monochrome BMP file.
   E. Render the scene using the Presentation render preset and a resolution of 320 × 480. Save the rendering as a BMP file.
   F. Open a word processor capable of importing BMP files, such as Microsoft Word or Wordpad.
   G. Write a memo related to the project. A sample appears below. The memo should discuss how you created the drawing, the BMP file, and the rendered file. Insert the BMP files as appropriate.
   F. Save the document as P18_04. Print the document.

MEMO

To:	Otto Desque
From:	Ima Drafter
Date:	Thursday, March 14
Subject:	Project Progress

Dear Otto,

I have completed the initial drawing. As you can see from the drawing shown here, the project is complying with design parameters. The drawing is ready for transfer to the engineering department for approval.

I have also included a rendered image of the project. The material spec'ed by the engineering department is represented in the rendering. This may help in evaluation of the design.

Respectfully,

Ima

5. Begin a new drawing.
   A. Insert the blocks you created in Problem 3. Arrange them in any order.
   B. Add any notes you need to identify this drawing as a sheet of library shapes. Be sure each shape is identified with its file name and location (path).
   C. Create a PDF file of the drawing.
   D. Save the drawing as P18_05.
   E. Open the PDF in Adobe Reader and print it. If Adobe Reader is not installed, obtain permission from your instructor or supervisor to download and install it.

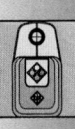

6. Add a raster image to one of your title block template drawings as a design element or a company logo. A sample is shown below. Import an existing raster image or create your own using a program such as Windows Paint. Save the template drawing.

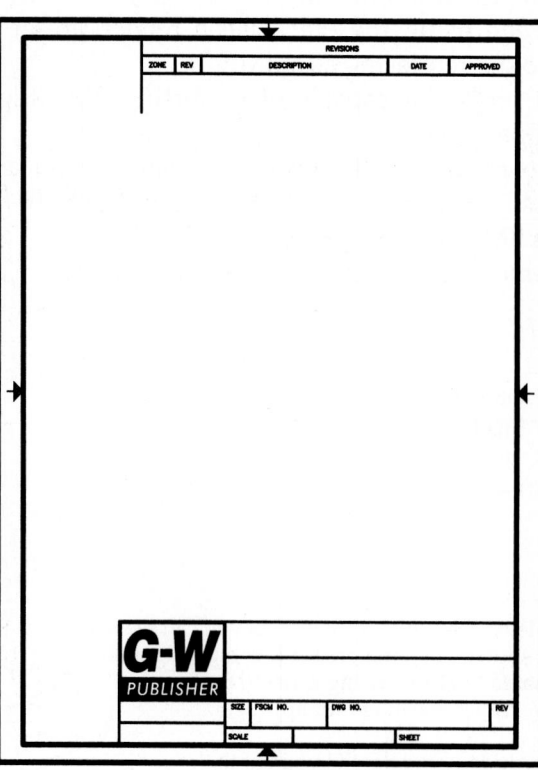

CHAPTER 19

Customizing the AutoCAD Environment

Learning Objectives

After completing this chapter, you will be able to:

✓ Set environment variables.
✓ Assign colors and fonts to the text and graphics windows.
✓ Control general AutoCAD system variables.
✓ Set options that control display quality and AutoCAD performance.
✓ Control shortcut menus.
✓ Modify program icon properties.
✓ Set up AutoCAD for multiple configurations.

AutoCAD provides a variety of options for customizing the user interface and working environment. These options permit users to configure the software to suit personal preferences. You can define colors for the individual window elements, assign preferred fonts to the command line window, control shortcut menus, and assign properties to program icons.

The options for customizing the AutoCAD user interface and working environment are found in the **Options** dialog box, **Figure 19-1.** This dialog box is commonly accessed by right-clicking in the drawing area with nothing selected and no command active and picking **Options...** from the shortcut menu.

Changes made in the **Options** dialog box do not take effect until either the **Apply** or **OK** button is picked. If you pick the **Cancel** button or the close button (**X**), all changes are discarded. Each time you change the options settings, the system registry is updated and the changes are used in this and subsequent drawing sessions. Settings that are stored within the drawing file have the AutoCAD icon next to them. These settings do not apply to other drawings. Settings without the icon indicate that the option affects all AutoCAD drawing sessions.

Type	
	OPTIONS
	OP
Pull-Down Menu	
Tools	
> Options...	

OPTIONS

Figure 19-1.
The **Options** dialog box is used to customize the AutoCAD working environment. Each tab contains a variety of options and settings.

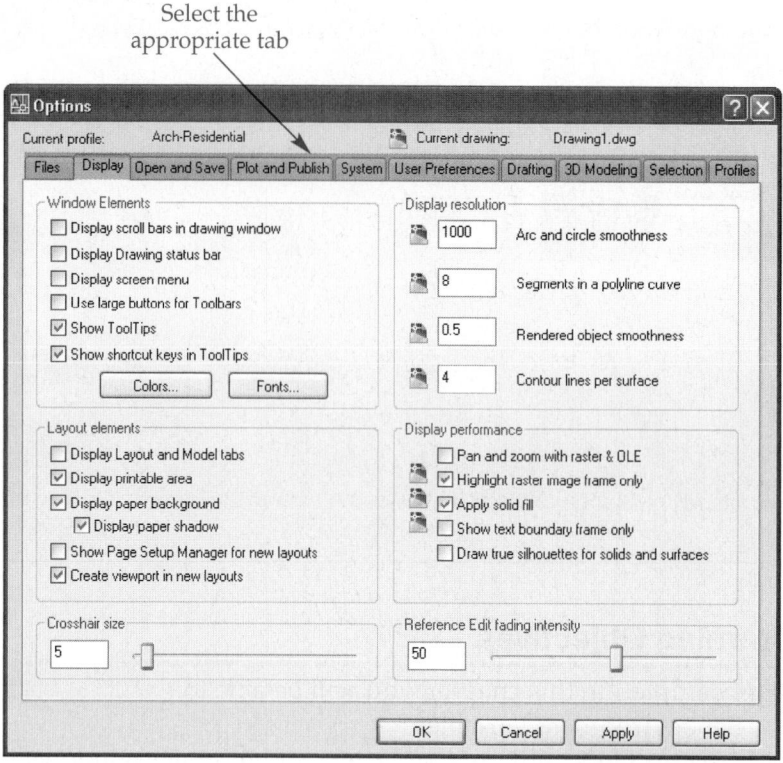

Select the appropriate tab

Setting AutoCAD Environment Variables

There are numerous settings that control the manner in which AutoCAD behaves in the Windows environment. These settings are made through the use of *environment variables.* Environment variables are used to specify such items as which folders to search for driver and menu files and the location of your temporary and support files. The default settings created during installation are usually adequate, but changing the settings may result in better performance. While several different options exist for setting many of the environment variables, the simplest method is to use the **Options** dialog box.

File Locations

When AutoCAD is used in a network environment, some files pertaining to AutoCAD may reside on a network drive, so all users can access them, and some files may reside in folders specifically created for a particular AutoCAD user. These files may include drawings containing blocks, external reference files, and custom menu files.

The **Files** tab of the **Options** dialog box is used to specify the path AutoCAD searches to find support files and driver files. It also contains the paths where certain types of files are saved, and where AutoCAD looks for specific types of files. Support files include text fonts, menus, AutoLISP files, ObjectARX files, blocks, linetypes, and hatch patterns.

The folder names shown under the Support File Search Path heading in the **Search paths, file names, and file locations:** list are automatically created by AutoCAD during the installation. For example, Figure 19-2 shows that the support files are stored in six different folders. Folders are searched in the order in which they are listed under Support File Search Path. As previously mentioned, some of these paths are created for a specific user. The first path listed is long and ultimately ends with the \Support folder. In the example shown, this path starts on the C: drive in a folder called \Documents and Settings. The folder listed immediately after the \Documents and Settings folder is the user-specific folder. The next folders to

Figure 19-2.
Folder paths can be customized in the **Files** tab of the **Options** dialog box.

Folder for specific user

Add a new folder to the selected path

Folders in support search path

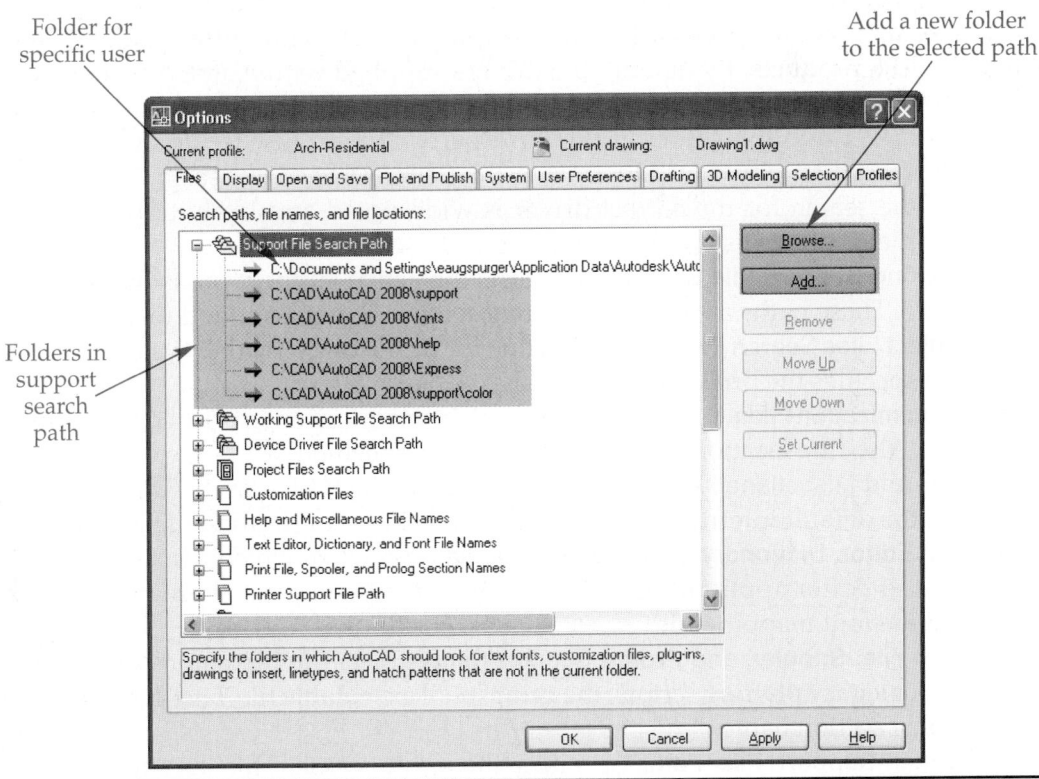

be searched are, in order, \Support, \Fonts, \Help, \Express, and \Support\Color. These paths are not user specific; they are located in the AutoCAD installation path.

You can add the path of any new folders you create that contain support files. As an example, suppose all of the blocks you typically use are stored in a separate folder named \Blocks. Unless this folder name is placed in the support files search path, AutoCAD will not be able to find your blocks when you attempt to insert them, unless you specify the entire folder path location. You can add this folder to the existing search path in two ways. The first method is to highlight the Support File Search Path heading and pick the **Add...** button. This places a new, empty listing under the heading. You can now type C:\BLOCKS to complete the entry. Alternately, instead of typing the path name, after picking **Add...** you can pick the **Browse...** button to display the **Browse for Folder** dialog box. You can then use this dialog box to select the desired folder. The new setting takes effect as soon as you pick **Apply** or the **OK** button and close the **Options** dialog box.

PROFESSIONAL TIP

In addition to the paths listed under Support File Search Path, AutoCAD will search two other folders. The folder that contains the AutoCAD executable file, acad.exe, (typically, C:\Program Files\ AutoCAD 2008) is searched as is the folder that contains the current drawing file. These folders are searched only if the desired file name is not found in any of the listed folders. It is not advisable to store files such as block files in the AutoCAD folder. However, if you store block files in the same folder as the current drawing, you do not need to add that folder to the search path.

Other File Settings

Another setting that can be specified in the **Files** tab is the location of device driver files. *Device drivers* are specifications for peripherals that work with AutoCAD and other Autodesk products. By default, the drivers supplied with AutoCAD are placed in the \Drv folder. If you purchase a third-party driver to use with AutoCAD, be sure to load the driver into this folder. If the third-party driver must reside in a different folder, you should specify that folder using the Device Driver File Search Path setting. Otherwise, the search for the correct driver is widespread and likely to take longer. Some other file locations listed in the **Files** tab include:

- **Working Support File Search Path.** Lists the active support paths AutoCAD is using. These paths are only for reference; they cannot be added to.
- **Project Files Search Path.** Sets the value for the **PROJECTNAME** system variable and specifies the project path names.
- **Customization Files.** Specifies the name of the main and enterprise customization files. Also, the location of custom icon files is specified.
- **Help and Miscellaneous File Names.** Specifies which files are used for the help file, the default Internet location, and where the configuration file is located.
- **Text Editor, Dictionary, and Font File Names.** Specifies which files are used for the text editor application, main and custom dictionaries, alternate font files, and the font mapping file.
- **Print File, Spooler, and Prolog Section Names.** Sets the file names for the plot file for legacy plotting scripts, the print spool executable file, and the PostScript prolog section name.
- **Printer Support File Path.** Specifies the print spooler file location, printer configuration search path, printer description file search path, and plot style table search path.
- **Automatic Save File Location.** Sets the path where the autosave (.sv$) file is stored. An autosave file is only created if the **Automatic save** option is checked in the **Open and Save** tab of the **Options** dialog box.
- **Color Book Locations.** Specifies the path for color book files that can be used when specifying colors in the **Select Color** dialog box.
- **Data Sources Location.** Specifies the path for database source files (.udl).
- **Template Settings.** Specifies the default location for drawing and sheet set template files and the file name for the defaults.
- **Tool Palettes File Locations.** Specifies the path for tool palette support files.
- **Authoring Palette File Locations.** Specifies the location of authoring palette files.
- **Log File Location.** Specifies the path for the AutoCAD log file. A log file is only created if the **Maintain a log file** option is checked in the **Open and Save** tab of the **Options** dialog box.
- **Plot and Publish Log File Location.** Specifies the path for the log file for "plot and publish" operations. A log file is only created if the **Automatically save plot and publish log** check box in the **Plot and Publish** tab of the **Options** dialog box is checked.
- **Temporary Drawing File Location.** Sets the folder where AutoCAD stores temporary drawing files.
- **Temporary External Reference File Location.** Indicates where temporary external reference files are placed.
- **Texture Maps Search Path.** Location of texture map files for rendering.
- **Web File Search Path.** Specifies the folders to search for files associated with photometric weblight lighting.
- **i-drop Associated File Location.** Specifies the folder used by default to store downloaded i-drop content.

Customizing the Graphics Window

Numerous options are available to customize the graphics window to your personal liking. Select the **Display** tab in the **Options** dialog box to view the display control options, Figure 19-3.

The **Window Elements** area has settings for turning the scroll bars and screen menu on or off, using large buttons for toolbars, showing tooltips, showing shortcut keys in tooltips, and selecting the color and font settings. At the bottom of the tab, the **Crosshair size** setting is a percentage of the drawing screen area. The higher the value, the further the crosshairs extend. The **Reference edit fading intensity** value determines the display intensity of the unselected objects in reference edit mode. A higher value means the unselected objects are less visible. Other options are discussed in the next sections.

Changing Colors

By customizing colors, you can add your personal touch and make AutoCAD stand out among other active Windows applications. AutoCAD provides this capability with the **Drawing Window Colors** dialog box, Figure 19-4. This dialog box is accessed by picking the **Colors...** button in the **Window Elements** area of the **Display** tab in the **Options** dialog box.

To change a color, first select a context. A *context* is one of the environments, or modes, in AutoCAD, such as the 3D perspective projection mode that is set current when a new drawing is started based on the acad3D.dwt template. The **Context:** list box contains the names of all contexts. The context that was current when the **Options** dialog box is opened is initially selected. A preview of the context and its settings is displayed in the **Preview:** area at the bottom of the dialog box.

Each context contains several interface elements. An *interface element* is an item that is visible, or can be made visible, in a given context, such as the grid axis, autosnap

---

Figure 19-3.
Use the **Display** tab to set up many of the visual elements of the AutoCAD environment.

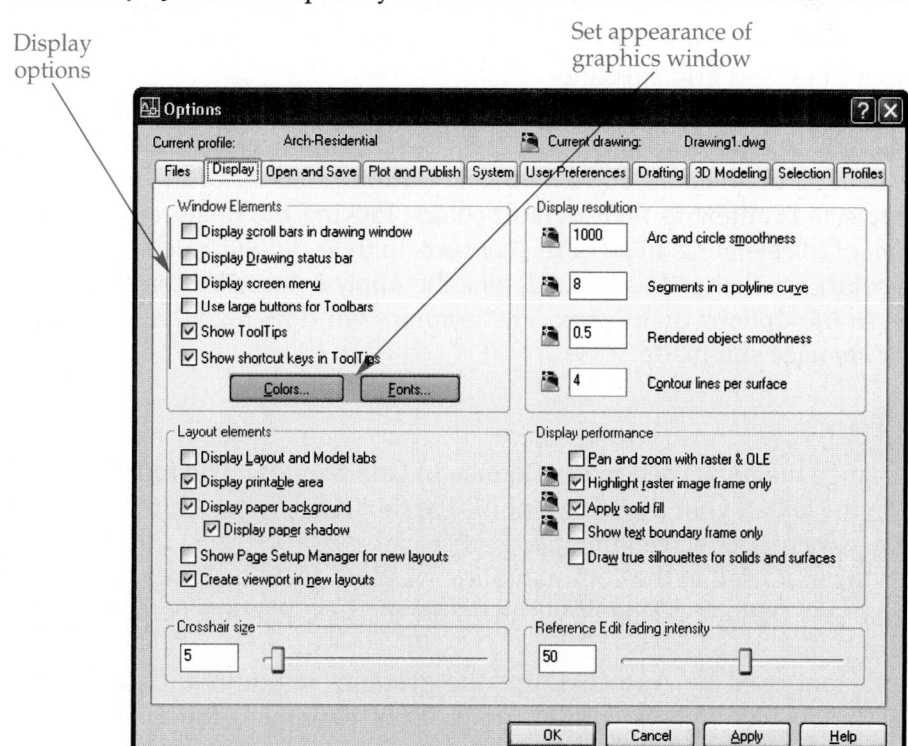

Display options

Set appearance of graphics window

Figure 19-4.
Change AutoCAD color settings using the **Drawing Window Colors** dialog box.

Select a context

Select an element

Select a color

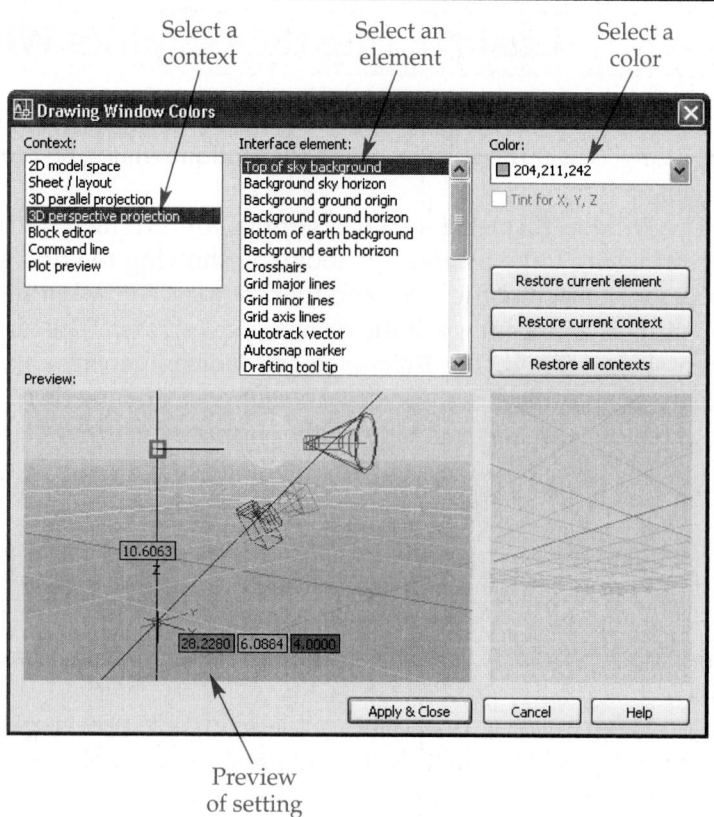

Preview of setting

marker, or light glyphs. Once a context is selected, pick the element to change in the **Interface element:** list.

With a context and element selected, the color of the element can be changed. Use the **Color:** drop-down list to change the color. If you pick the Select color… entry, the **Select Color** dialog box is displayed. Below the **Color:** drop-down list is the **Tint for X, Y, Z** check box. This check box is available when certain elements are selected. When checked, a tint is applied along the X, Y, and Z axes. The elements to which a tint can be applied are: crosshairs, autotrack vector, drafting tooltip background, grid major lines, grid minor lines, and grid axis lines.

Along the right side of the dialog box are buttons for restoring the default settings. Picking the **Restore current element** button resets the currently selected element to its default color. Picking the **Restore current context** button resets *all* of the elements of the currently selected context to their default colors. Picking the **Restore all contexts** button resets *all* of the elements in *all* of the contexts to their default colors.

Once the colors are changed as needed, pick the **Apply & Close** button. Then, pick the **OK** button in the **Options** dialog box. The graphics window regenerates and displays the color changes you made.

Changing Fonts

You can change the fonts used in the **Command Line** window. The font you select has no effect on the text in your drawings, nor is the font used in the AutoCAD dialog boxes, pull-down menus, or screen menus.

To change the font used in the command line window, pick the **Fonts…** button in the **Display** tab of the **Options** dialog box. The **Command Line Window Font** dialog box appears, **Figure 19-5.**

The default font used by AutoCAD for the graphics window is Courier New. The font style for Courier New is regular (not bold or italic) and the default size is

Figure 19-5.
The **Command Line** window can be changed to suit your preference.

Select a font · Select a style · Select a size

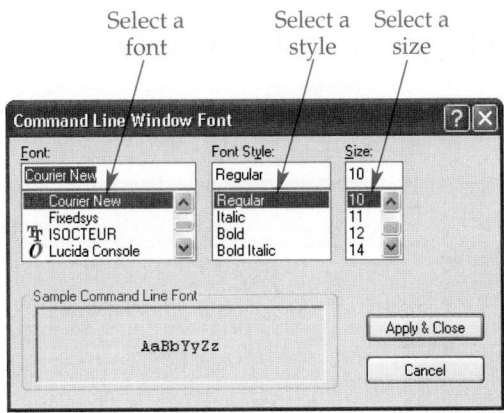

10 points. Select a new font from the **Font:** list. This list displays the system fonts available for use. Also, set a style and size. The **Sample Command Line Font** area displays a sample of the selected font. Once you have selected the desired font, font style, and font size for the **Command Line** window, pick the **Apply & Close** button to assign the new font.

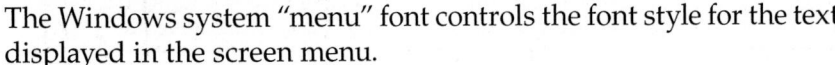

NOTE

The Windows system "menu" font controls the font style for the text displayed in the screen menu.

PROFESSIONAL TIP

The **UNDO** command does not affect changes made to your system using the **Options** dialog box. If you have made changes you do not want to save, pick **Cancel** to dismiss the **Options** dialog box. Picking **Cancel** does *not* dismiss changes that have been applied using the **Apply** button.

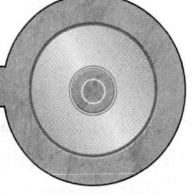

Exercise 19-1

Complete the exercise on the Student CD.

Layout Display Settings

The appearance of a layout tab is different than the appearance of the **Model** tab. The theory behind the default layout tab settings is to provide a picture of what the drawing will look like when plotted. You can see if the objects will fit on the paper or if some of the objects are outside of the margins. The following options, which are found in the **Layout elements** area of the **Display** tab in the **Options** dialog box, are illustrated in **Figure 19-6.**

- **Display Layout and Model tabs.** Displays the **Model** and layout tabs at the bottom of the drawing screen area. This is unchecked by default.

Figure 19-6.
Customizing the display of layouts. These options are set in the **Options** dialog box.

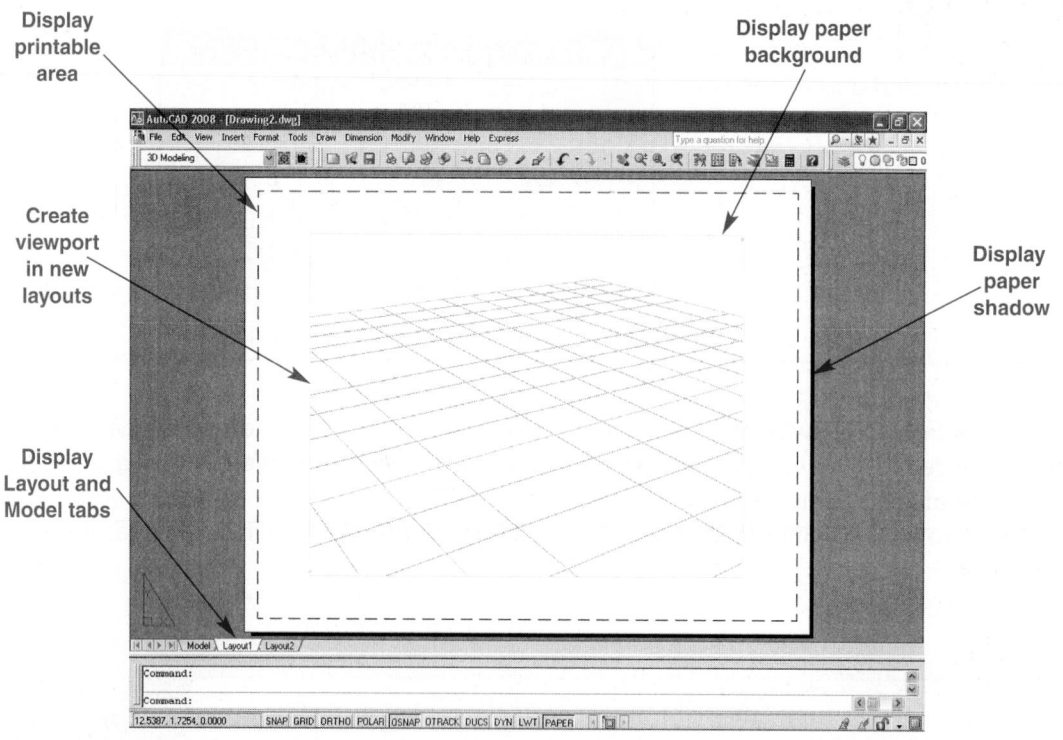

- **Display printable area.** The margins of the printable area are shown as dashed lines on the layout paper. Any portion of an object outside of the margins is not plotted.
- **Display paper background.** Displays the paper size specified in the page setup.
- **Display paper shadow.** Displays a shadow to the right and bottom of the paper. This option is only available if **Display paper background** is checked.
- **Show Page Setup Manager for new layouts.** Determines if the **Page Setup** dialog box is displayed when a new layout is selected or created. By default, this is unchecked.
- **Create viewport in new layouts.** Determines whether a viewport is automatically created when a new layout is selected or created. Many users uncheck this option since they will be creating their own floating viewports.

Display Performance Settings

The settings in the **Display resolution** and **Display performance** areas of the **Display** tab in the **Options** dialog box affect the performance of AutoCAD. The settings can affect regeneration time and realtime panning and zooming. The following options are available in the **Display resolution** area.

- **Arc and circle smoothness.** This setting controls the smoothness of circles, arcs, and ellipses. The default value is 1000; the range is from 1 to 20000. The system variable equivalent is **VIEWRES**.
- **Segments in a polyline curve.** This value determines how many line segments will be generated for each polyline curve. The default value is 8; the range is a nonzero value from –32768 to 32767. The system variable equivalent is **SPLINESEGS**.
- **Rendered object smoothness.** This setting controls the smoothness of curved solids when they are hidden, shaded, or rendered. This value is multiplied by the **Arc and circle smoothness** value. The default value is 0.5; the range is from 0.01 to 10. The system variable equivalent is **FACETRES**.

- **Contour lines per surface.** This value controls the number of contour lines per surface on solid objects. The default value is 4; the range is from 0 to 2047. The system variable equivalent is **ISOLINES**.

The following options are available in the **Display performance** area.

- **Pan and zoom with raster & OLE.** If this is checked, raster images are displayed when panning and zooming. If it is unchecked, only the frame is displayed. The system variable equivalent is **RTDISPLAY**.
- **Highlight raster image frame only.** If this is checked, only the frame around a raster image is highlighted when the image is selected. If this option is unchecked, the image displays a diagonal checkered pattern to indicate selection. The system variable equivalent is **IMAGEHLT**.
- **Apply solid fill.** Controls the display of solid fills in objects. Affected objects include hatches, wide polylines, solids, multilines, and traces. The system variable equivalent is **FILLMODE**.
- **Show text boundary frame only.** This setting controls the Quick Text mode. When checked, text is replaced by a rectangular frame. The system variable equivalent is **QTEXTMODE**.
- **Draw true silhouettes for solids and surfaces.** Controls whether or not the silhouette curves are displayed for solid objects. The system variable equivalent is **DISPSILH**.

NOTE

After changing display settings, use the **REGEN** or **REGENALL** command to make the settings take effect on the objects in the drawing.

PROFESSIONAL TIP

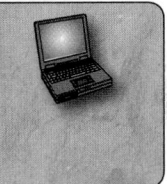

If you notice performance slowing down, you may want to adjust display settings. For example, if there is a lot of text in the drawing, you can activate Quick Text mode to improve performance. When the drawing is ready for plotting, deactivate Quick Text mode.

File Saving Options

The settings specified in the **Open and Save** tab of the **Options** dialog box deal with how drawing files are saved, safety precautions, xrefs, the loading of ObjectARX applications, and proxy objects. This tab is shown in **Figure 19-7.** The options in this tab are discussed in the next sections.

Default Settings for Saving Files

The settings in the **File Save** area determine the defaults for saving files. The setting in the **Save as:** drop-down list determines the default file type. You may want to change this setting if you are saving drawing files as a previous release of AutoCAD or saving drawings as DXF files.

The **Maintain visual fidelity for annotative objects** check box controls how annotative objects are displayed when the drawing is opened in AutoCAD 2007 or earlier versions. If you work primarily in model space, this can be left unchecked. If you use layouts and expect the drawing files to be opened in older versions of AutoCAD, this should be checked. When checked and the drawing is saved and then opened in an older version of AutoCAD, the scaled representations of annotative objects are divided into separate objects. These objects are stored in an anonymous block, saved on separate layers with names based on the layer's original name appended with a number. When the drawing is opened once again in AutoCAD 2008, the annotative objects are restored to normal. The system variable equivalent for this toggle is **SAVEFIDELITY**. Checking the check box sets this variable to 1 (on). Unchecking it sets the variable to 0 (off).

The **Incremental save percentage** value determines how much of the drawing is saved when a **SAVE** or **QSAVE** is performed. If the quantity of new data in a drawing file reaches the specified percentage, a full save is performed. To force a full save to be performed, set the value to 0.

If you pick the **Thumbnail Preview Settings...** button, the **Thumbnail Preview Settings** dialog box is displayed, Figure 19-8. If the **Save a thumbnail preview image** check box is checked, a preview image of the drawing will be displayed in the **Select File** dialog box when the drawing is selected for opening. The system variable equivalent for this setting is **RASTERPREVIEW**; 1 creates a preview.

When the **Generate Sheet, Sheet View, and Model View Thumbnails** check box is checked in the **Thumbnail Preview Settings** dialog box, the thumbnails in the **Sheet Set Manager** are updated based on the position of the slider below this check box. The slider can be set to one of three positions. A description of the current setting appears below the slider. When the slider is in the middle position (default), thumbnails are updated when they are accessed. When the slider is in the left-hand position, thumbnails must be updated manually. When the slider is in the right-hand position, the thumbnails are updated when the drawing is saved. The system variable equivalent is **UPDATETHUMBNAIL**. The settings are:

- **0.** The **Generate Sheet, Sheet View, and Model View Thumbnails** check box is unchecked.
- **7.** The check box is checked and the slider is in the left-hand position.

Figure 19-7.
The **Open and Save** tab settings control default save options, file safety features, xref options, and ObjectARX application options.

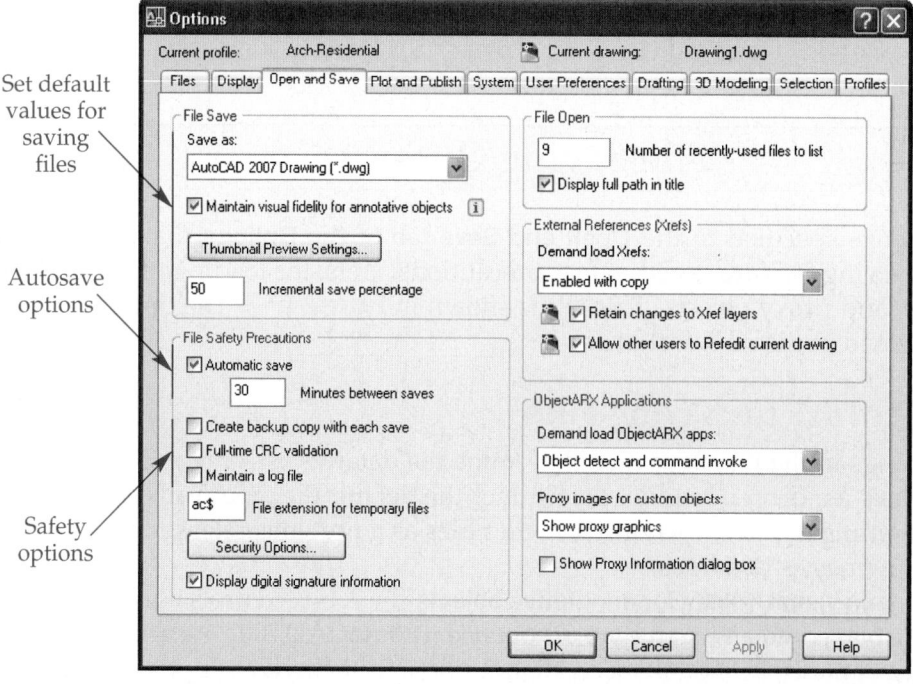

Figure 19-8.
The **Thumbnail Preview Settings** dialog box.

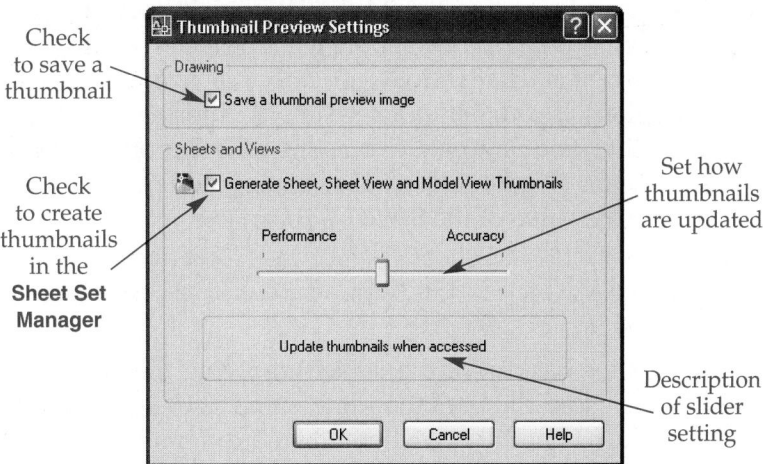

Check to save a thumbnail

Check to create thumbnails in the **Sheet Set Manager**

Set how thumbnails are updated

Description of slider setting

- **15.** The check box is checked and the slider is in the middle position.
- **23.** The check box is checked and the slider is in the right-hand position.

PROFESSIONAL TIP

To maintain forward compatibility of drawings, annotative objects should not be edited in older versions of AutoCAD. Doing so may compromise the annotative properties. For example, exploding an annotative block in an older version of AutoCAD then opening that drawing in AutoCAD 2008 results in each of the scaled representations becoming a separate annotative object.

Autosave Settings

When working in AutoCAD, data loss can occur due to a sudden power outage or an unforeseen system error. AutoCAD provides several safety precautions to help minimize data loss when these types of events occur. The settings for the precautions are found in the **File Safety Precautions** area in the **Open and Save** tab of the **Options** dialog box.

When the **Automatic save** check box is enabled, AutoCAD automatically creates a backup file at a specified time interval. The **Minutes between saves** edit box sets this interval. This is the value of the **SAVETIME** system variable. Removing the check sets **SAVETIME** to 0.

The automatic save feature does not overwrite the source drawing file with its incremental saves. Rather, AutoCAD saves temporary files. The path for autosave files is specified in the **Files** tab in the **Options** dialog box, as discussed earlier. The autosave file is stored in the specified location until the drawing is closed. When the drawing is closed, the autosave file is deleted. Autosave files have a .sv$ extension with the drawing name and some random numbers generated by AutoCAD. If AutoCAD unexpectedly quits, the autosave file is not deleted and can be renamed with a .dwg extension so it can be opened in AutoCAD.

The interval setting should be based on working conditions and file size. It is possible to adversely affect your productivity by setting your **SAVETIME** value too small. For example, in larger drawings, a save can take a significant amount of time. Ideally, it is best to set your **SAVETIME** variable to the greatest amount of time you can afford to repeat. While it may be acceptable to redo the last fifteen minutes or less of work, it is unlikely that you would feel the same about having to redo the last hour of work.

Backup Files

AutoCAD can create a backup of the current drawing file whenever the current drawing is saved. The backup file uses the same name as the drawing, but has a .bak file extension. The backup is not overwritten when a different drawing is opened or saved. When the **Create backup copy with each save** check box in the **Open and Save** tab of the **Options** dialog box is checked, the backup file feature is enabled. If not checked, the file is not backed up when you save. Unless you prefer to take unnecessary risks, it is usually best to have this feature enabled.

CRC Validation

A *cyclic redundancy check*, or CRC, verifies that the number of data bits sent is the same as the number received. **Full-time CRC validation** is a feature you can use when drawing files are being corrupted and you suspect a hardware or software problem. When using full-time CRC validation, the CRC check is done every time data are read into the drawing. This ensures that all data are correctly received.

Log Files

The log file can serve a variety of purposes. The source of drawing errors can be determined by reviewing the commands that produced the incorrect results. Additionally, log files can be reviewed by a CAD manager to determine the need for staff training or customization of the system.

When the **Maintain a log file** check box is activated in the **Open and Save** tab of the **Options** dialog box, AutoCAD creates a file named with the drawing name, a code, and the .log file extension. The name and location of the log file can be specified using the Log File Location listing in the **Files** tab of the **Options** dialog box. When activated, all prompts, messages, and responses that appear in the **Command Line** window are saved to this file. The log file status can also be set using the **LOGFILEON** and **LOGFILEOFF** commands.

File Opening Settings

The **File Open** area of the **Open and Save** tab in the **Options** dialog box contains two settings. The value in the **Number of recently-used files to list** text box controls the number of drawing files listed at the bottom of the **File** pull-down menu. This value can be from 0 to 9. The **Display full path in title** check box controls whether the entire drawing file path (when checked) or just the file name (when unchecked) is displayed in the title bar of the AutoCAD window.

External Reference Settings

The external reference options in the **Open and Save** tab of the **Options** dialog box are important if you are working with xrefs. These options are found in the **External Reference (Xrefs)** area of the tab. The **Demand load Xrefs:** setting can affect system performance and the ability for another user to edit a drawing currently referenced into another drawing. You can select Enabled, Disabled, or Enabled with copy from the drop-down list. This setting is also controlled by the **XLOADCTL** system variable.

If the **Retain changes to Xref layers** option is checked, xref layer settings are saved with the drawing file. The **VISRETAIN** system variable also controls this setting.

The **Allow other users to Refedit current drawing** setting controls whether or not the drawing can be edited in-place when it is referenced by another drawing. This setting is also controlled by the **XEDIT** system variable.

ObjectARX Options

The **ObjectARX Applications** area of the **Open and Save** tab of the **Options** dialog box controls the loading of ObjectARX applications and the displaying of proxy objects. The **Demand load ObjectARX apps:** setting specifies if and when AutoCAD loads third-party applications associated with objects in the drawing. The **Proxy images for custom objects:** setting controls how objects created by a third-party application are displayed. When a drawing with proxy objects is opened, the **Proxy Information** dialog box is displayed. To disable the dialog box, uncheck the **Show Proxy Information dialog box** option.

System Settings

Options for the pointing device, graphic settings, general system options, and dbConnect can be found in the **System** tab of the **Options** dialog box, Figure 19-9. These settings affect the interaction between AutoCAD and your operating system.

Figure 19-9.
General AutoCAD system options and hardware settings can be controlled in the **System** tab.

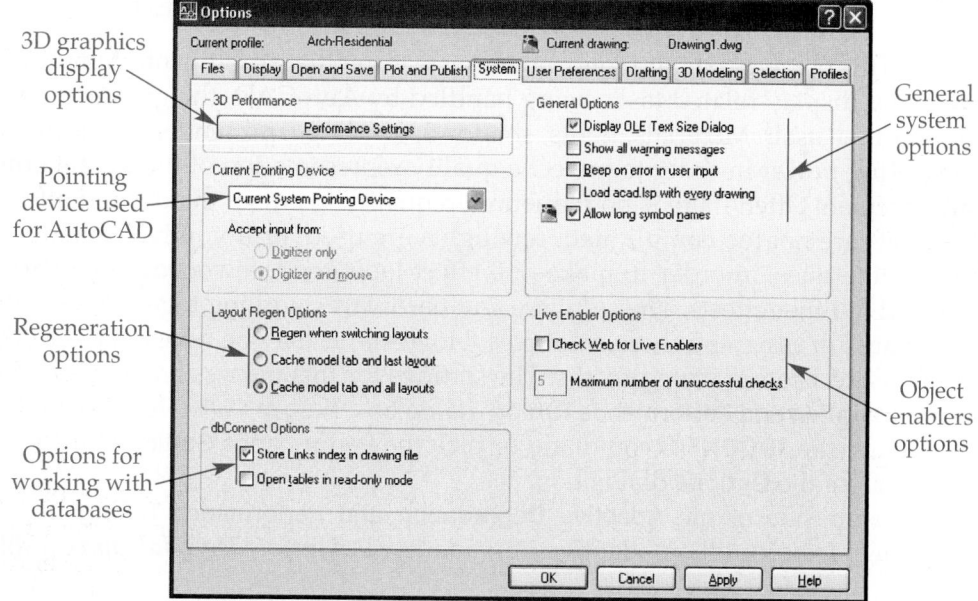

In the **3D Performance** area is the **Performance Settings** button. Selecting this button displays the **Adaptive Degradation and Performance Tuning** dialog box. The options available in this dialog box are discussed in the next section.

The **Current Pointing Device** area determines the pointing device used with AutoCAD. The default is the current system pointing device (usually your mouse). If you have a digitizer tablet, you will want to select the Wintab Compatible Digitizer option. You must configure your tablet before it can be used. For detailed instructions on using your tablet as a digitizing device, refer to Appendix B on the Student CD.

The **Layout Regen Options** setting determines what is regenerated and when it is regenerated when working with layout tabs. The **Live Enabler Options** determines if the Autodesk website is checked for object enablers. You can also specify the number of retries when checking. The following options are available in the **dbConnect Options** area.

- **Store Links index in drawing file.** When this option is checked, the database index is saved within the drawing file. This makes the link selection operation quicker, but increases the drawing file size.
- **Open tables in read-only mode.** Determines whether tables are opened in read-only mode.

The settings in the **General Options** area control general system functions. The following options are available.

- **Display OLE Text Size Dialog.** When inserting an OLE object, the **OLE Text Size** dialog box is displayed if this option is checked.
- **Show all warning messages.** Controls the display of dialog boxes that include a **Don't Display This Warning Again** option.
- **Beep on error in user input.** Specifies whether AutoCAD alerts you of incorrect user input with an audible beep.
- **Load acad.lsp with every drawing.** This setting turns the persistent AutoLISP feature on or off.
- **Allow long symbol names.** Determines if long symbol names can be used in AutoCAD. If this option is checked, up to 255 characters can be used for layers, dimension styles, blocks, linetypes, text styles, layouts, UCS names, views, and viewport configurations. If unchecked, symbol names are limited to 31 characters. The system variable is **EXTNAMES**.

3D Performance Settings

With all of the powerful 3D and solid modeling features that are built into AutoCAD, there are many display-related tasks being handled by AutoCAD, the graphics card, and the computer itself. Materials, lights, shadows, shading, and rendering require a lot of computing power in order to project a quality representation of the model onto the monitor screen. Often there is no reduction in quality to any of the desired effects if the materials are not too complicated, few lights are used, or if you have shadows turned off. Sometimes, in order to make one effect look good, fewer resources have to be assigned to other effects. The software and hardware, working together, usually do an adequate job assigning these resources. However, it may be necessary for you to assist in this decision-making process. The settings for this process are made in the **Adaptive Degradation and Performance Tuning** dialog box, Figure 19-10. To display this dialog box, enter the **3DCONFIG** command or pick the **Performance Settings** button in the **Systems** tab of the **Options** dialog box.

The left-hand side of the **Adaptive Degradation and Performance Tuning** dialog contains settings for controlling adaptive degradation. *Adaptive degradation* controls

Figure 19-10.
The **Adaptive
Degradation and
Performance Tuning**
dialog box is used to
turn on and prioritize
adaptive degradation.

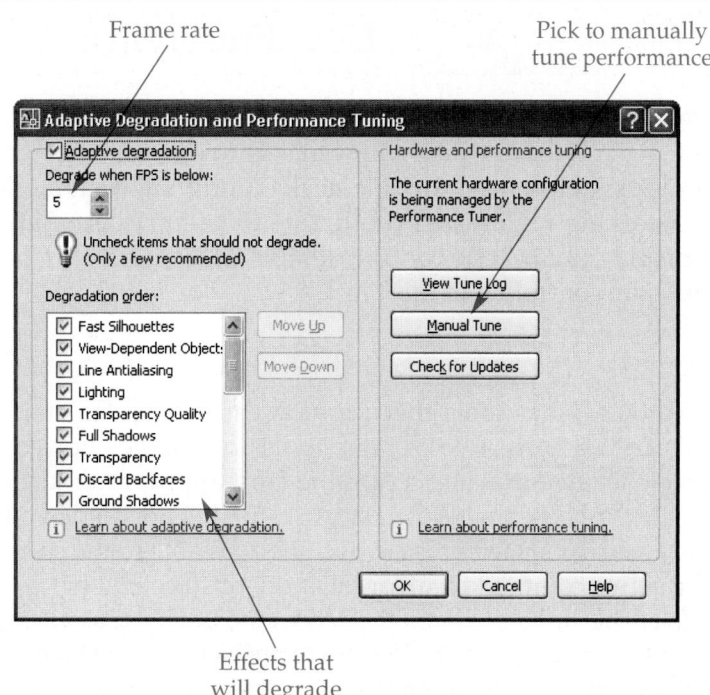

Frame rate

Pick to manually
tune performance

Effects that
will degrade

system performance by turning off features or preventing them from using resources. The check box at the top controls whether or not adaptive degradation is being used. When unchecked, adaptive degradation is turned off and all effects are using all resources. This may result in graphics lagging or becoming slow and "choppy" as you zoom and pan around your drawing. The orbiting commands are even more affected by this being turned off. By checking the check box, adaptive degradation is activated.

AutoCAD tracks its graphics performance in terms of frames per second (fps). Just below the **Adaptive degradation** check box is a text box for setting this value. You may enter a new value in the text box or use the arrows to increase or decrease the value. The higher the number, the sooner resources start being reassigned. If performance dips below this level, resources are taken away from the various effects that create the displayed graphics.

The effects that can be controlled while adaptive degradation is turned on are shown in the **Degradation order:** list box. Certain effects that you deem important can be unchecked so they are not degraded and operate using maximum resources. The top-to-bottom order in which the effects are listed determines the priority in which resources are removed. This order can be changed by selecting an effect and picking the **Move Up** or **Move Down** buttons on the right side of the list.

On the right side of the **Adaptive Degradation and Performance Tuning** dialog box is the **Hardware and performance tuning** area. Picking the **View Tune Log** button displays a log of any features or effects that have been turned off. Information regarding your computer, amount of RAM, and 3D graphics card are also shown. The log can be saved as a file. The **Manual Tune** button displays the **Manual Performance Tuning** dialog box. This dialog box allows control over hardware settings (hardware acceleration, graphics card driver name, and the effects the graphics card is capable of), general settings (discard back faces and quality of transparency), and dynamic tessellation settings (surface and curve tessellation settings and number of tessellations to cache).

When the settings have been adjusted as desired in the **Adaptive Degradation and Performance Tuning** dialog box, pick the **OK** button to return to the **Options** dialog box. Then, close the **Options** dialog box.

User Preferences

A variety of settings are found in the **User Preferences** tab of the **Options** dialog box. See Figure 19-11. AutoCAD allows users to optimize the way they work in AutoCAD by providing options for double-click editing, shortcut menu functions, **DesignCenter** units, working with fields, coordinate data entry, associative dimensions, hyperlink icon display, undo/redo control, default lineweight settings, and scale list settings. All of these are controlled in this tab.

Shortcut Menus and Double-Click Editing

AutoCAD has tools that provide easy access to commonly used editing commands and options. Two of these tools are double-click editing and shortcut menus. Double-clicking on an object calls the most appropriate editing tool for that object type, often the **Properties** window. Shortcut menus are displayed by right-clicking and are *context sensitive,* meaning the options available in the shortcut menu are determined by the active command, cursor location, or selected object.

To enable double-click editing, check the **Double click editing** check box in the **Windows Standard Behavior** area in the **User Preferences** tab of the **Options** dialog box. To enable shortcut menus, check the **Shortcut menus in drawing area** check box in the same area. Disabling the shortcut menus makes a right mouse click the equivalent of pressing the [Enter] key.

You can also customize the setting for the right mouse button. Pick the **Right-click Customization...** button to access the **Right-Click Customization** dialog box. See Figure 19-12. The **Turn on time-sensitive right-click:** check box controls the right-click behavior. A quick click is the same as pressing [Enter]. A longer click displays a shortcut menu. You can set the duration of the longer click in milliseconds. If the check box is checked, the **Default Mode** and **Command Mode** areas of the dialog box are disabled.

Different settings can be used for the three different shortcut menu modes. Each of the three menu modes has a separate area in the **Right-Click Customization** dialog box.

- **Default Mode.** In this mode, no objects are selected and no command is active. The **Repeat Last Command** option activates the last command issued. The **Shortcut Menu** option displays the shortcut menu.

Figure 19-11.
The **User Preferences** tab allows you to set up AutoCAD in a manner that works best for you.

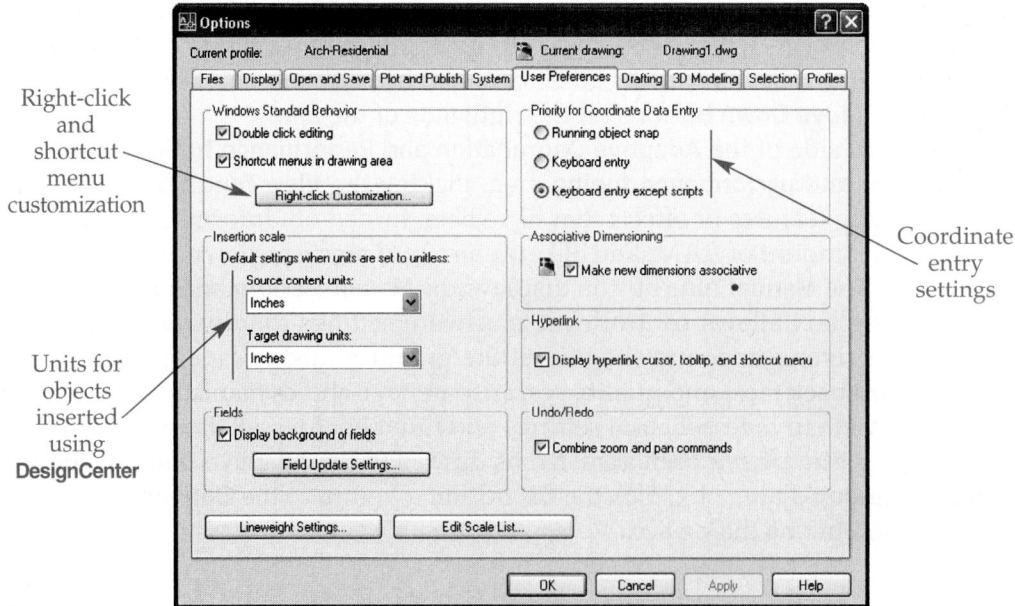

Figure 19-12.
Use this dialog box to customize the right mouse button.

Controls
right-click
behavior

Select
behavior for
each mode

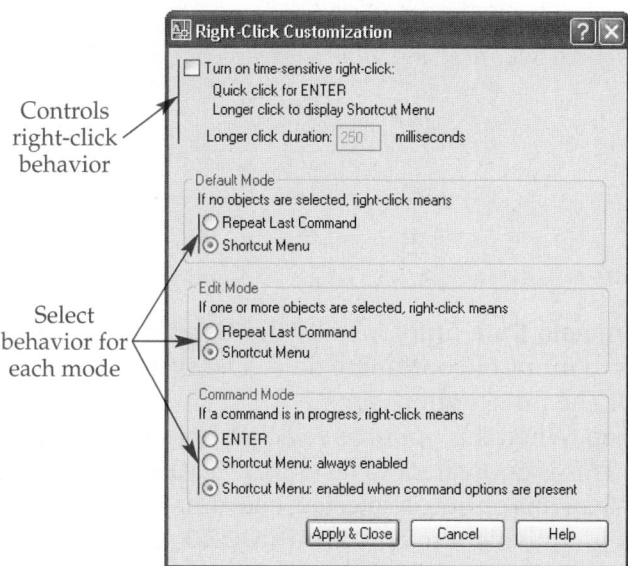

- **Edit Mode.** In this mode, an object is selected, but no command is active. The **Repeat Last Command** option activates the last command issued. The **Shortcut Menu** option displays the shortcut menu.
- **Command Mode.** In this mode, a command is active. The **ENTER** option makes a right-click the same as pressing [Enter]. The **Shortcut Menu: always enabled** option means that the shortcut menu is always displayed in command mode. The **Shortcut Menu: enabled when command options are present** option means the shortcut menu is only displayed when command options are available on the command line. When there are no command options, a right-click is the same as [Enter]. This is the default option.

Insertion Scale

In the **Insertion scale** area of the **User Preferences** tab, unit values can be set for objects when they are inserted into a drawing. This applies to "unitless" objects dragged from **DesignCenter** or inserted using the i-drop method. The **Source content units:** setting specifies the units for objects being inserted into the current drawing. The **Target drawing units:** setting determines the units in the current drawing. These settings are used when there are no units set with the **INSUNITS** system variable.

Fields

A *field* is a special type of text object that displays a specific property value, setting, or characteristic. Fields can display information related to a specific object, general drawing properties, or information related to the current user or computer system. The text displayed in the field can change if the value being displayed changes. Refer to *AutoCAD and Its Applications—Basics* for more information on using fields.

In the **Fields** area of the **User Preferences** tab, you can set whether or not a field is displayed with a nonplotting background. When the **Display background of fields** check box is checked, the field background is displayed in light gray.

Picking the **Field Update Settings...** button in the **Fields** area opens the **Field Update Settings** dialog box, **Figure 19-13.** In this dialog box, you can set when fields are automatically updated. The five options are **Open**, **Save**, **Plot**, **eTransmit**, and **Regen**. Check as many of the options as appropriate.

Figure 19-13.
Setting when fields
are automatically
updated.

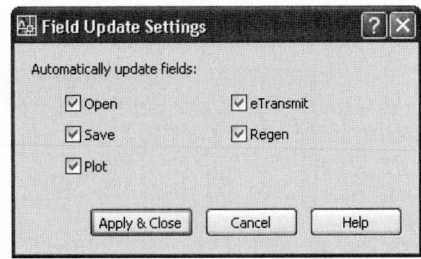

Coordinate Data Priority

The **Priority for Coordinate Data Entry** area of the **User Preferences** tab controls how AutoCAD responds to input of coordinate data. The system variable equivalent for this is **OSNAPCOORD**. The three options are:

- **Running object snap.** When this option is selected, object snaps always override coordinate entry. This is equivalent to an **OSNAPCOORD** setting of 0.
- **Keyboard entry.** When this option is selected, coordinate entry always overrides object snaps. This is equivalent to an **OSNAPCOORD** setting of 1.
- **Keyboard entry except scripts.** When this option is selected, coordinate entry will override object snaps except those object snaps contained within scripts. This is the default and equivalent to an **OSNAPCOORD** setting of 2.

Associative Dimensions

By default, all new dimensions are associative. This means that the dimension value automatically changes when a dimension's defpoints are moved. However, you can turn this option off in the **User Preferences** tab of the **Options** dialog box. When the **Make new dimensions associative** check box in the **Associative Dimensioning** area is unchecked, any dimensions drawn do *not* have associativity. This is equivalent to a **DIMASSOC** setting of 1.

Hyperlinks

In the **Hyperlink** area of the **User Preferences** tab, you can set whether or not the hyperlink cursor and tooltip are displayed when the cursor is over a hyperlink. If **Display hyperlink cursor, tooltip, and shortcut menu** is checked, the hyperlink icon appears next to the crosshairs when they are over an object containing a hyperlink. The tooltip is also displayed. Additional hyperlink options are available from the shortcut menu when an object with a hyperlink is selected.

Undo/Redo

The **Undo/Redo** area of the **User Preferences** tab allows you to control how multiple, consecutive zooms and pans are handled within the **UNDO** and **REDO** commands. By checking the **Combine zoom and pan commands** check box, back-to-back zooms and pans are considered a single operation for undo and redo purposes. In other words, performing an undo or redo undoes or redoes the entire zoom/pan sequence. Unchecking the check box allows each zoom or pan to be considered a separate operation.

Lineweight Settings and Edit Scale List

At the bottom of the **User Preferences** tab are the **Lineweight Settings...** and the **Edit Scale List...** buttons. The **Lineweight Settings...** button opens the **Lineweight Settings** dialog box in which you can change default lineweight settings. This is discussed in detail in *AutoCAD and Its Applications—Basics*.

Figure 19-14.
The **Edit Scales List** dialog box allows you to change the scale list that appears when using various viewport, page setup, and plot scaling dialog boxes.

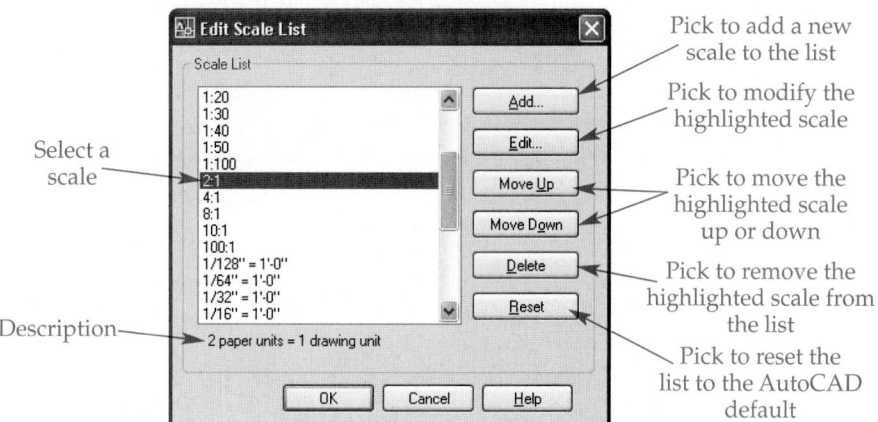

Select a scale

Description

Pick to add a new scale to the list

Pick to modify the highlighted scale

Pick to move the highlighted scale up or down

Pick to remove the highlighted scale from the list

Pick to reset the list to the AutoCAD default

A default list of scales appears in various dialog boxes related to viewports, page setups, and plot scaling. You can add custom scales to, or remove scales from, this list so that the list is more appropriate for your application. Picking the **Edit Scale List...** button at the bottom of the **User Preferences** tab displays the **Edit Scales List** dialog box. See **Figure 19-14.** The dialog box displays the current list of scales. The buttons on the right side of the dialog box allow you to add a new scale, edit an existing scale, move a scale up or down within the list, delete a scale, or reset the list to the default set of scales.

To add a scale, pick the **Add...** button. In the **Add Scale** dialog box that appears, enter a name for the scale in the **Name appearing in scale list:** text box. Then, in the **Scale Properties** area of the dialog box, enter values to indicate how many paper space units equals how many drawing units. Finally, pick the **OK** button to return to the **Edit Scale List** dialog box. The new scale appears in the list and is available wherever the scale list is displayed.

3D Display Properties

There are many ways to customize your system specifically for working in a 3D environment. The **3D Modeling** tab of the **Options** dialog box allows you to control the various settings having to do with working in 3D, **Figure 19-15.**

The **3D Crosshairs** area of the dialog box contains check boxes for displaying the Z axis on the crosshairs, labeling the axes of standard crosshairs, and labeling the axes of the dynamic UCS icon. There are three labeling possibilities from which to choose:
- X, Y, and Z.
- N (north), E (east), and z.
- Or you can specify custom labels for each axes.

The check boxes in the **Display UCS Icon** area determine if the UCS icon is displayed in 2D model space, 3D parallel projection, and 3D perspective projection. The **Dynamic Input** area has a check box for showing the Z field for dynamic input.

The setting in the **Visual Style while creating 3D objects** drop-down list in the **3D Objects** area determines which visual style is set current when objects are created. The **Deletion control while creating 3D objects** drop-down list determines how geometry is handled when creating 3D objects. For example, when **Delete profile curves** is selected, the profile and path curves are deleted after a sweep is created. The two sliders in the **3D Objects** area control set the **SURFU** and **SURFV** system variables for old-style surfaces.

Figure 19-15.
Use the **3D Modeling**
tab to customize
settings when
working in 3D.

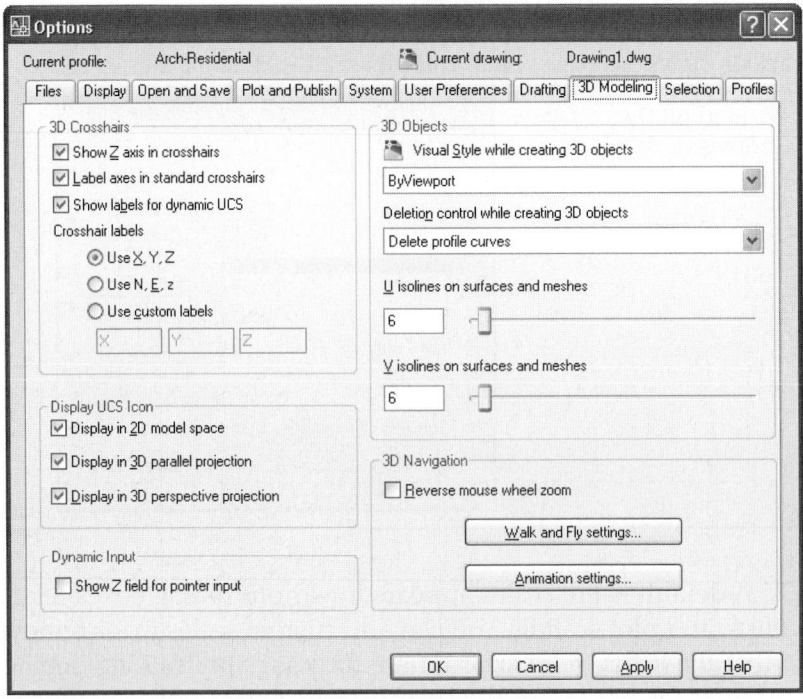

The **3D Navigation** area has a check box for reversing the zoom direction of the mouse wheel. There are also two buttons in this area that allow access to settings for walkthroughs/flybys and animations. Selecting the **Walk and Fly settings...** button opens the **Walk and Fly Settings** dialog box. This dialog box contains settings used when creating walkthroughs and flybys. Selecting the **Animation settings...** button opens the **Animation Settings** dialog box. This dialog box contains settings that control the actual animation of a walkthrough or flyby. Both of these dialog boxes are discussed in detail in Chapter 17.

Changing Program Properties

When AutoCAD is first installed on your computer, the installation program automatically creates the AutoCAD group and several program items and places a program icon on the Windows desktop. If desired, you can modify the program icon properties. These properties include such things as the file attributes, the folder where AutoCAD is started, and the icon for the shortcut.

To modify the AutoCAD program icon properties, right-click on the AutoCAD 2008 icon on the desktop and then select **Properties** from the shortcut menu. See **Figure 19-16.** You can also pick the icon and then use the [Alt]+[Enter] key combination. Either action displays the **AutoCAD 2008 Properties** dialog box, **Figure 19-17.** There are three main tabs: **General**, **Shortcut**, and **Compatibility**. Additional tabs, such as **Security**, may be listed, depending on your Windows setup. The options in the **Shortcut** tab are:

- **Target.** This text box contains the name of the executable program and its path. If the folder that contains the AutoCAD executable has changed, this line can be edited so the shortcut still links to the correct file. If you are not sure of the exact path, you can pick the **Find Target...** button at the bottom of the tab to locate the executable.
- **Start in.** This text box specifies the name of the folder where the AutoCAD program files are located. The folder specified in this text box becomes the current folder when AutoCAD is running. Any new files are placed here.

Figure 19-16.
This shortcut menu appears when you right-click on an icon (shortcut) on the Windows desktop.

Right-click on the icon to access the shortcut menu

Figure 19-17.
The **AutoCAD 2008 Properties** dialog box.

Current folder when program is running

Create shortcut key to start AutoCAD

Browse for location of executable file

Location of executable file

Select a new icon

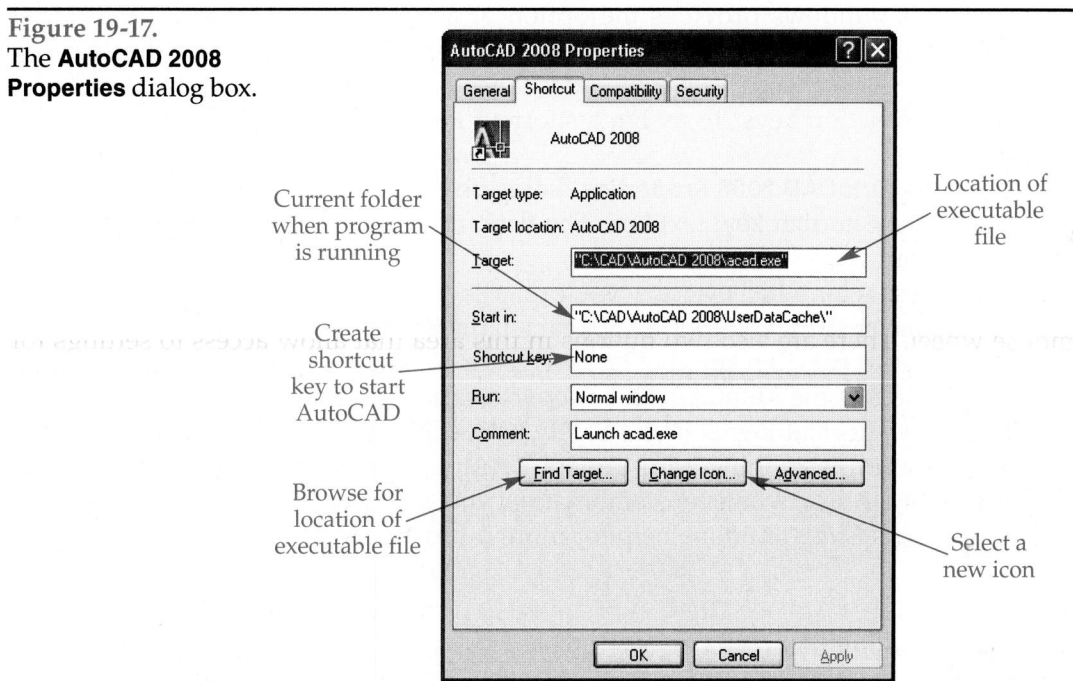

- **Shortcut key.** Microsoft Windows provides a special feature called an *application shortcut key.* This feature permits you to launch AutoCAD with a user-defined key combination. Assigning a shortcut key for AutoCAD is described later in this chapter.
- **Run.** This listing offers options to run the program in a normal, maximized, or minimized window. Do not run the program minimized, otherwise AutoCAD appears only as a button on the taskbar when you start it. You can easily restore or maximize it, but when it does not automatically appear on screen, it may be confusing to newer users.
- **Comment.** This is the tooltip displayed next to the cursor.

When you are finished making your changes, pick the **OK** button to exit the **AutoCAD 2008 Properties** dialog box. Any changes you make immediately take effect, so there is no need to restart Windows.

> **NOTE**
>
> Be sure to check with your instructor or system administrator before modifying the AutoCAD program properties.

Changing the AutoCAD Icon

The **AutoCAD 2008 Properties** dialog box provides the option to change the program icon for the shortcut. Use the following procedure to change the icon.

1. Pick the **Change Icon...** button in the **Shortcut** tab of the **AutoCAD 2008 Properties** dialog box. The **Change Icon** dialog box is then displayed.
2. To display icons for AutoCAD, use the **Browse...** button to find the file named acad.exe in the \AutoCAD 2008 folder. Pick the **Open** button to display the AutoCAD icons, as shown in Figure 19-18. You can also select any valid icon or library file.
3. Select the icon you wish to use and pick the **OK** button to exit the **Change Icon** dialog box. Your icon selection is now displayed at the top of the **AutoCAD 2008 Properties** dialog box. Pick **OK** to close the dialog box.

Defining a Shortcut Key

Microsoft Windows provides the option of assigning a shortcut key that starts an application. You can use any letter, number, or special character for a shortcut key. Whichever key you choose, Windows automatically adds a [Ctrl]+[Alt] in front of it. You can also use function keys. To assign a shortcut key for launching AutoCAD, do the following.

1. Open the **AutoCAD 2008 Properties** dialog box.
2. Pick in the **Shortcut key:** text box. The flashing vertical cursor appears at the end of the word None.
3. Now, press A (or whichever key you prefer).
4. The character string Ctrl + Alt + A appears in the **Shortcut key:** text box, Figure 19-19. If you press a function key, the Ctrl and Alt are not added.
5. Pick **OK** to exit the **AutoCAD 2008 Properties** dialog box.

Your new shortcut key is immediately active. Now, no matter which Windows-based application is running, you can start AutoCAD with the keyboard combination [Ctrl]+[Alt]+[A] (or whatever combination you specified). Refer to the Microsoft Windows *User's Guide* or online help for more information regarding shortcut keys.

Creating Alternate AutoCAD Configurations

The information you specify for AutoCAD regarding the pointing and printing devices is recorded in a configuration file. Your pointing and printing devices are specified in the **Options** dialog box, but the information is stored in the current configuration file. The default configuration file is acad2008.cfg. You can determine the current location for this configuration file by going to the Help and Miscellaneous File Names section of the **Files** tab in the **Options** dialog box. Each time you specify a new

Figure 19-18.
A new icon can be selected in the **Change Icon** dialog box.

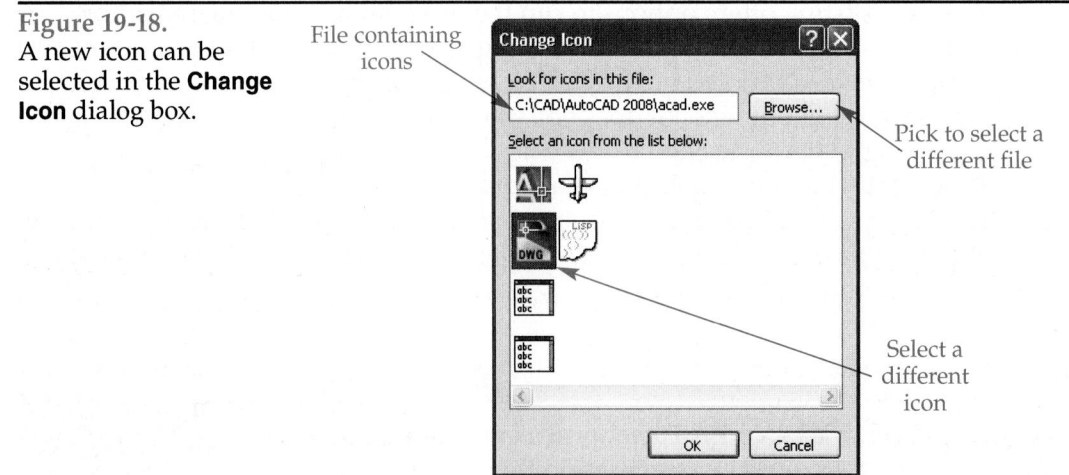

Figure 19-19.
Setting the [Ctrl]+[Alt]+[A] key combination to automatically start AutoCAD.

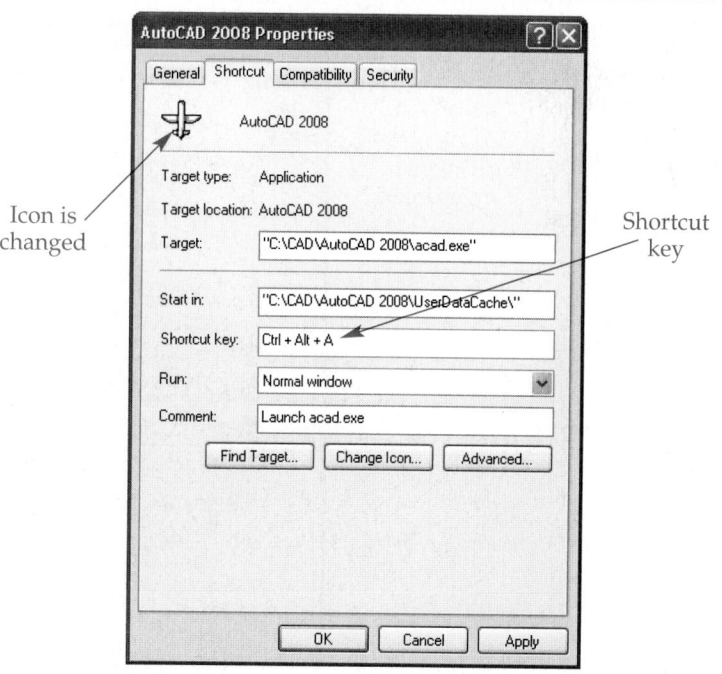

Icon is changed

Shortcut key

pointing or printing device, the existing acad2008.cfg file is overwritten with the new information.

Under most circumstances, a single configuration file is all that is necessary. Some users, however, may require multiple configurations. As an example, if you use a mouse most of the time, but sometimes need a digitizer tablet, you may find it convenient to set up AutoCAD to use multiple configurations. This can save you the time required to reconfigure AutoCAD each time you need to switch your pointing devices.

To save multiple configurations, you must specify a new location for AutoCAD to store the acad2008.cfg so that it does not overwrite the previous version. This way, you actually have more than one configuration file, with each file located in a specific folder. It is recommended that these folders be placed under the AutoCAD "user" folder so they are easy to locate. For this example, create a folder named \Altcfg. Now, find the acad2008.cfg file in its current folder and copy it to the new folder.

On the Windows desktop, press the [Ctrl] key and drag the **AutoCAD 2008** icon (shortcut) to create a copy. This new shortcut is for the new configuration. Open the **AutoCAD 2008 Properties** dialog box for the new shortcut and go to the **Shortcut** tab. In the **Target:** edit box, place /c after the existing target, followed by the directory path location for the alternate configuration. For example, in **Figure 19-20,** the configuration directory is entered as:

"C:\Program Files\AutoCAD 2008\acad.exe" /c "C:\Documents and Settings*username*\ Local Settings\Application Data\Autodesk\AutoCAD 2008\R17.1\enu\altcfg"

The *username* listing indicates the specific AutoCAD user. The new path must be placed in quotation marks due to the spaces in the path name. The /c is not in quotation marks. Command line switches (the /c) are separated by spaces. A space is interpreted as the end of the path name.

It is also recommended that you change the title of the shortcut icon on the desktop to match the configuration. For example, one shortcut icon could be called AutoCAD 2008 Original and the other could be called AutoCAD 2008 Alternate. Do this by rightclicking on the icon on the desktop and selecting **Rename**. Then, enter the new text.

When you start AutoCAD using the new shortcut, the alternate configuration file folder is used. This means that any configuration changes you make are stored in the new configuration file and do not affect other configurations.

Figure 19-20.
If multiple configurations are used, the location of the alternate configuration file must be specified in the **Target:** edit box.

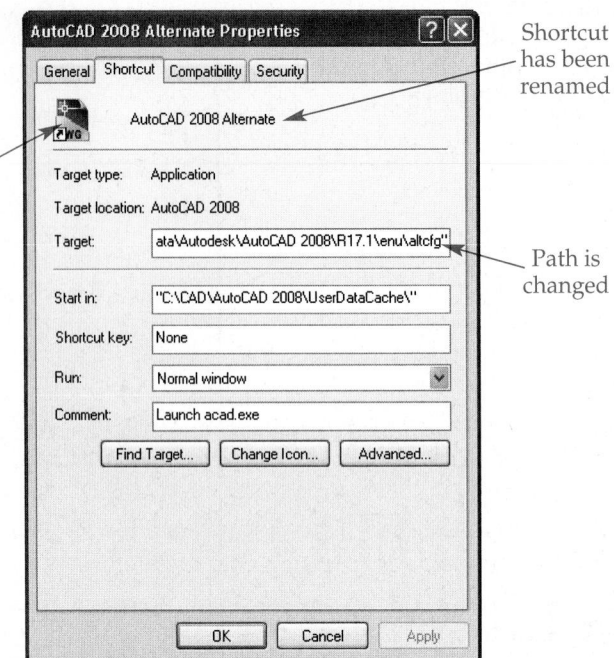

Icon is changed

Shortcut has been renamed

Path is changed

NOTE

You can set up unique shortcut keys for each AutoCAD shortcut on your desktop.

PROFESSIONAL TIP

A user profile can be directly accessed from an AutoCAD shortcut on the desktop using a /p switch and the exact profile name. For example, if you created a profile called Project 0256, the **Target:** text box in the **AutoCAD 2008 Properties** dialog box may read:

"C:\Program Files\AutoCAD 2008\acad.exe" /p "Project 0256"

Chapter Test

Answer the following questions. Write your answers on a separate sheet of paper or complete the electronic chapter test on the Student CD.

1. List three methods used to open the **Options** dialog box.
2. List the tabs found in the **Options** dialog box.
3. AutoCAD resides in the C:\Program Files\AutoCAD 2008 folder on your workstation. You have created two folders under \AutoCAD 2008 named \Projects and \Symbols. You want to store your drawings in the \Projects folder and your blocks in the \Symbols folder. What should you enter in the Support File Search Path area so these folders are added to the search path?
4. How do you open the **Drawing Window Colors** dialog box to change the color of AutoCAD screen elements?
5. For which AutoCAD feature(s) can you customize the font (not within a drawing)?
6. In which tab of the **Options** dialog box can you change settings for layout tabs?
7. Briefly describe how to turn on the automatic save feature and specify the save interval.

8. How do you select the folder in which the autosave file is saved?
9. What are the advantages of toggling the log file open?
10. Name the two commands that toggle the log file on and off.
11. How would you set the right mouse button to perform an [Enter], rather than displaying shortcut menus?
12. How do you open the **Edit Scales List** dialog box from within the **Options** dialog box?
13. Which file must be copied to a separate folder before creating an alternate AutoCAD configuration?

Drawing Problems

1. Using the methods described in this chapter, create an alternate configuration for AutoCAD dedicated to 3D modeling and rendering. Use the following instructions.
   A. Assign a different program icon for the 3D configuration.
   B. Name the program shortcut AutoCAD 3D.
   C. Define a shortcut key for the configuration.
   D. Add to the support path a folder that contains 3D shapes you have created.

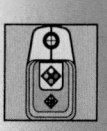

2. Create an alternate configuration for AutoCAD dedicated to dimensioning. Use the following instructions to complete this problem.
   A. Assign a different program icon for the dimensioning configuration.
   B. Name the program shortcut AutoCAD Dimensioning.
   C. Define a shortcut key for the configuration.

The **Dashboard** can be customized by adding control panels and then adding tools to them. Here, the **Customize User Interface** dialog box is shown with the custom control panel definition displayed. The custom control panel, below, allows this user to have only a single control panel displayed in the **Dashboard** while still having access to commands commonly used for 3D work.

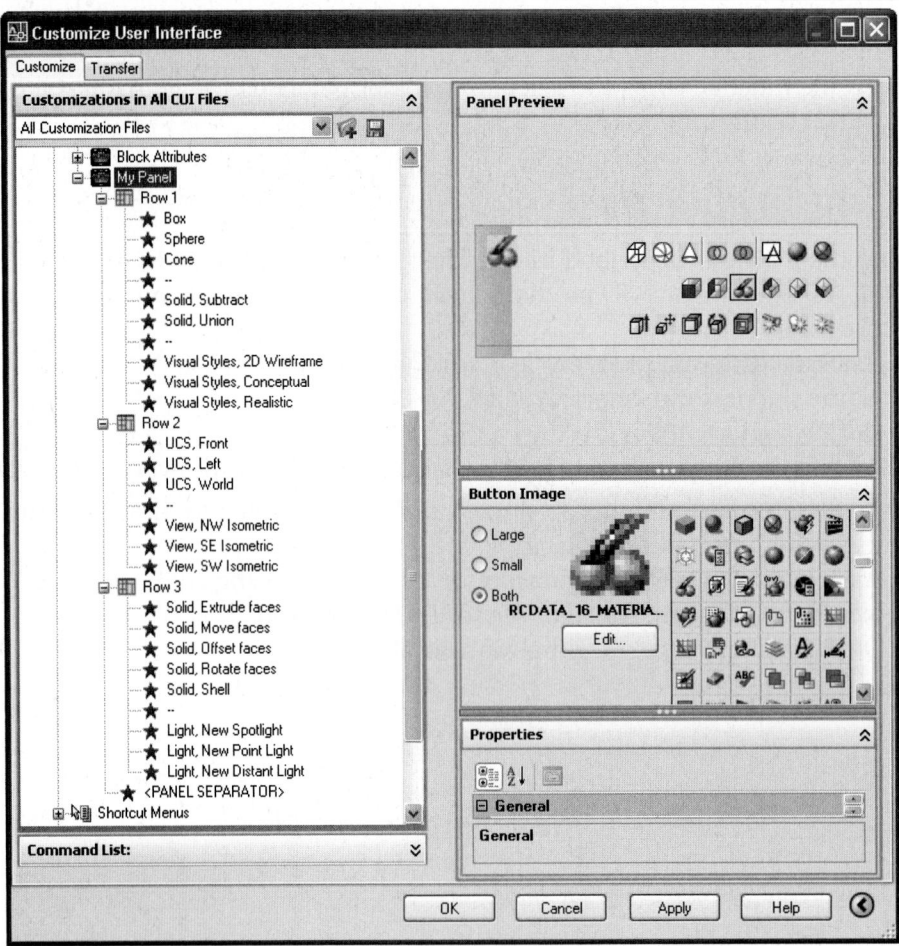

CHAPTER 20

Customizing Toolbars, Pull-Down Menus, and the Dashboard

Learning Objectives

After completing this chapter, you will be able to:
- ✓ Display and hide toolbars.
- ✓ Modify existing toolbars.
- ✓ Create new toolbars.
- ✓ Create custom commands.
- ✓ Add flyouts to toolbars.
- ✓ Explain how to customize pull-down menus.
- ✓ Add DIESEL expressions to pull-down menu names and custom commands.
- ✓ Customize control panels in the **Dashboard**.
- ✓ Create new **Dashboard** control panels.

One of the easiest ways to alter the AutoCAD environment is by customizing toolbars, pull-down menus, and the **Dashboard**. Existing toolbars and pull-down menus can be quickly modified by removing and adding commands. The control panels in the **Dashboard** can also be modified. New commands can also be created and assigned to an existing toolbar, pull-down menu, or **Dashboard** control panel. The most powerful aspect of customizing toolbars, pull-down menus, and **Dashboard** control panels is the ability to quickly create entirely new functions to help you in your work.

Working with Toolbars

Toolbars provide access to most AutoCAD commands with one or two quick "picks." This graphic interface provides much flexibility. Toolbars can be quickly and easily resized, repositioned, hidden from view, or made visible. Toolbars are moved, resized, docked, and floated in the same way as in all Windows-compatible software.

In addition to positioning and sizing toolbars, you can customize the toolbar interface. When a command is placed on a toolbar, it is represented by a button. You can add new command buttons or reposition existing command buttons for quicker access. Infrequently used commands can be removed from the toolbar or repositioned to a less prominent location. Entirely new toolbars can be created and filled with predefined or custom commands. Toolbars are customized using the **Customize User Interface** dialog box.

Toolbar Visibility

You can adjust the AutoCAD screen so that only the toolbars you need are visible. This helps conserve drawing window space. If too many toolbars are displayed, the drawing window can become small and crowded. When your drawing area is small, too much of your time is spent making display changes so you can clearly see parts of the drawing.

Figure 20-1 shows an example of a small and crowded drawing window. Also, look closely at the toolbars docked on the left side and top of the window. They are partially hidden from view. The length of some of the toolbars is longer than the available space. Remember this when arranging your toolbars. You should have access to all of the buttons. There is no way to "pan" a toolbar that is partially hidden from view.

AutoCAD provides a shortcut menu for fast and convenient control of toolbar visibility. To access the toolbars shortcut menu, point at any toolbar and right-click. As shown in **Figure 20-2**, a check mark is displayed next to the currently visible toolbars. Pick any toolbar name in the menu to toggle its visibility.

Another way to hide a floating toolbar is to pick its menu control button, **Figure 20-3.** If you wish to hide a docked toolbar, you can first move it away from the edge to make it a floating toolbar. Then, pick the menu control button. Remember, when you hide a previously docked toolbar in this manner, it will appear in the floating position when you again make it visible.

When using floating toolbars, it is also possible to overlap the toolbars to save screen space. To bring a toolbar to the front, simply pick on it. Be sure to leave part of each toolbar showing.

Figure 20-1.
Too many toolbars visible at once can cut down on the useful drawing area.

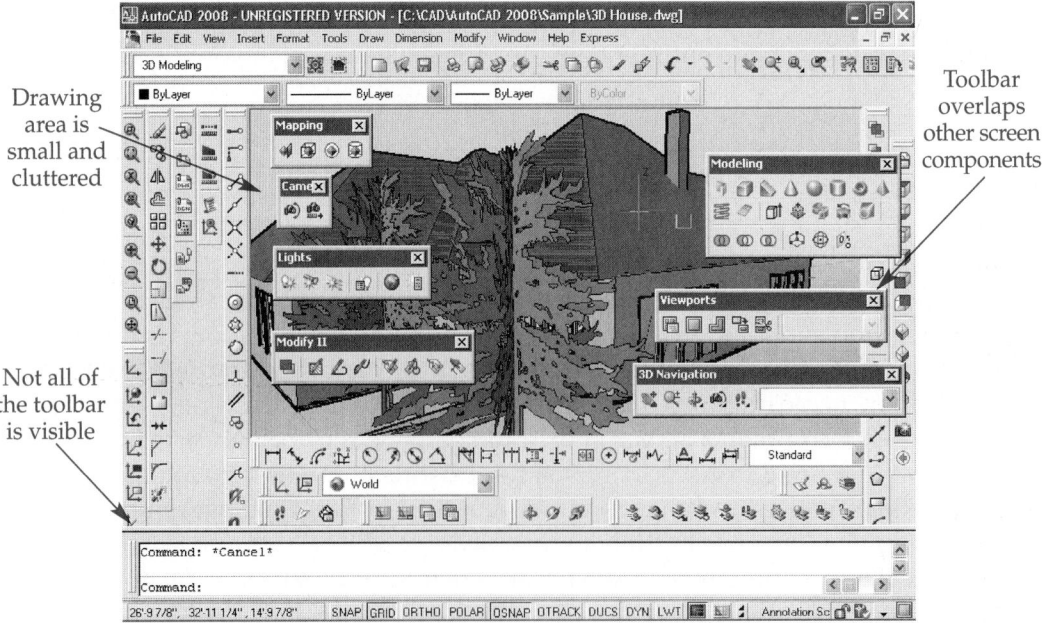

Drawing area is small and cluttered

Not all of the toolbar is visible

Toolbar overlaps other screen components

Toolbar Display Options

The **Display** tab of the **Options** dialog box contains three check boxes relating to toolbars. Located in the **Window Elements** area of the tab, these check boxes provide display options for toolbar buttons.

When the **Use large buttons for Toolbars** check box is checked, the size of toolbar buttons is increased from 16 × 16 pixels to 32 × 32 pixels. At higher screen resolutions, such as 1280 × 1024, the small buttons may be difficult to see. At lower screen resolutions, such as 800 × 600, the large buttons take up too much of the display area.

When the **Show ToolTips** check box is checked, the name of the button to which you are pointing is displayed next to the cursor. Below this check box is the **Show shortcut keys in ToolTips** check box. When this option is checked, the shortcut key combination for the command is displayed in the tooltip, if one is available. When tooltips are turned off, this option is grayed out.

Figure 20-2.
The toolbars shortcut menu is accessed by right-clicking on any toolbar.

Check marks identify the currently visible toolbars

Pick to access the **Customize User Interface** dialog box

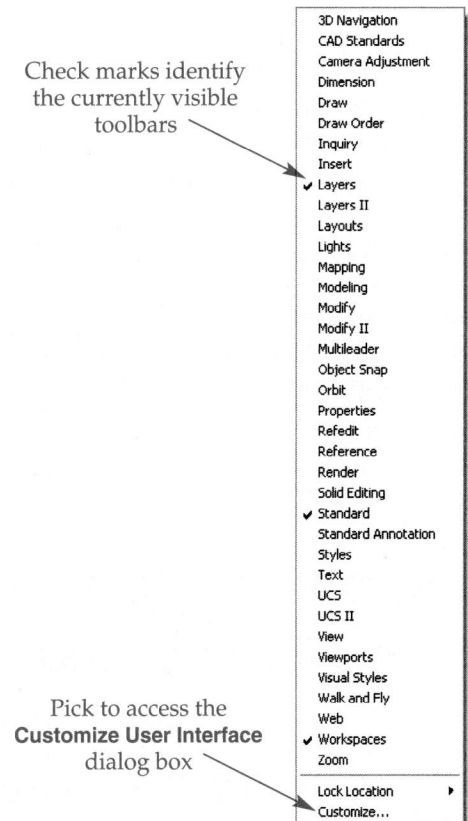

Figure 20-3.
Pick the menu control button to hide the toolbar.

Menu control button

Customizing Existing Toolbars

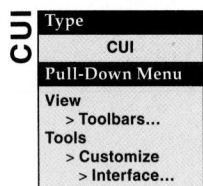

CUI

Type
CUI

Pull-Down Menu
View
> **Toolbars...**
Tools
> **Customize**
> **Interface...**

Toolbars and toolbar commands can be modified using the **Customize User Interface** dialog box, **Figure 20-4**. The changes made in this dialog box are saved in a customization file (.cui). By default, this is the acad.cui file. The **CUI** command opens the **Customize User Interface** dialog box. You can also pick **Customize...** from the shortcut menu displayed by right-clicking on a toolbar.

The upper-left pane of the **Customize User Interface** dialog box is initially labeled **Customizations in All CUI Files**. The drop-down list located below the pane name contains the name of the main CUI file and any other currently loaded CUI files. By default, the acad.cui, custom.cui, and acimpression.cui files are loaded. If the Express Tools are installed, the acetmain.cui file is also loaded. If you select a different entry from the drop-down list, the name of the pane changes to reflect the selection, either **Customizations in All CUI Files** or **Customizations in Main CUI**. By default, the customization file acad.cui is the main CUI file. In the box located below the drop-down list, the selected CUI file is displayed in a tree. The top level of the tree is the ACAD branch, which is the name of the selected customization file, and the AutoCAD logo icon is shown next to it. The tree under the ACAD branch lists the various customizable items. To see the list of available toolbars, expand the Toolbars branch, or node, by picking the plus sign located just to its left. Any other partially loaded CUI files that have toolbars in them will be listed under the Partial CUI Files item in the tree and can have their toolbar list similarly expanded. A partially loaded CUI file is one not designated as the main CUI file. Partial CUI files are discussed later in this chapter.

To delete a toolbar, select the toolbar in the Toolbars branch, right-click, and pick **Delete** from the shortcut menu. When prompted, pick the **Yes** button to indicate that you indeed want to delete the item (toolbar). Then, pick the **Apply** or **OK** button in the **Customize User Interface** dialog box to make the deletion permanent. However, a better method is to remove the toolbar from the workspace. In this way, the toolbar is still

Figure 20-4.
The **Customize User Interface** dialog box is used to edit existing toolbars, create new toolbars, create custom commands, and create button icons.

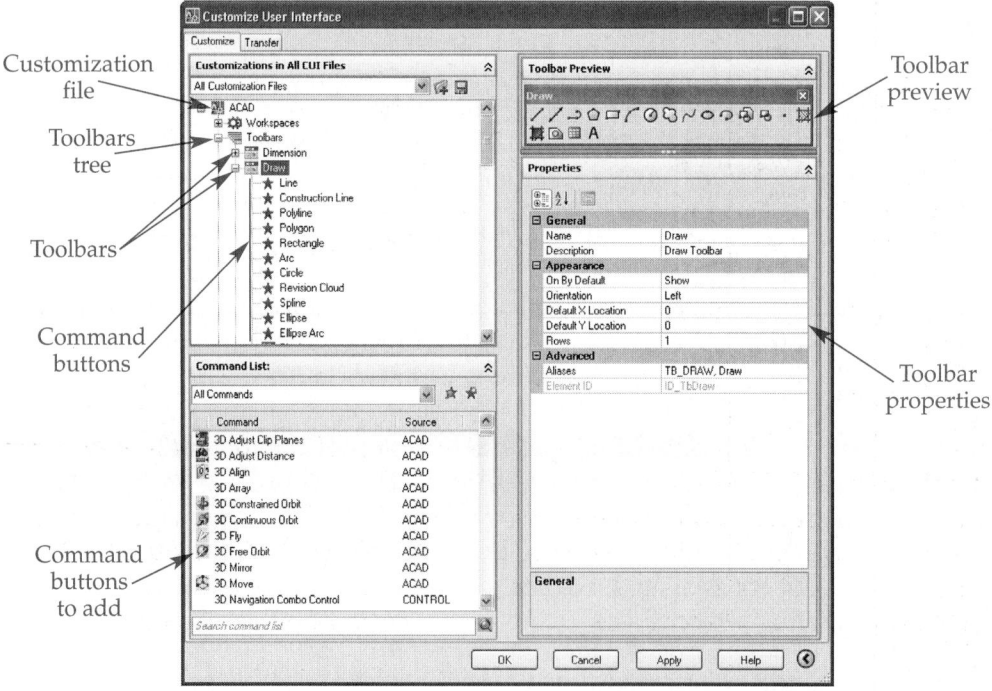

available to other workspaces. For a brief discussion, see the section Removing a Pull-Down or Cascading Menu later in this chapter. Also, refer to Chapter 23 for complete details on workspaces.

To rename a toolbar, select the toolbar in the Toolbars branch, right-click, and pick **Rename** from the shortcut menu. The existing name of the toolbar in the tree turns into an edit box with the current name highlighted. Type a new name in the edit box and press [Enter]. The new toolbar name is displayed in the tree. You can also rename a toolbar using the Name property in the **Properties** pane on the right-hand side of the dialog box. Pick the **Apply** or **OK** button in the **Customize User Interface** dialog box to make the change permanent.

You can modify existing toolbars by deleting and adding commands. Commands that are not available in the default toolbars can also be assigned to toolbars.

PROFESSIONAL TIP

All changes made in the **Customize User Interface** dialog box are saved in the CUI file, including pull-down menu, **Dashboard**, and shortcut key customizations. Customizing pull-down menus and the **Dashboard** are discussed later in this chapter. Customizing shortcut keys is discussed in Chapter 21.

Deleting a Toolbar Command

To delete a command from a toolbar, expand the tree for the toolbar containing the command to delete. All of the commands currently on that toolbar are displayed as branches below the toolbar name. Select the command you wish to delete, right-click, and pick **Remove** from the shortcut menu. Pick the **Apply** or **OK** button in the **Customize User Interface** dialog box to make the deletion permanent. The command is, however, still available in the **Command List:** pane of the **Customize User Interface** dialog box.

Adding a Toolbar Command

All commands are available in the **Command List:** pane of the **Customize User Interface** dialog box, including many commands and macros (custom commands) that are not found on the default toolbars. See **Figure 20-5.** All toolbars are listed in the Toolbars branch of the **Customizations in All CUI Files** pane.

To add a command to a toolbar, first expand the toolbar tree in the **Customizations in All CUI Files** pane for the toolbar to which you want the command added. Then, select a command from the **Command List:** pane. The list is alphabetized. If you hover the cursor over a command, the macro or command is displayed as help text. Also, you can search the list by picking the **Find command or text** button at the top of the **Command List:** pane. The drop-down list at the top of the pane can be used to filter the list so that only commands in a certain category appear in the list. See **Figure 20-6.**

Once the command is located, pick and hold on the command in the **Commands List:** pane and drag it into the **Customizations in All CUI Files** pane. A horizontal "I-bar" appears in the pane as you drag the command. This represents the location where the command button will be inserted. The top of the toolbar's branch represents the left-hand side (or top) of the toolbar. The bottom of the branch represents the right-hand side (or bottom) of the toolbar. Position the new command between the commands where you would like it to appear and release the left mouse button. The new command appears as a branch in the toolbar tree. Pick the **Apply** or **OK** button in the **Customize User Interface** dialog box to make the addition permanent.

Figure 20-5.
The **Commands List:** pane of the **Customize User Interface** dialog box displays all predefined and custom commands. These commands can be added to toolbars as buttons.

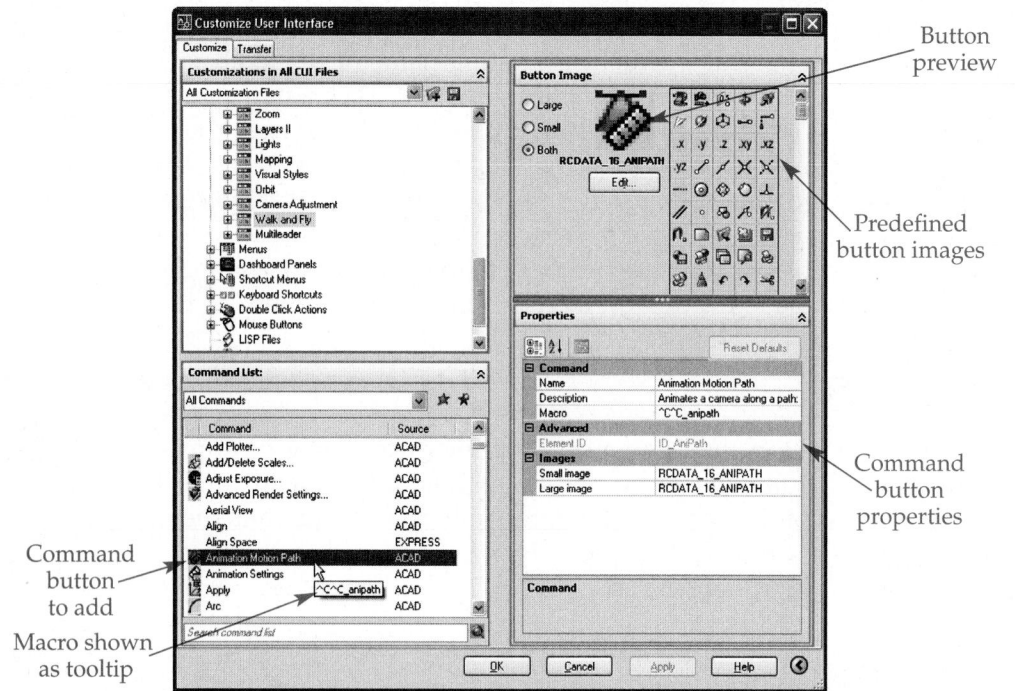

Button preview

Predefined button images

Command button properties

Command button to add

Macro shown as tooltip

> **NOTE**
>
> Selecting the **Cancel** button of the **Customize User Interface** dialog box after selecting the **Apply** button does *not* cancel the changes made before the **Apply** button was selected.

Figure 20-6.
Use the drop-down list to filter the commands shown in the **Command List:** pane.

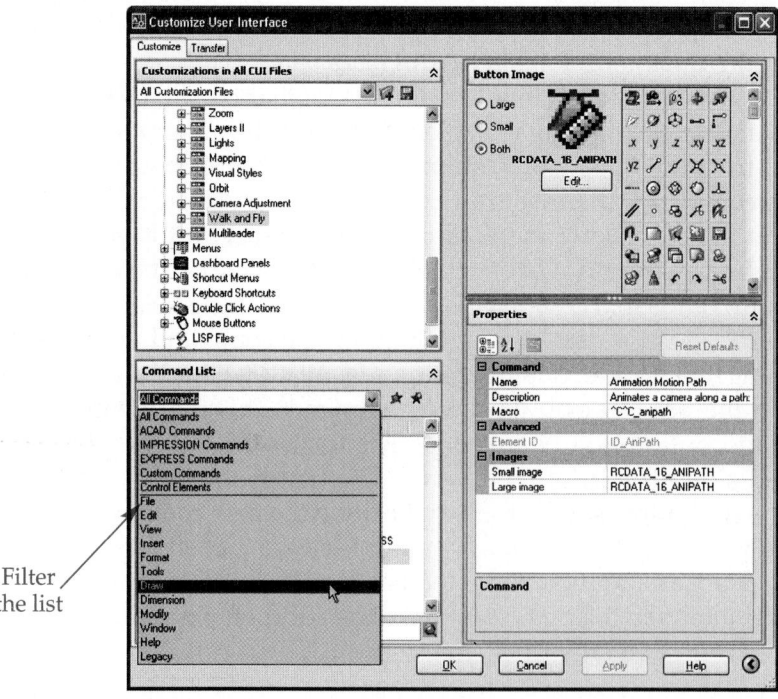

Filter the list

Moving and Copying Command Buttons

You can move and copy commands between toolbars. First, expand the tree for both toolbars in the upper-left pane of the **Customize User Interface** dialog box. To move a command from one toolbar to another, pick and hold on the button and drag it to the other toolbar. The horizontal "I-bar" cursor appears as you drag. Position the cursor between the commands where you want the new command to appear and release the left mouse button. The command is moved from the first toolbar to the second.

Use this same process to copy a command between toolbars, but hold the [Ctrl] key before you release the left mouse button. The command remains on the first toolbar and a copy is placed on the second toolbar.

You can also drag commands from the **Customize User Interface** dialog box and drop them onto toolbars that are displayed, or onto a tool palette. A button can be removed from a displayed toolbar while the **Customize User Interface** dialog box is open by dragging it into the drawing area and releasing. A message appears asking if you want to remove the button. Pick **OK** to remove the button. Buttons can also be rearranged on displayed toolbars while the **Customize User Interface** dialog box is open by simply dragging a button to a new position.

PROFESSIONAL TIP

When dragging a command to a tool palette, if the desired palette is not current (on top), simply pause the cursor over the palette name until the palette is made current. Tool palette customization is discussed in detail in Chapter 22.

Adding a Separator

A *separator* is a vertical or horizontal line that can be used in a toolbar (or pull-down menu) to create visual groupings of related commands. For example, look at the **Standard** toolbar above the drawing area. This toolbar contains several separators. There is a separator between the **Save** command button and the **Plot...** command button. There is another separator between the **Block Editor** button and the **Undo** button. These separators are vertical lines because the toolbar is docked along the top edge. If the toolbar is docked along the left or right side of the screen, the separators will be horizontal lines.

You can add separators to any toolbar. First, open the **Customize User Interface** dialog box. Then, in the **Customizations in All CUI Files** pane, expand the branch for the toolbar to which you want separators added. Next, right-click on the command in the tree below which you want the separator added. Select **Insert Separator** from the shortcut menu. A separator, represented by two dashes, appears in the tree below the selected command. When done adding separators, pick the **OK** button to close the **Customize User Interface** dialog box.

PROFESSIONAL TIP

A separator can be removed from a toolbar in the same manner as removing a button from a toolbar.

Partial CUI Files

A *partial CUI file* is any CUI file that is not the main CUI file. To load a partial CUI file, pick the Open... entry in the drop-down list in the **Customizations in All CUI Files** pane. Remember, the name of this pane may be different, depending on what is currently selected in the drop-down list. You can also pick the **Load partial customization file** button to the right of the drop-down list. Next, in the **Open** dialog box that is displayed, navigate to the folder where the CUI file is located, select the file, and pick the **Open** button. If the partial CUI file that has been opened contains any workspaces, the AutoCAD alert shown in Figure 20-7 is displayed. Any workspace information contained in the CUI file is not automatically available. Workspaces are covered in Chapter 23.

Once you open the CUI file, it is automatically selected in the drop-down list. The name of the pane changes to **Customizations in Main CUI**. Now, you can manage the items contained within the partial CUI.

If you select either the main CUI or All Customization Files in the drop-down list, the Partial CUI Files branch appears in the tree. Expanding this branch, you can see the partial CUI files that are loaded. Expanding the branch for a partial CUI file, you can see the items contained within the CUI file. These items can be copied from the partial CUI file to the main CUI file as needed.

To unload a partial CUI file, select All Customization Files in the drop-down list in the "customizations" pane. Then, expand the Partial CUI Files branch, right-click on the name of the CUI file, and select **Unload CUI File** from the shortcut menu. You can also unload a partial CUI file by typing MENULOAD or MENUUNLOAD at the Command: prompt. Then, in the **Load/Unload Customizations** dialog box, select the CUI file to unload and pick the **Unload** button.

QUICKCUI

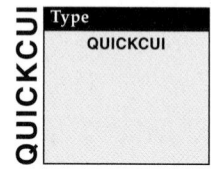

The **QUICKCUI** command opens a condensed version of the **Customize User Interface** dialog box. See Figure 20-8. The **Command List:** pane is the only visible pane. The "customizations" pane is shown minimized. The right-hand side of the dialog box is not visible, but can be displayed by picking the "expand" button at the lower-right corner. This simplified dialog can be accessed by typing QUICKCUI, right clicking on a toolbar button and selecting **Customize...** from the shortcut menu, right clicking on the title bar or a blank area of the tool palette and selecting **Customize Commands...** from the shortcut menu, or right clicking on a blank area of a tool palette and selecting **Customize Panels...** from the shortcut menu

The condensed dialog box allows you to more quickly perform drag-and-drop customizations. As discussed earlier, drag-and-drop operations can be done while the **Customize User Interface** dialog box is expanded. However, the expanded dialog box

Figure 20-7.
This warning appears when loading a partial CUI file that contains workspaces. Workspaces are covered in Chapter 23.

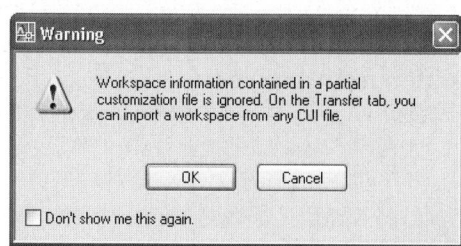

Figure 20-8.
The **QUICKCUI** command displays a condensed version of the **Customize User Interface** dialog box.

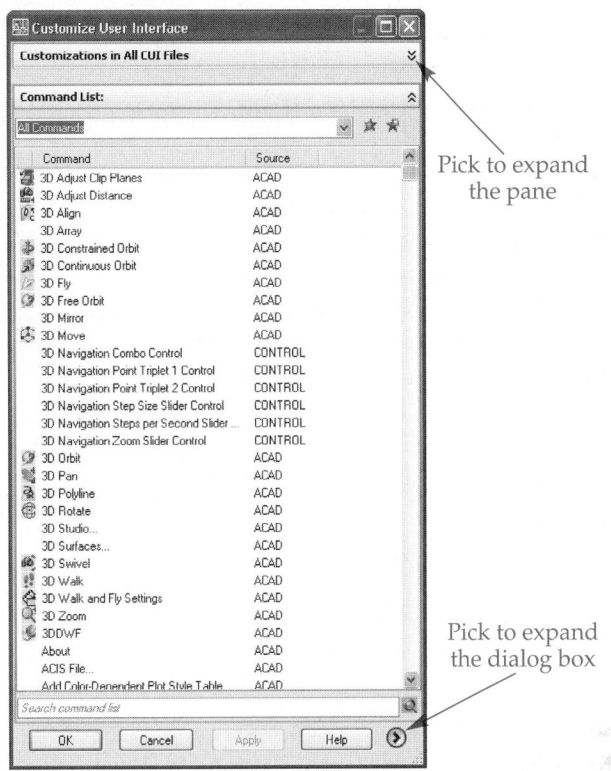

Pick to expand the pane

Pick to expand the dialog box

takes up most of the screen. The condensed version takes up less screen space, making more toolbars accessible. An advantage of the expanded **Customize User Interface** dialog box is that you can do drag-and-drop customization within the dialog box.

Creating New Toolbars and Commands

AutoCAD has many predefined toolbars. However, entirely new toolbars can be created and filled with predefined or custom commands. For ease of access, toolbars can be created containing commands related to specific projects or tasks. The **Customize User Interface** dialog box is used to create new toolbars and custom commands.

Creating a New Toolbar

To create a new toolbar, open the expanded **Customize User Interface** dialog box. Then, right-click on the Toolbars branch in the upper-left pane to display the shortcut menu. Pick **New Toolbar** in the shortcut menu. A new toolbar is added at the bottom of the Toolbars branch. An edit box is displayed in place of the toolbar name with a default name highlighted. Type a descriptive name for the toolbar and press [Enter].

After the new toolbar is named, it is highlighted in the Toolbars branch. The properties for the toolbar are displayed in the **Properties** pane of the **Customize User Interface** dialog box. See **Figure 20-9.** A preview of the toolbar also appears in the **Toolbar Preview** pane, but since the toolbar is empty, there is not currently a preview. You can change the name of the toolbar and add a description in the **General** category of the **Properties** pane. The description appears on the AutoCAD status line when the cursor is over the docked toolbar. In the **Appearance** category, you can specify the default settings for the toolbar, including whether it is displayed (Show) or hidden (Hide), floating or docked, the location of the toolbar's upper-left corner, and the number of rows for the toolbar. The settings in the **Advanced** category are used for programming applications.

Figure 20-9.
The properties of a toolbar can be changed in the **Properties** pane of the **Customize User Interface** dialog box.

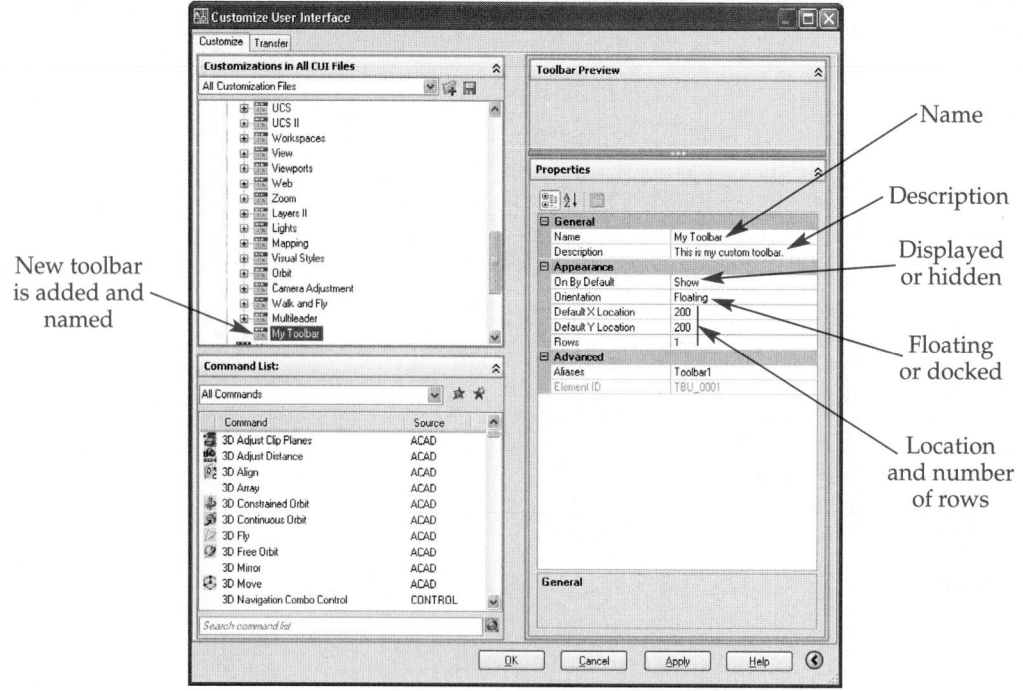

New toolbar is added and named

Name

Description

Displayed or hidden

Floating or docked

Location and number of rows

A new toolbar is now added and its properties are set. You can add commands to the new toolbar using the methods discussed earlier in this chapter.

Adding a Custom Command to a Toolbar

You are not limited to AutoCAD's predefined commands. *Custom commands* can be created and then added to toolbars, pull-down menus, tool palettes, and **Dashboard** control panels. First, however, you must create the new, custom command. To create a custom command, first pick the **Create a new command** button in the **Command List:** pane of the **Customize User Interface** dialog box. This button is to the right of the drop-down list. A new command is added to the list in the **Command List:** pane. Also, the **Button Image** and **Properties** panes are displayed for the new command. See **Figure 20-10.**

By default, the new command name is **Command**n, where n is a sequential number based on the number of new commands that have been added in this dialog box session. To give the command a descriptive name, highlight the command and pick in the Name: property edit box in the **General** category of the **Properties** pane. Then, type the new name and press [Enter]. The command name is what appears in the tooltip. The name should be logical and short, such as **Draw Box**.

The text that appears in the Description: property text box in the **General** category of the **Properties** pane appears on the AutoCAD status line when the cursor is over the button. This text, called the *help string,* should also be logical, but can be longer and more descriptive than the command name.

As an example, you will create a command that draws a rectangular border for an E-size sheet (44″ × 34″) using a wide polyline, sets the drawing limits, and finishes with **ZOOM Extents**. To start, create a new command and enter **E-Border** as the name. Also, enter Draws E-size border, sets limits, and zooms extents. for the Description: property. See **Figure 20-11.** In the next sections, you will complete the command and its associated button image.

Figure 20-10.
The first step in adding a custom command button to a toolbar is to create the custom command.

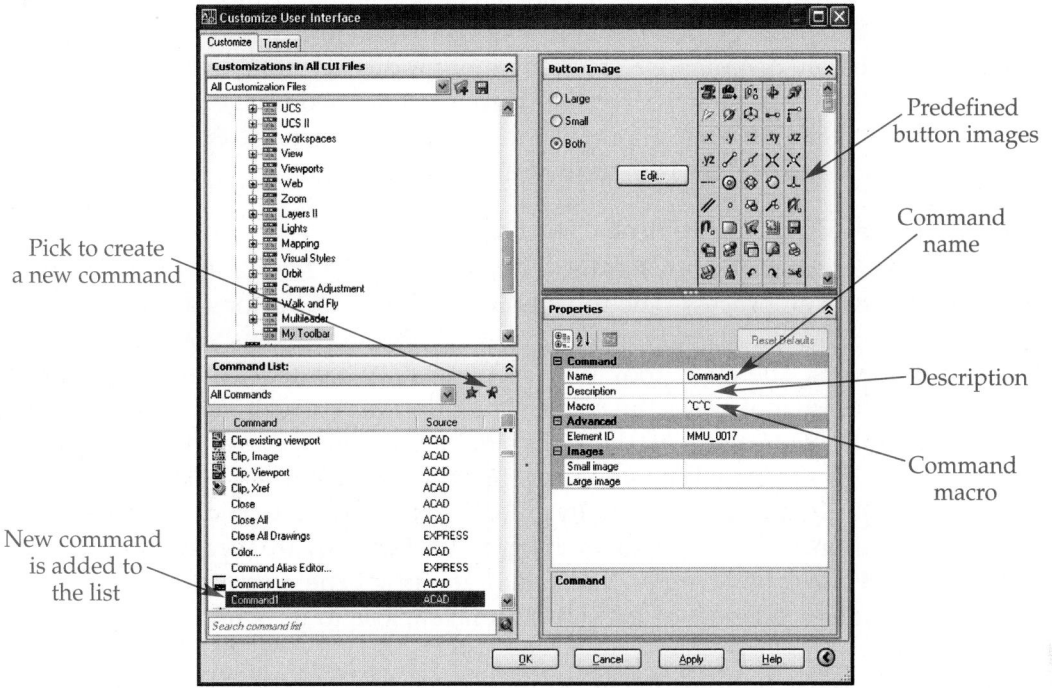

Predefined button images

Command name

Pick to create a new command

New command is added to the list

Description

Command macro

Figure 20-11.
The custom command is named and a help string is assigned to it.

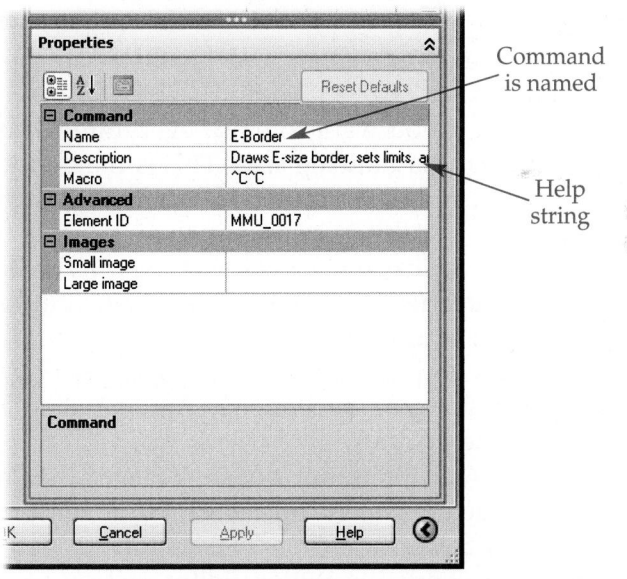

Command is named

Help string

Button image

The **Button Image** pane in the **Customize User Interface** dialog box is used to define the image that appears on the button. The image should graphically represent the function of the command. You can select one of the predefined images from the list. You can also right-click on the list of images and select **Import Image...** from the shortcut menu to import an image. A different image can be selected for large and small buttons, or you can use the same image for both button sizes. Pick the appropriate radio button in the pane and select an image. The name of the image appears in the **Images** category in the **Properties** pane. The small image also appears next to the command name in the **Command List:** pane.

However, confusion may arise if your custom command has the same button image as an existing AutoCAD command. It is best to create custom button images for use with your custom commands. You can either modify an existing button image or create a new image from scratch. In either case, a predefined image must be selected from the list of existing images. Then, pick the **Edit...** button in the **Button Image** pane to open the **Button Editor**. This is described in the next section.

Creating a custom button image

The **Button Editor** dialog box has basic "pixel-painting" tools and several features to simplify the editing process. The four tools are shown as buttons at the top of the dialog box. The pencil paints individual pixels. The line tool allows you to draw a line between two points. The circle tool allows you to draw center/radius style ellipses and circles. The erase tool clears the color from individual pixels. The current color is selected from the color palette on the right side of the dialog box and indicated by a depressed color button. Anything you draw appears in the current color.

Drawing a button image is usually much easier with the grid turned on. The grid provides outlines for each pixel in the graphic. Each square represents one pixel. Picking the **Grid** check box toggles the state of the grid. The area just above the **Grid** check box provides a preview of the button image, close to its actual size, while you draw the image.

When the toolbar buttons are set to their default, small size, the button editor provides a drawing area of 16 pixels × 16 pixels. If **Use large buttons for Toolbars** is turned on in the **Display** tab of the **Options** dialog, then the button image drawing area is 32 pixels × 32 pixels. Ideally, a button will have a separate image for each of the two button sizes.

There are several other tools available in the **Button Editor**. These include the following.

- **Clear.** If you want to erase everything and start over, pick the **Clear** button to clear the drawing area. This is the button you will use to clear the existing image and start a button image from scratch.
- **Open.** Use this button to open an existing bitmap (BMP) file, up to 380 × 380 pixels in size, that does not appear in the **Button Image** pane of the **Customize User Interface** dialog box. The image is automatically resized to fit the current button size.
- **Undo.** You can undo the last operation by picking this button. Only the last operation can be undone. An operation that has been undone cannot be redone.
- **Save As.** This button saves a file using the **Create File** dialog box. Use this when you do not want to alter the original button image.
- **Save.** Saves the current bitmap file.
- **Close.** Ends the **Button Editor** session. A message is displayed if you have unsaved changes.
- **Help.** Provides context-sensitive help.

Once a button image is saved, it appears at the bottom of the list of predefined images in the **Button Image** pane of the **Customize User Interface** dialog box. All images saved for use as button images must be stored where AutoCAD will find them. AutoCAD provides the \Icons folder within the user's support file search path. This is the default folder when using the **Save as...** button in the **Button Editor** dialog box. If you choose to use a different folder, it must be added to the support file search path, which is specified in the **Files** tab of the **Options** dialog box.

Rather than using an existing button image for the **E-Border** command, an entirely new button image will be created. With **E-Border** highlighted in the **Command List:** pane, select any one of the images in the **Button Image** pane and pick the **Edit...** button. The **Button Editor** dialog box is displayed. Now, select the **Clear** button to completely remove the existing image.

Figure 20-12A shows a 16 × 16 pixel image created for the **E-Border** button with the **Grid** option activated. Use the pencil and line tools to create this or a similar image. Save your button image with a name of E-border and store it in an appropriate location. Pick the **Close** button to return to the **Customize User Interface** dialog box. Your newly created image now appears at the bottom of the list of existing images in the **Button Image** pane, as shown in **Figure 20-12B**. However, it has not yet been associated with the button.

PROFESSIONAL TIP

Consider the needs of the persons who will be using your custom commands when you design button images. Simple, abstract designs may be recognizable to you because you created them. However, when someone else uses the toolbar, they may not recognize the purpose of the command by the button image. For example, the standard buttons in AutoCAD show a graphic that implies something about the command that the button executes. A custom command you create will be most effective if its button image graphically represents the actions the command will perform.

Associating a custom image with a command

There are two ways to associate a new, custom button image with a command. You can use the **Button Image** pane or the **Properties** pane in the **Customize User Interface** dialog box. Once a button image is associated with a command, the image is used for that command on *all* toolbars and menus where the command is inserted.

Once you have saved the custom button image, it appears in the list of predefined button images in the **Button Image** pane until the **Customize User Interface** dialog box

---

Figure 20-12.
A—A custom button image is created. B—The new button image has been created and appears in the list.

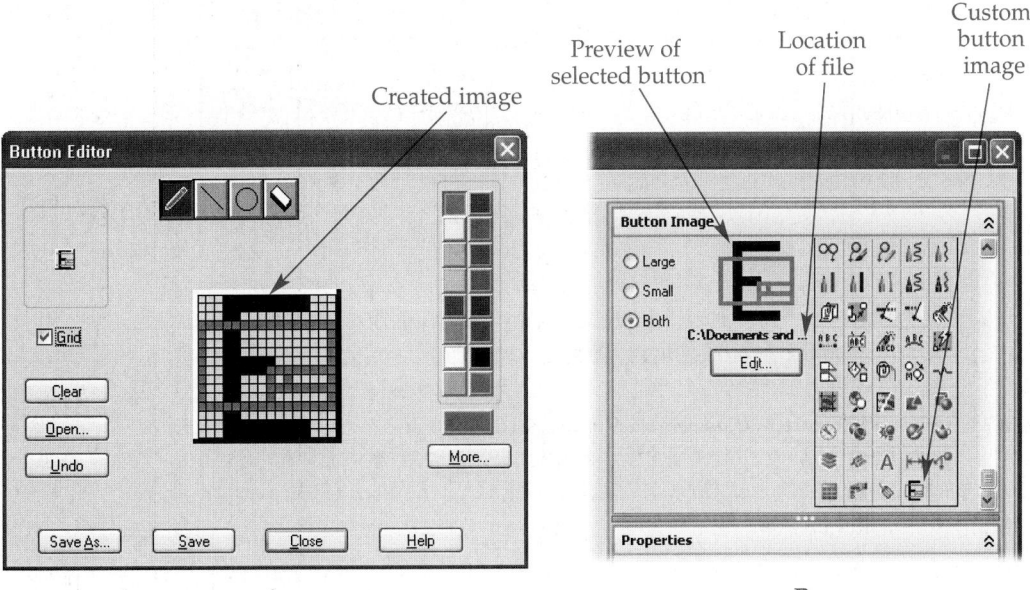

is closed. To assign the image to the command, first make sure the command is selected in the **Command List:** pane. Then, select the **Large**, **Small**, or **Both** radio button in the **Button Image** pane to determine for which size of button the image will be used. Next, pick the custom button image in the list of predefined button images. Finally, pick the **Apply** button at the bottom of the **Customize User Interface** dialog box to assign the image to the button.

You can also use the **Properties** pane to associate the saved custom button image file(s) with the command. Make sure the command is selected in the **Command List:** pane. Then, in the **Properties** pane, expand the **Images** category to display the Small image and Large image properties. If there is an image currently associated with the property, the path to the image is displayed in the text box. Pick in each property text box and type the path and file name of the saved image files. Alternately, you can pick the "browse" button (**...**) to open the **Select Image File** dialog box and locate the file. This button appears when the property is selected. Finally, pick the **Apply** button at the bottom of the **Customize User Interface** dialog box to assign the image(s) to the button.

If you only designate an image file for small buttons, the button for the command will be blank on a toolbar when you switch to large buttons. This is because no image has been designated for that size. Be sure to specify an image for both small and large buttons.

To add your custom button image to your custom **E-border** command, select the command in the **Command List:** pane. Then, use either the **Button Image** or **Properties** pane to associate your custom button image with the command. Use the same image for both small and large buttons. Then, pick the **Apply** button to associate the images with the command. Your custom button image is now displayed next to the custom **E-Border** command in the **Command List:** and **Button Image** panes, Figure 20-13. If you associated the image using the **Properties** pane, you may need to select the command in the **Command List:** pane to force the **Button Image** pane to update.

Figure 20-13.
The custom button image has been assigned to the custom command.

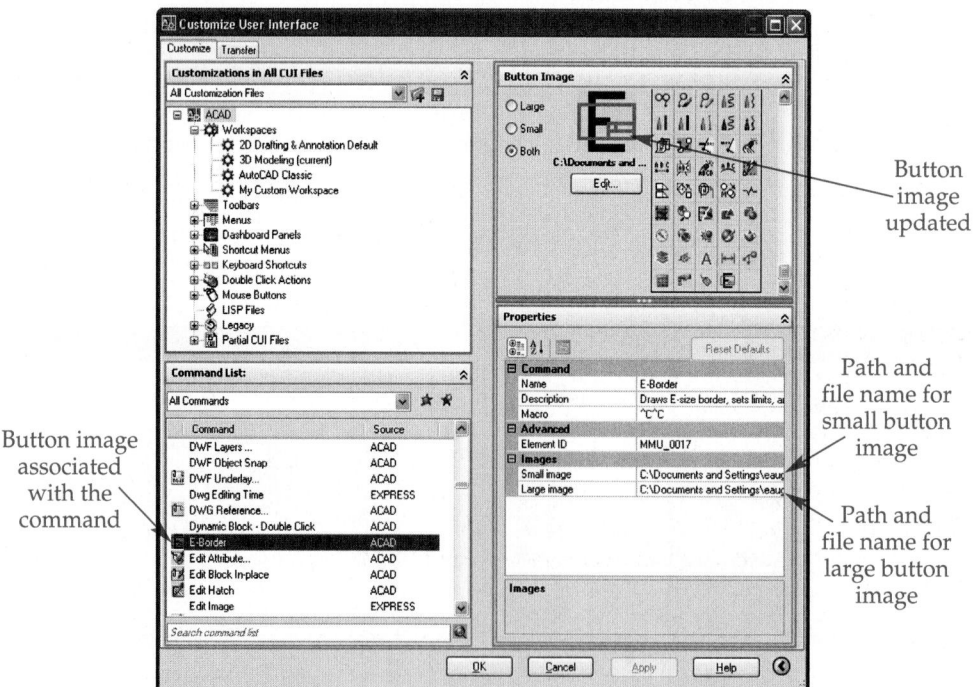

Button image updated

Path and file name for small button image

Path and file name for large button image

Button image associated with the command

Defining a custom command

Now, you need to define the action that the custom command will perform. A text string called a *macro* defines the action performed by the command. This text string appears in the Macro property text box in the **Macro** category in the **Properties** pane of the **Customize User Interface** dialog box. In many cases, this "command" is actually a macro that invokes more than one command. By default, the text ^C^C appears in the text box. The text ^C is a cancel command. This is the same as pressing the [Esc] key. The default text, then, represents two cancels.

Two cancels are required to be sure you begin at the Command: prompt. One cancel may not completely exit some commands. In this case, a second cancel is required to fully exit the command. Whenever a command is not required to operate transparently, it is best to begin the macro with two cancel keystrokes (^C^C) to fully exit any current command and return to the Command: prompt.

The macro must perfectly match the requirements of the activated commands. For example, if the **LINE** command is issued, the subsequent prompt expects a coordinate point to be entered. Any other data are inappropriate and will cause an error in the macro. It is best to manually "walk through" the desired macro, writing down each step and the data required by each prompt. The following command sequence creates the rectangular polyline border with a .015 line width.

```
Command: PLINE↵
Specify start point: 1,1↵
Current line-width is 0.0000
Specify next point or [Arc/Halfwidth/Length/Undo/Width]: W↵
Specify starting width <0.0000>: .015↵
Specify ending width <0.0150>: ↵
Specify next point or [Arc/Halfwidth/Length/Undo/Width]: 42,1↵
Specify next point or [Arc/Close/Halfwidth/Length/Undo/Width]: 42,32↵
Specify next point or [Arc/Close/Halfwidth/Length/Undo/Width]: 1,32↵
Specify next point or [Arc/Close/Halfwidth/Length/Undo/Width]: C↵
Command:
```

Creating the macro for your custom **E-Border** command involves duplicating these keystrokes, with a couple of differences. Some symbols are used in menu macros to represent keystrokes. For example, a cancel (^C) is not entered by pressing [Esc]. Instead, the [Shift]+[6] key combination is used to place the *caret* symbol, which is used to represent the [Ctrl] key in combination with the subsequent character (a C in this case). Another keystroke represented by a symbol is the [Enter] key. An [Enter] is placed in a macro as a semicolon (;). A space can also be used to designate [Enter]. However, the semicolon is more commonly used because it is very easy to count to make sure that the correct number of "enters" are supplied.

AutoCAD system variables and control characters can be used in menus. They can be included to increase the speed and usefulness of your menu commands. Become familiar with these variables so you can make use of them in your menus.

- **^B.** Snap mode toggle.
- **^C.** Cancel.
- **^D.** Dynamic UCS toggle.
- **^E.** Isoplane crosshair toggle.
- **^G.** Grid mode toggle.
- **^T.** Tablet toggle.
- **^H.** Issues a backspace.
- **^M.** Issues a return.
- **^O.** Ortho mode toggle.
- **^P. MENUECHO** system variable toggle.
- **^Q.** Toggles echoing of prompts, status listings, and input to the printer.
- **^V.** Switches current viewport.
- **^Z.** Suppresses the addition of the automatic [Enter] at the end of a command macro.

Keeping the above guidelines in mind, the following macro draws the polyline border.

^C^CPLINE;1,1;W;.015;;42,1;42,32;1,32;C;

Compare this with the command line entry example to identify each part of the macro.

The next steps that the command will perform are to set the limits and zoom to display the entire border. To do this at the command line requires the following entries.

Command: **LIMITS**⏎
Reset Model space limits:
Specify lower left corner or [ON/OFF] <0.0000,0.0000>: **0,0**⏎
Specify upper right corner <12.0000,9.0000>: **44,34**⏎
Command: **ZOOM**⏎
Specify corner of window, enter a scale factor (nX or nXP), or
[All/Center/Dynamic/Extents/Previous/Scale/Window/Object] <real time>: **E**⏎ *(this prompt will differ if the current view is perspective, but the entry is the same)*
Command:

Continue to develop the macro by adding the following text string (shown in color) immediately after the previous one.

^C^CPLINE;1,1;W;.015;;42,1;42,32;1,32;C;LIMITS;0,0;44,34;ZOOM;E

An "enter" is automatically issued at the end of the macro, so it is not necessary to place a semicolon at the end. The macro for the custom command is now complete.

To assign the macro to your custom **E-Border** command, first make sure the command is selected in the **Command List:** pane of the **Customize User Interface** dialog box. Then, pick in the Macro property text box in the **Properties** pane and enter the complete macro shown above. For a long macro such as this one, you can pick the button at the end of the text box (**...**) to display the **Long String Editor**. See Figure 20-14. Enter the macro in this dialog box and pick the **OK** button to return to the **Customize User Interface** dialog box. Finally, pick the **Apply** button to associate the macro with the custom command.

AutoCAD and Its Applications—Advanced

Figure 20-14.
The **Long String Editor** dialog box can be used to write longer macros. The text string will automatically "wrap" in this dialog box, which does not affect the macro.

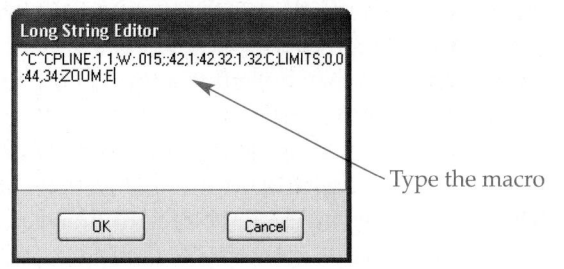

Type the macro

Placing a custom command on a toolbar

The custom command is now fully defined. The macro has been written and associated with the command. A custom button image has also been created and associated with the command. Now, you can add the custom command to a toolbar just as you would one of the predefined AutoCAD commands. Refer to the earlier section Adding a Toolbar Command. After doing so, the new command (button) should be fully functional when you exit the **Customize User Interface** dialog box. If you select the toolbar in the "customizations" pane in the **Customize User Interface** dialog box, a preview appears in the **Toolbar Preview** pane on the right-hand side of the dialog box. Once you close the dialog box, test the command button to make sure. Edit the macro in the **Customize User Interface** dialog box as needed.

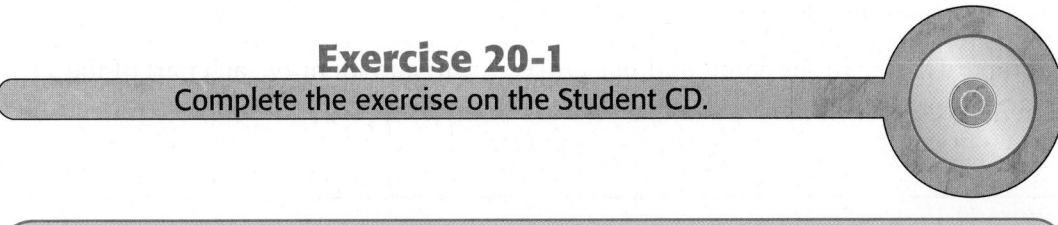

Exercise 20-1
Complete the exercise on the Student CD.

Working with Flyouts

A *flyout* is a single command button that can display a number of other command buttons, usually for related commands. A single pick on a flyout button activates the command associated with the currently visible toolbar button. When you pick and hold on a flyout button, the other commands in the flyout are displayed in a pop-up toolbar. A flyout is really a toolbar associated with a button on another toolbar.

To activate a command in the flyout other than the command "on top," pick the flyout and hold the mouse button to display the pop-up toolbar, move the cursor to the desired command, and then release the mouse button. This activates the command. Also, the selected command is displayed as the current command ("on top") in the flyout.

Creating custom toolbars can help save time and increase productivity. However, each displayed toolbar takes up some of the available screen area. If many toolbars are displayed at once, the drawing area can be drastically reduced, especially with low-resolution displays. You can conserve on-screen space by using flyouts in your custom toolbars. The following discussion shows how to create a custom toolbar flyout for 3D projects and add it to the **Modify** toolbar. If the **Modify** toolbar is not displayed, display it and dock it on the right side of the drawing area.

First, open the **Customize User Interface** dialog box. Then, expand the Toolbars branch in the **Customizations in All CUI Files** pane. Next, right-click on the Modify branch (or whichever toolbar you want the flyout added to), select **New Flyout** in the shortcut menu. A new toolbar is added to the bottom of the Modify branch. This is the "flyout toolbar." A toolbar with the same default name also appears in the Toolbars branch. This is the "source toolbar." Right-click on the new toolbar in the Modify branch and pick **Rename** from the shortcut menu. Change the toolbar name to **3D Tools**. This does not rename the *source* toolbar.

Next, drag and drop commands from the **Command List:** pane onto the new **3D Tools** toolbar. Use the drop-down list to filter the commands and select commands in the **Draw** and **View** categories. Refer to **Figure 20-15.** As you add command buttons to the flyout toolbar, the source toolbar is also updated. If you select the source toolbar in the Toolbars branch, you will see that the same commands are displayed in its branch. It is a good idea to rename the source toolbar to match the name of the flyout toolbar to avoid confusion.

If you want the new flyout to appear at the top (or left) of the **Modify** toolbar, drag it to the top position in the **Modify** branch. Then, select **OK** to exit the **Customize User Interface** dialog box and apply the changes. Now, when you pick the flyout button that you have added to the **Modify** toolbar, your custom **3D Tools** toolbar is displayed, as shown in **Figure 20-16.** When you point at the flyout button, the name and help string of the most recently used command (the "top" button) is displayed.

You can also turn any existing toolbar into a flyout on another existing toolbar. To do so, merely drag and drop the toolbar to be a flyout into the branch of the toolbar to contain the flyout. The original toolbar, the source, remains in the Toolbars branch. For example, to associate the **Modify II** toolbar with a flyout button on the **Modify** toolbar, select the **Modify II** toolbar in the Toolbars branch. Then, drag it to the Modify toolbar branch and drop it. If the Modify branch is not expanded, you can hold the cursor over the name for a second or two and the branch automatically expands. Now, move the **Modify II** toolbar into the desired location within the Modify toolbar branch.

Do not use a toolbar that contains drop-down controls, such as the **Layer Control** or **Dim Style Control**, as a flyout toolbar. The resulting flyout will not properly function.

Figure 20-15.
The **3D Tools** flyout placed in the **Modify** toolbar. Commands have been added to the **3D Tools** toolbar.

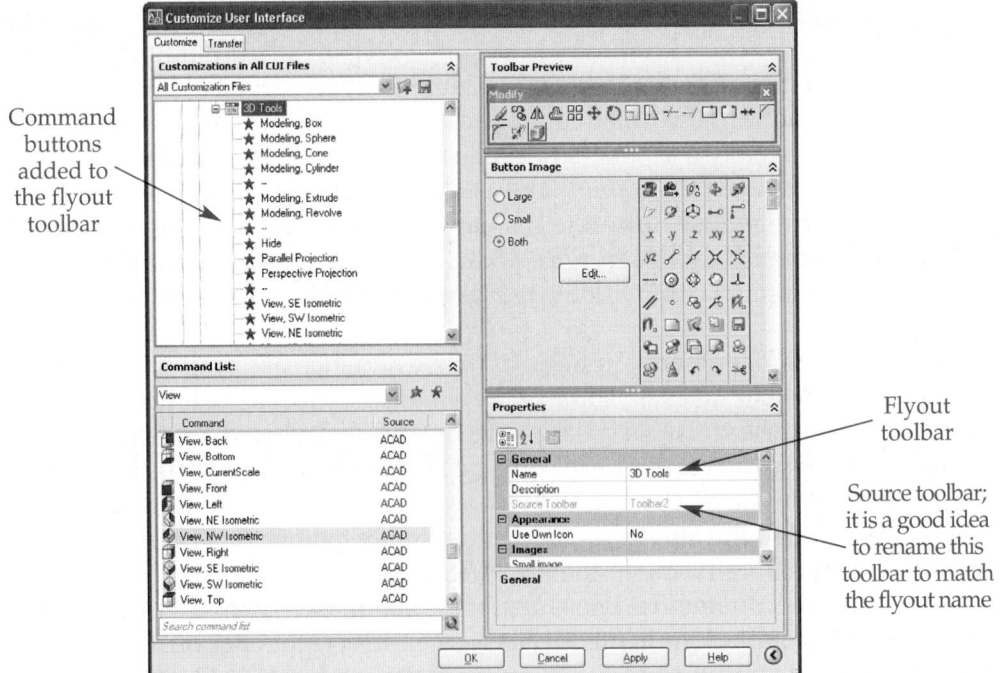

Command buttons added to the flyout toolbar

Flyout toolbar

Source toolbar; it is a good idea to rename this toolbar to match the flyout name

Figure 20-16.
A custom toolbar for working in 3D has been created and associated with a flyout in the **Modify** toolbar.

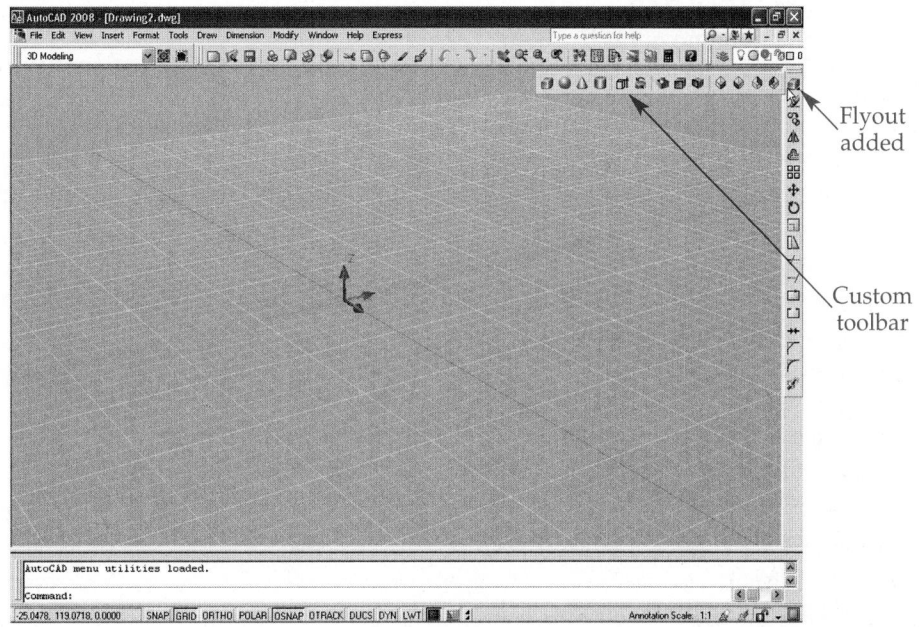

Flyout added

Custom toolbar

NOTE

You can delete a flyout toolbar from the toolbar branch within which it is contained. However, keep in mind that doing so does not delete the *source* toolbar, which is directly below the Toolbars branch.

PROFESSIONAL TIP

Remember, a flyout is really a toolbar associated with a button. You can display the source toolbar and float, dock, and reposition it as needed, just as you would any of AutoCAD's standard toolbars.

Exercise 20-2

Complete the exercise on the Student CD.

Working with Toolbars on the Command Line

Use the **-TOOLBAR** command to work with toolbars at the command line. This command is most useful when creating menu macros, script files, or AutoLISP functions to perform automated toolbar setups. When using this method, you are prompted for the toolbar name. The complete toolbar name consists of the menu group and toolbar name, separated by a period. For example, the toolbar name for the **Draw** toolbar is ACAD.DRAW. The menu group name can be omitted when only one menu is currently loaded or if the toolbar name is not duplicated in another menu group. After specifying the toolbar name (or selecting **ALL** for all toolbars), you can select an option.

Command: **-TOOLBAR.**↵
Enter toolbar name or [ALL]: **ACAD.DRAW**↵
Enter an option [Show/Hide/Left/Right/Top/Bottom/Float] <Show>:

These options are used to hide, show, or specify a location for the toolbar.

- **Show.** Makes the toolbar visible. Selecting this option is identical to placing a check mark next to a toolbar name in the shortcut menu displayed by right-clicking on any toolbar.
- **Hide.** Causes the toolbar to be invisible. Selecting this option is identical to removing the check mark next to the toolbar name in the shortcut menu displayed by right-clicking on any toolbar.
- **Left.** Places the toolbar in a docked position at the left side of the AutoCAD window.
- **Right.** Places the toolbar in a docked position at the right side of the AutoCAD window.
- **Top.** Places the toolbar in a docked position at the top of the AutoCAD window.
- **Bottom.** Places the toolbar in a docked position at the bottom of the AutoCAD window.
- **Float.** Places the toolbar as a floating toolbar.

For example, to dock the **Zoom** toolbar on the left side of the AutoCAD window, use the following command sequence.

Command: **-TOOLBAR.**↵
Enter toolbar name or [ALL]: **ACAD.ZOOM**↵
Enter an option [Show/Hide/Left/Right/Top/Bottom/Float] <Show>: **LEFT**↵
Enter new position (horizontal,vertical) <0,0>: ↵
Command:

The **Float** option places the toolbar in a floating position anchored at the pixels specified at the Position (screen coordinates) <0,0>: prompt. The anchor point of a floating toolbar is the upper-left corner. If you place the toolbar at 400,300, the upper-left corner of the toolbar is at this location. You are then asked to establish the shape of the new toolbar by specifying the number of rows of buttons for the toolbar. For example, the following sequence places the **Modeling** toolbar as shown in Figure 20-17.

Command: **-TOOLBAR.**↵
Enter toolbar name or [ALL]: **ACAD.MODELING.**↵
Enter an option [Show/Hide/Left/Right/Top/Bottom/Float] <Show>: **F.**↵
Enter new position (screen coordinates) <0,0>: **400,300.**↵
Enter number of rows for toolbar <1>: **2.**↵
Command:

Another capability of the **-TOOLBAR** command is to show or hide all toolbars at once. When prompted for the toolbar name, enter ALL. The only two options that appear are **Show** and **Hide**. If you use the **Hide** option, all toolbars are hidden. Then, you can use the **Customize User Interface** dialog box to display the toolbars you need. To display toolbars in this manner, you must add them to your workspace. Workspaces are discussed in Chapter 23.

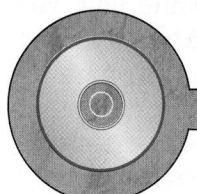

Exercise 20-3
Complete the exercise on the Student CD.

Figure 20-17.
Locating a floating toolbar at a 400,300 position using the **-TOOLBAR** command.

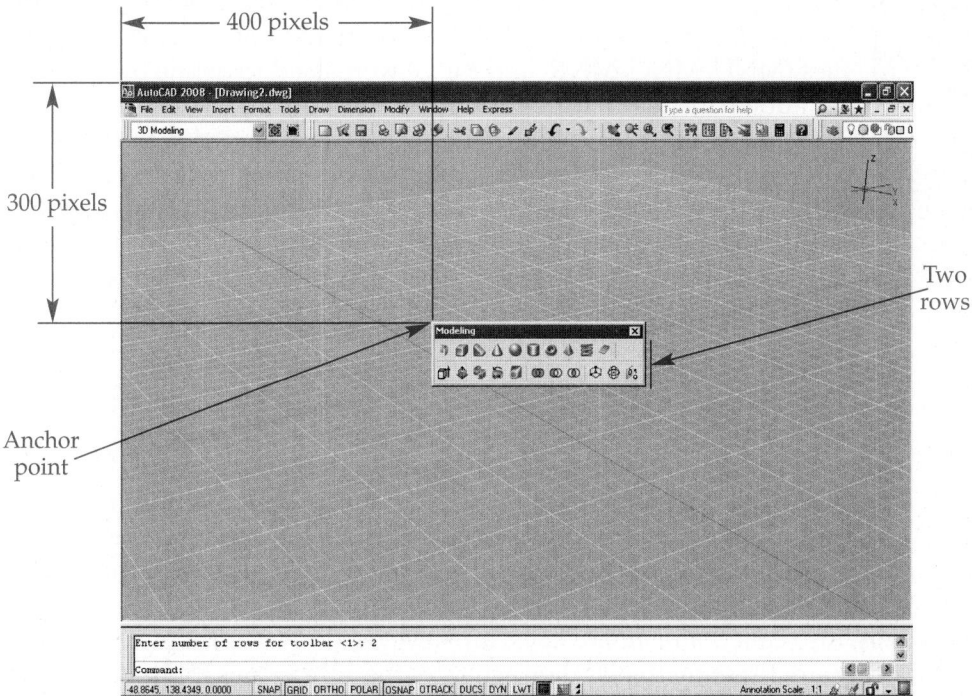

Customizing Pull-Down Menus

The names of the standard *pull-down menus* appear in the menu bar at the top of the AutoCAD graphics window. The menus are selected by placing the cursor over the menu name and picking. You can also use the access (mnemonic) keys to select menus.

Once you understand how pull-down menus are designed, you can customize existing menus and create your own. Some basic information about pull-down menus includes:

- The names of the pull-down menus appear along the menu bar just below the title bar of the AutoCAD window. By default, AutoCAD has 11 pull-down menus displayed.
- If no pull-down menus are defined in the current CUI file or workspace, AutoCAD inserts default **File**, **View**, **Window**, and **Help** menus. This is similar to how AutoCAD is displayed without a drawing open.
- The name of the pull-down menu should be as concise as possible. On low-resolution displays, long menu names may cause the menu bar to be displayed on two lines, which reduces the drawing area.
- Menu item names can be any length. The menu is displayed as wide as its longest menu item name.
- Each menu can have multiple cascading menus.
- A pull-down menu can have up to 999 items, including cascading menus.
- To create an access (mnemonic) key for a pull-down menu or menu item, place an ampersand (&) before the desired access key character. Access and shortcut keys are discussed in the next section.

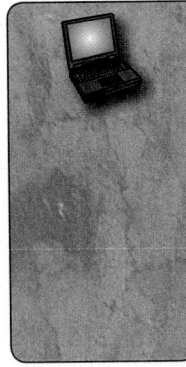
Shortcut and Access Keys

Before getting started with pull-down menu customization, it is important to understand the difference between shortcut keys and access keys. *Shortcut keys,* also called *accelerator keys,* are key combinations used to initiate a command. For example, [Ctrl]+[1] displays the **Properties** window (palette). Custom shortcut keys can be created to initiate specific AutoCAD commands or macros. Creating custom shortcut keys is covered in Chapter 21.

Access keys, also called *mnemonic keys,* are keys used to access a menu or menu item via the keyboard. Pressing the [Alt] key activates the access keys for the pull-down menus. The access keys are shown as underlined (underscored) letters. Most access keys (underscores) are not displayed in Windows 2000 and XP until the [Alt] key is depressed. While the access keys are on, notice that the letter M is underlined in the **Modify** menu name. Pressing the [M] key accesses the **Modify** pull-down menu. Any letter in the menu or menu item name can be defined as the access key, but an access key must be unique for a menu or submenu. Notice on the **Modify** pull-down menu that the M is used for **Match Properties**, so **Mirror** and **Move** use the i and v, respectively. The letter T can be used for both **Trim** and **Text** because **Text** is on the **Object** submenu, while **Trim** is in the "main" **Modify** menu. When creating custom pull-down menus, you can add custom access keys to the menu.

Creating a New Pull-Down Menu

A new pull-down menu is created within the **Customize User Interface** dialog box. First, a menu name is added to the Menus branch. Then, commands are added to the new menu. The process is basically the same as creating a new toolbar, as described earlier in this chapter. The basic procedure is:

1. Open the **Customize User Interface** dialog box.
2. In the **Customizations in All CUI Files** pane, expand the Menus branch. All of the existing pull-down menus are displayed.
3. Right-click on the Menus branch to display the shortcut menu. Pick **New Menu** from the shortcut menu. A new menu is added to the bottom of the list of existing menus. See **Figure 20-18A.** The name is highlighted in an edit box so the default name can be changed.

Figure 20-18.
A—Adding a new pull-down menu. B—Commands have been added to the new pull-down menu.

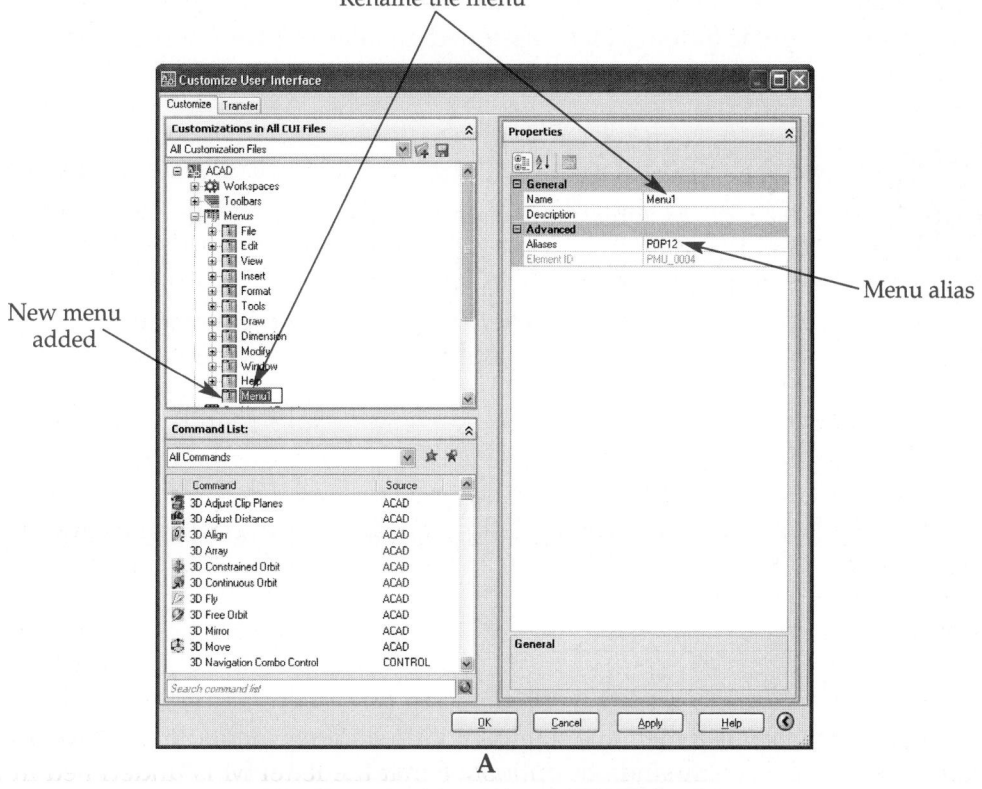

Rename the menu

New menu added

Menu alias

A

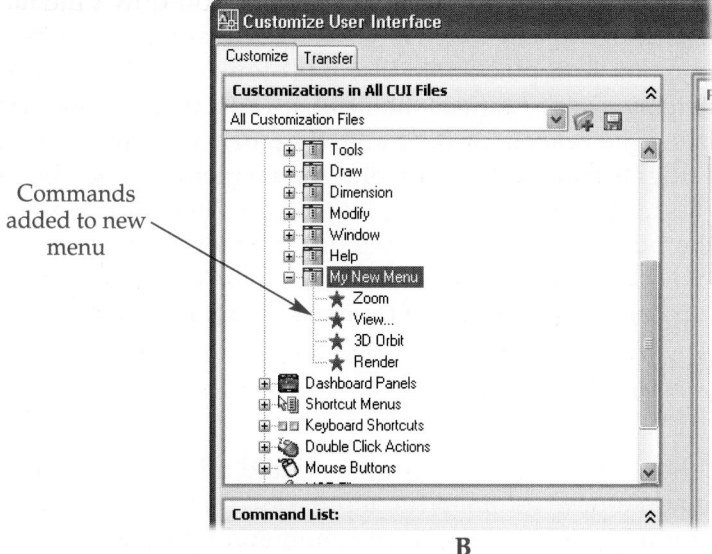

Commands added to new menu

B

4. Give the menu an appropriate name.
5. Drag the desired commands from the **Commands List:** pane and drop them into the new menu. See **Figure 20-18B.** When dragging the command to the new menu, be sure the arrow appears next to the new menu name before releasing the pick button.

When all of the desired commands have been added to the new menu, a separator can be used to create logical command groups within the menu. To add a separator, right-click on the command below which it should be inserted and select **Insert Separator** from the shortcut menu. A separator appears as two dashes in the tree. It can be moved around within the menu or between menus just as a command can be moved using the drag-and-drop method.

By default, AutoCAD has 11 pull-down menus. When adding a new pull-down menu, the new menu is automatically assigned an alias of POP*n*, where *n* is the next available integer.

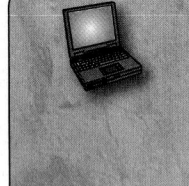

PROFESSIONAL TIP

The order in which pull-down menus appear in the **Menus** branch, from top to bottom, is the order in which they appear on the menu bar from left to right. You can drag menus to a new location in the tree to change the order in which menus appear on the menu bar, similar to how toolbar command buttons are rearranged on a toolbar.

Exercise 20-4

Complete the exercise on the Student CD.

Adding a Cascading Menu

A *cascading menu* is a menu contained within another menu. It can also be used to help group similar commands or options. For example, when **Circle** is selected in the **Draw** pull-down menu, a cascading menu appears that offers the different options for drawing a circle.

Adding a cascading menu to a pull-down menu is similar to adding a "main" menu. First, open the **Customize User Interface** dialog box. Then, in the **Customizations in All CUI Files** pane, expand the branch for the pull-down menu to which the cascading menu is to be added. Right-click on the command after which the cascading menu should appear. In the shortcut menu that is displayed, pick **New Sub-menu**. A new menu is added within the pull-down menu. Notice that the icon in the tree indicates this item is a menu, not a command. Now, the submenu can be renamed to an appropriate name. Finally, drag commands from the **Command List:** pane and drop them into the new menu. See Figure 20-19.

Adding a New Command to a Pull-Down Menu

Earlier, you learned how to create a new command and add it to a toolbar. This is the same basic way to add a new command to a pull-down menu. First, you must create the new, custom command. Once the custom command is created, drag it from the **Command List:** pane and drop it into the menu where you want it.

To create a custom command, first pick the **Create a new command** button in the **Command List:** pane of the **Customize User Interface** dialog box. A new command is added to the list in the **Command List:** pane. Also, the **Button Image** and **Properties** panes are displayed for the new command. Next, in the **Properties** pane, name the command and define the macro, as described earlier. Finally, assign button images to the command, if needed.

Marking Menu Items

Menu items can be marked with a check mark (✓) or, if an image is associated with the command, a border around the image. Marking is often related to an item that is toggled on or off, such as ortho or snap. When the item is on, it is marked. When the item is off, it is not marked. A marked item has a check mark, which is boxed, if no image is associated with it. If an image is associated with the item, the item is marked by placing a border around the image. To mark an item, place an exclamation point and period (!.) in front of its name in the **Customize User Interface** dialog box.

Menu items can also be grayed out. Any item that is grayed out cannot be selected in the menu. To gray out an item, place a tilde (~) in front of its name in the **Customize User Interface** dialog box.

Look at the sample menu and the resulting pull-down menu shown in Figure 20-20. When these characters are used in an item name, they permanently mark the item. However, as you will see in the next section, you can create smart menu items that can react to certain conditions. In this way, you can toggle between marked/unmarked and enabled/disabled menu items.

If you select the command in the Menu branch of the "customizations" pane, the **Properties** pane contains a **Display** category with a Name property, as shown in Figure 20-20. This is also true for commands selected in other branches, such as the Toolbars branch. The entry for the Name property is displayed in the menu. If you entered a special, marking character for the command name, it is displayed in this property. However, notice that the Command Name property in the **Command** category does not have the marking character. If you select the command in the **Command List:** pane, the **Properties** pane does not contain the **Display** category and the Command Name property does not have the marking character. The marking characters are only placed in the Name property of the **Display** category, which is only available if the command is selected in the tree in the "customizations" pane.

Creating Smart Pull-Down Menu Items

You can create "smart" pull-down menu labels by using a string expression language called *Direct Interpretively Evaluated String Expression Language (DIESEL).* A *string* is simply a group of characters that can be input from the keyboard or from the value of a system variable. DIESEL uses a string for its input and provides a string as output. In other words, you give DIESEL a value and it gives something back to you.

Adding a menu check mark is an excellent example of how DIESEL can be used for menu labels. For example, select **Lock Location** from the **Windows** pull-down menu.

Figure 20-19.
A—A cascading submenu has been added to the new pull-down menu. B—The menu displayed on the menu bar.

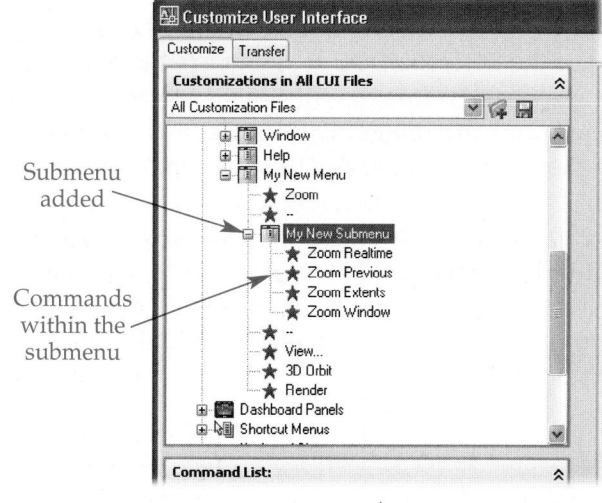

Submenu added

Commands within the submenu

A

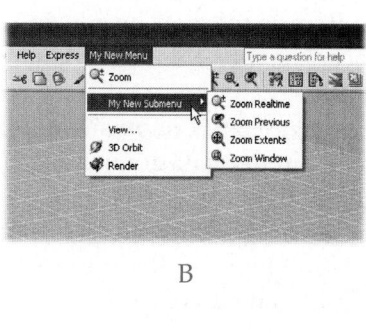

B

Figure 20-20.
Note the characters used to mark and gray out menu items.

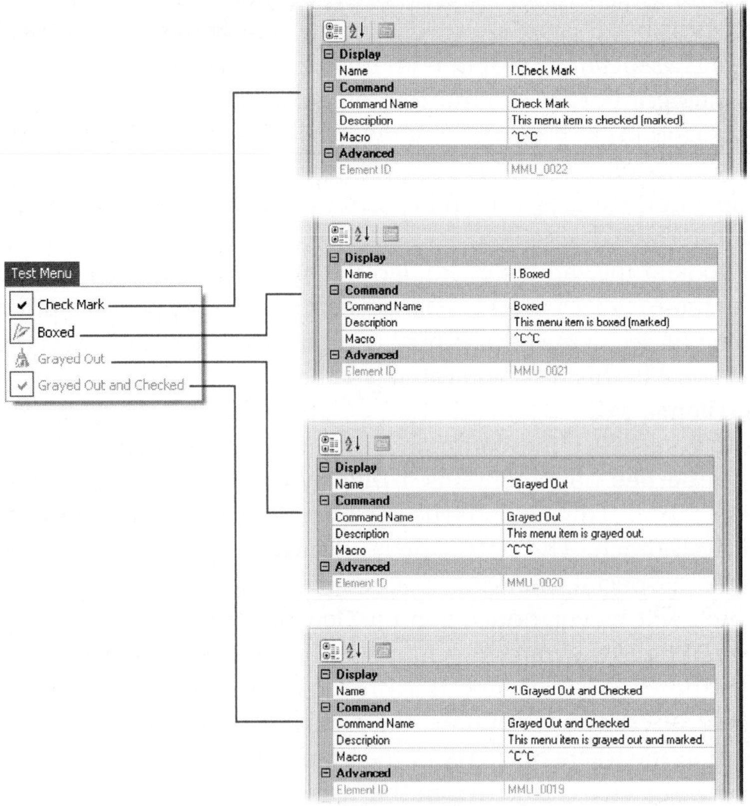

In the cascading menu that is displayed, a check mark appears next to any of the user interface items that are locked in place, such as floating toolbars, docked toolbars, floating windows (palettes), or docked windows (palettes). By default, none of these items are locked. Selecting **Docked Toolbars** in the cascading menu locks all docked toolbars in place. Notice the grab bars are removed from the ends of the docked toolbars. Also, a check mark is placed next to the item in the cascading menu. Selecting that item again unlocks the docked toolbars and removes the check mark from the menu label.

Suppose you want to create a pull-down menu item that allows the ortho mode to be toggled on and off with "on" indicated by a check mark. The command label for this menu item is:

$(if,$(getvar,orthomode),!.)&Ortho Toggle

The first dollar sign ($) signals the pull-down menu to evaluate a DIESEL expression. This expression gets the value (getvar) of the **ORTHOMODE** system variable and marks the item if the value is 1 (on). If you associate an image with this custom command, the item is marked by placing a box around the image. Otherwise, a check mark is placed next to the item name in the menu. The macro for this custom command is simply ^O.

Figure 20-21 shows two DIESEL expressions in menu labels and how they would appear in the pull-down menu. The pull-down menu shows that ortho mode is off and snap mode is on.

Adding DIESEL expressions to your menu labels can make them more powerful and "intelligent." Refer to the online documentation for a complete discussion of the DIESEL language.

Figure 20-21.
Note the DIESEL
expressions and the
resulting pull-down
menu items.

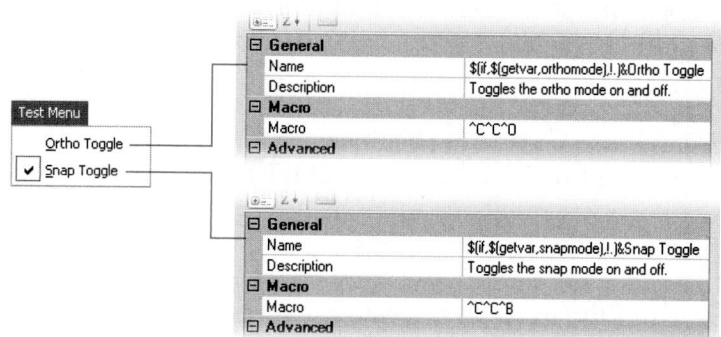

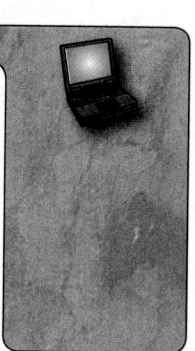

In the ortho toggle example, &Ortho Toggle must be placed at the end of the line for the Name property. However, notice in Figure 20-21 that the Command Name property is Ortho Toggle. This property is displayed when the command is selected in the Menu tree in the "customizations" pane. AutoCAD removes the special characters from the command name so that the custom command is sorted in the **Command List:** pane based on the name and appears with the other "o" commands. Keep this in mind when defining custom commands.

Referencing Other Pull-Down Menus

A menu pick can activate, or reference, another pull-down menu. A menu pick can also gray out or mark another pull-down menu item. The character codes shown in Figure 20-22 are used for these purposes.

When referencing other pull-down menus, you can combine the characters to gray out items or mark items. Study the following menu item examples. The first example activates and displays the twelfth menu in the menu section (alias POP12).

    $p12=*

The next menu item marks the fourth item in the twelfth menu (alias POP12).

    $p12.4=!.

This entry grays out the third item in the sixth menu (alias POP6).

    $p6.3=~

The following menu item marks the second item in the eighth menu (alias POP8) and grays it out.

    $p8.2=!.~

Figure 20-22.
Character codes used
for graying out or
marking another
pull-down menu
item.

Character String	Function
$p*n*=	Makes another pull-down menu current, where *n* is the number of the menu. Alternately, any specified alias for the menu can be referenced. The alias is listed in the Aliases property text box in the **Properties** pane of the **Customize User Interface** dialog box.
$p*n*=*	Displays the currently active pull-down menu.
$p*n*.1=	References a specific item number on another pull-down menu.

The next menu item removes all marks and any "gray out" from the second item in the eighth menu (alias POP8).

$p8.2=

Menu item numbering begins with the first line of the pull-down menu below the name and continues to the bottom of the menu. Separator lines are also counted when determining line numbers. AutoCAD numbers items consecutively through all menus without considering menu levels.

The following examples show how these techniques can be combined in macros. For each of the examples, create a new command and enter the information in the **Properties** pane of the **Customize User Interface** dialog box.

Name: Insert desk
Macro: ^C^C-insert;desk;\\\\$p12=*

Name: Setup .5
Macro: ^C^Cgrid;.5;snap;.25;$p12.1=!. $p12.2=!.~

Name: Defaults
Macro: ^C^Cgrid;off;snap;off;$p12.1= $p12.2=

Figure 20-23 shows an example containing similar macros and the resulting pull-down menu.

PROFESSIONAL TIP

The method for referencing other pull-down menus described here is called *absolute referencing.* Another method, called *relative referencing,* uses the customization group and element ID. A discussion of this method is beyond the scope of this text. Refer to the online documentation for more information on relative referencing.

Figure 20-23.
Note the macros used to control the fourth item in the pull-down menu. Also note that the separators count as an item.

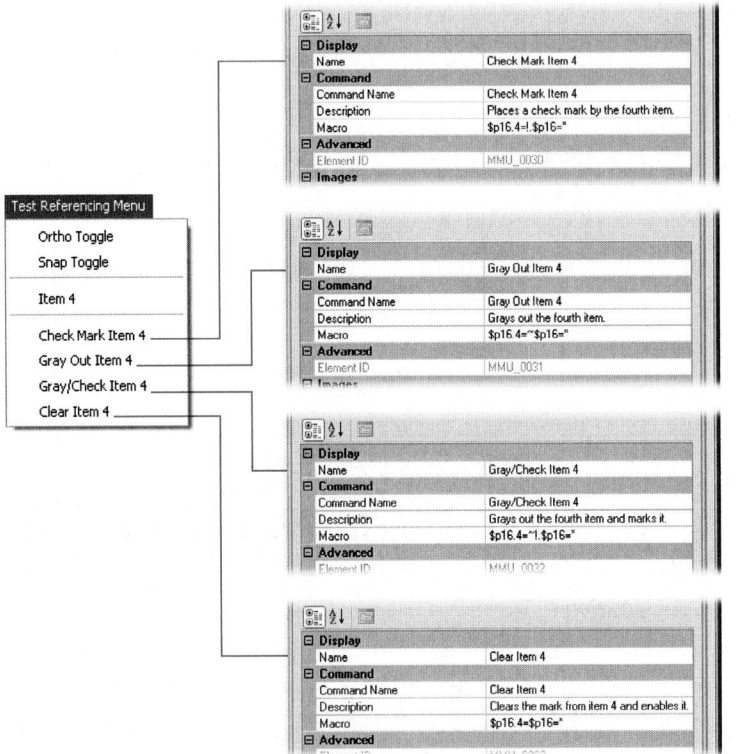

Removing a Pull-Down or Cascading Menu

If you want to permanently remove a pull-down or cascading menu, open the **Customize User Interface** dialog box. Then, expand the tree in the **Customizations in All CUI Files** pane to display the menu to be deleted. Right-click on the menu and pick **Delete** from the shortcut menu. You can also highlight the pull-down menu in the tree and press the [Delete] key. With either method, an AutoCAD alert appears asking you to confirm the deletion. Picking **Yes** in this alert box permanently deletes the menu from the user interface.

The above procedure is not recommended because the menu is permanently removed. To "restore" the menu in the future, it must be rebuilt. A better way to remove any unwanted pull-down menus is by deleting them from the workspace. Managing workspaces is covered in detail in Chapter 23. Briefly, to remove a pull-down menu from a workspace:

1. Open the **Customize User Interface** dialog box and expand the Workspaces branch in the **Customizations in All CUI Files** pane.
2. Select the workspace from which you wish to remove a pull-down menu.
3. In the **Workspace Contents** pane, expand the Menus branch.
4. Right-click on the menu you wish to remove and pick **Remove from Workspace** in the shortcut menu.
5. Exit the **Customize User Interface** dialog box.

Now, the pull-down menu is removed from the workspace, but it is still available to other workspaces. Refer to Chapter 23 for complete details on workspaces and managing workspaces.

Sample Pull-Down Menus

The following examples show how AutoCAD commands and options can be used to create pull-down menu items. Remember, an ampersand (&) preceding a character in a menu or item name defines the keyboard access (mnemonic) key used to enable it. The examples are listed using the following three-step process:

- Step 1. A description of the macro.
- Step 2. The key strokes required for the macro.
- Step 3. The name and macro for the new command as entered in the **Properties** pane of the **Customize User Interface** dialog box.

Example 1

1. This **HEXAGON** command will start the **POLYGON** command and draw a six-sided polygon inscribed in a circle.
2. **POLYGON.⏎**
   6.⏎
   (select center)
   I.⏎
3. Name: &Hexagon
   Macro: *^C^Cpolygon;6;\i

The asterisk in front of the ^C^C repeats the command continuously until it is canceled. The \ in front of i indicates that the macro will wait for user input, in this case the center of the polygon, before continuing.

A return can be represented in a command or macro by using either a space or a semicolon. Notice the following two macros. Both macros perform the same function.

```
*^C^Cpolygon 6 \i
*^C^Cpolygon;6;\i
```

The first example uses spaces and the second example uses semicolons to represent pressing the [Enter] key. The technique used is a matter of personal preference, but semicolons are recommended.

Example 2

1. This **DOT** command draws a solid dot that is .1 unit in diameter. Use the **DONUT** command. The inside diameter is 0 (zero) and the outside diameter is .1.
2. **DONUT.⏎**
   0.⏎
   .1.⏎
3. Name: &Dot
   Macro: ^C^Cdonut;0;.1

Example 3

1. This **X-POINT** command sets the **PDMODE** system variable to 3 and draws an X at the pick point. The command should repeat.
2. **PDMODE.⏎**
   3.⏎
   POINT.⏎
   (pick the point)
3. Name: &X-Point
   Macro: *^C^Cpdmode;3;point

Example 4

1. This command, named **NOTATION**, could be used by a drawing checker or instructor. It allows them to circle features on a drawing and then add a leader and text. It first sets the color to red, then draws a circle, snaps a leader to the nearest point that is picked on the circle, and prompts for the text. User input for text is provided, then a cancel [Esc] returns the Command: prompt and the color is set to ByLayer.
2. **-COLOR.⏎**
   RED.⏎
   CIRCLE.⏎
   (pick center point)
   (pick radius)
   LEADER.⏎
   NEA.⏎
   (pick a point on the circle)
   (pick end of leader)
   (press [Enter] for automatic shoulder)
   (enter text) ⏎
   (press [Enter] to cancel)
   -COLOR.⏎
   BYLAYER.⏎
3. Name: &Notation
   Macro: ^C^C-color;red;circle;\\leader;nea;\\;\;-color;bylayer

Example 5

1. This is a repeating command named **MULTISQUARE** that draws one-unit squares oriented at a 0° horizontal angle until the command is canceled.
2. **RECTANG.⏎**
   (pick lower-left corner)
   @1,1⏎
3. Name: &Multisquare
   Macro: *^C^Crectang;\@1,1

PROFESSIONAL TIP

Some commands, such as the **COLOR** command, display a dialog box. Menu macros can provide input to the command line, but cannot control dialog boxes. To access the command-line version of a command, prefix the command name with a hyphen (-), as shown in Example 4. However, not all commands that display a dialog box have a command-line equivalent.

Exercise 20-5
Complete the exercise on the Student CD.

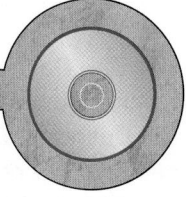

Some Notes about Pull-Down Menus

Here are a few more things to keep in mind when developing pull-down menus.
- Pull-down menus are disabled during **DTEXT** after the rotation angle is entered and during **SKETCH** after the record increment is set.
- A pull-down menu label can be as long as needed, but should be as brief as possible for easy reading. The pull-down menu width is automatically created to fit the width of the longest item.
- Pull-down menus that are longer than the screen display are truncated to fit on the screen.

Dashboard Customization

The **Dashboard** contains commands and tools that are grouped in *control panels*. A control panel has an identifying icon at one end that represents the tools available in the panel. The icon is located in a gray, vertical strip that turns orange when the panel is expanded to show additional tools. A control panel may contain rows of command buttons, drop-down lists, or sliders. You can pick and choose which panels are visible on the fly or control their visibility through the use of workspaces.

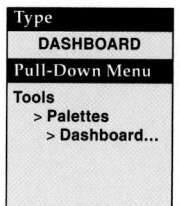

Type
DASHBOARD
Pull-Down Menu

Tools
> Palettes
  > Dashboard...

DASHBOARD

The **Dashboard** can be customized in a number of different ways. It can be horizontally resized. The vertical size is controlled by the number of displayed control panels. If the width of the **Dashboard** does not allow the display of the entire row of available tools, a small arrow appears at the right end of the row. Picking on this arrow and holding displays the hidden command buttons, similar to a flyout in a toolbar. See **Figure 20-24.**

Figure 20-24.
If the **Dashboard** is not wide enough to show an entire row of command buttons, a small arrow appears at the end of the row. Pick and hold the arrow to show the hidden buttons in a flyout.

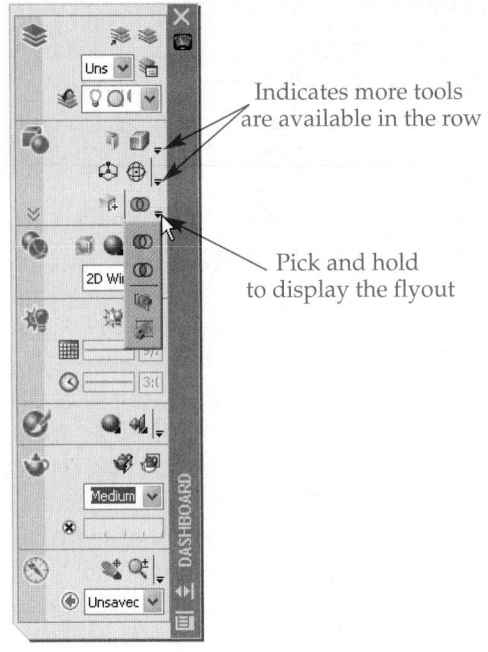

Indicates more tools are available in the row

Pick and hold to display the flyout

The **Dashboard** may also be docked or anchored just as the **Tool Palettes** window. Docking and anchoring is discussed in Chapter 22. In addition, the control panels in the **Dashboard** can be shown or hidden. New panels can be created. Commands can be added or removed from control panels.

Controlling the Display of the Control Panels

Right-click on the title bar of the **Dashboard** and select **Control Panels** from the shortcut menu. A cascading menu is displayed that contains the names of all available control panels. See Figure 20-25. These are the default control panels: **2D Draw**, **3D Make**, **3D Navigate**, **Visual Styles**, **Lights**, **Materials**, **Render**, **Layers**, **Annotation Scaling**, **Text**, **Dimensions**, **Multileaders**, **Tables**, **2D Navigate**, **Object Properties**, and **Block Attributes**. The currently displayed control panels have a check mark next to their name. Selecting a name from the cascading menu toggles the visibility of the control panel.

Figure 20-25.
Control panels can be displayed or hidden on the fly by right-clicking on the **Dashboard** title bar and selecting **Control panels** in the shortcut menu. A check mark appears next to the currently displayed control panels.

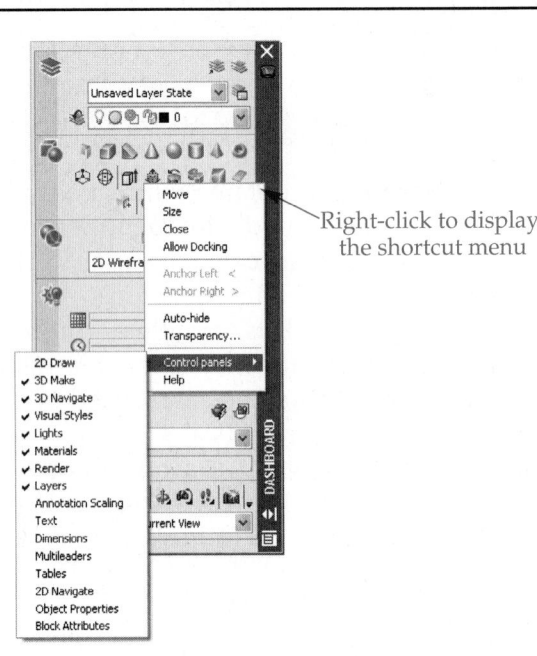

Right-click to display the shortcut menu

While the visibility of the control panels can be adjusted "on the fly" as described above, this can also be controlled through the use of workspaces. Workspaces are discussed in detail in Chapter 23. Briefly, change the visibility of control panels in a workspace as follows.

1. Open the **Customize User Interface** dialog box and expand the Workspaces branch in the **Customizations in All CUI Files** pane.
2. Select the workspace for which you wish to adjust control panel visibility.
3. In the **Workspace Contents** pane, pick the **Customize Workspace** button.
4. Expand the Dashboard Panels branch. The control panels visible in the workspace appear in the branch.
5. In the **Customizations in All CUI Files** pane, expand the Dashboard Panels branch. All available control panels appear in the branch. The currently displayed control panels have a check mark next to their name. See Figure 20-26.
6. Check the control panels to display and uncheck the control panels to hide.
7. In the **Workspace Contents** pane, pick the **Done** button, which replaced the **Customize Workspace** button.
8. Exit the **Customize User Interface** dialog box.

Control panels appear in the **Dashboard** in the order they are displayed in the tree in the **Workspace Contents** pane. As you add control panels to the workspace, they are added to the bottom of the Dashboard Panels branch. To rearrange the control panels, pick and drag them within the **Workspace Contents** pane. You do not need to be in "customization mode." You can also remove a control panel from the workspace by right-clicking on its name in the **Workspace Contents** pane and picking **Remove from Workspace** from the shortcut menu.

PROFESSIONAL TIP

Do not display too many control panels at one time. Remember, the **Dashboard** can only be horizontally resized. The vertical size of the dashboard is determined by the number of visible panels. Too many visible panels and the lower panels may extend off the bottom of the screen, making them inaccessible.

Figure 20-26.
Controlling control panel visibility by editing the workspace. Workspaces are covered in Chapter 23.

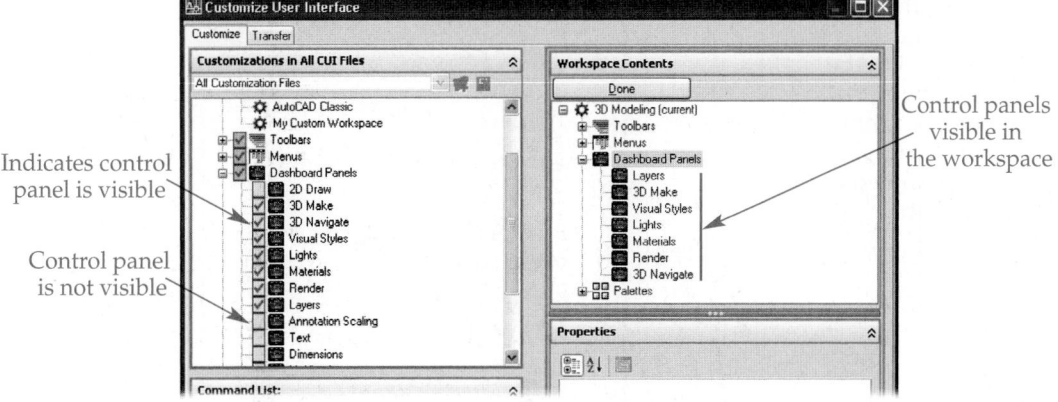

Understanding a Control Panel Definition

Before customizing control panels, look at the layout of existing control panels. Open the **Customize User Interface** dialog box. In the **Customizations in All CUI Files** pane, expand the Dashboard Panels branch. All of the available control panels are shown. Expand the 2D Draw branch. Notice that it consists of two rows and a panel separator. Now, expand the 3D Make branch. Notice that this control panel has three rows, a panel separator, and one more row. See **Figure 20-27.** Any row listed after the panel separator is only visible when the control panel is expanded. Remember, the vertical bar turns from gray to orange when a control panel is expanded. Notice that there are no rows listed after the panel separator in the 2D Draw branch. If this control panel is displayed, it is not expandable.

Next, expand the Row 1 branch in the 2D Draw branch. All of the commands available in the first row of the **2D Draw** control panel are listed. See **Figure 20-28.** In this case, they are the same commands that are available on the **Draw** toolbar, including the **Block** flyout. If you expand the Block branch, you will see that the commands available are the same as those found in the flyout on the **Draw** toolbar. Expand the Row 2 branch in the 2D Draw branch. Notice the available commands. In this case, they are the same commands available on the **Modify** toolbar.

Expand the Layers branch and each of the branches below it. Notice that this panel contains other types of tools in addition to standard command tools. See **Figure 20-29.** If you select the Layers branch, a preview of the control panel appears on the right side of the **Customize User Interface** dialog box in the **Panel Preview** pane. Also, notice the **Button Image** pane on the lower-right side of the dialog box. This is where the icon associated with the control panel is specified.

Customizing a Control Panel

To add a command to a control panel, open the **Customize User Interface** dialog box. In the **Customizations in All CUI Files** pane, expand the branches for the panel and row to which the command will be added. In the **Commands List:** pane, locate the command to add to the control panel. Select the command and drag it into position in the **Customizations in All CUI Files** pane. You can also drag a command into the **Panel Preview** pane and drop it into position there, rather than into the tree in the **Customizations in All CUI Files** pane.

A new row can be added to a control panel. In the **Customizations in All CUI Files** pane, right-click on the row after which you would like the new row added. Then,

Figure 20-27.
Notice how the **3D Make** control panel is represented in the tree. Any row below the separator is not shown until the control panel is expanded in the **Dashboard**.

Always visible

Visible in expanded control panel

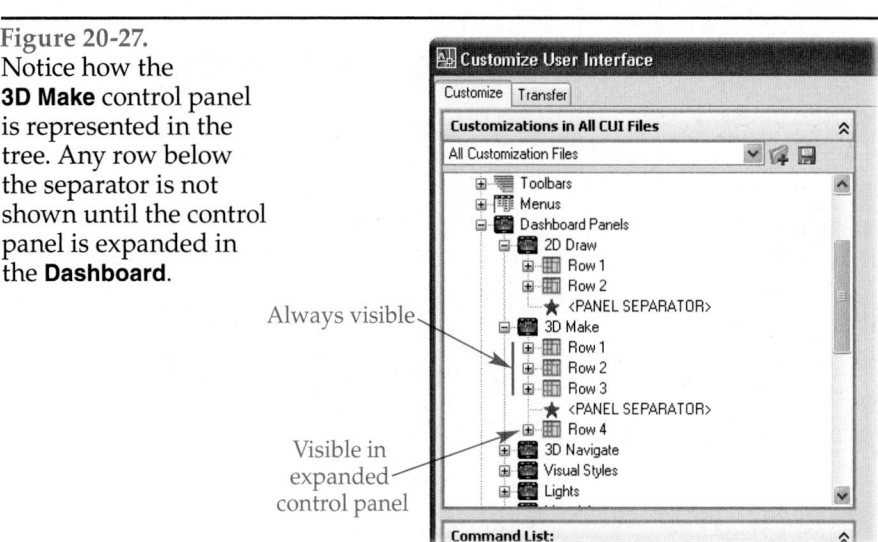

AutoCAD and Its Applications—Advanced

Figure 20-28.
A—How the **2D Draw** control panel is represented in the tree in the **Customize User Interface** dialog box. B—The **2D Draw** control panel is shown at the bottom of the **Dashboard**. Compare the buttons to the entries in the tree in the **Customize User Interface** dialog box.

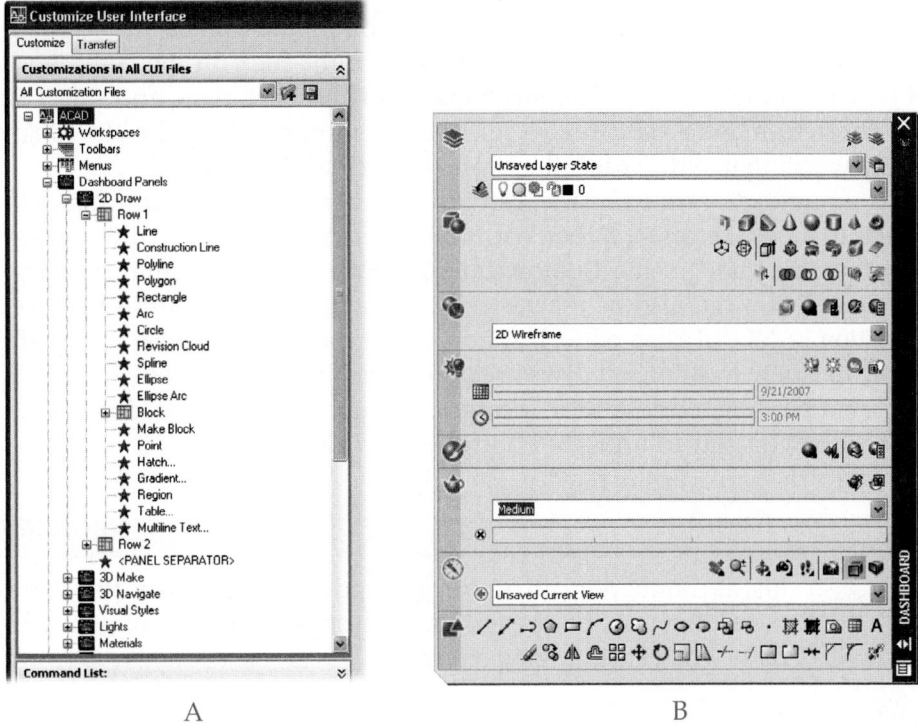

A   B

Figure 20-29.
Compare the preview of the control panel to how the control panel is represented in the tree in the **Customizations in All CUI** Files pane.

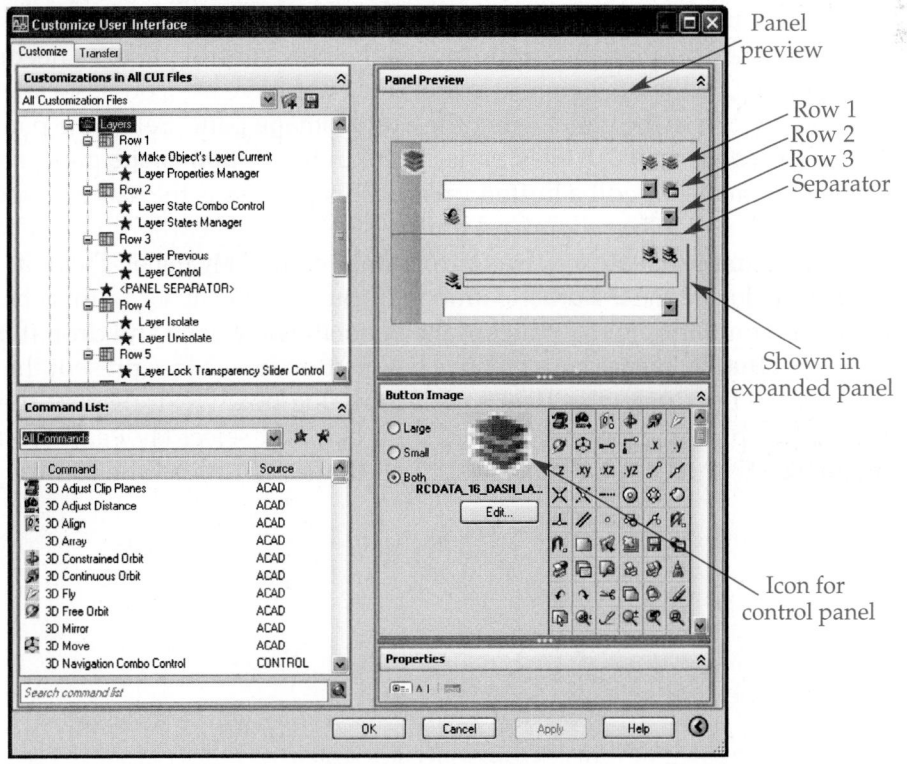

select **New Row** from the shortcut menu. Remember, any rows below the separator are not displayed until the panel is expanded. To add a new first row, right-click on the panel branch name and select **New Row** from the shortcut menu. The new row is added and all other rows are renumbered. The rows are always sequentially numbered beginning with one. Once a row is added, commands can be added to it.

To remove a command from a control panel, right-click on the command in the control panel's branch in the **Customizations in All CUI Files** pane and select **Remove** from the shortcut menu. You can also select the command and press the [Delete] key. There is no warning in either case; the command is simply removed.

The commands in a control panel can be rearranged. Select the command to move and drag it to a new location, either within its current row or in a different row. You can drag the command in the **Customizations in All CUI Files** pane or in the **Panel Preview** pane. Rows can also be rearranged by dragging them within the tree in the **Customization in All CUI Files** pane, but not within the **Panel Preview** pane. After you drag a row to a new location, all rows are automatically renumbered. The panel separator can also be dragged to a new location. Remember, rows listed after the panel separator are not displayed until the control panel is expanded.

PROFESSIONAL TIP

Just as commands can be dragged and dropped into the **Panel Preview** pane, they can be dragged and dropped into the **Toolbar Preview** pane when customizing a toolbar.

Creating a New Control Panel

To create a new control panel, open the **Customize User Interface** dialog box. Then, in the **Customizations in All CUI Files** pane, right-click on the Dashboard Panels branch and select **New Panel** from the shortcut menu. A new panel with the default name of Panel$x$ is added to the bottom of the Dashboard Panels branch. Enter a name for the new control panel, either in the tree or in the **Properties** pane. Expand the branch for the new control panel and notice that Row 1 and the panel separator are automatically added to it. Add commands and rows to the new control panel as needed.

By default, the new control panel does not have an icon associated with it. You can add an icon to the panel using the **Button Image** pane. Select the panel name in the **Customizations in All CUI Files** pane. Then, in the **Button Image** pane, select an image, import an image, or edit a button image. This process is the same as specifying a button image for a toolbar command button, as described earlier in this chapter.

For example, create a new control panel named My Panel. Then, in the **Command List:** pane, locate the **E-Border** command you created earlier in this chapter. Drag the command onto the control panel in the **Panel Preview** pane and drop it in the first row. Using the **Button Image** pane, create a new button image to represent the control panel. Then, close the **Customize User Interface** dialog box. Next, display the **Dashboard** if it is not displayed, right-click on the title bar, and select **My Panel** from the shortcut menu. See **Figure 20-30**. Finally, test the **E-Border** button on the control panel.

Figure 20-30.
A new, custom control panel has been created and added to the bottom of the **Dashboard**.

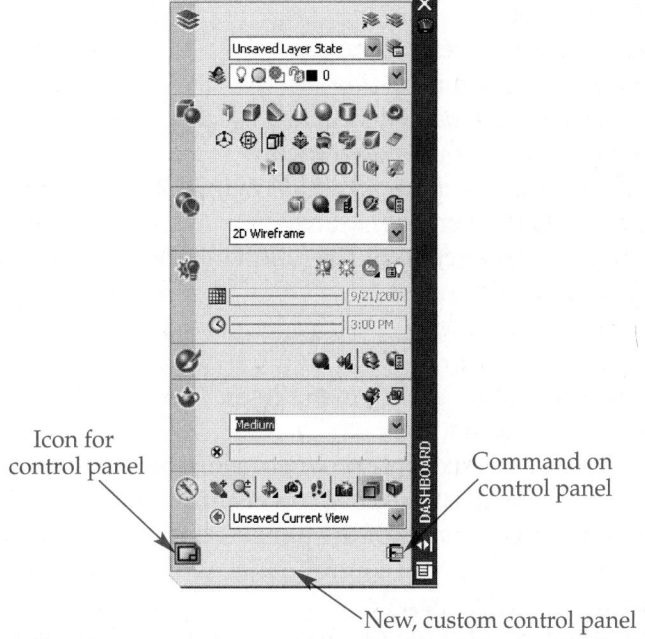

Icon for control panel

Command on control panel

New, custom control panel

Chapter Test

Answer the following questions. Write your answers on a separate sheet of paper or complete the electronic chapter test on the Student CD.

1. Name two ways to show or hide toolbars.
2. List three ways to access the **Customize User Interface** dialog box.
3. In which pane of the **Customize User Interface** dialog box can you find all predefined commands?
4. How do you copy an existing command button from one toolbar to another?
5. How do you remove a command button from a toolbar?
6. How can you copy an existing command button to a new location on the same toolbar?
7. What is the advantage offered by the **QUICKCUI** command vs. the **CUI** command?
8. How do you create a new toolbar?
9. How do you create a tooltip for a new command button?
10. How do you create a help string for a new command button?
11. How should you develop and test a new macro before entering it into a custom command definition?
12. Name two ways to specify an [Enter] in a macro. Which of the two methods is recommended?
13. Name the four tools that are provided in the **Button Editor** dialog box.
14. What is the default, small size (in pixels) of the button editor drawing area?
15. Where is the **Use large buttons for Toolbars** check box located? What function does this check box perform?
16. How do you insert a flyout into a toolbar?
17. How do you associate a toolbar with a flyout?
18. Explain how to display a toolbar without using a dialog box.
19. How many items can a pull-down menu contain?

20. Provide the character(s) required to perform the following functions in a pull-down menu.
    A. Gray out a menu item.
    B. Mark a menu item.
    C. Specify the menu access key.
21. How wide is a pull-down menu?
22. What is the function of the following DIESEL expression?
    $(if,$(getvar,snapmode),!.)Snap
23. What is the function of the following menu item characters?
    A. $p3=*
    B. $p4.1=~
    C. $p6.7=!.
24. Interpret the following menu item.
    ^C^Crectang;\@1,1
25. Name at least six control panels available on the **Dashboard**.
26. Name two ways to control the visibility of control panels on the **Dashboard**.
27. What is the purpose of the panel separator for a control panel?
28. When adding a new control panel, which two items are automatically added to the new control panel?
29. Briefly describe how to create a new **Dashboard** control panel.
30. How do you associate an icon with a custom control panel?

Drawing Problems

*Before customizing or creating any toolbars, pull-down menus, or **Dashboard** control panels, check with your instructor or supervisor for specific instructions or guidelines.*

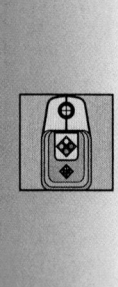

1. Create a new toolbar using the following information.
    A. Name the toolbar **Draw/Modify**.
    B. Copy at least three, but no more than six, commonly used drawing commands onto the new toolbar. Use only existing commands; do not create new ones.
    C. Copy at least three, but no more than six, commonly used editing commands onto the new toolbar. Use only existing commands; do not create new ones.
    D. Hide the default **Draw** and **Modify** toolbars from the display.
    E. Dock the new **Draw/Modify** toolbar at the upper-left side of the screen.

2. Create a new toolbar using the following information.
    A. Name the toolbar **My 3D Tools**.
    B. Copy the following commands from the **Modeling** toolbar onto the new toolbar.

Box	**Pyramid**
Cone	**Sphere**
Cylinder	**Torus**

    C. Copy the following commands from the **View** toolbar onto the new toolbar.

Top	**Bottom**	**Left**
Right	**Front**	**Back**

    D. Copy the following commands from the **UCS** toolbar onto the new toolbar.

3 Point	**Object**	**World**
Face UCS	**Origin**	**UCS Previous**

    E. Dock the toolbar in a location of your choice.

3. Create a new **Dashboard** control panel using the following information.
   A. Name the control panel **Paper Space Viewports**.
   B. The control panel should contain eight custom commands that use the **MVIEW** command to create paper space viewports:
      - **1 Viewport**—allow user to pick location
      - **1 Viewport (Fit)**
      - **2 Viewports (Horizontal)**—allow user to pick location
      - **2 Viewports (Vertical)**
      - **3 Viewports**—allow user to pick orientation and location
      - **3 Viewports (Right)**
      - **4 Viewports**—allow user to pick location
      - **4 Viewports (Fit)**
   C. Create a custom command that will switch from one viewport to another. Add this command to the new toolbar.
   D. Construct button graphics for the custom commands. Save the images in the default \Icons folder or create a new folder (be sure to add it to the AutoCAD support environment).
   E. Place a button on the control panel that executes the **PLOT** command.
   F. Position the control panel below the **Annotation Scaling** control panel.

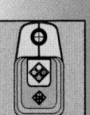

4. Create a new toolbar for inserting title block drawings. Name the toolbar **Title Blocks**.
   A. The toolbar should contain six custom commands that do the following.
      - Insert the ANSI A title block drawing (plot style of your choice)
      - Insert the ANSI B title block drawing (plot style of your choice)
      - Insert the ANSI C title block drawing (plot style of your choice)
      - Insert the ANSI D title block drawing (plot style of your choice)
      - Insert the ANSI E title block drawing (plot style of your choice)
      - Insert the Architectural title block drawing (plot style of your choice)
   B. Create button graphics for each of the custom commands. Save the images in a new folder and add the folder to the AutoCAD support environment.
   C. Dock the toolbar on the left side of the screen.

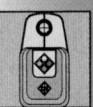

5. Add a flyout to the **Standard** toolbar that will display the toolbar created in Problem 4. Place the flyout next to the **Open** button.

6. Create a new dimensioning pull-down menu. Place as many dimensioning commands as you need in the menu. Use cascading menus if necessary. One or more of the cascading menus should be dimensioning variables. Include menu access (mnemonic) keys.

7. Create a pull-down menu for 3D objects. Include menu access (mnemonic) keys. The menu should include the following items.
   - At least three 3D solid objects
   - **HIDE** command
   - At least three visual style commands
   - **VPORTS** command
   - **3DORBIT** command

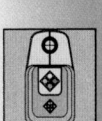

8. Create a new pull-down menu named **Special**. The menu should include the following drawing and editing commands.

LINE	MOVE
ARC	COPY
CIRCLE	STRETCH
POLYLINE	TRIM
POLYGON	EXTEND
RECTANGLE	CHAMFER
DTEXT	FILLET
ERASE	

Use cascading menus, if necessary. Include a separator line between the drawing and editing commands and specify appropriate menu access (mnemonic) keys.

9. Create a single pull-down menu to insert a variety of blocks or symbols. These symbols can be for any drawing discipline that suits your needs. Use cascading menus and menu access (mnemonic) keys, if necessary.

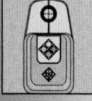

10. Create a new **Dashboard** control panel named **My 3D Tools**. Evaluate which tools you use most often for creating and rendering 3D models. Place these commands on the custom control panel, even if they are already contained on another control panel. The purpose of this new control panel is to streamline your modeling and rendering work. Create a custom button image to use as the icon for the control panel. Position the control panel at the top of the **Dashboard**.

Drawing Problems – Chapter 20

Customizing Shortcut Keys, Shortcut Menus, and Double-Click Actions

Learning Objectives

After completing this chapter, you will be able to:
- ✓ Assign shortcut keys to commands.
- ✓ Explain how shortcut menus function.
- ✓ Edit existing shortcut menus.
- ✓ Create custom shortcut menus.
- ✓ Describe double-click actions.
- ✓ Edit double-click actions.
- ✓ Create custom double-click actions.

AutoCAD has many tools that can be used in "heads-up design." Heads-up design is a concept of working in which your eyes remain focused on the drawing area. For example, when dynamic input is on, you do not need to look at the command line to see the options for the current command. The options are displayed near the cursor in the drawing area. AutoCAD's shortcut menus and double-click actions also contribute to heads-up design. Shortcut menus are displayed by right-clicking. Double-click actions are initiated when an object is double-clicked. Like many of the menus and toolbars in AutoCAD, shortcut menus and double-click actions can be customized.

In order to use the shortcut menu and double-click action customization techniques discussed in this chapter, shortcut menus and double-click editing need to be enabled. To do this, open the **Options** dialog box and select the **User Preferences** tab. Then, check the **Double click editing** and **Shortcut menus in drawing area** check boxes, as shown in Figure 21-1.

The use of shortcut menus can be further refined by picking the **Right-click Customization...** button that appears below the check boxes. This displays the **Right-Click Customization** dialog box. See Figure 21-2. The settings in this dialog box allow you to define what a right-click does when in default mode, edit mode, or command mode. For this chapter, pick the **Shortcut menu** radio buttons in the **Default Mode** and **Edit Mode** areas. Also, pick the **Shortcut Menu: always enabled** radio button in the **Command Mode** area. Then, close the **Right-Click Customization** and **Options** dialog boxes.

Figure 21-1.
The settings for
enabling shortcut
menus and
double-click editing
are found in the
Options dialog box.

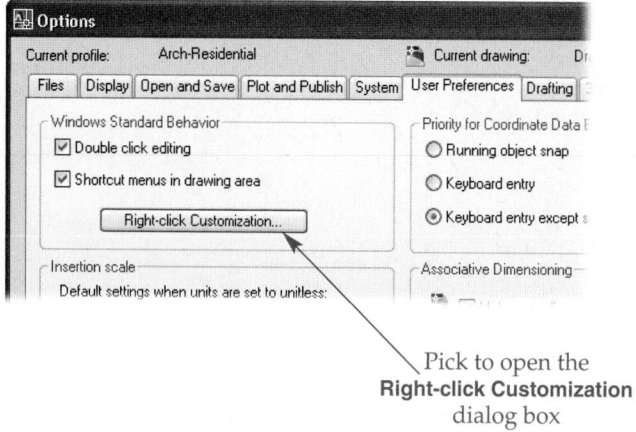

Pick to open the
Right-click Customization
dialog box

Figure 21-2.
The settings in the
**Right-Click
Customization** dialog
box allow you to
define what a
right-click does when
in default mode, edit
mode, or command
mode.

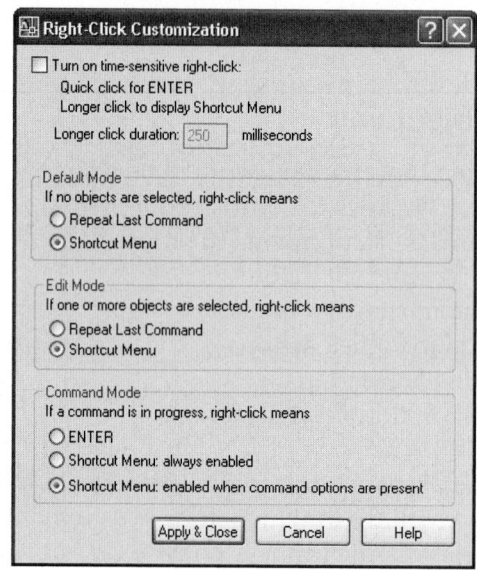

Customizing Shortcut Keys

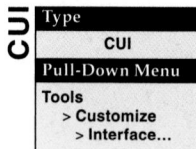

You can define your own custom shortcut keys (accelerator keys) for AutoCAD commands and custom macros. The **Customize User Interface** dialog box is used to define shortcut keys. To see the commands to which shortcut keys are assigned, expand the Keyboard Shortcuts branch in the **Customizations in All CUI Files** pane. Then, expand the Shortcut Keys branch. All commands that have a shortcut key assigned to them appear in this branch. See **Figure 21-3.**

When the Shortcut Keys branch is selected, the **Shortcuts** pane is displayed in the upper-right corner of the **Customize User Interface** dialog box. A command that has a shortcut key assigned to it can be selected in this pane to display the **Properties** pane.

Assigning a Shortcut Key

To assign a shortcut key to a command, first locate the command in the **Command List:** pane of the **Customize User Interface** dialog box. Next, drag the command into the Shortcut Keys branch in the **Customizations in All CUI Files** pane. The command is added to the list of shortcut keys (although it may not be immediately visible) and the **Properties** pane is displayed for the command. See **Figure 21-4.** In the **Access** category

Figure 21-3.
Shortcut keys are added to commands in the **Customize User Interface** dialog box.

Expand to see the commands to which shortcut keys are assigned

Shortcut key assignments

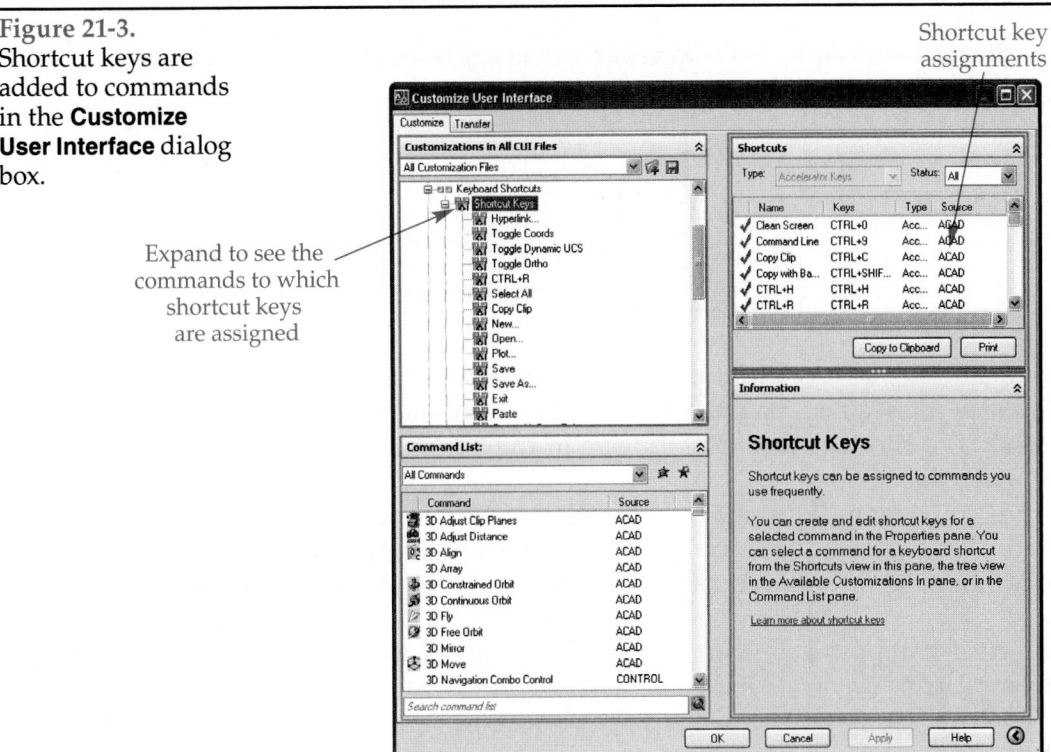

Figure 21-4.
Adding a shortcut key to the **RENDER** command.

Command is added to the Shortcut Keys branch

Define a shortcut key here

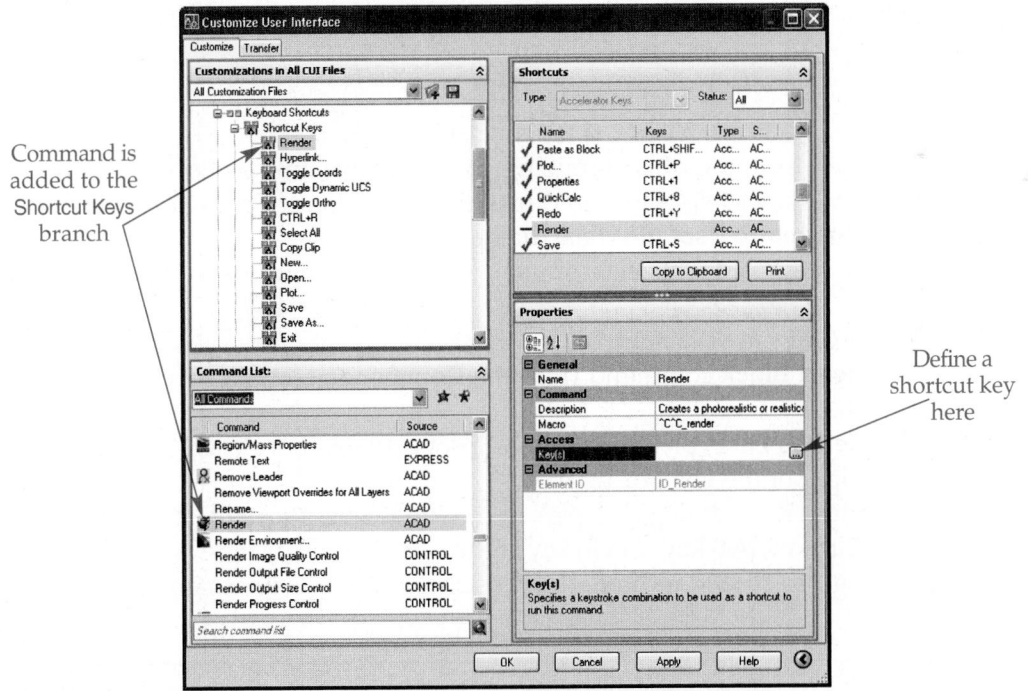

of the **Properties** pane, pick in the Key(s) property text box. Next, pick the button on the right of the text box (**...**) to display the **Shortcut Keys** dialog box. See **Figure 21-5.**

To assign a new shortcut key to the command, pick in the text box labeled **Press new shortcut key:** and press a combination of [Ctrl] + another key. If the shortcut key combination is currently assigned to another command, the name of the other

Figure 21-5.
The **Shortcut Keys** dialog box is where a shortcut key is specified for the command.

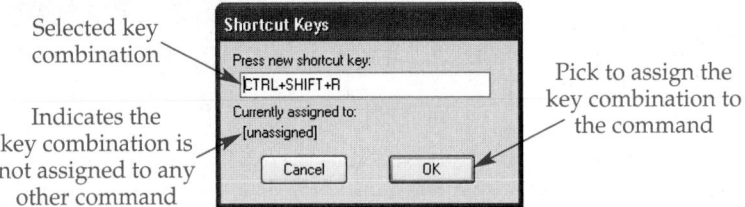

Selected key combination

Indicates the key combination is not assigned to any other command

Pick to assign the key combination to the command

command is displayed in the **Currently assigned to:** area. If the shortcut key combination is unassigned, pick the **OK** button to associate the shortcut key with the command. The shortcut key then appears in the Key(s) property in the **Customize User Interface** dialog box.

If you attempt to assign a shortcut key that is currently assigned to another command, an alert box appears indicating the shortcut assignment already exists and explaining the priority for using the shortcut. See **Figure 21-6.** It is not a good idea to have a shortcut key assigned to multiple commands. Be especially careful to ensure the standard Windows keyboard shortcuts are unique, such as [Ctrl]+[X] for cut, [Ctrl]+[C] for copy, and [Ctrl]+[V] for paste.

PROFESSIONAL TIP

In addition to [Ctrl]+*key*, a shortcut can be [Ctrl]+[Shift]+*key*, [Ctrl]+[Alt]+*key*, or [Ctrl]+[Shift]+[Alt]+*key*. The [Caps Lock] key must be off in order to specify the [Shift] key in the **Press new shortcut key:** text box.

Example Shortcut Key Assignment

To provide an example of customizing shortcut keys, this section shows how to assign the shortcut key [Ctrl]+[Alt]+[I] to the **INSERT** command. Do the following:
1. Open the **Customize User Interface** dialog box.
2. Expand the Keyboard Shortcuts branch in the **Customizations in All CUI Files** pane.
3. Expand the Shortcut Keys branch.
4. Drag the **Insert Block** command from the **Commands List:** pane into the Shortcut Keys branch.
5. In the **Properties** pane, pick in the Key(s) property text box. Then, pick the button on the far right of the text box (**...**).
6. In the **Shortcut Keys** dialog box, pick in the **Press new shortcut key:** text box.
7. Press the [Ctrl] key, [Alt] key, and [I] key at the same time. The message at the bottom of the dialog box should indicate that this shortcut key is unassigned.

Figure 21-6.
This warning appears if the shortcut key you are trying to assign to a command is already assigned to a different command. Avoid assigning a shortcut key to more than one command.

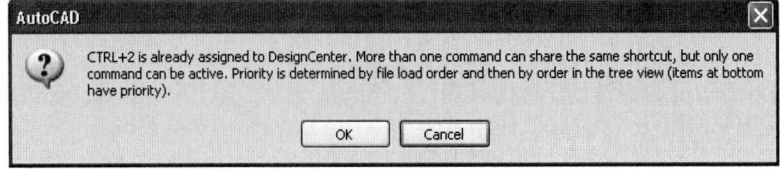

8. Pick the **OK** button to close the **Shortcut Keys** dialog box.
9. Pick the **OK** button to close the **Customize User Interface** dialog box and apply the change.
10. Test the [Ctrl]+[Alt]+[I] shortcut key. The **Insert** dialog box should appear when the shortcut key is used.

PROFESSIONAL TIP

Shortcut keys (accelerator keys) have some specific limitations. For example, a shortcut cannot pause for user input or use repeating commands. Be aware of this when assigning shortcut keys to custom commands.

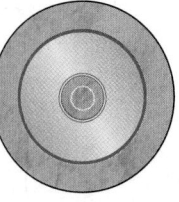

Exercise 21-1
Complete the exercise on the Student CD.

Examining Existing Shortcut Menus

Shortcut menus are context-sensitive menus that appear at the cursor location when using the right-hand button on the pointing device (right-clicking). *Context sensitive* means that the displayed shortcut menu is dependent on what is occurring at the time of the right-click. For example, if no command is active, there is no object selection, and you right-click in the drawing area, the shortcut menu shown in **Figure 21-7A** is displayed. If no command is active and you right-click in **Command Line** window, the shortcut menu shown in **Figure 21-7B** is displayed. If the **CIRCLE** command is active and you right-click in the drawing area before any point is selected, the shortcut menu shown in **Figure 21-7C** is displayed. Other menus appear when right-clicking in other situations, too, such as when grips are being used or when an object is selected in the drawing window. In the case of a selected object, the shortcut menu is based on the type of object that is selected.

Figure 21-7.
A—Displayed when no command is active and no object is selected. B—Displayed when no command is active and you right-click in the **Command Line** window. C—Displayed when the **CIRCLE** command is active and before any point is selected.

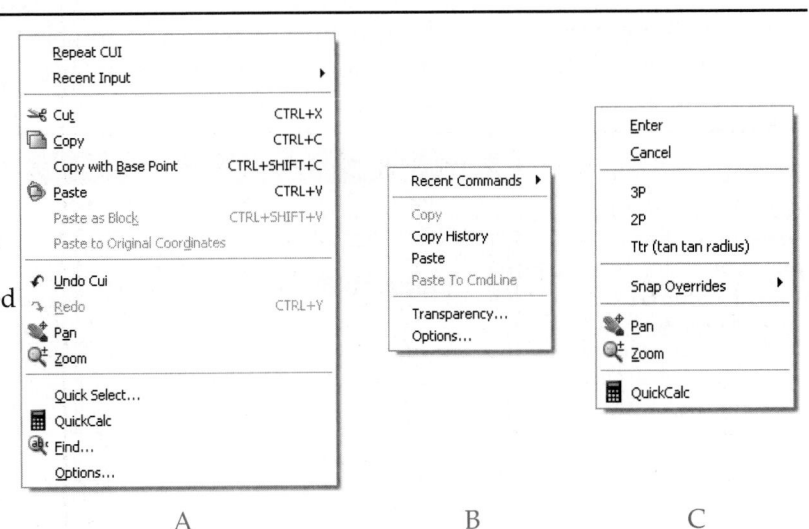

A   B   C

Figure 21-8.
Existing shortcut
menus are displayed
as branches in the
Shortcut Menus branch
in the **Customize User
Interface** dialog box.

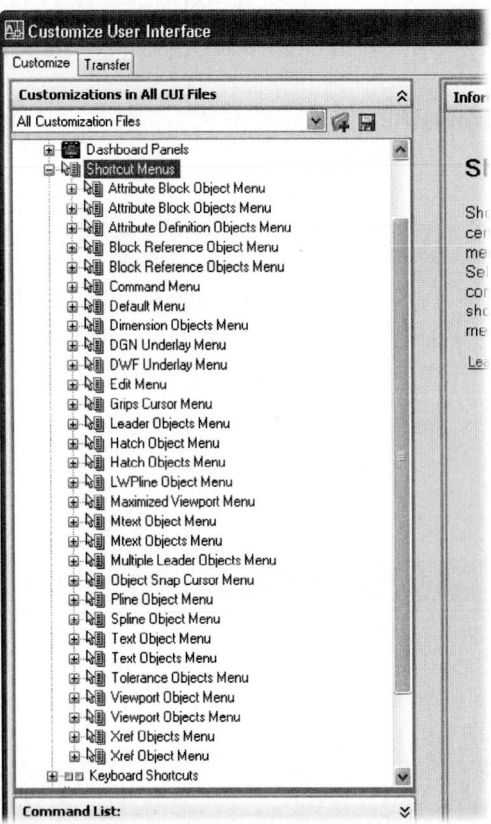

Before learning how to customize shortcut menus, take a look at the existing shortcut menus. Open the **Customize User Interface** dialog box and look at the **Customizations in All CUI Files** pane. The name of this pane is based on what is selected in the drop-down list. Expand the Shortcut Menus branch in the tree. All of the existing shortcut menu names are displayed as branches. See **Figure 21-8.** There are command-specific, object-specific, and generic shortcut menus. The generic shortcut menus are:

- **Command Menu.** This menu appears when right-clicking in the drawing window while a command is active. Any command options for the active command are inserted into this menu. See **Figure 21-9.**
- **Default Menu.** This menu appears when right-clicking in the drawing window while no command is active and no objects are selected. See **Figure 21-10.**
- **Edit Menu.** This menu appears when right-clicking in the drawing window when no command is active and an object is selected. In order for this menu to be displayed, the **PICKFIRST** system variable must be set to 1. If an object menu is available for the type of object selected, it is inserted into this menu. See **Figure 21-11.**

Figure 21-9.
A—The Command
Menu branch in the
**Customize User
Interface** dialog box.
B—The command
shortcut menu.

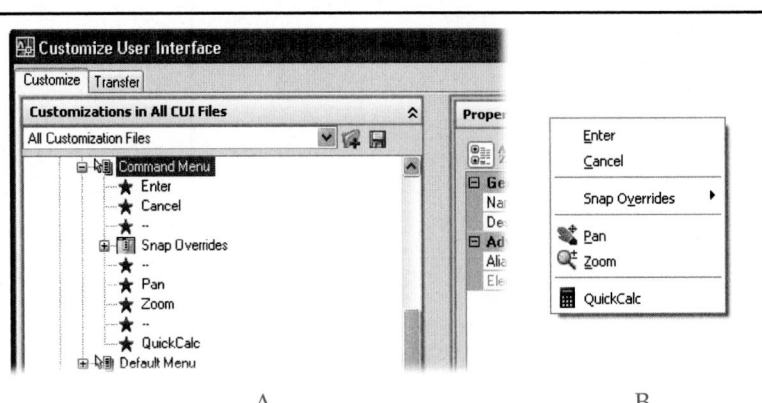

A

B

Figure 21-10.
A—The Default Menu branch in the **Customize User Interface** dialog box.
B—The default shortcut menu.

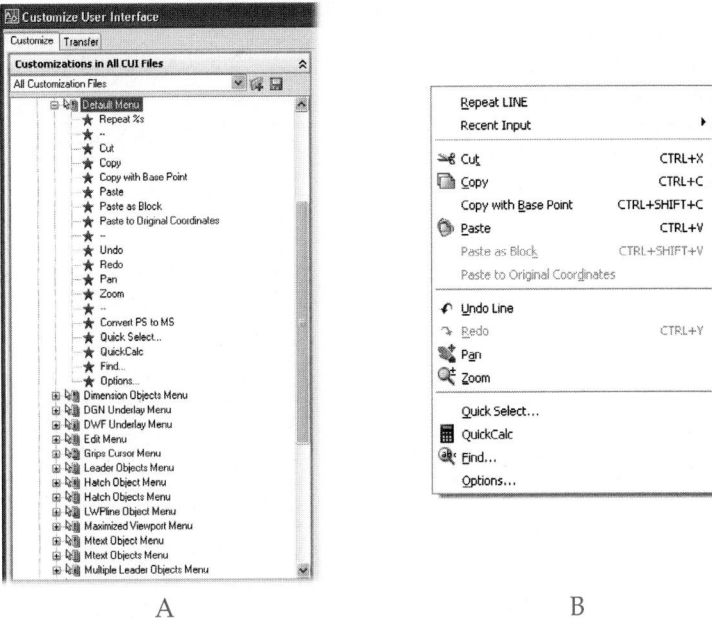

A   B

- **Grips Menu.** This menu appears when grips are being used. See **Figure 21-12.** An object must be selected and at least one grip must be hot.
- **Object Snap Cursor Menu.** This menu appears when holding the down [Shift] key and right-clicking. See **Figure 21-13.** It also appears as a cascading menu in the Command Menu.

The remaining menus are object-specific menus that appear when right-clicking while a certain type of object is selected. Notice that there are menu branches named Attribute Block Objects Menu, Block Reference Objects Menu, Dimension Objects Menu, Hatch Objects Menu, and others. These menus contain items that can be used on the type of object selected. For example, the menu branch Dimension Objects Menu contains commands for editing the dimension text position, the dimension text precision, and the dimension style.

Figure 21-11.
A—The Edit Menu branch in the **Customize User Interface** dialog box.
B—The edit shortcut menu.

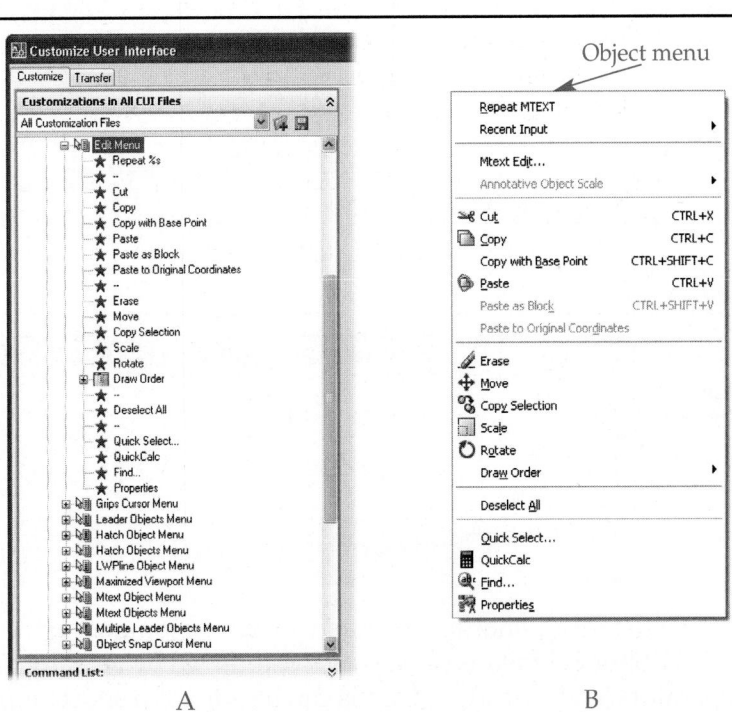

A   B

Figure 21-12.
A—The Grips Menu branch in the **Customize User Interface** dialog box. B—The grips shortcut menu.

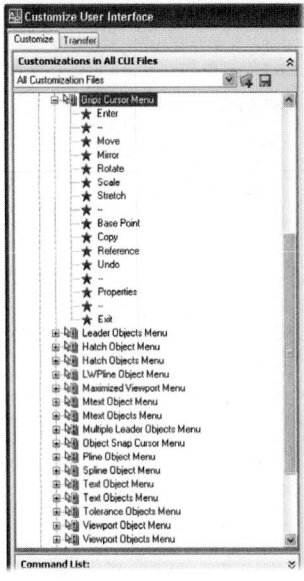

A

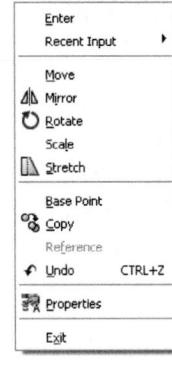

B

Figure 21-13.
A—The Object Snap Cursor Menu branch in the **Customize User Interface** dialog box. B—The object snap shortcut menu.

A

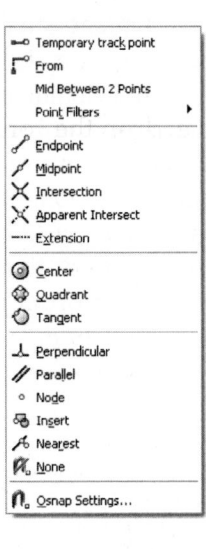

B

Exercise 21-2
Complete the exercise on the Student CD.

Customizing Shortcut Menus

The existing shortcut menus can be customized by adding or removing commands. Shortcut menus can also be customized by visually grouping commands using separators, and cascading menus can be added to shortcut menus.

AutoCAD and Its Applications—Advanced

To add a command to a shortcut menu, open the **Customize User Interface** dialog box and expand the branch for the shortcut menu you would like to customize in the **Customizations in All CUI Files** pane. Next, locate the command you wish to add in the **Command List:** pane. Then, drag the command into the desired position within the shortcut menu in the **Customizations in All CUI Files** pane and drop it when the bar appears.

To remove a command from a shortcut menu, expand the branch for the shortcut menu in the **Customizations in All CUI Files** pane. Highlight the command to be removed, right-click, and select **Remove** from the shortcut menu. You can also highlight the command and press the [Delete] key.

To add a separator to a shortcut menu, expand the branch for the shortcut menu in the **Customizations in All CUI Files** pane. Highlight the command *after* which you would like the separator to be added. Right-click and select **Add Separator** from the shortcut menu.

To rename a shortcut menu, highlight the branch in the **Customizations in All CUI Files** pane. Then, right-click and select **Rename** from the shortcut menu. Finally, type the new name and press [Enter]. The shortcut menu can also be renamed using the Name property in the **Properties** pane.

To add a cascading menu to a shortcut menu, expand the branch for the shortcut menu in the **Customizations in All CUI Files** pane. Highlight the command *after* which you would like the cascading menu to appear. Right-click and select **New Sub-menu** from the shortcut menu. A new shortcut menu branch with the default name of Menu*x* is added to the current shortcut menu. The new menu can be renamed. Now, in the **Command List:** pane, locate the commands you wish to add to the new shortcut menu. Drag the commands into the **Customizations in All CUI Files** pane and drop them next to the name of the new shortcut menu. When the arrow appears next to the new menu name, drop the command to add it to the new shortcut menu.

Creating a new, custom shortcut menu is a two-step process. First, make a new shortcut menu and then drag commands into it. Follow these steps to make a new shortcut menu:

1. Open the **Customize User Interface** dialog box.
2. In the **Customizations in All CUI Files** pane, right-click on the Shortcut Menus branch and select **New Shortcut Menu** in the shortcut menu that is displayed.
3. Enter a name for the shortcut menu.
4. In the **Properties** pane, add a description for the shortcut menu in the **General** category.
5. In the **Advanced** category of the **Properties** pane, add an alias. This alias is in addition to the automatic, sequential POP5*xx* alias that AutoCAD creates. Select the property, pick the **...** button at the right of the text box, and type the alias in the **Aliases** dialog box that appears. Each alias must be on its own line in this dialog box. Close the **Aliases** dialog box.
6. Drag commands from the **Command List:** pane into the new shortcut menu.
7. Pick the **Apply** or **OK** button to apply the changes.

There are two types of custom shortcut menus: object specific and command oriented. The next sections describe the two types of custom shortcut menus in detail.

Creating Object-Specific Shortcut Menus

When creating an object-specific shortcut menu, there can actually be two menus available. One menu is displayed for instances when just a single object of a given type is selected. The other menu is displayed when more than one object is selected.

The name assigned to the object menu should follow the same syntax used for naming AutoCAD's default object-specific menus: *object_type* **Object Menu** or *object_type* **Objects Menu** (with an S). In this way, when looking at the shortcut menus in the **Customizations in All CUI Files** pane in the **Customize User Interface** dialog box, you will easily recognize which object type that menu applies to and whether it is for multiple selected objects or a single selected object. The use of this syntax is optional. Menus can be named using whatever naming scheme you wish. However, it is recommended to follow the naming syntax described here.

The alias for the shortcut menu has a syntax that *must* be followed. It is this alias that AutoCAD uses in determining to which object or objects the menu applies. The syntax for the alias must take on the form of OBJECT_*type* or OBJECTS_*type* and must be exactly followed in order for AutoCAD to properly display the shortcut menu.

As an example, the following procedure creates a shortcut menu that allows access to the **LENGTHEN** and **BREAK** commands when a single line is selected.

1. Open the **Customize User Interface** dialog box.
2. Right-click on the Shortcut Menus branch in the **Customizations in All CUI Files** pane and select **New Shortcut Menu**.
3. Name the shortcut menu **Line Object Menu**.
4. In the **Properties** pane, select the Alias property in the **Advanced** category. Then, pick the **...** button to open the **Aliases** dialog box. On the second line, enter the alias OBJECT_LINE and then close the **Aliases** dialog box. Since the **LENGTHEN** and **BREAK** commands can only be applied to a single object, be sure to use the OBJECT_*type* syntax (without the S).
5. Drag the **LENGTHEN** and **BREAK** commands from the **Command List:** pane into the Line Object Menu branch in **Customizations in All CUI Files** pane. See **Figure 21-14A.**
6. Pick the **OK** button to close the **Customize User Interface** dialog box and apply the changes.

Now, draw a line, select it, and right-click. Notice that **Lengthen** and **Break** entries appear in the shortcut menu. See **Figure 21-14B.** Selecting either entry executes the command on the selected line.

Creating Command-Oriented Shortcut Menus

When a command is being executed, any command options appear in the shortcut menu. For example, when the **CIRCLE** command prompts for a radius, you can right-click and select **Diameter** from the shortcut menu. Custom shortcut menus can be created for use when certain commands are active. This allows you to add options to the

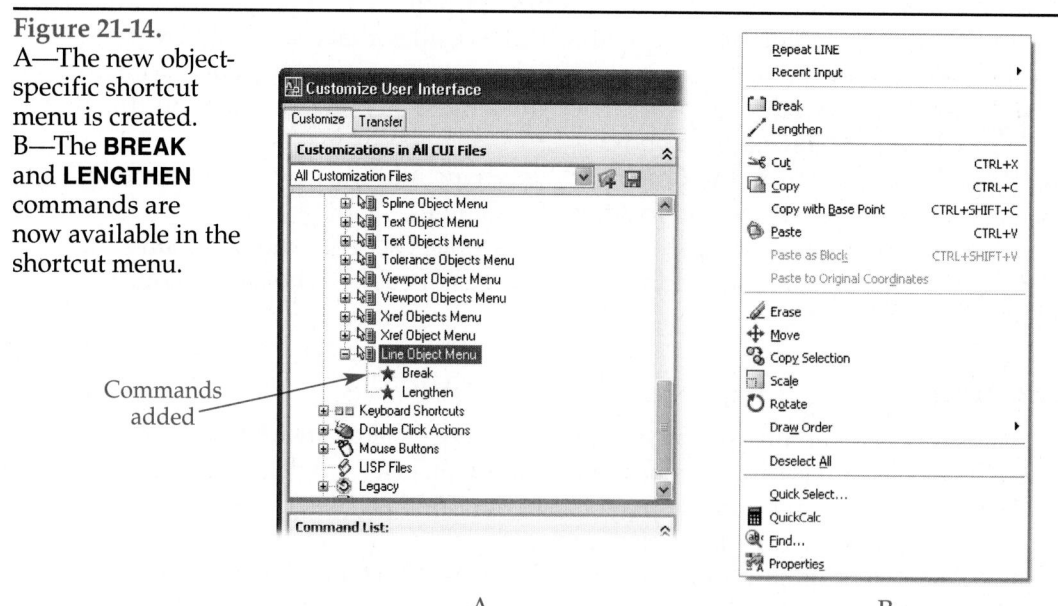

Figure 21-14.
A—The new object-specific shortcut menu is created. B—The **BREAK** and **LENGTHEN** commands are now available in the shortcut menu.

Commands added

A   B

shortcut menu that is displayed when a command is active. Quicker access to object snaps and object selection methods are just a couple of applications that custom, command-oriented shortcut menus could allow for within commonly used commands.

A command-oriented shortcut menu is created in the same way as an object-oriented shortcut menu, as discussed in the previous section. However, the syntax for the alias is slightly different. The alias must be in the form of COMMAND_*command_name*, where *command_name* is the name of the command with which you want the shortcut menu associated.

Also, if the command step does not have any default options, such as a Select objects: prompt, right-clicking is, by default, interpreted as the [Enter] key. Therefore, in the **Right-Click Customization** dialog box, the **Shortcut Menu: always enabled** radio button must be selected in the **Command Mode** area, as described earlier.

As an example, the following procedure creates a custom shortcut menu that displays **Previous**, **Last**, and **Fence** selection options at the Select objects: prompt for the **MOVE** command.

1. Open the **Customize User Interface** dialog box.
2. Make custom commands for the three selection options. Name the commands **Previous**, **Last**, and **Fence**. For the macros, remove the ^C^C that is automatically placed in the macro and type the selection option; for example, PREVIOUS for the **Previous** command.
3. Right-click on the Shortcut Menus branch in the **Customizations in All CUI Files** pane and select **New Shortcut Menu**.
4. Name the shortcut menu **Move Command Menu**.
5. In the **Properties** pane, select the Alias property in the **Advanced** category. Then, pick the **...** button to open the **Aliases** dialog box. On the second line, enter the alias COMMAND_MOVE and then close the **Aliases** dialog box. The syntax of COMMAND_*command_name* must be exactly followed in order for AutoCAD to properly display the shortcut menu.
6. Drag the **Previous**, **Last**, and **Fence** custom commands from the **Command List:** pane into the Move Command Menu branch in **Customizations in All CUI Files** pane. See **Figure 21-15A**.
7. Pick the **OK** button to close the **Customize User Interface** dialog box and apply the changes.

Now, initiate the **MOVE** command. At the Select objects: prompt, right-click and notice that **Previous**, **Last**, and **Fence** entries are available in the shortcut menu. See Figure 21-15B.

Figure 21-15.
A—The new command-specific shortcut menu is created. B—The **Previous**, **Last**, and **Fence** "command options" (actually, custom commands) are available in the shortcut menu.

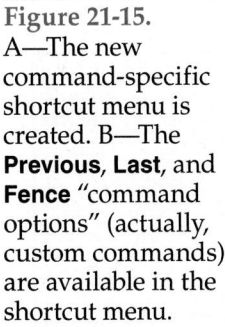

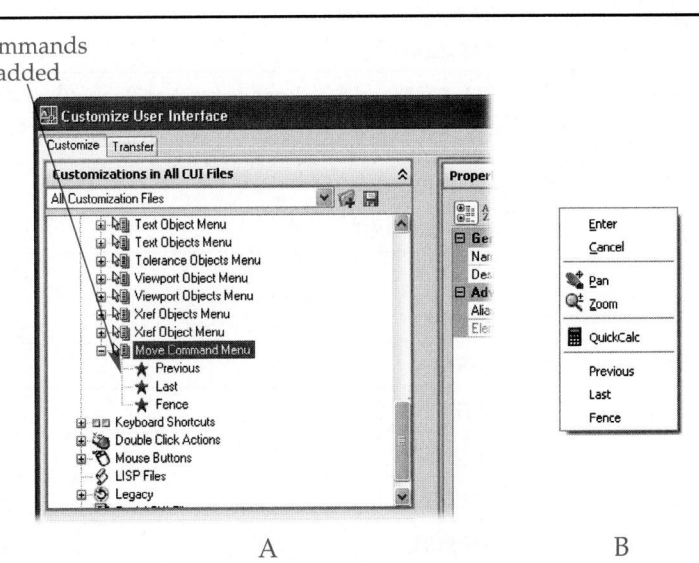

A   B

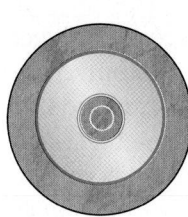

Exercise 21-3
Complete the exercise on the Student CD.

Customizing Double-Click Actions

By double-clicking on certain objects, an appropriate editing command is automatically executed. Which command is initiated is determined by the *double-click action* associated with the object type. Some AutoCAD objects have very specific editing tools available. For example, multiline text (mtext) objects are edited with the in-place text editor and hatches are edited in the **Hatch Edit** dialog box.

A list of AutoCAD objects that have default double-click actions associated with them, other than the **PROPERTIES** command, is shown in Figure 21-16. If you double-click on one of the object types listed in the table, the command or macro listed in the Associated Double-Click Action column is executed. If the object type is not listed in the table, it is likely the **Properties** window is displayed, by default, when the object is double-clicked. This is the double-click action associated with most objects.

Assigning Double-Click Actions

Double-click actions are assigned to specific object types in the **Customize User Interface** dialog box. In the **Customizations in All CUI Files** pane, expand the Double Click Actions branch. All of the AutoCAD object types are listed. See Figure 21-17. Expand each branch and notice that many double-click actions call the **Properties** window,

Figure 21-16.
AutoCAD objects to which a default double-click action other than **PROPERTIES** is assigned.

AutoCAD Object Type	Associated Double-Click Action
ATTDEF	DDEDIT
ATTBLOCKREF	EATTEDIT
ATTDYNBLOCKREF	EATTEDIT
BLOCKREF	$M=$(if,$(and,$(>,$(getvar,blockeditlock),0)),^C^C_properties,^C^C_bedit)
DYNBLOCKREF	$M=$(if,$(and,$(>,$(getvar,blockeditlock),0)),^C^C_properties,^C^C_bedit)
HATCH	HATCHEDIT
IMAGE	IMAGEADJUST
LWPOLYLINE	PEDIT
MLINE	MLEDIT
MTEXT	MTEDIT
POLYLINE	PEDIT
SPLINE	SPLINEDIT
TEXT	DDEDIT
XREF	REFEDIT

Figure 21-17.
All of the AutoCAD object types are displayed in the Double Click Actions branch in the **Customize User Interface** dialog box.

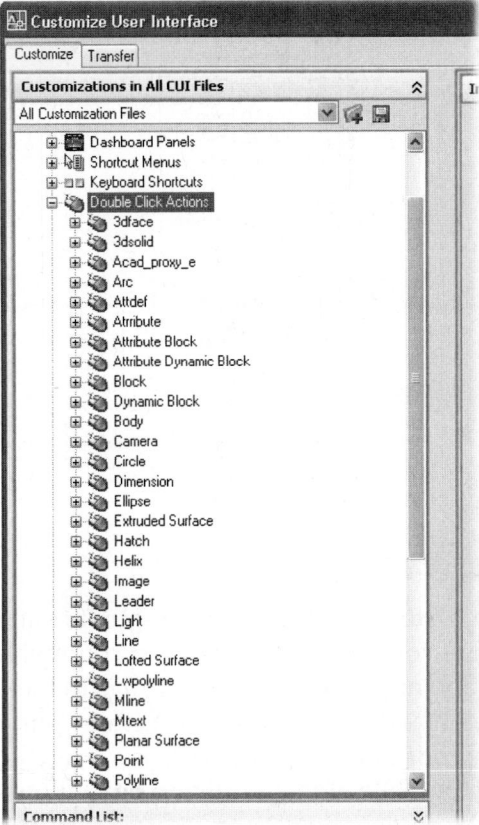

while the objects listed in the table in **Figure 21-16** have double-click actions that call the object-specific editing command.

Use the following procedure to change the double-click editing action associated with an object type. For this example, the **DDPTYPE** command will be associated with the point object type so the **Point Style** dialog box appears when a point object is double-clicked.

1. Open the **Customize User Interface** dialog box.
2. In the **Customizations in All CUI Files** pane, expand the Double Click Actions branch.
3. Expand the Point branch under the Double Click Actions branch. Notice that the **PROPERTIES** command is associated with the point object type.
4. In the **Command List:** pane, select the **Point Style...** command. This is the **DDPTYPE** command, as indicated in the **Properties** pane.
5. Drag the **Point Style...** command from the **Command List:** pane and drop it into the Point branch in the **Customizations in All CUI Files** pane. See **Figure 21-18.** The command replaces the existing command as there can only be one double-click action.
6. Pick the **OK** button to close the **Customize User Interface** dialog box and apply the change.

Now, draw a point using the **POINT** command. Double-click on the point and the **Point Style** dialog box appears. Select a new point style in the dialog box and pick the **OK** button. All existing points in the drawing should update to the new style. If not, use the **REGEN** command to update the display.

Chapter 21 Customizing Shortcut Keys, Shortcut Menus, and Double-Click Actions

Figure 21-18.
The double-click
action associated
with the point object
type is changed.

New double-click
action assigned

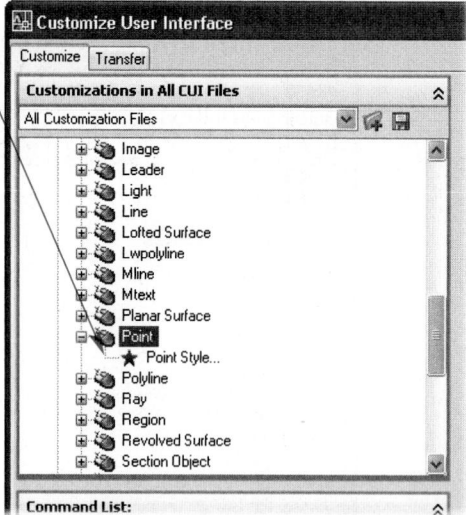

Custom Double-Click Action

You can also create a custom command and assign it to an object type as a double-click action. In this section, you will create a custom command for overriding dimension variables on the fly and applying the new settings to the dimension object that is double-clicked. Here is a breakdown of what the custom command will do:

* Cancel any commands in progress. (^C^C)
* Open the **Dimension Style Manager** dialog box, allowing the **Override** button to be used to make any changes or to create a new dimension style and set it current. The dialog box stays open until the **OK** button is picked. (dimstyle;)
* Execute a command-line version of the **DIMSTYLE** command. (-dimstyle;)
* Enter the **Apply** option. (a;)
* Select the previous selection set (the object that was double-clicked) and end the selection. (p;;)

Dimensioning variables can be overridden using the **Properties** window. However, using the **Dimension Style Manager** dialog box may be a more-familiar means to accomplish the overrides.

Follow these steps to create a custom command and assign it as a double-click action for the dimension object type:

1. Open the **Customize User Interface** dialog box.
2. Pick the **Create a new command** button in the **Command List:** pane.
3. Name the custom command **DblClkDimEdit**.
4. In the **Properties** pane, select the Macro property. Then, enter the macro ^C^Cdimstyle;-dimstyle;a;p;; in the text box. Use the **Long String Editor**, if needed.
5. In the **Customizations in All CUI Files** pane, expand the Double Click Actions branch and locate the Dimension branch below it. Notice that the **PROPERTIES** command is associated with the dimension object type.
6. In the **Command List:** pane, select the new **DblClkDimEdit** command and drag it into the Dimension branch in the **Customizations in All CUI Files** pane.
7. Pick the **OK** button to close the **Customize User Interface** dialog box and apply the change.

Now, place a dimension using the **DIMLINEAR** command. Next, double-click on the dimension. In the **Dimension Style Manager** dialog box, select the **Override...** button. In the **Override Current Style:** dialog box that is displayed, select the **Text** tab. Using the **Text color:** drop-down list, change the text color. Pick the **OK** button to close the **Override Current Style:** dialog box. Then, pick the **OK** button to close the **Dimension Style Manager** dialog box. The dimension text should assume the new color setting. If it does not, open the **Customize User Interface** dialog box and examine the custom command macro for any errors.

> **NOTE**
>
> After using the custom double-click action assigned to the dimension object type, the dimension overrides remain in effect for the next dimensions placed.

Chapter Test

Answer the following questions. Write your answers on a separate sheet of paper or complete the electronic chapter test on the Student CD.

1. What is the key combination called that allows you to press the [Ctrl] key and an additional key to execute a command?
2. How can you disable all shortcut menus and all double-click actions?
3. In which dialog box can you define what a right-click does when in default mode, edit mode, and command mode?
4. Why are shortcut menus *context sensitive?*
5. When does the command shortcut menu appear?
6. What must the **PICKFIRST** setting be in order for the edit shortcut menu to appear?
7. Briefly describe how to create a new shortcut menu.
8. Describe the syntax for the name of an object-specific shortcut menu.
9. Why is CIRCLE_OBJECT *not* a valid alias for a shortcut menu?
10. Describe the difference between an OBJECT_*type* shortcut menu and an OBJECTS_*type* shortcut menu.
11. What is the syntax for the alias for a command-specific shortcut menu?
12. List the steps to add an alias to a shortcut menu.
13. What is a *double-click action?*
14. What is the most common double-click action?
15. In which dialog box is a double-click action assigned?
16. List the basic steps for modifying the double-click action associated with an object.

Drawing Problems

Before customizing AutoCAD, check with your instructor or supervisor for specific instructions or guidelines.

1. Create a shortcut key for each of the drawing and editing commands listed below. Be sure not to use any existing shortcut keys.

LINE	**MOVE**
ARC	**COPY**
CIRCLE	**STRETCH**
POLYLINE	**TRIM**
POLYGON	**EXTEND**
RECTANGLE	**CHAMFER**
DTEXT	**FILLET**
ERASE	

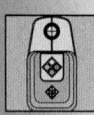

2. In this problem, create an object-specific shortcut menu. The shortcut menu should be displayed when an arc object is selected. The shortcut menu should contain the **LENGTHEN** and **BREAK** commands.

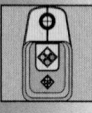

3. In this problem, create a command-specific shortcut menu. The shortcut menu should be displayed when the **CIRCLE** command is active. Add the **Tan, Tan, Tan** command available in the **Customize User Interface** dialog box to the shortcut menu. Add two selection options, such as **Last** or **Window**, as described in this chapter.

4. By default, double-clicking on a circle displays the **Properties** window. Take the steps necessary so that a **REGEN** is performed instead.

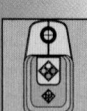

5. Create a custom command that changes the color of an object to blue. Then, assign this command as the double-click action for the hatch object type.

CHAPTER 22

Tool Palette Customization

Learning Objectives

After completing this chapter, you will be able to:

✓ Modify the appearance of the **Tool Palettes** window.
✓ Compare and contrast block insertion, hatch insertion, and command tools.
✓ Create new tool palettes from scratch and using **DesignCenter**.
✓ Add tools to existing tool palettes.
✓ Explain how tool palettes are formatted.
✓ Adjust the properties of tools.
✓ Create a flyout tool.
✓ Organize tool palette tabs into groups.
✓ Export and import tools and tool palettes.

Tool palettes are a user interface method for the easy insertion of blocks and hatch patterns, for command entry, and for attaching materials. Blocks and hatch patterns can be simply dragged and dropped from a tool palette directly into a drawing. In addition, tool palettes serve as a material library in AutoCAD. Tool palettes are contained within the **Tool Palettes** window.

Tool Palette Overview

The **TOOLPALETTES** command is used to display the **Tool Palettes** window. Notice that the **Tool Palettes** window has a number of tabs on its edge. Each of these tabs corresponds to a tool palette. To make a tool palette active, pick its tab. If there are more tabs than can be displayed, pick on the "stack" at the bottom of the tabs to display a shortcut menu in which you can select the tool palette to display. To use a tool on any tool palette, drag it from the tool palette and drop it into the drawing.

By default, the **Tool Palettes** window contains the **Modeling**, **Annotation**, **Architectural**, **Mechanical**, **Electrical**, **Civil**, **Structural**, **Hatches and Fills**, **Tables**, **Command Tool Samples**, **Leaders**, **Draw**, **Modify**, **Cameras**, **Visual Styles**, 22 material palettes, and five light palettes.

- **Modeling palette.** Contains tools for creating specific variations of some solid primitives.

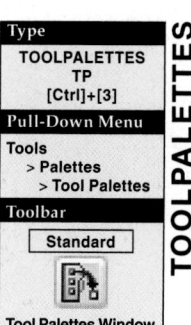

Type	
TOOLPALETTES	
TP	
[Ctrl]+[3]	

Pull-Down Menu

Tools
> Palettes
> Tool Palettes

Toolbar

Standard

Tool Palettes Window

TOOLPALETTES

- **Annotation palette.** Contains blocks that are typically inserted in paper space. Also contains two **UCS** commands and the **3DALIGN** command.
- **Architectural, Mechanical, Electrical, Civil, and Structural palettes.** Can be used to insert blocks that are meant to be used within the discipline for which the palette is named. Certain preset properties are already attached to the symbols, such as scale and rotation.
- **Hatches and Fills palette.** Contains some commonly used hatches and sample gradient fills that can be quickly inserted into a drawing.
- **Tables palette.** Allows you to insert sample tables in US customary (Imperial) and metric formats.
- **Command Tool Samples palette.** Allows you to execute certain commands by picking the tool.
- **Leaders palette.** Allows you to place leaders with or without text, or with various types of callout balloons in both US customary (Imperial) and metric scales.
- **Draw palette.** Contains the same tools found on the **Draw** toolbar and some tools for inserting blocks, attaching images, and attaching xrefs.
- **Modify palette.** Contains the same tools found on the **Modify** and **Modify II** toolbar.
- **Material palettes.** The tools in these palettes allow you to quickly drag and drop various materials into the drawing. The material palettes are AutoCAD's material library.
- **Light palettes.** Contain tools for inserting many types of lights.
- **Cameras palette.** Contains tools for inserting three different cameras into the drawing. The cameras have differing lens lengths and fields of view.
- **Visual Styles palette.** Contains tools for three variations of the default visual styles.

For detailed instruction on how tool palettes can be used to insert blocks and hatch patterns, see *AutoCAD and Its Applications—Basics.* This chapter describes how to customize existing tool palettes and create your own tool palettes.

Tool Palette Appearance

There are a number of methods to alter the appearance of the **Tool Palettes** window, either for productivity or personal preference. For example, the **Tool Palettes** tabs can be renamed. Right-click on the title of the tab and select **Rename Palette** from the shortcut menu. An edit box is displayed near the current name with the name highlighted. Type a new name and press [Enter] to rename the palettes. Other methods of changing the appearance of the **Tool Palettes** window are covered in this section.

Docking

By default, the **Tool Palettes** window is floating on the right side of the screen in the AutoCAD Classic and 2D Drafting & Annotation workspaces and docked on the right side of the screen in the 3D Modeling workspace. It can be moved to a new, floating location by picking and holding on the title bar, dragging the window to the desired location, and releasing the pick button. Moving the window to the far side of the drawing window forces the title bar to flip to the other side of the **Tool Palettes** window so that it is toward the outer edge of the drawing window.

By default, the **Tool Palettes** window can be docked, just like a toolbar. Moving the window outside of the drawing window to the left or right docks it. The **Tool Palettes** window cannot be docked at the top or bottom. To float the **Tool Palettes** window, pick and hold on the double bar that appears at the top of the docked window, move the window to a location inside of the drawing window, and release the pick button. To prevent docking, right-click on the **Tool Palettes** window title bar to display the shortcut menu. Select **Allow Docking** to remove the check mark. When a check mark appears next to **Allow Docking**, the window can be docked.

The **Tool Palettes** window can be resized just like standard windows. While floating, the top and bottom edges, the vertical area just below the tabs, and the corner just below that vertical area can be used to resize the window. While docked, only the right and left edges can be used for resizing. As with standard windows, move the cursor to one of the edges of the window until a double arrow appears. Then, press and hold the pick button, drag the edge until the window reaches the desired size, and release the pick button.

Transparency

Using the **Tool Palettes** window while it is floating may cause occasional visibility problems because it covers up part of the drawing window. However, the window can be made partially transparent so that the part of the drawing under the window can be seen. Transparency will not be active when the window is in a docked position. Hardware acceleration must be off to set transparency.

Right-click on the title bar of the **Tool Palettes** window and pick **Transparency...** from the shortcut menu. The **Transparency** dialog box is displayed, Figure 22-1. To enable transparency, uncheck the **Turn off window transparency** check box. This also enables the slider in the dialog box. The slider controls the level of transparency applied to the window. The further to the right that the slider is placed, the more transparent the **Tool Palettes** window, Figure 22-2. Placing the slider all of the way to the left actually makes the **Tool Palettes** window opaque.

If you find a particular level of transparency that you like, but would like to make the **Tool Palettes** window opaque for a short time while you perform an operation or two, you can just use the toggle to turn off transparency. Open the **Transparency** dialog box and check the **Turn off window transparency** check box. Then, when you want to go back to your previous level of transparency, simply open the **Transparency** dialog box again and uncheck the check box. You will not have to adjust the slider; just toggle the transparency back on.

PROFESSIONAL TIP

Although transparency allows you to *see* through the **Tool Palettes** window, you cannot *work* through it. You cannot access points behind the window because the cursor is actually on the **Tool Palettes** window, not on the drawing underneath it.

Autohide

As useful as the **Tool Palettes** window is, it does take up a large amount of valuable drawing area. The *autohide* feature, when enabled, compresses the **Tool Palettes** window so just the title bar appears when the cursor is not over the window, Figure 22-3. This allows the **Tool Palettes** window to take up less room when not being used.

To turn on autohide, right-click on the title bar of the **Tool Palettes** window or pick the **Properties** button at the bottom of the title bar to display the shortcut menu, Figure 22-4. Then, select **Auto-hide** from the shortcut menu. A check mark appears next to the menu item when autohide is enabled. You can also pick the **Auto-hide** button at the bottom of the **Tool Palettes** window title bar.

Figure 22-1.
The **Transparency** dialog box is used to control the transparency of the **Tool Palettes** window.

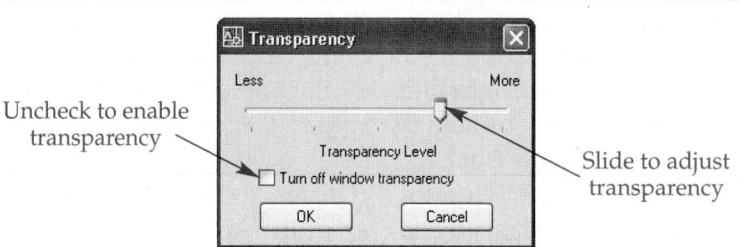

Uncheck to enable transparency

Slide to adjust transparency

Figure 22-2.
A—The **Tool Palettes** window has a low transparency setting. B—The **Tool Palettes** window has a high transparency setting.

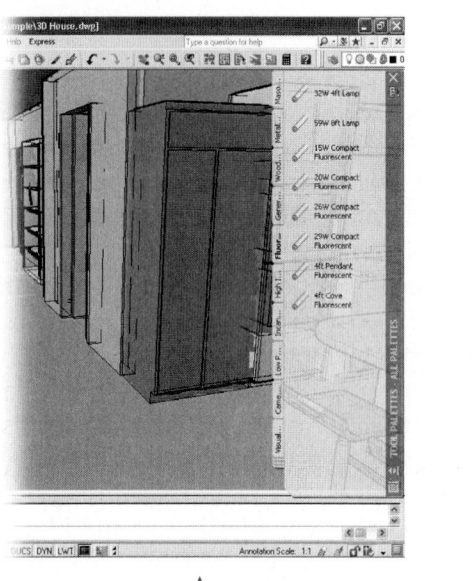
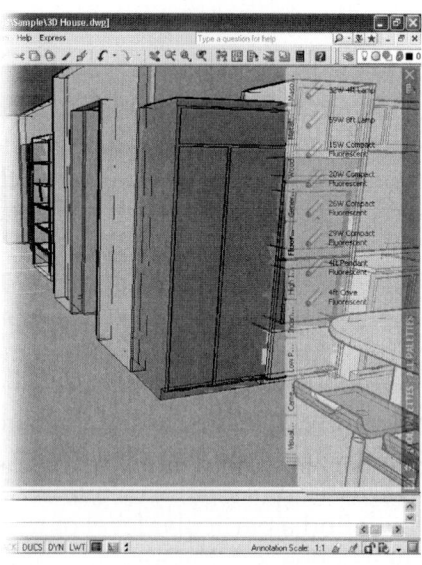

A   B

Figure 22-3.
When the autohide feature is enabled, the **Tool Palettes** window appears as only the title bar when the cursor is not over it.

Autohide is enabled

Figure 22-4.
Enabling autohide.

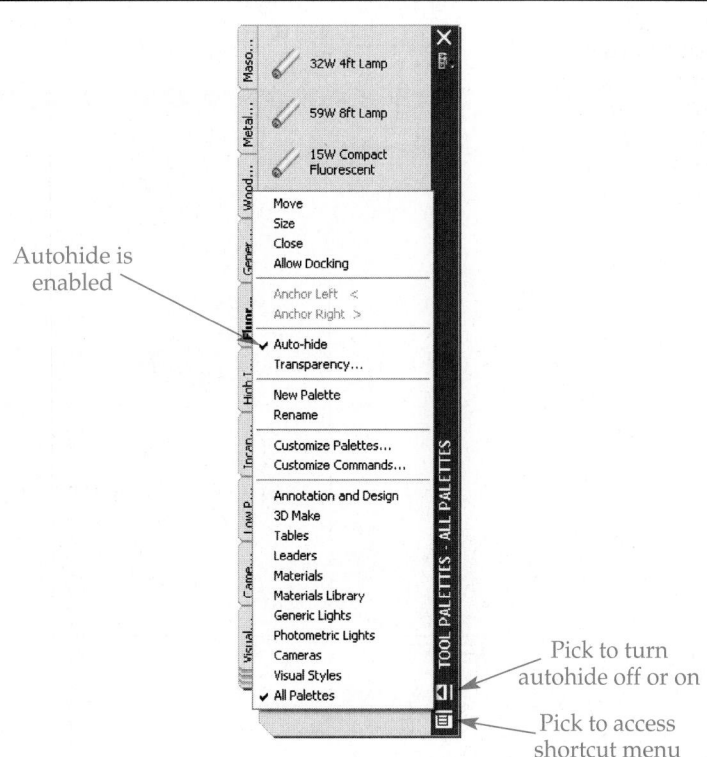

Autohide is enabled

Pick to turn autohide off or on

Pick to access shortcut menu

To use the **Tool Palettes** window when autohide is enabled, move the cursor over the title bar and the window expands to its normal size. The tool palettes can then be used in the standard way. After using the **Tool Palettes** window, it is again hidden shortly after the cursor is no longer over the window.

Anchoring

The **Tool Palettes** window can also be *anchored.* Anchoring is a combination of docking and autohide. When a tool palette is anchored, it is docked on the right or left side of the drawing area, but it is compressed to just a title bar. See **Figure 22-5.** To use the **Tool Palettes** window when it is anchored, move the cursor over the anchored title bar. The **Tool Palettes** window is then displayed floating next to the anchored window. It can be used just as if autohide is enabled. Once the cursor is moved off of the **Tool Palettes** window, the window is hidden.

To anchor the tool palette, docking must first be enabled. Then, right-click on the title bar of the **Tool Palettes** window or pick the **Properties** button at the bottom of the title bar to display the shortcut menu. Next, select either **Anchor Left <** or **Anchor Right >** in the shortcut menu. To return the window to floating mode, pick and drag the title bar back into the drawing area while the window is displayed.

PROFESSIONAL TIP

The **Properties** window, **DesignCenter**, and the **Dashboard** also have the anchoring feature. You can create a very productive drawing window arrangement by anchoring these windows along with the **Tool Palettes** window. Anchor the **Dashboard** and **Tool Palettes** window on one side of the drawing window and the **Properties** window and **DesignCenter** on the other side.

Figure 22-5.
When the **Tool Palettes** window is anchored, it is docked but compressed to just its title bar.

The window is anchored

Tool Appearance

The way in which the tools are shown in the palettes can be customized. To do so, right-click in a blank area of the current tool palette (not on the title bar). Then, select **View Options...** from the shortcut menu. The **View Options** dialog box is displayed, **Figure 22-6.**

The **Image Size:** area of the dialog box is used to set the size of the tool icons in the palette. Drag the slider to the left or right to change the size. Dragging the slider to the left decreases the size of the icon. Dragging the slider to the right increases the size of the icon. To the left of the slider is a preview that represents the size of the icon.

The **View Style:** area controls how the tools on the tool palettes are displayed. When the **Icon only** radio button is selected, the tools are represented as an image only, **Figure 22-7A.** Tooltips will be displayed if you hold your cursor over a tool. Selecting the **Icon with text** radio button represents the tools with an image and the tool name below the image, **Figure 22-7B.** When the **List view** radio button is selected, the tools are represented with an image and the tool name to the side of the image, **Figure 22-7C.** This is the default view style.

Figure 22-6.
The **View Options** dialog box is used to set how the tools appear in tool palettes.

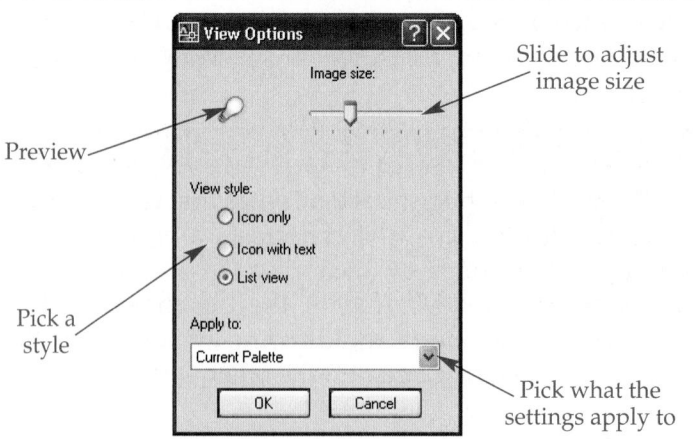

Slide to adjust image size

Preview

Pick a style

Pick what the settings apply to

Figure 22-7.
The various ways in which tools can appear in tool palettes. A—Icons only. B—Icons and text. C—As a list.

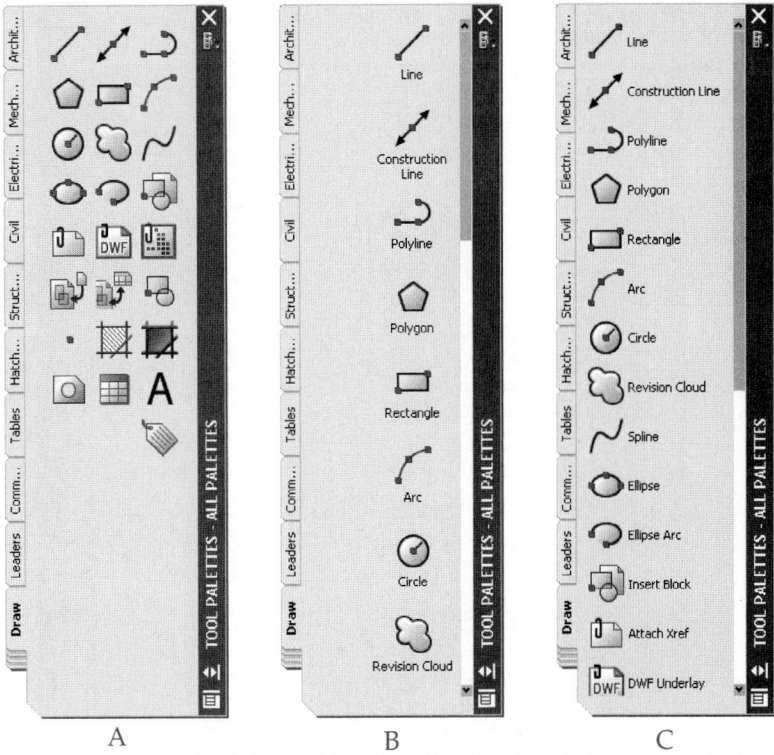

A   B   C

The **Apply to:** drop-down list at the bottom of the dialog box determines where the settings are applied. To have the settings applied to the current tool palette, select **Current Palette** from the drop-down list. To have the settings applied to all tool palettes, select **All Palettes** from the drop-down list. When finished making settings, pick the **OK** button to close the **View** options dialog box.

Exercise 22-1
Complete the exercise on the Student CD.

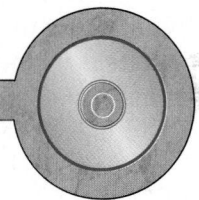

Commands in a Tool Palette

As indicated earlier, the **Tool Palettes** window not only offers a means to easily insert blocks and hatch patterns, it can be used to execute commands. Make the **Tool Palettes** window active and select the **Command Tool Samples** palette, **Figure 22-8**. The tools on this palette are provided to demonstrate how tool palettes can be customized by adding commands. This tool palette is provided with the intention that it will be customized by the user. Customizing tool palettes is discussed later in this chapter. The default tools provided are:

- **Line.** Executes the **LINE** command. Notice that this tool has a small triangle, or arrow, to the right of the icon. The arrow indicates that the tool acts as a *flyout tool,* similar to flyout toolbar buttons. Picking the arrow displays a graphic shortcut menu containing other command tools attached to this tool, as shown in **Figure 22-8**. Selecting a command tool from the shortcut menu executes

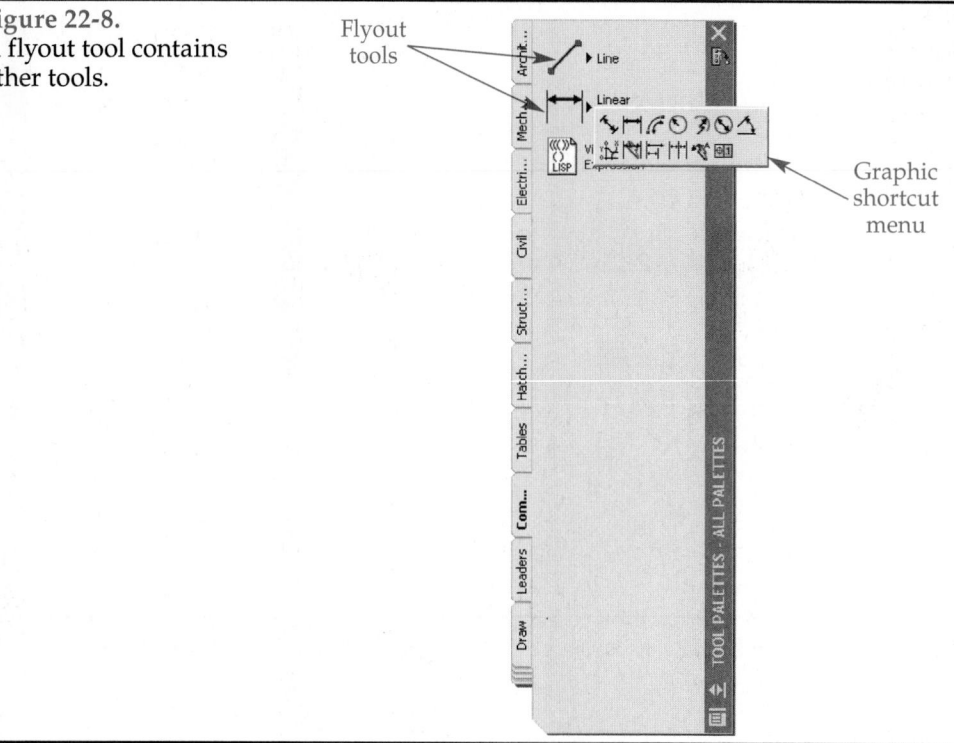

Figure 22-8.
A flyout tool contains other tools.

Flyout tools

Graphic shortcut menu

that command and causes that command image to become the default image displayed in the palette.

- **Linear Dimension.** Executes the **DIMLINEAR** command. This tool is also a flyout.
- **VisualLisp Expression.** Executes the AutoLISP expression (entget (car (entsel))). The entity data list for the selected entity is displayed on the command line. AutoLISP is discussed in Chapters 24 and 25.

While these three tools on the **Command Tools** palette can be productive tools, this palette is included to show you examples of ways in which tools can be customized to make you more productive in your own design environment. It is meant to be customized to your own needs.

Adding Tool Palettes

As discussed later in this chapter, you can add new tools to tool palettes. You can also create new tool palettes and then add tools to them. To add a new tool palette, right-click on a blank area of an existing tool palette or on the title bar of the **Tool Palettes** window. Then, select **New Palette** from the shortcut menu. A new, blank palette is added and a text box appears next to the name. Type the desired name for the new palette and press [Enter].

Notice the help link at the top of the new tool palette, Figure 22-9. This link offers assistance in customizing tool palettes. It will disappear once you add a tool to the tool palette.

The new tool palette can be reordered within the tabs by right-clicking on the tab to display the shortcut menu. Then, select **Move Up** or **Move Down** to reorder the palettes. You may need to do this several times in order to get the palette in the position you want. The other palettes can be reordered in this same manner.

AutoCAD and Its Applications—Advanced

Figure 22-9.
A new, blank tool palette has been created.

New palette named **Custom Palette**

Pick to access the online workshop

DesignCenter can be used to create a new palette fully populated with all of the blocks contained in a drawing. In the **Folders** tab of the **DesignCenter** window, navigate to the drawing from which you are making the tool palette, right-click on the drawing name, and select **Create Tool Palette** from the shortcut menu. A new tool palette is added to the **Tool Palettes** window with the same name as the drawing file.

For example, open **DesignCenter** and navigate to the Fasteners-US drawing located in the \Sample\DesignCenter folder. Right-click on the file name and select **Create Tool Palette** from the shortcut menu, **Figure 22-10A**. A tool palette named **Fasteners-US** is added to the **Tool Palettes** window. All of the blocks contained in the Fasteners-US drawing are available on the tool palette, **Figure 22-10B**.

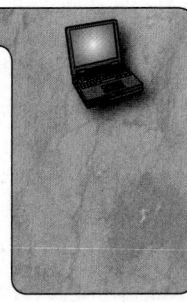

Type
ADCENTER
DC
ADC
[Ctrl]+[2]
Pull-Down Menu
Tools
> Palettes
> DesignCenter
Toolbar
Standard
DesignCenter

ADCENTER

NOTE

When using any "block insertion" tool from a tool palette, the block is actually being imported from the source drawing—the drawing from which the block tool on the palette was created. An error occurs if the source file has been moved or deleted. The source file must be restored to its original location to allow the tool to work, or the tool must be recreated from the source drawing in the drawing's new location.

Figure 22-10.
A—Creating a tool palette from the blocks contained within a drawing. B—The new tool palette is added.

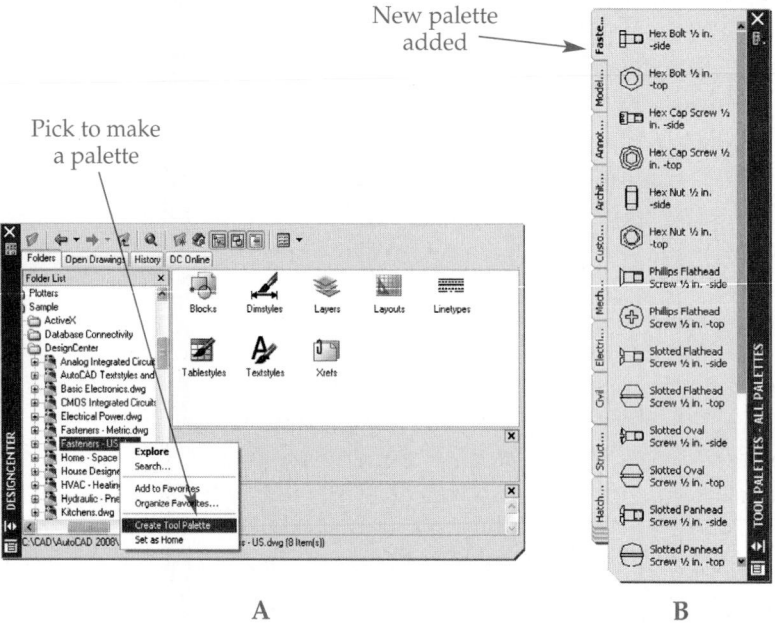

Pick to make a palette

New palette added

A   B

Adding Tools to a Tool Palette

Tools can be added to a tool palette in a variety of ways. Tools can be created from toolbar buttons, geometric objects in the current drawing, and objects in other drawings (via **DesignCenter**). Tools can also be copied to and pasted from the Windows clipboard. Once tools have been added to a tool palette, they can be arranged to suit your preference. Related tools can be separated into distinct areas on the tool palette and those areas can have text labels added to them.

PROFESSIONAL TIP

Tool palettes can be thought of as an extension of toolbars. You may want to add some of your favorite toolbar buttons to a tool palette.

Creating a Tool from a Toolbar Button

Toolbar buttons can be directly dragged and dropped onto a tool palette. To do this, the **Customize** dialog box for tool palettes must be open. This is *not* the **Customize User Interface** dialog box that is used to customize toolbars, pull-down menus, etc., as described in previous chapters.

To open the tool palette customization dialog box, right-click in any blank area on the tool palette or on the title bar of the **Tool Palettes** window. Then, select **Customize Palettes...** from the shortcut menu. This dialog box can also be opened by typing CUSTOMIZE. You do not actually use the **Customize** dialog box to copy a toolbar button to a tool palette, but the dialog box must be open. The **Customize** dialog box is discussed in detail later in this chapter.

Make sure the palette you want the button added to is current (on top). With the **Customize** dialog box open, move your cursor to the desired toolbar button. Flyout

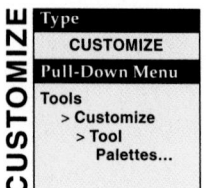

Type
CUSTOMIZE
Pull-Down Menu
Tools
> Customize
> Tool
Palettes...

CUSTOMIZE

buttons cannot be added to a tool palette. Pick and hold on the toolbar button and drag it to the desired location in the tool palette, **Figure 22-11**. A horizontal "I-bar" appears in the tool palette to indicate where the new tool will be inserted. Drop the toolbar button when it is in the desired position. The tool is inserted in the tool palette. Close the **Customize** dialog box.

Creating a Tool from an Object in the Current Drawing

Another way to add a drawing command to a tool palette is to drag an object in the current drawing, such as a line, hatch, block, dimension, camera, or light, and drop it onto the tool palette. The appropriate command to create that object is added to the tool palette.

First, ensure that the **PICKFIRST** system variable is set to 1. Also, make sure the tool palette to which you want the tool added to is current (on top). Next, with no command active, select the desired object. Move the cursor directly onto the selected object (not a grip). Then, press and hold down either the pick button or the right mouse button. Finally, drag the object to the desired position on the tool palette and drop it. The appropriate drawing command is inserted into the tool palette.

Using the Windows Clipboard to Create a Tool

The copy-and-paste feature of the Windows operating system is another way to transfer objects in the drawing to a tool palette. First, ensure that the **PICKFIRST** system variable is set to 1. Then, with no command active, right-click on the object and select **Copy** from the shortcut menu. Next, make the tool palette that you want the tool added to current. Finally, right-click on a blank area in the tool palette and select **Paste** from the shortcut menu. The appropriate command is added as the last tool on the tool palette.

The copy-and-paste technique can also be used to transfer tools from one tool palette to another. First, make the tool palette that contains the tool to be transferred current. Right-click on the tool to transfer and select **Copy** from the shortcut menu. If you want to *move* the tool from the first tool palette to the second, select **Cut** from the shortcut menu. Next, make the tool palette to which you want the tool transferred

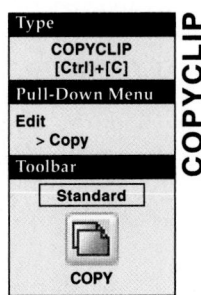

Figure 22-11.
Creating a tool on a tool palette from a toolbar button.

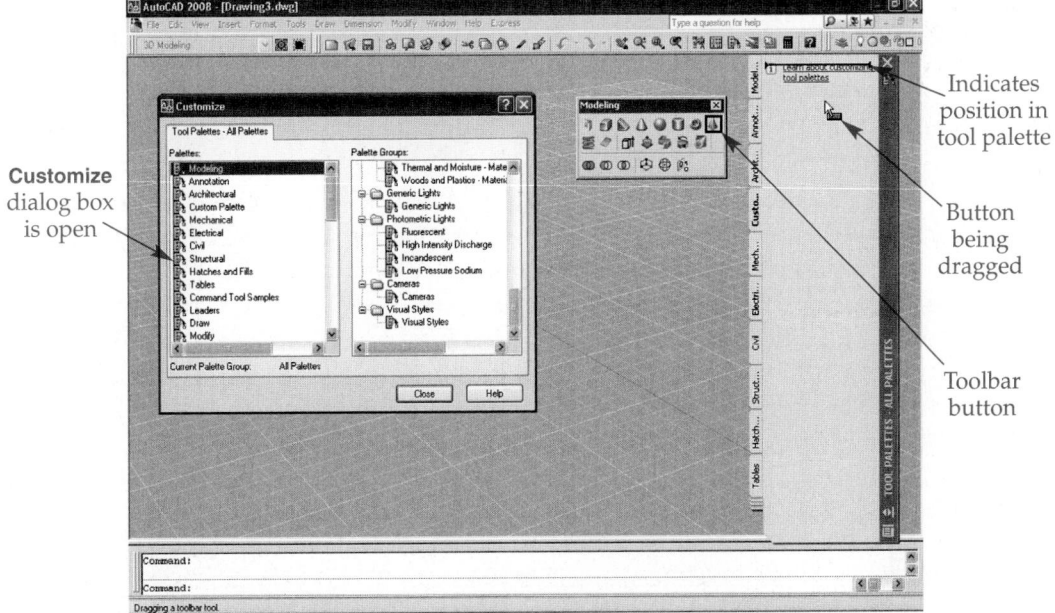

current. Right-click and select **Paste** from the shortcut menu. The tool is added to the second tool palette as the last tool on the palette.

Adding Block and Hatch Tools from DesignCenter

Earlier, you saw how to create a tool palette consisting of all of the blocks in a single drawing by using **DesignCenter**. It is also possible to add individual blocks from a drawing to a tool palette using **DesignCenter**. To do this, open the **DesignCenter** window. In the **Folders** tab, navigate to the drawing that contains the desired block. Expand that drawing's branch to see the named objects within the drawing. Select the Blocks branch. The blocks that are defined in the drawing appear on the right-hand side of the **DesignCenter** window. Make sure the tool palette you want the tool added to is current. Then, select the block in **DesignCenter** and drag it to the tool palette, Figure 22-12. Move the cursor to the desired position on the tool palette and drop the block. The new block tool is inserted in the tool palette.

A tool that inserts an entire drawing into the current drawing can also be added to a tool palette using **DesignCenter**. In **DesignCenter**, navigate to the drawing in the **Folders** tab. Select the drawing on the right-hand side of the **DesignCenter** window, drag it to the tool palette, and drop it in the desired position, Figure 22-13. The new block tool is inserted in the tool palette. When the new tool is used, the entire drawing is inserted into the current drawing as a block.

DesignCenter can also be used to add hatch patterns to a tool palette. Hatch pattern definitions are stored in two files—acad.pat and acadiso.pat. These files are located in the user's \Support folder. In the **Folders** tab of the **DesignCenter** window, navigate to the acad.pat file and select it. All of the hatch patterns defined within that file are shown on the right-hand side of the **DesignCenter** window, Figure 22-14. Make sure the tool palette you want the hatch pattern added to is current. Then, select the desired hatch pattern in **DesignCenter**, drag it to the tool palette, and drop it in the desired location. The new hatch tool is inserted in the tool palette.

Figure 22-12.
Adding an individual block contained within a drawing as a tool on a tool palette.

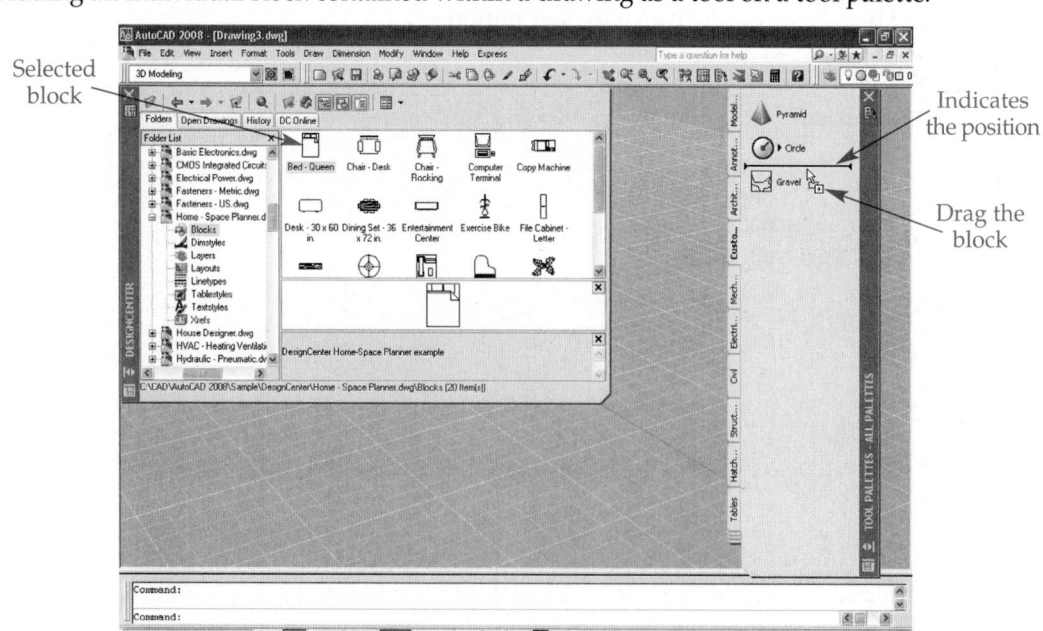

Adding Visual Style and Material Tools

Visual styles that are available in the drawing can be added as a tool to a tool palette. To do this, first make the tool palette to which you want the visual style added current. Then, open the **Visual Styles Manager**. Select the icon for the visual style at the top of the **Visual Style Manager**, drag it to the tool palette, and drop it into position. See **Figure 22-15**.

Materials that are available in the current drawing can also be added to a tool palette. This is how you create and manage a material library. First, make the tool palette to which you want the visual style added current. Then, open the **Materials** window. Select the material at the top of the **Materials** window, drag it to the tool palette, and drop it into position. See **Figure 22-16**.

Figure 22-13.
Adding an entire drawing as a tool on a tool palette.

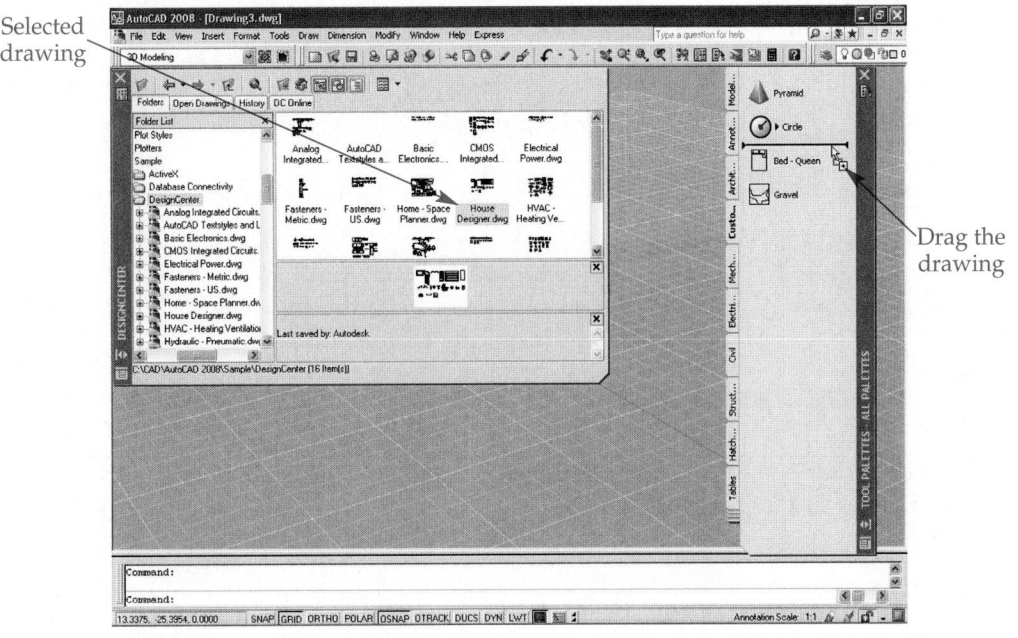

Figure 22-14.
Hatch patterns can be selected in **DesignCenter** and dragged to a tool palette to create a new tool.

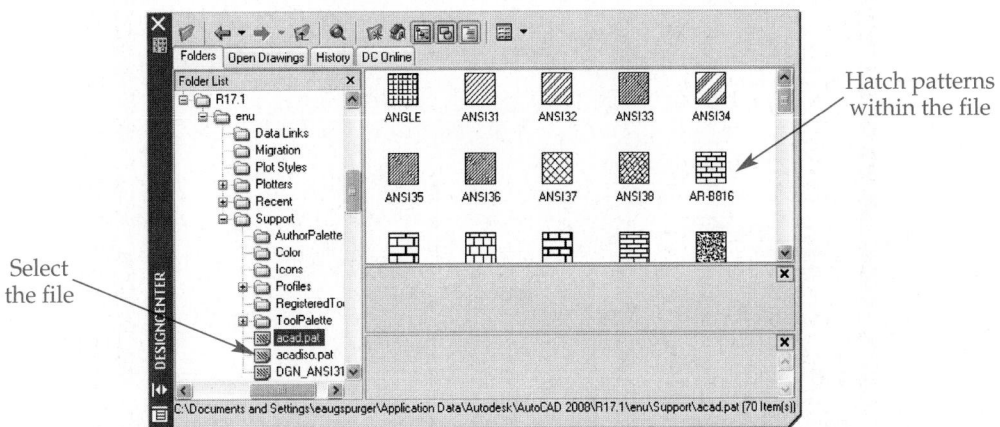

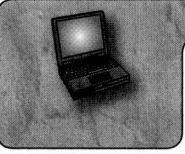
Figure 22-15.
Adding a visual style as a tool on a tool palette.

Select the visual style

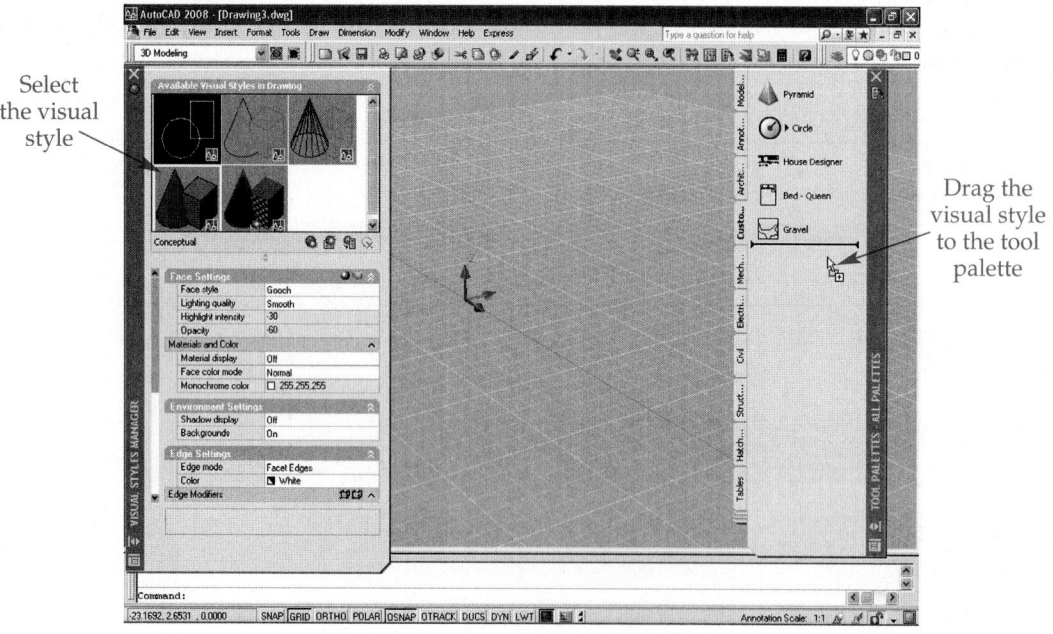

Drag the visual style to the tool palette

Figure 22-16.
Adding a material as a tool on a tool palette.

Select the material

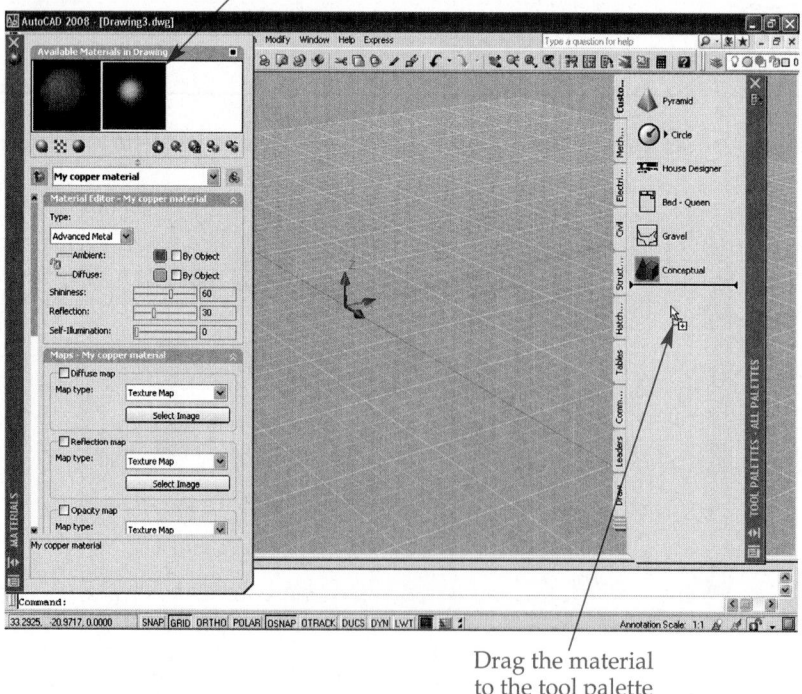

Drag the material to the tool palette

Rearranging Tools on a Tool Palette

The tools on a tool palette can be rearranged into a more productive order. To move a tool within a tool palette, simply select the tool and drag it to a new location. Remember, the horizontal I-bar indicates where the tool will be moved. In this way, you can place your drawing tools together, your block tools together, and so on.

You can further separate the tools within a tool palette by adding separator bars and text labels. Move the cursor so that it is between the two tools where you would like to add the separator. Then, right-click and select **Add Separator** from the shortcut menu. A horizontal bar is added to the tool palette. To add text to a tool palette, right-click between the two items where the label should be and select **Add Text** from the shortcut menu. A text box is displayed with the default text highlighted. Type the text that you want for the label and press [Enter]. The text label is added to the tool palette. Separators and text labels can be used together to make the visual grouping of tools even more apparent, **Figure 22-17.** You can move separators and text labels to different locations within the palette just as you can tools.

Exercise 22-2
Complete the exercise on the Student CD.

Modifying the Properties of a Tool

A tool on a tool palette can basically do one of these operations:
- Insert a block.
- Insert a hatch pattern.
- Insert a gradient fill.

Figure 22-17.
Separators and text labels can be added to tool palettes to help group tools.

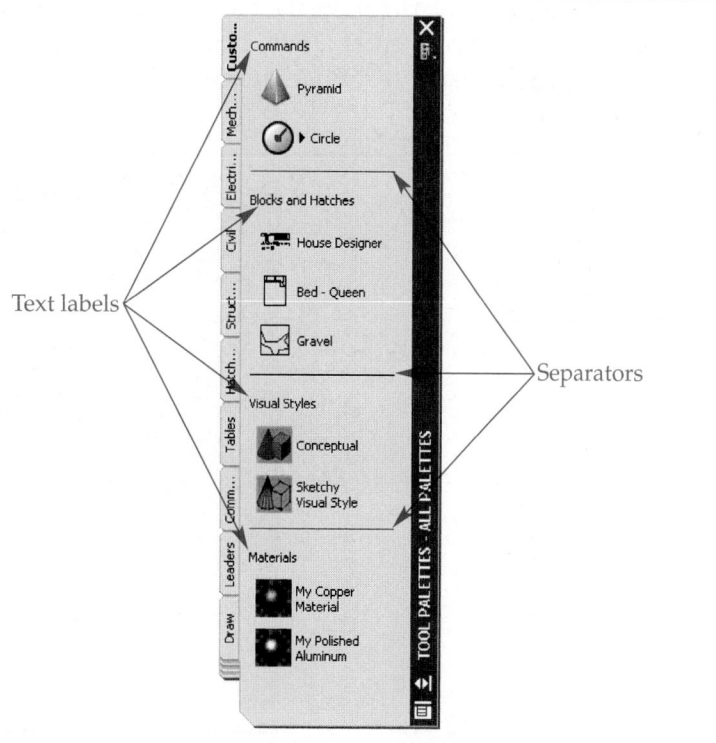

- Initiate a command.
- Insert a light.
- Insert a camera.
- Apply a visual style.
- Apply a material.

Another type of tool called a flyout is discussed later in this chapter. Each of these tools has general properties assigned to it, such as color, layer, or linetype. Each of these tools also has some tool-specific properties assigned to it, depending on the operation associated with the tool. Most of these assigned properties can be customized to your own needs.

For example, select the **Hatches and Fills** palette in the **Tool Palettes** window. Right-click on the **Curved** gradient tool and select **Properties** in the shortcut menu. The **Tool Properties** dialog box is displayed, **Figure 22-18.** Notice that the lower half of the dialog box is divided into two sections. The **General** category contains settings for properties such as Color, Layer, and Linetype. The **Pattern** category contains settings for properties specific to this tool's operation—inserting a gradient fill. Notice that properties such as Color 1, Color 2, and Gradient angle are shown. Other types of tools will have a different category in place of the **Pattern** category. Select the **Cancel** button to close the dialog box.

Now, select the **Command Tool Samples** palette in the **Tool Palettes** window, right-click on the **VisualLisp Expression** tool in the tool palette, and select **Properties** from the shortcut menu. The **Tool Properties** dialog box is displayed, **Figure 22-19.** This is the same dialog box displayed for the **Curved** gradient tool. However, in place of the **Pattern** category is the **Command** category. The settings in the **Command** category are specific to the **VisualLisp Expression** tool. Notice that the **General** category contains the same properties as for the **Curved** gradient tool. There are some other general properties listed that are not applicable to a gradient (Linetype scale, Text style, and Dimension style). Select the **Cancel** button to close the dialog box.

Customizing General Properties

The three items at the top of the **Tool Properties** dialog box are available for all types of tools. The **Image:** area shows the image that is assigned to the tool. This can be modified within the dialog box for command, camera, light, and visual style tools. The **Name:** text box displays the name of the tool. You can enter a new name for the tool. The **Description:** text box displays the current description of the tool. You can change the existing description or enter a new description. The name and description appear in the tooltip that is displayed when the cursor is held over the tool, **Figure 22-20.**

Figure 22-18.
Modifying the properties of a gradient fill tool.

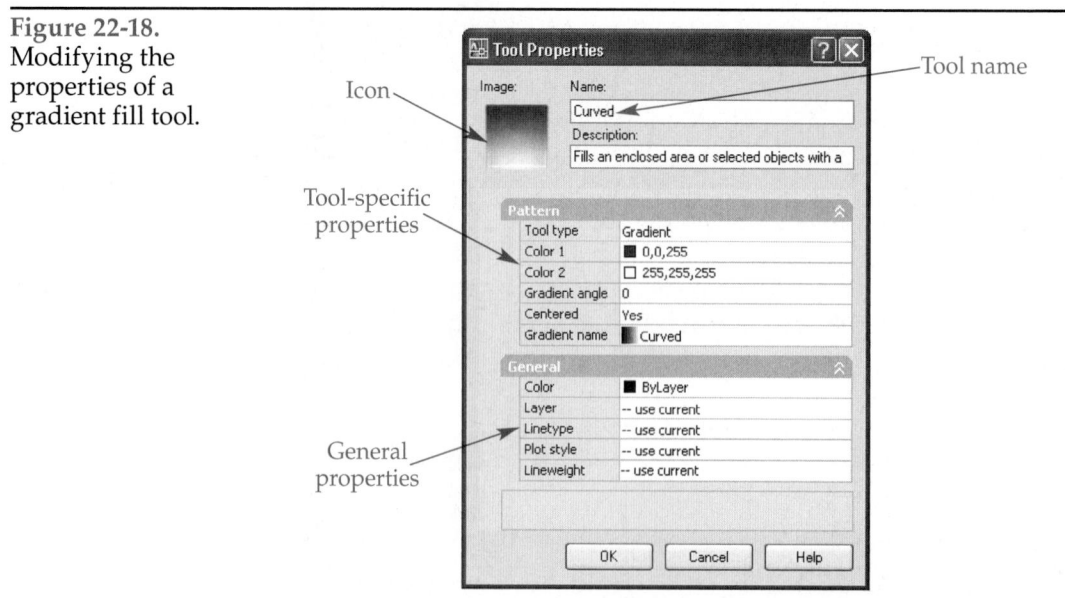

AutoCAD and Its Applications—Advanced

Figure 22-19.
Modifying the
properties of a
command tool.

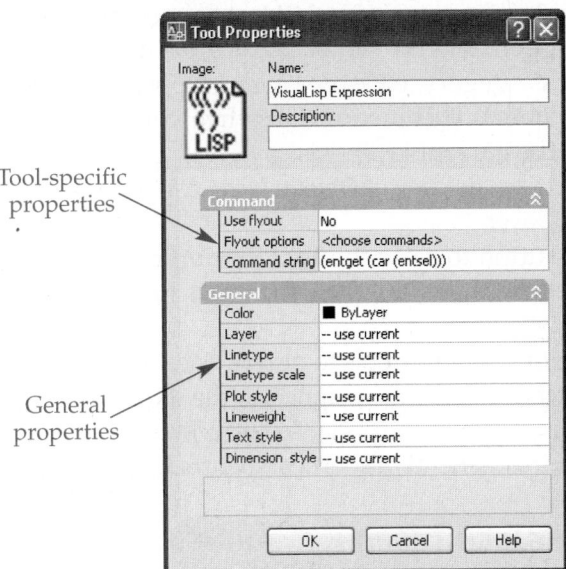

Tool-specific
properties

General
properties

Figure 22-20.
The Name: and
Description: property
settings in the **Tool
Properties** dialog box
are used as the tooltip
for the tool.

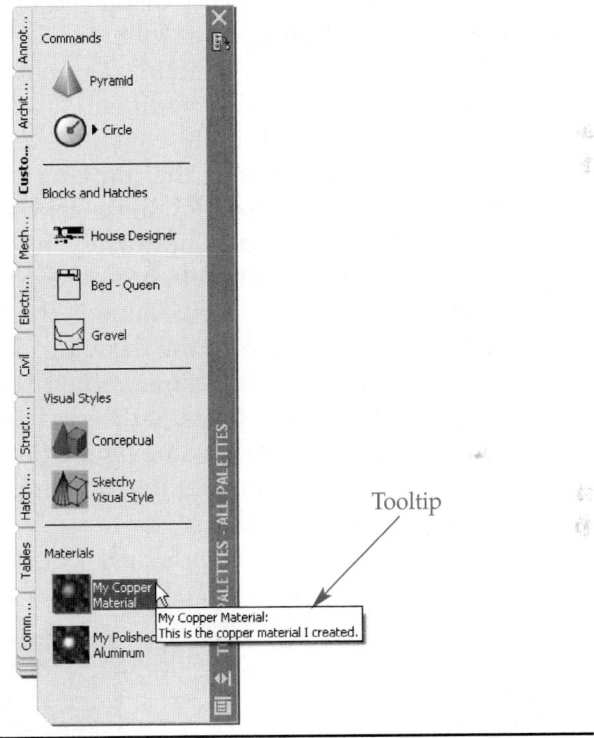

Tooltip

The **General** category in the **Tool Properties** dialog box can be used to assign specific values to the general properties that are a part of nearly all AutoCAD objects. The properties that can be customized are Color, Layer, Linetype, Linetype scale, Plot style, Lineweight, Text style, and Dimension style. Depending on the type of tool, some of these properties may not be available.

The values assigned in the **Tool Properties** dialog box override the current property settings in the drawing when the tool is used. For instance, create three layers called Object, Hidden, and Center in the current drawing. A separate line tool can now be created for each of these layers:

1. Create a new, blank palette named **Line Tools**.
2. Add three line tools to the tool palette by copying them from the **Command Tool Samples** palette.
3. Right-click on the first of these new line tools and select **Properties** from the shortcut menu to display the **Tool Properties** dialog box.

4. In the **Name:** text box, enter Line-Object as the name.

5. In the **Description:** text box, enter Draws a line on the Object layer. as the description.

6. In the **General** category, pick the Layer property. A drop-down list appears that is set to —use current. This means that when you draw a line using the tool, the line is drawn on the current layer.

7. In the drop-down list, select Object. Now, any lines drawn with the tool are placed on the Object layer.

8. Pick the **OK** button to close the **Tool Properties** dialog box and save the changes.

9. Repeat the above steps for the other two line tools setting them to Hidden and Center layers.

Now, use one of your new tools to draw a line. Notice that when you select the tool the current layer switches to the one assigned to the tool. When you finish using the tool, the current layer switches back to the previous layer. Try each of the other new tools. Experiment with some of the other general properties, such as Color, Linetype, and Lineweight.

Customizing Block Insertion Tools

When a block insertion tool is modified in the **Tool Properties** dialog box, properties specific to block insertion are displayed in a category labeled **Insert**, Figure 22-21. These properties are described as follows.

- **Name.** This property contains the name of the block to be inserted. The Name property is not usually modified.

- **Source file.** This property contains the name and path to the source drawing containing the block. If the drawing file has been moved to a new location, specify the correct location in the text box for this property. When you pick in the text box, an ellipses button (...) appears at the right-hand side of the box. You can pick this button to browse for the drawing file.

- **Scale.** The Scale property value is the scale that will be applied to the block when it is inserted into the drawing. The scale is applied equally in the X, Y, and Z directions. The default value is 1.000.

- **Auxiliary scale.** The block is inserted at a scale calculated by multiplying the Auxiliary scale property value by the Scale property value. This drop-down list allows you to apply either the dimension scale or the plot scale to the insertion scale. The default value is None.

Figure 22-21.
The **Tool Properties** dialog box for a block insertion tool.

Properties specific to block insertion

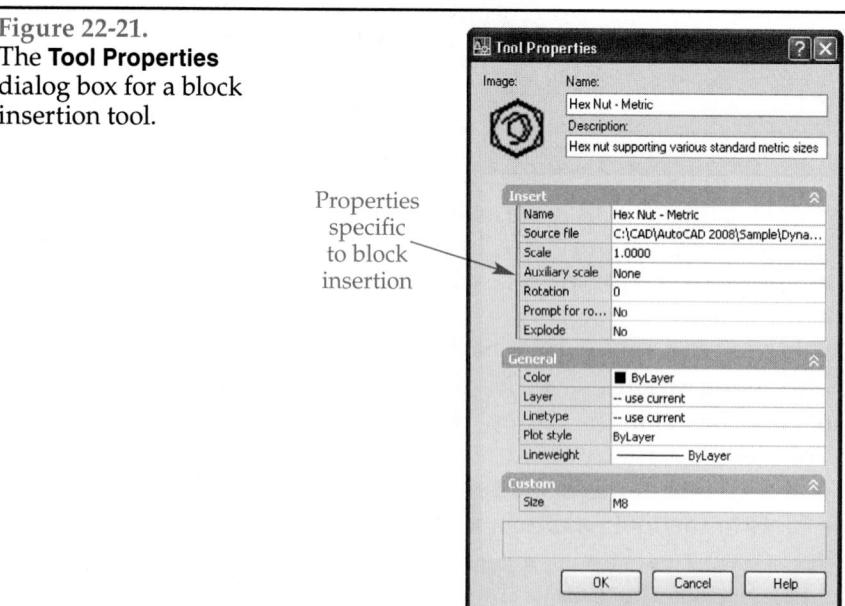

- **Rotation.** The rotation angle for the block when it is inserted is set by this property. The default value is 0.
- **Prompt for rotation.** This property determines whether or not the user is prompted for a rotation angle when the block is inserted. The default value in the drop-down list is No.
- **Explode.** This property determines whether or not the block is inserted as a block or as its component objects (exploded). The default value in the drop-down list is No, which means the block is inserted unexploded.

Customizing Hatch Pattern Tools

When a hatch pattern insertion tool is modified in the **Tool Properties** dialog box, properties specific to hatch patterns are displayed in the **Pattern** category, Figure 22-22. These properties are described as follows. Which properties are disabled or enabled is determined by the pattern type.

- **Tool type.** This property determines if the hatch pattern is a standard hatch or a gradient fill. Choosing Gradient in the drop-down list changes the rest of the properties found in this area of the dialog box. Gradient fill properties are discussed in the next section.
- **Type.** This property determines the type of hatch pattern. To change the type, select the property and then pick the ellipses button (...) at the right-hand end of the entry. The **Hatch Pattern Type** dialog box is displayed, Figure 22-23. In the **Pattern type:** drop-down list of this dialog box, select User-defined, Predefined, or Custom.

  If Predefined is selected, the **Pattern...** button and drop-down list are enabled. Select a pattern from the drop-down list or pick the button to select a pattern in the **Hatch Pattern Palette** dialog box. This is the same dialog box used with the **BHATCH** command.

  If User-defined is selected, the rest of the items in the dialog box are disabled. The properties for user-defined hatch patterns are set in the **Tool Properties** dialog box, as discussed in this section.

  Selecting Custom disables the **Pattern...** button and drop-down list and enables the **Custom Pattern:** text box. In this text box, enter the name of the custom pattern to use.

Figure 22-22.
The **Tool Properties** dialog box for a hatch insertion tool.

Properties specific to hatches

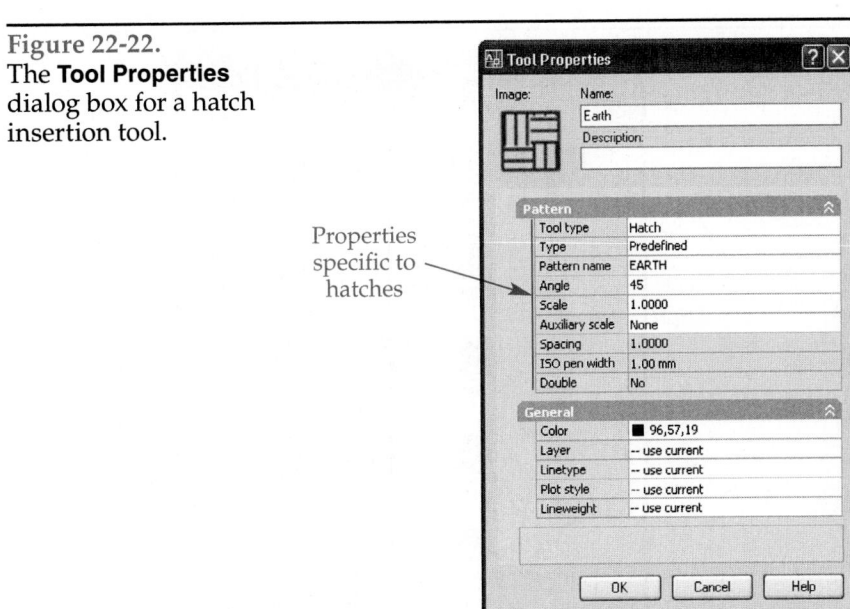

Figure 22-23.
The **Hatch Pattern Type** dialog box is used to determine the type of hatch. A predefined hatch pattern can also be selected in this dialog box.

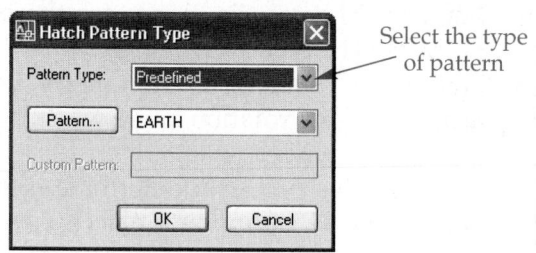

Select the type of pattern

- **Pattern name.** If the pattern type is set to Predefined, you can change the pattern using this property. Select the property and pick the ellipses button (...) to open the **Hatch Pattern Palette** dialog box, **Figure 22-24.** If you selected the pattern in the **Hatch Pattern Type** dialog box, you will not need to select it using this property. This property is "display only" when the type is set to User-defined or Custom.
- **Angle.** This property allows you to rotate the hatch pattern. The default value is 0.
- **Scale.** This property determines the scale to be applied to the hatch pattern. Pick in the text box and enter a scale factor for the pattern. The default value is 1.000.
- **Auxiliary scale.** The hatch is inserted at a scale calculated by multiplying the Auxiliary scale property value by the Scale property value. This drop-down list allows you to apply either the dimension scale or the plot scale to the insertion scale. The default value is None.
- **Spacing.** This property determines the spacing of lines in a user-defined hatch pattern. For other hatch pattern types, this property is "display only." To change the spacing, pick in the text box and enter the relative distance between lines. The default value is 1.000.
- **ISO pen width.** This property allows you to set the pen width for ISO hatch patterns. It is disabled for other hatch patterns. The default value in the drop-down list is 1.00 mm.
- **Double.** This property determines whether or not the user-defined hatch is a crosshatch pattern. The default value in the drop-down list is No.

Figure 22-24.
Selecting a predefined hatch pattern.

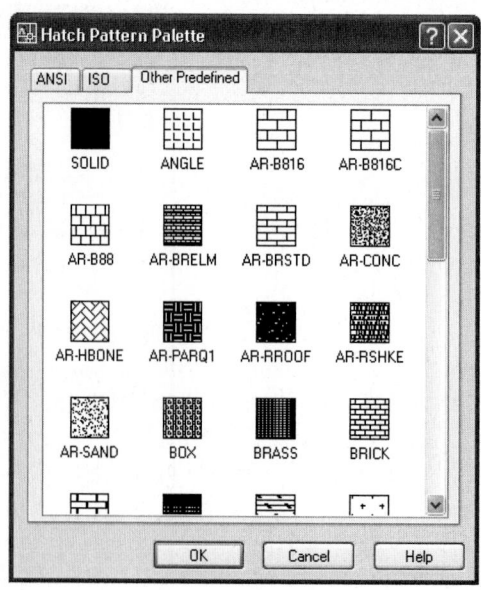

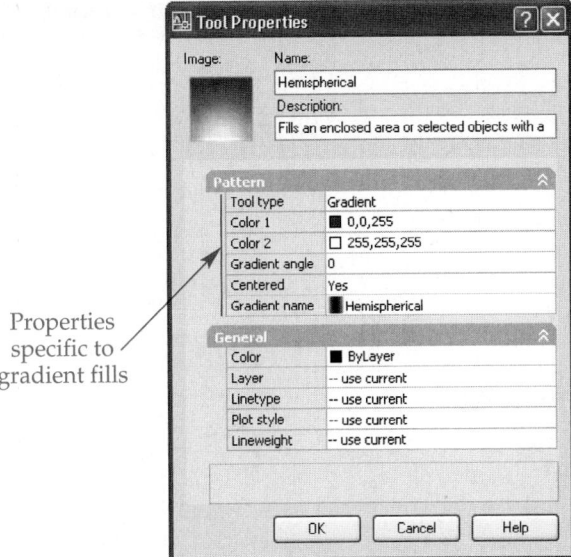

Figure 22-25.
The **Tool Properties** dialog box for a gradient fill hatch insertion tool.

Properties specific to gradient fills

Customizing Gradient Fill Tools

When a gradient fill hatch pattern insertion tool is modified in the **Tool Properties** dialog box, properties specific to gradient fills are displayed in the **Pattern** category, Figure 22-25. These properties are described as follows.

- **Tool type.** This property determines if the hatch pattern is a standard hatch or a gradient fill. Choosing Hatch in the drop-down list changes the rest of the properties found in this area of the dialog box, as described in the previous section.
- **Color 1.** This property is used to specify the first color of the gradient fill. Any AutoCAD or custom color can be selected using the drop-down list.
- **Color 2.** This property is used to specify the second color of the gradient fill. Any AutoCAD or custom color can be selected using the drop-down list.
- **Gradient angle.** The value of this property determines the angle of the gradient fill. Pick in the text box and enter the number of degrees for the angle of the gradient.
- **Centered.** This property determines whether or not the gradient fill is centered. The default value in the drop-down list is Yes.
- **Gradient name.** The type of gradient fill is set by this property. AutoCAD's preset gradient fills appear in the drop-down list. Select the type of gradient fill to use.

Customizing Command Tools

When a command tool is modified in the **Tool Properties** dialog box, properties specific to commands are displayed in the **Command** category, Figure 22-26. These properties are described as follows.

- **Use flyout.** This property determines whether or not the tool is a flyout. Flyouts are discussed later in this chapter.
- **Flyout options.** This property allows you to pick which commands are associated with the flyout, as discussed later.
- **Command string.** The command macro for the tool is entered in this text box, if the tool is not a flyout. Creating custom commands is discussed in Chapter 20. If the tool is a flyout, this text box is disabled.

For example, suppose you need a tool that will draw three concentric circles with diameters of .50, 1.00, and 1.50. Use the following procedure.

Figure 22-26.
The **Tool Properties** dialog box for a command tool.

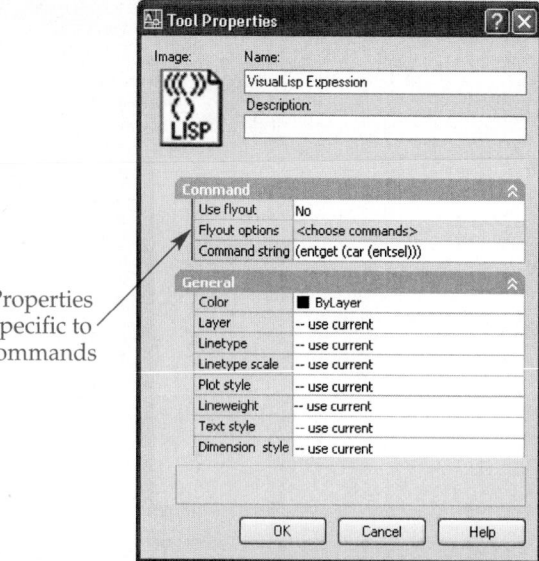

Properties specific to commands

1. In the current drawing, create a circle of any diameter at any location.
2. Drag and drop the circle onto a tool palette to create a new tool.
3. Right-click on the new **Circle** tool and select **Properties...** from the shortcut menu.
4. In the **Tool Properties** dialog box, change the following properties:
   Name: Triple Circle
   Description: Creates three concentric circles.
   Use Flyout: No
   Command string: ^C^Ccircle;\d;.50;circle;@;d;1.0;circle;@;d;1.5
5. Pick the **OK** button to close the **Tool Properties** dialog box.
6. Test the new tool.

Look closely at the command macro for the **Triple Circle** tool. Can you identify each component of the macro? If not, use the tool and then display the **AutoCAD Text Window** by pressing [F2]. Using the text window, determine what function each component of the macro performs.

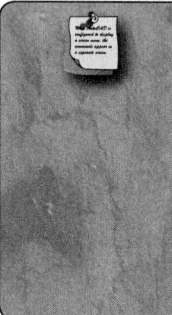

NOTE

The **VisualLisp Expression** tool included on the **Command Tool Samples** palette is not actually a "command" tool. It is merely there to let you know that you can use a command tool to execute Visual LISP expressions. Visual LISP functions can be added in the **Command string** text box in the **Tool Properties** dialog box. For more information on AutoLISP and Visual LISP, refer to Chapters 24 and 25 of this text and to the text *Visual LISP Programming* from Goodheart-Willcox Publisher.

Exercise 22-3
Complete the exercise on the Student CD.

Customizing Camera and Light Tools

Cameras and lights are stored in the drawing file. By placing camera and light tools on a tool palette, you can store your favorite settings for use in all drawings. Productivity is increased since you do not have to use **DesignCenter** to browse for your favorite cameras and lights within other drawings. In fact, AutoCAD provides several tool palettes with different light tools. These tools palettes are provided for lights:

- **Generic Lights**
- **Fluorescent**
- **High Intensity Discharge**
- **Incandescent**
- **Low Pressure Sodium**

AutoCAD also has a **Cameras** tool palette containing three camera tools. These tools are provided on the **Cameras** tool palette:

- **Normal Camera**
- **Wide-Angle Camera**
- **Extreme Wide-Angle Camera**

When customizing a camera or light tool, the **Tool Properties** dialog box provides all of the properties that are required to create a camera or light. See Figure 22-27. For detailed information about setting up lights and cameras, see Chapters 15 and 17.

Customizing Visual Style and Material Tools

When either a visual style or material tool is modified in the **Tool Properties** dialog box, properties specific to the type of tool appear in the dialog box. The properties available are identical to those available in the **Visual Style Manager** window or **Materials** window. See Figure 22-28. Refer to Chapter 13 for information on creating and modifying visual styles and Chapter 14 for information on creating and modifying materials.

NOTE

Modifying a material tool does not alter the material in the drawing if it has been attached to any objects.

Figure 22-27.
A—The **Tool Properties** dialog box for a light tool. B—The **Tool Properties** dialog box for a camera tool.

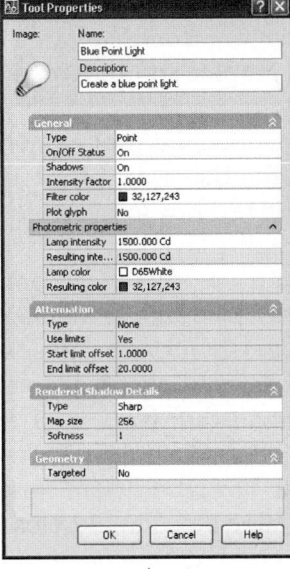

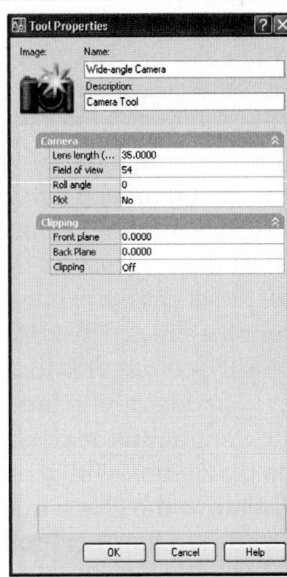

A

B

Figure 22-28.
A—The **Tool Properties** dialog box for a visual style tool. B—The **Tool Properties** dialog box for a material tool.

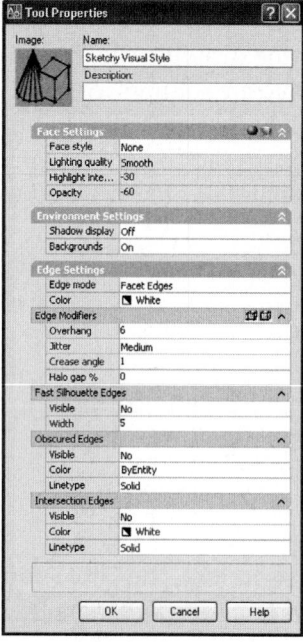

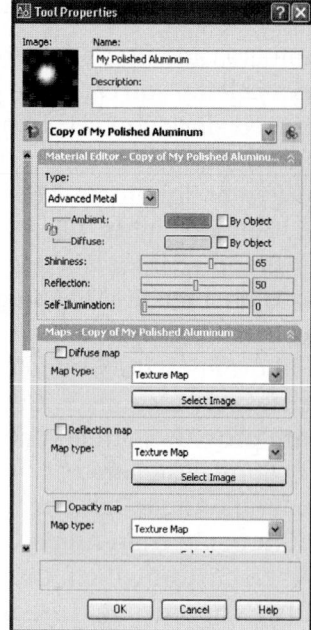

A

B

Changing a Tool Icon

You can change the icon associated with a tool. This can be done from within the **Tool Properties** dialog box or directly on the tool palette. Right-click on the icon, either in the dialog box or on the tool palette, and select **Specify Image...** from the shortcut menu. The **Select Image File** dialog box is displayed. This is a standard "open" dialog box. Navigate to the image file, select it, and pick the **Open** button. The icon displays the new image. To change an icon back to the original image, right-click on the icon (either in the dialog box or on the tool palette) and select **Remove specified image** from the shortcut menu. The icon returns to its original image.

Working with Flyouts

A command tool in a tool palette can be set to function as a flyout. A flyout tool is similar to a toolbar button flyout. The tool icon displays a small arrow to the right of the tool. When the arrow is picked, a graphic shortcut menu is displayed that contains the command tools in the flyout.

To set a command tool as a flyout, open the **Tool Properties** dialog box for the tool. Then, in the **Command** category, set the Use flyout property to Yes. The tool is now a flyout. Notice that the **Command** string text box in the dialog box is disabled. You must now select the commands that will be displayed in the flyout.

The Flyout options property is used to specify which commands will be displayed in the flyout for a tool. This property is disabled unless the Use flyout property is set to Yes. To choose the commands to appear in the flyout, select the property and pick the ellipses button (...) at the right-hand side. The **Flyout Options** dialog box appears, Figure 22-29.

The commands that will appear in the flyout tool are indicated in the **Flyout Options** dialog box with a check. To prevent a command from being displayed in the flyout, remove the check mark next to its name. Then, close the **Flyout Options** dialog box to return to the **Tool Properties** dialog box. Finally, close the **Tool Properties** dialog box and test the tool.

Figure 22-29.
A—The commands
available for a
dimensioning
command flyout
tool. B—The
commands available
for a drawing
command flyout tool.

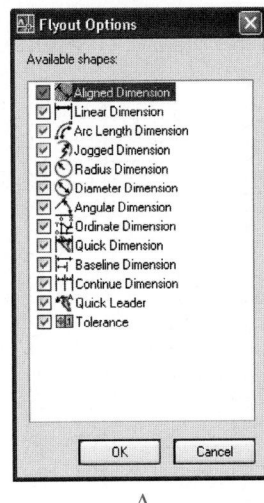
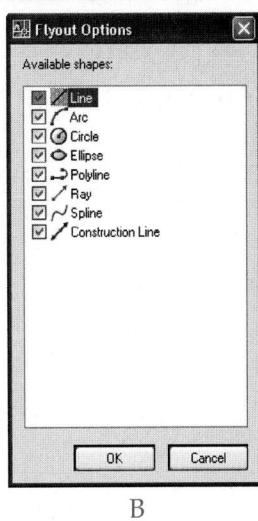

A   B

The commands displayed in the **Flyout Options** dialog box depend on which command tool is being modified. Figure 22-29A shows the commands available when a dimensioning command tool is modified. When a drawing command tool is modified, the commands shown in Figure 22-29B are available. These also act as the default tools for other commands, such as modify commands or custom commands.

PROFESSIONAL TIP

When a drawing or dimensioning command is added to a tool palette, the tool is automatically a flyout. It can then be modified to customize or remove its flyout capabilities.

Organizing Tool Palettes into Groups

Tool palettes are very useful, productive tools. You may find it beneficial to create many tool palettes to meet your design needs. However, having too many palettes visible at once can be counterproductive. The tool palette names become abbreviated in the **Tool Palettes** window or the tabs may be stacked on top of each other. This is the case if all of the default AutoCAD tool palettes are displayed. Fortunately, tool palettes can be divided into named groups and then a single group can be displayed.

By default, all of the tool palettes are shown in the **Tool Palettes** window, but the existing tool palettes are divided into named groups. Right-click on the title bar of **Tool Palettes** window and look at the shortcut menu. At the bottom of the shortcut menu, notice the **Annotation and Design**, **3D Make**, **Tables**, **Leaders**, **Materials**, **Materials Library**, **Generic Lights**, **Photometric Lights**, **Cameras**, **Visual Styles**, and **All Palettes** entries, Figure 22-30. The check mark next to **All Palettes** indicates that all of the defined tool palettes are being displayed. Select **Annotation and Design** from the shortcut menu and notice that only the block-related tool palettes are visible. Right-click on the title bar again and select **Materials Library** from the shortcut menu. Notice that only the tool palettes related to materials are displayed. These tool palettes represent AutoCAD's material library.

Figure 22-30.
Select a palette group to display or choose to display all palettes.

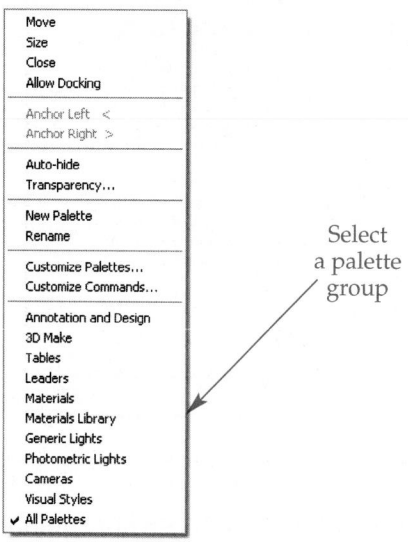

Select a palette group

CUSTOMIZE

Type
CUSTOMIZE
Pull-Down Menu
Tools
> Customize
> Tool
Palettes...

The **Customize** dialog box is used to make new palette groups or customize existing groups. To open this dialog box, right-click on the **Tool Palettes** window title bar and select **Customize Palettes...** from the shortcut menu. You can also type CUSTOMIZE. All of the currently defined tool palettes are listed in the **Palettes:** area on the left side of the dialog box, Figure 22-31. The currently defined palette groups are listed in the **Palette Groups:** area on the right side of the dialog box. Palette groups are shown as folders. The tool palettes contained within the group are shown in the tree below the folder. The current palette group is indicated at the bottom of the dialog box and by the bold folder name in the **Palette Groups:** area.

You can customize one of the existing palette groups by adding tool palettes to or removing tool palettes from the group. To remove a tool palette from a group, select the palette name under the group name in the **Palette Groups:** area. Then, press the [Delete] key or right-click and select **Remove** from the shortcut menu. To delete a palette group, select it in the **Palette Groups:** area and press the [Delete] key or right-click and select **Delete** from the shortcut menu. To add a palette to a group, simply select

Figure 22-31.
The **Customize** dialog box is used to create and manage palette groups.

Palettes

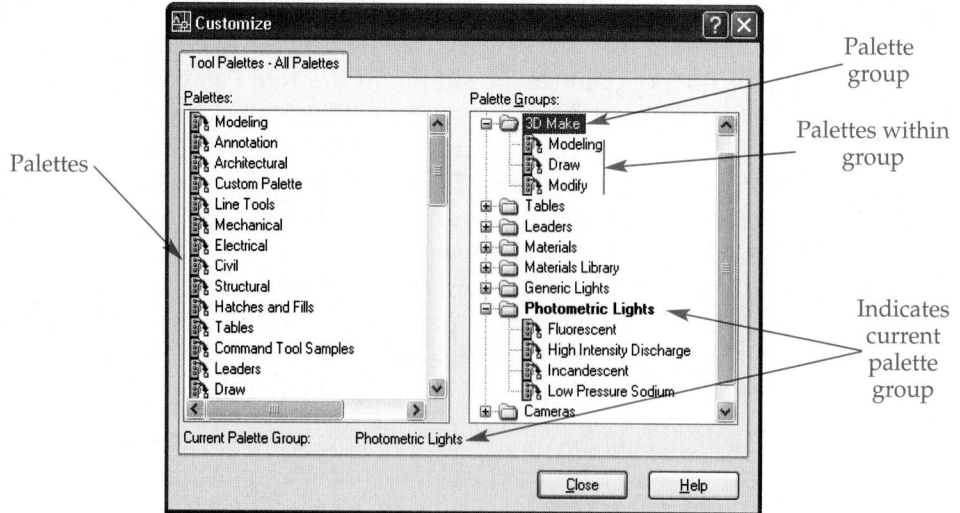

Palette group

Palettes within group

Indicates current palette group

the palette in the **Palettes:** area and drag it into the group in the **Palette Groups:** area. A tool palette can be a member of more than one palette group.

To create a new palette group, right-click in a blank area of the **Palette Groups:** area and select **New Group** from the shortcut menu. A new folder appears in the tree with the default name highlighted in a text box. Type a name for the new palette group and press [Enter]. Then, drag tool palettes from the **Palettes:** area and drop them into the new palette group.

The order in which tool palettes appear in the **Tool Palettes** window is determined by their positions in the tree. To reorder the tool palettes, simply drag them to different positions within the palette group. To reorder the palette groups, drag them to different positions within the tree in the **Palette Groups:** area. The order in which the palette groups appear in the **Palette Groups:** area determines the order in which they appear in the shortcut menu displayed by right-clicking on the **Tool Palettes** window title bar.

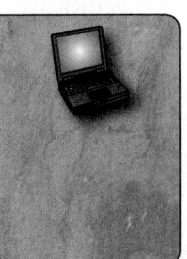

PROFESSIONAL TIP

When adding a palette group, be careful where you right-click. If you right-click within a group, the new palette group is nested within that group. A cascading menu appears in the shortcut menu displayed when right-clicking on the **Tool Palettes** window title bar. If you do not want the palette group nested, simply drag the group to the top of the tree in the **Customize** dialog box.

Saving and Sharing Tool Palettes and Palette Groups

Tool palettes and palette groups can be exported from and imported into AutoCAD. Both operations are performed in the **Customize** dialog box. Some precautions about tool palette files:

- Tool palette files can only be imported into the same version of AutoCAD as the version from which the file was exported.
- Tool palette files exported from AutoCAD and imported into AutoCAD LT may have tools that will not work or behave the same. For example, color property tools using a color other than an AutoCAD Color Index (ACI) color are converted to ByLayer in AutoCAD LT. Also, gradient fill tools convert to hatch tools in AutoCAD LT. Raster image tools do not work in AutoCAD LT.

To export a tool palette, right-click on the palette to be exported in the **Palettes:** area of the **Customize** dialog box and select **Export...** from the shortcut menu. To export a palette group, right-click on the name of the group in the **Palette Groups:** area and select **Export...** from the shortcut menu. The **Export Palette** or **Export Group** dialog box is displayed. This is a standard Windows "save" dialog box. Name the file, navigate to the folder where you want to save it, and pick the **Save** button. Tool palettes are saved with a .xtp file extension. Palette groups are saved with a .xgp file extension.

To import a tool palette, right-click in the **Palettes:** area of the **Customize** dialog box and select **Import...** from the shortcut menu. To import a palette group, right-click in the **Palette Groups:** area and select **Import...** from the shortcut menu. The **Import Palette** or **Import Group** dialog box is displayed. Navigate to the folder where the file is saved, select it, and pick the **Open** button. The imported tool palette is added to the **Palettes:** area. An imported palette group is added to the **Palette Groups:** area.

Chapter Test

Answer the following questions. Write your answers on a separate sheet of paper or complete the electronic chapter test on the Student CD.

1. Name three ways to open the **Tool Palettes** window.
2. How do you dock the **Tool Palettes** window?
3. When enabled, what does the autohide feature do to the **Tool Palettes** window? How is the **Tool Palettes** window accessed when autohide is enabled?
4. Name two ways to toggle the autohide feature on the **Tool Palettes** window.
5. Describe how anchoring the **Tool Palettes** window differs from using the autohide feature or docking it.
6. How do you activate the transparency feature for the **Tool Palettes** window?
7. Name the three view styles in which tools can be displayed in the **Tool Palettes** window.
8. How do you create a new, blank tool palette?
9. How do you add a tool palette that contains all of the blocks in a particular drawing?
10. Which dialog box must be open to create a tool on a tool palette from a toolbar button? How is it opened?
11. What are the names of the two files that store hatch pattern definitions?
12. How do you rearrange tools on a tool palette?
13. Name four of the general properties that can be customized on individual tools on a tool palette.
14. What is the purpose of the auxiliary scale property for block and hatch insertion tools?
15. What are the two types of patterns that can be inserted using a tool in a tool palette?
16. If you are creating a command tool that performs a custom function, where is the command macro entered?
17. Which two types of commands can be included in a flyout tool?
18. What is the purpose of creating tool palette groups?
19. What is the extension given to an exported tool palette file?
20. How do you import a tool palette file?

Drawing Problems

Before customizing or creating any tool palettes, check with your instructor or supervisor for specific instructions or guidelines.

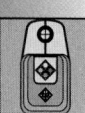

1. Design a complete tool palette system for your chosen discipline. Incorporate:
   - Multiple tool palettes
   - Block tools
   - Hatch tools
   - Drawing command tools (with and without flyouts)
   - Modification command tools
   - Inquiry command tools
   - Custom macro tools
   - Dimensioning command tools (with and without flyouts)
   A. On the tool palettes that use multiple types of command tools, use separators and text labels to group the types of tools.
   B. Create groups for the multiple tool palettes.

2. Export the tool palette groups created in problem 1. Copy the files to removable media or an archive drive.

CHAPTER 23

User Profiles and Workspaces

Learning Objectives

After completing this chapter, you will be able to:
- ✓ Describe user profiles.
- ✓ Create user profiles.
- ✓ Restore a user profile.
- ✓ Describe workspaces.
- ✓ Create workspaces.
- ✓ Customize a workspace.
- ✓ Restore a workspace.

In a school or company, there is often more than one person who will use the same AutoCAD workstation. Each drafter has a unique style for creating a drawing. While there are often general rules to follow, many times the method used to arrive at the end result is not important. As you learned in Chapters 19 through 22, there are many ways to customize AutoCAD. You can set screen colors and other features of the AutoCAD environment, create custom toolbars and pull-down menus, and customize legacy features. Many of these settings can be saved in a user profile or workspace. User profiles and workspaces allow you to quickly and easily restore a group of custom settings.

User Profiles

A *user profile* is a group of settings for devices and AutoCAD functions. Some of the settings and values a profile can contain are:
- Temporary drawing file location.
- Template drawing file location.
- Text display format.
- Startup dialog box display.
- Minutes between automatic saves.
- File extension for temporary files.
- AutoCAD screen menu display (on/off).
- Color and font settings for AutoCAD's text and graphics screens.
- Type of pointer and length of crosshairs.
- Default printer or plotter.

Multiple profiles can be saved by a single user for different applications, or several users can create individual profiles for their own use. A user profile should not be confused with settings found in a drawing. Template files are used to save settings relating to a drawing session, such as units, limits, object snap settings, drafting settings, grip settings, arc and circle smoothness, dimension styles, and text styles. A user profile, on the other hand, saves settings related to the performance and appearance of the software and hardware.

Creating a User Profile

A user profile is basically a collection of all things you have customized in AutoCAD, except toolbars, pull-down menus, and palettes, and **Dashboard** control panels. These customizations are usually done to make AutoCAD easier for you to use. For example, as you gain experience in AutoCAD, you realize that you:
- Like the crosshairs extending to the edges of the graphics window.
- Often use the **Inquiry** toolbar.
- Prefer the graphics window background color to be gray.

Through the course of several drawing sessions, you have customized AutoCAD to reflect these preferences. Now, so you do not lose your preferred settings, you should create a user profile.

First, open the **Options** dialog box and pick the **Profiles** tab, Figure 23-1. Pick the **Add to List...** button on the right side of the tab. The **Add Profile** dialog box is opened, Figure 23-2. Enter a name and description. Then, pick the **Apply & Close** button to close the **Add Profile** dialog box. The current settings are saved to the user profile and the new user profile is now listed in the **Profiles** tab of the **Options** dialog box. The user profile is saved and will be available in the current and future AutoCAD drawing sessions.

To change the name of a user profile, pick the **Rename...** button in the **Profiles** tab. In the **Change Profile** dialog box, enter a new name and description. To delete a user profile, highlight it in the **Profiles** tab and pick the **Delete** button. You cannot delete the current user profile. If you pick the **Reset** button, the highlighted user profile has all of its settings restored to AutoCAD defaults.

Figure 23-1.
Settings can be saved in a profile.

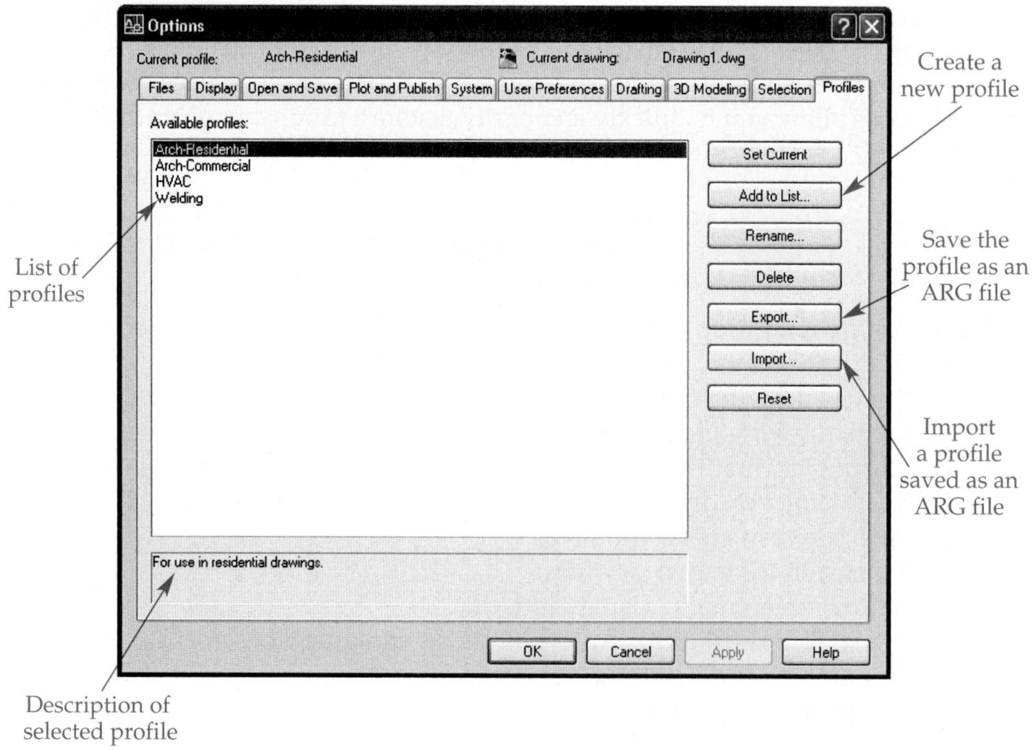

List of profiles

Create a new profile

Save the profile as an ARG file

Import a profile saved as an ARG file

Description of selected profile

Figure 23-2.
The **Add Profile** dialog box is used to create a new profile.

Enter name for new profile

Enter description for new profile

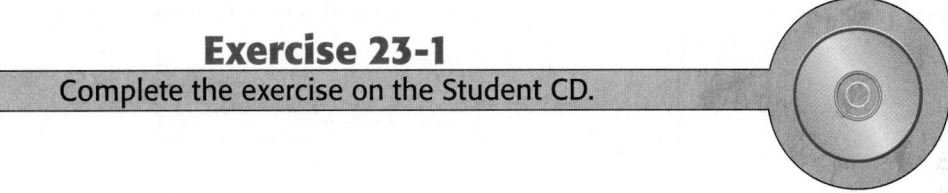

PROFESSIONAL TIP

Changes made to the environment (screen color, toolbar display, etc.) are automatically saved to the current profile.

Restoring a User Profile

Once a user profile is saved, it is available in the current and future AutoCAD drawing sessions. To set any saved user profile as the current user profile, first open the **Options** dialog box. The current profile is indicated at the top of the **Options** dialog box. Then, pick the **Profiles** tab. Highlight the name of the profile to restore in the **Available profiles:** list. Then, pick the **Set Current** button. You can also double-click on the name in the **Available profiles:** list to restore a profile. All of the settings in the user profile are applied while the **Options** dialog box is still open. Close the dialog box to return to the drawing editor.

Exercise 23-1
Complete the exercise on the Student CD.

Importing and Exporting User Profiles

A user profile can be exported and imported. You may want to do this to take your user profile to a different AutoCAD workstation. A user profile is saved as an ARG file.

To export a user profile, open the **Options** dialog box and pick the **Profiles** tab. Highlight the profile to export and pick the **Export...** button. The **Export Profiles** dialog box is opened, **Figure 23-3.** Then, select a folder and name the file. When you pick the **Save** button, the user profile is saved with the .arg file extension.

To import a user profile, pick the **Import...** button in the **Profiles** tab. The **Import Profile** dialog box is displayed. This is a standard "open" dialog box. Then, navigate to the appropriate folder and select the proper ARG file and pick the **Open** button. A second dialog box named **Import Profile** is displayed. See **Figure 23-4.** You can rename the user profile, change the description, and choose to include the file path. Pick the **Apply & Close** button to complete the process. The user profile is then available in the **Profiles** tab.

Figure 23-3.
The **Export Profile** dialog box is used to save a user profile as an ARG file, which can be transferred to another AutoCAD workstation.

Select a folder

Name the user profile

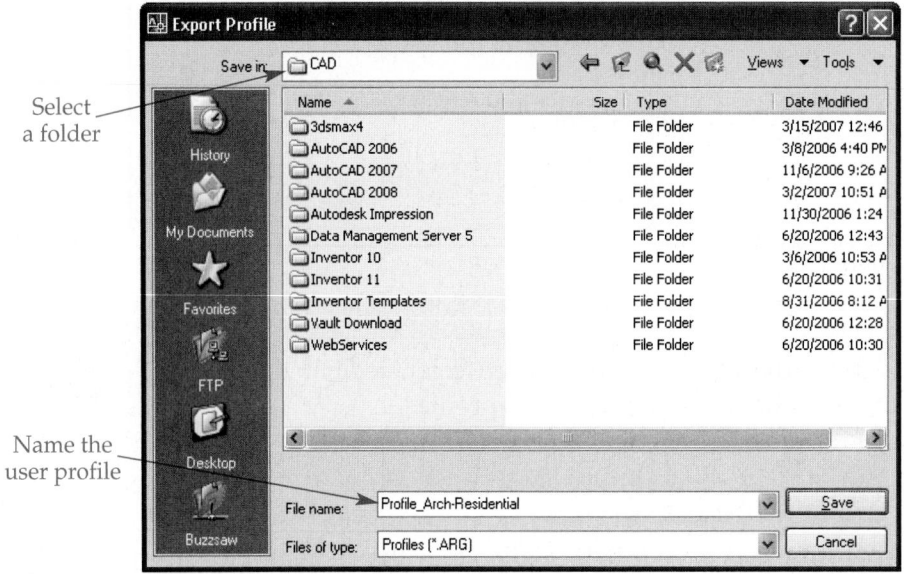

Figure 23-4.
Importing a user profile.

Profile name

Description

Check to include the path

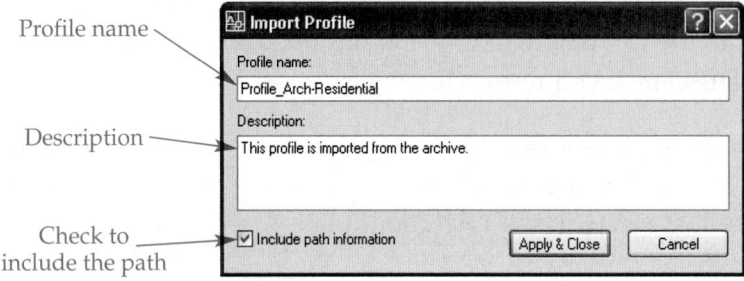

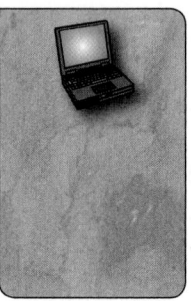

PROFESSIONAL TIP

A variety of settings can be changed in the **Options** dialog box. Settings that have the AutoCAD drawing icon located next to them can be stored in a template file (or drawing). Using the appropriate template file to begin a drawing automatically resets these settings. Settings within the **Options** dialog box that do not have the AutoCAD drawing icon next to them can typically be restored through the use of user profiles.

Exercise 23-2
Complete the exercise on the Student CD.

Workspaces

As you have seen, a user profile allows you to set and restore settings for screen colors, drafting settings, and file locations. On the other hand, a workspace allows you to set and restore settings for toolbars, pull-down menus, palettes (the **Dashboard**, **DesignCenter**, **Properties** window, **Tool Palettes** window, etc.), and **Dashboard** control panels, but it does not contain environmental settings. A *workspace* is a collection of displayed toolbars, palettes, **Dashboard** control panels, and pull-down menus and their configurations. A workspace stores not only which of these tools are visible, but also their on-screen locations.

PROFESSIONAL TIP

A user profile also stores which toolbars and palettes are displayed and their location. However, the configuration of the menu bar (pull-down menus) is not saved in a user profile. Also, if a workspace is restored, the settings for toolbar and palette display and location override the current user profile settings.

Creating a Workspace

AutoCAD has three default workspaces—AutoCAD Classic, 2D Drafting and Annotation, and 3D Modeling. When AutoCAD is launched, the workspace that was last active is restored. AutoCAD can be set up so that any changes made to toolbars, pull-down menus, and palettes are saved to this workspace. However, it is best to create your own workspaces.

The first step in setting up and storing your own workspace is to arrange the toolbars, tool palettes, and pull-down menus to your liking. Refer to Chapter 20 for information on customizing toolbars and pull-down menus. Next, use the **WSSAVE** command to open the **Save Workspace** dialog box, Figure 23-5. Enter a name for the workspace, such as Normal Design or Standard Arrangement, and then pick the **Save** button.

The current settings for toolbars, pull-down menus, and tool palettes are now stored in the new workspace, which is also made current. The current workspace is indicated in the workspace drop-down list in the **Workspaces** toolbar. The current workspace is also indicated by a check mark in the **Workspaces** cascading menu in the **Tools** pull-down menu.

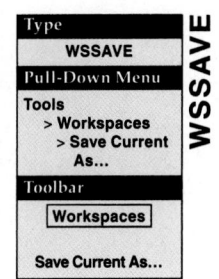

Type	
WSSAVE	
Pull-Down Menu	
Tools	
> Workspaces	
> Save Current	
As...	
Toolbar	
Workspaces	
Save Current As...	

WSSAVE

PROFESSIONAL TIP

Workspaces are saved in a CUI file. By default, they are saved to the main CUI file (acad.cui).

Figure 23-5.
Creating a new workspace.

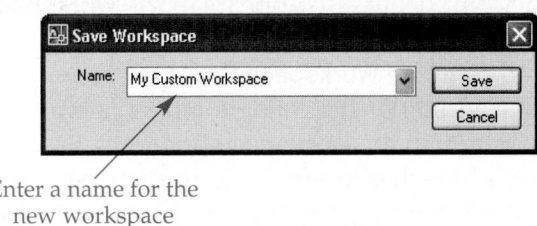

Enter a name for the new workspace

Restoring a Workspace

Once a workspace has been saved, it can easily be restored. A list of available workspaces appears in the drop-down list on the **Workspaces** toolbar and in the **Workspaces** cascading menu in the **Tools** pull-down menu. To select a different workspace, simply pick the name of the workspace in the drop-down list or cascading menu.

A workspace can also be restored using the command line:

```
Command: WORKSPACE↵
Enter workspace option [setCurrent/SAveas/Edit/Rename/Delete/SEttings/?]
<setCurrent>: C↵
Enter name of workspace to make current [?] <current>: MY CUSTOM
    WORKSPACE↵
Command:
```

Notice that you can manage workspaces using this command.

You can also use the **Customize User Interface** dialog box to restore a workspace. First, open the dialog box. Then, expand the Workspaces branch in the **Customizations in All CUI Files** pane. All of the workspaces defined in the default CUI file, and any open CUI files, are displayed in this branch. The label (current) follows the name of the current workspace. To restore a workspace, right-click on its name in the Workspaces branch and select **Set Current** from the shortcut menu. Its name is now followed by (current). Pick the **OK** button to close the **Customize User Interface** dialog box and make the workspace current.

PROFESSIONAL TIP

The **WSCURRENT** system variable indicates the current workspace. You can use this system variable to restore a workspace. Simply set the system variable to the name of the workspace you want to restore.

Customizing a Workspace

An existing workspace can be customized using the **Customize User Interface** dialog box. First, select the workspace to be customized in the Workspaces branch of the **Customizations in All CUI Files** pane. Remember, the name of this pane will change based on the selection in the drop-down list. The **Workspace Contents** pane at the upper-right corner of the dialog box displays the contents of the selected workspace. There are Toolbars, Menus, Dashboard Panels, and Palettes branches. Refer to **Figure 23-6.** Expand a branch to see which components the workspace contains.

To customize the workspace, pick the **Customize Workspace** button at the top of the **Workspace Contents** pane. The tree in the pane turns blue to indicate you are in customize mode and the button changes to the **Done** button. Also, notice that the tree in the **Customizations in All CUI Files** pane has changed. Several branches have disappeared and the Toolbars, Menus, and Dashboard Panels branches have a green check mark next to them. If you expand these branches, you will see that a green check mark also appears next to the components that currently are in the workspace. See **Figure 23-7.**

To add a component, pick the blank box in front of its name to place a check mark in the box. The component also appears in the **Workspace Contents** pane. To remove a component, pick the check mark in front of its name to clear the box. The component is also removed from the **Workspace Contents** pane.

When done adding or removing toolbars, menus, and **Dashboard** control panels, pick the **Done** button in the **Workspace Contents** pane. The tree is no longer displayed in blue. Also, all branches are once again displayed in the **Customizations in All CUI Files** pane. You can now expand the Toolbars branch in the **Workspace Contents** pane,

Figure 23-6.
You can customize existing workspaces.

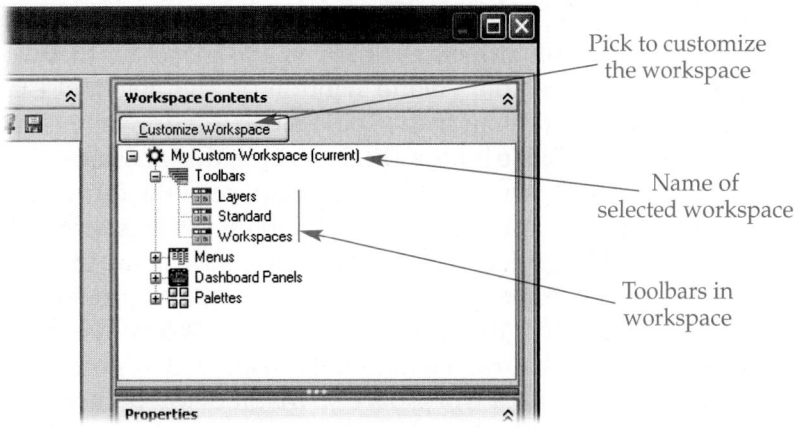

Pick to customize
the workspace

Name of
selected workspace

Toolbars in
workspace

Figure 23-7.
Specifying which toolbars, menus, and **Dashboard** control panels are included in the workspace.

Check mark indicates
the component
is in the workspace

No check mark
indicates it is not in
the current workspace

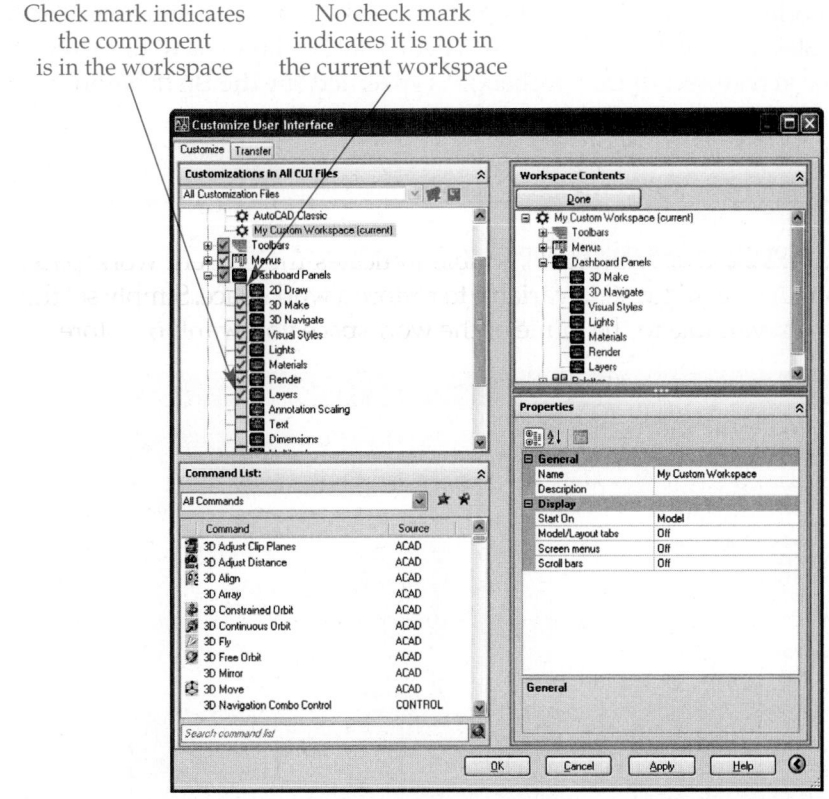

select a toolbar name, and use the **Properties** pane to adjust the toolbar's properties. For example, in the 3D Modeling workspace, the **Layers** toolbar is docked on the top of the screen by default. You can change it to a floating toolbar, specify the location of its anchor point, and set the number of rows for the toolbar in the **Properties** pane. You can also change the order in which pull-down menus appear on the menu bar by dragging them to a new location in the tree in the **Workspace Contents** pane. The top of the tree is the left-hand side of the menu bar.

You may have noticed that there is not a Palettes branch in the **Customizations in All CUI Files** pane. All palettes are automatically available in all workspaces. You can, however, specify whether a palette is displayed or hidden in a workspace. You can also change other properties of a palette, such as floating/docked status, its size, and whether or not the autohide feature is enabled. To change the properties of a palette, first select it in the Palettes branch in the **Workspace Contents** pane. Then, in the **Properties** pane, adjust the properties as needed. When you pick **OK** to close the **Customize User Interface** dialog box, the default properties of the palette are set for that workspace.

For example, the **Tool Palette** window in the AutoCAD Classic workspace is, by default, floating. You can hide the **Tool Palette** window when in the drawing editor by simply picking the **Close** button (**X**). However, this does not change the default setting for the workspace. If you restore the workspace in the future, the **Tool Palette** window will again be shown. You must alter the default settings for the **Tool Palette** window in the workspace. First, select Tool Palette in the Palettes branch in the **Workspace Contents** pane. Then, in the **Properties** pane, change the Show property to No. See **Figure 23-8**. Now, when you restore the workspace, the **Tool Palette** window will not be displayed by default. It can, of course, be manually displayed as needed.

You can also set up a workspace so that it displays model space or layout (paper) space when restored. By default, a workspace displays model space when it is set as current. To change this, highlight the workspace name in either the **Customizations in All CUI Files** pane or the **Workspace Contents** pane. Then, in the **Properties** pane, change the Start On property to Layout or Do not change. If Model is specified for the Start On property, model space is displayed when the workspace is restored. If Layout is specified for the Start On property, the most recently active layout tab is displayed when the workspace is restored. If Do not change is specified for the Start On property, the current tab remains active when the workspace is restored.

Figure 23-8.
Changing the default properties of a palette for a given workspace.

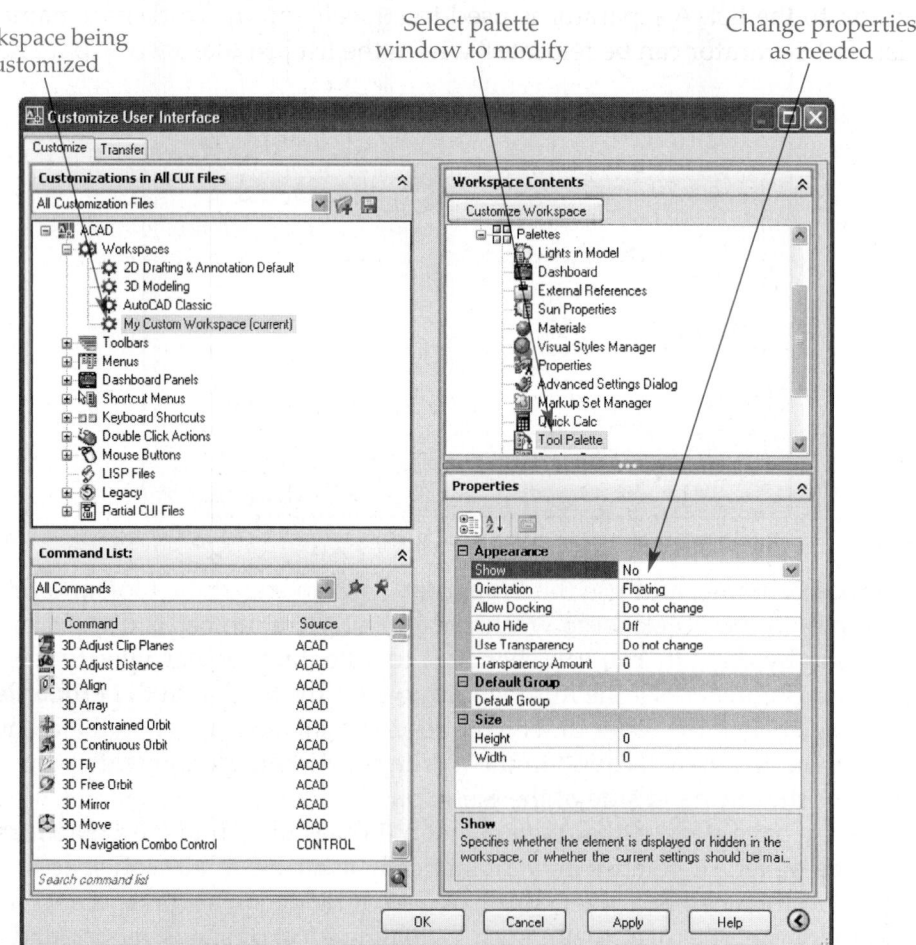

If the **Customize User Interface** dialog box is open, but you are not in customization mode, you can also remove a component from the workspace by right-clicking on it in the tree in the **Workspace Contents** pane and selecting **Remove from Workspace** in the shortcut menu. This is true for all component types except palettes, as all palettes are always available to all workspaces.

Workspace Settings

There are various settings related to workspaces. These are set in the **Workspace Settings** dialog box. See **Figure 23-9**. The **WSSETTINGS** command opens this dialog box. At the top of the **Workspace Settings** dialog box is the **My Workspace =** drop-down list. All saved workspaces in the CUI file appear in this list. The workspace that is selected in the list is defined as My Workspace. The workspace that is designated as My Workspace is restored when the **My Workspace** button on the **Workspaces** toolbar is picked. This can be useful if one person primarily uses a machine, but others may temporarily use the machine with their own workspace settings. You may also find this useful if you have more than one workspace, but use one more often than all of the others.

The **Menu Display and Order** area of the **Workspace Settings** dialog box contains a list of all workspaces saved in the CUI file. The order of this list determines the order of the list that appears in the **Workspaces** cascading menu in the **Tools** pull-down menu and in the drop-down list on the **Workspaces** toolbar. The order of the list can be modified by highlighting one of the workspaces and using the **Move Up** and **Move Down** buttons. The **Add Separator** button is used to add a horizontal line, or menu separator, to the list. A separator is used to logically group workspace names within the list. The separator can be relocated within the list just like a workspace name.

You can prevent a workspace name or separator from being displayed in the menu or drop-down list by removing the check box next to its name. The check box next to the current workspace and the workspace designated as My Workspace can be cleared. However, these workspaces will always be displayed in the menu and drop-down list.

At the bottom of the **Workspace Settings** dialog box is the **When Switching Workspaces** area. The radio buttons in this area determine whether or not changes

Type
WSSETTINGS
Pull-Down Menu
Tools
> Workspaces
> Workspace
Settings...
Toolbar
Workspaces
Workspace Settings...

Figure 23-9.
The **Workspace Settings** dialog box is used to set which workspace is My Workspace, specify which workspaces are shown in the menu and drop-down list and their order, and set whether or not changes are automatically saved when a different workspace is restored.

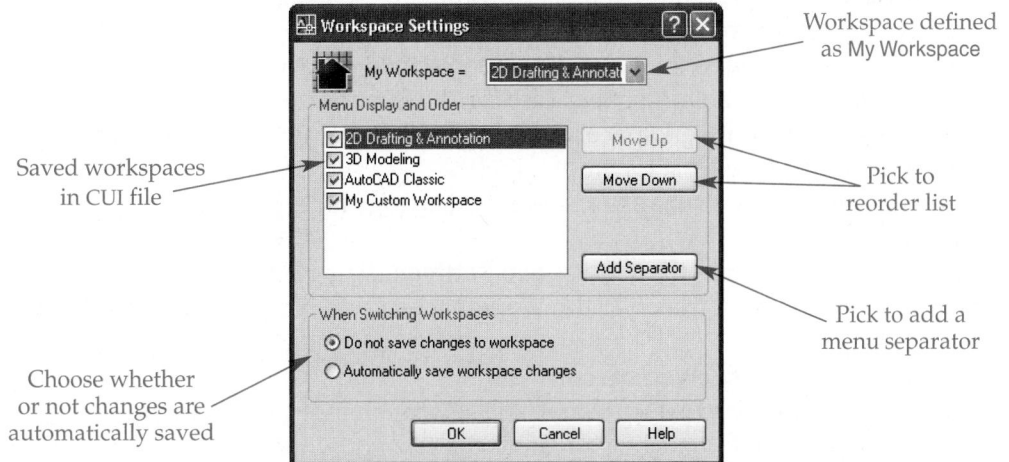

you have made to the arrangement or visibility of the toolbars since you last saved the workspace are saved when you switch to a different workspace. To retain the settings as you last saved them, pick the **Do not save changes to workspace** radio button. Changes made since the workspace was last saved are discarded when a different workspace is restored. If the **Automatically save workspace changes** radio button is on, any "as you work" toolbar changes are automatically saved to the workspace when a different workspace is restored.

At any time, you can manually save the settings to the current workspace. Pick the Save Current As... selection in the drop-down list on the **Workspace** toolbar. When the **Save Workspace** dialog box appears, select the current workspace from the drop-down list. Then, pick the **Save** button. An alert is displayed stating that a workspace with that name already exists and asking if you would like to replace it. Pick the **Yes** button to save the changes to the current workspace.

PROFESSIONAL TIP

Unlike a user profile, changes to the environment (toolbar display, menu bar configuration, etc.) are not necessarily automatically saved. To ensure the changes are only saved when you decide to save them, be sure the **Do not save workspace changes** radio button is on.

Exercise 23-3

Complete the exercise on the Student CD.

Chapter Test

Answer the following questions. Write your answers on a separate sheet of paper or complete the electronic chapter test on the Student CD.

1. What is a *user profile?*
2. How and why are profiles used?
3. What is the file extension used for a profile when it is exported?
4. In which dialog box is a user profile created?
5. How do you restore a user profile?
6. Why would you export a user profile?
7. Briefly describe how to import a user profile.
8. Define *workspace* as related to AutoCAD.
9. List three ways to open the **Save Workspace** dialog box.
10. How do you restore a workspace? List three methods.
11. When customizing a workspace, how do you determine which menus and toolbars are displayed?
12. Briefly describe how to change the default settings for a palette for a given workspace.
13. List three ways to open the **Workspace Settings** dialog box.
14. How do you add a separator to the **Workspaces** cascading menu in the **Tools** pull-down menu?
15. How do you define My Workspace?
16. Briefly describe how to set up AutoCAD so that changes made to the environment are automatically saved to the current workspace.

Drawing Problems

Before creating any user profiles or workspaces, check with your instructor or supervisor for specific instructions or guidelines.

1. Create two user profiles, one named Model Development for modeling and one named Rendering for visual styles and rendering.

   A. Display the toolbars that contain the commands needed for each type of work.
   B. Change the color of the drawing area as needed. For example, some drafters prefer a white background when drawing. However, a black background is often desired when shading and rendering the model.

2. Export the user profiles created in Problem #1 to ARG files. Then, delete each profile from AutoCAD. Restart AutoCAD and verify that the profiles are no longer available. Next, import each profile from file. Restore each profile to verify the settings.

3. Create two workspaces, one named Design Development and one named Dimensioning.
   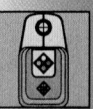
   A. For the Design Development workspace, display toolbars related to drawing and editing. Also, rearrange the pull-down menus to group the drawing and editing/modifying menus together. Remove any pull-down menus that are not needed.
   B. For the Dimensioning workspace, display the toolbars related to dimensioning the drawing. Also, remove drawing-related pull-down menus from the menu bar. You may consider removing editing/modifying pull-down menus.
   C. Create custom toolbars as needed. Include flyouts of other toolbars when advantageous.

4. Customize the two workspaces created in Problem #3.
   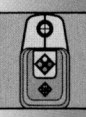
   A. Change default on/off status of any palettes to suit the purpose of the workspace. For example, you may want the **Dashboard**, **Tool Palette**, and **Properties** windows displayed for the Design Development workspace.
   B. Enable the autohide status of all displayed palettes.
   C. Change the Dimensioning workspace so that it starts in a layout.

5. Set up the workspaces from Problem #4 so that "on the fly" changes are automatically saved when a different workspace is made current.

Drawing Problems - Chapter 23

This LISP routine allows you to select a line and offset it a specified distance on each side of the original. The original line is deleted. As an example where this might be useful, you could draw the walls on a floor plan as single lines in the center of the walls. Then, use this program to create the final parallel lines. To run the program, type OL.

```
;;;
;;;
;;;  DBLOffset.lsp
;;;  by Craig P. Black
;;;  original release date: 7/29/06
;;;
;;;
;;;  This program offsets a selected line the same distance on each side of the original and deletes the
;;;  original
;;;
; Defines function name and localizes variables
(defun C:OL (/ OD LN EN PT ED OT FP EP LN-ANG ANG PT1 PT2)
   (setq OD (getdist "\nEnter offset distance: "))        ; Gets and stores offset distance
   (while (not LN)                                        ; Perform loop while no line is selected
      (setq LN (entsel "\nSelect line to offset: "))      ; Get and store LINE entity
      (if LN                                              ; If any entity is selected…
         (progn                                           ; Check it…
            (setq   EN (car LN)                           ; Extract and store the entity data
                    PT (cadr LN)                          ; Extract and store the selected point
                    ED (entget EN)                        ; Get and store entity data from entity name
                    OT (cdr (assoc 0 ED))                 ; Extract and store entity type
            )                                             ; End of setq
            (if (/= OT "LINE")                            ; If entity type is NOT a LINE…
               (progn; Do the following
                  (prompt "\nObject selected must be a LINE...")  ; Make user aware of error
                  (setq LN NIL)                           ; Reset entity type variable to nil
               )                                          ; End of progn
            )                                             ; End of if
         )                                                ; End of progn
      )                                                   ; End of if
   )                                                      ; End of while
                                                          ; The correct entity type has now been
                                                          ; confirmed
   (setq  FP    (cdr (assoc 10 ED))                       ; Extract first point of line from entity data
          EP    (cdr (assoc 11 ED))                       ; Extract end point of line from entity data
          LN-ANG (angle FP EP)                            ; Store angle between points
          ANG    (- LN-ANG (/ pi 2))                      ; Subtract 90 degrees/perpendicular
                                                          ; from/to known angle
          PT1   (polar FP ANG OD)                         ; Create and store point on one side of
                                                          ; object at offset distance
          PT2   (polar FP ANG (* OD -1))                  ; Create and store point on other side of
                                                          ; object at offset distance
   )                                                      ; End of setq
   (command "offset" OD PT PT1 PT PT2 "" "erase" PT "")   ; OFFSET, at offset distance, entity at PT
                                                          ; to PT1 then to PT2
   (princ)                                                ; Clean exit
)                                                         ; End of defun
```

CHAPTER 24

Introduction to AutoLISP

Learning Objectives

After completing this chapter, you will be able to:

- ✓ Locate, load, and run existing AutoLISP programs.
- ✓ Use basic AutoLISP functions on the command line.
- ✓ Define new AutoCAD commands.
- ✓ Write AutoLISP programs using the **Visual LISP Editor**.

What Is AutoLISP?

AutoLISP is a derivative, or dialect, of the LISP programming language. *LISP,* which is an acronym for *list processing,* is a high-level computer programming language used in artificial intelligence (AI) systems. In this reference, the term *high-level* does not mean *complex,* rather it means *powerful.* As a matter of fact, many AutoCAD users refer to AutoLISP as the "nonprogrammer's language" because it is easy to understand.

AutoLISP is specially designed by Autodesk to work with AutoCAD. It is a flexible language that allows the programmer to create custom commands and functions that can greatly increase productivity and drawing efficiency.

Knowing the basics of AutoLISP gives you a better understanding of how AutoCAD works. By learning just a few simple functions, you can create new commands that make a significant difference in your daily productivity. Read through this chapter slowly while you are at a computer. Type all of the examples and exercises as you read them. This is the best way to get a feel for AutoLISP.

AutoLISP and AutoCAD

AutoLISP can be used in several ways. It is a built-in feature of AutoCAD and is, therefore, available on the command line. When AutoLISP commands and functions are issued inside of parentheses on the command line, the AutoLISP interpreter automatically evaluates the entry and carries out the specified tasks. AutoLISP functions can also be incorporated into the AutoCAD menu as toolbar buttons, screen menu items, and tablet menu picks. In addition, AutoLISP command and function definitions can be saved in a file and then loaded into AutoCAD when needed. Items that are frequently used can be placed in the acad2008.lsp file, which is automatically loaded for the first drawing (by default) when AutoCAD starts. The acad2008doc.lsp file should contain functions that are to be available in all concurrent drawings during a session.

AutoCAD also provides an integrated development environment for editing called *Visual LISP*. Visual LISP and the **Visual LISP Editor** offer powerful features designed specifically for writing and editing AutoLISP programs.

The benefits of using AutoLISP are endless. A person with a basic understanding of AutoLISP can create new commands and functions to automate many routine tasks. After working through this chapter, you will be able to add greater capabilities to your screen, tablet, and toolbar menu macros. You can also enter simple AutoLISP expressions on the command line. More experienced programmers can create powerful programs that quickly complete very complex design requirements. Examples of possible new functions that might be designed using AutoLISP include:

- Automatic line breaks when inserting schematic symbols.
- Automatic creation of shapes with associated text objects.
- Parametric design applications that create geometry based on numeric entry.

NOTE

For additional information on using AutoLISP, refer to *Visual LISP Programming* available from Goodheart-Willcox Publisher, which provides complete coverage of AutoLISP and Visual LISP.

AutoLISP Basics

As stated earlier, LISP stands for list processing, which indicates that AutoLISP processes lists. In the LISP language, a *list* can be defined as any number of data enclosed in parentheses. Each item in a list must be separated from other items by a space.

When any entry is made on the command line, it is checked to see if the first character is a parenthesis. The opening parenthesis tells AutoCAD that an AutoLISP expression is being entered. AutoCAD then sends the expression to the AutoLISP interpreter for evaluation. The initial input can be supplied as direct keyboard entry or even a menu macro. The format for an AutoLISP expression, called *syntax*, is:

(*FunctionName AnyRequiredData*...)

The first item in the AutoLISP expression is a *function name*. A function in AutoLISP is similar to a command in AutoCAD. Some functions require additional information. For example, the addition function requires numeric data:

```
Command: (+ 2 4)↵
6
Command:
```

Any required or optional data for a function are called the *arguments*. Some functions use no arguments; others may require one or more. When entering an AutoLISP expression, it is important to *close* it using a closing parenthesis prior to pressing [Enter]. When you press [Enter], the AutoLISP interpreter checks to see that the number of opening and closing parentheses match. If they do not, you are prompted:

```
Command: (+ 2 4↵
(_>
```

The (_> indicates that you are missing one closing parenthesis. In this example, all that is necessary is to enter the single missing parenthesis and the function is complete.

```
(_>) ↵
6
Command:
```

When the AutoLISP interpreter evaluates an AutoLISP expression, it *returns* a value. An expression entered on the command line instructs the system to return its value to the command line, such as 6 in the previous example. If a different prompt is active, the returned value is used as input for that prompt. For example, this next sequence uses the result of adding two numbers as the input at the Specify radius of circle or [Diameter]: prompt. Checking the **CIRCLERAD** system variable verifies that the value returned by AutoLISP was in fact applied to the circle radius.

```
Command: C or CIRCLE↵
Specify center point for circle or [3P/2P/Ttr (tan tan radius)]: (pick a point)
Specify radius of circle or [Diameter]: (+ 14.25 3.0)↵
17.25
Command: CIRCLERAD↵
Enter new value for CIRCLERAD <17.2500>: ↵
```

Basic AutoLISP Functions

The best way to get started learning AutoLISP is to enter a few functions on the command line and see what they do. The following discussion includes basic AutoLISP functions that are part of the foundation for all AutoLISP programs. Practice using the functions as you read. Then, begin using them in menus and macros. At first, these functions and expressions will be entered on the command line. Later in this chapter, and in Chapter 25, you will learn about creating and using AutoLISP program files.

AutoLISP Math Functions

AutoLISP provides many different mathematical operators for performing calculations. All real number calculations in AutoLISP are accurate to 15 decimal places. AutoLISP distinguishes between real numbers and integers, handling each data type differently. *Real numbers* are numbers with a decimal point, such as 1.25, 7.0, and –0.438. *Integers* are whole numbers without a decimal point, such as 3, 91, and –115. If a mathematical expression has only integer arguments, the result is returned as an integer. If at least one real number is used, the result is returned as a real number. The following symbols are used for the four basic math functions.

Symbol	Function
+	Addition; returns the sum of all the supplied number arguments.
–	Subtraction; subtracts the sum of the second through the last number arguments from the first number argument and returns the result.
*	Multiplication; returns the product of all the supplied number arguments.
/	Division; divides the first number argument by the product of the second through the last number arguments.

Real numbers are technically defined as those that have no imaginary part. They include integers and fractions, as well as decimal numbers. In applications involving AutoLISP, and throughout this discussion, real numbers are always classified as those that have a decimal part.

The following examples illustrate AutoLISP math expressions entered on the command line. As you practice entering these expressions, use the following procedure.

1. Start with an open parenthesis.
2. Separate each item in the expression with a space.
3. End the expression with a closing parenthesis.

Using these steps, enter the following expressions on the command line. If you get lost at any time or do not return to the Command: prompt when expected, press the [Esc] key to cancel the AutoLISP entry.

```
Command: (+ 6 2).⏎
8
Command: (+ 6.0 2).⏎
8.0
Command: (– 15 9).⏎
6
Command: (* 4 6).⏎
24
Command: (/ 12 3).⏎
4
Command: (/ 12 3.2).⏎
3.75
Command: (/ 19 10).⏎
1
```

An "incorrect" answer is returned in the last example. The result of dividing 19 by 10 is 1.9. When only integers are supplied as arguments, the result is returned as an integer. If the result is rounded, it rounds to 2. However, the returned result is simply the integer portion of the actual answer. The result is not rounded, it is truncated. To get the correct result in division expressions such as the one above, specify at least one of the arguments as a real number.

```
Command: (/ 19.0 10).⏎
1.9
```

When entering real numbers between 1 and –1, you must include the leading zero. If the zero is not entered, you will get an error message:

```
Command: (+ .5 16).⏎
; error: misplaced dot on input
Command:
```

The correct entry is:

```
Command: (+ 0.5 16).⏎
16.5
```

Exercise 24-1

Complete the exercise on the Student CD.

Nested Expressions

The term *nested* refers to an expression that is used as part of another expression. For example, to add 15 to the product of 3.75 and 2.125, you can nest the multiplication expression within the AutoLISP addition expression. Notice the two closing parentheses:

```
Command: (+ 15 (* 3.75 2.125)).⏎
22.9688
```

Nested expressions are evaluated from the deepest nested level outward. In the previous expression, the multiplication operation is evaluated first and the result is applied to the addition operation. Here are some examples of nested expressions:

```
Command: (+ 24 (* 5 4)).⏎
44
Command: (* 12 (/ 60 20)).⏎
36
Command: (/ 39 (* 1.6 11)).⏎
2.21591
```

Significant Digits

AutoLISP performs all mathematical calculations to 15 decimal places, but only displays six significant digits. For example, take a close look at this expression:

```
Command: (+ 15 (* 3.75 2.125)).⏎
22.9688
```

The actual result is 22.96875, but AutoLISP displays only six significant digits on the command line and rounds the number for display only. This is true for large and small numbers alike. The next example shows how AutoLISP uses exponential notation to display larger numbers using only six digits:

```
Command: (* 1000 1575.25).⏎
1.57525e+006
```

This final example uses a numeric printing function (real to string) set to show eight decimal places in order to indicate that the number is not actually rounded and that no precision is lost:

```
Command: (rtos (+ 15 (* 3.75 2.125)) 2 8).⏎
"22.96875000"
```

Exercise 24-2
Complete the exercise on the Student CD.

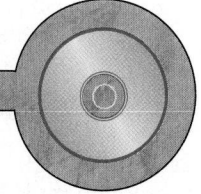

Variables

All programming languages make use of *variables* to temporarily store information. The variable name can be used in an expression anywhere in the program. When AutoLISP encounters a variable in an expression, it uses the value of the variable to evaluate the expression. An AutoLISP variable name cannot be made up of numeric characters only, nor can it contain any of the following characters.

- Open parenthesis (()
- Close parenthesis ())
- Period (.)

- Apostrophe (')
- Quotation marks ("")
- Semicolon (;)

The **(setq)** AutoLISP function is used to set variable values. A **(setq)** expression requires a variable name and value as arguments. The following example shows an expression that creates a variable named **A** and assigns it a value of 5.

Command: **(setq A 5)**↵
5

If you try to use an illegal variable name, an error message is returned. The following example tries to create a variable named **2** with an assigned value of 7. Since **2** is not a valid variable name, an error message is returned.

Command: **(setq 2 7)**↵
; error: syntax error

Once a valid variable name has been assigned a value, the variable can be used in subsequent AutoLISP expressions, or even directly accessed on the command line. To access a variable value on the command line, precede the variable name with an exclamation mark (!). For example:

Command: **C** *or* **CIRCLE**↵
Specify center point for circle or [3P/2P/Ttr (tan tan radius)]: *(pick a point)*
Specify radius of circle or [Diameter] <*current*>: **!A**↵
5
Command:

To use the value of a variable in any expression, simply include the variable in the appropriate location. The following sequence sets and uses a series of variables.

Command: **(setq A 5)**↵
5
Command: **(setq B (– A 1))**↵
4
Command: **(setq C (– A B))**↵
1
Command: **(setq D (* (+ A B) 2))**↵
18

Look closely at the example illustrated in Figure 24-1. Find the three separate expressions inside of parentheses. AutoLISP evaluates Expression 3 first. The result is applied to Expression 2, which is then evaluated. The result of Expression 2 is applied to Expression 1. The final evaluation determines the value of the variable **D**.

Figure 24-1.
Each AutoLISP expression must be enclosed within parentheses. In this evaluation of variable **D**, expression 3 is evaluated first, then expression 2, and finally expression 1.

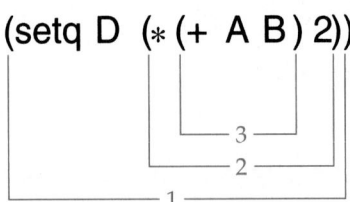

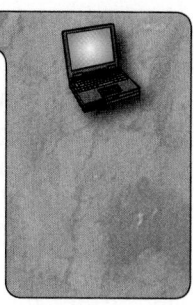

When working with AutoLISP on the command line, use AutoCAD's command line editing features to your best advantage. Remember that you can use the up and down arrow keys to display previously entered lines of code. Additionally, you can use the left and right arrow keys to position the cursor to delete or insert text within a line. You may also find it convenient to turn off dynamic input while entering AutoLISP expressions on the command line.

Exercise 24-3
Complete the exercise on the Student CD.

AutoLISP Program Files

Entering AutoLISP expressions on the command line is suitable for applications that are simple or unique. However, when more complex expressions are required or when the expressions you are using may be needed again, it is best to save them in an AutoLISP program file. This can be easily accomplished using the **Visual LISP Editor** provided with AutoCAD. AutoLISP programs can be more effectively developed using the **Visual LISP Editor**. Creating AutoLISP program files is discussed in the following sections.

A very common feature found in most AutoLISP programs is a function definition. A *function definition* is a collection of AutoLISP code that performs any number of tasks. The function is assigned a name that is used to activate the code. Some function definitions create new AutoCAD command names that can be entered at the command line.

Once written and saved, an AutoLISP program can be loaded and used whenever it is needed. By default, AutoCAD automatically loads the acad2008.lsp file, if it is located in the support file search path, when you first begin a drawing session. The acad2008doc.lsp file is loaded with each drawing that is opened. Any new AutoLISP commands or functions that you define in this file will be available in every drawing during a session.

An AutoLISP program file must be a "plain" text file. If you choose to edit your AutoLISP files with a word processing program such as Microsoft Word or WordPerfect, be sure to save the files as "text only." Word processing files use special codes that AutoLISP cannot understand. It is recommended that you use the **Visual LISP Editor** because it has tools specifically designed for use in writing and editing AutoLISP programs.

Introduction to the Visual LISP Editor

The **Visual LISP Editor** provides powerful editing features. The editor is an *integrated development environment (IDE)* that features AutoLISP development tools not available in standard text editing programs. The **Visual LISP Editor** is an application containing many powerful tools and features. The interactive nature of the **Visual LISP Editor** simplifies the task of creating AutoLISP program files. This section provides only a brief introduction to Visual LISP. For a more detailed discussion of the features and applications of Visual LISP, refer to *Visual LISP Programming* available from Goodheart-Willcox Publisher.

The **VLIDE** command is used to open the **Visual LISP Editor**. When the **Visual LISP Editor** is first displayed, it appears as shown in **Figure 24-2**. The windows within the editor can be minimized or maximized, and the editor itself can be temporarily closed to return to AutoCAD as necessary.

To create a new AutoLISP program using the **Visual LISP Editor**, pick the **New file** button, select **New File** from the editor's **File** pull-down menu, or press [Ctrl]+[N]. This opens a window for an untitled document on the **Visual LISP Editor** desktop. See **Figure 24-3**. The windows and features in the **Visual LISP Editor** are:

- **Desktop.** This is the main area of the editor window. It is similar to the main program window in AutoCAD and can be used to relocate toolbars or windowed components, such as the **Visual LISP Console** or a text editor window.
- **Text editor window.** Text editor windows are used to write and edit AutoLISP programs. Different windows can be used to create new files or view existing programs. The **Visual LISP Editor** provides interactive feedback as you enter material to help you avoid errors.
- **Visual LISP Console window.** This window provides several functions. You can use it to enter any AutoLISP expression to immediately see the results, or you can enter any AutoLISP variable to determine its value. You can also enter Visual LISP commands from this window and copy the text from the window to a text editor window.
- **Trace window.** This window is minimized when you first display the **Visual LISP Editor**. It records a history of the functions within your program and can be used to trace values when developing or debugging a program.

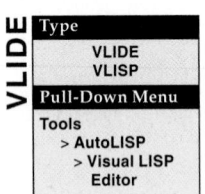

Figure 24-2.
The primary features of the **Visual LISP Editor**.

Pull-down menu bar

New file button

Activate AutoCAD button

Desktop

Enter an AutoLISP expression or variable

Status bar

Trace window (minimized)

Figure 24-3.
Picking the **New file** button or selecting **New File** from the **File** pull-down menu displays a text editor window in the **Visual LISP Editor**.

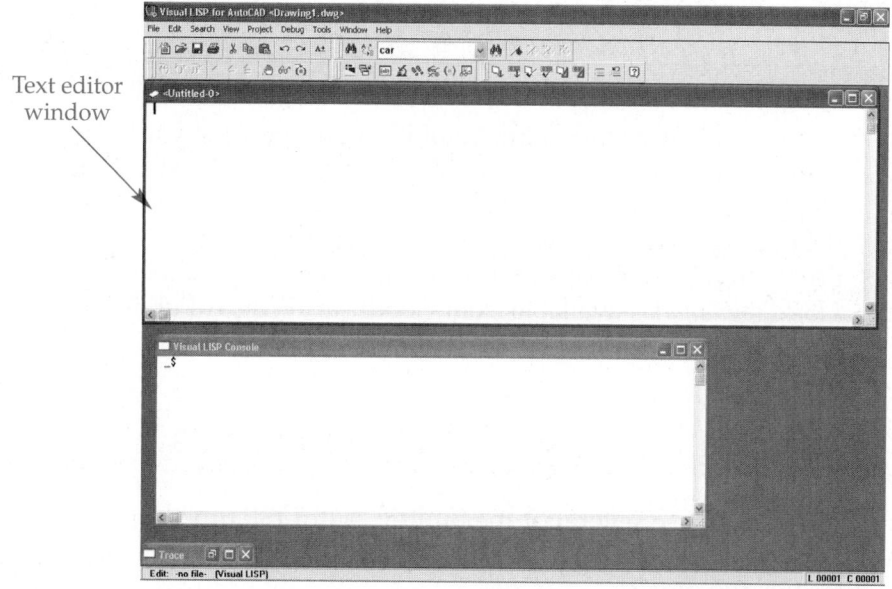

- **Status bar.** This area at the bottom of the **Visual LISP Editor** is similar to the status bar in AutoCAD's main program window. It provides feedback regarding the status of the current window or application being used.

Several visual aids are provided to help identify functions as you enter text. For example, as you construct the expressions that make up your program, a color coding system provides immediate feedback as you type. Text for any unrecognized items, such as a user variable or a portion of a function, is shown in black. For example, if you enter the **(setq)** function, the text is shown in black until you have entered the letters set. Because AutoLISP recognizes the text entry as the valid function **(set)**, a function not covered in this book, the color of the text is changed to blue. When you have entered the full **(setq)** function name, the text remains blue because AutoLISP also recognizes this function name. This can be very useful, because if you enter a function name and the text does not turn blue, you know that you have made an incorrect entry. The default color coding system used in the **Visual LISP Editor** appears in the following chart.

AutoLISP Text Elements	Associated Color
Built-in functions and protected symbols	Blue
Text strings	Magenta
Integers	Green
Real numbers	Teal
Comments	Purple on a gray background
Parentheses	Red
Unrecognized items	Black

Another valuable visual aid provided by the **Visual LISP Editor** is instant parenthesis matching. When you enter a closing parenthesis in an expression, the cursor jumps to the opening parenthesis and then returns back to the current position. If the closing parenthesis does not have a match, the cursor does not jump. This helps indicate that a matching parenthesis is needed.

Once you have entered one or more expressions in the **Visual LISP Editor**, you can save the file and then test the results in the **Visual LISP Console** window. Or, you can return to AutoCAD to test your results.

Defining New AutoCAD Commands

In this section, you will use several of the built-in AutoLISP functions to create a new AutoCAD command. The **(defun)** AutoLISP function (define function) is used for this. The syntax for this function is:

(defun *FunctionName* (*ArgumentList*)
(*Expression*)...
)

The function name can be any alphanumeric name and is subject to the same conditions as for any variable name assigned with the **(setq)** function. If you prefix the function name with **C:**, the name can be entered on the command line in AutoCAD.

You must include an argument list in every function definition, even if the list is empty. The argument list is used to declare local variables and, in more advanced applications, to indicate which arguments are required by a function. For many applications, the argument list is simply left empty.

Any number of expressions can be included in a function definition. All of the expressions contained in the definition are evaluated when the function name is called.

A very powerful, yet simple, application for a function definition is to create a short-cut command similar to one of the command aliases in the acad.pgp file. However, a short-cut command defined using AutoLISP can specify command options and even multiple commands to use. Remember that the command aliases defined in the acad.pgp file can only start a single command; they cannot specify any command options.

This first example shows the definition for a new function named **ZX**. The function issues the **ZOOM** command and performs the **Previous** option.

```
(defun C:ZX ()
   (command "ZOOM" "PREVIOUS")
)
```

To see this function work, enter the definition at the command line as:

Command: **(defun C:ZX () (command "zoom" "previous"))**↵
C:ZX

Notice that the new function name is returned by the **(defun)** function. The **C:** prefix indicates that it can be entered at the Command: prompt.

Command: **ZX**↵
Command: nil
Command:

When activated, defined functions return the value of the last expression evaluated in the definition. Since the **(command)** function always returns a value of "nil," this is returned when using the **ZX** function. The "nil" value has no effect. You can suppress it if you do not want it to appear each time you use a defined function. To suppress the value, add the **(princ)** function using no arguments to the end of the definition:

```
(defun C:ZX ()
  (command "ZOOM" "PREVIOUS")
  (princ)
)
```

Entering a function definition on the command line is an inconvenient way to define custom functions. By storing such definitions in a text file, they can be loaded whenever needed.

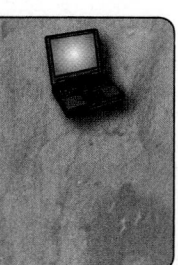

PROFESSIONAL TIP

When defining new command names, keep in mind that most AutoCAD users are one-handed typists because the other hand is used for the pointing device. For example, when deciding on the name for a function that performs a **ZOOM Previous**, it may be easier for the user to type the [Z]+[X] key combination rather than [Z]+[P]. The [Z] and [P] keys are in opposite corners of the keyboard.

Creating Your First AutoLISP Program

As discussed earlier, a typical use for an AutoLISP program file is to hold function definitions. An AutoLISP program file can contain a single function or it can contain several. Many AutoLISP programs are created to perform a single, specific task. Other AutoLISP programs hold a large number of function definitions, all of which become available when the program file is loaded. One common application for the acad2008doc.lsp file is to create a series of function definitions for shortcut commands used to speed up routine drafting tasks.

Writing the Program

To create your first AutoLISP program, open the **Visual LISP Editor** or another text editing application and start a new document (file). Begin by entering two function definitions into the program. The first is the **ZX** function from the previous example. The second defines a command named **FC** (fillet corner) that sets the fillet radius to 0 and allows the **FILLET** command to continue.

```
(defun C:ZX ()
  (command "ZOOM" "PREVIOUS")
  (princ)
)

(defun C:FC ()
  (command "FILLET" "RADIUS" 0 "FILLET" "MULTIPLE")
  (princ)
)
```

When using the **Visual LISP Editor**, the final closing parenthesis is not automatically "flush left." You will need to delete the spaces added. It is a good habit to place the final closing parenthesis "flush left" to help keep your program organized.

Adding the appropriate documentation to your program files is recommended. When a semicolon (;) is encountered in a program (except when it is part of a text string), any information to the right of the semicolon is ignored. This enables you to place *comments* and documentation in your AutoLISP programs. The example below shows the appropriate documentation for this program file, called myfirst.lsp.

```
; MyFirst.lsp
; by A. Novice

;C:ZX – To key ZOOM Previous command.
(defun C:ZX ()
   (command "ZOOM" "PREVIOUS")
   (princ)
)

;C:FC – Fillet Corner: Sets fillet radius to 0 and
;allows FILLET command to continue.
 (defun C:FC ()
    (command "FILLET" "RADIUS" 0 "FILLET")
    (princ)
)
```

After entering these functions and comments into the new LISP program, save the file as myfirst.lsp in the AutoCAD or your user's \Support folder.

Loading the Program

The **APPLOAD** command is used to load applications, such as AutoLISP program files, into AutoCAD. Once the command is selected in AutoCAD, the **Load/Unload Applications** dialog box appears, Figure 24-4. A list of currently loaded applications appears in the **Loaded Applications** tab. To load an application file, select it in the file selection window near the top of the dialog box. You can highlight any number of files in the file list. Picking the **Load** button loads the currently selected application file(s). If the **Add to History** check box is activated, the loaded file(s) will be added to the list in the **History list** tab. This tab provides convenient access to saved files during subsequent **APPLOAD** sessions and keeps you from having to search for frequently used files every time they are needed. Picking the **Unload** button removes any highlighted files from the **History list** tab or **Loaded Applications** tab.

You can also load an AutoLISP file by highlighting the file in Windows Explorer and dragging and dropping it into the AutoCAD drawing area. This method is extremely convenient if Windows Explorer is open.

The **(load)** function allows you to load an AutoLISP program file on the command line. This function requires an AutoLISP file name as its argument and requires that the name be enclosed in quotation marks. To load the myfirst.lsp file using the **(load)** function, the following sequence is used.

```
Command: (load "myfirst").⏎
C:FC
Command:
```

When the file has a .lsp file extension, it is not necessary to include the extension in the **(load)** expression. Therefore, you should use the standard .lsp file extension for all AutoLISP files you create. If you are loading an AutoLISP file that does not use a .lsp file extension, the actual extension must be included in the file name argument.

When an AutoLISP program file is loaded and no errors are encountered, the result of evaluating the last expression in the file is returned to the screen. In the example above, the last expression in the file is the definition for the **FC** function, so that function name is returned.

Figure 24-4.
The **Load/Unload Applications** dialog box is used to load AutoLISP program files into AutoCAD.

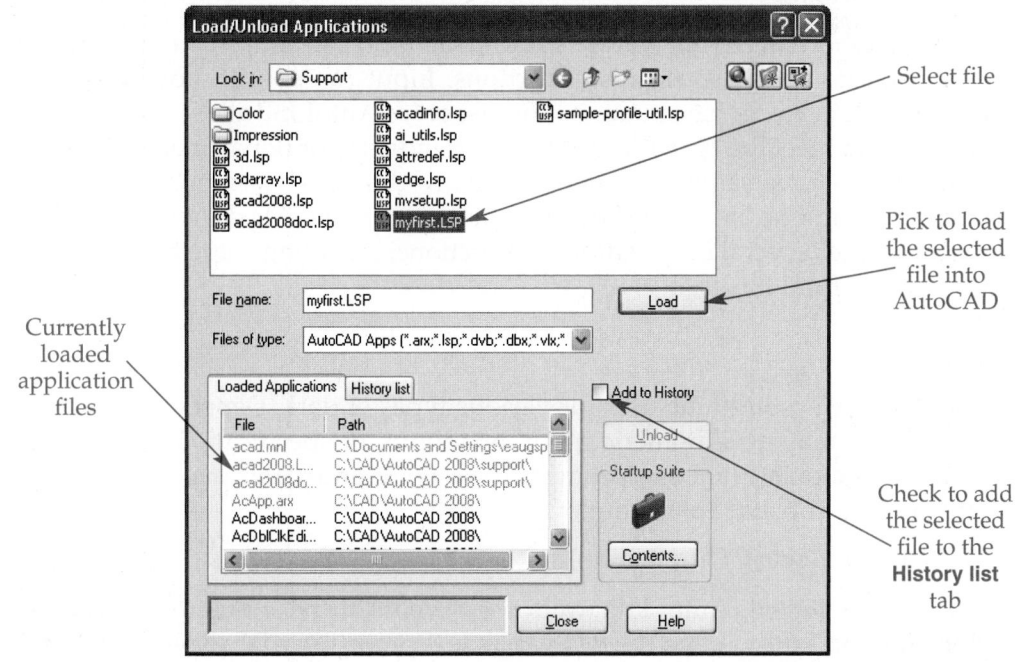

The **(load)** function locates AutoLISP files residing in the support file search path. To load a file that exists elsewhere, the path name must also be specified. In the following example, the myfirst.lsp file is stored in the C:\My Documents\AutoLISP folder.

Command: **(load "c:/my documents/autolisp/myfirst")**↵
C:FC

Notice that backslashes are not used in the path specification. In an AutoLISP text string, the backslash is used to specify special characters. For example, the string **\n** indicates a new line, or carriage return. When specifying file paths, you can use either forward slashes, as shown above, or double backslashes (\\). Therefore, in the example above, the file to load could also have been specified as c:\\my documents\\autolisp\\myfirst.

If you frequently load files that are in a folder not found in the support file search path, it may be helpful to include the folder in the path. This is done using the **Options** dialog box. After displaying this dialog box, pick the **Files** tab and select Support File Search Path. Then, pick the **Add...** button and enter the desired folder. Refer to Chapter 19 for detailed information.

As previously indicated, when you have defined one or more functions that you want to have available in all editing sessions, the definitions can be placed in the acad-2008doc.lsp file. If the acad2008doc.lsp file already exists on your system, consult your system administrator or instructor prior to directly editing this file. The acad2008.lsp and acad2008doc.lsp files are often used by third-party applications. Changing them or accidentally redefining existing commands or functions may render certain features unusable.

Exercise 24-4
Complete the exercise on the Student CD.

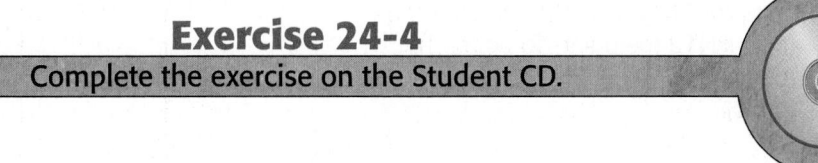

Creating Specialized Functions

Although shortcut commands are a powerful use for AutoLISP, AutoLISP can also be used to create highly specialized functions. Input can specify how the program should function in any given situation. This aspect of AutoLISP allows you to customize AutoCAD to meet the specific needs of your industry or department.

AutoLISP is a versatile tool, offering many different functions for effectively working with numeric data, text data, data files, and AutoCAD drawing objects. This section introduces several basic AutoLISP functions, including some that are used for acquiring input from the user.

Providing for User Input

AutoLISP can prompt the user for various types of data. Depending on its function, a program may need numeric input, text input, or specification of a coordinate location. The **(getpoint)** function prompts for a point entry and pauses the program until the point is entered. For example:

Command: **(setq PT1 (getpoint)).⏎**

After you press [Enter], AutoLISP waits for a value to be input for the **(getpoint)** function and stores the value in the **PT1** variable. A prompt can be added to the original expression to clarify it as follows.

Command: **(setq PT1 (getpoint "Enter a point: ")).⏎**
Enter a point:

Now, pick a point on screen. The coordinates for the selected point are assigned to **PT1** and displayed on the command line. If you know the coordinates, you can enter them at the keyboard.

The following example shows how closely AutoCAD and AutoLISP work together. First, define the two variables **PT1** and **PT2** as shown below. Then, enter the **LINE** command and use AutoLISP notation to return the values of **PT1** and **PT2** as the endpoints of the line.

Command: **(setq PT1 (getpoint "From point: ")).⏎**
From point: **2,2**⏎
(2.0 2.0 0.0)
Command: **(setq PT2 (getpoint "To point: ")).⏎**
To point: **6.25,2**⏎
(6.25 2.0 0.0)
Command: **LINE**⏎
Specify first point: **!PT1**⏎
(2.0 2.0 0.0)
Specify next point or [Undo]: **!PT2**⏎
(6.25 2.0 0.0)
Specify next point or [Undo]: ⏎

The following is a sample function definition named **1LINE** that uses expressions similar to those given in the previous example. This function will draw a line object based on user input.

```
(defun C:1LINE ()
    (setq PNT1 (getpoint "From point: "))
    (setq PNT2 (getpoint "To point: "))
    (command "LINE" PNT1 PNT2 "")
    (princ)
)
```

The **(command)** function is used to call AutoCAD commands from within AutoLISP. Typically, an AutoCAD command that is "started" within a program is also "ended" within the program. The pair of quotation marks near the end of the fourth line is equivalent to pressing [Enter] after the second point entry, thus ending the **LINE** command.

When developing AutoLISP routines, you may need to assign the length of a line or the distance between two points to a variable. The **(getdist)** function allows you to assign a distance to a variable. A command line prompt is not added to the following example; the "second point" prompt is automatic.

> Command: **(setq LGTH (getdist))**↵
> *(pick the first point)*
> Specify second point: *(pick the second point)*
> *distance*

Use object snaps as needed or enter absolute coordinates. After the second point is specified, the distance value is shown and assigned to the variable. In this example, the distance is assigned to the variable **LGTH**. You can confirm the setting by retrieving the value of the variable.

> Command: **!LGTH**↵
> *distance*

The **(distance)** function is similar to the **(getdist)** function. However, the **(distance)** function does not require picking two points. Instead, it measures the distance between two *existing* points. This function can be used to display a distance or to assign a distance to a variable.

> Command: **(distance PT1 PT2)**↵
> *distance between **PT1** and **PT2***

> Command: **(setq D1 (distance PT1 PT2))**↵
> *distance between **PT1** and **PT2***

The first example returns the distance between the previously defined points **PT1** and **PT2**. The second example displays the distance *and* applies it to the variable **D1**.

PROFESSIONAL TIP

The sample AutoLISP expressions in this section are entered at the command line. However, AutoLISP expressions are more effective as part of a saved program file.

Exercise 24-5

Complete the exercise on the Student CD.

Assigning Text Values to AutoLISP Applications

Values assigned to AutoLISP variables do not have to be numeric. In some applications, you may need to assign a word or line of text to a variable. To do so, use the **(setq)** function and enclose the word(s) in quotation marks.

> Command: **(setq W "What next?")**↵
> "What next?"

You can also assign a word or line of text to a variable with the **(getstring)** function. This function is similar to the **(getpoint)** function in that the user must enter a value.

> Command: **(setq E (getstring))**↵

Nothing is displayed on the command line because the optional prompt was not specified. AutoLISP is waiting for a "string" of characters. You can enter as many characters (numbers and letters) as needed. Once you press [Enter] or the spacebar, the string is entered and displayed. To allow spaces in the response, place the letter **T**, without quotation marks, after the **(getstring)** function:

> Command: **(setq E (getstring T))**↵
> **HI THERE.**↵
> "HI THERE"
> Command:

The **(prompt)** function can be used to simply display a message. The resulting message has no variable value. AutoLISP indicates this by printing nil after the prompt.

> Command: **(prompt "Select an object: ")**↵
> Select an object: nil

You can use prompts in AutoLISP programs to provide information or to prompt the user.

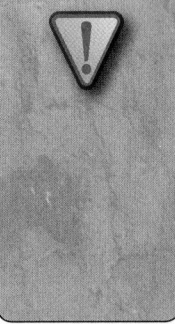

CAUTION

The symbol **T** is a built-in AutoLISP constant defined as a *protected symbol*. However, it is possible to change its value using the **(setq)** function. Do *not* change its value. Be certain not to use the variable name **T** for any of your own variables, or other functions referencing this symbol may not properly function. If it is accidentally changed, you can reset the value of **T** using the following expression.

> Command: **(setq T 'T)**↵

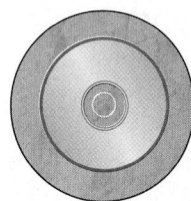

Exercise 24-6
Complete the exercise on the Student CD.

Basic AutoLISP Review

Before applying the functions you have learned to an AutoLISP program, take a few minutes to review the following list. These functions are used in the next chapter, which discusses more advanced AutoLISP applications.

- **(+), (−), (*), (/).** These are the basic math functions used in AutoLISP. They must be entered as the first part of an expression. For example, (+ 6 8).
- **(setq).** The **(setq)** function allows a value to be assigned to a variable. For example, the expression (setq CITY "San Francisco") sets the value San Francisco to the variable **CITY**.
- **!.** An exclamation point entered before a variable returns the value of the variable. For example, !CITY returns the value San Francisco for the above expression.

AutoCAD and Its Applications—Advanced

- **(getpoint).** This function allows you to define a point location by entering coordinates at the keyboard or using the pointing device. The resulting value can be applied to a variable. For example, the expression (setq A (getpoint)) assigns a point to the variable **A**.

- **(getdist).** This function returns the distance between two points entered at the keyboard or picked on screen. The value can be applied to a variable and a prompt can be used. For example, the expression (setq D2 (getdist "Pick two points:")) allows you to determine a distance and assign it to the variable **D2**.

- **(distance).** This function returns a distance between two existing points. For example, the expression (distance P1 P2) returns the distance between the defined points **P1** and **P2**. The distance can also be assigned to a variable. For example, (setq D (distance P1 P2)).

- **(getstring).** This function returns a word or string of characters entered by the user. The resulting text can be assigned to a variable. For example, the expression (getstring) waits for a string of characters and displays the string when [Enter] or the spacebar is pressed. Spaces are allowed in the text string if **T** follows the **(getstring)** function. For example, the expression (setq TXT (getstring T "Enter text:")) assigns the text entered, which can contain spaces, to the variable **TXT**.

- **(prompt).** Messages or prompts can be issued in a program using the **(prompt)** function. For example, the expression (prompt "Select an entity:") prints the Select an entity: prompt.

PROFESSIONAL TIP

Design your AutoLISP programs to closely resemble the AutoCAD interface. For example, it is easier for the user to read "back-to-back" prompts when the prompts appear on separate lines. Use the **\n** string to specify a new line for a prompt. For example:

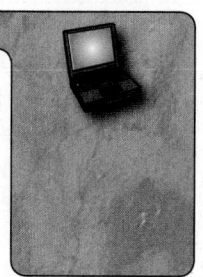

(setq PT2 (getpoint "\nTo point:"))

Exercise 24-7

Complete the exercise on the Student CD.

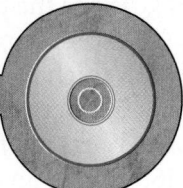

Chapter Test

Answer the following questions. Write your answers on a separate sheet of paper or complete the electronic chapter test on the Student CD.

1. What is the standard extension used for AutoLISP program files?
2. A comment is indicated in an AutoLISP file with a(n) _____.
3. When in the drawing area, what are three ways to load the contents of the AutoLISP file named chgtext.lsp?
4. Define the terms *integer* and *real number* as related to AutoLISP.
5. Write expressions in the proper AutoLISP format for the following arithmetic functions.
   A. 23 + 54
   B. 12.45 + 6.28
   C. 56 − 34
   D. 23.004 − 7.008
   E. 16 × 4.6
   F. 7.25 × 10.30
   G. 45 ÷ 23
   H. 147 ÷ 29.6
   I. 53 + (12 × 3.8)
   J. 567 ÷ (34 − 14)
6. Explain the purpose of the **(setq)** function.
7. Write the proper AutoLISP notation to assign the value of (67 − 34.5) to the variable **NUM1**.
8. What does the **(getpoint)** function allow you to do?
9. Which AutoLISP functions allow you to find the distance between two points? Describe the difference between the two functions.
10. Explain the purpose of the **(getstring)** function.
11. Write the proper AutoLISP notation for assigning the string This is a test: to the variable **TXT**.
12. How do you allow spaces in a string of text when using the **(getstring)** function?
13. Write the proper notation for using the **PLINE** command in an AutoLISP expression.
14. Which prefix must you enter before a function name in an expression to indicate it is accessible at the Command: prompt?
15. What is a *function definition?*
16. Define an *argument*.
17. Which AutoLISP function is used to create new AutoCAD commands?
18. What is the purpose of the **Visual LISP Editor**?
19. How is the **Visual LISP Editor** accessed?
20. When entering text in the **Visual LISP Editor**, which color indicates that you have entered a built-in function or a protected symbol?
21. Explain the purpose of the \n text string in AutoLISP.

Drawing Problems

*Write AutoLISP programs for the following problems. Use the **Visual LISP Editor**. Save the files as P24-(problem number) with the .lsp extension.*

1. Write an AutoLISP program to draw a rectangle. Use the **(getpoint)** function to set the opposite corners of the rectangle. Follow these guidelines:
   A. Set **P1** as the first corner.
   B. Set **P3** as the opposite corner.
   C. Use the **RECTANG** command to draw the rectangle using **P1** and **P3** in place of picking corners.
   D. The users should not be able to change any options in the **RECTANG** command.

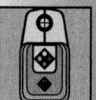

2. Create an AutoLISP program to draw a square. Follow these guidelines:
   A. Set a variable for the length of one side.
   B. Set the variable **P1** as the lower-left corner of the square.
   C. Use the **RECTANG** command to draw the square.

3. Revise the program in Problem 2 to draw a square with filleted corners.
   A. The fillet radius should be equal to 1/4 of the side length.
   B. After the fillet rectangle is drawn, reset the fillet radius so the next rectangle drawn with the **RECTANG** command does not automatically have fillets. Note: Use ^C to cancel a command that you do not want to complete. For example:

   (command "LINE" PT1 ^C)

4. Use the program in Problem 3 to create a new command that draws a square with thick lines.
   A. The line thickness should be a percentage of the fillet radius (between 5% and 10%).
   B. Reset the line thickness so that the next rectangle drawn with the **RECTANG** command does not automatically have thick lines. Note: Use ^C to cancel a command that you do not want to complete. For example:

   (command "LINE" PT1 ^C)

5. Write an AutoLISP program that allows the user to draw parallel rectangles.
   A. Provide a prompt that asks the user to enter an offset distance for a second rectangle to be placed inside the first rectangle.
   B. Use the **OFFSET** command to allow the user to draw the parallel rectangle inside the original without entering an offset distance.

AutoLISP programs do not need to be complex to be very useful. This program, which is fully documented, allows the user to select an arc and turn it into a circle. AutoCAD does not have the ability to extend an arc into a circle. At the bottom of the page, the program is shown as it appears in the **Visual LISP Editor**.

```lisp
;;;
;;;
;;;                    ARC2CIR.lsp
;;;                   by Craig P. Black
;;;              original release date: 6/7/xx
;;;
;;;
;;;   This program was written to handle AutoCAD's inability to
;;;   extend an arc into a circle. AutoCAD can trim a circle into
;;;   an arc, but not vice-versa.

(defun C:ARC2CIR                          ; defines a command named ARC2CIR
    (/ CMD ARC EDATA CPT RAD LYR)         ; localizes variables used in program
    (setq CMD (getvar "CMDECHO"))         ; stores value of cmdecho sysvar
    (setvar "CMDECHO" 0)                  ; sets cmdecho sysvar to off
    (setq ARC (entsel "\nSelect arc: "))  ; allows use to select an arc
    (setq EDATA (entget (car ARC)))       ; stores the data associated with the arc
    (setq CPT (assoc 10 EDATA))           ; stores the center point of the arc
    (setq RAD (assoc 40 EDATA))           ; stores the radius of the arc
    (setq LYR (assoc 8 EDATA))            ; stores the layer of the arc
    (entdel (car ARC))                    ; deletes the existing arc
    (entmake   (list                      ; creates a new entity
            (cons 0 "CIRCLE")             ; the entity will be a circle
            CPT                           ; the circle will use the arc's center point
            RAD                           ; the circle will use the arc's radius
            LYR                           ; the circle will use the arc's layer
        )
    )
    (princ)                               ; cleanly exits the program
)
```

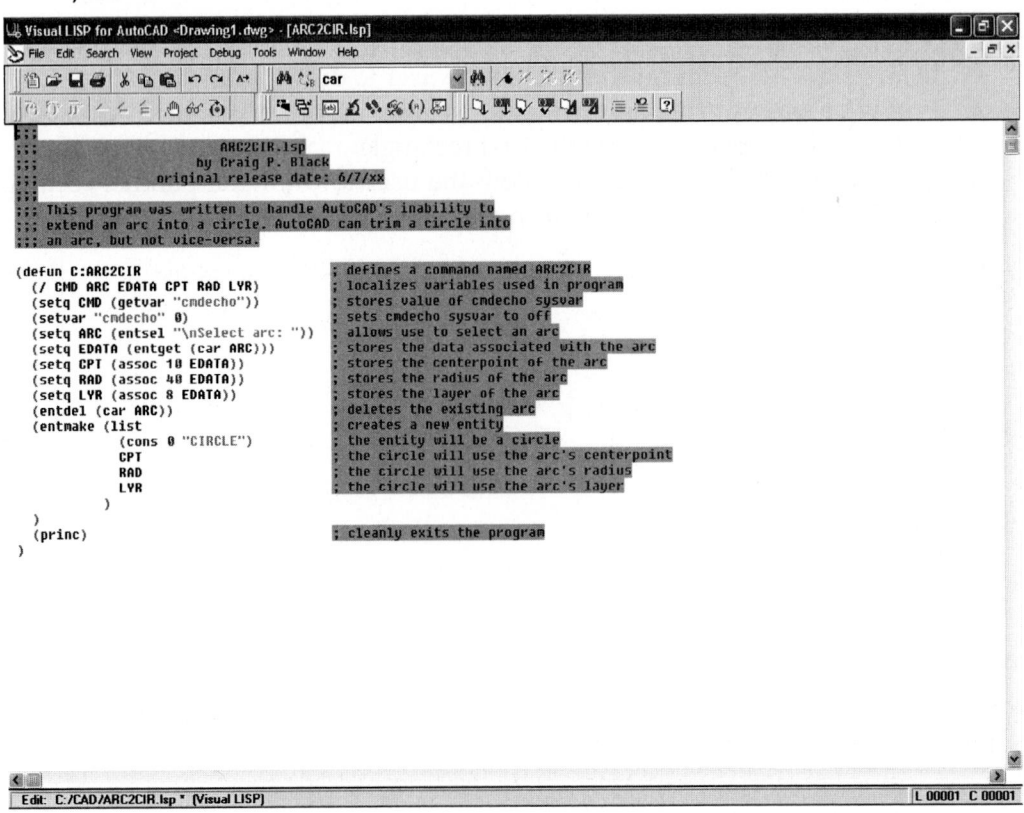

CHAPTER 25

Beyond AutoLISP Basics

Learning Objectives

After completing this chapter, you will be able to:
- ✓ Identify ways to provide for user input.
- ✓ Retrieve and use system variable values in AutoLISP programs.
- ✓ Work with lists using AutoLISP.
- ✓ Use angular input in AutoLISP programs.

As you practice using AutoLISP, you will develop ideas for programs that require additional commands and functions. Some of these programs may require that the user pick two corners of a windowed selection set. Another program may use existing points to draw a shape. You may also need to locate a point using polar coordinate notation or determine the angle of a line. All of these drawing tasks can be done with AutoLISP programs.

Providing for Additional User Input

The **(getreal)** function allows you to define a variable value by entering a real number at the keyboard. Remember, as defined by AutoLISP, real numbers are classified separately from integers. A real number is considered to be more precise than an integer because it has a decimal value.

The **(getreal)** function works with numbers as units. You cannot respond with a value of feet and inches. Once issued, the function waits for user input. A prompt can be included. The real number is returned after a response is entered. The **(getreal)** function can be used to set the value of a variable as follows.

```
Command: (setq X (getreal "Enter number: ")).↵
Enter number: 34.↵
34.0
```

The **(getcorner)** function allows the user to pick the opposite corner of a rectangle and define it as a point value. This is similar to placing a window around objects to define a selection set in a drawing. An existing point serves as the first corner of the rectangle. When locating the opposite corner, the screen cursor appears as a "rubber band" box similar to the window used when defining a selection set.

The **(getcorner)** function can also be used to set the value of a variable. The second corner can be picked with the pointing device or entered at the keyboard. The following is an example of using the **(getcorner)** function.

> Command: **(setq PT1 (getpoint "\nPick a point:"))**↵
> Pick a point: *(pick the point)*
> Command: **(setq PT2 (getcorner PT1 "\nPick the second corner:"))**↵
> Pick the second corner: *(pick the corner)*

Notice that the value of **PT1** is set first. The point represented by **PT1** becomes the base point for locating **PT2**. The two points (corners) located in this example can be used to construct an angled line, rectangle, or other shape. The points can also be applied to other functions.

Using the Values of System Variables

AutoCAD's system variables can be read and changed from within AutoLISP applications with the **(getvar)** and **(setvar)** functions. These functions can be useful if an application requires you to store the value of a system variable in an AutoLISP variable, change the system variable setting for your program, and then reset the system variable to its original value.

The **(getvar)** function is used to return the value of a system variable. In the following example, two system variable settings are saved as AutoLISP variable values.

> Command: **(setq V1 (getvar "TEXTSIZE"))**↵
> *current value of the* **TEXTSIZE** *system variable*
> Command: **(setq V2 (getvar "FILLETRAD"))**↵
> *current value of the* **FILLETRAD** *system variable*

The **(setvar)** function is used to change an AutoCAD system variable setting. You can assign a new value to a variable as follows.

> Command: **(setvar "TEXTSIZE" 0.25)**↵
> 0.25
> Command: **(setvar "FILLETRAD" 0.25)**↵
> 0.25

Remember, you need to add the 0 in front of .25 or an error is generated.

Suppose you need to save a current system variable setting, change the variable, and then reset the variable to its original value after the command is executed. The **(getvar)** function can be used to assign the original value to a variable, such as **V1** shown in the first example on the **TEXTSIZE** system variable above. When the program is complete, the **(setvar)** function can be used to reset **TEXTSIZE** to its original value.

> Command: **(setvar "TEXTSIZE" V1)**↵
> 0.125

This returns the value of **TEXTSIZE** to the value of the variable **V1**, which is the original system variable setting.

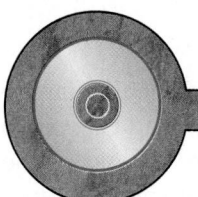

Exercise 25-1
Complete the exercise on the Student CD.

Working with Lists

In AutoLISP, a *list* is defined as a stored set of values that are enclosed in parentheses. Lists are commonly used to provide point locations and other data for use in functions. A list is created, for example, when you pick a point on screen in response to the **(getpoint)** function. The list is composed of three numbers—the X, Y, and Z coordinate values. You can tell it is a list because AutoLISP returns the numbers enclosed in parentheses. On the other hand, a number entered in response to the **(getreal)** function is returned as a real number (it is not enclosed in parentheses). A single number is not a list. The following expression returns a list.

> Command: **(setq P1 (getpoint "Enter point:"))**↵
> Enter point: *(pick a point)*
> (2.0 2.75 0.0)

The individual values in a list are called *atoms* and can be used in an AutoLISP program to create new points. The **(car)** function retrieves the first atom in a list. The variable **P1** in the example above is composed of the list (2.0 2.75 0.0). Thus, using the **(car)** function with the **P1** variable returns a value of 2.0.

> Command: **(car P1)**↵
> 2.0

The second atom in a list is retrieved with the **(cadr)** function. Find the second atom of the list stored in the variable **P1** by entering the following.

> Command: **(cadr P1)**↵
> 2.75

You can create a new list of two coordinates by extracting values from existing points using the **(car)** and **(cadr)** functions. This is done with the **(list)** function. Values returned by this function are placed inside of parentheses. The coordinates of the first variable, **P1**, can be combined with the coordinates of a second point variable, named **P2**, to form a third point variable, named **P3**. Study the following example and **Figure 25-1.** The coordinates stored in the variable **P1** are (2.0 2.75).

> Command: **(setq P2 (getcorner P1 "Enter second point: "))**↵
> Enter second point: **6,4.5**↵
> (6.0 4.5 0.0)
> Command: **(setq P3 (list (car P2)(cadr P1)))**↵
> (6.0 2.75)

In AutoLISP, a function is followed by an argument. An *argument* consists of data on or with which a function operates. An expression must be composed of only one function and any required arguments. Therefore, the functions **(car)** and **(cadr)** must be separated because they are two different expressions combined to make a list. The **(car)** value of the list stored in **P2** is to be the X value of **P3**, so it is given first. The **(cadr)** value of the list stored in **P1** is placed second because it is to be the Y value of **P3**. Notice the number of closing parentheses at the end of the expression.

Figure 25-1.
A third point identified as **P3** has been created using the **(car)** value of the list **P2** and the **(cadr)** value of the list **P1**.

+ **P2**
X = 6.0 **(car P2)**
Y = 4.5 **(cadr P2)**

+ **P1**
X = 2.0 **(car P1)**
Y = 2.75 **(cadr P1)**

+ **P3**
X = 6.0 **(car P2)**
Y = 2.75 **(cadr P1)**

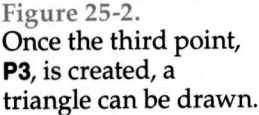

Figure 25-2.
Once the third point,
P3, is created, a
triangle can be drawn.

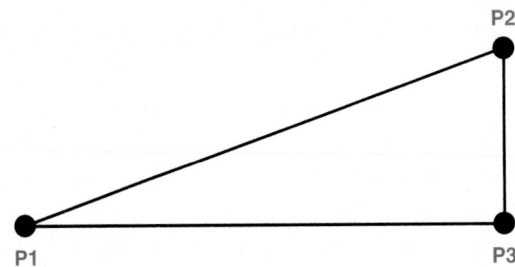

Now, with three points defined, there are many things you can do. For example, you can draw lines through the points to form a triangle, Figure 25-2. To do so, use the **(command)** function as follows.

Command: **(command "LINE" P1 P2 P3 "C")**↵

The **(car)** and **(cadr)** functions allow you to work with 2D coordinates. The **(caddr)** function allows you to use the third atom of a list. This can be the Z coordinate of a point. Enter the following at your keyboard.

Command: **(setq B (list 3 4 6))**↵
(3 4 6)

You have created a list of three atoms, or values, and assigned it to the variable **B**. The third value is retrieved with the **(caddr)** function.

Command: **(caddr B)**↵
6

Since 6 is a single value, not a list, it is not enclosed in parentheses. Now, use the **(car)** and **(cadr)** functions to find the other two atoms of the list.

Command: **(car B)**↵
3
Command: **(cadr B)**↵
4

The following is a short AutoLISP program that uses the **(car)** and **(cadr)** retrieval functions to place an X at the midpoint of two selected points.

```
(defun C:MDPNT ()
    (setq PT1 (getpoint "\nEnter the first point: "))
    (setq PT2 (getpoint "\nEnter the second point: "))
    (setq PT3 (list (/ (+ (car PT1) (car PT2)) 2) (/ (+ (cadr PT1) (cadr PT2)) 2)))
    (setvar "PDMODE" 3)
    (command "POINT" PT3)
)
```

The **(cdr)** function is also used to work with lists. It allows you to retrieve the second and remaining values of a list. Earlier in this discussion, the list (3 4 6) was assigned to variable **B**. In the following example, the **(cdr)** function is used to return the list (4 6).

Command: **(cdr B)**↵
(4 6)

This returns a list of two values, or coordinates, that can be further manipulated with the **(car)** and **(cadr)** functions. Study Figure 25-3 and the following examples.

Command: **(car (cdr B))**↵
4
Command: **(cadr (cdr B))**↵
6

Figure 25-3.
The **(cdr)** function
creates a list
containing the second
and remaining atoms
of a list. The new list
can be manipulated
as necessary with the
(car) and **(cadr)**
functions.

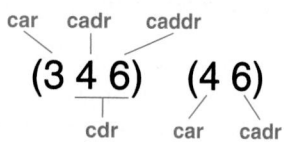

The first example is asking for the first atom—**(car)**—of the list generated from the last two atoms—**(cdr)**—of variable **B**. In the second example, the second atom— **(cadr)**—of the list generated from the last two atoms of variable **B** is returned.

The four functions used to manipulate lists—**(car)**, **(cadr)**, **(caddr)**, and **(cdr)**—may seem confusing at first. Practice using them to see how they work. Practice with a list of numbers, coordinate values, or text strings. Remember, text strings must be enclosed in quotation marks. Try the following examples to see what happens. Enter the expressions on the command line exactly as shown and press [Enter] at the end of each line.

```
(setq NOTES (list "DO" "RE" "MI"))
(car NOTES)
(cadr NOTES)
(caddr NOTES)
(cdr NOTES)
(setq LASTNOTES (cdr NOTES))
(car (cdr NOTES))
(cadr (cdr NOTES))
(car LASTNOTES)
(cadr LASTNOTES)
```

As you continue to work in AutoLISP, you will find many uses for the functions that allow you to work with lists. Remember the following review.

- **(car)**. Returns the first atom in a list.
- **(cadr)**. Returns the second atom in a list.
- **(caddr)**. Returns the third atom in a list.
- **(cdr)**. Returns the second and remaining atoms of a list. The returned values are placed in a list. If the original list contains two atoms, only the second atom is returned and it is placed in a list.
- **(list)**. Creates a list of all values entered as arguments to the function name.

Exercise 25-2

Complete the exercise on the Student CD.

Using Polar Coordinates and Angles

The ability to work with angles is vital if you plan to do much AutoLISP programming. Four functions—**(angle)**, **(polar)**, **(getangle)**, and **(getorient)**—allow you to use angles when writing program files. AutoLISP works with these functions using the radian system of angle measurement. This system of measurement is explained in the next section.

Measuring Angles in Radians

The **(angle)** function is used to calculate the angle in the XY plane of a line between two given points. The value of the angle is given in radians. *Radian angle measurement* is a system in which 180° equals "pi" (π). Pi is approximately equal to 3.14159.

AutoLISP functions use radians for angular measurement, but AutoCAD commands use degrees. Therefore, to use a radian angle in an AutoCAD command, it must first be converted to degrees. Conversely, a degree angle to be used by AutoLISP must be converted to radians. The following formulas are used for those conversions.

- To convert degrees to radians, use the formula:

(* pi (/ *ad* 180.0))

where *ad* = angle in degrees.

- To convert radians to degrees, use the formula:

(/ (* *ar* 180.0) pi)

where *ar* = angle in radians.

The following table gives common angles measured in degrees, the AutoLISP expressions used to convert the angular values to radian values, and the resulting values in radians to four decimal places.

Angle (degrees)	AutoLISP expression	Angle (radians)
0		0
30	(/ pi 6)	0.5236
45	(/ pi 4)	0.7854
60	(/ pi 3)	1.0472
90	(/ pi 2)	1.5708
135	(/ (* pi 3) 4)	2.3562
180	pi	3.1416
270	(/ (* pi 3) 2)	4.7124
360	(* pi 2)	6.2832

The following example illustrates how the angle between two points can be set to a variable, then converted to degrees.

```
Command: (setq P1 (getpoint "Enter first point: "))↵
Enter first point: 1.75,5.25↵
(1.75 5.25 0.0)
Command: (setq P2 (getpoint "Enter second point: "))↵
Enter second point: 6.75,7.25↵
(6.75 7.25 0.0)
Command: (setq A1 (angle P1 P2))↵
0.380506
```

The angle represented by the variable **A1** is measured in radians (0.380506). To convert this value to degrees, use the following expression.

```
Command: (/ (* A1 180.0) pi)↵
21.8014
Command: !A1↵
0.380506
```

The value 21.8014 is the angle in degrees between the coordinates in variables **P1** and **P2**. However, notice that this conversion does not set the variable **A1** to the value in degrees. Make the degree value permanent by assigning it to the variable using the following expression.

Command: **(setq A1 (/ (* A1 180.0) pi))**↵
21.8014
Command: **!A1**↵
21.8014

The variable **A1** now has a value of 21.8014.

Exercise 25-3
Complete the exercise on the Student CD.

Providing for Angular Input by the User

The **(getangle)** function allows the user to input an angular value for use in an application. This function is often used to set a variable that can be used by another function. The **(getangle)** function automatically issues a Specify second point: prompt. The following example illustrates how you can set a variable to an angular value that is input by the user.

Command: **(setq A (getangle "Pick first point: "))**↵
Pick first point: *(pick the first point)*
Specify second point: *(pick the second point)*
angle (in radians)

The angular value is given in radians. To convert it to degrees, use the formula presented in the previous section.

The **(getangle)** function uses the current **ANGBASE** (angle 0 direction) and **ANGDIR** (clockwise or counterclockwise) system variables. Therefore, if you have angles set to be measured from north (where **ANGBASE** = 90°), angles picked with the **(getangle)** function will be measured from north. If the **ANGDIR** system variable is set to measure angles clockwise, the **(getangle)** function will accept input of clockwise values, but returns counterclockwise values.

A companion function to **(getangle)** is **(getorient)**. It is used in exactly the same manner as the **(getangle)** function. However, **(getorient)** always measures angles counterclockwise from east (0°), regardless of the current **ANGBASE** and **ANGDIR** system variable settings.

Exercise 25-4
Complete the exercise on the Student CD.

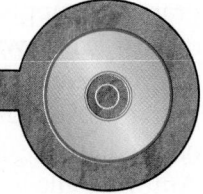

Using Polar Coordinates

The **(polar)** function allows you to specify a new point based on the angle and distance from an existing point. Three arguments are required for the **(polar)** function. The first argument must contain the coordinates of the base point from which you are locating the new point. The second argument is the angular direction (in radians) to go from the base point argument. The third argument is the distance value from the base point argument to the new point. The syntax for the **(polar)** function is:

(polar *base_point angle distance*)

For example, suppose you want to specify a point as **P1** and locate another point, **P2**, at a specific distance (three units) and angle (60°) from **P1**. Enter the following expressions.

```
Command: (setq P1 (getpoint "Enter point: "))↵
Enter point: 4.0,4.5↵
(4.0 4.5 0.0)
Command: (setq D (getdist P1 "Enter distance: "))↵
Enter distance: 3.0↵
3.0
Command: (setq A (/ pi 3))↵
1.0472
```

In this example, the desired angle is 60°. However, AutoLISP uses radians for angular values. Therefore, the degree value is converted to radians. The resulting value, 1.0472, is saved as the variable **A**. Next, use the **(polar)** function to locate the second point relative to **P1** at the specified angle and distance. A line can then be drawn from **P1** to **P2** using the **(command)** function. The sequence is:

```
Command: (setq P2 (polar P1 A D))↵
(5.5 7.09808 0.0)
Command: (command "LINE" P1 P2 "")↵
```

Exercise 25-5
Complete the exercise on the Student CD.

Locating AutoCAD's AutoLISP Files

One of the best ways to become familiar with AutoLISP is to enter expressions and programs into your computer. Look for programs in the books, magazines, newsgroups, and blogs that you read. Get a feel for how the functions and arguments go together and how they work in AutoCAD. Make a habit of reading through one of the AutoCAD journals and experiment with the AutoLISP routines printed in them. Also, refer to the online documentation for other samples.

AutoLISP files are typically saved with the .lsp extension. A variety of AutoLISP programs are supplied with AutoCAD. These are saved in the AutoCAD folder structure. You can use Windows Explorer to search the AutoCAD folder structure and list the .lsp files.

The AutoLISP files found in the \Support folder are standard files that support many of AutoCAD's built-in features. When the command that starts the function is entered, the associated program file is automatically loaded. For example, the 3darray.lsp AutoLISP file is found in the \Support folder. This routine makes it possible to create an arrangement of rows, columns, and levels of an object with the **3DARRAY** command.

PROFESSIONAL TIP

For easier access to any AutoLISP program file, add its folder in the Support File Search Path listing located in the **Files** tab of the **Options** dialog box.

Sample AutoLISP Programs

The following programs are provided for you to copy and add to your acad2008doc.lsp file or to your custom menus. Practice using the routines for a few minutes a couple of times a week. This will help you begin to better understand and use AutoLISP. Train yourself to learn a new function every week. Before long, you will be writing your own useful programs.

Erasing the Entire Screen

This program sets two variables to the minimum and maximum screen limits. It then erases everything within those limits and redraws the screen. Name this program zap.lsp.

```
;;; ERASES ENTIRE LIMITS.
(defun C:ZAP ()
    (setq LMIN (getvar "LIMMIN"))
    (setq LMAX (getvar "LIMMAX"))
    (command "ERASE" "C" LMIN LMAX "")
    (command "REDRAW")
)
```

Setting the Current Layer

Similar to the built-in **Make Object's Layer Current** button on the **Layers** toolbar, this program asks for the user to pick an object on the layer to be set current. The program finds the layer of the object picked and sets it current. Name this program lp.lsp.

```
;;; AUTHOR ROD RAWLS
(defun C:LP (/ E)
    (while (not (setq E (entsel "\nSelect object on target layer...")))
        (alert "No object selected!")
    )
    (setq LN (cdr (assoc 8 (entget (car E)))))
    (command "-LAYER" "S" LN "")
    (princ)
)
```

Cleaning Overlapping Corners

This program allows you to trim the overlapping ends of intersecting lines. You are requested to pick the two lines that intersect and overlap. The points you pick are on the portion to keep. The program does the rest. Name the program cleanc.lsp. Note: The value returned at the end of the program is the original **OSMODE** setting.

```
;;; AUTHOR: GEORGE HEAD
;;; PRINTED IN THE JANUARY 1998 ISSUE OF CADENCE MAGAZINE
(defun C:CLEANC (/ O1 P1 P2)
    (setq O1 (getvar "OSMODE"))
    (setvar "OSMODE" 512)
    (command "FILLET" "R" 0)
    (setq P1 (getpoint "\nPick a line "))
    (setq P2 (getpoint "\nPick other line "))
    (command "FILLET" P1 P2)
    (setvar "OSMODE" O1)
)
```

Calculating the Length of Lines

This program calculates the length of all lines on a specified layer. It can be used for estimating and material takeoffs. This program works only with lines, not with polylines. Name the program linear.lsp. After loading it into AutoCAD, respond to the first prompt by entering the name of the layer that contains the lines you wish to total. The calculation is given in current drawing units. Also, the layer name is case sensitive.

```
;;; AUTHOR: JOE PUCILOWSKI
;;; COMPANY: JOSEPH & ASSOCIATES
;;; REVISED BY CRAIG BLACK
;;; NOTE: THIS PROGRAM FIGURES THE TOTAL NUMBER OF LINEAR
;;; UNITS (FEET, INCHES, ETC.) OF LINES ON A SPECIFIC LAYER.
;;;
;;;
(defun C:LINEAR ()
   (setq   TOTAL    0
           E        (entnext)
           NUMLIN   0
           LAYPIK   (getstring T "\nAdd up lines on layer: ")
   )
   (if (tblsearch "LAYER" LAYPIK)
      (progn
         (while E
            (setq ENTTYP  (cdr  (assoc 0 (setq EG (entget E))))
                  LAYNAM  (cdr  (assoc 8 EG))
            )
            (if  (and
                     (equal ENTTYP "LINE")
                     (equal (strcase LAYNAM)
                            (strcase LAYPIK)
                     )
                 )
                 (progn
                    (setq  LINLEN (distance  (cdr  (assoc 10 EG))
                                             (cdr  (assoc 11 EG))
                           )
                           TOTAL    (+ TOTAL LINLEN)
                           NUMLIN (+ 1 NUMLIN)
                    )
                 )
            )
            (setq E (entnext E))
         )
         (princ (strcat "\nFound "
                        (itoa NUMLIN)
                        " lines on layer <"
                        LAYPIK
                        "> with a total of "
                        (rtos TOTAL)
                        " linear units."
                )
         )
      )
      (princ "\nLayer does not exist.")
   )
   (princ)
)
```

Changing the Grid Rotation

The first routine, titled **S**, rotates the grid to the angle between the X axis and any picked line. The second routine, **SS**, returns the grid to zero rotation. These functions are achieved by rotating the snap. Save the file as rotgrid.lsp.

```
;;; AUTHOR : EBEN KUNZ
;;; COMPANY: KUNA ASSOCIATES ARCHITECTS
;;; REVISED BY CRAIG BLACK
;;;
(defun C:S (/ PT1 PT2)
  (setq IOSMODEI (getvar "OSMODE"))
    (setvar "OSMODE" 0)
    (setvar "ORTHOMODE" 0)
    (setq PT1 (osnap (getpoint "\nPick line to match new Grid angle: \n") "NEA"))
    (setq PT2 (osnap PT1 "END"))
    (command "SNAP" "R" PT1 PT2)
    (setvar "SNAPMODE" 0)
  (setvar "OSMODE" IOSMODEI)
  (princ)
)
(defun C:SS ()
  (prompt "\nReturn Grid to zero.")
  (command "SNAP" "R" "" 0.0)
  (setvar "SNAPMODE" 0)
)
```

Moving Objects to a Selected Layer

This routine, named la.lsp, allows you to move objects to a layer by picking an object on the destination layer. After you select an object on the destination layer, you can select multiple objects using any AutoCAD selection method.

```
;;; AUTHOR: SHELDON MCCARTHY
;;; COMPANY: EPCM SERVICES LTD.
;;;
(defun C:LA ()
  (setq 1A
        (cdr  (assoc 8
                     (entget  (car
                               (entsel "Entity on destination layer: "
                               )
                              )
                     )
              )
        )
  )
  (prompt "Objects to change...")
  (ssget)
  (command     "CHANGE"
               "P"
               ""
               "P"
               "LA"
               1A
               ""
  )
)
```

Moving Objects to the Current Layer

This simple program, titled cl.lsp, quickly changes selected objects to the current layer. You can select multiple objects using any AutoCAD selection method.

```
;;; AUTHOR: BILL FANE
;;; COMPANY: WISER, INC.
;;;
;;;
(defun C:CL (/ THINGS)
   (setq THINGS (ssget))
   (command   "CHANGE"
              THINGS
              ""
              "P"
              "LA"
              (getvar "CLAYER")
              ""

   )
)
```

Chapter Test

Answer the following questions. Write your answers on a separate sheet of paper or complete the electronic chapter test on the Student CD.

1. Name the function that allows you to return a real number and use it as a variable value.
2. Which two functions allow you to work with system variables?
3. Define the following AutoLISP functions.
   A. **(car)**
   B. **(cadr)**
   C. **(cdr)**
   D. **(caddr)**
   E. **(list)**
4. Write the proper AutoLISP notation to return the last two atoms of the list (4 7 3) as a list.
5. Write an expression to set a variable named **A** to the result of Question 4.
6. Write an expression to return the second atom of the list created in Question 5.
7. Compare and contrast the **(getangle)** and **(getorient)** functions.
8. Write an expression to set the angle between points **P3** and **P4** to the variable **A**.
9. Which system of angular measurement does AutoLISP use?
10. Explain the purpose of the **(polar)** function.

Drawing Problems

*Write AutoLISP programs for the following problems. Use the **Visual LISP Editor**. Save the files as P25_(problem number) with the .lsp extension.*

1. Add the following capabilities to the right triangle function developed in Exercise 25-2.
   A. Use the **(getdist)** function instead of **(getcorner)**.
   B. Allow the angle of the hypotenuse to be picked.
   C. Allow the length of a side or the hypotenuse length to be picked.

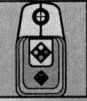

2. Create an AutoLISP program similar to that in Problem 1, but write it so that it draws an equilateral triangle (with equal angles and equal sides). Use the **(polar)** function.

3. Revise the program in Problem 1 in Chapter 24 to draw a rectangle using the **(getcorner)** function to find the second corner. Also, revise the program so that the **LINE** command is used instead of the **RECTANG** command.

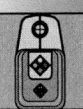

4. Add a **Fillet 0** command to your **Modify** pull-down menu. Use menu macros and AutoLISP expressions to create the command. Follow these guidelines:
   A. Retrieve the current fillet radius setting and assign it to an AutoLISP variable.
   B. Set the fillet radius to 0.
   C. Allow the user to select two lines and automatically enter a 0 radius fillet.
   D. Reset the fillet radius to the original value.
   E. Assign an appropriate mnemonic key to the new menu command.

5. Write an AutoLISP program that allows the user to measure the distance between two points using the **DIST** command. Use AutoLISP expressions to do the following.
   A. Assign the current unit precision for read-only linear units to an AutoLISP variable.
   B. Prompt for the desired unit precision from the user and store the value as a variable.
   C. Set the unit precision with the user-defined variable value.
   D. Allow the user to measure the distance between two selected points with the **DIST** command.
   E. Reset the unit precision to the original value.

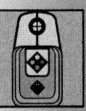

6. Write an AutoLISP program to draw a rectangle and place a circle having a user-specified diameter in the center of the rectangle.
   A. Incorporate the rectangle program from Problem 3.
   B. Use the **(angle)**, **(polar)**, and **(distance)** functions to find the center point of the rectangle.
   C. Prompt the user to enter the diameter of the circle.
   D. Use the **CIRCLE** command to draw the circle at the center point of the rectangle.

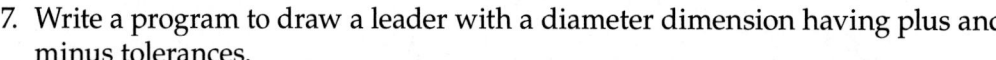

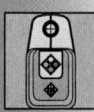

7. Write a program to draw a leader with a diameter dimension having plus and minus tolerances.
    A. Issue prompts that allow the user to set the **DIMTP** and **DIMTM** system variables and save the specified values to AutoLISP variables.
    B. Set the new values to the **DIMTP** and **DIMTM** system variables.
    C. Turn the **DIMTOL** system variable on.
    D. Activate the **DIMDIAMETER** command. Use the **(entsel)** function to set the selection specification to a variable as follows.

        (setq SC (entsel))

    E. Using the **(getpoint)** function, issue a prompt that allows the user to pick a location for the leader line and the default dimension text.
    F. Turn the **DIMTOL** system variable off.

8. Write an AutoLISP program to draw a leader with a bubble attached to the end.
    A. Prompt the user for the start point of the leader and set it to the variable **P1**.
    B. Prompt the user for the endpoint of the leader and set it to the variable **P2**.
    C. Prompt the user for the text height and set it to a variable.
    D. Issue a prompt that asks for the text string (specify a maximum of two characters) and set the resulting text to a variable.
    E. Calculate the circle diameter at three times the text height and set it to a variable.
    F. Set the center point of the circle to a point relative to **P2** using the **(polar)** function. Set the relative distance as the radius of the circle. Assign the center point to the variable **P3**.
    G. Use the **LEADER** command to draw a leader from **P1** to **P2**.
    H. Draw the leader line with no shoulder and no annotation text.
    I. Draw a circle with the center point at **P3**.
    J. Draw text in the center of the circle using the appropriate justification option of the **TEXT** command.

9. Develop a program that draws a line of text and places a box around it.
    A. Prompt the user for the text height and set it to the variable **TXHT**.
    B. Prompt the user for a point representing the lower-left corner of the box and set it to a variable.
    C. Prompt for the text string from the user.
    D. Set the text string length to the variable **LG1**. Use the **(strlen)** function. The following is an example of using this function.

        (setq TEXT (getstring T "Enter Text: "))
        (setq LG1 (strlen TEXT))

    E. Set the X length of the box to a variable using the expression:

        (* LG1 TXHT)

    F. Set the Y length of the box to a variable using the expression:

        (* 3 TXHT)

    G. Draw the box using the variables set in E and F.
    H. Calculate the center point of the box and set it to the variable **CEN1**.
    I. Draw the text string inside the box. Use the **MC** text justification option for point **CEN1**.

CHAPTER 26

Introduction to Dialog Control Language (DCL)

Learning Objectives

After completing this chapter, you will be able to:
- ✓ Describe the types of files that control dialog boxes.
- ✓ Define the components of a dialog box.
- ✓ Write a DCL file for a basic dialog box.
- ✓ Write an AutoLISP file to control a dialog box.
- ✓ Associate an action with a dialog box tile.

Programmable dialog boxes can be used to completely customize the interface of AutoLISP programs. These dialog boxes allow LISP programs to work like many of AutoCAD's built-in functions. Using dialog boxes improves efficiency and reduces data entry errors.

Dialog boxes minimize the amount of typing required by the user. Rather than answering a series of text prompts on the command line, the user selects options from the dialog box. Dialog box fields can be filled in by the user in any order. While the dialog box is still active, the user can revise values as necessary.

AutoLISP provides basic tools for controlling dialog boxes, but the dialog box itself must be defined using the *Dialog Control Language (DCL).* The definition is written to an ASCII file with a .dcl file extension. When creating and editing DCL files, the **Visual LISP Editor** provides many helpful tools, including color coding.

This chapter is only an introduction to DCL. It covers basic DCL file construction and a few common tile types. For more information, refer to the online help documentation.

DCL File Formats

A DCL file is formatted as an ASCII text file with a .dcl file extension. These files can have any valid file name, but a file name with 1 to 8 characters is recommended. Writing DCL is easy. Many of the components of a DCL file are normal English words.

The components of a dialog box—such as edit boxes, images, and drop-down lists—are referred to as *tiles.* Tiles are defined by specifying various *attribute* values. Each attribute controls a specific property of the tile, such as size, location, and default values.

When writing a DCL file, you do not use parentheses as you do with AutoLISP. When defining a dialog box or tile, all of the required attributes are placed within

Figure 26-1.
A portion of the
acad.dcl file.

```
acad_snap : dialog {                     Dialog definition
    label = "Drawing Aids";
    : row {                              Label attribute
        : column {                       adds a text string
            : boxed_column {
                label = "Modes";
                : toggle {               Key attribute
                    label = "&Ortho";    identifies a text string
                    key = "ortho";       that associates the dialog
                }                        tile with an AutoLISP
                : toggle {               function
                    label = "Solid &Fill";
                    key = "fill";
                }
```

{braces}. As with AutoLISP programs, indentation helps to separate individual elements, making the file more readable. Comments are preceded by two forward slashes (//). Semicolons are used at the end of an attribute definition line.

To view an example of DCL code, open the acad.dcl and base.dcl files in a text editor. These two files are found in the user's \Support folder, not the AutoCAD \Support folder. A portion of the acad.dcl file is shown in Figure 26-1.

CAUTION

The base.dcl file contains standard prototype definitions. The acad.dcl file contains definitions for all of the dialog boxes used by AutoCAD. Do *not* edit either one of these files! Altering them can cause AutoCAD's built-in dialog boxes to crash.

AutoLISP and DCL

A DCL file simply defines a dialog box. The dialog box cannot actually do anything without a controlling application. AutoLISP is frequently used to control dialog sessions. This section shows examples using the AutoLISP dialog handling functions.

In order to display a dialog box, the controlling AutoLISP application must first load the dialog definition. The AutoLISP **(load_dialog)** function loads the specified dialog definition file:

(load_dialog "*file name*.dcl")

The file name is enclosed in quotation marks. The **(load_dialog)** function returns a positive integer that identifies the loaded DCL file. If the attempted load was unsuccessful, a negative integer is returned.

The next step is to activate a specific dialog box definition contained within the DCL file. The AutoLISP **(new_dialog)** function activates the dialog box specified, where *dlgname* is the name of the dialog box:

(new_dialog *dlgname dcl_id*)

This function is case sensitive. Suppose the dialog definition is named main. Specifying Main or MAIN will not activate this dialog box since the text string does not match exactly. The *dcl_id* argument represents the integer value returned by **(load_dialog)**. This value is often assigned to a variable, as you will see later. The **(new_dialog)** function also supports additional, optional arguments, which are not discussed here.

To actually begin accepting input from the user, the AutoLISP **(start_dialog)** function must be used:

```
(start_dialog)
```

This function has no arguments. It allows input to be received from the dialog box initialized by the previous **(new_dialog)** expression.

With these basic AutoLISP functions, it is possible to display the dialog box shown in Figure 26-2. You will create this dialog box in the next section. After the AutoLISP program is written and saved, it can be loaded into AutoCAD using the load function or the **APPLOAD** command. Enter the controlling AutoLISP application named EXAMPLE1.LSP as follows.

```
(setq EX1_DCL_ID (load_dialog "EXAMPLE1.DCL"))
(if (not (new_dialog "main" EX1_DCL_ID))
  (exit)
)
(start_dialog)
```

Now, take a closer look at the controlling code for this dialog box:

```
(setq EX1_DCL_ID (load_dialog "EXAMPLE1.DCL"))
(if (not (new_dialog "main" EX1_DCL_ID))
  (exit)
)
(start_dialog)
```

This expression loads the dialog definition found in EXAMPLE1.DCL and assigns the value returned by **(load_dialog)** to the variable **EX1_DCL_ID**.

```
(setq EX1_DCL_ID (load_dialog "EXAMPLE1.DCL"))
(if (not (new_dialog "main" EX1_DCL_ID))
  (exit)
)
(start_dialog)
```

If **(new_dialog)** is unable to activate the specified dialog box for any reason, the expression in the next three lines exits (terminates) the application. This is an important safety feature. In many cases, loading an incorrect or incomplete definition can cause your system to lock up and may require the system to be rebooted.

```
(setq EX1_DCL_ID (load_dialog "EXAMPLE1.DCL"))
(if (not (new_dialog "main" EX1_DCL_ID))
  (exit)
)
(start_dialog)
```

The last expression opens the dialog box indicated by the previous **(new_dialog)** expression.

Once the descriptions within a specific DCL file are no longer needed, they can be removed from memory using the AutoLISP **(unload_dialog)** function.

```
(unload_dialog dcl_id)
```

Do not unload a dialog definition until your application is finished using the DCL file. Otherwise, your application may fail to properly function.

Figure 26-2.
A sample custom dialog box.

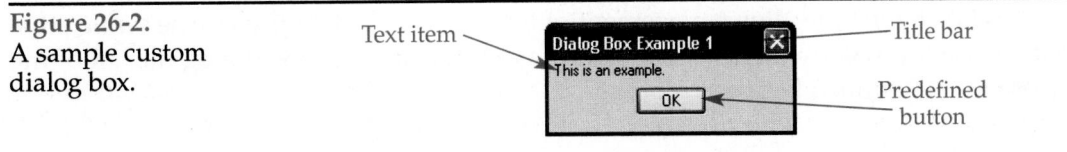

Your work in AutoCAD has provided you with a good background in how dialog boxes work. By now, you should be familiar with the use of buttons, edit boxes, radio buttons, and list boxes. This will be helpful as you design dialog interfaces for your AutoLISP programs.

DCL tiles are used individually or combined into structures called *clusters.* For example, a series of button tiles can be placed in a column tile to control the arrangement of the buttons in the dialog box. The primary tile is the dialog box itself.

The best way to begin understanding the format of a DCL file is to study a simple dialog box definition. The following DCL code defines the dialog box shown in Figure 26-2.

```
main : dialog {
   label  = "Dialog Box Example 1";
   : text_part {
         value = "This is an example.";
   }
   ok_only;
}
```

Now, take a closer look at the definition of this dialog box. The *dialog definition* is always the first tile definition.

```
main : dialog {
   label  = "Dialog Box Example 1";
   : text_part {
         value = "This is an example.";
   }
   ok_only;
}
```

Everything within the braces defines the features of the dialog box. The word "main" indicates the name of the dialog box within the code. This name is referenced by the controlling AutoLISP application. A colon (:) precedes all tile callouts. In the case of a dialog tile, the colon separates the name from the tile callout.

```
main : dialog {
   label = "Dialog Box Example 1";
   : text_part {
         value = "This is an example.";
   }
   ok_only;
}
```

The *label* attribute of the dialog tile controls the text that appears in the title bar of the dialog box. The line is terminated with a semicolon. All attribute lines must be terminated with a semicolon.

```
main : dialog {
   label  = "Dialog Box Example 1";
   : text_part {
         value = "This is an example.";
   }
   ok_only;
}
```

The *text_part* tile allows placement of text items in a dialog box. The *value* attribute is used to specify the text that is displayed. Just as with the dialog tile, all of the attributes are defined between braces.

```
main : dialog {
    label = "Dialog Box Example 1";
    : text_part {
            value = "This is an example.";
    }
    ok_only;
}
```

There are many predefined tiles and subassemblies in the base.dcl file. A *subassembly* is a cluster of predefined tiles, such as **ok_cancel** and **ok_help**. The **ok_only** tile places an **OK** button at the bottom of the dialog box, as shown in **Figure 26-2.** The statement is not preceded by a colon because it is not a specific definition. This line is terminated with a semicolon, just like an attribute. Braces are not required because the statement is a reference to a predefined tile, rather than a tile definition.

Once you have defined a dialog box, the definition must then be saved in a DCL file. For this example, the dialog definition above should be saved in the file **EXAMPLE1. DCL**. This is treated as any other support file and should be saved in the AutoCAD support path.

For examples of other DCL functions, look at the **Viewpoint Presets** dialog box shown in **Figure 26-3.** Various tiles of this dialog box are identified with the corresponding DCL code needed to define the tile. In older releases of AutoCAD, this dialog box was defined by a stand-alone DCL file named ddvpoint.dcl. However, this DCL file no longer exists as the dialog box is now defined by a different method.

Figure 26-3.
Some of the tile definitions and attributes associated with the **Viewpoint Presets** dialog box (this dialog box is no longer defined by a DCL file).

```
ddvpoint : dialog {
  aspect_ratio = 0;
  label = "Viewpoint Presets";
  fixed_height = true;
  fixed_width  = true;
  : column {
    : row {
      : text {
        label = "Set Viewing Angles";
        key = "ddvp_header";
      }
    }

  : row {
      fixed_width = true;
      fixed_height = true;
      : image_button {
        alignment = top;
        fixed_width = true;
        fixed_height = true;
        key = "ddvp_image";
        width  = 39;
        height = 12;
        color  = 0;
        is_tab_stop = false;
      }
    }

   : row {
      : button {
        label = "Set to Plan View";
        key = "ddvp_set_plan";
        mnemonic = "V";
      }
    }
  }
}
```

```
  : row {
      : radio_row {
        : radio_button {
          label = "Absolute to WCS";
          key = "ddvp_abs_wcs";
          mnemonic = "W";
          value = "1";
        }
        : radio_button {
          label = "Relative to UCS";
          key = "ddvp_rel_ucs";
          mnemonic = "U";
        }
      }
  }

  : row {
      : edit_box {
        label = "From:  X Axis:";
        mnemonic = "A";
        key = "ddvp_val_x";
        fixed_width = true;
        edit_width  = 6;
      }
      : edit_box {
        label = "XY Plane:";
        mnemonic = "P";
        key = "ddvp_val_xyp";
        fixed_width = true;
        edit_width  = 6;
      }
  }
```

```
spacer_1;
  ok_cancel_help_errtile;
}
```

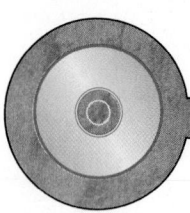

Exercise 26-1
Complete the exercise on the Student CD.

Associating Functions with Tiles

Most tiles can be associated with actions. These actions vary from run-time error checking to performing tasks outside of the dialog box session. The **(action_tile)** AutoLISP function provides the basic means of associating tiles with actions.

(action_tile "*key*" "*action-expression*")

The *key* references the attribute assigned in the DCL file. The *action-expression* is the AutoLISP expression performed when the action is called. When the desired action requires a large amount of AutoLISP code, it is best to define a function to perform the required tasks. This function is then called within the *action-expression*. Both the *key* and *action-expression* arguments are supplied as text strings.

In order to access a specific tile from AutoLISP, the key of the tile must be referenced. The key is specified as an attribute in the DCL file. Tiles that are static (no associated action) do not require keys. Any tile that must be referenced in any way— such as setting or retrieving a value, associating an action, or enabling/disabling the tile—requires a key.

The next example changes the previous dialog box by adding a button that displays the current time when picked. The new or changed DCL code is shown in color. Save this file as EXAMPLE2.DCL.

```
main : dialog {
    label = "Dialog Box Example 2";
    : text_part {
            value  = "";
              key  = "time";
    }
    : button {
              key  = "update";
            label  = "Display Current Time";
        mnemonic   = "C";
    }
    ok_only;
}
```

Notice the addition of a key attribute to the **text_part** tile. This allows access by the AutoLISP application while the dialog box is open. Another addition is the **button** tile. A **key** attribute is provided in the **button** tile so an association can be created in the AutoLISP program with an *action-expression* argument. The **label** attribute provides the text displayed on the button. The **mnemonic** attribute underlines the specified letter within the label to allow keyboard access. The AutoLISP application used to manage this dialog session is as follows. Save the program as EXAMPLE2.LSP.

```
            (setq EX2_DCL_ID (load_dialog "EXAMPLE2.DCL"))
            (if   (not (new_dialog "main" EX2_DCL_ID))
                  (exit)
            )
            (defun  UPDTILE ()
               (setq CDVAR (rtos (getvar "CDATE") 2 16)
                     CDTXT (strcat "Current Time: "
                        (substr CDVAR 10 2)
                        "."
                        (substr CDVAR 12 2)
                        "."
                        (substr CDVAR 14 2)
                        )
               )
               (set_tile "time" CDTXT)
            )
            (UPDTILE)
            (action_tile "update" "(UPDTILE)")
            (start_dialog)
```

The dialog box displayed by this code is shown in **Figure 26-4.** The "update" button displays the current time when the button is picked. The mnemonic character is displayed once the [Alt] key is pressed. Note: Some AutoLISP functions not covered in this text are used in the above programming to retrieve and display the current time.

Commands that change the display or require user input (outside of the dialog interface) cannot be used while a dialog box is active. These AutoLISP functions cannot be used with DCL:

command	**getangle**	**getpoint**	**grread**	**prompt**
entdel	**getcorner**	**getreal**	**grtext**	**redraw**
entmake	**getdist**	**getstring**	**grvecs**	**ssget** (interactive)
entmod	**getint**	**graphscr**	**menucmd**	**textpage**
entsel	**getkword**	**grclear**	**nentsel**	**textscr**
entupd	**getorient**	**grdraw**	**osnap**	

Figure 26-4.
The dialog box
defined by
EXAMPLE2.DCL
and controlled by
EXAMPLE2.LSP.

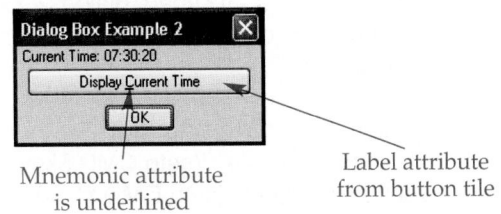

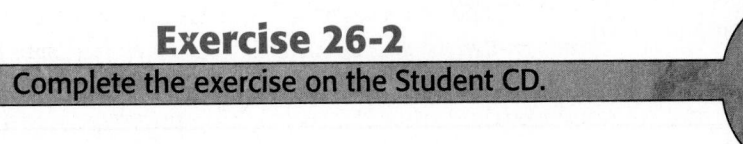

Mnemonic attribute
is underlined

Label attribute
from button tile

Exercise 26-2
Complete the exercise on the Student CD.

There are many types of DCL tiles available. You can provide edit boxes for users to directly enter information, such as numeric or text information. You can create lists and drop-down lists to allow users to choose from preset selections. You can also add buttons to provide a simple means of initiating an action.

Images can be used to enhance dialog boxes. For example, you can place company or personal logos in your dialog boxes. An interactive image, such as the one that appears in the **Viewpoint Presets** dialog box shown in Figure 26-3, can also be used. Tools such as text tiles, sliders, and clusters are used to control the layout of tiles in a dialog box.

A wide variety of attributes are available for controlling the appearance and function of a dialog session. In addition, several AutoLISP functions are provided to control your dialog session. You can disable or enable tiles and change the active tile. It is even possible to change the value or state of a tile based on an entry in another tile.

You have already seen two examples of dialog boxes created using DCL and AutoLISP. The following sections provide two additional applications that use various dialog boxes. Study these examples for additional insight into the creation of dialog boxes. Be sure to have an appropriate reference handy, such as the online documentation, to look up DCL and AutoLISP terms. You can adapt or modify these programs to produce dialog sessions of your own.

Dialog Example 3

Create the following DCL and AutoLISP programs. Save the programs as EXAMPLE3.DCL and EXAMPLE3.LSP. Then, load the AutoLISP program file. To open the dialog box, type DRAW. The dialog box is shown in Figure 26-5.

```
;EXAMPLE3.LSP
;This file displays the dialog box defined in EXAMPLE3.DCL and begins the
; selected drawing command as specified by the user.
;
(defun C:DRAW (/ EX3_DCL_ID)
  (setq EX3_DCL_ID (load_dialog "EXAMPLE3.DCL"))
  (if (not (new_dialog "draw" EX3_DCL_ID))
    (exit)
  )
  (action_tile "line" "(setq CMD $key) (done_dialog)")
  (action_tile "circle" "(setq CMD $key) (done_dialog)")
  (action_tile "arc" "(setq CMD $key) (done_dialog)")
  (action_tile "cancel" "(setq CMD nil) (done_dialog)")
  (start_dialog)
  (unload_dialog EX3_DCL_ID)
  (command CMD)
)
```

Figure 26-5.
The dialog box displayed using the EXAMPLE3 DCL and LSP files.

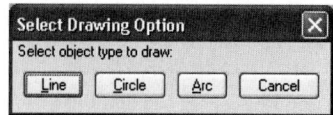

```
//EXAMPLE3.DCL
//Defines a dialog box that presents three drawing options to the user.
//
draw : dialog {
   label = "Select Drawing Option";
   :   text_part {
       label = "Select object type to draw: ";
   }
   : row {
      : button {
          key             = "line";
          label           = "Line";
          mnemonic        = "L";
          fixed_width     = true;
      }
      : button {
          key             = "circle";
          label           = "Circle";
          mnemonic        = "C";
          fixed_width     = true;
      }
      : button {
          key             = "arc";
          label           = "Arc";
          mnemonic        = "A";
          fixed_width     = true;
      }
      : button {
          key             = "cancel";
          label           = "Cancel";
          is_cancel       = true;
          fixed_width     = true;
      }
   }
}
```

Dialog Example 4

This example allows you to select a new current layer from a drop-down list in a dialog box. Save the files as EXAMPLE4.DCL and EXAMPLE4.LSP. Then, load the AutoLISP file. To access the dialog box, type GOFOR. The dialog box is shown in Figure 26-6.

```
;;EXAMPLE4.LSP
;;
(defun  CHECKOUT ()
  (setq LD (tblsearch "LAYER" (nth (atoi (get_tile "lyr_pop")) LL))
      LN (cdr (assoc 2 LD))
      LS (cdr (assoc 70 LD))
  )
  (if (and
        (/= 1 LS)
        (/= 65 LS)
      )
      (progn
        (setvar "CLAYER" (nth (atoi (get_tile "lyr_pop")) LL))
        (done_dialog)
      )
      (alert "Selected layer is frozen!")
) )
(defun C:GOFOR ()
  (setq EX4_DCL_ID (load_dialog "EXAMPLE4.DCL"))
  (if (not (new_dialog "fourth" EX4_DCL_ID)) (exit))
  (start_list "lyr_pop")
  (setq LL '()
      NL (tblnext "LAYER" T)
      IDX 0
  )
  (while   NL
        (if (= (getvar "CLAYER") (cdr (assoc 2 NL)))
          (setq CL IDX)
          (setq IDX (1+ IDX))
        )
        (setq LL (append LL (list (cdr (assoc 2 NL)))))
          NL (tblnext "LAYER")
  )    )
  (mapcar 'add_list LL)
  (end_list)
  (set_tile "lyr_pop" (itoa CL))
  (action_tile "lyr_pop" "(if (= $reason 4) (mode_tile \"accept\" 2))")
  (action_tile "accept" "(CHECKOUT)")
  (start_dialog)
  (unload_dialog EX4_DCL_ID)
  (princ)
)
```

```
//EXAMPLE4.DCL
// Presents a list of layers to the user.
fourth : dialog {
   label = "Select Layer";
   : popup_list {
      label            = "New Current Layer:";
      mnemonic      = "N";
      key              = "lyr_pop";
      allow_accept  = true;
      width            = 32;
   }
   ok_cancel;
}
```

Figure 26-6.
The dialog box
displayed using the
EXAMPLE4 DCL and
LSP files.

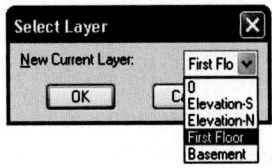

Chapter Test

Answer the following questions. Write your answers on a separate sheet of paper or complete the electronic chapter test on the Student CD.

1. What are the two types of files that must be created to construct a functioning dialog box?
2. When referring to a dialog box, what is a *tile?*
3. When defining a dialog or tile, inside of which character are all of the required attributes for a tile definition placed?
4. Which symbol indicates a comment inside of a DCL file?
5. Write the appropriate notation for the first line of a DCL file that defines a dialog box named **Test**.
6. Write the appropriate notation in a DCL file that defines the text in the title bar of a dialog box named **Select Application**.
7. Write the notation in a DCL file for defining a cluster of four buttons labeled **OK**, **Next**, **Cancel**, and **Help**.
8. Which type of file is commonly used to control a DCL file?
9. Write the notation that would appear in the file in question 8 that loads a dialog file named **PICKFILE**.
10. What is a *key* in a DCL file?
11. What is the function of a *mnemonic* attribute?
12. Write the proper DCL file notation for the first line that identifies a button.

Drawing Problems

1. Create a dialog box that contains the following items. Write the required DCL and AutoLISP files.
   A. Title bar—**Dialog Box Test**
   B. Label—**This is a test.**
   C. **OK** button

2. Create a dialog box that contains the following items. Write the required DCL and AutoLISP files.
   A. Title bar—**Date**
   B. Label—**Current date:**
   C. Action button—**Display Current Date**
   D. **OK** button

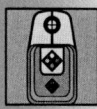

3. Create a dialog box that performs the following tasks. Then, write the required DCL and AutoLISP files.
   A. Displays the current date.
   B. Displays the current time.
   C. Contains buttons to display and update current date and time.
   D. Displays the current drawing name.
   E. Contains an **OK** button.

CHAPTER 27

Introduction to Visual Basic for Applications (VBA)

Learning Objectives

After completing this chapter, you will be able to:
- ✓ Explain object-oriented programming.
- ✓ Describe the AutoCAD object model.
- ✓ Change an object's properties.
- ✓ Use an object's methods.
- ✓ Use the **VBA Manager**.
- ✓ Develop a VBA project using the **Visual Basic Editor**.
- ✓ Explain the data types used in VBA.
- ✓ Store data in variables.
- ✓ Run a VBA macro.
- ✓ Create a form (dialog box) in a VBA project.

Visual Basic for Applications (VBA) is a version of Microsoft's Visual Basic (VB) programming language that is built into AutoCAD. All of the features of the full version of VB are included, in addition to functions and procedures that are specific to programming the AutoCAD application. This chapter is intended to give you an overview of the basics of VBA. You will learn how easy to use, and yet powerful, the language is. This chapter is by no means an in-depth look at VBA. For more complete discussions and study of VBA within AutoCAD, refer to *VBA for AutoCAD* published by The Goodheart-Willcox Company, Inc.

Object-Oriented Programming

VBA is an *object-oriented* programming language. Although lines, arcs, and circles are objects, AutoCAD entities are not the only objects. The many "parts" that make up the AutoCAD application itself are considered objects. The whole program and all that it is composed of are considered the *object model*. The AutoCAD object model contains all of the objects, and provides access to their methods, properties, and events, in a tree-like hierarchy. See **Figure 27-1**. To display this object model, select **Help>Additional Resources>Developer Help**. In the left-hand pane (**Contents** tab) of the help that is displayed, select **ActiveX and VBA Reference**. Finally, in the right-hand pane, select **Object Model**.

Figure 27-1.
The object model for AutoCAD.

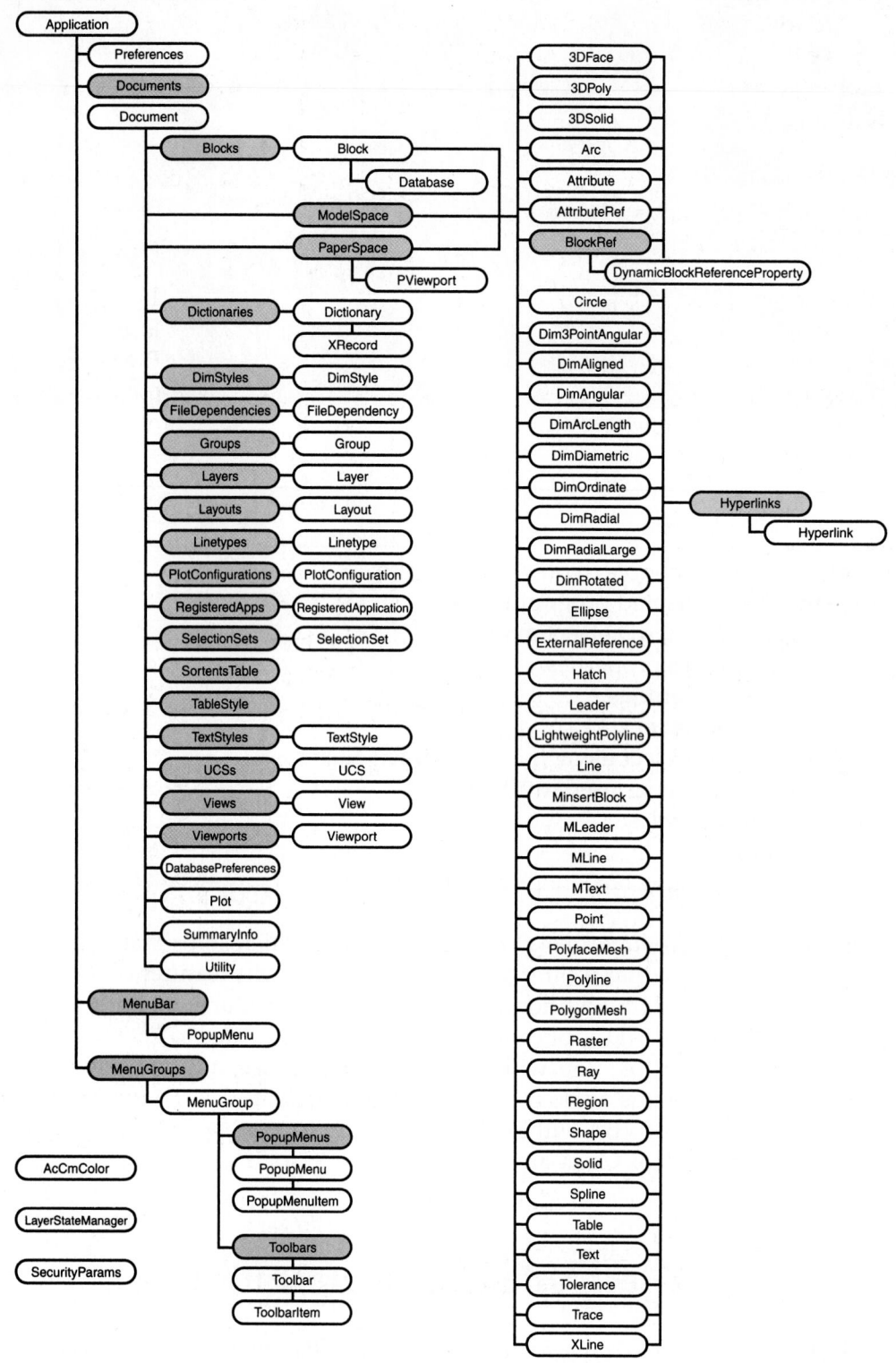

Notice that the AutoCAD **Application** object itself is the upper-most object in the hierarchy. The application is considered the *root* of the tree. Under the application are branches for **Preferences, Documents, Document, MenuBar,** and **MenuGroups**. Each of these is considered an object. Through the **Application** object and then through these five objects (branches of the tree), all of the methods, properties, and events can be accessed for all of the objects in the AutoCAD program.

For example, to change the size of the pick box to four, you must go through the hierarchy to get to that object's properties using the following code. Each level, or branch, of the object model is separated by a period.

    Application.Preferences.Selection.PickBoxSize = 4

The above code introduces another level in the hierarchy: **Selection**. The **Selection** object is a subobject of the **Preferences** object. The **Preferences** object holds those options in AutoCAD's **Options** dialog box that are stored in the registry. The **Preferences** object is made up of subobjects that represent each of the tabs in the **Options** dialog box. Working from AutoCAD's point of view, rather than VBA's point of view, the pick box size is set on the **Selection** tab of the **Options** dialog box in the AutoCAD application.

Methods, Properties, and Events

Each object within the object model has various methods, properties, and events associated with it. The set of available methods, properties, and events is unique for each object. However, some methods, properties, and events are available to multiple objects. Some objects do not have any methods, properties, or events available to them.

Methods are functions built into the objects that allow the object's properties to be modified. Some examples of methods that are available to a few objects include:
- The **Circle** object has a **Move** method, and 18 other methods.
- The **Layer** object has a **Delete** method, and three other methods.
- The **ModelSpace** object has an **AddLine** method, and 51 other methods.
- The **Document** object has a **Close** method, and 19 other methods.

Properties are the "settings" associated with an object, similar to the properties of AutoCAD entities that are found in the **Properties** dialog box. Other, non-AutoCAD-entity objects have properties, too. Some examples of properties that are associated with a few objects include:
- The **Circle** object has a **Layer** property, and 20 other properties.
- The **Layer** object has a **Freeze** property, and 19 other properties.
- The **ModelSpace** object has a **Count** property, and six other properties.
- The **Document** object has an **ActiveSpace** property, and 48 other properties.

Events are actions that occur while a VBA program or macro is running. An event can be monitored (continuously checked) and, if it occurs, another action can be triggered. An event can be as simple as the user picking the **OK** button to close a dialog box. For example, you can create a VBA program that changes the linetype scale setting when the user switches from model space to paper (layout) space. Some examples of events that are associated with a few objects include:
- The **Circle** object has a **Modified** event.
- The **Layer** object has a **Modified** event.
- The **ModelSpace** object has a **Modified** event.
- The **Document** object has a **LayoutSwitched** event, and 27 other events.

Events are beyond the scope of this text. For more information on using events in VBA macros, refer to *VBA for AutoCAD* published by The Goodheart-Willcox Company, Inc.

Exercise 27-1
Complete the exercise on the Student CD.

Understanding How a VBA Program Works

VBA programs are actually called projects. A *project* consists of the forms and modules necessary to obtain the desired outcome. VBA refers to dialog boxes as *forms. Modules* are the **Sub** procedures that actually contain the program code. *Sub procedures* are subroutines, or small programs, that can be called from within other procedures. A *macro* is a **Sub** that is declared as **Public**, meaning it will show up in AutoCAD's **Macros** dialog box. The terms *projects, modules, macros, subs,* and *forms* are used throughout this chapter.

Projects can be stored in two locations: in a file or in a drawing. A project stored in a drawing is considered *embedded.* That project is automatically loaded and its macros are available each time the drawing in which the project is embedded is opened. A project stored in a file has a .dvb file extension and must be loaded in order for its macros to be available in the drawing. A project stored as a DVB file is considered *global* as it can be loaded into any drawing from any computer that has access to the DVB file. If the project is saved as a file named acad.dvb, and the file is in the AutoCAD search path, it is loaded each time a drawing is opened. Interestingly, once a project has been loaded into one drawing, its macros are available to all open drawings, as long as the drawing into which the project was loaded remains open.

Using the VBA Manager

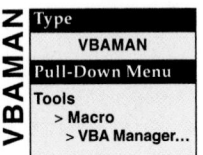

Type
VBAMAN
Pull-Down Menu
Tools
> Macro
> VBA Manager...

The **VBA Manager** dialog box allows a project to be loaded or embedded. See **Figure 27-2.** It also allows a project to be created or saved to a file. The **VBAMAN** command opens the dialog box.

The active drawing file is shown at the top of the dialog box. Any other open drawings are available within the drop-down list. Just below the drop-down list, the name of an embedded project is shown, if a project is embedded in that drawing. Only one project can be embedded in a drawing at a time.

The **Projects** area in the middle of the dialog box lists all of the projects that are currently loaded. This list shows the name and location of the project. If the project is stored as a DVB file, the file name and path are shown. If the project is embedded in a drawing, the drawing name and path are shown.

On the right side of the dialog box are several buttons. These buttons are described below.

- **Extract.** Picking this button removes the embedded project. A message box appears asking if you would like to save the project to a file before extracting it from the drawing.
- **Embed.** This button allows a project to be embedded in a drawing. A project must be selected from the **Projects** list and the drawing in which you want to embed the project must be selected in the **Drawing** drop-down list. Only one project can be embedded in a drawing at a time.

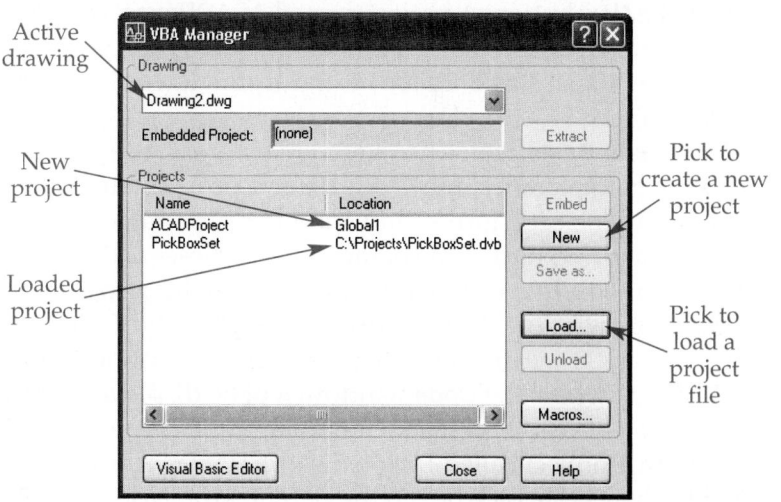

Figure 27-2.
The **VBA Manager** in AutoCAD.

Active drawing

New project

Loaded project

Pick to create a new project

Pick to load a project file

- **New.** Picking this button creates a new project and adds it to the **Projects** list. The new project has the default name ACADProject name and is generically listed as Global*n*, where *n* is a sequential integer. The project name can only be changed in the **Visual Basic Editor**, which is covered in the next section. The Global*n* location is updated when the project is saved as a file or embedded in a drawing.
- **Save as.** Use this button to save to a file the project highlighted in the **Projects** list. A standard Windows "save as" dialog box appears when the button is picked.
- **Load.** Picking this button displays a standard Windows "open" dialog box in which you can select a project file (DVB) to be loaded. The project is loaded into the drawing selected in the **Drawing** drop-down list.
- **Unload.** This button allows a project to be unloaded, making its macros unavailable. Highlight the project to unload in the **Projects** list and then pick this button.
- **Macros.** Picking this button closes the **VBA Manager** dialog box and opens the **Macros** dialog box. The available macros are listed in the **Macros** dialog box. The **Macros** dialog box has a **VBA Manager...** button that displays the **VBA Manager** dialog box.

There is also the **Visual Basic Editor** button in the lower-left corner of the **VBA Manager** dialog box. Picking this button opens the **Visual Basic Editor**, which is covered in the next section.

Using the Visual Basic Editor

The **Visual Basic Editor** is a full featured, built-in editor for VBA programming in AutoCAD. The **VBAIDE** command displays the **Visual Basic Editor**. It can also be opened by picking the **Visual Basic Editor** button from within the **VBA Manager** dialog box.

Now that you have been introduced to VBA terminology and have a basic understanding of how to manipulate projects, you will create a project to allow you to examine the **Visual Basic Editor**. To avoid confusion, first unload all loaded projects:

1. Open the **VBA Manager**.
2. Select a project in the **Projects** list.
3. Pick the **Unload** button.
4. Do the same for all other projects until the **Projects** list is empty.

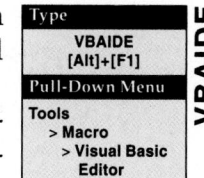

Type
VBAIDE
[Alt]+[F1]
Pull-Down Menu
Tools
> Macro
> Visual Basic
Editor

VBAIDE

5. Pick the **New** button. A project named ACADProject is added to the **Projects** list and its location is shown as Global*n*.
6. Pick the **Visual Basic Editor** button in the lower-left corner of the **VBA Manager** dialog box.

The **Visual Basic Editor** has several key areas. See **Figure 27-3.** At the upper, left is the **Project Explorer** window. All loaded projects are listed in this area, as well as the AutoCAD objects, forms, and modules associated with the project. The project name is shown and next to the name in parentheses is the project location. The objects, forms, and modules are shown in a tree below the project name. At the lower, left is the **Properties** window. This window is used to set the various object properties used in the program. It will be most often used when creating forms. The right-hand side is the "desktop" where the **Code** window will be displayed while writing the program.

You will create a short macro for enlarging the size of the pick box. The macro will be stored in a project called PickBoxSet.dvb. Later, you will add another macro to the project to change the pick box to the default size. Notice the **Project Explorer** window shows the project as ACADProject and the project location as Global*n*. Also, notice the ThisDrawing branch listed under the AutoCAD Objects branch in the tree. Continue as follows.

1. Select ACADProject in the **Project Explorer** window. Notice that ACADProject is now shown in the **Properties** window next to the (Name) property.
2. Pick in the text box next to the (Name) property in the **Properties** window, change the name to PickBoxSet, and press [Enter]. Notice that the **Project Explorer** window now shows the project name as PickBoxSet. This named the project within the drawing; it did *not* save the project to a file.
3. Select **Module** from the **Insert** pull-down menu in the **Visual Basic Editor**. The **Code** window is opened on the **Visual Basic Editor** desktop. Also, notice that a Modules branch has been added in the **Project Explorer** window and Module1 is listed in this branch. Module1 is highlighted in the **Project Explorer** window and listed in the **Properties** window.
4. In the **Properties** window, change the name of Module1 to PickBoxBig. Notice that the module name is updated in the **Project Explorer** window and in the title bar of the **Code** window.

Figure 27-3.
The **Visual Basic Editor**.

Project
Explorer
window

Properties
window

Code
window

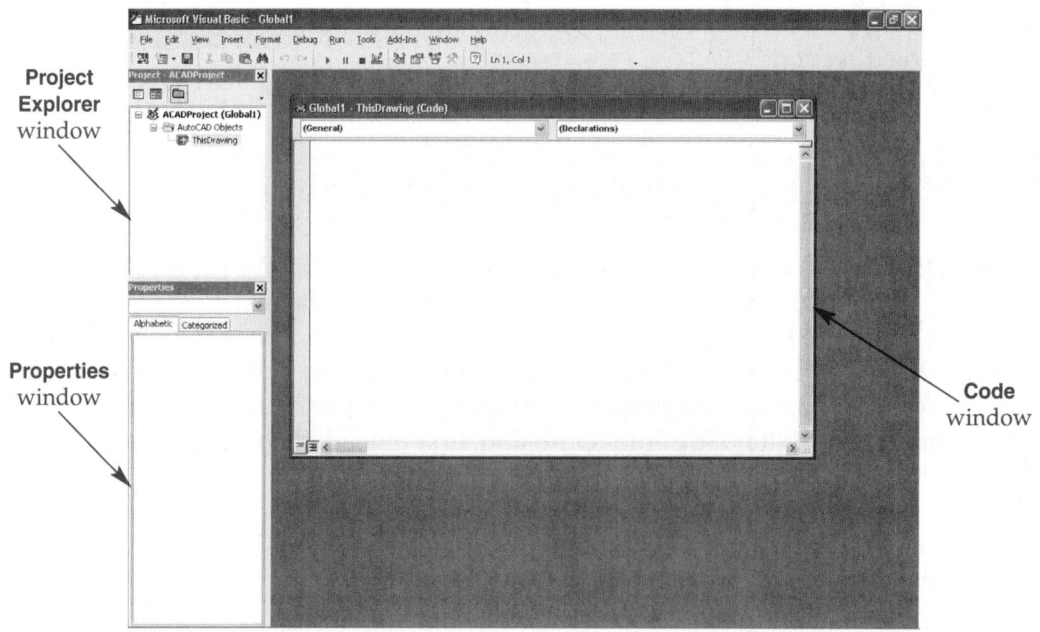

AutoCAD and Its Applications—Advanced

Figure 27-4.
Adding a procedure.

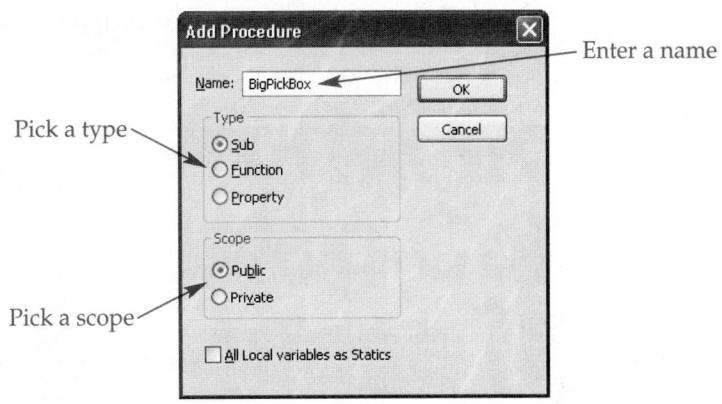

Enter a name

Pick a type

Pick a scope

5. Pick inside of the **Code** window. Notice the blinking, vertical cursor in the window, similar to how it would appear in a text editor.

6. Select **Procedure...** from the **Insert** pull-down menu in the **Visual Basic Editor**. The **Add Procedure** dialog box appears, **Figure 27-4.** Enter BigPickBox in the **Name:** text box. Pick the **Sub** and **Public** radio buttons. Then, pick the **OK** button to close the dialog box.

Notice that some code is automatically entered in the **Code** window. The Public Sub BigPickBox () line is the syntax for the beginning of a **Public Sub**. The End Sub line is the syntax used for the ending of a **Sub**. The remainder of the code for the **Sub** is entered between these two lines of code. Continue as follows.

7. On the first line after Public Sub BigPickBox (), type:

        Application.Preferences.Selection.PickBoxSize = 7

Notice that the editor has a feature called **Auto List Members**. After you type the period following the object name, a list of methods and procedures associated with that object appears. Typing the first letter of the method or property you want scrolls the list to that letter. You can continue typing or use the up and down arrow keys to highlight the word you want. When the word you want is highlighted, press the [Tab] key and the word is entered for you. If you want to select a method or property of the new object, type another period and the **Auto List Members** feature is displayed for the new object. This greatly reduces the amount of typing needed to get to nested objects. The module (macro) is now complete. Test the macro in AutoCAD:

8. Return to AutoCAD by picking the **View AutoCAD** button in the **Visual Basic Editor**. See **Figure 27-5.**

9. Determine the current setting for the **PICKBOX** system variable. If it is 7, change it to a different value.

10. Select **Tools>Macro>Macros...** to display the **Macros** dialog box. Notice that the BigPickBox macro is listed in the dialog box. See **Figure 27-6.** The name shows that it is a global macro, it is stored in a module named PickBoxBig, and the **Sub** is named BigPickBox.

11. With the macro highlighted, pick the **Run** button. Notice that the pick box is now slightly larger.

12. Verify the change to the **PICKBOX** system variable.

PROFESSIONAL TIP

Be sure that the **PICKFIRST** system variable is set to 1 (noun/verb selection enabled) so that the pick box is displayed with the crosshairs. Also, you can use a value higher in the macro to make the change in the pick box size easier to see.

Figure 27-5.
Picking the **View AutoCAD** button returns you to AutoCAD.

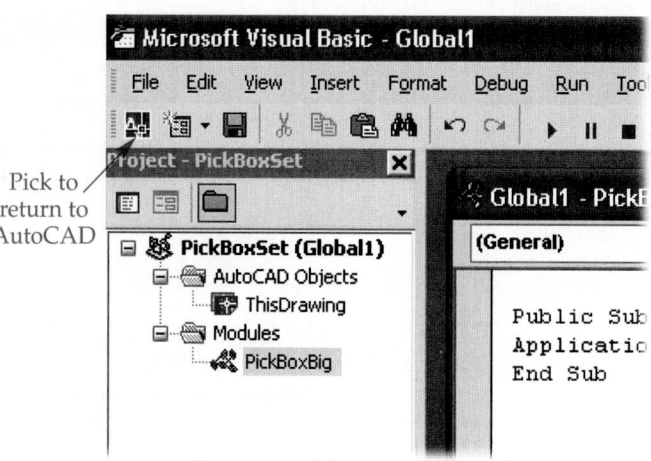

Pick to return to AutoCAD

Figure 27-6.
The **Macros** dialog box is used to select a macro to run.

Global macro   Module name   **Sub** name   Pick to run the macro

Select a macro

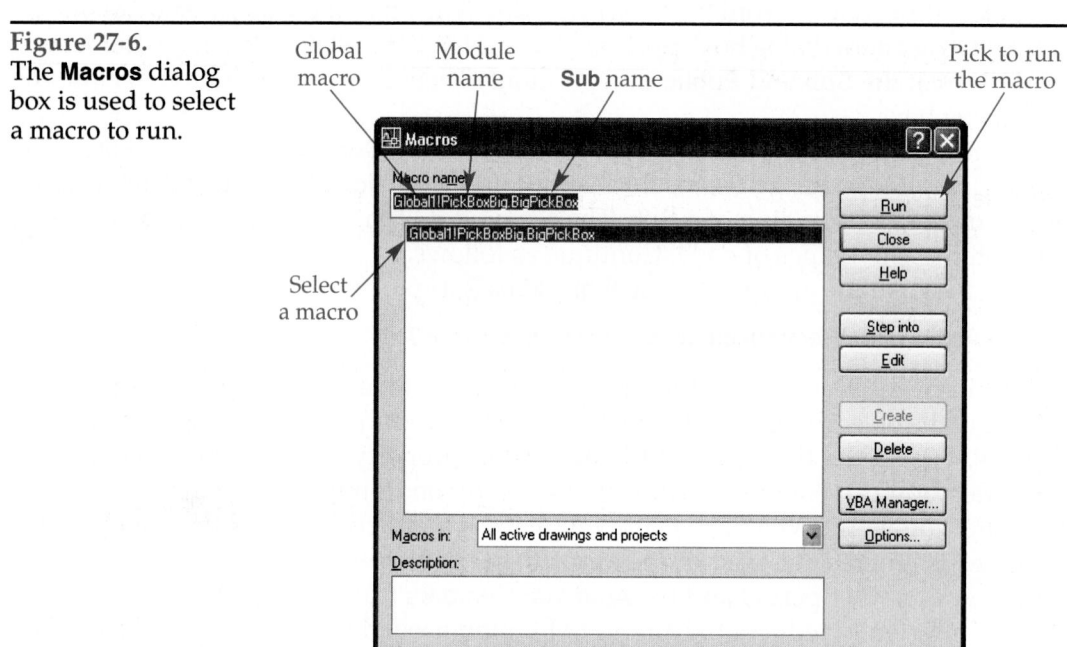

You have just created your first VBA macro! You will now add another module to change the pick box back to the default size, and then save the project as a DVB file. Follow these steps:

1. Display the **Visual Basic Editor**.
2. Pick inside of the **Code** window to make it active.
3. Select **Procedure...** from the **Insert** pull-down menu.
4. In the **Add Procedure** dialog box, enter NormPickBox as the name of the new **Sub**. Also, pick the **Sub** and **Public** radio buttons, then pick the **OK** button.
5. Enter the following code in the new **Sub**. Remember, type the code between the Public Sub and the End Sub lines.

```
Application.Preferences.Selection.PickBoxSize = 3
```

6. Display AutoCAD.
7. Select **Tools>Macro>Macros...** to display the **Macros** dialog box. Notice the new macro is now listed along with the first macro. Select the new macro and pick the **Run** button.
8. Notice that the pick box size is now set to the default size. The default **PICKBOX** value is 3.

9. Display the **Visual Basic Editor**.

10. Pick the **Save** button on the toolbar in the **Visual Basic Editor**. A standard Windows "save as" dialog box appears. Save the file under the name PickBoxSet in the folder of your choice. The .dvb extension is automatically added.

As you work through the rest of the chapter, enter each example in the **Code** window in the **Visual Basic Editor**. Then, test each example using **Macros** dialog box in AutoCAD.

Exercise 27-2
Complete the exercise on the Student CD.

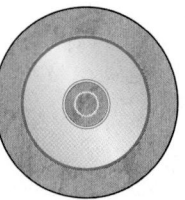

Dealing with Data Types

The concept of programming revolves around gathering, storing, and reusing data. The data used by programs come in various *data types.* In the previous project, the macro set the pick box size by providing an integer. An integer is considered a data type. As you learn to use VBA to manipulate the AutoCAD environment in other ways, and to create and modify AutoCAD entities, you will need to use other data types.

Although there are many data types available and needed while programming in VBA, only a few are often used while working in AutoCAD. The more common data types used in AutoCAD are strings, integers, real numbers, and variants. Integers and real numbers are broken down further into two types for each covering different ranges of numbers.

Data type	Range	Description
String		Text characters.
Integer	–32,768 to 32,767	Small integer values.
Long	–2,147,483,648 to 2,147,483,647	Large integer values.
Single	1.4E–45 to 3.4E+48	Single precision floating point numbers.
Double	4.94E–324 to 1.8E+308	Double precision floating point numbers.
Variant		Typically used to denote coordinates.

For the examples in the rest of this chapter, you will use the **String**, **Integer**, **Double**, and **Variant** data types. The practical applications for these data types are:

- **String.** Used for command names, prompts, AutoCAD system variables, and so on. When using strings within a program, the characters making up the string are enclosed in quotation marks "like this".
- **Integer.** Used for counting. Often, the program has to progress through a list in increments. Integers are used to do so.
- **Double.** Used for lengths; distances; and X, Y, or Z coordinate values (when separately dealing with X, Y, and Z).
- **Variant.** Used for point coordinates (when working with X, Y, and Z values together).

Using Variables

A *variable* is a named memory location that holds a value. The name given to a variable should have a prefix, based on the type of data that it is holding. Refer to the following table.

Data type	Prefix	Example
String	str	strFirstName
Integer	int	intCount
Double	dbl	dblDist1
Variant	var	varCenterPoint

In VBA, before a variable name is assigned a value, it must be *declared* as to which type of data will be stored. The syntax to do this is:

Dim *variable_name* As *data_type*

Applying this syntax to the examples in the above table:

```
Dim strFirstName As String
Dim intCount As Integer
Dim dblDist1 As Double
Dim varCenterPoint As Variant
```

Once a variable has been declared, a value can be assigned to it. This is accomplished with the = assignment operator. The syntax for assigning a value to a *data variable* is:

variable_name = value

Examples of how this looks in the **Code** window of the **Visual Basic Editor** are:

```
strFirstName = "John"
intCount = 10
dblDist1 = 135.75
```

Allowing for User Interaction

The last examples in the previous section are referred to as *hard coding* of variables. The variables are not really "variable," rather they are being directly set by the programmer. Look at this line of code:

```
strFirstName = "John"
```

This would work great if everyone in the world was named John. VBA provides methods that allow prompting the user for values and retrieving those values. There is a specific method for each data type that a program may need. To handle the **String**, **Integer**, **Real**, and **Variant** data types, there are the **GetString**, **GetInteger**, **GetReal**, and **GetPoint** methods, respectively.

There are also data conversion methods for changing the data type of a variable when this is necessary. Most of these methods are found in the **Utility** object, along with most of the user-interaction methods. The **Utility** object is a subobject of the **ActiveDocument** object, which, in turn, is a subobject of the **Application** object.

To make coding a little easier, the **ThisDrawing** object can be used as an alias for the **Application.ActiveDocument** object.

To store a string supplied by the user, the **Utility** object's **GetString** method is used. The **GetString** method has one required argument, which must come first, and one optional argument, which must come second. An *argument* is additional information that can be passed to the method. The arguments are listed within parentheses immediately after the method. Each argument is separated by a comma. This additional information is required in some instances and optional in other instances.

In the case of the **GetString** method, the first argument is a **TRUE** or **FALSE** test and determines whether or not the string that the user enters can contain spaces. Actually, it determines whether the space bar is interpreted as a space or as the [Enter] key. If the argument is **FALSE**, spaces are not allowed. If the user presses the space bar, the text input is ended. If the argument is **TRUE**, spaces are allowed in the input string.

The second argument for the **GetString** method is an optional prompt. If included, it must be a string. The provided string is displayed on the command line when the method is called. This can be used to let the user know what is expected of them. Even though this argument is optional, it is almost always included.

The following code gets a string input by the user and stores it in a variable. Notice that spaces are not allowed in the string.

```
Dim strName as String
strName = ThisDrawing.Utility.GetString(FALSE,"First name only: ")
```

Now that the value is stored, it can be used in some way. For the test macro, it will just be sent to the command line using the **Prompt** method. The **Prompt** method requires one argument, and that argument must be a string. The data stored in the strName variable represent a string, so pass this variable to the **Prompt** method:

```
ThisDrawing.Utility.Prompt (strName)
```

Another feature of the **Visual Basic Editor** becomes apparent as you enter functions that can have arguments passed to them. The **Auto Quick Info** feature displays information about the arguments as soon as you type the opening parenthesis. The argument that you are "working on" is in bold. Arguments that are optional are shown enclosed in brackets. Required arguments are shown without brackets.

The following shows additional example code for the **GetInteger**, **GetReal**, and **GetPoint** methods. For each method, the variable is passed to the **Prompt** variable.

```
Sub GetSamples ()

    Dim strName as String
    strName = ThisDrawing.Utility.GetString(FALSE,"First name only: ")
    ThisDrawing.Utility.Prompt (strName)

    Dim intNumber as Integer
    intNumber = ThisDrawing.Utility.GetInteger("Enter an integer: ")
    ThisDrawing.Utility.Prompt (intNumber)

    Dim dblNumber as Double
    dblNumber = ThisDrawing.Utility.GetReal("Enter a real number: ")
    ThisDrawing.Utility.Prompt (dblNumber)
```

```
Dim varPoint as Variant
varPoint = ThisDrawing.Utility.GetPoint(, "Pick a point: ")
ThisDrawing.Utility.Prompt (varPoint(0) & ", " & varPoint(1))
```

```
End Sub
```

Some items of note regarding the **GetPoint** code:

- The **GetPoint** method can have two arguments, but in this case only a prompt string argument needs to be supplied. However, this must be the second argument. The first argument is left blank, but still separated from the second argument with a comma.
- The **GetPoint** method returns (produces) a set of X, Y, and Z coordinates. These three values are stored in what is called an *array* in VBA, which is similar to an AutoLISP list. The items in an array are indexed beginning with 0, rather than 1. So, the X value is in the array at an index of 0, the Y value at index 1, and the Z value at index 2. Each item can be passed as an argument by using its index in the array. In the above example, the X and Y values are passed to the **Prompt** method.
- The **Prompt** method can only have one argument, a string, passed to it. Multiple strings can be *concatenated* (added together) using the ampersand (**&**). In the above example, only the X value varPoint(0) and Y value varPoint(1) are supplied, and they are separated by a comma and a space (", ").

Exercise 27-3
Complete the exercise on the Student CD.

Creating AutoCAD Entities

AutoCAD entities can be created using VBA. The following sample code creates a circle. Later in this section, sample code is provided that creates a line.

```
Sub CreateCircle()

Dim objCircle As AcadCircle
Dim varCP As Variant
Dim dblRadius As Double

varCP = ThisDrawing.Utility.GetPoint(, "Center point for circle: ")
dblRadius = ThisDrawing.Utility.GetReal("Enter circle radius: ")

Set objCircle = ThisDrawing.ModelSpace.AddCircle(varCP, dblRadius)

End Sub
```

The **Set** statement and **=** assignment operator are used to assign a reference to a particular object type. This is how you store a value in an *object variable*. The **AddCircle** method is used to create a circle, in this case as a member of the **ModelSpace** collection (created in model space). This example also introduces a new data type. **AcadCircle** is an object data type exclusive to AutoCAD. Variables for use with object data types have their names prefixed with obj. A list of all AutoCAD-specific object data types is located in the developer's help:

1. In AutoCAD, select **Help>Additional Resources>Developer Help**.
2. In the left-hand pane (**Contents** tab), select **ActiveX and VBA Reference**.

3. In the right-hand pane, select **Objects**.

4. The right-hand pane now displays a list of all AutoCAD-specific data types. Picking on an object name displays information specific to that data type.

The next example creates a line between two points that the user selects. This example is similar to the previous example.

```
Sub CreateLine()

Dim objLine As AcadLine
Dim varFP As Variant
Dim varNP As Variant

varFP = ThisDrawing.Utility.GetPoint(, "Select first point for line: ")
varNP = ThisDrawing.Utility.GetPoint(varFP, "Select last point for line: ")

Set objLine = ThisDrawing.ModelSpace.AddLine(varFP, varNP)

End Sub
```

The only new concept introduced in this macro is that the first selected point, which is stored in a variable as a **Variant** data type, is being passed as the first argument for the second use of the **GetPoint** method. By including this, a "drag line" is shown from the first point to the cursor location until the second point is picked or entered.

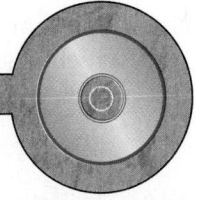

Exercise 27-4
Complete the exercise on the Student CD.

Editing AutoCAD Entities

Editing an AutoCAD entity typically involves changing one of its properties. In order to do that, the user must be allowed to select the entity. Then, the properties of the entity can be accessed. The **GetEntity** method allows the user to pick an entity, returns the object and the point used to select it, and provides for a prompt that can be used to let the user know what to do. The following code allows the user to specify a radius and then to select a circle to change.

```
Sub ChngCirRad()

Dim objCir As AcadCircle
Dim varPt As Variant
Dim dblCirRad As Double

dblCirRad = ThisDrawing.Utility.GetReal("Enter new circle radius: ")
ThisDrawing.Utility.GetEntity objCir, varPt, "Pick a circle: "

objCir.Radius = dblCirRad

End Sub
```

The **GetEntity** method assigns both the selected object and the selection point to the variable. This is similar to the argument-passing concept. A third argument is the prompting string. Notice how the **Radius** property of the variable objCir, which is an **AcadCircle** data type, is set equal to the value of the dblCirRad variable.

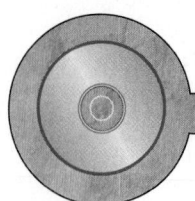

Exercise 27-5

Complete the exercise on the Student CD.

Creating a Dialog Box Using VBA

When programming using VBA, dialog boxes are called *forms.* The command buttons, option buttons, labels, text boxes, and other items that are found on forms are called *controls.* Adding forms to your programs, and controls to your forms, is rather easy. If you are familiar with AutoLISP and Dialog Control Language (DCL) programming, you will find VBA's approach to dialog box creation much simpler.

This section shows you how to add a form to a VBA project, use some of the available controls, add code to those controls, and create a macro that will call the dialog box. It is not meant to be an in-depth discussion of using forms and their many possible uses. When you have completed this section, you will have a good overview of the concepts of forms and controls, as well as created a very handy program. For more detailed information on VBA forms, refer to *VBA for AutoCAD* published by The Goodheart-Willcox Company, Inc.

The example in this section creates a program that adds and subtracts the areas of circles and polylines selected by the user. The program has a dialog box (form) interface, which has buttons to be used for adding and subtracting objects. The area of the last object selected is shown in the dialog box along with the running total area. See Figure 27-7.

Step 1: Begin a New Project

1. In AutoCAD, open the **VBA Manager** dialog box. Pick the **New** button. Make note of the location.
2. Pick the **Visual Basic Editor** button to open the **Visual Basic Editor.**
3. In the **Project Explorer** window, highlight the ACADProject that was just created. The location appears at the end of the name.
4. In the **Properties** window, pick in the (Name) property text box.
5. Change the name of the project to AreaCalc.
6. Pick the **Save** button on the toolbar in the **Visual Basic Editor** to save the project.
7. Name the project AreaCalc.dvb and put it in a folder of your choice. Notice that the location is changed in the **Project Explorer** window.

Figure 27-7.
This is the dialog box you will create using VBA.

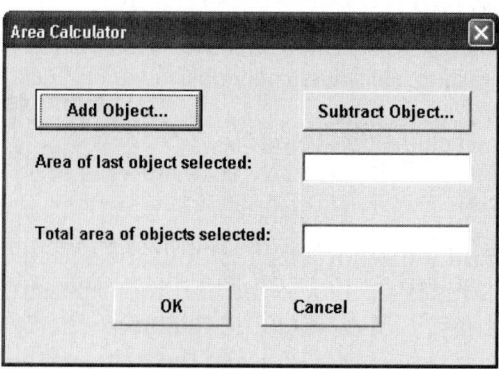

Step 2: Add a User Form

1. In the **Visual Basic Editor**, select **Insert>UserForm** from the pull-down menu. The **UserForm** window, containing a blank user form, is opened on the **Visual Basic Editor** desktop. A **Toolbox** window also appears, which contains controls that can be placed on the form.

2. The **Properties** window shows all of the various properties of the form. Change the (Name) property to frmAreaCalc. Also, change the Caption property to Area Calculator.

The Caption property is the name that appears in the title bar of the form (dialog box). The form is an object and, for the sake of clarity, is usually given a name with the standard form prefix frm. Other standard prefixes will be used later when you provide names for the controls that are placed on the form. The project should now look similar to **Figure 27-8**.

Step 3: Add Controls to the Form

1. From the **Toolbox** window, drag a **CommandButton** object onto the form and drop it anywhere. If you pause the cursor over an object in the **Toolbox** window, the name of the object is displayed as help text.

The default size of the command button may be quite large or small in comparison to the default size of the form. The form and controls can be resized. The controls can also be repositioned on the form.

2. In the **UserForm** window, pick on the form to make it the active object. Resizing grips appear along the edges and at the corners.

3. Move the cursor to the lower-right corner. When the standard Windows resizing cursor appears, drag the corner down and to the right to increase the size of the form.

4. From the **Toolbox** window, drag three more **CommandButton** objects, two **Label** objects, and two **TextBox** objects onto the form.

5. The controls can be moved around on the form by picking on the object and dragging it to a new location. Multiple controls can be selected by pressing the [Ctrl] key before picking the objects. Arrange the controls as shown in **Figure 27-9**.

Figure 27-8.
A new form has been added to the project. Its name and caption have been changed.

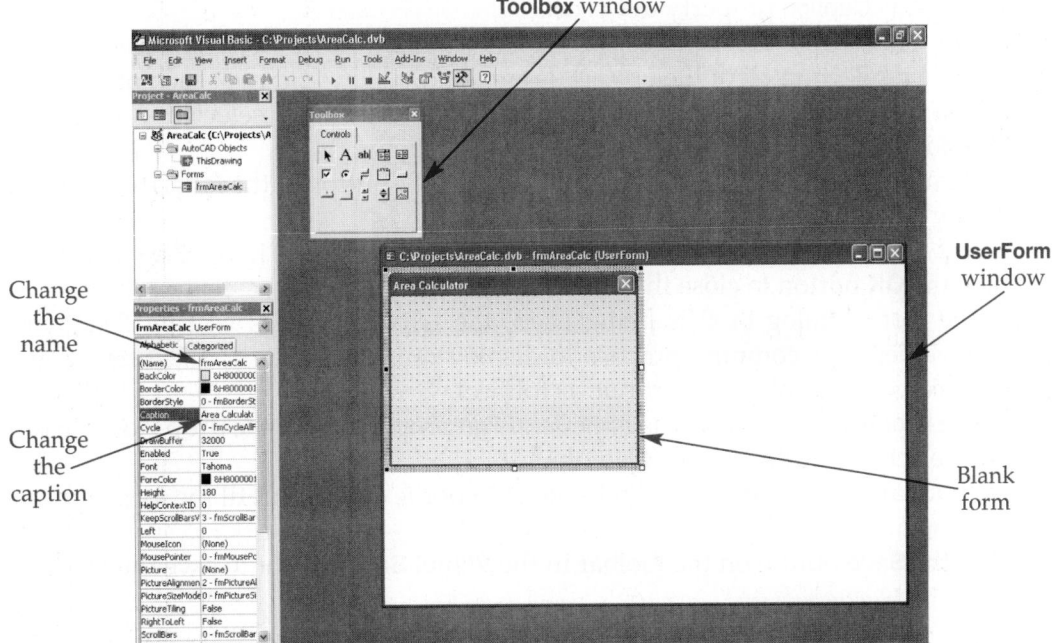

Figure 27-9.
Controls have been added to the form and arranged.

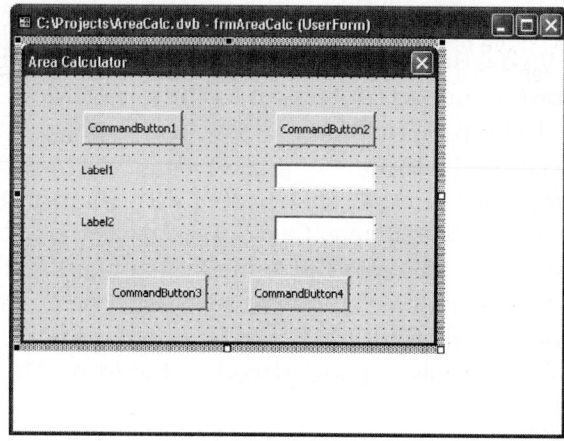

Step 4: Set the Properties of the Controls

1. Select the upper-left command button to make it active. Notice that its properties are now shown in the **Properties** window and the resizing grips are displayed on the object.
2. Change the Caption property to Add Object... and the (Name) property to btnAddObject. The btn prefix is used for the names of button objects.
3. Select the upper-right command button. Change its Caption property to Subtract Object... and its (Name) property to btnSubtractObject.
4. Change the (Name) property of the top label to lblLastArea and its Caption property to Area of last object selected:. The lbl prefix is used for the names of label objects.
5. Change the (Name) property of the bottom label to lblTotalArea and its Caption property to Total area of objects selected:.
6. Change the (Name) property of the top text box to txtLastArea. Leave its Text property blank. The txt prefix is used for the names of text box objects.
7. Change the (Name) property of the bottom text box to txtTotalArea. Leave its Text property blank.
8. Change the (Name) property of the bottom-left command button to btnExit. Change its Caption property to OK.
9. Change the (Name) property of the bottom-right command button to btnCancel. Change its Caption property to Cancel.

Next, you will change the font used to display text on the objects. This can be done "globally" by selecting all of the objects. Press the [Ctrl] key and pick each of the eight objects on the form. The properties that are common to the selected controls are displayed in the **Properties** window. Continue as follows.

10. Pick in the Font property text box and select the **...** button at the far right. The **Font** dialog box is displayed.
11. Select Arial in the **Font:** list, Bold in the **Font style:** list, and 10 in the **Size:** list. Then, pick the **OK** button to close the **Font** dialog box.

When the form (dialog box) is being used, the two text boxes will be displaying numeric values. It is common practice to display numeric data right justified. Select the two text box controls and continue as follows.

12. In the **Properties** window, select the TextAlign property. Pick the drop-down arrow and select 3–fmTextAlignRight from the list.
13. Individually select, resize, and relocate each of the controls until the form appears as shown in Figure 27-10.
14. Pick the **Save** button on the toolbar in the **Visual Basic Editor** to save the project.

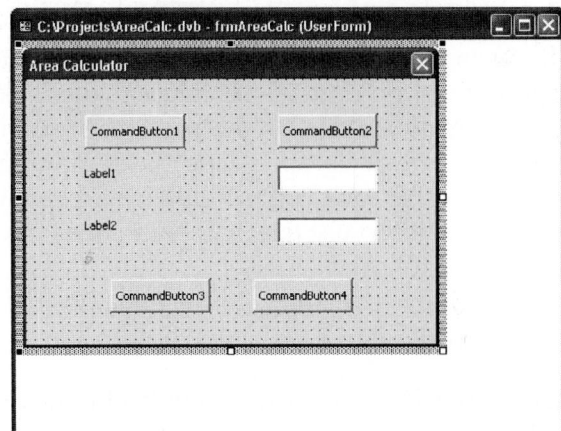

Figure 27-10.
The controls have been edited and resized.

Step 5: Add Code to the Form

So far, you have created the visual interface for the program, but the form cannot yet do anything. You are now ready to add code to the form. Double-click anywhere on the form (not on a control). This opens the **Code** window for the form where code can be added for the form itself and the objects (buttons, text boxes, etc.) it contains. The window contains some default code. This code is associated with an action, or event. In this case, the default code is a **Private Sub** associated with the action of picking (clicking) on the form. This default code should be removed since no actions will be performed when the form is picked.

1. Highlight all of the existing code and press the [Delete] key.
2. Be sure (General) is selected in the top-left drop-down list in the **Code** window and (Declarations) is selected in the top-right drop-down list.
3. Enter the following lines of code:

```
' Declaration of variables for use in the program
Dim objOBJ As AcadObject      ' The object (circle or polyline) that will be selected
Dim varPNT As Variant          ' The point that was used when selecting the object
Dim dblObjectArea As Double    ' The area of the selected object
Dim dblTotalArea As Double     ' The running total of the area of all the selected objects
Dim strType As String          ' The type of object (circle or polyline) that is selected
```

4. Pick the **Save** button on the toolbar in the **Visual Basic Editor** to save the project.

The code you just entered declares the variables needed to do the area calculations. Also, note the comments added to the code. Adding *comments* is very important because it informs you or anyone else reading the code as to the purpose of the code. Anything after an apostrophe (') is ignored by VBA. Comments are usually added to a line above code or at the end of a line of code, as shown above.

Step 6: Add Code to the Exit Button

1. With the **Code** window active, select btnExit in the upper-left drop-down list.

   The upper-right drop-down list changes to the Click action. A **Private Sub** is added that will be executed when the **Exit** button on the form is picked. Also, notice the horizontal line between the declarations and the beginning of the **Private Sub**. This automatically appears before each **Sub** to help visually separate the program into blocks. It is also common practice to use tabs and blank lines to visually separate logical blocks of code. Continue as follows.

2. On the blank line between the Private Sub line and the End Sub line, type:

   Unload Me

   This line of code closes the dialog box and removes from memory all of the code associated with the form.

3. Save the project.

Step 7: Add Code to the Cancel Button

1. Activate the **UserForm** window. This can be done by picking on the window (if it is visible) or selecting the window in the **Window** pull-down menu of the **Visual Basic Editor**.

2. Double-click on the btnCancel control. Make sure you do not double-click on the label displayed on the object.

   This displays the **Code** window and adds a **Private Sub** that will be executed when the **Cancel** button on the form is picked. In the last section, you used the left-hand drop-down list in the **Code** window to accomplish the same thing. Use whichever method you prefer. Continue as follows.

3. Add the Unload Me line of code to the **Private Sub**. The **Code** window should appear as shown in **Figure 27-11**.

4. Save the project.

Figure 27-11.
Variables have been declared and code has been added for the **Cancel** and **Exit** buttons.

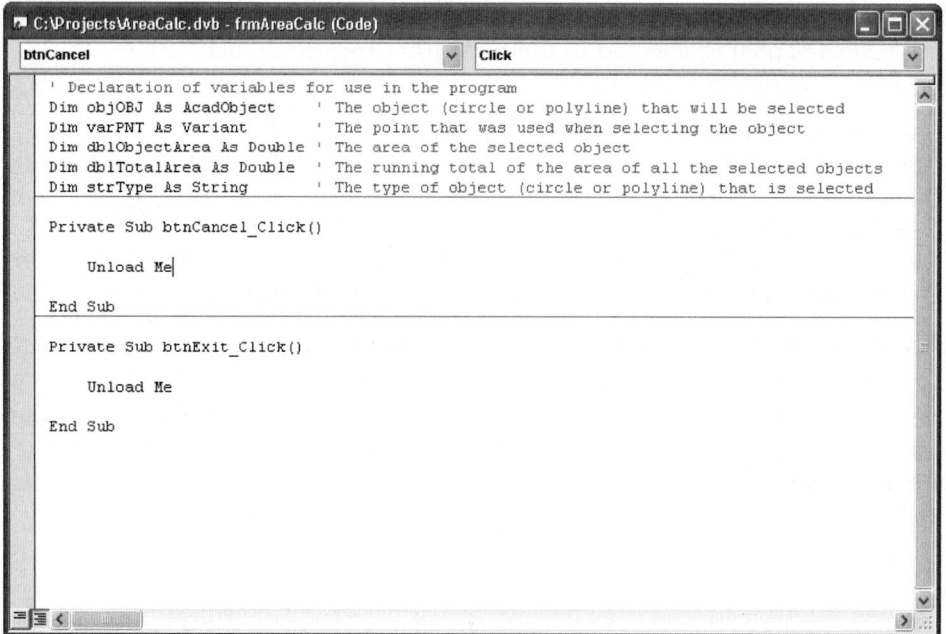

AutoCAD and Its Applications—Advanced

In the **Area Calculator** dialog box (form) you are creating, there will be no difference between the actions of the **OK** button and the **Cancel** button. Both are included for consistency, since most AutoCAD dialog boxes have an **OK** and a **Cancel** button. Users quickly become accustom to the consistent locations of features in the software. Try to mimic this with your programs, always including **OK** and **Cancel** buttons located near the bottom of the dialog box.

Step 8: Add Code to the Add Object... Button

1. Make the **UserForm** window active.
2. Double-click on the btnAddObject object. The **Code** window is displayed and a **Private Sub** is added that will be executed when the **Add Object...** button on the form is picked.
3. Between the Private Sub line and the End Sub line, type the following lines of code. Notice how blank lines and tabs are used to visually organize the code.

```
frmAreaCalc.Hide

ThisDrawing.Utility.GetEntity objOBJ, varPNT, "Pick a circle or a polyline: "
strType = objOBJ.ObjectName

If strType = "AcDbCircle" Or strType = "AcDbPolyline" Then
    dblObjectArea = objOBJ.Area
    dblTotalArea = dblObjectArea + dblTotalArea
    txtLastArea.Text = Str(dblObjectArea)
    txtTotalArea.Text = Str(dblTotalArea)
    frmAreaCalc.Show

Else

    MsgBox ("Object must be a circle or a polyline")
    frmAreaCalc.Show

Exit Sub

End If
```

4. Save the project.

Here is a description of each line of code for the **Add Object...** button:

```
frmAreaCalc.Hide
```

The **Hide** method of the frmAreaCalc object is used to temporarily hide the dialog box. This allows the user to work in the drawing area.

```
ThisDrawing.Utility.GetEntity objOBJ, varPNT, "Pick a circle or a polyline: "
```

The **GetEntity** method of the **Utility** object is used to get the object selected by the user. This method is discussed in detail earlier in the chapter.

```
strType = objOBJ.ObjectName
```

This line stores the **ObjectName** property of the selected AutoCAD object in the strType variable.

```
If strType = "AcDbCircle" Or strType = "AcDbPolyline" Then
```

This line is the first line of the **If** function. The **If** function checks a condition, and if the condition is true, it executes all of the code after the **Then** statement up to the **Else** statement. The **Else** statement is optional, so if an **Else** statement is not included, all of the code after the **Then** statement is executed until the **End If** statement is encountered. In the case of this program, the condition being tested is the object type. This check has to be performed since the **Area** property will be used and not all AutoCAD entities have an **Area** property.

At this point, the program branches. If the selected AutoCAD object is a circle or polyline, then the next line is executed. Otherwise, execution jumps to the **Else** statement.

        dblObjectArea = objOBJ.Area

This line stores the value of the selected object's **Area** property in the dblObjectArea variable.

        dblTotalArea = dblObjectArea + dblTotalArea

This line adds the value of the dblObjectArea variable to the value of the dblTotalArea variable and stores the result in the dblTotalArea variable. The first time this line is performed, the dblTotalArea variable does not have a value, so 0 is used.

        txtLastArea.Text = Str(dblObjectArea)

This line sets the **Text** property of the txtLastArea object (labeled **Area of last object selected:**). The text to appear in the text box is the value that is stored in the dblObjectArea variable. That variable is a numeric value, and text boxes can only display string values. The **Str** function is being used to convert the data type from a number to a string. This is done by passing the dblObjectArea variable as an argument to the **Str** function.

        txtTotalArea.Text = Str(dblTotalArea)

This line is doing the same as the previous line, but it applies to the txtTotalArea object (labeled **Total area of objects selected:**).

        frmAreaCalc.Show

The **Show** method of the frmAreaCalc object is used to display the dialog box.

If the selected AutoCAD object is not a circle or polyline, code execution jumps from the **If** statement to the **Else** statement:

        Else

This line begins the lines of code that are to be performed if the condition being checked is false. The condition being checked is whether or not the selected object is a circle or a polyline. If the selected object is not either of these object types, the **MsgBox** function is called.

        MsgBox ("Object must be a circle or a polyline")

The **MsgBox** function takes a string as an argument and shows that string as a message to the user in a small dialog box with an **OK** button at the bottom. The message informs the user that a circle or a polyline was not selected. When the user picks the **OK** button, the next line of code is executed.

        frmAreaCalc.Show

This line uses the **Show** method of the frmAreaCalc object to display the dialog box, allowing the user to pick the **Add Objects...** button to select another object or **Subtract Object...** button to remove and object.

```
Exit Sub
```

This line exits the **Sub** routine that was called when the user picked the **Add Object...** button the first time.

```
End If
```

This line signals the end of the code within the **If** function.

Step 9: Add Code to the Subtract Object... Button

1. Activate the **UserForm** window.
2. Double-click on the btnSubtractObject object. The **Code** window is displayed and a **Private Sub** is added that will be executed when the **Subtract Object...** button on the form is picked.
3. Between the Private Sub line and the End Sub line, type the following lines of code. Notice how blank lines and tabs are used to visually organize the code.

```
frmAreaCalc.Hide

ThisDrawing.Utility.GetEntity objOBJ, varPNT, "Pick a circle or a polyline: "
strType = objOBJ.ObjectName

If strType = "AcDbCircle" Or strType = "AcDbPolyline" Then
    dblObjectArea = objOBJ.Area
    dblTotalArea = dblTotalArea – dblObjectArea
    txtLastArea.Text = Str(dblObjectArea)
    txtTotalArea.Text = Str(dblTotalArea)
    frmAreaCalc.Show

Else

    MsgBox ("Object must be a circle or a polyline")
    frmAreaCalc.Show

Exit Sub

End If
```

The only difference between these lines of code and those for the **Add Object...** button is this line:

```
dblTotalArea = dblTotalArea – dblObjectArea
```

This line subtracts the area of the selected AutoCAD object from the total area.

4. Save the project.

NOTE

As you double-click to add code for the various objects on the form, the **Private Subs** are added to the **Code** window in alphabetical order. The **Private Subs** can be rearranged using cut-and-paste editing to more closely follow the flow of the program, if desired. For example, you may wish to rearrange the **Private Subs** for the controls on the frmAreaCalc form as:

```
Private Sub btnAddObject_Click()
    lines of code
End Sub

Private Sub btnSubtractObject_Click()
    lines of code
End Sub

Private Sub btnExit_Click()
    lines of code
End Sub

Private Sub btnCancel_Click()
    lines of code
End Sub
```

Step 10: Create a Macro to Call the Form

The form is complete, as is the code attached to the command button controls on the form. The last task is to create a macro to call the form so the dialog box will be displayed on the screen.

1. In the **Visual Basic Editor**, make sure the AreaCalc project is selected in the **Project Explorer** window.
2. Select **Insert>Module** from the pull-down menu.

The **Code** window for the module is opened on the **Visual Basic Editor** desktop. This is not the same **Code** window for the form, which is why it currently is blank. Also, notice that a Modules folder is added to the tree in the **Project Explorer** window, with Module1 listed below it. Continue as follows.

3. Select Module1 in the tree in the **Project Explorer** window.
4. In the **Properties** window, change the (Name) property to RunAreaCalc.
5. In the module **Code** window, type:

```
Public Sub RunAreaCalc()

    frmAreaCalc.Show

End Sub
```

6. Save the project.

Step 11: Load the Project and Run the Macro

If you have been following along with the text, the macro is available at this point and you can skip to step #3. Otherwise, the project needs to be loaded. In this case, begin with step #1.

1. Select **Tools>Macro>VBA Manager...** from the pull-down menu.
2. In the **VBA Manager** dialog box, pick the **Load...** button. Navigate to the AreaCalc.dvb file and open it. The project name and location are shown in the dialog box. If the file is already loaded, you do not need to reload it.
3. Switch to AutoCAD.
4. Draw a couple of circles, polylines, lines, and arcs.
5. Select **Tools>Macro>Macros...** to open the **Macros** dialog box. The macro that was created in the AreaCalc project is listed.
6. Highlight the RunAreaCalc macro and pick the **Run** button.

The form (**Area Calculator** dialog box) created in the project appears. Pick the **Add Object...** button; the dialog box is hidden. Select one of the circles you drew. The dialog box is displayed and the area of the circle appears in both text boxes in the dialog box. Pick the **Add Object...** button again and select a different circle. The area of that circle appears in the top text box and the combined area of the two circles appears in the bottom text box. Experiment with using the **Subtract Object...** button, selecting a line or arc, and using the **OK** and **Cancel** buttons.

CAUTION

This routine is not error proof. It will break down if you do not select an object when prompted to do so. Error checking is an important feature of programming. For information on adding error checking to your VBA programs, refer to *VBA for AutoCAD* published by The Goodheart-Willcox Company, Inc.

Running a VBA Macro from the Keyboard

One drawback of the VBA language is that there is no way to create a command out of a VBA macro or project. Additionally, there is no way to create a keyboard shortcut for a VBA macro or a project. There is, however, a way to create a command from a VBA project through the use of AutoLISP.

Create the following AutoLISP program using the **Visual LISP Editor**. A couple of AutoLISP functions are used that are not covered in this text. You can research these functions in the online documentation if you want to explore them deeper.

```
; For use with AreaCalc VBA project
(defun c:AreaCalc ()
    (vl-vbaload "c:/vba projects/AreaCalc.dvb")
    (vl-vbarun "RunAreaCalc")
    (princ)
)
```

The first line of code after the comment defines a function called **AreaCalc** that can be used on the command line. The second line of code after the comment loads a VBA project file. The path needs to match the location of your file, so adjust this line as needed. The next line runs the macro that calls the dialog box from the loaded project. The next line creates a clean exit from the AutoLISP program. The last line just closes the **(defun)** function. Now, this LISP program can be saved, loaded into AutoCAD, and run. Refer to Chapters 24 and 25 for more information.

Chapter Test

1. What does *VBA* stand for?
2. Briefly describe the AutoCAD object model.
3. What is the root object of the AutoCAD object model?
4. What are the five objects that branch from the root object in the AutoCAD object model?
5. Which branch off of the root allows access to most of the objects stored in AutoCAD's **Options** dialog box?
6. Which branch off of the root allows access to the objects stored in model space and paper space?
7. What is a VBA *method?*
8. What is a *property,* in terms of VBA?
9. What are *events,* in terms of VBA?
10. What is a VBA *project?*
11. What is a *form?*
12. Describe the difference between an *embedded* project and a *global* project.
13. How do you access to the **Macros** dialog box, **VBA Manager**, and **Visual Basic Editor** using AutoCAD's pull-down menus?
14. Describe the **Auto List Members** feature of the **Visual Basic Editor**.
15. Name six common data types used in VBA programming.
16. Define *variable.*
17. What is *declaring* a variable?
18. What does the term *hard coding* mean?
19. The **ThisDrawing** object is an alias for _____.
20. In which object are most of the user-interaction methods stored?
21. Name the methods that will obtain each of the following data types: **String, Integer, Real, Point.**
22. Given ThisDrawing.Utility.Prompt (strName), which term describes the (strName) portion of the code?
23. Describe the **Auto Quick Info** feature of the **Visual Basic Editor**.
24. Describe the difference between storing a value in an object variable versus storing a value in a data variable.
25. Command buttons, option buttons, labels, text boxes, and other items that are found on forms are called ____.

Drawing Problems

1. Create a VBA macro that will ask the user to select an object. Then, display a message box indicating the type of object selected. Name the macro P27_01_ObjectType.

2. Create a VBA macro that will ask the user to select a line. Then, display the length of the selected object in a message box. If the selected object is not a line, display a message informing the user of this. Name the macro P27_02_LineLength.

3. Create a VBA macro that will draw three circles.
    A. Draw the first circle using a center point and radius provided by the user.
    B. Draw the second circle using the same center point and a radius 25% larger than the first circle.
    C. Draw the third circle using the same center point and a radius 25% smaller than the first circle.
    D. Provide prompts for the user for the center point and radius.
    E. Name the macro P27_03_DrawCircles.

4. Create a VBA macro that will reduce the radius of a selected arc or circle to half of its original radius. If the selected object is not an arc or circle, display a message informing the user of this. Name the macro P27_04_ChangeRadius.

Index

measuring angles in
radians, 570–571
moving objects to current
layer, 576
moving objects to selected
layer, 575
nested expressions, 549
polar coordinates, 571–572
polar coordinates and
angles, 569–572
program files, 551
providing for additional
user input, 565–566
providing for angular
input, 571
providing for user input,
558–559
review, 560–561
sample programs, 573–576
setting current layer, 573
significant digits, 549
using values of system
variables, 566
variables, 549–551
Visual LISP Editor, 551–554
writing programs, 555–556
autosave settings, 433–434

B

Background dialog box, 357–359
backgrounds, 356–361
changing on existing
views, 360–361
gradient, 358
images, 358–359
solid, 356–357
sun and sky, 360
backup files, 434
banking, 150
base grip, 253
base surface, 174
bitmaps, 404
block insertion tools, 522–523
body editing, 233–236
check, 235
clean, 235
imprint, 233
separate, 233–234
shell, 234–235
Boolean operations, 49–50
Boundary Creation dialog box,
57–58
Button Editor dialog box, 461

C

caddr function, 568–569
cadr function, 567–569
camera and light tools, 527
CAMERADISPLAY system
variable, 387

CAMERAHEIGHT system
variable, 387
Camera Preview window,
387–388
cameras, 385–389
Camera tool palette, 387
changing views, 387–388
clipping planes, 388–389
creating for rendering, 379
system variables, 387
Camera tool palette, 387
car function, 567–569
cascading menus, 472, 477
cdr function, 568–569
chamfers, 174–175
Change Icon dialog box, 444
checker map, 315–316
clipping planes, 388–389
clusters, 582
colors,
edges, 211
faces, 232
graphics window, 427–428
materials, 309–310
command function, 572
Command Line Window Font
dialog box, 428–429
commands,
3DALIGN, 165–166
3DARRAY, 171–173
3DCONFIG, 436
3DCORBIT, 71
3DDISTANCE, 70
3DFLY, 390–396
3DFORBIT, 27, 66
3DMOVE, 167–168
3DORBIT, 27, 65–66, 77, 83
3DPOLY, 86
3DROTATE, 122, 168–170
3DSWIVEL, 70
3DWALK, 390–396
ACISIN, 272
ACISOUT, 272
ADCENTER, 513
ALIGN, 166–167
ANIPATH, 397
APPLOAD, 556, 581
AREA, 58
BOUNDARY, 57–58
BOX, 40
CAMERA, 379, 386
CHAMFER, 174–175
COMPILE, 121
CONE, 40–41
CONVTOSOLID, 132, 177–178
CONVTOSURFACE, 132,
176–177
COPYCLIP, 515–516
CUI, 452, 490
CUSTOMIZE, 514, 530
CYLINDER, 42–43, 119
DASHBOARD, 22, 479–485
defining new, 554–555
DISTANTLIGHT, 344–346

DTEXT, 121, 479
DXFIN, 414
DXFOUT, 413
ETRANSMIT, 418
EXPLODE, 218
EXPORT, 272, 416
EXTERNALREFERENCES,
404
EXTRUDE, 91–92, 118, 131–
135, 137–138
FILLET, 173–174
FLATSHOT, 262–263
FREESPOT, 349
GEOGRAPHICLOCATION,
341
HELIX, 54
HIDE, 28, 30–31, 121, 247,
281–282
IMAGEADJUST, 409–410
IMAGEATTACH, 405–406
IMAGECLIP, 408–409
IMAGEFRAME, 410
IMAGEQUALITY, 410
IMPORT, 272
IMPRINT, 233
INTERFERE, 52–54
INTERSECT, 51–52, 193
JOGSECTION, 255–256
LIGHT, 344
LIGHTLIST, 351–353
LIVESECTION, 256–258
LOFT, 133, 151–157
LOGFILEOFF, 434
LOGFILEON, 434
MASSPROP, 271
MATERIALATTACH, 302–303
MATERIALMAP, 328
MATERIALS, 304
MIRROR, 170
MIRROR3D, 170–171
MTEXT, 121
MVIEW, 110, 268
OFFSET, 227–228
OPTIONS, 423–424
PAN, 77
PEDIT, 86
PLAN, 64
PLANESURF, 48–49, 135, 194
PLINE, 86
PLOT, 416, 418
POINT, 85
POINTLIGHT, 346–347
POLYSOLID, 43–44
PRESSPULL, 217
PROPERTIES, 121, 163
PSFILL, 416
PSOUT, 416
PUBLISHTOWEB, 416
PYRAMID, 44–45
QUICKCUI, 456–457
REDRAW, 77
REGEN, 28, 77, 119, 431
REGENALL, 119, 431
REGION, 56–57